dont = whose; of whom; of which
from which
whence
about; of
whom

Helg ☑ W9-BSF-200

THE OXFORD PAPERBACK

French Dictionary and Grammar

trop - too (much)
au loin - far away
certes - indeed
aussi = also, too, as
well

celui / celle
celle-ci / là =
(dem. pron.)
he, she, that;
the one

soit = given;
suppose;
say

lorsque - when
quoique - whatever
aussitôt - immediately
aussitôt que - as soon as
tandis que - whereas, while
bien que - although
pourtant - yet
lequel / laquelle - which, who(m)
devoir - must do/be
donc - so; then; therefore
tant (de) - so much; many
malgré - in spite of; despite
malgré tout - after all
Même - same, even
quelque - some; any; a few

soit.. soit =
either... or

Helge Duncan

en depit = in spite of
pouvoir = might, power, authority
                force
avoir rien de = have nothing of

THE OXFORD PAPERBACK

French
Dictionary
and Grammar

WILLIAM ROWLINSON
MICHAEL JANES
EDWIN CARPENTER
DORA LATIRI-CARPENTER

Oxford New York
OXFORD UNIVERSITY PRESS

Oxford University Press, Walton Street, Oxford OX2 6DP

Oxford New York
Athens Auckland Bangkok Bombay
Calcutta Cape Town Dar es Salaam Delhi
Florence Hong Kong Istanbul Karachi
Kuala Lumpur Madras Madrid Melbourne
Mexico City Nairobi Paris Singapore
Taipei Tokyo Toronto

and associated companies in
Berlin Ibadan

Oxford is a trade mark of Oxford University Press

Grammar: © *Oxford University Press 1991*
Dictionary: © *Oxford University Press 1986, 1993*
This combined edition first published 1995

British Library Cataloguing in Publication Data
Data available

Library of Congress Cataloging in Publication Data
Data available
ISBN 0–19–864529–5

10 9 8 7 6 5

Printed in Great Britain by
Mackays of Chatham
Chatham, Kent

Contents

Grammar

William Rowlinson

Dictionary *289*

Michael Janes

Edwin Carpenter

Dora Latiri-Carpenter

Grammar

Contents

Verbs

TENSE FORMATION

The tenses of French verbs are either *simple*, in which case the verb is a single word, or *compound*, in which case it is normally formed from a part of the verb **avoir**, *to have*, followed by the past participle:

> simple tense: **je porte**, *I wear*
> compound tense: **j'ai porté**, *I have worn*

Regular verbs, what they are

Most French verbs are regular—that is they follow an entirely predictable pattern. The pattern they follow is determined by the way their infinitive ends. They divide into three groups (known as conjugations), each with its own infinitive ending:

> por**ter**, *to wear*, first conjugation
> fin**ir**, *to finish*, second conjugation
> ven**dre**, *to sell*, third conjugation

Most French verbs belong to the first conjugation, whose infinitives all end in **-er**. All invented new verbs are automatically first conjugation verbs. Verbs in the second conjugation all have an infinitive ending **-ir**, and those in the very small third conjugation all have an infinitive ending **-re**.

Irregular verbs, what they are

Some French verbs are irregular, following no pattern. In the simple tenses there is no way of predicting their stems (the part of the verb to which endings are added) or, quite frequently, the endings that are added to them. In the compound tenses, however, it is only the past participle which is irregular. So, for example, with **vouloir** (irregular), *to want*:

present (simple tense)	*perfect (compound tense)*
je veux	**j'ai voulu**
tu veux	**tu as voulu**
il veut	**il a voulu**
nous voulons	**nous avons voulu**
vous voulez	**vous avez voulu**
ils veulent	**ils ont voulu**

▶ There is a table of all the common irregular verbs with their conjugation on page 242.

Simple-tense formation, regular verbs

To form each simple tense a fixed set of endings is added to the verb's stem. The stem is the infinitive minus its **-er**, **-ir** or **-re** ending. Each conjugation has a different set of verb endings.

> **porter** → **port-** → **je** porte, *I wear*
> **finir** → **fin-** → **je** finis, *I finish*
> **vendre** → **vend-** → **je** vends, *I sell*

The ending of the verb corresponds to the subject of the verb:

> **je** finis, *I finish*
> **il** finit, *he finishes*

▶ The complete tense-formation of regular verbs is given on pp. 4–12, with the verb endings printed in bold.

Compound-tense formation, all verbs

To form a compound tense you need to know a verb's past participle. The past participle of a regular verb is formed by removing the **-er**, **-ir**, or **-re** of the infinitive. To this stem is added **-é** (first conjugation), **-i** (second conjugation), or **-u** (third conjugation):

infinitive		*past participle*
porter	→	por**té**
finir	→	fin**i**
vendre	→	vend**u**

The tenses of **avoir** used to form the compound tenses are:

> perfect tense:
> present of **avoir**: j'**ai** porté

> pluperfect tense:
> imperfect of **avoir**: j'**avais** porté

> future perfect tense:
> future of **avoir**: j'**aurai** porté

> conditional perfect tense:
> conditional of **avoir**: j'**aurais** porté

> past anterior tense:
> past historic of **avoir**: j'**eus** porté

> perfect subjunctive:
> present subjunctive of **avoir**: j'**aie** porté

> pluperfect subjunctive:
> imperfect subjunctive of **avoir**: j'**eusse** porté

▶ Some very common French verbs form their compound tenses with **être** instead of **avoir**. See p. 12.

▶ In all the compound tenses the past participle may sometimes agree with its subject or its direct object, in gender and in number. See p. 14.

CONJUGATION OF -er VERBS

(First-conjugation verbs)

In all tenses **elle** (*she*), **on** (*one*) and singular nouns are followed by the **il** form of the verb; **elles** (*they*, feminine) and plural nouns are followed by the **ils** form of the verb.

infinitive	**porter**, *to wear*
present participle	**portant**, *wearing*
past participle	**porté**, *worn*
imperative	**porte**, *wear...!*
	portons, *let's wear...*
	portez, *wear...!*

Simple tenses

present tense, *I wear, I am wearing*	je port**e** tu port**es** il port**e**	nous port**ons** vous port**ez** ils port**ent**
imperfect tense, *I wore, I was wearing,* *I used to wear*	je port**ais** tu port**ais** il port**ait**	nous port**ions** vous port**iez** ils port**aient**
past historic tense, *I wore*	je port**ai** tu port**as** il port**a**	nous port**âmes** vous port**âtes** ils port**èrent**
future tense, *I shall wear, I shall* *be wearing*	je port**erai** tu port**eras** il port**era**	nous port**erons** vous port**erez** ils port**eront**
conditional tense, *I should wear*	je port**erais** tu port**erais** il port**erait**	nous port**erions** vous port**eriez** ils port**eraient**
present subjunctive, *I wear, I may wear*	je port**e** tu port**es** il port**e**	nous port**ions** vous port**iez** ils port**ent**
imperfect subjunctive*, *I wore, I might wear*	je port**asse** tu port**asses** il port**ât**	nous port**assions** vous port**assiez** ils port**assent**

* archaic or literary

Compound tenses

perfect tense, *I wore, I have worn, I have been wearing*	j'**ai** porté	nous **avons** porté
	tu **as** porté	vous **avez** porté
	il **a** porté	ils **ont** porté
pluperfect tense, *I had worn, I had been wearing*	j'**avais** porté	nous **avions** porté
	tu **avais** porté	vous **aviez** porte
	il **avait** porté	ils **avaient** porté
future perfect tense, *I shall have worn, I shall have been wearing*	j'**aurai** porté	nous **aurons** porté
	tu **auras** porté	vous **aurez** porté
	il **aura** porté	ils **auront** porté
conditional perfect tense, *I should have worn*	j'**aurais** porté	nous **aurions** porté
	tu **aurais** porté	vous **auriez** porté
	il **aurait** porté	ils **auraient** porté
past anterior tense*, *I had worn*	j'**eus** porté	nous **eûmes** porté
	tu **eus** porté	vous **eûtes** porté
	il **eut** porté	ils **eurent** porté
perfect subjunctive, *I wore, I may have worn*	j'**aie** porté	nous **ayons** porté
	tu **aies** porté	vous **ayez** porté
	il **ait** porté	ils **aient** porté
pluperfect subjunctive*, *I had worn*	j'**eusse** porté	nous **eussions** porté
	tu **eusses** porté	vous **eussiez** porté
	il **eût** porté	ils **eussent** porté

Imperative of -er verbs

The **tu** form of the imperative of **-er** verbs (also verbs like **ouvrir**, see p. 29) has no **-s** except when followed by **y** or **en**:

> **donne-le-moi!**, *give it to me!*
> **donnes-en à ta sœur aussi!**, *give your sister some as well!*
> **vas-y!**, *go on!*

* archaic or literary

Spelling changes in some -er verbs

▶ Tenses with changes are given in detail in the verb tables on p. 239.

■ Verbs ending **-e[CONSONANT]er** change the **e** of the stem to **è** when a silent **e** follows:

> **mener → je mène**

They also make this change in the future and conditional, where the **e** that follows is soft rather than silent:

> **je mènerai; je mènerais**

■ verbs ending **-eter** and **-eler**, however, usually produce the open sound in the **e** by doubling the consonant:

> **jeter → je jette**
> **rappeler → je rappelle**

■ some verbs ending **-eter** and **-eler** follow the pattern of **mener**, changing the **e** to **è**:

> **acheter → j'achète**
> **geler → je gèle**

Most verbs that do this are, however, quite uncommon. The only ones you are at all likely to encounter are:

acheter, *buy*	**geler**, *freeze*
ciseler, *engrave*	**haleter**, *pant*
congeler, *(deep) freeze*	**modeler**, *model*
crocheter, *hook (up)*	**peler**, *peel*
déceler, *disclose*	**racheter**, *buy back,*
dégeler, *thaw*	*buy again*
démanteler, dismantle	

■ Verbs ending **-é[CONSONANT]er** change the **é** to **è** before a silent **e** in the same way, *except in the future and conditional tenses:*

espérer → **j'espère**, but
j'espérerai; j'espérerais

■ Verbs ending **-cer** and **-ger** change the **c** to **ç** and the **g** to **ge** before **a** and **o**. This keeps the **c** and the **g** soft:

commencer → **nous commençons**
manger → **nous mangeons**

■ Verbs ending **-oyer** and **-uyer** change the **y** to **i** before a silent **e**:

envoyer → **j'envoie**
appuyer → **j'appuie**

With verbs ending **-ayer** this change is optional:

payer → **je paie** or **je paye**

CONJUGATION OF -ir VERBS

(Second-conjugation verbs)

In all tenses **elle** (*she*), **on** (*one*), and singular nouns are followed by the **il** form of the verb; **elles** (*they*, feminine) and plural nouns are followed by the **ils** form of the verb.

infinitive	fin**ir**, *to finish*
present participle	fin**issant**, *finishing*
past participle	fin**i**, *finished*
imperative	fin**is**, *finish ...!*
	fin**issons**, *let's finish ...*
	fin**issez**, *finish ...!*

Simple tenses

present tense,	je fin**is**	nous fin**issons**
I finish, I am	tu fin**is**	vous fin**issez**
finishing	il fin**it**	ils fin**issent**

imperfect tense, I finished, I was finishing, I used to finish	je fin**issais** tu fin**issais** il fin**issait**	nous fin**issions** vous fin**issiez** ils fin**issaient**
past historic tense, I finished	je fin**is** tu fin**is** il fin**it**	nous fin**îmes** vous fin**îtes** ils fin**irent**
future tense, I shall finish, I shall be finishing	je fin**irai** tu fin**iras** il fin**ira**	nous fin**irons** vous fin**irez** ils fin**iront**
conditional tense, I should finish	je fin**irais** tu fin**irais** il fin**irait**	nous fin**irions** vous fin**iriez** ils fin**iraient**
present subjunctive, I finish, I may finish	je fin**isse** tu fin**isses** il fin**isse**	nous fin**issions** vous fin**issiez** ils fin**issent**
imperfect subjunctive*, I finished, I might finish	je fin**isse** tu fin**isses** il fin**ît**	nous fin**issions** vous fin**issiez** ils fin**issent**

Compound tenses

perfect tense, I finished, I have finished	j'**ai** fini tu **as** fini il **a** fini	nous **avons** fini vous **avez** fini ils **ont** fini
pluperfect tense, I had finished	j'**avais** fini tu **avais** fini il **avait** fini	nous **avions** fini vous **aviez** fini ils **avaient** fini
future perfect tense, I shall have finished	j'**aurai** fini tu **auras** fini il **aura** fini	nous **aurons** fini vous **aurez** fini ils **auront** fini
conditional perfect tense, I should have finished	j'**aurais** fini tu **aurais** fini il **aurait** fini	nous **aurions** fini vous **auriez** fini ils **auraient** fini

* archaic or literary

past anterior tense*, *I had finished*	j'**eus** fini tu **eus** fini il **eut** fini	nous **eûmes** fini vous **eûtes** fini ils **eurent** fini
perfect subjunctive, *I finished, I may* *have finished*	j'**ale** fini tu **ales** fini il **alt** fini	nous **ayons** fini vous **ayez** fini ils **alent** fini
pluperfect subjunctive*, *I had* *finished*	j'**eusse** fini tu **eusses** fini il **eût** fini	nous **eussions** fini vous **eussiez** fini ils **eussent** fini

CONJUGATION OF -re VERBS

(Third-conjugation verbs)

In all tenses **elle** (*she*), **on** (*one*), and singular nouns are followed by the **il** form of the verb; **elles** (*they*, feminine) and plural nouns are followed by the **ils** form of the verb.

infinitive	vend**re**, *to sell*
present participle	vend**ant**, *selling*
past participle	vend**u**, *sold*
imperative	vend**s**, *sell ...!* vend**ons**, *let's sell ...* vend**ez**, *sell ...!*

Simple tenses

present tense, *I sell, I am selling*	je vend**s** tu vend**s** il vend	nous vend**ons** vous vend**ez** ils vend**ent**
imperfect tense, *I sold, I was selling,* *I used to sell*	je vend**ais** tu vend**ais** il vend**ait**	nous vend**ions** vous vend**iez** ils vend**aient**

* archaic or literary

past historic tense, *I sold*	je vend**is**	nous vend**îmes**
	tu vend**is**	vous vend**îtes**
	il vend**it**	ils vend**irent**

future tense, *I shall sell, I shall be selling*	je vend**rai**	nous vend**rons**
	tu vend**ras**	vous vend**rez**
	il vend**ra**	ils vend**ront**

conditional tense, *I should sell*	je vend**rais**	nous vend**rions**
	tu vend**rais**	vous vend**riez**
	il vend**rait**	ils vend**raient**

present subjunctive, *I sell, I may sell*	je vend**e**	nous vend**ions**
	tu vend**es**	vous vend**iez**
	il vend**e**	ils vend**ent**

imperfect subjunctive*, *I sold, I might sell*	je vend**isse**	nous vend**issions**
	tu vend**isses**	vous vend**issiez**
	il vend**ît**	ils vend**issent**

Compound tenses

perfect tense, *I sold, I have sold, I have been selling*	j'**ai** vendu	nous **avons** vendu
	tu **as** vendu	vous **avez** vendu
	il **a** vendu	ils **ont** vendu

pluperfect tense, *I had sold, I had been selling*	j'**avais** vendu	nous **avions** vendu
	tu **avais** vendu	vous **aviez** vendu
	il **avait** vendu	ils **avaient** vendu

future perfect tense, *I shall have sold*	j'**aurai** vendu	nous **aurons** vendu
	tu **auras** vendu	vous **aurez** vendu
	il **aura** vendu	ils **auront** vendu

conditional perfect tense, *I should have sold*	j'**aurais** vendu	nous **aurions** vendu
	tu **aurais** vendu	vous **auriez** vendu
	il **aurait** vendu	ils **auraient** vendu

past anterior tense*, *I had sold*	j'**eus** vendu	nous **eûmes** vendu
	tu **eus** vendu	vous **eûtes** vendu
	il **eut** vendu	ils **eurent** vendu

* archaic or literary

perfect subjunctive, *I sold, I may have sold*	j'**aie** vendu	nous **ayons** vendu
	tu **aies** vendu	vous **ayez** vendu
	il **ait** vendu	ils **aient** vendu
pluperfect subjunctive*, *I had sold*	j'**eusse** vendu	nous **eussions** vendu
	tu **eusses** vendu	vous **eussiez** vendu
	il **eût** vendu	ils **eussent** vendu

COMPOUND TENSES

▶ For the formation of the compound tenses see p. 3.

Compound tenses formed with être

Although most verbs form their compound tenses with **avoir** as the auxiliary, two groups form these tenses with **être**: reflexive verbs and a small number of common verbs expressing motion or change of state.

■ Reflexive verbs

> **je me suis levé de bonne heure**, *I got up early*
> **tu t'étais couché tard?**, *you'd gone to bed late?*

▶ See p. 30 for the formation of reflexive verbs and p. 15 for their agreement.

■ 'Motion' verbs

This is a group of thirteen common (and a few more quite uncommon) verbs mainly expressing some kind of motion or change of state, and all intransitive (used without a direct object):

arriver, *arrive*	**il est arrivé**
partir, *set off*	**il est parti**
entrer, *enter*	**il est entré**
sortir, *go out*	**il est sorti**
aller, *go*	**il est allé**
venir, *come*	**il est venu**

* archaic or literary

monter, *go up*	**il est monté**
descendre, *go down*	**il est descendu**
mourir, *die*	**il est mort**
naître, *be born*	**il est né**
rester, *stay*	**il est resté**
tomber, *fall*	**il est tombé**
retourner, *return*	**il est retourné**

Accourir and **passer** used intransitively may take either **être** or **avoir**:

> **elle est accourue/elle a accouru**, *she ran up*

Except **convenir à** (*suit*), all compound verbs based on the above verbs also take **être** when used intransitively.

> **je suis parvenu à le faire**, *I managed to do it*
> **il est devenu soldat**, *he became a soldier*

but **cela ne lui a pas convenu**, *it didn't suit him*

▶ See p. 15 for the past-participle agreement with this group of verbs.

■ 'Motion' verbs used transitively

Some of the above verbs can also be used with a direct object (transitively). These verbs are:

> **descendre**, *to take down, to get down, to go down*
> **monter**, *to take up, to put up, to bring up, to go up*
> **entrer** (or more usually its compound, **rentrer**), *to put in, to let in, to bring in*
> **retourner**, *to turn (over)*
> **sortir**, *to take out, to bring out*

When they are used this way they take **avoir**, not **être**:

> **il a sorti un billet de cent francs de son portefeuille**, *he took a hundred-franc note from his wallet*
> **j'ai descendu l'escalier**, *I came down the stairs*

■ Verbs of motion and change of state other than those listed above always take **avoir**, whether used transitively or intransitively.

> **tu as beaucoup changé**, *you've changed a lot*

Past-participle agreement in compound tenses

■ Verbs conjugated with **avoir**

In most cases the past participle of a verb conjugated with **avoir** does not change at all. However, if an **avoir** verb has a direct object, and this precedes the verb, the past participle agrees with that object in gender and number, adding **-e** for feminine singular, **-s** for masculine plural and **-es** for feminine plural.

> **tes papiers, je les ai trouvés**, *those papers of yours, I found them*
> – agreement, because direct object **les** precedes the verb
> **voilà les papiers que tu as cherchés toute la matinée**, *there are the papers you've been looking for all morning*
> – agreement, because direct object **que**, referring to **les papiers**, precedes
> **quelle date as-tu choisie?**, *what date did you choose?*
> – agreement, because direct object **quelle date** precedes

Notice that there is no agreement with an indirect object, or with **en**, or with a direct object that does not precede the verb:

> **j'ai trouvé les papiers**, *I've found the papers*
> – no agreement, direct object **les papiers** follows

c'est à Sylvie que j'ai envoyé cet argent, *it's Sylvie I sent that money to*
- no agreement with **que**: it is the indirect object, standing for **à Sylvie**. The direct object **cet argent** follows.

les gâteaux? J'en ai mangé deux, *the cakes? I've eaten two of them*
- no agreement with **en**: it is not a true direct object

■ Verbs conjugated with **être**

□ Intransitive verbs of motion and change of state

The past participles of the thirteen 'motion' verbs and their compounds conjugated with **être** (see p. 12) agree with the subject in gender and number, adding **-e** for feminine singular, **-s** for masculine plural, **-es** for feminine plural:

elle est arrivée hier, *she arrived yesterday*
elles étaient parties bien avant midi, *they'd set off long before twelve o'clock*
ils seront déjà sortis, *they'll already have gone out*

□ Reflexive verbs

The past participles of reflexive verbs agree in gender and number with the preceding direct object, which in most cases will correspond to the subject:

elle s'est levée tard, *she got up late*
ils se sont dépêchés, *they hurried*

In some cases, however, the reflexive is an indirect object, and then there is no agreement:

elle s'est dit, « pourquoi pas? », *she said to herself, why not?*
ils se sont écrit toutes les semaines, *they wrote to each other every week*

> **elle s'est cassé la cheville**, *she broke her ankle*
> – **la cheville**, the ankle, is the direct object, **se** is
> an indirect object indicating whose ankle she
> broke

but notice:

> **quelle cheville s'est-il cassée?**, *which ankle has
> he broken?*
> – the agreement is with **quelle cheville**, which is
> the direct object, precedes, and is feminine.

■ Past participle used as an adjective

The past participle may also be used simply as an
adjective, in which case, like any other adjective, it agrees
with its noun:

> **elles sont épuisées mais contentes**, *they are
> exhausted but happy*

▶ See p. 38 for all the uses of the past participle.

USE OF TENSES

The present tense

French has only one form of the present tense,
corresponding to both the present simple and the present
continuous in English. So **je mange** translates both *I eat*
and *I am eating*. There is no possible translation of *I am
eating* using the present participle in French. If the
continuing nature of the action needs to be stressed, **être
en train de** is used:

> **mais je suis en train de déjeuner!**, *but I'm still
> eating my lunch!*

General uses of the present tense

■ As in English, the present is used not just to indicate
what is going on at the moment:

je mange un œuf, *I'm eating an egg*

but also what habitually occurs:

je mange toujours un œuf au petit déjeuner, *I always have an egg for breakfast*

■ It can also be used, again as in English, to indicate a future:

tu veux un œuf?, *are you having (going to have) an egg?*

■ The present tense is used much more frequently than in English to narrate a past series of events, not just in spoken French but in written French also:

1945. A Hiroshima, la bombe explose. Toute discussion est terminée ... *1945. In Hiroshima, the bomb exploded. All discussion was over*

This is called the historic present, and it is used to give more immediacy to past events. But see also p. 22.

Special uses of the present tense

■ Present tense with **depuis** (*for*), **depuis que** (*since*), **voilà ... que** (*since/for*) and **il y a ... que** (*since/for*)

□ **Depuis, depuis que**

With the preposition **depuis** and after the conjunction **depuis que** a French present tense is used where in English we should expect a perfect:

je suis ici depuis deux jours, *I've been here (for) two days*

je le vois beaucoup plus souvent depuis que sa femme est partie, *I've seen him a lot more often since his wife's gone*

With **depuis** plus a negative, however, the tense is the same as in English:

> **je ne l'ai pas vu depuis deux jours**, *I haven't seen him for two days*

And where the action is already completed the tense with **depuis** is also a past tense, as in English:

> **je l'ai terminé depuis deux heures**, *I finished it two hours ago*

▶ See also **depuis** + imperfect, p. 21.

□ **Voilà ... que, il y a ... que**

All that has been said above about **depuis** also holds good for the constructions **voilà ... que** and **il y a ... que** (*since/for*):

> **voilà (il y a) deux jours que je suis ici**, *I've been here for two days*
>
> **voilà (il y a) deux jours que je ne l'ai pas vu**, *I haven't seen him for two days (it's two days since I've seen him)*

■ Present tense with **venir de**

With **venir de** (*to have just* done something) we find a present tense of **venir** corresponding to a perfect in English:

> **je viens de déjeuner**, *I've just had lunch*

The literal sense of the French is 'I'm coming from having lunch' (present) rather than the English 'I have just had lunch' (perfect). This French construction ('I'm coming from') is a quite logical equivalent to **je vais déjeuner**, *I'm going to* have lunch (see p. 24).

▶ See also **venir de** + imperfect, p. 21.

The perfect tense

The perfect has two main uses in French; as a 'true' perfect and as a past narrative tense.

■ The 'true' perfect (= *I have done*)

As in English, the true perfect is used to speak of something that happened in the past and has some bearing on what is being talked about in the present:

> **j'ai mangé tous tes chocolats**, *I've eaten all your chocolates* (now there's going to be trouble!)
>
> **je suis déjà tombé trois fois**, *I've fallen over three times already* (and he's asking me to go on the ice again!)

It also corresponds to the English perfect continuous:

> **j'ai regardé la télévision tout l'après-midi**, *I've been watching television all afternoon*

Don't be tempted to use an imperfect for this—**je regardais la télévision** means *I was watching television* (when all at once something happened).

■ The past-action perfect (= *I did*)

In French, the perfect is also used for an action in past narrative, especially in speech, where English uses a simple past tense:

> **je me suis levé à sept heures, j'ai allumé la radio et je suis entré dans la salle de bains**, *I got up at seven o'clock, switched on the radio and went into the bathroom*

However, for repeated past actions, where the English simple past, *I went*, really means *I used to go* or *I would go*, French uses the imperfect:

> **on allait chaque année à Torremolinos. C'était affreux!**, *we went (= used to go) to Torremolinos every year. It was (= used to be) dreadful!*

▶ See general uses of the imperfect, below.

The imperfect tense

General uses of the imperfect

■ To indicate a repeated action:

> **il venait me chercher tous les matins à huit
> heures**, *he came and picked me up (used to
> come and pick me up; would come and pick me
> up) every morning at eight*

■ To indicate a continuing action (which is often then interrupted by a single action, for which the perfect or past historic is used):

> **j'épluchais des pommes de terre quand elle sonna
> à la porte**, *I was peeling potatoes when she
> rang the doorbell*

■ To indicate a continuing state of affairs:

> **j'ai regardé par la fenêtre. Il pleuvait**, *I looked out
> of the window. It was raining*

Imperfect or not? Choosing the right French past tense

In general, an English 'was ... ing' indicates an imperfect, and so does 'would ...', unless this has an 'if' involved or implied (*I wouldn't do that ... if I were you*), in which case the tense is the conditional—see p. 26. However, if a simple past tense is to be translated into French, you must consider whether this is one single action (past historic or perfect) or a repeated action (imperfect).

Special uses of the imperfect

■ Imperfect for a single action

More and more frequently the imperfect is used by modern writers at all levels (literature, magazines, newspapers) as a single-action tense to give greater

immediacy to an event. Here the newspaper *Le Figaro* is
recounting individual events—in the imperfect:

> **Côté cinéma, Bernard Borderie décidait de saisir
> la balle au bond. Il choisissait pour interpréter
> le rôle la toute jeune Michèle Mercier**. *For the
> film, Bernard Borderie decided to grab his
> opportunity. He chose a really young actress to
> play the part, Michèle Mercier.*

Clearly 'deciding' and 'choosing' were single, not
continous or repeated, actions. The feeling behind these
imperfect tenses seems to be: 'there he was, deciding,
choosing …' Though this use of the imperfect should be
recognized, it is not recommended that it be imitated.

■ Imperfect with **depuis** (*for*), **depuis que** (*since*), **voilà
… que** (*since/for*) and **il y avait … que** (*since/for*)

Where English uses a pluperfect continuous (*I had been
doing*) with these expressions, French uses an imperfect:

> **j'y étais depuis deux jours**, *I had been there (for)
> two days*
> **je le voyais beaucoup plus souvent depuis que sa
> femme était partie**, *I had been seeing him a lot
> more since his wife had gone*
> **il y avait deux jours que j'étais là**, *I had been there
> for two days*

All the other rules that apply to these expressions used
with the present (see pp. 17, 18) also apply when they are
used with the imperfect.

■ Imperfect with **venir de** (*to have just*)

Where English uses a simple past of *have just* …, French
uses an imperfect of **venir de**:

> **je venais de déjeuner**, *I had just had lunch*

▶ Compare **venir de** + present, p. 18.

■ Imperfect in **si** sentences

After **si** meaning *if*, the simple past in English always corresponds to an imperfect in French:

> **si j'avais ton numéro, je te téléphonerais**, *if I had your number I'd phone you*

Perfect or past historic are not possible after **si** meaning *if*; nor is the conditional, which you might be tempted to use because the main verb in such sentences is usually in the conditional.

However, as in English, the conditional can be used after **si** where it really means *whether*:

> **je ne savais pas s'il rappellerait**, *I didn't know if (whether) he would phone back*

▶ See also p. 26 for the conditional in **si** sentences.

The past historic tense

The past historic is mainly, though not exclusively, a written past narrative tense. In spoken French the perfect is usually used instead to recount past actions. However, the past historic can readily be heard in some French dialects and may also be used in standard spoken French where what is being narrated is clearly a self-contained story or a historical event.

Cases where the past historic is not used

■ The past historic is an alternative to the perfect as a narrative tense—it can never be substituted for the imperfect, or for the 'true' perfect (see p. 19).

■ In letter-writing and other personal writing the perfect, not the past historic, is normally used to narrate single actions in the past.

■ The present tense (known in this case as the historic present) may quite often be found with a past meaning, substituting for the past historic. The change to the present from the past historic (or vice versa, from the historic present to the past historic) is felt to lend more immediacy to a narrative at the point at which it occurs. The following example (here, historic present to past historic at the important moment) is taken from the magazine *Marie France*:

> Ensemble le soir, ils **font** la tournée des bistrots de la Butte, ce qui ne **va** pas sans dispute ni même sans coups ... A l'époque Picasso **est** un petit gars noiraud et rablé; immenses yeux noirs, larges épaules et des hanches fines ... Le coup de foudre **se produisit** sous une pluie battante: la jeune femme courait pour se mettre à l'abri, Picasso lui **barra** le passage en lui tendant un petit chat; elle **rit** et **accepta** sans plus de façon.
>
> *In the evenings they made the rounds of the Butte pubs together, not without rows, even blows. At the time Picasso was a swarthy, broad, stocky lad, with huge black eyes, big shoulders and narrow hips. Then, in a downpour of rain, came love at first sight: the girl was running for shelter, Picasso stood in her way offering her a kitten. She laughed, and accepted without more ado.*

The change to the past historic comes at **le coup de foudre se produisit**.

■ Future for past historic

The use of the future tense instead of the past historic for past narrative is a not uncommon journalistic device. See p. 25.

The future tense

Future tense and aller + infinitive

As well as the actual future tense (**je porterai** — *I shall wear*), there is a future formed with **aller**, just as in

English futurity may be expressed by 'I am going to':

> **je vais partir**, *I'm going to leave*

This is sometimes called the 'immediate future', but the ordinary future tense can also be used for immediate happenings, and **aller** + infinitive can be used for things well into the distant future:

> **le défilé aura lieu cet après-midi**, *the procession will take place this afternoon*
>
> **on va retourner à Torremolinos l'année prochaine**, *we're going to go to Torremolinos again next year*

In fact, **aller** + infinitive is used to stress present intention:

> **je vais lui téléphoner demain matin**, *I'm going to (I intend to) phone him tomorrow morning*

or the relationship of the future event to something that is happening in the present:

> **si tu ne fais pas attention, tu vas te couper le doigt**, *if you don't look out you'll cut our finger (a direct consequence of not watching what you're doing!)*

This will often involve an event not too far into the future, but this is not necessarily the case (note the Torremolinos example above).

Special uses of the future tense

■ Future after **quand, lorsque, dès que, aussitôt que, tant que, pendant que**

Clauses beginning *when* (**quand, lorsque**), *as soon as* (**aussitôt que, dès que**), *as long as* (**tant que**) or *whilst* (**pendant que**) have a present tense in English with futurity implied. In French the tense must be future:

> **dès que le magasin ouvrira, nous serons à votre
> service**, *as soon as the shop opens we shall be at
> your service*

With these time conjunctions French follows the strict
time-logic of the situation, so that in sentences such as
the following a future perfect must be used:

> **je te dirai quand elle sera partie**, *I'll tell you when
> she's gone* (logically, *when she will have gone*)

Note that this strict time-logic does not extend to the
conjunction **si**, *if*, which takes the same non-logical tense
as English:

> **s'il est là quand je reviendrai**, *if he's there when I
> get back* (present tense, **est**, not the more
> logical future)

■ Future as a past narrative tense

The use of the future for past narrative is also becoming
more common, especially in newspaper writing. The aim
is to heighten the effect with a sense of 'what was
destined to happen next was ...' This example comes
from *Le Figaro*:

> Michèle **fera** tout pour échapper à cette cage
> dorée. Elle **finira** par quitter la France, **tentera** une
> nouvelle carrière aux États-Unis, **se lancera** dans
> la production, **se ruinera** avec une régularité
> métronomique pour «monter» des films qui
> n'**aboutiront** guère.
>
> *Michèle did everything possible to escape from
> this gilded cage. She ended up leaving France,
> tried a new career in the United States, launched
> herself into production, ruined herself over and
> over again putting on films that had little success.*

An effect similar to that of the French could be
obtained in English using *was to* with each verb, but it

would be considerably more clumsy than the French futures are.

The conditional tenses (conditional and conditional perfect)

General uses of the conditional

■ The conditional can show future possibility (what might or might not happen if ...):

> **je ne ferais pas ça (si j'étais à ta place)**, *I shouldn't do that (if I were you)*

The 'if' clause may or may not be expressed.

■ The conditional can also show a 'future in the past'. In this use it indicates something that is to happen subsequently to some event narrated in a past tense (*would* is used for this in English):

> **elle m'a assuré qu'elle le ferait**, *she assured me she'd do it*

Conditional tenses used in si sentences

Conditional and conditional perfect tenses are very often found in sentences that include a clause beginning with **si**:

> **je serais content si elle venait**, *I'd be pleased if she came*
> **si elle était venue, j'aurais été tellement heureux**, *if she'd come I'd have been so happy*

The sequence is

> **si** + imperfect, + main clause conditional
> **si** + pluperfect, + main clause conditional perfect

▶ See also p. 22.

Special uses of the conditional tense

■ The conditional may express qualified possibility:

> **il serait peut-être temps de regarder votre avenir en face**, *it might perhaps be time to face your future*

■ The conditional may be used to avoid direct responsibility for the accuracy of a statement:

> **il y aurait quinze blessés**, *there are said to be (appear to be) fifteen injured*

■ The conditional may express a polite, hesitant request:

> **vous ne pourriez pas le revendre?**, *couldn't you perhaps sell it again?*

Literary tenses

One of the simple tenses, the imperfect subjunctive, and two of the compound tenses, the pluperfect subjunctive and the past anterior, are obsolescent or literary, to be recognized but not used.

The imperfect subjunctive

This is found in subjunctive clauses with a past meaning:

> **elle ne pensait pas qu'il le sût**, *she didn't think he knew it*

Everyday French would use a present subjunctive:

> **elle ne pensait pas qu'il le sache**

The pluperfect subjunctive

■ This is used where the verb has a pluperfect meaning:

> **il téléphona, bien qu'elle fût déjà partie**, *he telephoned, even though she had already left*

Here, everyday French would use a perfect subjunctive:

> **il téléphona, bien qu'elle soit déjà partie**

■ It is also used in literary French instead of the conditional perfect:

> **Rodrigue, qui l'eût cru? ... Chimène, qui l'eût dit? ...** *Rodrigue, who would have believed it?—Chimène, who would have said it?*
>
> (Corneille: *Le Cid*)

The past anterior

This is used with a pluperfect meaning after the conjunctions **quand, lorsque, dès que, aussitôt que,** but only when the verb in the main clause is in the past historic:

> **quand elle eut fini de parler, il se leva et sortit,** *when she had finished speaking, he got up and went out*

THE IMPERATIVE

The imperative is used to give orders or instructions or to express requests.

Formation of the imperative

The imperative has three forms, which are the same as the **tu, nous,** and **vous** parts of the present tense of the verb:

> **choisis,** *choose!*
> **choisissons,** *let's choose*
> **choisissez,** *choose!*

■ First conjugation (**-er**) verbs lose the final **-s** of the **tu** form of the imperative, unless followed by **y** or **en**:

> **donne-le-moi,** *give it to me*
> **donnes-en à ton amie,** *give some to your friend*
> **va dans ta chambre!,** *go to your room!*

So do irregular verbs whose **tu** form of the present ends
in **-es**:

> **ouvre la porte**, *open the door*

▶ For form, order and position of pronoun objects with
the imperative, see p. 106.

■ In the negative the **ne** and **pas** etc. go round the verb
in the usual way:

> **ne choisissez pas encore**, *don't choose yet*

■ Third-person commands (*let him/her/it/them ...*) are
expressed by using **que** plus the present subjunctive:

> **qu'il le trouve lui-même**, *let him find it himself!*

Alternatives to the imperative

An imperative need not be used to express a command.
There are a number of other ways of doing it.

■ Politer than the imperative is **voulez-vous
(veux-tu) ...**, *will you/would you ...*, or **auriez-vous
l'amabilité de ...**, *would you be so kind as to ...*:

> **voulez-vous chercher mon sac?**, *would you look
> for my bag?*
> **auriez-vous l'amabilité de me passer ma valise?**,
> *would you be so kind as to pass me my case?*

■ The imperative of **vouloir** plus the infinitive is found
as an alternative to the imperative in formal language and
in the ending to formal letters:

> **veuillez signer ici**, *kindly sign here*
> **Veuillez agréer, chère madame, l'expression de
> mes sentiments les plus distingués**, *Yours
> sincerely*

■ In official notices and in recipes an infinitive, or
défense de ..., or **... interdit** may be found instead of
an imperative:

> **ne pas se pencher au dehors**, *do not lean out*
> **défense de fumer**, *no smoking*
> **entrée interdite**, *no entry*

■ The future tense may also express a command, as in English:

> **vous ferez exactement ce que je vous dirai**, *you'll do exactly what I say*

REFLEXIVE VERBS

Reflexive verbs are verbs whose direct or indirect object is the same as their subject (*he scratches himself; she allows herself a chocolate*). In French they consist of a simple verb preceded by a reflexive pronoun:

> **il arrête le train**, *he stops the train*—simple verb
> **le train s'arrête**, *the train stops (itself)*—reflexive verb

■ The reflexive pronouns

Apart from **se**, they are the same as the ordinary object pronouns:

> **me**, *(to) myself*
> **te**, *(to) yourself*
> **se**, *(to) himself, (to) herself, (to) itself, (to) oneself, (to) themselves*
> **nous**, *(to) ourselves*
> **vous**, *(to) yourself, (to) yourselves*

Me, te, and **se** become **m', t',** and **s'** before a vowel or **h** 'mute'. **Te** becomes **toi** when used with the imperative (see p. 107).

The reflexive pronoun corresponding to **on** is **se**:

> **on s'y habitue**, *you get used to it*

□ The reflexive pronouns are the same whether they are

direct or indirect objects, and stand before the verb in
the same way as other object pronouns.

▶ For the order of object pronouns, including reflexives,
see p. 106.

☐ Reflexive pronouns in the plural—**nous, vous, se**—as
well as meaning *(to) ourselves, (to) yourselves, (to)
themselves,* can also mean *(to) one another* or *(to) each
other.* This includes **se** when it refers to **on** with a plural
meaning (*we, you, people,* etc.):

> **ils se détestent**, *they hate each other*
> **elles se téléphonent tous les soirs**, *they phone
> each other every evening*
> **on s'aime**, *we love one another*

If ambiguity might otherwise result, **l'un(e) l'autre /
les un(e)s les autres** is added, where the reflexive is a
direct object; or **l'un(e) à l'autre / les un(e)s aux
autres,** where the reflexive is an indirect object:

> **nous nous sommes demandé, si ...,** *we wondered
> (asked ourselves) whether ...*
> **nous nous sommes demandé l'un à l'autre, si ...,**
> *we asked each other, whether ...*

■ Compound tenses of reflexive verbs are formed with
être, not **avoir**.

In compound tenses the past participle of a reflexive
verb agrees with a preceding direct object. Since direct
object and subject are usually the same, this means that
the past participle of a reflexive verb appears to agree
with its subject. However, this is not always the case:

> **elle s'est lavée**, *she washed (herself)*
> **elle s'est lavé les cheveux**, *she washed her hair*

▶ See also p. 15.

■ A French reflexive verb may correspond to an English
one:

il se gratte, *he scratches himself*

but very often it does not:

elle s'assoit, *she sits down*
il se lave, *he washes*

■ Reflexive verbs are occasionally used in French where English uses a passive:

je m'étonne: je croyais que c'était gratuit, *I'm surprised, I thought it was free*
cela ne se vend pas ici, *it's not sold here*

► See p. 34 for this and other alternatives to the passive.

■ Reflexive verbs may sometimes have the sense of 'becoming':

je m'ennuie, *I'm getting bored*
elle s'impatientait, *she was becoming impatient*

THE PASSIVE

The passive forms of the tenses are those where the subject of the verb experiences the action rather than performs it (active: *he helped*; passive: *he was helped*).

Formation of the passive

The passive in English is formed with parts of the verb *to be* plus the past participle; in French it is formed in exactly the same way with parts of **être** plus the past participle:

elle est détestée, *she is hated*
il était protégé par sa femme, *he was protected by his wife*
la ville avait été abandonnée par ses habitants, *the town had been abandoned by its inhabitants*

In the passive the past participle always agrees with the subject, in the same way that an adjective would.

■ In English the 'doer' of the action is indicated by *by* (as in this sentence you're reading). This is **par**, or sometimes **de**, in French. **Par** is more specific:

> **il a été tué par sa femme**, *he was killed by his wife*
>
> **elle est bien vue de tout le monde**, *she is well regarded by everyone*

However, where *by* refers to the instrument used, rather than the person doing the action, **de** is always used in French:

> **il a été tué d'un coup de revolver**, *he was killed by a revolver shot*

■ In English, the indirect object of an active verb may be made into the subject of the corresponding passive verb:

> *someone gave the book to me → I was given the book*
>
> *Paul gave the book to me → I was given the book by Paul*

This is impossible in French. *I was given the book* can be translated using **on**:

> **on m'a donné le livre** (literally, *someone has given me the book*)

However, in the second example, *I was given the book by Paul*, where the 'doer' of the action is stated, the sentence has to remain active in French:

> **Paul m'a donné le livre**

Or, if the English sentence stresses 'Paul':

> **c'est Paul qui m'a donné le livre**

Alternatives to the passive

The passive is frequently avoided in French, especially when the 'doer' of the action is not mentioned.

■ Most frequently **on** is used:

> **on l'avait abandonné**, *it had been abandoned*

■ Sometimes a reflexive verb may be used:

> **cela ne se fait pas!**, *that's not done!*
> **la porte s'ouvre**, *the door is (being) opened* (**la porte est ouverte** would mean *the door is— already—open*)

■ Or an active form may be preferred where English would use a passive:

> **ta lettre les a bouleversés**, *they've been shattered by your letter*

■ Occasionally, where the subject is a person, **se faire** is used:

> **il s'est fait renvoyer en Espagne**, *he's been sent (got himself sent) back to Spain*
> **nous nous sommes fait renvoyer**, *we've been sacked*

PARTICIPLES

The present participle

Formation of the present participle

The present participle (in English, the *-ing* part of the verb) is formed in French by substituting **-ant** for **-ons** in the **nous** form of the present tense of the verb:

> **choisir → nous choisissons → choisissant**

There are only three present participles which are exceptions to this rule:

être: étant
avoir: ayant
savoir: sachant (but **savant** where the present
    participle is used as an adjective: **un phoque**
    savant, *a performing seal*)

Note also the two spellings of **fatiguant/fatigant**, the
second used adjectivally:

en fatiguant la salade, *whilst dressing the salad*
une journée fatigante, *an exhausting day*

Uses of the present participle

■ As an adjective

The present participle can be used as an adjective. When
it is so used, it behaves exactly as other adjectives. So it
agrees with its noun, and qualifying adverbs precede it:

l'année suivante, *the following year*
une femme incroyablement charmante, *an*
    incredibly charming woman

■ As a verb

The present participle can also be used verbally in a
phrase with or without **en** (= *in*, *by*, *whilst*). When the
present participle is used verbally, pronoun objects stand
in front of it and adverbs after it, just as with any other
part of the verb:

en la rencontrant un jour dans la rue, il lui a
    adressé la parole, *(on) meeting her one day in*
    the street, he spoke to her

Negatives go round it, as they go round other parts of
the verb:

ne sachant pas que vous étiez là, elle se tourna
    vers moi, *not knowing you were there, she*
    turned to me

In this verbal use the present participle, since it is not an adjective, does not take adjective agreements.

☐ With or without **en**

When the present participle is used verbally without **en**, the two actions (that of the present participle and that of the main verb) follow one another. When the participle is used with **en** the actions go on simultaneously:

> **se retournant, elle répondit ...**, *turning round, she replied ...*
>
> **en tombant, elle a entrainé une lampe**, *in falling (as she fell), she brought down a lamp*
>
> **comment s'est-elle fait mal? — En tombant**, *how did she hurt herself? By falling (When she fell)*

En with a present participle usually corresponds to the English *on ... ing, by ... ing, in ... ing, whilst ... ing*.

☐ With **tout en**

The addition of **tout** to the above construction (**tout en ...**) draws attention to the fact that the two actions were going on together, often over a period of time. **Tout en** is usually translated as *whilst*:

> **tout en me parlant, il allumait sa pipe**, *whilst (all the time he was) speaking to me, he was lighting his pipe*

Tout en can also have the meaning of *whilst* (*on the one hand*):

> **tout en reconnaissant ce que vous avez fait, je dois vous dire que ...**, *whilst recognizing what you have done, I have to tell you that ...*

☐ With verbs of motion

English can make a verbal phrase by using a verb of motion plus a preposition (*swim away, fly off, run out*).

French has no equivalent construction and uses a variety of strategies to deal with these concepts (**partir à la nage, s'envoler**, etc.). One of these is to make the preposition into a verb and then add a present participle with **en**: **sortir en courant**, *run out*. This present-participle construction is most frequently found with **courir**.

▶ See also translation problems, p. 233.

■ As a noun

Present participles are occasionally used as nouns. They add **-e** for feminine, **-(e)s** for plural forms: **l'occupant**, *occupier*; **la passante**, *(woman) passer-by*; **des anciens combattants**, *old soldiers*.

▶ The present participle can never be used in French with an auxiliary verb, as it is in English. *I am sleeping* has to be **je dors**. See p. 16.

The perfect participle

In English, the perfect participle is formed with the present participle of *to have* plus the past participle of the verb. In French the perfect participle is formed in an exactly parallel way, using the present participle of **avoir** plus the past participle of the verb:

> **ayant dit cela, elle s'assit**, *having said that, she sat down*

Verbs that form their compound tenses with **être** also form their perfect participle with **être**:

> **étant arrivée de très bonne heure, elle acheta un journal**, *having arrived very early, she bought a newspaper*
> **s'étant déjà baigné, il revint sur la terrasse de la villa**, *having already had his dip, he came back on to the terrace of the villa*

As the above examples show, the use of the perfect participle in French exactly parallels its use in English.

The past participle

Formation of the past participle

Past participles of regular verbs are formed by removing the ending of the infinitive (**-er**, **-ir**, **-re**) and adding **-é**, **-i**, **-u**:

> **porter → porté**, *carried*
> **choisir → choisi**, *chosen*
> **vendre → vendu**, *sold*

▶ For the past participles of irregular verbs see the verb list, p. 242.

Uses of the past participle

■ The past participle is used to form all the compound tenses.

▶ See p. 3 (compound tense formation), p. 14 (past-participle agreement).

■ The past participle is used with **être** to form the passive.

▶ See p. 32.

■ The past participle may be used adjectivally; it then agrees with its noun, takes an adverb qualification, etc., just like any other adjective:

> **elle était complètement épuisée**, *she was completely exhausted*

■ The past participle may also occasionally be used as a noun:

> **le reçu**, *receipt*
> **les rescapés**, *survivors*

■ French sometimes uses a past participle where English

would use a present participle. Mostly this is to describe positions of the body. Common examples are:

accoudé, *leaning (on one's elbows)*	**couché**, *lying (e.g. in bed)*
agenouillé, *kneeling*	**étendu**, *lying*
appuyé, *leaning*	*(outstretched)*
assis, *sitting*	**(sus)pendu**, *hanging*

une seule lampe était suspendue au plafond, *just one lamp was hanging from the ceiling*

il était agenouillé devant l'autel, *he was kneeling before the altar*

THE SUBJUNCTIVE

The subjunctive, expressing doubt or unreality, barely exists any longer in English (*if I were you*; *if that be so*; *would that he were*). In French, though some of its tenses are literary or archaic, it is still in constant use in both the spoken and the written language.

The subjunctive is found in subordinate clauses beginning with **que** meaning *that*, though by no means all such clauses have a subjunctive. The subjunctive in French originally showed the speaker's attitude to an event in the light of his or her emotion (doubt, disbelief, pleasure, etc.). Nowadays it has become fixed as the form used after certain verbs or certain conjunctions, most of which still express some sort of emotion. In only a limited number of cases, however, noted below, is there still a choice between using or not using the subjunctive.

Formation of the subjunctive

The subjunctive has four tenses in French. Of these only the present subjunctive and, on the not very frequent occasions where a perfect meaning is necessary, the perfect subjunctive are in modern everyday use. The tenses are formed as follows:

■ Present subjunctive

The present subjunctive is formed from the **ils** form of the present tense with endings as follows:

choisir → ils choisissent → choisiss-

je choisiss**e**	nous choisiss**ions**
tu choisiss**es**	vous choisiss**iez**
il choisiss**e**	ils choisiss**ent**

This normally produces, as with **choisir** above, **nous** and **vous** forms identical with those of the imperfect tense. In the few cases where this would not be so, **nous** and **vous** forms of the imperfect tense are used for present subjunctive **nous** and **vous**:

prendre → ils prennent → prenn-

je prenne	**nous prenions**
tu prennes	**vous preniez**
il prenne	ils prennent

The following verbs do not follow this pattern:

> **aller, avoir, être, faire, falloir, pouvoir, savoir, valoir, vouloir**

▶ For the subjunctive forms of these verbs, see the list of irregular verbs, p. 242.

■ Perfect subjunctive

Use the present subjunctive of **avoir** or **être** with the past participle of the verb:

j'aie choisi	**nous ayons** choisi
tu aies choisi	**vous ayez** choisi
il ait choisi	**ils aient** choisi
je **sois** arrivé(e)	**nous soyons** arrivé(e)s
tu **sois** arrivé(e)	**vous soyez** arrivé(e)(s)
il **soit** arrivé	**ils soient** arrivés

■ Imperfect subjunctive

The imperfect subjunctive is based on the past historic tense, as follows:

-er verbs (past historic: **je portai**):

je port**asse**	nous port**assions**
tu port**asses**	vous port**assiez**
il port**ât**	ils port**assent**

-ir and **-re** verbs (past historic: **je choisis, je vendis**):

je vend**isse**	nous vend**issions**
tu vend**isses**	vous vend**issiez**
il vend**ît**	ils vend**issent**

Irregular verbs that form their past historic with **-us** etc. form their imperfect subjunctive with **-usse**:

être:	je f**usse**	nous f**ussions**
	tu f**usses**	vous f**ussiez**
	il f**ût**	ils f**ussent**

▶ See the irregular verb list, p. 242.

■ Pluperfect subjunctive

Formed from the imperfect subjunctive of **avoir** or **être** plus the past participle:

> **j'eusse** choisi, etc.
> **je fusse** parti, etc.

■ Future subjunctive

This tense does not exist. To express future meanings in subjunctive clauses, **devoir** must be used. See p. 67.

Uses of the subjunctive

■ The subjunctive is used after certain verbs; the ones listed are those most frequently met:

☐ Verbs of expectancy, wishing, wanting

> **vouloir que**, *wish; want*
> **souhaiter que**, *wish*
> **attendre que**, *wait until*
> **désirer que**, *want*
> **préférer que**, *prefer*
> **aimer mieux que**, *prefer*
> **il est préférable que**, *it is preferable*
> **il vaut mieux que**, *it is better*
> **il est important que**, *it is important*
>
> **il est important que tu le saches**, *it's important that you know*

With verbs of wishing, preferring, etc., English very often uses an infinitive dependent on an object—*they prefer us to go*. This is impossible in French and must always be translated by a dependent clause (= *they prefer that we should go*):

> **ils préfèrent que nous partions**, *they prefer us to go*
> **que voulez-vous qu'on fasse pour les jeunes chômeurs?**, *what do you want us to do for the young unemployed?*

Note that **espérer que**, *hope*, does not take the subjunctive.

☐ Verbs of necessity

> **il faut que**, *must*
> **il est nécessaire/urgent que**, *it is necessary/ urgent*
>
> **il faut que vous vous débrouilliez tout seul**, *you must sort it out on your own*

☐ Verbs of ordering, forbidding, allowing

> **ordonner que**, *order*
> **dire que**, *tell*

défendre que, *forbid*
permettre que, *allow*
s'opposer à ce que, *be opposed (to someone doing ...)*

je ne permets pas que vous voyagiez seule, *I shall not allow you to travel alone*

With **dire que** there is a difference in meaning according to whether the subjunctive is used or not:

dites au messager qu'il part ce soir, *tell the courier he's leaving tonight* (piece of information)
dites au messager qu'il parte ce soir, *tell the courier to leave tonight* (command)

☐ Verbs of possibility

il est possible que, *it is possible*
il se peut que, *it is possible*
il semble que, *it seems*
il paraît que, *it seems*
il est peu probable que, *it is improbable*
il est impossible que, *it is impossible*

se peut-il qu'elle soit déjà là?, *is it possible that she's there already?*

Note that **il est probable que**, *it is probable*, and **il me semble/me paraît que**, *it seems to me*, do not generally take the subjunctive.

☐ Verbs of surprise and incomprehension

s'étonner que, *be surprised*
être surpris/étonné que, *be surprised*
quelle chance que, *what luck*
il me paraît curieux/surprenant/incroyable etc. **que**, *it seems odd/surprising/unbelievable*

je m'étonne qu'il y ait autant de chômeurs, *I'm surprised there are so many unemployed*

☐ Verbs of uncertainty

> **il n'est pas certain que**, *it is not certain*
> **il n'est pas évident/vrai que**, *it is not obvious/true*
> **je ne nie pas que**, *I don't deny*
> **mettons/supposons que**, *let us assume*
>
> **mettons que les réponses de ce sondage soient exactes**, *let us assume that the replies to this poll are correct*

☐ Verbs of doubt and disbelief

> **douter que**, *doubt*
> **il est douteux que**,
>   *it is doubtful*
>
> **penser que**, *think*
> **croire que**, *believe*
> **trouver**, *think*   in the
> **s'attendre à ce que**, *expect*   negative or
> **être sûr/certain**,   interrogative
>   *be sure/certain*
>
> **je ne crois pas qu'elle t'ait dit des choses pareilles**, *I don't believe she said things like that to you*

With the last five verbs above there is a difference in meaning according to whether the subjunctive is used or not:

> **je ne pense pas qu'il pleut**, *I don't think it's raining* (I'm fairly sure it isn't)
> **je ne pense pas qu'il pleuve**, *I don't <u>think</u> it's raining* (though it may be)

☐ Verbs of liking, pleasure, dislike, displeasure

> **aimer que**, *like*
> **adorer que**, *love*
> **ça me plaît que**, *I'm glad*
> **être content/heureux/enchanté que**, *be glad/ happy/delighted*
> **détester que**, *hate*

j'aime que vous chantiez comme ça, *I like you to sing like that*

☐ Verbs of regret and concern

regretter que, *be sorry*
être désolé que, *be sorry*
c'est dommage que, *it's a pity*
avoir peur que ... (ne), *be afraid*
craindre que ... (ne), *be afraid,* (and the related conjunctions **de peur que ... (ne), de crainte que ... (ne),** *for fear that*)
être fâché que, *be annoyed that*
avoir honte que, *be ashamed that*

je suis désolé qu'elle ne puisse pas venir, *I'm sorry she can't come*

▶ The use of **ne** with **avoir peur que, craindre que,** and **de peur/crainte que** is formal or literary. See p. 162.

■ The subjunctive is used after certain conjunctions. The common ones are:

☐ **bien que/quoique,** *although*

bien que tout le monde se connaisse au village, personne ne lui parlait, *although everyone knew each other in the village, no-one would speak to him*

☐ **afin que/pour que,** *so that; for*

ils ont tout fait pour qu'il vienne le plus souvent possible, *they did everything so (that) he would come as often as possible*

☐ **à moins que ... (ne),** *unless*

il y aura une catastrophe à moins que vous ne trouviez une solution rapidement, *there'll be a disaster unless you find a solution quickly*

▶ The use of **ne** (without **pas**, and with no negative

meaning) is still quite commonly found after **à moins que**, although even here it is tending to disappear except in formal or literary language. See p. 163.

☐ **que**, *whether*; **que … que**, *whether … whether*; **soit que … soit que**, *whether … whether* (literary)

> **les Français aiment le rock, qu'il soit hard ou qu'il ne le soit pas**, *the French like rock, whether it's hard or not*
> **qu'on parte ou non**, *whether we leave or not*

☐ **jusqu'à ce que / en attendant que**, *until*

> **restez là jusqu'à ce qu'elle vienne**, *wait there until she comes*

☐ **avant que … (ne)**, *before*

> **ne bougez pas avant qu'elle parte**, *don't move before she goes*

The subjunctive is nowadays very commonly also used after **après que**, *after*, though not in careful or literary French.

▶ The use of **ne** after **avant que** is formal or literary. See p. 163.

☐ **pourvu que / à condition que**, *provided that*

> **oui, pourvu que vous le disiez au patron**, *yes, provided that you tell the boss*

☐ **si … que**, *however*; **qui que**, *whoever*; **quoi que**, *whatever*

> **cet édifice, si imposant qu'il soit**, *this building, however impressive it may be*
> **qui qu'elle soit, quoi qu'elle dise, ne la crois pas**, *whoever she is, whatever she says, don't believe her*

▶ See also p. 233.

☐ **sans que**, *without*

> **faites-le, sans que nous en sachions rien**, *do it without us knowing anything about it*

☐ **de sorte que / de façon que / de manière que**, *so that* (= *with the inention that*)

> **on le fera, de sorte que vous puissiez voir toutes les possibilités**, *we'll do it, so that you can see all the possibilities*

Note that when these conjunctions express result, they are not followed by the subjunctive:

> **on l'a fait de sorte qu'ils ont pu voir toutes les possibilités**, *we did it in such a way that they could see all the possibilities*

■ The subjunctive is also used in the following cases:

☐ To relate back to a superlative, or to the adjectives **premier, dernier, seul, unique**, which convey a superlative idea

> **la Bretagne est la première province française qu'on ait dotée d'un programme d'action**, *Britanny is the first French province to have been provided with an action programme*

The subjunctive is not always found in these constructions.

☐ To express a 'required characteristic'

> **il cherchait quelque chose qui puisse le protéger**, *he was looking for something that could protect him*

With this construction the subjunctive is not used if the thing characterized is actually known to exist:

> **il cherchait la seule chose qui pouvait le protéger: son casque**, *he was looking for the only thing that could protect him, his helmet*

☐ To express a third person command

> **que le ciel soit loué!**, *heaven be praised!*

☐ In a second 'if' clause, where **que** is substituted for **si**

> **si tu veux nous accompagner, et que tu puisses être prêt avant huit heures, on t'emmènera**, *if you want to go with us, and you can be ready by eight o'clock, we'll take you*

The substitution of **que** for the second **si** is not obligatory; a second **si** would not be followed by the subjunctive.

☐ Instead of a conditional perfect in literary French. The tense used is the pluperfect subjunctive

> **il ne l'eût pas fait**, *he would not have done it*

Avoiding the subjunctive

Though the French use the subjunctive a great deal in everyday conversation, it is most frequently found after expressions of desire, necessity, and regret (**je veux que ...**, **il faut que ...**, **je suis désolé que ...**). Otherwise it tends to indicate high style, and expressions involving it are avoided wherever possible. So

> **il est possible qu'elle vienne aujourd'hui**, *it's possible that she'll come today*

becomes

> **peut-être qu'elle va venir aujourd'hui**, *perhaps she'll come today*

and

> **on le fera demain, à moins qu'elle ne vienne aujourd'hui**, *we'll do it tomorrow, unless she comes today*

becomes

> **on le fera demain, si elle ne vient pas aujourd'hui**, *we'll do it tomorrow, if she doesn't come today*

and

> **donne-le-lui avant qu'elle parte**, *give it to her before she goes*

becomes

> **donne-le-lui avant son départ**, *give it to her before her departure*

■ The subjunctive is also avoided where both verbs would have the same subject, by using the appropriate preposition and a dependent infinitive. English frequently does this too:

> **je suis désolé d'apprendre la mauvaise nouvelle de cette façon**, *I'm sorry to hear (that I should hear) the bad news in this way* (instead of '**je suis désolé que j'apprenne la mauvaise nouvelle de cette façon**')

▶ See p. 51 for the infinitive after verbs and pp. 51, 52 for the infinitive after adjectives.

■ In the same way, the subjunctive can be avoided with impersonal verbs by using a dependent infinitive:

> **il a fallu que je repense tout → il a fallu tout repenser**, *I had to rethink everything*

If there is any ambiguity about what the subject of the infinitive is, then a subjunctive clause must be used. The use of an indirect object with the main verb (**il m'a fallu tout repenser**) is literary.

THE INFINITIVE

The infinitive, what it is

Infinitives of French regular verbs end in **-er**, **-ir**, or **-re**, corresponding to the English *to ...* form of the verb:

> **porter**, *to wear*
> **choisir**, *to choose*
> **vendre**, *to sell*

The infinitive is the 'name' of the verb: it is really a sort of noun, and as such can be the subject or object of a verb, or stand after a preposition:

> **fumer, c'est dangereux**, *smoking is dangerous*
> **défense de fumer**, *no smoking*

Notice, in the examples above, that English usually uses the *-ing* form of the verb rather than the infinitive as the verbal noun.

Some infinitives have become true nouns and take an article. They are always masculine:

> **à prendre après manger**, *to be taken after meals* (**manger**, *to eat*)
> **un homme de savoir**, *a man of learning* (**savoir**, *to know*)

■ Pronoun objects stand in front of the infinitive:

> **pour le regarder**, *in order to look at it*

■ Both parts of a negative stand in front of the infinitive and its object pronouns:

un film à ne pas manquer, *a film not to be missed*
pour ne plus le regarder, *in order not to look at it any more*

The infinitive after a verb

Infinitives usually follow another verb, and in English they are joined to it by *to*. In French they are joined to it by **à, de,** or nothing at all. Which of these is used depends on the head verb, not on the infinitive, and it doesn't vary—it is always, for instance, **se mettre à** + infinitive (*begin to*), **essayer de** + infinitive (*try to*), **vouloir** + infinitive (*want to*).

▶ For the correct preposition to use with any verb (**à, de,** or nothing) see the alphabetical list on pp. 59–64.

■ It is normally impossible in French for an infinitive to depend on the object of another verb as it can in English:

> *I want Fred to listen to me*—Fred is the object of *want*, but Fred is also the subject of *listen*.

A subordinate clause has to be used for this in French (see p. 42):

> **je veux que Fred m'écoute**, *I want Fred to listen to me*

However, with a verb of perceiving (seeing, hearing, feeling, etc.) a construction similar to the English one is possible:

> **je l'ai regardé travailler**, *I watched him work*

▶ See also p. 232.

The infinitive after adjectives, nouns, and adverbs

Infinitives may also follow adjectives, nouns, and adverbial expressions of quantity (**beaucoup, trop,** etc.).

A preposition is used before the infinitive and in most cases this is **de**:

> **je suis étonné de te voir**, *I'm surprised to see you*
> **je n'ai pas le temps de te parler**, *I haven't the time to speak to you*

Sometimes, however, the infinitive has a passive sense (*to be done* rather than *to do*), and in this case **à** is used:

> **j'ai beaucoup à faire**, *I've a lot to do* (= *to be done*)
> **j'ai deux pièces à tapisser**, *I've two rooms to paper* (= *to be papered*)
> **c'est une pièce très difficile à tapisser**, *it's a very difficult room to paper* (= *to be papered*).
> Compare: **il est très difficile de tapisser cette pièce**, *it's very difficult to paper this room*

There are one or two exceptions to this. In spite of the following infinitive having an active sense, **à** is always used with:

> **disposé à**, *willing to*
> **lent à**, *slow to*
> **prêt à**, *ready to*
> **prompt à**, *prompt in*
>
> **vous êtes prêts à partir?**, *you're ready to go?*

and with **unique**, **seul**, **dernier** and the ordinal numbers:

> **il était le seul à venir**, *he was the only one to come*

The infinitive after prepositions

▶ For infinitives following **à** and **de**:
after verbs, see pp. 55 and 56;
after adjectives, nouns and adverbs, see p. 51.

Infinitives may also follow the prepositions **après**, **par**, **sans**, and **pour**, and many compound prepositions formed with **de** (**au lieu de**, **avant de**, etc.):

> **sans bouger**, *without moving*
> **pour sortir**, *in order to go out*
> **je commence par citer Molière**, *I shall begin by quoting Molière*

■ In English, the part of the verb which follows a preposition is in almost all cases the present participle (*without looking, after eating*). In French it is always an infinitive, except after **en** where the present participle is used: **en revenant**, *on coming back*. See p. 35.

■ Always after **après**, and sometimes, according to meaning, after other prepositions, a perfect infinitive is used:

> **après l'avoir mangé**, *after eating (having eaten) it*
> **il est en prison pour avoir volé une voiture**, *he's in prison for having stolen a car*

▶ For the perfect infinitive, see below.

Other uses of the infinitive

■ In literary French the infinitive may be found, preceded by **de**, instead of a past historic:

> **et Yves de répondre «Mais non»**, *and Yves replied 'Of course not'*

■ The infinitive may also be used as an imperative. See p. 29.

The perfect infinitive

The perfect infinitive is formed with the infinitive of **avoir** or **être** plus the past participle of the verb:

> **avoir porté**, *to have worn*
> **être parti**, *to have gone*
> **s'être dépêché**, *to have hurried*

Past participles make the same agreements as in the compound tenses of the verb.

As well as being used after **après** and other prepositions (see p. 53), the perfect infinitive is used after a number of verbs where logic demands it. Common ones are:

> **se souvenir de/se rappeler**, *remember*
> **remercier de**, *thank for*
> **regretter de/être désolé de**, *be sorry for*
> **pardonner (à quelqu'un) de**, *forgive (somebody) for*

Beware: the tense of the equivalent English verb may not be the logical one!

> **je me souviens de l'avoir dit**, *I remember saying (having said) it*
> **je vous remercie d'avoir téléphoné**, *thank you for phoning (having phoned)*
> **elle est désolée de nous avoir dérangés**, *she's sorry to have (for having) disturbed us*
> **pardonne-moi de t'avoir retardé**, *forgive me for holding you up (having held you up)*

PREPOSITIONS AFTER VERBS

Prepositions with infinitives

In English a verb is linked to a following infinitive either by *to* (*I hope to go*) or by nothing at all (*I must go*). The constructions are invariable, we always use *hope + to*, *must* + *nothing*, whatever the infinitive that follows. The same is true of French, except that in French there are three possibilities, **de**, **à**, and nothing.

■ Verb + **de** + infinitive:

il essaie de le faire, *he tries to do it*

This is by far the largest group and if a verb does not belong to one of the two other groups below, it should be assumed to take **de**.

■ Verb + nothing + infinitive

This is a relatively small group of rather common verbs. It includes:

☐ Verbs of expectancy (wanting, hoping)

j'espère vous revoir, *I hope to see you again*

☐ Verbs of perception (seeing, hearing, feeling)

l'entends-tu venir?, *can you hear him coming?*

☐ Verbs of liking and dislike

je déteste nager dans l'eau froide, *I hate swimming in cold water*

☐ The modal verbs (**vouloir, pouvoir**, etc. See p. 64)

je ne sais pas nager, *I can't swim*

☐ Intransitive verbs of motion (**aller, monter, sortir**, etc.)

va chercher ton père, *go and look for your father* (note that the *and* used in English with these verbs is not used in French)

Pour may also be used with these verbs to stress the purpose of the action:

Il est entré dans le garage pour chercher une pelle, *he went into the garage (in order) to look for a spade*

The most frequently met verbs taking an infinitive without a preposition are:

adorer, *adore*
aimer (mieux), *prefer*
aller, *go*
compter, *expect*
croire, *think*
descendre, *come down*
désirer, *want*
détester, *hate*
devoir, *have to*
écouter, *listen to*
entendre, *hear*
entrer, *come in*

envoyer, *send*
espérer, *hope*
faillir, *almost (do)*
faire, *have (done)*
falloir, *must*
laisser, *let*
monter, *go up*
oser, *dare*
paraître, *seem*
partir, *go off*
pouvoir, *can*
préférer, *prefer*

prétendre, *claim*
se rappeler, *remember*
regarder, *look at*
rentrer, *come in*
sembler, *seem*
(se) sentir, *feel*
sortir, *go out*
souhaiter, *wish*
valoir mieux, *be better*
venir, *come*
voir, *see*
vouloir, *want*

▶ For a fuller treatment of **faire** and **laisser** + infinitive see p. 71.

■ Verb + **à** + infinitive

This is also a small group of verbs. They are less heavily used, but still common. The **à** indicates aim or direction. The most frequently met verbs in this group are:

aider à, *help*
s'amuser à, *enjoy oneself*
apprendre à, *learn*
s'apprêter à, *get ready*
arriver à, *manage*
s'attendre à, *expect*
avoir à, *have*

chercher à, *try*
commencer à, *begin*
consentir à, *consent*
consister à, *consist (in)*
continuer à, *continue*
se décider à, *decide; make up one's mind*

demander à, *ask*
encourager à, *encourage*
enseigner à, *teach*
forcer à, *force*
s'habituer à, *get used*
hésiter à, *hesitate*
s'intéresser à, *be interested*
inviter à, *invite*

se mettre à, start	**perdre du temps à**, waste time	**renoncer à**, *give up*
obliger à, *force*	**persister à**, persist	**rester à**, *be left*
parvenir à, *manage*		**réussir à**, *manage*
passer du temps à, spend time	**pousser à**, *urge*	**servir à**, *be used*
penser à, *think*	**(se) préparer à**, prepare	**songer à**, *think*
		tarder à, *be late*
		tenir à, *be keen*

▶ See p. 59 for an alphabetical list of infinitive and noun constructions after verbs.

Prepositions with nouns and pronouns

Most French verbs have the same preposition before a following noun as their English equivalents. There are three main groups where this is not the case.

■ Verbs with a direct object where we should expect a preposition:

> **attendez-moi!**, *wait for me!*

The most frequently met verbs of this kind are:

approuver, *approve of*	**habiter**, *live at*
attendre, *wait for*	**mettre**, *put on*
chercher, *look for*	**payer**, *pay for*
demander, *ask for*	**regarder**, *look at*
écouter, *listen to*	**reprocher**, *blame for*
essayer, *try on*	

■ Verbs taking **de** where we should expect nothing:

> **elle joue du violon**, *she plays the violin*

The most frequently met verbs in this group are:

s'apercevoir de, *notice*	**discuter de**, *discuss*
s'approcher de, approach	**douter de**, *doubt*
avoir besoin de, *need*	**se douter de**, suspect
changer de, *change*	**s'emparer de**, *grab*

jouer de, *play*	**se méfier de**, *mistrust*
(*an instrument*)	**se servir de**, *use*
jouir de, *enjoy*	**se souvenir de**, *remember*
manquer de, *lack*	**se tromper de**, *mistake*

■ Verbs taking **à** where we should expect nothing:

elle joue au tennis, *she plays tennis*

The most frequently encountered verbs of this kind
are:

assister à, *attend*	**renoncer à**, *renounce*
convenir à, *suit*	**répondre à**, *answer*
se fier à, *trust*	**résister à**, *resist*
jouer à, *play* (*a game*)	**ressembler à**, *resemble*
nuire à, *harm*	**succéder à**, *succeed*
(dés)obéir à, (*dis*)*obey*	(*someone*)
pardonner à, *forgive*	**survivre à**, *outlive*
(dé)plaire à, (*dis*)*please*	**téléphoner à**, *telephone*

Also in this group are a number of verbs that take **à**
with the noun at the same time as an infinitive with **de**:

j'ai dit à Jean-Pierre de ne pas sortir, *I told Jean-*
Pierre not to go out

These verbs are:

commander à ... de,	**ordonner à ... de**,
order	*order*
conseiller à ... de,	**permettre à ... de**,
advise	*allow*
défendre à ... de,	**promettre à ... de**,
forbid	*promise*
demander à ... de, *ask*	**proposer à ... de**,
dire à ... de, *tell*	*suggest*

■ Verbs taking **à** or **de** where English has an entirely
different preposition:

je l'ai acheté au fermier, *I bought it from the farmer*

These verbs are:

acheter à, *buy from*
arracher à, *snatch from*
blâmer de, *blame for*
boire à, *drink from*
cacher à, *hide from*
croire à, *believe in*
demander à, *ask for ... from*
dépendre de, *depend on*
doter de, *equip with*
emprunter à, *borrow from*
enlever à, *take away from*
féliciter de, *congratulate on*
s'intéresser à, *be interested in*

louer de, *praise for*
manquer à, *be missed by*
penser à, *think about*
prendre à, *take from*
punir de, *punish for*
récompenser de, *reward for*
réfléchir à, *think about*
remercier de, *thank for*
rêver à, *dream about*
rire de, *laugh at*
servir à, *be used for*
songer à, *think about*
témoigner de, *bear witness to*
toucher à, *meddle with*
vivre de, *live on*
voler à, *steal from*

Alphabetical list of verb constructions with prepositions

The list includes both verbs + preposition + infinitive, and verbs + preposition + noun. Only 'problem' verbs are included. If a verb is not included, assume that:

■ with a noun it will take the same construction as in English

■ before an infinitive it will take **de**

Abbreviations used:

> qn—**quelqu'un**
> qch—**quelque chose**
> sb—somebody
> sth—something
> INF—infinitive

acheter à qn	*buy from sb*
adorer + INF	*adore to*
aider à + INF	*help to*
aimer + INF	*like to*
aimer mieux + INF	*prefer to*
aller + INF	*go and; be going to*
s'amuser à + INF	*have fun … ing*
s'apercevoir de qch	*notice sth*
apprendre qch à qn	*teach sb sth*
apprendre à qn à + INF	*teach sb to*
apprendre à + INF	*learn to*
s'apprêter à + INF	*prepare to*
s'approcher de qn	*approach sb*
arracher à qn	*snatch from sb*
arriver à + INF	*manage to*
assister à qch	*attend/witness sth*
attendre qn	*wait for sb*
s'attendre à + INF	*expect to*
avoir qch à + INF	*have sth to*
avoir besoin de + INF	*need to*
blâmer de qch	*blame for sth*
boire à qch	*drink from/to sth*
cacher à qn	*hide from sb*
changer de qch	*change sth*
chercher qch	*look for sth*
chercher à + INF	*try to*
commander à qn de + INF	*order sb to*
commencer à (sometimes **de**) + INF	*begin to*

compter + INF	*intend to*
conseiller à qn de + INF	*advise sb to*
consentir à + INF	*agree to*
consentir à qch	*agree to sth*
consister en/dans qch	*consist of sth*
consister à + INF	*consist in*
continuer à (sometimes **de**) + INF	*continue to*
convenir à qn	*suit sb*
croire qn	*believe sb*
croire à/en qn/qch	*believe in sb/sth; trust in sb/sth*
se décider à + INF	*decide to; make up your mind to*
défendre à qn de + INF	*forbid sb to*
demander qn/qch	*ask for sb/sth*
demander qch à qn	*ask sb for sth*
demander à + INF	*ask to*
demander à qn de + INF	*ask sb to*
dépendre de qn/qch	*depend on sb/sth*
déplaire à qn	*displease sb*
descendre + INF	*go down and*
désirer + INF	*want to*
désobéir à qn	*disobey sb*
détester + INF	*hate to; detest … ing*
devoir + INF	*have to*
dire à qn de + INF	*tell sb to*
discuter de qch	*discuss sth*
doter de qch	*equip with sth*
douter de qch	*doubt sth*
se douter de qch	*suspect sth*
écouter qn/qch	*listen to sb/sth*
écouter qn + INF	*listen to sb … ing*
s'emparer de qch	*grab sth*
emprunter à qn	*borrow from sb*
encourager à + INF	*encourage to*

enlever à qn	*take away from sb*
enseigner qch à qn	*teach sb sth*
entendre qn + INF	*hear sb ... ing*
entrer + INF	*go/come in and*
envoyer qn + INF	*send sb to*
espérer + INF	*hope to*
essayer qch	*try sth on*
se fâcher de qch	*be annoyed about sth*
se fâcher contre qn	*be annoyed with sb*
faillir + INF	*almost do sth*
falloir + INF (**il faut**, etc.)	*must*
féliciter qn de qch	*congratulate sb on sth*
se fier à qn	*trust sb*
forcer à + INF	*force to*
habiter + PLACE	*live at/in*
habituer qn à + INF	*get sb used to ... ing*
s'habituer à + INF	*get used to ... ing*
hésiter à + INF	*hesitate to*
s'intéresser à qn/qch	*be interested in sb/sth*
s'intéresser à + INF	*be interested in ... ing*
inviter qn à + INF	*invite sb to*
jouer à qch	*play (a game)*
jouer de qch	*play (an instrument)*
jouir de qch	*enjoy sth*
laisser + INF	*let*
louer de qch	*praise for sth*
manquer de qch	*lack sth*
manquer à qn	*be missed by sb*
se marier avec qn	*marry sb*
se méfier de qn	*mistrust sb*
mettre qch	*put sth on*
se mettre à + INF	*begin to*
monter + INF	*go up (stairs) and*
nuire à qch	*harm sth*
obéir à qn	*obey sb*
obliger qn à + INF	*force sb to*

ordonner à qn de + INF	*order sb to*
oser + INF	*dare to*
paraître + INF	*appear to*
pardonner qch à qn	*forgive sb for sth*
partir + INF	*go off and; go off to*
parvenir à + INF	*manage to*
passer du temps à + INF	*spend time ... ing*
payer qch	*pay for sth*
penser à qn/qch	*think about sb/sth*
penser à + INF	*think of ... ing*
perdre du temps à + INF	*waste time ... ing*
permettre à qn de + INF	*allow sb to*
persister à + INF	*persist in ... ing*
plaire à qn	*please sb*
pousser à + INF	*urge to*
pouvoir + INF	*be able to*
préférer + INF	*prefer to*
prendre à qn	*take from sb*
préparer qn à + INF	*prepare sb to*
se préparer à	*get ready to*
prétendre + INF	*claim to*
promettre à qn de + INF	*promise sb to*
proposer à qn de + INF	*suggest to sb that they should*
punir de qch	*punish for sth*
se rappeler + PERFECT INF	*remember ... ing*
(*sometimes* **de** + PERF INF)	
récompenser de qch	*reward for sth*
réfléchir à qch	*think about sth*
regarder qn/qch	*look at sb/sth*
regarder qn + INF	*watch sb ... ing*
remercier de qch	*thank for sth*
renoncer à qch	*give sth up*
renoncer à + INF	*give up ... ing*
rentrer + INF	*come (back) in to*
répondre à qn/qch	*answer sb/sth*
reprocher qch à qn	*blame sb for sth*

résister à qch	*resist sth*
ressembler à qn/qch	*be like sb/sth*
rester à + INF	*remain to*
réussir à + INF	*manage to*
rêver à qn/qch	*dream about sb/sth*
rire de qn/qch	*laugh at sb/sth*
sembler + INF	*seem to*
sentir qch + INF	*feel sth ... ing*
se sentir + INF	*feel oneself ... ing*
servir à qch	*be used for sth*
servir à + INF	*be used to*
se servir de qch	*use sth*
songer à qn/qch	*think about sb/sth*
songer à + INF	*think about ... ing*
sortir + INF	*go out and*
souhaiter + INF	*want to*
se souvenir de qn/qch	*remember sb/sth*
succéder à qn	*succeed sb*
survivre à qn	*outlive sb*
tarder à + INF	*delay ... ing*
téléphoner à qn	*telephone sb*
témoigner de qch	*bear witness to sth*
tenir à + INF	*be keen to*
toucher à qch	*meddle with sth*
se tromper de qch	*mistake sth; be wrong about sth*
valoir mieux + INF	*be better to*
venir + INF	*come and; come to*
vivre de qch	*live on sth*
voir qn + INF	*see sb ... ing*
voler à qn	*steal from sb*
vouloir + INF	*want to*

MODAL VERBS

The modal verbs (auxiliary verbs of 'mood' like *can*, *must*, *will*, in English) always have a dependent infinitive:

je veux parler, *I want to speak*

Even if this infinitive is occasionally not expressed, it is always implied: **je veux bien!**, for instance, is really **je veux bien faire ce que tu as proposé!**

In French the five modal verbs are:

> **devoir**, *must*
> **falloir (il faut)**, *have to*
> **pouvoir**, *be allowed to*
> **savoir**, *can*
> **vouloir**, *will*

The meanings given above are in fact not really adequate. These verbs have a number of different meanings and shades of meaning in different uses of their various tenses. These are explained below.

Devoir

In its basic meaning **devoir** implies obligation, inner conviction, moral necessity (compare **falloir**, below). Its English equivalent is *have to* or *must*:

> **je dois rentrer**, *I must (have to) go home*

■ Present

As well as *have to*, **devoir** in the present tense also has the sense of *should, is supposed to, is probably ... ing*:

> **il doit être là**, *he should be there (by now)*

It can also mean *am to*:

> **je dois aller à Paris demain**, *I'm to go to Paris tomorrow*

■ Imperfect

As well as *used to have to*, the imperfect of **devoir** can also mean *was to, was due to*:

> **on devait faire la vaisselle tous les matins avant
> sept heures**, *we used to have to wash up every
> morning before seven o'clock*
> **dans trois jours la guerre devait éclater**, *in three
> days war was to break out*

■ Perfect

The basic meaning of the perfect is *had to* (or *has had to*);
the perfect also means *must have*:

> **j'ai dû prendre le train**, *I had to (I've had to) take
> the train*
> **il a dû partir plus tôt**, *he must have left earlier*

■ Pluperfect

The pluperfect meaning is *had had to*, or *must have* (*must
have* is the same as the perfect—English has no separate
pluperfect form of *must*):

> **comme la voiture était en panne, j'avais dû
> prendre le train**, *as the car was off the road, I'd
> had to take the train*
> **elle nous répondit qu'il avait dû partir plus tôt**, *she
> replied that he must have left earlier*

■ Conditional

The conditional means *would have to*, and also *ought to* or
should:

> **s'il devenait président, on devrait quitter le pays**, *if
> he became president we should have to leave
> the country*
> **cela devrait faire votre affaire**, *that ought to
> (should) do the job for you*

■ Conditional perfect

The conditional perfect means *would have had to*, and
also *ought to have* or *should have*:

**s'il était devenu président, on aurait dû quitter le
pays**, *if he had become president we should
have had to leave the country*
il aurait dû répondre, *he ought to have (should
have) replied*

■ Present subjunctive

Verbs have no future subjunctive. The present
subjunctive of **devoir** is used where it is necessary to
give other verbs in the subjunctive a future meaning:

je suis désolé qu'elle doive te suivre par avion,
I'm sorry she's going to fly out after you (**qu'elle
te suive** could mean she's already set out)

■ Note that **devoir** can be used impersonally, in all
tenses, as an extension of **il y a**:

il doit y avoir trois cents personnes, *there must be
three hundred people*

■ Used without a dependent infinitive, **devoir** means *to
owe*. In this sense it is not a modal verb:

je vous dois mille francs, *I owe you a thousand
francs*

Falloir

The basic meaning of **falloir** is *must* or *have to*, implying
external necessity or constraint. Compare **devoir**, above.

**tu dois rentrer déjà? — Mais oui, il faut
absolument que je rentre: sinon, ma mère ne me
permettra pas de sortir demain**, *you must go
home already? — Yes, I've really got to or my
mother won't let me come out tomorrow*

■ **Falloir** is always an impersonal verb, used only in the
il form (**il faut**, **il fallait**, etc.). The person need not be
expressed at all if it is obvious who is involved:

> **Pierre, il faut téléphoner à ta grand–mère**, *you must phone your grandmother, Pierre*

The real subject can be expressed by a dative:

> **il me faut partir**, *I have to go*

but this is rather formal, and spoken French prefers a subjunctive clause if it is necessary to say who is involved:

> **il faut que je parte**, *I've got to go*

Pouvoir

Pouvoir means basically *can* or *be allowed to*. Parts of the English verb *can* are missing and *be able to* or *be allowed to* has sometimes to be substituted when translating.

> **peut-on sortir par ici?**, *can we (are we allowed to) go out this way?*
>
> **l'eau est bonne, on pourra nager**, *the water's fine, we'll be able to go swimming*

As well as *be allowed to* and *can*, **pouvoir** can also mean *may*, either as the politer form of *can*, or expressing possibility:

> **puis-je parler à votre patron?**, *may I speak to your boss?*
>
> **il peut toujours venir**, *he may still come*

Note too the reflexive form, **se pouvoir**:

> **cela se peut**, *that's possible*

■ Perfect

Means *was able to* or *could* (in a past sense), or *may have*:

> **je n'ai pas pu ouvrir la boîte**, *I couldn't open the tin*

> **elle a pu se tromper de train**, *she may have got the wrong train*

■ Conditional

Means *would be able to* or *could* (in a conditional sense), and also *might*:

> **si tu payais, je pourrais t'accompagner**, *if you paid I could (would be able to) come with you*
> **je crois qu'il pourrait neiger**, *I think it might snow*

■ Conditional perfect

Means *would have been able to* or *could have*, also *might have*:

> **si tu avais payé, j'aurais pu t'accompagner**, *if you'd paid, I could have (would have been able to) come with you*
> **elle aurait pu se présenter avant le début du spectacle**, *she might have turned up before the play started*

■ **Pouvoir** can be used impersonally as an extension of **il y a**:

> **il pourrait y en avoir mille**, *there might be a thousand of them*

■ With verbs of perception (**entendre, voir, sentir**) English uses *can* or *could* where French prefers the simple verb:

> **je le voyais atterrir**, *I could see it landing*

Savoir

Savoir means *can* in the sense of *know how to*. Compare **pouvoir** above.

> **l'eau est bonne, on peut nager — Mais moi, je ne sais pas nager**, *the water's fine, we can go swimming—But I can't swim*

■ Conditional

In careful or formal language, the negative conditional of **savoir** is used as a politer form of *I can't*. In this use the **pas** is always omitted:

> **je ne saurais faire cela**, *I don't really think I can do that*

With the full negative **je ne saurais pas** means *would not know how to*, *couldn't* (in a moral sense):

> **je ne saurais pas faire quelque chose comme ça**, *I couldn't do anything like that*

■ **Savoir** is most frequently found used without a dependent infinitive, meaning *to know*. In this use it is not a modal verb:

> **je sais qu'elle est là**, *I know she's there*

Vouloir

The basic meaning of **vouloir** is *to wish* or *want*:

> **je veux vous dire quelque chose**, *I want to tell you something*

It also means *will*, *be willing to*. **Bien** is used where English stresses *will*:

> **oui, je veux bien le faire**, *yes, I will do it*
> **la moto ne veut pas démarrer**, *the bike won't start*

It can also mean *attempt to* or *intend to*:

> **j'ai voulu l'embrasser**, *I tried to kiss her*
> **qu'est-ce qu'il veut faire?**, *what does he mean to do?*

■ Conditional, conditional perfect

As well as *should wish*, *should want* (conditional), and *should have wished*, *should have wanted* (conditional perfect), these tenses also have the meanings *should like* and *should have liked*:

> **je voudrais être à sa place**, *I'd like to be in her place*
>
> **j'aurais voulu la revoir**, *I'd have liked to see her again*

With this meaning **je voudrais** is a standard way of asking politely for things:

> **je voudrais deux cents grammes de pâté s'il vous plaît**, *I'd like two hundred grams of pâté, please*

■ Vouloir may also be used as a polite form of the imperative.

► See p. 29.

FAIRE + INFINITIVE AND SIMILAR CONSTRUCTIONS

Faire + infinitive

Faire + infinitive means *to have something done, to get something done, to get someone to do something*:

> **j'ai fait téléphoner à ses parents**, *I've got someone to phone his parents*
>
> **elle a fait enlever ce qui restait du repas**, *she had what was left of the meal taken away*

■ Position of objects with **faire** + infinitive

☐ Noun objects of either verb follow both verbs

> **tu as fait jouer Pierre?**, *you got Pierre to play?*
>
> **tu as fait repeindre la porte?**, *you've had the door painted?*

☐ Pronoun objects of either verb come before both verbs

> **tu l'as fait jouer?**, *you got him to play?*
> **tu l'as fait repeindre?**, *you've had it painted?*

☐ If both verbs need an object, the object of **faire** is indirect (**à ...**), since in French a double direct object is impossible.

> **la nouvelle a fait perdre son sang-froid à mon**
>   **père**, *the news made my father lose his temper*

■ **Faire** + reflexive verbs

If the dependent verb is reflexive it loses its object pronoun:

> **je les ai fait asseoir** (not **s'asseoir**), *I got them to*
>   *sit down*
> **elle les a fait taire**, *she shut them up*

So if you find a reflexive pronoun in this construction it must belong to **faire** (*have oneself ..., get oneself ...*):

> **elle s'est fait virer du lycée**, *she got herself thrown*
>   *out of school*

■ Agreement of past participle of **faire**

In the **faire** + infinitive construction the past participle **fait** is invariable: it never agrees with a preceding direct object. See the last two examples above (**je les ai fait ..., elle s'est fait ...**).

Laisser, voir, entendre, sentir + infinitive

■ **Laisser** + infinitive means *to let something be done* or *to let someone do something*:

> **tu l'as déjà laissé revenir?**, *you've let him come*
>   *back already?*

> **j'ai dû le laisser passer**, *I had to let him go through*

■ **Voir/entendre/sentir** + infinitive mean *to see/hear/ feel something happen*:

> **on l'a vu partir**, *we saw him go*
> **je me sens guérir**, *I can feel myself getting better*

■ All points made above with regard to **faire** concerning objects and past participle agreement may also apply to this group of verbs, though they are quite often ignored:

> **tu lui as laissé repeindre ta porte?**, or very often
> **tu l'as laissé repeindre ta porte?**, *you've let him paint your door?*

English equivalents of faire, etc. + infinitive

Some infinitive constructions of the verbs considered above are the equivalent of a simple verb or a verb plus preposition in English. The most common are:

> **entendre dire que**, *hear that*
> **entendre parler de**, *hear about*
> **faire entrer**, *let in; show in*
> **faire sortir**, *let out; show out*
> **faire venir**, *send for*
> **faire voir**, *show*
> **laisser tomber**, *drop*

Similar constructions with other verbs used with an infinitive are:

> **aller chercher**, *go for*
> **envoyer chercher**, *send for*
> **venir chercher**, *come for*
> **vouloir dire**, *mean*

IMPERSONAL VERBS

Impersonal verbs are verbs whose subject is **il** or **ce/ cela** meaning *it* or *there*.

Impersonal verbs with il

These are of two kinds: those that are always constructed with **il**, and those where **il** is simply a temporary subject so that the real subject can be held back until later in the sentence.

■ Real subject **il**

In this group are:

☐ Weather verbs, e.g.

> **il pleut**, *it's raining*
> **il neige**, *it's snowing*
> **il gèle**, *it's freezing*
> **il tonne**, *it's thundering*
> **il y a du brouillard**, *it's foggy*
> **il fait du vent**, *it's windy*
> **il fait beau**, *it's fine*
> **il fait mauvais**, *the weather's bad*
> **il fait chaud/froid**, *it's hot/cold*

☐ **Être** used with time of day

> **il est cinq heures**, *it's five o'clock*
> **il est midi et demi**, *it's half past twelve*
> **il est tard**, *it's late*

☐ **Il y a**, *there is, there are*

> **il y a trente mille personnes dans le stade**, *there are thirty thousand people in the stadium*

Il y a is always singular.

▶ **Il y a** can also be used with **devoir** and **pouvoir: il peut y avoir ...**, *there may be ...* See pp. 67 and 69.

☐ A large number of other impersonal expressions, of which some of the commonest are:

> **Il s'agit de**, *it's a question of; it's about*
> **Il m'est arrivé de**, *I happened to*
> **Il faut (que)**, *you (we, they, etc.) must/need*
> **Il paraît que**, *it appears that*
> **Il semble que**, *it seems that*
> **Il suffit de**, *you only have to*
> **Il vaut mieux**, *it's better to*

Notice also

> **Il était une fois**, *once upon a time*

■ **Il** to hold back the real subject

Any verb can be used in this way; it remains singular, agreeing with **il**, even if the real subject is plural:

> **Il pousse beaucoup de fleurs au Sahara**, *there are lots of flowers (that grow) in the Sahara*
> **Il reste encore dix minutes**, *there are ten minutes still left*
> **Il me manque dix francs**, *I need ten francs* (literally: *there is lacking to me ten francs*)

☐ The real subject may be a noun, as in the examples above; or it may be a clause

> **Il me brûlait les lèvres de demander à quoi ça servait**, *I was dying to ask what that was for*

☐ The real subject may be an infinitive clause, following an adjective plus **de**. The pattern is: **il est** + adjective + **de** + infinitive clause

> **Il est difficile de concevoir quelque chose de plus imposant**, *it is difficult to conceive of anything more impressive*

In spoken French **c'est** is often used instead of **il est** in this construction.

☐ The real subject may be a clause introduced by **que**, following an adjective. The pattern is: **il est** + adjective + **que** + clause

> **il est évident qu'elle mange trop**, *it's obvious that she eats too much*

Here too, **c'est** is often used instead of **il est** in spoken French.

Impersonal verbs with ce or cela/ça as subject

Ce (*it*) is used as the subject of **être**, and **cela/ça** (*it, that*) as the subject of any verb (including **être**), to stand for a previously expressed clause:

> **il est facile de mentir — Ah oui, c'est facile**, *it's easy to tell lies—Oh yes, it's easy* (**c'** refers back to **de mentir**)
>
> **si elle ment, c'est qu'elle ne veut pas vous parler de Jean-Claude**, *if she's lying, it's because she doesn't want to talk to you about Jean-Claude* (**c'** refers back to **si elle ment**)
>
> **tout ce que j'ai dit me paraît évident — Oui, cela prouve que tu es fou!**, *everything I've said seems obvious to me—Yes, that proves you're crazy!* (**cela** refers back to **tout ce que j'ai dit me paraît évident**)

C'est + adjective is also used extremely often in spoken French instead of **il est** + adjective:

> **c'est** (for: **il est**) **facile de mentir — Ah oui, c'est facile**

Articles

Articles are words like *a* and *the*. Nouns are rarely used without an article in French. If the noun has no article in English, it is most likely to have a definite article in French. There are, however, quite a number of exceptions to this—see below.

THE DEFINITE ARTICLE

The definite article (*the* in English) has four forms, **le**, **la**, or **l'** with singular nouns, **les** with plural nouns. **Le** is used before a masculine singular noun, **la** before a feminine singular noun, **l'** before a singular noun of either gender beginning with a vowel or **h** 'mute'*. **Les** is used before a plural noun of either gender:

> **le garçon**, *the boy*; **la fille**, *the girl*; **le haricot**, *the bean*
>
> **l'homme**, *the man*; **l'arbre**, *the tree*
>
> **les garçons**, *the boys*; **les filles**, *the girls*; **les haricots**, *the beans*;
>
> **les hommes**, *the men*; **les arbres**, *the trees*

Le and **les** compound with **à** and **de** to produce **au**, **aux** (*to the*) and **du**, **des** (*of the*), thus:

---

* In older French some **h**'s were pronounced and some were not, which accounts for **le haricot** and **l'homme**. There is no pronunciation difference in modern French (no **h**'s are pronounced), and there are no rules to decide whether an **h** is 'mute' or not.

$$à + le = au \qquad de + le = du$$
$$à + les = aux \qquad de + les = des$$

A la and **à l'**, **de la** and **de l'** do not change.

The same changes are found in the compound words **auquel, auxquels, auxquelles** (*to whom*; *to which*) and **duquel, desquels, desquelles** (*of whom*; *of which*).

Using the definite article

The definite article is used in French in a number of places where we should omit it in English.

■ When generalizing:

> **aimez-vous les animaux?**, *do you like animals?*
> (i.e. animals in general)

■ With abstract nouns:

> **c'est comme ça, la vie**, *life's like that*
> **l'amour de la patrie**, *love of country*

But not with abstract nouns after **avec** and **sans**:

> **avec difficulté**, *with difficulty*
> **sans occupation**, *unemployed*

■ With parts of the body, especially when used as the object of a verb:

> **levez le bras**, *raise your arm*

A reflexive indirect object pronoun is added in this construction when the action is done to, rather than with, the part of the body mentioned:

> **elle s'est lavé le visage**, *she has washed her face*

■ With names preceded by adjective or titles:

> **le vieux Corneille**, *old Corneille*
> **le président Mitterrand**, *President Mitterrand*

■ With names of countries, areas, mountains, lakes:

> **l'Angleterre**, *England*; **la Corse**, *Corsica* (but **en Angleterre**, **d'Angleterre**, *in/from England*; **en Corse**, **de Corse**, *in/from Corsica*); **le Mont-Blanc**, *Mont Blanc*; **le lac Trasimène**, *Lake Trasimeno*

■ With names of languages:

> **j'apprends le français**, *I'm learning French*
> **tu parles bien le français**, *you speak French well*

The article is omitted, however, after **parler** where the name of the language follows without any other qualification:

> **il parle français**, *he speaks French*

■ With days, mealtimes, seasons, religious festivals:

> **je déteste le lundi**, *I hate Monday(s)*
> **tu prends le petit déjeuner?**, *do you want breakfast?*
> **c'est l'hiver qui revient**, *winter's back*
> **le vendredi saint**, *Good Friday*
> **la Toussaint**, *All Saints' Day* (but the article is omitted with **Pâques**, *Easter*, and **Noël**, *Christmas*)

■ With school subjects and games:

> **aimes-tu les maths?**, *do you like maths?*
> **ici, on joue au rugby**, *here they play rugby*
> **il déteste les sports**, *he hates games*

Definite article for indefinite article

The definite article is used in a number of places where we should use the indefinite article (*a, an*).

■ When expressing quantity after price:

> **douze francs le kilo**, *twelve francs a kilo*
> **cent francs la bouteille**, *a hundred francs a bottle*

■ When expressing speed:

> **cent vingt kilomètres à l'heure**, *120 km an hour*
> (note the addition of **à** in French)

■ French also uses a definite article in a number of set expressions where in English we should use an indefinite article or no article at all:

> **il s'est couché le dernier/le premier**, *he went to bed last/first*
> **l'un d'eux**, *one of them*
> **au lit**, *in bed*
> **au régime**, *on a diet*
> **à la maison**, *at home*
> **à l'école**, *at school*
> **à l'église**, *in church*

Omission of the definite article

The definite article is omitted in French in forming an attributive noun (a noun used as an adjective):

> **du pâté de campagne**, *country pâté*
> **un tronc d'arbre**, *a tree trunk*
> **les fromages de France**, *French cheeses*

Compare these with:

> **un goût de la campagne**, *a taste of the countryside*
> **le tronc de l'arbre**, *the trunk of the tree*
> **le nord de la France**, *the north of France*

THE INDEFINITE AND PARTITIVE ARTICLES

It is convenient to consider these two forms of article together, since there is much similarity in their use in French.

The indefinite article, what it is

The indefinite article (*a, an, some/any* in English) has three forms: **un** with masculine singular nouns, **une** with feminine singular nouns, **des** with plural nouns:

> **un garçon**, *a boy*; **une fille**, *a girl*; **un haricot**, *a bean*
> **un homme**, *a man*; **un arbre**, *a tree*
> **des garçons**, *some boys*; **des arbres**, *some trees*

The partitive article, what it is

The partitive article (*some* in English, or *any* in questions and after negatives) has three forms, **du**, **de la**, and **de l'**. They are used before singular 'uncountable' nouns, i.e. nouns like *milk*, *sugar*, etc. that cannot normally be used in the plural. **Du** is used before a masculine noun, **de la** before a feminine noun, **de l'** before a noun of either gender beginning with a vowel or **h** 'mute':

> **du chocolat**, *some chocolate*
> **de la confiture**, *some jam*
> **de l'argent**, *some money*

The partitive is sometimes said to have a plural form, **des**. Strictly speaking, however, **des** is the plural of the indefinite article: the singular of **des vins** is **un vin**, not **du vin**.

Du/de la/des or le/la/les?

English sometimes does not use any article at all before nouns:

> **vous prenez du lait?**, *do you take milk?*
> **je déteste le lait**, *I hate milk*

This raises the problem of whether to use **du/de la/des** or **le/la/les** where English has a noun with no article. **Du/de la/des** particularizes, **le/la/les** generalizes: **du/de la/des** means 'some', **le/la/les** implies 'all'. So:

> **vous avez du jus d'orange?**, *do you have orange juice?* (i.e., some orange juice)
>
> **j'aime le jus d'orange**, *I like orange juice* (i.e., orange juice in general, all orange juice)
>
> **il y a des mouches dans ma soupe**, *there are flies in my soup* (some flies, not all the flies that exist)
>
> **je n'aime pas les mouches**, *I don't like flies* (all flies, any flies at all, not just some flies)

De for des, etc.

■ After a negative the indefinite article (**un/une/des**) and the partitive article (**du/de la/de l'**) become **de** (**d'** before a vowel or **h** 'mute'). English may use *any* for this:

> **j'ai du temps**, *I have time*
>
> **je n'ai pas de temps à perdre**, *I've no time (I haven't any time) to lose*
>
> **il n'y a pas de pellicule dans l'appareil-photo**, *there isn't any film in the camera*
>
> **je n'ai pas d'appareil-photo**, *I don't have (haven't got) a camera*

Ne ... que is not regarded as negative as far as this rule is concerned:

> **je n'ai qu'un très vieil appareil**, *I've only a very old camera*

A negative *is* followed by an indefinite or partitive article if what is negated is the identity of the noun:

> **ce n'est pas un train, c'est un tramway**, *it isn't a train, it's a tram*

■ The plural indefinite article **des** becomes **de** (**d'** before a vowel or **h** 'mute') when the noun following is preceded by an adjective:

> **j'ai eu d'incroyables difficultés**, *I've had unbelievable difficulties*

This rule is often ignored where the meaning of the phrase centres on the noun rather than the adjective:

> **des jolies filles**, *pretty girls*

It is always ignored where the adjective + noun pair forms a set expression:

> **des petits pois**, *peas*
> **des petits pains**, *bread rolls*

Before the adjective **autres**, however, you must keep to **d'**:

> **d'autres voyageurs ont dit …**, *other travellers have said …*

■ After the preposition **de** (*of*) the partitive article **du/de la/de l'** and the plural indefinite article **des** are always omitted:

> **j'ai besoin d'argent**, *I need (some) money*
> **c'était un grand cratère plein d'eau**, *it was a great crater full of (some) water*

This means that expressions of quantity, which all incorporate the preposition **de** (*of*), omit **du/de la/de l'/ des**:

> **un verre de vin**, *a glass of wine*
> **beaucoup de vin**, *a lot of wine*

But note that the definite article, meaning *the*, is NOT omitted in such cases:

> **j'ai acheté une bouteille du vin qu'il nous a fait goûter**, *I bought a bottle of the wine he let us taste*

Nor is the indefinite article in the singular omitted:

> **il lui restait quelques bouteilles d'un vin très ancien**, *he still had a few bottles of a very old wine*

The expressions of quantity **encore** (*more*) and **bien** (*many*) are intensifying adverbs not incorporating the preposition **de** and are followed by **du/de la/des**:

> **encore du pain, s'il vous plaît!**, *more bread please!*
> **bien des gens disent cela**, *many people say that*

Omission of the indefinite article

The indefinite article is omitted in French in the following cases where, in the singular, it would be used in English.

■ In apposition (i.e., where a second noun is placed directly after a first one in order to explain it):

> **M. Duval, ancien combattant de la guerre de quatorze-dix-huit**, *M. Duval, a veteran of the 14–18 war*

Definite articles, however, are not dropped in apposition:

> **M. Duval, l'ancien combattant dont nous parlons**, *M. Duval, the veteran we're speaking about*

■ After **il est/elle est/**NOUN **est**, followed by the name of a profession:

> **il est menuisier**, *he's a joiner*
> **son fils est avocat**, *his son's a lawyer*

But not after **c'est**:

> **c'est un menuisier**, *he's a joiner*

■ After **quel!**:

> **quel imbécile!**, *what a fool!*

■ After **sans**:

> **les voyageurs sans billet**, *passengers without a ticket*

The partitive article is also omitted in this case, as in English:

> **une journée sans vin est une journée sans soleil**, *a day without wine is a day without sunshine*

■ In lists, both the indefinite article and the partitive article may be omitted, as in English:

> **on y voyait des moutons**, *sheep could be seen there*

but:

> **on y voyait moutons, vaches, porcs, poules, tous mélangés**, *sheep, cattle, pigs, chickens could be seen there, all higgledy piggledy*

> **on nous offrait du mouton**, *we were offered lamb*

but:

> **on nous offrait mouton, porc, veau, bœuf ... toutes sortes de viandes**, *we were offered lamb, pork, veal, beef—all kinds of meat*

This use is rather literary.

Nouns

GENDER OF NOUNS

English has three genders: masculine, feminine, and
neuter (*he*, *she*, *it*). French has only two: masculine and
feminine. Most nouns denoting male people are
masculine, most denoting female people are feminine.
Names of inanimate objects may be either masculine or
feminine. Unlike English nouns, French nouns make
their gender obvious by means of the article in front of
them and the adjectives that go with them.

The rules for gender in French are very far from
watertight and there are many exceptions to all of them.
As an overall rule of thumb for an unknown noun: if it
ends in **-e** it is more likely to be feminine, if not it is
more likely to be masculine.

Masculine groups

■ Workers, traders, names of males, and many names of
animals are masculine:

> **le constructeur**, *builder*; **le boulanger**, *baker*; **le
> lion**, *lion*; **le fils**, *son*

Many but not all of these also have feminine forms: see
p. 93. **Une autruche** (*ostrich*), **la baleine** (*whale*), **la
girafe** (*giraffe*), **la panthère** (*panther*), **la souris**
(*mouse*), **la fourmi** (*ant*) are always feminine.

■ Days, months, seasons, weights, measures, numerals, fractions, points of the compass, languages are masculine:

> **le vendredi**, *Friday*; **(le) janvier**, *January*; **le printemps**, *spring*; **le kilo**, *kilo*; **le kilomètre**, *kilometre*; **le douze**, *twelve*; **le quart**, *quarter*; **le sud**, *south*; **le français**, *French*

Exceptions: **la livre**, *pound*; **la tonne**, (*metric*) *ton*; **la moitié**, *half*

■ Trees, shrubs, metals are masculine:

> **le hêtre**, *beech*; **le laurier**, *laurel*; **le fer**, *iron*

Exceptions: **la bruyère**, *heather*; **la ronce**, *bramble*; **une aubépine**, *hawthorn*

■ Countries, rivers, vegetables and fruit not ending **-e** are masculine:

> **le Japon**, *Japan*; **le Nil**, *Nile*; **le chou**, *cabbage*; **le citron**, *lemon*

■ Most nouns of English origin are masculine:

> **le baby-foot**, *pin-table football*; **le hit-parade**, *hit parade*

Exception: **une interview**, *interview*

■ Words not originally nouns, when used as nouns, are masculine:

> **un joli rose**, *a pretty pink*
> **un oui suivi d'un non**, *a yes followed by a no*
> **on peut apporter son manger**, *you may bring your own food*

Exception: adjectives and participles used as nouns have the gender that their ending shows. So: **le passant, la passante**, *passer-by*; **une allée**, *path*; **la nouvelle**, *piece of news*; **la sortie**, *way out*

■ Nouns with the following endings are masculine:

 -acle and -icle:

  le spectacle, *show*; **un article**, *article*

 -age:

  le garage

  Exceptions: **la cage**, *cage*; **une image**, *picture*;
   la nage, *swimming*; **la page**, *page*; **la plage**,
   beach; **la rage**, *rage, rabies*

 -ail:

  le travail, *work*

 -asme and -isme:

  le sarcasme, *sarcasm*; **le communisme**,
   communism

 -c:

  le lac, *lake*

 -é:

  le péché, *sin*

 -eau:

  le bateau, *boat*

  Exceptions: **une eau**, *water*; **la peau**, *skin*

 -ège:

  le collège, *secondary school*

 -ème:

  le poème, *poem*

  Exception: **la crème**, *cream*

 -er and -ier:

  le clocher, *steeple*; **le papier**, *paper*

  Exceptions: **la mer**, *sea*; **la cuiller**, *spoon* (also
   spelled, and always pronounced, **cuillère**)

 -ment:

  le sentiment, *sentiment*

  Exception: **la jument**, *mare*

 -oir:

  le couloir, *corridor*

 -ou:

  le trou, *hole*

■ Concrete nouns ending **-eur** are masculine:

> **le moteur**, *engine*

Abstract nouns ending **-eur** are feminine: **la grandeur**, *greatness*

■ Common traps! The following nouns ending **-e** look extremely feminine—they are all masculine:

> **le crime**, *crime*; **le disque**, *record*; **le groupe**, *group*; **le manque**, *lack*; **le mélange**, *mixture*; **le reste**, *remainder*; **le risque**, *risk*; **le silence**, *silence*; **le vice**, *vice*

Feminine groups

■ Feminine forms of traders, workers, animals; names of females:

> **la boulangère**, *baker*; **une électricienne**, *electrician*; **la lionne**, *lioness*; **la fille**, *girl*

Many feminine forms, for historical reasons, do not exist; many others (like **l'électricienne** above) are being newly coined; some (e.g. **la mairesse**, *mayoress*, i.e., *mayor's wife*) can still only refer to the wife of the male. In the animals group, no feminine forms exist of **un éléphant**, *elephant*, **un hippopotame**, *hippopotamus*, **le vautour**, *vulture*.

▶ See also p. 93 for the formation of feminine nouns.

■ Countries, rivers, vegetables and fruit ending **-e** are feminine:

> **la Hollande**, *Holland*; **la Tamise**, *Thames*; **la poire**, *pear*; **la carotte**, *carrot*; **la marguerite**, *daisy*

Exceptions: **le Mexique**, *Mexico*; **le Danube**; **le Rhône**; **le légume**, *vegetable*

■ Shops and trades, arts and sciences, religious festivals
are feminine:

> **la boucherie**, *butcher's*; **la menuiserie**, *joinery*; **la**
> **sculpture**, *sculpture*; **la chimie**, *chemistry*; **la**
> **Pentecôte**, *Whitsun*; **la Toussaint**, *All Saints' Day*

Exception: **un joyeux Noël**, *happy Christmas* (but, in
some parts of France, **à la Noël**, short for **à la fête**
(*festival*) **de Noël**)

■ Nouns with the following endings are feminine:

> **-ace**:
>> **la grâce**, *grace*
>> Exception: **un espace**, *space*
>
> **-ade**:
>> **la baignade**, *bathing*
>> Exceptions: **le grade**, *grade*; **le stade**, *stadium*
>
> **-ance** (and the similarly pronounced endings
> **-anse**, **-ence**, **ense**):
>> **la dépendance**, *dependence*; **la danse**, *dance*;
>> **la conscience**, *conscience*; **la défense**,
>> *defence*
>> Exception: **le silence**, *silence*
>
> **-che**:
>> **la tâche**, *task*
>> Exceptions: **le manche**, *handle*; **le reproche**,
>> *reproach*; **le caniche**, *poodle*
>
> **-ée**:
>> **la matinée**, *morning*
>> Exceptions: **le musée**, *museum*; **le lycée**,
>> *sixth-form college*
>
> **-elle**:
>> **la querelle**, *quarrel*
>
> **-ère**:
>> **la lumière**, *light*
>> Exceptions: **le frère**, *brother*; **le père**, *father*;
>> **le cimetière**, *cemetery*; **le mystère**, *mystery*;
>> **le caractère**, *character*; **le cratère**, *crater*

-esse:

    la faiblesse, *weakness*

-ie:

    la pluie, *rain*

    Exceptions: **le génie**, *genius*; **un incendie**, *fire*;
        le parapluie, *umbrella*

-ine and **-une**:

    la piscine, *swimming pool*; **la fortune**, *fortune*

-ion:

    la concentration, *concentration*

    Exceptions: **le camion**, *lorry*; **un espion**, *spy*

-ison (and **-aison**):

    la prison, *prison*; **la maison**, *house*

    Exceptions: **le bison**, *bison*; **le vison**, *mink*

-oire:

    la foire, *fair*

    Exceptions: **le laboratoire**, *laboratory*; **le**
        pourboire, *tip*; **un observatoire**,
        observatory; **l'ivoire**, *ivory*

-onne:

    la couronne, *crown*

-te (and **-tte**, **-ette**):

    la date, *date*; **la patte**, *paw*; **la buvette**, *bar*

    Exception: **le squelette**, *skeleton*

-té and **-tié**:

    la beauté, *beauty*; **la pitié**, *pity*

    Exceptions: **le côté**, *side*; **le comté**, *county*; **le**
        traité, *treaty*; **le pâté**, (*meat, fish*) *pâté*

-ure:

    la nature, *nature*

    Exceptions: **le murmure**, *murmur*; **le mercure**,
        mercury

Very many of the above are abstract nouns: most abstract nouns, whatever their endings, are in fact feminine.

■ Abstract nouns ending **-eur** are feminine:

    la chaleur, *heat*

Exceptions: **le bonheur**, *happiness*; **le malheur**, *unhappiness*; **un honneur**, *honour*; **le déshonneur**, *dishonour*; **le labeur**, *labour*

Concrete nouns ending **-eur** are masculine: **le carburateur**, *carburettor*

■ Common traps! The following nouns ending in a consonant look extremely masculine—they are all feminine:

la chair, *flesh*; **la clef**, *key*; **la croix**, *cross*; **la façon**, *way, manner*; **la faim**, *hunger*; **la soif**, *thirst*; **la souris**, *mouse*; **la vis**, *screw*

Nouns with different meanings according to gender

masculine	*feminine*
l'aide, *assistant (male)*	**l'aide**, *assistance; assistant (female)*
le crêpe, *crêpe*	**la crêpe**, *pancake*
le critique, *critic*	**la critique**, *criticism*
le faux, *forgery*	**la faux**, *scythe*
le livre, *book*	**la livre**, *pound*
le manche, *handle*	**la manche**, *sleeve* (**la Manche**, *English Channel*)
le manœuvre, *labourer*	**la manœuvre**, *manœuvre*
le mémoire, *memorandum*	**la mémoire**, *memory*
le mode, *method; way*	**la mode**, *fashion; manner*
le mort, *dead man*	**la mort**, *death*
le moule, *mould*	**la moule**, *mussel*
un office, *office; religious service*	**une office**, *pantry*

le page, *page(boy)*	**la page**, *page (of a book)*
le pendule, *pendulum*	**la pendule**, *clock*
le physique, *physique*	**la physique**, *physics*
le poêle, *stove*	**la poêle**, *frying pan*
le poste, *set (e.g. TV); (military) post; (fire, police) station*	**la poste**, *post (= mail); post office*
le somme, *nap*	**la somme**, *sum*
le tour, *trick; tour*	**la tour**, *tower*
le vapeur, *steamer (boat)*	**la vapeur**, *steam*
le vase, *vase*	**la vase**, *mud; silt*
le voile, *veil*	**la voile**, *sail*

Gender of compound nouns

There are many exceptions, but

■ Compounds of two nouns or a noun plus adjective take the gender of the (first) noun:

le chou-fleur, *cauliflower*

■ Compounds where the first element is part of a verb are masculine:

le tire-bouchon, *corkscrew*

■ When in doubt about the gender of a compound noun, choose masculine.

FEMININE OF NOUNS

Professions, positions, nationalities, names of relationships, domestic animals (and a few wild ones) mostly have both masculine and feminine forms according to sex:

le vendeur, *salesman*	**la vendeuse**, *saleswoman*
le Français, *Frenchman*	**la Française**, *Frenchwoman*
le cousin, (*male*) *cousin*	**la cousine**, (*female*) *cousin*
le chien, *dog*	**la chienne**, *bitch*

With professions and positions the feminine form quite often still means *wife of the* ..., though this is not the case with the newer professions:

> **la mairesse**, *mayoress; wife of the mayor*
> **l'informaticienne**, (*female*) *computer programmer*

With animals, where two forms exist, the masculine form is used as the general term; the feminine form is only used where a specific distinction of sex is being made. Exception: **la chèvre** (general term for *goat*; masculine is **le bouc**, *billy-goat*)

■ The regular feminine endings are:

masculine noun	*feminine form*
-e	no change
le Russe, *Russian*	**la Russe**
-er	**-ère**
un ouvrier, *worker*	**une ouvrière**
-eur	**-euse**
le dormeur, *sleeper*	**la dormeuse**
-f	**-ve**
le veuf, *widower*	**la veuve**
-en, -on, -et	**-enne, -onne, -ette**
le chien, *dog*	**la chienne**
le Breton, *Breton*	**la Bretonne**
le cadet, *junior*	**la cadette**
-teur	**-teuse**: where the noun is based on the present participle of a verb

-trice: in all other cases

le menteur, *lier*   **la menteuse** (p.p. **mentant**)

le directeur, *director*   **la directrice** (p.p. **dirigeant**)

-x   **-se**

un époux, *spouse,*   une épouse
husband

With other endings the feminine, where it exists, is
formed by adding **-e**:

un ami, *friend*   une amie

un Anglais, *Englishman*   une Anglaise

■ Nouns with an irregular feminine form:

masculine	*feminine*
un abbé, *abbot*	une abbesse
un ambassadeur, *ambassador*	une ambassadrice
un âne, *donkey*	une ânesse
le canard, *drake*	la canne, *duck*
le chat, *cat*	la chatte
le comte, *count*	la comtesse
le compagnon, *companion*	la compagne
le copain, *pal*	la copine
le dieu, *god*	la déesse
le dindon, *turkey*	la dinde
le duc, *duke*	la duchesse
un empereur, *emperor*	une impératrice
le fils, *son*	la fille, *daughter*
le Grec, *Greek*	la Grecque
le héros, *hero*	l'héroïne
l'hôte, *host*	l'hôtesse
un inspecteur, *inspector*	une inspectrice
le jumeau, *twin*	la jumelle

le loup, *wolf*	la louve
le maître, *master*	la maîtresse
le mulet, *mule*	la mule
le nègre (pejorative), *negro*	la négresse
le neveu, *nephew*	la nièce
le paysan, *peasant*	la paysanne
le pécheur, *sinner*	la pécheresse
le prêtre, *priest*	la prêtresse
le prince, *prince*	la princesse
le Suisse, *Swiss*	la Suissesse
le tigre, *tiger*	la tigresse
le traître, *traitor*	la traîtresse
le Turc, *Turk*	la Turque

■ Nouns with an entirely different feminine form.

As in English, the feminine form may be expressed by an entirely different word. Among the commonest of these are:

masculine	*feminine*
le cerf, *stag*	la biche, *hind*
le cheval, *horse*	la jument, *mare*
le coq, *cock*	la poule, *hen*
l'étalon, *stallion*	la jument, *mare*
le frère, *brother*	la sœur, *sister*
le garçon, *boy*	la fille, *girl*
l'homme, *man*	la femme, *woman*
le mari, *husband*	la femme, *wife*
l'oncle, *uncle*	la tante, *aunt*
le parrain, *godfather*	la marraine, *godmother*
le père, *father*	la mère, *mother*
le porc, *pig*	la truie, *sow*
le roi, *king*	la reine, *queen*
le serviteur, *servant*	la servante, *servant*
le taureau, *bull*	la vache, *cow*

■ Nouns unchanged in the feminine form:

un/une enfant, *child*

plus masculine nouns ending **-e**.

■ Nouns with only one gender, whatever the sex of the person they refer to:

un ange, *angel*	**le maire**, *mayor*
un amateur, *lover, amateur*	**le médecin**, *doctor*
un assassin, *killer*	**le ministre**, *minister*
un auteur, *author*	**le peintre**, *painter*
le cadre, *executive*	**la personne**, *person*
la connaissance, *aquaintance*	**le poète**, *poet*
le député, *MP*	**le possesseur**, *owner*
le docteur, *doctor*	**le professeur**, *(secondary) teacher* (but, slang **le/la prof**)
la dupe, *dupe*	
un écrivain, *writer*	**la recrue**, *recruit*
le facteur, *postman*	**la sentinelle**, *sentry*
le guide, *guide*	**le spectateur**, *spectator*
un imposteur, *imposter*	**le soldat**, *soldier*
un ingénieur, *engineer*	**le témoin**, *witness*
le juge, *judge*	**la vedette**, *star*
	la victime, *victim*

With professions, a specifically female form can be produced where needed by using **une femme** and adding the name of the profession attributively:

une femme auteur, *woman author, authoress*

Feminine forms of some of the above are now appearing in French (e.g., **une ministre**). They are not yet fully accepted and are at present best avoided.

For names of animals with only one gender (which is most animals), specifically male and female forms can be produced by using the adjectives **mâle, femelle**:

une souris mâle, *a male mouse*
un hamster femelle, *a female hamster*

PLURAL OF NOUNS
Plural formation

French nouns add **-s** to form their plural, except:

■ Nouns ending **-s**, **-x**, **-z** remain unchanged:

le tas, *heap*	**les tas**
la croix, *cross*	**les croix**
le nez, *nose*	**les nez**

■ Nouns ending **-au**, **-eau**, **-eu** add **-x**:

le tuyau, *drainpipe*	**les tuyaux**
le gâteau, *cake*	**les gâteaux**
ie neveu, *nephew*	**les neveux**

Exceptions: **le bleu** (*bruise*) → **les bleus**; **le pneu**
(*tyre*) → **les pneus**

■ Nouns ending **-al** change their ending to **-aux**:

le journal, *newspaper*	**les journaux**

Exceptions: **le bal** (*dance*) → **les bals**; **le festival**
(*festival*) → **les festivals**

■ Four nouns ending **-ail** change it to **-aux** instead of
adding **-s**:

le corail, *coral*	**les coraux**
l'émail, *enamel*	**les émaux**
le travail, *work*	**les travaux**
le vitrail, *stained-glass window*	**les vitraux**

■ Seven nouns ending **-ou** add **-x** instead of **-s**:

le bijou, *jewel*	**les bijoux**
le caillou, *pebble*	**les cailloux**
le chou, *cabbage*	**les choux**
le genou, *knee*	**les genoux**
le hibou, *owl*	**les hiboux**
le joujou, *toy*	**les joujoux**
le pou, *louse*	**les poux**

■ Letter names remain unchanged in the plural:

cela s'écrit avec deux p, *you write it with two p's*

■ Family names usually remain unchanged in the plural; famous historical names add an **-s**:

les Robinson, *the Robinsons*
les Bourbons, *the Bourbons*

■ Irregular plurals:

l'aïeul, *ancestor*	**les aïeux**
le bonhomme, *fellow*	**les bonshommes**
le ciel, *sky*	**les cieux**
l'œil, *eye*	**les yeux**
madame, *Mrs*	**mesdames**
mademoiselle, *Miss*	**mesdemoiselles**
monsieur, *Mr*	**messieurs**

■ The following nouns have an extra meaning in the plural:

le ciseau, *chisel*	**les ciseaux**, *chisels; scissors*
la lunette, *telescope*	**les lunettes**, *telescopes; spectacles*
la vacance, *vacancy*	**les vacances**, *vacancies; holidays*
la gage, *pledge*	**les gages**, *pledges; wages*
l'affaire, *affair*	**les affaires**, *affairs; business*

Plural of compound nouns

There are many exceptions, but the following rules may help.

■ Compound nouns written as a single word, the plural is **-s**:

> **le pourboire**, *tip*   **les pourboires**

■ Compound nouns formed of an adjective plus a noun or two nouns, both add **-s**:

> **la belle-mère**, *mother-in-law*   **les belles-mères**
> **le chou-fleur**, *cauliflower*   **les choux-fleurs**

■ Compound nouns formed of a noun plus a prepositional phrase, only the noun adds **-s**:

> **un arc-en-ciel**, *rainbow*   **des arcs-en-ciel**

■ Compound nouns formed of a noun preceded by a preposition, the plural is the same as the singular:

> **le hors-d'œuvre**, *starter*   **les hors-d'œuvre**

■ Compound nouns formed of a verb plus its object noun, the noun adds **-s**:

> **le tire-bouchon**, *corkscrew*   **les tire-bouchons**
> **un essuie-glace**, *windscreen-*   **des essuie-glaces**
> *wiper*

But many compounds of this kind do not change in the plural:

> **le coupe-circuit**, *circuit-*   **les coupe-circuit**
> *breaker*

■ Compound nouns formed without a noun component, the plural is the same as the singular:

> **le passe-partout**, *master key*   **les passe-partout**

Singular for plural

■ Plural (or usually plural) in English, but singular in French are:

> **le bétail**, *cattle*; **la famille**, *family*; **la police**, *police*

The verb that follows them must be singular:

> **la famille est à table**, *the family are sitting down to a meal*

■ Singular in English, but plural in French are:

> **les funérailles**, *funeral*; **les nouvelles**, *news*; and (usually) **les fiancailles**, *engagement*; **les progrès**, *progress*

The verb that follows them must be plural:

> **les funérailles sont lundi prochain**, *the funeral is next Monday*

Pronouns

SUBJECT PRONOUNS

The subject pronouns are

singular	*plural*
je, *I*	**nous**, *we*
tu, *you*	**vous**, *you*
il, *he, it*; **elle**, *she, it*	**ils**, **elles**, *they*

Je becomes **j'** before a word beginning with a vowel or **h** 'mute'.

■ **Il** is used for a person or a thing when referring to a masculine noun, **elle** when referring to a feminine noun.

■ **Ils** (*they*) is used to refer to more than one masculine (people or things) or a mixture of masculines and feminines, **elles** (*they*) to refer to more than one feminine.

■ **Vous** can be either plural:

> **toi et ta famille, vous êtes déjà allés en Corse?**, *have you and your family already been to Corsica?*

or a formal or polite form of the singular:

> **pourriez-vous ouvrir la fenêtre, monsieur?**, *will you please open the window (sir)?*

The polite **vous** is always used to strangers; **tu** is normally used to a close friend or colleague, a relation, a fellow-student. **Tu** is always used to address a child or an animal. Said to a stranger it may be purposely impolite. The same applies of course to all related forms (**ton, le tien**, etc.; **votre, le vôtre**, etc.).

■ The subject pronoun **on** takes the same form of the verb as **il**. It means *one* in the sense of 'people in general', and often corresponds to an indefinite *we* or *they* in English:

> **on part à trois heures trente-six**, *we leave at 3.36*
> **on écrit des choses vraiment incroyables**, *they write some really unbelievable things*

In spoken French **on** is almost always used instead of **nous**:

> **où on va ce soir?**, *where are we going tonight?*

On may be seen as feminine or plural when agreements are made, but it does not have to be:

> **ton père et moi, on était si fatigué(s)**, *we were so tired, your father and I*

▶ **On** is frequently used in French instead of the passive. See pp. 33, 34.

■ **Ce** (*this, that, it, those*) is used as an impersonal subject pronoun, but only with the verb **être**. In the plural **ce** is used with a plural form of **être** (**ce sont, c'étaient**, etc.):

> **c'est une Citroën**, *it's a Citroën*
> **ce sont des mouettes**, *those are seagulls*

With verbs other than **être** (and sometimes with **être** too), **cela** or the less formal **ça** is used:

> **ça (cela) ne se voit pas**, *that's (it's) not obvious*

▶ See also pp. 75, 76, and 225 for the use of **c'est** or **il est** + adjective and p. 84 and p. 224 for **c'est** or **il est** + noun.

▶ The stressed or disjunctive pronouns, **moi, toi**, etc. may also be used as subject pronouns in some circumstances. See p. 110.

OBJECT PRONOUNS

Forms of the object pronouns

■ The direct object pronouns are:

singular	*plural*
me, *me*	**nous**, *us*
te, *you*	**vous**, *you*
le, *him, it*; **la**, *her, it*	**les**, *them*

■ The indirect object pronouns are:

singular	*plural*
me, *to me*	**nous**, *to us*
te, *to you*	**vous**, *to you*
lui, *to him, to her, to it*	**leur**, *to them*

English often omits the *to* of the indirect object: *give it (to) me*. If you are not clear whether an English object without a *to* is indirect or not, simply insert the *to* and see if the sentence still makes sense.

■ The reflexive object pronouns are the same whether direct or indirect. They are:

singular	*plural*
me, (*to*) *myself*	**nous**, (*to*) *ourselves*
te, (*to*) *yourself*	**vous**, (*to*) *yourself/ yourselves*
se, (*to*) *him-/her-/itself*	**se**, (*to*) *themselves*

▶ For the use of the reflexive pronouns see p. 30.

■ **Me, te, le, la, se** become **m', t', l', l', s'** before a vowel or **h** 'mute'.

Me and **te** become **moi** and **toi** in the positive imperative (**m'** and **t'** before a vowel). See p. 28 (formation of the imperative) and p. 106 (pronouns with the imperative).

■ **Y** (*to it*, *there*) and **en** (*of it*, *some*) are also treated as object pronouns. See p. 107.

Position of object pronouns

Object pronouns stand immediately before the verb (this includes infinitives, present participles, **voici** and **voilà**):

> **je t'explique le problème**, *I'll explain the problem to you*
>
> **je vais t'expliquer le problème**, *I'm going to explain the problem to you*
>
> **en t'expliquant le problème**, *by explaining the problem to you*
>
> **le voilà, le problème**, *that's it, that's the problem*

In the compound tenses they stand immediately before the auxiliary verb (**avoir** or **être**):

> **l'as-tu trouvé?**, *have you found it?*
>
> **je l'ai trouvé dans l'armoire**, *I found it in the cupboard*

Since they stand immediately before the verb, object pronouns follow the **ne** of a negative:

> **je ne l'ai pas trouvé**, *I haven't found it*

▶ For the position of object pronouns with the imperative, see below.

Order of object pronouns

Where two object pronouns appear together they stand in this order:

me, m'				
te, t'	**le, l'**			
se, s'	**la, l'**	**lui**		
nous	**les**	**leur**	**y**	**en**
vous				

> **je te l'apporte**, *I'll bring it to you*
> **elle le lui a emprunté**, *she's borrowed it from him*
> **il n'y en a pas**, *there isn't any*

Pronouns from the first and third columns cannot appear together. In the rare cases where this would happen the dative object is expressed by **à** + a disjunctive pronoun:

> **je vais vous conduire à eux**, *I'm going to take you to them* (not '**vous leur**')

Order of pronouns with the imperative

■ With the negative imperative the order of pronouns is as above:

> **ne me l'explique pas!**, *don't explain it to me!*

■ With the positive imperative, object pronouns follow the verb, are hyphenated to it and to each other, and stand in the following order:

	moi, m'		
	toi, t'		
le	lui		
la	nous	y	en
les	vous		
	leur		

So:

donne-les-lui, *give them to him*
donnez-la-leur, *give it to them*

Me and **te** become **moi** and **toi** in the positive imperative; before **en** they become **m'** and **t'** and are not followed by a hyphen:

donne-les-moi, *give them to me*
donne-m'en, *give me some*

The pronouns y and en

■ **Y** stands for **à**, **sur** or **dans** + a thing or things. In this sense it usually means *to, at, in it/them*:

je m'y oppose formellement, *I'm absolutely opposed to it*
il ne s'y intéresse pas du tout, *he's not in the least interested in it*

It can also mean *there*, in which case it is really an adverb, though it still behaves as an object pronoun as far as its position in the sentence is concerned:

on y sera à l'ombre, *we'll be in the shade there*

■ **En** stands for **de** + a thing or things. In this sense it usually means *of, with, from it/them*:

nous en parlerons demain, *we'll speak of it tomorrow*

trois voyageurs en sont descendus, *three passengers got out of it*

It often means *of it*, *of them* with an expression of quantity:

j'en ai beaucoup, *I've got a lot of it*
il y en a trois, *there are three of them*

With expressions of quantity English frequently drops *of it/them*. This is impossible in French—the **en** must always be there:

il faudra en remplacer un, *you'll have to replace one* (*of them*)

With expressions of quantity, **en** can also stand for **de** + persons:

combien de frères as-tu? — J'en ai trois, *how many brothers have you?—I've got three*

En can also mean *some* or *any*:

tu en as? Alors, donne-m'en, *have you got any? Well, give me some*

Object pronouns to complete the sense

We have an example above (**il faudra en remplacer un**) of **en** used to complete the sense in French where in English *of it/them* is often omitted. This also occurs with the pronouns **le** (= *it*) and **y**:

je te l'ai dit, *I told you* (*so*)
vous êtes la fille de cet homme? — Non, je le lui ai déjà dit, *you are this man's daughter?—No, I've already told him* (*it*)
oui, j'y vais, *all right, I'm going* (*there*)
elle sera déjà partie, je le sais, *she'll have gone, I know* (*it*)

However, with **savoir** this **le** is very often dropped in a simple response to a statement:

> **elle est là — Oui, je (le) sais**, *she's there—Yes, I know*

DISJUNCTIVE PRONOUNS

The disjunctive, or stressed, pronouns are those that stand separated from ('disjoined from') verbs. There are no separate forms for these pronouns in English, ordinary subject or object pronouns being used. In French the disjunctive pronouns are:

moi, *me*	**nous**, *us*
toi, *you*	**vous**, *you*
lui, *him*	**eux**, *them* (masculine)
elle, *her*	**elles**, *them* (feminine)

The disjunctive corresponding to **on** is **soi**. It means *oneself*, *yourself*, and is only used after a preposition or **que** (see below). **Soi** in fact is the disjunctive that corresponds to all the indefinite pronouns (**chacun, tout le monde, personne**, etc.). See p. 127.

Disjunctives usually only refer to people, not to things. For the corresponding usage with things, see p. 112.

Use of the disjunctive pronouns

■ Disjunctives may stand completely alone in response to a question or statement:

> **qui l'a pris? — Moi!**, *who's taken it?—Me!*
> **tu l'as pris! — Moi?**, *you've taken it!—(What) me?*

■ They are used after prepositions:

>**comme nous**, *like us*
>**la plupart d'entre elles**, *most of them*
>**c'est à moi**, *it's mine* (*it belongs to me*)
>**chacun pour soi**, *each one for himself*

■ The preposition **à** plus a disjunctive pronoun is used with certain verbs instead of an indirect object, to refer to people. These verbs are:

>**penser/songer à**, *think about*
>**avoir affaire à**, *have business with; deal with*
>**prendre garde à**, *beware of*
>
>**je pense à toi**, *I'm thinking of you*

A disjunctive after **à** is also used with **venir** and **aller** where movement in space is indicated:

>**elle est venue à moi**, *she came to me*

but not otherwise:

>**ce kilt ne te va pas du tout**, *that kilt really doesn't suit you*

■ Disjunctive pronouns are used to specify the individual parts of a plural subject. A subject pronoun may or may not appear as well:

>**eux et moi, on se voit souvent**, *they and I see each other a lot*
>**les enfants et lui se taquinent toujours**, *he and the children always tease each other*
>**qui l'a fait, lui ou son copain?**, *who did it, he or his pal?*

■ They are used to give a subject or object pronoun more emphasis:

>**moi, je ne suis pas d'accord**, *I don't agree*
>**lui, je ne l'aime pas du tout**, *I don't like **him** at all*

■ They are used after **c'est, c'était**, etc. In this sense the disjunctives may refer to things as well as people:

> **c'est toi?** *it's you?*
> **c'est eux/elles!**, *it's them!*

In careful speech or writing **ce sont eux/elles** is used.

■ They are used after **que** in comparatives and after **ne ... que**, *only*, and **ne ... ni ... ni**, *neither ... nor*:

> **elle est plus jolie que moi**, *she's prettier than me*
> **on parle toujours des choses qui n'intéressent que soi**, *we always talk about things that only interest ourselves*

■ They are used before a relative pronoun:

> **lui, qui ne sait absolument rien, a été promu capitaine**, *he, who knows absolutely nothing, has been promoted captain*
> **elle m'aime, moi qui n'ai pas un sou**, *she loves me, I who haven't a penny*

This usage is rather literary.

■ They are used instead of subject pronouns with **aussi** and **seul**:

> **lui seul est resté dans la chambre**, *he alone remained in the room*
> **eux aussi l'ont essayé**, *they tried it too*

■ They combine with **-même** to produce emphatic forms:

moi-même, *myself*	**nous-mêmes**, *ourselves*
toi-même, *yourself*	**vous-même(s)**, *yourself; yourselves*
lui-même, *himself*	**eux-mêmes**, *themselves*
elle-même, *herself*	**elles-mêmes**,
soi-même, *onself* etc.	*themselves*

tu l'as vraiment fait toi-même?, *you really did it (all by) yourself?*

Substitutes for the disjunctive pronouns

The disjunctive pronouns are not normally used to refer to things. For a preposition + *it/them* an adverb is substituted:

sur lui → dessus, *on it*
dans lui → dedans, *in it*
derrière lui → derrière, *behind it*
après lui → après, *after it*
à côté de lui → à côté, *beside it*
etc.

qu'est-ce qu'il y a dessus? Et dedans?, *what's on it? And in it?*

Alternatively a demonstrative pronoun may be used:

je n'ai jamais eu une moto comme celle-là, *I've never had a bike like it*

RELATIVE PRONOUNS

Relative pronouns introduce a clause within the sentence and usually relate it back to a noun in the main clause. In English they are *who, whom, whose, which, that, what*. In French they are:

qui, *who, which, that*
que, *whom, which, that*

ce qui, ce que, *what*

lequel, *which*

de qui or **dont**, *of whom, whose*

>> **duquel** or **dont**, *of which, whose*
>> **à qui**, *to whom*
>> **auquel**, *to which*

and the less common

>> **ce dont**, *that of which*
>> **ce à quoi**, *that to which*

Que and **ce que** become **qu'** and **ce qu'** before a vowel. **Qui** and **ce qui** never change.

Relatives are sometimes omitted in English. In French this is not possible and it is important to recognize that a sentence like 'the man you want to see is here' has a hidden relative (*who* or *that*):

>> **le client que tu voulais voir est là**, *the customer (that/who) you wanted to see is here*

Qui and que

■ **Qui** is the subject of the clause it introduces, **que** is the direct object:

>> **la femme qui parle**, *the woman who is speaking*
>> **la femme que tu connais**, *the woman (that) you know*

So **que** will be followed by a subject noun or pronoun (**tu** above), and **qui** will be followed by a verb, possibly preceded by **ne** and/or an object pronoun.

■ **Que** may not be the object of the verb it introduces but of an infinitive depending on that verb. This is similar to English:

>> **la femme que tu espères épouser**, *the woman that you hope to marry* (you hope to marry her, you don't 'hope' her, so **que** is actually the object of **épouser**, not of **espères**)

■ After **que** a noun subject and the verb are often inverted if nothing else follows in that clause:

> **voilà la liste que réclame l'inspecteur**, *here's the list the inspector is asking for*

This does not happen with pronoun subjects, or if something else follows in the clause:

> **voilà la liste que vous demandez**, *here's the list you're asking for*
>
> **voilà la liste que l'inspecteur a demandée hier**, *here's the list the inspector asked for yesterday*

■ Beware! As well as being a relative, meaning *who, which, that*, **que** may also be a conjunction meaning *that* (this too may be omitted in English):

> **j'espère que tu te portes bien**, *I hope (that) you are well*

and it may also be part of a comparison, meaning *than*:

> **il est plus grand que toi**, *he's bigger than you*

Que = *what*, **qui** = *who*, and **lequel** = *which* may also introduce questions; here the question mark makes their meaning clear:

> **que dis-tu?**, *what are you saying?*

► See p. 118.

■ In order to avoid ambiguity **lequel** may sometimes be used instead of **qui/que**. This is because **lequel** shows gender and number:

> **j'ai écrit au père de sa femme, lequel est très riche**, *I've written to his wife's father, who is very rich*

► For the declension of **lequel** see p. 116.

Relative pronouns after prepositions

■ After prepositions **qui** is used for people (English *whom* or *that*). So *with/without/under whom* is **avec/sans/ sous qui**:

> **la femme avec qui je parle**, *the woman to whom I'm speaking* (*that I'm speaking to*)

Notice that in English (as in the bracketed version above) we try to avoid the old-fashioned and formal word *whom*. So we often use *that* as the relative and push the preposition to the end of the clause. This is impossible in French: the preposition must come immediately before the relative.

□ After the prepositions **parmi**, *among*, and **entre**, *between*, **lesquels/lesquelles** is used instead of **qui** for people

> **les mineurs parmi lesquels tu vis**, *the miners among whom you live*

▶ For the declension of **lequel** see p. 116.

□ **De + qui** usually becomes **dont**, *whose, of whom*.

The word order after **dont** (or **de qui** or **duquel**) is always subject, verb, rest of clause. This is not the case in English, where the object is placed immediately after the word *whose*:

> **voilà l'homme dont (de qui) tu as volé la voiture**, *there's the man whose car you stole*

English also drops the definite article (*whose car*) which French does not (**dont ... la voiture**).

Dont is used as the relative (for both people and things) with verbs that have an object preceded by **de**:

> **l'homme dont tu as besoin**, *the man you need* (= *of whom you have need*)

■ After prepositions **lequel** is used for things. So *with/without/under which* is **avec/sans/sous lequel**. **Lequel** declines as follows:

	singular	*plural*
masculine	**lequel**	**lesquels**
feminine	**laquelle**	**lesquelles**

Lequel agrees in gender and number with the noun it refers back to.

□ **Lequel** combines with the prepositions **à** and **de** to produce the forms **auquel, auxquels, à laquelle, auxquelles** and **duquel, desquels, de laquelle, desquelles**

> **les autorités auxquelles j'écris**, *the authorities I'm writing to*
> **le pays duquel je parle**, *the country I'm speaking about*

However, the simpler word **dont**, *of which, whose*, is often substituted for **duquel** etc.

> **le pays dont je parle**, *the country I'm speaking of*
> **la voiture dont il a volé la radio**, *the car whose radio he stole*

Similarly, **où**, *where*, is often used instead of **auquel, dans lequel, sur lequel**, etc. where the meaning allows it:

> **la maison où (dans laquelle) il a passé sa vie**, *the house where (in which) he spent his life*

▶ See p. 115 for the word order after **dont** and **duquel**.

■ In English *whose* can be used after a preposition: *the nurse, without whose efforts I shouldn't be here.* **Dont** cannot be used in this way in French: **de qui/duquel** must be used instead:

> **cette infirmière, sans les soins de qui je ne serais plus ici, ne travaille plus dans cet hôpital**, *that nurse, without whose efforts I should no longer be here, doesn't work in this hospital any more*

This construction is often clumsy in French, however, and is usually avoided:

> **sans les soins de cette infirmière, je ne serais plus ici; mais elle ne travaille plus dans cet hôpital**, *without that nurse's efforts I should no longer be here today; but she doesn't work in this hospital any more*

Ce qui, ce que, ce dont, ce à quoi

■ *What* as a relative is **ce qui** or **ce que**, **ce qui** being the subject form and **ce que** the object form, as with **qui** and **que**. These relative pronouns introduce noun clauses:

> **je ne comprends pas ce que tu dis**, *I don't understand what you're saying*

If the main verb following a noun clause introduced by **ce qui/ce que** is **être**, a comma and **ce** are introduced, like this:

> **ce qui est difficile, c'est de jouer de la cornemuse**, *what's difficult is playing the bagpipes*

This construction is extremely common.

■ **Ce qui** and **ce que** are used instead of **qui** and **que** as relatives after **tout**, *all*, *everything*:

> **tout ce que tu dis est incompréhensible**, *everything (that) you say is incomprehensible*

■ **Ce qui** and **ce que** can also mean *which*, where this refers to an idea rather than a specific thing:

> **il va jouer de la cornemuse, ce qui est très difficile**, *he's going to play the bagpipes, which is very difficult* (*which* refers not to bagpipes but to playing them)

After prepositions the form of the relative meaning *which*, and referring back to an idea, is **quoi**:

> **je lui ait tout expliqué, sans quoi il aurait été vraiment fâché**, *I've explained everything to him, without which he would have been really angry* (*which* refers to my having explained things to him)

■ When the verb used in the relative clause takes **à** or **de** before its object, *what* as a relative is **ce à quoi** (**à** verbs) or **ce dont** (**de** verbs):

> **ce à quoi je pense, c'est d'aller jouer à la pétanque**, *what I'm thinking of is going to play pétanque* (the verb is **penser à**)
> **je peux t'envoyer ce dont tu as besoin**, *I can send you what you need* (*what you have need of*) (the verb is **avoir besoin de**)

De quoi is sometimes used instead of **ce dont**:

> **je ne comprends pas de quoi tu parles**, *I don't understand what you're talking about*

INTERROGATIVE PRONOUNS

The interrogative pronouns in English are *who?*, *what?*, and *which?* In English they have the same forms in both direct and indirect questions:

> *who did it?*—direct question
> *I want to know who did it*—indirect question

In French they have somewhat different forms in direct and in indirect questions.

Interrogative pronouns in direct questions

Referring to people

■ As the subject of the sentence the interrogative pronoun referring to people is **qui est-ce qui** or just **qui**. Both mean *who*:

> **qui est-ce qui arrive?**, *who's coming?*
> **qui vous a dit ça?**, *who told you that?*

The interrogative pronoun **qui** is always masculine singular—even if you know that the people who turned up were feminine and plural, you still ask **qui est arrivé?**

■ As the object of the sentence the interrogative pronoun referring to people is **qui est-ce que** or just **qui**. Both mean *who* (in older or formal English, *whom*). The **que** changes to **qu'** before a vowel:

> **qui est-ce qu'on a élu?**, *who did they elect?*
> **qui as-tu envoyé?**, *who did you send?*

■ After a preposition the interrogative pronoun referring to people is **qui est-ce que** or just **qui**. Both mean *who(m)*. The **que** changes to **qu'** before a vowel:

> **pour qui avez-vous fait cela?**, *who did you do it for? (for whom did you do it?)*
> **de qui est-ce que tu parles?**, *who are you talking about? (about whom are you talking?)*

Notice that in English the preposition may (and usually does) go to the end of its clause. This is impossible in French—it must always stand before the interrogative pronoun.

■ The longer forms of the interrogatives are common in speech.

Referring to things

■ As the subject of the sentence the interrogative pronoun referring to things is **qu'est-ce qui**, *what*:

> **qu'est-ce qui arrive?**, *what's happening?*

Notice that there is no alternative form here.

■ As the object of the sentence the interrogative pronoun referring to things is **qu'est-ce que** or just **que**. Both mean *what*. In both, **que** changes to **qu'** before a vowel:

> **qu'est-ce qu'on a trouvé?**, *what did they find?*
> **qu'as-tu fait de mon pullover blanc?**, *what have you done with my white pullover?*

Notice also the form **qu'est-ce que c'est qu'un ...?** (sometimes shortened to **qu'est-ce qu'un ...?**) meaning *what's a ...?*

> **qu'est-ce c'est qu'un ornithorynque?**, *what's a duck-billed platypus?*

■ After a preposition the interrogative pronoun referring to things is **quoi**, *what*:

> **avec quoi as-tu fait cela?**, *what did you do that with? (with what did you do that?)*

■ The longer forms of the interrogatives are common in speech.

Interrogative pronouns in indirect questions

Referring to people

■ The interrogative pronoun in indirect questions referring to people is always **qui**, *who(m)*, whether it is used as subject, object or after a preposition:

> **je ne sais pas qui sera président**, *I've no idea who will be president*

je me demande qui vous allez choisir, *I wonder
who you'll choose*

dis-moi à qui tu penses, *tell me who you're
thinking of*

Referring to things

■ As the subject of an indirect question, the
interrogative pronoun referring to things is **ce qui**, *what*:

je ne sais pas ce qui se passe ici, *I don't know
what's happening here*

■ As the object of an indirect question, the interrogative
pronoun referring to things is **ce que**, *what*:

explique-moi ce que tu penses, *explain to me what
you're thinking*

■ After prepositions, the interrogative pronoun in an
indirect question referring to things is **quoi**, *what*:

demande-lui de quoi elle a besoin, *ask her what
she needs*

The interrogative pronoun lequel

■ **Lequel** means *which* as an interrogative pronoun. It
refers to both people and things and is used in both
direct and indirect questions. It agrees with the noun it
refers to in gender and number:

	singular	*plural*
masculine	**lequel**	**lesquels**
feminine	**laquelle**	**lesquelles**

Notice that both parts of the word change.

lequel des deux préfères-tu?, *which of the two do
you prefer?*

il a répondu à trois questions — lesquelles?, *he's
answered three questions—which (ones)?*

> **je ne sais pas lequel des deux je préfère**, *I don't know which of the two I prefer*

■ With the prepositions **à** and **de**, **lequel** forms the following compounds:

	singular	*plural*
masculine	**auquel, duquel**	**auxquels, desquels**
feminine	**à laquelle, de laquelle**	**auxquelles, desquelles**

> **auquel des trois donnez-vous votre voix?**, *which of the three do you give your vote to?*

The interrogative adjective quel

■ The interrogative adjective corresponding to all the above pronouns is **quel**, *which, what*. **Quel** agrees with its noun in gender and number:

	singular	*plural*
masculine	**quel**	**quels**
feminine	**quelle**	**quelles**

> **avec quelle main l'as-tu fait?**, *which hand did you do it with?*
>
> **quels gens fréquente-t-il?**, *what (kind of) people does he go around with?*
>
> **je me demande à quel quai il va arriver**, *I wonder which (what) platform it will arrive at*

■ With the verb **être**, **quel** may be divided from its noun by the verb:

> **quels sont ces gens?**, *what (kind of) people are these? (who are these people?)*

▶ For questions introduced by other question-words see p. 212. For the formation of direct and indirect questions see pp. 211 and 213.

POSSESSIVE PRONOUNS

■ The forms of the possessive pronouns (*mine, yours,* etc. in English) are:

masc. sing.	fem. sing.	masc. plural	fem. plural	
le mien	la mienne	les miens	les miennes	*mine*
le tien	la tienne	les tiens	les tiennes	*yours*
le sien	la sienne	les siens	les siennes	*his, hers, its*
le nôtre	la nôtre	les nôtres		*ours*
le vôtre	la vôtre	les vôtres		*yours*
le leur	la leur	les leurs		*theirs*

> **ma mère et la vôtre sont parties ensemble**, *my mother and yours left together*

With **à, le/les** becomes **au/aux**; with **de, le/les** becomes **du/des**:

> **cet élève est un des miens**, *this pupil is one of mine*

■ The possessive pronouns do not agree with the *owner* of the object, but with the object itself. So **le sien** means either *his* or *hers*, referring to a masculine object, and **la sienne** means either *his* or *hers* referring to a feminine object:

> **mon argent, je l'ai toujours, mais Marie a dépensé tout le sien**, *I've still got my money, but Marie's spent all hers*

■ The possessive pronoun corresponding to **on** and other indefinite pronouns is **le sien**:

> **on s'occupe des siens**, *you look after your own (people)*

■ *It's mine, it's yours*, etc. may also be translated into French by **c'est à moi, c'est à toi**, etc. This use of

à + disjunctive pronoun is only possible after **être**, where it is extremely common.

There is a slight difference in meaning between **c'est à moi** and **c'est le mien**. **C'est le mien** distinguishes between objects possessed: 'that one is mine, maybe some other is yours'; **c'est à moi** emphasizes the ownership of the object 'that's mine (so give it me!)'.

DEMONSTRATIVE PRONOUNS

The demonstrative pronouns—English *this* (*one*), *that* (*one*), *those*—point things out. In French they are **celui**, *this one here; that one there*, specifying, or **ceci/cela**, *this one/that one*, not specifying.

■ The forms of **celui** are:

	masculine	*feminine*	
singular	**celui**	**celle**	*this, that, the one*
plural	**ceux**	**celles**	*these, those*

They agree in gender and number with the noun they refer to.

■ **Celui** does not stand alone. It may be followed by a preposition, by **qui/que** or by **-ci/-là**.

Celui + preposition

The preposition most frequently found after **celui** is **de**. **Celui de** means *that of* and is the equivalent of the English **'s**:

> **celui de Nicole est cassé**, *Nicole's is broken*
> **la voiture? C'est celle de mon ami**, *the car? It's my friend's*

■ Other prepositions are also found after **celui**:

> **quel tapis? — Celui en laine**, *which carpet?—The woollen one* (*the one in wool*)

Celui à is frequently encountered when shopping:

> **quels abricots? — Ceux à neuf francs**, *which apricots?—The ones at nine francs*

Celui qui, celui que

Celui qui and **celui que** mean *the one who, the one that* or in the plural *those who, those that*. The **qui** and **que** are relative pronouns (see p. 112), so **celui qui** is the subject of its clause and is followed by a verb, **celui que** is the object and is followed by a pronoun or noun subject, and then the verb:

> **celle qui habitait à côté de Jean-Luc a déménagé,** *that woman who lived next to Jean-Luc has moved* **lesquels? Ceux que tu trouves difficiles?**, *which? Those you find difficult?*

■ The relatives **à qui** and **dont** are also found after **celui** when the verb that follows takes **à** or **de**:

> **celui à qui je pense**, *the one I'm thinking of* (**penser à**) **celle dont tu parles**, *the one you're talking about* (**parler de**)

Celui-ci, celui-là

Celui-ci means *this one*, **celui-là** means *that one* when you are making a specific contrast:

> **celui-ci est bleu, celui-là est plutôt vert**, *this one's blue, that one's more green*

Because **là** is often used to mean *here* as well as *there* in modern French, **celui-là** is losing its ability to point to something at a distance when it is not contrasted, as in the example above, with **celui-ci**. To indicate something at a distance, therefore, **celui là-bas**, *that one over there*, is now often used instead of **celui-là**.

■ **Celui-ci** can also mean *the latter*, **celui-là** *the former*:

> **tu connais Luc et son frère? Alors, celui-ci a demandé de tes nouvelles hier soir**, *you know Luc and his brother? Well, the latter asked (his brother asked) about you last night*

Notice that *the former/the latter* are only used in formal English, whereas **celui-là/celui-ci** can be used with this meaning in French at all levels.

Cela, ça, ceci

Sometimes called neuter demonstratives, **cela** (and its more colloquial form **ça**) means *that* or *this* or *it*, **ceci** means *this*. **Cela/ça** is used much more frequently than **ceci**.

■ **Cela/ça** and **ceci** may refer to ideas, **cela** to one already mentioned, **ceci** to one about to be produced:

> **j'ai entendu tout ce que tu as dit, mais cela est très difficile à comprendre**, *I've heard all you've been saying, but that's (it's) very difficult to understand*
> **ça se comprend!** *that's obvious!*
> **écoutez ceci**, *listen to this*

or they may refer to objects, so far unnamed in the case of **ceci**:

> **je t'ai apporté ceci, c'est un petit cadeau**, *I've brought you this, it's a little present*

already known in the case of **cela / ça**:

> **ça te plaît?**, *do you like it?*

■ Whereas **celui-là** distinguishes between a number of objects, **cela / ça** simply points. Compare:

> **cela m'appartient**, *that's mine* (pointing to a single object)
>
> **celui-là m'appartient**, *that one's mine* (pointing to one among a number of similar objects)

Ce

The pronoun **ce** is a weaker form of **cela / ceci**, used only with **être**, and meaning *it* or *that*:

> **qui est-ce? — C'est moi**, *who's that?—It's me*

Ce becomes **c'** before **e**, **ç** before **a**:

> **ç'a été le plus grand problème**, *that's been the greatest problem*

■ The pronoun **ce** when used as the subject of **être** can also be plural:

> **ce sont des baleines**, *those are whales*

▶ See pp. 224 and 225 for **c'est** versus **il est**.

INDEFINITE PRONOUNS

Indefinite pronouns (*somebody*, *something*, *anybody*, etc. in English) all take the third person (**il** form) of the verb in French, as in English. The forms of object pronouns, reflexives, possessives corresponding to indefinite pronouns are also the third person forms (**le, la, lui; se; son, sa, ses; le sien** and their plurals); the corresponding form of the disjunctive is **soi**:

> **chacun doit s'asseoir à sa propre place**,
> *everybody must sit down in his or her own place*

Some indefinites only function as pronouns, some can also be adjectives—see below. See also indefinite adjectives, p. 148.

Used only as pronouns

■ **Chacun** (fem. **chacune**), *each one, everybody*:

> **chacun doit prendre une feuille de papier**,
> *everybody must take a sheet of paper*

■ **Je ne sais quoi**, *something or other*

This phrase is used as if it were a simple pronoun. It may take an adjective, preceded by **de**:

> **elle a dit je ne sais quoi de complètement stupide**,
> *she said something or other completely stupid*

■ **N'importe qui**, *anyone (at all)*:

> **n'importe qui te dira ça**, *anyone (at all) will tell you that*
> **ne le dis pas à n'importe qui**, *don't tell just anyone*

■ **On**, *one, you, we, they, someone, people in general*:

> **on nous regarde**, *somebody's looking at us*
> **qu'est-ce qu'on va faire?**, *what are we going to do?*

▶ See also pp. 103, 109, and (**on** as a substitute for the passive) 34.

■ **Personne**, *nobody, not anybody*:

> **qui est là? — Personne**, *who's there—Nobody*
> **je n'y vois personne**, *I can't see anyone there*

Personne must have a **ne** with an associated verb, as in the second example above. See p. 159.

Any adjective with **personne** follows it, is masculine, and is preceded by **de**:

> **il n'y a personne de compétent**, *there is no one qualified*

■ **Quelque chose,** *something, anything*:

> **tu as vu quelque chose?**, *did you see anything?*
> **oui, il y a quelque chose qui bouge**, *yes, there's something moving*

Any adjective with **quelque chose** follows it, is masculine, and is preceded by **de**:

> **ça doit être quelque chose d'horrible!**, *it must be something horrible!*

The other **chose** compounds behave similarly:

> **autre chose**, *something else*
> **peu de chose**, *little*
> **pas grand-chose**, *not much*

■ **Quelqu'un,** *someone, anybody*:

> **il y a quelqu'un dans la grange**, *there's someone in the barn*
> **est-ce que tu entends quelqu'un?**, *can you hear anybody?*

Quelqu'un has masculine and feminine plural forms (**quelques-uns, quelques-unes**) but no feminine singular form (the masculine must be used even if you are aware that 'someone' is a woman):

> **il vit avec quelqu'un depuis trois ans**, *he's been living with somebody for three years*

The plural form, **quelques-un(e)s**, must have an **en** with its associated verb when it is used as the direct object:

> **ces dames-là? oui, j'en connais quelques-unes**, *those ladies? yes, I know some of them*

Any adjective with **quelqu'un** follows it and is preceded by **de**:

> **je cherche quelqu'un de beau**, *I'm looking for someone handsome*

■ **Quiconque**, *whoever; anybody*:

> **quiconque dit cela, ment!**, *whoever says that is lying!*
> **il joue mieux que quiconque**, *he plays better than anybody*

Qui que ce soit (qui/que) may be used, in rather less formal style, for **quiconque**. See p. 234.

■ **Rien**, *nothing, not anything*:

> **tu entends quelque chose? — Non, rien**, *can you hear anything?—No, nothing*
> **je n'entends absolument rien**, *I can hear absolutely nothing*

Rien must have a **ne** with an associated verb, as in the second example above. See p. 159.

Any adjective with **rien** follows it, is masculine, and is preceded by **de**:

> **ce n'est rien de spécial**, *it's nothing special*

■ **L'un** (fem. **l'une**), *(the) one*:

> **j'ai rencontré l'un d'eux en ville**, *I met one of them in town*
> **l'une chante, l'autre pas**, *one sings, the other doesn't*

As in the second example above, **l'un** is often followed later in the sentence by **l'autre**, *another, the other*. The plural is **les un(e)s ... les autres ...**

L'un(e) l'autre (plural **les un(e)s les autres**) is used to mean *one another, each other*:

> **ils se détestent l'un l'autre**, *they hate one another*

Used as both pronouns and adjectives

▶ For these indefinites used as adjectives, see p. 148.

■ **Aucun** (fem. **aucune**), *none, not any*:

> **tu as entendu ses disques? — Non, aucun**, *you've heard his records?—No, none of them*
> **il n'en a aucun**, *he hasn't any*

Aucun must have **en** before the verb when it is used as the direct object; it must also have a **ne** with an associated verb, as in the second example above. See p. 159.

Pas un (fem. **pas une**) and **nul** (fem. **nulle**) are found as alternatives to **aucun**, with the same meaning.

■ **Certains** (fem. **certaines**), *some (people)*:

> **certains ont dit qu'il a subtilisé l'argent**, *some people said he pinched the money*
> **certaines d'entre elles ont très bien parlé**, *some of them spoke very well*

Certain(e)s must have **en** before the verb when used as the direct object:

> **j'en connais certains**, *I know some of them*

■ **Plusieurs**, *several (people)*:

> **plusieurs sont venus sans savoir pourquoi**, *several came without knowing why*

Plusieurs must have **en** before the verb when used as the direct object:

> **il en a tué plusieurs**, *he killed several (of them)*

Any adjective with **plusieurs** follows it and is preceded by **de**:

> **il y en a plusieurs de verts**, *there are several green ones*

■ **Tous** (fem. **toutes**), *everybody, all*:

> **je vous connais tous**, *I know you all*
> **elles sont toutes là**, *they are all there*
> **tous sont venus à la réunion**, *all of them came to the meeting*

Tous usually follows the verb, as in the first two examples above, whether it refers to the subject or the object. It stands before the verb when it alone is the subject, as in the third example above.

■ **Tout**, *everything, all*:

> **tout est arrangé**, *all is arranged*
> **j'ai tout fait**, *I've done everything*

Adjectives

In French, adjectives are singular or plural and masculine or feminine according to the noun they refer to. To the basic masculine form **-e** is added to make the adjective feminine, **-s** to make it masculine plural, **-es** to make it feminine plural:

	singular	*plural*
masculine	**un stylo noir**, *a black pen*	**des stylos noirs**
feminine	**une boîte noire**, *a black box*	**des boîtes noires**

An adjective referring to two singular nouns is plural; if they are of different genders the adjective is masculine plural:

> **un complet et une cravate noirs**, *a black suit and tie*

Adjectives usually follow their noun; but see p. 138, position of adjectives.

FEMININE OF ADJECTIVES

Adjectives whose masculine form ends in **-e** remain unchanged in the feminine:

> **un stylo rouge**, *a red pen*
> **une boîte rouge**, *a red box*

otherwise all adjectives add **-e** to form their feminine.

■ Additional changes are made by adjectives with the following endings. Many of these changes are identical to those made by nouns to form their feminines—see p. 93.

masculine adjective	*feminine adjective*
-c	**-que**
public, *public*	**publique**
except:	
blanc, *white*	**blanche**
franc, *frank*	**franche**
grec, *Greek*	**grecque**
sec, *dry*	**sèche**
-er	**-ère**
dernier, *last*	**dernière**
-eur	**-euse**
trompeur, *deceptive*	**trompeuse**
except:	
inférieur, *lower*	**inférieure**
supérieur, *higher*	**supérieure**
intérieur, *inner*	**intérieure**
extérieur, *outer*	**extérieure**
majeur, *major*	**majeure**
mineur, *minor*	**mineure**
meilleur, *better*	**meilleure**
and see **-teur** below	

-f	-ve
informatif, *informative*	**informative**
except:	
bref, *brief*	**brève**
-gu	-guë (the tréma, ¨, indicates that the **e** is pronounced separately from the **u**)
aigu, *sharp*	**alguë**
-teur	-teuse: where the adjective is based on the present participle of a verb
menteur, *lying*	**menteuse** (**mentir**, p.p. **mentant**)
	-trice: in all other cases
conservateur, *conservative*	**conservatrice** (**conserver**, p.p. **conservant**).
-x	-se
heureux, *happy*	**heureuse**
except:	
doux, *gentle*	**douce**
faux, *false*	**fausse**
roux, *red-haired*	**rousse**
vieux, *old*	**vieille**

■ Adjectives with the following endings double the consonant of their ending before adding **-e**:

masculine	*feminine*
-el	-elle
officiel, *official*	**officielle**
-en	-enne
ancien, *former*	**ancienne**
-et	-ette
net, *clear*	**nette**
except:	
complet, *complete*	**complète**
concret, *concrete*	**concrète**

discret, *discreet*	discrète
inquiet, *worried*	inquiète
secret, *secret*	secrète
-eil	-eille
pareil, *similar*	pareille
-on	-onne
bon, *good*	bonne

■ The following adjectives have a special form used before a masculine singular noun beginning with a vowel or 'mute' **h**, and their feminine form is derived from this:

masculine	*masc. before vowel*	*feminine*
beau, *fine*	bel	belle
fou, *mad*	fol	folle
mou, *soft*	mol	molle
nouveau, *new*	nouvel	nouvelle
vieux, *old*	vieil	vieille

■ Other adjectives with irregular feminine forms:

masculine	*feminine*
bas, *low*	basse
bénin, *benign*	bénigne
épais, *thick*	épaisse
favori, *favourite*	favorite
frais, *fresh*	fraîche
gras, *greasy*	grasse
gros, *big*	grosse
gentil, *nice*	gentille
jumeau, *twin*	jumelle
las, *tired*	lasse
long, *long*	longue
malin, *cunning*	maligne
nul, *no*	nulle
paysan, *peasant*	paysanne
sot, *foolish*	sotte

■ The following adjectives are usually invariable — they make no agreement at all with either a feminine or a plural noun:

> **châtain**, *chestnut*
> **impromptu**, *impromptu*
> **k(h)aki**, *khaki*
> **marron**, *brown*
> **snob**, *snobbish*

and all compound colour-adjectives:

> **une voiture bleu clair**, *a light blue car*
> **une boîte vert foncé**, *a dark green box*

The following adjectives make plural but no feminine agreements:

> **chic** (m. and f. plural **chics**), *chic*
> **maximum** (m. and f. plural, **maximums**), *maximum*
> **minimum** (m. and f. plural **minimums**), *minimum*

PLURAL OF ADJECTIVES

■ All feminine and most masculine adjectives form their plural by adding **-s** to their singular form. This also applies where the feminine singular is irregular:

	singular	*plural*
masculine	**bon**, *good*	**bons**
feminine	**bonne**	**bonnes**

■ Adjectives ending as follows have irregular masculine plurals. Their feminine plurals are formed regularly by adding **-s** to the feminine singular.

masculine singular	*masculine plural*
-s, -x	no change
gris, *grey*	**gris**
faux, *false*	**faux**

-eau	-eaux
beau, *fine*	**beaux**
-al	-aux
brutal, *brutal*	**brutaux**
except:	
banal, *trite*	**banals**
fatal, *fatal*	**fatals**
final, *final*	**finals**
naval, *naval*	**navals**

▶ A number of adjectives are invariable, remaining unchanged in both their feminine and their plural forms. See p. 137.

POSITION OF ADJECTIVES

The usual position for an adjective in French is immediately after the noun:

> **une robe verte**, *a green dress*

Two or more adjectives after the noun are joined with **et**:

> **une robe verte et blanche**, *a green and white dress*

Adjectives are also found in front of the noun, however, and some adjectives are almost always found in this position:

> **une jolie robe verte et blanche**, *a pretty green and white dress*

Adjectives that commonly precede are:

> **beau**, *fine*
> **bon**, *good* (and **meilleur**, *better, best*)
> **court**, *short*

gentil, *nice*
grand, *big; tall*
gros, *big*
jeune, *young*
joli, *pretty*
long, *long*
mauvais, *bad* (and **pire**, *worse, worst*)
méchant, *nasty*
nouveau, *new*
petit, *little* (and **moindre**, *less, least*)
vaste, *vast*
vieux, *old*
vilain, *ugly*

If in doubt place these adjectives before the noun, and all others after.

■ Most adjectives can in fact be placed before or after their noun, with a small but distinct difference in meaning. Placing the adjective after the noun indicates an objective distinction, placing it before shows a subjective feeling. So:

> **le long de cette côte s'étire une interminable plage**, *along this coastline stretches an endless beach* (travel agent's language: 'endless' is gushing and imprecise—'that seems as though it might go on for ever'; **une plage interminable**, however, means that the beach is literally or apparently interminable (and therefore boring and tiresome)

This use of adjectives before the noun is very common in modern French writing at all levels to strengthen the emotional content. The effect is often lost in written English: in spoken English we usually get it by stressing the adjective in some way:

ces superbes peintures, *these superb paintings*
une fantastique reproduction, *a fantastic reproduction*
cette magnifique vallée, *this magnificent valley*
d'une rare qualité, *of a really rare quality*

The adjectives listed on p. 138 above are rarely used as distinguishers: this is why they usually go before the noun. Some adjectives, however, such as colour adjectives, are almost always used to make an objective distinction and so they normally follow the noun.

■ There are some adjectives whose position is completely fixed:

□ Numbers, both cardinal (*one*, *two*, *three*, etc.) and ordinal (*first*, *second*, *third*, etc.), always precede the noun.

les trois mousquetaires, *the three musketeers*
le quatrième mousquetaire, *the fourth musketeer*

But in the following cases where the number follows in English it also follows in French.

numéro deux, *number two*
page cinq, *page five*
Henri quatre, *Henri the Fourth*
acte trois, *act three*

□ Demonstrative, possessive, and interrogative adjectives always precede.

cet enfant-là, *that child*
son parapluie, *his umbrella*
quelle difficulté?, *what difficulty?*

□ Indefinite adjectives like **chaque**, *each*, **tel**, *such*, **autre**, *other*, always precede. See p. 148.

une telle personne, *such a person*
chaque enfant, *each child*

☐ Past participles used as adjectives always follow.

> **un verre cassé**, *a broken glass*

☐ Adjectives of nationality always follow.

> **la révolution française**, *the French revolution*

☐ Scientific and technical adjectives always follow.

> **l'acide chlorhydrique**, *hydrochloric acid*

☐ Adjectives with a qualifying phrase always follow.

> **un bon champignon**, *a good mushroom*
> **un champignon bon à manger**, *an edible mushroom*

■ A small number of adjectives have quite different meanings according to whether they precede or follow the noun. They are:

ancien, *former / ancient*

> **un ancien professeur**, *a former teacher*
> **des meubles anciens**, *very old furniture*

certain, *certain* (= *I'm not sure what*) / *definite*, (*absolutely*) *sure*

> **un certain jour de mai**, *a certain day* (*one day*) *in May*
> **une date certaine**, *a definite date*

cher, *dear* (= *emotionally important*) / *dear* (= *expensive*)

> **mon cher Charles**, *my dear Charles*
> **une lampe chère**, *an expensive lamp*

dernier, *last* (*of a sequence*) / *last* (= *just gone*)

> **le dernier chèque de mon chéquier**, *the last cheque in my chequebook*
> **dimanche dernier**, *last Sunday*

divers, *various/varying*

> **j'ai eu diverses difficultés,** *I've had various difficulties*
> **on m'a donné des réponses diverses,** *I've been given varying replies*

même, *same/very*

> **la même chose,** *the same thing*
> **l'homme même,** *the very man*

Même before the article or before a pronoun means *even*:

> **même cet homme-là,** *even that man*
> **même vous,** *even you*

pauvre, *poor (= to be pitied)/poor (= not rich)*

> **ce pauvre enfant!,** *that poor child!*
> **une famille pauvre,** *a poor family*

propre, *own/clean*

> **mes propres mains,** *my own hands*
> **les mains propres,** *clean hands*

seul, *only/alone*

> **la seule solution,** *the only solution*
> **le roi seul a le droit de décider,** *the king alone has the right to decide* (this use is the equivalent of 'only the king', and **seul le roi** is equally possible)

vrai, *real (= genuine)/true (= not fictitious)*

> **un vrai mystère,** *a real mystery*
> **une histoire vraie,** *a true story*

COMPARATIVE AND SUPERLATIVE OF ADJECTIVES

■ English has two ways to form the comparative and superlative of adjectives:

> *fine*: *finer* (comparative), *finest* (superlative)
> *difficult*: *more difficult* (comparative), *most difficult* (superlative)

French forms the comparative and superlative in one way only, with **plus** (comparative) and **le/la/les plus** (superlative):

> **beau**, **plus beau**, **le plus beau**, *fine, finer, finest*
>
> **la voile est un plus beau sport que le tennis**, *sailing is a finer sport than tennis*
>
> **c'est le plus beau sport du monde**, *it's the finest sport in the world*
>
> **difficile**, **plus difficile**, **le plus difficule**, *difficult, more difficult, most difficult*
>
> **c'est une activité encore plus difficile**, *it's an even more difficult activity*
>
> **c'est l'activité la plus difficile**, *it's the most difficult activity*

■ The comparative or superlative comes in the same position, before or after the noun, that the adjective itself would take, and agrees in the same way as an ordinary adjective does. Notice that where it comes after the noun, the superlative adjective has its own definite article, independently of any article that already stands with the noun:

> **cette activité la plus difficile de toutes**, *this most difficult of all activities*

A superlative adjective immediately after a possessive (**mon, ma, mes; ton, ta, tes,** etc.) drops its definite article:

> **sa plus jolie jupe,** *her prettiest skirt*

■ The following comparative and superlative adjectives are exceptional:

> **bon, meilleur, le meilleur,** *good, better, best*
>
> **mauvais, plus mauvais, le plus mauvais,** or **mauvais, pire, le pire (pire, le pire** are less common. They are mainly used in some set phrases: **le remède est pire que le mal,** *the cure is worse than the disease*)
>
> **petit, plus petit, le plus petit,** *small,* (*physically*) *smaller, smallest,* or **petit, moindre, le moindre,** *little, less* (= *of less importance*), *least*

■ Comparisons, as well as being expressed by **plus ... que,** *more ... than,* can also be expressed by:

> **moins ... que,** *less ... than*
>
> **ton journal est moins intéressant que le mien,** *your paper's less interesting than mine*
>
> **aussi ... que,** *as ... as*
>
> **elle est aussi riche que son père,** *she's as rich as her father*
>
> **pas aussi** (or **pas si**) **... que,** *not as ... as*
>
> **elle n'est pas (aus)si riche que son grand-père,** *she's not as rich as her grandfather*

■ *Than* after a comparative is **que:**

> **vous êtes plus jeune qui moi,** *you're younger than me*

As after a comparative is also **que**:

> **elle n'est pas si vieille que lui**, *she's not as old as him*

In after a superlative is **de**:

> **le plus grand bâtiment du monde**, *the biggest building in the world*

By with either a comparative or a superlative is **de**:

> **il est de beaucoup le plus beau**, *he's by far the most handsome*

■ **Le/la/les moins** can also be used, like **le/la/les plus**, as a superlative:

> **l'enfant le moins gâté**, *the least spoiled child*

■ Where **plus** and **moins** are used to compare nouns rather than adjectives they are followed by **de**:

> **tu as plus de force que moi**, *you have more strength than I*
> **la ville a moins d'habitants qu'auparavant**, *the town has fewer inhabitants than formerly*

To express equal quantity **autant de**, *as much as*, is used:

> **elle a autant d'argent que son petit ami**, *she has as much money as her boyfriend*

More than, *less than* plus a quantity is also **plus de**, **moins de**:

> **il a plus de soixante ans**, *he's more than sixty*

■ *More and more* is **de plus en plus**, *less and less* **de moins en moins**:

> **le temps devient de plus en plus orageux**, *the weather's getting more and more stormy*
> **j'ai de moins en moins d'argent**, *I've less and less money*

▶ For the use of the subjunctive in a clause following a superlative, see p. 47.

DEMONSTRATIVE, POSSESSIVE, AND INTERROGATIVE ADJECTIVES

Demonstrative adjectives (*this*, *that* in English) and possessive adjectives (*my*, *your*, *his*, *her*, etc. in English) stand in exactly the same relationship to nouns as do definite and indefinite articles. They are in fact sometimes known as demonstrative and possessive articles.

■ The demonstrative adjective in French is **ce** (masculine singular), **cet** (masculine singular before a vowel or 'mute' h), **cette** (feminine singular), **ces** (plural):

> **ce jeune homme**, *this young man*
> **cet homme**, *this man*
> **cette fille**, *this girl*
> **ces gens**, *these people*

Where it is necessary to differentiate between *this* and *that*, **-ci** and **-là** are added to the following noun:

> **ce jeune homme-ci**, *this young man*
> **ces gens-là**, *those people*

However, just as French tends to use **là**, *there*, much more than **ici**, *here*, so **ce ... -là** is used in modern French in many cases where English would use *this*, with **ce ... là-bas** used for the more distant object:

> **tu sais quel train tu prends? Celui-là? — Non, ce train là-bas**, *do you know which train you're getting? This one?—No, that train (there)*

■ The possessive adjectives are:

with masc. sing. noun	with fem. sing. noun	with plur. noun	
mon	**ma**	**mes**	*my*
ton	**ta**	**tes**	*your*
son	**sa**	**ses**	*his, her, its*
	notre	**nos**	*our*
	votre	**vos**	*your*
	leur	**leurs**	*their*

Mon, ton, and **son** are also used before a feminine singular noun beginning with a vowel or 'mute' **h**.

> **c'est ma cassette**, *it's my cassette*
> **c'est ton orange**, *it's your orange* (**orange** is feminine)
> **c'est son pullover**, *it's his/her pullover*

Notice that **son, sa, ses**, like the rest of the possessives, have the gender of the object possessed, not of the person owning it. So **son pullover** is *his* or *her pullover*, **sa cassette** *his* or *her cassette*. Where it is necessary to differentiate, **à lui/à elle** are added:

> **c'est sa cassette à lui**, *it's his cassette*

■ The interrogative adjective in French is **quel?**, *which, what?* It agrees in gender and number with the noun that follows:

	singular	plural
masculine	**quel**	**quels**
feminine	**quelle**	**quelles**

> **quelle robe vas-tu porter?**, *which dress are you going to wear?*

Quel can be used to introduce an indirect question:

> **je ne sais pas quelle robe porter**, *I don't know what dress to wear*
>
> **je me demande quelle robe Sophie va porter**, *I wonder what dress Sophie will wear*

■ **Quel ...!** may also be an exclamation, meaning in the singular *what a ...!*, *what ...!*, in the plural *what ...!*

> **quel bel enfant!**, *what a lovely child!*
>
> **quelle chance!**, *what luck!*
>
> **quelles vacances formidables!**, *what terrific holidays!*

INDEFINITE ADJECTIVES

Indefinite adjectives, as a group, include in English such words as *several*, *certain*, *such*. The indefinite adjectives in French are:

> **aucun, nul**, *no, not any*
>
> **autre**, *other*
>
> **certain**, *certain*
>
> **chaque**, *each*
>
> **même**, *same*
>
> **plusieurs**, *several*
>
> **quelque**, *some, any*
>
> **tel**, *such*
>
> **tout** (singular) *all, the whole of*; (plural) *all*; *every*

Chaque has no plural form, **plusieurs** no singular form. **Plusieurs** is unchanged in both masculine and feminine; **tel** and **tout** decline as follows:

	singular	*plural*
masculine	**tel; tout**	**tels; tous**
feminine	**telle; toute**	**telles; toutes**

Aucun and **nul** take **ne** with their verb, like negative adverbs: see p. 159.

■ **Chaque, plusieurs, quelque, aucun, nul**, and
certains (plural) are used without preceding article:

> **chaque employé recevra la même somme**, *each
> worker will be paid the same amount*
> **plusieurs d'entre eux sont là**, *several of them are
> there*
> **j'y vois quelques problèmes**, *I can see some
> problems there*
> **c'est à cause de certaines difficultés**, *it's because
> of certain difficulties*

■ **Tout** has the article following, as with *all* in English
(but unlike the English usage with *every*):

> **tout le temps**, *all the time*
> **tous les soirs**, *every evening*

In the singular **tout** may be used without article to mean
all, any:

> **cela exclut tout progrès dans cette affaire**, *that
> excludes any progress in this matter*

■ **Autre** and **tel** stand after the article like other
adjectives. Notice that this is not the case with *such* in
English:

> **les autres hommes**, *the other men*
> **un autre homme**, *another man*
> **un tel homme**, *such a man*

Such may also be used in English adverbially to qualify
another adjective: *she has such big eyes*. In French this
must be the adverb form **tellement**, or **si**, both of which
mean *such* or *so*:

> **ses yeux sont tellement grands**, *her eyes are so
> big*
> **elle a de si grands yeux**, *she has such big eyes*

■ **Même** has four meanings according to position:

☐ Before the article, *even*

> **même son secrétaire le dit**, *even his secretary says so*

☐ Before the noun, or after the verb, *same*

> **c'est exactement la même chose**, *it's exactly the same thing*
>
> **ces deux filles sont toujours les mêmes**, *those two girls are always the same*

☐ After the noun, *very*

> **ce sont les paroles mêmes du président**, *they are the president's very words*

☐ Attached to a pronoun with a hyphen, *self*

> **il l'a fait lui-même**, *he did it himself*

NOUNS USED ADJECTIVALLY (ATTRIBUTIVE NOUNS)

English frequently uses nouns as adjectives: *a coffee pot, a steel saucepan, a box girder, a cat flap*. These imply something like 'used for', 'made from', 'in the form of', 'used by'. In French the adjectival (or attributive) noun is placed after the main noun, and joined to it with a preposition which makes clear this relationship. The prepositions used are **de**, **à**, and **en**:

de

☐ *of, appropriate for, belonging to*

> **un match de tennis**, *a tennis match* (= a match of tennis)

la route de Manieu, *the Manieu road* (= *the road appropriate for Manieu*)

les feuilles d'automne, *autumn leaves* (= *the leaves of autumn*)

des poulets de batterie, *battery hens* (= *belonging to a battery*)

☐ *for the purpose of*

une salle d'attente, *a waiting room* (= *a room for the purpose of waiting*)

un effet de choc, *a shock effect* (= *an effect for the purpose of shocking*)

à

☐ *to contain, intended for*

un pot à café, *a coffee pot* (= *a pot to contain coffee*. Compare **un pot de café**, *a pot of coffee*)

une boîte aux lettres, *a letter box* (= *a box intended for letters*)

Verbal nouns (the *-ing* form in English, the infinitive in French) use **à** with this meaning to transform themselves into adjectives:

une salle à manger, *a dining room* (= *a room intended for eating*)

une machine à laver, *a washing machine* (= *a machine intended for washing*)

☐ *using, employing*

une poutre à caisson, *a box girder* (= *a girder using a box shape*)

un moulin à vent, *a windmill* (= *a mill that uses wind*)

☐ *with, possessing*

un chien à pedigree, *a pedigree dog* (= *a dog possessing pedigree*)

en

☐ *made from*

> **une casserole en acier**, *a steel saucepan* (= *a
> saucepan made from steel*)
> **un bracelet en or**, *a gold bracelet* (= *a bracelet
> made from gold*)

De is sometimes used in this way, too:

> **une barre de fer**, *an iron bar*

☐ *in the form of*

> **un escalier en spirale**, *a spiral staircase* (= *a
> staircase in the form of a spiral*)

■ Sometimes, especially with modern words, the
adjectival noun simply follows the main one, without any
preposition, though often with a hyphen:

> **une cocotte-minute**, *a pressure cooker* ('minute
> casserole')
> **une bande-annonce**, *a film trailer* ('advertisement
> reel')

Adverbs

FORMATION OF ADVERBS

Adverbs formed from adjectives

■ Most French adverbs are formed by adding **-ment** to the feminine form of the adjective:

> **égal**, *equal* → feminine: **égale**
> → adverb: **également**, *equally*

■ If the masculine form of the adjective ends in a vowel, **-ment** is added to this masculine form:

> **vrai**, *real* → **vraiment**, *really*
> **forcé**, *forced* → **forcément**, *'forcedly'*, *necessarily*

Nouveau, mou, and **fou,** however, base their adverbs on their differing feminine forms **nouvelle, molle,** and **folle:**

> **nouveau** → **nouvellement**, *newly*
> **mou** → **mollement**, *softly*
> **fou** → **follement**, *madly*

■ Adjectives ending **-ent** and **-ant** form adverbs ending **-emment** and **-amment** (both pronounced as if they were spelled **-amment**):

>récent → **récemment**, *recently*
>**constant** → **constamment**, *constantly*

Exceptions: **lent** → **lentement**, *slowly*; **présent** →
présentement, *presently*

■ A number of adjectives that do not end in **é** follow the
pattern of **forcément**:

>**aveugle** → **aveuglément**, *blindly*
>**commun** → **communément**, *communally*
>**confus** → **confusément**, *confusedly*
>**énorme** → **énormément**, *enormously*
>**exprès** → **expressément**, *explicitly*
>**impuni**, *unpunished* → **impunément**, *with impunity,
>   scot-free*
>**intense**, *intense* → **intensément**, *intensively*
>**précis** → **précisément**, *precisely*
>**profond** → **profondément**, *deeply*

■ The following adverbs are completely irregular in the
way they are formed from their adjectives:

>**bon** → **bien**, *well*
>**bref** → **brièvement**, *briefly*
>**continu** → **continûment**, *continuously*
>**gai** → **gaiement**, *gaily*
>**gentil** → **gentiment**, *kindly*
>**mauvais** → **mal**, *badly*
>**meilleur** → **mieux**, *better*
>**moindre** → **moins**, *less*
>**petit** → **peu**, *little*
>**traître** → **traîtreusement**, *treacherously*

Adverbs not formed from adjectives

There are also many adverbs in French which are not
formed from adjectives, mostly short words like **ainsi**,
donc, **dedans**:

ainsi c'est entendu?, *so it's agreed?*

Some of these relate to conjunctions:

ainsi, *thus*, conjunction → **ainsi**, *so*, adverb

some to prepositions:

dans, *in*, preposition → **dedans**, *inside*, adverb

some are independent:

donc, *then*, adverb

Adverb alternatives

■ Adjectives are used as adverbs in a number of fixed expressions:

bas, haut	**parler bas, parler haut**,	*speak softly/loudly*
bon, mauvais	**sentir bon, sentir mauvais**,	*smell good/bad*
cher	**coûter cher, payer cher**,	*cost/pay a lot*
court	**s'arrêter court, couper court**,	*stop/cut short*
dur	**travailler dur**,	*work hard*
juste / faux	**chanter juste, chanter faux**,	*sing in/out of tune*
net	**refuser net**,	*refuse point blank*

■ Adverb phrases commonly substitute for the longer and more cumbersome adverbs, and must be used where the adjective has no corresponding adverb, such as **content**, *happy*, *content*:

il me regarda d'un air content, *he looked at me contentedly*

— **Ah non, dit-il d'une voix triste**, *'Oh no,' he said sadly*

elle répondit à voix basse, *she answered softly*

je l'ai fait avec soin, *I did it carefully*

le régiment s'est battu avec beaucoup de courage, *the regiment fought very courageously*

elle l'a fait sans hésitation, *she did it unhesitatingly*

POSITION OF ADVERBS

Adverbs describe or modify a verb:

> **elle joue bien**, *she plays well* (adverb: **bien**)

or an adjective:

> **cela est complètement différent**, *that's completely different* (adverb: **complètement**)

or another adverb:

> **oui, très probablement**, *yes, very probably* (modifying adverb: **très**)

■ With adjectives and adverbs the modifying adverb stands immediately in front of the word it modifies, as in English. See the last two examples above.

■ With verbs:

□ In simple tenses adverbs usually stand immediately after the verb.

> **je connais intimement toute cette famille**, *I know all that family intimately*

□ In compound tenses adverbs follow the past participle if they take the stress.

> **je l'ai vu finalement**, *I saw him, in the end*
> **je lui ai finalement parlé**, *I finally spoke to him*

In practice this means that adverbs of place and precise adverbs of time (**aujourd'hui, demain, hier**, etc.) almost always stand after the past participle:

> **elle l'a mis là, sur le plancher**, *she's put it there, on the floor*
> **on l'a fait hier**, *we did it yesterday*

and short adverbs of degree (**bien, beaucoup, trop**, etc.) or imprecise adverbs of time (**déjà, souvent, bientôt**, etc.) stand before the past participle:

tu l'as très bien expliqué, *you explained it very well*

il est déjà arrivé, *he's already arrived*

☐ With a dependent infinitive the above points about adverbs with the past participle also apply.

je vais le faire finalement, *I'm finally going to do it*

je vais finalement lui parler, *I'm finally going to speak to him*

■ Adverbs, especially those of time and place, may be placed at the head of their clause for emphasis, as they sometimes are in English:

partout on voyait des coquelicots, *everywhere poppies could be seen*

jamais je n'aurais fait cela, *I'd never have done that*

■ Interrogative adverbs stand at the head of their clause, of course:

quand reviendra-t-elle?, *when will she come back?*

▶ For the word order after interrogative adverbs, see p. 212.

COMPARATIVE AND SUPERLATIVE OF ADVERBS

In English the comparative and superlative are:

easily →comparative: *more easily*
superlative: *most easily*

In French the comparative and superlative of adverbs are formed in a similar way to those of adjectives (for which see p. 143):

facilement, *easily*

comparative **plus facilement**, *more easily*
superlative **le plus facilement**, *most easily*

> **c'est comme ça que tu le feras le plus facilement**,
> *that's the way you'll do it most easily*

■ The superlative adverb always starts **le** (never **la** or **les**):

> **c'est elle qui le fera le plus facilement**, *she's the one who will do it most easily*

■ As with adjectives

> **moins ... que**, *less ... than*
> **aussi ... que**, *as ... as*
> **si ... que**, *as* (after a negative)

can be used to form comparatives in the same way as **plus ... que**:

> **elle part en vacances moins souvent que toi**, *she goes on holiday less often than you*
> **il ne conduit pas si vite que toi**, *he doesn't drive as fast as you*

Le moins ..., *the least ...*, can also be used in a similar way to **le plus ...**, *the most ...*, to form a superlative:

> **celui qui le fait le moins bien**, *the one who does it least well*

■ The following adverbs have irregular comparatives and superlatives:

beaucoup, *much*	**plus, le plus**, *more, the most*
bien, *well*	**mieux, le mieux**, *better, the best*
peu, *little*	**moins, le moins**, *less, the least*

The comparative adverb **pis**, *worse*, corresponding to the comparative adjective **pire**, is now only used in a few set expressions:

> **tant pis pour lui!**, *so much the worse for him!*

NEGATIVE ADVERBS

The negative adverbs in French are

> **aucun**, *no, none*
> **guère**, *hardly*
> **jamais**, *never*
> **ni**, *neither; nor*
> **nul**, *no*
> **nulle part**, *nowhere*
> **nullement**, *in no way*
> **pas**, *not*
> **personne**, *nobody*
> **plus**, *no longer*
> **que**, *only*
> **rien**, *nothing*

Negating a verb

The normal position for all the negative adverbs is after the verb in simple tenses, and before the past participle in compound tenses. In addition, they all have **ne** before the verb and any accompanying object pronouns. **Ne** becomes **n'** before a vowel or 'mute' **h**:

> **je ne le lui donne jamais**, *I never give it to him*
> **je n'ai rien dit**, *I haven't said anything*

■ **Nulle part** and **personne** normally come after the past participle in compound tenses:

> **ils n'ont vu personne**, *they haven't seen anyone*
> **on ne le trouve nulle part**, *it is not found anywhere*

■ Ni

□ With two objects: the **ni** is repeated in front of each object. Any pronoun object must be a disjunctive (see p. 111)

> **je n'ai rencontré ni lui ni sa femme**, *I met neither him nor his wife*

□ With two subjects: the **ni** is repeated in front of each subject. Any pronoun subject must be a disjunctive (see p. 111). The verb is usually plural

> **ni lui ni sa femme n'étaient là**, *neither he nor his wife was (were) there*

□ With two verbs: the **ne** is repeated

> **il ne fume ni ne boit**, *he neither smokes nor drinks*

Neither without *nor* is **non plus**:

> **moi non plus**, *me neither!*
> **je ne l'ai pas vu non plus**, *I haven't seen him either*

■ Que, *only*, qualifying an object stands in front of the object. A pronoun object must be a disjunctive (see p. 111):

> **je n'aime que lui**, *I love only him*
> **je n'ai vraiment regardé que l'acteur principal**, *I only really looked at the main actor*

Que can also be made to qualify a verb by using the verb as an infinitive in the construction **ne faire que**:

> **cet enfant ne fait que crier**, *that child only cries (does nothing but cry)*

Que can itself be negated with **pas**:

> **il n'y a pas que Pierre qui soit invité**, *it's not only Pierre who's been invited*

■ **Aucun** and **nul** are actually adjectives, agreeing with the noun they stand in front of. They are used only in the singular; **nul** has the feminine form **nulle**.

In all other respects **aucun** and **nul** are like the other negative adverbs.

■ **Personne, rien, ni … ni…, aucun …** and **nul …** can stand as the subject of the sentence. The **ne** still appears before the verb (but beware—there is no **pas**!):

> **personne ne l'a entendu**, *nobody's heard him*

See indefinite pronouns, pp. 127 ff.

Negating an infinitive

■ With an infinitive both the **ne** and the negative adverb stand in front of the infinitive and its pronoun objects:

> **je peux ne pas venir**, *I may possibly not come* (as opposed to **je ne peux pas venir**, *I can't come*)

except in the case of those negative adverbs which follow the past participle (**personne, nulle part, ni, que, aucun, nul**), which also follow the infinitive:

> **je suis désolé de ne voir personne**, *I'm very sorry not to see anyone*
> **j'espère ne trouver ni difficultés ni problèmes**, *I hope to find neither difficulties nor problems*

■ **Sans** + infinitive can stand with all the negative adverbs, without a **ne**:

> **sans rien voir**, *without seeing anything*

Double negative adverbs

Plus and **jamais** can qualify another negative adverb. They stand in front of it:

> **je ne vois plus personne**, *I don't see anybody any
> more*
> **je n'achète jamais rien**, *I never buy anything*

Negatives with other parts of the sentence

■ *Not* with parts of the sentence other than the verb is
either **pas** or **non**, or the stronger **non pas**. **Ne** does not
appear in this case:

> **je veux des pommes, et non pas des pommes de
> terre!**, *I want apples, not potatoes!*

■ Most of the negative adverbs can be used without **ne**
where no verb is expressed:

> **qui a téléphoné? — Personne**, *who phoned?—
> Nobody*
> **qu'est-ce que tu entends? — Plus rien**, *what can
> you hear?—Nothing any more*

Omission of ne and pas

■ **Ne** is omitted extremely frequently in spoken French:

> **Jean-Luc? Connais pas!**, *Jean-Luc? Don't know
> him!*
> **elle vient ce soir? — Oh, je sais pas**, *is she coming
> tonight?—Oh, I don't know*

■ **Pas** is omitted in literary French with the verbs
pouvoir, savoir, oser + infinitive

> **je ne savais comment répondre**, *I did not know
> how to reply*

Non-negative ne

A non-negative **ne** is used in careful speech in clauses
dependent on a number of expressions, mostly involving
the subjunctive. The commonest are:

■ Verbs of fearing: **avoir peur que, craindre que**

> **j'ai peur qu'elle ne soit déjà là**, *I'm afraid she may be there already*

■ Conjunctions: **avant que, à moins que, de peur que, de crainte que**

> **je l'ai fait de peur qu'elle ne le fasse elle-même**, *I did it for fear she (in case she) might do it herself*

■ Comparisons: **plus ... que, moins ... que**

> **il est moins habile que vous ne pensez**, *he is less clever than you think*

This **ne** has no negative meaning and is not used in everyday spoken French.

▶ See uses of the subjunctive, pp. 41 ff.

Prepositions

Prepositions—words like *in*, *on*, *over*—stand in front of a noun or pronoun to relate it to the rest of the sentence:

> **il chante toujours dans la salle de bain**, *he always sings in the bathroom* (preposition: **dans**, *in*)

■ Prepositions can also stand in front of a verb—*without looking*, *by singing*. In English this part of a verb is the *-ing* form. In French it is the infinitive:

> **sans regarder**, *without looking*

except with the preposition **en**, which is followed by a present participle:

> **en chantant**, *whilst singing*

■ The prepositions **à** and **de** combine with the definite article to form **au**, **aux** and **du**, **des**. See p. 77.

■ The prepositions **à**, **de**, and **en** are usually repeated if they refer to more than one noun or pronoun. This is often not the case in English:

> **j'ai parlé à lui et à ses voisins**, *I spoke to him and his neighbours*

ALPHABETICAL LIST OF FRENCH PREPOSITIONS AND THEIR USE

The use of prepositions differs considerably from language to language. Below we give an alphabetical list of those French prepositions that may give difficulty, with their main and subsidiary meanings and examples of their use. The principal meaning (or meanings) is given first, with other meanings following in alphabetical order.

In addition, on p. 185 there is an alphabetical list of English prepositions with their various French equivalents, for cross-reference to the French list.

à, *at*

at (place)

> **on se retrouve à la gare routiere**, *we'll meet at the bus station*
> **à la maison**, *at home*
> **à l'école**, *at school*
> **au travail**, *at work*

at (time)

> **à midi et à une heure**, *at noon and at one o'clock*
> **au crépuscule**, *at twilight*
> **à l'aube**, *at dawn*
> **à Noël**, *at Christmas*

at (numbers)

> **à cent kilomètres à l'heure**, (*at*) *100 km. an hour*
> **à très peu de distance**, *at a very little distance*
> **ceux à vingt francs**, *those at 20 francs*

belonging to (English uses the possessive pronoun):

> **c'est à lui** (= it belongs to him), *it's his*

▶ See p. 123.

by

> **tu le reconnaîtras à sa moustache**, *you'll recognize him by his moustache*
> **des dentelles faites à la main** (= by hand), *hand-made lace*
> **cela se vend au kilo**, *we sell that by the kilo*

for (English uses an attributive noun)

>>> **un réservoir à essence** (= a tank for petrol), *a petrol tank*
>>> **un verre à vin** (= a glass for wine), *a wineglass* (compare **un verre de vin**, *a glass of wine*)

from

>>> **il l'a pris à ton frère**, *he took it from your brother* (and similarly **arracher à**, *snatch from*, **acheter à**, *buy from*, **boire à**, *drink from*, **cacher à**, *hide from*, **emprunter à**, *borrow from*, **voler à**, *steal from*)

in (place)

>>> **à la campagne**, *in the country* (but **en ville**, *in town*)
>>> **à la main**, *in my* (*her, your, etc.*) *hand*
>>> **au lit**, *in bed*
>>> **au ciel**, *in the sky*
>>> **au soleil**, *in the sun*
>>> **à Marseille**, *in Marseilles*
>>> **aux États-Unis**, *in the United States*
>>> **au Mexique**, *in Mexico* (but **en** with feminine singular countries: **en France**)

in (time)

>>> **au petit matin**, *in the early morning* (but without an adjective '*in*' with parts of the day is just **le**: **le matin**, *in the morning*; **l'après-midi**, *in the afternoon*; **le soir**, *in the evening*)
>>> **au XXᵉ siècle**, *in the twentieth century*
>>> **au mois de mai**, *in* (*the month of*) *May* (but **en mai**, *in May*)
>>> **au printemps**, *in spring* (but **en** with the other seasons: **en été**, *in summer*)
>>> **à son tour**, *in* (*his*) *turn*

in (manner)

> **à voix basse**, *in a soft voice*
> **des champignons à la grecque**, *mushrooms cooked the Greek way*
> **des tripes à la mode de Caen**, *Caen-style tripe*

on

> **au menu**, *on the menu*
> **ces peintures au mur**, *those paintings on the wall*
> **marqué au front**, *marked on the forehead*
> **à bicyclette, à pied, à cheval**, *on a bicycle (by bicycle), on foot, on horseback*
> **à droite/gauche**, *on the right/left*
> **à la page dix-huit**, *on page 18*

to

> **je vais à la boulangerie**, *I'm going to the baker's*
> **elle va à Paris, aux États-Unis, au Portugal**, *she's going to Paris, the USA, Portugal* (but **en** with feminine singular countries: **elle va en Italie**, *she's going to Italy*)
> **j'ai parlé à ton professeur**, *I've spoken to your teacher*
> **du matin au soir**, *from morning to (till) night*

using (English usually has an attributive noun)

> **un moteur à essence** (= using petrol), *a petrol engine*
> **un moulin à vent** (= using wind), *a windmill*
> **une locomotive à vapeur** (= using steam), *a steam locomotive*

with (= *containing, having*—English may use an attributive noun)

> **une pâté aux truffes** (= a pâté with truffles), *truffle pâté*
> **un chien à pedigree** (= a dog with a pedigree), *a pedigree dog*

> **l'homme au parapluie**, *the man with the umbrella*
> **la femme aux yeux verts**, *the woman with green eyes*

▶ For uses of **à** with verbs see p. 56.

▶ For **à** used after adjectives, nouns, and adverbs see p. 51.

à part, *except*

▶ See **au dehors de**, below.

à travers, *through*

▶ See **par**, p. 180.

après, *after*

after (time)

> **après trois heures**, *after three o'clock*
> **après la guerre**, *after the war*

after (place)

> **la troisième maison après la mairie**, *the third house after the town hall*
> **elle court après lui**, *she's running after him*

according to (notice the **d'**)

> **d'après Le Figaro**, *according to Le Figaro*

▶ For **après** + perfect infinitive (*after ...ing*), see p. 53.

au-dehors de, *outside*

outside

> **ce chien reste au-dehors de la maison**, *that dog stays outside the house*

The shorter form **hors de** locates less precisely:

> **ceux qui habitent hors de la ville**, *those who live (somewhere) outside the town*

Hors de also means *out of*:

> **elle était hors d'haleine**, *she was out of breath*

and, in literary usage, **hors** means *except*:

> **nous y sommes tous allés hors lui**, *we all went except him*

Except is, however, now more usually **à part**:

> **personne à part sa mère**, *no one except her mother*

au-dessous de, *under(neath), below*

▶ See **sous**, p. 183.

au-dessus de, *over*

over, above (physically)

> **le ciel au-dessus de la montagne**, *the sky over (above) the mountains*

Over, above with motion is **par-dessus**:

> **sauter par-dessus un obstacle**, *to leap over an obstacle*

Where *over* implies *touching* it is **sur**:

> **une serviette sur le bras**, *with a towel over his arm*

above, over (= *more than*)

> **ne paie pas au-dessus de cent francs**, *don't pay above (more than) 100 francs*

auprès de, *beside*

beside (nearness)

> **elle se tenait auprès du lit**, *she was standing beside the bed*

beside (= *compared to*)

> **son frère jumeau n'est rien auprès de lui**, *his twin brother is nothing beside (compared to) him*

avant, *before*

before (time)

> **avant le commencement du jeu**, *before the beginning of the match*
> **avant de sortir**, *before going out* (note the **de** before an infinitive)

before (place in a sequence of places)

> **vous descendez avant Genève?**, *are you getting out before Geneva?*

The older, formal use of *before* to mean *in front of* is **devant**:

> **il s'agenouilla devant l'autel**, *he knelt before the altar*

avec, *with*

with (= *together with*)

> **tu viens avec nous?**, *are you coming with us?*

with (= *by means of*)

> **tu n'y arriveras pas avec un tire-bouchon**, *you won't manage it with a corkscrew*

chez, *at X's*

at (or to) the house or shop of (English usually uses a possessive)

> **on va chez l'épicier**, *we're going to the grocer's*
> **on se voit chez Chantal**, *see you at Chantal's*
> **faites comme chez vous**, *make yourself at home*

with (= as far as X is concerned)

> **c'est une habitude chez elle**, *with her it's a habit*

among

> **chez les Esquimaux on ne joue pas beaucoup au tennis**, *not much tennis is played among the Eskimos*

in (the works of)

> **on ne trouve pas ce mot chez Racine**, *that word isn't found in Racine*

contre, *against*

against (in both concrete and abstract senses)

> **l'échelle est contre le garage**, *the ladder is against the garage*
> **nous sommes tous contre la guerre**, *we are all against war*

for

> **tu veux échanger ça contre mon tourne-disques?**, *do you want to exchange that for my record player?*

dans, *in*

in, into (place)

> **on va dans le jardin**, *we're going into the garden*
> **il y a deux hommes dans sa vie**, *there are two men in her life*

in (time, = *at the end of*)

> **je serai de retour dans dix minutes**, *I'll be back in ten minutes* (= *ten minutes from now*)

In = *within the space of* is **en**:

> **je le ferai en dix minutes**, *I'll do it in (within the space of) ten minutes*

from

> **je l'ai pris dans le tiroir**, *I took it from the drawer*

▶ See also **à**, *from*, p. 166. The French have in mind the original position of the object, from which it is then taken, snatched, etc.

de, *of*

of (possession or relation—English often uses a possessive or an attributive noun)

> **la voiture de Pierre**, *Pierre's car (the car of Pierre)*
> **la première femme de mon oncle**, *my uncle's first wife (the first wife of my uncle)*
> **la porte du jardin**, *the garden gate (the gate of the garden)*
> **la route de Versailles**, *the Versailles road (the road of Versailles)*
> **une partie de plaisir**, *a pleasure party (a party of pleasure)*

>> **les vacances de Noël**, *the Christmas holidays (the holidays of Christmas)*

of (= *containing*)

>> **un verre de vin**, *a glass of wine*

of (appositional, = *that is*)

>> **au mois de septembre**, *in the month of September (the month that is September)*
>> **la ville de Paris**, *the city of Paris*

about (= *concerning*)

>> **elle est folle de ses animaux**, *she's mad about her animals*

by

>> **elle est Française de naissance**, *she's French by birth*
>> **il arriva accompagné de sa femme**, *he arrived accompanied by his wife*
>> **il a été blessé d'une balle**, *he has been hit by a bullet* (See p. 33 for the use of **de** with the passive)

from

>> **d'où vient-il?**, *where has he come from?*
>> **il revient de Paris**, *he's just come back from Paris*
>> **de temps en temps**, *from time to time*
>> **elle est différente de sa sœur**, *she's different from her sister*

in (manner)

>> **d'une voix tremblante**, *in a trembling voice* (but **à voix basse/haute**, *in a low/loud voice*)
>> **d'une manière impolie**, *in a rude manner*
>> **d'une façon stupide**, *in a stupid way*

Similarly,

>> **d'un air fâché**, *with an angry look*

in (after a superlative or superlative-type word—see p. 145)

> **le meilleur du monde**, *the best in the world*
> **le premier de sa classe**, *the first in its class*

made of (English usually uses an attributive noun)

> **un coussin de soie**, *a silk cushion* (*a cushion made of silk*)
> **un chapeau de paille**, *a straw hat* (*a hat made of straw*)

than (with a quantity following a comparison)

> **plus de cinq fois**, *more than five times*
> **les enfants de moins de treize ans**, *children below (of less than) thirteen years*

to

> **tu es libre de supposer n'importe quoi**, *you are free to assume anything at all*

with

> **il est couvert de boue**, *he's covered with mud*
> **elle pleure de joie**, *she is weeping with joy*
> **il nous questionna d'un air soupçonneux**, *he questioned us with a suspicious look*

De is also used, with no equivalent word in English, in the following cases.

■ After expressions of quantity (this includes **un million**, *million*, and **un milliard**, *billion*, but not other numbers):

> **beaucoup de monde**, *a lot of people*
> **trop de questions**, *too many questions*
> **un million de chiens**, *a million dogs*

▶ See p. 83.

■ After **quelque chose**, **rien**, **personne**, etc.:

>**quelque chose de beau**, *something beautiful*
>**rien de spécial**, *nothing special*

▶ See pp. 128 ff.

■ To join two nouns where the second is used adjectivally (the attributive noun):

>**la salle de bain**, *the bathroom*
>**la salle de séjour**, *the sitting room*

▶ For **de** with verbs see p. 55.
▶ For **de** used after adjectives, nouns, and adverbs see p. 51.

depuis, *since*

since (a place or a point in time)

>**tu n'as rien mangé depuis ton arrivée**, *you haven't eaten anything since your arrival* (*since you got here*)
>**c'est le premier péage depuis Lyon**, *it's the first toll point since Lyons*

for (a length of time)

>**elle regarde la télévision depuis une demi-heure**, *she's been watching television for half an hour*

▶ *For* with time may also be **pendant** or **pour**. See pp. 181, 182.
▶ For tenses with both the above meanings of **depuis** see pp. 17 and 21.

from (a place or a time), in **depuis ... jusqu'à**, *from ... to*

>**la côte méditerranéenne depuis Toulon jusqu'à Nice**, *the Mediterranean coast from Toulon to (as far as) Nice*

on est ouvert depuis huit heures du matin jusqu'à huit heures du soir, *we are open from eight in the morning until eight at night*

De ... à is less emphatic:

du matin au soir, *from morning to night*

from (a place, = *out from*)

le panorama depuis le sommet est extraordinaire, *the panorama from the summit is remarkable*

dès, *as soon as*

as soon as; no later than (with future time)

je le ferai dès demain, *I'll do it no later than tomorrow*
dès son arrivée, *as soon as she gets here*
dès maintenant, *from now on*

as far back as; ever since (a point in past time onwards)

dès cette époque elle donnait des signes de folie, *even at that period (as far back as that period) she was showing signs of madness*

devant, *in front of*

▶ See **avant**, p. 170.

en, *in*

En expresses *in* in a more abstract or less specific way than does **dans**. It is always used without an article:

en ville, *in town*
en question, *in question*

except in a very few set expressions beginning with a vowel or 'mute' **h**:

en l'absence de, *in the absence of*
en l'air, *in the air*
en l'an ..., *in (the year)* ...
en l'honneur de, *in honour of*

in

en réponse à votre lettre, *in reply to your letter*
en forme de collier, *in the form of a necklace*
elle sortit en colère, *she went out angry (in anger)*
la cuisine était peinte en vert, *the kitchen was painted (in) green*
habillé en short, *dressed in shorts*

in (time: months, seasons, years)

en février, *in February*
en été, en automne et en hiver, *in summer, autumn, and winter* (but **au printemps**, *in spring*)
en 1999, *in 1999* (but **en l'an 1999**—note the article)

in, into (languages)

en français, *in French*
traduisez ça en anglais, *translate that into English*

in, to (with feminine singular names of countries and of continents)

on va en France, *we're going to France*
nous vivons en Europe, *we live in Europe*

▶ Otherwise *in* or *to* with countries is **au/aux**. See **à**, pp. 166, 167.

in (time within which)

je le ferai en deux minutes, *I'll do it (I'll have it done) in two minutes*

In (= *at the end of which time*) is **dans**:

> **je le ferai dans deux minutes**, *I'll do it (I'll start the job) in two minutes*

▶ See **dans**, p. 172.

as (= *in the shape of, as if it were*)

> **Monsieur Charles, en parfait gentleman, les accueillit très poliment**, *Charles, as the perfect gentleman, welcomed them very politely*
> **il me traite toujours en enfant**, *he always treats me as a child*
> **elle était déguisée en duchesse**, *she was dressed as a duchess*

by (with a form of transport, usually when one is 'in' the vehicle)

> **nous y allons en avion**, *we're going by plane*
> **ceux qui roulent en auto et en moto**, *those who travel by car and by motorbike* (also **à moto**)

▶ See also **à** (p. 167) and **par** (p. 180) with this meaning.

by, whilst, on (followed by the present participle)

> **je l'ai rencontrée en sortant du supermarché**, *I met her (whilst I was) coming out of the supermarket*

▶ See present participle, p. 35.

in the form of (English sometimes uses an attributive noun)

> **des chaussettes en accordéon**, *wrinkled socks* (*in the form of an accordion*)
> **un escalier en spirale**, *a spiral staircase* (*in the form of a spiral*)

made of (English often uses an attributive noun)

> **une table en acajou**, *a mahogany table*

De is also used with this meaning (see p. 174). **En** tends to draw more attention to the material of which the article is made than does **de**:

>**une montre en or**, *a gold watch*

on

>**j'ai un chat qui me suit en promenade**, *I've a cat that follows me on my walks*
>**on part en vacances**, *we're leaving on holiday*

entre, *between*

between (two people or things)

>**entre lui et moi**, *between him and me*
>**entre dix heures et minuit**, *between ten o'clock and midnight*

among(*st*) (more than two people or things)

>**ici vous êtes entre amis**, *here you are among friends*
>**les gens parlaient entre eux**, *people were talking among themselves*

Among(*st*) is, however, more frequently **parmi**:

>**parmi tous ceux qui étaient là, elle était la seule à bouger**, *amongst all those who were there she was the only one to move*

of (after **de** (**d'entre**) in expressions of quantity before pronouns)

>**quatre d'entre eux**, *four of them*
>**beaucoup d'entre vous**, *many of you*

envers, *towards* (figurative)

▶ See **vers**, p. 185.

hors (de), *except; out of*

▶ See **au-dehors de**, p. 168.

par, *by*

by

> **on commence par discuter, on finit par se quereller**, *you begin by discussing, you end by falling out*
> **par la D565**, *by the D565 road*
> **par ici/là**, *(by) this/that way*

by (with passive)

> **elle a été blessée par son mari**, *she was injured by her husband*

▶ See passive, p. 33.

by (with a few forms of transport, as an alternative to **en**)

> **par le train**, *by train*
> **par le métro**, *by underground*
> **par avion**, *by plane*

from (= *out of*, reason)

> **elle ne fait rien par conviction**, *she does nothing from (out of) conviction*

on, to

> **il était étendu par terre**, *he was lying on the ground*
> **elle est tombée par terre**, *she fell over; she fell to the ground* (from a standing position). Compare: **tomber à terre**, *fall to the ground* (from a height)

on, in (weather)

> **par un jour froid d'hiver**, *on a cold winter's day*
> **par un temps superbe**, *in splendid weather*

per, a (after numbers)

>>> **cinquante fois par semaine**, *fifty times a week*
>>> **deux par personne**, *two per person*

through

>>> **elle m'a vu par la fenêtre**, *she saw me through the window*
>>> **il a longtemps erré par les rues de Paris**, *for a long time he wandered through the streets of Paris*

Through where some difficulty is implied is **à travers**:

>>> **il se fraya un chemin à travers la foule**, *he battled his way through the crowd*

via

>>> **tu peux passer par Lyon ou par Dijon**, *you can go via Lyons or Dijon*

parmi, *among(st)*

▶ See **entre**, p. 179.

pendant, *during*

during

>>> **pendant ma visite**, *during my visit*

for (a completed period of time in the past)

>>> **ce mois-ci il a chômé pendant treize jours**, *this month he was out of work for thirteen days*

▶ See also **pour** (p. 182) and **depuis** (p. 175) meaning *for* with time.

pour, *for*

for (= *in favour of*)

> **tu votes pour les socialistes?**, *are you voting for the socialists?*
>
> **il faut peser le pour et le contre**, *you've got to weigh the pros and cons*

for (= *on behalf of*)

> **morts pour la France**, *they died for France*
>
> **elle y répondra pour toi**, *she'll reply to it for you*

for (intention)

> **ceci est pour toi**, *this is for you*
>
> **l'avion part pour Paris à trois heures cinq**, *the plane leaves for Paris at 3.05*

for (= *because of*)

> **on vous donne une contravention pour avoir laissé votre voiture devant le commissariat**, *you've been given a parking ticket for having left (for leaving) your car in front of the police station*

for (= *in exchange for*)

> **qu'est-ce que tu me donnes pour mon vélo?**, *what will you give me for my bike?*

for (plus intended length of time)

> **tu y vas pour trois mois?**, *you're going for three months?*

▶ See also **depuis** (p. 175) and **pendant** (p. 181) meaning *for* with time.

for (+ an amount)

> **tu en as là pour vingt minutes**, *you've enough work there for twenty minutes*

> **pour cent francs de sans-plomb, s'il vous plait**, *100
> francs worth ('for 100 francs') of unleaded,
> please*

as for

> **pour ma part, je voudrais bien le faire**, *as far as
> I'm concerned (as for me), I'd like to do it*

Quant à is also used in this sense:

> **quant à vous**, *as for you*

per

> **dix pour cent**, *ten per cent*

to (= in order to)

> **pour faire fonctionner la pompe, il faut d'abord
> sortir le robinet**, *(in order) to operate the pump,
> the nozzle must first be withdrawn*

to (after **trop** + adjective, *too ...*, **assez** + adjective,
... enough, and the verb **suffire**, *to be enough*)

> **tu es trop jeune pour y entrer**, *you're too young to
> go in*
> **vous êtes assez informé pour savoir que ...**,
> *you're well enough informed to know that ...*
> **cela suffira pour vous donner une idée de ce que
> nous pensons**, *that will be enough to give you an
> idea of our thoughts*

quant à, *as for*

▶ See **pour**, above.

sous, *under*

under

> **ton hamster est sous ma chaise**, *your hamster is
> under my chair*

Au-dessous de, *under*, implies *completely under* (= *underneath*), or means *below* in figurative senses:

> **les chiffres sont au-dessous de ce qu'on attendait**, *the figures are below what we expected*

in

> **tu ne peux pas sortir sous la pluie**, *you can't go out in the rain*
>
> **nous nous reverrons sous peu**, *we'll see each other shortly (in a little while)*
>
> **ils vécurent sous le règne de Louis XIV**, *they lived in the reign of Louis XIV*

sur, *on*

on, on to

> **je l'ai laissé sur le fauteuil**, *I left it on the armchair*
>
> **monte sur l'échelle**, *climb up (on to) the ladder*
>
> **elle était sur le point de m'interrompre**, *she was about to interrupt me (on the point of interrupting me)*
>
> **assis sur le mur**, *sitting on the wall (on = hanging on is* **à**. *See p. 167)*
>
> **sur notre droite**, *on our right*
>
> **je n'ai pas d'argent sur moi**, *I haven't any money on me*

by

> **douze centimètres de haut sur dix centimètres de large**, *12 cm. high by 10 cm. wide*

over

> **son autorité sur vous est très restreinte**, *his authority over you is very limited*
>
> **le pont sur l'estuaire de la Seine**, *the bridge over the Seine estuary*

▶ See also **au-dessus de**, *over*, p. 169.

in

> **j'ai laissé la clé sur la porte**, *I've left the key in the door*

in, out of

> **une personne sur dix**, *one person in ten*
> **dix-neuf sur vingt**, *19 out of 20*

upon

> **sur quoi, elle claqua la porte**, *whereupon (upon which) she slammed the door*

vers, *towards*

towards (place or point in time)

> **il s'en va vers la plage**, *he goes off towards the beach*
> **vers la fin de l'après-midi**, *towards the end of the afternoon*

Towards (figurative) is **envers**:

> **il est très bien intentionné envers nous**, *he is very well intentioned towards us*

about (with time of day)

> **vers dix heures et demie**, *about half past ten*

CROSS-REFERENCE LIST OF ENGLISH PREPOSITIONS

Prepositions presenting problems of translation are listed. These prepositions are cross-referenced to the list of French prepositions starting on p. 164. It is dangerous to take a French meaning from this list without subsequently checking its usage in the French list.

about
    = *concerning*, **de**, 173
    + time of day, **vers**, 185

according to
    d'après, 168

after
    place, **après**, 168
    time, **après**, 168

against
    contre, 171

among(st)
    chez, 171
    entre, 179
    parmi, 179

as
    = *in the shape of, as if it were*, **en**, 178

as far back as
    dès, 176

as for
    pour, 183

as soon as
    dès, 176

at
    numbers, **à**, 165
    place, **à**, 165
    time, **à**, 165

at X's (house, shop)
    chez, 171

above
    au-dessus de, 169
    par-dessus, 169

under
  sous, 183
  au-dessous de, 184

underneath
  au-dessous de, 184

upon
  sur, 185

using
  à, 167

via
  par, 181

whilst
  + present participle, **en**, 178

with
  de, 174
  manner, **de**, 173
  = *as far as X is concerned*, **chez**, 171
  = *by means of*, **avec**, 170
  = *containing, having*, **à**, 167
  = *together with*, **avec**, 170

| Conjunctions

■ Conjunctions are joining-words. They may join nouns or pronouns:

> **lui et son chien**, *he and his dog* (conjunction: **et**)

or phrases:

> **en arrivant ou en partant**, *on arriving or leaving*
> (conjunction: **ou**)

or clauses:

> **elle chante, mais elle ne joue pas**, *she sings but*
> *she doesn't play* (conjunction: **mais**)

■ They may also introduce a subordinate clause:

> **je le ferai quand j'aurai de l'argent**, *I'll do it when*
> *I have money* (conjunction: **quand**)

Many of the conjunctions that introduce subordinate clauses in French are two-word phrases with **que** as the second word:

> **je lui ai téléphoné pendant qu'elle travaillait**,
> *I phoned her whilst she was working*
> (conjunction: **pendant que**)

Quite often the first word of the phrase is a preposition with the same English meaning as the conjunction:

> **avant**, *before*, preposition
> **avant que**, *before*, conjunction
>
> **sans**, *without*, preposition
> **sans que**, *without*, conjunction

It is important to distinguish these—the preposition

will stand before a noun or (sometimes) the infinitive of a verb:

> **sans effort**, *without effort*
> **sans me regarder**, *without looking at me*

The conjunction will introduce a subordinate clause:

> **je l'organiserai avant qu'on leur parle**, *I'll
> organize it before anyone speaks to them*

▶ Many subordinating conjunctions are followed by the subjunctive. See p. 45.

■ The following conjunctions may give problems:

□ **aussi**, *so, therefore*

After **aussi**, verb and pronoun subject are inverted:

> **elle n'y montrait aucun intérêt, aussi est-il parti
> sans plus rien dire**, *she wasn't showing any
> interest, so he left without saying anything more*

Aussi can of course also be an adverb, meaning *also*.

□ **ni**, *nor*

After **sans**, **ni** is used where in English we should use *or*:

> **sans père ni mère**, *without father or mother*

□ **où**, *where*

After definite expressions of time **où** is used where in English we should use *when* or *that* or nothing at all:

> **l'instant où elle s'est retournée**, *the moment
> (when, that) she turned round*

See also **que** below.

□ **que**, *that*

Que becomes **qu'** before a vowel in written French. In spoken French it frequently remains as **que**.

After indefinite expressions of time **que** is used where in English we use *when*

> **un jour qu'il faisait beau**, *one day when it was fine*

See also **où** above.

Que is often used to avoid repeating a conjunction

> **quand tu viendras à Dijon et que tu verras la maison, tu seras enchanté**, *when you come to Dijon and (when you) see the house you'll be delighted*

When **que** replaces the conjunction **si** in this way it is followed by the subjunctive. See p. 48.

Que in comparisons means *than*

> **il est plus fort que moi**, *he's stronger than me*

▶ **Que** can also be a relative pronoun. See p. 112.

■ Paired conjunctions.

These conjunctions are used in much the same way as in English. The common ones are:

ni ... ni, *neither ... nor*
non seulement ... mais encore, *not only ... but also*
et ... et, *both ... and*
ou (bien) ... ou (bien), *either ... or (else)*
soit ... soit, *either ... or*

> **je n'ai ni argent ni ma carte Visa**, *I've neither money nor my Visa card*
>
> **non seulement lui mais encore toute sa famille sont venus déjeuner**, *not only he but all his family came to lunch*
>
> **on lui a pris et son agenda et son sac à main**, *they took both her diary and her handbag*
>
> **ou vous lui demandez pardon, ou je vous tue**, *either you apologize to her or I kill you*

on voyagera soit par le train soit par avion, *they'll travel either by train or by plane*

The last three pairs are used mostly in written French, a simple **et, ou,** or **ou bien** being used in the spoken language.

▶ For the use of **ne** with **ni ... ni** see p. 160.

Numbers, Time, Quantities

CARDINAL NUMBERS

The cardinal numbers are

0	zéro	24	vingt-quatre
1	un(e)	25	vingt-cinq
2	deux	26	vingt-six
3	trois	27	vingt-sept
4	quatre	28	vingt-huit
5	cinq	29	vingt-neuf
6	six	30	trente
7	sept	31	trente et un(e)
8	huit	32	trente-deux
9	neuf	40	quarante
10	dix	41	quarante et un(e)
11	onze	50	cinquante
12	douze	51	cinquante et un(e)
13	treize	60	soixante
14	quatorze	61	soixante et un(e)
15	quinze	70	soixante-dix
16	seize	71	soixante et onze
17	dix-sept	72	soixante-douze
18	dix-huit	80	quatre vingts
19	dix-neuf	81	quatre-vingt-un(e)
20	vingt	82	quatre-vingt-deux
21	vingt et un(e)	90	quatre-vingt-dix
22	vingt-deux	91	quatre-vingt-onze
23	vingt-trois	92	quatre-vingt-douze

100	cent	2 000	deux mille
101	cent un(e)	1 000 000	un million
200	deux cents	1 000 200	un million deux
201	deux cent un(e)		cents
1 000	mille	2 000 000	deux millions
1 001	mille un(e)	1.000 000 000	un milliard
1 002	mille deux	2 000 000 000	deux milliards

Thousands and millions are written with spaces (formerly sometimes with full stops) rather than, as in English, with commas. The comma is used for a decimal point—see p. 215.

■ There is no **-s** on the plural of **vingt** and **cent** when these are followed by another number.

■ There is never an **-s** on the plural of **mille** meaning *thousands*. **Le mille**, meaning *mile*, takes a plural **-s**.

■ **Million** and **milliard** are nouns. With a noun immediately following, they take **de**:

> **un million de soldats**, *a million soldiers*

but

> **un million deux cent mille soldats**, *1,200,000 soldiers*

All other numbers are adjectives. They are invariable, except that those ending in **un** agree with a following feminine noun (changing to **une**).

■ There is no **un** before **cent**, **mille**, meaning *one hundred*, *one thousand*:

> **mille francs**, *one thousand francs*

There is no **et** after **cent** or **mille**:

> **cent douze**, *a hundred and twelve*
> **mille un**, *one thousand and one*

except in the book title, ***Les mille et une nuits***, *A Thousand and One Nights*.

■ Figures are grouped in twos when you speak telephone numbers:

> 33 56 08 = **trente-trois cinquante-six zéro huit**
> 445 35 71 = **quatre cent quarante-cinq trente-cinq soixante et onze**

■ In Belgium, Switzerland, and Canada **septante**, **octante** or **huitante**, and **nonante** are used for 70, 80, and 90.

■ The numbers **six** and **dix** have each three different pronunciations. Before a consonant the **-x** is not pronounced; before a vowel or **h** 'mute' it is pronounced **z**; where **six** and **dix** stand after the noun (**chapitre six**) or alone (**le dix**) the **-x** is pronounced **s**.

The final consonants of **cinq**, **huit**, and (usually) **neuf** are not pronounced before another consonant, except in dates.

The **f** of **neuf** is pronounced **v** before the words **ans**, *years*, and **heures**, *o'clock*; before other words beginning with a vowel or **h** 'mute' it is pronounced **f**.

The **t** of **vingt** is usually pronounced in the numbers 21–29; it is not pronounced in dates: **le vin[gt] août**.

■ Before **huit** and **onze**, **le** does not become **l'**:

> **tu as le huit de trèfle?**, *do you have the eight of clubs?*
> **le onze juin**, *the eleventh of June*

This also applies to the ordinal forms:

> **le huitième**, *the eighth*
> **le onzième**, *the eleventh*

ORDINAL NUMBERS

Ordinal numbers (*first*, *second*, *third*, etc.) are formed by removing the final **-e** of the cardinal number (if it ends in **-e**) and adding **-ième**:

8, **huit** → 8th, **huitième**
12, **douze** → 12th, **douzième**
21, **vingt et un** → 21st, **vingt et unième**

Exceptions:

premier (fem: **première**), 1st
cinquième, 5th
neuvième, 9th

> **la première fois**, *the first time* (but **la trente et**
> **unième fois**, *the thirty-first time*)
> **le cinquième article**, *the fifth article*
> **le vingt-neuvième livre**, *the twenty-ninth book*

■ **Second** (fem: **seconde**) is an alternative to
deuxième, mainly used where there is no reference to a
third or subsequent thing or person. Notice though:

> **je suis en seconde**, *I'm in the fifth form* (French
> secondary schools count their classes in the
> opposite order to English schools)

■ Ordinals may be abbreviated thus **1ᵉʳ, 2ᵉ, 3ᵉ**, etc., or
1°, 2°, 3°, etc. The latter is short for the Latin *primo,*
secundo, tertio, etc.

■ When cardinal and ordinal numbers are used together
the order is the reverse of that in English:

> **les cinq premiers mois**, *the first five months*

■ French uses cardinal numbers where we use ordinal
numbers for days of the month and numbers of kings:

> **le vingt mai**, *the twentieth of May*
> **Henri quatre**, *Henri the Fourth*

However, for *first* French uses **premier**:

> **le premier septembre**, *the first of September*
> **Charles premier**, *Charles the First*

French, like English, uses cardinals for act, scene,

volume, and chapter numbers, but in all these cases uses
premier for *one*:

> **acte premier**, *act one*
> **acte deux**, *act two*
> **chapitre premier**, *chapter one*

APPROXIMATE NUMBERS

Approximate numbers are formed in French by adding
-aine to the cardinal number (the final **-e**, if any, is first
dropped). They can only be based on 8, 15, tens up to
60, and 100. The resultant number is a feminine noun
and is followed by **de**:

> **une quinzaine de francs**, *about fifteen francs*
> **une vingtaine de personnes**, *about twenty (a score of) people*
> **une cinquantaine de cahiers**, *about fifty exercise books*

■ **Mille**, *thousand*, forms **un millier**:

> **un millier de bateaux**, *about a thousand boats*

■ These nouns can be used in the plural:

> **des centaines de voitures**, *hundreds of cars*

■ **Une douzaine**, *a dozen*, though precise, is formed in
the same way as the approximate numbers:

> **une douzaine d'œufs**, *a dozen eggs*

Une quinzaine can also be used precisely to mean *a
fortnight*, and **une huitaine** is sometimes found as an
alternative to **une semaine**, *a week*.

FRACTIONS

Ordinal numbers are used to express fractions, as in
English:

$^1/_5$ = **un cinquième**
$^3/_8$ = **trois huitièmes**

Exceptions:

un quart = $^1/_4$, **trois quarts** = $^3/_4$
un tiers = $^1/_3$, **deux tiers** = $^2/_3$
un demi = $^1/_2$

■ *Half* as a mathematical term is **le demi**:

les deux demis, *the two halves*

but in ordinary language, *half of* something is **la moitié de**:

la moitié du temps il ne fait rien, *half the time he does nothing*

Half as an adjective is **demi**. It is hyphenated to the noun and is invariable:

une demi-journée, *a half day*
une demi-heure, *a half hour* (but **un quart d'heure**, *quarter of an hour*)

La demie is *the half-hour*:

la demie sonne, *it's striking half past*

■ Decimals are expressed in French with a comma:

1·5 → **1,5 (un virgule cinq)**

■ The main mathematical signs are:

+ **plus**	÷ **divisé par**
− **moins**	^{2} **au carré**
× **fois**	% **pour cent**

trois plus deux égalent cinq, *three plus two equals five*
dix au carré, *ten squared*
onze pour cent, *eleven per cent*

TIME AND DATE

Time of day

Quelle heure est-il?, *what time is it?*
Avez-vous l'heure, monsieur/madame? (politer!)

Il est:

> **une heure**, *one o'clock*
> **une heure cinq**, *five past one*
> **deux heures**, *two o'clock*
> **deux heures et** (or **un**) **quart**, *quarter past two*
> **trois heures et demie, trois heures trente**, *half past three*
> **quatre heures moins le** (or **moins un**) **quart**, *quarter to four*
> **cinq heures moins une (minute)**, *a minute to five*
> **midi**, *noon*
> **midi et demi, midi trente**, *half past twelve*
> **minuit**, *midnight*
> **minuit et demi, minuit trente**, *half past twelve*

■ **Heure(s)** is used where English uses *o'clock*. **Et
demie** is used after hours, **et demi** after **midi, minuit**.
With quarters the article **le** is used after **moins** but not
after **et**.

■ The forms **trois heures trente**, etc. are adopted
from the twenty-four hour clock, used in timetables and
all official documents. This follows the pattern:

> **une heure dix**, 01h10
> **douze heures quarante-cinq**, 12h45
> **dix-neuf heures cinquante-cinq**, 19h55

■ French has no equivalents to *a.m.* and *p.m.* Where
necessary, **du matin**, *in the morning*, **de l'après-midi**,
in the afternoon, or **du soir**, *in the evening*, are added as
appropriate:

trois heures du matin, *3 a.m.*

■ *In the morning (afternoon, evening)* is simply **le matin (l'après-midi, le soir)**. *At night* is **la nuit**. *Every morning* (etc.) is **tous les matins**.

Prepositions etc. with times of day

à, *at, by*

> **alors, on se revoit à trois heures précises**, *right, we'll meet at three o'clock sharp*
> **on sera là à midi**, *we'll be there by twelve*

à partir de, *from*

> **je serai au bureau à partir de neuf heures et demie**, *I shall be in the office from 9.30*

au bout de, *after*

> **au bout d'un petit instant elle recommença**, *after a moment she began again*

de ... à, *from ... to*

> **le restaurant est ouvert de midi à deux heures et demie**, *the restaurant is open from 12 to 2.30*

environ, *about*

> **il est environ sept heures** (or **sept heures environ**), *it's about seven o'clock*

jusqu'à, *until*

> **jusqu'à quatre heures de l'après-midi**, *until 4 p.m.*

pas plus tard que, *no later than*

> **il faut y arriver pas plus tard que deux heures et demie**, *you must get there no later than half past two*

passé, *past*

> **il est huit heures passées**, *it's past eight o'clock*

vers, *about*

    il est parti vers les cinq heures, *he left about five*

Days, months, seasons

days of the week	*months of the year*
dimanche, *Sunday*	**janvier**, *January*
lundi, *Monday*	**février**, *February*
mardi, *Tuesday*	**mars**, *March*
mercredi, *Wednesday*	**avril**, *April*
jeudi, *Thursday*	**mai**, *May*
vendredi, *Friday*	**juin**, *June*
samedi, *Saturday*	**juillet**, *July*
	août, *August*
today, etc.	**septembre**, *September*
avant-hier, *the day before*	**octobre**, *October*
yesterday	**novembre**, *November*
hier, *yesterday*	**décembre**, *December*
aujourd'hui, *today*	
demain, *tomorrow*	*seasons*
après-demain, *the day after*	**le printemps**, *spring*
tomorrow	**l'été**, *summer*
la veille, *the day before*	**l'automne**, *autumn*
le lendemain, *the day after*	**l'hiver**, *winter*

Days, months, and seasons are all masculine and are spelt with a small letter.

Parts of the day

hier, *yesterday*	
ce (cet), *this*	**matin**, *morning*
demain, *tomorrow*	**après-midi**, *afternoon*
dimanche, *Sunday* (etc.)	**soir**, *evening*
le lendemain, *the day*	
after, in the ...	

> **on vous verra dimanche soir**, *we'll see you
>   Sunday evening*
> **cela est arrivé ce matin**, *that happened this
>   morning*
> **on s'est brouillés le lendemain soir**, *we quarrelled
>   the following evening*

The evening before is **la veille au soir**.

Cette nuit means either *tonight* or *last night*, according
to context:

> **tu dormiras bien cette nuit!**, *you'll sleep well
>   tonight!*
> **je n'ai pas dormi cette nuit**, *I didn't sleep last night*

Prepositions with days, months, seasons, etc.

■ *In* with months is **en** or **au mois de**:

> **en avril**, *in April*
> **au mois d'août**, *in August*

■ *In* with seasons is **en**, except **le printemps**:

> **en hiver**, *in winter*
> **au printemps**, *in spring*

■ *In* with years is **en** or **en l'an**. **Mil** is used instead of
mille in writing years:

> **en l'an mil neuf cent quarante-cinq**, *in 1945*

In spoken French **dix-neuf** (etc.) is very often used
for **mil neuf** (etc.):

> **en seize cent douze**, *in 1612*

In the eighties (etc.) is **dans les années quatre-vingt**
(note spelling here: no **-s**, hyphen).

■ *In* with centuries is **au**:

> **au vingtième siècle**, *in the twentieth century*

■ *On* with days in the plural is **le**:

> **il ne travaille que le mercredi**, *he only works on Wednesdays*

■ *On* with days in the singular is not translated:

> **elle arrive mercredi**, *she's coming on Wednesday*
> **elle arrive mercredi matin**, *she's coming on Wednesday morning*

The date

The date is expressed with **le**, plus a cardinal number (except for **premier**, *first*), plus the month. *On* before a date is not translated:

> **on sera à Paris le quatorze juillet**, *we are going to be in Paris on the fourteenth of July*
> **nous sommes le premier juin**, *today's the first of June*

When the day is expressed, the article before the date is usually dropped:

> **lundi, vingt mai** or **le lundi vingt mai**, *Monday the twentieth of May*

MEASUREMENT

Length, breadth, height

Quelle est $\left\{\begin{array}{l}\textbf{la longueur}\\\textbf{la largeur}\\\textbf{la hauteur}\end{array}\right\}$ **de cette pièce?**,

How $\left\{\begin{array}{l}long\\wide\\high\end{array}\right\}$ *is this room?*

— **Elle a trois mètres dix de** $\left\{\begin{array}{l}\textbf{long}\\\textbf{large}\\\textbf{haut}\end{array}\right\}$, *It's*

3.10 metres $\left\{\begin{array}{l}\textit{long}\\\textit{wide}\\\textit{high}\end{array}\right\}$

■ **Faire** can be used instead of **avoir**:

elle fait trois mètres de long, *it's three metres long*

■ *By* in measurements is **sur**:

cette pièce fait trois mètres sur quatre, *this room is three metres by four*

Other common ways of expressing dimension

■ **Long** (etc.) **de**:

cette poutre est longue de trois mètres, *this beam is three metres long*

une poutre longue de trois mètres, *a beam three metres long*

■ **De longueur** (etc.):

cette poutre a trois mètres de longueur, *this beam is three metres long*

une poutre de trois mètres de longueur, *a beam three metres long*

■ **D'une longueur** (etc.) **de**:

cette poutre est d'une longueur de trois mètres, *this beam is three metres long*

une poutre d'une longueur de trois mètres, *a beam three metres long*

The same constructions can be used with **profond/la profondeur**, *deep/depth*, and **épais/l'épaisseur**, *thick/*

thickness, except the **de long** construction, which cannot be used with **épais** and **profond**.

Personal measurements

Quelle taille faites-vous?, *What size are you?*

Combien mesurez-vous?, *What is your height?*

Quel est votre tour de $\left\{ \begin{array}{l} \textbf{poitrine} \\ \textbf{taille} \\ \textbf{hanches} \end{array} \right\}$ **?**, *What is your*

$\left\{ \begin{array}{l} bust \\ waist \\ hip \end{array} \right\}$ *size?*

Quelle pointure chaussez-vous/faites-vous?, *What is your shoe size?*

Notice the three meanings of **la taille**: *size, height, waist*. Only the context makes clear which is meant.

Word Order

Special cases (after direct speech; after **peut-être, à peine, aussi**; in exclamations; after **dont**) *210*
Word order in direct questions *211*
Word order in indirect questions *213*

Word order in French is generally the same as in English, except that:

■ Adjectives usually follow their nouns. See p. 138.

■ Object pronouns precede the verb. See p. 105.

■ Adverbs follow the verb. See p. 156.

■ Negatives stand in two parts around the verb. See p. 159.

■ The 'strong' position in the French sentence is at the end, so where there are, for instance, two or more adverb phrases, the more important one goes to the end. Thus the answer to **quand l'as-tu retrouvé?** (*when did you find it?*) might be:

> **je l'ai retrouvé dans la voiture hier soir**, *I found it last night in the car*

English usage varies, but the more important phrase tends to come first in English, straight after the verb, as in the above example.

■ Word order in direct and indirect questions is treated on pp. 211 and 213.

SPECIAL CASES

■ After direct speech, subject and 'saying' verb are inverted:

> «Bonjour, dit-il, ça va?», *'Hello,' he said, 'How are you?'*
>
> «Vraiment?» répondit l'agent, *'Really?' the policeman replied*

Notice what happens in compound tenses:

> «Bonjour, a-t-il dit, ça va?», *'Hello,' he said, 'How are you?'*
>
> «Vraiment?» a répondu l'agent, *'Really?' the policeman replied*

Although the pronoun inversion is like the question form (**a-t-il dit?**) the noun inversion is not (**l'agent a-t-il répondu?**).

■ In a clause beginning **peut-être**, *perhaps*, **à peine**, *scarcely*, or **aussi**, *therefore*, verb and subject pronoun are inverted:

> peut-être a-t-elle froid, *perhaps she's cold*
>
> à peine son père était-il arrivé que le repas commença, *his father had scarcely got there when the meal began*
>
> maintenant tu me dis la vérité, aussi suis-je content, *now you're telling me the truth, so I'm happy*

This inversion is literary, however. In everyday French it is avoided: **peut-être** would be placed after the verb, or the sentence would begin with **peut-être que**:

> elle a peut-être froid
>
> peut-être qu'elle a froid

A peine would similarly be placed after the verb, and **donc** would be substituted for **aussi**:

> **son père était à peine arrivé que le repas commença**
>
> **maintenant tu me dis la vérité, donc je suis content**

■ In exclamations after **comme** and **que** French has normal word order where English does not:

> **comme il est beau!**, *how handsome he is!*
> **que tu es bête!**, *how silly you are!*

■ After **dont** French always has normal word order where English sometimes does not:

> **le médecin dont tu connais la fille**, *the doctor whose daughter you know*
> **le médecin dont la fille est malade**, *the doctor whose daughter is ill*

▶ See also p. 115.

WORD ORDER IN DIRECT QUESTIONS

Simple questions

Simple questions are formed:

■ By a statement with an interrogative (rising) intonation. This is the commonest way to form a question in speech:

> **c'est une Française?**, *is she French?*

■ By prefixing **est-ce que** to the statement. This is also common in both speech and writing:

> **est-ce que vous prenez du sucre?**, *do you take sugar?*

■ By inverting verb and subject pronoun and putting a hyphen between them:

> **prenez-vous du café?**, *will you have some coffee?*

An extra **-t** is inserted where the verb ends in **-e** or **-a**:

> **a-t-il déjà dîné?**, *has he already eaten?*

In modern French there is, for most verbs, no inverted form of the interrogative with the **je** form of the present tense. **Est-ce que** or a simple question intonation is used.

Inversion is, however, still used with the **je** form of the present tense of **pouvoir**, **devoir**, **être**, and, occasionally, **avoir**:

> **puis-je vous revoir?**, *may I see you again?* (NB never '**peux-je**')
> **que dois-je dire?**, *what am I to say?*
> **suis-je encore de tes amis?**, *am I still one of your friends?*
> **ai-je tout corrigé?**, *have I marked everything?*

■ By stating the noun subject and then asking the question about it using a pronoun. This produces the sequence noun, verb, hyphen, pronoun:

> **votre chien est-il toujours malade?**, *is your dog still ill?*

This construction is literary and is hardly ever found in everyday French.

Questions following question words (interrogative adverbs)

Questions following words such as **pourquoi**, *why*, **quand**, *when*, **où**, *where*, etc. are formed:

■ With a statement pronounced with an interrogative (rising) intonation, following the question word:

où tu vas?, *where are you going?*

This construction is frowned upon in the written language but is extremely common in spoken French.

■ With the question word followed by **est-ce que** and a statement:

où est-ce que tu vas?, *where are you going?*

This is common in both written and spoken French.

■ With the question word followed by the verb, a hyphen and the subject pronoun:

comment as-tu fait cela?, *how did you do that?*

■ With the question word followed by the verb and the subject noun:

quand part le train de Marseille?, *when does the Marseilles train go?*

This form is not possible after **pourquoi** and often sounds clumsy in compound tenses. In these cases one of the other forms is used.

■ With the question word followed by the noun subject, the question then being asked about this using a pronoun:

pourquoi le train de Marseille part-il de cette voie?, *why does the Marseilles train leave from this platform?*

This construction is literary and is hardly ever found in everyday French.

▶ For questions introduced by the interrogative pronouns **qui, que**, etc. (*who, what*), see p. 119.

WORD ORDER IN INDIRECT QUESTIONS

An indirect question is one that is reported in some way (direct question: *why is he there?*, indirect question:

I don't know why he's there). As in English the word
order is: question word followed by normal order:

> **je ne sais pas pourquoi il est là**, *I don't know why*
> *he's there*

If the subject of the indirect question is a noun and the
verb would otherwise end the sentence, verb and noun
are inverted:

> **je me demande si ta copine est là**, *I wonder if*
> *your friend is there*
> **je me demande où est ta copine**, *I wonder where*
> *your friend is*

In this way French avoids leaving a weak word like **est**
in the strong position at the end of the sentence.

Punctuation

French punctuation is largely similar to English, with the following exceptions:

COMMAS

■ Commas are not used in writing large numbers in French. Where we would put a comma, modern French leaves a gap:

> English: 44,000,000   French: 44 000 000

■ Commas are used in decimals where we would use a decimal point or a full stop:

> English: 3·25 or 3.25   French: 3,25

CAPITAL LETTERS

Capitals are used much less frequently in French than in English. French uses small letters for:

■ Country adjectives:

> **il a l'air italien**, *he looks Italian*
> **une assiette anglaise**, *a plate of cold meats*

■ Language nouns:

> **elle parle français**, *she speaks French*

but not nouns of nationality:

> **c'est une Française**, *she's French*

■ Personal and professional titles, ranks:

> **monsieur Dubois** (but **M. Dubois**)
> **le docteur Artin**
> **le général Leclerc**

■ Street, square, avenue, etc., in names:

> **tu descends place de la Concorde**, *you get out at*
> *the Place de la Concorde*
> **la mer Méditerranée**, *the Mediterranean Sea*
> **elle demeure boulevard Raspail**, *she lives in the*
> *Boulevard Raspail*
> **7, rue Victor-Hugo**

■ Points of the compass:

> **le sud**, *the south*; **le nord**, *the north* (but **le Nord**,
> name of the region)

■ Names of days, months:

> **dimanche prochain**, *next Sunday*
> **en janvier dernier**, *last January*

■ Cheeses and wines named after places:

> **le camembert**, *Camembert*
> **le beaujolais**, *Beaujolais*

■ Quite often after an exclamation mark where the sense
is not complete. There are two examples in the Daudet
extract on p. 218 (in the section on inverted commas).

COLON AND DASH

Colon

The colon is used more frequently than in English.
As well as being used as a long pause, intermediate

between a semi-colon and a full stop (as in English), the colon is used where an amplification or explanation is to follow next. English often uses a dash for this, French hardly ever:

> **La seule solution: refaire le toit**, *The only solution—repair the roof*

Dash

■ Used at the beginning and end of parentheses, as in English:

> **Le patron parlait — il aimait beaucoup parler — et en même temps il tapait sur la table**, *The boss was speaking—he was very fond of speaking— and at the same time he was tapping on the table*

■ Used to mark off items in a list:

> **il sera nécessaire de**
> **— remplacer les poutres**
> **— refaire le toit**
> **— réparer les rebords des fenêtres**
> **— reconstruire les placards**

> *It will be necessary to*
> *replace the beams,*
> *redo the roof,*
> *repair the window-sills,*
> *remake the cupboards*

■ Used to indicate a change of speaker in direct speech (see below, inverted commas).

SUSPENSION POINTS (...)

These may indicate that the sentence breaks off, as in English. In French, they may also indicate that what is to

come next is comic, incongruous, or unexpected. English
often uses a dash here:

> **45 milliards de francs par mois ... la moitié du**
> **budget de l'État!**, *45 billion francs a year—half*
> *the national budget!*

INVERTED COMMAS

These are printed « » or " ". Single inverted commas
' ', are almost never used in French.

Inverted commas are placed at the beginning and end
of a section of dialogue. Within that dialogue change of
speaker is indicated by a new paragraph beginning with a
dash (—), but the inverted commas are not closed or
reopened. Short phrases indicating who is speaking,
together with any adverbial qualifications, (e.g.,
répondit-il d'un air distrait) are included within the
dialogue without closing or reopening the inverted
commas. Longer interpolations (of at least one complete
sentence) do entail closing and reopening the inverted
commas.

The following extract from Daudet's *Lettres de mon
moulin* illustrates all these points:

> **«C'est fini ... Je n'en fais plus.**
> **— Qu'est-ce qu'il y a donc, père Gaucher?**
> **demanda le prieur, qui se doutait bien un peu de**
> **ce qu'il y avait.**
> **— Ce qu'il y a, monseigneur? ... Il y a que je**
> **bois, que je bois comme un misérable ...**
> **— Mais je vous avais dit de compter vos**
> **gouttes.**
> **— Ah, bien oui! compter mes gouttes! c'est par**
> **gobelets qu'il faudrait compter maintenant ... Que**
> **le feu de Dieu me brûle si je m'en mêle encore!»**

C'est le chapitre qui ne riait plus.

«Mais, malheureux, vous nous ruinez! criait l'argentier en agitant son grand-livre.

— Préférez-vous que je me damne?»

'It's over. I'm not making any more.'

'What's the matter then, père Gaucher?' asked the prior, who rather suspected what the matter was.

'What's the matter, monseigneur? The matter is, I'm drinking, drinking like a scoundrel.'

'But I told you to count your sips.'

'Oh yes, count my sips! It's cupfuls I'd have to be counting now. May the fire of God consume me if I have anything more to do with it!'

Now it was the chapter who were no longer laughing.

'But, you wretched man, you're ruining us!' cried the treasurer, waving his ledger.

'Would you rather I damned myself?'

Translation Problems

The following list is alphabetical. It includes items not covered in the body of the grammar, or treated in a number of different places and more conveniently brought together here. Translation problems not covered here should be tackled via the index, or, in the case of prepositions, the alphabetical lists on pp. 185 (English) and 164 (French).

-ING

The *-ing* form of the verb is basically the present participle, but it has other uses in English, few of which correspond to the French.

■ *-ing* as adjective (the *-ing* word stands in front of a noun):

the setting sun
the deciding factor

In this case the French word will also be an adjective. It may be a present participle used as an adjective, as in English:

le soleil couchant, *the setting sun* (**se coucher**,
set →present participle **couchant**)

or it may be an ordinary adjective:

le facteur décisif, *the deciding factor*

▶ See present participle, p. 34.

■ *-ing* as a verb in a phrase:

he spoke, looking at me closely
getting off the bus, I saw Micheline

In this case the *-ing* word is translated by a present participle, usually preceded by **en**, *whilst*:

il parla, en me regardant de près, *he spoke,*
looking at me closely
en descendant de l'autobus, j'ai vu Micheline,
getting off the bus, I saw Micheline

This construction can only be used where both verbs have the same subject (*he* spoke and *he* looked at me, *I* got off and *I* saw her). Where the subjects are different, **qui** (or alternatively, after verbs of perception only, an infinitive) has to be used:

j'ai vu Micheline qui descendait de l'autobus, or
j'ai vu Micheline descendre de l'autobus, *I saw*
Micheline getting off the bus

In this case the subjects are different (*I* saw, but *Micheline* got off).

▶ For more detail see p. 35.

■ *-ing* after a preposition:

> *without stopping*
> *before eating*

This is an infinitive:

> **sans parler**, *without speaking*
> **avant de manger**, *before eating*

With some prepositions, notably **après**, *after*, the sense may demand a perfect infinitive:

> **après avoir mangé**, *after eating*
> **après être sorti**, *after going out*

After the preposition **en**, *whilst*, *by*, *in*, a present participle is used:

> **en tournant**, *whilst turning*

▶ For more detail see pp. 52 (infinitives after prepositions) and 53 (perfect infinitive).

■ *-ing* in 'continuous' tenses: *I am running, I was running, I shall be running, I have been running*, etc.

French does not use a present participle for these: *I run* and *I am running* are the same in French: **je cours**, *I have been running* and *I have run* are the same, **j'ai couru**. Only in the case of the imperfect does a special 'continuous' tense exist: **je courais**, *I was running*.

If the continuous nature of an action needs to be emphasized (which is not usually the case), **être en train de** is used:

> **je serai en train de déjeuner**, *I shall be eating my lunch*

▶ For more details see p. 16.

Superficially similar to the above are sentences such as 'she was leaning on the fence', 'he was lying on the ground'. In this case, however, French views *lying*, *leaning*, etc. as adjectives and uses **être** plus a past participle:

> **elle était accoudée sur la clôture**, *she was leaning on the fence*
>
> **il était couché par terre**, *he was lying on the ground*

▶ For further details see p. 39.

■ *-ing* after a verb:

> *he begins typing*
> *she stops telephoning*
> *they love swimming*

This is an infinitive in French, preceded by the preposition appropriate to the main verb:

> **il commence à taper à la machine**, *he begins typing*
> **elle s'arrête de téléphoner**, *she stops telephoning*
> **ils adorent nager**, *they love swimming*

■ *-ing* after a verb with an object:

> *he stops her telephoning*
> *she heard him laughing*

This is also an infinitive in French, preceded by the preposition appropriate to the main verb:

> **il l'empêche de téléphoner**, *he stops her telephoning*
> **elle l'a entendu rire**, *she heard him laughing*

▶ For the prepositions that verbs take before an infinitive see p. 51.

■ *-ing* as subject of the sentence (the verbal noun):

> *walking tires me*
> *telephoning is easier*

This is an infinitive in French:

> **me promener me fatigue**, *walking tires me*
> **téléphoner est plus simple**, *telephoning is easier*

However, French prefers to avoid this use of the infinitive at the beginning of the sentence, and usually makes the infinitive depend on the other verb:

> **ça me fatigue de me promener**, *it tires me to walk*
> **c'est plus simple de téléphoner**, *it's easier to telephone*

▶ See also the infinitive as verbal noun, p. 50.

■ *-ing* as a noun

English uses *-ing* nouns for many sorts of activity and sports. These are translated by other nouns in French:

> *fishing*, **la pêche**
> *swimming*, **la natation**
> *singing*, **le chant**
> *horse-riding*, **l'équitation**

IT IS

It is with nouns and adjectives

■ Where *it is* refers to a noun that has already been mentioned, it is translated by **il est** or **elle est** according to the gender of that noun:

> **la clé? Elle est sur la porte**, *the key? It's in the door*
> **ma nouvelle robe, ah oui, elle est bleue**, *my new dress, yes, it's blue*

■ Where *it is* introduces a noun or pronoun, it is translated by **c'est**, whatever the gender of the noun or pronoun. The plural (*those are*) is **ce sont**:

> **c'est une Citroën**, *it's a Citroën*
> **c'est moi!**, *it's me!*
> **ce sont des mouettes**, *those are seagulls*

C'est is similarly used to introduce adverbial expressions:

> **c'est à Noël qu'elle vient**, *it's at Christmas that she's coming*

■ Where *it is* refers back to something other than a noun (a noun clause, a previous sentence, etc.), **c'est** is used.

> **il parle italien? Oui, c'est possible**, *he speaks Italian? Yes, it's possible*

■ Where *it is* introduces an adjective followed by **que** or **de**, **il est** is used:

> **il est possible qu'il parle italien**, *it's possible that he speaks Italian*
> **il est difficile de traduire cela**, *it's difficult to translate that*

However, in the spoken language **c'est** is very often used in this case too:

> **c'est possible qu'il parle Italien**, *it's possible he speaks Italian*

■ In all cases except the last **cela est** may be used instead of **c'est**:

> **cela est possible**, *it's (that's) possible*

It is, with weather, time, etc.

■ *It* is **il** with:

☐ Weather verbs, both simple verbs

> **il pleut**, *it's raining*
> **il neige**, *it's snowing*

and those constructed with **faire**

> **il fait du vent**, *it's windy*
> **il fait beau**, *it's fine*

☐ Time of day

> **il est cinq heures**, *it's five o'clock*
> **il est midi et demi**, *it's half past twelve*

☐ The time expressions: **tard**, *late*, **tôt**, *early*, **temps**, *time*

> **il est tard**, *it's late*
> **il est temps de partir**, *it's time to go*
> **il est temps que tu partes**, *it's time you went*

■ With other time expressions **c'est** is used:

> **c'est dimanche**, *it's Sunday*
> **c'est janvier**, *it's January*
> **c'est le printemps**, *it's spring*
> **c'est le 18 mai**, *it's the 18th of May*

■ **Pouvoir**, *can*, and **devoir**, *ought to, should*, may be introduced into these constructions:

> **ce doit être possible**, *it ought to be possible*
> **il peut neiger**, *it may snow*

▶ For further details see impersonal verbs, pp. 74 ff.

JUST (adverb)

■ *just = exactly*: **juste**; **justement**

> **tu as juste trois minutes**, *you have just three minutes*
> **c'est juste au-dessus de la porte**, *it's just above the door*
> **on a sonné juste au moment où je me mettais dans le bain**, *someone rang the bell just when I was getting into the bath*
> **c'est justement ce que je dis toujours**, *that's just what I always say*

■ *just = only*: **seul; seulement**

> **un seul**, *just one*
> **seulement deux, trois**, etc., *just two, three*, etc.
> **une seule fois**, *just once*

■ *just* in *have/had just*: **venir de** + infinitive

> **je viens de le faire**, *I've just done it*
> **on venait de l'ouvrir**, *they had just opened it*

▶ See pp. 18 and 21 for more details on tenses with **venir de**.

■ *just* in *just as* (= *equally*): **tout**

> **cela est tout aussi difficile**, *that's just as difficult*

■ *just* with a following verb: **ne faire que** + infinitive

> **elle n'a fait que pleurer**, *she just cried*

-SELF

■ *-self* as direct or indirect object: reflexive pronoun (**me, te, se**, etc.) before verb:

> **il s'est distingué**, *he distinguished himself*
> **je me disais la même chose**, *I was saying the same thing to myself*

▶ For further details see reflexive pronouns, p. 30.

■ *-self* as a strengthener of the subject: disjunctive pronoun + **-même** (**moi-même, toi-même**, etc.) placed after verb:

> **tu l'as fait toi-même?**, *you did it yourself?*

▶ For further details see disjunctive pronouns, p. 109 and disjunctives with **-même**, p. 111.

■ *-self* after preposition: disjunctive pronoun (**moi, toi,** etc.) with or without **-même**:

> **je ne parle que pour moi,** *I can only speak for myself*
>
> **il n'écrit que pour lui-même,** *he writes only for himself*

■ *oneself* is **soi(-même)**:

> **on ne peut pas le garder pour soi(-même),** *one can't keep it for oneself*

▶ For further details on the use of **soi** see p. 109.

SINCE

■ Preposition: **depuis**

> **je t'attends depuis deux heures et demie,** *I've been waiting for you since half past two*
>
> **je t'attendais depuis deux heures et demie,** *I had been waiting for you since half past two*

The tenses with **depuis** are different from the English ones in positive statements: *have been … ing* = French present, *had been … ing* = French imperfect. With a negative the tense is the same as in English:

> **je ne l'ai pas vue depuis la boum,** *I haven't seen her since the party*

▶ **Depuis** can also mean *for*. For more details on tenses with **depuis** see pp. 17 and 21.

■ Adverb: **depuis**

> **tu l'a vue depuis?,** *have you seen her since?*

The adverb **depuis** does not affect the tense of the verb.

■ Time conjunction: **depuis que**

> **elle travaille depuis que son mari est mort**, *she has been working* (*has worked*) *ever since her husband died*
>
> **elle allait à pied depuis que la voiture avait fini par tomber en panne**, *she had been walking* (*ever*) *since the car had finally broken down*
>
> **je ne dors plus depuis qu'il est de retour**, *I'm not sleeping any more since he's back*

Tenses with **depuis que**, conjunction, are the same as with **depuis**, preposition, above.

▶ For further information on **depuis que** see pp. 17 and 21.

■ Conjunction expressing reason: **puisque**

> **puisqu'il est si impoli je ne lui parle plus**, *since he's so rude I don't speak to him any more*

SOON AND LATE

Soon, early

■ *soon*: **bientôt**

> **on sera bientôt là**, *we'll soon be there*

■ *soon* = *early*: **tôt**

> **on est arrivé beaucoup trop tôt**, *we got there much too soon* (*early*)

■ *early* = *in good time*: **de bonne heure**

> **on est arrivé de bonne heure**, *we got there early*

■ *sooner* = *earlier*: **plus tôt**

> **nous sommes arrivés plus tôt qu'eux**, *we arrived sooner* (*earlier*) *than they did*

■ *sooner = in preference; rather*: **plutôt**

plutôt lui que moi, *sooner him than me*

Late

■ *late*, time of day: **tard**

il est très tard, rentrons, *it's very late, let's go
home*

■ *late*, = *after the appropriate time*: **tard**

maintenant il est trop tard, *now it's too late*

■ *late*, referring to people: **en retard**

nous sommes en retard, *we're late*

■ *late*, adjective: **tardif**

à cette heure tardive, *at this late hour*

■ *late*, adjective, = *dead*: **feu**

le tombeau de feu son père, *his late father's grave*

Feu is invariable. Note its position.

TIME(S)

■ *time(s) = occasion(s)*: **la/les fois**

pour la première fois, *for the first time*

■ *time = length, amount of time*: **le temps**

malheureusement je n'ai pas le temps,
unfortunately I haven't got (the) time

■ *time = point in time*: **le moment**

tu es arrivé au bon moment?, *you got there at the
right moment?*

On time is **à l'heure**; *in (the nick of) time* is **à temps**:

> **tu dois arriver à l'heure**, *you must get there on time*
> **tu es arrivé juste à temps**, *you got there just in time*

■ *time = time of day*: **l'heure**

> **vous avez l'heure?**, *do you have the (right) time?*

■ *time = period*: **l'époque**

> **à cette époque j'étais toujours au lycée**, *at that time I was still at college*

TO BE

To be is translated by verbs other than **être** in the following cases:

■ Location: **se trouver**

> **le garage se trouve derrière la maison**, *the garage is (located) behind the house*

■ Physical states: **avoir**

> **j'ai chaud/froid/faim/soif/sommeil/peur/honte**, *I'm hot/cold/hungry/thirsty/tired/frightened/ashamed*

Similarly: *to be right/wrong* is **avoir raison/tort**.

■ Health: **aller**

> **comment allez-vous?**, *how are you?*
> **maman va beaucoup mieux**, *mother's much better*

■ Weather: **faire**

> **il fait chaud/froid/beau/mauvais/du vent/du brouillard**, *it's hot/cold/fine/bad/windy/foggy*

■ Age: **avoir**

> **elle a vingt et un ans**, *she's twenty-one (years old)*

▶ *I am to/I was to* is translated by **devoir**. See p. 65.

VERB + OBJECT + INFINITIVE

Sentences such as *I want her to go, I like her to talk*
cannot be translated directly into French, as, with the
exception of a very few verbs (see below), this
verb + object + infinitive construction does not exist in
French. A clause has to be used instead:

> **je veux qu'elle parte**, *I want her to go* (*'I want that
> she should go'*)
>
> **j'aime qu'il me gratte le dos**, *I like him to scratch
> my back* (*'I like that he scratches my back'*)

Both **vouloir que** and **aimer que** in the above examples
take the subjunctive.

A similar construction used in English with verbs of
perception consists of verb + object + infinitive/present
participle (*I hear him speak/speaking*). This construction,
with verbs of perception (**voir, entendre, sentir**, etc.),
can be translated directly into French. A dependent
infinitive is used:

> **je l'entends parler**, *I hear him speak(ing)*

▶ For further details see p. 42 (subjunctive) and p. 51
(dependent infinitive)

VERB + PREPOSITION COMBINATIONS

Many English verbs consist of a simple verb plus a
preposition (*cry out, run away, run back*). This verb-plus-
preposition construction is impossible in French and
such verbs, sometimes called phrasal verbs, have to be
translated in one of the following ways.

■ By a simple verb:

> **crispée de douleur, elle commença à crier**,
> *contorted with pain, she began to cry out* (*cry
> out*: **crier**)

> **à la nuit tombante ils se sont enfuis**, *at nightfall they ran away* (*run away*: **s'enfuir**)

■ By a verb based on the preposition, plus a dependent present participle (with **en**) or an adverb phrase:

> **ils sont retournés en courant**, *they ran back* (*run back*: **retourner en courant**, *'go back running'*)
> **ils sont partis à la hâte**, *they hurried off* (*hurry off*: **partir à la hâte**, *'go off in a hurry'*)

▶ For further details see p. 36.

■ Where the verb-phrase has an object, by a verb with a dependent infinitive:

> **laisse-le entrer!**, *let him in*

Several of these are based on **faire**:

> **faire entrer**, *show in*
> **faire sortir**, *show out*
> **faire venir**, *send for*

▶ See p. 73 for more details.

WHATEVER, WHOEVER

Whatever

■ Pronoun subject: **quoi que ce soit qui**; pronoun object: **quoi que** (both + subjunctive)

> **quoi que ce soit qui bouge, ne tirez pas!**, *whatever moves, don't shoot*
> **quoi que ce soit qui ronge votre parquet, ce ne sont pas des souris**, *whatever is eating your floorboards, it isn't mice*
> **quoi qu'il dise, je ne le crois pas**, *whatever he says* (*may say*), *I don't believe him*

■ Adjective: **quel que soit**

> **quel que soit la somme qu'on vous offre**, *whatever money you are offered*
>
> **ne renoncez pas, quelles que soient les difficultés**, *don't give up, whatever the difficulties may be*

■ *Anything whatever* is **quoi que ce soit**, used as if it were a pronoun:

> **il ne se plaint pas de quoi que ce soit**, *he doesn't complain about anything whatever (anything at all)*

Whoever

■ **Qui que ce soit qui** (subject), **qui que ce soit que** (object) both + subjunctive:

> **qui que ce soit qui vous ait dit cela, c'est complètement faux**, *whoever told you that, it's completely untrue*
>
> **qui que ce soit qu'on propose comme candidat, je ne voterai pas**, *whoever they put up as candidate, I shall not vote*

Quiconque may be used (without the subjunctive), in rather more formal style, for **qui que ce soit qui/que**. See p. 130.

Pronunciation Traps

To attempt to present the pronunciation of French as a whole in a grammar of this kind would be impossible and pointless. It is, however, useful to provide reference to those commonly used words whose pronunciation does not follow the usual patterns or with which learners consistently find pronunciation problems.

The following list gives such problem words alphabetically, with a very approximate imitated pronunciation followed by the exact pronunciation represented by the letters of the International Phonetic Alphabet. In general, related words show the same pronunciation changes (so **le sculpteur**, *sculptor*, is pronounced without a p, like **la sculpture**, listed below).

ail (m.), *garlic*	eye	aj
aile (f.), *wing*	el	ɛl
alcool (m.), *alcohol*	al-col	alkɔl
	(one o pronounced)	
amener, *bring*	am-nay	amne
Amiens (the town)	am-ya	amjɛ̃
automne (m.), *autumn*	oh-tonn	otɔn
	(m not pronounced)	
but, **automnal**,	oh-tom-nal	otɔmnal
autumnal	(m often pronounced)	
bœuf (m.), *beef; ox*	berf	bœf
but plural **bœufs**,	berh	bø
cattle; oxen		
cent un, *101*; **cent onze**	son-ern; son-onz	sɑ̃ œ̃; sɑ̃ ɔ̃:z
111	(t not pronounced)	
chef (m.), chief, *head*	shef	ʃɛf
but, **chef d'œuvre**,	shed-er-vr	ʃɛdœ:vɾ
masterpiece	(f not pronounced)	

Christ (m.), *Christ*	creased (t pronounced)	krist
but **Jésus Christ**	jay-zoo-cree (t not pronounced)	ʒezy kri
condamner, *condemn*	con-da-nay (m not pronounced)	kɔ̃dane
cuiller (also spelled **cuillère**), (f.) *spoon*	kwee-yair (r pronounced)	kɥijɛːr
dix, *10* (standing alone) (before a consonant) (before a vowel)	deese dee deez	dis di diz
dot, (f.) *dowry*	dot (t pronounced)	dɔt
emmener, *take away*	om-nay	ɑ̃mne
estomac (m.), *stomach*	esto-ma (c not pronounced)	ɛstɔma
eu, *had* (past participle of **avoir**)	ee (+ rounded lips)	y
fier, *proud*	fee-air (r pronounced)	fjɛːr
fils (m.), *son*	feese (s pronounced)	fis
but **fils** (m. pl.), *wires*	feel (s not pronounced)	fil
hais, **hait**, *hate(s)* (**je**, **tu** and **il** form of present, **haïr**)	eh (i not pronounced separately)	ɛ
hélas, *alas*	ay-lars (s pronounced)	elɑːs
jus (m.), *juice*	joo (s not pronounced)	ʒy
mademoiselle (f.), *miss*	mad-mwa-zel (first e not pronounced)	madmwazɛl
mille, *thousand*	meal (ll pronounced l)	mil

mœurs, (f. pl.), *manners*	merse (s usually pronounced)	mœrs
naïveté (f.), *naïvety*	na-eev-tay	naivte
neuf, *9*	nerf	nœf
but **neuf heures**	ner-vur	nœv œːr
and **neuf ans**	ner-von (f pronounced v)	nœv ã
notre, *our*; **votre**, *your*	notr; votr	nɔtr̩; vɔtr̩
but, **nôtre**, *ours*; **vôtre**, *yours*	note-r, vote-r (o lengthened)	noːtr̩; voːtr̩
œuf (m.), *egg*	erf	œf
but plural **œufs**, *eggs*	erh (fs not pronounced, vowel lengthened)	ɸ
oignon (m.), *onion*	on-yon	ɔɲɔ̃
os (m.), *bone*	os	ɔs
but plural **os**, *bones*	oh (s not pronounced, vowel lengthened)	o
poêle (m.), *stove*; (f.), *frying pan*	pwal	pwal
Reims, (*Rheims*, the town)	ranse	rɛ̃ːs
rhum (m.), *rum* and **Rome**, *Rome*	rom	rɔm
sandwich (m.), *sandwich*	*sond-witch*	sɑ̃dwitʃ
sceptique, *sceptical*	sep-teek (c not pronounced)	sɛptik
sculpture (f.), *sculpture*	skill-tour (p not pronounced)	skyltyːr
sens (m.), *sense*; *direction*	sonse (last s pronounced)	sɑ̃ːs

six, *6* (standing alone) cease   sis
   (before a consonant) sea   si
   (before a vowel)   seas   siz

six, *6* (standing alone)	cease	sis
(before a consonant)	sea	si
(before a vowel)	seas	siz
solennel, *solemn*	sol-a-nel	sɔlanɛl
	(first e pronounced a)	
tabac (m.),	ta-ba	taba
tobacco(nist's)	(c not pronounced)	
tiers (m.), *third*	tea-air	tjɛ:r
	(s not pronounced)	
vieille (f.), *old*	vyay	vjɛ:j
but **veille** (f.), *the day*	vay	vɛːj
before		
village (m.), *village*	vee-large	vila:ʒ
	(ll pronounced l)	
ville (f.), *town*	veel	vil
	(ll pronounced l)	
vingt, *20*	van	vɛ̃
but **vingt et un**, *21*	van-tay-ern	vɛ̃t e œ̃
vingt-deux, *22*, etc.	vant-der	vɛ̃t dø
	(t usually pronounced	
	from 21 on)	
wagon (m.), *carriage*	va-gon	vagɔ̃

Verb Tables

► See also pp. 7 and 8.

■ Verbs with infinitives ending -e[consonant]er:

□ changing the -e to -è before a mute or unstressed e.
See p. 7 for a list of verbs in this group. Model: **acheter**,
to buy:

present		past participle
j'achète	nous achetons	acheté
tu achètes	vous achetez	
il achète	ils achètent	

future	past historic
j'achèterai	j'achetai

□ doubling the consonant before a mute or unstressed
-e. Model: **jeter**, *to throw*:

present		past participle
je jette	nous jetons	jeté
tu jettes	vous jetez	
il jette	ils jettent	

future	past historic
je jetterai	je jetai

■ Verbs with infinitives ending **-é[consonant]er**:

The **é** changes to **è** before a mute **e**, but not in the future or conditional. Model: **préférer**, *to prefer*:

present		past participle
je préfère	**nous préférons**	**préféré**
tu préfères	**vous préférez**	
il préfère	**ils préfèrent**	

future	past historic
je préférerai	**je préférai**

■ Verbs with infinitives ending **-yer**:

The **y** changes to **i** before a mute or unstressed **e**. The change is optional with **-ayer** verbs. Model: **appuyer**, *to lean*:

present		past participle
j'appuie	**nous appuyons**	**appuyé**
tu appuies	**vous appuyez**	
il appuie	**ils appuient**	

future	past historic
j'appuierai	**j'appuyai**

■ Verbs with infinitives ending **-cer**:

The **c** changes to **ç** before **a** and **o**. Model: **commencer**, *to begin*:

present		past participle
je commence	**nous commençons**	**commencé**
tu commences	**vous commencez**	
il commence	**ils commencent**	

future		past historic
je commencerai		**je commençai**

present participle	imperfect	
commençant	**je commençais**	**nous commencions**
	tu commençais	**vous commenciez**
	il commençait	**ils commençaient**

■ Verbs with infinitives ending **-ger**:

The **g** changes to **ge** before **a** and **o**. Model: **manger**, *to eat*:

present		past participle
je mange	**nous mangeons**	**mangé**
tu manges	**vous mangez**	
il mange	**ils mangent**	

future	past historic
je mangerai	**je mangeai**

present participle	imperfect	
mangeant	**je mangeais**	**nous mangions**
	tu mangeais	**vous mangiez**
	il mangeait	**ils mangeaient**

IRREGULAR VERBS

Verbs, including common compound verbs, are in alphabetical order. Verbs marked * are less common: some parts of these verbs are very rarely met.

Verbs marked † form their compound tenses with **être**.

The parts given are the infinitive, the full present tense, the past participle (from which all compound tenses may be formed, see p. 3), the **je** form of the future (from which the rest of the future and the conditional may be formed), and the **je** form of the past historic (from which the rest of the past historic may be formed). The endings for these last three tenses are:

	future	conditional	past historic		
je	-ai	-ais	-ai	-is	-us
tu	-as	-ais	-as	-is	-us
il	-a	-ait	-a	-it	-ut
nous	-ons	-ions	-âmes	-îmes	-ûmes
vous	-ez	-iez	-âtes	-îtes	-ûtes
ils	-ont	-aient	-èrent	-irent	-urent

The conditional endings are added to the future stem to form the conditional; the same endings are added to the **nous** form of the present (without its **-ons**) to form the imperfect.

For the formation of the present and imperfect subjunctive see pp. 40 and 41.

infinitive; present	past participle	future	past historic
*acquérir *acquire*			
j'acquiers	acquis	j'acquerrai	j'acquis
tu acquiers			
il acquiert			
nous acquérons			
vous acquérez			
ils acquièrent			

accueillir, *welcome* → **cueillir**

admettre, *admit* → **mettre**

aller† *go*			
je vais	allé	j'irai	j'allai
tu vas			
il va			
nous allons			
vous allez			
ils vont			
pres. subjunctive: **j'aille, nous allions**			

apercevoir, *catch sight of* → **recevoir**

apparaître, *appear* → **connaître**

apprendre, *learn* → **prendre**

infinitive; present	past participle	future	past historic
s'asseoir† *sit down*			
je m'assieds	assis	je m'assiérai	je m'assis
tu t'assieds			
il s'assied			
nous nous asseyons			
vous vous asseyez			
ils s'asseyent			

more colloquial form of present: **je m'assois, tu t'assois, il s'assoit, nous nous assoyons, vous vous assoyez, ils s'assoient**

atteindre, *reach* → **peindre**

avoir *have*			
j'ai	eu	j'aurai	j'eus
tu as			
il a			
nous avons			
vous avez			
ils ont			

pres. subjunctive: **j'aie, nous ayons**, pres. participle: **ayant**, imperative: **aie, ayons, ayez**

*battre *beat*   regular except present: **je bats, tu bats, il bat, nous battons, vous battez, ils battent**

*se battre†, *fight* → **battre**

infinitive; present	past participle	future	past historic
boire *drink*			
je bois	bu	je boirai	je bus
tu bois			
il boit			
nous buvons			
vous buvez			
ils boivent			

*bouillir *boil*	regular except present: **je bous, tu bous, il bout, nous bouillons, vous bouillez, ils bouillent**		

* combattre, *combat* → **battre**

commettre, *commit* → **mettre**

comprendre, *understand* → **prendre**

* concevoir, *conceive* → **recevoir**

infinitive; present	past participle	future	past historic
conduire *drive*			
je conduis	conduit	je conduirai	je conduisis
tu conduis			
il conduit			
nous conduisons			
vous conduisez			
ils conduisent			
connaître *know*			
je connais	connu	je connaîtrai	je connus
tu connais			
il connaît			
nous connaissons			
vous connaissez			
ils connaissent			

infinitive; present	past participle	future	past historic

construire, *construct* → **conduire**

* **contraindre**, *restrict* → **peindre**

* **contredire**, *contradict* → **dire** (present: **vous contredisez**)

* **convaincre**, *convince* → **vaincre**

* **coudre** *sew*			
je couds	cousu	je coudrai	je cousis
tu couds			
il coud			
nous cousons			
vous cousez			
ils cousent			

courir *run*			
je cours	couru	je courrai	je courus
tu cours			
il court			
nous courons			
vous courez			
ils courent			

couvrir *cover*			
je couvre	couvert	je couvrirai	je couvris
tu couvres			
il couvre			
nous couvrons			
vous couvrez			
ils couvrent			

craindre, *fear* → **peindre**

infinitive; present	past participle	future	past historic
croire *believe*			
je crois	cru	**je croirai**	je crus
tu crois			
il croit			
nous croyons			
vous croyez			
ils croient			
* croître *grow*			
je croîs	crû	**je croîtrai**	past hist.
tu croîs	(f.: **crue**)		not used
il croît			
nous croissons			
vous croissez			
ils croissent			
* cueillir *gather*			
je cueille	cueilli	**je cueillerai**	je cueillis
tu cueilles			
il cueille			
nous cueillons			
vous cueillez			
ils cueillent			

* cuire, *cook* → **conduire**

décevoir, *deceive* → **recevoir**

découvrir, *discover* → **couvrir**

décrire, *describe* → **écrire**

* détruire, *destroy* → **conduire**

infinitive; present	past participle	future	past historic
devoir			
must; *owe*			
je dois	dû	je devrai	je dus
tu dois	(f.: **due**,		
il doit	m. pl.: **dus**,		
nous devons	f. pl.: **dues**)		
vous devez			
ils doivent			
dire			
say			
je dis	dit	je dirai	je dis
tu dis			
il dit			
nous disons			
vous dites			
ils disent			
dormir, *sleep* → **partir**			
écrire			
write			
j'écris	écrit	j'écrirai	j'écrivis
tu écris			
il écrit			
nous écrivons			
vous écrivez			
ils écrivent			

★ **élire**, *elect* → **lire**

★ **émouvoir**, *move*; *stir up* → **mouvoir** (past participle: **ému**)

★ **s'enquérir†**, *enquire* → **acquérir**

infinitive; present	past participle	future	past historic
envoyer *send*			
j'envoie	**envoyé**	**j'enverrai**	**j'envoyai**
tu envoies			
il envoie			
nous envoyons			
vous envoyez			
ils envoient			

éteindre, *switch off; put out* → **peindre**

être *be*			
je suis	**été**	**je serai**	**je fus**
tu es			
il est			
nous sommes			
vous êtes			
ils sont			

pres. subjunctive: **je sois, nous soyons,**
pres. participle: **étant,** imperative: **sois, soyons, soyez**

* étreindre, *embrace* → **peindre**

faire *do; make*			
je fais			
tu fais	**fait**	**je ferai**	**je fis**
il fait			
nous faisons			
vous faites			
ils font			

pres. subjunctive: **je fasse, nous fassions**

infinitive; present	past participle	future	past historic
falloir *must; be necessary*			
il faut	**fallu**	**il faudra**	**il fallut**
pres. subjunctive: **il faille**			
* fuir *flee*			
je fuis	**fui**	**je fuirai**	**je fuis**
tu fuis			
il fuit			
nous fuyons			
vous fuyez			
ils fuient			
* haïr *hate*			
je hais	**haï**	**je haïrai**	**je haïs**
tu hais			
il hait			
nous haïssons			
vous haïssez			
ils haïssent			

(past. historic: **nous haïmes**, **vous haïtes**, imperfect subjunctive: **il haït**—but all three forms are virtually unused)

* s'inscrire†, *have oneself registered* → **écrire**

interdire, *forbid* → **dire** (present: **vous interdisez**)

introduire, *introduce; put in* → **conduire**

joindre, *join* → **peindre**

infinitive; present	past participle	future	past historic
lire *read*			
je lis	**lu**	**je lirai**	**je lus**
tu lis			
il lit			
nous lisons			
vous lisez			
ils lisent			
* luire *shine*			
il luit	**lui**	**il luira**	past hist.
ils luisent	(no f.)		not used
mentir, *tell lies* → **partir**			
mettre *put*			
je mets	**mis**	**je mettrai**	**je mis**
tu mets			
il met			
nous mettons			
vous mettez			
ils mettent			
* moudre *grind*			
je mouds	**moulu**	**je moudrai**	**je moulus**
tu mouds			
il moud			
nous moulons			
vous moulez			
ils moulent			

infinitive; present	past participle	future	past historic
mourir† *die*			
je meurs	**mort**	je mourrai	je mourus
tu meurs			
il meurt			
nous mourons			
vous mourez			
ils meurent			
★ **mouvoir** *drive; propel*			
je meus	**mû**	je mouvrai	je mus
tu meus	(f. **mue**)		(rare)
il meut			
nous mouvons			
vous mouvez			
ils meuvent			

★ **naître**†, *be born* → **connaître** (past participle: **né**, past historic: **je naquis**)

★ **nuire**, *harm* → **cuire** (past participle: **nui**)

offrir, *offer* → **couvrir**

ouvrir, *open* → **couvrir**

★ **paître**, *graze* → **connaître** (no past participle or past historic)

paraître, *appear* → **connaître**

infinitive; present	past participle	future	past historic
partir† *leave*			
je pars	**parti**	**je partirai**	**je partis**
tu pars			
il part			
nous partons			
vous partez			
ils partent			
peindre *paint*			
je peins	**peint**	**je peindrai**	**je peignis**
tu peins			
il peint			
nous peignons			
vous peignez			
ils peignent			

* plaindre, *pity* **→ peindre**

* plaire *please*			
je plais	**plu**	**je plairai**	**je plus**
tu plais			
il plaît			
nous plaisons			
vous plaisez			
ils plaisent			

pleuvoir *rain*			
il pleut	**plu**	**il pleuvra**	**il plut**

pres. subjunctive: **il pleuve**

poursuivre, *pursue* **→ suivre**

infinitive; present	past participle	future	past historic
pouvoir *can; be able*			
je peux (puis-je?)	pu	je pourrai	je pus
tu peux			
il peut			
nous pouvons			
vous pouvez			
ils peuvent			
pres. subjunctive: **je puisse, nous puissions**			

prendre *take*			
je prends	pris	je prendrai	je pris
tu prends			
il prend			
nous prenons			
vous prenez			
ils prennent			

produire, *produce* → **conduire**

*promouvoir, *promote:* only infinitive and past participle (**promu**) used

recevoir *receive*			
je reçois	reçu	je recevrai	je reçus
tu reçois			
il reçoit			
nous recevons			
vous recevez			
ils reçoivent			

reconnaître, *recognize* → **connaître**

infinitive; present	past participle	future	past historic

* réduire, *reduce* → **conduire**

* se repentir†, *repent* → **partir**

* résoudre
  resolve

je résous	résolu	je	je résolus
tu résous		résoudrai	
il résout			
nous résolvons			
vous résolvez			
ils résolvent			

* restreindre, *restrain*; *limit* → **peindre**

rire
  laugh

je ris	ri	je rirai	je ris
tu ris			
il rit			
nous rions			
vous riez			
ils rient			

* rompre
  break

je romps	rompu	je romprai	je rompis
tu romps			
il rompt			
nous rompons			
vous rompez			
ils rompent			

infinitive; present	past participle	future	past historic
savoir			
know			
je sais	su	je saurai	je sus
tu sais			
il sait			
nous savons			
vous savez			
ils savent			

pres. subjunctive: **je sache, nous sachions**
pres. participle: **sachant**; used as adjective, **savant**
imperative: **sache, sachons, sachez**

---

* séduire, *seduce* → **conduire**

---

sentir, se sentir†, *feel* → **partir**

---

servir, *serve* → **partir**

---

sortir†, *go out* → **partir**

---

souffrir, *suffer* → **couvrir**

---

sourire, *smile* → **rire**

---

suffire, *be (quite) enough* → **lire**   (past participle: **suffi**, past historic: **je suffis**)

---

suivre			
follow			
je suis	suivi	je suivrai	je suivis
tu suis			
il suit			
nous suivons			
vous suivez			
ils suivent			

---

surprendre, *surprise* → **prendre**

---

* survivre, *survive* → **vivre**

infinitive; present	past participle	future	past historic

*se taire†, *be quiet* → **plaire** (present: **il se tait**)

tenir, *hold* → **venir**

traduire, *translate* → **conduire**

*vaincre *defeat*			
je vaincs	vaincu	je vaincrai	je vainquis
tu vaincs			
il vainc			
nous vainquons			
vous vainquez			
ils vainquent			

*valoir *be worth*			
je vaux	valu	je vaudrai	je valus
tu vaux			
il vaut			
nous valons			
vous valez			
ils valent			

pres. subjunctive: **je vaille, nous valions, ils vaillent**; forms other than **il** extremely uncommon in all tenses

venir† *come*			
je viens	venu	je viendrai	je vins
tu viens			tu vins
il vient			il vint
nous venons			nous vînmes
vous venez			vous vîntes
ils viennent			ils vinrent

infinitive; present	past participle	future	past historic
* vêtir *dress*			
je vêts	vêtu	je vêtirai	je vêtis
tu vêts			
il vêt			
nous vêtons			
vous vêtez			
ils vêtent			

(present **nous vêtissons, vous vêtissez, ils vêtissent,** present part. **vêtissant,** and imperfect **je vêtissais** etc. are also found)

vivre *live*			
je vis	vécu	je vivrai	je vécus
tu vis			
il vit			
nous vivons			
vous vivez			
ils vivent			

voir *see*			
je vois	vu	je verrai	je vis
tu vois			
il voit			
nous voyons			
vous voyez			
ils voient			

infinitive; present	past participle	future	past historic

vouloir
  want

je veux	voulu	je voudrai	je voulus
tu veux			
il veut			
nous voulons			
vous voulez			
ils veulent			

pres. subjunctive: **je veuille, nous voulions**
imperative: **veuille, veuillez** (= *would you kindly*)

Glossary of Grammatical Terms

Abstract Noun The name of something that is not a concrete object or person. Words such as *difficulty*, *hope*, *discussion* are abstract nouns.

Active See Passive.

Adjective A word describing a noun. *A big, blue, untidy painting*—*big*, *blue*, *untidy* are adjectives describing the noun *painting*.

Adverb A word that describes or modifies (i) a verb: *he did it gracefully* (adverb: *gracefully*), or (ii) an adjective: *a disgracefully large helping* (adverb: *disgracefully*), or (iii) another adverb: *she skated extraordinarily gracefully* (adverbs: *extraordinarily*, *gracefully*).

Agreement In French, adjectives agree with nouns, verbs agree with subject nouns or pronouns, pronouns agree with nouns, etc. This is a way of showing that something refers to or goes with something else. Agreement is by number (showing whether something is singular or plural) and by gender (showing whether something is masculine or feminine). For instance: **des chaussettes bleues**, *blue socks*: **-e** is added to the adjective because **chaussette** is feminine, **-s** is added to **bleue** because **chaussettes** is plural.

Apposition Two nouns or noun phrases are used together, the second one explaining the first: *the station master, a big man with a moustache, came in.* 'A big man with a moustache' is in apposition to 'the station master'.

Articles The little words like *a* and *the* that stand in front of nouns. In English, *the* is the definite article (it defines a particular item in a category: *the hat you've got on*); *a* or *an* is the indefinite article (it doesn't specify which item in a category: *wear a hat, any hat*); *some* is the partitive article (it specifies a part but not the whole of a category: *I'd like some mustard*).

Attributive Noun A noun used as an adjective: *a petrol pump*: 'petrol' is an attributive noun, telling us what sort of pump.

Auxiliary Verb A verb used to help form a compound tense. In *I am walking, he has walked* the auxiliary verbs are *to be* (*am*) and *to have* (*has*).

Cardinal Numbers The numbers used in counting (*one, two, three, four*, etc.). Compare with Ordinal Numbers.

Clause A self-contained section of a sentence containing a verb: *He came in and was opening his mail when the lights went out*—'he came in', 'and (he) was opening his mail', 'when the lights went out' are clauses.

Comparative With adjectives and adverbs, the form produced by adding *-er* or prefixing *more*: *bigger, more difficult, more easily*.

Compound Noun Noun formed from two or more separate words, usually hyphenated in French: **le tire-bou-chon**, *corkscrew*—both English and French words are compound nouns.

Compound Tense Tense of a verb formed by a part of that verb preceded by an auxiliary verb (*am, have, shall*, etc.): *am walking; have walked; shall walk*.

Compound Verb Verb formed by the addition of a prefix (*un-, over-, de-, dis-*, etc.) to another verb: simple verbs: *wind, take*; compound verbs: *unwind, overtake*.

Conditional Perfect Tense The tense used to express what might have happened (if something else had occurred) and formed in English with *should have* (*I* *should have walked, we should have walked*) or *would have* (*you would have walked, he would have walked, they would have walked*).

Conditional Tense The tense used to express what might happen (if something else occurred) and formed in English with *should* (*I should walk, we should walk*) or *would* (*you would walk, he would walk, they would walk*).

Conjugation The pattern which a type of verb follows. There is only one regular conjugation in English: *to walk*: present, *I walk, he walks*; past, *he walked*; perfect, *he has walked*, etc.

Conjunction A word like *and, but, when, because* that starts a clause and joins it to the rest of the sentence.

Consonant A letter representing a sound that can only be used in conjunction with a vowel. In French, the vowels are **a, e, i, o, u, y**. All the other letters of the alphabet are consonants.

Definite Article See Articles.

Demonstrative Adjective An adjective that is used to point out a particular thing: *I'll have that cake; this cake is terrible; give me those cakes*—*that, this, those* are demonstrative adjectives.

Demonstrative Article Alternative name for Demonstrative Adjective.

Demonstrative Pronoun A pronoun that is used to point out a particular thing: *I'll have that; this is terrible; give me those*—*that, this, those* are demonstrative pronouns.

Direct Object The noun or pronoun that experiences the action of the verb: *he hits me*, direct object: *me*. See also Indirect Object.

Disjunctive Pronoun Also called Stressed Pronoun. A pronoun that does not stand directly with a verb as its subject or object: *Who said that? Me!*—*me* is a disjunctive pronoun. Disjunctives in French have different forms from ordinary personal pronouns.

Ending See Stem.

Feminine See Gender.

First Conjugation Verb In French, a verb whose infinitive ends in **-er**.

First Person See Third Person.

Future Perfect Tense The tense used to express what, at some future time, will be a past occurrence. Formed in English with *shall have* (*I shall have walked, we shall have walked*) and *will have* (*you will have walked, he will have walked, they will have walked*).

Future Tense The tense used to express a future occurrence and formed in English with *shall* (*I shall walk, we shall walk*) or *will* (*you will walk, he will walk, they will walk*).

Gender In French, a noun or pronoun may be either masculine or feminine: this is known as the gender of the noun or pronoun. The gender may correspond to the sex of the thing named, or may not. In English gender only shows in pronouns (*he, she, it,* etc.) and corresponds to the sex of the thing named. See Agreement.

Historic Present Present tense used to relate past events, often in order to make the narrative more vivid: *So then I go into the kitchen and what do I see?*

Imperative The form of the verb that expresses a command. In English it is usually the same as the infinitive without *to*: infinitive, *to walk*, imperative, *walk!*

Imperfect Subjunctive One of the past tenses of the French subjunctive. See Subjunctive.

Imperfect Tense A French past tense formed by adding a set of endings (**-ais, -ais, -ait,** etc.) to the **nous** form of the present tense minus its **-ons**. Often corresponds to the English past continuous: **je marchais**, *I was walking*.

Impersonal Verb A verb whose subject is an imprecise *it* or *there*: *it is raining*; *there's no need for that*.

Indefinite Adjectives Adjectives such as *each*, *such*, *some*, *other*, *every*, *several*.

Indefinite Article See Articles.

Indefinite Pronouns Pronouns such as *somebody*, *anybody*, *something*, *anything*, *everybody*, *nobody*.

Indirect Object The noun or pronoun at which the direct object is aimed. In English it either has or can have *to* in front of it: *I passed it (to) him*, indirect object *(to) him*; *I gave her my address (I gave my address to her)*, indirect object *(to) her*. In these examples *it* and *my address* are direct objects. See Direct Object.

Indirect Question A question (without a question mark) in a subordinate clause. It is introduced by some such expression as *I wonder if*, *do you know where*, *I'll tell him when*. Direct question: *When is he coming?* Indirect question: *I don't know when he's coming*.

Infinitive The basic part of the verb from which other parts are derived. In English, it is normally preceded by *to*: *to walk*, *to run*.

Interrogative The question form of the verb.

Interrogative Adjective A question word (in English *which* ...? or *what* ...?) used adjectivally with a following noun: *which book do you mean?*

Interrogative Adverb An adverb that introduces a direct question, in English *why?*, *when?*, *how?*, etc. In indirect questions the same words function as conjunctions, joining the question to the main clause. *Why do you say that?*—direct question, *why* is an interrogative adverb; *I don't know why you say that*—indirect question, *why* is a conjunction.

Interrogative Pronoun A pronoun that asks a question, in English *who?* and *what?*

Intransitive Of verbs: having no direct object.

Irregular Verb In French, a verb that does not follow the pattern of one of the three regular conjugations.

Main Clause A clause within a sentence that could stand on its own and still make sense. For example: *He came in when he was ready. He came in* is a main clause (it makes sense standing on its own); *when he was ready* is a subordinate clause (it can't stand on its own and still make sense).

Masculine See Gender.

Modal Verbs (literally 'verbs of mood') These are the auxiliary verbs (other than *have* and *be*) that always appear with a dependent infinitive: *I can walk, I must walk, I will walk*—*can, must, will* are modal verbs.

Noun A word that names a person or thing. *Peter, box, glory, indecision* are nouns.

Noun Clause A clause that is the equivalent of a noun within the sentence: *I don't want to catch whatever you've got* (*whatever you've got* is a clause for which we might substitute a noun, e.g., *measles*).

Number With nouns, pronouns, etc.—the state of being either singular or plural. See Agreement.

Object See Direct Object and Indirect Object.

Ordinal (Number) A number such as *first, second, third, fourth*, normally used adjectivally about one thing in a series.

Partitive Article See Articles.

Passive The basic tenses of a verb are active. Passive tenses are the set of tenses that are used in order to make the person or thing experiencing the action of the verb (normally the object) into the subject of the verb. Active (basic tense): *I discover it*, passive: *it is discovered (by me)*; active: *he ate them*, passive: *they were eaten (by him)*.

Past Anterior Tense A French tense equivalent in time to the pluperfect, formed with the past historic of **avoir** or **être** + past participle: **j'eus marché**, *I had walked*.

Past Historic Tense A French past tense used in writing narrative instead of the perfect; often eqivalent to the English simple past tense: **je marchai**, *I walked*.

Past Participle The part of the verb used to form compound past tenses. In English, it usually ends in *-ed*; verb: *to walk*; past participle: *walked*; perfect tense: *I have walked*.

Perfect Continuous In English, the past tense formed using *was* + *-ing*, implying that something was continuing to occur: *I was walking*.

Perfect Infinitive The past form of the infinitive, formed in English from *to have* + past participle: *to have walked*.

Perfect Participle The part of the verb that in English is formed by *having* + past participle: *having walked away, he now came back*: *having walked* is a perfect participle.

Perfect Tense The past tense that, in English, is formed by using *have* + past participle: *I have walked*.

Personal Pronouns Subject and object pronouns referring to people or things (*he, him, she, her, it,* etc.).

Phrasal Verb In English, a verb made by combining a simple verb with a preposition: *run out, jump up, stand down*.

Phrase A self-contained section of a sentence that does not contain a full verb. *Being late as usual, he arrived at* *a quarter past eleven*: *at a quarter past eleven* is a phrase; present and past participles are not full verbs, so *being late as usual* is also a phrase. Compare Clause.

Pluperfect Continuous In English, the equivalent tense to the pluperfect using *had been* + *-ing*, implying that something had been going on (when something else happened), e.g.: *I had been walking for an hour, when ...*

Pluperfect Tense The past tense, that, in English, is formed by using *had* + past participle: *I had walked.*

Possessive Adjective An adjective that indicates possession; in English, *my*, *your*, *her*, etc.: *that is my book.*

Possessive Article Alternative name for Possessive Adjective.

Possessive Pronoun A pronoun that indicates possession; in English, *mine*, *yours*, *hers*, etc.: *that book is mine.*

Preposition A word like *in*, *over*, *near*, *across* that stands in front of a noun or pronoun relating it to the rest of the sentence.

Present Continuous See Present Tense.

Present Participle The part of the verb that in English ends in *-ing*: *to walk*: present participle, *walking.*

Present Tense The tense of the verb that refers to things now happening regularly (simple present: *I walk*), or happening at the moment (present continuous: *I am walking*).

Pronoun A word such as *he*, *she*, *which*, *mine* that stands instead of a noun (usually already mentioned).

Reflexive Verbs Verbs whose object is the same as their subject: *he likes himself*, *she can dress herself. Himself, herself* are reflexive pronouns.

Relative Pronoun A pronoun that introduces a subordinate clause and at the same time allows that clause to function as an adjective or noun. In English the relative pronouns are *who(m)*, *which*, *whose*, *that*, and *what*. *Tell me what you know!*: *what you know* is a noun clause and the direct object of *tell me*. It is introduced by the relative pronoun *what*. *That's the lad who stole my wallet*: *who stole my wallet* is an adjectival clause describing *lad*. It is introduced by the relative pronoun *who*.

Second Conjugation Verb In French, a verb whose infinitive ends in **-ir**.

Second Person See Third Person.

Simple Tense A one-word tense of a verb: *I walk, I run* (as opposed to a compound tense: *I am walking, I was running*).

Stem The part of a verb to which endings indicating tense, person, etc. are added. Verb: *to walk*: stem, *walk-*: *he walk-s, he walk-ed*, etc.

Stressed Pronouns See Disjunctive Pronouns.

Subject (of verb, clause, or sentence) The noun or pronoun that initiates the action of the verb: *George walked*, subject: *George*; *he hit George*, subject: *he*.

Subjunctive In French, a set of tenses that express doubt or unlikelihood. The subjunctive still exists in only a few expressions in English: *If I were you* [but I'm not], *I'd go now* (*I were* is subjunctive—the normal past tense is *I was*).

Subordinate Clause A clause in a sentence that depends, in order to make sense, on a main clause. See Main Clause.

Subordinating Conjunction The conjunction that introduces a subordinate clause.

Superlative With adjectives and adverbs, the form produced by adding *-est* or prefixing *most*: *biggest, most difficult, most easily*.

Tense The form of a verb that indicates when the action takes place (e.g., present tense: *I walk*; past tense: *I walked*).

Third Conjugation Verb In French, a verb whose infinitive ends in **-re**.

Third Person *He, she, it, they* (and their derivatives, like *him, his, her, their*), or any noun. The first person is *I* or *we* (and their derivatives), the second person is *you* (and its derivatives).

Transitive Of verbs: having a direct object.

Verb The word that tells you what the subject of the clause does: *he goes; she dislikes me; have you eaten it?, they know nothing*—*goes, dislikes, have eaten, know* are verbs.

Verbal Noun Part of the verb (in English, usually the present participle) used as a noun: *smoking is bad for you*: verbal noun, *smoking*.

Vowel A letter representing a sound that can be pronounced by itself without the addition of other sounds. In French the vowels are **a, e, i, o, u, y**.

| Index

English prepositions should be looked up in the alphabetical list on page 185.

French prepositions should be looked up in the alphabetical list on page 164.

Irregular verbs should be looked up in the alphabetical list on page 242.

The preposition a verb takes before an infinitive or noun will be found in the alphabetical list of verbs on page 59.

Words offering problems of pronunciation should be looked up in the alphabetical list on page 235.

Definitions of grammatical terms will be found in the glossary on page 260.

Dictionary

Preface

This is the second edition of *The Oxford Paperback French Dictionary*. It remains largely the work of Michael Janes, the compiler of the first edition, but some entries have been substantially revised and we have been able to incorporate a large proportion of new material. We hope to have kept to the aim of the original: to provide users requiring a compact dictionary with the maximum amount of useful material.

Dora Latiri-Carpenter
Edwin Carpenter

Introduction

When you look up a word, you will find a pronunciation, a grammatical part of speech, and the translation. Sometimes more than one translation is given, and material in brackets in *italics* is included to help you choose the right one. For example, under **cabin** you will see (*hut*) and (*in ship, aircraft*). When a word has more than one part of speech, this can affect the translation. For example **praise** is translated one way when it is a verb (*v.t.*) and another way when it is a noun (*n.*).

A swung dash (~) represents the entry word, or the part of it that comes before a vertical bar (as in **libert|y**). You will see it in examples using the entry word and words based on it. For example, under **good** you will find **as ~ as** and **~-looking**.

Translations are given in their basic form. You will find tables at the end showing verb forms. Irregular verbs are marked on the French to English side with †. This side also shows the plurals of nouns and the feminine forms of adjectives when they do not follow the normal rules.

Abbreviations · Abréviations

abbreviation	*abbr., abrév.*	abréviation
adjective(s)	*a. (adjs.)*	adjectif(s)
adverb(s)	*adv(s).*	adverbe(s)
American	*Amer.*	américain
anatomy	*anat.*	anatomie
approximately	*approx.*	approximativement
archaeology	*archaeol., archéol.*	archéologie
architecture	*archit.*	architecture
motoring	*auto.*	automobile
auxiliary	*aux.*	auxiliaire
aviation	*aviat.*	aviation
botany	*bot.*	botanique
computing	*comput.*	informatique
commerce	*comm.*	commerce
conjunction(s)	*conj(s).*	conjonction(s)
cookery	*culin.*	culinaire
electricity	*electr., électr.*	électricité
feminine	*f.*	féminin
familiar	*fam.*	familier
figurative	*fig.*	figuré
geography	*geog., géog.*	géographie
geology	*geol., géol.*	géologie
grammar	*gram.*	grammaire
humorous	*hum.*	humoristique
interjection(s)	*int(s).*	interjection(s)
invariable	*invar.*	invariable
legal, law	*jurid.*	juridique
language	*lang.*	langue
masculine	*m.*	masculin
medicine	*med., méd.*	médecine
military	*mil.*	militaire
music	*mus.*	musique
noun(s)	*n(s).*	nom(s)
nautical	*naut.*	nautique
oneself	*o.s.*	se, soi-même
proprietary term	*P.*	marque déposée
pejorative	*pej., péj.*	péjoratif
philosophy	*phil.*	philosophie
photography	*photo.*	photographie
plural	*pl.*	pluriel
politics	*pol.*	politique
possessive	*poss.*	possessif

past participle	*p.p.*	participe passé
prefix	*pref., préf.*	préfixe
preposition(s)	*prep(s)., prép(s).*	préposition(s)
present participle	*pres. p.*	participe présent
pronoun	*pron.*	pronom
relative pronoun	*pron. rel.*	pronom relatif
psychology	*psych.*	psychologie
past tense	*p.t.*	passé
something	*qch.*	quelque chose
someone	*qn.*	quelqu'un
railway	*rail.*	chemin de fer
religion	*relig.*	religion
relative pronoun	*rel. pron.*	pronom relatif
school, scholastic	*schol., scol.*	scolaire
singular	*sing.*	singulier
slang	*sl.*	argot
someone	*s.o.*	quelqu'un
something	*sth.*	quelque chose
technical	*techn.*	technique
television	*TV*	télévision
university	*univ.*	université
auxiliary verb	*v. aux.*	verbe auxiliaire
intransitive verb	*v.i.*	verbe intransitif
pronominal verb	*v. pr.*	verbe pronominal
transitive verb	*v.t.*	verbe transitif

Proprietary terms

This dictionary includes some words which are, or are asserted to be, proprietary terms or trade marks. The presence or absence of such assertions should not be regarded as affecting the legal status of any proprietary name or trade mark.

Pronunciation of French

Phonetic symbols

Vowels

i	v*ie*	y	vêt*u*
e	pr*é*	ø	p*eu*
ɛ	l*ai*t	œ	p*eu*r
a	pl*a*t	ə	d*e*
ɑ	b*a*s	ɛ̃	mat*in*
ɔ	m*o*rt	ɑ̃	s*an*s
o	m*o*t	ɔ̃	b*on*
u	gen*ou*	œ̃	l*un*di

Consonants and semi-consonants

p	*p*ayer	ʒ	*j*e
b	*b*on	m	*m*ain
t	*t*erre	n	*n*ous
d	*d*ans	l	*l*ong
k	*c*ou	r	*r*ue
g	*g*ant	ɲ	a*gn*eau
f	*f*eu	ŋ	campi*ng*
v	*v*ous	j	*y*eux
s	*s*ale	w	*ou*i
z	*z*éro	ɥ	h*u*ile
ʃ	*ch*at		

Note: ' before the pronunciation of a word beginning with*h* indicates no liaison or elision.

An asterisk immediately following an apostrophe in some words like **qu'*** shows that this form of the word is used before a vowel or mute 'h'.

FRANÇAIS–ANGLAIS
FRENCH–ENGLISH

A

a /a/ *voir* **avoir**.

à /a/ *prép.* (*à + le = au, à + les = aux*) in, at; (*direction*) to; (*temps*) at; (*jusqu'à*) to, till; (*date*) on; (*époque*) in; (*moyen*) by, on; (*prix*) for; (*appartenance*) of; (*mesure*) by. **donner**/*etc.* **à qn.,** give/*etc.* to s.o. **apprendre**/*etc.* **à faire,** learn/*etc.* to do. **l'homme à la barbe,** the man with the beard. **à la radio,** on the radio. **c'est à moi**/*etc.*, it is mine/*etc.* **c'est à vous**/*etc.* **de,** it is up to you/*etc.* to; (*en jouant*) it is your/*etc.* turn to. **à six km d'ici,** six km. away. **dix km à l'heure,** ten km. an *ou* per hour. **il a un crayon à la main,** he's got a pencil in his hand.

abaissement /abɛsmɑ̃/ *n.m.* (*baisse*) drop, fall.

abaisser /abese/ *v.t.* lower; (*levier*) pull *ou* push down; (*fig.*) humiliate. **s'~** *v. pr.* go down, drop; (*fig.*) humiliate o.s. **s'~ à,** stoop to.

abandon /abɑ̃dɔ̃/ *n.m.* abandonment; desertion; (*sport*) withdrawal; (*naturel*) abandon. **à l'~,** in a state of neglect. **~ner** /-ɔne/ *v.t.* abandon, desert; (*renoncer à*) give up, abandon; (*céder*) give (**à,** to). **s'~ner à,** give o.s. up to.

abasourdir /abazurdir/ *v.t.* stun.

abat-jour /abaʒur/ *n.m. invar.* lampshade.

abats /aba/ *n.m. pl.* offal.

abattement /abatmɑ̃/ *n.m.* dejection; (*faiblesse*) exhaustion; (*comm.*) allowance.

abattis /abati/ *n.m. pl.* giblets.

abattoir /abatwar/ *n.m.* slaughterhouse, abattoir.

abattre† /abatr/ *v.t.* knock down; (*arbre*) cut down; (*animal*) slaughter; (*avion*) shoot down; (*affaiblir*) weaken; (*démoraliser*) dishearten. **s'~** *v. pr.* come down, fall (down). **se laisser ~,** let things get one down.

abbaye /abei/ *n.f.* abbey.

abbé /abe/ *n.m.* priest; (*supérieur d'une abbaye*) abbot.

abcès /apsɛ/ *n.m.* abscess.

abdi|quer /abdike/ *v.t./i.* abdicate. **~cation** *n.f.* abdication.

abdom|en /abdɔmɛn/ *n.m.* abdomen. **~inal** (*m. pl.* **~inaux**) *a.* abdominal.

abeille /abɛj/ *n.f.* bee.

aberrant, ~e /abɛrɑ̃, -t/ *a.* absurd.

aberration /abɛrasjɔ̃/ *n.f.* aberration; (*idée*) absurd idea.

abêtir /abetir/ *v.t.* make stupid.

abhorrer /abɔre/ *v.t.* loathe, abhor.

abîme /abim/ *n.m.* abyss.

abîmer /abime/ *v.t.* damage, spoil. **s'~** *v. pr.* get damaged *ou* spoilt.

abject /abʒɛkt/ *a.* abject.

abjurer /abʒyre/ *v.t.* abjure.

ablation /ablasjɔ̃/ *n.f.* removal.

ablutions /ablysjɔ̃/ *n.f. pl.* ablutions.

aboiement /abwamɑ̃/ *n.m.* bark(ing). **~s,** barking.

abois (aux) /(oz)abwa/ *adv.* at bay.

aboll|ir /abɔlir/ *v.t.* abolish. **~ition** *n.f.* abolition.

abominable /abɔminabl/ *a.* abominable.

abond|ant, ~ante /abɔ̃dɑ̃, -t/ *a.* abundant, plentiful. **~amment** *adv.* abundantly. **~ance** *n.f.* abundance; (*prospérité*) affluence.

abonder /abɔ̃de/ *v.i.* abound (**en,** in). **~ dans le sens de qn.,** completely agree with s.o.

abonn|er (s') /(s)abɔne/ *v. pr.* subscribe (**à,** to). **~é, ~ée** *n.m., f.* subscriber; season-ticket holder. **~ement** *n.m.* (*à un journal*) subscription; (*de bus, théâtre, etc.*) season-ticket.

abord /abɔr/ *n.m.* access. **~s,** surroundings. **d'~,** first.

abordable /abɔrdabl/ *a.* (*prix*) reasonable; (*personne*) approachable.

abordage /abɔrdaʒ/ *n.m.* (*accident: naut.*) collision. **prendre à l'~,** (*navire*) board, attack.

aborder /abɔrde/ *v.t.* approach; (*lieu*) reach; (*problème etc.*) tackle. —*v.i.* reach land.

aborigène /abɔriʒɛn/ *n.m.* aborigine, aboriginal.

aboutir /abutir/ *v.i.* succeed, achieve a result. **~ à,** end (up) in, lead to. **n'~ à rien,** come to nothing.

aboutissement /abutismã/ *n.m.* outcome.

aboyer /abwaje/ *v.i.* bark.

abrasi|f, ~ve /abrazif, -v/ *a. & n.m.* abrasive.

abrégé /abreʒe/ *n.m.* summary.

abréger /abreʒe/ *v.t.* (*texte*) shorten, abridge; (*mot*) abbreviate, shorten; (*visite*) cut short.

abreuv|er /abrœve/ *v.t.* water; (*fig.*) overwhelm (**de,** with). **s'~er** *v. pr.* drink. **~oir** *n.m.* watering-place.

abréviation /abrevjasjɔ̃/ *n.f.* abbreviation.

abri /abri/ *n.m.* shelter. **à l'~,** under cover. **à l'~ de** sheltered from.

abricot /abriko/ *n.m.* apricot.

abriter /abrite/ *v.t.* shelter; (*recevoir*) house. **s'~** *v. pr.* (take) shelter.

abroger /abrɔʒe/ *v.t.* repeal.

abrupt /abrypt/ *a.* steep, sheer; (*fig.*) abrupt.

abruti, ~e /abryti/ *n.m., f.* (*fam.*) idiot.

abrutir /abrytir/ *v.t.* make *ou* drive stupid, dull the mind of.

absence /apsãs/ *n.f.* absence.

absent, ~e /apsã, -t/ *a.* absent, away; (*chose*) missing. —*n.m., f.* absentee. **il est toujours ~,** he's still away. **d'un air ~,** absently. **~éisme** /-teism/ *n.m.* absenteeism. **~éiste** /-teist/ *n.m./f.* absentee.

absenter (s') /(s)apsãte/ *v. pr.* go *ou* be away; (*sortir*) go out, leave.

absolu /apsɔly/ *a.* absolute. **~ment** *adv.* absolutely.

absolution /apsɔlysjɔ̃/ *n.f.* absolution.

absor|ber /apsɔrbe/ *v.t.* absorb; (*temps etc.*) take up. **~bant, ~bante** *a.* (*travail etc.*) absorbing; (*matière*) absorbent. **~ption** *n.f.* absorption.

absoudre /apsudr/ *v.t.* absolve.

absten|ir (s') /(s)apstənir/ *v. pr.* abstain. **s'~ir de,** refrain from. **~tion** /-ãsjɔ̃/ *n.f.* abstention.

abstinence /apstinãs/ *n.f.* abstinence.

abstr|aire /apstrɛr/ *v.t.* abstract. **~action** *n.f.* abstraction. **faire ~action de,** disregard. **~ait, ~aite** *a. & n.m.* abstract.

absurd|e /apsyrd/ *a.* absurd. **~ité** *n.f.* absurdity.

abus /aby/ *n.m.* abuse, misuse; (*injustice*) abuse. **~ de confiance,** breach of trust. **~ sexuel,** sexual abuse.

abuser /abyze/ *v.t.* deceive. —*v.i.* go too far. **s'~** *v. pr.* be mistaken. **~ de,** abuse, misuse; (*profiter de*) take advantage of; (*alcool etc.*) over-indulge in.

abusi|f, ~ve /abyzif, -v/ *a.* excessive; (*usage*) mistaken.

acabit /akabi/ *n.m.* **du même ~,** of that sort.

académicien, ~ne /akademisjɛ̃, -jɛn/ *n.m., f.* academician.

académ|ie /akademi/ *n.f.* academy; (*circonscription*) educational district. **A~ie,** Academy. **~ique** *a.* academic.

acajou /akaʒu/ *n.m.* mahogany.

acariâtre /akarjɑtr/ *a.* cantankerous.

accablement /akɑbləmã/ *n.m.* despondency.

accabl|er /akɑble/ *v.t.* overwhelm. **~er d'impôts,** burden with taxes. **~er d'injures,** heap insults upon. **~ant, ~ante** *a.* (*chaleur*) oppressive.

accalmie /akalmi/ *n.f.* lull.

accaparer /akapare/ *v.t.* monopolize; (*fig.*) take up all the time of.

accéder /aksede/ *v.i.* **~ à,** reach; (*pouvoir, requête, trône, etc.*) accede to.

accélér|er /akselere/ *v.i.* (*auto.*) accelerate. —*v.t.,* **s'~er** *v. pr.* speed up. **~ateur** *n.m.* accelerator. **~ation** *n.f.* acceleration; speeding up.

accent /aksã/ *n.m.* accent; (*sur une syllabe*) stress, accent; (*ton*) tone. **mettre l'~ sur,** stress.

accent|uer /aksãtɥe/ *v.t.* (*lettre, syllabe*) accent; (*fig.*) emphasize, accentuate. **s'~uer** *v. pr.* become more pronounced, increase. **~uation** *n.f.* accentuation.

accept|er /aksɛpte/ *v.t.* accept. **~er de,** agree to. **~able** *a.* acceptable. **~ation** *n.f.* acceptance.

acception /aksɛpsjɔ̃/ *n.f.* meaning.

accès /aksɛ/ *n.m.* access; (*porte*) entrance; (*de fièvre*) attack; (*de colère*) fit; (*de joie*) (out)burst. **les ~ de,** (*voies*) the approaches to. **facile d'~,** easy to get to.

accessible /aksesibl/ *a.* accessible; (*personne*) approachable.

accession /aksɛsjɔ̃/ *n.f.* **~ à,** accession to.

accessit /aksesit/ *n.m.* honourable mention.

accessoire /akseswar/ *a.* secondary. —*n.m.* accessory; (*théâtre*) prop.

accident /aksidã/ *n.m.* accident. **~ de train/d'avion,** train/plane crash. **par ~,** by accident. **~é** /-te/ *a.* damaged *ou* hurt (in an accident); (*terrain*) uneven, hilly.

accidentel, ∼le /aksidɑ̃tɛl/ a. accidental.

acclam|er /aklame/ v.t. cheer, acclaim. ∼ations n.f. pl. cheers.

acclimat|er /aklimate/ v.t., s'∼er v. pr. acclimatize; (*Amer.*) acclimate. ∼ation n.f. acclimatization; (*Amer.*) acclimation.

accolade /akɔlad/ n.f. embrace; (*signe*) brace, bracket.

accommodant, ∼e /akɔmɔdɑ̃, -t/ a. accommodating.

accommodement /akɔmɔdmɑ̃/ n.m. compromise.

accommoder /akɔmɔde/ v.t. adapt (à, to); (*cuisiner*) prepare; (*assaisonner*) flavour. s'∼ de, put up with.

accompagn|er /akɔ̃paɲe/ v.t. accompany. s'∼er de, be accompanied by. ∼ateur, ∼atrice n.m., f. (*mus.*) accompanist; (*guide*) guide. ∼ement n.m. (*mus.*) accompaniment.

accompli /akɔ̃pli/ a. accomplished.

accompl|ir /akɔ̃plir/ v.t. carry out, fulfil. s'∼ir v. pr. be carried out, happen. ∼issement n.m. fulfilment.

accord /akɔr/ n.m. agreement; (*harmonie*) harmony; (*mus.*) chord. être d'∼, agree (**pour**, to). se mettre d'∼, come to an agreement, agree. d'∼!, all right!, OK!

accordéon /akɔrdeɔ̃/ n.m. accordion.

accord|er /akɔrde/ v.t. grant; (*couleurs etc.*) match; (*mus.*) tune. s'∼er v. pr. agree. s'∼er avec, (*s'entendre avec*) get on with. ∼eur n.m. tuner.

accoster /akɔste/ v.t. accost; (*navire*) come alongside.

accotement /akɔtmɑ̃/ n.m. roadside, verge; (*Amer.*) shoulder.

accoter (s') /(s)akɔte/ v. pr. lean (à, against).

accouch|er /akuʃe/ v.i. give birth (de, to); (*être en travail*) be in labour. —v.t. deliver. ∼ement n.m. childbirth; (*travail*) labour. (*médecin*) ∼eur n.m. obstetrician. ∼euse n.f. midwife.

accoud|er (s') /(s)akude/ v. pr. lean (one's elbows) on. ∼oir n.m. armrest.

accoupl|er /akuple/ v.t. couple; (*faire copuler*) mate. s'∼er v. pr. mate. ∼ement n.m. mating; coupling.

accourir /akurir/ v.i. run up.

accoutrement /akutrəmɑ̃/ n.m. (strange) garb.

accoutumance /akutymɑ̃s/ n.f. habituation; (*méd.*) addiction.

accoutum|er /akutyme/ v.t. accustom. s'∼er v. pr. get accustomed. ∼é a. customary.

accréditer /akredite/ v.t. give credence to; (*personne*) accredit.

accro /akro/ n.m./f. (*drogué*) addict; (*amateur*) fan.

accroc /akro/ n.m. tear, rip; (*fig.*) hitch.

accroch|er /akrɔʃe/ v.t. (*suspendre*) hang up; (*attacher*) hook, hitch; (*déchirer*) catch; (*heurter*) hit; (*attirer*) attract. s'∼er v. pr. cling, hang on; (*se disputer*) clash. ∼age n.m. hanging; hooking; (*auto.*) collision; (*dispute*) clash; (*mil.*) encounter.

accroissement /akrwasmɑ̃/ n.m. increase (de, in).

accroître /akrwatr/ v.t., s'∼ v. pr. increase.

accroup|ir (s') /(s)akrupir/ v. pr. squat. ∼i a. squatting.

accru /akry/ a. increased, greater.

accueil /akœj/ n.m. reception, welcome.

accueill|ir† /akœjir/ v.t. receive, welcome; (*aller chercher*) meet. ∼ant, ∼ante a. friendly.

acculer /akyle/ v.t. corner. ∼ à, force ou drive into ou against ou close to.

accumul|er /akymyle/ v.t., s'∼er v. pr. accumulate, pile up. ∼ateur n.m. accumulator. ∼ation n.f. accumulation.

accus /aky/ n.m. pl. (*fam.*) battery.

accusation /akyzasjɔ̃/ n.f. accusation; (*jurid.*) charge. l'∼, (*magistrat*) the prosecution.

accus|er /akyze/ v.t. accuse (de, of); (*blâmer*) blame (de, for); (*jurid.*) charge (de, with); (*fig.*) show, emphasize. ∼er reception de, acknowledge receipt of. ∼ateur, ∼atrice a. incriminating; n.m., f. accuser. ∼é, ∼ée a. marked; n.m., f. accused.

acerbe /asɛrb/ a. bitter.

acéré /asere/ a. sharp.

achalandé /aʃalɑ̃de/ a. bien ∼, well-stocked.

acharn|é /aʃarne/ a. relentless, ferocious. ∼ement n.m. relentlessness.

acharner (s') /(s)aʃarne/ v. pr. s'∼ sur, set upon; (*poursuivre*) hound. s'∼ à faire, keep on doing.

achat /aʃa/ n.m. purchase. ∼s, shopping. faire l'∼ de, buy.

acheminer /aʃmine/ v.t. dispatch, convey. s'∼ vers, head for.

achet|er /aʃte/ v.t. buy ∼er à, buy from; (*pour*) buy for. ∼eur, ∼euse n.m., f. buyer; (*client de magasin*) shopper.

achèvement /aʃɛvmɑ̃/ n.m. completion.

achever /aʃve/ v.t. finish (off). **s'~** v. pr.
end.
acid|e /asid/ a. acid, sharp. —n.m. acid.
~ité n.f. acidity. **~ulé** a. slightly acid.
acier /asje/ n.m. steel. **aciérie** n.f.
steelworks.
acné /akne/ n.f. acne.
acolyte /akɔlit/ n.m. (péj.) associate.
acompte /akɔ̃t/ n.m. deposit, part-
payment.
à-côté /akote/ n.m. side-issue. **~s**,
(argent) extras.
à-coup /aku/ n.m. jolt, jerk. **par ~s**, by
fits and starts.
acoustique /akustik/ n.f. acoustics. —a.
acoustic.
acqu|érir† /akerir/ v.t. acquire, gain;
(biens) purchase, acquire. **~éreur** n.m.
purchaser. **~isition** n.f. acquisition;
purchase.
acquiescer /akjese/ v.i. acquiesce, agree.
acquis, ~e /aki, -z/ n.m. experience.
—a. acquired; (fait) established;
(faveurs) secured. **~ à**, (projet) in
favour of.
acquit /aki/ n.m. receipt. **par ~ de
conscience**, for peace of mind.
acquitt|er /akite/ v.t. acquit; (dette)
settle. **s'~er de**, (promesse, devoir)
carry ' out. **s'~er envers**, repay.
~ement n.m. acquittal; settlement.
âcre /ɑkr/ a. acrid.
acrobate /akrɔbat/ n.m./f. acrobat.
acrobatie /akrɔbasi/ n.f. acrobatics. **~
aérienne**, aerobatics. **acrobatique**
/-tik/ a. acrobatic.
acte /akt/ n.m. act, action, deed;
(théâtre) act; (de naissance, mariage)
certificate. **~s**, (compte rendu)
proceedings. **prendre ~ de**, note.
acteur /aktœr/ n.m. actor.
acti|f, ~ve /aktif, -v/ a. active. —n.m.
(comm.) assets. **avoir à son ~f**, have to
one's credit ou name. **~vement** adv.
actively.
action /aksjɔ̃/ n.f. action; (comm.) share;
(jurid.) action. **~naire** /-jɔnɛr/ n.m./f.
shareholder.
actionner /aksjɔne/ v.t. work, activate.
activer /aktive/ v.t. speed up; (feu)
boost. **s'~** v. pr. hurry, rush.
activiste /aktivist/ n.m./f. activist.
activité /aktivite/ n.f. activity. **en ~**,
active.
actrice /aktris/ n.f. actress.
actualiser /aktɥalize/ v.t. update.
actualité /aktɥalite/ n.f. topicality. **l'~**,
current events. **les ~s**, news. **d'~**,
topical.

actuel, ~le /aktɥɛl/ a. present;
(d'actualité) topical. **~lement** adv. at
the present time.
acuité /akɥite/ n.f. acuteness.
acupunct|ure /akypɔ̃ktyr/ n.f. acupunc-
ture. **~eur** n.m. acupuncturist.
adage /adaʒ/ n.m. adage.
adapt|er /adapte/ v.t. adapt; (fixer) fit.
s'~er v. pr. adapt (o.s.); (techn.) fit,
~ateur, ~atrice n.m., f. adapter; n.m.
(électr.) adapter. **~ation** n.f. adaptation.
additif /aditif/ n.m. (note) rider;
(substance) additive.
addition /adisjɔ̃/ n.f. addition; (au café
etc.) bill; (Amer.) check. **~nel, ~nelle**
/-jɔnɛl/ a. additional. **~ner** /-jɔne/ v.t.
add; (totaliser) add (up).
adepte /adɛpt/ n.m./f. follower.
adéquat, ~e /adekwa, -t/ a. suitable.
adhérent, ~e /aderɑ̃, -t/ n.m., f.
member.
adhé|rer /adere/ v.i. adhere, stick (à, to).
~rer à, (club etc.) be a member of;
(s'inscrire à) join. **~rence** n.f.
adhesion. **~sif, ~sive** a. & n.m.
adhesive. **~sion** n.f. membership;
(accord) adherence.
adieu (pl. **~x**) /adjø/ int. & n.m.
goodbye, farewell.
adipeu|x, ~se /adipø, -z/ a. fat; (tissu)
fatty.
adjacent, ~e /adʒasɑ̃, -t/ a. adjacent.
adjectif /adʒɛktif/ n.m. adjective.
adjoindre /adʒwɛ̃dr/ v.t. add, attach;
(personne) appoint. **s'~** v. pr. appoint.
adjoint, ~e /adʒwɛ̃, -t/ n.m., f. & a.
assistant. **~ au maire**, deputy mayor.
adjudant /adʒydɑ̃/ n.m. warrant-officer.
adjuger /adʒyʒe/ v.t. award; (aux
enchères) auction. **s'~** v. pr. take.
adjurer /adʒyre/ v.t. beseech.
admettre† /admɛtr/ v.t. let in, admit;
(tolérer) allow; (reconnaître) admit;
(candidat) pass.
administrati|f, ~ve /administratif,
-v/ a. administrative.
administr|er /administre/ v.t. run,
manage; (justice, biens, antidote, etc.)
administer. **~ateur, ~atrice** n.m., f.
administrator, director. **~ation** n.f. administration. **A~ation**, Civil Service.
admirable /admirabl/ a. admirable.
admirati|f, ~ve /admiratif, -v/ a.
admiring.
admir|er /admire/ v.t. admire. **~ateur,
~atrice** n.m., f. admirer. **~ation** n.f.
admiration.

admissible /admisibl/ *a.* admissible; (*candidat*) eligible.

admission /admisjɔ̃/ *n.f.* admission.

adolescen|t, ∼te /adɔlesɑ̃, -t/ *n.m., f.* adolescent. **∼ce** *n.f.* adolescence.

adonner (s') /(s)adɔne/ *v. pr.* **s'∼ à,** devote o.s. to; (*vice*) take to.

adopt|er /adɔpte/ *v.t.* adopt. **∼ion** /-psjɔ̃/ *n.f.* adoption.

adopti|f, ∼ve /adɔptif, -v/ *a.* (*enfant*) adopted; (*parents*) adoptive.

adorable /adɔrabl/ *a.* delightful, adorable.

ador|er /adɔre/ *v.t.* adore; (*relig.*) worship, adore. **∼ation** *n.f.* adoration; worship.

adosser /adɔse/ *v.t.* **s'∼** *v. pr.* lean back (**à, contre,** against).

adouci|r /adusir/ *v.t.* soften; (*boisson*) sweeten; (*personne*) mellow; (*chagrin*) ease. **s'∼r** *v. pr.* soften; mellow; ease; (*temps*) become milder. **∼ssant** *n.m.* (fabric) softener.

adresse /adrɛs/ *n.f.* address; (*habileté*) skill.

adresser /adrese/ *v.t.* send; (*écrire l'adresse sur*) address; (*remarque etc.*) address. **∼ la parole à,** speak to. **s'∼ à,** address; (*aller voir*) go and ask *ou* see; (*bureau*) enquire at; (*viser, intéresser*) be directed at.

adroit, ∼e /adrwa, -t/ *a.* skilful, clever. **∼ement** /-tmɑ̃/ *adv.* skilfully, cleverly.

aduler /adyle/ *v.t.* adulate.

adulte /adylt/ *n.m./f.* adult. —*a.* adult; (*plante, animal*) fully-grown.

adultère /adyltɛr/ *a.* adulterous. —*n.m.* adultery.

advenir /advənir/ *v.i.* occur.

adverbe /advɛrb/ *n.m.* adverb.

adversaire /advɛrsɛr/ *n.m.* opponent, adversary.

adverse /advɛrs/ *a.* opposing.

adversité /advɛrsite/ *n.f.* adversity.

aérateur /aeratœr/ *n.m.* ventilator.

aér|er /aere/ *v.t.* air; (*texte*) lighten. **s'∼er** *v. pr.* get some air. **∼ation** *n.f.* ventilation. **∼é** *a.* airy.

aérien, ∼ne /aerjɛ̃, -jɛn/ *a.* air; (*photo*) aerial; (*câble*) overhead; (*fig.*) airy.

aérobic /aerɔbik/ *m.* aerobics.

aérodrome /aerɔdrom/ *n.m.* aerodrome.

aérodynamique /aerɔdinamik/ *a.* streamlined, aerodynamic.

aérogare /aerɔgar/ *n.f.* air terminal.

aéroglisseur /aerɔglisœr/ *n.m.* hovercraft.

aérogramme /aerɔgram/ *n.m.* airmail letter; (*Amer.*) aerogram.

aéronautique /aerɔnotik/ *a.* aeronautical. —*n.f.* aeronautics.

aéronavale /aerɔnaval/ *n.f.* Fleet Air Arm; (*Amer.*) Naval Air Force.

aéroport /aerɔpɔr/ *n.m.* airport.

aéroporté /aerɔpɔrte/ *a.* airborne.

aérosol /aerɔsɔl/ *n.m.* aerosol.

aérospat|ial (*m. pl.* **∼iaux**) /aerɔspasjal, -jo/ *a.* aerospace.

affable /afabl/ *a.* affable.

affaibl|ir /afeblir/ *v.t.,* **s'∼ir** *v. pr.* weaken. **∼issement** *n.m.* weakening.

affaire /afɛr/ *n.f.* matter, affair; (*histoire*) affair; (*transaction*) deal; (*occasion*) bargain; (*firme*) business; (*jurid.*) case. **∼s,** affairs; (*comm.*) business; (*effets*) belongings. **avoir ∼ à,** (have to) deal with. **c'est mon ∼, ce sont mes ∼s,** that is my business. **faire l'∼,** do the job. **tirer qn. d'∼,** help s.o. out. **se tirer d'∼,** manage.

affair|er (s') /(s)afere/ *v. pr.* bustle about. **∼é** *a.* busy.

affaiss|er (s') /(s)afese/ *v. pr.* (*sol*) sink, subside; (*poutre*) sag; (*personne*) collapse. **∼ement** /-ɛsmɑ̃/ *n.m.* subsidence.

affaler (s') /(s)afale/ *v. pr.* slump (down), collapse.

affam|er /afame/ *v.t.* starve. **∼é** *a.* starving.

affect|é /afɛkte/ *a.* affected. **∼ation¹** *n.f.* affectation.

affect|er /afɛkte/ *v.t.* (*feindre, émouvoir*) affect; (*destiner*) assign; (*nommer*) appoint, post. **∼ation²** *n.f.* assignment; appointment, posting.

affecti|f, ∼ve /afɛktif, -v/ *a.* emotional.

affection /afɛksjɔ̃/ *n.f.* affection; (*maladie*) ailment. **∼ner** /-jɔne/ *v.t.* be fond of.

affectueu|x, ∼se /afɛktчø, -z/ *a.* affectionate.

affermir /afɛrmir/ *v.t.* strengthen.

affiche /afiʃ/ *n.f.* (public) notice; (*publicité*) poster; (*théâtre*) bill.

affich|er /afiʃe/ *v.t.* (*announce*) put up; (*événement*) announce; (*sentiment etc., comput.*) display. **∼age** *n.m.* billposting; (*électronique*) display.

affilée (d') /(d)afile/ *adv.* in a row, at a stretch.

affiler /afile/ *v.t.* sharpen.

affil|ier (s') /(s)afilje/ *v. pr.* become affiliated. **∼iation** *n.f.* affiliation.

affiner /afine/ *v.t.* refine.

affinité /afinite/ *n.f.* affinity.

affirmati|f, **~ve** /afirmatif, -v/ *a.* affirmative. **—***n.f.* affirmative.

affirm|er /afirme/ *v.t.* assert. **~ation** *n.f.* assertion.

affleurer /aflœre/ *v.i.* appear on the surface.

affliction /afliksjɔ̃/ *n.f.* affliction.

afflig|er /afliʒe/ *v.t.* grieve. **~é** *a.* distressed. **~é de,** afflicted with.

affluence /aflyɑ̃s/ *n.f.* crowd(s).

affluent /aflyɑ̃/ *n.m.* tributary.

affluer /aflye/ *v.i.* flood in; (*sang*) rush.

afflux /afly/ *n.m.* influx, flood; (*du sang*) rush.

affol|er /afɔle/ *v.t.* throw into a panic. **s'~er** *v. pr.* panic. **~ant,** **~ante** *a.* alarming. **~ement** *n.m.* panic.

affranch|ir /afrɑ̃ʃir/ *v.t.* stamp; (*à la machine*) frank; (*esclave*) emancipate; (*fig.*) free. **~issement** *n.m.* (*tarif*) postage.

affréter /afrete/ *v.t.* charter.

affreu|x, **~se** /afrø, -z/ *a.* (*laid*) hideous; (*mauvais*) awful. **~sement** *adv.* awfully, hideously.

affriolant, **~e** /afrijɔlɑ̃, -t/ *a.* enticing.

affront /afrɔ̃/ *n.m.* affront.

affront|er /afrɔ̃te/ *v.t.* confront. **s'~er** *v. pr.* confront each other. **~ement** *n.m.* confrontation.

affubler /afyble/ *v.t.* rig out (**de,** in).

affût /afy/ *n.m.* **à l'~,** on the watch (**de,** for).

affûter /afyte/ *v.t.* sharpen.

afin /afɛ̃/ *prép. & conj.* **~ de/que,** in order to/that.

africain, **~e** /afrikɛ̃, -ɛn/ *a. & n.m., f.* African.

Afrique /afrik/ *n.f.* Africa. **~ du Sud,** South Africa.

agacer /agase/ *v.t.* irritate, annoy.

âge /aʒ/ *n.m.* age. **quel ~ avez-vous?,** how old are you? **~ adulte,** adulthood. **~ mûr,** middle age. **d'un certain ~,** past one's prime.

âgé /aʒe/ *a.* elderly. **~ de cinq ans/***etc.*, five years/*etc.* old.

agence /aʒɑ̃s/ *n.f.* agency, bureau, office; (*succursale*) branch. **~ d'interim,** employment agency. **~ de voyages,** travel agency.

agenc|er /aʒɑ̃se/ *v.t.* organize, arrange. **~ement** *n.m.* organization.

agenda /aʒɛ̃da/ *n.m.* diary; (*Amer.*) datebook.

agenouiller (s') /(s)aʒnuje/ *v. pr.* kneel (down).

agent /aʒɑ̃/ *n.m.* agent; (*fonctionnaire*) official. **~ (de police),** policeman. **~ de change,** stockbroker.

agglomération /aglɔmerasjɔ̃/ *n.f.* built-up area, town.

aggloméré /aglɔmere/ *n.m.* (*bois*) chipboard.

agglomérer /aglɔmere/ *v.t.*, **s'~** *v. pr.* pile up.

agglutiner /aglytine/ *v.t.*, **s'~** *v. pr.* stick together.

aggraver /agrave/ *v.t.*, **s'~** *v. pr.* worsen.

agil|e /aʒil/ *a.* agile, nimble. **~ité** *n.f.* agility.

agir /aʒir/ *v.i. act.* **il s'agit de faire,** it is a matter of doing; (*il faut*) it is necessary to do. **dans ce livre il s'agit de,** this book is about. **dont il s'agit,** in question.

agissements /aʒismɑ̃/ *n.m. pl.* (*péj.*) dealings.

agité /aʒite/ *a.* restless, fidgety; (*troublé*) agitated; (*mer*) rough.

agit|er /aʒite/ *v.t.* (*bras etc.*) wave; (*liquide*) shake; (*troubler*) agitate; (*discuter*) debate. **s'~er** *v. pr.* bustle about; (*enfant*) fidget; (*foule, pensées*) stir. **~ateur,** **~atrice** *n.m., f.* agitator. **~ation** *n.f.* bustle; (*trouble*) agitation.

agneau (*pl.* **~x**) /aɲo/ *n.m.* lamb.

agonie /agɔni/ *n.f.* death throes.

agoniser /agɔnize/ *v.i.* be dying.

agraf|e /agraf/ *n.f.* hook; (*pour papiers*) staple. **~er** *v.t.* hook (up); staple. **~euse** *n.f.* stapler.

agrand|ir /agrɑ̃dir/ *v.t.* enlarge. **s'~ir** *v. pr.* expand, grow. **~issement** *n.m.* extension; (*de photo*) enlargement.

agréable /agreabl/ *a.* pleasant. **~ment** /-ɔmɑ̃/ *adv.* pleasantly.

agré|er /agree/ *v.t.* accept. **~er à,** please. **~é** *a.* authorized.

agrég|ation /agregasjɔ̃/ *n.f.* agrégation (*highest examination for recruitment of teachers*). **~é,** **~ée** /-ʒe/ *n.m., f.* agrégé (*teacher who has passed the agrégation*).

agrément /agremɑ̃/ *n.m.* charm; (*plaisir*) pleasure; (*accord*) assent.

agrémenter /agremɑ̃te/ *v.t.* embellish (**de,** with).

agrès /agrɛ/ *n.m. pl.* (gymnastics) apparatus.

agress|er /agrese/ *v.t.* attack. **~eur** /-esœr/ *n.m.* attacker; (*mil.*) aggressor. **~ion** /-esjɔ̃/ *n.f.* attack; (*mil.*) aggression.

agressi|f, **~ve** /agresif, -v/ *a.* aggressive. **~vité** *n.f.* aggressiveness.

agricole /agrikɔl/ *a.* agricultural; (*ouvrier etc.*) farm.

agriculteur /agrikyltœr/ *n.m.* farmer.

agriculture /agrikyltyr/ *n.f.* agriculture, farming.

agripper /agripe/ *v.t.*, **s'~ à**, grab, clutch.

agroalimentaire /agrɔalimɑ̃tɛr/ *n.m.* food industry.

agrumes /agrym/ *n.m. pl.* citrus fruit(s).

aguerrir /agerir/ *v.t.* harden.

aguets (aux) /(oz)agɛ/ *adv.* on the look-out.

aguicher /agiʃe/ *v.t.* entice.

ah /a/ *int.* ah, oh.

ahur|ir /ayrir/ *v.t.* dumbfound. **~issement** *n.m.* stupefaction.

ai /e/ *voir* **avoir**.

aide /ɛd/ *n.f.* help, assistance, aid. —*n.m./f.* assistant. **à l'~ de**, with the help of. **~ familiale**, home help. **~-mémoire** *n.m. invar.* handbook of facts. **~ sociale**, social security; (*Amer.*) welfare. **~ soignant**, **~ soignante** *n.m.*, *f.* auxiliary nurse. **venir en ~ à**, help.

aider /ede/ *v.t./i.* help, assist. **~ à faire**, help to do. **s'~ de**, use.

aïe /aj/ *int.* ouch, ow.

aïeul, **~e** /ajœl/ *n.m.*, *f.* grand-parent.

aïeux /ajø/ *n.m. pl.* forefathers.

aigle /ɛgl/ *n.m.* eagle.

aigr|e /ɛgr/ *a.* sour, sharp; (*fig.*) sharp. **~e-doux**, **~e-douce** *a.* bitter-sweet. **~eur** *n.f.* sourness; (*fig.*) sharpness. **~eurs d'estomac**, heartburn.

aigrir /egrir/ *v.t.* embitter; (*caractère*) sour. **s'~** *v. pr.* turn sour; (*personne*) become embittered.

aigu, **~ë** /egy/ *a.* acute; (*objet*) sharp; (*voix*) shrill. (*mus.*) **les ~s**, the high notes.

aiguillage /egɥijaʒ/ *n.m.* (*rail.*) points; (*rail.*, *Amer.*) switches.

aiguille /egɥij/ *n.f.* needle; (*de montre*) hand; (*de balance*) pointer.

aiguill|er /egɥije/ *v.t.* shunt; (*fig.*) steer. **~eur** *n.m.* pointsman; (*Amer.*) switchman. **~eur du ciel**, air traffic controller.

aiguillon /egɥijɔ̃/ *n.m.* (*dard*) sting; (*fig.*) spur. **~ner** /-jɔne/ *v.t.* spur on.

aiguiser /eg(ɥ)ize/ *v.t.* sharpen; (*fig.*) stimulate.

ail (*pl.* **~s**) /aj/ *n.m.* garlic.

aile /ɛl/ *n.f.* wing.

ailé /ele/ *a.* winged.

aileron /ɛlrɔ̃/ *n.m.* (*de requin*) fin.

ailier /elje/ *n.m.* winger; (*Amer.*) end.

aille /aj/ *voir* **aller**[1].

ailleurs /ajœr/ *adv.* elsewhere. **d'~**, besides, moreover. **par ~**, moreover, furthermore. **partout ~**, everywhere else.

ailloli /ajɔli/ *n.m.* garlic mayonnaise.

aimable /ɛmabl/ *a.* kind. **~ment** /-əmɑ̃/ *adv.* kindly.

aimant[1] /ɛmɑ̃/ *n.m.* magnet. **~er** /-te/ *v.t.* magnetize.

aimant[2], **~e** /ɛmɑ̃, -t/ *a.* loving.

aimer /eme/ *v.t.* like; (*d'amour*) love. **j'aimerais faire**, I'd like to do. **~ bien**, quite like. **~ mieux** *ou* **autant**, prefer.

aine /ɛn/ *n.f.* groin.

aîné, **~e** /ene/ *a.* eldest; (*entre deux*) elder. —*n.m.*, *f.* eldest (child); elder (child). **~s** *n.m. pl.* elders. **il est mon ~**, he is older than me *ou* my senior.

ainsi /ɛ̃si/ *adv.* thus; (*donc*) so. **~ que**, as well as; (*comme*) as. **et ~ de suite**, and so on. **pour ~ dire**, so to speak, as it were.

air /ɛr/ *n.m.* air; (*mine*) look, air; (*mélodie*) tune. **~ conditionné**, air-conditioning. **avoir l'~ de**, look like. **avoir l'~ de faire**, appear to be doing. **en l'~**, (up) in the air; (*promesses etc.*) empty.

aire /ɛr/ *n.f.* area. **~ d'atterrissage**, landing-strip.

aisance /ɛzɑ̃s/ *n.f.* ease; (*richesse*) affluence.

aise /ɛz/ *n.f.* joy. —*a.* **bien ~ de/que**, delighted about/that. **à l'~**, (*sur un siège*) comfortable; (*pas gêné*) at ease; (*fortuné*) comfortably off. **mal à l'~**, uncomfortable; ill at ease. **aimer ses ~s**, like one's comforts. **se mettre à l'~**, make o.s. comfortable.

aisé /eze/ *a.* easy; (*fortuné*) well-off. **~ment** *adv.* easily.

aisselle /ɛsɛl/ *n.f.* armpit.

ait /ɛ/ *voir* **avoir**.

ajonc /aʒɔ̃/ *n.m.* gorse.

ajourn|er /aʒurne/ *v.t.* postpone; (*assemblée*) adjourn. **~ement** *n.m.* postponement; adjournment.

ajout /aʒu/ *n.m.* addition.

ajouter /aʒute/ *v.t.*, **s'~** *v. pr.* add (à, to). **~ foi à**, lend credence to.

ajust|er /aʒyste/ *v.t.* adjust; (*coup*) aim; (*cible*) aim at; (*adapter*) fit. **s'~er** *v. pr.* fit. **~age** *n.m.* fitting. **~é** *a.* close-fitting. **~ement** *n.m.* adjustment. **~eur** *n.m.* fitter.

alambic /alɑ̃bik/ *n.m.* still.

alanguir (s') /(s)alɑ̃gir/ *v. pr.* grow languid.

alarme /alarm/ n.f. alarm. **donner l'~**, sound the alarm.

alarmer /alarme/ v.t. alarm. **s'~** v. pr. become alarmed (**de**, at).

alarmiste /alarmist/ a. & n.m. alarmist.

albâtre /albɑtr/ n.m. alabaster.

albatros /albatros/ n.m. albatross.

album /albɔm/ n.m. album.

albumine /albymin/ n.f. albumin.

alcali /alkali/ n.m. alkali.

alcool /alkɔl/ n.m. alcohol; (eau de vie) brandy. **~ à brûler**, methylated spirit. **~ique** a. & n.m./f. alcoholic. **~isé** a. (boisson) alcoholic. **~isme** n.m. alcoholism.

alcootest /alkɔtɛst/ n.m. (P.) breath test; (appareil) breathalyser.

alcôve /alkov/ n.f. alcove.

aléa /alea/ n.m. hazard.

aléatoire /aleatwar/ a. uncertain; (comput.) random.

alentour /alɑ̃tur/ adv. around. **~s** n.m. pl. surroundings. **aux ~s de**, round about.

alerte /alɛrt/ a. agile. —n.f. alert. **~ à la bombe**, bomb scare.

alerter /alɛrte/ v.t. alert.

algarade /algarad/ n.f. altercation.

alg|èbre /alʒɛbr/ n.f. algebra. **~ébrique** a. algebraic.

Alger /alʒe/ n.m./f. Algiers.

Algérie /alʒeri/ n.f. Algeria.

algérien, ~ne /alʒerjɛ̃, -jɛn/ a. & n.m., f. Algerian.

algue /alg/ n.f. seaweed. **les ~s**, (bot.) algae.

alias /aljas/ adv. alias.

alibi /alibi/ n.m. alibi.

aliéné, ~e /aljene/ n.m., f. insane person.

alién|er /aljene/ v.t. alienate; (céder) give up. **s'~er** v. pr. alienate. **~ation** n.f. alienation.

aligner /aliɲe/ v.t. (objets) line up, make lines of; (chiffres) string together. **~ sur**, bring into line with. **s'~** v. pr. line up. **s'~ sur**, align o.s. on. **alignement** /-əmɑ̃/ n.m. alignment.

aliment /alimɑ̃/ n.m. food. **~aire** /-tɛr/ a. food; (fig.) bread-and-butter.

aliment|er /alimɑ̃te/ v.t. feed; (fournir) supply; (fig.) sustain. **~ation** n.f. feeding; supply(ing); (régime) diet; (aliments) groceries.

alinéa /alinea/ n.m. paragraph.

aliter (s') /(s)alite/ v. pr. take to one's bed.

allaiter /alete/ v.t. feed. **~ au biberon**, bottle-feed. **~ au sein**, breast-feed; (Amer.) nurse.

allant /alɑ̃/ n.m. verve, drive.

allécher /aleʃe/ v.t. tempt.

allée /ale/ n.f. path, lane; (menant à une maïson) drive(way). **~s et venues**, comings and goings.

allégation /alegasjɔ̃/ n.f. allegation.

allég|er /aleʒe/ v.t. make lighter; (poids) lighten; (fig.) alleviate. **~é** a. (diététique) light.

allègre /alɛgr/ a. gay; (vif) lively, jaunty.

allégresse /alegrɛs/ n.f. gaiety.

alléguer /alege/ v.t. put forward.

Allemagne /almaɲ/ n.f. Germany. **~ de l'Ouest**, West Germany.

allemand, ~e /almɑ̃, -d/ a. & n.m., f. German. —n.m. (lang.) German.

aller¹† /ale/ v.i. (aux. être) go. **s'en ~** v. pr. go away. **~ à**, (convenir à) suit; (s'adapter à) fit. **~ faire**, be going to do. **comment allez-vous?**, (comment) ça va?, how are you? **ça va!**, all right! **il va bien**, he is well. **il va mieux**, he's better. **allez-y!**, go on! **allez!**, come on! **allons-y!**, let's go!

aller² /ale/ n.m. outward journey; **~ (simple)**, single (ticket); (Amer.) one-way (ticket). **~ (et) retour**, return journey; (Amer.) round trip; (billet) return (ticket); (Amer.) round trip (ticket).

allerg|ie /alɛrʒi/ n.f. allergy. **~ique** a. allergic.

alliage /aljaʒ/ n.m. alloy.

alliance /aljɑ̃s/ n.f. alliance; (bague) wedding-ring; (mariage) marriage.

allié, ~e /alje/ n.m., f. ally; (parent) relative (by marriage).

allier /alje/ v.t. combine; (pol.) ally. **s'~** v. pr. combine; (pol.) become allied; (famille) become related (**à**, to).

alligator /aligatɔr/ n.m. alligator.

allô /alo/ int. hallo, hello.

allocation /alɔkasjɔ̃/ n.f. allowance. **~ (de) chômage**, unemployment benefit. **~s familiales**, family allowance.

allocution /alɔkysjɔ̃/ n.f. speech.

allongé /alɔ̃ʒe/ a. elongated.

allongement /alɔ̃ʒmɑ̃/ n.m. lengthening.

allonger /alɔ̃ʒe/ v.t. lengthen; (bras, jambe) stretch (out). **s'~** v. pr. get longer; (s'étendre) stretch (o.s.) out.

allouer /alwe/ v.t. allocate.

allum|er /alyme/ v.t. light; (radio, lampe, etc.) turn on; (pièce) switch the light(s) on in; (fig.) arouse. **s'~er** v. pr. (lumière) come on. **~age** n.m. lighting;

(*auto.*) ignition. **～e-gaz** *n.m. invar.* gas lighter.

allumette /alymɛt/ *n.f.* match.

allure /alyr/ *n.f.* speed, pace; (*démarche*) walk; (*prestance*) bearing; (*air*) look. **à toute ～,** at full speed. **avoir de l'～,** have style.

allusion /alyzjɔ̃/ *n.f.* allusion (**à,** to); (*implicite*) hint (**à,** at). **faire ～ à,** allude to; hint at.

almanach /almana/ *n.m.* almanac.

aloi /alwa/ *n.m.* **de bon ～,** sterling; (*gaieté*) wholesome.

alors /alɔr/ *adv.* then. —*conj.* so, then. **～ que,** when, while; (*tandis que*) whereas. **ça ～!,** well! **et ～?,** so what?

alouette /alwɛt/ *n.f.* lark.

alourdir /alurdir/ *v.t.* weigh down.

aloyau (*pl.* **～x**) /alwajo/ *n.m.* sirloin.

alpage /alpaʒ/ *n.m.* mountain pasture.

Alpes /alp/ *n.f. pl.* **les ～,** the Alps.

alpestre /alpɛstr/ *a.* alpine.

alphab|et /alfabɛ/ *n.m.* alphabet. **～étique** *a.* alphabetical.

alphabétiser /alfabetize/ *v.t.* teach to read and write.

alphanumérique /alfanymerik/ *a.* alphanumeric.

alpin, ～e /alpɛ̃, -in/ *a.* alpine.

alpinis|te /alpinist/ *n.m./f.* mountaineer. **～me** *n.m.* mountaineering.

altér|er /altere/ *v.t.* falsify; (*abîmer*) spoil; (*donner soif à*) make thirsty. **s'～er** *v. pr.* deteriorate. **～ation** *n.f.* deterioration.

alternati|f, ～ve /altɛrnatif, -v/ *a.* alternating. —*n.f.* alternative. **～vement** *adv.* alternately.

altern|er /altɛrne/ *v.t./i.* alternate. **～ance** *n.f.* alternation. **en ～ance,** alternately. **～é** *a.* alternate.

Altesse /altɛs/ *n.f.* Highness.

alt|ier, ～ière /altje, -jɛr/ *a.* haughty.

altitude /altityd/ *n.f.* altitude, height.

alto /alto/ *n.m.* viola.

aluminium /alyminjɔm/ *n.m.* aluminium; (*Amer.*) aluminum.

alvéole /alveɔl/ *n.f.* (*de ruche*) cell.

amabilité /amabilite/ *n.f.* kindness.

amadouer /amadwe/ *v.t.* win over.

amaigr|ir /amegrir/ *v.t.* make thin(ner). **～issant, ～issante** *a.* (*régime*) slimming.

amalgam|e /amalgam/ *n.m.* combination. **～er** *v.t.* combine, amalgamate.

amande /amɑ̃d/ *n.f.* almond; (*d'un fruit à noyau*) kernel.

amant /amɑ̃/ *n.m.* lover.

amarr|e /amar/ *n.f.* (mooring) rope. **～es,** moorings. **～er** *v.t.* moor.

amas /ama/ *n.m.* heap, pile.

amasser /amase/ *v.t.* amass, gather; (*empiler*) pile up. **s'～** *v. pr.* pile up; (*gens*) gather.

amateur /amatœr/ *n.m.* amateur. **～ de,** lover of. **d'～,** amateur; (*péj.*) amateurish. **～isme** *n.m.* amateurism.

amazone (en) /(ɑ̃n)amazon/ *adv.* side-saddle.

Amazonie /amazɔni/ *n.f.* Amazonia.

ambages (sans) /(sɑ̃z)ɑ̃baʒ/ *adv.* in plain language.

ambassade /ɑ̃basad/ *n.f.* embassy.

ambassa|deur, ～drice /ɑ̃basadœr, -dris/ *n.m., f.* ambassador.

ambiance /ɑ̃bjɑ̃s/ *n.f.* atmosphere.

ambiant, ～e /ɑ̃bjɑ̃, -t/ *a.* surrounding.

ambigu, ～ë /ɑ̃bigy/ *a.* ambiguous. **～ité** /-ɥite/ *n.f.* ambiguity.

ambitieu|x, ～se /ɑ̃bisjø, -z/ *a.* ambitious.

ambition /ɑ̃bisjɔ̃/ *n.f.* ambition. **～ner** /-jɔne/ *v.t.* have as one's ambition (**de,** to).

ambivalent, ～e /ɑ̃bivalɑ̃, -t/ *a.* ambivalent.

ambre /ɑ̃br/ *n.m.* amber.

ambulanc|e /ɑ̃bylɑ̃s/ *n.f.* ambulance. **～ier, ～ière** *n.m., f.* ambulance driver.

ambulant, ～e /ɑ̃bylɑ̃, -t/ *a.* itinerant.

âme /ɑm/ *n.f.* soul. **～ sœur,** soul mate.

amélior|er /ameljɔre/ *v.t., s'～er** *v. pr.* improve. **～ation** *n.f.* improvement.

aménag|er /amenaʒe/ *v.t.* (*arranger*) fit out; (*transformer*) convert; (*installer*) fit up; (*territoire*) develop. **～ement** *n.m.* fitting out; conversion; fitting up; development; (*modification*) adjustment.

amende /amɑ̃d/ *n.f.* fine. **faire ～ honorable,** make an apology.

amend|er /amɑ̃de/ *v.t.* improve; (*jurid.*) amend. **s'～er** *v. pr.* mend one's ways. **～ement** *n.m.* (*de texte*) amendment.

amener /amne/ *v.t.* bring; (*causer*) bring about. **～ qn. à faire,** cause sb. to do. **s'～** *v. pr.* (*fam.*) come along.

amenuiser (s') /(s)amənɥize/ *v. pr.* dwindle.

amer, amère /amɛr/ *a.* bitter.

américain, ～e /amerikɛ̃, -ɛn/ *a. & n.m., f.* American.

Amérique /amerik/ *n.f.* America. **～ centrale/latine,** Central/Latin America. **～ du Nord/Sud,** North/South America.

amertume /amɛrtym/ *n.f.* bitterness.

ameublement /amœbləmɑ̃/ n.m. furniture.

ameuter /amøte/ v.t. draw a crowd of; (fig.) stir up.

ami, ~e /ami/ n.m., f. friend; (de la nature, des livres, etc.) lover. —a. friendly.

amiable /amjabl/ a. amicable. **à l'~** adv. amicably; a. amicable.

amiante /amjɑ̃t/ n.m. asbestos.

amic|al (m. pl. **~aux**) /amikal, -o/ a. friendly. **~alement** adv. in a friendly manner.

amicale /amikal/ n.f. association.

amidon /amidɔ̃/ n.m. starch. **~ner** /-ɔne/ v.t. starch.

amincir /amɛ̃sir/ v.t. make thinner. **s'~** v. pr. get thinner.

amir|al (pl. **~aux**) /amiral, -o/ n.m. admiral.

amitié /amitje/ n.f. friendship. **~s**, kind regards. **prendre en ~**, take a liking to.

ammoniac /amɔnjak/ n.m. (gaz) ammonia.

ammoniaque /amɔnjak/ n.f. (eau) ammonia.

amnésie /amnezi/ n.f. amnesia.

amnistie /amnisti/ n.f. amnesty.

amniocentèse /amniɔsɛ̃tɛz/ n.f. amniocentesis.

amocher /amɔʃe/ v.t. (fam.) mess up.

amoindrir /amwɛ̃drir/ v.t. diminish.

amollir /amɔlir/ v.t. soften.

amonceler /amɔ̃sle/ v.t., **s'~** v.pr. pile up.

amont (en) /(ɑ̃n)amɔ̃/ adv. upstream.

amorc|e /amɔrs/ n.f. bait; (début) start; (explosif) fuse, cap; (de pistolet d'enfant) cap. **~er** v.t. start; (hameçon) bait; (pompe) prime.

amorphe /amɔrf/ a. (mou) listless.

amortir /amɔrtir/ v.t. (choc) cushion; (bruit) deaden; (dette) pay off; (objet acheté) make pay for itself.

amortisseur /amɔrtisœr/ n.m. shock absorber.

amour /amur/ n.m. love. **pour l'~ de**, for the sake of. **~-propre** n.m. self-respect.

amouracher (s') /(s)amuraʃe/ v. pr. become infatuated (**de**, with).

amoureu|x, ~se /amurø, -z/ a. (ardent) amorous; (vie) love. —n.m., f. lover. **~x de qn.**, in love with s.o.

amovible /amɔvibl/ a. removable.

ampère /ɑ̃pɛr/ n.m. amp(ere).

amphibie /ɑ̃fibi/ a. amphibious.

amphithéâtre /ɑ̃fiteɑtr/ n.m. amphitheatre; (d'université) lecture hall.

ample /ɑ̃pl/ a. ample; (mouvement) broad. **~ment** /-əmɑ̃/ adv. amply.

ampleur /ɑ̃plœr/ n.f. extent, size; (de vêtement) fullness.

ampli /ɑ̃pli/ n.m. amplifier.

amplif|ier /ɑ̃plifje/ v.t. amplify; (fig.) expand, develop. **s'~ier** v.pr. expand, develop. **~icateur** n.m. amplifier.

ampoule /ɑ̃pul/ n.f. (électrique) bulb; (sur la peau) blister; (de médicament) phial.

ampoulé /ɑ̃pule/ a. turgid.

amput|er /ɑ̃pyte/ v.t. amputate; (fig.) reduce. **~ation** n.f. amputation; (fig.) reduction.

amuse-gueule /amyzgœl/ n.m. invar. appetizer.

amus|er /amyze/ v.t. amuse; (détourner l'attention de) distract. **s'~er** v. pr. enjoy o.s.; (jouer) play. **~ant, ~ante** a. (blague) funny; (soirée) enjoyable, entertaining. **~ement** n.m. amusement; (passe-temps) diversion. **~eur** n.m. (péj.) entertainer.

amygdale /amidal/ n.f. tonsil.

an /ɑ̃/ n.m. year. **avoir dix/etc. ans**, be ten/etc. years old.

anachronisme /anakrɔnism/ n.m. anachronism.

analgésique /analʒezik/ a. & n.m. analgesic.

analog|ie /analɔʒi/ n.f. analogy. **~ique** a. analogical, (comput.) analogue.

analogue /analɔg/ a. similar.

analphabète /analfabɛt/ a. & n.m./f. illiterate.

analy|se /analiz/ n.f. analysis; (de sang) test. **~ser** v.t. analyse. **~ste** n.m./f. analyst. **~tique** a. analytical.

ananas /anana(s)/ n.m. pineapple.

anarch|ie /anarʃi/ n.f. anarchy. **~ique** a. anarchic. **~iste** n.m./f. anarchist.

anatom|ie /anatɔmi/ n.f. anatomy. **~ique** a. anatomical.

ancestr|al (m. pl. **~aux**) /ɑ̃sɛstral, -o/ a. ancestral.

ancêtre /ɑ̃sɛtr/ n.m. ancestor.

anche /ɑ̃ʃ/ n.f. (mus.) reed.

anchois /ɑ̃ʃwa/ n.m. anchovy.

ancien, ~ne /ɑ̃sjɛ̃, -jɛn/ a. old; (de jadis) ancient; (meuble) antique; (précédent) former, ex-, old; (dans une fonction) senior. —n.m., f. senior; (par l'âge) elder. **~ combattant**, ex-serviceman. **~nement** /-jɛnmɑ̃/ adv. formerly. **~neté** /-jɛnte/ n.f. age; seniority.

ancr|e /ɑ̃kr/ n.f. anchor. **jeter/lever**

l'∼e, cast/weigh anchor. ∼er *v.t.*
anchor; (*fig.*) fix. s'∼er *v.pr.* anchor.
andouille /ãduj/ *n.f.* sausage filled with
chitterlings; (*idiot: fam.*) nitwit.
âne /ɑn/ *n.m.* donkey, ass; (*imbécile*)
ass.
anéantir /aneãtir/ *v.t.* destroy;
(*exterminer*) annihilate; (*accabler*)
overwhelm.
anecdot|e /anɛkdɔt/ *n.f.* anecdote.
∼**ique** *a.* anecdotal.
aném|ie /anemi/ *n.f.* anaemia. ∼**ié,**
∼**ique** *adjs.* anaemic.
ânerie /ɑnri/ *n.f.* stupidity; (*parole*)
stupid remark.
ânesse /ɑnɛs/ *n.f.* she-ass.
anesthés|ie /anɛstezi/ *n.f.* (*opération*)
anaesthetic. ∼**ique** *a.* & *n.m.* (*substance*) anaesthetic.
ang|e /ãʒ/ *n.m.* angel. **aux** ∼**es,** in
seventh heaven. ∼**élique** *a.* angelic.
angélus /ãʒelys/ *n.m.* angelus.
angine /ãʒin/ *n.f.* throat infection.
anglais, ∼**e** /ãglɛ, -z/ *a.* English. —*n.m.,*
f. Englishman, Englishwoman. —*n.m.*
(*lang.*) English.
angle /ãgl/ *n.m.* angle; (*coin*) corner.
Angleterre /ãglətɛr/ *n.f.* England.
anglicisme /ãglisism/ *n.m.* anglicism.
angliciste /ãglisist/ *n.m./f.* English
specialist.
anglo- /ãglɔ/ *préf.* Anglo-.
anglophone /ãglɔfɔn/ *a.* English-speak-
ing. —*n.m./f.* English speaker.
anglo-saxon, ∼**ne** /ãglɔsaksõ, -ɔn/ *a.*
& *n.m.,* f. Anglo-Saxon.
angoiss|e /ãgwas/ *n.f.* anxiety. ∼**ant,**
∼**ante** *a.* harrowing. ∼**é** *a.* anxious.
∼**er** *v.t.* make anxious.
anguille /ãgij/ *n.f.* eel.
anguleux, ∼**se** /ãgylø, -z/ *a.* (*traits*)
angular.
anicroche /anikrɔʃ/ *n.f.* snag.
anim|al (*pl.* ∼**aux**) /animal, -o/ *n.m.*
animal. —*a.* (*m. pl.* ∼**aux**) animal.
anima|teur, ∼**trice** /animatœr, -tris/
n.m., f. organizer, leader; (*TV*) host,
hostess.
anim|é /anime/ *a.* lively; (*affairé*) busy,
(*être*) animate. ∼**ation** *n.f.* liveliness;
(*affairement*) activity; (*cinéma*) anima-
tion.
animer /anime/ *v.t.* liven up; (*mener*)
lead; (*mouvoir, pousser*) drive;
(*encourager*) spur on. s'∼ *v. pr.* liven
up.
animosité /animozite/ *n.f.* animosity.
anis /anis/ *n.m.* (*parfum, boisson*)
aniseed.

ankylos|er (s') /(s)ãkiloze/ *v. pr.* go stiff.
∼**é** *a.* stiff.
anneau (*pl.* ∼**x**) /ano/ *n.m.* ring; (*de
chaîne*) link.
année /ane/ *n.f.* year.
annexe /anɛks/ *a.* attached; (*question*)
related; (*bâtiment*) adjoining. —*n.f.*
annexe; (*Amer.*) annex.
annex|er /anɛkse/ *v.t.* annex; (*document*)
attach. ∼**ion** *n.f.* annexation.
annihiler /aniile/ *v.t.* annihilate.
anniversaire /anivɛrsɛr/ *n.m.* birthday;
(*d'un événement*) anniversary. —*a.*
anniversary.
annonc|e /anõs/ *n.f.* announcement;
(*publicitaire*) advertisement; (*indice*)
sign. ∼**er** *v.t.* announce; (*dénoter*)
indicate. **s'**∼**er bien/mal,** look
good/bad. ∼**eur** *n.m.* advertiser;
(*speaker*) announcer.
Annonciation /anõsjasjõ/ *n.f.* l'∼, the
Annunciation.
annuaire /anɥɛr/ *n.m.* year-book. ∼
(**téléphonique**), (telephone) directory.
annuel, ∼**le** /anɥɛl/ *a.* annual, yearly.
∼**lement** *adv.* annually, yearly.
annuité /anɥite/ *n.f.* annual payment.
annulaire /anɥlɛr/ *n.m.* ringfinger.
annul|er /anyle/ *v.t.* cancel; (*contrat*)
nullify; (*jugement*) quash. **s'**∼**er** *v. pr.*
cancel each other out. ∼**ation** *n.f.* can-
cellation.
anodin, ∼**e** /anɔdɛ̃, -in/ *a.* insignificant; (*blessure*) harmless.
anomalie /anɔmali/ *n.f.* anomaly.
ânonner /anɔne/ *v.t./i.* mumble, drone.
anonymat /anɔnima/ *n.m.* anonymity.
anonyme /anɔnim/ *a.* anonymous.
anorak /anɔrak/ *n.m.* anorak.
anorexie /anɔreksi/ *n.f.* anorexia.
anorm|al (*m. pl.* ∼**aux**) /anɔrmal, -o/
a. abnormal.
anse /ãs/ *n.f.* handle; (*baie*) cove.
antagonis|me /ãtagɔnism/ *n.m.* an-
tagonism. ∼**te** *n.m./f.* antagonist; *a.*
antagonistic.
antan (d') /(d)ãtã/ *a.* of long ago.
antarctique /ãtarktik/ *a.* & *n.m.*
Antarctic.
antenne /ãten/ *n.f.* aerial; (*Amer.*)
antenna; (*d'insecte*) antenna; (*succursale*) agency; (*mil.*) outpost; (*auto.,
méd.*) emergency unit. **à l'**∼, on the air.
sur l'∼ **de,** on the wavelength of.
antérieur /ãterjœr/ *a.* previous, earlier;
(*placé devant*) front. ∼ **à,** prior to.
∼**ement** *adv.* earlier. ∼**ement à,** prior
to. **antériorité** /-jɔrite/ *n.f.* precedence.
anthologie /ãtɔlɔʒi/ *n.f.* anthology.

anthropolo|gie /ãtrɔpɔlɔʒi/ *n.f.* anthropology. **~gue** *n.m./f.* anthropologist.

anthropophage /ãtrɔpɔfaʒ/ *a.* cannibalistic. —*n.m./f.* cannibal.

anti- /ãti/ *préf.* anti-.

antiadhési|f, ~ve /ãtiadezif, -v/ *a.* non-stick.

antiaérien, ~ne /ãtiaerjɛ̃, -jɛn/ *a.* anti-aircraft. **abri ~,** air-raid shelter.

antiatomique /ãtiatɔmik/ *a.* **abri ~,** fall-out shelter.

antibiotique /ãtibjɔtik/ *n.m.* antibiotic.

anticancéreu|x, ~se /ãtikãserø, -z/ *a.* (anti-)cancer.

antichambre /ãtiʃãbr/ *n.f.* waiting-room, antechamber.

anticipation /ãtisipasjɔ̃/ *n.f.* **d'~,** (*livre, film*) science fiction. **par ~,** in advance.

anticipé /ãtisipe/ *a.* early.

anticiper /ãtisipe/ *v.t./i.* **~ (sur),** anticipate.

anticonceptionnel, ~le /ãtikɔ̃sɛpsjɔnɛl/ *a.* contraceptive.

anticorps /ãtikɔr/ *n.m.* antibody.

anticyclone /ãtisyklon/ *n.m.* anticyclone.

antidater /ãtidate/ *v.t.* backdate, antedate.

antidote /ãtidɔt/ *n.m.* antidote.

antigel /ãtiʒɛl/ *n.m.* antifreeze.

antihistaminique /ãtiistaminik/ *a.* & *n.m.* antihistamine.

antillais, ~e /ãtijɛ, -z/ *a.* & *n.m.,* f. West Indian.

Antilles /ãtij/ *n.f. pl.* **les ~,** the West Indies.

antilope /ãtilɔp/ *n.f.* antelope.

antimite /ãtimit/ *n.m.* moth repellent.

antipath|ie /ãtipati/ *n.f.* antipathy. **~ique** *a.* unpleasant.

antipodes /ãtipɔd/ *n.m. pl.* antipodes. **aux ~ de,** (*fig.*) poles apart from.

antiquaire /ãtikɛr/ *n.m./f.* antique dealer.

antiqu|e /ãtik/ *a.* ancient. **~ité** *n.f.* antiquity; (*objet*) antique.

antirouille /ãtiruj/ *a.* & *n.m.* rustproofing.

antisémit|e /ãtisemit/ *a.* anti-Semitic. **~isme** *n.m.* anti-Semitism.

antiseptique /ãtisɛptik/ *a.* & *n.m.* antiseptic.

antithèse /ãtitɛz/ *n.f.* antithesis.

antivol /ãtivɔl/ *n.m.* anti-theft lock *ou* device.

antre /ãtr/ *n.m.* den.

anus /anys/ *n.m.* anus.

anxiété /ãksjete/ *n.f.* anxiety.

anxieu|x, ~se /ãksjø, -z/ *a.* anxious. —*n.m., f.* worrier.

août /u(t)/ *n.m.* August.

apais|er /apeze/ *v.t.* calm down, (*douleur, colère*) soothe (*faim*) appease. **s'~er** *v. pr.* (*tempête*) die down. **~ement** *n.m.* appeasement; soothing. **~ements** *n.m. pl.* reassurances.

apanage /apanaʒ/ *n.m.* **l'~ de,** the privilege of.

aparté /aparte/ *n.m.* private exchange; (*théâtre*) aside. **en ~,** in private.

apath|ie /apati/ *n.f.* apathy. **~ique** *a.* apathetic.

apatride /apatrid/ *n.m./f.* stateless person.

apercevoir† /apɛrsəvwar/ *v.t.* see. **s'~ de,** notice. **s'~ que,** notice *ou* realize that.

aperçu /apɛrsy/ *n.m.* general view *ou* idea; (*intuition*) insight.

apéritif /aperitif/ *n.m.* aperitif.

à-peu-près /apøprɛ/ *n.m. invar.* approximation.

apeuré /apœre/ *a.* scared.

aphone /afɔn/ *a.* voiceless.

aphte /aft/ *n.m.* mouth ulcer.

apit|oyer /apitwaje/ *v.t.* move (to pity). **s'~oyer sur,** feel pity for. **~oiement** *n.m.* pity.

aplanir /aplanir/ *v.t.* level; (*fig.*) smooth out.

aplatir /aplatir/ *v.t.* flatten (out). **s'~** *v. pr.* (*s'allonger*) lie flat; (*s'humilier*) grovel; (*tomber: fam.*) fall flat on one's face.

aplomb /aplɔ̃/ *n.m.* balance; (*fig.*) self-possession. **d'~,** (*en équilibre*) steady, balanced.

apogée /apɔʒe/ *n.m.* peak.

apologie /apɔlɔʒi/ *n.f.* vindication.

a posteriori /apɔsterjɔri/ *adv.* after the event.

apostolique /apɔstɔlik/ *a.* apostolic.

apostroph|e /apɔstrɔf/ *n.f.* apostrophe; (*appel*) sharp address. **~er** *v.t.* address sharply.

apothéose /apɔteoz/ *n.f.* final triumph.

apôtre /apotr/ *n.m.* apostle.

apparaître† /aparɛtr/ *v.i.* appear. **il apparaît que,** it appears that.

apparat /apara/ *n.m.* pomp. **d'~,** ceremonial.

appareil /aparɛj/ *n.m.* apparatus; (*électrique*) appliance; (*anat.*) system; (*téléphonique*) phone; (*dentaire*) brace; (*auditif*) hearing-aid; (*avion*) plane; (*culin.*) mixture. **l'~ du parti,** the party machinery. **c'est Gabriel à l'~,** it's

Gabriel on the phone. ∿(-**photo**), camera. ∿ **électroménager,** household electrical appliance.

appareiller¹ /apareje/ *v.i.* (*navire*) cast off, put to sea.

appareiller² /apareje/ *v.t.* (*assortir*) match.

apparemment /aparamɑ̃/ *adv.* apparently.

apparence /aparɑ̃s/ *n.f.* appearance. **en** ∿, outwardly; (*apparemment*) apparently.

apparent, ∿e /aparɑ̃, -t/ *a.* apparent; (*visible*) conspicuous.

apparenté /aparɑ̃te/ *a.* related; (*semblable*) similar.

appariteur /aparitœr/ *n.m.* (*univ.*) attendant, porter.

apparition /aparisjɔ̃/ *n.f.* appearance. (*spectre*) apparition.

appartement /apartəmɑ̃/ *n.m.* flat; (*Amer.*) apartment.

appartenance /apartənɑ̃s/ *n.f.* membership (**à,** of), belonging (**à,** to).

appartenir† /apartənir/ *v.i.* belong (**à,** to). **il lui/vous**/*etc.* **appartient de,** it is up to him/you/*etc.* to.

appât /apɑ/ *n.m.* bait; (*fig.*) lure. ∿**er** /-te/ *v.t.* lure.

appauvrir /apovrir/ *v.t.* impoverish. **s'**∿ *v. pr.* grow impoverished.

appel /apɛl/ *n.m.* call; (*jurid.*) appeal; (*mil.*) call-up. **faire** ∿, appeal. **faire** ∿ **à,** (*recourir à*) call on; (*invoquer*) appeal to; (*évoquer*) call up; (*exiger*) call for. **faire l'**∿, (*scol.*) call the register; (*mil.*) take a roll-call. ∿ **d'offres,** (*comm.*) invitation to tender. **faire un** ∿ **de phares,** flash one's headlights.

appelé /aple/ *n.m.* conscript.

appel|er /aple/ *v.t.* call; (*nécessiter*) call for. **s'**∿**er** *v. pr.* be called. ∿**é à,** (*désigné à*) marked out for. **en** ∿**er à,** appeal to. **il s'appelle,** his name is. ∿**lation** /apelɑsjɔ̃/ *n.f.* designation.

appendic|e /apɛ̃dis/ *n.m.* appendix. ∿**ite** *n.f.* appendicitis.

appentis /apɑ̃ti/ *n.m.* lean-to.

appesantir /apəzɑ̃tir/ *v.t.* weigh down. **s'**∿ *v. pr.* grow heavier. **s'**∿ **sur,** dwell upon.

appétissant, ∿e /apetisɑ̃, -t/ *a.* appetizing.

appétit /apeti/ *n.m.* appetite.

applaud|ir /aplodir/ *v.t./i.* applaud. ∿**ir à,** applaud. ∿**issements** *n.m. pl.* applause.

applique /aplik/ *n.f.* wall lamp.

appliqué /aplike/ *a.* painstaking.

appliquer /aplike/ *v.t.* apply; (*loi*) enforce. **s'**∿ *v. pr.* apply o.s. (**à,** to). **s'**∿ **à,** (*concerner*) apply to. **applicable** /-abl/ *a.* applicable. **application** /-ɑsjɔ̃/ *n.f.* application.

appoint /apwɛ̃/ *n.m.* contribution. **d'**∿, extra. **faire l'**∿, give the correct money.

appointements /apwɛ̃tmɑ̃/ *n.m. pl.* salary.

apport /apɔr/ *n.m.* contribution.

apporter /apɔrte/ *v.t.* bring.

apposer /apoze/ *v.t.* affix.

appréciable /apresjabl/ *a.* appreciable.

appréc|ier /apresje/ *v.t.* appreciate; (*évaluer*) appraise. ∿**iation** *n.f.* appreciation; appraisal.

appréhen|der /apreɑ̃de/ *v.t.* dread, fear; (*arrêter*) apprehend. ∿**sion** *n.f.* apprehension.

apprendre† /aprɑ̃dr/ *v.t./i.* learn; (*être informé de*) hear of. ∿ **qch. à qn.,** teach s.o. sth.; (*informer*) tell s.o. sth. ∿ **à faire,** learn to do. ∿ **à qn. à faire,** teach s.o. to do. ∿ **que,** learn that; (*être informé*) hear that.

apprenti, ∿e /aprɑ̃ti/ *n.m., f.* apprentice.

apprentissage /aprɑ̃tisaʒ/ *n.m.* apprenticeship; (*d'un sujet*) learning.

apprêté /aprete/ *a.* affected.

apprêter /aprete/ *v.t./i.,* **s'**∿ *v. pr.* prepare.

apprivoiser /aprivwaze/ *v.t.* tame.

approba|teur, ∿**trice** /aprɔbatœr, -tris/ *a.* approving.

approbation /aprɔbɑsjɔ̃/ *n.f.* approval.

approchant, ∿e /aprɔʃɑ̃, -t/ *a.* close, similar.

approche /aprɔʃ/ *n.f.* approach.

approché /aprɔʃe/ *a.* approximate.

approcher /aprɔʃe/ *v.t.* (*objet*) move near(er) (**de,** to); (*personne*) approach. —*v.i.* ∿ (**de,** approach. **s'**∿ **de,** approach, move near(er) to.

approfond|ir /aprɔfɔ̃dir/ *v.t.* deepen; (*fig.*) go into thoroughly. ∿**i** *a.* thorough.

approprié /aprɔprije/ *a.* appropriate.

approprier (s') /(s)aprɔprije/ *v. pr.* appropriate.

approuver /apruve/ *v.t.* approve; (*trouver louable*) approve of; (*soutenir*) agree with.

approvisionn|er /aprɔvizjɔne/ *v.t.* supply. **s'**∿**er** *v. pr.* stock up. ∿**ement** *n.m.* supply.

approximati|f, ∿**ve** /aprɔksimatif, -v/ *a.* approximate. ∿**vement** *adv.* approximately.

approximation /aprɔksimɑsjɔ̃/ n.f. approximation.

appui /apɥi/ n.m. support; (de fenêtre) sill; (pour objet) rest. **à l'~ de,** in support of. **prendre ~,** support o.s. on.

appuie-tête /apɥitɛt/ n.m. headrest.

appuyer /apɥije/ v.t. lean, rest; (presser) press; (soutenir) support, back. —v.i. **~ sur,** press (on); (fig.) stress. **s'~ sur,** lean on; (compter sur) rely on.

âpre /apr/ a. harsh, bitter. **~ au gain,** grasping.

après /aprɛ/ prép. after; (au-delà de) beyond. —adv. after(wards); (plus tard) later. **~ avoir fait,** after doing. **~ qu'il est parti,** after he left. **~ coup,** after the event. **~ tout,** after all. **d'~,** (selon) according to. **~-demain** adv. the day after tomorrow. **~-guerre** n.m. postwar period. **~-midi** n.m./f. invar. afternoon. **~-rasage** n.m. aftershave. **~-ski** n.m. moonboot. **~-vente** a. after-sales.

a priori /aprijɔri/ adv. in principle, without going into the matter. —n.m. preconception.

à-propos /aprɔpo/ n.m. timeliness; (fig.) presence of mind.

apte /apt/ a. capable (à, of).

aptitude /aptityd/ n.f. aptitude, ability.

aquarelle /akwarɛl/ n.f. water-colour, aquarelle.

aquarium /akwarjɔm/ n.m. aquarium.

aquatique /akwatik/ a. aquatic.

aqueduc /akdyk/ n.m. aqueduct.

arabe /arab/ a. Arab; (lang.) Arabic; (désert) Arabian. —n.m./f. Arab. —n.m. (lang.) Arabic.

Arabie /arabi/ n.f. **~ Séoudite,** Saudi Arabia.

arable /arabl/ a. arable.

arachide /araʃid/ n.f. peanut.

araignée /arene/ n.f. spider.

arbitraire /arbitrɛr/ a. arbitrary.

arbitr|e /arbitr/ n.m. referee; (cricket, tennis) umpire; (maître) arbiter; (jurid.) arbitrator. **~age** n.m. arbitration; (sport) refereeing. **~er** v.t. (match) referee; (jurid.) arbitrate.

arborer /arbɔre/ v.t. display; (vêtement) sport.

arbre /arbr/ n.m. tree; (techn.) shaft.

arbrisseau (pl. **~x**) /arbriso/ n.m. shrub.

arbuste /arbyst/ n.m. bush.

arc /ark/ n.m. (arme) bow; (voûte) arch. **~ de cercle,** arc of a circle.

arcade /arkad/ n.f. arch. **~s,** arcade, arches.

arc-boutant (pl. **arcs-boutants**) /arkbutɑ̃/ n.m. flying buttress.

arc-bouter (s') /(s)arkbute/ v. pr. lean (for support), brace o.s.

arceau (pl. **~x**) /arso/ n.m. hoop; (de voûte) arch.

arc-en-ciel (pl. **arcs-en-ciel**) /arkɑ̃sjɛl/ n.m. rainbow.

archaïque /arkaik/ a. archaic.

arche /arʃ/ n.f. arch. **~ de Noé,** Noah's ark.

archéolo|gie /arkeɔlɔʒi/ n.f. archaeology. **~gique** a. archaeological. **~gue** n.m./f. archaeologist.

archer /arʃe/ n.m. archer.

archet /arʃe/ n.m. (mus.) bow.

archétype /arketip/ n.m. archetype.

archevêque /arʃɔvɛk/ n.m. archbishop.

archi- /arʃi/ préf. (fam.) tremendously.

archipel /arʃipɛl/ n.m. archipelago.

architecte /arʃitɛkt/ n.m. architect.

architecture /arʃitɛktyr/ n.f. architecture.

archiv|es /arʃiv/ n.f. pl. archives. **~iste** n.m./f. archivist.

arctique /arktik/ a. & n.m. Arctic.

ardemment /ardamɑ̃/ adv. ardently.

ard|ent, ~ente /ardɑ̃, -t/ a. burning; (passionné) ardent; (foi) fervent. **~eur** n.f. ardour; (chaleur) heat.

ardoise /ardwaz/ n.f. slate.

ardu /ardy/ a. arduous.

are /ar/ n.m. are (= 100 square metres).

arène /arɛn/ n.f. arena. **~(s),** (pour courses de taureaux) bullring.

arête /arɛt/ n.f. (de poisson) bone; (bord) ridge.

argent /arʒɑ̃/ n.m. money; (métal) silver. **~ comptant,** cash. **prendre pour ~ comptant,** take at face value. **~ de poche,** pocket money.

argenté /arʒɑ̃te/ a. silver(y); (métal) (silver-)plated.

argenterie /arʒɑ̃tri/ n.f. silverware.

argentin, ~e /arʒɑ̃tɛ̃, -in/ a. & n.m., f. Argentinian, Argentine.

Argentine /arʒɑ̃tin/ n.f. Argentina.

argil|e /arʒil/ n.f. clay. **~eux, ~euse** a. clayey.

argot /argo/ n.m. slang. **~ique** /-ɔtik/ a. (terme) slang; (style) slangy.

arguer /argɥe/ v.i. **~ de,** put forward as a reason.

argument /argymɑ̃/ n.m. argument. **~er** /-te/ v.i. argue.

aride /arid/ a. arid, barren.

aristocrate /aristɔkrat/ n.m./f. aristocrat.

aristocrat|ie /aristɔkrasi/ n.f. aristocracy. **~ique** /-atik/ a. aristocratic.

arithmétique /aritmetik/ n.f. arithmetic. —a. arithmetical.

armateur /armatœr/ n.m. shipowner.

armature /armatyr/ n.f. framework; (de tente) frame.

arme /arm/ n.f. arm, weapon. **~s**, (blason) arms. **~ à feu**, firearm.

armée /arme/ n.f. army. **~ de l'air**, Air Force. **~ de terre**, Army.

armement /arməmã/ n.m. arms.

armer /arme/ v.t. arm; (fusil) cock; (navire) equip; (renforcer) reinforce; (photo.) wind on. **~ de**, (garnir de) fit with. **s'~ de**, arm o.s. with.

armistice /armistis/ n.m. armistice.

armoire /armwar/ n.f. cupboard; (penderie) wardrobe; (Amer.) closet.

armoiries /armwari/ n.f. pl. (coat of) arms.

armure /armyr/ n.f. armour.

arnaque /arnak/ n.f. (fam.) swindling. **c'est de l'~**, it's a swindle ou con (fam.). **~r**, con (fam.).

arnica /arnika/ n.f. (méd.) arnica.

aromate /arɔmat/ n.m. herb, spice.

aromatique /arɔmatik/ a. aromatic.

aromatisé /arɔmatize/ a. flavoured.

arôme /arom/ n.m. aroma.

arpent|er /arpɑ̃te/ v.t. pace up and down; (terrain) survey. **~eur** n.m. surveyor.

arqué /arke/ a. arched; (jambes) bandy.

arraché (à l') /(al)araʃe/ adv. with a struggle, after a hard struggle.

arrache-pied (d') /(d)araʃpje/ adv. relentlessly.

arrach|er /araʃe/ v.t. pull out ou off; (plante) pull ou dig up; (cheveux, page) tear ou pull out; (par une explosion) blow off. **~er à**, (enlever à) snatch from; (fig.) force ou wrest from. **s'~er qch.**, fight over sth. **~age** /-aʒ/ n.m. pulling ou digging up.

arraisonner /arezɔne/ v.t. inspect.

arrangeant, ~e /arɑ̃ʒɑ̃, -t/ a. obliging.

arrangement /arɑ̃ʒmɑ̃/ n.m. arrangement.

arranger /arɑ̃ʒe/ v.t. arrange, fix up; (réparer) put right; (régler) sort out; (convenir à) suit. **s'~**, (se mettre d'accord) come to an arrangement; (se débrouiller) manage (**pour**, to).

arrestation /arɛstasjɔ̃/ n.f. arrest.

arrêt /arɛ/ n.m. stopping (**de**, of); (lieu) stop; (pause) pause; (jurid.) decree. **~s**, (mil.) arrest. **à l'~**, stationary. **faire un ~**, (make a) stop. **sans ~**,

without stopping. **~ maladie**, sick leave. **~ de travail**, (grève) stoppage; (méd.) sick leave. **rester** ou **tomber en ~**, stop short.

arrêté /arete/ n.m. order.

arrêter /arete/ v.t./i. stop; (date, regard) fix; (appareil) turn off; (appréhender) arrest. **s'~** v. pr. stop. **(s')~ de faire**, stop doing.

arrhes /ar/ n.f. pl. deposit.

arrière /arjɛr/ n.m. back, rear; (football) back. —a. invar. back, rear. **à l'~**, in ou at the back. **en ~**, behind; (marcher) backwards. **en ~ de**, behind. **~-boutique** n.f. back room (of the shop). **~-garde** n.f. rearguard. **~-goût** n.m. after-taste. **~-grand-mère** n.f. great-grandmother. **~-grand-père** (pl. **~-grands-pères**) n.m. great-grandfather. **~-pays** n.m. backcountry. **~-pensée** n.f. ulterior motive. **~-plan** n.m. background.

arriéré /arjere/ a. backward. —n.m. arrears.

arrimer /arime/ v.t. rope down; (cargaison) stow.

arrivage /arivaʒ/ n.m. consignment.

arrivant, ~e /arivɑ̃, -t/ n.m., f. new arrival.

arrivée /arive/ n.f. arrival; (sport) finish.

arriver /arive/ v.i. (aux. être) arrive, come; (réussir) succeed; (se produire) happen. **~ à**, (atteindre) reach. **~ à faire**, manage to do. **en ~ à faire**, get to the stage of doing. **il arrive que**, it happens that. **il lui arrive de faire**, he (sometimes) does.

arriviste /arivist/ n.m./f. self-seeker.

arrogan|t, ~te /arɔgɑ̃, -t/ a. arrogant. **~ce** n.f. arrogance.

arroger (s') /(s)arɔʒe/ v. pr. assume (without justification).

arrondir /arɔ̃dir/ v.t. (make) round; (somme) round off. **s'~** v. pr. become round(ed).

arrondissement /arɔ̃dismɑ̃/ n.m. district.

arros|er /aroze/ v.t. water; (repas) wash down; (rôti) baste; (victoire) celebrate with a drink. **~age** n.m. watering. **~oir** n.m. watering-can.

arsen|al (pl. **~aux**) /arsənal, -o/ n.m. arsenal; (naut.) dockyard.

arsenic /arsənik/ n.m. arsenic.

art /ar/ n.m. art. **~s et métiers**, arts and crafts. **~s ménagers**, domestic science.

artère /artɛr/ n.f. artery. (**grande**) **~**, main road.

artériel, ~le /arterjɛl/ a. arterial.

arthrite /artrit/ *n.f.* arthritis.

arthrose /artroz/ *n.f.* osteoarthritis.

artichaut /artiʃo/ *n.m.* artichoke.

article /artikl/ *n.m.* article; (*comm.*) item, article. **à l'~ de la mort,** at death's door. **~ de fond,** feature (article). **~s d'ameublement,** furnishings. **~s de voyage,** travel requisites *ou* goods.

articul|er /artikyle/ *v.t.,* **s'~er** *v. pr.* articulate. **~ation** *n.f.* articulation; (*anat.*) joint.

artifice /artifis/ *n.m.* contrivance.

artificiel, **~le** /artifisjɛl/ *a.* artificial. **~lement** *adv.* artificially.

artill|erie /artijri/ *n.f.* artillery. **~eur** *n.m.* gunner.

artisan /artizɑ̃/ *n.m.* artisan, craftsman. **l'~ de,** (*fig.*) the architect of. **~al** (*m. pl.* **~aux**) /-anal, -o/ *a.* of *ou* by craftsmen, craft; (*amateur*) homemade. **~at** /-ana/ *n.m.* craft; (*classe*) artisans.

artist|e /artist/ *n.m./f.* artist. **~ique** *a.* artistic.

as[1] /a/ *voir* **avoir.**

as[2] /as/ *n.m.* ace.

ascendant[1], **~e** /asɑ̃dɑ̃, -t/ *a.* ascending, upward.

ascendant[2] /asɑ̃dɑ̃/ *n.m.* influence. **~s,** ancestors.

ascenseur /asɑ̃sœr/ *n.m.* lift; (*Amer.*) elevator.

ascension /asɑ̃sjɔ̃/ *n.f.* ascent. **l' A~,** Ascension.

ascète /asɛt/ *n.m./f.* ascetic.

ascétique /asetik/ *a.* ascetic.

aseptique /asɛptik/ *a.* aseptic.

aseptis|er /asɛptize/ *v.t.* disinfect; (*stériliser*) sterilize. **~é** (*péj.*) sanitized.

asiatique /azjatik/ *a.* & *n.m./f.*, **Asiate** /azjat/ *n.m./f.* Asian.

Asie /azi/ *n.f.* Asia.

asile /azil/ *n.m.* refuge; (*pol.*) asylum; (*pour malades, vieillards*) home.

aspect /aspɛ/ *n.m.* appearance; (*fig.*) aspect. **à l'~ de,** at the sight of.

asperge /aspɛrʒ/ *n.f.* asparagus.

asper|ger /aspɛrʒe/ *v.t.* spray. **~sion** *n.f.* spray(ing).

aspérité /asperite/ *n.f.* bump, rough edge.

asphalt|e /asfalt/ *n.m.* asphalt. **~er** *v.t.* asphalt.

asphyxie /asfiksi/ *n.f.* suffocation.

asphyxier /asfiksje/ *v.t.,* **s'~** *v. pr.* suffocate, asphyxiate; (*fig.*) stifle.

aspic /aspik/ *n.m.* (*serpent*) asp.

aspirateur /aspiratœr/ *n.m.* vacuum cleaner.

aspir|er /aspire/ *v.t.* inhale; (*liquide*) suck up. —*v.i.* **~er à,** aspire to. **~ation** *n.f.* inhaling; suction; (*ambition*) aspiration.

aspirine /aspirin/ *n.f.* aspirin.

assagir /asaʒir/ *v.t.,* **s'~** *v. pr.* sober down.

assaill|ir /asajir/ *v.t.* assail. **~ant** *n.m.* assailant.

assainir /asenir/ *v.t.* clean up.

assaisonn|er /asɛzɔne/ *v.t.* season. **~ement** *n.m.* seasoning.

assassin /asasɛ̃/ *n.m.* murderer; (*pol.*) assassin.

assassin|er /asasine/ *v.t.* murder; (*pol.*) assassinate. **~at** *n.m.* murder; (*pol.*) assassination.

assaut /aso/ *n.m.* assault, onslaught. **donner l'~ à, prendre d'~,** storm.

assécher /aseʃe/ *v.t.* drain.

assemblée /asɑ̃ble/ *n.f.* meeting; (*gens réunis*) gathering; (*pol.*) assembly.

assembl|er /asɑ̃ble/ *v.t.* assemble, put together; (*réunir*) gather. **s'~er** *v. pr.* gather, assemble. **~age** *n.m.* assembly; (*combinaison*) collection; (*techn.*) joint. **~eur** *n.m.* (*comput.*) assembler.

assener /asene/ *v.t.* (*coup*) deal.

assentiment /asɑ̃timɑ̃/ *n.m.* assent.

asseoir† /aswar/ *v.t.* sit (down), seat; (*affermir*) establish; (*baser*) base. **s'~** *v. pr.* sit (down).

assermenté /asɛrmɑ̃te/ *a.* sworn.

assertion /asɛrsjɔ̃/ *n.f.* assertion.

asservir /asɛrvir/ *v.t.* enslave.

assez /ase/ *adv.* enough; (*plutôt*) quite, fairly. **~ grand/rapide** *etc.*, big/fast/ *etc.* enough (**pour,** to). **~ de,** enough. **j'en ai ~ (de),** I've had enough (of).

assid|u /asidy/ *a.* (*zélé*) assiduous; (*régulier*) regular. **~u auprès de,** attentive to. **~uité** /-ɥite/ *n.f.* assiduousness; regularity. **~ûment** *adv.* assiduously.

assiéger /asjeʒe/ *v.t.* besiege.

assiette /asjɛt/ *n.f.* plate; (*équilibre*) seat. **~ anglaise,** assorted cold meats. **~ creuse/plate,** soup-/dinner-plate. **ne pas être dans son ~,** feel out of sorts.

assiettée /asjete/ *n.f.* plateful.

assigner /asiɲe/ *v.t.* assign; (*limite*) fix.

assimil|er /asimile/ *v.t.,* **s'~er** *v. pr.* assimilate. **~er à,** liken to; (*classer*) class as. **~ation** *n.f.* assimilation; likening; classification.

assis, **~e** /asi, -z/ *voir* **asseoir.** —*a.* sitting (down), seated.

assise /asiz/ *n.f.* (*base*) foundation. ～s, (*tribunal*) assizes; (*congrès*) conference, congress.

assistance /asistãs/ *n.f.* audience; (*aide*) assistance. **l'A～ (publique)**, government child care service.

assistant, ～e /asistã, -t/ *n.m.*, *f.* assistant; (*univ.*) assistant lecturer. ～s, (*spectateurs*) members of the audience. ～ **social**, ～e **sociale**, social worker.

assist|er /asiste/ *v.t.* assist. —*v.i.* ～er à, attend, be (present) at; (*scène*) witness. ～é par ordinateur, computer-assisted.

association /asɔsjasjɔ̃/ *n.f.* association.

associé, ～e /asɔsje/ *n.m.*, *f.* partner, associate. —*a.* associate.

associer /asɔsje/ *v.t.* associate; (*mêler*) combine (à, with). ～ **qn. à**, (*projet*) involve s.o. in; (*bénéfices*) give s.o. a share of. **s'～** *v. pr.* (*sociétés personnes*) become associated, join forces (à, with); (*s'harmoniser*) combine (à, with). **s'～ à**, (*joie de qn.*) share in; (*opinion de qn.*) share; (*projet*) take part in.

assoiffé /aswafe/ *a.* thirsty.

assombrir /asɔ̃brir/ *v.t.* darken; (*fig.*) make gloomy. **s'～** *v. pr.* darken; become gloomy.

assommer /asɔme/ *v.t.* knock out; (*tuer*) kill; (*animal*) stun; (*fig.*) overwhelm; (*ennuyer: fam.*) bore.

Assomption /asɔ̃psjɔ̃/ *n.f.* Assumption.

assorti /asɔrti/ *a.* matching; (*objets variés*) assorted.

assort|ir /asɔrtir/ *v.t.* match (à, with, to). ～ir de, accompany with. **s'～ir (à)**, match. ～iment *n.m.* assortment.

assoup|ir (s') /(s)asupir/ *v. pr.* doze off; (*s'apaiser*) subside. ～i *a.* dozing.

assouplir /asuplir/ *v.t.* make supple; (*fig.*) make flexible.

assourdir /asurdir/ *v.t.* (*personne*) deafen; (*bruit*) deaden.

assouvir /asuvir/ *v.t.* satisfy.

assujettir /asyʒetir/ *v.t.* subject, subdue. ～ à, subject to.

assumer /asyme/ *v.t.* assume.

assurance /asyrãs/ *n.f.* (*self-*)assurance; (*garantie*) assurance; (*contrat*) insurance. ～-maladie *n.f.* health insurance. ～s sociales, National Insurance. ～-vie *n.f.* life assurance *ou* insurance.

assuré, ～e /asyre/ *a.* certain, assured; (*sûr de soi*) (self-)confident, assured. —*n.m.*, *f.* insured. ～ment *adv.* certainly.

assurer /asyre/ *v.t.* ensure; (*fournir*)

provide; (*exécuter*) carry out; (*comm.*) insure; (*stabiliser*) steady; (*frontières*) make secure. ～ à qn. que, assure s.o. that. ～ qn. de, assure s.o. of. ～ la gestion de, manage. **s'～ de/que**, make sure of/that. **s'～ qch.**, (*se procurer*) secure *ou* ensure sth. **assureur** /-œr/ *n.m.* insurer.

astérisque /asterisk/ *n.m.* asterisk.

asthm|e /asm/ *n.m.* asthma. ～atique *a.* & *n.m./f.* asthmatic.

asticot /astiko/ *n.m.* maggot.

astiquer /astike/ *v.t.* polish.

astre /astr/ *n.m.* star.

astreignant, ～e /astreɲã, -t/ *a.* exacting.

astreindre /astrɛ̃dr/ *v.t.* ～ **qn. à qch.**, force sth. on s.o. ～ **à faire**, force to do.

astringent, ～e /astrɛ̃ʒã, -t/ *a.* astringent.

astrolo|gie /astrɔlɔʒi/ *n.f.* astrology. ～gue *n.m./f.* astrologer.

astronaute /astronot/ *n.m./f.* astronaut.

astronom|ie /astronomi/ *n.f.* astronomy. ～e *n.m./f.* astronomer. ～ique *a.* astronomical.

astuce /astys/ *n.f.* smartness; (*truc*) trick; (*plaisanterie*) wisecrack.

astucieu|x, ～se /astysjø, -z/ *a.* smart, clever.

atelier /atəlje/ *n.m.* workshop; (*de peintre*) studio.

athé|e /ate/ *n.m./f.* atheist. —*a.* atheistic. ～isme *n.m.* atheism.

athl|ète /atlɛt/ *n.m./f.* athlete. ～étique *a.* athletic. ～étisme *n.m.* athletics.

atlantique /atlãtik/ *a.* Atlantic. —*n.m.* A～, Atlantic (Ocean).

atlas /atlas/ *n.m.* atlas.

atmosph|ère /atmɔsfɛr/ *n.f.* atmosphere. ～érique *a.* atmospheric.

atome /atom/ *n.m.* atom.

atomique /atɔmik/ *a.* atomic.

atomiseur /atɔmizœr/ *n.m.* spray.

atout /atu/ *n.m.* trump (card); (*avantage*) great asset.

âtre /atr/ *n.m.* hearth.

atroc|e /atrɔs/ *a.* atrocious. ～ité *n.f.* atrocity.

atroph|ie /atrɔfi/ *n.f.* atrophy. ～ié *a.* atrophied.

attabler (s') /(s)atable/ *v. pr.* sit down at table.

attachant, ～e /ataʃã, -t/ *a.* likeable.

attache /ataʃ/ *n.f.* (*agrafe*) fastener; (*lien*) tie.

attach|é /ataʃe/ *a.* **être ～é à**, (*aimer*) be attached to. —*n.m.*, *f.* (*pol.*) attaché.

~**é-case** *n.m.* attaché case. ~**ement** *n.m.* attachment.

attacher /ataʃe/ *v.t.* tie (up); (*ceinture, robe, etc.*) fasten; (*étiquette*) attach. ~ **à,** (*attribuer à*) attach to. —*v.i.* (*culin.*) stick. **s'**~ **à,** (*se lier à*) become attached to; (*se consacrer à*) apply o.s. to.

attaque /atak/ *n.f.* attack. ~ **(cérébrale),** stroke. **il va en faire une** ~, he'll have a fit. ~ **à main armée,** armed attack.

attaqu|er /atake/ *v.t./i.,* **s'**~**er à,** attack; (*problème, sujet*) tackle. ~**ant,** ~**ante** *n.m., f.* attacker; (*football*) striker; (*football, Amer.*) forward.

attardé /atarde/ *a.* backward; (*idées*) outdated; (*en retard*) late.

attarder (s') /(s)atarde/ *v. pr.* linger.

atteindre† /atɛdr/ *v.t.* reach; (*blesser*) hit; (*affecter*) affect.

atteint, ~**e** /atɛ̃, -t/ *a.* ~ **de,** suffering from.

atteinte /atɛ̃t/ *n.f.* attack (**à,** on). **porter** ~ **à,** make an attack on.

attel|er /atle/ *v.t.* (*cheval*) harness; (*remorque*) couple. **s'**~**er à,** get down to. ~**age** *n.m.* harnessing; coupling; (*bêtes*) team.

attelle /atɛl/ *n.f.* splint.

attenant, ~**e** /atnɑ̃, -t/ *a.* ~ **(à),** adjoining.

attendant (en) /(ɑ̃n)atɑ̃dɑ̃/ *adv.* meanwhile.

attendre /atɑ̃dr/ *v.t.* wait for; (*bébé*) expect; (*être le sort de*) await; (*escompter*) expect. —*v.i.* wait. ~ **que qn. fasse,** wait for s.o. to do. **s'**~ **à,** expect.

attendr|ir /atɑ̃drir/ *v.t.* move (to pity). **s'**~ *v. pr.* be moved to pity. ~**issant,** ~**issante** *a.* moving.

attendu /atɑ̃dy/ *a.* (*escompté*) expected; (*espéré*) long-awaited. ~ **que,** considering that.

attentat /atɑ̃ta/ *n.m.* murder attempt. ~ **(à la bombe),** (bomb) attack.

attente /atɑ̃t/ *n.f.* wait(ing); (*espoir*) expectation.

attenter /atɑ̃te/ *v.i.* ~ **à,** make an attempt on; (*fig.*) violate.

attenti|f, ~**ve** /atɑ̃tif, -v/ *a.* attentive; (*scrupuleux*) careful. ~**f à,** mindful of; (*soucieux*) careful of. ~**vement** *adv.* attentively.

attention /atɑ̃sjɔ̃/ *n.f.* attention; (*soin*) care. ~ **(à)!,** watch out (for)! **faire** ~ **à,** (*professeur*) pay attention to; (*marche*) mind. **faire** ~ **à faire,** be careful to do. ~**né** /-jɔne/ *a.* considerate.

attentisme /atɑ̃tism/ *n.m.* wait-and-see policy.

atténuer /atenɥe/ *v.t.* (*violence*) tone down; (*douleur*) ease; (*faute*) mitigate. **s'**~ *v. pr.* subside.

atterrer /atere/ *v.t.* dismay.

atterr|ir /aterir/ *v.i.* land. ~**issage** *n.m.* landing.

attestation /atɛstasjɔ̃/ *n.f.* certificate.

attester /atɛste/ *v.t.* testify to. ~ **que,** testify that.

attifé /atife/ *a.* (*fam.*) dressed up.

attirail /atiraj/ *n.m.* (*fam.*) gear.

attirance /atirɑ̃s/ *n.f.* attraction.

attirant, ~**e** /atirɑ̃, -t/ *a.* attractive.

attirer /atire/ *v.t.* draw, attract; (*causer*) bring. **s'**~ *v. pr.* bring upon o.s.; (*amis*) win.

attiser /atize/ *v.t.* (*feu*) poke; (*sentiment*) stir up.

attitré /atitre/ *a.* accredited; (*habituel*) usual.

attitude /atityd/ *n.f.* attitude; (*maintien*) bearing.

attraction /atraksjɔ̃/ *n.f.* attraction.

attrait /atrɛ/ *n.m.* attraction.

attrape-nigaud /atrapnigo/ *n.m.* (*fam.*) con.

attraper /atrape/ *v.t.* catch; (*habitude, style*) pick up; (*duper*) take in; (*gronder: fam.*) tell off.

attrayant, ~**e** /atrɛjɑ̃, -t/ *a.* attractive.

attrib|uer /atribɥe/ *v.t.* award; (*donner*) assign; (*imputer*) attribute. **s'**~**uer** *v. pr.* claim. ~**ution** *n.f.* awarding; assignment. ~**utions** *n.f. pl.* attributions.

attrister /atriste/ *v.t.* sadden.

attroup|er (s') /(s)atrupe/ *v. pr.* gather. ~**ement** *n.m.* crowd.

au /o/ *voir* **à.**

aubaine /obɛn/ *n.f.* (stroke of) good fortune.

aube /ob/ *n.f.* dawn, daybreak.

aubépine /obepin/ *n.f.* hawthorn.

auberg|e /obɛrʒ/ *n.f.* inn. ~**e de jeunesse,** youth hostel. ~**iste** *n.m./f.* innkeeper.

aubergine /obɛrʒin/ *n.f.* aubergine; (*Amer.*) egg-plant.

aucun, ~**e** /okœ̃, okyn/ *a.* no, not any; (*positif*) any. —*pron.* none, not any; (*positif*) any. ~ **des deux,** neither of the two. **d'**~**s,** some. ~**ement** /okynmɑ̃/ *adv.* not at all.

audace /odas/ *n.f.* daring; (*impudence*) audacity.

audacieu|x, ~**se** /odasjø, -z/ *a.* daring.

au-delà /odla/ *adv.,* ~ **de** *prép.* beyond.

au-dessous /odsu/ adv., ∼ **de** prép. below; (couvert par) under.

au-dessus /odsy/ adv., ∼ **de** prép. above.

au-devant (de) /odvã(də)/ prép. aller ∼ **de qn.**, go to meet s.o.

audience /odjãs/ n.f. audience; (d'un tribunal) hearing; (intérêt) attention.

Audimat /odimat/ n.m. (P.) **l'∼**, the TV ratings.

audiotypiste /odjotipist/ n.m./f. audio typist.

audio-visuel, ∼**le** /odjovizчɛl/ a. audio-visual.

audi|teur, ∼**trice** /oditœr, -tris/ n.m., f. listener.

audition /odisjɔ̃/ n.f. hearing; (théâtre, mus.) audition. ∼**ner** /-jɔne/ v.t./i. audition.

auditoire /oditwar/ n.m. audience.

auditorium /oditɔrjɔm/ n.m. (mus., radio) recording studio.

auge /oʒ/ n.f. trough.

augment|er /ogmɑ̃te/ v.t./i. increase; (employé) increase the pay of. ∼**ation** n.f. increase. ∼**ation (de salaire)**, (pay) rise; (Amer.) raise.

augure /ogyr/ n.m. (devin) oracle. **être de bon/mauvais ∼**, be a good/bad sign.

auguste /ogyst/ a. august.

aujourd'hui /oʒurdчi/ adv. today.

aumône /omon/ n.f. alms.

aumônier /omonje/ n.m. chaplain.

auparavant /oparavɑ̃/ adv. before(hand).

auprès (de) /oprɛ(də)/ prép. by, next to; (comparé à) compared with; (s'adressant à) to.

auquel /okɛl/ voir **lequel**.

aura, aurait /ora, orɛ/ voir **avoir**.

auréole /oreɔl/ n.f. halo.

auriculaire /orikylɛr/ n.m. little finger.

aurore /orɔr/ n.f. dawn.

ausculter /ɔskylte/ v.t. examine with a stethoscope.

auspices /ospis/ n.m. pl. auspices.

aussi /osi/ adv. too, also; (comparaison) as; (tellement) so. —conj. (donc) therefore. ∼ **bien que**, as well as.

aussitôt /osito/ adv. immediately. ∼ **que**, as soon as. ∼ **arrivé/levé/**etc., as soon as one has arrived/got up/etc.

aust|ère /ostɛr/ a. austere. ∼**érité** n.f. austerity.

austral (m. pl. ∼**s**) /ostral/ a. southern.

Australie /ɔstrali/ n.f. Australia.

australien, ∼**ne** /ostraljɛ̃, -jɛn/ a. & n.m., f. Australian.

autant /otɑ̃/ adv. (travailler, manger,

etc.) as much (**que**, as). ∼ **(de)**, (quantité) as much (**que**, as); (nombre) as many (**que**, as); (tant) so much; so many. ∼ **faire**, one had better do. **d'∼ plus que**, all the more since. **en faire ∼**, do the same. **pour ∼**, for all that.

autel /otɛl/ n.m. altar.

auteur /otœr/ n.m. author. **l'∼ du crime**, the person who committed the crime.

authentifier /otɑ̃tifje/ v.t. authenticate.

authenti|que /otɑ̃tik/ a. authentic. ∼**cité** n.f. authenticity.

auto /oto/ n.f. car. ∼**s tamponneuses**, dodgems, bumper cars.

auto- /oto/ préf. self-, auto-.

autobiographie /otobjɔgrafi/ n.f. autobiography.

autobus /otobys/ n.m. bus.

autocar /otokar/ n.m. coach.

autochtone /otɔktɔn/ n.m./f. native.

autocollant, ∼**e** /otɔkɔlɑ̃, -t/ a. self-adhesive. —n.m. sticker.

autocratique /otɔkratik/ a. autocratic.

autocuiseur /otɔkчizœr/ n.m. pressure cooker.

autodéfense /otɔdefɑ̃s/ n.f. self-defence.

autodidacte /otɔdidakt/ a. & n.m./f. self-taught (person).

auto-école /otɔekɔl/ n.f. driving school.

autographe /otɔgraf/ n.m. autograph.

automate /otɔmat/ n.m. automaton, robot.

automatique /otɔmatik/ a. automatic. ∼**ment** adv. automatically.

automat|iser /otɔmatize/ v.t. automate. ∼**ion** /-masjɔ̃/ n.f. ∼**isation** n.f. automation.

automne /otɔn/ n.m. autumn; (Amer.) fall.

automobil|e /otɔmɔbil/ a. motor, car. —n.f. (motor) car. **l'∼e**, (sport) motoring. ∼**iste** n.m./f. motorist.

autonom|e /otɔnɔm/ a. autonomous. ∼**ie** n.f. autonomy.

autopsie /otɔpsi/ n.f. post-mortem, autopsy.

autoradio /otɔradjo/ n.m. car radio.

autorail /otɔraj/ n.m. railcar.

autorisation /otɔrizasjɔ̃/ n.f. permission, authorization; (permis) permit.

autoris|er /otɔrize/ v.t. authorize, permit; (rendre possible) allow (of). ∼**é** a. (opinions) authoritative.

autoritaire /otɔritɛr/ a. authoritarian.

autorité /otɔrite/ n.f. authority. **faire ∼**, be authoritative.

autoroute /otɔrut/ n.f. motorway; (Amer.) highway.

auto-stop /otɔstɔp/ *n.m.* hitch-hiking. **faire de l'~,** hitch-hike. **prendre en ~,** give a lift to. **~peur, ~peuse** *n.m., f.* hitch-hiker.

autour /otur/ *adv.,* **~ de** *prép.* around. **tout ~,** all around.

autre /otr/ *a.* other. **un ~ jour/***etc.,* another day/*etc. —pron.* **un ~, une ~,** another (one). **l'~,** the other (one). **les autres,** the others; (*autrui*) others. **d'~s,** (some) others. **l'un l'~,** each other. **l'un et l'~,** both of them. **~ chose/part,** sth./somewhere else. **qn./rien d'~,** s.o./nothing else. **quoi d'~?,** what else? **d'~ part,** on the other hand. **vous ~s Anglais,** you English. **d'un jour/***etc.* **à l'~,** (*bientôt*) any day/*etc.* now. **entre ~s,** among other things.

autrefois /otrəfwa/ *adv.* in the past.

autrement /otrəmɑ̃/ *adv.* differently; (*sinon*) otherwise; (*plus*) far more. **~ dit,** in other words.

Autriche /otriʃ/ *n.f.* Austria.

autrichien, ~ne /otriʃjɛ̃, -jɛn/ *a. & n.m., f.* Austrian.

autruche /otryʃ/ *n.f.* ostrich.

autrui /otrɥi/ *pron.* others.

auvent /ovɑ̃/ *n.m.* canopy.

aux /o/ *voir* à.

auxiliaire /oksiljɛr/ *a.* auxiliary. *—n.m./f.* (*assistant*) auxiliary. *—n.m.* (*gram.*) auxiliary.

auxquel|s, ~les /okɛl/ *voir* lequel.

aval (en) /(ɑ̃n)aval/ *adv.* downstream.

avalanche /avalɑ̃ʃ/ *n.f.* avalanche.

avaler /avale/ *v.t.* swallow.

avance /avɑ̃s/ *n.f.* advance; (*sur un concurrent*) lead. **~ (de fonds),** advance. **à l'~, d'~,** in advance. **en ~,** early; (*montre*) fast. **en ~ (sur),** (*menant*) ahead (of).

avancement /avɑ̃smɑ̃/ *n.m.* promotion.

avanc|er /avɑ̃se/ *v.i.* move forward, advance; (*travail*) make progress; (*montre*) be fast; (*faire saillie*) jut out. *—v.t.* (*argent*) advance; (*montre*) put forward. **s'~er** *v. pr.* move forward, advance; (*se hasarder*) commit o.s. **~é, ~ée** *a.* advanced; *n.f.* projection.

avanie /avani/ *n.f.* affront.

avant /avɑ̃/ *prép & adv.* before. *—a. invar.* front. *—n.m.* front; (*football*) forward. **~ de faire,** before doing. **~ qu'il (ne) fasse,** before he does. **en ~,** (*mouvement*) forward. **en ~ (de),** (*position, temps*) in front (of). **~ peu,** before long. **~ tout,** above all. **bien ~ dans,** very deep(ly) *ou* far into. **~-bras**

n.m. invar. forearm. **~-centre** *n.m.* centre-forward. **~-coureur** *a. invar.* precursory, foreshadowing. **~-dernier, ~-dernière** *a. & n.m., f.* last but one. **~-garde** *n.f.* (*mil.*) vanguard; (*fig.*) avant-garde. **~-goût** *n.m.* foretaste. **~-guerre** *n.m.* pre-war period. **~-hier** /-tjɛr/ *adv.* the day before yesterday. **~-poste** *n.m.* outpost. **~-première** *n.f.* preview. **~-propos** *n.m.* foreword. **~-veille** *n.f.* two days before.

avantag|e /avɑ̃taʒ/ *n.m.* advantage; (*comm.*) benefit. **~er** *v.t.* favour; (*embellir*) show off to advantage.

avantageu|x, ~se /avɑ̃taʒø, -z/ *a.* attractive.

avar|e /avar/ *a.* miserly. *—n.m./f.* miser. **~e de,** sparing of. **~ice** *n.f.* avarice.

avarié /avarje/ *a.* (*aliment*) spoiled.

avaries /avari/ *n.f. pl.* damage.

avatar /avatar/ *n.m.* (*fam.*) misfortune.

avec /avɛk/ *prép.* with; (*envers*) towards. *—adv.* (*fam.*) with it *ou* them.

avenant, ~e /avnɑ̃, -t/ *a.* pleasing.

avenant (à l') /(al)avnɑ̃/ *adv.* in a similar style.

avènement /avɛnmɑ̃/ *n.m.* advent; (*d'un roi*) accession.

avenir /avnir/ *n.m.* future. **à l'~,** in future. **d'~,** with (future) prospects.

aventur|e /avɑ̃tyr/ *n.f.* adventure; (*sentimentale*) affair. **~eux, ~euse** *a.* adventurous; (*hasardeux*) risky. **~ier, ~ière** *n.m., f.* adventurer.

aventurer (s') /(s)avɑ̃tyre/ *v. pr.* venture.

avenue /avny/ *n.f.* avenue.

avérer (s') /(s)avere/ *v. pr.* prove (to be).

averse /avɛrs/ *n.f.* shower.

aversion /avɛrsjɔ̃/ *n.f.* aversion.

avert|ir /avɛrtir/ *v.t.* inform; (*mettre en garde, menacer*) warn. **~i** *a.* informed. **~issement** *n.m.* warning.

avertisseur /avɛrtisœr/ *n.m.* (*auto.*) horn. **~ d'incendie,** fire-alarm.

aveu (*pl.* **~x**) /avø/ *n.m.* confession. **de l'~ de,** by the admission of.

aveugl|e /avœgl/ *a.* blind. *—n.m./f.* blind man, blind woman. **~ement** *n.m.* blindness. **~ément** *adv.* blindly. **~er** *v.t.* blind.

aveuglette (à l') /(al)avœglɛt/ *adv.* (*à tâtons*) blindly.

avia|teur, ~trice /avjatœr, -tris/ *n.m., f.* aviator.

aviation /avjɑsjɔ̃/ *n.f.* flying; (*industrie*) aviation; (*mil.*) air force. **d'~,** air.

avid|e /avid/ *a.* greedy (**de,** for);

(*anxieux*) eager (**de**, for). **~e de faire**, eager to do. **~ité** *n.f.* greed; eagerness.

avilir /avilir/ *v.t.* degrade.

avion /avjɔ̃/ *n.m.* plane, aeroplane, aircraft; (*Amer.*) airplane. **~ à réaction**, jet.

aviron /avirɔ̃/ *n.m.* oar. **l'~**, (*sport*) rowing.

avis /avi/ *n.m.* opinion; (*renseignement*) notification; (*comm.*) advice. **à mon ~**, in my opinion. **changer d'~**, change one's mind. **être d'~ que**, be of the opinion that.

avisé /avize/ *a.* sensible. **bien/mal ~ de**, well-/ill-advised to.

aviser /avize/ *v.t.* notice; (*informer*) advise. —*v.i.* decide what to do (**à**, about). **s'~ de**, suddenly realize. **s'~ de faire**, take it into one's head to do.

aviver /avive/ *v.t.* revive.

avocat[1], **~e** /avɔka, -t/ *n.m.*, *f.* barrister; (*Amer.*) attorney; (*fig.*) advocate. **~ de la défense**, counsel for the defence.

avocat[2] /avɔka/ *n.m.* (*fruit*) avocado (pear).

avoine /avwan/ *n.f.* oats.

avoir† /avwar/ *v. aux.* have. —*v.t.* have; (*obtenir*) get; (*duper*: *fam.*) take in. —*n.m.* assets. **je n'ai pas de café**, I haven't (got) any coffee; (*Amer.*) I don't have any coffee. **est-ce que tu as du café?**, have you (got) any coffee?; (*Amer.*) do you have any coffee? **~ à faire**, have to do. **tu n'as qu'à l'appeler**, all you have to do is call her. **~ chaud/faim**/*etc.*, be hot/hungry/*etc.* **~ dix**/*etc.* **ans**, be ten/*etc.* years old. **~ lieu**, take place. **~ lieu de**, have good reason to. **en ~ contre qn.**, have a grudge against s.o. **en ~ assez**, have had enough. **en ~ pour une minute**/*etc.*, be busy for a minute/*etc.* **il en a pour cent francs**, it will cost him one hundred francs. **qu'est-ce que vous avez?**, what is the matter with you? **on m'a eu!**, I've been had.

avoisin|er /avwazine/ *v.t.* border on. **~ant**, **~ante** *a.* neighbouring.

avort|er /avɔrte/ *v.i.* (*projet etc.*) miscarry. **(se faire) ~er**, have an abortion. **~é** *a.* abortive. **~ement** *n.m.* (*méd.*) abortion.

avou|er /avwe/ *v.t.* confess (to). —*v.i.* confess. **~é** *a.* avowed; *n.m.* solicitor; (*Amer.*) attorney.

avril /avril/ *n.m.* April.

axe /aks/ *n.m.* axis; (*essieu*) axle; (*d'une*

politique) main line(s), basis. **~ (routier)**, main road.

axer /akse/ *v.t.* centre.

axiome /aksjom/ *n.m.* axiom.

ayant /ɛjɑ̃/ *voir* **avoir**.

azimuts /azimyt/ *n.m. pl.* **dans tous les ~**, (*fam.*) all over the place.

azote /azɔt/ *n.m.* nitrogen.

azur /azyr/ *n.m.* sky-blue.

B

ba-ba /beaba/ *n.m.* **le ~ (de)**, the basics (of).

baba /baba/ *n.m.* **~ (au rhum)**, rum baba. **en rester ~**, (*fam.*) be flabbergasted.

babil /babi(l)/ *n.m.* babble. **~ler** /-ije/ *v.i.* babble.

babines /babin/ *n.f. pl.* **se lécher les ~**, lick one's chops.

babiole /babjɔl/ *n.f.* knick-knack.

bâbord /babɔr/ *n.m.* port (side).

babouin /babwɛ̃/ *n.m.* baboon.

baby-foot /babifut/ *n.m. invar.* table football.

baby-sitt|er /bebisitœr/ *n.m.*/*f.* babysitter. **~ing** *n.m.* **faire du ~ing**, babysit.

bac[1] /bak/ *n.m.* = **baccalauréat**.

bac[2] /bak/ *n.m.* (*bateau*) ferry; (*récipient*) tub; (*plus petit*) tray.

baccalauréat /bakalɔrea/ *n.m.* school leaving certificate.

bâch|e /baʃ/ *n.f.* tarpaulin. **~er** *v.t.* cover (with a tarpaulin).

bachel|ier, **~ière** /baʃəlje, -jɛr/ *n.m.*, *f.* holder of the *baccalauréat*.

bachot /baʃo/ *n.m.* (*fam.*) = **baccalauréat**. **~er** /-ɔte/ *v.i.* cram (for an exam).

bâcler /bakle/ *v.t.* botch (up).

bactérie /bakteri/ *n.f.* bacterium.

badaud, **~e** /bado, -d/ *n.m.*, *f.* (*péj.*) onlooker.

badigeon /badiʒɔ̃/ *n.m.* whitewash. **~ner** /-ɔne/ *v.t.* whitewash; (*barbouiller*) daub.

badin, **~e** /badɛ̃, -in/ *a.* light-hearted.

badiner /badine/ *v.i.* joke (**sur, avec**, about).

badminton /badmintɔn/ *n.m.* badminton.

baffe /baf/ *n.f.* (*fam.*) slap.

baffle /bafl/ *n.m.* speaker.

bafouer /bafwe/ *v.t.* scoff at.

bafouiller /bafuje/ v.t./i. stammer.
bâfrer /bɑfre/ v.i. (fam.) gobble. se ∼
v.pr. stuff o.s.
bagage /bagaʒ/ n.m. bag; (fig.) (store of)
knowledge. ∼s, luggage, baggage. ∼s
à main, hand luggage.
bagarr∣e /bagar/ n.f. fight. ∼er v.i., se
∼er v. pr. fight.
bagatelle /bagatɛl/ n.f. trifle; (somme)
trifling amount.
bagnard /baɲar/ n.m. convict.
bagnole /baɲɔl/ n.f. (fam.) car.
bagou(t) /bagu/ n.m. avoir du ∼, have
the gift of the gab.
bagu∣e /bag/ n.f. (anneau) ring. ∼er v.t.
ring.
baguette /bagɛt/ n.f. stick; (de chef
d'orchestre) baton; (chinoise) chopstick; (magique) wand; (pain) stick of
bread. ∼ de tambour, drumstick.
baie /bɛ/ n.f. (géog.) bay; (fruit) berry.
∼ (vitrée), picture window.
baign∣er /beɲe/ v.t. bathe; (enfant) bath.
—v.i. ∼er dans, soak in; (être
enveloppé dans) be steeped in. se ∼er
v. pr. go swimming (ou bathing). ∼é
de, bathed in; (sang) soaked in. ∼ade
/bɛɲad/ n.f. bathing, swimming. ∼eur,
∼euse /bɛɲœr, -øz/ n.m., f. bather.
baignoire /bɛɲwar/ n.f. bath(-tub).
bail (pl. **baux** /baj, bo/ n.m. lease.
bâill∣er /baje/ v.i. yawn; (être ouvert)
gape. ∼ement n.m. yawn.
bailleur /bajœr/ n.m. ∼ de fonds,
(comm.) backer.
bâillon /bajɔ̃/ n.m. gag. ∼ner /bajɔne/
v.t. gag.
bain /bɛ̃/ n.m. bath; (de mer) bathe. ∼(s)
de soleil, sunbathing. ∼-marie (pl.
∼s-marie) n.m. double boiler. ∼ de
bouche, mouthwash. mettre qn. dans
le ∼, (compromettre) drop s.o. in it; (au
courant) put s.o. in the picture. se
remettre dans le ∼, get back into the
swim of things. prendre un ∼ de foule,
mingle with the crowd.
baiser /beze/ n.m. kiss. —v.t. (main)
kiss; (fam.) screw.
baisse /bɛs/ n.f. fall, drop. en ∼, falling.
baiss∣er /bese/ v.t. lower; (radio, lampe,
etc.) turn down. —v.i. go down, fall;
(santé, forces) fail. se ∼ v. pr. bend
down.
bajoues /baʒu/ n.f. pl. chops.
bakchich /bakʃiʃ/ n.m. (fam.) bribe.
bal (pl. ∼s) /bal/ n.m. dance; (habillé)
ball; (lieu) dance-hall. ∼ costumé,
fancy-dress ball.
balad∣e /balad/ n.f. stroll; (en auto)
drive. ∼er v.t. take for a stroll. se ∼er

v. pr. (go for a) stroll; (excursionner)
wander around. se ∼er (en auto), go
for a drive.
baladeur /baladœr/ n.m. personal
stereo.
balafr∣e /balafr/ n.f. gash; (cicatrice)
scar. ∼er v.t. gash.
balai /balɛ/ n.m. broom. ∼-brosse n.m.
garden broom.
balance /balɑ̃s/ n.f. scales. la B∼, Libra.
balancer /balɑ̃se/ v.t. swing; (doucement) sway; (lancer; fam.) chuck; (se
débarrasser de: fam.) chuck out. —v.i.
se ∼ v. pr. swing; sway. se ∼ de, (fam.)
not care about.
balancier /balɑ̃sje/ n.m. (d'horloge)
pendulum; (d'équilibriste) pole.
balançoire /balɑ̃swar/ n.f. swing;
(bascule) see-saw.
balay∣er /baleje/ v.t. sweep (up);
(chasser) sweep away; (se débarrasser
de) sweep aside. ∼age n.m. sweeping;
(cheveux) highlights. ∼eur, ∼euse
n.m., f. road sweeper.
balbut∣ier /balbysje/ v.t./i. stammer.
∼iement n.m. stammering.
balcon /balkɔ̃/ n.m. balcony; (théâtre)
dress circle.
baleine /balɛn/ n.f. whale.
balis∣e /baliz/ n.f. beacon; (bouée) buoy;
(auto.) (road) sign. ∼er v.t. mark out
(with beacons); (route) signpost.
balistique /balistik/ a. ballistic.
balivernes /balivern/ n.f. pl. balder-
dash.
ballade /balad/ n.f. ballad.
ballant, ∼e /balɑ̃, -t/ a. dangling.
ballast /balast/ n.m. ballast.
balle /bal/ n.f. (projectile) bullet; (sport)
ball; (paquet) bale.
ballerine /balrin/ n.f. ballerina.
ballet /balɛ/ n.m. ballet.
ballon /balɔ̃/ n.m. balloon; (sport) ball.
∼ de football, football.
ballonné /balɔne/ a. bloated.
ballot /balo/ n.m. bundle; (nigaud: fam.)
idiot.
ballottage /balɔtaʒ/ n.m. second ballot
(due to indecisive result).
ballotter /balɔte/ v.t./i. shake about, toss.
balnéaire /balneɛr/ a. seaside.
balourd, ∼e /balur, -d/ n.m., f. oaf.
—a. oafish.
balustrade /balystrad/ n.f. railing(s).
bambin /bɑ̃bɛ̃/ n.m. tot.
bambou /bɑ̃bu/ n.m. bamboo.
ban /bɑ̃/ n.m. round of applause. ∼s, (de
mariage) banns. mettre au ∼ de, cast
out from. publier les ∼s, have the
banns called.

banal (*m. pl.* ~s) /banal/ *a.* commonplace, banal. ~ité *n.f.* banality.

banane /banan/ *n.f.* banana.

banc /bɑ̃/ *n.m.* bench; (*de poissons*) shoal. ~ **des accusés**, dock. ~ **d'essai**, test bed; (*fig.*) testing-ground.

bancaire /bɑ̃kɛr/ *a.* banking; (*chèque*) bank.

bancal (*m. pl.* ~s) /bɑ̃kal/ *a.* wobbly; (*raisonnement*) shaky.

bandage /bɑ̃daʒ/ *n.m.* bandage. ~ **herniaire**, truss.

bande[1] /bɑ̃d/ *n.f.* (*de papier etc.*) strip; (*rayure*) stripe; (*de film*) reel; (*radio*) band; (*pansement*) bandage. ~ (**magnétique**), tape. ~ **dessinée**, comic strip. ~ **sonore**, sound-track. **par la** ~, indirectly.

bande[2] /bɑ̃d/ *n.f.* (*groupe*) bunch, band, gang.

bandeau (*pl.* ~x) /bɑ̃do/ *n.m.* headband; (*sur les yeux*) blindfold.

bander /bɑ̃de/ *v.t.* bandage; (*arc*) bend; (*muscle*) tense. ~ **les yeux à**, blindfold.

banderole /bɑ̃drɔl/ *n.f.* banner.

bandit /bɑ̃di/ *n.m.* bandit. ~**isme** /-tism/ *n.m.* crime.

bandoulière (en) /(ɑ̃)bɑ̃duljɛr/ *adv.* across one's shoulder.

banjo /bɑ̃(d)ʒo/ *n.m.* banjo.

banlieue /bɑ̃ljø/ *n.f.* suburbs. **de** ~**e**, suburban. ~**sard** /-zar, -zard/ *n.m.,f.* (suburban) commuter.

bannière /banjɛr/ *n.f.* banner.

bannir /banir/ *v.t.* banish.

banque /bɑ̃k/ *n.f.* bank; (*activité*) banking. ~ **d'affaires**, merchant bank.

banqueroute /bɑ̃krut/ *n.f.* (fraudulent) bankruptcy.

banquet /bɑ̃kɛ/ *n.m.* dinner; (*fastueux*) banquet.

banquette /bɑ̃kɛt/ *n.f.* seat.

banquier /bɑ̃kje/ *n.m.* banker.

bapt|ême /batɛm/ *n.m.* baptism; christening. ~**iser** *v.t.* baptize, christen; (*appeler*) christen.

baquet /bakɛ/ *n.m.* tub.

bar /bar/ *n.m.* (*lieu*) bar.

baragouin /baragwɛ̃/ *n.m.* gibberish, gabble. ~**er** /-wine/ *v.t./i.* gabble; (*langue*) speak a few words of.

baraque /barak/ *n.f.* hut, shed; (*boutique*) stall; (*maison: fam.*) house. ~**ments** *n.m. pl.* huts.

baratin /baratɛ̃/ *n.m.* (*fam.*) sweet *ou* smooth talk. ~**er** /-ine/ *v.t.* (*fam.*) chat up; (*Amer.*) sweet-talk.

barbar|e /barbar/ *a.* barbaric. —*n.m./f.* barbarian. ~**ie** *n.f.* (*cruauté*) barbarity.

barbe /barb/ *n.f.* beard. ~ **à papa**,

candy-floss; (*Amer.*) cotton candy. **la** ~!, (*fam.*) blast (it)! **quelle** ~!, (*fam.*) what a bore!

barbecue /barbəkju/ *n.m.* barbecue.

barbelé /barbəle/ *a.* **fil** ~, barbed wire.

barber /barbe/ *v.t.* (*fam.*) bore.

barbiche /barbiʃ/ *n.f.* goatee.

barbiturique /barbityrik/ *n.m.* barbiturate.

barboter[1] /barbɔte/ *v.i.* paddle, splash.

barboter[2] /barbɔte/ *v.t.* (*voler: fam.*) pinch.

barbouill|er /barbuje/ *v.t.* (*peindre*) daub; (*souiller*) smear; (*griffonner*) scribble. **avoir l'estomac** ~**é** *ou* **se sentir** ~**é** feel liverish.

barbu /barby/ *a.* bearded.

barda /barda/ *n.m.* (*fam.*) gear.

barder /barde/ *v.i.* **ça va** ~, (*fam.*) sparks will fly.

barème /barɛm/ *n.m.* list, table; (*échelle*) scale.

baril /bari(l)/ *n.m.* barrel; (*de poudre*) keg.

bariolé /barjɔle/ *a.* motley.

barman /barman/ *n.m.* barman; (*Amer.*) bartender.

baromètre /barɔmɛtr/ *n.m.* barometer.

baron, ~ne /barɔ̃, -ɔn/ *n.m., f.* baron, baroness.

baroque /barɔk/ *a.* (*fig.*) weird; (*archit., art*) baroque.

baroud /barud/ *n.m.* ~ **d'honneur**, gallant last fight.

barque /bark/ *n.f.* (small) boat.

barrage /baraʒ/ *n.m.* dam; (*sur route*) road-block.

barre /bar/ *n.f.* bar; (*trait*) line, stroke; (*naut.*) helm.

barreau (*pl.* ~x) /baro/ *n.m.* bar; (*d'échelle*) rung. **le** ~, (*jurid.*) the bar.

barrer /bare/ *v.t.* block; (*porte*) bar; (*rayer*) cross out; (*naut.*) steer. **se** ~ *v. pr.* (*fam.*) hop it.

barrette /barɛt/ *n.f.* (hair-)slide.

barricad|e /barikad/ *n.f.* barricade. ~**er** *v.t.* barricade. **se** ~**er** *v. pr.* barricade o.s.

barrière /barjɛr/ *n.f.* (*porte*) gate; (*clôture*) fence; (*obstacle*) barrier.

barrique /barik/ *n.f.* barrel.

baryton /baritɔ̃/ *n.m.* baritone.

bas, basse /bɑ, bɑs/ *a.* low; (*action*) base. —*n.m.* bottom; (*chaussette*) stocking. —*n.f.* (*mus.*) bass. —*adv.* low. **à** ~, down with. **au** ~ **mot**, at the lowest estimate. **en** ~, down below; (*dans une maison*) downstairs. **en** ~ **de**, at the bottom of. **plus** ~, further *ou* lower down. ~**-côté** *n.m.* (*de* *route*) verge; (*Amer.*) shoulder. ～ **de casse** *n.m. invar.* lower case. ～ **de laine,** nest-egg. ～**-fonds** *n.m. pl.* (*eau*) shallows; (*fig.*) dregs. ～ **morceaux,** (*viande*) cheap cuts. ～**-relief** *n.m.* low relief. ～**-ventre** *n.m.* lower abdomen. **mettre** ～, give birth (to).

basané /bazane/ *a.* tanned.

bascule /baskyl/ *n.f.* (*balance*) scales. **cheval/fauteuil à** ～, rocking-horse/ -chair.

basculer /baskyle/ *v.t./i.* topple over; (*benne*) tip up.

base /baz/ *n.f.* base; (*fondement*) basis; (*pol.*) rank and file. **de** ～, basic.

baser /baze/ *v.t.* base. **se** ～ **sur,** base o.s. on.

basilic /bazilik/ *n.m.* basil.

basilique /bazilik/ *n.f.* basilica.

basket(-ball) /baskɛt(bol)/ *n.m.* basket-ball.

basque /bask/ *a. & n.m./f.* Basque.

basse /bas/ *voir* **bas.**

basse-cour (*pl.* **basses-cours**) /baskur/ *n.f.* farmyard.

bassement /basmã/ *adv.* basely.

bassesse /basɛs/ *n.f.* baseness; (*action*) base act.

bassin /basɛ̃/ *n.m.* bowl; (*pièce d'eau*) pond; (*rade*) dock; (*géog.*) basin; (*anat.*) pelvis. ～ **houiller,** coalfield.

basson /basɔ̃/ *n.m.* bassoon.

bastion /bastjɔ̃/ *n.m.* bastion.

bat /ba/ *voir* **battre.**

bât /ba/ *n.m.* **là où le** ～ **blesse,** where the shoe pinches.

bataill|e /bataj/ *n.f.* battle; (*fig.*) fight. ～**er** *v.i.* fight.

bataillon /batajɔ̃/ *n.m.* battalion.

bâtard, ～**e** /batar, -d/ *n.m., f.* bastard. —*a.* (*solution*) hybrid.

bateau (*pl.* ～**x**) /bato/ *n.m.* boat. ～**-mouche** (*pl.* ～**x-mouches**) *n.m.* sightseeing boat.

bâti /bati/ *a.* **bien** ～, well-built.

batifoler /batifɔle/ *v.i.* fool about.

bâtiment /batimã/ *n.m.* building; (*navire*) vessel; (*industrie*) building trade.

bâtir /batir/ *v.t.* build; (*coudre*) baste.

bâtisse /batis/ *n.f.* (*péj.*) building.

bâton /batɔ̃/ *n.m.* stick. **à** ～**s rompus,** jumping from subject to subject. ～ **de rouge,** lipstick.

battage /bataʒ/ *n.m.* (*publicité: fam.*) (hard) plugging.

battant /batã/ *n.m.* (*vantail*) flap. **porte à deux** ～**s,** double door.

battement /batmã/ *n.m.* (*de cœur*) beat(ing); (*temps*) interval.

batterie /batri/ *n.f.* (*mil.*, *électr.*) battery; (*mus.*) drums. ～ **de cuisine,** pots and pans.

batteur /batœr/ *n.m.* (*mus.*) drummer; (*culin.*) whisk.

battre† /batr/ *v.t./i.* beat; (*blé*) thresh; (*cartes*) shuffle; (*parcourir*) scour; (*faire du bruit*) bang. **se** ～ *v. pr.* fight. ～ **des ailes,** flap its wings. ～ **des mains,** clap. ～ **en retraite,** beat a retreat. ～ **la semelle,** stamp one's feet. ～ **pavillon britannique**/*etc.,* fly the British/*etc.* flag. ～ **son plein,** be in full swing.

battue /baty/ *n.f.* (*chasse*) beat; (*de police*) search.

baume /bom/ *n.m.* balm.

bavard, ～**e** /bavar, -d/ *a.* talkative. —*n.m., f.* chatterbox.

bavard|er /bavarde/ *v.i.* chat; (*jacasser*) chatter, gossip. ～**age** *n.m.* chatter, gossip.

bav|e /bav/ *n.f.* dribble, slobber; (*de limace*) slime. ～**er** *v.i.* dribble, slobber. ～**eux,** ～**euse** *a.* dribbling; (*omelette*) runny.

bav|ette /bavɛt/ *n.f.,* ～**oir** *n.m.* bib. **tailler une** ～**ette,** (*fam.*) have a chat.

bavure /bavyr/ *n.f.* smudge; (*erreur*) mistake. ～ **policière,** (*fam.*) police cock-up. **sans** ～, flawless(ly).

bazar /bazar/ *n.m.* bazaar; (*objets: fam.*) clutter.

bazarder /bazarde/ *v.t.* (*vendre: fam.*) get rid of, flog.

BCBG *abrév.* (*bon chic bon genre*) posh.

BD *abrév.* (*bande dessinée*) comic strip.

béant, ～**e** /beã, -t/ *a.* gaping.

béat, ～**e** /bea, -t/ *a.* (*hum.*) blissful; (*péj.*) smug. ～**itude** /-tityd/ *n.f.* (*hum.*) bliss.

beau *ou* **bel*, belle** (*m. pl.* ～**x**) /bo, bɛl/ *a.* fine, beautiful; (*femme*) beautiful; (*homme*) handsome; (*grand*) big. —*n.f.* beauty; (*sport*) deciding game. **au** ～ **milieu,** right in the middle. **bel et bien,** well and truly. **de plus belle,** more than ever. **faire le** ～, sit up and beg. **on a** ～ **essayer/insister**/*etc.,* however much one tries/insists/*etc.,* it is no use trying/insisting/*etc.* ～**x-arts** *n.m. pl.* fine arts. ～**-fils** (*pl.* ～**x-fils**) *n.m.* son-in-law; (*remariage*) stepson. ～**-frère** (*pl.* ～**x-frères**) *n.m.* brother-in-law. ～**-père** (*pl.* ～**x-pères**) *n.m.* father-in-law; stepfather. ～**x-parents** *n.m. pl.* parents-in-law.

beaucoup /boku/ *adv.* a lot, very much. —*pron.* many (people). ～ **de,** (*nombre*) many; (*quantité*) a lot of. **pas ~ (de)**, not many; (*quantité*) not much. **~ plus**/*etc*., much more/*etc*. **~ trop**, much too much. **de ~**, by far.

beauté /bote/ *n.f.* beauty. **en ~**, magnificently. **tu es en ~**, you are looking good.

bébé /bebe/ *n.m.* baby. **~-éprouvette**, test-tube baby.

bec /bɛk/ *n.m.* beak; (*de plume*) nib; (*de bouilloire*) spout; (*de casserole*) lip; (*bouche*: *fam.*) mouth. **~-de-cane** (*pl.* **~s-de-cane**)door-handle. **~ degaz**, gas lamp (*in street*).

bécane /bekan/ *n.f.* (*fam.*) bike.

bécasse /bekas/ *n.f.* woodcock.

bêche /bɛʃ/ *n.f.* spade.

bêcher /beʃe/ *v.t.* dig.

bécoter /bekɔte/ *v.t.*, **se ~** *v. pr.* (*fam.*) kiss.

becquée /beke/ *n.f.* **donner la ~ à**, (*oiseau*) feed; (*fig.*) spoonfeed.

bedaine /bədɛn/ *n.f.* paunch.

bedeau (*pl.* **~x**) /bədo/ *n.m.* beadle.

bedonnant, ~e /bədɔnɑ̃, -t/ *a.* paunchy.

beffroi /befrwa/ *n.m.* belfry.

bégayer /begeje/ *v.t./i.* stammer.

bègue /bɛg/ *n.m./f.* stammerer. **être ~**, stammer.

bégueule /begœl/ *a.* prudish.

béguin /begɛ̃/ *n.m.* **avoir le ~ pour**, (*fam.*) have a crush on.

beige /bɛʒ/ *a. & n.m.* beige.

beignet /bɛɲɛ/ *n.m.* fritter.

bel /bɛl/ *voir* **beau**.

bêler /bele/ *v.i.* bleat.

belette /bəlɛt/ *n.f.* weasel.

belge /bɛlʒ/ *a. & n.m./f.* Belgian.

Belgique /bɛlʒik/ *n.f.* Belgium.

bélier /belje/ *n.m.* ram. **le B~**, Aries.

belle /bɛl/ *voir* **beau**.

belle|-fille (*pl.* **~s-filles**) /bɛlfij/ *n.f.* daughter-in-law; (*remariage*) stepdaughter. **~-mère** (*pl.* **~s-mères**) *n.f.* mother-in-law; stepmother. **~-sœur** (*pl.* **~s-sœurs**) *n.f.* sister-in-law.

belligérant, ~e /beliʒerɑ̃, -t/ *a. & n.m.* belligerent.

belliqueu|x, ~se /belikø, -z/ *a.* warlike.

belote /bəlɔt/ *n.f.* belote (*card game*).

belvédère /bɛlvedɛr/ *n.m.* (*lieu*) viewing spot, viewpoint.

bémol /bemɔl/ *n.m.* (*mus.*) flat.

bénédiction /benediksjɔ̃/ *n.f.* blessing.

bénéfice /benefis/ *n.m.* (*gain*) profit; (*avantage*) benefit.

bénéficiaire /benefisjɛr/ *n.m./f.* beneficiary.

bénéficier /benefisje/ *v.i.* **~ de**, benefit from; (*jouir de*) enjoy, have.

bénéfique /benefik/ *a.* beneficial.

Bénélux /benelyks/ *n.m.* Benelux.

benêt /bənɛ/ *n.m.* simpleton.

bénévole /benevɔl/ *a.* voluntary.

bén|in, ~igne /benɛ̃, -iɲ/ *a.* mild, slight; (*tumeur*) benign.

bén|ir /benir/ *v.t.* bless. **~it, ~ite** *a.* (*eau*) holy; (*pain*) consecrated.

bénitier /benitje/ *n.m.* stoup.

benjamin, ~e /bɛ̃ʒamɛ̃, -in/ *n.m., f.* youngest child.

benne /bɛn/ *n.f.* (*de grue*) scoop; (*amovible*) skip. **~ (basculante),** dump truck.

benzine /bɛ̃zin/ *n.f.* benzine.

béotien, ~ne /beɔsjɛ̃, -jɛn/ *n.m., f.* philistine.

béquille /bekij/ *n.f.* crutch; (*de moto*) stand.

bercail /bɛrkaj/ *n.m.* fold.

berceau (*pl.* **~x**) /bɛrso/ *n.m.* cradle.

bercer /bɛrse/ *v.t.* (*balancer*) rock; (*apaiser*) lull; (*leurrer*) delude.

berceuse /bɛrsøz/ *n.f.* lullaby.

béret /berɛ/ *n.m.* beret.

berge /bɛrʒ/ *n.f.* (*bord*) bank.

berg|er, ~ère /bɛrʒe, -ɛr/ *n.m., f.* shepherd, shepherdess. **~erie** *n.f.* sheep-fold.

berlingot /bɛrlɛ̃go/ *n.m.* boiled sweet; (*emballage*) carton.

berne (en) /(ɑ̃)bɛrn/ *adv.* at half-mast.

berner /bɛrne/ *v.t.* hoodwink.

besogne /bəzɔɲ/ *n.f.* task, job, chore.

besoin /bəzwɛ̃/ *n.m.* need. **avoir ~ de**, need. **au ~**, if need be.

best|ial (*m. pl.* **~iaux**) /bɛstjal, -jo/ *a.* bestial.

bestiaux /bɛstjo/ *n.m. pl.* livestock.

bestiole /bɛstjɔl/ *n.f.* creepy-crawly.

bétail /betaj/ *n.m.* farm animals.

bête[1] /bɛt/ *n.f.* animal. **~ noire**, pet hate, pet peeve. **~ sauvage**, wild beast. **chercher la petite ~**, be overfussy.

bête[2] /bɛt/ *a.* stupid. **~ment** *adv.* stupidly.

bêtise /betiz/ *n.f.* stupidity; (*action*) stupid thing.

béton /betɔ̃/ *n.m.* concrete. **~ armé**, reinforced concrete. **~nière** /-ɔnjɛr/ *n.f.* cement-mixer, concrete-mixer.

betterave /bɛtrav/ *n.f.* beetroot. **~ sucrière**, sugar-beet.

beugler /bøgle/ *v.i.* bellow, low; (*radio*) blare.

beur /bœr/ *n.m./f. & a.* (*fam.*) young French North African.

beurr|e /bœr/ *n.m.* butter. **~er** *v.t.*

butter. **~ier** *n.m.* butter-dish. **~é,** *a.*
buttered; (*fam.*) drunk.
bévue /bevy/ *n.f.* blunder.
biais /bjɛ/ *n.m.* (*fig.*) expedient; (*côté*)
angle. **de ~, en ~,** at an angle. **de ~,**
(*fig.*) indirectly.
biaiser /bjeze/ *v.i.* hedge.
bibelot /biblo/ *n.m.* curio.
biberon /bibrɔ̃/ *n.m.* (feeding-)bottle.
nourrir au ~, bottle-feed.
bible /bibl/ *n.f.* bible. **la B~,** the Bible.
bibliographie /biblijɔgrafi/ *n.f.* biblio-
graphy.
bibliophile /biblijɔfil/ *n.m./f.* book-
lover.
biblioth|èque /biblijɔtɛk/ *n.f.* library;
(*meuble*) bookcase; **~écaire** *n.m./f.*
librarian.
biblique /biblik/ *a.* biblical.
bic /bik/ *n.m.* (P.) biro (P.).
bicarbonate /bikarbɔnat/ *n.m.* **~ (de
soude),** bicarbonate (of soda).
biceps /bisɛps/ *n.m.* biceps.
biche /biʃ/ *n.f.* doe.
bichonner /biʃɔne/ *v.t.* doll up.
bicoque /bikɔk/ *n.f.* shack.
bicyclette /bisiklɛt/ *n.f.* bicycle.
bide /bid/ *n.m.* (*ventre*: *fam.*) belly;
(*théâtre*: *fam.*) flop.
bidet /bidɛ/ *n.m.* bidet.
bidon /bidɔ̃/ *n.m.* can. —*a. invar.* (*fam.*)
phoney. **c'est pas du ~,** (*fam.*) it's the
truth, it's for real.
bidonville /bidɔ̃vil/ *n.f.* shanty town.
bidule /bidyl/ *n.m.* (*fam.*) thing.
bielle /bjɛl/ *n.f.* connecting rod.
bien /bjɛ̃/ *adv.* well; (*très*) quite, very.
—*n.m.* good; (*patrimoine*) possession.
—*a. invar.* good; (*passable*) all right; (*en
forme*) well; (*à l'aise*) comfortable;
(*beau*) attractive; (*respectable*) nice, respectable. —*conj.* **~ que,** (al)though. **~
que ce soit/que ça ait,** although it is/it
has. **~ du,** (*quantité*) a lot of, much. **~
des,** (*nombre*) many. **il l'a ~ fait,**
(*intensif*) he did do it. **ce n'est pas ~ de,**
it is not right to. **~ sûr,** of course. **~s de
consommation,** consumer goods. **~-
aimé, ~-aimée** *a.* & *n.m.,* *f.* beloved. **~-
être** *n.m.* well-being. **~-fondé** *n.m.*
soundness. **~-pensant, ~-pensante** *a.*
& *n.m.,* *f.* (*péj.*) right-thinking.
bienfaisan|t, -te /bjɛ̃fəzɑ̃, -t/ *a.* benefi-
cial. **~ce** *n.f.* charity. **fête de ~ce,** fête.
bienfait /bjɛ̃fɛ/ *n.m.* (kind) favour;
(*avantage*) benefit.
bienfai|teur, ~trice /bjɛ̃fɛtœr, -tris/
n.m., f. benefactor.
bienheureu|x, ~se /bjɛ̃nœrø, -z/ *a.*
happy, blessed.

bienséan|t, ~te /bjɛ̃seɑ̃, -t/ *a.* proper.
~ce *n.f.* propriety.
bientôt /bjɛ̃to/ *adv.* soon. **à ~,** see you
soon.
bienveillan|t, ~te /bjɛ̃vɛjɑ̃, -t/ *a.*
kind(ly). **~ce** *n.f.* kind(li)ness.
bienvenu, ~e /bjɛ̃vny/ *a.* welcome.
—*n.f.* welcome.—*n.m.,* *f.* **être le ~,
être la ~e,** be welcome. **souhaiter la
~e à,** welcome.
bière /bjɛr/ *n.f.* beer; (*cercueil*) coffin. **~
blonde,** lager. **~ brune,** stout, brown
ale. **~ pression,** draught beer.
biffer /bife/ *v.t.* cross out.
bifteck /biftɛk/ *n.m.* steak.
bifur|quer /bifyrke/ *v.i.* branch off, fork.
~cation *n.f.* fork, junction.
bigam|e /bigam/ *a.* bigamous. —*n.m./f.*
bigamist. **~ie** *n.f.* bigamy.
bigarré /bigare/ *a.* motley.
big-bang /bigbɑ̃g/ *n.m.* big bang.
bigot, ~e /bigo, -ɔt/ *n.m., f.* religious
fanatic. —*a.* over-pious.
bigoudi /bigudi/ *n.m.* curler.
bijou (*pl.* **~x**) /biʒu/ *n.m.* jewel. **~terie**
n.f. (*boutique*) jeweller's shop;
(*comm.*) jewellery. **~tier, ~tière** *n.m.,*
f. jeweller.
bikini /bikini/ *n.m.* bikini.
bilan /bilɑ̃/ *n.m.* outcome; (*d'une
catastrophe*) (casualty) toll; (*comm.*)
balance sheet. **faire le ~ de,** assess. **~
de santé,** check-up.
bile /bil/ *n.f.* bile. **se faire de la ~,** (*fam.*)
worry.
bilieu|x, ~se /biljø, -z/ *a.* bilious. (*fig.*)
irascible.
bilingue /bilɛ̃g/ *a.* bilingual.
billard /bijar/ *n.m.* billiards; (*table*)
billiard-table.
bille /bij/ *n.f.* (*d'enfant*) marble; (*de
billard*) billiard-ball.
billet /bijɛ/ *n.m.* ticket; (*lettre*) note;
(*article*) column. **~ (de banque),**
(bank)note. **~ d'aller et retour,** return
ticket; (*Amer.*) round trip ticket. **~ de
faveur,** complimentary ticket. **~ aller
simple,** single ticket; (*Amer.*) one-way
ticket.
billetterie /bijɛtri/ *n.f.* cash dispenser.
billion /biljɔ̃/ *n.m.* billion (= 10^{12});
(*Amer.*) trillion.
billot /bijo/ *n.m.* block.
bimensuel, ~le /bimɑ̃sɥɛl/ *a.*
fortnightly, bimonthly.
bin|er /bine/ *v.t.* hoe. **~ette** *n.f.* hoe;
(*fam.*) face.
biochimie /bjoʃimi/ *n.f.* biochemistry.
biodégradable /bjɔdegradabl/ *a.*
biodegradable.

biograph|ie /bjɔgrafi/ n.f. biography. **~e** n.m./f. biographer.

biolog|ie /bjɔlɔʒi/ n.f. biology. **~ique** a. biological. **~iste** n.m./f. biologist.

bipède /bipɛd/ n.m. biped.

bis¹, bise /bi, biz/ a. greyish brown.

bis² /bis/ a.invar. (numéro) A, a. —n.m. & int. encore.

bisbille (en) /(ã)bisbij/ adv. (fam.) at loggerheads (**avec,** with).

biscornu /biskɔrny/ a. crooked; (bizarre) weird.

biscotte /biskɔt/ n.f. rusk.

biscuit /biskɥi/ n.m. (salé) biscuit; (Amer.) cracker; (sucré) biscuit; (Amer.) cookie. **~ de Savoie,** sponge-cake.

bise¹ /biz/ n.f. (fam.) kiss.

bise² /biz/ n.f. (vent) north wind.

bison /bizõ/ n.m. (American) buffalo, bison.

bisou /bizu/ n.m. (fam.) kiss.

bisser /bise/ v.t. encore.

bistouri /bisturi/ n.m. lancet.

bistre /bistr/ a. & n.m. dark brown.

bistro(t) /bistro/ n.m. café, bar.

bit /bit/ n.m. (comput.) bit.

bitume /bitym/ n.m. asphalt.

bizarre /bizar/ a. odd, peculiar. **~ment** adv. oddly. **~rie** n.f. peculiarity.

blafard, ~e /blafar, -d/ a. pale.

blagu|e /blag/ n.f. joke. **~e à tabac,** tobacco-pouch. **~er** v.i. joke; v.t. tease. **~eur, ~euse** n.m., f. joker; a. jokey.

blaireau (pl. **~x**) /blɛro/ n.m. shaving-brush; (animal) badger.

blâm|e /blɑm/ n.m. rebuke, blame. **~able** a. blameworthy. **~er** v.t. rebuke, blame.

blanc, blanche /blã, blãʃ/ a. white; (papier, page) blank. —n.m. white; (espace) blank. —n.m., f. white man, white woman. —n.f. (mus.) minim. **~ (de poulet),** breast, white meat (of the chicken). **le ~,** (linge) whites. **laisser en ~,** leave blank.

blancheur /blãʃœr/ n.f. whiteness.

blanch|ir /blãʃir/ v.t. whiten; (linge) launder; (personne: fig.) clear; (culin.) blanch. **~ir (à la chaux),** whitewash. —v.i. turn white. **~issage** n.m. laundering. **~isserie** n.f. laundry. **~isseur, ~isseuse** n.m., f. laundryman, laundress.

blasé /blaze/ a. blasé.

blason /blazõ/ n.m. coat of arms.

blasph|ème /blasfɛm/ n.m. blasphemy. **~ématoire** a. blasphemous. **~émer** v.t./i. blaspheme.

blatte /blat/ n.f. cockroach.

blazer /blɛzœr/ n.m. blazer.

blé /ble/ n.m. wheat.

bled /blɛd/ n.m. (fam.) dump, hole.

blême /blɛm/ a. (sickly) pale.

bless|er /blese/ v.t. injure, hurt; (par balle) wound; (offenser) hurt, wound. **se ~er** v. pr. injure ou hurt o.s. **~ant, ~ante** /blɛsã, -t/ a. hurtful. **~é, ~ée** n.m., f. casualty, injured person.

blessure /blesyr/ n.f. wound.

blet, ~te /blɛ, blɛt/ a. over-ripe.

bleu /blø/ a. blue; (culin.) very rare. **~ marine,** navy blue. —n.m. blue; (contusion) bruise. **~(s),** (vêtement) overalls. **~ir** v.t./i. turn blue.

bleuet /bløɛ/ n.m. cornflower.

bleuté /bløte/ a. slightly blue.

blind|er /blɛde/ v.t. armour(-plate); (fig.) harden. **~é** a. armoured; (fig.) immune (**contre,** to); n.m. armoured car, tank.

blizzard /blizar/ n.m. blizzard.

bloc /blɔk/ n.m. block; (de papier) pad; (système) unit; (pol.) bloc. **à ~,** hard, tight. **en ~,** all together. **~-notes** (pl. **~s-notes**) n.m. note-pad.

blocage /blɔkaʒ/ n.m. (des prix) freeze, freezing; (des roues) locking; (psych.) block.

blocus /blɔkys/ n.m. blockade.

blond, ~e /blõ, -d/ a. fair, blond. —n.m., f. fair-haired ou blond man ou woman. **~eur** /-dœr/ n.f. fairness.

bloquer /blɔke/ v.t. block; (porte, machine) jam; (freins) slam on; (roues) lock; (prix, crédits) freeze; (grouper) put together. **se ~** v. pr. jam; (roues) lock.

blottir (se) /(sə)blɔtir/ v. pr. snuggle, huddle.

blouse /bluz/ n.f. smock.

blouson /bluzõ/ n.m. lumber-jacket; (Amer.) windbreaker.

blue-jean /bludʒin/ n.m. jeans.

bluff /blœf/ n.m. bluff. **~er** v.t./i. bluff.

blush /blœʃ/ n.m. blusher.

boa /bɔa/ n.m. boa.

bobard /bɔbar/ n.m. (fam.) fib.

bobine /bɔbin/ n.f. reel; (sur machine) spool; (électr.) coil.

bobo /bobo/ n.m. (fam.) sore, cut. **avoir ~,** have a pain.

bocage /bɔkaʒ/ n.m. grove.

boc|al (pl. **~aux**) /bɔkal, -o/ n.m. jar.

bock /bɔk/ n.m. beer glass; (contenu) glass of beer.

body /bodi/ n.m. leotard.

bœuf (pl. **~s**) /bœf, bø/ n.m. ox; (viande) beef. **~s,** oxen.

bogue /bɔg/ n.m. (comput.) bug.

bohème /bɔɛm/ a. & n.m./f. unconventional.

boire† /bwar/ *v.t./i.* drink; (*absorber*) soak up. ~ **un coup**, have a drink.

bois¹ /bwa/ *voir* **boire**.

bois² /bwa/ *n.m.* (*matériau, forêt*) wood. **de ~, en ~,** wooden.

boisé /bwaze/ *a.* wooded.

bois|er /bwaze/ *v.t.* (*chambre*) panel. ~**eries** *n.f. pl.* panelling.

boisson /bwasɔ̃/ *n.f.* drink.

boit /bwa/ *voir* **boire**.

boîte /bwat/ *n.f.* box; (*de conserves*) tin, can; (*firme: fam.*) firm. ~ **à gants**, glove compartment. ~ **aux lettres**, letter-box. ~ **de nuit**, night-club. ~ **postale**, post-office box. ~ **de vitesses**, gear box.

boiter /bwate/ *v.i.* limp; (*meuble*) wobble.

boiteu|x, ~se /bwatø, -z/ *a.* lame; (*meuble*) wobbly; (*raisonnement*) shaky.

boîtier /bwatje/ *n.m.* case.

bol /bɔl/ *n.m.* bowl. **un ~ d'air**, a breath of fresh air. **avoir du ~,** (*fam.*) be lucky.

bolide /bɔlid/ *n.m.* racing car.

Bolivie /bɔlivi/ *n.f.* Bolivia.

bolivien, ~ne /bɔlivjɛ̃, -jɛn/ *a. & n.m., f.* Bolivian.

bombance /bɔ̃bɑ̃s/ *n.f.* **faire ~,** (*fam.*) revel.

bombard|er /bɔ̃barde/ *v.t.* bomb; (*par obus*) shell; (*nommer: fam.*) appoint unexpectedly (as). ~**er qn. de,** (*fig.*) bombard s.o. with. ~**ement** *n.m.* bombing; shelling. ~**ier** *n.m.* (*aviat.*) bomber.

bombe /bɔ̃b/ *n.f.* bomb; (*atomiseur*) spray, aerosol.

bombé /bɔ̃be/ *a.* rounded; (*route*) cambered.

bomber /bɔ̃be/ *v.t.* ~ **la poitrine**, throw out one's chest.

bon, bonne /bɔ̃, bɔn/ *a.* good; (*qui convient*) right; (*prudent*) wise. ~ **à/pour**, (*approprié*) fit to/for. **tenir ~,** stand firm. —*n.m.* (*billet*) voucher, coupon; (*comm.*) bond. **du ~,** some good. **pour de ~,** for good. **à quoi ~?,** what's the good *ou* point? **bonne année**, happy New Year. ~ **anniversaire**, happy birthday. ~ **appétit/voyage**, enjoy your meal/trip. **bonne chance/nuit**, good luck/night. **bonne femme**, (*péj.*) woman. **bonne-maman** (*pl.* **bonnes-mamans**) *n.f.* (*fam.*) granny. ~**-papa** (*pl.* ~**s-papas**) *n.m.* (*fam.*) grand-dad. ~ **sens**, common sense. ~ **vivant**, bon viveur. **de bonne heure**, early.

bonbon /bɔ̃bɔ̃/ *n.m.* sweet; (*Amer.*) candy. ~**nière** /-ɔnjɛr/ *n.f.* sweet box; (*Amer.*) candy box.

bonbonne /bɔ̃bɔn/ *n.f.* demijohn; (*de gaz*) canister.

bond /bɔ̃/ *n.m.* leap. **faire un ~,** leap in the air; (*de surprise*) jump.

bonde /bɔ̃d/ *n.f.* plug; (*trou*) plughole.

bondé /bɔ̃de/ *a.* packed.

bondir /bɔ̃dir/ *v.i.* leap; (*de surprise*) jump.

bonheur /bɔnœr/ *n.m.* happiness; (*chance*) (good) luck. **au petit ~,** haphazardly. **par ~,** luckily.

bonhomme¹ (*pl.* **bonshommes**) /bɔnɔm, bɔ̃zɔm/ *n.m.* fellow. ~ **de neige**, snowman.

bonhom|me² /bɔnɔm/ *a. invar.* good-hearted. ~**ie** *n.f.* good-heartedness.

bonifier (se) /(sə)bɔnifje/ *v. pr.* improve.

boniment /bɔnimɑ̃/ *n.m.* smooth talk.

bonjour /bɔ̃ʒur/ *n.m. & int.* hallo, hello, good morning *ou* afternoon.

bon marché /bɔ̃marʃe/ *a. invar.* cheap. —*adv.* cheap(ly).

bonne¹ /bɔn/ *a.f. voir* **bon**.

bonne² /bɔn/ *n.f.* (*domestique*) maid. ~ **d'enfants**, nanny.

bonnement /bɔnmɑ̃/ *adv.* **tout ~,** quite simply.

bonnet /bɔnɛ/ *n.m.* hat; (*de soutien-gorge*) cup. ~ **de bain**, swimming cap.

bonneterie /bɔnɛtri/ *n.f.* hosiery.

bonsoir /bɔ̃swar/ *n.m. & int.* good evening; (*en se couchant*) good night.

bonté /bɔ̃te/ *n.f.* kindness.

bonus /bɔnys/ *n.m.* (*auto.*) no claims bonus.

boom /bum/ *n.m.* (*comm.*) boom.

boots /buts/ *n.m. pl.* ankle boots.

bord /bɔr/ *n.m.* edge; (*rive*) bank. **à ~ (de),** on board. **au ~ de la mer**, at the seaside. **au ~ des larmes**, on the verge of tears. ~ **de la route**, roadside. ~ **du trottoir**, kerb; (*Amer.*) curb.

bordeaux /bɔrdo/ *n.m. invar.* Bordeaux (wine), claret. —*a. invar.* maroon.

bordée /bɔrde/ *n.f.* ~ **d'injures**, torrent of abuse.

bordel /bɔrdɛl/ *n.m.* brothel; (*désordre: fam.*) shambles.

border /bɔrde/ *v.t.* line, border; (*tissu*) edge; (*personne, lit*) tuck in.

bordereau (*pl.* ~**x**) /bɔrdəro/ *n.m.* (*liste*) note, slip; (*facture*) invoice.

bordure /bɔrdyr/ *n.f.* border. **en ~ de,** on the edge of.

borgne /bɔrɲ/ *a.* one-eyed; (*fig.*) shady.

borne /bɔrn/ *n.f.* boundary marker. ~ **(kilométrique)**, (*approx.*) milestone. ~**s**, limits.

borné /bɔrne/ *a.* narrow; (*personne*) narrow-minded.

borner /bɔrne/ *v.t.* confine. **se ~** *v. pr.* confine o.s. (**à**, to).

bosquet /bɔskɛ/ *n.m.* grove.

bosse /bos/ *n.f.* bump; (*de chameau*) hump. **avoir la ~ de**, (*fam.*) have a gift for. **avoir roulé sa ~**, have been around.

bosseler /bɔsle/ *v.t.* emboss; (*endommager*) dent.

bosser /bɔse/ *v.i.* (*fam.*) work (hard). —*v.t.* (*fam.*) work (hard) at.

bossu, ~e /bɔsy/ *n.m., f.* hunch-back.

botani|que /bɔtanik/ *n.f.* botany. —*a.* botanical. **~ste** *n.m./f.* botanist.

bott|e /bɔt/ *n.f.* boot; (*de fleurs, légumes*) bunch; (*de paille*) bundle, bale. **~es de caoutchouc,** wellingtons. **~ier** *n.m.* boot-maker.

botter /bɔte/ *v.t.* (*fam.*) **ça me botte,** I like the idea.

Bottin /bɔtɛ̃/ *n.m.* (P.) phone book.

bouc /buk/ *n.m.* (billy-)goat; (*barbe*) goatee. **~ émissaire,** scapegoat.

boucan /bukɑ̃/ *n.m.* (*fam.*) din.

bouche /buʃ/ *n.f.* mouth. **~ bée,** open-mouthed. **~ d'égout,** manhole. **~ d'incendie,** (fire) hydrant. **~ de métro,** entrance to the underground *ou* subway (*Amer.*). **~-à-bouche** *n.m.* mouth-to-mouth resuscitation.

bouché /buʃe/ *a.* **c'est ~,** (*profession, avenir*) it's a dead end.

bouchée /buʃe/ *n.f.* mouthful.

boucher¹ /buʃe/ *v.t.* block; (*bouteille*) cork. **se ~** *v. pr.* get blocked. **se ~ le nez,** hold one's nose.

bouch|er², ~ère /buʃe, -ɛr/ *n.m., f.* butcher. **~erie** *n.f.* butcher's (shop); (*carnage*) butchery.

bouche-trou /buʃtru/ *n.m.* stopgap.

bouchon /buʃɔ̃/ *n.m.* stopper; (*en liège*) cork; (*de bidon, tube*) cap; (*de pêcheur*) float; (*de circulation*: *fig.*) hold-up.

boucle /bukl/ *n.f.* (*de ceinture*) buckle; (*forme*) loop; (*de cheveux*) curl. **~ d'oreille,** ear-ring.

boucl|er /bukle/ *v.t.* fasten; (*terminer*) finish off; (*enfermer*: *fam.*) shut up; (*encercler*) seal off; (*budget*) balance. —*v.i.* curl. **~é a.** (*cheveux*) curly.

bouclier /buklije/ *n.m.* shield.

bouddhiste /budist/ *a. & n.m./f.* Buddhist.

boud|er /bude/ *v.i.* sulk. **~** clear of. **~erie** *n.f.* sulkiness. **~eur, ~euse** *a. & n.m., f.* sulky (person).

boudin /budɛ̃/ *n.m.* black pudding.

boudoir /budwar/ *n.m.* boudoir.

boue /bu/ *n.f.* mud.

bouée /bwe/ *n.f.* buoy. **~ de sauvetage,** lifebuoy.

boueu|x, ~se /bwø, -z/ *a.* muddy.

—*n.m.* dustman; (*Amer.*) garbage collector.

bouff|e /buf/ *n.f.* (*fam.*) food, grub. **~er** *v.t./i.* (*fam.*) eat; (*bâfrer*) gobble.

bouffée /bufe/ *n.f.* puff, whiff; (*méd.*) flush; (*d'orgueil*) fit.

bouffi /bufi/ *a.* bloated.

bouffon, ~ne /bufɔ̃, -ɔn/ *a.* farcical. —*n.m.* buffoon.

bouge /buʒ/ *n.m.* hovel; (*bar*) dive.

bougeoir /buʒwar/ *n.m.* candlestick.

bougeotte /buʒɔt/ *n.f.* **la ~,** (*fam.*) the fidgets.

bouger /buʒe/ *v.t./i.* move; (*agir*) stir. **se ~** *v. pr.* (*fam.*) move.

bougie /buʒi/ *n.f.* candle; (*auto.*) spark(ing)-plug.

bougon, ~ne /bugɔ̃, -ɔn/ *a.* grumpy. **~ner** /-ɔne/ *v.i.* grumble.

bouillabaisse /bujabɛs/ *n.f.* bouillabaisse.

bouillie /buji/ *n.f.* porridge; (*pour bébé*) baby food; (*péj.*) mush. **en ~,** crushed, mushy.

bouill|ir† /bujir/ *v.i.* boil. —*v.t.* **(faire) ~ir,** boil. **~ant, ~ante** *a.* boiling; (*très chaud*) boiling hot.

bouilloire /bujwar/ *n.f.* kettle.

bouillon /bujɔ̃/ *n.m.* (*aliment*) stock. **~ cube,** stock cube. **~ner** /-ɔne/ *v.i.* bubble.

bouillotte /bujɔt/ *n.f.* hot-water bottle.

boulang|er, ~ère /bulɑ̃ʒe, -ɛr/ *n.m., f.* baker. **~erie** *n.f.* bakery. **~erie-pâtisserie** *n.f.* baker's and confectioner's shop.

boule /bul/ *n.f.* ball; (*de machine à écrire*) golf ball. **~s,** (*jeu*) bowls. **jouer aux ~s,** play bowls. **une ~ dans la gorge,** lump in one's throat. **~ de neige,** snowball. **faire ~ de neige,** snowball.

bouleau (*pl.* **~x**) /bulo/ *n.m.* (silver) birch.

bouledogue /buldɔg/ *n.m.* bulldog.

boulet /bulɛ/ *n.m.* (*de canon*) cannon-ball; (*de forçat*: *fig.*) ball and chain.

boulette /bulɛt/ *n.f.* (*de papier*) pellet; (*aliment*) meat ball.

boulevard /bulvar/ *n.m.* boulevard.

boulevers|er /bulverse/ *v.t.* turn upside down; (*pays, plans*) disrupt; (*émouvoir*) distress, upset. **~ant, ~ante** *a.* deeply moving. **~ement** *n.m.* upheaval.

boulier /bulje/ *n.m.* abacus.

boulimie /bulimi/ *n.f.* compulsive eating; (*méd.*) bulimia.

boulon /bulɔ̃/ *n.m.* bolt.

boulot¹ /bulo/ *n.m.* (*travail*: *fam.*) work.

boulot², ~te /bulo, -ɔt/ *a.* (*rond*: *fam.*) dumpy.

boum /bum/ *n.m. & int.* bang. —*n.f.* (*réunion: fam.*) party.

bouquet /bukɛ/ *n.m.* (*de fleurs*) bunch, bouquet; (*d'arbres*) clump. **c'est le ~!**, (*fam.*) that's the last straw!

bouquin /bukɛ̃/ *n.m.* (*fam.*) book. **~er** /-ine/ *v.t./i.* (*fam.*) read. **~iste** /-inist/ *n.m./f.* second-hand bookseller.

bourbeu|x, ~se /burbø, -z/ *a.* muddy.

bourbier /burbje/ *n.m.* mire.

bourde /burd/ *n.f.* blunder.

bourdon /burdɔ̃/ *n.m.* bumble-bee.

bourdonn|er /burdɔne/ *v.i.* buzz. **~ement** *n.m.* buzzing.

bourg /bur/ *n.m.* (market) town.

bourgade /burgad/ *n.f.* village.

bourgeois, ~e /burʒwa, -z/ *a. & n.m., f.* middle-class (person); (*péj.*) bourgeois. **~ie** /-zi/ *n.f.* middle class(es).

bourgeon /burʒɔ̃/ *n.m.* bud. **~ner** /-ɔne/ *v.i.* bud.

bourgogne /burgɔɲ/ *n.m.* burgundy. —*n.f.* **la B~**, Burgundy.

bourlinguer /burlɛ̃ge/ *v.i.* (*fam.*) travel about.

bourrade /burad/ *n.f.* prod.

bourrage /buraʒ/ *n.m.* **~ de crâne**, brainwashing.

bourrasque /burask/ *n.f.* squall.

bourrati|f, ~ve /buratif, -v/ *a.* filling, stodgy.

bourreau (*pl.* **~x**) /buro/ *n.m.* executioner. **~ de travail**, workaholic.

bourrelet /burlɛ/ *n.m.* weather-strip, draught excluder; (*de chair*) roll of fat.

bourrer /bure/ *v.t.* cram (**de**, with); (*pipe*) fill. **~ de**, (*nourriture*) stuff with. **~ de coups**, thrash. **~ le crâne à qn.**, fill s.o.'s head with nonsense.

bourrique /burik/ *n.f.* ass.

bourru /bury/ *a.* surly.

bours|e /burs/ *n.f.* purse; (*subvention*) grant. **la B~e**, the Stock Exchange. **~ier, ~ière** *a.* Stock Exchange; *n.m., f.* holder of a grant.

boursoufler /bursufle/ *v.t., se ~ v. pr.* puff up, swell.

bouscul|er /buskyle/ *v.t.* (*pousser*) jostle; (*presser*) rush; (*renverser*) knock over. **~ade** *n.f.* rush; (*cohue*) crush.

bouse /buz/ *n.f.* (cow) dung.

bousiller /buzije/ *v.t.* (*fam.*) mess up.

boussole /busɔl/ *n.f.* compass.

bout /bu/ *n.m.* end; (*de langue, bâton*) tip; (*morceau*) bit. **à ~**, exhausted. **à ~ de souffle**, out of breath. **à ~ portant**, point-blank. **au ~ de**, (*après*) after. **~ filtre**, filter-tip. **venir à ~ de**, (*finir*) manage to finish.

boutade /butad/ *n.f.* jest; (*caprice*) whim.

boute-en-train /butɑ̃trɛ̃/ *n.m. invar.* joker, live wire.

bouteille /butɛj/ *n.f.* bottle.

boutique /butik/ *n.f.* shop; (*de mode*) boutique.

bouton /butɔ̃/ *n.m.* button; (*pustule*) pimple; (*pousse*) bud; (*de porte, radio, etc.*) knob. **~ de manchette**, cuff-link. **~-d'or** *n.m.* (*pl.* **~s-d'or**) buttercup. **~ner** /-ɔne/ *v.t.* button (up). **~nière** /-ɔnjɛr/ *n.f.* buttonhole. **~-pression** (*pl.* **~s-pression**) *n.m.* press-stud; (*Amer.*) snap.

boutonneu|x, ~se /butɔnø, -z/ *a.* pimply.

bouture /butyr/ *n.f.* (*plante*) cutting.

bovin, ~e /bɔvɛ̃, -in/ *a.* bovine. **~s** *n.m. pl.* cattle.

bowling /bɔliŋ/ *n.m.* bowling; (*salle*) bowling-alley.

box (*pl.* **~ ou boxes**) /bɔks/ *n.m.* lock-up garage; (*de dortoir*) cubicle; (*d'écurie*) (loose) box; (*jurid.*) dock.

box|e /bɔks/ *n.f.* boxing. **~er** *v.t./i.* box. **~eur** *n.m.* boxer.

boyau (*pl.* **~x**) /bwajo/ *n.m.* gut; (*corde*) catgut; (*galerie*) gallery; (*de bicyclette*) tyre; (*Amer.*) tire.

boycott|er /bɔjkɔte/ *v.t.* boycott. **~age** *n.m.* boycott.

BP *abrév.* (*boîte postale*) PO Box.

bracelet /braslɛ/ *n.m.* bracelet; (*de montre*) strap.

braconn|er /brakɔne/ *v.i.* poach. **~ier** *n.m.* poacher.

brad|er /brade/ *v.t.* sell off. **~erie** *n.f.* open-air sale.

braguette /bragɛt/ *n.f.* fly.

braille /braj/ *n.m. & a.* Braille.

brailler /braje/ *v.t./i.* bawl.

braire /brɛr/ *v.i.* bray.

braise /brɛz/ *n.f.* embers.

braiser /breze/ *v.t.* braise.

brancard /brɑ̃kar/ *n.m.* stretcher; (*bras*) shaft. **~ier** /-dje/ *n.m.* stretcher-bearer.

branch|e /brɑ̃ʃ/ *n.f.* branch. **~ages** *n.m. pl.* (cut) branches.

branché /brɑ̃ʃe/ *a.* (*fam.*) trendy.

branch|er /brɑ̃ʃe/ *v.t.* connect; (*électr.*) plug in. **~ement** *n.m.* connection.

branchies /brɑ̃ʃi/ *n.f. pl.* gills.

brandir /brɑ̃dir/ *v.t.* brandish.

branle /brɑ̃l/ *n.m.* **mettre en ~**, set in motion. **se mettre en ~**, get started. **~-bas (de combat)** *n.m. invar.* bustle.

branler /brɑ̃le/ *v.i.* be shaky. —*v.t.* shake.

braquer /brake/ *v.t.* aim; (*regard*) fix; (*roue*) turn; (*banque: fam.*) hold up. **~ qn. contre**, turn s.o. against. —*v.i.*

(*auto.*) turn (the wheel). —*v. pr.* **se ~**, dig one's heels in.

bras /brɑ/ *n.m.* arm. —*n.m. pl.* (*fig.*) labour, hands. **à ~-le-corps** *adv.* round the waist. **~ dessus bras dessous**, arm in arm. **~ droit**, (*fig.*) right-hand man. **en ~ de chemise**, in one's shirtsleeves.

brasier /brɑzje/ *n.m.* blaze.

brassard /brasar/ *n.m.* arm-band.

brasse /brɑs/ *n.f.* (breast-)stroke; (*mesure*) fathom.

brassée /brɑse/ *n.f.* armful.

brass|er /brase/ *v.t.* mix; (*bière*) brew; (*affaires*) handle a lot of. **~age** *n.m.* mixing; brewing. **~erie** *n.f.* brewery; (*café*) brasserie. **~eur** *n.m.* brewer. **~eur d'affaires**, big businessman.

brassière /brasjɛr/ *n.f.* (baby's) vest.

bravache /bravaʃ/ *n.m.* braggart.

bravade /bravad/ *n.f.* **par ~**, out of bravado.

brave /brav/ *a.* brave; (*bon*) good. **~ment** *adv.* bravely.

braver /brave/ *v.t.* defy.

bravo /bravo/ *int.* bravo. —*n.m.* cheer.

bravoure /bravur/ *n.f.* bravery.

break /brɛk/ *n.m.* estate car; (*Amer.*) station-wagon.

brebis /brəbi/ *n.f.* ewe. **~ galeuse**, black sheep.

brèche /brɛʃ/ *n.f.* gap, breach. **être sur la ~**, be on the go.

bredouille /brəduj/ *a.* empty-handed.

bredouiller /brəduje/ *v.t./i.* mumble.

bref, brève /brɛf, -v/ *a.* short, brief. —*adv.* in short. **en ~**, in short.

Brésil /brezil/ *n.m.* Brazil.

brésilien, ~ne /breziljɛ̃, -jɛn/ *a.* & *n.m., f.* Brazilian.

Bretagne /brətaɲ/ *n.f.* Brittany.

bretelle /brətɛl/ *n.f.* (shoulder-)strap; (*d'autoroute*) access road. **~s**, (*pour pantalon*) braces; (*Amer.*) suspenders.

breton, ~ne /brətɔ̃, -ɔn/ *a.* & *n.m., f.* Breton.

breuvage /brœvaʒ/ *n.m.* beverage.

brève /brɛv/ *voir* **bref**.

brevet /brəvɛ/ *n.m.* diploma. **~ (d'invention)**, patent.

brevet|er /brəvte/ *v.t.* patent. **~é** *a.* patented.

bribes /brib/ *n.f. pl.* scraps.

bric-à-brac /brikabrak/ *n.m. invar.* bric-à-brac.

bricole /brikɔl/ *n.f.* trifle.

bricol|er /brikɔle/ *v.i.* do odd (do-it-yourself) jobs. —*v.t.* fix (up). **~age** *n.m.* do-it-yourself (jobs). **~eur, ~euse** *n.m., f.* handyman, handywoman.

brid|e /brid/ *n.f.* bridle. **tenir en ~e**, keep in check. **~er** *v.t.* (*cheval*) bridle; (*fig.*) keep in check, bridle; (*culin.*) truss.

bridé /bride/ *a.* **yeux ~s**, slit eyes.

bridge /bridʒ/ *n.m.* (*cartes*) bridge.

brièvement /brijɛvmɑ̃/ *adv.* briefly. **~té** *n.f.* brevity.

brigad|e /brigad/ *n.f.* (*de police*) squad; (*mil.*) brigade; (*fig.*) team. **~ier** *n.m.* (*de police*) sergeant.

brigand /brigɑ̃/ *n.m.* robber. **~age** /-daʒ/ *n.m.* robbery.

briguer /brige/ *v.t.* seek (after).

brill|ant, ~ante /brijɑ̃, -t/ *a.* (*couleur*) bright; (*luisant*) shiny; (*remarquable*) brilliant. —*n.m.* (*éclat*) shine; (*diamant*) diamond. **~amment** *adv.* brilliantly.

briller /brije/ *v.i.* shine.

brim|er /brime/ *v.t.* bully, harass. **se sentir brimé**, feel put down. **~ade** *n.f.* vexation.

brin /brɛ̃/ *n.m.* (*de corde*) strand; (*de muguet*) sprig. **~ d'herbe**, blade of grass. **un ~ de**, a bit of.

brindille /brɛ̃dij/ *n.f.* twig.

bringuebaler /brɛ̃gbale/ *v.i.* (*fam.*) wobble about.

brio /brijo/ *n.m.* brilliance. **avec ~**, brilliantly.

brioche /brijɔʃ/ *n.f.* brioche (*small round sweet cake*); (*ventre: fam.*) paunch.

brique /brik/ *n.f.* brick.

briquer /brike/ *v.t.* polish.

briquet /brikɛ/ *n.m.* (cigarette-)lighter.

brisant /brizɑ̃/ *n.m.* reef.

brise /briz/ *n.f.* breeze.

bris|er /brize/ *v.t.* break. **se ~er** *v. pr.* break. **~e-lames** *n.m. invar.* breakwater. **~eur de grève** *n.m.* strikebreaker.

britannique /britanik/ *a.* British. —*n.m./f.* Briton. **les B~s**, the British.

broc /bro/ *n.m.* pitcher.

brocant|e /brɔkɑ̃t/ *n.f.* second-hand goods. **~eur, ~euse** *n.m., f.* second-hand goods dealer.

broche /brɔʃ/ *n.f.* brooch; (*culin.*) spit. **à la ~**, spit-roasted.

broché /brɔʃe/ *a.* paperback(ed).

brochet /brɔʃɛ/ *n.m.* (*poisson*) pike.

brochette /brɔʃɛt/ *n.f.* skewer.

brochure /brɔʃyr/ *n.f.* brochure, booklet.

brod|er /brɔde/ *v.t.* embroider. —*v.i.* (*fig.*) embroider the truth. **~erie** *n.f.* embroidery.

broncher /brɔ̃ʃe/ *v.i.* **sans ~**, without turning a hair.

bronch|es /brɔ̃ʃ/ *n.f. pl.* bronchial tubes. **~ite** *n.f.* bronchitis.

bronze /brɔ̃z/ *n.m.* bronze.

bronz|er /brɔ̃ze/ *v.i.*, **se ~er** *v. pr.* get a

(sun-)tan. ~age *n.m.* (sun-)tan. ~é *a.* (sun-)tanned.

brosse /brɔs/ *n.f.* brush. ~ **à dents,** toothbrush. ~ **à habits,** clothes-brush. **en** ~, (*coiffure*) in a crew cut.

brosser /brɔse/ *v.t.* brush; (*fig.*) paint. **se** ~ **les dents/les cheveux,** brush one's teeth/hair.

brouette /bruɛt/ *n.f.* wheelbarrow.

brouhaha /bruaa/ *n.m.* hubbub.

brouillard /brujar/ *n.m.* fog.

brouille /bruj/ *n.f.* quarrel.

brouill|er /bruje/ *v.t.* mix up; (*vue*) blur; (*œufs*) scramble; (*radio*) jam; (*amis*) set at odds. **se** ~**er** *v. pr.* become confused; (*ciel*) cloud over; (*amis*) fall out. ~**on**[1], *a.* untidy.

brouillon[2] /brujɔ̃/ *n.m.* (rough) draft.

broussailles /brusɑj/ *n.f. pl.* undergrowth.

brousse /brus/ *n.f.* **la** ~, the bush.

brouter /brute/ *v.t./i.* graze.

broutille /brutij/ *n.f.* trifle.

broyer /brwaje/ *v.t.* crush; (*moudre*) grind.

bru /bry/ *n.f.* daughter-in-law.

bruin|e /bruin/ *n.f.* drizzle. ~**er** *v.i.* drizzle.

bruire /bruir/ *v.i.* rustle.

bruissement /bruismã/ *n.m.* rustling.

bruit /brui/ *n.m.* noise; (*fig.*) rumour.

bruitage /bruitaʒ/ *n.m.* sound effects.

brûlant, ~**e** /brylã, -t/ *a.* burning (hot); (*sujet*) red-hot; (*ardent*) fiery.

brûlé /bryle/ *a.* (*démasqué: fam.*) blown. —*n.m.* burning. **ça sent le** ~, **I** can smell sth. burning.

brûle-pourpoint (à) /(a)brylpurpwɛ̃/ *adv.* point-blank.

brûl|er /bryle/ *v.t./i.* burn; (*essence*) use (up); (*signal*) go through *ou* past (without stopping); (*dévorer*: *fig.*) consume. **se** ~**er** *v. pr.* burn o.s. ~**eur** *n.m.* burner.

brûlure /brylyr/ *n.f.* burn. ~**s d'estomac,** heartburn.

brum|e /brym/ *n.f.* mist. ~**eux,** ~**euse** *a.* misty; (*idées*) hazy.

brun, ~**e** /brœ̃, bryn/ *a.* brown, dark. —*n.m.* brown. —*n.m., f.* dark-haired person. ~**ir** /brynir/ *v.i.* turn brown; (*se bronzer*) get a tan.

brunch /brœnʃ/ *n.m.* brunch.

brushing /brœʃiŋ/ *n.m.* blow-dry.

brusque /brysk/ *a.* (*soudain*) sudden, abrupt; (*rude*) abrupt. ~**ment** /-əmã/ *adv.* suddenly, abruptly.

brusquer /bryske/ *v.t.* rush.

brut /bryt/ *a.* (*diamant*) rough; (*soie*) raw; (*pétrole*) crude; (*comm.*) gross.

brut|al (*m. pl.* ~**aux**) /brytal, -o/ *a.* brutal. ~**aliser** *v.t.* treat roughly *ou* violently, manhandle. ~**alité** *n.f.* brutality.

brute /bryt/ *n.f.* brute.

Bruxelles /brysɛl/ *n.m./f.* Brussels.

bruy|ant, ~**ante** /bruijã, -t/ *a.* noisy. ~**amment** *adv.* noisily.

bruyère /bryjɛr/ *n.f.* heather.

bu /by/ *voir* **boire.**

bûche /byʃ/ *n.f.* log. ~ **de Noël,** Christmas log. (**se**) **ramasser une** ~, (*fam.*) come a cropper.

bûcher[1] /byʃe/ *n.m.* (*supplice*) stake.

bûch|er[2] /byʃe/ *v.t./i.* (*fam.*) slog away (at). ~**eur,** ~**euse** *n.m., f.* (*fam.*) slogger.

bûcheron /byʃrɔ̃/ *n.m.* woodcutter.

budg|et /bydʒɛ/ *n.m.* budget. ~**étaire** *a.* budgetary.

buée /bye/ *n.f.* mist, condensation.

buffet /byfɛ/ *n.m.* sideboard; (*réception*, *restaurant*) buffet.

buffle /byfl/ *n.m.* buffalo.

buis /bui/ *n.m.* (*arbre, bois*) box.

buisson /buisɔ̃/ *n.m.* bush.

buissonnière /buisɔnjɛr/ *a.f.* **faire l'école** ~, play truant.

bulbe /bylb/ *n.m.* bulb.

bulgare /bylgar/ *a. & n.m./f.* Bulgarian.

Bulgarie /bylgari/ *n.f.* Bulgaria.

bulldozer /byldozɛr/ *n.m.* bulldozer.

bulle /byl/ *n.f.* bubble.

bulletin /byltɛ̃/ *n.m.* bulletin, report; (*scol.*) report; (*billet*) ticket. ~ **d'information,** news bulletin. ~ **météorologique,** weather report. ~ (**de vote**), ballot-paper. ~ **de salaire,** pay-slip. ~**-réponse** *n.m.* (*pl.* ~**s-réponses**) reply slip.

buraliste /byralist/ *n.m./f.* tobacconist; (*à la poste*) clerk.

bureau (*pl.* ~**x**) /byro/ *n.m.* office; (*meuble*) desk; (*comité*) board. ~ **de location,** booking-office; (*théâtre*) box-office. ~ **de poste,** post office. ~ **de tabac,** tobacconist's (shop). ~ **de vote,** polling station.

bureaucrate /byrokrat/ *n.m./f.* bureaucrat.

bureaucrat|ie /byrokrasi/ *n.f.* bureaucracy. ~**ique** /-tik/ *a.* bureaucratic.

bureautique /byrotik/ *n.f.* office automation.

burette /byrɛt/ *n.f.* (*de graissage*) oilcan.

burin /byrɛ̃/ *n.m.* (cold) chisel.

burlesque /byrlɛsk/ *a.* ludicrous; (*théâtre*) burlesque.

bus /bys/ *n.m.* bus.
busqué /byske/ *a.* hooked.
buste /byst/ *n.m.* bust.
but /by(t)/ *n.m.* target; (*dessein*) aim,
goal; (*football*) goal. **avoir pour ~ de**,
aim to. **de ~ en blanc**, point-blank.
dans le ~ de, with the intention of.
butane /bytan/ *n.f.* butane, Calor gas
(P.).
buté /byte/ *a.* obstinate.
buter /byte/ *v.i.* **~ contre**, knock
against; (*problème*) come up against.
—*v.t.* antagonize. **se ~** *v. pr.*
(*s'entêter*) become obstinate.
buteur /bytœr/ *n.m.* striker.
butin /bytɛ̃/ *n.m.* booty, loot.
butiner /bytine/ *v.i.* gather nectar.
butoir /bytwar/ *n.m.* **~ (de porte)**,
doorstop.
butor /bytɔr/ *n.m.* (*péj.*) lout.
butte /byt/ *n.f.* mound. **en ~ à**, exposed
to.
buvard /byvar/ *n.m.* blotting-paper.
buvette /byvɛt/ *n.f.* (refreshment) bar.
buveu|r, **~se** /byvœr, -øz/ *n.m.*, *f.*
drinker.

C

c' /s/ *voir* **ce**[1].
ça /sa/ *pron.* it, that; (*pour désigner*) that;
(*plus près*) this. **ça va?**, (*fam.*) how's it
going? **ça va!**, (*fam.*) all right! **où ça?**,
(*fam.*) where? **quand ça?**, (*fam.*)
when? **c'est ça**, that's right.
çà /sa/ *adv.* **çà et là**, here and there.
caban|e /kaban/ *n.f.* hut; (*à outils*) shed.
~on *n.m.* hut; (*en Provence*) cottage.
cabaret /kabarɛ/ *n.m.* night-club.
cabas /kabɑ/ *n.m.* shopping bag.
cabillaud /kabijo/ *n.m.* cod.
cabine /kabin/ *n.f.* (*à la piscine*) cubicle;
(*à la plage*) (beach) hut; (*de bateau*)
cabin; (*de pilotage*) cockpit; (*de camion*)
cab; (*d'ascenseur*) cage. **~ (téléphonique)**, phone-booth, phone-box.
cabinet /kabinɛ/ *n.m.* (*de médecin*)
surgery; (*Amer.*) office; (*d'avocat*)
office; (*clientèle*) practice; (*pol.*)
Cabinet; (*pièce*) room. **~s**, (*toilettes*)
toilet. **~ de toilette**, toilet.
câble /kɑbl/ *n.m.* cable; (*corde*) rope.
câbler /kɑble/ *v.t.* cable.
cabosser /kabɔse/ *v.t.* dent.
cabot|age /kabɔtaʒ/ *n.m.* coastal naviga-
tion. **~eur** *n.m.* coaster.

cabotin, **~e** /kabɔtɛ̃, -in/ *n.m.*, *f.*
(*théâtre*) ham; (*fig.*) play-actor. **~age**
/-inaʒ/ *n.m.* ham acting; (*fig.*) play-
acting.
cabrer /kabre/ *v.t.*, **se ~** *v. pr.* (*cheval*)
rear up. **se ~ contre**, rebel against.
cabri /kabri/ *n.m.* kid.
cabriole /kabrijɔl/ *n.f.* (*culbute*) somersault. **faire des ~s**, caper about.
cacahuète /kakaɥɛt/ *n.f.* peanut.
cacao /kakao/ *n.m.* cocoa.
cachalot /kaʃalo/ *n.m.* sperm whale.
cache /kaʃ/ *n.m.* mask; (*photo.*) lens
cover.
cachemire /kaʃmir/ *n.m.* cashmere.
cach|er /kaʃe/ *v.t.* hide, conceal (**à**,
from). **se ~er** *v. pr.* hide; (*se trouver
caché*) be hidden. **~e-cache** *n.m. invar.*
hide-and-seek. **~e-nez** *n.m. invar.* scarf.
~e-pot *n.m.* cache-pot.
cachet /kaʃɛ/ *n.m.* seal; (*de la poste*)
postmark; (*comprimé*) tablet; (*d'artiste*)
fee; (*fig.*) style.
cacheter /kaʃte/ *v.t.* seal.
cachette /kaʃɛt/ *n.f.* hiding-place. **en ~**,
in secret.
cachot /kaʃo/ *n.m.* dungeon.
cachott|eries /kaʃɔtri/ *n.f. pl.* secrecy.
faire des ~eries, be secretive. **~ier**,
~ière *a.* secretive.
cacophonie /kakɔfɔni/ *n.f.* caco-
phony.
cactus /kaktys/ *n.m.* cactus.
cadavérique /kadaverik/ *a.* (*teint*)
deathly pale.
cadavre /kadavr/ *n.m.* corpse.
caddie /kadi/ *n.m.* trolley.
cadeau (*pl.* **~x**) /kado/ *n.m.* present,
gift. **faire un ~ à qn.**, give s.o. a
present.
cadenas /kadna/ *n.m.* padlock. **~ser**
/-ase/ *v.t.* padlock.
cadenc|e /kadɑ̃s/ *n.f.* rhythm, cadence;
(*de travail*) rate. **en ~e**, in time. **~é** *a.*
rhythmic(al).
cadet, **~te** /kadɛ, -t/ *a.* youngest;
(*entre deux*) younger. —*n.m.*, *f.*
youngest (child); younger (child).
cadran /kadrɑ̃/ *n.m.* dial. **~ solaire**,
sundial.
cadre /kadr/ *n.m.* frame; (*milieu*)
surroundings; (*limites*) scope; (*contexte*)
framework. —*n.m./f.* (*personne:
comm.*) executive. **les ~s**, (*comm.*) the
managerial staff.
cadrer /kadre/ *v.i.* **~ avec**, tally with.
—*v.t.* (*photo*) centre.
cadu|c, **~que** /kadyk/ *a.* obsolete.
cafard /kafar/ *n.m.* (*insecte*) cockroach.

avoir le ~, (*fam.*) be feeling low. **~er**
/-de/ *v.i.* (*fam.*) tell tales.
caf|é /kafe/ *n.m.* coffee; (*bar*) café. **~é**
au lait, white coffee. **~etière** *n.f.*
coffee-pot.
caféine /kafein/ *n.f.* caffeine.
cafouiller /kafuje/ *v.i.* (*fam.*) bumble,
flounder.
cage /kaʒ/ *n.f.* cage; (*d'escalier*) well;
(*d'ascenseur*) shaft.
cageot /kaʒo/ *n.m.* crate.
cagibi /kaʒibi/ *n.m.* storage room.
cagneu|x, **~se** /kaɲø, -z/ *a.* knock-
kneed.
cagnotte /kaɲɔt/ *n.f.* kitty.
cagoule /kagul/ *n.f.* hood.
cahier /kaje/ *n.m.* notebook; (*scol.*)
exercise-book.
cahin-caha /kaɛ̃kaa/ *adv.* aller **~,**
(*fam.*) jog along.
cahot /kao/ *n.m.* bump, jolt. **~er**
v.t./i. bump, jolt. **~eux,** **~euse** /kaotø,
-z/ *a.* bumpy.
caïd /kaid/ *n.m.* (*fam.*) big shot.
caille /kaj/ *n.f.* quail.
cailler /kaje/ *v.t./i.,* **se ~** *v. pr.* (*sang*)
clot; (*lait*) curdle.
caillot /kajo/ *n.m.* (blood) clot.
caillou (*pl.* **~x**) /kaju/ *n.m.* stone;
(*galet*) pebble. **~teux,** **~teuse** *a.*
stony. **~tis** *n.m.* gravel.
caisse /kɛs/ *n.f.* crate, case; (*tiroir,
machine*) till; (*guichet*) pay-desk;
(*bureau*) office; (*mus.*) drum. **~**
enregistreuse, cash register. **~**
d'épargne, savings bank. **~ de**
retraite, pension fund.
caiss|ier, **~ière** /kesje, -jɛr/ *n.m., f.*
cashier.
cajol|er /kaʒɔle/ *v.t.* coax. **~eries** *n.f. pl.*
coaxing.
cake /kɛk/ *n.m.* fruit-cake.
calamité /kalamite/ *n.f.* calamity.
calandre /kalɑ̃dr/ *n.f.* radiator grill.
calanque /kalɑ̃k/ *n.f.* creek.
calcaire /kalkɛr/ *a.* (*sol*) chalky; (*eau*)
hard.
calciné /kalsine/ *a.* charred.
calcium /kalsjɔm/ *n.m.* calcium.
calcul /kalkyl/ *n.m.* calculation; (*scol.*)
arithmetic; (*différentiel*) calculus. **~**
biliaire, gallstone.
calcul|er /kalkyle/ *v.t.* calculate. **~ateur**
n.m. (*ordinateur*) computer, calculator.
~atrice *n.f.* (*ordinateur*) calculator.
~ette *n.f.* (pocket) calculator.
cale /kal/ *n.f.* wedge; (*de navire*) hold. **~**
sèche, dry dock.
calé /kale/ *a.* (*fam.*) clever.

caleçon /kalsɔ̃/ *n.m.* underpants; (*de
femme*) leggings. **~ de bain,** (bathing)
trunks.
calembour /kalɑ̃bur/ *n.m.* pun.
calendrier /kalɑ̃drije/ *n.m.* calendar;
(*fig.*) timetable.
calepin /kalpɛ̃/ *n.m.* notebook.
caler /kale/ *v.t.* wedge; (*moteur*) stall.
—*v.i.* stall.
calfeutrer /kalføtre/ *v.t.* stop up the
cracks of.
calibr|e /kalibr/ *n.m.* calibre; (*d'un œuf,
fruit*) grade. **~er** *v.t.* grade.
calice /kalis/ *n.m.* (*relig.*) chalice; (*bot.*)
calyx.
califourchon (à) /(a)kalifurʃɔ̃/ *adv.*
astride. —*prép.* **à ~ sur,** astride.
câlin, ~e /kɑlɛ̃, -in/ *a.* endearing,
cuddly. **~er** /-ine/ *v.t.* cuddle.
calmant /kalmɑ̃/ *n.m.* sedative.
calm|e /kalm/ *a.* calm —*n.m.*
calm(ness). **du ~e!,** calm down! **~er**
v.t., **se ~er** *v. pr.* (*personne*) calm
(down); (*diminuer*) ease.
calomn|ie /kalɔmni/ *n.f.* slander; (*écrite*)
libel. **~ier** *v.t.* slander; libel. **~ieux,
~ieuse** *a.* slanderous; libellous.
calorie /kalɔri/ *n.f.* calorie.
calorifuge /kalɔrifyʒ/ *a.* (heat-)insulat-
ing. —*n.m.* lagging.
calot /kalo/ *n.m.* (*mil.*) forage-cap.
calotte /kalɔt/ *n.f.* (*relig.*) skullcap;
(*tape: fam.*) slap.
calqu|e /kalk/ *n.m.* tracing; (*fig.*) exact
copy. **~er** *v.t.* trace; (*fig.*) copy. **~er**
sur, model on.
calvaire /kalvɛr/ *n.m.* (*croix*) calvary;
(*fig.*) suffering.
calvitie /kalvisi/ *n.f.* baldness.
camarade /kamarad/ *n.m./f.* friend;
(*pol.*) comrade. **~ de jeu,** playmate.
~rie *n.f.* good companionship.
cambiste /kɑ̃bist/ *n.m./f.* foreign exchange dealer.
cambouis /kɑ̃bwi/ *n.m.* (engine) oil.
cambrer /kɑ̃bre/ *v.t.* arch. **se ~** *v. pr.*
arch one's back.
cambriol|er /kɑ̃brijɔle/ *v.t.* burgle.
~age *n.m.* burglary. **~eur,** **~euse**
n.m., f. burglar.
cambrure /kɑ̃bryr/ *n.f.* curve.
came /kam/ *n.f.* **arbe à ~s,** camshaft.
camée /kame/ *n.m.* cameo.
camelot /kamlo/ *n.m.* street vendor.
camelote /kamlɔt/ *n.f.* junk.
camembert /kamɑ̃bɛr/ *n.m.* Camembert
(cheese).
caméra /kamera/ *n.f.* (*cinéma,
télévision*) camera.

caméra|man (*pl.* ~**men**) /kameraman, -mɛn/ *n.m.* cameraman.

camion /kamjɔ̃/ *n.m.* lorry, truck. ~**-citerne** *n.m.* tanker. ~**nage** /-jɔnaʒ/ *n.m.* haulage. ~**nette** /-jɔnɛt/ *n.f.* van. ~**neur** /-jɔnœr/ *n.m.* lorry *ou* truck driver; (*entrepreneur*) haulage contractor.

camisole /kamizɔl/ *n.f.* ~ (**de force**), strait-jacket.

camoufl|er /kamufle/ *v.t.* camouflage. ~**age** *n.m.* camouflage.

camp /kɑ̃/ *n.m.* camp; (*sport*)side.

campagn|e /kɑ̃paɲ/ *n.f.* country(side); (*mil., pol.*) campaign. ~**ard, **~**arde** *a.* country; *n.m.*, *f.* countryman, countrywoman.

campanile /kɑ̃panil/ *n.m.* belltower.

camp|er /kɑ̃pe/ *v.i.* camp. —*v.t.* plant boldly; (*esquisser*) sketch. **se **~**er** *v. pr.* plant o.s. ~**ement** *n.m.* encampment. ~**eur, **~**euse** *n.m.*, *f.* camper.

camphre /kɑ̃fr/ *n.m.* camphor.

camping /kɑ̃piŋ/ *n.m.* camping. **faire du **~, go camping. ~**-car** *n.m.* campervan; (*Amer.*) motorhome. ~**-gaz** *n.m. invar.* (P.) camping-gaz. (**terrain de**) ~, campsite.

campus /kɑ̃pys/ *n.m.* campus.

Canada /kanada/ *n.m.* Canada.

canadien, **~ne** /kanadjɛ̃, -jɛn/ *a. & n.m.*, *f.* Canadian. —*n.f.* fur-lined jacket.

canaille /kanɑj/ *n.f.* rogue.

can|al (*pl.* ~**aux**) /kanal, -o/ *n.m.* (*artificiel*) canal; (*bras de mer*) channel; (*techn., TV*) channel. **par le **~**al de**, through.

canalisation /kanalizasjɔ̃/ *n.f.* (*tuyaux*) main(s).

canaliser /kanalize/ *v.t.* (*eau*) canalize; (*fig.*) channel.

canapé /kanape/ *n.m.* sofa.

canard /kanar/ *n.m.* duck; (*journal*: *fam.*) rag.

canari /kanari/ *n.m.* canary.

cancans /kɑ̃kɑ̃/ *n.m. pl.* malicious gossip.

canc|er /kɑ̃sɛr/ *n.m.* cancer. **le C**~**er**, Cancer. ~**éreux, **~**éreuse** *a.* cancerous. ~**érigène** *a.* carcinogenic.

cancre /kɑ̃kr/ *n.m.* dunce.

cancrelat /kɑ̃krəla/ *n.m.* cockroach.

candélabre /kɑ̃delabr/ *n.m.* candelabrum.

candeur /kɑ̃dœr/ *n.f.* naïvety.

candidat, **~e** /kɑ̃dida, -t/ *n.m.*, *f.* candidate; (*à un poste*) applicant, candidate (**à**, for). ~**ure** /-tyr/ *n.f.*

application; (*pol.*) candidacy. **poser sa **~ **pour**, apply for.

candide /kɑ̃did/ *a.* naïve.

cane /kan/ *n.f.* (female) duck. ~**ton** *n.m.* duckling.

canette /kanɛt/ *n.f.* (*de bière*) bottle.

canevas /kanva/ *n.m.* canvas; (*plan*) framework, outline.

caniche /kaniʃ/ *n.m.* poodle.

canicule /kanikyl/ *n.f.* hot summer days.

canif /kanif/ *n.m.* penknife.

canin, **~e** /kanɛ̃, -in/ *a.* canine. —*n.f.* canine (tooth).

caniveau (*pl.* ~**x**) /kanivo/ *n.m.* gutter.

cannabis /kanabis/ *n.m.* cannabis.

canne /kan/ *n.f.* (walking-)stick. ~ **à pêche**, fishing-rod. ~ **à sucre**, sugarcane.

cannelle /kanɛl/ *n.f.* cinnamon.

cannibale /kanibal/ *a. & n.m./f.* cannibal.

canoë /kanɔe/ *n.m.* canoe; (*sport*) canoeing.

canon /kanɔ̃/ *n.m.* (big) gun; (*d'une arme*) barrel; (*principe, règle*) canon. ~**nade** /-ɔnad/ *n.f.* gunfire. ~**nier** /-ɔnje/ *n.m.* gunner.

canot /kano/ *n.m.* boat. ~ **de sauvetage**, lifeboat. ~ **pneumatique**, rubber dinghy.

canot|er /kanɔte/ *v.i.* boat. ~**age** *n.m.* boating. ~**ier** *n.m.* boater.

cantate /kɑ̃tat/ *n.f.* cantata.

cantatrice /kɑ̃tatris/ *n.f.* opera singer.

cantine /kɑ̃tin/ *n.f.* canteen.

cantique /kɑ̃tik/ *n.m.* hymn.

canton /kɑ̃tɔ̃/ *n.m.* (*en France*) district; (*en Suisse*) canton.

cantonade (à la) /(ala)kɑ̃tɔnad/ *adv.* for all to hear.

cantonner /kɑ̃tɔne/ *v.t.* (*mil.*) billet. **se **~ **dans**, confine o.s. to.

cantonnier /kɑ̃tɔnje/ *n.m.* roadman, road mender.

canular /kanylar/ *n.m.* hoax.

caoutchou|c /kautʃu/ *n.m.* rubber; (*élastique*) rubber band. ~**c mousse**, foam rubber. ~**té** *a.* rubberized. ~**teux** *a.* rubbery.

cap /kap/ *n.m.* cape, headland; (*direction*) course. **doubler** *ou* **franchir le **~ **de**, go beyond (the point of). **mettre le **~ **sur**, steer a course for.

capable /kapabl/ *a.* able, capable. ~ **de qch.**, capable of sth. ~ **de faire**, able to do, capable of doing.

capacité /kapasite/ *n.f.* ability; (*contenance*) capacity.

cape /kap/ *n.f.* cape. **rire sous** ∼, laugh up one's sleeve.

capillaire /kapilɛr/ *a.* (*lotion, soins*) hair. (**vaisseau**) ∼, capillary.

capilotade (en) /(ɑ̃)kapilɔtad/ *adv.* (*fam.*) reduced to a pulp.

capitaine /kapitɛn/ *n.m.* captain.

capit|al, ∼**ale** (*m. pl.* ∼**aux**) /kapital, -o/ *a.* major, fundamental; (*peine, lettre*) capital. —*n.m.* (*pl.* ∼**aux**) (*comm.*) capital; (*fig.*) stock. ∼**aux**, (*comm.*) capital. —*n.f.* (*ville, lettre*) capital.

capitalis|te /kapitalist/ *a. & n.m./f.* capitalist. ∼**me** *n.m.* capitalism.

capiteu|x, ∼**se** /kapitø, -z/ *a.* heady.

capitonné /kapitɔne/ *a.* padded.

capitul|er /kapityle/ *v.i.* capitulate. ∼**ation** *n.f.* capitulation.

capor|al (*pl.* ∼**aux**) /kapɔral, -o/ *n.m.* corporal.

capot /kapo/ *n.m.* (*auto.*) bonnet; (*auto., Amer.*) hood.

capote /kapɔt/ *n.f.* (*auto.*) hood; (*auto., Amer.*) (*convertible*) top; (*fam.*) condom.

capoter /kapɔte/ *v.i.* overturn.

câpre /kɑpr/ *n.f.* (*culin.*) caper.

capric|e /kapris/ *n.m.* whim, caprice. ∼**ieux**, ∼**ieuse** *a.* capricious; (*appareil*) temperamental.

Capricorne /kaprikɔrn/ *n.m.* **le** ∼, Capricorn.

capsule /kapsyl/ *n.f.* capsule; (*de bouteille*) cap.

capter /kapte/ *v.t.* (*eau*) tap; (*émission*) pick up; (*fig.*) win, capture.

capti|f, ∼**ve** /kaptif, -v/ *a. & n.m., f.* captive.

captiver /kaptive/ *v.t.* captivate.

captivité /kaptivite/ *n.f.* captivity.

captur|e /kaptyr/ *n.f.* capture. ∼**er** *v.t.* capture.

capuch|e /kapyʃ/ *n.f.* hood. ∼**on** *n.m.* hood; (*de stylo*) cap.

caquet /kakɛ/ *n.m.* **rabattre le** ∼ **à qn.**, take s.o. down a peg or two.

caquet|er /kakte/ *v.i.* cackle. ∼**age** *n.m.* cackle.

car[1] /kar/ *conj.* because, for.

car[2] /kar/ *n.m.* coach; (*Amer.*) bus.

carabine /karabin/ *n.f.* rifle.

caracoler /karakɔle/ *v.i.* prance.

caract|ère /karaktɛr/ *n.m.* (*nature, lettre*) character. ∼**ères d'imprimerie**, block letters. ∼**ériel**, ∼**érielle** *a.* character; *n.m., f.* disturbed child.

caractérisé /karakterize/ *a.* well-defined.

caractériser /karakterize/ *v.t.* characterize. **se** ∼ **par**, be characterized by.

caractéristique /karakteristik/ *a. & n.f.* characteristic.

carafe /karaf/ *n.f.* carafe; (*pour le vin*) decanter.

caraïbe /karaib/ *a.* Caribbean. **les C**∼**s**, the Caribbean.

carambo1|er (se) /(sə)karɑ̃bɔle/ *v. pr.* (*voitures*) smash into each other. ∼**age** *n.m.* multiple smash-up.

caramel /karamɛl/ *n.m.* caramel. ∼**iser** *v.t./i.* caramelize.

carapace /karapas/ *n.f.* shell.

carat /kara/ *n.m.* carat.

caravane /karavan/ *n.f.* (*auto.*) caravan; (*auto., Amer.*) trailer; (*convoi*) caravan.

carbone /karbɔn/ *n.m.* carbon; (*double*) carbon (copy). (**papier**) ∼, carbon (paper).

carboniser /karbɔnize/ *v.t.* burn (to ashes).

carburant /karbyrɑ̃/ *n.m.* (motor) fuel.

carburateur /karbyratœr/ *n.m.* carburettor; (*Amer.*) carburetor.

carcan /karkɑ̃/ *n.m.* (*contrainte*) yoke.

carcasse /karkas/ *n.f.* carcass; (*d'immeuble, de voiture*) frame.

cardiaque /kardjak/ *a.* heart. —*n.m./f.* heart patient.

cardigan /kardigɑ̃/ *n.m.* cardigan.

cardin|al (*m. pl.* ∼**aux**) /kardinal, -o/ *a.* cardinal. —*n.m.* (*pl.* ∼**aux**) cardinal.

Carême /karɛm/ *n.m.* Lent.

carence /karɑ̃s/ *n.f.* inadequacy; (*manque*) deficiency.

caressant, ∼**e** /karɛsɑ̃, -t/ *a.* endearing.

caress|e /karɛs/ *n.f.* caress. ∼**er** /-ese/ *v.t.* caress, stroke; (*espoir*) cherish.

cargaison /kargɛzɔ̃/ *n.f.* cargo.

cargo /kargo/ *n.m.* cargo boat.

caricatur|e /karikatyr/ *n.f.* caricature. ∼**al** (*m. pl.* ∼**aux**) *a.* caricature-like.

car|ie /kari/ *n.f.* cavity. **la** ∼**ie** (**dentaire**), tooth decay. ∼**ié** *a.* (*dent*) decayed.

carillon /karijɔ̃/ *n.m.* chimes; (*horloge*) chiming clock. ∼**ner** /-jɔne/ *v.i.* chime, peal.

caritati|f, ∼**ve** /karitatif, -v/ *a.* **association** ∼**ve**, charity.

carlingue /karlɛ̃g/ *n.f.* (*d'avion*) cabin.

carnage /karnaʒ/ *n.m.* carnage.

carnass|ier, ∼**ière** /karnasje, -jɛr/ *a.* flesh-eating.

carnaval (*pl.* ∼**s**) /karnaval/ *n.m.* carnival.

carnet /karnɛ/ *n.m.* notebook; (*de tickets*

etc.) book. **~ de chèques,** cheque-book. **~ de notes,** school report.

carotte /karɔt/ *n.f.* carrot.

carotter /karɔte/ *v.t.* (*argot*) swindle. **~ qch. à qn.,** (*argot*) wangle sth. from s.o.

carpe /karp/ *n.f.* carp.

carpette /karpɛt/ *n.f.* rug.

carré /kare/ *a.* (*forme, mesure*) square; (*fig.*) straightforward. —*n.m.* square; (*de terrain*) patch.

carreau (*pl.* **~x**) /karo/ *n.m.* (window) pane; (*par terre, au mur*) tile; (*dessin*) check; (*cartes*) diamonds. **à ~x,** check(ed).

carrefour /karfur/ *n.m.* crossroads.

carrel|er /karle/ *v.t.* tile. **~age** *n.m.* tiling; (*sol*) tiles.

carrelet /karlɛ/ *n.m.* (*poisson*) plaice.

carrément /karemã/ *adv.* straight; (*dire*) straight out.

carrer (se) /(sə)kare/ *v. pr.* settle firmly (**dans,** in).

carrière /karjɛr/ *n.f.* career; (*terrain*) quarry.

carrossable /karɔsabl/ *a.* suitable for vehicles.

carrosse /karɔs/ *n.m.* (horse-drawn) coach.

carross|erie /karɔsri/ *n.f.* (*auto.*) body(work). **~ier** *n.m.* (*auto.*) body-builder.

carrure /karyr/ *n.f.* build; (*fig.*) calibre.

cartable /kartabl/ *n.m.* satchel.

carte /kart/ *n.f.* card; (*géog.*) map; (*naut.*) chart; (*au restaurant*) menu. **~s,** (*jeu*) cards. **à la ~,** (*manger*) à la carte. **~ blanche,** a free hand. **~ de crédit,** credit card. **~ des vins,** wine list. **~ de visite,** (business) card. **~ grise,** (car) registration card. **~ postale,** postcard.

cartel /kartɛl/ *n.m.* cartel.

cartilage /kartilaʒ/ *n.m.* cartilage.

carton /kartɔ̃/ *n.m.* cardboard; (*boîte*) (cardboard) box. **~ à dessin,** portfolio. **faire un ~,** (*fam.*) take a pot-shot. **~nage** /-ɔnaʒ/ *n.m.* cardboard packing. **~-pâte** *n.m.* pasteboard. **en ~-pâte,** cardboard.

cartonné /kartɔne/ *a.* (*livre*) hardback.

cartouch|e /kartuʃ/ *n.f.* cartridge; (*de cigarettes*) carton. **~ière** *n.f.* cartridge-belt.

cas /kɑ/ *n.m.* case. **au ~ où,** in case. **~ urgent,** emergency. **en aucun ~,** on no account. **en ~ de,** in the event of, in case of. **en tout ~,** in any case. **faire ~ de,** set great store by. **~ de conscience,** matter of conscience.

casan|ier, ~ière /kazanje, -jɛr/ *a.* home-loving.

casaque /kazak/ *n.f.* (*de jockey*) shirt.

cascade /kaskad/ *n.f.* waterfall; (*fig.*) spate.

cascad|eur, ~euse /kaskadœr, -øz/ *n.m., f.* stuntman, stuntgirl.

case /kɑz/ *n.f.* hut; (*compartiment*) pigeon-hole; (*sur papier*) square.

caser /kaze/ *v.t.* (*mettre*) put; (*loger*) put up; (*dans un travail*) find a job for; (*marier: péj.*) marry off.

caserne /kazɛrn/ *n.f.* barracks.

cash /kaʃ/ *adv.* **payer ~,** pay (in) cash.

casier /kazje/ *n.m.* pigeon-hole, compartment; (*meuble*) cabinet; (*à bouteilles*) rack. **~ judiciaire,** criminal record.

casino /kazino/ *n.m.* casino.

casqu|e /kask/ *n.m.* helmet; (*chez le coiffeur*) (hair-)drier. **~e (à écouteurs),** headphones. **~é** *a.* wearing a helmet.

casquette /kaskɛt/ *n.f.* cap.

cassant, ~e /kasã, -t/ *a.* brittle; (*brusque*) curt.

cassation /kasastjɔ̃/ *n.f.* **cour de ~,** appeal court.

casse /kɑs/ *n.f.* (*objets*) breakages. **mettre à la ~,** scrap.

cass|er /kase/ *v.t./i.* break; (*annuler*) annul. **se ~er** *v. pr.* break. **~er la tête à,** (*fam.*) give a headache to. **~e-cou** *n.m. invar.* daredevil. **~e-croûte** *n.m. invar.* snack. **~e-noisettes** *ou* **~e-noix** *n.m. invar.* nutcrackers. **~e-pieds** *n.m./f. invar.* (*fam.*) pain (in the neck). **~e-tête** *n.m. invar.* (*problème*) headache; (*jeu*) brain teaser.

casserole /kasrɔl/ *n.f.* saucepan.

cassette /kasɛt/ *n.f.* casket; (*de magnétophone*) cassette; (*de video*) video tape.

cassis[1] /kasis/ *n.m.* blackcurrant.

cassis[2] /kasi/ *n.m.* (*auto.*) dip.

cassoulet /kasulɛ/ *n.m.* stew (of beans and meat).

cassure /kasyr/ *n.f.* break.

caste /kast/ *n.f.* caste.

castor /kastɔr/ *n.m.* beaver.

castr|er /kastre/ *v.t.* castrate. **~ation** *n.f.* castration.

cataclysme /kataklism/ *n.m.* cataclysm.

catalogu|e /katalɔg/ *n.m.* catalogue. **~er** *v.t.* catalogue; (*personne: péj.*) label.

catalyseur /katalizœr/ *n.m.* catalyst.

cataphote /katafɔt/ *n.m.* reflector.

cataplasme /kataplasm/ *n.m.* poultice.

catapult|e /katapylt/ *n.f.* catapult. **~er**
v.t. catapult.
cataracte /katarakt/ *n.f.* cataract.
catastroph|e /katastrɔf/ *n.f.* disaster,
catastrophe. **~ique** *a.* catastrophic.
catch /katʃ/ *n.m.* (all-in) wrestling.
~eur, ~euse *n.m.*, *f.* (all-in) wrestler.
catéchisme /kateʃism/ *n.m.* catechism.
catégorie /kategɔri/ *n.f.* category.
catégorique /kategɔrik/ *a.* categorical.
cathédrale /katedral/ *n.f.* cathedral.
catholi|que /katɔlik/ *a.* Catholic.
~cisme *n.m.* Catholicism. **pas très
~que**, a bit fishy.
catimini (en) /(ɑ̃)katimini/ *adv.* on the
sly.
cauchemar /koʃmar/ *n.m.* nightmare.
cause /koz/ *n.f.* cause; (*jurid.*) case. **à ~
de**, because of. **en ~**, (*en jeu, concerné*)
involved. **pour ~ de**, on account
of.
caus|er /koze/ *v.t.* cause. —*v.i.* chat.
~erie *n.f.* talk. **~ette** *n.f.* **faire la
~ette**, have a chat.
caustique /kostik/ *a.* caustic.
caution /kosjɔ̃/ *n.f.* surety; (*jurid.*) bail;
(*appui*) backing; (*garantie*) deposit.
sous ~, on bail.
cautionn|er /kosjɔne/ *v.t.* guarantee;
(*soutenir*) back.
cavalcade /kavalkad/ *n.f.* (*fam.*) stampede, rush.
cavalerie /kavalri/ *n.f.* (*mil.*) cavalry;
(*au cirque*) horses.
caval|ier, ~ière /kavalje, -jɛr/ *a.*
offhand. —*n.m.*, *f.* rider; (*pour danser*)
partner. —*n.m.* (*échecs*) knight.
cave[1] /kav/ *n.f.* cellar.
cave[2] /kav/ *a.* sunken.
caveau (*pl.* **~x**) /kavo/ *n.m.* vault.
caverne /kavɛrn/ *n.f.* cave.
caviar /kavjar/ *n.m.* caviare.
cavité /kavite/ *n.f.* cavity.
CD (*abrév.*) (*compact disc*) CD.
ce[1]**, c'*** /sə, s/ *pron.* it, that. **c'est**, it *ou*
that is. **ce sont**, they are. **c'est moi**, it's
me. **c'est un chanteur/une chan-
teuse/***etc.*, he/she is a singer/*etc.* **ce qui,
ce que**, what. **ce que c'est bon/***etc.***!**,
how good/*etc.* it is! **tout ce qui, tout ce
que**, everything that.
ce[2] *ou* **cet***** /sə, sɛt, se/ *a.*
that; (*proximité*) this. **ces,** those;
(*proximité*) these.
CE *abrév.* (Communauté européenne)
EC.
ceci /səsi/ *pron.* this.
cécité /sesite/ *n.f.* blindness.
céder /sede/ *v.t.* give up. —*v.i.* (*se*

**rompre*) give way; (*se soumettre*) give
in.
cédille /sedij/ *n.f.* cedilla.
cèdre /sɛdr/ *n.m.* cedar.
CEE *abrév.* (*Communauté économique
européenne*) EEC.
ceinture /sɛ̃tyr/ *n.f.* belt; (*taille*) waist;
(*de bus, métro*) circle (line). **~ de
sauvetage**, lifebelt. **~ de sécurité**, seat-
belt.
ceinturer /sɛ̃tyre/ *v.t.* seize round the
waist; (*entourer*) surround.
cela /səla/ *pron.* it, that; (*pour désigner*)
that. **~ va de soi**, it is obvious.
célèbre /selɛbr/ *a.* famous.
célébrité /selebrite/ *n.f.* fame;
(*personne*) celebrity.
céleri /sɛlri/ *n.m.* (*en branches*) celery.
~(-rave), celeriac.
céleste /selɛst/ *a.* celestial.
célibat /seliba/ *n.m.* celibacy.
célibataire /selibatɛr/ *a.* unmarried.
—*n.m.* bachelor. —*n.f.* unmarried
woman.
celle, celles /sɛl/ *voir* **celui**.
cellier /selje/ *n.m.* store-room (*for wine*).
cellophane /selɔfan/ *n.f.* (P.) Cellophane
(P.).
cellul|e /selyl/ *n.f.* cell. **~aire** *a.* cell.
fourgon *ou* **voiture ~aire**, prison van.
celui, celle (*pl.* **ceux, celles**) /səlɥi, sɛl,
sø/ *pron.* the one. **~ de mon ami**, my
friend's. **~-ci**, this (one). **~-là**, that
(one). **ceux-ci**, these (ones). **ceux-là**,
those (ones).
cendr|e /sɑ̃dr/ *n.f.* ash. **~é** *a.* (*couleur*)
ashen. **blond ~é**, ash blond.
cendrier /sɑ̃drije/ *n.m.* ashtray.
censé /sɑ̃se/ *a.* **être ~ faire**, be supposed
to do.
censeur /sɑ̃sœr/ *n.m.* censor; (*scol.*)
assistant headmaster.
censur|e /sɑ̃syr/ *n.f.* censorship. **~er** *v.t.*
censor; (*critiquer*) censure.
cent (*pl.* **~s**) /sɑ̃/ (*generally* /sɑ̃t/ *pl.*
/sɑ̃z/ *before vowel*) *a. & n.m.* (a)
hundred. **~ un** /sɑ̃œ̃/ a hundred and
one.
centaine /sɑ̃tɛn/ *n.f.* hundred. **une ~
(de)**, (about) a hundred.
centenaire /sɑ̃tnɛr/ *n.m.* (*anniversaire*)
centenary.
centième /sɑ̃tjɛm/ *a. & n.m./f.*
hundredth.
centigrade /sɑ̃tigrad/ *a.* centigrade.
centilitre /sɑ̃tilitr/ *n.m.* centilitre.
centime /sɑ̃tim/ *n.m.* centime.

centimètre /sɑ̃timɛtr/ n.m. centimetre; (*ruban*) tape-measure.

centr|al, ∼**ale** (*m. pl.* ∼**aux**) /sɑ̃tral, -o/ a. central. —n.m. (*pl.* ∼**aux**). ∼**al (téléphonique),** (telephone) exchange. —n.f. power-station. ∼**aliser** v.t. centralize.

centr|e /sɑ̃tr/ n.m. centre. ∼**e-ville** n.m. town centre. ∼**er** v.t. centre.

centuple /sɑ̃typl/ n.m. **le** ∼ **(de),** a hundredfold. **au** ∼, a hundredfold.

cep /sɛp/ n.m. vine stock.

cépage /sepaʒ/ n.m. (variety of) vine.

cèpe /sɛp/ n.m. (edible) boletus.

cependant /səpɑ̃dɑ̃/ adv. however.

céramique /seramik/ n.f. ceramic; (*art*) ceramics.

cerceau (*pl.* ∼**x**) /sɛrso/ n.m. hoop.

cercle /sɛrkl/ n.m. circle; (*cerceau*) hoop. ∼ **vicieux,** vicious circle.

cercueil /sɛrkœj/ n.m. coffin.

céréale /sereal/ n.f. cereal.

cérébr|al (*m. pl.* ∼**aux**) /serebral, -o/ a. cerebral.

cérémonial (*pl.* ∼**s**) /seremɔnjal/ n.m. ceremonial.

cérémon|ie /seremɔni/ n.f. ceremony. ∼**ie(s),** (*façons*) fuss. ∼**ieux,** ∼**ieuse** a. ceremonious.

cerf /sɛr/ n.m. stag.

cerfeuil /sɛrfœj/ n.m. chervil.

cerf-volant (*pl.* **cerfs-volants**) /sɛrvɔlɑ̃/ n.m. kite.

ceris|e /sriz/ n.f. cherry. ∼**ier** n.m. cherry tree.

cerne /sɛrn/ n.m. ring.

cern|er /sɛrne/ v.t. surround; (*question*) define. **les yeux** ∼**és,** with rings under one's eyes.

certain, ∼**e** /sɛrtɛ̃, -ɛn/ a. certain; (*sûr*) certain, sure (**de,** of; **que,** that). —pron. ∼**s,** certain people. **d'un** ∼ **âge,** past one's prime. **un** ∼ **temps,** some time.

certainement /sɛrtɛnmɑ̃/ adv. certainly.

certes /sɛrt/ adv. indeed.

certificat /sɛrtifika/ n.m. certificate.

certif|ier /sɛrtifje/ v.t. certify. ∼**ier qch. à qn.,** assure s.o. of sth. ∼**ié** a. (*professeur*) qualified.

certitude /sɛrtityd/ n.f. certainty.

cerveau (*pl.* ∼**x**) /sɛrvo/ n.m. brain.

cervelas /sɛrvəla/ n.m. saveloy.

cervelle /sɛrvɛl/ n.f. (*anat.*) brain; (*culin.*) brains.

ces /se/ *voir* ce².

césarienne /sezarjɛn/ n.f. Caesarean (section).

cessation /sɛsasjɔ̃/ n.f. suspension.

cesse /sɛs/ n.f. **n'avoir de** ∼ **que,** have no rest until. **sans** ∼, incessantly.

cesser /sese/ v.t./i. stop. ∼ **de faire,** stop doing.

cessez-le-feu /seselfø/ n.m. invar. cease-fire.

cession /sɛsjɔ̃/ n.f. transfer.

c'est-à-dire /setadir/ conj. that is (to say).

cet, cette /sɛt/ *voir* ce².

ceux /sø/ *voir* celui.

chacal (*pl.* ∼**s**) /ʃakal/ n.m. jackal.

chacun, ∼**e** /ʃakœ̃, -yn/ pron. each (one), every one; (*tout le monde*) everyone.

chagrin /ʃagrɛ̃/ n.m. sorrow. **avoir du** ∼, be distressed. ∼**er** /-ine/ v.t. distress.

chahut /ʃay/ n.m. row, din. ∼**er** /-te/ v.i. make a row; v.t. be rowdy with. ∼**eur,** ∼**euse** /- tœr, -tøz/ n.m., f. rowdy.

chaîn|e /ʃɛn/ n.f. chain; (*de télévision*) channel. ∼**e de montagnes,** mountain range. ∼**e de montage/fabrication,** assembly/production line. ∼**e hi-fi,** hi-fi system. **en** ∼**e,** (*accidents*) multiple. ∼**ette** n.f. (small) chain. ∼**on** n.m. link.

chair /ʃɛr/ n.f. flesh. **bien en** ∼, plump. **en** ∼ **et en os,** in the flesh. ∼ **à saucisses,** sausage meat. **la** ∼ **de poule,** goose-flesh. —a. invar. (**couleur**) ∼, flesh-coloured.

chaire /ʃɛr/ n.f. (*d'église*) pulpit; (*univ.*) chair.

chaise /ʃɛz/ n.f. chair. ∼ **longue,** deck-chair.

chaland /ʃalɑ̃/ n.m. barge.

châle /ʃal/ n.m. shawl.

chalet /ʃalɛ/ n.m. chalet.

chaleur /ʃalœr/ n.f. heat; (*moins intense*) warmth; (*d'un accueil, d'une couleur*) warmth. ∼**eux,** ∼**euse** a. warm.

challenge /ʃalɑ̃ʒ/ n.m. contest.

chaloupe /ʃalup/ n.f. launch, boat.

chalumeau (*pl.* ∼**x**) /ʃalymo/ n.m. blowlamp; (*Amer.*) blowtorch.

chalut /ʃaly/ n.m. trawl-net ∼**ier** /-tje/ n.m. trawler.

chamailler (se) /(sə)ʃamaje/ v. pr. squabble.

chambarder /ʃɑ̃barde/ v.t. (*fam.*) turn upside down.

chambre /ʃɑ̃br/ n.f. (bed)room; (*pol., jurid.*) chamber. **faire** ∼ **à part,** sleep in different rooms. ∼ **à air,** inner tube. ∼ **d'amis,** spare *ou* guest room. ∼ **à coucher,** bedroom. ∼ **à un lit/deux lits,** single/double room. ∼ **forte,** strong-room.

chambrer /ʃɑ̃bre/ v.t. (vin) bring to room temperature.

chameau (pl. ~x) /ʃamo/ n.m. camel.

chamois /ʃamwa/ n.m. chamois. **peau de** ~, chamois leather.

champ /ʃɑ̃/ n.m. field. ~ **de bataille,** battlefield. ~ **de courses,** racecourse.

champagne /ʃɑ̃paɲ/ n.m. champagne.

champêtre /ʃɑ̃pɛtr/ a. rural.

champignon /ʃɑ̃piɲɔ̃/ n.m. mushroom; (moisissure) fungus. ~ **de Paris,** button mushroom.

champion, ~ne /ʃɑ̃pjɔ̃, -jɔn/ n.m., f. champion. **~nat** /-jɔna/ n.m. championship.

chance /ʃɑ̃s/ n.f. (good) luck; (possibilité) chance. **avoir de la** ~, be lucky. **quelle** ~!, what luck!

chanceler /ʃɑ̃sle/ v.i. stagger; (fig.) falter.

chancelier /ʃɑ̃səlje/ n.m. chancellor.

chanceu|x, ~se /ʃɑ̃sø, -z/ a. lucky.

chancre /ʃɑ̃kr/ n.m. canker.

chandail /ʃɑ̃daj/ n.m. sweater.

chandelier /ʃɑ̃dəlje/ n.m. candlestick.

chandelle /ʃɑ̃dɛl/ n.f. candle. **dîner aux** ~s, candlelight dinner.

change /ʃɑ̃ʒ/ n.m. (foreign) exchange.

changeant, ~e /ʃɑ̃ʒɑ̃, -t/ a. changeable.

changement /ʃɑ̃ʒmɑ̃/ n.m. change. ~ **de vitesses** (dispositif) gears.

changer /ʃɑ̃ʒe/ v.t./i. change. **se** ~ v. pr. change (one's clothes). ~ **de nom/voiture,** change one's name/car. ~ **de place/train,** change places/trains. ~ **de direction,** change direction. ~ **d'avis** ou **d'idée,** change one's mind. ~ **de vitesses,** change gear.

changeur /ʃɑ̃ʒœr/ n.m. ~ **automatique,** (money) change machine.

chanoine /ʃanwan/ n.m. canon.

chanson /ʃɑ̃sɔ̃/ n.f. song.

chant /ʃɑ̃/ n.m. singing; (chanson) song; (religieux) hymn.

chantage /ʃɑ̃taʒ/ n.m. blackmail. ~ **psychologique,** emotional blackmail.

chant|er /ʃɑ̃te/ v.t./i. sing. **si cela vous** ~**e,** (fam.) if you feel like it. **faire** ~, (délit) blackmail. **~eur, ~euse** n.m., f. singer.

chantier /ʃɑ̃tje/ n.m. building site. ~ **naval,** shipyard. **mettre en** ~, get under way, start.

chantonner /ʃɑ̃tɔne/ v.t./i. hum.

chanvre /ʃɑ̃vr/ n.m. hemp.

chao|s /kao/ n.m. chaos. **~tique** /kaɔtik/ a. chaotic.

chaparder /ʃaparde/ v.t. (fam.) filch.

chapeau (pl. ~x) /ʃapo/ n.m. hat. ~!, well done!

chapelet /ʃaplɛ/ n.m. rosary; (fig.) string.

chapelle /ʃapɛl/ n.f. chapel. ~ **ardente,** chapel of rest.

chapelure /ʃaplyr/ n.f. breadcrumbs.

chaperon /ʃaprɔ̃/ n.m. chaperon. **~ner** /-ɔne/ v.t. chaperon.

chapiteau (pl. ~x) /ʃapito/ n.m. (de cirque) big top; (de colonne) capital.

chapitre /ʃapitr/ n.m. chapter; (fig.) subject.

chapitrer /ʃapitre/ v.t. reprimand.

chaque /ʃak/ a. every, each.

char /ʃar/ n.m. (mil.) tank; (de carnaval) float; (charrette) cart; (dans l'antiquité) chariot.

charabia /ʃarabja/ n.m. (fam.) gibberish.

charade /ʃarad/ n.f. riddle.

charbon /ʃarbɔ̃/ n.m. coal. ~ **de bois,** charcoal. **~nages** /-ɔnaʒ/ n.m. pl. coalmines.

charcut|erie /ʃarkytri/ n.f. porkbutcher's shop; (aliments) (cooked) pork meats. **~ier, ~ière** n.m., f. porkbutcher.

chardon /ʃardɔ̃/ n.m. thistle.

charge /ʃarʒ/ n.f. load, burden; (mil., électr., jurid.) charge; (mission) responsibility. **~s,** expenses; (de locataire) service charges. **être à la** ~ **de,** be the responsibility of. **~s sociales,** social security contributions. **prendre en** ~, take charge of; (transporter) give a ride to.

chargé /ʃarʒe/ a. (journée) busy; (langue) coated. —n.m., f. ~ **de mission.** head of mission. ~ **d'affaires,** chargé d'affaires. ~ **de cours,** lecturer.

charger /ʃarʒe/ v.t. load; (attaquer) charge; (batterie) charge. —v.i. (attaquer) charge. **se** ~ **de,** take charge ou care of. ~ **qn. de,** weigh. s.o. down with; (tâche) entrust s.o. with. ~ **qn. de faire,** instruct s.o. to do. **chargement** /-əmɑ̃/ n.m. loading; (objets) load.

chariot /ʃarjo/ n.m. (à roulettes) trolley; (charrette) cart.

charitable /ʃaritabl/ a. charitable.

charité /ʃarite/ n.f. charity. **faire la** ~, give to charity. **faire la** ~ **à,** give to.

charlatan /ʃarlatɑ̃/ n.m. charlatan.

charmant, ~e /ʃarmɑ̃, -t/ a. charming.

charm|e /ʃarm/ n.m. charm. **~er** v.t. charm. **~eur, ~euse** n.m., f. charmer.

charnel, ~le /ʃarnɛl/ a. carnal.

charnier /ʃarnje/ n.m. mass grave.

charnière /ʃarnjɛr/ n.f. hinge. **à la ~ de,** at the meeting point between.

charnu /ʃarny/ a. fleshy.

charpent|e /ʃarpɑ̃t/ n.f. framework; (*carrure*) build. **~é** a. built.

charpentier /ʃarpɑ̃tje/ n.m. carpenter.

charpie (en) /(ɑ̃)ʃarpi/ adv. in(to) shreds.

charretier /ʃartje/ n.m. carter.

charrette /ʃarɛt/ n.f. cart.

charrier /ʃarje/ v.t. carry.

charrue /ʃary/ n.f. plough.

charte /ʃart/ n.f. charter.

charter /ʃartɛr/ n.m. charter flight.

chasse /ʃas/ n.f. hunting; (*au fusil*) shooting; (*poursuite*) chase; (*recherche*) hunt. **~ (d'eau),** (toilet) flush. **~ sous-marine,** underwater fishing.

châsse /ʃas/ n.f. shrine, reliquary.

chass|er /ʃase/ v.t./i. hunt; (*faire partir*) chase away; (*odeur, employé*) get rid of. **~e-neige** n.m. invar. snow-plough. **~eur, ~euse** n.m., f. hunter; n.m. page-boy; (*avion*) fighter.

châssis /ʃasi/ n.m. frame; (*auto.*) chassis.

chaste /ʃast/ a. chaste. **~té** /-əte/ n.f. chastity.

chat, ~te /ʃa, ʃat/ n.m., f. cat.

châtaigne /ʃatɛɲ/ n.f. chestnut.

châtaignier /ʃatɛɲe/ n.m. chestnut tree.

châtain /ʃatɛ̃/ a. invar. chestnut (brown).

château (pl. **~x**) /ʃato/ n.m. castle; (*manoir*) manor. **~ d'eau,** water-tower. **~ fort,** fortified castle.

châtelain, ~e /ʃatlɛ̃, -ɛn/ n.m., f. lord of the manor, lady of the manor.

châtier /ʃatje/ v.t. chastise; (*style*) refine.

châtiment /ʃatimɑ̃/ n.m. punishment.

chaton /ʃatɔ̃/ n.m. (*chat*) kitten.

chatouill|er /ʃatuje/ v.t. tickle. **~ement** n.m. tickling.

chatouilleu|x, ~se /ʃatujø, -z/ a. ticklish; (*susceptible*) touchy.

chatoyer /ʃatwaje/ v.i. glitter.

châtrer /ʃatre/ v.t. castrate.

chatte /ʃat/ voir **chat.**

chaud, ~e /ʃo, ʃod/ a. warm; (*brûlant*) hot; (*vif: fig.*) warm. —n.m. heat. **au ~,** in the warm(th). **avoir ~,** be warm; be hot. **il fait ~,** it is warm; it is hot. **pour te tenir ~,** to keep you warm. **~ement** /-dmɑ̃/ adv. warmly; (*disputé*) hotly.

chaudière /ʃodjɛr/ n.f. boiler.

chaudron /ʃodrɔ̃/ n.m. cauldron.

chauffage /ʃofaʒ/ n.m. heating. **~ central,** central heating.

chauffard /ʃofar/ n.m. (*péj.*) reckless driver.

chauff|er /ʃofe/ v.t./i. heat (up). **se ~er**

v. pr. warm o.s. (up). **~e-eau** n.m. invar. water-heater.

chauffeur /ʃofœr/ n.m. driver; (*aux gages de qn.*) chauffeur.

chaum|e /ʃom/ n.m. (*de toit*) thatch.

chaussée /ʃose/ n.f. road(way).

chauss|er /ʃose/ v.t. (*chaussures*) put on; (*enfant*) put shoes on (to). **se ~er** v. pr. put one's shoes on. **~er bien,** (*aller*) fit well. **~er du 35/etc.,** take a size 35/etc. shoe. **~e-pied** n.m. shoehorn. **~eur** n.m. shoemaker.

chaussette /ʃosɛt/ n.f. sock.

chausson /ʃosɔ̃/ n.m. slipper; (*de bébé*) bootee. **~ (aux pommes),** (apple) turnover.

chaussure /ʃosyr/ n.f. shoe. **~s de ski,** ski boots. **~s de marche,** hiking boots.

chauve /ʃov/ a. bald.

chauve-souris (pl. **chauves-souris**) /ʃovsuri/ n.f. bat.

chauvin, ~e /ʃovɛ̃, -in/ a. chauvinistic. —n.m., f. chauvinist. **~isme** /-inism/ n.m. chauvinism.

chaux /ʃo/ n.f. lime.

chavirer /ʃavire/ v.t./i. (*bateau*) capsize.

chef /ʃɛf/ n.m. leader, head; (*culin.*) chef; (*de tribu*) chief. **~ d'accusation,** (*jurid.*) charge. **~ d'équipe,** foreman; (*sport*) captain. **~ d'État,** head of State. **~ de famille,** head of the family. **~ de file,** (*pol.*) leader. **~ de gare,** station-master. **~ d'orchestre,** conductor. **~ de service,** department head. **~-lieu** (pl. **~s-lieux**) n.m. county town.

chef-d'œuvre (pl. **chefs-d'œuvre**) /ʃɛdœvr/ n.m. masterpiece.

cheik /ʃɛk/ n.m. sheikh.

chemin /ʃmɛ̃/ n.m. path, road; (*direction, trajet*) way. **beaucoup de ~ à faire,** a long way to go. **~ de fer,** railway. **en ou par ~ de fer,** by rail. **~ de halage,** towpath. **~ vicinal,** by-road. **se mettre en ~,** start out.

cheminée /ʃmine/ n.f. chimney; (*intérieure*) fireplace; (*encadrement*) mantelpiece; (*de bateau*) funnel.

chemin|er /ʃmine/ v.i. plod; (*fig.*) progress. **~ement** n.m. progress.

cheminot /ʃmino/ n.m. railwayman; (*Amer.*) railroad man.

chemis|e /ʃmiz/ n.f. shirt; (*dossier*) folder; (*de livre*) jacket. **~e de nuit,** night-dress. **~ette** n.f. short-sleeved shirt.

chemisier /ʃmizje/ n.m. blouse.

chen|al (pl. **~aux**) /ʃənal, -o/ n.m. channel.

chêne /ʃɛn/ n.m. oak.

chenil /ʃni(l)/ *n.m.* kennels.

chenille /ʃnij/ *n.f.* caterpillar.

chenillette /ʃnijɛt/ *n.f.* tracked vehicle.

cheptel /ʃɛptɛl/ *n.m.* livestock.

chèque /ʃɛk/ *n.m.* cheque. ~ **de voyage,** traveller's cheque.

chéquier /ʃekje/ *n.m.* cheque-book.

cher, chère /ʃɛr/ *a.* (*coûteux*) dear, expensive; (*aimé*) dear. —*adv.* (*coûter, payer*) a lot (of money). —*n.m., f.* **mon ~, ma chère,** my dear.

chercher /ʃɛrʃe/ *v.t.* look for; (*aide, paix, gloire*) seek. **aller ~,** go and get *ou* fetch, go for. ~ **à faire,** attempt to do. ~ **la petite bête,** be finicky.

chercheu|r, ~**se** /ʃɛrʃœr, -øz/ *n.m., f.* research worker.

chèrement /ʃɛrmã/ *adv.* dearly.

chéri, ~**e** /ʃeri/ *a.* beloved. —*n.m., f.* darling.

chérir /ʃerir/ *v.t.* cherish.

cherté /ʃɛrte/ *n.f.* high cost.

chéti|f, ~**ve** /ʃetif, -v/ *a.* puny.

chev|al (*pl.* ~**aux**) /ʃval, -o/ *n.m.* horse. ~**al (vapeur),** horsepower. **à ~al,** on horseback. **à ~al sur,** straddling. **faire du ~al,** ride (a horse). ~**al-d'arçons** *n.m. invar.* (*gymnastique*) horse.

chevaleresque /ʃvalrɛsk/ *a.* chivalrous.

chevalerie /ʃvalri/ *n.f.* chivalry.

chevalet /ʃvalɛ/ *n.m.* easel.

chevalier /ʃvalje/ *n.m.* knight.

chevalière /ʃvaljɛr/ *n.f.* signet ring.

chevalin, ~**e** /ʃvalɛ̃, -in/ *a.* (*boucherie*) horse; (*espèce*) equine.

chevauchée /ʃvoʃe/ *n.f.* (horse-)ride.

chevaucher /ʃvoʃe/ *v.t.* straddle. —*v.i.,* **se ~** *v. pr.* overlap.

chevelu /ʃəvly/ *a.* hairy.

chevelure /ʃəvlyr/ *n.f.* hair.

chevet /ʃvɛ/ *n.m.* **au ~ de,** at the bedside of.

cheveu (*pl.* ~**x**) /ʃvø/ *n.m.* (*poil*) hair. ~**x,** (*chevelure*) hair. **avoir les ~x longs,** have long hair.

cheville /ʃvij/ *n.f.* ankle; (*fiche*) peg, pin; (*pour mur*) (wall) plug.

chèvre /ʃɛvr/ *n.f.* goat.

chevreau (*pl.* ~**x**) /ʃəvro/ *n.m.* kid.

chevreuil /ʃəvrœj/ *n.m.* roe(-deer); (*culin.*) venison.

chevron /ʃəvrɔ̃/ *n.m.* (*poutre*) rafter. **à ~s,** herring-bone.

chevronné /ʃəvrɔne/ *a.* experienced, seasoned.

chevrotant, ~**e** /ʃəvrɔtã, -t/ *a.* quavering.

chewing-gum /ʃwiŋɡɔm/ *n.m.* chewing-gum.

chez /ʃe/ *prép.* at *ou* to the house of; (*parmi*) among; (*dans le caractère ou l'œuvre de*) in. ~ **le boucher**/*etc.*, at the butcher's/*etc.* ~ **soi,** at home; (*avec direction*) home. ~**-soi** *n.m. invar.* home.

chic /ʃik/ *a. invar.* smart; (*gentil*) kind. **sois ~,** do me a favour. —*n.m.* style. **avoir le ~ pour,** have the knack of. ~ **(alors)!,** great!

chicane /ʃikan/ *n.f.* zigzag. **chercher ~ à qn,** needle s.o.

chiche /ʃiʃ/ *a.* mean (**de,** with). ~ **(que je le fais)!,** (*fam.*) I bet you I will, can, *etc.*

chichis /ʃiʃi/ *n.m. pl.* (*fam.*) fuss.

chicorée /ʃikɔre/ *n.f.* (*frisée*) endive; (*à café*) chicory.

chien, ~**ne** /ʃjɛ̃, ʃjɛn/ *n.m.* dog. —*n.f.* dog, bitch. ~ **de garde,** watch-dog. ~**-loup** *n.m.* (*pl.* ~**s-loups**) wolfhound.

chiffon /ʃifɔ̃/ *n.m.* rag.

chiffonner /ʃifɔne/ *v.t.* crumple; (*préoccuper: fam.*) bother.

chiffonnier /ʃifɔnje/ *n.m.* rag-and-bone man.

chiffre /ʃifr/ *n.m.* figure; (*code*) code. ~**s arabes/romains,** Arabic/Roman numerals. ~ **d'affaires,** turnover.

chiffrer /ʃifre/ *v.t.* set a figure to, assess; (*texte*) encode. **se ~ à,** amount to.

chignon /ʃiɲɔ̃/ *n.m.* bun, chignon.

Chili /ʃili/ *n.m.* Chile.

chilien, ~**ne** /ʃiljɛ̃, -jɛn/ *a. & n.m., f.* Chilean.

chim|ère /ʃimɛr/ *n.f.* fantasy. ~**érique** *a.* fanciful.

chim|ie /ʃimi/ *n.f.* chemistry. ~**ique** *a.* chemical. ~**iste** *n.m./f.* chemist.

chimpanzé /ʃɛ̃pɑ̃ze/ *n.m.* chimpanzee.

Chine /ʃin/ *n.f.* China.

chinois, ~**e** /ʃinwa, -z/ *a. & n.m., f.* Chinese. —*n.m.* (*lang.*) Chinese.

chiot /ʃjo/ *n.m.* pup(py).

chiper /ʃipe/ *v.t.* (*fam.*) swipe.

chipoter /ʃipɔte/ *v.i.* (*manger*) nibble; (*discuter*) quibble.

chips /ʃips/ *n.m. pl.* crisps; (*Amer.*) chips.

chiquenaude /ʃiknod/ *n.f.* flick.

chiromanc|ie /kirɔmɑ̃si/ *n.f.* palmistry. ~**ien,** ~**ienne** *n.m., f.* palmist.

chirurgic|al (*m. pl.* ~**aux**) /ʃiryrʒikal, -o/ *a.* surgical.

chirurg|ie /ʃiryrʒi/ *n.f.* surgery. ~**ie esthétique,** plastic surgery. ~**ien** *n.m.* surgeon.

chlore /klɔr/ *n.m.* chlorine.

choc /ʃɔk/ *n.m.* (*heurt*) impact, shock; (*émotion*) shock; (*collision*) crash; (*affrontement*) clash; (*méd.*) shock.

chocolat /ʃɔkɔla/ *n.m.* chocolate; (*à boire*) drinking chocolate. ~ **au lait,** milk chocolate. ~**chaud,** hot chocolat.

chœur /kœr/ *n.m.* (*antique*) chorus; (*chanteurs, nef*) choir. **en ~,** in chorus.

chois|ir /ʃwazir/ *v.t.* choose, select. ~**i** *a.* carefully chosen; (*passage*) selected.

choix /ʃwa/ *n.m.* choice, selection. **au ~,** according to preference. **de ~,** choice. **de premier ~,** top quality.

choléra /kɔlera/ *n.m.* cholera.

chômage /ʃomaʒ/ *n.m.* unemployment. **en ~,** unemployed. **mettre en ~ technique,** lay off.

chôm|er /ʃome/ *v.i.* be unemployed; (*usine*) lie idle. ~**eur,** ~**euse** *n.m., f.,* unemployed person. **les ~eurs,** the unemployed.

chope /ʃɔp/ *n.f.* tankard.

choper /ʃɔpe/ *v.t.* (*fam.*) catch.

choquer /ʃɔke/ *v.t.* shock; (*commotionner*) shake.

choral, ~e (*m. pl.* ~**s**) /kɔral/ *a.* choral. —*n.f.* choir, choral society.

chorégraph|ie /kɔregrafi/ *n.f.* choreography. ~**e** *n.m./f.* choreographer.

choriste /kɔrist/ *n.m./f.* (*à l'église*) chorister; (*opéra, etc.*) member of the chorus *ou* choir.

chose /ʃoz/ *n.f.* thing. **(très) peu de ~,** nothing much.

chou (*pl.* ~**x**) /ʃu/ *n.m.* cabbage. ~ **(à la crème),** cream puff. ~**x de Bruxelles,** Brussels sprouts. **mon petit ~,** (*fam.*) my little dear.

choucas /ʃuka/ *n.m.* jackdaw.

chouchou, ~te /ʃuʃu, ‑t/ *n.m., f.* pet, darling. **le ~ du prof.,** the teacher's pet.

choucroute /ʃukrut/ *n.f.* sauerkraut.

chouette[1] /ʃwɛt/ *n.f.* owl.

chouette[2] /ʃwɛt/ *a.* (*fam.*) super.

chou-fleur (*pl.* **choux-fleurs**) /ʃuflœr/ *n.m.* cauliflower.

choyer /ʃwaje/ *v.t.* pamper.

chrétien, ~ne /kretjɛ̃, ‑jɛn/ *a. & n.m., f.* Christian.

Christ /krist/ *n.m.* **le ~,** Christ.

christianisme /kristjanism/ *n.m.* Christianity.

chrom|e /krom/ *n.m.* chromium, chrome. ~**é** *a.* chromium-plated.

chromosome /krɔmozom/ *n.m.* chromosome.

chronique|le /krɔnik/ *a.* chronic. —*n.f.* (*rubrique*) column; (*nouvelles*) news;

(*annales*) chronicle. ~**eur** *n.m.* columnist; (*historien*) chronicler.

chronolog|ie /krɔnɔlɔʒi/ *n.f.* chronology. ~**ique** *a.* chronological.

chronom|ètre /krɔnɔmɛtr/ *n.m.* stopwatch. ~**étrer** *v.t.* time.

chrysanthème /krizɑ̃tɛm/ *n.m.* chrysanthemum.

chuchot|er /ʃyʃɔte/ *v.t./i.* whisper. ~**ement** *n.m.* whisper(ing).

chuinter /ʃwɛ̃te/ *v.i.* hiss.

chut /ʃyt/ *int.* shush.

chute /ʃyt/ *n.f.* fall; (*déchet*) scrap. ~ **(d'eau),** waterfall. ~ **du jour,** nightfall. ~ **de pluie,** rainfall. **la ~ des cheveux,** hair loss.

chuter /ʃyte/ *v.i.* fall.

Chypre /ʃipr/ *n.f.* Cyprus.

-ci /si/ *adv.* (*après un nom précédé de ce, cette, etc.*) **cet homme-ci,** this man. **ces maisons-ci,** these houses.

ci- /si/ *adv.* here. **ci-après,** hereafter. **ci-contre,** opposite. **ci- dessous,** below. **ci-dessus,** above. **ci-gît,** here lies. **ci-inclus, ci-incluse, ci-joint, ci-jointe,** enclosed.

cible /sibl/ *n.f.* target.

ciboul|e /sibul/ *n.f.,* ~**ette** *n.f.* chive(s).

cicatrice /sikatris/ *n.f.* scar.

cicatriser /sikatrize/ *v.t.,* **se ~** *v. pr.* heal (up).

cidre /sidr/ *n.m.* cider.

ciel (*pl.* **cieux, ciels**) /sjɛl, sjø/ *n.m.* sky; (*relig.*) heaven. **cieux,** (*relig.*) heaven.

cierge /sjɛrʒ/ *n.m.* candle.

cigale /sigal/ *n.f.* cicada.

cigare /sigar/ *n.m.* cigar.

cigarette /sigarɛt/ *n.f.* cigarette.

cigogne /sigɔɲ/ *n.f.* stork.

cil /sil/ *n.m.* (eye)lash.

ciller /sije/ *v.i.* blink.

cime /sim/ *n.f.* peak, tip.

ciment /simɑ̃/ *n.m.* cement. ~**er** ‑ te/ *v.t.* cement.

cimetière /simtjɛr/ *n.m.* cemetery. ~ **de voitures,** breaker's yard.

cinéaste /sineast/ *n.m./f.* film-maker.

ciné-club /sineklœb/ *n.m.* film society.

cinéma /sinema/ *n.m.* cinema. ~**tographique** *a.* cinema.

cinémathèque /sinematɛk/ *n.f.* film library; (*salle*) film theatre.

cinéphile /sinefil/ *n.m./f.* film lover.

cinétique /sinetik/ *a.* kinetic.

cinglant, ~e /sɛ̃glɑ̃, ‑t/ *a.* biting.

cinglé /sɛ̃gle/ *a.* (*fam.*) crazy.

cingler /sɛ̃gle/ *v.t.* lash.

cinq /sɛ̃k/ *a. & n.m.* five. ~**ième** *a. & n.m./f.* fifth.

cinquantaine /sɛ̃kɑ̃tɛn/ *n.f.* une ~ (de), about fifty.

cinquant|e /sɛ̃kɑ̃t/ *a. & n.m.* fifty. ~**ième** *a. & n.m./f.* fiftieth.

cintre /sɛ̃tr/ *n.m.* coat-hanger; (*archit.*) curve.

cintré /sɛ̃tre/ *a.* (*chemise*) fitted.

cirage /siraʒ/ *n.m.* (wax) polish.

circoncision /sirkɔ̃sizjɔ̃/ *n.f.* circumcision.

circonférence /sirkɔ̃ferɑ̃s/ *n.f.* circumference.

circonflexe /sirkɔ̃flɛks/ *a.* circumflex.

circonscription /sirkɔ̃skripsjɔ̃/ *n.f.* district. ~ (**électorale**), constituency.

circonscrire /sirkɔ̃skrir/ *v.t.* confine; (*sujet*) define.

circonspect /sirkɔ̃spɛkt/ *a.* circumspect.

circonstance /sirkɔ̃stɑ̃s/ *n.f.* circumstance; (*occasion*) occasion. ~**s atténuantes**, mitigating circumstances.

circonstancié /sirkɔ̃stɑ̃sje/ *a.* detailed.

circonvenir /sirkɔ̃vnir/ *v.t.* circumvent.

circuit /sirkɥi/ *n.m.* circuit; (*trajet*) tour, trip.

circulaire /sirkylɛr/ *a. & n.f.* circular.

circul|er /sirkyle/ *v.i.* circulate; (*train, automobile, etc.*) travel; (*piéton*) walk. **faire** ~**er**, (*badauds*) move on. ~**ation** *n.f.* circulation; (*de véhicules*) traffic.

cire /sir/ *n.f.* wax.

ciré /sire/ *n.m.* oilskin; waterproof.

cir|er /sire/ *v.t.* polish, wax. ~**euse** *n.f.* (*appareil*) floor-polisher.

cirque /sirk/ *n.m.* circus; (*arène*) amphitheatre; (*désordre: fig.*) chaos.

cirrhose /siroz/ *n.f.* cirrhosis.

cisaille(s) /sizaj/ *n.f.* (*pl.*) shears.

ciseau (*pl.* ~**x**) /sizo/ *n.m.* chisel. ~**x**, scissors.

ciseler /sizle/ *v.t.* chisel.

citadelle /sitadɛl/ *n.f.* citadel.

citadin, ~**e** /sitadɛ̃, -in/ *n.m., f.* city dweller. —*a.* city.

cité /site/ *n.f.* city. ~ **ouvrière,** (workers') housing estate. ~ **universitaire,** (university) halls of residence. ~**-dortoir** *n.f.* (*pl.* ~**s-dortoirs**) dormitory town.

cit|er /site/ *v.t.* quote, cite; (*jurid.*) summon. ~**ation** *n.f.* quotation; (*jurid.*) summons.

citerne /sitɛrn/ *n.f.* tank.

cithare /sitar/ *n.f.* zither.

citoyen, ~**ne** /sitwajɛ̃, -jɛn/ *n.m., f.* citizen. ~**neté** /-jɛnte/ *n.f.* citizenship.

citron /sitrɔ̃/ *n.m.* lemon. ~ **vert,** lime. ~**nade** /-ɔnad/ *n.f.* lemon squash *ou* drink, (still) lemonade.

citrouille /sitruj/ *n.f.* pumpkin.

civet /sivɛ/ *n.m.* stew. ~ **de lièvre/lapin,** jugged hare/rabbit.

civette /sivɛt/ *n.f.* (*culin.*) chive(s).

civière /sivjɛr/ *n.f.* stretcher.

civil /sivil/ *a.* civil; (*non militaire*) civilian; (*poli*) civil. —*n.m.* civilian. **dans le** ~, in civilian life. **en** ~, in plain clothes.

civilisation /sivilizasjɔ̃/ *n.f.* civilization.

civiliser /sivilize/ *v.t.* civilize. **se** ~ *v. pr.* become civilized.

civi|que /sivik/ *a.* civic. ~**sme** *n.m.* civic sense.

clair /klɛr/ *a.* clear; (*éclairé*) light, bright; (*couleur*) light; (*liquide*) thin. —*adv.* clearly. —*n.m.* ~ **de lune,** moonlight. **le plus** ~ **de,** most of. ~**ement** *adv.* clearly.

claire-voie (à) /(a)klɛrvwa/ *adv.* with slits to let the light through.

clairière /klɛrjɛr/ *n.f.* clearing.

clairon /klɛrɔ̃/ *n.m.* bugle. ~**ner** /-ɔne/ *v.t.* trumpet (forth).

clairsemé /klɛrsəme/ *a.* sparse.

clairvoyant, ~**e** /klɛrvwajɑ̃, -t/ *a.* clear-sighted.

clamer /klame/ *v.t.* utter aloud.

clameur /klamœr/ *n.f.* clamour.

clan /klɑ̃/ *n.m.* clan.

clandestin, ~**e** /klɑ̃dɛstɛ̃, -in/ *a.* secret; (*journal*) underground. **passager** ~, stowaway.

clapet /klapɛ/ *n.m.* valve.

clapier /klapje/ *n.m.* (rabbit) hutch.

clapot|er /klapɔte/ *v.i.* lap. ~**is** *n.m.* lapping.

claquage /klakaʒ/ *n.m.* strained muscle.

claque /klak/ *n.f.* slap. **en avoir sa** ~ (**de**), (*fam.*) be fed up (with).

claqu|er /klake/ *v.i.* bang; (*porte*) slam, bang; (*fouet*) snap, crack; (*se casser: fam.*) conk out; (*mourir: fam.*) snuff it. —*v.t.* (*porte*) slam, bang; (*dépenser: fam.*) blow; (*fatiguer: fam.*) tire out. ~**er des doigts,** snap one's fingers. ~**er des mains,** clap one's hands. **il claque des dents,** his teeth are chattering. ~**ement** *n.m.* bang(ing); slam(ming); snap(ping).

claquettes /klakɛt/ *n.f. pl.* tap-dancing.

clarifier /klarifje/ *v.t.* clarify.

clarinette /klarinɛt/ *n.f.* clarinet.

clarté /klarte/ *n.f.* light, brightness; (*netteté*) clarity.

classe /klɑs/ *n.f.* class; (*salle: scol.*) class(-room). **aller en** ~, go to school. ~ **ouvrière/moyenne,** working/middle class. **faire la** ~, teach.

class|er /klase/ v.t. classify; (par mérite) grade; (papiers) file; (affaire) close. **se ~er premier/ dernier**, come first/last. **~ement** n.m. classification; grading; filing; (rang) place, grade; (de coureur) placing.

classeur /klɑsœr/ n.m. filing cabinet; (chemise) file.

classif|ier /klasifje/ v.t. classify. **~ication** n.f. classification.

classique /klasik/ a. classical; (de qualité) classic(al); (habituel) classic. —n.m. classic; (auteur) classical author.

clause /kloz/ n.f. clause.

claustration /klostrɑsjɔ̃/ n.f. confinement.

claustrophobie /klostrɔfɔbi/ n.f. claustrophobia.

clavecin /klavsɛ̃/ n.m. harpsichord.

clavicule /klavikyl/ n.f. collar-bone.

clavier /klavje/ n.m. keyboard.

claviste /klavist/ n.m./f. keyboarder.

clé, clef /kle/ n.f. key; (outil) spanner; (mus.) clef. —a. invar. key. **~ anglaise**, (monkey-)wrench. **~ de contact**, ignition key. **~ de voûte**, keystone. **prix ~s en main**, (voiture) on-the-road price.

clémen|t, **~te** /klemã, -t/ a. (doux) mild; (indulgent) lenient. **~ce** n.f. mildness; leniency.

clémentine /klemɑ̃tin/ n.f. clementine.

clerc /klɛr/ n.m. (d'avoué etc.) clerk; (relig.) cleric.

clergé /klɛrʒe/ n.m. clergy.

cléric|al (m. pl. **~aux**) /klerikal, -o/ a. clerical.

cliché /kliʃe/ n.m. cliché; (photo.) negative.

client, **~e** /klijã, -t/ n.m., f. customer; (d'un avocat) client; (d'un médecin) patient; (d'hôtel) guest. **~èle** /-tɛl/ n.f. customers, clientele; (d'un avocat) clientele, clients, practice; (d'un médecin) practice, patients; (soutien) custom.

cligner /kliɲe/ v.i. **~ des yeux**, blink. **~ de l'œil**, wink.

clignot|er /kliɲɔte/ v.i. blink; (lumière) flicker; (comme signal) flash. **~ant** n.m. (auto.) indicator; (auto., Amer.) directional signal.

climat /klima/ n.m. climate. **~ique** /-tik/ a. climatic.

climatis|ation /klimatizɑsjɔ̃/ n.f. air-conditioning. **~é** a. air-conditioned.

clin d'œil /klɛ̃dœj/ n.m. wink. **en un ~**, in a flash.

clinique /klinik/ a. clinical. —n.f. (private) clinic.

clinquant, **~e** /klɛ̃kã, -t/ a. showy.

clip /klip/ n.m. video.

clique /klik/ n.f. clique; (mus., mil.) band.

cliquet|er /klikte/ v.i. clink. **~is** n.m. clink(ing).

clitoris /klitɔris/ n.m. clitoris.

clivage /klivaʒ/ n.m. cleavage.

clochard, **~e** /klɔʃar, -d/ n.m., f. tramp.

cloche[1] /klɔʃ/ n.f. bell; (fam.) idiot. **~ à fromage**, cheese-cover. **~ette** n.f. bell.

cloche[2] /klɔʃ/ n.f. (fam.) idiot.

cloche-pied (à) /(a)klɔʃpje/ adv. hopping on one foot.

clocher[1] /klɔʃe/ n.m. bell-tower; (pointu) steeple. **de ~**, parochial.

clocher[2] /klɔʃe/ v.i. (fam.) be wrong.

cloison /klwazɔ̃/ n.f. partition; (fig.) barrier. **~ner** /-ɔne/ v.t. partition; (personne) cut off.

cloître /klwatr/ n.m. cloister.

cloîtrer (se) /(sə)klwatre/ v. pr. shut o.s. away.

clopin-clopant /klɔpɛ̃klɔpã/ adv. hobbling.

cloque /klɔk/ n.f. blister.

clore /klɔr/ v.t. close.

clos, **~e** /klo, -z/ a. closed.

clôtur|e /klotyr/ n.f. fence; (fermeture) closure. **~er** v.t. enclose; (festival, séance, etc.) close.

clou /klu/ n.m. nail; (furoncle) boil; (de spectacle) star attraction. **~ de girofle**, clove. **les ~s**, (passage) zebra ou pedestrian crossing. **~er** v.t. nail down; (fig.) pin down. **être cloué au lit**, be confined to one's bed. **~er le bec à qn.**, shut s.o. up.

clouté /klute/ a. studded.

clown /klun/ n.m. clown.

club /klœb/ n.m. club.

coaguler /kɔagyle/ v.t./i., **se ~** v. pr. coagulate.

coaliser (se) /(sə)kɔalize/ v. pr. join forces.

coalition /kɔalisjɔ̃/ n.f. coalition.

coasser /kɔase/ v.i. croak.

cobaye /kɔbaj/ n.m. guinea-pig.

coca /kɔka/ n.m. (P.) Coke.

cocagne /kɔkaɲ/ n.f. **pays de ~**, land of plenty.

cocaïne /kɔkain/ n.f. cocaine.

cocarde /kɔkard/ n.f. rosette.

cocard|ier, **~ière** /kɔkardje, -jɛr/ a. chauvinistic.

cocasse /kɔkas/ a. comical.

coccinelle /kɔksinɛl/ n.f. ladybird; (*Amer.*) ladybug; (*voiture*) beetle.

cocher¹ /kɔʃe/ v.t. tick (off), check.

cocher² /kɔʃe/ n.m. coachman.

cochon, ~ne /kɔʃɔ̃, -ɔn/ n.m. pig. —n.m., f. (*personne*: fam.) pig. —a. (fam.) filthy. **~nerie** /-ɔnri/ n.f. (*saleté*: fam.) filth; (*marchandise*: fam.) rubbish.

cocktail /kɔktɛl/ n.m. cocktail; (*réunion*) cocktail party.

cocon /kɔkɔ̃/ n.m. cocoon.

cocorico /kɔkɔriko/ n.m. cock-a-doodle-doo.

cocotier /kɔkɔtje/ n.m. coconut palm.

cocotte /kɔkɔt/ n.f. (*marmite*) casserole. **~ minute**, (P.) pressure-cooker. **ma ~**, (fam.) my sweet, my dear.

cocu /kɔky/ n.m. (fam.) cuckold.

code /kɔd/ n.m. code. **~s, phares ~**, dipped headlights. **~ de la route**, Highway Code. **se mettre en ~**, dip one's headlights.

coder /kɔde/ v.t. code.

codifier /kɔdifje/ v.t. codify.

coéquip|ier, ~ière /kɔekipje, -jɛr/ n.m., f. team-mate.

cœur /kœr/ n.m. heart; (*cartes*) hearts. **~ d'artichaut**, artichoke heart. **~ de palmier**, heart of palm. **à ~ ouvert**, (*opération*) open-heart; (*parler*) freely. **avoir bon ~**, be kind-hearted. **de bon ~**, with a good heart. **par ~**, by heart. **avoir mal au ~**, feel sick. **je veux en avoir le ~ net**, I want to be clear in my own mind (about it).

coexist|er /kɔɛgziste/ v.i. coexist. **~ence** n.f. coexistence.

coffre /kɔfr/ n.m. chest; (*pour argent*) safe; (*auto.*) boot; (*auto., Amer.*) trunk. **~-fort** (pl. **~s-forts**) n.m. safe.

coffrer /kɔfre/ v.t. (fam.) lock up.

coffret /kɔfrɛ/ n.m. casket, box.

cognac /kɔnak/ n.m. cognac.

cogner /kɔne/ v.t./i. knock. **se ~** v. pr. knock o.s.

cohabit|er /kɔabite/ v.i. live together. **~ation** n.f. living together.

cohérent, ~e /kɔerɑ̃, -t/ a. coherent.

cohésion /kɔezjɔ̃/ n.f. cohesion.

cohorte /kɔɔrt/ n.f. troop.

cohue /kɔy/ n.f. crowd.

coi, coite /kwa, -t/ a. silent.

coiffe /kwaf/ n.f. head-dress.

coiffer /kwafe/ v.t. do the hair of; (*chapeau*) put on; (*surmonter*) cap. **~er qn. d'un chapeau**, put a hat on s.o. **se ~er** v. pr. do one's hair. **~é de**, wearing. **bien/mal ~é**, with tidy/untidy

hair. **~eur, ~euse** n.m., f. hairdresser; n.f. dressing-table.

coiffure /kwafyr/ n.f. hairstyle; (*chapeau*) hat; (*métier*) hairdressing.

coin /kwɛ̃/ n.m. corner; (*endroit*) spot; (*cale*) wedge; (*pour graver*) die. **au ~ du feu**, by the fireside. **dans le ~**, locally. **du ~**, local. **le boulanger du ~**, the local baker.

coincer /kwɛ̃se/ v.t. jam; (*caler*) wedge; (*attraper*: fam.) catch. **se ~** v. pr. get jammed.

coïncid|er /kɔɛ̃side/ v.i. coincide. **~ence** n.f. coincidence.

coing /kwɛ̃/ n.m. quince.

coït /kɔit/ n.m. intercourse.

coite /kwat/ voir coi.

coke /kɔk/ n.m. coke.

col /kɔl/ n.m. collar; (*de bouteille*) neck; (*de montagne*) pass. **~ roulé**, polo-neck; (*Amer.*) turtle-neck. **~ de l'utérus**, cervix.

coléoptère /kɔleɔptɛr/ n.m. beetle.

colère /kɔlɛr/ n.f. anger; (*accès*) fit of anger. **en ~**, angry. **se mettre en ~**, lose one's temper.

colér|eux, ~euse /kɔlerø, -z/, **~ique** adjs. quick-tempered.

colibri /kɔlibri/ n.m. humming-bird.

colifichet /kɔlifiʃɛ/ n.m. trinket.

colimaçon (en) /(ɑ̃)kɔlimasɔ̃/ adv. spiral.

colin /kɔlɛ̃/ n.m. (*poisson*) hake.

colin-maillard /kɔlɛ̃majar/ n.m. **jouer à ~**, play blind man's buff.

colique /kɔlik/ n.f. diarrhoea; (*méd.*) colic.

colis /kɔli/ n.m. parcel.

collabor|er /kɔlabɔre/ v.i. collaborate (à, on). **~er à**, (*journal*) contribute to. **~ateur, ~atrice** n.m., f. collaborator; contributor. **~ation** n.f. collaboration (à, on); contribution (à, to).

collant, ~e /kɔlɑ̃, -t/ a. skin-tight; (*poisseux*) sticky. —n.m. (*bas*) tights; (*de danseur*) leotard.

collation /kɔlasjɔ̃/ n.f. light meal.

colle /kɔl/ n.f. glue; (*en pâte*) paste; (*problème*: fam.) poser; (*scol., argot*) detention.

collect|e /kɔlɛkt/ n.f. collection. **~er** v.t. collect.

collecteur /kɔlɛktœr/ n.m. (*égout*) main sewer.

collecti|f, ~ve /kɔlɛktif, -v/ a. collective; (*billet, voyage*) group. **~vement** adv. collectively.

collection /kɔlɛksjɔ̃/ n.f. collection.

collectionn|er /kɔlɛksjɔne/ v.t. collect. **~eur, ~euse** n.m., f. collector.

collectivité /kɔlɛktivite/ n.f. community.

collège /kɔlɛʒ/ n.m. (secondary) school; (assemblée) college. **~égien, ~é-gienne** n.m., f. schoolboy, schoolgirl.

collègue /kɔlɛg/ n.m./f. colleague.

coll|er /kɔle/ v.t. stick; (avec colle liquide) glue; (affiche) stick up; (mettre: fam.) stick; (scol., argot) keep in; (par une question: fam.) stump. —v.i. stick (à, to); (être collant) be sticky. **~er à**, (convenir à) fit, correspond to. **être ~é à**, (examen: fam.) fail.

collet /kɔlɛ/ n.m. (piège) snare. **~ monté**, prim and proper. **prendre qn. au ~**, collar s.o.

collier /kɔlje/ n.m. necklace; (de chien) collar.

colline /kɔlin/ n.f. hill.

collision /kɔlizjɔ̃/ n.f. (choc) collision; (lutte) clash. **entrer en ~ (avec)**, collide (with).

colloque /kɔlɔk/ n.m. symposium.

collyre /kɔlir/ n.m. eye drops.

colmater /kɔlmate/ v.t. seal; (trou) fill in.

colombe /kɔlɔ̃b/ n.f. dove.

Colombie /kɔlɔ̃bi/ n.f. Colombia.

colon /kɔlɔ̃/ n.m. settler.

colonel /kɔlɔnɛl/ n.m. colonel.

colon|ial, ~iale (m. pl. **~iaux**) /kɔlɔnjal, -jo/ a. & n.m., f. colonial.

colonie /kɔlɔni/ n.f. colony. **~ de vacances**, children's holiday camp.

coloniser /kɔlɔnize/ v.t. colonize.

colonne /kɔlɔn/ n.f. column. **~ vertébrale**, spine. **en ~ par deux**, in double file.

color|er /kɔlɔre/ v.t. colour; (bois) stain. **~ant** n.m. colouring. **~ation** n.f. (couleur) colour(ing).

colorier /kɔlɔrje/ v.t. colour (in).

coloris /kɔlɔri/ n.m. colour.

coloss|al (m. pl. **~aux**) /kɔlɔsal, -o/ a. colossal.

colosse /kɔlɔs/ n.m. giant.

colport|er /kɔlpɔrte/ v.t. hawk. **~eur, ~euse** n.m., f. hawker.

colza /kɔlza/ n.m. rape(-seed).

coma /kɔma/ n.m. coma. **dans le ~**, in a coma.

combat /kɔ̃ba/ n.m. fight; (sport) match. **~s**, fighting.

combati|f, ~ve /kɔ̃batif, -v/ a. eager to fight; (esprit) fighting.

combatt|re† /kɔ̃batr/ v.t./i. fight. **~ant,**

~ante n.m., f. fighter; (mil.) combatant.

combien /kɔ̃bjɛ̃/ adv. **~ (de)**, (quantité) how much; (nombre) how many; (temps) how long. **~ il a changé!**, (comme) how he has changed! **~y a-t-il d'ici à . . .?**, how far is it to . . .?

combinaison /kɔ̃binɛzɔ̃/ n.f. combination; (manigance) scheme; (de femme) slip; (bleu de travail) boiler suit; (Amer.) overalls; (de plongée) wetsuit. **~ d'aviateur**, flying-suit.

combine /kɔ̃bin/ n.f. trick; (fraude) fiddle.

combiné /kɔ̃bine/ n.m. (de téléphone) receiver.

combiner /kɔ̃bine/ v.t. (réunir) combine; (calculer) devise.

comble¹ /kɔ̃bl/ a. packed.

comble² /kɔ̃bl/ n.m. height. **~s**, (mansarde) attic, loft. **c'est le ~!**, that's the (absolute) limit!

combler /kɔ̃ble/ v.t. fill; (perte, déficit) make good; (désir) fulfil; (personne) gratify. **~ qn. de cadeaux/etc.**, lavish gifts/etc. on s.o.

combustible /kɔ̃bystibl/ n.m. fuel.

combustion /kɔ̃bystjɔ̃/ n.f. combustion.

comédie /kɔmedi/ n.f. comedy. **~ musicale**, musical. **jouer la ~**, put on an act.

comédien, ~ne /kɔmedjɛ̃, -jɛn/ n.m., f. actor, actress.

comestible /kɔmɛstibl/ a. edible. **~s** n.m. pl. foodstuffs.

comète /kɔmɛt/ n.f. comet.

comique /kɔmik/ a. comical; (genre) comic. —n.m. (acteur) comic; (comédie) comedy; (côté drôle) comical aspect.

comité /kɔmite/ n.m. committee.

commandant /kɔmɑ̃dɑ̃/ n.m. commander; (armée de terre) major. **~ (de bord)**, captain. **~ en chef**, Commander-in-Chief.

commande /kɔmɑ̃d/ n.f. (comm.) order. **~s**, (d'avion etc.) controls.

command|er /kɔmɑ̃de/ v.t. command; (acheter) order. —v.i. be in command. **~er à**, (maîtriser) control. **~er à qn. de**, command s.o. to. **~ement** n.m. command; (relig.) commandment.

commando /kɔmɑ̃do/ n.m. commando.

comme /kɔm/ conj. as. —prép. like. —adv. (exclamation) how. **~ ci comme ça**, so-so. **~ d'habitude, ~ à l'ordinaire**, as usual. **~ il faut**, proper(ly). **~ pour faire**, as if to do. **~ quoi**, to the effect that. **qu'avez-vous ~**

amis/*etc*.?, what have you in the way of friends/*etc*.? ~ **c'est bon!**, it's so good! ~ **il est mignon!** isn't he sweet!

commémor|er /kɔmemɔre/ *v.t.* commemorate. ~**ation** *n.f.* commemoration.

commenc|er /kɔmãse/ *v.t.* begin, start. ~**er à faire**, begin *ou* start to do. ~**ement** *n.m.* beginning, start.

comment /kɔmã/ *adv.* how. ~?, (*répétition*) pardon?; (*surprise*) what? ~ **est-il?**, what is he like? **le ~ et le pourquoi**, the whys and wherefores.

commentaire /kɔmãtɛr/ *n.m.* comment; (*d'un texte*) commentary.

comment|er /kɔmãte/ *v.t.* comment on. ~**ateur**, ~**atrice** *n.m.*, *f.* commentator.

commérages /kɔmeraʒ/ *n.m. pl.* gossip.

commerçant, ~**e** /kɔmɛrsã, -t/ *a.* (*rue*) shopping; (*personne*) business-minded. —*n.m.*, *f.* shopkeeper.

commerce /kɔmɛrs/ *n.m.* trade, commerce; (*magasin*) business. **faire du ~**, trade.

commerc|ial (*m. pl.* ~**iaux**) /kɔmɛrsjal, -jo/ *a.* commercial. ~**ialiser** *v.t.* market. ~**ialisable** *a.* marketable.

commère /kɔmɛr/ *n.f.* gossip.

commettre /kɔmɛtr/ *v.t.* commit.

commis /kɔmi/ *n.m.* (*de magasin*) assistant; (*de bureau*) clerk.

commissaire /kɔmisɛr/ *n.m.* (*sport*) steward. ~ **(de police)**, (*police*) superintendent. ~**-priseur** (*pl.* ~**s-priseurs**) *n.m.* auctioneer.

commissariat /kɔmisarja/ *n.m.* ~ **(de police)**, police station.

commission /kɔmisjɔ̃/ *n.f.* commission; (*course*) errand; (*message*) message. ~**s**, shopping. ~**naire** /-jɔnɛr/ *n.m.* errand-boy.

commod|e /kɔmɔd/ *a.* handy; (*facile*) easy. **pas ~e**, (*personne*) a difficult customer. —*n.f.* chest (of drawers). ~**ité** *n.f.* convenience.

commotion /kɔmosjɔ̃/ *n.f.* ~ **(cérébrale)**, concussion. ~**né** /-jɔne/ *a.* shaken.

commuer /kɔmɥe/ *v.t.* commute.

commun, ~**e** /kɔmœ̃, -yn/ *a.* common; (*effort*, *action*) joint; (*frais*, *pièce*) shared. —*n.f.* (*circonscription*) commune. ~**s** *n.m. pl.* outhouses, outbuildings. **avoir** *ou* **mettre en ~**, share. **le ~ des mortels**, ordinary mortals. ~**al** (*m. pl.* ~**aux**) /-ynal, -o/ *a.* of the commune, local. ~**ément** /-ynemã/ *adv.* commonly.

communauté /kɔmynote/ *n.f.* community. ~ **des biens** (*entre époux*) shared estate.

commune /kɔmyn/ *voir* **commun**.

communiant, ~**e** /kɔmynjã, -t/ *n.m.*, *f.* (*relig.*) communicant.

communicati|f, ~**ve** /kɔmynikatif, -v/ *a.* communicative.

communication /kɔmynikasjɔ̃/ *n.f.* communication; (*téléphonique*) call. ~ **interurbaine**, long-distance call.

commun|ier /kɔmynje/ *v.i.* (*relig.*) receive communion; (*fig.*) commune. ~**ion** *n.f.* communion.

communiqué /kɔmynike/ *n.m.* communiqué.

communiquer /kɔmynike/ *v.t.* pass on, communicate; (*mouvement*) impart. —*v.i.* communicate. **se ~ à**, spread to.

communis|te /kɔmynist/ *a.* & *n.m./f.* communist. ~**me** *n.m.* communism.

commutateur /kɔmytatœr/ *n.m.* (*électr.*) switch.

compact /kɔ̃pakt/ *a.* dense; (*voiture*) compact.

compact disc /kɔ̃paktdisk/ *n.m.* (P.) compact disc.

compagne /kɔ̃paɲ/ *n.f.* companion.

compagnie /kɔ̃paɲi/ *n.f.* company. **tenir ~ à**, keep company.

compagnon /kɔ̃paɲɔ̃/ *n.m.* companion; (*ouvrier*) workman. ~ **de jeu**, playmate.

comparaître /kɔ̃parɛtr/ *v.i.* (*jurid.*) appear (**devant**, before).

compar|er /kɔ̃pare/ *v.t.* compare. ~**er qch./qn. à** *ou* **et** compare sth./s.o. with *ou* and; **se ~er** *v. pr.* be compared. ~**able** *a.* comparable. ~**aison** *n.f.* comparison; (*littéraire*) simile. ~**atif**, ~**ative** *a.* & *n.m.* comparative. ~**é** *a.* comparative.

comparse /kɔ̃pars/ *n.m./f.* (*péj.*) stooge.

compartiment /kɔ̃partimã/ *n.m.* compartment. ~**er** /-te/ *v.t.* divide up.

comparution /kɔ̃parysjɔ̃/ *n.f.* (*jurid.*) appearance.

compas /kɔ̃pa/ *n.m.* (pair of) compasses; (*boussole*) compass.

compassé /kɔ̃pase/ *a.* stilted.

compassion /kɔ̃pasjɔ̃/ *n.f.* compassion.

compatible /kɔ̃patibl/ *a.* compatible.

compatir /kɔ̃patir/ *v.i.* sympathize. ~ **à**, share in.

compatriote /kɔ̃patrijɔt/ *n.m./f.* compatriot.

compens|er /kɔ̃pãse/ *v.t.* compensate for, make up for. ~**ation** *n.f.* compensation.

compère /kɔ̃pɛr/ *n.m.* accomplice.

compéten|t, **~te** /kɔpetɑ̃, -t/ *a.* competent. **~ce** *n.f.* competence.

compétiti|f, **~ve** /kɔpetitif, -v/ *a.* competitive.

compétition /kɔpetisjɔ̃/ *n.f.* competition; (*sportive*) event. **de ~**, competitive.

complainte /kɔplɛ̃t/ *n.f.* lament.

complaire (se) /(sə)kɔplɛr/ *v. pr.* **se ~ dans**, delight in.

complaisan|t, **~te** /kɔplɛzɑ̃, -t/ *a.* kind; (*indulgent*) indulgent. **~ce** *n.f.* kindness; indulgence.

complément /kɔplemɑ̃/ *n.m.* complement; (*reste*) rest. **~ (d'objet)**, (*gram.*) object. **~ d'information**, further information. **~aire** /-tɛr/ *a.* complementary; (*renseignements*) supplementary.

compl|et¹, **~ète** /kɔplɛ, -t/ *a.* complete; (*train, hôtel, etc.*) full. **~ètement** *adv.* completely.

complet² /kɔplɛ/ *n.m.* suit.

compléter /kɔplete/ *v.t.* complete; (*agrémenter*) complement. **se ~** *v. pr.* complement each other.

complex|e¹ /kɔplɛks/ *a.* complex. **~ité** *n.f.* complexity.

complex|e² /kɔplɛks/ *n.m.* (*sentiment, bâtiments*) complex. **~é** *a.* hung up.

complication /kɔplikasjɔ̃/ *n.f.* complication; (*complexité*) complexity.

complic|e /kɔplis/ *n.m.* accomplice. **~ité** *n.f.* complicity.

compliment /kɔplimɑ̃/ *n.m.* compliment. **~s**, (*félicitations*) congratulations. **~er** /-te/ *v.t.* compliment.

compliqu|er /kɔplike/ *v.t.* complicate. **se ~er** *v. pr.* become complicated. **~é** *a.* complicated.

complot /kɔplo/ *n.m.* plot. **~er** /-ɔte/ *v.t./i.* plot.

comporter¹ /kɔpɔrte/ *v.t.* contain; (*impliquer*) involve.

comport|er² (**se**) /(sə)kɔpɔrte/ *v. pr.* behave; (*joueur*) perform. **~ement** *n.m.* behaviour; (*de joueur*) performance.

composé /kɔpoze/ *a.* compound; (*guindé*) affected. —*n.m.* compound.

compos|er /kɔpoze/ *v.t.* make up, compose; (*chanson, visage*) compose; (*numéro*) dial. —*v.i.* (*scol.*) take an exam; (*transiger*) compromise. **se ~er de**, be made up or composed of. **~ant** *n.m.*, **~ante** *n.f.* component.

composi|teur, **~trice** /kɔpozitœr, -tris/ *n.m., f.* (*mus.*) composer.

composition /kɔpozisjɔ̃/ *n.f.* composition; (*examen*) test, exam.

composter /kɔpɔste/ *v.t.* (*billet*) punch.

compot|e /kɔpɔt/ *n.f.* stewed fruit. **~e de pommes**, stewed apples. **~ier** *n.m.* fruit dish.

compréhensible /kɔpreɑ̃sibl/ *a.* understandable.

compréhensi|f, **~ve** /kɔpreɑ̃sif, -v/ *a.* understanding.

compréhension /kɔpreɑ̃sjɔ̃/ *n.f.* understanding, comprehension.

comprendre† /kɔprɑ̃dr/ *v.t.* understand; (*comporter*) comprise. **ça se comprend**, that is understandable.

compresse /kɔprɛs/ *n.f.* compress.

compression /kɔprɛsjɔ̃/ *n.f.* (*physique*) compression, (*réduction*) reduction. **~ de personnel**, staff cuts.

comprimé /kɔprime/ *n.m.* tablet.

comprimer /kɔprime/ *v.t.* compress; (*réduire*) reduce.

compris, **~e** /kɔpri, -z/ *a.* included; (*d'accord*) agreed. **~ entre**, (contained) between. **service (non) ~**, service (not) included, (not) including service. **tout ~**, (all) inclusive. **y ~**, including.

compromettre /kɔprɔmɛtr/ *v.t.* compromise.

compromis /kɔprɔmi/ *n.m.* compromise.

comptab|le /kɔtabl/ *a.* accounting. —*n.m.* accountant. **~ilité** *n.f.* accountancy; (*comptes*) accounts; (*service*) accounts department.

comptant /kɔtɑ̃/ *adv.* (*payer*) (in) cash; (*acheter*) for cash.

compte /kɔt/ *n.m.* count; (*facture, à la banque, comptabilité*) account; (*nombre exact*) right number. **demander/rendre des ~s**, ask for/give an explanation. **à bon ~**, cheaply. **s'en tirer à bon ~**, get off lightly. **à son ~**, (*travailler*) for o.s., on one's own. **faire le ~ de**, count. **pour le ~ de**, on behalf of. **sur le ~ de**, about. **~ à rebours**, countdown. **~-gouttes** *n.m. invar.* (*méd.*) dropper. **au ~-gouttes**, (*fig.*) in dribs and drabs. **~ rendu**, report; (*de film, livre*) review. **~-tours** *n.m. invar.* rev counter.

compter /kɔte/ *v.t.* count; (*prévoir*) reckon; (*facturer*) charge for; (*avoir*) have; (*classer*) consider. —*v.i.* (*calculer, importer*) count. **~ avec**, reckon with. **~ faire**, expect to do. **~ parmi**, (*figurer*) be considered among. **~ sur**, rely on.

compteur /kɔtœr/ *n.m.* meter. **~ de vitesse**, speedometer.

comptine /kɔtin/ *n.f.* nursery rhyme.

comptoir /kɔ̃twar/ n.m. counter; (de café) bar.

compulser /kɔ̃pylse/ v.t. examine.

comt|e, ~esse /kɔ̃t, -ɛs/ n.m., f. count, countess.

comté /kɔ̃te/ n.m. county.

con, conne /kɔ̃, kɔn/ a. (argot) bloody foolish. —n.m., f. (argot) bloody fool.

concave /kɔ̃kav/ a. concave.

concéder /kɔ̃sede/ v.t. grant, concede.

concentr|er /kɔ̃sɑ̃tre/ v.t., **se ~er** v. pr. concentrate. **~ation** n.f. concentration. **~é** a. concentrated; (lait) condensed; (personne) absorbed; n.m. concentrate.

concept /kɔ̃sɛpt/ n.m. concept.

conception /kɔ̃sɛpsjɔ̃/ n.f. conception.

concerner /kɔ̃sɛrne/ v.t. concern. **en ce qui me concerne,** as far as I am concerned.

concert /kɔ̃sɛr/ n.m. concert. **de ~,** in unison.

concert|er /kɔ̃sɛrte/ v.t. organize, prepare. **se ~er** v. pr. confer. **~é** a. (plan etc.) planned.

concerto /kɔ̃sɛrto/ n.m. concerto.

concession /kɔ̃sesjɔ̃/ n.f. concession; (terrain) plot.

concessionnaire /kɔ̃sesjɔnɛr/ n.m./f. (authorized) dealer.

concevoir† /kɔ̃svwar/ v.t. (imaginer, engendrer) conceive; (comprendre) understand.

concierge /kɔ̃sjɛrʒ/ n.m./f. caretaker.

concile /kɔ̃sil/ n.m. council.

concil|ier /kɔ̃silje/ v.t. reconcile. **se ~ier** v. pr. (s'attirer) win (over). **~iation** n.f. conciliation.

concis, ~e /kɔ̃si, -z/ a. concise. **~ion** /-zjɔ̃/ n.f. concision.

concitoyen, ~ne /kɔ̃sitwajɛ̃, -jɛn/ n.m., f. fellow citizen.

concl|ure† /kɔ̃klyr/ v.t./i. conclude. **~ure à,** conclude in favour of. **~uant, ~uante** a. conclusive. **~usion** n.f. conclusion.

concocter /kɔ̃kɔkte/ v.t. (fam.) cook up.

concombre /kɔ̃kɔ̃br/ n.m. cucumber.

concorde /kɔ̃kɔrd/ n.f. concord.

concord|er /kɔ̃kɔrde/ v.i. agree. **~ance** n.f. agreement; (analogie) similarity. **~ant, ~ante** a. in agreement.

concourir /kɔ̃kurir/ v.i. compete. **~ à,** contribute towards.

concours /kɔ̃kur/ n.m. competition; (examen) competitive examination; (aide) aid; (de circonstances) combination.

concr|et, ~ète /kɔ̃krɛ, -t/ a. concrete. **~ètement** adv. in concrete terms.

concrétiser /kɔ̃kretize/ v.t. give concrete form to. **se ~** v. pr. materialize.

conçu /kɔ̃sy/ a. **bien/mal ~,** (appartement etc.) well/badly planned.

concubinage /kɔ̃kybinaʒ/ n.m. cohabitation.

concurrenc|e /kɔ̃kyrɑ̃s/ n.f. competition. **faire ~e à,** compete with. **jusqu'à ~e de,** up to. **~er** v.t. compete with.

concurrent, ~e /kɔ̃kyrɑ̃, -t/ n.m., f. competitor; (scol.) candidate. —a. competing.

condamn|er /kɔ̃dane/ v.t. (censurer, obliger) condemn; (jurid.) sentence; (porte) block up. **~ation** n.f. condemnation; (peine) sentence. **~é** a. (fichu) without hope, doomed.

condens|er /kɔ̃dɑ̃se/ v.t., **se ~er** v. pr. condense. **~ation** n.f. condensation.

condescendre /kɔ̃desɑ̃dr/ v.i. condescend (à, to).

condiment /kɔ̃dimɑ̃/ n.m. condiment.

condisciple /kɔ̃disipl/ n.m. classmate, schoolfellow.

condition /kɔ̃disjɔ̃/ n.f. condition. **~s,** (prix) terms. **à ~ de ou que,** provided (that). **sans ~,** unconditional(ly). **sous ~,** conditionally. **~nel, ~nelle** /-jɔnɛl/ a. conditional. **~nel** n.m. conditional (tense).

conditionnement /kɔ̃disjɔnmɑ̃/ n.m. conditioning; (emballage) packaging.

conditionner /kɔ̃disjɔne/ v.t. condition; (emballer) package.

condoléances /kɔ̃dɔleɑ̃s/ n.f. pl. condolences.

conduc|teur, ~trice /kɔ̃dyktœr, -tris/ n.m., f. driver.

conduire† /kɔ̃dɥir/ v.t. lead; (auto.) drive; (affaire) conduct. —v.i. drive. **se ~** v. pr. behave. **~ à,** (accompagner à) take to.

conduit /kɔ̃dɥi/ n.m. (anat.) duct.

conduite /kɔ̃dɥit/ n.f. conduct; (auto.) driving; (tuyau) main. **~ à droite,** (place) right-hand drive.

cône /kon/ n.m. cone.

confection /kɔ̃fɛksjɔ̃/ n.f. making. **de ~,** ready-made. **la ~,** the clothing industry. **~ner** /-jɔne/ v.t. make.

confédération /kɔ̃federasjɔ̃/ n.f. confederation.

conférenc|e /kɔ̃ferɑ̃s/ n.f. conference; (exposé) lecture. **~e au sommet,** summit conference. **~ier, ~ière** n.m., f. lecturer.

conférer /kɔ̃fere/ v.t. give; (décerner) confer.

confess|er /kɔ̃fese/ v.t., **se ~er** v. pr.

confess. ~eur *n.m.* confessor. ~ion *n.f.* confession; (*religion*) denomination. ~ionnal (*pl.* ~ionnaux) *n.m.* confessional. ~ionnel, ~ionnelle *a.* denominational.

confettis /kɔ̃feti/ *n.m. pl.* confetti.

confiance /kɔ̃fjɑ̃s/ *n.f.* trust. avoir ~ en, trust.

confiant, ~e /kɔ̃fjɑ̃, -t/ *a.* (*assure*) confident; (*sans défiance*) trusting. ~ en *ou* dans, confident in.

confiden|t, ~te /kɔ̃fidɑ̃, -t/ *n.m.*, *f.* confidant, confidante. ~ce *n.f.* confidence.

confidentiel, ~le /kɔ̃fidɑ̃sjɛl/ *a.* confidential.

confier /kɔ̃fje/ *v.t.* ~ à qn., entrust s.o. with; (*secret*) confide to s.o. se ~ à, confide in.

configuration /kɔ̃figyrasjɔ̃/ *n.f.* configuration.

confiner /kɔ̃fine/ *v.t.* confine. —*v.i.* ~ à, border on. se ~ *v. pr.* confine o.s. (à, dans, to).

confins /kɔ̃fɛ̃/ *n.m. pl.* confines.

confirm|er /kɔ̃firme/ *v.t.* confirm. ~ation *n.f.* confirmation.

confis|erie /kɔ̃fizri/ *n.f.* sweet shop. ~eries, confectionery. ~eur, ~euse *n.m.*, *f.* confectioner.

confis|quer /kɔ̃fiske/ *v.t.* confiscate. ~cation *n.f.* confiscation.

confit, ~e /kɔ̃fi, -t/ *a.* (*culin.*) candied. fruits ~s, crystallized fruits. —*n.m.* ~ d'oie, goose liver conserve.

confiture /kɔ̃fityr/ *n.f.* jam.

conflit /kɔ̃fli/ *n.m.* conflict.

confondre /kɔ̃fɔ̃dr/ *v.t.* confuse, mix up; (*consterner, étonner*) confound. se ~ *v. pr.* merge. se ~ en excuses, apologize profusely.

confondu /kɔ̃fɔ̃dy/ *a.* (*déconcerté*) overwhelmed, confounded.

conforme /kɔ̃fɔrm/ *a.* ~ à, in accordance with.

conformément /kɔ̃fɔrmemɑ̃/ *adv.* ~ à, in accordance with.

conform|er /kɔ̃fɔrme/ *v.t.* adapt. se ~er à, conform to. ~ité *n.f.* conformity.

conformis|te /kɔ̃fɔrmist/ *a. & n.m./f.* conformist. ~me *n.m.* conformism.

confort /kɔ̃fɔr/ *n.m.* comfort. tout ~, with all mod cons. ~able /-tabl/ *a.* comfortable.

confrère /kɔ̃frɛr/ *n.m.* colleague.

confrérie /kɔ̃freri/ *n.f.* brotherhood.

confront|er /kɔ̃frɔ̃te/ *v.t.* confront; (*textes*) compare. se ~er à *v. pr.* confront. ~ation *n.f.* confrontation.

confus, ~e /kɔ̃fy, -z/ *a.* confused; (*gêné*) embarrassed.

confusion /kɔ̃fyzjɔ̃/ *n.f.* confusion; (*gêné*) embarrassment.

congé /kɔ̃ʒe/ *n.m.* holiday; (*arrêt momentané*) time off; (*mil.*) leave; (*avis de départ*) notice. ~ de maladie, sick-leave. ~ de maternité, maternity leave. jour de ~, day off. prendre ~ de, take one's leave of.

congédier /kɔ̃ʒedje/ *v.t.* dismiss.

congel|er /kɔ̃ʒle/ *v.t.* freeze. les ~elés, frozen food. ~élateur *n.m.* freezer.

congénère /kɔ̃ʒenɛr/ *n.m./f.* fellow creature.

congénit|al (*m. pl.* ~aux) /kɔ̃ʒenital, -o/ *a.* congenital.

congère /kɔ̃ʒɛr/ *n.f.* snow-drift.

congestion /kɔ̃ʒɛstjɔ̃/ *n.f.* congestion. ~ cérébrale, stroke, cerebral haemorrhage. ~ner /-jɔne/ *v.t.* congest; (*visage*) flush.

congrégation /kɔ̃gregasjɔ̃/ *n.f.* congregation.

congrès /kɔ̃grɛ/ *n.m.* congress.

conifère /kɔnifɛr/ *n.m.* conifer.

conique /kɔnik/ *a.* conic(al).

conjectur|e /kɔ̃ʒɛktyr/ *n.f.* conjecture. ~er *v.t./i.* conjecture.

conjoint, ~e[1] /kɔ̃ʒwɛ̃, -t/ *n.m.*, *f.* spouse.

conjoint, ~e[2] /kɔ̃ʒwɛ̃, -t/ *a.* joint. ~ement /-tmɑ̃/ *adv.* jointly.

conjonction /kɔ̃ʒɔ̃ksjɔ̃/ *n.f.* conjunction.

conjonctivite /kɔ̃ʒɔ̃ktivit/ *n.f.* conjunctivitis.

conjoncture /kɔ̃ʒɔ̃ktyr/ *n.f.* circumstances; (*économique*) economic climate.

conjugaison /kɔ̃ʒygɛzɔ̃/ *n.f.* conjugation.

conjug|al (*m. pl.* ~aux) /kɔ̃ʒygal, -o/ *a.* conjugal.

conjuguer /kɔ̃ʒyge/ *v.t.* (*gram.*) conjugate; (*efforts*) combine. se ~ *v. pr.* (*gram.*) be conjugated.

conjur|er /kɔ̃ʒyre/ *v.t.* (*éviter*) avert; (*implorer*) entreat. ~ation *n.f.* conspiracy. ~é, ~ée *n.m.*, *f.* conspirator.

connaissance /kɔnɛsɑ̃s/ *n.f.* knowledge; (*personne*) acquaintance. ~s, (*science*) knowledge. faire la ~ de, meet; (*personne connue*) get to know. perdre ~, lose consciousness. sans ~, unconscious.

connaisseur /kɔnɛsœr/ *n.m.* connoisseur.

connaître† /kɔnɛtr/ *v.t.* know; (*avoir*) have. se ~ *v. pr.* (*se rencontrer*) meet.

faire ~, make known. **s'y ~ à** *ou* **en**, know (all) about.

conne|cter /kɔnɛkte/ *v.t.* connect. **~xion** *n.f.* connection.

connerie /kɔnri/ *n.f.* (*argot*) (*remarque*) rubbish. **faire une ~**, do sth. stupid. **dire une ~**, talk rubbish. **quelle ~!**, how stupid!

connivence /kɔnivãs/ *n.f.* connivance.

connotation /kɔnɔtasjɔ̃/ *n.f.* connotation.

connu /kɔny/ *a.* well-known.

conquér|ir /kɔ̃kerir/ *v.t.* conquer. **~ant**, **~ante** *n.m.*, *f.* conqueror.

conquête /kɔ̃kɛt/ *n.f.* conquest.

consacrer /kɔ̃sakre/ *v.t.* devote; (*relig.*) consecrate; (*sanctionner*) establish. **se ~** *v. pr.* devote o.s. (**à**, to).

consciemment /kɔ̃sjamɑ̃/ *adv.* consciously.

conscience /kɔ̃sjɑ̃s/ *n.f.* conscience; (*perception*) consciousness. **avoir/ prendre ~ de**, be/become aware of. **perdre ~**, lose consciousness. **avoir bonne/mauvaise ~**, have a clear/guilty conscience.

consciencieu|x, **~se** /kɔ̃sjɑ̃sjø, -z/ *a.* conscientious.

conscient, **~e** /kɔ̃sjɑ̃, -t/ *a.* conscious. **~ de**, aware *ou* conscious of.

conscrit /kɔ̃skri/ *n.m.* conscript.

consécration /kɔ̃sekrasjɔ̃/ *n.f.* consecration.

consécuti|f, **~ve** /kɔ̃sekytif, -v/ *a.* consecutive. **~f à**, following upon. **~vement** *adv.* consecutively.

conseil /kɔ̃sɛj/ *n.m.* (piece of) advice; (*assemblée*) council, committee; (*séance*) meeting; (*personne*) consultant. **~ d'administration**, board of directors. **~ des ministres**, Cabinet. **~ municipal**, town council.

conseiller[1] /kɔ̃seje/ *v.t.* advise. **~ à qn. de**, advise s.o. to. **~ qch. à qn.**, recommend sth to s.o.

conseill|er[2], **~ère** /kɔ̃seje, -ɛjɛr/ *n.m.*, *f.* adviser, counsellor. **~er municipal**, town councillor.

consent|ir /kɔ̃sɑ̃tir/ *v.i.* agree (**à**, to). **—** *v.t.* grant. **~ement** *n.m.* consent.

conséquence /kɔ̃sekɑ̃s/ *n.f.* consequence. **en ~**, consequently; (*comme il convient*) accordingly.

conséquent, **~e** /kɔ̃sekɑ̃, -t/ *a.* logical; (*important*: *fam.*) sizeable. **par ~**, consequently.

conserva|teur, **~trice** kɔ̃sɛrvatœr, -tris/ *a.* conservative. **—** *n.m.*, *f.* (*pol.*)

conservative. **—** *n.m.* (*de musée*) curator. **~tisme** *n.m.* conservatism.

conservatoire /kɔ̃sɛrvatwar/ *n.m.* academy.

conserve /kɔ̃sɛrv/ *n.f.* tinned *ou* canned food. **en ~**, tinned, canned.

conserv|er /kɔ̃sɛrve/ *v.t.* keep; (*en bon état*) preserve; (*culin.*) preserve. **se ~er** *v. pr.* (*culin.*) keep. **~ation** *n.f.* preservation.

considérable /kɔ̃siderabl/ *a.* considerable.

considération /kɔ̃siderasjɔ̃/ *n.f.* consideration; (*respect*) regard. **prendre en ~**, take into consideration.

considérer /kɔ̃sidere/ *v.t.* consider; (*respecter*) esteem. **~ comme**, consider to be.

consigne /kɔ̃siɲ/ *n.f.* (*de gare*) left luggage (office); (*Amer.*) (baggage) checkroom; (*scol.*) detention; (*somme*) deposit; (*ordres*) orders. **~ automatique**, (left-luggage) lockers; (*Amer.*) (baggage) lockers.

consigner /kɔ̃siɲe/ *v.t.* (*comm.*) charge a deposit on; (*écrire*) record; (*élève*) keep in; (*soldat*) confine.

consistan|t, **~te** /kɔ̃sistɑ̃, -t/ *a.* solid; (*épais*) thick. **~ce** *n.f.* consistency; (*fig.*) solidity.

consister /kɔ̃siste/ *v.i.* **~ en/dans**, consist of/in. **~ à faire**, consist in doing.

consœur /kɔ̃sœr/ *n.f.* colleague; fellow member.

consol|er /kɔ̃sɔle/ *v.t.* console. **se ~er** *v. pr.* be consoled (**de**, for). **~ation** *n.f.* consolation.

consolider /kɔ̃sɔlide/ *v.t.* strengthen; (*fig.*) consolidate.

consomma|teur, **~trice** /kɔ̃sɔmatœr, -tris/ *n.m.*, *f.* (*comm.*) consumer; (*dans un café*) customer.

consommé[1] /kɔ̃sɔme/ *a.* consummate.

consommé[2] /kɔ̃sɔme/ *n.m.* (*bouillon*) consommé.

consomm|er /kɔ̃sɔme/ *v.t.* consume; (*user*) use, consume; (*mariage*) consummate. **—** *v.i.* drink. **~ation** *n.f.* consumption; consummation; (*boisson*) drink. **de ~ation**, (*comm.*) consumer.

consonne /kɔ̃sɔn/ *n.f.* consonant.

consortium /kɔ̃sɔrsjɔm/ *n.m.* consortium.

conspir|er /kɔ̃spire/ *v.i.* conspire. **~ateur**, **~atrice** *n.m.*, *f.* conspirator. **~ation** *n.f.* conspiracy.

conspuer /kɔ̃spɥe/ *v.t.* boo.

const|ant, **~ante** /kɔ̃stɑ̃, -t/ *a.*

constant. —*n.f.* constant. **~amment**
/-amã/ *adv.* constantly. **~ance** *n.f.*
constancy.

constat /kɔ̃sta/ *n.m.* (official) report.

constat|er /kɔ̃state/ *v.t.* note; (*certifier*)
certify. **~ation** *n.f.* observation, statement of fact.

constellation /kɔ̃stelasjɔ̃/ *n.f.* constellation.

constellé /kɔ̃stele/ *a.* **~ de,** studded with.

constern|er /kɔ̃stɛrne/ *v.t.* dismay.
~ation *n.f.* dismay.

constip|é /kɔ̃stipe/ *a.* constipated; (*fig.*)
stilted. **~ation** *n.f.* constipation.

constitu|er /kɔ̃stitɥe/ *v.t.* make up,
constitute; (*organiser*) form; (*être*)
constitute. **se ~er prisonnier,** give o.s.
up. **~é de,** made up of.

constituti|f, **~ve** /kɔ̃stitytif, -v/ *a.*
constituent.

constitution /kɔ̃stitysjɔ̃/ *n.f.* formation;
(*d'une équipe*) composition; (*pol.,
méd.*) constitution. **~nel,** **~nelle**
/-jɔnɛl/ *a.* constitutional.

constructeur /kɔ̃stryktœr/ *n.m.* manu-
facturer.

constructi|f, **~ve** /kɔ̃stryktif, -v/ *a.*
constructive.

constr|uire† /kɔ̃strɥir/ *v.t.* build;
(*système, phrase, etc.*) construct.
~uction *n.f.* building; (*structure*)
construction.

consul /kɔ̃syl/ *n.m.* consul. **~aire** *a.*
consular. **~at** *n.m.* consulate.

consult|er /kɔ̃sylte/ *v.t.* consult. —*v.i.*
(*médecin*) hold surgery; (*Amer.*) hold
office hours. **se ~er** *v. pr.* confer.
~ation *n.f.* consultation; (*réception:
méd.*) surgery; (*Amer.*) office.

consumer /kɔ̃syme/ *v.t.* consume. **se ~**
v. pr. be consumed.

contact /kɔ̃takt/ *n.m.* contact; (*toucher*)
touch. **au ~ de,** on contact with;
(*personne*) by contact with, by seeing.
mettre/couper le ~, (*auto.*) switch
on/off the ignition. **prendre ~ avec,**
get in touch with. **~er** *v.t.* contact.

contag|ieux, **~ieuse** /kɔ̃taʒjø, -z/ *a.*
contagious. **~ion** *n.f.* contagion.

container /kɔ̃tɛnɛr/ *n.m.* container.

contamin|er /kɔ̃tamine/ *v.t.* con-
taminate. **~ation** *n.f.* contamination.

conte /kɔ̃t/ *n.m.* tale. **~ de fées,** fairy
tale.

contempl|er /kɔ̃tãple/ *v.t.* contemplate.
~ation *n.f.* contemplation.

contemporain, **~e** /kɔ̃tãpɔrɛ̃, -ɛn/ *a.*
& *n.m., f.* contemporary.

contenance /kɔ̃tnãs/ *n.f.* (*contenu*)

capacity; (*allure*) bearing; (*sang-froid*)
composure.

conteneur /kɔ̃tnœr/ *n.m.* container.

contenir† /kɔ̃tnir/ *v.t.* contain; (*avoir
une capacité de*) hold. **se ~** *v. pr.*
contain o.s.

content, **~e** /kɔ̃tã, -t/ *a.* pleased (**de,**
with). **~ de faire,** pleased to do.

content|er /kɔ̃tãte/ *v.t.* satisfy. **se ~er
de,** content o.s. with. **~ement** *n.m.*
contentment.

contentieux /kɔ̃tãsjø/ *n.m.* matters in
dispute; (*service*) legal department.

contenu /kɔ̃tny/ *n.m.* (*de contenant*)
contents; (*de texte*) content.

conter /kɔ̃te/ *v.t.* tell, relate.

contestataire /kɔ̃tɛstatɛr/ *n.m./f.* protester.

conteste (sans) /(sã)kɔ̃tɛst/ *adv.* indis-
putably.

contest|er /kɔ̃tɛste/ *v.t.* dispute;
(*s'opposer*) protest against. —*v.i.*
protest. **~able** *a.* debatable. **~ation** *n.f.*
dispute; (*opposition*) protest.

conteu|r, **~se** /kɔ̃tœr, -øz/ *n.m., f.*
story-teller.

contexte /kɔ̃tɛkst/ *n.m.* context.

contigu, **~ë** /kɔ̃tigy/ *a.* adjacent (**à,** to).

continent /kɔ̃tinã/ *n.m.* continent. **~al**
(*m. pl.* **~aux**) /-tal, -to/ *a.*
continental.

contingences /kɔ̃tɛ̃ʒɔ̃s/ *n.f. pl.* contin-
gencies.

contingent /kɔ̃tɛ̃ʒã/ *n.m.* (*mil.*) contingent; (*comm.*) quota.

continu /kɔ̃tiny/ *a.* continuous.

continuel, **~le** /kɔ̃tinɥɛl/ *a.* continual.
~lement *adv.* continually.

contin|uer /kɔ̃tinɥe/ *v.t.* continue. —*v.i.*
continue, go on. **~uer à** *ou* **de faire,**
carry on *ou* go on *ou* continue doing.
~uation *n.f.* continuation.

continuité /kɔ̃tinɥite/ *n.f.* continuity.

contorsion /kɔ̃tɔrsjɔ̃/ *n.f.* contortion. **se
~ner** *v. pr.* wriggle.

contour /kɔ̃tur/ *n.m.* outline, contour.
~s, (*d'une route etc.*) twists and turns,
bends.

contourner /kɔ̃turne/ *v.t.* go round;
(*difficulté*) get round.

contracepti|f, **~ve** /kɔ̃trasɛptif, -v/ *a.*
& *n.m.* contraceptive.

contraception /kɔ̃trasɛpsjɔ̃/ *n.f.* contraception.

contract|er /kɔ̃trakte/ *v.t.* (*maladie,
dette*) contract; (*muscle*) tense, contract; (*assurance*) take out. **se ~er** *v. pr.*
contract. **~é** *a.* tense. **~ion** /-ksjɔ̃/ *n.f.*
contraction.

contractuel, ∼le /kɔ̃traktɥɛl/ *n.m.*, *f.* (*agent*) traffic warden.

contradiction /kɔ̃tradiksjɔ̃/ *n.f.* contradiction.

contradictoire /kɔ̃tradiktwar/ *a.* contradictory; (*débat*) open.

contraignant, ∼e /kɔ̃trɛɲɑ̃, -t/ *a.* restricting.

contraindre† /kɔ̃trɛ̃dr/ *v.t.* compel.

contraint, ∼e /kɔ̃trɛ̃, -t/ *a.* constrained. —*n.f.* constraint.

contraire /kɔ̃trɛr/ *a. & n.m.* opposite. ∼ à, contrary to. au ∼, on the contrary. ∼ment *adv.* ∼ment à, contrary to.

contralto /kɔ̃tralto/ *n.m.* contralto.

contrar|ier /kɔ̃trarje/ *v.t.* annoy; (*action*) frustrate. ∼iété *n.f.* annoyance.

contrast|e /kɔ̃trast/ *n.m.* contrast. ∼er *v.i.* contrast.

contrat /kɔ̃tra/ *n.m.* contract.

contravention /kɔ̃travɑ̃sjɔ̃/ *n.f.* (parking-)ticket. en ∼, in contravention (à, of).

contre /kɔ̃tr(ə)/ *prép.* against; (*en échange de*) for. par ∼, on the other hand. tout ∼, close by. ∼-attaque *n.f.*, ∼-attaquer *v.t.* counter-attack. ∼-balancer *v.t.* counterbalance. ∼-courant *n.m.* aller à ∼-courant de, swim against the current of. ∼indiqué *a.* (*méd.*) contra-indicated; (*déconseillé*) not recommended. à ∼-jour *adv.* against the (sun)light. ∼-offensive *n.f.* counter-offensive. prendre le ∼-pied, do the opposite; (*opinion*) take the opposite view. à ∼-pied *adv.* (*sport*) on the wrong foot. ∼-plaqué *n.m.* plywood. ∼-révolution *n.f.* counter-revolution. ∼-torpilleur *n.m.* destroyer.

contreband|e /kɔ̃trəbɑ̃d/ *n.f.* contraband. faire la ∼e de, passer en ∼e, smuggle. ∼ier *n.m.* smuggler.

contrebas (en) /(ɑ̃)kɔ̃trəba/ *adv. & prép.* en ∼ (de), below.

contrebasse /kɔ̃trəbas/ *n.f.* double-bass.

contrecarrer /kɔ̃trəkare/ *v.t.* thwart.

contrecœur (à) /(a)kɔ̃trəkœr/ *adv.* reluctantly.

contrecoup /kɔ̃trəku/ *n.m.* consequence.

contredire† /kɔ̃trədir/ *v.t.* contradict. se ∼ *v. pr.* contradict o.s.

contrée /kɔ̃tre/ *n.f.* region, land.

contrefaçon /kɔ̃trəfasɔ̃/ *n.f.* (*objet imité*, *action*) forgery.

contrefaire /kɔ̃trəfɛr/ *v.t.* (*falsifier*) forge; (*parodier*) mimic; (*déguiser*) disguise.

contrefait, ∼e /kɔ̃trəfɛ, -t/ *a.* deformed.

contreforts /kɔ̃trəfɔr/ *n.m. pl.* foothills.

contremaître /kɔ̃trəmɛtr/ *n.m.* foreman.

contrepartie /kɔ̃trəparti/ *n.f.* compensation. en ∼, in exchange, in return.

contrepoids /kɔ̃trəpwa/ *n.m.* counterbalance.

contrer /kɔ̃tre/ *v.t.* counter.

contresens /kɔ̃trəsɑ̃s/ *n.m.* misinterpretation; (*absurdité*) nonsense. à ∼, the wrong way.

contresigner /kɔ̃trəsiɲe/ *v.t.* countersign.

contretemps /kɔ̃trətɑ̃/ *n.m.* hitch. à ∼, at the wrong time.

contrevenir /kɔ̃trəvnir/ *v.i.* ∼ à, contravene.

contribuable /kɔ̃tribɥabl/ *n.m./f.* taxpayer.

contribuer /kɔ̃tribɥe/ *v.t.* contribute (à, to, towards).

contribution /kɔ̃tribysjɔ̃/ *n.f.* contribution. ∼s, (*impôts*) taxes; (*administration*) tax office.

contrit, ∼e /kɔ̃tri, -t/ *a.* contrite.

contrôl|e /kɔ̃trol/ *n.m.* check; (*des prix, d'un véhicule*) control; (*poinçon*) hallmark; (*scol.*) test. ∼e continu, continuous assessment. ∼e de soi-même, self-control. ∼e des changes, exchange control. ∼e des naissances birth-control. ∼er *v.t.* check; (*surveiller, maîtriser*) control. se ∼er *v. pr.* control o.s.

contrôleu|r, ∼se /kɔ̃trolœr, -øz/ *n.m.*, *f.* (bus) conductor *ou* conductress; (*de train*) (ticket) inspector.

contrordre /kɔ̃trɔrdr/ *n.m.* change of orders.

controvers|e /kɔ̃trɔvɛrs/ *n.f.* controversy. ∼é *a.* controversial.

contumace (par) /(par)kɔ̃tymas/ *adv.* in one's absence.

contusion /kɔ̃tyzjɔ̃/ *n.f.* bruise. ∼né /-jɔne/ *a.* bruised.

convaincre† /kɔ̃vɛ̃kr/ *v.t.* convince. ∼ qn. de faire, persuade s.o. to do.

convalescen|t, ∼te /kɔ̃valesɑ̃, -t/ *a. & n.m.*, *f.* convalescent. ∼ce *n.f.* convalescence. être en ∼ce, convalesce.

convenable /kɔ̃vnabl/ *a.* (*correct*) decent, proper; (*approprié*) suitable.

convenance /kɔ̃vnɑ̃s/ *n.f.* à sa ∼, to one's satisfaction. les ∼s, the proprieties.

convenir† /kɔ̃vnir/ *v.i.* be suitable. ∼ à suit. ∼ de/que, (*avouer*) admit (to)/that. ∼ de qch., (*s'accorder sur*) agree on sth. ⁓ **de faire,** agree to do. **il convient de,** it is advisable to; (*selon les bienséances*) it would be right to.

convention /kɔ̃vɑ̃sjɔ̃/ *n.f.* convention. ⁓**s,** (*convenances*) convention. **de** ⁓, conventional. ⁓ **collective,** industrial agreement. ⁓**né** *a.* (*prix*) official; (*médecin*) health service (*not private*). ⁓**nel,** ⁓**nelle** /-jɔnɛl/ *a.* conventional.

convenu /kɔ̃vny/ *a.* agreed.

converger /kɔ̃vɛrʒe/ *v.i.* converge.

convers|er /kɔ̃vɛrse/ *v.i.* converse. ⁓**ation** *n.f.* conversation.

conver|tir /kɔ̃vɛrtir/ *v.t.* convert (**à,** to; **en,** into). **se** ⁓**tir** *v. pr.* be converted, convert. ⁓**sion** *n.f.* conversion. ⁓**tible** *a.* convertible.

convexe /kɔ̃vɛks/ *a.* convex.

conviction /kɔ̃viksjɔ̃/ *n.f.* conviction.

convier /kɔ̃vje/ *v.t.* invite.

convive /kɔ̃viv/ *n.m./f.* guest.

conviv|ial (*m. pl.* ⁓**iaux**) /kɔ̃vivjal, -jo/ *a.* convivial; (*comput.*) user-friendly.

convocation /kɔ̃vɔkasjɔ̃/ *n.f.* summons to attend; (*d'une assemblée*) convening; (*document*) notification to attend.

convoi /kɔ̃vwa/ *n.m.* convoy; (*train*) train. ⁓ (**funèbre**), funeral procession.

convoit|er /kɔ̃vwate/ *v.t.* desire, covet, envy. ⁓**ise** *n.f.* desire, envy.

convoquer /kɔ̃vɔke/ *v.t.* (*assemblée*) convene; (*personne*) summon.

convoy|er /kɔ̃vwaje/ *v.t.* escort. ⁓**eur** *n.m.* escort ship. ⁓**eur de fonds,** security guard.

convulsion /kɔ̃vylsjɔ̃/ *n.f.* convulsion.

cool /kul/ *a. invar.* cool, laidback.

coopérati|f, ⁓**ve** /kɔɔperatif, -v/ *a.* co-operative. —*n.f.* co-operative (society).

coopér|er /kɔɔpere/ *v.i.* co-operate (**à,** in). ⁓**ation** *n.f.* co-operation. **la C**⁓**ation,** civilian national service.

coopter /kɔɔpte/ *v.t.* co-opt.

coordination /kɔɔrdinasjɔ̃/ *n.f.* co-ordination.

coordonn|er /kɔɔrdɔne/ *v.t.* co-ordinate. ⁓**ées** *n.f. pl.* co-ordinates; (*adresse: fam.*) particulars.

copain /kɔpɛ̃/ *n.m.* (*fam.*) pal; (*petit ami*) boyfriend.

copeau (*pl.* ⁓**x**) /kɔpo/ *n.m.* (*lamelle de bois*) shaving.

cop|ie /kɔpi/ *n.f.* copy; (*scol.*) paper. ⁓**ier** *v.t./i.* copy. ⁓**ier sur,** (*scol.*) copy *ou* crib from.

copieu|x, ⁓**se** /kɔpjø, -z/ *a.* copious.

copine /kɔpin/ *n.f.* (*fam.*) pal; (*petite amie*) girlfriend.

coproduction /kɔprɔdyksjɔ̃/ *n.f.* co-production.

copiste /kɔpist/ *n.m./f.* copyist.

copropriété /kɔprɔprijete/ *n.f.* co-ownership.

copulation /kɔpylasjɔ̃/ *n.f.* copulation.

coq /kɔk/ *n.m.* cock. ⁓**-à-l'âne** *n.m. invar.* abrupt change of subject.

coque /kɔk/ *n.f.* shell; (*de bateau*) hull.

coquelicot /kɔkliko/ *n.m.* poppy.

coqueluche /kɔklyʃ/ *n.f.* whooping cough.

coquet, ⁓**te** /kɔkɛ, -t/ *a.* flirtatious; (*élégant*) pretty; (*somme: fam.*) tidy. ⁓**terie** /-tri/ *n.f.* flirtatiousness.

coquetier /kɔktje/ *n.m.* egg-cup.

coquillage /kɔkijaʒ/ *n.m.* shellfish; (*coquille*) shell.

coquille /kɔkij/ *n.f.* shell; (*faute*) misprint. ⁓ **Saint-Jacques,** scallop.

coquin, ⁓**e** /kɔkɛ̃, -in/ *a.* naughty. —*n.m., f.* rascal.

cor /kɔr/ *n.m.* (*mus.*) horn; (*au pied*) corn.

cor|ail (*pl.* ⁓**aux**) /kɔraj, -o/ *n.m.* coral.

Coran /kɔrɑ̃/ *n.m.* Koran.

corbeau (*pl.* ⁓**x**) /kɔrbo/ *n.m.* (*oiseau*) crow.

corbeille /kɔrbɛj/ *n.f.* basket. ⁓ **à papier,** waste-paper basket.

corbillard /kɔrbijar/ *n.m.* hearse.

cordage /kɔrdaʒ/ *n.m.* rope. ⁓**s,** (*naut.*) rigging.

corde /kɔrd/ *n.f.* rope; (*d'arc, de violon, etc.*) string. ⁓ **à linge,** washing line. ⁓ **à sauter,** skipping-rope. ⁓ **raide,** tight-rope. ⁓**s vocales,** vocal cords.

cordée /kɔrde/ *n.f.* roped party.

cord|ial (*m. pl.* ⁓**iaux**) /kɔrdjal, -jo/ *a.* warm, cordial. ⁓**ialité** *n.f.* warmth.

cordon /kɔrdɔ̃/ *n.m.* string, cord. ⁓**-bleu** (*pl.* ⁓**s-bleus**) *n.m.* first-rate cook. ⁓ **de police,** police cordon.

cordonnier /kɔrdɔnje/ *n.m.* shoe mender.

Corée /kɔre/ *n.f.* Korea.

coreligionnaire /kɔrəliʒjɔnɛr/ *n.m./f.* person of the same religion.

coriace /kɔrjas/ *a.* (*aliment*) tough. —*a. & n.m.* tenacious and tough (person).

corne /kɔrn/ *n.f.* horn.

cornée /kɔrne/ *n.f.* cornea.

corneille /kɔrnɛj/ *n.f.* crow.

cornemuse /kɔrnəmyz/ *n.f.* bagpipes.

corner[1] /kɔrne/ *v.t.* (*page*) make dog-eared. —*v.i.* (*auto.*) hoot; (*auto., Amer.*) honk.

corner[2] /kɔrnɛr/ *n.m.* (*football*) corner.

cornet /kɔrnɛ/ n.m. (paper) cone; (*crème glacée*) cornet, cone.

corniaud /kɔrnjo/ n.m. (*fam.*) nitwit.

corniche /kɔrniʃ/ n.f. cornice; (*route*) cliff road.

cornichon /kɔrniʃɔ̃/ n.m. gherkin.

corollaire /kɔrɔlɛr/ n.m. corollary.

corporation /kɔrpɔrasjɔ̃/ n.f. professional body.

corporel, ~le /kɔrpɔrɛl/ a. bodily; (*châtiment*) corporal.

corps /kɔr/ n.m. body; (*mil., pol.*) corps. **~ à corps,** hand to hand. **~ électoral,** electorate. **~ enseignant,** teaching profession. **faire ~ avec,** form part of.

corpulen|t, ~te /kɔrpylɑ̃, -t/ a. stout. **~ce** n.f. stoutness.

correct /kɔrɛkt/ a. proper, correct; (*exact*) correct; (*tenue*) decent. **~ement** adv. properly; correctly; decently.

correc|teur, ~trice /kɔrɛktœr, -tris/ n.m., f. (*d'épreuves*) proof-reader; (*scol.*) examiner. **~teur d'ortho-graphe,** spelling checker.

correction /kɔrɛksjɔ̃/ n.f. correction; (*punition*) beating.

corrélation /kɔrelasjɔ̃/ n.f. correlation.

correspondan|t, ~te /kɔrɛspɔ̃dɑ̃, -t/ a. corresponding. —n.m., f. correspondent; (*au téléphone*) caller. **~ce** n.f. correspondence; (*de train, d'autobus*) connection. **vente par ~ce,** mail order.

correspondre /kɔrɛspɔ̃dr/ v.i. (*s'accorder, écrire*) correspond; (*chambres*) communicate.

corrida /kɔrida/ n.f. bullfight.

corridor /kɔridɔr/ n.m. corridor.

corrig|er /kɔriʒe/ v.t. correct; (*devoir*) mark, correct; (*punir*) beat; (*guérir*) cure. **se ~er de,** cure o.s. of. **~é** n.m. (*scol.*) correct version, model answer.

corroborer /kɔrɔbɔre/ v.t. corroborate.

corro|der /kɔrɔde/ v.t. corrode. **~sion** /-ozjɔ̃/ n.f. corrosion.

corromp|re† /kɔrɔ̃pr/ v.t. corrupt; (*soudoyer*) bribe. **~u** a. corrupt.

corrosi|f, ~ve /kɔrozif, -v/ a. corrosive.

corruption /kɔrypsjɔ̃/ n.f. corruption.

corsage /kɔrsaʒ/ n.m. bodice; (*chemisier*) blouse.

corsaire /kɔrsɛr/ n.m. pirate.

Corse /kɔrs/ n.f. Corsica.

corse /kɔrs/ a. & n.m./f. Corsican.

corsé /kɔrse/ a. (*vin*) full-bodied; (*scabreux*) spicy.

corset /kɔrsɛ/ n.m. corset.

cortège /kɔrtɛʒ/ n.m. procession.

cortisone /kɔrtizɔn/ n.f. cortisone.

corvée /kɔrve/ n.f. chore.

cosaque /kɔzak/ n.m. Cossack.

cosmétique /kɔsmetik/ n.m. cosmetic.

cosmique /kɔsmik/ a. cosmic.

cosmonaute /kɔsmɔnot/ n.m./f. cosmonaut.

cosmopolite /kɔsmɔpɔlit/ a. cosmopolitan.

cosmos /kɔsmɔs/ n.m. (*espace*) (outer) space; (*univers*) cosmos.

cosse /kɔs/ n.f. (*de pois*) pod.

cossu /kɔsy/ a. (*gens*) well-to-do; (*demeure*) opulent.

costaud, ~e /kɔsto, -d/ a. (*fam.*) strong. —n.m. (*fam.*) strong man.

costum|e /kɔstym/ n.m. suit; (*théâtre*) costume. **~é** a. dressed up.

cote /kɔt/ n.f. (classification) mark; (*en Bourse*) quotation; (*de cheval*) odds (**de,** on); (*de candidat, acteur*) rating. **~ d'alerte,** danger level.

côte /kot/ n.f. (*littoral*) coast; (*pente*) hill; (*anat.*) rib; (*de porc*) chop. **~ à côte,** side by side. **la C~ d'Azur,** the (French) Riviera.

côté /kote/ n.m. side; (*direction*) way. **à ~,** nearby; (*voisin*) nextdoor. **à ~ de,** next to; (*comparé à*) compared to; (*cible*) wide of. **aux ~s de,** by the side of. **de ~,** aside; (*regarder*) sideways. **mettre de ~,** put aside. **de ce ~,** this way. **de chaque ~,** on each side. **de tous les ~s,** on every side; (*partout*) everywhere. **du ~ de,** towards; (*proximité*) near; (*provenance*) from.

coteau (*pl.* **~x**) /kɔto/ n.m. hill.

côtelette /kotlɛt/ n.f. chop.

coter /kɔte/ v.t. (*comm.*) quote; (*apprécier, noter*) rate.

coterie /kɔtri/ n.f. clique.

côt|ier, ~ière /kotje, -jɛr/ a. coastal.

cotis|er /kɔtize/ v.i. pay one's contributions (**à,** to); (*à un club*) pay one's subscription. **se ~er** v. pr. club together. **~ation** n.f. contribution(s); subscription.

coton /kɔtɔ̃/ n.m. cotton. **~ hydrophile,** cotton wool.

côtoyer /kotwaje/ v.t. skirt, run along; (*fréquenter*) rub shoulders with; (*fig.*) verge on.

cotte /kɔt/ n.f. (*d'ouvrier*) overalls.

cou /ku/ n.m. neck.

couchage /kuʃaʒ/ n.m. sleeping arrangements.

couchant /kuʃɑ̃/ n.m. sunset.

couche /kuʃ/ n.f. layer; (*de peinture*)

coat; (*de bébé*) nappy. ~s, (*méd.*) childbirth. ~s sociales, social strata.

coucher /kuʃe/ *n.m.* ~ (du soleil), sunset. —*v.t.* put to bed; (*loger*) put up; (*étendre*) lay down. ~ (par écrit), set down. —*v.i.* sleep. se ~ *v. pr.* go to bed; (*s'étendre*) lie down; (*soleil*) set. couché *a.* in bed; (*étendu*) lying down.

couchette /kuʃɛt/ *n.f.* (*rail.*) couchette; (*naut.*) bunk.

coucou /kuku/ *n.m.* cuckoo.

coude /kud/ *n.m.* elbow; (*de rivière etc.*) bend. ~ à coude, side by side.

cou-de-pied (*pl.* cous-de-pied) /kudpje/ *n.m.* instep.

coudoyer /kudwaje/ *v.t.* rub shoulders with.

coudre† /kudr/ *v.t./i.* sew.

couenne /kwan/ *n.f.* (*de porc*) rind.

couette /kwɛt/ *n.f.* duvet, continental quilt.

couffin /kufɛ̃/ *n.m.* Moses basket.

couiner /kwine/ *v.i.* squeak.

coulant, ~e /kulɑ̃, -t/ *a.* (*indulgent*) easy-going; (*fromage*) runny.

coulée /kule/ *n.f.* ~ de lave, lava flow.

couler¹ /kule/ *v.i.* flow, run; (*fromage, nez*) run; (*fuir*) leak. —*v.t.* (*sculpture, métal*) cast; (*vie*) pass, lead. se ~ *v. pr.* (*se glisser*) slip.

couler² /kule/ *v.t./i.* (*bateau*) sink.

couleur /kulœr/ *n.f.* colour; (*peinture*) paint; (*cartes*) suit. ~s, (*teint*) colour. de ~, (*homme, femme*) coloured. en ~s, (*télévision, film*) colour.

couleuvre /kulœvr/ *n.f.* (grass *ou* smooth) snake.

coulis /kuli/ *n.m.* (*culin.*) coulis.

couliss|e /kulis/ *n.f.* (*de tiroir etc.*) runner. ~es, (*théâtre*) wings. à ~e, (*porte, fenêtre*) sliding. ~er *v.i.* slide.

couloir /kulwar/ *n.m.* corridor; (*de bus*) gangway; (*sport*) lane.

coup /ku/ *n.m.* blow; (*choc*) knock; (*sport*) stroke; (*de crayon, chance, cloche*) stroke; (*de fusil, pistolet*) shot; (*fois*) time; (*aux échecs*) move. à ~ sûr, definitely. après ~, after the event. boire un ~, have a drink. ~ de chiffon, wipe (with a rag). ~ de coude, nudge. ~ de couteau, stab. ~ d'envoi, kick-off. ~ d'état (*pol.*) coup. ~ de feu, shot. ~ de fil, phone call. ~ de filet, haul. ~ de frein, sudden braking. ~ de grâce, coup de grâce. ~ de main, helping hand. avoir le ~ de main, have the knack. ~ d'œil, glance. ~ de pied, kick. ~ de poing, punch. ~ de sang, (*méd.*) stroke. ~ de soleil, sunburn. ~

de sonnette, ring (on a bell). ~ de téléphone, (tele)phone call. ~ de tête, wild impulse. ~ de théâtre, dramatic event. ~ de tonnerre, thunderclap. ~ de vent, gust of wind. ~ franc, free kick. ~ sur coup, in rapid succession. d'un seul ~, in one go. du premier ~, first go. sale ~, dirty trick. sous le ~ de, under the influence of. sur le ~, immediately. tenir le coup, take it.

coupable /kupabl/ *a.* guilty. —*n.m./f.* culprit.

coupe¹ /kup/ *n.f.* cup; (*de champagne*) goblet; (*à fruits*) dish.

coupe² /kup/ *n.f.* (*de vêtement etc.*) cut; (*dessin*) section. ~ de cheveux, haircut.

coupé /kupe/ *n.m.* (*voiture*) coupé.

coup|er /kupe/ *v.t./i.* cut; (*arbre*) cut down; (*arrêter*) cut off; (*voyage*) break; (*appétit*) take away; (*vin*) water down. ~er par, take a short cut via. se ~er *v. pr.* cut o.s.; (*routes*) intersect. ~er la parole à, cut short. ~e-papier *n.m. invar.* paper-knife.

couperosé /kuproze/ *a.* blotchy.

couple /kupl/ *n.m.* couple.

coupler /kuple/ *v.t.* couple.

couplet /kuplɛ/ *n.m.* verse.

coupole /kupɔl/ *n.f.* dome.

coupon /kupɔ̃/ *n.m.* (*étoffe*) remnant; (*billet, titre*) coupon.

coupure /kupyr/ *n.f.* cut; (*billet de banque*) note; (*de presse*) cutting. ~ (de courant), power cut.

cour /kur/ *n.f.* (court)yard; (*de roi*) court; (*tribunal*) court. ~ de récréation), playground. ~ martiale, court martial. faire la ~ à, court.

courag|e /kuraʒ/ *n.m.* courage. ~eux, ~euse *a.* courageous.

couramment /kuramɑ̃/ *adv.* frequently; (*parler*) fluently.

courant¹, ~e /kurɑ̃, -t/ *a.* standard, ordinary; (*en cours*) current.

courant² /kurɑ̃/ *n.m.* current; (*de mode, d'idées*) trend. ~ d'air, draught. dans le ~ de, in the course of. être/mettre au ~ de, know/tell about; (*à jour*) be/bring up to date on.

courbatur|e /kurbatyr/ *n.f.* ache. ~é *a.* aching.

courbe /kurb/ *n.f.* curve. —*a.* curved.

courber /kurbe/ *v.t./i.*, se ~ *v. pr.* bend.

coureu|r, ~se /kurœr, -øz/ *n.m., f.* (*sport*) runner. ~r automobile, racing driver. —*n.m.* womaniser.

courge /kurʒ/ *n.f.* marrow; (*Amer.*) squash.

courgette /kurʒɛt/ n.f. courgette; (*Amer.*) zucchini.

courir† /kurir/ v.i. run; (*se hâter*) rush; (*nouvelles etc.*) go round. —v.t. (*risque*) run; (*danger*) face; (*épreuve sportive*) run *ou* compete in; (*fréquenter*) do the rounds of; (*filles*) chase.

couronne /kurɔn/ n.f. crown; (*de fleurs*) wreath.

couronn|er /kurɔne/ v.t. crown. **~ement** n.m. coronation, crowning; (*fig.*) crowning achievement.

courrier /kurje/ n.m. post, mail; (*à écrire*) letters; (*de journal*) column.

courroie /kurwa/ n.f. strap; (*techn.*) belt.

courroux /kuru/ n.m. wrath.

cours /kur/ n.m. (*leçon*) class; (*série de leçons*) course; (*prix*) price; (*cote*) rate; (*déroulement, d'une rivière*) course; (*allée*) avenue. **au ~ de**, in the course of. **avoir ~**, (*monnaie*) be legal tender; (*fig.*) be current; (*scol.*) have a lesson. **~ d'eau**, river, stream. **~ du soir**, evening class. **~ magistral**, (*univ.*) lecture. **en ~**, current; (*travail*) in progress. **en ~ de route**, on the way.

course /kurs/ n.f. run(ning); (*épreuve de vitesse*) race; (*entre rivaux: fig.*) race; (*de projectile*) flight; (*voyage*) journey; (*commission*) errand. **~s**, (*achats*) shopping; (*de chevaux*) races.

cours|ier, **~ère** /kursje, -jɛr/ n.m., f. messenger.

court[1], **~e** /kur, -t/ a. short. —adv. short. **à ~ de**, short of. **pris de ~**, caught unawares. **~-circuit** (*pl.* **~s-circuits**) n.m. short circuit.

court[2] /kur/ n.m. **~ (de tennis)**, (tennis) court.

court|ier, **~ière** /kurtje, -jɛr/ n.m., f. broker.

courtisan /kurtizɑ̃/ n.m. courtier.

courtisane /kurtizan/ n.f. courtesan.

courtiser /kurtize/ v.t. court.

courtois, ~e /kurtwa, -z/ a. courteous. **~ie** /-zi/ n.f. courtesy.

couscous /kuskus/ n.m. couscous.

cousin, ~e /kuzɛ̃, -in/ n.m., f. cousin. **~ germain**, first cousin.

coussin /kusɛ̃/ n.m. cushion.

coût /ku/ n.m. cost.

couteau (*pl.* **~x**) /kuto/ n.m. knife. **~ à cran d'arrêt**, flick-knife.

coutellerie /kutɛlri/ n.f. (*magasin*) cutlery shop.

coût|er /kute/ v.t./i. cost. **~e que coûte**, at all costs. **au prix ~ant**, at cost (price). **~eux, ~euse** a. costly.

coutum|e /kutym/ n.f. custom. **~ier, ~ière** a. customary.

coutur|e /kutyr/ n.f. sewing; (*métier*) dressmaking; (*points*) seam. **~ier** n.m. fashion de-signer. **~ière** n.f. dressmaker.

couvée /kuve/ n.f. brood.

couvent /kuvɑ̃/ n.m. convent; (*de moines*) monastery.

couver /kuve/ v.t. (*œufs*) hatch; (*personne*) pamper; (*maladie*) be coming down with, be sickening for. —v.i. (*feu*) smoulder; (*mal*) be brewing.

couvercle /kuvɛrkl/ n.m. (*de marmite, boîte*) lid; (*d'objet allongé*) top.

couvert[1], **~e** /kuvɛr, -t/ a. covered (**de**, with); (*habillé*) covered up; (*ciel*) overcast. —n.m. (*abri*) cover. **à ~**, (*mil.*) under cover. **à ~ de**, (*fig.*) safe from.

couvert[2] /kuvɛr/ n.m. (*à table*) place-setting; (*prix*) cover charge. **~s**, (*couteaux etc.*) cutlery. **mettre le ~**, lay the table.

couverture /kuvɛrtyr/ n.f. cover; (*de lit*) blanket; (*toit*) roofing. **~ chauffante**, electric blanket.

couveuse /kuvøz/ n.f. **~ (artificielle)**, incubator.

couvreur /kuvrœr/ n.m. roofer.

couvr|ir† /kuvrir/ v.t. cover. **se ~ir** v. pr. (*s'habiller*) cover up; (*se coiffer*) put one's hat on; (*ciel*) become overcast. **~e-chef** n.m. hat. **~e-feu** (*pl.* **~e-feux**) n.m. curfew. **~e-lit** n.m. bedspread.

cow-boy /kɔbɔj/ n.m. cowboy.

crabe /krab/ n.m. crab.

crachat /kraʃa/ n.m. spit(tle).

cracher /kraʃe/ v.i. spit; (*radio*) crackle. —v.t. spit (out).

crachin /kraʃɛ̃/ n.m. drizzle.

crack /krak/ n.m. (*fam.*) wizard, ace, prodigy.

craie /krɛ/ n.f. chalk.

craindre† /krɛ̃dr/ v.t. be afraid of, fear; (*être sensible à*) be easily damaged by.

crainte /krɛ̃t/ n.f. fear. **de ~ de/que**, for fear of/that.

crainti|f, ~ve /krɛ̃tif, -v/ a. timid.

cramoisi /kramwazi/ a. crimson.

crampe /krɑ̃p/ n.f. cramp.

crampon /krɑ̃pɔ̃/ n.m. (*de chaussure*) stud.

cramponner (se) /(sə)krɑ̃pɔne/ v. pr. **se ~ à**, cling to.

cran /krɑ̃/ n.m. (*entaille*) notch; (*trou*) hole; (*courage: fam.*) pluck.

crâne /krɑn/ *n.m.* skull.

crâner /krɑne/ *v.i.* (*fam.*) swank.

crapaud /krapo/ *n.m.* toad.

crapul|e /krapyl/ *n.f.* villain. ～**eux**, ～**euse** *a.* sordid, foul.

craqu|er /krake/ *v.i.* crack, snap; (*plancher*) creak; (*couture*) split; (*fig.*) break down; (*céder*) give in. —*v.t.* ～**er une allumette,** strike a match. ～**ement** *n.m.* crack(ing), snap(ping); creak(ing); striking.

crass|e /kras/ *n.f.* grime. ～**eux**, ～**euse** *a.* grimy.

cratère /kratɛr/ *n.m.* crater.

cravache /kravaʃ/ *n.f.* horsewhip.

cravate /kravat/ *n.f.* tie.

crawl /krol/ *n.m.* (*nage*) crawl.

crayeu|x, ～**se** /krɛjø, -z/ *a.* chalky.

crayon /krɛjɔ̃/ *n.m.* pencil. ～ **(de couleur),** crayon. ～ **à bille,** ball-point pen. ～ **optique,** light pen.

créanc|ier, ～**ière** /kreɑ̃sje, -jɛr/ *n.m.*, *f.* creditor.

créa|teur, ～**trice** /kreatœr, -tris/ *a.* creative. —*n.m.*, *f.* creator.

création /kreasjɔ̃/ *n.f.* creation; (*comm.*) product.

créature /kreatyr/ *n.f.* creature.

crèche /krɛʃ/ *n.f.* day nursery; (*relig.*) crib.

crédibilité /kredibilite/ *n.f.* credibility.

crédit /kredi/ *n.m.* credit; (*banque*) bank. ～**s,** funds. **à** ～, on credit. **faire** ～, give credit (**à**, to). ～**er** /-te/ *v.t.* credit. ～**eur**, ～**euse** /-tœr, -tøz/ *a.* in credit.

credo /kredo/ *n.m.* creed.

crédule /kredyl/ *a.* credulous.

créer /kree/ *v.t.* create.

crémation /kremasjɔ̃/ *n.f.* cremation.

crème /krɛm/ *n.f.* cream; (*dessert*) cream dessert. —*a. invar.* cream. —*n.m.* **(café)** ～, white coffee. ～ **anglaise,** fresh custard. ～ **à raser,** shaving-cream.

crémeu|x, ～**se** /kremø, -z/ *a.* creamy.

crém|ier, ～**ière** /kremje, -jɛr/ *n.m.*, *f.* dairyman, dairywoman. ～**erie** /krɛmri/ *n.f.* dairy.

créneau (*pl.* ～**x**) /kreno/ *n.m.* ·(*trou, moment*) slot; (*dans le marché*) gap; **faire un** ～, park between two cars.

créole /kreol/ *n.m./f.* Creole.

crêpe¹ /krɛp/ *n.f.* (*galette*) pancake. ～**rie** *n.f.* pancake shop.

crêpe² /krɛp/ *n.m.* (*tissu*) crêpe; (*matière*) crêpe (rubber).

crépit|er /krepite/ *v.i.* crackle. ～**ement** *n.m.* crackling.

crépu /krepy/ *a.* frizzy.

crépuscule /krepyskyl/ *n.m.* twilight, dusk.

crescendo /kreʃɛndo/ *adv. & n.m. invar.* crescendo.

cresson /kresɔ̃/ *n.m.* (water)cress.

crête /krɛt/ *n.f.* crest; (*de coq*) comb.

crétin, ～**e** /kretɛ̃, -in/ *n.m.*, *f.* cretin.

creuser /krøze/ *v.t.* dig; (*évider*) hollow out; (*fig.*) go deeply into. **se** ～ **(la cervelle),** (*fam.*) rack one's brains.

creuset /krøze/ *n.m.* (*lieu*) melting-pot.

creu|x, ～**se** /krø, -z/ *a.* hollow; (*heures*) off-peak. —*n.m.* hollow; (*de l'estomac*) pit.

crevaison /krəvɛzɔ̃/ *n.f.* puncture.

crevasse /krəvas/ *n.f.* crack; (*de glacier*) crevasse; (*de la peau*) chap.

crevé /krəve/ *a.* (*fam.*) worn out.

crève-cœur /krɛvkœr/ *n.m. invar.* heart-break.

crever /krəve/ *v.t./i.* burst; (*pneu*) puncture burst; (*exténuer: fam.*) exhaust; (*mourir: fam.*) die; (*œil*) put out.

crevette /krəvɛt/ *n.f.* ～ **(grise),** shrimp. ～ **(rose),** prawn.

cri /kri/ *n.m.* cry; (*de douleur*) scream, cry.

criant, ～**e** /krijɑ̃, -t/ *a.* glaring.

criard, ～**e** /krijar, -d/ *a.* (*couleur*) garish; (*voix*) bawling.

crible /kribl/ *n.m.* sieve, riddle.

criblé /krible/ *a.* ～ **de,** riddled with.

cric /krik/ *n.m.* (*auto.*) jack.

crier /krije/ *v.i.* (*fort*) shout, cry (out); (*de douleur*) scream; (*grincer*) creak. —*v.t.* (*ordre*) shout (out).

crim|e /krim/ *n.m.* crime; (*meurtre*) murder. ～**inalité** *n.f.* crime. ～**inel**, ～**inelle** *a.* criminal; *n.m.*, *f.* criminal; (*assassin*) murderer.

crin /krɛ̃/ *n.m.* horsehair.

crinière /krinjɛr/ *n.f.* mane.

crique /krik/ *n.f.* creek.

criquet /krikɛ/ *n.m.* locust.

crise /kriz/ *n.f.* crisis; (*méd.*) attack; (*de colère*) fit. ～ **cardiaque,** heart attack. ～ **de foie,** bilious attack.

crisp|er /krispe/ *v.t./i.*, **se** ～**er** *v. pr.* tense; (*poings*) clench. ～**ation** *n.f.* tenseness; (*spasme*) twitch. ～**é** *a.* tense.

crisser /krise/ *v.i.* crunch; (*pneu*) screech.

crist|al (*pl.* ～**aux**) /kristal, -o/ *n.m.* crystal.

cristallin, ～**e** /kristalɛ̃, -in/ *a.* (*limpide*) crystal-clear.

cristalliser /kristalize/ *v.t./i.*, **se** ～ *v. pr.* crystallize.

critère /kritɛr/ *n.m.* criterion.
critique /kritik/ *a.* critical. —*n.f.* criticism; (*article*) review. —*n.m.* critic. **la ~,** (*personnes*) the critics.
critiquer /kritike/ *v.t.* criticize.
croasser /krɔase/ *v.i.* caw.
croc /kro/ *n.m.* (*dent*) fang; (*crochet*) hook.
croc-en-jambe (*pl.* **crocs-en-jambe**) /krɔkɑ̃ʒɑ̃b/ *n.m.* = **croche-pied.**
croche /krɔʃ/ *n.f.* quaver. **double ~,** semiquaver.
croche-pied /krɔʃpje/ *n.m.* **faire un ~ à,** trip up.
crochet /krɔʃɛ/ *n.m.* hook; (*détour*) detour; (*signe*) (square) bracket; (*tricot*) crochet. **faire au ~,** crochet.
crochu /krɔʃy/ *a.* hooked.
crocodile /krɔkɔdil/ *n.m.* crocodile.
crocus /krɔkys/ *n.m.* crocus.
croire† /krwar/ *v.t./i.* believe (**à, en,** in); (*estimer*) think, believe (**que,** that).
croisade /krwazad/ *n.f.* crusade.
croisé /krwaze/ *a.* (*veston*) double-breasted. —*n.m.* crusader.
croisée /krwaze/ *n.f.* window. **~ des chemins,** crossroads.
crois|er[1] /krwaze/ *v.t.,* **se ~er** *v. pr.* cross; (*passant, véhicule*) pass (each other). **(se) ~er les bras,** fold one's arms. **(se) ~er les jambes,** cross one's legs. **~ement** *n.m.* crossing; passing; (*carrefour*) crossroads.
crois|er[2] /krwaze/ *v.i.* (*bateau*) cruise. **~eur** *n.m.* cruiser. **~ière** *n.f.* cruise.
croissan|t[1], **~te** /krwasɑ̃, -t/ *a.* growing. **~ce** *n.f.* growth.
croissant[2] /krwasɑ̃/ *n.m.* crescent; (*pâtisserie*) croissant.
croître† /krwatr/ *v.i.* grow; (*lune*) wax.
croix /krwa/ *n.f.* cross. **~ gammée,** swastika. **C~-Rouge,** Red Cross.
croque-monsieur /krɔkməsjø/ *n.m. invar.* toasted ham and cheese sandwich.
croque-mort /krɔkmɔr/ *n.m.* undertaker's assistant.
croqu|er /krɔke/ *v.t./i.* crunch; (*dessiner*) sketch. **chocolat à ~er,** plain chocolate. **~ant, ~ante** *a.* crunchy.
croquet /krɔkɛ/ *n.m.* croquet.
croquette /krɔkɛt/ *n.f.* croquette.
croquis /krɔki/ *n.m.* sketch.
crosse /krɔs/ *n.f.* (*de fusil*) butt; (*d'évêque*) crook.
crotte /krɔt/ *n.f.* droppings.
crotté /krɔte/ *a.* muddy.
crottin /krɔtɛ̃/ *n.m.* (horse) dung.

crouler /krule/ *v.i.* collapse; (*être en ruines*) crumble.
croupe /krup/ *n.f.* rump; (*de colline*) brow. **en ~,** pillion.
croupier /krupje/ *n.m.* croupier.
croupir /krupir/ *v.i.* stagnate.
croustill|er /krustije/ *v.i.* be crusty. **~ant, ~ante** *a.* crusty; (*fig.*) spicy.
croûte /krut/ *n.f.* crust; (*de fromage*) rind; (*de plaie*) scab. **en ~,** (*culin.*) en croûte.
croûton /krutɔ̃/ *n.m.* (*bout de pain*) crust; (*avec potage*) croûton.
croyable /krwajabl/ *a.* credible.
croyan|t, ~te /krwajɑ̃, -t/ *n.m.,* f. believer. **~ce** *n.f.* belief.
CRS *abrév.* (*Compagnies républicaines de sécurité*) French state security police.
cru[1] /kry/ *voir* **croire.**
cru[2] /kry/ *a.* raw; (*lumière*) harsh; (*propos*) crude. —*n.m.* vineyard; (*vin*) wine.
crû /kry/ *voir* **croître.**
cruauté /kryote/ *n.f.* cruelty.
cruche /kryʃ/ *n.f.* pitcher.
cruc|ial (*m. pl.* **~iaux**) /krysjal, -jo/ *a.* crucial.
crucif|ier /krysifje/ *v.t.* crucify. **~ixion** *n.f.* crucifixion.
crucifix /krysifi/ *n.m.* crucifix.
crudité /krydite/ *n.f.* (*de langage*) crudeness. **~s,** (*culin.*) raw vegetables.
crue /kry/ *n.f.* rise in water level. **en ~,** in spate.
cruel, ~le /kryɛl/ *a.* cruel.
crûment /krymɑ̃/ *adv.* crudely.
crustacés /krystase/ *n.m. pl.* shellfish.
crypte /kript/ *n.f.* crypt.
Cuba /kyba/ *n.m.* Cuba.
cubain, ~e /kybɛ̃, -ɛn/ *a. & n.m.,* f. Cuban.
cub|e /kyb/ *n.m.* cube. —*a.* (*mètre etc.*) cubic. **~ique** *a.* cubic.
cueill|ir† /kœjir/ *v.t.* pick, gather; (*personne: fam.*) pick up. **~ette** *n.f.* picking, gathering.
cuill|er, ~ère /kɥijɛr/ *n.f.* spoon. **~er à soupe,** soup-spoon; (*mesure*) tablespoonful. **~erée** *n.f.* spoonful.
cuir /kɥir/ *n.m.* leather. **~ chevelu,** scalp.
cuirassé /kɥirase/ *n.m.* battleship.
cuire /kɥir/ *v.t./i.* cook; (*picoter*) smart. **~ (au four),** bake. **faire ~,** cook.
cuisine /kɥizin/ *n.f.* kitchen; (*art*) cookery, cooking; (*aliments*) cooking. **faire la ~,** cook.
cuisin|er /kɥizine/ *v.t./i.* cook;

(*interroger*: *fam*.) grill. ~ier, ~ière
n.m., *f*. cook; *n.f*. (*appareil*) cooker,
stove.

cuisse /kɥis/ *n.f*. thigh; (*de poulet,
mouton*) leg.

cuisson /kɥisɔ̃/ *n.m*. cooking.

cuit, ~e /kɥi, -t/ *a*. cooked. **bien** ~,
well done *ou* cooked. **trop** ~,
overdone.

cuivr|e /kɥivr/ *n.m*. copper. ~e **(jaune)**,
brass. ~es, (*mus*.) brass. ~é *a*.
coppery.

cul /ky/ *n.m*. (*derrière*: *fam*.) backside,
bum.

culasse /kylas/ *n.f*. (*auto*.) cylinder head;
(*arme*) breech.

culbut|e /kylbyt/ *n.f*. somersault; (*chute*)
tumble. ~er *v.i*. tumble; *v.t*. knock
over.

cul-de-sac (*pl*. **culs-de-sac**) /kydsak/
n.m. cul-de-sac.

culinaire /kylinɛr/ *a*. culinary; (*recette*)
cooking.

culminer /kylmine/ *v.i*. reach the highest
point.

culot[1] /kylo/ *n.m*. (*audace*: *fam*.) nerve,
cheek.

culot[2] /kylo/ *n.m*. (*fond*: *techn*.) base.

culotte /kylɔt/ *n.f*. (*de femme*) knickers;
(*Amer*.) panties. ~ **(de cheval)**, (riding)
breeches. ~ **courte**, short trousers.

culpabilité /kylpabilite/ *n.f*. guilt.

culte /kylt/ *n.m*. cult, worship; (*religion*)
religion; (*protestant*) service.

cultivé /kyltive/ *a*. cultured.

cultiv|er /kyltive/ *v.t*. cultivate;
(*plantes*) grow. ~ateur, ~atrice *n.m*.,
f. farmer.

culture /kyltyr/ *n.f*. cultivation; (*de
plantes*) growing; (*agriculture*) farming; (*éducation*) culture. ~s, (*terrains*)
lands under cultivation. ~ **physique**,
physical training.

culturel, ~le /kyltyrɛl/ *a*. cultural.

cumuler /kymyle/ *v.t*. (*fonctions*) hold
simultaneously.

cupide /kypid/ *a*. grasping.

cure /kyr/ *n.f*. (course of) treatment,
cure.

curé /kyre/ *n.m*. (parish) priest.

cur|er /kyre/ *v.t*. clean. **se** ~er **les
dents/ongles**, clean one's teeth/nails.
~e-dent *n.m*. toothpick. ~e-pipe *n.m*.
pipe-cleaner.

curieu|x, ~se /kyrjø, -z/ *a*. curious.
—*n.m*., *f*. (*badaud*) onlooker.
~sement *adv*. curiously.

curiosité /kyrjozite/ *n.f*. curiosity;
(*objet*) curio; (*spectacle*) unusual sight.

curriculum vitae /kyrikylɔm vite/ *n.m*.
invar. curriculum vitae.

curseur /kyrsœr/ *n.m*. cursor.

cutané /kytane/ *a*. skin.

cuve /kyv/ *n.f*. tank.

cuvée /kyve/ *n.f*. (*de vin*) vintage.

cuvette /kyvɛt/ *n.f*. bowl; (*de lavabo*)
(wash-)basin; (*des cabinets*) pan, bowl.

CV /seve/ *n.m*. CV.

cyanure /sjanyr/ *n.m*. cyanide.

cybernétique /sibɛrnetik/ *n.f*. cybernetics.

cycl|e /sikl/ *n.m*. cycle. ~ique *a*.
cyclic(al).

cyclis|te /siklist/ *n.m./f*. cyclist. —*a*.
cycle. ~me *n.m*. cycling.

cyclomoteur /syklɔmɔtœr/ *n.m*. moped.

cyclone /syklon/ *n.m*. cyclone.

cygne /siɲ/ *n.m*. swan.

cylindr|e /silɛ̃dr/ *n.m*. cylinder. ~ique *a*.
cylindrical.

cylindrée /silɛ̃dre/ *n.f*. (*de moteur*)
capacity.

cymbale /sɛ̃bal/ *n.f*. cymbal.

cystite /sistit/ *n.f*. cystitis.

cyni|que /sinik/ *a*. cynical. —*n.m*. cynic.
~sme *n.m*. cynicism.

cyprès /siprɛ/ *n.m*. cypress.

cypriote /siprijɔt/ *a*. & *n.m./f*. Cypriot.

D

d' /d/ *voir* **de**.

d'abord /dabɔr/ *adv*. first; (*au début*) at
first.

dactylo /daktilo/ *n.f*. typist. ~**(graphie)** *n.f*. typing. ~**graphe** *n.f*. typist.
~**graphier** *v.t*. type.

dada /dada/ *n.m*. hobby-horse.

dahlia /dalja/ *n.m*. dahlia.

daigner /deɲe/ *v.t*. deign.

daim /dɛ̃/ *n.m*. (fallow) deer; (*cuir*)
suede.

dall|e /dal/ *n.f*. paving stone, slab. ~age
n.m. paving.

daltonien, ~ne /daltɔnjɛ̃, -jɛn/ *a*.
colour-blind.

dame /dam/ *n.f*. lady; (*cartes, échecs*)
queen. ~s, (*jeu*) draughts; (*jeu*: *Amer*.)
checkers.

damier /damje/ *n.m*. draught-board;
(*Amer*.) checker-board. **à** ~, chequered.

damn|er /dɑne/ *v.t*. damn. ~ation *n.f*.
damnation.

dancing /dɑ̃siŋ/ *n.m*. dance-hall.

dandiner (se) /(sə)dɑ̃dine/ *v. pr.*
waddle.

Danemark /danmark/ *n.m.* Denmark.

danger /dɑ̃ʒe/ *n.m.* danger. **en ～,** in
danger. **mettre en ～,** endanger.

dangereu|x, ～se /dɑ̃ʒrø, -z/ *a.*
dangerous.

danois, ～e /danwa, -z/ *a.* Danish.
—*n.m., f.* Dane. —*n.m.* (*lang.*) Danish.

dans /dɑ̃/ *prép.* in; (*mouvement*) into; (*à
l'intérieur de*) inside, in; (*approximation*) about. **～ dix jours,** in ten
days' time. **prendre/boire/*etc.* ～,** take/
drink/*etc.* out of *ou* from.

dans|e /dɑ̃s/ *n.f.* dance; (*art*) dancing.
～er *v.t./i.* dance. **～eur, ～euse** *n.m., f.*
dancer.

dard /dar/ *n.m.* (*d'animal*) sting.

darne /darn/ *n.f.* steak (*of fish*).

dat|e /dat/ *n.f.* date. **～e limite,** deadline;
～e limite de vente, sell-by date; **～e de
péremption,** expiry date. **～er** *v.t./i.*
date. **à ～er de,** as from.

datt|e /dat/ *n.f.* (*fruit*) date. **～ier** *n.m.*
date-palm.

daube /dob/ *n.f.* casserole.

dauphin /dofɛ̃/ *n.m.* (*animal*) dolphin.

davantage /davɑ̃taʒ/ *adv.* more; (*plus
longtemps*) longer. **～ de,** more. **～ que,**
more than; longer than.

de, d'* /də, d/ *prép.* (*de + le = du, de + les
= des*) of; (*provenance*) from; (*moyen,
manière*) with; (*agent*) by. —*article*
some; (*interrogation*) any, some. **le
livre de mon ami,** my friend's book. **un
pont de fer,** an iron bridge. **dix mètres
de haut,** ten metres high. **du pain,**
(some) bread; **une tranche de pain,** a
slice of bread. **des fleurs,** (some)
flowers.

dé /de/ *n.m.* (*à jouer*) dice; (*à coudre*)
thimble. **dés,** (*jeu*) dice.

dealer /dilœr/ *n.m.* (*drug*) dealer.

débâcle /debakl/ *n.f.* (*mil.*) rout.

déball|er /debale/ *v.t.* unpack; (*montrer,
péj.*) spill out. **～age** *n.m.* unpacking.

débarbouiller /debarbuje/ *v.t.* wash the
face of. **se ～** *v. pr.* wash one's face.

débarcadère /debarkadɛr/ *n.m.* landing-stage.

débardeur /debardœr/ *n.m.* docker;
(*vêtement*) tank top.

débarqu|er /debarke/ *v.t./i.* disembark,
land; (*arriver: fam.*) turn up. **～ement**
n.m. disembarkation.

débarras /debara/ *n.m.* junk room. **bon
～!,** good riddance!

débarrasser /debarase/ *v.t.* clear (**de,**
of). **～ qn. de,** take from s.o.; (*défaut,*

ennemi) rid s.o. of. **se ～ de,** get rid of,
rid o.s. of.

débat /deba/ *n.m.* debate.

débattre†¹ /debatr/ *v.t.* debate. —*v.i.* **～
de,** discuss.

débattre†² (se) /(sə)debatr/ *v. pr.*
struggle (to get free).

débauch|e /deboʃ/ *n.f.* debauchery;
(*fig.*) profusion. **～er¹** *v.t.* debauch.

débaucher² /deboʃe/ *v.t.* (*licencier*) lay
off.

débile /debil/ *a.* weak; (*fam.*) stupid.
—*n.m./f.* moron.

débit /debi/ *n.m.* (rate of) flow; (*de
magasin*) turnover; (*élocution*) delivery;
(*de compte*) debit. **～ de tabac,**
tobacconist's shop; **～ de boissons,**
licensed premises.

débi|ter /debite/ *v.t.* cut up; (*fournir*)
produce; (*vendre*) sell; (*dire: péj.*)
spout; (*compte*) debit. **～teur, ～trice**
n.m., f. debtor; *a.* (*compte*) in debit.

débl|ayer /debleje/ *v.t.* clear. **～aiement,
～ayage** *n.m.* clearing.

déblo|quer /deblɔke/ *v.t.* (*prix, salaires*)
free. **～cage** *n.m.* freeing.

déboires /debwar/ *n.m. pl.* disappoint-
ments.

déboiser /debwaze/ *v.t.* clear (of
trees).

déboîter /debwate/ *v.i.* (*véhicule*) pull
out. —*v.t.* (*membre*) dislocate.

débord|er /deborde/ *v.i.* overflow. —*v.t.*
(*dépasser*) extend beyond. **～er de,**
(*joie etc.*) be overflowing with. **～é a**
snowed under (**de,** with). **～ement** *n.m.*
overflowing.

débouché /debuʃe/ *n.m.* opening;
(*carrière*) prospect; (*comm.*) outlet;
(*sortie*) end, exit.

déboucher /debuʃe/ *v.t.* (*bouteille*)
uncork; (*évier*) unblock. —*v.i.* emerge
(**de,** from). **～ sur,** (*rue*) lead into.

débourser /deburse/ *v.t.* pay out.

déboussolé /debusɔle/ *a.* (*fam.*) disorientated, disoriented.

debout /dəbu/ *adv.* standing; (*levé,
éveillé*) up. **être ～, se tenir ～,** be
standing, stand. **se mettre ～,** stand up.

déboutonner /debutɔne/ *v.t.* unbutton.
se ～ *v. pr.* unbutton o.s.; (*vêtement*)
come undone.

débraillé /debraje/ *a.* slovenly.

débrancher /debrɑ̃ʃe/ *v.t.* unplug,
disconnect.

débray|er /debreje/ *v.i.* (*auto.*) declutch;
(*faire grève*) stop work. **～age**
/debrɛjaʒ/ *n.m.* (*pédale*) clutch;
(*grève*) stoppage.

débris /debri/ *n.m. pl.* fragments; (*détritus*) rubbish, debris.

débrouill|er /debruje/ *v.t.* disentangle; (*problème*) sort out. **se ~er** *v. pr.* manage. **~ard, ~arde** *a.* (*fam.*) resourceful.

débroussailler /debrusaje/ *v.t.* clear (of brushwood).

début /deby/ *n.m.* beginning. **faire ses ~s,** (*en public*) make one's début.

début|er /debyte/ *v.i.* begin; (*dans un métier etc.*) start out. **~ant, ~ante** *n.m., f.* beginner.

déca /deka/ *n.m.* decaffeinated coffee.

décaféiné /dekafeine/ *a.* decaffeinated. **—n.m. du ~,** decaffeinated coffee.

deçà (en) /(ã)dəsa/ *adv.* this side. **—prép. en ~ de,** this side of.

décacheter /dekaʃte/ *v.t.* open.

décade /dekad/ *n.f.* ten days; (*décennie*) decade.

décaden|t, ~te /dekadã, -t/ *a.* decadent. **~ce** *n.f.* decadence.

décalcomanie /dekalkɔmani/ *n.f.* transfer; (*Amer.*) decal.

décal|er /dekale/ *v.t.* shift. **~age** *n.m.* (*écart*) gap. **~age horaire,** time difference.

décalquer /dekalke/ *v.t.* trace.

décamper /dekãpe/ *v.i.* clear off.

décanter /dekãte/ *v.t.* allow to settle. **se ~** *v. pr.* settle.

décap|er /dekape/ *v.t.* scrape down; (*surface peinte*) strip. **~ant** *n.m.* chemical agent; (*pour peinture*) paint stripper.

décapotable /dekapɔtabl/ *a.* convertible.

décapsul|er /dekapsyle/ *v.t.* take the cap off. **~eur** *n.m.* bottle-opener.

décarcasser (se) /(sə)dekarkase/ *v. pr.* (*fam.*) work o.s. to death.

décathlon /dekatlɔ̃/ *n.m.* decathlon.

décéd|er /desede/ *v.i.* die. **~é** *a.* deceased.

décel|er /desle/ *v.t.* detect; (*démontrer*) reveal. **~able** *a.* detectable.

décembre /desãbr/ *n.m.* December.

décennie /deseni/ *n.f.* decade.

déc|ent, ~ente /desã, -t/ *a.* decent. **~emment** /-amã/ *adv.* decently. **~ence** *n.f.* decency.

décentralis|er /desãtralize/ *v.t.* decentralize. **~ation** *n.f.* decentralization.

déception /desɛpsjɔ̃/ *n.f.* disappointment.

décerner /desɛrne/ *v.t.* award.

décès /desɛ/ *n.m.* death.

décev|oir† /desvwar/ *v.t.* disappoint. **~ant, e** *a.* disappointing.

déchaîn|er /deʃene/ *v.t.* (*violence etc.*) unleash; (*enthousiasme*) arouse a good deal of. **se ~er** *v. pr.* erupt. **~ement** /-ɛnmã/ *n.m.* (*de passions*) outburst.

décharge /deʃarʒ/ *n.f.* (*salve*) volley of shots. **~** (*électrique*), electrical discharge. **~** (*publique*), rubbish tip.

décharg|er /deʃarʒe/ *v.t.* unload; (*arme, accusé*) discharge. **~er de,** release from. **se ~er** *v. pr.* (*batterie, pile*) go flat. **~ement** *n.m.* unloading.

décharné /deʃarne/ *a.* bony.

déchausser (se) /(sə)deʃose/ *v. pr.* take off one's shoes; (*dent*) work loose.

dèche /dɛʃ/ *n.f.* **dans la ~,** broke.

déchéance /deʃeãs/ *n.f.* decay.

déchet /deʃɛ/ *n.m.* (*reste*) scrap; (*perte*) waste. **~s,** (*ordures*) refuse.

déchiffrer /deʃifre/ *v.t.* decipher.

déchiqueter /deʃikte/ *v.t.* tear to shreds.

déchir|ant, ~ante /deʃirã, -t/ *a.* heartbreaking. **~ement** *n.m.* heart-break; (*conflit*) split.

déchir|er /deʃire/ *v.t.* tear; (*lacérer*) tear up; (*arracher*) tear off *ou* out; (*diviser*) tear apart; (*oreilles: fig.*) split. **se ~er** *v. pr.* tear. **~ure** *n.f.* tear.

déch|oir /deʃwar/ *v.i.* demean o.s. **~oir de,** (*rang*) lose, fall from. **~u** *a.* fallen.

décibel /desibel/ *n.m.* decibel.

décid|er /deside/ *v.t.* decide on; (*persuader*) persuade. **~er que/de,** decide that/to. **—v.i.** decide. **~er de qch.,** decide on sth. **se ~er** *v. pr.* make up one's mind (**à,** to). **~é** *a.* (*résolu*) determined; (*fixé, marqué*) decided. **~ément** *adv.* really.

décim|al, ~ale (*m. pl.* **~aux**) /desimal, -o/ *a. & n.f.* decimal.

décimètre /desimɛtr/ *n.m.* decimetre.

décisi|f, ~ve /desizif, -v/ *a.* decisive.

décision /desizjɔ̃/ *n.f.* decision.

déclar|er /deklare/ *v.t.* declare; (*naissance*) register. **se ~er** *v. pr.* (*feu*) break out. **~er forfait,** (*sport*) withdraw. **~ation** *n.f.* declaration; (*commentaire politique*) statement. **~ation d'impôts,** tax return.

déclasser /deklase/ *v.t.* (*coureur*) relegate; (*hôtel*) downgrade.

déclench|er /deklãʃe/ *v.t.* (*techn.*) release, set off; (*lancer*) launch; (*provoquer*) trigger off. **se ~er** *v. pr.* (*techn.*) go off. **~eur** *n.m.* (*photo.*) trigger.

déclic /deklik/ *n.m.* click; (*techn.*) trigger mechanism.

déclin /deklɛ̃/ n.m. decline.

déclin|er¹ /dekline/ v.i. decline. **∼aison** n.f. (lang.) declension.

décliner² /dekline/ v.t. (refuser) decline; (dire) state.

déclivité /deklivite/ n.f. slope.

décocher /dekɔʃe/ v.t. (coup) fling; (regard) shoot.

décoder /dekɔde/ v.t. decode.

décoiffer /dekwafe/ v.t. (ébouriffer) disarrange the hair of.

décoincer /dekwɛ̃se/ v.t. free.

décoll|er¹ /dekɔle/ v.i. (avion) take off. **∼age** n.m. take-off.

décoller² /dekɔle/ v.t. unstick.

décolleté /dekɔlte/ a. low-cut. —n.m. low neckline.

décolor|er /dekɔlɔre/ v.t. fade; (cheveux) bleach. **se ∼er** v. pr. fade. **∼ation** n.f. bleaching.

décombres /dekɔ̃br/ n.m. pl. rubble.

décommander /dekɔmɑ̃de/ v.t. cancel.

décompos|er /dekɔ̃poze/ v.t. break up; (substance) decompose; (visage) contort. **se ∼er** v. pr. (pourrir) decompose. **∼ition** n.f. decomposition.

décompt|e /dekɔ̃t/ n.m. deduction; (détail) breakdown. **∼er** v.t. deduct.

déconcerter /dekɔ̃sɛrte/ v.t. disconcert.

décongel|er /dekɔ̃ʒle/ v.t. thaw. **∼ation** n.f. thawing.

décongestionner /dekɔ̃ʒɛstjɔne/ v.t. relieve congestion in.

déconseill|er /dekɔ̃seje/ v.t. **∼er qch. à qn.**, advise s.o. against sth. **∼é a.** not advisable, inadvisable.

décontenancer /dekɔ̃tnɑ̃se/ v.t. disconcert.

décontract|er /dekɔ̃trakte/ v.t., **se ∼** v. pr. relax. **∼é a.** relaxed.

déconvenue /dekɔ̃vny/ n.f. disappointment.

décor /dekɔr/ n.m. (paysage, théâtre) scenery; (cinéma) set; (cadre) setting; (de maison) décor.

décorati|f, ∼ve /dekɔratif, -v/ a. decorative.

décor|er /dekɔre/ v.t. decorate. **∼ateur, ∼atrice** n.m., f. (interior) decorator. **∼ation** n.f. decoration.

décortiquer /dekɔrtike/ v.t. shell; (fig.) dissect.

découdre (se) /(sə)dekudr/ v. pr. come unstitched.

découler /dekule/ v.i. **∼ de**, follow from.

découp|er /dekupe/ v.t. cut up; (viande) carve; (détacher) cut out. **se ∼er sur**, stand out against. **∼age** n.m. (image) cut-out.

décourag|er /dekuraʒe/ v.t. discourage. **se ∼er** v. pr. become discouraged. **∼ement** n.m. discouragement. **∼é a.** discouraged.

décousu /dekuzy/ a. (vêtement) falling apart; (idées etc.) disjointed.

découvert, ∼e /dekuvɛr, -t/ a. (tête etc.) bare; (terrain) open. —n.m. (de compte) overdraft. —n.f. discovery. **à ∼**, exposed; (fig.) openly. **à la ∼e de**, in search of.

découvrir† /dekuvrir/ v.t. discover; (enlever ce qui couvre) uncover; (voir) see; (montrer) reveal. **se ∼** v. pr. uncover o.s.; (se décoiffer) take one's hat off; (ciel) clear.

décrasser /dekrase/ v.t. clean.

décrépit, ∼e /dekrepi, -t/ a. decrepit. **∼ude** n.f. decay.

décret /dekrɛ/ n.m. decree. **∼er** /-ete/ v.t. decree.

décrié /dekrije/ v.t. decried.

décrire† /dekrir/ v.t. describe.

décrisp|er (se) /(sə)dekrispe/ v. pr. become less tense. **∼ation** n.f. lessening of tension.

décroch|er /dekrɔʃe/ v.t. unhook; (obtenir: fam.) get. —v.i. (abandonner: fam.) give up. **∼er (le téléphone)**, pick up the phone. **∼é a.** (téléphone) off the hook.

décroître /dekrwatr/ v.i. decrease.

décrue /dekry/ n.f. going down (of river water).

déçu /desy/ a. disappointed.

décupl|e /dekypl/ n.m. **au ∼e,** tenfold. **le ∼e de,** ten times. **∼er** v.t./i. increase tenfold.

dédaign|er /dedeɲe/ v.t. scorn. **∼er de faire**, consider it beneath one to do. **∼eux, ∼euse** /dedɛɲø, -z/ a. scornful.

dédain /dedɛ̃/ n.m. scorn.

dédale /dedal/ n.m. maze.

dedans /dədɑ̃/ adv. & n.m. inside. **au ∼ (de)**, inside. **en ∼**, on the inside.

dédicac|e /dedikas/ n.f. dedication, inscription. **∼er** v.t. dedicate, inscribe.

dédier /dedje/ v.t. dedicate.

dédommag|er /dedɔmaʒe/ v.t. compensate (de, for). **∼ement** n.m. compensation.

dédouaner /dedwane/ v.t. clear through customs.

dédoubler /deduble/ v.t. split into two. **∼ un train,** put on a relief train.

déd|uire† /dedɥir/ v.t. deduct;

(*conclure*) deduce. ~**uction** *n.f.* deduction; ~**uction d'impôts** tax deduction.

déesse /deɛs/ *n.f.* goddess.

défaillance /defajɑ̃s/ *n.f.* weakness; (*évanouissement*) black-out; (*panne*) failure.

défaill|ir /defajir/ *v.i.* faint; (*forces etc.*) fail. ~**ant**, ~**ante** *a.* (*personne*) faint; (*candidat*) defaulting.

défaire† /defɛr/ *v.t.* undo; (*valise*) unpack; (*démonter*) take down; (*débarrasser*) rid. **se** ~ *v. pr.* come undone. **se** ~ **de,** rid o.s. of.

défait, ~**e**[1] /defɛ, -t/ *a.* (*cheveux*) ruffled; (*visage*) haggard.

défaite[2] /defɛt/ *n.f.* defeat.

défaitisme /defetizm/ *n.m.* defeatism.

défaitiste /defetist/ *a. & n.m./f.* defeatist.

défalquer /defalke/ *v.t.* (*somme*) deduct.

défaut /defo/ *n.m.* fault, defect; (*d'un verre, diamant, etc.*) flaw; (*carence*) lack; (*pénurie*) shortage. **à** ~ **de,** for lack of. **en** ~, at fault. **faire** ~, (*argent etc.*) be lacking. **par** ~, (*jurid.*) in one's absence.

défav|eur /defavœr/ *n.f.* disfavour. ~**orable** *a.* unfavourable.

défavoriser /defavɔrize/ *v.t.* put at a disadvantage.

défection /defɛksjɔ̃/ *n.f.* desertion. **faire** ~, desert.

défect|ueux, ~**ueuse** /defɛktɥø, -z/ *a.* faulty, defective. ~**uosité** *n.f.* faultiness; (*défaut*) fault.

défendre /defɑ̃dr/ *v.t.* defend; (*interdire*) forbid. ~ **à qn. de,** forbid s.o. to. **se** ~ *v. pr.* defend o.s.; (*se débrouiller*) manage; (*se protéger*) protect o.s. **se** ~ **de,** (*refuser*) refrain from.

défense /defɑ̃s/ *n.f.* defence; (*d'éléphant*) tusk. ~ **de fumer/***etc.*, no smoking/*etc.*

défenseur /defɑ̃sœr/ *n.m.* defender.

défensi|f, ~**ve** /defɑ̃sif, -v/ *a. & n.f.* defensive.

déféren|t, ~**te** /deferɑ̃, -t/ *a.* deferential. ~**ce** *n.f.* deference.

déférer /defere/ *v.t.* (*jurid.*) refer. —*v.i.* ~ **à,** (*avis etc.*) defer to.

déferler /defɛrle/ *v.i.* (*vagues*) break; (*violence etc.*) erupt.

défi /defi/ *n.m.* challenge; (*refus*) defiance. **mettre au** ~, challenge.

déficeler /defisle/ *v.t.* untie.

déficience /defisjɑ̃s/ *n.f.* deficiency.

déficient /defisjɑ̃/ *a.* deficient.

déficit /defisit/ *n.m.* deficit. ~**aire** *a.* in deficit.

défier /defje/ *v.t.* challenge; (*braver*) defy. **se** ~ **de,** mistrust.

défilé[1] /defile/ *n.m.* procession; (*mil.*) parade; (*fig.*) (continual) stream. ~ **de mode,** fashion parade.

défilé[2] /defile/ *n.m.* (*géog.*) gorge.

défiler /defile/ *v.i.* march (past); (*visiteurs*) stream; (*images*) flash by. **se** ~ *v. pr.* (*fam.*) sneak off.

défini /defini/ *a.* definite.

définir /definir/ *v.t.* define.

définissable /definisabl/ *a.* definable.

définiti|f, ~**ve** /definitif, -v/ *a.* final; (*permanent*) definitive. **en** ~**ve,** in the final analysis. ~**vement** *adv.* definitively, permanently.

définition /definisjɔ̃/ *n.f.* definition; (*de mots croisés*) clue.

déflagration /deflagrasjɔ̃/ *n.f.* explosion.

déflation /deflasjɔ̃/ *n.f.* deflation. ~**niste** /-jɔnist/ *a.* deflationary.

défoncer /defɔ̃se/ *v.t.* (*porte etc.*) break down; (*route, terrain*) dig up; (*lit*) break the springs of. **se** ~ *v. pr.* (*fam.*) work like mad; (*drogué*) get high.

déform|er /deforme/ *v.t.* put out of shape; (*membre*) deform; (*faits, pensée*) distort. ~**ation** *n.f.* loss of shape; deformation; distortion.

défouler (se) /(sə)defule/ *v. pr.* let off steam.

défraîchir (se) /(sə)defreʃir/ *v. pr.* become faded.

défrayer /defreje/ *v.t.* (*payer*) pay the expenses of.

défricher /defriʃe/ *v.t.* clear (for cultivation).

défroisser /defrwase/ *v.t.* smooth out.

défunt, ~**e** /defœ̃, -t/ *a.* (*mort*) late. —*n.m., f.* deceased.

dégagé /degaʒe/ *a.* clear; (*ton*) free and easy.

dégag|er /degaʒe/ *v.t.* (*exhaler*) give off; (*désencombrer*) clear; (*délivrer*) free; (*faire ressortir*) bring out. —*v.i.* (*football*) kick the ball (down the pitch *ou* field). **se** ~**er** *v. pr.* free o.s.; (*ciel, rue*) clear; (*odeur etc.*) emanate. ~**ement** *n.m.* giving off; clearing; freeing; (*espace*) clearing; (*football*) clearance.

dégainer /degene/ *v.t./i.* draw.

dégarnir /degarnir/ *v.t.* clear, empty. **se** ~ *v. pr.* clear, empty; (*crâne*) go bald.

dégâts /dega/ *n.m. pl.* damage.

dégel /deʒɛl/ *n.m.* thaw. ~**er** /deʒle/ *v.t./i.* thaw (out). **(faire)** ~**er,** (*culin.*) thaw.

dégénér|er /deʒenere/ v.i. degenerate.
~é, ~ée a. & n.m., f. degenerate.
dégingandé /deʒɛ̃gɑ̃de/ a. gangling.
dégivrer /deʒivre/ v.t. (auto.) de-ice;
(frigo) defrost.
déglacer /deglase/ v.t. (culin.) deglaze.
déglingu|er /deglɛ̃ge/ (fam.) v.t. knock
about. se ~er v. pr. fall to bits. ~é adj.
falling to bits.
dégonfl|er /degɔ̃fle/ v.t. let down, deflate.
se ~er v. pr. (fam.) get cold feet. ~é a.
(pneu) flat; (lâche: fam.) yellow.
dégorger /degɔrʒe/ v.i. faire ~, (culin.)
soak.
dégouliner /deguline/ v.i. trickle.
dégourdi /degurdi/ a. smart.
dégourdir /degurdir/ v.t. (membre,
liquide) warm up. se ~ les jambes,
stretch one's legs.
dégoût /degu/ n.m. disgust.
dégoût|er /degute/ v.t. disgust. ~er qn.
de qch., put s.o. off sth. ~ant, ~ante a.
disgusting. ~é a. disgusted. ~é de, sick
of. faire le ~é, look disgusted.
dégradant /degradɑ̃/ a. degrading.
dégrader /degrade/ v.t. degrade;
(abîmer) damage. se ~ v. pr. (se
détériorer) deteriorate.
dégrafer /degrafe/ v.t. unhook.
degré /dəgre/ n.m. degree; (d'escalier)
step.
dégressi|f, ~ve /degresif, -v/ a.
gradually lower.
dégrèvement /degrɛvmɑ̃/ n.m. ~ fiscal
ou d'impôts, tax reduction.
dégrever /degrəve/ v.t. reduce the tax
on.
dégringol|er /degrɛ̃gɔle/ v.i. tumble
(down). —v.t. rush down. ~ade n.f.
tumble.
dégrossir /degrosir/ v.t. (bois) trim;
(projet) rough out.
déguerpir /degɛrpir/ v.i. clear off.
dégueulasse /degœlas/ a. (argot) disgusting, lousy.
dégueuler /degœle/ v.t. (argot) throw
up.
déguis|er /degize/ v.t. disguise. se ~er v.
pr. disguise o.s.; (au carnaval etc.)
dress up. ~ement n.m. disguise; (de
carnaval etc.) fancy dress.
dégust|er /degyste/ v.t. taste, sample;
(savourer) enjoy. ~ation n.f. tasting,
sampling.
déhancher (se) /(sə)deɑ̃ʃe/ v. pr. sway
one's hips.
dehors /dəɔr/ adv. & n.m. outside.
—n.m. pl. (aspect de qn.) exterior. au
~ (de), outside. en ~ de, outside;

(hormis) apart from. jeter/mettre/etc.
~, throw/put/etc. out.
déjà /deʒa/ adv. already; (avant) before,
already.
déjà-vu /deʒavy/ n.m. inv. déjà vu.
déjeuner /deʒœne/ v.i. (have) lunch; (le
matin) (have) breakfast. —n.m. lunch.
(petit) ~, breakfast.
déjouer /deʒwe/ v.t. thwart.
delà /dəla/ adv. & prép. au ~ (de), en ~
(de), par ~, beyond.
délabrer (se) /(sə)delɑbre/ v. pr. become
dilapidated.
délacer /delase/ v.t. undo.
délai /delɛ/ n.m. time-limit; (attente)
wait; (sursis) extension (of time). sans
~, without delay. dans les plus brefs
~s, as soon as possible.
délaisser /delese/ v.t. desert.
délass|er /delase/ v.t., se ~er v. pr.
relax. ~ement n.m. relaxation.
délation /delasjɔ̃/ n.f. informing.
délavé /delave/ a. faded.
délayer /deleje/ v.t. mix (with liquid);
(idée) drag out.
delco /dɛlkɔ/ n.m. (P., auto.) distributor.
délecter (se) /(sə)delɛkte/ v. pr. se ~ de,
delight in.
délégation /delegasjɔ̃/ n.f. delegation.
délégu|er /delege/ v.t. delegate. ~é, ~ée
n.m., f. delegate.
délibéré /delibere/ a. deliberate;
(résolu) determined. ~ment adv.
deliberately.
délibér|er /delibere/ v.i. deliberate.
~ation n.f. deliberation.
délicat, ~e /delika, -t/ a. delicate;
(plein de tact) tactful; (exigeant)
particular. ~ement /-tmɑ̃/ adv. deli-
cately; tactfully. ~esse /-tɛs/ n.f.
delicacy; tact. ~esses /-tɛs/ n.f. pl.
(kind) attentions.
délice /delis/ n.m. delight. ~s n.f. pl.
delights.
délicieu|x, ~se /delisjø, -z/ a. (au
goût) delicious; (charmant) delightful.
délié /delje/ a. fine, slender; (agile)
nimble.
délier /delje/ v.t. untie; (délivrer) free. se
~ v. pr. come untied.
délimit|er /delimite/ v.t. determine,
demarcate. ~ation n.f. demarcation.
délinquan|t, ~te /delɛ̃kɑ̃, -t/ a. &
n.m., f. delinquent. ~ce n.f. delin-
quency.
délire /delir/ n.m. delirium; (fig.) frenzy.
délir|er /delire/ v.i. be delirious (de,
with); (déraisonner) rave. ~ant,

~ante *a.* delirious; (*frénétique*) frenzied; (*fam.*) wild.

délit /deli/ *n.m.* offence, crime.

délivr|er /delivre/ *v.t.* free, release; (*pays*) deliver; (*remettre*) issue. **~ance** *n.f.* release; deliverance; issue.

déloger /delɔʒe/ *v.t.* force out.

déloy|al (*m. pl.* **~aux**) /delwajal, -jo/ *a.* disloyal; (*procédé*) unfair.

delta /dɛlta/ *n.m.* delta.

deltaplane /dɛltaplan/ *n.m.* hang-glider.

déluge /delyʒ/ *n.m.* flood; (*pluie*) downpour.

démagogie /demagɔʒi/ *n.f.* demagogy.

démagogue /demagɔg/ *n.m./f.* demagogue.

demain /dmɛ̃/ *adv.* tomorrow.

demande /dmɑ̃d/ *n.f.* request; (*d'emploi*) application; (*exigence*) demand. **~ en mariage,** proposal (of marriage).

demandé /dmɑ̃de/ *a.* in demand.

demander /dmɑ̃de/ *v.t.* ask for; (*chemin, heure*) ask; (*emploi*) apply for; (*nécessiter*) require. **~ que/si,** ask that/if. **~ qch. à qn.,** ask s.o. for sth. **~ à qn. de,** ask s.o. to. **~ en mariage,** propose to. **se ~ si/où/***etc.*, wonder if/where/*etc.*

demandeu|r, **~se** /dmɑ̃dœr, -øz/ *n.m., f.* **les ~rs d'emploi** job seekers.

démang|er /demɑ̃ʒe/ *v.t./i.* itch. **~eaison** *n.f.* itch(ing).

démanteler /demɑ̃tle/ *v.t.* break up.

démaquill|er (se) /(sə)demakije/ *v. pr.* remove one's make-up. **~ant** *n.m.* make-up remover.

démarcation /demarkasjɔ̃/ *n.f.* demarcation.

démarchage /demarʃaʒ/ *n.m.* door-to-door selling.

démarche /demarʃ/ *n.f.* walk, gait; (*procédé*) step. **faire des ~s auprès de,** make approaches to.

démarcheu|r, **~se** /demarʃœr, -øz/ *n.m., f.* (door-to-door) canvasser.

démarr|er /demare/ *v.i.* (*moteur*) start (up); (*partir*) move off; (*fig.*) get moving. *—v.t.* (*fam.*) get moving. **~age** *n.m.* start. **~eur** *n.m.* starter.

démasquer /demaske/ *v.t.* unmask.

démêlant /demelɑ̃/ *n.m.* conditioner.

démêler /demele/ *v.t.* disentangle.

démêlés /demele/ *n.m. pl.* trouble.

déménag|er /demenaʒe/ *v.i.* move (house). *—v.t.* (*meubles*) remove. **~ement** *n.m.* move; (*de meubles*) removal. **~eur** *n.m.* removal man; (*Amer.*) furniture mover.

démener (se) /(sə)demne/ *v. pr.* move about wildly; (*fig.*) exert o.s.

démen|t, **~te** /demɑ̃, -t/ *a.* insane. *—n.m., f.* lunatic. **~ce** *n.f.* insanity.

démenti /demɑ̃ti/ *n.m.* denial.

démentir /demɑ̃tir/ *v.t.* refute; (*ne pas être conforme à*) belie. **~ que,** deny that.

démerder (se) /(sə)demɛrde/ (*fam.*) manage.

démesuré /deməzyre/ *a.* inordinate.

démettre /demɛtr/ *v.t.* (*poignet etc.*) dislocate. **~ qn. de,** dismiss s.o. from. **se ~** *v. pr.* resign (**de,** from).

demeure /dəmœr/ *n.f.* residence. **mettre en ~ de,** order to.

demeurer /dəmœre/ *v.i.* live; (*rester*) remain.

demi, **~e** /dmi/ *a.* half(-). *—n.m., f.* half. *—n.m.* (*bière*) (half-pint) glass of beer; (*football*) half-back. *—n.f.* (*à l'horloge*) half-hour. **~-mesure** *n.f.* à **~,** half; (*ouvrir, fermer*) half-way. **à la ~e,** at half-past. **une heure et ~e,** an hour and a half; (*à l'horloge*) half past one. **une ~-journée/-livre/***etc.*, half a day/pound/*etc.*, a half-day/-pound/*etc.* **~-cercle** *n.m.* semicircle. **~-finale** *n.f.* semifinal. **~-frère** *n.m.* stepbrother. **~-heure** *n.f.* half-hour, half an hour. **~-jour** *n.m.* half-light. **~-mesure** *n.f.* half-measure. **à ~-mot** *adv.* without having to express every word. **~-pension** *n.f.* half-board. **~-pensionnaire** *n.m./f.* day-boarder. **~-sel** *a. invar.* slightly salted. **~-sœur** *n.f.* stepsister. **~-tarif** *n.m.* half-fare. **~-tour** *n.m.* about turn; (*auto.*) U-turn. **faire ~-tour,** turn back.

démis, **~e** /demi, -z/ *a.* dislocated. **~ de ses fonctions,** removed from his post.

démission /demisjɔ̃/ *n.f.* resignation. **~ner** /-jɔne/ *v.i.* resign.

démobiliser /demɔbilize/ *v.t.* demobilize.

démocrate /demɔkrat/ *n.m./f.* democrat. *—a.* democratic.

démocrat|ie /demɔkrasi/ *n.f.* democracy. **~ique** /-atik/ *a.* democratic.

démodé /demɔde/ *a.* old-fashioned.

démographi|e /demɔgrafi/ *n.f.* demography. **~que** *a.* demographic.

demoiselle /dəmwazɛl/ *n.f.* young lady; (*célibataire*) spinster. **~ d'honneur,** bridesmaid.

démol|ir /demɔlir/ *v.t.* demolish. **~ition** *n.f.* demolition.

démon /demɔ̃/ *n.m.* demon. **le D~,** the Devil.

démoniaque /demɔnjak/ *a.* fiendish.

démonstra|teur, **~trice** /demɔ̃stratœr, -tris/ *n.m., f.* demonstrator. **~tion** /-asjɔ̃/ *n.f.* demonstration; (*de force*) show.

démonstrati|f, **~ve** /demɔ̃stratif, -v/ *a.* demonstrative.

démonter /demɔ̃te/ *v.t.* take apart, dismantle; (*installation*) take down; (*fig.*) disconcert. **se ~** *v. pr.* come apart.

démontrer /demɔ̃tre/ *v.t.* show, demonstrate.

démoraliser /demɔralize/ *v.t.* demoralize.

démuni /demyni/ *a.* impoverished. **~ de,** without.

démunir /demynir/ *v.t.* **~ de,** deprive of. **se ~ de,** part with.

démystifier /demistifje/ *v.t.* enlighten.

dénaturer /denatyre/ *v.t.* (*faits etc.*) distort.

dénégation /denegasjɔ̃/ *n.f.* denial.

dénicher /deniʃe/ *v.t.* (*trouver*) dig up; (*faire sortir*) flush out.

dénigr|er /denigre/ *v.t.* denigrate. **~ement** *n.m.* denigration.

dénivellation /denivɛlasjɔ̃/ *n.f.* (*pente*) slope.

dénombrer /denɔ̃bre/ *v.t.* count; (*énumérer*) enumerate.

dénomination /denɔminasjɔ̃/ *n.f.* designation.

dénommé, **~e** /denɔme/ *n. m., f.* **le ~ X,** the said X.

dénonc|er /denɔ̃se/ *v.t.* denounce; (*scol.*) tell on. **se ~er** *v. pr.* give o.s. up. **~iateur,** **~iatrice** *n.m., f.* informer; (*scol.*) tell-tale. **~iation** *n.f.* denunciation.

dénoter /denɔte/ *v.t.* denote.

dénouement /denumɑ̃/ *n.m.* outcome; (*théâtre*) dénouement.

dénouer /denwe/ *v.t.* unknot, undo. **se ~** *v. pr.* (*nœud*) come undone.

dénoyauter /denwajote/ *v.t.* stone; (*Amer.*) pit.

denrée /dɑ̃re/ *n.f.* foodstuff.

dens|e /dɑ̃s/ *a.* dense. **~ité** *n.f.* density.

dent /dɑ̃/ *n.f.* tooth; (*de roue*) cog. **faire ses ~s,** teethe. **~aire** /-tɛr/ *a.* dental.

dentelé /dɑ̃tle/ *a.* jagged.

dentelle /dɑ̃tɛl/ *n.f.* lace.

dentier /dɑ̃tje/ *n.m.* denture.

dentifrice /dɑ̃tifris/ *n.m.* toothpaste.

dentiste /dɑ̃tist/ *n.m./f.* dentist.

dentition /dɑ̃tisjɔ̃/ *n.f.* teeth.

dénud|er /denyde/ *v.t.* bare. **~é a.** bare.

dénué /denɥe/ *a.* **~ de,** devoid of.

dénuement /denɥmɑ̃/ *n.m.* destitution.

déodorant /deɔdɔrɑ̃/ *a.m. & n.m.* (**produit**) **~,** deodorant.

déontologi|e /deɔ̃tɔlɔʒi/ *n.f.* code of practice. **~que** *a.* ethical.

dépann|er /depane/ *v.t.* repair; (*fig.*) help out. **~age** *n.m.* repair. **de ~age,** (*service etc.*) breakdown. **~euse** *n.f.* breakdown lorry; (*Amer.*) wrecker.

dépareillé /depareje/ *a.* odd, not matching.

départ /depar/ *n.m.* departure; (*sport*) start. **au ~,** at the outset.

départager /departaʒe/ *v.t.* settle the matter between.

département /departəmɑ̃/ *n.m.* department.

dépassé /depase/ *a.* outdated.

dépass|er /depase/ *v.t.* go past, pass; (*véhicule*) overtake; (*excéder*) exceed; (*rival*) surpass; (*dérouter: fam.*) be beyond. —*v.i.* stick out; (*véhicule*) overtake. **~ement** *n.m.* overtaking.

dépays|er /depeize/ *v.t.* disorientate, disorient. **~ant,** **~e** *a.* disorientating. **~ement** *n.m.* disorientation; (*changement*) change of scenery.

dépêch|e /depɛʃ/ *n.f.* dispatch. **~er**[1] /-eʃe/ *v.t.* dispatch.

dépêcher[2] (**se**) /(sə)depeʃe/ *v. pr.* hurry (up).

dépeindre /depɛ̃dr/ *v.t.* depict.

dépendance /depɑ̃dɑ̃s/ *n.f.* dependence; (*bâtiment*) outbuilding.

dépendre /depɑ̃dr/ *v.t.* take down. —*v.i.* depend (**de,** on). **~ de,** (*appartenir à*) belong to.

dépens (aux) /(o)depɑ̃/ *prép.* **aux ~ de,** at the expense of.

dépens|e /depɑ̃s/ *n.f.* expense; expenditure. **~er** *v.t./i.* spend; (*énergie etc.*) expend. **se ~er** *v. pr.* exert o.s.

dépens|ier, **~ière** /depɑ̃sje, -jɛr/ *a.* **être ~ier,** be a spendthrift.

dépérir /deperir/ *v.i.* wither.

dépêtrer (se) /(sə)depetre/ *v. pr.* get o.s. out (**de,** of).

dépeupler /depœple/ *v.t.* depopulate. **se ~** *v. pr.* become depopulated.

déphasé /defaze/ *a.* (*fam.*) out of touch.

dépilatoire /depilatwar/ *a. & n.m.* depilatory.

dépist|er /depiste/ *v.t.* detect; (*criminel*) track down; (*poursuivant*) throw off the scent. **~age** *n.m.* detection.

dépit /depi/ *n.m.* resentment. **en ~ de,** despite. **en ~ du bon sens,** against all common sense. **~é** /-te/ *a.* vexed.

déplacé /deplase/ *a.* out of place.

déplac|er /deplase/ *v.t.* move. **se ∼er** *v. pr.* move; (*voyager*) travel. **∼ement** *n.m.* moving; travel(-ling).

déplaire /depler/ *v.i.* **∼ à,** (*irriter*) displease. **ça me déplaît,** I dislike that.

déplaisant, **∼e** /deplɛzɑ̃, -t/ *a.* unpleasant, disagreeable.

déplaisir /deplezir/ *n.m.* displeasure.

dépliant /deplijɑ̃/ *n.m.* leaflet.

déplier /deplije/ *v.t.* unfold.

déplor|er /deplore/ *v.t.* (*trouver regrettable*) deplore; (*mort*) lament. **∼able** *a.* deplorable.

dépl|oyer /deplwaje/ *v.t.* (*ailes, carte*) spread; (*courage*) display; (*armée*) deploy. **∼oiement** *n.m.* display; deployment.

déport|er /deporte/ *v.t.* (*exiler*) deport; (*dévier*) carry off course. **∼ation** *n.f.* deportation.

déposer /depoze/ *v.t.* put down; (*laisser*) leave; (*passager*) drop; (*argent*) deposit; (*installation*) dismantle; (*plainte*) lodge; (*armes*) lay down; (*roi*) depose. —*v.i.* (*jurid.*) testify. **se ∼** *v. pr.* settle.

dépositaire /depoziter/ *n.m./f.* (*comm.*) agent.

déposition /depozisjɔ̃/ *n.f.* (*jurid.*) statement.

dépôt /depo/ *n.m.* (*garantie, lie*) deposit; (*entrepôt*) warehouse; (*d'autobus*) depot; (*d'ordures*) dump. **laisser en ∼,** give for safe keeping.

dépotoir /depotwar/ *n.m.* rubbish dump.

dépouille /depuj/ *n.f.* skin, hide. **∼ (mortelle),** mortal remains. **∼s,** (*butin*) spoils.

dépouiller /depuje/ *v.t.* go through; (*votes*) count; (*écorcher*) skin. **∼ de,** strip of.

dépourvu /depurvy/ *a.* **∼ de,** devoid of. **prendre au ∼,** catch unawares.

dépréc|ier /depresje/ *v.t.*, **se ∼ier** *v. pr.* depreciate. **∼iation** *n.f.* depreciation.

déprédations /depredasjɔ̃/ *n.f. pl.* damage.

dépr|imer /deprime/ *v.t.* depress. **∼ession** *n.f.* depression. **∼ession nerveuse,** nervous breakdown.

depuis /dəpɥi/ *prép.* since; (*durée*) for; (*à partir de*) from. —*adv.* (ever) since. **∼ que,** since. **∼ quand attendez-vous?,** how long have you been waiting?

députation /depytasjɔ̃/ *n.f.* deputation.

député, **∼e** /depyte/ *n.m.*, *f.* Member of Parliament.

déraciné, **∼e** /derasine/ *a.* & *n.m.*, *f.* rootless (person).

déraciner /derasine/ *v.t.* uproot.

déraill|er /deraje/ *v.i.* be derailed; (*fig., fam.*) be talking nonsense. **faire ∼er,** derail. **∼ement** *n.m.* derailment. **∼eur** *n.m.* (*de vélo*) gear mechanism, *dérailleur.*

déraisonnable /derɛzonabl/ *a.* unreasonable.

dérang|er /derɑ̃ʒe/ *v.t.* (*gêner*) bother, disturb; (*dérégler*) upset, disrupt. **se ∼er** *v. pr.* put o.s. out. **ça vous ∼e si . . .?,** do you mind if . . .? **∼ement** *n.m.* bother; (*désordre*) disorder, upset. **en ∼ement,** out of order.

dérap|er /derape/ *v.i.* skid; (*fig.*) get out of control. **∼age** *n.m.* skid.

déréglé /deregle/ *a.* (*vie*) dissolute; (*estomac*) upset; (*pendule*) (that is) not running properly.

dérégler /deregle/ *v.t.* put out of order. **se ∼** *v. pr.* go wrong.

dérision /derizjɔ̃/ *n.f.* mockery. **par ∼,** derisively. **tourner en ∼,** mock.

dérisoire /derizwar/ *a.* derisory.

dérivatif /derivatif/ *n.m.* distraction.

dériv|e /deriv/ *n.f.* **aller à la ∼e,** drift. **∼er**[1] *v.i.* (*bateau*) drift; *v.t.* (*détourner*) divert.

dériv|er[2] /derive/ *v.i.* **∼er de,** derive from. **∼é** *a.* derived; *n.m.* derivative; (*techn.*) by-product.

dermatolo|gie /dɛrmatɔlɔʒi/ *n.f.* dermatology. **∼gue** /-g/ *n.m./f.* dermatologist.

dern|ier, **∼ière** /dɛrnje, -jɛr/ *a.* last; (*nouvelles, mode*) latest; (*étage*) top. —*n.m.*, *f.* last (one). **ce ∼ier,** the latter. **en ∼ier,** last. **le ∼ier cri,** the latest fashion.

dernièrement /dɛrnjɛrmɑ̃/ *adv.* recently.

dérobé /derobe/ *a.* hidden. **à la ∼e,** stealthily.

dérober /derobe/ *v.t.* steal; (*cacher*) hide (à, from). **se ∼** *v. pr.* slip away. **se ∼ à,** (*obligation*) shy away from; (*se cacher à*) hide from.

dérogation /derɔgasjɔ̃/ *n.f.* exemption.

déroger /derɔʒe/ *v.i.* **∼ à,** go against.

dérouiller (se) /(sə)deruje/ *v. pr.* **se ∼ les jambes** to stretch one's legs.

déroul|er /derule/ *v.t.* (*fil etc.*) unwind. **se ∼er** *v. pr.* unwind; (*avoir lieu*) take place; (*récit, paysage*) unfold. **∼ement** *n.m.* (*d'une action*) development.

déroute /derut/ *n.f.* (*mil.*) rout.

dérouter /derute/ *v.t.* disconcert.

derrière /dɛrjɛr/ *prép.* & *adv.* behind.

—*n.m.* back, rear; (*postérieur*) behind. **de ~,** back, rear; (*pattes*) hind. **par ~,** (from) behind, at the back *ou* rear.

des /de/ *voir* **de**.

dès /dɛ/ *prép.* (right) from, from the time of. **~ lors,** from then on. **~ que,** as soon as.

désabusé /dezabyze/ *a.* disillusioned.

désaccord /dezakɔr/ *n.m.* disagreement. **~é** /-de/ *a.* out of tune.

désaffecté /dezafɛkte/ *a.* disused.

désaffection /dezafɛksjɔ̃/ *n.f.* alienation (**pour,** from).

désagréable /dezagreabl/ *a.* unpleasant.

désagréger (se) /(sə)dezagreʒe/ *v. pr.* disintegrate.

désagrément /dezagremɑ̃/ *n.m.* annoyance.

désaltérant /dezalterɑ̃/ *a.* thirst-quenching, refreshing.

désaltérer /dezaltere/ *v.i.,* **se ~** *v. pr.* quench one's thirst.

désamorcer /dezamɔrse/ *v.t.* (*situation, obus*) defuse.

désappr|ouver /dezapruve/ *v.t.* disapprove of. **~obation** *n.f.* disapproval.

désarçonner /dezarsɔne/ *v.t.* disconcert, throw; (*jockey*) unseat, throw.

désarmant /dezarmɑ̃/ *a.* disarming.

désarm|er /dezarme/ *v.t./i.* disarm. **~ement** *n.m.* (*pol.*) disarmament.

désarroi /dezarwa/ *n.m.* confusion.

désarticulé /dezartikyle/ *a.* dislocated.

désastr|e /dezastr/ *n.m.* disaster. **~eux, ~euse** *a.* disastrous.

désavantag|e /dezavɑ̃taʒ/ *n.m.* disadvantage. **~er** *v.t.* put at a disadvantage. **~eux, ~euse** *a.* disadvantageous.

désaveu (*pl.* **~x**) /dezavø/ *n.m.* repudiation.

désavouer /dezavwe/ *v.t.* repudiate.

désaxé, ~e /dezakse/ *a. & n.m., f.* unbalanced (person).

descendan|t, ~te /desɑ̃dɑ̃, -t/ *n.m., f.* descendant. **~ce** *n.f.* descent; (*enfants*) descendants.

descendre /desɑ̃dr/ *v.i.* (*aux. être*) go down; (*venir*) come down; (*passager*) get off *ou* out; (*nuit*) fall. **~ de,** (*être issu de*) be descended from. **~ à l'hôtel,** go to a hotel. —*v.t.* (*aux. avoir*) (*escalier etc.*) go *ou* come down; (*objet*) take down; (*abattre, fam.*) shoot down.

descente /desɑ̃t/ *n.f.* descent; (*pente*) (downward) slope; (*raid*) raid. **~ de lit,** bedside rug.

descripti|f, ~ve /dɛskriptif, -v/ *a.* descriptive.

description /dɛskripsjɔ̃/ *n.f.* description.

désemparé /dezɑ̃pare/ *a.* distraught.

désemplir /dezɑ̃plir/ *v.i.* **ne pas ~,** be always crowded.

désendettement /dezɑ̃dɛtmɑ̃/ *n.m.* getting out of debt.

désenfler /dezɑ̃fle/ *v.i.* go down.

déséquilibre /dezekilibr/ *n.m.* imbalance. **en ~,** unsteady.

déséquilibr|er /dezekilibre/ *v.t.* throw off balance. **~é, ~ée** *a. & n.m., f.* unbalanced (person).

désert¹ ~e /dezɛr, -t/ *a.* deserted.

désert² /dezɛr/ *n.m.* desert. **~ique** /-tik/ *a.* desert.

déserter /dezɛrte/ *v.t./i.* desert. **~eur** *n.m.* deserter. **~ion** /-ɛrsjɔ̃/ *n.f.* desertion.

désespér|er /dezɛspere/ *v.i.,* **se ~er** *v. pr.* despair. **~er de,** despair of. **~ant, ~ante** *a.* utterly disheartening. **~é** *a.* in despair; (*état, cas*) hopeless; (*effort*) desperate. **~ément** *adv.* desperately.

désespoir /dezɛspwar/ *n.m.* despair. **au ~,** in despair. **en ~ de cause,** as a last resort.

déshabill|er /dezabije/ *v.t.* **se ~er** *v. pr.* undress, get undressed. **~é** *a.* undressed; *n.m.* négligée.

déshabituer (se) /(sə)dezabitɥe/ *v. pr.* **se ~ de,** get out of the habit of.

désherb|er /dezɛrbe/ *v.t.* weed. **~ant** *n.m.* weed-killer.

déshérit|er /dezerite/ *v.t.* disinherit. **~é** *a.* (*région*) deprived. **les ~és** *n.m. pl.* the underprivileged.

déshonneur /dezɔnœr/ *n.m.* dishonour.

déshonor|er /dezɔnɔre/ *v.t.* dishonour. **~ant, ~ante** *a.* dishonourable.

déshydrater /dezidrate/ *v.t.,* **se ~** *v. pr.* dehydrate.

désigner /dezine/ *v.t.* (*montrer*) point to *ou* out; (*élire*) appoint; (*signifier*) indicate.

désillusion /dezilyzjɔ̃/ *n.f.* disillusionment.

désincrust|er /dezɛ̃kryste/ *v. pr.* (*chaudière*) descale; (*peau*) exfoliate. **~ant** *a.* **produit ~ant,** (skin) scrub.

désinence /dezinɑ̃s/ *n.f.* (*gram.*) ending.

désinfect|er /dezɛ̃fɛkte/ *v.t.* disinfect. **~ant** *n.m.* disinfectant.

désinfection /dezɛ̃fɛksjɔ̃/ *n.f.* disinfection.

désintégrer /dezɛ̃tegre/ *v.t.,* **se ~** *v. pr.* disintegrate.

désintéressé /dezɛ̃terese/ *a.* disinterested.

désintéresser (se) /(sə)dezɛ̃terese/ v. pr. se ~ de, lose interest in.

désintoxication /dezɛ̃tɔksikasjɔ̃/ n.f. detoxification. **cure de ~,** detoxication course.

désintoxiquer /dezɛ̃tɔksike/ v.t. cure of an addiction; (régime) purify.

désinvolt|e /dezɛ̃vɔlt/ a. casual. ~ure n.f. casualness.

désir /dezir/ n.m. wish, desire; (convoitise) desire.

désirer /dezire/ v.t. want; (convoiter) desire. ~ faire, want ou wish to do.

désireu|x, ~se /dezirø, -z/ a. ~x de, anxious to.

désist|er (se) /(sə)deziste/ v. pr. withdraw. ~ement n.m. withdrawal.

désobéir /dezɔbeir/ v.i. ~ (à), disobey.

désobéissan|t, ~te /dezɔbeisɑ̃, -t/ a. disobedient. ~ce n.f. disobedience.

désobligeant, ~e /dezɔbliʒɑ̃, -t/ a. disagreeable, unkind.

désodé /desɔde/ a. sodium-free.

désodorisant /dezɔdɔrizɑ̃/ n.m. air freshener.

désœuvr|é /dezœvre/ a. idle. ~ement n.m. idleness.

désolé /dezɔle/ a. (région) desolate.

désol|er /dezɔle/ v.t. distress. être ~é, (regretter) be sorry. ~ation n.f. distress.

désopilant, ~e /dezɔpilɑ̃, -t/ a. hilarious.

désordonné /dezɔrdɔne/ a. untidy; (mouvements) uncoordinated.

désordre /dezɔrdr/ n.m. disorder; (de vêtements, cheveux) untidiness. **mettre en ~,** make untidy.

désorganiser /dezɔrganize/ v.t. disorganize.

désorienté /dezɔrjɑ̃te/ a. disorientated.

désorienter /dezɔrjɑ̃te/ v.t. disorientate, disorient.

désormais /dezɔrmɛ/ adv. from now on.

désosser /dezɔse/ v.t. bone.

despote /dɛspɔt/ n.m. despot.

desquels, desquelles /dekɛl/ voir **lequel**.

dessécher /deseʃe/ v.t., se ~ v. pr. dry out ou up.

dessein /desɛ̃/ n.m. intention. **à ~,** intentionally.

desserrer /desere/ v.t. loosen. **sans ~ les dents,** without opening his/her mouth. se ~ v. pr. come loose.

dessert /desɛr/ n.m. dessert.

desserte /desɛrt/ n.f. (transports) service, servicing.

desservir /desɛrvir/ v.t./i. clear away; (autobus) provide a service to, serve.

dessin /desɛ̃/ n.m. drawing; (motif) design; (contour) outline. **~ animé,** (cinéma) cartoon. **~ humoristique,** cartoon.

dessin|er /desine/ v.t./i. draw; (fig.) outline. se ~er v. pr. appear, take shape. ~ateur, ~atrice n.m., f. artist; (industriel) draughtsman.

dessoûler /desule/ v.t./i. sober up.

dessous /dsu/ adv. underneath. —n.m. under-side, underneath. —n.m. pl. underclothes. **du ~,** bottom; (voisins) downstairs. **en ~, par ~,** underneath. **~-de-plat** n.m. invar. (heat-resistant) table-mat. **~-de-table** n.m. invar. backhander.

dessus /dsy/ adv. on top (of it), on it. —n.m. top. **du ~,** top; (voisins) upstairs. **en ~,** above. **par ~,** over (it). **avoir le ~,** get the upper hand. **~-de-lit** n.m. invar. bedspread.

destabilis|er /destabilize/ v.t. destabilize. ~ation n.f. destabilization.

destin /dɛstɛ̃/ n.m. (sort) fate; (avenir) destiny.

destinataire /dɛstinatɛr/ n.m./f. addressee.

destination /dɛstinasjɔ̃/ n.f. destination; (emploi) purpose. **à ~ de,** (going) to.

destinée /dɛstine/ n.f. (sort) fate; (avenir) destiny.

destin|er /dɛstine/ v.t. ~er à, intend for; (vouer) destine for; (affecter) earmark for. être ~é à faire, be intended to do; (condamné, obligé) be destined to do. se ~er à, (carrière) intend to take up.

destit|uer /dɛstitɥe/ v.t. dismiss (from office). ~ution n.f. dismissal.

destruc|teur, ~trice /dɛstryktœr, -tris/ a. destructive.

destruction /dɛstryksjɔ̃/ n.f. destruction.

dés|uet, ~uète /desɥɛ, -t/ a. outdated.

désunir /dezynir/ v.t. divide.

détachant /detaʃɑ̃/ n.m. stain-remover.

détach|é /detaʃe/ a. detached. ~ement n.m. detachment.

détacher /detaʃe/ v.t. untie; (ôter) remove, detach; (déléguer) send (on assignment ou secondment). se ~ v. pr. come off, break away; (nœud etc.) come undone; (ressortir) stand out.

détail /detaj/ n.m. detail; (de compte) breakdown; (comm.) retail. **au ~,** (vendre etc.) retail. **de ~,** (prix etc.) retail. **en ~,** in detail.

détaillé /detaje/ a. detailed.

détaill|er /detaje/ v.t. (articles) sell in small quantities, split up. ~ant, ~ante n.m., f. retailer.

détaler /detale/ v.i. (fam.) make tracks, run off.

détartrant /detartrɑ̃/ n.m. descaler.

détaxer /detakse/ v.t. reduce the tax on.

détect|er /detɛkte/ v.t. detect. **~eur** n.m. detector. **~ion** /-ksjɔ̃/ n.f. detection.

détective /detɛktiv/ n.m. detective.

déteindre /detɛ̃dr/ v.i. (couleur) run (sur, on to). **~ sur**, (fig.) rub off on.

détend|re /detɑ̃dr/ v.t. slacken; (ressort) release; (personne) relax. **se ~re** v. pr. become slack, slacken; be released; relax. **~u** a. (calme) relaxed.

détenir† /detnir/ v.t. hold; (secret, fortune) possess.

détente /detɑ̃t/ n.f. relaxation; (pol.) détente; (saut) spring; (gâchette) trigger; (relâchement) release.

déten|teur, ~trice /detɑ̃tœr, -tris/ n.m., f. holder.

détention /detɑ̃sjɔ̃/ n.f. **~ préventive**, custody.

détenu, ~e /detny/ n.m., f. prisoner.

détergent /detɛrʒɑ̃/ n.m. detergent.

détérior|er /deterjore/ v.t. damage. **se ~er** v. pr. deteriorate. **~ation** n.f. damaging; deterioration.

détermin|er /detɛrmine/ v.t. determine. **se ~er** v. pr. make up one's mind (à, to). **~ation** n.f. determination. **~é** a. (résolu) determined; (précis) definite.

déterrer /detere/ v.t. dig up.

détersif /detɛrsif/ n.m. detergent.

détestable /detɛstabl/ a. foul.

détester /detɛste/ v.t. hate. **se ~** v. pr. hate each other.

déton|er /detone/ v.i. explode, detonate. **~ateur** n.m. detonator. **~ation** n.f. explosion, detonation.

détonner /detone/ v.i. clash.

détour /detur/ n.m. bend; (crochet) detour; (fig.) roundabout means.

détourné /deturne/ a. roundabout.

détourn|er /deturne/ v.t. divert; (tête, yeux) turn away; (avion) hijack; (argent) embezzle. **se ~er de**, stray from. **~ement** n.m. hijack(ing); embezzlement.

détrac|teur, ~trice /detraktœr, -tris/ n.m., f. critic.

détraquer /detrake/ v.t. break, put out of order; (estomac) upset. **se ~** v. pr. (machine) go wrong.

détresse /detrɛs/ n.f. distress.

détriment /detrimɑ̃/ n.m. detriment.

détritus /detritys/ n.m. pl. rubbish.

détroit /detrwa/ n.m. strait.

détromper /detrɔ̃pe/ v.t. undeceive, enlighten.

détruire† /detrɥir/ v.t. destroy.

dette /dɛt/ n.f. debt.

deuil /dœj/ n.m. mourning; (perte) bereavement. **porter le ~**, be in mourning.

deux /dø/ a. & n.m. two. **~ fois**, twice. **tous (les) ~**, both. **~-pièces** n.m. invar. (vêtement) two-piece; (logement) two-room flat or apartment. **~-points** n.m. invar. (gram.) colon. **~-roues** n.m. invar. two-wheeled vehicle.

deuxième /døzjɛm/ a. & n.m./f. second. **~ment** adv. secondly.

dévaler /devale/ v.t./i. hurtle down.

dévaliser /devalize/ v.t. rob, clean out.

dévaloriser /devalɔrize/ v.t., **se ~** v. pr. reduce in value.

dévalorisant, ~e /devalɔrizɑ̃, -t/ a. demeaning.

déval|uer /devalɥe/ v.t., **se ~uer** v. pr. devalue. **~uation** n.f. devaluation.

devancer /dəvɑ̃se/ v.t. be ou go ahead of; (arriver) arrive ahead of; (prévenir) anticipate.

devant /dvɑ̃/ prép. in front of; (distance) ahead of; (avec mouvement) past; (en présence de) before; (face à) in the face of. —adv. in front; (à distance) ahead. —n.m. front. **prendre les ~s**, take the initiative. **de ~**, front. **par ~**, at ou from the front, in front. **aller au ~ de qn.**, go to meet sb. **aller au ~ des désirs de qn.**, anticipate sb.'s wishes.

devanture /dvɑ̃tyr/ n.f. shop front; (étalage) shop-window.

dévaster /devaste/ v.t. devastate.

déveine /devɛn/ n.f. bad luck.

développ|er /devlɔpe/ v.t., **se ~er** v. pr. develop. **~ement** n.m. development; (de photos) developing.

devenir† /dəvnir/ v.i. (aux. être) become. **qu'est-il devenu?**, what has become of him?

dévergondé /devɛrgɔ̃de/ a. shameless.

déverser /devɛrse/ v.t., **se ~** v. pr. empty out, pour out.

dévêtir /devetir/ v.t., **se ~** v. pr. undress.

déviation /devjasjɔ̃/ n.f. diversion.

dévier /devje/ v.t. divert; (coup) deflect. —v.i. (ballon, balle) veer; (personne) deviate.

devin /dəvɛ̃/ n.m. fortune-teller.

deviner /dvine/ v.t. guess; (apercevoir) distinguish.

devinette /dvinɛt/ n.f. riddle.

devis /dvi/ n.m. estimate.

dévisager /devizaʒe/ v.t. stare at.

devise /dviz/ n.f. motto. **~s**, (monnaie) (foreign) currency.

dévisser /devise/ *v.t.* unscrew.
dévitaliser /devitalize/ *v.t.* (*dent*) kill the nerve in.
dévoiler /devwale/ *v.t.* reveal.
devoir¹ /dvwar/ *n.m.* duty; (*scol.*) homework; (*fait en classe*) exercise.
devoir†² /dvwar/ *v.t.* owe. —*v. aux.* ~ faire, (*nécessité*) must do, have (got) to do; (*intention*) be due to do. ~ être, (*probabilité*) must be. **vous devriez,** you should. **il aurait dû,** he should have.
dévolu /devɔly/ *n.m.* **jeter son ~ sur,** set one's heart on. —*a.* ~ à, allotted to.
dévorer /devɔre/ *v.t.* devour.
dévot, ~e /devo, -ɔt/ *a.* devout.
dévotion /devosjɔ̃/ *n.f.* (*relig.*) devotion.
dévou|er (se) /(sə)devwe/ *v. pr.* devote o.s. (**à,** to); (*se sacrifier*) sacrifice o.s. ~é *a.* devoted. ~ement /-vumɑ̃/ *n.m.* devotion.
dextérité /dɛksterite/ *n.f.* skill.
diab|ète /djabɛt/ *n.m.* diabetes. ~étique *a. & n.m./f.* diabetic.
diab|le /djɑbl/ *n.m.* devil. ~olique *a.* diabolical.
diagnosti|c /djagnɔstik/ *n.m.* diagnosis. ~quer *v.t.* diagnose.
diagon|al, ~ale (*m. pl.* ~aux) /djagɔnal, -o/ *a. & n.f.* diagonal. **en ~ale,** diagonally.
diagramme /djagram/ *n.m.* diagram; (*graphique*) graph.
dialecte /djalɛkt/ *n.m.* dialect.
dialogu|e /djalɔg/ *n.m.* dialogue. ~er *v.i.* (*pol.*) have a dialogue.
diamant /djamɑ̃/ *n.m.* diamond.
diamètre /djamɛtr/ *n.m.* diameter.
diapason /djapazɔ̃/ *n.m.* tuning-fork.
diaphragme /djafragm/ *n.m.* diaphragm.
diapo /djapo/ *n.f.* (colour) slide.
diapositive /djapozitiv/ *n.f.* (colour) slide.
diarrhée /djare/ *n.f.* diarrhoea.
dictat|eur /diktatœr/ *n.m.* dictator. ~ure *n.f.* dictatorship.
dict|er /dikte/ *v.t.* dictate. ~ée *n.f.* dictation.
diction /diksjɔ̃/ *n.f.* diction.
dictionnaire /diksjɔnɛr/ *n.m.* dictionary.
dicton /diktɔ̃/ *n.m.* saying.
dièse /djɛz/ *n.m.* (*mus.*) sharp.
diesel /djezɛl/ *n.m. & a. invar.* diesel.
diète /djɛt/ *n.f.* (*régime*) diet.
diététicien, ~ne /djetetisjɛ̃, -jɛn/ *n.m., f.* dietician.
diététique /djetetik/ *n.f.* dietetics. —*a.* **produit** *ou* **aliment ~,** dietary product.

dieu (*pl.* ~x) /djø/ *n.m.* god. **D~,** God.
diffamatoire /difamatwar/ *a.* defamatory.
diffam|er /difame/ *v.t.* slander; (*par écrit*) libel. ~ation *n.f.* slander; libel.
différé (en) /(ɑ̃)difere/ *adv.* (*émission*) recorded.
différemment /diferamɑ̃/ *adv.* differently.
différence /diferɑ̃s/ *n.f.* difference. **à la ~ de,** unlike.
différencier /diferɑ̃sje/ *v.t.* differentiate. **se ~ de,** (*différer de*) differ from.
différend /diferɑ̃/ *n.m.* difference (of opinion).
différent, ~e /diferɑ̃, -t/ *a.* different (**de,** from).
différentiel, ~le /diferɑ̃sjɛl/ *a. & n.m.* differential.
différer¹ /difere/ *v.t.* postpone.
différer² /difere/ *v.i.* differ (**de,** from).
difficile /difisil/ *a.* difficult. ~ment *adv.* with difficulty.
difficulté /difikylte/ *n.f.* difficulty.
difform|e /difɔrm/ *a.* deformed. ~ité *n.f.* deformity.
diffus, ~e /dify, -z/ *a.* diffuse.
diffus|er /difyze/ *v.t.* broadcast; (*lumière, chaleur*) diffuse. ~ion *n.f.* broadcasting; diffusion.
dig|érer /diʒere/ *v.t.* digest; (*endurer: fam.*) stomach. ~este, ~estible *adjs.* digestible. ~estion *n.f.* digestion.
digesti|f, ~ve /diʒɛstif, -v/ *a.* digestive. —*n.m.* after-dinner liqueur.
digit|al (*m. pl.* ~aux) /diʒital, -o/ *a.* digital.
digne /diɲ/ *a.* (*noble*) dignified; (*honnête*) worthy. ~ **de,** worthy of. ~ **de foi,** trustworthy.
dignité /diɲite/ *n.f.* dignity.
digression /digresjɔ̃/ *n.f.* digression.
digue /dig/ *n.f.* dike.
diktat /diktat/ *n.m.* diktat.
dilapider /dilapide/ *v.t.* squander.
dilat|er /dilate/ *v.t.*, **se ~er** *v. pr.* dilate. ~ation /-asjɔ̃/ *n.f.* dilation.
dilemme /dilɛm/ *n.m.* dilemma.
dilettante /diletɑ̃t/ *n.m., f.* amateur.
diluant /dilɥɑ̃/ *n.m.* thinner.
diluer /dilɥe/ *v.t.* dilute.
diluvien, ~ne /dilɥvjɛ̃, -ɛn/ *a.* (*pluie*) torrential.
dimanche /dimɑ̃ʃ/ *n.m.* Sunday.
dimension /dimɑ̃sjɔ̃/ *n.f.* (*taille*) size; (*mesure*) dimension.
dimin|uer /diminɥe/ *v.t.* reduce, decrease; (*plaisir, courage, etc.*) lessen;

(*dénigrer*) lessen. —*v.i.* decrease. ~**ution** *n.f.* decrease (**de,** in).

diminutif /diminytif/ *n.m.* diminutive; (*surnom*) pet name *ou* form.

dinde /dɛ̃d/ *n.f.* turkey.

dindon /dɛ̃dɔ̃/ *n.m.* turkey.

dîn|er /dine/ *n.m.* dinner. —*v.i.* have dinner. ~**eur,** ~**euse** *n.m.,* f. diner.

dingue /dɛ̃g/ *a.* (*fam.*) crazy.

dinosaure /dinozɔr/ *n.m.* dinosaur.

diocèse /djɔsɛz/ *n.m.* diocese.

diphtérie /difteri/ *n.f.* diphtheria.

diphtongue /diftɔ̃g/ *n.f.* diphthong.

diplomate /diplɔmat/ *n.m.* diplomat. —*a.* diplomatic.

diplomat|ie /diplɔmasi/ *n.f.* diplomacy. ~**ique** /-atik/ *a.* diplomatic.

diplôm|e /diplom/ *n.m.* certificate, diploma; (*univ.*) degree. ~**é** *a.* qualified.

dire† /dir/ *v.t.* say; (*secret, vérité, heure*) tell; (*penser*) think. ~ **que,** say that. ~ **à qn. que/de,** tell s.o. that/to. se ~ *v. pr.* (*mot*) be said; (*fatigué etc.*) say that one is. **ça me/vous/***etc.* **dit de faire, I/you/***etc.* feel like doing. **on dirait que,** it would seem that, it seems that. **dis/dites donc!,** hey! —*n.m.* **au ~ de, selon les ~s de,** according to.

direct /dirɛkt/ *a.* direct. **en ~,** (*émission*) live. ~**ement** *adv.* directly.

direc|teur, ~**trice** /dirɛktœr, -tris/ *n.m.,* f. director; (*chef de service*) manager, manageress; (*d'école*) headmaster, headmistress.

direction /dirɛksjɔ̃/ *n.f.* (*sens*) direction; (*de société etc.*) management; (*auto.*) steering. **en ~ de,** (going to).

directive /dirɛktiv/ *n.f.* instruction.

dirigeant, ~**e** /diriʒɑ̃, -t/ *n.m.,* f. (*pol.*) leader; (*comm.*) manager. —*a.* (*classe*) ruling.

diriger /diriʒe/ *v.t.* run, manage, direct; (*véhicule*) steer; (*orchestre*) conduct; (*braquer*) aim; (*tourner*) turn. **se ~** *v. pr.* guide o.s. **se ~ vers,** make one's way to.

dirigis|me /diriʒism/ *n.m.* interventionism. ~**te** /-ist/ *a. & n.m./f.* interventionist.

dis /di/ *voir* **dire.**

discern|er /disɛrne/ *v.t.* discern. ~**ement** *n.m.* discernment.

disciple /disipl/ *n.m.* disciple.

disciplin|e /disiplin/ *n.f.* discipline. ~**aire** *a.* disciplinary. ~**er** *v.t.* discipline.

discontinu /diskɔ̃tiny/ *a.* intermittent.

discontinuer /diskɔ̃tinɥe/ *v.i.* **sans ~,** without stopping.

discordant, ~**e** /diskɔrdɑ̃, -t/ *a.* discordant.

discorde /diskɔrd/ *n.f.* discord.

discothèque /diskɔtɛk/ *n.f.* record library; (*club*) disco(thèque).

discount /diskunt/ *n.m.* discount.

discourir /diskurir/ *v.i.* (*péj.*) hold forth, ramble on.

discours /diskur/ *n.m.* speech.

discréditer /diskredite/ *v.t.* discredit.

discr|et, ~**ète** /diskrɛ, -t/ *a.* discreet. ~**ètement** *adv.* discreetly.

discrétion /diskresjɔ̃/ *n.f.* discretion. **à ~,** as much as one desires.

discrimination /diskriminasjɔ̃/ *n.f.* discrimination.

discriminatoire /diskriminatwar/ *a.* discriminatory.

disculper /diskylpe/ *v.t.* exonerate. **se ~** *v. pr.* prove o.s. innocent.

discussion /diskysjɔ̃/ *n.f.* discussion; (*querelle*) argument.

discuté /diskyte/ *a.* controversial.

discut|er /diskyte/ *v.t.* discuss; (*contester*) question. —*v.i.* (*parler*) talk; (*répliquer*) argue. ~**er de,** discuss. ~**able** *a.* debatable.

disette /dizɛt/ *n.f.* (food) shortage.

diseuse /dizøz/ *n.f.* **~ de bonne aventure,** fortune-teller.

disgrâce /disgras/ *n.f.* disgrace.

disgracieu|x, ~**se** /disgrasjø, -z/ *a.* ungainly.

disjoindre /disʒwɛ̃dr/ *v.t.* take apart. **se ~** *v. pr.* come apart.

dislo|quer /disloke/ *v.t.* (*membre*) dislocate; (*machine etc.*) break (apart). **se ~quer** *v. pr.* (*parti, cortège*) break up; (*meuble*) come apart. ~**cation** *n.f.* (*anat.*) dislocation.

dispar|aître† /disparɛtr/ *v.i.* disappear; (*mourir*) die. **faire ~aître,** get rid of. ~**ition** *n.f.* disappearance; (*mort*) death. ~**u,** ~**ue** *a.* (*soldat etc.*) missing; *n.m.,* f. missing person; (*mort*) dead person.

disparate /disparat/ *a.* ill-assorted.

disparité /disparite/ *n.f.* disparity.

dispensaire /dispɑ̃sɛr/ *n.m.* clinic.

dispense /dispɑ̃s/ *n.f.* exemption.

dispenser /dispɑ̃se/ *v.t.* exempt (**de,** from). **se ~ de (faire),** avoid (doing).

disperser /dispɛrse/ *v.t.* (*éparpiller*) scatter; (*répartir*) disperse. **se ~** *v. pr.* disperse.

disponib|le /dispɔnibl/ *a.* available. ~**ilité** *n.f.* availability.

dispos, ~e /dispo, -z/ *a.* **frais et** ~, fresh and alert.

disposé /dispoze/ *a.* **bien/mal** ~, in a good/bad mood. ~ **à,** prepared to. ~ **envers,** disposed towards.

disposer /dispoze/ *v.t.* arrange. ~ **à,** (*engager à*) incline to. —*v.i.* ~ **de,** have at one's disposal. **se** ~ **à,** prepare to.

dispositif /dispozitif/ *n.m.* device; (*plan*) plan of action. ~ **anti-parasite,** suppressor.

disposition /dispozisjɔ̃/ *n.f.* arrangement; (*humeur*) mood; (*tendance*) tendency. ~**s,** (*préparatifs*) arrangements; (*aptitude*) aptitude. **à la** ~ **de,** at the disposal of.

disproportionné /disprɔpɔrsjɔne/ *a.* disproportionate.

dispute /dispyt/ *n.f.* quarrel.

disputer /dispyte/ *v.t.* (*match*) play; (*course*) run in; (*prix*) fight for; (*gronder: fam.*) tell off. **se** ~ *v. pr.* quarrel; (*se battre pour*) fight over; (*match*) be played.

disquaire /diskɛr/ *n.m./f.* record dealer.

disqualif|ier /diskalifje/ *v.t.* disqualify. ~**ication** *n.f.* disqualification.

disque /disk/ *n.m.* (*mus.*) record; (*sport*) discus; (*cercle*) disc, disk. ~ **dur,** hard disk.

disquette /diskɛt/ *n.f.* (floppy) disk.

dissection /disɛksjɔ̃/ *n.f.* dissection.

dissemblable /disɑ̃blabl/ *a.* dissimilar.

disséminer /disemine/ *v.t.* scatter.

disséquer /diseke/ *v.t.* dissect.

dissertation /disɛrtasjɔ̃/ *n.f.* (*scol.*) essay.

disserter /disɛrte/ *v.i.* ~ **sur,** comment upon.

dissiden|t, ~**te** /disidɑ̃, -t/ *a. & n.m., f.* dissident. ~**ce** *n.f.* dissidence.

dissimul|er /disimyle/ *v.t.* conceal (**à,** from). **se** ~**er** *v. pr.* conceal o.s. ~**ation** *n.f.* concealment; (*fig.*) deceit.

dissipé /disipe/ *a.* (*élève*) unruly.

dissip|er /disipe/ *v.t.* (*fumée, crainte*) dispel; (*fortune*) squander; (*personne*) lead into bad ways. **se** ~**er** *v. pr.* disappear. ~**ation** *n.f.* squandering; (*indiscipline*) misbehaviour.

dissolution /disɔlysjɔ̃/ *n.f.* dissolution.

dissolvant /disɔlvɑ̃/ *n.m.* solvent; (*pour ongles*) nail polish remover.

dissonant, ~e /disɔnɑ̃, -t/ *a.* discordant.

dissoudre† /disudr/ *v.t.,* **se** ~ *v. pr.* dissolve.

dissua|der /disɥade/ *v.t.* dissuade (**de,** from). ~**sion** /-ɥazjɔ̃/ *n.f.* dissuasion. **force de** ~**sion,** deterrent force.

dissuasi|f, ~**ve** /disɥazif, -v/ *a.* dissuasive.

distance /distɑ̃s/ *n.f.* distance; (*écart*) gap. **à** ~, **at** *ou* from a distance.

distancer /distɑ̃se/ *v.t.* leave behind.

distant, ~e /distɑ̃, -t/ *a.* distant.

distendre /distɑ̃dr/ *v.t.,* **se** ~ *v. pr.* distend.

distill|er /distile/ *v.t.* distil. ~**ation** *n.f.* distillation.

distillerie /distilri/ *n.f.* distillery.

distinct, ~e /distɛ̃(kt), -ɛ̃kt/ *a.* distinct. ~**ement** /-ɛ̃ktəmɑ̃/ *adv.* distinctly.

distincti|f, ~**ve** /distɛ̃ktif, -v/ *a.* distinctive.

distinction /distɛ̃ksjɔ̃/ *n.f.* distinction.

distingué /distɛ̃ge/ *a.* distinguished.

distinguer /distɛ̃ge/ *v.t.* distinguish.

distraction /distraksjɔ̃/ *n.f.* absent-mindedness; (*oubli*) lapse; (*passe-temps*) distraction.

distraire† /distrɛr/ *v.t.* amuse; (*rendre inattentif*) distract. **se** ~ *v. pr.* amuse o.s.

distrait, ~e /distrɛ, -t/ *a.* absent-minded. ~**ement** *a.* absent-mindedly.

distrayant, ~e /distrɛjɑ̃, -t/ *a.* entertaining.

distrib|uer /distribɥe/ *v.t.* hand out, distribute; (*répartir, amener*) distribute; (*courrier*) deliver. ~**uteur** *n.m.* (*auto., comm.*) distributor. ~**uteur** (**automatique**)**,** vending-machine; (*de billets*) (cash) dispenser. ~**ution** *n.f.* distribution; (*du courrier*) delivery; (*acteurs*) cast.

district /distrikt/ *n.m.* district.

dit¹, dites /di, dit/ *voir* **dire.**

dit², ~e /di, dit/ *a.* (*décidé*) agreed; (*surnommé*) called.

diurétique /djyretik/ *a. & n.m.* diuretic.

diurne /djyrn/ *a.* diurnal.

divag|uer /divage/ *v.i.* rave. ~**ations** *n.f. pl.* ravings.

divan /divɑ̃/ *n.m.* divan.

divergen|t, ~**te** /divɛrʒɑ̃, -t/ *a.* divergent. ~**ce** *n.f.* divergence.

diverger /divɛrʒe/ *v.i.* diverge.

divers, ~e /divɛr, -s/ *a.* (*varié*) diverse; (*différent*) various. ~**ement** /-səmɑ̃/ *adv.* variously.

diversifier /divɛrsifje/ *v.t.* diversify.

diversion /divɛrsjɔ̃/ *n.f.* diversion.

diversité /divɛrsite/ *n.f.* diversity.

divert|ir /divɛrtir/ *v.t.* amuse. **se** ~**ir**

v. pr. amuse o.s. ~**issement** *n.m.* amusement.

dividende /dividɑ̃d/ *n.m.* dividend.

divin, ~**e** /divɛ̃, -in/ *a.* divine.

divinité /divinite/ *n.f.* divinity.

divis|er /divize/ *v.t.,* **se** ~**er** *v. pr.* divide. ~**ion** *n.f.* division.

divorc|e /divɔrs/ *n.m.* divorce. ~**é** ~**ée** *a.* divorced; *n.m., f.* divorcee. ~**er** *v.i.* ~**er (d'avec),** divorce.

divulguer /divylge/ *v.t.* divulge.

dix /dis/ (/di/ *before consonant,* /diz/ *before vowel*) *a. & n.m.* ten. ~**ième** /dizjɛm/ *a. & n.m./f.* tenth.

dix-huit /dizɥit/ *a. & n.m.* eighteen. ~**ième** *a. & n.m./f.* eighteenth.

dix-neu|f /diznœf/ *a. & n.m.* nineteen. ~**vième** *a. & n.m./f.* nineteenth.

dix-sept /disɛt/ *a. & n.m.* seventeen. ~**ième** *a. & n.m./f.* seventeenth.

dizaine /dizɛn/ *n.f.* (about) ten.

docile /dɔsil/ *a.* docile.

docilité /dɔsilite/ *n.f.* docility.

dock /dɔk/ *n.m.* dock.

docker /dɔkɛr/ *n.m.* docker.

doct|eur /dɔktœr/ *n.m.* doctor. ~**oresse** *n.f.* (*fam.*) lady doctor.

doctorat /dɔktɔra/ *n.m.* doctorate.

doctrine /dɔktrin/ *n.f.* doctrine. ~**aire** *a.* doctrinaire.

document /dɔkymɑ̃/ *n.m.* document. ~**aire** /-tɛr/ *a. & n.m.* documentary.

documentaliste /dɔkymɑ̃talist/ *n.m./f.* information officer.

document|er /dɔkymɑ̃te/ *v.t.* document. **se** ~**er** *v. pr.* collect information. ~**ation** *n.f.* information, literature. ~**é** *a.* well-documented.

dodo /dodo/ *n.m.* **faire** ~, (*langage enfantin*) go to byebyes.

dodu /dɔdy/ *a.* plump.

dogm|e /dɔgm/ *n.m.* dogma. ~**atique** *a.* dogmatic.

doigt /dwa/ *n.m.* finger. **un** ~ **de,** a drop of. **à deux** ~**s de,** a hair's breadth away from. ~ **de pied,** toe.

doigté /dwate/ *n.m.* (*mus.*) fingering, touch; (*adresse*) tact.

dois, doit /dwa/ *voir* **devoir**[2].

Dolby /dɔlbi/ *n.m. & a.* (P.) Dolby (P.).

doléances /dɔleɑ̃s/ *n.f. pl.* grievances.

dollar /dɔlar/ *n.m.* dollar.

domaine /dɔmɛn/ *n.m.* estate, domain; (*fig.*) domain.

dôme /dom/ *n.m.* dome.

domestique /dɔmɛstik/ *a.* domestic. —*n.m./f.* servant.

domestiquer /dɔmɛstike/ *v.t.* domesticate.

domicile /dɔmisil/ *n.m.* home. **à** ~, at home; (*livrer*) to the home.

domicilié /dɔmisilje/ *a.* resident.

domin|er /dɔmine/ *v.t./i.* dominate; (*surplomber*) tower over, dominate; (*équipe*) dictate the game (to). ~**ant,** ~**ante** *a.* dominant; *n.f.* dominant feature. ~**ation** *n.f.* domination.

domino /dɔmino/ *n.m.* domino.

dommage /dɔmaʒ/ *n.m.* (*tort*) harm. ~**(s),** (*dégâts*) damage. **c'est** ~, it's a pity. **quel** ~, what a shame. ~**s-intérêts** *n.m. pl.* (*jurid.*) damages.

dompt|er /dɔ̃te/ *v.t.* tame. ~**eur,** ~**euse** *n.m., f.* tamer.

don /dɔ̃/ *n.m.* (*cadeau, aptitude*) gift.

dona|teur, ~**trice** /dɔnatœr, -tris/ *n.m., f.* donor.

donation /dɔnasjɔ̃/ *n.f.* donation.

donc /dɔ̃(k)/ *conj.* so, then; (*par conséquent*) so, therefore.

donjon /dɔ̃ʒɔ̃/ *n.m.* (*tour*) keep.

donné /dɔne/ *a.* (*fixé*) given; (*pas cher: fam.*) dirt cheap. **étant** ~ **que,** given that.

données /dɔne/ *n.f. pl.* (*de science*) data; (*de problème*) facts.

donner /dɔne/ *v.t.* give; (*vieilles affaires*) give away; (*distribuer*) give out; (*récolte etc.*) produce; (*film*) show; (*pièce*) put on. —*v.i.* ~ **sur,** look out on to. ~ **dans,** (*piège*) fall into. **ça donne soif/faim,** it makes one thirsty/hungry. ~ **à réparer/**etc., take to be repaired/etc. ~ **lieu à,** give rise to. **se** ~ **à,** devote o.s. to. **se** ~ **du mal,** go to a lot of trouble (**pour faire,** to do).

donneu|r, ~**se** /dɔnœr, -øz/ *n.m., f.* (*de sang*) donor.

dont /dɔ̃/ *pron. rel.* (*chose*) whose, of which; (*personne*) whose; (*partie d'un tout*) of whom; (*chose*) of which; (*provenance*) from which; (*manière*) in which. **le père** ~ **la fille,** the father whose daughter. **ce** ~, what. ~ **il a besoin,** which he needs. **l'enfant** ~ **il est fier,** the child he is proud of. **trois enfants** ~ **deux sont jumeaux,** three children, two of whom are twins.

dopage /dɔpaʒ/ *n.m.* doping.

doper /dɔpe/ *v.t.* dope. **se** ~ *v. pr.* take dope.

doré /dɔre/ *a.* (*couleur d'or*) golden; (*avec dorure*) gold. **la bourgeoisie** ~**e** the affluent middle class.

dorénavant /dɔrenavɑ̃/ *adv.* henceforth.

dorer /dɔre/ *v.t.* gild; (*culin.*) brown.

dorloter /dɔrlɔte/ *v.t.* pamper.

dorm|ir† /dɔrmir/ *v.i.* sleep; (*être*

endormi) be asleep. **~eur, ~euse** *n.m.*, *f.* sleeper. **il dort debout**, he can't keep awake. **une histoire à ~ir debout**, a cock-and-bull story.

dortoir /dɔrtwar/ *n.m.* dormitory.

dorure /dɔryr/ *n.f.* gilding.

dos /do/ *n.m.* back; (*de livre*) spine. **à ~ de**, riding on. **de ~**, from behind. **~ crawlé**, backstroke.

dos|e /doz/ *n.f.* dose. **~age** *n.m.* (*mélange*) mixture. **faire le ~age de**, measure out; balance. **~er** *v.t.* measure out; (*équilibrer*) balance.

dossard /dɔsar/ *n.m.* (*sport*) number.

dossier /dɔsje/ *n.m.* (*documents*) file; (*de chaise*) back.

dot /dɔt/ *n.f.* dowry.

doter /dɔte/ *v.t.* **~ de**, equip with.

douan|e /dwan/ *n.f.* customs. **~ier, ~ière** *a.* customs; *n.m.*, *f.* customs officer.

doubl|e /dubl/ *a. & adv.* double. —*n.m.* (*copie*) duplicate; (*sosie*) double. **le ~e (de)**, twice as much *ou* as many (as). **le ~ emessieurs**, the men's doubles. **~e décimètre**, ruler. **~ement**[1] *adv.* doubly.

doubl|er /duble/ *v.t./i.* double; (*dépasser*) overtake; (*vêtement*) line; (*film*) dub; (*classe*) repeat; (*cap*) round. **~ement**[2] *n.m.* doubling. **~ure** *n.f.* (*étoffe*) lining; (*acteur*) understudy.

douce /dus/ *voir* **doux**.

douceâtre /dusɑtr/ *a.* sickly sweet.

doucement /dusmɑ̃/ *adv.* gently.

douceur /dusœr/ *n.f.* (*mollesse*) softness; (*de climat*) mildness; (*de personne*) gentleness; (*joie, plaisir*) sweetness. **~s**, (*friandises*) sweet things. **en ~**, smoothly.

douch|e /duʃ/ *n.f.* shower. **~er** *v.t.* give a shower to. **se ~er** *v. pr.* have *ou* take a shower.

doudoune /dudun/ *n.f.* (*fam.*) anorak.

doué /dwe/ *a.* gifted. **~ de**, endowed with.

douille /duj/ *n.f.* (*électr.*) socket.

douillet, ~te /dujɛ, -t/ *a.* cosy, comfortable; (*personne: péj.*) soft.

doul|eur /dulœr/ *n.f.* pain; (*chagrin*) grief. **~oureux, ~oureuse** *a.* painful. **la ~oureuse** *n.f.* the bill.

doute /dut/ *n.m.* doubt. **sans ~**, no doubt. **sans aucun ~**, without doubt.

douter /dute/ *v.i.* **~ de**, doubt. **se ~ de**, suspect.

douteu|x, ~se /dutø, -z/ *a.* doubtful.

Douvres /duvr/ *n.m./f.* Dover.

doux, douce /du, dus/ *a.* (*moelleux*) soft;

(*sucré*) sweet; (*clément, pas fort*) mild; (*pas brusque, bienveillant*) gentle.

douzaine /duzɛn/ *n.f.* about twelve; (*douze*) dozen. **une ~ d'œufs**/*etc.*, a dozen eggs/*etc.*

douz|e /duz/ *a. & n.m.* twelve. **~ième** *a. & n.m./f.* twelfth.

doyen, ~ne /dwajɛ̃, -jɛn/ *n.m.*, *f.* dean; (*en âge*) most senior person.

dragée /draʒe/ *n.f.* sugared almond.

dragon /dragɔ̃/ *n.m.* dragon.

dragu|e /drag/ *n.f.* (*bateau*) dredger. **~er** *v.t.* (*rivière*) dredge; (*filles: fam.*) chat up, try to pick up.

drain /drɛ̃/ *n.m.* drain.

drainer /drene/ *v.t.* drain.

dramatique /dramatik/ *a.* dramatic; (*tragique*) tragic. —*n.f.* (television) drama.

dramatiser /dramatize/ *v.t.* dramatize.

dramaturge /dramatyrʒ/ *n.m./f.* dramatist.

drame /dram/ *n.m.* drama.

drap /dra/ *n.m.* sheet; (*tissu*) (woollen) cloth. **~-housse** /draus/ *n.m.* fitted sheet.

drapeau (*pl.* **~x**) /drapo/ *n.m.* flag.

draper /drape/ *v.t.* drape.

dress|er /drese/ *v.t.* put up, erect; (*tête*) raise; (*animal*) train; (*liste*) draw up. **se ~er** *v. pr.* (*bâtiment etc.*) stand; (*personne*) draw o.s. up. **~er l'oreille**, prick up one's ears. **~age** /drɛsaʒ/ *n.m.* training. **~eur, ~euse** /drɛsœr, -øz/ *n.m.*, *f.* trainer.

dribbler /drible/ *v.t./i.* (*sport*) dribble.

drille /drij/ *n.m.* **un joyeux ~**, a cheery character.

drive /drajv/ *n.m.* (*comput.*) drive.

drogue /drɔg/ *n.f.* drug. **la ~**, drugs.

drogu|er /drɔge/ *v.t.* (*malade*) drug heavily, dose up; (*victime*) drug. **se ~er** *v. pr.* take drugs. **~é, ~ée** *n.m.*, *f.* drug addict.

drogu|erie /drɔgri/ *n.f.* hardware and chemist's shop; (*Amer.*) drugstore. **~iste** *n.m./f.* owner of a *droguerie*.

droit[1], **~e** /drwa, -t/ *a.* (*non courbe*) straight; (*loyal*) upright; (*angle*) right. —*adv.* straight. —*n.f.* straight line.

droit[2] **~e** /drwa, -t/ *a.* (*contraire de gauche*) right. **à ~e**, on the right; (*direction*) (to the) right. **la ~e**, the right (side); (*pol.*) the right (wing). **~ier, ~ière** /-tje, -tjɛr/ *a. & n.m.*, *f.* right-handed (person).

droit[3] /drwa/ *n.m.* right. **~(s)**, (*taxe*) duty; (*d'inscription*) fee(s). **le ~**, (*jurid.*) law. **avoir ~ à**, be entitled to.

avoir le ~ de, be allowed to. **être dans son ~,** be in the right. **~ d'auteur,** copyright. **~s d'auteur,** royalties.

drôle /drol/ *a.* funny. **~ d'air,** funny look. **~ment** *adv.* funnily; (*extrêmement: fam.*) dreadfully.

dromadaire /drɔmadɛr/ *n.m.* dromedary.

dru /dry/ *a.* thick. **tomber ~,** fall thick and fast.

drugstore /drœgstɔr/ *n.m.* drugstore.

du /dy/ *voir* **de**.

dû, due /dy/ *voir* **devoir**². —*a.* due. —*n.m.* due; (*argent*) dues. **du à,** due to.

duc, duchesse /dyk, dyʃɛs/ *n.m.*, *f.* duke, duchess.

duel /dɥɛl/ *n.m.* duel.

dune /dyn/ *n.f.* dune.

duo /dɥo/ *n.m.* (*mus.*) duet; (*fig.*) duo.

dup|e /dyp/ *n.f.* dupe. **~er** *v.t.* dupe.

duplex /dyplɛks/ *n.m.* split-level apartment; (*Amer.*) duplex; (*émission*) link-up.

duplicata /dyplikata/ *n.m. invar.* duplicate.

duplicité /dyplisite/ *n.f.* duplicity.

duquel /dykɛl/ *voir* **lequel**.

dur /dyr/ *a.* hard; (*sévère*) harsh, hard; (*viande*) tough, hard; (*col, brosse*) stiff. —*adv.* hard. —*n.m.* tough guy. **~ d'oreille,** hard of hearing.

durable /dyrabl/ *a.* lasting.

durant /dyrã/ *prép.* during; (*mesure de temps*) for.

durc|ir /dyrsir/ *v.t./i.,* **se ~ir** *v. pr.* harden. **~issement** *n.m.* hardening.

dure /dyr/ *n.f.* **à la ~,** the hard way.

durée /dyre/ *n.f.* length; (*période*) duration.

durement /dyrmã/ *adv.* harshly.

durer /dyre/ *v.i.* last.

dureté /dyrte/ *n.f.* hardness; (*sévérité*) harshness.

duvet /dyvɛ/ *n.m.* down; (*sac*) (down-filled) sleeping-bag.

dynami|que /dinamik/ *a.* dynamic. **~sme** *n.m.* dynamism.

dynamit|e /dinamit/ *n.f.* dynamite. **~er** *v.t.* dynamite.

dynamo /dinamo/ *n.f.* dynamo.

dynastie /dinasti/ *n.f.* dynasty.

dysenterie /disãtri/ *n.f.* dysentery.

E

eau (*pl.* **~x**) /o/ *n.f.* water. **~ courante/dormante,** running/still water. **~ de Cologne,** eau-de-Cologne. **~ dentifrice,** mouthwash. **~ de toilette,** toilet water. **~-de-vie** (*pl.* **~x-de-vie**) *n.f.* brandy. **~ douce/salée,** fresh/salt water. **~-forte** (*pl.* **~x-fortes**) *n.f.* etching. **~ potable,** drinking water. **~ de Javel,** bleach. **~ minérale,** mineral water. **~ gazeuse,** fizzy water. **~ plate,** still water. **~x usées,** dirty water. **tomber à l'~** (*fig.*) fall through. **prendre l'~,** take in water.

ébahi /ebai/ *a.* dumbfounded.

ébattre (s') /(s)ebatr/ *v. pr.* frolic.

ébauch|e /eboʃ/ *n.f.* outline. **~er** *v.t.* outline. **s'~er** *v. pr.* form.

ébène /ebɛn/ *n.f.* ebony.

ébéniste /ebenist/ *n.m.* cabinet-maker.

éberlué /ebɛrlɥe/ *a.* flabbergasted.

éblou|ir /ebluir/ *v.t.* dazzle. **~issement** *n.m.* dazzle, dazzling; (*malaise*) dizzy turn.

éboueur /ebwœr/ *n.m.* dustman; (*Amer.*) garbage collector.

ébouillanter /ebujãte/ *v.t.* scald.

éboul|er (s') /(s)ebule/ *v. pr.* crumble, collapse. **~ement** *n.m.* landslide. **~is** *n.m. pl.* fallen rocks and earth.

ébouriffé /eburife/ *a.* dishevelled.

ébranler /ebrãle/ *v.t.* shake. **s'~** *v. pr.* move off.

ébrécher /ebreʃe/ *v.t.* chip.

ébriété /ebrijete/ *n.f.* intoxication.

ébrouer (s') /(s)ebrue/ *v. pr.* shake o.s.

ébruiter /ebrɥite/ *v.t.* spread about.

ébullition /ebylisjɔ̃/ *n.f.* boiling. **en ~,** boiling.

écaille /ekaj/ *n.f.* (*de poisson*) scale; (*de peinture, roc*) flake; (*matière*) tortoiseshell.

écailler /ekaje/ *v.t.* (*poisson*) scale. **s'~** *v. pr.* flake (off).

écarlate /ekarlat/ *a. & n.f.* scarlet.

écarquiller /ekarkije/ *v.t.* **~ les yeux,** open one's eyes wide.

écart /ekar/ *n.m.* gap; (*de prix etc.*) difference; (*embardée*) swerve; (*conduite*) lapse (**de,** in). **à l'~,** out of the way. **tenir à l'~,** (*participant*) keep out of things. **à l'~ de,** away from.

écarté /ekarte/ *a.* (*lieu*) remote. **les jambes ~es,** (with) legs apart. **les bras ~s,** with one's arms out.

écartement /ekartəmã/ *n.m.* gap.

écarter /ekarte/ *v.t.* (*objets*) move apart; (*ouvrir*) open; (*éliminer*) dismiss. **~ qch. de,** move sth. away from. **~ qn. de,** keep s.o. away from. **s'~** *v. pr.* (*s'éloigner*) move away; (*quitter son* *chemin*) move aside. **s'~ de,** stray from.

ecchymose /ekimoz/ *n.f.* bruise.

ecclésiastique /eklezjastik/ *a.* ecclesiastical. —*n.m.* clergyman.

écervelé, **~e** /esɛrvəle/ *a.* scatterbrained. —*n.m., f.* scatter-brain.

échafaud|age /eʃafodaʒ/ *n.m.* scaffolding; (*amas*) heap. **~er** *v.t.* (*projets*) construct.

échalote /eʃalɔt/ *n.f.* shallot.

échang|e /eʃɑ̃ʒ/ *n.m.* exchange. **en ~e (de),** in exchange (for). **~er** *v.t.* exchange (**contre,** for).

échangeur /eʃɑ̃ʒœr/ *n.m.* (*auto.*) interchange.

échantillon /eʃɑ̃tijɔ̃/ *n.m.* sample. **~nage** /-jɔnaʒ/ *n.m.* range of samples.

échappatoire /eʃapatwar/ *n.f.* (clever) way out.

échappée /eʃape/ *n.f.* (*sport*) breakaway.

échappement /eʃapmɑ̃/ *n.m.* exhaust.

échapper /eʃape/ *v.i.* **~ à,** escape; (*en fuyant*) escape (from). **s'~** *v. pr.* escape. **~ des mains de** *ou* **à,** slip out of the hands of. **l'~ belle,** have a narrow *ou* lucky escape.

écharde /eʃard/ *n.f.* splinter.

écharpe /eʃarp/ *n.f.* scarf; (*de maire*) sash. **en ~,** (*bras*) in a sling.

échasse /eʃɑs/ *n.f.* stilt.

échassier /eʃasje/ *n.m.* wader.

échaud|er /eʃode/ *v.t.* **se faire ~er, être ~é,** get one's fingers burnt.

échauffer /eʃofe/ *v.t.* heat; (*fig.*) excite. **s'~** *v. pr.* warm up.

échauffourée /eʃofure/ *n.f.* (*mil.*) skirmish; (*bagarre*) scuffle.

échéance /eʃeɑ̃s/ *n.f.* due date (for payment); (*délai*) deadline; (*obligation*) (financial) commitment.

échéant (le cas) /(lǝkaz)eʃeɑ̃/ *adv.* if the occasion arises, possibly.

échec /eʃɛk/ *n.m.* failure. **~s,** (*jeu*) chess. **~ et mat,** checkmate. **en ~,** in check.

échelle /eʃɛl/ *n.f.* ladder; (*dimension*) scale.

échelon /eʃlɔ̃/ *n.m.* rung; (*de fonctionnaire*) grade; (*niveau*) level.

échelonner /eʃlɔne/ *v.t.* spread out, space out.

échevelé /eʃəvle/ *a.* dishevelled.

échine /eʃin/ *n.f.* backbone.

échiquier /eʃikje/ *n.m.* chessboard.

écho /eko/ *n.m.* echo. **~s,** (*dans la presse*) gossip.

échographie /ekɔgrafi/ *n.f.* ultrasound (scan).

échoir /eʃwar/ *v.i.* (*dette*) fall due; (*délai*) expire.

échoppe /eʃɔp/ *n.f.* stall.

échouer[1] /eʃwe/ *v.i.* fail.

échouer[2] /eʃwe/ *v.t.* (*bateau*) ground. —*v.i.,* **s'~** *v. pr.* run aground.

échu /eʃy/ *a.* (*delai*) expired.

éclabouss|er /eklabuse/ *v.t.* splash. **~ure** *n.f.* splash.

éclair /eklɛr/ *n.m.* (flash of) lightning; (*fig.*) flash; (*gâteau*) éclair. —*a. invar.* lightning.

éclairag|e /eklɛraʒ/ *n.m.* lighting; (*point de vue*) light. **~iste** /-aʒist/ *n.* lighting technician.

éclaircie /eklɛrsi/ *n.f.* sunny interval.

éclairc|ir /eklɛrsir/ *v.t.* make lighter; (*mystère*) clear up. **s'~ir** *v. pr.* (*ciel*) clear; (*mystère*) become clearer. **~issement** *n.m.* clarification.

éclairer /eklere/ *v.t.* light (up); (*personne*) give some light to; (*fig.*) enlighten; (*situation*) throw light on. —*v.i.* give light. **s'~** *v. pr.* become clearer. **s'~ à la bougie,** use candlelight.

éclaireu|r, **~se** /eklɛrœr, -øz/ *n.m., f.* (boy) scout, (girl) guide. —*n.m.* (*mil.*) scout.

éclat /ekla/ *n.m.* fragment; (*de lumière*) brightness; (*de rire*) (out)burst; (*splendeur*) brilliance.

éclatant, **~e** /eklatɑ̃, -t/ *a.* brilliant.

éclat|er /eklate/ *v.i.* burst; (*exploser*) go off; (*verre*) shatter; (*guerre*) break out; (*groupe*) split up. **~er de rire,** burst out laughing. **~ement** *n.m.* bursting; (*de bombe*) explosion; (*scission*) split.

éclipse /eklips/ *n.f.* eclipse.

éclipser /eklipse/ *v.t.* eclipse. **s'~** *v. pr.* slip away.

écl|ore /eklɔr/ *v.i.* (*œuf*) hatch; (*fleur*) open. **~osion** *n.f.* hatching; opening.

écluse /eklyz/ *n.f.* (*de canal*) lock.

écœurant, **~e** /ekœrɑ̃, -t/ *a.* (*gâteau*) sickly; (*fig.*) disgusting.

écœurer /ekœre/ *v.t.* sicken.

école /ekɔl/ *n.f.* school. **~ maternelle/primaire / secondaire,** nursery/ primary / secondary school. **~ normale,** teachers' training college.

écol|ier, **~ière** /ekɔlje, -jɛr/ *n.m., f.* schoolboy, schoolgirl.

écolo /ekɔlɔ/ *a. & n.m./f.* green.

écolog|ie /ekɔlɔʒi/ *n.f.* ecology. **~ique** *a.* ecological, green.

écologiste /ekɔlɔʒist/ n.m./f. ecologist.

econduire /ekɔ̃dɥir/ v.t. dismiss.

économat /ekɔnɔma/ n.m. bursary.

économe /ekɔnɔm/ a. thrifty. —n.m./f. bursar.

économ|ie /ekɔnɔmi/ n.f. economy. ～**ies**, (argent) savings. **une ～ie de**, (gain) a saving of. ～**ie politique**, economics. ～**ique** a. (pol.) economic; (bon marché) economical. ～**iser** v.t./i. save. ～**iste** n.m./f. economist.

écoper /ekɔpe/ v.t. bail out. ～ **(de)**, (fam.) get.

écorce /ekɔrs/ n.f. bark; (de fruit) peel.

écorch|er /ekɔrʃe/ v.t. graze; (animal) skin. **s'～er** v. pr. graze o.s. ～**ure** n.f. graze.

écossais, ～**e** /ekɔsɛ, -z/ a. Scottish. —n.m., f. Scot.

Écosse /ekɔs/ n.f. Scotland.

écosser /ekɔse/ v.t. shell.

écosystème /ekɔsistɛm/ n.m. ecosystem.

écouler[1] /ekule/ v.t. dispose of, sell.

écoul|er[2] **(s')** /(s)ekule/ v. pr. flow (out), run (off); (temps) pass. ～**ement** n.m. flow.

écourter /ekurte/ v.t. shorten.

écoute /ekut/ n.f. listening. **à l'～ (de)**, listening in (to). **aux ～s**, attentive. **heures de grande ～**, peak time. ～**s téléphoniques**, phone tapping.

écout|er /ekute/ v.t. listen to; (radio) listen (in) to. —v.i. listen. ～**eur** n.m. earphones; (de téléphone) receiver.

écran /ekrɑ̃/ n.m. screen. ～ **total**, sunblock.

écrasant, ～**e** /ekrazɑ̃, -t/ a. overwhelming.

écraser /ekraze/ v.t. crush; (piéton) run over. **s'～** v. pr. crash (contre, into).

écrémé /ekreme/ a. **lait ～**, skimmed milk. **lait demi-～**, semi-skimmed milk.

écrevisse /ekrəvis/ n.f. crayfish.

écrier (s') /(s)ekrije/ v. pr. exclaim.

écrin /ekrɛ̃/ n.m. case.

écrire† /ekrir/ v.t./i. write; (orthographier) spell. **s'～** v. pr. (mot) be spelt.

écrit /ekri/ n.m. document; (examen) written paper. **par ～**, in writing.

écriteau (pl. ～**x**) /ekrito/ n.m. notice.

écriture /ekrityr/ n.f. writing. ～**s**, (comm.) accounts. **l'É～ (sainte)**, the Scriptures.

écrivain /ekrivɛ̃/ n.m. writer.

écrou /ekru/ n.m. nut.

écrouer /ekrue/ v.t. imprison.

écrouler (s') /(s)ekrule/ v. pr. collapse.

écru /ekry/ a. (couleur) natural; (tissu) raw.

Écu /eky/ n.m. invar. ecu.

écueil /ekœj/ n.m. reef; (fig.) danger.

éculé /ekyle/ a. (soulier) worn at the heel; (fig.) well-worn.

écume /ekym/ n.f. foam; (culin.) scum.

écum|er /ekyme/ v.t. skim; (piller) plunder. —v.i. foam. ～**oire** n.f. skimmer.

écureuil /ekyrœj/ n.m. squirrel.

écurie /ekyri/ n.f. stable.

écuy|er, ～**ère** /ekɥije, -jɛr/ n.m., f. (horse) rider.

eczéma /ɛgzema/ n.m. eczema.

édenté /edɑ̃te/ a. toothless.

édifice /edifis/ n.m. building.

édif|ier /edifje/ v.t. construct; (porter à la vertu, éclairer) edify. ～**ication** n.f. construction; edification.

édit /edi/ n.m. edict.

édi|ter /edite/ v.t. publish; (annoter) edit. ～**teur**, ～**trice** n.m., f. publisher; editor.

édition /edisjɔ̃/ n.f. edition; (industrie) publishing.

éditor|ial (pl. ～**iaux**) /editɔrjal, -jo/ n.m. editorial.

édredon /edrədɔ̃/ n.m. eiderdown.

éducateur, ～**trice** /edykatœr, -tris/ n.m., f. teacher.

éducati|f, ～**ve** /edykatif, -v/ a. educational.

éducation /edykasjɔ̃/ n.f. education; (dans la famille) upbringing; (manières) manners. ～ **physique**, physical education.

édulcorant /edylkɔrɑ̃/ n.m. & a. **(produit) ～**, sweetener.

éduquer /edyke/ v.t. educate; (à la maison) bring up.

effac|é /efase/ a. (modeste) unassuming. ～**ement** n.m. unassuming manner; (suppression) erasure.

effacer /efase/ v.t. (gommer) rub out; (par lavage) wash out; (souvenir etc.) erase. **s'～** v. pr. fade; (s'écarter) step aside.

effar|er /efare/ v.t. alarm. ～**ement** n.m. alarm.

effaroucher /efaruʃe/ v.t. scare away.

effecti|f[1], ～**ve** /efɛktif, -v/ a. effective. ～**vement** adv. effectively; (en effet) indeed.

effectif[2] /efɛktif/ n.m. size, strength. ～**s**, numbers.

effectuer /efɛktɥe/ v.t. carry out, make.

efféminé /efemine/ a. effeminate.

effervescen|t, ～**te** /efɛrvesɑ̃, -t/ a.

comprimé ~**t,** effervescent tablet. ~**ce** *n.f.* excitement.

effet /efɛ/ *n.m.* effect; (*impression*) impression. ~**s,** (*habits*) clothes, things. **en** ~, indeed. **faire de l'**~, have an effect, be effective. **faire bon/mauvais** ~, make a good/bad impression.

efficac|e /efikas/ *a.* effective; (*personne*) efficient. ~**ité** *n.f.* effectiveness; efficiency.

effigie /efiʒi/ *n.f.* effigy.

effilocher (s') /(s)efilɔʃe/ *v. pr.* fray.

efflanqué /eflɑ̃ke/ *a.* emaciated.

effleurer /eflœre/ *v.t.* touch lightly; (*sujet*) touch on; (*se présenter à*) occur to.

effluves /eflyv/ *n.m. pl.* exhalations.

effondr|er (s') /(s)efɔ̃dre/ *v. pr.* collapse. ~**ement** *n.m.* collapse.

efforcer (s') /(s)efɔrse/ *v. pr.* try (hard) (**de,** to).

effort /efɔr/ *n.m.* effort.

effraction /efraksjɔ̃/ *n.f.* **entrer par** ~, break in.

effray|er /efreje/ *v.t.* frighten; (*décourager*) put off. **s'**~**er** *v. pr.* be frightened. ~**ant,** ~**ante** *a.* frightening; (*fig.*) frightful.

effréné /efrene/ *a.* wild.

effriter (s') /(s)efrite/ *v. pr.* crumble.

effroi /efrwa/ *n.m.* dread.

effronté /efrɔ̃te/ *a.* impudent.

effroyable /efrwajabl/ *a.* dreadful.

effusion /efyzjɔ̃/ *n.f.* ~ **de sang,** bloodshed.

ég|al, ~**ale** (*m. pl.* ~**aux**) /egal, -o/ *a.* equal; (*surface, vitesse*) even. —*n.m., f.* equal. **ça m'est/lui est** ~**al,** it is all the same to me/him. **sans égal,** matchless. **d'** ~ **à égal,** between equals.

également /egalmɑ̃/ *adv.* equally; (*aussi*) as well.

égaler /egale/ *v.t.* equal.

égaliser /egalize/ *v.t./i.* (*sport*) equalize; (*niveler*) level out; (*cheveux*) trim.

égalit|é /egalite/ *n.f.* equality; (*surface, d'humeur*) evenness. **à** ~**é** (**de points**), equal. ~**aire** *a.* egalitarian.

égard /egar/ *n.m.* regard. ~**s,** consideration. **à cet** ~, in this respect. **à l'** ~ **de,** with regard to; (*envers*) towards. **eu** ~ **à,** in view of.

égar|er /egare/ *v.t.* mislay; (*tromper*) lead astray. **s'**~**er** *v. pr.* get lost; (*se tromper*) go astray. ~**ement** *n.m.* loss; (*affolement*) confusion.

égayer /egeje/ *v.t.* (*personne*) cheer up; (*pièce*) brighten up.

égide /eʒid/ *n.f.* aegis.

églantier /eglɑ̃tje/ *n.m.* wild rose(-bush).

églefin /egləfɛ̃/ *n.m.* haddock.

église /egliz/ *n.f.* church.

égoïs|te /egɔist/ *a.* selfish. —*n.m./f.* egoist. ~**me** *n.m.* selfishness, egoism.

égorger /egɔrʒe/ *v.t.* slit the throat of.

égosiller (s') /(s)egozije/ *v. pr.* shout one's head off.

égout /egu/ *n.m.* sewer.

égoutt|er /egute/ *v.t./i.,* **s'**~**er** *v. pr.* (*vaisselle*) drain. ~**oir** *n.m.* draining-board; (*panier*) dish drainer.

égratign|er /egratiɲe/ *v.t.* scratch. ~**ure** *n.f.* scratch.

égrener /egrəne/ *v.t.* (*raisins*) pick off; (*notes*) sound one by one.

Égypte /eʒipt/ *n.f.* Egypt.

égyptien, ~**ne** /eʒipsjɛ̃, -jɛn/ *a. & n.m., f.* Egyptian.

eh /e/ *int.* hey. **eh bien,** well.

éjacul|er /eʒakyle/ *v.i.* ejaculate. ~**ation** *n.f.* ejaculation.

éjectable *a.* **siège** ~, ejector seat.

éjecter /eʒɛkte/ *v.t.* eject.

élabor|er /elabɔre/ *v.t.* elaborate. ~**ation** *n.f.* elaboration.

élaguer /elage/ *v.t.* prune.

élan¹ /elɑ̃/ *n.m.* (*sport*) run-up; (*vitesse*) momentum; (*fig.*) surge.

élan² /elɑ̃/ *n.m.* (*animal*) moose.

élancé /elɑ̃se/ *a.* slender.

élancement /elɑ̃smɑ̃/ *n.m.* twinge.

élancer (s') /(s)elɑ̃se/ *v. pr.* leap forward, dash; (*se dresser*) soar.

élarg|ir /elarʒir/ *v.t.,* **s'**~**ir** *v. pr.* widen. ~**issement** *n.m.* widening.

élasti|que /elastik/ *a.* elastic. —*n.m.* elastic band; (*tissu*) elastic. ~**cité** *n.f.* elasticity.

élec|teur, ~**trice** /elɛktœr, -tris/ *n.m., f.* voter, elector.

élection /elɛksjɔ̃/ *n.f.* election.

élector|al (*m. pl.* ~**aux**) /elɛktɔral, -o/ *a.* (*réunion etc.*) election; (*collège*) electoral.

électorat /elɛktɔra/ *n.m.* electorate, voters.

électricien /elɛktrisjɛ̃/ *n.m.* electrician.

électricité /elɛktrisite/ *n.f.* electricity.

électrifier /elɛktrifje/ *v.t.* electrify.

électrique /elɛktrik/ *a.* electric(al).

électrocuter /elɛktrɔkyte/ *v.t.* electrocute.

électroménager /elɛktrɔmenaʒe/ *n.m.* **l'**~, household appliances.

électron /elɛktrɔ̃/ *n.m.* electron.

électronique /elɛktrɔnik/ *a.* electronic. —*n.f.* electronics.

électrophone /elɛktrɔfɔn/ *n.m.* record-player.

élég|ant, **~ante** /elegɑ̃, -t/ *a.* elegant. **~amment** *adv.* elegantly. **~ance** *n.f.* elegance.

élément /elemɑ̃/ *n.m.* element; (*meuble*) unit. **~aire** /-tɛr/ *a.* elementary.

éléphant /elefɑ̃/ *n.m.* elephant.

élevage /ɛlvaʒ/ *n.m.* (stock-)breeding.

élévation /elevasjɔ̃/ *n.f.* raising; (*hausse*) rise; (*plan*) elevation.

élève /elɛv/ *n.m./f.* pupil.

élevé /ɛlve/ *a.* high; (*noble*) elevated. **bien ~,** well-mannered.

élever /ɛlve/ *v.t.* raise; (*enfants*) bring up, raise; (*animal*) breed. **s'~** *v. pr.* rise; (*dans le ciel*) soar up. **s'~ à,** amount to.

éleveu|r, **~se** /ɛlvœr, -øz/ *n.m., f.* (stock-)breeder.

éligible /eliʒibl/ *a.* eligible.

élimé /elime/ *a.* worn thin.

élimin|er /elimine/ *v.t.* eliminate. **~ation** *n.f.* elimination. **~atoire** *a.* eliminating; *n.f.* (*sport*) heat.

élire† /elir/ *v.t.* elect.

élite /elit/ *n.f.* élite.

elle /ɛl/ *pron.* she; (*complément*) her; (*chose*) it. **~-même** *pron.* herself; itself.

elles /ɛl/ *pron.* they; (*complément*) them. **~-mêmes** *pron.* themselves.

ellip|se /elips/ *n.f.* ellipse. **~tique** *a.* elliptical.

élocution /elɔkysjɔ̃/ *n.f.* diction.

élog|e /elɔʒ/ *n.m.* praise. **faire l'~e de,** praise. **~ieux,** **~ieuse** *a.* laudatory.

éloigné /elwaɲe/ *a.* distant. **~ de,** far away from. **parent ~,** distant relative.

éloign|er /elwaɲe/ *v.t.* take away *ou* remove (**de,** from); (*personne aimée*) estrange (**de,** from); (*danger*) ward off; (*visite*) put off. **s'~er** *v. pr.* go *ou* move away (**de,** from); (*affectivement*) become estranged (**de,** from). **~ement** *n.m.* removal; (*distance*) distance; (*oubli*) estrangement.

élongation /elɔ̃gasjɔ̃/ *n.f.* strained muscle.

éloquen|t, **~te** /elɔkɑ̃, -t/ *a.* eloquent. **~ce** *n.f.* eloquence.

élu, **~e** /ely/ *a.* elected. —*n.m., f.* (*pol.*) elected representative.

élucider /elyside/ *v.t.* elucidate.

éluder /elyde/ *v.t.* elude.

émacié /emasje/ *a.* emaciated.

ém|ail (*pl.* **~aux**) /emaj, -o/ *n.m.* enamel.

émaillé /emaje/ *a.* enamelled. **~ de,** studded with.

émancip|er /emɑ̃sipe/ *v.t.* emancipate. **s'~er** *v. pr.* become emancipated. **~ation** *n.f.* emancipation.

éman|er /emane/ *v.i.* emanate. **~ation** *n.f.* emanation.

émarger /emarʒe/ *v.t.* initial.

emball|er /ɑ̃bale/ *v.t.* pack, wrap; (*personne*: *fam.*) enthuse. **s'~er** *v. pr.* (*moteur*) race; (*emporter*: *fam.*) bolt; (*personne*) get carried away. **~age** *n.m.* package, wrapping.

embarcadère /ɑ̃barkadɛr/ *n.m.* landing-stage.

embarcation /ɑ̃barkasjɔ̃/ *n.f.* boat.

embardée /ɑ̃barde/ *n.f.* swerve.

embargo /ɑ̃bargo/ *n.m.* embargo.

embarqu|er /ɑ̃barke/ *v.t.* embark; (*charger*) load; (*emporter*: *fam.*) cart off. —*v.i.,* **s'~er** *v. pr.* board, embark. **s'~er dans,** embark upon. **~ement** *n.m.* embarkation; loading.

embarras /ɑ̃bara/ *n.m.* obstacle; (*gêne*) embarrassment; (*difficulté*) difficulty.

embarrasser /ɑ̃barase/ *v.t.* clutter (up); (*gêner dans les mouvements*) hinder; (*fig.*) embarrass. **s'~ de,** burden o.s. with.

embauch|e /ɑ̃boʃ/ *n.f.* hiring; (*emploi*) employment. **~er** *v.t.* hire, take on.

embauchoir /ɑ̃boʃwar/ *n.m.* shoe tree.

embaumer /ɑ̃bome/ *v.t./i.* (make) smell fragrant; (*cadavre*) embalm.

embellir /ɑ̃belir/ *v.t.* brighten up; (*récit*) embellish.

embêt|er /ɑ̃bete/ *v.t.* (*fam.*) annoy. **s'~er** *v. pr.* (*fam.*) get bored. **~ant,** **~ante** *a.* (*fam.*) annoying. **~ement** /ɑ̃bɛtmɑ̃/ *n.m.* (*fam.*) annoyance.

emblée (d') /(d)ɑ̃ble/ *adv.* right away.

emblème /ɑ̃blɛm/ *n.m.* emblem.

embobiner /ɑ̃bɔbine/ *v.t.* (*fam.*) get round.

emboîter /ɑ̃bwate/ *v.t.,* **s'~** *v. pr.* fit together. **(s')~ dans,** fit into. **~ le pas à qn.,** (*imiter*) follow suit.

embonpoint /ɑ̃bɔ̃pwɛ̃/ *n.m.* stoutness.

embouchure /ɑ̃buʃyr/ *n.f.* (*de fleuve*) mouth; (*mus.*) mouthpiece.

embourber (s') /(s)ɑ̃burbe/ *v. pr.* get bogged down.

embourgeoiser (s') /(s)ɑ̃burʒwaze/ *v. pr.* become middle-class.

embout /ɑ̃bu/ *n.m.* tip.

embouteillage /ɑ̃butɛjaʒ/ *n.m.* traffic jam.

emboutir /ɑ̃butir/ *v.t.* (*heurter*) crash into.

embranchement /ãbrãʃmã/ n.m. (de routes) junction.

embraser /ãbraze/ v.t. set on fire, fire. **s'~** v. pr. flare up.

embrass|er /ãbrase/ v.t. kiss; (adopter, contenir) embrace. **s'~er** v. pr. kiss. **~ades** n.f. pl. kissing.

embrasure /ãbrazyr/ n.f. opening.

embray|er /ãbreje/ v.i. let in the clutch. **~age** /ãbrɛjaʒ/ n.m. clutch.

embrigader /ãbrigade/ v.t. enrol.

embrocher /ãbrɔʃe/ v.t. (viande) spit.

embrouiller /ãbruje/ v.t. mix up; (fils) tangle. **s'~** v. pr. get mixed up.

embroussaillé /ãbrusaje/ a. (poils, chemin) bushy.

embryon /ãbrijɔ̃/ n.m. embryo. **~naire** /-jɔnɛr/ a. embryonic.

embûches /ãbyʃ/ n.f. pl. traps.

embuer /ãbɥe/ v.t. mist up.

embuscade /ãbyskad/ n.f. ambush.

embusquer (s') /(s)ãbyske/ v. pr. lie in ambush.

éméché /emeʃe/ a. tipsy.

émeraude /ɛmrod/ n.f. emerald.

émerger /emɛrʒe/ v.i. emerge; (fig.) stand out.

émeri /ɛmri/ n.m. emery.

émerveill|er /emɛrveje/ v.t. amaze. **s'~er de**, marvel at, be amazed at. **~ement** /-vɛjmã/ n.m. amazement, wonder.

émett|re† /emɛtr/ v.t. give out; (message) transmit; (timbre, billet) issue; (opinion) express. **~eur** n.m. transmitter.

émeut|e /emøt/ n.f. riot. **~ier**, **~ière** n.m., f. rioter.

émietter /emjete/ v.t., **s'~** v. pr. crumble.

émigrant, ~e /emigrã, -t/ n.m., f. emigrant.

émigr|er /emigre/ v.i. emigrate. **~ation** n.f. emigration.

émincer /emɛ̃se/ v.t. cut into thin slices.

émin|ent, ~ente /eminã, -t/ a. eminent. **~emment** /-amã/ adv. eminently. **~ence** n.f. eminence; (colline) hill. **~ence grise**, éminence grise.

émissaire /emisɛr/ n.m. emissary.

émission /emisjɔ̃/ n.f. emission; (de message) transmission; (de timbre) issue; (programme) broadcast.

emmagasiner /ãmagazine/ v.t. store.

emmanchure /ãmãʃyr/ n.f. armhole.

emmêler /ãmele/ v.t. tangle. **s'~** v. pr. get mixed up.

emménager /ãmenaʒe/ v.i. move in. **~ dans**, move into.

emmener /ãmne/ v.t. take; (comme prisonnier) take away.

emmerder /ãmɛrde/ v.t. (argot) bother. **s'~** v. pr. (argot) get bored.

emmitoufler /ãmitufle/ v.t., **s'~** v. pr. wrap up (warmly).

émoi /emwa/ n.m. excitement.

émoluments /emɔlymã/ n.m. pl. remuneration.

émonder /emɔ̃de/ v.t. prune.

émoti|f, ~ve /emɔtif, -v/ a. emotional.

émotion /emosjɔ̃/ n.f. emotion; (peur) fright. **~nel, ~nelle** /-jɔnɛl/ a. emotional.

émousser /emuse/ v.t. blunt.

émouv|oir /emuvwar/ v.t. move. **s'~oir** v. pr. be moved. **~ant, ~ante** a. moving.

empailler /ãpaje/ v.t. stuff.

empaqueter /ãpakte/ v.t. package.

emparer (s') /(s)ãpare/ v. pr. **s'~ de**, seize.

empâter (s') /(s)ãpate/ v. pr. fill out, grow fatter.

empêchement /ãpɛʃmã/ n.m. hitch, difficulty.

empêch|er /ãpeʃe/ v.t. prevent. **~ de faire**, prevent ou stop (from) doing. **il ne peut pas s'~ de penser**, he cannot help thinking. **(il) n'empêche que**, still.

empêch|eur, ~euse /ãpeʃœr, -øz/ n.m., f. **~eur de tourner en rond**, spoilsport.

empeigne /ãpɛɲ/ n.f. upper.

empereur /ãprœr/ n.m. emperor.

empeser /ãpoze/ v.t. starch.

empester /ãpɛste/ v.t. make stink, stink out; (essence etc.) stink of. —v.i. stink.

empêtrer (s') /(s)ãpetre/ v. pr. become entangled.

emphase /ãfaz/ n.f. pomposity.

empiéter /ãpjete/ v.i. **~ sur**, encroach upon.

empiffrer (s') /(s)ãpifre/ v. pr. (fam.) gorge o.s.

empiler /ãpile/ v.t., **s'~** v. pr. pile (up).

empire /ãpir/ n.m. empire; (fig.) control.

empirer /ãpire/ v.i. worsen.

empirique /ãpirik/ a. empirical.

emplacement /ãplasmã/ n.m. site.

emplâtre /ãplatr/ n.m. (méd.) plaster.

emplettes /ãplɛt/ n.f. pl. purchase. **faire des ~**, do one's shopping.

emplir /ãplir/ v.t., **s'~** v. pr. fill.

emploi /ãplwa/ n.m. use; (travail) job. **~ du temps**, timetable. **l'~**, (pol.) employment.

employ|er /ɑ̃plwaje/ v.t. use; (personne) employ. s'~er v. pr. be used. s'~er à, devote o.s. to. ~é, ~ée n.m., f. employee. ~eur, ~euse n.m., f. employer.

empocher /ɑ̃pɔʃe/ v.t. pocket.

empoigner /ɑ̃pwaɲe/ v.t. grab. s'~ v. pr. come to blows.

empoisonn|er /ɑ̃pwazɔne/ v.t. poison; (empuantir) stink out; (embêter: fam.) annoy. ~ement n.m. poisoning.

emport|é /ɑ̃pɔrte/ a. quicktempered. ~ement n.m. anger.

emporter /ɑ̃pɔrte/ v.t. take (away); (entraîner) carry away; (prix) carry off; (arracher) tear off. ~ un chapeau/etc. (vent) blow off a hat/etc. s'~ v. pr. lose one's temper. l'~, get the upper hand (sur, of). plat à ~, take-away.

empoté /ɑ̃pɔte/ a. silly.

empourpré /ɑ̃purpre/ a. crimson.

empreint /ɑ̃prɛ̃, -t/ a. ~ de, marked with. —n.f. mark. ~e (digitale), fingerprint. ~e de pas, footprint.

empress|er (s') /(s)ɑ̃prese/ v. pr. s'~er auprès de, be attentive to. s'~er de, hasten to. ~é a. eager, attentive. ~ement /ɑ̃presmɑ̃/ n.m. eagerness.

emprise /ɑ̃priz/ n.f. influence.

emprisonn|er /ɑ̃prizɔne/ v.t. imprison. ~ement n.m. imprisonment.

emprunt /ɑ̃prœ̃/ n.m. loan. faire un ~, take out a loan.

emprunté /ɑ̃prœ̃te/ a. awkward.

emprunt|er /ɑ̃prœ̃te/ v.t. borrow (à, from); (route) take; (fig.) assume. ~eur, ~euse n.m., f. borrower.

ému /emy/ a. moved; (apeuré) nervous; (joyeux) excited.

émulation /emylasjɔ̃/ n.f. emulation.

émule /emyl/ n.m./f. imitator.

émulsion /emylsjɔ̃/ n.f. emulsion.

en[1] /ɑ̃/ prép. in; (avec direction) to; (manière, état) in, on; (moyen de transport) by; (composition) made of. en cadeau/médecin/etc., as a present/doctor/etc. en guerre, at war. en faisant, by ou on ou while doing.

en[2] /ɑ̃/ pron. of it, of them; (moyen) with it; (cause) from it; (lieu) from there. en avoir/vouloir/etc., have/want/etc. some. ne pas en avoir/vouloir/etc., not have/want/etc. any. où en êtes-vous?, where are you up to?, how far have you got? j'en ai assez, I've had enough. en êtes-vous sûr?, are you sure?

encadr|er /ɑ̃kadre/ v.t. frame; (entourer d'un trait) circle; (entourer) surround.

~ement n.m. framing; (de porte) frame.

encaiss|er /ɑ̃kese/ v.t. (argent) collect; (chèque) cash; (coups: fam.) take. ~eur /ɑ̃kesœr/ n.m. debt-collector.

encart /ɑ̃kar/ n.m. ~ publicitaire, (advertising) insert.

en-cas /ɑ̃ka/ n.m. (stand-by) snack.

encastré /ɑ̃kastre/ a. built-in.

encaustiqu|e /ɑ̃kostik/ n.f. wax polish. ~er v.t. wax.

enceinte[1] /ɑ̃sɛ̃t/ a.f. pregnant. ~ de 3 mois, 3 months pregnant.

enceinte[2] /ɑ̃sɛ̃t/ n.f. enclosure. ~ (acoustique), loudspeaker.

encens /ɑ̃sɑ̃/ n.m. incense.

encercler /ɑ̃sɛrkle/ v.t. surround.

en haîn|er /ɑ̃ʃene/ v.t. chain (up); (coordonner) link (up). —v.i. continue. s'~er v. pr. be linked (up). ~ement /ɑ̃ʃenmɑ̃/ n.m. (suite) chain; (liaison) link(ing).

enchant|er /ɑ̃ʃɑ̃te/ v.t. delight; (ensorceler) enchant. ~é a. (ravi) delighted. ~ement n.m. delight; (magie) enchantment.

enchâsser /ɑ̃ʃase/ v.t. set.

enchère /ɑ̃ʃɛr/ n.f. bid. mettre ou vendre aux ~s, sell by auction.

enchevêtrer /ɑ̃ʃvetre/ v.t. tangle. s'~ v. pr. become tangled.

enclave /ɑ̃klav/ n.f. enclave.

enclencher /ɑ̃klɑ̃ʃe/ v.t. engage.

enclin, ~e /ɑ̃klɛ̃, -in/ a. ~ à, inclined to.

enclore /ɑ̃klɔr/ v.t. enclose.

enclos /ɑ̃klo/ n.m. enclosure.

enclume /ɑ̃klym/ n.f. anvil.

encoche /ɑ̃kɔʃ/ n.f. notch.

encoignure /ɑ̃kɔɲyr/ n.f. corner.

encoller /ɑ̃kɔle/ v.t. paste.

encolure /ɑ̃kɔlyr/ n.f. neck.

encombre n.m. sans ~, without any problems.

encombr|er /ɑ̃kɔ̃bre/ v.t. clutter (up); (gêner) hamper. s'~er de, burden o.s. with. ~ant, ~ante a. cumbersome. ~ement n.m. congestion; (auto.) traffic jam; (volume) bulk.

encontre de (à l') /(al)ɑ̃kɔ̃trədə/ prép. against.

encore /ɑ̃kɔr/ adv. (toujours) still; (de nouveau) again; (de plus) more; (aussi) also. ~ mieux/plus grand/etc., even better/larger/etc. ~ une heure/un café/etc., another hour/coffee/etc. pas ~, not yet. si ~, if only.

encourag|er /ɑ̃kuraʒe/ v.t. encourage. ~ement n.m. encouragement.

encourir /ākurir/ v.t. incur.

encrasser /ākrase/ v.t. clog up (with dirt).

encr|e /ākr/ n.f. ink. **~er** v.t. ink.

encrier /ākrije/ n.m. ink-well.

encroûter (s') /(s)ākrute/ v. pr. become doggedly set in one's ways. **s'~ dans,** sink into.

encyclopéd|ie /āsiklɔpedi/ n.f. encyclopaedia. **~ique** a. encyclopaedic.

endetter /ādete/ v.t., **s'~** v. pr. get into debt.

endeuiller /ādœje/ v.t. plunge into mourning.

endiablé /ādjable/ a. wild.

endiguer /ādige/ v.t. dam; (fig.) check.

endimanché /ādimāʃe/ a. in one's Sunday best.

endive /ādiv/ n.f. chicory.

endocrinolo|gie /ādɔkrinɔlɔʒi/ n.f. endocrinology. **~gue** n.m./f. endocrinologist.

endoctrin|er /ādɔktrine/ v.t. indoctrinate. **~ement** n.m. indoctrination.

endommager /ādɔmaʒe/ v.t. damage.

endorm|ir /ādɔrmir/ v.t. send to sleep; (atténuer) allay. **s'~ir** v. pr. fall asleep. **~i** a. asleep; (apathique) sleepy.

endosser /ādɔse/ v.t. (vêtement) put on; (assumer) assume; (comm.) endorse.

endroit /ādrwa/ n.m. place; (de tissu) right side. **à l'~,** the right way round, right side out.

end|uire /āduir/ v.t. coat. **~uit** n.m. coating.

endurance /ādyrās/ n.f. endurance.

endurant, ~e /ādyrā, -t/ a. tough.

endurci /ādyrsi/ a. célibataire **~,** confirmed bachelor.

endurcir /ādyrsir/ v.t. harden. **s'~** v. pr. become hard(ened).

endurer /ādyre/ v.t. endure.

énerg|ie /enɛrʒi/ n.f. energy; (techn.) power. **~étique** a. energy. **~ique** a. energetic.

énervant, ~e /enɛrvā, -t/ a. irritating, annoying.

énerver /enɛrve/ v.t. irritate. **s'~** v. pr. get worked up.

enfance /āfās/ n.f. childhood. **la petite ~,** infancy.

enfant /āfā/ n.m./f. child. **~ en bas âge,** infant. **~illage** /-tijaʒ/ n.m. childishness. **~in, ~ine** /-tē, -tin/ a. childlike; (puéril) childish; (jeu, langage) children's.

enfanter /āfāte/ v.t./i. give birth (to).

enfer /āfɛr/ n.m. hell.

enfermer /āfɛrme/ v.t. shut up. **s'~** v. pr. shut o.s. up.

enferrer (s') /(s)āfere/ v. pr. become entangled.

enfiévré /āfjevre/ a. feverish.

enfilade /āfilad/ n.f. string, row.

enfiler /āfile/ v.t. (aiguille) thread; (anneaux) string; (vêtement) slip on; (rue) take; (insérer) insert.

enfin /āfē/ adv. at last, finally; (en dernier lieu) finally; (somme toute) after all; (résignation, conclusion) well.

enflammer /āflame/ v.t. set fire to; (méd.) inflame. **s'~** v. pr. catch fire.

enfl|er /āfle/ v.t./i., **s'~er** v. pr. swell. **~é** a. swollen. **~ure** n.f. swelling.

enfoncer /āfɔse/ v.t. (épingle etc.) push ou drive in; (chapeau) push down; (porte) break down; (mettre) thrust, put. —v.i., **s'~** v. pr. sink (dans, into).

enfouir /āfwir/ v.t. bury.

enfourcher /āfurʃe/ v.t. mount.

enfourner /āfurne/ v.t. put in the oven.

enfreindre /āfrēdr/ v.t. infringe.

enfuir† (s') /(s)āfɥir/ v.t. run off.

enfumer /āfyme/ v.t. fill with smoke.

engagé /āgaʒe/ a. committed.

engageant, ~e /āgaʒā, -t/ a. attractive.

engag|er /āgaʒe/ v.t. (lier) bind, commit; (embaucher) take on; (commencer) start; (introduire) insert; (entraîner) involve; (encourager) urge; (investir) invest. **s'~er** v. pr. (promettre) commit o.s.; (commencer) start; (soldat) enlist; (concurrent) enter. **s'~er à faire,** undertake to do. **s'~er dans,** (voie) enter. **~ement** n.m. (promesse) promise; (pol., comm.) commitment; (début) start; (inscription: sport) entry.

engelure /āʒlyr/ n.f. chilblain.

engendrer /āʒādre/ v.t. beget; (causer) generate.

engin /āʒē/ n.m. machine; (outil) instrument; (projectile) missile. **~ explosif,** explosive device.

englober /āglɔbe/ v.t. include.

engloutir /āglutir/ v.t. swallow (up). **s'~** v. pr. (navire) be engulfed.

engorger /āgɔrʒe/ v.t. block.

engou|er (s') /(s)āgwe/ v. pr. **s'~er de,** become infatuated with. **~ement** /-umā/ n.m. infatuation.

engouffrer /āgufre/ v.t. devour. **s'~ dans,** rush into (with force).

engourd|ir /āgurdir/ v.t. numb. **s'~ir** v. pr. go numb. **~i** a. numb.

engrais /ãgrɛ/ *n.m.* manure; (*chimique*) fertilizer.

engraisser /ãgrese/ *v.t.* fatten. **s'~** *v. pr.* get fat.

engrenage /ãgrənaʒ/ *n.m.* gears; (*fig.*) chain (of events).

engueuler /ãgœle/ *v.t.* (*argot*) curse, swear at, hurl abuse at.

enhardir (s') /(s)ãardir/ *v. pr.* become bolder.

énième /ɛnjɛm/ *a.* (*fam.*) umpteenth.

énigm|e /enigm/ *n.f.* riddle, enigma. **~atique** *a.* enigmatic.

enivrer /ãnivre/ *v.t.* intoxicate. **s'~** *v. pr.* get drunk.

enjamb|er /ãʒãbe/ *v.t.* step over; (*pont*) span. **~ée** *n.f.* stride.

enjeu (*pl.* **~x**) /ãʒø/ *n.m.* stake(s).

enjôler /ãʒole/ *v.t.* wheedle.

enjoliver /ãʒɔlive/ *v.t.* embellish.

enjoliveur /ãʒɔlivœr/ *n.m.* hub-cap.

enjoué /ãʒwe/ *a.* cheerful.

enlacer /ãlase/ *v.t.* entwine.

enlaidir /ãledir/ *v.t.* make ugly. —*v.i.* grow ugly.

enlèvement /ãlɛvmã/ *n.m.* removal; (*rapt*) kidnapping.

enlever /ãlve/ *v.t.* (*emporter*) take (away), remove (**à**, from); (*vêtement*) take off, remove; (*tache, organe*) take out, remove; (*kidnapper*) kidnap; (*gagner*) win.

enliser (s') /(s)ãlize/ *v. pr.* get bogged down.

enluminure /ãlyminyr/ *n.f.* illumination.

enneig|é /ãneʒe/ *a.* snow-covered. **~ement** /ãneʒmã/ *n.m.* snow conditions.

ennemi /ɛnmi/ *n.m.* & *a.* enemy. **~ de**, (*fig.*) hostile to. **l'~ public numéro un**, public enemy number one.

ennui /ãnɥi/ *n.m.* boredom; (*tracas*) trouble, worry. **il a des ~s**, he's got problems.

ennuyer /ãnɥije/ *v.t.* bore; (*irriter*) annoy; (*préoccuper*) worry. **s'~** *v. pr.* get bored.

ennuyeu|x, ~se /ãnɥijø, -z/ *a.* boring; (*fâcheux*) annoying.

énoncé /enõse/ *n.m.* wording, text; (*gram.*) utterance.

énoncer /enõse/ *v.t.* express, state.

enorgueillir (s') /(s)ãnɔrgœjir/ *v. pr.* **s'~ de**, pride o.s. on.

énorm|e /enɔrm/ *a.* enormous. **~ément** *adv.* enormously. **~ément de**, an enormous amount of. **~ité** *n.f.*

enormous size; (*atrocité*) enormity; (*bévue*) enormous blunder.

enquérir (s') /(s)ãkerir/ *v. pr.* **s'~ de**, enquire about.

enquêt|e /ãkɛt/ *n.f.* investigation; (*jurid.*) inquiry; (*sondage*) survey. **mener l'~e**, lead the inquiry. **~er /-ete/** *v.i.* **~er (sur)**, investigate. **~eur, ~euse** *n.m., f.* investigator.

enquiquin|er /ãkikine/ *v.t.* (*fam.*) bother. **~ant, ~ante** *a.* irritating. **c'est ~ant**, it's a nuisance.

enraciné /ãrasine/ *a.* deep-rooted.

enrag|er /ãraʒe/ *v.i.* be furious. **faire ~er**, annoy. **~é** *a.* furious; (*chien*) mad; (*fig.*) fanatical. **~eant, ~eante** *a.* infuriating.

enrayer /ãreje/ *v.t.* check.

enregistr|er /ãrʒistre/ *v.t.* note, record; (*mus.*) record. **(faire) ~er**, (*bagages*) register, check in. **~ement** *n.m.* recording; (*des bagages*) registration.

enrhumer (s') /(s)ãryme/ *v. pr.* catch a cold.

enrich|ir /ãriʃir/ *v.t.* enrich. **s'~ir** *v. pr.* grow rich(er). **~issement** *n.m.* enrichment.

enrober /ãrɔbe/ *v.t.* coat (**de**, with).

enrôl|er /ãrole/ *v.t.*, **s'~** *v. pr.* enlist, enrol.

enrou|er (s') /(s)ãrwe/ *v. pr.* become hoarse. **~é** *a.* hoarse.

enrouler /ãrule/ *v.t.*, **s'~** *v. pr.* wind. **s'~ dans une couverture**, roll o.s. up in a blanket.

ensabler /ãsable/ *v.t.*, **s'~** *v. pr.* (*port*) silt up.

ensanglanté /ãsãglãte/ *a.* bloodstained.

enseignant, ~e /ãsɛɲã, -t/ *n.m., f.* teacher. —*a.* teaching.

enseigne /ãsɛɲ/ *n.f.* sign.

enseignement /ãsɛɲmã/ *n.m.* teaching; (*instruction*) education.

enseigner /ãseɲe/ *v.t./i.* teach. **~ qch. à qn.**, teach s.o. sth.

ensemble /ãsãbl/ *adv.* together. —*n.m.* unity; (*d'objets*) set; (*mus.*) ensemble; (*vêtements*) outfit. **dans l'~**, on the whole. **d'~**, (*idée etc.*) general. **l'~ de**, (*totalité*) all of, the whole of.

ensemencer /ãsmãse/ *v.t.* sow.

enserrer /ãsere/ *v.t.* grip (tightly).

ensevelir /ãsəvlir/ *v.t.* bury.

ensoleill|é /ãsɔleje/ *a.* sunny. **~ement** /ãsɔlejmã/ *n.m.* (period of) sunshine.

ensommeillé /ãsɔmeje/ *a.* sleepy.

ensorceler /ãsɔrsəle/ *v.t.* bewitch.

ensuite /ãsɥit/ *adv.* next, then; (*plus tard*) later.

ensuivre (s') /(s)ãsɥivr/ v. pr. follow. **et tout ce qui s'ensuit,** and so on.

entaill|e /ãtaj/ n.f. notch; (blessure) gash. **~er** v.t. notch; gash.

entamer /ãtame/ v.t. start; (inciser) cut into; (ébranler) shake.

entass|er /ãtase/ v.t., **s'~er** v. pr. pile up. **(s')~er dans,** cram (together) into. **~ement** n.m. (tas) pile.

entendement /ãtãdmã/ n.m. understanding. **ça dépasse l'~,** it defies one's understanding.

entendre /ãtãdr/ v.t. hear; (comprendre) understand; (vouloir) intend, mean; (vouloir dire) mean. **s'~** v. pr. (être d'accord) agree. **~ dire que,** hear that. **~ parler de,** hear of. **s'~ (bien),** get on (avec, with). **(cela) s'entend,** of course.

entendu /ãtãdy/ a. (convenu) agreed; (sourire, air) knowing. **bien ~,** of course. **(c'est) ~!,** all right!

entente /ãtãt/ n.f. understanding. **à double ~,** with a double meaning.

entériner /ãterine/ v.t. ratify.

enterr|er /ãtere/ v.t. bury. **~ement** /ãtɛrmã/ n.m. burial, funeral.

entêtant, ~e /ãtɛtã, -t/ a. heady.

en-tête /ãtɛt/ n.m. heading. **à ~,** headed.

entêt|é /ãtete/ a. stubborn. **~ement** /ãtɛtmã/ n.m. stubbornness.

entêter (s') /(s)ãtete/ v. pr. persist (à, dans, in).

enthousias|me /ãtuzjasm/ n.m. enthusiasm. **~mer** v.t. enthuse. **s'~mer pour,** enthuse over. **~te** a. enthusiastic.

enticher (s') /(s)ãtiʃe/ v. pr. **s'~ de,** become infatuated with.

ent|ier, ~ière /ãtje, -jɛr/ a. whole; (absolu) absolute; (entêté) unyielding. —n.m. whole. **en ~ier,** entirely. **~ièrement** adv. entirely.

entité /ãtite/ n.f. entity.

entonner /ãtɔne/ v.t. start singing.

entonnoir /ãtɔnwar/ n.m. funnel; (trou) crater.

entorse /ãtɔrs/ n.f. sprain. **~ à,** (loi) infringement of.

entortiller /ãtɔrtije/ v.t. wrap (up); (enrouler) wind, wrap; (duper) deceive.

entourage /ãturaʒ/ n.m. circle of family and friends; (bordure) surround.

entourer /ãture/ v.t. surround (de, with); (réconforter) rally round. **~ de,** (écharpe etc.) wrap round.

entracte /ãtrakt/ n.m. interval.

entraide /ãtrɛd/ n.f. mutual aid.

entraider (s') /(s)ãtrede/ v. pr. help each other.

entrailles /ãtraj/ n.f. pl. entrails.

entrain /ãtrɛ̃/ n.m. zest, spirit.

entraînant, ~e /ãtrɛnã, -t/ a. rousing.

entraînement /ãtrɛnmã/ n.m. (sport) training.

entraîn|er /ãtrene/ v.t. carry away ou along; (emmener, influencer) lead; (impliquer) entail; (sport) train; (roue) drive. **~eur** /ãtrɛnœr/ n.m. trainer.

entrav|e /ãtrav/ n.f. hindrance. **~er** v.t. hinder.

entre /ãtr(ə)/ prép. between; (parmi) among(st). **~ autres,** among other things. **l'un d'~ nous/vous/eux,** one of us/you/ them.

entrebâillé /ãtrəbaje/ a. ajar.

entrechoquer (s') /(s)ãtrəʃɔke/ v. pr. knock against each other.

entrecôte /ãtrəkot/ n.f. rib steak.

entrecouper /ãtrəkupe/ v.t. **~ de,** intersperse with.

entrecroiser (s') /(s)ãtrəkrwaze/ v. pr. (routes) intersect.

entrée /ãtre/ n.f. entrance; (accès) admission, entry; (billet) ticket; (culin.) first course; (de données: techn.) input. **~ interdite,** no entry.

entrefaites (sur ces) /(syrsez)ãtrəfɛt/ adv. at that moment.

entrefilet /ãtrəfilɛ/ n.m. paragraph.

entrejambe /ãtrəʒãb/ n.m. crotch.

entrelacer (s') /ãtrəlase/ v.t., **s'~** v. pr. intertwine.

entremêler /ãtrəmele/ v.t., **s'~** v. pr. (inter)mingle.

entremets /ãtrəmɛ/ n.m. dessert.

entremetteu|r, ~se /ãtrəmɛtœr, -øz/ n.m., f. (péj.) go-between.

entre|mettre (s') /(s)ãtrəmɛtr/ v. pr. intervene. **~mise** n.f. intervention. **par l'~mise de,** through.

entreposer /ãtrəpoze/ v.t. store.

entrepôt /ãtrəpo/ n.m. warehouse.

entreprenant, ~e /ãtrəprənã, -t/ a. (actif) enterprising; (séducteur) forward.

entreprendre† /ãtrəprãdr/ v.t. start on; (personne) buttonhole. **~ de faire,** undertake to do.

entrepreneur /ãtrəprənœr/ n.m. **~ (de bâtiments),** (building) contractor.

entreprise /ãtrəpriz/ n.f. undertaking; (société) firm.

entrer /ãtre/ v.i. (aux. être) go in, enter; (venir) come in, enter. **~ dans,** go ou come into, enter; (club) join. **~ en collision,** collide (avec, with). **faire ~,** (personne) show in. **laisser ~,** let in.

entresol /ãtrəsɔl/ n.m. mezzanine.

entre-temps /ɑ̃trətɑ̃/ adv. meanwhile.
entretenir† /ɑ̃trətnir/ v.t. maintain; (faire durer) keep alive. ∼ **qn. de,** converse with s.o. about. **s'**∼ v. pr. speak (**de,** about; **avec,** to).
entretien /ɑ̃trətjɛ̃/ n.m. maintenance; (discussion) talk; (audience pour un emploi) interview.
entrevoir /ɑ̃trəvwar/ v.t. make out; (brièvement) glimpse.
entrevue /ɑ̃trəvy/ n.f. interview.
entrouvrir /ɑ̃truvrir/ v.t. half-open.
énumér|er /enymere/ v.t. enumerate. ∼**ation** n.f. enumeration.
envah|ir /ɑ̃vair/ v.t. invade, overrun; (douleur, peur) overcome. ∼**isseur** n.m. invader.
enveloppe /ɑ̃vlɔp/ n.f. envelope; (emballage) covering; (techn.) casing.
envelopper /ɑ̃vlɔpe/ v.t. wrap (up); (fig.) envelop.
envenimer /ɑ̃vnime/ v.t. embitter. **s'**∼ v. pr. become embittered.
envergure /ɑ̃vɛrgyr/ n.f. wing-span; (importance) scope; (qualité) calibre.
envers /ɑ̃vɛr/ prép. toward(s), to. —n.m. (de tissu) wrong side. **à l'**∼, upside down; (pantalon) back to front; (chaussette) inside out.
enviable /ɑ̃vjabl/ a. enviable. **peu** ∼, unenviable.
envie /ɑ̃vi/ n.f. desire, wish; (jalousie) envy. **avoir** ∼ **de,** want, feel like. **avoir** ∼ **de faire,** want to do, feel like doing.
envier /ɑ̃vje/ v.t. envy.
envieu|x, ∼**se** /ɑ̃vjø, -z/ a. & n.m., f. envious (person).
environ /ɑ̃virɔ̃/ adv. (round) about. ∼**s** n.m. pl. surroundings. **aux** ∼**s de,** round about.
environnement /ɑ̃virɔnmɑ̃/ n.m. environment.
environn|er /ɑ̃virɔne/ v.t. surround. ∼**ant,** ∼**ante** a. surrounding.
envisager /ɑ̃vizaʒe/ v.t. consider. ∼ **de faire,** consider doing.
envoi /ɑ̃vwa/ n.m. dispatch; (paquet) consignment.
envol /ɑ̃vɔl/ n.m. flight; (d'avion) take-off.
envoler (s') /(s)ɑ̃vɔle/ v. pr. fly away; (avion) take off; (papiers) blow away.
envoûter /ɑ̃vute/ v.t. bewitch.
envoyé, ∼**e** /ɑ̃vwaje/ n.m., f. envoy; (de journal) correspondent.
envoyer† /ɑ̃vwaje/ v.t. send; (lancer) throw. ∼ **promener qn.,** give s.o. the brush-off.
enzyme /ɑ̃zim/ n.m. enzyme.

épagneul, ∼**e** /epaɲœl/ n.m., f. spaniel.
épais, ∼**se** /epɛ, -s/ a. thick. ∼**seur** /-sœr/ n.f. thickness.
épaissir /epesir/ v.t./i., **s'**∼ v. pr. thicken.
épanch|er (s') /(s)epɑ̃ʃe/ v. pr. pour out one's feelings; (liquide) pour out. ∼**ement** n.m. outpouring.
épanoui /epanwi/ a. (joyeux) beaming, radiant.
épan|ouir (s') /(s)epanwir/ v. pr. (fleur) open out; (visage) beam; (personne) blossom. ∼**ouissement** n.m. (éclat) blossoming, full bloom.
épargne /eparɲ/ n.f. saving; (somme) savings. **caisse d'**∼, savings bank.
épargn|er /eparɲe/ v.t./i. save; (ne pas tuer) spare. ∼**er qch. à qn.,** spare s.o. sth. ∼**ant,** ∼**ante** n.m., f. saver.
éparpiller /eparpije/ v.t. scatter. **s'**∼ v. pr. scatter; (fig.) dissipate one's efforts.
épars, ∼**e** /epar, -s/ a. scattered.
épat|er /epate/ v.t. (fam.) amaze. ∼**ant,** ∼**ante** a. (fam.) amazing.
épaule /epol/ n.f. shoulder.
épauler /epole/ v.t. (arme) raise; (aider) support.
épave /epav/ n.f. wreck.
épée /epe/ n.f. sword.
épeler /ɛple/ v.t. spell.
éperdu /epɛrdy/ a. wild, frantic. ∼**ment** adv. wildly, frantically.
éperon /eprɔ̃/ n.m. spur. ∼**ner** /-ɔne/ v.t. spur (on).
épervier /epɛrvje/ n.m. sparrow-hawk.
éphémère /efemɛr/ a. ephemeral.
éphéméride /efemerid/ n.f. tear-off calendar.
épi /epi/ n.m. (de blé) ear. ∼ **de cheveux,** tuft of hair.
épic|e /epis/ n.f. spice. ∼**é** a. spicy. ∼**er** v.t. spice.
épic|ier, ∼**ière** /episje, -jɛr/ n.m., f. grocer. ∼**erie** n.f. grocery shop; (produits) groceries.
épidémie /epidemi/ n.f. epidemic.
épiderme /epidɛrm/ n.m. skin.
épier /epje/ v.t. spy on.
épilep|sie /epilɛpsi/ n.f. epilepsy. ∼**tique** a. & n.m./f. epileptic.
épiler /epile/ v.t. remove unwanted hair from; (sourcils) pluck.
épilogue /epilɔg/ n.m. epilogue; (fig.) outcome.
épinard /epinar/ n.m. (plante) spinach. ∼**s,** (nourriture) spinach.
épin|e /epin/ n.f. thorn, prickle; (d'animal) prickle, spine. ∼**e dorsale,** backbone. ∼**eux,** ∼**euse** a. thorny.

épingl|e /epɛ̃gl/ n.f. pin. **~e de nourrice, ~e de sûreté,** safety-pin. **~er** v.t. pin; (arrêter: fam.) nab.

épique /epik/ a. epic.

épisod|e /epizɔd/ n.m. episode. **à ~es,** serialized. **~ique** a. occasional.

épitaphe /epitaf/ n.f. epitaph.

épithète /epitɛt/ n.f. epithet.

épître /epitr/ n.f. epistle.

éploré /eplore/ a. tearful.

épluche-légumes /eplyʃlegym/ n.m. invar. (potato) peeler.

épluch|er /eplyʃe/ v.t. peel; (examiner: fig.) scrutinize. **~age** n.m. peeling; (fig.) scrutiny. **~ure** n.f. piece of peel ou peeling. **~ures** n.f. pl. peelings.

épong|e /epɔ̃ʒ/ n.f. sponge. **~er** v.t. (liquide) sponge up; (surface) sponge (down); (front) mop; (dettes) wipe out.

épopée /epope/ n.f. epic.

époque /epɔk/ n.f. time, period. **à l'~,** at the time. **d'~,** period.

épouse /epuz/ n.f. wife.

épouser[1] /epuze/ v.t. marry.

épouser[2] /epuze/ v.t. (forme, idée) assume, embrace, adopt.

épousseter /epuste/ v.t. dust.

époustouflant, ~e /epustuflɑ̃, -t/ a. (fam.) staggering.

épouvantable /epuvɑ̃tabl/ a. appalling.

épouvantail /epuvɑ̃taj/ n.m. scarecrow.

épouvant|e /epuvɑ̃t/ n.f. terror. **~er** v.t. terrify.

époux /epu/ n.m. husband. **les ~,** the married couple.

éprendre (s') /(s)eprɑ̃dr/ v. pr. **s'~ de,** fall in love with.

épreuve /eprœv/ n.f. test; (sport) event; (malheur) ordeal; (photo.) print; (d'imprimerie) proof. **mettre à l'~,** put to the test.

éprouvé /epruve/ a. (well-)proven.

éprouv|er /epruve/ v.t. test; (ressentir) experience; (affliger) distress. **~ant, ~ante** a. testing.

éprouvette /epruvɛt/ n.f. test-tube. **bébé-~,** test-tube baby.

épuis|er /epɥize/ v.t. (fatiguer, user) exhaust. **s'~er** v. pr. become exhausted. **~é** a. exhausted; (livre) out of print. **~ement** n.m. exhaustion.

épuisette /epɥizɛt/ n.f. fishing-net.

épur|er /epyre/ v.t. purify; (pol.) purge. **~ation** n.f. purification; (pol.) purge.

équat|eur /ekwatœr/ n.m. equator. **~orial** (m. pl. **~oriaux**) a. equatorial.

équation /ekwasjɔ̃/ n.f. equation.

équerre /ekɛr/ n.f. (set) square. **d'~,** square.

équilibr|e /ekilibr/ n.m. balance. **être** ou **se tenir en ~e,** (personne) balance; (objet) be balanced. **~é** a. well-balanced. **~er** v.t. balance. **s'~er** v. pr. (forces etc.) counterbalance each other.

équilibriste /ekilibrist/ n.m./f. tightrope walker.

équinoxe /ekinɔks/ n.m. equinox.

équipage /ekipaʒ/ n.m. crew.

équipe /ekip/ n.f. team. **~ de nuit/jour,** night/day shift.

équipé /ekipe/ a. **bien/mal ~,** well/poorly equipped.

équipée /ekipe/ n.f. escapade.

équipement /ekipmɑ̃/ n.m. equipment. **~s,** (installations) amenities, facilities.

équiper /ekipe/ v.t. equip (de, with). **s'~** v. pr. equip o.s.

équip|ier, ~ière /ekipje, -jɛr/ n.m., f. team member.

équitable /ekitabl/ a. fair. **~ment** /-əmɑ̃/ adv. fairly.

équitation /ekitasjɔ̃/ n.f. (horse-)riding.

équité /ekite/ n.f. equity.

équivalen|t, ~te /ekivalɑ̃, -t/ a. equivalent. **~ce** n.f. equivalence.

équivaloir /ekivalwar/ v.i. **~ à,** be equivalent to.

équivoque /ekivɔk/ a. equivocal; (louche) questionable. **—n.f.** ambiguity.

érable /erabl/ n.m. maple.

érafl|er /erafle/ v.t. scratch. **~ure** n.f. scratch.

éraillé /eraje/ a. (voix) raucous.

ère /ɛr/ n.f. era.

érection /erɛksjɔ̃/ n.f. erection.

éreinter /erɛ̃te/ v.t. exhaust; (fig.) criticize severely.

ergoter /ɛrgɔte/ v.i. quibble.

ériger /eriʒe/ v.t. erect. **(s')~ en,** set (o.s.) up as.

ermite /ɛrmit/ n.m. hermit.

éroder /erɔde/ v.t. erode.

érosion /erozjɔ̃/ n.f. erosion.

éroti|que /erɔtik/ a. erotic. **~sme** n.m. eroticism.

errer /ɛre/ v.i. wander.

erreur /ɛrœr/ n.f. mistake, error. **dans l'~,** mistaken. **par ~,** by mistake. **~ judiciaire,** miscarriage of justice.

erroné /ɛrɔne/ a. erroneous.

ersatz /ɛrzats/ n.m. ersatz.

érudit, ~e /erydi, -t/ a. scholarly. **—n.m., f.** scholar. **~ion** /-sjɔ̃/ n.f. scholarship.

éruption /erypsjɔ̃/ n.f. eruption; (méd.) rash.

es /ɛ/ voir **être.**

escabeau (*pl.* **~x**) /ɛskabo/ *n.m.* step-ladder; (*tabouret*) stool.

escadre /ɛskadr/ *n.f.* (*naut.*) squadron.

escadrille /ɛskadrij/ *n.f.* (*aviat.*) flight, squadron.

escadron /ɛskadrɔ̃/ *n.m.* (*mil.*) squadron.

escalad|e /ɛskalad/ *n.f.* climbing; (*pol., comm.*) escalation. **~er** *v.t.* climb.

escalator /ɛskalatɔr/ *n.m.* (P.) escalator.

escale /ɛskal/ *n.f.* (*d'avion*) stopover; (*port*) port of call. **faire ~ à**, (*avion, passager*) stop over at; (*navire, passager*) put in at.

escalier /ɛskalije/ *n.m.* stairs. **~ mécanique** *ou* **roulant**, escalator.

escalope /ɛskalɔp/ *n.f.* escalope.

escamotable /ɛskamɔtabl/ *a.* (*techn.*) retractable.

escamoter /ɛskamɔte/ *v.t.* make vanish; (*éviter*) dodge.

escargot /ɛskargo/ *n.m.* snail.

escarmouche /ɛskarmuʃ/ *n.f.* skirmish.

escarpé /ɛskarpe/ *a.* steep.

escarpin /ɛskarpɛ̃/ *n.m.* pump.

escient /ɛsjɑ̃/ *n.m.* **à bon ~**, with good reason.

esclaffer (s') /(s)ɛsklafe/ *v. pr.* guffaw, burst out laughing.

esclandre /ɛsklɑ̃dr/ *n.m.* scene.

esclav|e /ɛsklav/ *n.m./f.* slave. **~age** *n.m.* slavery.

escompte /ɛskɔ̃t/ *n.m.* discount.

escompter /ɛskɔ̃te/ *v.t.* expect; (*comm.*) discount.

escort|e /ɛskɔrt/ *n.f.* escort. **~er** *v.t.* escort. **~eur** *n.m.* escort (ship).

escouade /ɛskwad/ *n.f.* squad.

escrim|e /ɛskrim/ *n.f.* fencing. **~eur, ~euse** *n.m., f.* fencer.

escrimer (s') /(s)ɛskrime/ *v. pr.* struggle.

escroc /ɛskro/ *n.m.* swindler.

escroqu|er /ɛskrɔke/ *v.t.* swindle. **~er qch. à qn.**, swindle s.o. out of sth. **~erie** *n.f.* swindle.

espace /ɛspas/ *n.m.* space. **~s verts**, gardens, parks.

espacer /ɛspase/ *v.t.* space out. **s'~** *v. pr.* become less frequent.

espadrille /ɛspadrij/ *n.f.* rope sandals.

Espagne /ɛspaɲ/ *n.f.* Spain.

espagnol, ~e /ɛspaɲɔl/ *a.* Spanish. —*n.m., f.* Spaniard. —*n.m.* (*lang.*) Spanish.

espagnolette /ɛspaɲɔlɛt/ *n.f.* (window) catch.

espèce /ɛspɛs/ *n.f.* kind, sort; (*race*) species. **~s**, (*argent*) cash. **~**

d'idiot/de brute/*etc.*!**,** you idiot/brute/ *etc.*!

espérance /ɛsperɑ̃s/ *n.f.* hope.

espérer /ɛspere/ *v.t.* hope for. **~ faire/que**, hope to do/that. —*v.i.* hope. **~ en**, have faith in.

espiègle /ɛspjɛgl/ *a.* mischievous.

espion, ~ne /ɛspjɔ̃, -jɔn/ *n.m., f.* spy.

espionn|er /ɛspjɔne/ *v.t./i.* spy (on). **~age** *n.m.* espionage, spying.

esplanade /ɛsplanad/ *n.f.* esplanade.

espoir /ɛspwar/ *n.m.* hope.

esprit /ɛspri/ *n.m.* spirit; (*intellect*) mind; (*humour*) wit. **perdre l'~**, lose one's mind. **reprendre ses ~s**, come to. **vouloir faire de l'~**, try to be witty.

Esquimau, ~de (*m. pl.* **~x**) /ɛskimo, -d/ *n.m., f.* Eskimo.

esquinter /ɛskɛ̃te/ *v.t.* (*fam.*) ruin.

esquiss|e /ɛskis/ *n.f.* sketch; (*fig.*) suggestion. **~er** *v.t.* sketch; (*geste etc.*) make an attempt at.

esquiv|e /ɛskiv/ *n.f.* (*sport*) dodge. **~er** *v.t.* dodge. **s'~er** *v. pr.* slip away.

essai /ɛse/ *n.m.* testing; (*épreuve*) test, trial; (*tentative*) try; (*article*) essay. **à l'~**, on trial.

essaim /ɛsɛ̃/ *n.m.* swarm. **~er** /ɛseme/ *v.i.* swarm; (*fig.*) spread.

essayage /ɛsɛjaʒ/ *n.m.* (*de vêtement*) fitting. **salon d'~**, fitting room.

essayer /ɛseje/ *v.t./i.* try; (*vêtement*) try (on); (*voiture etc.*) try (out). **~ de faire**, try to do.

essence¹ /ɛsɑ̃s/ *n.f.* (*carburant*) petrol; (*Amer.*) gas.

essence² /ɛsɑ̃s/ *n.f.* (*nature, extrait*) essence.

essentiel, ~le /ɛsɑ̃sjɛl/ *a.* essential. —*n.m.* **l'~**, the main thing; (*quantité*) the main part. **~lement** *adv.* essentially.

essieu (*pl.* **~x**) /ɛsjø/ *n.m.* axle.

essor /ɛsɔr/ *n.m.* expansion. **prendre son ~**, expand.

essor|er /ɛsɔre/ *v.t.* (*linge*) spin-dry; (*en tordant*) wring. **~euse** *n.f.* spin-drier.

essouffler *v.t.* make breathless. **s'~** *v. pr.* get out of breath.

ess|uyer¹ /ɛsɥije/ *v.t.* wipe. **s'~uyer** *v. pr.* dry *ou* wipe o.s. **~uie-glace** *n.m. invar.* windscreen wiper; (*Amer.*) windshield wiper. **~uie-mains** *n.m. invar.* hand-towel.

essuyer² /ɛsɥije/ *v.t.* (*subir*) suffer.

est¹ /ɛ/ *voir* **être**.

est² /ɛst/ *n.m.* east. —*a. invar.* east; (*partie*) eastern; (*direction*) easterly.

estampe /ɛstɑ̃p/ *n.f.* print.

estampille /ɛstɑ̃pij/ n.f. stamp.
esthète /ɛstɛt/ n.m./f. aesthete.
esthéticienne /ɛstetisjɛn/ n.f. beautician.
esthétique /ɛstetik/ a. aesthetic.
estimable /ɛstimabl/ a. worthy.
estimation /ɛstimasjɔ̃/ n.f. valuation.
estime /ɛstim/ n.f. esteem.
estim|er /ɛstime/ v.t. (objet) value; (calculer) estimate; (respecter) esteem; (considérer) consider. ~ation n.f. valuation; (calcul) estimation.
estiv|al (m. pl. ~aux) /ɛstival, -o/ a. summer. ~ant, ~ante n.m., f. summer visitor, holiday-maker.
estomac /ɛstɔma/ n.m. stomach.
estomaqué /ɛstɔmake/ a. (fam.) stunned.
estomper (s') /(s)ɛstɔpe/ v. pr. become blurred.
estrade /ɛstrad/ n.f. platform.
estragon /ɛstragɔ̃/ n.m. tarragon.
estrop|ier /ɛstrɔpje/ v.t. cripple; (fig.) mangle. ~ié, ~iée n.m., f. cripple.
estuaire /ɛstɥɛr/ n.m. estuary.
estudiantin, ~e /ɛstydjɑ̃tɛ̃, -in/ a. student.
esturgeon /ɛstyrʒɔ̃/ n.m. sturgeon.
et /e/ conj. and. **et moi/lui/**etc.**?**, what about me/him/etc.?
étable /etabl/ n.f. cow-shed.
établi[1] /etabli/ a. established. **un fait bien** ~, a well-established fact.
établi[2] /etabli/ n.m. work-bench.
établir /etablir/ v.t. establish; (liste, facture) draw up; (personne, camp, record) set up. **s'**~ v. pr. (personne) establish o.s. **s'**~ **épicier/**etc., set (o.s.) up as a grocer/etc. **s'**~ **à son compte**, set up on one's own.
établissement /etablismɑ̃/ n.m. (bâtiment, institution) establishment.
étage /etaʒ/ n.m. floor, storey; (de fusée) stage. **à l'**~, upstairs. **au premier** ~, on the first floor.
étager (s') /(s)etaʒe/ v. pr. rise at different levels.
étagère /etaʒɛr/ n.f. shelf; (meuble) shelving unit.
étai /etɛ/ n.m. prop, buttress.
étain /etɛ̃/ n.m. pewter.
étais, était /etɛ/ voir **être**.
étal (pl. ~s) /etal/ n.m. stall.
étalag|e /etalaʒ/ n.m. display; (vitrine) shop-window. **faire** ~**e de**, show off ~**iste** n.m./f. window-dresser.
étaler /etale/ v.t. spread; (journal) spread (out); (vacances) stagger; (exposer) display. **s'**~ v. pr. (s'étendre) stretch out; (tomber: fam.)

fall flat. **s'**~ **sur**, (paiement) be spread over.
étalon /etalɔ̃/ n.m. (cheval) stallion; (modèle) standard.
étanche /etɑ̃ʃ/ a. watertight; (montre) waterproof.
étancher /etɑ̃ʃe/ v.t. (soif) quench; (sang) stem.
étang /etɑ̃/ n.m. pond.
étant /etɑ̃/ voir **être**.
étape /etap/ n.f. stage; (lieu d'arrêt) stopover.
état /eta/ n.m. state; (liste) statement; (métier) profession; (nation) State. **en bon/mauvais** ~, in good/bad condition. **en** ~ **de**, in a position to. **hors d'**~ **de**, not in a position to. **en** ~ **de marche**, in working order. ~ **civil**, civil status. ~**-major** (pl. ~**s-majors**) n.m. (officiers) staff. **faire** ~ **de**, (citer) mention. **être dans tous ses** ~**s**, be in a state. ~ **des lieux**, inventory.
étatisé /etatize/ a. State-controlled.
États-Unis /etazyni/ n.m. pl. ~ **(d'Amérique)**, United States (of America).
étau (pl. ~**x**) /eto/ n.m. vice.
étayer /eteje/ v.t. prop up.
été[1] /ete/ voir **être**.
été[2] /ete/ n.m. summer.
étein|dre† /etɛ̃dr/ v.t. put out, extinguish; (lumière, radio) turn off. **s'**~**dre** v. pr. (feu) go out; (mourir) die. ~**t**, ~**te** /etɛ̃, -t/ a. (feu) out; (volcan) extinct.
étendard /etɑ̃dar/ n.m. standard.
étendre /etɑ̃dr/ v.t. spread; (journal, nappe) spread out; (bras, jambes) stretch (out); (linge) hang out; (agrandir) extend. **s'**~ v. pr. (s'allonger) stretch out; (se propager) spread; (plaine etc.) stretch. **s'**~ **sur**, (sujet) dwell on.
étendu, ~e /etɑ̃dy/ a. extensive. —n.f. area; (d'eau) stretch; (importance) extent.
éternel, ~**le** /etɛrnɛl/ a. eternal. ~**lement** adv. eternally.
éterniser (s') /(s)etɛrnize/ v. pr. (durer) drag on.
éternité /etɛrnite/ n.f. eternity.
étern|uer /etɛrnɥe/ v.i. sneeze. ~**uement** /-ymɑ̃/ n.m. sneeze.
êtes /ɛt/ voir **être**.
éthique /etik/ a. ethical. —n.f. ethics.
ethn|ie /ɛtni/ n.f. ethnic group. ~**ique** a. ethnic.
éthylisme /etilism/ n.m. alcoholism.
étinceler /etɛ̃sle/ v.i. sparkle.

étincelle /etɛ̃sɛl/ n.f. spark.

étioler (s') /(s)etjɔle/ v. pr. wilt.

étiqueter /etikte/ v.t. label.

étiquette /etikɛt/ n.f. label; (protocole) etiquette.

étirer /etire/ v.t., **s'~** v. pr. stretch.

étoffe /etɔf/ n.f. fabric.

étoffer /etɔfe/ v.t., **s'~** v. pr. fill out.

étoil|le /etwal/ n.f. star. **à la belle ~e**, in the open. **~e de mer**, starfish. **~é** a. starry.

étonn|er /etɔne/ v.t. amaze. **s'~er** v. pr. be amazed (de, at). **~ant, ~ante** a. amazing. **~ement** n.m. amazement.

étouffée /etufe/ n.f. **cuire à l'~**, braise.

étouff|er /etufe/ v.t./i. suffocate; (sentiment, révolte) stifle; (feu) smother; (bruit) muffle. **on ~e**, it is stifling. **s'~er** v. pr. suffocate; (en mangeant) choke. **~ant, ~ante** a. stifling.

étourd|i, ~ie /eturdi/ a. unthinking, scatter-brained. —n.m., f. scatter-brain. **~erie** n.f. thoughtlessness; (acte) thoughtless act.

étourd|ir /eturdir/ v.t. stun; (griser) make dizzy. **~issant, ~issante** a. stunning. **~issement** n.m. (syncope) dizzy spell.

étourneau (pl. **~x**) /eturno/ n.m. starling.

étrange /etrɑ̃ʒ/ a. strange. **~ment** adv. strangely. **~té** n.f. strangeness.

étrang|er, ~ère /etrɑ̃ʒe, -ɛr/ a. strange, unfamiliar; (d'un autre pays) foreign. —n.m., f. foreigner; (inconnu) stranger. **à l'~er**, abroad. **de l'~er**, from abroad.

étrangler /etrɑ̃gle/ v.t. strangle; (col) stifle. **s'~** v. pr. choke.

être† /ɛtr/ v.i. be. —v. aux. (avec aller, sortir, etc.) have. **~ donné/fait par**, (passif) be given/done by. —n.m. (personne, créature) being. **~ humain**, human being **~ médecin/tailleur**/etc., be a doctor/a tailor/etc. **~ à qn.**, be s.o.'s. **c'est à faire**, it needs to be ou should be done. **est-ce qu'il travaille?**, is he working?, does he work? **vous travaillez, n'est-ce pas?**, you are working, aren't you?, you work, don't you? **il est deux heures**/etc., it is two o'clock/etc. **nous sommes le six mai**, it is the sixth of May.

étrein|dre /etrɛ̃dr/ v.t. grasp; (ami) embrace. **~te** /-ɛ̃t/ n.f. grasp; embrace.

étrenner /etrene/ v.t. use for the first time.

étrennes /etrɛn/ n.f. pl. (cadeau) New Year's gift.

étrier /etrije/ n.m. stirrup.

étriqué /etrike/ a. tight; (fig.) small-minded.

étroit, ~e /etrwa, -t/ a. narrow; (vêtement) tight; (liens, surveillance) close. **à l'~**, cramped. **~ement** /-tmɑ̃/ adv. closely. **~esse** /-tɛs/ n.f. narrowness.

étude /etyd/ n.f. study; (bureau) office. **(salle d')~**, (scol.) prep room; (scol., Amer.) study hall. **à l'~**, under consideration. **faire des ~s (de)**, study.

étudiant, ~e /etydjɑ̃, -t/ n.m., f. student.

étudier /etydje/ v.t./i. study.

étui /etɥi/ n.m. case.

étuve /etyv/ n.f. steamroom. **quelle étuve!**, it's like a hothouse in here.

étuvée /etyve/ n.f. **cuire à l'~**, braise.

etymologie /etimɔlɔʒi/ n.f. etymology.

eu, eue /y/ voir **avoir**.

eucalyptus /økaliptys/ n.m. eucalyptus.

euphémisme /øfemism/ n.m. euphemism.

euphorie /øfɔri/ n.f. euphoria.

Europe /ørɔp/ n.f. Europe.

europé|en, ~ne /ørɔpeɛ̃, -ɛn/ a. & n.m., f. European.

euthanasie /øtanazi/ n.f. euthanasia.

eux /ø/ pron. they; (complément) them. **~-mêmes** pron. themselves.

évac|uer /evakɥe/ v.t. evacuate. **~uation** n.f. evacuation.

évad|er (s') /(s)evade/ v. pr. escape. **~é, ~ée** a. escaped; n.m., f. escaped prisoner.

éval|uer /evalɥe/ v.t. assess. **~uation** n.f. assessment.

évang|ile /evɑ̃ʒil/ n.m. gospel. **l'Évangile**, the Gospel. **~élique** a. evangelical.

évan|ouir (s') /(s)evanwir/ v. pr. faint; (disparaître) vanish. **~ouissement** n.m. (syncope) fainting fit.

évapor|er /evapɔre/ v.t., **s'~er** v. pr. evaporate. **~ation** n.f. evaporation.

évasi|f, ~ve /evazif, -v/ a. evasive.

évasion /evazjɔ̃/ n.f. escape; (par le rêve etc.) escapism.

éveil /evɛj/ n.m. awakening. **donner l'~ à**, arouse the suspicions of. **en ~**, alert.

éveill|er /eveje/ v.t. awake(n); (susciter) arouse. **s'~er** v. pr. awake(n); be aroused. **~é** a. awake; (intelligent) alert.

événement /evɛnmɑ̃/ n.m. event.

éventail /evɑ̃taj/ *n.m.* fan; (*gamme*) range.

éventaire /evɑ̃tɛr/ *n.m.* stall, stand.

éventé /evɑ̃te/ *a.* (*gâté*) stale.

éventrer /evɑ̃tre/ *v.t.* (*sac etc.*) rip open.

éventualité /evɑ̃tɥalite/ *n.f.* possibility. **dans cette ~**, in that event.

éventuel, ~le /evɑ̃tɥɛl/ *a.* possible. **~lement** *adv.* possibly.

évêque /evɛk/ *n.m.* bishop.

évertuer (s') /(s)evɛrtɥe/ *v. pr.* **s'~ à**, struggle hard to.

éviction /eviksjɔ̃/ *n.f.* eviction.

évidemment /evidamɑ̃/ *adv.* obviously; (*bien sûr*) of course.

évidence /evidɑ̃s/ *n.f.* obviousness; (*fait*) obvious fact. **être en ~**, be conspicuous. **mettre en ~**, (*fait*) highlight.

évident, ~e /evidɑ̃, -t/ *a.* obvious, evident.

évider /evide/ *v.t.* hollow out.

évier /evje/ *n.m.* sink.

évincer /evɛ̃se/ *v.t.* oust.

éviter /evite/ *v.t.* avoid (**de faire**, doing). **~ à qn.**, (*dérangement etc.*) spare s.o.

évoca|teur ~trice /evɔkatœr, -tris/ *a.* evocative.

évocation /evɔkasjɔ̃/ *n.f.* evocation.

évolué /evɔlɥe/ *a.* highly developed.

évol|uer /evɔlɥe/ *v.i.* develop; (*se déplacer*) move, manœuvre; (*Amer.*) maneuver. **~ution** *n.f.* development; (*d'une espèce*) evolution; (*déplacement*) movement.

évoquer /evɔke/ *v.t.* call to mind, evoke.

ex- /ɛks/ *préf.* ex-.

exacerber /ɛgzasɛrbe/ *v.t.* exacerbate.

exact, ~e /ɛgza(kt), -akt/ *a.* exact, accurate; (*correct*) correct; (*personne*) punctual. **~ement** /-ktəmɑ̃/ *adv.* exactly. **~itude** /-ktityd/ *n.f.* exactness; punctuality.

ex aequo /ɛgzeko/ *adv.* (*classer*) equal. **être ~**, be equally placed.

exagéré /ɛgzaʒere/ *a.* excessive.

exagér|er /ɛgzaʒere/ *v.t./i.* exaggerate; (*abuser*) go too far. **~ation** *n.f.* exaggeration.

exaltation /ɛgzaltasjɔ̃/ *n.f.* elation.

exalté, ~e /ɛgzalte/ *n.m.*, *f.* fanatic.

exalter /ɛgzalte/ *v.t.* excite; (*glorifier*) exalt.

examen /ɛgzamɛ̃/ *n.m.* examination; (*scol.*) exam(ination).

examin|er /ɛgzamine/ *v.t.* examine. **~ateur, ~atrice** *n.m.*, *f.* examiner.

exaspér|er /ɛgzaspere/ *v.t.* exasperate. **~ation** *n.f.* exasperation.

exaucer /ɛgzose/ *v.t.* grant; (*personne*) grant the wish(es) of.

excavateur /ɛkskavatœr/ *n.m.* digger.

excavation /ɛkskavasjɔ̃/ *n.f.* excavation.

excédent /ɛksedɑ̃/ *n.m.* surplus. **~ de bagages**, excess luggage. **~ de la balance commerciale**, trade surplus. **~aire** /-tɛr/ *a.* excess, surplus.

excéder[1] /ɛksede/ *v.t.* (*dépasser*) exceed.

excéder[2] /ɛksede/ *v.t.* (*agacer*) irritate.

excellen|t, ~te /ɛksɛlɑ̃, -t/ *a.* excellent. **~ce** *n.f.* excellence.

exceller /ɛksele/ *v.i.* excel (**dans**, in).

excentri|que /ɛksɑ̃trik/ *a. & n.m./f.* eccentric. **~cité** *n.f.* eccentricity.

excepté /ɛksɛpte/ *a. & prép.* except.

excepter /ɛksɛpte/ *v.t.* except.

exception /ɛksɛpsjɔ̃/ *n.f.* exception. **à l'~ de**, except for. **d'~**, exceptional. **faire ~**, be an exception. **~nel, ~nelle** /-jɔnɛl/ *a.* exceptional. **~nellement** /-jɔnɛlmɑ̃/ *adv.* exceptionally.

excès /ɛksɛ/ *n.m.* excess. **~ de vitesse**, speeding.

excessi|f, ~ve /ɛksesif, -v/ *a.* excessive. **~vement** *adv.* excessively.

excitant /ɛksitɑ̃/ *n.m.* stimulant.

excit|er /ɛksite/ *v.t.* excite; (*encourager*) exhort (**à**, to); (*irriter: fam.*) annoy. **~ation** *n.f.* excitement.

exclam|er (s') /(s)ɛksklame/ *v. pr.* exclaim. **~ation** *n.f.* exclamation.

exclu|re† /ɛksklyr/ *v.t.* exclude; (*expulser*) expel; (*empêcher*) preclude. **~sion** *n.f.* exclusion.

exclusi|f, ~ve /ɛksklyzif, -v/ *a.* exclusive. **~vement** *adv.* exclusively. **~vité** *n.f.* (*comm.*) exclusive rights. **en ~vité à**, (*film*) (showing) exclusively at.

excrément(s) /ɛkskremɑ̃/ *n.m.* (*pl.*). excrement.

excroissance /ɛkskrwasɑ̃s/ *n.f.* (out) growth, excrescence.

excursion /ɛkskyrsjɔ̃/ *n.f.* excursion; (*à pied*) hike.

excuse /ɛkskyz/ *n.f.* excuse. **~s**, apology. **faire des ~s**, apologize.

excuser /ɛkskyze/ *v.t.* excuse. **s'~** *v. pr.* apologize (**de**, for). **je m'excuse**, (*fam.*) excuse me.

exécrable /ɛgzekrabl/ *a.* abominable.

exécrer /ɛgzekre/ *v.t.* loathe.

exécut|er /ɛgzekyte/ *v.t.* carry out, execute; (*mus.*) perform; (*tuer*) execute. **~ion** /-sjɔ̃/ *n.f.* execution; (*mus.*) performance.

exécuti|f, ⁓ve /ɛgzekytif, -v/ *a. & n.m.* (*pol.*) executive.

exemplaire /ɛgzɑ̃plɛr/ *a.* exemplary. —*n.m.* copy.

exemple /ɛgzɑ̃pl/ *n.m.* example. **par ⁓,** for example. **donner l'⁓,** set an example.

exempt, ⁓e /ɛgzɑ̃, -t/ *a.* **⁓ de,** exempt from.

exempt|er /ɛgzɑ̃te/ *v.t.* exempt (**de,** from). **⁓ion** /-psjɔ̃/ *n.f.* exemption.

exercer /ɛgzɛrse/ *v.t.* exercise; (*influence, contrôle*) exert; (*métier*) work at; (*former*) train, exercise. **s'⁓** (**à**), practise.

exercice /ɛgzɛrsis/ *n.m.* exercise; (*mil.*) drill; (*de métier*) practice. **en ⁓,** in office; (*médecin*) in practice.

exhaler /ɛgzale/ *v.t.* emit.

exhausti|f, ⁓ve /ɛgzostif, -v/ *a.* exhaustive.

exhiber /ɛgzibe/ *v.t.* exhibit.

exhibitionniste /ɛgzibisjɔnist/ *n.m./f.* exhibitionist.

exhorter /ɛgzɔrte/ *v.t.* exhort (**à,** to).

exigence /ɛgziʒɑ̃s/ *n.f.* demand.

exig|er /ɛgziʒe/ *v.t.* demand. **⁓eant, ⁓eante** *a.* demanding.

exigu, ⁓ë /ɛgzigy/ *a.* tiny.

exil /ɛgzil/ *n.m.* exile. **⁓é, ⁓ée** *n.m., f.* exile. **⁓er** *v.t.* exile. **s'⁓er** *v. pr.* go into exile.

existence /ɛgzistɑ̃s/ *n.f.* existence.

exist|er /ɛgziste/ *v.i.* exist. **⁓ant, ⁓ante** *a.* existing.

exode /ɛgzɔd/ *n.m.* exodus.

exonér|er /ɛgzɔnere/ *v.t.* exempt (**de,** from). **⁓ation** *n.f.* exemption.

exorbitant, ⁓e /ɛgzɔrbitɑ̃, -t/ *a.* exorbitant.

exorciser /ɛgzɔrsize/ *v.t.* exorcize.

exotique /ɛgzɔtik/ *a.* exotic.

expansi|f, ⁓ve /ɛkspɑ̃sif, -v/ *a.* expansive.

expansion /ɛkspɑ̃sjɔ̃/ *n.f.* expansion.

expatr|ier (s') /(s)ɛkspatrije/ *v. pr.* leave one's country. **⁓ié, ⁓iée** *n.m., f.* expatriate.

expectative /ɛkspɛktativ/ *n.f.* **dans l'⁓,** still waiting.

expédient, ⁓e /ɛkspedjɑ̃, -t/ *a. & n.m.* expedient. **vivre d'⁓s,** live by one's wits. **user d'⁓s,** resort to expedients.

expéd|ier /ɛkspedje/ *v.t.* send, dispatch; (*tâche: péj.*) dispatch. **⁓iteur, ⁓itrice** *n.m., f.* sender. **⁓ition** *n.f.* dispatch; (*voyage*) expedition.

expéditi|f, ⁓ve /ɛkspeditif, -v/ *a.* quick.

expérience /ɛksperjɑ̃s/ *n.f.* experience; (*scientifique*) experiment.

expérimenté /ɛksperimɑ̃te/ *a.* experienced.

expériment|er /ɛksperimɑ̃te/ *v.t.* test, experiment with. **⁓al** (*m. pl.* **⁓aux**) *a.* experimental. **⁓ation** *n.f.* experimentation.

expert, ⁓e /ɛkspɛr, -t/ *a.* expert. —*n.m.* expert; (*d'assurances*) valuer; (*Amer.*) appraiser. **⁓-comptable** (*pl.* **⁓s-comptables**) *n.m.* accountant.

expertis|e /ɛkspɛrtiz/ *n.f.* expert appraisal. **⁓er** *v.t.* appraise.

expier /ɛkspje/ *v.t.* atone for.

expir|er /ɛkspire/ *v.i.* breathe out; (*finir, mourir*) expire. **⁓ation** *n.f.* expiry.

explicati|f, ⁓ve /ɛksplikatif, -v/ *a.* explanatory.

explication /ɛksplikɑsjɔ̃/ *n.f.* explanation; (*fig.*) discussion; (*scol.*) commentary. **⁓ de texte,** (*scol.*) literary commentary.

explicite /ɛksplisit/ *a.* explicit.

expliquer /ɛksplike/ *v.t.* explain. **s'⁓** *v. pr.* explain o.s.; (*discuter*) discuss things; (*être compréhensible*) be understandable.

exploit /ɛksplwa/ *n.m.* exploit.

exploitant /ɛksplwatɑ̃/ *n.m.* **⁓ (agricole),** farmer.

exploit|er /ɛksplwate/ *v.t.* (*personne*) exploit; (*ferme*) run; (*champs*) work. **⁓ation** *n.f.* exploitation; running; working; (*affaire*) concern. **⁓eur, ⁓euse** *n.m., f.* exploiter.

explor|er /ɛksplɔre/ *v.t.* explore. **⁓ateur, ⁓atrice** *n.m., f.* explorer. **⁓ation** *n.f.* exploration.

explos|er /ɛksploze/ *v.i.* explode. **faire ⁓er,** explode; (*bâtiment*) blow up. **⁓ion** *n.f.* explosion.

explosi|f, ⁓ve /ɛksplozif, -v/ *a. & n.m.* explosive.

export|er /ɛkspɔrte/ *v.t.* export. **⁓ateur, ⁓atrice** *n.m., f.* exporter; *a.* exporting. **⁓ation** *n.f.* export.

exposant, ⁓e /ɛkspozɑ̃, -t/ *n.m., f.* exhibitor.

exposé /ɛkspoze/ *n.m.* talk (**sur,** on); (*d'une action*) account. **faire l'⁓ de la situation,** give an account of the situation.

expos|er /ɛkspoze/ *v.t.* display, show; (*expliquer*) explain; (*soumettre, mettre en danger*) expose (**à,** to); (*vie*) endanger. **⁓é au nord/etc.,** facing north/etc. **s'⁓er à,** expose o.s. to.

exposition /ɛkspozisjɔ̃/ n.f. display; (*salon*) exhibition. ∼ à, exposure to.

exprès[1] /ɛksprɛ/ adv. specially; (*délibérément*) on purpose.

exprÌès[2], ∼**esse** /ɛksprɛs/ a. express. ∼**essément** adv. expressly.

exprès[3] /ɛkspres/ a. invar. & n.m. **lettre** ∼, express letter. (**par**) ∼, sent special delivery.

express /ɛkspres/ a. & n.m. invar. (**café**) ∼, espresso. (**train**) ∼, fast train.

expressi|f, ∼**ve** /ɛkspresif, -v/ a. expressive.

expression /ɛkspresjɔ̃/ n.f. expression. ∼ **corporelle**, physical expression.

exprimer /ɛksprime/ v.t. express. **s'**∼ v. pr. express o.s.

expuls|er /ɛkspylse/ v.t. expel; (*locataire*) evict; (*joueur*) send off. ∼**ion** n.f. expulsion; eviction.

expurger /ɛkspyrʒe/ v.t. expurgate.

exquis, ∼**e** /ɛkski, -z/ a. exquisite.

extase /ɛkstaz/ n.f. ecstasy.

extasier (s') /(s)ɛkstazje/ v. pr. **s'**∼ **sur**, be ecstatic about.

extensible /ɛkstɑ̃sibl/ a. expandable, extendible. **tissu** ∼, stretch fabric.

extensi|f, ∼**ve** /ɛkstɑ̃sif, -v/ a. extensive.

extension /ɛkstɑ̃sjɔ̃/ n.f. extension; (*expansion*) expansion.

exténuer /ɛkstenɥe/ v.t. exhaust.

extérieur /ɛksterjœr/ a. outside; (*signe, gaieté*) outward; (*politique*) foreign. —n.m. outside, exterior; (*de personne*) exterior. **à l'**∼ (**de**), outside. ∼**ement** adv. outwardly.

extérioriser /ɛksterjɔrize/ v.t. show, externalize.

extermin|er /ɛkstɛrmine/ v.t. exterminate. ∼**ation** n.f. extermination.

externe /ɛkstɛrn/ a. external. —n.m./f. (*scol.*) day pupil.

extincteur /ɛkstɛ̃ktœr/ n.m. fire extinguisher.

extinction /ɛkstɛ̃ksjɔ̃/ n.f. extinction. ∼ **de voix**, loss of voice.

extirper /ɛkstirpe/ v.t. eradicate.

extor|quer /ɛkstɔrke/ v.t. extort. ∼**sion** n.f. extortion.

extra /ɛkstra/ a. invar. first-rate. —n.m. invar. (*repas*) (special) treat.

extra- /ɛkstra/ préf. extra-.

extrad|er /ɛkstrade/ v.t. extradite. ∼**ition** n.f. extradition.

extr|aire† /ɛkstrer/ v.t. extract. ∼**action** n.f. extraction.

extrait /ɛkstrɛ/ n.m. extract.

extraordinaire /ɛkstraɔrdinɛr/ a. extraordinary.

extravagan|t, ∼**te** /ɛkstravagɑ̃, -t/ a. extravagant. ∼**ce** n.f. extravagance.

extraverti, ∼**e** /ɛkstravɛrti/ n.m., f. extrovert.

extrême /ɛkstrɛm/ a. & n.m. extreme. **E**∼**-Orient** n.m. Far East. ∼**ment** adv. extremely.

extrémiste /ɛkstremist/ n.m., f. extremist.

extrémité /ɛkstremite/ n.f. extremity, end; (*misère*) dire straits. ∼**s**, (*excès*) extremes.

exubéran|t, ∼**te** /ɛgzyberɑ̃, -t/ a. exuberant. ∼**ce** n.f. exuberance.

exulter /ɛgzylte/ v.i. exult.

exutoire /ɛgzytwar/ n.m. outlet.

F

F abrév. (*franc, francs*) franc, francs.

fable /fabl/ n.f. fable.

fabrique /fabrik/ n.f. factory.

fabri|quer /fabrike/ v.t. make; (*industriellement*) manufacture; (*fig.*) make up. ∼**cant**, ∼**cante** n.m., f. manufacturer. ∼**cation** n.f. making; manufacture.

fabul|er /fabyle/ v.i. fantasize. ∼**ation** n.f. fantasizing.

fabuleu|x, ∼**se** /fabylø, -z/ a. fabulous.

fac /fak/ n.f. (*fam.*) university.

façade /fasad/ n.f. front; (*fig.*) façade.

face /fas/ n.f. face; (*d'un objet*) side. **en** ∼ (**de**), **d'en** ∼, opposite. **en** ∼ **de**, (*fig.*) faced with. ∼ **à**, facing; (*fig.*) faced with. **faire** ∼ **à**, face.

facétie /fasesi/ n.f. joke.

facette /fasɛt/ n.f. facet.

fâch|er /faʃe/ v.t. anger. **se** ∼**er** v. pr. get angry; (*se brouiller*) fall out. ∼**é** a. angry; (*désolé*) sorry.

fâcheu|x, ∼**se** /faʃø, -z/ a. unfortunate.

facil|e /fasil/ a. easy; (*caractère*) easygoing. ∼**ement** adv. easily. ∼**ité** n.f. easiness; (*aisance*) ease; (*aptitude*) ability; (*possibilité*) facility. ∼**ités de paiement**, easy terms.

faciliter /fasilite/ v.t. facilitate.

façon /fasɔ̃/ n.f. way; (*de vêtement*) cut. ∼**s**, (*chichis*) fuss. **de cette** ∼, in this way. **de** ∼ **à**, so as to. **de toute** ∼, anyway.

façonner /fasɔne/ v.t. shape; (*faire*) make.

facteur[1] /faktœr/ *n.m.* postman.
facteur[2] /faktœr/ *n.m.* (*élément*) factor.
factice /faktis/ *a.* artificial.
faction /faksjɔ̃/ *n.f.* faction. **de ~,** (*mil.*) on guard.
factur|e /faktyr/ *n.f.* bill; (*comm.*) invoice. **~er** *v.t.* invoice.
facultati|f, ~ve /fakyltatif, -v/ *a.* optional.
faculté /fakylte/ *n.f.* faculty; (*possibilité*) power; (*univ.*) faculty.
fade /fad/ *a.* insipid.
fagot /fago/ *n.m.* bundle of firewood.
fagoter /fagɔte/ *v.t.* (*fam.*) rig out.
faibl|e /fɛbl/ *a.* weak; (*espoir, quantité, écart*) slight; (*revenu, intensité*) low. —*n.m.* weakling; (*penchant, défaut*) weakness. **~e d'esprit,** feeble-minded. **~esse** *n.f.* weakness. **~ir** *v.i.* weaken.
faïence /fajɑ̃s/ *n.f.* earthenware.
faille /faj/ *n.f.* (*géog.*) fault; (*fig.*) flaw.
faillir /fajir/ *v.i.* **j'ai failli acheter/***etc.*, I almost bought/*etc.*
faillite /fajit/ *n.f.* bankruptcy; (*fig.*) collapse.
faim /fɛ̃/ *n.f.* hunger. **avoir ~,** be hungry.
fainéant, ~e /feneɑ̃, -t/ *a.* idle. —*n.m., f.* idler.
faire† /fɛr/ *v.t.* make; (*activité*) do; (*rêve, chute, etc.*) have; (*dire*) say. **ça fait 20 F,** that's 20 F. **ça fait 3 ans,** it's been 3 years. —*v.i.* do; (*paraître*) look. **se ~,** *v. pr.* (*petit etc.*) make o.s.; (*amis, argent*) make; (*illusions*) have; (*devenir*) become. **~ du rugby/du violon/***etc.*, play rugby/the violin/*etc.* **~ construire/punir/***etc.*, have *ou* get built/punished/*etc.*, **~ pleurer/tomber/***etc.*, make cry/fall/*etc.* **se ~ tuer/***etc.*, get killed/*etc.* **se ~ couper les cheveux,** have one's hair cut. **il fait beau/chaud/***etc.*, it is fine/hot/*etc.* **~ l'idiot,** play the fool. **ne ~ que pleurer/***etc.*, (*faire continuellement*) do nothing but cry/*etc.* **ça ne fait rien,** it doesn't matter. **se ~ à,** get used to. **s'en ~,** worry. **ça se fait,** that is done. **~part** *n.m. invar.* announcement.
fais, fait[1] /fɛ/ *voir* **faire.**
faisable /fəzabl/ *a.* feasible.
faisan /fəzɑ̃/ *n.m.* pheasant.
faisandé /fəzɑ̃de/ *a.* high.
faisceau (*pl.* **~x**) /fɛso/ *n.m.* (*rayon*) beam; (*fagot*) bundle.
fait[2], **~e** /fɛ, fɛt/ *a.* done; (*fromage*) ripe. **~ pour,** made for. **tout ~,** ready made. **c'est bien ~ pour toi,** it serves you right.
fait[3] /fɛ/ *n.m.* fact; (*événement*) event. **au**

~ (de), informed (of). **de ce ~,** therefore. **du ~ de,** on account of. **~ divers,** (*trivial*) news item. **~ nouveau,** new development. **sur le ~,** in the act.
faîte /fɛt/ *n.m.* top; (*fig.*) peak.
faites /fɛt/ *voir* **faire.**
faitout /fɛtu/ *n.m.* stew-pot.
falaise /falɛz/ *n.f.* cliff.
falloir† /falwar/ *v.i.* **il faut qch./qn.,** we, you, *etc.* need sth./so. **il lui faut du pain,** he needs bread. **il faut rester,** we, you, *etc.* have to *ou* must stay. **il faut que j'aille,** I have to *ou* must go. **il faudrait que tu partes,** you should leave. **il aurait fallu le faire,** we, you, *etc.* should have done it. **il s'en faut de beaucoup que je sois,** I am far from being. **comme il faut,** properly; *a.* proper.
falot, ~e /falo, falɔt/ *a.* grey.
falsifier /falsifje/ *v.t.* falsify.
famélique /famelik/ *a.* starving.
fameu|x, ~se /famø, -z/ *a.* famous; (*excellent: fam.*) first-rate. **~sement** *adv.* (*fam.*) extremely.
famil|ial (*m. pl.* **~iaux**) /familjal, -jo/ *a.* family.
famil|iariser /familjarize/ *v.t.* familiarize (**avec,** with). **se ~iser** *v. pr.* familiarize o.s. **~isé** *a.* familiar. **~ité** *n.f.* familiarity.
famil|ier, ~ière /familje, -jɛr/ *a.* familiar; (*amical*) informal. —*n.m.* regular visitor. **~ièrement** *adv.* informally.
famille /famij/ *n.f.* family. **en ~,** with one's family.
famine /famin/ *n.f.* famine.
fanati|que /fanatik/ *a.* fanatical. —*n.m./f.* fanatic. **~sme** *n.m.* fanaticism.
faner (se) /(sə)fane/ *v. pr.* fade.
fanfare /fɑ̃far/ *n.f.* brass band; (*musique*) fanfare.
fanfaron, ~ne /fɑ̃farɔ̃, -ɔn/ *a.* boastful. —*n.m., f.* boaster.
fanion /fanjɔ̃/ *n.m.* pennant.
fantaisie /fɑ̃tezi/ *n.f.* imagination, fantasy; (*caprice*) whim. **(de) ~,** (*boutons etc.*) fancy.
fantaisiste /fɑ̃tezist/ *a.* unorthodox.
fantasme /fɑ̃tasm/ *n.m.* fantasy.
fantasque /fɑ̃task/ *a.* whimsical.
fantastique /fɑ̃tastik/ *a.* fantastic.
fantoche /fɑ̃tɔʃ/ *a.* puppet.
fantôme /fɑ̃tom/ *n.m.* ghost. —*a.* (*péj.*) bogus.
faon /fɑ̃/ *n.m.* fawn.

faramineux, **~se** /faraminø, -z/ a. astronomical.

farce[1] /fars/ n.f. (practical) joke; (théâtre) farce. **~eur**, **~euse** n.m., f. joker.

farce[2] /fars/ n.f. (hachis) stuffing. **~ir** v.t. stuff.

fard /far/ n.m. make-up. **piquer un ~,** blush. **~er** /-de/ v.t., **se ~er** v. pr. make up.

fardeau (pl. **~x**) /fardo/ n.m. burden.

farfelu, **~e** /farfəly/ a. & n.m., f. eccentric.

farine /farin/ n.f. flour. **~eux**, **~euse** a. floury. **les ~eux** n.m. pl. starchy food.

farouche /faruʃ/ a. shy; (peu sociable) unsociable; (violent) fierce. **~ment** adv. fiercely.

fascicule /fasikyl/ n.m. volume.

fascin|er /fasine/ v.t. fascinate. **~ation** n.f. fascination.

fascis|te /faʃist/ a. & n.m./f. fascist. **~me** n.m. fascism.

fasse /fas/ voir **faire**.

faste /fast/ n.m. splendour.

fast-food /fastfud/ n.m. fast-food place.

fastidieu|x, **~se** /fastidjø, -z/ a. tedious.

fat|al (m. pl. **~als**) /fatal/ a. inevitable; (mortel) fatal. **~alement** adv. inevitably. **~alité** n.f. (destin) fate.

fataliste /fatalist/ n.m./f. fatalist.

fatidique /fatidik/ a. fateful.

fatigant, **~e** /fatigã, -t/ a. tiring; (ennuyeux) tiresome.

fatigue /fatig/ n.f. fatigue, tiredness.

fatigu|er /fatige/ v.t. tire; (yeux, moteur) strain. —v.i. (moteur) labour. **se ~er** v. pr. get tired, tire (**de**, of). **~é** a. tired.

fatras /fatra/ n.m. jumble.

faubourg /fobur/ n.m. suburb.

fauché /foʃe/ a. (fam.) broke.

fauch|er /foʃe/ v.t. (herbe) mow; (voler: fam.) pinch. **~ qn.,** (véhicule, tir) mow s.o. down.

faucille /fosij/ n.f. sickle.

faucon /fokõ/ n.m. falcon, hawk.

faudra, **faudrait** /fodra, fodrɛ/ voir **falloir**.

faufiler (se) /(sə)fofile/ v. pr. edge one's way.

faune /fon/ n.f. wildlife, fauna.

faussaire /fosɛr/ n.m. forger.

fausse /fos/ voir **faux**[2].

faussement /fosmã/ adv. falsely, wrongly.

fausser /fose/ v.t. buckle; (fig.) distort. **~ compagnie à,** sneak away from.

fausseté /foste/ n.f. falseness.

faut /fo/ voir **falloir**.

faute /fot/ n.f. mistake; (responsabilité) fault; (délit) offence; (péché) sin. **en ~,** at fault. **~ de,** for want of. **~ de quoi,** failing which. **sans faute,** without fail, without failing. **~ de frappe,** typing error. **~ de goût,** bad taste. **~ professionelle,** professional misconduct.

fauteuil /fotœj/ n.m. armchair; (de président) chair; (théâtre) seat. **~ roulant,** wheelchair.

fauti|f, **~ve** /fotif, -v/ a. guilty; (faux) faulty. —n.m., f. guilty party.

fauve /fov/ a. (couleur) fawn. —n.m. wild cat.

faux[1] /fo/ n.f. scythe.

faux[2], **fausse** /fo, fos/ a. false; (falsifié) fake, forged; (numéro, calcul) wrong; (voix) out of tune. **c'est ~!,** that is wrong! **~ témoignage,** perjury. **faire ~ bond à qn.,** stand s.o. up. —adv. (chanter) out of tune. —n.m. forgery. **fausse alerte,** false alarm. **fausse couche,** miscarriage. **~-filet** n.m. sirloin. **~ frais,** n.m. pl. incidental expenses. **~-monnayeur** n.m. forger.

faveur /favœr/ n.f. favour. **de ~,** (régime) preferential. **en ~ de,** in favour of.

favorable /favorabl/ a. favourable.

favori, **~te** /favori, -t/ a. & n.m., f. favourite. **~tisme** n.m. favouritism.

favoriser /favorize/ v.t. favour.

fax /faks/ n.m. fax. **~er** v.t. fax.

fébrile /febril/ a. feverish.

fécond, **~e** /fekõ, -d/ a. fertile. **~er** /-de/ v.t. fertilize. **~ité** /-dite/ n.f. fertility.

fédér|al (m. pl. **~aux**) /federal, -o/ a. federal.

fédération /federasjõ/ n.f. federation.

fée /fe/ n.f. fairy.

féer|ie /fe(e)ri/ n.f. magical spectacle. **~ique** a. magical.

feindre† /fɛ̃dr/ v.t. feign. **~ de,** pretend to.

feinte /fɛ̃t/ n.f. feint.

fêler /fele/ v.t., **se ~** v. pr. crack.

félicit|er /felisite/ v.t. congratulate (**de**, on). **~ations** n.f. pl. congratulations (**pour**, on).

félin, **~e** /felɛ̃, -in/ a. & n.m. feline.

fêlure /felyr/ n.f. crack.

femelle /famɛl/ a. & n.f. female.

fémin|in, **~ine** /feminɛ̃, -in/ a. feminine; (sexe) female; (mode, équipe) women's. —n.m. feminine. **~ité** n.f. femininity.

féministe /feminist/ n.m./f. feminist.

femme /fam/ *n.f.* woman; (*épouse*) wife. **~ au foyer,** housewife. **~ de chambre,** chambermaid. **~ de ménage,** cleaning lady.

fémur /femyr/ *n.m.* thigh-bone.

fendiller /fɑ̃dije/ *v.t.,* **se ~** *v. pr.* crack.

fendre /fɑ̃dr/ *v.t.* (*couper*) split; (*fissurer*) crack; (*foule*) push through. **se ~** *v. pr.* crack.

fenêtre /fɑnɛtr/ *n.f.* window.

fenouil /fɑnuj/ *n.m.* fennel.

fente /fɑ̃t/ *n.f.* (*ouverture*) slit, slot; (*fissure*) crack.

féod|al (*m. pl.* **~aux**) /feɔdal, -o/ *a.* feudal.

fer /fɛr/ *n.m.* iron. **~ (à repasser),** iron. **~ à cheval,** horseshoe. **~-blanc** (*pl.* **~s-blancs**) *n.m.* tinplate. **~ de lance,** spearhead. **~ forgé,** wrought iron.

fera, ferait /fɑra, fɑrɛ/ *voir* **faire.**

férié /ferje/ *a.* **jour ~,** public holiday.

ferme[1] /fɛrm/ *a.* firm. —*adv.* (*travailler*) hard. **~ment** /-əmɑ̃/ *adv.* firmly.

ferme[2] /fɛrm/ *n.f.* farm; (*maison*) farm(house).

fermé /fɛrme/ *a.* closed; (*gaz, radio, etc.*) off.

ferment /fɛrmɑ̃/ *n.m.* ferment.

ferment|er /fɛrmɑ̃te/ *v.i.* ferment. **~ation** *n.f.* fermentation.

fermer /fɛrme/ *v.t./i.* close, shut; (*cesser d'exploiter*) close *ou* shut down; (*gaz, robinet*) turn off. **se ~** *v. pr.* close, shut.

fermeté /fɛrməte/ *n.f.* firmness.

fermeture /fɛrmətyr/ *n.f.* closing; (*dispositif*) catch. **~ annuelle,** annual closure. **~ éclair,** (P.) zip(-fastener); (*Amer.*) zipper.

ferm|ier, ~ière /fɛrmje, -jɛr/ *n.m.* farmer. —*n.f.* farmer's wife. —*a.* farm.

fermoir /fɛrmwar/ *n.m.* clasp.

féroc|e /ferɔs/ *a.* ferocious. **~ité** *n.f.* ferocity.

ferraille /fɛraj/ *n.f.* scrap-iron.

ferré /fɛre/ *a.* (*canne*) steel-tipped.

ferrer /fɛre/ *v.t.* (*cheval*) shoe.

ferronnerie /fɛrɔnri/ *n.f.* ironwork.

ferroviaire /fɛrɔvjɛr/ *a.* rail(way).

ferry(-boat) /fɛri(bot)/ *n.m.* ferry.

fertil|e /fɛrtil/ *a.* fertile. **~e en,** (*fig.*) rich in. **~iser** *v.t.* fertilize. **~ité** *n.f.* fertility.

féru, ~e /fery/ *a.* **~ de,** passionate about.

ferv|ent, ~ente /fɛrvɑ̃, -t/ *a.* fervent. —*n.m., f.* enthusiast (**de,** of). **~eur** *n.f.* fervour.

fesse /fɛs/ *n.f.* buttock.

fessée /fese/ *n.f.* spanking.

festin /fɛstɛ̃/ *n.m.* feast.

festival (*pl.* **~s**) /fɛstival/ *n.m.* festival.

festivités /fɛstivite/ *n.f. pl.* festivities.

festoyer /fɛstwaje/ *v.i.* feast.

fêtard /fɛtar/ *n.m.* merry-maker.

fête /fɛt/ *n.f.* holiday; (*religieuse*) feast; (*du nom*) name-day; (*réception*) party; (*en famille*) celebration; (*foire*) fair; (*folklorique*) festival. **~ des Mères,** Mother's Day. **~ foraine,** fun-fair. **faire la ~,** make merry. **les ~s (de fin d'année),** the Christmas season.

fêter /fete/ *v.t.* celebrate; (*personne*) give a celebration for.

fétiche /fetiʃ/ *n.m.* fetish; (*fig.*) mascot.

fétide /fetid/ *a.* fetid.

feu[1] (*pl.* **~x**) /fø/ *n.m.* fire; (*lumière*) light; (*de réchaud*) burner. **~x (rouges),** (traffic) lights. **à ~ doux/vif,** on a low/ high heat. **du ~,** (*pour cigarette*) a light. **au ~!,** fire! **~ d'artifice,** firework display. **~ de joie,** bonfire. **~ rouge/vert/orange,** red/green/amber *ou* yellow (*Amer.*). **~ de position,** sidelight. **mettre le ~ à,** set fire to. **prendre ~,** catch fire. **jouer avec le ~,** play with fire. **ne pas faire long ~,** not last.

feuillage /fœjaʒ/ *n.m.* foliage.

feuille /fœj/ *n.f.* leaf; (*de papier, bois, etc.*) sheet; (*formulaire*) form.

feuillet /fœjɛ/ *n.m.* leaf.

feuilleter /fœjte/ *v.t.* leaf through.

feuilleton /fœjtɔ̃/ *n.m.* (*à suivre*) serial; (*histoire complète*) series.

feuillu /fœjy/ *a.* leafy.

feutre /føtr/ *n.m.* felt; (*chapeau*) felt hat; (*crayon*) felt-tip (pen).

feutré /føtre/ *a.* (*bruit*) muffled.

fève /fɛv/ *n.f.* broad bean.

février /fevrije/ *n.m.* February.

fiable /fjabl/ *a.* reliable.

fiançailles /fjɑ̃saj/ *n.f. pl.* engagement.

fianc|er (se) /(sə)fjɑ̃se/ *v. pr.* become engaged (**avec,** to). **~é,** **~ée** *a.* engaged; *n.m.* fiancé; *n.f.* fiancée.

fiasco /fjasko/ *n.m.* fiasco.

fibre /fibr/ *n.f.* fibre. **~ de verre,** fibreglass.

ficeler /fisle/ *v.t.* tie up.

ficelle /fisɛl/ *n.f.* string.

fiche /fiʃ/ *n.f.* (index) card; (*formulaire*) form, slip; (*électr.*) plug.

ficher[1] /fiʃe/ *v.t.* (*enfoncer*) drive (**dans,** into).

ficher[2] /fiʃe/ *v.t.* (*faire: fam.*) do; (*donner: fam.*) give; (*mettre: fam.*) put. **se ~ de,** (*fam.*) make fun of. **~ le**

camp, (*fam.*) clear off. **il s'en fiche,** (*fam.*) he couldn't care less.

fichier /fiʃje/ *n.m.* file.

fichu /fiʃy/ *a.* (*mauvais: fam.*) rotten; (*raté: fam.*) done for. **mal ~,** (*fam.*) terrible.

ficti|f, ~ve /fiktif, -v/ *a.* fictitious.

fiction /fiksjɔ̃/ *n.f.* fiction.

fidèle /fidɛl/ *a.* faithful. —*n.m./f.* (*client*) regular; (*relig.*) believer. **~s,** (*à l'église*) congregation. **~ment** *adv.* faithfully.

fidélité /fidelite/ *n.f.* fidelity.

fier¹, fière /fjɛr/ *a.* proud (**de,** of). **fièrement** *adv.* proudly. **~té** *n.f.* pride.

fier² (se) /(sə)fje/ *v. pr.* **se ~ à,** trust.

fièvre /fjɛvr/ *n.f.* fever.

fiévreu|x, ~se /fjevrø, -z/ *a.* feverish.

figé /fiʒe/ *a.* fixed, set; (*manières*) stiff.

figer /fiʒe/ *v.t./i.,* **se ~** *v. pr.* congeal. **~ sur place,** petrify.

fignoler /fiɲɔle/ *v.t.* refine (upon), finish off meticulously.

figu|e /fig/ *n.f.* fig. **~ier** *n.m.* fig-tree.

figurant, ~e /figyrɑ̃, -t/ *n.m., f.* (*cinéma*) extra.

figure /figyr/ *n.f.* face; (*forme, personnage*) figure; (*illustration*) picture.

figuré /figyre/ *a.* (*sens*) figurative. **au ~,** figuratively.

figurer /figyre/ *v.i.* appear. —*v.t.* represent. **se ~** *v. pr.* imagine.

fil /fil/ *n.m.* thread; (*métallique, électrique*) wire; (*de couteau*) edge; (*à coudre*) cotton. **au ~ de,** with the passing of. **au ~ de l'eau,** with the current. **~ de fer,** wire. **au bout du ~,** on the phone.

filament /filamɑ̃/ *n.m.* filament.

filature /filatyr/ *n.f.* (*textile*) mill; (*surveillance*) shadowing.

file /fil/ *n.f.* line; (*voie: auto.*) lane. **~ (d'attente),** queue; (*Amer.*) line. **en ~ indienne,** in single file. **se mettre en ~,** line up.

filer /file/ *v.t.* spin; (*suivre*) shadow. **~ qch. à qn.,** (*fam.*) slip s.o. sth. —*v.i.* (*bas*) ladder, run; (*liquide*) run; (*aller vite: fam.*) speed along, fly by; (*partir: fam.*) dash off. **~ doux,** do as one's told. **~ à l'anglaise,** take French leave.

filet /filɛ/ *n.m.* net; (*d'eau*) trickle; (*de viande*) fillet. **~ (à bagages),** (luggage) rack. **~ à provisions,** string bag (*for shopping*).

fil|ial, ~iale (*m. pl.* **~iaux**) /filjal, -jo/ *a.* filial. —*n.f.* subsidiary (company).

filière /filjɛr/ *n.f.* (official) channels; (*de*

trafiquants) network. **passer par** *ou* **suivre la ~,** (*employé*) work one's way up.

filigrane /filigran/ *n.m.* watermark. **en ~,** between the lines.

filin /filɛ̃/ *n.m.* rope.

fille /fij/ *n.f.* girl; (*opposé à fils*) daughter. **~-mère** (*pl.* **~s-mères**) *n.f.* (*péj.*) unmarried mother.

fillette /fijɛt/ *n.f.* little girl.

filleul /fijœl/ *n.m.* godson. **~e** *n.f.* god-daughter.

film /film/ *n.m.* film. **~ d'épouvante/ muet/parlant,** horror/silent/talking film. **~ dramatique,** drama. **~er** *v.t.* film.

filon /filɔ̃/ *n.m.* (*géol.*) seam; (*situation*) source of wealth.

filou /filu/ *n.m.* crook.

fils /fis/ *n.m.* son.

filtr|e /filtr/ *n.m.* filter. **~er** *v.t./i.* filter; (*personne*) screen.

fin¹ /fɛ̃/ *n.f.* end. **à la ~,** finally. **en ~ de compte,** all things considered. **~ de semaine,** weekend. **mettre ~ à,** put an end to. **prendre ~,** come to an end.

fin², fine /fɛ̃, fin/ *a.* fine; (*tranche, couche*) thin; (*taille*) slim; (*plat*) exquisite; (*esprit, vue*) sharp. —*adv.* (*couper*) finely. **~es herbes,** herbs.

fin|al, ~ale (*m. pl.* **~aux** *ou* **~als**) /final, -o/ *a.* final. —*n.f.* (*sport*) final; (*gram.*) final syllable. —*n.m.* (*pl.* **~aux** *ou* **~als**) (*mus.*) finale. **~alement** *adv.* finally; (*somme toute*) after all.

finaliste /finalist/ *n.m./f.* finalist.

financ|e /finɑ̃s/ *n.f.* finance. **~er** *v.t.* finance. **~ier, ~ière** *a.* financial; *n.m.* financier.

finesse /finɛs/ *n.f.* fineness; (*de taille*) slimness; (*acuité*) sharpness. **~s,** (*de langue*) niceties.

fini /fini/ *a.* finished; (*espace*) finite. —*n.m.* finish.

finir /finir/ *v.t./i.* finish, end; (*arrêter*) stop; (*manger*) finish (up). **en ~ avec,** have done with. **~ par faire,** end up doing. **ça va mal ~,** it will turn out badly.

finition /finisjɔ̃/ *n.f.* finish.

finlandais, ~e /fɛ̃lɑ̃dɛ, -z/ *a.* Finnish. —*n.m., f.* Finn.

finlande /fɛ̃lɑ̃d/ *n.f.* Finland.

finnois, ~e /finwa, -z/ *a.* Finnish. —*n.m.* (*lang.*) Finnish.

fiole /fjɔl/ *n.f.* phial.

firme /firm/ *n.f.* firm.

fisc /fisk/ *n.m.* tax authorities. **~al** (*m. pl.*

~aux) a. tax, fiscal. ~alité n.f. tax system.

fission /fisjɔ̃/ n.f. fission.

fissur|e /fisyr/ n.f. crack. ~er v.t., se ~er v. pr. crack.

fiston /fistɔ̃/ n.m. (fam.) son.

fixation /fiksasjɔ̃/ n.f. fixing; (complexe) fixation.

fixe /fiks/ a. fixed; (stable) steady. à heure ~, at a set time. menu à prix ~, set menu.

fix|er /fikse/ v.t. fix. ~er (du regard), stare at. se ~er v. pr. (s'installer) settle down. être ~é, (personne) have made up one's mind.

flacon /flakɔ̃/ n.m. bottle.

flageolet /flaʒɔlɛ/ n.m. (haricot) (dwarf) kidney bean.

flagrant, ~e /flagrɑ̃, -t/ a. flagrant. en ~ délit, in the act.

flair /flɛr/ n.m. (sense of) smell; (fig.) intuition. ~er /flere/ v.t. sniff at; (fig.) sense.

flamand, ~e /flamɑ̃, -d/ a. Flemish. —n.m. (lang.) Flemish. —n.m., f. Fleming.

flamant /flamɑ̃/ n.m. flamingo.

flambant /flɑ̃bɑ̃/ adv. ~ neuf, brand-new.

flambé, ~e /flɑ̃be/ a. (culin.) flambé.

flambeau (pl. ~x) /flɑ̃bo/ n.m. torch.

flambée /flɑ̃be/ n.f. blaze; (fig.) explosion.

flamber /flɑ̃be/ v.i. blaze; (prix) shoot up. —v.t. (aiguille) sterilize; (volaille) singe.

flamboyer /flɑ̃bwaje/ v.i. blaze.

flamme /flam/ n.f. flame; (fig.) ardour. en ~s, ablaze.

flan /flɑ̃/ n.m. custard-pie.

flanc /flɑ̃/ n.m. side; (d'animal, d'armée) flank.

flancher /flɑ̃ʃe/ v.i. (fam.) give in.

Flandre(s) /flɑ̃dr/ n.f. (pl.) Flanders.

flanelle /flanɛl/ n.f. flannel.

flân|er /flɑne/ v.i. stroll. ~erie n.f. stroll.

flanquer /flɑ̃ke/ v.t. flank; (jeter: fam.) chuck; (donner: fam.) give. ~ à la porte, kick out.

flaque /flak/ n.f. (d'eau) puddle; (de sang) pool.

flash (pl. ~es) /flaʃ/ n.m. (photo.) flash; (information) news flash.

flasque /flask/ a. flabby.

flatt|er /flate/ v.t. flatter. se ~er de, pride o.s. on. ~erie n.f. flattery. ~eur, ~euse a. flattering; n.m., f. flatterer.

fléau (pl. ~x) /fleo/ n.m. (désastre) scourge; (personne) bane.

flèche /flɛʃ/ n.f. arrow; (de clocher) spire. monter en ~, spiral. partir en ~, shoot off.

flècher /fleʃe/ v.t. mark ou signpost (with arrows).

fléchette /fleʃɛt/ n.f. dart.

fléchir /fleʃir/ v.t. bend; (personne) move. —v.i. (faiblir) weaken; (poutre) sag, bend.

flegmatique /flɛgmatik/ a. phlegmatic.

flemm|e /flɛm/ n.f. (fam.) laziness. j'ai la ~e de faire, I can't be bothered doing. ~ard, ~arde a. (fam.) lazy; n.m., f. (fam.) lazy-bones.

flétrir /fletrir/ v.t., se ~ v. pr. wither.

fleur /flœr/ n.f. flower. à ~ de terre/d'eau, just above the ground/water. à ~s, flowery. ~ de l'âge, prime of life. en ~s, in flower.

fleur|ir /flœrir/ v.i. flower; (arbre) blossom; (fig.) flourish. —v.t. adorn with flowers. ~i a. flowery.

fleuriste /flœrist/ n.m./f. florist.

fleuve /flœv/ n.m. river.

flexible /flɛksibl/ a. flexible.

flexion /flɛksjɔ̃/ n.f. (anat.) flexing.

flic /flik/ n.m. (fam.) cop.

flipper /flipœr/ n.m. pinball (machine).

flirter /flœrte/ v.i. flirt.

flocon /flɔkɔ̃/ n.m. flake.

flopée /flɔpe/ n.f. (fam.) une ~ de, masses of.

floraison /flɔrɛzɔ̃/ n.f. flowering.

flore /flɔr/ n.f. flora.

florissant, ~e /flɔrisɑ̃, -t/ a. flourishing.

flot /flo/ n.m. flood, stream. être à ~, be afloat. les ~s, the waves.

flottant, ~e /flɔtɑ̃, -t/ a. (vêtement) loose; (indécis) indecisive.

flotte /flɔt/ n.f. fleet; (pluie: fam.) rain; (eau: fam.) water.

flottement /flɔtmɑ̃/ n.m. (incertitude) indecision.

flott|er /flɔte/ v.i. float; (drapeau) flutter; (nuage, parfum, pensées) drift; (pleuvoir: fam.) rain. ~eur n.m. float.

flou /flu/ a. out of focus; (fig.) vague.

fluct|uer /flyktɥe/ v.i. fluctuate. ~uation n.f. fluctuation.

fluet, ~te /flyɛ, -t/ a. thin.

fluid|e /flɥid/ a. & n.m. fluid. ~ité n.f. fluidity.

fluor /flyɔr/ n.m. (pour les dents) fluoride.

fluorescent, ~e /flyɔresɑ̃, -t/ a. fluorescent.

flût|e /flyt/ n.f. flute; (verre) champagne

glass. **~iste** *n.m./f.* flautist; (*Amer.*) flutist.

fluv|ial (*m. pl.* **~iaux**) /flyvjal, -jo/ *a.* river.

flux /fly/ *n.m.* flow. **~ et reflux,** ebb and flow.

FM /ɛfɛm/ *abrév. f.* FM.

foc /fɔk/ *n.m.* jib.

fœtus /fetys/ *n.m.* foetus.

foi /fwa/ *n.f.* faith. **être de bonne/mauvaise ~,** be acting in good/bad faith. **ma ~!,** well (indeed)! **digne de ~,** reliable.

foie /fwa/ *n.m.* liver. **~ gras,** foie gras.

foin /fwɛ̃/ *n.m.* hay. **faire tout un ~,** (*fam.*) make a fuss.

foire /fwar/ *n.f.* fair. **faire la ~,** (*fam.*) make merry.

fois /fwa/ *n.f.* time. **une ~,** once. **deux ~,** twice. **à la ~,** at the same time. **des ~,** (*parfois*) sometimes. **une ~ pour toutes,** once and for all.

foison /fwazɔ̃/ *n.f.* abundance. **à ~,** in abundance. **~ner** /-ɔne/ *v.i.* abound (**de,** in).

fol /fɔl/ *voir* **fou.**

folâtrer /fɔlɑtre/ *v.i.* frolic.

folichon, ~ne /fɔliʃɔ̃, -ɔn/ *a.* **pas ~,** (*fam.*) not much fun.

folie /fɔli/ *n.f.* madness; (*bêtise*) foolish thing, folly.

folklor|e /fɔlklɔr/ *n.m.* folklore. **~ique** *a.* folk; (*fam.*) picturesque.

folle /fɔl/ *voir* **fou.**

follement /fɔlmɑ̃/ *adv.* madly.

fomenter /fɔmɑ̃te/ *v.t.* foment.

fonc|er[1] /fɔ̃se/ *v.t./i.* darken. **~é** *a.* dark.

foncer[2] /fɔ̃se/ *v.i.* (*fam.*) dash along. **~ sur,** (*fam.*) charge at.

fonc|ier, ~ière /fɔ̃sje, -jɛr/ *a.* fundamental; (*comm.*) real estate. **~ièrement** *adv.* fundamentally.

fonction /fɔ̃ksjɔ̃/ *n.f.* function; (*emploi*) position. **~s,** (*obligations*) duties. **en ~ de,** according to. **~ publique,** civil service. **voiture de ~,** company car.

fonctionnaire /fɔ̃ksjɔnɛr/ *n.m./f.* civil servant.

fonctionnel, ~le /fɔ̃ksjɔnɛl/ *a.* functional.

fonctionn|er /fɔ̃ksjɔne/ *v.i.* work. **faire ~er,** work. **~ement** *n.m.* working.

fond /fɔ̃/ *n.m.* bottom; (*de salle, magasin, etc.*) back; (*essentiel*) basis; (*contenu*) content; (*plan*) background. **à ~,** thoroughly. **au ~,** basically. **de ~,** (*bruit*) background; (*sport*) long-distance. **de ~ en comble,** from top to bottom. **au** *ou* **dans le ~,** really.

fondament|al (*m. pl.* **~aux**) /fɔ̃damɑ̃tal, -o/ *a.* fundamental.

fondation /fɔ̃dasjɔ̃/ *n.f.* foundation.

fond|er /fɔ̃de/ *v.t.* found; (*baser*) base (**sur,** on). **(bien) ~é,** well-founded. **~é à,** justified in. **se ~er sur,** be guided by, place one's reliance on. **~ateur, ~atrice** *n.m., f.* founder.

fonderie /fɔ̃dri/ *n.f.* foundry.

fondre /fɔ̃dr/ *v.t./i.* melt; (*dans l'eau*) dissolve; (*mélanger*) merge. **se ~** *v. pr.* merge. **faire ~,** melt; dissolve. **~ en larmes,** burst into tears. **~ sur,** swoop on.

fondrière /fɔ̃drijɛr/ *n.f.* pot-hole.

fonds /fɔ̃/ *n.m.* fund. —*n.m. pl.* (*capitaux*) funds. **~ de commerce,** business.

fondu /fɔ̃dy/ *a.* melted; (*métal*) molten.

font /fɔ̃/ *voir* **faire.**

fontaine /fɔ̃tɛn/ *n.f.* fountain; (*source*) spring.

fonte /fɔ̃t/ *n.f.* melting; (*fer*) cast iron. **~ des neiges,** thaw.

foot /fut/ *n.m.* (*fam.*) football.

football /futbol/ *n.m.* football. **~eur** *n.m.* footballer.

footing /futiŋ/ *n.m.* fast walking.

forage /fɔraʒ/ *n.m.* drilling.

forain /fɔrɛ̃/ *n.m.* fairground entertainer. **(marchand) ~,** stall-holder (*at a fair or market*).

forçat /fɔrsa/ *n.m.* convict.

force /fɔrs/ *n.f.* force; (*physique*) strength; (*hydraulique etc.*) power. **~s,** (*physiques*) strength. **à ~ de,** by sheer force of. **de ~, par la ~,** by force. **~ de dissuasion,** deterrent. **~ de frappe,** strike force, deterrent. **~ de l'âge,** prime of life. **~s de l'ordre,** police (force).

forcé /fɔrse/ *a.* forced; (*inévitable*) inevitable.

forcément /fɔrsemɑ̃/ *adv.* necessarily; (*évidemment*) obviously.

forcené, ~e /fɔrsəne/ *a.* frenzied. —*n.m., f.* maniac.

forceps /fɔrsɛps/ *n.m.* forceps.

forcer /fɔrse/ *v.t.* force (**à faire,** to do); (*voix*) strain. —*v.i.* (*exagérer*) overdo it. **se ~** *v. pr.* force o.s.

forcir /fɔrsir/ *v.i.* fill out.

forer /fɔre/ *v.t.* drill.

forest|ier, ~ière /fɔrɛstje, -jɛr/ *a.* forest.

foret /fɔrɛ/ *n.m.* drill.

forêt /fɔrɛ/ *n.f.* forest.

forfait /fɔrfɛ/ *n.m.* (*comm.*) inclusive price. **~aire** /-tɛr/ *a.* (*prix*) inclusive.

forge /fɔrʒ/ *n.f.* forge.
forger /fɔrʒe/ *v.t.* forge; (*inventer*) make up.
forgeron /fɔrʒərɔ̃/ *n.m.* blacksmith.
formaliser (se) /(sə)fɔrmalize/ *v. pr.* take offence (**de,** at).
formalité /fɔrmalite/ *n.f.* formality.
format /fɔrma/ *n.m.* format.
formater /fɔrmate/ *v.t.* (*comput.*) format.
formation /fɔrmasjɔ̃/ *n.f.* formation; (*de médecin etc.*) training; (*culture*) education. **~ permanente** *ou* **continue,** continuing education. **~ professionnelle,** professional training.
forme /fɔrm/ *n.f.* form; (*contour*) shape, form. **~s,** (*de femme*) figure. **en ~,** (*sport*) in good shape, on form. **en ~ de,** in the shape of. **en bonne et due ~,** in due form.
formel, ~le /fɔrmɛl/ *a.* formal; (*catégorique*) positive. **~lement** *adv.* positively.
former /fɔrme/ *v.t.* form; (*instruire*) train. **se ~** *v. pr.* form.
formidable /fɔrmidabl/ *a.* fantastic.
formulaire /fɔrmylɛr/ *n.m.* form.
formul|e /fɔrmyl/ *n.f.* formula; (*expression*) expression; (*feuille*) form. **~e de politesse,** polite phrase, letter ending. **~er** *v.t.* formulate.
fort¹, ~e /fɔr, -t/ *a.* strong; (*grand*) big; (*pluie*) heavy; (*bruit*) loud; (*pente*) steep; (*élève*) clever. —*adv.* (*frapper*) hard; (*parler*) loud; (*très*) very; (*beaucoup*) very much. —*n.m.* strong point. **au plus ~ de,** at the height of. **c'est une ~e tête,** she/he's headstrong.
fort² /fɔr/ *n.m.* (*mil.*) fort.
forteresse /fɔrtərɛs/ *n.f.* fortress.
fortifiant /fɔrtifjɑ̃/ *n.m.* tonic.
fortif|ier /fɔrtifje/ *v.t.* fortify. **~ication** *n.f.* fortification.
fortiori /fɔrsjɔri/ **a ~,** even more so.
fortuit, ~e /fɔrtɥi, -t/ *a.* fortuitous.
fortune /fɔrtyn/ *n.f.* fortune. **de ~,** (*improvisé*) makeshift. **faire ~,** make one's fortune.
fortuné /fɔrtyne/ *a.* wealthy.
fosse /fos/ *n.f.* pit; (*tombe*) grave. **~ d'aisances,** cesspool. **~ d'orchestre,** orchestral pit. **~ septique,** septic tank.
fossé /fose/ *n.m.* ditch; (*fig.*) gulf.
fossette /fosɛt/ *n.f.* dimple.
fossile /fosil/ *n.m.* fossil.
fossoyeur /foswajœr/ *n.m.* gravedigger.
fou *ou* **fol*, folle** /fu, fɔl/ *a.* mad; (*course, regard*) wild; (*énorme: fam.*) tremendous. **~ de,** crazy about. —*n.m.*

madman; (*bouffon*) jester. —*n.f.* madwoman; (*fam.*) gay. **le ~ rire,** the giggles.
foudre /fudr/ *n.f.* lightning.
foudroy|er /fudrwaje/ *v.t.* strike by lightning; (*maladie etc.*) strike down; (*atterrer*) stagger. **~ant, ~ante** *a.* staggering; (*mort, maladie*) violent.
fouet /fwɛ/ *n.m.* whip; (*culin.*) whisk.
fouetter /fwete/ *v.t.* whip; (*crème etc.*) whisk.
fougère /fuʒɛr/ *n.f.* fern.
fougu|e /fug/ *n.f.* ardour. **~eux, ~euse** *a.* ardent.
fouill|e /fuj/ *n.f.* search; (*archéol.*) excavation. **~er** *v.t./i.* search; (*creuser*) dig. **~er dans,** (*tiroir*) rummage through.
fouillis /fuji/ *n.m.* jumble.
fouine /fwin/ *n.f.* beech-marten.
fouiner /fwine/ *v.i.* nose about.
foulard /fular/ *n.m.* scarf.
foule /ful/ *n.f.* crowd. **une ~ de,** (*fig.*) a mass of.
foulée /fule/ *n.f.* stride. **il l'a fait dans la ~,** he did it while he was at it.
fouler /fule/ *v.t.* press; (*sol*) tread. **se ~ le poignet/le pied** sprain one's wrist/foot. **ne pas se ~,** (*fam.*) not strain o.s.
foulure /fulyr/ *n.f.* sprain.
four /fur/ *n.m.* oven; (*de potier*) kiln; (*théâtre*) flop. **~ à micro-ondes,** microwave oven. **~ crématoire,** crematorium.
fourbe /furb/ *a.* deceitful.
fourbu /furby/ *a.* exhausted.
fourche /furʃ/ *n.f.* fork; (*à foin*) pitchfork.
fourchette /furʃɛt/ *n.f.* fork; (*comm.*) margin.
fourchu /furʃy/ *a.* forked.
fourgon /furgɔ̃/ *n.m.* van; (*wagon*) wagon. **~ mortuaire,** hearse.
fourgonnette /furgɔnɛt/ *n.f.* (small) van.
fourmi /furmi/ *n.f.* ant. **avoir des ~s,** have pins and needles.
fourmiller /furmije/ *v.i.* swarm (**de,** with).
fournaise /furnɛz/ *n.f.* (*feu, endroit*) furnace.
fourneau (*pl.* **~x**) /furno/ *n.m.* stove.
fournée /furne/ *n.f.* batch.
fourni /furni/ *a.* (*épais*) thick.
fourn|ir /furnir/ *v.t.* supply, provide; (*client*) supply; (*effort*) put in. **~ir à qn.,** supply s.o. with. **se ~ir chez,** shop at. **~isseur** *n.m.* supplier. **~iture** *n.f.* supply.

fourrage /furaʒ/ n.m. fodder.
fourré¹ /fure/ n.m. thicket.
fourré² /fure/ a. (*vêtement*) fur-lined; (*gâteau etc.*) filled (*with jam, cream, etc.*).
fourreau (pl. ~x) /furo/ n.m. sheath.
fourr|er /fure/ v.t. (*mettre: fam.*) stick. ~e-tout n.m. invar. (*sac*) holdall.
fourreur /furœr/ n.m. furrier.
fourrière /furjɛr/ n.f. (*lieu*) pound.
fourrure /furyr/ n.f. fur.
fourvoyer (se) /(sə)furvwaje/ v. pr. go astray.
foutaise /futɛz/ n.f. (*argot*) rubbish.
foutre /futr/ v.t. (*argot*) = **ficher²**.
foutu, ~e /futy/ a. (*argot*) = **fichu**.
foyer /fwaje/ n.m. home; (*âtre*) hearth; (*club*) club; (*d'étudiants*) hostel; (*théâtre*) foyer; (*photo.*) focus; (*centre*) centre.
fracas /fraka/ n.m. din; (*de train*) roar; (*d'objet qui tombe*) crash.
fracass|er /frakase/ v.t., **se** ~**er** v. pr. smash. ~**ant**, ~**ante** a. (*bruyant, violent*) shattering.
fraction /fraksjɔ̃/ n.f. fraction. ~**ner** /-jone/ v.t., **se** ~**ner** v. pr. split (up).
fractur|e /fraktyr/ n.f. fracture. ~**er** v.t. (*os*) fracture; (*porte etc.*) break open.
fragil|e /fraʒil/ a. fragile. ~**ité** n.f. fragility.
fragment /fragmã/ n.m. bit, fragment. ~**aire** /-tɛr/ a. fragmentary. ~**er** /-te/ v.t. split, fragment.
fraîche /frɛʃ/ *voir* **frais¹**.
fraîchement /frɛʃmã/ adv. (*récemment*) freshly; (*avec froideur*) coolly.
fraîcheur /frɛʃœr/ n.f. coolness; (*nouveauté*) freshness.
fraîchir /freʃir/ v.i. freshen.
frais¹, fraîche /frɛ, -ʃ/ a. fresh; (*temps, accueil*) cool; (*peinture*) wet. —adv. (*récemment*) newly. —n.m. **mettre au** ~, put in a cool place. **prendre le** ~, take a breath of cool air. ~ **et dispos**, fresh. **il fait** ~, it is cool.
frais² /frɛ/ n.m. pl. expenses; (*droits*) fees. ~ **généraux**, (*comm.*) overheads, running expenses. ~ **de scolarité**, school fees.
frais|e /frɛz/ n.f. strawberry. ~**ier** n.m. strawberry plant.
frambois|e /frãbwaz/ n.f. raspberry. ~**ier** n.m. raspberry bush.
fran|c¹, ~**che** /frã, -ʃ/ a. frank; (*regard*) open; (*net*) clear; (*cassure*) clean; (*libre*) free; (*véritable*) downright. ~**c-maçon** (pl. ~**cs-maçons**) n.m. Freemason. ~**c-maçon-**

nerie n.f. Freemasonry. ~**-parler** n.m. inv. outspokenness.
franc² /frã/ n.m. franc.
français, ~**e** /frãsɛ, -z/ a. French. —n.m., f. Frenchman, Frenchwoman. —n.m. (*lang.*) French.
France /frãs/ n.f. France.
franche /frãʃ/ *voir* **franc¹**.
franchement /frãʃmã/ adv. frankly; (*nettement*) clearly; (*tout à fait*) really.
franchir /frãʃir/ v.t. (*obstacle*) get over; (*traverser*) cross; (*distance*) cover; (*limite*) exceed.
franchise /frãʃiz/ n.f. frankness; (*douanière*) exemption (from duties).
franco /frãko/ adv. postage paid.
franco- /frãko/ préf. Franco-.
francophone /frãkɔfɔn/ a. French-speaking. —n.m./f. French speaker.
frange /frãʒ/ n.f. fringe.
franquette (à la bonne) /(alabɔn)frãkɛt/ adv. informally.
frappant, ~**e** /frapã, -t/ a. striking.
frappe /frap/ n.f. (*de courrier etc.*) typing; (*de dactylo*) touch.
frappé, ~**e** /frape/ a. chilled.
frapp|er /frape/ v.t./i. strike; (*battre*) hit, strike; (*monnaie*) mint; (*à la porte*) knock, bang. ~**é de panique**, panic-stricken.
frasque /frask/ n.f. escapade.
fratern|el, ~**elle** /fratɛrnɛl/ a. brotherly. ~**iser** v.i. fraternize. ~**ité** n.f. brotherhood.
fraude /frod/ n.f. fraud; (*à un examen*) cheating.
frauder /frode/ v.t./i. cheat.
frauduleu|x, ~**se** /frodylø, -z/ a. fraudulent.
frayer /freje/ v.t. open up. **se** ~ **un passage**, force one's way (**dans**, through).
frayeur /frejœr/ n.f. fright.
fredonner /frədɔne/ v.t. hum.
free-lance /frilãs/ a. & n.m./f. freelance.
freezer /frizœr/ n.m. freezer.
frégate /fregat/ n.f. frigate.
frein /frɛ̃/ n.m. brake. **mettre un** ~ **à**, curb. ~ **à main**, hand brake.
frein|er /frene/ v.t. slow down; (*modérer, enrayer*) curb. —v.i. (*auto.*) brake. ~**age** /frenaʒ/ n.m. braking.
frelaté /frəlate/ a. adulterated.
frêle /frɛl/ a. frail.
frelon /frəlɔ̃/ n.m. hornet.
freluquet /frəlykɛ/ n.m. (*fam.*) weed.
frémir /fremir/ v.i. shudder, shake; (*feuille, eau*) quiver.
frêne /frɛn/ n.m. ash.

fréné|sie /frenezi/ *n.f.* frenzy. **~tique** *a.* frenzied.

fréqu|ent, ~ente /frekɑ̃, -t/ *a.* frequent. **~emment** /-amɑ̃/ *adv.* frequently. **~ence** *n.f.* frequency.

fréquenté /frekɑ̃te/ *a.* crowded.

fréquent|er /frekɑ̃te/ *v.t.* frequent; (*école*) attend; (*personne*) see. **~ation** *n.f.* frequenting. **~ations** *n.f. pl.* acquaintances.

frère /frɛr/ *n.m.* brother.

fresque /frɛsk/ *n.f.* fresco.

fret /frɛ/ *n.m.* freight.

frétiller /fretije/ *v.i.* wriggle.

fretin /frətɛ̃/ *n.m.* **menu ~,** small fry.

friable /frijabl/ *a.* crumbly.

friand, ~e /frijɑ̃, -d/ *a.* **~ de,** fond of.

friandise /frijɑ̃diz/ *n.f.* sweet; (*Amer.*) candy; (*gâteau*) cake.

fric /frik/ *n.m.* (*fam.*) money.

fricassée /frikase/ *n.f.* casserole.

friche (en) /(ɑ̃)friʃ/ *adv.* fallow. **être en ~,** lie fallow.

friction /friksjɔ̃/ *n.f.* friction; (*massage*) rub-down. **~ner** /-jɔne/ *v.t.* rub (down).

frigidaire /friʒidɛr/ *n.m.* (P.) refrigerator.

frigid|e /friʒid/ *a.* frigid. **~ité** *n.f.* frigidity.

frigo /frigo/ *n.m.* (*fam.*) fridge.

frigorif|ier /frigɔrifje/ *v.t.* refrigerate. **~ique** *a.* (*vitrine etc.*) refrigerated.

frileu|x, ~se /frilø, -z/ *a.* sensitive to cold.

frime /frim/ *n.f.* (*fam.*) show off. **~r** *v.i.* (*fam.*) putting on a show.

frimousse /frimus/ *n.f.* (sweet) face.

fringale /frɛ̃gal/ *n.f.* (*fam.*) ravenous appetite.

fringant, ~e /frɛ̃gɑ̃, -t/ *a.* dashing.

fringues /frɛ̃g/ *n.f. pl.* (*fam.*) togs.

friper /fripe/ *v.t.,* **se ~** *v. pr.* crumple.

fripon, ~ne /fripɔ̃, -ɔn/ *n.m., f.* rascal. **—a.** rascally.

fripouille /fripuj/ *n.f.* rogue.

frire /frir/ *v.t./i.* fry. **faire ~,** fry.

frise /friz/ *n.f.* frieze.

fris|er /frize/ *v.t./i.* (*cheveux*) curl; (*personne*) curl the hair of. **~é** *a.* curly.

frisquet /friskɛ/ *a.m.* (*fam.*) chilly.

frisson /frisɔ̃/ *n.m.* (*de froid*) shiver; (*de peur*) shudder. **~ner** /-ɔne/ *v.i.* shiver; shudder.

frit, ~e /fri, -t/ *a.* fried. **—n.f.** chip. **avoir la ~e,** (*fam.*) feel good.

friteuse /fritøz/ *n.f.* (deep-)fryer.

friture /frityr/ *n.f.* fried fish; (*huile*) (frying) oil *ou* fat.

frivol|e /frivɔl/ *a.* frivolous. **~ité** *n.f.* frivolity.

froid, ~e /frwa, -d/ *a. & n.m.* cold. **avoir/prendre ~,** be/catch cold. **il fait ~,** it is cold. **~ement** /-dmɑ̃/ *adv.* coldly; (*calculer*) coolly. **~eur** /-dœr/ *n.f.* coldness.

froisser /frwase/ *v.t.* crumple; (*fig.*) offend. **se ~** *v. pr.* crumple; (*fig.*) take offence. **se ~ un muscle,** strain a muscle.

frôler /frole/ *v.t.* brush against, skim; (*fig.*) come close to.

fromag|e /frɔmaʒ/ *n.m.* cheese. **~er, ~ère** *a.* cheese; *n.m., f.* cheese maker; (*marchand*) cheesemonger.

froment /frɔmɑ̃/ *n.m.* wheat.

froncer /frɔ̃se/ *v.t.* gather. **~ les sourcils,** frown.

fronde /frɔ̃d/ *n.f.* sling; (*fig.*) revolt.

front /frɔ̃/ *n.m.* forehead; (*mil., pol.*) front. **de ~,** at the same time; (*de face*) head-on; (*côte à côte*) abreast. **faire ~ à,** face up to. **~al** (*m. pl.* **~aux**) /-tal, -to/ *a.* frontal.

frontali|er, ère /frɔ̃talje, -ɛr/ *a.* border. (**travailleur**) **~er,** commuter from across the border.

frontière /frɔ̃tjɛr/ *n.f.* border, frontier.

frott|er /frote/ *v.t./i.* rub; (*allumette*) strike. **~ement** *n.m.* rubbing.

frottis /frɔti/ *n.m.* **~ vaginal,** smear test.

frouss|e /frus/ *n.f.* (*fam.*) fear. **avoir la ~e,** (*fam.*) be scared. **~ard, ~arde** *n.m., f.* (*fam.*) coward.

fructifier /fryktifje/ *v.i.* **faire ~,** put to work.

fructueu|x, ~se /fryktɥø, -z/ *a.* fruitful.

frug|al (*m. pl.* **~aux**) /frygal, -o/ *a.* frugal. **~alité** *n.f.* frugality.

fruit /frɥi/ *n.m.* fruit. **des ~s,** (some) fruit. **~s de mer,** seafood. **~é** /-te/ *a.* fruity. **~ier, ~ière** /-tje, -tjɛr/ *a.* fruit; *n.m., f.* fruiterer.

fruste /fryst/ *a.* coarse.

frustr|er /frystre/ *v.t.* frustrate. **~ant, ~ante** *a.* frustrating. **~ation** *n.f.* frustration.

fuel /fjul/ *n.m.* fuel oil.

fugiti|f, ~ve /fyʒitif, -v/ *a.* (*passager*) fleeting. **—n.m., f.** fugitive.

fugue /fyg/ *n.f.* (*mus.*) fugue. **faire une ~,** run away.

fuir† /fɥir/ *v.i.* flee, run away; (*eau, robinet, etc.*) leak. **—v.t.** (*éviter*) shun.

fuite /fɥit/ *n.f.* flight; (*de liquide, d'une nouvelle*) leak. **en ~,** on the run. **mettre**

en ~, put to flight. **prendre la** ~, take (to) flight.

fulgurant, ~e /fylgyrã, -t/ *a.* (*vitesse*) lightning.

fumée /fyme/ *n.f.* smoke; (*vapeur*) steam.

fum|er /fyme/ *v.t./i.* smoke. ~e-**cigarette** *n.m. invar.* cigarette- holder. ~é *a.* (*poisson, verre*) smoked. ~eur, ~euse *n.m., f.* smoker.

fumet /fymɛ/ *n.m.* aroma.

fumeu|x, ~se /fymø, -z/ *a.* (*confus*) hazy.

fumier /fymje/ *n.m.* manure.

fumiste /fymist/ *n.m./f.* (*fam.*) shirker.

funambule /fynãbyl/ *n.m./f.* tightrope walker.

funèbre /fynɛbr/ *a.* funeral; (*fig.*) gloomy.

funérailles /fyneraj/ *n.f. pl.* funeral.

funéraire /fynerɛr/ *a.* funeral.

funeste /fynɛst/ *a.* fatal.

funiculaire /fynikylɛr/ *n.m.* funicular.

fur /fyr/ *n.m.* **au** ~ **et à mesure,** as one goes along, progressively. **au** ~ **et à mesure que,** as.

furet /fyrɛ/ *n.m.* ferret.

fureter /fyrte/ *v.i.* nose (about).

fureur /fyrœr/ *n.f.* fury; (*passion*) passion. **avec** ~, furiously; passionately. **mettre en** ~, infuriate. **faire** ~, be all the rage.

furibond, ~e /furibõ, -d/ *a.* furious.

furie /fyri/ *n.f.* fury; (*femme*) shrew.

furieu|x, ~se /fyrjø, -z/ *a.* furious.

furoncle /fyrõkl/ *n.m.* boil.

furti|f, ~ve /fyrtif, -v/ *a.* furtive.

fusain /fyzɛ̃/ *n.m.* (*crayon*) charcoal; (*arbre*) spindle-tree.

fuseau (*pl.* ~x) /fyzo/ *n.m.* ski trousers; (*pour filer*) spindle. ~ **horaire,** time zone.

fusée /fyze/ *n.f.* rocket.

fuselage /fyzlaʒ/ *n.m.* fuselage.

fuselé /fyzle/ *a.* slender.

fusible /fyzibl/ *n.m.* fuse.

fuser /fyze/ *v.i.* issue forth.

fusil /fyzi/ *n.m.* rifle, gun; (*de chasse*) shotgun. ~ **mitrailleur,** machine-gun.

fusill|er /fyzije/ *v.t.* shoot. ~ade *n.f.* shooting.

fusion /fyzjõ/ *n.f.* fusion; (*comm.*) merger. ~ner /-jɔne/ *v.t./i.* merge.

fut /fy/ *voir* **être.**

fût /fy/ *n.m.* (*tonneau*) barrel; (*d'arbre*) trunk.

futé /fyte/ *a.* cunning.

futil|e /fytil/ *a.* futile. ~ité *n.f.* futility.

futur /fytyr/ *a.* & *n.m.* future. ~e **femme/maman,** wife-/mother-to-be.

fuyant, ~e /fɥijã, -t/ *a.* (*front, ligne*) receding; (*personne*) evasive.

fuyard, ~e /fɥijar, -d/ *n.m., f.* runaway.

G

gabardine /gabardin/ *n.f.* gabardine; raincoat.

gabarit /gabari/ *n.m.* dimension; (*patron*) template; (*fig.*) calibre.

gâcher /gaʃe/ *v.t.* (*gâter*) spoil; (*gaspiller*) waste.

gâchette /gaʃɛt/ *n.f.* trigger.

gâchis /gaʃi/ *n.m.* waste.

gadoue /gadu/ *n.f.* sludge.

gaff|e /gaf/ *n.f.* blunder. **faire** ~e, (*fam.*) be careful (**à,** of). ~er *v.i.* blunder.

gag /gag/ *n.m.* gag.

gage /gaʒ/ *n.m.* pledge; (*de jeu*) forfeit. ~s, (*salaire*) wages. **en** ~ **de,** as a token of. **mettre en** ~, pawn.

gageure /gaʒyr/ *n.f.* wager (against all the odds).

gagn|er /gaɲe/ *v.t.* (*match, prix, etc.*) win; (*argent, pain*) earn; (*temps, terrain*) gain; (*atteindre*) reach; (*convaincre*) win over. —*v.i.* win; (*fig.*) gain. ~er **sa vie,** earn one's living. ~ant, ~ante, *a.* winning; *n.m., f.* winner. ~e-**pain** *n.m. invar.* job.

gai /ge/ *a.* cheerful; (*ivre*) merry. ~ement *adv.* cheerfully. ~eté *n.f.* cheerfulness. ~etés *n.f. pl.* delights.

gaillard, ~e /gajar, -d/ *a.* hale and hearty; (*grivois*) coarse. —*n.m.* hale and hearty fellow; (*type: fam.*) fellow.

gain /gɛ̃/ *n.m.* (*salaire*) earnings; (*avantage*) gain; (*économie*) saving. ~s, (*comm.*) profits; (*au jeu*) winnings.

gaine /gɛn/ *n.f.* (*corset*) girdle; (*étui*) sheath.

gala /gala/ *n.m.* gala.

galant, ~e /galã, -t/ *a.* courteous; (*scène, humeur*) romantic.

galaxie /galaksi/ *n.f.* galaxy.

galb|e /galb/ *n.m.* curve. ~é *a.* shapely.

gale /gal/ *n.f.* (*de chat etc.*) mange.

galéjade /galeʒad/ *n.f.* (*fam.*) tall tale.

galère /galɛr/ *n.f.* (*navire*) galley. **c'est la** ~!, (*fam.*) what an ordeal!

galérer /galere/ *v.i.* (*fam.*) have a hard time.

galerie /galri/ n.f. gallery; (théâtre) circle; (de voiture) roof- rack.

galet /galɛ/ n.m. pebble.

galette /galɛt/ n.f. flat cake.

galeu|x, ~se /galø, -z/ a. (animal) mangy.

galipette /galipɛt/ n.f. somersault.

Galles /gal/ n.f. pl. **le pays de ~,** Wales.

gallois, ~e /galwa, -z/ a. Welsh. —n.m., f. Welshman, Welshwoman. —n.m. (lang.) Welsh.

galon /galɔ̃/ n.m. braid; (mil.) stripe. **prendre du ~,** be promoted.

galop /galo/ n.m. gallop. **aller au ~,** gallop. **~ d'essai,** trial run. **~er** /-ɔpe/ v.i. (cheval) gallop; (personne) run.

galopade /galɔpad/ n.f. wild rush.

galopin /galɔpɛ̃/ n.m. (fam.) rascal.

galvaudé /galvode/ a. worthless.

gambad|e /gɑ̃bad/ n.f. leap. **~er** v.i. leap about.

gamelle /gamɛl/ n.f. (de soldat) mess bowl ou tin; (d'ouvrier) food-box.

gamin, ~e /gamɛ̃, -in/ a. playful. —n.m., f. (fam.) kid.

gamme /gam/ n.f. (mus.) scale; (série) range. **haut de ~,** up-market, top of the range. **bas de ~,** down-market, bottom of the range.

gang /gɑ̃g/ n.m. gang.

ganglion /gɑ̃glijɔ̃/ n.m. swelling.

gangrène /gɑ̃grɛn/ n.f. gangrene.

gangster /gɑ̃gstɛr/ n.m. gangster; (escroc) crook.

gant /gɑ̃/ n.m. glove. **~ de toilette,** face-flannel, face-cloth. **~é** /-gɑ̃te/ a. (personne) wearing gloves.

garag|e /garaʒ/ n.m. garage. **~iste** n.m. garage owner; (employé) garage mechanic.

garant, ~e /garɑ̃, -t/ n.m., f. guarantor. —n.m. guarantee. **se porter ~ de,** guarantee, vouch for.

garant|ie /garɑ̃ti/ n.f. guarantee; (protection) safeguard. **~ies,** (de police d'assurance) cover. **~ir** v.t. guarantee; (protéger) protect (de, from).

garce /gars/ n.f. (fam.) bitch.

garçon /garsɔ̃/ n.m. boy; (célibataire) bachelor. **~ (de café),** waiter. **~ d'honneur,** best man.

garçonnière /garsɔnjɛr/ n.f. bachelor flat.

garde[1] /gard/ n.f. guard; (d'enfants, de bagages) care; (service) guard (duty); (infirmière) nurse. **de ~,** on duty. **~ à vue,** (police) custody. **mettre en ~,**

warn. **prendre ~,** be careful (à, of). **(droit de) ~,** custody (de, of).

garde[2] /gard/ n.m. (personne) guard; (de propriété, parc) warden. **~ champêtre,** village policeman. **~ du corps,** bodyguard.

gard|er /garde/ v.t. (conserver, maintenir) keep; (vêtement) keep on; (surveiller) look after; (défendre) guard. **se ~er** v. pr. (denrée) keep. **~er le lit,** stay in bed. **se ~er de faire,** be careful not to do. **~e-à-vous** int. (mil.) attention. **~e-boue** n.m. invar. mudguard. **~e-chasse** (pl. **~es-chasses**) n.m. gamekeeper. **~e-fou** n.m. railing. **~e-manger** n.m. invar. (food) safe; (placard) larder. **~e-robe** n.f. wardrobe.

garderie /gardəri/ n.f. crèche.

gardien, ~ne /gardjɛ̃, -jɛn/ n.m., f. (de prison, réserve) warden; (d'immeuble) caretaker; (de musée) attendant; (garde) guard. **~ de but,** goalkeeper. **~ de la paix,** policeman. **~ de nuit,** night watchman. **~ne d'enfants,** child-minder.

gare[1] /gar/ n.f. (rail.) station. **~ routière,** coach station; (Amer.) bus station.

gare[2] /gar/ int. **~ (à toi),** watch out!

garer /gare/ v.t., **se ~** v. pr. park.

gargariser (se) /(sə)gargarize/ v. pr. gargle.

gargarisme /gargarism/ n.m. gargle.

gargouille /garguj/ n.f. (water-)spout; (sculptée) gargoyle.

gargouiller /garguje/ v.i. gurgle.

garnement /garnəmɑ̃/ n.m. rascal.

garn|ir /garnir/ v.t. fill; (décorer) decorate; (couvrir) cover; (doubler) line; (culin.) garnish. **~i** a. (plat) served with vegetables. **bien ~i,** (rempli) well-filled.

garnison /garnizɔ̃/ n.f. garrison.

garniture /garnityr/ n.f. (légumes) vegetables; (ornement) trimming; (de voiture) trim.

garrot /garo/ n.m. (méd.) tourniquet.

gars /gɑ/ n.m. (fam.) fellow.

gas-oil /gazɔjl/ n.m. diesel oil.

gaspill|er /gaspije/ v.t. waste. **~age** n.m. waste.

gastrique /gastrik/ a. gastric.

gastronom|e /gastrɔnɔm/ n.m./f. gourmet. **~ie** n.f. gastronomy.

gâteau (pl. **~x**) /gɑto/ n.m. cake. **~ sec,** biscuit; (Amer.) cookie. **un papa ~,** a doting dad.

gâter /gate/ v.t. spoil. **se** ~ v. pr. (*dent, viande*) go bad; (*temps*) get worse.

gâterie /gɑtri/ n.f. little treat.

gâteu|x, ~se /gɑtø, -z/ a. senile.

gauch|e¹ /goʃ/ a. left. **à ~e**, on the left; (*direction*) (to the) left. **la ~e**, the left (side); (*pol.*) the left (wing). **~er, ~ère** a. & n.m., f. left-handed (person). **~iste** a. & n.m./f. (*pol.*) leftist.

gauche² /goʃ/ a. (*maladroit*) awkward. **~rie** n.f. awkwardness.

gaufre /gofr/ n.f. waffle.

gaufrette /gofrɛt/ n.f. wafer.

gaulois, ~e /golwa, -z/ a. Gallic; (*fig.*) bawdy. **~**n.m., f. Gaul.

gausser (se) /(sə)gose/ v. pr. **se ~ de,** deride, scoff at.

gaver /gave/ v.t. force-feed; (*fig.*) cram. **se ~ de,** gorge o.s. with.

gaz /gɑz/ n.m. invar. gas. **~ lacrymogène,** tear-gas.

gaze /gɑz/ n.f. gauze.

gazelle /gɑzɛl/ n.f. gazelle.

gaz|er /gɑze/ v.i. (*fam.*) **ça ~e,** it's going all right.

gazette /gɑzɛt/ n.f. newspaper.

gazeu|x, ~se /gɑzø, -z/ a. (*boisson*) fizzy.

gazoduc /gɑzɔdyk/ n.m. gas pipeline.

gazomètre /gɑzɔmɛtr/ n.m. gasometer.

gazon /gɑzɔ̃/ n.m. lawn, grass.

gazouiller /gɑzuje/ v.i. (*oiseau*) chirp; (*bébé*) babble.

geai /ʒɛ/ n.m. jay.

géant, ~e /ʒeɑ̃, -t/ a. & n.m., f. giant.

geindre /ʒɛ̃dr/ v.i. groan.

gel /ʒɛl/ n.m. frost; (*pâte*) gel; (*comm.*) freezing.

gélatine /ʒelatin/ n.f. gelatine.

gel|er /ʒəle/ v.t./i. freeze. **on gèle,** it's freezing. **~é** a. frozen; (*membre abîmé*) frost-bitten. **~ée** n.f. frost; (*culin.*) jelly. **~ée blanche,** hoar-frost.

gélule /ʒelyl/ n.f. (*méd.*) capsule.

Gémeaux /ʒemo/ n.m. pl. Gemini.

gém|ir /ʒemir/ v.i. groan. **~issement** n.m. groan(ing).

gênant, ~e /ʒenɑ̃, -t/ a. embarrassing; (*irritant*) annoying.

gencive /ʒɑ̃siv/ n.f. gum.

gendarme /ʒɑ̃darm/ n.m. policeman, gendarme. **~rie** /-əri/ n.f. police force; (*local*) police station.

gendre /ʒɑ̃dr/ n.m. son-in-law.

gène /ʒɛn/ n.m. gene.

gêne /ʒɛn/ n.f. discomfort; (*confusion*) embarrassment; (*dérangement*) trouble. **dans la ~,** in financial straits.

généalogie /ʒenealɔʒi/ n.f. genealogy.

gên|er /ʒene/ v.t. bother, disturb; (*troubler*) embarrass; (*encombrer*) hamper; (*bloquer*) block. **~é** a. embarrassed.

génér|al (*m. pl.* **~aux**) /ʒeneral, -o/ a. general. **—**n.m. (*pl.* **~aux**) general. **en ~al,** in general. **~alement** adv. generally.

généralis|er /ʒeneralize/ v.t./i. generalize. **se ~er** v. pr. become general. **~ation** n.f. generalization.

généraliste /ʒeneralist/ n.m./f. general practitioner, GP.

généralité /ʒeneralite/ n.f. majority. **~s,** general points.

génération /ʒenerasjɔ̃/ n.f. generation.

génératrice /ʒeneratris/ n.f. generator.

généreu|x, ~se /ʒenerø, -z/ a. generous. **~sement** adv. generously.

générique /ʒenerik/ n.m. (*cinéma*) credits. **—**a. generic.

générosité /ʒenerozite/ n.f. generosity.

genêt /ʒənɛ/ n.m. (*plante*) broom.

génétique /ʒenetik/ a. genetic. **—**n.f. genetics.

Genève /ʒənɛv/ n.m./f. Geneva.

gén|ial (*m. pl.* **~iaux**) /ʒenjal, -jo/ a. brilliant; (*fam.*) fantastic.

génie /ʒeni/ n.m. genius. **~ civil,** civil engineering.

genièvre /ʒənjɛvr/ n.m. juniper.

génisse /ʒenis/ n.f. heifer.

génit|al (*m. pl.* **~aux**) /ʒenital, -o/ a. genital.

génocide /ʒenɔsid/ n.m. genocide.

génoise /ʒenwaz/ n.f. sponge (cake).

genou (*pl.* **~x**) /ʒnu/ n.m. knee. **à ~x,** kneeling. **se mettre à ~x,** kneel.

genre /ʒɑ̃r/ n.m. sort, kind; (*attitude*) manner; (*gram.*) gender. **~ de vie,** lifestyle.

gens /ʒɑ̃/ n.m./f. pl. people.

genti|l, ~lle /ʒɑ̃ti, -j/ a. kind, nice; (*agréable*) nice; (*sage*) good. **~llesse** /-jɛs/ n.f. kindness. **~ment** adv. kindly.

géograph|ie /ʒeɔgrafi/ n.f. geography. **~e** n.m./f. geographer. **~ique** a. geographical.

geôl|ier, ~ière /ʒolje, -jɛr/ n.m., f. gaoler, jailer.

géolo|gie /ʒeɔlɔʒi/ n.f. geology. **~gique** a. geological. **~gue** n.m./f. geologist.

géomètre /ʒeɔmɛtr/ n.m. surveyor.

géométr|ie /ʒeɔmetri/ n.f. geometry. **~ique** a. geometric.

géranium /ʒeranjɔm/ n.m. geranium.

géran|t, ~te /ʒerɑ̃, -t/ n.m., f. manager, manageress. **~t d'immeuble,** landlord's agent. **~ce** n.f. management.

gerbe /ʒɛrb/ n.f. (de fleurs, d'eau) spray; (de blé) sheaf.

gercé /ʒɛrse/ a. chapped.

ger|cer /ʒɛrse/ v.t./i., **se ～cer** v. pr. chap. **～çure** n.f. chap.

gérer /ʒere/ v.t. manage.

germain, ～e /ʒɛrmɛ̃, -ɛn/ a. **cousin ～,** first cousin.

germanique /ʒɛrmanik/ a. Germanic.

germ|e /ʒɛrm/ n.m. germ. **～er** v.i. germinate.

gésier /ʒezje/ n.m. gizzard.

gestation /ʒɛstɑsjɔ̃/ n.f. gestation.

geste /ʒɛst/ n.m. gesture.

gesticul|er /ʒɛstikyle/ v.i. gesticulate. **～ation** n.f. gesticulation.

gestion /ʒɛstjɔ̃/ n.f. management.

geyser /ʒɛzɛr/ n.m. geyser.

ghetto /ɡeto/ n.m. ghetto.

gibecière /ʒibsjɛr/ n.f. shoulder-bag.

gibet /ʒibɛ/ n.m. gallows.

gibier /ʒibje/ n.m. (animaux) game.

giboulée /ʒibule/ n.f. shower.

gicl|er /ʒikle/ v.i. squirt. **faire ～er,** squirt. **～ée** n.f. squirt.

gifle /ʒifl/ n.f. slap (in the face). **～er** v.t. slap.

gigantesque /ʒiɡɑ̃tɛsk/ a. gigantic.

gigot /ʒiɡo/ n.m. leg (of lamb).

gigoter /ʒiɡote/ v.i. (fam.) wriggle.

gilet /ʒile/ n.m. waistcoat; (cardigan) cardigan. **～ de sauvetage,** life-jacket.

gin /dʒin/ n.m. gin.

gingembre /ʒɛ̃ʒɑ̃br/ n.m. ginger.

gingivite /ʒɛ̃ʒivit/ n.f. gum infection.

girafe /ʒiraf/ n.f. giraffe.

giratoire /ʒiratwar/ a. **sens ～,** roundabout.

giroflée /ʒirɔfle/ n.f. wallflower.

girouette /ʒirwɛt/ n.f. weathercock, weather-vane.

gisement /ʒizmɑ̃/ n.m. deposit.

gitan, ～e /ʒitɑ̃, -an/ n.m., f. gypsy.

gîte /ʒit/ n.m. (maison) home; (abri) shelter. **～ rural,** holiday cottage.

givr|e /ʒivr/ n.m. (hoar-)frost. **～er** v.t., **se ～er** v. pr. frost (up).

givré /ʒivre/ a. (fam.) nuts.

glace /ɡlas/ n.f. ice; (crème) ice-cream; (vitre) window; (miroir) mirror; (verre) glass.

glac|er /ɡlase/ v.t. freeze; (gâteau, boisson) ice; (papier) glaze; (pétrifier) chill. **se ～er** v. pr. freeze. **～é** a. (vent, accueil) icy.

glac|ial (m. pl. **～iaux**) /ɡlasjal, -jo/ a. icy.

glacier /ɡlasje/ n.m. (géog.) glacier; (vendeur) ice-cream man.

glacière /ɡlasjɛr/ n.f. icebox.

glaçon /ɡlasɔ̃/ n.m. (pour boisson) ice-cube; (péj.) cold fish.

glaïeul /ɡlajœl/ n.m. gladiolus.

glaise /ɡlɛz/ n.f. clay.

gland /ɡlɑ̃/ n.m. acorn; (ornement) tassel.

glande /ɡlɑ̃d/ n.f. gland.

glander /ɡlɑ̃de/ v.i. (fam.) laze around.

glaner /ɡlane/ v.t. glean.

glapir /ɡlapir/ v.i. yelp.

glas /ɡlɑ/ n.m. knell.

glauque /ɡlok/ a. (fig.) gloomy.

glissant, ～e /ɡlisɑ̃, -t/ a. slippery.

gliss|er /ɡlise/ v.i. slide; (sur l'eau) glide; (déraper) slip; (véhicule) skid. **—v.t., se ～er** v. pr. slip (dans, into). **～ade** n.f. sliding; (endroit) slide. **～ement** n.m. sliding; gliding; (fig.) shift. **～ement de terrain,** landslide.

glissière /ɡlisjɛr/ n.f. groove. **à ～,** (porte, système) sliding.

glob|al (m. pl. **～aux**) /ɡlɔbal, -o/ a. (entier, général) overall. **～alement** adv. as a whole.

globe /ɡlɔb/ n.m. globe. **～ oculaire,** eyeball. **～ terrestre,** globe.

globule /ɡlɔbyl/ n.m. (du sang) corpuscle.

gloire /ɡlwar/ n.f. glory.

glorieu|x, ～se /ɡlɔrjø, -z/ a. glorious. **～sement** adv. gloriously.

glorifier /ɡlɔrifje/ v.t. glorify.

glose /ɡloz/ n.f. gloss.

glossaire /ɡlɔsɛr/ n.m. glossary.

glouss|er /ɡluse/ v.i. chuckle; (poule) cluck. **～ement** n.m. chuckle; cluck.

glouton, ～ne /ɡlutɔ̃, -ɔn/ a. gluttonous. **—n.m., f.** glutton.

gluant, ～e /ɡlyɑ̃, -t/ a. sticky.

glucose /ɡlykoz/ n.m. glucose.

glycérine /ɡliserin/ n.f. glycerine.

glycine /ɡlisin/ n.f. wisteria.

gnome /ɡnom/ n.m. gnome.

go /ɡo/ **tout de go,** straight out.

GO (abrév. grandes ondes) long wave.

goal /ɡol/ n.m. goalkeeper.

gobelet /ɡɔblɛ/ n.m. tumbler, mug.

gober /ɡɔbe/ v.t. swallow (whole). **je ne peux pas le ～,** (fam.) I can't stand him.

godasse /ɡɔdas/ n.f. (fam.) shoe.

godet /ɡɔdɛ/ n.m. (small) pot.

goéland /ɡɔelɑ̃/ n.m. (sea)gull.

goélette /ɡɔelɛt/ n.f. schooner.

gogo (à) /(a)ɡɔɡo/ adv. (fam.) galore, in abundance.

goguenard, ～e /ɡɔɡnar, -d/ a. mocking.

goguette (en) /(ɑ̃)gɔgɛt/ adv. (fam.) having a binge ou spree.

goinfr|e /gwɛfr/ n.m. (glouton: fam.) pig. **se ~er** v. pr. (fam.) stuff o.s. like a pig (**de**, with).

golf /gɔlf/ n.m. golf; golf course.

golfe /gɔlf/ n.m. gulf.

gomm|e /gɔm/ n.f. rubber; (Amer.) eraser; (résine) gum. **~er** v.t. rub out.

gond /gɔ̃/ n.m. hinge. **sortir de ses ~s,** go mad.

gondol|e /gɔ̃dɔl/ n.f. gondola. **~ier** n.m. gondolier.

gondoler (se) /(sə)gɔ̃dɔle/ v. pr. warp; (rire: fam.) split one's sides.

gonfl|er /gɔ̃fle/ v.t./i. swell; (ballon, pneu) pump up, blow up; (exagérer) inflate. **se ~er** v. pr. swell. **~é** a. swollen. **il est ~é,** (fam.) he's got a nerve. **~ement** n.m. swelling.

gorge /gɔrʒ/ n.f. throat; (poitrine) breast; (vallée) gorge.

gorgée /gɔrʒe/ n.f. sip, gulp.

gorg|er /gɔrʒe/ v.t. fill (**de**, with). **se ~er** v. pr. gorge o.s. (**de**, with). **~é de,** full of.

gorille /gɔrij/ n.m. gorilla; (garde: fam.) bodyguard.

gosier /gozje/ n.m. throat.

gosse /gɔs/ n.m./f. (fam.) kid.

gothique /gɔtik/ a. Gothic.

goudron /gudrɔ̃/ n.m. tar. **~ner** /-ɔne/ v.t. tar; (route) surface. **à faible teneur en ~,** low tar.

gouffre /gufr/ n.m. gulf, abyss.

goujat /guʒa/ n.m. lout, boor.

goulot /gulo/ n.m. neck. **boire au ~,** drink from the bottle.

goulu, **~e** /guly/ a. gluttonous. —n.m., f. glutton.

gourde /gurd/ n.f. (à eau) flask; (idiot: fam.) chump.

gourdin /gurdɛ̃/ n.m. club, cudgel.

gourer (se) /(sə)gure/ v. pr. (fam.) make a mistake.

gourmand, **~e** /gurmã, -d/ a. greedy. —n.m., f. glutton. **~ise** /-diz/ n.f. greed; (mets) delicacy.

gourmet /gurmɛ/ n.m. gourmet.

gourmette /gurmɛt/ n.f. chain bracelet.

gousse /gus/ n.f. **~ d'ail,** clove of garlic.

goût /gu/ n.m. taste.

goûter /gute/ v.t. taste; (apprécier) enjoy. —v.i. have tea. —n.m. tea, snack. **~ à** ou **~,** taste.

goutt|e /gut/ n.f. drop; (méd.) gout. **~er** v.i. drip.

goutte-à-goutte /gutagut/ n.m. drip.

gouttelette /gutlɛt/ n.f. droplet.

gouttière /gutjɛr/ n.f. gutter.

gouvernail /guvɛrnaj/ n.m. rudder; (barre) helm.

gouvernante /guvɛrnɑ̃t/ n.f. governess.

gouvernement /guvɛrnəmɑ̃/ n.m. government. **~al** (m. pl. **~aux**) /-tal, -to/ a. government.

gouvern|er /guvɛrne/ v.t./i. govern. **~eur** n.m. governor.

grâce /grɑs/ n.f. (charme) grace; (faveur) favour; (jurid.) pardon; (relig.) grace. **~ à,** thanks to.

gracier /grasje/ v.t. pardon.

gracieu|x, **~se** /grasjø, -z/ a. graceful; (gratuit) free. **~sement** adv. gracefully; free (of charge).

gradation /gradasjɔ̃/ n.f. gradation.

grade /grad/ n.m. rank. **monter en ~,** be promoted.

gradé /grade/ n.m. non-commissioned officer.

gradin /gradɛ̃/ n.m. tier, step. **en ~s,** terraced.

gradué /gradye/ a. graded, graduated.

graduel, **~le** /graduɛl/ a. gradual.

grad|uer /gradye/ v.t. increase gradually. **~uation** n.f. graduation.

graffiti /grafiti/ n.m. pl. graffiti.

grain /grɛ̃/ n.m. grain; (naut.) squall; (de café) bean; (de poivre) pepper corn. **~ de beauté,** beauty spot. **~ de raisin,** grape.

graine /grɛn/ n.f. seed.

graissage /grɛsaʒ/ n.m. lubrication.

graiss|e /grɛs/ n.f. fat; (lubrifiant) grease. **~er** v.t. grease. **~eux,** **~euse** a. greasy.

gramm|aire /gramɛr/ n.f. grammar. **~atical** (m. pl. **~aticaux**) a. grammatical.

gramme /gram/ n.m. gram.

grand, **~e** /grã, -d/ a. big, large; (haut) tall; (mérite, distance, ami) great; (bruit) loud; (plus âgé) big. —adv. (ouvrir) wide. **~ ouvert,** wide open. **voir ~,** think big. —n.m., f. (adulte) grown-up; (enfant) older child. **au ~ air,** in the open air. **au ~ jour,** in broad daylight; (fig.) in the open. **de ~e envergure,** large-scale. **en ~e partie,** largely. **~-angle,** n.m. wide angle. **~e banlieue,** outer suburbs. **G~e-Bretagne** n.f. Great Britain. **pas ~-chose,** not much. **~ ensemble,** housing estate. **~es lignes,** (rail.) main lines. **~ magasin,** department store. **~-mère** (pl. **~s-mères**) n.f. grandmother. **~s-parents** n.m. pl. grandparents. **~-père** (pl. **~s-pères**) n.m. grandfather. **~e**

personne, grown-up. ∼ **public,** general public. ∼**-rue** *n.f.* high street. ∼**e surface,** hypermarket. ∼**es vacances,** summer holidays.

grandeur /grɑ̃dœr/ *n.f.* greatness; (*dimension*) size. **folie des** ∼**s,** delusions of grandeur.

grandiose /grɑ̃djoz/ *a.* grandiose.

grandir /grɑ̃dir/ *v.i.* grow; (*bruit*) grow louder. —*v.t.* make taller.

grange /grɑ̃ʒ/ *n.f.* barn.

granit /granit/ *n.m.* granite.

granulé /granyle/ *n.m.* granule.

graphique /grafik/ *a.* graphic. —*n.m.* graph.

graphologie /grafɔlɔʒi/ *n.f.* graphology.

grappe /grap/ *n.f.* cluster. ∼ **de raisin,** bunch of grapes.

grappin /grapɛ̃/ *n.m.* **mettre le** ∼ **sur,** get one's claws into.

gras, ∼**se** /grɑ, -s/ *a.* fat; (*aliment*) fatty; (*surface*) greasy; (*épais*) thick; (*caractères*) bold. —*n.m.* (*culin.*) fat. **faire la** ∼**se matinée,** sleep late. ∼**sement payé,** highly paid.

gratification /gratifikasjɔ̃/ *n.f.* bonus, satisfaction.

gratifi|er /gratifje/ *v.t.* favour, reward (**de,** with). ∼**ant,** ∼**ante** *a.* rewarding.

gratin /gratɛ̃/ *n.m.* baked dish with cheese topping; (*élite: fam.*) upper crust.

gratis /gratis/ *adv.* free.

gratitude /gratityd/ *n.f.* gratitude.

gratt|er /grate/ *v.t./i.* scratch; (*avec un outil*) scrape. **se** ∼**er** *v. pr.* scratch o.s. **ça me** ∼**e,** (*fam.*) it itches. ∼**e-ciel** *n.m. invar.* skyscraper. ∼**-papier** *n.m. invar.* (*péj.*) pen pusher.

gratuit, ∼**e** /gratɥi, -t/ *a.* free; (*acte*) gratuitous. ∼**ement** -tmɑ̃/ *adv.* free (of charge).

gravats /grava/ *n.m. pl.* rubble.

grave /grav/ *a.* serious; (*solennel*) grave; (*voix*) deep; (*accent*) grave. ∼**ment** *adv.* seriously, gravely.

grav|er /grave/ *v.t.* engrave; (*sur bois*) carve. ∼**eur** *n.m.* engraver.

gravier /gravje/ *n.m.* gravel.

gravir /gravir/ *v.t.* climb.

gravitation /gravitasjɔ̃/ *n.f.* gravitation.

gravité /gravite/ *n.f.* gravity.

graviter /gravite/ *v.i.* revolve.

gravure /gravyr/ *n.f.* engraving; (*de tableau, photo*) print, plate.

gré /gre/ *n.m.* (*volonté*) will; (*goût*) taste. **à son** ∼, (*agir*) as one likes. **de bon** ∼, willingly. **bon** ∼ **mal gré,** like

it or not. **je vous en saurais** ∼, I'll be grateful for that.

grec, ∼**que** /grɛk/ *a. & n.m.,* f. Greek. —*n.m.* (*lang.*) Greek.

Grèce /grɛs/ *n.f.* Greece.

greff|e /grɛf/ *n.f.* graft; (*d'organe*) transplant. ∼**er** /grefe/ *v.t.* graft; transplant.

greffier /grefje/ *n.m.* clerk of the court.

grégaire /gregɛr/ *a.* gregarious.

grêle[1] /grɛl/ *a.* (*maigre*) spindly; (*voix*) shrill.

grêl|e[2] /grɛl/ *n.f.* hail. ∼**er** /grele/ *v.i.* hail. ∼**on** *n.m.* hailstone.

grelot /grəlo/ *n.m.* (little) bell.

grelotter /grəlɔte/ *v.i.* shiver.

grenade[1] /grənad/ *n.f.* (*fruit*) pomegranate.

grenade[2] /grənad/ *n.f.* (*explosif*) grenade.

grenat /grəna/ *a. invar.* dark red.

grenier /grənje/ *n.m.* attic; (*pour grain*) loft.

grenouille /grənuj/ *n.f.* frog.

grès /grɛ/ *n.m.* sandstone; (*poterie*) stoneware.

grésiller /grezije/ *v.i.* sizzle; (*radio*) crackle.

grève[1] /grɛv/ *n.f.* strike. **se mettre en** ∼, go on strike. ∼ **du zèle,** work-to-rule; (*Amer.*) rule-book slow-down. ∼ **de la faim,** hunger strike. ∼ **sauvage,** wildcat strike.

grève[2] /grɛv/ *n.f.* (*rivage*) shore.

gréviste /grevist/ *n.m./f.* striker.

gribouill|er /gribuje/ *v.t./i.* scribble. ∼**is** /-ji/ *n.m.* scribble.

grief /grijɛf/ *n.m.* grievance.

grièvement /grijɛvmɑ̃/ *adv.* seriously.

griff|e /grif/ *n.f.* claw; (*de couturier*) label. ∼**er** *v.t.* scratch, claw.

griffonner /grifɔne/ *v.t./i.* scrawl.

grignoter /griɲɔte/ *v.t./i.* nibble.

gril /gril/ *n.m.* grill, grid(iron).

grillade /grijad/ *n.f.* (*viande*) grill.

grillage /grijaʒ/ *n.m.* wire netting.

grille /grij/ *n.f.* railings; (*portail*) (metal) gate; (*de fenêtre*) bars; (*de cheminée*) grate; (*fig.*) grid.

grill|er /grije/ *v.t./i.* burn; (*ampoule*) blow; (*feu rouge*) go through. (**faire**) ∼**er,** (*pain*) toast; (*viande*) grill; (*café*) roast. ∼**e-pain** *n.m. invar.* toaster.

grillon /grijɔ̃/ *n.m.* cricket.

grimace /grimas/ *n.f.* (funny) face; (*de douleur, dégoût*) grimace.

grimer /grime/ *v.t.,* **se** ∼ *v. pr.* make up.

grimper /grɛ̃pe/ *v.t./i.* climb.

grinc|er /grɛ̃se/ *v.i.* creak. ∼**er des**

dents, grind one's teeth. **∼ement** n.m. creak(ing).

grincheu|x, ∼se /grɛ̃ʃø, -z/ a. grumpy.

gripp|e /grip/ n.f. influenza, flu. **être ∼é,** have (the) flu; (*mécanisme*) be seized up *ou* jammed.

gris, ∼e /gri, -z/ a. grey; (*saoul*) tipsy.

grisaille /grizɑj/ n.f. greyness, gloom.

grisonner /grizɔne/ v.i. go grey.

grisou /grizu/ n.m. **coup de ∼,** firedamp explosion.

grive /griv/ n.f. (*oiseau*) thrush.

grivois, ∼e /grivwa, -z/ a. bawdy.

grog /grɔg/ n.m. grog.

grogn|er /grɔɲe/ v.i. growl; (*fig.*) grumble. **∼ement** n.m. growl; grumble.

grognon, ∼ne /grɔɲɔ̃, -ɔn/ a. grumpy.

groin /grwɛ̃/ n.m. snout.

grommeler /grɔmle/ v.t./i. mutter.

grond|er /grɔ̃de/ v.i. rumble; (*chien*) growl; (*conflit etc.*) be brewing. —v.t. scold. **∼ement** n.m. rumbling; growling.

groom /grum/ n.m. page(-boy).

gros, ∼se /gro, -s/ a. big, large; (*gras*) fat; (*important*) great; (*épais*) thick; (*lourd*) heavy. —n.m., f. fat man, fat woman. —n.m. **le ∼ de,** the bulk of. **de ∼,** (*comm.*) wholesale. **en ∼,** roughly; (*comm.*) wholesale. **∼ bonnet,** (*fam.*) bigwig. **∼ lot,** jackpot. **∼ mot,** rude word. **∼ plan,** close-up. **∼ titre,** headline. **∼se caisse,** big drum.

groseille /grozɛj/ n.f. (red- *ou* white) currant. **∼ à maquereau,** gooseberry.

grosse /gros/ *voir* gros.

grossesse /groses/ n.f. pregnancy.

grosseur /grosœr/ n.f. (*volume*) size; (*enflure*) lump.

gross|ier, ∼ière /grosje, -jɛr/ a. coarse, rough; (*imitation, instrument*) crude; (*vulgaire*) coarse; (*insolent*) rude; (*erreur*) gross. **∼ièrement** adv. (*sommairement*) roughly; (*vulgairement*) coarsely. **∼ièreté** n.f. coarseness; crudeness; rudeness; (*mot*) rude word.

grossir /grosir/ v.t./i. swell; (*personne*) put on weight; (*au microscope*) magnify; (*augmenter*) grow; (*exagérer*) magnify.

grossiste /grosist/ n.m./f. wholesaler.

grosso modo /grosomodo/ adv. roughly.

grotesque /grotɛsk/ a. grotesque; (*ridicule*) ludicrous.

grotte /grɔt/ n.f. cave, grotto.

grouill|er /gruje/ v.i. be swarming (**de,** with). **∼ant, ∼ante** a. swarming.

groupe /grup/ n.m. group; (*mus.*) band.

∼ électrogène, generating set. **∼ scolaire,** school block.

group|er /grupe/ v.t., **se ∼er** v. pr. group (together). **∼ement** n.m. grouping.

grue /gry/ n.f. (*machine, oiseau*) crane.

grumeau (*pl.* **∼x**) /grymo/ n.m. lump.

grumeler /grymle/ n.m. (*cheese*).

gruyère /gryjɛr/ n.m. gruyère (cheese).

gué /ge/ n.m. ford. **passer** *ou* **traverser à ∼,** ford.

guenon /gənɔ̃/ n.f. female monkey.

guépard /gepar/ n.m. cheetah.

guêp|e /gɛp/ n.f. wasp. **∼ier** /gepje/ n.m. wasp's nest; (*fig.*) trap.

guère /gɛr/ adv. **(ne) ∼,** hardly. **il n'y a ∼ d'espoir,** there is no hope.

guéridon /geridɔ̃/ n.m. pedestal table.

guérill|a /gerija/ n.f. guerrilla warfare. **∼ero** /-jero/ n.m. guerrilla.

guér|ir /gerir/ v.t. (*personne, maladie, mal*) cure (**de,** of); (*plaie, membre*) heal. —v.i. get better; (*blessure*) heal. **∼ir de,** recover from. **∼ison** n.f. curing; healing; (*de personne*) recovery. **∼isseur, ∼isseuse** n.m., f. healer.

guérite /gerit/ n.f. (*mil.*) sentry-box.

guerre /gɛr/ n.f. war. **en ∼,** at war. **faire la ∼,** wage war (**à,** against). **∼ civile,** civil war. **∼ d'usure,** war of attrition.

guerr|ier, ∼ière /gɛrje, -jɛr/ a. warlike. —n.m., f. warrior.

guet /gɛ/ n.m. watch. **faire le ∼,** be on the watch. **∼-apens** /gɛtapɑ̃/ n.m. invar. ambush.

guetter /gete/ v.t. watch; (*attendre*) watch out for.

gueule /gœl/ n.f. mouth; (*figure: fam.*) face. **ta ∼!,** (*fam.*) shut up!

gueuler /gœle/ v.i. (*fam.*) bawl.

gueuleton /gœltɔ̃/ n.m. (*repas: fam.*) blow-out, slap-up meal.

gui /gi/ n.m. mistletoe.

guichet /giʃɛ/ n.m. window, counter; (*de gare*) ticket-office (window); (*de théâtre*) box-office (window).

guide /gid/ n.m. guide. —n.f. (*fille scout*) girl guide. **∼s** n.f. pl. (*rênes*) reins.

guider /gide/ v.t. guide.

guidon /gidɔ̃/ n.m. handlebars.

guignol /giɲɔl/ n.m. puppet; (*personne*) clown; (*spectacle*) puppet-show.

guili-guili /giligili/ n.m. (*fam.*) tickle. **faire ∼ à,** tickle.

guillemets /gijmɛ/ n.m. pl. quotation marks, inverted commas. **entre ∼,** in inverted commas.

guilleret, ～te /gijrɛ, -t/ a. sprightly, jaunty.

guillotine /gijɔtin/ n.f. guillotine. **～er** v.t. guillotine.

guimauve /gimov/ n.f. marshmallow. **c'est de la ～,** (fam.) it's mush.

guindé /gɛ̃de/ a. stilted.

guirlande /girlɑ̃d/ n.f. garland.

guise /giz/ n.f. **à sa ～,** as one pleases. **en ～ de,** by way of.

guitar|e /gitar/ n.f. guitar. **～iste** n.m./f. guitarist.

gus /gys/ n.m. (fam.) bloke.

guttur|al (m. pl. **～aux**) /gytyral, -o/ a. guttural.

gym /ʒim/ n.f. gym.

gymnas|e /ʒimnɑz/ n.m. gym(nasium). **～te** /-ast/ n.m./f. gymnast. **～tique** /-astik/ n.f. gymnastics.

gynécolo|gie /ʒinekɔlɔʒi/ n.f. gynaecology. **～gique** a. gynaecological. **～gue** n.m./f. gynaecologist.

gypse /ʒips/ n.m. gypsum.

H

habile /abil/ a. skilful, clever. **～té** n.f. skill.

habilité /abilite/ a. **～ à faire,** entitled to do.

habill|er /abije/ v.t. dress (**de,** in); (équiper) clothe; (recouvrir) cover (**de,** with). **s'～er** v. pr. dress (o.s.), get dressed; (se déguiser) dress up. **～é** a. (costume) dressy. **～ement** n.m. clothing.

habit /abi/ n.m. dress, outfit; (de cérémonie) tails. **～s,** clothes.

habitable /abitabl/ a. (in)habitable.

habitant, ～e /abitɑ̃, -t/ n.m., f. (de maison) occupant; (de pays) inhabitant.

habitat /abita/ n.m. housing conditions; (d'animal) habitat.

habitation /abitɑsjɔ̃/ n.f. living; (logement) house.

habit|er /abite/ v.i. live. —v.t. live in; (planète, zone) inhabit. **～é** a. (terre) inhabited.

habitude /abityd/ n.f. habit. **avoir l'～ de faire,** be used to doing. **d'～,** usually. **comme d'～,** as usual.

habitué, ～e /abitɥe/ n.m., f. regular visitor; (client) regular.

habituel, ～le /abitɥɛl/ a. usual. **～lement** adv. usually.

habituer /abitɥe/ v.t. **～ à,** accustom to. **s'～ à,** get used to.

hache /aʃ/ n.f. axe.

haché /aʃe/ a. (viande) minced; (phrases) jerky.

hacher /aʃe/ v.t. mince; (au couteau) chop.

hachette /aʃɛt/ n.f. hatchet.

hachis /aʃi/ n.m. minced meat; (Amer.) ground meat.

hachisch /aʃiʃ/ n.m. hashish.

hachoir /aʃwar/ n.m. (appareil) mincer; (couteau) chopper; (planche) chopping board.

hagard, ～e /agar, -d/ a. wild(-looking).

haie /'ɛ/ n.f. hedge; (rangée) row. **course de ～s,** hurdle race.

haillon /'ajɔ̃/ n.m. rag.

hain|e /'ɛn/ n.f. hatred. **～eux, ～euse** a. full of hatred.

haïr /'air/ v.t. hate.

hâl|e /'ɑl/ n.m. (sun-)tan. **～é** a. (sun-)tanned.

haleine /alɛn/ n.f. breath. **hors d'～,** out of breath. **travail de longue ～,** long job.

hal|er /'ale/ v.t. tow. **～age** n.m. towing.

haleter /'alte/ v.i. pant.

hall /'ol/ n.m. hall; (de gare) concourse.

halle /'al/ n.f. (covered) market. **～s,** (main) food market.

hallucination /alysinɑsjɔ̃/ n.f. hallucination.

halo /'alo/ n.m. halo.

halte /'alt/ n.f. stop; (repos) break; (escale) stopping place. —int. stop; (mil.) halt. **faire ～,** stop.

halt|ère /altɛr/ n.m. dumb-bell. **～érophilie** n.f. weight-lifting.

hamac /'amak/ n.m. hammock.

hamburger /ãburgœr/ n.m. hamburger.

hameau (pl. **～x**) /'amo/ n.m. hamlet.

hameçon /amsɔ̃/ n.m. (fish-)hook.

hanche /'ãʃ/ n.f. hip.

hand-ball /'ãdbal/ n.m. handball.

handicap /'ãdikap/ n.m. handicap. **～é, ～ée** a. & n.m., f. handicapped (person). **～er** v.t. handicap.

hangar /'ãgar/ n.m. shed; (pour avions) hangar.

hanneton /'antɔ̃/ n.m. May-bug.

hanter /'ãte/ v.t. haunt.

hantise /'ãtiz/ n.f. obsession (**de,** with).

happer /'ape/ v.t. snatch, catch.

haras /'ara/ n.m. stud-farm.

harasser /'arase/ v.t. exhaust.

harcèlement /arsɛlmã/ n.m. **～ sexuel,** sexual harassment.

harceler /'arsəle/ v.t. harass.
hardi /'ardi/ a. bold. ~esse /-djɛs/ n.f.
boldness. ~ment adv. boldly.
hareng /'arɑ̃/ n.m. herring.
hargn|e /'arɲ/ n.f. (aggressive) bad
temper. ~eux, ~euse a. bad-tempered.
haricot /'ariko/ n.m. bean. ~ vert,
French ou string bean; (Amer.) green
bean.
harmonica /armɔnika/ n.m. harmonica.
harmon|ie /armɔni/ n.f. harmony.
~ieux, ~ieuse a. harmonious.
harmoniser /armɔnize/ v.t., s'~ v. pr.
harmonize.
harnacher /'arnaʃe/ v.t. harness.
harnais /'arnɛ/ n.m. harness.
harp|e /'arp/ n.f. harp. ~iste n.m./f.
harpist.
harpon /'arpɔ̃/ n.m. harpoon. ~ner
/-ɔne/ v.t. harpoon; (arrêter: fam.)
detain.
hasard /'azar/ n.m. chance; (coïnci-
dence) coincidence. ~s, (risques)
hazards. au ~, (choisir etc.) at random;
(flâner) aimlessly. ~eux, ~euse /-dø,
-z/ a. risky.
hasarder /'azarde/ v.t. risk; (remarque)
venture. se ~ dans, risk going into. se
~ à faire, risk doing.
hâte /'at/ n.f. haste. à la ~, en ~,
hurriedly. avoir ~ de, be eager to.
hâter /'ate/ v.t. hasten. se ~ v. pr. hurry
(de, to).
hâti|f, ~ve /'atif, -v/ a. hasty;
(précoce) early.
hauss|e /'os/ n.f. rise (de, in). ~e des
prix, price rises. en ~e, rising. ~er v.t.
raise; (épaules) shrug. se ~er v. pr.
stand up, raise o.s. up.
haut, ~e /'o, 'ot/ a. high; (de taille) tall.
—adv. high; (parler) loud(ly); (lire)
aloud. —n.m. top. à ~e voix, aloud.
des ~s et des bas, ups and downs. en
~, (regarder, jeter) up; (dans une
maison) upstairs. en ~ (de), at the top
(of). ~ en couleur, colourful. plus ~,
further up, higher up; (dans un texte)
above. en ~ lieu, in high places. ~-de-
forme (pl. ~s-de-forme) n.m. top hat.
~-fourneau (pl. ~s-fourneaux) n.m.
blast-furnace. ~-le-cœur n.m. invar.
nausea. ~-parleur n.m. loudspeaker.
hautain, ~e /'otɛ̃, -ɛn/ a. haughty.
hautbois /'obwa/ n.m. oboe.
hautement /'otmɑ̃/ adv. highly.
hauteur /'otœr/ n.f. height; (colline)
hill; (arrogance) haughtiness. à la ~,
(fam.) up to it. à la ~ de, level with;
(tâche, situation) equal to.

hâve /'av/ a. gaunt.
havre /'avr/ n.m. haven.
Haye (La) /(la)'ɛ/ n.f. The Hague.
hayon /'ɛjɔ̃/ n.m. (auto.) rear opening,
tail-gate.
hebdo /ɛbdo/ n.m. (fam.) weekly.
hebdomadaire /ɛbdɔmadɛr/ a. & n.m.
weekly.
héberg|er /ebɛrʒe/ v.t. accommodate,
take in. ~ement n.m. accommodation.
hébété /ebete/ a. dazed.
hébraïque /ebraik/ a. Hebrew.
hébreu (pl. ~x) /ebrø/ a.m. Hebrew.
—n.m. (lang.) Hebrew. c'est de l'~!,
it's double Dutch.
hécatombe /ekatɔ̃b/ n.f. slaughter.
hectare /ɛktar/ n.m. hectare (= 10,000
square metres).
hégémonie /eʒemɔni/ n.f. hegemony.
hein /'ɛ̃/ int. (fam.) eh.
hélas /'elas/ int. alas. —adv. sadly.
héler /'ele/ v.t. hail.
hélice /elis/ n.f. propeller.
hélicoptère /elikɔptɛr/ n.m. helicopter.
helvétique /ɛlvetik/ a. Swiss.
hématome /ematom/ n.m. bruise.
hémisphère /emisfɛr/ n.m. hemisphere.
hémorragie /emɔraʒi/ n.f. haemorrhage.
hémorroïdes /emɔrɔid/ n.f. pl. piles,
haemorrhoids.
henn|ir /'enir/ v.i. neigh. ~issement
n.m. neigh.
hépatite /epatit/ n.f. hepatitis.
herbage /ɛrbaʒ/ n.m. pasture.
herb|e /ɛrb/ n.f. grass; (méd., culin.)
herb. en ~e, green; (fig.) budding.
~eux, ~euse a. grassy.
herbicide /ɛrbisid/ n.m. weed-killer.
hérédit|é /eredite/ n.f. heredity. ~aire a.
hereditary.
héré|sie /erezi/ n.f. heresy. ~tique a.
heretical; n.m./f. heretic.
hériss|er /'erise/ v.t., se ~er v. pr.
bristle. ~er qn., ruffle s.o. ~é a.
bristling (de, with).
hérisson /'erisɔ̃/ n.m. hedgehog.
héritage /eritaʒ/ n.m. inheritance;
(spirituel etc.) heritage.
hérit|er /erite/ v.t./i. inherit (de, from).
~er de qch., inherit sth. ~ier, ~ière
n.m., f. heir, heiress.
hermétique /ɛrmetik/ a. airtight; (fig.)
unfathomable. ~ment adv. hermetic-
ally.
hermine /ɛrmin/ n.f. ermine.
hernie /'ɛrni/ n.f. hernia.
héroïne[1] /erɔin/ n.f. (femme) heroine.
héroïne[2] /erɔin/ n.f. (drogue) heroin.

héroï|que /erɔik/ a. heroic. ∼**sme** n.m. heroism.

héron /'erɔ̃/ n.m. heron.

héros /'ero/ n.m. hero.

hésit|er /ezite/ v.i. hesitate (**à**, to). **en** ∼**ant**, hesitantly. ∼**ant**, ∼**ante** a. hesitant. ∼**ation** n.f. hesitation.

hétéro /etero/ n.m. & a. (fam.) straight.

hétéroclite /eterɔklit/ a. heterogeneous.

hétérogène /eterɔʒɛn/ a. heterogeneous.

hétérosexuel, ∼**le** /eterɔsɛksɥɛl/ n.m., f. & a. heterosexual.

hêtre /'ɛtr/ n.m. beech.

heure /œr/ n.f. time; (mesure de durée) hour; (scol.) period. **quelle** ∼ **est-il?**, what time is it? **il est dix**/etc. ∼**s**, it is ten/etc. o'clock. **à l'**∼, (venir, être) on time. **d'**∼ **en heure**, hourly. ∼ **avancée**, late hour. ∼ **d'affluence**, ∼ **de pointe**, rush-hour. ∼ **indue**, ungodly hour. ∼**s creuses**, off-peak periods. ∼**s supplémentaires**, overtime.

heureusement /œrøzmɑ̃/ adv. fortunately, luckily.

heureu|x, ∼**se** /œrø, -z/ a. happy; (chanceux) lucky, fortunate.

heurt /œr/ n.m. collision; (conflit) clash.

heurter /'œrte/ v.t. (cogner) hit; (mur etc.) bump into, hit; (choquer) offend. **se** ∼ **à**, bump into, hit; (fig.) come up against.

hexagone /ɛgzagɔn/ n.m. hexagon. **l'**∼, France.

hiberner /ibɛrne/ v.i. hibernate.

hibou (pl. ∼**x**) /'ibu/ n.m. owl.

hideu|x, ∼**se** /'idø, -z/ a. hideous.

hier /jɛr/ adv. yesterday. ∼ **soir**, last night, yesterday evening.

hiérarch|ie /'jerarʃi/ n.f. hierarchy. ∼**ique** a. hierarchical.

hi-fi /'ifi/ a. invar. & n.f. (fam.) hi-fi.

hilare /ilar/ a. merry.

hilarité /ilarite/ n.f. laughter.

hindou, ∼**e** /ɛ̃du/ a. & n.m., f. Hindu.

hippi|que /ipik/ a. horse, equestrian. ∼**sme** n.m. horse-riding.

hippodrome /ipɔdrom/ n.m. racecourse.

hippopotame /ipɔpɔtam/ n.m. hippopotamus.

hirondelle /irɔ̃dɛl/ n.f. swallow.

hirsute /irsyt/ a. shaggy.

hisser /'ise/ v.t. hoist, haul. **se** ∼ v. pr. raise o.s.

histoire /istwar/ n.f. (récit, mensonge) story; (étude) history; (affaire) business. ∼**(s)**, (chichis) fuss. ∼**s**, (ennuis) trouble.

historien, ∼**ne** /istɔrjɛ̃, -jɛn/ n.m., f. historian.

historique /istɔrik/ a. historical.

hiver /ivɛr/ n.m. winter. ∼**nal** (m. pl. ∼**naux**) a. winter; (glacial) wintry. ∼**ner** v.i. winter.

H.L.M. /'aʃɛlɛm/ n.m./f. (= habitation à loyer modéré) block of council flats; (Amer.) (government-sponsored) low-cost apartment building.

hocher /'ɔʃe/ v.t. ∼ **la tête**, (pour dire oui) nod; (pour dire non) shake one's head.

hochet /'ɔʃɛ/ n.m. rattle.

hockey /'ɔkɛ/ n.m. hockey. ∼ **sur glace**, ice hockey.

hold-up /'ɔldœp/ n.m. invar. (attaque) hold-up.

hollandais, ∼**e** /'ɔlɑ̃dɛ, -z/ a. Dutch. —n.m., f. Dutchman, Dutchwoman. —n.m. (lang.) Dutch.

Hollande /'ɔlɑ̃d/ n.f. Holland.

hologramme /ɔlɔgram/ n.m. hologram.

homard /'ɔmar/ n.m. lobster.

homéopathie /ɔmeɔpati/ n.f. homoeopathy.

homicide /ɔmisid/ n.m. homicide. ∼ **involontaire**, manslaughter.

hommage /ɔmaʒ/ n.m. tribute. ∼**s**, (salutations) respects. **rendre** ∼ **à**, pay tribute.

homme /ɔm/ n.m. man; (espèce) man(kind). ∼ **d'affaires**, businessman. ∼ **de la rue**, man in the street. ∼ **d'État**, statesman. ∼ **de paille**, stooge. ∼**-grenouille** (pl. ∼**s-grenouilles**) n.m. frogman. ∼ **politique**, politician.

homogène /ɔmɔʒɛn/ a. homogeneous. ∼**énéité** n.f. homogeneity.

homologue /ɔmɔlɔg/ n.m./f. counterpart.

homologué /ɔmɔlɔge/ a. (record) officially recognized; (tarif) official.

homologuer /ɔmɔlɔge/ v.t. recognize (officially), validate.

homonyme /ɔmɔnim/ n.m. (personne) namesake.

homosex|uel, ∼**uelle** /ɔmɔsɛksɥɛl/ a. & n.m., f. homosexual. ∼**ualité** n.f. homosexuality.

Hongrie /'ɔ̃gri/ n.f. Hungary.

hongrois, ∼**e** /'ɔ̃grwa, -z/ a. & n.m., f. Hungarian.

honnête /ɔnɛt/ a. honest; (satisfaisant) fair. ∼**ment** adv. honestly; fairly. ∼**té** n.f. honesty.

honneur /ɔnœr/ n.m. honour; (mérite) credit. **d'**∼, (invité, place) of honour; (membre) honorary. **en l'**∼ **de**, in honour of. **en quel** ∼**?**, (fam.) why? **faire** ∼ **à**, (équipe, famille) bring credit to.

honorable /ɔnɔrabl/ a. honourable; (*convenable*) respectable. **~ment** /-əmɑ̃/ adv. honourably; respectably.

honoraire /ɔnɔrɛr/ a. honorary. **~s** n.m. pl. fees.

honorer /ɔnɔre/ v.t. honour; (*faire honneur à*) do credit to. **s'~ de**, pride o.s. on.

honorifique /ɔnɔrifik/ a. honorary.

hont|e /'ɔ̃t/ n.f. shame. **avoir ~e**, be ashamed (**de**, of). **faire ~e à**, make ashamed. **~eux, ~euse** a. (*personne*) ashamed (**de**, of); (*action*) shameful. **~eusement** adv. shamefully.

hôpit|al (pl. **~aux**) /ɔpital, -o/ n.m. hospital.

hoquet /'ɔkɛ/ n.m. hiccup. **le ~**, (the) hiccups.

horaire /ɔrɛr/ a. hourly. **—**n.m. timetable. **~ flexible,** flexitime.

horizon /ɔrizɔ̃/ n.m. horizon; (*perspective*) view.

horizont|al (m. pl. **~aux**) /ɔrizɔ̃tal, -o/ a. horizontal. **~alement** adv. horizontally.

horloge /ɔrlɔʒ/ n.f. clock.

horlog|er, ~ère /ɔrlɔʒe, -ɛr/ n.m., f. watchmaker.

hormis /'ɔrmi/ prép. save.

hormon|al (m. pl. **~aux**) /ɔrmɔnal, -no/ a. hormonal, hormone.

hormone /ɔrmɔn/ n.f. hormone.

horoscope /ɔrɔskɔp/ n.m. horoscope.

horreur /ɔrœr/ n.f. horror. **avoir ~ de**, detest.

horrible /ɔribl/ a. horrible. **~ment** /-əmɑ̃/ adv. horribly.

horrifier /ɔrifje/ v.t. horrify.

hors /'ɔr/ prép. **~ de**, out of; (*à l'extérieur de*) outside. **~-bord** n.m. invar. speedboat. **~ d'atteinte**, out of reach. **~ d'haleine**, out of breath. **~-d'œuvre** n.m. invar. hors- d'œuvre. **~ de prix**, exorbitant. **~ de soi**, beside o.s. **~-jeu** a. invar. offside. **~-la-loi** n.m. invar. outlaw. **~ pair**, outstanding. **~-taxe** a. invar. duty-free.

hortensia /ɔrtɑ̃sja/ n.m. hydrangea.

horticulture /ɔrtikyltyr/ n.f. horticulture.

hospice /ɔspis/ n.m. home.

hospital|ier, ~ière[1] /ɔspitalje, -jɛr/ a. hospitable. **~ité** n.f. hospitality.

hospital|ier, ~ière[2] /ɔspitalje, -jɛr/ a. (*méd.*) hospital. **~iser** v.t. take to hospital.

hostie /ɔsti/ n.f. (*relig.*) host.

hostil|e /ɔstil/ a. hostile. **~ité** n.f. hostility.

hosto /ɔsto/ n.m. (*fam.*) hospital.

hôte /ot/ n.m. (*maître*) host; (*invité*) guest.

hôtel /otɛl/ n.m. hotel. **~ (particulier),** (private) mansion. **~ de ville,** town hall. **~ier, ~ière** /otəlje, -jɛr/ a. hotel; n.m., f. hotelier. **~lerie** n.f. hotel business; (*auberge*) country hotel.

hôtesse /otɛs/ n.f. hostess. **~ de l'air,** air hostess.

hotte /'ɔt/ n.f. basket; (*de cuisinière*) hood.

houblon /'ublɔ̃/ n.m. le **~**, hops.

houill|e /'uj/ n.f. coal. **~e blanche,** hydroelectric power. **~er, ~ère** a. coal; n.f. coalmine.

houl|e /'ul/ n.f. (*de mer*) swell. **~eux, ~euse** a. stormy.

houligan /uligɑ̃/ n.m. hooligan.

houppette /'upɛt/ n.f. powder-puff.

hourra /'ura/ n.m. & int. hurrah.

housse /'us/ n.f. dust-cover.

houx /'u/ n.m. holly.

hovercraft /ɔvɛrkraft/ n.m. hovercraft.

hublot /'yblo/ n.m. porthole.

huche /'yʃ/ n.f. **~ à pain,** breadbin.

huer /'ɥe/ v.t. boo. **huées** n.f. pl. boos.

huil|e /ɥil/ n.f. oil; (*personne: fam.*) bigwig. **~er** v.t. oil. **~eux, ~euse** a. oily.

huis /ɥi/ à **~ clos,** in camera.

huissier /ɥisje/ n.m. (*appariteur*) usher; (*jurid.*) bailiff.

huit /'ɥi(t)/ a. eight. **—**n.m. eight. **~ jours,** a week. **lundi en ~,** a week on Monday. **~aine** /'ɥitɛn/ n.f. (*semaine*) week. **~ième** /'ɥitjɛm/ a. & n.m./f. eighth.

huître /ɥitr/ n.f. oyster.

humain, ~e /ymɛ̃, ymɛn/ a. human; (*compatissant*) humane. **~ement** /ymɛnmɑ̃/ adv. humanly; humanely.

humanitaire /ymanitɛr/ a. humanitarian.

humanité /ymanite/ n.f. humanity.

humble /œ̃bl/ a. humble.

humecter /ymɛkte/ v.t. moisten.

humer /'yme/ v.t. smell.

humeur /ymœr/ n.f. mood; (*tempérament*) temper. **de bonne/mauvaise ~,** in a good/bad mood.

humid|e /ymid/ a. damp; (*chaleur, climat*) humid; (*lèvres, yeux*) moist. **~ité** n.f. humidity.

humil|ier /ymilje/ v.t. humiliate. **~iation** n.f. humiliation.

humilité /ymilite/ n.f. humility.

humorist|e /ymɔrist/ n.m./f. humorist. **~ique** a. humorous.

humour /ymur/ *n.m.* humour; (*sens*) sense of humour.

huppé /'ype/ *a.* (*fam.*) high-class.

hurl|er /'yrle/ *v.t./i.* howl. **~ement** *n.m.* howl(ing).

hurluberlu /yrlybɛrly/ *n.m.* scatter-brain.

hutte /'yt/ *n.f.* hut.

hybride /ibrid/ *a. & n.m.* hybrid.

hydratant, ~e /idratɑ̃, -t/ *a.* (*lotion*) moisturizing.

hydrate /idrat/ *n.m.* **~ de carbone,** carbohydrate.

hydraulique /idrolik/ *a.* hydraulic.

hydravion /idravjɔ̃/ *n.m.* seaplane.

hydro-electrique /idrɔelɛktrik/ *a.* hydroelectric.

hydrogène /idrɔʒɛn/ *n.m.* hydrogen.

hyène /jɛn/ *n.f.* hyena.

hyg|iène /iʒjɛn/ *n.f.* hygiene. **~iénique** /iʒjenik/ *a.* hygienic.

hymne /imn/ *n.m.* hymn. **~ national,** national anthem.

hyper- /ipɛr/ *préf.* hyper-.

hypermarché /ipɛrmarʃe/ *n.m.* (*supermarché*) hypermarket.

hypermétrope /ipɛrmetrɔp/ *a.* long-sighted.

hypertension /ipɛrtɑ̃sjɔ̃/ *n.f.* high blood-pressure.

hypno|se /ipnoz/ *n.f.* hypnosis. **~tique** /-ɔtik/ *a.* hypnotic. **~tisme** /-ɔtism/ *n.m.* hypnotism.

hypnotis|er /ipnɔtize/ *v.t.* hypnotize. **~eur** *n.m.* hypnotist.

hypocrisie /ipɔkrizi/ *n.f.* hypocrisy.

hypocrite /ipɔkrit/ *a.* hypocritical. —*n.m./f.* hypocrite.

hypoth|èque /ipɔtɛk/ *n.f.* mortgage. **~équer** *v.t.* mortgage.

hypoth|èse /ipɔtɛz/ *n.f.* hypothesis. **~étique** *a.* hypothetical.

hystér|ie /isteri/ *n.f.* hysteria. **~ique** *a.* hysterical.

I

iceberg /isbɛrg/ *n.m.* iceberg.

ici /isi/ *adv.* (*espace*) here; (*temps*) now. **d'~ demain,** by tomorrow. **d'~ là,** in the meantime. **d'~ peu,** shortly. **~ même,** in this very place.

icône /ikon/ *n.f.* icon.

idé|al (*m. pl.* **~aux**) /ideal, -o/ *a.* ideal. —*n.m.* (*pl.* **~aux**) ideal. **~aliser** *v.t.* idealize.

idéalis|te /idealist/ *a.* idealistic. —*n.m./f.* idealist. **~me** *n.m.* idealism.

idée /ide/ *n.f.* idea; (*esprit*) mind. **~ fixe,** obsession. **~ reçue,** conventional opinion.

identifi|er /idɑ̃tifje/ *v.t.*, **s'~ier** *v. pr.* identify (**à,** with). **~ication** *n.f.* identification.

identique /idɑ̃tik/ *a.* identical.

identité /idɑ̃tite/ *n.f.* identity.

idéolog|ie /ideɔlɔʒi/ *n.f.* ideology. **~ique** *a.* ideological.

idiom|e /idjom/ *n.m.* idiom. **~atique** /idjɔmatik/ *a.* idiomatic.

idiot, ~e /idjo, idjɔt/ *a.* idiotic. —*n.m., f.* idiot. **~ie** /idjɔsi/ *n.f.* idiocy; (*acte, parole*) idiotic thing.

idiotisme /idjɔtism/ *n.m.* idiom.

idolâtrer /idɔlatre/ *v.t.* idolize.

idole /idɔl/ *n.f.* idol.

idyll|e /idil/ *n.f.* idyll. **~ique** *a.* idyllic.

if /if/ *n.m.* (*arbre*) yew.

igloo /iglu/ *n.m.* igloo.

ignare /iɲar/ *a.* ignorant. —*n.m./f.* ignoramus.

ignifugé /iɲify3e/ *a.* fireproof.

ignoble /iɲɔbl/ *a.* vile.

ignoran|t, ~te /iɲɔrɑ̃, -t/ *a.* ignorant. —*n.m., f.* ignoramus. **~ce** *n.f.* ignorance.

ignorer /iɲɔre/ *v.t.* not know; (*personne*) ignore.

il /il/ *pron.* he; (*chose*) it. **il est vrai/***etc.* **que,** it is true/*etc.* that. **il neige/pleut/***etc.*, it is snowing/raining/*etc.* **il y a,** there is; (*pluriel*) there are; (*temps*) ago; (*durée*) for. **il y a 2 ans,** 2 years ago. **il y a plus d'une heure que j'attends,** I've been waiting for over an hour.

île /il/ *n.f.* island. **~ déserte,** desert island. **~ anglo-normandes,** Channel Islands. **~s Britanniques,** British Isles.

illég|al (*m. pl.* **~aux**) /ilegal, -o/ *a.* illegal. **~alité** *n.f.* illegality.

illégitim|e /ileʒitim/ *a.* illegitimate. **~ité** *n.f.* illegitimacy.

illettré, ~e /iletre/ *a. & n.m., f.* illiterate.

illicite /ilisit/ *a.* illicit.

illimité /ilimite/ *a.* unlimited.

illisible /ilizibl/ *a.* illegible; (*livre*) unreadable.

illogique /ilɔʒik/ *a.* illogical.

illumin|er /ilymine/ *v.t.*, **s'~er** *v. pr.* light up. **~ation** *n.f.* illumination. **~é a.** (*monument*) floodlit.

illusion /ilyzjɔ̃/ *n.f.* illusion. **se faire des ~s,** delude o.s. **~ner** /-jɔne/ *v.t.*

delude. **~niste** /-jɔnist/ *n.m./f.* conjuror.

illusoire /ilyzwar/ *a.* illusory.

illustre /ilystr/ *a.* illustrious.

illustr|er /ilystre/ *v.t.* illustrate. **s'~er** *v. pr.* become famous. **~ation** *n.f.* illustration. **~é** *a.* illustrated; *n.m.* illustrated magazine.

îlot /ilo/ *n.m.* island; (*de maisons*) block.

ils /il/ *pron.* they.

imag|e /imaʒ/ *n.f.* picture; (*métaphore*) image; (*reflet*) reflection. **~é** *a.* full of imagery.

imaginaire /imaʒinɛr/ *a.* imaginary.

imaginati|f, **~ve** /imaʒinatif, -v/ *a.* imaginative.

imagin|er /imaʒine/ *v.t.* imagine; (*inventer*) think up. **s'~er** *v. pr.* imagine (**que,** that). **~ation** *n.f.* imagination.

imbattable /ɛ̃batabl/ *a.* unbeatable.

imbécil|e /ɛ̃besil/ *a.* idiotic. *—n.m./f.* idiot. **~lité** *n.f.* idiocy; (*action*) idiotic thing.

imbib|er /ɛ̃bibe/ *v.t.* soak (**de,** with). **être ~é,** (*fam.*) be sozzled. **s'~er** *v. pr.* become soaked.

imbriqué /ɛ̃brike/ *a.* (*lié*) linked.

imbroglio /ɛ̃brɔglio/ *n.m.* imbroglio.

imbu /ɛ̃by/ *a.* **~ de,** full of.

imbuvable /ɛ̃byvabl/ *a.* undrinkable; (*personne: fam.*) insufferable.

imit|er /imite/ *v.t.* imitate; (*personnage*) impersonate; (*faire comme*) do the same as; (*document*) copy. **~ateur**, **~atrice** *n.m., f.* imitator; impersonator. **~ation** *n.f.* imitation; impersonation.

immaculé /imakyle/ *a.* spotless.

immangeable /ɛ̃mɑ̃ʒabl/ *a.* inedible.

immatricul|er /imatrikyle/ *v.t.* register. **(se) faire ~er,** register. **~ation** *n.f.* registration.

immature /imatyr/ *a.* immature.

immédiat, **~e** /imedja, -t/ *a.* immediate. *—n.m.* **dans l'~,** for the moment. **~ement** /-tmɑ̃/ *adv.* immediately.

immens|e /imɑ̃s/ *a.* immense. **~ément** *adv.* immensely. **~ité** *n.f.* immensity.

immer|ger /imɛrʒe/ *v.t.* immerse. **s'~ger** *v. pr.* submerge. **~sion** *n.f.* immersion.

immeuble /imœbl/ *n.m.* block of flats, building. **~ (de bureaux),** (office) building *ou* block.

immigr|er /imigre/ *v.i.* immigrate. **~ant**, **~ante** *a. & n.m., f.* immigrant. **~ation** *n.f.* immigration. **~é**, **~ée** *a. & n.m., f.* immigrant.

imminen|t, **~te** /iminɑ̃, -t/ *a.* imminent. **~ce** *n.f.* imminence.

immiscer (s') /(s)imise/ *v. pr.* interfere (**dans,** in).

immobil|e /imɔbil/ *a.* still, motionless. **~ité** *n.f.* stillness; (*inaction*) immobility.

immobil|ier, **~ière** /imɔbilje, -jɛr/ *a.* property. **agence ~ière,** estate agent's office; (*Amer.*) real estate office. **agent ~ier,** estate agent; (*Amer.*) real estate agent. **l'~ier,** property; (*Amer.*) real estate.

immobilis|er /imɔbilize/ *v.t.* immobilize; (*stopper*) stop. **s'~er** *v. pr.* stop. **~ation** *n.f.* immobilization.

immodéré /imɔdere/ *a.* immoderate.

immoler /imɔle/ *v.t.* sacrifice.

immonde /imɔ̃d/ *a.* filthy.

immondices /imɔ̃dis/ *n.f. pl.* refuse.

immor|al (*m. pl.* **~aux**) /imɔral, -o/ *a.* immoral. **~alité** *n.f.* immorality.

immortaliser /imɔrtalize/ *v.t.* immortalize.

immort|el, **~elle** /imɔrtɛl/ *a.* immortal. **~alité** *n.f.* immortality.

immuable /imɥabl/ *a.* unchanging.

immunis|er /imynize/ *v.t.* immunize. **~é contre,** (*à l'abri de*) immune to.

immunité /imynite/ *n.f.* immunity.

impact /ɛ̃pakt/ *n.m.* impact.

impair[1] /ɛ̃pɛr/ *a.* (*numéro*) odd.

impair[2] /ɛ̃pɛr/ *n.m.* blunder.

impardonnable /ɛ̃pardɔnabl/ *a.* unforgivable.

imparfait, **~e** /ɛ̃parfɛ, -t/ *a. & n.m.* imperfect.

impart|ial (*m. pl.* **~iaux**) /ɛ̃parsjal, -jo/ *a.* impartial. **~ialité** *n.f.* impartiality.

impasse /ɛ̃pas/ *n.f.* (*rue*) dead end; (*situation*) deadlock.

impassible /ɛ̃pasibl/ *a.* impassive.

impat|ient, **~iente** /ɛ̃pasjɑ̃, -t/ *a.* impatient. **~iemment** /-jamɑ̃/ *adv.* impatiently. **~ience** *n.f.* impatience.

impatienter /ɛ̃pasjɑ̃te/ *v.t.* annoy. **s'~** *v. pr.* lose patience (**contre,** with).

impayable /ɛ̃pɛjabl/ *a.* (killingly) funny, hilarious.

impayé /ɛ̃peje/ *a.* unpaid.

impeccable /ɛ̃pekabl/ *a.* impeccable.

impénétrable /ɛ̃penetrabl/ *a.* impenetrable.

impensable /ɛ̃pɑ̃sabl/ *a.* unthinkable.

impérati|f, **~ve** /ɛ̃peratif, -v/ *a.* imperative. *—n.m.* requirement; (*gram.*) imperative.

impératrice /ɛ̃peratris/ *n.f.* empress.

imperceptible /ɛ̃pɛrsɛptibl/ *a.* imperceptible.

imperfection /ɛ̃pɛrfɛksjɔ̃/ *n.f.* imperfection.

impér|ial (*m. pl.* ~**iaux**) /ɛ̃perjal, -jo/ *a.* imperial. ~**ialisme** *n.m.* imperialism.

impériale /ɛ̃perjal/ *n.f.* upper deck.

impérieu|x, ~**se** /ɛ̃perjø, -z/ *a.* imperious; (*pressant*) pressing.

impérissable /ɛ̃perisabl/ *a.* undying.

imperméable /ɛ̃pɛrmeabl/ *a.* impervious (**à**, to); (*manteau*, *tissu*) waterproof. —*n.m.* raincoat.

impersonnel, ~**le** /ɛ̃pɛrsɔnɛl/ *a.* impersonal.

impertinen|t, ~**te** /ɛ̃pɛrtinã, -t/ *a.* impertinent. ~**ce** *n.f.* impertinence.

imperturbable /ɛ̃pɛrtyrbabl/ *a.* unshakeable.

impét|ueux, ~**ueuse** /ɛ̃petɥø, -z/ *a.* impetuous. ~**uosité** *n.f.* impetuosity.

impitoyable /ɛ̃pitwajabl/ *a.* merciless.

implacable /ɛ̃plakabl/ *a.* implacable.

implant /ɛ̃plã/ *n.m.* implant.

implant|er /ɛ̃plãte/ *v.t.* establish. **s'**~**er** *v. pr.* become established. ~**ation** *n.f.* establishment.

implication /ɛ̃plikɑsjɔ̃/ *n.f.* implication.

implicite /ɛ̃plisit/ *a.* implicit.

impliquer /ɛ̃plike/ *v.t.* imply (**que**, that). ~ **dans**, implicate in.

implorer /ɛ̃plɔre/ *v.t.* implore.

impoli /ɛ̃pɔli/ *a.* impolite. ~**tesse** *n.f.* impoliteness; (*remarque*) impolite remark.

impondérable /ɛ̃pɔ̃derabl/ *a. & n.m.* imponderable.

impopulaire /ɛ̃pɔpylɛr/ *a.* unpopular.

importance /ɛ̃pɔrtãs/ *n.f.* importance; (*taille*) size; (*ampleur*) extent. **sans** ~, unimportant.

important, ~**e** /ɛ̃pɔrtã, -t/ *a.* important; (*en quantité*) considerable, sizeable, big. —*n.m.* **l'**~, the important thing.

import|er[1] /ɛ̃pɔrte/ *v.t.* (*comm.*) import. ~**ateur**, ~**atrice** *n.m.*, *f.* importer; *a.* importing. ~**ation** *n.f.* import.

import|er[2] /ɛ̃pɔrte/ *v.i.* matter, be important (**à**, to). **il** ~**e que**, it is important that. **n'**~**e**, **peu** ~**e**, it does not matter. **n'**~**e comment**, anyhow. **n'**~**e où**, anywhere. **n'**~**e qui**, anybody. **n'**~**e quoi**, anything.

importun, ~**e** /ɛ̃pɔrtœ̃, -yn/ *a.* troublesome. —*n.m.*, *f.* nuisance. ~**er** /-yne/ *v.t.* trouble.

imposant, ~**e** /ɛ̃pozã, -t/ *a.* imposing.

imposer /ɛ̃poze/ *v.t.* impose (**à**, on); (*taxer*) tax. **s'**~ *v. pr.* (*action*) be essential; (*se faire reconnaître*) stand out. **en** ~ **à qn.**, impress s.o.

imposition /ɛ̃pozisjɔ̃/ *n.f.* taxation. ~ **des mains**, laying-on of hands.

impossibilité /ɛ̃pɔsibilite/ *n.f.* impossibility. **dans l'**~ **de**, unable to.

impossible /ɛ̃pɔsibl/ *a. & n.m.* impossible. **faire l'**~, do the impossible.

impost|eur /ɛ̃pɔstœr/ *n.m.* impostor. ~**ure** *n.f.* imposture.

impôt /ɛ̃po/ *n.m.* tax. ~**s**, (*contributions*) tax(ation), taxes. ~ **sur le revenu**, income tax.

impotent, ~**e** /ɛ̃potã, -t/ *a.* crippled. —*n.m.*, *f.* cripple.

impraticable /ɛ̃pratikabl/ *a.* (*route*) impassable.

imprécis, ~**e** /ɛ̃presi, -z/ *a.* imprecise. ~**ion** /-zjɔ̃/ *n.f.* imprecision.

imprégner /ɛ̃preɲe/ *v.t.* fill (**de**, with); (*imbiber*) impregnate (**de**, with). **s'** ~ **de**, become filled with; (*s'imbiber*) become impregnated with.

imprenable /ɛ̃prǝnabl/ *a.* impregnable.

impresario /ɛ̃presarjo/ *n.m.* manager.

impression /ɛ̃presjɔ̃/ *n.f.* impression; (*de livre*) printing.

impressionn|er /ɛ̃presjɔne/ *v.t.* impress. ~**able** *a.* impressionable. ~**ant**, ~**ante** *a.* impressive.

imprévisible /ɛ̃previzibl/ *a.* unpredictable.

imprévoyant, ~**e** /ɛ̃prevwajã, -t/ *a.* improvident.

imprévu /ɛ̃prevy/ *a.* unexpected. —*n.m.* unexpected incident.

imprim|er /ɛ̃prime/ *v.t.* print; (*marquer*) imprint; (*transmettre*) impart. ~**ante** *n.f.* (*d'un ordinateur*) printer. ~**é** *a.* printed; *n.m.* (*formulaire*) printed form. ~**erie** *n.f.* (*art*) printing; (*lieu*) printing works. ~**eur** *n.m.* printer.

improbable /ɛ̃prɔbabl/ *a.* unlikely, improbable.

impromptu /ɛ̃prɔ̃pty/ *a. & adv.* impromptu.

impropr|e /ɛ̃prɔpr/ *a.* incorrect. ~**e à**, unfit for. ~**iété**, *n.f.* incorrectness; (*erreur*) error.

improvis|er /ɛ̃prɔvize/ *v.t./i.* improvise. ~**ation** *n.f.* improvisation.

improviste (à l') /(al)ɛ̃prɔvist/ *adv.* unexpectedly.

imprud|ent, ~**ente** /ɛ̃prydã, -t/ *a.* careless. **il est** ~**ent de**, it is unwise to. ~**emment** /-amã/ *adv.* carelessly. ~**ence** *n.f.* carelessness; (*acte*) careless action.

impuden|t, **∼te** /ɛ̃pydɑ̃, -t/ *a.*
impudent. **∼ce** *n.f.* impudence.
impudique /ɛ̃pydik/ *a.* immodest.
impuissan|t, **∼te** /ɛ̃pɥisɑ̃, -t/ *a.*
helpless; (*méd.*) impotent. **∼t à**,
powerless to. **∼ce** *n.f.* helplessness;
(*méd.*) impotence.
impulsi|f, **∼ve** /ɛ̃pylsif, -v/ *a.* impul-
sive.
impulsion /ɛ̃pylsjɔ̃/ *n.f.* (*poussée*,
influence) impetus; (*instinct*, *mouvement*) impulse.
impunément /ɛ̃pynemɑ̃/ *adv.* with
impunity.
impuni /ɛ̃pyni/ *a.* unpunished.
impunité /ɛ̃pynite/ *n.f.* impunity.
impur /ɛ̃pyr/ *a.* impure. **∼eté** *n.f.*
impurity.
imput|er /ɛ̃pyte/ *v.t.* **∼er à**, impute to.
∼able *a.* ascribable (**à**, to).
inabordable /inabɔrdabl/ *a.* (*prix*)
prohibitive.
inacceptable /inaksɛptabl/ *a.* unacceptable; (*scandaleux*) outrageous.
inaccessible /inaksesibl/ *a.* inaccessible.
inaccoutumé /inakutyme/ *a.* unaccustomed.
inachevé /inaʃve/ *a.* unfinished.
inacti|f, **∼ve** /inaktif, -v/ *a.* inactive.
inaction /inaksjɔ̃/ *n.f.* inactivity.
inadapté, **∼e** /inadapte/ *n.m.*, *f.*
(*psych.*) maladjusted person.
inadéquat, **∼e** /inadekwa, -t/ *a.*
inadequate.
inadmissible /inadmisibl/ *a.* unacceptable.
inadvertance /inadvɛrtɑ̃s/ *n.f.* **par ∼**,
by mistake.
inaltérable /inalterabl/ *a.* stable, that
does not deteriorate; (*sentiment*) unfailing.
inanimé /inanime/ *a.* (*évanoui*) unconscious; (*mort*) lifeless; (*matière*) inanimate.
inaperçu /inapɛrsy/ *a.* unnoticed.
inappréciable /inapresjabl/ *a.* invaluable.
inapte /inapt/ *a.* unsuited (**à**, to). **∼ à
faire**, incapable of doing.
inarticulé /inartikyle/ *a.* inarticulate.
inassouvi /inasuvi/ *a.* unsatisfied.
inattendu /inatɑ̃dy/ *a.* unexpected.
inattenti|f, **∼ve** /inatɑ̃tif, -v/ *a.*
inattentive (**à**, to).
inattention /inatɑ̃sjɔ̃/ *n.f.* inattention.
inaugur|er /inɔgyre/ *v.t.* inaugurate.
∼ation *n.f.* inauguration.
inaugur|al (*m. pl.* **∼aux**) /inɔgyral,
-o/ *a.* inaugural.

incalculable /ɛ̃kalkylabl/ *a.* incalculable.
incapable /ɛ̃kapabl/ *a.* incapable (**de
qch.**, of sth.). **∼ de faire**, unable to do,
incapable of doing. —*n.m./f.* incom-
petent.
incapacité /ɛ̃kapasite/ *n.f.* incapacity.
dans l'∼ de, unable to.
incarcérer /ɛ̃karsere/ *v.t.* incarcerate.
incarn|er /ɛ̃karne/ *v.t.* embody. **∼ation**
n.f. embodiment, incarnation. **∼é** *a.*
(*ongle*) ingrowing.
incartade /ɛ̃kartad/ *n.f.* indiscretion,
misdeed, prank.
incassable /ɛ̃kasabl/ *a.* unbreakable.
incendiaire /ɛ̃sɑ̃djɛr/ *a.* incendiary,
(*propos*) inflammatory. —*n.m./f.* arsonist.
incend|ie /ɛ̃sɑ̃di/ *n.m.* fire. **∼ie criminel**,
arson. **∼ier** *v.t.* set fire to.
incert|ain, **∼aine** /ɛ̃sɛrtɛ̃, -ɛn/ *a.*
uncertain; (*contour*) vague. **∼itude** *n.f.*
uncertainty.
incessamment /ɛ̃sɛsamɑ̃/ *adv.* shortly.
incessant, **∼e** /ɛ̃sɛsɑ̃, -t/ *a.* incessant.
incest|e /ɛ̃sɛst/ *n.m.* incest. **∼ueux**,
∼ueuse *a.* incestuous.
inchangé /ɛ̃ʃɑ̃ʒe/ *a.* unchanged.
incidence /ɛ̃sidɑ̃s/ *n.f.* effect.
incident /ɛ̃sidɑ̃/ *n.m.* incident. **∼
technique**, technical hitch.
incinér|er /ɛ̃sinere/ *v.t.* incinerate;
(*mort*) cremate. **∼ateur** *n.m.* in-
cinerator.
incis|er /ɛ̃size/ *v.t.* (*abcès etc.*) lance.
∼ion *n.f.* lancing; (*entaille*) incision.
incisi|f, **∼ve** /ɛ̃sizif, -v/ *a.* incisive.
incit|er /ɛ̃site/ *v.t.* incite (**à**, to). **∼ation**
n.f. incitement.
inclinaison /ɛ̃klinɛzɔ̃/ *n.f.* incline; (*de la
tête*) tilt.
inclination[1] /ɛ̃klinasjɔ̃/ *n.f.* (*penchant*)
inclination.
inclin|er /ɛ̃kline/ *v.t.* tilt, lean; (*courber*)
bend; (*inciter*) encourage (**à**, to). —*v.i.*
∼er à, be inclined to. **s'∼er** *v. pr.* (*se
courber*) bow down; (*céder*) give in;
(*chemin*) slope. **∼er la tête**,
(*approuver*) nod; (*révérence*) bow.
∼ation[2] *n.f.* (*de la tête*) nod; (*du buste*)
bow.
incl|ure /ɛ̃klyr/ *v.t.* include; (*enfermer*)
enclose. **jusqu'au lundi ∼us**, up to and
including Monday. **∼usion** *n.f.* inclu-
sion.
incognito /ɛ̃kɔnito/ *adv.* incognito.
incohéren|t, **∼te** /ɛ̃kɔerɑ̃, -t/ *a.*
incoherent. **∼ce** *n.f.* incoherence.

incollable /ɛ̃kɔlabl/ *a.* **il est ~**, he can't be stumped.

incolore /ɛ̃kɔlɔr/ *a.* colourless; (*crème*, *verre*) clear.

incomber /ɛ̃kɔ̃be/ *v.i.* **il vous**/*etc.* **incombe de**, it is your/*etc.* responsibility to.

incombustible /ɛ̃kɔ̃bystibl/ *a.* incombustible.

incommode /ɛ̃kɔmɔd/ *a.* awkward.

incommoder /ɛ̃kɔmɔde/ *v.t.* inconvenience.

incomparable /ɛ̃kɔ̃parabl/ *a.* incomparable.

incompatib|le /ɛ̃kɔ̃patibl/ *a.* incompatible. **~ilité** *n.f.* incompatibility.

incompéten|t, **~te** /ɛ̃kɔ̃petɑ̃, -t/ *a.* incompetent. **~ce** *n.f.* incompetence.

incompl|et, **~ète** /ɛ̃kɔ̃plɛ, -t/ *a.* incomplete.

incompréhensible /ɛ̃kɔ̃preɑ̃sibl/ *a.* incomprehensible.

incompréhension /ɛ̃kɔ̃preɑ̃sjɔ̃/ *n.f.* lack of understanding.

incompris, **~e** /ɛ̃kɔ̃pri, -z/ *a.* misunderstood.

inconcevable /ɛ̃kɔ̃svabl/ *a.* inconceivable.

inconciliable /ɛ̃kɔ̃siljabl/ *a.* irreconcilable.

inconditionnel, **~le** /ɛ̃kɔ̃disjɔnɛl/ *a.* unconditional.

inconduite /ɛ̃kɔ̃dɥit/ *n.f.* loose behaviour.

inconfort /ɛ̃kɔ̃fɔr/ *n.m.* discomfort. **~able** /-tabl/ *a.* uncomfortable.

incongru /ɛ̃kɔ̃gry/ *a.* unseemly.

inconnu, **~e** /ɛ̃kɔny/ *a.* unknown (**à**, to). —*n.m.*, *f.* stranger. —*n.m.* **l'~**, the unknown. —*n.f.* unknown (quantity).

inconsc|ient, **~iente** /ɛ̃kɔ̃sjɑ̃, -t/ *a.* unconscious (**de**, of); (*fou*) mad. —*n.m.* (*psych.*) subconscious. **~iemment** /-jamɑ̃/ *adv.* unconsciously. **~ience** *n.f.* unconsciousness; (*folie*) madness.

inconsidéré /ɛ̃kɔ̃sidere/ *a.* thoughtless.

inconsistant, **~e** /ɛ̃kɔ̃sistɑ̃, -t/ *a.* (*fig.*) flimsy.

inconsolable /ɛ̃kɔ̃sɔlabl/ *a.* inconsolable.

inconstan|t, **~te** /ɛ̃kɔ̃stɑ̃, -t/ *a.* fickle. **~ce** *n.f.* fickleness.

incontest|able /ɛ̃kɔ̃tɛstabl/ *a.* indisputable. **~é** *a.* undisputed.

incontinen|t, **~te** /ɛ̃kɔ̃tinɑ̃, -t/ *a.* incontinent. **~ce** *n.f.* incontinence.

incontrôlable /ɛ̃kɔ̃trolabl/ *a.* unverifiable.

inconvenan|t, **~te** /ɛ̃kɔ̃vnɑ̃, -t/ *a.* improper. **~ce** *n.f.* impropriety.

inconvénient /ɛ̃kɔ̃venjɑ̃/ *n.m.* disadvantage; (*risque*) risk; (*objection*) objection.

incorpor|er /ɛ̃kɔrpɔre/ *v.t.* incorporate; (*mil.*) enlist. **~ation** *n.f.* incorporation; (*mil.*) enlistment.

incorrect /ɛ̃kɔrɛkt/ *a.* (*faux*) incorrect; (*malséant*) improper; (*impoli*) impolite.

incorrigible /ɛ̃kɔriʒibl/ *a.* incorrigible.

incrédul|e /ɛ̃kredyl/ *a.* incredulous. **~ité** *n.f.* incredulity.

increvable /ɛ̃krəvabl/ *a.* (*fam.*) tireless.

incriminer /ɛ̃krimine/ *v.t.* incriminate.

incroyable /ɛ̃krwajabl/ *a.* incredible.

incroyant, **~e** /ɛ̃krwajɑ̃, -t/ *n.m.*, *f.* non-believer.

incrust|er /ɛ̃kryste/ *v.t.* (*décorer*) inlay (**de**, with). **s'~er** (*invité*: *péj.*) take root. **~ation** *n.f.* inlay.

incubateur /ɛ̃kybatœr/ *n.m.* incubator.

inculp|er /ɛ̃kylpe/ *v.t.* charge (**de**, with). **~ation** *n.f.* charge. **~é**, **~ée** *n.m.*, *f.* accused.

inculquer /ɛ̃kylke/ *v.t.* instil (**à**, into).

inculte /ɛ̃kylt/ *a.* uncultivated; (*personne*) uneducated.

incurable /ɛ̃kyrabl/ *a.* incurable.

incursion /ɛ̃kyrsjɔ̃/ *n.f.* incursion.

incurver /ɛ̃kyrve/ *v.t.*, **s'~** *v. pr.* curve.

Inde /ɛ̃d/ *n.f.* India.

indécen|t, **~te** /ɛ̃desɑ̃, -t/ *a.* indecent. **~ce** *n.f.* indecency.

indéchiffrable /ɛ̃deʃifrabl/ *a.* indecipherable.

indécis, **~e** /ɛ̃desi, -z/ *a.* indecisive; (*qui n'a pas encore pris de décision*) undecided. **~ion** /-izjɔ̃/ *n.f.* indecision.

indéfendable /ɛ̃defɑ̃dabl/ *a.* indefensible.

indéfini /ɛ̃defini/ *a.* indefinite; (*vague*) undefined. **~ment** *adv.* indefinitely. **~ssable** *a.* indefinable.

indélébile /ɛ̃delebil/ *a.* indelible.

indélicat, **~e** /ɛ̃delika, -t/ *a.* (*malhonnête*) unscrupulous.

indemne /ɛ̃dɛmn/ *a.* unharmed.

indemniser /ɛ̃dɛmnize/ *v.t.* compensate (**de**, for).

indemnité /ɛ̃dɛmnite/ *n.f.* indemnity; (*allocation*) allowance. **~s de licenciement**, redundancy payment.

indéniable /ɛ̃denjabl/ *a.* undeniable.

indépend|ant, **~ante** /ɛ̃depɑ̃dɑ̃, -t/ *a.* independent. **~amment** *adv.* independently. **~amment de**, apart from. **~ance** *n.f.* independence.

indescriptible /ɛ̃dɛskriptibl/ *a.* indescribable.

indésirable /ɛ̃dezirabl/ *a.* & *n.m./f.* undesirable.

indestructible /ɛ̃dɛstryktibl/ *a.* indestructible.

indétermination /ɛ̃detɛrminasjɔ̃/ *n.f.* indecision.

indéterminé /ɛ̃detɛrmine/ *a.* unspecified.

index /ɛ̃dɛks/ *n.m.* forefinger; (*liste*) index. **∼er** *v.t.* index.

indic /ɛ̃dik/ (*fam.*) grass.

indica|teur, ∼trice /ɛ̃dikatœr, -tris/ *n.m.,* *f.* (police) informer. —*n.m.* (*livre*) guide; (*techn.*) indicator. **∼teur des chemins de fer,** railway timetable. **∼teur des rues,** street directory.

indicati|f, ∼ve /ɛ̃dikatif, -v/ *a.* indicative (**de,** of). —*n.m.* (*radio*) signature tune; (*téléphonique*) dialling code; (*gram.*) indicative.

indication /ɛ̃dikasjɔ̃/ *n.f.* indication; (*renseignement*) information; (*directive*) instruction.

indice /ɛ̃dis/ *n.m.* sign; (*dans une enquête*) clue; (*des prix*) index; (*de salaire*) rating.

indien, ∼ne /ɛ̃djɛ̃, -jɛn/ *a.* & *n.m.,* *f.* Indian.

indifféremment /ɛ̃diferamɑ̃/ *adv.* equally.

indifféren|t, ∼te /ɛ̃diferɑ̃, -t/ *a.* indifferent (**à,** to). **ça m'est ∼t,** it makes no difference to me. **∼ce** *n.f.* indifference.

indigène /ɛ̃diʒɛn/ *a.* & *n.m./f.* native.

indigen|t, ∼te /ɛ̃diʒɑ̃, -t/ *a.* poor **∼ce** *n.f.* poverty.

indigeste /ɛ̃diʒɛst/ *a.* indigestible. **∼ion** *n.f.* indigestion.

indignation /ɛ̃diɲasjɔ̃/ *n.f.* indignation.

indign|e /ɛ̃diɲ/ *a.* unworthy (**de,** of); (*acte*) vile. **∼ité** *n.f.* unworthiness; (*acte*) vile act.

indigner /ɛ̃diɲe/ **s'∼** *v. pr.* become indignant (**de,** at).

indiquer /ɛ̃dike/ *v.t.* show, indicate; (*renseigner sur*) point out, tell; (*déterminer*) give, state, appoint. **∼er du doigt,** point to *ou* out *ou* at. **∼é** *a.* (*heure*) appointed; (*opportun*) appropriate; (*conseillé*) recommended.

indirect /ɛ̃dirɛkt/ *a.* indirect.

indiscipliné /ɛ̃disipline/ *a.* unruly.

indiscr|et, ∼ète /ɛ̃diskrɛ, -t/ *a.* inquisitive. **∼étion** *n.f.* indiscretion; inquisitiveness.

indiscutable /ɛ̃diskytabl/ *a.* unquestionable.

indispensable /ɛ̃dispɑ̃sabl/ *a.* indispensable. **il est ∼ qu'il vienne,** it is essential that he comes.

indispos|er /ɛ̃dispoze/ *v.t.* make unwell. **∼er** (*mécontenter*) antagonize. **∼é** *a.* unwell. **∼ition** *n.f.* indisposition.

indistinct, ∼e /ɛ̃distɛ̃(kt), -ɛ̃kt/ *a.* indistinct. **∼ement** /-ɛ̃ktəmɑ̃/ *adv.* indistinctly; (*également*) without distinction.

individ|u /ɛ̃dividy/ *n.m.* individual. **∼ualiste** *n.m./f.* individualist.

individuel, ∼le /ɛ̃dividɥɛl/ *a.* individual; (*opinion*) personal. **chambre ∼le,** single room. **maison ∼le,** private house. **∼lement** *adv.* individually.

indivisible /ɛ̃divizibl/ *a.* indivisible.

indolen|t, ∼te /ɛ̃dɔlɑ̃, -t/ *a.* indolent. **∼ce** *n.f.* indolence.

indolore /ɛ̃dɔlɔr/ *a.* painless.

Indonésie /ɛ̃dɔnezi/ *n.f.* Indonesia.

Indonésien, ∼ne /ɛ̃dɔnezjɛ̃, -jɛn/ *a.* & *n.m.,* *f.* Indonesian.

indu, ∼e /ɛ̃dy/ *a.* **à une heure ∼e,** at some ungodly hour.

induire /ɛ̃dɥir/ *v.t.* infer (**de,** from). **∼ en erreur,** mislead.

indulgen|t, ∼te /ɛ̃dylʒɑ̃, -t/ *a.* indulgent; (*clément*) lenient. **∼ce** *n.f.* indulgence; leniency.

industr|ie /ɛ̃dystri/ *n.f.* industry. **∼ialisé** *a.* industrialized.

industriel, ∼le /ɛ̃dystrijɛl/ *a.* industrial. —*n.m.* industrialist. **∼lement** *adv.* industrially.

inébranlable /inebrɑ̃labl/ *a.* unshakeable.

inédit, ∼e /inedi, -t/ *a.* unpublished; (*fig.*) original.

inefficace /inefikas/ *a.* ineffective.

inég|al (*m. pl.* **∼aux**) /inegal, -o/ *a.* unequal; (*irrégulier*) uneven. **∼alé** *a.* unequalled. **∼alable** *a.* matchless. **∼alité** *n.f.* (*injustice*) inequality; (*irrégularité*) unevenness; (*différence*) difference (**de,** between).

inéluctable /inelyktabl/ *a.* inescapable.

inept|e /inɛpt/ *a.* inept, absurd. **∼ie** /inɛpsi/ *n.f.* ineptitude.

inépuisable /inepɥizabl/ *a.* inexhaustible.

inert|e /inɛrt/ *a.* inert; (*mort*) lifeless. **∼ie** /inɛrsi/ *n.f.* inertia.

inespéré /inɛspere/ *a.* unhoped for.

inestimable /inɛstimabl/ *a.* priceless.

inévitable /inevitabl/ *a.* inevitable.

inexact, ∼e /inɛgza(kt), -akt/ *a.*

(*imprécis*) inaccurate; (*incorrect*) incorrect.

inexcusable /inɛkskyzabl/ *a.* unforgivable.

inexistant, ~e /inɛgzistɑ̃, -t/ *a.* nonexistent.

inexorable /inɛgzɔrabl/ *a.* inexorable.

inexpérience /inɛksperjɑ̃s/ *n.f.* inexperience.

inexpli|cable /inɛksplikabl/ *a.* inexplicable. **~qué** *a.* unexplained.

in extremis /inɛkstremis/ *adv. & a.* (*par nécessité*) (taken/done etc.) as a last resort; (*au dernier moment*) (at the) last minute.

inextricable /inɛkstrikabl/ *a.* inextricable.

infaillible /ɛ̃fajibl/ *a.* infallible.

infâme /ɛ̃fam/ *a.* vile.

infamie /ɛ̃fami/ *n.f.* infamy; (*action*) vile action.

infanterie /ɛ̃fɑ̃tri/ *n.f.* infantry.

infantile /ɛ̃fɑ̃til/ *a.* infantile.

infantilisme /ɛ̃fɑ̃tilism/ *n.m.* infantilism. **faire de l'~**, be childish.

infarctus /ɛ̃farktys/ *n.m.* coronary (thrombosis).

infatigable /ɛ̃fatigabl/ *a.* tireless.

infatué /ɛ̃fatɥe/ *a.* **~ de sa personne**, full of himself.

infect /ɛ̃fɛkt/ *a.* revolting.

infect|er /ɛ̃fɛkte/ *v.t.* infect. **s'~er** *v. pr.* become infected. **~ion** /-ksjɔ̃/ *n.f.* infection.

infectieu|x, ~se /ɛ̃fɛksjø, -z/ *a.* infectious.

inférieur, ~e /ɛ̃ferjœr/ *a.* (*plus bas*) lower; (*moins bon*) inferior (**à**, to). —*n.m., f.* inferior. **~ à**, (*plus petit que*) smaller than.

infériorité /ɛ̃ferjɔrite/ *n.f.* inferiority.

infern|al (*m. pl.* **~aux**) /ɛ̃fɛrnal, -o/ *a.* infernal.

infester /ɛ̃fɛste/ *v.t.* infest.

infid|èle /ɛ̃fidɛl/ *a.* unfaithful. **~élité** *n.f.* unfaithfulness; (*acte*) infidelity.

infiltr|er (s') /(s)ɛ̃filtre/ *v. pr.* **s'~er (dans)**, (*personnes, idées, etc.*) infiltrate; (*liquide*) percolate. **~ation** *n.f.* infiltration.

infime /ɛ̃fim/ *a.* tiny, minute.

infini /ɛ̃fini/ *a.* infinite. —*n.m.* infinity. **à l'~**, endlessly. **~ment** *adv.* infinitely.

infinité /ɛ̃finite/ *n.f.* **une ~ de**, an infinite amount of.

infinitésimal /ɛ̃finitezimal/ *a.* infinitesimal.

infinitif /ɛ̃finitif/ *n.m.* infinitive.

infirm|e /ɛ̃firm/ *a. & n.m./f.* disabled (person). **~ité** *n.f.* disability.

infirmer /ɛ̃firme/ *v.t.* invalidate.

infirm|erie /ɛ̃firməri/ *n.f.* sickbay, infirmary. **~ier** *n.m.* (male) nurse. **~ière** *n.f.* nurse. **~ière-chef**, sister.

inflammable /ɛ̃flamabl/ *a.* (in)flammable.

inflammation /ɛ̃flamasjɔ̃/ *n.f.* inflammation.

inflation /ɛ̃flasjɔ̃/ *n.f.* inflation.

inflexible /ɛ̃flɛksibl/ *a.* inflexible.

inflexion /ɛ̃flɛksjɔ̃/ *n.f.* inflexion.

infliger /ɛ̃fliʒe/ *v.t.* inflict; (*sanction*) impose.

influen|ce /ɛ̃flyɑ̃s/ *n.f.* influence. **~çable** *a.* easily influenced. **~cer** *v.t.* influence.

influent, ~e /ɛ̃flyɑ̃, -t/ *a.* influential.

influer /ɛ̃flye/ *v.i.* **~ sur**, influence.

info /ɛ̃fo/ *n.f.* (some) news. **les ~s**, the news.

informa|teur, ~trice /ɛ̃fɔrmatœr, -tris/ *n.m., f.* informant.

informaticien, ~ne /ɛ̃fɔrmatisjɛ̃, -jɛn/ *n.m., f.* computer scientist.

information /ɛ̃fɔrmasjɔ̃/ *n.f.* information; (*jurid.*) inquiry. **une ~**, (some) information; (*nouvelle*) (some) news. **les ~s**, the news.

informati|que /ɛ̃fɔrmatik/ *n.f.* computer science; (*techniques*) data processing. **~ser** *v.t.* computerize.

informe /ɛ̃fɔrm/ *a.* shapeless.

informer /ɛ̃fɔrme/ *v.t.* inform (**de**, about, of). **s'~** *v. pr.* enquire (**de**, about).

infortune /ɛ̃fɔrtyn/ *n.f.* misfortune.

infraction /ɛ̃fraksjɔ̃/ *n.f.* offence. **~ à**, breach of.

infranchissable /ɛ̃frɑ̃ʃisabl/ *a.* impassable; (*fig.*) insuperable.

infrarouge /ɛ̃fraruʒ/ *a.* infra-red.

infrastructure /ɛ̃frastryktyr/ *n.f.* infrastructure.

infructueu|x, ~se /ɛ̃fryktɥø, -z/ *a.* fruitless.

infus|er /ɛ̃fyze/ *v.t./i.* infuse, brew. **~ion** *n.f.* herb-tea, infusion.

ingénier (s') /(s)ɛ̃ʒenje/ *v. pr.* **s'~ à**, strive to.

ingénieur /ɛ̃ʒenjœr/ *n.m.* engineer.

ingén|ieux, ~ieuse /ɛ̃ʒenjø, -z/ *a.* ingenious. **~iosité** *n.f.* ingenuity.

ingénu /ɛ̃ʒeny/ *a.* naive.

ingér|er (s') /(s)ɛ̃ʒere/ *v. pr.* **s'~er dans**, interfere in. **~ence** *n.f.* interference.

ingrat, ~e /ɛ̃gra, -t/ *a.* ungrateful; (*pénible*) thankless; (*disgracieux*) unattractive. **~itude** /-tityd/ *n.f.* ingratitude.

ingrédient /ɛ̃gredjɑ̃/ *n.m.* ingredient.
ingurgiter /ɛ̃gyrʒite/ *v.t.* swallow.
inhabité /inabite/ *a.* uninhabited.
inhabituel, ~**le** /inabitɥɛl/ *a.* unusual.
inhalation /inalasjɔ̃/ *n.f.* inhaling.
inhérent, ~**e** /inerɑ̃, -t/ *a.* inherent (**à,** in).
inhibition /inibisjɔ̃/ *n.f.* inhibition.
inhospital|ier, ~**ière** /inɔspitalje, -jɛr/ *a.* inhospitable.
inhumain, ~**e** /inymɛ̃, -ɛn/ *a.* inhuman.
inhum|er /inyme/ *v.t.* bury. ~**ation** *n.f.* burial.
inimaginable /inimaʒinabl/ *a.* unimaginable.
inimitié /inimitje/ *n.f.* enmity.
ininterrompu /inɛ̃tɛrɔ̃py/ *a.* continuous, uninterrupted.
iniqu|e /inik/ *a.* iniquitous. ~**ité** *n.f.* iniquity.
init|ial (*m. pl.* ~**iaux**) /inisjal, -jo/ *a.* initial. ~**ialement** *adv.* initially.
initiale /inisjal/ *n.f.* initial.
initialis|er /inisjalize/ (*comput.*) format. ~**ation** *n.f.* formatting.
initiative /inisjativ/ *n.f.* initiative.
init|ier /inisje/ *v.t.* initiate (**à,** into). **s'**~**ier** *v. pr.* become initiated (**à,** into). ~**iateur,** ~**iatrice** *n.m., f.* initiator. ~**iation** *n.f.* initiation.
inject|er /ɛ̃ʒɛkte/ *v.t.* inject. ~**é de sang,** bloodshot. ~**ion** -ksjɔ̃/ *n.f.* injection.
injur|e /ɛ̃ʒyr/ *n.f.* insult. ~**ier** *v.t.* insult. ~**ieux,** ~**ieuse** *a.* insulting.
injust|e /ɛ̃ʒyst/ *a.* unjust, unfair. ~**ice** *n.f.* injustice.
inlassable /ɛ̃lasabl/ *a.* tireless.
inné /ine/ *a.* innate, inborn.
innocen|t, ~**te** /inɔsɑ̃, -t/ *a. & n.m., f.* innocent. ~**ce** *n.f.* innocence.
innocenter /inɔsɑ̃te/ *v.t.* (*disculper*) clear, prove innocent.
innombrable /inɔ̃brabl/ *a.* countless.
innov|er /inɔve/ *v.i.* innovate. ~**ateur,** ~**atrice** *n.m., f.* innovator. ~**ation** *n.f.* innovation.
inoccupé /inɔkype/ *a.* unoccupied.
inoculer /inɔkyle/ *v.t.* inoculate.
inodore /inɔdɔr/ *a.* odourless.
inoffensi|f, ~**ve** /inɔfɑ̃sif, -v/ *a.* harmless.
inond|er /inɔ̃de/ *v.t.* flood; (*mouiller*) soak; (*envahir*) inundate (**de,** with). ~**é de soleil,** bathed in sunlight. ~**ation** *n.f.* flood; (*action*) flooding.
inopérant, ~**e** /inɔperɑ̃, -t/ *a.* inoperative.
inopiné /inɔpine/ *a.* unexpected.

inopportun, ~**e** /inɔpɔrtœ̃, -yn/ *a.* inopportune.
inoubliable /inublijabl/ *a.* unforgettable.
inouï /inwi/ *a.* incredible.
inox /inɔks/ *n.m.* (P.) stainless steel.
inoxydable /inɔksidabl/ *a.* **acier** ~**,** stainless steel.
inqualifiable /ɛ̃kalifjabl/ *a.* unspeakable.
inqu|iet, ~**iète** /ɛ̃kjɛ, -ɛ̃kjɛt/ *a.* worried. —*n.m., f.* worrier.
inquiét|er /ɛ̃kjete/ *v.t.* worry. **s'**~**er** worry (**de,** about). ~**ant,** ~**ante** *a.* worrying.
inquiétude /ɛ̃kjetyd/ *n.f.* anxiety, worry.
inquisition /ɛ̃kizisjɔ̃/ *n.f.* inquisition.
insaisissable /ɛ̃sezisabl/ *a.* indefinable.
insalubre /ɛ̃salybr/ *a.* unhealthy.
insanité /ɛ̃sanite/ *n.f.* insanity.
insatiable /ɛ̃sasjabl/ *a.* insatiable.
insatisfaisant, ~**e** /ɛ̃satisfəzɑ̃, -t/ *a.* unsatisfactory.
insatisfait, ~**e** /ɛ̃satisfɛ, -t/ *a.* (*mécontent*) dissatisfied; (*frustré*) unfulfilled.
inscription /ɛ̃skripsjɔ̃/ *n.f.* inscription; (*immatriculation*) enrolment.
inscrire† /ɛ̃skrir/ *v.t.* write (down); (*graver, tracer*) inscribe; (*personne*) enrol; (*sur une liste*) put down. **s'**~ *v. pr.* put one's name down. **s'**~ **à,** (*école*) enrol at; (*club, parti*) join; (*examen*) enter for. **s'**~ **dans le cadre de,** come within the framework of.
insecte /ɛ̃sɛkt/ *n.m.* insect.
insecticide /ɛ̃sɛktisid/ *n.m.* insecticide.
insécurité /ɛ̃sekyrite/ *n.f.* insecurity.
insensé /ɛ̃sɑ̃se/ *a.* mad.
insensib|le /ɛ̃sɑ̃sibl/ *a.* insensitive (**à,** to); (*graduel*) imperceptible. ~**ilité** *n.f.* insensitivity.
inséparable /ɛ̃separabl/ *a.* inseparable.
insérer /ɛ̃sere/ *v.t.* insert. **s'**~ **dans,** be part of.
insidieu|x, ~**se** /ɛ̃sidjø, -z/ *a.* insidious.
insigne /ɛ̃siɲ/ *n.m.* badge. ~**(s),** (*d'une fonction*) insignia.
insignifian|t, ~**te** /ɛ̃siɲifjɑ̃, -t/ *a.* insignificant. ~**ce** *n.f.* insignificance.
insinuation /ɛ̃sinɥasjɔ̃/ *n.f.* insinuation.
insinuer /ɛ̃sinɥe/ *v.t.* insinuate. **s'**~ **dans,** penetrate.
insipide /ɛ̃sipid/ *a.* insipid.
insistan|t, ~**te** /ɛ̃sistɑ̃, -t/ *a.* insistent. ~**ce** *n.f.* insistence.
insister /ɛ̃siste/ *v.i.* insist (**pour faire,** on doing). ~ **sur,** stress.

insolation /ɛ̃sɔlasjɔ̃/ *n.f.* (*méd.*) sunstroke.

insolen|t, ~te /ɛ̃sɔlɑ̃, -t/ *a.* insolent. **~ce** *n.f.* insolence.

insolite /ɛ̃sɔlit/ *a.* unusual.

insoluble /ɛ̃sɔlybl/ *a.* insoluble.

insolvable /ɛ̃sɔlvabl/ *a.* insolvent.

insomnie /ɛ̃sɔmni/ *n.f.* insomnia.

insonoriser /ɛ̃sɔnɔrize/ *v.t.* soundproof.

insoucian|t, ~te /ɛ̃susjɑ̃, -t/ *a.* carefree. **~ce** *n.f.* unconcern.

insoumission /ɛ̃sumisjɔ̃/ *n.f.* rebelliousness.

insoupçonnable /ɛ̃supsɔnabl/ *a.* undetectable.

insoutenable /ɛ̃sutnabl/ *a.* unbearable; (*argument*) untenable.

inspec|ter /ɛ̃spɛkte/ *v.t.* inspect. **~teur, ~trice** *n.m., f.* inspector. **~tion** /-ksjɔ̃/ *n.f.* inspection.

inspir|er /ɛ̃spire/ *v.t.* inspire. —*v.i.* breathe in. **~er à qn.**, inspire s.o. with. **s'~er de**, be inspired by. **~ation** *n.f.* inspiration; (*respiration*) breath.

instab|le /ɛ̃stabl/ *a.* unstable; (*temps*) unsettled; (*meuble, équilibre*) unsteady. **~ilité** *n.f.* instability; unsteadiness.

install|er /ɛ̃stale/ *v.t.* install; (*gaz, meuble*) put in; (*étagère*) put up; (*équiper*) fit out. **s'~er** *v. pr.* settle (down); (*emménager*) settle in. **s'~er comme**, set o.s. up as. **~ation** *n.f.* installation; (*de local*) fitting out; (*de locataire*) settling in. **~ations** *n.f. pl.* (*appareils*) fittings.

instance /ɛ̃stɑ̃s/ *n.f.* authority; (*prière*) entreaty. **avec ~**, with insistence. **en ~**, pending. **en ~ de**, in the course of, on the point of.

instant /ɛ̃stɑ̃/ *n.m.* moment, instant. **à l'~**, this instant.

instantané /ɛ̃stɑ̃tane/ *a.* instantaneous; (*café*) instant.

instar /ɛ̃star/ *n.m.* **à l'~ de**, like.

instaur|er /ɛ̃stɔre/ *v.t.* institute. **~ation** *n.f.* institution.

instiga|teur, ~trice /ɛ̃stigatœr, -tris/ *n.m., f.* instigator. **~tion** /-asjɔ̃/ *n.f.* instigation.

instinct /ɛ̃stɛ̃/ *n.m.* instinct. **d'~**, instinctively.

instincti|f, ~ve /ɛ̃stɛ̃ktif, -v/ *a.* instinctive. **~vement** *adv.* instinctively.

instit /ɛ̃stit/ *n.m./f.* (*fam.*) teacher.

instituer /ɛ̃stitɥe/ *v.t.* establish.

institut /ɛ̃stity/ *n.m.* institute. **~ de beauté**, beauty parlour. **~ univer**sitaire de technologie, polytechnic, technical college.

institu|teur, ~trice /ɛ̃stitytœr, -tris/ *n.m., f.* primary-school teacher.

institution /ɛ̃stitysjɔ̃/ *n.f.* institution; (*école*) private school.

instructi|f, ~ve /ɛ̃stryktif, -v/ *a.* instructive.

instruction /ɛ̃stryksjɔ̃/ *n.f.* education; (*document*) directive. **~s**, (*ordres, mode d'emploi*) instructions.

instruire† /ɛ̃strɥir/ *v.t.* teach, educate. **~ de**, inform of. **s'~** *v. pr.* educate o.s. **s'~ de**, enquire about.

instruit, ~e /ɛ̃strɥi, -t/ *a.* educated.

instrument /ɛ̃strymɑ̃/ *n.m.* instrument; (*outil*) implement.

insu /ɛ̃sy/ *n.m.* **à l'~ de**, without the knowledge of.

insubordination /ɛ̃sybɔrdinasjɔ̃/ *n.f.* insubordination.

insuffisan|t, ~te /ɛ̃syfizɑ̃, -t/ *a.* inadequate; (*en nombre*) insufficient. **~ce** *n.f.* inadequacy.

insulaire /ɛ̃sylɛr/ *a.* island. —*n.m./f.* islander.

insuline /ɛ̃sylin/ *n.f.* insulin.

insult|e /ɛ̃sylt/ *n.f.* insult. **~er** *v.t.* insult.

insupportable /ɛ̃sypɔrtabl/ *a.* unbearable.

insurg|er (s') /(s)ɛ̃syrʒe/ *v. pr.* rebel. **~é, ~ée** *a.* & *n.m., f.* rebel.

insurmontable /ɛ̃syrmɔ̃tabl/ *a.* insurmountable.

insurrection /ɛ̃syrɛksjɔ̃/ *n.f.* insurrection.

intact /ɛ̃takt/ *a.* intact.

intangible /ɛ̃tɑ̃ʒibl/ *a.* intangible.

intarissable /ɛ̃tarisabl/ *a.* inexhaustible.

intégr|al (*m. pl.* **~aux**) /ɛ̃tegral, -o/ *a.* complete; (*édition*) unabridged. **~alement** *adv.* in full. **~alité** *n.f.* whole. **dans son ~alité**, in full.

intégrant, ~e /ɛ̃tegrɑ̃, -t/ *a.* **faire partie ~e de**, be part and parcel of.

intègre /ɛ̃tɛgr/ *a.* upright.

intégr|er /ɛ̃tegre/ *v.t.*, **s'~er** *v. pr.* integrate. **~ation** *n.f.* integration.

intégri|ste /ɛ̃tegrist/ *a.* fundamentalist. **~sme** /-sm/ *n.m.* fundamentalism.

intégrité /ɛ̃tegrite/ *n.f.* integrity.

intellect /ɛ̃telɛkt/ *n.m.* intellect. **~uel, ~uelle** *a.* & *n.m., f.* intellectual.

intelligence /ɛ̃teliʒɑ̃s/ *n.f.* intelligence; (*compréhension*) understanding; (*complicité*) complicity.

intellig|ent, ~ente /ɛ̃teliʒɑ̃, -t/ *a.* intelligent. **~emment** /-amɑ̃/ *adv.* intelligently.

intelligible /ɛ̃teliʒibl/ a. intelligible.

intempéries /ɛ̃tɑ̃peri/ n.f. pl. severe weather.

intempesti|f, **~ve** /ɛ̃tɑ̃pɛstif, -v/ a. untimely.

intenable /ɛ̃tnabl/ a. unbearable; (*enfant*) impossible.

intendan|t, **~te** /ɛ̃tɑ̃dɑ̃, -t/ n.m. (*mil.*) quartermaster. —n.m., f. (*scol.*) bursar. **~ce** n.f. (*scol.*) bursar's office.

intens|e /ɛ̃tɑ̃s/ a. intense; (*circulation*) heavy. **~ément** adv. intensely. **~ifier** v.t., s'**~ifier** v. pr. intensify. **~ité** n.f. intensity.

intensi|f, **~ve** /ɛ̃tɑ̃sif, -v/ a. intensive.

intenter /ɛ̃tɑ̃te/ v.t. **~ un procès** ou **une action**, institute proceedings (**à**, **contre**, against).

intention /ɛ̃tɑ̃sjɔ̃/ n.f. intention (**de faire**, of doing). **à l'~ de qn.**, for s.o. **~né** /-jɔne/ a. **bien/mal ~né**, well-/ill-intentioned.

intentionnel, **~le** /ɛ̃tɑ̃sjɔnɛl/ a. intentional.

inter- /ɛ̃tɛr/ préf. inter-.

interaction /ɛ̃tɛraksjɔ̃/ n.f. interaction.

intercaler /ɛ̃tɛrkale/ v.t. insert.

intercéder /ɛ̃tɛrsede/ v.i. intercede (**en faveur de**, on behalf of).

intercept|er /ɛ̃tɛrsɛpte/ v.t. intercept. **~ion** /-psjɔ̃/ n.f. interception.

interchangeable /ɛ̃tɛrʃɑ̃ʒabl/ a. interchangeable.

interdiction /ɛ̃tɛrdiksjɔ̃/ n.f. ban. **~ de fumer**, no smoking.

interdire† /ɛ̃tɛrdir/ v.t. forbid; (*officiellement*) ban, prohibit. **~ à qn. de faire**, forbid s.o. to do.

interdit, **~e** /ɛ̃tɛrdi, -t/ a. (*étonné*) nonplussed.

intéressant, **~e** /ɛ̃teresɑ̃, -t/ a. interesting; (*avantageux*) attractive.

intéressé, **~e** /ɛ̃terese/ a. (**en cause**) concerned; (*pour profiter*) self-interested. —n.m., f. person concerned.

intéresser /ɛ̃terese/ v.t. interest; (*concerner*) concern. s'**~ à**, be interested in.

intérêt /ɛ̃terɛ/ n.m. interest; (*égoïsme*) self-interest. **~(s)**, (*comm.*) interest. **vous avez ~ à**, it is in your interest to.

interférence /ɛ̃tɛrferɑ̃s/ n.f. interference.

intérieur /ɛ̃terjœr/ a. inner, inside; (*vol, politique*) domestic; (*vie, calme*) inner. —n.m. interior; (*de boîte, tiroir*) inside. **à l'~ (de)**, inside; (*fig.*) within. **~ement** adv. inwardly.

intérim /ɛ̃terim/ n.m. interim. **assurer l'~**, deputize (**de**, for). **par ~**, acting. **faire de l'~**, temp. **~aire** a. temporary, interim.

interjection /ɛ̃tɛrʒɛksjɔ̃/ n.f. interjection.

interlocu|teur, **~trice** /ɛ̃tɛrlɔkytœr, -tris/ n.m., f. **son ~teur**, the person one is speaking to.

interloqué /ɛ̃tɛrlɔke/ a. **être ~**, be taken aback.

intermède /ɛ̃tɛrmɛd/ n.m. interlude.

intermédiaire /ɛ̃tɛrmedjɛr/ a. intermediate. —n.m./f. intermediary.

interminable /ɛ̃tɛrminabl/ a. endless.

intermittence /ɛ̃tɛrmitɑ̃s/ n.f. **par ~**, intermittently.

intermittent, **~e** /ɛ̃tɛrmitɑ̃, -t/ a. intermittent.

internat /ɛ̃tɛrna/ n.m. boarding-school.

internation|al (m. pl. **~aux**) /ɛ̃tɛrnasjɔnal, -o/ a. international.

interne /ɛ̃tɛrn/ a. internal. —n.m./f. (*scol.*) boarder.

intern|er /ɛ̃tɛrne/ v.t. (*pol.*) intern; (*méd.*) confine. **~ement** n.m. (*pol.*) internment.

interpell|er /ɛ̃tɛrpale/ v.t. shout to; (*apostropher*) shout at; (*interroger*) question. **~ation** n.f. (*pol.*) questioning.

interphone /ɛ̃tɛrfɔn/ n.m. intercom.

interposer (s') /(s)ɛ̃tɛrpoze/ v. pr. intervene.

interpr|ète /ɛ̃tɛrprɛt/ n.m./f. interpreter; (*artiste*) performer. **~étariat** n.m. interpreting.

interprét|er /ɛ̃tɛrprete/ v.t. interpret; (*jouer*) play; (*chanter*) sing. **~ation** n.f. interpretation; (*d'artiste*) performance.

interroga|teur, **~trice** /ɛ̃tɛrɔgatœr, -tris/ a. questioning.

interrogati|f, **~ve** /ɛ̃tɛrɔgatif, -v/ a. interrogative.

interrogatoire /ɛ̃tɛrɔgatwar/ n.m. interrogation.

interro|ger /ɛ̃tɛrɔʒe/ v.t. question; (*élève*) test. **~gateur**, **~gatrice** a. questioning. **~gation** n.f. question; (*action*) questioning; (*épreuve*) test.

interr|ompre† /ɛ̃tɛrɔ̃pr/ v.t. break off, interrupt; (*personne*) interrupt. **s'~ompre** v. pr. break off. **~upteur** n.m. switch. **~uption** n.f. interruption; (*arrêt*) break.

intersection /ɛ̃tɛrsɛksjɔ̃/ n.f. intersection.

interstice /ɛ̃tɛrstis/ n.m. crack.

interurbain /ɛ̃tɛryrbɛ̃/ *n.m.* long-distance telephone service.

intervalle /ɛ̃tɛrval/ *n.m.* space; (*temps*) interval. **dans l'~**, in the meantime.

interven|ir† /ɛ̃tɛrvənir/ *v.i.* intervene; (*survenir*) occur; (*méd.*) operate. **~tion** /-vɑ̃sjɔ̃/ *n.f.* intervention; (*méd.*) operation.

intervertir /ɛ̃tɛrvɛrtir/ *v.t.* invert.

interview /ɛ̃tɛrvju/ *n.f.* interview. **~er** /-ve/ *v.t.* interview.

intestin /ɛ̃tɛstɛ̃/ *n.m.* intestine.

intim|e /ɛ̃tim/ *a.* intimate; (*fête, vie*) private; (*dîner*) quiet. —*n.m./f.* intimate friend. **~ement** *adv.* intimately. **~ité** *n.f.* intimacy; (*vie privée*) privacy.

intimid|er /ɛ̃timide/ *v.t.* intimidate. **~ation** *n.f.* intimidation.

intituler /ɛ̃tityle/ *v.t.* entitle. **s'~** *v. pr.* be entitled.

intolérable /ɛ̃tɔlerabl/ *a.* intolerable.

intoléran|t, **~te** /ɛ̃tɔlerɑ̃, -t/ *a.* intolerant. **~ce** *n.f.* intolerance.

intonation /ɛ̃tɔnasjɔ̃/ *n.f.* intonation.

intox /ɛ̃tɔks/ *n.m.* (*fam.*) brainwashing.

intoxi|quer /ɛ̃tɔsike/ *v.t.* poison; (*pol.*) brainwash. **~cation** *n.f.* poisoning; (*pol.*) brainwashing.

intraduisible /ɛ̃tradɥizibl/ *a.* untranslatable.

intraitable /ɛ̃tretabl/ *a.* inflexible.

intransigean|t, **~te** /ɛ̃trɑ̃siʒɑ̃, -t/ *a.* intransigent. **~ce** *n.f.* intransigence.

intransiti|f, **~ve** /ɛ̃trɑ̃zitif, -v/ *a.* intransitive.

intraveineu|x, **~se** /ɛ̃travɛnø, -z/ *a.* intravenous.

intrépide /ɛ̃trepid/ *a.* fearless.

intrigu|e /ɛ̃trig/ *n.f.* intrigue; (*théâtre*) plot. **~er** *v.t./i.* intrigue.

intrinsèque /ɛ̃trɛ̃sɛk/ *a.* intrinsic.

introduction /ɛ̃trɔdyksjɔ̃/ *n.f.* introduction.

introduire† /ɛ̃trɔdɥir/ *v.t.* introduce, bring in; (*insérer*) put in, insert. **~ qn.**, show s.o. in. **s'~ dans**, get into, enter.

introspecti|f, **~ve** /ɛ̃trɔspɛktif, -v/ *a.* introspective.

introuvable /ɛ̃truvabl/ *a.* that cannot be found.

introverti, **~e** /ɛ̃trɔverti/ *n.m.*, *f.* introvert. —*a.* introverted.

intrus, **~e** /ɛ̃try, -z/ *n.m.*, *f.* intruder. **~ion** /-zjɔ̃/ *n.f.* intrusion.

intuiti|f, **~ve** /ɛ̃tɥitif, -v/ *a.* intuitive.

intuition /ɛ̃tɥisjɔ̃/ *n.f.* intuition.

inusable /inyzabl/ *a.* hard-wearing.

inusité /inyzite/ *a.* little used.

inutil|e /inytil/ *a.* useless; (*vain*) needless. **~ement** *adv.* needlessly. **~ité** *n.f.* uselessness.

inutilisable /inytilizabl/ *a.* unusable.

invalid|e /ɛ̃valid/ *a.* & *n.m./f.* disabled (person). **~ité** *n.f.* disablement.

invariable /ɛ̃varjabl/ *a.* invariable.

invasion /ɛ̃vazjɔ̃/ *n.f.* invasion.

invectiv|e /ɛ̃vɛktiv/ *n.f.* invective. **~er** *v.t.* abuse.

invend|able /ɛ̃vɑ̃dabl/ *a.* unsaleable. **~u** *a.* unsold.

inventaire /ɛ̃vɑ̃tɛr/ *n.m.* inventory. **faire l'~ de**, take stock of.

invent|er /ɛ̃vɑ̃te/ *v.t.* invent. **~eur** *n.m.* inventor. **~ion** /ɛ̃vɑ̃sjɔ̃/ *n.f.* invention.

inventi|f, **~ve** /ɛ̃vɑ̃tif, -v/ *a.* inventive.

inverse /ɛ̃vɛrs/ *a.* opposite; (*ordre*) reverse. —*n.m.* reverse. **~ment** /-əmɑ̃/ *adv.* conversely.

invers|er /ɛ̃vɛrse/ *v.t.* reverse, invert. **~ion** *n.f.* inversion.

investigation /ɛ̃vɛstigasjɔ̃/ *n.f.* investigation.

invest|ir /ɛ̃vɛstir/ *v.t.* invest. **~issement** *n.m.* (*comm.*) investment.

investiture /ɛ̃vɛstityr/ *n.f.* nomination.

invétéré /ɛ̃vetere/ *a.* inveterate.

invincible /ɛ̃vɛ̃sibl/ *a.* invincible.

invisible /ɛ̃vizibl/ *a.* invisible.

invit|er /ɛ̃vite/ *v.t.* invite (à, to). **~ation** *n.f.* invitation. **~é**, **~ée** *n.m.*, *f.* guest.

invivable /ɛ̃vivabl/ *a.* unbearable.

involontaire /ɛ̃vɔlɔ̃tɛr/ *a.* involuntary.

invoquer /ɛ̃vɔke/ *v.t.* call upon, invoke; (*alléguer*) plead.

invraisembl|able /ɛ̃vrɛsɑ̃blabl/ *a.* improbable; (*incroyable*) incredible. **~ance** *n.f.* improbability.

invulnérable /ɛ̃vylnerabl/ *a.* invulnerable.

iode /jɔd/ *n.m.* iodine.

ion /jɔ̃/ *n.m.* ion.

ira, irait /ira, irɛ/ *voir* **aller**[1].

Irak /irak/ *n.m.* Iraq. **~ien**, **~ienne** *a.* & *n.m.*, *f.* Iraqi.

Iran /irɑ̃/ *n.m.* Iran. **~ien**, **~ienne** /iranjɛ̃, -jɛn/ *a.* & *n.m.*, *f.* Iranian.

irascible /irasibl/ *a.* irascible.

iris /iris/ *n.m.* iris.

irlandais, **~e** /irlɑ̃dɛ, -z/ *a.* Irish. —*n.m.*, *f.* Irishman, Irishwoman.

Irlande /irlɑ̃d/ *n.f.* Ireland.

iron|ie /irɔni/ *n.f.* irony. **~ique** *a.* ironic(al).

irraisonné /irɛzɔne/ *a.* irrational.

irrationnel, **~le** /irasjɔnɛl/ *a.* irrational.

irréalisable /irealizabl/ *a.* (*projet*) unworkable.

irrécupérable /irekyperabl/ *a.* irretrievable, beyond recall.

irréel, ~le /ireɛl/ *a.* unreal.

irréfléchi /irefleʃi/ *a.* thoughtless.

irréfutable /irefytabl/ *a.* irrefutable.

irrégul|ier, ~ière /iregylje, -jɛr/ *a.* irregular. **~arité** *n.f.* irregularity.

irrémédiable /iremedjabl/ *a.* irreparable.

irremplaçable /irãplasabl/ *a.* irreplaceable.

irréparable /ireparabl/ *a.* beyond repair.

irréprochable /ireprɔʃabl/ *a.* flawless.

irrésistible /irezistibl/ *a.* irresistible; (*drôle*) hilarious.

irrésolu /irezɔly/ *a.* indecisive.

irrespirable /irɛspirabl/ *a.* stifling.

irresponsable /irɛspɔ̃sabl/ *a.* irresponsible.

irréversible /irevɛrsibl/ *a.* irreversible.

irrévocable /irevɔkabl/ *a.* irrevocable.

irrigation /irigɑsjɔ̃/ *n.f.* irrigation.

irriguer /irige/ *v.t.* irrigate.

irrit|er /irite/ *v.t.* irritate. **s'~er de,** be annoyed at. **~able** *a.* irritable. **~ation** *n.f.* irritation.

irruption /irypsjɔ̃/ *n.f.* **faire ~ dans,** burst into.

Islam /islam/ *n.m.* Islam.

islamique /islamik/ *a.* Islamic.

islandais, ~e /islɑ̃dɛ, -z/ *a.* Icelandic. —*n.m., f.* Icelander. —*n.m.* (*lang.*) Icelandic.

Islande /islɑ̃d/ *n.f.* Iceland.

isolé /izɔle/ *a.* isolated. **~ment** *adv.* in isolation.

isol|er /izɔle/ *v.t.* isolate; (*électr.*) insulate. **s'~er** *v. pr.* isolate o.s. **~ant** *n.m.* insulating material. **~ation** *n.f.* insulation. **~ement** *n.m.* isolation.

isoloir /izɔlwar/ *n.m.* polling booth.

Isorel /izɔrɛl/ *n.m.* (P.) hardboard.

isotope /izɔtɔp/ *n.m.* isotope.

Israël /israɛl/ *n.m.* Israel.

israélien, ~ne /israeljɛ̃, -jɛn/ *a. & n.m., f.* Israeli.

israélite /israelit/ *a.* Jewish. —*n.m./f.* Jew, Jewess.

issu /isy/ *a.* **être ~ de,** come from.

issue /isy/ *n.f.* exit; (*résultat*) outcome; (*fig.*) solution. **à l'~ de,** at the conclusion of. **rue** *ou* **voie sans ~,** dead end.

isthme /ism/ *n.m.* isthmus.

Italie /itali/ *n.f.* Italy.

italien, ~ne /italjɛ̃, -jɛn/ *a. & n.m., f.* Italian. —*n.m.* (*lang.*) Italian.

italique /italik/ *n.m.* italics.

itinéraire /itinerɛr/ *n.m.* itinerary, route.

itinérant, ~e /itinerã, -t/ *a.* itinerant.

I.U.T. /iyte/ *n.m.* (*abrév.*) polytechnic.

I.V.G. /iveʒe/ *n.f.* (*abrév.*) abortion.

ivoire /ivwar/ *n.m.* ivory.

ivr|e /ivr/ *a.* drunk. **~esse** *n.f.* drunkenness. **~ogne** *n.m.* drunk(ard).

J

j' /ʒ/ *voir* **je.**

jacasser /ʒakase/ *v.i.* chatter.

jachère (en) /(ã)ʒaʃɛr/ *adv.* fallow.

jacinthe /ʒasɛ̃t/ *n.f.* hyacinth.

jade /ʒad/ *n.m.* jade.

jadis /ʒadis/ *adv.* long ago.

jaillir /ʒajir/ *v.i.* (*liquide*) spurt (out); (*lumière*) stream out; (*apparaître, fuser*) burst forth.

jais /ʒɛ/ *n.m.* **(noir) de ~,** jet-black.

jalon /ʒalɔ̃/ *n.m.* (*piquet*) marker. **~ner** /-ɔne/ *v.t.* mark (out).

jalou|x, ~se /ʒalu, -z/ *a.* jealous. **~ser** *v.t.* be jealous of. **~sie** *n.f.* jealousy; (*store*) (venetian) blind.

jamais /ʒamɛ/ *adv.* ever. **(ne) ~,** never. **il ne boit ~,** he never drinks. **à ~,** for ever. **si ~,** if ever.

jambe /ʒɑ̃b/ *n.f.* leg.

jambon /ʒɑ̃bɔ̃/ *n.m.* ham. **~neau** (*pl. ~neaux*) /-ɔno/ *n.m.* knuckle of ham.

jante /ʒɑ̃t/ *n.f.* rim.

janvier /ʒɑ̃vje/ *n.m.* January.

Japon /ʒapɔ̃/ *n.m.* Japan.

japonais, ~e /ʒaponɛ, -z/ *a. & n.m., f.* Japanese. —*n.m.* (*lang.*) Japanese.

japper /ʒape/ *v.i.* yelp.

jaquette /ʒakɛt/ *n.f.* (*de livre, femme*) jacket; (*d'homme*) morning coat.

jardin /ʒardɛ̃/ *n.m.* garden. **~ d'enfants,** nursery (school). **~ public,** public park.

jardin|er /ʒardine/ *v.i.* garden. **~age** *n.m.* gardening. **~ier, ~ière** *n.m., f.* gardener; *n.f.* (*meuble*) plant-stand. **~ière de légumes,** mixed vegetables.

jargon /ʒargɔ̃/ *n.m.* jargon.

jarret /ʒarɛ/ *n.m.* back of the knee.

jarretelle /ʒartɛl/ *n.f.* suspender; (*Amer.*) garter.

jarretière /ʒartjɛr/ *n.f.* garter.

jaser /ʒaze/ *v.i.* jabber.

jasmin /ʒasmɛ̃/ *n.m.* jasmine.

jatte /ʒat/ *n.f.* bowl.

jaug|e /ʒoʒ/ *n.f.* capacity; (*de navire*) tonnage; (*compteur*) gauge. **~er** *v.t.* gauge.

jaun|e /ʒon/ *a. & n.m.* yellow; (*péj.*) scab. **~e d'œuf,** (egg) yolk. **rire ~e,** laugh on the other side of one's face. **~ir** *v.t./i.* turn yellow.

jaunisse /ʒonis/ *n.f.* jaundice.

javelot /ʒavlo/ *n.m.* javelin.

jazz /dʒaz/ *n.m.* jazz.

J.C. /ʒezykri/ *n.m.* (*abrév.*) **500 avant/après ~,** 500 B.C./A.D.

je, j'* /ʒə, ʒ/ *pron.* I.

jean /dʒin/ *n.m.* jeans.

jeep /(d)ʒip/ *n.f.* jeep.

jerrycan /(d)ʒerikan/ *n.m.* jerrycan.

jersey /ʒɛrzɛ/ *n.m.* jersey.

Jersey /ʒɛrzɛ/ *n.f.* Jersey.

Jésus /ʒezy/ *n.m.* Jesus.

jet¹ /ʒɛ/ *n.m.* throw; (*de liquide, vapeur*) jet. **~ d'eau,** fountain.

jet² /dʒɛt/ *n.m.* (*avion*) jet.

jetable /ʒətabl/ *a.* disposable.

jetée /ʒte/ *n.f.* pier.

jeter /ʒte/ *v.t.* throw; (*au rebut*) throw away; (*regard, ancre, lumière*) cast; (*cri*) utter; (*bases*) lay. **~ un coup d'œil,** have *ou* take a look (**à,** at). **se ~ contre,** (*heurter*) bash into. **se ~ dans,** (*fleuve*) flow into. **se ~ sur,** (*se ruer sur*) rush at.

jeton /ʒtɔ̃/ *n.m.* token; (*pour compter*) counter.

jeu (*pl.* **~x**) /ʒø/ *n.m.* game; (*amusement*) play; (*au casino etc.*) gambling; (*théâtre*) acting; (*série*) set; (*de lumière, ressort*) play. **en ~,** (*honneur*) at stake; (*forces*) at work. **~ de cartes,** (*paquet*) pack of cards. **~ d'échecs,** (*boîte*) chess set. **~ de mots,** pun. **~ télévisé,** television quiz.

jeudi /ʒødi/ *n.m.* Thursday.

jeun (à) /(a)ʒœ̃/ *adv.* **être/rester à ~,** be/stay without food; **comprimé à prendre à ~,** tablet to be taken on an empty stomach.

jeune /ʒœn/ *a.* young. —*n.m./f.* young person. **~ fille,** girl. **~s mariés,** newlyweds. **les ~s,** young people.

jeûn|e /ʒøn/ *n.m.* fast. **~er** *v.i.* fast.

jeunesse /ʒœnɛs/ *n.f.* youth; (*apparence*) youthfulness. **la ~,** (*jeunes*) the young.

joaill|ier, **~ière** /ʒɔaje, -jɛr/ *n.m., f.* jeweller. **~erie** *n.f.* jewellery; (*magasin*) jeweller's shop.

job /dʒɔb/ *n.m.* (*fam.*) job.

jockey /ʒɔkɛ/ *n.m.* jockey.

joie /ʒwa/ *n.f.* joy.

joindre† /ʒwɛ̃dr/ *v.t.* join (**à,** to);

(*contacter*) contact; (*mains, pieds*) put together; (*efforts*) combine; (*dans une enveloppe*) enclose. **se ~ à,** join.

joint, ~e /ʒwɛ̃, -t/ *a.* (*efforts*) joint; (*pieds*) together. —*n.m.* joint; (*ligne*) join; (*de robinet*) washer. **~ure** /-tyr/ *n.f.* joint; (*ligne*) join.

joker /ʒɔkɛr/ *n.m.* (*carte*) joker.

joli /ʒɔli/ *a.* pretty, nice; (*somme, profit*) nice. **c'est du ~!,** (*ironique*) charming! **c'est bien ~ mais,** that is all very well but. **~ment** *adv.* prettily; (*très: fam.*) awfully.

jonc /ʒɔ̃/ *n.m.* (bul)rush.

jonch|er /ʒɔ̃ʃe/ *v.t.,* **~é de,** littered with.

jonction /ʒɔ̃ksjɔ̃/ *n.f.* junction.

jongl|er /ʒɔ̃gle/ *v.i.* juggle. **~eur, ~euse** *n.m., f.* juggler.

jonquille /ʒɔ̃kij/ *n.f.* daffodil.

Jordanie /ʒɔrdani/ *n.f.* Jordan.

joue /ʒu/ *n.f.* cheek.

jou|er /ʒwe/ *v.t./i.* play; (*théâtre*) act; (*au casino etc.*) gamble; (*fonctionner*) work; (*film, pièce*) put on; (*cheval*) back; (*être important*) count. **~er à** *ou* **de,** play. **~er la comédie,** put on an act. **bien ~é!,** well done!

jouet /ʒwɛ/ *n.m.* toy; (*personne, fig.*) plaything; (*victime*) victim.

joueu|r, ~se /ʒwœr, -øz/ *n.m., f.* player; (*parieur*) gambler.

joufflu /ʒufly/ *a.* chubby-cheeked; (*visage*) chubby.

joug /ʒu/ *n.m.* yoke.

jouir /ʒwir/ *v.i.* (*sexe*) come. **~ de,** enjoy.

jouissance /ʒwisɑ̃s/ *n.f.* pleasure; (*usage*) use (**de qch.,** of sth.).

joujou (*pl.* **~x**) /ʒuʒu/ *n.m.* (*fam.*) toy.

jour /ʒur/ *n.m.* day; (*opposé à nuit*) day(time); (*lumière*) daylight; (*aspect*) light; (*ouverture*) gap. **de nos ~s,** nowadays. **du ~ au lendemain,** overnight. **il fait ~,** it is (day)light. **~ chômé** *ou* **férié,** public holiday. **~ de fête,** holiday. **~ ouvrable, ~ de travail,** working day. **mettre à ~,** update. **mettre au ~,** uncover. **au grand ~,** in the open. **donner le ~,** give birth. **voir le ~,** be born. **vivre au ~ le jour,** live from day to day.

journ|al (*pl.* **~aux**) /ʒurnal, -o/ *n.m.* (news)paper; (*spécialisé*) journal; (*intime*) diary; (*radio*) news. **~al de bord,** log-book.

journal|ier, ~ière /ʒurnalje, -jɛr/ *a.* daily.

journalis|te /ʒurnalist/ *n.m./f.* journalist. **~me** *n.m.* journalism.

journée /ʒurne/ *n.f.* day.
journellement /ʒurnɛlmã/ *adv.* daily.
jov|ial (*m. pl.* **~iaux**) /ʒɔvjal, -jo/ *a.* jovial.
joyau (*pl.* **~x**) /ʒwajo/ *n.m.* gem.
joyeu|x, **~se** /ʒwajø, -z/ *a.* merry, joyful. **~x anniversaire**, happy birthday. **~sement** *adv.* merrily.
jubilé /ʒybile/ *n.m.* jubilee.
jubil|er /ʒybile/ *v.i.* be jubilant. **~ation** *n.f.* jubilation.
jucher /ʒyʃe/ *v.t.*, **se ~** *v. pr.* perch.
judaï|que /ʒydaik/ *a.* Jewish. **~sme** *n.m.* Judaism.
judas /ʒyda/ *n.m.* peep-hole.
judiciaire /ʒydisjɛr/ *a.* judicial.
judicieu|x, **~se** /ʒydisjø, -z/ *a.* judicious.
judo /ʒydo/ *n.m.* judo.
juge /ʒyʒ/ *n.m.* judge; (*arbitre*) referee. **~ de paix**, Justice of the Peace. **~ de touche**, linesman.
jugé (au) /(o)ʒyʒe/ *adv.* by guesswork.
jugement /ʒyʒmã/ *n.m.* judgement; (*criminel*) sentence.
jugeote /ʒyʒɔt/ *n.f.* (*fam.*) gumption, common sense.
juger /ʒyʒe/ *v.t./i.* judge; (*estimer*) consider (**que**, that). **~ de**, judge.
juguler /ʒygyle/ *v.t.* stifle, check.
jui|f, **~ve** /ʒɥif, -v/ *a.* Jewish. —*n.m.*, *f.* Jew, Jewess.
juillet /ʒɥijɛ/ *n.m.* July.
juin /ʒɥɛ̃/ *n.m.* June.
jules /ʒyl/ *n.m.* (*fam.*) guy.
jum|eau, **~elle** (*m. pl.* **~eaux**) /ʒymo, -ɛl/ *a.* & *n.m.*, *f.* twin. **~elage** *n.m.* twinning. **~eler** *v.t.* (*villes*) twin.
jumelles /ʒymɛl/ *n.f. pl.* binoculars.
jument /ʒymã/ *n.f.* mare.
jungle /ʒœ̃gl/ *n.f.* jungle.
junior /ʒynjɔr/ *n.m./f.* & *a.* junior.
junte /ʒœ̃t/ *n.f.* junta.
jupe /ʒyp/ *n.f.* skirt.
jupon /ʒypɔ̃/ *n.m.* slip, petticoat.
juré, **~e** /ʒyre/ *n.m.*, *f.* juror. —*a.* sworn.
jurer /ʒyre/ *v.t.* swear (**que**, that). —*v.i.* (*pester*) swear; (*contraster*) clash (**avec**, with). **~ de qch./de faire**, swear to sth./to do.
juridiction /ʒyridiksjɔ̃/ *n.f.* jurisdiction; (*tribunal*) court of law.
juridique /ʒyridik/ *a.* legal.
juriste /ʒyrist/ *n.m./f.* legal expert.
juron /ʒyrɔ̃/ *n.m.* swear-word.
jury /ʒyri/ *n.m.* jury.
jus /ʒy/ *n.m.* juice; (*de viande*) gravy. **~ de fruit**, fruit juice.

jusque /ʒysk(ə)/ *prép.* **jusqu'à**, (up) to, as far as; (*temps*) until, till; (*limite*) up to; (*y compris*) even. **jusqu'à ce que**, until. **jusqu'à présent**, until now. **jusqu'en**, until. **jusqu'où?**, how far? **~ dans**, **~ sur**, as far as.
juste /ʒyst/ *a.* fair, just; (*légitime*) just; (*correct*, *exact*) right; (*vrai*) true; (*vêtement*) tight; (*quantité*) on the short side. **le ~ milieu**, the happy medium. —*adv.* rightly, correctly; (*chanter*) in tune; (*seulement*, *exactement*) just. (**un peu**) **~**, (*calculer*, *mesurer*) a bit fine *ou* close. **au ~**, exactly. **c'était ~**, (*presque raté*) it was a close thing.
justement /ʒystəmã/ *adv.* just; (*avec justice ou justesse*) justly.
justesse /ʒystɛs/ *n.f.* accuracy. **de ~**, just, narrowly.
justice /ʒystis/ *n.f.* justice; (*autorités*) law; (*tribunal*) court.
justif|ier /ʒystifje/ *v.t.* justify. —*v.i.* **~ier de**, prove. **se ~ier** *v. pr.* justify o.s. **~iable** *a.* justifiable. **~ication** *n.f.* justification.
juteu|x, **~se** /ʒytø, -z/ *a.* juicy.
juvénile /ʒyvenil/ *a.* youthful.
juxtaposer /ʒykstapoze/ *v.t.* juxtapose.

K

kaki /kaki/ *a. invar.* & *n.m.* khaki.
kaléidoscope /kaleidɔskɔp/ *n.m.* kaleidoscope.
kangourou /kãguru/ *n.m.* kangaroo.
karaté /karate/ *n.m.* karate.
kart /kart/ *n.m.* go-cart.
kascher /kaʃɛr/ *a. invar.* kosher.
képi /kepi/ *n.m.* kepi.
kermesse /kɛrmɛs/ *n.f.* fair; (*de charité*) fête.
kérosène /kerozɛn/ *n.m.* kerosene, aviation fuel.
kibboutz /kibuts/ *n.m.* kibbutz.
kidnapp|er /kidnape/ *v.t.* kidnap. **~eur**, **~euse** *n.m.*, *f.* kidnapper.
kilo /kilo/ *n.m.* kilo.
kilogramme /kilɔgram/ *n.m.* kilogram.
kilohertz /kilɛrts/ *n.m.* kilohertz.
kilom|ètre /kilɔmɛtr/ *n.m.* kilometre. **~étrage** *n.m.* (*approx.*) mileage.
kilowatt /kilɔwat/ *n.m.* kilowatt.
kinésithérapie /kineziterapi/ *n.f.* physiotherapy.
kiosque /kjɔsk/ *n.m.* kiosk. **~ à musique**, bandstand.

kit /kit/ *n.m.* **meubles en** ∼, flat-pack furniture.
kiwi /kiwi/ *n.m.* kiwi (*fruit*, *bird*).
klaxon /klaksɔn/ *n.m.* (P.) (*auto.*) horn. ∼**ner** /-e/ *v.i.* sound one's horn.
knock-out /nɔkawt/ *n.m.* knock-out.
ko /kao/ *n.m.* (*comput.*) k.
K.O. /kao/ *a. invar.* (knocked) out.
k-way /kawe/ *n.m. invar.* (P.) cagoule.
kyste /kist/ *n.m.* cyst.

L

l', la /l, la/ *voir* **le.**
là /la/ *adv.* there; (*ici*) here; (*chez soi*) in; (*temps*) then. **c'est là que,** this is where. **là où,** where. **là-bas** *adv.* over there. **là-dedans** *adv.* inside, in there. **là-dessous** *adv.* underneath, under there. **là-dessus** *adv.* on there. **là-haut** *adv.* up there; (*à l'étage*) upstairs.
-là /la/ *adv.* (*après un nom précédé de ce, cette, etc.*) **cet homme-là,** that man. **ces maisons-là,** those houses.
label /labɛl/ *n.m.* (*comm.*) seal.
labeur /labœr/ *n.m.* toil.
labo /labo/ *n.m.* (*fam.*) lab.
laboratoire /labɔratwar/ *n.m.* laboratory.
laborieu|x, ∼**se** /labɔrjø, -z/ *a.* laborious; (*personne*) industrious; (*dur*) heavy going. **classes/masses** ∼**ses,** working classes/masses.
labour /labur/ *n.m.* ploughing; (*Amer.*) plowing. ∼**er** *v.t./i.* plough; (*Amer.*) plow; (*déchirer*) rip at. ∼**eur** *n.m.* ploughman; (*Amer.*) plowman.
labyrinthe /labirɛ̃t/ *n.m.* maze.
lac /lak/ *n.m.* lake.
lacer /lase/ *v.t.* lace up.
lacérer /lasere/ *v.t.* tear (up).
lacet /lasɛ/ *n.m.* (*shoe-*)lace; (*de route*) sharp bend, zigzag.
lâche /lɑʃ/ *a.* cowardly; (*détendu*) loose. —*n.m./f.* coward. ∼**ment** *adv.* in a cowardly way.
lâcher /lɑʃe/ *v.t.* let go of; (*abandonner*) give up; (*laisser*) leave; (*libérer*) release; (*parole*) utter; (*desserrer*) loosen. —*v.i.* give way. ∼ **prise,** let go.
lâcheté /lɑʃte/ *n.f.* cowardice.
laconique /lakɔnik/ *a.* laconic.
lacrymogène /lakrimɔʒɛn/ *a.* **gaz** ∼, tear gas. **grenade** ∼, tear gas grenade.
lacté /lakte/ *a.* milk.
lacune /lakyn/ *n.f.* gap.

ladite /ladit/ *voir* **ledit.**
lagune /lagyn/ *n.f.* lagoon.
laïc /laik/ *n.m.* layman.
laid, ∼**e** /lɛ, lɛd/ *a.* ugly; (*action*) vile. ∼**eur** /lɛdœr/ *n.f.* ugliness.
lain|e /lɛn/ *n.f.* wool. **de** ∼**e,** woollen. ∼**age** *n.m.* woollen garment.
laïque /laik/ *a.* secular; (*habit, personne*) lay. —*n.m./f.* layman, laywoman.
laisse /lɛs/ *n.f.* lead, leash.
laisser /lese/ *v.t.* leave. ∼ **qn. faire,** let s.o. do. ∼ **qch. à qn.,** let s.o. have sth., leave s.o. sth. ∼ **tomber,** drop. se ∼ **aller,** let o.s. go. ∼**-aller** *n.m. invar.* carelessness. **laissez-passer** *n.m. invar.* pass.
lait /lɛ/ *n.m.* milk. **frère/sœur de** ∼, foster-brother/-sister. ∼**age** /lɛtaʒ/ *n.m.* milk product. ∼**eux,** ∼**euse** /lɛtø, -z/ *a.* milky.
lait|ier, ∼**ière** /letje, lɛtjɛr/ *a.* dairy. —*n.m., f.* dairyman, dairywoman. —*n.m.* (*livreur*) milkman. ∼**erie** /lɛtri/ *n.f.* dairy.
laiton /lɛtɔ̃/ *n.m.* brass.
laitue /lety/ *n.f.* lettuce.
laïus /lajys/ *n.m.* (*péj.*) big speech.
lama /lama/ *n.m.* llama.
lambeau (*pl.* ∼**x**) /lɑ̃bo/ *n.m.* shred. **en** ∼**x,** in shreds.
lambris /lɑ̃bri/ *n.m.* panelling.
lame /lam/ *n.f.* blade; (*lamelle*) strip; (*vague*) wave. ∼ **de fond,** ground swell.
lamelle /lamɛl/ *n.f.* (thin) strip.
lamentable /lamɑ̃tabl/ *a.* deplorable.
lament|er (se) /(sə)lamɑ̃te/ *v. pr.* moan. ∼**ation(s)** *n.f.* (*pl.*) moaning.
laminé /lamine/ *a.* laminated.
lampadaire /lɑ̃padɛr/ *n.m.* standard lamp; (*de rue*) street lamp.
lampe /lɑ̃p/ *n.f.* lamp; (*de radio*) valve; (*Amer.*) vacuum tube. ∼ **(de poche),** torch; (*Amer.*) flashlight. ∼ **de chevet,** bedside lamp.
lampion /lɑ̃pjɔ̃/ *n.m.* (Chinese) lantern.
lance /lɑ̃s/ *n.f.* spear; (*de tournoi*) lance; (*tuyau*) hose. ∼ **d'incendie,** fire hose.
lancée /lɑ̃se/ *n.f.* **continuer sur sa** ∼, keep going.
lanc|er /lɑ̃se/ *v.t.* throw; (*avec force*) hurl; (*navire, idée, personne*) launch; (*émettre*) give out; (*regard*) cast; (*moteur*) start. **se** ∼**er** *v. pr.* (*sport*) gain momentum; (*se précipiter*) rush. **se** ∼**er dans,** launch into. —*n.m.* throw; (*action*) throwing. ∼**ement** *n.m.* throwing; (*de navire*) launching. ∼**e-**

missiles *n.m. invar.* missile launcher.
~e-pierres *n.m. invar.* catapult.
lancinant, ~e /lãsinã, -t/ *a.* haunting; (*douleur*) throbbing.
landau /lãdo/ *n.m.* pram; (*Amer.*) baby carriage.
lande /lãd/ *n.f.* heath, moor.
langage /lãgaʒ/ *n.m.* language.
langoureu|x, ~se /lãgurø, -z/ *a.* languid.
langoust|e /lãgust/ *n.f.* (spiny) lobster. **~ine** *n.f.* (Norway) lobster.
langue /lãg/ *n.f.* tongue; (*idiome*) language. **il m'a tiré la ~,** he stuck out his tongue out at me. **de ~ anglaise/française,** English-/French-speaking. **~ maternelle,** mother tongue.
languette /lãgɛt/ *n.f.* tongue.
langueur /lãgœr/ *n.f.* languor.
langu|ir /lãgir/ *v.i.* languish; (*conversation*) flag. **faire ~ir qn.,** keep s.o. waiting. **se ~ir de,** miss. **~issant, ~issante** *a.* languid.
lanière /lanjɛr/ *n.f.* strap.
lanterne /lãtɛrn/ *n.f.* lantern; (*électrique*) lamp; (*de voiture*) sidelight.
laper /lape/ *v.t./i.* lap.
lapider /lapide/ *v.t.* stone.
lapin /lapɛ̃/ *n.m.* rabbit. **poser un ~ à qn.,** stand s.o. up.
laps /laps/ *n.m.* **~ de temps,** lapse of time.
lapsus /lapsys/ *n.m.* slip (of the tongue).
laquais /lakɛ/ *n.m.* lackey.
laqu|e /lak/ *n.f.* lacquer. **~er** *v.t.* lacquer.
laquelle /lakɛl/ *voir* **lequel.**
larcin /larsɛ̃/ *n.m.* theft.
lard /lar/ *n.m.* (pig's) fat; (*viande*) bacon.
large /larʒ/ *a.* wide, broad; (*grand*) large; (*non borné*) broad; (*généreux*) generous. —*adv.* (*mesurer*) broadly; (*voir*) big. —*n.m.* **de ~,** (*mesure*) wide. **le ~,** (*mer*) the open sea. **au ~ de,** (*en face de: naut.*) off. **~ d'esprit,** broad-minded. **~ment** /-əmã/ *adv.* widely; (*ouvrir*) wide; (*amplement*) amply; (*généreusement*) generously; (*au moins*) easily.
largesse /larʒɛs/ *n.f.* generosity.
largeur /larʒœr/ *n.f.* width, breadth; (*fig.*) breadth.
larguer /large/ *v.t.* drop. **~ les amarres,** cast off.
larme /larm/ *n.f.* tear; (*goutte: fam.*) drop.
larmoyant, ~e /larmwajã, -t/ *a.* tearful.

larron /larɔ̃/ *n.m.* thief.
larve /larv/ *n.f.* larva.
larvé /larve/ *a.* latent.
laryngite /larɛ̃ʒit/ *n.f.* laryngitis.
larynx /larɛ̃ks/ *n.m.* larynx.
las, ~se /la, las/ *a.* weary.
lasagnes /lazaɲ/ *n.f. pl.* lasagne.
lasci|f, ~ve /lasif, -v/ *a.* lascivious.
laser /lazɛr/ *n.m.* laser.
lasse /las/ *voir* **las.**
lass|er /lase/ *v.t.* weary. **se ~** *v. pr.* weary (**de,** of).
lassitude /lasityd/ *n.f.* weariness.
lasso /laso/ *n.m.* lasso.
latent, ~e /latã, -t/ *a.* latent.
latér|al (*m. pl.* **~aux**) /lateral, -o/ *a.* lateral.
latex /latɛks/ *n.m.* latex.
latin, ~e /latɛ̃, -in/ *a. & n.m., f.* Latin. —*n.m.* (*lang.*) Latin.
latitude /latityd/ *n.f.* latitude.
latrines /latrin/ *n.f. pl.* latrine(s).
latte /lat/ *n.f.* lath; (*de plancher*) board.
lauréat, ~e /lɔrea, -t/ *a.* prize-winning. —*n.m., f.* prize-winner.
laurier /lɔrje/ *n.m.* laurel; (*culin.*) bay-leaves.
lavable /lavabl/ *a.* washable.
lavabo /lavabo/ *n.m.* wash-basin. **~s,** toilet(s).
lavage /lavaʒ/ *n.m.* washing. **~ de cerveau,** brainwashing.
lavande /lavãd/ *n.f.* lavender.
lave /lav/ *n.f.* lava.
lav|er /lave/ *v.t.* wash; (*injure etc.*) avenge. **se ~er** *v. pr.* wash (o.s.). (**se**) **~er de,** clear (o.s.) of. **~e-glace** *n.m.* windscreen washer. **~eur de carreaux,** window-cleaner. **~e-vaisselle** *n.m. invar.* dishwasher.
laverie /lavri/ *n.f.* **~ (automatique),** launderette; (*Amer.*) laundromat.
lavette /lavɛt/ *n.f.* dishcloth; (*péj.*) wimp.
lavoir /lavwar/ *n.m.* wash-house.
laxati|f, ~ve /laksatif, -v/ *a. & n.m.* laxative.
laxisme /laksism/ *n.m.* laxity.
layette /lɛjɛt/ *n.f.* baby clothes.
le *ou* **l'*, la** *ou* **l'*** (*pl.* **les**) /lə, l/, /la, le/ *article* the; (*mesure*) a, per. —*pron.* (*homme*) him; (*femme*) her; (*chose, animal*) it. **les** *pron.* them. **aimer le thé/la France,** like tea/France. **le matin,** in the morning. **il sort le mardi,** he goes out on Tuesdays. **levez le bras,** raise your arm. **je le connais,** I know him. **je le sais,** I know (it).
lécher /leʃe/ *v.t.* lick.

lèche-vitrines /lɛʃvitrin/ *n.m.* **faire du** ∼, go window-shopping.

leçon /ləsɔ̃/ *n.f.* lesson. **faire la** ∼ **à**, lecture.

lec|teur, ∼**trice** /lɛktœr, -tris/ *n.m.*, *f.* reader; (*univ.*) foreign language assistant. ∼**teur de cassettes,** cassette player. ∼**teur de disquettes,** (disk) drive.

lecture /lɛktyr/ *n.f.* reading.

ledit, ladite (*pl.* **lesdit(e)s**) /lədi, ladit, ledi(t)/ *a.* the aforesaid.

lég|al (*m. pl.* ∼**aux**) /legal, -o/ *a.* legal. ∼**alement** *adv.* legally. ∼**aliser** *v.t.* legalize. ∼**alité** *n.f.* legality; (*loi*) law.

légation /legɑsjɔ̃/ *n.f.* legation.

légend|e /leʒɑ̃d/ *n.f.* (*histoire, inscription*) legend. ∼**aire** *a.* legendary.

lég|er, ∼**ère** /leʒe, -ɛr/ *a.* light; (*bruit, faute, maladie*) slight; (*café, argument*) weak; (*imprudent*) thoughtless; (*frivole*) fickle. **à la** ∼**ère,** thoughtlessly. ∼**èrement** /-ɛrmɑ̃/ *adv.* lightly; (*agir*) thoughtlessly; (*un peu*) slightly. ∼**èreté** /-ɛrte/ *n.f.* lightness; thoughtlessness.

légion /leʒjɔ̃/ *n.f.* legion. **une** ∼ **de,** a crowd of. ∼**naire** /-jɔnɛr/ *n.m.* (*mil.*) legionnaire.

législati|f, ∼**ve** /leʒislatif, -v/ *a.* legislative.

législation /leʒislɑsjɔ̃/ *n.f.* legislation.

legislature /leʒislatyr/ *n.f.* term of office.

légitim|e /leʒitim/ *a.* legitimate. **en état de** ∼**e défense,** acting in self-defence. ∼**ité** *n.f.* legitimacy.

legs /lɛg/ *n.m.* legacy.

léguer /lege/ *v.t.* bequeath.

légume /legym/ *n.m.* vegetable.

lendemain /lɑ̃dmɛ̃/ *n.m.* **le** ∼, the next day, the day after; (*fig.*) the future. **le** ∼ **de,** the day after. **le** ∼ **matin/soir,** the next morning/evening.

lent, ∼**e** /lɑ̃, lɑ̃t/ *a.* slow. ∼**ement** /lɑ̃tmɑ̃/ *adv.* slowly. ∼**eur** /lɑ̃tœr/ *n.f.* slowness.

lentille¹ /lɑ̃tij/ *n.f.* (*plante*) lentil.

lentille² /lɑ̃tij/ *n.f.* (*verre*) lens; ∼**s de contact,** (*contact*) lenses.

léopard /leɔpar/ *n.m.* leopard.

lèpre /lɛpr/ *n.f.* leprosy.

lequel, laquelle (*pl.* **lesquel(le)s**) /ləkɛl, lakɛl, lekɛl/ *pron.* (*à + lequel = auquel, à + lesquel(le)s = auxquel(le)s; de + lequel = duquel, de + lesquel(le)s = desquel(le)s*) which; (*interrogatif*) which (one); (*personne*) who; (*complément indirect*) whom.

les /le/ *voir* **le**.

lesbienne /lɛsbjɛn/ *n.f.* lesbian.

léser /leze/ *v.t.* wrong.

lésiner /lezine/ *v.i.* **ne pas** ∼ **sur,** not stint on.

lésion /lezjɔ̃/ *n.f.* lesion.

lesquels, lesquelles /lekɛl/ *voir* **lequel**.

lessive /lesiv/ *n.f.* washing-powder; (*linge, action*) washing.

lest /lɛst/ *n.m.* ballast. **jeter du** ∼, (*fig.*) climb down. ∼**er** *v.t.* ballast.

leste /lɛst/ *a.* nimble; (*grivois*) coarse.

léthargi|e /letarʒi/ *n.f.* lethargy. ∼**ique** *a.* lethargic.

lettre /lɛtr/ *n.f.* letter. **à la** ∼, literally. **en toutes** ∼**s,** in full. ∼ **exprès,** express letter. **les** ∼**s,** (*univ.*) (the) arts.

lettré /letre/ *a.* well-read.

leucémie /løsemi/ *n.f.* leukaemia.

leur /lœr/ *a.* (*f. invar.*) their. —*pron.* (to) them. **le** ∼, **la** ∼, **les** ∼**s,** theirs.

leurr|e /lœr/ *n.m.* illusion; (*duperie*) deception. ∼**er** *v.t.* delude.

levain /ləvɛ̃/ *n.m.* leaven.

levé /ləve/ *a.* (*debout*) up.

levée /ləve/ *n.f.* lifting; (*de courrier*) collection; (*de troupes, d'impôts*) levying.

lever /ləve/ *v.t.* lift (up), raise; (*interdiction*) lift; (*séance*) close; (*armée, impôts*) levy. —*v.i.* (*pâte*) rise. **se** ∼ *v. pr.* get up; (*soleil, rideau*) rise; (*jour*) break. —*n.m.* **au** ∼, on getting up. ∼ **du jour,** daybreak. ∼ **du rideau,** (*théâtre*) curtain (up). ∼ **du soleil,** sunrise.

levier /ləvje/ *n.m.* lever.

lèvre /lɛvr/ *n.f.* lip.

lévrier /levrije/ *n.m.* greyhound.

levure /ləvyr/ *n.f.* yeast. ∼ **alsacienne** *ou* **chimique,** baking powder.

lexicographie /lɛksikɔgrafi/ *n.f.* lexicography.

lexique /lɛksik/ *n.m.* vocabulary; (*glossaire*) lexicon.

lézard /lezar/ *n.m.* lizard.

lézard|e /lezard/ *n.f.* crack. **se** ∼**er** *v. pr.* crack.

liaison /ljɛzɔ̃/ *n.f.* connection; (*transport*) link; (*contact*) contact; (*gram., mil.*) liaison; (*amoureuse*) affair.

liane /ljan/ *n.f.* creeper.

liasse /ljas/ *n.f.* bundle, wad.

Liban /libɑ̃/ *n.m.* Lebanon.

libanais, ∼**e** /libanɛ, -z/ *a. & n.m.,* *f.* Lebanese.

libell|er /libele/ *v.t.* (*chèque*) write; (*lettre*) draw up. ∼**é à l'ordre de,** made out to.

libellule /libelyl/ n.f. dragonfly.
libér|al (m. pl. ~aux) /liberal, -o/ a.
liberal. **les professions** ~ales the
professions. ~alement adv. liberally.
~alisme n.m. liberalism. ~alité n.f.
liberality.
libér|er /libere/ v.t. (personne) free,
release; (pays) liberate, free. **se** ~er v.
pr. free o.s. ~ateur, ~atrice a.
liberating; n.m., f. liberator. ~ation n.f.
release; (de pays) liberation.
liberté /libɛrte/ n.f. freedom, liberty;
(loisir) free time. **en** ~ **provisoire,** on
bail. **être/mettre en** ~, be/set free.
libertin, ~e /libɛrtɛ̃, -in/ a. & n.m., f.
libertine.
librair|e /librɛr/ n.m./f. bookseller. ~ie
/-eri/ n.f. bookshop.
libre /libr/ a. free; (place, pièce) vacant,
free; (passage) clear; (école) private
(usually religious). ~ **de qch./de faire,**
free from sth./to do. ~-**échange** n.m.
free trade. ~**ment** /-əmɑ̃/ adv. freely.
~-**service** (pl. ~s-services) n.m. self-
service.
Libye /libi/ n.f. Libya.
libyen, ~**ne** /libjɛ̃, -jɛn/ a. & n.m., f.
Libyan.
licence /lisɑ̃s/ n.f. licence; (univ.)
degree.
licencié, ~**e** /lisɑ̃sje/ n.m., f. ~ **ès**
lettres/sciences, Bachelor of Arts/
Science.
licenc|ier /lisɑ̃sje/ v.t. make redundant,
(pour faute) dismiss. ~**iements** n.m. pl.
redundancies.
licencieu|x, ~**se** /lisɑ̃sjø, -z/ a.
licentious, lascivious.
lichen /likɛn/ n.m. lichen.
licite /lisit/ a. lawful.
licorne /likɔrn/ n.f. unicorn.
lie /li/ n.f. dregs.
liège /ljɛʒ/ n.m. cork.
lien /ljɛ̃/ n.m. (rapport) link; (attache)
bond, tie; (corde) rope.
lier /lje/ v.t. tie (up), bind; (relier) link;
(engager, unir) bind. ~ **conversation,**
strike up a conversation. **se** ~ **avec,**
make friends with. **ils sont très liés,**
they are very close.
lierre /ljɛr/ n.m. ivy.
lieu (pl. ~**x**) /ljø/ n.m. place. ~**x,**
(locaux) premises; (d'un accident)
scene. **au** ~ **de,** instead of. **avoir** ~,
take place. **tenir** ~ **de,** serve as. **en**
premier ~, firstly. **en dernier** ~,
lastly. ~ **commun,** commonplace.
lieutenant /ljøtnɑ̃/ n.m. lieutenant.
lièvre /ljɛvr/ n.m. hare.

ligament /ligamɑ̃/ n.m. ligament.
ligne /liɲ/ n.f. line; (trajet) route;
(formes) lines; (de femme) figure. **en**
~, (joueurs etc.) lined up; (personne au
téléphone) on the phone.
lignée /liɲe/ n.f. ancestry, line.
ligoter /ligɔte/ v.t. tie up.
ligu|e /lig/ n.f. league. **se** ~**er** v. pr. form
a league (**contre,** against).
lilas /lila/ n.m. & a. invar. lilac.
limace /limas/ n.f. slug.
limande /limɑ̃d/ n.f. (poisson) dab.
lim|e /lim/ n.f. file. ~**e à ongles,** nail file.
~**er** v.t. file.
limier /limje/ n.m. bloodhound;
(policier) sleuth.
limitation /limitasjɔ̃/ n.f. limitation. ~
de vitesse, speed limit.
limit|e /limit/ n.f. limit; (de jardin,
champ) boundary. —a. (vitesse, âge)
maximum. **cas** ~**e,** borderline case.
date ~**e,** deadline. ~**er** v.t. limit;
(délimiter) form the border of.
limoger /limɔʒe/ v.t. dismiss.
limon /limɔ̃/ n.m. stilt.
limonade /limɔnad/ n.f. lemonade.
limpid|e /lɛ̃pid/ a. limpid, clear. ~**ité** n.f.
clearness.
lin /lɛ̃/ n.m. (tissu) linen.
linceul /lɛ̃sœl/ n.m. shroud.
linéaire /lineɛr/ a. linear.
linge /lɛ̃ʒ/ n.m. linen; (lessive) washing;
(torchon) cloth. ~ (**de corps**),
underwear. ~**rie** n.f. underwear.
lingot /lɛ̃go/ n.m. ingot.
linguiste /lɛ̃gɥist/ n.m./f. linguist.
linguistique /lɛ̃gɥistik/ a. linguistic.
—n.f. linguistics.
lino /lino/ n.m. lino.
linoléum /linɔleɔm/ n.m. linoleum.
lion, ~**ne** /ljɔ̃, ljɔn/ n.m., f. lion, lioness.
le L~, Leo.
lionceau (pl. ~**x**) /ljɔ̃so/ n.m. lion cub.
liquéfier /likefje/ v.t., **se** ~ v. pr. liquefy.
liqueur /likœr/ n.f. liqueur.
liquide /likid/ a. & n.m. liquid. (**argent**)
~, ready money. **payer en** ~, pay
cash.
liquid|er /likide/ v.t. liquidate; (vendre)
sell. ~**ation** n.f. liquidation; (vente)
(clearance) sale.
lire[1]† /lir/ v.t./i. read.
lire[2] /lir/ n.f. lira.
lis[1] /li/ voir **lire**[1].
lis[2] /lis/ n.m. (fleur) lily.
lisible /lizibl/ a. legible; (roman etc.)
readable.
lisière /lizjɛr/ n.f. edge.
liss|e /lis/ a. smooth. ~**er** v.t. smooth.

liste /list/ *n.f.* list. ∼ **électorale,** register of voters.

listing /listiŋ/ *n.m.* printout.

lit¹ /li/ *voir* **lire**¹.

lit² /li/ *n.m.* (*de personne, fleuve*) bed. **se mettre au** ∼, get into bed. ∼ **de camp,** camp-bed. ∼ **d'enfant,** cot. ∼ **d'une personne,** single bed.

litanie /litani/ *n.f.* litany.

litchi /litʃi/ *n.m.* litchi.

literie /litri/ *n.f.* bedding.

litière /litjɛr/ *n.f.* (*paille*) litter.

litige /litiʒ/ *n.m.* dispute.

litre /litr/ *n.m.* litre.

littéraire /literɛr/ *a.* literary.

littér|al (*m. pl.* ∼**aux**) /literal, -o/ *a.* literal. ∼**alement** *adv.* literally.

littérature /literatyr/ *n.f.* literature.

littor|al (*pl.* ∼**aux**) /litoral, -o/ *n.m.* coast.

liturg|ie /lityrʒi/ *n.f.* liturgy. ∼**ique** *a.* liturgical.

livide /livid/ *a.* (*blême*) pallid.

livraison /livrɛzɔ̃/ *n.f.* delivery.

livre¹ /livr/ *n.m.* book. ∼ **de bord,** log-book. ∼ **de compte,** books. ∼ **de poche,** paperback.

livre² /livr/ *n.f.* (*monnaie, poids*) pound.

livrée /livre/ *n.f.* livery.

livr|er /livre/ *v.t.* deliver; (*abandonner*) give over (**à,** to); (*secret*) give away. ∼**é à soi-même,** left to o.s. **se** ∼**er à,** give o.s. over to; (*actes, boisson*) indulge in; (*se confier à*) confide in; (*effectuer*) carry out.

livret /livrɛ/ *n.m.* book; (*mus.*) libretto. ∼ **scolaire,** school report (book).

livreu|r, ∼**se** /livrœr, -øz/ *n.m., f.* delivery boy *ou* girl.

lobe /lɔb/ *n.m.* lobe.

loc|al¹ (*m. pl.* ∼**aux**) /lɔkal, -o/ *a.* local. ∼**alement** *adv.* locally.

loc|al² (*pl.* ∼**aux**) /lɔkal, -o/ *n.m.* premises. ∼**aux,** premises.

localisé /lɔkalize/ *a.* localized.

localité /lɔkalite/ *n.f.* locality.

locataire /lɔkatɛr/ *n.m./f.* tenant; (*de chambre, d'hôtel*) lodger.

location /lɔkasjɔ̃/ *n.f.* (*de maison*) renting; (*de voiture*) hiring, renting; (*de place*) booking, reservation; (*guichet*) booking office; (*théâtre*) box office; (*par propriétaire*) renting out; hiring out. **en** ∼, (*voiture*) on hire, rented.

lock-out /lɔkawt/ *n.m. invar.* lockout.

locomotion /lɔkɔmosjɔ̃/ *n.f.* locomotion.

locomotive /lɔkɔmɔtiv/ *n.f.* engine, locomotive.

locution /lɔkysjɔ̃/ *n.f.* phrase.

logarithme /lɔgaritm/ *n.m.* logarithm.

loge /lɔʒ/ *n.f.* (*de concierge*) lodge; (*d'acteur*) dressing-room; (*de spectateur*) box.

logement /lɔʒmɑ̃/ *n.m.* accommodation; (*appartement*) flat; (*habitat*) housing.

log|er /lɔʒe/ *v.t.* accommodate. —*v.i.,* **se** ∼**er** *v. pr.* live. **trouver à se** ∼**er,** find accommodation. **être** ∼**é,** live. **se** ∼**er dans,** (*balle*) lodge itself in.

logeu|r, ∼**se** /lɔʒœr, -øz/ *n.m., f.* landlord, landlady.

logiciel /lɔʒisjɛl/ *n.m.* software.

logique /lɔʒik/ *a.* logical. —*n.f.* logic. ∼**ment** *adv.* logically.

logis /lɔʒi/ *n.m.* dwelling.

logistique /lɔʒistik/ *n.f.* logistics.

logo /lɔgo/ *n.m.* logo.

loi /lwa/ *n.f.* law.

loin /lwɛ̃/ *adv.* far (away). **au** ∼, far away. **de** ∼, from far away; (*de beaucoup*) by far. ∼ **de là,** far from it. **plus** ∼, further. **il revient de** ∼, (*fig.*) he had a close shave.

lointain, ∼**e** /lwɛ̃tɛ̃, -ɛn/ *a.* distant. —*n.m.* distance.

loir /lwar/ *n.m.* dormouse.

loisir /lwazir/ *n.m.* (*spare*) time. ∼**s,** spare time; (*distractions*) spare time activities. **à** ∼, at one's leisure.

londonien, ∼**ne** /lɔ̃dɔnjɛ̃, -jɛn/ *a.* London. —*n.m., f.* Londoner.

Londres /lɔ̃dr/ *n.m./f.* London.

long, ∼**ue** /lɔ̃, lɔ̃g/ *a.* long. —*n.m.* **de** ∼, (*mesure*) long. **à la** ∼**ue,** in the end. **à** ∼ **terme,** long-term. **de** ∼ **en large,** back and forth. ∼ **à faire,** a long time doing. (**tout**) **le** ∼ **de,** (all) along.

longer /lɔ̃ʒe/ *v.t.* go along; (*limiter*) border.

longévité /lɔ̃ʒevite/ *n.f.* longevity.

longiligne /lɔ̃ʒiliɲ/ *a.* tall and slender.

longitude /lɔ̃ʒityd/ *n.f.* longitude.

longtemps /lɔ̃tɑ̃/ *adv.* a long time. **avant** ∼, before long. **trop** ∼, too long. **ça prendra** ∼, it will take a long time.

longue /lɔ̃g/ *voir* **long.**

longuement /lɔ̃gmɑ̃/ *adv.* at length.

longueur /lɔ̃gœr/ *n.f.* length. ∼**s,** (*de texte etc.*) over-long parts. **à** ∼ **de journée,** all day long. ∼ **d'onde,** wavelength.

longue-vue /lɔ̃gvy/ *n.f.* telescope.

look /luk/ *n.m.* (*fam.*) look, image.

lopin /lɔpɛ̃/ *n.m.* ∼ **de terre,** patch of land.

loquace /lɔkas/ *a.* talkative.

loque /lɔk/ *n.f.* ∼**s,** rags. ∼ (**humaine**), (human) wreck.

loquet /lɔkɛ/ *n.m.* latch.

lorgner /lɔrɲe/ *v.t.* eye.

lors de /lɔrdə/ *prép.* at the time of.

lorsque /lɔrsk(ə)/ *conj.* when.

losange /lozɑ̃ʒ/ *n.m.* diamond.

lot /lo/ *n.m.* prize; (*portion, destin*) lot.

loterie /lɔtri/ *n.f.* lottery.

lotion /losjɔ̃/ *n.f.* lotion.

lotissement /lɔtismɑ̃/ *n.m.* (*à construire*) building plot; (*construit*) (housing) development.

louable /lwabl/ *a.* praiseworthy.

louange /lwɑ̃ʒ/ *n.f.* praise.

louche¹ /luʃ/ *a.* shady, dubious.

louche² /luʃ/ *n.f.* ladle.

loucher /luʃe/ *v.i.* squint.

louer¹ /lwe/ *v.t.* (*maison*) rent; (*voiture*) hire, rent; (*place*) book, reserve; (*propriétaire*) rent out; hire out. **à ~,** to let, for rent (*Amer.*)

louer² /lwe/ *v.t.* (*approuver*) praise (**de,** for). **se ~ de,** congratulate o.s. on.

loufoque /lufɔk/ *a.* (*fam.*) crazy.

loup /lu/ *n.m.* wolf.

loupe /lup/ *n.f.* magnifying glass.

louper /lupe/ *v.t.* (*fam.*) miss.

lourd, ~e /lur, -d/ *a.* heavy; (*chaleur*) close; (*faute*) gross. **~ de consé-quences,** with dire consequences. **~ement** /-dəmɑ̃/ *adv.* heavily. **~eur** /-dœr/ *n.f.* heaviness.

lourdaud, ~e /lurdo, -d/ *a.* loutish. —*n.m., f.* lout, oaf.

loutre /lutr/ *n.f.* otter.

louve /luv/ *n.f.* she-wolf.

louveteau (*pl.* **~x**) /luvto/ *n.m.* wolf cub; (*scout*) Cub (Scout).

louvoyer /luvwaje/ *v.i.* (*fig.*) sidestep the issue; (*naut.*) tack.

loy|al (*m. pl.* **~aux**) /lwajal, -o/ *a.* loyal; (*honnête*) fair. **~alement** *adv.* loyally; fairly. **~auté** *n.f.* loyalty; fairness.

loyer /lwaje/ *n.m.* rent.

lu /ly/ *voir* **lire**¹.

lubie /lybi/ *n.f.* whim.

lubrif|ier /lybrifje/ *v.t.* lubricate. **~iant** *n.m.* lubricant.

lubrique /lybrik/ *a.* lewd.

lucarne /lykarn/ *n.f.* skylight.

lucid|e /lysid/ *a.* lucid. **~ité** *n.f.* lucidity.

lucrati|f, ~ve /lykratif, -v/ *a.* lucrative. **à but non ~f,** non-profit-making.

lueur /lɥœr/ *n.f.* (faint) light, glimmer; (*fig.*) glimmer, gleam.

luge /lyʒ/ *n.f.* toboggan.

lugubre /lygybr/ *a.* gloomy.

lui /lɥi/ *pron.* him; (*sujet*) he; (*chose*) it; (*objet indirect*) (to) him; (*femme*) (to)

her; (*chose*) (to) it. **~-même** *pron.* himself; itself.

luire† /lɥir/ *v.i.* shine; (*reflet humide*) glisten; (*reflet chaud, faible*) glow.

lumbago /lɔ̃bago/ *n.m.* lumbago.

lumière /lymjɛr/ *n.f.* light. **~s,** (*connaissances*) knowledge. **faire (toute) la ~ sur,** clear up.

luminaire /lyminɛr/ *n.m.* lamp.

lumineu|x, ~se /lyminø, -z/ *a.* luminous; (*éclairé*) illuminated; (*source, rayon*) (of) light; (*vif*) bright.

lunaire /lynɛr/ *a.* lunar.

lunatique /lynatik/ *a.* temperamental.

lunch /lœntʃ/ *n.m.* buffet lunch.

lundi /lœdi/ *n.m.* Monday.

lune /lyn/ *n.f.* moon. **~ de miel,** honeymoon.

lunette /lynɛt/ *n.f.* **~s,** glasses; (*de protection*) goggles. **~ arrière,** (*auto.*) rear window. **~s de soleil,** sunglasses.

luron /lyrɔ̃/ *n.m.* **gai** *ou* **joyeux ~,** (*fam.*) quite a lad.

lustre /lystr/ *n.m.* (*éclat*) lustre; (*objet*) chandelier.

lustré /lystre/ *a.* shiny.

luth /lyt/ *n.m.* lute.

lutin /lytɛ̃/ *n.m.* goblin.

lutrin /lytrɛ̃/ *n.m.* lectern.

lutt|e /lyt/ *n.f.* fight, struggle; (*sport*) wrestling. **~er** *v.i.* fight, struggle; (*sport*) wrestle. **~eur, ~euse** *n.m., f.* fighter; (*sport*) wrestler.

luxe /lyks/ *n.m.* luxury. **de ~,** luxury; (*produit*) de luxe.

Luxembourg /lyksɑ̃bur/ *n.m.* Luxemburg.

lux|er /lykse/ *v.t.* **se ~er le genou,** dislocate one's knee. **~ation** *n.f.* dislocation.

luxueu|x, ~se /lyksɥø, -z/ *a.* luxurious.

luxure /lyksyr/ *n.f.* lust.

luxuriant, ~e /lyksyrjɑ̃, -t/ *a.* luxuriant.

luzerne /lyzɛrn/ *n.f.* (*plante*) lucerne, alfalfa.

lycée /lise/ *n.m.* (secondary) school. **~n, ~nne** /-ɛ̃, -ɛn/ *n.m., f.* pupil (at secondary school).

lynch|er /lɛ̃ʃe/ *v.t.* lynch. **~age** *n.m.* lynching.

lynx /lɛ̃ks/ *n.m.* lynx.

lyophilis|er /ljɔfilize/ *v.t.* freeze-dry. **~é** *a.* freeze-dried.

lyre /lir/ *n.f.* lyre.

lyri|que /lirik/ *a.* (*poésie*) lyric; (*passionné*) lyrical. **artiste/théâtre**

~**que**, opera singer/-house. ~**sme** *n.m.* lyricism.
lys /lis/ *n.m.* lily.

M

m' /m/ *voir* **me**.
ma /ma/ *voir* **mon**.
maboul /mabul/ *a.* (*fam.*) mad.
macabre /makabr/ *a.* gruesome, macabre.
macadam /makadam/ *n.m.* (*goudronné*) Tarmac (P.).
macaron /makarɔ̃/ *n.m.* (*gâteau*) macaroon; (*insigne*) badge.
macaronis /makarɔni/ *n.m. pl.* macaroni.
macédoine /masedwan/ *n.f.* mixed vegetables. ~ **de fruits**, fruit salad.
macérer /masere/ *v.t./i.* soak; (*dans du vinaigre*) pickle.
mâchefer /mɑʃfɛr/ *n.m.* clinker.
mâcher /mɑʃe/ *v.t.* chew. **ne pas** ~ **ses mots**, not mince one's words.
machiavélique /makjavelik/ *a.* machiavellian.
machin /maʃɛ̃/ *n.m.* (*chose: fam.*) thing; (*personne: fam.*) what's-his-name.
machin|al (*m. pl.* ~**aux**) /maʃinal, -o/ *a.* automatic. ~**alement** *adv.* automatically.
machinations /maʃinasjɔ̃/ *n.f. pl.* machinations.
machine /maʃin/ *n.f.* machine; (*d'un train, navire*) engine. ~ **à écrire**, typewriter. ~ **à laver/coudre**, washing-/sewing-machine. ~ **à sous**, fruit machine; (*Amer.*) slot-machine. ~**outil** (*pl.* ~**s-outils**) *n.f.* machine tool. ~**rie** *n.f.* machinery.
machiner /maʃine/ *v.t.* plot.
machiniste /maʃinist/ *n.m.* (*théâtre*) stage-hand; (*conducteur*) driver.
macho /ma(t)ʃo/ *n.m.* (*fam.*) macho.
mâchoire /mɑʃwar/ *n.f.* jaw.
mâchonner /mɑʃɔne/ *v.t.* chew at.
maçon /masɔ̃/ *n.m.* builder; (*poseur de briques*) bricklayer. ~**nerie** /-ɔnri/ *n.f.* brickwork; (*pierres*) stonework, masonry.
maçonnique /masɔnik/ *a.* Masonic.
macrobiotique /makrɔbjɔtik/ *a.* macrobiotic.
maculer /makyle/ *v.t.* stain.
Madagascar /madagaskar/ *n.f.* Madagascar.

madame (*pl.* **mesdames**) /madam, medam/ *n.f.* madam. **M**~ **Dupont**, Mrs Dupont. **bonsoir, mesdames**, good evening, ladies.
madeleine /madlɛn/ *n.f.* madeleine (*small shell-shaped sponge-cake*).
mademoiselle (*pl.* **mesdemoiselles**) /madmwazɛl, medmwazɛl/ *n.f.* miss. **M**~ *ou* **Mlle Dupont**, Miss Dupont. **bonsoir, mesdemoiselles**, good evening, ladies.
madère /madɛr/ *n.m.* (*vin*) Madeira.
madone /madɔn/ *n.f.* madonna.
madrig|al (*pl.* ~**aux**) /madrigal, -o/ *n.m.* madrigal.
maestro /maɛstro/ *n.m.* maestro.
maf(f)ia /mafja/ *n.f.* Mafia.
magasin /magazɛ̃/ *n.m.* shop, store; (*entrepôt*) warehouse; (*d'une arme etc.*) magazine.
magazine /magazin/ *n.m.* magazine; (*émission*) programme.
Maghreb /magrɛb/ *n.m.* North Africa. ~**in**, ~**ine** *a. & n.m., f.* North African.
magicien, ~**ne** /maʒisjɛ̃, -jɛn/ *n.m., f.* magician.
magie /maʒi/ *n.f.* magic.
magique /maʒik/ *a.* magic; (*mystérieux*) magical.
magistr|al (*m. pl.* ~**aux**) /maʒistral, -o/ *a.* masterly; (*grand: hum.*) colossal. ~**alement** *adv.* in a masterly fashion.
magistrat /maʒistra/ *n.m.* magistrate.
magistrature /maʒistratyr/ *n.f.* judiciary.
magnanim|e /maɲanim/ *a.* magnanimous. ~**ité** *n.f.* magnanimity.
magnat /magna/ *n.m.* tycoon, magnate.
magner (se) /(sə)maɲe/ *v. pr.* (*argot*) hurry.
magnésie /maɲezi/ *n.f.* magnesia.
magnéti|que /maɲetik/ *a.* magnetic. ~**ser** *v.t.* magnetize. ~**sme** *n.m.* magnetism.
magnétophone /maɲetɔfɔn/ *n.m.* tape recorder. ~ **à cassettes**, cassette recorder.
magnétoscope /maɲetɔskɔp/ *n.m.* video-recorder.
magnifi|que /maɲifik/ *a.* magnificent. ~**cence** *n.f.* magnificence.
magnolia /maɲɔlja/ *n.m.* magnolia.
magot /mago/ *n.m.* (*fam.*) hoard (of money).
magouill|er /maguje/ *v.i.* (*fam.*) scheming. ~**eur**, ~**euse** *n.m., f.* (*fam.*) schemer. ~**e** *n.f.* (*fam.*) scheming.
magret /magrɛ/ *n.m.* ~ **de canard**, steaklet of duck.

mai /mɛ/ *n.m.* May.

maigr|e /mɛgr/ *a.* thin; (*viande*) lean; (*yaourt*) low-fat; (*fig.*) poor, meagre. **faire ∼e,** abstain from meat. **∼ement** *adv.* poorly. **∼eur** *n.f.* thinness; leanness; (*fig.*) meagreness.

maigrir /megrir/ *v.i.* get thin(ner); (*en suivant un régime*) slim. —*v.t.* make thin(ner).

maille /maj/ *n.f.* stitch; (*de filet*) mesh. **∼ filée,** ladder, run.

maillet /majɛ/ *n.m.* mallet.

maillon /majɔ̃/ *n.m.* link.

maillot /majo/ *n.m.* (*de sport*) jersey. **∼ (de corps),** vest. **∼ (de bain),** (swimming) costume.

main /mɛ̃/ *n.f.* hand. **avoir la ∼ heureuse,** be lucky. **donner la ∼ à qn.,** hold s.o.'s hand. **en ∼s propres,** in person. **en bonnes ∼s,** in good hands. **∼ courante,** handrail. **∼-d'œuvre** (*pl.* **∼s-d'œuvre**) *n.f.* labour; (*ensemble d'ouvriers*) labour force. **∼-forte** *n.f. invar.* assistance. **se faire la ∼,** get the hang of it. **perdre la ∼,** lose one's touch. **sous la ∼,** to hand. **vol/attaque à ∼ armée,** armed robbery/attack.

mainmise /mɛ̃miz/ *n.f.* **∼ sur,** complete hold on.

maint, ∼e /mɛ̃, mɛ̃t/ *a.* many a. **∼s,** many. **à ∼es reprises,** on many occasions.

maintenant /mɛ̃tnɑ̃/ *adv.* now; (*de nos jours*) nowadays.

maintenir† /mɛ̃tnir/ *v.t.* keep, maintain; (*soutenir*) hold up; (*affirmer*) maintain. **se ∼** *v. pr.* (*continuer*) persist; (*rester*) remain.

maintien /mɛ̃tjɛ̃/ *n.m.* (*attitude*) bearing; (*conservation*) maintenance.

maire /mɛr/ *n.m.* mayor.

mairie /meri/ *n.f.* town hall; (*administration*) town council.

mais /mɛ/ *conj.* but. **∼ oui, ∼ si,** of course. **∼ non,** definitely not.

maïs /mais/ *n.m.* (*à cultiver*) maize; (*culin.*) sweet corn; (*Amer.*) corn.

maison /mɛzɔ̃/ *n.f.* house; (*foyer*) home; (*immeuble*) building. **∼ (de commerce),** firm. —*a. invar.* (*culin.*) home-made. **à la ∼,** at home. **rentrer** *ou* **aller à la ∼,** go home. **∼ des jeunes,** youth centre. **∼ de repos, ∼ de convalescence,** convalescent home. **∼ de retraite,** old people's home. **∼ mère,** parent company.

maisonnée /mɛzɔne/ *n.f.* household.

maisonnette /mɛzɔnɛt/ *n.f.* small house, cottage.

maître /mɛtr/ *n.m.* master. **∼ (d'école),** schoolmaster. **∼ de,** in control of. **se rendre ∼ de,** gain control of; (*incendie*) bring under control. **∼ assistant/de conférences,** junior/senior lecturer. **∼ chanteur,** blackmailer. **∼ d'hôtel,** head waiter; (*domestique*) butler. **∼ nageur,** swimming instructor.

maîtresse /mɛtrɛs/ *n.f.* mistress. **∼ (d'école),** schoolmistress. —*a.f.* (*idée, poutre, qualité*) main. **∼ de,** in control of.

maîtris|e /metriz/ *n.f.* mastery; (*univ.*) master's degree. **∼e (de soi),** self-control. **∼er** *v.t.* master; (*incendie*) control; (*personne*) subdue. **se ∼er** *v. pr.* control o.s.

maïzena /maizena/ *n.f.* (P.) cornflour.

majesté /maʒɛste/ *n.f.* majesty.

majestueu|x, ∼se /maʒɛstɥø, -z/ *a.* majestic. **∼sement** *adv.* majestically.

majeur /maʒœr/ *a.* major; (*jurid.*) of age. —*n.m.* middle finger. **en ∼e partie,** mostly. **la ∼e partie de,** most of.

major|er /maʒɔre/ *v.t.* increase. **∼ation** *n.f.* increase (**de,** in).

majorit|é /maʒɔrite/ *n.f.* majority. **en ∼é,** chiefly. **∼aire** *a.* majority. **être ∼aire,** be in the majority.

Majorque /maʒɔrk/ *n.f.* Majorca.

majuscule /maʒyskyl/ *a.* capital. —*n.f.* capital letter.

mal¹ /mal/ *adv.* badly; (*incorrectement*) wrong(ly). **∼ (à l'aise),** uncomfortable. **aller ∼,** (*malade*) be bad. **c'est ∼ de,** it is wrong *ou* bad to. **∼ entendre/comprendre,** not hear/understand properly. **∼ famé,** of ill repute. **∼ fichu,** (*personne: fam.*) feeling lousy. **∼ en point,** in a bad state. **pas ∼,** not bad; quite a lot.

mal² (*pl.* **maux**) /mal, mo/ *n.m.* evil; (*douleur*) pain, ache; (*maladie*) disease; (*effort*) trouble; (*dommage*) harm; (*malheur*) misfortune. **avoir ∼ à la tête/aux dents/à la gorge,** have a headache/a toothache/a sore throat. **avoir le ∼ de mer/du pays,** be seasick/homesick. **faire du ∼ à,** hurt, harm. **se donner du ∼ pour faire qch.,** go to a lot of trouble to do sth.

malade /malad/ *a.* sick, ill; (*bras, gorge*) bad; (*plante*) diseased. **tu es complètement ∼!,** (*fam.*) you're mad. —*n.m./f.* sick person; (*d'un médecin*) patient.

maladie /maladi/ *n.f.* illness, disease.

maladi|f, ∼ve /maladif, -v/ *a.* sickly; (*peur*) morbid.

maladresse /maladrɛs/ n.f. clumsiness; (erreur) blunder.

maladroit, ~e /maladrwa, -t/ a. & n.m., f. clumsy (person).

malais, ~e[1] /malɛ, -z/ a. & n.m., f. Malay.

malaise[2] /malɛz/ n.m. feeling of faintness ou dizziness; (fig.) uneasiness, malaise.

malaisé /maleze/ a. difficult.

malaria /malarja/ n.f. malaria.

Malaysia /malɛzja/ n.f. Malaysia.

malaxer /malakse/ v.t. (pétrir) knead; (mêler) mix.

malchanc|e /malʃɑ̃s/ n.f. misfortune. ~eux, ~euse a. unlucky.

malcommode /malkɔmɔd/ a. awkward.

mâle /mɑl/ a. male; (viril) manly. —n.m. male.

malédiction /malediksjɔ̃/ n.f. curse.

maléfice /malefis/ n.m. evil spell.

maléfique /malefik/ a. evil.

malencontreu|x, ~se /malɑ̃kɔ̃trø, -z/ a. unfortunate.

malentendant, ~e a. & n.m., f. hard of hearing.

malentendu /malɑ̃tɑ̃dy/ n.m. misunderstanding.

malfaçon /malfasɔ̃/ n.f. fault.

malfaisant, ~e /malfəzɑ̃, -t/ a. harmful.

malfaiteur /malfɛtœr/ n.m. criminal.

malformation /malfɔrmasjɔ̃/ n.f. malformation.

malgache /malgaʃ/ a. & n.m./f. Malagasy.

malgré /malgre/ prép. in spite of, despite. ~ tout, after all.

malhabile /malabil/ a. clumsy.

malheur /malœr/ n.m. misfortune; (accident) accident. faire un ~, be a big hit.

malheureu|x, ~se /malœrø, -z/ a. unhappy; (regrettable) unfortunate; (sans succès) unlucky; (insignifiant) wretched. —n.m., f. (poor) wretch. ~sement adv. unfortunately.

malhonnête /malɔnɛt/ a. dishonest. ~té n.f. dishonesty; (action) dishonest action.

malic|e /malis/ n.f. mischievousness; (méchanceté) malice. ~ieux, ~ieuse a. mischievous.

mal|in, ~igne /malɛ̃, -iɲ/ a. clever, smart; (méchant) malicious; (tumeur) malignant; (difficile: fam.) difficult. ~ignité n.f. malignancy.

malingre /malɛ̃gr/ a. puny.

malintentionné /malɛ̃tɑ̃sjɔne/ a. malicious.

malle /mal/ n.f. (valise) trunk; (auto.) boot; (auto., Amer.) trunk.

malléable /maleabl/ a. malleable.

mallette /malɛt/ n.f. (small) suitcase.

malmener /malmøne/ v.t. manhandle, handle roughly.

malnutrition /malnytrisjɔ̃/ n.f. malnutrition.

malodorant, ~e /malɔdɔrɑ̃, -t/ a. smelly, foul-smelling.

malotru /malɔtry/ n.m. boor.

malpoli /malpoli/ a. impolite.

malpropre /malprɔpr/ a. dirty. ~té /-əte/ n.f. dirtiness.

malsain, ~e /malsɛ̃, -ɛn/ a. unhealthy.

malt /malt/ n.m. malt.

maltais, ~e /maltɛ, -z/ a. & n.m., f. Maltese.

Malte /malt/ n.f. Malta.

maltraiter /maltrete/ v.t. ill-treat.

malveillan|t, ~te /malvɛjɑ̃, -t/ a. malevolent. ~ce n.f. malevolence.

maman /mamɑ̃/ n.f. mum(my), mother.

mamelle /mamɛl/ n.f. teat.

mamelon /mamlɔ̃/ n.m. (anat.) nipple; (colline) hillock.

mamie /mami/ n.f. (fam.) granny.

mammifère /mamifɛr/ n.m. mammal.

mammouth /mamut/ n.m. mammoth.

manche[1] /mɑ̃ʃ/ n.f. sleeve; (sport, pol.) round. la M~, the Channel.

manche[2] /mɑ̃ʃ/ n.m. (d'un instrument) handle. ~ à balai, broomstick.

manchette /mɑ̃ʃɛt/ n.f. cuff; (de journal) headline.

manchot[1], ~e /mɑ̃ʃo, -ɔt/ a. & n.m., f. one-armed (person); (sans bras) armless (person).

manchot[2] /mɑ̃ʃo/ n.m. (oiseau) penguin.

mandarin /mɑ̃darɛ̃/ n.m. (fonctionnaire) mandarin.

mandarine /mɑ̃darin/ n.f. tangerine, mandarin (orange).

mandat /mɑ̃da/ n.m. (postal) money order; (pol.) mandate; (procuration) proxy; (de police) warrant. ~aire /-tɛr/ n.m. (représentant) representative. ~er /-te/ v.t. (pol.) delegate.

manège /manɛʒ/ n.m. riding-school; (à la foire) merry-go-round; (manœuvre) wiles, ploy.

manette /manɛt/ n.f. lever; (comput.) joystick.

mangeable /mɑ̃ʒabl/ a. edible.

mangeoire /mɑ̃ʒwar/ n.f. trough.

mang|er /mɑ̃ʒe/ v.t./i. eat; (fortune) go

through; (*ronger*) eat into. —*n.m.* food.
donner à ~er à, feed. **~eur, ~euse**
n.m., f. eater.

mangue /mɑ̃g/ *n.f.* mango.

maniable /manjabl/ *a.* easy to handle.

maniaque /manjak/ *a.* fussy. —*n.m./f.*
fuss-pot; (*fou*) maniac. **un ~ de**, a
maniac for.

manie /mani/ *n.f.* habit; obsession.

man|ier /manje/ *v.t.* handle. **~iement**
n.m. handling.

manière /manjɛr/ *n.f.* way, manner. **~s**,
(*politesse*) manners; (*chichis*) fuss. **de
cette ~**, in this way. **de ~ à**, so as to. **de
toute ~**, anyway, in any case.

maniéré /manjere/ *a.* affected.

manif /manif/ *n.f.* (*fam.*) demo.

manifestant, ~e /manifɛstɑ̃, -t/ *n.m.,
f.* demonstrator.

manifeste /manifɛst/ *a.* obvious. —*n.m.*
manifesto.

manifest|er[1] /manifɛste/ *v.t.* show,
manifest. **se ~er** *v. pr.* (*sentiment*)
show itself; (*apparaître*) appear.
~ation[1] *n.f.* expression, demonstration, manifestation; (*de maladie*) appearance.

manifest|er[2] /manifɛste/ *v.i.* (*pol.*)
demonstrate. **~ation**[2] *n.f.* (*pol.*)
demonstration; (*événement*) event.

maniganc|e /manigɑ̃s/ *n.f.* little plot.
~er *v.t.* plot.

manipul|er /manipyle/ *v.t.* handle;
(*péj.*) manipulate. **~ation** *n.f.* handling; (*péj.*) manipulation.

manivelle /manivɛl/ *n.f.* crank.

manne /man/ *n.f.* (*aubaine*) god-send.

mannequin /mankɛ̃/ *n.m.* (*personne*)
model; (*statue*) dummy.

manœuvr|e[1] /manœvr/ *n.f.* manœuvre.
~er *v.t./i.* manœuvre; (*machine*)
operate.

manœuvre[2] /manœvr/ *n.m.* (*ouvrier*)
labourer.

manoir /manwar/ *n.m.* manor.

manque /mɑ̃k/ *n.m.* lack (**de**, of); (*vide*)
gap. **~s**, (*défauts*) faults. **~ à gagner**,
loss of profit. **en (état de) ~**, having
withdrawal symptoms.

manqué /mɑ̃ke/ *a.* (*écrivain etc.*) failed.
garçon ~, tomboy.

manquement /mɑ̃kmɑ̃/ *n.m.* **~ à**,
breach of.

manquer /mɑ̃ke/ *v.t.* miss; (*gâcher*)
spoil; (*examen*) fail. —*v.i.* be short *ou*
lacking; (*absent*) be absent; (*en moins,
disparu*) be missing; (*échouer*) fail. **~
à**, (*devoir*) fail in. **~ de**, be short of,
lack. **il/ça lui manque**, he misses

him/it. **~ (de) faire**, (*faillir*) nearly do.
ne pas ~ de, not fail to.

mansarde /mɑ̃sard/ *n.f.* attic.

manteau (*pl.* **~x**) /mɑ̃to/ *n.m.* coat.

manucur|e /manykyr/ *n.m./f.* manicurist.
~er *v.t.* manicure.

manuel, ~le /manɥɛl/ *a.* manual.
—*n.m.* (*livre*) manual. **~lement** *adv.*
manually.

manufactur|e /manyfaktyr/ *n.f.* factory.
~é *a.* manufactured.

manuscrit, ~e /manyskri, -t/ *a.*
handwritten. —*n.m.* manuscript.

manutention /manytɑ̃sjɔ̃/ *n.f.* handling.

mappemonde /mapmɔ̃d/ *n.f.* world
map; (*sphère*) globe.

maquereau (*pl.* **~x**) /makro/ *n.m.*
(*poisson*) mackerel; (*fam.*) pimp.

maquette /makɛt/ *n.f.* (*scale*) model;
(*mise en page*) paste-up.

maquill|er /makije/ *v.t.* make up;
(*truquer*) fake. **se ~er** *v. pr.* make (o.s.)
up. **~age** *n.m.* make-up.

maquis /maki/ *n.m.* (*paysage*) scrub;
(*mil.*) Maquis, underground.

maraîch|er, ~ère /mareʃe, -ɛʃɛr/
n.m., f. market gardener; (*Amer.*) truck
farmer. **cultures ~ères**, market gar-
dening.

marais /marɛ/ *n.m.* marsh.

marasme /marasm/ *n.m.* slump.

marathon /maratɔ̃/ *n.m.* marathon.

marbre /marbr/ *n.m.* marble.

marc /mar/ *n.m.* (*eau-de-vie*) marc. **~
de café**, coffee-grounds.

marchand, ~e /marʃɑ̃, -d/ *n.m., f.*
trader; (*de charbon, vins*) merchant.
—*a.* (*valeur*) market. **~ de couleurs**,
ironmonger; (*Amer.*) hardware merchant. **~ de journaux**, newsagent. **~
de légumes**, greengrocer. **~ de
poissons**, fishmonger.

marchand|er /marʃɑ̃de/ *v.t.* haggle
over. —*v.i.* haggle. **~age** *n.m.*
haggling.

marchandise /marʃɑ̃diz/ *n.f.* goods.

marche /marʃ/ *n.f.* (*démarche, trajet*)
walk; (*rythme*) pace; (*mil., mus.*)
march; (*d'escalier*) step; (*sport*) walking; (*de machine*) working; (*de
véhicule*) running. **en ~**, (*train etc.*)
moving. **faire ~ arrière**, (*véhicule*)
reverse. **mettre en ~**, start (up). **se
mettre en ~**, start moving.

marché /marʃe/ *n.m.* market; (*contrat*)
deal. **faire son ~**, do one's shopping. **~
aux puces**, flea market. **M~ commun**,
Common Market. **~ noir**, black
market.

marchepied /marʃəpje/ *n.m. (de train, camion)* step.

march|er /marʃe/ *v.i.* walk; *(aller)* go; *(fonctionner)* work, run; *(prospérer)* go well; *(consentir: fam.)* agree. ~**er (au pas)**, *(mil.)* march. **faire** ~**er qn.**, pull s.o.'s leg. ~**eur, ~euse** *n.m., f.* walker.

mardi /mardi/ *n.m.* Tuesday. **M**~ **gras**, Shrove Tuesday.

mare /mar/ *n.f. (étang)* pond; *(flaque)* pool.

marécag|e /mareka3/ *n.m.* marsh. ~**eux, ~euse** *a.* marshy.

maréch|al *(pl.* ~**aux)** /mareʃal, -o/ *n.m.* marshal. ~**al-ferrant** *(pl.* ~**aux-ferrants)** blacksmith.

marée /mare/ *n.f. (poissons)* fresh fish. ~ **haute/basse**, high/low tide. ~ **noire**, oil-slick.

marelle /marɛl/ *n.f.* hopscotch.

margarine /margarin/ *n.f.* margarine.

marge /mar3/ *n.f.* margin. **en** ~ **de**, *(à l'écart de)* on the fringes(s) of. ~ **bénéficiaire**, profit margin.

margin|al *(pl.* ~**aux)** /mar3inal, -o/ *a.* marginal. —*n.m., f.* drop-out.

marguerite /margərit/ *n.f.* daisy; *(qui imprime)* daisy-wheel.

mari /mari/ *n.m.* husband.

mariage /marja3/ *n.m.* marriage; *(cérémonie)* wedding.

marié, ~**e** /marje/ *a.* married. —*n.m.* (bride)groom. —*n.f.* bride. **les** ~**s**, the bride and groom.

marier /marje/ *v.t.* marry. **se** ~ *v. pr.* get married, marry. **se** ~ **avec**, marry, get married to.

marin, ~**e** /marɛ̃, -in/ *a.* sea. —*n.m.* sailor. —*n.f.* navy. ~**e marchande**, merchant navy.

mariner /marine/ *v.t./i.* marinate. **faire** ~, *(fam.)* keep hanging around.

marionnette /marjɔnɛt/ *n.f.* puppet; *(à fils)* marionette.

maritalement /maritalmɑ̃/ *adv.* as husband and wife.

maritime /maritim/ *a.* maritime, coastal; *(droit, agent)* shipping.

mark /mark/ *n.m.* mark.

marmaille /marmaj/ *n.f. (enfants: fam.)* brats.

marmelade /marməlad/ *n.f.* stewed fruit. ~ **(d'oranges)**, marmalade.

marmite /marmit/ *n.f.* (cooking-)pot.

marmonner /marmɔne/ *v.t./i.* mumble.

marmot /marmo/ *n.m. (fam.)* kid.

marmotter /marmɔte/ *v.t./i.* mumble.

Maroc /marɔk/ *n.m.* Morocco.

marocain, ~**e** /marɔkɛ̃, -ɛn/ *a.* & *n.m.*, *f.* Moroccan.

maroquinerie /marɔkinri/ *n.f. (magasin)* leather goods shop.

marotte /marɔt/ *n.f.* fad, craze.

marquant, ~**e** /markɑ̃, -t/ *a.* *(remarquable)* outstanding; *(qu'on n'oublie pas)* significant.

marque /mark/ *n.f.* mark; *(de produits)* brand, make. **à vos** ~**s!**, *(sport)* on your marks! **de** ~, *(comm.)* brand-name; *(fig.)* important. ~ **de fabrique**, trade mark. ~ **déposée**, registered trade mark.

marqué /marke/ *a.* marked.

marquer /marke/ *v.t.* mark; *(indiquer)* show; *(écrire)* note down; *(point, but)* score; *(joueur)* mark; *(animal)* brand. —*v.i.* *(trace)* leave a mark; *(événement)* stand out.

marqueterie /markɛtri/ *n.f.* marquetry.

marquis, ~**e**[1] /marki, -z/ *n.m., f.* marquis, marchioness.

marquise[2] /markiz/ *n.f. (auvent)* glass awning.

marraine /marɛn/ *n.f.* godmother.

marrant, ~**e** /marɑ̃, -t/ *a. (fam.)* funny.

marre /mar/ *adv.* **en avoir** ~, *(fam.)* be fed up **(de**, with).

marrer (se) /(sə)mare/ *v. pr. (fam.)* laugh, have a (good) laugh.

marron /marɔ̃/ *n.m.* chestnut; *(couleur)* brown; *(coup: fam.)* thump. —*a. invar.* brown. ~ **d'Inde**, horse-chestnut.

mars /mars/ *n.m.* March.

marsouin /marswɛ̃/ *n.m.* porpoise.

marteau *(pl.* ~**x)** /marto/ *n.m.* hammer. ~ **(de porte)**, (door) knocker. ~ **piqueur** *ou* **pneumatique**, pneumatic drill. **être** ~, *(fam.*mad.)

marteler /martəle/ *v.t.* hammer.

mart|ial *(m. pl.* ~**iaux)** /marsjal, -jo/ *a.* martial.

martien, ~**ne** /marsjɛ̃, -jɛn/ *a.* & *n.m.*, *f.* Martian.

martyr, ~**e**[1] /martir/ *n.m., f.* martyr. —*a.* martyred. ~**iser** *v.t.* martyr; *(fig.)* batter.

martyre[2] /martir/ *n.m. (souffrance)* martyrdom.

marxis|te /marksist/ *a.* & *n.m./f.* Marxist. ~**me** *n.m.* Marxism.

mascara /maskara/ *n.m.* mascara.

mascarade /maskarad/ *n.f.* masquerade.

mascotte /maskɔt/ *n.f.* mascot.

masculin, ~**e** /maskylɛ̃, -in/ *a.* masculine; *(sexe)* male; *(mode, équipe)*

men's. —*n.m.* masculine. **∼ité** /-inite/
n.f. masculinity.
maso /mazo/ *n.m./f.* (*fam.*) masochist.
—*a. invar.* masochistic.
masochis|te /mazɔʃist/ *n.m./f.* maso-
chist. —*a.* masochistic. **∼me** *n.m.*
masochism.
masqu|e /mask/ *n.m.* mask. **∼er** *v.t.*
(*cacher*) hide, conceal (**à,** from);
(*lumière*) block (off).
massacr|e /masakr/ *n.m.* massacre. **∼er**
v.t. massacre; (*abîmer: fam.*) spoil.
massage /masaʒ/ *n.m.* massage.
masse /mas/ *n.f.* (*volume*) mass; (*gros
morceau*) lump, mass; (*outil*) sledge-
hammer. **en ∼,** (*vendre*) in bulk;
(*venir*) in force; (*production*) mass. **la
∼,** (*foule*) the masses. **une ∼ de,**
(*fam.*) masses of.
masser[1] /mase/ *v.t.*, **se ∼** *v. pr.* (*gens,
foule*) mass.
mass|er[2] /mase/ *v.t.* (*pétrir*) massage.
∼eur, ∼euse *n.m., f.* masseur,
masseuse.
massi|f, ∼ve /masif, -v/ *a.* massive;
(*or, argent*) solid. —*n.m.* (*de fleurs*)
clump; (*géog.*) massif. **∼vement** *adv.*
(*en masse*) in large numbers.
massue /masy/ *n.f.* club, bludgeon.
mastic /mastik/ *n.m.* putty.
mastiquer /mastike/ *v.t.* (*mâcher*)
chew.
masturb|er (se) /(sə)mastyrbe/ *v. pr.*
masturbate. **∼ation** *n.f.* masturbation.
masure /mazyr/ *n.f.* hovel.
mat /mat/ *a.* (*couleur*) matt; (*bruit*) dull.
être ∼, (*aux échecs*) be checkmate.
mât /mɑ/ *n.m.* mast; (*pylône*) pole.
match /matʃ/ *n.m.* match; (*Amer.*) game.
(**faire**) **∼ nul,** tie, draw. **∼ aller,** first
leg. **∼ retour,** return match.
matelas /matla/ *n.m.* mattress. **∼
pneumatique,** air mattress.
matelassé /matlase/ *a.* padded; (*tissu*)
quilted.
matelot /matlo/ *n.m.* sailor.
mater /mate/ *v.t.* (*personne*) subdue;
(*réprimer*) stifle.
matérialiser (se) /(sə)materjalize/ *v. pr.*
materialize.
matérialiste /materjalist/ *a.* materialis-
tic. —*n.m./f.* materialist.
matériaux /materjo/ *n.m. pl.* materials.
matériel, ∼le /materjɛl/ *a.* material.
—*n.m.* equipment, materials; (*d'un
ordinateur*) hardware.
maternel, ∼le /matɛrnɛl/ *a.* motherly,
maternal; (*rapport de parenté*) maternal. —*n.f.* nursery school.

maternité /matɛrnite/ *n.f.* maternity
hospital; (*état de mère*) motherhood.
mathémati|que /matematik/ *a.* mathe-
matical. —*n.f. pl.* mathematics. **∼cien,
∼cienne** *n.m., f.* mathematician.
maths /mat/ *n.f. pl.* (*fam.*) maths.
matière /matjɛr/ *n.f.* matter; (*produit*)
material; (*sujet*) subject. **en ∼ de,** as
regards. **∼ plastique,** plastic. **∼s
grasses,** fat. **à 0% de ∼s grasses,** fat
free. **∼s premières,** raw materials.
matin /matɛ̃/ *n.m.* morning. **de bon ∼,**
early in the morning.
matin|al (*m. pl.* **∼aux**) /matinal, -o/ *a.*
morning; (*de bonne heure*) early. **être
∼,** be up early.
matinée /matine/ *n.f.* morning;
(*spectacle*) matinée.
matou /matu/ *n.m.* tom-cat.
matraqu|e /matrak/ *n.f.* (*de police*)
truncheon; (*Amer.*) billy (club). **∼er**
v.t. club, beat; (*message*) plug.
matrice /matris/ *n.f.* (*techn.*) matrix.
matrimon|ial (*m. pl.* **∼iaux**) /matri-
mɔnjal, -jo/ *a.* matrimonial.
maturité /matyrite/ *n.f.* maturity.
maudire† /modir/ *v.t.* curse.
maudit, ∼e /modi, -t/ *a.* (*fam.*)
damned.
maugréer /mogree/ *v.i.* grumble.
mausolée /mozɔle/ *n.m.* mausoleum.
maussade /mosad/ *a.* gloomy.
mauvais, ∼e /mɔvɛ, -z/ *a.* bad;
(*erroné*) wrong; (*malveillant*) evil;
(*désagréable*) nasty, bad; (*mer*) rough.
—*n.m.* **il fait ∼,** the weather is bad. **le
∼ moment,** the wrong time. **∼e herbe,**
weed. **∼e langue,** gossip. **∼e passe,**
tight spot. **∼ traitements,** ill-treatment.
mauve /mov/ *a. & n.m.* mauve.
mauviette /movjɛt/ *n.f.* weakling.
maux /mo/ *voir* **mal**[2].
maxim|al (*m. pl.* **∼aux**) /maksimal,
-o/ *a.* maximum.
maxime /maksim/ *n.f.* maxim.
maximum /maksimɔm/ *a. & n.m.*
maximum. **au ∼,** as much as possible;
(*tout au plus*) at most.
mayonnaise /majɔnɛz/ *n.f.* mayonnaise.
mazout /mazut/ *n.m.* (fuel) oil.
me, m'* /mə, m/ *pron.* me; (*indirect*)
(to) me; (*réfléchi*) myself.
méandre /meɑ̃dr/ *n.m.* meander.
mec /mɛk/ *n.m.* (*fam.*) bloke, guy.
mécanicien /mekanisjɛ̃/ *n.m.* mechanic;
(*rail.*) train driver.
mécani|que /mekanik/ *a.* mechanical;
(*jouet*) clockwork. **problème ∼que,**
engine trouble. —*n.f.* mechanics;

(*mécanisme*) mechanism. **~ser** *v.t.* mechanize.

mécanisme /mekanism/ *n.m.* mechanism.

méch|ant, ~ante /meʃɑ̃, -t/ *a.* (*cruel*) wicked; (*désagréable*) nasty; (*enfant*) naughty; (*chien*) vicious; (*sensationnel*: *fam.*) terrific. —*n.m.*, *f.* (*enfant*) naughty child. **~amment** *adv.* wickedly. **~anceté** *n.f.* wickedness; (*action*) wicked action.

mèche /mɛʃ/ *n.f.* (*de cheveux*) lock; (*de bougie*) wick; (*d'explosif*) fuse. **de ~ avec,** in league with.

méconnaissable /mekɔnɛsabl/ *a.* unrecognizable.

méconn|aître /mekɔnɛtr/ *v.t.* be ignorant of; (*mésestimer*) underestimate. **~aissance** *n.f.* ignorance. **~u** *a.* unrecognized.

mécontent, ~e /mekɔ̃tɑ̃, -t/ *a.* dissatisfied (**de,** with); (*irrité*) annoyed (**de,** at, with). **~ement** /-tmɑ̃/ *n.m.* dissatisfaction; annoyance. **~er** /-te/ *v.t.* dissatisfy; (*irriter*) annoy.

médaill|e /medaj/ *n.f.* medal; (*insigne*) badge; (*bijou*) medallion. **~é, ~ée** *n.m., f.* medal holder.

médaillon /medajɔ̃/ *n.m.* medallion; (*bijou*) locket.

médecin /mɛdsɛ̃/ *n.m.* doctor.

médecine /mɛdsin/ *n.f.* medicine.

média /medja/ *n.m.* medium. **les ~s,** the media.

média|teur, ~trice /medjatœr, -tris/ *n.m., f.* mediator.

médiation /medjasjɔ̃/ *n.f.* mediation.

médiatique /medjatik/ *a.* **événement/personnalité ~,** media event/personality.

médic|al (*m. pl.* **~aux**) /medikal, -o/ *a.* medical.

médicament /medikamɑ̃/ *n.m.* medicine.

médicin|al (*m. pl.* **~aux**) /medisinal, -o/ *a.* medicinal.

médico-lég|al (*m. pl.* **~aux**) /mediko-legal, -o/ *a.* forensic.

médiév|al (*m. pl.* **~aux**) /medjeval, -o/ *a.* medieval.

médiocr|e /medjɔkr/ *a.* mediocre, poor. **~ement** *adv.* (*peu*) not very; (*mal*) in a mediocre way. **~ité** *n.f.* mediocrity.

médire /medir/ *v.i.* **~ de,** speak ill of.

médisance /medizɑ̃s/ *n.f.* **~(s),** malicious gossip.

méditati|f, ~ve /meditatif, -v/ *a.* (*pensif*) thoughtful.

médit|er /medite/ *v.t./i.* meditate. **~er de,** plan to. **~ation** *n.f.* meditation.

Méditerranée /mediterane/ *n.f.* **la ~,** the Mediterranean.

méditerranéen, ~ne /mediteraneɛ̃, -ɛn/ *a.* Mediterranean.

médium /medjɔm/ *n.m.* (*personne*) medium.

méduse /medyz/ *n.f.* jellyfish.

meeting /mitiŋ/ *n.m.* meeting.

méfait /mefɛ/ *n.m.* misdeed. **les ~s de,** (*conséquences*) the ravages of.

méfian|t, ~te /mefjɑ̃, -t/ *a.* distrustful. **~ce** *n.f.* distrust.

méfier (se) /(sə)mefje/ *v. pr.* be wary *ou* careful. **se ~ de,** distrust, be wary of.

mégarde (par) /(par)megard/ *adv.* by accident, accidentally.

mégère /meʒɛr/ *n.f.* (*femme*) shrew.

mégot /mego/ *n.m.* (*fam.*) cigarette-end.

meilleur, ~e /mejœr/ *a. & adv.* better (**que,** than). **le ~ livre**/*etc.*, the best book/*etc.* **mon ~ ami**/*etc.*, my best friend/*etc.* **~ marché,** cheaper. —*n.m., f.* **le ~/la ~e,** the best (one).

mélancol|ie /melɑ̃kɔli/ *n.f.* melancholy. **~ique** *a.* melancholy.

mélang|e /melɑ̃ʒ/ *n.m.* mixture, blend. **~er** *v.t.,* **se ~er** *v. pr.* mix, blend; (*embrouiller*) mix up.

mélasse /melas/ *n.f.* treacle; (*Amer.*) molasses.

mêlée /mele/ *n.f.* scuffle; (*rugby*) scrum.

mêler /mele/ *v.t.* mix (**à,** with); (*qualités*) combine; (*embrouiller*) mix up; (**à,** (*impliquer dans*) involve in. **se ~** *v. pr.* mix; combine. **se ~ à,** (*se joindre à*) join. **se ~ de,** meddle in. **mêle-toi de ce qui te regarde,** mind your own business.

méli-mélo /melimelo/ *n.m.* (*pl.* **mélis-mélos**) jumble.

mélo /melo/ (*fam.*) *n.m.* melodrama. —*a. invar.* melodramatic.

mélod|ie /melɔdi/ *n.f.* melody. **~ieux, ~ieuse** *a.* melodious. **~ique** *a.* melodic.

mélodram|e /melɔdram/ *n.m.* melodrama. **~atique** *a.* melodramatic.

mélomane /melɔman/ *n.m./f.* music lover.

melon /mlɔ̃/ *n.m.* melon. **(chapeau) ~,** bowler (hat).

membrane /mɑ̃bran/ *n.f.* membrane.

membre[1] /mɑ̃br/ *n.m.* limb.

membre[2] /mɑ̃br/ *n.m.* (*adhérent*) member.

même /mɛm/ *a.* same. **ce livre**/*etc.* **~,** this very book/*etc.* **la bonté**/*etc.* **~,** kindness/*etc.* itself. —*pron.* **le ~/la ~,** the same (one). —*adv.* even. **à ~,** (*sur*) directly on. **à ~ de,** in a position to. **de ~,** (*aussi*) too; (*de la même façon*) likewise. **de ~ que,** just as. **en ~ temps,** at the same time.

mémé /meme/ *n.f.* (*fam.*) granny.

mémo /memo/ *n.m.* memo.

mémoire /memwar/ *n.f.* memory. —*n.m.* (*requête*) memorandum; (*univ.*) dissertation. **~s,** (*souvenirs écrits*) memoirs. **à la ~ de,** to the memory of. **de ~,** from memory. **~ morte/vive,** (*comput.*) ROM/RAM.

mémorable /memɔrabl/ *a.* memorable.

mémorandum /memɔrɑ̃dɔm/ *n.m.* memorandum.

menac|e /mɔnas/ *n.f.* threat. **~er** *v.t.* threaten (**de faire,** to do).

ménage /menaʒ/ *n.m.* (married) couple; (*travail*) housework. **se mettre en ~,** set up house. **scène de ~,** scene. **dépenses du ~,** household expenditure.

ménagement /menaʒmɑ̃/ *n.m.* care and consideration.

ménag|er¹, **~ère** /menaʒe, -ɛr/ *a.* household, domestic. **travaux ~ers,** housework. **~ère** *n.f.* housewife.

ménager² /menaʒe/ *v.t.* treat with tact; (*utiliser*) be sparing in the use of; (*organiser*) prepare (carefully).

ménagerie /menaʒri/ *n.f.* menagerie.

mendiant, ~e /mɑ̃djɑ̃, -t/ *n.m., f.* beggar.

mendicité /mɑ̃disite/ *n.f.* begging.

mendier /mɑ̃dje/ *v.t.* beg for. —*v.i.* beg.

menées /mɔne/ *n.f. pl.* schemings.

mener /mɔne/ *v.t.* lead; (*entreprise, pays*) run. —*v.i.* lead. **~ à,** (*accompagner à*) take to. **~ à bien,** see through.

meneur /mɔnœr/ *n.m.* (*chef*) (ring)leader. **~ de jeu,** compère; (*Amer.*) master of ceremonies.

méningite /menɛ̃ʒit/ *n.f.* meningitis.

ménopause /menopoz/ *n.f.* menopause.

menotte /mɔnɔt/ *n.f.* (*fam.*) hand. **~s,** handcuffs.

mensong|e /mɑ̃sɔ̃ʒ/ *n.m.* lie; (*action*) lying. **~er, ~ère** *a.* untrue.

menstruation /mɑ̃stryɑsjɔ̃/ *n.f.* menstruation.

mensualité /mɑ̃syalite/ *n.f.* monthly payment.

mensuel, ~le /mɑ̃syɛl/ *a. & n.m.* monthly. **~lement** *adv.* monthly.

mensurations /mɑ̃syrɑsjɔ̃/ *n.f. pl.* measurements.

ment|al (*m. pl.* **~aux**) /mɑ̃tal, -o/ *a.* mental.

mentalité /mɑ̃talite/ *n.f.* mentality.

menteu|r, ~se /mɑ̃tœr, -øz/ *n.m., f.* liar. —*a.* untruthful.

menthe /mɑ̃t/ *n.f.* mint.

mention /mɑ̃sjɔ̃/ *n.f.* mention; (*annotation*) note; (*scol.*) grade. **~ bien,** (*scol.*) distinction. **~ner** /-jɔne/ *v.t.* mention.

mentir† /mɑ̃tir/ *v.i.* lie.

menton /mɑ̃tɔ̃/ *n.m.* chin.

mentor /mɛ̃tɔr/ *n.m.* mentor.

menu¹ /mɔny/ *n.m.* (*carte*) menu; (*repas*) meal.

menu² /mɔny/ *a.* (*petit*) tiny; (*fin*) fine; (*insignifiant*) minor. —*adv.* (*couper*) fine.

menuis|ier /mɔnɥizje/ *n.m.* carpenter, joiner. **~erie** *n.f.* carpentry, joinery.

méprendre (se) /(sə)meprɑ̃dr/ *v. pr.* se **~ sur,** be mistaken about.

mépris /mepri/ *n.m.* contempt, scorn (**de,** for). **au ~ de,** in defiance of.

méprisable /meprizabl/ *a.* despicable.

méprise /mepriz/ *n.f.* mistake.

mépris|er /meprize/ *v.t.* scorn, despise. **~ant, ~ante** *a.* scornful.

mer /mɛr/ *n.f.* sea; (*marée*) tide. **en haute ~,** on the open sea.

mercenaire /mɛrsɔnɛr/ *n.m. & a.* mercenary.

merci /mɛrsi/ *int.* thank you, thanks (**de, pour,** for). —*n.f.* mercy. **~ beaucoup, ~ bien,** thank you very much.

merc|ier, ~ière /mɛrsje, -jɛr/ *n.m., f.* haberdasher; (*Amer.*) notions merchant. **~erie** *n.f.* haberdashery; (*Amer.*) notions store.

mercredi /mɛrkrɔdi/ *n.m.* Wednesday. **~ des Cendres,** Ash Wednesday.

mercure /mɛrkyr/ *n.m.* mercury.

merde /mɛrd/ *n.f.* (*fam.*) shit. **être dans la ~,** be in a mess.

mère /mɛr/ *n.f.* mother. **~ de famille,** mother.

méridien /meridjɛ̃/ *n.m.* meridian.

méridion|al, ~ale (*m. pl.* **~aux**) /meridjɔnal, -o/ *a.* southern. —*n.m., f.* southerner.

meringue /mɔrɛ̃g/ *n.f.* meringue.

mérite /merit/ *n.m.* merit. **il n'a aucun ~,** that's as it should be. **il a du ~,** it's very much to his credit.

mérit|er /merite/ *v.t.* deserve. **~ant, ~ante** *a.* deserving.

méritoire /meritwar/ *a.* commendable.

merlan /mɛrlɑ̃/ *n.m.* whiting.

merle /mɛrl/ *n.m.* blackbird.

merveille /mɛrvɛj/ *n.f.* wonder, marvel.

à ~, wonderfully. **faire des** ~**s,** work wonders.

merveilleu|x, ~**se** /mɛrvɛjø, -z/ *a.* wonderful, marvellous. ~**sement** *adv.* wonderfully.

mes /me/ *voir* **mon.**

mésange /mezãʒ/ *n.f.* tit(mouse).

mésaventure /mezavãtyr/ *n.f.* misadventure.

mesdames /medam/ *voir* **madame.**

mesdemoiselles /medmwazɛl/ *voir* **mademoiselle.**

mésentente /mezãtãt/ *n.f.* disagreement.

mesquin, ~**e** /mɛskɛ̃, -in/ *a.* mean. ~**erie** /-inri/ *n.f.* meanness.

mess /mɛs/ *n.m.* (*mil.*) mess.

messag|e /mesaʒ/ *n.m.* message. ~**er,** ~**ère** *n.m., f.* messenger.

messe /mɛs/ *n.f.* (*relig.*) mass.

Messie /mesi/ *n.m.* Messiah.

messieurs /mesjø/ *voir* **monsieur.**

mesure /məzyr/ *n.f.* measurement; (*quantité, étalon*) measure; (*disposition*) measure, step; (*cadence*) time; (*modération*) moderation. à ~ **que,** as. **dans la** ~ **où,** in so far as. **dans une certaine** ~, to some extent. **en** ~ **de,** in a position to.

mesuré /məzyre/ *a.* measured; (*personne*) moderate.

mesurer /məzyre/ *v.t.* measure; (*juger*) assess; (*argent, temps*) ration. **se** ~ **avec,** pit o.s. against.

met /mɛ/ *voir* **mettre.**

métabolisme /metabɔlism/ *n.m.* metabolism.

mét|al (*pl.* ~**aux**) /metal, -o/ *n.m.* metal. ~**allique** *a.* (*objet*) metal; (*éclat etc.*) metallic.

métallurg|ie /metalyrʒi/ *n.f.* (*industrie*) steel *ou* metal industry. ~**iste** *n.m.* steel *ou* metal worker.

métamorphos|e /metamɔrfoz/ *n.f.* metamorphosis. ~**er** *v.t.,* **se** ~**er** *v. pr.* transform.

métaphor|e /metafɔr/ *n.f.* metaphor. ~**ique** *a.* metaphorical.

météo /meteo/ *n.f.* (*bulletin*) weather forecast.

météore /meteɔr/ *n.m.* meteor.

météorolog|ie /meteɔrɔlɔʒi/ *n.f.* meteorology; (*service*) weather bureau. ~**ique** *a.* weather; (*études etc.*) meteorological.

méthod|e /metɔd/ *n.f.* method; (*ouvrage*) course, manual. ~**ique** *a.* methodical.

méticuleu|x, ~**se** /metikylø, -z/ *a.* meticulous.

métier /metje/ *n.m.* job; (*manuel*) trade; (*intellectuel*) profession; (*expérience*) skill. ~ **(à tisser),** loom. **remettre sur le** ~, keep going back to the drawing-board.

métis, ~**se** /metis/ *a. & n.m., f.* half-caste.

métrage /metraʒ/ *n.m.* length. **court** ~, short film. **long** ~, full-length film.

mètre /mɛtr/ *n.m.* metre; (*règle*) rule. ~ **ruban,** tape-measure.

métreur /metrœr/ *n.m.* quantity surveyor.

métrique /metrik/ *a.* metric.

métro /metro/ *n.m.* underground; (*à Paris*) Métro.

métropol|e /metrɔpɔl/ *n.f.* metropolis; (*pays*) mother country. ~**itain,** ~**itaine** *a.* metropolitan.

mets¹ /mɛ/ *n.m.* dish.

mets² /mɛ/ *voir* **mettre.**

mettable /metabl/ *a.* wearable.

metteur /metœr/ *n.m.* ~ **en scène,** (*théâtre*) producer; (*cinéma*) director.

mettre† /mɛtr/ *v.t.* put; (*vêtement*) put on; (*radio, chauffage, etc.*) put *ou* switch on; (*table*) lay; (*pendule*) set; (*temps*) take; (*installer*) put in; (*supposer*) suppose. **se** ~ *v. pr.* put o.s.; (*objet*) go; (*porter*) wear. ~ **bas,** give birth. ~ **qn. en boîte,** pull s.o.'s leg. ~ **en cause** *ou* **en question,** question. ~ **en colère,** make angry. ~ **en valeur,** highlight. (*un bien*) exploit. **se** ~ **à,** (*entrer dans*) get *ou* go into. **se** ~ **à faire,** start doing. **se** ~ **à l'aise,** make o.s. comfortable. **se** ~ **à table,** sit down at the table. **se** ~ **au travail,** set to work. (**se**) ~ **en ligne,** line up. **se** ~ **dans tous ses états,** get into a state. **se** ~ **du sable dans les yeux,** get sand in one's eyes.

meuble /mœbl/ *n.m.* piece of furniture. ~**s,** furniture.

meublé /mœble/ *n.m.* furnished flatlet.

meubler /mœble/ *v.t.* furnish; (*fig.*) fill. **se** ~ *v. pr.* buy furniture.

meugl|er /mœgle/ *v.i.* moo. ~**ement(s)** *n.m.* (*pl.*) mooing.

meule /møl/ *n.f.* (*de foin*) haystack; (*à moudre*) millstone.

meun|ier, ~**ière** /mønje, -jɛr/ *n.m., f.* miller.

meurs, meurt /mœr/ *voir* **mourir.**

meurtr|e /mœrtr/ *n.m.* murder. ~**ier,** ~**ière** *a.* deadly; *n.m.* murderer; *n.f.* murderess.

meurtr|ir /mœrtrir/ *v.t.* bruise. ~**issure** *n.f.* bruise.

meute /møt/ *n.f.* (*troupe*) pack.

mexicain, ∼e /mɛksikɛ̃, -ɛn/ *a.* & *n.m., f.* Mexican.

Mexique /mɛksik/ *n.m.* Mexico.

mi- /mi/ *préf.* mid-, half-. **à mi-chemin**, half-way. **à mi-côte**, half-way up the hill. **la mi-juin**/*etc.*, mid-June/*etc.*

miaou /mjau/ *n.m.* mew.

miau∣ler /mjole/ *v.i.* mew. ∼**ement** *n.m.* mew.

miche /miʃ/ *n.f.* round loaf.

micro /mikro/ *n.m.* microphone, mike; (*comput.*) micro.

micro- /mikro/ *préf.* micro-.

microbe /mikrɔb/ *n.m.* germ.

microfilm /mikrɔfilm/ *n.m.* microfilm.

micro-onde /mikrɔɔd/ *n.f.* microwave. **un (four à)** ∼**s**, microwave (oven).

microphone /mikrɔfɔn/ *n.m.* microphone.

microplaquette /mikrɔplakɛt/ *n.f.* (micro)chip.

microprocesseur /mikrɔprɔsɛsœr/ *n.m.* microprocess.

microscop∣e /mikrɔskɔp/ *n.m.* microscope. ∼**ique** *a.* microscopic.

microsillon /mikrɔsijɔ̃/ *n.m.* long-playing record.

midi /midi/ *n.m.* twelve o'clock, midday, noon; (*déjeuner*) lunch-time; (*sud*) south. **le M**∼, the South of France.

mie /mi/ *n.f.* soft part (of the loaf). **un pain de** ∼, a sandwich loaf.

miel /mjɛl/ *n.m.* honey.

miel∣eux, ∼se /mjɛlø, -z/ *a.* unctuous.

mien, ∼ne /mjɛ̃, mjɛn/ *pron.* **le** ∼, **la** ∼**ne, les** ∼**(ne)s**, mine.

miette /mjɛt/ *n.f.* crumb; (*fig.*) scrap. **en** ∼**s**, in pieces.

mieux /mjø/ *adv.* & *a. invar.* better (**que**, than). **le** *ou* **la** *ou* **les** ∼, (the) best. —*n.m.* best; (*progrès*) improvement. **faire de son** ∼, do one's best. **tu ferais** ∼ **de faire**, you would be better off doing. **le** ∼ **serait de**, the best thing would be to.

mièvre /mjɛvr/ *a.* genteel and insipid.

mignon, ∼ne /miɲɔ̃, -ɔn/ *a.* pretty.

migraine /migrɛn/ *n.f.* headache.

migration /migrasjɔ̃/ *n.f.* migration.

mijoter /miʒɔte/ *v.t./i.* simmer; (*tramer: fam.*) cook up.

mil /mil/ *n.m.* a thousand.

milic∣e /milis/ *n.f.* militia. ∼**ien** *n.m.* militiaman.

milieu (*pl.* ∼**x**) /miljø/ *n.m.* middle; (*environnement*) environment; (*groupe*) circle; (*voie*) middle way; (*criminel*) underworld. **au** ∼ **de**, in the middle of.

en plein *ou* **au beau** ∼ **de,** right in the middle (of).

militaire /militɛr/ *a.* military. —*n.m.* soldier.

milit∣er /milite/ *v.i.* be a militant. ∼**er pour**, militate in favour of. ∼**ant**, ∼**ante** *n.m., f.* militant.

milk-shake /milkʃɛk/ *n.m.* milk shake.

mille[1] /mil/ *a.* & *n.m. invar.* a thousand. **deux** ∼, two thousand. **dans le** ∼, bang on target.

mille[2] /mil/ *n.m.* ∼ **(marin)**, (nautical) mile.

mi.lénaire /milenɛr/ *n.m.* millennium.

mille-pattes /milpat/ *n.m. invar.* centipede.

millésime /milezim/ *n.m.* year.

millésimé /milezime/ *a.* **vin** ∼, vintage wine.

millet /mijɛ/ *n.m.* millet.

milliard /miljar/ *n.m.* thousand million, billion. ∼**aire** /-dɛr/ *n.m./f.* multimillionaire.

millier /milje/ *n.m.* thousand. **un** ∼ **(de)**, about a thousand.

millimètre /milimɛtr/ *n.m.* millimetre.

million /miljɔ̃/ *n.m.* million. **deux** ∼**s (de)**, two million. ∼**naire** /-jɔnɛr/ *n.m./f.* millionaire.

mim∣e /mim/ *n.m./f.* (*personne*) mime. —*n.m.* (*art*) mime. ∼**er** *v.t.* mime; (*singer*) mimic.

mimique /mimik/ *n.f.* (expressive) gestures.

mimosa /mimoza/ *n.m.* mimosa.

minable /minabl/ *a.* shabby.

minaret /minarɛ/ *n.m.* minaret.

minauder /minode/ *v.i.* simper.

minc∣e /mɛ̃s/ *a.* thin; (*svelte, insignifiant*) slim. —*int.* dash (it). ∼**ir** *v.i.* get slimmer. **ça te** ∼**it**, it makes you look slimmer. ∼**eur** *n.f.* thinness; slimness.

mine[1] /min/ *n.f.* expression; (*allure*) appearance. **avoir bonne** ∼, look well. **faire** ∼ **de**, make as if to.

mine[2] /min/ *n.f.* (*exploitation, explosif*) mine; (*de crayon*) lead. ∼ **de charbon**, coal-mine.

miner /mine/ *v.t.* (*saper*) undermine; (*garnir d'explosifs*) mine. **minerai** /minrɛ/ *n.m.* ore.

minér∣al (*m. pl.* ∼**aux**) /mineral, -o/ *a.* mineral. —*n.m.* (*pl.* ∼**aux**) mineral.

minéralogique /mineralɔʒik/ *a.* **plaque** ∼, number/license (*Amer.*) plate.

minet, ∼te /minɛ, -t/ *n.m., f.* (*chat: fam.*) puss(y).

mineur[1], ~e /minœr/ a. minor; (*jurid.*) under age. —*n.m., f.* (*jurid.*) minor.

mineur[2] /minœr/ *n.m.* (*ouvrier*) miner.

mini- /mini/ *préf.* mini-.

miniature /minjatyr/ *n.f. & a.* miniature.

minibus /minibys/ *n.m.* minibus.

min|ier, ~**ière** /minje, -jɛr/ a. mining.

minim|al (*m. pl.* ~**aux**) /minimal, -o/ a. minimum.

minime /minim/ a. minor. —*n.m./f.* (*sport*) junior.

minimiser /minimize/ *v.t.* minimize.

minimum /minimɔm/ a. & n.m. minimum. **au** ~, (*pour le moins*) at the very least.

mini-ordinateur /miniɔrdinatœr/ *n.m.* minicomputer.

minist|ère /ministɛr/ *n.m.* ministry; (*gouvernement*) government. ~**ère de l'Intérieur**, Home Office; (*Amer.*) Department of the Interior. ~**ériel**, ~**érielle** a. ministerial, government.

ministre /ministr/ *n.m.* minister. ~ **de l'Intérieur**, Home Secretary; (*Amer.*) Secretary of the Interior.

Minitel /minitɛl/ *n.m.* (P.) Minitel (*telephone videotext system*).

minorer /minɔre/ *v.t.* reduce.

minorit|é /minɔrite/ *n.f.* minority. ~**aire** a. minority. **être** ~**aire**, be in the minority.

minuit /minɥi/ *n.m.* midnight.

minuscule /minyskyl/ a. minute. —*n.f.* (*lettre*) ~, small letter.

minut|e /minyt/ *n.f.* minute. ~**er** *v.t.* time (to the minute).

minuterie /minytri/ *n.f.* time-switch.

minutie /minysi/ *n.f.* meticulousness.

minutieu|x, ~**se** /minysjø, -z/ a. meticulous. ~**sement** adv. meticulously.

mioche /mjɔʃ/ *n.m., f.* (*fam.*) youngster, kid.

mirabelle /mirabɛl/ *n.f.* (mirabelle) plum.

miracle /mirɑkl/ *n.m.* miracle.

miraculeu|x, ~**se** /mirakylø, -z/ a. miraculous. ~**sement** adv. miraculously.

mirage /miraʒ/ *n.m.* mirage.

mire /mir/ *n.f.* (*fig.*) centre of attraction; (TV) test card.

miro /miro/ a. *invar.* (*fam.*) short-sighted.

mirobolant, ~**e** /mirɔbɔlɑ̃, -t/ a. (*fam.*) marvellous.

miroir /mirwar/ *n.m.* mirror.

miroiter /mirwate/ *v.i.* gleam, shimmer.

mis, ~**e**[1] /mi, miz/ *voir* **mettre**. —*a.* **bien** ~, well-dressed.

misanthrope /mizɑ̃trɔp/ *n.m.* misanthropist. —*a.* misanthropic.

mise[2] /miz/ *n.f.* (*argent*) stake; (*tenue*) attire. ~ **à feu**, blast-off. ~ **au point**, adjustment; (*fig.*) clarification. ~ **de fonds**, capital outlay. ~ **en garde**, warning. ~ **en scène**, (*théâtre*) production; (*cinéma*) direction.

miser /mize/ *v.t.* (*argent*) bet, stake (**sur**, on). ~ **sur**, (*compter sur: fam.*) bank on.

misérable /mizerabl/ a. miserable, wretched; (*indigent*) poverty-stricken; (*minable*) seedy. —*n.m./f.* wretch.

mis|ère /mizɛr/ *n.f.* (grinding) poverty; (*malheur*) misery. ~**éreux**, ~**éreuse** *n.m., f.* pauper.

miséricorde /mizerikɔrd/ *n.f.* mercy.

missel /misɛl/ *n.m.* missal.

missile /misil/ *n.m.* missile.

mission /misjɔ̃/ *n.m.* mission. ~**naire** /-jɔnɛr/ *n.m./f.* missionary.

missive /misiv/ *n.f.* missive.

mistral /mistral/ *n.m. invar.* (*vent*) mistral.

mitaine /mitɛn/ *n.f.* mitten.

mit|e /mit/ *n.f.* (clothes-)moth. ~**é** a. moth-eaten.

mi-temps /mitɑ̃/ *n.f. invar.* (*repos: sport*) half-time; (*période: sport*) half. **à** ~, part time.

miteu|x, ~**se** /mitø, -z/ a. shabby.

mitigé /mitiʒe/ a. (*modéré*) lukewarm.

mitonner /mitɔne/ *v.t.* cook slowly with care; (*fig.*) cook up.

mitoyen, ~**ne** /mitwajɛ̃, -ɛn/ a. **mur** ~, party wall.

mitrailler /mitraje/ *v.t.* machine-gun; (*fig.*) bombard.

mitraill|ette /mitrajɛt/ *n.f.* sub-machine-gun. ~**euse** *n.f.* machine-gun.

mi-voix (à) /(a)mivwa/ adv. in an undertone.

mixeur /miksœr/ *n.m.* liquidizer, blender.

mixte /mikst/ a. mixed; (*usage*) dual; (*tribunal*) joint; (*école*) co-educational.

mixture /mikstyr/ *n.f.* (*péj.*) mixture.

mobile[1] /mɔbil/ a. mobile; (*pièce*) moving; (*feuillet*) loose. —*n.m.* (*art*) mobile.

mobile[2] /mɔbil/ *n.m.* (*raison*) motive.

mobilier /mɔbilje/ *n.m.* furniture.

mobilis|er /mɔbilize/ *v.t.* mobilize. ~**ation** *n.f.* mobilization.

mobilité /mɔbilite/ *n.f.* mobility.

mobylette /mɔbilɛt/ *n.f.* (P.) moped.

mocassin /mɔkasɛ̃/ n.m. moccasin.

moche /mɔʃ/ a. (laid: fam.) ugly; (mauvais: fam.) lousy.

modalité /mɔdalite/ n.f. mode.

mode¹ /mɔd/ n.f. fashion; (coutume) custom. à la ~, fashionable.

mode² /mɔd/ n.m. method, mode; (genre) way. ~ d'emploi, directions (for use).

modèle /mɔdɛl/ n.m. & a. model. ~ réduit, (small-scale) model.

modeler /mɔdle/ v.t. model (sur, on). se ~ sur, model o.s. on.

modem /mɔdɛm/ n.m. modem.

modéré, ~e /mɔdere/ a. & n.m., f. moderate. ~ment adv. moderately.

modér|er /mɔdere/ v.t. moderate. se ~er v. pr. restrain o.s. ~ateur, ~atrice a. moderating. ~ation n.f. moderation.

modern|e /mɔdɛrn/ a. modern. —n.m. modern style. ~iser v.t. modernize.

modest|e /mɔdɛst/ a. modest. ~ement adv. modestly. ~ie n.f. modesty.

modif|ier /mɔdifje/ v.t. modify. se ~ier v. pr. alter. ~ication n.f. modification.

modique /mɔdik/ a. low.

modiste /mɔdist/ n.f. milliner.

module /mɔdyl/ n.m. module.

modul|er /mɔdyle/ v.t./i. modulate. ~ation n.f. modulation.

moelle /mwal/ n.f. marrow. ~ épinière, spinal cord.

moelleu|x, ~se /mwalø, -z/ a. soft; (onctueux) smooth.

mœurs /mœr(s)/ n.f. pl. (morale) morals; (habitudes) customs; (manières) ways.

moi /mwa/ pron. me; (indirect) (to) me; (sujet) I. —n.m. self. ~-même pron. myself.

moignon /mwaɲɔ̃/ n.m. stump.

moindre /mwɛ̃dr/ a. (moins grand) less(er). le ou la ~, les ~s, the slightest, the least.

moine /mwan/ n.m. monk.

moineau (pl. ~x) /mwano/ n.m. sparrow.

moins /mwɛ̃/ adv. less (que, than). —prép. (soustraction) minus. ~ de, (quantité) less, not so much (que, as); (objets, personnes) fewer, not so many (que, as). ~ de dix francs/d'une livre/etc., less than ten francs/one pound/etc. le ou la ou les ~, the least. le ~ grand/haut, the smallest/lowest. au ~, du ~, at least. de ~, less. en ~, less; (manquant) missing. une heure ~ dix, ten to one. à ~ que, unless. de ~ en moins, less and less.

mois /mwa/ n.m. month.

moise /mɔiz/ n.m. Moses basket.

mois|i /mwazi/ a. mouldy. —n.m. mould. de ~i, (odeur, goût) musty. ~ir v.i. go mouldy. ~issure n.f. mould.

moisson /mwasɔ̃/ n.f. harvest.

moissonn|er /mwasɔne/ v.t. harvest, reap. ~eur, ~euse n.m., f. harvester. ~euse-batteuse (pl. ~euses-batteuses) n.f. combine harvester.

moit|e /mwat/ a. sticky, clammy. ~eur n.f. stickiness.

moitié /mwatje/ n.f. half; (milieu) halfway mark. à ~, half-way. à ~ vide/fermé/etc., half empty/ closed/etc. à ~ prix, (at) half-price. la ~ de, half (of). ~ moitié, half-and-half.

moka /mɔka/ n.m. (gâteau) coffee cream cake.

mol /mɔl/ voir mou.

molaire /mɔlɛr/ n.f. molar.

molécule /mɔlekyl/ n.f. molecule.

molester /mɔlɛste/ v.t. manhandle, rough up.

molle /mɔl/ voir mou.

moll|ement /mɔlmɑ̃/ adv. softly; (faiblement) feebly. ~esse n.f. softness; (faiblesse, indolence) feebleness.

mollet /mɔlɛ/ n.m. (de jambe) calf.

molletonné /mɔltɔne/ a. (fleece-)lined.

mollir /mɔlir/ v.i. soften; (céder) yield.

mollusque /mɔlysk/ n.m. mollusc.

môme /mom/ n.m./f. (fam.) kid.

moment /mɔmɑ̃/ n.m. moment; (période) time. (petit) ~, short while. au ~ où, when. par ~s, now and then. du ~ où ou que, seeing that. en ce ~, at the moment.

momentané /mɔmɑ̃tane/ a. momentary. ~ment adv. momentarily; (en ce moment) at present.

momie /mɔmi/ n.f. mummy.

mon, ma ou mon* (pl. mes) /mɔ̃, ma, mɔ̃n, me/ a. my.

Monaco /mɔnako/ n.f. Monaco.

monarchie /mɔnarʃi/ n.f. monarchy.

monarque /mɔnark/ n.m. monarque.

monastère /mɔnastɛr/ n.m. monastery.

monceau (pl. ~x) /mɔ̃so/ n.m. heap, pile.

mondain, ~e /mɔ̃dɛ̃, -ɛn/ a. society, social.

monde /mɔ̃d/ n.m. world. du ~, (a lot of) people; (quelqu'un) somebody. le (grand) ~, (high) society. se faire un ~ de qch., make a great deal of fuss about sth.

mond|ial (m. pl. ~iaux) /mɔ̃djal, -jo/

a. world; (*influence*) worldwide. ∼**ialement** *adv.* the world over.

monégasque /mɔnegask/ *a. & n.m./f.* Monegasque.

monétaire /mɔnetɛr/ *a.* monetary.

moni|teur, ∼**trice** /mɔnitœr, -tris/ *n.m.*, *f.* instructor, instructress; (*de colonie de vacances*) supervisor; (*Amer.*) (camp) counselor.

monnaie /mɔnɛ/ *n.f.* currency; (*pièce*) coin; (*appoint*) change. **faire la** ∼ **de**, get change for. **faire à qn. la** ∼ **de**, give s.o. change for. **menue** *ou* **petite** ∼, small change.

monnayer /mɔneje/ *v.t.* convert into cash.

mono /mɔno/ *a. invar.* mono.

monocle /mɔnɔkl/ *n.m.* monocle.

monocorde /mɔnɔkɔrd/ *a.* monotonous.

monogramme /mɔnɔgram/ *n.m.* monogram.

monologue /mɔnɔlɔg/ *n.m.* monologue.

monopol|e /mɔnɔpɔl/ *n.m.* monopoly. ∼**iser** *v.t.* monopolize.

monosyllabe /mɔnɔsilab/ *n.m.* monosyllable.

monoton|e /mɔnɔtɔn/ *a.* monotonous. ∼**ie** *n.f.* monotony.

monseigneur /mɔ̃sɛɲœr/ *n.m.* Your *ou* His Grace.

monsieur (*pl.* **messieurs**) /mɔsjø, mesjø/ *n.m.* gentleman. **M**∼ **ou M. Dupont**, Mr Dupont. **Messieurs** *ou* **MM. Dupont**, Messrs Dupont. **oui** ∼, yes; (*avec déférence*) yes, sir.

monstre /mɔ̃str/ *n.m.* monster. —*a.* (*fam.*) colossal.

monstr|ueux, ∼**ueuse** /mɔ̃stryø, -z/ *a.* monstrous. ∼**uosité** *n.f.* monstrosity.

mont /mɔ̃/ *n.m.* mount. **par** ∼**s et par vaux**, up hill and down dale.

montage /mɔ̃taʒ/ *n.m.* (*assemblage*) assembly; (*cinéma*) editing.

montagn|e /mɔ̃taɲ/ *n.f.* mountain; (*région*) mountains. ∼**es russes**, roller-coaster. ∼**ard**, ∼**arde** *n.m.*, *f.* mountain dweller. ∼**eux**, ∼**euse** *a.* mountainous.

montant[1], ∼**e** /mɔ̃tã, -t/ *a.* rising; (*col*) high-necked.

montant[2] /mɔ̃tã/ *n.m.* amount; (*pièce de bois*) upright.

mont-de-piété (*pl.* **monts-de-piété**) /mɔ̃dpjete/ *n.m.* pawnshop.

monte-charge /mɔ̃tʃarʒ/ *n.m. invar.* service lift; (*Amer.*) dumb waiter.

montée /mɔ̃te/ *n.f.* ascent, climb; (*de prix*) rise; (*côte*) hill. **au milieu de la**

∼, halfway up. **à la** ∼ **de lait,** when the milk comes.

monter /mɔ̃te/ *v.i.* (*aux. être*) go *ou* come up; (*grimper*) climb; (*prix, mer*) rise. ∼ **à**, (*cheval*) mount. ∼ **dans**, (*train, avion*) get on to; (*voiture*) get into. ∼ **sur**, (*colline*) climb up; (*trône*) ascend. —*v.t.* (*aux. avoir*) go *ou* come up; (*objet*) take *ou* bring up; (*cheval, garde*) mount; (*société*) start up. ∼ **à cheval**, (*sport*) ride. ∼ **en flèche**, soar. ∼ **en graine**, go to seed.

monteu|r, ∼**se** /mɔ̃tœr, -øz/ *n.m.*, *f.* (*techn.*) fitter; (*cinéma*) editor.

monticule /mɔ̃tikyl/ *n.m.* mound.

montre /mɔ̃tr/ *n.f.* watch. ∼**-bracelet** (*pl.* ∼**s-bracelets**) *n.f.* wrist-watch. **faire** ∼ **de**, show.

montrer /mɔ̃tre/ *v.t.* show (**à**, to). **se** ∼ *v. pr.* show o.s.; (*être*) be; (*s'avérer*) prove to be. ∼ **du doigt**, point to.

monture /mɔ̃tyr/ *n.f.* (*cheval*) mount; (*de lunettes*) frame; (*de bijou*) setting.

monument /mɔnymã/ *n.m.* monument. ∼ **aux morts**, war memorial. ∼**al** (*m. pl.* ∼**aux**) /-tal, -to/ *a.* monumental.

moqu|er (**se**) /(sə)mɔke/ *v. pr.* **se** ∼**er de**, make fun of. **je m'en** ∼**e**, (*fam.*) I couldn't care less. ∼**erie** *n.f.* mockery. ∼**eur**, ∼**euse** *a.* mocking.

moquette /mɔkɛt/ *n.f.* fitted carpet; (*Amer.*) wall-to-wall carpeting.

mor|al, ∼**ale** (*m. pl.* ∼**aux**) /mɔral, -o/ *a.* moral. —*n.m.* (*pl.* ∼**aux**) morale. —*n.f.* moral code; (*mœurs*) morals; (*de fable*) moral. **avoir le** ∼**al**, be on form. **ça m'a remonté le** ∼**al**, it gave me a boost. **faire la** ∼**ale à**, lecture. ∼**alement** *adv.* morally. ∼**alité** *n.f.* morality; (*de fable*) moral.

moralisa|teur, ∼**trice** /mɔralizatœr, -tris/ *a.* moralizing.

morbide /mɔrbid/ *a.* morbid.

morceau (*pl.* ∼**x**) /mɔrso/ *n.m.* piece, bit; (*de sucre*) lump; (*de viande*) cut; (*passage*) passage. **manger un** ∼, have a bite to eat. **mettre en** ∼**x**, smash *ou* tear *etc.* to bits.

morceler /mɔrsəle/ *v.t.* fragment.

mordant, ∼**e** /mɔrdã, -t/ *a.* scathing; (*froid*) biting. —*n.m.* (*énergie*) vigour, punch.

mordiller /mɔrdije/ *v.t.* nibble at.

mord|re /mɔrdr/ *v.t./i.* bite. ∼**re sur**, overlap into. ∼**re à l'hameçon**, bite. ∼**u**, ∼**ue** *n.m.*, *f.* (*fam.*) fan; *a.* bitten. ∼**u de**, (*fam.*) crazy about.

morfondre (**se**) /(sə)mɔrfɔ̃dr/ *v. pr.* mope, wait anxiously.

morgue¹ /mɔrg/ n.f. morgue, mortuary.
morgue² /mɔrg/ n.f. (attitude) haughtiness.
moribond, ∼e /mɔribɔ̃, -d/ a. dying.
morne /mɔrn/ a. dull.
morose /mɔroz/ a. morose.
morphine /mɔrfin/ n.f. morphine.
mors /mɔr/ n.m. (de cheval) bit.
morse¹ /mɔrs/ n.m. walrus.
morse² /mɔrs/ n.m. (code) Morse code.
morsure /mɔrsyr/ n.f. bite.
mort¹ /mɔr/ n.f. death.
mort², ∼e /mɔr, -t/ a. dead. —n.m., f. dead man, dead woman. **les** ∼**s**, the dead. ∼ **de fatigue**, dead tired. ∼-**né** a. stillborn.
mortadelle /mɔrtadɛl/ n.f. mortadella.
mortalité /mɔrtalite/ n.f. death rate.
mortel, ∼**le** /mɔrtɛl/ a. mortal; (accident) fatal; (poison, silence) deadly. —n.m., f. mortal. ∼**lement** adv. mortally.
mortier /mɔrtje/ n.m. mortar.
mortifié /mɔrtifje/ a. mortified.
mortuaire /mɔrtɥɛr/ a. (cérémonie) funeral; (avis) death.
morue /mɔry/ n.f. cod.
mosaïque /mɔzaik/ n.f. mosaic.
Moscou /mɔsku/ n.m./f. Moscow.
mosquée /mɔske/ n.f. mosque.
mot /mo/ n.m. word; (lettre, message) line, note. ∼ **d'ordre**, watchword. ∼ **de passe**, password. ∼**s croisés**, crossword (puzzle).
motard /mɔtar/ n.m. biker; (policier) police motorcyclist.
motel /mɔtɛl/ n.m. motel.
moteur¹ /mɔtœr/ n.m. engine, motor. **barque à** ∼, motor launch.
mo|teur², ∼**trice** /mɔtœr, -tris/ a. (nerf) motor; (force) driving. **à 4 roues motrices**, 4-wheel drive.
motif /mɔtif/ n.m. reason; (jurid.) motive; (dessin) pattern.
motion /mosjɔ̃/ n.f. motion.
moti|ver /mɔtive/ v.t. motivate; (justifier) justify. ∼**ation** n.f. motivation.
moto /mɔto/ n.f. motor cycle. ∼**cycliste** n.m./f. motorcyclist.
motorisé /mɔtɔrize/ a. motorized.
motrice /mɔtris/ voir **moteur²**.
motte /mɔt/ n.f. lump; (de beurre) slab; (de terre) clod. ∼ **de gazon**, turf.
mou ou **mol***, **molle** /mu, mɔl/ a. soft; (péj.) flabby; (faible, indolent) feeble. —n.m. **du** ∼, slack. **avoir du** ∼, be slack.
mouchard, ∼**e** /muʃar, -d/ n.m., f.

informer; (scol.) sneak. ∼**er** /-de/ v.t. (fam.) inform on.
mouche /muʃ/ n.f. fly.
moucher (se) /(sə)muʃe/ v. pr. blow one's nose.
moucheron /muʃrɔ̃/ n.m. midge.
moucheté /muʃte/ a. speckled.
mouchoir /muʃwar/ n.m. hanky; handkerchief; (en papier) tissue.
moudre /mudr/ v.t. grind.
moue /mu/ n.f. long face. **faire la** ∼, pull a long face.
mouette /mwɛt/ n.f. (sea)gull.
moufle /mufl/ n.f. (gant) mitten.
mouill|er /muje/ v.t. wet, make wet. se ∼**er** v. pr. get (o.s.) wet. ∼**er (l'ancre)**, anchor. ∼**é** a. wet.
moulage /mulaʒ/ n.m. cast.
moul|e¹ /mul/ n.m. mould. ∼**er** v.t. mould; (statue) cast. ∼**e à gâteau**, cake tin. ∼**e à tarte**, flan dish.
moule² /mul/ n.f. (coquillage) mussel.
moulin /mulɛ̃/ n.m. mill; (moteur: fam.) engine. ∼ **à vent**, windmill.
moulinet /mulinɛ/ n.m. (de canne à pêche) reel. **faire des** ∼**s avec qch.**, twirl sth. around.
moulinette /mulinɛt/ n.f. (P.) purée maker.
moulu /muly/ a. ground; (fatigué: fam.) dead beat.
moulure /mulyr/ n.f. moulding.
mourant, ∼**e** /murɑ̃, -t/ a. dying. —n.m., f. dying person.
mourir† /murir/ v.i. (aux. être) die. ∼ **d'envie de**, be dying to. ∼ **de faim**, be starving. ∼ **d'ennui**, be dead bored.
mousquetaire /muskətɛr/ n.m. musketeer.
mousse¹ /mus/ n.f. moss; (écume) froth, foam; (de savon) lather; (dessert) mousse. ∼ **à raser**, shaving cream.
mousse² /mus/ n.m. ship's boy.
mousseline /muslin/ n.f. muslin; (de soie) chiffon.
mousser /muse/ v.i. froth, foam; (savon) lather.
mousseu|x, ∼**se** /musø, -z/ a. frothy. —n.m. sparkling wine.
mousson /musɔ̃/ n.f. monsoon.
moustach|e /mustaʃ/ n.f. moustache. ∼**es**, (d'animal) whiskers. ∼**u** a. wearing a moustache.
moustiquaire /mustikɛr/ n.f. mosquito-net.
moustique /mustik/ n.m. mosquito.
moutarde /mutard/ n.f. mustard.
mouton /mutɔ̃/ n.m. sheep; (peau) sheepskin; (viande) mutton.

mouvant, ~e /muvᾶ, -t/ *a.* changing; (*terrain*) shifting.

mouvement /muvmᾶ/ *n.m.* movement; (*agitation*) bustle; (*en gymnastique*) exercise; (*impulsion*) impulse; (*tendance*) tendency. **en ~,** in motion.

mouvementé /muvmᾶte/ *a.* eventful.

mouvoir† /muvwar/ *v.t.* (*membre*) move. **se ~** *v. pr.* move.

moyen¹, ~ne /mwajɛ̃, -jɛn/ *a.* average; (*médiocre*) poor. —*n.f.* average; (*scol.*) pass-mark. **de taille ~ne,** medium-sized. **~ âge,** Middle Ages. **~ne d'âge,** average age. **M~-Orient** *n.m.* Middle East. **~nement** /-jɛnmᾶ/ *adv.* moderately.

moyen² /mwajɛ̃/ *n.m.* means, way. **~s,** means; (*dons*) abilities. **au ~ de,** by means of. **il n'y a pas ~ de,** it is not possible to.

moyennant /mwajɛnᾶ/ *prép.* (*pour*) for; (*grâce à*) with.

moyeu (*pl.* **~x**) /mwajø/ *n.m.* hub.

mû, mue¹ /my/ *a.* driven (**par,** by).

mucoviscidose /mykɔvisidoz/ *n.f.* cystic fibrosis.

mue² /my/ *n.f.* moulting; (*de voix*) breaking of the voice.

muer /mɥe/ *v.i.* moult; (*voix*) break. **se ~ en,** change into.

muesli /mysli/ *n.m.* muesli.

muet, ~te /mɥɛ, -t/ *a.* (*personne*) dumb; (*fig.*) speechless (**de,** with); (*silencieux*) silent. —*n.m., f.* dumb person.

mufle /myfl/ *n.m.* nose, muzzle; (*personne: fam.*) boor, lout.

mugir /myʒir/ *v.i.* (*vache*) moo; (*bœuf*) bellow; (*fig.*) howl.

muguet /mygɛ/ *n.m.* lily of the valley.

mule /myl/ *n.f.* (she-)mule; (*pantoufle*) mule.

mulet /mylɛ/ *n.m.* (he-)mule.

multi- /mylti/ *préf.* multi-.

multicolore /myltikɔlɔr/ *a.* multi-coloured.

multinational, ~ale (*m. pl.* **~aux**) /myltinasjɔnal, -o/ *a. & n.f.* multinational.

multiple /myltipl/ *a. & n.m.* multiple.

multiplicité /myltiplisite/ *n.f.* multiplicity, abundance.

multiplier /myltiplije/ *v.t.,* **se ~ier** *v. pr.* multiply. **~ication** *n.f.* multiplication.

multitude /myltityd/ *n.f.* multitude, mass.

municipal (*m. pl.* **~aux**) /mynisipal, -o/ *a.* municipal; (*conseil*) town. **~alité** *n.f.* (*ville*) municipality; (*conseil*) town council.

munir /mynir/ *v.t.* **~ de,** provide with. **se ~ de,** provide o.s. with.

munitions /mynisjɔ̃/ *n.f. pl.* ammunition.

mur /myr/ *n.m.* wall. **~ du son,** sound barrier.

mûr /myr/ *a.* ripe; (*personne*) mature.

muraille /myrɑj/ *n.f.* (high) wall.

mural, ~aux (*m. pl.* **~aux**) /myral, -o/ *a.* wall; (*tableau*) mural.

mûre /myr/ *n.f.* blackberry.

muret /myrɛ/ *n.m.* low wall.

mûrir /myrir/ *v.t./i.* ripen; (*abcès*) come to a head; (*personne, projet*) mature.

murmure /myrmyr/ *n.m.* murmur. **~er** *v.t./i.* murmur.

musc /mysk/ *n.m.* musk.

muscade /myskad/ *n.f.* **noix (de) ~,** nutmeg.

muscle /myskl/ *n.m.* muscle. **~é** *a.* muscular, brawny.

musculaire /myskylɛr/ *a.* muscular. **~ature** *n.f.* muscles.

museau (*pl.* **~x**) /myzo/ *n.m.* muzzle; (*de porc*) snout.

musée /myze/ *n.m.* museum; (*de peinture*) art gallery.

museler /myzle/ *v.t.* muzzle.

muselière /myzaljɛr/ *n.f.* muzzle.

musette /myzɛt/ *n.f.* haversack.

muséum /myzeɔm/ *n.m.* (natural history) museum.

musical (*m. pl.* **~aux**) /myzikal, -o/ *a.* musical.

music-hall /myzikol/ *n.m.* variety theatre.

musicien, ~ne /myzisjɛ̃, -jɛn/ *a.* musical. —*n.m., f.* musician.

musique /myzik/ *n.f.* music; (*orchestre*) band.

musulman, ~e /myzylmᾶ, -an/ *a. & n.m., f.* Muslim.

mutation /mytɑsjɔ̃/ *n.f.* change; (*biologique*) mutation.

muter /myte/ *v.t.* transfer.

mutiler /mytile/ *v.t.* mutilate. **~ation** *n.f.* mutilation. **~é, ~ée** *a. & n.m., f.* disabled (person).

mutin, ~in /mytɛ̃, -in/ *a.* saucy. —*n.m., f.* rebel.

mutiner (se) /(sə)mytine/ *v. pr.* mutiny. **~é** *a.* mutinous. **~erie** *n.f.* mutiny.

mutisme /mytism/ *n.m.* silence.

mutuel, ~le /mytɥɛl/ *a.* mutual. —*n.f.* Friendly Society; (*Amer.*) benefit society. **~lement** *adv.* mutually; (*l'un l'autre*) each other.

myop|e /mjɔp/ *a.* short-sighted. **~ie** *n.f.* short-sightedness.

myosotis /mjozɔtis/ *n.m.* forget-me-not.

myriade /mirjad/ *n.f.* myriad.

myrtille /mirtij/ *n.f.* bilberry; (*Amer.*) blueberry.

mystère /mistɛr/ *n.m.* mystery.

mystérieu|x, ~se /misterjø, -z/ *a.* mysterious.

mystif|ier /mistifje/ *v.t.* deceive, hoax. **~ication** *n.f.* hoax.

mysti|que /mistik/ *a.* mystic(al). —*n.m./f.* mystic. —*n.f.* (*puissance*) mystique. **~cisme** *n.m.* mysticism.

myth|e /mit/ *n.m.* myth. **~ique** *a.* mythical.

mytholog|ie /mitolɔʒi/ *n.f.* mythology. **~ique** *a.* mythological.

mythomane /mitɔman/ *n.m./f.* compulsive liar (and fantasizer).

N

n' /n/ *voir* **ne.**

nacr|e /nakr/ *n.f.* mother-of-pearl. **~é** *a.* pearly.

nage /naʒ/ *n.f.* swimming; (*manière*) (swimming) stroke. **à la ~,** by swimming. **traverser à la ~,** swim across. **en ~,** sweating.

nageoire /naʒwar/ *n.f.* fin.

nag|er /naʒe/ *v.t./i.* swim. **~eur, ~euse** *n.m., f.* swimmer.

naguère /nagɛr/ *adv.* some time ago.

naï|f, ~ve /naif, -v/ *a.* naïve.

nain, ~e /nɛ̃, nɛn/ *n.m., f. & a.* dwarf.

naissance /nesɑ̃s/ *n.f.* birth. **donner ~ à,** give birth to, (*fig.*) give rise to.

naître† /nɛtr/ *v.i.* be born; (*résulter*) arise (**de,** from). **faire ~,** (*susciter*) give rise to.

naïveté /naivte/ *n.f.* naïvety.

nana /nana/ *n.f.* (*fam.*) girl.

nanti /nɑ̃ti/ *n.m.* **les ~s,** the affluent.

nantir /nɑ̃tir/ *v.t.* **~ de,** provide with.

naphtaline /naftalin/ *n.f.* mothballs.

nappe /nap/ *n.f.* table-cloth; (*de pétrole, gaz*) layer. **~ phréatique,** ground water.

napperon /naprɔ̃/ *n.m.* (cloth) table-mat.

narcotique /narkɔtik/ *a. & n.m.* narcotic.

narguer /narge/ *v.t.* mock.

narine /narin/ *n.f.* nostril.

narquois, ~e /narkwa, -z/ *a.* derisive.

narr|er /nare/ *v.t.* narrate. **~ateur,**
~atrice *n.m., f.* narrator. **~ation** *n.f.* narrative; (*action*) narration; (*scol.*) composition.

nas|al (*m. pl.* **~aux**) /nazal, -o/ *a.* nasal.

naseau (*pl.* **~x**) /nazo/ *n.m.* nostril.

nasiller /nazije/ *v.i.* have a nasal twang.

nat|al (*m. pl.* **~als**) /natal/ *a.* native.

natalité /natalite/ *n.f.* birth rate.

natation /natasjɔ̃/ *n.f.* swimming.

nati|f, ~ve /natif, -v/ *a.* native.

nation /nɑsjɔ̃/ *n.f.* nation.

nation|al, ~ale (*m. pl.* **~aux**) /nasjɔnal, -o/ *a.* national. —*n.f.* A road; (*Amer.*) highway. **~aliser** *v.t.* nationalize. **~alisme** *n.m.* nationalism.

nationalité /nasjɔnalite/ *n.f.* nationality.

Nativité /nativite/ *n.f.* **la ~,** the Nativity.

natte /nat/ *n.f.* (*de cheveux*) plait; (*tapis de paille*) mat.

naturaliser /natyralize/ *v.t.* naturalize.

nature /natyr/ *n.f.* nature. —*a. invar.* (*eau, omelette, etc.*) plain. **de ~ à,** likely to. **payer en ~,** pay in kind. **~ morte,** still life.

naturel, ~le /natyrɛl/ *a.* natural. —*n.m.* nature; (*simplicité*) naturalness. **~lement** *adv.* naturally.

naufrag|e /nofraʒ/ *n.m.* (ship)-wreck. **faire ~e,** be shipwrecked; (*bateau*) be wrecked. **~é, ~ée** *a. & n.m., f.* shipwrecked (person).

nauséabond, ~e /nozeabɔ̃, -d/ *a.* nauseating.

nausée /noze/ *n.f.* nausea.

nautique /notik/ *a.* nautical; (*sports*) aquatic.

naval (*m. pl.* **~s**) /naval/ *a.* naval.

navet /navɛ/ *n.m.* turnip; (*film, tableau*) dud.

navette /navɛt/ *n.f.* shuttle (service). **faire la ~,** shuttle back and forth.

navigable /navigabl/ *a.* navigable.

navig|uer /navige/ *v.i.* sail; (*piloter*) navigate. **~ateur** *n.m.* seafarer; (*d'avion*) navigator. **~ation** *n.f.* navigation; (*trafic*) shipping.

navire /navir/ *n.m.* ship.

navré /navre/ *a.* sorry (**de,** to).

navrer /navre/ *v.t.* upset.

ne, n'* /nə, n/ *adv.* **ne pas,** not. **ne jamais,** never. **ne plus,** (*temps*) no longer, not any more. **ne que,** only. **je crains qu'il ne parte,** (*sans valeur négative*) I am afraid he will leave.

né, née /ne/ *voir* **naître.** —*a. & n.m., f.* born. **il est né,** he was born. **premier-/dernier-né,** first-/last-born. **née Martin,** née Martin.

néanmoins /neɑ̃mwɛ̃/ *adv.* nevertheless.

néant /neɑ̃/ *n.m.* nothingness; (*aucun*) none.

nébuleu|x, ~**se** /nebylø, -z/ *a.* nebulous.

nécessaire /neseser/ *a.* necessary. —*n.m.* (*sac*) bag; (*trousse*) kit. **le** ~, (*l'indispensable*) the necessities. **faire le** ~, do what is necessary. ~**ment** *adv.* necessarily.

nécessité /nesesite/ *n.f.* necessity.

nécessiter /nesesite/ *v.t.* necessitate.

nécrologie /nekrɔlɔʒi/ *n.f.* obituary.

néerlandais, ~**e** /neɛrlɑ̃dɛ, -z/ *a.* Dutch. —*n.m.,* *f.* Dutchman, Dutchwoman. —*n.m.* (*lang.*) Dutch.

nef /nɛf/ *n.f.* nave.

néfaste /nefast/ *a.* harmful (**à,** to); (*funeste*) ill-fated.

négati|f, ~**ve** /negatif, -v/ *a. & n.m.,* *f.* negative.

négation /negɑsjɔ̃/ *n.f.* negation.

négligé /negliʒe/ *a.* (*tenue, travail*) slovenly. —*n.m.* (*tenue*) négligé.

négligeable /negliʒabl/ *a.* negligible, insignificant.

négligen|t, ~**te** /negliʒɑ̃, -t/ *a.* careless, negligent. ~**ce** *n.f.* carelessness, negligence; (*erreur*) omission.

négliger /negliʒe/ *v.t.* neglect; (*ne pas tenir compte de*) disregard. **se** ~ *v. pr.* neglect o.s.

négoc|e /negɔs/ *n.m.* business. ~**iant,** ~**iante** *n.m.,* *f.* merchant.

négoc|ier /negɔsje/ *v.t./i.* negotiate. ~**iable** *a.* negotiable. ~**iateur,** ~**iatrice** *n.m.,* *f.* negotiator. ~**iation** *n.f.* negotiation.

nègre[1] /nɛgr/ *a.* (*musique etc.*) Negro.

nègre[2] /nɛgr/ *n.m.* (*écrivain*) ghost writer.

neig|e /nɛʒ/ *n.f.* snow. ~**eux,** ~**euse** *a.* snowy.

neiger /neʒe/ *v.i.* snow.

nénuphar /nenyfar/ *n.m.* waterlily.

néologisme /neɔlɔʒism/ *n.m.* neologism.

néon /neɔ̃/ *n.m.* neon.

néo-zélandais, ~**e** /neɔzelɑ̃dɛ, -z/ *a.* New Zealand. —*n.m.,* *f.* New Zealander.

nerf /nɛr/ *n.m.* nerve; (*vigueur: fam.*) stamina.

nerv|eux, ~**euse** /nɛrvø, -z/ *a.* nervous; (*irritable*) nervy; (*centre, cellule*) nerve-; (*voiture*) responsive. ~**eusement** *adv.* nervously. ~**osité** *n.f.* nervousness; (*irritabilité*) touchiness.

nervure /nɛrvyr/ *n.f.* (*bot.*) vein.

net, ~**te** /nɛt/ *a.* (*clair, distinct*) clear; (*propre*) clean; (*soigné*) neat; (*prix, poids*) net. —*adv.* (*s'arrêter*) dead; (*refuser*) flatly; (*parler*) plainly; (*se casser*) clean. ~**tement** *adv.* clearly; (*certainement*) definitely.

netteté /nɛtte/ *n.f.* clearness.

nettoy|er /nɛtwaje/ *v.t.* clean. ~**age** *n.m.* cleaning. ~**age à sec,** dry-cleaning.

neuf[1] /nœf/ (/nœv/ *before heures, ans*) *a. & n.m.* nine.

neu|f[2], ~**ve** /nœf, -v/ *a. & n.m.* new. **remettre à** ~**f,** brighten up. **du** ~**f,** (*fait nouveau*) some new development.

neutr|e /nøtr/ *a.* neutral; (*gram.*) neuter. —*n.m.* (*gram.*) neuter. ~**alité** *n.f.* neutrality.

neutron /nøtrɔ̃/ *n.m.* neutron.

neuve /nœv/ *voir* **neuf**[2].

neuvième /nœvjɛm/ *a. & n.m./f.* ninth.

neveu (*pl.* ~**x**) /nəvø/ *n.m.* nephew.

névros|e /nevroz/ *n.f.* neurosis. ~**é,** ~**ée** *a. & n.m.,* *f.* neurotic.

nez /ne/ *n.m.* nose. ~ **à nez,** face to face. ~ **épaté,** flat nose. ~ **retroussé,** turned-up nose. **avoir du** ~, have flair.

ni /ni/ *conj.* neither, nor. **ni grand ni petit,** neither big nor small. **ni l'un ni l'autre ne fument,** neither (one nor the other) smokes.

niais, ~**e** /njɛ, -z/ *a.* silly. —*n.m.,* *f.* simpleton. ~**erie** /-zri/ *n.f.* silliness.

niche /niʃ/ *n.f.* (*de chien*) kennel; (*cavité*) niche; (*farce*) trick.

nichée /niʃe/ *n.f.* brood.

nicher /niʃe/ *v.i.* nest. **se** ~ *v. pr.* nest; (*se cacher*) hide.

nickel /nikɛl/ *n.m.* nickel. **c'est** ~**!,** (*fam.*) it's spotless.

nicotine /nikɔtin/ *n.f.* nicotine.

nid /ni/ *n.m.* nest. ~ **de poule,** pot-hole.

nièce /njɛs/ *n.f.* niece.

nier /nje/ *v.t.* deny.

nigaud, ~**e** /nigo, -d/ *a.* silly. —*n.m.,* *f.* silly idiot.

nippon, ~**e** /nipɔ̃, -ɔn/ *a. & n.m.,* *f.* Japanese.

niveau (*pl.* ~**x**) /nivo/ *n.m.* level; (*compétence*) standard. **au** ~, up to standard. ~ **à bulle,** spirit-level. ~ **de vie,** standard of living.

nivel|er /nivle/ *v.t.* level. ~**lement** /-ɛlmɑ̃/ *n.m.* levelling.

noble /nɔbl/ *a.* noble. —*n.m./f.* nobleman, noblewoman.

noblesse /nɔblɛs/ *n.f.* nobility.

noce /nɔs/ *n.f.* (*personnes*) wedding guests. ~**s,** wedding. **faire la** ~, (*fam.*) make merry.

noci|f, **∼ve** /nɔsif, -v/ *a.* harmful.
noctambule /nɔktãbyl/ *n.m./f.* night-owl, late-night reveller.
nocturne /nɔktyrn/ *a.* nocturnal.
Noël /nɔɛl/ *n.m.* Christmas.
nœud[1] /nø/ *n.m.* knot; (*ornemental*) bow. **∼s**, (*fig.*) ties. **∼ coulant**, noose. **∼ papillon**, bow-tie.
nœud[2] /nø/ *n.m.* (*naut.*) knot.
noir, ∼e /nwar/ *a.* black; (*obscur, sombre*) dark; (*triste*) gloomy. —*n.m.* black; (*obscurité*) dark. **travail au ∼**, moonlighting. —*n.m.*, *f.* (*personne*) Black. —*n.f.* (*mus.*) crotchet. **∼ceur** *n.f.* blackness; (*indignité*) vileness.
noircir /nwarsir/ *v.t./i.*, **se ∼** *v. pr.* blacken.
nois|ette /nwazɛt/ *n.f.* hazel-nut; (*de beurre*) knob. **∼etier** *n.m.* hazel tree.
noix /nwa/ *n.f.* nut; (*du noyer*) walnut; (*de beurre*) knob. **∼ de cajou**, cashew nut. **∼ de coco**, coconut. **à la ∼**, (*fam.*) useless.
nom /nɔ̃/ *n.m.* name; (*gram.*) noun. **au ∼ de**, on behalf of. **∼ de famille**, surname. **∼ de jeune fille**, maiden name. **∼ propre**, proper noun.
nomade /nɔmad/ *a.* nomadic. —*n.m./f.* nomad.
no man's land /nomanslãd/ *n.m. invar.* no man's land.
nombre /nɔ̃br/ *n.m.* number. **au ∼ de**, (*parmi*) among; (*l'un de*) one of. **en (grand) ∼**, in large numbers.
nombreu|x, **∼se** /nɔ̃brø, -z/ *a.* numerous; (*important*) large.
nombril /nɔ̃bri/ *n.m.* navel.
nomin|al (*m. pl.* **∼aux**) /nɔminal, -o/ *a.* nominal.
nomination /nɔminasjɔ̃/ *n.f.* appointment.
nommément /nɔmemã/ *adv.* by name.
nommer /nɔme/ *v.t.* name; (*élire*) appoint. **se ∼** *v. pr.* (*s'appeler*) be called.
non /nɔ̃/ *adv.* no; (*pas*) not. —*n.m. invar.* no. **∼ (pas) que**, not that. **il vient, ∼?**, he is coming, isn't he? **moi ∼ plus**, neither am, do, can, *etc.* I.
non- /nɔ̃/ *préf.* non-. **∼-fumeur**, non-smoker.
nonante /nɔnãt/ *a. & n.m.* ninety.
nonchalance /nɔ̃ʃalãs/ *n.f.* nonchalance.
non-sens /nɔsãs/ *n.m.* absurdity.
non-stop /nɔnstɔp/ *a. invar.* non-stop.
nord /nɔr/ *n.m.* north. —*a. invar.* north; (*partie*) northern; (*direction*) northerly. **au ∼ de**, to the north of. **∼-africain**, **∼-africaine** *a. & n.m.*, *f.* North

African. **∼-est** *n.m.* north-east. **∼-ouest** *n.m.* north-west.
nordique /nɔrdik/ *a. & n.m./f.* Scandinavian.
norm|al, **∼ale** (*m. pl.* **∼aux**) /nɔrmal, -o/ *a.* normal. —*n.f.* normality; (*norme*) norm; (*moyenne*) average. **∼alement** *adv.* normally.
normand, ∼e /nɔrmã, -d/ *a. & n.m.*, *f.* Norman.
Normandie /nɔrmãdi/ *n.f.* Normandy.
norme /nɔrm/ *n.f.* norm; (*de production*) standard.
Norvège /nɔrvɛʒ/ *n.f.* Norway.
norvégien, ∼ne /nɔrveʒjɛ̃, -jɛn/ *a. & n.m.*, *f.* Norwegian.
nos /no/ *voir* **notre**.
nostalg|ie /nɔstalʒi/ *n.f.* nostalgia. **∼ique** *a.* nostalgic.
notable /nɔtabl/ *a. & n.m.* notable.
notaire /nɔtɛr/ *n.m.* notary.
notamment /nɔtamã/ *adv.* notably.
notation /nɔtasjɔ̃/ *n.f.* notation; (*remarque*) remark.
note /nɔt/ *n.f.* (*remarque*) note; (*chiffrée*) mark; (*facture*) bill; (*mus.*) note. **∼ (de service)**, memorandum. **prendre ∼ de**, take note of.
not|er /nɔte/ *v.t.* note, notice; (*écrire*) note (down); (*devoir*) mark. **bien/mal ∼é**, (*employé etc.*) highly/poorly rated.
notice /nɔtis/ *n.f.* note; (*mode d'emploi*) directions.
notif|ier /nɔtifje/ *v.t.* notify (à, to). **∼ication** *n.f.* notification.
notion /nɔsjɔ̃/ *n.f.* notion.
notoire /nɔtwar/ *a.* well-known; (*criminel*) notorious.
notre (*pl.* **nos**) /nɔtr, no/ *a.* our.
nôtre /notr/ *pron.* **le** *ou* **la ∼**, **les ∼s**, ours.
nouer /nwe/ *v.t.* tie, knot; (*relations*) strike up.
noueu|x, **∼se** /nwø, -z/ *a.* gnarled.
nougat /nuga/ *n.m.* nougat.
nouille /nuj/ *n.f.* (*idiot: fam.*) idiot.
nouilles /nuj/ *n.f. pl.* noodles.
nounours /nunurs/ *n.m.* teddy bear.
nourri /nuri/ *a.* (*fig.*) intense. **logé ∼**, bed and board. **∼ au sein**, breastfed.
nourrice /nuris/ *n.f.* child-minder; (*qui allaite*) wet-nurse.
nourr|ir /nurir/ *v.t.* feed; (*faire vivre*) feed, provide for; (*sentiment: fig.*) nourish. —*v.i.* be nourishing. **se ∼ir** *v. pr.* eat. **se ∼ir de**, feed on. **∼issant, ∼issante** *a.* nourishing.
nourrisson /nurisɔ̃/ *n.m.* infant.
nourriture /nurityr/ *n.f.* food.

nous /nu/ *pron.* we; (*complément*) us; (*indirect*) (to) us; (*réfléchi*) ourselves; (*l'un l'autre*) each other. **~-mêmes** *pron.* ourselves.

nouveau *ou* **nouvel***, **nouvelle**[1] (*m. pl.* **~x**) /nuvo, nuvɛl/ *a. & n.m.* new. —*n.m., f.* (*élève*) new boy, new girl. **de ~, à ~**, again. **du ~**, (*fait nouveau*) some new development. **nouvel an**, new year. **~x mariés**, newly-weds. **~né, ~née** *a.* new-born; *n.m., f.* newborn baby. **~ venu, nouvelle venue**, newcomer. **Nouvelle Zélande**, New Zealand.

nouveauté /nuvote/ *n.f.* novelty; (*chose*) new thing.

nouvelle[2] /nuvɛl/ *n.f.* (*piece of news*); (*récit*) short story. **~s**, news.

nouvellement /nuvɛlmã/ *adv.* newly, recently.

novembre /nɔvᾶbr/ *n.m.* November.

novice /nɔvis/ *a.* inexperienced. —*n.m./f.* novice.

noyade /nwajad/ *n.f.* drowning.

noyau (*pl.* **~x**) /nwajo/ *n.m.* (*de fruit*) stone; (*de cellule*) nucleus; (*groupe*) group; (*centre*: *fig.*) core.

noyauter /nwajote/ *v.t.* (*organisation*) infiltrate.

noyer[1] /nwaje/ *v.t.* drown; (*inonder*) flood. **se ~er** *v. pr.* drown; (*volontairement*) drown o.s. **se ~er dans un verre d'eau**, make a mountain out of a molehill. **~é, ~ée** *n.m., f.* drowning person; (*mort*) drowned person.

noyer[2] /nwaje/ *n.m.* (*arbre*) walnut-tree.

nu /ny/ *a.* naked; (*mains, mur, fil*) bare. —*n.m.* nude. **se mettre à nu**, (*fig.*) bare one's heart. **mettre à nu**, lay bare. **nu-pieds** *adv.* barefoot; *n.m. pl.* beach shoes. **nu- tête** *adv.* bareheaded. **à l'œil nu**, to the naked eye.

nuage /nɥaʒ/ *n.m.* cloud. **~eux, ~euse** *a.* cloudy.

nuance /nɥᾶs/ *n.f.* shade; (*de sens*) nuance; (*différence*) difference.

nuancer /nɥᾶse/ *v.t.* (*opinion*) qualify.

nucléaire /nykleɛr/ *a.* nuclear.

nudis|te /nydist/ *n.m./f.* nudist. **~me** *n.m.* nudism.

nudité /nydite/ *n.f.* (*de personne*) nudity; (*de chambre etc.*) bareness.

nuée /nɥe/ *n.f.* (*foule*) host.

nues /ny/ *n.f. pl.* **tomber des ~**, be amazed. **porter aux ~**, extol.

nuire† /nɥir/ *v.i.* **~ à**, harm.

nuisible /nɥizibl/ *a.* harmful.

nuit /nɥi/ *n.f.* night. **cette ~**, tonight; (*hier*) last night. **il fait ~**, it is dark. **~ blanche**, sleepless night. **la ~, de ~**, at night. **~ de noces**, wedding night.

nul, ~le /nyl/ *a.* (*aucun*) no; (*zéro*) nil; (*qui ne vaut rien*) useless; (*non valable*) null. **match ~**, draw. **~ en**, no good at. —*pron.* no one. **~ autre**, no one else. **~le part**, nowhere. **~lement** *adv.* not at all. **~lité** *n.f.* uselessness; (*personne*) useless person.

numéraire /nymerɛr/ *n.m.* cash.

numér|al (*pl.* **~aux**) /nymeral, -o/ *n.m.* numeral.

numérique /nymerik/ *a.* numerical; (*montre, horloge*) digital.

numéro /nymero/ *n.m.* number; (*de journal*) issue; (*spectacle*) act. **~ter** /-ɔte/ *v.t.* number.

nuque /nyk/ *n.f.* nape (of the neck).

nurse /nœrs/ *n.f.* (*children's*) nurse.

nutriti|f, ~ve /nytritif, -v/ *a.* nutritious; (*valeur*) nutritional.

nutrition /nytrisjɔ̃/ *n.f.* nutrition.

nylon /nilɔ̃/ *n.m.* nylon.

nymphe /nɛ̃f/ *n.f.* nymph.

O

oasis /ɔazis/ *n.f.* oasis.

obéir /ɔbeir/ *v.i.* obey. **~ à**, obey. **être obéi**, be obeyed.

obéissan|t, ~te /ɔbeisᾶ, -t/ *a.* obedient. **~ce** *n.f.* obedience.

obèse /ɔbɛz/ *a.* obese.

obésité /ɔbezite/ *n.f.* obesity.

object|er /ɔbʒɛkte/ *v.t.* put forward (as an excuse). **~er que**, object that. **~ion** /-ksjɔ̃/ *n.f.* objection.

objecteur /ɔbʒɛktœr/ *n.m.* **~ de conscience**, conscientious objector.

objecti|f, ~ve /ɔbʒɛktif, -v/ *a.* objective. —*n.m.* objective; (*photo.*) lens. **~vement** *adv.* objectively. **~vité** *n.f.* objectivity.

objet /ɔbʒɛ/ *n.m.* object; (*sujet*) subject. **être** *ou* **faire l'~ de**, be the subject of; (*recevoir*) receive. **~ d'art**, objet d'art. **~s de toilette**, toilet requisites. **~s trouvés**, lost property; (*Amer.*) lost and found.

obligation /ɔbligasjɔ̃/ *n.f.* obligation; (*comm.*) bond. **être dans l'~ de**, be under obligation to.

obligatoire /ɔbligatwar/ *a.* compulsory.

⁓**ment** *adv.* of necessity; (*fam.*) inevitably.

obligean|t, ⁓**te** /ɔbliʒɑ̃, -t/ *a.* obliging, kind. ⁓**ce** *n.f.* kindness.

oblig|er /ɔbliʒe/ *v.t.* compel, oblige (**à faire,** to do); (*aider*) oblige. **être** ⁓**é de,** have to. ⁓**é à qn.,** obliged to s.o. (**de,** for).

oblique /ɔblik/ *a.* oblique. **regard** ⁓, sidelong glance. **en** ⁓, at an angle.

obliquer /ɔblike/ *v.i.* turn off (**vers,** towards).

oblitérer /ɔblitere/ *v.t.* (*timbre*) cancel.

oblong, ⁓**ue** /ɔblɔ̃, -g/ *a.* oblong.

obnubilé, ⁓**e** /ɔbnybile/ *a.* obsessed.

obsc|ène /ɔpsɛn/ *a.* obscene. ⁓**énité** *n.f.* obscenity.

obscur /ɔpskyr/ *a.* dark; (*confus, humble*) obscure.

obscurantisme /ɔpskyrɑ̃tizm/ *n.m.* obscurantism.

obscurcir /ɔpskyrsir/ *v.t.* darken; (*fig.*) obscure. **s'**⁓ *v. pr.* (*ciel etc.*) darken.

obscurité /ɔpskyrite/ *n.f.* dark(-ness); (*passage, situation*) obscurity.

obséd|er /ɔpsede/ *v.t.* obsess. ⁓**ant,** ⁓**ante** *a.* obsessive. ⁓**é,** ⁓**ée** *n.m., f.* maniac.

obsèques /ɔpsɛk/ *n.f. pl.* funeral.

observation /ɔpsɛrvasjɔ̃/ *n.f.* observation; (*reproche*) criticism; (*obéissance*) observance. **en** ⁓, under observation.

observatoire /ɔpsɛrvatwar/ *n.m.* observatory; (*mil.*) observation post.

observ|er /ɔpsɛrve/ *v.t.* observe; (*surveiller*) watch, observe. **faire** ⁓**er qch.,** point sth. out (**à,** to). ⁓**ateur,** ⁓**atrice** *a.* observant; *n.m., f.* observer.

obsession /ɔpsesjɔ̃/ *n.f.* obsession.

obstacle /ɔpstakl/ *n.m.* obstacle; (*cheval*) jump; (*athlète*) hurdle. **faire** ⁓ **à,** stand in the way of.

obstétrique /ɔpstetrik/ *n.f.* obstetrics.

obstin|é /ɔpstine/ *a.* obstinate. ⁓**ation** *n.f.* obstinacy.

obstiner (s') /(s)ɔpstine/ *v. pr.* persist (**à,** in).

obstruction /ɔpstryksjɔ̃/ *n.f.* obstruction. **faire de l'**⁓, obstruct.

obstruer /ɔpstrye/ *v.t.* obstruct.

obten|ir† /ɔptənir/ *v.t.* get, obtain. ⁓**tion** /-ɑ̃sjɔ̃/ *n.f.* obtaining.

obturateur /ɔptyratœr/ *n.m.* (*photo.*) shutter.

obtus, ⁓**e** /ɔpty, -z/ *a.* obtuse.

obus /ɔby/ *n.m.* shell.

occasion /ɔkazjɔ̃/ *n.f.* opportunity (**de faire,** of doing); (*circonstance*) occasion; (*achat*) bargain; (*article non neuf*) second-hand buy. **à l'**⁓, sometimes. **d'**⁓, second-hand. ⁓**nel,** ⁓**nelle** /-jɔnɛl/ *a.* occasional.

occasionner /ɔkazjɔne/ *v.t.* cause.

occident /ɔksidɑ̃/ *n.m.* west. ⁓**al,** ⁓**ale** (*m. pl.* ⁓**aux**) /-tal, -to/ *a.* western. —*n.m., f.* westerner.

occulte /ɔkylt/ *a.* occult.

occupant, ⁓**e** /ɔkypɑ̃, -t/ *n.m., f.* occupant. —*n.m.* (*mil.*) forces of occupation.

occupation /ɔkypasjɔ̃/ *n.f.* occupation.

occupé /ɔkype/ *a.* busy; (*place, pays*) occupied; (*téléphone*) engaged; (*Amer.*) busy.

occuper /ɔkype/ *v.t.* occupy; (*poste*) hold. **s'**⁓ *v. pr.* (*s'affairer*) keep busy (**à faire,** doing). **s'**⁓ **de,** (*personne, problème*) take care of; (*bureau, firme*) be in charge of.

occurrence (en l') /(ɑ̃l)ɔkyrɑ̃s/ *adv.* in this case.

océan /ɔseɑ̃/ *n.m.* ocean.

ocre /ɔkr/ *a. invar.* ochre.

octane /ɔktan/ *n.m.* octane.

octante /ɔktɑ̃t/ *a.* (*régional*) eighty.

octave /ɔktav/ *n.f.* (*mus.*) octave.

octet /ɔktɛ/ *n.m.* byte.

octobre /ɔktɔbr/ *n.m.* October.

octogone /ɔktɔgɔn/ *n.m.* octagon.

octroyer /ɔktrwaje/ *v.t.* grant.

oculaire /ɔkylɛr/ *a.* ocular.

oculiste /ɔkylist/ *n.m./f.* eye-specialist.

ode /ɔd/ *n.f.* ode.

odeur /ɔdœr/ *n.f.* smell.

odieu|x, ⁓**se** /ɔdjø, -z/ *a.* odious.

odorant, ⁓**e** /ɔdɔrɑ̃, -t/ *a.* sweet-smelling.

odorat /ɔdɔra/ *n.m.* (sense of) smell.

œcuménique /ekymenik/ *a.* ecumenical.

œil (*pl.* **yeux**) /œj, jø/ *n.m.* eye. **à l'**⁓, (*fam.*) free. **à mes yeux,** in my view. **faire de l'**⁓ **à,** make eyes at. **faire les gros yeux à,** scowl at. **ouvrir l'**⁓, keep one's eye open. **fermer l'**⁓, shut one's eyes. ⁓ **poché,** black eye. **yeux bridés,** slit eyes.

œillade /œjad/ *n.f.* wink.

œillères /œjɛr/ *n.f. pl.* blinkers.

œillet /œjɛ/ *n.m.* (*plante*) carnation; (*trou*) eyelet.

œuf (*pl.* ⁓**s**) /œf, ø/ *n.m.* egg. ⁓ **à la coque/dur/sur le plat,** boiled/hard-boiled/fried egg.

œuvre /œvr/ *n.f.* (*ouvrage, travail*) work. ⁓ **d'art,** work of art. ⁓ (**de bienfaisance**), charity. **être à l'**⁓, be at work. **mettre en** ⁓, (*moyens*) implement.

œuvrer /œvre/ *v.i.* work.

off /ɔf/ *a. invar.* **voix** ~, voice off.

offense /ɔfɑ̃s/ *n.f.* insult; (*péché*) offence.

offens|er /ɔfɑ̃se/ *v.t.* offend. **s'~er de**, take offence at. ~**ant**, ~**ante** *a.* offensive.

offensi|f, ~**ve** /ɔfɑ̃sif, -v/ *a. & n.f.* offensive.

offert, ~**e** /ɔfɛr, -t/ *voir* **offrir**.

office /ɔfis/ *n.m.* office; (*relig.*) service; (*de cuisine*) pantry. **d'~**, automatically.

officiel, ~**le** /ɔfisjɛl/ *a. & n.m., f.* official. ~**lement** *adv.* officially.

officier¹ /ɔfisje/ *n.m.* officer.

officier² /ɔfisje/ *v.i.* (*relig.*) officiate.

officieu|x, ~**se** /ɔfisjø, -z/ *a.* unofficial. ~**sement** *adv.* unofficially.

offrande /ɔfrɑ̃d/ *n.f.* offering.

offrant /ɔfrɑ̃/ *n.m.* **au plus** ~, to the highest bidder.

offre /ɔfr/ *n.f.* offer; (*aux enchères*) bid. **l'~ et la demande**, supply and demand. ~**s d'emploi**, jobs advertised, (*rubrique*) situations vacant.

offrir† /ɔfrir/ *v.t.* offer (**de faire**, to do); (*cadeau*) give; (*acheter*) buy. **s'~** *v. pr.* offer o.s. (**comme**, as); (*spectacle*) present itself; (*s'acheter*) treat o.s. to. ~ **à boire à**, (*chez soi*) give a drink to; (*au café*) buy a drink for.

offusquer /ɔfyske/ *v.t.* offend.

ogive /ɔʒiv/ *n.f.* (*atomique etc.*) warhead.

ogre /ɔgr/ *n.m.* ogre.

oh /o/ *int.* oh.

oie /wa/ *n.f.* goose.

oignon /ɔɲɔ̃/ *n.m.* (*légume*) onion; (*de tulipe etc.*) bulb.

oiseau (*pl.* ~**x**) /wazo/ *n.m.* bird.

oisi|f, ~**ve** /wazif, -v/ *a.* idle. ~**veté** *n.f.* idleness.

O.K. /ɔke/ *int.* O.K.

oléoduc /ɔleɔdyk/ *n.m.* oil pipeline.

oliv|e /ɔliv/ *n.f. & a. invar.* olive. ~**ier** *n.m.* olive-tree.

olympique /ɔlɛ̃pik/ *a.* Olympic.

ombrag|e /ɔ̃braʒ/ *n.m.* shade. **prendre** ~**e de**, take offence at. ~**é** *a.* shady. ~**eux**, ~**euse** *a.* easily offended.

ombre /ɔ̃br/ *n.f.* (*pénombre*) shade; (*contour*) shadow; (*soupçon: fig.*) hint, shadow. **dans l'~**, (*secret*) in the dark. **faire de l'~ à qn.**, be in s.o.'s light.

ombrelle /ɔ̃brɛl/ *n.f.* parasol.

omelette /ɔmlɛt/ *n.f.* omelette.

omettre† /ɔmɛtr/ *v.t.* omit.

omission /ɔmisjɔ̃/ *n.f.* omission.

omnibus /ɔmnibys/ *n.m.* stopping train.

omoplate /ɔmɔplat/ *n.f.* shoulder-blade.

on /ɔ̃/ *pron.* we, you, one; (*les gens*) people, they; (*quelqu'un*) someone. **on dit**, people say, they say, it is said (**que**, that).

once /ɔ̃s/ *n.f.* ounce.

oncle /ɔ̃kl/ *n.m.* uncle.

onctueu|x, ~**se** /ɔ̃ktɥø, -z/ *a.* smooth.

onde /ɔ̃d/ *n.f.* wave. ~**s courtes/longues**, short/long wave. **sur les** ~**s**, on the radio.

ondée /ɔ̃de/ *n.f.* shower.

on-dit /ɔ̃di/ *n.m. invar.* **les** ~, rumour.

ondul|er /ɔ̃dyle/ *v.i.* undulate; (*cheveux*) be wavy. ~**ation** *n.f.* wave, undulation. ~**é** *a.* (*chevelure*) wavy.

onéreu|x, ~**se** /ɔnerø, -z/ *a.* costly.

ongle /ɔ̃gl/ *n.m.* (finger-)nail. **se faire les** ~**s**, do one's nails.

ont /ɔ̃/ *voir* **avoir**.

ONU *abrév.* (*Organisation des nations unies*) UN.

onyx /ɔniks/ *n.m.* onyx.

onz|e /ɔ̃z/ *a. & n.m.* eleven. ~**ième** *a. & n.m./f.* eleventh.

opale /ɔpal/ *n.f.* opal.

opa|que /ɔpak/ *a.* opaque. ~**cité** *n.f.* opaqueness.

open /ɔpɛn/ *n.m.* open (champion-ship).

opéra /ɔpera/ *n.m.* opera; (*édifice*) opera-house. ~**-comique** (*pl.* ~**s-comiques**) *n.m.* light opera.

opérateur /ɔperatœr/ *n.m.* (*caméra-man*) cameraman.

opération /ɔperasjɔ̃/ *n.f.* operation; (*comm.*) deal.

opérationnel, ~**le** /ɔperasjɔnɛl/ *a.* operational.

opératoire /ɔperatwar/ *a.* (*méd.*) surgical. **bloc** ~, operating suite.

opérer /ɔpere/ *v.t.* (*personne*) operate on; (*kyste etc.*) remove; (*exécuter*) carry out, make. **se faire** ~, have an operation. —*v.i.* (*méd.*) operate; (*faire effet*) work. **s'~** *v. pr.* (*se produire*) occur.

opérette /ɔperɛt/ *n.f.* operetta.

opiner /ɔpine/ *v.i.* nod.

opiniâtre /ɔpinjɑtr/ *a.* obstinate.

opinion /ɔpinjɔ̃/ *n.f.* opinion.

opium /ɔpjɔm/ *n.m.* opium.

opportun, ~**e** /ɔpɔrtœ̃, -yn/ *a.* opportune. ~**ité** /-ynite/ *n.f.* opportuneness.

opposant, ~**e** /ɔpozɑ̃, -t/ *n.m., f.* opponent.

opposé /ɔpoze/ *a.* (*sens, angle, etc.*) opposite; (*factions*) opposing; (*intérêts*) conflicting. —*n.m.* opposite. **à l'~**, (*opinion etc.*) contrary (**de,** to). **être ~ à,** be opposed to.

opposer /ɔpoze/ *v.t.* (*objets*) place opposite each other; (*personnes*) oppose; (*contraster*) contrast; (*résistance, argument*) put up. **s'~** *v. pr.* (*personnes*) confront each other; (*styles*) contrast. **s'~ à,** oppose.

opposition /ɔpozisjɔ̃/ *n.f.* opposition. **par ~ à,** in contrast with. **entrer en ~ avec,** come into conflict with. **faire ~ à un chèque,** stop a cheque.

oppress|er /ɔprese/ *v.t.* oppress. **~ant, ~ante** *a.* oppressive. **~eur** *n.m.* oppressor. **~ion** *n.f.* oppression.

opprimer /ɔprime/ *v.t.* oppress.

opter /ɔpte/ *v.i.* **~ pour,** opt for.

opticien, ~ne /ɔptisjɛ̃, -jɛn/ *n.m., f.* optician.

optimis|te /ɔptimist/ *n.m./f.* optimist. **—a.** optimistic. **~me** *n.m.* optimism.

optimum /ɔptimɔm/ *a. & n.m.* optimum.

option /ɔpsjɔ̃/ *n.f.* option.

optique /ɔptik/ *a.* (*verre*) optical. **—n.f.** (*perspective*) perspective.

opulen|t, ~te /ɔpylɑ̃, -t/ *a.* opulent. **~ce** *n.f.* opulence.

or[1] /ɔr/ *n.m.* gold. **d'~,** golden. **en or,** gold; (*occasion*) golden.

or[2] /ɔr/ *conj.* now, well.

oracle /ɔrakl/ *n.m.* oracle.

orag|e /ɔraʒ/ *n.m.* (thunder)storm. **~eux, ~euse** *a.* stormy.

oraison /ɔrɛzɔ̃/ *n.f.* prayer.

or|al (*m. pl.* **~aux**) /ɔral, -o/ *a.* oral. **—n.m.** (*pl.* **~aux**) oral.

orang|e /ɔrɑ̃ʒ/ *n.f. & a. invar.* orange. **~é** *a.* orange-coloured. **~er** *n.m.* orange-tree.

orangeade /ɔrɑ̃ʒad/ *n.f.* orangeade.

orateur /ɔratœr/ *n.m.* speaker.

oratorio /ɔratɔrjo/ *n.m.* oratorio.

orbite /ɔrbit/ *n.f.* orbit; (*d'œil*) socket.

orchestr|e /ɔrkɛstr/ *n.m.* orchestra; (*de jazz*) band; (*parterre*) stalls. **~er** *v.t.* orchestrate.

orchidée /ɔrkide/ *n.f.* orchid.

ordinaire /ɔrdinɛr/ *a.* ordinary; (*habituel*) usual; (*qualité*) standard. **—n.m. l'~,** the ordinary; (*nourriture*) the standard fare. **d'~, à l'~,** usually. **~ment** *adv.* usually.

ordinateur /ɔrdinatœr/ *n.m.* computer.

ordination /ɔrdinasjɔ̃/ *n.f.* (*relig.*) ordination.

ordonnance /ɔrdɔnɑ̃s/ *n.f.* (*ordre, décret*) order; (*de médecin*) prescription; (*soldat*) orderly.

ordonné /ɔrdɔne/ *a.* tidy.

ordonner /ɔrdɔne/ *v.t.* order (**à qn. de,** s.o. to); (*agencer*) arrange; (*méd.*) prescribe; (*prêtre*) ordain.

ordre /ɔrdr/ *n.m.* order; (*propreté*) tidiness. **aux ~s de qn.,** at s.o.'s disposal. **avoir de l'~,** be tidy. **de premier ~,** first-rate. **l'~ du jour,** (*programme*) agenda. **mettre en ~,** tidy (up). **de premier ~,** first rate. **jusqu'à nouvel ~,** until further notice. **un ~ de grandeur,** an approximate idea.

ordure /ɔrdyr/ *n.f.* filth. **~s,** (*détritus*) rubbish; (*Amer.*) garbage. **~s ménagères,** household refuse.

oreille /ɔrɛj/ *n.f.* ear.

oreiller /ɔreje/ *n.m.* pillow.

oreillons /ɔrejɔ̃/ *n.m. pl.* mumps.

orfèvr|e /ɔrfɛvr/ *n.m.* goldsmith, silversmith. **~erie** *n.f.* goldsmith's *ou* silversmith's trade.

organe /ɔrgan/ *n.m.* organ; (*porte-parole*) mouthpiece.

organigramme /ɔrganigram/ *n.m.* flow chart.

organique /ɔrganik/ *a.* organic.

organisation /ɔrganizasjɔ̃/ *n.f.* organization.

organis|er /ɔrganize/ *v.t.* organize. **s'~er** *v. pr.* organize o.s. **~ateur, ~atrice** *n.m., f.* organizer.

organisme /ɔrganism/ *n.m.* body, organism.

organiste /ɔrganist/ *n.m./f.* organist.

orgasme /ɔrgasm/ *n.m.* orgasm.

orge /ɔrʒ/ *n.f.* barley.

orgelet /ɔrʒəlɛ/ *n.m.* (*furoncle*) sty.

orgie /ɔrʒi/ *n.f.* orgy.

orgue /ɔrg/ *n.m.* organ. **~s** *n.f. pl.* organ. **~ de Barbarie,** barrel-organ.

orgueil /ɔrgœj/ *n.m.* pride.

orgueilleu|x, ~se /ɔrgœjø, -z/ *a.* proud.

Orient /ɔrjɑ̃/ *n.m.* **l'~,** the Orient.

orientable /ɔrjɑ̃tabl/ *a.* adjustable.

orient|al, ~ale (*m. pl.* **~aux**) /ɔrjɑ̃tal, -o/ *a.* eastern; (*de l'Orient*) oriental. **—n.m., f.** Oriental.

orientation /ɔrjɑ̃tasjɔ̃/ *n.f.* direction; (*d'une politique*) course; (*de maison*) aspect. **~ professionnelle,** careers advisory service.

orienté /ɔrjɑ̃te/ *a.* (*partial*) slanted, tendentious.

orienter /ɔrjɑ̃te/ *v.t.* position; (*personne*) direct. **s'~** *v. pr.* (*se repérer*) find one's bearings. **s'~ vers,** turn towards.

orifice /ɔrifis/ *n.m.* orifice.

origan /ɔrigɑ̃/ *n.m.* oregano.

originaire /ɔriʒinɛr/ *a*. être ∼ **de**, be a native of.

origin|al, ∼ale (*m. pl.* ∼**aux**) /ɔriʒinal, -o/ *a*. original; (*curieux*) eccentric. —*n.m.* original. —*n.m., f*. eccentric. ∼**alité** *n.f.* originality; eccentricity.

origine /ɔriʒin/ *n.f.* origin. à l'∼, originally. d'∼, (*pièce, pneu*) original.

originel, ∼le /ɔriʒinɛl/ *a*. original.

orme /ɔrm/ *n.m.* elm.

ornement /ɔrnəmã/ *n.m.* ornament. ∼**al** (*m. pl.* ∼**aux**) /-tal, -to/ *a*. ornamental.

orner /ɔrne/ *v.t.* decorate.

ornière /ɔrnjɛr/ *n.f.* rut.

ornithologie /ɔrnitɔlɔʒi/ *n.f.* ornithology.

orphelin, ∼e /ɔrfəlɛ̃, -in/ *n.m., f*. orphan. —*a*. orphaned. ∼**at** /-ina/ *n.m.* orphanage.

orteil /ɔrtɛj/ *n.m.* toe.

orthodox|e /ɔrtɔdɔks/ *a*. orthodox. ∼**ie** *n.f.* orthodoxy.

orthographe /ɔrtɔgraf/ *n.f.* spelling. ∼**ier** *v.t.* spell.

orthopédique /ɔrtɔpedik/ *a*. orthopaedic.

ortie /ɔrti/ *n.f.* nettle.

os (*pl.* **os**) /ɔs, o/ *n.m.* bone.

OS *abrév. voir* **ouvrier spécialisé**.

oscar /ɔskar/ *n.m.* award; (*au cinéma*) oscar.

oscill|er /ɔsile/ *v.i.* sway; (*techn.*) oscillate; (*hésiter*) waver, fluctuate. ∼**ation** *n.f.* (*techn.*) oscillation; (*variation*) fluctuation.

oseille /ozɛj/ *n.f.* (*plante*) sorrel.

os|er /oze/ *v.t./i.* dare. ∼**é** *a*. daring.

osier /ozje/ *n.m.* wicker.

ossature /ɔsatyr/ *n.f.* frame.

ossements /ɔsmã/ *n.m. pl.* bones.

osseu|x, ∼se /ɔsø, -z/ *a*. bony; (*tissu*) bone.

ostensible /ɔstãsibl/ *a*. conspicuous, obvious.

ostentation /ɔstãtasjɔ̃/ *n.f.* ostentation.

ostéopathe /ɔsteɔpat/ *n.m./f.* osteopath.

otage /ɔtaʒ/ *n.m.* hostage.

otarie /ɔtari/ *n.f.* sea-lion.

ôter /ote/ *v.t.* remove (à **qn.**, from s.o.); (*déduire*) take away.

otite /ɔtit/ *n.f.* ear infection.

ou /u/ *conj.* or. **ou bien**, or else. **vous ou moi**, either you or me.

où /u/ *adv. & pron.* where; (*dans lequel*) in which; (*sur lequel*) on which; (*auquel*) at which. d'**où**, from which; (*pour cette raison*) hence. d'**où?**, from

where? **par où**, through which. **par où?**, which way? **où qu'il soit**, wherever he may be. **au prix où c'est**, at those prices. **le jour où**, the day when.

ouate /wat/ *n.f.* cotton wool; (*Amer.*) absorbent cotton.

oubli /ubli/ *n.m.* forgetfulness; (*trou de mémoire*) lapse of memory; (*négligence*) oversight. l'∼, (*tomber dans, sauver de*) oblivion.

oublier /ublije/ *v.t.* forget. s'∼ *v. pr.* forget o.s.; (*chose*) be forgotten.

oublieu|x, ∼se /ublijø, -z/ *a*. forgetful (**de**, of).

ouest /wɛst/ *n.m.* west. —*a. invar.* west; (*partie*) western; (*direction*) westerly.

ouf /uf/ *int.* phew.

oui /wi/ *adv.* yes.

ouï-dire (**par**) /(par)widir/ *adv.* by hearsay.

ouïe /wi/ *n.f.* hearing.

ouïes /wi/ *n.f. pl.* gills.

ouille /uj/ *int.* ouch.

ouïr /wir/ *v.t.* hear.

ouragan /uragã/ *n.m.* hurricane.

ourler /urle/ *v.t.* hem.

ourlet /urlɛ/ *n.m.* hem.

ours /urs/ *n.m.* bear. ∼ **blanc**, polar bear. ∼ **en peluche**, teddy bear. ∼ **mal léché**, boor.

ouste /ust/ *int.* (*fam.*) scram.

outil /uti/ *n.m.* tool.

outillage /utijaʒ/ *n.m.* tools; (*d'une usine*) equipment.

outiller /utije/ *v.t.* equip.

outrage /utraʒ/ *n.m.* (*grave*) insult.

outrag|er /utraʒe/ *v.t.* offend. ∼**eant, ∼eante** *a*. offensive.

outranc|e /utrãs/ *n.f.* excess. à ∼**e**, to excess; (*guerre*) all-out. ∼**ier, ∼ière** *a*. excessive.

outre /utr/ *prép.* besides. **en** ∼, besides. ∼-**mer** *adv.* overseas. ∼ **mesure**, excessively.

outrepasser /utrəpase/ *v.t.* exceed.

outrer /utre/ *v.t.* exaggerate; (*indigner*) incense.

outsider /awtsajdœr/ *n.m.* outsider.

ouvert, ∼e /uvɛr, -t/ *voir* **ouvrir**. —*a*. open; (*gaz, radio, etc.*) on. ∼**ement** /-təmã/ *adv.* openly.

ouverture /uvɛrtyr/ *n.f.* opening; (*mus.*) overture; (*photo.*) aperture. ∼**s**, (*offres*) overtures. ∼ **d'esprit**, open-mindedness.

ouvrable /uvrabl/ *a*. **jour** ∼, working day.

ouvrag|e /uvraʒ/ *n.m.* (*travail, livre*)

work; (*couture*) needlework. ~é *a.* finely worked.

ouvreuse /uvrøz/ *n.f.* usherette.

ouvr|ier, ~**ière** /uvrije, -jɛr/ *n.m.*, *f.* worker. —*a.* working-class; (*conflit*) industrial; (*syndicat*) workers'. ~**ier qualifié/spécialisé,** skilled/unskilled worker.

ouvr|ir† /uvrir/ *v.t.* open (up); (*gaz, robinet, etc.*) turn *ou* switch on. —*v.i.* open (up). **s'~ir** *v. pr.* open (up). **s'~ir à qn.,** open one's heart to s.o. ~**e-boîte(s)** *n.m.* tin-opener. ~**e-bouteille(s)** *n.m.* bottle-opener.

ovaire /ɔvɛr/ *n.m.* ovary.

ovale /ɔval/ *a. & n.m.* oval.

ovation /ɔvasjɔ̃/ *n.f.* ovation.

overdose /ɔvɛrdoz/ *n.f.* overdose.

ovni /ɔvni/ *n.m.* (*abrév.*) UFO.

ovule /ɔvyl/ *n.f.* (*à féconder*) egg; (*gynécologique*) pessary.

oxyder (s') /(s)ɔkside/ *v. pr.* become oxidized.

oxygène /ɔksiʒɛn/ *n.m.* oxygen.

oxygéner (s') /(s)ɔksiʒene/ *v. pr.* (*fam.*) get some fresh air.

ozone /ozon/ *n.f.* ozone. **la couche d'~,** the ozone layer.

P

pacemaker /pesmekœr/ *n.m.* pacemaker.

pachyderme /paʃidɛrm/ *n.m.* elephant.

pacifier /pasifje/ *v.t.* pacify.

pacifique /pasifik/ *a.* peaceful; (*personne*) peaceable; (*géog.*) Pacific. —*n.m.* **P~,** Pacific (Ocean).

pacifiste /pasifist/ *n.m./f.* pacifist.

pacotille /pakɔtij/ *n.f.* trash.

pacte /pakt/ *n.m.* pact.

pactiser /paktize/ *v.i.* ~ **avec,** be in league *ou* agreement with.

paddock /padɔk/ *n.m.* paddock.

pag|aie /pagɛ/ *n.f.* paddle. ~**ayer** *v.i.* paddle.

pagaille /pagaj/ *n.f.* mess, shambles.

page /paʒ/ *n.f.* page. **être à la ~,** be up to date.

pagode /pagɔd/ *n.f.* pagoda.

paie /pɛ/ *n.f.* pay.

paiement /pɛmã/ *n.m.* payment.

païen, ~**ne** /pajɛ̃, -jɛn/ *a. & n.m.*, *f.* pagan.

paillasse /pajas/ *n.f.* straw mattress; (*dans un laboratoire*) draining-board.

paillasson /pajasɔ̃/ *n.m.* doormat.

paille /paj/ *n.f.* straw; (*défaut*) flaw.

paillette /pajɛt/ *n.f.* (*sur robe*) sequin; (*de savon*) flake. ~**s d'or,** gold-dust.

pain /pɛ̃/ *n.m.* bread: (*unité*) loaf (of bread); (*de savon etc.*) bar. ~ **d'épice,** gingerbread. ~ **grillé,** toast.

pair[1] /pɛr/ *a.* (*nombre*) even.

pair[2] /pɛr/ *n.m.* (*personne*) peer. **au ~,** (*jeune fille etc.*) au pair. **aller de ~,** go together (**avec,** with).

paire /pɛr/ *n.f.* pair.

paisible /pezibl/ *a.* peaceful.

paître /pɛtr/ *v.i.* (*brouter*) graze.

paix /pɛ/ *n.f.* peace; (*papier*) peace treaty.

Pakistan /pakistɑ̃/ *n.m.* Pakistan.

pakistanais, ~**e** /pakistanɛ, -z/ *a. & n.m.*, *f.* Pakistani.

palace /palas/ *n.m.* luxury hotel.

palais[1] /palɛ/ *n.m.* palace. **P~ de Justice,** Law Courts. ~ **des sports,** sports stadium.

palais[2] /palɛ/ *n.m.* (*anat.*) palate.

palan /palɑ̃/ *n.m.* hoist.

pâle /pal/ *a.* pale.

Palestine /palɛstin/ *n.f.* Palestine.

palestinien, ~**ne** /palɛstinjɛ̃, -jɛn/ *a. & n.m.*, *f.* Palestinian.

palet /palɛ/ *n.m.* (*hockey*) puck.

paletot /palto/ *n.m.* thick jacket.

palette /palɛt/ *n.f.* palette.

pâleur /palœr/ *n.f.* paleness.

palier /palje/ *n.m.* (*d'escalier*) landing; (*étape*) stage; (*de route*) level stretch.

pâlir /palir/ *v.t./i.* (turn) pale.

palissade /palisad/ *n.f.* fence.

pallier /palje/ *v.t.* alleviate.

palmarès /palmarɛs/ *n.m.* list of prize-winners.

palm|e /palm/ *n.f.* palm leaf; (*symbole*) palm; (*de nageur*) flipper. ~**ier** *n.m.* palm(-tree).

palmé /palme/ *a.* (*patte*) webbed.

pâlot, ~**te** /palo, -ɔt/ *a.* pale.

palourde /palurd/ *n.f.* clam.

palper /palpe/ *v.t.* feel.

palpit|er /palpite/ *v.i.* (*battre*) pound, palpitate; (*frémir*) quiver. ~**ations** *n.f. pl.* palpitations. ~**ant,** ~**ante** *a.* thrilling.

paludisme /palydism/ *n.m.* malaria.

pâmer (se) /(sə)pame/ *v. pr.* swoon.

pamphlet /pɑ̃flɛ/ *n.m.* satirical pamphlet.

pamplemousse /pɑ̃pləmus/ *n.m.* grape-fruit.

pan[1] /pɑ̃/ *n.m.* piece; (*de chemise*) tail.

pan² /pɑ̃/ *int.* bang.
panacée /panase/ *n.f.* panacea.
panache /panaʃ/ *n.m.* plume; (*bravoure*) gallantry; (*allure*) panache.
panaché /panaʃe/ *a.* (*bariolé, mélangé*) motley. **glace** ~**e**, mixed-flavour ice cream. —*n.m.* shandy. **bière** ~**e, demi** ~**,** shandy.
pancarte /pɑ̃kart/ *n.f.* sign; (*de manifestant*) placard.
pancréas /pɑ̃kreas/ *n.m.* pancreas.
pané /pane/ *a.* breaded.
panier /panje/ *n.m.* basket. ~ **à provisions,** shopping basket. ~ **à salade,** (*fam.*) police van.
panique /panik/ *n.f.* panic. (*fam.*) ~**er** *v.i.* panic.
panne /pan/ *n.f.* breakdown. **être en** ~**,** have broken down. **être en** ~ **sèche,** have run out of petrol *ou* gas (*Amer.*). ~ **d'électricité** *ou* **de courant,** power failure.
panneau (*pl.* ~**x**) /pano/ *n.m.* sign; (*publicitaire*) hoarding; (*de porte etc.*) panel. ~ **(d'affichage),** notice-board. ~ **(de signalisation),** road sign.
panoplie /panɔpli/ *n.f.* (*jouet*) outfit; (*gamme*) range.
panoram|a /panɔrama/ *n.m.* panorama. ~**ique** *a.* panoramic.
panse /pɑ̃s/ *n.f.* paunch.
pans|er /pɑ̃se/ *v.t.* (*plaie*) dress; (*personne*) dress the wound(s) of; (*cheval*) groom. ~**ement** *n.m.* dressing. ~**ement adhésif,** stickingplaster.
pantalon /pɑ̃talɔ̃/ *n.m.* (pair of) trousers. ~**s,** trousers.
panthère /pɑ̃tɛr/ *n.f.* panther.
pantin /pɑ̃tɛ̃/ *n.m.* puppet.
pantomime /pɑ̃tɔmim/ *n.f.* mime; (*spectacle*) mime show.
pantoufle /pɑ̃tufl/ *n.f.* slipper.
paon /pɑ̃/ *n.m.* peacock.
papa /papa/ *n.m.* dad(dy). **de** ~**,** (*fam.*) old-time.
papauté /papote/ *n.f.* papacy.
pape /pap/ *n.m.* pope.
paperass|e /papras/ *n.f.* ~**e(s),** (*péj.*) papers. ~**erie** *n.f.* (*péj.*) papers; (*tracasserie*) red tape.
papet|ier, -ière /paptje, -jɛr/ *n.m., f.* stationer. ~**erie** /papetri/ *n.f.* (*magasin*) stationer's shop.
papier /papje/ *n.m.* paper; (*formulaire*) form. ~**s (d'identité),** (identity) papers. ~ **à lettres,** writing-paper. ~ **aluminium,** tin foil. ~ **buvard,** blotting-paper. ~ **calque,** tracing-

paper. ~ **carbone,** carbon paper. ~ **collant,** sticky paper. ~ **de verre,** sandpaper. ~ **hygiénique,** toilet-paper. ~ **journal,** newspaper. ~ **mâché,** papier mâché. ~ **peint,** wallpaper.
papillon /papijɔ̃/ *n.m.* butterfly; (*contravention*) parking-ticket. ~ **(de nuit),** moth.
papot|er /papɔte/ *v.i.* prattle. ~**age** *n.m.* prattle.
paprika /paprika/ *n.m.* paprika.
Pâque /pɑk/ *n.f.* Passover.
paquebot /pakbo/ *n.m.* liner.
pâquerette /pɑkrɛt/ *n.f.* daisy.
Pâques /pɑk/ *n.f. pl. & n.m.* Easter.
paquet /pakɛ/ *n.m.* packet; (*de cartes*) pack; (*colis*) parcel. **un** ~ **de,** (*tas*) a mass of.
par /par/ *prép.* by; (*à travers*) through; (*motif*) out of, from; (*provenance*) from. **commencer/finir** ~ **qch.,** begin/end with sth. **commencer/finir** ~ **faire,** begin by/end up (by) doing. ~ **an/mois/**etc., a *ou* per year/ month/*etc.* ~ **avion,** (*lettre*) (by) airmail. ~**-ci,** **par-là,** here and there. ~ **contre,** on the other hand. ~ **hasard,** by chance. ~ **ici/là,** this/that way. ~ **inadvertance,** inadvertently. ~ **intermittence,** intermittently. ~ **l'intermédiaire de,** through. ~ **jour,** a day. ~ **malheur** *ou* **malchance,** unfortunately. ~ **miracle,** miraculously. ~ **moments,** at times. ~ **opposition à,** as opposed to. ~ **personne,** each, per person.
parabole /parabɔl/ *n.f.* (*relig.*) parable; (*maths*) parabola.
paracétamol /parasetamɔl/ *n.m.* paracetamol.
parachever /paraʃve/ *v.t.* perfect.
parachut|e /paraʃyt/ *n.m.* parachute. ~**er** *v.t.* parachute. ~**iste** *n.m./f.* parachutist; (*mil.*) paratrooper.
parad|e /parad/ *n.f.* parade; (*sport*) parry; (*réplique*) reply. ~**er** *v.i.* show off.
paradis /paradi/ *n.m.* paradise. ~ **fiscal,** tax haven.
paradox|e /paradɔks/ *n.m.* paradox. ~**al** (*m. pl.* ~**aux**) *a.* paradoxical.
paraffine /parafin/ *n.f.* paraffin wax.
parages /paraʒ/ *n.m. pl.* area, vicinity.
paragraphe /paragraf/ *n.m.* paragraph.
paraître† /parɛtr/ *v.i.* appear; (*sembler*) seem, appear; (*ouvrage*) be published, come out. **faire** ~**,** (*ouvrage*) bring out.
parallèle /paralɛl/ *a.* parallel; (*illégal*) unofficial. —*n.m.* parallel. **faire un** ~ **entre,** draw a parallel between. **faire le**

~, make a connection. —*n.f.* parallel (line). ~**ment** *adv.* parallel (**à**, to).

paraly|ser /paralize/ *v.t.* paralyse. ~**sie** *n.f.* paralysis. ~**tique** *a.* & *n.m./f.* paralytic.

paramètre /parametr/ *n.m.* parameter.

paranoïa /paranɔja/ *n.f.* paranoia.

parapet /parapε/ *n.m.* parapet.

paraphe /paraf/ *n.m.* signature.

paraphrase /parafraz/ *n.f.* paraphrase.

parapluie /paraplчi/ *n.m.* umbrella.

parasite /parazit/ *n.m.* parasite. ~**s**, (*radio*) interference.

parasol /parasɔl/ *n.m.* sunshade.

paratonnerre /paratɔnεr/ *n.m.* lightning-conductor *ou* -rod.

paravent /paravɑ̃/ *n.m.* screen.

parc /park/ *n.m.* park; (*de bétail*) pen; (*de bébé*) play-pen; (*entrepôt*) depot. ~ **de stationnement,** car-park.

parcelle /parsεl/ *n.f.* fragment; (*de terre*) plot.

parce que /parsk(ə)/ *conj.* because.

parchemin /parʃəmε̃/ *n.m.* parchment.

parcimon|ie /parsimɔni/ *n.f.* **avec** ~**ie,** parsimoniously. ~**ieux,** ~**ieuse** *a.* parsimonious.

parcmètre /parkmεtr/ *n.m.* parking-meter.

parcourir† /parkurir/ *v.t.* travel *ou* go through; (*distance*) travel; (*des yeux*) glance at *ou* over.

parcours /parkur/ *n.m.* route; (*voyage*) journey.

par-delà /pardəla/ *prép.* & *adv.* beyond.

par-derrière /pardεrjεr/ *prép.* & *adv.* behind, at the back *ou* rear (of).

par-dessous /pardsu/ *prép.* & *adv.* under(neath).

pardessus /pardəsy/ *n.m.* overcoat.

par-dessus /pardsy/ *prép.* & *adv.* over. ~ **bord,** overboard. ~ **le marché,** into the bargain. ~ **tout,** above all.

par-devant /pardvɑ̃/ *adv.* at *ou* from the front, in front.

pardon /pardɔ̃/ *n.m.* forgiveness. (**je vous demande**) ~**!,** (I am) sorry!; (*pour demander qch.*) excuse me!

pardonn|er /pardɔne/ *v.t.* forgive. ~**er qch. à qn.,** forgive s.o. for sth. ~**able** *a.* forgivable.

paré /pare/ *a.* ready.

pare-balles /parbal/ *a. invar.* bullet-proof.

pare-brise /parbriz/ *n.m. invar.* windscreen; (*Amer.*) windshield.

pare-chocs /parʃɔk/ *n.m. invar.* bumper.

pareil, ~**le** /parεj/ *a.* similar (**à** to); (*tel*) such (a). —*n.m., f.* equal. —*adv.* (*fam.*)

the same. **c'est** ~, it is the same. **vos** ~**s,** (*péj.*) those of your type, those like you. ~**lement** *adv.* the same.

parement /parmɑ̃/ *n.m.* facing.

parent, ~**e** /parɑ̃, -t/ *a.* related (**de,** to). —*n.m., f.* relative, relation. ~**s** (*père et mère*) *n.m. pl.* parents. ~ **seul,** single parent.

parenté /parɑ̃te/ *n.f.* relationship.

parenthèse /parɑ̃tεz/ *n.f.* bracket, parenthesis; (*fig.*) digression.

parer¹ /pare/ *v.t.* (*coup*) parry. —*v.i.* ~ **à,** deal with. ~ **au plus pressé,** tackle the most urgent things first.

parer² /pare/ *v.t.* (*orner*) adorn.

paress|e /parεs/ *n.f.* laziness. ~**er** /-ese/ *v.i.* laze (about). ~**eux,** ~**euse** *a.* lazy; *n.m., f.* lazybones.

parfaire /parfεr/ *v.t.* perfect.

parfait, ~**e** /parfε, -t/ *a.* perfect. ~**ement** /-tmɑ̃/ *adv.* perfectly; (*bien sûr*) certainly.

parfois /parfwa/ *adv.* sometimes.

parfum /parfœ̃/ *n.m.* scent; (*substance*) perfume, scent; (*goût*) flavour.

parfum|er /parfyme/ *v.t.* perfume; (*gâteau*) flavour. **se** ~**er** *v. pr.* put on one's perfume. ~**é** *a.* fragrant; (*savon*) scented. ~**erie** *n.f.* (*produits*) perfumes; (*boutique*) perfume shop.

pari /pari/ *n.m.* bet.

par|ier /parje/ *v.t.* bet. ~**ieur,** ~**ieuse** *n.m., f.* punter, better.

Paris /pari/ *n.m./f.* Paris.

parisien, ~**ne** /parizjε̃, -jεn/ *a.* Paris, Parisian. —*n.m., f.* Parisian.

parit|é /parite/ *n.f.* parity. ~**aire** *a.* (*commission*) joint.

parjur|e /parʒyr/ *n.m.* perjury. —*n.m./f.* perjurer. **se** ~**er** *v. pr.* perjure o.s.

parking /parkiŋ/ *n.m.* car-park; (*Amer.*) parking-lot; (*stationnement*) parking.

parlement /parləmɑ̃/ *n.m.* parliament. ~**aire** /-tεr/ *a.* parliamentary; *n.m./f.* Member of Parliament; (*fig.*) negotiator. ~**er** /-te/ *v.i.* negotiate.

parl|er /parle/ *v.i.* talk, speak (**à,** to). —*v.t.* (*langue*) speak; (*politique, affaires, etc.*) talk. **se** ~**er** *v. pr.* (*langue*) be spoken. —*n.m.* speech; (*dialecte*) dialect. ~**ant,** ~**ante** *a.* (*film*) talking; (*fig.*) eloquent. ~**eur,** ~**euse** *n.m., f.* talker.

parloir /parlwar/ *n.m.* visiting room.

parmi /parmi/ *prép.* among(st).

parod|ie /parɔdi/ *n.f.* parody. ~**ier** *v.t.* parody.

paroi /parwa/ *n.f.* wall; (*cloison*) partition (wall). ~ **rocheuse,** rock face.

paroiss|e /parwas/ *n.f.* parish. **~ial** (*m. pl.* **~iaux**) *a.* parish. **~ien, ~ienne** *n.m.*, *f.* parishioner.

parole /parɔl/ *n.f.* (*mot, promesse*) word; (*langage*) speech. **demander la ~,** ask to speak. **prendre la ~,** (begin to) speak. **tenir ~,** keep one's word. **croire qn. sur ~,** take s.o.'s word for it.

paroxysme /parɔksism/ *n.m.* height, highest point.

parquer /parke/ *v.t.*, **se ~** *v. pr.* (*auto.*) park. **~ des réfugiés,** pen up refugees.

parquet /parkɛ/ *n.m.* floor; (*jurid.*) public prosecutor's department.

parrain /parɛ̃/ *n.m.* godfather; (*fig.*) sponsor. **~er** /-ene/ *v.t.* sponsor.

pars, part[1] /par/ *voir* **partir.**

parsemer /parsəme/ *v.t.* strew (**de, with**).

part[2] /par/ *n.f.* share, part. **à ~,** (*de côté*) aside; (*séparément*) apart; (*excepté*) apart from. **d'autre ~,** on the other hand; (*de plus*) moreover. **de la ~ de,** from. **de toutes ~s,** from all sides. **de ~ et d'autre,** on both sides. **d'une ~,** on the one hand. **faire ~ à qn.,** inform s.o. (**de,** of). **faire la ~ des choses,** make allowances. **prendre ~ à,** take part in; (*joie, douleur*) share. **pour ma ~,** as for me.

partag|e /partaʒ/ *n.m.* dividing; sharing out; (*part*) share. **~er** *v.t.* divide; (*distribuer*) share out; (*avoir en commun*) share. **se ~er qch.,** share sth.

partance (en) /(ã)partãs/ *adv.* about to depart.

partant /partã/ *n.m.* (*sport*) starter.

partenaire /partənɛr/ *n.m./f.* partner.

parterre /partɛr/ *n.m.* flower-bed; (*théâtre*) stalls.

parti /parti/ *n.m.* (*pol.*) party; (*en mariage*) match; (*décision*) decision. **~ pris,** prejudice. **prendre ~ pour,** side with. **j'en prends mon ~,** I've come to terms with that.

part|ial (*m. pl.* **~iaux**) /parsjal, -jo/ *a.* biased. **~ialité** *n.f.* bias.

participe /partisip/ *n.m.* (*gram.*) participle.

particip|er /partisipe/ *v.i.* **~er à,** take part in, participate in; (*profits, frais*) share; (*spectacle*) appear in. **~ant, ~ante** *n.m.*, *f.* participant (**à,** in); (*à un concours*) entrant. **~ation** *n.f.* participation; sharing; (*comm.*) interest. (*d'un artiste*) appearance.

particularité /partikylarite/ *n.f.* particularity.

particule /partikyl/ *n.f.* particle.

particul|ier, ~ière /partikylje, -jɛr/ *a.* (*spécifique*) particular; (*bizarre*) peculiar; (*privé*) private. —*n.m.* private individual. **en ~ier,** in particular; (*en privé*) in private. **~ier à,** peculiar to. **~ièrement** *adv.* particularly.

partie /parti/ *n.f.* part; (*cartes, sport*) game; (*jurid.*) party; (*sortie*) outing, party. **une ~ de pêche,** a fishing trip. **en ~,** partly. **faire ~ de,** be part of; (*adhérer à*) belong to. **en grande ~,** largely. **~ intégrante,** integral part.

partiel, ~le /parsjɛl/ *a.* partial. —*n.m.* (*univ.*) class examination. **~lement** *adv.* partially, partly.

partir† /partir/ *v.i.* (*aux. être*) go; (*quitter un lieu*) leave, go; (*tache*) come out; (*bouton*) come off; (*coup de feu*) go off; (*commencer*) start. **à ~ de,** from.

partisan, ~e /partizã, -an/ *n.m.*, *f.* supporter. —*n.m.* (*mil.*) partisan. **être ~ de,** be in favour of.

partition /partisjɔ̃/ *n.f.* (*mus.*) score.

partout /partu/ *adv.* everywhere. **~ où,** wherever.

paru /pary/ *voir* **paraître.**

parure /paryr/ *n.f.* adornment; (*bijoux*) jewellery; (*de draps*) set.

parution /parysjɔ̃/ *n.f.* publication.

parvenir† /parvənir/ *v.i.* (*aux. être*) **~ à,** reach; (*résultat*) achieve. **~ à faire,** manage to do. **faire ~,** send.

parvenu, ~e /parvəny/ *n.m.*, *f.* upstart.

parvis /parvi/ *n.m.* (*place*) square.

pas[1] /pɑ/ *adv.* not. **(ne) ~,** not. **je ne sais ~,** I do not know. **~ de sucre/livres/***etc.***,** no sugar/books/*etc.* **~ du tout,** not at all. **~ encore,** not yet. **~ mal,** not bad; (*beaucoup*) quite a lot (**de,** of). **~ vrai?,** (*fam.*) isn't that so?

pas[2] /pɑ/ *n.m.* step; (*bruit*) footstep; (*trace*) footprint; (*vitesse*) pace; (*de vis*) thread. **à deux ~ (de),** close by. **au ~,** at a walking pace; (*véhicule*) very slowly. **au ~ (cadencé),** in step. **à ~ de loup,** stealthily. **faire les cent ~,** walk up and down. **faire les premiers ~,** take the first steps. **sur le ~ de la porte,** on the doorstep.

passable /pɑsabl/ *a.* tolerable. **mention ~,** pass mark.

passage /pɑsaʒ/ *n.m.* passing, passage; (*traversée*) crossing; (*visite*) visit; (*chemin*) way, passage; (*d'une œuvre*) passage. **de ~,** (*voyageur*) visiting; (*amant*) casual. **~ à niveau,** level crossing. **~ clouté,** pedestrian crossing. **~ interdit,** (*panneau*) no thoroughfare. **~ souterrain,** subway; (*Amer.*) underpass.

passag|er, ~ère /pɑsaʒe, -ɛr/ *a.* temporary. —*n.m.*, *f.* passenger. **~er clandestin,** stowaway.

passant, ~e /pɑsɑ̃, -t/ *a.* (*rue*) busy. —*n.m.*, *f.* passer-by. —*n.m.* (*anneau*) loop.

passe /pɑs/ *n.f.* pass. **bonne/ mauvaise ~,** good/bad patch. **en ~ de,** on the road to. **~-droit,** *n.m.* special privilege. **~-montagne** *n.m.* Balaclava. **~-partout** *n.m. invar.* master-key; *a. invar.* for all occasions. **~-temps** *n.m. invar.* pastime.

passé /pɑse/ *a.* (*révolu*) past; (*dernier*) last; (*fini*) over; (*fané*) faded. —*prép.* after. —*n.m.* past. **~ de mode,** out of fashion.

passeport /pɑspɔr/ *n.m.* passport.

passer /pɑse/ *v.i.* (*aux. être ou avoir*) pass; (*aller*) go; (*venir*) come; (*temps*) pass (by), go by; (*film*) be shown; (*couleur*) fade. —*v.t.* (*aux. avoir*) pass, cross; (*donner*) pass, hand; (*mettre*) put; (*oublier*) overlook; (*enfiler*) slip on; (*dépasser*) go beyond; (*temps*) spend, pass; (*film*) show; (*examen*) take; (*commande*) place; (*soupe*) strain. **se ~** *v. pr.* happen, take place. **laisser ~,** let through; (*occasion*) miss. **~ à tabac,** (*fam.*) beat up. **~ devant,** (*édifice*) go past. **~ en fraude,** smuggle. **~ outre,** take no notice (**à,** of). **~ par,** go through. **~ pour,** (*riche etc.*) be taken to be. **~ sur,** (*détail*) pass over. **~ l'aspirateur,** hoover, vacuum. **~ un coup de fil à qn.,** give s.o. a ring. **je vous passe Mme X,** (*par le standard*) I'm putting you through to Mrs X; (*en donnant l'appareil*) I'll hand you over to Mrs X. **se ~ de,** go ou do without.

passerelle /pɑsrɛl/ *n.f.* footbridge; (*pour accéder à un avion, à un navire*) gangway.

pass|eur, ~euse /pɑsœr, œz/ *n.m.*, *f.* smuggler.

passible /pɑsibl/ *a.* **~ de,** liable to.

passi|f, ~ve /pɑsif, -v/ *a.* passive. —*n.m.* (*comm.*) liabilities. **~vité** *n.f.* passiveness.

passion /pɑsjɔ̃/ *n.f.* passion.

passionn|er /pɑsjɔne/ *v.t.* fascinate. **se ~er pour,** have a passion for. **~é** *a.* passionate. **être ~é de,** have a passion for. **~ément** *adv.* passionately.

passoire /pɑswar/ *n.f.* (*à thé*) strainer; (*à légumes*) colander.

pastel /pastɛl/ *n.m. & a. invar.* pastel.

pastèque /pastɛk/ *n.f.* watermelon.

pasteur /pastœr/ *n.m.* (*relig.*) minister.

pasteurisé /pastœrize/ *a.* pasteurized.

pastiche /pastiʃ/ *n.m.* pastiche.

pastille /pastij/ *n.f.* (*bonbon*) pastille, lozenge.

pastis /pastis/ *n.m.* aniseed liqueur.

patate /patat/ *n.f.* (*fam.*) potato. **~ (douce),** sweet potato.

patauger /patoʒe/ *v.i.* splash about.

pâte /pɑt/ *n.f.* paste; (*farine*) dough; (*à tarte*) pastry; (*à frire*) batter. **~s (alimentaires),** pasta. **~ à modeler,** Plasticine (P.). **~ dentifrice,** toothpaste.

pâté /pɑte/ *n.m.* (*culin.*) pâté; (*d'encre*) ink-blot. **~ de maisons,** block of houses; (*de sable*) sand-pie. **~ en croûte,** meat pie.

pâtée /pɑte/ *n.f.* feed, mash.

patelin /patlɛ̃/ *n.m.* (*fam.*) village.

patent, ~e[1] /patɑ̃, -t/ *a.* patent.

patent|e[2] /patɑ̃t/ *n.f.* trade licence. **~é** *a.* licensed.

patère /patɛr/ *n.f.* (*coat*) peg.

patern|el, ~elle /patɛrnɛl/ *a.* paternal. **~ité** *n.f.* paternity.

pâteu|x, ~se /pɑtø, -z/ *a.* pasty; (*langue*) coated.

pathétique /patetik/ *a.* moving. —*n.m.* pathos.

patholog|ie /patɔlɔʒi/ *n.f.* pathology. **~ique** *a.* pathological.

pat|ient, ~iente /pasjɑ̃, -t/ *a. & n.m.*, *f.* patient. **~iemment** /-jamɑ̃/ *adv.* patiently. **~ience** *n.f.* patience.

patienter /pasjɑ̃te/ *v.i.* wait.

patin /patɛ̃/ *n.m.* skate. **~ à roulettes,** roller-skate.

patin|er /patine/ *v.i.* skate; (*voiture*) spin. **~age** *n.m.* skating. **~eur, ~euse** *n.m.*, *f.* skater.

patinoire /patinwar/ *n.f.* skating-rink.

pâtir /pɑtir/ *v.i.* suffer (**de,** from).

pâtiss|ier, ~ière /pɑtisje, -jɛr/ *n.m.*, *f.* pastry-cook, cake-shop owner. **~erie** *n.f.* cake shop; (*gâteau*) pastry; (*art*) cake making.

patois /patwa/ *n.m.* patois.

patraque /patrak/ *a.* (*fam.*) peaky, out of sorts.

patrie /patri/ *n.f.* homeland.

patrimoine /patrimwan/ *n.m.* heritage.

patriot|e /patrijɔt/ *a.* patriotic. —*n.m./f.* patriot. **~ique** *a.* patriotic. **~isme** *n.m.* patriotism.

patron[1]**, ~ne** /patrɔ̃, -ɔn/ *n.m.*, *f.*

employer, boss; (*propriétaire*) owner, boss; (*saint*) patron saint. ∼al (*m. pl.* ∼aux) /-ɔnal, -o/ *a.* employers'. ∼at /-ɔna/ *n.m.* employers.

patron[2] /patrɔ̃/ *n.m.* (*couture*) pattern.

patronage /patrɔnaʒ/ *n.m.* patronage; (*foyer*) youth club.

patronner /patrɔne/ *v.t.* support.

patrouill|e /patruj/ *n.f.* patrol. ∼er *v.i.* patrol.

patte /pat/ *n.f.* leg; (*pied*) foot; (*de chat*) paw. ∼s, (*favoris*) sideburns.

pâturage /pɑtyraʒ/ *n.m.* pasture.

pâture /pɑtyr/ *n.f.* food.

paume /pom/ *n.f.* (*de main*) palm.

paumé, ∼e /pome/ *n.m.*, *f.* (*fam.*) wretch, loser.

paumer /pome/ *v.t.* (*fam.*) lose.

paupière /popjɛr/ *n.f.* eyelid.

pause /poz/ *n.f.* pause; (*halte*) break.

pauvre /povr/ *a.* poor. —*n.m./f.* poor man, poor woman. ∼ment /-əmɑ̃/ *adv.* poorly. ∼té /-əte/ *n.f.* poverty.

pavaner (se) /(sə)pavane/ *v. pr.* strut.

pav|er /pave/ *v.t.* pave; (*chaussée*) cobble. ∼é *n.m.* paving-stone; cobble(stone).

pavillon[1] /pavijɔ̃/ *n.m.* house; (*de gardien*) lodge.

pavillon[2] /pavijɔ̃/ *n.m.* (*drapeau*) flag.

pavoiser /pavwaze/ *v.t.* deck with flags. —*v.i.* put out the flags.

pavot /pavo/ *n.m.* poppy.

payant, ∼e /pɛjɑ̃, -t/ *a.* (*billet*) for which a charge is made; (*spectateur*) (fee-)paying; (*rentable*) profitable.

payer /peje/ *v.t./i.* pay; (*service, travail, etc.*) pay for; (*acheter*) buy (à, for). se ∼ *v. pr.* (*s'acheter*) buy o.s. faire ∼ à qn., (*cent francs etc.*) charge s.o. (pour, for). se ∼ la tête de, make fun of. il me le paiera!, he'll pay for this.

pays /pei/ *n.m.* country; (*région*) region; (*village*) village. du ∼, local. les P∼-Bas, the Netherlands. le ∼ de Galles, Wales.

paysage /peizaʒ/ *n.m.* landscape.

paysan, ∼ne /peizɑ̃, -an/ *n.m.*, f. farmer, country person; (*péj.*) peasant. —*a.* (*agricole*) farming; (*rural*) country.

PCV (en) /(ɑ̃)peseve/ *adv.* appeler *ou* téléphoner en ∼, reverse the charges; (*Amer.*) call collect.

PDG *abrév. voir* **président directeur général.**

péage /peaʒ/ *n.m.* toll; (*lieu*) toll-gate.

peau (*pl.* ∼x) /po/ *n.f.* skin; (*cuir*) hide. ∼ de chamois, chamois(-leather). ∼

de mouton, sheepskin. être bien/mal dans sa ∼, be/not be at ease with oneself.

pêche[1] /pɛʃ/ *n.f.* peach.

pêche[2] /pɛʃ/ *n.f.* (*activité*) fishing; (*poissons*) catch. ∼ à la ligne, angling.

péché /peʃe/ *n.m.* sin.

péch|er /peʃe/ *v.i.* sin. ∼er par timidité/*etc.*, be too timid/*etc.* ∼eur, ∼eresse *n.m.*, f. sinner.

pêch|er /peʃe/ *v.t.* (*poisson*) catch; (*dénicher: fam.*) dig up. —*v.i.* fish. ∼eur *n.m.* fisherman; (à la ligne) angler.

pécule /pekyl/ *n.m.* (*économies*) savings.

pécuniaire /pekynjɛr/ *a.* financial.

pédago|gie /pedagɔʒi/ *n.f.* education. ∼gique *a.* educational. ∼gue *n.m./f.* teacher.

pédal|e /pedal/ *n.f.* pedal. ∼er *v.i.* pedal.

pédalo /pedalo/ *n.m.* pedal boat.

pédant, ∼e /pedɑ̃, -t/ *a.* pedantic.

pédé /pede/ *n.m.* (*argot*) queer, fag (*Amer.*).

pédestre /pedɛstr/ *a.* faire de la randonnée ∼, go walking *ou* hiking.

pédiatre /pedjatr/ *n.m./f.* paediatrician.

pédicure /pedikyr/ *n.m./f.* chiropodist.

pedigree /pedigri/ *n.m.* pedigree.

pègre /pɛgr/ *n.f.* underworld.

peign|e /pɛɲ/ *n.m.* comb. ∼er /peɲe/ *v.t.* comb; (*personne*) comb the hair of. se ∼er *v. pr.* comb one's hair.

peignoir /pɛɲwar/ *n.m.* dressing-gown.

peindre† /pɛ̃dr/ *v.t.* paint.

peine /pɛn/ *n.f.* sadness, sorrow; (*effort, difficulté*) trouble; (*punition*) punishment; (*jurid.*) sentence. avoir de la ∼, feel sad. faire de la ∼ à, hurt. ce n'est pas la ∼ de faire, it is not worth (while) doing. se donner *ou* prendre la ∼ de faire, go to the trouble of doing. ∼ de mort death penalty.

peine (à) /(a)pɛn/ *adv.* hardly.

peiner /pene/ *v.i.* struggle. —*v.t.* sadden.

peintre /pɛ̃tr/ *n.m.* painter. ∼ en bâtiment, house painter.

peinture /pɛ̃tyr/ *n.f.* painting; (*matière*) paint. ∼ à l'huile, oil-painting.

péjorati|f, ∼ve /peʒɔratif, -v/ *a.* pejorative.

pelage /pəlaʒ/ *n.m.* coat, fur.

pêle-mêle /pɛlmɛl/ *adv.* in a jumble.

peler /pəle/ *v.t./i.* peel.

pèlerin /pɛlrɛ̃/ *n.m.* pilgrim. ∼age /-inaʒ/ *n.m.* pilgrimage.

pèlerine /pɛlrin/ *n.f.* cape.

pélican /pelikɑ̃/ *n.m.* pelican.

pelle /pɛl/ n.f. shovel; (d'enfant) spade. ~**tée** n.f. shovelful.

pellicule /pelikyl/ n.f. film. ~**s**, (cheveux) dandruff.

pelote /pəlɔt/ n.f. ball; (d'épingles) pincushion.

peloton /plɔtɔ̃/ n.m. troop, squad; (sport) pack. ~ **d'exécution**, firing-squad.

pelotonner (se) /(sə)plɔtɔne/ v. pr. curl up.

pelouse /pluz/ n.f. lawn.

peluche /plyʃ/ n.f. (tissu) plush; (jouet) cuddly toy. **en ~**, (lapin, chien) fluffy, furry.

pelure /plyr/ n.f. peeling.

pén|al (m. pl. ~**aux**) /penal, -o/ a. penal. ~**aliser** v.t. penalize. ~**alité** n.f. penalty.

penalt|y (pl. ~**ies**) /penalti/ n.m. penalty (kick).

penaud, ~e /pəno, -d/ a. sheepish.

penchant /pɑ̃ʃɑ̃/ n.m. inclination; (goût) liking (**pour**, for).

pench|er /pɑ̃ʃe/ v.t. tilt. —v.i. lean (over), tilt. **se ~er** v. pr. lean (forward). ~**er pour**, favour. **se ~er sur**, (problème etc.) examine.

pendaison /pɑ̃dɛzɔ̃/ n.f. hanging.

pendant[1] /pɑ̃dɑ̃/ prép. (au cours de) during; (durée) for. ~ **que**, while.

pendant[2], ~**e** /pɑ̃dɑ̃, -t/ a. hanging; (question etc.) pending. —n.m. (contrepartie) matching piece (**de**, to). **faire ~ à**, match. ~ **d'oreille**, drop earring.

pendentif /pɑ̃dɑ̃tif/ n.m. pendant.

penderie /pɑ̃dri/ n.f. wardrobe.

pend|re /pɑ̃dr/ v.t./i. hang. **se ~re** v. pr. hang (**à**, from); (se tuer) hang o.s. ~**re la crémaillère**, have a house-warming. ~**u, ~ue** a. hanging (**à**, from); n.m., f. hanged man, hanged woman.

pendul|e /pɑ̃dyl/ n.f. clock. —n.m. pendulum. ~**ette** n.f. (travelling) clock.

pénétr|er /penetre/ v.i. ~**er (dans)**, enter. —v.t. penetrate. **se ~er de**, become convinced of. ~**ant, ~ante** a. penetrating.

pénible /penibl/ a. difficult; (douloureux) painful; (fatigant) tiresome. ~**ment** /-əmɑ̃/ adv. with difficulty; (cruellement) painfully.

péniche /peniʃ/ n.f. barge.

pénicilline /penisilin/ n.f. penicillin.

péninsule /penɛ̃syl/ n.f. peninsula.

pénis /penis/ n.m. penis.

pénitence /penitɑ̃s/ n.f. (peine) penance; (regret) penitence; (fig.) punishment. **faire ~**, repent.

péniten|cier /penitɑ̃sje/ n.m. penitentiary. ~**tiaire** /-sjɛr/ a. prison.

pénombre /penɔ̃br/ n.f. half-light.

pensée[1] /pɑ̃se/ n.f. thought.

pensée[2] /pɑ̃se/ n.f. (fleur) pansy.

pens|er /pɑ̃se/ v.t./i. think. ~**er à**, (réfléchir à) think about; (se souvenir de, prévoir) think of. ~**er faire**, think of doing. **faire ~er à**, remind one of. ~**eur** n.m. thinker.

pensi|f, ~ve /pɑ̃sif, -v/ a. pensive.

pension /pɑ̃sjɔ̃/ n.f. (scol.) boarding-school; (repas, somme) board; (allocation) pension. ~ **(de famille)**, guest-house. ~ **alimentaire**, (jurid.) alimony. ~**naire** /-jɔnɛr/ n.m./f. boarder; (d'hôtel) guest. ~**nat** /-jɔna/ n.m. boarding-school.

pente /pɑ̃t/ n.f. slope. **en ~**, sloping.

Pentecôte /pɑ̃tkot/ n.f. **la ~**, Whitsun.

pénurie /penyri/ n.f. shortage.

pépé /pepe/ n.m. (fam.) grandad.

pépier /pepje/ v.i. chirp.

pépin /pepɛ̃/ n.m. (graine) pip; (ennui, fam.) hitch; (parapluie; fam.) brolly.

pépinière /pepinjɛr/ n.f. (tree) nursery.

perçant, ~e /pɛrsɑ̃, -t/ a. (froid) piercing; (regard) keen.

percée /pɛrse/ n.f. opening; (attaque) breakthrough.

perce-neige /pɛrsəneʒ/ n.m./f. invar. snowdrop.

percepteur /pɛrsɛptœr/ n.m. tax-collector.

perceptible /pɛrsɛptibl/ a. perceptible.

perception /pɛrsɛpsjɔ̃/ n.f. perception; (d'impôts) collection.

percer /pɛrse/ v.t. pierce; (avec perceuse) drill; (mystère) penetrate. —v.i. break through; (dent) come through.

perceuse /pɛrsøz/ n.f. drill.

percevoir† /pɛrsəvwar/ v.t. perceive; (impôt) collect.

perche /pɛrʃ/ n.f. (bâton) pole.

perch|er /pɛrʃe/ v.t., **se ~er** v. pr. perch. ~**oir** n.m. perch.

percolateur /pɛrkɔlatœr/ n.m. percolator.

percussion /pɛrkysjɔ̃/ n.f. percussion.

percuter /pɛrkyte/ v.t. strike; (véhicule) crash into.

perd|re /pɛrdr/ v.t./i. lose; (gaspiller) waste; (ruiner) ruin. **se ~re** v. pr. get lost; (rester inutilisé) go to waste. ~**ant, ~ante** a. losing; n.m., f. loser. ~**u** a. (endroit) isolated; (moments) spare; (malade) finished.

perdreau (pl. ~**x**) /pɛrdro/ n.m. (young) partridge.

perdrix /pɛrdri/ *n.f.* partridge.

père /pɛr/ *n.m.* father. ~ **de famille**, father, family man. ~ **spirituel**, father figure. **le** ~ **Noël**, Father Christmas, Santa Claus.

péremptoire /perãptwar/ *a.* peremptory.

perfection /pɛrfɛksjɔ̃/ *n.f.* perfection.

perfectionn|er /pɛrfɛksjɔne/ *v.t.* improve. **se** ~**er en anglais**/*etc.*, improve one's English/*etc.* ~**é á** *a.* sophisticated. ~**ement** *n.m.* improvement.

perfectionniste /pɛrfɛksjɔnist/ *n.m./f.* perfectionist.

perfid|e /pɛrfid/ *a.* perfidious, treacherous. ~**ie** *n.f.* perfidy.

perfor|er /pɛrfɔre/ *v.t.* perforate; (*billet, bande*) punch. ~**ateur** *n.m.* (*appareil*) punch. ~**ation** *n.f.* perforation; (*trou*) hole.

performan|ce /pɛrfɔrmãs/ *n.f.* performance. ~**t, ~te** *a.* high-performance, successful.

perfusion /pɛrfyzjɔ̃/ *n.f.* drip. **mettre qn. sous** ~, put s.o. on a drip.

péricliter /periklite/ *v.i.* decline, be in rapid decline.

péridural /peridyral/ *a.* (**anesthésie**) ~**e**, epidural.

péril /peril/ *n.m.* peril.

périlleu|x, ~se /perijø, -z/ *a.* perilous.

périmé /perime/ *a.* expired; (*désuet*) outdated.

périmètre /perimetr/ *n.m.* perimeter.

périod|e /perjɔd/ *n.f.* period. ~**ique** *a.* periodic(al); *n.m.* (*journal*) periodical.

péripétie /peripesi/ *n.f.* (unexpected) event, adventure.

périphér|ie /periferi/ *n.f.* periphery; (*banlieue*) outskirts. ~**ique** *a.* peripheral; *n.m.* (**boulevard**) ~**ique**, ring road.

périple /peripl/ *n.m.* journey.

pér|ir /perir/ *v.i.* perish, die. ~**issable** *a.* perishable.

périscope /periskɔp/ *n.m.* periscope.

perle /pɛrl/ *n.f.* (*bijou*) pearl; (*boule, de sueur*) bead.

permanence /pɛrmanãs/ *n.f.* permanence; (*bureau*) duty office; (*scol.*) study room. **de** ~, on duty. **en** ~, permanently. **assurer une** ~, keep the office open.

permanent, ~e /pɛrmanã, -t/ *a.* permanent; (*spectacle*) continuous; (*comité*) standing. —*n.f.* (*coiffure*) perm.

perméable /pɛrmeabl/ *a.* permeable; (*personne*) susceptible (à, to).

permettre† /pɛrmetr/ *v.t.* allow, permit. ~ **à qn. de**, allow *ou* permit s.o. to. **se** ~ **de**, take the liberty to.

permis, ~e /pɛrmi, -z/ *a.* allowed. —*n.m.* licence, permit. ~ **(de conduire)**, driving-licence.

permission /pɛrmisjɔ̃/ *n.f.* permission. **en** ~, (*mil.*) on leave.

permut|er /pɛrmyte/ *v.t.* change round. ~**ation** *n.f.* permutation.

pernicieu|x, ~se /pɛrnisjø, -z/ *a.* pernicious.

Pérou /peru/ *n.m.* Peru.

perpendiculaire /pɛrpãdikylɛr/ *a.* & *n.f.* perpendicular.

perpétrer /pɛrpetre/ *v.t.* perpetrate.

perpétuel, ~le /pɛrpetɥel/ *a.* perpetual.

perpétuer /pɛrpetɥe/ *v.t.* perpetuate.

perpétuité (à) /(a)pɛrpetɥite/ *adv.* for life.

perplex|e /pɛrplɛks/ *a.* perplexed. ~**ité** *n.f.* perplexity.

perquisition /pɛrkizisjɔ̃/ *n.f.* (police) search. ~**ner** /-jɔne/ *v.t./i.* search.

perron /pɛrɔ̃/ *n.m.* (front) steps.

perroquet /pɛrɔke/ *n.m.* parrot.

perruche /perys̆/ *n.f.* budgerigar.

perruque /peryk/ *n.f.* wig.

persan, ~e /pɛrsã, -an/ *a.* & *n.m.* (*lang.*) Persian.

persécut|er /pɛrsekyte/ *v.t.* persecute. ~**ion** /-ysjɔ̃/ *n.f.* persecution.

persévér|er /pɛrsevere/ *v.i.* persevere. ~**ance** *n.f.* perseverance.

persienne /pɛrsjɛn/ *n.f.* (outside) shutter.

persil /pɛrsi/ *n.m.* parsley.

persistan|t, ~te /pɛrsistã, -t/ *a.* persistent; (*feuillage*) evergreen. ~**ce** *n.f.* persistence.

persister /pɛrsiste/ *v.i.* persist (à faire, in doing).

personnage /pɛrsɔnaʒ/ *n.m.* character; (*important*) personality.

personnalité /pɛrsɔnalite/ *n.f.* personality.

personne /pɛrsɔn/ *n.f.* person. ~**s**, people. —*pron.* (*quelqu'un*) anybody. (ne) ~, nobody.

personnel, ~le /pɛrsɔnel/ *a.* personal; (*égoïste*) selfish. —*n.m.* staff. ~**lement** *adv.* personally.

personnifier /pɛrsɔnifje/ *v.t.* personify.

perspective /pɛrspɛktiv/ *n.f.* (*art*) perspective; (*vue*) view; (*possibilité*) prospect; (*point de vue*) viewpoint, perspective.

perspicac|e /pɛrspikas/ *a.* shrewd. ~**ité** *n.f.* shrewdness.

persua|der /pɛrsɥade/ *v.t.* persuade (**de**

faire, to do). **~sion** /-ɥazjɔ̃/ *n.f.* persuasion.

persuasi|f, **~ve** /pɛrsɥazif, -v/ *a.* persuasive.

perte /pɛrt/ *n.f.* loss; (*ruine*) ruin. **à ~ de vue**, as far as the eye can see. **~ de**, (*temps, argent*) waste of. **~ sèche**, total loss. **~s**, (*méd.*) discharge.

pertinen|t, **~te** /pɛrtinɑ̃, -t/ *a.* pertinent; (*esprit*) judicious. **~ce** *n.f.* pertinence.

perturb|er /pɛrtyrbe/ *v.t.* disrupt; (*personne*) perturb. **~ateur**, **~atrice** *a.* disruptive; *n.m., f.* disruptive element. **~ation** *n.f.* disruption.

pervenche /pɛrvɑ̃ʃ/ *n.f.* periwinkle; (*fam.*) traffic warden.

pervers, **~e** /pɛrvɛr, -s/ *a.* perverse; (*dépravé*) perverted. **~ion** /-sjɔ̃/ *n.f.* perversion.

pervert|ir /pɛrvɛrtir/ *v.t.* pervert. **~i**, **~ie** *n.m./f.* pervert.

pes|ant, **~ante** /pəzɑ̃, -t/ *a.* heavy. **~amment** *adv.* heavily. **~anteur** *n.f.* heaviness. **la ~anteur**, (*force*) gravity.

pèse-personne /pɛzpɛrsɔn/ *n.m.* (bathroom) scales.

pes|er /pəze/ *v.t./i.* weigh. **~er sur**, bear upon. **~ée** *n.f.* weighing; (*effort*) pressure.

peseta /pezeta/ *n.f.* peseta.

pessimis|te /pesimist/ *a.* pessimistic. **—***n.m.* pessimist. **~me** *n.m.* pessimism.

peste /pɛst/ *n.f.* plague; (*personne*) pest.

pester /pɛste/ *v.i.* **~ (contre)**, curse.

pestilentiel, **~le** /pɛstilɑ̃sjɛl/ *a.* fetid, stinking.

pet /pɛ/ *n.m.* fart.

pétale /petal/ *n.m.* petal.

pétanque /petɑ̃k/ *n.f.* bowls.

pétarader /petarade/ *v.i.* backfire.

pétard /petar/ *n.m.* banger.

péter /pete/ *v.i.* fart; (*fam.*) go bang; (*casser: fam.*) snap.

pétill|er /petije/ *v.i.* (*feu*) crackle; (*champagne, yeux*) sparkle. **~er d'intelligence**, sparkle with intelligence. **~ant**, **~ante** *a.* (*gazeux*) fizzy.

petit, **~e** /pti, -t/ *a.* small; (*avec nuance affective*) little; (*jeune*) young, small; (*faible*) slight; (*mesquin*) petty. **—***n.m., f.* little child; (*scol.*) junior. **~s**, (*de chat*) kittens; (*de chien*) pups. **en ~**, in miniature. **~ ami**, boy-friend. **~e amie**, girl-friend. **~ à petit**, little by little. **~es annonces**, small ads. **~e cuiller**, teaspoon. **~ déjeuner**, breakfast. **le ~ écran**, the small screen,

television. **~-enfant** (*pl.* **~s-enfants**) *n.m.* grandchild. **~e-fille** (*pl.* **~es-filles**) *n.f.* granddaughter. **~-fils** (*pl.* **~s-fils**) *n.m.* grandson. **~ pois** (*pl.* **~s-pois**) *n.m.* garden pea.

petitesse /ptitɛs/ *n.f.* smallness; (*péj.*) meanness.

pétition /petisjɔ̃/ *n.f.* petition.

pétrifier /petrifje/ *v.t.* petrify.

pétrin /petrɛ̃/ *n.m.* (*situation*: *fam.*) **dans le ~**, in a fix.

pétrir /petrir/ *v.t.* knead.

pétrol|e /petrɔl/ *n.m.* (*brut*) oil; (*pour lampe etc.*) paraffin. **lampe à ~e**, oil lamp. **~ier**, **~ière** *a.* oil; *n.m.* (*navire*) oil-tanker.

pétulant, **~e** /petylɑ̃, -t/ *a.* exuberant, full of high spirits.

peu /pø/ *adv.* **~ (de)**, (*quantité*) little, not much; (*nombre*) few, not many. **~ intéressant/***etc.***, not very interesting/***etc.* **—***pron. etc.—n.m.* little. **un ~ (de)**, a little. **à ~ près**, more or less. **de ~**, only just. **~ à peu**, gradually. **~ après/avant**, shortly after/ before. **~ de chose**, not much. **~ nombreux**, few. **~ souvent**, seldom. **pour ~ que**, as long as.

peuplade /pœplad/ *n.f.* tribe.

peuple /pœpl/ *n.m.* people.

peupler /pœple/ *v.t.* populate.

peuplier /pøplije/ *n.m.* poplar.

peur /pœr/ *n.f.* fear. **avoir ~**, be afraid (**de**, of). **de ~ de**, for fear of. **faire ~ à**, frighten. **~eux**, **~euse** *a.* fearful, timid.

peut /pø/ *voir* **pouvoir**[1].

peut-être /pøtɛtr/ *adv.* perhaps, maybe. **~ que**, perhaps, maybe.

peux /pø/ *voir* **pouvoir**[1].

pèze /pɛz/ *n.m.* (*fam.*) **du ~**, money, dough.

phallique /falik/ *a.* phallic.

phantasme /fɑ̃tasm/ *n.m.* fantasy.

phare /far/ *n.m.* (*tour*) lighthouse; (*de véhicule*) headlight. **~ antibrouillard**, fog lamp.

pharmaceutique /farmasøtik/ *a.* pharmaceutical.

pharmac|ie /farmasi/ *n.f.* (*magasin*) chemist's (shop); (*Amer.*) pharmacy; (*science*) pharmacy; (*armoire*) medicine cabinet. **~ien**, **~ienne** *n.m., f.* chemist, pharmacist.

pharyngite /farɛ̃ʒit/ *n.f.* pharyngitis.

phase /faz/ *n.f.* phase.

phénomène /fenɔmɛn/ *n.m.* phenomenon; (*original*: *fam.*) eccentric.

philanthrop|e /filɑ̃trɔp/ *n.m./f.* philanthropist. **~ique** *a.* philanthropic.

philatél|ie /filateli/ *n.f.* philately. **~iste** *n.m./f.* philatelist.

philharmonique /filarmɔnik/ *a.* philharmonic.

Philippines /filipin/ *n.f. pl.* **les ~,** the Philippines.

philosoph|e /filozɔf/ *n.m./f.* philosopher. —*a.* philosophical. **~ie** *n.f.* philosophy. **~ique** *a.* philosophical.

phobie /fɔbi/ *n.f.* phobia.

phonétique /fɔnetik/ *a.* phonetic.

phoque /fɔk/ *n.m.* (*animal*) seal.

phosphate /fɔsfat/ *n.m.* phosphate.

phosphore /fɔsfɔr/ *n.m.* phosphorus.

photo /fɔto/ *n.f.* photo; (*art*) photography. **prendre en ~,** take a photo of. **~ d'identité,** passport photograph.

photocop|ie /fɔtɔkɔpi/ *n.f.* photocopy. **~ier** *v.t.* photocopy. **~ieuse** *n.f.* photocopier.

photogénique /fɔtɔʒenik/ *a.* photogenic.

photograph|e /fɔtɔgraf/ *n.m./f.* photographer. **~ie** *n.f.* photograph; (*art*) photography. **~ier** *v.t.* take a photo of. **~ique** *a.* photographic.

phrase /fraz/ *n.f.* sentence.

physicien, ~ne /fizisjɛ̃, -jɛn/ *n.m., f.* physicist.

physiologie /fizjɔlɔʒi/ *n.f.* physiology.

physionomie /fizjɔnɔmi/ *n.f.* face.

physique[1] /fizik/ *a.* physical. —*n.m.* physique. **au ~,** physically. **~ment** *adv.* physically.

physique[2] /fizik/ *n.f.* physics.

piailler /pjɑje/ *v.i.* squeal, squawk.

pian|o /pjano/ *n.m.* piano. **~iste** *n.m./f.* pianist.

pianoter /pjanɔte/ *v.t.* (*air*) tap out. —*v.i.* (**sur, on**) (*ordinateur*) tap away; (*table*) tap one's fingers.

pic /pik/ *n.m.* (*outil*) pickaxe; (*sommet*) peak; (*oiseau*) woodpecker. **à ~,** (*verticalement*) sheer; (*couler*) straight to the bottom; (*arriver*) just at the right time.

pichenette /piʃnɛt/ *n.f.* flick.

pichet /piʃɛ/ *n.m.* jug.

pickpocket /pikpɔkɛt/ *n.m.* pickpocket.

pick-up /pikœp/ *n.m. invar.* record-player.

picorer /pikɔre/ *v.t./i.* peck.

picot|er /pikɔte/ *v.t.* prick; (*yeux*) make smart. **~ement** *n.m.* pricking; smarting.

pie /pi/ *n.f.* magpie.

pièce /pjɛs/ *n.f.* piece; (*chambre*) room; (*pour raccommoder*) patch; (*écrit*) document. **~ (de monnaie),** coin. **~ (de théâtre),** play. **dix francs/*etc.* (la)**

~, ten francs/*etc.* each. ~ de rechange, spare part. **~ détachée,** part. **~ d'identité,** identity paper. **~ montée,** tiered cake. **~s justificatives,** supporting documents. **deux/trois** *etc.* **~s,** two-/three-/*etc.* room flat *ou* apartment (*Amer.*).

pied /pje/ *n.m.* foot; (*de meuble*) leg; (*de lampe*) base; (*de salade*) plant. **à ~,** on foot. **au ~ de la lettre,** literally. **avoir ~,** have a footing. **avoir les ~s plats,** have flat feet. **comme un ~,** (*fam.*) terribly. **mettre sur ~,** set up. **~ bot,** club-foot. **sur un ~ d'égalité,** on an equal footing. **mettre les ~s dans le plat,** put one's foot in it. **c'est le ~!,** (*fam.*) it's great!

piédest|al (*pl.* **~aux**) /pjedɛstal, -o/ *n.m.* pedestal.

piège /pjɛʒ/ *n.m.* trap.

piég|er /pjeʒe/ *v.t.* trap; (*avec explosifs*) booby-trap. **lettre/voiture ~ée,** letter-/car-bomb.

pierr|e /pjɛr/ *n.f.* stone. **~e d'achoppement,** stumbling-block. **~e de touche,** touchstone. **~e précieuse,** precious stone. **~e tombale,** tombstone. **~eux, ~euse** *a.* stony.

piété /pjete/ *n.f.* piety.

piétiner /pjetine/ *v.i.* stamp one's feet; (*ne pas avancer: fig.*) mark time. —*v.t.* trample (on).

piéton /pjetɔ̃/ *n.m.* pedestrian. **~nier, ~nière** /-ɔnje, -jɛr/ *a.* pedestrian.

piètre /pjɛtr/ *a.* wretched.

pieu (*pl.* **~x**) /pjø/ *n.m.* post, stake.

pieuvre /pjœvr/ *n.f.* octopus.

pieu|x, ~se /pjø, -z/ *a.* pious.

pif /pif/ *n.m.* (*fam.*) nose.

pigeon /piʒɔ̃/ *n.m.* pigeon.

piger /piʒe/ *v.t./i.* (*fam.*) understand, get (it).

pigment /pigmã/ *n.m.* pigment.

pignon /piɲɔ̃/ *n.m.* (*de maison*) gable.

pile /pil/ *n.f.* (*tas, pilier*) pile; (*électr.*) battery; (*atomique*) pile. —*adv.* (*s'arrêter: fam.*) dead. **à dix heures ~,** (*fam.*) at ten on the dot. **~ ou face?,** heads or tails?

piler /pile/ *v.t.* pound.

pilier /pilje/ *n.m.* pillar.

pill|er /pije/ *v.t.* loot. **~age** *n.m.* looting. **~ard, ~arde** *n.m., f.* looter.

pilonner /pilɔne/ *v.t.* pound.

pilori /pilɔri/ *n.m.* **mettre** *ou* **clouer au ~,** pillory.

pilot|e /pilɔt/ *n.m.* pilot; (*auto.*) driver. —*a.* pilot. **~er** *v.t.* (*aviat., naut.*) pilot; (*auto.*) drive; (*fig.*) guide.

pilule /pilyl/ *n.f.* pill. **la ~**, the pill.

piment /pimɑ̃/ *n.m.* pepper, pimento; (*fig.*) spice. **~é** /-te/ *a.* spicy.

pimpant, ~e /pɛ̃pɑ̃, -t/ *a.* spruce.

pin /pɛ̃/ *n.m.* pine.

pinard /pinar/ *n.m.* (*vin*: *fam.*) plonk, cheap wine.

pince /pɛ̃s/ *n.f.* (*outil*) pliers; (*levier*) crowbar; (*de crabe*) pincer; (*à sucre*) tongs. **~ (à épiler)**, tweezers. **~ (à linge)**, (clothes-)peg.

pinceau (*pl.* **~x**) /pɛ̃so/ *n.m.* paintbrush.

pinc|er /pɛ̃se/ *v.t.* pinch; (*arrêter*: *fam.*) pinch. **se ~er le doigt**, catch one's finger. **~é** *a.* (*ton*, *air*) stiff. **~ée** *n.f.* pinch (**de**, of).

pince-sans-rire /pɛ̃sɑ̃rir/ *a. invar.* po-faced. **c'est un ~**, he's po-faced.

pincettes /pɛ̃sɛt/ *n.f. pl.* (fire) tongs.

pinède /pined/ *n.f.* pine forest.

pingouin /pɛ̃gwɛ̃/ *n.m.* penguin.

ping-pong /piŋpɔ̃g/ *n.m.* table tennis, ping-pong.

pingre /pɛ̃gr/ *a.* miserly.

pinson /pɛ̃sɔ̃/ *n.m.* chaffinch.

pintade /pɛ̃tad/ *n.f.* guinea-fowl.

pioch|e /pjɔʃ/ *n.f.* pick(axe). **~er** *v.t./i.* dig; (*étudier*: *fam.*) study hard, slog away (at).

pion /pjɔ̃/ *n.m.* (*de jeu*) piece; (*échecs*) pawn; (*scol.*, *fam.*) supervisor.

pionnier /pjɔnje/ *n.m.* pioneer.

pipe /pip/ *n.f.* pipe. **fumer la ~**, smoke a pipe.

pipe-line /piplin/ *n.m.* pipeline.

piquant, ~e /pikɑ̃, -t/ *a.* (*barbe etc.*) prickly; (*goût*) pungent; (*détail etc.*) spicy. **—n.m.** (*de plante*) prickle; (*de hérisson*) spine, prickle; (*fig.*) piquancy.

pique /pik/ *n.f.* (*arme*) pike.

pique /pik/ *n.m.* (*cartes*) spades.

pique-niqu|e /piknik/ *n.m.* picnic. **~er** *v.i.* picnic.

piquer /pike/ *v.t.* prick; (*langue*) burn, sting; (*abeille etc.*) sting; (*serpent etc.*) bite; (*enfoncer*) stick; (*coudre*) (machine-)stitch; (*curiosité*) excite; (*crise*) have; (*voler*: *fam.*) pinch. **—v.i.** (*avion*) dive; (*goût*) be hot. **~ une tête**, plunge headlong. **se ~ de**, pride o.s. on.

piquet /pike/ *n.m.* stake; (*de tente*) peg. **au ~**, (*scol.*) in the corner. **~ de grève**, (strike) picket.

piqûre /pikyr/ *n.f.* prick; (*d'abeille etc.*) sting; (*de serpent etc.*) bite; (*point*) stitch; (*méd.*) injection, shot (*Amer.*) **faire une ~ à qn.**, give s.o. an injection.

pirate /pirat/ *n.m.* pirate. **~ de l'air**, hijacker. **~rie** *n.f.* piracy.

pire /pir/ *a.* worse (**que**, than). **le ~ livre/**etc., the worst book/etc. **—n.m. le ~**, the worst (thing). **au ~**, at worst.

pirogue /pirɔg/ *n.f.* canoe, dug-out.

pirouette /pirwɛt/ *n.f.* pirouette.

pis /pi/ *n.m.* (*de vache*) udder.

pis /pi/ *a. invar. & adv.* worse. **aller de mal en ~**, go from bad to worse.

pis-aller /pizale/ *n.m. invar.* stopgap, temporary expedient.

piscine /pisin/ *n.f.* swimming-pool. **~ couverte**, indoor swimming-pool.

pissenlit /pisɑ̃li/ *n.m.* dandelion.

pistache /pistaʃ/ *n.f.* pistachio.

piste /pist/ *n.f.* track; (*de personne, d'animal*) track, trail; (*aviat.*) runway; (*de cirque*) ring; (*de ski*) run; (*de patinage*) rink; (*de danse*) floor; (*sport*) race-track. **~ cyclable**, cycle-track; (*Amer.*) bicycle path.

pistolet /pistɔlɛ/ *n.m.* gun, pistol; (*de peintre*) spray-gun.

piston /pistɔ̃/ *n.m.* (*techn.*) piston. **il a un ~**, (*fam.*) somebody is pulling strings for him.

pistonner /pistɔne/ *v.t.* (*fam.*) recommend, pull strings for.

piteu|x, ~se /pitø, -z/ *a.* pitiful.

pitié /pitje/ *n.f.* pity. **il me fait ~, j'ai ~ de lui**, I pity him.

piton /pitɔ̃/ *n.m.* (*à crochet*) hook; (*sommet pointu*) peak.

pitoyable /pitwajabl/ *a.* pitiful.

pitre /pitr/ *n.m.* clown. **faire le ~**, clown around.

pittoresque /pitɔrɛsk/ *a.* picturesque.

pivot /pivo/ *n.m.* pivot. **~er** /-ɔte/ *v.i.* revolve; (*personne*) swing round.

pizza /pidza/ *n.f.* pizza.

placage /plakaʒ/ *n.m.* (*en bois*) veneer; (*sur un mur*) facing.

placard /plakar/ *n.m.* cupboard; (*affiche*) poster. **~er** /-de/ *v.t.* (*affiche*) post up; (*mur*) cover with posters.

place /plas/ *n.f.* place; (*espace libre*) room, space; (*siège*) seat, place; (*prix d'un trajet*) fare; (*esplanade*) square; (*emploi*) position; (*de parking*) space. **à la ~ de**, instead of. **en ~, à sa ~**, in its place. **faire ~ à**, give way to. **sur ~**, on the spot. **remettre qn. à sa ~**, put s.o. in his place. **ça prend de la ~**, it takes up a lot of room. **se mettre à la ~ de qn.** put oneself in s.o.'s shoes *ou* place.

placebo /plasebo/ *n.m.* placebo.

placenta /plasɛ̃ta/ *n.m.* placenta.

plac|er /plase/ *v.t.* place; (*invité, spectateur*) seat; (*argent*) invest. **se ~er** *v. pr.* (*personne*) take up a position; (*troisième etc.: sport*) come (in); (*à un endroit*) to go and stand (**à**, in). **～é** *a.* (*sport*) placed. **bien ～é pour,** in a position to. **～ement** *n.m.* (*d'argent*) investment.

placide /plasid/ *a.* placid.

plafond /plafɔ̃/ *n.m.* ceiling.

plage /plaʒ/ *n.f.* beach; (*station*) (seaside) resort; (*aire*) area.

plagiat /plaʒja/ *n.m.* plagiarism.

plaid /plɛd/ *n.m.* travelling-rug.

plaider /plede/ *v.t./i.* plead.

plaid|oirie /plɛdwari/ *n.f.* (*defence*) speech. **～oyer** *n.m.* plea.

plaie /plɛ/ *n.f.* wound; (*personne: fam.*) nuisance.

plaignant, ～e /plɛɲɑ̃, -t/ *n.m., f.* plaintiff.

plaindre† /plɛ̃dr/ *v.t.* pity. **se ～** *v. pr.* complain (**de,** about). **se ～ de,** (*souffrir de*) complain of.

plaine /plɛn/ *n.f.* plain.

plaint|e /plɛ̃t/ *n.f.* complaint; (*gémissement*) groan. **～if, ～ive** *a.* plaintive.

plaire† /plɛr/ *v.i.* **～ à,** please. **ça lui plaît,** he likes it. **elle lui plaît,** he likes her. **ça me plaît de faire,** I like *ou* enjoy doing. **s'il vous plaît,** please. **se ～** *v. pr.* (*à Londres etc.*) like *ou* enjoy it.

plaisance /plɛzɑ̃s/ *n.f.* **la (navigation de) ～,** yachting.

plaisant, ～e /plɛzɑ̃, -t/ *a.* pleasant; (*drôle*) amusing.

plaisant|er /plɛzɑ̃te/ *v.i.* joke. **～erie** *n.f.* joke. **～in** *n.m.* joker.

plaisir /plezir/ *n.m.* pleasure. **faire ～ à,** please. **pour le ～,** for fun *ou* pleasure.

plan¹ /plɑ̃/ *n.m.* plan; (*de ville*) map; (*surface, niveau*) plane. **～ d'eau,** expanse of water. **premier ～,** foreground. **dernier ～,** background.

plan², ～e /plɑ̃, -an/ *a.* flat.

planche /plɑ̃ʃ/ *n.f.* board, plank; (*gravure*) plate; (*de potager*) bed. **～ à repasser,** ironing-board. **～ à voile,** sailboard; (*sport*) windsurfing.

plancher /plɑ̃ʃe/ *n.m.* floor.

plancton /plɑ̃ktɔ̃/ *n.m.* plankton.

plan|er /plane/ *v.i.* glide. **～ sur,** (*mystère, danger*) hang over. **～eur** *n.m.* (*avion*) glider.

planète /planɛt/ *n.f.* planet.

planif|ier /planifje/ *v.t.* plan. **～ication** *n.f.* planning.

planqu|e /plɑ̃k/ *n.f.* (*fam.*) hideout; (*emploi: fam.*) cushy job. **～er** *v.t.,* **se ～er** *v. pr.* hide.

plant /plɑ̃/ *n.m.* seedling; (*de légumes*) bed.

plante /plɑ̃t/ *n.f.* plant. **～ des pieds,** sole (of the foot).

plant|er /plɑ̃te/ *v.t.* (*plante etc.*) plant; (*enfoncer*) drive in; (*installer*) put up; (*mettre*) put. **rester ～é,** stand still, remain standing. **～ation** *n.f.* planting; (*de tabac etc.*) plantation.

plantureu|x, ～se /plɑ̃tyrø, -z/ *a.* abundant; (*femme*) buxom.

plaque /plak/ *n.f.* plate; (*de marbre*) slab; (*insigne*) badge; (*commémorative*) plaque. **～ chauffante,** hotplate. **～ minéralogique,** number-plate.

plaqu|er /plake/ *v.t.* (*bois*) veneer; (*aplatir*) flatten; (*rugby*) tackle; (*abandonner: fam.*) ditch. **～er qch. sur** *ou* **contre,** make sth. stick to. **～age** *n.m.* (*rugby*) tackle.

plasma /plasma/ *n.m.* plasma.

plastic /plastik/ *n.m.* plastic explosive.

plastique /plastik/ *a. & n.m.* plastic. **en ～,** plastic.

plastiquer /plastike/ *v.t.* blow up.

plat¹, ～e /pla, -t/ *a.* flat. **—n.m.** (*de la main*) flat. **à ～** *adv.* (*poser*) flat; *a.* (*batterie, pneu*) flat. **à ～ ventre,** flat on one's face.

plat² /pla/ *n.m.* (*culin.*) dish; (*partie de repas*) course.

platane /platan/ *n.m.* plane(-tree).

plateau (*pl. ～x*) /plato/ *n.m.* tray; (*d'électrophone*) turntable, deck; (*de balance*) pan; (*géog.*) plateau. **～ de fromages,** cheeseboard.

plateau-repas (*pl. plateaux-repas*) *n.m.* tray meal.

plate-bande (*pl. plates-bandes*) /platbɑ̃d/ *n.f.* flower-bed.

plate-forme (*pl. plates-formes*) /platfɔrm/ *n.f.* platform.

platine¹ /platin/ *n.m.* platinum.

platine² /platin/ *n.f.* (*de tourne-disque*) turntable.

platitude /platityd/ *n.f.* platitude.

platonique /platonik/ *a.* platonic.

plâtr|e /plɑtr/ *n.m.* plaster; (*méd.*) (plaster) cast. **～er** *v.t.* plaster; (*membre*) put in plaster.

plausible /plozibl/ *a.* plausible.

plébiscite /plebisit/ *n.m.* plebiscite.

plein, ～e /plɛ̃, plɛn/ *a.* full (**de,** of); (*total*) complete. **—n.m.** **faire le ～ (d'essence),** fill up (the tank). **à ～,** to the full. **à ～ temps,** full-time. **en ～ air,** in the open air. **en ～ milieu/visage,** right in the middle/the face. **en ～e nuit**/*etc.,* in the middle of the night/*etc.* **～ les mains,** all over one's hands.

pleinement /plɛnmɑ̃/ *adv.* fully.

pléthore /pletɔr/ *n.f.* over-abundance, plethora.

pleurer /plœre/ *v.i.* cry, weep (**sur,** over); (*yeux*) water. —*v.t.* mourn.

pleurésie /plœrezi/ *n.f.* pleurisy.

pleurnicher /plœrniʃe/ *v.i.* (*fam.*) snivel.

pleurs (en) /(ɑ̃)plœr/ *adv.* in tears.

pleuvoir† /pløvwar/ *v.i.* rain; (*fig.*) rain *ou* shower down. **il pleut,** it is raining. **il pleut à verse** *ou* **à torrents,** it is pouring.

pli /pli/ *n.m.* fold; (*de jupe*) pleat; (*de pantalon*) crease; (*enveloppe*) cover; (*habitude*) habit. (**faux**) **∼,** crease.

pliant, ∼e /plijɑ̃, -t/ *a.* folding; (*parapluie*) telescopic. —*n.m.* folding stool, camp-stool.

plier /plije/ *v.t.* fold; (*courber*) bend; (*personne*) submit (**à,** to). —*v.i.* bend; (*personne*) submit. **se ∼** *v. pr.* fold. **se ∼ à,** submit to.

plinthe /plɛ̃t/ *n.f.* skirting-board; (*Amer.*) baseboard.

plisser /plise/ *v.t.* crease; (*yeux*) screw up; (*jupe*) pleat.

plomb /plɔ̃/ *n.m.* lead; (*fusible*) fuse. **∼s,** (*de chasse*) lead shot. **de** *ou* **en ∼,** lead. **de ∼,** (*ciel*) leaden.

plomb|er /plɔ̃be/ *v.t.* (*dent*) fill. **∼age** *n.m.* filling.

plomb|ier /plɔ̃bje/ *n.m.* plumber. **∼erie** *n.f.* plumbing.

plongeant, ∼e /plɔ̃ʒɑ̃, -t/ *a.* (*vue*) from above; (*décolleté*) plunging.

plongeoir /plɔ̃ʒwar/ *n.m.* diving-board.

plongeon /plɔ̃ʒɔ̃/ *n.m.* dive.

plong|er /plɔ̃ʒe/ *v.i.* dive; (*route*) plunge. —*v.t.* plunge. **se ∼er** *v. pr.* plunge (**dans,** into). **∼é dans,** (*lecture*) immersed in. **∼ée** *n.f.* diving. **en ∼ée** (*sous-marin*) submerged. **∼eur, ∼euse** *n.m.,* *f.* diver; (*employé*) dishwasher.

plouf /pluf/ *n.m.* & *int.* splash.

ployer /plwaje/ *v.t./i.* bend.

plu /ply/ *voir* **plaire, pleuvoir.**

pluie /plɥi/ *n.f.* rain; (*averse*) shower. **∼ battante/diluvienne,** driving/torrential rain.

plumage /plymaʒ/ *n.m.* plumage.

plume /plym/ *n.f.* feather; (*stylo*) pen; (*pointe*) nib.

plumeau (*pl.* **∼x**) /plymo/ *n.m.* feather duster.

plumer /plyme/ *v.t.* pluck.

plumier /plymje/ *n.m.* pencil box.

plupart /plypar/ *n.f.* most. **la ∼ des,** (*gens, cas, etc.*) most. **la ∼ du temps,** most of the time. **pour la ∼,** for the most part.

pluriel, ∼le /plyrjɛl/ *a.* & *n.m.* plural. **au ∼,** (*nom*) plural.

plus[1] /ply/ *adv. de négation.* (**ne**) **∼,** (*temps*) no longer, not any more. (**ne**) **∼ de,** (*quantité*) no more. **je n'y vais ∼,** I do not go there any longer *ou* any more. (**il n'y a**) **∼ de pain,** (there is) no more bread.

plus[2] /ply/ (/plyz/ *before vowel,* /plys/ *in final position*) *adv.* more (**que,** than). **∼ âgé/tard/***etc.*, older/later/*etc.* **∼ beau/** *etc.*, more beautiful/*etc.* **le ∼,** the most. **le ∼ beau/***etc.*, the most beautiful; (*de deux*) the more beautiful. **le ∼ de,** (*gens etc.*) most. **∼ de,** (*pain etc.*) more; (*dix jours etc.*) more than. **il est ∼ de huit heures/***etc.* it is after eight/*etc.* o'clock. **de ∼,** more (**que,** than); (*en outre*) moreover. (**âgés**) **de ∼ de** (*huit ans etc.*) over, more than. **de ∼ en plus,** more and more. **en ∼,** extra. **en ∼ de,** in addition to. **∼ ou moins,** more or less.

plus[3] /plys/ *conj.* plus.

plusieurs /plyzjœr/ *a.* & *pron.* several.

plus-value /plyvaly/ *n.f.* (*bénéfice*) profit.

plutôt /plyto/ *adv.* rather (**que,** than).

pluvieu|x, ∼se /plyvjø, -z/ *a.* rainy.

pneu (*pl.* **∼s**) /pnø/ *n.m.* tyre; (*lettre*) express letter. **∼matique** *a.* inflatable.

pneumonie /pnømɔni/ *n.f.* pneumonia.

poche /pɔʃ/ *n.f.* pocket; (*sac*) bag. **∼s,** (*sous les yeux*) bags.

pocher /pɔʃe/ *v.t.* (*œuf*) poach.

pochette /pɔʃɛt/ *n.f.* pack(et), envelope; (*sac*) bag, pouch; (*d'allumettes*) book; (*de disque*) sleeve; (*mouchoir*) pocket handkerchief. **∼ surprise,** lucky bag.

podium /pɔdjɔm/ *n.m.* rostrum.

poêle[1] /pwal/ *n.f.* **∼ (à frire),** frying-pan.

poêle[2] /pwal/ *n.m.* stove.

poème /pɔɛm/ *n.m.* poem.

poésie /pɔezi/ *n.f.* poetry; (*poème*) poem.

poète /pɔɛt/ *n.m.* poet.

poétique /pɔetik/ *a.* poetic.

poids /pwa/ *n.m.* weight. **∼ coq/ lourd/plume,** bantamweight/heavy-weight/featherweight. **∼ lourd,** (*camion*) lorry, juggernaut; (*Amer.*) truck.

poignant, ∼e /pwaɲɑ̃, -t/ *a.* poignant.

poignard /pwaɲar/ *n.m.* dagger. **∼er** /-de/ *v.t.* stab.

poigne /pwaɲ/ *n.f.* grip. **avoir de la ∼,** have an iron fist.

poignée /pwaɲe/ *n.f.* handle; (*quantité*) handful. **~ de main**, handshake.

poignet /pwaɲɛ/ *n.m.* wrist; (*de chemise*) cuff.

poil /pwal/ *n.m.* hair; (*pelage*) fur; (*de brosse*) bristle. **~s,** (*de tapis*) pile. **à ~,** (*fam.*) naked. **~u** *a.* hairy.

poinçon /pwɛ̃sɔ̃/ *n.m.* awl; (*marque*) hallmark. **~ner** /-ɔne/ *v.t.* (*billet*) punch. **~neuse** /-ɔnøz/ *n.f.* punch.

poing /pwɛ̃/ *n.m.* fist.

point[1] /pwɛ̃/ *n.m.* point; (*note: scol.*) mark; (*tache*) spot, dot; (*de couture*) stitch. **~ (final),** full stop, period. **à ~,** (*culin.*) medium; (*arriver*) at the right time. **faire le ~,** take stock. **mettre au ~,** (*photo.*) focus; (*technique*) perfect; (*fig.*) clear up. **deux ~s,** colon. **~ culminant,** peak. **~ de repère,** landmark. **~s de suspension,** suspension points. **~ de suture,** (*méd.*) stitch. **~ de vente,** retail outlet. **~ de vue,** point of view. **~ d'interrogation/ d'exclamation,** question/exclamation-mark. **~ du jour,** daybreak. **~ mort,** (*auto.*) neutral. **~ virgule,** semicolon. **sur le ~ de,** about to.

point[2] /pwɛ̃/ *adv.* (**ne**) **~,** not.

pointe /pwɛ̃t/ *n.f.* point, tip; (*clou*) tack; (*de grille*) spike; (*fig.*) touch (**de,** of). **de ~,** (*industrie*) highly advanced. **en ~,** pointed. **heure de ~,** peak hour. **sur la ~ des pieds,** on tiptoe.

pointer[1] /pwɛte/ *v.t.* (*cocher*) tick off. **—v.i.** (*employé*) clock in *ou* out. **se ~** *v. pr.* (*fam.*) turn up.

pointer[2] /pwɛte/ *v.t.* (*diriger*) point, aim.

pointillé /pwɛ̃tije/ *n.m.* dotted line. **—a.** dotted.

pointilleu|x, **~se** /pwɛ̃tijø, -z/ *a.* fastidious, particular.

pointu /pwɛ̃ty/ *a.* pointed; (*aiguisé*) sharp.

pointure /pwɛ̃tyr/ *n.f.* size.

poire /pwar/ *n.f.* pear.

poireau (*pl.* **~x**) /pwaro/ *n.m.* leek.

poireauter /pwarote/ *v.i.* (*fam.*) hang about.

poirier /pwarje/ *n.m.* pear-tree.

pois /pwa/ *n.m.* pea; (*dessin*) dot.

poison /pwazɔ̃/ *n.m.* poison.

poisseu|x, **~se** /pwasø, -z/ *a.* sticky.

poisson /pwasɔ̃/ *n.m.* fish. **~ rouge,** goldfish. **~ d'avril,** April fool. **les P~s,** Pisces.

poissonn|ier, **~ière** /pwasɔnje, -jɛr/ *n.m., f.* fishmonger. **~erie** *n.f.* fish shop.

poitrail /pwatraj/ *n.m.* breast.

poitrine /pwatrin/ *n.f.* chest; (*seins*) bosom; (*culin.*) breast.

poivr|e /pwavr/ *n.m.* pepper. **~é** *a.* peppery. **~ière** *n.f.* pepper-pot.

poivron /pwavrɔ̃/ *n.m.* pepper, capsicum.

poivrot, **~e** /pwavro, -ɔt/ *n.m., f.* (*fam.*) drunkard.

poker /pɔkɛr/ *n.m.* poker.

polaire /pɔlɛr/ *a.* polar.

polariser /pɔlarize/ *v.t.* polarize.

polaroïd /pɔlarɔid/ *n.m.* (P.) Polaroid (P.).

pôle /pol/ *n.m.* pole.

polémique /pɔlemik/ *n.f.* argument. **—a.** controversial.

poli /pɔli/ *a.* (*personne*) polite. **~ment** *adv.* politely.

polic|e[1] /pɔlis/ *n.f.* police; (*discipline*) (law and) order. **~ier,** **~ière** *a.* police; (*roman*) detective; *n.m.* policeman.

police[2] /pɔlis/ *n.f.* (*d'assurance*) policy.

polio(myélite) /pɔljɔ(mjelit)/ *n.f.* polio(myelitis).

polir /pɔlir/ *v.t.* polish.

polisson, **~ne** /pɔlisɔ̃, -ɔn/ *a.* naughty. **—n.m., f.** rascal.

politesse /pɔlitɛs/ *n.f.* politeness; (*parole*) polite remark.

politicien, **~ne** /pɔlitisjɛ̃, -jɛn/ *n.m., f.* (*péj.*) politician.

politi|que /pɔlitik/ *a.* political. **—n.f.** politics; (*ligne de conduite*) policy. **~ser** *v.t.* politicize.

pollen /pɔlɛn/ *n.m.* pollen.

polluant, **~e** /pɔlyɑ̃, -t/ *a.* polluting. **—n.m.** pollutant.

poll|uer /pɔlɥe/ *v.t.* pollute. **~ution** *n.f.* pollution.

polo /pɔlo/ *n.m.* polo; (*vêtement*) sports shirt, tennis shirt.

Pologne /pɔlɔɲ/ *n.f.* Poland.

polonais, **~e** /pɔlɔnɛ, -z/ *a.* Polish. **—n.m., f.** Pole. **—n.m.** (*lang.*) Polish.

poltron, **~ne** /pɔltrɔ̃, -ɔn/ *a.* cowardly. **—n.m., f.** coward.

polycopier /pɔlikɔpje/ *v.t.* duplicate, stencil.

polygamie /pɔligami/ *n.f.* polygamy.

polyglotte /pɔliglɔt/ *n.m./f.* polyglot.

polyvalent, **~e** /pɔlivalɑ̃, -t/ *a.* varied; (*personne*) versatile.

pommade /pɔmad/ *n.f.* ointment.

pomme /pɔm/ *n.f.* apple; (*d'arrosoir*) rose. **~ d'Adam,** Adam's apple. **~ de pin,** pine cone. **~ de terre,** potato. **~s frites,** chips; (*Amer.*) French fries. **tomber dans les ~s,** (*fam.*) pass out.

pommeau (*pl.* ⁓x) /pɔmo/ *n.m.* (*de canne*) knob.

pommette /pɔmɛt/ *n.f.* cheek-bone.

pommier /pɔmje/ *n.m.* apple-tree.

pompe /pɔ̃p/ *n.f.* pump; (*splendeur*) pomp. ⁓ **à incendie**, fire-engine. ⁓s **funèbres**, undertaker's.

pomper /pɔ̃pe/ *v.t.* pump; (*copier: fam.*) copy, crib. ⁓ **l'air à qn.**, (*fam.*) get on s.o.'s nerves.

pompeu|x, ⁓**se** /pɔ̃pø, -z/ *a.* pompous.

pompier /pɔ̃pje/ *n.m.* fireman.

pompiste /pɔ̃pist/ *n.m./f.* petrol pump attendant; (*Amer.*) gas station attendant.

pompon /pɔ̃pɔ̃/ *n.m.* pompon.

pomponner /pɔ̃pɔne/ *v.t.* deck out.

poncer /pɔ̃se/ *v.t.* rub down.

ponctuation /pɔ̃ktɥasjɔ̃/ *n.f.* punctuation.

ponct|uel, ⁓**uelle** /pɔ̃ktɥɛl/ *a.* punctual. ⁓**ualité** *f.* punctuality.

ponctuer /pɔ̃ktɥe/ *v.t.* punctuate.

pondéré /pɔ̃dere/ *a.* level-headed.

pondre /pɔ̃dr/ *v.t./i.* lay.

poney /pɔnɛ/ *n.m.* pony.

pont /pɔ̃/ *n.m.* bridge; (*de navire*) deck; (*de graissage*) ramp. **faire le** ⁓, take the extra day(s) off (*between holidays*). ⁓ **aérien**, airlift. ⁓**levis** (*pl.* ⁓**s-levis**) *n.m.* drawbridge.

ponte /pɔ̃t/ *n.f.* laying (of eggs).

pontife /pɔ̃tif/ *n.m.* (**souverain**) ⁓, pope.

pontific|al (*m. pl.* ⁓**aux**) /pɔ̃tifikal, -o/ *a.* papal.

pop /pɔp/ *n.m. & a. invar.* (*mus.*) pop.

popote /pɔpɔt/ *n.f.* (*fam.*) cooking.

populace /pɔpylas/ *n.f.* (*péj.*) rabble.

popul|aire /pɔpylɛr/ *a.* popular; (*expression*) colloquial; (*quartier*, *origine*) working-class. ⁓**arité** *n.f.* popularity.

population /pɔpylasjɔ̃/ *n.f.* population.

populeu|x, ⁓**se** /pɔpylø, -z/ *a.* populous.

porc /pɔr/ *n.m.* pig; (*viande*) pork.

porcelaine /pɔrsəlɛn/ *n.f.* china, porcelain.

porc-épic (*pl.* **porcs-épics**) /pɔrkepik/ *n.m.* porcupine.

porche /pɔrʃ/ *n.m.* porch.

porcherie /pɔrʃəri/ *n.f.* pigsty.

por|e /pɔr/ *n.m.* pore. ⁓**eux**, ⁓**euse** *a.* porous.

pornograph|ie /pɔrnɔgrafi/ *n.f.* pornography. ⁓**ique** *a.* pornographic.

port[1] /pɔr/ *n.m.* port, harbour. **à bon** ⁓, safely. ⁓ **maritime**, seaport.

port[2] /pɔr/ *n.m.* (*transport*) carriage; (*d'armes*) carrying; (*de barbe*) wearing.

portail /pɔrtaj/ *n.m.* portal.

portant, ⁓**e** /pɔrtɑ̃, -t/ *a.* **bien/mal** ⁓, in good/bad health.

portati|f, ⁓**ve** /pɔrtatif, -v/ *a.* portable.

porte /pɔrt/ *n.f.* door; (*passage*) doorway; (*de jardin, d'embarquement*) gate. **mettre à la** ⁓, throw out. ⁓ **d'entrée**, front door. ⁓**-fenêtre** (*pl.* ⁓**s-fenêtres**) *n.f.* French window.

porté /pɔrte/ *a.* ⁓ **à**, inclined to. ⁓ **sur**, fond of.

portée /pɔrte/ *n.f.* (*d'une arme*) range; (*de voûte*) span; (*d'animaux*) litter; (*impact*) significance; (*mus.*) stave. **à** ⁓ **de**, within reach of. **à** ⁓ **de (la) main**, within (arm's) reach. **hors de** ⁓ **(de)**, out of reach (of). **à la** ⁓ **de qn.** at s.o.'s level.

portefeuille /pɔrtəfœj/ *n.m.* wallet; (*de ministre*) portfolio.

portemanteau (*pl.* ⁓x) /pɔrtmɑ̃to/ *n.m.* coat *ou* hat stand.

port|er /pɔrte/ *v.t.* carry; (*vêtement*, *bague*) wear; (*fruits*, *responsabilité*, *nom*) bear; (*coup*) strike; (*amener*) bring; (*inscrire*) enter. —*v.i.* (*bruit*) carry; (*coup*) hit home. ⁓**er sur**, rest on; (*concerner*) bear on. **se** ⁓**er bien**, be *ou* feel well. **se** ⁓**er candidat**, stand as a candidate. ⁓**er aux nues**, praise to the skies. ⁓**e-avions** *n.m. invar.* aircraft-carrier. ⁓**e-bagages** *n.m. invar.* luggage rack. ⁓**e-bonheur** *n.m. invar.* (*objet*) charm. ⁓**e-clefs** *n.m. invar.* key-ring. ⁓**e-documents** *n.m. invar.* attaché case, document wallet. ⁓**e-monnaie** *n.m. invar.* purse. ⁓**e-parole** *n.m. invar.* spokesman. ⁓**e-voix** *n.m. invar.* megaphone.

porteu|r, ⁓**se** /pɔrtœr, -øz/ *n.m.*, *f.* (*de nouvelles*) bearer; (*méd.*) carrier. —*n.m.* (*rail.*) porter.

portier /pɔrtje/ *n.m.* door-man.

portière /pɔrtjɛr/ *n.f.* door.

portillon /pɔrtijɔ̃/ *n.m.* gate.

portion /pɔrsjɔ̃/ *n.f.* portion.

portique /pɔrtik/ *n.m.* portico; (*sport*) crossbar.

porto /pɔrto/ *n.m.* port (wine).

portrait /pɔrtrɛ/ *n.m.* portrait. ⁓**-robot** (*pl.* ⁓**s-robots**) *n.m.* identikit, photofit.

portuaire /pɔrtɥer/ *a.* port.

portugais, ⁓**e** /pɔrtygɛ, -z/ *a. & n.m.*, *f.* Portuguese. —*n.m.* (*lang.*) Portuguese.

Portugal /pɔrtygal/ *n.m.* Portugal.

pose /poz/ *n.f.* installation; (*attitude*) pose; (*photo.*) exposure.

posé /poze/ *a.* calm, serious.

poser /poze/ *v.t.* put (down); (*installer*) install, put in; (*fondations*) lay; (*question*) ask; (*problème*) pose. —*v.i.* (*modèle*) pose. **se** ~ *v. pr.* (*avion, oiseau*) land; (*regard*) alight; (*se présenter*) arise. ~ **sa candidature,** apply (à, for).

positi|f, ~**ve** /pozitif, -v/ *a.* positive.

position /pozisjɔ̃/ *n.f.* position; (*banque*) balance (of account). **prendre** ~, take a stand.

posologie /pozɔlɔʒi/ *n.f.* directions for use.

poss|éder /posede/ *v.t.* possess; (*propriété*) own, possess. ~**esseur** *n.m.* possessor; owner.

possessi|f, ~**ve** /posesif, -v/ *a.* possessive.

possession /posesjɔ̃/ *n.f.* possession. **prendre** ~ **de,** take possession of.

possibilité /posibilite/ *n.f.* possibility.

possible /posibl/ *a.* possible. —*n.m.* **le** ~, what is possible. **dès que** ~, as soon as possible. **faire son** ~, do one's utmost. **le plus tard/etc.** ~, as late/etc. as possible. **pas** ~, impossible; (*int.*) really!

post- /post/ *préf.* post-.

post|al (*m. pl.* ~**aux**) /postal, -o/ *a.* postal.

poste¹ /post/ *n.f.* (*service*) post; (*bureau*) post office. ~ **aérienne,** airmail. **mettre à la** ~, post. ~ **restante,** poste restante.

poste² /post/ *n.m.* (*lieu, emploi*) post; (*de radio, télévision*) set; (*téléphone*) extension (number). ~ **d'essence,** petrol *ou* gas (*Amer.*) station. ~ **d'incendie,** fire point. ~ **de pilotage,** cockpit. ~ **de police,** police station. ~ **de secours,** first-aid post.

poster¹ /poste/ *v.t.* (*lettre, personne*) post.

poster² /postɛr/ *n.m.* poster.

postérieur /posterjœr/ *a.* later; (*partie*) back. ~ **à,** after. —*n.m.* (*fam.*) posterior.

postérité /posterite/ *n.f.* posterity.

posthume /postym/ *a.* posthumous.

postiche /postiʃ/ *a.* false.

post|ier, ~**ière** /postje, -jɛr/ *n.m., f.* postal worker.

post-scriptum /postskriptɔm/ *n.m. invar.* postscript.

postul|er /postyle/ *v.t./i.* apply (à *ou* **pour,** for); (*principe*) postulate. ~**ant,** ~**ante** *n.m., f.* applicant.

posture /postyr/ *n.f.* posture.

pot /po/ *n.m.* pot; (*en carton*) carton; (*en verre*) jar; (*chance: fam.*) luck; (*boisson: fam.*) drink. ~**-au-feu** /potofø/ *n.m. invar.* (*plat*) stew. ~ **d'échappement,** exhaust-pipe. ~**-de-vin** (*pl.* ~**s-de-vin**) *n.m.* bribe. ~**-pourri,** (*pl.* ~**s-pourris**) *n.m.* pot pourri.

potable /potabl/ *a.* drinkable. **eau** ~, drinking water.

potage /potaʒ/ *n.m.* soup.

potag|er, ~**ère** /potaʒe, -ɛr/ *a.* vegetable. —*n.m.* vegetable garden.

pote /pot/ *n.m.* (*fam.*) chum.

poteau (*pl.* ~**x**) /poto/ *n.m.* post; (*télégraphique*) pole. ~ **indicateur,** signpost.

potelé /potle/ *a.* plump.

potence /potãs/ *n.f.* gallows.

potentiel, ~**le** /potãsjɛl/ *a. & n.m.* potential.

pot|erie /potri/ *n.f.* pottery; (*objet*) piece of pottery. ~**ier** *n.m.* potter.

potins /potɛ̃/ *n.m. pl.* gossip.

potion /posjɔ̃/ *n.f.* potion.

potiron /potirɔ̃/ *n.m.* pumpkin.

pou (*pl.* ~**x**) /pu/ *n.m.* louse.

poubelle /pubɛl/ *n.f.* dustbin; (*Amer.*) garbage can.

pouce /pus/ *n.m.* thumb; (*de pied*) big toe; (*mesure*) inch.

poudr|e /pudr/ *n.f.* powder. ~**e** (à canon), gunpowder. **en** ~**e,** (*lait*) powdered; (*chocolat*) drinking. ~**er** *v.t.* powder. ~**eux,** ~**euse** *a.* powdery.

poudrier /pudrije/ *n.m.* (powder) compact.

poudrière /pudrijɛr/ *n.f.* (*région: fig.*) powder-keg.

pouf /puf/ *n.m.* pouffe.

pouffer /pufe/ *v.i.* guffaw.

pouilleu|x, ~**se** /pujø, -z/ *a.* filthy.

poulailler /pulaje/ *n.m.* (hen-)coop.

poulain /pulɛ̃/ *n.m.* foal; (*protégé*) protégé.

poule /pul/ *n.f.* hen; (*culin.*) fowl; (*femme: fam.*) tart; (*rugby*) group.

poulet /pulɛ/ *n.m.* chicken.

pouliche /puliʃ/ *n.f.* filly.

poulie /puli/ *n.f.* pulley.

pouls /pu/ *n.m.* pulse.

poumon /pumɔ̃/ *n.m.* lung.

poupe /pup/ *n.f.* stern.

poupée /pupe/ *n.f.* doll.

poupon /pupɔ̃/ *n.m.* baby. ~**nière** /-ɔnjɛr/ *n.f.* crèche, day nursery.

pour /pur/ *prép.* for; (*envers*) to; (à la

place de) on behalf of; (*comme*) as. ~ **cela,** for that reason. ~ **cent,** per cent. ~ **de bon,** for good. ~ **faire,** (in order) to do. ~ **que,** so that. ~ **moi,** as for me. ~ **petit**/*etc.* **qu'il soit,** however small/*etc.* he may be. **trop poli**/*etc.* ~, too polite/*etc.* to. **le ~ et le contre,** the pros and cons. ~ **ce qui est de,** as for.

pourboire /purbwar/ *n.m.* tip.

pourcentage /pursɑ̃taʒ/ *n.m.* percentage.

pourchasser /purʃase/ *v.t.* pursue.

pourparlers /purparle/ *n.m. pl.* talks.

pourpre /purpr/ *a. & n.m.* crimson; (*violet*) purple.

pourquoi /purkwa/ *conj. & adv.* why. —*n.m. invar.* reason.

pourra, pourrait /pura, purɛ/ *voir* **pouvoir**[1].

pourr|ir /purir/ *v.t./i.* rot. ~**i** *a.* rotten. ~**iture** *n.f.* rot.

poursuite /pursɥit/ *n.f.* pursuit (**de,** of). ~**s,** (*jurid.*) legal action.

poursuiv|re† /pursɥivr/ *v.t.* pursue; (*continuer*) continue (with). ~**re (en justice),** (*au criminel*) prosecute; (*au civil*) sue. —*v.i.,* **se ~re** *v. pr.* continue. ~**ant,** ~**ante** *n.m., f.* pursuer.

pourtant /purtɑ̃/ *adv.* yet.

pourtour /purtur/ *n.m.* perimeter.

pourv|oir† /purvwar/ *v.t.* ~**oir de,** provide with. —*v.i.* ~**oir à,** provide for. ~**u de,** supplied with. —*v. pr.* **se** ~**oir de** (*argent*) provide o.s. with. ~**oyeur,** ~**oyeuse** *n.m., f.* supplier.

pourvu que /purvyk(ə)/ *conj.* (*condition*) provided (that); (*souhait*) let us hope (that). **pourvu qu'il ne soit rien arrivé,** I hope nothing's happened.

pousse /pus/ *n.f.* growth; (*bourgeon*) shoot.

poussé /puse/ *a.* (*études*) advanced.

poussée /puse/ *n.f.* pressure; (*coup*) push; (*de prix*) upsurge; (*méd.*) outbreak.

pousser /puse/ *v.t.* push; (*du coude*) nudge; (*cri*) let out; (*soupir*) heave; (*continuer*) continue; (*exhorter*) urge (**à,** to); (*forcer*) drive (**à,** to); (*amener*) bring (**à,** to). —*v.i.* push; (*grandir*) grow. **faire ~** (*cheveux*) let grow; (*plante*) grow. **se ~** *v. pr.* move over *ou* up.

poussette /pusɛt/ *n.f.* push-chair; (*Amer.*) (baby) stroller.

pouss|ière /pusjɛr/ *n.f.* dust. ~**iéreux,** ~**iéreuse** *a.* dusty.

poussi|f, ~**ve** /pusif, -v/ *a.* short-winded, wheezing.

poussin /pusɛ̃/ *n.m.* chick.

poutre /putr/ *n.f.* beam: (*en métal*) girder.

pouvoir[1]† /puvwar/ *v. aux.* (*possibilité*) can, be able; (*permission, éventualité*) may, can. **il peut/pouvait/pourrait venir,** he can/could/might come. **je n'ai pas pu,** I could not. **j'ai pu faire,** (*réussi à*) I managed to do. **je n'en peux plus,** I am exhausted. **il se peut que,** it may be that.

pouvoir[2] /puvwar/ *n.m.* power; (*gouvernement*) government. **au ~,** in power. ~**s publics,** authorities.

prairie /preri/ *n.f.* meadow.

praline /pralin/ *n.f.* sugared almond.

praticable /pratikabl/ *a.* practicable.

praticien, ~**ne** /pratisjɛ̃, -jɛn/ *n.m., f.* practitioner.

pratiquant, ~**e** /pratikɑ̃, -t/ *a.* practising. —*n.m., f.* churchgoer.

pratique /pratik/ *a.* practical. —*n.f.* practice; (*expérience*) experience. **la ~ du golf/du cheval,** golfing/riding. ~**ment** *adv.* in practice; (*presque*) practically.

pratiquer /pratike/ *v.t./i.* practise; (*sport*) play; (*faire*) make.

pré /pre/ *n.m.* meadow.

pré- /pre/ *préf.* pre-.

préalable /prealabl/ *a.* preliminary, prior. —*n.m.* precondition. **au ~,** first.

préambule /preɑ̃byl/ *n.m.* preamble.

préau (*pl.* ~**x**) /preo/ *n.m.* (*scol.*) playground shelter.

préavis /preavi/ *n.m.* (advance) notice.

précaire /prekɛr/ *a.* precarious.

précaution /prekosjɔ̃/ *n.f.* (*mesure*) precaution; (*prudence*) caution.

précéd|ent, ~**ente** /presedɑ̃, -t/ *a.* previous. —*n.m.* precedent. ~**emment** /-amɑ̃/ *adv.* previously.

précéder /presede/ *v.t./i.* precede.

précepte /presɛpt/ *n.m.* precept.

précep|teur, ~**trice** /preseptœr, -tris/ *n.m., f.* tutor.

prêcher /preʃe/ *v.t./i.* preach.

précieu|x, ~**se** /presjø, -z/ *a.* precious.

précipice /presipis/ *n.m.* abyss, chasm.

précipit|é /presipite/ *a.* hasty. ~**amment** *adv.* hastily. ~**ation** *n.f.* haste.

précipiter /presipite/ *v.t.* throw, precipitate; (*hâter*) hasten. **se ~** *v. pr.* rush (**sur,** at, on to); (*se jeter*) throw o.s; (*s'accélérer*) speed up.

précis, ~**e** /presi, -z/ *a.* precise; (*mécanisme*) accurate. —*n.m.* summary. **dix heures**/*etc.* ~**es,** ten o'clock/*etc.* sharp. ∼**ément** /-zemã/ *adv.* precisely.

préciser /presize/ *v.t./i.* specify; (*pensée*) be more specific about. **se** ∼ *v. pr.* become clear(er).

précision /presizjɔ̃/ *n.f.* precision; (*détail*) detail.

précoce /prekɔs/ *a.* early; (*enfant*) precocious. ∼**ité** *n.f.* earliness; precociousness.

préconçu /prekɔ̃sy/ *a.* preconceived.

préconiser /prekɔnize/ *v.t.* advocate.

précurseur /prekyrsœr/ *n.m.* forerunner.

prédécesseur /predesesœr/ *n.m.* predecessor.

prédicateur /predikatœr/ *n.m.* preacher.

prédilection /predilɛksjɔ̃/ *n.f.* preference.

préd|ire† /predir/ *v.t.* predict. ∼**iction** *n.f.* prediction.

prédisposer /predispoze/ *v.t.* predispose.

prédominant, ∼**e** /predɔminã, -t/ *a.* predominant.

prédominer /predɔmine/ *v.i.* predominate.

préfabriqué /prefabrike/ *a.* prefabricated.

préface /prefas/ *n.f.* preface.

préfecture /prefɛktyr/ *n.f.* prefecture. ∼ **de police,** police headquarters.

préférence /preferãs/ *n.f.* preference. **de** ∼, preferably. **de** ∼ **à,** in preference to.

préférentiel, ∼**le** /preferãsjɛl/ *a.* preferential.

préfér|er /prefere/ *v.t.* prefer (à, to). **je ne préfère pas,** I'd rather not. ∼**er faire,** prefer to do. ∼**able** *a.* preferable. ∼**é,** ∼**ée** *a. & n.m.,* f. favourite.

préfet /prefɛ/ *n.m.* prefect. ∼ **de police,** prefect *ou* chief of police.

préfixe /prefiks/ *n.m.* prefix.

préhistorique /preistɔrik/ *a.* prehistoric.

préjudic|e /preʒydis/ *n.m.* harm, prejudice. **porter** ∼**e à,** harm. ∼**iable** *a.* harmful.

préjugé /preʒyʒe/ *n.m.* prejudice. **avoir un** ∼ **contre,** be prejudiced against. **sans** ∼**s,** without prejudices.

préjuger /preʒyʒe/ *v.i.* ∼ **de,** prejudge.

prélasser (se) /(sə)prelɑse/ *v. pr.* loll (about).

prél|ever /prelve/ *v.t.* deduct (**sur,** from); (*sang*) take. ∼**èvement** *n.m.* deduction. ∼**èvement de sang,** blood sample.

préliminaire /preliminɛr/ *a. & n.m.* preliminary. ∼**s,** (*sexuels*) foreplay.

prélude /prelyd/ *n.m.* prelude.

prématuré /prematyre/ *a.* premature. —*n.m.* premature baby.

prémédit|er /premedite/ *v.t.* premeditate. ∼**ation** *n.f.* premeditation.

prem|ier, ∼**ière** /prəmje, -jɛr/ *a.* first; (*rang*) front, first; (*enfance*) early; (*nécessité, souci*) prime; (*qualité*) top, prime; (*état*) original. —*n.m.,* f. first (one). —*n.m.* (*date*) first; (*étage*) first floor. —*n.f.* (*rail.*) first class; (*exploit jamais vu*) first; (*cinéma, théâtre*) première. **de** ∼**ier ordre,** first-rate. **en** ∼**ier,** first. ∼**ier jet,** first draft. ∼**ier ministre,** Prime Minister.

premièrement /prəmjɛrmã/ *adv.* firstly.

prémisse /premis/ *n.f.* premiss.

prémonition /premɔnisjɔ̃/ *n.f.* premonition.

prémunir /premynir/ *v.t.* protect (**contre,** against).

prenant, ∼**e** /prənã, -t/ *a.* (*activité*) engrossing; (*enfant*) demanding.

prénatal (*m. pl.* ∼**s**) /prenatal/ *a.* antenatal; (*Amer.*) prenatal.

prendre† /prãdr/ *v.t.* take; (*attraper*) catch, get; (*acheter*) get; (*repas*) have; (*engager, adopter*) take on; (*poids*) put on; (*chercher*) pick up; (*panique, colère*) take hold of. —*v.i.* (*liquide*) set; (*feu*) catch; (*vaccin*) take. **se** ∼ **pour,** think one is. **s'en** ∼ **à,** attack; (*rendre responsable*) blame. **s'y** ∼, set about (it).

preneu|r, ∼**se** /prənœr, -øz/ *n.m.,* f. buyer. **être** ∼ **r,** be willing to buy. **trouver** ∼**r,** find a buyer.

prénom /prenɔ̃/ *n.m.* first name. ∼**mer** /-ɔme/ *v.t.* call. **se** ∼**mer** *v. pr.* be called.

préoccup|er /preɔkype/ *v.t.* worry; (*absorber*) preoccupy. **se** ∼**er de,** be worried about; be preoccupied about. ∼**ation** *n.f.* worry; (*idée fixe*) preoccupation.

préparatifs /preparatif/ *n.m. pl.* preparations.

préparatoire /preparatwar/ *a.* preparatory.

prépar|er /prepare/ *v.t.* prepare; (*repas, café*) make. **se** ∼**er** *v. pr.* prepare o.s.; (*être proche*) be brewing. ∼**er à qn.,** (*surprise*) have (got) in store for s.o. ∼**ation** *n.f.* preparation.

prépondéran|t, ∼**te** /prepɔ̃derã, -t/ *a.* dominant. ∼**ce** *n.f.* dominance.

prépos|er /prepoze/ *v.t.* put in charge (**à,** of). ∼**é,** ∼**ée** *n.m.,* f. employee; (*des postes*) postman, postwoman.

préposition /prepozisjɔ̃/ n.f. preposition.

préretraite /preretret/ n.f. early retirement.

prérogative /prerɔgativ/ n.f. prerogative.

près /prɛ/ adv. near, close. ~ **de**, near (to), close to; (presque) nearly. **à cela** ~, apart from that. **de** ~, closely.

présag|e /prezaʒ/ n.m. foreboding, omen. ~**er** v.t. forebode.

presbyte /prɛsbit/ a. long-sighted, far-sighted.

presbytère /prɛsbitɛr/ n.m. presbytery.

prescr|ire† /prɛskrir/ v.t. prescribe. ~**iption** n.f. prescription.

préséance /preseɑ̃s/ n.f. precedence.

présence /prezɑ̃s/ n.f. presence; (scol.) attendance.

présent, ~**e** /prezɑ̃, -t/ a. present. —n.m. (temps, cadeau) present. **à** ~, now.

présent|er /prezɑ̃te/ v.t. present; (personne) introduce (**à**, to); (montrer) show. **se** ~**er** v. pr. introduce o.s. (**à**, to); (aller) go; (apparaître) appear; (candidat) come forward; (occasion etc.) arise. ~**er bien**, have a pleasing appearance. **se** ~**er à**, (examen) sit for; (élection) stand for. **se** ~**er bien**, look good. ~**able** a. presentable. ~**ateur**, ~**atrice** n.m., f. presenter. ~**ation** n.f. presentation; introduction.

préservatif /prezɛrvatif/ n.m. condom.

préserv|er /prezɛrve/ v.t. protect. ~**ation** n.f. protection, preservation.

présiden|t, ~**te** /prezidɑ̃, -t/ n.m., f. president; (de firme, comité) chairman, chairwoman. ~**t directeur général**, managing director. ~**ce** n.f. presidency; chairmanship.

présidentiel, ~**le** /prezidɑ̃sjɛl/ a. presidential.

présider /prezide/ v.t. preside over. —v.i. preside.

présomption /prezɔ̃psjɔ̃/ n.f. presumption.

présomptueu|x, ~**se** /prezɔ̃ptɥø, -z/ a. presumptuous.

presque /prɛsk(ə)/ adv. almost, nearly. ~ **jamais**, hardly ever. ~ **rien**, hardly anything. ~ **pas (de)**, hardly any.

presqu'île /prɛskil/ n.f. peninsula.

pressant, ~**e** /prɛsɑ̃, -t/ a. pressing, urgent.

presse /prɛs/ n.f. (journaux, appareil) press.

pressent|ir /presɑ̃tir/ v.t. sense. ~**iment** n.m. presentiment.

press|er /prese/ v.t. squeeze, press; (appuyer sur, harceler) press; (hâter) hasten; (inciter) urge (**de**, to). —v.i. (temps) press; (affaire) be pressing. **se** ~**er** v. pr. (se hâter) hurry; (se grouper) crowd. ~**é** a. in a hurry; (orange, citron) freshly squeezed. ~**e-papiers** n.m. invar. paperweight.

pressing /presiŋ/ n.m. (magasin) dry-cleaner's.

pression /presjɔ̃/ n.f. pressure. —n.m./f. (bouton) press-stud; (Amer.) snap.

pressoir /preswar/ n.m. press.

pressuriser /presyrize/ v.t. pressurize.

prestance /prɛstɑ̃s/ n.f. (imposing) presence.

prestation /prɛstasjɔ̃/ n.f. allowance; (d'artiste etc.) performance.

prestidigita|teur, ~**trice** /prɛstidiʒitatœr, -tris/ n.m., f. conjuror. ~**tion** /-asjɔ̃/ n.f. conjuring.

prestig|e /prɛstiʒ/ n.m. prestige. ~**ieux**, ~**ieuse** a. prestigious.

présumer /prezyme/ v.t. presume. ~ **que**, assume that. ~ **de**, overrate.

prêt¹, ~**e** /prɛ, -t/ a. ready (**à qch.**, for sth., **à faire**, to do). ~**-à-porter** /prɛ(t)aporte/ n.m. invar. ready-to-wear clothes.

prêt² /prɛ/ n.m. loan.

prétendant /pretɑ̃dɑ̃/ n.m. (amoureux) suitor.

prétend|re /pretɑ̃dr/ v.t. claim (**que**, that); (vouloir) intend. ~**re qn. riche**/etc., claim that s.o. is rich/etc. ~**u** a. so-called. ~**ument** adv. supposedly, allegedly.

prétent|ieux, ~**ieuse** /pretɑ̃sjø, -z/ a. pretentious. ~**ion** n.f. pretentiousness; (exigence) claim.

prêt|er /prete/ v.t. lend (**à**, to); (attribuer) attribute. —v.i. ~**er à**, lead to. ~**er attention**, pay attention. ~**er serment**, take an oath. ~**eur**, ~**euse** /pretœr, -øz/ n.m., f. (money-)lender. ~**eur sur gages**, pawnbroker.

prétext|e /pretɛkst/ n.m. pretext, excuse. ~**er** v.t. plead.

prêtre /prɛtr/ n.m. priest.

prêtrise /pretriz/ n.f. priesthood.

preuve /prœv/ n.f. proof. **faire** ~ **de**, show. **faire ses** ~**s**, prove one's ou its worth.

prévaloir /prevalwar/ v.i. prevail.

prévenan|t, ~**te** /prevnɑ̃, -t/ a. thoughtful. ~**ce(s)** n.f. (pl.) thoughtfulness.

prévenir† /prevnir/ v.t. (menacer)

warn; (*informer*) tell; (*éviter, anticiper*)
forestall.

préventi|f, **∼ve** /prevãtif, -v/ *a.*
preventive.

prévention /prevãsjɔ̃/ *n.f.* prevention;
(*préjuge*) prejudice. **∼ routière,** road
safety.

prévenu, **∼e** /prɛvny/ *n.m., f.* defen-
dant.

prév|oir† /prevwar/ *v.t.* foresee; (*temps*)
forecast; (*organiser*) plan for), provide
for; (*envisager*) allow (for). **∼u pour,**
(*jouet etc.*) designed for. **∼isible** *a.*
foreseeable. **∼ision** *n.f.* prediction;
(*météorologique*) forecast.

prévoyan|t, **∼te** /prevwajã, -t/ *a.*
showing foresight. **∼ce** *n.f.* foresight.

prier /prije/ *v.i.* pray. —*v.t.* pray to;
(*implorer*) beg (**de,** to); (*demander à*)
ask (**de,** to). **je vous en prie,** please; (*il
n'y a pas de quoi*) don't mention it.

prière /prijɛr/ *n.f.* prayer; (*demande*)
request. **∼ de,** (*vous êtes prié de*) will
you please.

primaire /primɛr/ *a.* primary.

primauté /primote/ *n.f.* primacy.

prime /prim/ *n.f.* free gift; (*d'employé*)
bonus; (*subvention*) subsidy; (*d'assurance*) premium.

primé /prime/ *a.* prize-winning.

primer /prime/ *v.t./i.* excel.

primeurs /primœr/ *n.f. pl.* early fruit and
vegetables.

primevère /primvɛr/ *n.f.* primrose.

primiti|f, **∼ve** /primitif, -v/ *a.*
primitive; (*originel*) original. —*n.m., f.*
primitive.

primord|ial (*m. pl.* **∼iaux**) /primɔrdjal,
-jo/ *a.* essential.

princ|e /prɛ̃s/ *n.m.* prince. **∼esse** *n.f.*
princess. **∼ier, ∼ière** *a.* princely.

princip|al (*m. pl.* **∼aux**) /prɛ̃sipal, -o/
a. main, principal. —*n.m.* (*pl.* **∼aux**)
headmaster; (*chose*) main thing.
∼alement *adv.* mainly.

principauté /prɛ̃sipote/ *n.f.* principality.

principe /prɛ̃sip/ *n.m.* principle. **en ∼,**
theoretically; (*d'habitude*) as a rule.

printan|ier, ∼ière /prɛ̃tanje, -jɛr/ *a.*
spring(-like).

printemps /prɛ̃tã/ *n.m.* spring.

priorit|é /prijɔrite/ *n.f.* priority; (*auto.*)
right of way. **∼aire** *a.* priority. **être
∼aire,** have priority.

pris, **∼e**[1] /pri, -z/ *voir* **prendre.** —*a.*
(*place*) taken; (*personne, journée*)
busy; (*gorge*) infected. **∼ de,** (*peur,
fièvre, etc.*) stricken with. **∼ de
panique,** panic-stricken.

prise[2] /priz/ *n.f.* hold, grip; (*animal etc.
attrapé*) catch; (*mil.*) capture. **∼ (de
courant),** (*mâle*) plug; (*femelle*)
socket. **aux ∼s avec,** at grips with. **∼
de conscience,** awareness. **∼ de
contact,** first contact, initial meeting. **∼
de position,** stand. **∼ de sang,** blood
test.

priser /prize/ *v.t.* (*estimer*) prize.

prisme /prism/ *n.m.* prism.

prison /prizɔ̃/ *n.f.* prison, gaol, jail;
(*réclusion*) imprisonment. **∼nier,
∼nière** /-ɔnje, -jɛr/ *n.m., f.* prisoner.

privé /prive/ *a.* private. —*n.m.* (*comm.*)
private sector. **en ∼, dans le ∼,** in
private.

priv|er /prive/ *v.t.* **er de,** deprive of. **se
∼er de,** go without. **∼ation** *n.f.*
deprivation; (*sacrifice*) hardship.

privil|ège /privilɛʒ/ *n.m.* privilege.
∼égié, ∼égiée *a. & n.m., f.* privileged
(person).

prix /pri/ *n.m.* price; (*récompense*) prize.
à tout ∼, at all costs. **au ∼ de,** (*fig.*) at
the expense of. **∼ coûtant, ∼ de
revient,** cost price. **à ∼ fixe,** set price.

pro- /prɔ/ *préf.* pro-.

probab|le /prɔbabl/ *a.* probable, likely.
∼ilité *n.f.* probability. **∼lement** *adv.*
probably.

probant, **∼e** /prɔbã, -t/ *a.* convincing,
conclusive.

probité /prɔbite/ *n.f.* integrity.

problème /prɔblɛm/ *n.m.* problem.

procéd|er /prɔsede/ *v.i.* proceed. **∼er à,**
carry out. **∼é** *n.m.* process; (*conduite*)
behaviour.

procédure /prɔsedyr/ *n.f.* procedure.

procès /prɔsɛ/ *n.m.* (*criminel*) trial;
(*civil*) lawsuit, proceedings. **∼-verbal**
(*pl.* **∼-verbaux**) *n.m.* report; (*contravention*) ticket.

procession /prɔsesjɔ̃/ *n.f.* procession.

processus /prɔsesys/ *n.m.* process.

prochain, **∼e** /prɔʃɛ̃, -ɛn/ *a.* (*suivant*)
next; (*proche*) imminent; (*avenir*) near.
je descends à la ∼e, I'm getting off at
the next stop. —*n.m.* fellow. **∼ement**
/-ɛnmã/ *adv.* soon.

proche /prɔʃ/ *a.* near, close; (*avoisinant*)
neighbouring; (*parent, ami*) close. **∼
de,** close *ou* near to. **de ∼ en proche,**
gradually. **dans un ∼ avenir,** in the
near future. **être ∼, (*imminent*)** be
approaching. **∼s** *n.m. pl.* close
relations. **P∼-Orient** *n.m.* Near East.

proclam|er /prɔklame/ *v.t.* declare,
proclaim. **∼ation** *n.f.* declaration,
proclamation.

procréation /prɔkreasjɔ̃/ n.f. procreation.

procuration /prɔkyrasjɔ̃/ n.f. proxy.

procurer /prɔkyre/ v.t. bring (**à**, to). **se ∼** v. pr. obtain.

procureur /prɔkyrœr/ n.m. public prosecutor.

prodig|e /prɔdiʒ/ n.m. marvel; (personne) prodigy. **enfant/musicien ∼e**, child/musical prodigy. **∼ieux, ∼ieuse** a. tremendous, prodigious.

prodigu|e /prɔdig/ a. wasteful. **fils ∼e**, prodigal son. **∼er** v.t. **∼er à**, lavish on.

producti|f, ∼ve /prɔdyktif, -v/ a. productive. **∼vité** n.f. productivity.

prod|uire† /prɔdɥir/ v.t. produce. **se ∼uire** v. pr. (survenir) happen; (acteur) perform. **∼ucteur, ∼uctrice** a. producing; n.m., f. producer. **∼uction** n.f. production; (produit) product.

produit /prɔdɥi/ n.m. product. **∼s**, (de la terre) produce. **∼ chimique**, chemical. **∼s alimentaires**, foodstuffs. **∼ de consommation**, consumer goods. **∼ national brut**, gross national product.

proéminent, ∼e /prɔeminɑ̃, -t/ a. prominent.

prof /prɔf/ n.m. (fam.) teacher.

profane /prɔfan/ a. secular. —n.m./f. lay person.

profaner /prɔfane/ v.t. desecrate.

proférer /prɔfere/ v.t. utter.

professer[1] /prɔfese/ v.t. (déclarer) profess.

professer[2] /prɔfese/ v.t./i. (enseigner) teach.

professeur /prɔfesœr/ n.m. teacher; (univ.) lecturer; (avec chaire) professor.

profession /prɔfesjɔ̃/ n.f. occupation; (intellectuelle) profession. **∼nel, ∼nelle** /-jɔnɛl/ a. professional; (école) vocational; n.m., f. professional.

professorat /prɔfesɔra/ n.m. teaching.

profil /prɔfil/ n.m. profile.

profiler (se) /(sə)prɔfile/ v. pr. be outlined.

profit /prɔfi/ n.m. profit. **au ∼ de**, in aid of. **∼able** /-tabl/ a. profitable.

profiter /prɔfite/ v.i. **∼ à**, benefit. **∼ de**, take advantage of.

profond, ∼e /prɔfɔ̃, -d/ a. deep; (sentiment, intérêt) profound; (causes) underlying. **au plus ∼ de**, in the depths of. **∼ément** /-demɑ̃/ adv. deeply; (différent, triste) profoundly; (dormir) soundly. **∼eur** /-dœr/ n.f. depth.

profusion /prɔfyzjɔ̃/ n.f. profusion.

progéniture /prɔʒenityr/ n.f. offspring.

programmation /prɔgramasjɔ̃/ n.f. programming.

programm|e /prɔgram/ n.m. programme; (matières: scol.) syllabus; (informatique) program. **∼e (d'études)**, curriculum. **∼er** v.t. (ordinateur, appareil) program; (émission) schedule. **∼eur, ∼euse** n.m., f. computer programmer.

progrès /prɔgrɛ/ n.m. & n.m. pl. progress. **faire des ∼**, make progress.

progress|er /prɔgrese/ v.i. progress. **∼ion** /-ɛsjɔ̃/ n.f. progression.

progressi|f, ∼ve /prɔgresif, -v/ a. progressive. **∼vement** adv. progressively.

progressiste /prɔgresist/ a. progressive.

prohib|er /prɔibe/ v.t. prohibit. **∼ition** n.f. prohibition.

prohibiti|f, ∼ve /prɔibitif, -v/ a. prohibitive.

proie /prwa/ n.f. prey. **en ∼ à**, tormented by.

projecteur /prɔʒɛktœr/ n.m. floodlight; (mil.) searchlight; (cinéma) projector.

projectile /prɔʒɛktil/ n.m. missile.

projection /prɔʒɛksjɔ̃/ n.f. projection; (séance) show.

projet /prɔʒɛ/ n.m. plan; (ébauche) draft. **∼ de loi**, bill.

projeter /prɔʒte/ v.t. plan (**de, to**); (film) project, show; (jeter) hurl, project.

prolét|aire /prɔletɛr/ n.m./f. proletarian. **∼ariat** n.m. proletariat. **∼arien, ∼arienne** a. proletarian.

prolifér|er /prɔlifere/ v.i. proliferate. **∼ation** n.f. proliferation.

prolifique /prɔlifik/ a. prolific.

prologue /prɔlɔg/ n.m. prologue.

prolongation /prɔlɔ̃gasjɔ̃/ n.f. extension. **∼s**, (football) extra time.

prolong|er /prɔlɔ̃ʒe/ v.t. prolong. **se ∼er** v. pr. continue, extend. **∼é a**. prolonged. **∼ement** n.m. extension.

promenade /prɔmnad/ n.f. walk; (à bicyclette, à cheval) ride; (en auto) drive, ride. **faire une ∼**, go for a walk.

promen|er /prɔmne/ v.t. take for a walk. **∼er sur qch.**, (main, regard) run over sth. **se ∼er** v. pr. walk. (aller) **se ∼er**, go for a walk. **∼eur, ∼euse** n.m., f. walker.

promesse /prɔmɛs/ n.f. promise.

promett|re† /prɔmɛtr/ v.t./i. promise. **∼re (beaucoup)**, be promising. **se ∼re de**, resolve to. **∼eur, ∼euse** a. promising.

promontoire /prɔmɔ̃twar/ *n.m.* headland.

promoteur /prɔmɔtœr/ *n.m.* (*immobilier*) property developer.

prom|ouvoir /prɔmuvwar/ *v.t.* promote. **être ∼u,** be promoted. **∼otion** *n.f.* promotion; (*univ.*) year; (*comm.*) special offer.

prompt, ∼e /prɔ̃, -t/ *a.* swift.

prôner /prone/ *v.t.* extol; (*préconiser*) preach, advocate.

pronom /prɔnɔ̃/ *n.m.* pronoun. **∼inal** (*m. pl.* **∼inaux**) /-ɔminal, -o/ *a.* pronominal.

prononc|er /prɔnɔ̃se/ *v.t.* pronounce; (*discours*) make. **se ∼er** *v. pr.* (*mot*) be pronounced; (*personne*) make a decision (**pour,** in favour of). **∼é** *a.* pronounced. **∼iation** *n.f.* pronunciation.

pronosti|c /prɔnɔstik/ *n.m.* forecast; (*méd.*) prognosis. **∼quer** *v.t.* forecast.

propagande /prɔpagɑ̃d/ *n.f.* propaganda.

propag|er /prɔpaʒe/ *v.t.,* **se ∼er** *v. pr.* spread. **∼ation** /-gasjɔ̃/ *n.f.* spread(ing).

proph|ète /prɔfɛt/ *n.m.* prophet. **∼étie** /-esi/ *n.f.* prophecy. **∼étique** *a.* prophetic. **∼étiser** *v.t./i.* prophesy.

propice /prɔpis/ *a.* favourable.

proportion /prɔpɔrsjɔ̃/ *n.f.* proportion; (*en mathématiques*) ratio. **toutes ∼s gardées,** making appropriate allowances. **∼né** /-jɔne/ *a.* proportionate (**à,** to). **∼nel, ∼nelle** /-jɔnɛl/ *a.* proportional. **∼ner** /-jɔne/ *v.t.* proportion.

propos /prɔpo/ *n.m.* intention; (*sujet*) subject. **—** *n.m. pl.* (*paroles*) remarks. **à ∼,** at the right time; (*dans un dialogue*) by the way. **à ∼ de,** about. **à tout ∼,** at every possible occasion.

propos|er /prɔpoze/ *v.t.* propose; (*offrir*) offer. **se ∼er** *v. pr.* volunteer (**pour,** to); (*but*) set o.s. **se ∼er de faire,** propose to do. **∼ition** *n.f.* proposal; (*affirmation*) proposition; (*gram.*) clause.

propre¹ /prɔpr/ *a.* clean; (*soigné*) neat; (*honnête*) decent. **mettre au ∼,** write out again neatly. **c'est du ∼!** (*ironique*) well done! **∼ment¹** /-əmɑ̃/ *adv.* cleanly; neatly; decently.

propre² /prɔpr/ *a.* (*à soi*) own; (*sens*) literal. **∼ à,** (*qui convient*) suited to; (*spécifique*) peculiar to. **∼-à-rien** *n.m./f.* good-for-nothing. **∼ment²** /-əmɑ̃/ *adv.* strictly. **le bureau/**etc.**∼ment dit,** the office/etc. itself.

propreté /prɔprəte/ *n.f.* cleanliness; (*netteté*) neatness.

propriétaire /prɔprijetɛr/ *n.m./f.* owner; (*comm.*) proprietor; (*qui loue*) landlord, landlady.

propriété /prɔprijete/ *n.f.* property; (*droit*) ownership.

propuls|er /prɔpylse/ *v.t.* propel. **∼ion** *n.f.* propulsion.

prorata /prɔrata/ *n.m. invar.* **au ∼ de,** in proportion to.

proroger /prɔrɔʒe/ *v.t.* (*contrat*) defer; (*passeport*) extend.

prosaïque /prozaik/ *a.* prosaic.

proscr|ire /prɔskrir/ *v.t.* proscribe. **∼it, ∼ite** *a.* proscribed; *n.m., f.* (*exilé*) exile.

prose /proz/ *n.f.* prose.

prospec|ter /prɔspɛkte/ *v.t.* prospect. **∼teur, ∼trice** *n.m., f.* prospector. **∼tion** /-ksjɔ̃/ *n.f.* prospecting.

prospectus /prɔspɛktys/ *n.m.* leaflet.

prosp|ère /prɔspɛr/ *a.* flourishing, thriving. **∼érer** *v.i.* thrive, prosper. **∼érité** *n.f.* prosperity.

prostern|er (se) /(sə)prɔstɛrne/ *v. pr.* bow down. **∼é** *a.* prostrate.

prostit|uée /prɔstitɥe/ *n.f.* prostitute. **∼ution** *n.f.* prostitution.

prostré /prɔstre/ *a.* prostrate.

protagoniste /prɔtagɔnist/ *n.m.* protagonist.

protec|teur, ∼trice /prɔtɛktœr, -tris/ *n.m., f.* protector. **—***a.* protective.

protection /prɔtɛksjɔ̃/ *n.f.* protection; (*fig.*) patronage.

protég|er /prɔteʒe/ *v.t.* protect; (*fig.*) patronize. **se ∼er** *v. pr.* protect o.s. **∼é** *n.m.* protégé. **∼ée** *n.f.* protégée.

protéine /prɔtein/ *n.f.* protein.

protestant, ∼e /prɔtɛstɑ̃, -t/ *a. & n.m., f.* Protestant.

protest|er /prɔtɛste/ *v.t./i.* protest. **∼ation** *n.f.* protest.

protocole /prɔtɔkɔl/ *n.m.* protocol.

prototype /prɔtɔtip/ *n.m.* prototype.

protubéran|t, ∼te /prɔtyberɑ̃, -t/ *a.* bulging. **∼ce,** *n.f.* protuberance.

proue /pru/ *n.f.* bow, prow.

prouesse /prues/ *n.f.* feat, exploit.

prouver /pruve/ *v.t.* prove.

provenance /prɔvnɑ̃s/ *n.f.* origin. **en ∼ de,** from.

provençal, ∼ale (*m. pl.* **∼aux**) /prɔvɑ̃sal, -o/ *a. & n.m., f.* Provençal.

Provence /prɔvɑ̃s/ *n.f.* Provence.

provenir† /prɔvnir/ *v.i.* **∼ de,** come from.

proverb|e /prɔvɛrb/ *n.m.* proverb. **∼ial** (*m. pl.* **∼iaux**) *a.* proverbial.

providence /prɔvidɑ̃s/ *n.f.* providence.
provinc|e /prɔvɛ̃s/ *n.f.* province. **de** ~**e**, provincial. **la** ~**e**, the provinces. ~**ial**, ~**iale** (*m. pl.* ~**iaux**) *a. & n.m., f.* provincial.
proviseur /prɔvizœr/ *n.m.* headmaster, principal.
provision /prɔvizjɔ̃/ *n.f.* supply, store; (*dans un compte*) funds; (*acompte*) deposit. ~**s**, (*vivres*) provisions. **panier à** ~**s**, shopping basket.
provisoire /prɔvizwar/ *a.* temporary. ~**ment** *adv.* temporarily.
provo|quer /prɔvɔke/ *v.t.* cause; (*exciter*) arouse; (*défier*) provoke. ~**cant**, ~**cante** *a.* provocative. ~**cation** *n.f.* provocation.
proximité /prɔksimite/ *n.f.* proximity. **à** ~ **de**, close to.
prude /pryd/ *a.* prudish. —*n.f.* prude.
prud|ent, ~**ente** /prydɑ̃, -t/ *a.* cautious; (*sage*) wise. **soyez** ~**ent**, be careful. ~**emment** /-amɑ̃/ *adv.* cautiously; wisely. ~**ence** *n.f.* caution; wisdom.
prune /pryn/ *n.f.* plum.
pruneau (*pl.* ~**x**) /pryno/ *n.m.* prune.
prunelle[1] /prynɛl/ *n.f.* (*pupille*) pupil.
prunelle[2] /prynɛl/ *n.f.* (*fruit*) sloe.
psaume /psom/ *n.m.* psalm.
pseudo- /psødɔ/ *préf.* pseudo-.
pseudonyme /psødɔnim/ *n.m.* pseudonym.
psychanalys|e /psikanaliz/ *n.f.* psychoanalysis. ~**er** *v.t.* psychoanalyse. ~**te** /-st/ *n.m./f.* psychoanalyst.
psychiatr|e /psikjatr/ *n.m./f.* psychiatrist. ~**ie** *n.f.* psychiatry. ~**ique** *a.* psychiatric.
psychique /psiʃik/ *a.* mental, psychological.
psycholo|gie /psikɔlɔʒi/ *n.f.* psychology. ~**gique** *a.* psychological. ~**gue** *n.m./f.* psychologist.
psychosomatique /psikɔsɔmatik/ *a.* psychosomatic.
psychothérapie /psikɔterapi/ *n.f.* psychotherapy.
PTT *abrév.* (*Postes, Télécommunications et Télédiffusion*) Post Office.
pu /py/ *voir* **pouvoir**[1].
puant, ~**e** /pɥɑ̃, -t/ *a.* stinking. ~**eur** /-tœr/ *n.f.* stink.
pub /pyb/ *n.f.* **la** ~, advertising. **une** ~, an advert.
puberté /pybɛrte/ *n.f.* puberty.
publi|c, ~**que** /pyblik/ *a.* public. —*n.m.* public; (*assistance*) audience. **en** ~**c**, in public.

publicit|é /pyblisite/ *n.f.* publicity, advertising; (*annonce*) advertisement. ~**aire** *a.* publicity.
publ|ier /pyblije/ *v.t.* publish. ~**ication** *n.f.* publication.
publiquement /pyblikmɑ̃/ *adv.* publicly.
puce[1] /pys/ *n.f.* flea. **marché aux** ~**s**, flea market.
puce[2] /pys/ *n.f.* (*électronique*) chip.
pud|eur /pydœr/ *n.f.* modesty. ~**ique** *a.* modest.
pudibond, ~**e** /pydibɔ̃, -d/ *a.* prudish.
puer /pɥe/ *v.i.* stink. —*v.t.* stink of.
puéricultrice /pɥerikyltris/ *n.f.* children's nurse.
puéril /pɥeril/ *a.* puerile.
pugilat /pyʒila/ *n.m.* fight.
puis /pɥi/ *adv.* then.
puiser /pɥize/ *v.t.* draw (**qch. dans**, sth. from). —*v.i.* ~ **dans qch.**, dip into sth.
puisque /pɥisk(ə)/ *conj.* since, as.
puissance /pɥisɑ̃s/ *n.f.* power. **en** ~ *a.* potential; *adv.* potentially.
puiss|ant, ~**ante** /pɥisɑ̃, -t/ *a.* powerful. ~**amment** *adv.* powerfully.
puits /pɥi/ *n.m.* well; (*de mine*) shaft.
pull-(over) /pyl(ɔvɛr)/ *n.m.* pullover, jumper.
pulpe /pylp/ *n.f.* pulp.
pulsation /pylsasjɔ̃/ *n.f.* (heart-)beat.
pulvéris|er /pylverize/ *v.t.* pulverize; (*liquide*) spray. ~**ateur** *n.m.* spray.
punaise /pynɛz/ *n.f.* (*insecte*) bug; (*clou*) drawing-pin; (*Amer.*) thumbtack.
punch[1] /pɔ̃ʃ/ *n.m.* punch.
punch[2] /pœnʃ/ *n.m.* **avoir du** ~, have drive.
pun|ir /pynir/ *v.t.* punish. ~**ition** *n.f.* punishment.
punk /pœnk/ *a. invar.* punk.
pupille[1] /pypij/ *n.f.* (*de l'œil*) pupil.
pupille[2] /pypij/ *n.m./f.* (*enfant*) ward.
pupitre /pypitr/ *n.m.* (*scol.*) desk. ~ **à musique**, music stand.
pur /pyr/ *a.* pure; (*whisky*) neat. ~**ement** *adv.* purely. ~**eté** *n.f.* purity. ~**-sang** *n.m. invar.* (*cheval*) thoroughbred.
purée /pyre/ *n.f.* purée; (*de pommes de terre*) mashed potatoes.
purgatoire /pyrgatwar/ *n.m.* purgatory.
purg|e /pyrʒ/ *n.f.* purge. ~**er** *v.t.* (*pol., méd.*) purge; (*peine: jurid.*) serve.
purif|ier /pyrifje/ *v.t.* purify. ~**ication** *n.f.* purification.
purin /pyrɛ̃/ *n.m.* (liquid) manure.

puritain, ~**e** /pyritɛ̃, -ɛn/ *n.m.*, *f.* puritan. —*a.* puritanical.

pus /py/ *n.m.* pus.

pustule /pystyl/ *n.f.* pimple.

putain /pytɛ̃/ *n.f.* (*fam.*) whore.

putréfier (se) /(sə)pytrefje/ *v. pr.* putrefy.

putsch /putʃ/ *n.m.* putsch.

puzzle /pœzl/ *n.m.* jigsaw (puzzle).

P-V *abrév.* (*procès-verbal*) ticket, traffic fine.

pygmée /pigme/ *n.m.* pygmy.

pyjama /piʒama/ *n.m.* pyjamas. **un** ~, a pair of pyjamas.

pylône /pilon/ *n.m.* pylon.

pyramide /piramid/ *n.f.* pyramid.

Pyrénées /pirene/ *n.f. pl.* **les** ~, the Pyrenees.

pyromane /pirɔman/ *n.m./f.* arsonist.

Q

QG *abrév.* (*quartier général*) HQ.

QI *abrév.* (*quotient intellectuel*) IQ.

qu' /k/ *voir* que.

quadrill|er /kadrije/ *v.t.* (*zone*) comb, control. ~**age** *n.m.* (*mil.*) control. ~**é** *a.* (*papier*) squared.

quadrupède /kadrypɛd/ *n.m.* quadruped.

quadrupl|e /kadrypl/ *a.* & *n.m.* quadruple. ~**er** *v.t./i.* quadruple. ~**és**, ~**ées** *n.m.*, *f. pl.* quadruplets.

quai /ke/ *n.m.* (*de gare*) platform; (*de port*) quay; (*de rivière*) embankment.

qualificatif /kalifikatif/ *n.m.* (*épithète*) term.

qualif|ier /kalifje/ *v.t.* (*décrire*) describe (**de**, as). **se** ~**ier** *v. pr.* qualify (**pour**, for). ~**ication** *n.f.* qualification; description. ~**ié** *a.* qualified; (*main d'œuvre*) skilled.

qualit|é /kalite/ *n.f.* quality; (*titre*) occupation. **en** ~**é de**, in one's capacity as. ~**atif**, ~**ative** *a.* qualitative.

quand /kɑ̃/ *conj.* & *adv.* when. ~ **même**, all the same. ~ **(bien) même,** even if.

quant (à) /kɑ̃t(a)/ *prép.* as for.

quant-à-soi /kɑ̃taswa/ *n.m.* **rester sur son** ~, stand aloof.

quantit|é /kɑ̃tite/ *n.f.* quantity. **une** ~**é de**, a lot of. **des** ~**és**, masses. ~**atif,** ~**ative** *a.* quantitative.

quarantaine /karɑ̃tɛn/ *n.f.* (*méd.*) quarantine. **une** ~ **(de),** about forty.

quarant|e /karɑ̃t/ *a.* & *n.m.* forty. ~**ième** *a.* & *n.m./f.* fortieth.

quart /kar/ *n.m.* quarter; (*naut.*) watch. ~ **(de litre),** quarter litre. ~ **de finale,** quarter-final. ~ **d'heure,** quarter of an hour.

quartier /kartje/ *n.m.* neighbourhood, district; (*de lune, bœuf*) quarter; (*de fruit*) segment. ~**s**, (*mil.*) quarters. **de** ~, **du** ~, local. ~ **général,** headquarters. **avoir** ~ **libre,** be free.

quartz /kwarts/ *n.m.* quartz.

quasi- /kazi/ *préf.* quasi-.

quasiment /kazimɑ̃/ *adv.* almost.

quatorz|e /katɔrz/ *a.* & *n.m.* fourteen. ~**ième** *a.* & *n.m./f.* fourteenth.

quatre /katr(ə)/ *a.* & *n.m.* four. ~**vingt(s)** *a.* & *n.m.* eighty. ~**-vingt-dix** *a.* & *n.m.* ninety.

quatrième /katrijɛm/ *a.* & *n.m./f.* fourth. ~**ment** *adv.* fourthly.

quatuor /kwatɥɔr/ *n.m.* quartet.

que, qu'* /kə, k/ *conj.* that; (*comparaison*) than. **qu'il vienne,** let him come. **qu'il vienne ou non,** whether he comes or not. **ne faire** ~ **demander**/*etc.*, only ask/*etc.* —*adv.* **(ce)** ~ **tu es bête, qu'est-ce** ~ **tu es bête,** how silly you are. ~ **de,** what a lot of. —*pron. rel.* (*personne*) that, whom; (*chose*) that, which; (*temps, moment*) when; (*interrogatif*) what. **un jour**/*etc.* ~, one day/*etc.* when. ~ **faites-vous?, qu'est-ce** ~ **vous faites?,** what are you doing?

Québec /kebɛk/ *n.m.* Quebec.

quel, ~**le** /kɛl/ *a.* what; (*interrogatif*) which, what; (*qui*) who. —*pron.* which. ~ **dommage,** what a pity. ~ **qu'il soit,** (*chose*) whatever *ou* whichever it may be; (*personne*) whoever he may be.

quelconque /kɛlkɔ̃k/ *a.* any, some; (*banal*) ordinary; (*médiocre*) poor.

quelque /kɛlkə/ *a.* some. ~**s**, a few, some. —*adv.* (*environ*) some. **et** ~, (*fam.*) and a bit. ~ **chose,** something; (*interrogation*) anything. ~ **part,** somewhere. ~ **peu,** somewhat.

quelquefois /kɛlkəfwa/ *adv.* sometimes.

quelques|-uns, ~**-unes** /kɛlkəzœ̃, -yn/ *pron.* some, a few.

quelqu'un /kɛlkœ̃/ *pron.* someone, somebody; (*interrogation*) anyone, anybody.

quémander /kemɑ̃de/ *v.t.* beg for.

qu'en-dira-t-on /kɑ̃diratɔ̃/ *n.m. invar.* **le** ~, gossip.

querell|e /kɔrɛl/ *n.f.* quarrel. **~eur,**
~euse *a.* quarrelsome.

quereller (se) /(sə)kɔrele/ *v. pr.* quarrel.

question /kɛstjɔ̃/ *n.f.* question; (*affaire*)
matter, question. **en ~,** in question; (*en
jeu*) at stake. **il est ~ de,** (*cela
concerne*) it is about; (*on parle de*) there
is talk of. **il n'en est pas ~,** it is out of
the question. **~ner** /-jɔne/ *v.t.* question.

questionnaire /kɛstjɔnɛr/ *n.m.* questionnaire.

quêt|e /kɛt/ *n.f.* (*relig.*) collection. **en ~e**
de, in search of. **~er** /kete/ *v.i.* collect
money; *v.t.* seek.

quetsche /kwɛtʃ/ *n.f.* (sort of dark red)
plum.

queue /kø/ *n.f.* tail; (*de poêle*) handle;
(*de fruit*) stalk; (*de fleur*) stem; (*file*)
queue; (*file: Amer.*) line; (*de train*) rear.
faire la ~, queue (up); (*Amer.*) line up.
~ de cheval, pony-tail.

qui /ki/ *pron. rel.* (*personne*) who;
(*chose*) which, that; (*interrogatif*) who;
(*après prép.*) whom; (*quiconque*)
whoever. **à ~ est ce stylo**/*etc.*?, whose
pen/*etc.* is this? **qu'est-ce ~?,** what? **~**
est-ce qui?, who? **~ que ce soit,**
anyone.

quiche /kiʃ/ *n.f.* quiche.

quiconque /kikɔ̃k/ *pron.* whoever;
(*n'importe qui*) anyone.

quiétude /kjetyd/ *n.f.* quiet.

quignon /kiɲɔ̃/ *n.m.* **~ de pain,** chunk of
bread.

quille[1] /kij/ *n.f.* (*de bateau*) keel.

quille[2] /kij/ *n.f.* (*jouet*) skittle.

quincaill|ier, **~ière** /kɛ̃kaje, -jɛr/
n.m., *f.* hardware dealer. **~erie** *n.f.*
hardware; (*magasin*) hardware shop.

quinine /kinin/ *n.f.* quinine.

quinquenn|al (*m. pl.* **~aux**) /kɛ̃kenal,
-o/ *a.* five-year.

quint|al (*pl.* **~aux**) /kɛ̃tal, -o/ *n.m.*
quintal (= *100 kg.*).

quinte /kɛ̃t/ *n.f.* **~ de toux,** coughing fit.

quintette /kɛ̃tɛt/ *n.m.* quintet.

quintupl|e /kɛ̃typl/ *a.* fivefold. —*n.m.*
quintuple. **~er** *v.t./i.* increase fivefold.
~és, **~ées,** *n.m.,* *f. pl.* quintuplets.

quinzaine /kɛ̃zɛn/ *n.f.* **une ~ (de),** about
fifteen.

quinz|e /kɛ̃z/ *a. & n.m.* fifteen. **~e jours,**
two weeks. **~ième** *a. & n.m./f.*
fifteenth.

quiproquo /kiprɔko/ *n.m.* misunderstanding.

quittance /kitɑ̃s/ *n.f.* receipt.

quitte /kit/ *a.* quits (**envers,** with). **~ à**
faire, even if it means doing.

quitter /kite/ *v.t.* leave; (*vêtement*) take
off. **se ~** *v. pr.* part.

quoi /kwa/ *pron.* what; (*après prép.*)
which. **de ~ vivre/manger**/*etc.*,
(*assez*) enough to live on/to eat/*etc.* **de**
~ écrire, sth. to write with, what is
necessary to write with. **~ que,**
whatever. **~ que ce soit,** anything.

quoique /kwak(ə)/ *conj.* (al)though.

quolibet /kɔlibɛ/ *n.m.* gibe.

quorum /kɔrɔm/ *n.m.* quorum.

quota /kɔta/ *n.m.* quota.

quote-part (*pl.* **quotes-parts**) /kɔtpar/
n.f. share.

quotidien, **~ne** /kɔtidjɛ̃, -jɛn/ *a.* daily;
(*banal*) everyday. —*n.m.* daily (paper).
~nement /- jɛnmɑ̃/ *adv.* daily.

quotient /kɔsjɑ̃/ *n.m.* quotient.

R

rab /rab/ *n.m.* (*fam.*) extra. **il y en a en**
~, there's some over.

rabâcher /rabaʃe/ *v.t.* keep repeating.

rabais /rabɛ/ *n.m.* (price) reduction.

rabaisser /rabese/ *v.t.* (*déprécier*)
belittle; (*réduire*) reduce.

rabat /raba/ *n.m.* flap. **~-joie** *n.m. invar.*
killjoy.

rabattre /rabatr/ *v.t.* pull *ou* put down;
(*diminuer*) reduce; (*déduire*) take off.
se ~ *v. pr.* (*se refermer*) close;
(*véhicule*) cut in, turn sharply. **se ~ sur,**
fall back on.

rabbin /rabɛ̃/ *n.m.* rabbi.

rabibocher /rabibɔʃe/ *v.t.* (*fam.*) reconcile.

rabiot /rabjo/ *n.m.* (*fam.*) = **rab**.

râblé /rable/ *a.* stocky, sturdy.

rabot /rabo/ *n.m.* plane. **~er** /-ɔte/ *v.t.*
plane.

raboteu|x, **~se** /rabɔtø, -z/ *a.* uneven.

rabougri /rabugri/ *a.* stunted.

rabrouer /rabrue/ *v.t.* snub.

racaille /rakɑj/ *n.f.* rabble.

raccommoder /rakɔmɔde/ *v.t.* mend;
(*personnes: fam.*) reconcile.

raccompagner /rakɔ̃paɲe/ *v.t.* see *ou*
take back (home).

raccord /rakɔr/ *n.m.* link; (*de papier
peint*) join. **~ (de peinture),** touch-
up.

raccord|er /rakɔrde/ *v.t.* connect, join.
~ement *n.m.* connection.

raccourci /rakursi/ *n.m.* short cut. **en ~,**
in brief.

raccourcir /rakursir/ v.t. shorten. —v.i. get shorter.

raccrocher /rakrɔʃe/ v.t. hang back up; (personne) grab hold of; (relier) connect. ~ (le récepteur), hang up. se ~ à, cling to; (se relier à) be connected to ou with.

rac|e /ras/ n.f. race; (animale) breed. de ~e, pure-bred. ~ial (m. pl. ~iaux) a. racial.

rachat /raʃa/ n.m. buying (back); (de pécheur) redemption.

racheter /raʃte/ v.t. buy (back); (davantage) buy more; (nouvel objet) buy another; (pécheur) redeem. se ~ v. pr. make amends.

racine /rasin/ n.f. root. ~ carrée/cubique, square/cube root.

racis|te /rasist/ a. & n.m./f. racist. ~me n.m. racism.

racket /rakɛt/ n.m. racketeering.

raclée /rakle/ n.f. (fam.) thrashing.

racler /rakle/ v.t. scrape. se ~ la gorge, clear one's throat.

racol|er /rakɔle/ v.t. solicit; (marchand, parti) drum up. ~age n.m. soliciting.

racontars /rakɔ̃tar/ n.m. pl. (fam.) gossip, stories.

raconter /rakɔ̃te/ v.t. (histoire) tell, relate; (vacances etc.) tell about. ~ à qn. que, tell s.o. that, say to s.o. that.

racorni /rakɔrni/ a. hard(ened).

radar /radar/ n.m. radar.

rade /rad/ n.f. harbour. en ~, (personne: fam.) stranded, behind.

radeau (pl. ~x) /rado/ n.m. raft.

radiateur /radjatœr/ n.m. radiator; (électrique) heater.

radiation /radjɑsjɔ̃/ n.f. (énergie) radiation.

radic|al (m. pl. ~aux) /radikal, -o/ a. radical. —n.m. (pl. ~aux) radical.

radier /radje/ v.t. cross off.

radieu|x, ~se /radjø, -z/ a. radiant.

radin, ~e /radɛ̃, -in/ a. (fam.) stingy.

radio /radjo/ n.f. radio; (radiographie) X-ray.

radioacti|f, ~ve /radjɔaktif, -v/ a. radioactive. ~vité n.f. radioactivity.

radiocassette /radjokasɛt/ n.f. radio-cassette-player.

radiodiffus|er /radjodifyze/ v.t. broadcast. ~ion n.f. broadcasting.

radiograph|ie /radjografi/ n.f. (photographie) X-ray. ~ier v.t. X-ray. ~ique a. X-ray.

radiologue /radjolɔg/ n.m./f. radiographer.

radiophonique /radjofɔnik/ a. radio.

radis /radi/ n.m. radish. **ne pas avoir un ~**, be broke.

radoter /radɔte/ v.i. (fam.) talk drivel.

radoucir (se) /(sə)radusir/ v. pr. calm down; (temps) become milder.

rafale /rafal/ n.f. (de vent) gust; (tir) burst of gunfire.

raffermir /rafɛrmir/ v.t. strengthen. se ~ v. pr. become stronger.

raffin|é /rafine/ a. refined. ~ement n.m. refinement.

raffin|er /rafine/ v.t. refine. ~age n.m. refining. ~erie n.f. refinery.

raffoler /rafole/ v.i. ~ de, be extremely fond of.

raffut /rafy/ n.m. (fam.) din.

rafiot /rafjo/ n.m. (fam.) boat.

rafistoler /rafistole/ v.t. (fam.) patch up.

rafle /rafl/ n.f. (police) raid.

rafler /rafle/ v.t. grab, swipe.

rafraîch|ir /rafreʃir/ v.t. cool (down); (raviver) brighten up; (personne, mémoire) refresh. se ~ir v. pr. (se laver) freshen up; (boire) refresh o.s.; (temps) get cooler. ~issant, ~issante a. refreshing.

rafraîchissement /rafreʃismɑ̃/ n.m. (boisson) cold drink. ~s, (fruits etc.) refreshments.

ragaillardir /ragajardir/ v.t. (fam.) buck up. se ~ v. pr. buck up.

rag|e /raʒ/ n.f. rage; (maladie) rabies. **faire ~e**, rage. **~e de dents**, raging toothache. ~er v.i. rage. ~eur, ~euse a. ill-tempered. ~eant, ~eante a. maddening.

ragot(s) /rago/ n.m. (pl.) (fam.) gossip.

ragoût /ragu/ n.m. stew.

raid /rɛd/ n.m. (mil.) raid; (sport) rally.

raid|e /rɛd/ a. stiff; (côte) steep; (corde) tight; (cheveux) straight. —adv. (en pente) steeply. ~eur n.f. stiffness, steepness.

raidir /redir/ v.t., se ~ v. pr. stiffen; (position) harden; (corde) tighten.

raie¹ /rɛ/ n.f. line; (bande) strip; (de cheveux) parting.

raie² /rɛ/ n.f. (poisson) skate.

raifort /rɛfɔr/ n.m. horse-radish.

rail /raj/ n.m. (barre) rail. **le ~**, (transport) rail.

raill|er /raje/ v.t. mock (at). ~erie n.f. mocking remark. ~eur, ~euse a. mocking.

rainure /renyr/ n.f. groove.

raisin /rezɛ̃/ n.m. ~(s), grapes. ~ sec, raisin.

raison /rezɔ̃/ n.f. reason. **à ~ de**, at the

rate of. **avec** ∼, rightly. **avoir** ∼, be right (**de faire**, to do). **avoir** ∼ **de qn.**, get the better of s.o. **donner** ∼ **à**, prove right. **en** ∼ **de**, (*cause*) because of. ∼ **de plus**, all the more reason. **perdre la** ∼, lose one's mind.

raisonnable /rɛzɔnabl/ *a.* reasonable, sensible.

raisonn|er /rɛzɔne/ *v.i.* reason. —*v.t.* (*personne*) reason with. ∼**ement** *n.m.* reasoning; (*propositions*) argument.

rajeunir /raʒœnir/ *v.t.* make (look) younger; (*moderniser*) modernize; (*méd.*) rejuvenate. —*v.i.* look younger.

rajout /raʒu/ *n.m.* addition. ∼**er** /-te/ *v.t.* add.

rajust|er /raʒyste/ *v.t.* straighten; (*salaires*) (re)adjust. ∼**ement** *n.m.* (re)adjustment.

râl|e /ral/ *n.m.* (*de blessé*) groan. ∼**er** *v.i.* groan; (*protester*: *fam.*) moan.

ralent|ir /ralɑ̃tir/ *v.t./i.*, **se** ∼**ir** *v.pr.* slow down. ∼**i** *a.* slow; *n.m.* (*cinéma*) slow motion. **être** *ou* **tourner au** ∼**i**, tick over, idle.

rall|ier /ralje/ *v.t.* rally; (*rejoindre*) rejoin. **se** ∼**ier** *v.pr.* rally. **se** ∼**ier à**, (*avis*) come over to. ∼**iement** *n.m.* rallying.

rallonge /ralɔ̃ʒ/ *n.f.* (*de table*) extension. ∼ **de**, (*supplément de*) extra.

rallonger /ralɔ̃ʒe/ *v.t.* lengthen.

rallumer /ralyme/ *v.t.* light (up) again; (*lampe*) switch on again; (*ranimer*: *fig.*) revive.

rallye /rali/ *n.m.* rally.

ramadan /ramadɑ̃/ *n.m.* Ramadan.

ramassé /ramase/ *a.* squat; (*concis*) concise.

ramass|er /ramase/ *v.t.* pick up; (*récolter*) gather; (*recueillir*) collect. **se** ∼**er** *v.pr.* draw o.s. together, curl up. ∼**age** *n.m.* (*cueillette*) gathering. ∼**age scolaire**, school bus service.

rambarde /rɑ̃bard/ *n.f.* guardrail.

rame /ram/ *n.f.* (*aviron*) oar; (*train*) train; (*perche*) stake.

rameau (*pl.* ∼**x**) /ramo/ *n.m.* branch.

ramener /ramne/ *v.t.* bring back. ∼ **à**, (*réduire à*) reduce to. **se** ∼ *v.pr.* (*fam.*) turn up. **se** ∼ **à**, (*problème*) come down to.

ram|er /rame/ *v.i.* row. ∼**eur**, ∼**euse** *n.m.*, *f.* rower.

ramif|ier (se) /(sə)ramifje/ *v.pr.* ramify. ∼**ication** *n.f.* ramification.

ramollir /ramɔlir/ *v.t.*, **se** ∼ *v.pr.* soften.

ramon|er /ramɔne/ *v.t.* sweep. ∼**eur** *n.m.* (chimney-)sweep.

rampe /rɑ̃p/ *n.f.* banisters; (*pente*) ramp. ∼ **de lancement**, launching pad.

ramper /rɑ̃pe/ *v.i.* crawl.

rancard /rɑ̃kar/ *n.m.* (*fam.*) appointment.

rancart /rɑ̃kar/ *n.m.* **mettre** *ou* **jeter au** ∼, (*fam.*) scrap.

ranc|e /rɑ̃s/ *a.* rancid. ∼**ir** *v.i.* go *ou* turn rancid.

rancœur /rɑ̃kœr/ *n.f.* resentment.

rançon /rɑ̃sɔ̃/ *n.f.* ransom. ∼**ner** /-ɔne/ *v.t.* hold to ransom.

rancun|e /rɑ̃kyn/ *n.f.* grudge. **sans** ∼!, no hard feelings. ∼**ier**, ∼**ière** *a.* vindictive.

randonnée /rɑ̃dɔne/ *n.f.* walk; (*en auto*, *vélo*) ride.

rang /rɑ̃/ *n.m.* row; (*hiérarchie*, *condition*) rank. **se mettre en** ∼, line up. **au premier** ∼, in the first row; (*fig.*) at the forefront. **de second** ∼, (*péj.*) second-rate.

rangée /rɑ̃ʒe/ *n.f.* row.

rang|er /rɑ̃ʒe/ *v.t.* put away; (*chambre etc.*) tidy (up); (*disposer*) place; (*véhicule*) park. **se** ∼**er** *v.pr.* (*véhicule*) park; (*s'écarter*) stand aside; (*s'assagir*) settle down. **se** ∼**er à**, (*avis*) accept. ∼**ement** *n.m.* (*de chambre*) tidying (up); (*espace*) storage space.

ranimer /ranime/ *v.t.*, **se** ∼ *v.pr.* revive.

rapace[1] /rapas/ *n.m.* bird of prey.

rapace[2] /rapas/ *a.* grasping.

rapatr|ier /rapatrije/ *v.t.* repatriate. ∼**iement** *n.m.* repatriation.

râp|e /rap/ *n.f.* (*culin.*) grater; (*lime*) rasp. ∼**er** *v.t.* grate; (*bois*) rasp.

râpé /rape/ *a.* threadbare. **c'est** ∼!, (*fam.*) that's right out!

rapetisser /raptise/ *v.t.* make smaller. —*v.i.* get smaller.

râpeu|x, ∼**se** /rapø, -z/ *a.* rough.

rapid|e /rapid/ *a.* fast, rapid. —*n.m.* (*train*) express (train); (*cours d'eau*) rapids *pl.* ∼**ement** *adv.* fast, rapidly. ∼**ité** *n.f.* speed.

rapiécer /rapjese/ *v.t.* patch.

rappel /rapɛl/ *n.m.* recall; (*deuxième avis*) reminder; (*de salaire*) back pay; (*méd.*) booster.

rappeler /raple/ *v.t.* call back; (*diplomate*, *réserviste*) recall; (*évoquer*) remind, recall. ∼ **qch. à qn.**, (*redire*) remind s.o. of sth. **se** ∼ *v.pr.* remember, recall.

rapport /rapɔr/ *n.m.* connection; (*compte rendu*) report; (*profit*) yield.

~s, (*relations*) relations. **en ~ avec**, (*accord*) in keeping with. **mettre/se mettre en ~ avec**, put/get in touch with. **par ~ à**, in relation to. ~s (*sexuels*), intercourse.

rapport|er /rapɔrte/ *v.t.* bring back; (*profit*) bring in; (*dire, répéter*) report. —*v.i.* (*comm.*) bring in a good return; (*mouchard: fam.*) tell. **se ~er à**, relate to. **s'en ~er à**, rely on. ~**eur**, ~**euse** *n.m., f.* (*mouchard*) tell-tale; *n.m.* (*instrument*) protractor.

rapproch|er /raprɔʃe/ *v.t.* bring closer (**de**, to); (*réconcilier*) bring together; (*comparer*) compare. **se ~er** *v. pr.* get *ou* come closer (**de**, to); (*personnes, pays*) come together; (*s'apparenter*) be close (**de**, to). ~**é** *a.* close. ~**ement** *n.m.* reconciliation; (*rapport*) connection; (*comparaison*) parallel.

rapt /rapt/ *n.m.* abduction.

raquette /rakɛt/ *n.f.* (*de tennis*) racket; (*de ping-pong*) bat.

rare /rar/ *a.* rare; (*insuffisant*) scarce. ~**ment** *adv.* rarely, seldom. ~**té** *n.f.* rarity; scarcity; (*objet*) rarity.

raréfier (se) /(sə)rarefje/ *v. pr.* (*nourriture etc.*) become scarce.

ras, ~**e** /rɑ, rɑz/ *a.* (*herbe, poil*) short. **à ~ de**, very close to. **en avoir ~ le bol**, (*fam.*) be really fed up. ~**e campagne**, open country. **coupé à ~**, cut short. **à ~ bord**, to the brim. **pull ~ du cou**, round-neck pull-over. ~-**le-bol** *n.m.* (*fam.*) anger. **en avoir ~ le bol**, be fed-up.

ras|er /rɑze/ *v.t.* shave; (*cheveux, barbe*) shave off; (*frôler*) skim; (*abattre*) raze; (*ennuyer: fam.*) bore. **se ~er** *v. pr.* shave. ~**age** *n.m.* shaving. ~**eur**, ~**euse** *n.m., f.* (*fam.*) bore.

rasoir /rɑzwar/ *n.m.* razor.

rassas|ier /rasazje/ *v.t.* satisfy. **être ~ié de**, have had enough of.

rassembl|er /rasɑ̃ble/ *v.t.* gather; (*courage*) muster. **se ~er** *v. pr.* gather. ~**ement** *n.m.* gathering.

rasseoir (se) /(sə)raswar/ *v. pr.* sit down again.

rass|is, ~**ise** *ou* ~**ie** /rasi, -z/ *a.* (*pain*) stale.

rassurer /rasyre/ *v.t.* reassure.

rat /ra/ *n.m.* rat.

ratatiner (se) /(sə)ratatine/ *v. pr.* shrivel up.

rate /rat/ *n.f.* spleen.

râteau (*pl.* ~**x**) /rɑto/ *n.m.* rake.

râtelier /rɑtəlje/ *n.m.*; (*fam.*) dentures.

rat|er /rate/ *v.t./i.* miss; (*gâcher*) spoil;

(*échouer*) fail. **c'est ~é**, that's right out. ~**é**, ~**ée** *n.m., f.* (*personne*) failure. **avoir des ~és**, (*auto.*) backfire.

ratif|ier /ratifje/ *v.t.* ratify. ~**ication** *n.f.* ratification.

ratio /rasjo/ *n.m.* ratio.

ration /rasjɔ̃/ *n.f.* ration.

rationaliser /rasjɔnalize/ *v.t.* rationalize.

rationnel, ~**le** /rasjɔnɛl/ *a.* rational.

rationn|er /rasjɔne/ *v.t.* ration. ~**ement** *n.m.* rationing.

ratisser /ratise/ *v.t.* rake; (*fouiller*) comb.

rattacher /rataʃe/ *v.t.* tie up again; (*relier*) link; (*incorporer*) join.

rattrapage /ratrapaʒ/ *n.m.* ~ **scolaire**, remedial classes.

rattraper /ratrape/ *v.t.* catch; (*rejoindre*) catch up with; (*retard, erreur*) make up for. **se ~** *v. pr.* catch up; (*se dédommager*) make up for it. **se ~ à**, catch hold of.

ratur|e /ratyr/ *n.f.* deletion. ~**er** *v.t.* delete.

rauque /rok/ *a.* raucous, harsh.

ravager /ravaʒe/ *v.t.* devastate, ravage.

ravages /ravaʒ/ *n.m. pl.* **faire des ~**, wreak havoc.

raval|er /ravale/ *v.t.* (*façade etc.*) clean; (*humilier*) lower (**à**, down to). ~**ement** *n.m.* cleaning.

ravi /ravi/ *a.* delighted (**que**, that).

ravier /ravje/ *n.m.* hors-d'œuvre dish.

ravigoter /ravigɔte/ *v.t.* (*fam.*) buck up.

ravin /ravɛ̃/ *n.m.* ravine.

ravioli /ravjɔli/ *n.m. pl.* ravioli.

ravir /ravir/ *v.t.* delight. ~ **à qn.**, (*enlever*) rob s.o. of.

raviser (se) /(sə)ravize/ *v. pr.* change one's mind.

ravissant, ~**e** /ravisɑ̃, -t/ *a.* beautiful.

ravisseu|r, ~**se** /ravisœr, -øz/ *n.m., f.* kidnapper.

ravitaill|er /ravitaje/ *v.t.* provide with supplies; (*avion*) refuel. **se ~er** *v. pr.* stock up. ~**ement** *n.m.* provision of supplies (**de**, to), refuelling; (*denrées*) supplies.

raviver /ravive/ *v.t.* revive.

rayé /reje/ *a.* striped.

rayer /reje/ *v.t.* scratch; (*biffer*) cross out.

rayon /rɛjɔ̃/ *n.m.* ray; (*planche*) shelf; (*de magasin*) department; (*de roue*) spoke; (*de cercle*) radius. ~ **d'action**, range. ~ **de miel**, honeycomb. ~ **X**, X-ray. **en connaître un ~**, (*fam.*) know one's stuff.

rayonn|er /rɛjɔne/ *v.i.* radiate; (*de joie*)

beam; (*se déplacer*) tour around (*from a central point*). **∼ement** *n.m.* (*éclat*) radiance; (*influence*) influence; (*radiations*) radiation.

rayure /rejyr/ *n.f.* scratch; (*dessin*) stripe. **à ∼s,** striped.

raz-de-marée /rɑdmare/ *n.m. invar.* tidal wave. **∼ électoral,** landslide.

re- /rə/ *préf.* re-.

ré- /re/ *préf.* re-.

réacteur /reaktœr/ *n.m.* jet engine; (*nucléaire*) reactor.

réaction /reaksjɔ̃/ *n.f.* reaction. **∼ en chaîne,** chain reaction. **∼naire** /-jɔnɛr/ *a. & n.m./f.* reactionary.

réadapter /readapte/ *v.t.,* **se ∼** *v. pr.* readjust (**à,** to).

réaffirmer /reafirme/ *v.t.* reaffirm.

réagir /reaʒir/ *v.i.* react.

réalis|er /realize/ *v.t.* carry out; (*effort, bénéfice, achat*) make; (*rêve*) fulfil; (*film*) produce, direct; (*capital*) realize; (*se rendre compte de*) realize. **se ∼er** *v. pr.* materialize. **∼ateur, ∼atrice** *n.m., f.* (*cinéma*) director; (*TV*) producer. **∼ation** *n.f.* realization; (*œuvre*) achievement.

réalis|te /realist/ *a.* realistic. —*n.m./f.* realist. **∼me** *n.m.* realism.

réalité /realite/ *n.f.* reality.

réanim|er /reanime/ *v.t.* resuscitate. **∼ation** *n.f.* resuscitation. **service de ∼ation,** intensive care.

réapparaître /reaparɛtr/ *v.i.* reappear.

réarm|er (se) /(sə)rearme/ *v. pr.* rearm. **∼ement** *n.m.* rearmament.

rébarbati|f, ∼ve /rebarbatif, -v/ *a.* forbidding, off-putting.

rebâtir /rəbatir/ *v.t.* rebuild.

rebelle /rəbɛl/ *a.* rebellious; (*soldat*) rebel. —*n.m./f.* rebel.

rebeller (se) /(sə)rəbele/ *v. pr.* rebel, hit back defiantly.

rébellion /rebeljɔ̃/ *n.f.* rebellion.

rebiffer (se) /(sə)rəbife/ *v. pr.* (*fam.*) rebel.

rebond /rəbɔ̃/ *n.m.* bounce; (*par ricochet*) rebound. **∼ir** /-ḑir/ *v.i.* bounce; rebound.

rebondi /rəbɔ̃di/ *a.* chubby.

rebondissement /rəbɔ̃dismã/ *n.m.* (new) development.

rebord /rəbɔr/ *n.m.* edge. **∼ de la fenêtre,** window-ledge.

rebours (à) /(a)rəbur/ *adv.* the wrong way.

rebrousse-poil (à) /(a)rəbruspwal/ *adv.* (*fig.*) **prendre qn. ∼,** rub s.o. up the wrong way.

rebrousser /rəbruse/ *v.t.* **∼ chemin,** turn back.

rebuffade /rəbyfad/ *n.f.* rebuff.

rébus /rebys/ *n.m.* rebus.

rebut /rəby/ *n.m.* **mettre** *ou* **jeter au ∼,** scrap.

rebut|er /rəbyte/ *v.t.* put off. **∼ant, ∼ante** *a.* off-putting.

récalcitrant, ∼e /rekalsitrã, -t/ *a.* stubborn.

recal|er /rəkale/ *v.t.* (*fam.*) fail. **se faire ∼er** *ou* **être ∼é,** fail.

récapitul|er /rekapityle/ *v.t./i.* recapitulate. **∼ation** *n.f.* recapitulation.

recel /rəsɛl/ *n.m.* receiving. **∼er** /rəs(ə)le/ *v.t.* (*objet volé*) receive; (*cacher*) conceal.

récemment /resamã/ *adv.* recently.

recens|er /rəsɑ̃se/ *v.t.* (*population*) take a census of; (*objets*) list. **∼ement** *n.m.* census; list.

récent, ∼e /resã, -t/ *a.* recent.

récépissé /resepise/ *n.m.* receipt.

récepteur /reseptœr/ *n.m.* receiver.

récepti|f, ∼ve /reseptif, -v/ *a.* receptive.

réception /resɛpsjɔ̃/ *n.f.* reception. **∼ de,** (*lettre etc.*) receipt of. **∼niste** /-jɔnist/ *n.m./f.* receptionist.

récession /resesjɔ̃/ *n.f.* recession.

recette /rəsɛt/ *n.f.* (*culin.*) recipe; (*argent*) takings. **∼s,** (*comm.*) receipts.

receveu|r, ∼se /rəsvœr, -øz/ *n.m., f.* (*des impôts*) tax collector.

recevoir† /rəsvwar/ *v.t.* receive; (*client, malade*) see; (*obtenir*) get, receive. **être reçu (à),** pass. —*v.i.* (*médecin*) receive patients. **se ∼** *v. pr.* (*tomber*) land.

rechange (de) /(də)rəʃɑ̃ʒ/ *a.* (*roue, vêtements, etc.*) spare; (*solution etc.*) alternative.

réchapper /reʃape/ *v.i.* **∼ de** *ou* **à,** come through, survive.

recharg|e /rəʃarʒ/ *n.f.* (*de stylo*) refill. **∼er** *v.t.* refill; (*batterie*) recharge.

réchaud /reʃo/ *n.m.* stove.

réchauff|er /reʃofe/ *v.t.* warm up. **se ∼er** *v. pr.* warm o.s. up; (*temps*) get warmer. **∼ement** *n.m.* (*de température*) rise (**de,** in).

rêche /rɛʃ/ *a.* rough.

recherche /rəʃɛrʃ/ *n.f.* search (**de,** for); (*raffinement*) elegance. **∼s,** (*univ.*) research. **∼s,** (*enquête*) investigations.

recherch|er /rəʃɛrʃe/ *v.t.* search for. **∼é** *a.* in great demand; (*élégant*) elegant. **∼é pour meurtre,** wanted for murder.

rechigner /rəʃiɲe/ *v.i.* **∼ à,** balk at.

rechut|e /rəʃyt/ n.f. (méd.) relapse. **~er** v.i. relapse.

récidiv|e /residiv/ n.f. second offence. **~er** v.i. commit a second offence.

récif /resif/ n.m. reef.

récipient /resipjɑ̃/ n.m. container.

réciproque /resiprɔk/ a. mutual, reciprocal. **~ment** adv. each other; (inversement) conversely.

récit /resi/ n.m. (compte rendu) account, story; (histoire) story.

récital (pl. **~s**) /resital/ n.m. recital.

récit|er /resite/ v.t. recite. **~ation** n.f. recitation.

réclame /reklam/ n.f. **faire de la ~**, advertise. **en ~**, on offer.

réclam|er /reklame/ v.t. call for, demand; (revendiquer) claim. —v.i. complain. **~ation** n.f. complaint.

reclus, ~e /rəkly, -z/ n.m., f. recluse. —a. cloistered.

réclusion /reklyzjɔ̃/ n.f. imprisonment.

recoin /rəkwɛ̃/ n.m. nook.

récolt|e /rekɔlt/ n.f. (action) harvest; (produits) crop, harvest; (fig.) crop. **~er** v.t. harvest, gather; (fig.) collect.

recommand|er /rəkɔmɑ̃de/ v.t. recommend; (lettre) register. **envoyer en ~é**, send registered. **~ation** n.f. recommendation.

recommence|r /rəkɔmɑ̃se/ v.t./i. (reprendre) begin ou start again; (refaire) repeat. **ne ~ pas**, don't do it again.

récompens|e /rekɔ̃pɑ̃s/ n.f. reward; (prix) award. **~er** v.t. reward (de, for).

réconcil|ier /rekɔ̃silje/ v.t. reconcile. **se ~ier** v. pr. become reconciled (avec, with). **~iation** n.f. reconciliation.

reconduire† /rəkɔ̃dɥir/ v.t. see home; (à la porte) show out; (renouveler) renew.

réconfort /rekɔ̃fɔr/ n.m. comfort. **~er** /-te/ v.t. comfort.

reconnaissable /rəkɔnɛsabl/ a. recognizable.

reconnaissan|t, ~te /rəkɔnɛsɑ̃, -t/ a. grateful (de, for). **~ce** n.f. gratitude; (fait de reconnaître) recognition; (mil.) reconnaissance.

reconnaître† /rəkɔnɛtr/ v.t. recognize; (admettre) admit (que, that); (mil.) reconnoitre; (enfant, tort) acknowledge.

reconstituant /rəkɔ̃stitɥɑ̃/ n.m. tonic.

reconstituer /rəkɔ̃stitɥe/ v.t. reconstitute; (crime) reconstruct.

reconstr|uire† /rəkɔ̃strɥir/ v.t. rebuild. **~uction** n.f. rebuilding.

reconversion /rəkɔ̃vɛrsjɔ̃/ n.f. (de main-d'œuvre) redeployment.

recopier /rəkɔpje/ v.t. copy out.

record /rəkɔr/ n.m. & a. invar. record.

recoupe|r /rəkupe/ v.t. confirm. **se ~** v. pr. check, tally, match up. **par ~ment**, by making connections.

recourbé /rəkurbe/ a. curved; (nez) hooked.

recourir /rəkurir/ v.i. **~ à**, resort to.

recours /rəkur/ n.m. resort. **avoir ~ à**, have recourse to, resort to.

recouvrer /rəkuvre/ v.t. recover.

recouvrir† /rəkuvrir/ v.t. cover.

récréation /rekreasjɔ̃/ n.f. recreation; (scol.) playtime.

récrier (se) /(sə)rekrije/ v. pr. cry out.

récrimination /rekriminasjɔ̃/ n.f. recrimination.

recroqueviller (se) /(sə)rəkrɔkvije/ v. pr. curl up.

recrudescence /rəkrydesɑ̃s/ n.f. new outbreak.

recrue /rəkry/ n.f. recruit.

recrut|er /rəkryte/ v.t. recruit. **~ement** n.m. recruitment.

rectang|le /rɛktɑ̃gl/ n.m. rectangle. **~ulaire** a. rectangular.

rectif|ier /rɛktifje/ v.t. correct, rectify. **~ication** n.f. correction.

recto /rɛkto/ n.m. front of the page.

reçu /rəsy/ voir recevoir. —n.m. receipt. —a. accepted; (candidat) successful.

recueil /rəkœj/ n.m. collection.

recueill|ir† /rəkœjir/ v.t. collect; (prendre chez soi) take in. **se ~ir** v. pr. meditate. **~ement** n.m. meditation. **~i** a. meditative.

recul /rəkyl/ n.m. retreat; (éloignement) distance; (déclin) decline. **(mouvement de) ~**, backward movement. **~ade** n.f. retreat.

reculé /rəkyle/ a. (région) remote.

reculer /rəkyle/ v.t./i. move back; (véhicule) reverse; (armée) retreat; (diminuer) decline; (différer) postpone. **~ devant**, (fig.) shrink from.

reculons (à) /(a)rəkylɔ̃/ adv. backwards.

récupér|er /rekypere/ v.t./i. recover; (vieux objets) salvage. **~ation** n.f. recovery; salvage.

récurer /rekyre/ v.t. scour. **poudre à ~**, scouring powder.

récuser /rekyze/ v.t. challenge. **se ~** v. pr. state that one is not qualified to judge.

recycl|er /rəsikle/ v.t. (personne) retrain; (chose) recycle. **se ~er** v. pr. retrain. **~age** n.m. retraining; recycling.

rédac|teur, ~trice /redaktœr, -tris/

n.m., f. writer, editor. **le ~teur en chef,** the editor (in chief).

rédaction /redaksjɔ̃/ *n.f.* writing; (*scol.*) composition; (*personnel*) editorial staff.

reddition /redisjɔ̃/ *n.f.* surrender.

redemander /rədmɑ̃de/ *v.t.* ask again for; ask for more of.

redevable /rədvabl/ *a.* **être ~ à qn. de,** (*argent*) owe sb; (*fig.*) be indebted to s.o. for.

redevance /rədvɑ̃s/ *n.f.* (*de télévision*) licence fee.

rédiger /rediʒe/ *v.t.* write; (*contrat*) draw up.

redire† /rədir/ *v.t.* repeat. **avoir** *ou* **trouver à ~ à,** find fault with.

redondant, ~e /rədɔ̃dɑ̃, -t/ *a.* superfluous.

redonner /rədɔne/ *v.t.* give back; (*davantage*) give more.

redoubl|er /rəduble/ *v.t./i.* increase; (*classe: scol.*) repeat. **~er de prudence**/*etc.*, be more careful/*etc.* **~ement** *n.m.* (*accroissement*) increase (de, in).

redout|er /rədute/ *v.t.* dread. **~able** *a.* formidable.

redoux /rədu/ *n.m.* milder weather.

redress|er /rədrese/ *v.t.* straighten (out *ou* up); (*situation*) right, redress. **se ~er** *v. pr.* (*personne*) straighten (o.s.) up; (*se remettre debout*) stand up; (*pays, économie*) recover. **~ement** /rədrɛsmɑ̃/ *n.m.* (*relèvement*) recovery.

réduction /redyksjɔ̃/ *n.f.* reduction.

réduire† /reduir/ *v.t.* reduce (**à,** to). **se ~ à,** (*revenir à*) come down to.

réduit¹, ~e /redui, -t/ *a.* (*objet*) small-scale; (*limité*) limited.

réduit² /redui/ *n.m.* recess.

réédu|quer /reedyke/ *v.t.* (*personne*) rehabilitate; (*membre*) re-educate. **~cation** *n.f.* rehabilitation; re-education.

réel, ~le /reɛl/ *a.* real. —*n.m.* reality. **~lement** *adv.* really.

réexpédier /reɛkspedje/ *v.t.* forward; (*retourner*) send back.

refaire† /rəfɛr/ *v.t.* do again; (*erreur, voyage*) make again; (*réparer*) do up, redo.

réfection /refɛksjɔ̃/ *n.f.* repair.

réfectoire /refɛktwar/ *n.m.* refectory.

référence /referɑ̃s/ *n.f.* reference.

référendum /referɛ̃dɔm/ *n.m.* referendum.

référer /refere/ *v.i.* **en ~ à,** refer the matter to. **se ~ à,** refer to.

refermer /rəfɛrme/ *v.t.,* **se ~,** *v. pr.* close (again).

refiler /rəfile/ *v.t.* (*fam.*) palm off (**à,** on).

réfléch|ir /refleʃir/ *v.i.* think (**à,** about). —*v.t.* reflect. **se ~ir** *v. pr.* be reflected. **~i** *a.* (*personne*) thoughtful; (*verbe*) reflexive.

refl|et /rəflɛ/ *n.m.* reflection; (*lumière*) light. **~éter** /-ete/ *v.t.* reflect. **se ~éter** *v. pr.* be reflected.

réflexe /reflɛks/ *a. & n.m.* reflex.

réflexion /reflɛksjɔ̃/ *n.f.* reflection; (*pensée*) thought, reflection. **à la ~,** on second thoughts.

refluer /rəflye/ *v.i.* flow back; (*foule*) retreat.

reflux /rəfly/ *n.m.* (*de marée*) ebb.

refondre /rəfɔ̃dr/ *v.t.* recast.

réform|e /reform/ *n.f.* reform. **~ateur, ~atrice** *n.m., f.* reformer. **~er** *v.t.* reform; (*soldat*) invalid (out of the army).

refoul|er /rəfule/ *v.t.* (*larmes*) force back; (*désir*) repress. **~é** *a.* repressed. **~ement** *n.m.* repression.

réfractaire /refraktɛr/ *a.* **être ~ à,** resist.

refrain /rəfrɛ̃/ *n.m.* chorus. **le même ~,** the same old story.

refréner /rəfrene/ *v.t.* curb, check.

réfrigér|er /refriʒere/ *v.t.* refrigerate. **~ateur** *n.m.* refrigerator.

refroid|ir /rəfrwadir/ *v.t./i.* cool (down). **se ~ir** *v. pr.* (*personne, temps*) get cold; (*ardeur*) cool (off). **~issement** *n.m.* cooling; (*rhume*) chill.

refuge /rəfyʒ/ *n.m.* refuge; (*chalet*) mountain hut.

réfug|ier (se) /(sə)refyʒje/ *v. pr.* take refuge. **~ié, ~iée** *n.m., f.* refugee.

refus /rəfy/ *n.m.* refusal. **ce n'est pas de ~,** I wouldn't say no. **~er** /-ze/ *v.t.* refuse (**de,** to); (*recaler*) fail. **se ~er à,** (*évidence etc.*) reject.

réfuter /refyte/ *v.t.* refute.

regagner /rəgaɲe/ *v.t.* regain; (*revenir à*) get back to.

regain /rəgɛ̃/ *n.m.* **~ de,** renewal of.

régal (*pl. ~s*) /regal/ *n.m.* treat. **~er** *v.t.* treat (**de,** to). **se ~er** *v. pr.* treat o.s. (**de,** to).

regard /rəgar/ *n.m.* (*expression, coup d'œil*) look; (*fixe*) stare; (*vue, œil*) eye. **au ~ de,** in regard to. **en ~ de,** compared with.

regardant, ~e /rəgardɑ̃, -t/ *a.* careful (with money). **peu ~ (sur),** not fussy (about).

regarder /rəgarde/ v.t. look at; (*observer*) watch; (*considérer*) consider; (*concerner*) concern. **∼ (fixement)**, stare at. —v.i. look. **∼ à**, (*qualité etc.*) pay attention to. **∼ vers**, (*maison*) face. **se ∼** v. pr. (*personnes*) look at each other.

régates /regat/ n.f. pl. regatta.

régénérer /reʒenere/ v.t. regenerate.

régen|t, ∼te /reʒɑ̃, -t/ n.m., f. regent. **∼ce** n.f. regency.

régenter /reʒɑ̃te/ v.t. rule.

reggae /rege/ n.m. reggae.

régie /reʒi/ n.f. (*entreprise*) public corporation; (*radio, TV*) control room; (*cinéma, théâtre*) production.

regimber /rəʒɛ̃be/ v.i. balk.

régime /reʒim/ n.m. (*organisation*) system; (*pol.*) regime; (*méd.*) diet; (*de moteur*) speed; (*de bananes*) bunch. **se mettre au ∼**, go on a diet.

régiment /reʒimɑ̃/ n.m. regiment.

région /reʒjɔ̃/ n.f. region. **∼al** (*m. pl. ∼aux*) /-jɔnal, -o/ a. regional.

régir /reʒir/ v.t. govern.

régisseur /reʒisœr/ n.m. (*théâtre*) stage-manager; (*cinéma, TV*) assistant director.

registre /rəʒistr/ n.m. register.

réglage /reglaʒ/ n.m. adjustment.

règle /regl/ n.f. rule; (*instrument*) ruler. **∼s**, (*de femme*) period. **en ∼**, in order. **∼ à calculer**, slide-rule.

réglé /regle/ a. (*vie*) ordered; (*arrangé*) settled.

règlement /regləmɑ̃/ n.m. regulation; (*règles*) regulations; (*solution, paiement*) settlement. **∼aire** /-tɛr/ a. (*uniforme*) regulation.

réglement|er /regləmɑ̃te/ v.t. regulate. **∼ation** n.f. regulation.

régler /regle/ v.t. settle; (*machine*) adjust; (*programmer*) set; (*facture*) settle; (*personne*) settle up with; (*papier*) rule. **∼ son compte à**, settle a score with.

réglisse /reglis/ n.f. liquorice.

règne /rɛɲ/ n.m. reign; (*végétal, animal, minéral*) kingdom.

régner /reɲe/ v.i. reign.

regorger /rəɡɔrʒe/ v.i. **∼ de**, be overflowing with.

regret /rəɡrɛ/ n.m. regret. **à ∼**, with regret.

regrett|er /rəɡrete/ v.t. regret; (*personne*) miss. **∼able** a. regrettable.

regrouper /rəɡrupe/ v.t., group together. **se ∼** v. pr. gather (together).

régulariser /regylarize/ v.t. regularize.

régulation /regylasjɔ̃/ n.f. regulation.

régul|ier, ∼ière /regylje, -jɛr/ a. regular; (*qualité, vitesse*) steady, even; (*ligne, paysage*) even; (*légal*) legal; (*honnête*) honest. **∼arité** n.f. regularity; steadiness; evenness. **∼ièrement** adv. regularly; (*d'ordinaire*) normally.

réhabilit|er /reabilite/ n.f. rehabilitate. **∼ation** n.f. rehabilitation.

rehausser /rəose/ v.t. raise; (*faire valoir*) enhance.

rein /rɛ̃/ n.m. kidney. **∼s**, (*dos*) back.

réincarnation /reɛ̃karnasjɔ̃/ n.f. reincarnation.

reine /rɛn/ n.f. queen. **∼-claude** n.f. greengage.

réinsertion /reɛ̃sɛrsjɔ̃/ n.f. reintegration, rehabilitation.

réintégrer /reɛ̃tegre/ v.t. (*lieu*) return to; (*jurid.*) reinstate.

réitérer /reitere/ v.t. repeat.

rejaillir /rəʒajir/ v.i. **∼ sur**, rebound on.

rejet /rəʒɛ/ n.m. rejection.

rejeter /rəʒte/ v.t. throw back; (*refuser*) reject; (*vomir*) bring up; (*déverser*) discharge. **∼ une faute/etc. sur qn.**, shift the blame for a mistake/etc. on to s.o.

rejeton(s) /rəʒtɔ̃/ n.m. (pl.) (*fam.*) offspring.

rejoindre† /rəʒwɛ̃dr/ v.t. go back to, rejoin; (*rattraper*) catch up with; (*rencontrer*) join, meet. **se ∼** v. pr. (*personnes*) meet; (*routes*) join, meet.

réjoui /reʒwi/ a. joyful.

réjou|ir /reʒwir/ v.t. delight. **se ∼ir** v. pr. be delighted (**de qch.**, at sth.). **∼issances** n.f. pl. festivities. **∼issant, ∼issante** a. cheering.

relâche /rəlɑʃ/ n.m. (*repos*) respite. **faire ∼**, (*théâtre*) close.

relâché /rəlɑʃe/ a. lax.

relâch|er /rəlɑʃe/ v.t. slacken; (*personne*) release; (*discipline*) relax. **se ∼er** v. pr. slacken. **∼ement** n.m. slackening.

relais /rəlɛ/ n.m. relay. **∼ (routier)**, roadside café.

relanc|e /rəlɑ̃s/ n.f. boost. **∼er** v.t. boost, revive; (*renvoyer*) throw back.

relati|f, ∼ve /rəlatif, -v/ a. relative.

relation /rəlasjɔ̃/ n.f. relation(ship); (*ami*) acquaintance; (*récit*) account. **∼s**, relation. **en ∼ avec qn.**, in touch with s.o.

relativement /rəlativmɑ̃/ adv. relatively. **∼ à**, in relation to.

relativité /rəlativite/ *n.f.* relativity.

relax|er (se) /(sə)rəlakse/ *v. pr.* relax. **~ation** *n.f.* relaxation. **~é** *a.* (*fam.*) laid-back.

relayer /rəleje/ *v.t.* relieve; (*émission*) relay. **se ~** *v. pr.* take over from one another.

reléguer /rəlege/ *v.t.* relegate.

relent /rəlɑ̃/ *n.m.* stink.

relève /rəlɛv/ *n.f.* relief. **prendre** *ou* **assurer la ~,** take over (**de,** from).

relevé /rəlve/ *n.m.* list; (*de compte*) statement; (*de compteur*) reading. —*a.* spicy.

relever /rəlve/ *v.t.* pick up; (*personne tombée*) help up; (*remonter*) raise; (*col*) turn up; (*manches*) roll up; (*sauce*) season; (*goût*) bring out; (*compteur*) read; (*défi*) accept; (*relayer*) relieve; (*remarquer, noter*) note; (*rebâtir*) rebuild. —*v.i.* **~ de,** (*dépendre de*) be the concern of; (*méd.*) recover from. **se ~** *v. pr.* (*personne*) get up (again); (*pays, économie*) recover.

relief /rəljɛf/ *n.m.* relief. **mettre en ~,** highlight.

relier /rəlje/ *v.t.* link (**à,** to); (*ensemble*) link together; (*livre*) bind.

religieu|x, ~se /rəliʒjø, -z/ *a.* religious. —*n.m.* monk. —*n.f.* nun; (*culin.*) choux bun.

religion /rəliʒjɔ̃/ *n.f.* religion.

reliquat /rəlika/ *n.m.* residue.

relique /rəlik/ *n.f.* relic.

reliure /rəljyr/ *n.f.* binding.

reluire /rəlɥir/ *v.i.* shine. **faire ~,** shine.

reluisant, ~e /rəlɥizɑ̃, -t/ *a.* **peu** *ou* **pas ~,** not brilliant.

reman|ier /rəmanje/ *v.t.* revise; (*ministère*) reshuffle. **~iement** *n.m.* revision; reshuffle.

remarier (se) /(sə)rəmarje/ *v. pr.* remarry.

remarquable /rəmarkabl/ *a.* remarkable.

remarque /rəmark/ *n.f.* remark; (*par écrit*) note.

remarquer /rəmarke/ *v.t.* notice; (*dire*) say. **faire ~,** point out (**à,** to). **se faire ~,** attract attention. **remarque(z),** mind you.

remblai /rɑ̃blɛ/ *n.m.* embankment.

rembourrer /rɑ̃bure/ *v.t.* pad.

rembours|er /rɑ̃burse/ *v.t.* repay; (*billet, frais*) refund. **~ement** *n.m.* repayment; refund.

remède /rəmɛd/ *n.m.* remedy; (*médicament*) medicine.

remédier /rəmedje/ *v.i.* **~ à,** remedy.

remémorer (se) /(sə)rəmemɔre/ *v. pr.* recall.

remerc|ier /rəmɛrsje/ *v.t.* thank (**de,** for); (*licencier*) dismiss. **~iements** *n.m. pl.* thanks.

remettre† /rəmɛtr/ *v.t.* put back; (*vêtement*) put back on; (*donner*) hand (over); (*devoir, démission*) hand in; (*restituer*) give back; (*différer*) put off; (*ajouter*) add; (*se rappeler*) remember; (*peine*) remit. **se ~** *v. pr.* (*guérir*) recover. **se ~ à,** go back to. **se ~ à faire,** start doing again. **s'en ~ à,** leave it to. **~ en cause** *ou* **en question,** call into question.

réminiscence /reminisɑ̃s/ *n.f.* reminiscence.

remise¹ /rəmiz/ *n.f.* (*abri*) shed.

remise² /rəmiz/ *n.f.* (*rabais*) discount; (*livraison*) delivery; (*ajournement*) postponement. **~ en cause** *ou* **en question,** calling into question.

remiser /rəmize/ *v.t.* put away.

rémission /remisjɔ̃/ *n.f.* remission.

remontant /rəmɔ̃tɑ̃/ *n.m.* tonic.

remontée /rəmɔ̃te/ *n.f.* ascent; (*d'eau, de prix*) rise. **~ mécanique,** ski-lift.

remont|er /rəmɔ̃te/ *v.i.* go *ou* come (back) up; (*prix, niveau*) rise *ou* (*revenir*) go back. —*v.t.* (*rue etc.*) go *ou* come (back) up; (*relever*) raise; (*montre*) wind up; (*objet démonté*) put together again; (*personne*) buck up. **~e-pente** *n.m.* ski-lift.

remontoir /rəmɔ̃twar/ *n.m.* winder.

remontrer /rəmɔ̃tre/ *v.t.* show again. **en ~ à qn.,** go one up on s.o.

remords /rəmɔr/ *n.m.* remorse. **avoir un** *ou* **des ~,** feel remorse.

remorqu|e /rəmɔrk/ *n.f.* (*véhicule*) trailer. **en ~e,** on tow. **~er** *v.t.* tow.

remorqueur /rəmɔrkœr/ *n.m.* tug.

remous /rəmu/ *n.m.* eddy; (*de bateau*) backwash; (*fig.*) turmoil.

rempart /rɑ̃par/ *n.m.* rampart.

remplaçant, ~e /rɑ̃plasɑ̃, -t/ *n.m.,* *f.* replacement; (*joueur*) reserve.

remplac|er /rɑ̃plase/ *v.t.* replace. **~ement** *n.m.* replacement.

rempli /rɑ̃pli/ *a.* full (**de,** of).

rempl|ir /rɑ̃plir/ *v.t.* fill (up); (*formulaire*) fill (in *ou* out); (*tâche, condition*) fulfil. **se ~ir** *v. pr.* fill (up). **~issage** *n.m.* filling; (*de texte*) padding.

remporter /rɑ̃pɔrte/ *v.t.* take back; (*victoire*) win.

remuant, ~e /rəmɥɑ̃, -t/ *a.* restless.

remue-ménage /rəmymenaʒ/ *n.m. invar.* commotion, bustle.

remuer /rəmɥe/ v.t./i. move; (thé, café) stir; (gigoter) fidget. **se** ~ v. pr. move.

rémunér|er /remynere/ v.t. pay. ~**ation** n.f. payment.

renâcler /rənɑkle/ v.i. snort. ~ **à**, balk at, jib at.

ren|aître /rənɛtr/ v.i. be reborn; (sentiment) be revived. ~**aissance** n.f. rebirth.

renard /rənar/ n.m. fox.

renchérir /rɑ̃ʃerir/ v.i. become dearer. ~ **sur**, go one better than.

rencontr|e /rɑ̃kɔ̃tr/ n.f. meeting; (de routes) junction; (mil.) encounter; (match) match; (Amer.) game. ~**er** v.t. meet; (heurter) strike; (trouver) find. **se** ~**er** v. pr. meet.

rendement /rɑ̃dmɑ̃/ n.m. yield; (travail) output.

rendez-vous /rɑ̃devu/ n.m. appointment; (d'amoureux) date; (lieu) meeting-place. **prendre** ~ **(avec)**, make an appointment (with).

rendormir (se) /(sə)rɑ̃dərmir/ v. pr. go back to sleep.

rendre /rɑ̃dr/ v.t. give back, return; (donner en retour) return; (monnaie) give; (hommage) pay; (justice) dispense; (jugement) pronounce. ~ **heureux/possible/etc.**, make happy/possible/etc. —v.i. (terres) yield; (vomir) vomit. **se** ~ v. pr. (capituler) surrender; (aller) go (à, to); (ridicule, utile, etc.) make o.s. ~ **compte de**, report on. ~ **des comptes à**, be accountable to. ~ **justice à qn.**, do s.o. justice. ~ **service (à)**, help. ~ **visite à**, visit. **se** ~ **compte de**, realize.

rendu /rɑ̃dy/ a. **être** ~, (arrivé) have arrived.

rêne /rɛn/ n.f. rein.

renégat, ~**e** /rənega, -t/ n.m., f. renegade.

renfermé /rɑ̃fɛrme/ n.m. stale smell. **sentir le** ~, smell stale. —a. withdrawn.

renfermer /rɑ̃fɛrme/ v.t. contain. **se** ~ **(en soi-même)**, withdraw (into o.s.).

renfl|é /rɑ̃fle/ a. bulging. ~**ement** n.m. bulge.

renflouer /rɑ̃flue/ v.t. refloat.

renfoncement /rɑ̃fɔ̃smɑ̃/ n.m. recess.

renforcer /rɑ̃fɔrse/ v.t. reinforce.

renfort /rɑ̃fɔr/ n.m. reinforcement. **de** ~, (armée, personnel) back-up. **à grand** ~ **de**, with a great deal of.

renfrogn|er (se) /(sə)rɑ̃frɔɲe/ v. pr. scowl. ~**é** a. surly, sullen.

rengaine /rɑ̃gɛn/ n.f. (péj.) **la même** ~, the same old story.

renier /rənje/ v.t. (personne, pays) disown, deny; (foi) renounce.

renifler /rənifle/ v.t./i. sniff.

renne /rɛn/ n.m. reindeer.

renom /rənɔ̃/ n.m. renown; (réputation) reputation. ~**mé** /-ɔme/ a. famous. ~**mée** /-ɔme/ n.f. fame; reputation.

renonc|er /rənɔ̃se/ v.i. ~**er à**, (habitude, ami, etc.) give up, renounce. ~**er à faire**, give up (all thought of) doing. ~**ement** n.m., ~**iation** n.f. renunciation.

renouer /rənwe/ v.t. tie up (again); (reprendre) renew. —v.i. ~ **avec**, start up again with.

renouveau (pl. ~**x**) /rənuvo/ n.m. revival.

renouvel|er /rənuvle/ v.t. renew; (réitérer) repeat. **se** ~**er** v. pr. be renewed; be repeated. ~**lement** /-vɛlmɑ̃/ n.m. renewal.

rénov|er /renɔve/ v.t. (édifice) renovate; (institution) reform. ~**ation** n.f. renovation; reform.

renseignement /rɑ̃sɛɲmɑ̃/ n.m. ~**(s)**, information. **(bureau des)** ~**s**, information desk.

renseigner /rɑ̃seɲe/ v.t. inform, give information to. **se** ~ v. pr. enquire, make enquiries, find out.

rentab|le /rɑ̃tabl/ a. profitable. ~**ilité** n.f. profitability.

rent|e /rɑ̃t/ n.f. (private) income; (pension) pension, annuity. ~**ier**, ~**ière** n.m., f. person of private means.

rentrée /rɑ̃tre/ n.f. return; **la** ~ **parlementaire**, the reopening of Parliament; (scol.) start of the new year.

rentrer /rɑ̃tre/ (aux. être) v.i. go ou come back home, return home; (entrer) go ou come in; (entrer à nouveau) go ou come back in; (revenu) come in; (élèves) go back. ~ **dans**, (heurter) smash into. —v.t. (aux. avoir) bring in; (griffes) draw in; (vêtement) tuck in ou **dans l'ordre**, be back to normal. ~ **dans ses frais**, break even.

renverse (à la) /(ala)rɑ̃vɛrs/ adv. backwards.

renvers|er /rɑ̃vɛrse/ v.t. knock over ou down; (piéton) knock down; (liquide) upset, spill; (mettre à l'envers) turn upside down; (gouvernement) overturn; (inverser) reverse. **se** ~**er** v. pr. (véhicule) overturn; (verre, vase) fall over. ~**ement** n.m. (pol.) overthrow.

renv|oi /rɑ̃vwa/ *n.m.* return; dismissal; expulsion; postponement; reference; (*rot*) belch. **~oyer†** *v.t.* send back, return; (*employé*) dismiss; (*élève*) expel; (*ajourner*) postpone; (*référer*) refer; (*réfléchir*) reflect.

réorganiser /reɔrganize/ *v.t.* reorganize.

réouverture /reuvɛrtyr/ *n.f.* reopening.

repaire /rəpɛr/ *n.m.* den.

répandre /repɑ̃dr/ *v.t.* (*liquide*) spill; (*étendre, diffuser*) spread; (*lumière, sang*) shed; (*odeur*) give off. **se ~** *v. pr.* spread; (*liquide*) spill. **se ~ en,** (*injures etc.*) pour forth, launch forth into.

répandu /repɑ̃dy/ *a.* (*courant*) widespread.

répar|er /repare/ *v.t.* repair, mend; (*faute*) make amends for; (*remédier à*) put right. **~ateur** *n.m.* repairer. **~ation** *n.f.* repair; (*compensation*) compensation.

repartie /rəparti/ *n.f.* retort. **avoir (le sens) de la ~,** be good at repartee.

repartir† /rəpartir/ *v.i.* start (up) again; (*voyageur*) set off again; (*s'en retourner*) go back.

répart|ir /repartir/ *v.t.* distribute; (*partager*) share out; (*étaler*) spread. **~ition** *n.f.* distribution.

repas /rəpa/ *n.m.* meal.

repass|er /rəpase/ *v.i.* come *ou* go back. —*v.t.* (*linge*) iron; (*leçon*) go over; (*examen*) retake, (*film*) show again. **~age** *n.m.* ironing.

repêcher /rəpeʃe/ *v.t.* fish out; (*candidat*) allow to pass.

repentir /rəpɑ̃tir/ *n.m.* repentance. **se ~** *v. pr.* (*relig.*) repent (*de,* of). **se ~ de,** (*regretter*) regret.

répercu|ter /repɛrkyte/ *v.t.* (*bruit*) echo. **se ~ter** *v. pr.* echo. **se ~ter sur,** have repercussions on. **~ssion** *n.f.* repercussion.

repère /rəpɛr/ *n.m.* mark; (*jalon*) marker; (*fig.*) landmark.

repérer /rəpere/ *v.t.* locate, spot. **se ~** *v. pr.* find one's bearings.

répert|oire /repɛrtwar/ *n.m.* index; (*artistique*) repertoire. **~orier** *v.t.* index.

répéter /repete/ *v.t.* repeat. —*v.t./i.* (*théâtre*) rehearse. **se ~** *v. pr.* be repeated; (*personne*) repeat o.s.

répétition /repetisjɔ̃/ *n.f.* repetition; (*théâtre*) rehearsal.

repiquer /rəpike/ *v.t.* (*plante*) plant out.

répit /repi/ *n.m.* rest, respite.

replacer /rəplase/ *v.t.* replace.

repl|i /rəpli/ *n.m.* fold; (*retrait*) withdrawal. **~ier** *v.t.* fold (up); (*ailes, jambes*) tuck in. **se ~ier** *v. pr.* withdraw (**sur soi-même,** into o.s.).

répliqu|e /replik/ *n.f.* reply; (*riposte*) retort; (*discussion*) objection; (*théâtre*) line(s); (*copie*) replica. **~er** *v.t./i.* reply; (*riposter*) retort; (*objecter*) answer back.

répondant, ~e /repɔ̃dɑ̃, -t/ *n.m., f.* guarantor. **avoir du ~,** have money behind one.

répondeur /repɔ̃dœr/ *n.m.* answering machine.

répondre /repɔ̃dr/ *v.t.* (*remarque etc.*) reply with. **~ que,** answer *ou* reply that. —*v.i.* answer, reply; (*être insolent*) answer back; (*réagir*) respond (**à,** to). **~ à,** answer. **~ de,** answer for.

réponse /repɔ̃s/ *n.f.* answer, reply; (*fig.*) response.

report /rəpɔr/ *n.m.* (*transcription*) transfer; (*renvoi*) postponement.

reportage /rəpɔrtaʒ/ *n.m.* report; (*en direct*) commentary; (*par écrit*) article.

reporter¹ /rəpɔrte/ *v.t.* take back; (*ajourner*) put off; (*transcrire*) transfer. **se ~ à,** refer to.

reporter² /rəpɔrtɛr/ *n.m.* reporter.

repos /rəpo/ *n.m.* rest; (*paix*) peace; (*tranquillité*) peace and quiet; (*moral*) peace of mind.

repos|er /rəpoze/ *v.t.* put down again; (*délasser*) rest. —*v.i.* rest (**sur,** on). **se ~er** *v. pr.* rest. **se ~er sur,** rely on. **~ant, ~ante** *a.* restful. **laisser ~er,** (*pâte*) leave to stand.

repoussant, ~e /rəpusɑ̃, -t/ *a.* repulsive.

repousser /rəpuse/ *v.t.* push back; (*écarter*) push away; (*dégoûter*) repel; (*décliner*) reject; (*ajourner*) put back. —*v.i.* grow again.

répréhensible /repreɑ̃sibl/ *a.* blameworthy.

reprendre† /rəprɑ̃dr/ *v.t.* take back; (*retrouver*) regain; (*souffle*) get back; (*évadé*) recapture; (*recommencer*) resume; (*redire*) repeat; (*modifier*) alter; (*blâmer*) reprimand. **~ du pain/etc.,** take some more bread/etc. —*v.i.* (*recommencer*) resume; (*affaires*) pick up. **se ~** *v. pr.* (*se ressaisir*) pull o.s. together; (*se corriger*) correct o.s. **on ne m'y reprendra pas,** I won't be caught out again.

représailles /rəprezaj/ *n.f. pl.* reprisals.

représentati|f, ~ve /rəprezɑ̃tatif, -v/ *a.* representative.

représent|er /rəprezɑ̃te/ *v.t.* represent;

(*théâtre*) perform. **se ~er** *v. pr.*
(*s'imaginer*) imagine. **~ant, ~ante**
n.m., f. representative. **~ation** *n.f.*
representation; (*théâtre*) performance.
réprimand|e /reprimɑ̃d/ *n.f.* reprimand.
~er *v.t.* reprimand.
répr|imer /reprime/ *v.t.* (*peuple*) repress
(*sentiment*) suppress. **~ession** *n.f.*
repression.
repris /rəpri/ *n.m.* **~ de justice,** ex-
convict.
reprise /rəpriz/ *n.f.* resumption;
(*théâtre*) revival; (*télévision*) repeat;
(*de tissu*) darn, mend; (*essor*) recovery;
(*comm.*) part-exchange, trade-in. **à**
plusieurs ~s, on several occasions.
repriser /rəprize/ *v.t.* darn, mend.
réprobation /reprɔbasjɔ̃/ *n.f.* condem-
nation.
reproch|e /rəprɔʃ/ *n.m.* reproach, blame.
~er *v.t.* **~er qch. à qn.,** reproach *ou*
blame s.o. for sth.
reprod|uire† /rəprɔdɥir/ *v.t.* reproduce.
se ~uire *v. pr.* reproduce; (*arriver*)
recur. **~ucteur, ~uctrice** *a.* reproduc-
tive. **~uction** *n.f.* reproduction.
réprouver /repruve/ *v.t.* condemn.
reptile /rɛptil/ *n.m.* reptile.
repu /rəpy/ *a.* satiated.
républi|que /repyblik/ *n.f.* republic.
~que populaire, people's republic.
~cain, ~caine *a.* & *n.m., f.* republican.
répudier /repydje/ *v.t.* repudiate.
répugnance /repyɲɑ̃s/ *n.f.* repugnance;
(*hésitation*) reluctance.
répugn|er /repyɲe/ *v.i.* **~er à,** be
repugnant to. **~er à faire,** be reluctant
to do. **~ant, ~ante** *a.* repulsive.
répulsion /repylsjɔ̃/ *n.f.* repulsion.
réputation /repytasjɔ̃/ *n.f.* reputation.
réputé /repyte/ *a.* renowned (**pour,** for).
~ pour être, reputed to be.
requérir /rəkerir/ *v.t.* require, demand.
requête /rəkɛt/ *n.f.* request; (*jurid.*)
petition.
requiem /rekɥijɛm/ *n.m. invar.* requiem.
requin /rəkɛ̃/ *n.m.* shark.
requis, ~e /rəki, -z/ *a.* required.
réquisition /rekizisjɔ̃/ *n.f.* requisition.
~ner /-jɔne/ *v.t.* requisition.
rescapé, ~e /rɛskape/ *n.m., f.* survivor.
—*a.* surviving.
rescousse /rɛskus/ *n.f.* **à la ~,** to the
rescue.
réseau (*pl.* **~x**) /rezo/ *n.m.* network.
réservation /rezɛrvasjɔ̃/ *n.f.* reservation.
bureau de ~, booking office.
réserve /rezɛrv/ *n.f.* reserve; (*restriction*)
reservation, reserve; (*indienne*) reser-

vation; (*entrepôt*) store-room. **en ~,** in
reserve. **les ~s,** (*mil.*) the reserves.
réserv|er /rezɛrve/ *v.t.* reserve; (*place*)
book, reserve. **se ~er le droit de,**
reserve the right to. **~é** *a.* (*personne,*
place) reserved.
réserviste /rezɛrvist/ *n.m.* reservist.
réservoir /rezɛrvwar/ *n.m.* tank; (*lac*)
reservoir.
résidence /rezidɑ̃s/ *n.f.* residence.
résident, ~e /rezidɑ̃, -t/ *n.m., f.*
resident foreigner. **~iel, ~ielle** /-sjɛl/
a. residential.
résider /rezide/ *v.i.* reside.
résidu /rezidy/ *n.m.* residue.
résign|er (se) /(sə)reziɲe/ *v. pr.* **se ~er à**
faire, resign o.s. to doing. **~ation** *n.f.*
resignation.
résilier /rezilje/ *v.t.* terminate.
résille /rezij/ *n.f.* (hair)net.
résine /rezin/ *n.f.* resin.
résistance /rezistɑ̃s/ *n.f.* resistance; (*fil*
électrique) element.
résistant, ~e /rezistɑ̃, -t/ *a.* tough.
résister /reziste/ *v.i.* resist. **~ à,** resist;
(*examen, chaleur*) stand up to.
résolu /rezɔly/ *voir* **résoudre. —***a.*
resolute. **~ à,** resolved to. **~ment** *adv.*
resolutely.
résolution /rezɔlysjɔ̃/ *n.f.* (*fermeté*)
resolution; (*d'un problème*) solving.
résonance /rezɔnɑ̃s/ *n.f.* resonance.
résonner /rezɔne/ *v.i.* resound.
résor|ber /rezɔrbe/ *v.t.* reduce. **se ~ber**
v. pr. be reduced. **~ption** *n.f.* reduction.
résoudre† /rezudr/ *v.t.* solve; (*décider*)
decide on. **se ~ à,** resolve to.
respect /rɛspɛ/ *n.m.* respect.
respectab|le /rɛspɛktabl/ *a.* respectable.
~ilité *n.f.* respectability.
respecter /rɛspɛkte/ *v.t.* respect. **faire**
~, (*loi, décision*) enforce.
respecti|f, ~ve /rɛspɛktif, -v/ *a.*
respective. **~vement** *adv.* respectively.
respectueu|x, ~se /rɛspɛktɥø, -z/ *a.*
respectful.
respir|er /rɛspire/ *v.i.* breathe; (*se*
reposer) get one's breath. **—***v.t.*
breathe; (*exprimer*) radiate. **~ation** *n.f.*
breathing; (*haleine*) breath. **~atoire** *a.*
breathing.
resplend|ir /rɛsplɑ̃dir/ *v.i.* shine (**de,**
with). **~issant, ~issante** *a.* radiant.
responsabilité /rɛspɔ̃sabilite/ *n.f.*
responsibility; (*légale*) liability.
responsable /rɛspɔ̃sabl/ *a.* responsible
(**de,** for). **~ de,** (*chargé de*) in charge
of. **—***n.m./f.* person in charge;
(*coupable*) person responsible.

resquiller /rɛskije/ v.i. (fam.) get in without paying; (dans la queue) jump the queue.

ressaisir (se) /(sə)rəsezir/ v. pr. pull o.s. together.

ressasser /rəsase/ v.t. keep going over.

ressembl|er /rəsɑ̃ble/ v.i. ~er à, resemble, look like. se ~er v. pr. look alike. ~ance n.f. resemblance. ~ant, ~ante a. (portrait) true to life; (pareil) alike.

ressemeler /rəsəmle/ v.t. sole.

ressentiment /rəsɑ̃timɑ̃/ n.m. resentment.

ressentir /rəsɑ̃tir/ v.t. feel. se ~ de, feel the effects of.

resserre /rəsɛr/ n.f. shed.

resserrer /rəsere/ v.t. tighten; (contracter) contract. se ~ v. pr. tighten; contract; (route etc.) narrow.

resservir /rəsɛrvir/ v.i. come in useful (again).

ressort /rəsɔr/ n.m. (objet) spring; (fig.) energy. du ~ de, within the jurisdiction ou scope of. en dernier ~, in the last resort.

ressortir† /rəsɔrtir/ v.i. go ou come back out; (se voir) stand out. faire ~, bring out. ~ de, (résulter) result ou emerge from.

ressortissant, ~e /rəsɔrtisɑ̃, -t/ n.m., f. national.

ressource /rəsurs/ n.f. resource. ~s, resources.

ressusciter /resysite/ v.i. come back to life.

restant, ~e /rɛstɑ̃, -t/ a. remaining. —n.m. remainder.

restaur|ant /rɛstɔrɑ̃/ n.m. restaurant. ~ateur, ~atrice n.m., f. restaurant owner.

restaur|er /rɛstɔre/ v.t. restore. se ~er v. pr. eat. ~ation n.f. restoration; (hôtellerie) catering.

reste /rɛst/ n.m. rest; (d'une soustraction) remainder. ~s, remains (de, of); (nourriture) leftovers. un ~ de pain/etc., some left-over bread/etc. au ~, du ~, moreover, besides.

rest|er /rɛste/ v.i. (aux. être) stay, remain; (subsister) be left, remain. il ~e du pain/etc., there is some bread/etc. left (over). il me ~e du pain, I have some bread left (over). il me ~e à, it remains for me to. en ~er à, go no further than. en ~er là, stop there.

restitu|er /rɛstitɥe/ v.t. (rendre) return, restore; (son) reproduce. ~ution n.f. return.

restreindre† /rɛstrɛ̃dr/ v.t. restrict. se ~ v. pr. (dans les dépenses) cut down.

restricti|f, ~ve /rɛstriktif, -v/ a. restrictive.

restriction /rɛstriksjɔ̃/ n.f. restriction.

résultat /rezylta/ n.m. result.

résulter /rezylte/ v.i. ~ de, result from.

résum|er /rezyme/ v.t., se ~er v. pr. summarize. ~é n.m. summary. en ~é, in short.

résurrection /rezyrɛksjɔ̃/ n.f. resurrection; (renouveau) revival.

rétabl|ir /retablir/ v.t. restore; (personne) restore to health. se ~ir v. pr. be restored; (guérir) recover. ~issement n.m. restoring; (méd.) recovery.

retaper /rətape/ v.t. (maison etc.) do up. se ~ v. pr. (guérir) get back on one's feet.

retard /rətar/ n.m. lateness; (sur un programme) delay; (infériorité) backwardness. avoir du ~, be late; (montre) be slow. en ~, late; (retardé) backward. en ~ sur, behind. rattraper ou combler son ~, catch up.

retardataire /rətardatɛr/ n.m./f. latecomer. —a. (arrivant) late.

retardé /rətarde/ a. backward.

retardement (à) /(a)rətardəmɑ̃/ a. (bombe etc.) delayed-action.

retarder /rətarde/ v.t. delay; (sur un programme) set back; (montre) put back. —v.i. (montre) be slow; (fam.) be out of touch.

retenir† /rətnir/ v.t. hold back; (souffle, attention, prisonnier) hold; (eau, chaleur) retain, hold; (larmes) hold back; (garder) keep; (retarder) detain; (réserver) book; (se rappeler) remember; (déduire) deduct; (accepter) accept. se ~ v. pr. (se contenir) restrain o.s. se ~ à, hold on to. se ~ de, stop o.s. from.

rétention /retɑ̃sjɔ̃/ n.f. retention.

retent|ir /rətɑ̃tir/ v.i. ring out (de, with). ~issant, ~issante a. resounding. ~issement n.m. (effet, répercussion) effect.

retenue /rətny/ n.f. restraint; (somme) deduction; (scol.) detention.

réticen|t, ~te /retisɑ̃, -t/ a. (hésitant) reluctant; (réservé) reticent. ~ce n.f. reluctance; reticence.

rétif, ~ve /retif, -v/ a. restive, recalcitrant.

rétine /retin/ n.f. retina.

retiré /rətire/ a. (vie) secluded; (lieu) remote.

retirer /rǝtire/ v.t. (sortir) take out; (ôter) take off; (argent, candidature) withdraw; (avantage) derive. ~ à qn., take away from s.o. se ~ v. pr. withdraw, retire.

retombées /rǝtɔ̃be/ n.f. pl. fall-out.

retomber /rǝtɔ̃be/ v.i. fall; (à nouveau) fall again. ~ dans, (erreur etc.) fall back into.

rétorquer /retɔrke/ v.t. retort.

rétorsion /retɔrsjɔ̃/ n.f. **mesures de ~**, retaliation.

retouch|e /rǝtuʃ/ n.f. touch-up; alteration. ~er v.t. touch up; (vêtement) alter.

retour /rǝtur/ n.m. return. **être de ~**, be back (de, from). ~ **en arrière**, flashback. **par ~ du courrier**, by return of post. **en ~**, in return.

retourner /rǝturne/ v.t. (aux. avoir) turn over; (vêtement) turn inside out; (lettre, compliment) return; (émouvoir: fam.) upset. —v.i. (aux. être) go back, return. **se ~** v. pr. turn round; (dans son lit) twist and turn. **s'en ~**, go back. **se ~ contre**, turn against.

retracer /rǝtrase/ v.t. retrace.

rétracter /retrakte/ v.t., **se ~** v. pr. retract.

retrait /rǝtrɛ/ n.m. withdrawal; (des eaux) ebb, receding. **être (situé) en ~**, be set back.

retraite /rǝtrɛt/ n.f. retirement; (pension) (retirement) pension; (fuite, refuge) retreat. **mettre à la ~**, pension off. **prendre sa ~**, retire.

retraité, ~e /rǝtrete/ a. retired. —n.m., f. (old-age) pensioner, senior citizen.

retrancher /rǝtrɑ̃ʃe/ v.t. remove; (soustraire) deduct. **se ~** v. pr. (mil.) entrench o.s. **se ~ derrière/dans**, take refuge behind/in.

retransm|ettre /rǝtrɑ̃smɛtr/ v.t. broadcast. **~ission** n.f. broadcast.

rétrécir /retresir/ v.t. narrow; (vêtement) take in. —v.i. (tissu) shrink. **se ~**, (rue) narrow.

rétrib|uer /retribɥe/ v.t. pay. **~ution** n.f. payment.

rétroactif, ~ve /retrɔaktif, -v/ a. retrospective. **augmentation à effet ~f**, backdated pay rise.

rétrograd|e /retrɔgrad/ a. retrograde. **~er** v.i. (reculer) fall back, recede; v.t. demote.

rétrospectivement /retrɔspɛktivmɑ̃/ adv. in retrospect.

retrousser /rǝtruse/ v.t. pull up.

retrouvailles /rǝtruvaj/ n.f. pl. reunion.

retrouver /rǝtruve/ v.t. find (again); (rejoindre) meet (again); (forces, calme) regain; (se rappeler) remember. **se ~** v. pr. find o.s. (back); (se réunir) meet (again). **s'y ~**, (s'orienter, comprendre) find one's way; (rentrer dans ses frais) break even.

rétroviseur /retrɔvizœr/ n.m. (auto.) (rear-view) mirror.

réunion /reynjɔ̃/ n.f. meeting; (d'objets) collection.

réunir /reynir/ v.t. gather, collect; (rapprocher) bring together; (convoquer) call together; (raccorder) join; (qualités) combine. **se ~** v. pr. meet.

réussi /reysi/ a. successful.

réussir /reysir/ v.i. succeed, be successful (à faire, in doing). **~ à qn.**, work well for s.o.; (climat etc.) agree with s.o. —v.t. make a success of.

réussite /reysit/ n.f. success; (jeu) patience.

revaloir /rǝvalwar/ v.t. **je vous revaudrai cela**, (en mal) I'll pay you back for this; (en bien) I'll repay you some day.

revaloriser /rǝvalɔrize/ v.t. (monnaie) revalue; (salaires) raise.

revanche /rǝvɑ̃ʃ/ n.f. revenge; (sport) return ou revenge match. **en ~**, on the other hand.

rêvasser /rɛvase/ v.i. day-dream.

rêve /rɛv/ n.m. dream. **faire un ~**, have a dream.

revêche /rǝvɛʃ/ a. ill-tempered.

réveil /revɛj/ n.m. waking up, (fig.) awakening; (pendule) alarm-clock.

réveill|er /reveje/ v.t., **se ~er** v. pr. wake (up); (fig.) awaken. **~é** a. awake. **~e-matin** n.m. invar. alarm-clock.

réveillon /revɛjɔ̃/ n.m. (Noël) Christmas Eve; (nouvel an) New Year's Eve. **~ner** /-jɔne/ v.i. celebrate the réveillon.

révél|er /revele/ v.t. reveal. **se ~er** v. pr. be revealed. **se ~er facile/etc.**, prove easy/etc. **~ateur, ~atrice** a. revealing. —n.m. (photo) developer. **~ation** n.f. revelation.

revenant /rǝvnɑ̃/ n.m. ghost.

revendi|quer /rǝvɑ̃dike/ v.t. claim. **~catif, ~cative** a. (mouvement etc.) in support of one's claims. **~cation** n.f. claim; (action) claiming.

revend|re /rǝvɑ̃dr/ v.t. sell (again). **~eur, ~euse** n.m., f. dealer.

revenir† /rǝvnir/ v.i. (aux. être) come back, return (à, to). **~ à**, (activité) go back to; (se résumer à) come down to;

(*échoir à*) fall to; (*coûter*) cost. ~ **de**, (*maladie, surprise*) get over. ~ **sur ses pas**, retrace one's steps. **faire** ~, (*culin.*) brown. **ça me revient**, it comes back to me.

revente /rəvãt/ *n.f.* resale.

revenu /rəvny/ *n.m.* income; (*d'un état*) revenue.

rêver /reve/ *v.t./i.* dream (**à** *ou* **de**, of).

réverbération /reverberasjɔ̃/ *n.f.* reflection, reverberation.

réverbère /reverbɛr/ *n.m.* street lamp.

révérenc|e /reverãs/ *n.f.* reverence; (*salut d'homme*) bow; (*salut de femme*) curtsy. ~**ieux**, ~**ieuse** *a.* reverent.

révérend, ~e /reverã, -d/ *a.* & *n.m.* reverend.

rêverie /rɛvri/ *n.f.* day-dream; (*activité*) day-dreaming.

revers /rəver/ *n.m.* reverse; (*de main*) back; (*d'étoffe*) wrong side; (*de veste*) lapel; (*tennis*) backhand; (*fig.*) setback.

réversible /reversibl/ *a.* reversible.

revêt|ir /rəvetir/ *v.t.* cover; (*habit*) put on; (*prendre, avoir*) assume. ~**ement** /-vɛtmã/ *n.m.* covering; (*de route*) surface.

rêveu|r, ~se /rɛvœr, -øz/ *a.* dreamy. —*n.m., f.* dreamer.

revigorer /rəvigɔre/ *v.t.* revive.

revirement /rəvirmã/ *n.m.* sudden change.

révis|er /revize/ *v.t.* revise; (*véhicule*) overhaul. ~**ion** *n.f.* revision; overhaul.

revivre† /rəvivr/ *v.i.* live again. —*v.t.* relive. **faire** ~, revive.

révocation /revɔkasjɔ̃/ *n.f.* repeal; (*d'un fonctionnaire*) dismissal.

revoir† /rəvwar/ *v.t.* see (again); (*réviser*) revise. **au** ~, goodbye.

révolte /revɔlt/ *n.f.* revolt.

révolt|er /revɔlte/ *v.t.*, **se** ~**er** *v. pr.* revolt. ~**ant, ~ante** *a.* revolting. ~**é, ~ée** *n.m., f.* rebel.

révolu /revɔly/ *a.* past.

révolution /revɔlysjɔ̃/ *n.f.* revolution. ~**naire** /-jɔnɛr/ *a.* & *n.m./f.* revolutionary. ~**ner** /- jɔne/ *v.t.* revolutionize.

revolver /revɔlver/ *n.m.* revolver, gun.

révoquer /revɔke/ *v.t.* repeal; (*fonctionnaire*) dismiss.

revue /rəvy/ *n.f.* (*examen, défilé*) review; (*magazine*) magazine; (*spectacle*) variety show.

rez-de-chaussée /redʃose/ *n.m. invar.* ground floor; (*Amer.*) first floor.

RF *abrév.* (*République Française*) French Republic.

rhabiller (se) /(sə)rabije/ *v. pr.* get dressed (again), dress (again).

rhapsodie /rapsɔdi/ *n.f.* rhapsody.

rhétorique /retɔrik/ *n.f.* rhetoric. —*a.* rhetorical.

rhinocéros /rinɔserɔs/ *n.m.* rhinoceros.

rhubarbe /rybarb/ *n.f.* rhubarb.

rhum /rɔm/ *n.m.* rum.

rhumatis|me /rymatism/ *n.m.* rheumatism. ~**ant, ~ante** /-zã, -t/ *a.* rheumatic.

rhume /rym/ *n.m.* cold. ~ **des foins**, hay fever.

ri /ri/ *voir* **rire**.

riant, ~e /rjã, -t/ *a.* cheerful.

ricaner /rikane/ *v.i.* snigger, giggle.

riche /riʃ/ *a.* rich (**en**, in). —*n.m./f.* rich person. ~**ment** *adv.* richly.

richesse /riʃɛs/ *n.f.* wealth; (*de sol, décor*) richness. ~**s**, wealth.

ricoch|er /rikɔʃe/ *v.i.* rebound, ricochet. ~**et** *n.m.* rebound, ricochet. **par** ~**er**, indirectly.

rictus /riktys/ *n.m.* grin, grimace.

rid|e /rid/ *n.f.* wrinkle; (*sur l'eau*) ripple. ~**er** *v.t.* wrinkle; (*eau*) ripple.

rideau (*pl.* ~**x**) /rido/ *n.m.* curtain; (*métallique*) shutter; (*fig.*) screen. ~ **de fer**, (*pol.*) Iron Curtain.

ridicul|e /ridikyl/ *a.* ridiculous. —*n.m.* absurdity. **le** ~**e**, ridicule. ~**iser** *v.t.* ridicule.

rien /rjɛ̃/ *pron.* (**ne**) ~, nothing. —*n.m.* trifle. **de** ~**!**, don't mention it! ~ **d'autre/de plus**, nothing else/more. ~ **du tout**, nothing at all. ~ **que**, just, only. **trois fois** ~, next to nothing. **il n'y est pour** ~, he has nothing to do with it. **en un** ~ **de temps**, in next to no time. ~ **à faire**, it's no good!

rieu|r, ~se /rjœr, rjøz/ *a.* merry.

rigid|e /riʒid/ *a.* rigid; (*muscle*) stiff. ~**ité** *n.f.* rigidity; stiffness.

rigole /rigɔl/ *n.f.* channel.

rigol|er /rigɔle/ *v.i.* laugh; (*s'amuser*) have some fun; (*plaisanter*) joke. ~**ade** *n.f.* fun.

rigolo, ~te /rigɔlo, -ɔt/ *a.* (*fam.*) funny. —*n.m., f.* (*fam.*) joker.

rigoureu|x, ~se /rigurø, -z/ *a.* rigorous; (*hiver*) harsh. ~**sement** *adv.* rigorously.

rigueur /rigœr/ *n.f.* rigour. **à la** ~, at a pinch. **être de** ~, be the rule. **tenir** ~ **à qn. de qch.**, hold sth. against s.o.

rim|e /rim/ *n.f.* rhyme. ~**er** *v.i.* rhyme (**avec**, with). **cela ne** ~**e à rien**, it makes no sense.

rin|cer /rɛ̃se/ v.t. rinse. ~**cage** n.m. rinse; (action) rinsing. ~**ce-doigts** n.m. invar. finger-bowl.

ring /riŋ/ n.m. boxing ring.

ripost|e /ripɔst/ n.f. retort; (mil.) reprisal. ~**er** v.i. retaliate; v.t. retort (**que**, that). ~**er à**, (attaque) counter; (insulte etc.) reply to.

rire† /rir/ v.i. laugh (**de**, at); (plaisanter) joke; (s'amuser) have fun. **c'était pour** ~, it was a joke. —n.m. laugh. ~**s, le** ~, laughter.

risée /rize/ n.f. **la** ~ **de**, the laughing-stock of.

risible /rizibl/ a. laughable.

risqu|e /risk/ n.m. risk. ~**é** a. risky; (osé) daring. ~**er** v.t. risk. ~**er de faire**, stand a good chance of doing. **se** ~**er à/dans**, venture to/into.

rissoler /risɔle/ v.t./i. brown. (**faire**) ~, brown.

ristourne /risturn/ n.f. discount.

rite /rit/ n.m. rite; (habitude) ritual.

rituel, ~**le** /rituɛl/ a. & n.m. ritual.

rivage /rivaʒ/ n.m. shore.

riv|al, ~ale (m. pl. ~**aux**) /rival, -o/ n.m., f. rival. —a. rival. ~**aliser** v.i. compete (**avec**, with). ~**alité** n.f. rivalry.

rive /riv/ n.f. (de fleuve) bank; (de lac) shore.

riv|er /rive/ v.t. rivet. ~**er son clou à qn.**, shut s.o. up. ~**et** n.m. rivet.

riverain, ~**e** /rivrɛ̃, -ɛn/ a. riverside. —n.m., f. riverside resident; (d'une rue) resident.

rivière /rivjɛr/ n.f. river.

rixe /riks/ n.f. brawl.

riz /ri/ n.m. rice. ~**ière** /rizjɛr/ n.f. paddy(-field), rice field.

robe /rɔb/ n.f. (de femme) dress; (de juge) robe; (de cheval) coat. ~ **de chambre**, dressing-gown.

robinet /rɔbinɛ/ n.m. tap; (Amer.) faucet.

robot /rɔbo/ n.m. robot.

robuste /rɔbyst/ a. robust. ~**sse** /-ɛs/ n.f. robustness.

roc /rɔk/ n.m. rock.

rocaill|e /rɔkaj/ n.f. rocky ground; (de jardin) rockery. ~**eux, ~euse** a. (terrain) rocky.

roch|e /rɔʃ/ n.f. rock. ~**eux, ~euse** a. rocky.

rocher /rɔʃe/ n.m. rock.

rock /rɔk/ n.m. (mus.) rock.

rod|er /rɔde/ v.t. (auto.) run in; (auto., Amer.) break in. **être** ~**é**, (personne) be broken in. ~**age** n.m. running in; breaking in.

rôd|er /rode/ v.i. roam; (suspect) prowl. ~**eur, ~euse** n.m., f. prowler.

rogne /rɔɲ/ n.f. (fam.) anger.

rogner /rɔɲe/ v.t. trim; (réduire) cut. ~ **sur**, cut down on.

rognon /rɔɲɔ̃/ n.m. (culin.) kidney.

rognures /rɔɲyr/ n.f. pl. scraps.

roi /rwa/ n.m. king. **les Rois mages**, the Magi. **la fête des Rois**, Twelfth Night.

roitelet /rwatlɛ/ n.m. wren.

rôle /rol/ n.m. role, part.

romain, ~**e** /rɔmɛ̃, -ɛn/ a. & n.m., f. Roman. —n.f. (laitue) cos.

roman /rɔmɑ̃/ n.m. novel; (fig.) story; (genre) fiction.

romance /rɔmɑ̃s/ n.f. sentimental ballad.

romanc|ier, ~**ière** /rɔmɑ̃sje/, /-jɛr/ n.m., f. novelist.

romanesque /rɔmanɛsk/ a. romantic; (fantastique) fantastic. **œuvres** ~**s**, novels, fiction.

romanichel, ~**le** /rɔmaniʃɛl/ n.m., f. gypsy.

romanti|que /rɔmɑ̃tik/ a. & n.m./f. romantic. ~**sme** n.m. romanticism.

rompre† /rɔ̃pr/ v.t./i. break; (relations) break off; (fiancés) break it off. **se** ~ v. pr. break.

rompu /rɔ̃py/ a. (exténué) exhausted.

ronces /rɔ̃s/ n.f. pl. brambles.

ronchonner /rɔ̃ʃɔne/ v.i. (fam.) grumble.

rond, ~**e¹** /rɔ̃, rɔ̃d/ a. round; (gras) plump; (ivre: fam.) tight. —n.m. (cercle) ring; (tranche) slice. **il n'a pas un** ~, (fam.) he hasn't got a penny. **en** ~, in a circle. ~**ement** /rɔ̃dmɑ̃/ adv. briskly; (franchement) straight. ~**eur** /rɔ̃dœr/ n.f. roundness; (franchise) frankness; (embonpoint) plumpness. ~**-point** (pl. ~**s-points**) n.m. roundabout; (Amer.) traffic circle.

ronde² /rɔ̃d/ n.f. round(s); (de policier) beat; (mus.) semibreve.

rondelet, ~**te** /rɔ̃dlɛ, -t/ a. chubby.

rondelle /rɔ̃dɛl/ n.f. (techn.) washer; (tranche) slice.

rondin /rɔ̃dɛ̃/ n.m. log.

ronfl|er /rɔ̃fle/ v.i. snore; (moteur) hum. ~**ement(s)** n.m. (pl.) snoring; humming.

rong|er /rɔ̃ʒe/ v.t. gnaw (at); (vers, acide) eat into; (personne: fig.) consume. **se** ~**er les ongles**, bite one's nails. ~**eur** n.m. rodent.

ronronn|er /rɔ̃rɔne/ v.i. purr. ~**ement** n.m. purr(ing).

roquette /rɔkɛt/ *n.f.* rocket.

rosace /rɔzas/ *n.f.* (*d'église*) rose window.

rosaire /rozɛr/ *n.m.* rosary.

rosbif /rɔsbif/ *n.m.* roast beef.

rose /roz/ *n.f.* rose. —*a.* pink; (*situation, teint*) rosy. —*n.m.* pink.

rosé /roze/ *a.* pinkish; (*vin*) rosé. —*n.m.* rosé.

roseau (*pl.* ~**x**) /rozo/ *n.m.* reed.

rosée /roze/ *n.f.* dew.

roseraie /rozrɛ/ *n.f.* rose garden.

rosette /rozɛt/ *n.f.* rosette.

rosier /rozje/ *n.m.* rose-bush, rose tree.

rosse /rɔs/ *a.* (*fam.*) nasty.

rosser /rose/ *v.t.* thrash.

rossignol /rɔsiɲɔl/ *n.m.* nightingale.

rot /ro/ *n.m.* (*fam.*) burp.

rotati|f, ~ve /rɔtatif, -v/ *a.* rotary.

rotation /rɔtasjɔ̃/ *n.f.* rotation.

roter /rote/ *v.i.* (*fam.*) burp.

rotin /rɔtɛ̃/ *n.m.* (rattan) cane.

rôt|ir /rotir/ *v.t./i.*, **se ~ir** *v. pr.* roast. **~i** *n.m.* roasting meat; (*cuit*) roast. **~i de porc**, roast pork.

rôtisserie /rotisri/ *n.f.* grill-room.

rôtissoire /rotiswar/ *n.f.* (roasting) spit.

rotule /rɔtyl/ *n.f.* kneecap.

roturi|er, ère /rɔtyrje, -ɛr/ *n.m., f.* commoner.

rouage /rwaʒ/ *n.m.* (*techn.*) (working) part. **~s**, (*d'une organisation*: *fig.*) wheels.

roucouler /rukule/ *v.i.* coo.

roue /ru/ *n.f.* wheel. **~ (dentée)**, cog (-wheel). **~ de secours**, spare wheel.

roué /rwe/ *a.* wily, calculating.

rouer /rwe/ *v.t.* **~ de coups**, thrash.

rouet /rwe/ *n.m.* spinning-wheel.

rouge /ruʒ/ *a.* red; (*fer*) red-hot. —*n.m.* red; (*vin*) red wine; (*fard*) rouge. **~ (à lèvres)**, lipstick. —*n.m./f.* (*pol.*) red. **~-gorge** (*pl.* **~s-gorges**) *n.m.* robin.

rougeole /ruʒɔl/ *n.f.* measles.

rougeoyer /ruʒwaje/ *v.i.* glow (red).

rouget /ruʒɛ/ *n.m.* red mullet.

rougeur /ruʒœr/ *n.f.* redness; (*tache*) red blotch; (*gêne, honte*) red face.

rougir /ruʒir/ *v.t./i.* turn red; (*de honte*) blush.

rouill|e /ruj/ *n.f.* rust. **~é** *a.* rusty. **~er** *v.i.*, **se ~er** *v. pr.* get rusty, rust.

roulant, ~e /rulã, -t/ *a.* (*meuble*) on wheels; (*escalier*) moving.

rouleau (*pl.* ~**x**) /rulo/ *n.m.* roll; (*outil, vague*) roller. **~ à pâtisserie**, rolling-pin. **~ compresseur**, steamroller.

roulement /rulmã/ *n.m.* rotation; (*bruit*) rumble; (*succession de personnes*) turnover; (*de tambour*) roll. **~ à billes**, ball-bearing. **par ~**, in rotation.

rouler /rule/ *v.t./i.* roll; (*ficelle, manches*) roll up; (*duper*: *fam.*) cheat; (*véhicule, train*) go, travel; (*conducteur*) drive. **se ~ dans** *v. pr.* roll (over) in.

roulette /rulɛt/ *n.f.* (*de meuble*) castor; (*de dentiste*) drill; (*jeu*) roulette. **comme sur des ~s**, very smoothly.

roulis /ruli/ *n.m.* rolling.

roulotte /rulɔt/ *n.f.* caravan.

roumain, ~e /rumɛ̃, -ɛn/ *a. & n.m., f.* Romanian.

Roumanie /rumani/ *n.f.* Romania.

roupiller /rupije/ *v.i.* (*fam.*) sleep.

rouquin, ~e /rukɛ̃, -in/ *a.* (*fam.*) red-haired. —*n.m., f.* (*fam.*) redhead.

rouspéter /ruspete/ *v.i.* (*fam.*) grumble, moan, complain.

rousse /rus/ *voir* **roux**.

roussir /rusir/ *v.t.* scorch. —*v.i.* turn brown.

route /rut/ *n.f.* road; (*naut., aviat.*) route; (*direction*) way; (*voyage*) journey; (*chemin*: *fig.*) path. **en ~**, on the way. **en ~!**, let's go! **mettre en ~**, start. **~ nationale**, trunk road, main road. **se mettre en ~**, set out.

rout|ier, ~ière /rutje, -jɛr/ *a.* road. —*n.m.* long-distance lorry driver *ou* truck driver (*Amer.*); (*restaurant*) roadside café.

routine /rutin/ *n.f.* routine.

rouvrir /ruvrir/ *v.t.*, **se ~ir** *v. pr.* reopen, open again.

rou|x, ~sse /ru, rus/ *a.* red, reddish-brown; (*personne*) red-haired. —*n.m., f.* redhead.

roy|al (*m. pl.* ~**aux**) /rwajal, -jo/ *a.* royal; (*total*: *fam.*) thorough. **~alement** *adv.* royally.

royaume /rwajom/ *n.m.* kingdom. **R~-Uni** *n.m.* United Kingdom.

royauté /rwajote/ *n.f.* royalty.

ruade /ryad, rɥad/ *n.f.* kick.

ruban /rybã/ *n.m.* ribbon; (*de magnétophone*) tape; (*de chapeau*) band. **~ adhésif**, sticky tape.

rubéole /rybeɔl/ *n.f.* German measles.

rubis /rybi/ *n.m.* ruby; (*de montre*) jewel.

rubrique /rybrik/ *n.f.* heading; (*article*) column.

ruche /ryʃ/ *n.f.* beehive.

rude /ryd/ *a.* rough; (*pénible*) tough; (*grossier*) crude; (*fameux*: *fam.*) tremendous. **~ment** *adv.* (*frapper etc.*) hard; (*traiter*) harshly; (*très*: *fam.*) awfully.

rudiment|s /rydimã/ *n.m. pl.* rudiments.
~**aire** /-tɛr/ *a.* rudimentary.
rudoyer /rydwaje/ *v.t.* treat harshly.
rue /ry/ *n.f.* street.
ruée /rɥe/ *n.f.* rush.
ruelle /rɥɛl/ *n.f.* alley.
ruer /rɥe/ *v.i.* (*cheval*) kick. **se** ~
dans/vers, rush into/towards. **se** ~ **sur,**
pounce on.
rugby /rygbi/ *n.m.* Rugby.
rugby|man (*pl.* ~**men**) /rygbiman,
-mɛn/ *n.m.* Rugby player.
rug|ir /ryʒir/ *v.i.* roar. ~**issement** *n.m.*
roar.
rugueu|x, ~**se** /rygø, -z/ *a.* rough.
ruin|e /rɥin/ *n.f.* ruin. **en** ~**e(s),** in ruins.
~**er** *v.t.* ruin.
ruineu|x, ~**se** /rɥinø, -z/ *a.* ruinous.
ruisseau (*pl.* ~**x**) /rɥiso/ *n.m.* stream;
(*rigole*) gutter.
ruisseler /rɥisle/ *v.i.* stream.
rumeur /rymœr/ *n.f.* (*nouvelle*) rumour;
(*son*) murmur, hum; (*protestation*)
rumblings.
ruminer /rymine/ *v.t./i.* (*herbe*)
ruminate; (*méditer*) meditate.
rupture /ryptyr/ *n.f.* break; (*action*)
breaking; (*de contrat*) breach; (*de
pourparlers*) breakdown.
rur|al (*m. pl.* ~**aux**) /ryral, -o/ *a.* rural.
rus|e /ryz/ *n.f.* cunning; (*perfidie*)
trickery. **une** ~**e,** a trick, a ruse. ~**é** *a.*
cunning.
russe /rys/ *a.* & *n.m./f.* Russian. —*n.m.*
(*lang.*) Russian.
Russie /rysi/ *n.f.* Russia.
rustique /rystik/ *a.* rustic.
rustre /rystr/ *n.m.* lout, boor.
rutilant, ~**e** /rytilã, -t/ *a.* sparkling,
gleaming.
rythm|e /ritm/ *n.m.* rhythm; (*vitesse*)
rate; (*de la vie*) pace. ~**é,** ~**ique** *adjs.*
rhythmical.

S

s' /s/ *voir* **se.**
sa /sa/ *voir* **son**[1].
SA *abrév.* (*société anonyme*) PLC.
sabbat /saba/ *n.m.* sabbath. ~**ique** *a.*
année ~**ique,** sabbatical year.
sabl|e /sabl/ *n.m.* sand. ~**es mouvants,**
quicksands. ~**er** *v.t.* sand. ~**er le
champagne,** drink champagne. ~**eux,**
~**euse,** ~**onneux,** ~**onneuse** *adjs.*
sandy.

sablier /sablije/ *n.m.* (*culin.*) egg-timer.
saborder /saborde/ *v.t.* (*navire, projet*)
scuttle.
sabot /sabo/ *n.m.* (*de cheval etc.*) hoof;
(*chaussure*) clog; (*de frein*) shoe. ~ **de
Denver,** (wheel) clamp.
sabot|er /sabote/ *v.t.* sabotage; (*bâcler*)
botch. ~**age** *n.m.* sabotage; (*acte*) act
of sabotage. ~**eur,** ~**euse** *n.m.,* f.
saboteur.
sabre /sabr/ *n.m.* sabre.
sac /sak/ *n.m.* bag; (*grand, en toile*) sack.
mettre à ~, (*maison*) ransack; (*ville*)
sack. ~ **à dos,** rucksack. ~ **à main,**
handbag. ~ **de couchage,** sleeping-
bag. **mettre dans le même** ~, lump
together.
saccad|e /sakad/ *n.f.* jerk. ~**é** *a.* jerky.
saccager /sakaʒe/ *v.t.* (*ville, pays*) sack;
(*maison*) ransack; (*ravager*) wreck.
saccharine /sakarin/ *n.f.* saccharin.
sacerdoce /saserdɔs/ *n.m.* priesthood;
(*fig.*) vocation.
sachet /saʃɛ/ *n.m.* (small) bag; (*de
médicament etc.*) sachet. ~ **de thé,** tea-
bag.
sacoche /sakɔʃ/ *n.f.* bag; (*d'élève*)
satchel; (*de moto*) saddle-bag.
sacquer /sake/ *v.t.* (*fam.*) sack. **je ne
peux pas le** ~, I can't stand him.
sacr|e /sakr/ *n.m.* (*de roi*) coronation;
(*d'évêque*) consecration. ~**er** *v.t.*
crown; consecrate.
sacré /sakre/ *a.* sacred; (*maudit: fam.*)
damned.
sacrement /sakrəmã/ *n.m.* sacrament.
sacrifice /sakrifis/ *n.m.* sacrifice.
sacrifier /sakrifje/ *v.t.* sacrifice. ~ **à,**
conform to. **se** ~ *v. pr.* sacrifice o.s.
sacrilège /sakrilɛʒ/ *n.m.* sacrilege. —*a.*
sacrilegious.
sacristain /sakristɛ̃/ *n.m.* sexton.
sacristie /sakristi/ *n.f.* (*protestante*)
vestry; (*catholique*) sacristy.
sacro-saint, ~**e** /sakrɔsɛ̃, -t/ *a.*
sacrosanct.
sadi|que /sadik/ *a.* sadistic. —*n.m./f.*
sadist. ~**sme** *n.m.* sadism.
safari /safari/ *n.m.* safari.
sagace /sagas/ *a.* shrewd.
sage /saʒ/ *a.* wise; (*docile*) good. —*n.m.*
wise man. ~**-femme** (*pl.* ~**s-femmes**)
n.f. midwife. ~**ment** *adv.* wisely;
(*docilement*) quietly. ~**sse** /-ɛs/ *n.f.*
wisdom.
Sagittaire /saʒitɛr/ *n.m.* **le** ~, Sagittarius.
Sahara /saara/ *n.m.* **le** ~, the Sahara
(desert).

saignant, ~e /sɛɲɑ̃, -t/ *a.* (*culin.*) rare.
saign|er /seɲe/ *v.t./i.* bleed. ~**er du nez,** have a nosebleed. ~**ée** *n.f.* bleeding. ~**ement** *n.m.* bleeding. ~**ement de nez,** nosebleed.
saill|ie /saji/ *n.f.* projection. **faire** ~**ie,** project. ~**ant,** ~**ante** *a.* projecting; (*remarquable*) salient.
sain, ~e /sɛ̃, sɛn/ *a.* healthy; (*moralement*) sane. ~ **et sauf,** safe and sound. ~**ement** /sɛnmɑ̃/ *adv.* healthily; (*juger*) sanely.
saindoux /sɛ̃du/ *n.m.* lard.
saint, ~e /sɛ̃, sɛ̃t/ *a.* holy; (*bon, juste*) saintly. ~e, *f.* saint. **S**~**e-Esprit** *n.m.* Holy Spirit. **S**~**e-Siège** *n.m.* Holy See. **S**~**-Sylvestre** *n.f.* New Year's Eve. **S**~**e Vierge,** Blessed Virgin.
sainteté /sɛ̃tte/ *n.f.* holiness; (*d'un lieu*) sanctity.
sais /sɛ/ *voir* **savoir**.
saisie /sezi/ *n.f.* (*jurid.*) seizure; (*comput.*) keyboarding. ~ **de données,** data capture.
sais|ir /sezir/ *v.t.* grab (hold of), seize; (*occasion, biens*) seize; (*comprendre*) grasp; (*frapper*) strike; (*comput.*) keyboard, capture. ~**i de,** (*peur*) stricken by, overcome by. **se** ~**ir de,** seize. ~**issant,** ~**issante** *a.* (*spectacle*) gripping.
saison /sɛzɔ̃/ *n.f.* season. **la morte** ~**,** the off season. ~**nier,** ~**nière** /-ɔnje, -jɛr/ *a.* seasonal.
sait /sɛ/ *voir* **savoir**.
salad|e /salad/ *n.f.* salad; (*laitue*) lettuce; (*désordre: fam.*) mess. ~**ier** *n.m.* salad bowl.
salaire /salɛr/ *n.m.* wages, salary.
salami /salami/ *n.m.* salami.
salarié, ~e /salarje/ *a.* wage-earning. —*n.m., f.* wage-earner.
salaud /salo/ *n.m.* (*argot*) bastard.
sale /sal/ *a.* dirty, filthy; (*mauvais*) nasty.
sal|er /sale/ *v.t.* salt. ~**é** *a.* (*goût*) salty; (*plat*) salted; (*viande, poisson*) salt; (*grivois: fam.*) spicy; (*excessif: fam.*) steep.
saleté /salte/ *n.f.* dirtiness; (*crasse*) dirt; (*action*) dirty trick; (*obscénité*) obscenity. ~(s), (*camelote*) rubbish. ~s, (*détritus*) mess.
salière /saljɛr/ *n.f.* salt-cellar.
salin, ~e /salɛ̃, -in/ *a.* saline.
sal|ir /salir/ *v.t.* (make) dirty; (*réputation*) tarnish. **se** ~**ir** *v. pr.* get dirty. ~**issant,** ~**issante** *a.* dirty; (*étoffe*) easily dirtied.

salive /saliv/ *n.f.* saliva.
salle /sal/ *n.f.* room; (*grande, publique*) hall; (*d'hôpital*) ward; (*théâtre, cinéma*) auditorium. ~ **à manger,** dining-room. ~ **d'attente,** waiting-room. ~ **de bains,** bathroom. ~ **de séjour,** living-room. ~ **de classe,** class-room. ~ **d'embarquement,** departure lounge. ~ **d'opération,** operating theatre. ~ **des ventes,** saleroom.
salon /salɔ̃/ *n.m.* lounge; (*de coiffure, beauté*) salon; (*exposition*) show. ~ **de thé,** tea-room.
salope /salɔp/ *n.f.* (*argot*) bitch.
saloperie /salɔpri/ *n.f.* (*fam.*) (*action*) dirty trick; (*chose de mauvaise qualité*) rubbish.
salopette /salɔpɛt/ *n.f.* dungarees; (*d'ouvrier*) overalls.
salsifis /salsifi/ *n.m.* salsify.
saltimbanque /saltɛ̃bɑ̃k/ *n.m./f.* (street *ou* fairground) acrobat.
salubre /salybr/ *a.* healthy.
saluer /salɥe/ *v.t.* greet; (*en partant*) take one's leave of; (*de la tête*) nod to; (*de la main*) wave to; (*mil.*) salute.
salut /saly/ *n.m.* greeting; (*de la tête*) nod; (*de la main*) wave; (*mil.*) salute; (*sauvegarde, rachat*) salvation. —*int.* (*bonjour: fam.*) hallo; (*au revoir: fam.*) bye-bye.
salutaire /salytɛr/ *a.* salutary.
salutation /salytɑsjɔ̃/ *n.f.* greeting. **veuillez agréer, Monsieur, mes** ~**s distingués,** yours faithfully.
salve /salv/ *n.f.* salvo.
samedi /samdi/ *n.m.* Saturday.
sanatorium /sanatɔrjɔm/ *n.m.* sanatorium.
sanctifier /sɑ̃ktifje/ *v.t.* sanctify.
sanction /sɑ̃ksjɔ̃/ *n.f.* sanction. ~**ner** /-jɔne/ *v.t.* sanction; (*punir*) punish.
sanctuaire /sɑ̃ktɥɛr/ *n.m.* sanctuary.
sandale /sɑ̃dal/ *n.f.* sandal.
sandwich /sɑ̃dwitʃ/ *n.m.* sandwich.
sang /sɑ̃/ *n.m.* blood. ~**-froid** *n.m. invar.* calm, self-control. **se faire du mauvais** ~ *ou* **un** ~ **d'encre** be worried stiff.
sanglant, ~e /sɑ̃glɑ̃, -t/ *a.* bloody.
sangl|e /sɑ̃gl/ *n.f.* strap. ~**er** *v.t.* strap.
sanglier /sɑ̃glije/ *n.m.* wild boar.
sanglot /sɑ̃glo/ *n.m.* sob. ~**er** /-ɔte/ *v.i.* sob.
sangsue /sɑ̃sy/ *n.f.* leech.
sanguin, ~e /sɑ̃gɛ̃, -in/ *a.* (*groupe etc.*) blood; (*caractère*) fiery.
sanguinaire /sɑ̃ginɛr/ *a.* bloodthirsty.
sanitaire /sanitɛr/ *a.* health; (*conditions*)

sanitary; (*appareils, installations*) bathroom, sanitary. ~s *n.m. pl.* bathroom.

sans /sã/ *prép.* without. ~ **que vous le sachiez,** without your knowing. ~**-abri** /sãzabri/ *n.m./f. invar.* homeless person. ~ **ça,** ~ **quoi,** otherwise. ~ **arrêt,** nonstop. ~ **encombre/faute/tarder,** without incident/fail/delay. ~**fin/goût/limite,** endless/tasteless/limitless. ~**-gêne** *a. invar.* inconsiderate, thoughtless; *n.m. invar.* thoughtlessness. ~ **importance / pareil / précédent / travail,** unimportant/unparalleled/unprecedented/unemployed. ~ **plus,** but no more than that, but nothing more.

santé /sãte/ *n.f.* health. **à ta** *ou* **votre** ~, cheers!

saoul, ~**e** /su, sul/ *voir* **soûl.**

saper /sape/ *v.t.* undermine.

sapeur /sapœr/ *n.m.* (*mil.*) sapper. ~**-pompier** (*pl.* ~**s-pompiers**) *n.m.* fireman.

saphir /safir/ *n.m.* sapphire.

sapin /sapɛ̃/ *n.m.* fir(-tree). ~ **de Noël,** Christmas tree.

sarbacane /sarbakan/ *n.f.* (*jouet*) peashooter.

sarcas|me /sarkasm/ *n.m.* sarcasm. ~**tique** *a.* sarcastic.

sarcler /sarkle/ *v.t.* weed.

sardine /sardin/ *n.f.* sardine.

sardonique /sardɔnik/ *a.* sardonic.

sarment /sarmã/ *n.m.* vine shoot.

sas /sɑ(s)/ *n.m.* (*naut., aviat.*) airlock.

satané /satane/ *a.* (*fam.*) blasted.

satanique /satanik/ *a.* satanic.

satellite /satelit/ *n.m.* satellite.

satin /satɛ̃/ *n.m.* satin.

satir|e /satir/ *n.f.* satire. ~**ique** *a.* satirical.

satisfaction /satisfaksjɔ̃/ *n.f.* satisfaction.

satis|faire† /satisfɛr/ *v.t.* satisfy. —*v.i.* ~**faire à,** satisfy. ~**faisant,** ~**faisante** *a.* (*acceptable*) satisfactory. ~**fait,** ~**faite** *a.* satisfied (**de,** with).

satur|er /satyre/ *v.t.* saturate. ~**ation** *n.f.* saturation.

sauc|e /sos/ *n.f.* sauce; (*jus de viande*) gravy. ~**er** *v.t.* (*plat*) wipe. **se faire** ~**er** (*fam.*) get soaked. ~**e tartare,** tartar sauce. ~**ière** *n.f.* sauce-boat.

saucisse /sosis/ *n.f.* sausage.

saucisson /sosisɔ̃/ *n.m.* (slicing) sausage.

sauf¹ /sof/ *prép.* except. ~ **erreur/imprévu,** barring error/the unforeseen. ~ **avis contraire,** unless you hear otherwise.

sau|f², ~**ve** /sof, sov/ *a.* safe, unharmed. ~**f-conduit** *n.m.* safe conduct.

sauge /soʒ/ *n.f.* (*culin.*) sage.

saugrenu /sogrəny/ *a.* preposterous, ludicrous.

saule /sol/ *n.m.* willow. ~ **pleureur,** weeping willow.

saumon /somɔ̃/ *n.m.* salmon. —*a. invar.* salmon-pink.

saumure /somyr/ *n.f.* brine.

sauna /sona/ *n.m.* sauna.

saupoudrer /sopudre/ *v.t.* sprinkle (**de,** with).

saut /so/ *n.m.* jump, leap. **faire un** ~ **chez qn.,** pop round to s.o.'s (place). **le** ~, (*sport*) jumping. ~ **en hauteur/longueur,** high/long jump. ~ **périlleux,** somersault. **au** ~ **du lit,** on getting up.

sauté /sote/ *a. & n.m.* (*culin.*) sauté.

saut|er /sote/ *v.i.* jump, leap; (*exploser*) blow up; (*fusible*) blow; (*se détacher*) come off. —*v.t.* jump (over); (*page, classe*) skip. **faire** ~**er,** (*détruire*) blow up; (*fusible*) blow; (*casser*) break; (*culin.*) sauté; (*renvoyer: fam.*) kick out. ~**er à la corde,** skip. ~**er aux yeux,** be obvious. ~**e-mouton** *n.m.* leap-frog. ~**er au cou de qn.,** fling one's arms round s.o. ~**er sur une occasion,** jump at an opportunity.

sauterelle /sotrɛl/ *n.f.* grasshopper.

sautiller /sotije/ *v.i.* hop.

sauvage /sovaʒ/ *a.* wild; (*primitif, cruel*) savage; (*farouche*) unsociable; (*illégal*) unauthorized. —*n.m./f.* unsociable person; (*brute*) savage. ~**rie** *n.f.* savagery.

sauve /sov/ *voir* **sauf².**

sauvegard|e /sovgard/ *n.f.* safeguard; (*comput.*) backup. ~**er** *v.t.* safeguard; (*comput.*) save.

sauv|er /sove/ *v.t.* save; (*d'un danger*) rescue, save; (*matériel*) salvage. **se** ~**er** *v. pr.* (*fuir*) run away; (*partir: fam.*) be off. ~**e-qui-peut** *n.m. invar.* stampede. ~**etage** *n.m.* rescue; salvage. ~**eteur** *n.m.* rescuer. ~**eur** *n.m.* saviour.

sauvette (à la) /(ala)sovɛt/ *adv.* hastily; (*vendre*) illicitly.

savamment /savamã/ *adv.* learnedly; (*avec habileté*) skilfully.

savan|t, ~**e** /savã, -t/ *a.* learned; (*habile*) skilful. —*n.m.* scientist.

saveur /savœr/ *n.f.* flavour; (*fig.*) savour.

savoir† /savwar/ *v.t.* know; (*apprendre*) hear. **elle sait conduire/nager,** she can drive/swim. —*n.m.* learning. **à** ~, namely. **faire** ~ **à qn. que,** inform s.o.

that. **je ne saurais pas,** I could not, I cannot. **(pas) que je sache,** (not) as far as I know.

savon /savɔ̃/ *n.m.* soap. **passer un ∼ à qn.,** (*fam.*) give s.o. a dressing down. **∼ner** /-ɔne/ *v.t.* soap. **∼nette** /-ɔnɛt/ *n.f.* bar of soap. **∼neux, ∼neuse** /-ɔnø, -z/ *a.* soapy.

savour|er /savure/ *v.t.* savour. **∼eux, ∼euse** *a.* tasty; (*fig.*) spicy.

saxo(phone) /saksɔ(fɔn)/ *n.m.* sax- (ophone).

scabreu|x, ∼se /skabrø, -z/ *a.* risky; (*indécent*) obscene.

scandal|e /skãdal/ *n.m.* scandal; (*tapage*) uproar; (*en public*) noisy scene. **faire ∼e,** shock people. **faire un ∼e,** make a scene. **∼eux, ∼euse** *a.* scandalous. **∼iser** *v.t.* scandalize, shock.

scander /skãde/ *v.t.* (*vers*) scan; (*slogan*) chant.

scandinave /skãdinav/ *a.* & *n.m./f.* Scandinavian.

Scandinavie /skãdinavi/ *n.f.* Scan- dinavia.

scarabée /skarabe/ *n.m.* beetle.

scarlatine /skarlatin/ *n.f.* scarlet fever.

scarole /skarɔl/ *n.f.* endive.

sceau (*pl.* **∼x**) /so/ *n.m.* seal.

scélérat /selera/ *n.m.* scoundrel.

scell|er /sele/ *v.t.* seal; (*fixer*) cement. **∼és** *n.m. pl.* seals.

scénario /senarjo/ *n.m.* scenario.

scène /sɛn/ *n.f.* scene; (*estrade, art dramatique*) stage. **mettre en ∼,** (*pièce*) stage. **∼ de ménage,** domestic scene.

scepti|que /sɛptik/ *a.* sceptical. —*n.m./f.* sceptic. **∼cisme** *n.m.* scepticism.

sceptre /sɛptr/ *n.m.* sceptre.

schéma /ʃema/ *n.m.* diagram. **∼tique** *a.* diagrammatic; (*sommaire*) sketchy.

schisme /ʃism/ *n.m.* schism.

schizophrène /skizɔfrɛn/ *a.* & *n.m./f.* schizophrenic.

sciatique /sjatik/ *n.f.* sciatica.

scie /si/ *n.f.* saw.

sciemment /sjamã/ *adv.* knowingly.

scien|ce /sjãs/ *n.f.* science; (*savoir*) knowledge. **∼ce-fiction** *n.f.* science fiction. **∼tifique** *a.* scientific; *n.m./f.* scientist.

scier /sje/ *v.t.* saw.

scinder /sɛ̃de/ *v.t./i.*, **se ∼** *v. pr.* split.

scintill|er /sɛ̃tije/ *v.i.* glitter; (*étoile*) twinkle. **∼ement** *n.m.* glittering; twinkling.

scission /sisjɔ̃/ *n.f.* split.

sciure /sjyr/ *n.f.* sawdust.

sclérose /skleroz/ *n.f.* sclerosis. **∼ en plaques,** multiple sclerosis.

scol|aire /skɔlɛr/ *a.* school. **∼arisation** *n.f.*, **∼arité** *n.f.* schooling. **∼arisé** *a.* provided with schooling.

scorbut /skɔrbyt/ *n.m.* scurvy.

score /skɔr/ *n.m.* score.

scories /skɔri/ *n.f. pl.* slag.

scorpion /skɔrpjɔ̃/ *n.m.* scorpion. **le S∼,** Scorpio.

scotch[1] /skɔtʃ/ *n.m.* (*boisson*) Scotch (whisky).

scotch[2] /skɔtʃ/ *n.m.* (P.) Sellotape (P.); (*Amer.*) Scotch (tape) (P.).

scout, ∼e /skut/ *n.m.* & *a.* scout.

script /skript/ *n.m.* (*cinéma*) script; (*écriture*) printing. **∼-girl,** continuity girl.

scrupul|e /skrypyl/ *n.m.* scruple. **∼eusement** *adv.* scrupulously. **∼eux, ∼euse** *a.* scrupulous.

scruter /skryte/ *v.t.* examine, scrutin- ize.

scrutin /skrytɛ̃/ *n.m.* (*vote*) ballot; (*opération électorale*) poll.

sculpt|er /skylte/ *v.t.* sculpture; (*bois*) carve (**dans,** out of). **∼eur** *n.m.* sculptor. **∼ure** *n.f.* sculpture.

se, s'* /sə, s/ *pron.* himself; (*femelle*) herself; (*indéfini*) oneself; (*non humain*) itself; (*pl.*) themselves; (*réciproque*) each other, one another. **se parler,** (*à soi-même*) talk to o.s.; (*réciproque*) talk to each other. **se faire,** (*passif*) be done. **se laver les mains,** (*possessif*) wash one's hands.

séance /seãs/ *n.f.* session; (*cinéma, théâtre*) show. **∼ de pose,** sitting. **∼ tenante,** forthwith.

seau (*pl.* **∼x**) /so/ *n.m.* bucket, pail.

sec, sèche /sɛk, sɛʃ/ *a.* dry; (*fruits*) dried; (*coup, bruit*) sharp; (*cœur*) hard; (*whisky*) neat; (*Amer.*) straight. —*n.* **à ∼,** (*sans eau*) dry; (*sans argent*) broke. **au ∼,** in a dry place. —*n.f.* (*fam.*) (*cigarette*) fag.

sécateur /sekatœr/ *n.m.* (*pour les haies*) shears; (*petit*) secateurs.

sécession /sesesjɔ̃/ *n.f.* secession. **faire ∼,** secede.

sèche /sɛʃ/ *voir* **sec. ∼ment** *adv.* drily.

sèche-cheveux /sɛʃʃəvø/ *n.m. invar.* hair-drier.

sécher /seʃe/ *v.t./i.* dry; (*cours: fam.*) skip; (*ne pas savoir: fam.*) be stumped. **se ∼** *v. pr.* dry o.s.

sécheresse /seʃrɛs/ *n.f.* dryness; (*temps sec*) drought.

séchoir /seʃwar/ *n.m.* drier.

second, ∼e¹ /sgɔ̃, -d/ *a.* & *n.m.*, *f.* second. —*n.m.* (*adjoint*) second in command; (*étage*) second floor, (*Amer.*) third floor. —*n.f.* (*transport*) second class.

secondaire /sgɔ̃dɛr/ *a.* secondary.

seconde² /sgɔ̃d/ *n.f.* (*instant*) second.

seconder /sgɔ̃de/ *v.t.* assist.

secouer /skwe/ *v.t.* shake; (*poussière, torpeur*) shake off. **se** ∼, (*fam.*) (*se dépêcher*) get a move on; (*réagir*) shake o.s. up.

secour|ir /skurir/ *v.t.* assist, help. ∼**able** *a.* helpful. ∼**iste** *n.m./f.* first-aid worker.

secours /skur/ *n.m.* assistance, help. —*n.m. pl.* (*méd.*) first aid. **au** ∼!, help! **de** ∼, emergency; (*équipe, opération*) rescue.

secousse /skus/ *n.f.* jolt, jerk; (*électrique*) shock; (*séisme*) tremor.

secr|et, ∼**ète** /sɔkrɛ, -t/ *a.* secret. —*n.m.* secret; (*discrétion*) secrecy. **le** ∼**et professionnel,** professional secrecy. ∼**et de Polichinelle,** open secret. **en** ∼**et,** in secret, secretly.

secrétaire /skretɛr/ *n.m./f.* secretary. ∼ **de direction,** executive secretary. —*n.m.* (*meuble*) writing-desk. ∼ **d'État,** junior minister.

secrétariat /skretarja/ *n.m.* secretarial work; (*bureau*) secretary's office; (*d'un organisme*) secretariat.

sécrét|er /sekrete/ *v.t.* secrete. ∼**ion** /-sjɔ̃/ *n.f.* secretion.

sect|e /sɛkt/ *n.f.* sect. ∼**aire** *a.* sectarian.

secteur /sɛktœr/ *n.m.* area; (*mil., comm.*) sector; (*circuit: électr.*) mains. ∼ **primaire/secondaire/tertiaire,** primary/secondary/tertiary industry.

section /sɛksjɔ̃/ *n.f.* section; (*transports publics*) fare stage; (*mil.*) platoon. ∼**ner** /-jone/ *v.t.* sever.

sécu /seky/ *n.f.* (*fam.*) **la** ∼, the social security services.

séculaire /sekylɛr/ *a.* age-old.

sécul|ier, ∼**ière** /sekylje, -jɛr/ *a.* secular.

sécuriser /sekyrize/ *v.t.* reassure.

sécurité /sekyrite/ *n.f.* security; (*absence de danger*) safety. **en** ∼, safe, secure. **S**∼ **sociale,** social services, social security services.

sédatif /sedatif/ *n.m.* sedative.

sédentaire /sedɑ̃tɛr/ *a.* sedentary.

sédiment /sedimɑ̃/ *n.m.* sediment.

séditieu|x, ∼**se** /sedisjø, -z/ *a.* seditious.

sédition /sedisjɔ̃/ *n.f.* sedition.

séd|uire† /sedɥir/ *v.t.* charm; (*plaire à*) appeal to; (*abuser de*) seduce. ∼**ucteur,** ∼**uctrice** *a.* seductive; *n.m.*, *f.* seducer. ∼**uction** *n.f.* seduction; (*charme*) charm. ∼**uisant,** ∼**uisante** *a.* attractive.

segment /sɛgmɑ̃/ *n.m.* segment.

ségrégation /segregɑsjɔ̃/ *n.f.* segregation.

seigle /sɛgl/ *n.m.* rye.

seigneur /sɛɲœr/ *n.m.* lord. **le S**∼, the Lord.

sein /sɛ̃/ *n.m.* breast; (*fig.*) bosom. **au** ∼ **de,** in the midst of.

Seine /sɛn/ *n.f.* Seine.

séisme /seism/ *n.m.* earthquake.

seiz|e /sɛz/ *a.* & *n.m.* sixteen. ∼**ième** *a.* & *n.m./f.* sixteenth.

séjour /seʒur/ *n.m.* stay; (*pièce*) living-room. ∼**ner** *v.i.* stay.

sel /sɛl/ *n.m.* salt; (*piquant*) spice.

sélect /selɛkt/ *a.* select.

sélecti|f, ∼**ve** /selɛktif, -v/ *a.* selective.

sélection /selɛksjɔ̃/ *n.f.* selection. ∼**ner** /-jone/ *v.t.* select.

self(-service) /sɛlf(sɛrvis)/ *n.m.* self-service.

selle /sɛl/ *n.f.* saddle.

seller /sele/ *v.t.* saddle.

sellette /sɛlɛt/ *n.f.* **sur la** ∼, (*question*) under examination; (*personne*) in the hot seat.

selon /slɔ̃/ *prép.* according to (**que,** whether).

semaine /smɛn/ *n.f.* week. **en** ∼, in the week.

sémantique /semɑ̃tik/ *a.* semantic. —*n.f.* semantics.

sémaphore /semafɔr/ *n.m.* (*appareil*) semaphore.

semblable /sɑ̃blabl/ *a.* similar (**à,** to). **de** ∼**s propos**/*etc.*, (*tels*) such remarks/ *etc.* —*n.m.* fellow (creature).

semblant /sɑ̃blɑ̃/ *n.m.* **faire** ∼ **de,** pretend to. **un** ∼ **de,** a semblance of.

sembl|er /sɑ̃ble/ *v.i.* seem (**à,** to; **que,** that). **il me** ∼**e que,** it seems to me that.

semelle /smɛl/ *n.f.* sole.

semence /smɑ̃s/ *n.f.* seed; (*clou*) tack. ∼**s,** (*graines*) seed.

sem|er /sme/ *v.t.* sow; (*jeter, parsemer*) strew; (*répandre*) spread; (*personne: fam.*) lose. ∼**eur,** ∼**euse** *n.m.*, *f.* sower.

semestr|e /smɛstr/ *n.m.* half-year; (*univ.*) semester. ∼**iel,** ∼**ielle** *a.* half-yearly.

semi- /səmi/ *préf.* semi-.

séminaire /seminɛr/ *n.m.* (*relig.*) semi-nary; (*univ.*) seminar.

semi-remorque /səmirəmɔrk/ *n.m.* ar-ticulated lorry; (*Amer.*) semi(-trailer).

semis /smi/ *n.m.* (*terrain*) seed-bed; (*plant*) seedling.

sémit|e /semit/ *a.* Semitic. —*n.m./f.* Semite. ∼**ique** *a.* Semitic.

semonce /səmɔ̃s/ *n.f.* reprimand. **coup de** ∼, warning shot.

semoule /smul/ *n.f.* semolina.

sénat /sena/ *n.m.* senate. ∼**eur** /-tœr/ *n.m.* senator.

sénil|e /senil/ *a.* senile. ∼**ité** *n.f.* senil-ity.

sens /sɑ̃s/ *n.m.* sense; (*signification*) meaning, sense; (*direction*) direction. **à mon** ∼, to my mind. **à** ∼ **unique**, (*rue etc.*) one-way. **ça n'a pas de** ∼, that does not make sense. ∼ **commun**, common sense. ∼ **giratoire**, round-about; (*Amer.*) rotary. ∼ **interdit**, no entry; (*rue*) one-way street. **dans le** ∼ **des aiguilles d'une montre**, clockwise. ∼ **dessus dessous**, upside down.

sensation /sɑ̃sɑsjɔ̃/ *n.f.* feeling, sensa-tion. **faire** ∼, create a sensation. ∼**nel**, ∼**nelle** /-jɔnɛl/ *a.* sensational.

sensé /sɑ̃se/ *a.* sensible.

sensibiliser /sɑ̃sibilize/ *v.t.* ∼ **à**, make sensitive to.

sensib|le /sɑ̃sibl/ *a.* sensitive (**à**, to); (*appréciable*) noticeable. ∼**ilité** *n.f.* sensitivity. ∼**lement** *adv.* noticeably; (*à peu prés*) more or less.

sensoriel, ∼**le** /sɑ̃sɔrjɛl/ *a.* sensory.

sens|uel, ∼**uelle** /sɑ̃sɥɛl/ *a.* sensuous; (*sexuel*) sensual. ∼**ualité** *n.f.* sensuous-ness; sensuality.

sentenc|e /sɑ̃tɑ̃s/ *n.f.* sentence. ∼**ieux**, ∼**ieuse** *a.* sententious.

senteur /sɑ̃tœr/ *n.f.* scent.

sentier /sɑ̃tje/ *n.m.* path.

sentiment /sɑ̃timɑ̃/ *n.m.* feeling. **avoir le** ∼ **de**, be aware of.

sentiment|al (*m. pl.* ∼**aux**) /sɑ̃timɑ̃tal, -o/ *a.* sentimental. ∼**alité** *n.f.* sentimentality.

sentinelle /sɑ̃tinɛl/ *n.f.* sentry.

sentir† /sɑ̃tir/ *v.t.* feel; (*odeur*) smell; (*goût*) taste; (*pressentir*) sense. ∼ **la lavande**/*etc.*, smell of lavender/*etc.* —*v.i.* smell. **je ne peux pas le** ∼, (*fam.*) I can't stand him. **se** ∼ **fier/mieux/***etc.*, feel proud/better/*etc.*

séparatiste /separatist/ *a.* & *n.m./f.* separatist.

séparé /separe/ *a.* separate; (*conjoints*) separated. ∼**ment** *adv.* separately.

sépar|er /separe/ *v.t.* separate; (*en deux*) split. **se** ∼**er** *v. pr.* separate, part (**de**, from); (*se détacher*) split. **se** ∼**er de**, (*se défaire de*) part with. ∼**ation** *n.f.* separation.

sept /sɛt/ *a.* & *n.m.* seven.

septante /sɛptɑ̃t/ *a.* & *n.m.* (*en Belgique, Suisse*) seventy.

septembre /sɛptɑ̃br/ *n.m.* September.

septentrion|al (*m. pl.* ∼**aux**) /sɛptɑ̃tri-jɔnal, -o/ *a.* northern.

septième /sɛtjɛm/ *a.* & *n.m./f.* seventh.

sépulcre /sepylkr/ *n.m.* (*relig.*) sepulchre.

sépulture /sepyltyr/ *n.f.* burial; (*lieu*) burial place.

séquelles /sekɛl/ *n.f. pl.* (*maladie*) after-effects; (*fig.*) aftermath.

séquence /sekɔ̃s/ *n.f.* sequence.

séquestrer /sekɛstre/ *v.t.* confine (il-legally); (*biens*) impound.

sera, serait /sra, srɛ/ *voir* **être**.

serein, ∼**e** /sərɛ̃, -ɛn/ *a.* serene.

sérénade /serenad/ *n.f.* serenade.

sérénité /serenite/ *n.f.* serenity.

sergent /sɛrʒɑ̃/ *n.m.* sergeant.

série /seri/ *n.f.* series; (*d'objets*) set. **de** ∼, (*véhicule etc.*) standard. **fabrication** *ou* **production en** ∼, mass production.

sérieu|x, ∼**se** /serjø, -z/ *a.* serious; (*digne de foi*) reliable; (*chances, raison*) good. —*n.m.* seriousness. **garder/perdre son** ∼**x**, keep/be unable to keep a straight face. **prendre au** ∼**x**, take seriously. ∼**sement** *adv.* seri-ously.

serin /srɛ̃/ *n.m.* canary.

seringue /srɛ̃g/ *n.f.* syringe.

serment /sɛrmɑ̃/ *n.m.* oath; (*promesse*) pledge.

sermon /sɛrmɔ̃/ *n.m.* sermon. ∼**ner** /-ɔne/ *v.t.* (*fam.*) lecture.

séropositi|f, ∼**ve** /serɔpozitif, -v/ *a.* HIV-positive.

serpe /sɛrp/ *n.f.* bill(hook).

serpent /sɛrpɑ̃/ *n.m.* snake. ∼ **à son-nettes**, rattlesnake.

serpenter /sɛrpɑ̃te/ *v.i.* meander.

serpentin /sɛrpɑ̃tɛ̃/ *n.m.* streamer.

serpillière /sɛrpijɛr/ *n.f.* floor-cloth.

serre[1] /sɛr/ *n.f.* (*local*) greenhouse.

serre[2] /sɛr/ *n.f.* (*griffe*) claw.

serré /sere/ *a.* (*habit, nœud, programme*) tight; (*personnes*) packed, crowded; (*lutte, mailles*) close; (*cœur*) heavy.

serrer /sere/ *v.t.* (*saisir*) grip; (*presser*) squeeze; (*vis, corde, ceinture*) tighten; (*poing, dents*) clench; (*pieds*) pinch. ∼ **qn. dans ses bras**, hug. ∼ **les rangs**, close ranks. ~ **qn.**, (*vêtement*) be tight on s.o. —*v.i.* ~ **à droite**, keep over to the right. **se** ~ *v. pr.* (*se rapprocher*) squeeze (up) (**contre**, against). ~ **de près**, follow closely. ~ **la main à**, shake hands with.

serrur|e /seryr/ *n.f.* lock. ~**ier** *n.m.* locksmith.

sertir /sɛrtir/ *v.t.* (*bijou*) set.

sérum /serɔm/ *n.m.* serum.

servante /sɛrvɑ̃t/ *n.f.* (maid)servant.

serveu|r, ~**se** /sɛrvœr, -øz/ *n.m.*, *f.* waiter, waitress; (*au bar*) barman, barmaid.

serviable /sɛrvjabl/ *a.* helpful.

service /sɛrvis/ *n.m.* service; (*fonction, temps de travail*) duty; (*pourboire*) service (charge). ~ (**non**) **compris**, service (not) included. **être de** ~, be on duty. **pendant le** ~, (when) on duty. **rendre un** ~/**mauvais** ~ **à qn.**, do s.o. a favour/disservice. ~ **d'ordre**, (*policiers*) police. ~ **après-vente**, after-sales service. ~ **militaire**, military service.

serviette /sɛrvjɛt/ *n.f.* (*de toilette*) towel; (*sac*) briefcase. ~ (**de table**), serviette; (*Amer.*) napkin. ~ **hygiénique**, sanitary towel.

servile /sɛrvil/ *a.* servile.

servir† /sɛrvir/ *v.t.i./i.* serve; (*être utile*) be of use, serve. ~ **qn.** (**à table**), wait on s.o. **ça sert à**, (*outil, récipient, etc.*) it is used for. **ça me sert à/de**, I use it for/as. ~ **de**, serve as, be used as. ~ **à qn. de guide**/*etc.*, act as a guide/*etc.* for s.o. **se** ~ *v. pr.* (*à table*) help o.s. (**de**, to). **se** ~ **de**, use.

serviteur /sɛrvitœr/ *n.m.* servant.

servitude /sɛrvityd/ *n.f.* servitude.

ses /se/ *voir* **son**[1]

session /sesjɔ̃/ *n.f.* session.

seuil /sœj/ *n.m.* doorstep; (*entrée*) doorway; (*fig.*) threshold.

seul, ~**e** /sœl/ *a.* alone, on one's own; (*unique*) only. **un** ~ **travail**/*etc.*, only one job/*etc.* **pas un** ~ **ami**/*etc.*, not a single friend/*etc.* **parler tout** ~, talk to o.s. **faire qch. tout** ~, do sth. on one's own. —*n.m.*, *f.* **le** ~, **la** ~**e**, the only one. **un** ~, **une** ~**e**, only one. **pas un** ~, not (a single) one.

seulement /sœlmɑ̃/ *adv.* only.

sève /sɛv/ *n.f.* sap.

sév|ère /sevɛr/ *a.* severe. ~**èrement** *adv.* severely. ~**érité** /-erite/ *n.f.* severity.

sévices /sevis/ *n.m. pl.* cruelty.

sévir /sevir/ *v.i.* (*fléau*) rage. ~ **contre**, punish.

sevrer /səvre/ *v.t.* wean.

sex|e /sɛks/ *n.m.* sex; (*organes*) sex organs. ~**isme** *n.m.* sexism. ~**iste** *a.* sexist.

sex|uel, ~**uelle** /sɛksyɛl/ *a.* sexual. ~**ualité** *n.f.* sexuality.

seyant, ~**e** /sejɑ̃, -t/ *a.* becoming.

shampooing /ʃɑ̃pwɛ̃/ *n.m.* shampoo.

shérif /ʃerif/ *n.m.* sheriff.

short /ʃɔrt/ *n.m.* (pair of) shorts.

si[1] (**s'** *before il, ils*) /si, s/ *conj.* if; (*interrogation indirecte*) if, whether. **si on partait?**, (*suggestion*) what about going? **s'il vous** *ou* **te plaît**, please. **si oui**, if so. **si seulement**, if only.

si[2] /si/ *adv.* (*tellement*) so; (*oui*) yes. **un si bon repas**, such a good meal. **pas si riche que**, not as rich as. **si habile qu'il soit**, however skilful he may be. **si bien que**, with the result that.

siamois, ~**e** /sjamwa, -z/ *a.* Siamese.

Sicile /sisil/ *n.f.* Sicily.

sida /sida/ *n.m.* (*méd.*) AIDS.

sidéré /sidere/ *a.* staggered.

sidérurgie /sideryrʒi/ *n.f.* iron and steel industry.

siècle /sjɛkl/ *n.m.* century; (*époque*) age.

siège /sjɛʒ/ *n.m.* seat; (*mil.*) siege. ~ **éjectable**, ejector seat. ~ **social**, head office, headquarters.

siéger /sjeʒe/ *v.i.* (*assemblée*) sit.

sien, ~**ne** /sjɛ̃, sjɛn/ *pron.* **le** ~, **la** ~**ne**, **les** ~(**ne**)**s**, his; (*femme*) hers; (*chose*) its. **les** ~**s**, (*famille*) one's family.

sieste /sjɛst/ *n.f.* nap; (*en Espagne*) siesta. **faire la** ~, have an afternoon nap.

siffl|er /sifle/ *v.i.* whistle; (*avec un sifflet*) blow one's whistle; (*serpent, gaz*) hiss. —*v.t.* (*air*) whistle; (*chien*) whistle to *ou* for; (*acteur*) hiss; (*signaler*) blow one's whistle for. ~**ement** *n.m.* whistling. **un** ~**ement**, a whistle.

sifflet /siflɛ/ *n.m.* whistle. ~**s**, (*huées*) boos.

siffloter /siflɔte/ *v.t./i.* whistle.

sigle /sigl/ *n.m.* abbreviation, acronym.

sign|al (*pl.* ~**aux**) /siɲal, -o/ *n.m.* signal. ~**aux lumineux**, (*auto.*) traffic signals.

signal|er /siɲale/ *v.t.* indicate; (*par une sonnerie, un écriteau*) signal; (*dénoncer, mentionner*) report; (*faire remarquer*) point out. **se** ~**er par**, distinguish o.s. by. ~**ement** *n.m.* description.

signalisation /siɲalizasjɔ̃/ *n.f.* signalling, signposting; (*signaux*) signals.

signataire /siɲatɛr/ n.m./f. signatory.
signature /siɲatyr/ n.f. signature; (*action*) signing.
signe /siɲ/ n.m. sign; (*de ponctuation*) mark. **faire ~ à**, beckon (**de**, to); (*contacter*) contact. **faire ~ que non**, shake one's head. **faire ~ que oui**, nod.
signer /siɲe/ v.t. sign. **se ~** v. pr. (*relig.*) cross o.s.
signet /siɲe/ m. bookmark.
significati|f, **~ve** /siɲifikatif, -v/ a. significant.
signification /siɲifikasjɔ̃/ n.f. meaning.
signifier /siɲifje/ v.t. mean, signify; (*faire connaître*) make known (**à**, to).
silenc|e /silɑ̃s/ n.m. silence; (*mus.*) rest. **garder le ~e**, keep silent. **~ieux**, **~ieuse** a. silent; n.m. (*auto.*) silencer; (*auto., Amer.*) muffler.
silex /silɛks/ n.m. flint.
silhouette /silwɛt/ n.f. outline, silhouette.
silicium /silisjɔm/ n.m. silicon.
sillage /sijaʒ/ n.m. (*trace d'eau*) wake.
sillon /sijɔ̃/ n.m. furrow; (*de disque*) groove.
sillonner /sijɔne/ v.t. criss-cross.
silo /silo/ n.m. silo.
simagrées /simagre/ n.f. pl. fuss, pretence.
simil|aire /similɛr/ a. similar. **~itude** n.f. similarity.
simple /sɛ̃pl/ a. simple; (*non double*) single. —n.m. (*tennis*) singles. **~ d'esprit** n.m./f. simpleton. **~ soldat**, private. **~ment** /-əmɑ̃/ adv. simply.
simplicité /sɛ̃plisite/ n.f. simplicity; (*naïveté*) simpleness.
simplif|ier /sɛ̃plifje/ v.t. simplify. **~ication** n.f. simplification.
simpliste /sɛ̃plist/ a. simplistic.
simulacre /simylakr/ n.m. pretence, sham.
simul|er /simyle/ v.t. simulate. **~ateur** m. (*appareil*) simulator. **~ation** n.f. simulation.
simultané /simyltane/ a. simultaneous. **~ment** adv. simultaneously.
sinc|ère /sɛ̃sɛr/ a. sincere. **~èrement** adv. sincerely. **~érité** n.f. sincerity.
singe /sɛ̃ʒ/ n.m. monkey, ape.
singer /sɛ̃ʒe/ v.t. mimic, ape.
singeries /sɛ̃ʒri/ n.f. pl. antics.
singulariser (se) /(sə)sɛ̃gylarize/ v. pr. make o.s. conspicuous.
singul|ier, **~ière** /sɛ̃gylje, -jɛr/ a. peculiar, remarkable; (*gram.*) singular. —n.m. (*gram.*) singular. **~arité** n.f.

peculiarity. **~ièrement** adv. peculiarly; (*beaucoup*) remarkably.
sinistre¹ /sinistr/ a. sinister.
sinistr|e² /sinistr/ n.m. disaster; (*incendie*) blaze; (*dommages*) damage. **~é** a. disaster-stricken; n.m., f. disaster victim.
sinon /sinɔ̃/ conj. (*autrement*) otherwise; (*sauf*) except (**que**, that); (*si ce n'est*) if not.
sinueu|x, **~se** /sinɥø, -z/ a. winding; (*fig.*) tortuous.
sinus /sinys/ n.m. (*anat.*) sinus.
sionisme /sjɔnism/ n.m. Zionism.
siphon /sifɔ̃/ n.m. siphon; (*de WC*) U-bend.
sirène¹ /sirɛn/ n.f. (*appareil*) siren.
sirène² /sirɛn/ n.f. (*femme*) mermaid.
sirop /siro/ n.m. syrup; (*boisson*) cordial.
siroter /sirɔte/ v.t. sip.
sirupeu|x, **~se** /sirypø, -z/ a. syrupy.
sis, **~e** /si, siz/ a. situated.
sismique /sismik/ a. seismic.
site /sit/ n.m. setting; (*pittoresque*) beauty spot; (*emplacement*) site; (*monument etc.*) place of interest.
sitôt /sito/ adv. **~ entré**/*etc.*, immediately after coming in/*etc.* **~ que**, as soon as. **pas de ~**, not for a while.
situation /sitɥasjɔ̃/ n.f. situation, position. **~ de famille**, marital status.
situ|er /sitɥe/ v.t. situate, locate. **se ~er** v. pr. (*se trouver*) be situated. **~é** a. situated.
six /sis/ (/si/ *before consonant*, /siz/ *before vowel*) a. & n.m. six. **~ième** /sizjɛm/ a. & n.m./f. sixth.
sketch (pl. **~es**) /skɛtʃ/ n.m. (*théâtre*) sketch.
ski /ski/ n.m. (*patin*) ski; (*sport*) skiing. **faire du ~**, ski. **~ de fond**, cross-country skiing. **~ nautique**, water-skiing.
sk|ier /skje/ v.i. ski. **~ieur**, **~ieuse** n.m., f. skier.
slalom /slalɔm/ n.m. slalom.
slave /slav/ a. Slav; (*lang.*) Slavonic. —n.m./f. Slav.
slip /slip/ n.m. (*d'homme*) (under)pants; (*de femme*) knickers; (*Amer.*) panties. **~ de bain**, (swimming) trunks; (*du bikini*) briefs.
slogan /slɔgɑ̃/ n.m. slogan.
smoking /smɔkiŋ/ n.m. evening *ou* dinner suit, dinner-jacket.
snack(-bar) /snak(bar)/ n.m. snack-bar.
snob /snɔb/ n.m./f. snob. —a. snobbish. **~isme** n.m. snobbery.

sobr|e /sɔbr/ a. sober. **~iété** n.f. sobriety.

sobriquet /sɔbrikɛ/ n.m. nickname.

sociable /sɔsjabl/ a. sociable.

soc|ial (m. pl. **~iaux**) /sɔsjal, -jo/ a. social.

socialis|te /sɔsjalist/ n.m./f. socialist. **~me** n.m. socialism.

société /sɔsjete/ n.f. society; (compagnie, firme) company.

sociolo|gie /sɔsjɔlɔʒi/ n.f. sociology. **~gique** a. sociological. **~gue** n.m./f. sociologist.

socle /sɔkl/ n.m. (de colonne, statue) plinth; (de lampe) base.

socquette /sɔkɛt/ n.f. ankle sock.

soda /sɔda/ n.m. (fizzy) drink.

sodium /sɔdjɔm/ n.m. sodium.

sœur /sœr/ n.f. sister.

sofa /sɔfa/ n.m. sofa.

soi /swa/ pron. oneself. **en ~**, in itself. **~-disant** a. invar. so-called; (qui se veut tel) self-styled; adv. supposedly.

soie /swa/ n.f. silk.

soif /swaf/ n.f. thirst. **avoir ~**, be thirsty. **donner ~ à**, make thirsty.

soigné /swaɲe/ a. tidy, neat; (bien fait) careful.

soigner /swaɲe/ v.t. look after, take care of; (tenue, style) take care over; (maladie) treat. **se ~** v. pr. look after o.s.

soigneu|x, ~se /swaɲø, -z/ a. careful (de, about); (ordonné) tidy. **~sement** adv. carefully.

soi-même /swamɛm/ pron. oneself.

soin /swɛ̃/ n.m. care; (ordre) tidiness. **~s**, care; (méd.) treatment. **avoir ou prendre ~ de qn./de faire**, take care of s.o./to do. **premiers ~s**, first aid.

soir /swar/ n.m. evening.

soirée /sware/ n.f. evening; (réception) party. **~ dansante**, dance.

soit /swa/ voir **être**. —conj. (à savoir) that is to say. **~ . . . soit**, either . . . or.

soixantaine /swasãtɛn/ n.f. une **~ (de)**, about sixty.

soixant|e /swasãt/ a. & n.m. sixty. **~e-dix** a. & n.m. seventy. **~e-dixième** a. & n.m./f. seventieth. **~ième** a. & n.m./f. sixtieth.

soja /sɔʒa/ n.m. (graines) soya beans; (plante) soya.

sol /sɔl/ n.m. ground; (de maison) floor; (terrain agricole) soil.

solaire /sɔlɛr/ a. solar; (huile, filtre) sun. **les rayons ~s**, the sun's rays.

soldat /sɔlda/ n.m. soldier.

solde¹ /sɔld/ n.f. (salaire) pay.

solde² /sɔld/ n.m. (comm.) balance. **~s**, (articles) sale goods. **en ~**, (acheter etc.) at sale price. **les ~s**, the sales.

solder /sɔlde/ v.t. reduce; (liquider) sell off at sale price; (compte) settle. **se ~ par**, (aboutir à) end in.

sole /sɔl/ n.f. (poisson) sole.

soleil /sɔlɛj/ n.m. sun; (chaleur) sunshine; (fleur) sunflower. **il y a du ~**, it is sunny.

solennel /sɔlanɛl/ a. solemn.

solennité /sɔlanite/ n.f. solemnity.

solex /sɔleks/ n.m. (P.) moped.

solfège /sɔlfɛʒ/ n.m. elementary musical theory.

solid|aire /sɔlidɛr/ a. (mécanismes) interdependent; (couple) (mutually) supportive; (ouvriers) who show solidarity. **~arité** n.f. solidarity.

solidariser (se) /(sə)sɔlidarize/ v. pr. show solidarity (avec, with).

solid|e /sɔlid/ a. solid. —n.m. (objet) solid; (corps) sturdy. **~ement** adv. solidly. **~ité** n.f. solidity.

solidifier /sɔlidifje/ v.t., **se ~** v. pr. solidify.

soliste /sɔlist/ n.m./f. soloist.

solitaire /sɔlitɛr/ a. solitary. —n.m./f. (ermite) hermit; (personne insociable) loner.

solitude /sɔlityd/ n.f. solitude.

solive /sɔliv/ n.f. joist.

sollicit|er /sɔlisite/ v.t. request; (attirer, pousser) prompt; (tenter) tempt; (faire travailler) make demands on. **~ation** n.f. earnest request.

sollicitude /sɔlisityd/ n.f. concern.

solo /sɔlo/ n.m. & a. invar. (mus.) solo.

solstice /sɔlstis/ n.m. solstice.

soluble /sɔlybl/ a. soluble.

solution /sɔlysjɔ̃/ n.f. solution.

solvable /sɔlvabl/ a. solvent.

solvant /sɔlvã/ n.m. solvent.

sombre /sɔ̃br/ a. dark; (triste) sombre.

sombrer /sɔ̃bre/ v.i. sink (dans, into).

sommaire /sɔmɛr/ a. summary; (tenue, repas) scant. —n.m. summary.

sommation /sɔmasjɔ̃/ n.f. (mil.) warning; (jurid.) summons.

somme¹ /sɔm/ n.f. sum. **en ~, ~ toute**, in short. **faire la ~ de**, add (up), total (up).

somme² /sɔm/ n.m. (sommeil) nap.

sommeil /sɔmɛj/ n.m. sleep; (besoin de dormir) drowsiness. **avoir ~**, be ou feel sleepy. **~ler** /-mɛje/ v.i. doze; (fig.) lie dormant.

sommelier /sɔmǝlje/ n.m. wine waiter.

sommer /sɔme/ v.t. summon.

sommes /sɔm/ *voir* être.

sommet /sɔmɛ/ *n.m.* top; (*de montagne*) summit; (*de triangle*) apex; (*gloire*) height.

sommier /sɔmje/ *n.m.* base (of bed).

somnambule /sɔmnãbyl/ *n.m.* sleep-walker.

somnifère /sɔmnifɛr/ *n.m.* sleeping-pill.

somnolen|t, ~**te** /sɔmnɔlã, -t/ *a.* drowsy. ~**ce** *n.f.* drowsiness.

somnoler /sɔmnɔle/ *v.i.* doze.

sompt|ueux, ~**ueuse** /sɔ̃ptɥø, -z/ *a.* sumptuous. ~**uosité** *n.f.* sumptuousness.

son¹, sa *ou* **son*** (*pl.* **ses**) /sɔ̃, sa, sɔ̃, se/ *a.* his; (*femme*) her; (*chose*) its; (*indéfini*) one's.

son² /sɔ̃/ *n.m.* (*bruit*) sound.

son³ /sɔ̃/ *n.m.* (*de blé*) bran.

sonar /sɔnar/ *n.* Sonar.

sonate /sɔnat/ *n.f.* sonata.

sonde /sɔ̃d/ *n.f.* (*pour les forages*) drill; (*méd.*) probe.

sond|er /sɔ̃de/ *v.t.* sound; (*terrain*) drill; (*personne*) sound out. ~**age** *n.m.* sounding; drilling. ~**age (d'opinion),** (opinion) poll.

song|e /sɔ̃ʒ/ *n.m.* dream. ~**er** *v.i.* dream; *v.t.* ~**er** que, think that. ~**er à,** think about. ~**eur,** ~**euse** *a.* pensive.

sonnantes /sɔnãt/ *a.f. pl.* **à six/***etc.* **heures** ~, on the stroke of six/*etc.*

sonné /sɔne/ *a.* (*fam.*) crazy; (*fatigué*) knocked out.

sonn|er /sɔne/ *v.t./i.* ring; (*clairon, glas*) sound; (*heure*) strike; (*domestique*) ring for. **midi** ~**é,** well past noon. ~**er de,** (*clairon etc.*) sound, blow.

sonnerie /sɔnri/ *n.f.* ringing; (*de clairon*) sound; (*mécanisme*) bell.

sonnet /sɔnɛ/ *n.m.* sonnet.

sonnette /sɔnɛt/ *n.f.* bell.

sonor|e /sɔnɔr/ *a.* resonant; (*onde, effets, etc.*) sound. ~**ité** *n.f.* resonance; (*d'un instrument*) tone.

sonoris|er /sɔnɔrize/ *v.t.* (*salle*) wire for sound. ~**ation** *n.f.* (*matériel*) sound equipment.

sont /sɔ̃/ *voir* être.

sophistiqué /sɔfistike/ *a.* sophisticated.

soporifique /sɔpɔrifik/ *a.* soporific.

sorbet /sɔrbɛ/ *n.m.* sorbet.

sorcellerie /sɔrsɛlri/ *n.f.* witchcraft.

sorc|ier /sɔrsje/ *n.m.* sorcerer. ~**ière** *n.f.* witch.

sordide /sɔrdid/ *a.* sordid; (*lieu*) squalid.

sort /sɔr/ *n.m.* (*destin, hasard*) fate; (*condition*) lot; (*maléfice*) spell. **tirer (qch.) au** ~, draw lots (for sth.).

sortant, ~**e** /sɔrtã, -t/ *a.* (*président etc.*) outgoing.

sorte /sɔrt/ *n.f.* sort, kind. **de** ~ **que,** so that. **en quelque** ~, in a way. **faire en** ~ **que,** see to it that.

sortie /sɔrti/ *n.f.* departure, exit; (*porte*) exit; (*promenade, dîner*) outing; (*invective*) outburst; (*parution*) appearance; (*de disque, gaz*) release; (*d'un ordinateur*) output. ~**s,** (*argent*) outgoings.

sortilège /sɔrtilɛʒ/ *n.m.* (magic) spell.

sortir† /sɔrtir/ *v.i.* (*aux. être*) go out, leave; (*venir*) come out; (*aller au spectacle etc.*) go out; (*livre, film*) come out; (*plante*) come up. ~ **de,** (*pièce*) leave; (*milieu social*) come from; (*limites*) go beyond. —*v.t.* (*aux. avoir*) take out; (*livre, modèle*) bring out; (*dire: fam.*) come out with. ~ **d'affaire, (s')en** ~, get out of an awkward situation. ~ **du commun** *ou* **de l'ordinaire,** be out of the ordinary.

sosie /sɔzi/ *n.m.* double.

sot, ~**te** /so, sɔt/ *a.* foolish.

sottise /sɔtiz/ *n.f.* foolishness; (*action, remarque*) foolish thing.

sou /su/ *n.m.* ~**s,** money. **pas un** ~, not a penny. **sans le** ~, without a penny. **près de ses** ~**s,** tight-fisted.

soubresaut /subrəso/ *n.m.* (sudden) start.

souche /suʃ/ *n.f.* (*d'arbre*) stump; (*de famille, vigne*) stock; (*de carnet*) counterfoil. **planté comme une** ~, standing like an idiot.

souci¹ /susi/ *n.m.* (*inquiétude*) worry; (*préoccupation*) concern. **se faire du** ~, worry.

souci² /susi/ *n.m.* (*plante*) marigold.

soucier (se) /(sə)susje/ *v. pr.* **se** ~ **de,** be concerned about.

soucieu|x, ~**se** /susjø, -z/ *a.* concerned (**de,** about).

soucoupe /sukup/ *n.f.* saucer. ~ **volante,** flying saucer.

soudain, ~**e** /sudɛ̃, -ɛn/ *a.* sudden. —*adv.* suddenly. ~**ement** /-ɛnmã/ *adv.* suddenly. ~**eté** /-ɛnte/ *n.f.* suddenness.

soude /sud/ *n.f.* soda.

soud|er /sude/ *v.t.* solder, (*à la flamme*) weld. **se** ~**er** *v. pr.* (*os*) knit (together). ~**ure** *n.f.* soldering, welding; (*substance*) solder.

soudoyer /sudwaje/ *v.t.* bribe.

souffle /sufl/ *n.m.* blow, puff; (*haleine*) breath; (*respiration*) breathing; (*explosion*) blast; (*vent*) breath of air.

soufflé /sufle/ *n.m.* (*culin.*) soufflé.

souffl|er /sufle/ *v.i.* blow; (*haleter*) puff. —*v.t.* (*bougie*) blow out; (*poussière, fumée*) blow; (*par explosion*) destroy; (*chuchoter*) whisper. **~er son rôle à,** prompt. **~eur, ~euse** *n.m., f.* (*théâtre*) prompter.

soufflet /suflɛ/ *n.m.* (*instrument*) bellows.

souffrance /sufrãs/ *n.f.* suffering. **en ~,** (*affaire*) pending.

souffr|ir† /sufrir/ *v.i.* suffer (**de,** from). —*v.t.* (*endurer*) suffer; (*admettre*) admit of. **il ne peut pas le ~ir,** he cannot stand *ou* bear him. **~ant, ~ante** *a.* unwell.

soufre /sufr/ *n.m.* sulphur.

souhait /swɛ/ *n.m.* wish. **nos ~s de,** (*vœux*) good wishes for. **à vos ~s!,** bless you!

souhait|er /swete/ *v.t.* (*bonheur etc.*) wish for. **~er qch. à qn.,** wish s.o. sth. **~er que/faire,** hope that/to do. **~able** /swetabl/ *a.* desirable.

souiller /suje/ *v.t.* soil.

soûl, ~e /su, sul/ *a.* drunk. —*n.m.* **tout son ~,** as much as one can.

soulag|er /sulaʒe/ *v.t.* relieve. **~ement** *n.m.* relief.

soûler /sule/ *v.t.* make drunk. **se ~** *v. pr.* get drunk.

soulèvement /sulɛvmã/ *n.m.* uprising.

soulever /sulve/ *v.t.* lift, raise; (*exciter*) stir; (*question, poussière*) raise. **se ~** *v. pr.* lift *ou* raise o.s. up; (*se révolter*) rise up.

soulier /sulje/ *n.m.* shoe.

souligner /suliɲe/ *v.t.* underline; (*taille, yeux*) emphasize.

soum|ettre† /sumɛtr/ *v.t.* (*dompter, assujettir*) subject (**à,** to); (*présenter*) submit (**à,** to). **se ~ettre** *v. pr.* submit (**à,** to). **~is, ~ise** *a.* submissive. **~ission** *n.f.* submission.

soupape /supap/ *n.f.* valve.

soupçon /supsõ/ *n.m.* suspicion. **un ~ de,** (*fig.*) a touch of. **~ner** /-ɔne/ *v.t.* suspect. **~neux, ~neuse** /-ɔnø, -z/ *a.* suspicious.

soupe /sup/ *n.f.* soup.

souper /supe/ *n.m.* supper. —*v.i.* have supper.

soupeser /supəze/ *v.t.* judge the weight of; (*fig.*) weigh up.

soupière /supjɛr/ *n.f.* (soup) tureen.

soupir /supir/ *n.m.* sigh. **pousser un ~,** heave a sigh. **~er** *v.i.* sigh.

soupir|ail (*pl.* **~aux**) /supiraj, -o/ *n.m.* small basement window.

soupirant /supirã/ *n.m.* suitor.

souple /supl/ *a.* supple; (*règlement, caractère*) flexible. **~sse** /-ɛs/ *n.f.* suppleness; flexibility.

source /surs/ *n.f.* source; (*eau*) spring. **de ~ sûre,** from a reliable source. **~ thermale,** hot springs.

sourcil /sursi/ *n.m.* eyebrow.

sourciller /sursije/ *v.i.* **sans ~,** without batting an eyelid.

sourd, ~e /sur, -d/ *a.* deaf; (*bruit, douleur*) dull; (*inquiétude, conflit*) silent, hidden. —*n.m., f.* deaf person. **faire la ~e oreille,** turn a deaf ear. **~muet** (*pl.* **~s-muets**), **~e-muette** (*pl.* **~es-muettes**) *a.* deaf and dumb; *n.m., f.* deaf mute.

sourdine /surdin/ *n.f.* (*mus.*) mute. **en ~,** quietly.

souricière /surisjɛr/ *n.f.* mousetrap; (*fig.*) trap.

sourire /surir/ *n.m.* smile. **garder le ~,** keep smiling. —*v.i.* smile (**à,** at). **~ à,** (*fortune*) smile on.

souris /suri/ *n.f.* mouse.

sournois, ~e /surnwa, -z/ *a.* sly, underhand. **~ement** /-zmã/ *adv.* slyly.

sous /su/ *prép.* under, beneath. **~ la main,** handy. **~ la pluie,** in the rain. **~ peu,** shortly. **~ terre,** underground.

sous- /su/ *préf.* (*subordination*) sub-; (*insuffisance*) under-.

sous-alimenté /suzalimãte/ *a.* undernourished.

sous-bois /subwa/ *n.m. invar.* undergrowth.

souscr|ire /suskrir/ *v.i.* **~ire à,** subscribe to. **~iption** *n.f.* subscription.

sous-direct|eur, ~rice /sudirɛktœr, -ris/ *n.m., f.* assistant manager.

sous-entend|re /suzãtãdr/ *v.t.* imply. **~u** *n.m.* insinuation.

sous-estimer /suzɛstime/ *v.t.* underestimate.

sous-jacent, ~e /suʒasã, -t/ *a.* underlying.

sous-marin, ~e /sumarɛ̃, -in/ *a.* underwater. —*n.m.* submarine.

sous-officier /suzɔfisje/ *n.m.* non-commissioned officer.

sous-préfecture /suprefɛktyr/ *n.f.* subprefecture.

sous-produit /suprɔdɥi/ *n.m.* by-product.

sous-programme /suprɔgram/ *n.m.* subroutine.

soussigné, ~e /susiɲe/ *a. & n.m., f.* undersigned.

sous-sol /susɔl/ *n.m.* (*cave*) basement.
sous-titr|e /sutitr/ *n.m.* subtitle. **~er** *v.t.* subtitle.
soustr|aire† /sustrɛr/ *v.t.* remove; (*déduire*) subtract. **se ~aire à,** escape from. **~action** *n.f.* (*déduction*) subtraction.
sous-trait|er /sutrete/ *v.t.* subcontract. **~ant** *n.m.* subcontractor.
sous-verre /suvɛr/ *n.m. invar.* picture frame, glass mount.
sous-vêtement /suvɛtmɑ̃/ *n.m.* undergarment. **~s,** underwear.
soutane /sutan/ *n.f.* cassock.
soute /sut/ *n.f.* (*de bateau*) hold. **~ à charbon,** coal-bunker.
soutenir† /sutnir/ *v.t.* support; (*fortifier, faire durer*) sustain; (*résister à*) withstand. **~ que,** maintain that. **se ~** *v. pr.* (*se tenir debout*) support o.s.
soutenu /sutny/ *a.* (*constant*) sustained; (*style*) lofty.
souterrain, **~e** /sutɛrɛ̃, -ɛn/ *a.* underground. —*n.m.* underground passage, subway.
soutien /sutjɛ̃/ *n.m.* support. **~-gorge** (*pl.* **~s-gorge**) *n.m.* bra.
soutirer /sutire/ *v.t.* **~ à qn.,** extract from s.o.
souvenir[1] /suvnir/ *n.m.* memory, recollection; (*objet*) memento; (*cadeau*) souvenir. **en ~ de,** in memory of.
souvenir[2]† (se) /(sə)suvnir/ *v. pr.* **se ~ de,** remember. **se ~ que,** remember that.
souvent /suvɑ̃/ *adv.* often.
souverain, **~e** /suvrɛ̃, -ɛn/ *a.* sovereign; (*extrême*: péj.) supreme. —*n.m., f.* sovereign. **~eté** /-ɛnte/ *n.f.* sovereignty.
soviétique† /sɔvjetik/ *a.* Soviet. —*n.m./f.* Soviet citizen.
soyeu|x, **~se** /swajø, -z/ *a.* silky.
spacieu|x, **~se** /spasjø, -z/ *a.* spacious.
spaghetti /spageti/ *n.m. pl.* spaghetti.
sparadrap /sparadra/ *n.m.* sticking-plaster; (*Amer.*) adhesive tape *ou* bandage.
spasm|e /spasm/ *n.m.* spasm. **~odique** *a.* spasmodic.
spat|ial (*m. pl.* **~iaux**) /spasjal, -jo/ *a.* space.
spatule /spatyl/ *n.f.* spatula.
speaker, **~ine** /spikœr, -rin/ *n.m., f.* announcer.
spéc|ial (*m. pl.* **~iaux**) /spesjal, -jo/ *a.* special; (*singulier*) peculiar. **~ialement** *adv.* especially; (*exprès*) specially.

spécialis|er (se) /(sə)spesjalize/ *v. pr.* specialize (**dans,** in). **~ation** *n.f.* specialization.
spécialiste /spesjalist/ *n.m./f.* specialist.
spécialité /spesjalite/ *n.f.* speciality; (*Amer.*) specialty.
spécif|ier /spesifje/ *v.t.* specify. **~ication** *n.f.* specification.
spécifique /spesifik/ *a.* specific.
spécimen /spesimɛn/ *n.m.* specimen.
spectacle /spɛktakl/ *n.m.* sight, spectacle; (*représentation*) show.
spectaculaire /spɛktakylɛr/ *a.* spectacular.
specta|teur, **~trice** /spɛktatœr, -tris/ *n.m., f.* onlooker; (*sport*) spectator. **les ~teurs,** (*théâtre*) the audience.
spectre /spɛktr/ *n.m.* (*revenant*) spectre; (*images*) spectrum.
spécul|er /spekyle/ *v.i.* speculate. **~ateur,** **~atrice** *n.m., f.* speculator. **~ation** *n.f.* speculation.
spéléologie /speleɔlɔʒi/ *n.f.* cave exploration, pot-holing; (*Amer.*) spelunking.
sperme /spɛrm/ *n.m.* sperm.
sph|ère /sfɛr/ *n.f.* sphere. **~érique** *a.* spherical.
sphinx /sfɛ̃ks/ *n.m.* sphinx.
spirale /spiral/ *n.f.* spiral.
spirite /spirit/ *n.m./f.* spiritualist.
spirituel, **~le** /spirityɛl/ *a.* spiritual; (*amusant*) witty.
spiritueux /spirityø/ *n.m.* (*alcool*) spirit.
splend|ide /splɑ̃did/ *a.* splendid. **~eur** *n.f.* splendour.
spongieu|x, **~se** /spɔ̃ʒjø, -z/ *a.* spongy.
sponsor /spɔ̃sɔr/ *n.m.* sponsor. **~iser** *v.t.* sponsor.
spontané /spɔ̃tane/ *a.* spontaneous. **~ité** *n.f.* spontaneity. **~ment** *adv.* spontaneously.
sporadique /spɔradik/ *a.* sporadic.
sport /spɔr/ *n.m.* sport. —*a. invar.* (*vêtements*) casual. **veste/voiture de ~,** sports jacket/car.
sporti|f, **~ve** /spɔrtif, -v/ *a.* sporting; (*physique*) athletic; (*résultats*) sports. —*n.m.* sportsman. —*n.f.* sportswoman.
spot /spɔt/ *n.m.* spotlight; (*publicitaire*) ad.
spray /sprɛ/ *n.m.* spray; (*méd.*) inhaler.
sprint /sprint/ *n.m.* sprint. **~er** *v.i.* sprint. *n.m.* /-œr/ sprinter.
square /skwar/ *n.m.* (public) garden.
squash /skwaʃ/ *n.m.* squash.
squatter /skwatœr/ *n.m.* squatter. **~iser** *v.t.* squat in.
squelett|e /skəlɛt/ *n.m.* skeleton. **~ique**

/-etik/ a. skeletal; (maigre) all skin and bone.

stabiliser /stabilize/ v.t. stabilize.

stab|le /stabl/ a. stable. ∼ilité n.f. stability.

stade¹ /stad/ n.m. (sport) stadium.

stade² /stad/ n.m. (phase) stage.

stag|e /staʒ/ n.m. course. ∼iaire a. & n.m./f. course member; (apprenti) trainee.

stagn|er /stagne/ v.i. stagnate. ∼ant, ∼ante a. stagnant. ∼ation n.f. stagnation.

stand /stɑ̃d/ n.m. stand, stall. ∼ de tir, (shooting-)range.

standard¹ /stɑ̃dar/ n.m. switchboard. ∼iste /-dist/ n.m./f. switchboard operator.

standard² /stɑ̃dar/ a. invar. standard. ∼iser /-dize/ v.t. standardize.

standing /stɑ̃diŋ/ n.m. status, standing. de ∼, (hôtel etc.) luxury.

star /star/ n.f. (actrice) star.

starter /starter/ n.m. (auto.) choke.

station /stasjɔ̃/ n.f. station; (halte) stop. ∼ balnéaire, seaside resort. ∼ debout, standing position. ∼ de taxis, taxi rank; (Amer.) taxi stand. ∼-service (pl. ∼s-service) n.f. service station. ∼ thermale, spa.

stationnaire /stasjɔner/ a. stationary.

stationn|er /stasjɔne/ v.i. park. ∼ement n.m. parking.

statique /statik/ a. static.

statistique /statistik/ n.f. statistic; (science) statistics. —a. statistical.

statue /staty/ n.f. statue.

statuer /statɥe/ v.i. ∼ sur, rule on.

statu quo /statykwo/ n.m. status quo.

stature /statyr/ n.f. stature.

statut /staty/ n.m. status. ∼s, (règles) statutes. ∼aire /-tɛr/ a. statutory.

steak /stɛk/ n.m. steak.

stencil /stɛnsil/ n.m. stencil.

sténo /steno/ n.f. (personne) stenographer; (sténographie) shorthand.

sténodactylo /stenɔdaktilo/ n.f. shorthand typist; (Amer.) stenographer.

sténographie /stenɔgrafi/ n.f. shorthand.

stéréo /stereo/ n.f. & a. invar. stereo. ∼phonique /-eɔfɔnik/ a. stereophonic.

stéréotyp|e /stereɔtip/ n.m. stereotype. ∼é a. stereotyped.

stéril|e /steril/ a. sterile. ∼ité n.f. sterility.

stérilet /sterilɛ/ n.m. coil, IUD.

stérilis|er /sterilize/ v.t. sterilize. ∼ation n.f. sterilization.

stéroïde /sterɔid/ a. & n.m. steroid.

stéthoscope /stetɔskɔp/ n.m. stethoscope.

stigmat|e /stigmat/ n.m. mark, stigma. ∼iser v.t. stigmatize.

stimul|er /stimyle/ v.t. stimulate. ∼ant n.m. stimulus; (médicament) stimulant. ∼ateur cardiaque, pacemaker. ∼ation n.f. stimulation.

stipul|er /stipyle/ v.t. stipulate. ∼ation n.f. stipulation.

stock /stɔk/ n.m. stock. ∼er v.t. stock. ∼iste n.m. stockist; (Amer.) dealer.

stoïque /stɔik/ a. stoical. —n.m./f. stoic.

stop /stɔp/ int. stop. —n.m. stop sign; (feu arrière) brake light. faire du ∼, (fam.) hitch-hike.

stopper /stɔpe/ v.t./i. stop; (vêtement) mend, reweave.

store /stɔr/ n.m. blind; (Amer.) shade; (de magasin) awning.

strabisme /strabism/ n.m. squint.

strapontin /strapɔ̃tɛ̃/ n.m. folding seat, jump seat.

stratagème /strataʒɛm/ n.m. stratagem.

stratég|ie /strateʒi/ n.f. strategy. ∼ique a. strategic.

stress /stres/ n. stress, ∼ant a. stressful. ∼er v.t. put under stress.

strict /strikt/ a. strict; (tenue, vérité) plain. le ∼ minimum, the absolute minimum. ∼ement adv. strictly.

strident, ∼e /stridɑ̃, -t/ a. shrill.

str|ie /stri/ n.f. streak. ∼ier v.t. streak.

strip-tease /striptiz/ n.m. strip-tease.

strophe /strɔf/ n.f. stanza, verse.

structur|e /stryktyr/ n.f. structure. ∼al (m. pl. ∼aux) a. structural. ∼er v.t. structure.

studieu|x, ∼se /stydjø, -z/ a. studious; (période) devoted to study.

studio /stydjo/ n.m. (d'artiste, de télévision, etc.) studio; (logement) studio flat, bed-sitter.

stupéf|ait, ∼aite /stypefɛ, -t/ a. amazed. ∼action n.f. amazement.

stupéf|ier /stypefje/ v.t. amaze. ∼iant, ∼iante a. amazing; n.m. drug, narcotic.

stupeur /stypœr/ n.f. amazement; (méd.) stupor.

stupid|e /stypid/ a. stupid. ∼ité n.f. stupidity.

styl|e /stil/ n.m. style. ∼isé a. stylized.

stylé /stile/ a. well-trained.

styliste /stilist/ n.m./f. fashion designer.

stylo /stilo/ n.m. pen. ∼ (à) bille, ball-point pen. ∼ (à) encre, fountain-pen.

su /sy/ voir savoir.

suave /sɥav/ a. sweet.

subalterne /sybaltɛrn/ a. & n.m./f. subordinate.

subconscient, ~e /sypkɔ̃sjɑ̃, -t/ a. & n.m. subconscious.

subdiviser /sybdivize/ v.t. subdivide.

subir /sybir/ v.t. suffer; (traitement, expériences) undergo.

subit, ~e /sybi, -t/ a. sudden. **~ement** /-tmɑ̃/ adv. suddenly.

subjecti|f, ~ve /sybʒɛktif, -v/ a. subjective. **~vité** n.f. subjectivity.

subjonctif /sybʒɔ̃ktif/ a. & n.m. subjunctive.

subjuguer /sybʒyge/ v.t. (charmer) captivate.

sublime /syblim/ a. sublime.

submer|ger /sybmɛrʒe/ v.t. submerge; (fig.) overwhelm. **~sion** n.f. submersion.

subordonné, ~e /sybɔrdɔne/ a. & n.m., f. subordinate.

subord|onner /sybɔrdɔne/ v.t. subordinate (à, to). **~ination** n.f. subordination.

subreptice /sybrɛptis/ a. surreptitious.

subside /sybzid/ n.m. grant.

subsidiare /sypsidjɛr/ a. subsidiary.

subsist|er /sybziste/ v.i. subsist; (durer, persister) exist. **~ance** n.f. subsistence.

substance /sypstɑ̃s/ n.f. substance.

substantiel, ~le /sypstɑ̃sjɛl/ a. substantial.

substantif /sypstɑ̃tif/ n.m. noun.

substit|uer /sypstitɥe/ v.t. substitute (à, for). **se ~uer à**, (remplacer) substitute for; (évincer) take over from. **~ut** n.m. substitute; (jurid.) deputy public prosecutor. **~ution** n.f. substitution.

subterfuge /syptɛrfyʒ/ n.m. subterfuge.

subtil /syptil/ a. subtle. **~ité** n.f. subtlety.

subtiliser /syptilize/ v.t. **~ qch. (à qn.)**, spirit sth. away (from s.o.).

subvenir /sybvənir/ v.i. **~ à**, provide for.

subvention /sybvɑ̃sjɔ̃/ n.f. subsidy. **~ner** /-jɔne/ v.t. subsidize.

subversi|f, ~ve /sybvɛrsif, -v/ a. subversive.

subversion /sybvɛrsjɔ̃/ n.f. subversion.

suc /syk/ n.m. juice.

succédané /syksedane/ n.m. substitute (de, for).

succéder /syksede/ v.i. **~ à**, succeed. **se ~ v. pr.** succeed one another.

succès /syksɛ/ n.m. success. **à ~**, (film, livre, etc.) successful. **avoir du ~**, be a success.

successeur /syksesœr/ n.m. successor.

successi|f, ~ve /syksesif, -v/ a. successive. **~vement** adv. successively.

succession /syksesjɔ̃/ n.f. succession; (jurid.) inheritance.

succinct, ~e /syksɛ̃, -t/ a. succinct.

succomber /sykɔ̃be/ v.i. die. **~ à**, succumb to.

succulent, ~e /sykylɑ̃, -t/ a. succulent.

succursale /sykyrsal/ n.f. (comm.) branch.

sucer /syse/ v.t. suck.

sucette /sysɛt/ n.f. (bonbon) lollipop; (tétine) dummy; (Amer.) pacifier.

sucr|e /sykr/ n.m. sugar. **~e d'orge**, barley sugar. **~e en poudre**, caster sugar; (Amer.) finely ground sugar. **~e glace**, icing sugar. **~e roux**, brown sugar. **~ier, ~ière** a. sugar; n.m. (récipient) sugar-bowl.

sucr|er /sykre/ v.t. sugar, sweeten. **~é** a. sweet; (additionné de sucre) sweetened.

sucreries /sykrəri/ n.f. pl. sweets.

sud /syd/ n.m. south. —a. invar. south; (partie) southern; (direction) southerly. **~-africain, ~-africaine** a. & n.m., f. South African. **~-est** n.m. south-east. **~-ouest** n.m. south-west.

Suède /sɥɛd/ n.f. Sweden.

suédois, ~e /sɥedwa, -z/ a. Swedish. —n.m., f. Swede. —n.m. (lang.) Swedish.

suer /sɥe/ v.t./i. sweat. **faire ~ qn.**, (fam.) get on s.o.'s nerves.

sueur /sɥœr/ n.f. sweat. **en ~**, sweating.

suff|ire† /syfir/ v.i. be enough (à qn., for s.o.). **il ~it de faire**, one only has to do. **il ~it d'une goutte pour**, a drop is enough to. **~ire à**, (besoin) satisfy. **~ire à soi-même**, be self-sufficient.

suffis|ant, ~ante /syfizɑ̃, -t/ a. sufficient; (vaniteux) conceited. **~amment** adv. sufficiently. **~amment de**, sufficient. **~ance** n.f. (vanité) conceit.

suffixe /syfiks/ n.m. suffix.

suffoquer /syfɔke/ v.t./i. choke, suffocate.

suffrage /syfraʒ/ n.m. (voix: pol.) vote; (modalité) suffrage.

sugg|érer /sygʒere/ v.t. suggest. **~estion** /-ʒɛstjɔ̃/ n.f. suggestion.

suggesti|f, ~ve /sygʒɛstif, -v/ a. suggestive.

suicid|e /sɥisid/ n.m. suicide. **~aire** a. suicidal.

suicid|er (se) /(sə)sɥiside/ v. pr. commit suicide. **~é, ~ée** n.m., f. suicide.

suie /sɥi/ *n.f.* soot.

suint|er /sɥɛ̃te/ *v.i.* ooze. **~ement** *n.m.* oozing.

suis /sɥi/ *voir* **être, suivre.**

Suisse /sɥis/ *n.f.* Switzerland.

suisse /sɥis/ *a. & n.m.* Swiss. **~sse** /-ɛs/ *n.f.* Swiss (woman).

suite /sɥit/ *n.f.* continuation, rest; (*d'un film*) sequel; (*série*) series; (*appartement, escorte*) suite; (*résultat*) consequence; (*cohérence*) order. **~s,** (*de maladie*) after-effects. **à la ~, de ~,** (*successivement*) in succession. **à la ~ de,** (*derrière*) behind. **à la ~ de, par ~ de,** as a result of. **faire ~ (à),** follow. **par la ~,** afterwards. **~ à votre lettre du,** further to your letter of the.

suivant¹, ~e /sɥivɑ̃, -t/ *a.* following, next. *—n.m., f.* following *ou* next person.

suivant² /sɥivɑ̃/ *prép.* (*selon*) according to.

suivi /sɥivi/ *a.* steady, sustained; (*cohérent*) consistent. **peu/très ~,** (*cours*) poorly-/well-attended.

suivre† /sɥivr/ *v.t./i.* follow; (*comprendre*) keep up (with), follow. **se ~** *v. pr.* follow each other. **faire ~,** (*courrier etc.*) forward.

sujet¹, ~te /syʒɛ, -t/ *a.* **~ à,** liable *ou* subject to. *—n.m., f.* (*gouverné*) subject.

sujet² /syʒɛ/ *n.m.* (*matière, individu*) subject; (*motif*) cause; (*gram.*) subject. **au ~ de,** about.

sulfurique /sylfyrik/ *a.* sulphuric.

sultan /syltɑ̃/ *n.m.* sultan.

summum /sɔmɔm/ *n.m.* height.

super /sypɛr/ *n.m.* (*essence*) four-star, premium (*Amer.*). *—a. invar.* (*fam.*) great. *—adv.* (*fam.*) ultra, fantastically.

superbe /sypɛrb/ *a.* superb.

supercherie /sypɛrʃəri/ *n.f.* trickery.

supérette /sypɛrɛt/ *n.f.* minimarket.

superficie /sypɛrfisi/ *n.f.* area.

superficiel, ~le /sypɛrfisjɛl/ *a.* superficial.

superflu /sypɛrfly/ *a.* superfluous. *—n.m.* (*excédent*) surplus.

supérieur, ~e /sypɛrjœr/ *a.* (*plus haut*) upper; (*quantité, nombre*) greater (à, than); (*études, principe*) higher (à, than); (*meilleur, hautain*) superior (à, to). *—n.m., f.* superior.

supériorité /sypɛrjɔrite/ *n.f.* superiority.

superlati|f, ~ve /sypɛrlatif, -v/ *a. & n.m.* superlative.

supermarché /sypɛrmarʃe/ *n.m.* supermarket.

superposer /sypɛrpoze/ *v.t.* superimpose.

superproduction /sypɛrprɔdyksjɔ̃/ *n.f.* (*film*) spectacular.

superpuissance /sypɛrpɥisɑ̃s/ *n.f.* superpower.

supersonique /sypɛrsɔnik/ *a.* supersonic.

superstit|ion /sypɛrstisjɔ̃/ *n.f.* superstition. **~ieux, ~ieuse** *a.* superstitious.

superviser /sypɛrvize/ *v.t.* supervise.

supplanter /syplɑ̃te/ *v.t.* supplant.

suppléan|t, ~te /sypleɑ̃, -t/ *n.m., f. & a.* (**professeur**) **~t,** supply teacher; (**juge**) **~t,** deputy (judge). **~ce** *n.f.* (*fonction*) temporary appointment.

suppléer /syplee/ *v.t.* (*remplacer*) replace; (*ajouter*) supply. *—v.i.* **~ à,** (*compenser*) make up for.

supplément /syplemɑ̃/ *n.m.* (*argent*) extra charge; (*de frites, légumes*) extra portion. **en ~,** extra. **un ~ de,** (*travail etc.*) extra. **payer pour un ~ de bagages,** pay extra for excess luggage. **~aire** /-tɛr/ *a.* extra, additional.

supplic|e /syplis/ *n.m.* torture. **~ier** *v.t.* torture.

supplier /syplije/ *v.t.* beg, beseech (**de,** to).

support /sypɔr/ *n.m.* support; (*publicitaire: fig.*) medium.

support|er¹ /sypɔrte/ *v.t.* (*endurer*) bear; (*subir*) suffer; (*soutenir*) support; (*résister à*) withstand. **~able** *a.* bearable.

supporter² /sypɔrtɛr/ *n.m.* (*sport*) supporter.

suppos|er /sypoze/ *v.t.* suppose; (*impliquer*) imply. **à ~er que,** supposing that. **~ition** *n.f.* supposition.

suppositoire /sypozitwar/ *n.m.* suppository.

suppr|imer /syprime/ *v.t.* get rid of, remove; (*annuler*) cancel; (*mot*) delete. **~imer à qn.,** (*enlever*) take away from s.o. **~ession** *n.f.* removal; cancellation; deletion.

suprématie /sypremasi/ *n.f.* supremacy.

suprême /syprɛm/ *a.* supreme.

sur /syr/ *prép.* on, upon; (*pardessus*) over; (*au sujet de*) about, on; (*proportion*) out of; (*mesure*) by. **aller/tourner/***etc.* **~,** go/turn/*etc.* towards. **mettre/jeter/***etc.* **~,** put/throw/*etc.* on to. **~-le-champ** *adv.* immediately. **~ le qui-vive,** on the alert. **~ mesure,** made to measure. **~ place,** on the spot. **~ ce,** hereupon.

sur- /syr/ *préf.* over-.

sûr /syr/ *a.* certain, sure; (*sans danger*) safe; (*digne de confiance*) reliable; (*main*) steady; (*jugement*) sound.

surabondance /syrabɔ̃dɑ̃s/ *n.f.* super-abundance.

suranné /syrane/ *a.* outmoded.

surcharg|e /syrʃarʒ/ *n.f.* overloading; (*poids*) extra load. **⁓er** *v.t.* overload; (*texte*) alter.

surchauffer /syrʃofe/ *v.t.* overheat.

surchoix /syrʃwa/ *a. invar.* of finest quality.

surclasser /syrklase/ *v.t.* outclass.

surcroît /syrkrwa/ *n.m.* increase (**de**, in), additional amount (**de**, of). **de ⁓**, in addition.

surdité /syrdite/ *n.f.* deafness.

sureau (*pl.* **⁓x**) /syro/ *n.m.* (*arbre*) elder.

surélever /syrɛlve/ *v.t.* raise.

sûrement /syrmɑ̃/ *adv.* certainly; (*sans danger*) safely.

surench|ère /syrɑ̃ʃɛr/ *n.f.* higher bid. **⁓érir** *v.i.* bid higher (**sur**, than).

surestimer /syrɛstime/ *v.t.* overestimate.

sûreté /syrte/ *n.f.* safety; (*garantie*) surety; (*d'un geste*) steadiness. **être en ⁓**, be safe. **S⁓ (nationale)**, *division of French Ministère de l'Intérieur in charge of police.*

surexcité /syrɛksite/ *a.* very excited.

surf /syrf/ *n.m.* surfing.

surface /syrfas/ *n.f.* surface. **faire ⁓**, (*sous-marin etc.*) surface. **en ⁓**, (*fig.*) superficially.

surfait, **⁓e** /syrfɛ, -t/ *a.* overrated.

surgelé /syrʒəle/ *a.* (deep-)frozen. **(aliments) ⁓s**, frozen food.

surgir /syrʒir/ *v.i.* appear (suddenly); (*difficulté*) arise.

surhomme /syrɔm/ *n.m.* superman.

surhumain, **⁓e** /syrymɛ̃, -ɛn/ *a.* superhuman.

surlendemain /syrlɑ̃dmɛ̃/ *n.m.* **le ⁓**, two days later. **le ⁓ de**, two days after.

surligneur /syrliɲœr/ *n.m.* highlighter (pen).

surmen|er /syrməne/ *v.t.*, **se ⁓er** *v. pr.* overwork. **⁓age** *n.m.* overworking; (*méd.*) overwork.

surmonter /syrmɔ̃te/ *v.t.* (*vaincre*) overcome, surmount; (*être au-dessus de*) surmount, top.

surnager /syrnaʒe/ *v.i.* float.

surnaturel, **⁓le** /syrnatyrɛl/ *a.* supernatural.

surnom /syrnɔ̃/ *n.m.* nickname. **⁓mer** /-ɔme/ *v.t.* nickname.

surnombre (en) /(ɑ̃)syrnɔ̃br/ *adv.* too many. **il est en ⁓**, he is one too many.

surpasser /syrpase/ *v.t.* surpass.

surpeuplé /syrpœple/ *a.* overpopulated.

surplomb /syrplɔ̃/ *n.m.* **en ⁓**, overhanging. **⁓er** /-be/ *v.t./i.* overhang.

surplus /syrply/ *n.m.* surplus.

surpr|endre† /syrprɑ̃dr/ *v.t.* (*étonner*) surprise; (*prendre au dépourvu*) catch, surprise; (*entendre*) overhear. **⁓enant**, **⁓enante** *a.* surprising. **⁓is**, **⁓ise** *a.* surprised (**de**, at).

surprise /syrpriz/ *n.f.* surprise. **⁓-partie** (*pl.* **⁓s-parties**) *n.f.* party.

surréalisme /syrrealism/ *n.m.* sur-realism.

sursaut /syrso/ *n.m.* start, jump. **en ⁓**, with a start. **⁓ de**, (*regain*) burst of. **⁓er** /-te/ *v.i.* start, jump.

sursis /syrsi/ *n.m.* reprieve; (*mil.*) deferment. **deux ans (de prison) avec ⁓**, a two-year suspended sentence.

surtaxe /syrtaks/ *n.f.* surcharge.

surtout /syrtu/ *adv.* especially, mainly; (*avant tout*) above all. **⁓ pas**, certainly not.

surveillant, **⁓e** /syrvɛjɑ̃, -t/ *n.m.*, *f.* (*de prison*) warder; (*au lycée*) supervisor (in charge of discipline).

surveill|er /syrveje/ *v.t.* watch; (*travaux*, *élèves*) supervise. **⁓ance** *n.f.* watch; supervision; (*de la police*) surveillance.

survenir /syrvənir/ *v.i.* occur, come about; (*personne*) turn up; (*événement*) take place.

survêtement /syrvɛtmɑ̃/ *n.m.* (*sport*) track suit.

survie /syrvi/ *n.f.* survival.

survivance /syrvivɑ̃s/ *n.f.* survival.

surviv|re† /syrvivr/ *v.i.* survive. **⁓re à**, (*conflit etc.*) survive; (*personne*) out-live. **⁓ant** *a.* surviving; *n.m.*, *f.* survivor.

survol /syrvɔl/ *n.m.* **le ⁓ de**, flying over. **⁓er** *v.t.* fly over; (*livre*) skim through.

survolté /syrvɔlte/ *a.* (*surexcité*) worked up.

susceptib|le /sysɛptibl/ *a.* touchy. **⁓le de faire**, (*possibilité*) liable to do; (*capacité*) able to do. **⁓ilité** *n.f.* susceptibility.

susciter /sysite/ *v.t.* (*éveiller*) arouse; (*occasionner*) create.

suspect, **⁓e** /syspɛ, -ɛkt/ *a.* (*témoignage*) suspect; (*individu*) suspicious. **⁓ de**, suspected of. —*n.m.*, *f.* suspect. **⁓er** /-ɛkte/ *v.t.* suspect.

suspend|re /syspɑ̃dr/ *v.t.* (*arrêter*, *différer*, *destituer*) suspend; (*accrocher*) hang (up). se ∼re à, hang from. ∼u à, hanging from.

suspens (en) /(ɑ̃)syspɑ̃/ adv. (affaire) in abeyance; (dans l'indécision) in suspense.

suspense /syspɑ̃s/ n.m. suspense.

suspension /syspɑ̃sjɔ̃/ n.f. suspension; (lustre) chandelier.

suspicion /syspisjɔ̃/ n.f. suspicion.

susurrer /sysyre/ v.t./i. murmur.

suture /sytyr/ n.f. **point de** ∼, stitch.

svelte /svɛlt/ a. slender.

S.V.P. abrév. voir **s'il vous plaît.**

sweat-shirt /switʃœrt/ n.m. sweat-shirt.

syllabe /silab/ n.f. syllable.

symbol|e /sɛ̃bɔl/ n.m. symbol. ∼**ique** a. symbolic(al). ∼**iser** v.t. symbolize.

symétr|ie /simetri/ n.f. symmetry. ∼**ique** a. symmetrical.

sympa /sɛ̃pa/ a. invar. (fam.) nice. **sois** ∼, be a pal.

sympath|ie /sɛ̃pati/ n.f. (goût) liking; (affinité) affinity; (condoléances) sympathy. ∼**ique** a. nice, pleasant.

sympathis|er /sɛ̃patize/ v.i. get on well (avec, with). ∼**ant**, ∼**ante** n.m., f. sympathizer.

symphon|ie /sɛ̃fɔni/ n.f. symphony. ∼**ique** a. symphonic; (orchestre) symphony.

symposium /sɛ̃pozjɔm/ n.m. symposium.

sympt|ôme /sɛ̃ptom/ n.m. symptom. ∼**omatique** /-ɔmatik/ a. symptomatic.

synagogue /sinagɔg/ n.f. synagogue.

synchroniser /sɛ̃krɔnize/ v.t. synchronize.

syncope /sɛ̃kɔp/ n.f. (méd.) black-out.

syncoper /sɛ̃kɔpe/ v.t. syncopate.

syndic /sɛ̃dik/ n.m. ∼ **(d'immeuble)**, managing agent.

syndic|at /sɛ̃dika/ n.m. (trade) union. ∼**at d'initiative,** tourist office. ∼**al** (m. pl. ∼**aux**) a. (trade-)union. ∼**aliste** n.m./f. trade-unionist; a. (trade-)union.

syndiqué, ∼**e** /sɛ̃dike/ n.m., f. (trade-) union member.

syndrome /sɛ̃drom/ n.m. syndrome.

synonyme /sinɔnim/ a. synonymous. —n.m. synonym.

syntaxe /sɛ̃taks/ n.f. syntax.

synthèse /sɛ̃tɛz/ n.f. synthesis.

synthétique /sɛ̃tetik/ a. synthetic.

synthé(tiseur) /sɛ̃te(tizœr)/ n.m. synthesizer.

syphilis /sifilis/ n.f. syphilis.

Syrie /siri/ n.f. Syria.

syrien, ∼**ne** /sirjɛ̃, -jɛn/ a. & n.m., f. Syrian.

systématique /sistematik/ a. systematic. ∼**ment** adv. systematically.

système /sistɛm/ n.m. system. **le** ∼ **D,** coping with problems.

T

t' /t/ voir **te.**

ta /ta/ voir **ton**[1].

tabac /taba/ n.m. tobacco; (magasin) tobacconist's shop. —a. invar. buff. ∼ **à priser,** snuff.

tabasser /tabase/ v.t. (fam.) beat up.

table /tabl/ n.f. table. **à** ∼**!,** come and eat! **faire** ∼ **rase,** make a clean sweep (de, of). ∼ **de nuit,** bedside table. ∼ **des matières,** table of contents. ∼ **roulante,** (tea-)trolley; (Amer.) (serving) cart.

tableau (pl. ∼**x**) /tablo/ n.m. picture; (peinture) painting; (panneau) board; (graphique) chart; (liste) list. ∼ **(noir),** blackboard. ∼ **d'affichage,** noticeboard. ∼ **de bord,** dashboard.

tabler /table/ v.i. ∼ **sur,** count on.

tablette /tablɛt/ n.f. shelf. ∼ **de chocolat,** bar of chocolate.

tablier /tablije/ n.m. apron; (de pont) platform; (de magasin) shutter.

tabloïd(e) /tablɔid/ a. & n.m. tabloïd.

tabou /tabu/ n.m. & a. taboo.

tabouret /taburɛ/ n.m. stool.

tabulateur /tabylatœr/ n.m. tabulator.

tac /tak/ n.m. **du** ∼ **au tac,** tit for tat.

tache /taʃ/ n.f. mark, spot; (salissure) stain. **faire** ∼ **d'huile,** spread. ∼ **de rousseur,** freckle.

tâche /taʃ/ n.f. task, job.

tacher /taʃe/ v.t. stain. **se** ∼ v. pr. (personne) get stains on one's clothes.

tâcher /taʃe/ v.i. ∼ **de faire,** try to do.

tacheté /taʃte/ a. spotted.

tacite /tasit/ a. tacit.

taciturne /tasityrn/ a. taciturn.

tact /takt/ n.m. tact.

tactile /taktil/ a. tactile.

tactique /taktik/ a. tactical. —n.f. tactics. **une** ∼, a tactic.

taie /tɛ/ n.f. ∼ **d'oreiller,** pillowcase.

taillader /tɑjade/ v.t. gash, slash.

taille[1] /tɑj/ n.f. (milieu du corps) waist; (hauteur) height; (grandeur) size. **de** ∼, sizeable. **être de** ∼ **à faire,** be up to doing.

taill|e[2] /tɑj/ n.f. cutting; pruning;

(*forme*) cut. **~er** *v.t.* cut; (*arbre*) prune; (*crayon*) sharpen; (*vêtement*) cut out. **se ~er** *v. pr.* (*argot*) clear off. **~e-crayon(s)** *n.m. invar.* pencil-sharpener.

tailleur /tajœr/ *n.m.* tailor; (*costume*) lady's suit. **en ~**, cross-legged.

taillis /taji/ *n.m.* copse.

taire† /tɛr/ *v.t.* say nothing about. **se ~** *v. pr.* be silent *ou* quiet; (*devenir silencieux*) fall silent. **faire ~**, silence.

talc /talk/ *n.m.* talcum powder.

talent /talɑ̃/ *n.m.* talent. **~ueux, ~ueuse** /-tɥø, -z/ *a.* talented.

taloche /talɔʃ/ *n.f.* (*fam.*) slap.

talon /talɔ̃/ *n.m.* heel; (*de chèque*) stub.

talonner /talɔne/ *v.t.* follow hard on the heels of.

talus /taly/ *n.m.* embankment.

tambour /tɑ̃bur/ *n.m.* drum; (*personne*) drummer; (*porte*) revolving door.

tambourin /tɑ̃burɛ̃/ *n.m.* tambourine.

tambouriner /tɑ̃burine/ *v.t./i.* drum (**sur**, on).

tamis /tami/ *n.m.* sieve. **~er** /-ze/ *v.t.* sieve.

Tamise /tamiz/ *n.f.* Thames.

tamisé /tamize/ *a.* (*lumière*) subdued.

tampon /tɑ̃pɔ̃/ *n.m.* (*pour boucher*) plug; (*ouate*) wad, pad; (*timbre*) stamp; (*de train*) buffer. **~ (hygiénique)**, tampon.

tamponner /tɑ̃pɔne/ *v.t.* crash into; (*timbrer*) stamp; (*plaie*) dab; (*mur*) plug. **se ~** *v. pr.* (*véhicules*) crash into each other.

tandem /tɑ̃dɛm/ *n.m.* (*bicyclette*) tandem; (*personnes*: *fig.*) duo.

tandis que /tɑ̃dik(ə)/ *conj.* while.

tangage /tɑ̃gaʒ/ *n.m.* pitching.

tangente /tɑ̃ʒɑ̃t/ *n.f.* tangent.

tangible /tɑ̃ʒibl/ *a.* tangible.

tango /tɑ̃go/ *n.m.* tango.

tanguer /tɑ̃ge/ *v.i.* pitch.

tanière /tanjɛr/ *n.f.* den.

tank /tɑ̃k/ *n.m.* tank.

tann|er /tane/ *v.t.* tan. **~é** *a.* (*visage*) tanned, weather-beaten.

tant /tɑ̃/ *adv.* (*travailler, manger, etc.*) so much. **~ (de)**, (*quantité*) so much; (*nombre*) so many. **~ que**, as long as; (*autant que*) as much as. **en ~ que**, (*comme*) as. **~ mieux!**, fine!, all the better! **~ pis!**, too bad!

tante /tɑ̃t/ *n.f.* aunt.

tantôt /tɑ̃to/ *adv.* sometimes; (*cet après-midi*) this afternoon.

tapag|e /tapaʒ/ *n.m.* din. **~eur, ~euse** *a.* rowdy; (*tape-à-l'œil*) flashy.

tapant, ~e /tapɑ̃, -t/ *a.* **à deux/trois/***etc.* **heures ~es** at exactly two/three/*etc.* o'clock.

tape /tap/ *n.f.* slap. **~-à-l'œil** *a. invar.* flashy, tawdry.

taper /tape/ *v.t.* bang; (*enfant*) slap; (*emprunter*: *fam.*) touch for money. **~ (à la machine)**, type. —*v.i.* (*cogner*) bang; (*soleil*) beat down. **~ dans**, (*puiser dans*) dig into. **~ sur**, thump; (*critiquer*: *fam.*) knock. **se ~** *v. pr.* (*repas*: *fam.*) put away; (*corvée*: *fam.*) do.

tap|ir (se) /(sə)tapir/ *v. pr.* crouch. **~i** *a.* crouching.

tapis /tapi/ *n.m.* carpet; (*petit*) rug; (*aux cartes*) baize. **~ de bain**, bath mat. **~-brosse** *n.m.* doormat. **~ de sol**, groundsheet. **~ roulant** (*pour objets*) conveyor belt.

tapiss|er /tapise/ *v.t.* (wall)paper; (*fig.*) cover (**de**, with). **~erie** *n.f.* tapestry; (*papier peint*) wallpaper. **~ier, ~ière** *n.m., f.* (*décorateur*) interior decorator; (*qui recouvre un siège*) upholsterer.

tapoter /tapɔte/ *v.t.* tap, pat.

taquin, ~e /takɛ̃, -in/ *a.* fond of teasing. —*n.m., f.* tease(r). **~er** /-ine/ *v.t.* tease. **~erie(s)** /-inri/ *n.f.* (*pl.*) teasing.

tarabiscoté /tarabiskɔte/ *a.* over-elaborate.

tard /tar/ *adv.* late. **au plus ~**, at the latest. **plus ~**, later. **sur le ~**, late in life.

tard|er /tarde/ *v.i.* (*être lent à venir*) be a long time coming. **~er (à faire)**, take a long time (doing), delay (doing). **sans (plus) ~er**, without (further) delay. **il me ~e de**, I long to.

tardi|f, ~ve /tardif, -v/ *a.* late; (*regrets*) belated.

tare /tar/ *n.f.* (*défaut*) defect.

taré /tare/ *a.* cretin.

targette /tarʒɛt/ *n.f.* bolt.

targuer (se) /(sə)targe/ *v. pr.* **se ~ de**, boast about.

tarif /tarif/ *n.m.* tariff; (*de train, taxi*) fare. **~s postaux**, postage *ou* postal rates. **~aire** *a.* tariff.

tarir /tarir/ *v.t./i.*, **se ~** *v. pr.* dry up.

tartare /tartar/ *a.* (*culin.*) tartar.

tarte /tart/ *n.f.* tart; (*Amer.*) (open) pie. —*a. invar.* (*sot*: *fam.*) stupid; (*laid*: *fam.*) ugly.

tartin|e /tartin/ *n.f.* slice of bread. **~e beurrée**, slice of bread and butter. **~er** *v.t.* spread.

tartre /tartr/ *n.m.* (*bouilloire*) fur, calcium deposit; (*dents*) tartar.

tas /tɑ/ *n.m.* pile, heap. **un** *ou* **des ~ de,** (*fam.*) lots of.

tasse /tɑs/ *n.f.* cup. **~ à thé,** teacup.

tasser /tɑse/ *v.t.* pack, squeeze; (*terre*) pack (down). **se ~** *v. pr.* (*terrain*) sink; (*se serrer*) squeeze up.

tâter /tate/ *v.t.* feel; (*fig.*) sound out. —*v.i.* **~ de,** try out.

tatillon, ~ne /tatijɔ̃, -jɔn/ *a.* finicky.

tâtonn|er /tɑtɔne/ *v.i.* grope about. **~ements** *n.m. pl.* (*essais*) trial and error.

tâtons (à) /(a)tɑtɔ̃/ *adv.* **avancer** *ou* **marcher à ~,** grope one's way along.

tatou|er /tatwe/ *v.t.* tattoo. **~age** *n.m.* (*dessin*) tattoo.

taudis /todi/ *n.m.* hovel.

taule /tol/ *n.f.* (*fam.*) prison.

taup|e /top/ *n.f.* mole. **~inière** *n.f.* molehill.

taureau (*pl.* **~x**) /tɔro/ *n.m.* bull. **le T~,** Taurus.

taux /to/ *n.m.* rate.

taverne /tavɛrn/ *n.f.* tavern.

tax|e /taks/ *n.f.* tax. **~e sur la valeur ajoutée,** value added tax. **~er** *v.t.* tax; (*produit*) fix the price of. **~er qn. de,** accuse s.o. of.

taxi /taksi/ *n.m.* taxi(-cab); (*personne*: *fam.*) taxi-driver.

taxiphone /taksifɔn/ *n.m.* pay phone.

Tchécoslovaquie /tʃekɔslɔvaki/ *n.f.* Czechoslovakia.

tchèque /tʃɛk/ *a. & n.m./f.* Czech.

te, t'* /tə, t/ *pron.* you; (*indirect*) (to) you; (*réfléchi*) yourself.

technicien, ~ne /tɛknisjɛ̃, -jɛn/ *n.m., f.* technician.

technique /tɛknik/ *a.* technical. —*n.f.* technique. **~ment** *adv.* technically.

technolog|ie /tɛknɔlɔʒi/ *n.f.* technology. **~ique** *a.* technological.

teck /tɛk/ *n.m.* teak.

tee-shirt /tiʃœrt/ *n.m.* tee-shirt.

teindre† /tɛ̃dr/ *v.t.* dye. **se ~ les cheveux** *v. pr.* dye one's hair.

teint /tɛ̃/ *n.m.* complexion.

teint|e /tɛ̃t/ *n.f.* shade, tint. **une ~e de,** (*fig.*) a tinge of. **~er** *v.t.* (*papier, verre, etc.*) tint; (*bois*) stain.

teintur|e /tɛ̃tyr/ *n.f.* dyeing; (*produit*) dye. **~erie** *n.f.* (*boutique*) drycleaner's. **~ier, ~ière** *n.m., f.* drycleaner.

tel, ~le /tɛl/ *a.* such. **un ~ livre**/*etc.*, such a book/*etc.* **un ~ chagrin**/*etc.*,

such sorrow/*etc.* **~ que,** such as, like; (*ainsi que*) (just) as. **~ ou tel,** suchand-such. **~ quel,** (just) as it is.

télé /tele/ *n.f.* (*fam.*) TV.

télécommande /telekɔmɑ̃d/ *n.f.* remote control.

télécommunications /telekɔmynikasjɔ̃/ *n.f. pl.* telecommunications.

télécopi|e /telekɔpi/ *n.f.* tele(fax). **~eur** *n.m.* fax machine.

téléfilm /telefilm/ *n.m.* (tele)film.

télégramme /telegram/ *n.m.* telegram.

télégraph|e /telegraf/ *n.m.* telegraph. **~ier** *v.t./i.* **~ier (à),** cable. **~ique** *a.* telegraphic; (*fil, poteau*) telegraph.

téléguid|er /telegide/ *v.t.* control by radio. **~é** *a.* radio-controlled.

télématique /telematik/ *n.f.* computer communications.

télépathe /telepat/ *a. & n.m., f.* psychic.

télépathie /telepati/ *n.f.* telepathy.

téléphérique /teleferik/ *n.m.* cablecar.

téléphon|e /telefɔn/ *n.m.* (tele)phone. **~e rouge,** (*pol.*) hot line. **~er** *v.t./i.* **~er (à),** (tele)phone. **~ique** *a.* (tele)phone. **~iste** *n.m./f.* operator.

télescop|e /telɛskɔp/ *n.m.* telescope. **~ique** *a.* telescopic.

télescoper /telɛskɔpe/ *v.t.* smash into. **se ~** *v. pr.* (*véhicules*) smash into each other.

télésiège /telesjɛʒ/ *n.m.* chair-lift.

téléski /teleski/ *n.m.* ski tow.

téléspecta|teur, ~trice /telespɛktatœr, -tris/ *n.m., f.* (television) viewer.

télévente /televɑ̃t/ *n.f.* telesales.

télévis|é /televize/ *a.* **émission ~ée,** television programme. **~eur** *n.m.* television set.

télévision /televizjɔ̃/ *n.f.* television.

télex /telɛks/ *n.m.* telex.

télexer /telɛkse/ *v.t.* telex.

telle /tɛl/ *voir* **tel.**

tellement /tɛlmɑ̃/ *adv.* (*tant*) so much; (*si*) so. **~ de,** (*quantité*) so much; (*nombre*) so many.

témér|aire /temerɛr/ *a.* rash. **~ité** *n.f.* rashness.

témoignage /temwaɲaʒ/ *n.m.* testimony, evidence; (*récit*) account. **~ de,** (*sentiment*) token of.

témoigner /temwaɲe/ *v.i.* testify (**de,** to). —*v.t.* show. **~ que,** testify that.

témoin /temwɛ̃/ *n.m.* witness; (*sport*) baton. **être ~ de,** witness. **~ oculaire,** eyewitness.

tempe /tɑ̃p/ *n.f.* (*anat.*) temple.

tempérament /tɑ̃peramɑ̃/ *n.m.* tem-

perament; (*physique*) constitution. **à ~,**
(*acheter*) on hire-purchase; (*Amer.*) on
the instalment plan.
température /tɑ̃peratyr/ *n.f.* temperature.
tempér|er /tɑ̃pere/ *v.t.* temper. **~é** *a.*
(*climat*) temperate.
tempête /tɑ̃pɛt/ *n.f.* storm. **~ de neige,**
snowstorm.
tempêter /tɑ̃pete/ *v.i.* (*crier*) rage.
temple /tɑ̃pl/ *n.m.* temple; (*protestant*)
church.
temporaire /tɑ̃pɔrɛr/ *a.* temporary.
~ment *adv.* temporarily.
temporel, ~le /tɑ̃pɔrɛl/ *a.* temporal.
temporiser /tɑ̃pɔrize/ *v.i.* play for
time.
temps[1] /tɑ̃/ *n.m.* time; (*gram.*) tense;
(*étape*) stage. **à ~ partiel/plein,** part-/
full-time. **ces derniers ~,** lately. **dans
le ~,** at one time. **dans quelque ~,** in a
while. **de ~ en temps,** from time to
time. **~ d'arrêt,** pause. **avoir tout son
~,** have plenty of time.
temps[2] /tɑ̃/ *n.m.* (*atmosphère*) weather.
~ de chien, filthy weather. **quel ~ fait-
il?,** what's the weather like?
tenace /tənas/ *a.* stubborn.
ténacité /tenasite/ *n.f.* stubbornness.
tenaille(s) /tənaj/ *n.f.* (*pl.*) pincers.
tenanc|ier, ~ière /tənɑ̃sje, -jɛr/ *n.m.,
f.* keeper (**de,** of).
tenant /tənɑ̃/ *n.m.* (*partisan*) supporter;
(*d'un titre*) holder.
tendance /tɑ̃dɑ̃s/ *n.f.* tendency;
(*opinions*) leanings; (*évolution*) trend.
avoir ~ à, have a tendency to, tend to.
tendon /tɑ̃dɔ̃/ *n.m.* tendon.
tendre[1] /tɑ̃dr/ *v.t.* stretch; (*piège*) set;
(*bras*) stretch out; (*main*) hold out;
(*cou*) crane; (*tapisserie*) hang. **~ à qn.,**
hold out to s.o. —*v.i.* **~ à,** tend to. **~
l'oreille,** prick up one's ears.
tendre[2] /tɑ̃dr/ *a.* tender; (*couleur, bois*)
soft. **~ment** /-əmɑ̃/ *adv.* tenderly.
~sse /-ɛs/ *n.f.* tenderness.
tendu /tɑ̃dy/ *a.* (*corde*) tight; (*personne,
situation*) tense; (*main*) outstretched.
tén|èbres /tenɛbr/ *n.f. pl.* darkness.
~ébreux, ~ébreuse *a.* dark.
teneur /tənœr/ *n.f.* content.
tenir† /tənir/ *v.t.* hold; (*pari, promesse,
hôtel*) keep; (*place*) take up; (*propos*)
utter; (*rôle*) play. **~ de,** (*avoir reçu de*)
have got from. **~ pour,** regard as. **~
propre/chaud/***etc.*, keep clean/warm/
etc. —*v.i.* hold. **~ à,** be attached to. **~ à
faire,** be anxious to do. **~ dans,** fit into.
~ de qn., take after s.o. **se ~** *v. pr.*

(*rester*) remain; (*debout*) stand; (*avoir
lieu*) be held. **se ~ à,** hold on to. **se ~
bien,** behave o.s. **s'en ~ à,** (*se limiter
à*) confine o.s. to. **~ bon,** stand firm. **~
compte de,** take into account. **~ le
coup,** hold out. **~ tête à,** stand up to.
tiens!, (*surprise*) hey!

tennis /tenis/ *n.m.* tennis; (*terrain*)
tennis-court. —*n.m. pl.* (*chaussures*)
sneakers. **~ de table,** table tennis.
ténor /tenɔr/ *n.m.* tenor.
tension /tɑ̃sjɔ̃/ *n.f.* tension. **avoir de la
~,** have high blood-pressure.
tentacule /tɑ̃takyl/ *n.m.* tentacle.
tentative /tɑ̃tativ/ *n.f.* attempt.
tente /tɑ̃t/ *n.f.* tent.
tenter[1] /tɑ̃te/ *v.t.* try (**de faire,** to do).
tent|er[2] /tɑ̃te/ *v.t.* (*allécher*) tempt. **~é
de,** tempted to. **~ation** *n.f.* temptation.
tenture /tɑ̃tyr/ *n.f.* (*wall*) hanging. **~s,**
drapery.
tenu /təny/ *voir* **tenir.** —*a.* **bien ~,**
well-kept. **~ de,** obliged to.
ténu /teny/ *a.* (*fil etc.*) fine; (*cause,
nuance*) tenuous.
tenue /təny/ *n.f.* (*habillement*) dress; (*de
sport*) clothes; (*de maison*) upkeep;
(*conduite*) (good) behaviour; (*maintien*)
posture. **~ de soirée,** evening dress.
ter /tɛr/ *a. invar.* (*numéro*) B, b.
térébenthine /terebɑ̃tin/ *n.f.* turpentine.
tergiverser /tɛrʒivɛrse/ *v.i.* procrastinate.
terme /tɛrm/ *n.m.* (*mot*) term; (*date
limite*) time-limit; (*fin*) end; (*date de
loyer*) term. **à long/court ~,** long-/
short-term. **en bons ~s,** on good terms
(**avec,** with).
termin|al, ~ale (*m. pl.* **~aux**)
/tɛrminal, -o/ *a.* terminal. (**classe**)
~ale, sixth form; (*Amer.*) twelfth
grade. —*n.m.* (*pl.* **~aux**) terminal.
termin|er /tɛrmine/ *v.t./i.* finish; (*soirée,
débat*) end, finish. **se ~er** *v. pr.* end
(**par,** with). **~aison** *n.f.* (*gram.*)
ending.
terminologie /tɛrminɔlɔʒi/ *n.f.* terminology.
terminus /tɛrminys/ *n.m.* terminus.
terne /tɛrn/ *a.* dull, drab.
ternir /tɛrnir/ *v.t./i.*, **se ~** *v. pr.* tarnish.
terrain /terɛ̃/ *n.m.* ground; (*parcelle*)
piece of land; (*à bâtir*) plot. **~
d'aviation,** airfield. **~ de camping,**
campsite. **~ de golf,** golf-course. **~ de
jeu,** playground. **~ vague,** waste
ground; (*Amer.*) vacant lot.
terrasse /teras/ *n.f.* terrace; (*de café*)
pavement area.

terrassement /tɛrasmã/ *n.m.* excavation.

terrasser /tɛrase/ *v.t.* (*adversaire*) floor; (*maladie*) strike down.

terrassier /tɛrasje/ *n.m.* navvy, labourer, ditch-digger.

terre /tɛr/ *n.f.* (*planète*, *matière*) earth; (*étendue*, *pays*) land; (*sol*) ground; (*domaine*) estate. **à ~,** (*naut.*) ashore. **par ~,** (*tomber*, *jeter*) to the ground; (*s'asseoir*, *poser*) on the ground. **~ (cuite),** terracotta. **~-à-terre** *a. invar.* matter-of-fact, down-to-earth. **~-plein** *n.m.* platform, (*auto.*) central reservation. **la ~ ferme,** dry land. **~ glaise,** clay.

terreau /tɛro/ *n.m. invar.* compost.

terrer (se) /(sə)tɛre/ *v. pr.* hide o.s., dig o.s. in.

terrestre /tɛrɛstr/ *a.* land; (*de notre planète*) earth's; (*fig.*) earthly.

terreur /tɛrœr/ *n.f.* terror.

terreu|x, **~se** /tɛrø, -z/ *a.* earthy; (*sale*) grubby.

terrible /tɛribl/ *a.* terrible; (*formidable*: *fam.*) terrific.

terrien, **~ne** /tɛrjɛ̃, -jɛn/ *n.m.*, *f.* earth-dweller.

terrier /tɛrje/ *n.m.* (*trou de lapin etc.*) burrow; (*chien*) terrier.

terrifier /tɛrifje/ *v.t.* terrify.

terrine /tɛrin/ *n.f.* (*culin.*) terrine.

territ|oire /tɛritwar/ *n.m.* territory. **~orial** (*m. pl.* **~oriaux**) *a.* territorial.

terroir /tɛrwar/ *n.m.* (*sol*) soil; (*région*) region. **du ~,** country.

terroriser /tɛrɔrize/ *v.t.* terrorize.

terroris|te /tɛrɔrist/ *n.m./f.* terrorist. **~me** *n.m.* terrorism.

tertre /tɛrtr/ *n.m.* mound.

tes /te/ *voir* **ton¹**.

tesson /tesɔ̃/ *n.m.* **~ de bouteille,** piece of broken bottle.

test /tɛst/ *n.m.* test. **~er** *v.t.* test.

testament /tɛstamã/ *n.m.* (*jurid.*) will; (*politique*, *artistique*) testament. **Ancien/Nouveau T~,** Old/New Testament.

testicule /tɛstikyl/ *n.m.* testicle.

tétanos /tetanos/ *n.m.* tetanus.

têtard /tɛtar/ *n.m.* tadpole.

tête /tɛt/ *n.f.* head; (*figure*) face; (*cheveux*) hair; (*cerveau*) brain. **à la ~ de,** at the head of. **à ~ reposée,** in a leisurely moment. **de ~,** (*calculer*) in one's head. **en ~,** (*sport*) in the lead. **faire la ~,** sulk. **faire une ~,** (*football*) head the ball. **tenir ~ à qn.,** stand up to s.o. **une forte ~,** a rebel. **la ~ la première,** head first. **il n'en fait qu'à sa ~,** he does just as he pleases. **de la ~ aux pieds,** from head to toe. **~-à-queue** *n.m. invar.* (*auto.*) spin. **~-à-tête** *n.m. invar.* tête-à-tête. **en ~-à-tête,** in private.

tétée /tete/ *n.f.* feed.

téter /tete/ *v.t./i.* suck.

tétine /tetin/ *n.f.* (*de biberon*) teat; (*sucette*) dummy; (*Amer.*) pacifier.

têtu /tety/ *a.* stubborn.

texte /tɛkst/ *n.m.* text; (*de leçon*) subject; (*morceau choisi*) passage.

textile /tɛkstil/ *n.m.* & *a.* textile.

textuel, **~le** /tɛkstɥɛl/ *a.* literal.

texture /tɛkstyr/ *n.f.* texture.

thaïlandais, **~e** /tailãdɛ, -z/ *a. & n.m.*, *f.* Thai.

Thaïlande /tailãd/ *n.f.* Thailand.

thé /te/ *n.m.* tea.

théâtr|al (*m. pl.* **~aux**) /teatral, -o/ *a.* theatrical.

théâtre /teatr/ *n.m.* theatre; (*jeu forcé*) play-acting; (*d'un crime*) scene. **faire du ~,** act.

théière /tejɛr/ *n.f.* teapot.

thème /tɛm/ *n.m.* theme; (*traduction*: *scol.*) prose.

théolog|ie /teɔlɔʒi/ *n.f.* theology. **~ien** *n.m.* theologian. **~ique** *a.* theological.

théorème /teɔrɛm/ *n.m.* theorem.

théor|ie /teɔri/ *n.f.* theory. **~icien,** **~icienne** *n.m.*, *f.* theorist. **~ique** *a.* theoretical. **~iquement,** *adv.* theoretically.

thérap|ie /terapi/ *n.f.* therapy. **~eutique** *a.* therapeutic.

thermique /tɛrmik/ *a.* thermal.

thermomètre /tɛrmɔmɛtr/ *n.m.* thermometer.

thermonucléaire /tɛrmɔnykleɛr/ *a.* thermonuclear.

thermos /tɛrmos/ *n.m./f.* (P.) Thermos (P.) (flask).

thermostat /tɛrmɔsta/ *n.m.* thermostat.

thésauriser /tezɔrize/ *v.t./i.* hoard.

thèse /tɛz/ *n.f.* thesis.

thon /tɔ̃/ *n.m.* (*poisson*) tuna.

thrombose /trɔ̃boz/ *n.f.* thrombosis.

thym /tɛ̃/ *n.m.* thyme.

thyroïde /tirɔid/ *n.f.* thyroid.

tibia /tibja/ *n.m.* shin-bone.

tic /tik/ *n.m.* (*contraction*) twitch; (*manie*) mannerism.

ticket /tikɛ/ *n.m.* ticket.

tic-tac /tiktak/ *n.m. invar.* (*de pendule*) ticking. **faire ~,** go tick tock.

tiède /tjɛd/ *a.* lukewarm; (*atmosphère*)

mild. **tiédeur** /tjedœr/ n.f. lukewarm-ness; mildness.

tiédir /tjedir/ v.t./i. **(faire)** ~, warm slightly.

tien, ~ne /tjɛ̃, tjɛn/ pron. le ~, la ~ne, les ~(ne)s, yours. à la ~ ne!, cheers!

tiens, tient /tjɛ̃/ voir tenir.

tiercé /tjɛrse/ n.m. place-betting.

tier|s, ~ce /tjɛr, -s/ a. third. —n.m. (fraction) third; (personne) third party. **T~s-Monde** n.m. Third World.

tifs /tif/ n.m. pl. (fam.) hair.

tige /tiʒ/ n.f. (bot.) stem, stalk; (en métal) shaft.

tignasse /tiɲas/ n.f. mop of hair.

tigre /tigr/ n.m. tiger. ~sse /-ɛs/ n.f. tigress.

tigré /tigre/ a. (rayé) striped; (chat) tabby.

tilleul /tijœl/ n.m. lime(-tree), linden (-tree); (infusion) lime tea.

timbale /tɛ̃bal/ n.f. (gobelet) (metal) tumbler.

timbr|e /tɛ̃br/ n.m. stamp; (sonnette) bell; (de voix) tone. ~e- poste (pl. ~es-poste) n.m. postage stamp. ~er v.t. stamp.

timbré /tɛ̃bre/ a. (fam.) crazy.

timid|e /timid/ a. timid. ~ité n.f. timidity.

timoré /timɔre/ a. timorous.

tintamarre /tɛ̃tamar/ n.m. din.

tint|er /tɛ̃te/ v.i. ring; (clefs) jingle. ~ement n.m. ringing; jingling.

tique /tik/ n.f. (insecte) tick.

tir /tir/ n.m. (sport) shooting; (action de tirer) firing; (feu, rafale) fire. ~ à l'arc, archery. ~ forain, shooting-gallery.

tirade /tirad/ n.f. soliloquy.

tirage /tiraʒ/ n.m. (de photo) printing; (de journal) circulation; (de livre) edition; (de loterie) draw; (de cheminée) draught. ~ au sort, drawing lots.

tirail|er /tiraje/ v.t. pull (away) at; (harceler) plague. ~é entre, (possibilités etc.) torn between. ~ement n.m. (douleur) gnawing pain; (conflit) conflict.

tiré /tire/ a. (traits) drawn.

tire-bouchon /tirbuʃɔ̃/ n.m. cork-screw.

tire-lait /tirlɛ/ n.m. breastpump.

tirelire /tirlir/ n.f. money-box; (Amer.) coin-bank.

tirer /tire/ v.t. pull; (navire) tow, tug; (langue) stick out; (conclusion, trait, rideaux) draw; (coup de feu) fire; (gibier) shoot, (photo) print. ~ de, (sortir) take ou get out of; (extraire)

extract from; (plaisir, nom) derive from. —v.i. shoot, fire (sur, at). ~ sur, (couleur) verge on; (corde) pull at. se ~ v. pr. (fam.) clear off. se ~ de, get out of. s'en ~, (en réchapper) pull through; (réussir: fam.) cope. ~ à sa fin, be drawing to a close. ~ au clair, clarify. ~ au sort, draw lots (for). ~ parti de, take advantage of. ~ profit de, profit from.

tiret /tirɛ/ n.m. dash.

tireur /tirœr/ n.m. gunman. ~ d'élite, marksman. ~ isolé, sniper.

tiroir /tirwar/ n.m. drawer. ~-caisse (pl. ~s-caisses) n.m. till.

tisane /tizan/ n.f. herb-tea.

tison /tizɔ̃/ n.m. ember.

tisonnier /tizɔnje/ n.m. poker.

tiss|er /tise/ v.t. weave. ~age n.m. weaving. ~erand /tisrɑ̃/ n.m. weaver.

tissu /tisy/ n.m. fabric, material; (biologique) tissue. un ~ de, (fig.) a web of. ~-éponge (pl. ~s-éponge) n.m. towelling.

titre /titr/ n.m. title; (diplôme) qualification; (comm.) bond. ~s, (droits) claims. (gros) ~s, headlines. à ce ~, (pour cette qualité) as such. à ~ d'exemple, as an example. à juste ~, rightly. à ~ privé, in a private capacity. ~ de propriété, title-deed.

titré /titre/ a. titled.

titrer /titre/ v.t. (journal) give as a headline.

tituber /titybe/ v.i. stagger.

titul|aire /titylɛr/ a. être ~aire, have tenure. être ~aire de, hold. —n.m./f. (de permis etc.) holder. ~ariser v.t. give tenure to.

toast /tost/ n.m. piece of toast; (allocution) toast.

toboggan /tɔbɔgɑ̃/ n.m. (traîneau) toboggan; (glissière) slide; (auto.) flyover; (auto., Amer.) overpass.

toc /tɔk/ int. ~ toc! knock knock!

tocsin /tɔksɛ̃/ n.m. alarm (bell).

toge /tɔʒ/ n.f. (de juge etc.) gown.

tohu-bohu /tɔybɔy/ n.m. hubbub.

toi /twa/ pron. you; (réfléchi) yourself. lève-~, stand up.

toile /twal/ n.f. cloth; (sac, tableau) canvas; (coton) cotton. ~ d'araignée, (spider's) web; (délabrée) cobweb. ~ de fond, backdrop, backcloth.

toilette /twalɛt/ n.f. washing; (habille-ment) clothes, dress. ~s, (cabinets) toilet(s). de ~, (articles, savon, etc.) toilet. faire sa ~, wash (and get ready).

toi-même /twamɛm/ pron. yourself.

toiser /twaze/ v.t. ~ **qn.**, look s.o. up and down.

toison /twazɔ̃/ n.f. (*laine*) fleece.

toit /twa/ n.m. roof. ~ **ouvrant**, (*auto.*) sun-roof.

toiture /twatyr/ n.f. roof.

tôle /tol/ n.f. (*plaque*) iron sheet. ~ **ondulée**, corrugated iron.

tolérable /tɔlerabl/ a. tolerable.

toléran|t, ~**te** /tɔlerɑ̃, -t/ a. tolerant. ~**ce** n.f. tolerance; (*importations: comm.*) allowance.

tolérer /tɔlere/ v.t. tolerate; (*importations: comm.*) allow.

tollé /tɔle/ n.m. hue and cry.

tomate /tɔmat/ n.f. tomato.

tombe /tɔ̃b/ n.f. grave; (*avec monument*) tomb.

tombeau (*pl.* ~**x**) /tɔ̃bo/ n.m. tomb.

tombée /tɔ̃be/ n.f. ~ **de la nuit**, nightfall.

tomber /tɔ̃be/ v.i. (*aux. être*) fall; (*fièvre, vent*) drop; (*enthousiasme*) die down. **faire** ~, knock over; (*gouvernement*) bring down. **laisser** ~, drop; (*abandonner*) let down. **laisse** ~!, forget it! ~ **à l'eau**, (*projet*) fall through. ~ **bien** *ou* **à point**, come at the right time. ~ **en panne**, break down. ~ **en syncope**, faint. ~ **sur**, (*trouver*) run across.

tombola /tɔ̃bɔla/ n.f. tombola; (*Amer.*) lottery.

tome /tom/ n.m. volume.

ton[1], **ta** *ou* **ton*** (*pl.* **tes**) /tɔ̃, ta, tɔ̃, te/ a. your.

ton[2] /tɔ̃/ n.m. tone; (*gamme: mus.*) key; (*hauteur de la voix*) pitch. **de bon** ~, in good taste.

tonalité /tɔnalite/ n.f. tone; (*téléphone*) dialling tone; (*téléphone: Amer.*) dial tone.

tond|re /tɔ̃dr/ v.t. (*herbe*) mow; (*mouton*) shear; (*cheveux*) clip. ~**euse** n.f. shears; clippers. ~**euse (à gazon)**, (lawn-)mower.

tongs /tɔ̃g/ n.f. pl. flip-flops.

tonifier /tɔnifje/ v.t. tone up.

tonique /tɔnik/ a. & n.m. tonic.

tonne /tɔn/ n.f. ton(ne).

tonneau (*pl.* ~**x**) /tɔno/ n.m. (*récipient*) barrel; (*naut.*) ton; (*culbute*) somersault.

tonnelle /tɔnɛl/ n.f. bower.

tonner /tɔne/ v.i. thunder.

tonnerre /tɔnɛr/ n.m. thunder.

tonte /tɔ̃t/ n.f. (*de gazon*) mowing; (*de moutons*) shearing.

tonton /tɔ̃tɔ̃/ n.m. (*fam.*) uncle.

tonus /tɔnys/ n.m. energy.

top /tɔp/ n.m. (*signal pour marquer un instant précis*) stroke.

topo /tɔpo/ n.m. (*fam.*) talk, oral report.

toquade /tɔkad/ n.f. craze; (*pour une personne*) infatuation.

toque /tɔk/ n.f. (fur) hat; (*de jockey*) cap; (*de cuisinier*) hat.

toqué /tɔke/ a. (*fam.*) crazy.

torche /tɔrʃ/ n.f. torch.

torcher /tɔrʃe/ v.t. (*fam.*) wipe.

torchon /tɔrʃɔ̃/ n.m. cloth, duster; (*pour la vaisselle*) tea-towel; (*Amer.*) dish-towel.

tordre /tɔrdr/ v.t. twist; (*linge*) wring. **se** ~ v. pr. twist, bend; (*de douleur*) writhe. **se** ~ (**de rire**), split one's sides.

tordu /tɔrdy/ a. twisted, bent; (*esprit*) warped.

tornade /tɔrnad/ n.f. tornado.

torpeur /tɔrpœr/ n.f. lethargy.

torpill|e /tɔrpij/ n.f. torpedo. ~**er** v.t. torpedo.

torréfier /tɔrefje/ v.t. roast.

torrent /tɔrɑ̃/ n.m. torrent. ~**iel**, ~**ielle** /-sjɛl/ a. torrential.

torride /tɔrid/ a. torrid.

torsade /tɔrsad/ n.f. twist.

torse /tɔrs/ n.m. chest; (*sculpture*) torso.

tort /tɔr/ n.m. wrong. **à** ~, wrongly. **à** ~ **et à travers**, without thinking. **avoir** ~, be wrong (**de faire**, to do). **donner** ~ **à**, prove wrong. **être dans son** ~, be in the wrong. **faire** (**du**) ~ **à**, harm.

torticolis /tɔrtikɔli/ n.m. stiff neck.

tortiller /tɔrtije/ v.t. twist, twirl. **se** ~ v. pr. wriggle, wiggle.

tortionnaire /tɔrsjɔnɛr/ n.m. torturer.

tortue /tɔrty/ n.f. tortoise; (*de mer*) turtle.

tortueu|x, ~**se** /tɔrtɥø, -z/ a. (*explication*) tortuous; (*chemin*) twisting.

tortur|e(s) /tɔrtyr/ n.f. (*pl.*) torture. ~**er** v.t. torture.

tôt /to/ adv. early. **plus** ~, earlier. **au plus** ~, at the earliest. **le plus** ~ **possible**, as soon as possible. ~ **ou tard**, sooner or later.

tot|al (*m. pl.* ~**aux**) /tɔtal, -o/ a. total. —n.m. (*pl.* ~**aux**) total. —adv. (*fam.*) to conclude, in short. **au** ~**al**, all in all. ~**alement** adv. totally. ~**aliser** v.t. total.

totalitaire /tɔtalitɛr/ a. totalitarian.

totalité /tɔtalite/ n.f. entirety. **la** ~ **de**, all of.

toubib /tubib/ n.m. (*fam.*) doctor.

touchant, ~**e** /tuʃɑ̃, -t/ a. (*émouvant*) touching.

touche /tuʃ/ n.f. (*de piano*) key; (*de*

peintre) touch. **(ligne de)** ~, touch-line. **une** ~ **de**, a touch of.

toucher[1] /tuʃe/ *v.t.* touch; (*émouvoir*) move, touch; (*contacter*) get in touch with; (*cible*) hit; (*argent*) draw; (*chèque*) cash; (*concerner*) affect. —*v.i.* ~ **à**, touch; (*question*) touch on; (*fin, but*) approach. **je vais lui en** ~ **un mot**, I'll talk to him about it. **se** ~ *v. pr.* (*lignes*) touch.

toucher[2] /tuʃe/ *n.m.* (*sens*) touch.

touffe /tuf/ *n.f.* (*de poils, d'herbe*) tuft; (*de plantes*) clump.

touffu /tufy/ *a.* thick, bushy; (*fig.*) complex.

toujours /tuʒur/ *adv.* always; (*encore*) still; (*en tout cas*) anyhow. **pour** ~, for ever.

toupet /tupɛ/ *n.m.* (*culot: fam.*) cheek, nerve.

toupie /tupi/ *n.f.* (*jouet*) top.

tour[1] /tur/ *n.f.* tower; (*immeuble*) tower block; (*échecs*) rook.

tour[2] /tur/ *n.m.* (*mouvement, succession, tournure*) turn; (*excursion*) trip; (*à pied*) walk; (*en auto*) drive; (*artifice*) trick; (*circonférence*) circumference; (*techn.*) lathe. ~ **(de piste)**, lap. **à** ~ **de rôle**, in turn. **à mon**/*etc.* ~, when it is my/*etc.* turn. **c'est mon**/*etc.* ~ **de**, it is my/*etc.* turn to. **faire le** ~ **de**, go round; (*question*) survey. ~ **de contrôle**, control tower. ~ **d'horizon**, survey. ~ **de passe-passe**, sleight of hand. ~ **de taille**, waist measurement; (*ligne*) waistline.

tourbe /turb/ *n.f.* peat.

tourbillon /turbijɔ̃/ *n.m.* whirlwind; (*d'eau*) whirlpool; (*fig.*) whirl, swirl. ~**ner** /-jone/ *v.i.* whirl, swirl.

tourelle /turɛl/ *n.f.* turret.

tourisme /turism/ *n.m.* tourism. **faire du** ~, do some sightseeing.

tourist|e /turist/ *n.m./f.* tourist. ~**ique** *a.* tourist; (*route*) scenic.

tourment /turmɑ̃/ *n.m.* torment. ~**er** /-te/ *v.t.* torment. **se** ~**er** *v. pr.* worry.

tournage /turnaʒ/ *n.m.* (*cinéma*) shooting.

tournant[1], ~**e** /turnɑ̃, -t/ *a.* (*qui pivote*) revolving.

tournant[2] /turnɑ̃/ *n.m.* bend; (*fig.*) turning-point.

tourne-disque /turnədisk/ *n.m.* record-player.

tournée /turne/ *n.f.* (*voyage, consommations*) round; (*théâtre*) tour. **faire la** ~, make the rounds (**de**, of). **je paye** *ou* **j'offre la** ~, I'll buy this round.

tourner /turne/ *v.t.* turn; (*film*) shoot, make. —*v.i.* turn; (*toupie, tête*) spin; (*moteur, usine*) run. **se** ~ *v. pr.* turn. ~ **au froid**, turn cold. ~ **autour de**, go round; (*personne, maison*) hang around; (*terre*) revolve round; (*question*) centre on. ~ **de l'œil**, (*fam.*) faint. ~ **en dérision**, mock. ~ **en ridicule**, ridicule. ~ **le dos à**, turn one's back on. ~ **mal**, turn out badly.

tournesol /turnəsɔl/ *n.m.* sunflower.

tournevis /turnəvis/ *n.m.* screwdriver.

tourniquet /turnikɛ/ *n.m.* (*barrière*) turnstile.

tournoi /turnwa/ *n.m.* tournament.

tournoyer /turnwaje/ *v.i.* whirl.

tournure /turnyr/ *n.f.* turn; (*locution*) turn of phrase.

tourte /turt/ *n.f.* pie.

tourterelle /turtərɛl/ *n.f.* turtle-dove.

Toussaint /tusɛ̃/ *n.f.* **la** ~, All Saints' Day.

tousser /tuse/ *v.i.* cough.

tout[1], ~**e** (*pl.* **tous, toutes** /tu, tut/ *a.* all; (*n'importe quel*) any; (*tout à fait*) entirely. ~ **le pays**/*etc.*, the whole country/*etc.*, all the country/*etc.* ~**e la nuit/journée**, the whole night/day. ~ **un paquet**, a whole pack. **tous les jours/mois**/*etc.*, every day/month/*etc.* —*pron.* everything, all. **tous** /tus/, **toutes**, all. **prendre** ~, take everything, take it all. ~ **ce que**, all that. ~ **le monde**, everyone. **tous les deux, toutes les deux**, both of them. **tous les trois**, all three (of them). —*adv.* (*très*) very; (*tout à fait*) quite. ~ **au bout/début**/*etc.*, right at the end/beginning/*etc.* **le** ~ **premier**, the very first. **en chantant/marchant**/*etc.*, while singing/walking/*etc.* ~ **à coup**, all of a sudden. ~ **à fait**, quite, completely. ~ **à l'heure**, in a moment; (*passé*) a moment ago. ~ **au** *ou* **le long de**, throughout. ~ **au plus/moins**, at most/least. ~ **de même**, all the same. ~ **de suite**, straight away. ~ **entier**, whole. ~ **le contraire**, quite the opposite. ~ **neuf**, brand-new. ~ **nu**, stark naked. ~ **près**, nearby. ~**puissant**, ~**e-puissante** *a.* omnipotent. ~ **seul**, alone. ~ **terrain** *a. invar.* all terrain.

tout[2] /tu/ *n.m.* (*ensemble*) whole. **en** ~, in all. **pas du** ~!, not at all!

tout-à-l'égout /tutalegu/ *n.m.* main drainage.

toutefois /tutfwa/ *adv.* however.

toux /tu/ *n.f.* cough.
toxicomane /tɔksikɔman/ *n.m./f.* drug addict.
toxine /tɔksin/ *n.f.* toxin.
toxique /tɔksik/ *a.* toxic.
trac /trak/ *n.m.* le ~, nerves; (*théâtre*) stage fright.
tracas /traka/ *n.m.* worry. ~ser /-se/ *v.t.*, se ~ser *v. pr.* worry.
trace /tras/ *n.f.* trace, mark; (*d'animal, de pneu*) tracks; (*vestige*) trace. sur la ~ de, on the track of. ~s de pas, footprints.
tracé /trase/ *n.m.* (*ligne*) line; (*plan*) layout.
tracer /trase/ *v.t.* draw, trace; (*écrire*) write; (*route*) mark out.
trachée(-artère) /traʃe(artɛr)/ *n.f.* windpipe.
tract /trakt/ *n.m.* leaflet.
tractations /traktɑsjɔ̃/ *n.f. pl.* dealings.
tracteur /traktœr/ *n.m.* tractor.
traction /traksjɔ̃/ *n.f.* (*sport*) press-up, push-up.
tradition /tradisjɔ̃/ *n.f.* tradition. ~nel, ~nelle /-jɔnɛl/ *a.* traditional.
trad|uire† /traduir/ *v.t.* translate; (*sentiment*) express. ~uire en justice, take to court. ~ucteur, ~uctrice *n.m., f.* translator. ~uction *n.f.* translation.
trafic /trafik/ *n.m.* (*commerce, circulation*) traffic.
trafiqu|er /trafike/ *v.i.* traffic. —*v.t.* (*fam.*) (*vin*) doctor; (*moteur*) fiddle with. ~ant, ~ante *n.m., f.* trafficker; (*d'armes, de drogues*) dealer.
tragédie /traʒedi/ *n.f.* tragedy.
tragique /traʒik/ *a.* tragic. ~ment *adv.* tragically.
trah|ir /trair/ *v.t.* betray. ~ison *n.f.* betrayal; (*crime*) treason.
train /trɛ̃/ *n.m.* (*rail.*) train; (*allure*) pace. en ~, (*en forme*) in shape. en ~ de faire, (busy) doing. mettre en ~, start up. ~ d'atterrissage, undercarriage. ~ électrique, (*jouet*) electric train set. ~ de vie, lifestyle.
traînard, ~e /trɛnar, -d/ *n.m., f.* slowcoach; (*Amer.*) slowpoke; (*en marchant*) straggler.
traîne /trɛn/ *n.f.* (*de robe*) train. à la ~, lagging behind; (*en remorque*) in tow.
traineau (*pl.* ~x) /trɛno/ *n.m.* sledge.
traînée /trɛne/ *n.f.* (*trace*) trail; (*bande*) streak; (*femme: péj.*) slut.
traîner /trɛne/ *v.t.* drag (along); (*véhicule*) pull. —*v.i.* (*pendre*) trail; (*rester en arrière*) trail behind; (*flâner*) hang about; (*papiers, affaires*) lie

around. ~ (en longueur), drag on. se ~ *v. pr.* (*par terre*) crawl. (faire) ~ en longueur, drag out. ~ les pieds, drag one's feet. ça n'a pas traîné!, that didn't take long.
train-train /trɛ̃trɛ̃/ *n.m.* routine.
traire† /trɛr/ *v.t.* milk.
trait /trɛ/ *n.m.* line; (*en dessinant*) stroke; (*caractéristique*) feature, trait; (*acte*) act. ~s, (*du visage*) features. avoir ~ à, relate to. d'un ~, (*boire*) in one gulp. ~ d'union, hyphen; (*fig.*) link.
traite /trɛt/ *n.f.* (*de vache*) milking; (*comm.*) draft. d'une (seule) ~, in one go, at a stretch.
traité /trete/ *n.m.* (*pacte*) treaty; (*ouvrage*) treatise.
traitement /trɛtmɑ̃/ *n.m.* treatment; (*salaire*) salary. ~ de données, data processing. ~ de texte, word processing.
traiter /trete/ *v.t.* treat; (*affaire*) deal with; (*données, produit*) process. ~ qn. de lâche/*etc.*, call s.o. a coward/*etc.* —*v.i.* deal (avec, with). ~ de, (*sujet*) deal with.
traiteur /trɛtœr/ *n.m.* caterer; (*boutique*) delicatessen.
traître, ~sse /trɛtr, -ɛs/ *a.* treacherous. —*n.m./f.* traitor.
trajectoire /traʒɛktwar/ *n.f.* path.
trajet /traʒɛ/ *n.m.* (*à parcourir*) distance; (*voyage*) journey; (*itinéraire*) route.
trame /tram/ *n.f.* (*de tissu*) weft; (*de récit etc.*) framework. usé jusqu'à la ~, threadbare.
trame|r /trame/ *v.t.* plot; (*complot*) hatch. qu'est ce qui se ~?, what's brewing?
tramway /tramwɛ/ *n.m.* tram; (*Amer.*) streetcar.
tranchant, ~e /trɑ̃ʃɑ̃, -t/ *a.* sharp; (*fig.*) cutting. —*n.m.* cutting edge. à double ~, two-edged.
tranche /trɑ̃ʃ/ *n.f.* (*rondelle*) slice; (*bord*) edge; (*partie*) portion.
tranchée /trɑ̃ʃe/ *n.f.* trench.
tranch|er¹ /trɑ̃ʃe/ *v.t.* cut; (*question*) decide. —*v.i.* (*décider*) decide. ~é *a.* (*net*) clear-cut.
trancher² /trɑ̃ʃe/ *v.i.* (*contraster*) contrast (sur, with).
tranquill|e /trɑ̃kil/ *a.* quiet; (*esprit*) at rest; (*conscience*) clear. être/laisser ~e, be/leave in peace. ~ement *adv.* quietly. ~ité *n.f.* (peace and) quiet; (*d'esprit*) peace of mind.

tranquillisant /trɑ̃kilizɑ̃/ *n.m.* tranquillizer.

tranquilliser /trɑ̃kilize/ *v.t.* reassure.

transaction /trɑ̃zaksjɔ̃/ *n.f.* transaction.

transat /trɑ̃zat/ *n.m.* (*fam.*) deck-chair.

transatlantique /trɑ̃zatlɑ̃tik/ *n.m.* transatlantic liner. —*a.* transatlantic.

transborder /trɑ̃sbɔrde/ *v.t.* transfer, transship.

transcend|er /trɑ̃sɑ̃de/ *v.t.* transcend. ~**ant**, ~**ante** *a.* transcendent.

transcr|ire /trɑ̃skrir/ *v.t.* transcribe. ~**iption** *n.f.* transcription; (*copie*) transcript.

transe /trɑ̃s/ *n.f.* **en** ~, in a trance; (*fig.*) very excited.

transférer /trɑ̃sfere/ *v.t.* transfer.

transfert /trɑ̃sfɛr/ *n.m.* transfer.

transform|er /trɑ̃sfɔrme/ *v.t.* change; (*radicalement*) transform; (*vêtement*) alter. **se** ~**er** *v. pr.* change; be transformed. (**se**) ~**er en**, turn into. ~**ateur** *n.m.* transformer. ~**ation** *n.f.* change; transformation.

transfuge /trɑ̃sfyʒ/ *n.m.* renegade.

transfusion /trɑ̃sfyzjɔ̃/ *n.f.* transfusion.

transgresser /trɑ̃sgrese/ *v.t.* disobey.

transiger /trɑ̃siʒe/ *v.i.* compromise. **ne pas** ~ **sur**, not compromise on.

transi /trɑ̃zi/ *a.* chilled to the bone.

transistor /trɑ̃zistɔr/ *n.m.* (*dispositif, poste de radio*) transistor.

transit /trɑ̃zit/ *n.m.* transit. ~**er** *v.t./i.* pass in transit.

transiti|f, ~**ve** /trɑ̃zitif, -v/ *a.* transitive.

transi|tion /trɑ̃zisjɔ̃/ *n.f.* transition. ~**toire** *a.* (*provisoire*) transitional.

translucide /trɑ̃slysid/ *a.* translucent.

transm|ettre† /trɑ̃smɛtr/ *v.t.* pass on; (*techn.*) transmit; (*radio*) broadcast. ~**ission** *n.f.* transmission; (*radio*) broadcasting.

transparaître /trɑ̃sparɛtr/ *v.i.* show (through).

transparen|t, ~**te** /trɑ̃sparɑ̃, -t/ *a.* transparent. ~**ce** *n.f.* transparency.

transpercer /trɑ̃spɛrse/ *v.t.* pierce.

transpir|er /trɑ̃spire/ *v.i.* perspire. ~**ation** *n.f.* perspiration.

transplant|er /trɑ̃splɑ̃te/ *v.t.* (*bot., med.*) transplant. ~**ation** *n.f.* (*bot.*) transplantation; (*méd.*) transplant.

transport /trɑ̃spɔr/ *n.m.* transport(ation); (*sentiment*) rapture. **les** ~**s**, transport. **les** ~**s en commun**, public transport.

transport|er /trɑ̃spɔrte/ *v.t.* transport; (*à la main*) carry. **se** ~**er** *v. pr.* take o.s. (**à**, to). ~**eur** *n.m.* haulier; (*Amer.*) trucker.

transposer /trɑ̃spoze/ *v.t.* transpose.

transvaser /trɑ̃svaze/ *v.t.* decant.

transvers|al (*m. pl.* ~**aux**) /trɑ̃vɛrsal, -o/ *a.* cross, transverse.

trap|èze /trapɛz/ *n.m.* (*sport*) trapeze. ~**éziste** /-ezist/ *n.m./f.* trapeze artist.

trappe /trap/ *n.f.* trapdoor.

trappeur /trapœr/ *n.m.* trapper.

trapu /trapy/ *a.* stocky.

traquenard /traknar/ *n.m.* trap.

traquer /trake/ *v.t.* track down.

traumatis|me /tromatism/ *n.m.* trauma. ~**ant**, ~**ante** /-zɑ̃, -t/ *a.* traumatic. ~**er** /-ze/ *v.t.* traumatize.

trav|ail (*pl.* ~**aux**) /travaj, -o/ *n.m.* work; (*emploi, poste*) job; (*façonnage*) working. ~**aux**, work. **en** ~**ail**, (*femme*) in labour. ~**ail à la chaîne**, production line work. ~**ail à la pièce** *ou* **à la tâche**, piece-work. ~**ail au noir**, (*fam.*) moonlighting. ~**aux forcés**, hard labour. ~**aux manuels**, handicrafts. ~**aux ménagers**, housework.

travaill|er /travaje/ *v.i.* work; (*se déformer*) warp. ~**er à**, (*livre etc.*) work on. —*v.t.* (*façonner*) work; (*étudier*) work at *ou* on; (*tourmenter*) worry. ~**eur**, ~**euse** *n.m.*, *f.* worker; *a.* hardworking.

travailliste /travajist/ *a.* Labour. —*n.m./f.* Labour party member.

travers /travɛr/ *n.m.* (*défaut*) failing. **à** ~, through. **au** ~ (**de**), through. **de** ~, (*chapeau, nez*) crooked; (*mal*) badly, the wrong way; (*regarder*) askance. **en** ~ (**de**), across.

traverse /travɛrs/ *n.f.* (*rail.*) sleeper; (*rail., Amer.*) tie.

traversée /travɛrse/ *n.f.* crossing.

traverser /travɛrse/ *v.t.* cross; (*transpercer*) go (right) through; (*période, forêt*) go *ou* pass through.

traversin /travɛrsɛ̃/ *n.m.* bolster.

travesti /travɛsti/ *n.m.* transvestite.

travestir /travɛstir/ *v.t.* disguise; (*vérité*) misrepresent.

trébucher /trebyʃe/ *v.i.* stumble, trip (over). **faire** ~, trip (up).

trèfle /trɛfl/ *n.m.* (*plante*) clover; (*cartes*) clubs.

treillage /trejaʒ/ *n.m.* trellis.

treillis[1] /treji/ *n.m.* trellis; (*en métal*) wire mesh.

treillis[2] /treji/ *n.m.* (*tenue militaire*) combat uniform.

treiz|e /trɛz/ *a. & n.m.* thirteen. ~**ième** *a. & n.m./f.* thirteenth.

tréma /trema/ n.m. diaeresis.
trembl|er /trɑ̃ble/ v.i. shake, tremble; (lumière, voix) quiver. ∼ement n.m. shaking; (frisson) shiver. ∼ement de terre, earthquake.
trembloter /trɑ̃blɔte/ v.i. quiver.
trémousser (se) /(sə)tremuse/ v. pr. wriggle, wiggle.
trempe /trɑ̃p/ n.f. (caractère) calibre.
tremper /trɑ̃pe/ v.t./i. soak; (plonger) dip; (acier) temper. **mettre à ∼ ou faire ∼**, soak. **∼ dans**, (fig.) be involved in. **se ∼** v. pr. (se baigner) have a dip.
trempette /trɑ̃pɛt/ n.f. **faire ∼**, have a little dip.
tremplin /trɑ̃plɛ̃/ n.m. springboard.
trentaine /trɑ̃tɛn/ n.f. **une ∼ (de)**, about thirty. **il a la ∼**, he's about thirty.
trent|e /trɑ̃t/ a. & n.m. thirty. **∼ième** a. & n.m./f. thirtieth. **se mettre sur son ∼e et un**, put on one's Sunday best. **tous les ∼e-six du mois**, once in a blue moon.
trépider /trepide/ v.i. vibrate.
trépied /trepje/ n.m. tripod.
trépigner /trepiɲe/ v.i. stamp one's feet.
très /trɛ/ (/trɛz/ before vowel) adv. very. **∼ aimé/estimé**, much liked/esteemed.
trésor /trezɔr/ n.m. treasure; (ressources: comm.) finances. **le T∼**, the revenue department.
trésorerie /trezɔrri/ n.f. (bureaux) accounts department; (du Trésor) revenue office; (argent) finances; (gestion) accounts.
trésor|ier, **∼ière** /trezɔrje, -jɛr/ n.m., f. treasurer.
tressaill|ir /tresajir/ v.i. shake, quiver; (sursauter) start. **∼ement** n.m. quiver, start.
tressauter /tresote/ v.i. (sursauter) start, jump.
tresse /trɛs/ n.f. braid, plait.
tresser /trese/ v.t. braid, plait.
tréteau (pl. **∼x**) /treto/ n.m. trestle. **∼x**, (théâtre) stage.
treuil /trœj/ n.m. winch.
trêve /trɛv/ n.f. truce; (fig.) respite. **∼ de plaisanteries**, enough of this joking.
tri /tri/ n.m. (classement) sorting; (sélection) selection. **faire le ∼ de**, sort; select. **∼age** /-jaʒ/ n.m. sorting.
triang|le /trijɑ̃gl/ n.m. triangle. **∼ulaire** a. triangular.
trib|al (m. pl. **∼aux**) /tribal, -o/ a. tribal.
tribord /tribɔr/ n.m. starboard.
tribu /triby/ n.f. tribe.

tribulations /tribylɑsjɔ̃/ n.f. pl. tribulations.
tribun|al (m. pl. **∼aux**) /tribynal, -o/ n.m. court. **∼al d'instance**, magistrates' court.
tribune /tribyn/ n.f. (public) gallery; (dans un stade) grandstand; (d'orateur) rostrum; (débat) forum.
tribut /triby/ n.m. tribute.
tributaire /tribytɛr/ a. **∼ de**, dependent on.
trich|er /triʃe/ v.i. cheat. **∼erie** n.f. cheating. **une ∼erie**, piece of trickery. **∼eur**, **∼euse** n.m., f. cheat.
tricolore /trikɔlɔr/ a. three-coloured; (français) red, white and blue; (français: fig.) French.
tricot /triko/ n.m. knitting; (pull) sweater. **en ∼**, knitted. **∼ de corps**, vest; (Amer.) undershirt. **∼er** /-ɔte/ v.t./i. knit.
trictrac /triktrak/ n.m. backgammon.
tricycle /trisikl/ n.m. tricycle.
trier /trije/ v.t. (classer) sort; (choisir) select.
trilogie /trilɔʒi/ n.f. trilogy.
trimbaler /trɛ̃bale/ v.t., **se ∼** v. pr. (fam.) trail around.
trimer /trime/ v.i. (fam.) slave.
trimestr|e /trimɛstr/ n.m. quarter; (scol.) term. **∼iel**, **∼ielle** a. quarterly; (bulletin) end-of-term.
tringle /trɛ̃gl/ n.f. rod.
Trinité /trinite/ n.f. **la ∼**, (dogme) the Trinity; (fête) Trinity.
trinquer /trɛ̃ke/ v.i. clink glasses.
trio /trijo/ n.m. trio.
triomph|e /trijɔ̃f/ n.m. triumph. **∼al** (m. pl. **∼aux**) a. triumphant.
triomph|er /trijɔ̃fe/ v.i. triumph (de, over); (jubiler) be triumphant. **∼ant**, **∼ante** a. triumphant.
trip|es /trip/ n.f. pl. (mets) tripe; (entrailles: fam.) guts.
triple /tripl/ a. triple, treble. —n.m. **le ∼**, three times as much (de, as). **∼ment** /-əmɑ̃/ adv. trebly.
tripl|er /triple/ v.t./i. triple, treble. **∼és**, **∼ées** n.m., f. pl. triplets.
tripot /tripo/ n.m. gambling den.
tripoter /tripɔte/ v.t. (fam.) fiddle with. —v.i. (fam.) fiddle about.
trique /trik/ n.f. cudgel.
trisomique /trizɔmik/ a. **enfant ∼**, Down's (syndrome) child.
triste /trist/ a. sad; (rue, temps, couleur) gloomy; (lamentable) wretched, dreadful. **∼ment** /- əmɑ̃/ adv. sadly. **∼sse** /-ɛs/ n.f. sadness; gloominess.

triv|ial (*m. pl.* ∼**iaux**) /trivjal, -jo/ *a.* coarse. ∼**ialité** *n.f.* coarseness.

troc /trɔk/ *n.m.* exchange; (*comm.*) barter.

troène /trɔɛn/ *n.m.* (*bot.*) privet.

trognon /trɔɲɔ̃/ *n.m.* (*de pomme*) core.

trois /trwɑ/ *a. & n.m.* three. **hôtel** ∼**étoiles,** three-star hotel. ∼**ième** /-zjɛm/ *a. & n.m./f.* third. ∼**ièmement** /-zjɛmmɑ̃/ *adv.* thirdly.

trombe /trɔ̃b/ *n.f.* ∼ **d'eau,** downpour.

trombone /trɔ̃bɔn/ *n.m.* (*mus.*) trombone; (*agrafe*) paper-clip.

trompe /trɔ̃p/ *n.f.* (*d'éléphant*) trunk; (*mus.*) horn.

tromp|er /trɔ̃pe/ *v.t.* deceive, mislead; (*déjouer*) elude. **se** ∼**er** *v. pr.* be mistaken. **se** ∼**er de route/train/**etc., take the wrong road/train/etc. ∼**erie** *n.f.* deception. ∼**eur,** ∼**euse** *a.* (*personne*) deceitful; (*chose*) deceptive.

trompette /trɔ̃pɛt/ *n.f.* trumpet.

tronc /trɔ̃/ *n.m.* trunk; (*boîte*) collection box.

tronçon /trɔ̃sɔ̃/ *n.m.* section. ∼**ner** /-ɔne/ *v.t.* cut into sections.

trôn|e /tron/ *n.m.* throne. ∼**er** *v.i.* occupy the place of honour.

tronquer /trɔ̃ke/ *v.t.* truncate.

trop /tro/ *adv.* (*grand, loin, etc.*) too; (*boire, marcher, etc.*) too much. ∼ (**de**), (*quantité*) too much; (*nombre*) too many. **c'est** ∼ **chauffé,** it's overheated. **de** ∼, **en** ∼, too much; too many. **il a bu un verre de** ∼, he's had one too many. **de** ∼, (*intrus*) in the way. ∼**-plein** *n.m.* excess; (*dispositif*) overflow.

trophée /trɔfe/ *n.m.* trophy.

tropic|al (*m. pl.* ∼**aux**) /trɔpikal, -o/ *a.* tropical.

tropique /trɔpik/ *n.m.* tropic. ∼**s,** tropics.

troquer /trɔke/ *v.t.* exchange; (*comm.*) barter (**contre,** for).

trot /tro/ *n.m.* trot. **aller au** ∼, trot. **au** ∼, (*fam.*) on the double.

trotter /trɔte/ *v.i.* trot.

trotteuse /trɔtøz/ *n.f.* (*aiguille de montre*) second hand.

trottiner /trɔtine/ *v.i.* patter along.

trottinette /trɔtinɛt/ *n.f.* (*jouet*) scooter.

trottoir /trɔtwar/ *n.m.* pavement; (*Amer.*) sidewalk. ∼ **roulant,** moving walkway.

trou /tru/ *n.m.* hole; (*moment*) gap; (*lieu: péj.*) dump. ∼ (**de mémoire**), lapse (of memory). ∼ **de la serrure,** keyhole. **faire son** ∼, carve one's niche.

trouble /trubl/ *a.* (*eau, image*) unclear; (*louche*) shady. —*n.m.* agitation. ∼**s,** (*pol.*) disturbances; (*méd.*) trouble.

troubl|er /truble/ *v.t.* disturb; (*eau*) make cloudy; (*inquiéter*) trouble. ∼**ant,** ∼**ante** *a.* disturbing. **se** ∼**er** *v. pr.* (*personne*) become flustered. ∼**e-fête** *n.m./f. invar.* killjoy.

trouée /true/ *n.f.* gap, open space; (*mil.*) breach (**dans,** in).

trouer /true/ *v.t.* make a hole *ou* holes in. **mes chaussures se sont trouées,** my shoes have got holes in them.

trouille /truj/ *n.f.* **avoir la** ∼, (*fam.*) be scared.

troupe /trup/ *n.f.* troop; (*d'acteurs*) troupe. ∼**s,** (*mil.*) troops.

troupeau (*pl.* ∼**x**) /trupo/ *n.m.* herd; (*de moutons*) flock.

trousse /trus/ *n.f.* case, bag; (*de réparations*) kit. **aux** ∼**s de,** on the tail of. ∼ **de toilette,** toilet bag.

trousseau (*pl.* ∼**x**) /truso/ *n.m.* (*de clefs*) bunch; (*de mariée*) trousseau.

trouvaille /truvɑj/ *n.f.* find.

trouver /truve/ *v.t.* find; (*penser*) think. **aller/venir** ∼, (*rendre visite à*) go/come and see. **se** ∼ *v. pr.* find o.s.; (*être*) be; (*se sentir*) feel. **il se trouve que,** it happens that. **se** ∼ **mal,** faint.

truand /tryɑ̃/ *n.m.* gangster.

truc /tryk/ *n.m.* (*moyen*) way; (*artifice*) trick; (*chose: fam.*) thing. ∼**age** *n.m.* = **truquage.**

truchement /tryʃmɑ̃/ *n.m.* **par le** ∼ **de,** through.

truculent, ∼**e** /trykylɑ̃, -t/ *a.* colourful.

truelle /tryɛl/ *n.f.* trowel.

truffe /tryf/ *n.f.* (*champignon, chocolat*) truffle; (*nez*) nose.

truffer /tryfe/ *v.t.* (*fam.*) fill, pack (**de,** with).

truie /trɥi/ *n.f.* (*animal*) sow.

truite /trɥit/ *n.f.* trout.

truqu|er /tryke/ *v.t.* fix, rig; (*photo, texte*) fake. ∼**age** *n.m.* fixing; faking; (*cinéma*) special effect.

trust /trœst/ *n.m.* (*comm.*) trust.

tsar /tsar/ *n.m.* tsar, czar.

tsigane /tsigan/ *a. & n.m./f.* (Hungarian) gypsy.

tu[1] /ty/ *pron.* (*parent, ami, enfant, etc.*) you.

tu[2] /ty/ *voir* **taire.**

tuba /tyba/ *n.m.* (*mus.*) tuba; (*sport*) snorkel.

tube /tyb/ *n.m.* tube.

tubercul|eux, ∼**euse** /tybɛrkylø, -z/ *a.*

être ∼eux, have tuberculosis. ∼ose *n.f.*
tuberculosis.
tubulaire /tybylɛr/ *a.* tubular.
tubulure /tybylyr/ *n.f.* tubing.
tu|er /tɥe/ *v.t.* kill; (*d'une balle*) shoot,
kill; (*épuiser*) exhaust. **se ∼er** *v. pr.* kill
o.s.; (*accident*) be killed. ∼**ant,** ∼**ante,**
a. exhausting. ∼**é,** ∼**ée** *n.m., f.* person
killed. ∼**eur,** ∼**euse** *n.m., f.* killer.
tuerie /tyri/ *n.f.* slaughter.
tue-tête (à) /(a)tytɛt/ *adv.* at the top of
one's voice.
tuile /tɥil/ *n.f.* tile; (*malchance*: *fam.*)
(stroke of) bad luck.
tulipe /tylip/ *n.f.* tulip.
tuméfié /tymefje/ *a.* swollen.
tumeur /tymœr/ *n.f.* tumour.
tumult|e /tymylt/ *n.m.* commotion;
(*désordre*) turmoil. ∼**ueux,** ∼**ueuse** *a.*
turbulent.
tunique /tynik/ *n.f.* tunic.
Tunisie /tynizi/ *n.f.* Tunisia.
tunisien, ∼**ne** /tynizjɛ̃, -jɛn/ *a. & n.m.,*
f. Tunisian.
tunnel /tynɛl/ *n.m.* tunnel.
turban /tyrbɑ̃/ *n.m.* turban.
turbine /tyrbin/ *n.f.* turbine.
turbo /tyrbo/ *a.* turbo. *n.f.* (*voiture*)
turbo.
turbulen|t, ∼**te** /tyrbylɑ̃, -t/ *a.*
boisterous, turbulent. ∼**ce** *n.f.* turbulence.
tur|c, ∼**que** /tyrk/ *a.* Turkish. —*n.m., f.*
Turk. —*n.m.* (*lang.*) Turkish.
turf /tyrf/ *n.m.* **le ∼,** the turf. ∼**iste**
n.m./f. racegoer.
Turquie /tyrki/ *n.f.* Turkey.
turquoise /tyrkwaz/ *a. invar.* turquoise.
tutelle /tytɛl/ *n.f.* (*jurid.*) guardianship;
(*fig.*) protection.
tu|teur, ∼**trice** /tytœr, -tris/ *n.m., f.*
(*jurid.*) guardian. —*n.m.* (*bâton*)
stake.
tut|oyer /tytwaje/ *v.t.* address familiarly
(using *tu*). ∼**oiement** *n.m.* use of
(familiar) *tu*.
tuyau (*pl.* ∼**x**) /tɥijo/ *n.m.* pipe;
(*conseil*: *fam.*) tip. ∼ **d'arrosage,**
hose-pipe. ∼**ter** *v.t.* (*fam.*) give a tip to.
∼**terie** *n.f.* piping.
TVA *abrév.* (*taxe sur la valeur ajoutée*)
VAT.
tympan /tɛ̃pɑ̃/ *n.m.* ear-drum.
type /tip/ *n.m.* (*modèle*) type; (*traits*)
features; (*individu*: *fam.*) bloke, guy.
—*a. invar.* typical. **le ∼ même de,** a
classic example of.
typhoïde /tifɔid/ *n.f.* typhoid (fever).
typhon /tifɔ̃/ *n.m.* typhoon.

typhus /tifys/ *n.m.* typhus.
typique /tipik/ *a.* typical. ∼**ment** *adv.*
typically.
tyran /tirɑ̃/ *n.m.* tyrant.
tyrann|ie /tirani/ *n.f.* tyranny. ∼**ique** *a.*
tyrannical. ∼**iser** *v.t.* oppress, tyran-
nize.

U

ulcère /ylsɛr/ *n.m.* ulcer.
ulcérer /ylsere/ *v.t.* (*vexer*) embitter,
gall.
ULM *abrév. m.* (*ultraléger motorisé*)
microlight.
ultérieur /ylterjœr/ *a.,* ∼**ement** *adv.*
later.
ultimatum /yltimatɔm/ *n.m.* ultimatum.
ultime /yltim/ *a.* final.
ultra /yltra/ *n.m./f.* hardliner.
ultra- /yltra/ *préf.* ultra-.
un, une /œ̃, yn/ *a.* one; (*indéfini*) a, an.
un enfant, /œ̃nɑ̃fɑ̃/ a child. —*pron. &*
n.m., f. one. **l'un,** one. **les uns,** some.
l'un et l'autre, both. **l'un l'autre, les**
uns les autres, each other. **l'un ou**
l'autre, either. **la une,** (*de journal*)
front page. **un autre,** another. **un par**
un, one by one.
unanim|e /ynanim/ *a.* unanimous. ∼**ité**
n.f. unanimity. **à l'∼ité,** unanimously.
uni /yni/ *a.* united; (*couple*) close;
(*surface*) smooth; (*sans dessins*) plain.
unième /ynjɛm/ *a.* -first. **vingt et ∼,**
twenty-first. **cent ∼,** one hundred and
first.
unif|ier /ynifje/ *v.t.* unify. ∼**ication** *n.f.*
unification.
uniform|e /ynifɔrm/ *n.m.* uniform. —*a.*
uniform. ∼**ément** *adv.* uniformly.
∼**iser** *v.t.* standardize. ∼**ité** *n.f.*
uniformity.
unilatér|al (*m. pl.* ∼**aux**) /ynilateral,
-o/ *a.* unilateral.
union /ynjɔ̃/ *n.f.* union. **l'U∼ soviétique,**
the Soviet Union.
unique /ynik/ *a.* (*seul*) only; (*prix, voie*)
one; (*incomparable*) unique. **enfant ∼,**
only child. **sens ∼,** one-way street.
∼**ment** *adv.* only, solely.
unir /ynir/ *v.t.,* **s'∼** *v. pr.* unite, join.
unisson (à l') /(al)ynisɔ̃/ *adv.* in unison.
unité /ynite/ *n.f.* unit; (*harmonie*) unity.
univers /ynivɛr/ *n.m.* universe.
universel, ∼**le** /ynivɛrsɛl/ *a.* universal.

universit|é /yniversite/ *n.f.* university. **~aire** *a.* university; *n.m./f.* academic.

uranium /yranjɔm/ *n.m.* uranium.

urbain, ~e /yrbɛ̃, -ɛn/ *a.* urban.

urbanisme /yrbanism/ *n.m.* town planning; (*Amer.*) city planning.

urgence /yrʒɑ̃s/ *n.f.* (*cas*) emergency; (*de situation, tâche, etc.*) urgency. **d'~** *a.* emergency; *adv.* urgently.

urgent, ~e /yrʒɑ̃, -t/ *a.* urgent.

urger /yrʒe/ *v.i.* **ça urge!**, (*fam.*) it's getting urgent.

urin|e /yrin/ *n.f.* urine. **~er** *v.i.* urinate.

urinoir /yrinwar/ *n.m.* urinal.

urne /yrn/ *n.f.* (*électorale*) ballot-box; (*vase*) urn. **aller aux ~s**, go to the polls.

URSS *abrév.* (*Union des Républiques Socialistes Soviétiques*) USSR.

urticaire /yrtikɛr/ *n.f.* **une crise d'~**, nettle rash.

us /ys/ *n.m. pl.* **les us et coutumes,** habits and customs.

usage /yzaʒ/ *n.m.* use; (*coutume*) custom; (*de langage*) usage. **à l'~ de**, for. **d'~**, (*habituel*) customary. **faire ~ de**, make use of.

usagé /yzaʒe/ *a.* worn.

usager /yzaʒe/ *n.m.* user.

usé /yze/ *a.* worn (out); (*banal*) trite.

user /yze/ *v.t.* wear (out); (*consommer*) use (up). **—v.i. ~ de**, use. **s'~** *v. pr.* (*tissu etc.*) wear (out).

usine /yzin/ *n.f.* factory; (*de métallurgie*) works.

usité /yzite/ *a.* common.

ustensile /ystɑ̃sil/ *n.m.* utensil.

usuel, ~le /yzɥɛl/ *a.* ordinary, everyday.

usufruit /yzyfrɥi/ *n.m.* usufruct.

usure /yzyr/ *n.f.* (*détérioration*) wear (and tear).

usurper /yzyrpe/ *v.t.* usurp.

utérus /yterys/ *n.m.* womb, uterus.

utile /ytil/ *a.* useful. **~ment** *adv.* usefully.

utilis|er /ytilize/ *v.t.* use. **~able** *a.* usable. **~ation** *n.f.* use.

utilitaire /ytilitɛr/ *a.* utilitarian.

utilité /ytilite/ *n.f.* use(fulness).

utop|ie /ytɔpi/ *n.f.* Utopia; (*idée*) Utopian idea. **~ique** *a.* Utopian.

UV *abrév. f.* (*unité de valeur*) (*scol.*) credit.

V

va /va/ *voir* **aller**[1].

vacanc|e /vakɑ̃s/ *n.f.* (*poste*) vacancy. **~es**, holiday(s); (*Amer.*) vacation. **en ~es**, on holiday. **~ier, ~ière** *n.m., f.* holiday-maker; (*Amer.*) vacationer.

vacant, ~e /vakɑ̃, -t/ *a.* vacant.

vacarme /vakarm/ *n.m.* uproar.

vaccin /vaksɛ̃/ *n.m.* vaccine; (*inoculation*) vaccination.

vaccin|er /vaksine/ *v.t.* vaccinate. **~ation** *n.f.* vaccination.

vache /vaʃ/ *n.f.* cow. **—a.** (*méchant: fam.*) nasty. **~ment** *adv.* (*très: fam.*) damned; (*pleuvoir, manger, etc.: fam.*) a hell of a lot. **~rie** *n.f.* (*fam.*) nastiness; (*chose: fam.*) nasty thing.

vacill|er /vasije/ *v.i.* sway, wobble; (*lumière*) flicker; (*fig.*) falter. **~ant, ~ante** *a.* (*mémoire, démarche*) shaky.

vadrouiller /vadruje/ *v.i.* (*fam.*) wander about.

va-et-vient /vaevjɛ̃/ *n.m. invar.* to and fro (motion); (*de personnes*) comings and goings.

vagabond, ~e /vagabɔ̃, -d/ *n.m., f.* (*péj.*) vagrant, vagabond. **~er** /-de/ *v.i.* wander.

vagin /vaʒɛ̃/ *n.m.* vagina.

vagir /vaʒir/ *v.i.* cry.

vague[1] /vag/ *a.* vague. **—n.m.** vagueness. **il est resté dans le ~**, he was vague about it. **~ment** *adv.* vaguely.

vague[2] /vag/ *n.f.* wave. **~ de fond,** ground swell. **~ de froid,** cold spell. **~ de chaleur,** hot spell.

vaill|ant, ~ante /vajɑ̃, -t/ *a.* brave; (*vigoureux*) healthy. **~amment** /-amɑ̃/ *adv.* bravely.

vaille /vaj/ *voir* **valoir**.

vain, ~e /vɛ̃, vɛn/ *a.* vain. **en ~**, in vain. **~ement** /vɛnmɑ̃/ *adv.* vainly.

vain|cre† /vɛ̃kr/ *v.t.* defeat; (*surmonter*) overcome. **~cu, ~cue** *n.m., f.* (*sport*) loser. **~queur** *n.m.* victor; (*sport*) winner.

vais /vɛ/ *voir* **aller**[1].

vaisseau (*pl.* **~x**) /vɛso/ *n.m.* ship; (*veine*) vessel. **~ spatial,** space-ship.

vaisselle /vɛsɛl/ *n.f.* crockery; (*à laver*) dishes. **faire la ~**, do the washing-up, wash the dishes. **produit pour la ~,** washing-up liquid.

val (*pl.* **~s** *ou* **vaux**) /val, vo/ *n.m.* valley.

valable /valabl/ *a.* valid; (*de qualité*) worthwhile.

valet /valɛ/ *n.m.* (*cartes*) jack. **~ (de chambre),** manservant. **~ de ferme,** farm-hand.

valeur /valœr/ *n.f.* value; (*mérite*) worth, value. **~s**, (*comm.*) stocks and shares. **avoir de la ~**, be valuable.

valid|e /valid/ *a.* (*personne*) fit; (*billet*) valid. **~er** *v.t.* validate. **~ité** *n.f.* validity.

valise /valiz/ *n.f.* (suit)case. **faire ses ~s**, pack (one's bags).

vallée /vale/ *n.f.* valley.

vallon /valɔ̃/ *n.m.* (small) valley. **~né** /-ɔne/ *a.* undulating.

valoir† /valwar/ *v.i.* be worth; (*s'appliquer*) apply. **~ qch.**, be worth sth.; (*être aussi bon que*) be as good as sth. —*v.t.* **~ qch. à qn.**, bring s.o. sth. **se ~** *v. pr.* (*être équivalents*) be as good as each other. **faire ~**, put forward to advantage; (*droit*) assert. **~ la peine**, **~ le coup**, be worth it. **ça ne vaut rien**, it is no good. **il vaudrait mieux faire**, we'd better do. **ça ne me dit rien qui vaille**, I don't think much of it.

valoriser /valɔrize/ *v.t.* add value to. **se sentir valorisé**, feel valued.

vals|e /vals/ *n.f.* waltz. **~er** *v.i.* waltz.

valve /valv/ *n.f.* valve.

vampire /vɑ̃pir/ *n.m.* vampire.

van /vɑ̃/ *n.m.* van.

vandal|e /vɑ̃dal/ *n.m./f.* vandal. **~isme** *n.m.* vandalism.

vanille /vanij/ *n.f.* vanilla.

vanit|é /vanite/ *n.f.* vanity. **~eux**, **~euse** *a.* vain, conceited.

vanne /van/ *n.f.* (*d'écluse*) sluice(-gate); (*fam.*) joke.

vant|ail (*pl.* **~aux**) /vɑ̃taj, -o/ *n.m.* door, flap.

vantard, **~e** /vɑ̃tar, -d/ *a.* boastful; *n.m.*, *f.* boaster. **~ise** /-diz/ *n.f.* boastfulness; (*acte*) boast.

vanter /vɑ̃te/ *v.t.* praise. **se ~** *v. pr.* boast (**de**, about).

va-nu-pieds /vanypje/ *n.m./f. invar.* vagabond, beggar.

vapeur[1] /vapœr/ *n.f.* (*eau*) steam; (*brume*, *émanation*) vapour.

vapeur[2] /vapœr/ *n.m.* (*bateau*) steamer.

vaporeu|x, **~se** /vapɔrø, -z/ *a.* hazy; (*léger*) filmy, flimsy.

vaporis|er /vapɔrize/ *v.t.* spray. **~ateur** *n.m.* spray.

vaquer /vake/ *v.i.* **~ à**, attend to.

varappe /varap/ *n.f.* rock climbing.

vareuse /varøz/ *n.f.* (*d'uniforme*) tunic.

variable /varjabl/ *a.* variable; (*temps*) changeable.

variante /varjɑ̃t/ *n.f.* variant.

varicelle /varisɛl/ *n.f.* chicken-pox.

varices /varis/ *n.f. pl.* varicose veins.

var|ier /varje/ *v.t./i.* vary. **~iation** *n.f.* variation. **~ié** *a.* (*non monotone*, *étendu*) varied; (*divers*) various.

variété /varjete/ *n.f.* variety. **~s**, (*spectacle*) variety.

variole /varjɔl/ *n.f.* smallpox.

vase[1] /vɑz/ *n.m.* vase.

vase[2] /vɑz/ *n.f.* (*boue*) silt, mud.

vaseu|x, **~se** /vɑzø, -z/ *a.* (*confus*: *fam.*) woolly, hazy.

vasistas /vazistas/ *n.m.* fanlight, hinged panel (*in door or window*).

vaste /vast/ *a.* vast, huge.

vaudeville /vodvil/ *n.m.* vaudeville, light comedy.

vau-l'eau (à) /(a)volo/ *adv.* downhill.

vaurien, **~ne** /vorjɛ̃, -jɛn/ *n.m.*, *f.* good-for-nothing.

vautour /votur/ *n.m.* vulture.

vautrer (se) /(sə)votre/ *v. pr.* sprawl. **se ~ dans**, (*vice*, *boue*) wallow in.

va-vite (à la) /(ala)vavit/ *adv.* (*fam.*) in a hurry.

veau (*pl.* **~x**) /vo/ *n.m.* calf; (*viande*) veal; (*cuir*) calfskin.

vécu /veky/ *voir* **vivre**. —*a.* (*réel*) true, real.

vedette[1] /vədɛt/ *n.f.* (*artiste*) star. **en ~**, (*objet*) in a prominent position; (*personne*) in the limelight.

vedette[2] /vədɛt/ *n.f.* (*bateau*) launch.

végét|al (*m. pl.* **~aux**) /veʒetal, -o/ *a.* plant. —*n.m.* (*pl.* **~aux**) plant.

végétalien, **~ne** /veʒetaljɛ̃, -jɛn/ *n.m.*, *f. & a.* vegan.

végétarien, **~ne** /veʒetarjɛ̃, -jɛn/ *a. & n.m.*, *f.* vegetarian.

végétation /veʒetasjɔ̃/ *n.f.* vegetation. **~s**, (*méd.*) adenoids.

végéter /veʒete/ *v.i.* vegetate.

véhémen|t, **~te** /veemɑ̃, -t/ *a.* vehement. **~ce** *n.f.* vehemence.

véhicul|e /veikyl/ *n.m.* vehicle. **~er** *v.t.* convey.

veille[1] /vɛj/ *n.f.* **la ~ (de)**, the day before. **la ~ de Noël**, Christmas Eve. **à la ~ de**, on the eve of.

veille[2] /vɛj/ *n.f.* (*état*) wakefulness.

veillée /veje/ *n.f.* evening (gathering); (*mortuaire*) vigil, wake.

veiller /veje/ *v.i.* stay up *ou* awake. **~ à**, attend to. **~ sur**, watch over. —*v.t.* (*malade*) watch over.

veilleur /vɛjœr/ *n.m.* **~ de nuit**, night-watchman.

veilleuse /vɛjøz/ *n.f.* night-light; (*de véhicule*) sidelight; (*de réchaud*) pilot-light. **mettre qch. en ~**, put sth. on the back burner.

veinard, ~e /vɛnar, -d/ *n.m.*, *f.* (*fam.*) lucky devil.

veine¹ /vɛn/ *n.f.* (*anat.*) vein; (*nervure*, *filon*) vein.

veine² /vɛn/ *n.f.* (*chance: fam.*) luck. **avoir de la ~,** (*fam.*) be lucky.

velcro /vɛlkrɔ/ *n.m.* (P.) velcro.

véliplanchiste /veliplɑ̃ʃist/ *n.m./f.* windsurfer.

vélo /velo/ *n.m.* bicycle, bike; (*activité*) cycling.

vélodrome /velodrom/ *n.m.* velodrome, cycle-racing track.

vélomoteur /velomotœr/ *n.m.* moped.

velours /vlur/ *n.m.* velvet. **~ côtelé, ~ à côtes,** corduroy.

velouté /velute/ *a.* smooth. —*n.m.* smoothness.

velu /vǝly/ *a.* hairy.

venaison /vǝnɛzɔ̃/ *n.f.* venison.

vendang|es /vɑ̃dɑ̃ʒ/ *n.f. pl.* grape harvest. **~er** *v.i.* pick the grapes. **~eur, ~euse** *n.m., f.* grape-picker.

vendetta /vɑ̃dɛta/ *n.f.* vendetta.

vendeu|r, ~se /vɑ̃dœr, -øz/ *n.m., f.* shop assistant; (*marchand*) salesman, saleswoman; (*jurid.*) vendor, seller.

vendre /vɑ̃dr/ *v.t.,* **se ~** *v. pr.* sell. **à ~,** for sale.

vendredi /vɑ̃drǝdi/ *n.m.* Friday. **V~ saint,** Good Friday.

vénéneu|x, ~se /venenø, -z/ *a.* poisonous.

vénérable /venerabl/ *a.* venerable.

vénérer /venere/ *v.t.* revere.

vénérien, ~ne /venerjɛ̃, -jɛn/ *a.* venereal.

vengeance /vɑ̃ʒɑ̃s/ *n.f.* revenge, vengeance.

veng|er /vɑ̃ʒe/ *v.t.* avenge. **se ~er** *v. pr.* take (one's) revenge (**de,** for). **~eur, ~eresse** *a.* vengeful; *n.m., f.* avenger.

ven|in /vǝnɛ̃/ *n.m.* venom. **~imeux, ~imeuse** *a.* poisonous, venomous.

venir† /vǝnir/ *v.i.* (*aux. être*) come (**de,** from). **~ faire,** come to do. **venez faire,** come and do. **~ de faire,** to have just done. **il vient/venait d'arriver,** he has/had just arrived. **en ~ à,** (*question, conclusion, etc.*) come to. **en ~ aux mains,** come to blows. **faire ~,** send for. **il m'est venu à l'esprit** *ou* **à l'idée que,** it occurred to me that.

vent /vɑ̃/ *n.m.* wind. **être dans le ~,** (*fam.*) be with it. **il fait du ~,** it is windy.

vente /vɑ̃t/ *n.f.* sale. **~ (aux enchères),** auction. **en ~,** on *ou* for sale. **~ de charité,** (charity) bazaar.

ventil|er /vɑ̃tile/ *v.t.* ventilate. **~ateur** *n.m.* fan, ventilator. **~ation** *n.f.* ventilation.

ventouse /vɑ̃tuz/ *n.f.* (*dispositif*) suction pad; (*pour déboucher l'évier etc.*) plunger.

ventre /vɑ̃tr/ *n.m.* belly, stomach; (*utérus*) womb. **avoir/prendre du ~,** have/develop a paunch.

ventriloque /vɑ̃trilɔk/ *n.m./f.* ventriloquist.

ventru /vɑ̃try/ *a.* pot-bellied.

venu /vǝny/ *voir* **venir.** —*a.* **bien ~,** (*à propos*) timely. **mal ~,** untimely. **être mal ~ de faire,** have no grounds for doing.

venue /vǝny/ *n.f.* coming.

vêpres /vɛpr/ *n.f. pl.* vespers.

ver /vɛr/ *n.m.* worm; (*des fruits, de la viande*) maggot; (*du bois*) woodworm. **~ luisant,** glow-worm. **~ à soie,** silkworm. **~ solitaire,** tapeworm. **~ de terre,** earthworm.

véranda /verɑ̃da/ *n.f.* veranda.

verb|e /vɛrb/ *n.m.* (*gram.*) verb. **~al** (*m. pl.* **~aux**) *a.* verbal.

verdâtre /vɛrdɑtr/ *a.* greenish.

verdict /vɛrdikt/ *n.m.* verdict.

verdir /vɛrdir/ *v.i.* turn green.

verdoyant, ~e /vɛrdwajɑ̃, -t/ *a.* green, verdant.

verdure /vɛrdyr/ *n.f.* greenery.

véreu|x, ~se /verø, -z/ *a.* maggoty, wormy; (*malhonnête: fig.*) shady.

verger /vɛrʒe/ *n.m.* orchard.

vergla|s /vɛrgla/ *n.m.* (black) ice; (*Amer.*) sleet. **~cé** *a.* icy.

vergogne (sans) /(sɑ̃)vɛrgɔɲ/ *a.* shameless. —*adv.* shamelessly.

véridique /veridik/ *a.* truthful.

vérif|ier /verifje/ *v.t.* check, verify; (*compte*) audit; (*confirmer*) confirm. **~ication** *n.f.* check(ing), verification.

véritable /veritabl/ *a.* true, real; (*authentique*) real. **~ment** /- ǝmɑ̃/ *adv.* really.

vérité /verite/ *n.f.* truth; (*de tableau, roman*) trueness to life. **en ~,** in fact.

vermeil, ~le /vɛrmɛj/ *a.* bright red.

vermicelle(s) /vɛrmisɛl/ *n.m.* (*pl.*) vermicelli.

vermine /vɛrmin/ *n.f.* vermin.

vermoulu /vɛrmuly/ *a.* wormeaten.

vermouth /vɛrmut/ *n.m.* (*apéritif*) vermouth.

verni /vɛrni/ *a.* (*fam.*) lucky. **chaussures ~es,** patent (leather) shoes.

vernir /vɛrnir/ *v.t.* varnish.

vernis /vɛrni/ *n.m.* varnish; (*de poterie*)

glaze. ~ **à ongles,** nail polish *ou* varnish.

vernissage /vɛrnisaʒ/ *n.m.* (*exposition*) preview.

vernisser /vɛrnise/ *v.t.* glaze.

verra, verrait /vɛra, vɛrɛ/ *voir* **voir**.

verre /vɛr/ *n.m.* glass. **prendre** *ou* **boire un ~,** have a drink. **~ de contact,** contact lens. **~ dépoli/grossissant,** frosted/magnifying glass. **~rie** *n.f.* (*objets*) glassware.

verrière /vɛrjɛr/ *n.f.* (*toit*) glass roof; (*paroi*) glass wall.

verrou /vɛru/ *n.m.* bolt. **sous les ~s,** behind bars.

verrouiller /vɛruje/ *v.t.* bolt.

verrue /vɛry/ *n.f.* wart.

vers[1] /vɛr/ *prép.* towards; (*temps*) about.

vers[2] /vɛr/ *n.m.* (*ligne*) line. **les ~,** (*poésie*) verse.

versant /vɛrsɑ̃/ *n.m.* slope, side.

versatile /vɛrsatil/ *a.* fickle.

verse (à) /(a)vɛrs/ *adv.* in torrents.

versé /vɛrse/ *a.* **~ dans,** versed in.

Verseau /vɛrso/ *n.m.* **le ~,** Aquarius.

vers|er /vɛrse/ *v.t./i.* pour; (*larmes, sang*) shed; (*basculer*) overturn; (*payer*) pay. **~ement** *n.m.* payment.

verset /vɛrsɛ/ *n.m.* (*relig.*) verse.

version /vɛrsjɔ̃/ *n.f.* version; (*traduction*) translation.

verso /vɛrso/ *n.m.* back (of the page).

vert, ~e /vɛr, -t/ *a.* green; (*vieillard*) sprightly. —*n.m.* green.

vertèbre /vɛrtɛbr/ *n.f.* vertebra.

vertement /vɛrtəmɑ̃/ *adv.* sharply.

vertic|al, ~ale (*m. pl.* **~aux**) /vɛrtikal, -o/ *a. & n.f.* vertical. **à la ~ale, ~alement** *adv.* vertically.

vertig|e /vɛrtiʒ/ *n.m.* dizziness. **~es,** dizzy spells. **avoir le** *ou* **un ~e,** feel dizzy. **~ineux, ~ineuse** *a.* dizzy; (*très grand*) staggering.

vertu /vɛrty/ *n.f.* virtue. **en ~ de,** by virtue of. **~eux, ~euse** /-tɥø, -z/ *a.* virtuous.

verve /vɛrv/ *n.f.* spirit, wit.

verveine /vɛrvɛn/ *n.f.* verbena.

vésicule /vezikyl/ *n.f.* **~ biliaire,** gall-bladder.

vessie /vesi/ *n.f.* bladder.

veste /vɛst/ *n.f.* jacket.

vestiaire /vɛstjɛr/ *n.m.* cloakroom; (*sport*) changing-room.

vestibule /vɛstibyl/ *n.m.* hall.

vestige /vɛstiʒ/ *n.m.* (*objet*) relic; (*trace*) vestige.

veston /vɛstɔ̃/ *n.m.* jacket.

vêtement /vɛtmɑ̃/ *n.m.* article of clothing. **~s,** clothes.

vétéran /veterɑ̃/ *n.m.* veteran.

vétérinaire /veterinɛr/ *n.m./f.* vet, veterinary surgeon, (*Amer.*) veterinarian.

vétille /vetij/ *n.f.* trifle.

vêt|ir /vetir/ *v.t.,* **se ~ir** *v. pr.* dress. **~u** *a.* dressed (**de,** in).

veto /veto/ *n.m. invar.* veto.

vétuste /vetyst/ *a.* dilapidated.

veu|f, ~ve /vœf, -v/ *a.* widowed. —*n.m.* widower. —*n.f.* widow.

veuille /vœj/ *voir* **vouloir**.

veule /vøl/ *a.* feeble.

veut, veux /vø/ *voir* **vouloir**.

vexation /vɛksɑsjɔ̃/ *n.f.* humiliation.

vex|er /vɛkse/ *v.t.* upset, hurt. **se ~er** *v. pr.* be upset, be hurt. **~ant, ~ante** *a.* upsetting.

via /vja/ *prép.* via.

viable /vjabl/ *a.* viable.

viaduc /vjadyk/ *n.m.* viaduct.

viande /vjɑ̃d/ *n.f.* meat.

vibr|er /vibre/ *v.i.* vibrate; (*être ému*) thrill. **~ant, ~ante** *a.* (*émouvant*) vibrant. **~ation** *n.f.* vibration.

vicaire /vikɛr/ *n.m.* curate.

vice /vis/ *n.m.* (*moral*) vice; (*défectuosité*) defect.

vice- /vis/ *préf.* vice-.

vice versa /vis(e)vɛrsa/ *adv.* vice versa.

vicier /visje/ *v.t.* taint.

vicieu|x, ~se /visjø, -z/ *a.* depraved. —*n.m., f.* pervert.

vicin|al (*pl.* **~aux**) /visinal, -o/ *a.m.* **chemin ~al,** by-road, minor road.

vicomte /vikɔ̃t/ *n.m.* viscount.

victime /viktim/ *n.f.* victim; (*d'un accident*) casualty.

vict|oire /viktwar/ *n.f.* victory; (*sport*) win. **~orieux, ~orieuse** *a.* victorious; (*équipe*) winning.

victuailles /viktɥaj/ *n.f. pl.* provisions.

vidang|e /vidɑ̃ʒ/ *n.f.* emptying; (*auto.*) oil change; (*dispositif*) waste pipe. **~er** *v.t.* empty.

vide /vid/ *a.* empty. —*n.m.* emptiness, void; (*trou, manque*) gap; (*espace sans air*) vacuum. **à ~,** empty.

vidéo /video/ *a. invar.* video. **jeu ~,** video game. **~cassette** *n.f.* video(tape). **~thèque** *n.f.* video library.

vide-ordures /vidɔrdyr/ *n.m. invar.* (rubbish) chute.

vider /vide/ *v.t.* empty; (*poisson*) gut; (*expulser: fam.*) throw out. **~ les lieux,** vacate the premises. **se ~** *v. pr.* empty.

videur /vidœr/ *n.m.* bouncer.

vie /vi/ n.f. life; (durée) lifetime. à ∼, pour la ∼, for life. donner la ∼ à, give birth to. en ∼, alive. ∼ chère, high cost of living.

vieil /vjɛj/ voir vieux.

vieillard /vjɛjar/ n.m. old man.

vieille /vjɛj/ voir vieux.

vieillesse /vjɛjɛs/ n.f. old age.

vieill|ir /vjɛjir/ v.i. grow old, age; (mot, idée) become old-fashioned. —v.t. age. ∼issement n.m. ageing.

viens, vient /vjɛ̃/ voir venir.

vierge /vjɛrʒ/ n.f. virgin. la V∼, Virgo. —a. virgin; (feuille, film) blank.

vieux ou vieil*, vieille (m. pl. vieux) /vjø, vjɛj/ a. old. —n.m. old man. —n.f. old woman. les ∼, old people. mon ∼, (fam.) old man ou boy. ma vieille, (fam.) old girl, dear. vieille fille, (péj.) spinster. ∼ garçon, bachelor. ∼ jeu a. invar. old-fashioned.

vif, vive /vif, viv/ a. lively; (émotion, vent) keen; (froid) biting; (lumière) bright; (douleur, parole) sharp; (souvenir, style, teint) vivid; (succès, impatience) great. brûler/enterrer ∼, burn/bury alive. de vive voix, personally. avoir les nerfs à ∼, be on edge.

vigie /viʒi/ n.f. look-out.

vigilan|t, ∼te /viʒilɑ̃, -t/ a. vigilant. ∼ce n.f. vigilance.

vigne /viɲ/ n.f. (plante) vine; (vignoble) vineyard.

vigneron, ∼ne /viɲrɔ̃, -ɔn/ n.m., f. wine-grower.

vignette /viɲɛt/ n.f. (étiquette) label; (auto.) road tax sticker.

vignoble /viɲɔbl/ n.m. vineyard.

vigoureu|x, ∼se /vigurø, -z/ a. vigorous, sturdy.

vigueur /vigœr/ n.f. vigour. être/entrer en ∼, (loi) be/come into force. en ∼, (terme) in use.

VIH abrév. (virus d'immunodéficience humaine) HIV.

vil /vil/ a. vile, base.

vilain, ∼e /vilɛ̃, -ɛn/ a. (mauvais) nasty; (laid) ugly.

villa /vila/ n.f. (detached) house.

village /vilaʒ/ n.m. village.

villageois, ∼e /vilaʒwa, -z/ a. village. —n.m., f. villager.

ville /vil/ n.f. town; (importante) city. ∼ d'eaux, spa.

vin /vɛ̃/ n.m. wine. ∼ d'honneur, reception. ∼ ordinaire, table wine.

vinaigre /vinɛgr/ n.m. vinegar.

vinaigrette /vinɛgrɛt/ n.f. oil and vinegar dressing, vinaigrette.

vindicati|f, ∼ve /vɛ̃dikatif, -v/ a. vindictive.

vingt /vɛ̃/ (/vɛ̃t/ before vowel and in numbers 22–29) a. & n.m. twenty. ∼ième a. & n.m./f. twentieth.

vingtaine /vɛ̃tɛn/ n.f. une ∼ (de), about twenty.

vinicole /vinikɔl/ a. wine(-growing).

vinyle /vinil/ n.m. vinyl.

viol /vjɔl/ n.m. (de femme) rape; (de lieu, loi) violation.

violacé /vjɔlase/ a. purplish.

viol|ent, ∼ente /vjɔlɑ̃, -t/ a. violent. ∼emment /-amɑ̃/ adv. violently. ∼ence n.f. violence; (acte) act of violence.

viol|er /vjɔle/ v.t. rape; (lieu, loi) violate. ∼ation n.f. violation.

violet, ∼te /vjɔlɛ, -t/ a. & n.m. purple. —n.f. violet.

violon /vjɔlɔ̃/ n.m. violin. ∼iste /-ɔnist/ n.m./f. violinist. ∼ d'Ingres, hobby.

violoncell|e /vjɔlɔ̃sɛl/ n.m. cello. ∼iste /-elist/ n.m./f. cellist.

vipère /vipɛr/ n.f. viper, adder.

virage /viraʒ/ n.m. bend; (de véhicule) turn; (changement d'attitude: fig.) change of course.

virée /vire/ n.f. (fam.) trip, outing.

vir|er /vire/ v.i. turn. ∼er de bord, tack. ∼er au rouge/etc., turn red/etc. —v.t. (argent) transfer; (expulser: fam.) throw out. ∼ement n.m. (comm.) (credit) transfer.

virevolter /virvɔlte/ v.i. spin round, swing round.

virginité /virʒinite/ n.f. virginity.

virgule /virgyl/ n.f. comma; (dans un nombre) (decimal) point.

viril /viril/ a. manly, virile. ∼ité n.f. manliness, virility.

virtuel, ∼le /virtɥɛl/ a. virtual. ∼lement adv. virtually.

virtuos|e /virtɥoz/ n.m./f. virtuoso. ∼ité n.f. virtuosity.

virulen|t, ∼te /virylɑ̃, -t/ a. virulent. ∼ce n.f. virulence.

virus /virys/ n.m. virus.

vis¹ /vi/ voir vivre, voir.

vis² /vis/ n.f. screw.

visa /viza/ n.m. visa.

visage /vizaʒ/ n.m. face.

vis-à-vis /vizavi/ adv. face to face, opposite. ∼ de, opposite; (à l'égard de) with respect to. —n.m. invar. (personne) person opposite.

viscères /visɛr/ n.m. pl. intestines.

visées /vize/ n.f. pl. aim. avoir des ∼ sur, have designs on.

viser /vize/ v.t. aim at; (*concerner*) be aimed at; (*timbrer*) stamp. —v.i. aim. ~ à, aim at; (*mesure, propos*) be aimed at.

visib|le /vizibl/ a. visible. ~ilité n.f. visibility. ~lement adv. visibly.

visière /vizjɛr/ n.f. (*de casquette*) peak; (*de casque*) visor.

vision /vizjɔ̃/ n.f. vision.

visionnaire /vizjɔnɛr/ a. & n.m./f. visionary.

visionn|er /vizjɔne/ v.t. view. ~euse n.f. (*appareil*) viewer.

visite /vizit/ n.f. visit; (*examen*) examination; (*personne*) visitor. **heures de ~,** visiting hours. ~ **guidée,** guided tour. **rendre ~ à,** visit. **être en ~ (chez qn.),** be visiting (s.o.).

visit|er /vizite/ v.t. visit; (*examiner*) examine. ~eur, ~euse n.m., f. visitor.

vison /vizɔ̃/ n.m. mink.

visqueu|x, ~se /viskø, -z/ a. viscous.

visser /vise/ v.t. screw (on).

visuel, ~le /vizɥɛl/ a. visual.

vit /vi/ voir **vivre, voir.**

vit|al (m. pl. ~aux) /vital, -o/ a. vital. ~alité n.f. vitality.

vitamine /vitamin/ n.f. vitamin.

vite /vit/ adv. fast, quickly; (*tôt*) soon. ~!, quick! **faire ~,** be quick.

vitesse /vitɛs/ n.f. speed; (*régime: auto.*) gear. **à toute ~,** at top speed. **en ~,** in a hurry, quickly.

vitic|ole /vitikɔl/ a. wine. ~ulteur n.m. wine-grower. ~ulture n.f. wine-growing.

vitrage /vitraʒ/ n.m. (*vitres*) windows. **double-~,** double glazing.

vitr|ail (pl. ~aux) /vitraj, -o/ n.m. stained-glass window.

vitr|e /vitr/ n.f. (window) pane; (*de véhicule*) window. ~é a. glass, glazed. ~er v.t. glaze.

vitrine /vitrin/ n.f. (shop) window; (*meuble*) display cabinet.

vivable /vivabl/ a. **ce n'est pas ~,** it's unbearable.

vivace /vivas/ a. (*plante, sentiment*) perennial.

vivacité /vivasite/ n.f. liveliness; (*agilité*) quickness; (*d'émotion, de l'air*) keenness; (*de souvenir, style, teint*) vividness.

vivant, ~e /vivɑ̃, -t/ a. (*doué de vie, en usage*) living; (*en vie*) alive, living; (*actif, vif*) lively. —n.m. **un bon ~,** a bon viveur. **de son ~,** in one's lifetime. **les ~s,** the living.

vivats /viva/ n.m. pl. cheers.

vive¹ /viv/ voir **vif.**

vive² /viv/ int. ~ **le roi/président/etc.!,** long live the king/president/etc.!

vivement /vivmɑ̃/ adv. (*vite, sèchement*) sharply; (*avec éclat*) vividly; (*beaucoup*) greatly. ~ **la fin!,** roll on the end, I'll be glad when it's the end!

vivier /vivje/ n.m. fish-pond.

vivifier /vivifje/ v.t. invigorate.

vivisection /vivisɛksjɔ̃/ n.f. vivisection.

vivoter /vivɔte/ v.i. plod on, get by.

vivre† /vivr/ v.i. live. ~ **de,** (*nourriture*) live on. —v.t. (*vie*) live; (*période, aventure*) live through. ~s n.m. pl. supplies. **faire ~,** (*famille etc.*) support. ~ **encore,** be still alive.

vlan /vlɑ̃/ int. bang.

vocabulaire /vɔkabylɛr/ n.m. vocabulary.

voc|al (m. pl. ~aux) /vɔkal, -o/ a. vocal.

vocalise /vɔkaliz/ n.f. voice exercise.

vocation /vɔkɑsjɔ̃/ n.f. vocation.

vociférer /vɔsifere/ v.t./i. scream.

vodka /vɔdka/ n.f. vodka.

vœu (pl. ~x) /vø/ n.m. (*souhait*) wish; (*promesse*) vow.

vogue /vɔg/ n.f. fashion, vogue.

voguer /vɔge/ v.i. sail.

voici /vwasi/ prép. here is, this is; (*au pluriel*) here are, these are. **me ~,** here I am. ~ **un an,** (*temps passé*) a year ago. ~ **un an que,** it is a year since.

voie /vwa/ n.f. (*route*) road; (*chemin*) way; (*moyen*) means, way; (*partie de route*) lane; (*rails*) track; (*quai*) platform. **en ~ de,** in the process of. **en ~ de développement,** (*pays*) developing. **par la ~ des airs,** by air. ~ **de dégagement,** slip-road. ~ **ferrée,** railway; (*Amer.*) railroad. ~ **lactée,** Milky Way. ~ **navigable,** waterway. ~ **publique,** public highway. ~ **sans issue,** cul-de-sac, dead end. **sur la bonne ~,** (*fig.*) well under way. **mettre sur une ~ de garage,** (*fig.*) sideline.

voilà /vwala/ prép. there is, that is; (*au pluriel*) there are, those are; (*voici*) here is; here are. **le ~,** there he is. ~!, right!; (*en offrant qch.*) there you are! ~ **un an,** (*temps passé*) a year ago. ~ **un an que,** it is a year since.

voilage /vwalaʒ/ n.m. net curtain.

voile¹ /vwal/ n.f. (*de bateau*) sail; (*sport*) sailing.

voile² /vwal/ n.m. veil; (*tissu léger et fin*) net.

voil|er[1] /vwale/ *v.t.* veil. **se ∼er** *v. pr.* (*devenir flou*) become hazy. **∼é** *a.* (*terme, femme*) veiled; (*flou*) hazy.

voiler[2] /vwale/ *v.t.,* **se ∼** *v. pr.* (*roue etc.*) buckle.

voilier /vwalje/ *n.m.* sailing-ship.

voilure /vwalyr/ *n.f.* sails.

voir† /vwar/ *v.t./i.* see. **se ∼** *v. pr.* (*être visible*) show; (*se produire*) be seen; (*se trouver*) find o.s.; (*se fréquenter*) see each other. **ça n'a rien à ∼ avec,** that has nothing to do with. **faire ∼, laisser ∼,** show. **je ne peux pas le ∼,** (*fam.*) I cannot stand him. **∼ trouble,** have blurred vision. **voyons!,** (*irritation*) come on!

voire /vwar/ *adv.* indeed.

voirie /vwari/ *n.f.* (*service*) highway maintenance. **travaux de ∼,** road-works.

voisin, ∼e /vwazɛ̃, -in/ *a.* (*proche*) neighbouring; (*adjacent*) next (**de,** to); (*semblable*) similar (**de,** to). —*n.m., f.* neighbour. **le ∼,** the man next door.

voisinage /vwazinaʒ/ *n.m.* neighbourhood; (*proximité*) proximity.

voiture /vwatyr/ *n.f.* (motor) car; (*wagon*) coach, carriage. **en ∼!,** all aboard! **∼ à cheval,** horse-drawn carriage. **∼ de course,** racing-car. **∼ d'enfant,** pram; (*Amer.*) baby carriage. **∼ de tourisme,** private car.

voix /vwa/ *n.f.* voice; (*suffrage*) vote. **à ∼ basse,** in a whisper.

vol[1] /vɔl/ *n.m.* (*d'avion, d'oiseau*) flight; (*groupe d'oiseaux etc.*) flock, flight. **à ∼ d'oiseau,** as the crow flies. **∼ libre,** hang-gliding. **∼ plané,** gliding.

vol[2] /vɔl/ *n.m.* (*délit*) theft; (*hold-up*) robbery. **∼ à la tire,** pickpocketing.

volage /vɔlaʒ/ *a.* fickle.

volaille /vɔlaj/ *n.f.* **la ∼,** (*poules etc.*) poultry. **une ∼,** a fowl.

volant /vɔlɑ̃/ *n.m.* (steering-)wheel; (*de jupe*) flounce.

volcan /vɔlkɑ̃/ *n.m.* volcano. **∼ique** /-anik/ *a.* volcanic.

volée /vɔle/ *n.f.* flight; (*oiseaux*) flight, flock; (*de coups, d'obus*) volley. **à toute ∼,** with full force. **de ∼, à la ∼,** in flight.

voler[1] /vɔle/ *v.i.* (*oiseau etc.*) fly.

vol|er[2] /vɔle/ *v.t./i.* steal (**à,** from). **il ne l'a pas ∼é,** he deserved it. **∼er qn.,** rob s.o. **∼eur, ∼euse** *n.m., f.* thief; *a.* thieving.

volet /vɔlɛ/ *n.m.* (*de fenêtre*) shutter; (*de document*) (folded *ou* tear-off) section. **trié sur le ∼,** hand-picked.

voleter /vɔlte/ *v.i.* flutter.

volière /vɔljɛr/ *n.f.* aviary.

volontaire /vɔlɔ̃tɛr/ *a.* voluntary; (*personne*) determined. —*n.m./f.* volunteer. **∼ment** *adv.* voluntarily; (*exprès*) intentionally.

volonté /vɔlɔ̃te/ *n.f.* (*faculté, intention*) will; (*souhait*) wish; (*énergie*) will-power. **à ∼,** (*à son gré*) at will. **bonne ∼,** goodwill. **mauvaise ∼,** ill will. **faire ses quatre ∼s,** do exactly as one pleases.

volontiers /vɔlɔ̃tje/ *adv.* (*de bon gré*) with pleasure, willingly, gladly; (*ordinairement*) readily.

volt /vɔlt/ *n.m.* volt. **∼age** *n.m.* voltage.

volte-face /vɔltəfas/ *n.f. invar.* about-face. **faire ∼,** turn round.

voltige /vɔltiʒ/ *n.f.* acrobatics.

voltiger /vɔltiʒe/ *v.i.* flutter.

volubile /vɔlybil/ *a.* voluble.

volume /vɔlym/ *n.m.* volume.

volumineu|x, ∼se /vɔlyminø, -z/ *a.* bulky.

volupt|é /vɔlypte/ *n.f.* sensual pleasure. **∼ueux, ∼ueuse** *a.* voluptuous.

vom|ir /vɔmir/ *v.t./i.* vomit. **∼i** *n.m.* vomit. **∼issement(s)** *n.m.* (*pl.*) vomiting.

vont /vɔ̃/ *voir* **aller**[1].

vorace /vɔras/ *a.* voracious.

vos /vo/ *voir* **votre.**

vote /vɔt/ *n.m.* (*action*) voting; (*d'une loi*) passing; (*suffrage*) vote.

vot|er /vɔte/ *v.i.* vote. —*v.t.* vote for; (*adopter*) pass; (*crédits*) vote. **∼ant, ∼ante** *n.m., f.* voter.

votre (*pl.* **vos**) /vɔtr, vo/ *a.* your.

vôtre /votr/ *pron.* **le** *ou* **la ∼, les ∼s,** yours.

vou|er /vwe/ *v.t.* dedicate (**à,** to); (*promettre*) vow. **∼é à l'échec,** doomed to failure.

vouloir† /vulwar/ *v.t.* want (**faire,** to do). **ça ne veut pas bouger/etc.,** it will not move/etc. **je voudrais/voudrais bien venir/etc.,** I should *ou* would like/really like to come/etc. **je veux bien venir/etc.,** I am happy to come/etc. **voulez-vous attendre/etc.?,** will you wait/etc.? **veuillez attendre/etc.,** kindly wait/etc. **∼ absolument faire,** insist on doing. **comme** *ou* **si vous voulez,** if you like *ou* wish. **en ∼ à qn.,** have a grudge against s.o.; (*être en colère contre*) be annoyed with s.o. **qu'est ce qu'il me veut?,** what does he want with me? **ne pas ∼ de qch./qn.,** not want sth./s.o. **∼ dire,** mean. **∼ du bien à,** wish well.

voulu /vuly/ *a.* (*délibéré*) intentional; (*requis*) required.

vous /vu/ *pron.* (*sujet, complément*) you; (*indirect*) (to) you; (*réfléchi*) yourself; (*pl.*) yourselves; (*l'un l'autre*) each other. **~-même** *pron.* yourself. **~-mêmes** *pron.* yourselves.

voûte /vut/ *n.f.* (*plafond*) vault; (*porche*) archway.

voûté /vute/ *a.* bent, stooped. **il a le dos ~,** he's stooped.

vouv|oyer /vuvwaje/ *v.t.* address politely (using *vous*). **~oiement** *n.m.* use of (polite) *vous*.

voyage /vwaja3/ *n.m.* journey, trip; (*par mer*) voyage. **~(s),** (*action*) travelling. **~ d'affaires,** business trip. **~ de noces,** honeymoon. **~ organisé,** (package) tour.

voyag|er /vwaja3e/ *v.i.* travel. **~eur, ~euse** *n.m., f.* traveller.

voyant[1], **~e** /vwajɑ̃, -t/ *a.* gaudy. —*n.f.* (*femme*) clairvoyant.

voyant[2] /vwajɑ̃/ *n.m.* (*signal*) (warning) light.

voyelle /vwajɛl/ *n.f.* vowel.

voyeur /vwajœr/ *n.m.* voyeur.

voyou /vwaju/ *n.m.* hooligan.

vrac (en) /(ɑ̃)vrak/ *adv.* in disorder; (*sans emballage, au poids*) loose, in bulk.

vrai /vrɛ/ *a.* true; (*réel*) real. —*n.m.* truth. **à ~ dire,** to tell the truth.

vraiment /vrɛmɑ̃/ *adv.* really.

vraisembl|able /vrɛsɑ̃blabl/ *a.* likely. **~ablement** *adv.* very likely. **~ance** *n.f.* likelihood, plausibility.

vrille /vrij/ *n.f.* (*aviat.*) spin.

vromb|ir /vrɔ̃bir/ *v.i.* hum. **~issement** *n.m.* humming.

VRP *abrév. m.* (*voyageur représentant placier*) rep.

vu /vy/ *voir* **voir.** —*a.* **bien/mal ~,** well/not well thought of. —*prép.* in view of. **~ que,** seeing that.

vue /vy/ *n.f.* (*spectacle*) sight; (*sens*) (eye)sight; (*panorama, idée*) view. **avoir en ~,** have in mind. **à ~,** (*tirer, payable*) at sight. **de ~,** by sight. **perdre de ~,** lose sight of. **en ~,** (*proche*) in sight; (*célèbre*) in the public eye. **en ~ de faire,** with a view to doing.

vulg|aire /vylgɛr/ *a.* (*grossier*) vulgar; (*ordinaire*) common. **~arité** *n.f.* vulgarity.

vulgariser /vylgarize/ *v.t.* popularize.

vulnérab|le /vylnerabl/ *a.* vulnerable. **~ilité** *n.f.* vulnerability.

vulve /vylv/ *n.f.* vulva.

W

wagon /vagɔ̃/ *n.m.* (*de voyageurs*) carriage; (*Amer.*) car; (*de marchandises*) wagon; (*Amer.*) freight car. **~-lit** (*pl.* **~s-lits**) *n.m.* sleeping-car, sleeper. **~-restaurant** (*pl.* **~s-restaurants**) *n.m.* dining-car.

walkman /wɔkman/ *n.m.* (P.) walkman.

wallon, ~ne /walɔ̃, -ɔn/ *a. & n.m., f.* Walloon.

waters /watɛr/ *n.m. pl.* toilet.

watt /wat/ *n.m.* watt.

w.-c. /(dublə)vese/ *n.m. pl.* toilet.

week-end /wikɛnd/ *n.m.* weekend.

western /wɛstɛrn/ *n.m.* western.

whisk|y (*pl.* **~ies**) /wiski/ *n.m.* whisky.

X

xénophob|e /ksenɔfɔb/ *a.* xenophobic. —*n.m./f.* xenophobe. **~ie** *n.f.* xenophobia.

xérès /kserɛs/ *n.m.* sherry.

xylophone /ksilɔfɔn/ *n.m.* xylophone.

Y

y /i/ *adv. & pron.* there; (*dessus*) on it; (*pl.*) on them; (*dedans*) in it; (*pl.*) in them. **s'y habituer,** (*à cela*) get used to it. **s'y attendre,** expect it. **y penser,** think of it. **il y entra,** (*dans cela*) he entered it. **j'y vais,** I'm on my way. **ça y est,** that is it. **y être pour qch.,** have sth. to do with it.

yacht /jɔt/ *n.m.* yacht.

yaourt /jaur(t)/ *n.m.* yoghurt. **~ière** /-tjɛr/ *n.f.* yoghurt maker.

yeux /jø/ *voir* **œil.**

yiddish /(j)idiʃ/ *n.m.* Yiddish.

yoga /jɔga/ *n.m.* yoga.

yougoslave /jugɔslav/ *a. & n.m./f.* Yugoslav.

Yougoslavie /jugɔslavi/ *n.f.* Yugoslavia.

yo-yo /jojo/ *n.m. invar.* (P.) yo-yo (P.).

yuppie /jøpi/ *n.m./f.* yuppie.

Z

zèbre /zɛbr/ *n.m.* zebra.
zébré /zebre/ *a.* striped.
zèle /zɛl/ *n.m.* zeal.
zélé /zele/ *a.* zealous.
zénith /zenit/ *n.m.* zenith.
zéro /zero/ *n.m.* nought, zero; (*température*) zero; (*dans un numéro*) 0; (*football*) nil; (*football: Amer.*) zero; (*personne*) nonentity. **(re)partir de ~,** start from scratch.
zeste /zɛst/ *n.m.* peel. **un ~ de,** (*fig.*) a pinch of.
zézayer /zezeje/ *v.i.* lisp.

zigzag /zigzag/ *n.m.* zigzag. **en ~,** zigzag. **~uer** /-e/ *v.i.* zigzag.
zinc /zɛ̃g/ *n.m.* (*métal*) zinc; (*comptoir*: *fam.*) bar.
zizanie /zizani/ *n.f.* **semer la ~,** put the cat among the pigeons.
zizi /zizi/ *n.m.* (*fam.*) willy.
zodiaque /zɔdjak/ *n.m.* zodiac.
zona /zona/ *n.m.* (*méd.*) shingles.
zone /zon/ *n.f.* zone, area; (*faubourgs*) shanty town. **~ bleue,** restricted parking zone.
zoolog|ie /zɔɔlɔʒi/ *n.f.* zoology. **~ique** *a.* zoological. **~iste** *n.m./f.* zoologist.
zoom /zum/ *n.m.* zoom lens.
zut /zyt/ *int.* blast (it), (oh) hell.

ANGLAIS–FRANÇAIS
ENGLISH–FRENCH

A

a /eɪ, *unstressed* ə/ *a.* (*before vowel* **an** /æn, ən/) un(e). **I'm a painter,** je suis peintre. **ten pence a kilo,** dix pence le kilo. **once a year,** une fois par an.

aback /ə'bæk/ *adv.* **taken ~,** déconcerté, interdit.

abandon /ə'bændən/ *v.t.* abandonner. —*n.* désinvolture *f.* **~ed** *a.* (*behaviour*) débauché. **~ment** *n.* abandon *m.*

abashed /ə'bæʃt/ *a.* confus.

abate /ə'beɪt/ *v.i.* se calmer. —*v.t.* diminuer. **~ment** *n.* diminution *f.*

abattoir /'æbətwɑː(r)/ *n.* abattoir *m.*

abbey /'æbɪ/ *n.* abbaye *f.*

abb|ot /'æbət/ *n.* abbé *m.* **~ess** *n.* abbesse *f.*

abbreviat|e /ə'briːvɪeɪt/ *v.t.* abréger. **~ion** /-'eɪʃn/ *n.* abréviation *f.*

abdicat|e /'æbdɪkeɪt/ *v.t./i.* abdiquer. **~ion** /-'keɪʃn/ *n.* abdication *f.*

abdom|en /'æbdəmən/ *n.* abdomen *m.* **~inal** /-'dɒmɪnl/ *a.* abdominal.

abduct /æb'dʌkt/ *v.t.* enlever. **~ion** /-kʃn/ *n.* rapt *m.* **~or** *n.* ravisseur|r, -se *m., f.*

aberration /æbə'reɪʃn/ *n.* aberration *f.*

abet /ə'bet/ *v.t.* (*p.t.* **abetted**) (*jurid.*) encourager.

abeyance /ə'beɪəns/ *n.* **in ~,** (*matter*) en suspens; (*custom*) en désuétude.

abhor /əb'hɔː(r)/ *v.t.* (*p.t.* **abhorred**) exécrer. **~rence** /-'hɒrəns/ *n.* horreur *f.* **~rent** /-'hɒrənt/ *a.* exécrable.

abide /ə'baɪd/ *v.t.* supporter. **~ by,** respecter.

abiding /ə'baɪdɪŋ/ *a.* éternel.

ability /ə'bɪlətɪ/ *n.* aptitude *f.* (**to do,** à faire); (*talent*) talent *m.*

abject /'æbdʒekt/ *a.* abject.

ablaze /ə'bleɪz/ *a.* en feu. **~ with,** (*anger etc.: fig.*) enflammé de.

abl|e /'eɪbl/ *a.* (**-er, -est**) capable (**to,** de). **be ~e,** pouvoir; (*know how to*) savoir. **~y** *adv.* habilement.

ablutions /ə'bluːʃnz/ *n. pl.* ablutions *f. pl.*

abnormal /æb'nɔːml/ *a.* anormal. **~ity** /-'mælətɪ/ *n.* anomalie *f.* **~ly** *adv.* (*unusually*) exceptionnellement.

aboard /ə'bɔːd/ *adv.* à bord. —*prep.* à bord de.

abode /ə'bəʊd/ (*old use*) demeure *f.* **of no fixed ~,** sans domicile fixe.

aboli|sh /ə'bɒlɪʃ/ *v.t.* supprimer, abolir. **~tion** /æbə'lɪʃn/ *n.* suppression *f.,* abolition *f.*

abominable /ə'bɒmɪnəbl/ *a.* abominable.

abominat|e /ə'bɒmɪneɪt/ *v.t.* exécrer. **~ion** /-'neɪʃn/ *n.* abomination *f.*

aboriginal /æbə'rɪdʒənl/ *a. & n.* aborigène (*m.*).

aborigines /æbə'rɪdʒəniːz/ *n. pl.* aborigènes *m. pl.*

abort /ə'bɔːt/ *v.t.* faire avorter. —*v.i.* avorter. **~ive** *a.* (*attempt etc.*) manqué.

abortion /ə'bɔːʃn/ *n.* avortement *m.* **have an ~,** se faire avorter.

abound /ə'baʊnd/ *v.i.* abonder (**in,** en).

about /ə'baʊt/ *adv.* (*approximately*) environ; (*here and there*) çà et là; (*all round*) partout, autour; (*nearby*) dans les parages; (*of rumour*) en circulation. —*prep.* au sujet de; (*round*) autour de; (*somewhere in*) dans. **~-face,** **~-turn** *ns.* (*fig.*) volte-face *f. invar.* **~ here,** par ici. **be ~ to do,** être sur le point de faire. **how or what ~ leaving,** si on partait. **what's the film ~?,** quel est le sujet du film? **talk ~,** parler de.

above /ə'bʌv/ *adv.* au-dessus; (*on page*) ci-dessus. —*prep.* au-dessus de. **he is not ~ lying,** il n'est pas incapable de mentir. **~ all,** par-dessus tout. **~-board** *a.* honnête. **~-mentioned** *a.* mentionné ci-dessus.

abrasion /ə'breɪʒn/ *n.* frottement *m.*; (*injury*) écorchure *f.*

abrasive /ə'breɪsɪv/ *a.* abrasif; (*manner*) brusque. —*n.* abrasif *m.*

abreast /ə'brest/ *adv.* de front. **keep ~ of,** se tenir au courant de.

abridge /ə'brɪdʒ/ v.t. abréger. ∼ment n. abrégement m., réduction f.; (abridged text) abrégé m.
abroad /ə'brɔːd/ adv. à l'étranger; (far and wide) de tous côtés.
abrupt /ə'brʌpt/ a. (sudden, curt) brusque; (steep) abrupt. ∼ly adv. (suddenly) brusquement; (curtly, rudely) avec brusquerie. ∼ness n. brusquerie f.
abscess /'æbses/ n. abcès m.
abscond /əb'skɒnd/ v.i. s'enfuir.
abseil /'æbseɪl/ v.i. descendre en rappel.
absen|t¹ /'æbsənt/ a. absent; (look etc.) distrait. ∼ce n. absence f.; (lack) manque m. **in the** ∼**ce of,** à défaut de. ∼tly adv. distraitement. ∼t-minded a. distrait. ∼t-mindedness n. distraction f.
absent² /əb'sent/ v. pr. ∼ **o.s.,** s'absenter.
absentee /æbsən'tiː/ n. absent(e) m. (f.). ∼ism n. absentéisme m.
absolute /'æbsəluːt/ a. absolu; (coward etc.: fam.) véritable. ∼ly adv. absolument.
absolution /æbsə'luːʃn/ n. absolution f.
absolve /əb'zɒlv/ v.t. (from sin) absoudre (from, de); (from vow etc.) délier (from, de).
absor|b /əb'sɔːb/ v.t. absorber. ∼ption n. absorption f.
absorbent /əb'sɔːbənt/ a. absorbant. ∼ **cotton,** (Amer.) coton hydrophile m.
abst|ain /əb'steɪn/ v.i. s'abstenir (from, de). ∼ention /-'stenʃn/ n. abstention f.; (from drink) abstinence f.
abstemious /əb'stiːmɪəs/ a. sobre.
abstinen|ce /'æbstɪnəns/ n. abstinence f. ∼t a. sobre.
abstract¹ /'æbstrækt/ a. abstrait. —n. (quality) abstrait m.; (summary) résumé m.
abstract² /əb'strækt/ v.t. retirer, extraire. ∼ion /-kʃn/ n. extraction f.; (idea) abstraction f.
abstruse /əb'struːs/ a. obscur.
absurd /əb'sɜːd/ a. absurde. ∼ity n. absurdité f.
abundan|t /ə'bʌndənt/ a. abondant. ∼ce n. abondance f. ∼tly adv. (entirely) tout à fait.
abuse¹ /ə'bjuːz/ v.t. (misuse) abuser de; (ill-treat) maltraiter; (insult) injurier.
abus|e² /ə'bjuːs/ n. (misuse) abus m. (of, de); (insults) injures f. pl. ∼ive a. injurieux. **get** ∼**ive,** devenir grossier.
abut /ə'bʌt/ v.i. (p.t. abutted) être contigu (on, à).

abysmal /ə'bɪzməl/ a. (great) profond; (bad: fam.) exécrable.
abyss /ə'bɪs/ n. abîme m.
academic /ækə'demɪk/ a. universitaire; (scholarly) intellectuel; (pej.) théorique. —n. universitaire m./f. ∼ally /-lɪ/ adv. intellectuellement.
academ|y /ə'kædəmɪ/ n. (school) école f. **A∼y,** (society) Académie f. ∼ician /-'mɪʃn/ n. académicien(ne) m. (f.).
accede /ək'siːd/ v.i. ∼ **to,** (request, post, throne) accéder à.
accelerat|e /ək'seləreɪt/ v.t. accélérer. —v.i. (speed up) s'accélérer; (auto.) accélérer. ∼ion /-'reɪʃn/ n. accélération f.
accelerator /ək'seləreɪtə(r)/ n. (auto.) accélérateur m.
accent¹ /'æksənt/ n. accent m.
accent² /æk'sent/ v.t. accentuer.
accentuat|e /ək'sentʃueɪt/ v.t. accentuer. ∼ion /-'eɪʃn/ n. accentuation f.
accept /ək'sept/ v.t. accepter. ∼able a. acceptable. ∼ance n. acceptation f.; (approval, favour) approbation f.
access /'ækses/ n. accès m. (**to sth.,** à qch.; **to s.o.,** auprès de qn.). ∼ible /ək'sesəbl/ a. accessible. ∼ **road,** route d'accès f.
accession /æk'seʃn/ n. accession f.; (thing added) nouvelle acquisition f.
accessory /ək'sesərɪ/ a. accessoire. —n. accessoire m.; (person: jurid.) complice m./f.
accident /'æksɪdənt/ n. accident m.; (chance) hasard m. ∼al /-'dentl/ a. accidentel, fortuit. ∼ally /-'dentəlɪ/ adv. involontairement. ∼-prone, qui attire les accidents.
acclaim /ə'kleɪm/ v.t. acclamer. —n. acclamation(s) f. (pl.).
acclimat|e /'æklɪmeɪt/ v.t./i. (Amer.) (s')acclimater. ∼ion /-'meɪʃn/ n. (Amer.) acclimatation f.
acclimatiz|e /ə'klaɪmətaɪz/ v.t./i. (s')acclimater. ∼ation /-'zeɪʃn/ n. acclimatation f.
accommodat|e /ə'kɒmədeɪt/ v.t. loger, avoir de la place pour; (adapt) adapter; (supply) fournir; (oblige) obliger. ∼ing a. obligeant. ∼ion /-'deɪʃn/ n. (living premises) logement m.; (rented rooms) chambres f. pl.
accompan|y /ə'kʌmpənɪ/ v.t. accompagner. ∼iment n. accompagnement m. ∼ist n. accompagnateur, -trice m., f.
accomplice /ə'kʌmplɪs/ n. complice m./f.

accomplish /əˈkʌmplɪʃ/ v.t. (perform) accomplir; (achieve) réaliser. ~ed a. accompli. ~ment n. accomplissement m. ~ments n. pl. (abilities) talents m. pl.

accord /əˈkɔːd/ v.i. concorder. —v.t. accorder. —n. accord m. **of one's own ~,** de sa propre initiative. ~ance n. **in ~ance with,** conformément à.

according /əˈkɔːdɪŋ/ adv. ~ **to,** selon, suivant. ~ly adv. en conséquence.

accordion /əˈkɔːdɪən/ n. accordéon m.

accost /əˈkɒst/ v.t. aborder.

account /əˈkaʊnt/ n. (comm.) compte m.; (description) compte rendu m.; (importance) importance f. —v.t. considérer. ~ **for,** rendre compte de, expliquer. **on ~ of,** à cause de. **on no ~,** en aucun cas. **take into ~,** tenir compte de. ~able a. responsable (for, de; to, envers). ~ability /-əˈbɪlətɪ/ n. responsabilité f.

accountan|t /əˈkaʊntənt/ n. comptable m./f., expert-comptable m. ~cy n. comptabilité f.

accredited /əˈkredɪtɪd/ a. accrédité.

accrue /əˈkruː/ v.i. s'accumuler. ~ **to,** (come to) revenir à.

accumulat|e /əˈkjuːmjʊleɪt/ v.t./i. (s')accumuler. ~ion /-ˈleɪʃn/ n. accumulation f.

accumulator /əˈkjuːmjʊleɪtə(r)/ n. (battery) accumulateur m.

accura|te /ˈækjərət/ a. exact, précis. ~cy n. exactitude f., précision f. ~tely adv. exactement, avec précision.

accus|e /əˈkjuːz/ v.t. accuser. **the ~ed,** l'accusé(e) m.(f.). ~ation /ækjuːˈzeɪʃn/ n. accusation f.

accustom /əˈkʌstəm/ v.t. accoutumer. ~ed a. accoutumé. **become ~ed to,** s'accoutumer à.

ace /eɪs/ n. (card, person) as m.

ache /eɪk/ n. douleur f., mal m. —v.i. faire mal. **my leg ~s,** ma jambe me fait mal, j'ai mal à la jambe.

achieve /əˈtʃiːv/ v.t. réaliser, accomplir; (success) obtenir. ~ment n. réalisation f. (of, de); (feat) exploit m., réussite f.

acid /ˈæsɪd/ a. & n. acide (m.). ~ity /əˈsɪdətɪ/ n. acidité f. ~ **rain,** pluies acides f. pl.

acknowledge /əkˈnɒlɪdʒ/ v.t. reconnaître. ~ **(receipt of),** accuser réception de. ~ment n. reconnaissance f.; accusé de réception m.

acme /ˈækmɪ/ n. sommet m.

acne /ˈæknɪ/ n. acné f.

acorn /ˈeɪkɔːn/ n. (bot.) gland m.

acoustic /əˈkuːstɪk/ a. acoustique. ~s n. pl. acoustique f.

acquaint /əˈkweɪnt/ v.t. ~ **s.o. with sth.,** mettre qn. au courant de qch. **be ~ed with,** (person) connaître; (fact) savoir. ~ance n. (knowledge, person) connaissance f.

acquiesce /ækwɪˈes/ v.i. consentir. ~nce n. consentement m.

acqui|re /əˈkwaɪə(r)/ v.t. acquérir; (habit) prendre. ~sition /ækwɪˈzɪʃn/ n. acquisition f. ~sitive /əˈkwɪzɪtɪv/ a. avide, âpre au gain.

acquit /əˈkwɪt/ v.t. (p.t. **acquitted**) acquitter. ~ **o.s. well,** bien s'en tirer. ~tal n. acquittement m.

acre /ˈeɪkə(r)/ n. (approx.) demi-hectare m. ~age n. superficie f.

acrid /ˈækrɪd/ a. âcre.

acrimon|ious /ækrɪˈməʊnɪəs/ a. acerbe, acrimonieux. ~y /ˈækrɪmənɪ/ n. acrimonie f.

acrobat /ˈækrəbæt/ n. acrobate m./f. ~ic /-ˈbætɪk/ a. acrobatique. ~ics /-ˈbætɪks/ n. pl. acrobatie f.

acronym /ˈækrənɪm/ n. sigle m.

across /əˈkrɒs/ adv. & prep. (side to side) d'un côté à l'autre (de); (on other side) de l'autre côté (from, de); (crosswise) en travers (de), à travers. **go or walk ~,** traverser.

acrylic /əˈkrɪlɪk/ a. & n. acrylique (m.).

act /ækt/ n. (deed, theatre) acte m.; (in variety show) numéro m.; (decree) loi f. —v.i. agir; (theatre) jouer; (function) marcher; (pretend) jouer la comédie. —v.t. (part, role) jouer. ~ **as,** servir de. ~ing a. (temporary) intérimaire; n. (theatre) jeu m.

action /ˈækʃn/ n. action f.; (mil.) combat m. **out of ~,** hors de service. **take ~,** agir.

activate /ˈæktɪveɪt/ v.t. (machine) actionner; (reaction) activer.

activ|e /ˈæktɪv/ a. actif; (interest) vif; (volcano) en activité. ~ism n. activisme m. ~ist n. activiste m./f. ~ity /-ˈtɪvətɪ/ n. activité f.

ac|tor /ˈæktə(r)/ n. acteur m. ~tress n. actrice f.

actual /ˈæktʃʊəl/ a. réel; (example) concret. **the ~ pen which,** (the house itself) dans la maison elle-même. **no ~ promise,** pas de promesse en tant que telle. ~ity /-ˈælətɪ/ n. réalité f. ~ly adv. (in fact) en réalité, réellement.

actuary /'æktʃʊərɪ/ n. actuaire m./f.
acumen /'ækjʊmen, Amer. ə'kju:mən/ n. perspicacité f.
acupuncture /'ækjʊpʌŋktʃə(r)/ n. acupuncture f. **~ist** n. acupuncteur m.
acute /ə'kju:t/ a. aigu; (mind) pénétrant; (emotion) intense, vif; (shortage) grave. **~ly** adv. vivement. **~ness** n. intensité f.
ad /æd/ n. (fam.) annonce f.
AD abbr. après J.-C.
adamant /'ædəmənt/ a. inflexible.
Adam's apple /'ædəmz'æpl/ n. pomme d'Adam f.
adapt /ə'dæpt/ v.t./i. (s')adapter. **~ation** /-'teɪʃn/ n. adaptation f. **~or** n. (electr.) adaptateur m.; (for two plugs) prise multiple f.
adaptab|le /ə'dæptəbl/ a. souple; (techn.) adaptable. **~ility** /-'bɪlətɪ/ n. souplesse f.
add /æd/ v.t./i. ajouter. **~** (up), (total) additionner. **~ up to**, (total) s'élever à. **~ing machine**, machine à calculer f.
adder /'ædə(r)/ n. vipère f.
addict /'ædɪkt/ n. intoxiqué(e) m. (f.); (fig.) fanatique m./f.
addict|ed /ə'dɪktɪd/ a. **~ed to**, (drink) adonné à. **be ~ed to**, (fig.) être un fanatique de. **~ion** /-kʃn/ n. (med.) dépendance f.; (fig.) manie f. **~ive** a. (drug etc.) qui crée une dépendance.
addition /ə'dɪʃn/ n. addition f. **in ~**, en outre. **~al** /-ʃənl/ a. supplémentaire.
additive /'ædɪtɪv/ n. additif m.
address /ə'dres/ n. adresse f.; (speech) allocution f. **—v.t.** adresser; (speak to) s'adresser à. **~ee** /ædre'si:/ n. destinataire m./f.
adenoids /'ædɪnɔɪdz/ n. pl. végétations (adénoïdes) f. pl.
adept /'ædept, Amer. ə'dept/ a. & n. expert (at, en) (m.).
adequa|te /'ædɪkwət/ a. suffisant; (satisfactory) satisfaisant. **~cy** n. quantité suffisante f.; (of person) compétence f. **~tely** adv. suffisamment.
adhere /əd'hɪə(r)/ v.i. adhérer (to, à). **~ to**, (fig.) respecter. **~nce** /-rəns/ n. adhésion f.
adhesion /əd'hi:ʒn/ n. (grip) adhérence f.; (support: fig.) adhésion f.
adhesive /əd'hi:sɪv/ a. & n. adhésif (m.).
ad infinitum /ædɪnfɪ'naɪtəm/ adv. à l'infini.
adjacent /ə'dʒeɪsnt/ a. contigu (to, à).
adjective /'ædʒɪktɪv/ n. adjectif m.

adjoin /ə'dʒɔɪn/ v.t. être contigu à.
adjourn /ə'dʒɜ:n/ v.t. ajourner. **—v.t./i.** **~ (the meeting)**, suspendre la séance. **~ to**, (go) se retirer à.
adjudicate /ə'dʒu:dɪkeɪt/ v.t./i. juger.
adjust /ə'dʒʌst/ v.t. (machine) régler; (prices) (r)ajuster; (arrange) rajuster, arranger. **—v.t./i.** **~ (o.s.) to**, s'adapter à. **~able** a. réglable. **~ment** n. (techn.) réglage m.; (of person) adaptation f.
ad lib /æd'lɪb/ v.i. (p.t. **ad libbed**) (fam.) improviser.
administer /əd'mɪnɪstə(r)/ v.t. administrer.
administration /ədmɪnɪ'streɪʃn/ n. administration f.
administrative /əd'mɪnɪstrətɪv/ a. administratif.
administrator /əd'mɪnɪstreɪtə(r)/ n. administrateur, -trice m., f.
admirable /'ædmərəbl/ a. admirable.
admiral /'ædmərəl/ n. amiral m.
admir|e /əd'maɪə(r)/ v.t. admirer. **~ation** /ædmə'reɪʃn/ n. admiration f. **~er** n. admirateur, -trice m., f.
admissible /əd'mɪsəbl/ a. admissible.
admission /əd'mɪʃn/ n. admission f.; (to museum, theatre, etc.) entrée f.; (confession) aveu m.
admit /əd'mɪt/ v.t. (p.t. **admitted**) laisser entrer; (acknowledge) reconnaître, admettre. **~ to**, avouer. **~tance** n. entrée f. **~tedly** adv. il est vrai (que).
admonish /əd'mɒnɪʃ/ v.t. réprimander.
ado /ə'du:/ n. **without more ~**, sans plus de cérémonies.
adolescen|t /ædə'lesnt/ n. & a. adolescent(e) (m. (f.)). **~ce** n. adolescence f.
adopt /ə'dɒpt/ v.t. adopter. **~ed** a. (child) adoptif. **~ion** /-pʃn/ n. adoption f.
adoptive /ə'dɒptɪv/ a. adoptif.
ador|e /ə'dɔ:(r)/ v.t. adorer. **~able** a. adorable. **~ation** /ædə'reɪʃn/ n. adoration f.
adorn /ə'dɔ:n/ v.t. orner. **~ment** n. ornement m.
adrift /ə'drɪft/ a. & adv. à la dérive.
adroit /ə'drɔɪt/ a. adroit.
adulation /ædjʊ'leɪʃn/ n. adulation f.
adult /'ædʌlt/ a. & n. adulte (m./f.). **~hood** n. condition d'adulte f.
adulterate /ə'dʌltəreɪt/ v.t. falsifier, frelater, altérer.
adulter|y /ə'dʌltərɪ/ n. adultère m. **~er**, **~ess** ns. époulx, -se adultère m., f. **~ous** a. adultère.
advance /əd'vɑ:ns/ v.t. avancer. **—v.i.** (s')avancer; (progress) avancer. **—n.**

avance *f.* —*a.* (*payment*) anticipé. **in
~,** à l'avance. **~d** *a.* avancé; (*studies*)
supérieur. **~ment** *n.* avancement *m.*

advantage /əd'vɑːntɪdʒ/ *n.* avantage *m.*
take ~ of, profiter de; (*person*)
exploiter. **~ous** /ædvən'teɪdʒəs/ *a.*
avantageux.

advent /'ædvənt/ *n.* arrivée *f.*

Advent /'ædvənt/ *n.* Avent *m.*

adventur|e /əd'ventʃə(r)/ *n.* aventure *f.*
~er *n.* explora|teur, -trice *m.*, *f.*; (*pej.*)
aventurlier, -ière *m.*, *f.* **~ous** *a.*
aventureux.

adverb /'ædvɜːb/ *n.* adverbe *m.*

adversary /'ædvəsərɪ/ *n.* adversaire *m./f.*

advers|e /'ædvɜːs/ *a.* défavorable. **~ity**
/əd'vɜːsətɪ/ *n.* adversité *f.*

advert /'ædvɜːt/ *n.* (*fam.*) annonce *f.*;
(*TV*) pub *f.*, publicité *f.* **~isement**
/əd'vɜːtɪsmənt/ *n.* publicité *f.*; (*in
paper etc.*) annonce *f.*

advertis|e /'ædvətaɪz/ *v.t./i.* faire de la
publicité (pour); (*sell*) mettre une
annonce (pour vendre). **~ for,** (*seek*)
chercher (par voie d'annonce). **~ing** *n.*
publicité *f.* **~er** /-ə(r)/ *n.* annonceur *m.*

advice /əd'vaɪs/ *n.* conseil(s) *m.* (*pl.*);
(*comm.*) avis *m.* **some ~, a piece of ~,**
un conseil.

advis|e /əd'vaɪz/ *v.t.* conseiller; (*inform*)
aviser. **~e against,** déconseiller. **~able**
a. conseillé, prudent (**to,** de). **~er** *n.* conseiller, -ère *m.*, *f.* **~ory** *a.* consultatif.

advocate[1] /'ædvəkət/ *n.* (*jurid.*) avocat
m. **~s of,** les défenseurs de.

advocate[2] /'ædvəkeɪt/ *v.t.* recommander.

aegis /'iːdʒɪs/ *n.* **under the ~ of,** sous
l'égide de *f.*

aeon /'iːən/ *n.* éternité *f.*

aerial /'eərɪəl/ *a.* aérien. —*n.* antenne *f.*

aerobatics /eərə'bætɪks/ *n. pl.* acrobatie
aérienne *f.*

aerobics /eə'rəʊbɪks/ *n.* aérobic *m.*

aerodrome /'eərədrəʊm/ *n.* aérodrome
m.

aerodynamic /eərəʊdaɪ'næmɪk/ *a.*
aérodynamique.

aeroplane /'eərəpleɪn/ *n.* avion *m.*

aerosol /'eərəsɒl/ *n.* atomiseur *m.*

aesthetic /iːs'θetɪk, *Amer.* es'θetɪk/ *a.*
esthétique.

afar /ə'fɑː(r)/ *adv.* **from ~,** de loin.

affable /'æfəbl/ *a.* affable.

affair /ə'feə(r)/ *n.* (*matter*) affaire *f.*;
(*romance*) liaison *f.*

affect /ə'fekt/ *v.t.* affecter. **~ation**
/æfek'teɪʃn/ *n.* affectation *f.* **~ed** *a.*
affecté.

affection /ə'fekʃn/ *n.* affection *f.*

affectionate /ə'fekʃənət/ *a.* affectueux.

affiliat|e /ə'fɪlɪeɪt/ *v.t.* affilier. **~ed
company,** filiale *f.* **~ion** /-'eɪʃn/ *n.*
affiliation *f.*

affinity /ə'fɪnətɪ/ *n.* affinité *f.*

affirm /ə'fɜːm/ *v.t.* affirmer. **~ation**
/æfə'meɪʃn/ *n.* affirmation *f.*

affirmative /ə'fɜːmətɪv/ *a.* affirmatif.
—*n.* affirmative *f.*

affix /ə'fɪks/ *v.t.* apposer.

afflict /ə'flɪkt/ *v.t.* affliger. **~ion** /-kʃn/
n. affliction *f.*, détresse *f.*

affluen|t /'æflʊənt/ *a.* riche. **~ce** *n.*
richesse *f.*

afford /ə'fɔːd/ *v.t.* avoir les moyens
d'acheter; (*provide*) fournir. **~ to do,**
avoir les moyens de faire; (*be able*) se
permettre de faire. **can you ~ the
time?,** avez-vous le temps?

affray /ə'freɪ/ *n.* rixe *f.*

affront /ə'frʌnt/ *n.* affront *m.* —*v.t.*
insulter.

afield /ə'fiːld/ *adv.* **far ~,** loin.

afloat /ə'fləʊt/ *adv.* à flot.

afoot /ə'fʊt/ *adv.* **sth. is ~,** il se trame *or*
se prépare qch.

aforesaid /ə'fɔːsed/ *a.* susdit.

afraid /ə'freɪd/ *a.* **be ~,** avoir peur (**of,
to,** de; **that,** que); (*be sorry*) regretter. **I
am ~ that,** (*regret to say*) je regrette de
dire que.

afresh /ə'freʃ/ *adv.* de nouveau.

Africa /'æfrɪkə/ *n.* Afrique *f.* **~n** *a. & n.*
africain(e) (*m.* (*f.*)).

after /'ɑːftə(r)/ *adv. & prep.* après.
—*conj.* après que. **~ doing,** après avoir
fait. **~ all** après tout. **~-effect** *n.* suite *f.*
~-sales service, service après-vente *m.*
~ the manner of, d'après. **be ~,** (*seek*)
chercher.

aftermath /'ɑːftəmɑːθ/ *n.* suites *f. pl.*

afternoon /ɑːftə'nuːn/ *n.* après-midi
m./f. invar.

afters /'ɑːftəz/ *n. pl.* (*fam.*) dessert *m.*

aftershave /'ɑːftəʃeɪv/ *n.* lotion après-
rasage *f.*

afterthought /'ɑːftəθɔːt/ *n.* réflexion
après coup *f.* **as an ~,** en y repensant.

afterwards /'ɑːftəwədz/ *adv.* après, par
la suite.

again /ə'gen/ *adv.* de nouveau, encore
une fois; (*besides*) en outre. **do ~, see
~/etc.,** refaire, revoir/etc.

against /ə'genst/ *prep.* contre. **~ the
law,** illégal.

age /eɪdʒ/ *n.* âge *m.* —*v.t./i.* (*pres. p.*
ageing) vieillir. **~ group,** tranche
d'âge *f.* **~ limit,** limite d'âge *f.* **for ~s,**

(*fam.*) une éternité. **of ~,** (*jurid.*) majeur. **ten years of ~,** âgé de dix ans. **~less** *a.* toujours jeune.

aged[1] /eɪdʒd/ *a.* **~ six,** âgé de six ans.

aged[2] /'eɪdʒɪd/ *a.* âgé, vieux.

agen|cy /'eɪdʒənsɪ/ *n.* agence *f.*; (*means*) entremise *f.* **~t** *n.* agent *m.*

agenda /ə'dʒendə/ *n.* ordre du jour *m.*

agglomeration /əglɒmə'reɪʃn/ *n.* agglomération *f.*

aggravat|e /'ægrəveɪt/ *v.t.* (*make worse*) aggraver; (*annoy: fam.*) exaspérer. **~ion** /-'veɪʃn/ *n.* aggravation *f.*; exaspération *f.*; (*trouble: fam.*) ennuis *m. pl.*

aggregate /'ægrɪgət/ *a. & n.* total (*m.*).

aggress|ive /ə'gresɪv/ *a.* agressif. **~ion** /-ʃn/ *n.* agression *f.* **~iveness** *n.* agressivité *f.* **~or** *n.* agresseur *m.*

aggrieved /ə'griːvd/ *a.* peiné.

aghast /ə'gɑːst/ *a.* horrifié.

agil|e /'ædʒaɪl, *Amer.* 'ædʒl/ *a.* agile. **~ity** /ə'dʒɪlətɪ/ *n.* agilité *f.*

agitat|e /'ædʒɪteɪt/ *v.t.* agiter. **~ion** /-'teɪʃn/ *n.* agitation *f.* **~or** *n.* agitateur, -trice *m., f.*

agnostic /æg'nɒstɪk/ *a. & n.* agnostique (*m./f.*).

ago /ə'gəʊ/ *adv.* il y a. **a month ~,** il y a un mois. **long ~,** il y a long-temps. **how long ~?,** il y a combien de temps?

agog /ə'gɒg/ *a.* impatient, en émoi.

agon|y /'ægənɪ/ *n.* grande souffrance *f.*; (*mental*) angoisse *f.* **~ize** *v.i.* souffrir. **~ize over,** se torturer l'esprit pour. **~ized** *a.* angoissé. **~izing** *a.* angoissant.

agree /ə'griː/ *v.i.* être *or* se mettre d'accord (**on,** sur); (*of figures*) concorder. **—***v.t.* (*date*) convenir de. **~ that,** reconnaître que. **~ to do,** accepter de faire. **~ to sth.,** accepter qch. **onions don't ~ with me,** je ne digère pas les oignons. **~d** *a.* (*time, place*) convenu. **be ~d,** être d'accord.

agreeable /ə'griːəbl/ *a.* agréable. **be ~,** (*willing*) être d'accord.

agreement /ə'griːmənt/ *n.* accord *m.* **in ~,** d'accord.

agricultur|e /'ægrɪkʌltʃə(r)/ *n.* agriculture *f.* **~al** /-'kʌltʃərəl/ *a.* agricole.

aground /ə'graʊnd/ *adv.* **run ~,** (*of ship*) (s')échouer.

ahead /ə'hed/ *adv.* (*in front*) en avant, devant; (*in advance*) à l'avance. **~ of s.o.,** devant qn.; en avance sur qn. **~ of time,** en avance. **straight ~,** tout droit.

aid /eɪd/ *v.t.* aider. **—***n.* aide *f.* **in ~ of,** au profit de.

aide /eɪd/ *n.* aide *m./f.*

AIDS /eɪdz/ *n.* (*med.*) sida *m.*

ail /eɪl/ *v.t.* **what ~s you?,** qu'avez-vous? **~ing** *a.* souffrant. **~ment** *n.* maladie *f.*

aim /eɪm/ *v.t.* diriger; (*gun*) braquer (**at,** sur); (*remark*) destiner. **—***v.i.* viser. **—***n.* but *m.* **~ at,** viser. **~ to,** avoir l'intention de. **take ~,** viser. **~less** *a.,* **~lessly** *adv.* sans but.

air /eə(r)/ *n.* air *m.* **—***v.t.* aérer; (*views*) exposer librement. **—***a.* (*base etc.*) aérien. **~-bed** *n.* matelas pneumatique *m.* **~-conditioned** *a.* climatisé. **~-conditioning** *n.* climatisation *f.* **~ force/hostess,** armée/hôtesse de l'air *f.* **~ letter,** aérogramme *m.* **~mail,** poste aérienne *f.* **by ~mail,** par avion. **~ raid,** attaque aérienne *f.* **~ terminal,** aérogare *f.* **~ traffic controller,** aiguilleur du ciel *m.* **by ~,** par avion. **in the ~,** (*rumour*) répandu; (*plan*) incertain. **on the ~,** sur l'antenne.

airborne /'eəbɔːn/ *a.* en (cours de) vol; (*troops*) aéroporté.

aircraft /'eəkrɑːft/ *n. invar.* avion *m.* **~-carrier** *n.* porte-avions *m. invar.*

airfield /'eəfiːld/ *n.* terrain d'aviation *m.*

airgun /'eəgʌn/ *n.* carabine à air comprimé *f.*

airlift /'eəlɪft/ *n.* pont aérien *m.* **—***v.t.* transporter par pont aérien.

airline /'eəlaɪn/ *n.* ligne aérienne *f.* **~r** /-ə(r)/ *n.* avion de ligne *m.*

airlock /'eəlɒk/ *n.* (*in pipe*) bulle d'air *f.*; (*chamber: techn.*) sas *m.*

airman /'eəmən/ *n.* (*pl.* **-men**) aviateur *m.*

airplane /'eəpleɪn/ *n.* (*Amer.*) avion *m.*

airport /'eəpɔːt/ *n.* aéroport *m.*

airsickness /'eəsɪknɪs/ *n.* mal de l'air *m.*

airtight /'eətaɪt/ *a.* hermétique.

airways /'eəweɪz/ *n. pl.* compagnie d'aviation *f.*

airworthy /'eəwɜːðɪ/ *a.* en état de navigation.

airy /'eərɪ/ *a.* (**-ier, -iest**) bien aéré; (*manner*) désinvolte.

aisle /aɪl/ *n.* (*of church*) nef latérale *f.*; (*gangway*) couloir *m.*

ajar /ə'dʒɑː(r)/ *adv. & a.* entr'ouvert.

akin /ə'kɪn/ *a.* **~ to,** apparenté à.

alabaster /'æləbɑːstə(r)/ *n.* albâtre *m.*

à la carte /ɑːlɑː'kɑːt/ *adv. & a.* (*culin.*) à la carte.

alacrity /ə'lækrətɪ/ *n.* empressement *m.*

alarm /ə'lɑːm/ *n.* alarme *f.*; (*clock*) réveil *m.* **—***v.t.* alarmer. **~-clock** *n.*

réveil *m*., réveille-matin *m. invar.* ∼**ist**
n. alarmiste *m./f.*

alas /ə'læs/ *int.* hélas.

albatross /'ælbətrɒs/ *n.* albatros *m.*

album /'ælbəm/ *n.* album *m.*

alcohol /'ælkəhɒl/ *n.* alcool *m.* ∼**ic**
/-'hɒlɪk/ *a.* alcoolique; (*drink*) al-
coolisé; *n.* alcoolique *m./f.* ∼**ism**
n. alcoolisme *m.*

alcove /'ælkəʊv/ *n.* alcôve *f.*

ale /eɪl/ *n.* bière *f.*

alert /ə'lɜːt/ *a.* (*lively*) vif; (*watchful*)
vigilant. —*n.* alerte *f.* —*v.t.* alerter. ∼
s.o. to, prévenir qn. de. **on the** ∼, sur le
qui-vive. ∼**ness** *n.* vivacité *f.*; vigilance
f.

A-level /'eɪlevl/ *n.* baccalauréat *m.*

algebra /'ældʒɪbrə/ *n.* algèbre *f.* ∼**ic**
/-'breɪk/ *a.* algébrique.

Algeria /æl'dʒɪərɪə/ *n.* Algérie *f.* ∼**n** *a.*
& *n.* algérien(ne) (*m.* (*f.*)).

algorithm /'ælgərɪðm/ *n.* algorithme *m.*

alias /'eɪlɪəs/ *n.* (*pl.* -**ases**) faux nom *m.*
—*adv.* alias.

alibi /'ælɪbaɪ/ *n.* (*pl.* -**is**) alibi *m.*

alien /'eɪlɪən/ *n.* & *a.* étranger, -ère (*m.,*
f.) (**to**, à).

alienat|e /'eɪlɪəneɪt/ *v.t.* aliéner. ∼**e**
one's friends/*etc.*, s'aliéner ses
amis/*etc.* ∼**ion** /-'neɪʃn/ *n.* aliénation *f.*

alight[1] /ə'laɪt/ *v.i.* (*person*) descendre;
(*bird*) se poser.

alight[2] /ə'laɪt/ *a.* en feu, allumé.

align /ə'laɪn/ *v.t.* aligner. ∼**ment** *n.*
alignement *m.*

alike /ə'laɪk/ *a.* semblable. —*adv.* de la
même façon. **look** *or* **be** ∼, se
ressembler.

alimony /'ælɪmənɪ, *Amer.* -məʊnɪ/ *n.*
pension alimentaire *f.*

alive /ə'laɪv/ *a.* vivant. ∼ **to**, sensible à,
sensibilisé à. ∼ **with**, grouillant de.

alkali /'ælkəlaɪ/ *n.* (*pl.* -**is**) alcali *m.*

all /ɔːl/ *a.* tout(e), tous, toutes. —*pron.*
tous, toutes; (*everything*) tout. —*adv.*
tout. ∼ (**the**) **men**, tous les hommes. ∼
of it, (le) tout. ∼ **of us**, nous tous. ∼
but, presque. ∼ **for sth.**, à fond pour
qch. ∼ **in**, (*exhausted*) épuisé. ∼**in**-*a.*
tout compris. ∼**in wrestling**, catch *m.*
∼ **out**, à fond. ∼-**out** *a.* (*effort*)
maximum. ∼ **over**, partout (sur *or*
dans); (*finished*) fini. ∼ **right**, bien;
(*agreeing*) bon! ∼ **round**, dans tous les
domaines; (*for all*) pour tous. ∼-**round**
a. général. ∼ **there**, (*alert*) éveillé. ∼
the better, tant mieux. ∼ **the same**,
tout de même. **the best of** ∼, le
meilleur.

allay /ə'leɪ/ *v.t.* calmer.

allegation /ælɪ'geɪʃn/ *n.* allégation *f.*

allege /ə'ledʒ/ *v.t.* prétendre. ∼**dly** /-ɪdlɪ/
adv. d'après ce qu'on dit.

allegiance /ə'liːdʒəns/ *n.* fidélité *f.*

allerg|y /'ælədʒɪ/ *n.* allergie *f.* ∼**ic**
/ə'lɜːdʒɪk/ *a.* allergique (**to**, à).

alleviate /ə'liːvɪeɪt/ *v.t.* alléger.

alley /'ælɪ/ *n.* (*street*) ruelle *f.*

alliance /ə'laɪəns/ *n.* alliance *f.*

allied /'ælaɪd/ *a.* allié.

alligator /'ælɪgeɪtə(r)/ *n.* alligator *m.*

allocat|e /'æləkeɪt/ *v.t.* (*assign*) attribuer;
(*share out*) distribuer. ∼**ion** /-'keɪʃn/ *n.*
allocation *f.*

allot /ə'lɒt/ *v.t.* (*p.t.* **allotted**) attribuer.
∼**ment** *n.* attribution *f.*; (*share*) partage
m.; (*land*) parcelle de terre *f.* (*louée*
pour la culture).

allow /ə'laʊ/ *v.t.* permettre; (*grant*)
accorder; (*reckon on*) prévoir; (*agree*)
reconnaître. ∼ **s.o. to**, permettre à qn.
de. ∼ **for**, tenir compte de.

allowance /ə'laʊəns/ *n.* allocation *f.*,
indemnité *f.* **make** ∼**s for**, être
indulgent envers; (*take into account*)
tenir compte de.

alloy /'ælɔɪ/ *n.* alliage *m.*

allude /ə'luːd/ *v.i.* ∼ **to**, faire allusion à.

allure /ə'lʊə(r)/ *v.t.* attirer.

allusion /ə'luːʒn/ *n.* allusion *f.*

ally[1] /'ælaɪ/ *n.* allié(e) *m.* (*f.*).

ally[2] /ə'laɪ/ *v.t.* allier. ∼ **o.s. with**, s'allier
à *or* avec.

almanac /'ɔːlmənæk/ *n.* almanach *m.*

almighty /ɔːl'maɪtɪ/ *a.* tout-puissant;
(*very great: fam.*) sacré, formidable.

almond /'ɑːmənd/ *n.* amande *f.*

almost /'ɔːlməʊst/ *adv.* presque.

alms /ɑːmz/ *n.* aumône *f.*

alone /ə'ləʊn/ *a.* & *adv.* seul.

along /ə'lɒŋ/ *prep.* le long de. —*adv.*
come ∼, venir. **go** *or* **walk** ∼, passer.
all ∼, (*time*) tout le temps, depuis le
début. ∼ **with**, avec.

alongside /əlɒŋ'saɪd/ *adv.* (*naut.*) bord à
bord. **come** ∼, accoster. —*prep.* le long
de.

aloof /ə'luːf/ *adv.* à l'écart. —*a.* distant.
∼**ness** *n.* réserve *f.*

aloud /ə'laʊd/ *adv.* à haute voix.

alphabet /'ælfəbet/ *n.* alphabet *m.* ∼**ical**
/-'betɪkl/ *a.* alphabétique.

alpine /'ælpaɪn/ *a.* (*landscape*) alpestre;
(*climate*) alpin.

Alpine /'ælpaɪn/ *a.* des Alpes.

Alps /ælps/ *n. pl.* the ∼, les Alpes *f. pl.*

already /ɔːl'redɪ/ *adv.* déjà.

alright /ɔːl'raɪt/ *a.* & *adv.* = **all right**.

Alsatian /æl'seɪʃn/ n. (*dog*) berger allemand m.

also /'ɔːlsəʊ/ adv. aussi.

altar /'ɔːltə(r)/ n. autel m.

alter /'ɔːltə(r)/ v.t./i. changer. ∼**ation** /-'reɪʃn/ n. changement m.; (*to garment*) retouche f.

alternate[1] /ɔːl'tɜːnət/ a. alterné, alternatif; (*Amer.*) = **alternative. on** ∼ **days**/*etc.*, (*first one then the other*) tous les deux jours/*etc.* ∼**ly** adv. tour à tour.

alternate[2] /'ɔːltəneɪt/ v.i. alterner. —v.t. faire alterner.

alternative /ɔːl'tɜːnətɪv/ a. autre; (*policy*) de rechange. —n. alternative f., choix m. ∼**ly** adv. comme alternative. **or** ∼**ly**, ou alors.

alternator /'ɔːltəneɪtə(r)/ n. alternateur m.

although /ɔːl'ðəʊ/ conj. bien que.

altitude /'æltɪtjuːd/ n. altitude f.

altogether /ɔːltə'geðə(r)/ adv. (*completely*) tout à fait; (*on the whole*) à tout prendre.

aluminium /æljʊ'mɪnɪəm/ (*Amer.* **aluminum** /ə'luːmɪnəm/) n. aluminium m.

always /'ɔːlweɪz/ adv. toujours.

am /æm/ see **be**.

a.m. /eɪ'em/ adv. du matin.

amalgamate /ə'mælgəmeɪt/ v.t./i. (s')amalgamer; (*comm.*) fusionner.

amass /ə'mæs/ v.t. amasser.

amateur /'æmətə(r)/ n. amateur m. —a. (*musician etc.*) amateur invar. ∼**ish** a. (*pej.*) d'amateur. ∼**ishly** adv. en amateur.

amaz|e /ə'meɪz/ v.t. étonner. ∼**ed** a. étonné. ∼**ement** n. étonnement m. ∼**ingly** adv. étonnamment.

ambassador /æm'bæsədə(r)/ n. ambassadeur m.

amber /'æmbə(r)/ n. ambre m.; (*auto.*) feu orange m.

ambigu|ous /æm'bɪgjʊəs/ a. ambigu. ∼**ity** /-'gjuːətɪ/ n. ambiguïté f.

ambiti|on /æm'bɪʃn/ n. ambition f. ∼**ous** a. ambitieux.

ambivalent /æm'bɪvələnt/ a. ambigu, ambivalent.

amble /'æmbl/ v.i. marcher sans se presser, s'avancer lentement.

ambulance /'æmbjʊləns/ n. ambulance f.

ambush /'æmbʊʃ/ n. embuscade f. —v.t. tendre une embuscade à.

amenable /ə'miːnəbl/ a. obligeant. ∼ **to,** (*responsive*) sensible à.

amend /ə'mend/ v.t. modifier, corriger. ∼**ment** n. (*to rule*) amendement m.

amends /ə'mendz/ n. pl. **make** ∼, réparer son erreur.

amenities /ə'miːnətɪz/ n. pl. (*pleasant features*) attraits m. pl.; (*facilities*) aménagements m. pl.

America /ə'merɪkə/ n. Amérique f. ∼**n** a. & n. américain(e) (m. (f.)).

amiable /'eɪmɪəbl/ a. aimable.

amicable /'æmɪkəbl/ a. amical.

amid(st) /ə'mɪd(st)/ prep. au milieu de.

amiss /ə'mɪs/ a. & adv. mal. **sth.** ∼, qch. qui ne va pas. **take sth.** ∼, être offensé par qch.

ammonia /ə'məʊnɪə/ n. (*gas*) ammoniac m.; (*water*) ammoniaque f.

ammunition /æmjʊ'nɪʃn/ n. munitions f. pl.

amnesia /æm'niːzɪə/ n. amnésie f.

amnesty /'æmnəstɪ/ n. amnistie f.

amok /ə'mɒk/ adv. **run** ∼, devenir fou furieux; (*crowd*) se déchaîner.

among(st) /ə'mʌŋ(st)/ prep. parmi, entre. ∼ **the crowd,** (*in the middle of*) parmi la foule. ∼ **the English**/*etc.*, (*race, group*) chez les Anglais/*etc.* ∼ **ourselves**/*etc.*, entre nous/*etc.*

amoral /eɪ'mɒrəl/ a. amoral.

amorous /'æmərəs/ a. amoureux.

amorphous /ə'mɔːfəs/ a. amorphe.

amount /ə'maʊnt/ n. quantité f.; (*total*) montant m.; (*sum of money*) somme f. —v.i. ∼ **to,** (*add up to*) s'élever à; (*be equivalent to*) revenir à.

amp /æmp/ n. (*fam.*) ampère m.

ampere /'æmpeə(r)/ n. ampère m.

amphibi|an /æm'fɪbɪən/ n. amphibie m. ∼**ous** a. amphibie.

ampl|e /'æmpl/ a. (**-er, -est**) (*enough*) (bien) assez de; (*large, roomy*) ample. ∼**y** adv. amplement.

amplif|y /'æmplɪfaɪ/ v.t. amplifier. ∼**ier** n. amplificateur m.

amputat|e /'æmpjʊteɪt/ v.t. amputer. ∼**ion** /-'teɪʃn/ n. amputation f.

amuck /ə'mʌk/ see **amok**.

amuse /ə'mjuːz/ v.t. amuser. ∼**ment** n. amusement m., divertissement m. ∼**ment arcade,** salle de jeux f.

an /æn, *unstressed* ən/ see **a**.

anachronism /ə'nækrənɪzəm/ n. anachronisme m.

anaem|ia /ə'niːmɪə/ n. anémie f. ∼**ic** a. anémique.

anaesthetic /ænɪs'θetɪk/ n. anesthésique m. **give an** ∼, faire une anesthésie (**to,** à).

analogue, analog /'ænəlɒg/ a. analogique.

analogy /ə'næɫədʒɪ/ n. analogie f.

analys|e (*Amer.* **analyze**) /'ænəlaɪz/ v.t. analyser. **~t** /-ɪst/ n. analyste m./f.

analysis /ə'næləsɪs/ n. (*pl.* **-yses** /-əsiːz/) analyse f.

analytic(al) /ænə'lɪtɪk(l)/ a. analytique.

anarch|y /'ænəkɪ/ n. anarchie f. **~ist** n. anarchiste m./f.

anathema /ə'næθəmə/ n. **that is ~ to me**, j'ai cela en abomination.

anatom|y /ə'nætəmɪ/ n. anatomie f. **~ical** /ænə'tɒmɪkl/ a. anatomique.

ancest|or /'ænsestə(r)/ n. ancêtre m. **~ral** /-'sestrəl/ a. ancestral.

anchor /'æŋkə(r)/ n. ancre f. —v.t. mettre à l'ancre. —v.i. jeter l'ancre.

anchovy /'æntʃəvɪ/ n. anchois m.

ancient /'eɪnʃənt/ a. ancien.

ancillary /æn'sɪlərɪ/ a. auxiliaire.

and /ænd, *unstressed* ən(d)/ conj. et. **go ~ see him**, allez le voir. **richer ~ richer**, de plus en plus riche.

anecdote /'ænɪkdəʊt/ n. anecdote f.

anemia /ə'niːmɪə/ n. (*Amer.*) = **anaemia**.

anesthetic /ænɪs'θetɪk/ (*Amer.*) = **anaesthetic**.

anew /ə'njuː/ adv. de *or* à nouveau.

angel /'eɪndʒl/ n. ange m. **~ic** /æn'dʒelɪk/ a. angélique.

anger /'æŋgə(r)/ n. colère f. —v.t. mettre en colère, fâcher.

angle[1] /'æŋgl/ n. angle m.

angle[2] /'æŋgl/ v.i. pêcher (à la ligne). **~ for**, (*fig.*) quêter. **~r** /-ə(r)/ n. pêcheulr, -se m., f.

Anglican /'æŋglɪkən/ a. & n. anglican(e) (m. (f.)).

Anglo- /'æŋgləʊ/ pref. anglo-.

Anglo-Saxon /'æŋgləʊ'sæksn/ a. & n. anglo-saxon(ne) (m. (f.)).

angr|y /'æŋgrɪ/ a. (**-ier**, **-iest**) fâché, en colère. **get ~y**, se fâcher, se mettre en colère (**with**, contre). **make s.o. ~y**, mettre qn. en colère. **~ily** adv. en colère.

anguish /'æŋgwɪʃ/ n. angoisse f.

angular /'æŋgjʊlə(r)/ a. (*features*) anguleux.

animal /'ænɪml/ n. & a. animal (m.).

animate[1] /'ænɪmət/ a. animé.

animat|e[2] /'ænɪmeɪt/ v.t. animer. **~ion** /-'meɪʃn/ n. animation f.

animosity /ænɪ'mɒsətɪ/ n. animosité f.

aniseed /'ænɪsiːd/ n. anis m.

ankle /'æŋkl/ n. cheville f. **~ sock**, socquette f.

annex /ə'neks/ v.t. annexer. **~ation** /ænek'seɪʃn/ n. annexion f.

annexe /'æneks/ n. annexe f.

annihilate /ə'naɪəleɪt/ v.t. anéantir.

anniversary /ænɪ'vɜːsərɪ/ n. anniversaire m.

announce /ə'naʊns/ v.t. annoncer. **~ment** n. annonce f. **~r** /-ə(r)/ n. (*radio, TV*) speaker(ine) m. (f.).

annoy /ə'nɔɪ/ v.t. agacer, ennuyer. **~ance** n. contrariété f. **~ed** a. fâché (**with**, contre). **get ~ed**, se fâcher. **~ing** a. ennuyeux.

annual /'ænjʊəl/ a. annuel. —n. publication annuelle f. **~ly** adv. annuellement.

annuity /ə'njuːətɪ/ n. rente (viagère) f.

annul /ə'nʌl/ v.t. (*p.t.* **annulled**) annuler. **~ment** n. annulation f.

anomal|y /ə'nɒməlɪ/ n. anomalie f. **~ous** a. anormal.

anonym|ous /ə'nɒnɪməs/ a. anonyme. **~ity** /ænə'nɪmətɪ/ n. anonymat m.

anorak /'ænəræk/ n. anorak m.

another /ə'nʌðə(r)/ a. & pron. un(e) autre. **~ coffee**, (*one more*) encore un café. **~ ten minutes**, encore dix minutes, dix minutes de plus.

answer /'ɑːnsə(r)/ n. réponse f.; (*solution*) solution f. —v.t. répondre à; (*prayer*) exaucer. —v.i. répondre. **~ the door**, ouvrir la porte. **~ back**, répondre. **~ for**, répondre de. **~ to**, (*superior*) dépendre de; (*description*) répondre à **~able** a. responsable (**for**, de; **to**, devant). **~ing machine**, répondeur m.

ant /ænt/ n. fourmi f.

antagonis|m /æn'tægənɪzəm/ n. antagonisme m. **~tic** /-'nɪstɪk/ a. antagoniste.

antagonize /æn'tægənaɪz/ v.t. provoquer l'hostilité de.

Antarctic /æn'tɑːktɪk/ a. & n. antarctique (m.).

ante- /'æntɪ/ pref. anti-, anté-.

antelope /'æntɪləʊp/ n. antilope f.

antenatal /'æntɪneɪtl/ a. prénatal.

antenna /æn'tenə/ n. (*pl.* **-ae** /-iː/) (*of insect*) antenne f.; (*pl.* **-as**; *aerial*; *Amer.*) antenne f.

anthem /'ænθəm/ n. (*relig.*) motet m.; (*of country*) hymne national m.

anthology /æn'θɒlədʒɪ/ n. anthologie f.

anthropolog|y /ænθrə'pɒlədʒɪ/ n. anthropologie f. **~ist** n. anthropologue m./f.

anti- /'æntɪ/ pref. anti-. **~-aircraft** a. antiaérien.

antibiotic /æntɪbaɪ'ɒtɪk/ n. antibiotique m.

antibody /'æntɪbɒdɪ/ n. anticorps m.

antic /'æntɪk/ n. bouffonnerie f.

anticipat|e /æn'tɪsɪpeɪt/ v.t. (foresee, expect) prévoir, s'attendre à; (forestall) devancer. ∼ion /-'peɪʃn/ n. attente f. in ∼ion of, en prévision or attente de.

anticlimax /æntɪ'klaɪmæks/ n. (let-down) déception f. it was an ∼, ça n'a pas répondu à l'attente.

anticlockwise /æntɪ'klɒkwaɪz/ adv. & a. dans le sens inverse des aiguilles d'une montre.

anticyclone /æntɪ'saɪkləʊn/ n. anticyclone m.

antidote /'æntɪdəʊt/ n. antidote m.

antifreeze /'æntɪfriːz/ n. antigel m.

antihistamine /æntɪ'hɪstəmiːn/ n. antihistaminique m.

antipathy /æn'tɪpəθɪ/ n. antipathie f.

antiquated /'æntɪkweɪtɪd/ a. vieillot, suranné.

antique /æn'tiːk/ a. (old) ancien; (from antiquity) antique. —n. objet ancien m., antiquité f. ∼ dealer, antiquaire m./f. ∼ shop, magasin d'antiquités m.

antiquity /æn'tɪkwətɪ/ n. antiquité f.

anti-Semiti|c /æntɪsɪ'mɪtɪk/ a. antisémite. ∼sm /-'semɪtɪzəm/ n. antisémitisme m.

antiseptic /æntɪ'septɪk/ a. & n. antiseptique (m.).

antisocial /æntɪ'səʊʃl/ a. asocial, antisocial; (unsociable) insociable.

antithesis /æn'tɪθəsɪs/ n. (pl. -eses /-əsiːz/) antithèse f.

antlers /'æntləz/ n. pl. bois m. pl.

anus /'eɪnəs/ n. anus m.

anvil /'ænvɪl/ n. enclume f.

anxiety /æŋ'zaɪətɪ/ n. (worry) anxiété f.; (eagerness) impatience f.

anxious /'æŋkʃəs/ a. (troubled) anxieux; (eager) impatient (to, de). ∼ly adv. anxieusement; impatiemment.

any /'enɪ/ a. (some) du, de l', de la, des; (after negative) de, d'; (every) tout; (no matter which) n'importe quel. at ∼ moment, à tout moment. have you ∼ water?, avez-vous de l'eau? —pron. (no matter which one) n'importe lequel; (someone) quelqu'un; (any amount of it or them) en. I do not have ∼, je n'en ai pas. did you see ∼ of them?, en avez-vous vu? —adv. (a little) un peu. do you have ∼ more?, en avez-vous encore? do you have ∼ more tea?, avez-vous encore du thé? not ∼, nullement. I don't do it ∼ more, je ne le fais plus.

anybody /'enɪbɒdɪ/ pron. n'importe qui;

(somebody) quelqu'un; (after negative) personne. he did not see ∼, il n'a vu personne.

anyhow /'enɪhaʊ/ adv. de toute façon; (badly) n'importe comment.

anyone /'enɪwʌn/ pron. = **anybody**.

anything /'enɪθɪŋ/ pron. n'importe quoi; (something) quelque chose; (after negative) rien. he did not see ∼, il n'a rien vu. ∼ but, (cheap etc.) nullement. ∼ you do, tout ce que tu fais.

anyway /'enɪweɪ/ adv. de toute façon.

anywhere /'enɪweə(r)/ adv. n'importe où; (somewhere) quelque part; (after negative) nulle part. he does not go ∼, il ne va nulle part. ∼ you go, partout où tu vas, où que tu ailles. ∼ else, partout ailleurs.

apart /ə'pɑːt/ adv. (on or to one side) à part; (separated) séparé; (into pieces) en pièces. ∼ from, à part, excepté. ten metres ∼, (distant) à dix mètres l'un de l'autre. come ∼, (break) tomber en morceaux; (machine) se démonter. legs ∼, les jambes écartées. keep ∼, séparer. take ∼, démonter.

apartment /ə'pɑːtmənt/ n. (Amer.) appartement m. ∼s, logement m.

apath|y /'æpəθɪ/ n. apathie f. ∼etic /-'θetɪk/ a. apathique.

ape /eɪp/ n. singe m. —v.t. singer.

aperitif /ə'perətɪf/ n. apéritif m.

aperture /'æpətʃə(r)/ n. ouverture f.

apex /'eɪpeks/ n. sommet m.

apiece /ə'piːs/ adv. chacun.

apologetic /əpɒlə'dʒetɪk/ a. (tone etc.) d'excuse. be ∼, s'excuser. ∼ally /-lɪ/ adv. en s'excusant.

apologize /ə'pɒlədʒaɪz/ v.i. s'excuser (for, de; to, auprès de).

apology /ə'pɒlədʒɪ/ n. excuses f. pl.; (defence of belief) apologie f.

Apostle /ə'pɒsl/ n. apôtre m.

apostrophe /ə'pɒstrəfɪ/ n. apostrophe f.

appal /ə'pɔːl/ v.t. (p.t. **appalled**) épouvanter. ∼ling a. épouvantable.

apparatus /æpə'reɪtəs/ n. (machine & anat.) appareil m.

apparel /ə'pærəl/ n. habillement m.

apparent /ə'pærənt/ a. apparent. ∼ly adv. apparemment.

appeal /ə'piːl/ n. appel m.; (attractiveness) attrait m., charme m. —v.i. (jurid.) faire appel. ∼ to s.o., (beg) faire appel à qn.; (attract) plaire à qn. ∼ to s.o. for sth., demander qch. à qn. ∼ing a. (attractive) attirant.

appear /ə'pɪə(r)/ v.i. apparaître; (arrive) se présenter; (seem, be published) paraître; (*theatre*) jouer. ∼ **on TV**, passer à la télé. ∼**ance** *n.* apparition *f.*; (*aspect*) apparence *f.*

appease /ə'piːz/ *v.t.* apaiser.

appendicitis /əpendɪ'saɪtɪs/ *n.* appendicite *f.*

appendix /ə'pendɪks/ *n.* (*pl.* -**ices** /-ɪsiːz/) appendice *m.*

appetite /'æpɪtaɪt/ *n.* appétit *m.*

appetizer /'æpɪtaɪzə(r)/ *n.* (*snack*) amuse-gueule *m. invar.*; (*drink*) apéritif *m.*

appetizing /'æpɪtaɪzɪŋ/ *a.* appétissant.

applau|d /ə'plɔːd/ *v.t./i.* applaudir; (*decision*) applaudir à. ∼**se** *n.* applaudissements *m. pl.*

apple /'æpl/ *n.* pomme *f.* ∼**-tree** *n.* pommier *m.*

appliance /ə'plaɪəns/ *n.* appareil *m.*

applicable /'æplɪkəbl/ *a.* applicable.

applicant /'æplɪkənt/ *n.* candidat(e) *m.* (*f.*) (**for**, à).

application /æplɪ'keɪʃn/ *n.* application *f.*; (*request, form*) demande *f.*; (*for job*) candidature *f.*

apply /ə'plaɪ/ *v.t.* appliquer. —*v.i.* ∼ **to**, (*refer*) s'appliquer à; (*ask*) s'adresser à. ∼ **for**, (*job*) postuler pour; (*grant*) demander. ∼ **o.s. to**, s'appliquer à. **applied** *a.* appliqué.

appoint /ə'pɔɪnt/ *v.t.* (*to post*) nommer; (*fix*) désigner. **well-**∼**ed** *a.* bien équipé. ∼**ment** *n.* nomination *f.*; (*meeting*) rendez-vous *m. invar.*; (*job*) poste *m.* **make an** ∼**ment**, prendre rendez-vous (**with**, avec).

apportion /ə'pɔːʃn/ *v.t.* répartir.

apprais|e /ə'preɪz/ *v.t.* évaluer. ∼**al** *n.* évaluation *f.*

appreciable /ə'priːʃəbl/ *a.* appréciable.

appreciat|e /ə'priːʃɪeɪt/ *v.t.* (*like*) apprécier; (*understand*) comprendre; (*be grateful for*). être reconnaissant de. —*v.i.* prendre de la valeur. ∼**ion** /-'eɪʃn/ *n.* appréciation *f.*; (*gratitude*) reconnaissance *f.*; (*rise*) augmentation *f.* ∼**ive** /ə'priːʃɪətɪv/ *a.* reconnaissant; (*audience*) enthousiaste.

apprehen|d /æprɪ'hend/ *v.t.* (*arrest, fear*) appréhender; (*understand*) comprendre. ∼**sion** *n.* appréhension *f.*

apprehensive /æprɪ'hensɪv/ *a.* inquiet. **be** ∼ **of**, craindre.

apprentice /ə'prentɪs/ *n.* apprenti *m.* —*v.t.* mettre en apprentissage. ∼**ship** *n.* apprentissage *m.*

approach /ə'prəʊtʃ/ *v.t.* (s')approcher de; (*accost*) aborder; (*with request*) s'adresser à. —*v.i.* (s')approcher. —*n.*

approche *f.* **an** ∼ **to**, (*problem*) une façon d'aborder; (*person*) une démarche auprès de. ∼**able** *a.* accessible; (*person*) abordable.

appropriate[1] /ə'prəʊprɪət/ *a.* approprié, propre. ∼**ly** *adv.* à propos.

appropriate[2] /ə'prəʊprɪeɪt/ *v.t.* s'approprier.

approval /ə'pruːvl/ *n.* approbation *f.* **on** ∼, à *or* sous condition.

approv|e /ə'pruːv/ *v.t./i.* approuver. ∼**e of**, approuver. ∼**ingly** *adv.* d'un air *or* d'un ton approbateur.

approximate[1] /ə'prɒksɪmət/ *a.* approximatif. ∼**ly** *adv.* approximativement.

approximat|e[2] /ə'prɒksɪmeɪt/ *v.i.* ∼**e to**, se rapprocher de. ∼**ion** /-'meɪʃn/ *n.* approximation *f.*

apricot /'eɪprɪkɒt/ *n.* abricot *m.*

April /'eɪprəl/ *n.* avril *m.* **make an** ∼ **fool of**, faire un poisson d'avril à.

apron /'eɪprən/ *n.* tablier *m.*

apse /æps/ *n.* (*of church*) abside *f.*

apt /æpt/ *a.* (*suitable*) approprié; (*pupil*) doué. **be** ∼ **to**, avoir tendance à. ∼**ly** *adv.* à propos.

aptitude /'æptɪtjuːd/ *n.* aptitude *f.*

aqualung /'ækwəlʌŋ/ *n.* scaphandre autonome *m.*

aquarium /ə'kweərɪəm/ *n.* (*pl.* -**ums**) aquarium *m.*

Aquarius /ə'kweərɪəs/ *n.* le Verseau.

aquatic /ə'kwætɪk/ *a.* aquatique; (*sport*) nautique.

aqueduct /'ækwɪdʌkt/ *n.* aqueduc *m.*

Arab /'ærəb/ *n. & a.* arabe (*m./f.*). ∼**ic** *a.* & *n.* (*lang.*) arabe (*m.*). ∼**ic numerals**, chiffres arabes *m. pl.*

Arabian /ə'reɪbɪən/ *a.* arabe.

arable /'ærəbl/ *a.* arable.

arbiter /'ɑːbɪtə(r)/ *n.* arbitre *m.*

arbitrary /'ɑːbɪtrərɪ/ *a.* arbitraire.

arbitrat|e /'ɑːbɪtreɪt/ *v.i.* arbitrer. ∼**ion** /-'treɪʃn/ *n.* arbitrage *m.* ∼**or** *n.* arbitre *m.*

arc /ɑːk/ *n.* arc *m.*

arcade /ɑː'keɪd/ *n.* (*shops*) galerie *f.*; (*arches*) arcades *f. pl.*

arch[1] /ɑːtʃ/ *n.* arche *f.*; (*in church etc.*) arc *m.*; (*of foot*) voûte plantaire *f.* —*v.t./i.* (s')arquer.

arch[2] /ɑːtʃ/ *a.* (*playful*) malicieux.

arch- /ɑːtʃ/ *pref.* (*hypocrite etc.*) grand, achevé.

archaeolog|y /ɑːkɪ'ɒlədʒɪ/ *n.* archéologie *f.* ∼**ical** /-ə'lɒdʒɪkl/ *a.* archéologique. ∼**ist** *n.* archéologue *m./f.*

archaic /ɑːˈkeɪɪk/ a. archaïque.
archbishop /ɑːtʃˈbɪʃəp/ n. archevêque m.
archeology /ɑːkɪˈɒlədʒɪ/ n. (Amer.) = **archaeology**.
archer /ˈɑːtʃə(r)/ n. archer m. ⁓y n. tir à l'arc m.
archetype /ˈɑːkɪtaɪp/ n. archétype m., modèle m.
archipelago /ɑːkɪˈpeləgəʊ/ n. (pl. -os) archipel m.
architect /ˈɑːkɪtekt/ n. architecte m.
architectur|e /ˈɑːkɪtektʃə(r)/ n. architecture f. ⁓al /-ˈtektʃərəl/ a. architectural.
archiv|es /ˈɑːkaɪvz/ n. pl. archives f. pl. ⁓ist /-ɪvɪst/ n. archiviste m./f.
archway /ˈɑːtʃweɪ/ n. voûte f.
Arctic /ˈɑːktɪk/ a. & n. arctique (m.). **arctic** a. glacial.
ardent /ˈɑːdnt/ a. ardent. ⁓ly adv. ardemment.
ardour /ˈɑːdə(r)/ n. ardeur f.
arduous /ˈɑːdjʊəs/ a. ardu.
are /ɑː(r)/ see **be**.
area /ˈeərɪə/ n. (surface) superficie f.; (region) région f.; (district) quartier m.; (fig.) domaine m. **parking/picnic** ⁓, aire de parking/de pique-nique f.
arena /əˈriːnə/ n. arène f.
aren't /ɑːnt/ = **are not**.
Argentin|a /ɑːdʒənˈtiːnə/ n. Argentine f. ⁓e /ˈɑːdʒəntaɪn/, ⁓ian /-ˈtɪnɪən/ a. & n. argentin(e) (m. (f.)).
argu|e /ˈɑːgjuː/ v.i. (quarrel) se disputer; (reason) argumenter. —v.t. (debate) discuter. ⁓e that, alléguer que. ⁓able /-ʊəbl/ a. le cas selon certains. ⁓ably adv. selon certains.
argument /ˈɑːgjʊmənt/ n. dispute f.; (reasoning) argument m.; (discussion) débat m. ⁓ative /-ˈmentətɪv/ a. raisonneur, contrariant.
arid /ˈærɪd/ a. aride.
Aries /ˈeərɪːz/ n. le Bélier.
arise /əˈraɪz/ v.i. (p.t. arose, p.p. arisen) se présenter; (old use) se lever. ⁓ from, résulter de.
aristocracy /ærɪˈstɒkrəsɪ/ n. aristocratie f.
aristocrat /ˈærɪstəkræt, Amer. əˈrɪstəkræt/ n. aristocrate m./f. ⁓ic /-ˈkrætɪk/ a. aristocratique.
arithmetic /əˈrɪθmətɪk/ n. arithmétique f.
ark /ɑːk/ n. (relig.) arche f.
arm¹ /ɑːm/ n. bras m. ⁓ **in arm**, bras dessus bras dessous. ⁓-**band** n. brassard m.

arm² /ɑːm/ v.t. armer. ⁓ed **robbery**, vol à main armée m.
armament /ˈɑːməmənt/ n. armement m.
armchair /ˈɑːmtʃeə(r)/ n. fauteuil m.
armistice /ˈɑːmɪstɪs/ n. armistice m.
armour /ˈɑːmə(r)/ n. armure f.; (on tanks etc.) blindage m. ⁓-**clad**, ⁓ed adjs. blindé.
armoury /ˈɑːmərɪ/ n. arsenal m.
armpit /ˈɑːmpɪt/ n. aisselle f.
arms /ɑːmz/ n. pl. (weapons) armes f. pl. ⁓ **dealer**, trafiquant d'armes m.
army /ˈɑːmɪ/ n. armée f.
aroma /əˈrəʊmə/ n. arôme m. ⁓**tic** /ærəˈmætɪk/ a. aromatique.
arose /əˈrəʊz/ see **arise**.
around /əˈraʊnd/ adv. (tout) autour; (here and there) çà et là. —prep. autour de. ⁓ **here**, par ici.
arouse /əˈraʊz/ v.t. (awaken, cause) éveiller; (excite) exciter.
arrange /əˈreɪndʒ/ v.t. arranger; (time, date) fixer. ⁓ **to**, s'arranger pour. ⁓**ment** n. arrangement m. **make** ⁓**ments**, prendre des dispositions.
array /əˈreɪ/ v.t. (mil.) déployer; (dress) vêtir. —n. **an** ⁓ **of**, (display) un étalage impressionnant de.
arrears /əˈrɪəz/ n. pl. arriéré m. **in** ⁓, (rent) arriéré. **he is in** ⁓, il a des paiements en retard.
arrest /əˈrest/ v.t. arrêter; (attention) retenir. —n. arrestation f. **under** ⁓, en état d'arrestation.
arrival /əˈraɪvl/ n. arrivée f. **new** ⁓, nouveau venu m., nouvelle venue f.
arrive /əˈraɪv/ v.i. arriver.
arrogan|t /ˈærəgənt/ a. arrogant. ⁓**ce** n. arrogance f. ⁓**tly** adv. avec arrogance.
arrow /ˈærəʊ/ n. flèche f.
arse /ɑːs/ n. (sl.) cul m. (sl.).
arsenal /ˈɑːsənl/ n. arsenal m.
arsenic /ˈɑːsnɪk/ n. arsenic m.
arson /ˈɑːsn/ n. incendie criminel m. ⁓**ist** n. incendiaire m./f.
art /ɑːt/ n. art m.; (fine arts) beaux-arts m. pl. ⁓**s**, (univ.) lettres f. pl. ⁓ **gallery**, (public) musée (d'art) m.; (private) galerie (d'art) f. ⁓ **school**, école des beaux-arts f.
artefact /ˈɑːtɪfækt/ n. objet fabriqué m.
arter|y /ˈɑːtərɪ/ n. artère f. ⁓**ial** /-ˈtɪərɪəl/ a. artériel. ⁓**ial road**, route principale f.
artful /ˈɑːtfl/ a. astucieux, rusé. ⁓**ness** n. astuce f.
arthriti|s /ɑːˈθraɪtɪs/ n. arthrite f. ⁓**c** /-ɪtɪk/ a. arthritique.
artichoke /ˈɑːtɪtʃəʊk/ n. artichaut m.

article /'ɑːtɪkl/ *n.* article *m.* ~ **of clothing**, vêtement *m.* ~**d** *a.* (*jurid.*) en stage.

articulate[1] /ɑːˈtɪkjʊlət/ *a.* (*person*) capable de s'exprimer clairement; (*speech*) distinct.

articulat|e[2] /ɑːˈtɪkjʊleɪt/ *v.t./i.* articuler. ~**ed lorry**, semi-remorque *m.* ~**ion** /-ˈleɪʃn/ *n.* articulation *f.*

artifice /'ɑːtɪfɪs/ *n.* artifice *m.*

artificial /ɑːtɪˈfɪʃl/ *a.* artificiel. ~**ity** /-ʃɪˈælətɪ/ *n.* manque de naturel *m.*

artillery /ɑːˈtɪlərɪ/ *n.* artillerie *f.*

artisan /ɑːtɪˈzæn/ *n.* artisan *m.*

artist /'ɑːtɪst/ *n.* artiste *m./f.* ~**ic** /-ˈtɪstɪk/ *a.* artistique. ~**ry** *n.* art *m.*

artiste /ɑːˈtiːst/ *n.* (*entertainer*) artiste *m./f.*

artless /'ɑːtlɪs/ *a.* ingénu, naïf.

artwork /'ɑːtwɜːk/ *n.* (*of book*) illustrations *f. pl.*

as /æz, *unstressed* əz/ *adv. & conj.* comme; (*while*) pendant que. **as you get older**, en vieillissant. **as she came in**, en entrant. **as a mother**, en tant que mère. **as a gift**, en cadeau. **as from Monday**, à partir de lundi. **as tall as**, aussi grand que. ~ **for, as to**, quant à ~ **if**, comme si. **you look as if you're tired**, vous avez l'air (d'être) fatigué. **as much, as many**, autant (as, que). **as soon as**, aussitôt que. **as well**, aussi (as, bien que). **as wide as possible**, aussi large que possible.

asbestos /æzˈbestɒs/ *n.* amiante *f.*

ascend /əˈsend/ *v.t.* gravir; (*throne*) monter sur. —*v.i.* monter. ~**ant** *n.* **be in the** ~**ant**, monter.

ascent /əˈsent/ *n.* (*climbing*) ascension *f.*; (*slope*) côte *f.*

ascertain /æsəˈteɪn/ *v.t.* s'assurer de. ~ **that**, s'assurer que.

ascetic /əˈsetɪk/ *a.* ascétique. —*n.* ascète *m./f.*

ascribe /əˈskraɪb/ *v.t.* attribuer.

ash[1] /æʃ/ *n.* ~(-**tree**), frêne *m.*

ash[2] /æʃ/ *n.* cendre *f.* **Ash Wednesday**, Mercredi des Cendres *m.* ~**en** *a.* cendreux.

ashamed /əˈʃeɪmd/ *a.* **be** ~, avoir honte (**of**, de).

ashore /əˈʃɔː(r)/ *adv.* à terre.

ashtray /'æʃtreɪ/ *n.* cendrier *m.*

Asia /'eɪʃə, *Amer.* 'eɪʒə/ *n.* Asie *f.* ~**n** *a. & n.* asiatique (*m./f.*). **the** ~**n community**, la communauté indo-pakistanaise. ~**tic** /-ɪˈætɪk/ *a.* asiatique.

aside /əˈsaɪd/ *adv.* de côté. —*n.* aparté *m.* ~ **from**, à part.

ask /ɑːsk/ *v.t./i.* demander; (*a question*) poser; (*invite*) inviter. ~ **s.o. sth.**, demander qch. à qn. ~ **s.o. to do**, demander à qn. de faire. ~ **about**, (*thing*) se renseigner sur; (*person*) demander des nouvelles de. ~ **for**, demander.

askance /əˈskæns/ *adv.* **look** ~ **at**, regarder avec méfiance.

askew /əˈskjuː/ *adv. & a.* de travers.

asleep /əˈsliːp/ *a.* endormi; (*numb*) engourdi. —*adv.* **fall** ~, s'endormir.

asparagus /əˈspærəgəs/ *n.* (*plant*) asperge *f.*; (*culin.*) asperges *f. pl.*

aspect /'æspekt/ *n.* aspect *m.*; (*direction*) orientation *f.*

aspersions /əˈspɜːʃnz/ *n. pl.* **cast** ~ **on**, calomnier.

asphalt /'æsfælt, *Amer.* 'æsfɔːlt/ *n.* asphalte *m.* —*v.t.* asphalter.

asphyxiat|e /əsˈfɪksɪeɪt/ *v.t./i.* (s')asphyxier. ~**ion** /-ˈeɪʃn/ *n.* asphyxie *f.*

aspir|e /əsˈpaɪə(r)/ *v.i.* ~**e to**, aspirer à. ~**ation** /æspəˈreɪʃn/ *n.* aspiration *f.*

aspirin /'æsprɪn/ *n.* aspirine *f.*

ass /æs/ *n.* âne *m.*; (*person: fam.*) idiot(e) *m.* (*f.*).

assail /əˈseɪl/ *v.t.* assaillir. ~**ant** *n.* agresseur *m.*

assassin /əˈsæsɪn/ *n.* assassin *m.*

assassinat|e /əˈsæsɪneɪt/ *v.t.* assassiner. ~**ion** /-ˈneɪʃn/ *n.* assassinat *m.*

assault /əˈsɔːlt/ *n.* (*mil.*) assaut *m.*; (*jurid.*) agression *f.* —*v.t.* (*person: jurid.*) agresser.

assembl|e /əˈsembl/ *v.t.* (*things*) assembler; (*people*) rassembler. —*v.i.* s'assembler, se rassembler. ~**age** *n.* assemblage *m.*

assembly /əˈsemblɪ/ *n.* assemblée *f.* ~ **line**, chaîne de montage *f.*

assent /əˈsent/ *n.* assentiment *m.* —*v.i.* consentir.

assert /əˈsɜːt/ *v.t.* affirmer; (*one's rights*) revendiquer. ~**ion** /-ʃn/ *n.* affirmation *f.* ~**ive** *a.* affirmatif, péremptoire.

assess /əˈses/ *v.t.* évaluer; (*payment*) déterminer le montant de. ~**ment** *n.* évaluation *f.* ~**or** *n.* (*valuer*) expert *m.*

asset /'æset/ *n.* (*advantage*) atout *m.* ~**s**, (*comm.*) actif *m.*

assiduous /əˈsɪdjʊəs/ *a.* assidu.

assign /əˈsaɪn/ *v.t.* (*allot*) assigner. ~ **s.o. to**, (*appoint*) affecter qn. à.

assignment /əˈsaɪnmənt/ *n.* (*task*) mission *f.*, tâche *f.*; (*schol.*) rapport *m.*

assimilat|e /əˈsɪməleɪt/ *v.t./i.* (s')assimiler. ~**ion** /-ˈleɪʃn/ *n.* assimilation *f.*

assist /ə'sɪst/ v.t./i. aider. ⏤**ance** n. aide f.

assistant /ə'sɪstənt/ n. aide m./f.; (in shop) vendeur, -se m., f. —a. (manager etc.) adjoint.

associate¹ /ə'səʊʃɪeɪt/ v.t. associer. —v.i. ⏤**e with**, fréquenter. ⏤**ion** /-'eɪʃn/ n. association f.

associate² /ə'səʊʃɪət/ n. & a. associé(e) (m. (f.)).

assort|ed /ə'sɔːtɪd/ a. divers; (foods) assortis. ⏤**ment** n. assortiment m. **an** ⏤**ment of guests**/etc., des invités/etc. divers.

assume /ə'sjuːm/ v.t. supposer, présumer; (power, attitude) prendre; (role, burden) assumer.

assumption /ə'sʌmpʃn/ n. (sth. supposed) supposition f.

assurance /ə'ʃʊərəns/ n. assurance f.

assure /ə'ʃʊə(r)/ v.t. assurer. ⏤**d** a. assuré. ⏤**dly** /-rɪdlɪ/ adv. assurément.

asterisk /'æstərɪsk/ n. astérisque m.

astern /ə'stɜːn/ adv. à l'arrière.

asthma /'æsmə/ n. asthme m. ⏤**tic** /-'mætɪk/ a. & n. asthmatique (m./f.).

astonish /ə'stɒnɪʃ/ v.t. étonner. ⏤**ingly** adv. étonnamment. ⏤**ment** n. étonnement m.

astound /ə'staʊnd/ v.t. stupéfier.

astray /ə'streɪ/ adv. & a. **go** ⏤, s'égarer. **lead** ⏤, égarer.

astride /ə'straɪd/ adv. & prep. à califourchon (sur).

astrolog|y /ə'strɒlədʒɪ/ n. astrologie f. ⏤**er** n. astrologue m.

astronaut /'æstrənɔːt/ n. astronaute m./f.

astronom|y /ə'strɒnəmɪ/ n. astronomie f. ⏤**er** n. astronome m. ⏤**ical** /æstrə'nɒmɪkl/ a. astronomique.

astute /ə'stjuːt/ a. astucieux. ⏤**ness** n. astuce f.

asylum /ə'saɪləm/ n. asile m.

at /æt, unstressed ət/ prep. à. **at the doctor's**/etc., chez le médecin/etc. **surprised at**, (cause) étonné de. **angry at**, fâché contre. **not at all**, pas du tout. **no wind**/etc. **at all**, (of any kind) pas le moindre vent/etc. **at night**, la nuit. **at once**, tout de suite; (simultaneously) à la fois. ⏤ **sea**, en mer. **at times**, parfois.

ate /et/ see **eat**.

atheis|t /'eɪθɪɪst/ n. athée m./f. ⏤**m** /-zəm/ n. athéisme m.

athlet|e /'æθliːt/ n. athlète m./f. ⏤**ic** /-'letɪk/ a. athlétique. ⏤**ics** /-'letɪks/ n. pl. athlétisme m.

Atlantic /ət'læntɪk/ a. atlantique. —n. ⏤ **(Ocean)**, Atlantique m.

atlas /'ætləs/ n. atlas m.

atmospher|e /'ætməsfɪə(r)/ n. atmosphère f. ⏤**ic** /-'ferɪk/ a. atmosphérique.

atoll /'ætɒl/ n. atoll m.

atom /'ætəm/ n. atome m. ⏤**ic** /ə'tɒmɪk/ a. atomique. ⏤**(ic) bomb**, bombe atomique f.

atomize /'ætəmaɪz/ v.t. atomiser. ⏤**r** /-ə(r)/ n. atomiseur m.

atone /ə'təʊn/ v.i. ⏤ **for**, expier. ⏤**ment** n. expiation f.

atrocious /ə'trəʊʃəs/ a. atroce.

atrocity /ə'trɒsətɪ/ n. atrocité f.

atrophy /'ætrəfɪ/ n. atrophie f. —v.t./i. (s')atrophier.

attach /ə'tætʃ/ v.t./i. (s')attacher; (letter) joindre (**to**, à). ⏤**ed** a. **be** ⏤**ed to**, (like) être attaché à. **the** ⏤**ed letter**, la lettre ci-jointe. ⏤**ment** n. (accessory) accessoire m.; (affection) attachement m.

attaché /ə'tæʃeɪ/ n. (pol.) attaché(e) m. (f.). ⏤ **case**, mallette f.

attack /ə'tæk/ n. attaque f.; (med.) crise f. —v.t. attaquer. ⏤**er** n. agresseur m., attaquant(e) m. (f.).

attain /ə'teɪn/ v.t. atteindre (à); (gain) acquérir. ⏤**able** a. accessible. ⏤**ment** n. acquisition f. (**of**, de). ⏤**ments**, réussites f. pl.

attempt /ə'tempt/ v.t. tenter. —n. tentative f. **an** ⏤ **on s.o.'s life**, un attentat contre qn.

attend /ə'tend/ v.t. assister à; (class) suivre; (school, church) aller à; (escort) accompagner. —v.i. assister. ⏤ **(to)**, (look after) s'occuper de. ⏤**ance** n. présence f.; (people) assistance f.

attendant /ə'tendənt/ n. employé(e) m. (f.); (servant) serviteur m. —a. concomitant.

attention /ə'tenʃn/ n. attention f.; ⏤**!**, (mil.) garde-à-vous! **pay** ⏤, faire or prêter attention (**to**, à).

attentive /ə'tentɪv/ a. attentif; (considerate) attentionné. ⏤**ly** adv. attentivement. ⏤**ness** n. attention f.

attenuate /ə'tenjʊeɪt/ v.t. atténuer.

attest /ə'test/ v.t./i. ⏤ **(to)**, attester. ⏤**ation** /æte'steɪʃn/ n. attestation f.

attic /'ætɪk/ n. grenier m.

attitude /'ætɪtjuːd/ n. attitude f.

attorney /ə'tɜːnɪ/ n. mandataire m.; (Amer.) avocat m.

attract /ə'trækt/ v.t. attirer. ⏤**ion** /-kʃn/ n. attraction f.; (charm) attrait m.

attractive /ə'træktɪv/ a. attrayant, séduisant. ⏤**ly** adv. agréablement. ⏤**ness** n. attrait m., beauté f.

attribute[1] /ə'trıbju:t/ v.t. ~ **to,** attribuer à.

attribute[2] /'ætrıbju:t/ n. attribut m.

attrition /ə'trıʃn/ n. **war of** ~, guerre d'usure f.

aubergine /'əʊbəʒi:n/ n. aubergine f.

auburn /'ɔːbən/ a. châtain roux invar.

auction /'ɔːkʃn/ n. vente aux enchères f.—v.t. vendre aux enchères. ~**eer** /-ə'nıə(r)/ n. commissaire-priseur m.

audaci|ous /ɔː'deıʃəs/ a. audacieux. ~**ty** /-æsətı/ n. audace f.

audible /'ɔːdəbl/ a. audible.

audience /'ɔːdıəns/ n. auditoire m.; (theatre, radio) public m.; (interview) audience f.

audio typist /'ɔːdıəʊ'taıpıst/ n. audiotypiste m./f.

audio-visual /ɔːdıəʊ'vıʒʊəl/ a. audio-visuel.

audit /'ɔːdıt/ n. vérification des comptes f. —v.t. vérifier.

audition /ɔː'dıʃn/ n. audition f. —v.t./i. auditionner.

auditor /'ɔːdıtə(r)/ n. commissaire aux comptes m.

auditorium /ɔːdı'tɔːrıəm/ n. (of theatre etc.) salle f.

augur /'ɔːgə(r)/ v.i. ~ **well/ill,** être de bon/mauvais augure.

August /'ɔːgəst/ n. août m.

aunt /ɑːnt/ n. tante f.

au pair /əʊ'peə(r)/ n. jeune fille au pair f.

aura /'ɔːrə/ n. atmosphère f.

auspices /'ɔːspısız/ n. pl. auspices m. pl., égide f.

auspicious /ɔː'spıʃəs/ a. favorable.

auster|e /ɔː'stıə(r)/ a. austère. ~**ity** /-erətı/ n. austérité f.

Australia /ɒ'streılıə/ n. Australie f. ~**n** a. & n. australien(ne) (m. (f.)).

Austria /'ɒstrıə/ n. Autriche f. ~**n** a. & n. autrichien(ne) (m. (f.)).

authentic /ɔː'θentık/ a. authentique. ~**ity** /-ən'tısətı/ n. authenticité f.

authenticate /ɔː'θentıkeıt/ v.t. authen-tifier.

author /'ɔːθə(r)/ n. auteur m. ~**ship** n. (origin) paternité f.

authoritarian /ɔːθɒrı'teərıən/ a. autori-taire.

authorit|y /ɔː'θɒrətı/ n. autorité f.; (permission) autorisation f. ~**ative** /-ıtatıv/ a. (credible) qui fait autorité; (trusted) autorisé; (manner) autoritaire.

authoriz|e /'ɔːθəraız/ v.t. autoriser. ~**ation** /-'zeıʃn/ n. autorisation f.

autistic /ɔː'tıstık/ a. autistique.

autobiography /ɔːtəbaı'ɒgrəfı/ n. autobiographie f.

autocrat /'ɔːtəkræt/ n. autocrate m. ~**ic** /-'krætık/ a. autocratique.

autograph /'ɔːtəgrɑːf/ n. autographe m. —v.t. signer, dédicacer.

auto-immune /ɔːtəʊ'mju:n/ a. auto-immune.

automat|e /'ɔːtəmeıt/ v.t. automatiser. ~**ion** /-'meıʃn/ n. automatisation f.

automatic /ɔːtə'mætık/ a. automatique. —n. (auto.) voiture automatique f. ~**ally** /-klı/ adv. automatiquement.

automobile /'ɔːtəməbi:l/ n. (Amer.) auto(mobile) f.

autonom|y /ɔː'tɒnəmı/ n. autonomie f. ~**ous** a. autonome.

autopsy /'ɔːtɒpsı/ n. autopsie f.

autumn /'ɔːtəm/ n. automne m. ~**al** /-'tʌmnəl/ a. automnal.

auxiliary /ɔːg'zılıərı/ a. & n. auxiliaire (m./f.) ~ (**verb**), auxiliaire m.

avail /ə'veıl/ v.t. ~ **o.s. of,** profiter de. —n. **of no** ~, inutile. **to no** ~, sans résultat.

availab|le /ə'veıləbl/ a. disponible. ~**ility** /-'bılətı/ n. disponibilité f.

avalanche /'ævəlɑːnʃ/ n. avalanche f.

avant-garde /ævã'gɑːd/ a. d'avant-garde.

avaric|e /'ævərıs/ n. avarice f. ~**ious** /-'rıʃəs/ a. avare.

avenge /ə'vendʒ/ v.t. venger. ~ **o.s.,** se venger (**on,** de).

avenue /'ævənju:/ n. avenue f.; (line of approach: fig.) voie f.

average /'ævərıdʒ/ n. moyenne f. —a. moyen. —v.t./i. faire la moyenne de; (produce, do) faire en moyenne. **on** ~, en moyenne.

avers|e /ə'vɜːs/ a. **be** ~**e to,** répugner à. ~**ion** /-ʃn/ n. aversion f.

avert /ə'vɜːt/ v.t. (turn away) détourner; (ward off) éviter.

aviary /'eıvıərı/ n. volière f.

aviation /eıvı'eıʃn/ n. aviation f.

avid /'ævıd/ a. avide.

avocado /ævə'kɑːdəʊ/ n. (pl. -os) avocat m.

avoid /ə'vɔıd/ v.t. éviter. ~**able** a. évitable. ~**ance** n. **the** ~**ance of s.o./sth. is . . .,** éviter qn./qch., c'est . . .

await /ə'weıt/ v.t. attendre.

awake /ə'weık/ v.t./i. (p.t. awoke, p.p. awoken) (s')éveiller. —a. **be** ~, ne pas dormir, être (r)éveillé.

awaken /ə'weıkən/ v.t./i. (s')éveiller.

award /ə'wɔːd/ v.t. attribuer. —n. récompense f., prix m.; (scholarship) bourse *f*. **pay** ~, augmentation (salariale) *f*.

aware /ə'weə(r)/ *a*. averti. **be** ~ **of**, (*danger*) être conscient de; (*fact*) savoir. **become** ~ **of**, prendre conscience de. ~**ness** *n*. conscience *f*.

awash /ə'wɒʃ/ *a*. inondé (**with**, de).

away /ə'weɪ/ *adv*. (*far*) (au) loin; (*absent*) absent, parti; (*persistently*) sans arrêt; (*entirely*) complètement. ~ **from**, loin de. **move** ~, s'écarter; (*to new home*) déménager. **six kilometres** ~, à six kilomètres (de distance). **take** ~, emporter. —*a*. & *n*. ~ (**match**), match à l'extérieur *m*.

awe /ɔ:/ *n*. crainte (révérencielle) *f*. ~-**inspiring**, ~**some** *adjs*. terrifiant; (*sight*) imposant. ~**struck** *a*. terrifié.

awful /'ɔ:fl/ *a*. affreux. ~**ly** /'ɔ:flɪ/ *adv*. (*badly*) affreusement; (*very*: *fam*.) rudement.

awhile /ə'waɪl/ *adv*. quelque temps.

awkward /'ɔ:kwəd/ *a*. difficile; (*inconvenient*) inopportun; (*clumsy*) maladroit; (*embarrassing*) gênant; (*embarrassed*) gêné. ~**ly** *adv*. maladroitement; avec gêne. ~**ness** *n*. maladresse *f*.; (*discomfort*) gêne *f*.

awning /'ɔ:nɪŋ/ *n*. auvent *m*.; (*of shop*) store *m*.

awoke, awoken /ə'wəʊk, ə'wəʊkən/ *see* **awake**.

awry /ə'raɪ/ *adv*. **go** ~, mal tourner. **sth. is** ~, qch. ne va pas.

axe, (*Amer*.) **ax** /æks/ *n*. hache *f*. —*v.t*. (*pres. p*. **axing**) réduire; (*eliminate*) supprimer; (*employee*) renvoyer.

axiom /'æksɪəm/ *n*. axiome *m*.

axis /'æksɪs/ *n*. (*pl*. **axes** /-si:z/) axe *m*.

axle /'æksl/ *n*. essieu *m*.

ay(e) /aɪ/ *adv*. & *n*. oui (*m. invar*.).

B

BA *abbr. see* **Bachelor of Arts**.

babble /'bæbl/ *v.i*. babiller; (*stream*) gazouiller. —*n*. babillage *m*.

baboon /bə'bu:n/ *n*. babouin *m*.

baby /'beɪbɪ/ *n*. bébé *m*. ~ **carriage**, (*Amer*.) voiture d'enfant *f*. ~-**sit** *v.i*. garder les enfants. ~-**sitter** *n*. baby-sitter *m./f*.

babyish /'beɪbɪʃ/ *a*. enfantin.

bachelor /'bætʃələ(r)/ *n*. célibataire *m*. **B**~ **of Arts/Science**, licencié(e) ès lettres/sciences *m*. (*f*.).

back /bæk/ *n*. (*of person, hand, page, etc*.) dos *m*.; (*of house*) derrière *m*.; (*of vehicle*) arrière *m*.; (*of room*) fond *m*.; (*of chair*) dossier *m*.; (*football*) arrière *m*. —*a*. de derrière, arrière *invar*.; (*taxes*) arriéré. —*adv*. en arrière; (*returned*) de retour, rentré. —*v.t*. (*support*) appuyer; (*bet on*) miser sur; (*vehicle*) faire reculer. —*v.i*. (*of person, vehicle*) reculer. **at the** ~ **of beyond**, au diable. **at the** ~ **of the book**, à la fin du livre. **come** ~, revenir. **give** ~, rendre. **take** ~, reprendre. **I want it** ~, je veux le récupérer. **in** ~ **of**, (*Amer*.) derrière. ~-**bencher** *n*. (*pol*.) membre sans portefeuille *m*. ~ **down**, abandonner, se dégonfler. ~ **number**, vieux numéro *m*. ~ **out**, se dégager, se dégonfler; (*auto*.) sortir en reculant. ~-**pedal** *v.i*. pédaler en arrière; (*fig*.) faire machine arrière (**on**, à propos de). ~ **up**, (*support*) appuyer. ~-**up** *n*. appui *m*.; (*Amer*., *fam*.) embouteillage *m*.; (*comput*.) sauvegarde *f*.; *a*. de réserve; (*comput*.) de sauvegarde.

backache /'bækeɪk/ *n*. mal de reins *m*., mal aux reins *m*.

backbiting /'bækbaɪtɪŋ/ *n*. médisance *f*.

backbone /'bækbəʊn/ *n*. colonne vertébrale *f*.

backdate /bæk'deɪt/ *v.t*. antidater; (*arrangement*) rendre rétroactif.

backer /'bækə(r)/ *n*. partisan *m*.; (*comm*.) bailleur de fonds *m*.

backfire /bæk'faɪə(r)/ *v.i*. (*auto*.) pétarader; (*fig*.) mal tourner.

backgammon /bæk'gæmən/ *n*. trictrac *m*.

background /'bækgraʊnd/ *n*. fond *m*., arrière-plan *m*.; (*context*) contexte *m*.; (*environment*) milieu *m*.; (*experience*) formation *f*. —*a*. (*music, noise*) de fond.

backhand /'bækhænd/ *n*. revers *m*. ~**ed** *a*. équivoque. ~**ed stroke**, revers *m*. ~**er** *n*. revers *m*.; (*bribe*: *sl*.) pot de vin *m*.

backing /'bækɪŋ/ *n*. appui *m*.

backlash /'bæklæʃ/ *n*. choc en retour *m*., répercussions *f. pl*.

backlog /'bæklɒg/ *n*. accumulation (de travail) *f*.

backpack /'bækpæk/ *n*. sac à dos *m*.

backside /'bæksaɪd/ *n*. (*buttocks*: *fam*.) derrière *m*.

backstage /bæk'steɪdʒ/ *a*. & *adv*. dans les coulisses.

backstroke /'bækstrəʊk/ *n*. dos crawlé *m*.

backtrack /'bæktræk/ *v.i.* rebrousser chemin; (*change one's opinion*) faire marche arrière.

backward /'bækwəd/ *a.* (*step etc.*) en arrière; (*retarded*) arriéré.

backwards /'bækwədz/ *adv.* en arrière; (*walk*) à reculons; (*read*) à l'envers; (*fall*) à la renverse. **go ∼ and forwards,** aller et venir.

backwater /'bækwɔːtə(r)/ *n.* (*pej.*) trou perdu *m.*

bacon /'beɪkən/ *n.* lard *m.*; (*in rashers*) bacon *m.*

bacteria /bæk'tɪərɪə/ *n. pl.* bactéries *f. pl.* ∼**l** *a.* bactérien.

bad /bæd/ *a.* (**worse, worst**) mauvais; (*wicked*) méchant; (*ill*) malade; (*accident*) grave; (*food*) gâté. **feel ∼,** se sentir mal. **go ∼,** se gâter. ∼ **language,** gros mots *m. pl.* ∼-**mannered** *a.* mal élevé. ∼-**tempered** *a.* grincheux. ∼**ly** *adv.* mal; (*hurt*) grièvement. **too ∼!,** tant pis; (*I'm sorry*) dommage! **want ∼ly,** avoir grande envie de.

badge /bædʒ/ *n.* insigne *m.*; (*of identity*) plaque *f.*

badger /'bædʒə(r)/ *n.* blaireau *m.* —*v.t.* harceler.

badminton /'bædmɪntən/ *n.* badminton *m.*

baffle /'bæfl/ *v.t.* déconcerter.

bag /bæg/ *n.* sac *m.* ∼**s,** (*luggage*) bagages *m.pl.*; (*under eyes*) poches *f. pl.* —*v.t.* (*p.t.* **bagged**) mettre en sac; (*take: fam.*) s'adjuger. ∼**s of,** (*fam.*) beaucoup de.

baggage /'bægɪdʒ/ *n.* bagages *m. pl.* ∼ **reclaim,** livraison des bagages *f.*

baggy /'bægɪ/ *a.* trop grand.

bagpipes /'bægpaɪps/ *n. pl.* cornemuse *f.*

Bahamas /bə'hɑːməz/ *n. pl.* **the ∼,** les Bahamas *f. pl.*

bail[1] /beɪl/ *n.* caution *f.* **on ∼,** sous caution. —*v.t.* mettre en liberté (provisoire) sous caution. ∼ **out,** (*fig.*) sortir d'affaire.

bail[2] /beɪl/ *n.* (*cricket*) bâtonnet *m.*

bail[3] /beɪl/ *v.t.* (*naut.*) écoper.

bailiff /'beɪlɪf/ *n.* huissier *m.*

bait /beɪt/ *n.* appât *m.* —*v.t.* appâter; (*fig.*) tourmenter.

bak|e /beɪk/ *v.t.* (faire) cuire (au four). —*v.i.* cuire (au four); (*person*) faire du pain or des gâteaux. ∼**ed beans,** haricots blancs à la tomate *m.pl.* ∼**ed potato,** pomme de terre en robe des champs *f.* ∼**er** *n.* boulanger, -ère *m.*, *f.*

∼**ing** *n.* cuisson *f.* ∼**ing-powder** *n.* levure *f.*

bakery /'beɪkərɪ/ *n.* boulangerie *f.*

Balaclava /bælə'klɑːvə/ *n.* ∼ **(helmet),** passe-montagne *m.*

balance /'bæləns/ *n.* équilibre *m.*; (*scales*) balance *f.*; (*outstanding sum: comm.*) solde *m.*; (*of payments, of trade*) balance *f.*; (*remainder*) reste *m.*; (*money in account*) position *f.* —*v.t.* tenir en équilibre; (*weigh up & comm.*) balancer; (*budget*) équilibrer; (*to compensate*) contrebalancer. —*v. i.* être en équilibre. ∼**d** *a.* équilibré.

balcony /'bælkənɪ/ *n.* balcon *m.*

bald /bɔːld/ *a.* (**-er, -est**) chauve; (*tyre*) lisse; (*fig.*) simple. ∼**ing** *a.* **be ∼ing,** perdre ses cheveux. ∼**ness** *n.* calvitie *f.*

bale[1] /beɪl/ *n.* (*of cotton*) balle *f.*; (*of straw*) botte *f.*

bale[2] /beɪl/ *v.i.* ∼ **out,** sauter en parachute.

baleful /'beɪlfʊl/ *a.* sinistre.

balk /bɔːk/ *v.t.* contrecarrer. —*v.i.* ∼ **at,** reculer devant.

ball[1] /bɔːl/ *n.* (*golf, tennis, etc.*) balle *f.*; (*football*) ballon *m.*; (*croquet, billiards, etc.*) boule *f.*; (*of wool*) pelote *f.*; (*sphere*) boule *f.* ∼-**bearing** *n.* roulement à billes *m.* ∼-**cock** *n.* robinet à flotteur *m.* ∼-**point** *n.* stylo à bille *m.*

ball[2] /bɔːl/ *n.* (*dance*) bal *m.*

ballad /'bæləd/ *n.* ballade *f.*

ballast /'bæləst/ *n.* lest *m.*

ballerina /bælə'riːnə/ *n.* ballerine *f.*

ballet /'bæleɪ/ *n.* ballet *m.*

ballistic /bə'lɪstɪk/ *a.* ∼ **missile,** engin balistique *m.*

balloon /bə'luːn/ *n.* ballon *m.*

ballot /'bælət/ *n.* scrutin *m.* ∼-**(paper),** bulletin de vote *m.* ∼-**box** *n.* urne *f.* —*v.i.* (*p.t.* **balloted**) (*pol.*) voter. —*v.t.* (*members*) consulter par voie de scrutin.

ballroom /'bɔːlrʊm/ *n.* salle de bal *f.*

ballyhoo /bælɪ'huː/ *n.* (*publicity*) battage *m.*; (*uproar*) tapage *m.*

balm /bɑːm/ *n.* baume *m.* ∼**y** *a.* (*fragrant*) embaumé; (*mild*) doux; (*crazy: sl.*) dingue.

baloney /bə'ləʊnɪ/ *n.* (*sl.*) idioties *f. pl.*, calembredaines *f. pl.*

balustrade /bælə'streɪd/ *n.* balustrade *f.*

bamboo /bæm'buː/ *n.* bambou *m.*

ban /bæn/ *v.t.* (*p.t.* **banned**) interdire. ∼ **from,** exclure de. —*n.* interdiction *f.*

banal /bə'nɑːl, *Amer.* 'beɪnl/ *a.* banal. ∼**ity** /-'ælətɪ/ *n.* banalité *f.*

banana /bə'nɑːnə/ n. banane f.

band /bænd/ n. (*strip, group of people*) bande f.; (*mus.*) orchestre m.; (*pop group*) groupe m. (*mil.*) fanfare f. —v.i. ~ **together**, se liguer.

bandage /'bændɪdʒ/ n. pansement m. —v.t. bander, panser.

bandit /'bændɪt/ n. bandit m.

bandstand /'bændstænd/ n. kiosque à musique m.

bandwagon /'bændwægən/ n. **climb on the ~**, prendre le train en marche.

bandy[1] /'bændɪ/ v.t. ~ **about**, (*rumours, ideas, etc.*) faire circuler.

bandy[2] /'bændɪ/ a. (**-ier, -iest**) qui a les jambes arquées.

bang /bæŋ/ n. (*blow, noise*) coup (violent) m.; (*explosion*) détonation f.; (*of door*) claquement m. —v.t./i. frapper; (*door*) claquer. —*int.* vlan. —*adv.* (*fam.*) exactement. ~ **in the middle,** en plein milieu. ~ **one's head,** se cogner la tête. ~**s,** frange f.

banger /'bæŋə(r)/ n. (*firework*) pétard m.; (*culin., sl.*) saucisse f. (**old**) ~, (*car: sl.*) guimbarde f.

bangle /'bæŋgl/ n. bracelet m.

banish /'bænɪʃ/ v.t. bannir.

banisters /'bænɪstəz/ n. pl. rampe (d'escalier) f.

banjo /'bændʒəʊ/ (*pl.* **-os**) banjo m.

bank[1] /bæŋk/ n. (*of river*) rive f.; (*of earth*) talus m.; (*of sand*) banc m. —v.t. (*earth*) amonceler; (*fire*) couvrir. —v.i. (*aviat.*) virer.

bank[2] /bæŋk/ n. banque f. —v.t. mettre en banque. —v.i. ~ **with,** avoir un compte à. ~ **account,** compte en banque m. ~ **card,** carte bancaire f. ~ **holiday,** jour férié m. ~ **on,** compter sur. ~ **statement,** relevé de compte m.

bank|ing /'bæŋkɪŋ/ n. opérations bancaires f. pl.; (*as career*) la banque. ~**er** n. banquier m.

banknote /'bæŋknəʊt/ n. billet de banque m.

bankrupt /'bæŋkrʌpt/ a. **be ~,** être en faillite. **go ~,** faire faillite. —n. failli(e) m. (*f.*). —v.t. mettre en faillite. ~**cy** n. faillite f.

banner /'bænə(r)/ n. bannière f.

banns /bænz/ n. pl. bans m. pl.

banquet /'bæŋkwɪt/ n. banquet m.

banter /'bæntə(r)/ n. plaisanterie f. —v.i. plaisanter.

bap /bæp/ n. petit pain m.

baptism /'bæptɪzəm/ n. baptême m.

Baptist /'bæptɪst/ n. baptiste m./f.

baptize /bæp'taɪz/ v.t. baptiser.

bar /bɑː(r)/ n. (*of metal*) barre f.; (*on window & jurid.*) barreau m.; (*of chocolate*) tablette f.; (*pub*) bar m.; (*counter*) comptoir m., bar m.; (*division: mus.*) mesure f.; (*fig.*) obstacle m. —v.t. (*p.t.* **barred**) (*obstruct*) barrer; (*prohibit*) interdire; (*exclude*) exclure. —*prep.* sauf. ~ **code,** code-barres m. invar. ~ **of soap,** savonnette f.

Barbados /bɑː'beɪdɒs/ n. Barbade f.

barbarian /bɑː'beərɪən/ n. barbare m./f.

barbari|c /bɑː'bærɪk/ a. barbare. ~**ty** /-ətɪ/ n. barbarie f.

barbarous /'bɑːbərəs/ a. barbare.

barbecue /'bɑːbɪkjuː/ n. barbecue m. —v.t. griller, rôtir (au barbecue).

barbed /bɑːbd/ a. ~ **wire,** fil de fer barbelé m.

barber /'bɑːbə(r)/ n. coiffeur m. (*pour hommes*).

barbiturate /bɑː'bɪtjʊrət/ n. barbiturique m.

bare /beə(r)/ a. (**-er, -est**) (*not covered or adorned*) nu; (*cupboard*) vide; (*mere*) simple. —v.t. mettre à nu.

barefaced /'beəfeɪst/ a. éhonté.

barefoot /'beəfʊt/ a. nu-pieds invar., pieds nus.

barely /'beəlɪ/ adv. à peine.

bargain /'bɑːgɪn/ n. (*deal*) marché m.; (*cheap thing*) occasion f. —v.i. négocier; (*haggle*) marchander. **not ~ for,** ne pas s'attendre à.

barge /bɑːdʒ/ n. chaland m. —v.i. ~ **in,** interrompre; (*into room*) faire irruption.

baritone /'bærɪtəʊn/ n. baryton m.

bark[1] /bɑːk/ n. (*of tree*) écorce f.

bark[2] /bɑːk/ n. (*of dog*) aboiement m. —v.i. aboyer.

barley /'bɑːlɪ/ n. orge f. ~ **sugar,** sucre d'orge m.

barmaid /'bɑːmeɪd/ n. serveuse f.

barman /'bɑːmən/ n. (*pl.* **-men**) barman m.

barmy /'bɑːmɪ/ a. (*sl.*) dingue.

barn /bɑːn/ n. grange f.

barometer /bə'rɒmɪtə(r)/ n. baromètre m.

baron /'bærən/ n. baron m. ~**ess** n. baronne f.

baroque /bə'rɒk, Amer. bə'rəʊk/ a. & n. baroque (m.).

barracks /'bærəks/ n. pl. caserne f.

barrage /'bærɑːʒ, Amer. bə'rɑːʒ/ n. (*barrier*) barrage m.; (*mil.*) tir de barrage m.; (*of complaints*) série f.

barrel /'bærəl/ *n.* tonneau *m.*; (*of oil*) baril *m.*; (*of gun*) canon *m.* ∼-**organ** *n.* orgue de Barbarie *m.*

barren /'bærən/ *a.* stérile.

barricade /bærɪ'keɪd/ *n.* barricade *f.* —*v.t.* barricader.

barrier /'bærɪə(r)/ *n.* barrière *f.*

barring /'bɑːrɪŋ/ *prep.* sauf.

barrister /'bærɪstə(r)/ *n.* avocat *m.*

barrow /'bærəʊ/ *n.* charrette à bras *f.*; (*wheelbarrow*) brouette *f.*

bartender /'bɑːtendə(r)/ *n.* (*Amer.*) barman *m.*

barter /'bɑːtə(r)/ *n.* troc *m.*, échange *m.* —*v.t.* troquer, échanger (**for**, contre).

base /beɪs/ *n.* base *f.* —*v.t.* baser (**on**, sur; **in**, à). —*a.* bas, ignoble. ∼**less** *a.* sans fondement.

baseball /'beɪsbɔːl/ *n.* base-ball *m.*

baseboard /'beɪsbɔːd/ *n.* (*Amer.*) plinthe *f.*

basement /'beɪsmənt/ *n.* sous-sol *m.*

bash /bæʃ/ *v.t.* cogner. —*n.* coup (violent) *m.* **have a** ∼ **at**, (*sl.*) s'essayer à. ∼**ed** *a.* enfoncé.

bashful /'bæʃfl/ *a.* timide.

basic /'beɪsɪk/ *a.* fondamental, élémentaire. **the** ∼**s**, les élements de base *m. pl.* ∼**ally** -klɪ/ *adv.* au fond.

basil /'bæzɪl, *Amer.* 'beɪzl/ *n.* basilic *m.*

basin /'beɪsn/ *n.* (*for liquids*) cuvette *f.*; (*for food*) bol *m.*; (*for washing*) lavabo *m.*; (*of river*) bassin *m.*

basis /'beɪsɪs/ *n.* (*pl.* **bases** /-siːz/) base *f.*

bask /bɑːsk/ *v.i.* se chauffer.

basket /'bɑːskɪt/ *n.* corbeille *f.*; (*with handle*) panier *m.*

basketball /'bɑːskɪtbɔːl/ *n.* basket(ball) *m.*

Basque /bɑːsk/ *a.* & *n.* basque (*m./f.*).

bass[1] /beɪs/ *a.* (*mus.*) bas, grave. —*n.* (*pl.* **basses**) basse *f.*

bass[2] /bæs/ *n. invar.* (*freshwater fish*) perche *f.*; (*sea*) bar *m.*

bassoon /bə'suːn/ *n.* basson *m.*

bastard /'bɑːstəd/ *n.* bâtard(e) *m.* (*f.*); (*sl.*) sallaud, -ope *m.*, *f.*

baste[1] /beɪst/ *v.t.* (*sew*) bâtir.

baste[2] /beɪst/ *v.t.* (*culin.*) arroser.

bastion /'bæstɪən/ *n.* bastion *m.*

bat[1] /bæt/ *n.* (*cricket etc.*) batte *f.*; (*table tennis*) raquette *f.* —*v.t.* (*p.t.* **batted**) (*ball*) frapper. **not** ∼ **an eyelid**, ne pas sourciller.

bat[2] /bæt/ *n.* (*animal*) chauve-souris *f.*

batch /bætʃ/ *n.* (*of people*) fournée *f.*; (*of papers*) paquet *m.*; (*of goods*) lot *m.*

bated /'beɪtɪd/ *a.* **with** ∼ **breath**, en retenant son souffle.

bath /bɑːθ/ *n.* (*pl.* **-s** /bɑːðz/) bain *m.*; (*tub*) baignoire *f.* (**swimming**) ∼**s**, piscine *f.* —*v.t.* donner un bain à —*a.* de bain. **have a** ∼, prendre un bain. ∼ **mat**, tapis de bain *f.*

bathe /beɪð/ *v.t.* baigner. —*v.i.* se baigner; (*Amer.*) prendre un bain. —*n.* bain (de mer) *m.* ∼**r** /-ə(r)/ *n.* baigneulr, -se *m.*, *f.*

bathing /'beɪðɪŋ/ *n.* baignade *f.* ∼-**costume** *n.* maillot de bain *m.*

bathrobe /'bæθrəʊb/ *m.* (*Amer.*) robe de chambre *f.*

bathroom /'bɑːθrʊm/ *n.* salle de bains *f.*

baton /'bætən/ *n.* (*mil.*) bâton *m.*; (*mus.*) baguette *f.*

battalion /bə'tæljən/ *n.* bataillon *m.*

batter /'bætə(r)/ *v.t.* (*strike*) battre; (*ill-treat*) maltraiter. —*n.* (*culin.*) pâte (à frire) *f.* ∼**ed** *a.* (*pan, car*) cabossé; (*face*) meurtri. ∼**ing** *n.* **take a** ∼**ing**, subir des coups.

battery /'bætərɪ/ *n.* (*mil., auto.*) batterie *f.*; (*of torch, radio*) pile *f.*

battle /'bætl/ *n.* bataille *f.*; (*fig.*) lutte *f.* —*v.i.* se battre.

battlefield /'bætlfiːld/ *n.* champ de bataille *m.*

battlements /'bætlmənts/ *n. pl.* (*crenellations*) créneaux *m. pl.*; (*wall*) remparts *m. pl.*

battleship /'bætlʃɪp/ *n.* cuirassé *m.*

baulk /bɔːk/ *v.t./i.* = **balk**.

bawd|y /'bɔːdɪ/ *a.* (**-ier, -iest**) paillard. ∼**iness** *n.* paillardise *f.*

bawl /bɔːl/ *v.t./i.* brailler.

bay[1] /beɪ/ *n.* (*bot.*) laurier *m.* ∼-**leaf** *n.* feuille de laurier *f.*

bay[2] /beɪ/ *n.* (*geog., archit.*) baie *f.*; (*area*) aire *f.* ∼ **window**, fenêtre en saillie *f.*

bay[3] /beɪ/ *n.* (*bark*) aboiement *m.* —*v.i.* aboyer. **at** ∼, aux abois. **keep** *or* **hold at** ∼, tenir à distance.

bayonet /'beɪənɪt/ *n.* baïonnette *f.*

bazaar /bə'zɑː(r)/ *n.* (*shop, market*) bazar *m.*; (*sale*) vente *f.*

BC *abbr.* (*before Christ*) avant J.-C.

be /biː/ *v.i.* (*present tense* **am, are, is**; *p.t.* **was, were**; *p.p.* **been**) être. **be hot/right**/*etc.*, avoir chaud/raison/*etc.* **he is 30,** (*age*) il a 30 ans. **it is fine/cold**/*etc.*, (*weather*) il fait beau/froid/*etc.* **I'm a painter—are you?**, je suis peintre—ah oui?, **how are you?**, (*health*) comment allez-vous? **he is to leave**, (*must*) il doit partir; (*will*) il va partir, il est prévu qu'il parte. **how much is it?**, (*cost*) ça fait *or* c'est combien? **be reading/walking**/*etc.*, (*aux.*) lire/marcher/*etc.* **the child was found,** l'enfant a été retrouvé, on a retrouvé l'enfant. **have been to,** avoir été à, être allé à.

beach /biːtʃ/ *n.* plage *f.*

beacon /ˈbiːkən/ *n.* (*lighthouse*) phare *m.*; (*marker*) balise *f.*

bead /biːd/ *n.* perle *f.*

beak /biːk/ *n.* bec *m.*

beaker /ˈbiːkə(r)/ *n.* gobelet *m.*

beam /biːm/ *n.* (*timber*) poutre *f.*; (*of light*) rayon *m.*; (*of torch*) faisceau *m.* —*v.i.* (*radiate*) rayonner. —*v.t.* (*broadcast*) diffuser. ~**ing** *a.* radieux.

bean /biːn/ *n.* haricot *m.*; (*of coffee*) grain *m.*

bear¹ /beə(r)/ *n.* ours *m.*

bear² /beə(r)/ *v.t.* (*p.t.* **bore**, *p.p.* **borne**) (*carry, show, feel*) porter; (*endure, sustain*) supporter; (*child*) mettre au monde. —*v.i.* ~ **left**/*etc.*, (*go*) prendre à gauche/*etc.* ~ **in mind,** tenir compte de. ~ **on,** se rapporter à. ~ **out,** corroborer. ~ **up!,** courage! ~**able** *a.* supportable. ~**er** *n.* porteulr, -se *m.*, *f.*

beard /bɪəd/ *n.* barbe *f.* ~**ed** *a.* barbu.

bearing /ˈbeərɪŋ/ *n.* (*behaviour*) maintien *m.*; (*relevance*) rapport *m.* **get one's** ~**s,** s'orienter.

beast /biːst/ *n.* bête *f.*; (*person*) brute *f.*

beastly /ˈbiːstlɪ/ *a.* (**-ier, -iest**) (*fam.*) détestable.

beat /biːt/ *v.t./i.* (*p.t.* **beat**, *p.p.* **beaten**) battre. —*n.* (*of drum, heart*) battement *m.*; (*mus.*) mesure *f.*; (*of policeman*) ronde *f.* ~ **a retreat,** battre en retraite. ~ **it!,** dégage! ~ **s.o. down,** faire baisser son prix à qn. ~ **off the competition,** éliminer la concurrence. ~ **up,** tabasser. **it** ~**s me,** (*fam.*) ça me dépasse. ~**er** *n.* batteur *m.* ~**ing** *n.* raclée *f.*

beautician /bjuːˈtɪʃn/ *n.* esthéticien(ne) *m.* (*f.*).

beautiful /ˈbjuːtɪfl/ *a.* beau. ~**ly** /-flɪ/ *adv.* merveilleusement.

beautify /ˈbjuːtɪfaɪ/ *v.t.* embellir.

beauty /ˈbjuːtɪ/ *n.* beauté *f.* ~ **parlour,** institut de beauté *m.* ~ **spot,** grain de beauté *m.*; (*fig.*) site pittoresque *m.*

beaver /ˈbiːvə(r)/ *n.* castor *m.*

became /bɪˈkeɪm/ *see* **become.**

because /bɪˈkɒz/ *conj.* parce que. ~ **of,** à cause de.

beck /bek/ *n.* **at the** ~ **and call of,** aux ordres de.

beckon /ˈbekən/ *v.t./i.* ~ **(to),** faire signe à.

become /bɪˈkʌm/ *v.t./i.* (*p.t.* **became**, *p.p.* **become**) devenir; (*befit*) convenir à. **what has** ~ **of her?,** qu'est-elle devenue?

becoming /bɪˈkʌmɪŋ/ *a.* (*seemly*) bienséant; (*clothes*) seyant.

bed /bed/ *n.* lit *m.*; (*layer*) couche *f.*; (*of sea*) fond *m.*; (*of flowers*) parterre *m.* **go to** ~, (aller) se coucher. —*v.i.* (*p.t.* **bedded**). ~ **down,** se coucher. ~**ding** *n.* literie *f.*

bedbug /ˈbedbʌg/ *n.* punaise *f.*

bedclothes /ˈbedkləʊðz/ *n. pl.* couvertures *f. pl.* et draps *m. pl.*

bedevil /bɪˈdevl/ *v.t.* (*p.t.* **bedevilled**) (*confuse*) embrouiller; (*plague*) tourmenter.

bedlam /ˈbedləm/ *n.* chahut *m.*

bedraggled /bɪˈdrægld/ *a.* (*untidy*) débraillé.

bedridden /ˈbedrɪdn/ *a.* cloué au lit.

bedroom /ˈbedrʊm/ *n.* chambre (à coucher) *f.*

bedside /ˈbedsaɪd/ *n.* chevet *m.* ~ **book,** livre de chevet *m.*

bedsit, bedsitter /ˈbedsɪt, -ˈsɪtə(r)/ *ns.* (*fam.*) *n.* chambre meublée *f.*, studio *m.*

bedspread /ˈbedspred/ *n.* dessus-de-lit *m. invar.*

bedtime /ˈbedtaɪm/ *n.* heure du coucher *f.*

bee /biː/ *n.* abeille *f.* **make a** ~**-line for,** aller tout droit vers.

beech /biːtʃ/ *n.* hêtre *m.*

beef /biːf/ *n.* bœuf *m.* —*v.i.* (*grumble*: *sl.*) rouspéter.

beefburger /ˈbiːfbɜːgə(r)/ *n.* hamburger *m.*

beefeater /ˈbiːfiːtə(r)/ *n.* hallebardier *m.*

beefy /ˈbiːfɪ/ *a.* (**-ier, -iest**) musclé.

beehive /ˈbiːhaɪv/ *n.* ruche *f.*

been /biːn/ *see* **be.**

beer /bɪə(r)/ *n.* bière *f.*

beet /biːt/ *n.* (*plant*) betterave *f.*

beetle /ˈbiːtl/ *n.* scarabée *m.*

beetroot /ˈbiːtruːt/ *n. invar.* (*culin.*) betterave *f.*

befall /bɪˈfɔːl/ *v.t.* (*p.t.* **befell**, *p.p.* **befallen**) arriver à.

befit /bɪˈfɪt/ (*v.t.* (*p.t.* **befitted**) convenir à, seoir à.

before /bɪˈfɔː(r)/ *prep.* (*time*) avant; (*place*) devant. —*adv.* avant; (*already*) déjà. —*conj.* ~ **leaving,** avant de partir. ~ **he leaves,** avant qu'il (ne) parte. **the day** ~, la veille. **two days** ~, deux jours avant.

beforehand /bɪˈfɔːhænd/ *adv.* à l'avance, avant.

befriend /brˈfrend/ *v.t.* offrir son amitié à, aider.

beg /beg/ *v.t.* (*p.t.* **begged**) (*entreat*) supplier (**to do,** de faire). **~ (for),** (*money, food*) mendier; (*request*) solliciter, demander. —*v.i.* **~ (for alms),** mendier. **it is going ~ging,** personne n'en veut.

began /brˈgæn/ *see* **begin.**

beggar /ˈbegə(r)/ *n.* mendiant(e) *m.* (*f.*); (*sl.*) individu *m.*

begin /brˈgɪn/ *v.t./i.* (*p.t.* **began,** *p.p.* **begun,** *pres. p.* **beginning**) commencer (**to do,** à faire). **~ner** *n.* débutant(e) *m.* (*f.*). **~ning** *n.* commencement *m.*, début *m.*

begrudge /brˈgrʌdʒ/ *v.t.* (*envy*) envier; (*give unwillingly*) donner à contrecœur. **~ doing,** faire à contrecœur.

beguile /brˈgaɪl/ *v.t.* tromper.

begun /brˈgʌn/ *see* **begin.**

behalf /brˈhɑːf/ *n.* **on ~ of,** pour; (*as representative*) au nom de, pour (le compte de).

behave /brˈheɪv/ *v.i.* se conduire. **~ (o.s.),** se conduire bien.

behaviour, (*Amer.*) **behavior** /brˈheɪvjə(r)/ *n.* conduite *f.*, comportement *m.*

behead /brˈhed/ *v.t.* décapiter.

behind /brˈhaɪnd/ *prep.* derrière; (*in time*) en retard sur. —*adv.* derrière; (*late*) en retard. —*n.* (*buttocks*) derrière *m.* **leave ~,** oublier.

behold /brˈhəʊld/ *v.t.* (*p.t.* **beheld**) (*old use*) voir.

beige /beɪʒ/ *a. & n.* beige (*m.*).

being /ˈbiːɪŋ/ *n.* (*person*) être *m.* **bring into ~,** créer. **come into ~,** prendre naissance.

belated /brˈleɪtɪd/ *a.* tardif.

belch /beltʃ/ *v.i.* faire un renvoi. —*v.t.* **~ out,** (*smoke*) vomir. —*n.* renvoi *m.*

belfry /ˈbelfrɪ/ *n.* beffroi *m.*

Belgi|um /ˈbeldʒəm/ *n.* Belgique *f.* **~an** *a. & n.* belge (*m./f.*).

belie /brˈlaɪ/ *v.t.* démentir.

belief /brˈliːf/ *n.* croyance *f.*; (*trust*) confiance *f.*; (*faith: relig.*) foi *f.*

believ|e /brˈliːv/ *v.t./i.* croire. **~e in,** croire à; (*deity*) croire en. **~able** *a.* croyable. **~er** *n.* croyant(e) *m.* (*f.*).

belittle /brˈlɪtl/ *v.t.* déprécier.

bell /bel/ *n.* cloche *f.*; (*small*) clochette *f.*; (*on door*) sonnette *f.*; (*of phone*) sonnerie *f.*

belligerent /brˈlɪdʒərənt/ *a. & n.* belligérant(e) (*m.* (*f.*)).

bellow /ˈbeləʊ/ *v.t./i.* beugler.

bellows /ˈbeləʊz/ *n. pl.* soufflet *m.*

belly /ˈbelɪ/ *n.* ventre *m.* **~-ache** *n.* mal au ventre *m.*

bellyful /ˈbelɪfʊl/ *n.* **have a ~,** en avoir plein le dos.

belong /brˈlɒŋ/ *v.i.* **~ to,** appartenir à; (*club*) être membre de.

belongings /brˈlɒŋɪŋz/ *n. pl.* affaires *f. pl.*

beloved /brˈlʌvɪd/ *a. & n.* bien-aimé(e) (*m.* (*f.*)).

below /brˈləʊ/ *prep.* au-dessous de; (*fig.*) indigne de. —*adv.* en dessous; (*on page*) ci-dessous.

belt /belt/ *n.* ceinture *f.*; (*techn.*) courroie *f.*; (*fig.*) région *f.* —*v.t.* (*hit: sl.*) rosser. —*v.i.* (*rush: sl.*) filer à toute allure.

beltway /ˈbeltweɪ/ *n.* (*Amer.*) périphérique *m.*

bemused /brˈmjuːzd/ *a.* (*confused*) stupéfié; (*thoughtful*) pensif.

bench /bentʃ/ *n.* banc *m.*; (*working-table*) établi *m.* **the ~,** (*jurid.*) la magistrature (assise). **~-mark** *n.* repère *m.*

bend /bend/ *v.t./i.* (*p.t.* **bent**) (se) courber; (*arm, leg*) plier. —*n.* courbe *f.*; (*in road*) virage *m.*; (*of arm, knee*) pli *m.* **~ down or over,** se pencher.

beneath /brˈniːθ/ *prep.* sous, au-dessous de; (*fig.*) indigne de. —*adv.* (au-)dessous.

benefactor /ˈbenɪfæktə(r)/ *n.* bien-faiteur, -trice *m.*, *f.*

beneficial /benɪˈfɪʃl/ *a.* avantageux, favorable.

benefit /ˈbenɪfɪt/ *n.* avantage *m.*; (*allowance*) allocation *f.* —*v.t.* (*p.t.* **benefited,** *pres. p.* **benefiting**) (*be useful to*) profiter à; (*do good to*) faire du bien à. **~ from,** tirer profit de.

benevolen|t /brˈnevələnt/ *a.* bienveillant. **~ce** *n.* bienveillance *f.*

benign /brˈnaɪn/ *a.* (*kindly*) bienveillant; (*med.*) bénin.

bent /bent/ *see* **bend.** —*n.* (*talent*) aptitude *f.*; (*inclination*) penchant *m.* —*a.* tordu; (*sl.*) corrompu. **~ on doing,** décidé à faire.

bequeath /brˈkwiːð/ *v.t.* léguer.

bequest /brˈkwest/ *n.* legs *m.*

bereave|d /brˈriːvd/ *a.* **the ~d wife/***etc.***,** la femme/*etc.* du disparu. **~ment** *n.* deuil *m.*

beret /ˈbereɪ/ *n.* béret *m.*

Bermuda /bəˈmjuːdə/ *n.* Bermudes *f. pl.*

berry /ˈberɪ/ *n.* baie *f.*

berserk /bəˈsɜːk/ *a.* **go ~,** devenir fou furieux.

berth /bɜːθ/ *n.* (*in train, ship*) couchette

f.; (*anchorage*) mouillage *m.* —*v.i.* mouiller. **give a wide ∼ to**, éviter.

beseech /bɪˈsiːtʃ/ *v.t.* (*p.t.* **besought**) implorer, supplier.

beset /bɪˈset/ *v.t.* (*p.t.* **beset**, *pres. p.* **besetting**) (*attack*) assaillir; (*surround*) entourer.

beside /bɪˈsaɪd/ *prep.* à côté de. ∼ **o.s.**, hors de soi. ∼ **the point**, sans rapport.

besides /bɪˈsaɪdz/ *prep.* en plus de; (*except*) excepté. —*adv.* en plus.

besiege /bɪˈsiːdʒ/ *v.t.* assiéger.

best /best/ *a.* meilleur. **the ∼ book***/etc.*, le meilleur livre*/etc.* —*adv.* (**the**) ∼, (*sing etc.*) le mieux. —*n.* **the ∼** (**one**), le meilleur, la meilleure. ∼ **man**, garçon d'honneur *m.* **the ∼ part of,** la plus grande partie de. **the ∼ thing is to . . .**, le mieux est de . . . **do one's ∼,** faire de son mieux. **make the ∼ of,** s'accommoder de.

bestow /bɪˈstəʊ/ *v.t.* accorder.

best-seller /bestˈselə(r)/ *n.* best-seller *m.*, succès de librairie *m.*

bet /bet/ *n.* pari *m.* —*v.t./i.* (*p.t.* **bet** *or* **betted,** *pres. p.* **betting**) parier.

betray /bɪˈtreɪ/ *v.t.* trahir. ∼**al** *n.* trahison *f.*

better /ˈbetə(r)/ *a.* meilleur. —*adv.* mieux. —*v.t.* (*improve*) améliorer; (*do better than*) surpasser. —*n.* **one's ∼s,** ses supérieurs *m. pl.* **be ∼ off,** (*financially*) avoir plus d'argent. **he's ∼ off at home,** il est mieux chez lui. **I had ∼ go,** je ferais mieux de partir. **the ∼ part of,** la plus grande partie de. **get ∼,** s'améliorer; (*recover*) se remettre. **get the ∼ of,** l'emporter sur. **so much the ∼,** tant mieux.

betting-shop /ˈbetɪŋʃɒp/ *n.* bureau de P.M.U. *m.*

between /bɪˈtwiːn/ *prep.* entre. —*adv.* **in ∼,** au milieu.

beverage /ˈbevərɪdʒ/ *n.* boisson *f.*

bevy /ˈbevɪ/ *n.* essaim *m.*

beware /bɪˈweə(r)/ *v.i.* prendre garde (**of,** à).

bewilder /bɪˈwɪldə(r)/ *v.t.* désorienter, embarrasser. ∼**ment** *n.* désorientation *f.*

bewitch /bɪˈwɪtʃ/ *v.t.* enchanter.

beyond /bɪˈjɒnd/ *prep.* au-delà de; (*doubt, reach*) hors de; (*besides*) excepté. —*adv.* au-delà. **it is ∼ me,** ça me dépasse.

bias /ˈbaɪəs/ *n.* (*inclination*) penchant *m.*; (*prejudice*) préjugé *m.* —*v.t.* (*p.t.* **biased**) influencer. ∼**ed** *a.* partial.

bib /bɪb/ *n.* bavoir *m.*

Bible /ˈbaɪbl/ *n.* Bible *f.*

biblical /ˈbɪblɪkl/ *a.* biblique.

bicarbonate /baɪˈkɑːbənət/ *n.* bicarbonate *m.*

biceps /ˈbaɪseps/ *n.* biceps *m.*

bicker /ˈbɪkə(r)/ *v.i.* se chamailler.

bicycle /ˈbaɪsɪkl/ *n.* bicyclette *f.* —*v.i.* faire de la bicyclette.

bid[1] /bɪd/ *n.* (*at auction*) offre *f.*, enchère *f.*; (*attempt*) tentative *f.* —*v.t./i.* (*p.t. & p.p.* **bid,** *pres. p.* **bidding**) (*offer*) faire une offre *or* une enchère (de). **the highest ∼der,** le plus offrant.

bid[2] /bɪd/ *v.t.* (*p.t.* **bade** /bæd/, *p.p.* **bidden** *or* **bid,** *pres. p.* **bidding**) ordonner; (*say*) dire. ∼**ding** *n.* ordre *m.*

bide /baɪd/ *v.t.* ∼ **one's time,** attendre le bon moment.

biennial /baɪˈenɪəl/ *a.* biennal.

bifocals /baɪˈfəʊklz/ *n. pl.* lunettes bifocales *f. pl.*

big /bɪɡ/ *a.* (**bigger, biggest**) grand; (*in bulk*) gros; (*generous: sl.*) généreux: —*adv.* (*fam.*) en grand; (*earn: fam.*) gros. ∼ **business,** les grandes affaires. ∼**-headed** *a.* prétentieux. ∼ **shot,** (*sl.*) huile *f.* **think ∼,** (*fam.*) voir grand.

bigam|y /ˈbɪɡəmɪ/ *n.* bigamie *f.* ∼**ist** *n.* bigame *m./f.* ∼**ous** *a.* bigame.

bigot /ˈbɪɡət/ *n.* fanatique *m./f.* ∼**ed** *a.* fanatique. ∼**ry** *n.* fanatisme *m.*

bike /baɪk/ *n.* (*fam.*) vélo *m.*

bikini /bɪˈkiːnɪ/ *n.* (*pl.* **-is**) bikini *m.*

bilberry /ˈbɪlbərɪ/ *n.* myrtille *f.*

bile /baɪl/ *n.* bile *f.*

bilingual /baɪˈlɪŋɡwəl/ *a.* bilingue.

bilious /ˈbɪlɪəs/ *a.* bilieux.

bill[1] /bɪl/ *n.* (*invoice*) facture *f.*; (*in hotel, for gas, etc.*) note *f.*; (*in restaurant*) addition *f.*; (*of sale*) acte *m.*; (*pol.*) projet de loi *m.*; (*banknote: Amer.*) billet de banque *m.* —*v.t.* (*person: comm.*) envoyer la facture à; (*theatre*) **on the ∼,** à l'affiche.

bill[2] /bɪl/ *n.* (*of bird*) bec *m.*

billboard /ˈbɪlbɔːd/ *n.* panneau d'affichage *m.*

billet /ˈbɪlɪt/ *n.* cantonnement *m.* —*v.t.* (*p.t.* **billeted**) cantonner (**on,** chez).

billfold /ˈbɪlfəʊld/ *n.* (*Amer.*) porte-feuille *m.*

billiards /ˈbɪljədz/ *n.* billard *m.*

billion /ˈbɪljən/ *n.* billion *m.*; (*Amer.*) milliard *m.*

billy-goat /ˈbɪlɪɡəʊt/ *n.* bouc *m.*

bin /bɪn/ *n.* (*for rubbish, litter*) boîte (à ordures) *f.*, poubelle *f.*; (*for bread*) huche *f.*, coffre *m.*

binary /ˈbaɪnərɪ/ *a.* binaire.

bind /baɪnd/ v.t. (p.t. **bound**) lier; (*book*) relier; (*jurid.*) obliger. —n. (*bore: sl.*) plaie f. **be ~ing on,** être obligatoire pour.

binding /'baɪndɪŋ/ n. reliure f.

binge /bɪndʒ/ n. **go on a ~,** (*spree: sl.*) faire la bringue.

bingo /'bɪŋgəʊ/ n. loto m.

binoculars /bɪ'nɒkjʊləz/ n. pl. jumelles f. pl.

biochemistry /baɪəʊ'kemɪstrɪ/ n. biochimie f.

biodegradable /baɪəʊdɪ'greɪdəbl/ a. biodégradable.

biograph|y /baɪ'ɒgrəfɪ/ n. biographie f. **~er** n. biographe m./f.

biolog|y /baɪ'ɒlədʒɪ/ n. biologie f. **~ical** /-ə'lɒdʒɪkl/ a. biologique. **~ist** n. biologiste m./f.

biorhythm /'baɪəʊrɪðəm/ n. biorythme m.

birch /bɜːtʃ/ n. (*tree*) bouleau m.; (*whip*) verge f., fouet m.

bird /bɜːd/ n. oiseau m.; (*fam.*) individu m.; (*girl: sl.*) poule f.

Biro /'baɪərəʊ/ n. (pl. **-os**) (P.) stylo à bille m., Bic m. (P.).

birth /bɜːθ/ n. naissance f. **give ~,** accoucher. **~ certificate,** acte de naissance m. **~-control** n. contrôle des naissances m. **~-rate** n. natalité f.

birthday /'bɜːθdeɪ/ n. anniversaire m.

birthmark /'bɜːθmɑːk/ n. tache de vin f., envie f.

biscuit /'bɪskɪt/ n. biscuit m.; (*Amer.*) petit pain (au lait) m.

bisect /baɪ'sekt/ v.t. couper en deux.

bishop /'bɪʃəp/ n. évêque m.

bit¹ /bɪt/ n. morceau m.; (*of horse*) mors m.; (*of tool*) mèche f. **a ~,** (*a little*) un peu.

bit² /bɪt/ *see* **bite**.

bit³ /bɪt/ n. (*comput.*) bit m., élement binaire m.

bitch /bɪtʃ/ n. chienne f.; (*woman: fam.*) garce f. —v.i. (*grumble: fam.*) râler. **~y** a. (*fam.*) vache.

bite /baɪt/ v.t./i. (p.t. **bit**, p.p. **bitten**) mordre. —n. morsure f.; (*by insect*) piqûre f.; (*mouthful*) bouchée f. **~ one's nails,** se ronger les ongles. **have a ~,** manger un morceau.

biting /'baɪtɪŋ/ a. mordant.

bitter /'bɪtə(r)/ a. amer; (*weather*) glacial, âpre. —n. bière anglaise f. **~ly** adv. amèrement. **it is ~ly cold,** il fait un temps glacial. **~ness** n. amertume f.

bitty /'bɪtɪ/ a. décousu.

bizarre /bɪ'zɑː(r)/ a. bizarre.

blab /blæb/ v.i. (p.t. **blabbed**) jaser.

black /blæk/ a. (**-er, -est**) noir. —n. (*colour*) noir m. **B~,** (*person*) Noir(e) m. (f.). —v.t. noircir; (*goods*) boycotter. **~ and blue,** couvert de bleus. **~ eye,** œil poché m. **~ ice,** verglas m. **~ list,** liste noire f. **~ market,** marché noir m. **~ sheep,** brebis galeuse f. **~ spot,** point noir m.

blackberry /'blækbərɪ/ n. mûre f.

blackbird /'blækbɜːd/ n. merle m.

blackboard /'blækbɔːd/ n. tableau noir m.

blackcurrant /'blækkʌrənt/ n. cassis m.

blacken /'blækən/ v.t./i. noircir.

blackhead /'blækhed/ n. point noir m.

blackleg /'blækleg/ n. jaune m.

blacklist /'blæklɪst/ v.t. mettre sur la liste noire *or* à l'index.

blackmail /'blækmeɪl/ n. chantage m. —v.t. faire chanter. **~er** n. maître-chanteur m.

blackout /'blækaʊt/ n. panne d'électricité f.; (*med.*) syncope f.

blacksmith /'blæksmɪθ/ n. forgeron m.

bladder /'blædə(r)/ n. vessie f.

blade /bleɪd/ n. (*of knife etc.*) lame f.; (*of propeller, oar*) pale f. **~ of grass,** brin d'herbe m.

blame /bleɪm/ v.t. accuser. —n. faute f. **~ s.o. for sth.,** reprocher qch. à qn. **he is to ~,** il est responsable (**for,** de). **~less** a. irréprochable.

bland /blænd/ a. (**-er, -est**) (*gentle*) doux; (*insipid*) fade.

blank /blæŋk/ a. blanc; (*look*) vide; (*cheque*) en blanc. —n. blanc m. **~ (cartridge),** cartouche à blanc f.

blanket /'blæŋkɪt/ n. couverture f.; (*layer, fig.*) couche f. —v.t. (p.t. **blanketed**) recouvrir.

blare /bleə(r)/ v.t./i. beugler. —n. vacarme m., beuglement m.

blarney /'blɑːnɪ/ n. boniment m.

blasé /'blɑːzeɪ/ a. blasé.

blasphem|y /'blæsfəmɪ/ n. blasphème m. **~ous** a. blasphématoire; (*person*) blasphémateur.

blast /blɑːst/ n. explosion f.; (*wave of air*) souffle m.; (*of wind*) rafale f.; (*noise from siren etc.*) coup m. —v.t. (*blow up*) faire sauter. —int. (*fam.*) maudit, fichu. **~-furnace** n. haut fourneau m. **~ off,** être mis à feu. **~-off** n. mise à feu f.

blatant /'bleɪtnt/ a. (*obvious*) flagrant; (*shameless*) éhonté.

blaze¹ /bleɪz/ n. flamme f.; (*conflagration*) incendie m.; (*fig.*) éclat *m.* —*v.i.* (*fire*) flamber; (*sky, eyes, etc.*) flamboyer.

blaze² /bleɪz/ *v.t.* ~ **a trail**, montrer *or* marquer la voie.

blazer /'bleɪzə(r)/ *n.* blazer *m.*

bleach /bliːtʃ/ *n.* décolorant *m.*; (*for domestic use*) eau de Javel *f.* —*v.t./i.* blanchir; (*hair*) décolorer.

bleak /bliːk/ *a.* (**-er, -est**) morne.

bleary /'blɪərɪ/ *a.* (*eyes*) voilé.

bleat /bliːt/ *n.* bêlement *m.* —*v.i.* bêler.

bleed /bliːd/ *v.t./i.* (*p.t.* **bled**) saigner.

bleep /bliːp/ *n.* bip *m.* —*v.i.* bip *m.*

blemish /'blemɪʃ/ *n.* tare *f.*, défaut *m.*; (*on reputation*) tache *f.* —*v.t.* entacher.

blend /blend/ *v.t./i.* (se) mélanger. —*n.* mélange *m.* ~**er** *n.* mixer *n.*

bless /bles/ *v.t.* bénir. **be** ~**ed with,** avoir le bonheur de posséder. ~**ing** *n.* bénédiction *f.*; (*benefit*) avantage *m.*; (*stroke of luck*) chance *f.*

blessed /'blesɪd/ *a.* (*holy*) saint; (*damned: fam.*) sacré.

blew /bluː/ *see* **blow¹**.

blight /blaɪt/ *n.* (*disease: bot.*) rouille *f.*; (*fig.*) fléau *m.*

blind /blaɪnd/ *a.* aveugle. —*v.t.* aveugler. —*n.* (*on window*) store *m.*; (*deception*) feinte *f.* **be** ~ **to,** ne pas voir. ~ **alley,** impasse *f.* ~ **corner,** virage sans visibilité *m.* ~ **man,** aveugle *m.* ~ **spot,** (*auto.*) angle mort *m.* ~**ers** *n. pl.* (*Amer.*) œillères *f. pl.* ~**ly** *adv.* aveuglément. ~**ness** *n.* cécité *f.*

blindfold /'blaɪndfəʊld/ *a. & adv.* les yeux bandés. —*n.* bandeau *m.* —*v.t.* bander les yeux à.

blink /blɪŋk/ *v.i.* cligner des yeux; (*of light*) clignoter.

blinkers /'blɪŋkəz/ *n. pl.* œillères *f. pl.*

bliss /blɪs/ *n.* félicité *f.* ~**ful** *a.* bienheureux. ~**fully** *adv.* joyeusement, merveilleusement.

blister /'blɪstə(r)/ *n.* ampoule *f.* (*on paint*) cloque *f.* —*v.i.* se couvrir d'ampoules; cloquer.

blithe /blaɪð/ *a.* joyeux.

blitz /blɪts/ *n.* (*aviat.*) raid éclair *m.* —*v.t.* bombarder.

blizzard /'blɪzəd/ *n.* tempête de neige *f.*

bloated /'bləʊtɪd/ *a.* gonflé.

bloater /'bləʊtə(r)/ *n.* hareng saur *m.*

blob /blɒb/ *n.* (*drop*) (grosse) goutte *f.*; (*stain*) tache *f.*

bloc /blɒk/ *n.* bloc *m.*

block /blɒk/ *n.* bloc *m.*; (*buildings*) pâté de maisons *m.*; (*in pipe*) obstruction *f.* ~ (**of flats**), immeuble *m.* —*v.t.* bloquer. ~ **letters,** majuscules *f. pl.*

~**age** *n.* obstruction *f.* ~**-buster** *n.* gros succès *m.*

blockade /blɒ'keɪd/ *n.* blocus *m.* —*v.t.* bloquer.

bloke /bləʊk/ *n.* (*fam.*) type *m.*

blond /blɒnd/ *a. & n.* blond (*m.*).

blonde /blɒnd/ *a. & n.* blonde (*f.*).

blood /blʌd/ *n.* sang *m.* —*a.* (*donor, bath, etc.*) de sang; (*bank, poisoning, etc.*) du sang; (*group, vessel*) sanguin. ~**-curdling** *a.* à tourner le sang. ~**less** *a.* (*fig.*) pacifique. ~**-pressure** *n.* tension artérielle *f.* ~ **test,** prise de sang *f.*

bloodhound /'blʌdhaʊnd/ *n.* limier *m.*

bloodshed /'blʌdʃed/ *n.* effusion de sang *f.*

bloodshot /'blʌdʃɒt/ *a.* injecté de sang.

bloodstream /'blʌdstriːm/ *n.* sang *m.*

bloodthirsty /'blʌdθɜːstɪ/ *a.* sanguinaire.

bloom /bluːm/ *n.* fleur *f.* —*v.i.* fleurir; (*fig.*) s'épanouir.

bloomer /'bluːmə(r)/ *n.* (*sl.*) gaffe *f.*

blossom /'blɒsəm/ *n.* fleur(s) *f.* (*pl.*). —*v.i.* fleurir; (*person: fig.*) s'épanouir.

blot /blɒt/ *n.* tache *f.* —*v.t.* (*p.t.* **blotted**) tacher; (*dry*) sécher. ~ **out,** effacer. ~**ter,** ~**ting-paper** *ns.* buvard *m.*

blotch /blɒtʃ/ *n.* tache *f.* ~**y** *a.* couvert de taches.

blouse /blaʊz/ *n.* chemisier *m.*

blow¹ /bləʊ/ *v.t./i.* (*p.t.* **blew,** *p.p.* **blown**) souffler; (*fuse*) (faire) sauter; (*squander: sl.*) claquer; (*opportunity: sl.*) rater. ~ **one's nose,** se moucher. ~ **a whistle,** siffler. ~ **away** *or* **off,** emporter. ~**-dry** *v.t.* sécher; *n.* brushing *m.* ~ **out,** (*candle*) souffler. ~**-out** *n.* (*of tyre*) éclatement *m.* ~ **over,** passer. ~ **up,** (faire) sauter; (*tyre*) gonfler; (*photo.*) aggrandir.

blow² /bləʊ/ *n.* coup *m.*

blowlamp /'bləʊlæmp/ *n.* chalumeau *m.*

blown /bləʊn/ *see* **blow¹**.

blowtorch /'bləʊtɔːtʃ/ *n.* (*Amer.*) chalumeau *m.*

blowy /'bləʊɪ/ *a.* **it is** ~, il y a du vent.

bludgeon /'blʌdʒən/ *n.* gourdin *m.* —*v.t.* matraquer.

blue /bluː/ *a.* (**-er, -est**) bleu; (*film*) porno. —*n.* bleu *m.* **come out of the** ~, être inattendu. **have the** ~**s,** avoir le cafard.

bluebell /'bluːbel/ *n.* jacinthe des bois *f.*

bluebottle /'bluːbɒtl/ *n.* mouche à viande *f.*

blueprint /'bluːprɪnt/ n. plan m.

bluff¹ /blʌf/ v.t./i. bluffer. —n. bluff m. **call, s.o.'s ~**, dire chiche à qn.

bluff² /blʌf/ a. (person) brusque.

blunder /'blʌndə(r)/ v.i. faire une gaffe; (move) avancer à tâtons. —n. gaffe f.

blunt /blʌnt/ a. (knife) émoussé; (person) brusque. —v.t. émousser. **~ly** adv. carrément. **~ness** n. brusquerie f.

blur /blɜː(r)/ n. tache floue f. —v.t. (p.t. **blurred**) rendre flou.

blurb /blɜːb/ n. résumé publicitaire m.

blurt /blɜːt/ v.t. **~ out**, lâcher, dire.

blush /blʌʃ/ v.i. rougir. —n. rougeur f. **~er** n. blush m.

bluster /'blʌstə(r)/ v.i. (wind) faire rage; (swagger) fanfaronner. **~y** a. à bourrasques.

boar /bɔː(r)/ n. sanglier m.

board /bɔːd/ n. planche f.; (for notices) tableau m.; (food) pension f.; (committee) conseil m. —v.t./i. (bus, train) monter dans; (naut.) monter à bord (de). **~ of directors**, conseil d'administration m. **go by the ~**, passer à l'as. **full ~**, pension complète f. **half ~**, demi-pension f. **on ~**, à bord. **~ up**, boucher. **~ with**, être en pension chez. **~er** n. pensionnaire m./f. **~ing-house** n. pension (de famille) f. **~ing-school** n. pensionnat m., pension f.

boast /bəʊst/ v.i. se vanter (**about**, de). —v.t. s'enorgueillir de. —n. vantardise f. **~er** n. vantard(e) m. (f.). **~ful** a. vantard. **~fully** adv. en se vantant.

boat /bəʊt/ n. bateau m.; (small) canot m. **in the same ~**, logé à la même enseigne. **~ing** n. canotage m.

boatswain /'bəʊsn/ n. maître d'équipage m.

bob¹ /bɒb/ v.i. (p.t. **bobbed**). **~ up and down**, monter et descendre.

bob² /bɒb/ n. invar. (sl.) shilling m.

bobby /'bɒbɪ/ n. (fam.) flic m.

bobsleigh /'bɒbsleɪ/ n. bob(-sleigh) m.

bode /bəʊd/ v.i. **~ well/ill**, être de bon/mauvais augure.

bodily /'bɒdɪlɪ/ a. physique, corporel. —adv. physiquement; (in person) en personne.

body /'bɒdɪ/ n. corps m.; (mass) masse f.; (organization) organisme m. **~(work)**, (auto.) carrosserie f. **the main ~ of**, le gros de. **~-builder** n. culturiste m./f. **~-building** n. culturisme m.

bodyguard /'bɒdɪgɑːd/ n. garde du corps m.

bog /bɒg/ n. marécage m. —v.t. (p.t. **bogged**). **get ~ged down**, s'embourber.

boggle /'bɒgl/ v.i. **the mind ~s**, on est stupéfait.

bogus /'bəʊgəs/ a. faux.

bogy /'bəʊgɪ/ n. (annoyance) embêtement m. **~(man)**, croquemitaine m.

boil¹ /bɔɪl/ n. furoncle m.

boil² /bɔɪl/ v.t./i. (faire) bouillir. **bring to the ~**, porter à ébullition. **~ down to**, se ramener à. **~ over**, déborder. **~ing hot**, bouillant. **~ing point**, point d'ébullition m. **~ed** a. (egg) à la coque; (potatoes) à l'eau.

boiler /'bɔɪlə(r)/ n. chaudière f. **~ suit**, bleu (de travail) m.

boisterous /'bɔɪstərəs/ a. tapageur.

bold /bəʊld/ a. (-er, -est) hardi; (cheeky) effronté; (type) gras. **~ness** n. hardiesse f.

Bolivia /bə'lɪvɪə/ n. Bolivie f. **~n** a. & n. bolivien(ne) (m. (f.)).

bollard /'bɒləd/ n. (on road) borne f.

bolster /'bəʊlstə(r)/ n. traversin m. —v.t. soutenir.

bolt /bəʊlt/ n. verrou m.; (for nut) boulon m.; (lightning) éclair m. —v.t. (door etc.) verrouiller; (food) engouffrer. —v.i. se sauver. **~ upright**, tout droit.

bomb /bɒm/ n. bombe f. —v.t. bombarder. **~ scare**, alerte à la bombe f. **~er** n. (aircraft) bombardier m.; (person) plastiqueur m.

bombard /bɒm'bɑːd/ v.t. bombarder.

bombastic /bɒm'bæstɪk/ a. grandiloquent.

bombshell /'bɒmʃel/ n. **be a ~**, tomber comme une bombe.

bona fide /bəʊnə'faɪdɪ/ a. de bonne foi.

bond /bɒnd/ n. (agreement) engagement m.; (link) lien m.; (comm.) obligation f., bon m. **in ~**, (entreposé) en douane.

bondage /'bɒndɪdʒ/ n. esclavage m.

bone /bəʊn/ n. os m.; (of fish) arête f. —v.t. désosser. **~-dry** a. tout à fait sec. **~ idle**, paresseux comme une couleuvre.

bonfire /'bɒnfaɪə(r)/ n. feu m.; (for celebration) feu de joie m.

bonnet /'bɒnɪt/ n. (hat) bonnet m.; (of vehicle) capot m.

bonus /'bəʊnəs/ n. prime f.

bony /'bəʊnɪ/ a. (-ier, -iest) (thin) osseux; (meat) plein d'os; (fish) plein d'arêtes.

boo /buː/ int. hou. —v.t./i. huer. —n. huée f.

boob /buːb/ n. (blunder: sl.) gaffe f.
—v.i. (sl.) gaffer.

booby-trap /'buːbɪtræp/ n. engin piégé
m. —v.t. (p.t. -**trapped**) piéger.

book /bʊk/ n. livre m.; (of tickets etc.)
carnet m. ∼**s**, (comm.) comptes m. pl.
—v.t. (reserve) réserver; (driver) faire
un P.V. à; (player) prendre le nom de;
(write down) inscrire. —v.i. retenir des
places. ∼**able** a. qu'on peut retenir.
(**fully**) ∼**ed**, complet. ∼**ing office**,
guichet m.

bookcase /'bʊkkeɪs/ n. bibliothèque f.

bookkeeping /'bʊkkiːpɪŋ/ n. comptabilité f.

booklet /'bʊklɪt/ n. brochure f.

bookmaker /'bʊkmeɪkə(r)/ n. bookmaker m.

bookseller /'bʊkselə(r)/ n. libraire m./f.

bookshop /'bʊkʃɒp/ n. librairie f.

bookstall /'bʊkstɔːl/ n. kiosque (à
journaux) m.

boom /buːm/ v.i. (gun, wind, etc.)
gronder; (trade) prospérer. —n.
grondement m.; (comm.) boom m.,
prospérité f.

boon /buːn/ n. (benefit) aubaine f.

boost /buːst/ v.t. stimuler; (morale)
remonter; (price) augmenter; (publicize)
faire de la réclame pour. —n. **give a** ∼
to, = **boost.**

boot /buːt/ n. (knee-length); botte f.;
(ankle-length) chaussure (montante) f.;
(for walking) chaussure de marche
f.; (sport) chaussure de sport f.;
(of vehicle) coffre m. —v.t./i. ∼
up, (comput.) démarrer, lancer (le
programme). **get the** ∼, (sl.) être mis à
la porte.

booth /buːð/ n. (for telephone) cabine f.;
(at fair) baraque f.

booty /'buːtɪ/ n. butin m.

booze /buːz/ v.i. (fam.) boire
(beaucoup). —n. (fam.) alcool m.;
(spree) beuverie f.

border /'bɔːdə(r)/ n. (edge) bord m.;
(frontier) frontière f.; (in garden)
bordure f. —v.i. ∼ **on,** (be next to,
come close to) être voisin de, avoisiner.

borderline /'bɔːdəlaɪn/ n. ligne de
démarcation f. ∼ **case,** cas limite m.

bore¹ /bɔː(r)/ see **bore²**.

bore² /bɔː(r)/ v.t./i. (techn.) forer.

bore³ /bɔː(r)/ v.t. ennuyer. —n. raseur,
-se m., f.; (thing) ennui m. **be** ∼**d,**
s'ennuyer. ∼**dom** n. ennui m. **boring** a.
ennuyeux.

born /bɔːn/ a. né. **be** ∼, naître.

borne /bɔːn/ see **bear²**.

borough /'bʌrə/ n. municipalité f.

borrow /'bɒrəʊ/ v.t. emprunter (**from,**
à). ∼**ing** n. emprunt m.

bosom /'bʊzəm/ n. sein m. ∼ **friend,**
ami(e) intime m. (f.).

boss /bɒs/ n. (fam.) patron(ne) m. (f.)
—v.t. ∼ (**about**), (fam.) donner des
ordres à, régenter.

bossy /'bɒsɪ/ a. autoritaire.

botan|y /'bɒtənɪ/ n. botanique f. ∼**ical**
/bə'tænɪkl/ a. botanique. ∼**ist** n.
botaniste m./f.

botch /bɒtʃ/ v.t. bâcler, saboter.

both /bəʊθ/ a. les deux. —pron. tous or
toutes (les) deux, l'un(e) et l'autre.
—adv. à la fois. ∼ **the books,** les deux
livres. **we** ∼ **agree,** nous sommes tous
les deux d'accord. **I bought** ∼ (**of
them**), j'ai acheté les deux. **I saw** ∼ **of
you,** je vous ai vus tous les deux.
∼ **Paul and Anne,** (et) Paul et
Anne.

bother /'bɒðə(r)/ v.t. (annoy, worry)
ennuyer; (disturb) déranger. —v.i. se
déranger. —n. ennui m.; (effort) peine
f. **don't** ∼ (**calling**), ce n'est pas la
peine (d'appeler). **don't** ∼ **about us,** ne
t'inquiète pas pour nous. **I can't be**
∼**ed,** j'ai la flemme. **it's no** ∼, ce n'est
rien.

bottle /'bɒtl/ n. bouteille f.; (for baby)
biberon m. —v.t. mettre en bouteille(s).
∼ **bank,** collecteur (de verre usagé) m.
∼**-opener** n. ouvre-bouteille(s) m. ∼
up, contenir.

bottleneck /'bɒtlnek/ n. (traffic jam)
bouchon m.

bottom /'bɒtəm/ n. fond m.; (of hill,
page, etc.) bas m.; (buttocks) derrière
m. —a. inférieur, du bas. ∼**less** a.
insondable.

bough /baʊ/ n. rameau m.

bought /bɔːt/ see **buy.**

boulder /'bəʊldə(r)/ n. rocher m.

boulevard /'buːləvɑːd/ n. boulevard m.

bounce /baʊns/ v.i. rebondir; (person)
faire des bonds, bondir; (cheques: sl.)
être refusé. —v.t. faire rebondir. —n.
rebond m.

bouncer /'baʊnsə(r)/ n. videur m.

bound¹ /baʊnd/ v.i. (leap) bondir. —n.
bond m.

bound² /baʊnd/ see **bind.** —a. **be** ∼
for, être en route pour, aller. vers. ∼ **to,**
(obliged) obligé de; (certain) sûr de.

boundary /'baʊndrɪ/ n. limite f.

bound|s /baʊndz/ n. pl. limites f. pl. **out
of** ∼**s,** interdit. ∼**ed by,** limité par.
∼**less** a. sans bornes.

bouquet /bʊˈkeɪ/ n. bouquet m.

bout /baʊt/ n. période f.; (med.) accès m.; (boxing) combat m.

boutique /buːˈtiːk/ n. boutique (de mode) f.

bow[1] /bəʊ/ n. (weapon) arc m.; (mus.) archet m.; (knot) nœud m. ~-**legged** a. aux jambes arquées. ~-**tie** n. nœud papillon m.

bow[2] /baʊ/ n. (with head) salut m.; (with body) révérence f. —v.t./i. (s')incliner.

bow[3] /baʊ/ n. (naut.) proue f.

bowels /ˈbaʊəlz/ n. pl. intestins m. pl.; (fig.) entrailles f. pl.

bowl[1] /bəʊl/ n. cuvette f.; (for food) bol m.; (for soup etc.) assiette creuse f.

bowl[2] /bəʊl/ n. (ball) boule f. —v.t./i. (cricket) lancer. ~ **over,** bouleverser. ~**ing** n. jeu de boules m. ~**ing-alley** n. bowling m.

bowler[1] /ˈbəʊlə(r)/ n. (cricket) lanceur m.

bowler[2] /ˈbəʊlə(r)/ n. ~ (**hat**), (chapeau) melon m.

box[1] /bɒks/ n. boîte f.; (cardboard) carton m. (theatre) loge f. —v.t. mettre en boîte. **the** ~, (fam.) la télé. ~ **in,** enfermer. ~-**office** n. bureau de location m. **Boxing Day,** le lendemain de Noël.

box[2] /bɒks/ v.t./i. (sport) boxer. ~ **s.o.'s ears,** gifler qn. ~**ing** n. boxe f.; a. de boxe.

boy /bɔɪ/ n. garçon m. ~-**friend** n. (petit) ami m. ~**hood** n. enfance f. ~**ish** a. enfantin, de garçon.

boycott /ˈbɔɪkɒt/ v.t. boycotter. —n. boycottage m.

bra /brɑː/ n. soutien-gorge m.

brace /breɪs/ n. (fastener) attache f.; (dental) appareil m.; (for bit) vilbrequin m. ~**s,** (for trousers) bretelles f. pl. —v.t. soutenir. ~ **o.s.,** rassembler ses forces.

bracelet /ˈbreɪslɪt/ n. bracelet m.

bracing /ˈbreɪsɪŋ/ a. vivifiant.

bracken /ˈbrækən/ n. fougère f.

bracket /ˈbrækɪt/ n. (for shelf etc.) tasseau m., support m.; (group) tranche f. (**round**) ~, (printing sign) parenthèse f. (**square**) ~, crochet m. —v.t. (p.t. **bracketed**) mettre entre parenthèses or crochets.

brag /bræg/ v.i. (p.t. **bragged**) se vanter.

braid /breɪd/ n. (trimming) galon m.; (of hair) tresse f.

Braille /breɪl/ n. braille m.

brain /breɪn/ n. cerveau m. ~**s,** (fig.) intelligence f. —v.t. assommer. ~-**child** n. invention personnelle f. ~-**drain** n. exode des cerveaux m. ~**less** a. stupide.

brainwash /ˈbreɪnwɒʃ/ v.t. faire un lavage de cerveau à.

brainwave /ˈbreɪnweɪv/ n. idée géniale f., trouvaille f.

brainy /ˈbreɪnɪ/ a. (-**ier,** -**iest**) intelligent.

braise /breɪz/ v.t. braiser.

brake /breɪk/ n. (auto & fig.) frein m. —v.t./i. freiner. ~ **fluid,** liquide de frein m. ~ **light,** feu de stop m. ~ **lining,** garniture de frein f.

bramble /ˈbræmbl/ n. ronce f.

bran /bræn/ n. (husks) son m.

branch /brɑːntʃ/ n. branche f.; (of road) embranchement m.; (comm.) succursale f.; (of bank) agence f. —v.i. ~ (**off**), bifurquer.

brand /brænd/ n. marque f. —v.t. ~ **s.o. as,** donner à qn. la réputation de. ~-**new** a. tout neuf.

brandish /ˈbrændɪʃ/ v.t. brandir.

brandy /ˈbrændɪ/ n. cognac m.

brash /bræʃ/ a. effronté.

brass /brɑːs/ n. cuivre m. **get down to** ~ **tacks,** en venir aux choses sérieuses. **the** ~, (mus.) les cuivres m. pl. **top** ~, (sl.) gros bonnets m. pl.

brassière /ˈbræsɪə(r), Amer. brəˈzɪər/ n. soutien-gorge m.

brat /bræt/ n. (child: pej.) môme m./f.; (ill-behaved) garnement m.

bravado /brəˈvɑːdəʊ/ n. bravade f.

brave /breɪv/ a. (-**er,** -**est**) courageux, brave. —n. (American Indian) brave m. —v.t. braver. ~**ry** /-ərɪ/ n. courage m.

bravo /ˈbrɑːvəʊ/ int. bravo.

brawl /brɔːl/ n. bagarre f. —v.i. se bagarrer.

brawn /brɔːn/ n. muscles m. pl. ~**y** a. musclé.

bray /breɪ/ n. braiment m. —v.i. braire.

brazen /ˈbreɪzn/ a. effronté.

brazier /ˈbreɪzɪə(r)/ n. brasero m.

Brazil /brəˈzɪl/ n. Brésil m. ~**ian** a. & n. brésilien(ne) (m. (f.)).

breach /briːtʃ/ n. violation f.; (of contract) rupture f.; (gap) brèche f. —v.t. ouvrir une brèche dans.

bread /bred/ n. pain m. ~ **and butter,** tartine f. ~-**bin,** (Amer.) ~-**box** ns. boîte à pain f. ~-**winner** n. soutien de famille m.

breadcrumbs /ˈbredkrʌmz/ n. pl. (culin.) chapelure f.

breadline /ˈbredlaɪn/ n. **on the** ~, dans l'indigence.

breadth /bretθ/ n. largeur f.
break /breɪk/ v.t. (p.t. **broke**, p.p.
broken) casser; (smash into pieces)
briser; (vow, silence, rank, etc.) rompre;
(law) violer; (a record) battre; (news)
révéler; (journey) interrompre; (heart,
strike, ice) briser. —v.i. (se) casser; se
briser. —n. cassure f., rupture f.; (in
relationship, continuity) rupture f.;
(interval) interruption f.; (at school)
récréation f., récré f.; (for coffee) pause
f.; (luck: fam.) chance f. ~ **one's arm**,
se casser le bras. ~ **away from**, quitter.
~ **down** v.i. (collapse) s'effondrer;
(fail) échouer; (machine) tomber en
panne; v.t. (door) enfoncer; (analyse)
analyser. ~ **even**, rentrer dans ses frais.
~**in** n. cambriolage m. ~ **into**, cambrioler. ~ **off**, (se) détacher; (suspend)
rompre; (stop talking) s'interrompre. ~
out, (fire, war, etc.) éclater. ~ **up**,
(end) (faire) cesser; (couple) rompre;
(marriage) (se) briser; (crowd) (se)
disperser; (schools) entrer en vacances.
~**able** a. cassable. ~**age** n. casse f.
breakdown /'breɪkdaʊn/ n. (techn.)
panne f.; (med.) dépression f.; (of
figures) analyse f. —a. (auto.) de
dépannage.
breaker /'breɪkə(r)/ n. (wave) brisant m.
breakfast /'brekfəst/ n. petit déjeuner
m.
breakthrough /'breɪkθruː/ n. percée f.
breakwater /'breɪkwɔːtə(r)/ n. brise-
lames m. invar.
breast /brest/ n. sein m.; (chest) poitrine
f. ~**-feed** v.t. (p.t. **-fed**) allaiter. ~**-
stroke** n. brasse f.
breath /breθ/ n. souffle m., haleine f. **out
of** ~, essoufflé. **under one's** ~, tout
bas. ~**less** a. essoufflé.
breathalyser /'breθəlaɪzə(r)/ n. alcootest m.
breath|e /briːð/ v.t./i. respirer. ~ **in**,
inspirer. ~ **out**, expirer. ~**ing** n.
respiration f.
breather /'briːðə(r)/ n. moment de repos
m.
breathtaking /'breθteɪkɪŋ/ a. à vous
couper le souffle.
bred /bred/ see **breed**.
breeches /'brɪtʃɪz/ n. pl. culotte f.
breed /briːd/ v.t. (p.t. **bred**) élever; (give
rise to) engendrer. —v.i. se reproduire.
—n. race f. ~**er** n. éleveur m. ~**ing** n.
élevage m.; (fig.) éducation f.
breez|e /briːz/ n. brise f. ~**y** a. (weather)
frais; (cheerful) jovial; (casual) désinvolte.

Breton /'bretn/ a. & n. breton(ne) (m.
(f.)).
brevity /'brevəti/ n. brièveté f.
brew /bruː/ v.t. (beer) brasser; (tea)
faire infuser. —v.i. fermenter; infuser;
(fig.) se préparer. —n. décoction f.
~**er** n. brasseur m. ~**ery** n. brasserie f.
bribe /braɪb/ n. pot-de-vin m. —v.t.
soudoyer, acheter. ~**ry** /-ərɪ/ n.
corruption f.
brick /brɪk/ n. brique f.
bricklayer /'brɪkleɪə(r)/ n. maçon m.
bridal /'braɪdl/ a. nuptial.
bride /braɪd/ n. mariée f.
bridegroom /'braɪdgrʊm/ n. marié m.
bridesmaid /'braɪdzmeɪd/ n. demoiselle
d'honneur f.
bridge¹ /brɪdʒ/ n. pont m.; (naut.)
passerelle f.; (of nose) arête f. —v.t. ~
a gap, combler une lacune.
bridge² /brɪdʒ/ n. (cards) bridge m.
bridle /'braɪdl/ n. bride f. —v.t. brider.
~**-path** n. allée cavalière f.
brief¹ /briːf/ a. (-er, -est) bref. ~**ly** adv.
brièvement. ~**ness** n. brièveté f.
brief² /briːf/ n. instructions f. pl.; (jurid.)
dossier m. —v.t. donner des instruc-
tions à. ~**ing** n. briefing m.
briefcase /'briːfkeɪs/ n. serviette f.
briefs /briːfs/ n. pl. slip m.
brigad|e /brɪ'geɪd/ n. brigade f. ~**ier**
/-ə'dɪə(r)/ n. général de brigade m.
bright /braɪt/ a. (-er, -est) brillant, vif;
(day, room) clair; (cheerful) gai;
(clever) intelligent. ~**ly** adv. brillam-
ment. ~**ness** n. éclat m.
brighten /'braɪtn/ v.t. égayer. —v.i.
(weather) s'éclaircir; (of face)
s'éclairer.
brillian|t /'brɪljənt/ a. brillant; (light)
éclatant; (very good: fam.) super. ~**ce**
n. éclat m.
brim /brɪm/ n. bord m. —v.i. (p.t.
brimmed). ~ **over**, déborder.
brine /braɪn/ n. saumure f.
bring /brɪŋ/ v.t. (p.t. **brought**) (thing)
apporter; (person, vehicle) amener. ~
about, provoquer. ~ **back**, rapporter;
ramener. ~ **down**, faire tomber; (shoot
down, knock down) abattre. ~ **forward**, avancer. ~ **off**, réussir. ~ **out**,
(take out) sortir; (show) faire ressortir;
(book) publier. ~ **round** or **to**, ranimer.
~ **to bear**, (pressure etc.) exercer. ~
up, élever; (med.) vomir; (question)
soulever.
brink /brɪŋk/ n. bord m.
brisk /brɪsk/ a. (-er, -est) vif. ~**ness** n.
vivacité f.

bristl|e /'brɪsl/ n. poil m. —v.i. se hérisser. **∼ing with,** hérissé de.

Britain /'brɪtn/ n. Grande-Bretagne f.

British /'brɪtɪʃ/ a. britannique. **the ∼,** les Britanniques m. pl.

Briton /'brɪtn/ n. Britannique m./f.

Brittany /'brɪtənɪ/ n. Bretagne f.

brittle /'brɪtl/ a. fragile.

broach /brəʊtʃ/ v.t. entamer.

broad /brɔːd/ a. (**-er, -est**) large; (daylight, outline) grand. **∼ bean,** fève f. **∼-minded** a. large d'esprit. **∼ly** adv. en gros.

broadcast /'brɔːdkɑːst/ v.t./i. (p.t. **broadcast**) diffuser; (person) parler à la télévision or à la radio. —n. émission f.

broaden /'brɔːdn/ v.t./i. (s')élargir.

broccoli /'brɒkəlɪ/ n. invar. brocoli m.

brochure /'brəʊʃə(r)/ n. brochure f.

broke /brəʊk/ see **break.** —a. (penniless: sl.) fauché.

broken /'brəʊkən/ see **break.** —a. **∼ English,** mauvais anglais m. **∼-hearted** a. au cœur brisé.

broker /'brəʊkə(r)/ n. courtier m.

brolly /'brɒlɪ/ n. (fam.) pépin m.

bronchitis /brɒŋ'kaɪtɪs/ n. bronchite f.

bronze /brɒnz/ n. bronze m. —v.t./i. (se) bronzer.

brooch /brəʊtʃ/ n. broche f.

brood /bruːd/ n. nichée f., couvée f. —v.i. couver; (fig.) méditer tristement. **∼y** a. mélancolique.

brook¹ /brʊk/ n. ruisseau m.

brook² /brʊk/ v.t. souffrir.

broom /bruːm/ n. balai m.

broomstick /'bruːmstɪk/ n. manche à balai m.

broth /brɒθ/ n. bouillon m.

brothel /'brɒθl/ n. maison close f.

brother /'brʌðə(r)/ n. frère m. **∼hood** n. fraternité f. **∼-in-law** n. (pl. **∼s-in-law**) beau-frère m. **∼ly** a. fraternel.

brought /brɔːt/ see **bring.**

brow /braʊ/ n. front m.; (of hill) sommet m.

browbeat /'braʊbiːt/ v.t. (p.t. **-beat,** p.p. **-beaten**) intimider.

brown /braʊn/ a. (**-er, -est**) marron (invar.); (cheveux) brun. —n. marron m.; brun m. —v.t./i. brunir; (culin.) (faire) dorer. **be ∼ed off,** (sl.) en avoir ras le bol. **∼ bread,** pain bis m. **∼ sugar,** cassonade f.

Brownie /'braʊnɪ/ n. jeannette f.

browse /braʊz/ v.i. feuilleter; (animal) brouter.

bruise /bruːz/ n. bleu m. —v.t. (hurt)

faire un bleu à; (fruit) abîmer. **∼d** a. couvert de bleus.

brunch /brʌntʃ/ n. petit déjeuner copieux m. (pris comme déjeuner).

brunette /bruː'net/ n. brunette f.

brunt /brʌnt/ n. **the ∼ of,** le plus fort de.

brush /brʌʃ/ n. brosse f.; (skirmish) accrochage m.; (bushes) broussailles f. pl. —v.t. brosser. **∼ against,** effleurer. **∼ aside,** écarter. **give s.o. the ∼-off,** (reject: fam.) envoyer promener qn. **∼ up (on),** se remettre à.

Brussels /'brʌslz/ n. Bruxelles m./f. **∼ sprouts,** choux de Bruxelles m. pl.

brutal /'bruːtl/ a. brutal. **∼ity** /-'tælətɪ/ n. brutalité f.

brute /bruːt/ n. brute f. **by ∼ force,** par la force.

B.Sc. abbr. see **Bachelor of Science.**

bubble /'bʌbl/ n. bulle f. —v.i. bouillonner. **∼ bath,** bain moussant m. **∼ over,** déborder.

buck¹ /bʌk/ n. mâle m. —v.i. ruer. **∼ up,** (sl.) prendre courage; (hurry: sl.) se grouiller.

buck² /bʌk/ n. (Amer., sl.) dollar m.

buck³ /bʌk/ n. **pass the ∼,** rejeter la responsabilité (**to,** sur).

bucket /'bʌkɪt/ n. seau m. **∼ shop,** agence de charters f.

buckle /'bʌkl/ n. boucle f. —v.t./i. (fasten) (se) boucler; (bend) voiler. **∼ down to,** s'atteler à.

bud /bʌd/ n. bourgeon m. —v.i. (p.t. **budded**) bourgeonner.

Buddhis|t /'bʊdɪst/ a. & n. bouddhiste (m./f.) **∼m** /-ɪzəm/ n. bouddhisme m.

budding /'bʌdɪŋ/ a. (talent etc.) naissant; (film star etc.) en herbe.

buddy /'bʌdɪ/ n. (fam.) copain m.

budge /bʌdʒ/ v.t./i. (faire) bouger.

budgerigar /'bʌdʒərɪgɑː(r)/ n. perruche f.

budget /'bʌdʒɪt/ n. budget m. —v.i. (p.t. **budgeted**). **∼ for,** prévoir (dans son budget).

buff /bʌf/ n. (colour) chamois m.; (fam.) fanatique m./f.

buffalo /'bʌfələʊ/ n. (pl. **-oes** or **-o**) buffle m.; (Amer.) bison m.

buffer /'bʌfə(r)/ n. tampon m. **∼ zone,** zone tampon f.

buffet¹ /'bʊfeɪ/ n. (meal, counter) buffet m. **∼ car,** buffet m.

buffet² /'bʌfɪt/ n. (blow) soufflet m. —v.t. (p.t. **buffeted**) souffleter.

buffoon /bə'fuːn/ n. bouffon m.

bug /bʌg/ n. (insect) punaise f.; (any small insect) bestiole f.; (germ: sl.)

microbe *m.*; (*device*: *sl.*) micro *m.*; (*defect*: *sl.*) défaut *m.* —*v.t.* (*p.t.* **bugged**) mettre des micros dans; (*Amer.*, *sl.*) embêter.

buggy /'bʌgɪ/ *n.* (*child's*) poussette *f.*

bugle /'bju:gl/ *n.* clairon *m.*

build /bɪld/ *v.t./i.* (*p.t.* **built**) bâtir, construire. —*n.* carrure *f.* ~ **up**, (*increase*) augmenter, monter; (*accumulate*) (s')accumuler. ~**-up** *n.* accumulation *f.*; (*fig.*) publicité *f.* ~**er** *n.* entrepreneur *m.*; (*workman*) ouvrier *m.*

building /'bɪldɪŋ/ *n.* bâtiment *m.*; (*dwelling*) immeuble *m.* ~ **society**, caisse d'épargne-logement *f.*

built /bɪlt/ *see* **build.** ~**-in** *a.* encastré. ~**-up area**, agglomération *f.*, zone urbanisée *f.*

bulb /bʌlb/ *n.* oignon *m.*; (*electr.*) ampoule *f.* ~**ous** *a.* bulbeux.

Bulgaria /bʌl'geərɪə/ *n.* Bulgarie *f.* ~**n** *a.* & *n.* bulgare (*m./f.*).

bulg|e /bʌldʒ/ *n.* renflement *m.* —*v.i.* se renfler, être renflé. **be** ~**ing with**, être gonflé *or* bourré de.

bulimia /bju:'lɪmɪə/ *n.* boulimie *f.*

bulk /bʌlk/ *n.* grosseur *f.* **in** ~, en gros; (*loose*) en vrac. the ~ **of**, la majeure partie de. ~**y** *a.* gros.

bull /bʊl/ *n.* taureau *m.* ~**'s-eye** *n.* centre (de la cible) *m.*

bulldog /'bʊldɒg/ *n.* bouledogue *m.*

bulldoze /'bʊldəʊz/ *v.t.* raser au bulldozer. ~**r** /-ə(r)/ *n.* bulldozer *m.*

bullet /'bʊlɪt/ *n.* balle *f.* ~**-proof** *a.* pare-balles *invar.*; (*vehicle*) blindé.

bulletin /'bʊlətɪn/ *n.* bulletin *m.*

bullfight /'bʊlfaɪt/ *n.* corrida *f.* ~**er** *n.* torero *m.*

bullion /'bʊljən/ *n.* or *or* argent en lingots *m.*

bullring /'bʊlrɪŋ/ *n.* arène *f.*

bully /'bʊlɪ/ *n.* brute *f.*; tyran *m.* —*v.t.* (*treat badly*) brutaliser; (*persecute*) tyranniser; (*coerce*) forcer (**into**, à).

bum¹ /bʌm/ *n.* (*sl.*) derrière *m.*

bum² /bʌm/ *n.* (*Amer.*, *sl.*) vagabond(e) *m.* (*f.*).

bumble-bee /'bʌmblbi:/ *n.* bourdon *m.*

bump /bʌmp/ *n.* choc *m.*; (*swelling*) bosse *f.* —*v.t./i.* cogner, heurter. ~ **along**, cahoter. ~ **into**, (*hit*) rentrer dans; (*meet*) tomber sur. ~**y** *a.* cahoteux.

bumper /'bʌmpə(r)/ *n.* pare-chocs *m.* *invar.* —*a.* exceptionnel.

bumptious /'bʌmpʃəs/ *a.* prétentieux.

bun /bʌn/ *n.* (*cake*) petit pain au lait *m.*; (*hair*) chignon *m.*

bunch /bʌntʃ/ *n.* (*of flowers*) bouquet *m.*; (*of keys*) trousseau *m.*; (*of people*) groupe *m.*; (*of bananas*) régime *m.* ~ **of grapes**, grappe de raisin *f.*

bundle /'bʌndl/ *n.* paquet *m.* —*v.t.* mettre en paquet; (*push*) pousser.

bung /bʌŋ/ *n.* bonde *f.* —*v.t.* boucher; (*throw*: *sl.*) flanquer.

bungalow /'bʌŋgələʊ/ *n.* bungalow *m.*

bungle /'bʌŋgl/ *v.t.* gâcher.

bunion /'bʌnjən/ *n.* (*med.*) oignon *m.*

bunk¹ /bʌŋk/ *n.* couchette *f.* ~**-beds** *n. pl.* lits superposés *m. pl.*

bunk² /bʌŋk/ *n.* (*nonsense*: *sl.*) foutaise(s) *f.* (*pl.*).

bunker /'bʌŋkə(r)/ *n.* (*mil.*) bunker *m.*

bunny /'bʌnɪ/ *n.* (*children's use*) (Jeannot) lapin *m.*

buoy /bɔɪ/ *n.* bouée *f.* —*v.t.* ~ **up**, (*hearten*) soutenir, encourager.

buoyan|t /'bɔɪənt/ *a.* (*cheerful*) gai. ~**cy** *n.* gaieté *f.*

burden /'bɜ:dn/ *n.* fardeau *m.* —*v.t.* accabler. ~**some** *a.* lourd.

bureau /'bjʊərəʊ/ *n.* (*pl.* **-eaux** /-əʊz/) bureau *m.*

bureaucracy /bjʊə'rɒkrəsɪ/ *n.* bureaucratie *f.*

bureaucrat /'bjʊərəkræt/ *n.* bureaucrate *m./f.* ~**ic** /-'krætɪk/ *a.* bureaucratique.

burglar /'bɜ:glə(r)/ *n.* cambrioleur *m.* ~**ize** *v.t.* (*Amer.*) cambrioler. ~ **alarm**, alarme *f.* ~**y** *n.* cambriolage *m.*

burgle /'bɜ:gl/ *v.t.* cambrioler.

Burgundy /'bɜ:gəndɪ/ *n.* (*wine*) bourgogne *m.*

burial /'berɪəl/ *n.* enterrement *m.*

burlesque /bɜ:'lesk/ *n.* (*imitation*) parodie *f.*

burly /'bɜ:lɪ/ *a.* (**-ier**, **-iest**) costaud, solidement charpenté.

Burm|a /'bɜ:mə/ *n.* Birmanie *f.* ~**ese** /-'mi:z/ *a.* & *n.* birman(e) (*m.* (*f.*)).

burn /bɜ:n/ *v.t./i.* (*p.t.* **burned** *or* **burnt**) brûler. —*n.* brûlure *f.* ~ **down** *or* **be** ~**ed down**, être réduit en cendres. ~**er** *n.* brûleur *m.* ~**ing** *a.* (*fig.*) brûlant.

burnish /'bɜ:nɪʃ/ *v.t.* polir.

burnt /bɜ:nt/ *see* **burn.**

burp /bɜ:p/ *n.* (*fam.*) rot *m.* —*v.i.* (*fam.*) roter.

burrow /'bʌrəʊ/ *n.* terrier *m.* —*v.t.* creuser.

bursar /'bɜ:sə(r)/ *n.* économe *m./f.*

bursary /'bɜ:sərɪ/ *n.* bourse *f.*

burst /bɜ:st/ *v.t./i.* (*p.t.* **burst**) crever, (faire) éclater. —*n.* explosion *f.*; (*of laughter*) éclat *m.*; (*surge*) élan *m.* **be** ~**ing with**, déborder de. ~ **into**, faire irruption dans. **~ into tears,** fondre en larmes. **~ out laughing,** éclater de rire. **~ pipe,** conduite qui a éclaté *f.*

bury /'berɪ/ *v.t.* (*person etc.*) enterrer; (*hide, cover*) enfouir; (*engross, thrust*) plonger.

bus /bʌs/ *n.* (*pl.* **buses**) (auto)bus *m.* —*v.t.* transporter en bus. —*v.i.* (*p.t.* **bussed**) prendre l'autobus. **~-stop** *n.* arrêt d'autobus *m.*

bush /bʊʃ/ *n.* buisson *m.*; (*land*) brousse *f.* **~y** *a.* broussailleux.

business /'bɪznɪs/ *n.* (*task, concern*) affaire *f.*; (*commerce*) affaires *f. pl.*; (*line of work*) mêtier *m.*; (*shop*) commerce *m.* **he has no ~ to,** il n'a pas le droit de. **mean ~,** être sérieux. **that's none of your ~!,** ça ne vous regarde pas! **~man,** homme d'affaires *m.*

businesslike /'bɪznɪslaɪk/ *a.* sérieux.

busker /'bʌskə(r)/ *n.* musicien(ne) des rues *m. (f.).*

bust[1] /bʌst/ *n.* buste *m.*; (*bosom*) poitrine *f.*

bust[2] /bʌst/ *v.t./i.* (*p.t.* **busted** *or* **bust**) (*burst: sl.*) crever; (*break: sl.*) (se) casser. —*a.* (*broken, finished: sl.*) fichu. **~-up** *n.* (*sl.*) engueulade *f.* **go ~,** (*sl.*) faire faillite.

bustl|e /'bʌsl/ *v.i.* s'affairer. —*n.* affairement *m.*, remue-ménage *m.* **~ing** *a.* (*place*) bruyant, animé.

bus|y /'bɪzɪ/ *a.* (**-ier, -iest**) occupé; (*street*) animé; (*day*) chargé. —*v.t.* **~y o.s. with,** s'occuper à. **~ily** *adv.* activement.

busybody /'bɪzɪbɒdɪ/ *n.* **be a ~,** faire la mouche du coche.

but /bʌt, *unstressed* bət/ *conj.* mais. —*prep.* sauf. —*adv.* (*only*) seulement. **~ for,** sans. **nobody ~,** personne d'autre que. **nothing ~,** rien que.

butane /'bjuːteɪn/ *n.* butane *m.*

butcher /'bʊtʃə(r)/ *n.* boucher *m.* —*v.t.* massacrer. **~y** *n.* boucherie *f.*, massacre *m.*

butler /'bʌtlə(r)/ *n.* maître d'hôtel *m.*

butt /bʌt/ *n.* (*of gun*) crosse *f.*; (*of cigarette*) mégot *m.*; (*target*) cible *f.*; (*barrel*) tonneau; (*Amer., fam.*) derrière *m.* —*v.i.* **~ in,** interrompre.

butter /'bʌtə(r)/ *n.* beurre *m.* —*v.t.* beurrer. **~-bean** *n.* haricot blanc *m.* **~-fingers** *n.* maladroit(e) *m. (f.).*

buttercup /'bʌtəkʌp/ *n.* bouton-d'or *m.*

butterfly /'bʌtəflaɪ/ *n.* papillon *m.*

buttock /'bʌtək/ *n.* fesse *f.*

button /'bʌtn/ *n.* bouton *m.* —*v.t./i.* **~ (up),** (se) boutonner.

buttonhole /'bʌtnhəʊl/ *n.* boutonnière *f.* —*v.t.* accrocher.

buttress /'bʌtrɪs/ *n.* contrefort *m.* —*v.t.* soutenir.

buxom /'bʌksəm/ *a.* bien en chair.

buy /baɪ/ *v.t.* (*p.t.* **bought**) acheter (**from,** à); (*believe: sl.*) croire, avaler. —*n.* achat *m.* **~ sth for s.o.** acheter qch. à qn., prendre qch. pour qn. **~er** *n.* acheteulr, -se *m., f.*

buzz /bʌz/ *n.* bourdonnement *m.* —*v.i.* bourdonner. **~ off,** (*sl.*) ficher le camp. **~er** *n.* sonnerie *f.*

by /baɪ/ *prep.* par, de; (*near*) à côté de; (*before*) avant; (*means*) en, à, par. **by bike,** à vélo. **by car,** en auto. **by day,** de jour. **by the kilo,** au kilo. **by running/**etc., en courant/*etc.* **by sea,** par mer. **by that time,** à ce moment-là. **by the way,** à propos. —*adv.* (*near*) tout près. **by and large,** dans l'ensemble. **by-election** *n.* élection partielle *f.* **~-law** *n.* arrêté *m.*; (*of club etc.*) statut *m.* **by o.s.,** tout seul. **by-product** *n.* sous-produit *m.*; (*fig.*) conséquence. **by-road** *n.* chemin de traverse *m.*

bye(-bye) /baɪ('baɪ)/ *int.* (*fam.*) au revoir, salut.

bypass /'baɪpɑːs/ *n.* (*auto.*) route qui contourne *f.*; (*med.*) pontage *m.* —*v.t.* contourner.

bystander /'baɪstændə(r)/ *n.* spectalteur, -trice *m., f.*

byte /baɪt/ *n.* octet *m.*

byword /'baɪwɜːd/ *n.* **be a ~ for,** être connu pour.

C

cab /kæb/ *n.* taxi *m.*; (*of lorry, train*) cabine *f.*

cabaret /'kæbəreɪ/ *n.* spectacle (de cabaret) *m.*

cabbage /'kæbɪdʒ/ *n.* chou *m.*

cabin /'kæbɪn/ *n.* (*hut*) cabane *f.*; (*in ship, aircraft*) cabine *f.*

cabinet /'kæbɪnɪt/ *n.* (petite) armoire *f.*, meuble de rangement *m.*; (*for filing*) classeur *m.* **C~,** (*pol.*) cabinet *m.* **~-maker** *n.* ébéniste *m.*

cable /'keɪbl/ *n.* câble *m.* —*v.t.* câbler. **~-car** *n.* téléphérique *m.* **~ railway,** funiculaire *m.*

caboose /kə'buːs/ *n.* (*rail., Amer.*) fourgon *m.*

cache /kæʃ/ *n.* (*place*) cachette *f.* **a ~ of arms,** des armes cachées.

cackle /'kækl/ *n.* caquet *m.* —*v.i.* caqueter.

cactus /'kæktəs/ *n.* (*pl.* **-ti** /-taɪ/ *or* **-tuses**) cactus *m.*

caddie /'kædɪ/ *n.* (*golf*) caddie *m.*

caddy /'kædɪ/ *n.* boîte à thé *f.*

cadence /'keɪdns/ *n.* cadence *f.*

cadet /kə'det/ *n.* élève officier *m.*

cadge /kædʒ/ *v.t.* se fairer payer, écornifler. —*v.i.* quémander. **~ money from,** taper. **~r** /-ə(r)/ *n.* écornifleulr, -se *m.*, *f.*

Caesarean /sɪ'zeərɪən/ *a.* **~ (section),** césarienne *f.*

café /'kæfeɪ/ *n.* café(-restaurant) *m.*

cafeteria /kæfɪ'tɪərɪə/ *n.* cafétéria *f.*

caffeine /'kæfiːn/ *n.* caféine *f.*

cage /keɪdʒ/ *n.* cage *f.* —*v.t.* mettre en cage.

cagey /'keɪdʒɪ/ *a.* (*secretive: fam.*) peu communicatif.

cagoule /kə'guːl/ *n.* K-way *n.* (P.).

Cairo /'kaɪərəʊ/ *n.* le Caire *m.*

cajole /kə'dʒəʊl/ *v.t.* **~ s.o. into doing,** faire l'enjoleur pour que qn. fasse.

cake /keɪk/ *n.* gâteau *m.* **~d** *a.* durci. **~d with,** raidi par.

calamit|y /kə'læmətɪ/ *n.* calamité *f.* **~ous** *a.* désastreux.

calcium /'kælsɪəm/ *n.* calcium *m.*

calculat|e /'kælkjʊleɪt/ *v.t./i.* calculer; (*Amer.*) supposer. **~ed** *a.* (*action*) délibéré. **~ing** *a.* calculateur. **~ion** /-'leɪʃn/ *n.* calcul *m.* **~or** *n.* calculatrice *f.*

calculus /'kælkjʊləs/ *n.* (*pl.* **-li** /-laɪ/ *or* **-luses**) calcul *m.*

calendar /'kælɪndə(r)/ *n.* calendrier *m.*

calf¹ /kɑːf/ *n.* (*pl.* **calves**) (*young cow or bull*) veau *m.*

calf² /kɑːf/ *n.* (*pl.* **calves**) (*of leg*) mollet *m.*

calibre /'kælɪbə(r)/ *n.* calibre *m.*

calico /'kælɪkəʊ/ *n.* calicot *m.*

call /kɔːl/ *v.t./i.* appeler. **~ (in or round),** (*visit*) passer. —*n.* appel *m.*; (*of bird*) cri *m.*; (*visit*) visite *f.* **be ~ed,** (*named*) s'appeler. **be on ~,** être de garde. **~ back,** rappeler; (*visit*) repasser. **~-box** *n.* cabine téléphonique *f.* **~ for,** (*require*) demander; (*fetch*) passer prendre. **~-girl** *n.* call-girl *f.* **~ off,** annuler. **~ out (to),** appeler. **~ on,** (*visit*) passer chez; (*appeal to*) faire appel à. **~ up,** appeler (au téléphone); (*mil.*) mobiliser, appeler. **~er** *n.* visiteulr, -se *m.*, *f.*; (*on phone*) personne qui appelle *f.* **~ing** *n.* vocation *f.*

callous /'kæləs/ *a.*, **~ly** *adv.* sans pitié. **~ness** *n.* manque de pitié *m.*

callow /'kæləʊ/ *a.* (**-er, -est**) inexpérimenté.

calm /kɑːm/ *a.* (**-er, -est**) calme. —*n.* calme *m.* —*v.t./i.* **~ (down),** (se) calmer. **~ness** *n.* calme *m.*

calorie /'kælərɪ/ *n.* calorie *f.*

camber /'kæmbə(r)/ *n.* (*of road*) bombement *m.*

camcorder /'kæmkɔːdə(r)/ *n.* caméscope *m.*

came /keɪm/ *see* **come.**

camel /'kæml/ *n.* chameau *m.*

cameo /'kæmɪəʊ/ *n.* (*pl.* **-os**) camée *m.*

camera /'kæmərə/ *n.* appareil(-photo) *m.*; (*for moving pictures*) caméra *f.* **in ~,** à huis clos. **~man** *n.* (*pl.* **-men**) caméraman *m.*

camouflage /'kæməflɑːʒ/ *n.* camouflage *m.* —*v.t.* camoufler.

camp¹ /kæmp/ *n.* camp *m.* —*v.i.* camper. **~-bed** *n.* lit de camp *m.* **~er** *n.* campeulr, -se *m.*, *f.* **~er(-van),** camping-car *m.* **~ing** *n.* camping *m.*

camp² /kæmp/ *a.* (*mannered*) affecté; (*vulgar*) de mauvais goût.

campaign /kæm'peɪn/ *n.* campagne *f.* —*v.i.* faire campagne.

campsite /'kæmpsaɪt/ *n.* (*for holiday-makers*) camping *m.*

campus /'kæmpəs/ *n.* (*pl.* **-puses**) campus *m.*

can¹ /kæn/ *n.* bidon *m.*; (*sealed container for food*) boîte *f.* —*v.t.* (*p.t.* **canned**) mettre en boîte. **~ it!,** (*Amer., sl.*) ferme-la! **~ned music,** musique de fond enregistrée *f.* **~-opener** *n.* ouvre-boîte(s) *m.*

can² /kæn, *unstressed* kən/ *v. aux.* (*be able to*) pouvoir; (*know how to*) savoir.

Canad|a /'kænədə/ *n.* Canada *m.* **~ian** /kə'neɪdɪən/ *a. & n.* canadien(ne) (*m.* (*f.*).

canal /kə'næl/ *n.* canal *m.*

canary /kə'neərɪ/ *n.* canari *m.*

cancel /'kænsl/ *v.t./i.* (*p.t.* **cancelled**) (*call off, revoke*) annuler; (*cross out*) barrer; (*a stamp*) oblitérer. **~ out,** (se) neutraliser. **~lation** /-ə'leɪʃn/ *n.* annulation *f.*; oblitération *f.*

cancer /'kænsə(r)/ *n.* cancer *m.* **~ous** *a.* cancéreux.

Cancer /'kænsə(r)/ *n.* le Cancer.

candid /'kændɪd/ *a.* franc. **~ness** *n.* franchise *f.*

candida|te /'kændɪdeɪt/ *n.* candidat(e) *m.* (*f.*). **~cy** /-əsɪ/ *n.* candidature *f.*

candle /'kændl/ n. bougie f., chandelle f.; (in church) cierge m.
candlestick /'kændlstık/ n. bougeoir m., chandelier m.
candour, (Amer.) **candor** /'kændə(r)/ n. franchise f.
candy /'kændı/ n. (Amer.) bonbon(s) m. (pl.). **~-floss** n. barbe à papa f.
cane /keın/ n. canne f.; (for baskets) rotin m.; (for punishment: schol.) baguette f., bâton m. —v.t. donner des coups de baguette or de bâton à, fustiger.
canine /'keınaın/ a. canin.
canister /'kænıstə(r)/ n. boîte f.
cannabis /'kænəbıs/ n. cannabis m.
cannibal /'kænıbl/ n. cannibale m./f. **~ism** n. cannibalisme m.
cannon /'kænən/ n. (pl. ~ or ~s) canon m. **~-ball** n. boulet de canon m.
cannot /'kænət/ = can not.
canny /'kænı/ a. rusé, madré.
canoe /kə'nu:/ n. (sport) canoë m., kayak m. —v.i. faire du canoë or du kayak. **~ist** n. canoéiste m./f.
canon /'kænən/ n. (clergyman) chanoine m.; (rule) canon m.
canonize /'kænənaız/ v.t. canoniser.
canopy /'kænəpı/ n. dais m.; (over doorway) marquise f.
can't /ka:nt/ = can not.
cantankerous /kæn'tæŋkərəs/ a. acariâtre, grincheux.
canteen /kæn'ti:n/ n. (restaurant) cantine f.; (flask) bidon m.
canter /'kæntə(r)/ n. petit galop m. —v.i. aller au petit galop.
canvas /'kænvəs/ n. toile f.
canvass /'kænvəs/ v.t./i. (comm., pol.) solliciter des commandes or des voix (de). **~ing** n. (comm.) démarchage m.; (pol.) démarchage électoral m. **~ opinion,** sonder l'opinion.
canyon /'kænjən/ n. cañon m.
cap /kæp/ n. (hat) casquette f.; (of bottle, tube) bouchon m.; (of beer or milk bottle) capsule f.; (of pen) capuchon m.; (for toy gun) amorce f. —v.t. (p.t. **capped**) (bottle) capsuler; (outdo) surpasser. **~ped with,** coiffé de.
capab|le /'keıpəbl/ a. (person) capable (of, de), compétent. **be ~le of,** (of situation, text, etc.) être susceptible de. **~ility** /-'bılətı/ n. capacité f. **~ly** adv. avec compétence.
capacity /kə'pæsətı/ n. capacité f. **in one's ~ as,** en sa qualité de.
cape¹ /keıp/ n. (cloak) cape f.
cape² /keıp/ n. (geog.) cap m.

caper¹ /'keıpə(r)/ v.i. gambader. —n. (prank) farce f.; (activity: sl.) affaire f.
caper² /'keıpə(r)/ n. (culin.) câpre f.
capital /'kæpıtl/ a. capital. —n. (town) capitale f.; (money) capital m. **~ (letter),** majuscule f.
capitalis|t /'kæpıtəlıst/ a. & n. capitaliste (m./f.). **~m** /-zəm/ n. capitalisme m.
capitalize /'kæpıtəlaız/ v.i. **~ on,** tirer profit de.
capitulat|e /kə'pıtʃʊleıt/ v.i. capituler. **~ion** /-'leıʃn/ n. capitulation f.
capricious /kə'prıʃəs/ a. capricieux.
Capricorn /'kæprıkɔ:n/ n. le Capricorne.
capsize /kæp'saız/ v.t./i. (faire) chavirer.
capsule /'kæpsju:l/ n. capsule f.
captain /'kæptın/ n. capitaine m.
caption /'kæpʃn/ n. (for illustration) légende f.; (heading) sous-titre m.
captivate /'kæptıveıt/ v.t. captiver.
captiv|e /'kæptıv/ a. & n. captif, -ve (m., f.). **~ity** /-'tıvətı/ n. captivité f.
capture /'kæptʃə(r)/ v.t. (person, animal) prendre, capturer; (attention) retenir. —n. capture f.
car /ka:(r)/ n. voiture f. **~ ferry,** ferry m. **~-park** n. parking m. **~ phone,** téléphone de voiture m. **~-wash** n. station de lavage f., lave-auto m.
carafe /kə'ræf/ n. carafe f.
caramel /'kærəmel/ n. caramel m.
carat /'kærət/ n. carat m.
caravan /'kærəvæn/ n. caravane f.
carbohydrate /ka:bəʊ'haıdreıt/ n. hydrate de carbone m.
carbon /'ka:bən/ n. carbone m. **~ copy, ~ paper,** carbone m.
carburettor, (Amer.) **carburetor** /ka:bju'retə(r)/ n. carburateur m.
carcass /'ka:kəs/ n. carcasse f.
card /ka:d/ n. carte f. **~-index** n. fichier m.
cardboard /'ka:dbɔ:d/ n. carton m.
cardiac /'ka:dıæk/ a. cardiaque.
cardigan /'ka:dıgən/ n. cardigan m.
cardinal /'ka:dınl/ a. cardinal. —n. (relig.) cardinal m.
care /keə(r)/ n. (attention) soin m., attention f.; (worry) souci m.; (protection) garde f. —v.i. **~ about,** s'intéresser à. **~ for,** s'occuper de; (invalid) soigner. **~ to or for,** aimer, vouloir. **I don't ~,** ça m'est égal. **take ~ of,** s'occuper de. **take ~ (of yourself),** prends soin de toi. **take ~ to do sth.,** faire bien attention à faire qch.
career /kə'rıə(r)/ n. carrière f. —v.i. aller à toute vitesse.

carefree /'keəfriː/ a. insouciant.

careful /'keəfl/ a. soigneux; (*cautious*) prudent. (**be**) ∼!, (fais) attention! ∼**ly** adv. avec soin.

careless /'keəlɪs/ a. négligent; (*work*) peu soigné. ∼ **about**, peu soucieux de. ∼**ly** adv. négligemment. ∼**ness** n. négligence f.

caress /kə'res/ n. caresse f. —v.t. caresser.

caretaker /'keəteɪkə(r)/ n. gardien(ne) m. (f.). —a. (*president*) par intérim.

cargo /'kɑːgəʊ/ n. (pl. **-oes**) cargaison f. ∼ **boat**, cargo m.

Caribbean /kærɪ'biːən/ a. caraïbe. —n. **the** ∼, (*sea*) la mer des Caraïbes; (*islands*) les Antilles f. pl.

caricature /'kærɪkətjʊə(r)/ n. caricature f. —v.t. caricaturer.

caring /'keərɪŋ/ a. (*mother, son, etc.*) aimant. —n. affection f.

carnage /'kɑːnɪdʒ/ n. carnage m.

carnal /'kɑːnl/ a. charnel.

carnation /kɑː'neɪʃn/ n. œillet m.

carnival /'kɑːnɪvl/ n. carnaval m.

carol /'kærəl/ n. chant (de Noël) m.

carp[1] /kɑːp/ n. invar. carpe f.

carp[2] /kɑːp/ v.i. ∼ (**at**), critiquer.

carpent|er /'kɑːpɪntə(r)/ n. charpentier m.; (*for light woodwork, furniture*) menuisier m. ∼**ry** n. charpenterie f.; menuiserie f.

carpet /'kɑːpɪt/ n. tapis m. —v.t. (p.t. **carpeted**) recouvrir d'un tapis. ∼-**sweeper** n. balai mécanique m. **on the** ∼, (*fam.*) sur la sellette.

carriage /'kærɪdʒ/ n. (*rail & horse-drawn*) voiture f.; (*of goods*) transport m.; (*cost*) port m.

carriageway /'kærɪdʒweɪ/ n. chaussée f.

carrier /'kærɪə(r)/ n. transporteur m.; (*med.*) porteulr, -se m., f. ∼ (**bag**), sac en plastique m.

carrot /'kærət/ n. carotte f.

carry /'kærɪ/ v.t./i. porter; (*goods*) transporter; (*involve*) comporter; (*motion*) voter. **be carried away**, s'emballer. ∼-**cot** n. porte-bébé m. ∼ **off**, enlever; (*prize*) remporter. ∼ **on**, continuer; (*behave: fam.*) se conduire (mal). ∼ **out**, (*an order, plan*) exécuter; (*duty*) accomplir; (*task*) effectuer.

cart /kɑːt/ n. charrette f. —v.t. transporter; (*heavy object: sl.*) trimballer.

cartilage /'kɑːtɪlɪdʒ/ n. cartilage m.

carton /'kɑːtn/ n. (*box*) carton m.; (*of yoghurt, cream*) pot m.; (*of cigarettes*) cartouche f.

cartoon /kɑː'tuːn/ n. dessin (humoristique) m.; (*cinema*) dessin animé m. ∼**ist** n. dessinalteur, -trice m., f.

cartridge /'kɑːtrɪdʒ/ n. cartouche f.

carve /kɑːv/ v.t. tailler; (*meat*) découper.

cascade /kæs'keɪd/ n. cascade f. —v.i. tomber en cascade.

case[1] /keɪs/ n. cas m.; (*jurid.*) affaire f.; (*phil.*) arguments m. pl. **in** ∼ **he comes**, au cas où il viendrait. **in** ∼ **of fire**, en cas d'incendie. **in** ∼ **of any problems**, au cas où il y aurait un problème. **in that** ∼, à ce moment-là.

case[2] /keɪs/ n. (*crate*) caisse f.; (*for camera, cigarettes, spectacles, etc.*) étui m.; (*suitcase*) valise f.

cash /kæʃ/ n. argent m. —a. (*price etc.*) (au) comptant. —v.t. encaisser. ∼ **a cheque**, (*person*) encaisser un chèque; (*bank*) payer un chèque. **pay** ∼, payer comptant. **in** ∼, en espèces. ∼ **desk**, caisse f. ∼ **dispenser**, distributeur de billets m. ∼-**flow** n. cash-flow m. ∼ **in (on)**, profiter (de). ∼ **register**, caisse enregistreuse f.

cashew /'kæʃuː/ n. noix de cajou f.

cashier /kæ'ʃɪə(r)/ n. caisslier, -ière m., f.

cashmere /'kæʃmɪə(r)/ n. cachemire m.

casino /kə'siːnəʊ/ n. (pl. **-os**) casino m.

cask /kɑːsk/ n. tonneau m.

casket /'kɑːskɪt/ n. (*box*) coffret m.; (*coffin: Amer.*) cercueil m.

casserole /'kæsərəʊl/ n. (*utensil*) cocotte f.; (*stew*) daube f.

cassette /kə'set/ n. cassette f.

cast /kɑːst/ v.t. (p.t. **cast**) (*throw*) jeter; (*glance, look*) jeter; (*shadow*) projeter; (*vote*) donner; (*metal*) couler. ∼ (**off**), (*shed*) se dépouiller de. —n. (*theatre*) distribution f.; (*of dice*) coup m.; (*mould*) moule m.; (*med.*) plâtre m. ∼ **iron**, fonte f. ∼-**iron** a. de fonte; (*fig.*) solide. ∼-**offs** n. pl. vieux vêtements m. pl.

castanets /kæstə'nets/ n. pl. castagnettes f. pl.

castaway /'kɑːstəweɪ/ n. naufragé(e) m. (f.).

caste /kɑːst/ n. caste f.

castle /'kɑːsl/ n. château m.; (*chess*) tour f.

castor /'kɑːstə(r)/ n. (*wheel*) roulette f. ∼ **sugar**, sucre en poudre m.

castrat|e /kæ'streɪt/ v.t. châtrer. ∼**ion** /-ʃn/ n. castration f.

casual /'kæʒʊəl/ a. (*remark*) fait au hasard; (*meeting*) fortuit; (*attitude*) désinvolte; (*work*) temporaire;

(*clothes*) sport *invar.* **~ly** *adv.* par hasard; (*carelessly*) avec désinvolture.

casualty /'kæʒuəltɪ/ *n.* (*dead*) mort(e) *m.* (*f.*); (*injured*) blessé(e) *m.* (*f.*); (*accident victim*) accidenté(e) *m.* (*f.*).

cat /kæt/ *n.* chat *m.* **C~'s-eyes** *n. pl.* (P.) catadioptres *m. pl.*

catalogue /'kætəlɒg/ *n.* catalogue *m.* —*v.t.* cataloguer.

catalyst /'kætəlɪst/ *n.* catalyseur *m.*

catapult /'kætəpʌlt/ *n.* lance-pierres *m.* *invar.* —*v.t.* catapulter.

cataract /'kætərækt/ *n.* (*waterfall & med.*) cataracte *f.*

catarrh /kə'tɑː(r)/ *n.* rhume *m.*, catarrhe *m.*

catastroph|e /kə'tæstrəfɪ/ *n.* catastrophe *f.* **~ic** /kætə'strɒfɪk/ *a.* catastrophique.

catch /kætʃ/ *v.t.* (*p.t.* **caught**) attraper; (*grab*) prendre, saisir; (*catch unawares*) surprendre; (*jam, trap*) prendre; (*understand*) saisir. —*v.i.* prendre; (*get stuck*) se prendre (**in,** dans). —*n.* capture *f.*, prise *f.*; (*on door*) loquet *m.*; (*fig.*) piège *m.* **~ fire,** prendre feu. **~ on,** (*fam.*) prendre, devenir populaire. **~ out,** prendre en faute. **~-phrase** *n.* slogan *m.* **~ sight of,** apercevoir. **~ s.o.'s eye,** attirer l'attention de qn. **~ up,** se rattraper. **~ up (with),** rattraper.

catching /'kætʃɪŋ/ *a.* contagieux.

catchment /'kætʃmənt/ *n.* **~ area,** région desservie *f.*

catchy /'kætʃɪ/ *a.* facile à retenir.

categorical /kætɪ'gɒrɪkl/ *a.* catégorique.

category /'kætɪgərɪ/ *n.* catégorie *f.*

cater /'keɪtə(r)/ *v.i.* s'occuper de la nourriture. **~ for,** (*pander to*) satisfaire; (*of magazine etc.*) s'adresser à. **~er** *n.* traiteur *m.*

caterpillar /'kætəpɪlə(r)/ *n.* chenille *f.*

cathedral /kə'θiːdrəl/ *n.* cathédrale *f.*

catholic /'kæθəlɪk/ *a.* universel. **C~** *a.* & *n.* catholique (*m./f.*). **C~ism** /kə'θɒlɪsɪzəm/ *n.* catholicisme *m.*

cattle /'kætl/ *n. pl.* bétail *m.*

catty /'kætɪ/ *a.* méchant.

caucus /'kɔːkəs/ *n.* comité électoral *m.*

caught /kɔːt/ *see* **catch.**

cauliflower /'kɒlɪflauə(r)/ *n.* chou-fleur *m.*

cause /kɔːz/ *n.* cause *f.*; (*reason*) raison *f.*, motif *m.* —*v.t.* causer. **~ sth. to grow/move/etc.,** faire pousser/bouger/etc. qch.

causeway /'kɔːzweɪ/ *n.* chaussée *f.*

cauti|on /'kɔːʃn/ *n.* prudence *f.*; (*warning*) avertissement *m.* —*v.t.*

avertir. **~ous** *a.* prudent. **~ously** *adv.* prudemment.

cavalier /kævə'lɪə(r)/ *a.* cavalier.

cavalry /'kævəlrɪ/ *n.* cavalerie *f.*

cave /keɪv/ *n.* caverne *f.*, grotte *f.* —*v.i.* **~ in,** s'effondrer; (*agree*) céder.

caveman /'keɪvmæn/ *n.* (*pl.* **-men**) homme des cavernes *m.*

cavern /'kævən/ *n.* caverne *f.*

caviare, *Amer.* **caviar** /'kævɪɑː(r)/ *n.* caviar *m.*

caving /'keɪvɪŋ/ *n.* spéléologie *f.*

cavity /'kævətɪ/ *n.* cavité *f.*

cavort /kə'vɔːt/ *v.i.* gambader.

CD /siː'diː/ *n.* compact disc *m.*

cease /siːs/ *v.t./i.* cesser. **~-fire** *n.* cessez-le-feu *m.* *invar.* **~less** *a.* incessant.

cedar /'siːdə(r)/ *n.* cèdre *m.*

cede /siːd/ *v.t.* céder.

cedilla /sɪ'dɪlə/ *n.* cédille *f.*

ceiling /'siːlɪŋ/ *n.* plafond *m.*

celebrat|e /'selɪbreɪt/ *v.t.* (*perform, glorify*) célébrer; (*event*) fêter, célébrer. —*v.i.* **we shall ~e,** on va fêter ça. **~ion** /-'breɪʃn/ *n.* fête *f.*

celebrated /'selɪbreɪtɪd/ *a.* célèbre.

celebrity /sɪ'lebrətɪ/ *n.* célébrité *f.*

celery /'selərɪ/ *n.* céleri *m.*

cell /sel/ *n.* cellule *f.*; (*electr.*) élément *m.*

cellar /'selə(r)/ *n.* cave *f.*

cell|o /'tʃeləʊ/ *n.* (*pl.* **-os**) violoncelle *m.* **~ist** *n.* violoncelliste *m./f.*

Cellophane /'seləfeɪn/ *n.* (P.) cellophane *f.* (P.).

Celt /kelt/ *n.* Celte *m./f.* **~ic** *a.* celtique, celte.

cement /sɪ'ment/ *n.* ciment *m.* —*v.t.* cimenter. **~-mixer** *n.* bétonnière *f.*

cemetery /'semətrɪ/ *n.* cimetière *m.*

censor /'sensə(r)/ *n.* censeur *m.* —*v.t.* censurer. **the ~,** la censure. **~ship** *n.* censure *f.*

censure /'senʃə(r)/ *n.* blâme *m.* —*v.t.* blâmer.

census /'sensəs/ *n.* recensement *m.*

cent /sent/ *n.* (*coin*) cent *m.*

centenary /sen'tiːnərɪ, *Amer.* 'sentənərɪ/ *n.* centenaire *m.*

centigrade /'sentɪgreɪd/ *a.* centigrade.

centilitre, *Amer.* **centiliter** /'sentɪliːtə(r)/ *n.* centilitre *m.*

centimetre, *Amer.* **centimeter** /'sentɪmiːtə(r)/ *n.* centimètre *m.*

centipede /'sentɪpiːd/ *n.* millepattes *m.* *invar.*

central /'sentrəl/ *a.* central. **~ heating,** chauffage central *m.* **~ize** *v.t.* centraliser. **~ly** *adv.* (*situated*) au centre.

centre /'sentə(r)/ *n.* centre *m.* —*v.t.* (*p.t.* **centred**) centrer. —*v.i.* ∼ **on**, tourner autour de.

centrifugal /sen'trɪfjʊɡl/ *a.* centrifuge.

century /'sentʃərɪ/ *n.* siècle *m.*

ceramic /sɪ'ræmɪk/ *a.* (*art*) céramique; (*object*) en céramique.

cereal /'sɪərɪəl/ *n.* céréale *f.*

cerebral /'serɪbrəl, *Amer.* sə'ri:brəl/ *a.* cérébral.

ceremonial /serɪ'məʊnɪəl/ *a.* de cérémonie. —*n.* cérémonial *m.*

ceremon|y /'serɪmənɪ/ *n.* cérémonie *f.* ∼**ious** /-'məʊnɪəs/ *a.* solennel.

certain /'sɜːtn/ *a.* certain. **for** ∼, avec certitude. **make** ∼ **of,** s'assurer de. ∼**ly** *adv.* certainement. ∼**ty** *n.* certitude *f.*

certificate /sə'tɪfɪkət/ *n.* certificat *m.*

certify /'sɜːtɪfaɪ/ *v.t.* certifier.

cervical /sɜː'vaɪkl/ *a.* cervical.

cessation /se'seɪʃn/ *n.* cessation *f.*

cesspit, cesspool /'sespɪt, 'sespuːl/ *ns.* fosse d'aisances *f.*

chafe /tʃeɪf/ *v.t.* frotter (contre).

chaff /tʃɑːf/ *v.t.* taquiner.

chaffinch /'tʃæfɪntʃ/ *n.* pinson *m.*

chagrin /'ʃæɡrɪn/ *n.* vif dépit *m.*

chain /tʃeɪn/ *n.* chaîne *f.* —*v.t.* enchaîner. ∼ **reaction,** réaction en chaîne *f.* ∼**-smoke** *v.i.* fumer de manière ininterrompue. ∼ **store,** magasin à succursales multiples *m.*

chair /tʃeə(r)/ *n.* chaise *f.*; (*armchair*) fauteuil *m.*; (*univ.*) chaire *f.* —*v.t.* (*preside over*) présider.

chairman /'tʃeəmən/ *n.* (*pl.* **-men**) président(e) *m.* (*f.*).

chalet /'ʃæleɪ/ *n.* chalet *m.*

chalk /tʃɔːk/ *n.* craie *f.* ∼**y** *a.* crayeux.

challeng|e /'tʃælɪndʒ/ *n.* défi *m.*; (*task*) gageure *f.* —*v.t.* (*summon*) défier (**to do,** de faire); (*question truth of*) contester. ∼**er** *n.* (*sport*) challenger *m.* ∼**ing** *a.* stimulant.

chamber /'tʃeɪmbə(r)/ *n.* (*old use*) chambre *f.* ∼ **music,** musique de chambre *f.* ∼**-pot** *n.* pot de chambre *m.*

chambermaid /'tʃeɪmbəmeɪd/ *n.* femme de chambre *f.*

chamois /'ʃæmɪ/ *n.* ∼**(-leather),** peau de chamois *f.*

champagne /ʃæm'peɪn/ *n.* champagne *m.*

champion /'tʃæmpɪən/ *n.* champion(ne) *m.* (*f.*). —*v.t.* défendre. ∼**ship** *n.* championnat *m.*

chance /tʃɑːns/ *n.* (*luck*) hasard *m.*; (*opportunity*) occasion *f.*; (*likelihood*) chances *f. pl.*; (*risk*) risque *m.* —*a.*

fortuit. —*v.t.* ∼ **doing,** prendre le risque de faire. ∼ **it,** risquer le coup. **by** ∼**,** par hasard. **by any** ∼**,** par hasard. ∼**s are that,** il est probable que.

chancellor /'tʃɑːnsələ(r)/ *n.* chancelier *m.* **C**∼ **of the Exchequer,** Chancelier de l'Échiquier.

chancy /'tʃɑːnsɪ/ *a.* risqué.

chandelier /ʃændə'lɪə(r)/ *n.* lustre *m.*

change /tʃeɪndʒ/ *v.t.* (*alter*) changer; (*exchange*) échanger (**for,** contre); (*money*) changer. ∼ **trains/one's dress/**etc., (*by substitution*) changer de train/de robe/*etc.* —*v.i.* changer; (*change clothes*) se changer. —*n.* changement *m.*; (*money*) monnaie *f.* **a** ∼ **for the better,** une amélioration. **a** ∼ **for the worse,** un changement en pire. ∼ **into,** se transformer en; (*clothes*) mettre. **a** ∼ **of clothes,** des vêtements de rechange. ∼ **one's mind,** changer d'avis. ∼ **over,** passer (**to,** à). **for a** ∼**,** pour changer. ∼**-over** *n.* passage *m.* ∼**able** *a.* changeant; (*weather*) variable. ∼**ing** *a.* changeant. ∼**ing room,** (*in shop*) cabine d'essayage; (*sport.*) vestiaire *m.*

channel /'tʃænl/ *n.* chenal *m.*; (*TV*) chaîne *f.*; (*medium, agency*) canal *m.*; (*groove*) rainure *f.* —*v.t.* (*p.t.* **channelled**) (*direct*) canaliser. **the (English) C**∼**,** la Manche. **the C**∼ **Islands,** les îles anglo-normandes *f. pl.*

chant /tʃɑːnt/ *n.* (*relig.*) psalmodie *f.*; (*of demonstrators*) chant (scandé) *m.* —*v.t./i.* psalmodier; scander (des slogans).

chao|s /'keɪɒs/ *n.* chaos *m.* ∼**tic** /-'ɒtɪk/ *a.* chaotique.

chap /tʃæp/ *n.* (*man: fam.*) type *m.*

chapel /'tʃæpl/ *n.* chapelle *f.*; (*Nonconformist*) église (nonconformiste) *f.*

chaperon /'ʃæpərəʊn/ *n.* chaperon *m.* —*v.t.* chaperonner.

chaplain /'tʃæplɪn/ *n.* aumônier *m.*

chapped /tʃæpt/ *a.* gercé.

chapter /'tʃæptə(r)/ *n.* chapitre *m.*

char[1] /tʃɑː(r)/ *n.* (*fam.*) femme de ménage *f.*

char[2] /tʃɑː(r)/ *v.t.* (*p.t.* **charred**) carboniser.

character /'kærəktə(r)/ *n.* caractère *m.*; (*in novel, play*) personnage *m.* **of good** ∼**,** de bonne réputation. ∼**ize** *v.t.* caractériser.

characteristic /kærəktə'rɪstɪk/ *a. & n.* caractéristique (*f.*). ∼**ally** *adv.* typiquement.

charade /ʃəˈrɑːd/ n. charade f.

charcoal /ˈtʃɑːkəʊl/ n. charbon (de bois) m.

charge /tʃɑːdʒ/ n. prix m.; (mil.) charge f.; (jurid.) inculpation f., accusation f.; (task, custody) charge f. ~s, frais m. pl. —v.t. faire payer; (ask) demander (for, pour); (enemy, gun) charger; (jurid.) inculper, accuser (**with**, de). —v.i. foncer, se précipiter. ~ **card,** carte d'achat f. ~ **it to my account,** mettez-le sur mon compte. **in** ~ **of,** responsable de. **take** ~ **of,** prendre en charge, se charger de. ~**able to,** (comm.) aux frais de.

charisma /kəˈrɪzmə/ n. magnétisme m. ~**tic** /kærɪzˈmætɪk/ a. charismatique.

charit|y /ˈtʃærətɪ/ n. charité f.; (society) fondation charitable f. ~**able** a. charitable.

charlatan /ˈʃɑːlətən/ n. charlatan m.

charm /tʃɑːm/ n. charme m.; (trinket) amulette f. —v.t. charmer. ~**ing** a. charmant.

chart /tʃɑːt/ n. (naut.) carte (marine) f.; (table) tableau m., graphique m. —v.t. (route) porter sur la carte.

charter /ˈtʃɑːtə(r)/ n. charte f. ~ (**flight**), charter m. —v.t. affréter. ~**ed accountant,** expert-comptable m.

charwoman /ˈtʃɑːwʊmən/ n. (pl. **-women**) femme de ménage f.

chase /tʃeɪs/ v.t. poursuivre. —v.i. courir (**after**, après). —n. chasse f. ~ **away** or **off,** chasser.

chasm /ˈkæzəm/ n. abîme m.

chassis /ˈʃæsɪ/ n. châssis m.

chaste /tʃeɪst/ a. chaste.

chastise /tʃæˈstaɪz/ v.t. châtier.

chastity /ˈtʃæstətɪ/ n. chasteté f.

chat /tʃæt/ n. causette f. —v.i. (p.t. **chatted**) bavarder. **have a** ~, bavarder. ~ **show,** talk-show m. ~ **up,** (fam.) draguer. ~**ty** a. bavard.

chatter /ˈtʃætə(r)/ n. bavardage m. —v.i. bavarder. **his teeth are** ~**ing,** il claque des dents.

chatterbox /ˈtʃætəbɒks/ n. bavard(e) m. (f.).

chauffeur /ˈʃəʊfə(r)/ n. chauffeur (de particulier) m.

chauvinis|t /ˈʃəʊvɪnɪst/ n. chauvin(e) m. (f.). **male** ~**t,** (pej.) phallocrate m. ~**m** /-zəm/ n. chauvinisme m.

cheap /tʃiːp/ a. (**-er, -est**) bon marché invar.; (fare, rate) réduit; (worthless) sans valeur. ~**er,** meilleur marché invar. ~(**ly**) adv. à bon marché. ~**ness** n. bas prix m.

cheapen /ˈtʃiːpən/ v.t. déprécier.

cheat /tʃiːt/ v.i. tricher; (by fraud) frauder. v.t. (defraud) frauder; (deceive) tromper. —n. escroc m.

check¹ /tʃek/ v.t./i. vérifier; (tickets) contrôler; (stop) enrayer, arrêter; (restrain) contenir; (rebuke) réprimander; (tick off: Amer.) cocher. —n. vérification f.; contrôle m.; (curb) frein m.; (chess) échec m.; (bill: Amer.) addition f.; (cheque: Amer.) chèque m. ~ **in,** signer le registre; (at airport) passer à l'enregistrement. ~**in** n. enregistrement m. ~**list** n. liste récapitulative f. ~ **out,** régler sa note. ~**out** n. caisse f. ~**point** n. contrôle m. ~ **up,** vérifier. ~ **up on,** (detail) vérifier; (situation) s'informer sur. ~**up** n, examen médical m.

check² /tʃek/ n. (pattern) carreaux m. pl. ~**ed** a. à carreaux.

checking /ˈtʃekɪŋ/ a. ~ **account,** (Amer.) compte courant m.

checkmate /ˈtʃekmeɪt/ n. échec et mat m.

checkroom /ˈtʃekrʊm/ n. (Amer.) vestiaire m.

cheek /tʃiːk/ n. joue f.; (impudence) culot m. ~**y** a. effronté.

cheer /tʃɪə(r)/ n. gaieté f. ~**s,** acclamations f. pl.; (when drinking) à votre santé. —v.t. acclamer, applaudir. ~ (**up**), (gladden) remonter le moral à. ~ **up,** prendre courage. ~**ful** a. gai. ~**fulness** n. gaieté f.

cheerio /tʃɪərɪˈəʊ/ int. (fam.) salut.

cheese /tʃiːz/ n. fromage m.

cheetah /ˈtʃiːtə/ n. guépard m.

chef /ʃef/ n. (cook) chef m.

chemical /ˈkemɪkl/ a. chimique. —n. produit chimique m.

chemist /ˈkemɪst/ n. pharmacien(ne) m. (f.); (scientist) chimiste m./f. ~**'s shop,** pharmacie f. ~**ry** n. chimie f.

cheque /tʃek/ n. chèque m. ~**-book** n. chéquier m. ~ **card,** carte bancaire f.

chequered /ˈtʃekəd/ a. (pattern) à carreaux; (fig.) mouvementé.

cherish /ˈtʃerɪʃ/ v.t. chérir; (hope) nourrir, caresser.

cherry /ˈtʃerɪ/ n. cerise f.

chess /tʃes/ n. échecs m. pl. ~**-board** n. échiquier m.

chest /tʃest/ n. (anat.) poitrine f.; (box) coffre m. ~ **of drawers,** commode f.

chestnut /ˈtʃesnʌt/ n. châtaigne f.; (edible) marron m., châtaigne f.

chew /tʃuː/ v.t. mâcher. ~**ing-gum** n. chewing-gum m.

chic /ʃiːk/ a. chic invar.

chick /tʃɪk/ n. poussin m.
chicken /'tʃɪkɪn/ n. poulet m. —a. (sl.) froussard. —v.i. ~ out, (sl.) se dégonfler. ~-pox n. varicelle f.
chick-pea /'tʃɪkpiː/ n. pois chiche m.
chicory /'tʃɪkərɪ/ n. (for salad) endive f.; (in coffee) chicorée f.
chief /tʃiːf/ n. chef m. —a. principal. ~ly adv. principalement.
chilblain /'tʃɪlbleɪn/ n. engelure f.
child /tʃaɪld/ n. (pl. children /'tʃɪldrən/) enfant m./f. ~hood n. enfance f. ~ish a. enfantin. ~less a. sans enfants. ~like a. innocent, candide. ~-minder n. nourrice f.
childbirth /'tʃaɪldbɜːθ/ n. accouchement m.
Chile /'tʃɪlɪ/ n. Chili m. ~an a. & n. chilien(ne) (m. (f.)).
chill /tʃɪl/ n. froid m.; (med.) refroidissement m. —a. froid. —v.t. (person) donner froid à; (wine) rafraîchir; (food) mettre au frais. ~y a. froid; (sensitive to cold) frileux. be or feel ~y, avoir froid.
chilli /'tʃɪlɪ/ n. (pl. -ies) piment m.
chime /tʃaɪm/ n. carillon m. —v.t./i. carillonner.
chimney /'tʃɪmnɪ/ n. cheminée f. ~-sweep n. ramoneur m.
chimpanzee /tʃɪmpæn'ziː/ n. chimpanzé m.
chin /tʃɪn/ n. menton m.
china /'tʃaɪnə/ n. porcelaine f.
China /'tʃaɪnə/ n. Chine f. ~ese /-'niːz/ a. & n. chinois(e) (m. (f.)).
chink¹ /tʃɪŋk/ n. (slit) fente f.
chink² /tʃɪŋk/ n. tintement m. —v.t./i. (faire) tinter.
chip /tʃɪp/ n. (on plate etc.) ébréchure f.; (piece) éclat m.; (of wood) copeau m.; (culin.) frite f.; (microchip) microplaquette f., puce f. —v.t./i. (p.t. chipped) (s')ébrécher. ~ in, (fam.) dire son mot; (with money: fam.) contribuer. (potato) ~s, (Amer.) chips m. pl.
chipboard /'tʃɪpbɔːd/ n. aggloméré m.
chiropodist /kɪ'rɒpədɪst/ n. pédicure m./f.
chirp /tʃɜːp/ n. pépiement m. —v.i. pépier.
chirpy /'tʃɜːpɪ/ a. gai.
chisel /'tʃɪzl/ n. ciseau m. —v.t. (p.t. chiselled) ciseler.
chit /tʃɪt/ n. note f., mot m.
chit-chat /'tʃɪttʃæt/ n. bavardage m.
chivalr|y /'ʃɪvlrɪ/ n. galanterie f. ~ous a. chevaleresque.
chives /tʃaɪvz/ n. pl. ciboulette f.
chlorine /'klɔːriːn/ n. chlore m.

choc-ice /'tʃɒkaɪs/ n. esquimau m.
chock /tʃɒk/ n. cale f. ~-a-block, ~-full adjs. archiplein.
chocolate /'tʃɒklət/ n. chocolat m.
choice /tʃɔɪs/ n. choix m. —a. de choix.
choir /'kwaɪə(r)/ n. chœur m.
choirboy /'kwaɪəbɔɪ/ n. jeune choriste m.
choke /tʃəʊk/ v.t./i. (s')étrangler. —n. starter m. ~ (up), boucher.
cholera /'kɒlərə/ n. choléra m.
cholesterol /kə'lestərɒl/ n. cholestérol m.
choose /tʃuːz/ v.t./i. (p.t. chose, p.p. chosen) choisir. ~ to do, décider de faire.
choosy /'tʃuːzɪ/ a. (fam.) exigeant.
chop /tʃɒp/ v.t./i. (p.t. chopped) (wood) couper (à la hache); (food) hacher. —n. (meat) côtelette f. ~ down, abattre. ~per n. hachoir m.; (sl.) hélicoptère m. ~ping-board n. planche à découper f.
choppy /'tʃɒpɪ/ a. (sea) agité.
chopstick /'tʃɒpstɪk/ n. baguette f.
choral /'kɔːrəl/ a. choral.
chord /kɔːd/ n. (mus.) accord m.
chore /tʃɔː(r)/ n. travail (routinier) m.; (unpleasant task) corvée f.
choreography /kɒrɪ'ɒgrəfɪ/ n. chorégraphie f.
chortle /'tʃɔːtl/ n. gloussement m. —v.i. glousser.
chorus /'kɔːrəs/ n. chœur m.; (of song) refrain m.
chose, chosen /tʃəʊz, 'tʃəʊzn/ see choose.
Christ /kraɪst/ n. le Christ m.
christen /'krɪsn/ v.t. baptiser. ~ing n. baptême m.
Christian /'krɪstʃən/ a. & n. chrétien(ne) (m. (f.)). ~ name, prénom m. ~ity /-strɪ'ænətɪ/ n. christianisme m.
Christmas /'krɪsməs/ n. Noël m. —a. (card, tree, etc.) de Noël. ~-box n. étrennes f. pl. ~ Day/Eve, le jour/la veille de Noël.
chrome /krəʊm/ n. chrome m.
chromium /'krəʊmɪəm/ n. chrome m.
chromosome /'krəʊməsəʊm/ n. chromosome m.
chronic /'krɒnɪk/ a. (situation, disease) chronique; (bad: fam.) affreux.
chronicle /'krɒnɪkl/ n. chronique f.
chronolog|y /krə'nɒlədʒɪ/ n. chronologie f. ~ical /krɒnə'lɒdʒɪkl/ a. chronologique.
chrysanthemum /krɪ'sænθəməm/ n. chrysanthème m.
chubby /'tʃʌbɪ/ a. (-ier, -iest) dodu, potelé.

chuck /tʃʌk/ v.t. (fam.) lancer. ~ **away** or **out**, (fam.) balancer.

chuckle /'tʃʌkl/ n. gloussement m. —v.i. glousser, rire.

chuffed /tʃʌft/ a. (sl.) bien content.

chum /tʃʌm/ n. copain, -ine m., f. ~**my** a. amical. ~**my with**, copain avec.

chunk /tʃʌŋk/ n. (gros) morceau m.

chunky /'tʃʌŋkɪ/ a. trapu.

church /tʃɜ:tʃ/ n. église f.

churchyard /'tʃɜ:tʃjɑ:d/ n. cimetière m.

churlish /'tʃɜ:lɪʃ/ a. grossier.

churn /'tʃɜ:n/ n. baratte f.; (milk-can) bidon m. —v.t. baratter. ~ **out**, produire (en série).

chute /ʃu:t/ n. glissière f.; (for rubbish) vide-ordures m. invar.

chutney /'tʃʌtnɪ/ n. condiment (de fruits) m.

cider /'saɪdə(r)/ n. cidre m.

cigar /sɪ'gɑ:(r)/ n. cigare m.

cigarette /sɪgə'ret/ n. cigarette f. ~ **end**, mégot m. ~**-holder** n. fume-cigarette m. invar.

cinder /'sɪndə(r)/ n. cendre f.

cine-camera /'sɪnɪkæmərə/ n. caméra f.

cinema /'sɪnəmə/ n. cinéma m.

cinnamon /'sɪnəmən/ n. cannelle f.

cipher /'saɪfə(r)/ n. (numeral, code) chiffre m.; (person) nullité f.

circle /'sɜ:kl/ n. cercle m.; (theatre) balcon m. —v.t. (go round) faire le tour de; (word, error, etc.) entourer d'un cercle. —v.i. décrire des cercles.

circuit /'sɜ:kɪt/ n. circuit m. ~**-breaker** n. disjoncteur m.

circuitous /sɜ:'kju:ɪtəs/ a. indirect.

circular /'sɜ:kjʊlə(r)/ a. & n. circulaire (f.).

circulat|e /'sɜ:kjʊleɪt/ v.t./i. (faire) circuler. ~**ion** /-'leɪʃn/ n. circulation f.; (of newspaper) tirage m.

circumcis|e /'sɜ:kəmsaɪz/ v.t. circoncire. ~**ion** /-'sɪʒn/ n. circoncision f.

circumference /sɜ:'kʌmfərəns/ n. circonférence f.

circumflex /'sɜ:kəmfleks/ n. circonflexe m.

circumspect /'sɜ:kəmspekt/ a. circonspect.

circumstance /'sɜ:kəmstəns/ n. circonstance f. ~**s**, (financial) situation financière f.

circus /'sɜ:kəs/ n. cirque m.

cistern /'sɪstən/ n. réservoir m.

citadel /'sɪtədel/ n. citadelle f.

cit|e /saɪt/ v.t. citer. ~**ation** /-'teɪʃn/ n. citation f.

citizen /'sɪtɪzn/ n. citoyen(ne) m. (f.); (of

town) habitant(e) m. (f.). ~**ship** n. citoyenneté f.

citrus /'sɪtrəs/ a. ~ **fruit(s)**, agrumes m. pl.

city /'sɪtɪ/ n. (grande) ville f. **the C~**, la Cité de Londres.

civic /'sɪvɪk/ a. civique. ~ **centre**, centre administratif m. ~**s** n. pl. instruction civique f.

civil /'sɪvl/ a. civil; (rights) civique; (defence) passif. ~ **engineer**, ingénieur civil m. **C~ Servant**, fonctionnaire m./f. **C~ Service**, fonction publique f. ~ **war**, guerre civile f. ~**ity** /sɪ'vɪlətɪ/ n. civilité f.

civilian /sɪ'vɪlɪən/ a. & n. civil(e) (m. (f.)).

civiliz|e /'sɪvəlaɪz/ v.t. civiliser. ~**ation** /-'zeɪʃn/ n. civilisation f.

civvies /'sɪvɪz/ n. pl. **in** ~, (sl.) en civil.

clad /klæd/ a. ~ **in**, vêtu de.

claim /kleɪm/ v.t. revendiquer, réclamer; (assert) prétendre. —n. revendication f., prétention f.; (assertion) affirmation f.; (for insurance) réclamation f.; (right) droit m.

claimant /'kleɪmənt/ n. (of social benefits) demandeur m.

clairvoyant /kleə'vɔɪənt/ n. voyant(e) m. (f.).

clam /klæm/ n. palourde f.

clamber /'klæmbə(r)/ v.i. grimper.

clammy /'klæmɪ/ a. (-ier, -iest) moite.

clamour /'klæmə(r)/ n. clameur f., cris m. pl. —v.i. ~ **for**, demander à grands cris.

clamp /klæmp/ n. agrafe f.; (large) crampon m.; (for carpentry) serre-joint(s) m.; (for car) sabot de Denver m. —v.t. serrer; (car) mettre un sabot de Denver à. ~ **down on**, sévir contre.

clan /klæn/ n. clan m.

clandestine /klæn'destɪn/ a. clandestin.

clang /klæŋ/ n. son métallique m.

clanger /'klæŋə(r)/ n. (sl.) bévue f.

clap /klæp/ v.t./i. (p.t. **clapped**) applaudir; (put forcibly) mettre. —n. applaudissement m.; (of thunder) coup m. ~ **one's hands**, battre des mains.

claptrap /'klæptræp/ n. baratin m.

claret /'klærət/ n. bordeaux rouge m.

clarif|y /'klærɪfaɪ/ v.t./i. (se) clarifier. ~**ication** /-ɪ'keɪʃn/ n. clarification f.

clarinet /klærɪ'net/ n. clarinette f.

clarity /'klærətɪ/ n. clarté f.

clash /klæʃ/ n. choc m.; (fig.) conflit m. —v.i. (metal objects) s'entrechoquer; (fig.) se heurter.

clasp /klɑ:sp/ n. (fastener) fermoir m., agrafe f. —v.t. serrer.

class /klɑːs/ n. classe f. —v.t. classer.
classic /'klæsɪk/ a. & n. classique (m.).
~s, (univ.) les humanités f. pl. **~al** a.
classique.
classif|y /'klæsɪfaɪ/ v.t. classifier.
~ication /-ɪ'keɪʃn/ n. classification f.
~ied a. (information etc.) secret. **~ied
advertisement**, petite annonce f.
classroom /'klɑːsrʊm/ n. salle de classe
f.
classy /'klɑːsɪ/ a. (sl.) chic invar.
clatter /'klætə(r)/ n. cliquetis m. —v.i.
cliqueter.
clause /klɔːz/ n. clause f.; (gram.)
proposition f.
claustrophob|ia /klɔːstrə'fəʊbɪə/ n.
claustrophobie f. **~ic** a. & n.
claustrophobe (m./f.).
claw /klɔː/ n. (of animal, small bird)
griffe f.; (of bird of prey) serre f.; (of
lobster) pince f. —v.t. griffer.
clay /kleɪ/ n. argile f.
clean /kliːn/ a. (-er, -est) propre; (shape,
stroke, etc.) net. —adv. complètement.
—v.t. nettoyer. —v.i. **~ up**, faire le
nettoyage. **~ one's teeth**, se brosser les
dents. **~-shaven** a. glabre. **~er** n. (at
home) femme de ménage f.;
(industrial) agent de nettoyage m./f.;
(of clothes) teinturier, -ière m., f. **~ly**
adv. proprement; (sharply) nettement.
cleanliness /'klenlɪnɪs/ n. propreté f.
cleans|e /klenz/ v.t. nettoyer; (fig.)
purifier. **~ing cream**, crème démaquil-
lante f.
clear /klɪə(r)/ a. (-er, -est) clair; (glass)
transparent; (profit) net; (road) dégagé.
—adv. complètement. —v.t. (free)
dégager (of, de); (table) débarrasser;
(building) évacuer; (cheque) encaisser;
(jump over) franchir; (debt) liquider;
(jurid.) disculper. **~ (away or off)**,
(remove) enlever. —v.i. (fog) se dissiper.
~ of, (away from) à l'écart de. **~ off or
out**, (sl.) décamper. **~ out**, (clean)
nettoyer. **~ up**, (tidy) ranger; (mystery)
éclaircir; (of weather) s'éclaircir. **make
sth. ~**, être très clair sur qch. **~-cut** a. net.
~ly adv. clairement.
clearance /'klɪərəns/ n. (permission)
autorisation f.; (space) dégagement m.
~ sale, liquidation f.
clearing /'klɪərɪŋ/ n. clairière f.
clearway /'klɪəweɪ/ n. route à stationnement interdit f.
cleavage /'kliːvɪdʒ/ n. clivage m.;
(breasts) décolleté m.
clef /klef/ n. (mus.) clé f.
cleft /kleft/ n. fissure f.

clemen|t /'klemənt/ a. clément. **~cy** n.
clémence f.
clench /klentʃ/ v.t. serrer.
clergy /'klɜːdʒɪ/ n. clergé m. **~man** n.
(pl. -men) ecclésiastique m.
cleric /'klerɪk/ n. clerc m. **~al** a. (relig.)
clérical; (of clerks) de bureau,
d'employé.
clerk /klɑːk, Amer. klɜːk/ n. employé(e)
de bureau m. (f.). (Amer.) (sales) **~**,
vendeur, -se m., f.
clever /'klevə(r)/ a. (-er, -est) intelligent; (skilful) habile. **~ly** adv.
intelligemment; habilement. **~ness** n.
intelligence f.
cliché /'kliːʃeɪ/ n. cliché m.
click /klɪk/ n. déclic m. —v.i. faire un
déclic; (people: sl.) s'entendre. se
plaire. —v.t. (heels, tongue) faire
claquer.
client /'klaɪənt/ n. client(e) m. (f.).
clientele /kliːɒn'tel/ n. clientèle f.
cliff /klɪf/ n. falaise f.
climat|e /'klaɪmɪt/ n. climat m. **~ic**
/-'mætɪk/ a. climatique.
climax /'klaɪmæks/ n. point culminant
m.; (sexual) orgasme m.
climb /klaɪm/ v.t. (stairs) monter,
grimper; (tree, ladder) monter or
grimper à; (mountain) faire l'ascension
de. —v.i. monter, grimper. —n. montée
f. **~ down**, (fig.) reculer. **~-down**, n.
recul m. **~er** n. (sport) alpiniste m./f.
clinch /klɪntʃ/ v.t. (a deal) conclure.
cling /klɪŋ/ v.i. (p.t. clung) se
cramponner (to, à); (stick) coller. **~-
film** n. (P.) film adhésif.
clinic /'klɪnɪk/ n. centre médical m.;
(private) clinique f.
clinical /'klɪnɪkl/ a. clinique.
clink /klɪŋk/ n. tintement m. —v.t./i.
(faire) tinter.
clinker /'klɪŋkə(r)/ n. mâchefer m.
clip¹ /klɪp/ n. (for paper) trombone m.;
(for hair) barrette f.; (for tube) collier
m. —v.t. (p.t. clipped) attacher (to, à).
clip² /klɪp/ v.t. (p.t. clipped) (cut)
couper. —n. coupe f.; (of film) extrait
m.; (blow: fam.) taloche f. **~ping** n.
coupure f.
clippers /'klɪpəz/ n. pl. tondeuse f.; (for
nails) coupe-ongles m.
clique /kliːk/ n. clique f.
cloak /kləʊk/ n. (grande) cape f.,
manteau ample m.
cloakroom /'kləʊkrʊm/ n. vestiaire m.;
(toilet) toilettes f. pl.
clobber /'klɒbə(r)/ n. (sl.) affaires f. pl.
—v.t. (hit: sl.) rosser.

clock /klɒk/ n. pendule f.; (large) horloge f. —v.i. ~ **in** or **out**, pointer. ~ **up,** (miles etc.: fam.) faire. ~**-tower** n. clocher m.

clockwise /'klɒkwaɪz/ a. & adv. dans le sens des aiguilles d'une montre.

clockwork /'klɒkwɜːk/ n. mécanisme m. —a. mécanique.

clog /klɒg/ n. sabot m. —v.t./i. (p.t. **clogged**) (se) boucher.

cloister /'klɔɪstə(r)/ n. cloître m.

close[1] /kləʊs/ a. (**-er, -est**) (near) proche (**to,** de); (link, collaboration) étroit; (examination) attentif; (friend) intime; (order, match) serré; (weather) lourd. ~ **together,** (crowded) serrés. —adv. (tout) près. —n. (street) impasse f. ~ **by, ~ at hand,** tout près. ~**-up** n. gros plan m. **have a ~ shave,** l'échapper belle. **keep a ~ watch on,** surveiller de près. ~**ly** adv. (follow) de près. ~**ness** n. proximité f.

close[2] /kləʊz/ v.t. fermer. —v.i. se fermer; (of shop etc.) fermer; (end) (se) terminer. —n. fin f. ~**d shop,** organisation qui exclut les travailleurs non syndiqués f.

closet /'klɒzɪt/ n. (Amer.) placard m.

closure /'kləʊʒə(r)/ n. fermeture f.

clot /klɒt/ n. (of blood) caillot m.; (in sauce) grumeau m. —v.t./i. (p.t. **clotted**) (se) coaguler.

cloth /klɒθ/ n. tissu m.; (duster) linge m.; (table-cloth) nappe f.

cloth|e /kləʊð/ v.t. vêtir. ~**ing** n. vêtements m. pl.

clothes /kləʊðz/ n. pl. vêtements m. pl., habits m. pl. ~**-brush** n. brosse à habits f. ~**-hanger** n. cintre m. ~**-line** n. corde à linge f. ~**-peg,** (Amer.) ~**-pin** ns. pince à linge f.

cloud /klaʊd/ n. nuage m. —v.i. se couvrir (de nuages); (become gloomy) s'assombrir. ~**y** a. (sky) couvert; (liquid) trouble.

cloudburst /'klaʊdbɜːst/ n. trombe d'eau f.

clout /klaʊt/ n. (blow) coup de poing m.; (power: fam.) pouvoir effectif m. —v.t. frapper.

clove /kləʊv/ n. clou de girofle m. ~ **of garlic,** gousse d'ail f.

clover /'kləʊvə(r)/ n. trèfle m.

clown /klaʊn/ n. clown m. —v.i. faire le clown.

cloy /klɔɪ/ v.t. écœurer.

club /klʌb/ n. (group) club m.; (weapon) massue f. ~**s,** (cards) trèfle m. —v.t./i. (p.t. **clubbed**) matraquer. **(golf) ~,** club

(de golf) m. ~ **together,** (share costs) se cotiser.

cluck /klʌk/ v.i. glousser.

clue /kluː/ n. indice m.; (in crossword) définition f. **I haven't a ~,** (fam.) je n'en ai pas la moindre idée.

clump /klʌmp/ n. massif m.

clums|y /'klʌmzɪ/ a. (**-ier, -iest**) maladroit; (tool) peu commode. ~**iness** n. maladresse f.

clung /klʌŋ/ see **cling.**

cluster /'klʌstə(r)/ n. (petit) groupe m. —v.i. se grouper.

clutch /klʌtʃ/ v.t. (hold) serrer fort; (grasp) saisir. —v.i. ~ **at,** (try to grasp) essayer de saisir. —n. étreinte f.; (auto.) embrayage m.

clutter /'klʌtə(r)/ n. désordre m., fouillis m. —v.t. encombrer.

coach /kəʊtʃ/ n. autocar m.; (of train) wagon m.; (horse-drawn) carrosse m.; (sport) entraîneur, -se m., f. —v.t. donner des leçons (particulières) à; (sport) entraîner.

coagulate /kəʊ'ægjʊleɪt/ v.t./i. (se) coaguler.

coal /kəʊl/ n. charbon m. ~**-mine** n. mine de charbon f.

coalfield /'kəʊlfiːld/ n. bassin houiller m.

coalition /kəʊə'lɪʃn/ n. coalition f.

coarse /kɔːs/ a. (**-er, -est**) grossier. ~**ness** n. caractère grossier m.

coast /kəʊst/ n. côte f. —v.i. (car, bicycle) descendre en roue libre. ~**al** a. côtier.

coaster /'kəʊstə(r)/ n. (ship) caboteur m.; (mat) dessous de verre m.

coastguard /'kəʊstgɑːd/ n. gardecôte m.

coastline /'kəʊstlaɪn/ n. littoral m.

coat /kəʊt/ n. manteau m.; (of animal) pelage m.; (of paint) couche f. —v.t. enduire, couvrir; (with chocolate) enrober (**with,** de). ~**-hanger** n. cintre m. ~ **of arms,** armoiries f. pl. ~**ing** n. couche f.

coax /kəʊks/ v.t. amadouer.

cob /kɒb/ n. (of corn) épi m.

cobble[1] /'kɒbl/ n. pavé m. ~**-stone** n. pavé m.

cobble[2] /'kɒbl/ v.t. rapetasser.

cobbler /'kɒblə(r)/ n. (old use) cordonnier m.

cobweb /'kɒbweb/ n. toile d'araignée f.

cocaine /kəʊ'keɪn/ n. cocaïne f.

cock /kɒk/ n. (oiseau) mâle m.; (rooster) coq m.; (tap) robinet m.; (gun) armer; (ears) dresser. ~**-and-bull story,** histoire à dormir debout f. ~**-eyed** a. (askew: sl.) de travers. ~**-up** n. (sl.) pagaille f.

cockerel /'kɒkərəl/ n. jeune coq m.
cockle /'kɒkl/ n. (culin.) coque f.
cockney /'kɒknɪ/ n. Cockney m./f.
cockpit /'kɒkpɪt/ n. poste de pilotage m.
cockroach /'kɒkrəʊtʃ/ n. cafard m.
cocksure /kɒk'ʃʊə(r)/ a. sûr de soi.
cocktail /'kɒkteɪl/ n. cocktail m. ∼ **party,** cocktail m. **fruit** ∼, macédoine (de fruits) f.
cocky /'kɒkɪ/ a. (**-ier, -iest**) trop sûr de soi, arrogant.
cocoa /'kəʊkəʊ/ n. cacao m.
coconut /'kəʊkənʌt/ n. noix de coco f.
cocoon /kə'kuːn/ n. cocon m.
COD abbr. (cash on delivery) paiement à la livraison m.
cod /kɒd/ n. invar. morue f. ∼**-liver oil,** huile de foie de morue f.
coddle /'kɒdl/ v.t. dorloter.
code /kəʊd/ n. code m. —v.t. coder.
codify /'kəʊdɪfaɪ/ v.t. codifier.
coeducational /kəʊedʒʊ'keɪʃənl/ a. (school, teaching) mixte.
coerce /kəʊ'ɜːs/ v.t. contraindre. ∼**ion** /-ʃn/ n. contrainte f.
coexist /kəʊɪg'zɪst/ v.i. coexister. ∼**ence** n. coexistence f.
coffee /'kɒfɪ/ n. café m. ∼ **bar,** café m., cafétéria f. ∼**-pot** n. cafetière f. ∼**table** n. table basse f.
coffer /'kɒfə(r)/ n. coffre m.
coffin /'kɒfɪn/ n. cercueil m.
cog /kɒg/ n. dent f.; (fig.) rouage m.
cogent /'kəʊdʒənt/ a. convaincant; (relevant) pertinent.
cognac /'kɒnjæk/ n. cognac m.
cohabit /kəʊ'hæbɪt/ v.i. vivre en concubinage.
coherent /kəʊ'hɪərənt/ a. cohérent.
coil /kɔɪl/ v.t./i. (s')enrouler. —n. rouleau m.; (one ring) spire f.; (contraceptive) stérilet m.
coin /kɔɪn/ n. pièce (de monnaie) f. —v.t. (word) inventer. ∼**age** n. monnaie f.; (fig.) invention ∼**-box** n. téléphone public m.
coincide /kəʊɪn'saɪd/ v.i. coïncider.
coinciden|ce /kəʊ'ɪnsɪdəns/ n. coïncidence f. ∼**tal** /-'dentl/ a. dû à une coïncidence.
coke /kəʊk/ n. coke m.
colander /'kʌləndə(r)/ n. passoire f.
cold /kəʊld/ a. (**-er, -est**) froid. **be** or **feel** ∼, avoir froid. **it is** ∼, il fait froid. —n. froid m.; (med.) rhume m. ∼**-blooded** a. sans pitié. ∼ **cream,** crème de beauté f. **get** ∼ **feet,** se dégonfler. ∼**-shoulder** v.t. snober. ∼ **sore,** bouton de fièvre m. ∼**ness** n. froideur f.

coleslaw /'kəʊlslɔː/ n. salade de chou cru f.
colic /'kɒlɪk/ n. coliques f. pl.
collaborat|e /kə'læbəreɪt/ v.i. collaborer. ∼**ion** /-'reɪʃn/ n. collaboration f. ∼**or** n. collaborateur, -trice m., f.
collage /'kɒlɑːʒ/ n. collage m.
collapse /kə'læps/ v.i. s'effondrer; (med.) avoir un malaise. —n. effondrement m.
collapsible /kə'læpsəbl/ a. pliant.
collar /'kɒlə(r)/ n. col m.; (of dog) collier m. —v.t. (take: sl.) piquer. ∼**-bone** n. clavicule f.
collateral /kə'lætərəl/ n. nantissement m.
colleague /'kɒliːg/ n. collègue m./f.
collect /kə'lekt/ v.t. rassembler; (pick up) ramasser; (call for) passer prendre; (money, rent) encaisser; (taxes) percevoir; (as hobby) collectionner. —v.i. se rassembler; (dust) s'amasser. —adv. ∼, (Amer.) téléphoner en PCV. ∼**ion** /-kʃn/ n. collection f.; (in church) quête f.; (of mail) levée f. ∼**or** n. (as hobby) collectionneur, -se m., f.
collective /kə'lektɪv/ a. collectif.
college /'kɒlɪdʒ/ n. (for higher education) institut m., école f.; (within university) collège m. **be at** ∼, être en faculté.
collide /kə'laɪd/ v.i. entrer en collision (with, avec).
colliery /'kɒlɪərɪ/ n. houillère f.
collision /kə'lɪʒn/ n. collision f.
colloquial /kə'ləʊkwɪəl/ a. familier. ∼**ism** n. expression familière f.
collusion /kə'luːʒn/ n. collusion f.
colon /'kəʊlən/ n. (gram.) deux-points m. invar.; (anat.) côlon m.
colonel /'kɜːnl/ n. colonel m.
colonize /'kɒlənaɪz/ v.t. coloniser.
colon|y /'kɒlənɪ/ n. colonie f. ∼**ial** /kə'ləʊnɪəl/ a. & n. colonial(e) (m. (f.)).
colossal /kə'lɒsl/ a. colossal.
colour /'kʌlə(r)/ n. couleur f. —a. (photo etc.) en couleur; (TV set) couleur invar. —v.t. colorer; (with crayon) colorier. ∼**-blind** a. daltonien. ∼**-fast** a. grand teint. invar. ∼**ful** a. coloré; (person) haut en couleur. ∼**ing** n. (of skin) teint m.; (in food) colorant m.
coloured /'kʌləd/ a. (person, pencil) de couleur. —n. personne de couleur f.
colt /kəʊlt/ n. poulain m.
column /'kɒləm/ n. colonne f.

columnist /'kɒləmnɪst/ n. journaliste chroniqueur m.

coma /'kəʊmə/ n. coma m.

comb /kəʊm/ n. peigne m. —v.t. peigner; (search) ratisser. ~ one's hair, se peigner.

combat /'kɒmbæt/ n. combat m. —v.t. (p.t. **combated**) combattre. ~ant /-ətənt/ n. combattant(e) m. (f.).

combination /kɒmbɪ'neɪʃn/ n. combinaison f.

combine[1] /kəm'baɪn/ v.t./i. (se) combiner, (s')unir.

combine[2] /'kɒmbaɪn/ n. (comm.) trust m., cartel m. ~ **harvester**, moissonneuse-batteuse f.

combustion /kəm'bʌstʃən/ n. combustion f.

come /kʌm/ v.i. (p.t. **came**, p.p. **come**) venir; (occur) arriver; (sexually) jouir. ~ **about**, arriver. ~ **across**, rencontrer or trouver par hasard. ~ **away** or **off**, se détacher, partir. ~ **back**, revenir. ~-**back** n. rentrée f.; (retort) réplique f. ~ **by**, obtenir. ~ **down**, descendre; (price) baisser. ~-**down** n. humiliation f. ~ **forward**, se présenter. ~ **from**, être de. ~ **in**, entrer. ~ **in for**, recevoir. ~ **into**, (money) hériter de. ~ **off**, (succeed) réussir; (fare) s'en tirer. ~ **on**, (actor) entrer en scène; (light) s'allumer; (improve) faire des progrès. ~ **on!**, allez! ~ **out**, sortir. ~ **round** or **to**, revenir à soi. ~ **through**, s'en tirer (indemne de). ~ **to**, (amount) revenir à; (decision, conclusion) arriver à. ~ **up**, monter; (fig.) se présenter. ~ **up against**, rencontrer. **get one's** ~-**uppance** n. (fam.) finir par recevoir ce qu'on mérite. ~ **up with**, (find) trouver; (produce) produire.

comedian /kə'miːdɪən/ n. comique m.

comedy /'kɒmədɪ/ n. comédie f.

comely /'kʌmlɪ/ a. (-ier, -iest) (old use) avenant, beau.

comet /'kɒmɪt/ n. comète f.

comfort /'kʌmfət/ n. confort m.; (consolation) réconfort m. —v.t. consoler. **one's** ~**s**, ses aises. ~**able** a. (chair, car, etc.) confortable; (person) à l'aise, bien; (wealthy) aisé.

comforter /'kʌmfətə(r)/ n. (baby's dummy) sucette f.; (quilt: Amer.) édredon m.

comfy /'kʌmfɪ/ a. (fam.) = **comfortable**.

comic /'kɒmɪk/ a. comique. —n. (person) comique m.; (periodical) comic m. ~ **strip**, bande dessinée f. ~**al** a. comique.

coming /'kʌmɪŋ/ n. arrivée f. —a. à venir. ~**s and goings**, allées et venues f. pl.

comma /'kɒmə/ n. virgule f.

command /kə'mɑːnd/ n. (authority) commandement m.; (order) ordre m.; (mastery) maîtrise f. —v.t. commander (s.o. to, à qn. de); (be able to use) disposer de; (require) nécessiter; (respect) inspirer. ~**er** n. commandant m. ~**ing** a. imposant.

commandeer /kɒmən'dɪə(r)/ v.t. réquisitionner.

commandment /kə'mɑːndmənt/ n. commandement m.

commando /kə'mɑːndəʊ/ n. (pl. **-os**) commando m.

commemorat|**e** /kə'meməreɪt/ v.t. commémorer. ~**ion** /-'reɪʃn/ n. commémoration f. ~**ive** /-ətɪv/ a. commémoratif.

commence /kə'mens/ v.t./i. commencer. ~**ment** n. commencement m.; (univ., Amer.) cérémonie de distribution des diplômes f.

commend /kə'mend/ v.t. (praise) louer; (entrust) confier. ~**able** a. louable. ~**ation** /kɒmen'deɪʃn/ n. éloge m.

commensurate /kə'menʃərət/ a. proportionné.

comment /'kɒment/ n. commentaire m. —v.i. faire des commentaires. ~ **on**, commenter.

commentary /'kɒməntrɪ/ n. commentaire m.; (radio, TV) reportage m.

commentat|**e** /'kɒmənteɪt/ v.i. faire un reportage. ~**or** n. commentalteur, -trice m., f.

commerce /'kɒmɜːs/ n. commerce m.

commercial /kə'mɜːʃl/ a. commercial; (traveller) de commerce. —n. publicité f. ~**ize** v.t. commercialiser.

commiserat|**e** /kə'mɪzəreɪt/ v.i. compatir (with, avec). ~**ion** /-'reɪʃn/ n. commisération f.

commission /kə'mɪʃn/ n. commission f.; (order for work) commande f. —v.t. (order) commander; (mil.) nommer officier. ~ **to do**, charger de faire. **out of** ~, hors service. ~**er** n. préfet (de police) m.; (in E.C.) commissaire m.

commissionaire /kəmɪʃə'neə(r)/ n. commissionnaire m.

commit /kə'mɪt/ v.t. (p.t. **committed**) commettre; (entrust) confier. ~ **o.s.**, s'engager. ~ **perjury**, se parjurer. ~ **suicide**, se suicider. ~ **to memory**, apprendre par cœur. ~**ment** n. engagement m.

committee /kə'mɪtɪ/ n. comité m.
commodity /kə'mɒdətɪ/ n. produit m.,
article m.
common /'kɒmən/ a. **(-er, -est)** (shared
by all) commun; (usual) courant,
commun; (vulgar) vulgaire, commun.
—n. terrain communal m. ∿ **law**, droit
coutumier m. **C∿ Market**, Marché
Commun m. ∿**-room** n. (schol.) salle
commune f. ∿ **sense**, bon sens m.
House of C∿s, Chambre des Communes f. **in** ∿, en commun. ∿**ly** adv.
communément.
commoner /'kɒmənə(r)/ n. roturier,
-ière m., f.
commonplace /'kɒmənpleɪs/ a. banal.
—n. banalité f.
Commonwealth /'kɒmənwelθ/ n. **the**
∿, le Commonwealth m.
commotion /kə'məʊʃn/ n. agitation f.,
remue-ménage m. invar.
communal /'kɒmjʊnl/ a. (shared)
commun; (life) collectif.
commune /'kɒmjuːn/ n. (group) communauté f.
communicat|e /kə'mjuːnɪkeɪt/ v.t./i.
communiquer. ∿**ion** /-'keɪʃn/ n. communication f. ∿**ive** /-ətɪv/ a. communicatif.
communion /kə'mjuːnɪən/ n. communion f.
communiqué /kə'mjuːnɪkeɪ/ n. communiqué m.
Communis|t /'kɒmjʊnɪst/ a. & n.
communiste (m./f.) ∿**m** /-zəm/ n.
communisme m.
community /kə'mjuːnɪtɪ/ n. communauté f.
commutation /kɒmjuː'teɪʃn/ n. ∿
ticket, carte d'abonnement f.
commute /kə'mjuːt/ v.i. faire la navette.
—v.t. (jurid.) commuer. ∿**r** /-ə(r)/ n.
banlieusard(e) m. (f.).
compact¹ /kəm'pækt/ a. compact.
∿ /'kɒmpækt/ **disc,** (disque) compact
m.
compact² /'kɒmpækt/ n. (lady's case)
poudrier m.
companion /kəm'pænjən/ n. compl
agnon, -agne m., f. ∿**ship** n.
camaraderie f.
company /'kʌmpənɪ/ n. (companionship, firm) compagnie f.; (guests)
invité(e)s m. (f.) pl.
comparable /'kɒmpərəbl/ a. comparable.
compar|e /kəm'peə(r)/ v.t. comparer
(with, to, à). ∿**ed with** or **to,** en
comparaison de. —v.i. être comparable.

∿**ative** /-'pærətɪv/ a. (study, form)
comparatif; (comfort etc.) relatif.
∿**atively** /-'pærətɪvlɪ/ adv. relativement.
comparison /kəm'pærɪsn/ n. comparaison f.
compartment /kəm'pɑːtmənt/ n. compartiment m.
compass /'kʌmpəs/ n. (for direction)
boussole f.; (scope) portée f. ∿**(es),**
(for drawing) compas m.
compassion /kəm'pæʃn/ n. compassion
f. ∿**ate** a. compatissant.
compatib|le /kəm'pætəbl/ a. compatible.
∿**ility** /-'bɪlətɪ/ n. compatibilité f.
compatriot /kəm'pætrɪət/ n. compatriote m./f.
compel /kəm'pel/ v.t. (p.t. **compelled**)
contraindre. ∿**ling** a. irrésistible.
compendium /kəm'pendɪəm/ n. abrégé
m., résumé m.
compensat|e /'kɒmpənseɪt/ v.t./i.
(financially) dédommager **(for,** de).
∿**e for sth.,** compenser qch. ∿**ion**
/-'seɪʃn/ n. compensation f.; (financial) dédommagement m.
compete /kəm'piːt/ v.i. concourir. ∿
with, rivaliser avec.
competen|t /'kɒmpɪtənt/ a. compétent.
∿**ce** n. compétence f.
competition /kɒmpə'tɪʃn/ n. (contest)
concours m.; (sport) compétition f.;
(comm.) concurrence f.
competitive /kəm'petətɪv/ a. (prices)
concurrentiel, compétitif. ∿ **examination,** concours m.
competitor /kəm'petɪtə(r)/ n. concurrent(e) m. (f.).
compile /kəm'paɪl/ v.t. (list) dresser;
(book) rédiger. ∿**r** /-ə(r)/ n. rédaclteur,
-trice m., f.
complacen|t /kəm'pleɪsnt/ a. content de
soi. ∿**cy** contentement de soi m.
complain /kəm'pleɪn/ v.i. se plaindre
(about, of, de).
complaint /kəm'pleɪnt/ n. plainte f.; (in
shop etc.) réclamation f.; (illness)
maladie f.
complement /'kɒmplɪmənt/ n. complément m. —v.t. compléter. ∿**ary**
/-'mentrɪ/ a. complémentaire.
complet|e /kəm'pliːt/ a. complet;
(finished) achevé; (downright) parfait.
—v.t. achever; (a form) remplir. ∿**ely**
adv. complètement. ∿**ion** /-ʃn/ n.
achèvement m.
complex /'kɒmpleks/ a. complexe. —n.
(psych., archit.) complexe m. ∿**ity**
/kəm'pleksətɪ/ n. complexité f.

complexion /kəm'plekʃn/ n. (of face) teint m.; (fig.) caractère m.

compliance /kəm'plaɪəns/ n. (agreement) conformité f.

complicat|e /'kɒmplɪkeɪt/ v.t. compliquer. ~ed a. compliqué. ~ion /-'keɪʃn/ n. complication f.

complicity /kəm'plɪsətɪ/ n. complicité f.

compliment /'kɒmplɪmənt/ n. compliment m. —v.t. /'kɒmplɪment/ complimenter.

complimentary /kɒmplɪ'mentrɪ/ a. (offert) à titre gracieux; (praising) flatteur.

comply /kəm'plaɪ/ v.i. ~ with, se conformer à, obéir à.

component /kəm'pəʊnənt/ n. (of machine etc.) pièce f.; (chemical substance) composant m.; (element: fig.) composante f. —a. constituant.

compose /kəm'pəʊz/ v.t. composer. ~ o.s., se calmer. ~d a. calme. ~r /-ə(r)/ n. (mus.) compositeur m.

composition /kɒmpə'zɪʃn/ n. composition f.

compost /'kɒmpɒst, Amer. 'kɒmpəʊst/ n. compost m.

composure /kəm'pəʊʒə(r)/ n. calme m.

compound[1] /'kɒmpaʊnd/ n. (substance, word) composé m.; (enclosure) enclos m. —a. composé.

compound[2] /kəm'paʊnd/ v.t. (problem etc.) aggraver.

comprehen|d /kɒmprɪ'hend/ v.t. comprendre. ~sion n. compréhension f.

comprehensive /kɒmprɪ'hensɪv/ a. étendu, complet; (insurance) tous-risques invar. ~ school, collège d'enseignement secondaire m.

compress /kəm'pres/ v.t. comprimer. ~ion /-ʃn/ n. compression f.

comprise /kəm'praɪz/ v.t. comprendre, inclure.

compromise /'kɒmprəmaɪz/ n. compromis m. —v.t. compromettre. —v.i. transiger, trouver un compromis. not ~ on, ne pas transiger sur.

compulsion /kəm'pʌlʃn/ n. contrainte f.

compulsive /kəm'pʌlsɪv/ a. (psych.) compulsif; (liar, smoker) invétéré.

compulsory /kəm'pʌlsərɪ/ a. obligatoire.

compunction /kəm'pʌŋkʃn/ n. scrupule m.

computer /kəm'pjuːtə(r)/ n. ordinateur m. ~ science, informatique f. ~ize v.t. informatiser.

comrade /'kɒmr(e)ɪd/ n. camarade m./f. ~ship n. camaraderie f.

con[1] /kɒn/ v.t. (p.t. conned) (sl.) rouler,

escroquer (**out of,** de). —n. (sl.) escroquerie f. ~ **s.o. into doing,** arnaquer qn. en lui faisant faire. ~ **man,** (sl₂) escroc m.

con[2] /kɒn/ see pro.

concave /'kɒŋkeɪv/ a. concave.

conceal /kən'siːl/ v.t. dissimuler. ~ment n. dissimulation f.

concede /kən'siːd/ v.t. concéder. —v.i. céder.

conceit /kən'siːt/ n. suffisance f. ~ed a. suffisant.

conceivabl|e /kən'siːvəbl/ a. concevable. ~y adv. this may ~y be done, il est concevable que cela puisse se faire.

conceive /kən'siːv/ v.t./i. concevoir. ~ of, concevoir.

concentrat|e /'kɒnsntreɪt/ v.t./i. (se) concentrer. ~ion /-'treɪʃn/ n. concentration f.

concept /'kɒnsept/ n. concept m. ~ual /kən'septʃʊəl/ a. notionnel.

conception /kən'sepʃn/ n. conception f.

concern /kən'sɜːn/ n. (interest, business) affaire f.; (worry) inquiétude f.; (firm: comm.) entreprise f., affaire f. —v.t. concerner. ~ **o.s. with, be ~ed with,** s'occuper de. ~**ing** prep. en ce qui concerne.

concerned /kən'sɜːnd/ a. inquiet.

concert /'kɒnsət/ n. concert m. in ~, ensemble.

concerted /kən'sɜːtɪd/ a. concerté.

concertina /kɒnsə'tiːnə/ n. concertina m.

concerto /kən'tʃeətəʊ/ n. (pl. -os) concerto m.

concession /kən'seʃn/ n. concession f.

conciliation /kənsɪlɪ'eɪʃn/ n. conciliation f.

concise /kən'saɪs/ a. concis. ~ly adv. avec concision. ~ness n. concision f.

conclu|de /kən'kluːd/ v.t. conclure. —v.i. se terminer. ~**ding** a. final. ~sion n. conclusion f.

conclusive /kən'kluːsɪv/ a. concluant. ~ly adv. de manière concluante.

concoct /kən'kɒkt/ v.t. confectionner; (invent: fig.) fabriquer. ~ion /-kʃn/ n. mélange m.

concourse /'kɒŋkɔːs/ n. (rail.) hall m.

concrete /'kɒŋkriːt/ n. béton m. —a. concret. —v.t. bétonner. ~-mixer n. bétonnière f.

concur /kən'kɜː(r)/ v.i. (p.t. concurred) être d'accord.

concurrently /kən'kʌrəntlɪ/ adv. simultanément.

concussion /kən'kʌʃn/ n. commotion (cérébrale) f.

condemn /kən'dem/ v.t. condamner. **~ation** /kɒndem'neɪʃn/ n. condamnation f.

condens|e /kən'dens/ v.t./i. (se) condenser. **~ation** /kɒnden'seɪʃn/ n. condensation f.; (mist) buée f.

condescend /kɒndɪ'send/ v.i. condescendre.

condiment /'kɒndɪmənt/ n. condiment m.

condition /kən'dɪʃn/ n. condition f. —v.t. conditionner. **on ~ that,** à condition que. **~al** a. conditionnel. **be ~al upon,** dépendre de. **~er** n. après-shampooing m.

condolences /kən'dəʊlənsɪz/ n. pl. condoléances f. pl.

condom /'kɒndɒm/ n. préservatif m.

condominium /kɒndə'mɪnɪəm/ n. (Amer.) copropriété f.

condone /kən'dəʊn/ v.t. pardonner, fermer les yeux sur.

conducive /kən'djuːsɪv/ a. **~ to,** favorable à.

conduct¹ /kən'dʌkt/ v.t. conduire; (orchestra) diriger.

conduct² /'kɒndʌkt/ n. conduite f.

conduct|or /kən'dʌktə(r)/ n. chef d'orchestre m.; (of bus) receveur m.; (on train: Amer.) chef de train m.; (electr.) conducteur m. **~ress** n. receveuse f.

cone /kəʊn/ n. cône m.; (of ice-cream) cornet m.

confectioner /kən'fekʃənə(r)/ n. confiseur, -se m., f. **~y** n. confiserie f.

confederation /kənfedə'reɪʃn/ n. confédération f.

confer /kən'fɜː(r)/ v.t./i. (p.t. **conferred**) conférer.

conference /'kɒnfərəns/ n. conférence f.

confess /kən'fes/ v.t./i. avouer; (relig.) (se) confesser. **~ion** /-ʃn/ n. confession f.; (of crime) aveu m.

confessional /kən'feʃənl/ n. confessionnal m.

confetti /kən'fetɪ/ n. confettis m. pl.

confide /kən'faɪd/ v.t. confier. —v.i. **~ in,** se confier à.

confiden|t /'kɒnfɪdənt/ a. sûr. **~ce** n. (trust) confiance f.; (boldness) confiance en soi f.; (secret) confidence f. **~ce trick,** escroquerie f. **in ~ce,** en confidence.

confidential /kɒnfɪ'denʃl/ a. confidentiel.

configure /kən'fɪgə(r)/ v.t. (comput.) configurer.

confine /kən'faɪn/ v.t. enfermer; (limit) limiter. **~d space,** espace réduit. **~d to,** limité à. **~ment** n. détention f.; (med.) couches f. pl.

confines /'kɒnfaɪnz/ n. pl. confins m. pl.

confirm /kən'fɜːm/ v.t. confirmer. **~ation** /kɒnfə'meɪʃn/ n. confirmation f. **~ed** a. (bachelor) endurci; (smoker) invétéré.

confiscat|e /'kɒnfɪskeɪt/ v.t. confisquer. **~ion** /-'keɪʃn/ n. confiscation f.

conflagration /kɒnflə'greɪʃn/ n. incendie m.

conflict¹ /'kɒnflɪkt/ n. conflit m.

conflict² /kən'flɪkt/ v.i. (statements, views) être en contradiction (with, avec); (appointments) tomber en même temps (with, que). **~ing** a. contradictoire.

conform /kən'fɔːm/ v.t./i. (se) conformer. **~ist** n. conformiste m./f.

confound /kən'faʊnd/ v.t. confondre. **~ed** a. (fam.) sacré.

confront /kən'frʌnt/ v.t. affronter. **~ with,** confronter avec. **~ation** /kɒnfrʌn'teɪʃn/ n. confrontation f.

confus|e /kən'fjuːz/ v.t. embrouiller; (mistake, confound) confondre. **become ~ed,** s'embrouiller. **I am ~ed,** je m'y perds. **~ing** a. déroutant. **~ion** /-ʒn/ n. confusion f.

congeal /kən'dʒiːl/ v.t./i. (se) figer.

congenial /kən'dʒiːnɪəl/ a. sympathique.

congenital /kən'dʒenɪtl/ a. congénital.

congest|ed /kən'dʒestɪd/ a. encombré; (med.) congestionné. **~ion** /-stʃən/ n. (traffic) encombrement(s) m. (pl.); (med.) congestion f.

conglomerate /kən'glɒmərət/ n. (comm.) conglomérat m.

congratulat|e /kən'grætjʊleɪt/ v.t. féliciter (on, de). **~ions** /-'leɪʃnz/ n. pl. félicitations f. pl.

congregat|e /'kɒngrɪgeɪt/ v.i. se rassembler. **~ion** /-'geɪʃn/ n. assemblée f.

congress /'kɒngres/ n. congrès m. **C~,** (Amer.) le Congrès.

conic(al) /'kɒnɪk(l)/ a. conique.

conifer /'kɒnɪfə(r)/ n. conifère m.

conjecture /kən'dʒektʃə(r)/ n. conjecture f. —v.t./i. conjecturer.

conjugal /'kɒndʒʊgl/ a. conjugal.

conjugat|e /'kɒndʒʊgeɪt/ v.t. conjuguer. **~ion** /-'geɪʃn/ n. conjugaison f.

conjunction /kən'dʒʌŋkʃn/ n. conjonction f. **in ~ with,** conjointement avec.

conjunctivitis /kɒndʒʌŋktɪ'vaɪtɪs/ n. conjonctivite f.

conjur|e /'kʌndʒə(r)/ v.i. faire des tours de passe-passe. —v.t. **~e up,** faire apparaître. **~or** *n.* prestidigitalteur, -trice *m.*, *f.*

conk /kɒŋk/ *v.i.* **~ out,** (*sl.*) tomber en panne.

conker /ˈkɒŋkə(r)/ *n.* (*horse-chestnut fruit*: *fam.*) marron *m.*

connect /kəˈnekt/ *v.t./i.* (se) relier; (*in mind*) faire le rapport entre; (*install, wire up to mains*) brancher. **~ with,** (*of train*) assurer la correspondance avec. **~ed** *a.* lié. **be ~ed with,** avoir rapport à; (*deal with*) avoir des rapports avec.

connection /kəˈnekʃn/ *n.* rapport *m.*; (*rail.*) correspondance *f.*; (*phone call*) communication *f.*; (*electr.*) contact *m.*; (*joining piece*) raccord *m.* **~s,** (*comm.*) relations *f. pl.*

connive /kəˈnaɪv/ *v.i.* **~e at,** se faire le complice de. **~ance** *n.* connivence *f.*

connoisseur /ˌkɒnəˈsɜː(r)/ *n.* connaisseur *m.*

connote /kəˈnəʊt/ *v.t.* connoter. **~ation** /ˌkɒnəˈteɪʃn/ *n.* connotation *f.*

conquer /ˈkɒŋkə(r)/ *v.t.* vaincre; (*country*) conquérir. **~or** *n.* conquérant *m.*

conquest /ˈkɒŋkwest/ *n.* conquête *f.*

conscience /ˈkɒnʃəns/ *n.* conscience *f.*

conscientious /ˌkɒnʃɪˈenʃəs/ *a.* consciencieux.

conscious /ˈkɒnʃəs/ *a.* conscient; (*deliberate*) voulu. **~ly** *adv.* consciemment. **~ness** *n.* conscience *f.*; (*med.*) connaissance *f.*

conscript¹ /kənˈskrɪpt/ *v.t.* recruter par conscription. **~ion** /-pʃn/ *n.* conscription *f.*

conscript² /ˈkɒnskrɪpt/ *n.* conscrit *m.*

consecrate /ˈkɒnsɪkreɪt/ *v.t.* consacrer.

consecutive /kənˈsekjʊtɪv/ *a.* consécutif. **~ly** *adv.* consécutivement.

consensus /kənˈsensəs/ *n.* consensus *m.*

consent /kənˈsent/ *v.i.* consentir (**to,** à). —*n.* consentement *m.*

consequence /ˈkɒnsɪkwəns/ *n.* conséquence *f.*

consequent /ˈkɒnsɪkwənt/ *a.* résultant. **~ly** *adv.* par conséquent.

conservation /ˌkɒnsəˈveɪʃn/ *n.* préservation *f.* **~ area,** zone classée *f.*

conservationist /ˌkɒnsəˈveɪʃənɪst/ *n.* défenseur de l'environnement *m.*

conservative /kənˈsɜːvətɪv/ *a.* conservateur; (*estimate*) modeste. **C~** *a. & n.* conservateur, -trice (*m.* (*f.*)).

conservatory /kənˈsɜːvətrɪ/ *n.* (*greenhouse*) serre *f.*; (*room*) véranda *f.*

conserve /kənˈsɜːv/ *v.t.* conserver; (*energy*) économiser.

consider /kənˈsɪdə(r)/ *v.t.* considérer; (*allow for*) tenir compte de; (*possibility*) envisager (**doing,** de faire). **~ation** /-ˈreɪʃn/ *n.* considération *f.*; (*respect*) égard(s) *m.* (*pl.*). **~ing** *prep.* compte tenu de.

considerabl|e /kənˈsɪdərəbl/ *a.* considérable; (*much*) beaucoup de. **~y** *adv.* beaucoup, considérablement.

considerate /kənˈsɪdərət/ *a.* prévenant, attentionné.

consign /kənˈsaɪn/ *v.t.* (*entrust*) confier; (*send*) expédier. **~ment** *n.* envoi *m.*

consist /kənˈsɪst/ *v.i.* consister (**of,** en; **in doing,** à faire).

consisten|t /kənˈsɪstənt/ *a.* cohérent. **~t with,** conforme à. **~cy** *n.* (*of liquids*) consistance *f.*; (*of argument*) cohérence *f.* **~tly** *adv.* régulièrement.

consol|e /kənˈsəʊl/ *v.t.* consoler. **~ation** /ˌkɒnsəˈleɪʃn/ *n.* consolation *f.*

consolidat|e /kənˈsɒlɪdeɪt/ *v.t./i.* (se) consolider. **~ion** /-ˈdeɪʃn/ *n.* consolidation *f.*

consonant /ˈkɒnsənənt/ *n.* consonne *f.*

consort¹ /ˈkɒnsɔːt/ *n.* époux *m.*, épouse *f.*

consort² /kənˈsɔːt/ *v.i.* **~ with,** fréquenter.

consortium /kənˈsɔːtɪəm/ *n.* (*pl.* **-tia**) consortium *m.*

conspicuous /kənˈspɪkjʊəs/ *a.* (*easily seen*) en évidence; (*showy*) voyant; (*noteworthy*) remarquable.

conspiracy /kənˈspɪrəsɪ/ *n.* conspiration *f.*

conspire /kənˈspaɪə(r)/ *v.i.* (*person*) comploter (**to do,** de faire), conspirer; (*events*) conspirer (**to do,** à faire).

constable /ˈkʌnstəbl/ *n.* agent de police *m.*, gendarme *m.*

constant /ˈkɒnstənt/ *a.* incessant; (*unchanging*) constant; (*friend*) fidèle. —*n.* constante *f.* **~ly** *adv.* constamment.

constellation /ˌkɒnstəˈleɪʃn/ *n.* constellation *f.*

consternation /ˌkɒnstəˈneɪʃn/ *n.* consternation *f.*

constipat|e /ˈkɒnstɪpeɪt/ *v.t.* constiper. **~ion** /-ˈpeɪʃn/ *n.* constipation *f.*

constituency /kənˈstɪtjʊənsɪ/ *n.* circonscription électorale *f.*

constituent /kənˈstɪtjʊənt/ *a.* constitutif. —*n.* élément constitutif *m.*; (*pol.*) élec|teur, -trice *m.*, *f.*

constitut|e /ˈkɒnstɪtjuːt/ *v.t.* constituer. **~ion** /-ˈtjuːʃn/ *n.* constitution *f.*

~ional /-'tju:ʃənl/ *a.* constitutionnel; *n.* promenade *f.*

constrain /kən'streın/ *v.t.* contraindre.

constraint /kən'streınt/ *n.* contrainte *f.*

constrict /kən'strıkt/ *v.t.* resserrer; (*movement*) gêner. **~ion** /-kʃn/ *n.* resserrement *m.*

construct /kən'strʌkt/ *v.t.* construire. **~ion** /-kʃn/ *n.* construction *f.* **~ion worker,** ouvrier de bâtiment *m.*

constructive /kən'strʌktɪv/ *a.* constructif.

construe /kən'stru:/ *v.t.* interpréter.

consul /'kɒnsl/ *n.* consul *m.* **~ar** /-jʊlə(r)/ *a.* consulaire.

consulate /'kɒnsjʊlət/ *n.* consulat *m.*

consult /kən'sʌlt/ *v.t.* consulter. —*v.i.* **~ with,** conférer avec. **~ation** /kɒnsl'teıʃn/ *n.* consultation *f.*

consultant /kən'sʌltənt/ *n.* conseilller, -ère *m.*, *f.*; (*med.*) spécialiste *m./f.*

consume /kən'sju:m/ *v.t.* consommer; (*destroy*) consumer. **~r** /-ə(r)/ *n.* consommalteur, -trice *m.*, *f. a.* (*society*) de consommation.

consumerism /kən'sju:mərızəm/ *n.* protection des consommateurs *f.*

consummate /'kɒnsəmeıt/ *v.t.* consommer.

consumption /kən'sʌmpʃn/ *n.* consommation *f.*; (*med.*) phtisie *f.*

contact /'kɒntækt/ *n.* contact *m.*; (*person*) relation *f.* —*v.t.* contacter. **~ lenses,** lentilles (de contact) *f. pl.*

contagious /kən'teıdʒəs/ *a.* contagieux.

contain /kən'teın/ *v.t.* contenir. **~ o.s.,** se contenir. **~er** *n.* récipient *m.*; (*for transport*) container *m.*

contaminat|e /kən'tæmıneıt/ *v.t.* contaminer. **~ion** /-'neıʃn/ *n.* contamination *f.*

contemplat|e /'kɒntempleıt/ *v.t.* (*gaze at*) contempler; (*think about*) envisager. **~ion** /-'pleıʃn/ *n.* contemplation *f.*

contemporary /kən'temprərı/ *a. & n.* contemporain(e) (*m.* (*f.*)).

contempt /kən'tempt/ *n.* mépris *m.* **~ible** *a.* méprisable. **~uous** /-tʃʊəs/ *a.* méprisant.

contend /kən'tend/ *v.t.* soutenir. —*v.i.* **~ with,** (*compete*) rivaliser avec; (*face*) faire face à. **~er** *n.* adversaire *m./f.*

content[1] /kən'tent/ *a.* satisfait. —*v.t.* contenter. **~ed** *a.* satisfait. **~ment** *n.* contentement *m.*

content[2] /'kɒntent/ *n.* (*of letter*) contenu *m.*; (*amount*) teneur *f.* **~s,** contenu *m.*

contention /kən'tenʃn/ *n.* dispute *f.*; (*claim*) affirmation *f.*

contest[1] /'kɒntest/ *n.* (*competition*) concours *m.*; (*fight*) combat *m.*

contest[2] /kən'test/ *v.t.* contester; (*compete for or in*) disputer. **~ant** *n.* concurrent(e) *m.* (*f.*).

context /'kɒntekst/ *n.* contexte *m.*

continent /'kɒntınənt/ *n.* continent *m.* **the C~,** l'Europe (continentale) *f.* **~al** /-'nentl/ *a.* continental; européen. **~al quilt,** couette *f.*

contingen|t /kən'tındʒənt/ *a.* **be ~t upon,** dépendre de. —*n.* (*mil.*) contingent *m.* **~cy** *n.* éventualité *f.* **~cy plan,** plan d'urgence *m.*

continual /kən'tınjʊəl/ *a.* continuel. **~ly** *adv.* continuellement.

continu|e /kən'tınju:/ *v.t./i.* continuer; (*resume*) reprendre. **~ance** *n.* continuation *f.* **~ation** /-ʊ'eıʃn/ *n.* continuation *f.*; (*after interruption*) reprise *f.*; (*new episode*) suite *f.* **~ed** *a.* continu.

continuity /kɒntı'nju:ətı/ *n.* continuité *f.*

continuous /kən'tınjʊəs/ *a.* continu. **~ stationery,** papier continu *m.* **~ly** *adv.* sans interruption, continûment.

contort /kən'tɔ:t/ *v.t.* tordre. **~ o.s.,** se contorsionner. **~ion** /-ʃn/ *n.* torsion *f.*; contorsion *f.* **~ionist** /-ʃənıst/ *n.* contorsionniste *m./f.*

contour /'kɒntʊə(r)/ *n.* contour *m.*

contraband /'kɒntrəbænd/ *n.* contrebande *f.*

contraception /kɒntrə'sepʃn/ *n.* contraception *f.*

contraceptive /kɒntrə'septıv/ *a. & n.* contraceptif (*m.*).

contract[1] /'kɒntrækt/ *n.* contrat *m.*

contract[2] /kən'trækt/ *v.t./i.* (se) contracter. **~ion** /-kʃn/ *n.* contraction *f.*

contractor /kən'træktə(r)/ *n.* entrepreneur *m.*

contradict /kɒntrə'dıkt/ *v.t.* contredire. **~ion** /-kʃn/ *n.* contradiction *f.* **~ory** *a.* contradictoire.

contralto /kən'træltəʊ/ *n.* (*pl.* **-os**) contralto *m.*

contraption /kən'træpʃn/ *n.* (*fam.*) engin *m.*, truc *m.*

contrary[1] /'kɒntrərı/ *a.* contraire (**to,** à). —*n.* contraire *m.* —*adv.* **~ to,** contrairement à. **on the ~,** au contraire.

contrary[2] /kən'treərı/ *a.* entêté.

contrast[1] /'kɒntrɑ:st/ *n.* contraste *m.*

contrast[2] /kən'trɑ:st/ *v.t./i.* contraster. **~ing** *a.* contrasté.

contraven|e /kɒntrə'vi:n/ *v.t.* enfreindre. **~tion** /-'venʃn/ *n.* infraction *f.*

contribut|e /kən'trɪbjuːt/ v.t. donner. —v.i. ~**e to,** contribuer à; (take part) participer à; (newspaper) collaborer à. ~**ion** /kɒntrɪ'bjuːʃn/ n. contribution f. ~**or** n. collaborateur, -trice m., f.

contrivance /kən'traɪvəns/ n. (device) appareil m., truc m.

contrive /kən'traɪv/ v.t. imaginer. ~ **to do,** trouver moyen de faire. ~**d** a. tortueux.

control /kən'trəʊl/ v.t. (p.t. controlled) (a firm etc.) diriger; (check) contrôler; (restrain) maîtriser. —n. contrôle m.; (mastery) maîtrise f. ~**s,** commandes f. pl.; (knobs) boutons m. pl. ~ **tower,** tour de contrôle f. **have under** ~, (event) avoir en main. **in** ~ **of,** maître de.

controversial /kɒntrə'vɜːʃl/ a. discutable, discuté.

controversy /'kɒntrəvɜːsɪ/ n. controverse f.

conurbation /kɒnɜː'beɪʃn/ n. agglomération f., conurbation f.

convalesce /kɒnvə'les/ v.i. être en convalescence. ~**nce** n. convalescence f. ~**nt** a. & n. convalescent(e) (m. (f.)). ~**nt home,** maison de convalescence f.

convector /kən'vektə(r)/ n. radiateur à convection m.

convene /kən'viːn/ v.t. convoquer. —v.i. se réunir.

convenience /kən'viːnɪəns/ n. commodité f. ~**s,** toilettes f. pl. **all modern** ~**s,** tout le confort moderne. **at your** ~, quand cela vous conviendra, à votre convenance. ~ **foods,** plats tout préparés m. pl.

convenient /kən'viːnɪənt/ a. commode, pratique; (time) bien choisi. **be** ~ **for,** convenir à. ~**ly** adv. (arrive) à propos. ~**ly situated,** bien situé.

convent /'kɒnvənt/ n. couvent m.

convention /kən'venʃn/ n. (assembly, agreement) convention f.; (custom) usage m. ~**al** a. conventionnel.

converge /kən'vɜːdʒ/ v.i. converger.

conversant /kən'vɜːsnt/ a. **be** ~ **with,** connaître; (fact) savoir; (machinery) s'y connaître en.

conversation /kɒnvə'seɪʃn/ n. conversation f. ~**al** a. (tone etc.) de la conversation; (French etc.) de tous les jours. ~**alist** n. causeur, -se m., f.

converse¹ /kən'vɜːs/ v.i. s'entretenir, converser (**with,** avec).

converse² /'kɒnvɜːs/ a. & n. inverse (m.). ~**ly** adv. inversement.

conver|t¹ /kən'vɜːt/ v.t. convertir; (house) aménager. —v.i. ~**t into,** se transformer en. ~**sion** /-ʃn/ n. conversion f. ~**tible** a. convertible. —n. (car) décapotable f.

convert² /'kɒnvɜːt/ n. converti(e) m. (f.).

convex /'kɒnveks/ a. convexe.

convey /kən'veɪ/ v.t. (wishes, order) transmettre; (goods, people) transporter; (idea, feeling) communiquer. ~**ance** n. transport m. ~**or belt,** tapis roulant m.

convict¹ /kən'vɪkt/ v.t. déclarer coupable. ~**ion** /-kʃn/ n. condamnation f.; (opinion) conviction f.

convict² /'kɒnvɪkt/ n. prisonnier, ère m., f.

convinc|e /kən'vɪns/ v.t. convaincre. ~**ing** a. convaincant.

convivial /kən'vɪvɪəl/ a. joyeux.

convoke /kən'vəʊk/ v.t. convoquer.

convoluted /'kɒnvəluːtɪd/ a. (argument etc.) compliqué.

convoy /'kɒnvɔɪ/ n. convoi m.

convuls|e /kən'vʌls/ v.t. convulser; (fig.) bouleverser. **be** ~**ed with laughter,** se tordre de rire. ~**ion** /-ʃn/ n. convulsion f.

coo /kuː/ v.i. roucouler.

cook /kʊk/ v.t./i. (faire) cuire; (of person) faire la cuisine. —n. cuisinier, -ière m., f. ~ **up,** (fam.) fabriquer. ~**ing** n. cuisine f.; a. de cuisine.

cooker /'kʊkə(r)/ n. (stove) cuisinière f.; (apple) pomme à cuire f.

cookery /'kʊkərɪ/ n. cuisine f. ~ **book,** livre de cuisine m.

cookie /'kʊkɪ/ n. (Amer.) biscuit m.

cool /kuːl/ a. (-er, -est) frais; (calm) calme; (unfriendly) froid. —n. fraîcheur f.; (calmness: sl.) sang-froid m. —v.t./i. rafraîchir. **in the** ~, au frais. ~ **box,** glacière f. ~**er** n. (for food) glacière f.; ~**ly** adv. calmement; froidement. ~**ness** n. fraîcheur f.; froideur f.

coop /kuːp/ n. poulailler m. —v.t. ~ **up,** enfermer.

co-operat|e /kəʊ'ɒpəreɪt/ v.i. coopérer. ~**ion** /-'reɪʃn/ n. coopération f.

co-operative /kəʊ'ɒpərətɪv/ a. coopératif. —n. coopérative f.

co-opt /kəʊ'ɒpt/ v.t. coopter.

co-ordinat|e /kəʊ'ɔːdɪneɪt/ v.t. coordonner. ~**ion** /-'neɪʃn/ n. coordination f.

cop /kɒp/ v.t. (p.t. copped) (sl.) piquer. —n. (policeman: sl.) flic m. ~ **out,** (sl.) se dérober. ~**-out** n. (sl.) dérobade f.

cope /kəʊp/ *v.i.* assurer. **∼ with,** s'en sortir avec.

copious /'kəʊpɪəs/ *a.* copieux.

copper¹ /'kɒpə(r)/ *n.* cuivre *m.*; (*coin*) sou *m.* —*a.* de cuivre.

copper² /'kɒpə(r)/ *n.* (*sl.*) flic *m.*

coppice, copse /'kɒpɪs, kɒps/ *ns.* taillis *m.*

copulat|e /'kɒpjʊleɪt/ *v.i.* s'accoupler. **∼ion** /-'leɪʃn/ *n.* copulation *f.*

copy /'kɒpɪ/ *n.* copie *f.*; (*of book, newspaper*) exemplaire *m.*; (*print*: *photo.*) épreuve *f.* —*v.t./i.* copier. **∼-writer** *n.* rédacteur-concepteur *m.*, rédactrice-conceptrice *f.*

copyright /'kɒpɪraɪt/ *n.* droit d'auteur *m.*, copyright *m.*

coral /'kɒrəl/ *n.* corail *m.*

cord /kɔːd/ *n.* (petite) corde *f.*; (*of curtain, pyjamas, etc.*) cordon *m.*; (*electr.*) cordon électrique *m.*; (*fabric*) velours côtelé *m.*

cordial /'kɔːdɪəl/ *a.* cordial. —*n.* (*fruit-flavoured drink*) sirop *m.*

cordon /'kɔːdn/ *n.* cordon *m.* —*v.t.* **∼ off,** mettre un cordon autour de.

corduroy /'kɔːdərɔɪ/ *n.* velours côtelé *m.*, velours à côtes *m.*

core /kɔː(r)/ *n.* (*of apple*) trognon *m.*; (*of problem*) cœur *m.*; (*techn.*) noyau *m.* —*v.t.* vider.

cork /kɔːk/ *n.* liège *m.*; (*for bottle*) bouchon *m.* —*v.t.* boucher.

corkscrew /'kɔːkskruː/ *n.* tire-bouchon *m.*

corn¹ /kɔːn/ *n.* blé *m.*; (*maize*: *Amer.*) maïs *m.*; (*seed*) grain *m.* **∼-cob** *n.* épi de maïs *m.*

corn² /kɔːn/ *n.* (*hard skin*) cor *m.*

cornea /'kɔːnɪə/ *n.* cornée *f.*

corned /kɔːnd/ *a.* **∼ beef,** corned-beef *m.*

corner /'kɔːnə(r)/ *n.* coin *m.*; (*bend in road*) virage *m.*; (*football*) corner *m.* —*v.t.* coincer, acculer; (*market*) accaparer. —*v.i.* prendre un virage. **∼-stone** *n.* pierre angulaire *f.*

cornet /'kɔːnɪt/ *n.* cornet *m.*

cornflakes /'kɔːnfleɪks/ *n. pl.* corn flakes *m. pl.*

cornflour /'kɔːnflaʊə(r)/ *n.* farine de maïs *f.*

cornice /'kɔːnɪs/ *n.* corniche *f.*

cornstarch /'kɔːnstɑːtʃ/ *n.* *Amer.* = **cornflour.**

cornucopia /kɔːnjʊ'kəʊpɪə/ *n.* corne d'abondance *f.*

Corn|wall /'kɔːnwəl/ *n.* Cornouailles *f.* **∼ish** *a.* de Cornouailles.

corny /'kɔːnɪ/ *a.* (**-ier, -iest**) (*trite*: *fam.*) rebattu; (*mawkish*: *fam.*) à l'eau de rose.

corollary /kə'rɒlərɪ, *Amer.* 'kɒrələrɪ/ *n.* corollaire *m.*

coronary /'kɒrənərɪ/ *n.* infarctus *m.*

coronation /kɒrə'neɪʃn/ *n.* couronnement *m.*

coroner /'kɒrənə(r)/ *n.* coroner *m.*

corporal¹ /'kɔːpərəl/ *n.* caporal *m.*

corporal² /'kɔːpərəl/ *a.* **∼ punishment,** châtiment corporel *m.*

corporate /'kɔːpərət/ *a.* en commun; (*body*) constitué.

corporation /kɔːpə'reɪʃn/ *n.* (*comm.*) société *f.*; (*of town*) municipalité *f.*

corps /kɔː(r)/ *n.* (*pl.* corps /kɔːz/) corps *m.*

corpse /kɔːps/ *n.* cadavre *m.*

corpulent /'kɔːpjʊlənt/ *a.* corpulent.

corpuscle /'kɔːpʌsl/ *n.* globule *m.*

corral /kə'rɑːl/ *n.* (*Amer.*) corral *m.*

correct /kə'rekt/ *a.* (*right*) exact, juste, correct; (*proper*) correct. **you are ∼,** vous avez raison. —*v.t.* corriger. **∼ion** /-kʃn/ *n.* correction *f.*

correlat|e /'kɒrəleɪt/ *v.t./i.* (faire) correspondre. **∼ion** /-'leɪʃn/ *n.* corrélation *f.*

correspond /kɒrɪ'spɒnd/ *v.i.* correspondre. **∼ence** *n.* correspondance *f.* **∼ence course,** cours par correspondance *m.* **∼ent** *n.* correspondant(e) *m.(f.).*

corridor /'kɒrɪdɔː(r)/ *n.* couloir *m.*

corroborate /kə'rɒbəreɪt/ *v.t.* corroborer.

corro|de /kə'rəʊd/ *v.t./i.* (se) corroder. **∼sion** *n.* corrosion *f.*

corrosive /kə'rəʊsɪv/ *a.* corrosif.

corrugated /'kɒrəgeɪtɪd/ *a.* ondulé. **∼ iron,** tôle ondulée *f.*

corrupt /kə'rʌpt/ *a.* corrompu. —*v.t.* corrompre. **∼ion** /-pʃn/ *n.* corruption *f.*

corset /'kɔːsɪt/ *n.* (*boned*) corset *m.*; (*elasticated*) gaine *f.*

Corsica /'kɔːsɪkə/ *n.* Corse *f.*

cortisone /'kɔːtɪzəʊn/ *n.* cortisone *f.*

cos /kɒs/ *n.* laitue romaine *f.*

cosh /kɒʃ/ *n.* matraque *f.* —*v.t.* matraquer.

cosmetic /kɒz'metɪk/ *n.* produit de beauté *m.* —*a.* cosmétique; (*fig., pej.*) superficiel.

cosmic /'kɒzmɪk/ *a.* cosmique.

cosmonaut /'kɒzmənɔːt/ *n.* cosmonaute *m./f.*

cosmopolitan /kɒzmə'pɒlɪt(ə)n/ *a. & n.* cosmopolite (*m./f.*).

cosmos /'kɒzmɒs/ n. cosmos m.

Cossack /'kɒsæk/ n. cosaque m.

cosset /'kɒsɪt/ v.t. (p.t. **cosseted**) dorloter.

cost /kɒst/ v.t. (p.t. **cost**) coûter; (p.t. **costed**) établir le prix de. —n. coût m. ∼s, (jurid.) dépens m. pl. **at all** ∼s, à tout prix. **to one's** ∼, à ses dépens. ∼-**effective** a. rentable. ∼-**effectiveness** n. rentabilité f. ∼ **price**, prix de revient m. ∼ **of living**, coût de la vie.

co-star /'kəʊstɑː(r)/ n. partenaire m./f.

costly /'kɒstlɪ/ a. (-**ier**, -**iest**) coûteux; (valuable) précieux.

costume /'kɒstjuːm/ n. costume m.; (for swimming) maillot m. ∼ **jewellery**, bijoux de fantaisie m. pl.

cosy /'kəʊzɪ/ a. (-**ier**, -**iest**) confortable, intime. —n. couvrethéière m. ∼**iness** n. confort m.

cot /kɒt/ n. lit d'enfant m.; (camp-bed: Amer.) lit de camp m.

cottage /'kɒtɪdʒ/ n. petite maison de campagne f.; (thatched) chaumière f. ∼ **cheese**, fromage blanc (maigre) m. ∼ **industry**, activité artisanale f. ∼ **pie**, hachis Parmentier m.

cotton /'kɒtn/ n. coton m.; (for sewing) fil (à coudre) m. —v.i. ∼ **on**, (sl.) piger. ∼ **candy**, (Amer.) barbe à papa f. ∼ **wool**, coton hydrophile m.

couch /kaʊtʃ/ n. divan m. —v.t. (express) formuler.

couchette /kuː'ʃet/ n. couchette f.

cough /kɒf/ v.i. tousser. —n. toux f. ∼ **up**, (sl.) cracher, payer.

could /kʊd, unstressed kəd/ p.t. of **can**[2].

couldn't /'kʊdnt/ = **could not**.

council /'kaʊnsl/ n. conseil m. ∼ **house**, maison construite par la municipalité f., (approx.) H.L.M. m./f.

councillor /'kaʊnsələ(r)/ n. conseilller, -ère municipal(e) m., f.

counsel /'kaʊnsl/ n. conseil m. invar. (jurid.) avocat(e) m. (f.). ∼**lor** n. conseilller, -ère m., f.

count[1] /kaʊnt/ v.t./i. compter. —n. compte m. ∼ **on**, compter sur.

count[2] /kaʊnt/ n. (nobleman) comte m.

countdown /'kaʊntdaʊn/ n. compte à rebours m.

countenance /'kaʊntɪnəns/ n. mine f. —v.t. admettre, approuver.

counter[1] /'kaʊntə(r)/ n. comptoir m.; (in bank etc.) guichet m.; (token) jeton m.

counter[2] /'kaʊntə(r)/ adv. ∼ **to**, à l'encontre de. —a. opposé. —v.t. opposer; (blow) parer. —v.i. riposter.

counter- /'kaʊntə(r)/ pref. contre-.

counteract /kaʊntər'ækt/ v.t. neutraliser.

counter-attack /'kaʊntərətæk/ n. contre-attaque f. —v.t./i. contre-attaquer.

counterbalance /'kaʊntəbæləns/ n. contrepoids m. —v.t. contre-balancer.

counter-clockwise /kaʊntə'klɒkwaɪz/ a. & adv. (Amer.) dans le sens inverse des aiguilles d'une montre.

counterfeit /'kaʊntəfɪt/ a. & n. faux (m.). —v.t. contrefaire.

counterfoil /'kaʊntəfɔɪl/ n. souche f.

countermand /kaʊntə'mɑːnd/ v.t. annuler.

counterpart /'kaʊntəpɑːt/ n. équivalent m.; (person) homologue m./f.

counter-productive /kaʊntəprə'dʌktɪv/ a. (measure) qui produit l'effet contraire.

countersign /'kaʊntəsaɪn/ v.t. contresigner.

counter-tenor /'kaʊntətenə(r)/ n. haute-contre m.

countess /'kaʊntɪs/ n. comtesse f.

countless /'kaʊntlɪs/ a. innombrable.

countrified /'kʌntrɪfaɪd/ a. rustique.

country /'kʌntrɪ/ n. (land, region) pays m.; (homeland) patrie f.; (countryside) campagne f. ∼ **dance**, danse folklorique f.

countryman /'kʌntrɪmən/ n. (pl. -**men**) campagnard m.; (fellow citizen) compatriote m.

countryside /'kʌntrɪsaɪd/ n. campagne f.

county /'kaʊntɪ/ n. comté m.

coup /kuː/ n. (achievement) joli coup m.; (pol.) coup d'état m.

coupé /'kuːpeɪ/ n. (car) coupé m.

couple /'kʌpl/ n. (people, animals) couple m. —v.t./i. (s')accoupler. **a** ∼ **(of)**, (two or three) deux ou trois.

coupon /'kuːpɒn/ n. coupon m.; (for shopping) bon or coupon de réduction m.

courage /'kʌrɪdʒ/ n. courage m. ∼**ous** /kə'reɪdʒəs/ a. courageux.

courgette /kʊə'ʒet/ n. courgette f.

courier /'kʊrɪə(r)/ n. messager, -ère m., f.; (for tourists) guide m.

course /kɔːs/ n. cours m.; (for training) stage m.; (series) série f.; (culin.) plat m.; (for golf) terrain m.; (at sea) itinéraire m. **change** ∼, changer de cap. ∼ **(of action)**, façon de faire f. **during the** ∼ **of**, pendant. **in due** ∼, en temps utile. **of** ∼, bien sûr.

court /kɔːt/ n. cour f.; (tennis) court m. —v.t. faire la cour à; (danger) rechercher. ～ **martial**, (pl. **courts martial**) conseil de guerre m. ～-**martial** v.t. (p.t. -**martialled**) faire passer en conseil de guerre. ～-**house** n. (Amer.) palais de justice m. ～ **shoe**, escarpin m. **go to** ～, aller devant les tribunaux.

courteous /ˈkɜːtɪəs/ a. courtois.

courtesy /ˈkɜːtəsɪ/ n. courtoisie f. **by** ～ **of**, avec la permission de.

courtier /ˈkɔːtɪə(r)/ n. (old use) courtisan m.

courtroom /ˈkɔːtrʊm/ n. salle de tribunal f.

courtyard /ˈkɔːtjɑːd/ n. cour f.

cousin /ˈkʌzn/ n. cousin(e) m. (f.). **first** ～, cousin(e) germain(e) m. (f.).

cove /kəʊv/ n. anse f., crique f.

covenant /ˈkʌvənənt/ n. convention f.

Coventry /ˈkɒvntrɪ/ n. **send to** ～, mettre en quarantaine.

cover /ˈkʌvə(r)/ v.t. couvrir. —n. (for bed, book, etc.) couverture f.; (lid) couvercle m.; (for furniture) housse f.; (shelter) abri m. ～ **charge**, couvert m. ～ **up**, cacher; (crime) couvrir. ～ **up for**, couvrir. ～-**up** n. tentative pour cacher la vérité f. **take** ～, se mettre à l'abri. ～**ing** n. enveloppe f. ～**ing letter**, lettre f. (jointe à un document).

coverage /ˈkʌvərɪdʒ/ n. reportage m.

coveralls /ˈkʌvərɔːlz/ (Amer.) bleu de travail m.

covert /ˈkʌvət, Amer. /ˈkəʊvɜːrt/ a. (activity) secret; (threat) voilé (look) dérobé.

covet /ˈkʌvɪt/ v.t. convoiter.

cow /kaʊ/ n. vache f.

coward /ˈkaʊəd/ n. lâche m./f. ～**ly** a. lâche.

cowardice /ˈkaʊədɪs/ n. lâcheté f.

cowboy /ˈkaʊbɔɪ/ n. cow-boy m.

cower /ˈkaʊə(r)/ v.i. se recroqueviller (sous l'effet de la peur).

cowshed /ˈkaʊʃed/ n. étable f.

cox /kɒks/ n. barreur m. —v.t. barrer.

coxswain /ˈkɒksn/ n. barreur m.

coy /kɔɪ/ a. (-**er**, -**est**) (faussement) timide, qui fait le or la timide.

cozy /ˈkəʊzɪ/ Amer. = **cosy**.

crab /kræb/ n. crabe m. —v.i. (p.t. **crabbed**) rouspéter. ～-**apple** n. pomme sauvage f.

crack /kræk/ n. fente f.; (in glass) fêlure f.; (noise) craquement m.; (joke: sl.) plaisanterie f. —a. (fam.) d'élite, —v.t./i. (break partially) (se) fêler;

(split) (se) fendre; (nut) casser; (joke) raconter; (problem) résoudre. ～ **down on**, (fam.) sévir contre. ～ **up**, (fam.) craquer. **get** ～**ing**, (fam.) s'y mettre.

cracked /krækt/ a. (sl.) cinglé.

cracker /ˈkrækə(r)/ n. pétard m.; (culin.) biscuit (salé) m.

crackers /ˈkrækəz/ a. (sl.) cinglé.

crackle /ˈkrækl/ v.i. crépiter. —n. crépitement m.

crackpot /ˈkrækpɒt/ n. (sl.) cinglé(e) m. (f.).

cradle /ˈkreɪdl/ n. berceau m. —v.t. bercer.

craft[1] /krɑːft/ n. métier artisanal m.; (technique) art m.; (cunning) ruse f.

craft[2] /krɑːft/ n. invar. (boat) bateau m.

craftsman /ˈkrɑːftsmən/ n. (pl. -**men**) artisan m. ～**ship** n. art m.

crafty /ˈkrɑːftɪ/ a. (-**ier**, -**iest**) rusé.

crag /kræg/ n. rocher à pic m. ～**gy** a. à pic; (face) rude.

cram /kræm/ v.t./i. (p.t. **crammed**). ～ **(for an exam)**, bachoter. ～ **into**, (pack) (s')entasser dans. ～ **with**, (fill) bourrer de.

cramp /kræmp/ n. crampe f.

cramped /kræmpt/ a. à l'étroit.

cranberry /ˈkrænbərɪ/ n. canneberge f.

crane /kreɪn/ n. grue f. —v.t. (neck) tendre.

crank[1] /kræŋk/ n. (techn.) manivelle f.

crank[2] /kræŋk/ n. excentrique m./f. ～**y** a. excentrique; (Amer.) grincheux.

cranny /ˈkrænɪ/ n. fissure f.

craps /kræps/ n. **shoot** ～, (Amer.) jouer aux dés.

crash /kræʃ/ n. accident m.; (noise) fracas m.; (of thunder) coup m.; (of firm) faillite f. —v.t./i. avoir un accident (avec); (of plane) s'écraser; (two vehicles) se percuter. —a. (course) intensif. ～-**helmet** n. casque (anti-choc) m. ～ **into**, rentrer dans. ～-**land** v.i. atterrir en catastrophe.

crass /kræs/ a. grossier.

crate /kreɪt/ n. cageot m.

crater /ˈkreɪtə(r)/ n. cratère m.

cravat /krəˈvæt/ n. foulard m.

crav|e /kreɪv/ v.t./i. ～**e (for)**, désirer ardemment. ～**ing** n. envie irrésistible f.

crawl /krɔːl/ v.i. ramper; (vehicle) se traîner. —n. (pace) pas m.; (swimming) crawl m. **be** ～**ing with**, grouiller de.

crayfish /ˈkreɪfɪʃ/ n. invar. écrevisse f.

crayon /ˈkreɪən/ n. crayon m.

craze /kreɪz/ n. engouement m.

crazed /kreɪzd/ a. affolé.

craz|y /ˈkreɪzɪ/ a. (-**ier**, -**iest**) fou. ～**y**

about, (*person*) fou.de; (*thing*) fana *or* fou de. **∿iness** *n.* folie *f.* **∿y paving,** dallage irrégulier *m.*

creak /kri:k/ *n.* grincement *m.* —*v.i.* grincer. **∿y** *a.* grinçant.

cream /kri:m/ *n.* crème *f.* —*a.* crème *invar.* —*v.t.* écrémer. **∿ cheese,** fromage frais *m.* **∿ off,** se servir en prenant. **∿y** *a.* crémeux.

crease /kri:s/ *n.* pli *m.* —*v.t./i.* (se) froisser.

creat|e /kri:'eɪt/ *v.t.* créer. **∿ion** /-ʃn/ *n.* création *f.* **∿ive** *a.* créateur. **∿or** *n.* créalteur, -trice *m., f.*

creature /'kri:tʃə(r)/ *n.* créature *f.*

crèche /kreʃ/ *n.* garderie *f.*

credence /'kri:dns/ *n.* **give ∿ to,** ajouter foi à.

credentials /krɪ'denʃlz/ *n. pl.* (*identity*) pièces d'identité *f. pl.*; (*competence*) références *f. pl.*

credib|le /'kredəbl/ *a.* (*excuse etc.*) croyable, plausible. **∿ility** /-'bɪlətɪ/ *n.* crédibilité *f.*

credit /'kredɪt/ *n.* crédit *m.*; (*honour*) honneur *m.* **in ∿,** créditeur. **∿s,** (*cinema*) générique *m.* —*a.* (*balance*) créditeur. —*v.t.* (*p.t.* **credited**) croire; (*comm.*) créditer. **∿ card,** carte de crédit *f.* **∿ note,** (*comm.*) avoir *m.* **∿ s.o. with,** attribuer à qn. **∿-worthy** *a.* solvable. **∿or** *n.* créanclier, -ière *m., f.*

creditable /'kredɪtəbl/ *a.* méritoire, honorable.

credulous /'kredjʊləs/ *a.* crédule.

creed /kri:d/ *n.* credo *m.*

creek /kri:k/ *n.* crique *f.*; (*Amer.*) ruisseau *m.* **up the ∿,** (*sl.*) dans le pétrin.

creep /kri:p/ *v.i.* (*p.t.* **crept**) ramper; (*fig.*) se glisser. —*n.* (*person: sl.*) pauvre type *m.* **give s.o. the ∿s,** faire frissonner qn. **∿er** *n.* liane *f.* **∿y** *a.* qui fait frissonner.

cremat|e /krɪ'meɪt/ *v.t.* incinérer. **∿ion** /-ʃn/ *n.* incinération *f.*

crematorium /kremə'tɔ:rɪəm/ *n.* (*pl.* **-ia**) crématorium *m.*

Creole /'kri:əʊl/ *n.* créole *m./f.*

crêpe /kreɪp/ *n.* crêpe *m.* **∿ paper,** papier crêpon *m.*

crept /krept/ *see* **creep.**

crescendo /krɪ'ʃendəʊ/ *n.* (*pl.* **-os**) crescendo *m.*

crescent /'kresnt/ *n.* croissant *m.*; (*fig.*) rue en demi-lune *f.*

cress /kres/ *n.* cresson *m.*

crest /krest/ *n.* crête *f.*; (*coat of arms*) armoiries *f. pl.*

Crete /kri:t/ *n.* Crète *f.*

cretin /'kretɪn, *Amer.* 'kri:tn/ *n.* crétin(e) *m.* (*f.*). **∿ous** *a.* crétin.

crevasse /krɪ'væs/ *n.* crevasse *f.*

crevice /'krevɪs/ *n.* fente *f.*

crew /kru:/ *n.* équipage *m.*; (*gang*) équipe *f.* **∿ cut,** coupe en brosse *f.* **∿ neck,** (col) ras du cou *m.*

crib¹ /krɪb/ *n.* lit d'enfant *m.*

crib² /krɪb/ *v.t./i.* (*p.t.* **cribbed**) copier. —*n.* (*schol., fam.*) traduction *f.*, aide-mémoire *m. invar.*

crick /krɪk/ *n.* (*in neck*) torticolis *m.*

cricket¹ /'krɪkɪt/ *n.* (*sport*) cricket *m.* **∿er** *n.* joueur de cricket *m.*

cricket² /'krɪkɪt/ *n.* (*insect*) grillon *m.*

crime /kraɪm/ *n.* crime *m.*; (*minor*) délit *m.*; (*acts*) criminalité *f.*

criminal /'krɪmɪnl/ *a. & n.* criminel(le) (*m.* (*f.*)).

crimp /krɪmp/ *v.t.* (*hair*) friser.

crimson /'krɪmzn/ *a. & n.* cramoisi (*m.*).

cring|e /krɪndʒ/ *v.i.* reculer; (*fig.*) s'humilier. **∿ing** *a.* servile.

crinkle /'krɪŋkl/ *v.t./i.* (se) froisser. —*n.* pli *m.*

cripple /'krɪpl/ *n.* infirme *m./f.* —*v.t.* estropier; (*fig.*) paralyser.

crisis /'kraɪsɪs/ *n.* (*pl.* **crises** /-si:z/) crise *f.*

crisp /krɪsp/ *a.* (**-er, -est**) (*culin.*) croquant; (*air, reply*) vif. **∿s** *n. pl.* chips *m. pl.*

criss-cross /'krɪskrɒs/ *a.* entrecroisé. —*v.t./i.* (s')entrecroiser.

criterion /kraɪ'tɪərɪən/ *n.* (*pl.* **-ia**) critère *m.*

critic /'krɪtɪk/ *n.* critique *m.* **∿al** *a.* critique. **∿ally** *adv.* d'une manière critique; (*ill*) gravement.

criticism /'krɪtɪsɪzəm/ *n.* critique *f.*

criticize /'krɪtɪsaɪz/ *v.t./i.* critiquer.

croak /krəʊk/ *n.* (*bird*) croassement; (*frog*) coassement *m.* —*v.i.* croasser; coasser.

crochet /'krəʊʃeɪ/ *n.* crochet *m.* —*v.t.* faire au crochet.

crockery /'krɒkərɪ/ *n.* vaisselle *f.*

crocodile /'krɒkədaɪl/ *n.* crocodile *m.*

crocus /'krəʊkəs/ *n.* (*pl.* **-uses**) crocus *m.*

crony /'krəʊnɪ/ *n.* copain, -ine *m., f.*

crook /krʊk/ *n.* (*criminal: fam.*) escroc *m.*; (*stick*) houlette *f.*

crooked /'krʊkɪd/ *a.* tordu; (*winding*) tortueux; (*askew*) de travers; (*dishonest: fig.*) malhonnête. **∿ly** *adv.* de travers.

croon /kru:n/ *v.t./i.* chantonner.

crop /krɒp/ n. récolte f.; (fig.) quantité f. —v.t. (p.t. **cropped**) couper. —v.i. ∼ **up**, se présenter.

croquet /'krəʊkeɪ/ n. croquet m.

croquette /krəʊ'ket/ n. croquette f.

cross /krɒs/ n. croix f.; (hybrid) hybride m. —v.t./i. traverser; (legs, animals) croiser; (cheque) barrer; (paths) se croiser. —a. en colère, fâché (**with**, contre). ∼-**check** v.t. vérifier (pour confirmer). ∼-**country (running),** cross m. ∼ **off** or **out**, rayer. ∼ **s.o.'s mind,** venir à l'esprit de qn. **talk at** ∼ **purposes,** parler sans se comprendre. ∼**ly** adv. avec colère.

crossbar /'krɒsbɑː(r)/ n. barre transversale f.

cross-examine /krɒsɪg'zæmɪn/ v.t. faire subir un examen contradictoire à.

cross-eyed /'krɒsaɪd/ a. **be** ∼, loucher.

crossfire /'krɒsfaɪə(r)/ n. feux croisés m. pl.

crossing /'krɒsɪŋ/ n. (by boat) traversée f.; (on road) passage clouté m.

cross-reference /krɒs'refrəns/ n. renvoi m.

crossroads /'krɒsrəʊdz/ n. carrefour m.

cross-section /krɒs'sekʃn/ n. coupe transversale f.; (sample: fig.) échantillon m.

cross-wind /'krɒswɪnd/ n. vent de travers m.

crosswise /'krɒswaɪz/ adv. en travers.

crossword /'krɒswɜːd/ n. mots croisés m. pl.

crotch /krɒtʃ/ n. (of garment) entrejambes m. invar.

crotchet /'krɒtʃɪt/ n. (mus.) noire f.

crotchety /'krɒtʃɪtɪ/ a. grincheux.

crouch /kraʊtʃ/ v.i. s'accroupir.

crow /krəʊ/ n. corbeau m. —v.i. (of cock) (p.t. **crew**) chanter; (fig.) jubiler. **as the** ∼ **flies,** à vol d'oiseau. ∼'**s feet,** pattes d'oie f. pl.

crowbar /'krəʊbɑː(r)/ n. pied-de-biche m.

crowd /kraʊd/ n. foule f. —v.i. affluer. —v.t. remplir. ∼ **into,** (s')entasser dans. ∼**ed** a. plein.

crown /kraʊn/ n. couronne f.; (top part) sommet m. —v.t. couronner. **C**∼ **Court,** Cour d'assises f. **C**∼ **prince,** prince héritier m.

crucial /'kruːʃl/ a. crucial.

crucifix /'kruːsɪfɪks/ n. crucifix m.

cruci|fy /'kruːsɪfaɪ/ v.t. crucifier. ∼**ixion** /-'fɪkʃn/ n. crucifixion f.

crude /kruːd/ a. (-er, -est) (raw) brut; (rough, vulgar) grossier.

cruel /krʊəl/ a. (**crueller, cruellest**) cruel. ∼**ty** n. cruauté f.

cruet /'kruːɪt/ n. huilier m.

cruis|e /kruːz/ n. croisière f. —v.i. (ship) croiser; (tourists) faire une croisière; (vehicle) rouler. ∼**er** n. croiseur m. ∼**ing speed,** vitesse de croisière f.

crumb /krʌm/ n. miette f.

crumble /'krʌmbl/ v.t./i. (s')effriter; (bread) (s')émietter; (collapse) s'écrouler.

crummy /'krʌmɪ/ a. (-ier, -iest) (sl.) moche, minable.

crumpet /'krʌmpɪt/ n. (culin.) petite crêpe (grillée) f.

crumple /'krʌmpl/ v.t./i. (se) froisser.

crunch /krʌntʃ/ v.t. croquer. —n. (event) moment critique m. **when it comes to the** ∼, quand ça devient sérieux.

crusade /kruː'seɪd/ n. croisade f. ∼**r** /-ə(r)/ n. (knight) croisé m.; (fig.) militant(e) m. (f.).

crush /krʌʃ/ v.t. écraser; (clothes) froisser. —n. (crowd) presse f. **a** ∼ **on,** (sl.) le béguin pour.

crust /krʌst/ n. croûte f. ∼**y** a. croustillant.

crutch /krʌtʃ/ n. béquille f.; (crotch) entre-jambes m. invar.

crux /krʌks/ n. **the** ∼ **of,** (problem etc.) le nœud de.

cry /kraɪ/ n. cri m. —v.i. (weep) pleurer; (call out) crier. ∼-**baby** n. pleurnicheu|r, -se m., f. ∼ **off,** abandonner.

crying /'kraɪɪŋ/ a. (evil etc.) flagrant. **a** ∼ **shame,** une vraie honte.

crypt /krɪpt/ n. crypte f.

cryptic /'krɪptɪk/ a. énigmatique.

crystal /'krɪstl/ n. cristal m. ∼-**clear** a. parfaitement clair. ∼**lize** v.t./i. (se) cristalliser.

cub /kʌb/ n. petit m. **Cub (Scout),** louveteau m.

Cuba /'kjuːbə/ n. Cuba m. ∼**n** a. & n. cubain(e) (m. (f.)).

cubby-hole /'kʌbɪhəʊl/ n. cagibi m.

cub|e /kjuːb/ n. cube m. ∼**ic** a. cubique; (metre etc.) cube.

cubicle /'kjuːbɪkl/ n. (in room, hospital, etc.) box m.; (at swimming-pool) cabine f.

cuckoo /'kʊkuː/ n. coucou m.

cucumber /'kjuːkʌmbə(r)/ n. concombre m.

cuddl|e /'kʌdl/ v.t. câliner. —v.i. (kiss and) ∼**e,** s'embrasser. —n. caresse f. ∼**y** a. câlin, caressant.

cudgel /'kʌdʒl/ n. gourdin m.

cue[1] /kju:/ *n.* signal *m.*; (*theatre*) réplique *f.*

cue[2] /kju:/ *n.* (*billiards*) queue *f.*

cuff /kʌf/ *n.* manchette *f.*; (*Amer.*) revers *m.* —*v.t.* gifler. **~-link** *n.* bouton de manchette *m.* **off the ~**, impromptu.

cul-de-sac /'kʌldəsæk/ *n.* (*pl.* **culs-de-sac**) impasse *f.*

culinary /'kʌlɪnərɪ/ *a.* culinaire.

cull /kʌl/ *v.t.* (*select*) choisir; (*kill*) abattre sélectivement.

culminat|e /'kʌlmɪneɪt/ *v.i.* **~e in**, se terminer par. **~ion** /-'neɪʃn/ *n.* point culminant *m.*

culprit /'kʌlprɪt/ *n.* coupable *m./f.*

cult /kʌlt/ *n.* culte *m.* **~ movie**, film culte.

cultivat|e /'kʌltɪveɪt/ *v.t.* cultiver. **~ion** /-'veɪʃn/ *n.* culture *f.*

cultural /'kʌltʃərəl/ *a.* culturel.

culture /'kʌltʃə(r)/ *n.* culture *f.* **~d** *a.* cultivé.

cumbersome /'kʌmbəsəm/ *a.* encombrant.

cumulative /'kju:mjʊlətɪv/ *a.* cumulatif.

cunning /'kʌnɪŋ/ *a.* rusé. —*n.* astuce *f.*, ruse *f.*

cup /kʌp/ *n.* tasse *f.*; (*prize*) coupe *f.* **Cup final**, finale de la coupe *f.* **~ size**, profondeur de bonnet *f.* **~-tie** *n.* match de coupe *m.*

cupboard /'kʌbəd/ *n.* placard *m.*, armoire *f.*

cupful /'kʌpfʊl/ *n.* tasse *f.*

Cupid /'kju:pɪd/ *n.* Cupidon *m.*

curable /'kjʊərəbl/ *a.* guérissable.

curate /'kjʊərət/ *n.* vicaire *m.*

curator /kjʊə'reɪtə(r)/ *n.* (*of museum*) conservateur *m.*

curb[1] /kɜ:b/ *n.* (*restraint*) frein *m.* —*v.t.* (*desires etc.*) refréner; (*price increase etc.*) freiner.

curb[2], (*Amer.*) **kerb**:/kɜ:b/ *n.* bord du trottoir *m.*

curdle /'kɜ:dl/ *v.t./i.* (se) cailler.

curds /kɜ:dz/ *n. pl.* lait caillé *m.*

cure[1] /kjʊə(r)/ *v.t.* guérir; (*fig.*) éliminer. —*n.* (*recovery*) guérison *f.*; (*remedy*) remède *m.*

cure[2] /kjʊə(r)/ *v.t.* (*culin.*) fumer; (*in brine*) saler.

curfew /'kɜ:fju:/ *n.* couvre-feu *m.*

curio /'kjʊərɪəʊ/ *n.* (*pl.* **-os**) curiosité *f.*, bibelot *m.*

curi|ous /'kjʊərɪəs/ *a.* curieux. **~osity** /-'ɒsɪtɪ/ *n.* curiosité *f.*

curl /kɜ:l/ *v.t./i.* (*hair*) boucler. —*n.* boucle *f.* **~ up**, se pelotonner; (*shrivel*) se racornir.

curler /'kɜ:lə(r)/ *n.* bigoudi *m.*

curly /'kɜ:lɪ/ *a.* (**-ier, -iest**) bouclé.

currant /'kʌrənt/ *n.* raisin de Corinthe *m.*; (*berry*) groseille *f.*

currency /'kʌrənsɪ/ *n.* (*money*) monnaie *f.*; (*acceptance*) cours *m.* **foreign ~**, devises étrangères *f. pl.*

current /'kʌrənt/ *a.* (*common*) courant; (*topical*) actuel; (*year etc.*) en cours. —*n.* courant *m.* **~ account**, compte courant *m.* **~ events**, l'actualité *f.* **~ly** *adv.* actuellement.

curriculum /kə'rɪkjʊləm/ *n.* (*pl.* **-la**) programme scolaire *m.* **~ vitae**, curriculum vitae *m.*

curry[1] /'kʌrɪ/ *n.* curry *m.*, cari *m.*

curry[2] /'kʌrɪ/ *v.t.* **~ favour with**, chercher les bonnes grâces de.

curse /kɜ:s/ *n.* malédiction *f.*; (*oath*) juron *m.* —*v.t.* maudire. —*v.i.* (*swear*) jurer.

cursor /'kɜ:sə(r)/ *n.* curseur *m.*

cursory /'kɜ:sərɪ/ *a.* (trop) rapide.

curt /kɜ:t/ *a.* brusque.

curtail /kɜ:'teɪl/ *v.t.* écourter, raccourcir; (*expenses etc.*) réduire.

curtain /'kɜ:tn/ *n.* rideau *m.*

curtsy /'kɜ:tsɪ/ *n.* révérence *f.* —*v.i.* faire une révérence.

curve /kɜ:v/ *n.* courbe *f.* —*v.t./i.* (se) courber; (*of road*) tourner.

cushion /'kʊʃn/ *n.* coussin *m.* —*v.t.* (*a blow*) amortir; (*fig.*) protéger.

cushy /'kʊʃɪ/ *a.* (**-ier, -iest**) (*job etc.*: *fam.*) pépère.

custard /'kʌstəd/ *n.* crème anglaise *f.*; (*set*) crème renversée *f.*

custodian /kʌ'stəʊdɪən/ *n.* gardien(ne) *m.* (*f.*).

custody /'kʌstədɪ/ *n.* garde *f.*; (*jurid.*) détention préventive *f.*

custom /'kʌstəm/ *n.* coutume *f.*; (*patronage*: *comm.*) clientèle *f.* **~-built, ~-made** *adjs.* fait *etc.* sur commande. **~ary** *a.* d'usage.

customer /'kʌstəmə(r)/ *n.* client(e) *m.* (*f.*); (*fam.*) **an odd/a difficult ~**, un individu curieux/difficile.

customize /'kʌstəmaɪz/ *v.t.* personnaliser.

customs /'kʌstəmz/ *n. pl.* douane *f.* —*a.* douanier. **~ officer**, douanier *m.*

cut /kʌt/ *v.t./i.* (*p.t.* **cut**, *pres. p.* **cutting**) couper; (*hedge, jewel*) tailler; (*prices etc.*) réduire. —*n.* coupure *f.*; (*of clothes*) coupe *f.*; (*piece*) morceau *m.*; réduction *f.* **~ back** *or* **down (on)**, réduire. **~-back** *n.* réduction *f.* **~ in**, (*auto.*) se rabattre. **~ off**, couper; (*fig.*)

isoler. ～ **out,** découper; (*leave out*) supprimer. ～-**price** *a.* à prix réduit. ～ **short,** (*visit*) écourter. ～ **up,** couper; (*carve*) découper. ～ **up about,** démoralisé par.

cute /kjuːt/ *a.* (**-er, -est**) (*fam.*) astucieux; (*Amer.*) mignon.

cuticle /'kjuːtɪkl/ *n.* petites peaux *f. pl.* (*de l' ongle*).

cutlery /'kʌtlərɪ/ *n.* couverts *m. pl.*

cutlet /'kʌtlɪt/ *n.* côtelette *f.*

cutting /'kʌtɪŋ/ *a.* cinglant. —*n.* (*from newspaper*) coupure *f.*; (*plant*) bouture *f.* ～ **edge,** tranchant *m.*

CV *abbr. see* **curriculum vitae.**

cyanide /'saɪənaɪd/ *n.* cyanure *m.*

cybernetics /saɪbə'netɪks/ *n.* cybernétique *f.*

cycl|e /'saɪkl/ *n.* cycle *m.*; (*bicycle*) vélo *m.* —*v.i.* aller à vélo. ～**ing** *n.* cyclisme *m.* ～**ist** *n.* cycliste *m./f.*

cyclic(al) /'saɪklɪk(l)/ *a.* cyclique.

cyclone /'saɪkləʊn/ *n.* cyclone *m.*

cylind|er /'sɪlɪndə(r)/ *n.* cylindre *m.* ～**rical** /-'lɪndrɪkl/ *a.* cylindrique.

cymbal /'sɪmbl/ *n.* cymbale *f.*

cynic /'sɪnɪk/ *n.* cynique *m./f.* ～**al** *a.* cynique. ～**ism** /-sɪzəm/ *n.* cynisme *m.*

cypress /'saɪprəs/ *n.* cyprès *m.*

Cypr|us /'saɪprəs/ *n.* Chypre *f.* ～**iot** /'sɪprɪət/ *a.* & *n.* cypriote (*m./f.*).

cyst /sɪst/ *n.* kyste *m.* ～**ic fibrosis,** mucoviscidose *f.*

cystitis /sɪst'aɪtɪs/ *n.* cystite *f.*

czar /zɑː(r)/ *n.* tsar *m.*

Czech /tʃek/ *a.* & *n.* tchèque (*m./f.*).

Czechoslovak /tʃekə'sləʊvæk/ *a.* & *n.* tchécoslovaque (*m./f.*). ～**ia** /-slə 'vækɪə/ *n.* Tchécoslovaquie *f.*

D

dab /dæb/ *v.t.* (*p.t.* **dabbed**) tamponner. —*n.* **a** ～ **of,** un petit coup de; (*fam.*) **be a** ～ **hand at,** avoir le coup de main pour. ～ **sth. on,** appliquer qch. à petits coups sur.

dabble /'dæbl/ *v.i.* ～ **in,** se mêler un peu de. ～**r** /-ə(r)/ *n.* amateur *m.*

dad /dæd/ *n.* (*fam.*) papa *m.* ～**dy** *n.* (*children's use*) papa *m.*

daffodil /'dæfədɪl/ *n.* jonquille *f.*

daft /dɑːft/ *a.* (**-er, -est**) idiot.

dagger /'dægə(r)/ *n.* poignard *m.*

dahlia /'deɪlɪə/ *n.* dahlia *m.*

daily /'deɪlɪ/ *a.* quotidien. —*adv.* tous les jours. —*n.* (*newspaper*) quotidien *m.*; (*charwoman: fam.*) femme de ménage *f.*

dainty /'deɪntɪ/ *a.* (**-ier, -iest**) délicat.

dairy /'deərɪ/ *n.* (*on farm*) laiterie *f.*; (*shop*) crémerie *f.* —*a.* laitier.

daisy /'deɪzɪ/ *n.* pâquerette *f.* ～ **wheel,** marguerite *f.*

dale /deɪl/ *n.* vallée *f.*

dam /dæm/ *n.* barrage *m.* —*v.t.* (*p.t.* **dammed**) endiguer.

damag|e /'dæmɪdʒ/ *n.* dégâts *m. pl.,* dommages *m. pl.*; (*harm: fig.*) préjudice *m.* ～**es,** (*jurid.*) dommages et intérêts *m. pl.* —*v.t.* abîmer; (*fig.*) nuire à. ～**ing** *a.* nuisible.

dame /deɪm/ *n.* (*old use*) dame *f.*; (*Amer., sl.*) fille *f.*

damn /dæm/ *v.t.* (*relig.*) damner; (*swear at*) maudire; (*condemn: fig.*) condamner. —*int.* zut, merde. —*n.* **not care a** ～, s'en foutre. —*a.* sacré. —*adv.* rudement. ～**ation** /-'neɪʃn/ *n.* damnation *f.*

damp /dæmp/ *n.* humidité *f.* —*a.* (**-er, -est**) humide. —*v.t.* humecter; (*fig.*) refroidir. ～**en** *v.t.* = **damp.** ～**ness** *n.* humidité *f.*

dance /dɑːns/ *v.t./i.* danser. —*n.* danse *f.*; (*gathering*) bal *m.* ～ **hall,** dancing *m.,* salle de danse *f.* ～**r** /-ə(r)/ *n.* danseur, -se *m., f.*

dandelion /'dændɪlaɪən/ *n.* pissenlit *m.*

dandruff /'dændrʌf/ *n.* pellicules *f. pl.*

dandy /'dændɪ/ *n.* dandy *m.*

Dane /deɪn/ *n.* Danois(e) *m.* (*f.*).

danger /'deɪndʒə(r)/ *n.* danger *m.*; (*risk*) risque *m.* **be in** ～ **of,** risquer de. ～**ous** *a.* dangereux.

dangle /'dæŋgl/ *v.t./i.* (se) balancer, (laisser) pendre. ～ **sth. in front of s.o.,** (*fig.*) faire miroiter qch. à qn.

Danish /'deɪnɪʃ/ *a.* danois. —*n.* (*lang.*) danois *m.*

dank /dæŋk/ *a.* (**-er, -est**) humide et froid.

dapper /'dæpə(r)/ *a.* élégant.

dare /deə(r)/ *v.t.* ～ (**to**) **do,** oser faire. ～ **s.o. to do,** défier qn. de faire. —*n.* défi *m.* **I** ～ **say,** je suppose (**that,** que).

daredevil /'deədevl/ *n.* casse-cou *m. invar.*

daring /'deərɪŋ/ *a.* audacieux.

dark /dɑːk/ *a.* (**-er, -est**) obscur, sombre, noir; (*colour*) foncé, sombre; (*skin*) brun, foncé; (*gloomy*) sombre. —*n.* noir *m.*; (*nightfall*) tombée de la nuit *f.* ～ **horse,** individu aux talents inconnus *m.* ～-**room** *n.* chambre noire *f.* **in the**

~, (*fig.*) dans l'ignorance (**about,** de). **~ness** *n.* obscurité *f.*

darken /'dɑːkən/ *v.t./i.* (s')assombrir.

darling /'dɑːlɪŋ/ *a. & n.* chéri(e) (*m.* (*f.*)).

darn /dɑːn/ *v.t.* repriser.

dart /dɑːt/ *n.* fléchette *f.* **~s,** (*game*) fléchettes *f. pl.* —*v.i.* s'élancer.

dartboard /'dɑːtbɔːd/ *n.* cible *f.*

dash /dæʃ/ *v.i.* (*hurry*) se dépêcher; (*forward etc.*) se précipiter. —*v.t.* jeter (avec violence); (*hopes*) briser. —*n.* ruée *f.*; (*stroke*) tiret *m.* **a ~ of,** un peu de. **~ off,** (*leave*) partir en vitesse.

dashboard /'dæʃbɔːd/ *n.* tableau de bord *m.*

dashing /'dæʃɪŋ/ *a.* fringant.

data /'deɪtə/ *n. pl.* données *f. pl.* **~ processing,** traitement des données *m.*

database /'deɪtəbeɪs/ *n.* base de données *f.*

date[1] /deɪt/ *n.* date *f.*; (*meeting: fam.*) rendez-vous *m.* —*v.t./i.* dater; (*go out with: fam.*) sortir avec. **~ from,** dater de. **out of ~,** (*old-fashioned*) démodé; (*passport*) périmé. **to ~,** à ce jour. **up to ~,** (*modern*) moderne; (*list*) à jour. **~d** /-ɪd/ *a.* démodé.

date[2] /deɪt/ *n.* (*fruit*) datte *f.*

daub /dɔːb/ *v.t.* barbouiller.

daughter /'dɔːtə(r)/ *n.* fille *f.* **~-in-law** *n.* (*pl.* **~s-in-law**) belle-fille *f.*

daunt /dɔːnt/ *v.t.* décourager.

dauntless /'dɔːntlɪs/ *a.* intrépide.

dawdle /'dɔːdl/ *v.i.* lambiner. **~r** /-ə(r)/ *n.* lambin(e) *m.* (*f.*).

dawn /dɔːn/ *n.* aube *f.* —*v.i.* poindre; (*fig.*) naître. **it ~ed on me,** je m'en suis rendu compte.

day /deɪ/ *n.* jour *m.*; (*whole day*) journée *f.*; (*period*) époque *f.* **~-break** *n.* point du jour *m.* **~-dream** *n.* rêverie *f.*; *v.i.* rêvasser. **the ~ before,** la veille. **the following** *or* **next ~,** le lendemain.

daylight /'deɪlaɪt/ *n.* jour *m.*

daytime /'deɪtaɪm/ *n.* jour *m.*, journée *f.*

daze /deɪz/ *v.t.* étourdir; (*with drugs*) hébéter. —*n.* **in a ~,** étourdi; hébété.

dazzle /'dæzl/ *v.t.* éblouir.

deacon /'diːkən/ *n.* diacre *m.*

dead /ded/ *a.* mort; (*numb*) engourdi. —*adv.* complètement. —*n.* **in the ~ of,** au cœur de. **the ~,** les morts. **~ beat,** éreinté. **~ end,** impasse *f.* **~-end job,** travail sans avenir *m.* **a ~ loss,** (*thing*) une perte de temps; (*person*) une catastrophe. **~-pan** *a.* impassible. **in ~ centre,** au beau milieu. **stop ~,** s'arrêter net. **the race was a ~ heat,** ils ont été classés ex aequo.

deaden /'dedn/ *v.t.* (*sound, blow*) amortir; (*pain*) calmer.

deadline /'dedlaɪn/ *n.* date limite *f.*

deadlock /'dedlɒk/ *n.* impasse *f.*

deadly /'dedlɪ/ *a.* (**-ier, -iest**) mortel; (*weapon*) meurtrier.

deaf /def/ *a.* (**-er, -est**) sourd. **the ~ and dumb,** les sourds-muets. **~-aid** *n.* appareil acoustique *m.* **~ness** *n.* surdité *f.*

deafen /'defn/ *v.t.* assourdir.

deal /diːl/ *v.t.* (*p.t.* **dealt**) donner; (*a blow*) porter. —*v.i.* (*trade*) commercer. —*n.* affaire *f.*; (*cards*) donne *f.* **a great** *or* **good ~,** beaucoup (**of,** de). **~ in,** faire le commerce de. **~ with,** (*handle, manage*) s'occuper de; (*be about*) traiter de. **~er** *n.* marchand(e) *m.* (*f.*); (*agent*) concessionnaire *m./f.*

dealings /'diːlɪŋz/ *n. pl.* relations *f. pl.*

dean /diːn/ *n.* doyen *m.*

dear /dɪə(r)/ *a.* (**-er, -est**) cher. —*n.* (**my**) **~,** mon cher, ma chère; (*darling*) (mon) chéri, (ma) chérie. —*adv.* cher. —*int.* **oh ~!,** oh mon Dieu! **~ly** *adv.* tendrement; (*pay*) cher.

dearth /dɜːθ/ *n.* pénurie *f.*

death /deθ/ *n.* mort *f.* **~ certificate,** acte de décès *m.* **~ duty,** droits de succession *m. pl.* **~ penalty,** peine de mort *f.* **it is a ~-trap,** (*place, vehicle*) il y a danger de mort. **~ly** *a.* de mort, mortel.

debar /dɪ'bɑː(r)/ *v.t.* (*p.t.* **debarred**) exclure.

debase /dɪ'beɪs/ *v.t.* avilir.

debat|e /dɪ'beɪt/ *n.* discussion *f.*, débat *m.* —*v.t.* discuter. **~e whether,** se demander si. **~able** *a.* discutable.

debauch /dɪ'bɔːtʃ/ *v.t.* débaucher. **~ery** *n.* débauche *f.*

debilitate /dɪ'bɪlɪteɪt/ *v.t.* débiliter.

debility /dɪ'bɪlətɪ/ *n.* débilité *f.*

debit /'debɪt/ *n.* débit *m.* **in ~,** débiteur. —*a.* (*balance*) débiteur. —*v.t.* (*p.t.* **debited**) débiter.

debris /'debriː/ *n.* débris *m. pl.*

debt /det/ *n.* dette *f.* **in ~,** endetté. **~or** *n.* débiteur, -trice *m.*, *f.*

debunk /diː'bʌŋk/ *v.t.* (*fam.*) démythifier.

decade /'dekeɪd/ *n.* décennie *f.*

decaden|t /'dekədənt/ *a.* décadent. **~ce** *n.* décadence *f.*

decaffeinated /diː'kæfɪneɪtɪd/ *a.* décaféiné.

decanter /dɪ'kæntə(r)/ *n.* carafe *f.*

decathlon /dɪ'kæθlən/ *n.* décathlon *m.*

decay /dɪ'keɪ/ *v.i.* se gâter, pourrir; (*fig.*)

décliner. —*n.* pourriture *f.*; (*of tooth*) carie *f.*; (*fig.*) déclin *m.*
deceased /dɪˈsiːst/ *a.* décédé. —*n.* défunt(e) *m.* (*f.*).
deceit /dɪˈsiːt/ *n.* tromperie *f.* **∼ful** *a.* trompeur. **∼fully** *adv.* d'une manière trompeuse.
deceive /dɪˈsiːv/ *v.t.* tromper.
December /dɪˈsembə(r)/ *n.* décembre *m.*
decen|t /ˈdiːsnt/ *a.* décent, convenable; (*good*: *fam.*) (assez) bon; (*kind*: *fam.*) gentil. **∼cy** *n.* décence *f.* **∼tly** *adv.* décemment.
decentralize /diːˈsentrəlaɪz/ *v.t.* décentraliser.
decept|ive /dɪˈseptɪv/ *a.* trompeur. **∼ion** /-pʃn/ *n.* tromperie *f.*
decibel /ˈdesɪbel/ *n.* décibel *m.*
decide /dɪˈsaɪd/ *v.t./i.* décider; (*question*) régler. **∼ on,** se décider pour. **∼ to do,** décider de faire. **∼d** /-ɪd/ *a.* (*firm*) résolu; (*clear*) net. **∼dly** /-ɪdlɪ/ *adv.* résolument; nettement.
deciduous /dɪˈsɪdjʊəs/ *a.* à feuillage caduc.
decimal /ˈdesɪml/ *a.* décimal. —*n.* décimale *f.* **∼ point,** virgule *f.*
decimate /ˈdesɪmeɪt/ *v.t.* décimer.
decipher /dɪˈsaɪfə(r)/ *v.t.* déchiffrer.
decision /dɪˈsɪʒn/ *n.* décision *f.*
decisive /dɪˈsaɪsɪv/ *a.* (*conclusive*) décisif; (*firm*) décidé. **∼ly** *adv.* d'une façon décidée.
deck /dek/ *n.* pont *m.*; (*of cards*: *Amer.*) jeu *m.* **∼-chair** *n.* chaise longue *f.* **top ∼,** (*of bus*) impériale *f.*
declar|e /dɪˈkleə(r)/ *v.t.* déclarer. **∼ation** /deklə'reɪʃn/ *n.* déclaration *f.*
decline /dɪˈklaɪn/ *v.t./i.* refuser (poliment); (*deteriorate*) décliner; (*fall*) baisser. —*n.* déclin *m.*; baisse *f.*
decode /diːˈkəʊd/ *v.t.* décoder.
decompos|e /diːkəmˈpəʊz/ *v.t./i.* (se) décomposer. **∼ition** /-ɒmpəˈzɪʃn/ *n.* décomposition *f.*
décor /ˈdeɪkɔː(r)/ *n.* décor *m.*
decorat|e /ˈdekəreɪt/ *v.t.* décorer; (*room*) peindre *or* tapisser. **∼ion** /-ˈreɪʃn/ *n.* décoration *f.* **∼ive** /-ətɪv/ *a.* décoratif.
decorator /ˈdekəreɪtə(r)/ *n.* peintre en bâtiment *m.* (**interior**) **∼,** décoraleur, -trice d'appartements *m.*, *f.*
decorum /dɪˈkɔːrəm/ *n.* décorum *m.*
decoy[1] /ˈdiːkɔɪ/ *n.* (*bird*) appeau *m.*; (*trap*) piège *m.*, leurre *m.*
decoy[2] /dɪˈkɔɪ/ *v.t.* attirer, appâter.
decrease /dɪˈkriːs/ *v.t./i.* diminuer. —*n.* /ˈdiːkriːs/ diminution *f.*
decree /dɪˈkriː/ *n.* (*pol.*, *relig.*) décret *m.*;

(*jurid.*) jugement *m.* —*v.t.* (*p.t.* **decreed**) décréter.
decrepit /dɪˈkrepɪt/ *a.* (*building*) délabré; (*person*) décrépit.
decry /dɪˈkraɪ/ *v.t.* dénigrer.
dedicat|e /ˈdedɪkeɪt/ *v.t.* dédier. **∼e o.s. to,** se consacrer à. **∼ed** *a.* dévoué. **∼ion** /-ˈkeɪʃn/ *n.* dévouement *m.*; (*in book*) dédicace *f.*
deduce /dɪˈdjuːs/ *v.t.* déduire.
deduct /dɪˈdʌkt/ *v.t.* déduire; (*from wages*) retenir. **∼ion** /-kʃn/ *n.* déduction *f.*; retenue *f.*
deed /diːd/ *n.* acte *m.*
deem /diːm/ *v.t.* juger.
deep /diːp/ *a.* (-er, -est) profond. —*adv.* profondément. **∼ in thought,** absorbé dans ses pensées. **∼ into the night,** tard dans la nuit. **∼-freeze** *n.* congélateur *m.*; *v.t.* congeler. **∼-fry,** frire. **∼ly** *adv.* profondément.
deepen /ˈdiːpən/ *v.t.* approfondir. —*v.i.* devenir plus profond; (*mystery, night*) s'épaissir.
deer /dɪə(r)/ *n. invar.* cerf *m.*; (*doe*) biche *f.*
deface /dɪˈfeɪs/ *v.t.* dégrader.
defamation /defəˈmeɪʃn/ *n.* diffamation *f.*
default /dɪˈfɔːlt/ *v.i.* (*jurid.*) faire défaut. —*n.* **by ∼,** (*jurid.*) par défaut. **win by ∼,** gagner par forfait. —*a.* (*comput.*) par défaut.
defeat /dɪˈfiːt/ *v.t.* vaincre; (*thwart*) faire échouer. —*n.* défaite *f.*; (*of plan etc.*) échec *m.*
defect[1] /ˈdiːfekt/ *n.* défaut *m.* **∼ive** /dɪˈfektɪv/ *a.* défectueux.
defect[2] /dɪˈfekt/ *v.i.* faire défection. **∼ to,** passer à. **∼or** *n.* transfuge *m./f.*
defence /dɪˈfens/ *n.* défense *f.* **∼less** *a.* sans défense.
defend /dɪˈfend/ *v.t.* défendre. **∼ant** *n.* (*jurid.*) accusé(e) *m.* (*f.*). **∼er,** défenseur *m.*
defense /dɪˈfens/ *n. Amer.* = **defence.**
defensive /dɪˈfensɪv/ *a.* défensif. —*n.* défensive *f.*
defer /dɪˈfɜː(r)/ *v.t.* (*p.t.* **deferred**) (*postpone*) différer, remettre.
deferen|ce /ˈdefərəns/ *n.* déférence *f.* **∼tial** /-ˈrenʃl/ *a.* déférent.
defian|ce /dɪˈfaɪəns/ *n.* défi *m.* **in ∼ce of,** au mépris de. **∼t** *a.* de défi. **∼tly** *adv.* d'un air de défi.
deficien|t /dɪˈfɪʃnt/ *a.* insuffisant. **be ∼t in,** manquer de. **∼cy** *n.* insuffisance *f.*; (*fault*) défaut *m.*
deficit /ˈdefɪsɪt/ *n.* déficit *m.*

defile /dɪ'faɪl/ v.t. souiller.

define /dɪ'faɪn/ v.t. définir.

definite /'defɪnɪt/ a. précis; (obvious) net; (firm) catégorique; (certain) certain. **~ly** adv. certainement; (clearly) nettement.

definition /defɪ'nɪʃn/ n. définition f.

definitive /dɪ'fɪnɪtɪv/ a. définitif.

deflat|e /dɪ'fleɪt/ v.t. dégonfler. **~ion** /-ʃn/ n. dégonflement m.; (comm.) déflation f.

deflect /dɪ'flekt/ v.t./i. (faire) dévier.

deforestation /diːfɒrɪ'steɪʃn/ n. déforestation.

deform /dɪ'fɔːm/ v.t. déformer. **~ed** a. difforme. **~ity** n. difformité f.

defraud /dɪ'frɔːd/ v.t. (state, customs) frauder. **~** s.o. of sth., escroquer qch. à qn.

defray /dɪ'freɪ/ v.t. payer.

defrost /diː'frɒst/ v.t. dégivrer.

deft /deft/ a. (-er, -est) adroit. **~ness** n. adresse f.

defunct /dɪ'fʌŋkt/ a. défunt.

defuse /diː'fjuːz/ v.t. désamorcer.

defy /dɪ'faɪ/ v.t. défier; (attempts) résister à.

degenerate¹ /dɪ'dʒenəreɪt/ v.i. dégénérer (**into**, en).

degenerate² /dɪ'dʒenərət/ a. & n. dégénéré(e) (m. (f.)).

degrad|e /dɪ'greɪd/ v.t. dégrader. **~ation** /degrə'deɪʃn/ n. dégradation f.; (state) déchéance f.

degree /dɪ'griː/ n. degré m.; (univ.) diplôme universitaire m.; (Bachelor's degree) licence f. **higher ~**, (univ.) maîtrise f. or doctorat m. **to such a ~ that**, à tel point que.

dehydrate /diː'haɪdreɪt/ v.t./i. (se) déshydrater.

de-ice /diː'aɪs/ v.t. dégivrer.

deign /deɪn/ v.t. **~ to do**, daigner faire.

deity /'diːɪtɪ/ n. divinité f.

deject|ed /dɪ'dʒektɪd/ a. abattu. **~ion** /-kʃn/ n. abattement m.

delay /dɪ'leɪ/ v.t. retarder. —v.i. tarder. —n. (lateness, time overdue) retard m.; (waiting) délai m. **~ doing**, attendre pour faire.

delectable /dɪ'lektəbl/ a. délectable, très agréable.

delegate¹ /'delɪgət/ n. délégué(e) m. (f.).

delegat|e² /'delɪgeɪt/ v.t. déléguer. **~ion** /-'geɪʃn/ n. délégation f.

delet|e /dɪ'liːt/ v.t. effacer; (with line) barrer. **~ion** /-ʃn/ n. suppression f.; (with line) rature f.

deliberate¹ /dɪ'lɪbərət/ a. délibéré;

(steps, manner) mesuré. **~ly** adv. exprès, délibérément.

deliberat|e² /dɪ'lɪbəreɪt/ v.i. délibérer. —v.t. considérer. **~ion** /-'reɪʃn/ n. délibération f.

delica|te /'delɪkət/ a. délicat. **~cy** n. délicatesse f.; (food) mets délicat or raffiné m.

delicatessen /delɪkə'tesn/ n. épicerie fine f., charcuterie f.

delicious /dɪ'lɪʃəs/ a. délicieux.

delight /dɪ'laɪt/ n. grand plaisir m., joie f., délice m. (f. in pl.); (thing) délice m. (f. in pl.). —v.t. réjouir. —v.i. **~ in**, prendre plaisir à. **~ed** a. ravi. **~ful** a. charmant, très agréable.

delinquen|t /dɪ'lɪŋkwənt/ a. & n. délinquant(e) (m. (f.)) **~cy** n. délinquance f.

deliri|ous /dɪ'lɪrɪəs/ a. **be ~ous**, délirer. **~um** n. délire m.

deliver /dɪ'lɪvə(r)/ v.t. (message) remettre; (goods) livrer; (letters) distribuer; (free) délivrer; (utter) prononcer; (med.) accoucher; (a blow) porter. **~ance** n. délivrance f. **~y** n. livraison f.; distribution f.; accouchement m.

delta /'deltə/ n. delta m.

delu|de /dɪ'luːd/ v.t. tromper. **~de o.s.**, se faire des illusions. **~sion** /-ʒn/ n. illusion f.

deluge /'deljuːdʒ/ n. déluge m. —v.t. inonder (**with**, de).

de luxe /də'lʌks/ a. de luxe.

delve /delv/ v.i. fouiller.

demagogue /'deməgɒg/ n. démagogue m./f.

demand /dɪ'mɑːnd/ v.t. exiger; (in negotiations) réclamer. —n. exigence f.; (claim) revendication f.; (comm.) demande f. **in ~**, recherché. **on ~**, à la demande. **~ing** a. exigeant.

demarcation /diːmɑː'keɪʃn/ n. démarcation f.

demean /dɪ'miːn/ v.t. **~ o.s.**, s'abaisser, s'avilir.

demeanour, (Amer.) **demeanor** /dɪ'miːnə(r)/ n. comportement m.

demented /dɪ'mentɪd/ a. dément.

demerara /deməˈreərə/ n. (brown sugar) cassonade f.

demise /dɪ'maɪz/ n. décès m.

demo /'deməʊ/ n. (pl. **-os**) (demonstration: fam.) manif f.

demobilize /diː'məʊbəlaɪz/ v.t. démobiliser.

democracy /dɪ'mɒkrəsɪ/ n. démocratie f.

democrat /'deməkræt/ *n.* démocrate *m./f.* **~ic** /-'krætɪk/ *a.* démocratique.

demoli|sh /dɪ'mɒlɪʃ/ *v.t.* démolir. **~tion** /demə'lɪʃn/ *n.* démolition *f.*

demon /'diːmən/ *n.* démon *m.*

demonstrat|e /'demənstreɪt/ *v.t.* démontrer. —*v.i.* (*pol.*) manifester. **~ion** /-'streɪʃn/ *n.* démonstration *f.*; (*pol.*) manifestation *f.* **~or** *n.* manifestant(e) *m.* (*f.*).

demonstrative /dɪ'mɒnstrətɪv/ *a.* démonstratif.

demoralize /dɪ'mɒrəlaɪz/ *v.t.* démoraliser.

demote /dɪ'məʊt/ *v.t.* rétrograder.

demure /dɪ'mjʊə(r)/ *a.* modeste.

den /den/ *n.* antre *m.*

denial /dɪ'naɪəl/ *n.* dénégation *f.*; (*statement*) démenti *m.*

denigrate /'denɪgreɪt/ *v.t.* dénigrer.

denim /'denɪm/ *n.* toile de coton *f.* **~s**, (*jeans*) blue-jeans *m. pl.*

Denmark /'denmɑːk/ *n.* Danemark *m.*

denomination /dɪnɒmɪ'neɪʃn/ *n.* (*relig.*) confession *f.*; (*money*) valeur *f.*

denote /dɪ'nəʊt/ *v.t.* dénoter.

denounce /dɪ'naʊns/ *v.t.* dénoncer.

dens|e /dens/ *a.* (-**er**, -**est**) dense; (*person*) obtus. **~ely** *adv.* (*packed etc.*) très. **~ity** *n.* densité *f.*

dent /dent/ *n.* bosse *f.* —*v.t.* cabosser. **there is a ~ in the car door,** la portière est cabossée.

dental /'dentl/ *a.* dentaire. **~ floss,** fil dentaire *m.* **~ surgeon,** dentiste *m./f.*

dentist /'dentɪst/ *n.* dentiste *m./f.* **~ry** *n.* art dentaire *m.*

dentures /'dentʃəz/ *n. pl.* dentier *m.*

denude /dɪ'njuːd/ *v.t.* dénuder.

denunciation /dɪnʌnsɪ'eɪʃn/ *n.* dénonciation *f.*

deny /dɪ'naɪ/ *v.t.* nier (**that,** que); (*rumour*) démentir; (*disown*) renier; (*refuse*) refuser.

deodorant /diː'əʊdərənt/ *n. & a.* déodorant (*m.*).

depart /dɪ'pɑːt/ *v.i.* partir. **~ from,** (*deviate*) s'écarter de.

department /dɪ'pɑːtmənt/ *n.* département *m.*; (*in shop*) rayon *m.*; (*in office*) service *m.* **D~ of Health,** ministère de la santé *m.* **~ store,** grand magasin *m.*

departure /dɪ'pɑːtʃə(r)/ *n.* départ *m.* **a ~ from,** (*custom, diet, etc.*) une entorse à.

depend /dɪ'pend/ *v.i.* dépendre (**on,** de). **it (all) ~s,** ça dépend. **~ on,** (*rely on*) compter sur. **~ing on the weather,** selon le temps qu'il fera. **~able** *a.* sûr.

~ence *n.* dépendance *f.* **~ent** *a.* dépendant. **be ~ent on,** dépendre de.

dependant /dɪ'pendənt/ *n.* personne à charge *f.*

depict /dɪ'pɪkt/ *v.t.* (*describe*) dépeindre; (*in picture*) représenter.

deplete /dɪ'pliːt/ *v.t.* (*reduce*) réduire; (*use up*) épuiser.

deplor|e /dɪ'plɔː(r)/ *v.t.* déplorer. **~able** *a.* déplorable.

deploy /dɪ'plɔɪ/ *v.t.* déployer.

depopulate /diː'pɒpjʊleɪt/ *v.t.* dépeupler.

deport /dɪ'pɔːt/ *v.t.* expulser. **~ation** /diːpɔː'teɪʃn/ *n.* expulsion *f.*

depose /dɪ'pəʊz/ *v.t.* déposer.

deposit /dɪ'pɒzɪt/ *v.t.* (*p.t.* **deposited**) déposer. —*n.* dépôt *m.*; (*of payment*) acompte *m.*; (*to reserve*) arrhes *f. pl.*; (*against damage*) caution *f.*; (*on bottle etc.*) consigne *f.*; (*of mineral*) gisement *m.* **~ account,** compte dépôt *m.* **~or** *n.* (*comm.*) déposant(e) *m.* (*f.*), épargnant(e) *m.* (*f.*).

depot /'depəʊ, *Amer.* 'diːpəʊ/ *n.* dépôt *m.*; (*Amer.*) gare (routière) *f.*

deprav|e /dɪ'preɪv/ *v.t.* dépraver. **~ity** /-'prævətɪ/ *n.* dépravation *f.*

deprecate /'deprəkeɪt/ *v.t.* désapprouver.

depreciat|e /dɪ'priːʃɪeɪt/ *v.t./i.* (se) déprécier. **~ion** /-'eɪʃn/ *n.* dépréciation *f.*

depress /dɪ'pres/ *v.t.* (*sadden*) déprimer; (*push down*) appuyer sur. **become ~ed,** déprimer. **~ing** *a.* déprimant. **~ion** /-ʃn/ *n.* dépression *f.*

deprivation /deprɪ'veɪʃn/ *n.* privation *f.*

deprive /dɪ'praɪv/ *v.t.* **~ of,** priver de. **~d** *a.* (*child etc.*) déshérité.

depth /depθ/ *n.* profondeur *f.* **be out of one's ~,** perdre pied; (*fig.*) être perdu. **in the ~s of,** au plus profond de.

deputation /depjʊ'teɪʃn/ *n.* députation *f.*

deputize /'depjʊtaɪz/ *v.i.* assurer l'intérim (**for,** de). —*v.t.* (*Amer.*) déléguer, nommer.

deputy /'depjʊtɪ/ *n.* suppléant(e) *m.* (*f.*) —*a.* adjoint. **~ chairman,** vice-président *m.*

derail /dɪ'reɪl/ *v.t.* faire dérailler. **be ~ed,** dérailler. **~ment** *n.* déraillement *m.*

deranged /dɪ'reɪndʒd/ *a.* (*mind*) dérangé.

derelict /'derəlɪkt/ *a.* abandonné.

deri|de /dɪ'raɪd/ *v.t.* railler. **~sion** /-'rɪʒn/ *n.* dérision *f.* **~sive** *a.* (*laughter, person*) railleur.

derisory /dɪ'raɪsərɪ/ *a.* (*scoffing*) railleur; (*offer etc.*) dérisoire.

derivative /dɪ'rɪvətɪv/ *a. & n.* dérivé (*m.*).

deriv|e /dɪ'raɪv/ *v.t.* **~e from,** tirer de. —*v.i.* **~e from,** dériver de. **~ation** /derɪ'veɪʃn/ *n.* dérivation *f.*

derogatory /dɪ'rɒgətrɪ/ *a.* (*word*) péjoratif; (*remark*) désobligeant.

derv /dɜːv/ *n.* gas-oil *m.*, gazole *m.*

descend /dɪ'send/ *v.t./i.* descendre. **be ~ed from,** descendre de. **~ant** *n.* descendant(e) *m.* (*f.*).

descent /dɪ'sent/ *n.* descente *f.*; (*lineage*) origine *f.*

descri|be /dɪ'skraɪb/ *v.t.* décrire. **~ption** /-'skrɪpʃn/ *n.* description *f.* **~ptive** /-'skrɪptɪv/ *a.* descriptif.

desecrat|e /'desɪkreɪt/ *v.t.* profaner. **~ion** /-'kreɪʃn/ *n.* profanation *f.*

desert[1] /'dezət/ *n.* désert *m.* —*a.* désertique. **~ island,** île déserte *f.*

desert[2] /dɪ'zɜːt/ *v.t./i.* déserter. **~ed** *a.* désert. **~er** *n.* déserteur *m.* **~ion** /-ʃn/ *n.* désertion *f.*

deserts /dɪ'zɜːts/ *n. pl.* one's **~,** ce qu'on mérite.

deserv|e /dɪ'zɜːv/ *v.t.* mériter (**to,** de). **~edly** /-ɪdlɪ/ *adv.* à juste titre. **~ing** *a.* (*person*) méritant; (*action*) méritoire.

design /dɪ'zaɪn/ *n.* (*sketch*) dessin *m.*, plan *m.*; (*construction*) conception *f.*; (*pattern*) motif *m.*; (*style of dress*) modèle *m.*; (*aim*) dessein *m.* —*v.t.* (*sketch*) dessiner; (*devise, intend*) concevoir. **~er** *n.* dessinateur, -trice *m.*, *f.*; (*of fashion*) styliste *m./f.*

designat|e /'dezɪgneɪt/ *v.t.* désigner. **~ion** /-'neɪʃn/ *n.* désignation *f.*

desir|e /dɪ'zaɪə(r)/ *n.* désir *m.* —*v.t.* désirer. **~able** *a.* désirable. **~ability** /-ə'bɪlətɪ/ *n.* attrait *m.*

desk /desk/ *n.* bureau *m.*; (*of pupil*) pupitre *m.*; (*in hotel*) réception *f.*; (*in bank*) caisse *f.*

desolat|e /'desələt/ *a.* (*place*) désolé; (*bleak: fig.*) morne. **~ion** /-'leɪʃn/ *n.* désolation *f.*

despair /dɪ'speə(r)/ *n.* désespoir *m.* —*v.i.* désespérer (**of,** de).

despatch /dɪ'spætʃ/ *v.t.* = **dispatch.**

desperate /'despərət/ *a.* désespéré; (*criminal*) prêt à tout. **be ~ for,** avoir une envie folle de. **~ly** *adv.* désespérément; (*worried*) terriblement; (*ill*) gravement.

desperation /despə'reɪʃn/ *n.* désespoir *m.* **in** *or* **out of ~,** en désespoir de cause.

despicable /dɪ'spɪkəbl/ *a.* méprisable, infâme.

despise /dɪ'spaɪz/ *v.t.* mépriser.

despite /dɪ'spaɪt/ *prep.* malgré.

despond|ent /dɪ'spɒndənt/ *a.* découragé. **~cy** *n.* découragement *m.*

despot /'despɒt/ *n.* despote *m.*

dessert /dɪ'zɜːt/ *n.* dessert *m.* **~spoon** *n.* cuiller à dessert *f.* **~spoonful** *n.* cuillerée à soupe *f.*

destination /destɪ'neɪʃn/ *n.* destination *f.*

destine /'destɪn/ *v.t.* destiner.

destiny /'destɪnɪ/ *n.* destin *m.*

destitute /'destɪtjuːt/ *a.* indigent. **~ of,** dénué de.

destr|oy /dɪ'strɔɪ/ *v.t.* détruire; (*animal*) abattre. **~uction** *n.* destruction *f.* **~uctive** *a.* destructeur.

destroyer /dɪ'strɔɪə(r)/ *n.* (*warship*) contre-torpilleur *m.*

detach /dɪ'tætʃ/ *v.t.* détacher. **~able** *a.* détachable. **~ed** *a.* détaché. **~ed house,** maison individuelle *f.*

detachment /dɪ'tætʃmənt/ *n.* détachement *m.*

detail /'diːteɪl/ *n.* détail *m.* —*v.t.* exposer en détail; (*troops*) détacher. **go into ~,** entrer dans le détail. **~ed** *a.* détaillé.

detain /dɪ'teɪn/ *v.t.* retenir; (*in prison*) détenir. **~ee** /diːteɪ'niː/ *n.* détenu(e) *m.* (*f.*).

detect /dɪ'tekt/ *v.t.* découvrir; (*perceive*) distinguer; (*tumour*) dépister; (*mine*) détecter. **~ion** /-kʃn/ *n.* découverte *f.*; dépistage *m.*; détection *f.* **~or** *n.* détecteur *m.*

detective /dɪ'tektɪv/ *n.* policier *m.*; (*private*) détective *m.*

detention /dɪ'tenʃn/ *n.* détention *f.*; (*schol.*) retenue *f.*

deter /dɪ'tɜː(r)/ *v.t.* (*p.t.* **deterred**) dissuader (**from,** de).

detergent /dɪ'tɜːdʒənt/ *a. & n.* détergent (*m.*).

deteriorat|e /dɪ'tɪərəreɪt/ *v.i.* se détériorer. **~ion** /-'reɪʃn/ *n.* détérioration *f.*

determin|e /dɪ'tɜːmɪn/ *v.t.* déterminer. **~e to do,** décider de faire. **~ation** /-'neɪʃn/ *n.* détermination *f.* **~ed** *a.* déterminé. **~ed to do,** décidé à faire.

deterrent /dɪ'terənt, *Amer.* dɪ'tɜːrənt/ *n.* force de dissuasion *f.*

detest /dɪ'test/ *v.t.* détester. **~able** *a.* détestable.

detonat|e /'detəneɪt/ *v.t./i.* (faire) détoner. **~ion** /-'neɪʃn/ *n.* détonation *f.* **~or** *n.* détonateur *m.*

detour /'diːtʊə(r)/ *n.* détour *m.*

detract /dɪ'trækt/ v.i. ~ **from,** (*lessen*) diminuer.

detriment /'detrɪmənt/ n. détriment m. ~**al** /-'mentl/ a. préjudiciable (**to,** à).

devalu|e /di:'vælju:/ v.t. dévaluer. ~**ation** /-ju'eɪʃn/ n. dévaluation f.

devastat|e /'devəsteɪt/ v.t. dévaster; (*overwhelm*: *fig.*) accabler. ~**ing** a. accablant.

develop /dɪ'veləp/ v.t./i. (p.t. **developed**) (se) développer; (*contract*) contracter; (*build on, transform*) exploiter, aménager; (*change*) évoluer; (*appear*) se manifester. ~ **into,** devenir. ~**ing country,** pays en voie de développement m. ~**ment** n. développement m. (**housing**) ~, lotissement m. (**new**) ~**ment,** fait nouveau m.

deviant /'di:vɪənt/ a. anormal. —n. (*psych.*) déviant m.

deviat|e /'di:vɪeɪt/ v.i. dévier. ~**e from,** (*norm*) s'écarter de. ~**ion** /-'eɪʃn/ n. déviation f.

device /dɪ'vaɪs/ n. appareil m.; (*scheme*) procédé m.

devil /'devl/ n. diable m. ~**ish** a. diabolique.

devious /'di:vɪəs/ a. tortueux. **he is** ~, il a l'esprit tortueux.

devise /dɪ'vaɪz/ v.t. inventer; (*plan, means*) combiner, imaginer.

devoid /dɪ'vɔɪd/ a. ~ **of,** dénué de.

devolution /di:və'lu:ʃn/ n. décentralisation f.; (*of authority, power*) délégation f. (**to,** à).

devot|e /dɪ'vəʊt/ v.t. consacrer. ~**ed** a. dévoué. ~**edly** adv. avec dévouement. ~**ion** /-ʃn/ n. dévouement m.; (*relig.*) dévotion f. ~**ions,** (*relig.*) dévotions f. pl.

devotee /devə'ti:/ n. ~ **of,** passionné(e) de m. (f.).

devour /dɪ'vaʊə(r)/ v.t. dévorer.

devout /dɪ'vaʊt/ a. fervent.

dew /dju:/ n. rosée f.

dexterity /dek'sterətɪ/ n. dextérité f.

diabet|es /daɪə'bi:ti:z/ n. diabète m. ~**ic** /-'betɪk/ a. & n. diabétique (m./f.).

diabolical /daɪə'bɒlɪkl/ a. diabolique; (*bad*: *fam.*) atroce.

diagnose /'daɪəgnəʊz/ v.t. diagnostiquer.

diagnosis /daɪəg'nəʊsɪs/ n. (pl. **-oses** /-si:z/) diagnostic m.

diagonal /daɪ'ægənl/ a. diagonal. —n. diagonale f. ~**ly** adv. en diagonale.

diagram /'daɪəgræm/ n. schéma m.

dial /'daɪəl/ n. cadran m. —v.t. (p.t. **dialled**) (*number*) faire; (*person*)

appeler. ~**ling code,** (*Amer.*) ~ **code,** indicatif m. ~**ling tone,** (*Amer.*) ~ **tone,** tonalité f.

dialect /'daɪəlekt/ n. dialecte m.

dialogue /'daɪəlɒg/ n. dialogue m.

diameter /daɪ'æmɪtə(r)/ n. diamètre m.

diamond /'daɪəmənd/ n. diamant m.; (*shape*) losange m.; (*baseball*) terrain m. ~**s,** (*cards*) carreau m.

diaper /'daɪəpə(r)/ n. (*baby's nappy*: *Amer.*) couche f.

diaphragm /'daɪəfræm/ n. diaphragme m.

diarrhoea, (*Amer.*) **diarrhea** /daɪə'rɪə/ n. diarrhée f.

diary /'daɪərɪ/ n. (*for appointments etc.*) agenda m.; (*appointments*) emploi du temps m. (*for private thoughts*) journal intime m.

dice /daɪs/ n. invar. dé m. —v.t. (*food*) couper en dés.

dicey /'daɪsɪ/ a. (*fam.*) risqué.

dictat|e /dɪk'teɪt/ v.t./i. dicter. ~**ion** /-ʃn/ n. dictée f.

dictates /'dɪkteɪts/ n. pl. préceptes m. pl.

dictator /dɪk'teɪtə(r)/ n. dictateur m. ~**ship** n. dictature f.

dictatorial /dɪktə'tɔ:rɪəl/ a. dictatorial.

diction /'dɪkʃn/ n. diction f.

dictionary /'dɪkʃənrɪ/ n. dictionnaire m.

did /dɪd/ see **do.**

diddle /'dɪdl/ v.t. (*sl.*) escroquer.

didn't /'dɪdnt/ = **did not.**

die[1] /daɪ/ v.i. (*pres. p.* **dying**) mourir. ~ **down,** diminuer. ~ **out,** disparaître. **be dying to do/for,** mourir d'envie de faire/de.

die[2] /daɪ/ n. (*metal mould*) matrice f., étampe f.

die-hard /'daɪhɑ:d/ n. réactionnaire m./f.

diesel /'di:zl/ n. diesel m. ~ **engine,** moteur diesel m.

diet /'daɪət/ n. (*habitual food*) alimentation f.; (*restricted*) régime m. —v.i. suivre un régime.

diet|etic /daɪə'tetɪk/ a. diététique. ~**ician** n. diététicien(ne) m. (f.).

differ /'dɪfə(r)/ v.i. différer (**from,** de); (*disagree*) ne pas être d'accord.

differen|t /'dɪfrənt/ a. différent. ~**ce** n. différence f.; (*disagreement*) différend m. ~**tly** adv. différemment (**from,** de).

differential /dɪfə'renʃl/ a. & n. différentiel (m.).

differentiate /dɪfə'renʃɪeɪt/ v.t. différencier. —v.i. faire la différence (**between,** entre).

difficult /'dɪfɪkəlt/ a. difficile. ~**y** n. difficulté f.

diffiden|t /'dıfıdənt/ a. qui manque d'assurance. **~ce** n. manque d'assurance m.

diffuse¹ /dı'fjuːs/ a. diffus.

diffus|e² /dı'fjuːz/ v.t. diffuser. **~ion** /-ʒn/ n. diffusion f.

dig /dıg/ v.t./i. (p.t. **dug**, pres. p. **digging**) creuser; (thrust) enfoncer. —n. (poke) coup de coude m.; (remark) coup de patte m.; (archaeol.) fouilles f. pl. **~s**, (lodgings: fam.) chambre meublée f. **~** (over), bêcher. **~** up, déterrer.

digest¹ /dı'dʒest/ v.t./i. digérer. **~ible** a. digestible. **~ion** /-stʃən/ n. digestion f.

digest² /'daıdʒest/ n. sommaire m.

digestive /dı'dʒestıv/ a. digestif.

digger /'dıgə(r)/ n. (techn.) pelleteuse f., excavateur m.

digit /'dıdʒıt/ n. chiffre m.

digital /'dıdʒıtl/ a. (clock) numérique, à affichage numérique; (recording) numérique.

dignif|y /'dıgnıfaı/ v.t. donner de la dignité à. **~ied** a. digne.

dignitary /'dıgnıtərı/ n. dignitaire m.

dignity /'dıgnıtı/ n. dignité f.

digress /daı'gres/ v.i. faire une digression. **~ from**, s'écarter de. **~ion** /-ʃn/ n. digression f.

dike /daık/ n. digue f.

dilapidated /dı'læpıdeıtıd/ a. délabré.

dilat|e /daı'leıt/ v.t./i. (se) dilater. **~ion** /-ʃn/ n. dilatation f.

dilatory /'dılətərı/ a. dilatoire.

dilemma /dı'lemə/ n. dilemme m.

dilettante /dılı'tæntı/ n. dilettante m./f.

diligen|t /'dılıdʒənt/ a. assidu. **~ce** n. assiduité f.

dilly-dally /'dılıdælı/ v.i. (fam.) lanterner.

dilute /daı'ljuːt/ v.t. diluer.

dim /dım/ a. (**dimmer, dimmest**) (weak) faible; (dark) sombre; (indistinct) vague; (fam.) stupide. —v.t./i. (p.t. **dimmed**) (light) (s')atténuer. **~ly** adv. (shine) faiblement; (remember) vaguement. **~mer** n. **~** (**switch**), variateur d'intensité m. **~ness** n. faiblesse f.; (of room etc.) obscurité f.

dime /daım/ n. (in USA, Canada) pièce de dix cents f.

dimension /daı'menʃn/ n. dimension f.

diminish /dı'mınıʃ/ v.t./i. diminuer.

diminutive /dı'mınjʊtıv/ a. minuscule. —n. diminutif m.

dimple /'dımpl/ n. fossette f.

din /dın/ n. vacarme m.

dine /daın/ v.i. dîner. **~r** /-ə(r)/ n. dîneu|r, -se m., f.; (rail.) wagon-restaurant m.; (Amer.) restaurant à service rapide m.

dinghy /'dıŋgı/ n. canot m.; (inflatable) canot pneumatique m.

ding|y /'dındʒı/ a. (-ier, -iest) miteux, minable. **~iness** n. aspect miteux or minable m.

dining-room /'daınıŋrʊm/ n. salle à manger f.

dinner /'dınə(r)/ n. (evening meal) dîner m.; (lunch) déjeuner m. **~-jacket** n. smoking m. **~ party**, dîner m.

dinosaur /'daınəsɔː(r)/ n. dinosaure m.

dint /dınt/ n. by **~** of, à force de.

diocese /'daıəsıs/ n. diocèse m.

dip /dıp/ v.t./i. (p.t. **dipped**) plonger. —n. (slope) déclivité f.; (in sea) bain rapide m. **~ into**, (book) feuilleter; (savings) puiser dans. **~ one's headlights**, se mettre en code.

diphtheria /dıf'θıərıə/ n. diphtérie f.

diphthong /'dıfθɒŋ/ n. diphtongue f.

diploma /dı'pləʊmə/ n. diplôme m.

diplomacy /dı'pləʊməsı/ n. diplomatie f.

diplomat /'dıpləmæt/ n. diplomate m./f. **~ic** /-'mætık/ a. (pol.) diplomatique; (tactful) diplomate.

dire /daıə(r)/ a. (-er, -est) affreux; (need, poverty) extrême.

direct /dı'rekt/ a. direct. —adv. directement. —v.t. diriger; (letter, remark) adresser; (a play) mettre en scène. **~ s.o. to**, indiquer à qn. le chemin de; (order) signifier à qn. de. **~ness** n. franchise f.

direction /dı'rekʃn/ n. direction f.; (theatre) mise en scène f. **~s**, indications f. pl. **ask ~s**, demander le chemin. **~s for use**, mode d'emploi m.

directly /dı'rektlı/ adv. directement; (at once) tout de suite. —conj. dès que.

director /dı'rektə(r)/ n. direc|teur, -trice m., f.; (theatre) metteur en scène m.

directory /dı'rektərı/ n. (phone book) annuaire m.

dirt /dɜːt/ n. saleté f.; (earth) terre f. **~ cheap**, (sl.) très bon marché invar. **~-track** n. (sport) cendrée f.

dirty /'dɜːtı/ a. (-ier, -iest) sale; (word) grossier. **get ~**, se salir. —v.t./i. (se) salir.

disability /dısə'bılətı/ n. handicap m.

disable /dıs'eıbl/ v.t. rendre infirme. **~d** a. handicapé.

disadvantage /dısəd'vɑːntıdʒ/ n. désavantage m. **~d** a. déshérité.

disagree /dısə'gri:/ v.i. ne pas être d'accord (**with**, avec). ∼ **with s.o.**, (*food*, *climate*) ne pas convenir à qn. ∼**ment** n. désaccord m.; (*quarrel*) différend m.

disagreeable /dısə'gri:əbl/ a. désagréable.

disappear /dısə'pıə(r)/ v.i. disparaître. ∼**ance** n. disparition f.

disappoint /dısə'pɔınt/ v.t. décevoir. ∼**ing** a. décevant. ∼**ed** a. déçu. ∼**ment** n. déception f.

disapprov|**e** /dısə'pru:v/ v.i. ∼**e (of)**, désapprouver. ∼**al** n. désapprobation f.

disarm /dıs'ɑ:m/ v.t./i. désarmer. ∼**ament** n. désarmement m.

disarray /dısə'reı/ n. désordre m.

disassociate /dısə'səʊʃıeıt/ v.t. = **dissociate**.

disast|**er** /dı'zɑ:stə(r)/ n. désastre m. ∼**rous** a. désastreux.

disband /dıs'bænd/ v.t./i. (se) disperser.

disbelief /dısbı'li:f/ n. incrédulité f.

disc /dısk/ n. disque m.; (*comput.*) = **disk**. ∼ **brake**, frein à disque m. ∼ **jockey**, disc-jockey m., animateur m.

discard /dı'skɑ:d/ v.t. se débarrasser de; (*beliefs etc.*) abandonner.

discern /dı'sɜ:n/ v.t. discerner. ∼**ible** a. perceptible. ∼**ing** a. perspicace.

discharge[1] /dıs'tʃɑ:dʒ/ v.t. (*unload*) décharger; (*liquid*) déverser; (*duty*) remplir; (*dismiss*) renvoyer; (*prisoner*) libérer. —v.i. (*of pus*) s'écouler.

discharge[2] /'dıstʃɑ:dʒ/ n. (*med.*) écoulement m.; (*dismissal*) renvoi m.; (*electr.*) décharge m.

disciple /dı'saıpl/ n. disciple m.

disciplin|**e** /'dısıplın/ n. discipline f. —v.t. discipliner; (*punish*) punir. ∼**ary** a. disciplinaire.

disclaim /dıs'kleım/ v.t. désavouer. ∼**er** n. correctif m., précision f.

disclos|**e** /dıs'kləʊz/ v.t. révéler. ∼**ure** /-ʒə(r)/ n. révélation f.

disco /'dıskəʊ/ n. (pl. **-os**) (*club*: *fam.*) discothèque f., disco m.

discol|**our** /dıs'kʌlə(r)/ v.t./i. (se) décolorer. ∼**oration** /-'reıʃn/ n. décoloration f.

discomfort /dıs'kʌmfət/ n. gêne f.

disconcert /dıskən'sɜ:t/ v.t. déconcerter.

disconnect /dıskə'nekt/ v.t. détacher; (*unplug*) débrancher; (*cut off*) couper.

discontent /dıskən'tent/ n. mécontentement m. ∼**ed** a. mécontent.

discontinue /dıskən'tınju:/ v.t. interrompre, cesser.

discord /'dıskɔ:d/ n. discorde f.; (*mus.*) dissonance f. ∼**ant** /-'skɔ:dənt/ a. discordant.

discothèque /'dıskətek/ n. discothèque f.

discount[1] /'dıskaʊnt/ n. rabais m.

discount[2] /dıs'kaʊnt/ v.t. ne pas tenir compte de.

discourage /dı'skʌrıdʒ/ v.t. décourager.

discourse /'dıskɔ:s/ n. discours m.

discourteous /dıs'kɜ:tıəs/ a. impoli, peu courtois.

discover /dı'skʌvə(r)/ v.t. découvrir. ∼**y** n. découverte f.

discredit /dıs'kredıt/ v.t. (*p.t.* **discredited**) discréditer. —n. discrédit m.

discreet /dı'skri:t/ a. discret. ∼**ly** adv. discrètement.

discrepancy /dı'skrepənsı/ n. contradiction f., incohérence f.

discretion /dı'skreʃn/ n. discrétion f.

discriminat|**e** /dı'skrımıneıt/ v.t./i. distinguer. ∼**e against**, faire de la discrimination contre. ∼**ing** a. (*person*) qui a du discernement. ∼**ion** /-'neıʃn/ n. discernement m.; (*bias*) discrimination f.

discus /'dıskəs/ n. disque m.

discuss /dı'skʌs/ v.t. (*talk about*) discuter de; (*argue about*, *examine critically*) discuter. ∼**ion** /-ʃn/ n. discussion f.

disdain /dıs'deın/ n. dédain m. ∼**ful** a. dédaigneux.

disease /dı'zi:z/ n. maladie f. ∼**d** a. malade.

disembark /dısım'bɑ:k/ v.t./i. débarquer.

disembodied /dısım'bɒdıd/ a. désincarné.

disenchant /dısın'tʃɑ:nt/ v.t. désenchanter. ∼**ment** n. désenchantement m.

disengage /dısın'geıdʒ/ v.t. dégager; (*mil.*) retirer. —v.i. (*mil.*) retirer; (*auto.*) débrayer. ∼**ment** n. dégagement m.

disentangle /dısın'tæŋgl/ v.t. démêler.

disfavour, (*Amer.*) **disfavor** /dıs-'feıvə(r)/ n. défaveur f.

disfigure /dıs'fıgə(r)/ v.t. défigurer.

disgrace /dıs'greıs/ n. (*shame*) honte f.; (*disfavour*) disgrâce f. —v.t. déshonorer. ∼**d** a. (*in disfavour*) disgracié. ∼**ful** a. honteux.

disgruntled /dıs'grʌntld/ a. mécontent.

disguise /dıs'gaız/ v.t. déguiser. —n. déguisement m. **in** ∼, déguisé.

disgust /dıs'gʌst/ n. dégoût m. —v.t. dégoûter. ∼**ing** a. dégoûtant.

dish /dɪʃ/ n. plat m. —v.t. ∼ **out**, (fam.) distribuer. ∼ **up,** servir. **the** ∼**es,** (crockery) la vaisselle.

dishcloth /'dɪʃklɒθ/ n. lavette f.; (for drying) torchon m.

dishearten /dɪs'hɑːtn/ v.t. décourager.

dishevelled /dɪ'ʃevld/ a. échevelé.

dishonest /dɪs'ɒnɪst/ a. malhonnête. ∼**y** n. malhonnêteté f.

dishonour, (Amer.) **dishonor** /dɪs'ɒnə(r)/ n. déshonneur m. —v.t. déshonorer. ∼**able** a. déshonorant. ∼**ably** adv. avec déshonneur.

dishwasher /'dɪʃwɒʃə(r)/ n. lave-vaisselle m. invar.

disillusion /dɪsɪ'luːʒn/ v.t. désillusionner. ∼**ment** n. désillusion f.

disincentive /dɪsɪn'sentɪv/ n. **be a** ∼ **to,** décourager.

disinclined /dɪsɪn'klaɪnd/ a. ∼ **to,** peu disposé à.

disinfect /dɪsɪn'fekt/ v.t. désinfecter. ∼**ant** n. désinfectant m.

disinherit /dɪsɪn'herɪt/ v.t. déshériter.

disintegrate /dɪs'ɪntɪgreɪt/ v.t./i. (se) désintégrer.

disinterested /dɪs'ɪntrəstɪd/ a. désintéressé.

disjointed /dɪs'dʒɔɪntɪd/ a. (talk) décousu.

disk /dɪsk/ n. (Amer.) = **disc;** (comput.) disque m. ∼ **drive,** drive m., lecteur de disquettes m.

diskette /dɪ'sket/ n. disquette f.

dislike /dɪs'laɪk/ n. aversion f. —v.t. ne pas aimer.

dislocat|e /'dɪsləkeɪt/ v.t. (limb) disloquer. ∼**ion** /-'keɪʃn/ n. dislocation f.

dislodge /dɪs'lɒdʒ/ v.t. (move) déplacer; (drive out) déloger.

disloyal /dɪs'lɔɪəl/ a. déloyal. ∼**ty** n. déloyauté f.

dismal /'dɪzməl/ a. morne, triste.

dismantle /dɪs'mæntl/ v.t. démonter, défaire.

dismay /dɪs'meɪ/ n. consternation f. —v.t. consterner.

dismiss /dɪs'mɪs/ v.t. renvoyer; (appeal) rejeter; (from mind) écarter. ∼**al** n. renvoi m.

dismount /dɪs'maʊnt/ v.i. descendre, mettre pied à terre.

disobedien|t /dɪsə'biːdɪənt/ a. désobéissant. ∼**ce** n. désobéissance f.

disobey /dɪsə'beɪ/ v.t. désobéir à —v.i. désobéir.

disorder /dɪs'ɔːdə(r)/ n. désordre m.; (ailment) trouble(s) m. (pl.). ∼**ly** a. désordonné.

disorganize /dɪs'ɔːgənaɪz/ v.t. désorganiser.

disorientate /dɪs'ɔːrɪənteɪt/ v.t. désorienter.

disown /dɪs'əʊn/ v.t. renier.

disparaging /dɪ'spærɪdʒɪŋ/ a. désobligeant. ∼**ly** adv. de façon désobligeante.

disparity /dɪ'spærətɪ/ n. disparité f., écart m.

dispassionate /dɪ'spæʃənət/ a. impartial; (unemotional) calme.

dispatch /dɪ'spætʃ/ v.t. (send, complete) expédier; (troops) envoyer. —n. expédition f.; (report) dépêche f. ∼**-rider** n. estafette f.

dispel /dɪ'spel/ v.t. (p.t. **dispelled**) dissiper.

dispensary /dɪ'spensərɪ/ n. pharmacie f., officine f.

dispense /dɪ'spens/ v.t. distribuer; (medicine) préparer. —v.i. ∼ **with,** se passer de. ∼**r** /-ə(r)/ n. (container) distributeur m.

dispers|e /dɪ'spɜːs/ v.t./i. (se) disperser. ∼**al** n. dispersion f.

dispirited /dɪ'spɪrɪtɪd/ a. découragé, abattu.

displace /dɪs'pleɪs/ v.t. déplacer.

display /dɪ'spleɪ/ v.t. montrer, exposer; (feelings) manifester. —n. exposition f.; manifestation f.; (comm.) étalage m.; (of computer) visuel m.

displeas|e /dɪs'pliːz/ v.t. déplaire à. ∼**ed with,** mécontent de. ∼**ure** /-'pleʒə(r)/ n. mecontentement m.

disposable /dɪ'spəʊzəbl/ a. à jeter.

dispos|e /dɪ'spəʊz/ v.t. disposer. —v.i. ∼**e of,** se débarrasser de. **well** ∼**ed to,** bien disposé envers. ∼**al** n. (of waste) évacuation f. **at s.o.'s** ∼**al,** à la disposition de qn.

disposition /dɪspə'zɪʃn/ n. disposition f.; (character) naturel m.

disproportionate /dɪsprə'pɔːʃənət/ a. disproportionné.

disprove /dɪs'pruːv/ v.t. réfuter.

dispute /dɪ'spjuːt/ v.t. contester. —n. discussion f.; (pol.) conflit m. **in** ∼, contesté.

disqualif|y /dɪs'kwɒlɪfaɪ/ v.t. rendre inapte; (sport) disqualifier. ∼**y from driving,** retirer le permis à. ∼**ication** /-ɪ'keɪʃn/ n. disqualification f.

disquiet /dɪs'kwaɪət/ n. inquiétude f. ∼**ing** a. inquiétante.

disregard /dɪsrɪ'gɑːd/ v.t. ne pas tenir compte de. —n. indifférence f. **(for,** à).

disrepair /dɪsrɪ'peə(r)/ n. mauvais état m., délabrement m.

disreputable /dɪs'repjʊtəbl/ a. peu recommandable.

disrepute /dɪsrɪ'pjuːt/ n. discrédit m.

disrespect /dɪsrɪ'spekt/ n. manque de respect m. **~ful** a. irrespectueux.

disrupt /dɪs'rʌpt/ v.t. (*disturb, break up*) perturber; (*plans*) déranger. **~ion** /-pʃn/ n. perturbation f. **~ive** a. perturbateur.

dissatisf|ied /dɪs'sætɪsfaɪd/ a. mécontent. **~action** /dɪsætɪs'fækʃn/ n. mécontentement m.

dissect /dɪ'sekt/ v.t. disséquer. **~ion** /-kʃn/ n. dissection f.

disseminate /dɪ'semɪneɪt/ v.t. disséminer.

dissent /dɪ'sent/ v.i. différer (**from,** de). —n. dissentiment m.

dissertation /dɪsə'teɪʃn/ n. (*univ.*) mémoire m.

disservice /dɪs'sɜːvɪs/ n. mauvais service m.

dissident /'dɪsɪdənt/ a. & n. dissident(e) (m. (f.)).

dissimilar /dɪ'sɪmɪlə(r)/ a. dissemblable, différent.

dissipate /'dɪsɪpeɪt/ v.t./i. (se) dissiper; (*efforts*) gaspiller. **~d** /-ɪd/ a. (*person*) débauché.

dissociate /dɪ'səʊʃɪeɪt/ v.t. dissocier. **~ o.s. from,** se désolidariser de.

dissolute /'dɪsəljuːt/ a. dissolu.

dissolution /dɪsə'luːʃn/ n. dissolution f.

dissolve /dɪ'zɒlv/ v.t./i. (se) dissoudre.

dissuade /dɪ'sweɪd/ v.t. dissuader.

distance /'dɪstəns/ n. distance f. **from a ~,** de loin. **in the ~,** au loin.

distant /'dɪstənt/ a. éloigné, lointain; (*relative*) éloigné; (*aloof*) distant.

distaste /dɪs'teɪst/ n. dégoût m. **~ful** a. désagréable.

distemper /dɪ'stempə(r)/ n. (*paint*) badigeon m.; (*animal disease*) maladie f. —v.t. badigeonner.

distend /dɪ'stend/ v.t./i. (se) distendre.

distil /dɪ'stɪl/ v.t. (p.t. **distilled**) distiller. **~lation** /-'leɪʃn/ n. distillation f.

distillery /dɪ'stɪlərɪ/ n. distillerie f.

distinct /dɪ'stɪŋkt/ a. distinct; (*marked*) net. **as ~ from,** par opposition à. **~ion** /-kʃn/ n. distinction f.; (*in exam*) mention très bien f. **~ive** a. distinctif. **~ly** adv. (*see*) distinctement; (*forbid*) expressément; (*markedly*) nettement.

distinguish /dɪ'stɪŋgwɪʃ/ v.t./i. distinguer. **~ed** a. distingué.

distort /dɪ'stɔːt/ v.t. déformer. **~ion** /-ʃn/ n. distorsion f.; (*of facts*) déformation f.

distract /dɪ'strækt/ v.t. distraire. **~ed** a. (*distraught*) éperdu. **~ing** a. gênant. **~ion** /-kʃn/ n. (*lack of attention, entertainment*) distraction f.

distraught /dɪ'strɔːt/ a. éperdu.

distress /dɪ'stres/ n. douleur f.; (*poverty, danger*) détresse f. —v.t. peiner. **~ing** a. pénible.

distribut|e /dɪ'strɪbjuːt/ v.t. distribuer. **~ion** /-'bjuːʃn/ n. distribution f. **~or** n. distributeur m.

district /'dɪstrɪkt/ n. région f.; (*of town*) quartier m.

distrust /dɪs'trʌst/ n. méfiance f. —v.t. se méfier de.

disturb /dɪ'stɜːb/ v.t. déranger; (*alarm, worry*) troubler. **~ance** n. dérangement m. (**of,** de); (*noise*) tapage m. **~ances** n. pl. (*pol.*) troubles m. pl. **~ed** a. troublé; (*psychologically*) perturbé. **~ing** a. troublant.

disused /dɪs'juːzd/ a. désaffecté.

ditch /dɪtʃ/ n. fossé m. —v.t. (*sl.*) abandonner.

dither /'dɪðə(r)/ v.i. hésiter.

ditto /'dɪtəʊ/ adv. idem.

divan /dɪ'væn/ n. divan m.

div|e /daɪv/ v.i. plonger; (*rush*) se précipiter. —n. plongeon m.; (*of plane*) piqué m.; (*place: sl.*) bouge m. **~er** n. plongeu|r, -se m., f. **~ing-board** n. plongeoir m. **~ing-suit** n. tenue de plongée f.

diverge /daɪ'vɜːdʒ/ v.i. diverger.

divergent /daɪ'vɜːdʒənt/ a. divergent.

diverse /daɪ'vɜːs/ a. divers.

diversify /daɪ'vɜːsɪfaɪ/ v.t. diversifier.

diversity /daɪ'vɜːsətɪ/ n. diversité f.

diver|t /daɪ'vɜːt/ v.t. détourner; (*traffic*) dévier. **~sion** /-ʃn/ n. détournement m.; (*distraction*) diversion f.; (*of traffic*) déviation f.

divest /daɪ'vest/ v.t. **~ of,** (*strip of*) priver de, déposséder de.

divide /dɪ'vaɪd/ v.t./i. (se) diviser.

dividend /'dɪvɪdend/ n. dividende m.

divine /dɪ'vaɪn/ a. divin.

divinity /dɪ'vɪnətɪ/ n. divinité f.

division /dɪ'vɪʒn/ n. division f.

divorce /dɪ'vɔːs/ n. divorce m. (**from,** d'avec). —v.t./i. divorcer (d'avec). **~d** a. divorcé.

divorcee /dɪvɔː'siː, Amer. dɪvɔː'seɪ/ n. divorcé(e) m. (f.).

divulge /daɪ'vʌldʒ/ v.t. divulguer.

DIY abbr. see **do-it-yourself.**

dizz|y /'dɪzɪ/ a. (-ier, -iest) vertigineux.
be or **feel ~y**, avoir le vertige. **~iness**
n. vertige m.

do /duː/ v.t./i. (3 sing. present tense **does**;
p.t. **did**; p.p., **done**) faire; (progress, be
suitable) aller; (be enough) suffire;
(swindle; sl.) avoir. **do well/badly**, se
débrouiller bien/mal. **do the house**,
peindre ou nettoyer etc. la maison. **well
done!**, bravo! **well done**, (culin.) bien
cuit. **done for**, (fam.) fichu. —v. aux.
do you see?, voyez-vous? **do you live
here?**—oui. **I do live here**, si, j'habite ici.
I do not smoke, je ne fume pas. **don't
you?, doesn't he?**, etc., n'est-ce pas?
—n. (pl. **dos** or **do's**) soirée f., fête f.
dos and don'ts, choses à faire et à ne
pas faire. **do away with**, supprimer. **do
in**, (sl.) tuer. **do-it-yourself** n.
bricolage m.; a. (shop, book) de
bricolage. **do out**, (clean) nettoyer. **do
up**, (fasten) fermer; (house) refaire. **it's
to ~ with the house**, c'est à propos de
la maison. **it's nothing to do with me**,
ça n'a rien à voir avec moi. **I could do
with a holiday**, j'aurais bien besoin de
vacances. **~ without**, se passer de.

docile /'dəʊsaɪl/ a. docile.

dock[1] /dɒk/ n. dock m. —v.t./i. (se)
mettre à quai. **~er** n. docker m.

dock[2] /dɒk/ n. (jurid.) banc des accusés
m.

dock[3] /dɒk/ v.t. (money) retrancher.

dockyard /'dɒkjɑːd/ n. chantier naval m.

doctor /'dɒktə(r)/ n. médecin m.,
docteur m.; (univ.) docteur m. —v.t.
(cat) châtrer; (fig.) altérer.

doctorate /'dɒktərət/ n. doctorat m.

doctrine /'dɒktrɪn/ n. doctrine f.

document /'dɒkjʊmənt/ n. document m.
~ary /-'mentrɪ/ a. & n. documentaire
(m.). **~ation** /-'eɪʃn/ n. documentation
f.

doddering /'dɒdərɪŋ/ a. gâteux.

dodge /dɒdʒ/ v.t. esquiver. —v.i. faire
un saut de côté —n. (fam.) truc m.

dodgems /'dɒdʒəmz/ n. pl. autos
tamponneuses f. pl.

dodgy /'dɒdʒɪ/ a. (-ier, -iest) (fam.:
difficult) épineux, délicat; (dangerous)
douteux.

doe /dəʊ/ n. (deer) biche f.

does /dʌz/ see do.

doesn't /'dʌznt/ = does not.

dog /dɒg/ n. chien m. —v.t. (p.t.
dogged) poursuivre. **~-collar** n. (fam.)
(faux) col d'ecclésiastique m. **~-eared**
a. écorné.

dogged /'dɒgɪd/ a. obstiné.

dogma /'dɒgmə/ n. dogme m. **~tic**
/-'mætɪk/ a. dogmatique.

dogsbody /'dɒgzbɒdɪ/ n. factotum m.,
bonne à tout faire f.

doily /'dɔɪlɪ/ n. napperon m.

doings /'duːɪŋz/ n. pl. (fam.) activités f.
pl., occupations f. pl.

doldrums /'dɒldrəmz/ n. pl. **be in the
~**, (person) avoir le cafard.

dole /dəʊl/ v.t. **~ out**, distribuer. —n.
(fam.) indemnité de chômage f. **on the
~**, (fam.) au chômage.

doleful /'dəʊlfl/ a. triste, morne.

doll /dɒl/ n. poupée f. —v.t. **~ up**,
(fam.) bichonner.

dollar /'dɒlə(r)/ n. dollar m.

dollop /'dɒləp/ n. (of food etc.: fam.)
gros morceau m.

dolphin /'dɒlfɪn/ n. dauphin m.

domain /də'meɪn/ n. domaine m.

dome /dəʊm/ n. dôme m.

domestic /də'mestɪk/ a. familial; (trade,
flights, etc.) intérieur; (animal) domestique. **~ science**, arts ménagers m. pl.
~ated /-keɪtɪd/ a. (animal) domestiqué.

domesticity /dɒme'stɪsətɪ/ n. vie de
famille f.

dominant /'dɒmɪnənt/ a. dominant.

dominat|e /'dɒmɪneɪt/ v.t./i. dominer.
~ion /-'neɪʃn/ n. domination f.

domineering /dɒmɪ'nɪərɪŋ/ a. domi-
nateur, autoritaire.

dominion /də'mɪnjən/ n. (British pol.)
dominion m.

domino /'dɒmɪnəʊ/ n. (pl. -oes) domino
m. **~es**, (game) dominos m. pl.

don[1] /dɒn/ v.t. (p.t. **donned**) revêtir,
endosser.

don[2] /dɒn/ n. professeur d'université m.

donat|e /dəʊ'neɪt/ v.t. faire don de. **~ion**
/-ʃn/ n. don m.

done /dʌn/ see do.

donkey /'dɒŋkɪ/ n. âne m. **the ~-work** le
sale boulot.

donor /'dəʊnə(r)/ n. donateur, -trice m.,
f.; (of blood) donneur, -se m., f.

don't /dəʊnt/ = do not.

doodle /'duːdl/ v.i. griffonner.

doom /duːm/ n. (ruin) ruine f.; (fate)
destin m. —v.t. **be ~ed to**, être destiné
or condamné à. **~ed (to failure)**, voué
à l'échec.

door /dɔː(r)/ n. porte f.; (of vehicle)
portière f., porte f.

doorbell /'dɔːbel/ n. sonnette f.

doorman /'dɔːmən/ n. (pl. -men) portier
m.

doormat /'dɔːmæt/ n. paillasson m.

doorstep /'dɔːstep/ n. pas de (la) porte m., seuil m.

doorway /'dɔːweɪ/ n. porte f.

dope /dəʊp/ n. (fam.) drogue f.; (idiot: sl.) imbécile m./f.; —v.t. doper. **~y** a. (foolish: sl.) imbécile.

dormant /'dɔːmənt/ a. en sommeil.

dormitory /'dɔːmɪtrɪ, Amer. 'dɔːmɪtɔːrɪ/ n. dortoir m.; (univ., Amer.) résidence f.

dormouse /'dɔːmaʊs/ n. (pl. -mice) loir m.

dos|e /dəʊs/ n. dose f. **~age** n. dose f.; (on label) posologie f.

doss /dɒs/ v.i. (sl.) roupiller. **~-house** n. asile de nuit m.

dossier /'dɒsɪə(r)/ n. dossier m.

dot /dɒt/ n. point m. **on the ~,** (fam.) à l'heure pile. **~-matrix** a. (printer) matriciel.

dote /dəʊt/ v.i. **~ on,** être gaga de.

dotted /dɒtɪd/ a. (fabric) à pois. **~ line,** ligne en pointillés f. **~ with,** parsemé de.

dotty /'dɒtɪ/ a. (-ier, -iest) (fam.) cinglé, dingue.

double /'dʌbl/ a. double; (room, bed) pour deux personnes. —adv. deux fois. —n. double m.; (stuntman) doublure f. **~s,** (tennis) double m. —v.t./i. doubler; (fold) plier en deux. **at** or **on the ~,** au pas de course. **~ the size,** deux fois plus grand: **pay ~,** payer le double. **~-bass** n. (mus.) contrebasse f. **~-breasted** a. croisé. **~-check** v.t. revérifier. **~ chin,** double menton m. **~-cross** v.t. tromper. **~-dealing** n. double jeu m. **~-decker** n. autobus à impériale m. **~ Dutch,** de l'hébreu m.

doubly /'dʌblɪ/ adv. doublement.

doubt /daʊt/ n. doute m. —v.t. douter de. **~ if** or **that,** douter que. **~ful** a. incertain, douteux; (person) qui a des doutes. **~less** adv. sans doute.

dough /dəʊ/ n. pâte f.; (money: sl.) fric m.

doughnut /'dəʊnʌt/ n. beignet m.

douse /daʊs/ v.t. arroser; (light, fire) éteindre.

dove /dʌv/ n. colombe f.

Dover /'dəʊvə(r)/ n. Douvres m./f.

dovetail /'dʌvteɪl/ v.t./i. (s')ajuster.

dowdy /'daʊdɪ/ a. (-ier, -iest) (clothes) sans chic, monotone.

down[1] /daʊn/ n. (fluff) duvet m.

down[2] /daʊn/ adv. en bas; (of sun) couché; (lower) plus bas. —prep. en bas de; (along) le long de. —v.t. (knock down, shoot down) abattre; (drink) vider. **come** or **go ~,** descendre. **go ~**

to the post office, aller à la poste. **~-and-out** n. clochard(e) m. (f.). **~-hearted** a. découragé. **~-market** a. bas de gamme. **~ payment,** acompte m. **~-to-earth** a. terre-à-terre invar. **~ under,** aux antipodes. **~ with,** à bas.

downcast /'daʊnkɑːst/ a. démoralisé.

downfall /'daʊnfɔːl/ n. chute f.

downgrade /daʊn'greɪd/ v.t. déclasser.

downhill /daʊn'hɪl/ adv. **go ~,** descendre; (pej.) baisser.

downpour /'daʊnpɔː(r)/ n. grosse averse f.

downright /'daʊnraɪt/ a. (utter) véritable; (honest) franc. —adv. carrément.

downs /daʊnz/ n. pl. région de collines f.

downstairs /daʊn'steəz/ adv. en bas. —a. d'en bas.

downstream /'daʊnstriːm/ adv. en aval.

downtown /'daʊntaʊn/ a. (Amer.) du centre de la ville. **~ Boston**/etc., le centre de Boston/etc.

downtrodden /'daʊntrɒdn/ a. opprimé.

downward /'daʊnwəd/ a. & adv., **~s** adv. vers le bas.

dowry /'daʊərɪ/ n. dot f.

doze /dəʊz/ v.i. sommeiller. **~ off,** s'assoupir. —n. somme m.

dozen /'dʌzn/ n. douzaine f. **a ~ eggs,** une douzaine d'œufs. **~s of,** (fam.) des dizaines de.

Dr abbr. (Doctor) Docteur.

drab /dræb/ a. terne.

draft[1] /drɑːft/ n. (outline) brouillon m.; (comm.) traite f. —v.t. faire le brouillon de; (draw up) rédiger. **the ~,** (mil., Amer.) la conscription. **a ~ treaty,** un projet de traité.

draft[2] /drɑːft/ n. (Amer.) = draught.

drag /dræg/ v.t./i. (p.t. dragged) traîner; (river) draguer; (pull away) arracher. —n. (task: fam.) corvée f.; (person: fam.) raseulr, -se m., f. **in ~,** en travesti. **~ on,** s'éterniser.

dragon /'drægən/ n. dragon m.

dragon-fly /'drægənflaɪ/ n. libellule f.

drain /dreɪn/ v.t. (land) drainer; (vegetables) égoutter; (tank, glass) vider; (use up) épuiser. **~ (off),** (liquid) faire écouler. —v.i. **~ (off),** (of liquid) s'écouler. —n. (sewer) égout m. **~(-pipe),** tuyau d'écoulement m. **be a ~ on,** pomper. **~ing-board** n. égouttoir m.

drama /'drɑːmə/ n. art dramatique m., théâtre m.; (play, event) drame m. **~tic** /drə'mætɪk/ a. (situation) dramatique; (increase) spectaculaire. **~tist**

/'dræmətɪst/ n. dramaturge m. ~**tize**
/'dræmətaɪz/ v.t. adapter pour la scène;
(fig.) dramatiser.

drank /dræŋk/ see drink.

drape /dreɪp/ v.t. draper. ~**s** n. pl.
(Amer.) rideaux m. pl.

drastic /'dræstɪk/ a. sévère.

draught /drɑːft/ n. courant d'air m. ~**s**,
(game) dames f. pl. ~ **beer**, bière (à la)
pression f. ~**y** a. plein de courants
d'air.

draughtsman /'drɑːftsmən/ n. (pl.
-men) dessinateur, -trice industriel(le)
m., f.

draw /drɔː/ v.t. (p.t. **drew**, p.p. **drawn**)
(pull) tirer; (attract) attirer; (pass)
passer; (picture) dessiner; (line) tracer.
—v.i. dessiner; (sport) faire match nul;
(come, move) venir. —n. (sport) match
nul m.; (in lottery) tirage au sort m. ~
back, (recoil) reculer. ~ **in**, (days)
diminuer. ~ **near**, (s')approcher (**to**,
de). ~ **out**, (money) retirer. ~ **up** v.i.
(stop) s'arrêter; v.t. (document) dresser;
(chair) approcher.

drawback /'drɔːbæk/ n. inconvénient m.

drawbridge /'drɔːbrɪdʒ/ n. pont-levis m.

drawer /drɔː(r)/ n. tiroir m.

drawers /drɔːz/ n. pl. culotte f.

drawing /'drɔːɪŋ/ n. dessin m. ~**-board**
n. planche à dessin f. ~**pin** n. punaise
f. ~**-room** n. salon m.

drawl /drɔːl/ n. voix traînante f.

drawn /drɔːn/ see draw. —a. (features)
tiré; (match) nul.

dread /dred/ n. terreur f., crainte f. —v.t.
redouter.

dreadful /'dredfl/ a. épouvantable,
affreux. ~**ly** adv. terriblement.

dream /driːm/ n. rêve m. —v.t./i. (p.t.
dreamed or **dreamt**) rêver. —a.
(ideal) de ses rêves. ~ **up**, imaginer.
~**er** n. rêveur, -se m., f. ~**y** a. rêveur.

drear|y /'drɪərɪ/ a. (-ier, -iest) triste;
(boring) monotone. ~**iness** n. tristesse
f.; monotonie f.

dredge /dredʒ/ n. drague f. —v.t./i.
draguer. ~**r** /-ə(r)/ n. dragueur m.

dregs /dregz/ n. pl. lie f.

drench /drentʃ/ v.t. tremper.

dress /dres/ n. robe f.; (clothing) tenue f.
—v.t./i. (s')habiller; (food) assaisonner; (wound) panser. ~ **circle**, premier
balcon m. ~ **rehearsal**, répétition
générale f. ~ **up as**, se déguiser en. **get**
~**ed**, s'habiller.

dresser /'dresə(r)/ n. buffet m.; (actor's)
habilleur, -se m., f.

dressing /'dresɪŋ/ n. (sauce) assaisonne-

ment m.; (bandage) pansement m. ~**-
gown** n. robe de chambre f. ~**-room** n.
(sport) vestiaire m.; (theatre) loge f. ~**-
table** n. coiffeuse f.

dressmak|er /'dresmeɪkə(r)/ n. coutu-
rière f. ~**ing** n. couture f.

dressy /'dresɪ/ a. (-ier, -iest) chic invar.

drew /druː/ see draw.

dribble /'drɪbl/ v.i. couler goutte à
goutte; (person) baver; (football)
dribbler.

dribs and drabs /drɪbzn'dræbz/ n. pl.
petites quantités f. pl.

dried /draɪd/ a. (fruit etc.) sec.

drier /'draɪə(r)/ n. séchoir m.

drift /drɪft/ v.i. aller à la dérive; (pile up)
s'amonceler. —n. dérive f.; amoncelle-
ment m.; (of events) tournure f.;
(meaning) sens m. ~ **towards**, glisser
vers. (snow) ~, congère f. ~**er** n.
personne sans but dans la vie f.

driftwood /'drɪftwʊd/ n. bois flotté m.

drill /drɪl/ n. (tool) perceuse f.; (for
teeth) roulette f.; (training) exercice m.;
(procedure: fam.) marche à suivre f.
(pneumatic) ~, marteau piqueur m.
—v.t. percer; (train) entraîner. —v.i.
être à l'exercice.

drily /'draɪlɪ/ adv. sèchement.

drink /drɪŋk/ v.t./i. (p.t. **drank**, p.p.
drunk) boire. —n. (liquid) boisson f.;
(glass of alcohol) verre m. **a** ~ **of**
water, un verre d'eau. ~**able** a. (not
unhealthy) potable; (palatable) buva-
ble. ~**er** n. buveur, -se m., f. ~**ing**
water, eau potable f.

drip /drɪp/ v.i. (p.t. **dripped**)
(dé)goutter; (washing) s'égoutter. —n.
goutte f.; (person: sl.) lavette f. ~**-dry**
v.t. laisser égoutter; a. sans repassage.

dripping /'drɪpɪŋ/ n. (Amer. ~**s**) graisse
de rôti f.

drive /draɪv/ v.t. (p.t. **drove**, p.p. **driven**)
chasser, pousser; (vehicle) conduire;
(machine) actionner. —v.i. conduire.
—n. promenade en voiture f.; (private
road) allée f.; (fig.) énergie f.; (psych.)
instinct m.; (pol.) campagne f.; (auto.)
traction; (golf, comput.) drive m. **it's a**
two-hour ~, c'est deux heures en
voiture. ~ **at**, en venir à. ~ **away**, (of
car) partir. ~ **in**, (force in) enfoncer. ~
mad, rendre fou. **left-hand** ~, conduite
à gauche f.

drivel /'drɪvl/ n. radotage m.

driver /'draɪvə(r)/ n. conducteur, -trice
m., f., chauffeur m. ~**'s license**
(Amer.), permis de conduire m.

driving /'draɪvɪŋ/ n. conduite f. ~

licence, permis de conduire *m.* ∼ **rain,** pluie battante *f.* ∼ **school,** auto-école *f.* **take one's** ∼ **test,** passer son permis.

drizzle /'drɪzl/ *n.* bruine *f.* —*v.i.* bruiner.

dromedary /'drɒmədərɪ/, (*Amer.*) 'drɒmədərɪ/ *n.* dromadaire *m.*

drone /drəʊn/ *n.* (*noise*) bourdonnement *m.*; (*bee*) faux bourdon *m.* —*v.i.* bourdonner; (*fig.*) parler d'une voix monotone.

drool /druːl/ *v.i.* baver (**over,** sur).

droop /druːp/ *v.i.* pencher, tomber.

drop /drɒp/ *n.* goutte *f.*; (*fall, lowering*) chute *f.* —*v.t./i.* (*p.t.* **dropped**) (laisser) tomber; (*decrease, lower*) baisser. ∼ (**off**), (*person from car*) déposer. ∼ **a line,** écrire un mot (**to,** à). ∼ **in,** passer (**on,** chez). ∼ **off,** (*doze*) s'assoupir. ∼ **out,** se retirer (**of,** de); (*of student*) abandonner. ∼**out** *n.* marginal(e) *m.* (*f.*), raté(e) *m.* (*f.*).

droppings /'drɒpɪŋz/ *n. pl.* crottes *f. pl.*

dross /drɒs/ *n.* déchets *m. pl.*

drought /draʊt/ *n.* sécheresse *f.*

drove /drəʊv/ *see* **drive.**

droves /drəʊvz/ *n. pl.* foule(s) *f.* (*pl.*).

drown /draʊn/ *v.t./i.* (se) noyer.

drowsy /'draʊzɪ/ *a.* somnolent. **be** *or* **feel** ∼, avoir envie de dormir.

drudge /drʌdʒ/ *n.* esclave du travail *m.* ∼**ry** /-ərɪ/ *n.* travail pénible et ingrat *m.*

drug /drʌg/ *n.* drogue *f.*; (*med.*) médicament *m.* —*v.t.* (*p.t.* **drugged**) droguer. ∼ **addict,** drogué(e) *m.* (*f.*). ∼**gist** *n.* pharmacien, -ne *m.*, *f.*

drugstore /'drʌgstɔː(r)/ *n.* (*Amer.*) drugstore(ne) *m.*(*f.*).

drum /drʌm/ *n.* tambour *m.*; (*for oil*) bidon *m.* ∼**s,** batterie *f.* —*v.i.* (*p.t.* **drummed**) tambouriner. —*v.t.* ∼ **into s.o.,** répéter sans cesse à qn. ∼ **up,** (*support*) susciter; (*business*) créer. ∼**mer** *n.* tambour *m.*; (*in pop group*) batteur *m.*

drumstick /'drʌmstɪk/ *n.* baguette de tambour *f.*; (*of chicken*) pilon *m.*

drunk /drʌŋk/ *see* **drink.** —*a.* ivre. **get** ∼, s'enivrer. —*n.*, ∼**ard** *n.* ivrogne(sse) *m.* (*f.*). ∼**en** *a.* ivre; (*habitually*) ivrogne. ∼**enness** *n.* ivresse *f.*

dry /draɪ/ *a.* (**drier, driest**) sec; (*day*) sans pluie. —*v.t./i.* (faire) sécher. **be** *or* **feel** ∼, avoir soif. ∼**-clean** *v.t.* nettoyer à sec. ∼**-cleaner** *n.* teinturier *m.* ∼ **run,** galop d'essai *m.* ∼ **up,** (*dry dishes*) essuyer la vaisselle; (*of supplies*) (se) tarir; (*be silent: fam.*) se taire. ∼**ness** *n.* sécheresse *f.*

dual /'djuːəl/ *a.* double. ∼ **carriageway,** route à quatre voies *f.* ∼**-purpose** *a.* qui fait double emploi.

dub /dʌb/ *v.t.* (*p.t.* **dubbed**) (*film*) doubler; (*nickname*) surnommer.

dubious /'djuːbɪəs/ *a.* (*pej.*) douteux. **be** ∼ **about sth.,** (*person*) avoir des doutes sur qch.

duchess /'dʌtʃɪs/ *n.* duchesse *f.*

duck /dʌk/ *n.* canard *m.* —*v.i.* se baisser subitement. —*v.t.* (*head*) baisser; (*person*) plonger dans l'eau. ∼**ling** *n.* caneton *m.*

duct /dʌkt/ *n.* conduit *m.*

dud /dʌd/ *a.* (*tool etc.: sl.*) mal fichu; (*coin: sl.*) faux; (*cheque: sl.*) sans provision. —*n.* **be a** ∼, (*not work: sl.*) ne pas marcher.

dude /duːd/ *n.* (*Amer.*) dandy *m.*

due /djuː/ *a.* (*owing*) dû; (*expected*) attendu; (*proper*) qui convient. —*adv.* ∼ **east**/*etc.*, droit vers l'est/*etc.* —*n.* dû *m.* ∼**s,** droits *m. pl.*; (*of club*) cotisation *f.* ∼ **to,** à cause de; (*caused by*) dû à. **she's** ∼ **to leave now,** c'est prévu qu'elle parte maintenant. **in** ∼ **course,** (*eventually*) avec le temps; (*at the right time*) en temps et lieu.

duel /'djuːəl/ *n.* duel *m.*

duet /djuː'et/ *n.* duo *m.*

duffle /'dʌfl/ *a.* ∼ **bag,** sac de marin *m.* ∼ **coat,** duffel-coat *m.*

dug /dʌg/ *see* **dig.**

duke /djuːk/ *n.* duc *m.*

dull /dʌl/ *a.* (**-er, -est**) ennuyeux; (*colour*) terne; (*weather*) morne; (*sound*) sourd; (*stupid*) bête; (*blunt*) émoussé. —*v.t.* (*pain*) amortir; (*mind*) engourdir.

duly /'djuːlɪ/ *adv.* comme il convient; (*in due time*) en temps voulu.

dumb /dʌm/ *a.* (**-er, -est**) muet; (*stupid: fam.*) bête.

dumbfound /dʌm'faʊnd/ *v.t.* sidérer, ahurir.

dummy /'dʌmɪ/ *n.* (*comm.*) article factice *m.*; (*of tailor*) mannequin *m.*; (*of baby*) sucette *f.* —*a.* factice. ∼ **run,** galop d'essai *m.*

dump /dʌmp/ *v.t.* déposer; (*abandon: fam.*) se débarrasser de; (*comm.*) dumper. —*n.* tas d'ordures *m.*; (*refuse tip*) décharge *f.*; (*mil.*) dépôt *m.*; (*dull place: fam.*) trou *m.* **be in the** ∼**s,** (*fam.*) avoir le cafard.

dumpling /'dʌmplɪŋ/ *n.* boulette de pâte *f.*

dumpy /'dʌmpɪ/ *a.* (**-ier, -iest**) boulot, rondelet.

dunce /dʌns/ n. cancre m., âne m.
dune /djuːn/ n. dune f.
dung /dʌŋ/ n. (excrement) bouse f., crotte f.; (manure) fumier m.
dungarees /dʌŋɡəˈriːz/ n. pl. (overalls) salopette f.; (jeans: Amer.) jean m.
dungeon /ˈdʌndʒən/ n. cachot m.
dunk /dʌŋk/ v.t. tremper.
dupe /djuːp/ v.t. duper. —n. dupe f.
duplex /ˈdjuːpleks/ n. duplex m.
duplicate[1] /ˈdjuːplɪkət/ n. double m. —a. identique.
duplicat|e[2] /ˈdjuːplɪkeɪt/ v.t. faire un double de; (on machine) polycopier. ~or n. duplicateur m.
duplicity /djuːˈplɪsətɪ/ n. duplicité f.
durable /ˈdjʊərəbl/ a. (tough) résistant; (enduring) durable.
duration /djʊˈreɪʃn/ n. durée f.
duress /djʊˈres/ n. contrainte f.
during /ˈdjʊərɪŋ/ prep. pendant.
dusk /dʌsk/ n. crépuscule m.
dusky /ˈdʌskɪ/ a. (-ier, -iest) foncé.
dust /dʌst/ n. poussière f. —v.t. épousseter; (sprinkle) saupoudrer (with, de). ~-jacket n. jaquette f.
dustbin /ˈdʌstbɪn/ n. poubelle f.
duster /ˈdʌstə(r)/ n. chiffon m.
dustman /ˈdʌstmən/ n. (pl. -men) éboueur m.
dustpan /ˈdʌstpæn/ n. pelle à poussière f.
dusty /ˈdʌstɪ/ a. (-ier, -iest) poussiéreux.
Dutch /dʌtʃ/ a. hollandais. —n. (lang.) hollandais m. go ~, partager les frais. ~man n. Hollandais m. ~woman n. Hollandaise f.
dutiful /ˈdjuːtɪfl/ a. obéissant.
dut|y /ˈdjuːtɪ/ n. devoir m.; (tax) droit m. ~ies, (of official etc.) fonctions f. pl. ~y-free a. hors-taxe. on ~y, de service.
duvet /ˈduːveɪ/ n. couette f.
dwarf /dwɔːf/ n. (pl. -fs) nain(e) m. (f.). —v.t. rapetisser.
dwell /dwel/ v.i. (p.t. dwelt) demeurer. ~ on, s'étendre sur. ~er n. habitant(e) m. (f.). ~ing n. habitation f.
dwindle /ˈdwɪndl/ v.i. diminuer.
dye /daɪ/ v.t. (pres. p. dyeing) teindre. —n. teinture f.
dying /ˈdaɪɪŋ/ a. mourant; (art) qui se perd.
dynamic /daɪˈnæmɪk/ a. dynamique.
dynamism /ˈdaɪnəmɪzəm/ n. dynamisme m.
dynamite /ˈdaɪnəmaɪt/ n. dynamite f. —v.t. dynamiter.

dynamo /ˈdaɪnəməʊ/ n. (pl. -os) dynamo f.
dynasty /ˈdɪnəstɪ, Amer. ˈdaɪnəstɪ/ n. dynastie f.
dysentery /ˈdɪsəntrɪ/ n. dysenterie f.
dyslexi|a /dɪsˈleksɪə/ n. dyslexie f. ~c a. & n. dyslexique (m./f.)

E

each /iːtʃ/ a. chaque. —pron. chacun(e). ~ one, chacun(e). ~ other, l'un(e) l'autre, les un(e)s les autres. know ~ other, se connaître. love ~ other, s'aimer. a pound ~, (get) une livre chacun; (cost) une livre chaque.
eager /ˈiːɡə(r)/ a. impatient (to, de); (supporter, desire) ardent. be ~ to, (want) avoir envie de. ~ for, avide de. ~ly adv. avec impatience or ardeur. ~ness n. impatience f., désir m., ardeur f.
eagle /ˈiːɡl/ n. aigle m.
ear[1] /ɪə(r)/ n. oreille f. ~-drum n. tympan m. ~-ring n. boucle d'oreille f.
ear[2] /ɪə(r)/ n. (of corn) épi m.
earache /ˈɪəreɪk/ n. mal à l'oreille m., mal d'oreille m.
earl /ɜːl/ n. comte m.
earlier /ˈɜːlɪə(r)/ a. (in series) précédent; (in history) plus ancien, antérieur; (in future) plus avancé. —adv. précedemment; antérieurement; avant.
early /ˈɜːlɪ/ (-ier, -iest) adv. tôt, de bonne heure; (ahead of time) en avance. —a. premier; (hour) matinal; (fruit) précoce; (retirement) anticipé. have an ~ dinner, dîner tôt. in ~ summer, au début de l'été.
earmark /ˈɪəmɑːk/ v.t. destiner, réserver (for, à).
earn /ɜːn/ v.t. gagner; (interest: comm.) rapporter. ~ s.o. sth., (bring) valoir qch. à qn.
earnest /ˈɜːnɪst/ a. sérieux. in ~, sérieusement.
earnings /ˈɜːnɪŋz/ n. pl. salaire m.; (profits) bénéfices m. pl.
earphone /ˈɪəfəʊn/ n. écouteur m.
earshot /ˈɪəʃɒt/ n. within ~, à portée de voix.
earth /ɜːθ/ n. terre f. —v.t. (electr.) mettre à la terre. why/how/where on ~ ...?, pourquoi/comment/où diable ...? ~ly a. terrestre.
earthenware /ˈɜːθnweə(r)/ n. faïence f.

earthquake /'ɜ:θkweɪk/ n. tremblement de terre m.

earthy /'ɜ:θɪ/ a. (of earth) terreux; (coarse) grossier.

earwig /'ɪəwɪg/ n. perce-oreille m.

ease /i:z/ n. aisance f., facilité f.; (comfort) bien-être m. —v.t./i. (se) calmer; (relax) (se) détendre; (slow down) ralentir; (slide) glisser. **at ～**, à l'aise; (mil.) au repos. **with ～**, aisément.

easel /'i:zl/ n. chevalet m.

east /i:st/ n. est m. —a. d'est. —adv. vers l'est. **the E～**, (Orient) l'Orient m. **～erly** a. d'est. **～ern** a. de l'est, oriental. **～ward** a. à l'est. **～wards** adv. vers l'est.

Easter /'i:stə(r)/ n. Pâques f. pl. (or m. sing.). **～ egg**, œuf de Pâques m.

easy /'i:zɪ/ a. (-ier, -iest) facile; (relaxed) aisé. **～ chair**, fauteuil m. **go ～ with**, (fam.) y aller doucement avec. **take it ～**, ne pas se fatiguer. **easily** adv. facilement.

easygoing /i:zɪ'gəʊɪŋ/ a. (with people) accommodant; (relaxed) décontracté.

eat /i:t/ v.t./i. (p.t. ate, p.p. eaten) manger. **～ into**, ronger. **～able** a. mangeable. **～er** n. mangeulr, -se m., f.

eau-de-Cologne /əʊdəkə'ləʊn/ n. eau de Cologne f.

eaves /i:vz/ n. pl. avant-toit m.

eavesdrop /'i:vzdrɒp/ v.i. (p.t. -dropped). **～ (on)**, écouter en cachette.

ebb /eb/ n. reflux m. —v.i. refluer; (fig.) décliner.

ebony /'ebənɪ/ n. ébène f.

ebullient /ɪ'bʌlɪənt/ a. exubérant.

EC abbr. (European Community) CE.

eccentric /ɪk'sentrɪk/ a. & n. excentrique (m./f.). **～ity** /eksen'trɪsətɪ/ n. excentricité f.

ecclesiastical /ɪkliːzɪ'æstɪkl/ a. ecclésiastique.

echo /'ekəʊ/ n. (pl. -oes) écho m. —v.t./i. (p.t. echoed, pres. p. echoing) (se) répercuter; (fig.) répéter.

eclipse /ɪ'klɪps/ n. éclipse f. —v.t. éclipser.

ecolog|y /i:'kɒlədʒɪ/ n. écologie f. **～ical** /i:kə'lɒdʒɪkl/ a. écologique.

economic /i:kə'nɒmɪk/ a. économique; (profitable) rentable. **～al** a. économique; (person) économe. **～s** n. économie politique f.

economist /ɪ'kɒnəmɪst/ n. économiste m./f.

econom|y /ɪ'kɒnəmɪ/ n. économie f. **～ize** v.i. **～ (on)**, économiser.

ecosystem /'ikəʊsɪstəm/ n. écosystème m.

ecstasy /'ekstəsɪ/ n. extase f.

ECU /'eɪkjuː/ n. ÉCU m.

eczema /'eksɪmə/ n. eczéma m.

eddy /'edɪ/ n. tourbillon m.

edge /edʒ/ n. bord m.; (of town) abords m. pl.; (of knife) tranchant m. —v.t. border. —v.i. (move) se glisser. **have the ～ on**, (fam.) l'emporter sur. **on ～**, énervé.

edgeways /'edʒweɪz/ adv. de côte. **I can't get a word in ～**, je ne peux pas placer un mot.

edging /'edʒɪŋ/ n. bordure f.

edgy /'edʒɪ/ a. énervé.

edible /'edɪbl/ a. mangeable; (not poisonous) comestible.

edict /'i:dɪkt/ n. décret m.

edifice /'edɪfɪs/ n. édifice m.

edify /'edɪfaɪ/ v.t. édifier.

edit /'edɪt/ v.t. (p.t. edited) (newspaper) diriger; (prepare text of) mettre au point, préparer; (write) rédiger; (cut) couper.

edition /ɪ'dɪʃn/ n. édition f.

editor /'edɪtə(r)/ n. (writer) rédaclteur, -trice m., f.; (annotator) éditleur, -trice m., f. **the ～ (in chief)**, le rédacteur en chef. **～ial** /-'tɔ:rɪəl/ a. de la rédaction; n. éditorial m.

educat|e /'edʒʊkeɪt/ v.t. instruire; (mind, public) éduquer. **～ed** a. instruit. **～ion** /-'keɪʃn/ n. éducation f.; (schooling) enseignement m. **～ional** /-'keɪʃənl/ a. pédagogique, éducatif.

EEC abbr. (European Economic Community) CEE f.

eel /i:l/ n. anguille f.

eerie /'ɪərɪ/ a. (-ier, -iest) sinistre.

effect /ɪ'fekt/ n. effet m. —v.t. effectuer. **come into ～**, entrer en vigueur. **in ～**, effectivement. **take ～**, agir.

effective /ɪ'fektɪv/ a. efficace; (striking) frappant; (actual) effectif. **～ly** adv. efficacement; de manière frappante; effectivement. **～ness** n. efficacité f.

effeminate /ɪ'femɪnət/ a. efféminé.

effervescent /efə'vesnt/ a. effervescent.

efficien|t /ɪ'fɪʃnt/ a. efficace; (person) compétent. **～cy** n. efficacité f.; compétence f. **～tly** adv. efficacement.

effigy /'efɪdʒɪ/ n. effigie f.

effort /'efət/ n. effort m. **～less** a. facile.

effrontery /ɪ'frʌntərɪ/ n. effronterie f.

effusive /ɪ'fju:sɪv/ a. expansif.

e.g. /i:'dʒi:/ abbr. par exemple.

egalitarian /ɪɡælɪ'teərɪən/ a. égalitaire. —n. égalitariste m./f.

egg[1] /eg/ *n.* œuf *m.* **~-cup** *n.* coquetier *m.* **~-plant** *n.* aubergine *f.*

egg[2] /eg/ *v.t.* **~ on**, (*fam.*) inciter.

eggshell /ˈegʃel/ *n.* coquille d'œuf *f.*

ego /ˈiːgəʊ/ *n.* (*pl.* **-os**) moi *m.* **~(t)ism** *n.* égoïsme *m.* **~(t)ist** *n.* égoïste *m./f.*

Egypt /ˈiːdʒɪpt/ *n.* Égypte *f.* **~ian** /ɪˈdʒɪpʃn/ *a. & n.* égyptien(ne) (*m.* (*f.*)).

eh /eɪ/ *int.* (*fam.*) hein.

eiderdown /ˈaɪdədaʊn/ *n.* édredon *m.*

eight /eɪt/ *a. & n.* huit (*m.*). **eighth** /eɪtθ/ *a. & n.* huitième (*m./f.*).

eighteen /eɪˈtiːn/ *a. & n.* dix-huit (*m.*). **~th** *a. & n.* dix-huitième (*m./f.*).

eight|y /ˈeɪtɪ/ *a. & n.* quatre-vingts (*m.*) **~ieth** *a. & n.* quatre-vingtième (*m./f.*).

either /ˈaɪðə(r)/ *a. & pron.* l'un(e) ou l'autre; (*with negative*) ni l'un(e) ni l'autre; (*each*) chaque. —*adv.* non plus. —*conj.* **~ . . . or**, ou (bien) . . . ou (bien); (*with negative*) ni . . . ni.

eject /ɪˈdʒekt/ *v.t.* éjecter. **~or seat**, siège éjectable *m.*

eke /iːk/ *v.t.* **~ out**, faire durer; (*living*) gagner difficilement.

elaborate[1] /ɪˈlæbərət/ *a.* compliqué, recherché.

elaborate[2] /ɪˈlæbəreɪt/ *v.t.* élaborer. —*v.i.* préciser. **~ on**, s'étendre sur.

elapse /ɪˈlæps/ *v.i.* s'écouler.

elastic /ɪˈlæstɪk/ *a. & n.* élastique (*m.*). **~ band**, élastique *m.* **~ity** /elæˈstɪsətɪ/ *n.* élasticité *f.*

elated /ɪˈleɪtɪd/ *a.* fou de joie.

elbow /ˈelbəʊ/ *n.* coude *m.* **~ room**, possibilité de manœuvre *f.*

elder[1] /ˈeldə(r)/ *a. & n.* aîné(e) (*m.* (*f.*)).

elder[2] /ˈeldə(r)/ *n.* (*tree*) sureau *m.*

elderly /ˈeldəlɪ/ *a.* (assez) âgé.

eldest /ˈeldɪst/ *a. & n.* aîné(e) (*m.* (*f.*)).

elect /ɪˈlekt/ *v.t.* élire. —*a.* (*president etc.*) futur. **~ to do**, choisir de faire. **~ion** /-kʃn/ *n.* élection *f.*

elector /ɪˈlektə(r)/ *n.* électeur, -trice *m.*, *f.* **~al** *a.* électoral. **~ate** *n.* électorat *m.*

electric /ɪˈlektrɪk/ *a.* électrique. **~ blanket**, couverture chauffante *f.* **~al** *a.* électrique.

electrician /ɪlekˈtrɪʃn/ *n.* électricien *m.*

electricity /ɪlekˈtrɪsətɪ/ *n.* électricité *f.*

electrify /ɪˈlektrɪfaɪ/ *v.t.* électrifier; (*excite*) électriser.

electrocute /ɪˈlektrəkjuːt/ *v.t.* électrocuter.

electron /ɪˈlektrɒn/ *n.* électron *m.*

electronic /ɪlekˈtrɒnɪk/ *a.* électronique. **~s** *n.* électronique *f.*

elegan|t /ˈelɪgənt/ *a.* élégant. **~ce** *n.* élégance *f.* **~tly** *adv.* élégamment.

element /ˈelɪmənt/ *n.* élément *m.*; (*of heater etc.*) résistance *f.* **~ary** /-ˈmentrɪ/ *a.* élémentaire.

elephant /ˈelɪfənt/ *n.* éléphant *m.*

elevat|e /ˈelɪveɪt/ *v.t.* élever. **~ion** /-ˈveɪʃn/ *n.* élévation *f.*

elevator /ˈeləveɪtə(r)/ *n.* (*Amer.*) ascenseur *m.*

eleven /ɪˈlevn/ *a. & n.* onze (*m.*). **~th** *a. & n.* onzième (*m./f.*).

elf /elf/ *n.* (*pl.* **elves**) lutin *m.*

elicit /ɪˈlɪsɪt/ *v.t.* obtenir (**from**, de).

eligible /ˈelɪdʒəbl/ *a.* admissible (**for**, à). **be ~ for**, (*entitled to*) avoir droit à.

eliminat|e /ɪˈlɪmɪneɪt/ *v.t.* éliminer. **~ion** /-ˈneɪʃn/ *n.* élimination *f.*

élit|e /eɪˈliːt/ *n.* élite *f.* **~ist** *a. & n.* élitiste (*m./f.*).

ellip|se /ɪˈlɪps/ *n.* ellipse *f.* **~tical** *a.* elliptique.

elm /elm/ *n.* orme *m.*

elocution /eləˈkjuːʃn/ *n.* élocution *f.*

elongate /ˈiːlɒŋgeɪt/ *v.t.* allonger.

elope /ɪˈləʊp/ *v.i.* s'enfuir. **~ment** *n.* fugue (amoureuse) *f.*

eloquen|t /ˈeləkwənt/ *a.* éloquent. **~ce** *n.* éloquence *f.* **~tly** *adv.* avec éloquence.

else /els/ *adv.* d'autre. **everybody ~**, tous les autres. **nobody ~**, personne d'autre. **nothing ~**, rien d'autre. **or ~**, ou bien. **somewhere ~**, autre part. **~where** *adv.* ailleurs.

elucidate /ɪˈluːsɪdeɪt/ *v.t.* élucider.

elude /ɪˈluːd/ *v.t.* échapper à; (*question*) éluder.

elusive /ɪˈluːsɪv/ *a.* insaisissable.

emaciated /ɪˈmeɪʃɪeɪtɪd/ *a.* émacié.

emanate /ˈeməneɪt/ *v.i.* émaner.

emancipat|e /ɪˈmænsɪpeɪt/ *v.t.* émanciper. **~ion** /-ˈpeɪʃn/ *n.* émancipation *f.*

embalm /ɪmˈbɑːm/ *v.t.* embaumer.

embankment /ɪmˈbæŋkmənt/ *n.* (*of river*) quai *m.*; (*of railway*) remblai *m.*, talus *m.*

embargo /ɪmˈbɑːgəʊ/ *n.* (*pl.* **-oes**) embargo *m.*

embark /ɪmˈbɑːk/ *v.t./i.* (s')embarquer. **~ on**, (*business etc.*) se lancer dans; (*journey*) commencer. **~ation** /embɑːˈkeɪʃn/ *n.* embarquement *m.*

embarrass /ɪmˈbærəs/ *v.t.* embarrasser, gêner. **~ment** *n.* embarras *m.*, gêne *f.*

embassy /ˈembəsɪ/ *n.* ambassade *f.*

embed /ɪmˈbed/ *v.t.* (*p.t.* **embedded**) encastrer.

embellish /ɪmˈbelɪʃ/ *v.t.* embellir. **~ment** *n.* enjolivement *m.*

embers /ˈembəz/ *n. pl.* braise *f.*

embezzle /ɪm'bezl/ v.t. détourner. ∼**ment** n. détournement de fonds m. ∼**r** /-ə(r)/ n. escroc m.

embitter /ɪm'bɪtə(r)/ v.t. (person) aigrir; (situation) envenimer.

emblem /'embləm/ n. emblème m.

embod|y /ɪm'bɒdɪ/ v.t. incarner, exprimer; (include) contenir. ∼**iment** n. incarnation f.

emboss /ɪm'bɒs/ v.t. (metal) repousser; (paper) gaufrer.

embrace /ɪm'breɪs/ v.t./i. (s')embrasser. —n. étreinte f.

embroider /ɪm'brɔɪdə(r)/ v.t. broder. ∼**y** n. broderie f.

embroil /ɪm'brɔɪl/ v.t. mêler (**in**, à).

embryo /'embrɪəʊ/ n. (pl. -os) embryon m. ∼**nic** /-'ɒnɪk/ a. embryonnaire.

emend /ɪ'mend/ v.t. corriger.

emerald /'emərəld/ n. émeraude f.

emerge /ɪ'mɜːdʒ/ v.i. apparaître. ∼**nce** /-əns/ n. apparition f.

emergency /ɪ'mɜːdʒənsɪ/ n. (crisis) crise f.; (urgent case: med.) urgence f. —a. d'urgence. ∼ **exit**, sortie de secours f. ∼ **landing**, atterrissage forcé. **in an** ∼, en cas d'urgence.

emery /'emərɪ/ n. émeri m.

emigrant /'emɪɡrənt/ n. émigrant(e) m. (f.).

emigrat|e /'emɪɡreɪt/ v.i. émigrer. ∼**ion** /-'ɡreɪʃn/ n. émigration f.

eminen|t /'emɪnənt/ a. éminent. ∼**ce** n. éminence f. ∼**tly** adv. éminemment, parfaitement.

emissary /'emɪsərɪ/ n. émissaire m.

emi|t /ɪ'mɪt/ v.t. (p.t. emitted) émettre. ∼**ssion** n. émission f.

emotion /ɪ'məʊʃn/ n. émotion f. ∼**al** a. (person, shock) émotif; (speech, scene) émouvant.

emotive /ɪ'məʊtɪv/ a. émotif.

emperor /'empərə(r)/ n. empereur m.

emphasis /'emfəsɪs/ n. (on word) accent m. **lay** ∼ **on**, mettre l'accent sur.

emphasize /'emfəsaɪz/ v.t. souligner; (syllable) insister sur.

emphatic /ɪm'fætɪk/ a. catégorique; (manner) énergique.

empire /'empaɪə(r)/ n. empire m.

employ /ɪm'plɔɪ/ v.t. employer. ∼**er** n. employeur, -se m., f. ∼**ment** n. emploi m. ∼**ment agency**, agence de placement f.

employee /emplɔɪ'iː/ n. employé(e) m. (f.).

empower /ɪm'paʊə(r)/ v.t. autoriser (**to do**, à faire).

empress /'emprɪs/ n. impératrice f.

empt|y /'emptɪ/ a. (-ier, -est) vide; (promise) vain. —v.t./i. (se) vider. ∼**y-handed** a. les mains vides. **on an** ∼**y stomach**, à jeun. ∼**ies** n. pl. bouteilles vides f. pl. ∼**iness** n. vide m.

emulat|e /'emjʊleɪt/ v.t. imiter. ∼**ion** /-'leɪʃn/ n. (comput.) émulation f.

emulsion /ɪ'mʌlʃn/ n. émulsion f. ∼ (**paint**), peinture-émulsion f.

enable /ɪ'neɪbl/ v.t. ∼ **s.o. to**, permettre à qn. de.

enact /ɪ'nækt/ v.t. (law) promulguer; (scene) représenter.

enamel /ɪ'næml/ n. émail m. —v.t. (p.t. enamelled) émailler.

enamoured /ɪ'næməd/ a. **be** ∼ **of**, aimer beaucoup, être épris de.

encampment /ɪn'kæmpmənt/ n. campement m.

encase /ɪn'keɪs/ v.t. (cover) recouvrir (**in**, de); (enclose) enfermer (**in**, dans).

enchant /ɪn'tʃɑːnt/ v.t. enchanter. ∼**ing** a. enchanteur. ∼**ment** n. enchantement m.

encircle /ɪn'sɜːkl/ v.t. encercler.

enclave /'enkleɪv/ n. enclave f.

enclose /ɪn'kləʊz/ v.t. (land) clôturer; (with letter) joindre. ∼**d** a. (space) clos; (market) couvert; (with letter) ci-joint.

enclosure /ɪn'kləʊʒə(r)/ n. enceinte f.; (comm.) pièce jointe f.

encompass /ɪn'kʌmpəs/ v.t. (include) inclure.

encore /'ɒŋkɔː(r)/ int. & n. bis (m.).

encounter /ɪn'kaʊntə(r)/ v.t. rencontrer. —n. rencontre f.

encourage /ɪn'kʌrɪdʒ/ v.t. encourager. ∼**ment** n. encouragement m.

encroach /ɪn'krəʊtʃ/ v.i. ∼ **upon**, empiéter sur.

encumber /ɪn'kʌmbə(r)/ v.t. encombrer.

encyclical /ɪn'sɪklɪkl/ n. encyclique f.

encyclopaed|ia, encycloped|ia /ɪnsaɪklə'piːdɪə/ n. encyclopédie f. ∼**ic** a. encyclopédique.

end /end/ n. fin f.; (farthest part) bout m. —v.t./i. (se) terminer. ∼ **up doing**, finir par faire. **come to an** ∼, prendre fin. ∼-**product**, produit fini m. **in the** ∼, finalement. **no** ∼ **of**, (fam.) énormément de. **on** ∼, (upright) debout; (in a row) de suite. **put an** ∼ **to**, mettre fin à.

endanger /ɪn'deɪndʒə(r)/ v.t. mettre en danger.

endear|ing /ɪn'dɪərɪŋ/ a. attachant. ∼**ment** n. parole tendre f.

endeavour, (Amer.) **endeavor** /ɪn'devə(r)/ n. effort m. —v.i. s'efforcer (**to**, de).

ending /'endɪŋ/ n. fin f.

endive /'endɪv/ n. chicorée f.

endless /'endlɪs/ a. interminable; (*times*) innombrable; (*patience*) infini.

endorse /ɪn'dɔːs/ v.t. (*document*) endosser; (*action*) approuver. ~**ment** n. (*auto.*) contravention f.

endow /ɪn'daʊ/ v.t. doter. ~**ed with**, doté de. ~**ment** n. dotation f. (**of**, de).

endur|e /ɪn'djʊə(r)/ v.t. supporter. —v.i. durer. ~**able** a. supportable. ~**ance** n. endurance f. ~**ing** a. durable.

enemy /'enəmɪ/ n. & a. ennemi(e) (m. (f.)).

energetic /enə'dʒetɪk/ a. énergique.

energy /'enədʒɪ/ n. énergie f.

enforce /ɪn'fɔːs/ v.t. appliquer, faire respecter; (*impose*) imposer (**on**, à). ~**d** a. forcé.

engage /ɪn'ɡeɪdʒ/ v.t. engager. —v.i. ~ **in**, prendre part à. ~**d** a. fiancé; (*busy*) occupé. **get** ~**d**, se fiancer. ~**ment** n. fiançailles f. pl.; (*meeting*) rendez-vous m.; (*undertaking*) engagement m.

engaging /ɪn'ɡeɪdʒɪŋ/ a. engageant, séduisant.

engender /ɪn'dʒendə(r)/ v.t. engendrer.

engine /'endʒɪn/ n. moteur m.; (*of train*) locomotive f.; (*of ship*) machine f. ~**-driver** n. mécanicien m.

engineer /endʒɪ'nɪə(r)/ n. ingénieur m.; (*appliance repairman*) dépanneur m. —v.t. (*contrive: fam.*) machiner. ~**ing** n. (*mechanical*) mécanique f.; (*road-building etc.*) génie m.

England /'ɪŋɡlənd/ n. Angleterre f.

English /'ɪŋɡlɪʃ/ a. anglais. —n. (*lang.*) anglais m. ~**-speaking** a. anglophone. **the** ~, les Anglais m. pl. ~**man** n. Anglais m. ~**woman** n. Anglaise f.

engrav|e /ɪn'ɡreɪv/ v.t. graver. ~**ing** n. gravure f.

engrossed /ɪn'ɡrəʊst/ a. absorbé (**in**, par).

engulf /ɪn'ɡʌlf/ v.t. engouffrer.

enhance /ɪn'hɑːns/ v.t. rehausser; (*price, value*) augmenter.

enigma /ɪ'nɪɡmə/ n. énigme f. ~**tic** /enɪɡ'mætɪk/ a. énigmatique.

enjoy /ɪn'dʒɔɪ/ v.t. aimer (*doing*, faire); (*benefit from*) jouir de. ~ **o.s.**, s'amuser. ~ **your meal**, bon appétit! ~**able** a. agréable. ~**ment** n. plaisir m.

enlarge /ɪn'lɑːdʒ/ v.t./i. (s')agrandir. ~ **upon**, s'étendre sur. ~**ment** n. agrandissement m.

enlighten /ɪn'laɪtn/ v.t. éclairer. ~**ment** n. édification f.; (*information*) éclaircissements m. pl.

enlist /ɪn'lɪst/ v.t. (*person*) recruter; (*fig.*) obtenir. —v.i. s'engager.

enliven /ɪn'laɪvn/ v.t. animer.

enmity /'enmɪtɪ/ n. inimitié f.

enormity /ɪ'nɔːmətɪ/ n. énormité f.

enormous /ɪ'nɔːməs/ a. énorme. ~**ly** adv. énormément.

enough /ɪ'nʌf/ adv. & n. assez. —a. assez de. ~ **glasses/time/**etc., assez de verres/de temps/etc. **have** ~ **of**, en avoir assez de.

enquir|e /ɪn'kwaɪə(r)/ v.t./i. demander. ~**e about**, se renseigner sur. ~**y** n. demande de renseignements f.

enrage /ɪn'reɪdʒ/ v.t. mettre en rage, rendre furieux.

enrich /ɪn'rɪtʃ/ v.t. enrichir.

enrol, (*Amer.*) **enroll** /ɪn'rəʊl/ v.t./i. (*p.t.* **enrolled**) (s')inscrire. ~**ment** n. inscription f.

ensconce /ɪn'skɒns/ v.t. ~ **o.s.**, bien s'installer.

ensemble /ɒn'sɒmbl/ n. (*clothing & mus.*) ensemble m.

ensign /'ensən, 'ensaɪn/ n. (*flag*) pavillon m.

enslave /ɪn'sleɪv/ v.t. asservir.

ensue /ɪn'sjuː/ v.i. s'ensuivre.

ensure /ɪn'ʃʊə(r)/ v.t. assurer. ~ **that**, (*ascertain*) s'assurer que.

entail /ɪn'teɪl/ v.t. entraîner.

entangle /ɪn'tæŋɡl/ v.t. emmêler.

enter /'entə(r)/ v.t. (*room, club, race, etc.*) entrer dans; (*note down, register*) inscrire; (*data*) entrer, saisir. —v.i. entrer (**into**, dans). ~ **for**, s'inscrire à.

enterprise /'entəpraɪz/ n. entreprise f.; (*boldness*) initiative f.

enterprising /'entəpraɪzɪŋ/ a. entreprenant.

entertain /entə'teɪn/ v.t. amuser, divertir; (*guests*) recevoir; (*ideas*) considérer. ~**er** n. artiste m./f. ~**ing** a. divertissant. ~**ment** n. amusement m., divertissement m.; (*performance*) spectacle m.

enthral, (*Amer.*) **enthrall** /ɪn'θrɔːl/ v.t. (*p.t.* **enthralled**) captiver.

enthuse /ɪn'θjuːz/ v.i. ~ **over**, s'enthousiasmer pour.

enthusiasm /ɪn'θjuːzɪæzəm/ n. enthousiasme m.

enthusiast /ɪn'θjuːzɪæst/ n. fervent(e) m. (f.), passionné(e) m. (f.) (**for**, de). ~**ic** /-'æstɪk/ a. (*supporter*) enthousiaste. **be** ~**ic about**, être enthousiasmé par. ~**ically** adv. /-'æstɪklɪ/ adv. avec enthousiasme.

entice /ɪn'taɪs/ v.t. attirer. ~ **to do**,

entraîner à faire. **~ment** *n.* (*attraction*) attrait *m.*

entire /ɪnˈtaɪə(r)/ *a.* entier. **~ly** *adv.* entièrement.

entirety /ɪnˈtaɪərətɪ/ *n.* **in its ~**, en entier.

entitle /ɪnˈtaɪtl/ *v.t.* donner droit à (**to sth.**, à qch.; **to do**, de faire). **~d** *a.* (*book*) intitulé. **be ~d to sth.**, avoir droit à qch. **~ment** *n.* droit *m.*

entity /ˈentətɪ/ *n.* entité *f.*

entrails /ˈentreɪlz/ *n. pl.* entrailles *f. pl.*

entrance[1] /ˈentrəns/ *n.* (*entering, way in*) entrée *f.* (**to**, de); (*right to enter*) admission *f.* —*a.* (*charge, exam*) d'entrée.

entrance[2] /ɪnˈtrɑːns/ *v.t.* transporter.

entrant /ˈentrənt/ *n.* (*sport*) concurrent(e) *m.* (*f.*); (*in exam*) candidat(e) *m.* (*f.*).

entreat /ɪnˈtriːt/ *v.t.* supplier.

entrenched /ɪnˈtrentʃt/ *a.* ancré.

entrepreneur /ɒntrəprəˈnɜː(r)/ *n.* entrepreneur *m.*

entrust /ɪnˈtrʌst/ *v.t.* confier.

entry /ˈentrɪ/ *n.* (*entrance*) entrée *f.*; (*word on list*) mot inscrit *m.* **~ form**, feuille d'inscription *f.*

enumerate /ɪˈnjuːməreɪt/ *v.t.* énumérer.

enunciate /ɪˈnʌnsɪeɪt/ *v.t.* (*word*) articuler; (*ideas*) énoncer.

envelop /ɪnˈveləp/ *v.t.* (*p.t.* **enveloped**) envelopper.

envelope /ˈenvələʊp/ *n.* enveloppe *f.*

enviable /ˈenvɪəbl/ *a.* enviable.

envious /ˈenvɪəs/ *a.* envieux (**of sth.**, de qch.). **~ of s.o.**, jaloux de qn. **~ly** *adv.* avec envie.

environment /ɪnˈvaɪərənmənt/ *n.* milieu *m.*; (*ecological*) environnement *m.* **~al** /-ˈmentl/ *a.* du milieu; de l'environnement. **~alist** *n.* spécialiste de l'environnement *m./f.*

envisage /ɪnˈvɪzɪdʒ/ *v.t.* envisager.

envoy /ˈenvɔɪ/ *n.* envoyé(e) *m.* (*f.*).

envy /ˈenvɪ/ *n.* envie *f.* —*v.t.* envier.

enzyme /ˈenzaɪm/ *n.* enzyme *m.*

ephemeral /ɪˈfemərəl/ *a.* éphémère.

epic /ˈepɪk/ *n.* épopée *f.* —*a.* épique.

epidemic /epɪˈdemɪk/ *n.* épidémie *f.*

epilep|sy /ˈepɪlepsɪ/ *n.* épilepsie *f.* **~tic** /-ˈleptɪk/ *a. & n.* épileptique (*m./f.*).

episode /ˈepɪsəʊd/ *n.* épisode *m.*

epistle /ɪˈpɪsl/ *n.* épître *f.*

epitaph /ˈepɪtɑːf/ *n.* épitaphe *f.*

epithet /ˈepɪθet/ *n.* épithète *f.*

epitom|e /ɪˈpɪtəmɪ/ *n.* (*embodiment*) modèle *m.*; (*summary*) résumé *m.* **~ize** *v.t.* incarner.

epoch /ˈiːpɒk/ *n.* époque *f.* **~-making** *a.* qui fait époque.

equal /ˈiːkwəl/ *a. & n.* égal(e) (*m.f.*). —*v.t.* (*p.t.* **equalled**) égaler. **~ opportunities/rights**, égalité des chances/droits *f.* **~ to**, (*task*) à la hauteur de. **~ity** /ɪˈkwɒlətɪ/ *n.* égalité *f.* **~ly** *adv.* également; (*just as*) tout aussi.

equalize /ˈiːkwəlaɪz/ *v.t./i.* égaliser. **~r** /-ə(r)/ *n.* (*goal*) but égalisateur *m.*

equanimity /ekwəˈnɪmətɪ/ *n.* égalité d'humeur *f.*, calme *m.*

equate /ɪˈkweɪt/ *v.t.* assimiler, égaler (**with**, à).

equation /ɪˈkweɪʒn/ *n.* équation *f.*

equator /ɪˈkweɪtə(r)/ *n.* équateur *m.* **~ial** /ekwəˈtɔːrɪəl/ *a.* équatorial.

equilibrium /iːkwɪˈlɪbrɪəm/ *n.* équilibre *m.*

equinox /ˈiːkwɪnɒks/ *n.* équinoxe *m.*

equip /ɪˈkwɪp/ *v.t.* (*p.t.* **equipped**) équiper (**with**, de). **~ment** *n.* équipement *m.*

equitable /ˈekwɪtəbl/ *a.* équitable.

equity /ˈekwɪtɪ/ *n.* équité *f.*

equivalen|t /ɪˈkwɪvələnt/ *a. & n.* équivalent (*m.*). **~ce** *n.* équivalence *f.*

equivocal /ɪˈkwɪvəkl/ *a.* équivoque.

era /ˈɪərə/ *n.* ère *f.*, époque *f.*

eradicate /ɪˈrædɪkeɪt/ *v.t.* supprimer, éliminer.

erase /ɪˈreɪz/ *v.t.* effacer. **~r** /-ə(r)/ *n.* (*rubber*) gomme *f.*

erect /ɪˈrekt/ *a.* droit. —*v.t.* ériger. **~ion** /-kʃn/ *n.* érection *f.*

ermine /ˈɜːmɪn/ *n.* hermine *f.*

ero|de /ɪˈrəʊd/ *v.t.* ronger. **~sion** *n.* érosion *f.*

erotic /ɪˈrɒtɪk/ *a.* érotique. **~ism** /-sɪzəm/ *n.* érotisme *m.*

err /ɜː(r)/ *v.i.* (*be mistaken*) se tromper; (*sin*) pécher.

errand /ˈerənd/ *n.* course *f.*

erratic /ɪˈrætɪk/ *a.* (*uneven*) irrégulier; (*person*) capricieux.

erroneous /ɪˈrəʊnɪəs/ *a.* erroné.

error /ˈerə(r)/ *n.* erreur *f.*

erudit|e /ˈeruːdaɪt, *Amer.* ˈerjʊdaɪt/ *a.* érudit. **~ion** /-ˈdɪʃn/ *n.* érudition *f.*

erupt /ɪˈrʌpt/ *v.i.* (*volcano*) entrer en éruption; (*fig.*) éclater. **~ion** /-pʃn/ *n.* éruption *f.*

escalat|e /ˈeskəleɪt/ *v.t./i.* (s')intensifier; (*of prices*) monter en flèche. **~ion** /-ˈleɪʃn/ *n.* escalade *f.*

escalator /ˈeskəleɪtə(r)/ *n.* escalier mécanique *m.*, escalator *m.*

escapade /eskəˈpeɪd/ *n.* fredaine *f.*

escape /ɪˈskeɪp/ *v.i.* s'échapper (**from a**

place, d'un lieu); (*prisoner*) s'évader.
—*v.t.* échapper à. —*n.* fuite *f.*, évasion
f.; (*of gas etc.*) fuite *f.* ~ **from s.o.,**
échapper à qn. ~ **to,** s'enfuir dans. **have
a lucky** *or* **narrow** ~, l'échapper belle.

escapism /ɪ'skeɪpɪzəm/ *n.* évasion (de la
réalité) *f.*

escort[1] /'eskɔːt/ *n.* (*guard*) escorte *f.*; (*of
lady*) cavalier *m.*

escort[2] /ɪ'skɔːt/ *v.t.* escorter.

Eskimo /'eskɪməʊ/ *n.* (*pl.* **-os**)
Esquimau(de) *m.* (*f.*).

especial /ɪ'speʃl/ *a.* particulier. ~**ly** *adv.*
particulièrement.

espionage /'espɪɒnɑːʒ/ *n.* espionnage *m.*

esplanade /esplə'neɪd/ *n.* esplanade *f.*

espresso /e'spresəʊ/ *n.* (*pl.* **-os**) (café)
express *m.*

essay /'eseɪ/ *n.* essai *m.*; (*schol.*) rédacton
f.; (*univ.*) dissertation *f.*

essence /'esns/ *n.* essence *f.*; (*main
point*) essentiel *m.*

essential /ɪ'senʃl/ *a.* essentiel. —*n. pl.*
the ~**s,** l'essentiel *m.* ~**ly** *adv.*
essentiellement.

establish /ɪ'stæblɪʃ/ *v.t.* établir;
(*business, state*) fonder. ~**ment** *n.*
établissement *m.*; fondation *f.* **the
E**~**ment,** les pouvoirs établis.

estate /ɪ'steɪt/ *n.* (*land*) propriété *f.*;
(*possessions*) biens *m. pl.*; (*inheritance*) succession *f.*; (*district*) cité *f.*,
complexe *m.* ~ **agent,** agent immobilier *m.* ~ **car,** break *m.*

esteem /ɪ'stiːm/ *v.t.* estimer. —*n.* estime *f.*

esthetic /es'θetik/ *a.* (*Amer.*) =
aesthetic.

estimate[1] /'estɪmət/ *n.* (*calculation*)
estimation *f.*; (*comm.*) devis *m.*

estimate[2] /'estɪmeɪt/ *v.t.* estimer. ~**ion**
/-'meɪʃn/ *n.* jugement *m.*; (*high regard*)
estime *f.*

estuary /'estʃʊərɪ/ *n.* estuaire *m.*

etc. /et'setərə/ *adv.* etc.

etching /'etʃɪŋ/ *n.* eau-forte *f.*

eternal /ɪ'tɜːnl/ *a.* éternel.

eternity /ɪ'tɜːnətɪ/ *n.* éternité *f.*

ether /'iːθə(r)/ *n.* éther *m.*

ethic /'eθɪk/ *n.* éthique *f.* ~**s,** moralité *f.*
~**al** *a.* éthique.

ethnic /'eθnɪk/ *a.* ethnique.

ethos /'iːθɒs/ *n.* génie *m.*

etiquette /'etɪket/ *n.* étiquette *f.*

etymology /etɪ'mɒlədʒɪ/ *n.* étymologie *f.*

eucalyptus /juːkə'lɪptəs/ *n.* (*pl.* **-tuses**)
eucalyptus *m.*

eulogy /'juːlədʒɪ/ *n.* éloge *m.*

euphemism /'juːfəmɪzəm/ *n.* euphémisme *m.*

euphoria /juː'fɔːrɪə/ *n.* euphorie *f.*

eurocheque /'jʊərəʊtʃek/ *n.* eurochèque
m.

Europe /'jʊərəp/ *n.* Europe *f.* ~**an**
/-'pɪən/ *a.* & *n.* européen(ne) (*m.* (*f.*)).
E~**an Community,** Communauté
Européenne *f.*

euthanasia /juːθə'neɪzɪə/ *n.* euthanasie *f.*

evacuat|e /ɪ'vækjʊeɪt/ *v.t.* évacuer. ~**ion**
/-'eɪʃn/ *n.* évacuation *f.*

evade /ɪ'veɪd/ *v.t.* esquiver. ~ **tax,**
frauder le fisc.

evaluate /ɪ'væljʊeɪt/ *v.t.* évaluer.

evangelical /iːvæn'dʒelɪkl/ *a.* évan-
gélique.

evangelist /ɪ'vændʒəlɪst/ *n.* évangéliste
m.

evaporat|e /ɪ'væpəreɪt/ *v.i.* s'évaporer.
~**ed milk,** lait concentré *m.* ~**ion**
/-'reɪʃn/ *n.* évaporation *f.*

evasion /ɪ'veɪʒn/ *n.* fuite *f.* (**of,** devant);
(*excuse*) subterfuge *m.* **tax** ~, fraude
fiscale.

evasive /ɪ'veɪsɪv/ *a.* évasif.

eve /iːv/ *n.* veille *f.* (**of,** de).

even /'iːvn/ *a.* régulier; (*surface*) uni;
(*equal, unvarying*) égal; (*number*) pair.
—*v.t./i.* ~ (**out** *or* **up**), (s')égaliser.
—*adv.* même. ~ **better/***etc.*, (*still*)
encore mieux/*etc.* **get** ~ **with,** se
venger de. ~**ly** *adv.* régulièrement;
(*equally*) de manière égale.

evening /'iːvnɪŋ/ *n.* soir *m.*; (*whole
evening, event*) soirée *f.*

event /ɪ'vent/ *n.* événement *m.*; (*sport*)
épreuve *f.* **in the** ~ **of,** en cas de. ~**ful**
a. mouvementé.

eventual /ɪ'ventʃʊəl/ *a.* final, définitif.
~**ity** /-'ælətɪ/ *n.* éventualité *f.* ~**ly** *adv.*
en fin de compte; (*in future*) un jour ou
l'autre.

ever /'evə(r)/ *adv.* jamais; (*at all times*)
toujours. ~ **since** *prep.* & *adv.* depuis
(ce moment-là); *conj.* depuis que. ~ **so,**
(*fam.*) vraiment.

evergreen /'evəgriːn/ *n.* arbre à feuilles
persistantes *m.*

everlasting /evə'lɑːstɪŋ/ *a.* éternel.

every /'evrɪ/ *a.* chaque. ~ **one,**
chacun(e). ~ **other day,** un jour sur
deux, tous les deux jours.

everybody /'evrɪbɒdɪ/ *pron.* tout le
monde.

everyday /'evrɪdeɪ/ *a.* quotidien.

everyone /'evrɪwʌn/ *pron.* tout le
monde.

everything /'evrɪθɪŋ/ *pron.* tout.

everywhere /'evrɪweə(r)/ *adv.* partout.
~ **he goes,** partout où il va.

evict /ɪ'vɪkt/ v.t. expulser. ∼ion /-kʃn/ n. expulsion f.

evidence /'evɪdəns/ n. (proof) preuve(s) f. (pl.); (certainty) évidence f.; (signs) signes m. pl.; (testimony) témoignage m. give ∼, témoigner. in ∼, en vue.

evident /'evɪdənt/ a. évident. ∼ly adv. de toute évidence.

evil /'iːvl/ a. mauvais. —n. mal m.

evo|ke /ɪ'vəʊk/ v.t. évoquer. ∼cative /ɪ'vɒkətɪv/ a. évocateur.

evolution /iːvə'luːʃn/ n. évolution f.

evolve /ɪ'vɒlv/ v.i. se développer, évoluer. —v.t. développer.

ewe /juː/ n. brebis f.

ex- /eks/ pref. ex-, ancien.

exacerbate /ɪg'zæsəbeɪt/ v.t. exacerber.

exact¹ /ɪg'zækt/ a. exact. ∼ly adv. exactement. ∼ness n. exactitude f.

exact² /ɪg'zækt/ v.t. exiger (from, de). ∼ing a. exigeant.

exaggerat|e /ɪg'zædʒəreɪt/ v.t./i. exagérer. ∼ion /-'reɪʃn/ n. exagération f.

exalted /ɪg'zɔːltɪd/ a. (in rank) de haut rang; (ideal) élevé.

exam /ɪg'zæm/ n. (fam.) examen m.

examination /ɪgzæmɪ'neɪʃn/ n. examen m.

examine /ɪg'zæmɪn/ v.t. examiner; (witness etc.) interroger. ∼r /-ə(r)/ n. examina|teur, -trice m., f.

example /ɪg'zɑːmpl/ n. exemple m. for ∼, par exemple. make an ∼ of, punir pour l'exemple.

exasperat|e /ɪg'zæspəreɪt/ v.t. exaspérer. ∼ion /-'reɪʃn/ n. exaspération f.

excavat|e /'ekskəveɪt/ v.t. creuser; (uncover) déterrer. ∼ions /-'veɪʃnz/ n. pl. (archaeol.) fouilles f. pl.

exceed /ɪk'siːd/ v.t. dépasser. ∼ingly adv. extrêmement.

excel /ɪk'sel/ v.i. (p.t. excelled) exceller. —v.t. surpasser.

excellen|t /'eksələnt/ a. excellent. ∼ce n. excellence f. ∼tly adv. admirablement, parfaitement.

except /ɪk'sept/ prep. sauf, excepté. —v.t. excepter. ∼ for, à part. ∼ing prep. sauf, excepté.

exception /ɪk'sepʃn/ n. exception f. take ∼ to, s'offenser de.

exceptional /ɪk'sepʃənl/ a. exceptionnel. ∼ly adv. exceptionnellement.

excerpt /'eksɜːpt/ n. extrait m.

excess¹ /ɪk'ses/ n. excès m.

excess² /'ekses/ a. excédentaire. ∼ fare, supplément m. ∼ luggage, excédent de bagages m.

excessive /ɪk'sesɪv/ a. excessif. ∼ly adv. excessivement.

exchange /ɪks'tʃeɪndʒ/ v.t. échanger. —n. échange m.; (between currencies) change m. ∼ rate, taux d'échange m. (telephone) ∼, central (téléphonique) m.

exchequer /ɪks'tʃekə(r)/ n. (British pol.) Échiquier m.

excise /'eksaɪz/ n. impôt (indirect) m.

excit|e /ɪk'saɪt/ v.t. exciter; (enthuse) enthousiasmer. ∼able a. excitable. ∼ed a. excité. get ∼ed, s'exciter. ∼ement n. excitation f. ∼ing a. passionnant.

exclaim /ɪk'skleɪm/ v.t./i. exclamer, s'écrier.

exclamation /eksklə'meɪʃn/ n. exclamation f. ∼ mark or point (Amer.), point d'exclamation m.

exclu|de /ɪk'skluːd/ v.t. exclure. ∼sion n. exclusion f.

exclusive /ɪk'skluːsɪv/ a. (rights etc.) exclusif; (club etc.) sélect; (news item) en exclusivité. ∼ of service/etc., service/etc. non compris. ∼ly adv. exclusivement.

excrement /'ekskrəmənt/ n. excrément(s) m. (pl.).

excruciating /ɪk'skruːʃɪeɪtɪŋ/ a. atroce, insupportable.

excursion /ɪk'skɜːʃn/ n. excursion f.

excus|e¹ /ɪk'skjuːz/ v.t. excuser. ∼e from, (exempt) dispenser de. ∼e me!, excusez-moi!, pardon! ∼able a. excusable.

excuse² /ɪk'skjuːs/ n. excuse f.

ex-directory /eksdɪ'rektərɪ/ a. qui n'est pas dans l'annuaire.

execute /'eksɪkjuːt/ v.t. exécuter.

execution /eksɪ'kjuːʃn/ n. exécution f. ∼er n. bourreau m.

executive /ɪg'zekjʊtɪv/ n. (pouvoir) exécutif m.; (person) cadre m. —a. exécutif.

exemplary /ɪg'zemplərɪ/ a. exemplaire.

exemplify /ɪg'zemplɪfaɪ/ v.t. illustrer.

exempt /ɪg'zempt/ a. exempt (from, de). —v.t. exempter. ∼ion /-pʃn/ n. exemption f.

exercise /'eksəsaɪz/ n. exercice m. —v.t. exercer; (restraint, patience) faire preuve de. —v.i. prendre de l'exercice. ∼ book, cahier m.

exert /ɪg'zɜːt/ v.t. exercer. ∼ o.s., se dépenser, faire des efforts. ∼ion /-ʃn/ n. effort m.

exhaust /ɪg'zɔːst/ v.t. épuiser. —n. (auto.) (pot d')échappement m. ∼ed a. épuisé. ∼ion /-stʃən/ n. épuisement m.

exhaustive /ɪgˈzɔːstɪv/ a. complet.
exhibit /ɪgˈzɪbɪt/ v.t. exposer; (fig.) faire preuve de. —n. objet exposé m. ∿or n. exposant(e) m. (f.).
exhibition /eksɪˈbɪʃn/ n. exposition f.; (act of showing) démonstration f. ∿ist n. exhibitionniste m./f.
exhilarat|e /ɪgˈzɪləreɪt/ v.t. transporter de joie; (invigorate) stimuler. ∿ing a. euphorisant. ∿ion /-ˈreɪʃn/ n. joie f.
exhort /ɪgˈzɔːt/ v.t. exhorter (to, à).
exhume /eksˈhjuːm/ v.t. exhumer.
exile /ˈeksaɪl/ n. exil m.; (person) exilé(e) m. (f.). —v.t. exiler.
exist /ɪgˈzɪst/ v.i. exister. ∿ence n. existence f. **be in** ∿ence, exister. ∿ing a. actuel.
exit /ˈeksɪt/ n. sortie f. —v.t./i. (comput.) sortir (de).
exodus /ˈeksədəs/ n. exode m.
exonerate /ɪgˈzɒnəreɪt/ v.t. disculper, innocenter.
exorbitant /ɪgˈzɔːbɪtənt/ a. exorbitant.
exorcize /ˈeksɔːsaɪz/ v.t. exorciser.
exotic /ɪgˈzɒtɪk/ a. exotique.
expand /ɪkˈspænd/ v.t./i. (develop) (se) développer; (extend) (s')étendre; (metal, liquid) (se) dilater. ∿sion n. développement m.; dilatation f.; (pol., comm.) expansion f.
expanse /ɪkˈspæns/ n. étendue f.
expatriate /eksˈpætrɪət, Amer. eksˈpeɪtrɪət/ a. & n. expatrié(e) (m. (f.)).
expect /ɪkˈspekt/ v.t. attendre, s'attendre à; (suppose) supposer; (demand) exiger; (baby) attendre. ∿ **to do,** compter faire. ∿ation /ekspekˈteɪʃn/ n. attente f.
expectan|t /ɪkˈspektənt/ a. ∿t look, air d'attente m. ∿t mother, future maman f. ∿cy n. attente f.
expedient /ɪkˈspiːdɪənt/ a. opportun. —n. expédient m.
expedite /ˈekspɪdaɪt/ v.t. hâter.
expedition /ekspɪˈdɪʃn/ n. expédition f.
expel /ɪkˈspel/ v.t. (p.t. **expelled**) expulser; (from school) renvoyer.
expend /ɪkˈspend/ v.t. dépenser. ∿able a. remplaçable.
expenditure /ɪkˈspendɪtʃə(r)/ n. dépense(s) f. (pl.).
expense /ɪkˈspens/ n. dépense f.; frais m. pl. **at s.o.'s** ∿, aux dépens de qn. ∿ **account,** note de frais f.
expensive /ɪkˈspensɪv/ a. cher, coûteux; (tastes, habits) de luxe. ∿ly adv. coûteusement.
experience /ɪkˈspɪərɪəns/ n. expérience f.; (adventure) aventure f. —v.t.

(undergo) connaître; (feel) éprouver. ∿d a. expérimenté.
experiment /ɪkˈsperɪmənt/ n. expérience f. —v.i. faire une expérience. ∿al /-ˈmentl/ a. expérimental.
expert /ˈekspɜːt/ n. expert(e) m. (f.). —a. expert. ∿ly adv. habilement.
expertise /ekspɜːˈtiːz/ n. compétence f. (in, en).
expir|e /ɪkˈspaɪə(r)/ v.i. expirer. ∿ed a. périmé. ∿y n. expiration f.
expl|ain /ɪkˈspleɪn/ v.t. expliquer. ∿anation /ekspləˈneɪʃn/ n. explication f. ∿anatory /-ˈænətərɪ/ a. explicatif.
expletive /ɪkˈspliːtɪv, Amer. ˈeksplətɪv/ n. juron m.
explicit /ɪkˈsplɪsɪt/ a. explicite.
explo|de /ɪkˈspləʊd/ v.t./i. (faire) exploser. ∿sion n. explosion f. ∿sive a. & n. explosif (m.).
exploit[1] /ˈeksplɔɪt/ n. exploit m.
exploit[2] /ɪkˈsplɔɪt/ v.t. exploiter. ∿ation /eksplɔɪˈteɪʃn/ n. exploitation f.
exploratory /ɪkˈsplɒrətrɪ/ a. (talks: pol.) exploratoire.
explor|e /ɪkˈsplɔː(r)/ v.t. explorer; (fig.) examiner. ∿ation /ekspləˈreɪʃn/ n. exploration f. ∿er n. explorateur, -trice m., f.
exponent /ɪkˈspəʊnənt/ n. interprète m. (of, de).
export[1] /ɪkˈspɔːt/ v.t. exporter. ∿er n. exportateur m.
export[2] /ˈekspɔːt/ n. exportation f.
expos|e /ɪkˈspəʊz/ v.t. exposer; (disclose) dévoiler. ∿ure /-ʒə(r)/ n. exposition f.; (photo.) pose f. **die of** ∿ure, mourir de froid.
expound /ɪkˈspaʊnd/ v.t. exposer.
express[1] /ɪkˈspres/ a. formel, exprès; (letter) exprès invar. —adv. (by express post) (par) exprès. —n. (train) rapide m.; (less fast) express m. ∿ly adv. expressément.
express[2] /ɪkˈspres/ v.t. exprimer. ∿ion /-ʃn/ n. expression f. ∿ive a. expressif.
expressway /ɪkˈspresweɪ/ n. voie express f.
expulsion /ɪkˈspʌlʃn/ n. expulsion f.; (from school) renvoi m.
expurgate /ˈekspəgeɪt/ v.t. expurger.
exquisite /ˈekskwɪzɪt/ a. exquis. ∿ly adv. d'une façon exquise.
ex-serviceman /eksˈsɜːvɪsmən/ n. (pl. -men) ancien combattant m.
extant /ekˈstænt/ a. existant.
extempore /ekˈstempərɪ/ a. & adv. impromptu.
exten|d /ɪkˈstend/ v.t. (increase)

étendre, agrandir; (*arm, leg*) étendre; (*prolong*) prolonger; (*house*) agrandir; (*grant*) offrir. —*v.i.* (*stretch*) s'étendre; (*in time*) se prolonger. ∿**sion** *n.* (*of line, road*) prolongement *m.*; (*in time*) prolongation *f.*; (*building*) annexe *f.*; (*of phone*) appareil supplémentaire *m.*; (*phone number*) poste *m.*; (*cable, hose, etc.*) rallonge *f.*

extensive /ɪk'stensɪv/ *a.* vaste; (*study*) profond; (*damage etc.*) important. ∿**ly** *adv.* (*much*) beaucoup; (*very*) très.

extent /ɪk'stent/ *n.* (*size, scope*) étendue *f.*; (*degree*) mesure *f.* **to some** ∿, dans une certaine mesure. **to such an** ∿ **that,** à tel point que.

extenuating /ɪk'stenjʊeɪtɪŋ/ *a.* ∿ **circumstances,** circonstances atténuantes.

exterior /ɪk'stɪərɪə(r)/ *a. & n.* extérieur (*m.*).

exterminat|e /ɪk'stɜ:mɪneɪt/ *v.t.* exterminer. ∿**ion** /-'neɪʃn/ *n.* extermination *f.*

external /ɪk'stɜ:nl/ *a.* extérieur; (*cause, medical use*) externe. ∿**ly** *adv.* extérieurement.

extinct /ɪk'stɪŋkt/ *a.* (*species*) disparu; (*volcano, passion*) éteint. ∿**ion** /-kʃn/ *n.* extinction *f.*

extinguish /ɪk'stɪŋgwɪʃ/ *v.t.* éteindre. ∿**er** *n.* extincteur *m.*

extol /ɪk'stəʊl/ *v.t.* (*p.t.* **extolled**) exalter, chanter les louanges de.

extort /ɪk'stɔ:t/ *v.t.* extorquer (**from,** à). ∿**ion** /-ʃn/ *n.* (*jurid.*) extorsion (de fonds) *f.*

extortionate /ɪk'stɔ:ʃənət/ *a.* exorbitant.

extra /'ekstrə/ *a.* de plus, supplémentaire. —*adv.* plus (que d'habitude). ∿ **strong,** extra-fort. —*n.* (*additional thing*) supplément *m.*; (*cinema*) figurant(e) *m.* (*f.*). ∿ **charge,** supplément *m.* ∿ **time,** (*football*) prolongation *f.*

extra- /'ekstrə/ *pref.* extra-.

extract[1] /ɪk'strækt/ *v.t.* extraire; (*promise, tooth*) arracher; (*fig.*) obtenir. ∿**ion** /-kʃn/ *n.* extraction *f.*

extract[2] /'ekstrækt/ *n.* extrait *m.*

extra-curricular /ekstrəkə'rɪkjʊlə(r)/ *a.* parascolaire.

extradit|e /'ekstrədaɪt/ *v.t.* extrader. ∿**ion** /-'dɪʃn/ *n.* extradition *f.*

extramarital /ekstrə'mærɪtl/ *a.* extra-conjugal.

extramural /ekstrə'mjʊərəl/ *a.* (*univ.*) hors faculté.

extraordinary /ɪk'strɔ:dnrɪ/ *a.* extraordinaire.

extravagan|t /ɪk'strævəgənt/ *a.* extravagant; (*wasteful*) prodigue. ∿**ce** *n.* extravagance *f.*; prodigalité *f.*

extrem|e /ɪk'stri:m/ *a. & n.* extrême (*m.*). ∿**ely** *adv.* extrêmement. ∿**ist** *n.* extrémiste *m./f.*

extremity /ɪk'stremətɪ/ *n.* extrémité *f.*

extricate /'ekstrɪkeɪt/ *v.t.* dégager.

extrovert /'ekstrəvɜ:t/ *n.* extraverti(e) *m.* (*f.*).

exuberan|t /ɪg'zju:bərənt/ *a.* exubérant. ∿**ce** *n.* exubérance *f.*

exude /ɪg'zju:d/ *v.t.* (*charm etc.*) dégager.

exult /ɪg'zʌlt/ *v.i.* exulter.

eye /aɪ/ *n.* œil *m.* (*pl.* yeux). —*v.t.* (*p.t.* **eyed,** *pres. p.* **eyeing**) regarder. **keep an** ∿ **on,** surveiller. ∿**-catching** *a.* qui attire l'attention. ∿**-opener** *n.* révélation *f.* ∿**-shadow** *n.* ombre à paupières *f.*

eyeball /'aɪbɔ:l/ *n.* globe oculaire *m.*

eyebrow /'aɪbraʊ/ *n.* sourcil *m.*

eyeful /'aɪfʊl/ *n.* **get an** ∿, (*fam.*) se rincer l'œil.

eyelash /'aɪlæʃ/ *n.* cil *m.*

eyelet /'aɪlɪt/ *n.* œillet *m.*

eyelid /'aɪlɪd/ *n.* paupière *f.*

eyesight /'aɪsaɪt/ *n.* vue *f.*

eyesore /'aɪsɔ:(r)/ *n.* horreur *f.*

eyewitness /'aɪwɪtnɪs/ *n.* témoin oculaire *m.*

F

fable /'feɪbl/ *n.* fable *f.*

fabric /'fæbrɪk/ *n.* (*cloth*) tissu *m.*

fabrication /fæbrɪ'keɪʃn/ *n.* (*invention*) invention *f.*

fabulous /'fæbjʊləs/ *a.* fabuleux; (*marvellous: fam.*) formidable.

façade /fə'sɑ:d/ *n.* façade *f.*

face /feɪs/ *n.* visage *m.*, figure *f.*; (*aspect*) face *f.*; (*of clock*) cadran *m.* ∿ **en face de;** (*risk*) devoir affronter; (*confront*) faire face à, affronter. —*v.i.* se tourner; (*of house*) être exposé. ∿**-flannel** *n.* gant de toilette *m.* ∿**-lift** *n.* lifting *m.* **give a** ∿**-lift to,** donner un coup de neuf à. ∿ **value,** (*comm.*) valeur nominale. **take sth. at** ∿ **value,** prendre qch. au premier degré. ∿ **to face,** face à face. ∿ **up/down,** tourné vers le haut/bas. ∿ **up to,** faire face à. **in the** ∿ **of,** ∿**d with,** face à. **make a (funny)** ∿, faire une grimace.

faceless /'feɪslɪs/ *a.* anonyme.

facet /'fæsɪt/ n. facette f.
facetious /fə'siːʃəs/ a. facétieux.
facial /'feɪʃl/ a. de la face, facial. —n.
soin du visage m.
facile /'fæsaɪl, Amer. 'fæsl/ a. facile,
superficiel.
facilitate /fə'sɪlɪteɪt/ v.t. faciliter.
facilit|y /fə'sɪlətɪ/ n. facilité f. **~ies**,
(equipment) équipements m. pl.
facing /'feɪsɪŋ/ n. parement m. —prep.
en face de. —a. en face.
facsimile /fæk'sɪmǝlɪ/ n. facsimilé m. **~
transmission**, télécopiage m.
fact /fækt/ n. fait m. **as a matter of ~, in
~**, en fait.
faction /'fækʃn/ n. faction f.
factor /'fæktə(r)/ n. facteur m.
factory /'fæktərɪ/ n. usine f.
factual /'fæktʃʊəl/ a. basé sur les faits.
faculty /'fækltɪ/ n. faculté f.
fad /fæd/ n. manie f., folie f.
fade /feɪd/ v.i. (sound) s'affaiblir;
(memory) s'évanouir; (flower) se faner;
(material) déteindre; (colour) passer.
fag /fæg/ n. (chore: fam.) corvée f.;
(cigarette: sl.) sèche f.; (homosexual:
Amer., sl.) pédé m.
fagged /fægd/ a. (tired) éreinté.
fail /feɪl/ v.i. échouer; (grow weak)
(s'af)faiblir; (run short) manquer; (engine
etc.) tomber en panne. —v.t. (exam)
échouer à; (candidate) refuser, recaler;
(disappoint) décevoir. **~ s.o.**, (of words
etc.) manquer à qn. **~ to do**, (not do) ne
pas faire; (not be able) ne pas réussir à
faire. **without ~**, à coup sûr.
failing /'feɪlɪŋ/ n. défaut m. —prep. à
défaut de.
failure /'feɪljə(r)/ n. échec m.; (person)
raté(e) m. (f.); (breakdown) panne f. **~
to do**, (inability) incapacité de faire f.
faint /feɪnt/ a. (-er, -est) léger, faible.
—v.i. s'évanouir. —n. évanouissement
m. **feel ~**, (ill) se trouver mal. **I haven't
the ~est idea**, je n'en ai pas la moindre
idée. **~-hearted** a. timide. **~ly** adv.
(weakly) faiblement; (slightly) légèrement. **~ness** n. faiblesse f.
fair[1] /feə(r)/ n. foire f. **~-ground** n.
champ de foire m.
fair[2] /feə(r)/ a. (-er, -est) (hair, person)
blond; (skin etc.) clair; (just) juste,
équitable; (weather) beau; (amount,
quality) raisonnable. —adv. (play)
loyalement. **~ play**, le fair-play. **~ly**
adv. (justly) équitablement; (rather)
assez. **~ness** n. justice f.
fairy /'feərɪ/ n. fée f. **~ story, ~-tale** n.
conte de fées m.

faith /feɪθ/ n. foi. f. **~-healer** n.
guérisseulr, -se m., f.
faithful /'feɪθfl/ a. fidèle. **~ly** adv.
fidèlement. **~ness** n. fidélité f.
fake /feɪk/ n. (forgery) faux m.; (person)
imposteur m. **it is a ~**, c'est faux. —a.
faux. —v.t. (copy) faire un faux de;
(alter) falsifier, truquer; (illness)
simuler.
falcon /'fɔːlkən/ n. faucon m.
fall /fɔːl/ v.i. (p.t. **fell**, p.p. **fallen**)
tomber. —n. chute f.; (autumn: Amer.)
automne m. **Niagara F~s**, chutes de
Niagara. **~ back on**, se rabattre sur. **~
behind**, prendre du retard. **~ down** or
off, tomber. **~ for**, (person: fam.)
tomber amoureux de; (a trick: fam.) se
laisser prendre à. **~ in**, (mil.) se mettre
en rangs. **~ off**, (decrease) diminuer.
~ out, se brouiller (**with**, avec). **~-out**
n. retombées f. pl. **~ over**, tomber (par
terre). **~ short**, être insuffisant. **~
through**, (plans) tomber à l'eau. **~**
fallacy /'fæləsɪ/ n. erreur f.
fallible /'fæləbl/ a. faillible.
fallow /'fæləʊ/ a. en jachère.
false /fɔːls/ a. faux. **~hood** n. mensonge
m. **~ly** adv. faussement. **~ness** n.
fausseté f.
falsetto /fɔːl'setəʊ/ n. (pl. -os) fausset m.
falsify /'fɔːlsɪfaɪ/ v.t. falsifier.
falter /'fɔːltə(r)/ v.i. vaciller; (nerve)
faire défaut.
fame /feɪm/ n. renommée f.
famed /feɪmd/ a. renommé.
familiar /fə'mɪlɪə(r)/ a. familier. **be ~
with**, connaître. **~ity** /-'ærətɪ/ n.
familiarité f. **~ize** v.t. familiariser.
family /'fæməlɪ/ n. famille f. —a. de
famille, familial.
famine /'fæmɪn/ n. famine f.
famished /'fæmɪʃt/ a. affamé.
famous /'feɪməs/ a. célèbre. **~ly** adv.
(very well: fam.) à merveille.
fan[1] /fæn/ n. ventilateur m.; (hand-held)
éventail m. —v.t. (p.t. **fanned**) éventer;
(fig.) attiser. —v.i. **~ out**, se déployer
en éventail. **~ belt**, courroie de
ventilateur f.
fan[2] /fæn/ n. (of person) fan m./f.,
admirateur, -trice m., f.; (enthusiast)
fervent(e) m. (f.), passionné(e) m. (f.).
fanatic /fə'nætɪk/ n. fanatique m./f. **~al**
a. fanatique. **~ism** /-sɪzəm/ n.
fanatisme m.
fancier /'fænsɪə(r)/ n. (dog/etc.) ~,
amateur de chiens/etc.) m.
fanciful /'fænsɪfl/ a. fantaisiste.
fancy /'fænsɪ/ n. (whim, fantasy)

fantaisie *f.*; (*liking*) goût *m.* —*a.* (*buttons etc.*) fantaisie *invar.*; (*prices*) extravagant; (*impressive*) impressionnant. —*v.t.* s'imaginer; (*want: fam.*) avoir envie de; (*like: fam.*) aimer. **take a ~ to s.o.**, se prendre d'affection pour qn. **it took my ~,** ça m'a plu. **~ dress,** déguisement *m.*

fanfare /'fænfeə(r)/ *n.* fanfare *f.*

fang /fæŋ/ *n.* (*of dog etc.*) croc *m.*; (*of snake*) crochet *m.*

fanlight /'fænlaɪt/ *n.* imposte *f.*

fantastic /fæn'tæstɪk/ *a.* fantastique.

fantas|y /'fæntəsɪ/ *n.* fantaisie *f.*; (*daydream*) fantasme *m.* **~ize** *v.i.* faire des fantasmes.

far /fɑː(r)/ *adv.* loin; (*much*) beaucoup; (*very*) très. —*a.* lointain; (*end, side*) autre. **~ away, ~ off,** au loin. **as ~ as,** (*up to*) jusqu'à. **as ~ as I know,** autant que je sache. **~-away** *a.* lointain. **by ~,** de loin. **~ from,** loin de. **the Far East,** l'Extrême-Orient *m.* **~-fetched** *a.* bizarre, exagéré. **~-reaching** *a.* de grande portée.

farc|e /fɑːs/ *n.* farce *f.* **~ical** *a.* ridicule, grotesque.

fare /feə(r)/ *n.* (*prix du*) billet *m.*; (*food*) nourriture *f.* —*v.i.* (*progress*) aller; (*manage*) se débrouiller.

farewell /feə'wel/ *int.* & *n.* adieu (*m.*).

farm /fɑːm/ *n.* ferme *f.* —*v.t.* cultiver. —*v.i.* être fermier. **~ out,** céder en sous-traitance. **~ worker,** ouvrier, -ère agricole *m.*, *f.* **~er** *n.* fermier *m.* **~ing** *n.* agriculture *f.*

farmhouse /'fɑːmhaʊs/ *n.* ferme *f.*

farmyard /'fɑːmjɑːd/ *n.* basse-cour *f.*

fart /fɑːt/ *v.i.* péter. —*n.* pet *m.*

farth|er /'fɑːðə(r)/ *adv.* plus loin. —*a.* plus éloigné. **~est** *adv.* le plus loin; *a.* le plus éloigné.

fascinat|e /'fæsɪneɪt/ *v.t.* fasciner. **~ion** /-'neɪʃn/ *n.* fascination *f.*

Fascis|t /'fæʃɪst/ *n.* fasciste *m./f.* **~m** /-zəm/ *n.* fascisme *m.*

fashion /'fæʃn/ *n.* (*current style*) mode *f.*; (*manner*) façon *f.* —*v.t.* façonner. **~ designer,** styliste *m./f.* **in ~,** à la mode. **out of ~,** démodé. **~able** *a.*, **~ably** *adv.* à la mode.

fast[1] /fɑːst/ *a.* (**-er, -est**) rapide; (*colour*) grand teint *invar.*, fixe; (*firm*) fixe, solide. —*adv.* vite; (*firmly*) ferme. **be ~,** (*clock etc.*) avancer. **~ asleep,** profondément endormi. **~ food,** fast food *m.* restauration rapide *f.*

fast[2] /fɑːst/ *v.i.* (*go without food*) jeûner. —*n.* jeûne *m.*

fasten /'fɑːsn/ *v.t./i.* (s')attacher. **~er, ~ing** *ns.* attache *f.*, fermeture *f.*

fastidious /fə'stɪdɪəs/ *a.* difficile.

fat /fæt/ *n.* graisse *f.*; (*on meat*) gras *m.* —*a.* (**fatter, fattest**) gros, gras; (*meat*) gras; (*sum, volume: fig.*) gros. **a ~ lot,** (*sl.*) bien peu (**of,** de). **~-head** *n.* (*fam.*) imbécile *m.*,*f.* **~ness** *n.* corpulence *f.*

fatal /'feɪtl/ *a.* mortel; (*fateful, disastrous*) fatal. **~ity** /fə'tælətɪ/ *n.* mort *m.* **~ly** *adv.* mortellement.

fatalist /'feɪtəlɪst/ *n.* fataliste *m./f.*

fate /feɪt/ *n.* (*controlling power*) destin *m.*, sort *m.*; (*one's lot*) sort *m.* **~ful** *a.* fatidique.

fated /'feɪtɪd/ *a.* destiné (**to,** à).

father /'fɑːðə(r)/ *n.* père *m.* **~-in-law** *n.* (*pl.* **~s-in-law**) beau-père *m.* **~hood** *n.* paternité *f.* **~ly** *a.* paternel.

fathom /'fæðəm/ *n.* brasse *f.* (= *1,8 m.*). —*v.t.* **~ (out),** comprendre.

fatigue /fə'tiːg/ *n.* fatigue *f.* —*v.t.* fatiguer.

fatten /'fætn/ *v.t./i.* engraisser. **~ing** *a.* qui fait grossir.

fatty /'fætɪ/ *a.* gras; (*tissue*) adipeux. —*n.* (*person: fam.*) gros(se) *m.* (*f.*).

fatuous /'fætʃʊəs/ *a.* stupide.

faucet /'fɔːsɪt/ *n.* (*Amer.*) robinet *m.*

fault /fɔːlt/ *n.* (*defect, failing*) défaut *m.*; (*blame*) faute *f.*; (*geol.*) faille *f.* —*v.t.* **~ sth./s.o.,** trouver des défauts à qch./chez qn. **at ~,** fautif. **find ~ with,** critiquer. **~less** *a.* irréprochable. **~y** *a.* défectueux.

fauna /'fɔːnə/ *n.* faune *f.*

favour, (*Amer.*) **favor** /'feɪvə(r)/ *n.* faveur *f.* —*v.t.* favoriser; (*support*) être en faveur de; (*prefer*) préférer. **do s.o. a ~,** rendre service à qn. **in ~ of,** pour. **~able** *a.* favorable. **~ably** *adv.* favorablement.

favourit|e /'feɪvərɪt/ *a.* & *n.* favori(te) (*m.* (*f.*)). **~ism** *n.* favoritisme *m.*

fawn[1] /fɔːn/ *n.* faon *m.* —*a.* fauve.

fawn[2] /fɔːn/ *v.i.* **~ on,** flatter bassement, flagorner.

fax /fæks/ *n.* fax *m.*, télécopie *f.* —*v.t.* faxer, envoyer par télécopie. **~ machine,** télécopieur *m.*

FBI *abbr.* (*Federal Bureau of Investigation*) (*Amer.*) service d'enquêtes du Ministère de la Justice *m.*

fear /fɪə(r)/ *n.* crainte *f.*, peur *f.*; (*fig.*) risque *m.* —*v.t.* craindre. **for ~ of/that,** de peur de/que. **~ful** *a.* (*terrible*) affreux; (*timid*) craintif. **~less** *a.* intrépide. **~lessness** *n.* intrépidité *f.*

fearsome /'fɪəsəm/ a. redoutable.

feasib|le /'fi:zəbl/ a. faisable; (*likely*) plausible. **~ility** /-'bɪlətɪ/ n. possibilité f.; plausibilité f.

feast /fi:st/ n. festin m.; (*relig.*) fête f. —v.i. festoyer. —v.t. régaler. **~ on,** se régaler de.

feat /fi:t/ n. exploit m.

feather /'feðə(r)/ n. plume f. —v.t. **~ one's nest,** s'enrichir. **~ duster,** plumeau m.

featherweight /'feðəweɪt/ n. poids plume m. invar.

feature /'fi:tʃə(r)/ n. caractéristique f.; (*of person, face*) trait m.; (*film*) long métrage m.; (*article*) article vedette m. —v.t. représenter; (*give prominence to*) mettre en vedette. —v.i. figurer (**in,** dans).

February /'februərɪ/ n. février m.

feckless /'feklɪs/ a. inepte.

fed /fed/ see **feed**. —a. be **~ up,** (*fam.*) en avoir marre (**with,** de).

federa|l /'fedərəl/ a. fédéral. **~tion** /-'reɪʃn/ n. fédération f.

fee /fi:/ n. (*for entrance*) prix m. **~(s),** (*of doctor etc.*) honoraires m. pl.; (*of actor, artist*) cachet m.; (*for tuition*) frais m. pl.; (*for enrolment*) droits m. pl.

feeble /'fi:bl/ a. (**-er, -est**) faible. **~-minded** a. faible d'esprit.

feed /fi:d/ v.t. (p.t. **fed**) nourrir, donner à manger à; (*suckle*) allaiter; (*supply*) alimenter. —v.i. se nourrir (**on,** de). —n. nourriture f.; (*of baby*) tétée f. **~ in information,** rentrer des données. **~er** n. alimentation. f.

feedback /'fi:dbæk/ n. réaction(s) f. (pl.); (*med., techn.*) feed-back m.

feel /fi:l/ v.t. (p.t. **felt**) (*touch*) tâter; (*be conscious of*) sentir; (*emotion*) ressentir; (*experience*) éprouver; (*think*) estimer. —v.i. (*tired, lonely, etc.*) se sentir. **~ hot/thirsty/**etc., avoir chaud/soif/etc. **~ as if,** avoir l'impression que. **~ awful,** (*ill*) se sentir malade. **~ like,** (*want: fam.*) avoir envie de.

feeler /'fi:lə(r)/ n. antenne f. **put out a ~,** lancer un ballon d'essai.

feeling /'fi:lɪŋ/ n. sentiment m.; (*physical*) sensation f.

feet /fi:t/ see **foot**.

feign /feɪn/ v.t. feindre.

feint /feɪnt/ n. feinte f.

felicitous /fə'lɪsɪtəs/ a. heureux.

feline /'fi:laɪn/ a. félin.

fell[1] /fel/ v.t. (*cut down*) abattre.

fell[2] /fel/ see **fall**.

fellow /'feləʊ/ n. compagnon m.,

camarade m.; (*of society*) membre m.; (*man: fam.*) type m. **~-countryman** n. compatriote m. **~-passenger, ~-traveller** n. compagnon de voyage m. **~-ship** n. camaraderie f.; (*group*) association f.

felony /'felənɪ/ n. crime m.

felt[1] /felt/ n. feutre m. **~-tip** n. feutre m.

felt[2] /felt/ see **feel**.

female /'fi:meɪl/ a. (*animal etc.*) femelle; (*voice, sex, etc.*) féminin. —n. femme f.; (*animal*) femelle f.

feminin|e /'femənɪn/ a. & n. féminin (m.). **~ity** /-'nɪnətɪ/ n. féminité f.

feminist /'femɪnɪst/ n. féministe m./f.

fenc|e /fens/ n. barrière f.; (*person: jurid.*) receleulr, -se m., f. —v.t. **~e (in),** clôturer. —v.i. (*sport*) faire de l'escrime. **~er** n. escrimeulr, -se m., f. **~ing** n. escrime f.

fend /fend/ v.i. **~ for o.s.,** se débrouiller tout seul. —v.t. **~ off,** (*blow, attack*) parer.

fender /'fendə(r)/ n. (*for fireplace*) garde-feu m. invar.; (*mudguard: Amer.*) garde-boue m. invar.

fennel /'fenl/ n. (*culin.*) fenouil m.

ferment[1] /fə'ment/ v.t./i. (faire) fermenter. **~ation** /fɜ:men'teɪʃn/ n. fermentation f.

ferment[2] /'fɜ:ment/ n. ferment m.; (*excitement: fig.*) agitation f.

fern /fɜ:n/ n. fougère f.

feroc|ious /fə'rəʊʃəs/ a. féroce. **~ity** /-'rɒsətɪ/ n. férocité f.

ferret /'ferɪt/ n. (*animal*) furet m. —v.i. (p.t. **ferreted**) fureter. —v.t. **~ out,** dénicher.

ferry /'ferɪ/ n. ferry m., bac m. —v.t. transporter.

fertil|e /'fɜ:taɪl, Amer. 'fɜ:tl/ a. fertile; (*person, animal*) fécond. **~ity** /fə'tɪlətɪ/ n. fertilité f.; fécondité f. **~ize** /-əlaɪz/ v.t. fertiliser; féconder.

fertilizer /'fɜ:təlaɪzə(r)/ n. engrais m.

fervent /'fɜ:vənt/ a. fervent.

fervour /'fɜ:və(r)/ n. ferveur f.

fester /'festə(r)/ v.i. (*wound*) suppurer; (*fig.*) rester sur le cœur.

festival /'festɪvl/ n. festival m.; (*relig.*) fête f.

festiv|e /'festɪv/ a. de fête, gai. **~e season,** période des fêtes f. **~ity** /fe'stɪvətɪ/ n. réjouissances f. pl.

festoon /fe'stu:n/ v.i. **~ with,** orner de.

fetch /fetʃ/ v.t. (*go for*) aller chercher; (*bring person*) amener; (*bring thing*) apporter; (*be sold for*) rapporter.

fête /feɪt/ n. fête f. —v.t. fêter.

fetid /'fetɪd/ a. fétide.

fetish /'fetɪʃ/ n. (object) fétiche m.; (psych.) obsession f.

fetter /'fetə(r)/ v.t. enchaîner. ~s n. pl. chaînes f. pl.

feud /fjuːd/ n. querelle f.

feudal /'fjuːdl/ a. féodal.

fever /'fiːvə(r)/ n. fièvre f. ~ish a. fiévreux.

few /fjuː/ a. & n. peu (de). ~ **books**, peu de livres. **they are** ~, ils sont peu nombreux. **a** ~ a. quelques; n. quelques-un(e)s. **a good** ~, **quite a** ~, (fam.) bon nombre (de). ~er a. & n. moins (de). **be** ~er, être moins nombreux (than, que). ~est a. & n. le moins (de).

fiancé /fɪ'ɒnseɪ/ n. fiancé m.

fiancée /fɪ'ɒnseɪ/ n. fiancée f.

fiasco /fɪ'æskəʊ/ n. (pl. -os) fiasco m.

fib /fɪb/ n. mensonge m. ~ber n. menteulr, -se m., f.

fibre, Amer. **fiber** /'faɪbə(r)/ n. fibre f. ~ **optics**, fibres optiques.

fibreglass, Amer. **fiberglass** /'faɪbəɡlɑːs/ n. fibre de verre f.

fickle /'fɪkl/ a. inconstant.

fiction /'fɪkʃn/ n. fiction f. (works of) ~, romans m. pl. ~al a. fictif.

fictitious /fɪk'tɪʃəs/ a. fictif.

fiddle /'fɪdl/ n. (fam.) violon m.; (swindle: sl.) combine f. —v.i. (sl.) frauder. —v.t. (sl.) falsifier. ~ **with**, (fam.) tripoter. ~r /-ə(r)/ n. (fam.) violoniste m./f.

fidelity /fɪ'delətɪ/ n. fidélité f.

fidget /'fɪdʒɪt/ v.i. (p.t. **fidgeted**) remuer sans cesse. —n. **be a** ~, être remuant. ~ **with**, tripoter. ~y a. remuant.

field /fiːld/ n. champ m.; (sport) terrain m.; (fig.) domaine m. —v.t. (ball: cricket) bloquer. ~-**day** n. grande occasion f. ~-**glasses** n. pl. jumelles f. pl. F~ **Marshal**, maréchal m.

fieldwork /'fiːldwɜːk/ n. travaux pratiques m. pl.

fiend /fiːnd/ n. démon m. ~ish a. diabolique.

fierce /fɪəs/ a. (-er, -est) féroce; (storm, attack) violent. ~ness n. férocité f.; violence f.

fiery /'faɪərɪ/ a. (-ier, -iest) (hot) ardent; (spirited) fougueux.

fiesta /fɪ'estə/ n. fiesta f.

fifteen /fɪf'tiːn/ a. & n. quinze (m.). ~th a. & n. quinzième (m./f.).

fifth /fɪfθ/ a. & n. cinquième (m./f.). ~ **column**, cinquième colonne f.

fift|y /'fɪftɪ/ a. & n. cinquante (m.). ~ieth

a. & n. cinquantième (m./f.). **a** ~y-**fifty chance**, (equal) une chance sur deux.

fig /fɪɡ/ n. figue f.

fight /faɪt/ v.i. (p.t. **fought**) se battre; (struggle: fig.) lutter; (quarrel) se disputer. —v.t. se battre avec; (evil etc.: fig.) lutter contre. —n. (struggle) lutte f.; (quarrel) dispute f.; (brawl) bagarre f.; (mil.) combat m. ~ **back**, se défendre. ~ **off**, surmonter. ~ **over sth.**, se disputer qch. ~ **shy of**, fuir devant. ~er n. (brawler, soldier) combattant m.; (fig.) battant m.; (aircraft) chasseur m. ~ing n. combats m. pl.

figment /'fɪɡmənt/ n. invention f.

figurative /'fɪɡjərətɪv/ a. figuré.

figure /'fɪɡə(r)/ n. (number) chiffre m.; (diagram) figure f.; (shape) forme f.; (body) ligne f. ~s, arithmétique f. —v.t. s'imaginer. —v.i. (appear) figurer. ~ **out**, comprendre. ~-**head** n. (person with no real power) prête-nom m. ~ **of speech**, façon de parler f. **that** ~s, (Amer., fam.) c'est logique.

filament /'fɪləmənt/ n. filament m.

filch /fɪltʃ/ v.t. voler, piquer.

fil|e¹ /faɪl/ n. (tool) lime f. —v.t. limer. ~ings n. pl. limaille f.

fil|e² /faɪl/ n. dossier m., classeur m.; (comput.) fichier m.; (row) file f. —v.t. (papers) classer; (jurid.) déposer. —v.i. ~e **in**, entrer en file. ~e **past**, défiler devant. ~ing **cabinet**, classeur m.

fill /fɪl/ v.t./i. (se) remplir. —n. **eat one's** ~, manger à sa faim. **have had one's** ~, en avoir assez. ~ **in** or **up**, (form) remplir. ~ **out**, (get fat) grossir. ~ **up**, (auto.) faire le plein (d'essence).

fillet /'fɪlɪt, Amer. fɪ'leɪ/ n. filet m. —v.t. (p.t. **filleted**) découper en filets.

filling /'fɪlɪŋ/ n. (of tooth) plombage m.; (of sandwich) garniture f. ~ **station**, station-service f.

filly /'fɪlɪ/ n. pouliche f.

film /fɪlm/ n. film m.; (photo.) pellicule f. —v.t. filmer. ~-**goer** n. cinéphile m./f. ~ **star**, vedette de cinéma f.

filter /'fɪltə(r)/ n. filtre m.; (traffic signal) flèche f. —v.t./i. filtrer; (of traffic) suivre la flèche. ~ **coffee**, café-filtre m. ~-**tip** n. bout filtre m.

filth /fɪlθ, ~iness n. (filθ, fɪlθɪnəs/ n. saleté f. ~y a. sale.

fin /fɪn/ n. (of fish, seal) nageoire f.; (of shark) aileron m.

final /'faɪnl/ a. dernier; (conclusive) définitif. —n. (sport) finale f. ~ist n.

finaliste *m./f.* ~**ly** *adv.* (*lastly, at last*) enfin, finalement; (*once and for all*) définitivement.

finale /fɪ'nɑːlɪ/ *n.* (*mus.*) final(e) *m.*

finalize /'faɪnəlaɪz/ *v.t.* mettre au point, fixer.

finan|ce /'faɪnæns/ *n.* finance *f.* —*a.* financier. —*v.t.* financer. ~**ier** /-'nænsɪə(r)/ *n.* financier *m.*

financial /faɪ'nænʃl/ *a.* financier. ~**ly** *adv.* financièrement.

find /faɪnd/ *v.t.* (*p.t.* **found**) trouver; (*sth. lost*) retrouver. —*n.* trouvaille *f.* ~ **out** *v.t.* découvrir; *v.i.* se renseigner (**about,** sur). ~**ings** *n. pl.* conclusions *f. pl.*

fine[1] /faɪn/ *n.* amende *f.* —*v.t.* condamner à une amende.

fine[2] /faɪn/ *a.* (**-er, -est**) fin; (*excellent*) beau. —*adv.* (très) bien; (*small*) fin. ~ **arts,** beaux-arts *m. pl.* ~**ly** *adv.* (*admirably*) magnifiquement; (*cut*) fin.

finery /'faɪnərɪ/ *n.* atours *m. pl.*

finesse /fɪ'nes/ *n.* finesse *f.*

finger /'fɪŋgə(r)/ *n.* doigt *m.* —*v.t.* palper. ~**-nail** *n.* ongle *m.* ~**-stall** *n.* doigtier *m.*

fingerprint /'fɪŋgəprɪnt/ *n.* empreinte digitale *f.*

fingertip /'fɪŋgətɪp/ *n.* bout du doigt *m.*

finicking, finicky /'fɪnɪkɪŋ, 'fɪnɪkɪ/ *adjs.* méticuleux.

finish /'fɪnɪʃ/ *v.t./i.* finir. —*n.* fin *f.*; (*of race*) arrivée *f.*; (*appearance*) finition *f.* ~ **doing,** finir de faire. ~ **up doing,** finir par faire. ~ **up in,** (*land up in*) se retrouver à.

finite /'faɪnaɪt/ *a.* fini.

Fin|land /'fɪnlənd/ *n.* finlande *f.* ~**n** *n.* finlandais(e) *m.* (*f.*). ~**nish** *a.* finlandais; *n.* (*lang.*) finnois *m.*

fir /fɜː(r)/ *n.* sapin *m.*

fire /'faɪə(r)/ *n.* feu *m.*; (*conflagration*) incendie *m.*; (*heater*) radiateur *m.* —*v.t.* (*bullet etc.*) tirer; (*dismiss*) renvoyer; (*fig.*) enflammer. —*v.i.* tirer (**at,** sur). ~ **a gun,** tirer un coup de revolver *or* de fusil. **set** ~ **to,** mettre le feu à. ~ **alarm,** avertisseur d'incendie *m.* ~ **brigade,** pompiers *m. pl.* ~**-engine** *n.* voiture de pompiers *f.* ~**-escape** *n.* escalier de secours *m.* ~ **extinguisher,** extincteur d'incendie *m.* ~ **station,** caserne de pompiers *f.*

firearm /'faɪərɑːm/ *n.* arme à feu *f.*

firecracker /'faɪəkrækə(r)/ *n.* (*Amer.*) pétard *m.*

firelight /'faɪəlaɪt/ *n.* lueur du feu *f.*

fireman /'faɪəmən/ *n.* (*pl.* **-men**) pompier *m.*

fireplace /'faɪəpleɪs/ *n.* cheminée *f.*

fireside /'faɪəsaɪd/ *n.* coin du feu *m.*

firewood /'faɪəwʊd/ *n.* bois de chauffage *m.*

firework /'faɪəwɜːk/ *n.* feu d'artifice *m.*

firing-squad /'faɪərɪŋskwɒd/ *n.* peloton d'exécution *m.*

firm[1] /fɜːm/ *n.* firme *f.*, société *f.*

firm[2] /fɜːm/ *a.* (**-er, -est**) ferme; (*belief*) solide. ~**ly** *adv.* fermement. ~**ness** *n.* fermeté *f.*

first /fɜːst/ *a.* premier. —*n.* premier, -ière *m.*, *f.* —*adv.* d'abord, première-ment; (*arrive etc.*) le premier, la première. **at** ~, d'abord. **at** ~ **hand,** de première main. **at** ~ **sight,** à première vue. ~ **aid,** premiers soins *m. pl.* ~**-class** *a.* de première classe. ~ **floor,** (*Amer.*) rez-de-chaussée *m. invar.* ~ (**gear**), première (vitesse) *f.* **F**~ **Lady,** (*Amer.*) épouse du Président *f.* ~ **name,** prénom *m.* ~ **of all,** tout d'abord. ~**-rate** *a.* de premier ordre. ~**ly** *adv.* premièrement.

fiscal /'fɪskl/ *a.* fiscal.

fish /fɪʃ/ *n.* (*usually invar.*) poisson *m.* —*v.i.* pêcher. ~ **for,** (*cod etc.*) pêcher. ~ **out,** (*from water*) repêcher; (*take out: fam.*) sortir. ~ **shop,** poissonnerie *f.* ~**ing** *n.* pêche *f.* **go** ~**ing,** aller à la pêche. ~**ing rod,** canne à pêche *f.* ~**y** *a.* de poisson; (*fig.*) louche.

fisherman /'fɪʃəmən/ *n.* (*pl.* **-men**) *n.* pêcheur *m.*

fishmonger /'fɪʃmʌŋgə(r)/ *n.* pois-sonnier, -ière *m.*, *f.*

fission /'fɪʃn/ *n.* fission *f.*

fist /fɪst/ *n.* poing *m.*

fit[1] /fɪt/ *n.* (*bout*) accès *m.*, crise *f.*

fit[2] /fɪt/ *a.* (**fitter, fittest**) en bonne santé; (*proper*) convenable; (*good enough*) bon; (*able*) capable. —*v.t./i.* (*p.t.* **fitted**) (*clothes*) aller (à); (*match*) s'accorder (avec); (*put or go in or on*) (s')adapter (**to,** à); (*into space*) aller; (*install*) poser. —*n.* **be a good** ~, (*dress*) être à la bonne taille. **in no** ~ **state to do,** pas en état de faire. ~ **in,** *v.t.* caser; *v.i.* (*newcomer*) s'intégrer. ~ **out,** ~ **up,** équiper. ~**ness** *n.* santé *f.*; (*of remark*) justesse *f.*

fitful /'fɪtfl/ *a.* irrégulier.

fitment /'fɪtmənt/ *n.* meuble fixe *m.*

fitted /'fɪtɪd/ *a.* (*wardrobe*) encastré. ~ **carpet,** moquette *f.*

fitting /'fɪtɪŋ/ *a.* approprié. —*n.* essayage *m.* ~ **room,** cabine d'essayage *f.*

fittings /'fɪtɪŋz/ *n. pl.* (*in house*) installations *f. pl.*

five /faɪv/ *a. & n.* cinq (*m.*).

fiver /'faɪvə(r)/ *n.* (*fam.*) billet de cinq livres *m.*

fix /fɪks/ *v.t.* (*make firm, attach, decide*) fixer; (*mend*) réparer; (*deal with*) arranger. —*n.* **in a ~,** dans le pétrin. ~ **s.o. up with sth.,** trouver qch. à qn. **~ed** *a.* fixe.

fixation /fɪk'seɪʃn/ *n.* fixation *f.*

fixture /'fɪkstʃə(r)/ *n.* (*sport*) match *m.* **~s,** (*in house*) installations *f. pl.*

fizz /fɪz/ *v.i.* pétiller. —*n.* pétillement *m.* **~y** *a.* gazeux.

fizzle /'fɪzl/ *v.i.* pétiller. ~ **out,** (*plan etc.*) finir en queue de poisson.

flab /flæb/ *n.* (*fam.*) corpulence *f.* **~by** /'flæbɪ/ *a.* flasque.

flabbergast /'flæbəgɑːst/ *v.t.* sidérer, ahurir.

flag¹ /flæg/ *n.* drapeau *m.*; (*naut.*) pavillon *m.* —*v.t.* (*p.t.* **flagged**). ~ (**down**), faire signe de s'arrêter à. **~-pole** *n.* mât *m.*

flag² /flæg/ *v.i.* (*p.t.* **flagged**) (*weaken*) faiblir; (*sick person*) s'affaiblir; (*droop*) dépérir.

flagon /'flægən/ *n.* bouteille *f.*

flagrant /'fleɪgrənt/ *a.* flagrant.

flagstone /'flægstəʊn/ *n.* dalle *f.*

flair /fleə(r)/ *n.* flair *m.*

flak /flæk/ *n.* (*fam.*) critiques *f. pl.*

flak|e /fleɪk/ *n.* flocon *m.*; (*of paint, metal*) écaille *f.* —*v.i.* s'écailler. **~y** *a.* (*paint*) écailleux.

flamboyant /flæm'bɔɪənt/ *a.* (*colour*) éclatant; (*manner*) extravagant.

flame /fleɪm/ *n.* flamme *f.* —*v.i.* flamber. **burst into ~s,** exploser. **go up in ~s,** brûler.

flamingo /flə'mɪŋgəʊ/ *n.* (*pl.* **-os**) flamant (rose) *m.*

flammable /'flæməbl/ *a.* inflammable.

flan /flæn/ *n.* tarte *f.*; (*custard tart*) flan *m.*

flank /flæŋk/ *n.* flanc *m.* —*v.t.* flanquer.

flannel /'flænl/ *n.* flannelle *f.*; (*for face*) gant de toilette *m.*

flannelette /flænə'let/ *n.* pilou *m.*

flap /flæp/ *v.i./t.* (*p.t.* **flapped**) battre. ~ **its wings,** battre des ailes. —*n.* (*of pocket*) rabat *m.*; (*of table*) abattant *m.* **get into a ~,** (*fam.*) s'affoler.

flare /fleə(r)/ *v.i.* ~ **up,** s'enflammer, flamber; (*fighting*) éclater; (*person*) s'emporter. —*n.* flamboiement *m.*; (*mil.*) fusée éclairante *f.*; (*in skirt*) évasement *m.* **~d** *a.* (*skirt*) évasé.

flash /flæʃ/ *v.i.* briller; (*on and off*)

clignoter. —*v.t.* faire briller; (*aim torch*) diriger (**at**, sur); (*flaunt*) étaler. —*n.* éclair *m.*, éclat *m.*; (*of news, camera*) flash *m.* **in a ~,** en un éclair. ~ **one's headlights,** faire un appel de phares. ~ **past,** passer à toute vitesse.

flashback /'flæʃbæk/ *n.* retour en arrière *m.*

flashlight /'flæʃlaɪt/ *n.* (*torch*) lampe électrique *f.*

flashy /'flæʃɪ/ *a.* voyant.

flask /flɑːsk/ *n.* flacon *m.*; (*vacuum flask*) thermos *m./f. invar.* (P.).

flat /flæt/ *a.* (**flatter, flattest**) plat; (*tyre*) à plat; (*refusal*) catégorique; (*fare, rate*) fixe. —*adv.* (*say*) carrément. —*n.* (*rooms*) appartement *m.*; (*tyre: fam.*) crevaison *f.*; (*mus.*) bémol *m.* ~ **out,** (*drive*) à toute vitesse; (*work*) d'arrache-pied. **~-pack** *a.* en kit. **~ly** *adv.* catégoriquement. **~ness** *n.* égalité *f.*

flatten /'flætn/ *v.t./i.* (s')aplatir.

flatter /'flætə(r)/ *v.t.* flatter. **~er** *n.* flatteur, -se *m., f.* **~ing** *a.* flatteur. **~y** *n.* flatterie *f.*

flatulence /'flætjʊləns/ *n.* flatulence *f.*

flaunt /flɔːnt/ *v.t.* étaler, afficher.

flautist /'flɔːtɪst/ *n.* flûtiste *m./f.*

flavour, (*Amer.*) **flavor** /'fleɪvə(r)/ *n.* goût *m.*; (*of ice-cream etc.*) parfum *m.* —*v.t.* parfumer, assaisonner. **~ing** *n.* arôme synthétique *m.*

flaw /flɔː/ *n.* défaut *m.* **~ed** *a.* imparfait. **~less** *a.* parfait.

flax /flæks/ *n.* lin *m.* **~en** *a.* de lin.

flea /fliː/ *n.* puce *f.* ~ **market,** marché aux puces *m.*

fleck /flek/ *n.* petite tache *f.*

fled /fled/ *see* **flee.**

fledged /fledʒd/ *a.* **fully-~,** (*doctor etc.*) diplômé; (*member, citizen*) à part entière.

flee /fliː/ *v.i.* (*p.t.* **fled**) s'enfuir. —*v.t.* s'enfuir de; (*danger*) fuir.

fleece /fliːs/ *n.* toison *f.* —*v.t.* voler.

fleet /fliːt/ *n.* (*naut., aviat.*) flotte *f.* **a ~ of vehicles,** un parc automobile.

fleeting /'fliːtɪŋ/ *a.* très bref.

Flemish /'flemɪʃ/ *a.* flamand. —*n.* (*lang.*) flamand *m.*

flesh /fleʃ/ *n.* chair *f.* **one's (own) ~ and blood,** les siens *m. pl.* **~y** *a.* charnu.

flew /fluː/ *see* **fly².**

flex¹ /fleks/ *v.t.* (*knee etc.*) fléchir; (*muscle*) faire jouer.

flex² /fleks/ *n.* (*electr.*) fil souple *m.*

flexib|le /'fleksəbl/ *a.* flexible. **~ility** /-'bɪlətɪ/ *n.* flexibilité *f.*

flexitime /'fleksɪtaɪm/ n. horaire variable m.

flick /flɪk/ n. petit coup m. —v.t. donner un petit coup à. **~-knife** n. couteau à cran d'arrêt m. **~ through,** feuilleter.

flicker /'flɪkə(r)/ v.i. vaciller. —n. vacillement m.; (light) lueur f.

flier /'flaɪə(r)/ n. = **flyer.**

flies /flaɪz/ n. pl. (on trousers: fam.) braguette f.

flight[1] /flaɪt/ n. (of bird, plane, etc.) vol m. **~-deck** n. poste de pilotage m. **~ of stairs,** escalier m.

flight[2] /flaɪt/ n. (fleeing) fuite f. **put to ~,** mettre en fuite. **take ~,** prendre la fuite.

flimsy /'flɪmzɪ/ a. (-ier, -iest) (pej.) mince, peu solide.

flinch /flɪntʃ/ v.i. (wince) broncher; (draw back) reculer.

fling /flɪŋ/ v.t. (p.t. **flung**) jeter. —n. have a ~, faire la fête.

flint /flɪnt/ n. silex m.; (for lighter) pierre f.

flip /flɪp/ v.t. (p.t. **flipped**) donner un petit coup à. —n. chiquenaude f. **~ through,** feuilleter. **~-flops** n. pl. tongs f. pl.

flippant /'flɪpənt/ a. désinvolte.

flipper /'flɪpə(r)/ n. (of seal etc.) nageoire f.; (of swimmer) palme f.

flirt /flɜːt/ v.i. flirter. —n. flirteur, -se m., f. **~ation** /-'teɪʃn/ n. flirt m.

flit /flɪt/ v.i. (p.t. **flitted**) voltiger.

float /fləʊt/ v.t./i. (faire) flotter. —n. flotteur m.; (cart) char m.

flock /flɒk/ n. (of sheep etc.) troupeau m.; (of people) foule f. —v.i. venir en foule.

flog /flɒg/ v.t. (p.t. **flogged**) (beat) fouetter; (sell: sl.) vendre.

flood /flʌd/ n. inondation f.; (fig.) flot m. —v.t. inonder. —v.i. (building etc.) être inondé; (river) déborder; (people: fig.) affluer.

floodlight /'flʌdlaɪt/ n. projecteur m. —v.t. (p.t. **floodlit**) illuminer.

floor /flɔː(r)/ n. sol m., plancher m.; (for dancing) piste f.; (storey) étage m. —v.t. (knock down) terrasser; (baffle) stupéfier. **~-board** n. planche f.

flop /flɒp/ v.i. (p.t. **flopped**) s'agiter faiblement; (drop) s'affaler; (fail: sl.) échouer. —n. (sl.) échec m., fiasco m. **~py** a. lâche, flasque. **~py (disk),** disquette f.

flora /'flɔːrə/ n. flore f.

floral /'flɔːrəl/ a. floral.

florid /'flɒrɪd/ a. fleuri.

florist /'flɒrɪst/ n. fleuriste m./f.

flounce /flaʊns/ n. volant m.

flounder[1] /'flaʊndə(r)/ v.i. patauger (avec difficulté).

flounder[2] /'flaʊndə(r)/ n. (fish: Amer.) flet m., plie f.

flour /'flaʊə(r)/ n. farine f. **~y** a. farineux.

flourish /'flʌrɪʃ/ v.i. prospérer. —v.t. brandir. —n. geste élégant m.; (curve) floriture f.

flout /flaʊt/ v.t. faire fi de.

flow /fləʊ/ v.i. couler; (circulate) circuler; (traffic) s'écouler; (hang loosely) flotter. —n. (of liquid, traffic) écoulement m.; (of tide) flux m.; (of orders, words: fig.) flot m. **~ chart,** organigramme m. **~ in,** affluer. **~ into,** (of river) se jeter dans.

flower /'flaʊə(r)/ n. fleur f. —v.i. fleurir. **~-bed** n. plate-bande f. **~ed** a. à fleurs. **~y** a. fleuri.

flown /fləʊn/ see **fly**[2].

flu /fluː/ n. (fam.) grippe f.

fluctuat|e /'flʌktʃʊeɪt/ v.i. varier. **~ion** /-'eɪʃn/ n. variation f.

flue /fluː/ n. (duct) tuyau m.

fluen|t /'fluːənt/ a. (style) aisé. **be ~t (in a language),** parler (une langue) couramment. **~cy** n. facilité f. **~tly** adv. avec facilité; (lang.) couramment.

fluff /flʌf/ n. peluche(s) f. (pl.); (down) duvet m. **~y** a. pelucheux.

fluid /'fluːɪd/ a. & n. fluide (m.).

fluke /fluːk/ n. coup de chance m.

flung /flʌŋ/ see **fling.**

flunk /flʌŋk/ v.t./i. (Amer., fam.) être collé (à).

fluorescent /flʊə'resnt/ a. fluorescent.

fluoride /'flʊəraɪd/ n. (in toothpaste, water) fluor m.

flurry /'flʌrɪ/ n. (squall) rafale f.; (fig.) agitation f.

flush[1] /flʌʃ/ v.i. rougir. —v.t. nettoyer à grande eau. —n. (blush) rougeur f.; (fig.) excitation f. —a. **~ with,** (level with) au ras de. **~ the toilet,** tirer la chasse d'eau.

flush[2] /flʌʃ/ v.t. **~ out,** chasser.

fluster /'flʌstə(r)/ v.t. énerver.

flute /fluːt/ n. flûte f.

flutter /'flʌtə(r)/ v.i. voleter; (of wings) battre. —n. (of wings) battement m.; (fig.) agitation f.; (bet: fam.) pari m.

flux /flʌks/ n. changement continuel m.

fly[1] /flaɪ/ n. mouche f.

fly[2] /flaɪ/ v.i. (p.t. **flew,** p.p. **flown**) voler; (of passengers) voyager en avion; (of flag) flotter; (rush) filer. —v.t. (aircraft) piloter; (passengers, goods)

transporter par avion; (*flag*), arborer.
—*n.* (*of trousers*) braguette *f.* ~ **off**,
s'envoler.

flyer /'flaɪə(r)/ *n.* aviateur *m.*; (*circular*:
Amer.) prospectus *m.*

flying /'flaɪɪŋ/ *a.* (*saucer etc.*) volant.
—*n.* (*activity*) aviation *f.* ~ **buttress**,
arc-boutant *m.* **with ~ colours**, haut la
main. ~ **start**, excellent départ *m.* ~
visit, visite éclair *f.* (*a. invar.*).

flyover /'flaɪəʊvə(r)/ *n.* (*road*) toboggan
m., saut-de-mouton *m.*

flyweight /'flaɪweɪt/ *n.* poids mouche *m.*

foal /fəʊl/ *n.* poulain *m.*

foam /fəʊm/ *n.* écume *f.*, mousse *f.*
—*v.i.* écumer, mousser. ~ (**rubber**) *n.*
caoutchouc mousse *m.*

fob /fɒb/ *v.t.* (*p.t.* **fobbed**) ~ **off on** (**to**)
s.o., (*palm off*) refiler à qn. ~ **s.o. off
with**, forcer qn. à se contenter de.

focal /'fəʊkl/ *a.* focal.

focus /'fəʊkəs/ *n.* (*pl.* **-cuses** *or* **-ci** /-saɪ/)
foyer *m.*; (*fig.*) centre *m.* —*v.t./i.* (*p.t.*
focused) (faire) converger; (*instrument*) mettre au point; (*with camera*)
faire la mise au point (**on**, sur); (*fig.*)
(se) concentrer. **be in/out of** ~, être/ne
pas être au point.

fodder /'fɒdə(r)/ *n.* fourrage *m.*

foe /fəʊ/ *n.* ennemi(e) *m.(f.)*.

foetus /'fiːtəs/ *n.* (*pl.* **-tuses**) fœtus *m.*

fog /fɒg/ *n.* brouillard *m.* —*v.t./i.* (*p.t.*
fogged) (*window etc.*) (s')embuer. ~**-
horn** *n.* (*naut.*) corne de brume *f.* ~**gy**
a. brumeux. **it is** ~**gy**, il fait du
brouillard.

fog(e)y /'fəʊgɪ/ *n.* (**old**) ~, vieille
baderne *f.*

foible /'fɔɪbl/ *n.* faiblesse *f.*

foil[1] /fɔɪl/ *n.* (*tin foil*) papier
d'aluminium *m.*; (*fig.*) repoussoir *m.*

foil[2] /fɔɪl/ *v.t.* (*thwart*) déjouer.

foist /fɔɪst/ *v.t.* imposer (**on**, à).

fold[1] /fəʊld/ *v.t./i.* (se) plier; (*arms*)
croiser; (*fail*) s'effondrer. —*n.* pli *m.*
~**er** *n.* (*file*) chemise *f.*; (*leaflet*)
dépliant *m.* ~**ing** *a.* pliant.

fold[2] /fəʊld/ *n.* (*for sheep*) parc à
moutons *m.*; (*relig.*) bercail *m.*

foliage /'fəʊlɪɪdʒ/ *n.* feuillage *m.*

folk /fəʊk/ *n.* gens *m. pl.* ~**s**, parents *m.
pl.* —*a.* folklorique.

folklore /'fəʊklɔː(r)/ *n.* folklore *m.*

follow /'fɒləʊ/ *v.t./i.* suivre. **it** ~**s that**, il
s'ensuit que. ~ **suit**, en faire autant. ~
up, (*letter etc.*) donner suite à. ~**er** *n.*
partisan *m.* ~**ing** *n.* partisans *m. pl.*; *a.*
suivant; *prep.* à la suite de.

folly /'fɒlɪ/ *n.* sottise *f.*

foment /fəʊ'ment/ *v.t.* fomenter.

fond /fɒnd/ *a.* (**-er**, **-est**) (*loving*)
affectueux; (*hope*) cher. **be ~ of**, aimer.
~**ness** *n.* affection *f.*; (*for things*)
attachement *m.*

fondle /'fɒndl/ *v.t.* caresser.

food /fuːd/ *n.* nourriture *f.* —*a.*
alimentaire. **French ~**, la cuisine
française. ~ **processor**, robot
(ménager) *m.*

fool /fuːl/ *n.* idiot(e) *m. (f.)*. —*v.t.* duper.
—*v.i.* ~ **around**, faire l'idiot.

foolhardy /'fuːlhɑːdɪ/ *a.* téméraire.

foolish /'fuːlɪʃ/ *a.* idiot. ~**ly** *adv.*
sottement. ~**ness** *n.* sottise *f.*

foolproof /'fuːlpruːf/ *a.* infaillible.

foot /fʊt/ *n.* (*pl.* **feet**) pied *m.*; (*measure*)
pied *m.* (= *30.48 cm.*); (*of stairs*, *page*)
bas *m.* —*v.t.* (*bill*) payer. ~**-bridge** *n.*
passerelle *f.* **on ~**, à pied. **on** *or* **to one's
feet**, debout. **under s.o.'s feet**, dans les
jambes de qn.

footage /'fʊtɪdʒ/ *n.* (*of film*) métrage *m.*

football /'fʊtbɔːl/ *n.* (*ball*) ballon *m.*;
(*game*) football *m.* ~ **pools**, paris sur
les matchs de football *m. pl.* ~**er** *n.*
footballeur *m.*

foothills /'fʊthɪlz/ *n. pl.* contreforts *m.
pl.*

foothold /'fʊthəʊld/ *n.* prise *f.*

footing /'fʊtɪŋ/ *n.* prise (de pied) *f.*,
équilibre *m.*; (*fig.*) situation *f.* **on an
equal ~**, sur un pied d'égalité.

footlights /'fʊtlaɪts/ *n. pl.* rampe *f.*

footman /'fʊtmən/ *n.* (*pl.* **-men**) valet de
pied *m.*

footnote /'fʊtnəʊt/ *n.* note (en bas de la
page) *f.*

footpath /'fʊtpɑːθ/ *n.* sentier *m.*; (*at the
side of the road*) chemin *m.*

footprint /'fʊtprɪnt/ *n.* empreinte (de
pied) *f.*

footsore /'fʊtsɔː(r)/ *a.* **be ~**, avoir les
pieds douloureux.

footstep /'fʊtstep/ *n.* pas *m.*

footwear /'fʊtweə(r)/ *n.* chaussures *f. pl.*

for /fɔː(r), *unstressed* fə(r)/ *prep.* pour;
(*during*) pendant; (*before*) avant.
—*conj.* car. **a liking** ~, le goût de. **look
~**, chercher. **pay ~**, payer. **he has been
away ~**, il est absent depuis. **he
stopped ~ ten minutes**, il s'est arrêté
(pendant) dix minutes. **it continues ~
ten kilometres**, ça continue pendant dix
kilomètres. ~ **ever**, pour toujours. ~
good, pour de bon. ~ **all my work**,
malgré mon travail.

forage /'fɒrɪdʒ/ *v.i.* fourrager. —*n.*
fourrage *m.*

foray /'fɒreɪ/ n. incursion f.

forbade /fə'bæd/ see **forbid**.

forbear /fɔː'beə(r)/ v.t./i. (p.t. **forbore**, p.p. **forborne**) s'abstenir. ~**ance** n. patience f.

forbid /fə'bɪd/ v.t. (p.t. **forbade**, p.p. **forbidden**) interdire, défendre (**s.o. to do**, à qn. de faire). ~ **s.o. sth.**, interdire or défendre qch. à qn. **you are ~den to leave**, il vous est interdit de partir.

forbidding /fə'bɪdɪŋ/ a. menaçant.

force /fɔːs/ n. force f. —v.t. forcer. ~ **into**, faire entrer de force. ~ **on**, imposer à. **come into** ~, entrer en vigueur. **the ~s**, les forces armées f. pl. ~**d** a. forcé. ~**ful** a. énergique.

force-feed /'fɔːsfiːd/ v.t. (p.t. **-fed**) nourrir de force.

forceps /'fɔːseps/ n. invar. forceps m.

forcible /'fɔːsəbl/ a., ~**y** adv. de force.

ford /fɔːd/ n. gué m. —v.t. passer à gué.

fore /fɔː(r)/ a. antérieur. —n. **to the** ~, en évidence.

forearm /'fɔːrɑːm/ n. avant-bras m. invar.

foreboding /fɔː'bəʊdɪŋ/ n. pressentiment m.

forecast /'fɔːkɑːst/ v.t. (p.t. **forecast**) prévoir. —n. prévision f.

forecourt /'fɔːkɔːt/ n. (of garage) devant m.; (of station) cour f.

forefathers /'fɔːfɑːðəz/ n. pl. aïeux m. pl.

forefinger /'fɔːfɪŋɡə(r)/ n. index m.

forefront /'fɔːfrʌnt/ n. premier rang m.

foregone /'fɔːɡɒn/ a. ~ **conclusion**, résultat à prévoir m.

foreground /'fɔːɡraʊnd/ n. premier plan m.

forehead /'fɒrɪd/ n. front m.

foreign /'fɒrən/ a. étranger; (trade) extérieur; (travel) à l'étranger. ~**er** n. étranger, -ère m., f.

foreman /'fɔːmən/ n. (pl. **-men**) contremaître m.

foremost /'fɔːməʊst/ a. le plus éminent. —adv. **first and** ~, tout d'abord.

forename /'fɔːneɪm/ n. prénom m.

forensic /fə'rensɪk/ a. médicolégal. ~ **medicine**, médecine légale f.

foreplay /'fɔːpleɪ/ n. préliminaires m. pl.

forerunner /'fɔːrʌnə(r)/ n. précurseur m.

foresee /fɔː'siː/ v.t. (p.t. **-saw**, p.p. **-seen**) prévoir. ~**able** a. prévisible.

foreshadow /fɔː'ʃædəʊ/ v.t. présager, laisser prévoir.

foresight /'fɔːsaɪt/ n. prévoyance f.

forest /'fɒrɪst/ n. forêt f.

forestall /fɔː'stɔːl/ v.t. devancer.

forestry /'fɒrɪstrɪ/ n. sylviculture f.

foretaste /'fɔːteɪst/ n. avant-goût m.

foretell /fɔː'tel/ v.t. (p.t. **foretold**) prédire.

forever /fə'revə(r)/ adv. toujours.

forewarn /fɔː'wɔːn/ v.t. avertir.

foreword /'fɔːwɜːd/ n. avant-propos m. invar.

forfeit /'fɔːfɪt/ n. (penalty) peine f.; (in game) gage m. —v.t. perdre.

forgave /fə'ɡeɪv/ see **forgive**.

forge[1] /fɔːdʒ/ v.i. ~ **ahead**, aller de l'avant, avancer.

forge[2] /fɔːdʒ/ n. forge f. —v.t. (metal, friendship) forger; (copy) contrefaire, falsifier. ~**r** /-ə(r)/ n. faussaire m. ~**ry** /-ərɪ/ n. faux m., contrefaçon f.

forget /fə'ɡet/ v.t./i. (p.t. **forgot**, p.p. **forgotten**) oublier. ~**-me-not** n. myosotis m. ~ **o.s.**, s'oublier. ~**ful** a. distrait. ~**ful of**, oublieux de.

forgive /fə'ɡɪv/ v.t. (p.t. **forgave**, p.p. **forgiven**) pardonner (**s.o. for sth.**, qch. à qn.). ~**ness** n. pardon m.

forgo /fɔː'ɡəʊ/ v.t. (p.t. **forwent**, p.p. **forgone**) renoncer à.

fork /fɔːk/ n. fourchette f.; (for digging etc.) fourche f.; (in road) bifurcation f. —v.i. (road) bifurquer. ~**-lift truck**, chariot élévateur m. ~ **out**, (sl.) payer. ~**ed** a. fourchu.

forlorn /fə'lɔːn/ a. triste, abandonné. ~ **hope**, mince espoir m.

form /fɔːm/ n. forme f.; (document) formulaire m.; (schol.) classe f. —v.t./i. (se) former. **on** ~, en forme.

formal /'fɔːml/ a. officiel, en bonne et due forme; (person) compassé, cérémonieux; (dress) de cérémonie; (denial, grammar) formel; (language) soutenu. ~**ity** /-'mælətɪ/ n. cérémonial m.; (requirement) formalité f. ~**ly** adv. officiellement.

format /'fɔːmæt/ n. format m. —v.t. (p.t. **formatted**) (disk) initialiser, formater.

formation /fɔː'meɪʃn/ n. formation f.

formative /'fɔːmətɪv/ a. formateur.

former /'fɔːmə(r)/ a. ancien; (first of two) premier. —n. **the** ~, celui-là, celle-là. ~**ly** adv. autrefois.

formidable /'fɔːmɪdəbl/ a. redoutable, terrible.

formula /'fɔːmjʊlə/ n. (pl. **-ae** /-iː/ or **-as**) formule f.

formulate /'fɔːmjʊleɪt/ v.t. formuler.

forsake /fə'seɪk/ v.t. (p.t. **forsook**, p.p. **forsaken**) abandonner.

fort /fɔːt/ n. (mil.) fort m.

forte /'fɔːteɪ/ n. (talent) fort m.

forth /fɔːθ/ *adv.* en avant. **and so ~,** et ainsi de suite. **go back and ~,** aller et venir.

forthcoming /fɔːθ'kʌmɪŋ/ *a.* à venir, prochain; (*sociable*: *fam.*) communicatif.

forthright /'fɔːθraɪt/ *a.* direct.

forthwith /fɔːθ'wɪθ/ *adv.* sur-le-champ.

fortif|y /'fɔːtɪfaɪ/ *v.t.* fortifier. **~ication** /-ɪ'keɪʃn/ *n.* fortification *f.*

fortitude /'fɔːtɪtjuːd/ *n.* courage *m.*

fortnight /'fɔːtnaɪt/ *n.* quinze jours *m. pl.*, quinzaine *f.* **~ly** *a.* bimensuel; *adv.* tous les quinze jours.

fortress /'fɔːtrɪs/ *n.* forteresse *f.*

fortuitous /fɔː'tjuːɪtəs/ *a.* fortuit.

fortunate /'fɔːtʃənət/ *a.* heureux. **be ~,** avoir de la chance. **~ly** *adv.* heureusement.

fortune /'fɔːtʃuːn/ *n.* fortune *f.* **~-teller** *n.* diseuse de bonne aventure *f.* **have the good ~ to,** avoir la chance de.

fort|y /'fɔːtɪ/ *a. & n.* quarante (*m.*). **~y winks,** un petit somme. **~ieth** *a. & n.* quarantième (*m./f.*).

forum /'fɔːrəm/ *n.* forum *m.*

forward /'fɔːwəd/ *a.* en avant; (*advanced*) précoce; (*pert*) effronté. —*n.* (*sport*) avant *m.* —*adv.* en avant. —*v.t.* (*letter*) faire suivre; (*goods*) expédier; (*fig.*) favoriser. **come ~,** se présenter. **go ~,** avancer. **~ness** *n.* précocité *f.*

forwards /'fɔːwədz/ *adv.* en avant.

fossil /'fɒsl/ *n. & a.* fossile (*m.*).

foster /'fɒstə(r)/ *v.t.* (*promote*) encourager; (*child*) élever. **~-child** *n.* enfant adoptif *m.* **~-mother** *n.* mère adoptive *f.*

fought /fɔːt/ *see* **fight**.

foul /faʊl/ *a.* (**-er, -est**) (*smell, weather, etc.*) infect; (*place, action*) immonde; (*language*) ordurier. —*n.* (*football*) faute *f.* —*v.t.* souiller, encrasser. **~-mouthed** *a.* au langage ordurier. **~ play,** jeu irrégulier *m.*; (*crime*) acte criminel *m.* **~ up,** (*sl.*) gâcher.

found¹ /faʊnd/ *see* **find**.

found² /faʊnd/ *v.t.* fonder. **~ation** /-'deɪʃn/ *n.* fondation *f.*; (*basis*) fondement *m.*; (*make-up*) fond de teint *m.* **~er¹** *n.* fondateur, -trice *m., f.*

founder² /'faʊndə(r)/ *v.i.* sombrer.

foundry /'faʊndrɪ/ *n.* fonderie *f.*

fountain /'faʊntɪn/ *n.* fontaine *f.* **~-pen** *n.* stylo à encre *m.*

four /fɔː(r)/ *a. & n.* quatre (*m.*). **~fold** *a.* quadruple; *adv.* au quadruple. **~th** *a. & n.* quatrième (*m./f.*). **~-wheel drive,**

quatre roues motrices; (*car*) quatre-quatre *f.*

foursome /'fɔːsəm/ *n.* partie à quatre *f.*

fourteen /fɔː'tiːn/ *a. & n.* quatorze (*m.*). **~th** *a. & n.* quatorzième (*m./f.*).

fowl /faʊl/ *n.* volaille *f.*

fox /fɒks/ *n.* renard *m.* —*v.t.* (*baffle*) mystifier; (*deceive*) tromper.

foyer /'fɔɪeɪ/ *n.* (*hall*) foyer *m.*

fraction /'frækʃn/ *n.* fraction *f.*

fracture /'fræktʃə(r)/ *n.* fracture *f.* —*v.t./i.* (se) fracturer.

fragile /'frædʒaɪl, *Amer.* 'frædʒəl/ *a.* fragile.

fragment /'frægmənt/ *n.* fragment *m.* **~ary** *a.* fragmentaire.

fragran|t /'freɪgrənt/ *a.* parfumé. **~ce** *n.* parfum *m.*

frail /freɪl/ *a.* (**-er, -est**) frêle.

frame /freɪm/ *n.* charpente *f.*; (*of picture*) cadre *m.*; (*of window*) châssis *m.*; (*of spectacles*) monture *f.* —*v.t.* encadrer; (*fig.*) formuler; (*jurid., sl.*) monter un coup contre. **~ of mind,** humeur *f.*

framework /'freɪmwɜːk/ *n.* structure *f.*; (*context*) cadre *m.*

franc /fræŋk/ *n.* franc *m.*

France /frɑːns/ *n.* France *f.*

franchise /'fræntʃaɪz/ *n.* (*pol.*) droit de vote *m.*; (*comm.*) franchise *f.*

Franco- /'fræŋkəʊ/ *pref.* franco-.

frank¹ /fræŋk/ *a.* franc. **~ly** *adv.* franchement. **~ness** *n.* franchise *f.*

frank² /fræŋk/ *v.t.* affranchir.

frantic /'fræntɪk/ *a.* frénétique. **~ with,** fou de.

fratern|al /frə'tɜːnl/ *a.* fraternel. **~ity** *n.* (*bond*) fraternité *f.*; (*group, club*) confrérie *f.*

fraternize /'frætənaɪz/ *v.i.* fraterniser (**with,** avec).

fraud /frɔːd/ *n.* (*deception*) fraude *f.*; (*person*) imposteur *m.* **~ulent** *a.* frauduleux.

fraught /frɔːt/ *a.* (*tense*) tendu. **~ with,** chargé de.

fray¹ /freɪ/ *n.* rixe *f.*

fray² /freɪ/ *v.t./i.* (s')effilocher.

freak /friːk/ *n.* phénomène *m.* —*a.* anormal. **~ish** *a.* anormal.

freckle /'frekl/ *n.* tache de rousseur *f.* **~d** *a.* couvert de taches de rousseur.

free /friː/ *a.* (**freer** /'friːə(r)/, **freest** /'friːɪst/) libre; (*gratis*) gratuit; (*lavish*) généreux. —*v.t.* (*p.t.* **freed**) libérer; (*clear*) dégager. **~ enterprise,** la libre entreprise. **a ~ hand,** carte blanche *f.* **~ kick,** coup franc *m.* **~lance** *a. & n.*

free-lance (*m./f.*), indépendant(e) *m.*, *f.* ∼ **(of charge)**, gratuit(ement). ∼-**range** *a.* (*eggs*) de ferme. ∼-**wheel** *v.i.* descendre en roue libre. ∼-**wheeling** *a.* sans contraintes. ∼**ly** *adv.* librement.

freedom /ˈfriːdəm/ *n.* liberté *f.*

Freemason /ˈfriːmeɪsn/ *n.* franc-maçon *m.* ∼**ry** *n.* francmaçonnerie *f.*

freeway /ˈfriːweɪ/ *n.* (*Amer.*) autoroute *f.*

freez|e /friːz/ *v.t./i.* (*p.t.* **froze**, *p.p.* **frozen**) (*culin.*) (se) congeler; (*wages etc.*) bloquer. —*n.* gel *m.*; blocage *m.* ∼**e-dried** *a.* lyophilisé. ∼**er** *n.* congélateur *m.* ∼**ing** *a.* glacial. **below** ∼**ing**, au-dessous de zéro.

freight /freɪt/ *n.* fret *m.* ∼**er** *n.* (*ship*) cargo *m.*

French /frentʃ/ *a.* français. —*n.* (*lang.*) français *m.* ∼ **bean,** haricot vert *m.* ∼ **fries,** frites *f. pl.* ∼-**speaking** *a.* francophone. ∼ **window** *n.* porte-fenêtre *f.* **the** ∼, les Français *m. pl.* ∼**man** *n.* Français *m.* ∼**woman** *n.* Française *f.*

frenz|y /ˈfrenzɪ/ *n.* frénésie *f.* ∼**ied** *a.* frénétique.

frequen|t¹ /ˈfriːkwənt/ *a.* fréquent. ∼**cy** *n.* fréquence *f.* ∼**tly** *adv.* fréquemment.

frequent² /frɪˈkwent/ *v.t.* fréquenter.

fresco /ˈfreskəʊ/ *n.* (*pl.* -**os**) fresque *f.*

fresh /freʃ/ *a.* (-**er**, -**est**) frais; (*different, additional*) nouveau; (*cheeky: fam.*) culotté. ∼**ly** *adv.* nouvellement. ∼**ness** *n.* fraîcheur *f.*

freshen /ˈfreʃn/ *v.i.* (*weather*) fraîchir. ∼ **up,** (*person*) se rafraîchir.

fresher /ˈfreʃə(r)/ *n.*, **freshman** /ˈfreʃmən/ *n.* (*pl.* -**men**) bizuth *m./f.*

freshwater /ˈfreʃwɔːtə(r)/ *a.* d'eau douce.

fret /fret/ *v.i.* (*p.t.* **fretted**) se tracasser. ∼**ful** *a.* ronchon, insatisfait.

friar /ˈfraɪə(r)/ *n.* moine *m.*, frère *m.*

friction /ˈfrɪkʃn/ *n.* friction *f.*

Friday /ˈfraɪdɪ/ *n.* vendredi *m.*

fridge /frɪdʒ/ *n.* frigo *m.*

fried /fraɪd/ *see* **fry.** —*a.* frit. ∼ **eggs,** œufs sur le plat *m. pl.*

friend /frend/ *n.* ami(e) *m.* (*f.*). ∼**ship** *n.* amitié *f.*

friend|ly /ˈfrendlɪ/ *a.* (-**ier**, -**iest**) amical, gentil. **F**∼**y Society,** mutuelle *f.*, société de prévoyance *f.* ∼**iness** *n.* gentillesse *f.*

frieze /friːz/ *n.* frise *f.*

frigate /ˈfrɪgət/ *n.* frégate *f.*

fright /fraɪt/ *n.* peur *f.*; (*person, thing*) horreur *f.* ∼**ful** *a.* affreux. ∼**fully** *adv.* affreusement.

frighten /ˈfraɪtn/ *v.t.* effrayer. ∼ **off,** faire fuir. ∼**ed** *a.* effrayé. **be** ∼**ed,** avoir peur (**of,** de). ∼**ing** *a.* effrayant.

frigid /ˈfrɪdʒɪd/ *a.* froid, glacial; (*psych.*) frigide. ∼**ity** /-ˈdʒɪdətɪ/ *n.* frigidité *f.*

frill /frɪl/ *n.* (*trimming*) fanfreluche *f.* **with no** ∼**s,** très simple.

fringe /frɪndʒ/ *n.* (*edging, hair*) frange *f.*; (*of area*) bordure *f.*; (*of society*) marge *f.* ∼ **benefits,** avantages sociaux *m. pl.*

frisk /frɪsk/ *v.t.* (*search*) fouiller.

frisky /ˈfrɪskɪ/ *a.* (-**ier**, -**iest**) fringant, frétillant.

fritter¹ /ˈfrɪtə(r)/ *n.* beignet *m.*

fritter² /ˈfrɪtə(r)/ *v.t.* ∼ **away,** gaspiller.

frivol|ous /ˈfrɪvələs/ *a.* frivole. ∼**ity** /-ˈvɒlətɪ/ *n.* frivolité *f.*

frizzy /ˈfrɪzɪ/ *a.* crépu, crêpelé.

fro /frəʊ/ *see* **to and fro.**

frock /frɒk/ *n.* robe *f.*

frog /frɒg/ *n.* grenouille *f.* **a** ∼ **in one's throat,** un chat dans la gorge.

frogman /ˈfrɒgmən/ *n.* (*pl.* -**men**) homme-grenouille *m.*

frolic /ˈfrɒlɪk/ *v.i.* (*p.t.* **frolicked**) s'ébattre. —*n.* ébats *m. pl.*

from /frɒm, *unstressed* frəm/ *prep.* de; (*with time, prices, etc.*) à partir de, de; (*habit, conviction, etc.*) par; (*according to*) d'après. **take** ∼ **s.o.,** prendre à qn. **take** ∼ **one's pocket,** prendre dans sa poche.

front /frʌnt/ *n.* (*of car, train, etc.*) avant *m.*; (*of garment, building*) devant *m.*; (*mil., pol.*) front *m.*; (*of book, pamphlet, etc.*) début *m.*; (*appearance: fig.*) façade *f.* —*a.* de devant, avant *invar.*; (*first*) premier. ∼ **door,** porte d'entrée *f.* ∼-**wheel drive,** traction avant *f.* **in** ∼ (**of**), devant. ∼**age** *n.* façade *f.* ∼**al** *a.* frontal; (*attack*) de front.

frontier /ˈfrʌntɪə(r)/ *n.* frontière *f.*

frost /frɒst/ *n.* gel *m.*, gelée *f.*; (*on glass etc.*) givre *m.* —*v.t./i.* (se) givrer. ∼-**bite** *n.* gelure *f.* ∼-**bitten** *a.* gelé. ∼**ed** *a.* (*glass*) dépoli. ∼**ing** *n.* (*icing: Amer.*) glace *f.* ∼**y** *a.* (*weather, welcome*) glacial; (*window*) givré.

froth /frɒθ/ *n.* mousse *f.*, écume *f.* —*v.i.* mousser, écumer. ∼**y** *a.* mousseux.

frown /fraʊn/ *v.i.* froncer les sourcils. —*n.* froncement de sourcils *m.* ∼ **on,** désapprouver.

froze /frəʊz/ *see* **freeze.**

frozen /ˈfrəʊzn/ *see* **freeze.** —*a.* congelé.

frugal /ˈfruːgl/ *a.* (*person*) économe;

(*meal*, *life*) frugal. ~**ly** *adv*. (*live*) simplement.

fruit /fruːt/ *n*. fruit *m*.; (*collectively*) fruits *m. pl*. ~ **machine**, machine à sous *f*. ~ **salad**, salade de fruits *f*. ~**erer** *n*. fruitier, -ière *m.*, *f*. ~**y** *a*. (*taste*) fruité.

fruit|ful /ˈfruːtfl/ *a*. (*discussions*) fructueux. ~**less** *a*. stérile.

fruition /fruːˈɪʃn/ *n*. **come to** ~, se réaliser.

frustrat|e /frʌˈstreɪt/ *v.t*. (*plan*) faire échouer; (*person: psych.*) frustrer; (*upset: fam.*) exaspérer. ~**ion** /-ʃn/ *n*. (*psych.*) frustration *f*.; (*disappointment*) déception *f*.

fry[1] /fraɪ/ *v.t./i*. (*p.t.* **fried**) (faire) frire. ~**ing-pan** *n*. poêle (à frire) *f*.

fry[2] /fraɪ/ *n*. **the small** ~, le menu fretin.

fuddy-duddy /ˈfʌdɪdʌdɪ/ *n*. **be a** ~, (*sl.*) être vieux jeu *invar*.

fudge /fʌdʒ/ *n*. (sorte de) caramel mou *m*. —*v.t*. se dérober à.

fuel /ˈfjuːəl/ *n*. combustible *m*.; (*for car engine*) carburant *m*. —*v.t*. (*p.t.* **fuelled**) alimenter en combustible.

fugitive /ˈfjuːdʒətɪv/ *n. & a*. fugitif, -ve (*m.*, *f.*).

fugue /fjuːg/ *n*. (*mus.*) fugue *f*.

fulfil /fʊlˈfɪl/ *v.t*. (*p.t.* **fulfilled**) accomplir, réaliser; (*condition*) remplier. ~ **o.s.**, s'épanouir. ~**ling** *a*. satisfaisant. ~**ment** *n*. réalisation *f*.; épanouissement *m*.

full /fʊl/ *a*. (-**er**, -**est**) plein (**of**, de); (*bus*, *hotel*) complet; (*programme*) chargé; (*name*) complet; (*skirt*) ample. —*n*. **in** ~, intégral(ement). **to the** ~, complètement. **be** ~ (**up**), n'avoir plus faim. ~ **back**, (*sport*) arrière *m*. ~ **moon**, pleine lune *f*. ~-**scale** *a*. (*drawing etc.*) grandeur nature *invar*.; (*fig.*) de grande envergure. **at** ~ **speed**, à toute vitesse. ~ **stop**, point *m*. ~-**time** *a. & adv*. à plein temps. ~**y** *adv*. complètement.

fulsome /ˈfʊlsəm/ *a*. excessif.

fumble /ˈfʌmbl/ *v.i*. tâtonner, fouiller. ~ **with**, tripoter.

fume /fjuːm/ *v.i*. rager. ~**s** *n. pl*. exhalaisons *f. pl.*, vapeurs *f. pl*.

fumigate /ˈfjuːmɪgeɪt/ *v.t*. désinfecter.

fun /fʌn/ *n*. amusement *m*. **be** ~, être chouette. **for** ~, pour rire. ~-**fair** *n*. fête foraine *f*. **make** ~ **of**, se moquer de.

function /ˈfʌŋkʃn/ *n*. (*purpose, duty*) fonction *f*.; (*event*) réception *f*. —*v.i*. fonctionner. ~**al** *a*. fonctionnel.

fund /fʌnd/ *n*. fonds *m*. —*v.t*. fournir les fonds pour.

fundamental /fʌndəˈmentl/ *a*. fondamental. ~**ist** *n*. intégriste *m./f*. ~**ism** *n*. intégrisme *m*.

funeral /ˈfjuːnərəl/ *n*. enterrement *m*., funérailles *f. pl*. —*a*. funèbre.

fungus /ˈfʌŋgəs/ *n*. (*pl*. -**gi** /-gaɪ/) (*plant*) champignon *m*.; (*mould*) moisissure *f*.

funicular /fjuːˈnɪkjʊlə(r)/ *n*. funiculaire *m*.

funk /fʌŋk/ *m*. **be in a** ~, (*afraid: sl.*) avoir la frousse; (*depressed: Amer., sl.*) être déprimé.

funnel /ˈfʌnl/ *n*. (*for pouring*) entonnoir *m*.; (*of ship*) cheminée *f*.

funn|y /ˈfʌnɪ/ *a*. (-**ier**, -**iest**) drôle; (*odd*) bizarre. ~**y business**, quelque chose de louche. ~**ily** *adv*. drôlement; bizarrement.

fur /fɜː(r)/ *n*. fourrure *f*.; (*in kettle*) tartre *m*.

furious /ˈfjʊərɪəs/ *a*. furieux. ~**ly** *adv*. furieusement.

furnace /ˈfɜːnɪs/ *n*. fourneau *m*.

furnish /ˈfɜːnɪʃ/ *v.t*. (*with furniture*) meubler; (*supply*) fournir. ~**ings** *n. pl*. ameublement *m*.

furniture /ˈfɜːnɪtʃə(r)/ *n*. meubles *m. pl.*, mobilier *m*.

furrow /ˈfʌrəʊ/ *n*. sillon *m*.

furry /ˈfɜːrɪ/ *a*. (*animal*) à fourrure; (*toy*) en peluche.

furth|er /ˈfɜːðə(r)/ *a*. plus éloigné; (*additional*) supplémentaire. —*adv*. plus loin; (*more*) davantage. —*v.t*. avancer. ~**er education**, formation continue *f*. ~**est** *a*. le plus éloigné; *adv*. le plus loin.

furthermore /ˈfɜːðəmɔː(r)/ *adv*. en outre, de plus.

furtive /ˈfɜːtɪv/ *a*. furtif.

fury /ˈfjʊərɪ/ *n*. fureur *f*.

fuse[1] /fjuːz/ *v.t./i*. (*melt*) fondre; (*unite: fig.*) fusionner. —*n*. fusible *m*., plomb *m*. ~ **the lights** *etc*., faire sauter les plombs.

fuse[2] /fjuːz/ *n*. (*of bomb*) amorce *f*.

fuselage /ˈfjuːzəlɑːʒ/ *n*. fuselage *m*.

fusion /ˈfjuːʒn/ *n*. fusion *f*.

fuss /fʌs/ *n*. (*when upset*) histoire(s) *f*. (*pl.*); (*when excited*) agitation *f*. —*v.i*. s'agiter. **make a** ~, faire des histoires; s'agiter; (*about food*) faire des chichis. **make a** ~ **of**, faire grand cas de. ~**y** *a*. (*finicky*) tatillon; (*hard to please*) difficile.

futile /ˈfjuːtaɪl/ *a*. futile, vain.

future /ˈfjuːtʃə(r)/ *a*. futur. —*n*. avenir *m*.; (*gram.*) futur *m*. **in** ~, à l'avenir.

fuzz /fʌz/ n. (*fluff*, *growth*) duvet m.; (*police*: *sl.*) flics m. pl.
fuzzy /'fʌzɪ/ a. (*hair*) crépu; (*photograph*) flou; (*person*: *fam.*) à l'esprit confus.

G

gabardine /gæbə'diːn/ n. gabardine f.
gabble /'gæbl/ v.t./i. bredouiller. —n. baragouin m.
gable /'geɪbl/ n. pignon m.
gad /gæd/ v.i. (*p.t.* gadded). ∼ about, se promener, aller çà et là.
gadget /'gædʒɪt/ n. gadget m.
Gaelic /'geɪlɪk/ n. gaélique m.
gaffe /gæf/ n. (*blunder*) gaffe f.
gag /gæg/ n. bâillon m.; (*joke*) gag m. —v.t. (*p.t.* gagged) bâillonner.
gaiety /'geɪətɪ/ n. gaieté f.
gaily /'geɪlɪ/ adv. gaiement.
gain /geɪn/ v.t. gagner; (*speed*, *weight*) prendre. —v.i. (*of clock*) avancer. —n. acquisition f.; (*profit*) gain m. ∼ful a. profitable.
gait /geɪt/ n. démarche f.
gala /'gɑːlə/ n. (*festive occasion*) gala m.; (*sport*) concours m.
galaxy /'gæləksɪ/ n. galaxie f.
gale /geɪl/ n. tempête f.
gall /gɔːl/ n. bile f.; (*fig.*) fiel m.; (*impudence*: *sl.*) culot m. ∼-bladder n. vésicule biliaire f.
gallant /'gælənt/ a. (*brave*) courageux; (*chivalrous*) galant. ∼ry n. courage m.
galleon /'gæliən/ n. galion m.
gallery /'gælərɪ/ n. galerie f. (art) ∼, (*public*) musée m.
galley /'gælɪ/ n. (*ship*) galère f.; (*kitchen*) cambuse f.
Gallic /'gælɪk/ a. français. ∼ism /-sɪzəm/ n. gallicisme m.
gallivant /gælɪ'vænt/ v.i. (*fam.*) se promener, aller çà et là.
gallon /'gælən/ n. gallon m. (*imperial* = 4.546 litres; *Amer.* = 3.785 litres).
gallop /'gæləp/ n. galop m. —v.i. (*p.t.* galloped) galoper.
gallows /'gæləʊz/ n. potence f.
galore /gə'lɔː(r)/ adv. en abondance, à gogo.
galosh /gə'lɒʃ/ n. (*overshoe*) caoutchouc m.
galvanize /'gælvənaɪz/ v.t. galvaniser.
gambit /'gæmbɪt/ n. (**opening**) ∼,

(*move*) première démarche f.; (*ploy*) stratagème m.
gamble /'gæmbl/ v.t./i. jouer. —n. (*venture*) entreprise risquée f.; (*bet*) pari m.; (*risk*) risque m. ∼e on, miser sur. ∼er n. joueur, -se m., f. ∼ing n. le jeu.
game¹ /geɪm/ n. jeu m.; (*football*) match m.; (*tennis*) partie f.; (*animals*, *birds*) gibier m. —a. (*brave*) brave. ∼ for, prêt à.
game² /geɪm/ a. (*lame*) estropié.
gamekeeper /'geɪmkiːpə(r)/ n. garde-chasse m.
gammon /'gæmən/ n. jambon fumé m.
gamut /'gæmət/ n. gamme f.
gamy /'geɪmɪ/ a. faisandé.
gang /gæŋ/ n. bande f.; (*of workmen*) équipe f. —v.i. ∼ up, se liguer (**on**, **against**, contre).
gangling /'gæŋglɪŋ/ a. dégingandé, grand et maigre.
gangrene /'gæŋgriːn/ n. gangrène f.
gangster /'gæŋstə(r)/ n. gangster m.
gangway /'gæŋweɪ/ n. passage m.; (*aisle*) allée f.; (*of ship*) passerelle f.
gaol /dʒeɪl/ n. & v.t. = **jail**.
gap /gæp/ n. trou m., vide m.; (*in time*) intervalle m.; (*in education*) lacune f.; (*difference*) écart m.
gape /geɪp/ v.i. rester bouche bée. ∼ing a. béant.
garage /'gærɑːʒ, *Amer.* gə'rɑːʒ/ n. garage m. —v.t. mettre au garage.
garb /gɑːb/ n. costume m.
garbage /'gɑːbɪdʒ/ n. ordures f. pl.
garble /'gɑːbl/ v.t. déformer.
garden /'gɑːdn/ n. jardin m. —v.i. jardiner. ∼er n. jardinier, -ière m., f. ∼ing n. jardinage m.
gargle /'gɑːgl/ v.i. se gargariser. —n. gargarisme m.
gargoyle /'gɑːgɔɪl/ n. gargouille f.
garish /'geərɪʃ/ a. voyant, criard.
garland /'gɑːlənd/ n. guirlande f.
garlic /'gɑːlɪk/ n. ail m.
garment /'gɑːmənt/ n. vêtement m.
garnish /'gɑːnɪʃ/ v.t. garnir (**with**, de). —n. garniture f.
garret /'gærət/ n. mansarde f.
garrison /'gærɪsn/ n. garnison f.
garrulous /'gærələs/ a. loquace.
garter /'gɑːtə(r)/ n. jarretière f. ∼-belt n. porte-jarretelles n.m. invar.
gas /gæs/ n. (*pl.* gases) gaz m.; (*med.*) anesthésique m.; (*petrol*: *Amer.*, *fam.*) essence f. —a. (*mask*, *pipe*) à gaz. —v.t. asphyxier; (*mil.*) gazer. —v.i. (*fam.*) bavarder.

gash /gæʃ/ n. entaille f. —v.t. entailler.
gasket /'gæskɪt/ n. (auto.) joint de culasse m.; (for pressure cooker) rondelle f.
gasoline /'gæsəli:n/ n. (petrol: Amer.) essence f.
gasp /gɑ:sp/ v.i. haleter; (in surprise: fig.) avoir le souffle coupé. —n. halètement m.
gassy /'gæsɪ/ a. gazeux.
gastric /'gæstrɪk/ a. gastrique.
gastronomy /gæ'strɒnəmɪ/ n. gastronomie f.
gate /geɪt/ n. porte f.; (of metal) grille f.; (barrier) barrière f.
gatecrash /'geɪtkræʃ/ v.t./i. venir sans invitation (à). ∼er n. intrus(e) m.(f.).
gateway /'geɪtweɪ/ n. porte f.
gather /'gæðə(r)/ v.t. (people, objects) rassembler; (pick up) ramasser; (flowers) cueillir; (fig.) comprendre; (sewing) froncer. —v.i. (people) se rassembler; (crowd) se former; (pile up) s'accumuler. ∼ **speed**, prendre de la vitesse. ∼ing n. rassemblement m.
gaudy /'gɔ:dɪ/ a. (-ier, -iest) voyant, criard.
gauge /geɪdʒ/ n. jauge f., indicateur m. —v.t. jauger, évaluer.
gaunt /gɔ:nt/ a. (lean) émacié; (grim) lugubre.
gauntlet /'gɔ:ntlɪt/ n. **run the ∼ of,** subir (l'assaut de).
gauze /gɔ:z/ n. gaze f.
gave /geɪv/ see **give.**
gawky /'gɔ:kɪ/ a. (-ier, -iest) gauche, maladroit.
gawp (or **gawk**) /gɔ:p, gɔ:k/ v.i. ∼ (at), regarder bouche bée.
gay /geɪ/ a. (-er, -est) (joyful) gai; (fam.) gay invar. —n. gay m./f.
gaze /geɪz/ v.i. ∼ (at), regarder (fixement). —n. regard (fixe) m.
gazelle /gə'zel/ n. gazelle f.
gazette /gə'zet/ n. journal (officiel) m.
GB abbr. see **Great Britain.**
gear /gɪə(r)/ n. équipement m.; (techn.) engrenage m.; (auto.) vitesse f. —v.t. adapter. ∼-**lever,** (Amer.) ∼-**shift** ns. levier de vitesse m. **in ∼,** en prise. **out of ∼,** au point mort.
gearbox /'gɪəbɒks/ n. (auto.) boîte de vitesses f.
geese /gi:s/ see **goose.**
gel /dʒel/ n. gelée f.; (for hair) gel m.
gelatine /'dʒeləti:n/ n. gélatine f.
gelignite /'dʒelɪgnaɪt/ n. nitroglycérine f.
gem /dʒem/ n. pierre précieuse f.

Gemini /'dʒemɪnaɪ/ n. les Gémeaux m. pl.
gender /'dʒendə(r)/ n. genre m.
gene /dʒi:n/ n. gène m.
genealogy /dʒi:nɪ'ælədʒɪ/ n. généalogie f.
general /'dʒenrəl/ a. général. —n. général m. ∼ **election,** élections législatives f. pl. ∼ **practitioner,** (med.) généraliste m. **in ∼,** en général. ∼**ly** adv. généralement.
generaliz|e /'dʒenrəlaɪz/ v.t./i. généraliser. ∼**ation** /-'zeɪʃn/ n. généralisation f.
generate /'dʒenəreɪt/ v.t. produire.
generation /dʒenə'reɪʃn/ n. génération f.
generator /'dʒenəreɪtə(r)/ n. (electr.) groupe électrogène m.
gener|ous /'dʒenərəs/ a. généreux; (plentiful) copieux. ∼**osity** /-'rɒsətɪ/ n. générosité f.
genetic /dʒɪ'netɪk/ a. génétique. ∼**s** n. génétique f.
Geneva /dʒɪ'ni:və/ n. Genève m./f.
genial /'dʒi:nɪəl/ a. affable, sympathique; (climate) doux.
genital /'dʒenɪtl/ a. génital. ∼**s** n. pl. organes génitaux m. pl.
genius /'dʒi:nɪəs/ n. (pl. -uses) génie m.
genocide /'dʒenəsaɪd/ n. génocide m.
gent /dʒent/ n. (sl.) monsieur m.
genteel /dʒen'ti:l/ a. distingué.
gentl|e /'dʒentl/ a. (-er, -est) (mild, kind) doux; (slight) léger; (hint) discret. ∼**eness** n. douceur f. ∼**y** adv. doucement.
gentleman /'dʒentlmən/ n. (pl. -men) (man) monsieur m.; (well-bred) gentleman m.
genuine /'dʒenjʊɪn/ a. (true) véritable; (person, belief) sincère.
geograph|y /dʒɪ'ɒgrəfɪ/ n. géographie f. ∼**er** n. géographe m./f. ∼**ical** /dʒɪə'græfɪkl/ a. géographique.
geolog|y /dʒɪ'ɒlədʒɪ/ n. géologie f. ∼**ical** /dʒɪə'lɒdʒɪkl/ a. géologique. ∼**ist** n. géologue m./f.
geometr|y /dʒɪ'ɒmətrɪ/ n. géométrie f. ∼**ic(al)** /dʒɪə'metrɪk(l)/ a. géométrique.
geranium /dʒə'reɪnɪəm/ n. géranium m.
geriatric /dʒerɪ'ætrɪk/ a. gériatrique.
germ /dʒɜ:m/ n. (rudiment, seed) germe m.; (med.) microbe m.
German /'dʒɜ:mən/ a. & n. allemand(e) (m. (f.)); (lang.) allemand m. ∼ **measles,** rubéole f. ∼ **shepherd,** (dog: Amer.) berger allemand m. ∼**ic** /dʒə'mænɪk/ a. germanique. ∼**y** n. Allemagne f.

germinate /'dʒɜːmɪneɪt/ v.t./i. (faire) germer.

gestation /dʒe'steɪʃn/ n. gestation f.

gesticulate /dʒe'stɪkjʊleɪt/ v.i. gesticuler.

gesture /'dʒestʃə(r)/ n. geste m.

get /get/ v.t. (p.t. & p.p. **got**, p.p. Amer. **gotten**, pres. p. **getting**) avoir, obtenir, recevoir; (catch) prendre; (buy) acheter, prendre; (find) trouver; (fetch) aller chercher; (understand: sl.) comprendre. ~ **s.o. to do sth.**, faire faire qch. à qn. ~ **sth. done**, faire faire qch. **did you ~ that number?**, tu as relevé le numéro? —v.i. aller, arriver (**to**, à); (become) devenir; (start) se mettre (**to**, à); (manage) parvenir (**to**, à). ~ **married/ready/**etc., se marier/se préparer/etc. ~ **promoted/hurt/**etc., être promu/blessé/etc. ~ **arrested/ robbed/**etc., se faire arrêter/ voler/etc. **you ~ to use the computer**, vous utilisez l'ordinateur. **it's ~ting to be annoying**, ça commence à être agaçant. ~ **about**, (person) se déplacer. ~ **across**, (cross) traverser. ~ **along** or **by**, (manage) se débrouiller. ~ **along** or **on**, (progress) avancer. ~ **along** or **on with**, s'entendre avec. ~ **at**, (reach) parvenir à. **what are you ~ting at?**, où veux-tu en venir? ~ **away**, partir; (escape) s'échapper. ~ **back** v.i. revenir; v.t. (recover) récupérer. ~ **by** or **through**, (pass) passer. ~ **down** v.t./i. descendre; (depress) déprimer. ~ **in**, entrer, arriver. ~ **into**, (car) monter dans; (dress) mettre. ~ **into trouble**, avoir des ennuis. ~ **off** v.i. (from bus etc.) descendre; (leave) partir, (jurid.) être acquitté; v.t. (remove) enlever. ~ **on**, (on train etc.) monter; (succeed) réussir. ~ **on with**, (job) attaquer; (person) s'entendre avec. ~ **out**, sortir. ~ **out of**, (fig.) se soustraire à. ~ **over**, (illness) se remettre de. ~ **round**, (rule) contourner; (person) entortiller. ~ **through**, (finish) finir. ~ **up** v.i. se lever; v.t. (climb, bring) monter. ~-**up** n. (clothes: fam.) mise f.

getaway /'getəweɪ/ n. fuite f.

geyser /'giːzə(r)/ n. chauffe-eau m. invar.; (geol.) geyser m.

Ghana /'ɡɑːnə/ n. Ghana m.

ghastly /'ɡɑːstlɪ/ a. (-ier, -iest) affreux; (pale) blême.

gherkin /'ɡɜːkɪn/ n. cornichon m.

ghetto /'ɡetəʊ/ n. (pl. -os) ghetto m.

ghost /ɡəʊst/ n. fantôme m. ~**ly** a. spectral.

giant /'dʒaɪənt/ n. & a. géant (m.).

gibberish /'dʒɪbərɪʃ/ n. baragouin m., charabia m.

gibe /dʒaɪb/ n. raillerie f. —v.i. ~ (**at**), railler.

giblets /'dʒɪblɪts/ n. pl. abattis m. pl., abats m. pl.

giddy /'ɡɪdɪ/ a. (-ier, -iest) vertigineux. **be** or **feel ~y**, avoir le vertige. ~**iness** n. vertige m.

gift /ɡɪft/ n. cadeau m.; (ability) don m. ~-**wrap** v.t. (p.t. -**wrapped**) faire un paquet-cadeau de.

gifted /'ɡɪftɪd/ a. doué.

gig /ɡɪɡ/ n. (fam.) concert m.

gigantic /dʒaɪ'ɡæntɪk/ a. gigantesque.

giggle /'ɡɪɡl/ v.i. ricaner (sottement), glousser. —n. ricanement m. **the ~s**, le fou rire.

gild /ɡɪld/ v.t. dorer.

gill /dʒɪl/ n. (approx.) décilitre (imperial = 0.15 litre; Amer. = 0.12 litre).

gills /ɡɪlz/ n. pl. ouïes f. pl.

gilt /ɡɪlt/ a. doré. —n. dorure f. ~-**edged** a. (comm.) de tout repos.

gimmick /'ɡɪmɪk/ n. truc m.

gin /dʒɪn/ n. gin m.

ginger /'dʒɪndʒə(r)/ n. gingembre m. —a. roux. ~ **ale**, ~ **beer**, boisson gazeuse au gingembre f.

gingerbread /'dʒɪndʒəbred/ n. pain d'épice m.

gingerly /'dʒɪndʒəlɪ/ adv. avec précaution.

gipsy /'dʒɪpsɪ/ n. = **gypsy**.

giraffe /dʒɪ'rɑːf/ n. girafe f.

girder /'ɡɜːdə(r)/ n. poutre f.

girdle /'ɡɜːdl/ n. (belt) ceinture f.; (corset) gaine f.

girl /ɡɜːl/ n. (petite) fille f.; (young woman) (jeune) fille f. ~-**friend** n. amie f.; (of boy) petite amie f. ~**hood** n. enfance f., jeunesse f. ~**ish** a. de (jeune) fille.

giro /'dʒaɪərəʊ/ n. (pl. -os) virement bancaire m.; (cheque: fam.) mandat m.

girth /ɡɜːθ/ n. circonférence f.

gist /dʒɪst/ n. essentiel m.

give /ɡɪv/ v.t. (p.t. **gave**, p.p. **given**) donner; (gesture) faire; (laugh, sigh, etc.) pousser. ~ **s.o. sth.**, donner qch. à qn. —v.i. donner; (yield) céder; (stretch) se détendre. —n. élasticité f. ~ **away**, donner; (secret) trahir. ~ **back**, rendre. ~ **in**, (yield) se rendre. ~ **off**, dégager. ~ **out** v.t. distribuer; v.i. (become used up) s'épuiser. ~ **over**, (devote) consacrer; (stop: fam.) cesser. ~ **up** v.t./i. (renounce) renoncer (à);

(*yield*) céder. **~ o.s. up**, se rendre. **~ way**, céder; (*collapse*) s'effondrer.

given /'gɪvn/ *see* **give**. —*a.* donné. **~ name**, prénom *m.*

glacier /'glæsɪə(r), *Amer.* 'gleɪʃər/ *n.* glacier *m.*

glad /glæd/ *a.* content. **~ly** *adv.* avec plaisir.

gladden /'glædn/ *v.t.* réjouir.

gladiolus /glædɪ'əʊləs/ *n.* (*pl.* **-li** /-laɪ/) glaïeul *m.*

glam|our /'glæmə(r)/ *n.* enchantement *m.*, séduction *f.* **~orize** *v.t.* rendre séduisant. **~orous** *a.* séduisant, ensorcelant.

glance /glɑːns/ *n.* coup d'œil *m.* —*v.i.* **~ at**, jeter un coup d'œil à.

gland /glænd/ *n.* glande *f.*

glar|e /gleə(r)/ *v.i.* briller très fort. —*n.* éclat (aveuglant) *m.*; (*stare: fig.*) regard furieux *m.* **~e at**, regarder d'un air furieux. **~ing** *a.* éblouissant; (*obvious*) flagrant.

glass /glɑːs/ *n.* verre *m.*; (*mirror*) miroir *m.* **~es**, (*spectacles*) lunettes *f. pl.* **~y** *a.* vitreux.

glaze /gleɪz/ *v.t.* (*door etc.*) vitrer; (*pottery*) vernisser. —*n.* vernis *m.*

gleam /gliːm/ *n.* lueur *f.* —*v.i.* luire.

glean /gliːn/ *v.t.* glaner.

glee /gliː/ *n.* joie *f.* **~ club**, chorale *f.* **~ful** *a.* joyeux.

glen /glen/ *n.* vallon *m.*

glib /glɪb/ *a.* (*person: pej.*) qui a la parole facile *or* du bagou; (*reply, excuse*) désinvolte, spécieux. **~ly** *adv.* avec désinvolture.

glide /glaɪd/ *v.i.* glisser; (*of plane*) planer. **~r** /-ə(r)/ *n.* planeur *m.*

glimmer /'glɪmə(r)/ *n.* lueur *f.* —*v.i.* luire.

glimpse /glɪmps/ *n.* aperçu *m.* **catch a ~ of**, entrevoir.

glint /glɪnt/ *n.* éclair *m.* —*v.i.* étinceler.

glisten /'glɪsn/ *v.i.* briller, luire.

glitter /'glɪtə(r)/ *v.i.* scintiller. —*n.* scintillement *m.*

gloat /gləʊt/ *v.i.* jubiler (**over**, à l'idée de).

global /'gləʊbl/ *a.* (*world-wide*) mondial; (*all-embracing*) global.

globe /gləʊb/ *n.* globe *m.*

gloom /gluːm/ *n.* obscurité *f.*; (*sadness: fig.*) tristesse *f.* **~y** *a.* triste; (*pessimistic*) pessimiste.

glorif|y /'glɔːrɪfaɪ/ *v.t.* glorifier. **a ~ied waitress**/*etc.*, à peine plus qu'une serveuse/*etc.*

glorious /'glɔːrɪəs/ *a.* splendide; (*deed, hero, etc.*) glorieux.

glory /'glɔːrɪ/ *n.* gloire *f.*; (*beauty*) splendeur *f.* —*v.i.* **~ in**, s'enorgueillir de.

gloss /glɒs/ *n.* lustre *m.*, brillant *m.* —*a.* brillant. —*v.i.* **~ over**, (*make light of*) glisser sur; (*cover up*) dissimuler. **~y** *a.* brillant.

glossary /'glɒsərɪ/ *n.* glossaire *m.*

glove /glʌv/ *n.* gant *m.* **~ compartment**, (*auto.*) vide-poches *m. invar.* **~d** *a.* ganté.

glow /gləʊ/ *v.i.* rougeoyer; (*person, eyes*) rayonner. —*n.* rougeoiement *m.*, éclat *m.* **~ing** *a.* (*account etc.*) enthousiaste.

glucose /'gluːkəʊs/ *n.* glucose *m.*

glue /gluː/ *n.* colle *f.* —*v.t.* (*pres. p.* **gluing**) coller.

glum /glʌm/ *a.* (**glummer, glummest**) triste, morne.

glut /glʌt/ *n.* surabondance *f.*

glutton /'glʌtn/ *n.* glouton(ne) *m.* (*f.*). **~ous** *a.* glouton. **~y** *n.* gloutonnerie *f.*

glycerine /'glɪsəriːn/ *n.* glycérine *f.*

gnarled /nɑːld/ *a.* noueux.

gnash /næʃ/ *v.t.* **~ one's teeth**, grincer des dents.

gnat /næt/ *n.* (*fly*) cousin *m.*

gnaw /nɔː/ *v.t./i.* ronger.

gnome /nəʊm/ *n.* gnome *m.*

go /gəʊ/ *v.i.* (*p.t.* **went**, *p.p.* **gone**) aller; (*leave*) partir; (*work*) marcher; (*become*) devenir; (*be sold*) se vendre; (*vanish*) disparaître. **my coat's gone**, mon manteau n'est plus là. **~ via Paris**, passer par Paris. **~ by car/on foot**, aller en voiture/à pied. **~ for a walk/ride**, aller se promener/ faire un tour en voiture. **go red/dry**/*etc.*, rougir/tarir/*etc.* **don't ~ telling him**, ne va pas lui dire. **~ riding/shopping**/*etc.*, faire du cheval/les courses/*etc.* —*n.* (*pl.* **goes**) (*try*) coup *m.*; (*success*) réussite *f.*; (*turn*) tour *m.*; (*energy*) dynamisme *m.* **have a ~**, essayer. **be ~ing to do**, aller faire. **~ across**, traverser. **~ ahead!**, allez-y! **~-ahead** *n.* feu vert *m.*; *a.* dynamique. **~ away**, s'en aller. **~ back**, retourner; (*go home*) rentrer. **~ back on**, (*promise etc.*) revenir sur. **~ bad** *or* **off**, se gâter. **~-between** *n.* intermédiaire *m./f.* **~ by**, (*pass*) passer. **~ down**, descendre; (*sun*) se coucher. **~ for**, aller chercher; (*like*) aimer; (*attack: sl.*) attaquer. **~ in**, (r)entrer. **~ in for**, (*exam*) se présenter à. **~ into**, entrer dans; (*subject*) examiner. **~-kart** *n.* kart *m.* **~ off**, partir; (*explode*) sauter; (*ring*) sonner; (*take place*) se dérouler; (*dislike*) revenir de. ∼ **on,** continuer; (*happen*) se passer. ∼ **out,** sortir; (*light, fire*) s'éteindre. ∼ **over,** (*cross*) traverser; (*pass*) passer. ∼ **over** *or* **through,** (*check*) vérifier; (*search*) fouiller. ∼ **round,** (*be enough*) suffire. ∼**-slow** *n.* grève perlée *f.* ∼ **through,** (*suffer*) subir. ∼ **under,** (*sink*) couler; (*fail*) échouer. ∼ **up,** monter. ∼ **without,** se passer de. **on the** ∼, actif.

goad /gəʊd/ *v.t.* aiguillonner.

goal /gəʊl/ *n.* but *m.* ∼**-post** *n.* poteau de but *m.*

goalkeeper /'gəʊlkiːpə(r)/ *n.* gardien de but *m.*

goat /gəʊt/ *n.* chèvre *f.*

goatee /gəʊ'tiː/ *n.* barbiche *f.*

gobble /'gɒbl/ *v.t.* engouffrer.

goblet /'gɒblɪt/ *n.* verre à pied *m.*

goblin /'gɒblɪn/ *n.* lutin *m.*

God /gɒd/ *n.* Dieu *m.* ∼**-forsaken** *a.* perdu.

god /gɒd/ *n.* dieu *m.* ∼**dess** *n.* déesse *f.* ∼**ly** *a.* dévot.

god|child /'gɒdtʃaɪld/ *n.* (*pl.* **-children**) filleul(e) *m.* (*f.*). ∼**daughter** *n.* filleule *f.* ∼**father** *n.* parrain *m.* ∼**mother** *n.* marraine *f.* ∼**son** *n.* filleul *m.*

godsend /'gɒdsend/ *n.* aubaine *f.*

goggle /'gɒgl/ *v.i.* ∼ (**at**), regarder avec de gros yeux.

goggles /'gɒglz/ *n. pl.* lunettes (protectrices) *f. pl.*

going /'gəʊɪŋ/ *n.* **it is slow/hard** ∼, c'est lent/difficile. —*a.* (*price, rate*) actuel. ∼**s-on** *n. pl.* activités (bizarres) *f. pl.*

gold /gəʊld/ *n.* or *m.* —*a.* en or, d'or. ∼**-mine** *n.* mine d'or *f.*

golden /'gəʊldən/ *a.* d'or; (*in colour*) doré; (*opportunity*) unique. ∼ **wedding,** noces d'or *f. pl.*

goldfish /'gəʊldfɪʃ/ *n. invar.* poisson rouge *m.*

gold-plated /gəʊld'pleɪtɪd/ *a.* plaqué or.

goldsmith /'gəʊldsmɪθ/ *n.* orfèvre *m.*

golf /gɒlf/ *n.* golf *m.* ∼ **ball,** balle de golf *f.*; (*on typewriter*) boule *f.* ∼**-course** *n.* terrain de golf *m.* ∼**er** *n.* joueulr, -se de golf *m., f.*

gondol|a /'gɒndələ/ *n.* gondole *f.* ∼**ier** /-'lɪə(r)/ *n.* gondolier *m.*

gone /gɒn/ *see* **go.** —*a.* parti. ∼ **six o'clock,** six heures passées. **the butter's all** ∼, il n'y a plus de beurre.

gong /gɒŋ/ *n.* gong *m.*

good /gʊd/ *a.* (**better, best**) bon; (*weather*) beau; (*well-behaved*) sage. —*n.* bien *m.* **as** ∼ **as,** (*almost*) pratiquement. **that's** ∼ **of you,** c'est

gentil (de ta part). **be** ∼ **with,** savoir s'y prendre avec. **do** ∼, faire du bien. **feel** ∼, se sentir bien. ∼**-for-nothing** *a.* & *n.* propre à rien (*m./f.*). **G∼ Friday,** Vendredi saint *m.* ∼**-afternoon,** ∼ **morning** *ints.* bonjour. ∼**-evening** *int.* bonsoir. ∼**-looking** *a.* beau. ∼**-natured** *a.* gentil. ∼ **name,** réputation *f.* ∼**-night** *int.* bonsoir, bonne nuit. **it is** ∼ **for you,** ça vous fait du bien. **is it any** ∼?, est-ce que c'est bien? **it's no** ∼, ça ne vaut rien. **it is no** ∼ **shouting**/*etc.*, ça ne sert à rien de crier/*etc.* **for** ∼, pour toujours. ∼**ness** *n.* bonté *f.* **my** ∼**ness!,** mon Dieu!

goodbye /gʊd'baɪ/ *int.* & *n.* au revoir (*m. invar.*).

goods /gʊdz/ *n. pl.* marchandises *f. pl.*

goodwill /gʊd'wɪl/ *n.* bonne volonté *f.*

goody /'gʊdɪ/ *n.* (*fam.*) bonne chose *f.* ∼**-goody** *n.* petit(e) saint(e) *m.* (*f.*).

gooey /'guːɪ/ *a.* (*sl.*) poisseux.

goof /guːf/ *v.i.* (*Amer.*) gaffer.

goose /guːs/ *n.* (*pl.* **geese**) oie *f.* ∼**-flesh,** ∼**-pimples** *ns.* chair de poule *f.*

gooseberry /'gʊzbərɪ/ *n.* groseille à maquereau *f.*

gore[1] /gɔː(r)/ *n.* (*blood*) sang *m.*

gore[2] /gɔː(r)/ *v.t.* encorner.

gorge /gɔːdʒ/ *n.* (*geog.*) gorge *f.* —*v.t.* ∼ **o.s.,** se gorger.

gorgeous /'gɔːdʒəs/ *a.* magnifique, splendide, formidable.

gorilla /gə'rɪlə/ *n.* gorille *m.*

gormless /'gɔːmlɪs/ *a.* (*sl.*) stupide.

gorse /gɔːs/ *n. invar.* ajonc(s) *m.* (*pl.*).

gory /'gɔːrɪ/ *a.* (**-ier, -iest**) sanglant; (*horrific: fig.*) horrible.

gosh /gɒʃ/ *int.* mince (alors).

gospel /'gɒspl/ *n.* évangile *m.* **the G∼,** l'Évangile *m.*

gossip /'gɒsɪp/ *n.* bavardage(s) *m.* (*pl.*), commérage(s) *m.* (*pl.*); (*person*) bavard(e) *m.* (*f.*). —*v.i.* (*p.t.* **gossiped**) bavarder. ∼**y** *a.* bavard.

got /gɒt/ *see* **get.** —**have** ∼, avoir. **have** ∼ **to do,** devoir faire.

Gothic /'gɒθɪk/ *a.* gothique.

gouge /gaʊdʒ/ *v.t.* ∼ **out,** arracher.

gourmet /'gʊəmeɪ/ *n.* gourmet *m.*

gout /gaʊt/ *n.* (*med.*) goutte *f.*

govern /'gʌvn/ *v.t./i.* gouverner. ∼**ess** /-ənɪs/ *n.* gouvernante *f.* ∼**or** /-ənə(r)/ *n.* gouverneur *m.*

government /'gʌvənmənt/ *n.* gouvernement *m.* ∼**al** /-'mentl/ *a.* gouvernemental.

gown /gaʊn/ *n.* robe *f.*; (*of judge, teacher*) toge *f.*

GP *abbr. see* **general practitioner.**

grab /græb/ *v.t.* (*p.t.* **grabbed**) saisir.

grace /greis/ *n.* grâce *f.* —*v.t.* (*honour*) honorer; (*adorn*) orner. **~ful** *a.* gracieux.

gracious /'greiʃəs/ *a.* (*kind*) bienveillant; (*elegant*) élégant.

gradation /grə'deiʃn/ *n.* gradation *f.*

grade /greid/ *n.* catégorie *f.*; (*of goods*) qualité *f.*; (*on scale*) grade *m.*; (*school mark*) note *f.*; (*class: Amer.*) classe *f.* —*v.t.* classer; (*school work*) noter. **~ crossing,** (*Amer.*) passage à niveau *m.* **~ school,** (*Amer.*) école primaire *f.*

gradient /'greidiənt/ *n.* (*slope*) inclinaison *f.*

gradual /'grædʒʊəl/ *a.* progressif, graduel. **~ly** *adv.* progressivement, peu à peu.

graduate[1] /'grædʒʊət/ *n.* (*univ.*) diplômé(e) *m.* (*f.*).

graduate[2] /'grædʒʊeit/ *v.i.* obtenir son diplôme. —*v.t.* graduer. **~ion** /-'eiʃn/ *n.* remise de diplômes *f.*

graffiti /grə'fi:ti:/ *n. pl.* graffiti *m. pl.*

graft[1] /grɑ:ft/ *n.* (*med., bot.*) greffe *f.* (*work*) boulot. —*v.t.* greffer; (*work*) trimer.

graft[2] /grɑ:ft/ *n.* (*bribery: fam.*) corruption *f.*

grain /grein/ *n.* (*seed, quantity, texture*) grain *m.*; (*in wood*) fibre *f.*

gram /græm/ *n.* gramme *m.*

gramm|ar /'græmə(r)/ *n.* grammaire *f.* **~atical** /grə'mætikl/ *a.* grammatical.

grand /grænd/ *a.* (*-er, -est*) magnifique; (*duke, chorus*) grand. **~ piano,** piano à queue *m.*

grandad /'grændæd/ *n.* (*fam.*) papy *m.*

grand|child /'græn(d)tʃaild/ *n.* (*pl.* **-children**) petit(e)-enfant *m.* (*f.*). **~daughter** *n.* petite-fille *f.* **~father** *n.* grand-père *m.* **~mother** *n.* grand-mère *f.* **~parents** *n. pl.* grands-parents *m. pl.* **~son** *n.* petit-fils *m.*

grandeur /'grændʒə(r)/ *n.* grandeur *f.*

grandiose /'grændiəus/ *a.* grandiose.

grandma /'grændmɑ:/ *n.* **= granny.**

grandstand /'græn(d)stænd/ *n.* tribune *f.*

granite /'grænit/ *n.* granit *m.*

granny /'græni/ *n.* (*fam.*) grandmaman *f.*, mémé *f.*, mamie *f.*

grant /grɑ:nt/ *v.t.* (*give*) accorder; (*request*) accéder à; (*admit*) admettre (**that,** que). —*n.* subvention *f.*; (*univ.*) bourse *f.* **take sth. for ~ed,** considérer qch. comme une chose acquise.

granulated /'grænjʊleitid/ *a.* **~ sugar,** sucre semoule *m.*

granule /'grænju:l/ *n.* granule *m.*

grape /greip/ *n.* grain de raisin *m.* **~s,** raisin(s) *m.* (*pl.*).

grapefruit /'greipfru:t/ *n. invar.* pamplemousse *m.*

graph /grɑ:f/ *n.* graphique *m.*

graphic /'græfik/ *a.* (*arts etc.*) graphique; (*fig.*) vivant, explicite. **~s** *n. pl.* (*comput.*) graphiques *m. pl.*

grapple /'græpl/ *v.i.* **~ with,** affronter, être aux prises avec.

grasp /grɑ:sp/ *v.t.* saisir. —*n.* (*hold*) prise *f.*; (*strength of hand*) poigne *f.*; (*reach*) portée *f.*; (*fig.*) compréhension *f.*

grasping /'grɑ:spiŋ/ *a.* rapace.

grass /grɑ:s/ *n.* herbe *f.* **~ roots,** peuple *m.*; (*pol.*) base *f.* **~-roots** *a.* populaire. **~y** *a.* herbeux.

grasshopper /'grɑ:shɒpə(r)/ *n.* sauterelle *f.*

grassland /'grɑ:slænd/ *n.* prairie *f.*

grate[1] /greit/ *n.* (*fireplace*) foyer *m.*; (*frame*) grille *f.*

grate[2] /greit/ *v.t.* râper. —*v.i.* grincer. **~r** /-ə(r)/ *n.* râpe *f.*

grateful /'greitfl/ *a.* reconnaissant. **~ly** *adv.* avec reconnaissance.

gratif|y /'grætifai/ *v.t.* satisfaire; (*please*) faire plaisir à **~ied** *a.* très heureux. **~ying** *a.* agréable.

grating /'greitiŋ/ *n.* grille *f.*

gratis /'greitis, 'grætis/ *a. & adv.* gratis (*a. invar.*).

gratitude /'grætitju:d/ *n.* gratitude *f.*

gratuitous /grə'tju:itəs/ *a.* gratuit.

gratuity /grə'tju:əti/ *n.* (*tip*) pourboire *m.*; (*bounty: mil.*) prime *f.*

grave[1] /greiv/ *n.* tombe *f.* **~-digger** *n.* fossoyeur *m.*

grave[2] /greiv/ *a.* (*-er, -est*) (*serious*) grave. **~ly** *adv.* gravement.

grave[3] /grɑ:v/ *a.* **~ accent,** accent grave *m.*

gravel /'grævl/ *n.* gravier *m.*

gravestone /'greivstəun/ *n.* pierre tombale *f.*

graveyard /'greivjɑ:d/ *n.* cimetière *m.*

gravitat|e /'græviteit/ *v.i.* graviter. **~ion** /-'teiʃn/ *n.* gravitation *f.*

gravity /'grævəti/ *n.* (*seriousness*) gravité *f.*; (*force*) pesanteur *f.*

gravy /'greivi/ *n.* jus (de viande) *m.*

gray /grei/ *a. & n.* **= grey.**

graze[1] /greiz/ *v.t./i.* (*eat*) paître.

graze[2] /greiz/ *v.t.* (*touch*) frôler; (*scrape*) écorcher. —*n.* écorchure *f.*

greas|e /griːs/ *n.* graisse *f.* —*v.t.* graisser. **~e-proof paper,** papier sulfurisé *m.* **~y** *a.* graisseux.

great /greɪt/ *a.* (**-er, -est**) grand; (*very good: fam.*) magnifique. **~ Britain,** Grande-Bretagne *f.* **~grandfather** *n.* arrière-grandpère *m.* **~grandmother** *n.* arrière-grand-mère *f.* **~ly** *adv.* (*very*) très; (*much*) beaucoup. **~ness** *n.* grandeur *f.*

Greece /griːs/ *n.* Grèce *f.*

greed /griːd/ *n.* avidité *f.*; (*for food*) gourmandise *f.* **~y** *a.* avide; gourmand.

Greek /griːk/ *a. & n.* grec(que) (*m.* (*f.*)); (*lang.*) grec *m.*

green /griːn/ *a.* (**-er, -est**) vert; (*fig.*) naïf. —*n.* vert *m.*; (*grass*) pelouse *f.*; (*golf*) green *m.* **~s,** légumes verts *m. pl.* **~ belt,** ceinture verte *f.* **~ light,** feu vert *m.* **~ery** *n.* verdure *f.*

greengage /ˈgriːngeɪdʒ/ *n.* (*plum*) reine-claude *f.*

greengrocer /ˈgriːngrəʊsə(r)/ *n.* marchand(e) de fruits et légumes *m.* (*f.*).

greenhouse /ˈgriːnhaʊs/ *n.* serre *f.*

greet /griːt/ *v.t.* (*receive*) accueillir; (*address politely*) saluer. **~ing** *n.* accueil *m.* **~ings** *n. pl.* compliments *m. pl.*; (*wishes*) vœux *m. pl.* **~ings card,** carte de vœux *f.*

gregarious /grɪˈɡeərɪəs/ *a.* (*instinct*) grégaire; (*person*) sociable.

grenade /grɪˈneɪd/ *n.* grenade *f.*

grew /gruː/ *see* **grow.**

grey /greɪ/ *a.* (**-er, -est**) gris; (*fig.*) triste. —*n.* gris *m.* **go ~,** (*hair, person*) grisonner.

greyhound /ˈɡreɪhaʊnd/ *n.* lévrier *m.*

grid /grɪd/ *n.* grille *f.*; (*network: electr.*) réseau *m.*; (*culin.*) gril *m.*

grief /griːf/ *n.* chagrin *m.* **come to ~,** (*person*) avoir un malheur; (*fail*) tourner mal.

grievance /ˈgriːvns/ *n.* grief *m.*

grieve /griːv/ *v.t./i.* (s')affliger. **~ for,** pleurer.

grill /grɪl/ *n.* (*cooking device*) gril *m.*; (*food*) grillade *f.*; (*auto.*) calandre *f.* —*v.t./i.* griller; (*interrogate*) cuisiner.

grille /grɪl/ *n.* grille *f.*

grim /grɪm/ *a.* (**grimmer, grimmest**) sinistre.

grimace /grɪˈmeɪs/ *n.* grimace *f.* —*v.i.* grimacer.

grim|e /graɪm/ *n.* crasse *f.* **~y** *a.* crasseux.

grin /grɪn/ *v.i.* (*p.t.* **grinned**) sourire. —*n.* (*large*) sourire *m.*

grind /graɪnd/ *v.t.* (*p.t.* **ground**) écraser;

(*coffee*) moudre; (*sharpen*) aiguiser. —*n.* corvée *f.* **~ one's teeth,** grincer des dents. **~ to a halt,** devenir paralysé.

grip /grɪp/ *v.t.* (*p.t.* **gripped**) saisir; (*interest*) passionner. —*n.* prise *f.*; (*strength of hand*) poigne *f.*; (*bag*) sac de voyage *m.* **come to ~s,** en venir aux prises.

gripe /graɪp/ *n.* **~s,** (*med.*) coliques *f. pl.* —*v.i.* (*grumble: sl.*) râler.

grisly /ˈgrɪzlɪ/ *a.* (**-ier, -iest**) macabre, horrible.

gristle /ˈgrɪsl/ *n.* cartilage *m.*

grit /grɪt/ *n.* gravillon *m.*, sable *m.*; (*fig.*) courage *m.* —*v.t.* (*p.t.* **gritted**) (*road*) sabler; (*teeth*) serrer.

grizzle /ˈgrɪzl/ *v.i.* (*cry*) pleurnicher.

groan /grəʊn/ *v.i.* gémir. —*n.* gémissement *m.*

grocer /ˈɡrəʊsə(r)/ *n.* épicier, -ière *m.*, *f.* **~ies** *n. pl.* (*goods*) épicerie *f.* **~y** *n.* (*shop*) épicerie *f.*

grog /grɒg/ *n.* grog *m.*

groggy /ˈɡrɒgɪ/ *a.* (*weak*) faible; (*unsteady*) chancelant; (*ill*) mal fichu.

groin /grɔɪn/ *n.* aine *f.*

groom /gruːm/ *n.* marié *m.*; (*for horses*) valet d'écurie *m.* —*v.t.* (*horse*) panser; (*fig.*) préparer.

groove /gruːv/ *n.* (*for door etc.*) rainure *f.*; (*in record*) sillon *m.*

grope /grəʊp/ *v.i.* tâtonner. **~ for,** chercher à tâtons.

gross /grəʊs/ *a.* (**-er, -est**) (*coarse*) grossier; (*comm.*) brut. —*n. invar.* grosse *f.* **~ly** *adv.* grossièrement; (*very*) extrêmement.

grotesque /grəʊˈtesk/ *a.* grotesque, horrible.

grotto /ˈgrɒtəʊ/ *n.* (*pl.* **-oes**) grotte *f.*

grotty /ˈgrɒtɪ/ *a.* (*sl.*) moche.

grouch /graʊtʃ/ *v.i.* (*grumble: fam.*) rouspéter, râler.

ground[1] /graʊnd/ *n.* terre *f.*, sol *m.*; (*area*) terrain *m.*; (*reason*) raison *f.*; (*electr., Amer.*) masse *f.* **~s,** terres *f. pl.*, parc *m.*; (*of coffee*) marc *m.* —*v.t./i.* (*naut.*) échouer; (*aircraft*) retenir au sol. **on the ~,** par terre. **lose ~,** perdre du terrain. **~ floor,** rez-de-chaussée *m. invar.* **~ rule,** règle de base *f.* **~less** *a.* sans fondement. **~ swell,** lame de fond *f.*

ground[2] /graʊnd/ *see* **grind.** —*a.* **~ beef,** (*Amer.*) bifteck haché *m.*

grounding /ˈgraʊndɪŋ/ *n.* connaissances (de base) *f. pl.*

groundsheet /ˈgraʊndʃiːt/ *n.* tapis de sol *m.*

groundwork /'graʊndwɜːk/ *n.* travail préparatoire *m.*

group /gruːp/ *n.* groupe *m.* —*v.t./i.* (se) grouper.

grouse[1] /graʊs/ *n. invar.* (*bird*) coq de bruyère *m.*, grouse *f.*

grouse[2] /graʊs/ *v.i.* (*grumble: fam.*) rouspéter, râler.

grove /grəʊv/ *n.* bocage *m.*

grovel /'grɒvl/ *v.i.* (*p.t.* **grovelled**) ramper. **~ling** *a.* rampant.

grow /grəʊ/ *v.i.* (*p.t.* **grew**, *p.p.* **grown**) grandir; (*of plant*) pousser; (*become*) devenir. —*v.t.* cultiver. **~ up**, devenir adulte, grandir. **~er** *n.* cultivateur, -trice *m.*, *f.* **~ing** *a.* grandissant.

growl /graʊl/ *v.i.* grogner. —*n.* grognement *m.*

grown /grəʊn/ *see* **grow**. —*a.* adulte. **~-up** *a.* & *n.* adulte (*m./f.*).

growth /grəʊθ/ *n.* croissance *f.*; (*in numbers*) accroissement *m.*; (*of hair, tooth*) pousse *f.*; (*med.*) tumeur *f.*

grub /grʌb/ *n.* (*larva*) larve *f.*; (*food: sl.*) bouffe *f.*

grubby /'grʌbɪ/ *a.* (**-ier, -iest**) sale.

grudge /grʌdʒ/ *v.t.* **~ doing**, faire à contrecœur. **~ s.o. sth.**, (*success, wealth*) en vouloir à qn. de qch. —*n.* rancune *f.* **have a ~ against**, en vouloir à. **grudgingly** *adv.* à contrecœur.

gruelling /'gruːəlɪŋ/ *a.* exténuant.

gruesome /'gruːsəm/ *a.* macabre.

gruff /grʌf/ *a.* (**-er, -est**) bourru.

grumble /'grʌmbl/ *v.i.* ronchonner, grogner (**at**, après).

grumpy /'grʌmpɪ/ *a.* (**-ier, -iest**) grincheux, grognon.

grunt /grʌnt/ *v.i.* grogner. —*n.* grognement *m.*

guarant|ee /gærən'tiː/ *n.* garantie *f.* —*v.t.* garantir. **~or** *n.* garant(e) *m.* (*f.*).

guard /gɑːd/ *v.t.* protéger; (*watch*) surveiller. —*v.i.* **~ against**, se protéger contre. —*n.* (*vigilance, mil., group*) garde *f.*; (*person*) garde *m.*; (*on train*) chef de train *m.* **~ian** *n.* gardien(ne) *m.* (*f.*); (*of orphan*) tulteur, -trice *m.*, *f.*

guarded /'gɑːdɪd/ *a.* prudent.

guerrilla /gə'rɪlə/ *n.* guérillero *m.* **~ warfare**, guérilla *f.*

guess /ges/ *v.t./i.* deviner; (*suppose*) penser. —*n.* conjecture *f.*

guesswork /'geswɜːk/ *n.* conjectures *f. pl.*

guest /gest/ *n.* invité(e) *m.* (*f.*); (*in hotel*) client(e) *m.* (*f.*). **~-house** *n.* pension *f.* **~-room** *n.* chambre d'ami *f.*

guffaw /gə'fɔː/ *n.* gros rire *m.* —*v.i.* s'esclaffer, rire bruyamment.

guidance /'gaɪdns/ *n.* (*advice*) conseils *m. pl.*; (*information*) information *f.*

guide /gaɪd/ *n.* (*person, book*) guide *m.* —*v.t.* guider. **~d** /-ɪd/ *a.* **~d missile**, missile téléguidé *m.* **~-dog** *n.* chien d'aveugle *m.* **~-lines** *n. pl.* grandes lignes *f. pl.*

Guide /gaɪd/ *n.* (*girl*) guide *f.*

guidebook /'gaɪdbʊk/ *n.* guide *m.*

guild /gɪld/ *n.* corporation *f.*

guile /gaɪl/ *n.* ruse *f.*

guillotine /'gɪləˌtiːn/ *n.* guillotine *f.*; (*for paper*) massicot *m.*

guilt /gɪlt/ *n.* culpabilité *f.* **~y** *a.* coupable.

guinea-pig /'gɪnɪpɪg/ *n.* cobaye *m.*

guinea-fowl /'gɪnɪfaʊl/ *n.* pintade *f.*

guise /gaɪz/ *n.* apparence *f.*

guitar /gɪ'tɑː(r)/ *n.* guitare *f.* **~ist** *n.* guitariste *m./f.*

gulf /gʌlf/ *n.* (*part of sea*) golfe *m.*; (*hollow*) gouffre *m.*

gull /gʌl/ *n.* mouette *f.*, goéland *m.*

gullet /'gʌlɪt/ *n.* gosier *m.*

gullible /'gʌləbl/ *a.* crédule.

gully /'gʌlɪ/ *n.* (*ravine*) ravine *f.*; (*drain*) rigole *f.*

gulp /gʌlp/ *v.t.* **~ (down)**, avaler en vitesse. —*v.i.* (*from fear etc.*) avoir un serrement de gorge. —*n.* gorgée *f.*

gum[1] /gʌm/ *n.* (*anat.*) gencive *f.*

gum[2] /gʌm/ *n.* (*from tree*) gomme *f.*; (*glue*) colle *f.*; (*for chewing*) chewing-gum *m.* —*v.t.* (*p.t.* **gummed**) gommer.

gumboil /'gʌmbɔɪl/ *n.* abcès dentaire *m.*

gumboot /'gʌmbuːt/ *n.* botte de caoutchouc *f.*

gumption /'gʌmpʃn/ *n.* (*fam.*) initiative *f.*, courage *m.*, audace *f.*

gun /gʌn/ *n.* (*pistol*) revolver *m.*; (*rifle*) fusil *m.*; (*large*) canon *m.* —*v.t.* (*p.t.* **gunned**). **~ down**, abattre. **~ner** *n.* artilleur *m.*

gunfire /'gʌnfaɪə(r)/ *n.* fusillade *f.*

gunge /gʌndʒ/ *n.* (*sl.*) crasse *f.*

gunman /'gʌnmən/ *n.* (*pl.* **-men**) bandit armé *m.*

gunpowder /'gʌnpaʊdə(r)/ *n.* poudre à canon *f.*

gunshot /'gʌnʃɒt/ *n.* coup de feu *m.*

gurgle /'gɜːgl/ *n.* glouglou *m.* —*v.i.* glouglouter.

guru /'gʊruː/ *n.* (*pl.* **-us**) gourou *m.*

gush /gʌʃ/ *v.i.* **~ (out)**, jaillir. —*n.* jaillissement *m.*

gust /gʌst/ *n.* rafale *f.*; (*of smoke*) bouffée *f.* **~y** *a.* venteux.

gusto /'gʌstəʊ/ n. enthousiasme m.

gut /gʌt/ n. boyau m. ∼s, boyaux m. pl., ventre m.; (courage: fam.) cran m. —v.t. (p.t. gutted) (fish) vider; (of fire) dévaster.

gutter /'gʌtə(r)/ n. (on roof) gouttière f.; (in street) caniveau m.

guttural /'gʌtərəl/ a. guttural.

guy /gaɪ/ n. (man: fam.) type m.

guzzle /'gʌzl/ v.t./i. (eat) bâfrer; (drink: Amer.) boire d'un trait.

gym /dʒɪm/ n. (fam.) gymnase m.; (fam.) gym(nastique) f. ∼-slip n. tunique f. ∼nasium n. gymnase m.

gymnast /'dʒɪmnæst/ n. gymnaste m./f. ∼ics /-'næstɪks/ n. pl. gymnastique f.

gynaecolog|y /gaɪnɪ'kɒlədʒɪ/ n. gynécologie f. ∼ist n. gynécologue m./f.

gypsy /'dʒɪpsɪ/ n. bohémien(ne) m. (f.).

gyrate /dʒaɪ'reɪt/ v.i. tournoyer.

H

haberdashery /hæbə'dæʃərɪ/ n. mercerie f.

habit /'hæbɪt/ n. habitude f.; (costume: relig.) habit m. **be in/get into the ∼ of,** avoir/prendre l'habitude de.

habit|able /'hæbɪtəbl/ a. habitable. ∼ation /-'teɪʃn/ n. habitation f.

habitat /'hæbɪtæt/ n. habitat m.

habitual /hə'bɪtʃʊəl/ a. (usual) habituel; (smoker, liar) invétéré. ∼ly adv. habituellement.

hack¹ /hæk/ n. (old horse) haridelle f.; (writer) nègre m., écrivailleur, -se m., f.

hack² /hæk/ v.t. hacher, tailler.

hackneyed /'hæknɪd/ a. rebattu.

had /hæd/ see **have.**

haddock /'hædək/ n. invar. églefin m. **smoked ∼,** haddock m.

haemorrhage /'hemərɪdʒ/ n. hémorragie f.

haemorrhoids /'hemərɔɪdz/ n. pl. hémorroïdes f. pl.

hag /hæg/ n. (vieille) sorcière f.

haggard /'hægəd/ a. (person) qui a le visage défait; (face, look) défait, hagard.

haggle /'hægl/ v.i. marchander. ∼ over, (object) marchander; (price) discuter.

Hague (The) /(ðə)'heɪg/ n. La Haye.

hail¹ /heɪl/ v.t. (greet) saluer; (taxi) héler. —v.i. ∼ from, venir de.

hail² /heɪl/ n. grêle f. —v.i. grêler.

hailstone /'heɪlstəʊn/ n. grêlon m.

hair /heə(r)/ n. (on head) cheveux m. pl.; (on body, of animal) poils m. pl.; (single strand on head) cheveu m.; (on body) poil m. ∼-do n. (fam.) coiffure f. ∼-drier n. séchoir à (cheveux) m. ∼-grip n. pince à cheveux f. ∼-raising a. horrifique. ∼ remover, dépilatoire m. ∼-style n. coiffure f.

hairbrush /'heəbrʌʃ/ n. brosse à cheveux f.

haircut /'heəkʌt/ n. coupe de cheveux f. **have a ∼,** se faire couper les cheveux.

hairdresser /'heədresə(r)/ n. coiffeur, -se m., f.

hairpin /'heəpɪn/ n. épingle à cheveux f.

hairy /'heərɪ/ a. (-ier, -iest) poilu; (terrifying: sl.) horrifique.

hake /heɪk/ n. invar. colin m.

hale /heɪl/ a. vigoureux.

half /hɑːf/ n. (pl. **halves**) moitié f., demi(e) m. (f.). —a. demi. —adv. à moitié. ∼ **a dozen,** une demi-douzaine. ∼ **an hour,** une demi-heure. **four and a ∼,** quatre et demi(e). ∼ **and half,** moitié moitié. **in ∼,** en deux. ∼-**back** n. (sport) demi m. ∼-**caste** n. métis(se) m. (f.). ∼-**hearted** a. tiède. **at ∼-mast** adv. en berne. ∼ **measure,** demi-mesure f. ∼ **price,** moitié prix. ∼-**term** n. congé de (de)mi-trimestre m. ∼-**time** n. mi-temps f. ∼-**way** adv. à mi-chemin. ∼-**wit** n. imbécile m./f.

halibut /'hælɪbət/ n. invar. (fish) flétan m.

hall /hɔːl/ n. (room) salle f.; (entrance) vestibule m.; (mansion) manoir m.; (corridor) couloir m. ∼ **of residence,** foyer d'étudiants m.

hallelujah /hælɪ'luːjə/ int. & n. = **alleluia.**

hallmark /'hɔːlmɑːk/ n. (on gold etc.) poinçon m.; (fig.) sceau m.

hallo /hə'ləʊ/ int. & n. bonjour (m.). ∼!, (on telephone) allô!; (in surprise) tiens!

hallow /'hæləʊ/ v.t. sanctifier.

Hallowe'en /hæləʊ'iːn/ n. la veille de la Toussaint.

hallucination /həluːsɪ'neɪʃn/ n. hallucination f.

halo /'heɪləʊ/ n. (pl. -oes) auréole f.

halt /hɔːlt/ n. halte f. —v.t./i. (s')arrêter.

halve /hɑːv/ v.t. diviser en deux; (time etc.) réduire de moitié.

ham /hæm/ n. jambon m.; (theatre: sl.) cabotin(e) m. (f.). ∼-**fisted** a. maladroit.

hamburger /'hæmbɜːgə(r)/ n. hamburger m.

hamlet /'hæmlɪt/ n. hameau m.
hammer /'hæmə(r)/ n. marteau m. —v.t./i. marteler, frapper; (defeat) battre à plate couture. ~ out, (differences) arranger; (agreement) arriver à.
hammock /'hæmək/ n. hamac m.
hamper[1] /'hæmpə(r)/ n. panier m.
hamper[2] /'hæmpə(r)/ v.t. gêner.
hamster /'hæmstə(r)/ n. hamster m.
hand /hænd/ n. main f.; (of clock) aiguille f.; (writing) écriture f.; (worker) ouvrier, -ière m., f.; (cards) jeu m. —v.t. donner. **at ~,** proche. **~-baggage** n. bagages à main m. pl. **give s.o. a ~,** donner un coup de main à qn. **~ in** or **over,** remettre. **~ out,** distribuer. **~-out** n. prospectus m.; (money) aumône f. **on ~,** disponible. **on one's ~s,** (fig.) sur les bras. **on the one ~ . . . on the other ~,** d'une part . . . d'autre part. **to ~,** à portée de la main.
handbag /'hændbæg/ n. sac à main m.
handbook /'hændbʊk/ n. manuel m.
handbrake /'hændbreɪk/ n. frein à main m.
handcuffs /'hændkʌfs/ n. pl. menottes f. pl.
handful /'hændfʊl/ n. poignée f. **he's a ~!,** c'est du boulot!
handicap /'hændɪkæp/ n. handicap m. —v.t. (p.t. handicapped) handicaper.
handicraft /'hændɪkrɑːft/ n. travaux manuels m. pl., artisanat m.
handiwork /'hændɪwɜːk/ n. ouvrage m.
handkerchief /'hæŋkətʃɪf/ n. (pl. -fs) mouchoir m.
handle /'hændl/ n. (of door etc.) poignée f.; (of implement) manche m.; (of cup etc.) anse f.; (of pan etc.) queue f.; (for turning) manivelle f. —v.t. manier; (deal with) s'occuper de; (touch) toucher à.
handlebar /'hændlbɑː(r)/ n. guidon m.
handshake /'hændʃeɪk/ n. poignée de main f.
handsome /'hænsəm/ a. (good-looking) beau; (generous) généreux; (large) considérable.
handwriting /'hændraɪtɪŋ/ n. écriture f.
handy /'hændɪ/ a. (-ier, -iest) (useful) commode, utile; (person) adroit; (near) accessible.
handyman /'hændɪmæn/ n. (pl. -men) bricoleur m.; (servant) homme à tout faire m.
hang /hæŋ/ v.t. (p.t. hung) suspendre, accrocher; (p.t. hanged) (criminal)

pendre. —v.i. pendre. —n. **get the ~ of doing,** trouver le truc pour faire. **~ about,** traîner. **~-gliding** n. vol libre m. **~ on,** (hold out) tenir bon; (wait: sl.) attendre. **~ out** v.i. pendre; (live: sl.) crécher; (spend time: sl.) passer son temps; v.t. (washing) étendre. **~ up,** (telephone) raccrocher. **~-up** n. (sl.) complexe m.
hangar /'hæŋə(r)/ n. hangar m.
hanger /'hæŋə(r)/ n. (for clothes) cintre m. **~-on** n. parasite m.
hangover /'hæŋəʊvə(r)/ n. (after drinking) gueule de bois f.
hanker /'hæŋkə(r)/ v.i. **~ after,** avoir envie de. **~ing** n. envie f.
hanky-panky /'hæŋkɪpæŋkɪ/ n. (trickery: sl.) manigances f. pl.
haphazard /hæp'hæzəd/ a., **~ly** adv. au petit bonheur, au hasard.
hapless /'hæplɪs/ a. infortuné.
happen /'hæpən/ v.i. arriver, se passer. **it so ~s that,** il se trouve que. **he ~s to know that,** il se trouve qu'il sait que. **~ing** n. événement m.
happ|y /'hæpɪ/ a. (-ier, -iest) heureux. **I'm not ~y about the idea,** je n'aime pas trop l'idée. **~y with sth.,** satisfait de qch. **~y medium** or **mean,** juste milieu m. **~ily** adv. joyeusement; (fortunately) heureusement. **~iness** n. bonheur m. **~y-go-lucky** a. insouciant.
harass /'hærəs/ v.t. harceler. **~ment** n. harcèlement m.
harbour, (Amer.) **harbor** /'hɑːbə(r)/ n. port m. —v.t. (shelter) héberger.
hard /hɑːd/ a. (-er, -est) dur; (difficult) difficile, dur. —adv. dur; (think) sérieusement; (pull) fort. **~ and fast,** concret. **~-boiled egg,** œuf dur m. **~ by,** tout près. **~ disk,** disque dur m. **~ done by,** mal traité. **~-headed** a. réaliste. **~ of hearing,** dur d'oreille. **the ~ of hearing,** les malentendants m. pl. **~-line** a. pur et dur. **~ shoulder,** accotement stabilisé m. **~ up,** (fam.) fauché. **~-wearing** a. solide. **~-working** a. travailleur. **~ness** n. dureté f.
hardboard /'hɑːdbɔːd/ n. Isorel m. (P.).
harden /'hɑːdn/ v.t./i. durcir.
hardly /'hɑːdlɪ/ adv. à peine. **~ ever,** presque jamais.
hardship /'hɑːdʃɪp/ n. **~(s),** épreuves f. pl., souffrance f.
hardware /'hɑːdweə(r)/ n. (metal goods) quincaillerie f.; (machinery, of computer) matériel m.
hardy /'hɑːdɪ/ a. (-ier, -iest) résistant.

hare /heə(r)/ n. lièvre m. ∼ **around,** courir partout. ∼**-brained** a. écervelé.

hark /hɑːk/ v.i. écouter. ∼ **back to,** revenir sur.

harm /hɑːm/ n. (hurt) mal m.; (wrong) tort m. —v.t. (hurt) faire du mal à; (wrong) faire du tort à; (object) endommager. **there is no** ∼ **in,** il n'y a pas de mal à. ∼**ful** a. nuisible. ∼**less** a. inoffensif.

harmonica /hɑːˈmɒnɪkə/ n. harmonica m.

harmon|y /ˈhɑːmənɪ/ n. harmonie f. ∼**ious** /-ˈməʊnɪəs/ a. harmonieux. ∼**ize** v.t./i. (s')harmoniser.

harness /ˈhɑːnɪs/ n. harnais m. —v.t. (horse) harnacher; (control) maîtriser; (use) exploiter.

harp /hɑːp/ n. harpe f. —v.i. ∼ **on (about),** rabâcher. ∼**ist** n. harpiste m./f.

harpoon /hɑːˈpuːn/ n. harpon m.

harpsichord /ˈhɑːpsɪkɔːd/ n. clavecin m.

harrowing /ˈhærəʊɪŋ/ a. déchirant, qui déchire le cœur.

harsh /hɑːʃ/ a. (-er, -est) dur, rude; (taste) âpre; (sound) rude, âpre. ∼**ly** adv. durement. ∼**ness** n. dureté f.

harvest /ˈhɑːvɪst/ n. moisson f., récolte f. **the wine** ∼, les vendanges f. pl. —v.t. moissonner, récolter. ∼**er** n. moissonneuse f.

has /hæz/ see have.

hash /hæʃ/ n. (culin.) hachis m.; (fig.) gâchis m. **make a** ∼ **of,** (bungle: sl.) saboter.

hashish /ˈhæʃiːʃ/ n. ha(s)chisch m.

hassle /ˈhæsl/ n. (fam.) difficulté(s) f. (pl.); (bother, effort: fam.) mal m., peine f.; (quarrel: fam.) chamaillerie f. —v.t. (harass: fam.) harceler.

haste /heɪst/ n. hâte f. **in** ∼, à la hâte. **make** ∼, se hâter.

hasten /ˈheɪsn/ v.t./i. (se) hâter.

hast|y /ˈheɪstɪ/ a. (-ier, -iest) précipité. ∼**ily** adv. à la hâte.

hat /hæt/ n. chapeau m. **a** ∼ **trick,** trois succès consécutifs.

hatch[1] /hætʃ/ n. (for food) passeplat m.; (naut.) écoutille f.

hatch[2] /hætʃ/ v.t./i. (faire) éclore.

hatchback /ˈhætʃbæk/ n. voiture avec hayon arrière f.

hatchet /ˈhætʃɪt/ n. hachette f.

hate /heɪt/ n. haine f. —v.t. haïr. ∼**ful** a. haïssable.

hatred /ˈheɪtrɪd/ n. haine f.

haughty /ˈhɔːtɪ/ a. (-ier, -iest) hautain.

haul /hɔːl/ v.t. traîner, tirer. —n. (of thieves) butin m.; (catch) prise f.;

(journey) voyage m. ∼**age** n. camionnage m. ∼**ier** n. camionneur m.

haunch /hɔːntʃ/ n. **on one's** ∼**es,** accroupi.

haunt /hɔːnt/ v.t. hanter. —n. endroit favori m.

have /hæv/ v.t. (3 sing. present tense **has**; p.t. **had**) avoir; (meal, bath, etc.) prendre; (walk, dream, etc.) faire. —v. aux. avoir; (with aller, partir, etc. & pronominal verbs) être. ∼ **it out with,** s'expliquer avec. ∼ **just done,** venir de faire. ∼ **sth. done,** faire faire qch. ∼ **to do,** devoir faire. **the** ∼**s and have-nots,** les riches et les pauvres m. pl.

haven /ˈheɪvn/ n. havre m., abri m.

haversack /ˈhævəsæk/ n. musette f.

havoc /ˈhævək/ n. ravages m. pl.

haw /hɔː/ see **hum**.

hawk[1] /hɔːk/ n. faucon m.

hawk[2] /hɔːk/ v.t. colporter. ∼**er** n. colporteur, -se m., f.

hawthorn /ˈhɔːθɔːn/ n. aubépine f.

hay /heɪ/ n. foin m. ∼ **fever,** rhume des foins m.

haystack /ˈheɪstæk/ n. meule de foin f.

haywire /ˈheɪwaɪə(r)/ a. **go** ∼, (plans) se désorganiser; (machine) se détraquer.

hazard /ˈhæzəd/ n. risque m. —v.t. risquer, hasarder. ∼ **warning lights,** feux de détresse m. pl. ∼**ous** a. hasardeux, risqué.

haze /heɪz/ n. brume f.

hazel /ˈheɪzl/ n. (bush) noisetier m. ∼**nut** n. noisette f.

hazy /ˈheɪzɪ/ a. (-ier, -iest) (misty) brumeux; (fig.) flou, vague.

he /hiː/ pron. il; (emphatic) lui. —n. mâle m.

head /hed/ n. tête f.; (leader) chef m.; (of beer) mousse f. —a. principal. ∼ **être à la tête de.** —v.i. ∼ **for,** se diriger vers. ∼**-dress** n. coiffure f.; (lady's) coiffe f. ∼**-on** a. & adv. de plein fouet. ∼ **first,** la tête la première. ∼**s or tails?,** pile ou face? ∼ **office,** siège m. ∼ **rest,** appui-tête m. ∼ **the ball,** faire une tête. ∼ **waiter,** maître d'hôtel m. ∼**er** n. (football) tête f.

headache /ˈhedeɪk/ n. mal de tête m.

heading /ˈhedɪŋ/ n. titre m.; (subject category) rubrique f.

headlamp /ˈhedlæmp/ n. phare m.

headland /ˈhedlənd/ n. cap m.

headlight /ˈhedlaɪt/ n. phare m.

headline /ˈhedlaɪn/ n. titre m.

headlong /ˈhedlɒŋ/ adv. (in a rush) à toute allure.

head|master /ˈhedˈmɑːstə(r)/ n. (of school) directeur m. ∼**mistress** n. directrice f.

headphone /ˈhedfəʊn/ n. écouteur m. ∼**s**, casque (à écouteurs) m.

headquarters /ˈhedkwɔːtəz/ n. pl. siège m., bureau central m.; (mil.) quartier général m.

headstrong /ˈhedstrɒŋ/ a. têtu.

headway /ˈhedweɪ/ n. progrès m. (pl.) **make** ∼, faire des progrès.

heady /ˈhedɪ/ a. (**-ier, -iest**) (wine) capiteux; (exciting) grisant.

heal /hiːl/ v.t./i. guérir.

health /helθ/ n. santé f. ∼ **centre**, dispensaire m. ∼ **foods**, aliments diététiques m. pl. ∼ **insurance**, assurance médicale f. ∼**y** a. sain; (person) en bonne santé.

heap /hiːp/ n. tas m. —v.t. entasser. ∼**s of**, (fam.) des tas de.

hear /hɪə(r)/ v.t./i. (p.t. **heard** /hɜːd/) entendre. **hear, hear!**, bravo! ∼ **from**, recevoir des nouvelles de. ∼ **of** or **about**, entendre parler de. **not** ∼ **of**, (refuse to allow) ne pas entendre parler de. ∼**ing** n. ouïe f.; (of witness) audition f.; (of case) audience f. ∼**ing-aid** n. appareil acoustique m.

hearsay /ˈhɪəseɪ/ n. ouï-dire m. invar. **from** ∼, par ouï-dire.

hearse /hɜːs/ n. corbillard m.

heart /hɑːt/ n. cœur m. ∼**s**, (cards) cœur m. **at** ∼, au fond. **by** ∼, par cœur. ∼ **attack**, crise cardiaque f. ∼**-break** n. chagrin m. ∼**-breaking** a. navrant. **be** ∼**-broken**, avoir le cœur brisé. ∼**-to-heart** a. à cœur ouvert. **lose** ∼, perdre courage.

heartache /ˈhɑːteɪk/ n. chagrin m.

heartburn /ˈhɑːtbɜːn/ n. brûlures d'estomac f. pl.

hearten /ˈhɑːtn/ v.t. encourager.

heartfelt /ˈhɑːtfelt/ a. sincère.

hearth /hɑːθ/ n. foyer m.

heartless /ˈhɑːtlɪs/ a. cruel.

heart|y /ˈhɑːtɪ/ a. (**-ier, -iest**) (sincere) chaleureux; (meal) gros. ∼**ily** adv. (eat) avec appétit.

heat /hiːt/ n. chaleur f.; (excitement: fig.) feu m.; (contest) éliminatoire f. —v.t./i. chauffer. ∼ **stroke**, insolation f. ∼ **up**, (food) réchauffer. ∼ **wave**, vague de chaleur f. ∼**er** n. radiateur m. ∼**ing** n. chauffage m.

heated /ˈhiːtɪd/ a. (fig.) passionné.

heath /hiːθ/ n. (area) lande f.

heathen /ˈhiːðn/ n. païen(ne) m. (f.).

heather /ˈheðə(r)/ n. bruyère f.

heave /hiːv/ v.t./i. (lift) (se) soulever; (a sigh) pousser; (throw: fam.) lancer; (retch) avoir des nausées.

heaven /ˈhevn/ n. ciel m. ∼**ly** a. céleste; (pleasing: fam.) divin.

heav|y /ˈhevɪ/ a. (**-ier, -iest**) lourd; (cold, work, etc.) gros; (traffic) dense. ∼**y goods vehicle**, poids lourd m. ∼**y-handed** a. maladroit. ∼**ily** adv. lourdement; (smoke, drink) beaucoup.

heavyweight /ˈhevɪweɪt/ n. poids lourd m.

Hebrew /ˈhiːbruː/ a. hébreu (m. only), hébraïque. —n. (lang.) hébreu m.

heckle /ˈhekl/ v.t. (speaker) interrompre, interpeller.

hectic /ˈhektɪk/ a. très bousculé, trépidant, agité.

hedge /hedʒ/ n. haie f. —v.t. entourer. —v.i. (in answering) répondre évasivement. ∼ **one's bets**, protéger ses arrières.

hedgehog /ˈhedʒhɒg/ n. hérisson m.

heed /hiːd/ v.t. faire attention à. —n. **pay** ∼ **to**, faire attention à. ∼**less** a. ∼**less of**, inattentif à.

heel /hiːl/ n. talon m.; (man: sl.) salaud m. **down at** ∼, (Amer.) **down at the** ∼**s**, miteux.

hefty /ˈheftɪ/ a. (**-ier, -iest**) gros, lourd.

heifer /ˈhefə(r)/ n. génisse f.

height /haɪt/ n. hauteur f.; (of person) taille f.; (of plane, mountain) altitude f.; (of fame, glory) apogée m.; (of joy, folly, pain) comble m.

heighten /ˈhaɪtn/ v.t. (raise) rehausser; (fig.) augmenter.

heinous /ˈheɪnəs/ a. atroce.

heir /eə(r)/ n. héritier m. ∼**ess** n. héritière f.

heirloom /ˈeəluːm/ n. bijou (meuble, tableau, etc.) de famille m.

held /held/ see **hold**[1].

helicopter /ˈhelɪkɒptə(r)/ n. hélicoptère m.

heliport /ˈhelɪpɔːt/ n. héliport m.

hell /hel/ n. enfer m. ∼**-bent** a. acharné (on, à). ∼**ish** a. infernal.

hello /həˈləʊ/ int. & n. = **hallo**.

helm /helm/ n. (of ship) barre f.

helmet /ˈhelmɪt/ n. casque m.

help /help/ v.t./i. aider. —n. aide f.; (employees) personnel m.; (charwoman) femme de ménage f. ∼ **o.s. to**, se servir de. **he cannot** ∼ **laughing**, il ne peut pas s'empêcher de rire. ∼**er** n. aide m./f. ∼**ful** a. utile; (person) serviable. ∼**less** a. impuissant.

helping /'helpɪŋ/ n. portion f.

helter-skelter /heltə'skeltə(r)/ n. toboggan m. —adv. pêle-mêle.

hem /hem/ n. ourlet m. —v.t. (p.t. **hemmed**) ourler. ～ **in,** enfermer.

hemisphere /'hemɪsfɪə(r)/ n. hémisphère m.

hemorrhage /'hemərɪdʒ/ n. (Amer.) = **haemorrhage**.

hemorrhoids /'hemərɔɪdz/ n. pl. (Amer.) = **haemorrhoids**.

hen /hen/ n. poule f.

hence /hens/ adv. (for this reason) d'où; (from now) d'ici. ～**forth** adv. désormais.

henchman /'hentʃmən/ n. (pl. -**men**) acolyte m., homme de main m.

henpecked /'henpekt/ a. dominé or harcelé par sa femme.

hepatitis /hepə'taɪtɪs/ n. hépatite f.

her /hɜː(r)/ pron. la, l'*; (after prep.) elle. (to) ～, lui. **I know** ～, je la connais. —a. son, sa, pl. ses.

herald /'herəld/ v.t. annoncer.

herb /hɜːb, Amer. ɜːb/ n. herbe f. ～**s,** (culin.) fines herbes f. pl.

herd /hɜːd/ n. troupeau m. —v.t./i. ～ **together,** (s')entasser.

here /hɪə(r)/ adv. ici. ～!, (take this) tenez! ～ **is,** ～ **are,** voici. **I'm** ～, je suis là. ～**abouts** adv. par ici.

hereafter /hɪər'ɑːftə(r)/ adv. après; (in book) ci-après.

hereby /hɪə'baɪ/ adv. par le présent acte; (in letter) par la présente.

hereditary /hɪ'redɪtərɪ/ a. héréditaire.

heredity /hɪ'redɪtɪ/ n. hérédité f.

here|sy /'herəsɪ/ n. hérésie f. ～**tic** n. hérétique m./f.

herewith /hɪə'wɪð/ adv. (comm.) avec ceci, ci-joint.

heritage /'herɪtɪdʒ/ n. patrimoine m., héritage m.

hermit /'hɜːmɪt/ n. ermite m.

hernia /'hɜːnɪə/ n. hernie f.

hero /'hɪərəʊ/ n. (pl. -**oes**) héros m. ～**ine** /'herəʊɪn/ n. héroïne f. ～**ism** /'herəʊɪzəm/ n. héroïsme m.

heroic /hɪ'rəʊɪk/ a. héroïque.

heroin /'herəʊɪn/ n. héroïne f.

heron /'herən/ n. héron m.

herpes /'hɜːpiːz/ n. herpès m.

herring /'herɪŋ/ n. hareng m.

hers /hɜːz/ poss. pron. le sien, la sienne, les sien(ne)s. **it is** ～, c'est à elle or le sien.

herself /hɜː'self/ pron. elle-même; (reflexive) se; (after prep.) elle.

hesitant /'hezɪtənt/ a. hésitant.

hesitat|e /'hezɪteɪt/ v.i. hésiter. ～**ion** /-'teɪʃn/ n. hésitation f.

het /het/ a. ～ **up,** (sl.) énervé.

heterosexual /hetərəʊ'seksjʊəl/ a. & n. hétérosexuel(le) (m. (f.)).

hexagon /'heksəgən/ n. hexagone m. ～**al** /-'ægənl/ a. hexagonal.

hey /heɪ/ int. dites donc.

heyday /'heɪdeɪ/ n. apogée m.

HGV abbr. see **heavy goods vehicle**.

hi /haɪ/ int. (greeting: Amer.) salut.

hibernat|e /'haɪbəneɪt/ v.i. hiberner. ～**ion** /-'neɪʃn/ n. hibernation f.

hiccup /'hɪkʌp/ n. hoquet m. —v.i. hoqueter. (**the**) ～**s,** le hoquet.

hide[1] /haɪd/ v.t. (p.t. **hid,** p.p. **hidden**) cacher (**from,** à). —v.i. se cacher (**from,** de). **go into hiding,** se cacher. ～**-out** n. (fam.) cachette f.

hide[2] /haɪd/ n. (skin) peau f.

hideous /'hɪdɪəs/ a. (dreadful) atroce; (ugly) hideux.

hiding /'haɪdɪŋ/ n. (thrashing: fam.) correction f.

hierarchy /'haɪərɑːkɪ/ n. hiérarchie f.

hi-fi /'haɪfaɪ/ a. & n. hi-fi a. & f. invar.; (machine) chaîne hi-fi f.

high /haɪ/ a. (-**er,** -**est**) haut; (price, number) élevé; (priest, speed) grand; (voice) aigu. —n. **a** (**new**) ～, (recorded level) un record. —adv. haut. ～ **chair,** chaise haute f. ～**-handed** a. autoritaire. ～**-jump,** saut en hauteur m. ～**-level** a. de haut niveau. ～**-rise building,** tour f. ～ **road,** grand-route f. ～ **school,** lycée m. **in the** ～ **season,** en pleine saison. ～**-speed** a. ultra-rapide. ～ **spot,** (fam.) point culminant m. ～ **street,** grand-rue f. ～**-strung** a. (Amer.) nerveux. ～ **tea,** goûter-dîner m. ～**er education,** enseignement supérieur m.

highbrow /'haɪbraʊ/ a. & n. intellectuel(le) (m. (f.)).

highlight /'haɪlaɪt/ n. (vivid moment) moment fort m. ～**s,** (in hair) balayage m. **recorded** ～**s,** extraits enregistrés m. pl. —v.t. (emphasize) souligner.

highly /'haɪlɪ/ adv. extrêmement; (paid) très bien. ～**-strung** a. nerveux. **speak/think** ～ **of,** dire/penser du bien de.

Highness /'haɪnɪs/ n. Altesse f.

highway /'haɪweɪ/ n. route nationale f. ～ **code,** code de la route m.

hijack /'haɪdʒæk/ v.t. détourner. —n. détournement m. ～**er** n. pirate (de l'air) m.

hike /haɪk/ n. randonnée f. —v.i. faire de

la randonnée. **price** ∼, hausse de prix *f.*
∼**r** /-ə(r)/ *n.* randonneur, -se *m., f.*
hilarious /hɪˈleərɪəs/ *a.* (*funny*)
désopilant.
hill /hɪl/ *n.* colline *f.*; (*slope*) côte *f.* ∼**y**
a. accidenté.
hillside /ˈhɪlsaɪd/ *n.* coteau *m.*
hilt /hɪlt/ *n.* (*of sword*) garde *f.* **to the** ∼,
tout à fait, au maximum.
him /hɪm/ *pron.* le, l'*; (*after prep.*) lui.
(**to**) ∼, lui. **I know** ∼, je le connais.
himself /hɪmˈself/ *pron.* lui-même;
(*reflexive*) se; (*after prep.*) lui.
hind /haɪnd/ *a.* de derrière.
hind|er /ˈhɪndə(r)/ *v.t.* (*hamper*) gêner;
(*prevent*) empêcher. ∼**rance** *n.*
obstacle *m.*, gêne *f.*
hindsight /ˈhaɪndsaɪt/ *n.* **with** ∼,
rétrospectivement.
Hindu /hɪnˈduː/ *a. & n.* hindou(e) (*m.*
(*f.*)). ∼**ism** /ˈhɪnduːɪzəm/ *n.* hin-
douisme *m.*
hinge /hɪndʒ/ *n.* charnière *f.* —*v.i.* ∼ **on**,
(*depend on*) dépendre de.
hint /hɪnt/ *n.* allusion *f.*; (*advice*) conseil
m. —*v.t.* laisser entendre. —*v.i.* ∼ **at**,
faire allusion à.
hip /hɪp/ *n.* hanche *f.*
hippie /ˈhɪpɪ/ *n.* hippie *m./f.*
hippopotamus /hɪpəˈpɒtəməs/ *n.* (*pl.*
-**muses**) hippopotame *m.*
hire /ˈhaɪə(r)/ *v.t.* (*thing*) louer; (*person*)
engager. —*n.* location *f.* ∼**-car** *n.*
voiture de location *f.* ∼**-purchase** *n.*
achat à crédit *m.*, vente à crédit *f.*
his /hɪz/ *a.* son, sa, *pl.* ses. —*poss. pron.*
le sien, la sienne, les sien(ne)s. **it is** ∼,
c'est à lui *or* le sien.
hiss /hɪs/ *n.* sifflement *m.* —*v.t./i.* siffler.
historian /hɪˈstɔːrɪən/ *n.* historien(ne) *m.*
(*f.*).
histor|y /ˈhɪstərɪ/ *n.* histoire *f.* **make** ∼**y**,
entrer dans l'histoire. ∼**ic(al)**
/hɪˈstɒrɪk(l)/ *a.* historique.
hit /hɪt/ *v.t.* (*p.t.* **hit**, *pres. p.* **hitting**)
frapper; (*knock against, collide with*)
heurter; (*find*) trouver; (*affect, reach*)
toucher. —*v.i.* ∼ **on**, (*find*) tomber sur.
—*n.* (*blow*) coup *m.*; (*fig.*) succès *m.*;
(*song*) tube *m.* ∼ **it off**, s'entendre bien
(**with**, avec). ∼**-or-miss** *a.* fait au petit
bonheur.
hitch /hɪtʃ/ *v.t.* (*fasten*) accrocher. —*n.*
(*snag*) anicroche *f.* ∼ **a lift**, ∼**-hike** *v.i.*
faire de l'auto-stop. ∼**-hiker** *n.* auto-
stoppeur, -se *m., f.* ∼ **up**, (*pull up*)
remonter.
hi-tech /haɪˈtek/ *a. & n.* high-tech (*m.*)
invar.

hitherto /hɪðəˈtuː/ *adv.* jusqu'ici.
HIV *abbr.* HIV. ∼**-positive** *a.*
séropositif.
hive /haɪv/ *n.* ruche *f.* —*v.t.* ∼ **off**,
séparer; (*industry*) vendre.
hoard /hɔːd/ *v.t.* amasser. —*n.*
réserve(s) *f.* (*pl.*); (*of money*) magot *m.*,
trésor *m.*
hoarding /ˈhɔːdɪŋ/ *n.* panneau
d'affichage *m.*
hoar-frost /ˈhɔːfrɒst/ *n.* givre *m.*
hoarse /hɔːs/ *a.* (-**er**, -**est**) enroué. ∼**ness**
n. enrouement *m.*
hoax /həʊks/ *n.* canular *m.* —*v.t.* faire un
canular à.
hob /hɒb/ *n.* plaque chauffante *f.*
hobble /ˈhɒbl/ *v.i.* clopiner.
hobby /ˈhɒbɪ/ *n.* passe-temps *m. invar.*
∼**-horse** *n.* (*fig.*) dada *m.*
hob-nob /ˈhɒbnɒb/ *v.i.* (*p.t.* **hob-
nobbed**) ∼ **with**, frayer avec.
hock¹ /hɒk/ *n.* vin du Rhin *m.*
hock² /hɒk/ *v.t.* (*pawn: sl.*) mettre au
clou.
hockey /ˈhɒkɪ/ *n.* hockey *m.*
hoe /həʊ/ *n.* binette *f.* —*v.t.* (*pres. p.*
hoeing) biner.
hog /hɒg/ *n.* cochon *m.* —*v.t.* (*p.t.*
hogged) (*fam.*) accaparer.
hoist /hɔɪst/ *v.t.* hisser. —*n.* palan *m.*
hold¹ /həʊld/ *v.t.* (*p.t.* **held**) tenir;
(*contain*) contenir; (*interest, breath,
etc.*) retenir; (*possess*) avoir; (*believe*)
maintenir. —*v.i.* (*of rope, weather,
etc.*) tenir. —*n.* prise *f.* **get** ∼ **of**, saisir;
(*fig.*) trouver. **on** ∼, en suspens. ∼
back, (*contain*) retenir; (*hide*) cacher.
∼ **down**, (*job*) garder; (*in struggle*)
retenir. ∼ **on**, (*stand firm*) tenir bon;
(*wait*) attendre. ∼ **on to**, (*keep*) garder;
(*cling to*) se cramponner à. ∼ **one's
tongue**, se taire. ∼ **out** *v.t.* (*offer*)
offrir; *v.i.* (*resist*) tenir le coup. ∼ (**the
line**), **please**, ne quittez pas. ∼ **up**,
(*support*) soutenir; (*delay*) retarder;
(*rob*) attaquer. ∼**-up** *n.* retard *m.*; (*of
traffic*) bouchon *m.*; (*robbery*) hold-up
m. invar. **not** ∼ **with**, désapprouver.
∼**er** *n.* détenteur, -trice *m., f.*; (*of post*)
titulaire *m./f.*; (*for object*) support
m.
hold² /həʊld/ *n.* (*of ship*) cale *f.*
holdall /ˈhəʊldɔːl/ *n.* (*bag*) fourre-tout
m. invar.
holding /ˈhəʊldɪŋ/ *n.* (*possession, land*)
possession *f.* ∼ **company**, holding *m.*
hole /həʊl/ *n.* trou *m.* —*v.t.* trouer.
holiday /ˈhɒlədeɪ/ *n.* vacances *f. pl.*;
(*public*) jour férié *m.*; (*day off*) congé

m. —*v.i.* passer ses vacances. —*a.* de vacances. **~-maker** *n.* vacancier, -ière *m., f.*

holiness /'həʊlɪnɪs/ *n.* sainteté *f.*

holistic /həʊ'lɪstɪk/ *a.* holistique.

Holland /'hɒlənd/ *n.* Hollande *f.*

hollow /'hɒləʊ/ *a.* creux; (*fig.*) faux. —*n.* creux *m.* —*v.t.* creuser.

holly /'hɒlɪ/ *n.* houx *m.*

holster /'həʊlstə(r)/ *n.* étui de revolver *m.*

holy /'həʊlɪ/ *a.* (**-ier, -iest**) saint, sacré; (*water*) bénit. **H~ Ghost, H~ Spirit,** Saint-Esprit *m.*

homage /'hɒmɪdʒ/ *n.* hommage *m.*

home /həʊm/ *n.* maison *f.*, foyer *m.*; (*institution*) maison *f.*; (*country*) pays natal *m.* —*a.* de la maison, du foyer; (*of family*) de famille; (*pol.*) national, intérieur; (*match, visit*) à domicile. —*adv.* (**at**) **~**, à la maison, chez soi. **come** or **go ~,** rentrer; (*from abroad*) rentrer dans son pays. **feel at ~ with,** être à l'aise avec. **H~ Counties,** région autour de Londres *f.* **~-made** *a.* (*food*) fait maison; (*clothes*) fait à la maison. **H~ Office,** ministère de l'Intérieur *m.* **H~ Secretary,** ministre de l'Intérieur *m.* **~ town,** ville natale *f.* **~ truth,** vérité bien sentie *f.* **~less** *a.* sans abri.

homeland /'həʊmlænd/ *n.* patrie *f.*

homely /'həʊmlɪ/ *a.* (**-ier, -iest**) simple; (*person: Amer.*) assez laid.

homesick /'həʊmsɪk/ *a.* **be ~,** avoir le mal du pays.

homeward /'həʊmwəd/ *a.* (*journey*) de retour.

homework /'həʊmwɜ:k/ *n.* devoirs *m. pl.*

homicide /'hɒmɪsaɪd/ *n.* homicide *m.*

homœopath|y /həʊmɪ'ɒpəθɪ/ *n.* homéopathie *f.* **~ic** *a.* homéopathique.

homogeneous /hɒmə'dʒi:nɪəs/ *a.* homogène.

homosexual /hɒmə'sekʃʊəl/ *a.* & *n.* homosexuel(le) (*m.* (*f.*)).

honest /'ɒnɪst/ *a.* honnête; (*frank*) franc. **~ly** *adv.* honnêtement; franchement. **~y** *n.* honnêteté *f.*

honey /'hʌnɪ/ *n.* miel *m.*; (*person: fam.*) chéri(e) *m.* (*f.*).

honeycomb /'hʌnɪkəʊm/ *n.* rayon de miel *m.*

honeymoon /'hʌnɪmu:n/ *n.* lune de miel *f.*

honk /hɒŋk/ *v.i.* klaxonner.

honorary /'ɒnərərɪ/ *a.* (*person*) honoraire; (*duties*) honorifique.

honour, (*Amer.*) **honor** /'ɒnə(r)/ *n.* honneur *m.* —*v.t.* honorer. **~able** *a.* honorable.

hood /hʊd/ *n.* capuchon *m.*; (*car roof*) capote *f.*; (*car engine cover: Amer.*) capot *m.*

hoodlum /'hu:dləm/ *n.* voyou *m.*

hoodwink /'hʊdwɪŋk/ *v.t.* tromper.

hoof /hu:f/ *n.* (*pl.* **-fs**) sabot *m.*

hook /hʊk/ *n.* crochet *m.*; (*on garment*) agrafe *f.*; (*for fishing*) hameçon *m.* —*v.t./i.* (s')accrocher; (*garment*) (s')agrafer. **off the ~,** tiré d'affaire; (*phone*) décroché.

hooked /hʊkt/ *a.* crochu. **~ on,** (*sl.*) adonné à.

hooker /'hʊkə(r)/ *n.* (*rugby*) talonneur *m.*; (*Amer., sl.*) prostituée *f.*

hookey /'hʊkɪ/ *n.* **play ~,** (*Amer., sl.*) faire l'école buissonnière.

hooligan /'hu:lɪgən/ *n.* houligan *m.*

hoop /hu:p/ *n.* (*toy etc.*) cerceau *m.*

hooray /hu:'reɪ/ *int.* & *n.* = **hurrah.**

hoot /hu:t/ *n.* (h)ululement *m.*; coup de klaxon *m.*; huée *f.* —*v.i.* (*owl*) (h)ululer; (*of car*) klaxonner; (*jeer*) huer. **~er** *n.* klaxon *m.* (P.); (*of factory*) sirène *f.*

Hoover /'hu:və(r)/ *n.* (P.) aspirateur *m.* —*v.t.* passer à l'aspirateur.

hop[1] /hɒp/ *v.i.* (*p.t.* **hopped**) sauter (à cloche-pied). —*n.* saut *m.*; (*flight*) étape *f.* **~ in,** (*fam.*) monter. **~ it,** (*sl.*) décamper. **~ out,** (*fam.*) descendre.

hop[2] /hɒp/ *n.* **~(s),** houblon *m.*

hope /həʊp/ *n.* espoir *m.* —*v.t./i.* espérer. **~ for,** espérer (avoir). **I ~ so,** je l'espère. **~ful** *a.* encourageant. **be ~ful (that),** avoir bon espoir (que). **~fully** *adv.* avec espoir; (*it is hoped*) on l'espère. **~less** *a.* sans espoir; (*useless: fig.*) nul. **~lessly** *adv.* sans espoir de.

hopscotch /'hɒpskɒtʃ/ *n.* marelle *f.*

horde /hɔ:d/ *n.* horde *f.*, foule *f.*

horizon /hə'raɪzn/ *n.* horizon *m.*

horizontal /hɒrɪ'zɒntl/ *a.* horizontal.

hormone /'hɔ:məʊn/ *n.* hormone *f.*

horn /hɔ:n/ *n.* corne *f.*; (*of car*) klaxon *m.* (P.); (*mus.*) cor *m.* —*v.i.* **~ in,** (*sl.*) interrompre. **~y** *a.* (*hands*) calleux.

hornet /'hɔ:nɪt/ *n.* frelon *m.*

horoscope /'hɒrəskəʊp/ *n.* horoscope *m.*

horrible /'hɒrəbl/ *a.* horrible.

horrid /'hɒrɪd/ *a.* horrible.

horrific /hə'rɪfɪk/ *a.* horrifiant.

horr|or /'hɒrə(r)/ *n.* horreur *f.* —*a.* (*film etc.*) d'épouvante. **~ify** *v.t.* horrifier.

hors-d'œuvre /ɔ:'dɜ:vrə/ *n.* hors d'œuvre *m. invar.*

horse /hɔːs/ n. cheval m. ～-**chestnut** n. marron (d'Inde) m. ～-**race** n. course de chevaux f. ～-**radish** n. raifort m. ～ **sense**, (fam.) bon sens m.

horseback /'hɔːsbæk/ n. **on** ～, à cheval.

horseman /'hɔːsmən/ n. (pl. -**men**) cavalier m.

horsepower /'hɔːspauə(r)/ n. (unit) cheval (vapeur) m.

horseshoe /'hɔːsʃuː/ n. fer à cheval m.

horsy /'hɔːsɪ/ a. (face etc.) chevalin.

horticultur|e /'hɔːtɪkʌltʃə(r)/ n. horticulture f. ～**al** /-'kʌltʃərəl/ a. horticole.

hose /həuz/ n. (tube) tuyau m. —v.t. arroser. ～-**pipe** n. tuyau m.

hosiery /'həuzɪərɪ/ n. bonneterie f.

hospice /'hɒspɪs/ n. hospice m.

hospit|able /hɒ'spɪtəbl/ a. hospitalier. ～**ably** adv. avec hospitalité. ～**ality** /-'tælətɪ/ n. hospitalité f.

hospital /'hɒspɪtl/ n. hôpital m.

host[1] /həust/ n. (to guests) hôte m.; (on TV) animateur m. ～**ess** n. hôtesse f.

host[2] /həust/ n. **a** ～ **of**, une foule de.

host[3] /həust/ n. (relig.) hostie f.

hostage /'hɒstɪdʒ/ n. otage m.

hostel /'hɒstl/ n. foyer m. (**youth**) ～, auberge (de jeunesse) f.

hostil|e /'hɒstaɪl, Amer. /'hɒstl/a. hostile. ～**ity** /hɒ'stɪlətɪ/ n. hostilité f.

hot /hɒt/ a. (**hotter, hottest**) chaud; (culin.) épicé; (news) récent. **be** or **feel** ～, avoir chaud. **it is** ～, il fait chaud. —v.t./i. (p.t. **hotted**) ～ **up**, (fam.) chauffer. ～ **dog**, hot-dog m. ～ **line**, téléphone rouge m. ～ **shot**, (Amer., sl.) crack m. ～-**water bottle**, bouillotte f. **in** ～ **water**, (fam.) dans le pétrin. ～**ly** adv. vivement.

hotbed /'hɒtbed/ n. foyer m.

hotchpotch /'hɒtʃpɒtʃ/ n. fatras m.

hotel /həu'tel/ n. hôtel m. ～**ier** /-ɪeɪ/ n. hôtelier, -ière m., f.

hothead /'hɒthed/ n. tête brûlée f. ～**ed** a. impétueux.

hotplate /'hɒtpleɪt/ n. plaque chauffante f.

hound /haund/ n. chien courant m. —v.t. poursuivre.

hour /'auə(r)/ n. heure f. ～**ly** a. & adv. toutes les heures. ～**ly rate**, tarif horaire m. **paid** ～**ly**, payé à l'heure.

house[1] /haus/ n. (pl. -s /'hauzɪz/) n. maison f.; (theatre) salle f.; (pol.) chambre f. ～-**proud** a. méticuleux. ～-**warming** n. pendaison de la crémaillère f.

house[2] /hauz/ v.t. loger; (of building) abriter; (keep) garder.

housebreaking /'hausbreɪkɪŋ/ n. cambriolage m.

housecoat /'hauskəut/ n. blouse f., tablier m.

household /'haushəuld/ n. (house, family) ménage m. —a. ménager. ～**er** n. occupant(e) m. (f.); (owner) propriétaire m./f.

housekeep|er /'hauskiːpə(r)/ n. gouvernante f. ～**ing** n. ménage m.

housewife /'hauswaɪf/ n. (pl. -**wives**) ménagère f.

housework /'hauswɜːk/ n. ménage m. travaux de ménage m. pl.

housing /'hauzɪŋ/ n. logement m. ～ **association**, service de logement m. ～ **development**, cité f.

hovel /'hɒvl/ n. taudis m.

hover /'hɒvə(r)/ v.i. (bird, threat, etc.) planer; (loiter) rôder.

hovercraft /'hɒvəkrɑːft/ n. aéroglisseur m.

how /hau/ adv. comment. ～ **long/tall is . . .?**, quelle est la longueur/hauteur de . . .? ～ **pretty!**, comme or que c'est joli! ～ **about a walk?**, si on faisait une promenade? ～ **are you?**, comment allez-vous? ～ **do you do?**, (introduction) enchanté. ～ **many?**, ～ **much?**, combien?

however /hau'evə(r)/ adv. de quelque manière que; (nevertheless) cependant. ～ **small/delicate**/etc. **it may be**, quelque petit/délicat/etc. que ce soit.

howl /haul/ n. hurlement m. —v.i. hurler.

howler /'haulə(r)/ n. (fam.) bévue f.

HP abbr. see **hire-purchase**.

hp abbr. see **horsepower**.

HQ abbr. see **headquarters**.

hub /hʌb/ n. moyeu m.; (fig.) centre m. ～-**cap** n. enjoliveur m.

hubbub /'hʌbʌb/ n. vacarme m.

huddle /'hʌdl/ v.i. se blottir.

hue[1] /hjuː/ n. (colour) teinte f.

hue[2] /hjuː/ n. ～ **and cry**, clameur f.

huff /hʌf/ n. **in a** ～, fâché, vexé.

hug /hʌg/ v.t. (p.t. **hugged**) serrer dans ses bras; (keep close to) serrer. —n. étreinte f.

huge /hjuːdʒ/ a. énorme. ～**ly** adv. énormément.

hulk /hʌlk/ n. (of ship) épave f.; (person) mastodonte m.

hull /hʌl/ n. (of ship) coque f.

hullo /hə'ləu/ int. & n. = **hallo**.

hum /hʌm/ v.t./i. (p.t. **hummed**)

(*person*) fredonner; (*insect*) bourdonner; (*engine*) vrombir. —*n.* bourdonnement *m.*; vrombissement *m.* ∼ **and haw,** hésiter.

human /'hjuːmən/ *a.* humain. —*n.* être humain *m.* ∼**itarian** /-'mænɪ'teərɪən/ *a.* humanitaire.

humane /hjuː'meɪn/ *a.* humain, plein d'humanité.

humanity /hjuː'mænətɪ/ *n.* humanité *f.*

humbl|e /'hʌmbl/ *a.* (**-er, -est**) humble. —*v.t.* humilier. ∼**y** *adv.* humblement.

humbug /'hʌmbʌg/ *n.* (*false talk*) hypocrisie *f.*

humdrum /'hʌmdrʌm/ *a.* monotone.

humid /'hjuːmɪd/ *a.* humide. ∼**ity** /-'mɪdətɪ/ *n.* humidité *f.*

humiliat|e /hjuː'mɪlɪeɪt/ *v.t.* humilier. ∼**ion** /-'eɪʃn/ *n.* humiliation *f.*

humility /hjuː'mɪlətɪ/ *n.* humilité *f.*

humorist /'hjuːmərɪst/ *n.* humoriste *m./f.*

hum|our, (*Amer.*) **hum|or** /'hjuːmə(r)/ *n.* humour *m.*; (*mood*) humeur *f.* —*v.t.* ménager. ∼**orous** *a.* humoristique; (*person*) plein d'humour. ∼**orously** *adv.* avec humour.

hump /hʌmp/ *n.* bosse *f.* —*v.t.* voûter. **the** ∼, (*sl.*) le cafard.

hunch[1] /hʌntʃ/ *v.t.* voûter.

hunch[2] /hʌntʃ/ *n.* petite idée *f.*

hunchback /'hʌntʃbæk/ *n.* bossu(e) *m.* (*f.*).

hundred /'hʌndrəd/ *a. & n.* cent (*m.*). ∼**s of,** des centaines de. ∼**fold** *a.* centuple; *adv.* au centuple. ∼**th** *a. & n.* centième (*m./f.*).

hundredweight /'hʌndrədweɪt/ *n.* 50.8 kg.; (*Amer.*) 45.36 kg.

hung /hʌŋ/ *see* **hang**.

Hungar|y /'hʌŋgərɪ/ *n.* Hongrie *f.* ∼**ian** /-'geərɪən/ *a. & n.* hongrois(e) (*m.* (*f.*)).

hunger /'hʌŋgə(r)/ *n.* faim *f.* —*v.i.* ∼ **for,** avoir faim de. ∼**-strike** *n.* grève de la faim *f.*

hungr|y /'hʌŋgrɪ/ *a.* (**-ier, -iest**) affamé. **be** ∼**y,** avoir faim. ∼**ily** *adv.* avidement.

hunk /hʌŋk/ *n.* gros morceau *m.*

hunt /hʌnt/ *v.t./i.* chasser. —*n.* chasse *f.* ∼ **for,** chercher. ∼**er** *n.* chasseur *m.* ∼**ing** *n.* chasse *f.*

hurdle /'hɜːdl/ *n.* (*sport*) haie *f.*; (*fig.*) obstacle *m.*

hurl /hɜːl/ *v.t.* lancer.

hurrah, hurray /hʊ'rɑː, hʊ'reɪ/ *int. & n.* hourra (*m.*).

hurricane /'hʌrɪkən, *Amer.* 'hʌrɪkeɪn/ *n.* ouragan *m.*

hurried /'hʌrɪd/ *a.* précipité. ∼**ly** *adv.* précipitamment.

hurry /'hʌrɪ/ *v.i.* se dépêcher, se presser. —*v.t.* presser, activer. —*n.* hâte *f.* **in a** ∼, pressé.

hurt /hɜːt/ *v.t./i.* (*p.t.* **hurt**) faire mal (à); (*injure, offend*) blesser. —*a.* blessé. —*n.* mal *m.* ∼**ful** *a.* blessant.

hurtle /'hɜːtl/ *v.t.* lancer. —*v.i.* ∼ **along,** avancer à toute vitesse.

husband /'hʌzbənd/ *n.* mari *m.*

hush /hʌʃ/ *v.t.* faire taire. —*n.* silence *m.* ∼**-hush** *a.* (*fam.*) ultra-secret. ∼ **up,** (*news etc.*) étouffer.

husk /hʌsk/ *n.* (*of grain*) enveloppe *f.*

husky /'hʌskɪ/ *a.* (**-ier, -iest**) (*hoarse*) rauque; (*burly*) costaud. —*n.* chien de traîneau *m.*

hustle /'hʌsl/ *v.t.* (*push, rush*) bousculer. —*v.i.* (*work busily: Amer.*) se démener. —*n.* bousculade *f.* ∼ **and bustle,** agitation *f.*

hut /hʌt/ *n.* cabane *f.*

hutch /hʌtʃ/ *n.* clapier *m.*

hyacinth /'haɪəsɪnθ/ *n.* jacinthe *f.*

hybrid /'haɪbrɪd/ *a. & n.* hybride (*m.*).

hydrangea /haɪ'dreɪndʒə/ *n.* hortensia *m.*

hydrant /'haɪdrənt/ *n.* (**fire**) ∼, bouche d'incendie *f.*

hydraulic /haɪ'drɔːlɪk/ *a.* hydraulique.

hydroelectric /haɪdrəʊɪ'lektrɪk/ *a.* hydro-électrique.

hydrofoil /'haɪdrəʊfɔɪl/ *n.* hydroptère *m.*

hydrogen /'haɪdrədʒən/ *n.* hydrogène *m.* ∼ **bomb,** bombe à hydrogène *f.*

hyena /haɪ'iːnə/ *n.* hyène *f.*

hygiene /'haɪdʒiːn/ *n.* hygiène *f.*

hygienic /haɪ'dʒiːnɪk/ *a.* hygiénique.

hymn /hɪm/ *n.* cantique *m.*, hymne *m.*

hype /haɪp/ *n.* tapage publicitaire *m.* —*v.t.* faire du tapage autour de.

hyper- /'haɪpə(r)/ *pref.* hyper-.

hypermarket /'haɪpəmɑːkɪt/ *n.* hypermarché *m.*

hyphen /'haɪfn/ *n.* trait d'union *m.* ∼**ate** *v.t.* mettre un trait d'union à.

hypno|sis /hɪp'nəʊsɪs/ *n.* hypnose *f.* ∼**tic** /-'nɒtɪk/ *a.* hypnotique.

hypnot|ize /'hɪpnətaɪz/ *v.t.* hypnotiser. ∼**ism** *n.* hypnotisme *m.*

hypochondriac /haɪpə'kɒndrɪæk/ *n.* malade imaginaire *m./f.*

hypocrisy /hɪ'pɒkrəsɪ/ *n.* hypocrisie *f.*

hypocrit|e /'hɪpəkrɪt/ *n.* hypocrite *m./f.* ∼**ical** /-'krɪtɪkl/ *a.* hypocrite.

hypodermic /haɪpə'dɜːmɪk/ *a.* hypodermique. —*n.* seringue hypodermique *f.*

hypothermia /haɪpəˈθɜːmɪə/ n. hypothermie f.

hypthe|sis /haɪˈpɒθəsɪs/ n. (pl. **-theses** /-siːz/) hypothèse f. ~**tical** /-əˈθetɪkl/ a. hypothétique.

hyster|ia /hɪˈstɪərɪə/ n. hystérie f. ~**ical** /-erɪkl/ a. hystérique; (person) surexcité.

hysterics /hɪˈsterɪks/ n. pl. crise de nerfs or de rire f.

I

I /aɪ/ pron. je, j'*; (stressed) moi.

ice /aɪs/ n. glace f.; (on road) verglas m. —v.t. (cake) glacer. —v.i. ~ (**up**), (window) se givrer; (river) geler. ~**cream** n. glace f. ~**cube** n. glaçon m. ~ **hockey**, hockey sur glace m. ~ **lolly**, glace (sur bâtonnet) f. ~ **rink**, patinoire f. ~ **skate**, patin à glace m.

iceberg /ˈaɪsbɜːg/ n. iceberg m.

icebox /ˈaɪsbɒks/ n. (Amer.) réfrigérateur m.

Iceland /ˈaɪslənd/ n. Islande f. ~**er** n. Islandais(e) m. (f.). ~**ic** /-ˈlændɪk/ a. islandais; n. (lang.) islandais m.

icicle /ˈaɪsɪkl/ n. glaçon m.

icing /ˈaɪsɪŋ/ n. (sugar) glace f.

icon /ˈaɪkɒn/ n. icône f.

icy /ˈaɪsɪ/ a. (**-ier**, **-iest**) (hands, wind) glacé; (road) verglacé; (manner, welcome) glacial.

idea /aɪˈdɪə/ n. idée f.

ideal /aɪˈdɪəl/ a. idéal. —n. idéal m. ~**ize** v.t. idéaliser. ~**ly** adv. idéalement.

idealis|t /aɪˈdɪəlɪst/ n. idéaliste m./f. ~**m** /-zəm/ n. idéalisme m. ~**tic** /-ˈlɪstɪk/ a. idéaliste.

identical /aɪˈdentɪkl/ a. identique.

identif|y /aɪˈdentɪfaɪ/ v.t. identifier. —v.i. ~**y with**, s'identifier à. ~**ication** /-ɪˈkeɪʃn/ n. identification f.; (papers) une pièce d'identité.

identikit /aɪˈdentɪkɪt/ n. ~ **picture**, portrait-robot m.

identity /aɪˈdentətɪ/ n. identité f.

ideolog|y /aɪdɪˈɒlədʒɪ/ n. idéologie f. ~**ical** /-əˈlɒdʒɪkl/ a. idéologique.

idiocy /ˈɪdɪəsɪ/ n. idiotie f.

idiom /ˈɪdɪəm/ n. expression idiomatique f.; (language) idiome m. ~**atic** /-ˈmætɪk/ a. idiomatique.

idiosyncrasy /ɪdɪəˈsɪŋkrəsɪ/ n. particularité f.

idiot /ˈɪdɪət/ n. idiot(e) m. (f.). ~**ic** /-ˈɒtɪk/ a. idiot.

idle /ˈaɪdl/ a. (**-er**, **-est**) désœuvré, oisif; (lazy) paresseux; (unemployed) sans travail; (machine) au repos; (fig.) vain. —v.i. (engine) tourner au ralenti. —v.t. ~ **away**, gaspiller. ~**ness** n. oisiveté f. ~**r** /-ə(r)/ n. oisilf, -ve m., f.

idol /ˈaɪdl/ n. idole f. ~**ize** v.t. idolâtrer.

idyllic /ɪˈdɪlɪk, Amer. aɪˈdɪlɪk/ a. idyllique.

i.e. abbr. c'est-à-dire.

if /ɪf/ conj. si.

igloo /ˈɪgluː/ n. igloo m.

ignite /ɪgˈnaɪt/ v.t./i. (s')enflammer.

ignition /ɪgˈnɪʃn/ n. (auto.) allumage m. ~ **key**, clé de contact. ~ (**switch**), contact m.

ignoran|t /ˈɪgnərənt/ a. ignorant (**of**, de). ~**ce** n. ignorance f. ~**tly** adv. par ignorance.

ignore /ɪgˈnɔː(r)/ v.t. ne faire or prêter aucune attention à; (person in street etc.) faire semblant de ne pas voir; (facts) ne pas tenir compte de.

ilk /ɪlk/ n. (kind: fam.) acabit m.

ill /ɪl/ a. malade; (bad) mauvais. —adv. mal. —n. mal m. ~**advised** a. peu judicieux. ~ **at ease**, mal à l'aise. ~**bred** a. mal élevé. ~**fated** a. malheureux. ~**feeling**, ressentiment m. ~**gotten** a. mal acquis. ~**natured** a. désagréable. ~**treat** v.t. maltraiter. ~ **will**, malveillance f.

illegal /ɪˈliːgl/ a. illégal.

illegible /ɪˈledʒəbl/ a. illisible.

illegitima|te /ɪlɪˈdʒɪtɪmət/ a. illégitime. ~**cy** n. illégitimité f.

illitera|te /ɪˈlɪtərət/ a. & n. illettré(e) (m. (f.)), analphabète m./f. ~**cy** n. analphabétisme m.

illness /ˈɪlnɪs/ n. maladie f.

illogical /ɪˈlɒdʒɪkl/ a. illogique.

illuminat|e /ɪˈluːmɪneɪt/ v.t. éclairer; (decorate with lights) illuminer. ~**ion** /-ˈneɪʃn/ n. éclairage m.; illumination f.

illusion /ɪˈluːʒn/ n. illusion f.

illusory /ɪˈluːsərɪ/ a. illusoire.

illustrat|e /ˈɪləstreɪt/ v.t. illustrer. ~**ion** /-ˈstreɪʃn/ n. illustration f. ~**ive** /-ətɪv/ a. qui illustre.

illustrious /ɪˈlʌstrɪəs/ a. illustre.

image /ˈɪmɪdʒ/ n. image f. (**public**) ~, (of firm, person) image de marque f. ~**ry** /-ərɪ/ n. images f. pl.

imaginary /ɪˈmædʒɪnərɪ/ a. imaginaire.

imaginat|ion /ɪmædʒɪˈneɪʃn/ n. imagination f. ~**ive** /ɪˈmædʒɪnətɪv/ a. plein d'imagination.

imagin|e /ı'mædʒın/ v.t. (picture to o.s.) (s')imaginer; (suppose) imaginer. **~able** a. imaginable.

imbalance /ım'bæləns/ n. déséquilibre m.

imbecile /'ımbəsi:l/ n. & a. imbécile (m./f.).

imbue /ım'bju:/ v.t. imprégner.

imitat|e /'ımıteıt/ v.t. imiter. **~ion** /-'teıʃn/ n. imitation f. **~or** n. imitateur, -trice m., f.

immaculate /ı'mækjʊlət/ a. (room, dress, etc.) impeccable.

immaterial /ımə'tıərıəl/ a. sans importance (**to,** pour; **that,** que).

immature /ımə'tjʊə(r)/ a. pas mûr; (person) immature.

immediate /ı'mi:dıət/ a. immédiat. **~ly** adv. immédiatement; conj. dès que.

immens|e /ı'mens/ a. immense. **~ely** adv. extrêmement, immensément. **~ity** n. immensité f.

immers|e /ı'mɜ:s/ v.t. plonger, immerger. **~ion** /-ɜ:ʃn/ n. immersion f. **~ion heater**, chauffe-eau (électrique) m. invar.

immigr|ate /'ımıgreıt/ v.i. immigrer. **~ant** n. & a. immigré(e) (m. (f.)); (newly-arrived) immigrant(e) (m. (f.)). **~ation** /-'greıʃn/ n. immigration f. **go through ~ation**, passer le contrôle des passeports.

imminen|t /'ımınənt/ a. imminent. **~ce** n. imminence f.

immobil|e /ı'məʊbaıl, Amer. ı'məʊbl/ a. immobile. **~ize** /-əlaız/ v.t. immobiliser.

immoderate /ı'mɒdərət/ a. immodéré.

immoral /ı'mɒrəl/ a. immoral. **~ity** /ımə'rælətı/ n. immoralité f.

immortal /ı'mɔ:tl/ a. immortel. **~ity** /-'tælətı/ n. immortalité f. **~ize** v.t. immortaliser.

immun|e /ı'mju:n/ a. immunisé (**from, to,** contre). **~ity** n. immunité f.

immuniz|e /'ımjʊnaız/ v.t. immuniser. **~ation** /-'zeıʃn/ n. immunisation f.

imp /ımp/ n. lutin m.

impact /'ımpækt/ n. impact m.

impair /ım'peə(r)/ v.t. détériorer.

impart /ım'pɑ:t/ v.t. communiquer, transmettre.

impartial /ım'pɑ:ʃl/ a. impartial. **~ity** /-ı'ælətı/ n. impartialité f.

impassable /ım'pɑ:səbl/ a. (barrier etc.) infranchissable; (road) impraticable.

impasse /'æmpɑ:s, Amer. 'ımpæs/ n. impasse f.

impassioned /ım'pæʃnd/ n. passionné.

impassive /ım'pæsıv/ a. impassible.

impatien|t /ım'peıʃnt/ a. impatient. **get ~t,** s'impatienter. **~ce** n. impatience f. **~tly** adv. impatiemment.

impeccable /ım'pekəbl/ a. impeccable.

impede /ım'pi:d/ v.t. gêner.

impediment /ım'pedımənt/ n. obstacle m. (**speech**) **~,** défaut d'élocution m.

impel /ım'pel/ v.t. (p.t. **impelled**) pousser, forcer (**to do,** à faire).

impending /ım'pendıŋ/ a. imminent.

impenetrable /ım'penıtrəbl/ a. impénétrable.

imperative /ım'perətıv/ a. nécessaire; (need etc.) impérieux. —n. (gram.) impératif m.

imperceptible /ımpə'septəbl/ a. imperceptible.

imperfect /ım'pɜ:fıkt/ a. imparfait; (faulty) défectueux. **~ion** /-ə'fekʃn/ n. imperfection f.

imperial /ım'pıərıəl/ a. impérial; (measure) légal (au Royaume-Uni). **~ism** n. impérialisme m.

imperil /ım'perəl/ v.t. (p.t. **imperilled**) mettre en péril.

imperious /ım'pıərıəs/ a. impérieux.

impersonal /ım'pɜ:sənl/ a. impersonnel.

impersonat|e /ım'pɜ:səneıt/ v.t. se faire passer pour; (mimic) imiter. **~ion** /-'neıʃn/ n. imitation f. **~or** n. imitateur, -trice m., f.

impertinen|t /ım'pɜ:tınənt/ a. impertinent. **~ce** n. impertinence f. **~tly** adv. avec impertinence.

impervious /ım'pɜ:vıəs/ a. **~ to,** imperméable à.

impetuous /ım'petʃʊəs/ a. impétueux.

impetus /'ımpıtəs/ n. impulsion f.

impinge /ım'pındʒ/ v.i. **~ on,** affecter; (encroach) empiéter sur.

impish /'ımpıʃ/ a. espiègle.

implacable /ım'plækəbl/ a. implacable.

implant /ım'plɑ:nt/ v.t. implanter. —n. implant m.

implement[1] /'ımplımənt/ n. (tool) outil m.; (utensil) ustensile m.

implement[2] /'ımplıment/ v.t. exécuter, mettre en pratique.

implicat|e /'ımplıkeıt/ v.t. impliquer. **~ion** /-'keıʃn/ n. implication f.

implicit /ım'plısıt/ a. (implied) implicite; (unquestioning) absolu.

implore /ım'plɔ:(r)/ v.t. implorer.

impl|y /ım'plaı/ v.t. (assume, mean) impliquer; (insinuate) laisser entendre. **~ied** a. implicite.

impolite /ımpə'laıt/ a. impoli.

imponderable /ɪm'pɒndərəbl/ a. & n. impondérable (m.).

import¹ /ɪm'pɔ:t/ v.t. importer. ∼ation /-'teɪʃn/ n. importation f. ∼er n. importalteur, -trice m., f.

import² /'ɪmpɔ:t/ n. (article) importation f.; (meaning) sens m.

importan|t /ɪm'pɔ:tnt/ a. important. ∼ce n. importance f.

impos|e /ɪm'pəʊz/ v.t. imposer. —v.i. ∼e on, abuser de l'amabilité de. ∼ition /-ə'zɪʃn/ n. imposition f.; (fig.) dérangement m.

imposing /ɪm'pəʊzɪŋ/ a. imposant.

impossib|le /ɪm'pɒsəbl/ a. impossible. ∼ility /-'bɪlətɪ/ n. impossibilité f.

impostor /ɪm'pɒstə(r)/ n. imposteur m.

impoten|t /'ɪmpətənt/ a. impuissant. ∼ce n. impuissance f.

impound /ɪm'paʊnd/ v.t. confisquer, saisir.

impoverish /ɪm'pɒvərɪʃ/ v.t. appauvrir.

impracticable /ɪm'præktɪkəbl/ a. impraticable.

impractical /ɪm'præktɪkl/ a. peu pratique.

imprecise /ɪmprɪ'saɪs/ a. imprécis.

impregnable /ɪm'pregnəbl/ a. imprenable; (fig.) inattaquable.

impregnate /'ɪmpregneɪt/ v.t. imprégner (with, de).

impresario /ɪmprɪ'sɑ:rɪəʊ/ n. (pl. -os) impresario m.

impress /ɪm'pres/ v.t. impressionner; (imprint) imprimer. ∼ on s.o., faire comprendre à qn.

impression /ɪm'preʃn/ n. impression f. ∼able a. impressionnable.

impressive /ɪm'presɪv/ a. impressionnant.

imprint¹ /'ɪmprɪnt/ n. empreinte f.

imprint² /ɪm'prɪnt/ v.t. imprimer.

imprison /ɪm'prɪzn/ v.t. emprisonner. ∼ment n. emprisonnement m., prison f.

improbab|le /ɪm'prɒbəbl/ a. (not likely) improbable; (incredible) invraisemblable. ∼ility /-'bɪlətɪ/ n. improbabilité f.

impromptu /ɪm'prɒmptju:/ a. & adv. impromptu.

improp|er /ɪm'prɒpə(r)/ a. inconvenant, indécent; (wrong) incorrect. ∼riety /-ə'praɪətɪ/ n. inconvenance f.

improve /ɪm'pru:v/ v.t./i. (s')améliorer. ∼ment n. amélioration f.

improvis|e /'ɪmprəvaɪz/ v.t./i. improviser. ∼ation /-'zeɪʃn/ n. improvisation f.

imprudent /ɪm'pru:dnt/ a. imprudent.

impuden|t /'ɪmpjʊdənt/ a. impudent. ∼ce n. impudence f.

impulse /'ɪmpʌls/ n. impulsion f. on ∼, sur un coup de tête.

impulsive /ɪm'pʌlsɪv/ a. impulsif. ∼ly adv. par impulsion.

impunity /ɪm'pju:nətɪ/ n. impunité f. with ∼, impunément.

impur|e /ɪm'pjʊə(r)/ a. impur. ∼ity n. impureté f.

impute /ɪm'pju:t/ v.t. imputer.

in /ɪn/ prep. dans, à, en. —adv. (inside) dedans; (at home) là, à la maison; (in fashion) à la mode. **in the box/garden**, dans la boîte/le jardin. **in Paris/school**, à Paris/l'école. **in town**, en ville. **in the country**, à la campagne. **in winter/English**, en hiver/anglais. **in India**, en Inde. **in Japan**, au Japon. **in a firm manner/voice**, d'une manière/voix ferme. **in blue**, en bleu. **in ink**, à l'encre. **in uniform**, en uniforme. **in a skirt**, en jupe. **in a whisper**, en chuchotant. **in a loud voice**, d'une voix forte. **in winter**, en hiver. **in spring**, au printemps. **in an hour**, (at end of) au bout d'une heure. **in an hour('s time)**, dans une heure. **in (the space of) an hour**, en une heure. **in doing**, en faisant. **in the evening**, le soir. **one in ten**, un sur dix. **in between**, entre les deux; (time) entretemps. **the best in**, le meilleur de. **we are in for**, on va avoir. **in-laws** n. pl. (fam.) beaux-parents m. pl. ∼-**patient** n. malade hospitalisé(e) m.(f.). **the ins and outs of**, les tenants et aboutissants de. **in so far as**, dans la mesure où.

inability /ɪnə'bɪlətɪ/ n. incapacité f. (**to do**, de faire).

inaccessible /ɪnæk'sesəbl/ a. inaccessible.

inaccurate /ɪn'ækjərət/ a. inexact.

inaction /ɪn'ækʃn/ n. inaction f.

inactiv|e /ɪn'æktɪv/ a. inactif. ∼ity /-'tɪvətɪ/ n. inaction f.

inadequa|te /ɪn'ædɪkwət/ a. insuffisant. ∼cy n. insuffisance f.

inadmissible /ɪnəd'mɪsəbl/ a. inadmissible.

inadvertently /ɪnəd'vɜ:təntlɪ/ adv. par mégarde.

inadvisable /ɪnəd'vaɪzəbl/ a. déconseillé, pas recommandé.

inane /ɪ'neɪn/ a. inepte.

inanimate /ɪn'ænɪmət/ a. inanimé.

inappropriate /ɪnə'prəʊprɪət/ a. inopportun; (term) inapproprié.

inarticulate /ɪnɑ:'tɪkjʊlət/ a. qui a du mal à s'exprimer.

inasmuch as /ɪnəz'mʌtʃəz/ adv. en ce sens que; (because) vu que.

inattentive /ɪnə'tentɪv/ a. inattentif.
inaudible /ɪn'ɔːdɪbl/ a. inaudible.
inaugural /ɪ'nɔːgjʊrəl/ a. inaugural.
inaugurat|e /ɪ'nɔːgjʊreɪt/ v.t. (open, begin) inaugurer; (person) investir. **~ion** /-'reɪʃn/ n. inauguration f.; investiture f.
inauspicious /ɪnɔː'spɪʃəs/ a. peu propice.
inborn /ɪn'bɔːn/ a. inné.
inbred /ɪn'bred/ a. (inborn) inné.
inc. abbr. (incorporated) S.A.
incalculable /ɪn'kælkjʊləbl/ a. incalculable.
incapable /ɪn'keɪpəbl/ a. incapable.
incapacit|y /ɪnkə'pæsətɪ/ n. incapacité f. **~ate** v.t. rendre incapable (de travailler etc.).
incarcerate /ɪn'kɑːsəreɪt/ v.t. incarcérer.
incarnat|e /ɪn'kɑːneɪt/ a. incarné. **~ion** /-'neɪʃn/ n. incarnation f.
incendiary /ɪn'sendɪərɪ/ a. incendiaire. —n. (bomb) bombe incendiaire f.
incense[1] /'ɪnsens/ n. encens m.
incense[2] /ɪn'sens/ v.t. mettre en fureur.
incentive /ɪn'sentɪv/ n. motivation f.; (payment) prime (d'encouragement) f.
inception /ɪn'sepʃn/ n. début m.
incessant /ɪn'sesnt/ a. incessant. **~ly** adv. sans cesse.
incest /'ɪnsest/ n. inceste m. **~uous** /ɪn'sestjʊəs/ a. incestueux.
inch /ɪntʃ/ n. pouce m. (= 2.54 cm.). —v.i. avancer doucement.
incidence /'ɪnsɪdəns/ n. fréquence f.
incident /'ɪnsɪdənt/ n. incident m.; (in play, film, etc.) épisode m.
incidental /ɪnsɪ'dentl/ a. accessoire. **~ly** adv. accessoirement; (by the way) à propos.
incinerat|e /ɪn'sɪnəreɪt/ v.t. incinérer. **~or** n. incinérateur m.
incipient /ɪn'sɪpɪənt/ a. naissant.
incision /ɪn'sɪʒn/ n. incision f.
incisive /ɪn'saɪsɪv/ a. incisif.
incite /ɪn'saɪt/ v.t. inciter, pousser. **~ment** n. incitation f.
inclement /ɪn'klemənt/ a. inclément, rigoureux.
inclination /ɪnklɪ'neɪʃn/ n. (propensity, bowing) inclination f.
incline[1] /ɪn'klaɪn/ v.t./i. incliner. **be ~d to**, avoir tendance à.
incline[2] /'ɪnklaɪn/ n. pente f.
inclu|de /ɪn'kluːd/ v.t. comprendre, inclure. **~ding** prep. (y) compris. **~sion** n. inclusion f.
inclusive /ɪn'kluːsɪv/ a. & adv. inclus, compris. **be ~ of**, comprendre, inclure.
incognito /ɪnkɒg'niːtəʊ/ adv. incognito.

incoherent /ɪnkəʊ'hɪərənt/ a. incohérent.
income /'ɪnkʌm/ n. revenu m. **~ tax**, impôt sur le revenu m.
incoming /'ɪnkʌmɪŋ/ a. (tide) montant; (tenant etc.) nouveau.
incomparable /ɪn'kɒmprəbl/ a. incomparable.
incompatible /ɪnkəm'pætəbl/ a. incompatible.
incompeten|t /ɪn'kɒmpɪtənt/ a. incompétent. **~ce** n. incompétence f.
incomplete /ɪnkəm'pliːt/ a. incomplet.
incomprehensible /ɪnkɒmprɪ'hensəbl/ a. incompréhensible.
inconceivable /ɪnkən'siːvəbl/ a. inconcevable.
inconclusive /ɪnkən'kluːsɪv/ a. peu concluant.
incongruous /ɪn'kɒŋgrʊəs/ a. déplacé, incongru.
inconsequential /ɪnkɒnsɪ'kwenʃl/ a. sans importance.
inconsiderate /ɪnkən'sɪdərət/ a. (person) qui ne se soucie pas des autres; (act) irréfléchi.
inconsisten|t /ɪnkən'sɪstənt/ a. (treatment) sans cohérence, inconséquent; (argument) contradictoire; (performance) irrégulier. **~t with**, incompatible avec. **~cy** n. inconséquence f. contradiction f.; irrégularité f.
inconspicuous /ɪnkən'spɪkjʊəs/ a. peu en évidence.
incontinen|t /ɪn'kɒntɪnənt/ a. incontinent. **~ce** n. incontinence f.
inconvenien|t /ɪnkən'viːnɪənt/ a. incommode, peu pratique; (time) mal choisi. **be ~t for**, ne pas convenir à. **~ce** n. dérangement m.; (drawback) inconvénient m.; v.t. déranger.
incorporate /ɪn'kɔːpəreɪt/ v.t. incorporer; (include) contenir.
incorrect /ɪnkə'rekt/ a. inexact.
incorrigible /ɪn'kɒrɪdʒəbl/ a. incorrigible.
incorruptible /ɪnkə'rʌptəbl/ a. incorruptible.
increas|e[1] /ɪn'kriːs/ v.t./i. augmenter. **~ing** a. croissant. **~ingly** adv. de plus en plus.
increase[2] /'ɪnkriːs/ n. augmentation f. (in, of, de). **be on the ~**, augmenter.
incredible /ɪn'kredəbl/ a. incroyable.
incredulous /ɪn'kredjʊləs/ a. incrédule.
increment /'ɪnkrəmənt/ n. augmentation f.
incriminat|e /ɪn'krɪmɪneɪt/ v.t. incriminer. **~ing** a. compromettant.

incubat|e /'ɪnkjʊbeɪt/ v.t. (eggs) couver. **∼ion** /-'beɪʃn/ n. incubation f. **∼or** n. couveuse f.

inculcate /'ɪnkʌlkeɪt/ v.t. inculquer.

incumbent /ɪn'kʌmbənt/ n. (pol., relig.) titulaire m./f.

incur /ɪn'kɜ:(r)/ v.t. (p.t. **incurred**) encourir; (debts) contracter; (anger) s'exposer à.

incurable /ɪn'kjʊərəbl/ a. incurable.

incursion /ɪn'kɜ:ʃn/ n. incursion f.

indebted /ɪn'detɪd/ a. **∼ to s.o.,** redevable à qn. (**for,** de).

indecen|t /ɪn'di:snt/ a. indécent. **∼cy** n. indécence f.

indecision /ɪndɪ'sɪʒn/ n. indécision f.

indecisive /ɪndɪ'saɪsɪv/ a. indécis; (ending) peu concluant.

indeed /ɪn'di:d/ adv. en effet, vraiment.

indefensible /ɪndɪ'fensɪbl/ a. indéfendable.

indefinable /ɪndɪ'faɪnəbl/ a. indéfinissable.

indefinite /ɪn'defɪnɪt/ a. indéfini; (time) indéterminé. **∼ly** adv. indéfiniment.

indelible /ɪn'delɪbl/ a. indélébile.

indemni|fy /ɪn'demnɪfaɪ/ v.t. (compensate) indemniser (**for,** de); (safeguard) garantir. **∼ty** /-nətɪ/ n. indemnité f.; garantie f.

indent /ɪn'dent/ v.t. (text) renfoncer. **∼ation** /-'teɪʃn/ n. (outline) découpure f.

independen|t /ɪndɪ'pendənt/ a. indépendant. **∼ce** n. indépendance f. **∼tly** adv. de façon indépendante. **∼tly of,** indépendamment de.

indescribable /ɪndɪ'skraɪbəbl/ a. indescriptible.

indestructible /ɪndɪ'strʌktəbl/ a. indestructible.

indeterminate /ɪndɪ'tɜ:mɪnət/ a. indéterminé.

index /'ɪndeks/ n. (pl. **indexes**) (figure) indice m.; (in book) index m.; (in library) catalogue m. —v.t. classer. **∼ card,** fiche f. **∼ finger** index m. **∼-linked** a. indexé.

India /'ɪndɪə/ n. Inde f. **∼n** a. & n. indien(ne) (m. (f.)). **∼n summer,** été de la Saint-Martin m.

indicat|e /'ɪndɪkeɪt/ v.t. indiquer. **∼ion** /-'keɪʃn/ n. indication f. **∼or** n. (device) indicateur m.; (on vehicle) clignotant m.; (board) tableau m.

indicative /ɪn'dɪkətɪv/ a. indicatif. —n. (gram.) indicatif m.

indict /ɪn'daɪt/ v.t. accuser. **∼ment** n. accusation f.

indifferen|t /ɪn'dɪfrənt/ a. indifférent; (not good) médiocre. **∼ce** n. indifférence f.

indigenous /ɪn'dɪdʒɪnəs/ a. indigène.

indigest|ion /ɪndɪ'dʒestʃən/ n. indigestion f. **∼ible** /-təbl/ a. indigeste.

indign|ant /ɪn'dɪgnənt/ a. indigné. **∼ation** /-'neɪʃn/ n. indignation f.

indigo /'ɪndɪgəʊ/ n. indigo m.

indirect /ɪndɪ'rekt/ a. indirect. **∼ly** adv. indirectement.

indiscr|eet /ɪndɪ'skri:t/ a. indiscret; (not wary) imprudent. **∼etion** /-eʃn/ n. indiscrétion f.

indiscriminate /ɪndɪ'skrɪmɪnət/ a. qui manque de discernement; (random) fait au hasard. **∼ly** adv. sans discernement; au hasard.

indispensable /ɪndɪ'spensəbl/ a. indispensable.

indispos|ed /ɪndɪ'spəʊzd/ a. indisposé, souffrant. **∼ition** /-ə'zɪʃn/ n. indisposition f.

indisputable /ɪndɪ'spju:təbl/ a. incontestable.

indistinct /ɪndɪ'stɪŋkt/ a. indistinct.

indistinguishable /ɪndɪ'stɪŋwɪʃəbl/ a. indifférenciable.

individual /ɪndɪ'vɪdʒʊəl/ a. individuel. —n. individu m. **∼ist** n. individualiste m./f. **∼ity** /-'ælətɪ/ n. individualité f. **∼ly** adv. individuellement.

indivisible /ɪndɪ'vɪzəbl/ a. indivisible.

indoctrinat|e /ɪn'dɒktrɪneɪt/ v.t. endoctriner. **∼ion** /-'neɪʃn/ n. endoctrinement m.

indolen|t /'ɪndələnt/ a. indolent. **∼ce** n. indolence f.

indomitable /ɪn'dɒmɪtəbl/ a. indomptable.

Indonesia /ɪndəʊ'ni:zɪə/ n. Indonésie f. **∼n** a. & n. indonésien(ne) (m. (f.)).

indoor /'ɪndɔ:(r)/ a. (clothes etc.) d'intérieur; (under cover) couvert. **∼s** /ɪn'dɔ:z/ adv. à l'intérieur.

induce /ɪn'dju:s/ v.t. (influence) persuader; (cause) provoquer. **∼ment** n. encouragement m.

induct /ɪn'dʌkt/ v.t. investir, installer; (mil., Amer.) incorporer.

indulge /ɪn'dʌldʒ/ v.t. (desires) satisfaire; (person) se montrer indulgent pour, gâter. —v.i. **∼ in,** se livrer à, s'offrir.

indulgen|t /ɪn'dʌldʒənt/ a. indulgent. **∼ce** n. indulgence f.; (treat) gâterie f.

industrial /ɪn'dʌstrɪəl/ a. industriel; (unrest etc.) ouvrier; (action) revendicatif; (accident) du travail. **∼ist** n.

industriel(le) *m.(f.)*. **~ized** *a.* industrialisé.

industrious /ɪn'dʌstrɪəs/ *a.* travailleur, appliqué.

industry /'ɪndəstrɪ/ *n.* industrie *f.*; (*zeal*) application *f.*

inebriated /ɪ'niːbrɪeɪtɪd/ *a.* ivre.

inedible /ɪn'edɪbl/ *a.* (*food*) immangeable.

ineffective /ɪnɪ'fektɪv/ *a.* inefficace; (*person*) incapable.

ineffectual /ɪnɪ'fektʃʊəl/ *a.* inefficace; (*person*) incapable.

inefficien|t /ɪnɪ'fɪʃnt/ *a.* inefficace; (*person*) incompétent. **~cy** *n.* inefficacité *f.*; incompétence *f.*

ineligible /ɪn'elɪdʒəbl/ *a.* inéligible. **be ~ for,** ne pas avoir droit à.

inept /ɪ'nept/ *a.* (*absurd*) inepte; (*out of place*) mal à propos.

inequality /ɪnɪ'kwɒlətɪ/ *n.* inégalité *f.*

inert /ɪ'nɜːt/ *a.* inerte.

inertia /ɪ'nɜːʃə/ *n.* inertie *f.*

inescapable /ɪnɪ'skeɪpəbl/ *a.* inéluctable.

inevitabl|e /ɪn'evɪtəbl/ *a.* inévitable. **~y** *adv.* inévitablement.

inexact /ɪnɪg'zækt/ *a.* inexact.

inexcusable /ɪnɪk'skjuːzəbl/ *a.* inexcusable.

inexhaustible /ɪnɪg'zɔːstəbl/ *a.* inépuisable.

inexorable /ɪn'eksərəbl/ *a.* inexorable.

inexpensive /ɪnɪk'spensɪv/ *a.* bon marché *invar.*, pas cher.

inexperience /ɪnɪk'spɪərɪəns/ *n.* inexpérience *f.* **~d** *a.* inexpérimenté.

inexplicable /ɪnɪk'splɪkəbl/ *a.* inexplicable.

inextricable /ɪnɪk'strɪkəbl/ *a.* inextricable.

infallib|le /ɪn'fæləbl/ *a.* infaillible. **~ility** /-'bɪlətɪ/ *n.* infaillibilité *f.*

infam|ous /'ɪnfəməs/ *a.* infâme. **~y** *n.* infamie *f.*

infan|t /'ɪnfənt/ *n.* (*baby*) nourrisson *m.*; (*at school*) petit(e) enfant *m.(f.)*. **~cy** *n.* petite enfance *f.*; (*fig.*) enfance *f.*

infantile /'ɪnfəntaɪl/ *a.* infantile.

infantry /'ɪnfəntrɪ/ *n.* infanterie *f.*

infatuat|ed /ɪn'fætʃʊeɪtɪd/ *a.* **~ed with,** engoué de. **~ion** /-'eɪʃn/ *n.* engouement *m.*, béguin *m.*

infect /ɪn'fekt/ *v.t.* infecter. **~ s.o. with,** communiquer à qn. **~ion** /-kʃn/ *n.* infection *f.*

infectious /ɪn'fekʃəs/ *a.* (*med.*) infectieux; (*fig.*) contagieux.

infer /ɪn'fɜː(r)/ *v.t.* (*p.t.* **inferred**)

déduire. **~ence** /'ɪnfərəns/ *n.* déduction *f.*

inferior /ɪn'fɪərɪə(r)/ *a.* inférieur (**to,** à); (*work, product*) de qualité inférieure. —*n.* inférieur(e) *m.* (*f.*). **~ity** /-'ɒrətɪ/ *n.* infériorité *f.*

infernal /ɪn'fɜːnl/ *a.* infernal. **~ly** *adv.* (*fam.*) atrocement.

inferno /ɪn'fɜːnəʊ/ *n.* (*pl.* **-os**) (*hell*) enfer *m.*; (*blaze*) incendie *m.*

infertil|e /ɪn'fɜːtaɪl, *Amer.* ɪn'fɜːtl/ *a.* infertile. **~ity** /-ə'tɪlətɪ/ *n.* infertilité *f.*

infest /ɪn'fest/ *v.t.* infester.

infidelity /ɪnfɪ'delətɪ/ *n.* infidélité *f.*

infighting /'ɪnfaɪtɪŋ/ *n.* querelles internes *f. pl.*

infiltrat|e /'ɪnfɪltreɪt/ *v.t./i.* s'infiltrer (dans). **~ion** /-'treɪʃn/ *n.* infiltration *f.*

infinite /'ɪnfɪnɪt/ *a.* infini. **~ly** *adv.* infiniment.

infinitesimal /ɪnfɪnɪ'tesɪml/ *a.* infinitésimal.

infinitive /ɪn'fɪnɪtɪv/ *n.* infinitif *m.*

infinity /ɪn'fɪnətɪ/ *n.* infinité *f.*

infirm /ɪn'fɜːm/ *a.* infirme. **~ity** *n.* infirmité *f.*

infirmary /ɪn'fɜːmərɪ/ *n.* hôpital *m.*; (*sick-bay*) infirmerie *f.*

inflam|e /ɪn'fleɪm/ *v.t.* enflammer. **~mable** /-æməbl/ *a.* inflammable. **~mation** /-ə'meɪʃn/ *n.* inflammation *f.*

inflammatory /ɪn'flæmətrɪ/ *a.* incendiaire.

inflat|e /ɪn'fleɪt/ *v.t.* (*balloon, prices, etc.*) gonfler. **~able** *a.* gonflable.

inflation /ɪn'fleɪʃn/ *n.* inflation *f.* **~ary** *a.* inflationniste.

inflection /ɪn'flekʃn/ *n.* inflexion *f.*; (*suffix: gram.*) désinence *f.*

inflexible /ɪn'fleksəbl/ *a.* inflexible.

inflict /ɪn'flɪkt/ *v.t.* infliger (**on,** à).

influence /'ɪnflʊəns/ *n.* influence *f.* —*v.t.* influencer. **under the ~,** (*drunk: fam.*) en état d'ivresse.

influential /ɪnflʊ'enʃl/ *a.* influent.

influenza /ɪnflʊ'enzə/ *n.* grippe *f.*

influx /'ɪnflʌks/ *n.* afflux *m.*

inform /ɪn'fɔːm/ *v.t.* informer (**of,** de). **keep ~ed,** tenir au courant. **~ant** *n.* informalteur, -trice *m.,* *f.* **~er** *n.* indicaleur, -trice *m.,* *f.*

informal /ɪn'fɔːml/ *a.* (*simple*) simple, sans cérémonie; (*unofficial*) officieux; (*colloquial*) familier. **~ity** /-'mælətɪ/ *n.* simplicité *f.* **~ly** *adv.* sans cérémonie.

information /ɪnfə'meɪʃn/ *n.* renseignement(s) *m. (pl.)*, information(s) *f. (pl.)*.

some ∿, un renseignement. ∿ **technology**, informatique *f.*

informative /ɪnˈfɔːmətɪv/ *a.* instructif.

infra-red /ɪnfrəˈred/ *a.* infrarouge.

infrastructure /ˈɪnfrəstrʌktʃə(r)/ *n.* infrastructure *f.*

infrequent /ɪnˈfriːkwənt/ *a.* peu fréquent. ∿**ly** *adv.* rarement.

infringe /ɪnˈfrɪndʒ/ *v.t.* contrevenir à. ∿ **on**, empiéter sur. ∿**ment** *n.* infraction *f.*

infuriate /ɪnˈfjʊərɪeɪt/ *v.t.* exaspérer, rendre furieux.

infus|e /ɪnˈfjuːz/ *v.t.* infuser. ∿**ion** /-ʒn/ *n.* infusion *f.*

ingen|ious /ɪnˈdʒiːnɪəs/ *a.* ingénieux. ∿**uity** /-ˈnjuːətɪ/ *n.* ingéniosité *f.*

ingenuous /ɪnˈdʒenjʊəs/ *a.* ingénu.

ingot /ˈɪŋɡət/ *n.* lingot *m.*

ingrained /ɪnˈɡreɪnd/ *a.* enraciné.

ingratiate /ɪnˈɡreɪʃɪeɪt/ *v.t.* ∿ **o.s. with**, gagner les bonnes grâces de.

ingratitude /ɪnˈɡrætɪtjuːd/ *n.* ingratitude *f.*

ingredient /ɪnˈɡriːdɪənt/ *n.* ingrédient *m.*

inhabit /ɪnˈhæbɪt/ *v.t.* habiter. ∿**able** *a.* habitable. ∿**ant** *n.* habitant(e) *m.* (*f.*).

inhale /ɪnˈheɪl/ *v.t.* inhaler; (*tobacco smoke*) avaler. ∿**r** *n.* spray *m.*

inherent /ɪnˈhɪərənt/ *a.* inhérent. ∿**ly** *adv.* en soi, intrinsèquement.

inherit /ɪnˈherɪt/ *v.t.* hériter (de). ∿**ance** *n.* héritage *m.*

inhibit /ɪnˈhɪbɪt/ *v.t.* (*hinder*) gêner; (*prevent*) empêcher. **be** ∿**ed**, avoir des inhibitions. ∿**ion** /-ˈbɪʃn/ *n.* inhibition *f.*

inhospitable /ɪnhɒˈspɪtəbl/ *a.* inhospitalier.

inhuman /ɪnˈhjuːmən/ *a.* (*brutal, not human*) inhumain. ∿**ity** /-ˈmænətɪ/ *n.* inhumanité *f.*

inhumane /ɪnhjuːˈmeɪn/ *a.* (*unkind*) inhumain.

inimitable /ɪˈnɪmɪtəbl/ *a.* inimitable.

iniquit|ous /ɪˈnɪkwɪtəs/ *a.* inique. ∿**y** /-ətɪ/ *n.* iniquité *f.*

initial /ɪˈnɪʃl/ *n.* initiale *f.* —*v.t.* (*p.t.* **initialled**) parapher. —*a.* initial. ∿**ly** *adv.* initialement.

initiat|e /ɪˈnɪʃɪeɪt/ *v.t.* (*begin*) amorcer; (*scheme*) lancer; (*person*) initier (**into**, à). ∿**ion** /-ˈeɪʃn/ *n.* initiation *f.*; (*start*) amorce *f.*

initiative /ɪˈnɪʃətɪv/ *n.* initiative *f.*

inject /ɪnˈdʒekt/ *v.t.* injecter; (*new element*: *fig.*) insuffler. ∿**ion** /-kʃn/ *n.* injection *f.*, piqûre *f.*

injunction /ɪnˈdʒʌŋkʃn/ *n.* (*court order*) ordonnance *f.*

injure /ˈɪndʒə(r)/ *v.t.* blesser; (*do wrong to*) nuire à.

injury /ˈɪndʒərɪ/ *n.* (*physical*) blessure *f.*; (*wrong*) préjudice *m.*

injustice /ɪnˈdʒʌstɪs/ *n.* injustice *f.*

ink /ɪŋk/ *n.* encre *f.* ∿-**well** *n.* encrier *m.* ∿**y** *a.* taché d'encre.

inkling /ˈɪŋklɪŋ/ *n.* petite idée *f.*

inland /ˈɪnlənd/ *a.* l'intérieur. —*adv.* /ɪnˈlænd/ à l'intérieur. **I**∿ **Revenue**, fisc *m.*

in-laws /ˈɪnlɔːz/ *n. pl.* (*parents*) beaux-parents; (*family*) belle-famille *f.*

inlay[1] /ɪnˈleɪ/ *v.t.* (*p.t.* **inlaid**) incruster.

inlay[2] /ˈɪnleɪ/ *n.* incrustation *f.*

inlet /ˈɪnlet/ *n.* bras de mer *m.*; (*techn.*) arrivée *f.*

inmate /ˈɪnmeɪt/ *n.* (*of asylum*) interné(e) *m.* (*f.*); (*of prison*) détenu(e) *m.* (*f.*).

inn /ɪn/ *n.* auberge *f.*

innards /ˈɪnədz/ *n. pl.* (*fam.*) entrailles *f. pl.*

innate /ɪˈneɪt/ *a.* inné.

inner /ˈɪnə(r)/ *a.* intérieur, interne; (*fig.*) profond, intime. ∿ **city**, quartiers défavorisés *m. pl.* ∿**most** *a.* le plus profond. ∿ **tube**, chambre à air *f.*

innings /ˈɪnɪŋz/ *n. invar.* tour de batte *m.*; (*fig.*) tour *m.*

innkeeper /ˈɪnkiːpə(r)/ *n.* aubergiste *m./f.*

innocen|t /ˈɪnəsnt/ *a. & n.* innocent(e) (*m.* (*f.*)). ∿**ce** *n.* innocence *f.*

innocuous /ɪˈnɒkjʊəs/ *a.* inoffensif.

innovat|e /ˈɪnəveɪt/ *v.i.* innover. ∿**ion** /-ˈveɪʃn/ *n.* innovation *f.* ∿**or** *n.* innovateur, -trice *m.*, *f.*

innuendo /ɪnjuːˈendəʊ/ *n.* (*pl.* -**oes**) insinuation *f.*

innumerable /ɪˈnjuːmərəbl/ *a.* innombrable.

inoculat|e /ɪˈnɒkjʊleɪt/ *v.t.* inoculer. ∿**ion** /-ˈleɪʃn/ *n.* inoculation *f.*

inoffensive /ɪnəˈfensɪv/ *a.* inoffensif.

inoperative /ɪnˈɒpərətɪv/ *a.* inopérant.

inopportune /ɪnˈɒpətjuːn/ *a.* inopportun.

inordinate /ɪˈnɔːdɪnət/ *a.* excessif. ∿**ly** *adv.* excessivement.

input /ˈɪnpʊt/ *n.* (*data*) données *f. pl.*; (*computer process*) entrée *f.*; (*power*: *electr.*) énergie *f.*

inquest /ˈɪnkwest/ *n.* enquête *f.*

inquire /ɪnˈkwaɪə(r)/ *v.t./i.* = **enquire**.

inquiry /ɪnˈkwaɪərɪ/ *n.* enquête *f.*

inquisition /ɪnkwɪˈzɪʃn/ *n.* inquisition *f.*

inquisitive /ɪnˈkwɪzətɪv/ *a.* curieux; (*prying*) indiscret.

inroad /'ɪnrəʊd/ *n.* incursion *f.*

insan|e /ɪn'seɪn/ *a.* fou. ~**ity** /ɪn'sænətɪ/ *n.* folie *f.*, démence *f.*

insanitary /ɪn'sænɪtrɪ/ *a.* insalubre, malsain.

insatiable /ɪn'seɪʃəbl/ *a.* insatiable.

inscri|be /ɪn'skraɪb/ *v.t.* inscrire; (*book*) dédicacer. ~**ption** /-ɪpʃn/ *n.* inscription *f.*; dédicace *f.*

inscrutable /ɪn'skruːtəbl/ *a.* impénétrable.

insect /'ɪnsekt/ *n.* insecte *m.*

insecticide /ɪn'sektɪsaɪd/ *n.* insecticide *m.*

insecur|e /ɪnsɪ'kjʊə(r)/ *a.* (*not firm*) peu solide; (*unsafe*) peu sûr; (*worried*) anxieux. ~**ity** *n.* insécurité *f.*

insemination /ɪnsemɪ'neɪʃn/ *n.* insémination *f.*

insensible /ɪn'sensəbl/ *a.* insensible; (*unconscious*) inconscient.

insensitive /ɪn'sensətɪv/ *a.* insensible.

inseparable /ɪn'seprəbl/ *a.* inséparable.

insert[1] /ɪn'sɜːt/ *v.t.* insérer. ~**ion** /-ʃn/ *n.* insertion *f.*

insert[2] /'ɪnsɜːt/ *n.* insertion *f.*; (*advertising*) encart *m.*

in-service /'ɪnsɜːvɪs/ *a.* (*training*) continu.

inshore /ɪn'ʃɔː(r)/ *a.* côtier.

inside /ɪn'saɪd/ *n.* intérieur *m.* ~(**s**), (*fam.*) entrailles *f. pl.* —*a.* intérieur. —*adv.* à l'intérieur, dedans. —*prep.* à l'intérieur de; (*of time*) en moins de. ~ **out**, à l'envers; (*thoroughly*) à fond.

insidious /ɪn'sɪdɪəs/ *a.* insidieux.

insight /'ɪnsaɪt/ *n.* (*perception*) perspicacité *f.*; (*idea*) aperçu *m.*

insignia /ɪn'sɪgnɪə/ *n. pl.* insignes *m. pl.*

insignificant /ɪnsɪg'nɪfɪkənt/ *a.* insignifiant.

insincer|e /ɪnsɪn'sɪə(r)/ *a.* peu sincère. ~**ity** /-'serətɪ/ *n.* manque de sincérité *m.*

insinuat|e /ɪn'sɪnjʊeɪt/ *v.t.* insinuer. ~**ion** /-'eɪʃn/ *n.* insinuation *f.*

insipid /ɪn'sɪpɪd/ *a.* insipide.

insist /ɪn'sɪst/ *v.t./i.* insister. ~ **on**, affirmer; (*demand*) exiger. ~ **on doing**, insister pour faire.

insisten|t /ɪn'sɪstənt/ *a.* insistant. ~**ce** *n.* insistance *f.* ~**tly** *adv.* avec insistance.

insole /'ɪnsəʊl/ *n.* (*separate*) semelle *f.*

insolen|t /'ɪnsələnt/ *a.* insolent. ~**ce** *n.* insolence *f.*

insoluble /ɪn'sɒljʊbl/ *a.* insoluble.

insolvent /ɪn'sɒlvənt/ *a.* insolvable.

insomnia /ɪn'sɒmnɪə/ *n.* insomnie *f.* ~**c** /-ɪæk/ *n.* insomniaque *m./f.*

inspect /ɪn'spekt/ *v.t.* inspecter; (*tickets*) contrôler. ~**ion** /-kʃn/ *n.* inspection *f.*; contrôle *m.* ~**or** *n.* inspecteur, -trice *m.*, *f.*; (*on train*, *bus*) contrôleur, -se *m.*, *f.*

inspir|e /ɪn'spaɪə(r)/ *v.t.* inspirer. ~**ation** /-ə'reɪʃn/ *n.* inspiration *f.*

instability /ɪnstə'bɪlətɪ/ *n.* instabilité *f.*

install /ɪn'stɔːl/ *v.t.* installer. ~**ation** /-ə'leɪʃn/ *n.* installation *f.*

instalment /ɪn'stɔːlmənt/ *n.* (*payment*) acompte *m.*, versement *m.*; (*of serial*) épisode *m.*

instance /'ɪnstəns/ *n.* exemple *m.*; (*case*) cas *m.* **for** ~, par exemple. **in the first** ~, en premier lieu.

instant /'ɪnstənt/ *a.* immédiat; (*food*) instantané. —*n.* instant *m.* ~**ly** *adv.* immédiatement.

instantaneous /ɪnstən'teɪnɪəs/ *a.* instantané.

instead /ɪn'sted/ *adv.* plutôt. ~ **of doing**, au lieu de faire. ~ **of s.o.**, à la place de qn.

instep /'ɪnstep/ *n.* cou-de-pied *m.*

instigat|e /'ɪnstɪgeɪt/ *v.t.* provoquer. ~**ion** /-'geɪʃn/ *n.* instigation *f.* ~**or** *n.* instigateur, -trice *m.*, *f.*

instil /ɪn'stɪl/ *v.t.* (*p.t.* **instilled**) inculquer; (*inspire*) insuffler.

instinct /'ɪnstɪŋkt/ *n.* instinct *m.* ~**ive** /ɪn'stɪŋktɪv/ *a.* instinctif.

institut|e /'ɪnstɪtjuːt/ *n.* institut *m.* —*v.t.* instituer; (*inquiry etc.*) entamer. ~**ion** /-'tjuːʃn/ *n.* institution *f.*; (*school*, *hospital*) établissement *m.*

instruct /ɪn'strʌkt/ *v.t.* instruire; (*order*) ordonner. ~ **s.o. in sth.**, enseigner qch. à qn. ~ **s.o. to do**, ordonner à qn. de faire. ~**ion** /-kʃn/ *n.* instruction *f.* ~**ions** /-kʃnz/ *n. pl.* (*for use*) mode d'emploi *m.* ~**ive** *a.* instructif. ~**or** *n.* professeur *m.*; (*skiing*, *driving*) moniteur, -trice *m.*, *f.*

instrument /'ɪnstrʊmənt/ *n.* instrument *m.* ~ **panel**, tableau de bord *m.*

instrumental /ɪnstrʊ'mentl/ *a.* instrumental. **be** ~ **in**, contribuer à. ~**ist** *n.* instrumentaliste *m./f.*

insubordinat|e /ɪnsə'bɔːdɪnət/ *a.* insubordonné. ~**ion** /-'neɪʃn/ *n.* insubordination *f.*

insufferable /ɪn'sʌfrəbl/ *a.* intolérable, insupportable.

insufficient /ɪnsə'fɪʃnt/ *a.* insuffisant. ~**ly** *adv.* insuffisamment.

insular /'ɪnsjʊlə(r)/ *a.* insulaire; (*mind*, *person*: *fig.*) borné.

insulat|e /'ɪnsjʊleɪt/ *v.t.* (*room*, *wire*,

etc.) isoler. **~ing tape,** chatterton *m.*
~ion /-'leɪʃn/ *n.* isolation *f.*

insulin /'ɪnsjʊlɪn/ *n.* insuline *f.*

insult¹ /ɪn'sʌlt/ *v.t.* insulter.

insult² /'ɪnsʌlt/ *n.* insulte *f.*

insuperable /ɪn'sju:prəbl/ *a.* insurmontable.

insur|e /ɪn'ʃʊə(r)/ *v.t.* assurer. **~e that,** (*ensure*: *Amer.*) s'assurer que. **~ance** *n.* assurance *f.*

insurmountable /ɪnsə'maʊntəbl/ *a.* insurmontable.

insurrection /ɪnsə'rekʃn/ *n.* insurrection *f.*

intact /ɪn'tækt/ *a.* intact.

intake /'ɪnteɪk/ *n.* admission(s) *f.* (*pl.*); (*techn.*) prise *f.*

intangible /ɪn'tændʒəbl/ *a.* intangible.

integral /'ɪntɪgrəl/ *a.* intégral. **be an ~ part of,** faire partie intégrante de.

integrat|e /'ɪntɪgreɪt/ *v.t./i.* (s')intégrer. **~ion** /-'greɪʃn/ *n.* intégration *f.*; (*racial*) déségrégation *f.*

integrity /ɪn'tegrətɪ/ *n.* intégrité *f.*

intellect /'ɪntəlekt/ *n.* intelligence *f.* **~ual** /-'lektʃʊəl/ *a.* & *n.* intellectuel(le) (*m.* (*f.*)).

intelligen|t /ɪn'telɪdʒənt/ *a.* intelligent. **~ce** *n.* intelligence *f.*; (*mil.*) renseignements *m. pl.* **~tly** *adv.* intelligemment.

intelligentsia /ɪntelɪ'dʒentsɪə/ *n.* intelligentsia *f.*

intelligible /ɪn'telɪdʒəbl/ *a.* intelligible.

intemperance /ɪn'tempərəns/ *n.* (*drunkenness*) ivrognerie *f.*

intend /ɪn'tend/ *v.t.* destiner. **~ to do,** avoir l'intention de faire. **~ed** *a.* (*deliberate*) intentionnel; (*planned*) prévu; *n.* (*future spouse*: *fam.*) promis(e) *m.* (*f.*).

intens|e /ɪn'tens/ *a.* intense; (*person*) passionné. **~ely** *adv.* (*to live etc.*) intensément; (*very*) extrêmement. **~ity** *n.* intensité *f.*

intensif|y /ɪn'tensɪfaɪ/ *v.t.* intensifier. **~ication** /-ɪ'keɪʃn/ *n.* intensification *f.*

intensive /ɪn'tensɪv/ *a.* intensif. **in ~ care,** en réanimation.

intent /ɪn'tent/ *n.* intention *f.* **—a.** attentif. **~ on,** absorbé par. **~ on doing,** résolu à faire. **~ly** *adv.* attentivement.

intention /ɪn'tenʃn/ *n.* intention *f.* **~al** *a.* intentionnel.

inter /ɪn'tɜ:(r)/ *v.t.* (*p.t.* **interred**) enterrer.

inter- /'ɪntə(r)/ *pref.* inter-.

interact /ɪntə'rækt/ *v.i.* avoir une action réciproque. **~ion** /-kʃn/ *n.* interaction *f.*

intercede /ɪntə'si:d/ *v.i.* intercéder.

intercept /ɪntə'sept/ *v.t.* intercepter. **~ion** /-pʃn/ *n.* interception *f.*

interchange /'ɪntətʃeɪndʒ/ *n.* (*road junction*) échangeur *m.*

interchangeable /ɪntə'tʃeɪndʒəbl/ *a.* interchangeable.

intercom /'ɪntəkɒm/ *n.* interphone *m.*

interconnected /ɪntəkə'nektɪd/ *a.* (*facts, events, etc.*) lié.

intercourse /'ɪntəkɔ:s/ *n.* (*sexual, social*) rapports *m. pl.*

interest /'ɪntrəst/ *n.* intérêt *m.*; (*stake*) intérêts *m. pl.* **—v.t.** intéresser. **~ rates,** taux d'intérêt *m. pl.* **~ed** *a.* intéressé. **be ~ed in,** s'intéresser à. **~ing** *a.* intéressant.

interface /'ɪntəfeɪs/ *n.* (*comput.*) interface *f.*; (*fig.*) zone de rencontre *f.*

interfer|e /ɪntə'fɪə(r)/ *v.i.* se mêler des affaires des autres. **~e in,** s'ingérer dans. **~e with,** (*plans*) créer un contretemps avec; (*work*) s'immiscer dans; (*radio*) faire des interférences avec; (*lock*) toucher à. **~ence** *n.* ingérence *f.*; (*radio*) parasites *m. pl.*

interim /'ɪntərɪm/ *n.* intérim *m.* **—a.** intérimaire.

interior /ɪn'tɪərɪə(r)/ *n.* intérieur *m.* **—a.** intérieur.

interjection /ɪntə'dʒekʃn/ *n.* interjection *f.*

interlinked /ɪntə'lɪŋkt/ *a.* lié.

interlock /ɪntə'lɒk/ *v.t./i.* (*techn.*) (s')emboîter, (s')enclencher.

interloper /'ɪntələʊpə(r)/ *n.* intrus(e) *m.* (*f.*).

interlude /'ɪntəlu:d/ *n.* intervalle *m.*; (*theatre, mus.*) intermède *m.*

intermarr|iage /ɪntə'mærɪdʒ/ *n.* mariage entre membres de races différentes *m.* **~y** *v.i.* se marier (entre eux).

intermediary /ɪntə'mi:dɪərɪ/ *n.* & *n.* intermédiaire (*m./f.*).

intermediate /ɪntə'mi:dɪət/ *a.* intermédiaire; (*exam etc.*) moyen.

interminable /ɪn'tɜ:mɪnəbl/ *a.* interminable.

intermission /ɪntə'mɪʃn/ *n.* pause *f.*; (*theatre etc.*) entracte *m.*

intermittent /ɪntə'mɪtnt/ *a.* intermittent. **~ly** *adv.* par intermittence.

intern¹ /ɪn'tɜ:n/ *v.t.* interner. **~ee** /-'ni:/ *n.* interné(e) *m.* (*f.*). **~ment** *n.* internement *m.*

intern² /'ɪntɜ:n/ *n.* (*doctor*: *Amer.*) interne *m./f.*

internal /ɪn'tɜ:nl/ *a.* interne; (*domestic*:

pol.) intérieur. **I~ Revenue**, (*Amer.*) fisc *m*. **~ly** *adv*. intérieurement.

international /ɪntəˈnæʃnəl/ *a*. & *n*. international (*m*.).

interplay /ˈɪntəpleɪ/ *n*. jeu *m*., interaction *f*.

interpolate /ɪnˈtɜːpəleɪt/ *v.t*. interpoler.

interpret /ɪnˈtɜːprɪt/ *v.t*. interpréter. —*v.i*. faire l'interprète. **~ation** /-ˈteɪʃn/ *n*. interprétation *f*. **~er** *n*. interprète *m./f*.

interrelated /ɪntərɪˈleɪtɪd/ *a*. en corrélation, lié.

interrogat|e /ɪnˈterəgeɪt/ *v.t*. interroger. **~ion** /-ˈgeɪʃn/ *n*. interrogation *f*. (**of**, de); (*session of questions*) interrogatoire *m*.

interrogative /ɪntəˈrɒgətɪv/ *a*. & *n*. interrogatif (*m*.).

interrupt /ɪntəˈrʌpt/ *v.t*. interrompre. **~ion** /-pʃn/ *n*. interruption *f*.

intersect /ɪntəˈsekt/ *v.t./i*. (*lines, roads*) (se) couper. **~ion** /-kʃn/ *n*. intersection *f*.; (*crossroads*) croisement *m*.

interspersed /ɪntəˈspɜːst/ *a*. (*scattered*) dispersé. **~ with**, parsemé de.

intertwine /ɪntəˈtwaɪn/ *v.t./i*. (s')entrelacer.

interval /ˈɪntəvl/ *n*. intervalle *m*.; (*theatre*) entracte *m*. **at ~s**, par intervalles.

interven|e /ɪntəˈviːn/ *v.i*. intervenir; (*of time*) s'écouler (**between**, entre); (*happen*) survenir. **~tion** /-ˈvenʃn/ *n*. intervention *f*.

interview /ˈɪntəvjuː/ *n*. (*with reporter*) interview *f*.; (*for job etc*.) entrevue *f*. —*v.t*. interviewer. **~er** *n*. interviewer *m*.

intestin|e /ɪnˈtestɪn/ *n*. intestin *m*. **~al** *a*. intestinal.

intima|te¹ /ˈɪntɪmət/ *a*. intime; (*detailed*) profond. **~cy** *n*. intimité *f*. **~tely** *adv*. intimement.

intimate² /ˈɪntɪmeɪt/ *v.t*. (*state*) annoncer; (*imply*) suggérer.

intimidat|e /ɪnˈtɪmɪdeɪt/ *v.t*. intimider. **~ion** /-ˈdeɪʃn/ *n*. intimidation *f*.

into /ˈɪntuː, *unstressed* ˈɪntə/ *prep*. (*put, go, fall, etc*.) dans; (*divide, translate, etc*.) en.

intolerable /ɪnˈtɒlərəbl/ *a*. intolérable.

intoleran|t /ɪnˈtɒlərənt/ *a*. intolérant. **~ce** *n*. intolérance *f*.

intonation /ɪntəˈneɪʃn/ *n*. intonation *f*.

intoxicat|e /ɪnˈtɒksɪkeɪt/ *v.t*. enivrer. **~ed** *a*. ivre. **~ion** /-ˈkeɪʃn/ *n*. ivresse *f*.

intra- /ˈɪntrə/ *pref*. intra-.

intractable /ɪnˈtræktəbl/ *a*. très difficile.

intransigent /ɪnˈtrænsɪdʒənt/ *a*. intransigeant.

intransitive /ɪnˈtrænsətɪv/ *a*. (*verb*) intransitif.

intravenous /ɪntrəˈviːnəs/ *a*. (*med.*) intraveineux.

intrepid /ɪnˈtrepɪd/ *a*. intrépide.

intrica|te /ˈɪntrɪkət/ *a*. complexe. **~cy** *n*. complexité *f*.

intrigu|e /ɪnˈtriːg/ *v.t./i*. intriguer. —*n*. intrigue *f*. **~ing** *a*. très intéressant; (*curious*) curieux.

intrinsic /ɪnˈtrɪnsɪk/ *a*. intrinsèque. **~ally** /-klɪ/ *adv*. intrinsèquement.

introduce /ɪntrəˈdjuːs/ *v.t*. (*bring in, insert*) introduire; (*programme, question*) présenter. **~ s.o. to**, (*person*) présenter qn. à; (*subject*) faire connaître à qn.

introduct|ion /ɪntrəˈdʌkʃn/ *n*. introduction *f*.; (*to person*) présentation *f*. **~ory** /-tərɪ/ *a*. (*letter, words*) d'introduction.

introspective /ɪntrəˈspektɪv/ *a*. introspectif.

introvert /ˈɪntrəvɜːt/ *n*. introverti(e) *m*. (*f*.).

intru|de /ɪnˈtruːd/ *v.i*. (*person*) s'imposer (**on s.o.**, à qn.), déranger. **~der** *n*. intrus(e) *m*. (*f*.). **~sion** *n*. intrusion *f*.

intuit|ion /ɪntjuːˈɪʃn/ *n*. intuition *f*. **~ive** /ɪnˈtjuːɪtɪv/ *a*. intuitif.

inundat|e /ˈɪnʌndeɪt/ *v.t*. inonder (**with**, de). **~ion** /-ˈdeɪʃn/ *n*. inondation *f*.

invade /ɪnˈveɪd/ *v.t*. envahir. **~r** /-ə(r)/ *n*. envahisseur, -se *m*., *f*.

invalid¹ /ˈɪnvəlɪd/ *n*. malade *m./f*.; (*disabled*) infirme *m./f*.

invalid² /ɪnˈvælɪd/ *a*. non valable. **~ate** *v.t*. invalider.

invaluable /ɪnˈvæljʊəbl/ *a*. inestimable.

invariab|le /ɪnˈveərɪəbl/ *a*. invariable. **~y** *adv*. invariablement.

invasion /ɪnˈveɪʒn/ *n*. invasion *f*.

invective /ɪnˈvektɪv/ *n*. invective *f*.

inveigh /ɪnˈveɪ/ *v.i*. invectiver.

inveigle /ɪnˈveɪgl/ *v.t*. persuader.

invent /ɪnˈvent/ *v.t*. inventer. **~ion** /-enʃn/ *n*. invention *f*. **~ive** *a*. inventif. **~or** *n*. inven|teur, -trice *m*., *f*.

inventory /ˈɪnvəntrɪ/ *n*. inventaire *m*.

inverse /ɪnˈvɜːs/ *a*. & *n*. inverse (*m*.). **~ly** *adv*. inversement.

inver|t /ɪnˈvɜːt/ *v.t*. intervertir. **~ted commas**, guillemets *m*. *pl*. **~sion** *n*. inversion *f*.

invest /ɪnˈvest/ *v.t*. investir; (*time, effort, fig.*) consacrer. —*v.i*. faire un investissement. **~ in**, (*buy: fam*.) se payer.

∼**ment** *n.* investissement *m.* ∼**or** *n.* actionnaire *m./f.*; (*saver*) épargnant(e) *m.* (*f.*).

investigat|e /ɪn'vestɪgeɪt/ *v.t.* étudier; (*crime etc.*) enquêter sur. ∼**ion** /-'geɪʃn/ *n.* investigation *f.* **under** ∼**ion**, à l'étude. ∼**or** *n.* (*police*) enquêteulr, -se *m.*, *f.*

inveterate /ɪn'vetərət/ *a.* invétéré.

invidious /ɪn'vɪdɪəs/ *a.* (*hateful*) odieux; (*unfair*) injuste.

invigilat|e /ɪn'vɪdʒɪleɪt/ *v.i.* (*schol.*) être de surveillance. ∼**or** *n.* surveillant(e) *m.* (*f.*).

invigorate /ɪn'vɪgəreɪt/ *v.t.* vivifier; (*encourage*) stimuler.

invincible /ɪn'vɪnsəbl/ *a.* invincible.

invisible /ɪn'vɪzəbl/ *a.* invisible.

invit|e /ɪn'vaɪt/ *v.t.* inviter; (*ask for*) demander. ∼**ation** /ɪnvɪ'teɪʃn/ *n.* invitation *f.* ∼**ing** *a.* (*meal, smile, etc.*) engageant.

invoice /'ɪnvɔɪs/ *n.* facture *f.* —*v.t.* facturer.

invoke /ɪn'vəʊk/ *v.t.* invoquer.

involuntary /ɪn'vɒləntrɪ/ *a.* involontaire.

involve /ɪn'vɒlv/ *v.t.* entraîner; (*people*) faire participer. ∼**d** *a.* (*complex*) compliqué; (*at stake*) en jeu. **be** ∼**d in,** (*work*) participer à; (*crime*) être mêlé à. ∼**ment** *n.* participation *f.* (**in,** à).

invulnerable /ɪn'vʌlnərəbl/ *a.* invulnérable.

inward /'ɪnwəd/ *a. & adv.* vers l'intérieur (*feeling etc.*) intérieur. ∼**ly** *adv.* intérieurement. ∼**s** *adv.* vers l'intérieur.

iodine /'aɪədiːn/ *n.* iode *m.*; (*antiseptic*) teinture d'iode *f.*

iota /aɪ'əʊtə/ *n.* (*amount*) brin *m.*

IOU /aɪəʊ'juː/ *abbr.* (*I owe you*) reconnaissance de dette *f.*

IQ /aɪ'kjuː/ *abbr.* (*intelligence quotient*) QI *m.*

Iran /ɪ'rɑːn/ *n.* Iran *m.* ∼**ian** /ɪ'reɪnɪən/ *a. & n.* iranien(ne) (*m.* (*f.*)).

Iraq /ɪ'rɑːk/ *n.* Irak *m.* ∼**i** *a. & n.* irakien(ne) (*m.* (*f.*)).

irascible /ɪ'ræsəbl/ *a.* irascible.

irate /aɪ'reɪt/ *a.* en colère, furieux.

ire /'aɪə(r)/ *n.* courroux *m.*

Ireland /'aɪələnd/ *n.* Irlande *f.*

iris /'aɪərɪs/ *n.* (*anat., bot.*) iris *m.*

Irish /'aɪərɪʃ/ *a.* irlandais. —*n.* (*lang.*) irlandais *m.* ∼**man** *n.* Irlandais *m.* ∼**woman** *n.* Irlandaise *f.*

irk /ɜːk/ *v.t.* ennuyer. ∼**some** *a.* ennuyeux.

iron /'aɪən/ *n.* fer *m.*; (*appliance*) fer (à repasser) *m.* —*a.* de fer. —*v.t.* repasser. **I**∼ **Curtain,** rideau de fer *m.* ∼ **out,** faire disparaître. ∼**ing-board** *n.* planche à repasser *f.*

ironic(al) /aɪ'rɒnɪk(l)/ *a.* ironique.

ironmonger /'aɪənmʌŋgə(r)/ *n.* quincaillier *m.* ∼**y** *n.* quincaillerie *f.*

ironwork /'aɪənwɜːk/ *n.* ferronnerie *f.*

irony /'aɪərənɪ/ *n.* ironie *f.*

irrational /ɪ'ræʃənl/ *a.* irrationnel; (*person*) pas rationnel.

irreconcilable /ɪrekən'saɪləbl/ *a.* irréconciliable; (*incompatible*) inconciliable.

irrefutable /ɪ'refjʊtəbl/ *a.* irréfutable.

irregular /ɪ'regjʊlə(r)/ *a.* irrégulier. ∼**ity** /-'lærətɪ/ *n.* irrégularité *f.*

irrelevan|t /ɪ'reləvənt/ *a.* sans rapport (**to,** avec). ∼**ce** *n.* manque de rapport *m.*

irreparable /ɪ'repərəbl/ *a.* irréparable, irrémédiable.

irreplaceable /ɪrɪ'pleɪsəbl/ *a.* irremplaçable.

irrepressible /ɪrɪ'presəbl/ *a.* irrépressible.

irresistible /ɪrɪ'zɪstəbl/ *a.* irrésistible.

irresolute /ɪ'rezəluːt/ *a.* irrésolu.

irrespective /ɪrɪ'spektɪv/ *a.* ∼ **of,** sans tenir compte de.

irresponsible /ɪrɪ'spɒnsəbl/ *a.* irresponsable.

irretrievable /ɪrɪ'triːvəbl/ *a.* irréparable.

irreverent /ɪ'revərənt/ *a.* irrévérencieux.

irreversible /ɪrɪ'vɜːsəbl/ *a.* irréversible; (*decision*) irrévocable.

irrevocable /ɪ'revəkəbl/ *a.* irrévocable.

irrigat|e /'ɪrɪgeɪt/ *v.t.* irriguer. ∼**ion** /-'geɪʃn/ *n.* irrigation *f.*

irritable /'ɪrɪtəbl/ *a.* irritable.

irritat|e /'ɪrɪteɪt/ *v.t.* irriter. **be** ∼**ed by,** être enervé par. ∼**ing** *a.* énervant. ∼**ion** /-'teɪʃn/ *n.* irritation *f.*

is /ɪz/ *see* be.

Islam /'ɪzlɑːm/ *n.* Islam *m.* ∼**ic** /ɪz'læmɪk/ *a.* islamique.

island /'aɪlənd/ *n.* île *f.* **traffic** ∼, refuge *m.* ∼**er** *n.* insulaire *m./f.*

isle /aɪl/ *n.* île *f.*

isolat|e /'aɪsəleɪt/ *v.t.* isoler. ∼**ion** /-'leɪʃn/ *n.* isolement *m.*

isotope /'aɪsətəʊp/ *n.* isotope *m.*

Israel /'ɪzreɪl/ *n.* Israël *m.* ∼**i** /ɪz'reɪlɪ/ *a. & n.* israélien(ne) (*m.* (*f.*)).

issue /'ɪʃuː/ *n.* question *f.*; (*outcome*) résultat *m.*; (*of magazine etc.*) numéro *m.*; (*of stamps etc.*) émission *f.*; (*offspring*) descendance *f.* —*v.t.* distribuer, donner; (*stamps etc.*) émettre; (*book*) publier; (*order*) donner. —*v.i.* ∼ **from**, sortir de. **at** ∼, en cause. **take** ∼, engager une controverse.

isthmus /'ɪsməs/ *n.* isthme *m.*

it /ɪt/ *pron.* (*subject*) il, elle; (*object*) le, la, l'*; (*impersonal subject*) il; (*nonspecific*) ce, c'*, cela, ça. **it is,** (*quiet, my book, etc.*) c'est. **it is/cold/warm/late/** *etc.*, il fait froid/chaud/tard/*etc.* **that's it,** c'est ça. **who is it?**, qui est-ce? **of it, from it,** en. **in it, at it, to it,** y.

IT *abbr. see* **information technology.**

italic /ɪ'tælɪk/ *a.* italique. ∼**s** *n. pl.* italique *m.*

Ital|y /'ɪtəlɪ/ *n.* Italie *f.* ∼**ian** /ɪ'tælɪən/ *a.* & *n.* italien(ne) (*m.* (*f.*)); (*lang.*) italien *m.*

itch /ɪtʃ/ *n.* démangeaison *f.* —*v.i.* démanger. **my arm** ∼**es**, mon bras me démange. **I am** ∼**ing to**, ça me démange de. ∼**y** *a.* qui démange.

item /'aɪtəm/ *n.* article *m.*, chose *f.*; (*on agenda*) question *f.* **news** ∼, nouvelle *f.* ∼**ize** *v.t.* détailler.

itinerant /aɪ'tɪnərənt/ *a.* itinérant; (*musician, actor*) ambulant.

itinerary /aɪ'tɪnərərɪ/ *n.* itinéraire *m.*

its /ɪts/ *a.* son, sa, *pl.* ses.

it's /ɪts/ = **it is, it has.**

itself /ɪt'self/ *pron.* lui-même, elle-même; (*reflexive*) se.

IUD *abbr.* (*intrauterine device*) stérilet *m.*

ivory /'aɪvərɪ/ *n.* ivoire *m.* ∼ **tower,** tour d'ivoire *f.*

ivy /'aɪvɪ/ *n.* lierre *m.*

J

jab /dʒæb/ *v.t.* (*p.t.* **jabbed**) (*thrust*) enfoncer; (*prick*) piquer. —*n.* coup *m.*; (*injection*) piqûre *f.*

jabber /'dʒæbə(r)/ *v.i.* jacasser, bavarder; (*indistinctly*) bredouiller. —*n.* bavardage *m.*

jack /dʒæk/ *n.* (*techn.*) cric *m.*; (*cards*) valet *m.*; (*plug*) fiche *f.* —*v.t.* ∼ **up,** soulever (avec un cric).

jackal /'dʒækɔːl/ *n.* chacal *m.*

jackass /'dʒækæs/ *n.* âne *m.*

jackdaw /'dʒækdɔː/ *n.* choucas *m.*

jacket /'dʒækɪt/ *n.* veste *f.*, veston *m.*; (*of book*) jaquette *f.*

jack-knife /'dʒæknaɪf/ *n.* couteau pliant *m.* —*v.i.* (*lorry*) faire un tête-à-queue.

jackpot /'dʒækpɒt/ *n.* gros lot *m.* **hit the** ∼, gagner le gros lot.

Jacuzzi /dʒə'kuːzɪ/ *n.* (P.) bain à remous *m.*

jade /dʒeɪd/ *n.* (*stone*) jade *m.*

jaded /'dʒeɪdɪd/ *a.* las; (*appetite*) blasé.

jagged /'dʒægɪd/ *a.* dentelé.

jail /dʒeɪl/ *n.* prison *f.* —*v.t.* mettre en prison. ∼**er** *n.* geôlier *m.*

jalopy /dʒə'lɒpɪ/ *n.* vieux tacot *m.*

jam¹ /dʒæm/ *n.* confiture *f.*

jam² /dʒæm/ *v.t./i.* (*p.t.* **jammed**) (*wedge, become wedged*) (se) coincer; (*cram*) (s')entasser; (*street etc.*) encombrer; (*thrust*) enfoncer; (*radio*) brouiller. —*n.* foule *f.*; (*of traffic*) embouteillage *m.*; (*situation: fam.*) pétrin *m.* ∼**-packed** *a.* (*fam.*) bourré.

Jamaica /dʒə'meɪkə/ *n.* Jamaïque *f.*

jangle /'dʒæŋgl/ *n.* cliquetis *m.* —*v.t./i.* (faire) cliqueter.

janitor /'dʒænɪtə(r)/ *n.* concierge *m.*

January /'dʒænjʊərɪ/ *n.* janvier *m.*

Japan /dʒə'pæn/ *n.* Japon *m.* ∼**ese** /dʒæpə'niːz/ *a.* & *n.* japonais(e) (*m.* (*f.*)); (*lang.*) japonais *m.*

jar¹ /dʒɑː(r)/ *n.* pot *m.*, bocal *m.*

jar² /dʒɑː(r)/ *v.i.* (*p.t.* **jarred**) grincer; (*of colours etc.*) jurer. —*v.t.* ébranler. —*n.* son discordant *m.* ∼**ring** *a.* discordant.

jargon /'dʒɑːgən/ *n.* jargon *m.*

jasmine /'dʒæsmɪn/ *n.* jasmin *m.*

jaundice /'dʒɔːndɪs/ *n.* jaunisse *f.*

jaundiced /'dʒɔːndɪst/ *a.* (*envious*) envieux; (*bitter*) aigri.

jaunt /dʒɔːnt/ *n.* (*trip*) balade *f.*

jaunty /'dʒɔːntɪ/ *a.* (**-ier, -iest**) (*cheerful, sprightly*) allègre.

javelin /'dʒævlɪn/ *n.* javelot *m.*

jaw /dʒɔː/ *n.* mâchoire *f.* —*v.i.* (*talk: sl.*) jacasser.

jay /dʒeɪ/ *n.* geai *m.* ∼**-walk** *v.i.* traverser la chaussée imprudemment.

jazz /dʒæz/ *n.* jazz *m.* —*v.t.* ∼ **up,** animer. ∼**y** *a.* tape-à-l'œil *invar.*

jealous /'dʒeləs/ *a.* jaloux. ∼**y** *n.* jalousie *f.*

jeans /dʒiːnz/ *n. pl.* (blue-)jean *m.*

jeep /dʒiːp/ *n.* jeep *f.*

jeer /dʒɪə(r)/ *v.t./i.* ∼ (**at**), railler; (*boo*) huer. —*n.* raillerie *f.*; huée *f.*

jell /dʒel/ *v.i.* (*set: fam.*) prendre. ∼**ied** *a.* en gelée.

jelly /'dʒelɪ/ *n.* gelée *f.*

jellyfish /'dʒelɪfɪʃ/ *n.* méduse *f.*

jeopard|y /'dʒepədɪ/ *n.* péril *m.* ∼**ize** *v.t.* mettre en péril.

jerk /dʒɜːk/ *n.* secousse *f.*; (*fool: sl.*)

idiot *m.*; (*creep: sl.*) salaud *m.* —*v.t.* donner une secousse à. ~ily *adv.* par saccades. ~y *a.* saccadé.

jersey /'dʒɜːzɪ/ *n.* (*garment*) chandail *m.*, tricot *m.*; (*fabric*) jersey *m.*

jest /dʒest/ *n.* plaisanterie *f.* —*v.i.* plaisanter. ~er *n.* bouffon *m.*

Jesus /'dʒiːzəs/ *n.* Jésus *m.*

jet¹ /dʒet/ *n.* (*mineral*) jais *m.* ~-**black** *a.* de jais.

jet² /dʒet/ *n.* (*stream*) jet *m.*; (*plane*) avion à réaction *m.*, jet *m.* ~ **lag**, fatigue due au décalage horaire *f.* ~-**propelled** *a.* à réaction.

jettison /'dʒetɪsn/ *v.t.* jeter à la mer; (*aviat.*) larguer; (*fig.*) abandonner.

jetty /'dʒetɪ/ *n.* (*breakwater*) jetée *f.*

Jew /dʒuː/ *n.* Juif *m.* ~ess *n.* Juive *f.*

jewel /'dʒuːəl/ *n.* bijou *m.* ~led *a.* orné de bijoux. ~ler *n.* bijoutlier, -ière *m.*, *f.* ~lery *n.* bijoux *m. pl.*

Jewish /'dʒuːɪʃ/ *a.* juif.

Jewry /'dʒʊərɪ/ *n.* les Juifs *m. pl.*

jib /dʒɪb/ *v.i.* (*p.t.* **jibbed**) regimber (**at,** devant). —*n.* (*sail*) foc *m.*

jibe /dʒaɪb/ *n.* = **gibe.**

jiffy /'dʒɪfɪ/ *n.* (*fam.*) instant *m.*

jig /dʒɪg/ *n.* (*dance*) gigue *f.*

jiggle /'dʒɪgl/ *v.t.* secouer légèrement.

jigsaw /'dʒɪgsɔː/ *n.* puzzle *m.*

jilt /dʒɪlt/ *v.t.* laisser tomber.

jingle /'dʒɪŋgl/ *v.t./i.* (faire) tinter. —*n.* tintement *m.*; (*advertising*) jingle *m.*, sonal *m.*

jinx /dʒɪŋks/ *n.* (*person: fam.*) porte-malheur *m. invar.*; (*spell: fig.*) mauvais sort *m.*

jitter|s /'dʒɪtəz/ *n. pl.* **the ~s,** (*fam.*) la frousse *f.* ~**y** /-ərɪ/ *a.* **be ~y,** (*fam.*) avoir la frousse.

job /dʒɒb/ *n.* travail *m.*; (*post*) poste *m.* **have a ~ doing,** avoir du mal à faire. **it is a good ~ that,** heureusement que. ~**less** *a.* sans travail, au chômage.

jobcentre /'dʒɒbsentə(r)/ *n.* agence (nationale) pour l'emploi *f.*

jockey /'dʒɒkɪ/ *n.* jockey *m.* —*v.i.* (*manœuvre*) manœuvrer.

jocular /'dʒɒkjʊlə(r)/ *a.* jovial.

jog /dʒɒg/ *v.t.* (*p.t.* **jogged**) pousser; (*memory*) rafraîchir. —*v.i.* faire du jogging. ~**ging** *n.* jogging *m.*

join /dʒɔɪn/ *v.t.* joindre, unir; (*club*) devenir membre de; (*political group*) adhérer à; (*army*) s'engager dans. ~ **s.o.,** (*in activity*) se joindre à qn.; (*meet*) rejoindre qn. —*v.i.* (*roads etc.*) se rejoindre. —*n.* joint *m.* ~ **in,** participer (à). ~ **up,** (*mil.*) s'engager.

joiner /'dʒɔɪnə(r)/ *n.* menuisier *m.*

joint /dʒɔɪnt/ *a.* (*account, venture*) commun. —*n.* (*join*) joint *m.*; (*anat.*) articulation *f.*; (*culin.*) rôti *m.*; (*place: sl.*) boîte *f.* ~ **author,** coauteur *m.* **out of ~,** déboîté. ~**ly** *adv.* conjointement.

joist /dʒɔɪst/ *n.* solive *f.*

jok|e /dʒəʊk/ *n.* plaisanterie *f.*; (*trick*) farce *f.* —*v.i.* plaisanter. **it's no ~e,** ce n'est pas drôle. ~**er** *n.* blagueur, -se *m.*, *f.*; (*pej.*) petit malin *m.*; (*cards*) joker *m.* ~**ingly** *adv.* pour rire.

joll|y /'dʒɒlɪ/ *a.* (**-ier, -iest**) gai. —*adv.* (*fam.*) rudement. ~**ification** /-fɪ'keɪʃn/, ~**ity** *ns.* réjouissances *f. pl.*

jolt /dʒəʊlt/ *v.t./i.* (*vehicle, passenger*) cahoter; (*shake*) secouer. —*n.* cahot *m.*; secousse *f.*

Jordan /'dʒɔːdn/ *n.* Jordanie *f.*

jostle /'dʒɒsl/ *v.t./i.* (*push*) bousculer; (*push each other*) se bousculer.

jot /dʒɒt/ *n.* brin *m.* —*v.t.* (*p.t.* **jotted**) ~ **down,** noter. ~**ter** *n.* (*pad*) bloc-notes *m.*

journal /'dʒɜːnl/ *n.* journal *m.* ~**ism** *n.* journalisme *m.* ~**ist** *n.* journaliste *m./f.* ~**ese** /-'liːz/ *n.* jargon des journalistes *m.*

journey /'dʒɜːnɪ/ *n.* voyage *m.*; (*distance*) trajet *m.* —*v.i.* voyager.

jovial /'dʒəʊvɪəl/ *a.* jovial.

joy /dʒɔɪ/ *n.* joie *f.* ~**-riding** *n.* courses en voitures volées *f. pl.* ~**ful,** ~**ous** *adjs.* joyeux.

joystick /'dʒɔɪstɪk/ *n.* (*comput.*) manette *f.*

jubil|ant /'dʒuːbɪlənt/ *a.* débordant de joie. **be ~ant,** jubiler. ~**ation** /-'leɪʃn/ *n.* jubilation *f.*

jubilee /'dʒuːbɪliː/ *n.* jubilé *m.*

Judaism /'dʒuːdeɪɪzəm/ *n.* judaïsme *m.*

judder /'dʒʌdə(r)/ *v.i.* vibrer. —*n.* vibration *f.*

judge /dʒʌdʒ/ *n.* juge *m.* —*v.t.* juger. **judging by,** à juger de. ~**ment** *n.* jugement *m.*

judic|iary /dʒuː'dɪʃərɪ/ *n.* magistrature *f.* ~**ial** *a.* judiciaire.

judicious /dʒuː'dɪʃəs/ *a.* judicieux.

judo /'dʒuːdəʊ/ *n.* judo *m.*

jug /dʒʌg/ *n.* cruche *f.*, pichet *m.*

juggernaut /'dʒʌgənɔːt/ *n.* (*lorry*) poids lourd *m.*, mastodonte *m.*

juggle /'dʒʌgl/ *v.t./i.* jongler (avec). ~**r** /-ə(r)/ *n.* jongleur, -se *m.*, *f.*

juic|e /dʒuːs/ *n.* jus *m.* ~**y** *a.* juteux; (*details etc.: fam.*) croustillant.

juke-box /'dʒuːkbɒks/ *n.* juke-box *m.*

July /dʒuː'laɪ/ *n.* juillet *m.*

jumble /'dʒʌmbl/ v.t. mélanger. —n. (*muddle*) fouillis m. ~ **sale**, vente (de charité) f.

jumbo /'dʒʌmbəʊ/ a. ~ **jet**, avion géant m., jumbo-jet m.

jump /dʒʌmp/ v.t./i. sauter; (*start*) sursauter; (*of price etc.*) faire un bond. —n. saut m.; sursaut m.; (*increase*) hausse f. ~ **at**, sauter sur. ~**-leads** n. pl. câbles de démarrage m. pl. ~ **the gun**, agir prématurément. ~ **the queue**, resquiller.

jumper /'dʒʌmpə(r)/ n. pull(-over) m.; (*dress: Amer.*) robe chasuble f.

jumpy /'dʒʌmpɪ/ a. nerveux.

junction /'dʒʌŋkʃn/ n. jonction f.; (*of roads etc.*) embranchement m.

juncture /'dʒʌŋktʃə(r)/ n. moment m.; (*state of affairs*) conjoncture f.

June /dʒuːn/ n. juin m.

jungle /'dʒʌŋgl/ n. jungle f.

junior /'dʒuːnɪə(r)/ a. (*in age*) plus jeune (**to**, que); (*in rank*) subalterne; (*school*) élémentaire; (*executive, doctor*) jeune. —n. cadet(te) m. (f.); (*schol.*) petit(e) élève m.(f.; (*sport*) junior m./f.

junk /dʒʌŋk/ n. bric-à-brac m. invar.; (*poor material*) camelote f. —v.t. (*Amer., sl.*) balancer. ~ **food**, saloperies f. pl. ~**-shop** n. boutique de brocanteur f.

junkie /'dʒʌŋkɪ/ n. (*sl.*) drogué(e) m. (f.).

junta /'dʒʌntə/ n. junte f.

jurisdiction /dʒʊərɪs'dɪkʃn/ n. juridiction f.

jurisprudence /dʒʊərɪs'pruːdəns/ n. jurisprudence f.

juror /'dʒʊərə(r)/ n. juré m.

jury /'dʒʊərɪ/ n. jury m.

just /dʒʌst/ a. (*fair*) juste. —adv. juste, exactement; (*only, slightly*) juste; (*simply*) tout simplement. **he has/had** ~ **left**/*etc.*, il vient/venait de partir/*etc.* **have** ~ **missed**, avoir manqué de peu. **it's** ~ **a cold**, ce n'est qu'un rhume. ~ **as tall**/*etc.*, tout aussi grand/*etc.* (**as**, que). ~ **as well**, heureusement (que). ~ **listen!**, écoutez donc! ~**ly** adv. avec justice.

justice /'dʒʌstɪs/ n. justice f. **J**~ **of the Peace**, juge de paix.

justifiab|le /dʒʌstɪ'faɪəbl/ a. justifiable. ~**y** adv. avec raison.

justif|y /'dʒʌstɪfaɪ/ v.t. justifier. ~**ication** /-ɪ'keɪʃn/ n. justification f.

jut /dʒʌt/ v.i. (p.t. jutted). ~ **out**, faire saillie, dépasser.

juvenile /'dʒuːvənaɪl/ a. (*youthful*) juvénile; (*childish*) puéril; (*delinquent*) jeune; (*court*) pour enfants. —n. jeune m./f.

juxtapose /dʒʌkstə'pəʊz/ v.t. juxtaposer.

K

kaleidoscope /kə'laɪdəskəʊp/ n. kaléidoscope.

kangaroo /kæŋgə'ruː/ n. kangourou m.

karate /kə'rɑːtɪ/ n. karaté m.

kebab /kə'bæb/ n. brochette f.

keel /kiːl/ n. (*of ship*) quille f. —v.i. ~ **over**, chavirer.

keen /kiːn/ a. (**-er, -est**) (*interest, wind, feeling, etc.*) vif; (*mind, analysis*) pénétrant; (*edge, appetite*) aiguisé; (*eager*) enthousiaste. **be** ~ **on**, (*person, thing: fam.*) aimer beaucoup. **be** ~ **to do** or **on doing**, tenir beaucoup à faire. ~**ly** adv. vivement; avec enthousiasme. ~**ness** n. vivacité f.; enthousiasme m.

keep /kiːp/ v.t. (p.t. **kept**) garder; (*promise, shop, diary, etc.*) tenir; (*family*) entretenir; (*animals*) élever; (*rule etc.*) respecter; (*celebrate*) célébrer; (*delay*) retenir; (*prevent*) empêcher; (*conceal*) cacher. —v.i. (*food*) se garder; (*remain*) rester. ~ (**on**), continuer (**doing**, à faire). —n. subsistance f.; (*of castle*) donjon m. **for** ~**s**, (*fam.*) pour toujours. ~ **back** v.t. retenir; v.i. ne pas s'approcher. ~ **s.o. from doing**, empêcher qn. de faire. ~ **in/out**, empêcher d'entrer/de sortir. ~ **up**, (se) maintenir. ~ **up** (**with**), suivre. ~**er** n. gardien(ne) m. (f.). ~**-fit** n. exercices physiques m. pl.

keeping /'kiːpɪŋ/ n. garde f. **in** ~ **with**, en accord avec.

keepsake /'kiːpseɪk/ n. (*thing*) souvenir m.

keg /keg/ n. tonnelet m.

kennel /'kenl/ n. niche f.

Kenya /'kenjə/ n. Kenya m.

kept /kept/ see **keep**.

kerb /kɜːb/ n. bord du trottoir m.

kerfuffle /kə'fʌfl/ n. (*fuss: fam.*) histoire(s) f. (pl.).

kernel /'kɜːnl/ n. amande f.

kerosene /'kerəsiːn/ n. (*aviation fuel*) kérosène m.; (*paraffin*) pétrole (lampant) m.

ketchup /'ketʃəp/ n. ketchup m.

kettle /'ketl/ n. bouilloire f.

key /kiː/ n. clef f.; (of piano etc.) touche f. —a. clef (f. invar.). ~-**ring** n. porte-clefs m. invar. —v.t. ~ **in**, (comput.) saisir. ~ **up**, surexciter.

keyboard /'kiːbɔːd/ n. clavier m.

keyhole /'kiːhəʊl/ n. trou de la serrure m.

keynote /'kiːnəʊt/ n. (of speech etc.) note dominante f.

keystone /'kiːstəʊn/ n. (archit., fig.) clef de voûte f.

khaki /'kɑːkɪ/ a. kaki invar.

kibbutz /kɪ'bʊts/ n. (pl. -im /-iːm/) n. kibboutz m.

kick /kɪk/ v.t./i. donner un coup de pied (à); (of horse) ruer. —n. coup de pied m.; ruade f.; (of gun) recul m.; (thrill: fam.) malin) plaisir m. ~-**off** n. coup d'envoi m. ~ **out**, (fam.) flanquer dehors. ~ **up**, (fuss, racket: fam.) faire.

kid /kɪd/ n. (goat, leather) chevreau m.; (child: sl.) gosse m./f. —v.t./i. (p.t. **kidded**) blaguer.

kidnap /'kɪdnæp/ v.t. (p.t. **kidnapped**) enlever, kidnapper. ~**ping** n. enlèvement m.

kidney /'kɪdnɪ/ n. rein m.; (culin.) rognon m.

kill /kɪl/ v.t. tuer; (fig.) mettre fin à. —n. mise à mort f. ~**er** n. tueulr, -se m., f. ~**ing** n. massacre m., meurtre m.; a. (funny: fam.) tordant; (tiring: fam.) tuant.

killjoy /'kɪldʒɔɪ/ n. rabat-joie m. invar., trouble-fête m./f. invar.

kiln /kɪln/ n. four m.

kilo /'kiːləʊ/ n. (pl. -os) kilo m.

kilobyte /'kɪləbaɪt/ n. kilo-octet m.

kilogram /'kɪləgræm/ n. kilogramme m.

kilohertz /'kɪləhɜːts/ n. kilohertz m.

kilometre /'kɪləmiːtə(r)/ n. kilomètre m.

kilowatt /'kɪləwɒt/ n. kilowatt m.

kilt /kɪlt/ n. kilt m.

kin /kɪn/ n. parents m. pl.

kind[1] /kaɪnd/ n. genre m., sorte f., espèce f. **in** ~, en nature f. ~ **of**, (somewhat: fam.) un peu. **be two of a** ~, se rassembler.

kind[2] /kaɪnd/ a. (-**er**, -**est**) gentil, bon. ~-**hearted** a. bon. ~**ness** n. bonté f.

kindergarten /'kɪndəgɑːtn/ n. jardin d'enfants m.

kindle /'kɪndl/ v.t./i. (s')allumer.

kindly /'kaɪndlɪ/ a. (-**ier**, -**iest**) bienveillant. —adv. avec bonté. ~ **wait**/etc., voulez-vous avoir la bonté d'attendre/ etc.

kindred /'kɪndrɪd/ a. apparenté. ~ **spirit**, personne qui a les mêmes goûts f., âme sœur f.

kinetic /kɪ'netɪk/ a. cinétique.

king /kɪŋ/ n. roi m. ~-**size(d)** a. géant.

kingdom /'kɪŋdəm/ n. royaume m.; (bot.) règne m.

kingfisher /'kɪŋfɪʃə(r)/ n. martin-pêcheur m.

kink /kɪŋk/ n. (in rope) entortillement m., déformation f.; (fig.) perversion f. ~**y** a. (fam.) perverti.

kiosk /'kiːɒsk/ n. kiosque m. **telephone** ~, cabine téléphonique f.

kip /kɪp/ n. (sl.) roupillon m. —v.i. (p.t. **kipped**) (sl.) roupiller.

kipper /'kɪpə(r)/ n. hareng fumé m.

kirby-grip /'kɜːbɪgrɪp/ n. pince à cheveux f.

kiss /kɪs/ n. baiser m. —v.t./i. (s')embrasser.

kit /kɪt/ n. équipement m.; (clothing) affaires f. pl.; (set of tools etc.) trousse f.; (for assembly) kit m. —v.t. (p.t. **kitted**) ~ **out**, équiper.

kitbag /'kɪtbæg/ n. sac m. (de marin etc.).

kitchen /'kɪtʃɪn/ n. cuisine f. ~ **garden**, jardin potager m.

kitchenette /kɪtʃɪ'net/ n. kitchenette f.

kite /kaɪt/ n. (toy) cerf-volant m.

kith /kɪθ/ n. ~ **and kin**, parents et amis m. pl.

kitten /'kɪtn/ n. chaton m.

kitty /'kɪtɪ/ n. (fund) cagnotte f.

knack /næk/ n. truc m., chic m.

knapsack /'næpsæk/ n. sac à dos m.

knave /neɪv/ n. (cards) valet m.

knead /niːd/ v.t. pétrir.

knee /niː/ n. genou m.

kneecap /'niːkæp/ n. rotule f.

kneel /niːl/ v.i. (p.t. **knelt**). ~ (**down**), s'agenouiller.

knell /nel/ n. glas m.

knew /njuː/ see **know**.

knickers /'nɪkəz/ n. pl. (woman's undergarment) culotte f., slip m.

knife /naɪf/ n. (pl. **knives**) couteau m. —v.t. poignarder.

knight /naɪt/ n. chevalier m.; (chess) cavalier m. —v.t. faire or armer chevalier. ~**hood** n. titre de chevalier m.

knit /nɪt/ v.t./i. (p.t. **knitted** or **knit**) tricoter; (bones etc.) (se) souder. ~ **one's brow**, froncer les sourcils. ~**ting** n. tricot m.

knitwear /'nɪtweə(r)/ n. tricots m. pl.

knob /nɒb/ n. bouton m.

knock /nɒk/ v.t./i. frapper, cogner; (*criticize*: *sl.*) critiquer. —n. coup m. ∼ **about** v.t. malmener; v.i. vadrouiller. ∼ **down**, (*chair*, *pedestrian*) renverser; (*demolish*) abattre; (*reduce*) baisser. ∼**-down** a. (*price*) très bas. ∼**-kneed** a. cagneux. ∼ **off** v.t. faire tomber; (*fam.*) expédier; v.i. (*fam.*) s'arrêter de travailler. ∼ **out**, (*by blow*) assommer; (*tire*) épuiser. ∼**-out** n. (*boxing*) knock-out m. ∼ **over**, renverser. ∼ **up**, (*meal etc.*) préparer en vitesse. ∼**er** n. heurtoir m.

knot /nɒt/ n. nœud m. —v.t. (*p.t.* **knotted**) nouer. ∼**ty** /'nɒtɪ/ a. noueux; (*problem*) épineux.

know /nəʊ/ v.t./i. (*p.t.* **knew**, *p.p.* **known**) savoir (**that**, que); (*person*, *place*) connaître. ∼ **how to do**, savoir comment faire. —n. **in the** ∼, (*fam.*) dans le secret, au courant. ∼ **about**, (*cars etc.*) s'y connaître en. ∼**-all**, (*Amer.*) ∼**-it-all** n. je-sais-tout m./f. ∼**-how** n. technique f. ∼ **of**, connaître, avoir entendu parler de. ∼**ingly** adv. (*consciously*) sciemment.

knowledge /'nɒlɪdʒ/ n. connaissance f.; (*learning*) connaissances f. pl. ∼**able** a. bien informé.

known /nəʊn/ see **know**. —a. connu; (*recognized*) reconnu.

knuckle /'nʌkl/ n. articulation du doigt f. —v.i. ∼ **under**, se soumettre.

Koran /kə'rɑːn/ n. Coran m.

Korea /kə'rɪə/ n. Corée f.

kosher /'kəʊʃə(r)/ a. kascher *invar.*

kowtow /kaʊ'taʊ/ v.i. se prosterner (**to**, devant).

kudos /'kjuːdɒs/ n. (*fam.*) gloire f.

Kurd /kɜːd/ a. & n. kurde m./f.

L

lab /læb/ n. (*fam.*) labo m.

label /'leɪbl/ n. étiquette f. —v.t. (*p.t.* **labelled**) étiqueter.

laboratory /lə'bɒrətrɪ, *Amer.* 'læbrətɔːrɪ/ n. laboratoire m.

laborious /lə'bɔːrɪəs/ a. laborieux.

labour /'leɪbə(r)/ n. travail m.; (*workers*) main-d'œuvre f. —v.i. peiner. —v.t. trop insister sur. **in** ∼, en train d'accoucher, en couches. ∼**ed** a. laborieux.

Labour /'leɪbə(r)/ n. le parti travailliste m. —a. travailliste.

labourer /'leɪbərə(r)/ n. manœuvre m.; (*on farm*) ouvrier agricole m.

labyrinth /'læbərɪnθ/ n. labyrinthe m.

lace /leɪs/ n. dentelle f.; (*of shoe*) lacet m. —v.t. (*fasten*) lacer; (*drink*) arroser. ∼**-ups** n. pl. chaussures à lacets f. pl.

lacerate /'læsəreɪt/ v.t. lacérer.

lack /læk/ n. manque m. —v.t. manquer de. **be** ∼**ing**, manquer (**in**, de). **for** ∼ **of**, faute de.

lackadaisical /lækə'deɪzɪkl/ a. indolent, apathique.

lackey /'lækɪ/ n. laquais m.

laconic /lə'kɒnɪk/ a. laconique.

lacquer /'lækə(r)/ n. laque f.

lad /læd/ n. garçon m., gars m.

ladder /'lædə(r)/ n. échelle f.; (*in stocking*) maille filée f. —v.t./i. (*stocking*) filer.

laden /'leɪdn/ a. chargé (**with**, de).

ladle /'leɪdl/ n. louche f.

lady /'leɪdɪ/ n. dame f. ∼ **friend**, amie f. ∼**-in-waiting** n. dame d'honneur f. **young** ∼, jeune femme *or* fille f. ∼**like** a. distingué.

lady|bird /'leɪdɪbɜːd/ n. coccinelle f. ∼**bug** n. (*Amer.*) coccinelle f.

lag[1] /læg/ v.i. (*p.t.* **lagged**) traîner. —n. (*interval*) décalage m.

lag[2] /læg/ v.t. (*p.t.* **lagged**) (*pipes*) calorifuger.

lager /'lɑːgə(r)/ n. bière blonde f.

lagoon /lə'guːn/ n. lagune f.

laid /leɪd/ see **lay**[2]. —∼**-back** a. (*fam.*) cool.

lain /leɪn/ see **lie**[2].

lair /leə(r)/ n. tanière f.

laity /'leɪətɪ/ n. laïques m. pl.

lake /leɪk/ n. lac m.

lamb /læm/ n. agneau m.

lambswool /'læmzwʊl/ n. laine d'agneau f.

lame /leɪm/ a. (-er, -est) boiteux; (*excuse*) faible. ∼**ly** adv. (*argue*) sans conviction. ∼ **duck**, canard boiteux m.

lament /lə'ment/ n. lamentation f. —v.t./i. se lamenter (sur). ∼**able** a. lamentable.

laminated /'læmɪneɪtɪd/ a. laminé.

lamp /læmp/ n. lampe f.

lamppost /'læmppəʊst/ n. réverbère m.

lampshade /'læmpʃeɪd/ n. abat-jour m. *invar.*

lance /lɑːns/ n. lance f. —v.t. (*med.*) inciser.

lancet /'lɑːnsɪt/ n. bistouri m.

land /lænd/ n. terre f.; (*plot*) terrain m.; (*country*) pays m. —a. terrestre;

(*policy, reform*) agraire. —*v.t./i.* débarquer; (*aircraft*) (se) poser, (faire) atterrir; (*fall*) tomber; (*obtain*) décrocher; (*put*) mettre; (*a blow*) porter. ~**-locked** *a.* sans accès à la mer. ~ **up,** se retrouver.

landed /'lændɪd/ *a.* foncier.

landing /'lændɪŋ/ *n.* débarquement *m.*; (*aviat.*) atterrissage *m.*; (*top of stairs*) palier *m.* ~**-stage** *n.* débarcadère *m.* ~**-strip** *n.* piste d'atterrissage *f.*

land‖lady /'lændleɪdɪ/ *n.* propriétaire *f.*; (*of inn*) patronne *f.* ~**lord** *n.* propriétaire *m.*; patron *m.*

landmark /'lændmɑːk/ *n.* (point de) repère *m.*

landscape /'læn(d)skeɪp/ *n.* paysage *m.* —*v.t.* aménager.

landslide /'lændslaɪd/ *n.* glissement de terrain *m.*; (*pol.*) raz-de-marée (électoral) *m. invar.*

lane /leɪn/ *n.* (*path, road*) chemin *m.*; (*strip of road*) voie *f.*; (*of traffic*) file *f.*; (*aviat.*) couloir *m.*

language /'læŋgwɪdʒ/ *n.* langue *f.*; (*speech, style*) langage *m.* ~ **laboratory,** laboratoire de langue *m.*

languid /'læŋgwɪd/ *a.* languissant.

languish /'læŋgwɪʃ/ *v.i.* languir.

lank /læŋk/ *a.* grand et maigre.

lanky /'læŋkɪ/ *a.* (**-ier, -iest**) dégingandé, grand et maigre.

lanolin /'lænəʊlɪn/ *n.* lanoline *f.*

lantern /'læntən/ *n.* lanterne *f.*

lap[1] /læp/ *n.* genoux *m. pl.*; (*sport*) tour (de piste) *m.* —*v.t./i.* (*p.t.* **lapped**) ~ **over,** (se) chevaucher.

lap[2] /læp/ *v.t.* (*p.t.* **lapped**). ~ **up,** laper. —*v.i.* (*waves*) clapoter.

lapel /lə'pel/ *n.* revers *m.*

lapse /læps/ *v.i.* (*decline*) se dégrader; (*expire*) se périmer. —*n.* défaillance *f.*, erreur *f.*; (*of time*) intervalle *m.* ~ **into,** retomber dans.

larceny /'lɑːsənɪ/ *n.* vol simple *m.*

lard /lɑːd/ *n.* saindoux *m.*

larder /'lɑːdə(r)/ *n.* garde-manger *m. invar.*

large /lɑːdʒ/ *a.* (**-er, -est**) grand, gros. **at** ~, en liberté. **by and** ~, en général. ~**ly** *adv.* en grande mesure. ~**ness** *n.* grandeur *f.*

lark[1] /lɑːk/ *n.* (*bird*) alouette *f.*

lark[2] /lɑːk/ *n.* (*bit of fun: fam.*) rigolade *f.* —*v.i.* (*fam.*) rigoler.

larva /'lɑːvə/ *n.* (*pl.* **-vae** /-viː/) larve *f.*

laryngitis /lærɪn'dʒaɪtɪs/ *n.* laryngite *f.*

larynx /'lærɪŋks/ *n.* larynx *m.*

lasagne /lə'zænjə/ *n.* lasagne *f.*

lascivious /lə'sɪvɪəs/ *a.* lascif.

laser /'leɪzə(r)/ *n.* laser *m.* ~ **printer,** imprimante laser *f.*

lash /læʃ/ *v.t.* fouetter. —*n.* coup de fouet *m.*; (*eyelash*) cil *m.* ~ **out,** (*spend*) dépenser follement. ~ **out against,** attaquer.

lashings /'læʃɪŋz/ *n. pl.* ~ **of,** (*cream etc.: sl.*) des masses de.

lass /læs/ *n.* jeune fille *f.*

lasso /læ'suː/ *n.* (*pl.* **-os**) lasso *m.*

last[1] /lɑːst/ *a.* dernier. —*adv.* en dernier; (*most recently*) la dernière fois. —*n.* dernier, -ière *m., f.*; (*remainder*) reste *m.* **at (long)** ~, enfin. ~**-ditch** *a.* ultime. ~**-minute** *a.* de dernière minute. ~ **night,** hier soir. **the** ~ **straw,** le comble. **the** ~ **word,** le mot de la fin. **on its** ~ **legs,** sur le point de rendre l'âme. ~**ly** *adv.* en dernier lieu.

last[2] /lɑːst/ *v.i.* durer. ~**ing** *a.* durable.

latch /lætʃ/ *n.* loquet *m.*

late /leɪt/ *a.* (**-er, -est**) (*not on time*) en retard; (*recent*) récent; (*former*) ancien; (*hour, fruit, etc.*) tardif; (*deceased*) défunt. **the late Mrs X,** feu Mme X. ~**st** /-ɪst/, (*last*) dernier. —*adv.* (*not early*) tard; (*not on time*) en retard. **in** ~ **July,** fin juillet. **of** ~, dernièrement. ~**ness** *n.* retard *m.*; (*of event*) heure tardive *f.*

latecomer /'leɪtkʌmə(r)/ *n.* retardataire *m./f.*

lately /'leɪtlɪ/ *adv.* dernièrement.

latent /'leɪtnt/ *a.* latent.

lateral /'lætərəl/ *a.* latéral.

lathe /leɪð/ *n.* tour *m.*

lather /'lɑːðə(r)/ *n.* mousse *f.* —*v.t.* savonner. —*v.i.* mousser.

Latin /'lætɪn/ *n.* (*lang.*) latin *m.* —*a.* latin. ~ **America,** Amérique latine *f.*

latitude /'lætɪtjuːd/ *n.* latitude *f.*

latrine /lə'triːn/ *n.* latrines *f. pl.*

latter /'lætə(r)/ *a.* dernier. —*n.* **the** ~, celui-ci, celle-ci. ~**-day** *a.* moderne. ~**ly** *adv.* dernièrement.

lattice /'lætɪs/ *n.* treillage *m.*

laudable /'lɔːdəbl/ *a.* louable.

laugh /lɑːf/ *v.i.* rire (**at,** de). —*n.* rire *m.* ~**able** *a.* ridicule. ~**ing-stock** *n.* objet de risée *m.*

laughter /'lɑːftə(r)/ *n.* (*act*) rire *m.*; (*sound of laughs*) rires *m. pl.*

launch[1] /lɔːntʃ/ *v.t.* lancer. —*n.* lancement *m.* ~ **(out) into,** se lancer dans. ~**ing pad,** aire de lancement *f.*

launch[2] /lɔːntʃ/ *n.* (*boat*) vedette *f.*

launder /'lɔːndə(r)/ *v.t.* blanchir.

launderette /lɔːn'dret/ n. laverie automatique f.

laundry /'lɔːndrɪ/ n. (*place*) blanchisserie f.; (*clothes*) linge m.

laurel /'lɒrəl/ n. laurier m.

lava /'lɑːvə/ n. lave f.

lavatory /'lævətrɪ/ n. cabinets m. pl.

lavender /'lævəndə(r)/ n. lavande f.

lavish /'lævɪʃ/ a. (*person*) prodigue; (*plentiful*) copieux; (*lush*) somptueux. —v.t. prodiguer (**on**, à). **~ly** adv. copieusement.

law /lɔː/ n. loi f.; (*profession, subject of study*) droit m. **~-abiding** a. respectueux des lois. **~ and order**, l'ordre public. **~ful** a. légal. **~fully** adv. légalement. **~less** a. sans loi.

lawcourt /'lɔːkɔːt/ n. tribunal m.

lawn /lɔːn/ n. pelouse f., gazon m. **~-mower** n. tondeuse à gazon f. **~ tennis**, tennis (sur gazon) m.

lawsuit /'lɔːsuːt/ n. procès m.

lawyer /'lɔːjə(r)/ n. avocat m.

lax /læks/ a. négligent; (*morals etc.*) relâché. **~ity** n. négligence f.

laxative /'læksətɪv/ n. laxatif m.

lay[1] /leɪ/ a. (*non-clerical*) laïque; (*opinion etc.*) d'un profane.

lay[2] /leɪ/ v.t. (*p.t.* **laid**) poser, mettre; (*trap*) tendre; (*table*) mettre; (*plan*) former; (*eggs*) pondre. —v.i. pondre. **~ aside**, mettre de côté. **~ down**, (dé)poser; (*condition*) (im)poser. **~ hold of**, saisir. **~ off** v.t. (*worker*) licencier; v.i. (*fam.*) arrêter. **~-off** n. licenciement m. **~ on**, (*provide*) fournir. **~ out**, (*design*) dessiner; (*display*) disposer; (*money*) dépenser. **~ up**, (*store*) amasser. **~ waste**, ravager.

lay[3] /leɪ/ *see* **lie**[2].

layabout /'leɪəbaʊt/ n. fainéant(e) m. (f.).

lay-by /'leɪbaɪ/ n. (*pl.* **-bys**) petite aire de stationnement f.

layer /'leɪə(r)/ n. couche f.

layman /'leɪmən/ n. (*pl.* **-men**) profane m.

layout /'leɪaʊt/ n. disposition f.

laze /leɪz/ v.i. paresser.

lazy /'leɪzɪ/ a. (**-ier, -iest**) paresseux. **~iness** n. paresse f. **~y-bones** n. flemmard(e) m. (f.).

lead[1] /liːd/ v.t./i. (*p.t.* **led**) mener; (*team etc.*) diriger; (*life*) mener; (*induce*) amener. **~ to**, conduire à, mener à. —n. avance f.; (*clue*) indice m.; (*leash*) laisse f.; (*theatre*) premier rôle m.; (*wire*) fil m.; (*example*) exemple m. **in the ~**, en tête. **~ away**, emmener. **~ up to**, (*come to*) en venir à; (*precede*) précéder.

lead[2] /led/ n. plomb m.; (*of pencil*) mine f. **~en** a. (*sky*) de plomb (*humour*) lourd.

leader /'liːdə(r)/ n. chef m.; (*of country, club, etc.*) dirigeant(e) m. (f.); (*leading article*) éditorial m. **~ship** n. direction f.

leading /'liːdɪŋ/ a. principal. **~ article**, éditorial m.

leaf /liːf/ n. (*pl.* **leaves**) feuille f.; (*of table*) rallonge f. —v.i. **~ through**, feuilleter. **~y** a. feuillu.

leaflet /'liːflɪt/ n. prospectus m.

league /liːg/ n. ligue f.; (*sport*) championnat m. **in ~ with**, de mèche avec.

leak /liːk/ n. fuite f. —v.i. fuir; (*news: fig.*) s'ébruiter. —v.t. répandre; (*fig.*) divulguer. **~age** n. fuite f. **~y** a. qui a une fuite.

lean[1] /liːn/ a. (**-er, -est**) maigre. —n. (*of meat*) maigre m. **~ness** n. maigreur f.

lean[2] /liːn/ v.t./i. (*p.t.* **leaned** or **leant** /lent/) (*rest*) (s')appuyer; (*slope*) pencher. **~ out**, se pencher à l'extérieur. **~ over**, (*of person*) se pencher. **~-to** n. appentis m.

leaning /'liːnɪŋ/ a. penché. —n. tendance f.

leap /liːp/ v.i. (*p.t.* **leaped** or **leapt** /lept/) bondir. —n. bond m. **~-frog** n. saute-mouton m. invar.; v.i. (*p.t.* **-frogged**) sauter (**over**, par-dessus). **~ year**, année bissextile f.

learn /lɜːn/ v.t./i. (*p.t.* **learned** or **learnt**) apprendre (**to do**, à faire). **~er** n. débutant(e) m. (f.).

learn|ed /'lɜːnɪd/ a. érudit. **~ing** n. érudition f., connaissances f. pl.

lease /liːs/ n. bail m. —v.t. louer à bail.

leaseback /'liːsbæk/ n. cession-bail f.

leash /liːʃ/ n. laisse f.

least /liːst/ a. **the ~**, (*smallest amount of*) le moins de; (*slightest*) le or la moindre. —n. le moins. —adv. le moins; (*with adjective*) le or la moins. **at ~**, au moins.

leather /'leðə(r)/ n. cuir m.

leave /liːv/ v.t. (*p.t.* **left**) laisser; (*depart from*) quitter. —n. (*holiday*) congé m.; (*consent*) permission f. **be left (over)**, rester. **~ alone**, (*thing*) ne pas toucher à; (*person*) laisser tranquille. **~ behind**, laisser. **~ out**, omettre. **on ~**, (*mil.*) en permission. **take one's ~**, prendre congé (**of**, de).

leavings /'li:vɪŋz/ n. pl. restes m. pl.
Leban|on /'lebənən/ n. Liban m. ᵔese
/-'niːz/ a. & n. libanais(e) (m. (f.)).
lecher /'letʃə(r)/ n. débauché m. ᵔous a.
lubrique. ᵔy n. lubricité f.
lectern /'lektən/ n. lutrin m.
lecture /'lektʃə(r)/ n. cours m., conférence f.; (rebuke) réprimande f.
—v.t./i. faire un cours or une
conférence (à); (rebuke) réprimander.
ᵔr /-ə(r)/ n. conférenclier, -ière m., f.,
(univ.) enseignant(e) m. (f.).
led /led/ see **lead¹**.
ledge /ledʒ/ n. (window) rebord m.;
(rock) saillie f.
ledger /'ledʒə(r)/ n. grand livre m.
lee /liː/ n. côté sous le vent m.
leech /liːtʃ/ n. sangsue f.
leek /liːk/ n. poireau m.
leer /lɪə(r)/ v.i. ᵔ (at), lorgner. —n.
regard sournois m.
leeway /'liːweɪ/ n. (naut.) dérive f.; (fig.)
liberté d'action f. **make up** ᵔ, rattraper
le retard.
left¹ /left/ see **leave**. ᵔ **luggage (office)**,
consigne f. ᵔ-**overs** n. pl. restes
m. pl.
left² /left/ a. gauche. —adv. à gauche.
—n. gauche f. ᵔ-**hand** a. à or de
gauche. ᵔ-**handed** a. gaucher. ᵔ-**wing**
a. (pol.) de gauche.
leftist /'leftɪst/ n. gauchiste m./f.
leg /leg/ n. jambe f.; (of animal) patte f.;
(of table) pied m.; (of chicken) cuisse f.;
(of lamb) gigot m.; (of journey) étape f.
ᵔ-**room** n. place pour les jambes f. ᵔ-
warmers n. pl. jambières f. pl.
legacy /'legəsɪ/ n. legs m.
legal /'liːgl/ a. légal; (affairs etc.)
juridique. ᵔity /liː'gælətɪ/ n. légalité f.
ᵔly adv. légalement.
legalize /'liːgəlaɪz/ v.t. légaliser.
legend /'ledʒənd/ n. légende f. ᵔary a.
légendaire.
leggings /'legɪŋz/ n. pl. collant sans pieds
m.
legib|le /'ledʒəbl/ a. lisible. ᵔility
/-'bɪlətɪ/ n. lisibilité f. ᵔly adv.
lisiblement.
legion /'liːdʒən/ n. légion f. ᵔnaire n.
légionnaire m. ᵔnaire's **disease**,
maladie du légionnaire f.
legislat|e /'ledʒɪsleɪt/ v.i. légiférer. ᵔion
/-'leɪʃn/ n. (body of laws) législation f.;
(law) loi f.
legislat|ive /'ledʒɪslətɪv/ a. législatif.
ᵔure /-eɪtʃə(r)/ n. corps législatif m.
legitima|te /lɪ'dʒɪtɪmət/ a. légitime. ᵔcy
n. légitimité f.

leisure /'leʒə(r)/ n. loisir(s) m. (pl.). **at
one's** ᵔ, à tête reposée. ᵔ **centre**,
centre de loisirs m. ᵔly a. lent; adv.
sans se presser.
lemon /'lemən/ n. citron m.
lemonade /lemə'neɪd/ n. (fizzy)
limonade f.; (still) citronnade f.
lend /lend/ v.t. (p.t. lent) prêter;
(contribute) donner. ᵔ **itself to**, se
prêter à. ᵔer n. prêteulr, -se m., f. ᵔing
n. prêt m.
length /leŋθ/ n. longueur f.; (in time)
durée f.; (section) morceau m. **at** ᵔ, (at
last) enfin. **at (great)** ᵔ, longuement.
ᵔy a. long.
lengthen /'leŋθən/ v.t./i. (s')allonger.
lengthways /'leŋθweɪz/ adv. dans le sens
de la longueur.
lenien|t /'liːnɪənt/ a. indulgent. ᵔcy n.
indulgence f. ᵔtly adv. avec indulgence.
lens /lenz/ n. lentille f.; (of spectacles)
verre m.; (photo.) objectif m.
lent /lent/ see **lend**.
Lent /lent/ n. Carême m.
lentil /'lentl/ n. (bean) lentille f.
Leo /'liːəʊ/ n. le Lion.
leopard /'lepəd/ n. léopard m.
leotard /'liːətɑːd/ n. body m.
leper /'lepə(r)/ n. lépreulx, -se m., f.
leprosy /'leprəsɪ/ n. lèpre f.
lesbian /'lezbɪən/ n. lesbienne f. —a.
lesbien.
lesion /'liːʒn/ n. lésion f.
less /les/ a. (in quantity etc.) moins de
(than, que). —adv., n. & prep. moins.
ᵔ **than**, (with numbers) moins de.
work/etc. ᵔ **than**, travailler/etc. moins
que. **ten pounds**/etc. ᵔ, dix livres/etc.
de moins. ᵔ **and less**, de moins en
moins. ᵔer a. moindre.
lessen /'lesn/ v.t./i. diminuer.
lesson /'lesn/ n. leçon f.
lest /lest/ conj. de peur que or de.
let /let/ v.t. (p.t. let, pres. p. letting)
laisser; (lease) louer. —v. aux. ᵔ **us
do**, ᵔ**'s do**, faisons. ᵔ **him do**, qu'il
fasse. ᵔ **me know the results**, informe-
moi des résultats. —n. location f. ᵔ
alone, (thing) ne pas toucher à;
(person) laisser tranquille; (never
mind) encore moins. ᵔ **down**, baisser;
(deflate) dégonfler; (fig.) décevoir. ᵔ-
down n. déception f. ᵔo g v.t. lâcher;
v.i. lâcher prise. ᵔ **sb. in/out**, laisser or
faire entrer/sortir qn. ᵔ **a dress out**,
élargir une robe. ᵔ **o.s. in for**, (task)
s'engager à; (trouble) s'attirer. ᵔ **off**,
(explode, fire) faire éclater or partir;

(*excuse*) dispenser; (*not punish*) ne pas punir. ～ **up**, (*fam.*) s'arrêter. ～**up** *n.* répit *m.*

lethal /ˈliːθl/ *a.* mortel; (*weapon*) meurtrier.

letharg|y /ˈleθədʒɪ/ *n.* léthargie *f.* ～**ic** /lɪˈθɑːdʒɪk/ *a.* léthargique.

letter /ˈletə(r)/ *n.* lettre *f.* ～**-bomb** *n.* lettre piégée *f.* ～**-box** *n.* boîte à *or* aux lettres *f.* ～**ing** *n.* (*letters*) caractères *m. pl.*

lettuce /ˈletɪs/ *n.* laitue *f.*, salade *f.*

leukaemia /luːˈkiːmɪə/ *n.* leucémie *f.*

level /ˈlevl/ *a.* plat, uni; (*on surface*) horizontal; (*in height*) au même niveau (**with**, que); (*in score*) à égalité. —*n.* niveau *m.* (**spirit**) ～, niveau à bulle *m.* —*v.t.* (*p.t.* **levelled**) niveler; (*aim*) diriger. **be on the** ～, (*fam.*) être franc. ～ **crossing**, passage à niveau *m.* ～**-headed** *a.* équilibré.

lever /ˈliːvə(r)/ *n.* levier *m.* —*v.t.* soulever au moyen d'un levier.

leverage /ˈliːvərɪdʒ/ *n.* influence *f.*

levity /ˈlevətɪ/ *n.* légèreté *f.*

levy /ˈlevɪ/ *v.t.* (*tax*) (pré)lever. —*n.* impôt *m.*

lewd /ljuːd/ *a.* (**-er**, **-est**) obscène.

liable /ˈlaɪəbl/ *a.* **be** ～ **to do**, avoir tendance à faire, pouvoir faire. ～ **to**, (*illness etc.*) sujet à; (*fine*) passible de. ～ **for**, responsable de.

liabilit|y /laɪəˈbɪlətɪ/ *n.* responsabilité *f.*; (*fam.*) handicap *m.* ～**ies**, (*debts*) dettes *f. pl.*

liais|e /lɪˈeɪz/ *v.i.* (*fam.*) faire la liaison. ～**on** /-ɒn/ *n.* liaison *f.*

liar /ˈlaɪə(r)/ *n.* menteu|r, -se *m.*, *f.*

libel /ˈlaɪbl/ *n.* diffamation *f.* —*v.t.* (*p.t.* **libelled**) diffamer.

liberal /ˈlɪbərəl/ *a.* libéral; (*generous*) généreux, libéral. ～**ly** *adv.* libéralement.

Liberal /ˈlɪbərəl/ *a.* & *n.* (*pol.*) libéral(e) (*m.* (*f.*)).

liberat|e /ˈlɪbəreɪt/ *v.t.* libérer. ～**ion** /-ˈreɪʃn/ *n.* libération *f.*

libert|y /ˈlɪbətɪ/ *n.* liberté *f.* **at** ～**y to**, libre de. **take** ～**ies**, prendre des libertés.

libido /lɪˈbiːdəʊ/ *n.* libido *f.*

Libra /ˈliːbrə/ *n.* la Balance.

librar|y /ˈlaɪbrərɪ/ *n.* bibliothèque *f.* ～**ian** /-ˈbreərɪən/ *n.* bibliothécaire *m./f.*

libretto /lɪˈbretəʊ/ *n.* (*pl.* **-os**) (*mus.*) livret *m.*

Libya /ˈlɪbɪə/ *n.* Libye *f.* ～**n** *a.* & *n.* libyen(ne) (*m.* (*f.*)).

lice /laɪs/ *see* **louse**.

licence, *Amer.* **license**[1] /ˈlaɪsns/ *n.*

permis *m.*; (*for television*) redevance *f.*; (*comm.*) licence *f.*; (*liberty*: *fig.*) licence *f.* ～ **plate**, plaque minéralogique *f.*

license[2] /ˈlaɪsns/ *v.t.* accorder un permis à, autoriser.

licentious /laɪˈsenʃəs/ *a.* licencieux.

lichen /ˈlaɪkən/ *n.* lichen *m.*

lick /lɪk/ *v.t.* lécher; (*defeat*: *sl.*) rosser. —*n.* coup de langue *m.* ～ **one's chops**, se lécher les babines.

licorice /ˈlɪkərɪs/ *n.* (*Amer.*) réglisse *f.*

lid /lɪd/ *n.* couvercle *m.*

lido /ˈlaɪdəʊ/ *n.* (*pl.* **-os**) piscine en plein air *f.*

lie[1] /laɪ/ *n.* mensonge *m.* —*v.i.* (*p.t.* **lied**, *pres. p.* **lying**) (*tell lies*) mentir. **give the** ～ **to**, démentir.

lie[2] /laɪ/ *v.i.* (*p.t.* **lay**, *p.p.* **lain**, *pres. p.* **lying**) s'allonger; (*remain*) rester; (*be*) se trouver, être; (*in grave*) reposer. **be lying**, être allongé. ～ **down**, s'allonger. ～ **in**, **have a** ～**-in**, faire la grasse matinée. ～ **low**, se cacher.

lieu /ljuː/ *n.* **in** ～ **of**, au lieu de.

lieutenant /lefˈtenənt, *Amer.* luːˈtenənt/ *n.* lieutenant *m.*

life /laɪf/ *n.* (*pl.* **lives**) vie *f.* ～ **cycle**, cycle de vie *m.* ～**-guard** *n.* sauveteur *m.* ～ **insurance**, assurance-vie *f.* ～**-jacket**, ～ **preserver**, *n.* gilet de sauvetage *m.* ～**-size(d)** *a.* grandeur nature *invar.* ～**-style** *n.* style de vie *m.*

lifebelt /ˈlaɪfbelt/ *n.* bouée de sauvetage *f.*

lifeboat /ˈlaɪfbəʊt/ *n.* canot de sauvetage *m.*

lifebuoy /ˈlaɪfbɔɪ/ *n.* bouée de sauvetage *f.*

lifeless /ˈlaɪflɪs/ *a.* sans vie.

lifelike /ˈlaɪflaɪk/ *a.* très ressemblant.

lifelong /ˈlaɪflɒŋ/ *a.* de toute la vie.

lifetime /ˈlaɪftaɪm/ *n.* vie *f.* **in one's** ～, de son vivant.

lift /lɪft/ *v.t.* lever; (*steal*: *fam.*) voler. —*v.i.* (*of fog*) se lever. —*n.* (*in building*) ascenseur *m.* **give a** ～ **to**, emmener (en voiture). ～**-off** *n.* (*aviat.*) décollage *m.*

ligament /ˈlɪgəmənt/ *n.* ligament *m.*

light[1] /laɪt/ *n.* lumière *f.*; (*lamp*) lampe *f.*; (*for fire, on vehicle, etc.*) feu *m.*; (*headlight*) phare *m.* —*a.* (*not dark*) clair. —*v.t.* (*p.t.* **lit** *or* **lighted**) allumer; (*room etc.*) éclairer; (*match*) frotter. **bring to** ～, révéler. **come to** ～, être révélé. **have you got a** ～?, vous avez du feu? ～ **bulb**, ampoule *f.* ～ **pen**, crayon optique *m.* ～ **up** *v.i.* s'allumer;

v.t. (*room*) éclairer. **~-year** *n.* année lumière *f.*

light² /laɪt/ *a.* (**-er, -est**) (*not heavy*) léger. **~-fingered** *a.* chapardeur. **~-headed** *a.* (*dizzy*) qui a un vertige; (*frivolous*) étourdi. **~-hearted** *a.* gai. **~ly** *adv.* légèrement. **~ness** *n.* légèreté *f.*

lighten¹ /'laɪtn/ *v.t.* (*give light to*) éclairer; (*make brighter*) éclaircir.

lighten² /'laɪtn/ *v.t.* (*make less heavy*) alléger.

lighter /'laɪtə(r)/ *n.* briquet *m.*; (*for stove*) allume-gaz *m. invar.*

lighthouse /'laɪthaʊs/ *n.* phare *m.*

lighting /'laɪtɪŋ/ *n.* éclairage *m.* **~ technician**, éclairagiste *m./f.*

lightning /'laɪtnɪŋ/ *n.* éclair(s) *m.* (*pl.*), foudre *f.* **—**a. éclair *invar.*

lightweight /'laɪtweɪt/ *a.* léger. **—**n. (*boxing*) poids léger *m.*

like¹ /laɪk/ *a.* semblable, pareil. **—**prep. comme. **—**conj. (*fam.*) comme. **—**n. pareil *m.* **be ~-minded**, avoir les mêmes sentiments. **the ~s of you**, des gens comme vous.

like² /laɪk/ *v.t.* aimer (bien). **~s** *n. pl.* goûts *m. pl.* **I should ~**, je voudrais, j'aimerais. **would you ~?**, voulez-vous? **~able** *a.* sympathique.

likely /'laɪklɪ/ *a.* (**-ier, -iest**) probable. **—**adv. probablement. **he is ~y to do**, il fera probablement. **not ~y!**, (*fam.*) pas question! **~ihood** *n.* probabilité *f.*

liken /'laɪkən/ *v.t.* comparer.

likeness /'laɪknɪs/ *n.* ressemblance *f.*

likewise /'laɪkwaɪz/ *adv.* de même.

liking /'laɪkɪŋ/ *n.* (*for thing*) penchant *m.*; (*for person*) affection *f.*

lilac /'laɪlək/ *n.* lilas *m.* **—**a. lilas *invar.*

lily /'lɪlɪ/ *n.* lis *m.*, lys *m.* **~ of the valley**, muguet *m.*

limb /lɪm/ *n.* membre *m.* **out on a ~**, isolé (et vulnérable).

limber /'lɪmbə(r)/ *v.i.* **~ up**, faire des exercices d'assouplissement.

limbo /'lɪmbəʊ/ *n.* **be in ~**, (*forgotten*) être tombé dans l'oubli.

lime¹ /laɪm/ *n.* chaux *f.*

lime² /laɪm/ *n.* (*fruit*) citron vert *m.*

lime³ /laɪm/ *n.* **~(-tree)**, tilleul *m.*

limelight /'laɪmlaɪt/ *n.* **in the ~**, en vedette.

limerick /'lɪmərɪk/ *n.* poème humoristique *m.* (*de cinq vers*).

limit /'lɪmɪt/ *n.* limite *f.* **—**v.t. limiter. **~ed company**, société anonyme *f.* **~ation** /-'teɪʃn/ *n.* limitation *f.* **~less** *a.* sans limites.

limousine /'lɪməziːn/ *n.* (*car*) limousine *f.*

limp¹ /lɪmp/ *v.i.* boiter. **—**n. **have a ~**, boiter.

limp² /lɪmp/ *a.* (**-er, -est**) mou.

limpid /'lɪmpɪd/ *a.* limpide.

linctus /'lɪŋktəs/ *n.* sirop *m.*

line¹ /laɪn/ *n.* ligne *f.*; (*track*) voie *f.*; (*wrinkle*) ride *f.*; (*row*) rangée *f.*, file *f.*; (*of poem*) vers *m.*; (*rope*) corde *f.*; (*of goods*) gamme *f.*; (*queue: Amer.*) queue *f.* **—**v.t. (*paper*) régler; (*streets etc.*) border. **be in ~ for**, avoir de bonnes chances d'avoir. **in ~ with**, en accord avec. **stand in ~**, faire la queue. **~ up**, (s')aligner; (*in queue*) faire la queue. **~ sth. up**, prévoir qch.

line² /laɪn/ *v.t.* (*garment*) doubler; (*fill*) remplir, garnir.

lineage /'lɪnɪɪdʒ/ *n.* lignée *f.*

linear /'lɪnɪə(r)/ *a.* linéaire.

linen /'lɪnɪn/ *n.* (*sheets etc.*) linge *m.*; (*material*) lin *m.*, toile de lin *f.*

liner /'laɪnə(r)/ *n.* paquebot *m.*

linesman /'laɪnzmən/ *n.* (*football*) juge de touche *m.*

linger /'lɪŋgə(r)/ *v.i.* s'attarder; (*smells etc.*) persister.

lingerie /'lænʒərɪ/ *n.* lingerie *f.*

lingo /'lɪŋgəʊ/ *n.* (*pl.* **-os**) (*hum., fam.*) jargon *m.*

linguist /'lɪŋgwɪst/ *n.* linguiste *m./f.*

linguistic /lɪŋ'gwɪstɪk/ *a.* linguistique. **~s** *n.* linguistique *f.*

lining /'laɪnɪŋ/ *n.* doublure *f.*

link /lɪŋk/ *n.* lien *m.*; (*of chain*) maillon *m.* **—**v.t. relier; (*relate*) (re)lier. **~ up**, (*of roads*) se rejoindre. **~age** *n.* lien *m.* **~-up** *n.* liaison *f.*

links /lɪŋks/ *n. invar.* terrain de golf *m.*

lino /'laɪnəʊ/ *n.* (*pl.* **-os**) lino *m.*

linoleum /lɪ'nəʊlɪəm/ *n.* linoléum *m.*

lint /lɪnt/ *n.* (*med.*) tissu ouaté *m.*; (*fluff*) peluche(s) *f.* (*pl.*).

lion /'laɪən/ *n.* lion *m.* **take the ~'s share**, se tailler la part du lion. **~ess** *n.* lionne *f.*

lip /lɪp/ *n.* lèvre *f.*; (*edge*) rebord *m.* **~-read** *v.t./i.* lire sur les lèvres. **pay ~-service to**, n'approuver que pour la forme.

lipsalve /'lɪpsælv/ *n.* baume pour les lèvres *m.*

lipstick /'lɪpstɪk/ *n.* rouge (à lèvres) *m.*

liquefy /'lɪkwɪfaɪ/ *v.t./i.* (se) liquéfier.

liqueur /lɪ'kjʊə(r)/ *n.* liqueur *f.*

liquid /'lɪkwɪd/ *n. & a.* liquide (*m.*). **~ize** *v.t.* passer au mixeur. **~izer** *n.* mixeur *m.*

liquidat|e /'lɪkwɪdeɪt/ v.t. liquider. ~**ion** /-'deɪʃn/ n. liquidation f. **go into** ~**ion,** déposer son bilan.

liquor /'lɪkə(r)/ n. alcool m.

liquorice /'lɪkərɪs/ n. réglisse f.

lira /'lɪərə/ n. (pl. **lire** /'lɪəreɪ/ or **liras**) lire f.

lisp /lɪsp/ n. zézaiement m. —v.i. zézayer. **with a** ~, en zézayant.

list[1] /lɪst/ n. liste f. —v.t. dresser la liste de.

list[2] /lɪst/ v.i. (ship) gîter.

listen /'lɪsn/ v.i. écouter. ~ **to,** ~ **in (to),** écouter. ~**er** n. auditeur, -trice m./f.

listless /'lɪstlɪs/ a. apathique.

lit /lɪt/ see **light**[1].

litany /'lɪtənɪ/ n. litanie f.

liter /'liːtə(r)/ see **litre**.

literal /'lɪtərəl/ a. littéral; (person) prosaïque. ~**ly** adv. littéralement.

literary /'lɪtərərɪ/ a. littéraire.

litera|te /'lɪtərət/ a. qui sait lire et écrire. ~**cy** n. capacité de lire et écrire f.

literature /'lɪtrətʃə(r)/ n. littérature f.; (fig.) documentation f.

lithe /laɪð/ a. souple, agile.

litigation /lɪtɪ'geɪʃn/ n. litige m.

litre, (Amer.) **liter** /'liːtə(r)/ n. litre m.

litter /'lɪtə(r)/ n. détritus m. pl., papiers m. pl.; (animals) portée f. —v.t. éparpiller; (make untidy) laisser des détritus dans. ~**bin** n. poubelle f. ~**ed with,** jonché de.

little /'lɪtl/ a. petit; (not much) peu de. —n. peu m. —adv. peu. **a** ~, un peu (de).

liturgy /'lɪtədʒɪ/ n. liturgie f.

live[1] /laɪv/ a. vivant; (wire) sous tension; (broadcast) en direct. **be a** ~ **wire,** être très dynamique.

live[2] /lɪv/ v.t./i. vivre; (reside) habiter, vivre. ~ **down,** faire oublier. ~ **it up,** mener la belle vie. ~ **on,** (feed o.s. on) vivre de; (continue) survivre. ~ **up to,** se montrer à la hauteur de.

livelihood /'laɪvlɪhʊd/ n. moyens d'existence m. pl.

livel|y /'laɪvlɪ/ a. (**-ier, -iest**) vif, vivant. ~**iness** n. vivacité f.

liven /'laɪvn/ v.t./i. ~ **up,** (s')animer; (cheer up) (s')égayer.

liver /'lɪvə(r)/ n. foie m.

livery /'lɪvərɪ/ n. livrée f.

livestock /'laɪvstɒk/ n. bétail m.

livid /'lɪvɪd/ a. livide; (angry: fam.) furieux.

living /'lɪvɪŋ/ a. vivant. —n. vie f. **make a** ~, gagner sa vie. ~ **conditions,**

conditions de vie f. pl. ~**-room** n. salle de séjour f.

lizard /'lɪzəd/ n. lézard m.

llama /'lɑːmə/ n. lama m.

load /ləʊd/ n. charge f.; (loaded goods) chargement m., charge f.; (weight, strain) poids m. ~**s of,** (fam.) des masses de. —v.t. charger. ~**ed** a. (dice) pipé; (wealthy: sl.) riche.

loaf[1] /ləʊf/ n. (pl. **loaves**) pain m.

loaf[2] /ləʊf/ v.i. ~ (**about),** fainéanter. ~**er** n. fainéant(e) m. (f.).

loam /ləʊm/ n. terreau m.

loan /ləʊn/ n. prêt m.; (money borrowed) emprunt m. —v.t. (lend: fam.) prêter.

loath /ləʊθ/ a. peu disposé (**to,** à).

loath|e /ləʊð/ v.t. détester. ~**ing** n. dégoût m. ~**some** a. dégoûtant.

lobby /'lɒbɪ/ n. entrée f., vestibule m.; (pol.) lobby m., groupe de pression m. —v.t. faire pression sur.

lobe /ləʊb/ n. lobe m.

lobster /'lɒbstə(r)/ n. homard m.

local /'ləʊkl/ a. local; (shops etc.) du quartier. —n. personne du pays f.; (pub: fam.) pub du coin m. ~ **government,** administration locale f. ~**ly** adv. localement; (nearby) dans les environs.

locale /ləʊ'kɑːl/ n. lieu m.

locality /ləʊ'kælətɪ/ n. (district) région f.; (position) lieu m.

localized /'ləʊkəlaɪzd/ a. localisé.

locat|e /ləʊ'keɪt/ v.t. (situate) situer; (find) repérer. ~**ion** /-ʃn/ n. emplacement m. **on** ~**ion,** (cinema) en extérieur.

lock[1] /lɒk/ n. mèche (de cheveux) f.

lock[2] /lɒk/ n. (of door etc.) serrure f.; (on canal) écluse f. —v.t./i. fermer à clef; (wheels: auto.) (se) bloquer. ~ **in or up,** (person) enfermer. ~ **out,** (by mistake) enfermer dehors. ~**-out** n. lockout m. invar. ~**-up** n. (shop) boutique f.; (garage) box m.

locker /'lɒkə(r)/ n. casier m.

locket /'lɒkɪt/ n. médaillon m.

locksmith /'lɒksmɪθ/ n. serrurier m.

locomotion /ləʊkə'məʊʃn/ n. locomotion f.

locomotive /'ləʊkəməʊtɪv/ n. locomotive f.

locum /'ləʊkəm/ n. (doctor etc.) remplaçant(e) m. (f.).

locust /'ləʊkəst/ n. criquet m., sauterelle f.

lodge /lɒdʒ/ n. (house) pavillon (de gardien or de chasse) m.; (of porter) loge f. —v.t. loger; (money, complaint) déposer. —v.i. être logé (**with,** chez);

(*become fixed*) se loger. ~r /-ə(r)/ *n.*
locataire *m./f.*, pensionnaire *m./f.*
lodgings /'lɒdʒɪŋz/ *n.* chambre
(meublée) *f.*; (*flat*) logement *m.*
loft /lɒft/ *n.* grenier *m.*
lofty /'lɒftɪ/ *a.* (**-ier, -iest**) (*tall*, *noble*)
élevé; (*haughty*) hautain.
log /lɒg/ *n.* (*of wood*) bûche *f.* ~(**-book**),
(*naut.*) journal de bord *m.*; (*auto.*)
(*équivalent de la*) carte grise *f.* —*v.t.*
(*p.t.* **logged**) noter; (*distance*) parcourir. ~ **on**, entrer. ~ **off**, sortir.
logarithm /'lɒgərɪðəm/ *n.* logarithme *m.*
loggerheads /'lɒgəhedz/ *n. pl.* **at** ~, en
désaccord.
logic /'lɒdʒɪk/ *a.* logique. ~**al** *a.* logique.
~**ally** *adv.* logiquement.
logistics /lə'dʒɪstɪks/ *n.* logistique *f.*
logo /'ləʊgəʊ/ *n.* (*pl.* **-os**) (*fam.*)
emblème *m.*
loin /lɔɪn/ *n.* (*culin.*) filet *m.* ~**s**, reins *m.
pl.*
loiter /'lɔɪtə(r)/ *v.i.* traîner.
loll /lɒl/ *v.i.* se prélasser.
loll|ipop /'lɒlɪpɒp/ *n.* sucette *f.* ~**y** *n.*
(*fam.*) sucette *f.*; (*sl.*) fric *m.*
London /'lʌndən/ *n.* Londres *m./f.* ~**er**
n. Londonien(ne) *m.* (*f.*).
lone /ləʊn/ *a.* solitaire. ~**r** /-ə(r)/ *n.*
solitaire *m./f.* ~**some** *a.* solitaire.
lonely /'ləʊnlɪ/ *a.* (**-ier, -iest**) solitaire;
(*person*) seul, solitaire.
long[1] /lɒŋ/ *a.* (**-er, -est**) long. —*adv.*
longtemps. **how** ~ **is?**, quelle est la
longueur de?; (*in time*) quelle est la
durée de? **how** ~**?**, combien de temps?
he will not be ~, il n'en a pas pour
longtemps. **a** ~ **time**, longtemps. **as** *or*
so ~ **as**, pourvu que. **before** ~, avant
peu. **I no** ~**er do**, je ne fais plus. ~**-
distance** *a.* (*flight*) sur long parcours;
(*phone call*) interurbain. ~ **face**,
grimace *f.* ~ **johns**, (*fam.*) caleçon
long *m.* ~ **jump**, saut en longueur *m.*
~**-playing record**, microsillon *m.* ~
range *a.* à longue portée; (*forecast*) à
long terme. ~**-sighted** *a.* presbyte. ~**-
standing** *a.* de longue date. ~**-
suffering** *a.* très patient. ~**-term** *a.* à
long terme. ~ **wave**, grandes ondes *f.
pl.* ~**-winded** *a.* (*speaker etc.*)
verbeux.
long[2] /lɒŋ/ *v.i.* avoir bien *or* très envie
(**for, to, de**). ~ **for s.o.**, (*pine for*)
languir après qn. ~**ing** *n.* envie *f.*;
(*nostalgia*) nostalgie *f.*
longevity /lɒn'dʒevətɪ/ *n.* longévité *f.*
longhand /'lɒŋhænd/ *n.* écriture
courante *f.*

longitude /'lɒndʒɪtjuːd/ *n.* longitude *f.*
loo /luː/ *n.* (*fam.*) toilettes *f. pl.*
look /lʊk/ *v.t./i.* regarder; (*seem*) avoir
l'air. —*n.* regard *m.*; (*appearance*) air
m., aspect *m.* (**good**) ~**s**, beauté *f.* ~
after, s'occuper de, soigner. ~ **at**,
regarder. ~ **back on**, repenser à. ~
down on, mépriser. ~ **for**, chercher. ~
forward to, attendre avec impatience.
~ **in on**, passer voir. ~ **into**, examiner.
~ **like**, ressembler à, avoir l'air de. ~
out, faire attention. ~ **out for**,
chercher; (*watch*) guetter. ~**-out** *n.*
(*mil.*) poste de guet *m.*; (*person*)
guetteur *m.* **be on the** ~**-out for**,
rechercher. ~ **round**, se retourner. ~
up, (*word*) chercher; (*visit*) passer voir.
~ **up to**, respecter. ~**-alike** *n.* sosie *m.*
~**ing-glass** *n.* glace *f.*
loom[1] /luːm/ *n.* métier à tisser *m.*
loom[2] /luːm/ *v.i.* surgir; (*event etc.: fig.*)
paraître imminent.
loony /'luːnɪ/ *n. & a.* (*sl.*) fou, folle (*m.*,
f.).
loop /luːp/ *n.* boucle *f.* —*v.t.* boucler.
loophole /'luːphəʊl/ *n.* (*in rule*)
échappatoire *f.*
loose /luːs/ *a.* (**-er, -est**) (*knot etc.*)
desserré; (*page etc.*) détaché; (*clothes*)
ample, lâche; (*tooth*) qui bouge; (*lax*)
relâché; (*not packed*) en vrac; (*inexact*)
vague; (*pej.*) immoral. **at a** ~ **end**,
(*Amer.*) **at** ~ **ends**, désœuvré. **come** ~,
bouger. ~**ly** *adv.* sans serrer; (*roughly*)
vaguement.
loosen /'luːsn/ *v.t.* (*slacken*) desserrer;
(*untie*) défaire.
loot /luːt/ *n.* butin *m.* —*v.t.* piller. ~**er** *n.*
pillard(e) *m.* (*f.*). ~**ing** *n.* pillage *m.*
lop /lɒp/ *v.t.* (*p.t.* **lopped**) ~ **off**, couper.
lop-sided /lɒp'saɪdɪd/ *a.* de travers.
lord /lɔːd/ *n.* seigneur *m.*; (*British title*)
lord *m.* **the L**~, le Seigneur. (**good**)
L~**!**, mon Dieu! ~**ly** *a.* noble;
(*haughty*) hautain.
lore /lɔː(r)/ *n.* traditions *f. pl.*
lorry /'lɒrɪ/ *n.* camion *m.*
lose /luːz/ *v.t./i.* (*p.t.* **lost**) perdre. **get
lost**, se perdre. ~**r** /-ə(r)/ *n.* perdant(e)
m. (*f.*).
loss /lɒs/ *n.* perte *f.* **be at a** ~, être
perplexe. **be at a** ~ **to**, être incapable
de. **heat** ~, déperdition de chaleur *f.*
lost /lɒst/ *see* **lose**. —*a.* perdu. ~
property, (*Amer.*) ~ **and found**, objets
trouvés *m. pl.*
lot[1] /lɒt/ *n.* (*fate*) sort *m.*; (*at auction*) lot
m.; (*land*) lotissement *m.*
lot[2] /lɒt/ *n.* **the** ~, (le) tout *m.*; (*people*)

tous *m. pl.*, toutes *f. pl.* **a ~ (of), ~s (of)**, (*fam.*) beaucoup (de). **quite a ~ (of)**, (*fam.*) pas mal (de).
lotion /'ləʊʃn/ *n.* lotion *f.*
lottery /'lɒtərɪ/ *n.* loterie *f.*
loud /laʊd/ *a.* (**-er, -est**) bruyant, fort. —*adv.* fort. **~ hailer**, portevoix *m. invar.* **out ~**, tout haut. **~ly** *adv.* fort.
loudspeaker /laʊd'spiːkə(r)/ *n.* haut-parleur *m.*
lounge /laʊndʒ/ *v.i.* paresser. —*n.* salon *m.* **~ suit**, costume *m.*
louse /laʊs/ *n.* (*pl.* **lice**) pou *m.*
lousy /'laʊzɪ/ *a.* (**-ier, -iest**) pouilleux; (*bad: sl.*) infect.
lout /laʊt/ *n.* rustre *m.*
lovable /'lʌvəbl/ *a.* adorable.
love /lʌv/ *n.* amour *m.*; (*tennis*) zéro *m.* —*v.t.* aimer; (*like greatly*) aimer (beaucoup) (**to do**, faire). **in ~**, amoureux (**with**, de). **~ affair**, liaison amoureuse *f.* **~ life**, vie amoureuse *f.* **make ~**, faire l'amour.
lovely /'lʌvlɪ/ *a.* (**-ier, -iest**) joli; (*delightful: fam.*) très agréable.
lover /'lʌvə(r)/ *n.* amant *m.*; (*devotee*) amateur *m.* (**of**, de).
lovesick /'lʌvsɪk/ *a.* amoureux.
loving /'lʌvɪŋ/ *a.* affectueux.
low[1] /ləʊ/ *v.i.* meugler.
low[2] /ləʊ/ *a. & adv.* (**-er, -est**) bas. —*n.* (*low pressure*) dépression *f.* **reach a (new) ~**, atteindre son niveau le plus bas. **~ in sth.**, à faible teneur en qch. **~-calorie** *a.* basses-calories. **~-cut** *a.* décolleté. **~-down** *a.* méprisable; *n.* (*fam.*) renseignements *m. pl.* **~-fat** *a.* maigre. **~-key** *a.* modéré; (*discreet*) discret. **~-lying** *a.* à faible altitude.
lowbrow /'ləʊbraʊ/ *a.* peu intellectuel.
lower /'ləʊə(r)/ *a. & adv. see* **low**[2]. —*v.t.* baisser. **~ o.s.**, s'abaisser.
lowlands /'ləʊləndz/ *n. pl.* plaine(s) *f.* (*pl.*).
lowly /'ləʊlɪ/ *a.* (**-ier, -iest**) humble.
loyal /'lɔɪəl/ *a.* loyal. **~ly** *adv.* loyalement. **~ty** *n.* loyauté *f.*
lozenge /'lɒzɪndʒ/ *n.* (*shape*) losange *m.*; (*tablet*) pastille *f.*
LP *abbr. see* **long-playing record.**
Ltd. *abbr.* (*Limited*) SA.
lubricate /'luːbrɪkeɪt/ *v.t.* graisser, lubrifier. **~ant** *n.* lubrifiant *m.* **~ation** /-'keɪʃn/ *n.* graissage *m.*
lucid /'luːsɪd/ *a.* lucide. **~ity** /luː'sɪdətɪ/ *n.* lucidité *f.*
luck /lʌk/ *n.* chance *f.* **bad ~**, malchance *f.* **good ~!**, bonne chance!
luck|y /'lʌkɪ/ *a.* (**-ier, -iest**) qui a de la chance, heureux; (*event*) heureux; (*number*) qui porte bonheur. **it's ~y that**, c'est une chance que. **~ily** *adv.* heureusement.
lucrative /'luːkrətɪv/ *a.* lucratif.
ludicrous /'luːdɪkrəs/ *a.* ridicule.
lug /lʌg/ *v.t.* (*p.t.* **lugged**) traîner.
luggage /'lʌgɪdʒ/ *n.* bagages *m. pl.* **~-rack** *n.* porte-bagages *m. invar.*
lukewarm /'luːkwɔːm/ *a.* tiède.
lull /lʌl/ *v.t.* (*soothe, send to sleep*) endormir. —*n.* accalmie *f.*
lullaby /'lʌləbaɪ/ *n.* berceuse *f.*
lumbago /lʌm'beɪgəʊ/ *n.* lumbago *m.*
lumber /'lʌmbə(r)/ *n.* bric-à-brac *m. invar.*; (*wood*) bois de charpente *m.* —*v.t.* **~ s.o. with**, (*chore etc.*) coller à qn.
lumberjack /'lʌmbədʒæk/ *n.* (*Amer.*) bûcheron *m.*
luminous /'luːmɪnəs/ *a.* lumineux.
lump /lʌmp/ *n.* morceau *m.*; (*swelling on body*) grosseur *f.*; (*in liquid*) grumeau *m.* —*v.t.* **~ together**, réunir. **~ sum**, somme globale *f.* **~y** *a.* (*sauce*) grumeleux; (*bumpy*) bosselé.
lunacy /'luːnəsɪ/ *n.* folie *f.*
lunar /'luːnə(r)/ *a.* lunaire.
lunatic /'luːnətɪk/ *n.* fou, folle *m., f.*
lunch /lʌntʃ/ *n.* déjeuner *m.* —*v.i.* déjeuner. **~ box**, cantine *f.*
luncheon /'lʌntʃən/ *n.* déjeuner *m.* **~ meat**, (*approx.*) saucisson *m.* **~ voucher**, chèque-repas *m.*
lung /lʌŋ/ *n.* poumon *m.*
lunge /lʌndʒ/ *n.* mouvement brusque en avant *m.* —*v.i.* s'élancer (**at**, sur).
lurch[1] /lɜːtʃ/ *n.* **leave in the ~**, planter là, laisser en plan.
lurch[2] /lɜːtʃ/ *v.i.* (*person*) tituber.
lure /lʊə(r)/ *v.t.* appâter, attirer. —*n.* (*attraction*) attrait *m.*, appât *m.*
lurid /'lʊərɪd/ *a.* choquant, affreux; (*gaudy*) voyant.
lurk /lɜːk/ *v.i.* se cacher; (*in ambush*) s'embusquer; (*prowl*) rôder. **a ~ing suspicion**, un petit soupçon.
luscious /'lʌʃəs/ *a.* appétissant.
lush /lʌʃ/ *a.* luxuriant. —*n.* (*Amer., fam.*) ivrogne(sse) *m.* (*f.*).
lust /lʌst/ *n.* luxure *f.*; (*fig.*) convoitise *f.* —*v.i.* **~ after**, convoiter.
lustre /'lʌstə(r)/ *n.* lustre *m.*
lusty /'lʌstɪ/ *a.* (**-ier, -iest**) robuste.
lute /luːt/ *n.* (*mus.*) luth *m.*
Luxemburg /'lʌksəmbɜːg/ *n.* Luxembourg *m.*
luxuriant /lʌg'ʒʊərɪənt/ *a.* luxuriant.
luxurious /lʌg'ʒʊərɪəs/ *a.* luxueux.

luxury /'lʌkʃərɪ/ n. luxe m. —a. de luxe.

lying /'laɪɪŋ/ see lie¹, lie². —n. le mensonge m.

lynch /lɪntʃ/ v.t. lyncher.

lynx /lɪŋks/ n. lynx m.

lyric /'lɪrɪk/ a. lyrique. ~s n. pl. paroles f. pl. ~al a. lyrique. ~ism /-sɪzəm/ n. lyrisme m.

M

MA abbr. see **Master of Arts.**

mac /mæk/ n. (fam.) imper m.

macaroni /mækə'rəʊnɪ/ n. macaronis m. pl.

macaroon /mækə'ruːn/ n. macaron m.

mace /meɪs/ n. (staff) masse f.

Mach /mɑːk/ n. ~ (number), (nombre de) Mach m.

machiavellian /mækɪə'velɪən/ a. machiavélique.

machinations /mækɪ'neɪʃnz/ n. pl. machinations f. pl.

machine /mə'ʃiːn/ n. machine f. —v.t. (sew) coudre à la machine; (techn.) usiner. ~ **code**, code machine m. ~-**gun** n. mitrailleuse f.; v.t. (p.t. -**gunned**) mitrailler. ~-**readable** a. en langage machine. ~ **tool**, machine-outil f.

machinery /mə'ʃiːnərɪ/ n. machinerie f.; (working parts & fig.) mécanisme(s) m. (pl.).

machinist /mə'ʃiːnɪst/ n. (operator) opéralteur, -trice sur machine m., f.; (on sewing-machine) piqueulr, -se m., f.

macho /'mætʃəʊ/ n. (pl. -os) macho m. —a. macho invar.

mackerel /'mækrəl/ n. invar. (fish) maquereau m.

mackintosh /'mækɪntɒʃ/ n. imperméable m.

macrobiotic /mækrəʊbaɪ'ɒtɪk/ a. macrobiotique.

mad /mæd/ a. (**madder, maddest**) fou; (foolish) insensé; (dog etc.) enragé; (angry: fam.) furieux. **be ~ about**, se passionner pour; (person) être fou de. **drive s.o. ~**, rendre qn. fou. **like ~**, comme un fou. ~**ly** adv. (interested, in love, etc.) follement; (frantically) comme un fou. ~**ness** n. folie f.

Madagascar /mædə'gæskə(r)/ n. Madagascar f.

madam /'mædəm/ n. madame f.; (unmarried) mademoiselle f.

madden /'mædn/ v.t. exaspérer.

made /meɪd/ see **make.** ~ **to measure**, fait sur mesure.

Madeira /mə'dɪərə/ n. (wine) madère m.

madhouse /'mædhaʊs/ n. (fam.) maison de fous f.

madman /'mædmən/ n. (pl. -**men**) fou m.

madrigal /'mædrɪgl/ n. madrigal m.

magazine /mægə'ziːn/ n. revue f., magazine m.; (of gun) magasin m.

magenta /mə'dʒentə/ a. magenta (invar.).

maggot /'mægət/ n. ver m., asticot m. ~**y** a. véreux.

magic /'mædʒɪk/ n. magie f. —a. magique. ~**al** a. magique.

magician /mə'dʒɪʃn/ n. magicien(ne) m. (f.).

magistrate /'mædʒɪstreɪt/ n. magistrat m.

magnanim|ous /mæg'nænɪməs/ a. magnanime. ~**ity** /-ə'nɪmətɪ/ n. magnanimité f.

magnate /'mægneɪt/ n. magnat m.

magnesia /mæg'niːʃə/ n. magnésie f.

magnet /'mægnɪt/ n. aimant m. ~**ic** /-'netɪk/ a. magnétique. ~**ism** n. magnétisme m. ~**ize** v.t. magnétiser.

magneto /mæg'niːtəʊ/ n. (pl. **os**) magnéto m.

magnificen|t /mæg'nɪfɪsnt/ a. magnifique. ~**ce** n. magnificence f.

magnif|y /'mægnɪfaɪ/ v.t. grossir; (sound) amplifier; (fig.) exagérer. ~**ication** /-ɪ'keɪʃn/ n. grossissement m.; amplification f. ~**ier** n., ~**ying glass**, loupe f.

magnitude /'mægnɪtjuːd/ n. (importance) ampleur f.; (size) grandeur f.

magnolia /mæg'nəʊlɪə/ n. magnolia m.

magnum /'mægnəm/ n. magnum m.

magpie /'mægpaɪ/ n. pie f.

mahogany /mə'hɒgənɪ/ n. acajou m.

maid /meɪd/ n. (servant) bonne f.; (girl: old use) jeune fille f.

maiden /'meɪdn/ n. (old use) jeune fille f. —a. (aunt) célibataire; (voyage) premier. ~ **name**, nom de jeune fille m. ~**hood** n. virginité f. ~**ly** a. virginal.

mail¹ /meɪl/ n. poste f.; (letters) courrier m. —a. (bag, van) postal. —v.t. envoyer par la poste. **mail box**, boîte à lettres f. ~**ing list**, liste d'adresses f. ~ **order**, vente par correspondance f. ~ **shot**, publipostage m.

mail² /meɪl/ n. (armour) cotte de mailles f.

mailman /'meɪlmæn/ n. (pl. **-men**) (Amer.) facteur m.

maim /meɪm/ v.t. mutiler.

main[1] /meɪn/ a. principal. —n. **in the ~,** en général. **~ line,** grande ligne f. **a ~ road,** une grande route. **~ly** adv. principalement, surtout.

main[2] /meɪn/ n. **(water/gas) ~,** conduite d'eau/de gaz f. **the ~s,** (electr.) le secteur.

mainframe n. unité centrale f.

mainland /'meɪnlənd/ n. continent m.

mainspring /'meɪnsprɪŋ/ n. ressort principal m.; (motive: fig.) mobile principal m.

mainstay /'meɪnsteɪ/ n. soutien m.

mainstream /'meɪnstriːm/ n. tendance principale f., ligne f.

maintain /meɪn'teɪn/ v.t. (continue, keep, assert) maintenir; (house, machine, family) entretenir; (rights) soutenir.

maintenance /'meɪntənəns/ n. (care) entretien m.; (continuation) maintien m.; (allowance) pension alimentaire f.

maisonette /meɪzə'net/ n. duplex m.

maize /meɪz/ n. maïs m.

majestic /mə'dʒestɪk/ a. majestueux.

majesty /'mædʒəstɪ/ n. majesté f.

major /'meɪdʒə(r)/ a. majeur. —n. commandant m. —v.i. **~ in,** (univ., Amer.) se spécialiser en. **~ road,** route à priorité f.

Majorca /mə'dʒɔːkə/ n. Majorque f.

majority /mə'dʒɒrətɪ/ n. majorité f. —a. majoritaire. **the ~ of people,** la plupart des gens.

make /meɪk/ v.t./i. (p.t. **made**) faire; (manufacture) fabriquer; (friends) se faire; (money) gagner, se faire; (decision) prendre; (destination) arriver à; (cause to be) rendre. **~ s.o. do sth.,** faire faire qch. à qn.; (force) obliger qn. à faire qch. —n. fabrication f.; (brand) marque f. **be made of,** être fait de. **~ o.s. at home,** se mettre à l'aise. **~ s.o. happy,** rendre qn. heureux. **~ it,** arriver; (succeed) réussir. **I ~ it two o'clock,** j'ai deux heures. **I ~ it 150,** d'après moi, ça fait 150. **I cannot ~ anything of it,** je n'y comprends rien. **can you ~ Friday?,** vendredi, c'est possible? **~ as if to,** faire mine de. **~ believe,** faire semblant. **~-believe,** a. feint, illusoire; n. fantaisie f. **~ do,** (manage) se débrouiller (with, avec). **~ do with,** (content o.s.) se contenter de. **~ for,** se diriger vers. (cause) tendre à créer. **~**

good v.i. réussir; v.t. compenser; (repair) réparer. **~ off,** filer (with, avec). **~ out** v.t. distinguer; (understand) comprendre; (draw up) faire; (assert) prétendre; v.i. (fam.) se débrouiller. **~ over,** céder (to, à); (convert) transformer. **~ up** v.t. faire, former; (story) inventer; (deficit) combler; v.i. se réconcilier. **~ up (one's face),** se maquiller. **~-up** n. maquillage m.; (of object) constitution f.; (psych.) caractère m. **~ up for,** compenser; (time) rattraper. **~ up one's mind,** se décider. **~ up to,** se concilier les bonnes grâces de.

maker /'meɪkə(r)/ n. fabricant m.

makeshift /'meɪkʃɪft/ n. expédient m. —a. provisoire.

making /'meɪkɪŋ/ n. **be the ~ of,** faire le succès de. **he has the ~s of,** il a l'étoffe de.

maladjusted /mælə'dʒʌstɪd/ a. inadapté.

maladministration /mælədmɪnɪ'streɪʃn/ n. mauvaise gestion f.

malaise /mæ'leɪz/ n. malaise m.

malaria /mə'leərɪə/ n. malaria f.

Malay /mə'leɪ/ a. & n. malais(e) (m. (f.)). **~sia** n. Malaysia f.

Malaya /mə'leɪə/ n. Malaisie f.

male /meɪl/ a. (voice, sex) masculin; (bot., techn.) mâle. —n. mâle m.

malevolen|t /mə'levələnt/ a. malveillant. **~ce** n. malveillance f.

malform|ation /mælfɔː'meɪʃn/ n. malformation f. **~ed** a. difforme.

malfunction /mæl'fʌŋkʃn/ n. mauvais fonctionnement m. —v.i. mal fonctionner.

malice /'mælɪs/ n. méchanceté f.

malicious /mə'lɪʃəs/ a. méchant. **~ly** adv. méchamment.

malign /mə'laɪn/ a. pernicieux. —v.t. calomnier.

malignan|t /mə'lɪgnənt/ a. malveillant; (tumour) malin. **~cy** n. malveillance f.; malignité f.

malinger /mə'lɪŋgə(r)/ v.i. feindre la maladie. **~er** n. simulateur, -trice m., f.

mall /mɔːl/ n. **(shopping) ~,** centre commercial m.

malleable /'mælɪəbl/ a. malléable.

mallet /'mælɪt/ n. maillet m.

malnutrition /mælnjuː'trɪʃn/ n. sous-alimentation f.

malpractice /mæl'præktɪs/ n. faute professionnelle f.

malt /mɔːlt/ n. malt m. **~ whisky,** whisky pur malt m.

Malt|a /'mɔːltə/ n. Malte f. ~**ese** /-'tiːz/ a. & n. maltais(e) (m. (f.)).

maltreat /mæl'triːt/ v.t. maltraiter. ~**ment** n. mauvais traitement m.

mammal /'mæml/ n. mammifère m.

mammoth /'mæməθ/ n. mammouth m. —a. monstre.

man /mæn/ n. (pl. **men**) homme m.; (in sports team) joueur m.; (chess) pièce f. —v.t. (p.t. **manned**) pourvoir en hommes; (ship) armer; (guns) servir; (be on duty at) être de service à ~-**hour** n. heure de main-d'œuvre f. ~ **in the street**, homme de la rue m. ~-**made** a. artificiel. ~-**sized** a. grand. ~ **to man**, d'homme à homme. ~**ned space flight**, vol spatial habité m.

manage /'mænɪdʒ/ v.t. diriger; (shop, affairs) gérer; (handle) manier. **I could ~ another drink**, (fam.) je prendrais bien encore un verre. **can you ~ Friday?**, vendredi, c'est possible? —v.i. se débrouiller. ~ **to do**, réussir à faire. ~**able** a. (tool, size, person, etc.) maniable; (job) faisable. ~**ment** n. direction f.; (of shop) gestion f. **managing director**, directeur général m.

manager /'mænɪdʒə(r)/ n. direc|teur, -trice m.f.; (of shop) gérant(e) m.(f.); (of actor) impresario m. ~**ess** /-'res/ n. directrice f.; gérante f. ~**ial** /-'dʒɪərɪəl/ a. directorial. ~**ial staff**, cadres m. pl.

mandarin /'mændərɪn/ n. mandarin m.; (orange) mandarine f.

mandate /'mændeɪt/ n. mandat m.

mandatory /'mændətrɪ/ a. obligatoire.

mane /meɪn/ n. crinière f.

manful /'mænfl/ a. courageux.

manganese /mæŋgə'niːz/ n. manganèse m.

mangetout /mɑːnʒ'tuː/ n. mange-tout m. invar.

mangle[1] /'mæŋgl/ n. (for wringing) essoreuse f.; (for smoothing) calandre f.

mangle[2] /'mæŋgl/ v.t. mutiler.

mango /'mæŋgəʊ/ n. (pl. -**oes**) mangue f.

manhandle /'mænhændl/ v.t. maltraiter, malmener.

manhole /'mænhəʊl/ n. trou d'homme m., regard m.

manhood /'mænhʊd/ n. âge d'homme m.; (quality) virilité f.

mania /'meɪnɪə/ n. manie f. ~**c** /-ɪæk/ n. maniaque m./f., fou m., folle f.

manic-depressive /'mænɪkdɪ'presɪv/ a & n. maniaco-dépressif(-ive) (m. (f.)).

manicur|e /'mænɪkjʊə(r)/ n. soin des mains m. —v.t. soigner, manucurer. ~**ist** n. manucure m./f.

manifest /'mænɪfest/ a. manifeste. —v.t. manifester. ~**ation** /-'steɪʃn/ n. manifestation f.

manifesto /mænɪ'festəʊ/ n. (pl. -**os**) manifeste m.

manifold /'mænɪfəʊld/ a. multiple. —n. (auto.) collecteur m.

manipulat|e /mə'nɪpjʊleɪt/ v.t. (tool, person) manipuler. ~**ion** /-'leɪʃn/ n. manipulation f.

mankind /mæn'kaɪnd/ n. genre humain m.

manly /'mænlɪ/ a. viril.

manner /'mænə(r)/ n. manière f.; (attitude) attitude f.; (kind) sorte f. ~**s**, (social behaviour) manières f. pl. ~**ed** a. maniéré.

mannerism /'mænərɪzəm/ n. trait particulier m.

manœuvre /mə'nuːvə(r)/ n. manœuvre f. —v.t./i. manœuvrer.

manor /'mænə(r)/ n. manoir m.

manpower /'mænpaʊə(r)/ n. main-d'œuvre f.

manservant /'mænsɜːvənt/ n. (pl. **menservants**) domestique m.

mansion /'mænʃn/ n. château m.

manslaughter /'mænslɔːtə(r)/ n. homicide involontaire m.

mantelpiece /'mæntlpiːs/ n. (shelf) cheminée f.

manual /'mænjʊəl/ a. manuel. —n. (handbook) manuel m.

manufacture /mænjʊ'fæktʃə(r)/ v.t. fabriquer. —n. fabrication f. ~**r** /-ə(r)/ n. fabricant m.

manure /mə'njʊə(r)/ n. fumier m.; (artificial) engrais m.

manuscript /'mænjʊskrɪpt/ n. manuscrit m.

many /'menɪ/ a. & n. beaucoup (de). **a great** or **good ~**, un grand nombre (de). ~ **a**, bien des.

Maori /'maʊrɪ/ a. maori. —n. Maori(e) m. (f.).

map /mæp/ n. carte f.; (of streets etc.) plan m. —v.t. (p.t. **mapped**) faire la carte de. ~ **out**, (route) tracer; (arrange) organiser.

maple /'meɪpl/ n. érable m.

mar /mɑː(r)/ v.t. (p.t. **marred**) gâter; (spoil beauty of) déparer.

marathon /'mærəθən/ n. marathon m.

marble /'mɑːbl/ n. marbre m.; (for game) bille f.

March /mɑːtʃ/ n. mars m.

march /mɑːtʃ/ *v.i.* (*mil.*) marcher (au pas). ∼ **off**/*etc.*, partir/*etc.* allégrement. —*v.t.* ∼ **off**, (*lead away*) emmener. —*n.* marche *f.* ∼**-past** *n.* défilé *m.*

mare /meə(r)/ *n.* jument *f.*

margarine /mɑːdʒəˈriːn/ *n.* margarine *f.*

margin /ˈmɑːdʒɪn/ *n.* marge *f.* ∼**al** *a.* marginal; (*increase etc.*) léger, faible. ∼**al seat**, (*pol.*) siège chaudement disputé *m.* ∼**alize** *v.t.* marginaliser. ∼**ally** *adv.* très légèrement.

marigold /ˈmærɪɡəʊld/ *n.* souci *m.*

marijuana /mærɪˈwɑːnə/ *n.* marijuana *f.*

marina /məˈriːnə/ *n.* marina *f.*

marinate /ˈmærɪneɪt/ *v.t.* mariner.

marine /məˈriːn/ *a.* marin. —*n.* (*shipping*) marine *f.*; (*sailor*) fusilier marin *m.*

marionette /mærɪəˈnet/ *n.* marionnette *f.*

marital /ˈmærɪtl/ *a.* conjugal. ∼ **status**, situation de famille *f.*

maritime /ˈmærɪtaɪm/ *a.* maritime.

marjoram /ˈmɑːdʒərəm/ *n.* marjolaine *f.*

mark[1] /mɑːk/ *n.* (*currency*) mark *m.*

mark[2] /mɑːk/ *n.* marque *f.*; (*trace*) trace *f.*, marque *f.*; (*schol.*) note *f.*; (*target*) but *m.* —*v.t.* marquer; (*exam*) corriger. ∼ **out**, délimiter; (*person*) désigner. ∼ **time**, marquer le pas. ∼**er** *n.* marque *f.* ∼**ing** *n.* (*marks*) marques *f.pl.*

marked /mɑːkt/ *a.* marqué. ∼**ly** /-ɪdlɪ/ *adv.* visiblement.

market /ˈmɑːkɪt/ *n.* marché *m.* —*v.t.* (*sell*) vendre; (*launch*) commercialiser. ∼ **garden**, jardin maraîcher *m.* ∼**place** *n.* marché *m.* ∼ **research**, étude de marché *f.* ∼ **value**, valeur marchande *f.* **on the** ∼, en vente. ∼**ing** *n.* marketing *m.*

marksman /ˈmɑːksmən/ *n.* (*pl.* **-men**) tireur d'élite *m.*

marmalade /ˈmɑːməleɪd/ *n.* confiture d'oranges *f.*

maroon /məˈruːn/ *n.* bordeaux *m. invar.* —*a.* bordeaux *invar.*

marooned /məˈruːnd/ *a.* abandonné; (*snow-bound etc.*) bloqué.

marquee /mɑːˈkiː/ *n.* grande tente *f.*; (*awning: Amer.*) marquise *f.*

marquis /ˈmɑːkwɪs/ *n.* marquis *m.*

marriage /ˈmærɪdʒ/ *n.* mariage *m.* ∼**able** *a.* nubile, mariable.

marrow /ˈmærəʊ/ *n.* (*of bone*) moelle *f.*; (*vegetable*) courge *f.*

marr|y /ˈmærɪ/ *v.t.* épouser; (*give or unite in marriage*) marier. —*v.i.* se marier. ∼**ied** *a.* marié; (*life*) conjugal. **get** ∼**ied**, se marier (**to**, avec).

Mars /mɑːz/ *n.* (*planet*) Mars *f.*

marsh /mɑːʃ/ *n.* marais *m.* ∼**y** *a.* marécageux.

marshal /ˈmɑːʃl/ *n.* maréchal *m.*; (*at event*) membre du service d'ordre *m.* —*v.t.* (*p.t.* **marshalled**) rassembler.

marshmallow /mɑːʃˈmæləʊ/ *n.* guimauve *f.*

martial /ˈmɑːʃl/ *a.* martial. ∼ **law**, loi martiale *f.*

martyr /ˈmɑːtə(r)/ *n.* martyr(e) *m.* (*f.*). —*v.t.* martyriser. ∼**dom** *n.* martyre *m.*

marvel /ˈmɑːvl/ *n.* merveille *f.* —*v.i.* (*p.t.* **marvelled**) s'émerveiller (**at**, de).

marvellous /ˈmɑːvələs/ *a.* merveilleux.

Marxis|t /ˈmɑːksɪst/ *a.* & *n.* marxiste (*m./f.*). ∼**m** /-zəm/ *n.* marxisme *m.*

marzipan /ˈmɑːzɪpæn/ *n.* pâte d'amandes *f.*

mascara /mæˈskɑːrə/ *n.* mascara *m.*

mascot /ˈmæskət/ *n.* mascotte *f.*

masculin|e /ˈmæskjʊlɪn/ *a.* & *n.* masculin (*m.*). ∼**ity** /-ˈlɪnətɪ/ *n.* masculinité *f.*

mash /mæʃ/ *n.* pâtée *f.*; (*potatoes: fam.*) purée *f.* —*v.t.* écraser. ∼**ed potatoes**, purée (de pommes de terre) *f.*

mask /mɑːsk/ *n.* masque *m.* —*v.t.* masquer.

masochis|t /ˈmæsəkɪst/ *n.* masochiste *m./f.* ∼**m** /-zəm/ *n.* masochisme *m.*

mason /ˈmeɪsn/ *n.* (*builder*) maçon *m.* ∼**ry** *n.* maçonnerie *f.*

Mason /ˈmeɪsn/ *n.* maçon *m.* ∼**ic** /məˈsɒnɪk/ *a.* maçonnique

masquerade /mɑːskəˈreɪd/ *n.* mascarade *f.* —*v.i.* ∼ **as**, se faire passer pour.

mass[1] /mæs/ *n.* (*relig.*) messe *f.*

mass[2] /mæs/ *n.* masse *f.* —*v.t./i.* (se) masser. ∼**-produce** *v.t.* fabriquer en série. **the** ∼**es**, les masses *f.pl.* **the** ∼ **media**, les media *m.pl.*

massacre /ˈmæsəkə(r)/ *n.* massacre *m.* —*v.t.* massacrer.

massage /ˈmæsɑːʒ, *Amer.* məˈsɑːʒ/ *n.* massage *m.* —*v.t.* masser.

masseu|r /mæˈsɜː(r)/ *n.* masseur *m.* ∼**se** /-ɜːz/ *n.* masseuse *f.*

massive /ˈmæsɪv/ *a.* (*large*) énorme; (*heavy*) massif.

mast /mɑːst/ *n.* mât *m.*; (*for radio, TV*) pylône *m.*

master /ˈmɑːstə(r)/ *n.* maître *m.*; (*in secondary school*) professeur *m.* —*v.t.* maîtriser. ∼**-key** *n.* passe-partout *m. invar.* ∼**-mind** *n.* (*of scheme etc.*) cerveau *m.*; *v.t.* diriger. **M**∼ **of Arts**/*etc.*, titulaire d'une maîtrise ès lettres/*etc. m./f.* **~-stroke** *n.* coup de maître *m.* **~y** *n.* maîtrise *f.*

masterly /'mɑːstəlɪ/ *a.* magistral.

masterpiece /'mɑːstəpiːs/ *n.* chef-d'œuvre *m.*

mastiff /'mæstɪf/ *n.* dogue *m.*

masturbat|e /'mæstəbeɪt/ *v.i.* se masturber. **~ion** /-'beɪʃn/ *n.* masturbation *f.*

mat /mæt/ *n.* (petit) tapis *m.*, natte *f.*; (*at door*) paillasson *m.*

match[1] /mætʃ/ *n.* allumette *f.*

match[2] /mætʃ/ *n.* (*sport*) match *m.*; (*equal*) égal(e) *m.* (*f.*); (*marriage*) mariage *m.*; (*s.o. to marry*) parti *m.* —*v.t.* opposer; (*go with*) aller avec; (*cups etc.*) assortir; (*equal*) égaler. **be a ~ for,** pouvoir tenir tête à. —*v.i.* (*be alike*) être assorti. **~ing** *a.* assorti.

matchbox /'mætʃbɒks/ *n.* boîte à allumettes *f.*

mate[1] /meɪt/ *n.* camarade *m./f.*; (*of animal*) compagnon *m.*, compagne *f.*; (*assistant*) aide *m./f.* —*v.t./i.* (s')accoupler (**with,** avec).

mate[2] /meɪt/ *n.* (*chess*) mat *m.*

material /mə'tɪərɪəl/ *n.* matière *f.*; (*fabric*) tissu *m.*; (*documents, for building*) matériau(x) *m.* (*pl.*). **~s,** (*equipment*) matériel *m.* —*a.* matériel; (*fig.*) important. **~istic** /-'lɪstɪk/ *a.* matérialiste.

materialize /mə'tɪərɪəlaɪz/ *v.i.* se matérialiser, se réaliser.

maternal /mə'tɜːnl/ *a.* maternel.

maternity /mə'tɜːnətɪ/ *n.* maternité *f.* —*a.* (*clothes*) de grossesse. **~ hospital,** maternité *f.* **~ leave,** congé maternité *m.*

mathematic|s /mæθə'mætɪks/ *n. & n. pl.* mathématiques *f. pl.* **~ian** /-ə'tɪʃn/ *n.* mathématicien(ne) *m.* (*f.*). **~al** *a.* mathématique.

maths /mæθs/ (*Amer.* **math** /mæθ/) *n. & n. pl.* (*fam.*) maths *f. pl.*

matinée /'mætɪneɪ/ *n.* matinée *f.*

mating /'meɪtɪŋ/ *n.* accouplement *m.* **~ season,** saison des amours *f.*

matriculat|e /mə'trɪkjʊleɪt/ *v.t./i.* (s')inscrire. **~ion** /-'leɪʃn/ *n.* inscription *f.*

matrimon|y /'mætrɪmənɪ/ *n.* mariage *m.* **~ial** /-'məʊnɪəl/ *a.* matrimonial.

matrix /'meɪtrɪks/ *n.* (*pl.* **matrices** /-ɪsiːz/) matrice *f.*

matron /'meɪtrən/ *n.* (*married, elderly*) dame âgée *f.*; (*in hospital: former use*) infirmière-major *f.* **~ly** *a.* d'âge mûr; (*manner*) très digne.

matt /mæt/ *a.* mat.

matted /'mætɪd/ *a.* (*hair*) emmêlé.

matter /'mætə(r)/ *n.* (*substance*) matière *f.*; (*affair*) affaire *f.*; (*pus*) pus *m.* —*v.i.* importer. **as a ~ of fact,** en fait. **it does not ~,** ça ne fait rien. **~-of-fact** *a.* terre à terre *invar.* **no ~ what happens,** quoi qu'il arrive. **what is the ~?,** qu'est-ce qu'il y a?

mattress /'mætrɪs/ *n.* matelas *m.*

matur|e /mə'tjʊə(r)/ *a.* mûr. —*v.t./i.* (se) mûrir. **~ity** *n.* maturité *f.*

maul /mɔːl/ *v.t.* déchiqueter.

Mauritius /mə'rɪʃəs/ *n.* île Maurice *f.*

mausoleum /mɔːsə'lɪəm/ *n.* mausolée *m.*

mauve /məʊv/ *a. & n.* mauve (*m.*).

maverick /'mævərɪk/ *n.* non-conformiste.

maxim /'mæksɪm/ *n.* maxime *f.*

maxim|um /'mæksɪməm/ *a. & n.* (*pl.* **-ima**) maximum (*m.*). **~ize** *v.t.* porter au maximum.

may /meɪ/ *v. aux.* (*p.t.* **might**) pouvoir. **he ~/might come,** il peut/pourrait venir. **you might have,** vous auriez pu. **you ~ leave,** vous pouvez partir. **~ I smoke?,** puis-je fumer? **~ he be happy,** qu'il soit heureux. **I ~** *or* **might as well stay,** je ferais aussi bien de rester.

May /meɪ/ *n.* mai *m.* **~ Day,** le Premier Mai.

maybe /'meɪbiː/ *adv.* peut-être.

mayhem /'meɪhem/ *n.* (*havoc*) ravages *m. pl.*

mayonnaise /meɪə'neɪz/ *n.* mayonnaise *f.*

mayor /meə(r)/ *n.* maire *m.* **~ess** *n.* (*wife*) femme du maire *f.*

maze /meɪz/ *n.* labyrinthe *m.*

MBA (*abbr.*) (*Master of Business Administration*) magistère en gestion commerciale.

me /miː/ *pron.* me, m'*; (*after prep.*) moi. **(to) ~,** me, m'*. **he knows ~,** il me connaît.

meadow /'medəʊ/ *n.* pré *m.*

meagre /'miːgə(r)/ *a.* maigre.

meal[1] /miːl/ *n.* repas *m.*

meal[2] /miːl/ *n.* (*grain*) farine *f.*

mealy-mouthed /miːlɪ'maʊðd/ *a.* mielleux.

mean[1] /miːn/ *a.* (**-er, -est**) (*poor*) misérable; (*miserly*) avare; (*unkind*) méchant. **~ness** *n.* avarice *f.*; méchanceté *f.*

mean[2] /miːn/ *a.* moyen. —*n.* milieu *m.*; (*average*) moyenne *f.* **in the ~ time,** en attendant.

mean[3] /miːn/ *v.t.* (*p.t.* **meant** /ment/)

vouloir dire, signifier; (*involve*)
entraîner. **I ~ that!**, je suis sérieux. **be
meant for**, être destiné à. **~ to do**, avoir
l'intention de faire.

meander /mɪ'ændə(r)/ *v.i.* faire des
méandres.

meaning /'mi:nɪŋ/ *n.* sens *m.*,
signification *f.* **~ful** *a.* significatif.
~less *a.* denué de sens.

means /mi:nz/ *n.* moyen(s) *m.* (*pl.*). **by
~ of sth.**, au moyen de qch. —*n. pl.*
(*wealth*) moyens financiers *m. pl.* **by all
~**, certainement. **by no ~**, nullement.

meant /ment/ *see* **mean**².

mean|time /'mi:ntaɪm/, **~while** *advs.*
en attendant.

measles /'mi:zlz/ *n.* rougeole *f.*

measly /'mi:zlɪ/ *a.* (*sl.*) minable.

measurable /'meʒərəbl/ *a.* mesurable.

measure /'meʒə(r)/ *n.* mesure *f.*; (*ruler*)
règle *f.* —*v.t./i.* mesurer. **~ up to**, être à
la hauteur de. **~d** *a.* mesuré. **~ment** *n.*
mesure *f.*

meat /mi:t/ *n.* viande *f.* **~y** *a.* de viande;
(*fig.*) substantiel.

mechanic /mɪ'kænɪk/ *a.* mécanicien(ne)
m. (*f.*).

mechanic|al /mɪ'kænɪkl/ *d.* mécanique.
~s *n.* (*science*) mécanique *f.*; *n. pl.*
mécanisme *m.*

mechan|ism /'mekənɪzəm/ *n.* méca-
nisme *m.* **~ize** *v.t.* mécaniser.

medal /'medl/ *n.* médaille *f.* **~list** *n.*
médaillé(e) *m.* (*f.*). **be a gold ~list**, être
médaille d'or.

medallion /mɪ'dælɪən/ *n.* (*medal,
portrait, etc.*) médaillon *m.*

meddle /'medl/ *v.i.* (*interfere*) se mêler
(**in**, de); (*tinker*) toucher (**with**, à).
~some *a.* importun.

media /'mi:dɪə/ *see* **medium**. —*n. pl.*
the ~, les media *m. pl.* **talk to the ~**,
parler à la presse.

median /'mi:dɪən/ *a.* médian. —*n.*
médiane *f.*

mediat|e /'mi:dɪeɪt/ *v.i.* servir d'inter-
médiaire. **~ion** /-'eɪʃn/ *n.* médiation *f.*
~or *n.* média|teur, -trice *m.*, *f.*

medical /'medɪkl/ *a.* médical; (*student*)
en médecine. —*n.* (*fam.*) visite
médicale *f.*

medicat|ed /'medɪkeɪtɪd/ *a.* médical.
~ion /-'keɪʃn/ *n.* médicaments *m. pl.*

medicin|e /'medsn/ *n.* (*science*)
médecine *f.*; (*substance*) médicament
m. **~al** /mɪ'dɪsɪnl/ *a.* médicinal.

medieval /medɪ'i:vl/ *a.* médiéval.

mediocr|e /mi:dɪ'əʊkə(r)/ *a.* médiocre.
~ity /-'ɒkrətɪ/ *n.* médiocrité *f.*

meditat|e /'medɪteɪt/ *v.t./i.* méditer.
~ion /-'teɪʃn/ *n.* méditation *f.*

Mediterranean /medɪtə'reɪnɪən/ *a.*
méditerranéen. —*n.* **the ~**, la Méditerranée *f.*

medium /'mi:dɪəm/ *n.* (*pl.* **media**)
milieu *m.*; (*for transmitting data etc.*)
support *m.*; (*pl.* **mediums**) (*person*)
médium *m.* —*a.* moyen.

medley /'medlɪ/ *n.* mélange *m.*; (*mus.*)
pot-pourri *m.*

meek /mi:k/ *a.* (**-er, -est**) doux.

meet /mi:t/ *v.t.* (*p.t.* **met**) rencontrer;
(*see again*) retrouver; (*fetch*) (aller)
chercher; (*be introduced to*) faire la
connaissance de; (*face*) faire face à;
(*requirement*) satisfaire. —*v.i.* se
rencontrer; (*see each other again*) se
retrouver; (*in session*) se réunir.

meeting /'mi:tɪŋ/ *n.* réunion *f.*; (*between
two people*) rencontre *f.*

megalomania /megələʊ'meɪnɪə/ *n.*
mégalomanie *f.* **~c** /-æk/ *n.*
mégalomane *m./f.*

megaphone /'megəfəʊn/ *n.* portevoix *m.*
invar.

melamine /'meləmi:n/ *n.* mélamine *f.*

melanchol|y /'melənkəlɪ/ *n.* mélancolie
f. —*a.* mélancolique. **~ic** /-'kɒlɪk/ *a.*
mélancolique.

mellow /'meləʊ/ *a.* (**-er, -est**) (*fruit*)
mûr; (*sound, colour*) moelleux, doux;
(*person*) mûri. —*v.t./i.* (*mature*) mûrir;
(*soften*) (s')adoucir.

melodious /mɪ'ləʊdɪəs/ *a.* mélodieux.

melodrama /'melədra:mə/ *n.* mélo-
drame *m.* **~tic** /-ə'mætɪk/ *a.*
mélodramatique.

melod|y /'melədɪ/ *n.* mélodie *f.* **~ic**
/mɪ'lɒdɪk/ *a.* mélodique.

melon /'melən/ *n.* melon *m.*

melt /melt/ *v.t./i.* (faire) fondre. **~ing-
pot** *n.* creuset *m.*

member /'membə(r)/ *n.* membre *m.*
M~ of Parliament, député *m.* **~ship**
n. adhésion *f.*; (*members*) membres *m.
pl.*; (*fee*) cotisation *f.*

membrane /'membreɪn/ *n.* membrane *f.*

memento /mɪ'mentəʊ/ *n.* (*pl.* **-oes**)
(*object*) souvenir *m.*

memo /'meməʊ/ *n.* (*pl.* **-os**) (*fam.*) note
f.

memoir /'memwɑ:(r)/ *n.* (*record, essay*)
mémoire *m.*

memorable /'memərəbl/ *a.* mémorable.

memorandum /memə'rændəm/ *n.* (*pl.*
-ums) note *f.*

memorial /mɪ'mɔ:rɪəl/ *n.* monument *m.*
—*a.* commémoratif.

memorize /'meməraɪz/ v.t. apprendre par cœur.

memory /'memərɪ/ n. (mind, in computer) mémoire f.; (thing remembered) souvenir m. **from ~**, de mémoire. **in ~ of**, à la mémoire de.

men /men/ see **man**.

menac|e /'menəs/ n. menace f.; (nuisance) peste f. —v.t. menacer. **~ing** a. menaçant.

menagerie /mɪ'nædʒərɪ/ n. ménagerie f.

mend /mend/ v.t. réparer; (darn) raccommoder. —n. raccommodage m. **~ one's ways**, s'amender. **on the ~**, en voie de guérison.

menial /'miːnɪəl/ a. servile.

meningitis /menɪn'dʒaɪtɪs/ n. méningite f.

menopause /'menəpɔːz/ n. ménopause f.

menstruation /menstrʊ'eɪʃn/ n. menstruation f.

mental /'mentl/ a. mental; (hospital) psychiatrique. **~ block**, blocage m.

mentality /men'tælətɪ/ n. mentalité f.

menthol /'menθɒl/ n. menthol m. —a. mentholé.

mention /'menʃn/ v.t. mentionner. —n. mention f. **don't ~ it!**, il n'y a pas de quoi!, je vous en prie!

mentor /'mentɔː(r)/ n. mentor m.

menu /'menjuː/ n. (food, on computer) menu m.; (list) carte f.

MEP (abbr.) (member of the European Parliament) député européen m.

mercenary /'mɜːsɪnərɪ/ a. & n. mercenaire (m.).

merchandise /'mɜːtʃəndaɪz/ n. marchandises f. pl.

merchant /'mɜːtʃənt/ n. marchand m. —a. (ship, navy) marchand. **~ bank**, banque de commerce f.

merciful /'mɜːsɪfl/ a. miséricordieux. **~ly** adv. (fortunately: fam.) Dieu merci.

merciless /'mɜːsɪlɪs/ a. impitoyable, implacable.

mercury /'mɜːkjʊrɪ/ n. mercure m.

mercy /'mɜːsɪ/ n. pitié f. **at the ~ of**, à la merci de.

mere /mɪə(r)/ a. simple. **~ly** adv. simplement.

merest /'mɪərɪst/ a. moindre.

merge /mɜːdʒ/ v.t./i. (se) mêler (with, à); (companies: comm.) fusionner. **~r** /-ə(r)/ n. fusion f.

meridian /mə'rɪdɪən/ n. méridien m.

meringue /mə'ræŋ/ n. meringue f.

merit /'merɪt/ n. mérite m. —v.t. (p.t. **merited**) mériter.

mermaid /'mɜːmeɪd/ n. sirène f.

merriment /'merɪmənt/ n. gaieté. f.

merry /'merɪ/ a. (-ier, -iest) gai. **make ~**, faire la fête. **~-go-round** n. manège m. **~-making** n. réjouissances f. pl.

merrily adv. gaiement.

mesh /meʃ/ n. maille f.; (fabric) tissu à mailles m.; (network) réseau m.

mesmerize /'mezməraɪz/ v.t. hypnotiser.

mess /mes/ n. désordre m., gâchis m.; (dirt) saleté f.; (mil.) mess m. —v.t. **~ up**, gâcher. —v.i. **~ about**, s'amuser; (dawdle) traîner. **~ with**, (tinker with) tripoter. **make a ~ of**, gâcher.

message /'mesɪdʒ/ n. message m.

messenger /'mesɪndʒə(r)/ n. messager m.

Messrs /'mesəz/ n. pl. **~ Smith**, Messieurs or MM. Smith.

messy /'mesɪ/ a. (-ier, -iest) en désordre; (dirty) sale.

met /met/ see **meet**.

metabolic /metə'bɒlɪk/ adj. métabolique.

metabolism /mɪ'tæbəlɪzəm/ n. métabolisme m.

metal /'metl/ n. métal m. —a. de métal. **~lic** /mɪ'tælɪk/ a. métallique; (paint, colour) métallisé.

metallurgy /mɪ'tælədʒɪ, Amer. 'metəlɜːdʒɪ/ n. métallurgie f.

metamorphosis /metə'mɔːfəsɪs/ n. (pl. -phoses /-siːz/) métamorphose f.

metaphor /'metəfə(r)/ n. métaphore f. **~ical** /-'fɒrɪkl/ a. métaphorique.

mete /miːt/ v.t. **~ out**, donner, distribuer; (justice) rendre.

meteor /'miːtɪə(r)/ n. météore m.

meteorite /'miːtɪəraɪt/ n. météorite m.

meteorolog|y /miːtɪə'rɒlədʒɪ/ n. météorologie f. **~ical** /-ə'lɒdʒɪkl/ a. météorologique.

meter¹ /'miːtə(r)/ n. compteur m.

meter² /'miːtə(r)/ n. (Amer.) = **metre**.

method /'meθəd/ n. méthode f.

methodical /mɪ'θɒdɪkl/ a. méthodique.

Methodist /'meθədɪst/ n. & a. méthodiste (m./f.).

methodology /meθə'dɒlədʒɪ/ n. méthodologie f.

methylated /'meθɪleɪtɪd/ a. **~ spirit**, alcool à brûler m.

meticulous /mɪ'tɪkjʊləs/ a. méticuleux.

metre /'miːtə(r)/ n. mètre m.

metric /'metrɪk/ a. métrique. **~ation** /-'keɪʃn/ n. adoption du système métrique f.

metropol|is /mə'trɒpəlɪs/ n. (city)

métropole *f.* **~itan** /metrə'pɒlitən/ *a.* métropolitain.

mettle /'metl/ *n.* courage *m.*

mew /mjuː/ *n.* miaulement *m.* —*v.i.* miauler.

mews /mjuːz/ *n. pl.* (*dwellings*) appartements chic aménagés dans des anciennes écuries *m. pl.*

Mexic|o /'meksikəʊ/ *n.* Mexique *m.* **~an** *a. & n.* mexicain(e) (*m. (f.)*).

miaow /miː'aʊ/ *n. & v.i.* = **mew.**

mice /mais/ *see* **mouse.**

mickey /'miki/ *n.* **take the ~ out of,** (*sl.*) se moquer de.

micro- /'maikrəʊ/ *pref.* micro-.

microbe /'maikrəʊb/ *n.* microbe *m.*

microchip /'maikrəʊtʃip/ *n.* microplaquette *f.*, puce *f.*

microclimate /'maikrəʊklaimət/ *n.* microclimat *n.*

microcomputer /maikrəʊkəm'pjuːtə(r)/ *n.* micro(-ordinateur) *m.*

microcosm /'maikrəʊkɒzm/ *n.* microcosme *m.*

microfilm /'maikrəʊfilm/ *n.* microfilm *m.*

microlight /'maikrəʊlait/ *n.* U.L.M. *m.*

microphone /'maikrəfəʊn/ *n.* microphone *m.*

microprocessor /maikrəʊ'prəʊsesə(r)/ *n.* microprocesseur *m.*

microscop|e /'maikrəskəʊp/ *n.* microscope *m.* **~ic** /-'skɒpik/ *a.* microscopique.

microwave /'maikrəʊweiv/ *n.* micro-onde *f.* **~ oven,** four à micro-ondes *m.*

mid /mid/ *a.* **in ~ air**/*etc.*, en plein ciel/*etc.* **in ~ March**/*etc.*, à la mi-mars/*etc.* **in ~ ocean**/*etc.*, au milieu de l'océan/*etc.*

midday /mid'dei/ *n.* midi *m.*

middle /'midl/ *a.* du milieu; (*quality*) moyen. —*n.* milieu *m.* **in the ~ of,** au milieu de. **~-aged** *a.* d'un certain âge. **M~ Ages,** moyen âge *m.* **~ class,** classe moyenne *f.* **~-class** *a.* bourgeois. **M~ East,** Proche-Orient *m.*

middleman /'midlmæn/ *n.* (*pl.* **-men**) intermédiaire *m.*

middling /'midliŋ/ *a.* moyen.

midge /midʒ/ *n.* moucheron *m.*

midget /'midʒit/ *n.* nain(e) *m. (f.)*. —*a.* minuscule.

Midlands /'midləndz/ *n. pl.* région du centre de l'Angleterre *f.*

midnight /'midnait/ *n.* minuit *f.*

midriff /'midrif/ *n.* ventre *m.*

midst /midst/ *n.* **in the ~ of,** au milieu de. **in our ~,** parmi nous.

midsummer /mid'sʌmə(r)/ *n.* milieu de l'été *m.*; (*solstice*) solstice d'été *m.*

midway /midwei/ *adv.* à mi-chemin.

midwife /'midwaif/ *n.* (*pl.* **-wives**) sage-femme *f.*

might[1] /mait/ *n.* puissance *f.* **~y** *a.* puissant; (*very great: fam.*) très grand; *adv.* (*fam.*) rudement.

might[2] /mait/ *see* **may.**

migraine /'miːgrein, *Amer.* 'maigrein/ *n.* migraine *f.*

migrant /'maigrənt/ *a. & n.* (*bird*) migrateur (*m.*); (*worker*) migrant(e) (*m. (f.)*).

migrat|e /mai'greit/ *v.i.* émigrer. **~ion** /-ʃn/ *n.* migration *f.*

mike /maik/ *n.* (*fam.*) micro *m.*

mild /maild/ *a.* (**-er, -est**) doux; (*illness*) bénin. **~ly** *adv.* doucement. **to put it ~ly,** pour ne rien exagérer. **~ness** *n.* douceur *f.*

mildew /'mildjuː/ *n.* moisissure *f.*

mile /mail/ *n.* mille *m.* (= *1.6 km.*). **~s too big**/*etc.*, (*fam.*) beaucoup trop grand/*etc.* **~age** *n.* (*loosely*) kilométrage *m.*

milestone /'mailstəʊn/ *n.* borne *f.*; (*event, stage: fig.*) jalon *m.*

militant /'militənt/ *a. & n.* militant(e) (*m. (f.)*).

military /'militri/ *a.* militaire.

militate /'militeit/ *v.i.* militer.

militia /mi'liʃə/ *n.* milice *f.*

milk /milk/ *n.* lait *m.* —*a.* (*product*) laitier. —*v.t.* (*cow etc.*) traire; (*fig.*) exploiter. **~ shake,** milk-shake *m.* **~y** *a.* (*diet*) lacté; (*colour*) laiteux; (*tea etc.*) au lait. **M~y Way,** Voie lactée *f.*

milkman /'milkmən, *Amer.* 'milkmæn/ *n.* (*pl.* **-men**) laitier *m.*

mill /mil/ *n.* moulin *m.*; (*factory*) usine *f.* —*v.t.* moudre. —*v.i.* **~ around,** tourner en rond; (*crowd*) grouiller. **~er** *n.* meunier *m.*

millennium /mi'leniəm/ *n.* (*pl.* **-ums**) millénaire *m.*

millet /'milit/ *n.* millet *m.*

milli- /'mili/ *pref.* milli-.

millimetre /'milimiːtə(r)/ *n.* millimètre *m.*

milliner /'milinə(r)/ *n.* modiste *f.*

million /'miljən/ *n.* million *m.* **a ~ pounds,** un million de livres. **~aire** /-'neə(r)/ *n.* millionnaire *m.*

millstone /'milstəʊn/ *n.* meule *f.*; (*burden: fig.*) boulet *m.*

milometer /mai'lɒmitə(r)/ *n.* compteur kilométrique *m.*

mime /maɪm/ n. (*actor*) mime m./f.; (*art*) (art du) mime m. —v.t./i. mimer.

mimic /'mɪmɪk/ v.t. (*p.t.* **mimicked**) imiter. —n. imitalteur, -trice m., f. ~ry n. imitation f.

mince /mɪns/ v.t. hacher. —n. viande hachée f. ~ **pie,** tarte aux fruits confits f. **not to** ~ **matters,** ne pas mâcher ses mots. ~**r** /-ə(r)/ n. (*machine*) hachoir m.

mincemeat /'mɪnsmiːt/ n. hachis de fruits confits m. **make** ~ **of,** anéantir, pulvériser.

mind /maɪnd/ n. esprit m.; (*sanity*) raison f.; (*opinion*) avis m. —v.t. (*have charge of*) s'occuper de; (*heed*) faire attention à. **be on s.o.'s** ~, préoccuper qn. **bear that in** ~, ne l'oubliez pas. **change one's** ~, changer d'avis. **make up one's** ~, se décider (**to,** à). **I do not** ~ **the noise**/*etc.*, le bruit/*etc.* ne me dérange pas. **I do not** ~, ça m'est égal. **would you** ~ **checking?,** je peux vous demander de vérifier? ~**ful** a. attentif (**of,** à). ~**less** a. irréfléchi.

minder /'maɪndə(r)/ n. (*for child*) gardien(ne) m. (f.); (*for protection*) ange gardien m.

mine¹ /maɪn/ poss. pron. le mien, la mienne, les mien(ne)s. **it is** ~, c'est à moi *or* le mien.

min|e² /maɪn/ n. mine f. —v.t. extraire; (*mil.*) miner. ~**er** n. mineur m. ~**ing** n. exploitation minière f.; a. minier.

minefield /'maɪnfiːld/ n. champ de mines m.

mineral /'mɪnərəl/ n. & a. minéral (m.). ~ (**water**), (*fizzy soft drink*) boisson gazeuse f. ~ **water,** (*natural*) eau minérale f.

minesweeper /'maɪnswiːpə(r)/ n. (*ship*) dragueur de mines m.

mingle /'mɪŋgl/ v.t./i. (se) mêler (**with,** à).

mingy /'mɪndʒɪ/ a. (*fam.*) radin.

mini- /'mɪnɪ/ pref. mini-.

miniatur|e /'mɪnɪtʃə(r)/ a. & n. miniature (f.). ~**ize** v.t. miniaturiser.

minibus /'mɪnɪbʌs/ n. minibus m.

minicab /'mɪnɪkæb/ n. taxi m.

minim /'mɪnɪm/ n. blanche f.

minim|um /'mɪnɪməm/ a. & n. (*pl.* **-ima**) minimum (m.). ~**al** a. minimal. ~**ize** v.t. minimiser.

minist|er /'mɪnɪstə(r)/ n. ministre m. ~**erial** /-'stɪərɪəl/ a. ministériel. ~**ry** n. ministère m.

mink /mɪŋk/ n. vison m.

minor /'maɪnə(r)/ a. petit, mineur. —n. (*jurid.*) mineur(e) m. (f.).

minority /maɪ'nɒrətɪ/ n. minorité f. —a. minoritaire.

mint¹ /mɪnt/ n. **the M**~, l'Hôtel de la Monnaie m. **a** ~, une fortune. —v.t. frapper. **in** ~ **condition,** à l'état neuf.

mint² /mɪnt/ n. (*plant*) menthe f.; (*sweet*) pastille de menthe f.

minus /'maɪnəs/ prep. moins; (*without*: *fam.*) sans. —n. (*sign*) moins m. ~ **sign,** moins m.

minute¹ /'mɪnɪt/ n. minute f. ~**s,** (*of meeting*) procès-verbal m.

minute² /maɪ'njuːt/ a. (*tiny*) minuscule; (*detailed*) minutieux.

mirac|le /'mɪrəkl/ n. miracle m. ~**ulous** /mɪ'rækjʊləs/ a. miraculeux.

mirage /'mɪrɑːʒ/ n. mirage m.

mire /maɪə(r)/ n. fange f.

mirror /'mɪrə(r)/ n. miroir m., glace f. —v.t. refléter.

mirth /mɜːθ/ n. gaieté f.

misadventure /mɪsəd'ventʃə(r)/ n. mésaventure f.

misanthropist /mɪs'ænθrəpɪst/ n. misanthrope m./f.

misapprehension /mɪsæprɪ'henʃn/ n. malentendu m.

misbehav|e /mɪsbɪ'heɪv/ v.i. se conduire mal. ~**iour** n. mauvaise conduite f.

miscalculat|e /mɪs'kælkjʊleɪt/ v.t. mal calculer. —v.i. se tromper. ~**ion** /-'leɪʃn/ n. erreur de calcul f.

miscarr|y /mɪs'kærɪ/ v.i. faire une fausse couche. ~**iage** /-ɪdʒ/ n. fausse couche f. ~**iage of justice,** erreur judiciaire f.

miscellaneous /mɪsə'leɪnɪəs/ a. divers.

mischief /'mɪstʃɪf/ n. (*foolish conduct*) espièglerie f.; (*harm*) mal m. **get into** ~, faire des sottises.

mischievous /'mɪstʃɪvəs/ a. espiègle; (*malicious*) méchant.

misconception /mɪskən'sepʃn/ n. idée fausse f.

misconduct /mɪs'kɒndʌkt/ n. mauvaise conduite f.

misconstrue /mɪskən'struː/ v.t. mal interpréter.

misdeed /mɪs'diːd/ n. méfait m.

misdemeanour /mɪsdɪ'miːnə(r)/ n. (*jurid.*) délit m.

misdirect /mɪsdɪ'rekt/ v.t. (*person*) mal renseigner.

miser /'maɪzə(r)/ n. avare m./f. ~**ly** a. avare.

miserable /'mɪzrəbl/ a. (*sad*) malheureux; (*wretched*) misérable; (*unpleasant*) affreux.

misery /'mɪzərɪ/ n. (*unhappiness*) malheur m.; (*pain*) souffrances f. pl.; (*poverty*) misère f.; (*person*: *fam.*) grincheulx, -se m., f.

misfire /mɪs'faɪə(r)/ v.i. (*plan etc.*) rater; (*engine*) avoir des ratés.

misfit /'mɪsfɪt/ n. inadapté(e) m. (f.).

misfortune /mɪs'fɔːtʃuːn/ n. malheur m.

misgiving /mɪs'ɡɪvɪŋ/ n. (*doubt*) doute m.; (*apprehension*) crainte f.

misguided /mɪs'ɡaɪdɪd/ a. (*foolish*) imprudent; (*mistaken*) erroné. **be ~,** (*person*) se tromper.

mishap /'mɪshæp/ n. mésaventure f., contretemps m.

misinform /mɪsɪn'fɔːm/ v.t. mal renseigner.

misinterpret /mɪsɪn'tɜːprɪt/ v.t. mal interpréter.

misjudge /mɪs'dʒʌdʒ/ v.t. mal juger.

mislay /mɪs'leɪ/ v.t. (*p.t.* mislaid) égarer.

mislead /mɪs'liːd/ v.t. (*p.t.* misled) tromper. **~ing** a. trompeur.

mismanage /mɪs'mænɪdʒ/ v.t. mal gérer. **~ment** n. mauvaise gestion f.

misnomer /mɪs'nəʊmə(r)/ n. terme impropre m.

misplace /mɪs'pleɪs/ v.t. mal placer; (*lose*) égarer.

misprint /'mɪsprɪnt/ n. faute d'impression f., coquille f.

misread /mɪs'riːd/ v.t. (*p.t.* misread /mɪs'red/) mal lire; (*intentions*) mal comprendre.

misrepresent /mɪsreprɪ'zent/ v.t. présenter sous un faux jour.

miss[1] /mɪs/ v.t./i. manquer; (*deceased person etc.*) regretter. **he ~es her/Paris/***etc.***,** elle/Paris/*etc.* lui manque. **I ~ you,** tu me manques. **you're ~ing the point,** vous n'avez rien compris. —n. coup manqué m. **it was a near ~,** on l'a échappé belle *or* de peu. **~ out,** omettre. **~ out on sth,** rater qch.

miss[2] /mɪs/ n. (*pl.* misses) mademoiselle f. (*pl.* mesdemoiselles). **M~ Smith,** Mademoiselle *or* Mlle Smith.

misshapen /mɪs'ʃeɪpən/ a. difforme.

missile /'mɪsaɪl/ n. (*mil.*) missile m.; (*object thrown*) projectile m.

missing /'mɪsɪŋ/ a. (*person*) disparu; (*thing*) qui manque. **something's ~,** il manque quelque chose.

mission /'mɪʃn/ n. mission f.

missionary /'mɪʃənrɪ/ n. missionnaire m./f.

missive /'mɪsɪv/ n. missive f.

misspell /mɪs'spel/ v.t. (*p.t.* misspelt *or* misspelled) mal écrire.

mist /mɪst/ n. brume f.; (*on window*) buée f. —v.t./i. (s')embuer.

mistake /mɪ'steɪk/ n. erreur f. —v.t. (*p.t.* mistook, *p.p.* mistaken) mal comprendre; (*choose wrongly*) se tromper de. **by ~,** par erreur. **make a ~,** faire une erreur. **~ for,** prendre pour. **~n** /-ən/ a. erroné. **be ~n,** se tromper. **~nly** /-ənlɪ/ adv. par erreur.

mistletoe /'mɪsltəʊ/ n. gui m.

mistreat /mɪs'triːt/ v.t. maltraiter.

mistress /'mɪstrɪs/ n. maîtresse f.

mistrust /mɪs'trʌst/ v.t. se méfier de. —n. méfiance f.

misty /'mɪstɪ/ a. (**-ier, -iest**) brumeux; (*window*) embué.

misunderstand /mɪsʌndə'stænd/ v.t. (*p.t.* -stood) mal comprendre. **~ing** n. malentendu m.

misuse[1] /mɪs'juːz/ v.t. mal employer; (*power etc.*) abuser de.

misuse[2] /mɪs'juːs/ n. mauvais emploi m.; (*unfair use*) abus m.

mitigat|**e** /'mɪtɪɡeɪt/ v.t. atténuer. **~ing circumstances,** circonstances atténuantes f.pl.

mitten /'mɪtn/ n. moufle f.

mix /mɪks/ v.t./i. (se) mélanger. —n. mélange m. **~ up,** mélanger; (*bewilder*) embrouiller; (*mistake, confuse*) confondre (**with,** avec). **~-up** n. confusion f. **~ with,** (*people*) fréquenter. **~er** n. (*culin.*) mélangeur m. **be a good ~er,** être sociable. **~er tap,** mélangeur m.

mixed /mɪkst/ a. (*school etc.*) mixte; (*assorted*) assorti. **be ~-up,** (*fam.*) avoir des problèmes.

mixture /'mɪkstʃə(r)/ n. mélange m.; (*for cough*) sirop m.

moan /məʊn/ n. gémissement m. —v.i. gémir; (*complain*) grogner. **~er** n. (*grumbler*) grognon m.

moat /məʊt/ n. douve(s) f. (*pl.*).

mob /mɒb/ n. (*crowd*) cohue f.; (*gang*: *sl.*) bande f. —v.t. (*p.t.* mobbed) assiéger.

mobil|**e** /'məʊbaɪl/ a. mobile. **~e home,** caravane f. **~e,** n. mobile m. **~ity** /-'bɪlətɪ/ n. mobilité f.

mobiliz|**e** /'məʊbɪlaɪz/ v.t./i. mobiliser. **~ation** /-'zeɪʃn/ n. mobilisation f.

moccasin /'mɒkəsɪn/ n. mocassin m.

mock /mɒk/ v.t./i. se moquer (de). —a. faux. **~-up** n. maquette f.

mockery /'mɒkərɪ/ n. moquerie f. **a ~ of,** une parodie de.

mode /məʊd/ n. (*way, method*) mode m.; (*fashion*) mode f.

model /'mɒdl/ n. modèle m.; (*of toy*) modèle réduit m.; (*artist's*) modèle m.; (*for fashion*) mannequin m. —a. modèle; (*car etc.*) modèle réduit invar. —v.t. (*p.t.* **modelled**) modeler; (*clothes*) présenter. —v.i. être mannequin; (*pose*) poser. **∼ling** n. métier de mannequin m.

modem /'məʊdem/ n. modem m.

moderate¹ /'mɒdərət/ a. & n. modéré(e) (m. (f.)). **∼ly** adv. (*in moderation*) modérément; (*fairly*) moyennement.

moderate² /'mɒdəreɪt/ v.t./i. (se) modérer. **∼ion** /-'reɪʃn/ n. modération f. **in ∼ion,** avec modération.

modern /'mɒdn/ a. moderne. **∼ languages,** langues vivantes f. pl. **∼ize** v.t. moderniser.

modest /'mɒdɪst/ a. modeste. **∼y** n. modestie f.

modicum /'mɒdɪkəm/ n. **a ∼ of,** un peu de.

modif|y /'mɒdɪfaɪ/ v.t. modifier. **∼ication** /-ɪ'keɪʃn/ n. modification f.

modular /'mɒdjʊlə(r)/ a. modulaire.

modulat|e /'mɒdjʊleɪt/ v.t./i. moduler. **∼ion** /-'leɪʃn/ n. modulation f.

module /'mɒdju:l/ n. module m.

mohair /'məʊheə(r)/ n. mohair m.

moist /mɔɪst/ a. (**-er, -est**) humide, moite. **∼ure** /'mɔɪstʃə(r)/ n. humidité f. **∼urizer** /'mɔɪstʃəraɪzə(r)/ n. produit hydratant.

moisten /'mɔɪsn/ v.t. humecter.

molar /'məʊlə(r)/ n. molaire f.

molasses /mə'læsɪz/ n. mélasse f.

mold /məʊld/ (*Amer.*) = **mould**.

mole¹ /məʊl/ n. grain de beauté m.

mole² /məʊl/ n. (*animal*) taupe f.

molecule /'mɒlɪkju:l/ n. molécule f.

molest /mə'lest/ v.t. (*pester*) importuner; (*ill-treat*) molester.

mollusc /'mɒləsk/ n. mollusque m.

mollycoddle /'mɒlɪkɒdl/ v.t. dorloter, chouchouter.

molten /'məʊltən/ a. en fusion.

mom /mɒm/ n. (*Amer.*) maman f.

moment /'məʊmənt/ n. moment m.

momentar|y /'məʊməntrɪ, *Amer.* -terɪ/ a. momentané. **∼ily** (*Amer.* /-'terəlɪ/) adv. momentanément; (*soon: Amer.*) très bientôt.

momentous /mə'mentəs/ a. important.

momentum /mə'mentəm/ n. élan m.

Monaco /'mɒnəkəʊ/ n. Monaco f.

monarch /'mɒnək/ n. monarque m. **∼y** n. monarchie f.

monast|ery /'mɒnəstrɪ/ n. monastère m. **∼ic** /mə'næstɪk/ a. monastique.

Monday /'mʌndɪ/ n. lundi m.

monetarist /'mʌnɪtərɪst/ n. monétariste m./f.

monetary /'mʌnɪtrɪ/ a. monétaire.

money /'mʌnɪ/ n. argent m. **∼s,** sommes d'argent f. pl. **∼-box** n. tirelire f. **∼-lender** n. prêteur, -se m., f. **∼ order,** mandat m. **∼-spinner** n. mine d'or f.

mongrel /'mʌŋɡrəl/ n. (chien) bâtard m.

monitor /'mɒnɪtə(r)/ n. (*pupil*) chef de classe m.; (*techn.*) moniteur m. —v.t. contrôler; (*a broadcast*) écouter.

monk /mʌŋk/ n. moine m.

monkey /'mʌŋkɪ/ n. singe m. **∼-nut** n. cacahuète f. **∼-wrench** n. clef à molette f.

mono /'mɒnəʊ/ n. (pl. **-os**) mono f. —a. mono invar.

monochrome /'mɒnəkrəʊm/ a. & n. (en) noir et blanc (m.).

monogram /'mɒnəɡræm/ n. monogramme m.

monologue /'mɒnəlɒɡ/ n. monologue m.

monopol|y /mə'nɒpəlɪ/ n. monopole m. **∼ize** v.t. monopoliser.

monotone /'mɒnətəʊn/ n. ton uniforme m.

monoton|ous /mə'nɒtənəs/ a. monotone. **∼y** n. monotonie f.

monsoon /mɒn'su:n/ n. mousson f.

monst|er /'mɒnstə(r)/ n. monstre m. **∼rous** a. monstrueux.

monstrosity /mɒn'strɒsətɪ/ n. monstruosité f.

month /mʌnθ/ n. mois m.

monthly /'mʌnθlɪ/ a. mensuel. —adv. mensuellement. —n. (*periodical*) mensuel m.

monument /'mɒnjʊmənt/ n. monument m. **∼al** /-'mentl/ a. monumental.

moo /mu:/ n. meuglement m. —v.i. meugler.

mooch /mu:tʃ/ v.i. (*sl.*) flâner. —v.t. (*Amer., sl.*) se procurer.

mood /mu:d/ n. humeur f. **in a good/bad ∼,** de bonne/mauvaise humeur. **∼y** a. d'humeur changeante; (*sullen*) maussade.

moon /mu:n/ n. lune f.

moon|light /'mu:nlaɪt/ n. clair de lune m. **∼lit** a. éclairé par la lune.

moonlighting /'mu:nlaɪtɪŋ/ n. (*fam.*) travail au noir m.

moor¹ /mʊə(r)/ n. lande f.

moor² /mʊə(r)/ v.t. amarrer. **∼ings** n. pl. (*chains etc.*) amarres f. pl.; (*place*) mouillage m.

moose /muːs/ *n. invar.* élan *m.*
moot /muːt/ *a.* discutable. —*v.t.* (*question*) soulever.
mop /mɒp/ *n.* balai à franges *m.* —*v.t.* (*p.t.* **mopped**). ~ (**up**), éponger. ~ **of** hair, tignasse *f.*
mope /məʊp/ *v.i.* se morfondre.
moped /'məʊped/ *n.* cyclomoteur *m.*
moral /'mɒrəl/ *a.* moral. —*n.* morale *f.* ~s, moralité *f.* ~ize *v.i.* moraliser. ~ly *adv.* moralement.
morale /mə'rɑːl/ *n.* moral *m.*
morality /mə'ræləti/ *n.* moralité *f.*
morass /mə'ræs/ *n.* marais *m.*
morbid /'mɔːbid/ *a.* morbide.
more /mɔː(r)/ *a.* (*a greater amount of*) plus de (**than**, que). —*n.* & *adv.* plus (**than**, que). (**some**) ~ **tea/pens**/*etc.*, (*additional*) encore du thé/des stylos/*etc.* **no** ~ **bread**/*etc.*, plus de pain/*etc.* **I want no** ~, **I do not want any** ~, je n'en veux plus. ~ **or less**, plus ou moins.
moreover /mɔː'rəʊvə(r)/ *adv.* de plus, en outre.
morgue /mɔːg/ *n.* morgue *f.*
moribund /'mɒrɪbʌnd/ *a.* moribond.
morning /'mɔːnɪŋ/ *n.* matin *m.*; (*whole morning*) matinée *f.*
Morocc|o /mə'rɒkəʊ/ *n.* Maroc *m.* ~**an** *a.* & *n.* marocain(e) (*m.* (*f.*)).
moron /'mɔːrɒn/ *n.* crétin(e) *m.* (*f.*).
morose /mə'rəʊs/ *a.* morose.
morphine /'mɔːfiːn/ *n.* morphine *f.*
Morse /mɔːs/ *n.* ~ (**code**), morse *m.*
morsel /'mɔːsl/ *n.* petit morceau *m.*; (*of food*) bouchée *f.*
mortal /'mɔːtl/ *a.* & *n.* mortel(le) (*m.*(*f.*)). ~**ity** /mɔː'tæləti/ *n.* mortalité *f.*
mortar /'mɔːtə(r)/ *n.* mortier *m.*
mortgage /'mɔːgɪdʒ/ *n.* crédit immobilier *m.* —*v.t.* hypothéquer.
mortify /'mɔːtɪfaɪ/ *v.t.* mortifier.
mortise /'mɔːtɪs/ *n.* ~ **lock** serrure encastrée *f.*
mortuary /'mɔːtʃərɪ/ *n.* morgue *f.*
mosaic /məʊ'zeɪɪk/ *n.* mosaïque *f.*
Moscow /'mɒskəʊ/ *n.* Moscou *m.*/*f.*
Moses /'məʊzɪz/ *a.* ~ **basket**, moïse *m.*
mosque /mɒsk/ *n.* mosquée *f.*
mosquito /mə'skiːtəʊ/ *n.* (*pl.* **-oes**) moustique *m.*
moss /mɒs/ *n.* mousse *f.* ~**y** *a.* moussu.
most /məʊst/ *a.* (*the greatest amount of*) le plus de; (*the majority of*) la plupart de. —*n.* le plus. —*adv.* (le) plus; (*very*) fort. ~ **of**, la plus grande partie de; (*majority*) la plupart de. **at** ~, tout au

plus. **for the** ~ **part,** pour la plupart. **make the** ~ **of,** profiter de. ~**ly** *adv.* surtout.
motel /məʊ'tel/ *n.* motel *m.*
moth /mɒθ/ *n.* papillon de nuit *m.*; (*in cloth*) mite *f.* ~**-ball** *n.* boule de naphtaline *f.*; *v.t.* mettre en réserve. ~**eaten** *a.* mité.
mother /'mʌðə(r)/ *n.* mère *f.* —*v.t.* entourer de soins maternels, materner. ~**hood** *n.* maternité *f.* ~**-in-law** *n.* (*pl.* ~**s-in-law**) belle-mère *f.* ~**-of-pearl** *n.* nacre *f.* **M**~**'s Day,** la fête des mères. ~**-to-be** *n.* future maman *f.* ~ **tongue,** langue maternelle *f.*
motherly /'mʌðəlɪ/ *a.* maternel.
motif /məʊ'tiːf/ *n.* motif *m.*
motion /'məʊʃn/ *n.* mouvement *m.*; (*proposal*) motion *f.* —*v.t.*/*i.* ~ (**to**) **s.o. to,** faire signe à qn. de. ~**less** *a.* immobile. ~ **picture,** (*Amer.*) film *m.*
motivat|e /'məʊtɪveɪt/ *v.t.* motiver. ~**ion** /-'veɪʃn/ *n.* motivation *f.*
motive /'məʊtɪv/ *n.* motif *m.*
motley /'mɒtlɪ/ *a.* bigarré.
motor /'məʊtə(r)/ *n.* moteur *m.*; (*car*) auto *f.* —*a.* (*anat.*) moteur; (*boat*) à moteur. —*v.i.* aller en auto. ~ **bike,** (*fam.*) moto *f.* ~ **car,** auto *f.* ~ **cycle,** motocyclette *f.* ~**-cyclist** *n.* motocycliste *m.*/*f.* ~ **home,** (*Amer.*) camping-car *m.* ~**ing** *n.* (*sport*) l'automobile *f.* ~**ized** *a.* motorisé ~ **vehicle,** véhicule automobile *m.*
motorist /'məʊtərɪst/ *n.* automobiliste *m.*/*f.*
motorway /'məʊtəweɪ/ *n.* auto-route *f.*
mottled /'mɒtld/ *a.* tacheté.
motto /'mɒtəʊ/ *n.* (*pl.* **-oes**) devise *f.*
mould[1] /məʊld/ *n.* moule *m.* —*v.t.* mouler; (*influence*) former. ~**ing** *n.* (*on wall etc.*) moulure *f.*
mould[2] /məʊld/ *n.* (*fungus, rot*) moisissure *f.* ~**y** *a.* moisi.
moult /məʊlt/ *v.i.* muer.
mound /maʊnd/ *n.* monticule *m.*, tertre *m.*; (*pile: fig.*) tas *m.*
mount[1] /maʊnt/ *n.* (*hill*) mont *m.*
mount[2] /maʊnt/ *v.t.*/*i.* monter. —*n.* monture *f.* ~ **up,** s'accumuler; (*add up*) chiffrer (**to,** à).
mountain /'maʊntɪn/ *n.* montagne *f.* ~ **bike,** (vélo) tout terrain *m.*, vtt *m.* ~**ous** *a.* montagneux.
mountaineer /maʊntɪ'nɪə(r)/ *n.* alpiniste *m.*/*f.* ~**ing** *n.* alpinisme *m.*
mourn /mɔːn/ *v.t.*/*i.* ~ (**for**), pleurer. ~**er** *n.* personne qui suit le cortège funèbre *f.* ~**ing** *n.* deuil *m.*

mournful /'mɔːnfl/ a. triste.

mouse /maʊs/ n. (pl. **mice**) souris f.

mousetrap /'maʊstræp/ n. souricière f.

mousse /muːs/ n. mousse f.

moustache /mə'stɑːʃ, Amer. 'mʌstæʃ/ n. moustache f.

mousy /'maʊsɪ/ a. (hair) d'un brun terne; (fig.) timide.

mouth /maʊθ/ n. bouche f.; (of dog, cat, etc.) gueule f. ∼-organ n. harmonica m.

mouthful /'maʊθfʊl/ n. bouchée f.

mouthpiece /'maʊθpiːs/ n. (mus.) embouchure f.; (person: fig.) porte-parole m. invar.

mouthwash /'maʊθwɒʃ/ n. eau dentifrice f.

mouthwatering /'maʊθwɔːtərɪŋ/ a. qui fait venir l'eau à la bouche.

movable /'muːvəbl/ a. mobile.

move /muːv/ v.t./i. remuer, (se) déplacer, bouger; (incite) pousser; (emotionally) émouvoir; (propose) proposer; (depart) partir; (act) agir. ∼ (out), déménager. —n. mouvement m.; (in game) coup m.; (player's turn) tour m.; (procedure: fig.) démarche f.; (house change) déménagement m. ∼ back, (faire) reculer. ∼ forward or on, (faire) avancer. ∼ in, emménager. ∼ over, se pousser. on the ∼, en marche.

movement /'muːvmənt/ n. mouvement m.

movie /'muːvɪ/ n. (Amer.) film m. the ∼s, le cinéma. ∼ camera, (Amer.) caméra f.

moving /'muːvɪŋ/ a. en mouvement; (touching) émouvant.

mow /məʊ/ v.t. (p.p. **mowed** or **mown**) (corn etc.) faucher; (lawn) tondre. ∼ down, faucher. ∼er n. (for lawn) tondeuse f.

MP abbr. see **Member of Parliament**.

Mr /'mɪstə(r)/ n. (pl. **Messrs**). ∼ Smith, Monsieur or M. Smith.

Mrs /'mɪsɪz/ n. (pl. **Mrs**). ∼ Smith, Madame or Mme Smith. the ∼ Smith, Mesdames or Mmes Smith.

Ms /mɪz/ n. (title of married or unmarried woman). ∼ Smith, Madame or Mme Smith.

much /mʌtʃ/ a. beaucoup de. —adv. & n. beaucoup.

muck /mʌk/ n. fumier m.; (dirt: fam.) saleté f. —v.i. ∼ about, (sl.) s'amuser. ∼ about with, (sl.) tripoter. ∼ in, (sl.) participer. —v.t. ∼ up, (sl.) gâcher. ∼y a. sale.

mucus /'mjuːkəs/ n. mucus m.

mud /mʌd/ n. boue f. ∼dy a. couvert de boue.

muddle /'mʌdl/ v.t. embrouiller. —v.i. ∼ through, se débrouiller. —n. désordre m., confusion f.; (mix-up) confusion f.

mudguard /'mʌdgɑːd/ n. garde-boue m. invar.

muff /mʌf/ n. manchon m.

muffin /'mʌfɪn/ n. muffin m. (petit pain rond et plat).

muffle /'mʌfl/ v.t. emmitoufler; (sound) assourdir. ∼r /-ə(r)/ n. (scarf) cache-nez m. invar.; (Amer.: auto.) silencieux m.

mug /mʌg/ n. tasse f.; (in plastic, metal) gobelet m.; (for beer) chope f.; (face: sl.) gueule f.; (fool: sl.) idiot(e) m.(f.) —v.t. (p.t. **mugged**) agresser. ∼ger n. agresseur m. ∼ging n. agression f.

muggy /'mʌgɪ/ a. lourd.

mule /mjuːl/ n. (male) mulet m.; (female) mule f.

mull[1] /mʌl/ v.t. (wine) chauffer.

mull[2] /mʌl/ v.t. ∼ over, ruminer.

multi- /'mʌltɪ/ pref. multi-.

multicoloured /'mʌltɪkʌləd/ a. multicolore.

multifarious /mʌltɪ'feərɪəs/ a. divers.

multinational /mʌltɪ'næʃnəl/ a. & n. multinational(e) (f.).

multiple /'mʌltɪpl/ a. & n. multiple (m.). ∼ sclerosis, sclérose en plaques f.

multiply /'mʌltɪplaɪ/ v.t./i. (se) multiplier. ∼ication /-ɪ'keɪʃn/ n. multiplication f.

multistorey /mʌltɪ'stɔːrɪ/ a. (car park) à étages.

multitude /'mʌltɪtjuːd/ n. multitude f.

mum[1] /mʌm/ a. keep ∼, (fam.) garder le silence.

mum[2] /mʌm/ n. (fam.) maman f.

mumble /'mʌmbl/ v.t./i. marmotter, marmonner.

mummy[1] /'mʌmɪ/ n. (embalmed body) momie f.

mummy[2] /'mʌmɪ/ n. (mother: fam.) maman f.

mumps /mʌmps/ n. oreillons m. pl.

munch /mʌntʃ/ v.t./i. mastiquer.

mundane /mʌn'deɪn/ a. banal.

municipal /mjuː'nɪsɪpl/ a. municipal. ∼ity /-'pælətɪ/ n. municipalité f.

munitions /mjuː'nɪʃnz/ n. pl. munitions f. pl.

mural /'mjʊərəl/ a. mural. —n. peinture murale f.

murder /'mɜːdə(r)/ n. meurtre m. —v.t.

assassiner; (*ruin*: *fam.*) massacrer. ∼**er**
n. meurtrier *m.*, assassin *m.* ∼**ous** *a.*
meurtrier.

murky /'mɜːkɪ/ *a.* (**-ier, -iest**) (*night,
plans, etc.*) sombre, ténébreux; (*liquid*)
épais, sale.

murmur /'mɜːmə(r)/ *n.* murmure *m.*
—*v.t./i.* murmurer.

muscle /'mʌsl/ *n.* muscle *m.* —*v.i.* ∼ **in**,
(*sl.*) s'introduire de force (**on,** dans).

muscular /'mʌskjʊlə(r)/ *a.* musculaire;
(*brawny*) musclé.

muse /mjuːz/ *v.i.* méditer.

museum /mjuːˈzɪəm/ *n.* musée *m.*

mush /mʌʃ/ *n.* (*pulp, soft food*) bouillie
f. ∼**y** *a.* mou.

mushroom /'mʌʃrʊm/ *n.* champignon
m. —*v.i.* pousser comme des champi-
gnons.

music /'mjuːzɪk/ *n.* musique *f.* ∼**al** *a.*
musical; (*instrument*) de musique;
(*talented*) doué pour la musique; *n.*
comédie musicale *f.*

musician /mjuːˈzɪʃn/ *n.* musicien(ne) *m.*
(*f.*).

musk /mʌsk/ *n.* musc *m.*

Muslim /'mʊzlɪm/ *a.* & *n.* musulman(e)
(*m.* (*f.*)).

muslin /'mʌzlɪn/ *n.* mousseline *f.*

mussel /'mʌsl/ *n.* moule *f.*

must /mʌst/ *v. aux.* devoir. **you** ∼ **go,**
vous devez partir, il faut que vous
partiez. **he** ∼ **be old,** il doit être vieux. **I**
∼ **have done it,** j'ai dû le faire. —*n.* be
a ∼, (*fam.*) être un must.

mustard /'mʌstəd/ *n.* moutarde *f.*

muster /'mʌstə(r)/ *v.t./i.* (se) rassembler.

musty /'mʌstɪ/ *a.* (**-ier, -iest**) (*room,
etc.*) qui sent le moisi; (*smell, taste*) de
moisi.

mutant /'mjuːtənt/ *a.* & *n.* mutant. (*m.*)

mutation /mjuːˈteɪʃn/ *n.* mutation *f.*

mute /mjuːt/ *a.* & *n.* muet(te) (*m.* (*f.*)).
∼**d** /-ɪd/ *a.* (*colour, sound*) sourd,
atténué; (*criticism*) voilé.

mutilat|e /'mjuːtɪleɪt/ *v.t.* mutiler. ∼**ion**
/-'leɪʃn/ *n.* mutilation *f.*

mutin|y /'mjuːtɪnɪ/ *n.* mutinerie *f.* —*v.i.*
se mutiner. ∼**ous** *a.* (*sailor etc.*)
mutiné; (*fig.*) rebelle.

mutter /'mʌtə(r)/ *v.t./i.* marmonner,
murmurer.

mutton /'mʌtn/ *n.* mouton *m.*

mutual /'mjuːtʃʊəl/ *a.* mutuel; (*common
to two or more*: *fam.*) commun. ∼**ly**
adv. mutuellement.

muzzle /'mʌzl/ *n.* (*snout*) museau *m.*;
(*device*) muselière *f.*; (*of gun*) gueule *f.*
—*v.t.* museler.

my /maɪ/ *a.* mon, ma, *pl.* mes.

myopic /maɪˈɒpɪk/ *a.* myope.

myself /maɪˈself/ *pron.* moi-même;
(*reflexive*) me, m'*; (*after prep.*) moi.

mysterious /mɪˈstɪərɪəs/ *a.* mystérieux.

mystery /'mɪstərɪ/ *n.* mystère *m.*

mystic /'mɪstɪk/ *a.* & *n.* mystique (*m./f.*).
∼**al** *a.* mystique. ∼**ism** /-sɪzəm/ *n.*
mysticisme *m.*

mystify /'mɪstɪfaɪ/ *v.t.* laisser perplexe.

mystique /mɪˈstiːk/ *n.* mystique *f.*

myth /mɪθ/ *n.* mythe *m.* ∼**ical** *a.*
mythique.

mythology /mɪˈθɒlədʒɪ/ *n.* mythologie *f.*

N

nab /næb/ *v.t.* (*p.t.* **nabbed**) (*arrest*: *sl.*)
épingler, attraper.

nag /næg/ *v.t./i.* (*p.t.* **nagged**) critiquer;
(*pester*) harceler.

nagging /'nægɪŋ/ *a.* persistant.

nail /neɪl/ *n.* clou *m.*; (*of finger, toe*)
ongle *m.* —*v.t.* clouer. ∼**-brush** *n.*
brosse à ongles *f.* ∼**-file** *n.* lime à ongles
f. ∼ **polish,** vernis à ongles *m.* **on the**
∼, (*pay*) sans tarder, tout de suite.

naïve /naɪˈiːv/ *a.* naïf.

naked /'neɪkɪd/ *a.* nu. **to the** ∼ **eye,** à
l'œil nu. ∼**ly** *adv.* à nu. ∼**ness** *n.* nudité
f.

name /neɪm/ *n.* nom *m.*; (*fig.*) réputation
f. —*v.t.* nommer; (*fix*) fixer. **be** ∼**d
after,** porter le nom de. ∼**less** *a.* sans
nom, anonyme.

namely /'neɪmlɪ/ *adv.* à savoir.

namesake /'neɪmseɪk/ *n.* (*person*)
homonyme *m.*

nanny /'nænɪ/ *n.* nounou *f.* ∼**-goat** *n.*
chèvre *f.*

nap /næp/ *n.* somme *m.* —*v.i.* (*p.t.*
napped) faire un somme. **catch** ∼**ping,**
prendre au dépourvu.

nape /neɪp/ *n.* nuque *f.*

napkin /'næpkɪn/ *n.* (*at meals*) serviette
f.; (*for baby*) couche *f.*

nappy /'næpɪ/ *n.* couche *f.*

narcotic /nɑːˈkɒtɪk/ *a.* & *n.* narcotique
(*m.*).

narrat|e /nəˈreɪt/ *v.t.* raconter. ∼**ion**
/-ʃn/ *n.* narration *f.* ∼**or** *n.* narral-
teur, -trice *m.*, *f.*

narrative /'nærətɪv/ *n.* récit *m.*

narrow /'nærəʊ/ *a.* (**-er, -est**) étroit.
—*v.t./i.* (se) rétrécir; (*limit*) (se) limiter.
∼ **down the choices,** limiter les choix.

~ly adv. étroitement; (just) de justesse. ~-minded a. à l'esprit étroit; (ideas etc.) étroit. ~ness n. étroitesse f.

nasal /'neɪzl/ a. nasal.

nast|y /'nɑːstɪ/ a. (-ier, -iest) mauvais, désagréable; (malicious) méchant. ~ily adv. désagréablement; méchamment. ~iness n. (malice) méchanceté f.

nation /'neɪʃn/ n. nation f. ~-wide a. dans l'ensemble du pays.

national /'næʃnəl/ a. national. —n. ressortissant(e) m. (f.). ~ anthem, hymne national m. ~ism n. nationalisme m. ~ize v.t. nationaliser. ~ly adv. à l'échelle nationale.

nationality /næʃə'nælətɪ/ n. nationalité f.

native /'neɪtɪv/ n. (local inhabitant) autochtone m./f.; (non-European) indigène m./f. —a. indigène; (country) natal; (inborn) inné. be a ~ of, être originaire de. ~ language, langue maternelle f. ~ speaker of French, personne de langue maternelle française f.

Nativity /nə'tɪvətɪ/ n. the ~, la Nativité f.

natter /'nætə(r)/ v.i. bavarder.

natural /'nætʃrəl/ a. naturel. ~ history, histoire naturelle f. ~ist n. naturaliste m./f. ~ly adv. (normally, of course) naturellement; (by nature) de nature.

naturaliz|e /'nætʃrəlaɪz/ v.t. naturaliser. ~ation /-'zeɪʃn/ n. naturalisation f.

nature /'neɪtʃə(r)/ n. nature f.

naught /nɔːt/ n. (old use) rien m.

naught|y /'nɔːtɪ/ a. (-ier, -iest) vilain, méchant; (indecent) grivois. ~ily adv. mal.

nause|a /'nɔːsɪə/ n. nausée f. ~ous a. nauséabond.

nauseate /'nɔːsɪeɪt/ v.t. écœurer.

nautical /'nɔːtɪkl/ a. nautique.

naval /'neɪvl/ a. (battle etc.) naval; (officer) de marine.

nave /neɪv/ n. (of church) nef f.

navel /'neɪvl/ n. nombril m.

navigable /'nævɪɡəbl/ a. navigable.

navigat|e /'nævɪɡeɪt/ v.t. (sea etc.) naviguer sur; (ship) piloter. —v.i. naviguer. ~ion /-'ɡeɪʃn/ n. navigation f. ~or n. navigateur m.

navvy /'nævɪ/ n. terrassier m.

navy /'neɪvɪ/ n. marine f. ~ (blue), bleu marine invar.

near /nɪə(r)/ adv. près. —prep. près de. —a. proche. —v.t. approcher de. draw ~, (s')approcher (to, de). ~ by adv. tout près. N~ East, Proche-Orient m.

~ to, près de. ~ness n. proximité f. ~-sighted a. myope.

nearby /nɪə'baɪ/ a. proche.

nearly /'nɪəlɪ/ adv. presque. I ~ forgot, j'ai failli oublier. not ~ as pretty/etc. as, loin d'être aussi joli/etc. que.

nearside /'nɪəsaɪd/ a. (auto.) du côté du passager.

neat /niːt/ a. (-er, -est) soigné, net; (room etc.) bien rangé; (clever) habile; (whisky, brandy, etc.) sec. ~ly adv. avec soin; habilement. ~ness n. netteté f.

nebulous /'nebjʊləs/ a. nébuleux.

necessar|y /'nesəsərɪ/ a. nécessaire. ~ies n. pl. nécessaire m. ~ily adv. nécessairement.

necessitate /nɪ'sesɪteɪt/ v.t. nécessiter.

necessity /nɪ'sesətɪ/ n. nécessité f.; (thing) chose indispensable f.

neck /nek/ n. cou m.; (of dress) encolure f. ~ and neck, à égalité.

necklace /'neklɪs/ n. collier m.

neckline /'neklaɪn/ n. encolure f.

necktie /'nektaɪ/ n. cravate f.

nectarine /'nektərɪn/ n. brugnon m., nectarine f.

need /niːd/ n. besoin m. —v.t. avoir besoin de; (demand) demander. you ~ not come, vous n'êtes pas obligé de venir. ~less a. inutile. ~lessly adv. inutilement.

needle /'niːdl/ n. aiguille f. —v.t. (annoy: fam.) asticoter, agacer.

needlework /'niːdlwɜːk/ n. couture f.; (object) ouvrage (à l'aiguille) m.

needy /'niːdɪ/ a. (-ier, -iest) nécessiteux, indigent.

negation /nɪ'ɡeɪʃn/ n. négation f.

negative /'neɡətɪv/ a. négatif. —n. (of photograph) négatif m.; (word: gram.) négation f. **in the** ~, (answer) par la négative; (gram.) à la forme négative. ~ly adv. négativement.

neglect /nɪ'ɡlekt/ v.t. négliger, laisser à l'abandon. —n. manque de soins m. (state of) ~, abandon m. ~ to do, négliger de faire. ~ful a. négligent.

négligé /'neɡlɪʒeɪ/ n. négligé m.

negligen|t /'neɡlɪdʒənt/ a. négligent. ~ce a. négligence f.

negligible /'neɡlɪdʒəbl/ a. négligeable.

negotiable /nɪ'ɡəʊʃəbl/ a. négociable.

negotiat|e /nɪ'ɡəʊʃɪeɪt/ v.t./i. négocier. ~ion /-'eɪʃn/ n. négociation f. ~or n. négociateur, -trice m., f.

Negr|o /'niːɡrəʊ/ n. (pl. -oes) Noir m. —a. noir; (art, music) nègre. ~ess n. Noire f.

neigh /neɪ/ n. hennissement m. —v.i.
hennir.

neighbour, Amer. **neighbor** /'neɪbə(r)/
n. voisin(e) m. (f.). ～**hood** n. voisinage
m., quartier m. **in the ～hood of,** aux
alentours de. ～**ing** a. voisin.

neighbourly /'neɪbəlɪ/ a. amical.

neither /'naɪðə(r)/ a. & pron. aucun(e)
des deux, ni l'un(e) ni l'autre. —adv. ni.
—conj. (ne) non plus. ～ **big nor small,**
ni grand ni petit. ～ **am I coming,** je ne
viendrai pas non plus.

neon /'ni:ɒn/ n. néon m. —a. (lamp etc.)
au néon.

nephew /'nevju:, Amer. 'nefju:/ n. neveu
m.

nerve /nɜ:v/ n. nerf m.; (courage)
courage m.; (calm) sang-froid m.;
(impudence: fam.) culot m. ～**s,** (before
exams etc.) le trac m. ～**-racking** a.
éprouvant.

nervous /'nɜ:vəs/ a. nerveux. **be** or **feel**
～, (afraid) avoir peur. ～ **breakdown,**
dépression nerveuse f. ～**ly** adv.
(tensely) nerveusement; (timidly)
craintivement. ～**ness** n. nervosité f.;
(fear) crainte f.

nervy /'nɜ:vɪ/ a. = **nervous**; (Amer.,
fam.) effronté.

nest /nest/ n. nid m. —v.i. nicher. ～**-egg**
n. pécule m.

nestle /'nesl/ v.i. se blottir.

net¹ /net/ n. filet m. —v.t. (p.t. netted)
prendre au filet. ～**ting** n. (nets) filets m.
pl.; (wire) treillis m.; (fabric) voile m.

net² /net/ a. (weight etc.) net.

netball /'netbɔ:l/ n. netball m.

Netherlands /'neðələndz/ n. pl. **the ～,**
les Pays-Bas m. pl.

nettle /'netl/ n. ortie f.

network /'netwɜ:k/ n. réseau m.

neuralgia /njʊə'rældʒə/ n. névralgie f.

neuro|sis /njʊə'rəʊsɪs/ n. (pl. -oses
/-si:z/) névrose f. ～**tic** /-'rɒtɪk/ a.
& n. névrosé(e) (m. (f.)).

neuter /'nju:tə(r)/ a. & n. neutre (m.).
—v.t. (castrate) castrer.

neutral /'nju:trəl/ a. neutre. ～ **(gear),**
(auto.) point mort m. ～**ity** /-'trælətɪ/ n.
neutralité f.

neutron /'nju:trɒn/ n. neutron m. ～
bomb, bombe à neutrons f.

never /'nevə(r)/ adv. (ne) jamais; (not:
fam.) (ne) pas. **he ～ refuses,** il ne
refuse jamais. **I ～ saw him,** (fam.) je
ne l'ai pas vu. ～ **again,** plus jamais. ～
mind, (don't worry) ne vous en faites
pas; (it doesn't matter) peu importe. ～**-
ending** a. interminable.

nevertheless /nevəðə'les/ adv. néanmoins, toutefois.

new /nju:/ a. (**-er, -est**) nouveau; (brand-
new) neuf. ～**-born** a. nouveau-né. ～**-
laid egg,** œuf frais m. ～ **moon,**
nouvelle lune f. ～ **year,** nouvel an m.
New Year's Day, le jour de l'an. **New
Year's Eve,** la Saint-Sylvestre. **New
Zealand,** Nouvelle-Zélande f. **New
Zealander,** Néo-Zélandais(e) m. (f.).
～**ness** n. nouveauté f.

newcomer /'nju:kʌmə(r)/ n. nouveau
venu m., nouvelle venue f.

newfangled /nju:'fæŋgld/ a. (pej.)
moderne, neuf.

newly /'nju:lɪ/ adv. nouvellement. ～**-
weds** n. pl. nouveaux mariés m. pl.

news /nju:z/ n. nouvelle(s) f. (pl.);
(radio, press) informations f. pl.; (TV)
actualités f. pl., informations f. pl. ～
agency, agence de presse f. ～**caster,**
～**-reader** ns. présentalteur, trice m.,f.

newsagent /'nju:zeɪdʒənt/ n. mar-
chand(e) de journaux m.(f.).

newsletter /'nju:zletə(r)/ n. bulletin m.

newspaper /'nju:speɪpə(r)/ n. journal
m.

newsreel /'nju:zri:l/ n. actualités f. pl.

newt /nju:t/ n. triton m.

next /nekst/ a. prochain; (adjoining)
voisin; (following) suivant. —adv. la
prochaine fois; (afterwards) ensuite.
—n. suivant(e) m.(f.). ～**-door** a.
(**to,** de). ～**-door** a. d'à côté. ～ **of kin,**
parent le plus proche m. ～ **to,** à côté de.

nib /nɪb/ n. bec m., plume f.

nibble /'nɪbl/ v.t./i. grignoter.

nice /naɪs/ a. (**-er, -est**) agréable, bon;
(kind) gentil; (pretty) joli; (respectable) bien invar.; (subtle) délicat. ～**ly**
adv. agréablement; gentiment; (well)
bien.

nicety /'naɪsətɪ/ n. subtilité f.

niche /nɪtʃ, ni:ʃ/ n. (recess) niche f.;
(fig.) place f., situation f.

nick /nɪk/ n. petite entaille f. —v.t.
(steal, arrest: sl.) piquer. **in the ～ of
time,** juste à temps.

nickel /'nɪkl/ n. nickel m.; (Amer.) pièce
de cinq cents f.

nickname /'nɪkneɪm/ n. surnom m.;
(short form) diminutif m. —v.t.
surnommer.

nicotine /'nɪkəti:n/ n. nicotine f.

niece /ni:s/ n. nièce f.

nifty /'nɪftɪ/ a. (sl.) chic invar.

Nigeria /naɪ'dʒɪərɪə/ n. Nigéria m./f. ～**n**
a. & n. nigérian(e) (m. (f.)).

niggardly /'nɪgədlɪ/ a. chiche.

niggling /'nɪglɪŋ/ a. (*person*) tatillon; (*detail*) insignifiant.

night /naɪt/ n. nuit f.; (*evening*) soir m. —a. de nuit. **~-cap** n. boisson f. (*avant d'aller se coucher*). **~-club** n. boîte de nuit f. **~-dress**, **~-gown**, **~ie** ns. chemise de nuit f. **~-life** n. vie nocturne f. **~-school** n. cours du soir m. pl. **~- time** n. nuit f. **~- watchman** n. veilleur de nuit m.

nightfall /'naɪtfɔːl/ n. tombée de la nuit f.

nightingale /'naɪtɪŋgeɪl/ n. rossignol m.

nightly /'naɪtlɪ/ a. & adv. (de) chaque nuit or soir.

nightmare /'naɪtmeə(r)/ n. cauchemar m.

nil /nɪl/ n. rien m.; (*sport*) zéro m. —a. (*chances, risk, etc.*) nul.

nimble /'nɪmbl/ a. (-er, -est) agile.

nine /naɪn/ a. & n. neuf (m.). **~th** a. & n. neuvième (m./f.).

nineteen /naɪn'tiːn/ a. & n. dix-neuf (m.). **~th** a. & n. dix-neuvième (m./f.).

ninety /'naɪntɪ/ a. & n. quatre-vingt-dix (m.). **~tieth** a. & n. quatre-vingt-dixième (m./f.).

nip /nɪp/ v.t./i. (p.t. nipped) (*pinch*) pincer; (*rush: sl.*) courir. **~ out/back/**etc., sortir/rentrer/ etc. rapidement. —n. pincement m.; (*cold*) fraîcheur f.

nipper /'nɪpə(r)/ n. (sl.) gosse m./f.

nipple /'nɪpl/ n. bout de sein m.; (*of baby's bottle*) tétine f.

nippy /'nɪpɪ/ a. (-ier, -iest) (*fam.*) alerte; (*chilly: fam.*) frais.

nitrogen /'naɪtrədʒən/ n. azote m.

nitwit /'nɪtwɪt/ n. (*fam.*) imbécile m./f.

no /nəʊ/ a. aucun(e); pas de. —adv. non. —n. (pl. noes) non m. invar. **~ man/**etc., aucun homme/etc. **~ money/time/**etc., pas d'argent/de temps/etc. **~ man's land**, no man's land m. **~ one = nobody. ~ smoking/entry**, défense de fumer/ d'entrer. **~ way!**, (*fam.*) pas question!

noble /'nəʊbl/ a. (-er, -est) noble. **~ility** /-'bɪlətɪ/ n. noblesse f.

nobleman /'nəʊblmən/ n. (pl. -men) noble m.

nobody /'nəʊbədɪ/ pron. (ne) personne. —n. nullité f. **he knows ~**, il ne connaît personne. **~ is there**, personne n'est là.

nocturnal /nɒk'tɜːnl/ a. nocturne.

nod /nɒd/ v.t./i. (p.t. nodded). **~ (one's head)**, faire un signe de tête. **~ off**, s'endormir. —n. signe de tête m.

noise /nɔɪz/ n. bruit m. **~less** a. silencieux.

noisy /'nɔɪzɪ/ a. (-ier, -iest) bruyant. **~ily** adv. bruyamment.

nomad /'nəʊmæd/ n. nomade m./f. **~ic** /-'mædɪk/ a. nomade.

nominal /'nɒmɪnl/ a. symbolique, nominal; (*value*) nominal. **~ly** adv. nominalement.

nominate /'nɒmɪneɪt/ v.t. nommer; (*put forward*) proposer. **~ion** /-'neɪʃn/ n. nomination f.

non- /nɒn/ pref. non-. **~-iron** a. qui ne se repasse pas. **~-skid** a. antidérapant. **~-stick** a. à revêtement antiadhésif.

non-commissioned /nɒnkə'mɪʃnd/ a. **~ officer**, sous-officier m.

non-committal /nɒnkə'mɪtl/ a. évasif.

nondescript /'nɒndɪskrɪpt/ a. indéfinissable.

none /nʌn/ pron. aucun(e). **~ of us**, aucun de nous. **I have ~**, je n'en ai pas. **~ of the money was used**, l'argent n'a pas du tout été utilisé. —adv. **~ too**, (ne) pas tellement. **he is ~ the happier**, il n'en est pas plus heureux.

nonentity /nɒ'nentətɪ/ n. nullité f.

non-existent /nɒnɪg'zɪstənt/ a. inexistant.

nonplussed /nɒn'plʌst/ a. perplexe, déconcerté.

nonsense /'nɒnsəns/ n. absurdités f. pl. **~ical** /-'sensɪkl/ a. absurde.

non-smoker /nɒn'sməʊkə(r)/ n. nonfumeur m.

non-stop /nɒn'stɒp/ a. (*train, flight*) direct. —adv. sans arrêt.

noodles /'nuːdlz/ n. pl. nouilles f. pl.

nook /nʊk/ n. (re)coin m.

noon /nuːn/ n. midi m.

noose /nuːs/ n. nœud coulant m.

nor /nɔː(r)/ adv. ni. —conj. (ne) non plus. **~ shall I come**, je ne viendrai pas non plus.

norm /nɔːm/ n. norme f.

normal /'nɔːml/ a. normal. **~ity** /nɔː'mælətɪ/ n. normalité f. **~ly** adv. normalement.

Norman /'nɔːmən/ a. & n. normand(e) (m.(f.)). **~dy** n. Normandie f.

north /nɔːθ/ n. nord m. —a. nord invar., du nord. —adv. vers le nord. **N~ America**, Amérique du Nord f. **N~ American** a. & n. nord-américain(e) (m. (f.)). **~-east** n. nord-est m. **~erly** /'nɔːðəlɪ/ a. du nord. **~ward** a. au nord. **~wards** adv. vers le nord. **~-west** n. nord-ouest m.

northern /'nɔːðən/ a. du nord. **~er** n. habitant(e) du nord m. (f.).

Norway /'nɔːweɪ/ n. Norvège f. **~egian**

/nɔː'wiːdʒən/ a. & n. norvégien(ne) (m. (f.)).

nose /nəʊz/ n. nez m. —v.i. ∼ **about,** fouiner.

nosebleed /'nəʊzbliːd/ n. saignement de nez m.

nosedive /'nəʊzdaɪv/ n. piqué m. —v.i. descendre en piqué.

nostalg|ia /nɒ'stældʒə/ n. nostalgie f. ∼**ic** a. nostalgique.

nostril /'nɒstrəl/ n. narine f.; (of horse) naseau m.

nosy /'nəʊzi/ a. (**-ier, -iest**) (fam.) curieux, indiscret.

not /nɒt/ adv. (ne) pas. **I do ∼ know,** je ne sais pas. ∼ **at all,** pas du tout. ∼ **yet,** pas encore. **I suppose ∼,** je suppose que non.

notable /'nəʊtəbl/ a. notable. —n. (person) notable m.

notably /'nəʊtəbli/ adv. notamment.

notary /'nəʊtəri/ n. notaire m.

notation /nəʊ'teɪʃn/ n. notation f.

notch /nɒtʃ/ n. entaille f. —v.t. ∼ **up,** (score etc.) marquer.

note /nəʊt/ n. note f.; (banknote) billet m.; (short letter) mot m. —v.t. noter; (notice) remarquer.

notebook /'nəʊtbʊk/ n. carnet m.

noted /'nəʊtɪd/ a. connu (**for,** pour).

notepaper /'nəʊtpeɪpə(r)/ n. papier à lettres m.

noteworthy /'nəʊtwɜːði/ a. remarquable.

nothing /'nʌθɪŋ/ pron. (ne) rien. —n. rien m.; (person) nullité f. —adv. nullement. **he eats ∼,** il ne mange rien. ∼ **big/etc.,** rien de grand/etc. ∼ **else,** rien d'autre. ∼ **much,** pas grand-chose. **for ∼,** pour rien, gratis.

notice /'nəʊtɪs/ n. avis m., annonce f.; (poster) affiche f. (**advance**) préavis m. **at short ∼,** dans des délais très brefs. **give in one's ∼,** donner sa démission. —v.t. remarquer, observer. ∼**-board** n. tableau d'affichage m. **take ∼,** faire attention (**of,** à).

noticeab|le /'nəʊtɪsəbl/ a. visible. ∼**y** adv. visiblement.

notif|y /'nəʊtɪfaɪ/ v.t. (inform) aviser; (make known) notifier. ∼**ication** /-ɪ'keɪʃn/ n. avis m.

notion /'nəʊʃn/ n. idée, notion f. ∼**s,** (sewing goods etc.: Amer.) mercerie f.

notor|ious /nəʊ'tɔːrɪəs/ a. (tristement) célèbre. ∼**iety** /-ə'raɪətɪ/ n. notoriété f. ∼**iously** adv. notoirement.

notwithstanding /nɒtwɪθ'stændɪŋ/ prep. malgré. —adv. néanmoins.

nougat /'nuːgɑː/ n. nougat m.

nought /nɔːt/ n. zéro m.

noun /naʊn/ n. nom m.

nourish /'nʌrɪʃ/ v.t. nourrir. ∼**ing** a. nourrissant. ∼**ment** n. nourriture f.

novel /'nɒvl/ n. roman m. —a. nouveau. ∼**ist** n. romancier, -ière m., f. ∼**ty** n. nouveauté f.

November /nəʊ'vembə(r)/ n. novembre m.

novice /'nɒvɪs/ n. novice m./f.

now /naʊ/ adv. maintenant. —conj. maintenant que. **just ∼,** maintenant; (a moment ago) tout à l'heure. ∼ **and again,** ∼ **and then,** de temps à autre.

nowadays /'naʊədeɪz/ adv. de nos jours.

nowhere /'nəʊweə(r)/ adv. nulle part.

nozzle /'nɒzl/ n. (tip) embout m.; (of hose) lance f.

nuance /'njuːɑːns/ n. nuance f.

nuclear /'njuːklɪə(r)/ a. nucléaire.

nucleus /'njuːklɪəs/ n. (pl. **-lei** /-lɪaɪ/) noyau m.

nud|e /njuːd/ a. nu. —n. nu m. **in the ∼e,** tout nu. ∼**ity** n. nudité f.

nudge /nʌdʒ/ v.t. pousser du coude. —n. coup de coude m.

nudis|t /'njuːdɪst/ n. nudiste m./f. ∼**m** /-zəm/ n. nudisme m.

nuisance /'njuːsns/ n. (thing, event) ennui m.; (person) peste f. **be a ∼,** être embêtant.

null /nʌl/ a. nul. ∼**ify** v.t. infirmer.

numb /nʌm/ a. engourdi. —v.t. engourdir.

number /'nʌmbə(r)/ n. nombre m.; (of ticket, house, page, etc.) numéro m. —v.t. numéroter; (count, include) compter. **a ∼ of people,** plusieurs personnes. ∼**-plate** n. plaque d'immatriculation f.

numeral /'njuːmərəl/ n. chiffre m.

numerate /'njuːmərət/ a. qui sait calculer.

numerical /njuː'merɪkl/ a. numérique.

numerous /'njuːmərəs/ a. nombreux.

nun /nʌn/ n. religieuse f.

nurs|e /nɜːs/ n. infirmière f., infirmier m.; (nanny) nurse f. —v.t. soigner; (hope etc.) nourrir. ∼**ing home,** clinique f.

nursemaid /'nɜːsmeɪd/ n. bonne d'enfants f.

nursery /'nɜːsəri/ n. chambre d'enfants f.; (for plants) pépinière f. (**day**) ∼, crèche f. ∼ **rhyme,** chanson enfantine f., comptine f. ∼ **school,** (école) maternelle f. ∼ **slope,** piste facile f.

nurture /'nɜːtʃə(r)/ v.t. élever.

nut /nʌt/ n. (walnut, Brazil nut, etc.)

noix f.; (*hazelnut*) noisette f.; (*peanut*) cacahuète f.; (*techn.*) écrou m.; (*sl.*) idiot(e) m. (f.).
nutcrackers /'nʌtkrækəz/ n. pl. casse-noix m. invar.
nutmeg /'nʌtmeg/ n. muscade f.
nutrient /'njuːtrɪənt/ n. substance nutritive f.
nutrit|ion /njuː'trɪʃn/ n. nutrition f. **~ious** a. nutritif.
nuts /nʌts/ a. (*crazy: sl.*) cinglé.
nutshell /'nʌtʃel/ n. coquille de noix f. **in a ~**, en un mot.
nuzzle /'nʌzl/ v.i. **~ up to**, coller son museau à.
nylon /'naɪlɒn/ n. nylon m. **~s**, bas nylon m. pl.

O

oaf /əʊf/ n. (*pl.* **oafs**) lourdaud(e) m. (f.).
oak /əʊk/ n. chêne m.
OAP abbr. (*old-age pensioner*) retraité(e) m. (f.), personne âgée f.
oar /ɔː(r)/ n. aviron m., rame f.
oasis /əʊ'eɪsɪs/ n. (*pl.* **oases** /-siːz/) oasis f.
oath /əʊθ/ n. (*promise*) serment m.; (*swear-word*) juron m.
oatmeal /'əʊtmiːl/ n. farine d'avoine f., flocons d'avoine m. pl.
oats /əʊts/ n. pl. avoine f.
obedien|t /ə'biːdɪənt/ a. obéissant. **~ce** n. obéissance f. **~tly** adv. docilement, avec soumission.
obes|e /əʊ'biːs/ a. obèse. **~ity** n. obésité f.
obey /ə'beɪ/ v.t./i. obéir (à).
obituary /ə'bɪtʃʊərɪ/ n. nécrologie f.
object[1] /'ɒbdʒɪkt/ n. (*thing*) objet m.; (*aim*) but m., objet m.; (*gram.*) complément (d'objet) m. **money**/*etc.* **is no ~**, l'argent/*etc.* ne pose pas de problèmes.
object[2] /əb'dʒekt/ v.i. protester. —v.t. **~ that**, objecter que. **~ to**, (*behaviour*) désapprouver; (*plan*) protester contre. **~ion** /-kʃn/ n. objection f.; (*drawback*) inconvénient m.
objectionable /əb'dʒekʃnəbl/ a. désagréable.
objectiv|e /əb'dʒektɪv/ a. objectif. —n. objectif m. **~ity** /ɒbdʒek'tɪvətɪ/ n. objectivité f.
obligat|e /'ɒblɪgeɪt/ v.t. obliger. **~ion**

/-'geɪʃn/ n. obligation f. **under an ~ion to s.o.**, redevable à qn. (**for**, de).
obligatory /ə'blɪgətrɪ/ a. obligatoire.
oblig|e /ə'blaɪdʒ/ v.t. obliger. **~e to do**, obliger à faire. **~ed** a. obligé (**to**, de). **~ed to s.o.**, redevable à qn. **~ing** a. obligeant. **~ingly** adv. obligeamment.
oblique /ə'bliːk/ a. oblique; (*reference etc.: fig.*) indirect.
obliterat|e /ə'blɪtəreɪt/ v.t. effacer. **~ion** /-'reɪʃn/ n. effacement m.
oblivion /ə'blɪvɪən/ n. oubli m.
oblivious /ə'blɪvɪəs/ a. (*unaware*) inconscient (**to**, **of**, de).
oblong /'ɒblɒŋ/ a. oblong. —n. rectangle m.
obnoxious /əb'nɒkʃəs/ a. odieux.
oboe /'əʊbəʊ/ n. hautbois m.
obscen|e /əb'siːn/ a. obscène. **~ity** /-'enətɪ/ n. obscénité f.
obscur|e /əb'skjʊə(r)/ a. obscur. —v.t. obscurcir; (*conceal*) cacher. **~ely** adv. obscurément. **~ity** n. obscurité f.
obsequious /əb'siːkwɪəs/ a. obséquieux.
observan|t /əb'zɜːvənt/ a. observateur. **~ce** n. observance f.
observatory /əb'zɜːvətrɪ/ n. observatoire m.
observ|e /əb'zɜːv/ v.t. observer; (*remark*) remarquer. **~ation** /ɒbzə'veɪʃn/ n. observation f. **~er** n. observateur, -trice m., f.
obsess /əb'ses/ v.t. obséder. **~ion** /-ʃn/ n. obsession f. **~ive** a. obsédant; (*psych.*) obsessionnel.
obsolete /'ɒbsəliːt/ a. dépassé.
obstacle /'ɒbstəkl/ n. obstacle m.
obstetric|s /əb'stetrɪks/ n. obstétrique f. **~ian** /ɒbstɪ'trɪʃn/ n. médecin accoucheur m.
obstina|te /'ɒbstɪnət/ a. obstiné. **~cy** n. obstination f. **~tely** adv. obstinément.
obstruct /əb'strʌkt/ v.t. (*block*) boucher; (*congest*) encombrer; (*hinder*) entraver. **~ion** /-kʃn/ n. (*act*) obstruction f.; (*thing*) obstacle m.; (*traffic jam*) encombrement m.
obtain /əb'teɪn/ v.t. obtenir. —v.i. avoir cours. **~able** a. disponible.
obtrusive /əb'truːsɪv/ a. importun; (*thing*) trop en évidence.
obtuse /əb'tjuːs/ a. obtus.
obviate /'ɒbvɪeɪt/ v.t. éviter.
obvious /'ɒbvɪəs/ a. évident, manifeste. **~ly** adv. manifestement.
occasion /ə'keɪʒn/ n. occasion f.; (*big event*) événement m. —v.t. occasionner. **on ~**, à l'occasion.

occasional /əˈkeɪʒənl/ *a.* fait, pris, *etc.* de temps en temps; (*visitor etc.*) qui vient de temps en temps. **~ly** *adv.* de temps en temps. **very ~ly**, rarement.

occult /ɒˈkʌlt/ *a.* occulte.

occupation /ɒkjʊˈpeɪʃn/ *n.* (*activity, occupying*) occupation *f.*; (*job*) métier *m.*, profession *f.* **~al** *a.* professionnel, du métier. **~al therapy** ergothérapie *f.*

occup|y /ˈɒkjʊpaɪ/ *v.i.* occuper. **~ant, ~ier** *ns.* occupant(e) *m.* (*f.*).

occur /əˈkɜː(r)/ *v.i.* (*p.t.* **occurred**) se produire; (*arise*) se présenter. **~ to s.o.**, venir à l'esprit de qn.

occurrence /əˈkʌrəns/ *n.* événement *m.* **a frequent ~**, une chose qui arrive souvent.

ocean /ˈəʊʃn/ *n.* océan *m.*

o'clock /əˈklɒk/ *adv.* **it is six ~**/*etc.*, il est six heures/*etc.*

octagon /ˈɒktəgən/ *n.* octogone *m.*

octane /ˈɒkteɪn/ *n.* octane *m.*

octave /ˈɒktɪv/ *n.* octave *f.*

October /ɒkˈtəʊbə(r)/ *n.* octobre *m.*

octopus /ˈɒktəpəs/ *n.* (*pl.* **-puses**) pieuvre *f.*

odd /ɒd/ *a.* (**-er, -est**) bizarre; (*number*) impair; (*left over*) qui reste; (*not of set*) dépareillé; (*occasional*) fait, pris, *etc.* de temps en temps. **~ jobs**, menus travaux *m. pl.* **twenty ~**, vingt et quelques. **~ity** *n.* bizarrerie *f.*; (*thing*) curiosité *f.* **~ly** *adv.* bizarrement.

oddment /ˈɒdmənt/ *n.* fin de série *f.*

odds /ɒdz/ *n. pl.* chances *f. pl.*; (*in betting*) cote *f.* (**on**, de). **at ~**, en désaccord. **it makes no ~**, ça ne fait rien. **~ and ends**, des petites choses.

ode /əʊd/ *n.* ode *f.*

odious /ˈəʊdɪəs/ *a.* odieux.

odour, *Amer.* **odor** /ˈəʊdə(r)/ *n.* odeur *f.* **~less** *a.* inodore.

of /ɒv, *unstressed* əv/ *prep.* de. **of the**, du, de la, *pl.* des. **of it, of them**, en. **a friend of mine**, un de mes amis. **six of them**, six d'entre eux. **the fifth of June**/*etc.*, le cinq juin/*etc.* **a litre of water**, un litre d'eau; **made of steel**, en acier.

off /ɒf/ *adv.* parti, absent; (*switched off*) éteint; (*tap*) fermé; (*taken off*) enlevé, détaché; *cancelled*) annulé. —*prep.* de; (*distant from*) éloigné de. **go ~**, (*leave*) partir; (*milk*) tourner; (*food*) s'abîmer. **be better ~**, (*in a better position, richer*) être mieux. **a day ~**, un jour de congé. **20% ~**, une réduction de 20%. **take sth. ~**, (*a surface*) prendre qch. sur. **~-beat** *a.* original. **on the ~**

chance (that), au cas où. **~ colour**, (*ill*) patraque. **~ color**, (*improper: Amer.*) scabreux. **~-licence** *n.* débit de vins *m.* **~-line** *a.* autonome; (*switched off*) déconnecté. **~-load** *v.t.* décharger. **~-peak** *a.* (*hours*) creux; (*rate*) des heures creuses. **~-putting** *a.* (*fam.*) rebutant. **~-stage** *a. & adv.* dans les coulisses. **~-white** *a.* blanc cassé *invar.*

offal /ˈɒfl/ *n.* abats *m. pl.*

offence /əˈfens/ *n.* délit *m.* **give ~ to**, offenser. **take ~**, s'offenser (**at**, de).

offend /əˈfend/ *v.t.* offenser; (*fig.*) choquer. **be ~ed**, s'offenser (**at**, de). **~er** *n.* délinquant(e) *m.* (*f.*).

offensive /əˈfensɪv/ *a.* offensant; (*disgusting*) dégoûtant; (*weapon*) offensif. —*n.* offensive *f.*

offer /ˈɒfə(r)/ *v.t.* (*p.t.* **offered**) offrir. —*n.* offre *f.* **on ~**, en promotion. **~ing** *n.* offrande *f.*

offhand /ɒfˈhænd/ *a.* désinvolte. —*adv.* à l'improviste.

office /ˈɒfɪs/ *n.* bureau *m.*; (*duty*) fonction *f.*; (*surgery: Amer.*) cabinet *m.* —*a.* de bureau. **good ~s**, bons offices *m. pl.* **in ~**, au pouvoir. **~ building**, immeuble de bureaux *m.*

officer /ˈɒfɪsə(r)/ *n.* (*army etc.*) officier *m.*; (*policeman*) agent *m.*

official /əˈfɪʃl/ *a.* officiel. —*n.* officiel *m.*; (*civil servant*) fonctionnaire *m./f.* **~ly** *adv.* officiellement.

officiate /əˈfɪʃɪeɪt/ *v.i.* (*priest*) officier; (*president*) présider.

officious /əˈfɪʃəs/ *a.* trop zélé.

offing /ˈɒfɪŋ/ *n.* **in the ~**, en perspective.

offset /ˈɒfset/ *v.t.* (*p.t.* **-set**, *pres. p.* **-setting**) compenser.

offshoot /ˈɒfʃuːt/ *n.* (*bot.*) rejeton *m.*; (*fig.*) ramification *f.*

offshore /ɒfˈʃɔː(r)/ *a.* (*waters*) côtier; (*exploration*) en mer; (*banking*) dans les paladis fiscaux.

offside /ɒfˈsaɪd/ *a.* (*sport*) hors jeu *invar.*; (*auto.*) du côté du conducteur.

offspring /ˈɒfsprɪŋ/ *n. invar.* progéniture *f.*

often /ˈɒfn/ *adv.* souvent. **how ~?**, combien de fois? **every so ~**, de temps en temps.

ogle /ˈəʊgl/ *v.t.* lorgner.

ogre /ˈəʊgə(r)/ *n.* ogre *m.*

oh /əʊ/ *int.* oh, ah.

oil /ɔɪl/ *n.* huile *f.*; (*petroleum*) pétrole *m.*; (*for heating*) mazout *m.* —*v.t.* graisser. **~-painting** *n.* peinture à l'huile *f.* **~-tanker** *n.* pétrolier *m.* **~y** *a.* graisseux.

oilfield /'ɔɪlfiːld/ n. gisement pétrolifère m.

oilskins /'ɔɪlskɪnz/ n. pl. ciré m.

ointment /'ɔɪntmənt/ n. pommade f., onguent m.

OK /əʊ'keɪ/ a. & adv. (fam.) bien.

old /əʊld/ a. (-er, -est) vieux; (person) vieux, âgé; (former) ancien. **how ~ is he?**, quel âge a-t-il? **he is eight years ~**, il a huit ans. **of ~**, jadis. **~ age**, vieillesse f. **old-age pensioner**, retraité(e) m. (f.) **~ boy**, ancien élève m.; (fellow: fam.) vieux m. **~er**, **~est**, (son etc.) aîné. **~fashioned** a. démodé; (person) vieux jeu invar. **~ maid**, vieille fille f. **~ man**, vieillard m., vieux m. **~time** a. ancien. **~ woman**, vieille f.

olive /'ɒlɪv/ n. olive f. —a. olive invar. **~ oil**, huile d'olive f.

Olympic /ə'lɪmpɪk/ a. olympique. **~s** n. pl., **~ Games**, Jeux olympiques m. pl.

omelette /'ɒmlɪt/ n. omelette f.

omen /'əʊmen/ n. augure m.

ominous /'ɒmɪnəs/ a. de mauvais augure; (fig.) menaçant.

omi|t /ə'mɪt/ v.t. (p.t. omitted) omettre. **~ssion** n. omission f.

on /ɒn/ prep. sur. —adv. en avant; (switched on) allumé; (tap) ouvert; (machine) en marche; (put on) mis. **on foot/time/etc.**, à pied/l'heure/etc. **on arriving**, en arrivant. **on Tuesday**, mardi. **on Tuesdays**, le mardi. **walk/etc. on**, continuer à marcher/etc. **be on**, (of film) passer. **the meeting/deal is still on**, la réunion/le marché est maintenu(e). **be on at**, (fam.) être après. **on and off**, de temps en temps.

once /wʌns/ adv. une fois; (formerly) autrefois. —conj. une fois que. **all at ~**, tout à coup. **~-over** n. (fam.) coup d'œil rapide m.

oncoming /'ɒnkʌmɪŋ/ a. (vehicle etc.) qui approche.

one /wʌn/ a. & n. un(e) (m. (f.)). —pron. un(e) m. (f.); (impersonal) on. **~ (and only)**, seul (et unique). **a big/red/etc. ~**, un(e) grand(e)/rouge/etc. **this/that ~**, celui-ci/-là, celle-ci/-là. **~ another**, l'un(e) l'autre. **~-eyed**, borgne. **~-off** a. (fam.), **~ of a kind**, (Amer.) unique, exceptionnel. **~-sided** a. (biased) partial; (unequal) inégal. **~-way** a. (street) à sens unique; (ticket) simple.

oneself /wʌn'self/ pron. soi-même; (reflexive) se.

ongoing /'ɒngəʊɪŋ/ a. qui continue à évoluer.

onion /'ʌnjən/ n. oignon m.

onlooker /'ɒnlʊkə(r)/ n. spectalteur, -trice m., f.

only /'əʊnlɪ/ a. seul. **an ~ son/etc.**, un fils/etc. unique. —adv. & conj. seulement. **he ~ has six**, il n'en a que six, il en a six seulement. **~ too**, extrêmement.

onset /'ɒnset/ n. début m.

onslaught /'ɒnslɔːt/ n. attaque f.

onus /'əʊnəs/ n. **the ~ is on me/etc.**, c'est ma/etc. responsabilité (**to, de**).

onward(s) /'ɒnwəd(z)/ adv. en avant.

onyx /'ɒnɪks/ n. onyx m.

ooze /uːz/ v.i. suinter.

opal /'əʊpl/ n. opale f.

opaque /əʊ'peɪk/ a. opaque.

open /'əʊpən/ a. ouvert; (view) dégagé; (free to all) public; (undisguised) manifeste; (question) en attente. —v.t./i. (s')ouvrir; (of shop, play) ouvrir. **in the ~ air**, en plein air. **~-ended** a. sans limite (de durée etc.); (system) qui peut évoluer. **~-heart** a. (surgery) à cœur ouvert. **keep ~ house**, tenir table ouverte. **~ out or up**, (s')ouvrir. **~-minded** à l'esprit ouvert. **~-plan** a. sans cloisons. **~ secret**, secret de Polichinelle m.

opener /'əʊpənə(r)/ n. ouvre-boîte(s) m., ouvre-bouteille(s) m.

opening /'əʊpənɪŋ/ n. ouverture f.; (job) débouché m., poste vacant m.

openly /'əʊpənlɪ/ adv. ouvertement.

opera /'ɒpərə/ n. opéra m. **~-glasses** n. pl. jumelles f. pl. **~tic** /ɒpə'rætɪk/ a. d'opéra.

operat|e /'ɒpəreɪt/ v.t./i. opérer; (techn.) (faire) fonctionner. **~e on**, (med.) opérer. **~ing theatre**, salle d'opération f. **~ion** /-'reɪʃn/ n. opération f. **have an ~ion**, se faire opérer. **in ~ion**, en vigueur; (techn.) en service. **~or** n. opéralteur, -trice m., f.; (telephonist) standardiste m./f.

operational /ɒpə'reɪʃənl/ a. opérationnel.

operative /'ɒpərətɪv/ a. (med.) opératoire; (law etc.) en vigueur.

operetta /ɒpə'retə/ n. opérette f.

opinion /ə'pɪnjən/ n. opinion f., avis m. **~ated** a. dogmatique.

opium /'əʊpɪəm/ n. opium m.

opponent /ə'pəʊnənt/ n. adversaire m./f.

opportune /'ɒpətjuːn/ a. opportun.

opportunist /ɒpə'tjuːnɪst/ n. opportuniste m./f.

opportunity /ɒpə'tjuːnətɪ/ n. occasion f. (**to do**, de faire).

oppos|e /ə'pəʊz/ v.t. s'opposer à. ∼**ed to,** opposé à. ∼**ing** a. opposé.

opposite /'ɒpəzɪt/ a. opposé. —n. contraire m., opposé m. —adv. en face. —prep. ∼ **(to),** en face de. **one's** ∼ **number,** son homologue m./f.

opposition /ɒpə'zɪʃn/ n. opposition f.; (mil.) résistance f.

oppress /ə'pres/ v.t. opprimer. ∼**ion** /-ʃn/ n. oppression f. ∼**ive** a. (cruel) oppressif; (heat) oppressant. ∼**or** n. oppresseur m.

opt /ɒpt/ v.i. ∼ **for,** opter pour. ∼ **out,** refuser de participer **(of,** à). ∼ **to do,** choisir de faire.

optical /'ɒptɪkl/ a. optique. ∼ **illusion,** illusion d'optique f.

optician /ɒp'tɪʃn/ n. opticien(ne) m. (f.).

optimis|t /'ɒptɪmɪst/ n. optimiste m./f. ∼**m** /-zəm/ n. optimisme m. ∼**tic** /-'mɪstɪk/ a. optimiste. ∼**tically** /-'mɪstɪklɪ/ adv. avec optimisme.

optimum /'ɒptɪməm/ a. & n. (pl. -ima) optimum (m.).

option /'ɒpʃn/ n. choix m., option f.

optional /'ɒpʃənl/ a. facultatif. ∼ **extras,** accessoires en option m. pl.

opulen|t /'ɒpjʊlənt/ a. opulent. ∼**ce** n. opulence f.

or /ɔ:(r)/ conj. ou; (with negative) ni.

oracle /'ɒrəkl/ n. oracle m.

oral /'ɔ:rəl/ a. oral. —n. (examination: fam.) oral m.

orange /'ɒrɪndʒ/ n. (fruit) orange f. —a. (colour) orange invar.

orangeade /ɒrɪndʒ'eɪd/ n. orangeade f.

orator /'ɒrətə(r)/ n. orateur, -trice m., f. ∼**y** /-trɪ/ n. rhétorique f.

oratorio /ɒrə'tɔ:rɪəʊ/ n. (pl. -os) oratorio m.

orbit /'ɔ:bɪt/ n. orbite f. —v.t. graviter autour de, orbiter.

orchard /'ɔ:tʃəd/ n. verger m.

orchestra /'ɔ:kɪstrə/ n. orchestre m. ∼ **stalls** (Amer.), fauteuils d'orchestre m. pl. ∼**l** /-'kestrəl/ a. orchestral.

orchestrate /'ɔ:kɪstreɪt/ v.t. orchestrer.

orchid /'ɔ:kɪd/ n. orchidée f.

ordain /ɔ:'deɪn/ v.t. décréter **(that,** que); (relig.) ordonner.

ordeal /ɔ:'di:l/ n. épreuve f.

order /'ɔ:də(r)/ n. ordre m.; (comm.) commande f. —v.t. ordonner; (goods etc.) commander. **in** ∼, (tidy) en ordre; (document) en règle; (fitting) de règle. **in** ∼ **that,** pour que. **in** ∼ **to,** pour. ∼ **s.o. to,** ordonner à qn. de.

orderly /'ɔ:dəlɪ/ a. (tidy) ordonné; (not unruly) discipliné. —n. (mil.) planton m.; (med.) garçon de salle m.

ordinary /'ɔ:dɪnrɪ/ a. (usual) ordinaire; (average) moyen.

ordination /ɔ:dɪ'neɪʃn/ n. (relig.) ordination f.

ore /ɔ:(r)/ n. mineral m.

organ /'ɔ:gən/ n. organe m.; (mus.) orgue m. ∼**ist** n. organiste m./f.

organic /ɔ:'gænɪk/ a. organique.

organism /'ɔ:gənɪzəm/ n. organisme m.

organiz|e /'ɔ:gənaɪz/ v.t. organiser. ∼**ation** /-'zeɪʃn/ n. organisation f. ∼**er** n. organisa|teur, -trice m., f.

orgasm /'ɔ:gæzəm/ n. orgasme m.

orgy /'ɔ:dʒɪ/ n. orgie f.

Orient /'ɔ:rɪənt/ n. **the** ∼, l'Orient m. ∼**al** /-'entl/ a. Oriental(e) m. (f.).

oriental /ɔ:rɪ'entl/ a. oriental.

orient(at|e /'ɔ:rɪənt(eɪt)/ v.t. orienter. ∼**ion** /-'teɪʃn/ n. orientation f.

orifice /'ɒrɪfɪs/ n. orifice m.

origin /'ɒrɪdʒɪn/ n. origine f.

original /ə'rɪdʒənl/ a. (first) originel; (not copied) original. ∼**ity** /-'nælətɪ/ n. originalité f. ∼**ly** adv. (at the outset) à l'origine; (write etc.) originalement.

originat|e /ə'rɪdʒɪneɪt/ v.i. (plan) prendre naissance. —v.t. être l'auteur de. ∼**e from,** provenir de; (person) venir de. ∼**or** n. auteur m.

ornament /'ɔ:nəmənt/ n. (decoration) ornement m.; (object) objet décoratif m. ∼**al** /-'mentl/ a. ornemental. ∼**ation** /-en'teɪʃn/ n. ornementation f.

ornate /ɔ:'neɪt/ a. richement orné.

ornithology /ɔ:nɪ'θɒlədʒɪ/ n. ornithologie f.

orphan /'ɔ:fn/ n. orphelin(e) m. (f.). —v.t. rendre orphelin. ∼**age** n. orphelinat m.

orthodox /'ɔ:θədɒks/ a. orthodoxe. ∼**y** n. orthodoxie f.

orthopaedic /ɔ:θə'pi:dɪk/ a. orthopédique.

oscillate /'ɒsɪleɪt/ v.i. osciller.

ostensibl|e /ɒs'tensəbl/ a. apparent, prétendu. ∼**y** adv. apparemment, prétendument.

ostentati|on /ɒsten'teɪʃn/ n. ostentation f. ∼**ous** a. prétentieux.

osteopath /'ɒstɪəpæθ/ n. ostéopathe m./f.

ostracize /'ɒstrəsaɪz/ v.t. frapper d'ostracisme.

ostrich /'ɒstrɪtʃ/ n. autruche f.

other /'ʌðə(r)/ a. autre. —n. & pron. autre m./f. —adv. ∼ **than,** autrement que; (except) à part. **(some)** ∼**s,** d'autres. **the** ∼ **one,** l'autre m./f.

otherwise /'ʌðəwaɪz/ adv. autrement.

otter /'ɒtə(r)/ n. loutre f.

ouch /aʊtʃ/ int. aïe!

ought /ɔːt/ v. aux. devoir. **you ~ to stay,** vous devriez rester. **he ~ to succeed,** il devrait réussir. **I ~ to have done it,** j'aurais dû le faire.

ounce /aʊns/ n. once f. (= 28.35 g.).

our /'aʊə(r)/ a. notre, pl. nos.

ours /'aʊəz/ poss. le or la nôtre, les nôtres.

ourselves /aʊə'selvz/ pron. nous-mêmes; (reflexive & after prep.) nous.

oust /aʊst/ v.t. évincer.

out /aʊt/ adv. dehors; (sun) levé. **be ~,** (person, book) être sorti; (light) être éteint; (flower) être épanoui; (tide) être bas; (secret) se savoir; (wrong) se tromper. **be ~ to do,** être résolu à faire. **run**/etc. **~,** sortir en courant/etc. **~-and-out** a. absolu. **~ of,** hors de; (without) sans, à court de. **~ of pity**/etc., par pitié/etc. **made ~ of,** fait en or de. **take ~ of,** prendre dans. **5 ~ of 6,** 5 sur 6. **~ of date,** démodé; (not valid) périmé. **~ of doors,** dehors. **~ of hand,** (situation) dont on n'est plus maître. **~ of line,** (impertinent: Amer.) incorrect. **~ of one's mind,** fou. **~ of order,** (broken) en panne. **~ of place,** (object, remark) déplacé. **~ of the way,** écarté. **get ~ of the way!** écarte-toi! **~ of work,** sans travail. **~-patient** n. malade en consultation externe m./f.

outbid /aʊt'bɪd/ v.t. (p.t. **-bid,** pres. p. **-bidding**) enchérir sur.

outboard /'aʊtbɔːd/ a. (motor) hors-bord invar.

outbreak /'aʊtbreɪk/ n. (of war etc.) début m.; (of violence, boils) éruption f.

outburst /'aʊtbɜːst/ n. explosion f.

outcast /'aʊtkɑːst/ n. paria m.

outclass /aʊt'klɑːs/ v.t. surclasser.

outcome /'aʊtkʌm/ n. résultat m.

outcrop /'aʊtkrɒp/ n. affleurement m.

outcry /'aʊtkraɪ/ n. tollé m.

outdated /aʊt'deɪtɪd/ a. démodé.

outdo /aʊt'duː/ v.t. (p.t. **-did,** p.p. **-done**) surpasser.

outdoor /'aʊtdɔː(r)/ a. de or en plein air. **~s** /-'dɔːz/ adv. dehors.

outer /'aʊtə(r)/ a. extérieur. **~ space,** espace (cosmique) m.

outfit /'aʊtfɪt/ n. (articles) équipement m.; (clothes) tenue f.; (group: fam.) équipe f. **~ter** n. spécialiste de confection m./f.

outgoing /'aʊtgəʊɪŋ/ a. (minister, tenant) sortant; (sociable) ouvert. **~s** n. pl. dépenses f. pl.

outgrow /aʊt'grəʊ/ v.t. (p.t. **-grew,** p.p. **-grown**) (clothes) devenir trop grand pour; (habit) dépasser.

outhouse /'aʊthaʊs/ n. appentis m.; (of mansion) dépendance f.; (Amer.) cabinets extérieurs m. pl.

outing /'aʊtɪŋ/ n. sortie f.

outlandish /aʊt'lændɪʃ/ a. bizarre, étrange.

outlaw /'aʊtlɔː/ n. hors-la-loi m. invar. —v.t. proscrire.

outlay /'aʊtleɪ/ n. dépenses f. pl.

outlet /'aʊtlet/ n. (for water, gases) sortie f.; (for goods) débouché m.; (for feelings) exutoire m.

outline /'aʊtlaɪn/ n. contour m.; (summary) esquisse f. **(main) ~s,** grandes lignes f. pl. —v.t. tracer le contour de; (summarize) exposer sommairement.

outlive /aʊt'lɪv/ v.t. survivre à.

outlook /'aʊtlʊk/ n. perspective f.

outlying /'aʊtlaɪɪŋ/ a. écarté.

outmoded /aʊt'məʊdɪd/ a. démodé.

outnumber /aʊt'nʌmbə(r)/ v.t. surpasser en nombre.

outpost /'aʊtpəʊst/ n. avant-poste m.

output /'aʊtpʊt/ n. rendement m.; (comput.) sortie f. —v.t./i. (comput.) sortir.

outrage /'aʊtreɪdʒ/ n. atrocité f.; (scandal) scandale m. —v.t. (morals) outrager; (person) scandaliser.

outrageous /aʊt'reɪdʒəs/ a. scandaleux, atroce.

outright /aʊt'raɪt/ adv. complètement; (at once) sur le coup; (frankly) carrément. —a. /'aʊtraɪt/ complet; (refusal) net.

outset /'aʊtset/ n. début m.

outside¹ /aʊt'saɪd/ n. extérieur m. —adv. (au) dehors. —prep. en dehors de; (in front of) devant.

outside² /'aʊtsaɪd/ a. extérieur.

outsider /aʊt'saɪdə(r)/ n. étranger, -ère m., f.; (sport) outsider m.

outsize /'aʊtsaɪz/ a. grande taille invar.

outskirts /'aʊtskɜːts/ n. pl. banlieue f.

outspoken /aʊt'spəʊkən/ a. franc.

outstanding /aʊt'stændɪŋ/ a. exceptionnel; (not settled) en suspens.

outstretched /əʊt'stretʃt/ a. (arm) tendu.

outstrip /aʊt'strɪp/ v.t. (p.t. **-stripped**) devancer, surpasser.

outward /'aʊtwəd/ a. & adv. vers l'extérieur; (sign etc.) extérieur;

(*journey*) d'aller. **~ly** *adv.* extérieurement. **~s** *adv.* vers l'extérieur.

outweigh /aʊt'weɪ/ *v.t.* (*exceed in importance*) l'emporter sur.

outwit /aʊt'wɪt/ *v.t.* (*p.t.* **-witted**) duper, être plus malin que.

oval /'əʊvl/ *n. & a.* ovale (*m.*).

ovary /'əʊvərɪ/ *n.* ovaire *m.*

ovation /ə'veɪʃn/ *n.* ovation *f.*

oven /'ʌvn/ *n.* four *m.*

over /'əʊvə(r)/ *prep.* sur, au-dessus de; (*across*) de l'autre côté de; (*during*) pendant; (*more than*) plus de. —*adv.* (par-)dessus; (*ended*) fini; (*past*) passé; (*too*) trop; (*more*) plus. **jump**/*etc.* **~**, sauter/*etc.* par-dessus. **~ the radio**, à la radio. **ask ~**, inviter chez soi. **he has some ~**, il lui en reste. **all ~ (the table)**, partout (sur la table). **~ and above**, en plus de. **~ and over**, à maintes reprises. **~ here**, par ici. **~ there**, là-bas.

over- /'əʊvə(r)/ *pref.* sur-, trop.

overall[1] /'əʊvərɔːl/ *n.* blouse *f.* **~s**, bleu(s) de travail *m.* (*pl.*).

overall[2] /əʊvər'ɔːl/ *a.* global, d'ensemble; (*length, width*) total. —*adv.* globalement.

overawe /əʊvər'ɔː/ *v.t.* intimider.

overbalance /əʊvə'bæləns/ *v.t./i.* (faire) basculer.

overbearing /əʊvə'beərɪŋ/ *a.* autoritaire.

overboard /'əʊvəbɔːd/ *adv.* pardessus bord.

overbook /əʊvə'bʊk/ *v.t.* accepter trop de réservations pour.

overcast /'əʊvəkɑːst/ *a.* couvert.

overcharge /əʊvə'tʃɑːdʒ/ *v.t.* **~ s.o. (for)**, faire payer trop cher à qn.

overcoat /'əʊvəkəʊt/ *n.* pardessus *m.*

overcome /əʊvə'kʌm/ *v.t.* (*p.t.* **-came**, *p.p.* **-come**) triompher de; (*difficulty*) surmonter, triompher de. **~ by**, accablé de.

overcrowded /əʊvə'kraʊdɪd/ *a.* bondé; (*country*) surpeuplé.

overdo /əʊvə'duː/ *v.t.* (*p.t.* **-did**, *p.p.* **-done**) exagérer; (*culin.*) trop cuire. **~ it**, (*overwork*) se surmener.

overdose /'əʊvədəʊs/ *n.* overdose *f.*, surdose *f.*

overdraft /'əʊvədrɑːft/ *n.* découvert *m.*

overdraw /əʊvə'drɔː/ *v.t.* (*p.t.* **-drew**, *p.p.* **-drawn**) (*one's account*) mettre à découvert.

overdrive /'əʊvədraɪv/ *n.* surmultipliée *f.*

overdue /əʊvə'djuː/ *a.* en retard; (*belated*) tardif; (*bill*) impayé.

overestimate /əʊvər'estɪmeɪt/ *v.t.* surestimer.

overexposed /əʊvərɪk'spəʊzd/ *a.* surexposé.

overflow[1] /əʊvə'fləʊ/ *v.i.* déborder.

overflow[2] /'əʊvəfləʊ/ *n.* (*outlet*) trop-plein *m.*

overgrown /əʊvə'grəʊn/ *a.* (*garden etc.*) envahi par la végétation.

overhang /əʊvə'hæŋ/ *v.t.* (*p.t.* **-hung**) surplomber. —*v.i.* faire saillie.

overhaul[1] /əʊvə'hɔːl/ *v.t.* réviser.

overhaul[2] /'əʊvəhɔːl/ *n.* révision *f.*

overhead[1] /əʊvə'hed/ *adv.* audessus; (*in sky*) dans le ciel.

overhead[2] /'əʊvəhed/ *a.* aérien. **~s** *n. pl.* frais généraux *m. pl.* **~ projector**, rétroprojecteur *m.*

overhear /əʊvə'hɪə(r)/ *v.t.* (*p.t.* **-heard**) surprendre, entendre.

overjoyed /əʊvə'dʒɔɪd/ *a.* ravi.

overland *a.* /'əʊvəlænd/, *adv.* /əʊvə'lænd/ par voie de terre.

overlap /əʊvə'læp/ *v.t./i.* (*p.t.* **-lapped**) (se) chevaucher.

overleaf /əʊvə'liːf/ *adv.* au verso.

overload /əʊvə'ləʊd/ *v.t.* surcharger.

overlook /əʊvə'lʊk/ *v.t.* oublier, négliger; (*of window, house*) donner sur; (*of tower*) dominer.

overly /'əʊvəlɪ/ *adv.* excessivement.

overnight /əʊvə'naɪt/ *adv.* (pendant) la nuit; (*instantly; fig.*) du jour au lendemain. —*a.* /'əʊvənaɪt/ (*train etc.*) de nuit; (*stay etc.*) d'une nuit; (*fig.*) soudain.

overpay /əʊvə'peɪ/ *v.t.* (*p.t.* **-paid**) (*person*) surpayer.

overpower /əʊvə'paʊə(r)/ *v.t.* subjuguer; (*opponent*) maîtriser; (*fig.*) accabler. **~ing** *a.* irrésistible; (*heat, smell*) accablant.

overpriced /əʊvə'praɪst/ *a.* trop cher.

overrate /əʊvə'reɪt/ *v.t.* surestimer. **~d** /-ɪd/ *a.* surfait.

overreach /əʊvə'riːtʃ/ *v.* **~ o.s.**, trop entreprendre.

overreact /əʊvərɪ'ækt/ *v.i.* réagir excessivement.

overrid|e /əʊvə'raɪd/ *v.t.* (*p.t.* **-rode**, *p.p.* **-ridden**) passer outre à. **~ing** *a.* prépondérant; (*importance*) majeur.

overripe /'əʊvəraɪp/ *a.* trop mûr.

overrule /əʊvə'ruːl/ *v.t.* rejeter.

overrun /əʊvə'rʌn/ *v.t.* (*p.t.* **-ran**, *p.p.* **-run**, *pres. p.* **-running**) envahir; (*a limit*) aller au-delà de. —*v.i.* (*meeting*) durer plus longtemps que prévu.

overseas /əʊvə'siːz/ *a.* d'outre-mer,

étranger. —*adv.* outre-mer, à l'étranger.

oversee /əʊvə'siː/ *v.t.* (*p.t.* **-saw**, *p.p.* **-seen**) surveiller. ~**r** /'əʊvəsɪə(r)/ *n.* contremaître *m.*

overshadow /əʊvə'ʃædəʊ/ *v.t.* (*darken*) assombrir; (*fig.*) éclipser.

overshoot /əʊvə'ʃuːt/ *v.t.* (*p.t.* **-shot**) dépasser.

oversight /'əʊvəsaɪt/ *n.* omission *f.*

oversleep /əʊvə'sliːp/ *v.i.* (*p.t.* **-slept**) se réveiller trop tard.

overt /'əʊvɜːt/ *a.* manifeste.

overtake /əʊvə'teɪk/ *v.t./i.* (*p.t.* **-took**, *p.p.* **-taken**) dépasser; (*vehicle*) doubler, dépasser; (*surprise*) surprendre.

overtax /əʊvə'tæks/ *v.t.* (*strain*) fatiguer; (*taxpayer*) surimposer.

overthrow /əʊvə'θrəʊ/ *v.t.* (*p.t.* **-threw**, *p.p.* **-thrown**) renverser.

overtime /'əʊvətaɪm/ *n.* heures supplémentaires *f. pl.*

overtone /'əʊvətəʊn/ *n.* nuance *f.*

overture /'əʊvətjʊə(r)/ *n.* ouverture *f.*

overturn /əʊvə'tɜːn/ *v.t./i.* (se) renverser.

overweight /əʊvə'weɪt/ *a.* be ~, peser trop.

overwhelm /əʊvə'welm/ *v.t.* accabler; (*defeat*) écraser; (*amaze*) bouleverser. ~**ing** *a.* accablant; (*victory*) écrasant; (*urge*) irrésistible.

overwork /əʊvə'wɜːk/ *v.t./i.* (se) surmener. —*n.* surmenage *m.*

overwrought /əʊvə'rɔːt/ *a.* à bout.

ow|e /əʊ/ *v.t.* devoir. ~**ing** *a.* dû. ~**ing to**, à cause de.

owl /aʊl/ *n.* hibou *m.*

own[1] /əʊn/ *a.* propre. **a house**/*etc.* **of one's** ~, sa propre maison/*etc.*, une maison/*etc.* à soi. **get one's** ~ **back**, (*fam.*) prendre sa revanche. **hold one's** ~, bien se défendre. **on one's** ~, tout seul.

own[2] /əʊn/ *v.t.* posséder. ~ **up (to)**, (*fam.*) avouer. ~**er** *n.* propriétaire *m./f.* ~**ership** *n.* possession *f.* (**of**, de); (*right*) propriété *f.*

ox /ɒks/ *n.* (*pl.* **oxen**) bœuf *m.*

oxygen /'ɒksɪdʒən/ *n.* oxygène *m.*

oyster /'ɔɪstə(r)/ *n.* huître *f.*

ozone /'əʊzəʊn/ *n.* ozone *m.* ~ **layer**, couche d'ozone *f.*

P

pace /peɪs/ *n.* pas *m.*; (*speed*) allure *f.*; —*v.t.* (*room etc.*) arpenter. —*v.i.* ~

(**up and down**), faire les cent pas. **keep** ~ **with**, suivre.

pacemaker /'peɪsmeɪkə(r)/ *n.* (*med.*) stimulateur cardiaque *m.*

Pacific /pə'sɪfɪk/ *a.* pacifique. —*n.* ~ (**Ocean**), Pacifique *m.*

pacifist /'pæsɪfɪst/ *n.* pacifiste *m./f.*

pacif|y /'pæsɪfaɪ/ *v.t.* (*country*) pacifier; (*person*) apaiser. ~**ier** *n.* (*Amer.*) sucette *f.*

pack /pæk/ *n.* paquet *m.*; (*mil.*) sac *m.*; (*of hounds*) meute *f.*; (*of thieves*) bande *f.*; (*of lies*) tissu *m.* —*v.t.* emballer; (*suitcase*) faire; (*box, room*) remplir; (*press down*) tasser. —*v.i.* ~ (**one's bags**), faire ses valises. ~ **into**, (*cram*) (s')entasser dans. ~ **off**, expédier. **send** ~**ing**, envoyer promener. ~**ed** *a.* (*crowded*) bondé. ~**ed lunch**, repas froid *m.* ~**ing** *n.* (*action, material*) emballage *m.* ~**ing case**, caisse *f.*

package /'pækɪdʒ/ *n.* paquet *m.* —*v.t.* empaqueter. ~ **deal**, forfait *m.* ~ **tour**, voyage organisé *m.*

packet /'pækɪt/ *n.* paquet *m.*

pact /pækt/ *n.* pacte *m.*

pad[1] /pæd/ *n.* bloc(-notes) *m.*; (*for ink*) tampon *m.* (**launching**) ~, rampe (de lancement) *f.* —*v.t.* (*p.t.* **padded**) rembourrer; (*text: fig.*) délayer. ~**ding** *n.* rembourrage *m.*; délayage *m.*

pad[2] /pæd/ *v.i.* (*p.t.* **padded**) (*walk*) marcher à pas feutrés.

paddle[1] /'pædl/ *n.* pagaie *f.* —*v.t.* ~ **a canoe**, pagayer. ~**-steamer** *n.* bateau à roues *m.*

paddl|e[2] /'pædl/ *v.i.* barboter, se mouiller les pieds. ~**ing pool**, pataugeoire *f.*

paddock /'pædək/ *n.* paddock *m.*

paddy(-field) /'pædɪ(fiːld)/ *n.* rizière *f.*

padlock /'pædlɒk/ *n.* cadenas *m.* —*v.t.* cadenasser.

paediatrician /piːdɪə'trɪʃn/ *n.* pédiatre *m./f.*

pagan /'peɪgən/ *a. & n.* païen(ne) (*m. (f.)*).

page[1] /peɪdʒ/ *n.* (*of book etc.*) page *f.*

page[2] /peɪdʒ/ *n.* (*in hotel*) chasseur *m.* (*at wedding*) page *m.* —*v.t.* (faire) appeler.

pageant /'pædʒənt/ *n.* spectacle (historique) *m.* ~**ry** *n.* pompe *f.*

pagoda /pə'gəʊdə/ *n.* pagode *f.*

paid /peɪd/ *see* **pay**. —*a.* **put** ~ **to**, (*fam.*) mettre fin à.

pail /peɪl/ *n.* seau *m.*

pain /peɪn/ n. douleur f. ∿s, efforts m.
pl. —v.t. (grieve) peiner. **be in** ∿,
souffrir. **take** ∿s **to**, se donner du mal
pour. ∿-**killer** n. analgésique m. ∿**less**
a. indolore.
painful /ˈpeɪnfl/ a. douloureux;
(laborious) pénible.
painstaking /ˈpeɪnzteɪkɪŋ/ a. assidu,
appliqué.
paint /peɪnt/ n. peinture f. ∿s, (in tube,
box) couleurs f. pl. —v.t./i. peindre.
∿**er** n. peintre m. ∿**ing** n. peinture f.
paintbrush /ˈpeɪntbrʌʃ/ n. pinceau m.
paintwork /ˈpeɪntwɜːk/ n. peintures f.
pl.
pair /peə(r)/ n. paire f.; (of people)
couple m. **a** ∿ **of trousers**, un pantalon.
—v.i. ∿ **off**, (at dance etc.) former un
couple.
pajamas /pəˈdʒɑːməz/ n.pl. (Amer.)
pyjama m.
Pakistan /pɑːkɪˈstɑːn/ n. Pakistan. m.
∿**i** a. & n. pakistanais(e) (m. (f.)).
pal /pæl/ n. (fam.) coplain, -ine m., f.
palace /ˈpælɪs/ n. palais m.
palat|e /ˈpælət/ n. (of mouth) palais m.
∿**able** a. agréable au goût.
palatial /pəˈleɪʃl/ a. somptueux.
palaver /pəˈlɑːvə(r)/ n. (fuss: fam.)
histoire(s) f. (pl.).
pale /peɪl/ a. (-er, -est) pâle. —v.i. pâlir.
∿**ness** n. pâleur f.
Palestin|e /ˈpælɪstaɪn/ n. Palestine f.
∿**ian** /-ˈstɪnɪən/ a. & n. palestinien(ne)
(m. (f.)).
palette /ˈpælɪt/ n. palette f.
pall /pɔːl/ v.i. devenir insipide.
pallet /ˈpælɪt/ n. palette f.
pallid /ˈpælɪd/ a. pâle.
palm /pɑːm/ n. (of hand) paume f.;
(tree) palmier m.; (symbol) palme f.
—v.t. ∿ **off**, (thing) refiler, coller (on,
à); (person) coller. **P**∿ **Sunday**,
dimanche des Rameaux.
palmist /ˈpɑːmɪst/ n. chiromancien(ne)
m. (f.).
palpable /ˈpælpəbl/ a. manifeste.
palpitat|e /ˈpælpɪteɪt/ v.i. palpiter. ∿**ion**
/-ˈteɪʃn/ n. palpitation f.
paltry /ˈpɔːltrɪ/ a. (-ier, -iest) dérisoire,
piètre.
pamper /ˈpæmpə(r)/ v.t. dorloter.
pamphlet /ˈpæmflɪt/ n. brochure f.
pan /pæn/ n. casserole f.; (for frying)
poêle f.; (of lavatory) cuvette f. —v.t.
(p.t. **panned**) (fam.) critiquer.
panacea /pænəˈsɪə/ n. panacée f.
panache /pəˈnæʃ/ n. panache m.
pancake /ˈpænkeɪk/ n. crêpe f.

pancreas /ˈpæŋkrɪəs/ n. pancréas m.
panda /ˈpændə/ n. panda m. ∿ **car**,
voiture pie (de la police) f.
pandemonium /pændɪˈməʊnɪəm/ n.
tumulte m., chaos m.
pander /ˈpændə(r)/ v.i. ∿ **to**, (person,
taste) flatter bassement.
pane /peɪn/ n. carreau m., vitre f.
panel /ˈpænl/ n. (of door etc.) panneau
m.; (jury) jury m.; (speakers: TV)
invités m. pl. (instrument) ∿, tableau
de bord m. ∿ **of experts**, groupe
d'experts m. ∿**led** a. lambrissé. ∿**ling**
n. lambrissage m. ∿**list** n. (TV)
invité(e) (de tribune) m. (f.).
pang /pæŋ/ n. pincement au cœur m. ∿s,
(of hunger, death) affres f. pl. ∿s **of**
conscience, remords m. pl.
panic /ˈpænɪk/ n. panique f. —v.t./ i.
(p.t. **panicked**) (s')affoler, paniquer.
∿-**stricken** a. pris de panique, affolé.
panorama /pænəˈrɑːmə/ n. panorama
m.
pansy /ˈpænzɪ/ n. (bot.) pensée f.
pant /pænt/ v.i. haleter.
panther /ˈpænθə(r)/ n. panthère f.
panties /ˈpæntɪz/ n. pl. (fam.) slip m.,
culotte f. (de femme).
pantihose /ˈpæntɪhəʊz/ n. (Amer.)
collant m.
pantomime /ˈpæntəmaɪm/ n. (show)
spectacle de Noël m.; (mime) pantomime f.
pantry /ˈpæntrɪ/ n. office m.
pants /pænts/ n. pl. (underwear: fam.)
slip m.; (trousers: fam. & Amer.)
pantalon m.
papacy /ˈpeɪpəsɪ/ n. papauté f.
papal /ˈpeɪpl/ a. papal.
paper /ˈpeɪpə(r)/ n. papier m.;
(newspaper) journal m.; (exam)
épreuve f.; (essay) exposé m.;
(wallpaper) papier peint m. (identity)
∿s papiers (d'identité) m. pl. —v.t.
(room) tapisser. **on** ∿, par écrit. ∿-**clip**
n. trombone m.
paperback /ˈpeɪpəbæk/ a. & n. ∿
(book), livre broché m.
paperweight /ˈpeɪpəweɪt/ n. presse-
papiers m. invar.
paperwork /ˈpeɪpəwɜːk/ n. paperasserie
f.
paprika /ˈpæprɪkə/ n. paprika m.
par /pɑː(r)/ n. **be below** ∿, ne pas être en
forme. **on a** ∿ **with**, à égalité avec.
parable /ˈpærəbl/ n. parabole f.
parachut|e /ˈpærəʃuːt/ n. parachute m.
—v.i. descendre en parachute. ∿**ist** n.
parachutiste m./f.

parade /pə'reɪd/ *n.* (*procession*) défilé *m.*; (*ceremony, display*) parade *f.*; (*street*) avenue *f.* —*v.i.* défiler. —*v.t.* faire parade de.

paradise /'pærədaɪs/ *n.* paradis *m.*

paradox /'pærədɒks/ *n.* paradoxe *m.* ∼**ical** /-'dɒksɪkl/ *a.* paradoxal.

paraffin /'pærəfɪn/ *n.* pétrole (lampant) *m.*; (*wax*) paraffine *f.*

paragon /'pærəgən/ *n.* modèle *m.*

paragraph /'pærəgrɑːf/ *n.* paragraphe *m.*

parallel /'pærəlel/ *a.* parallèle. —*n.* (*line*) parallèle *f.*; (*comparison & geog.*) parallèle *m.* —*v.t.* (*p.t.* **paralleled**) être semblable à; (*match*) égaler.

paralyse /'pærəlaɪz/ *v.t.* paralyser.

paraly|**sis** /pə'ræləsɪs/ *n.* paralysie *f.* ∼**tic** /pærə'lɪtɪk/ *a. & n.* paralytique (*m./f.*).

paramedic /pærə'medɪk/ *n.* auxiliaire médical(e) *m.* (*f.*).

parameter /pə'ræmɪtə(r)/ *n.* paramètre *m.*

paramount /'pærəmaʊnt/ *a.* primordial, fondamental.

paranoi|**a** /pærə'nɔɪə/ *n.* paranoïa *f.* ∼**d** *a.* paranoïaque; (*fam.*) parano *invar.*

parapet /'pærəpɪt/ *n.* parapet *m.*

paraphernalia /pærəfə'neɪlɪə/ *n.* attirail *m.*, équipement *m.*

paraphrase /'pærəfreɪz/ *n.* paraphrase *f.* —*v.t.* paraphraser.

parasite /'pærəsaɪt/ *n.* parasite *m.*

parasol /'pærəsɒl/ *n.* ombrelle *f.*; (*on table, at beach*) parasol *m.*

paratrooper /'pærətruːpə(r)/ *n.* (*mil.*) parachutiste *m/f.*

parcel /'pɑːsl/ *n.* colis *m.*, paquet *m.* —*v.t.* (*p.t.* **parcelled**). ∼ **out**, diviser en parcelles.

parch /pɑːtʃ/ *v.t.* dessécher. **be** ∼**ed**, (*person*) avoir très soif.

parchment /'pɑːtʃmənt/ *n.* parchemin *m.*

pardon /'pɑːdn/ *n.* pardon *m.*; (*jurid.*) grâce *m.* —*v.t.* (*p.t.* **pardoned**) pardonner (**s.o. for sth.**, qch. à qn.); gracier. **I beg your** ∼, pardon.

pare /peə(r)/ *v.t.* (*clip*) rogner; (*peel*) éplucher.

parent /'peərənt/ *n.* père *m.*, mère *f.* ∼**s**, parents *m. pl.* ∼**al** /pə'rentl/ *a.* des parents. ∼**hood** *n.* l'état de parent *m.*

parenthesis /pə'renθəsɪs/ *n.* (*pl.* **-theses** /-siːz/) parenthèse *f.*

Paris /'pærɪs/ *n.* Paris *m./f.* ∼**ian** /pə'rɪzɪən, *Amer.* pə'riːʒn/ *a. & n.* parisien(ne) (*m.* (*f.*)).

parish /'pærɪʃ/ *n.* (*relig.*) paroisse *f.*; (*municipal*) commune *f.* ∼**ioner** /pə'rɪʃənə(r)/ *n.* paroissien(ne) *m.* (*f.*).

parity /'pærətɪ/ *n.* parité *f.*

park /pɑːk/ *n.* parc *m.* —*v.t./i.* (se) garer; (*remain parked*) stationner. ∼**ing-lot** *n.* (*Amer.*) parking *m.* ∼**ing-meter** *n.* parcmètre *m.* ∼**ing ticket,** procès-verbal *m.*

parka /'pɑːkə/ *n.* parka *m./f.*

parlance /'pɑːləns/ *n.* langage *m.*

parliament /'pɑːləmənt/ *n.* parlement *m.* ∼**ary** /-'mentrɪ/ *a.* parlementaire.

parlour, (*Amer.*) **parlor** /'pɑːlə(r)/ *n.* salon *m.*

parochial /pə'rəʊkɪəl/ *a.* (*relig.*) paroissial; (*fig.*) borné, provincial.

parody /'pærədɪ/ *n.* parodie *f.* —*v.t.* parodier.

parole /pə'rəʊl/ *n.* **on** ∼, en liberté conditionnelle.

parquet /'pɑːkeɪ/ *n.* parquet *m.*

parrot /'pærət/ *n.* perroquet *m.*

parry /'pærɪ/ *v.t.* (*sport*) parer; (*question etc.*) esquiver. —*n.* parade *f.*

parsimonious /pɑːsɪ'məʊnɪəs/ *a.* parcimonieux.

parsley /'pɑːslɪ/ *n.* persil *m.*

parsnip /'pɑːsnɪp/ *n.* panais *m.*

parson /'pɑːsn/ *n.* pasteur *m.*

part /pɑːt/ *n.* partie *f.*; (*of serial*) épisode *m.*; (*of machine*) pièce *f.*; (*theatre*) rôle *m.*; (*side in dispute*) parti *m.* —*a.* partiel. —*adv.* en partie. —*v.t./i.* (*separate*) (se) séparer. **in** ∼, en partie. **on the** ∼ **of,** de la part de. ∼**-exchange** *n.* reprise *f.* ∼ **of speech,** catégorie grammaticale *f.* ∼**-time** *a. & adv.* à temps partiel. ∼ **with,** se séparer de. **take** ∼ **in,** participer à. **in these** ∼**s,** dans la région, dans le coin.

partake /pɑː'teɪk/ *v.i.* (*p.t.* **-took**, *p.p.* **-taken**) participer (**in,** à).

partial /'pɑːʃl/ *a.* partiel; (*biased*) partial. **be** ∼ **to,** avoir une prédilection pour. ∼**ity** /-ɪ'ælətɪ/ *n.* (*bias*) partialité *f.*; (*fondness*) prédilection *f.* ∼**ly** *adv.* partiellement.

particip|**ate** /pɑː'tɪsɪpeɪt/ *v.i.* participer (**in,** à). ∼**ant** *n.* participant(e) *m.* (*f.*). ∼**ation** /-'peɪʃn/ *n.* participation *f.*

participle /'pɑːtɪsɪpl/ *n.* participe *m.*

particle /'pɑːtɪkl/ *n.* particule *f.*

particular /pə'tɪkjʊlə(r)/ *a.* particulier; (*fussy*) difficile; (*careful*) méticuleux. **that** ∼ **man,** cet homme-là en particulier. ∼**s** *n. pl.* détails *m. pl.* **in** ∼, en particulier. **~ly** adv. particulièrement.

parting /'pɑ:tɪŋ/ n. séparation f.; (in hair) raie f. —a. d'adieu.

partisan /pɑ:tɪ'zæn, Amer. 'pɑ:tɪzn/ n. partisan(e) m. (f.).

partition /pɑ:'tɪʃn/ n. (of room) cloison f.; (pol.) partage m., partition f. —v.t. (room) cloisonner; (country) partager.

partly /'pɑ:tlɪ/ adv. en partie.

partner /'pɑ:tnə(r)/ n. associé(e) m. (f.); (sport) partenaire m./f. **~ship** n. association f.

partridge /'pɑ:trɪdʒ/ n. perdrix f.

party /'pɑ:tɪ/ n. fête f.; (formal) réception f.; (for young people) boum f.; (group) groupe m., équipe f.; (pol.) parti m.; (jurid.) partie f. **~ line,** (telephone) ligne commune f.

pass /pɑ:s/ v.t./i. (p.t. passed) passer; (overtake) dépasser; (in exam) être reçu (à); (approve) accepter, autoriser; (remark) faire; (judgement) prononcer; (law, bill) voter. **~ (by),** (building) passer devant; (person) croiser. —n. (permit) laissez-passer m. invar.; (ticket) carte (d'abonnement) f.; (geog.) col m.; (sport) passe f. **~ (mark),** (in exam) moyenne f. **make a ~ at,** (fam.) faire des avances à. **~ away,** mourir. **~ out** or **round,** distribuer. **~ out,** (faint: fam.) s'évanouir. **~ over,** (overlook) passer sur. **~ up,** (forego: fam.) laisser passer.

passable /'pɑ:səbl/ a. (adequate) passable; (road) praticable.

passage /'pæsɪdʒ/ n. (way through, text, etc.) passage m.; (voyage) traversée f.; (corridor) couloir m.

passenger /'pæsɪndʒə(r)/ n. passagler, -ère m., f.; (in train) voyageulr, -se m., f.

passer-by /pɑ:sə'baɪ/ n. (pl. **passers-by**) passant(e) m. (f.).

passing /'pɑ:sɪŋ/ a. (fleeting) fugitif, passager.

passion /'pæʃn/ n. passion f. **~ate** a. passionné. **~ately** adv. passionnément.

passive /'pæsɪv/ a. passif. **~ness** n. passivité f.

Passover /'pɑ:səʊvə(r)/ n. Pâque f.

passport /'pɑ:spɔ:t/ n. passeport m.

password /'pɑ:swɜ:d/ n. mot de passe m.

past /pɑ:st/ a. passé; (former) ancien. —n. passé m. —prep. au-delà de; (in front of) devant. —adv. devant. **the ~ months,** ces derniers mois. **~ midnight,** minuit passé. **10 ~ 6,** six heures dix.

pasta /'pæstə/ n. pâtes f. pl.

paste /peɪst/ n. (glue) colle f.; (dough) pâte f.; (of fish, meat) pâté m.; (jewellery) strass m. —v.t. coller.

pastel /'pæstl/ n. pastel m. —a. pastel invar.

pasteurize /'pæstʃəraɪz/ v.t. pasteuriser.

pastiche /pæ'sti:ʃ/ n. pastiche m.

pastille /'pæstl/ n. pastille f.

pastime /'pɑ:staɪm/ n. passetemps m. invar.

pastoral /'pɑ:stərəl/ a. pastoral.

pastry /'peɪstrɪ/ n. (dough) pâte f.; (tart) pâtisserie f.

pasture /'pɑ:stʃə(r)/ n. pâturage m.

pasty[1] /'pæstɪ/ n. petit pâté m.

pasty[2] /'peɪstɪ/ a. pâteux.

pat /pæt/ v.t. (p.t. **patted**) tapoter. —n. petite tape f. —adv. & a. à propos; (ready) tout prêt.

patch /pætʃ/ n. pièce f.; (over eye) bandeau m.; (spot) tache f.; (of vegetables) carré m. —v.t. **~ up,** rapiécer; (fig.) régler. **bad ~,** période difficile f. **not be a ~ on,** ne pas arriver à la cheville de. **~y** a. inégal.

patchwork /'pætʃwɜ:k/ n. patchwork m.

pâté /'pæteɪ/ n. pâté m.

patent /'peɪtnt/ a. patent. —n. brevet (d'invention) m. —v.t. breveter. **~ leather,** cuir verni m. **~ly** adv. manifestement.

paternal /pə'tɜ:nl/ a. paternel.

paternity /pə'tɜ:nətɪ/ n. paternité f.

path /pɑ:θ/ n. (pl. **-s** /pɑ:ðz/) sentier m., chemin m.; (in park) allée f.; (of rocket) trajectoire f.

pathetic /pə'θetɪk/ a. pitoyable; (bad: fam.) minable.

pathology /pə'θɒlədʒɪ/ n. pathologie f.

pathos /'peɪθɒs/ n. pathétique m.

patience /'peɪʃns/ n. patience f.

patient /'peɪʃnt/ a. patient. —n. malade m./f., patient(e) m. (f.). **~ly** adv. patiemment.

patio /'pætɪəʊ/ n. (pl. **-os**) patio m.

patriot /'pætrɪət, 'peɪtrɪət/ n. patriote m./f. **~ic** /-'ɒtɪk/ a. patriotique; (person) patriote. **~ism** n. patriotisme m.

patrol /pə'trəʊl/ n. patrouille f. —v.t./i. patrouiller (dans). **~ car,** voiture de police f.

patrolman /pə'trəʊlmən/ n. (pl. **-men** /-men/) (Amer.) agent de police m.

patron /'peɪtrən/ n. (of the arts) mécène m. (customer) client(e) m. (f.). **~ saint,** saint(e) patron(ne) m. (f.).

patron|age /'pætrənɪdʒ/ n. clientèle f.; (support) patronage m. **~ize** v.t. être client de; (*fig.*) traiter avec condescendance.

patter¹ /'pætə(r)/ n. (*of steps*) bruit m.; (*of rain*) crépitement m.

patter² /'pætə(r)/ n. (*speech*) baratin m.

pattern /'pætn/ n. motif m., dessin m.; (*for sewing*) patron m.; (*procedure, type*) schéma m.; (*example*) exemple m.

paunch /pɔːntʃ/ n. panse f.

pauper /'pɔːpə/ n. indigent(e) m. (f.), pauvre m., pauvresse f.

pause /pɔːz/ n. pause f. —v.i. faire une pause; (*hesitate*) hésiter.

pav|e /peɪv/ v.t. paver. ~**e the way,** ouvrir la voie (**for,** à). ~**ing-stone** n. pavé m.

pavement /'peɪvmənt/ n. trottoir m.; (*Amer.*) chaussée f.

pavilion /pə'vɪljən/ n. pavillon m.

paw /pɔː/ n. patte f. —v.t. (*of animal*) donner des coups de patte à; (*touch: fam.*) tripoter.

pawn¹ /pɔːn/ n. (*chess & fig.*) pion m.

pawn² /pɔːn/ v.t. mettre en gage. —n. **in** ~, en gage. ~**-shop** n. mont-de-piété m.

pawnbroker /'pɔːnbrəʊkə(r)/ n. prêteur sur gages m.

pay /peɪ/ v.t./i. (*p.t.* **paid**) payer; (*yield: comm.*) rapporter; (*compliment, visit*) faire. —n. salaire m., paie f. **in the** ~ **of,** à la solde de. ~ **attention,** faire attention (**to,** à). ~ **back,** rembourser. ~ **for,** payer. ~ **homage,** rendre hommage (**to,** à). ~ **in,** verser (**to,** à). ~ **off,** (finir de) payer; (*succeed: fam.*) être payant. ~ **out,** payer, verser.

payable /'peɪəbl/ a. payable.

payment /'peɪmənt/ n. paiement m.; (*regular*) versement m. (*reward*) récompense f.

payroll /'peɪrəʊl/ n. registre du personnel m. **be on the** ~ **of,** être membre du personnel du.

pea /piː/ n. (petit) pois m. ~**-shooter** n. sarbacane f.

peace /piːs/ n. paix f. ~ **of mind,** tranquillité d'esprit f. ~**able** a. pacifique.

peaceful /'piːsfl/ a. paisible; (*intention, measure*) pacifique.

peacemaker /'piːsmeɪkə(r)/ n. conciliateur, -trice m., f.

peach /piːtʃ/ n. pêche f.

peacock /'piːkɒk/ n. paon m.

peak /piːk/ n. sommet m.; (*of mountain*) pic m.; (*maximum*) maximum m. ~ **hours,** heures de pointe f. pl. ~**ed cap,** casquette f.

peaky /'piːkɪ/ a. (*pale*) pâlot; (*puny*) chétif; (*ill*) patraque.

peal /piːl/ n. (*of bells*) carillon m.; (*of laughter*) éclat m.

peanut /'piːnʌt/ n. cacahuète f. ~**s,** (*money: sl.*) une bagatelle.

pear /peə(r)/ n. poire f.

pearl /pɜːl/ n. perle f. ~**y** a. nacré.

peasant /'peznt/ n. paysan(ne) m. (f.).

peat /piːt/ n. tourbe f.

pebble /'pebl/ n. caillou m.; (*on beach*) galet m.

peck /pek/ v.t./i. (*food etc.*) picorer; (*attack*) donner des coups de bec (à). —n. coup de bec m. **a** ~ **on the cheek,** une bise.

peckish /'pekɪʃ/ a. **be** ~, (*fam.*) avoir faim.

peculiar /pɪ'kjuːlɪə(r)/ a. (*odd*) bizarre; (*special*) particulier (**to,** à). ~**ity** /-'ærətɪ/ n. bizarrerie f.

pedal /'pedl/ n. pédale f. —v.i. pédaler.

pedantic /pɪ'dæntɪk/ a. pédant.

peddle /'pedl/ v.t. colporter; (*drugs*) revendre.

pedestal /'pedɪstl/ n. piédestal m.

pedestrian /pɪ'destrɪən/ n. piéton m. —a. (*precinct, street*) piétonnier; (*fig.*) prosaïque. ~ **crossing,** passage piétons m.

pedigree /'pedɪɡriː/ n. (*of person*) ascendance f.; (*of animal*) pedigree m. —a. (*cattle etc.*) de race.

pedlar /'pedlə(r)/ n. camelot m.; (*door-to-door*) colporteur, -se m., f.

pee /piː/ v.i. (*fam.*) faire pipi.

peek /piːk/ v.i. & n. = **peep**¹.

peel /piːl/ n. épluchure(s) f. (*pl.*); (*of orange*) écorce f. —v.t. (*fruit, vegetables*) éplucher. —v.i. (*of skin*) peler; (*of paint*) s'écailler. ~**ings** n. pl. épluchures f. pl.

peep¹ /piːp/ v.i. jeter un coup d'œil (furtif) (**at,** à). —n. coup d'œil (furtif) m. ~**-hole** n. judas m. **P**~**ing Tom,** voyeur m.

peep² /piːp/ v.i. (*chirp*) pépier.

peer¹ /pɪə(r)/ v.i. ~ (**at**), regarder attentivement, scruter.

peer² /pɪə(r)/ n. (*equal, noble*) pair m. ~**age** n. pairie f.

peeved /piːvd/ a. (*sl.*) irrité.

peevish /'piːvɪʃ/ a. grincheux.

peg /peɡ/ n. cheville f.; (*for clothes*) pince à linge f.; (*to hang coats etc.*) patère f.; (*for tent*) piquet m. —v.t. (*p.t.* **pegged**) (*prices*) stabiliser. **buy off the** ~, acheter en prêt-à-porter.

pejorative /pɪ'dʒɒrətɪv/ a. péjoratif.

pelican /'pelɪkən/ n. pélican m. ~ **crossing**, passage clouté (avec feux de signalisation) m.

pellet /'pelɪt/ n. (round mass) boulette f.; (for gun) plomb m.

pelt[1] /pelt/ n. (skin) peau f.

pelt[2] /pelt/ v.t. bombarder (with, de). —v.i. pleuvoir à torrents.

pelvis /'pelvɪs/ n. (anat.) bassin m.

pen[1] /pen/ n. (for sheep etc.) enclos m.; (for baby, cattle) parc m.

pen[2] /pen/ n. stylo m.; (to be dipped in ink) plume f. —v.t. (p.t. **penned**) écrire. ~**-friend** n. correspondant(e) n. (f.). ~**-name** n. pseudonyme m.

penal /'piːnl/ a. pénal. ~**ize** v.t. pénaliser; (fig.) handicaper.

penalty /'penltɪ/ n. peine f.; (fine) amende f.; (sport) pénalité f.

penance /'penəns/ n. pénitence f.

pence /pens/ see penny.

pencil /'pensl/ n. crayon m. —v.t. (p.t. **pencilled**) crayonner. ~ **in**, noter provisoirement. ~**-sharpener** n. taille-crayon(s) m.

pendant /'pendənt/ n. pendentif m.

pending /'pendɪŋ/ a. en suspens. —prep. (until) en attendant.

pendulum /'pendjʊləm/ n. pendule m.; (of clock) balancier m.

penetrat|e /'penɪtreɪt/ v.t. (enter) pénétrer dans; (understand, permeate) pénétrer. —v.i. pénétrer. ~**ing** a. pénétrant. ~**ion** /-'treɪʃn/ n. pénétration f.

penguin /'peŋgwɪn/ n. manchot m., pingouin m.

penicillin /penɪ'sɪlɪn/ n. pénicilline f.

peninsula /pə'nɪnsjʊlə/ n. péninsule f.

penis /'piːnɪs/ n. pénis m.

peniten|t /'penɪtənt/ a. & n. pénitent(e) (m. (f.)). ~**ce** n. pénitence f.

penitentiary /penɪ'tenʃərɪ/ n. (Amer.) prison f., pénitencier m.

penknife /'pennaɪf/ n. (pl. **-knives**) canif m.

pennant /'penənt/ n. flamme f.

penniless /'penɪlɪs/ a. sans le sou.

penny /'penɪ/ n. (pl. **pennies** or **pence**) penny m.; (fig.) sou m.

pension /'penʃn/ n. pension f.; (for retirement) retraite f. —v.t. ~ **off**, mettre à la retraite. ~ **scheme**, caisse de retraite f. ~**able** a. qui a droit à une retraite. ~**er** n. (old-age) ~**er**, retraité(e) m. (f.), personne âgée f.

pensive /'pensɪv/ a. pensif.

Pentecost /'pentɪkɒst/ n. Pentecôte f. ~**al** a. pentecôtiste.

penthouse /'penthaʊs/ n. appartement de luxe m. (sur le toit d'un immeuble).

pent-up /'pentʌp/ a. refoulé.

penultimate /pen'ʌltɪmət/ a. avant-dernier.

people /'piːpl/ n. pl. gens m. pl., personnes f. pl. —n. peuple m. —v.t. peupler. **English**/etc. ~, les Anglais/etc. m. pl. ~ **say**, on dit.

pep /pep/ n. entrain m. —v.t. ~ **up**, donner de l'entrain à. ~ **talk**, discours d'encouragement m.

pepper /'pepə(r)/ n. poivre m.; (vegetable) poivron m. —v.t. (culin.) poivrer. ~**y** a. poivré.

peppermint /'pepəmɪnt/ n. (plant) menthe poivrée f.; (sweet) bonbon à la menthe m.

per /pɜː(r)/ prep. par. ~ **annum**, par an. ~ **cent**, pour cent. ~ **kilo**/etc., le kilo/etc. **ten km.** ~ **hour**, dix km à l'heure.

perceive /pə'siːv/ v.t. percevoir; (notice) s'apercevoir de. ~ **that**, s'apercevoir que.

percentage /pə'sentɪdʒ/ n. pourcentage m.

perceptible /pə'septəbl/ a. perceptible.

percept|ion /pə'sepʃn/ n. perception f. ~**ive** /-tɪv/ a. pénétrant.

perch /pɜːtʃ/ n. (of bird) perchoir m. —v.i. (se) percher.

percolat|e /'pɜːkəleɪt/ v.t. passer. —v.i. filtrer. ~**or** n. cafetière f.

percussion /pə'kʌʃn/ n. percussion f.

peremptory /pə'remptərɪ/ a. péremptoire.

perennial /pə'renɪəl/ a. perpétuel; (plant) vivace.

perfect[1] /'pɜːfɪkt/ a. parfait. ~**ly** adv. parfaitement.

perfect[2] /pə'fekt/ v.t. parfaire, mettre au point. ~**ion** /-kʃn/ n. perfection f. **to** ~**ion**, à la perfection. ~**ionist** /-kʃənɪst/ n. perfectionniste m./f.

perforat|e /'pɜːfəreɪt/ v.t. perforer. ~**ion** /-'reɪʃn/ n. perforation f.; (line of holes) pointillé m.

perform /pə'fɔːm/ v.t. exécuter, faire; (a function) remplir; (mus., theatre) interpréter, jouer. —v.i. jouer; (behave, function) se comporter. ~**ance** n. exécution f.; interprétation f.; (of car, team) performance f.; (show) représentation f.; séance f.; (fuss) histoire f. ~**er** n. artiste m./f.

perfume /'pɜːfjuːm/ n. parfum m.

perfunctory /pə'fʌŋktərɪ/ a. négligent, superficiel.

perhaps /pə'hæps/ *adv.* peut-être.

peril /'perəl/ *n.* péril *m.* ~**ous** *a.* périlleux.

perimeter /pə'rɪmɪtə(r)/ *n.* périmètre *m.*

period /'pɪərɪəd/ *n.* période *f.*, époque *f.*; (*era*) époque *f.*; (*lesson*) cours *m.*; (*gram.*) point *m.*; (*med.*) règles *f. pl.* —*a.* d'époque. ~**ic** /-'ɒdɪk/ *a.* périodique. ~**ically** /-'ɒdɪklɪ/ *adv.* périodiquement.

periodical /pɪərɪ'ɒdɪkl/ *n.* périodique *m.*

peripher|y /pə'rɪfərɪ/ *n.* périphérie *f.* ~**al** *a.* périphérique; (*of lesser importance*: *fig.*) accessoire; *n.* (*comput.*) périphérique *m.*

periscope /'perɪskəʊp/ *n.* périscope *m.*

perish /'perɪʃ/ *v.i.* périr; (*rot*) se détériorer. ~**able** *a.* périssable.

perjur|e /'pɜːdʒə(r)/ *v. pr.* ~**e o.s.,** se parjurer. ~**y** *n.* parjure *m.*

perk[1] /pɜːk/ *v.t./i.* ~ **up**, (*fam.*) (se) remonter. ~**y** *a.* (*fam.*) gai.

perk[2] /pɜːk/ *n.* (*fam.*) avantage *m.*

perm /pɜːm/ *n.* permanente *f.* —*v.t.* **have one's hair** ~**ed,** se faire faire une permanente.

permanen|t /'pɜːmənənt/ *a.* permanent. ~**ce** *n.* permanence *f.* ~**tly** *adv.* à titre permanent.

permeable /'pɜːmɪəbl/ *a.* perméable.

permeate /'pɜːmɪeɪt/ *v.t.* imprégner, se répandre dans.

permissible /pə'mɪsəbl/ *a.* permis.

permission /pə'mɪʃn/ *n.* permission *f.*

permissive /pə'mɪsɪv/ *a.* tolérant, laxiste. ~**ness** *n.* laxisme *m.*

permit[1] /pə'mɪt/ *v.t.* (*p.t.* **permitted**) permettre (**s.o. to,** à qn. de), autoriser (**s.o. to,** qn. à).

permit[2] /pə'mɪt/ *n.* permis *m.*; (*pass*) laissez-passer *m. invar.*

permutation /pɜːmjʊ'teɪʃn/ *n.* permutation *f.*

pernicious /pə'nɪʃəs/ *a.* nocif, pernicieux; (*med.*) pernicieux.

peroxide /pə'rɒksaɪd/ *n.* eau oxygénée *f.*

perpendicular /pɜːpən'dɪkjʊlə(r)/ *a. & n.* perpendiculaire (*f.*).

perpetrat|e /'pɜːpɪtreɪt/ *v.t.* perpétrer. ~**or** *n.* auteur *m.*

perpetual /pə'petʃʊəl/ *a.* perpétuel.

perpetuate /pə'petʃʊeɪt/ *v.t.* perpétuer.

perplex /pə'pleks/ *v.t.* rendre perplexe. ~**ed** *a.* perplexe. ~**ing** *a.* déroutant. ~**ity** *n.* perplexité *f.*

persecut|e /'pɜːsɪkjuːt/ *v.t.* persécuter. ~**ion** /-'kjuːʃn/ *n.* persécution *f.*

persever|e /pɜːsɪ'vɪə(r)/ *v.i.* persévérer. ~**ance** *n.* persévérance *f.*

Persian /'pɜːʃn/ *a. & n.* (*lang.*) persan (*m.*). ~ **Gulf,** golfe persique *m.*

persist /pə'sɪst/ *v.i.* persister (**in doing,** à faire). ~**ence** *n.* persistance *f.* ~**ent** *a.* (*cough, snow, etc.*) persistant; (*obstinate*) obstiné; (*continual*) continuel. ~**ently** *adv.* avec persistance.

person /'pɜːsn/ *n.* personne *f.* **in** ~, en personne. ~**able** *a.* beau.

personal /'pɜːsənl/ *a.* personnel; (*hygiene, habits*) intime; (*secretary*) particulier. ~**ly** *adv.* personnellement. ~ **stereo,** baladeur *m.*

personality /pɜːsə'nælətɪ/ *n.* personnalité *f.*; (*on TV*) vedette *f.*

personify /pə'sɒnɪfaɪ/ *v.t.* personnifier.

personnel /pɜːsə'nel/ *n.* personnel *m.*

perspective /pə'spektɪv/ *n.* perspective *f.*

Perspex /'pɜːspeks/ *n.* (P.) plexiglas *m.* (P.).

perspir|e /pə'spaɪə(r)/ *v.i.* transpirer. ~**ation** /-ə'reɪʃn/ *n.* transpiration *f.*

persua|de /pə'sweɪd/ *v.t.* persuader (**to, de**). ~**sion** /-eɪʒn/ *n.* persuasion *f.*

persuasive /pə'sweɪsɪv/ *a.* (*person, speech, etc.*) persuasif. ~**ly** *adv.* d'une manière persuasive.

pert /pɜːt/ *a.* (*saucy*) impertinent; (*lively*) plein d'entrain. ~**ly** *adv.* avec impertinence.

pertain /pə'teɪn/ *v.i.* ~ **to,** se rapporter à.

pertinent /'pɜːtɪnənt/ *a.* pertinent. ~**ly** *adv.* pertinemment.

perturb /pə'tɜːb/ *v.t.* troubler.

Peru /pə'ruː/ *n.* Pérou *m.* ~**vian** *a. & n.* péruvien(ne) (*m.* (*f.*)).

perus|e /pə'ruːz/ *v.t.* lire (attentivement). ~**al** *n.* lecture *f.*

perva|de /pə'veɪd/ *v.t.* imprégner, envahir. ~**sive** *a.* (*mood, dust*) envahissant.

pervers|e /pə'vɜːs/ *a.* (*stubborn*) entêté; (*wicked*) pervers. ~**ity** *n.* perversité *f.*

perver|t[1] /pə'vɜːt/ *v.t.* pervertir. ~**sion** *n.* perversion *f.*

perver|t[2] /'pɜːvɜːt/ *n.* perverti(e) *m.* (*f.*), dépravé(e) *m.* (*f.*).

peseta /pə'seɪtə/ *n.* peseta *f.*

pessimis|t /'pesɪmɪst/ *n.* pessimiste *m./f.* ~**m** /-zəm/ *n.* pessimisme *m.* ~**tic** /-'mɪstɪk/ *a.* pessimiste. ~**tically** /-'mɪstɪklɪ/ *adv.* avec pessimisme.

pest /pest/ *n.* insecte *or* animal nuisible *m.*; (*person: fam.*) enquiquineu|r, -se *m.*, *f.*

pester /'pestə(r)/ *v.t.* harceler.

pesticide /'pestisaid/ *n.* pesticide *m.*, insecticide *m.*

pet /pet/ *n.* animal (domestique) *m.*; (*favourite*) chouchou(te) *m.* (*f.*). —*a.* (*tame*) apprivoisé. —*v.t.* (*p.t.* petted) caresser; (*sexually*) peloter. ~ **hate,** bête noire *f.* ~ **name,** diminutif *m.*

petal /'petl/ *n.* pétale *m.*

peter /'pi:tə(r)/ *v.i.* ~ **out,** (*supplies*) s'épuiser; (*road*) finir.

petite /pə'ti:t/ *a.* (*woman*) menue.

petition /pı'tıʃn/ *n.* pétition *f.* —*v.t.* adresser une pétition à.

petrify /'petrıfaı/ *v.t.* pétrifier; (*scare; fig.*) pétrifier de peur.

petrol /'petrəl/ *n.* essence *f.* ~ **bomb,** cocktail molotov *m.* ~ **station,** station-service *f.* ~ **tank,** réservoir d'essence.

petroleum /pı'trəuliəm/ *n.* pétrole *m.*

petticoat /'petıkəut/ *n.* jupon *m.*

petty /'petı/ *a.* (**-ier, -iest**) (*minor*) petit; (*mean*) mesquin. ~ **cash,** petite caisse *f.*

petulan|t /'petjulənt/ *a.* irritable. ~**ce** *n.* irritabilité *f.*

pew /pju:/ *n.* banc (d'église) *m.*

pewter /'pju:tə(r)/ *n.* étain *m.*

phallic /'fælık/ *a.* phallique.

phantom /'fæntəm/ *n.* fantôme *m.*

pharmaceutical /fɑ:mə'sju:tıkl/ *a.* pharmaceutique.

pharmac|y /'fɑ:məsı/ *n.* pharmacie *f.* ~**ist** *n.* pharmacien(ne) *m.* (*f.*).

pharyngitis /færın'dʒaıtıs/ *n.* pharyngite *f.*

phase /feız/ *n.* phase *f.* —*v.t.* ~ **in/out,** introduire/retirer progressivement.

pheasant /'feznt/ *n.* faisan *m.*

phenomen|on /fı'nɒmınən/ *n.* (*pl.* **-ena**) phénomène *m.* ~**al** *a.* phénoménal.

phew /fju:/ *int.* ouf.

phial /'faıəl/ *n.* fiole *f.*

philanderer /fı'lændərə(r)/ *n.* coureur (de femmes) *m.*

philanthrop|ist /fı'lænθrəpıst/ *n.* philanthrope *m./f.* ~**ic** /-ən'θrɒpık/ *a.* philanthropique.

philatel|y /fı'lætəlı/ *n.* philatélie *f.* ~**ist** *n.* philatéliste *m./f.*

philharmonic /fılɑ:'mɒnık/ *a.* philharmonique.

Philippines /'fılıpi:nz/ *n. pl.* **the** ~, les Philippines *f. pl.*

philistine /'fılıstaın, *Amer.* 'fılısti:n/ *n.* philistin *m.*

philosoph|y /fı'lɒsəfı/ *n.* philosophie *f.* ~**er** *n.* philosophe *m./f.* ~**ical** /-ə'sɒfıkl/ *a.* philosophique; (*resigned*) philosophe.

phlegm /flem/ *n.* (*med.*) mucosité *f.*

phlegmatic /fleg'mætık/ *a.* flegmatique.

phobia /'fəubıə/ *n.* phobie *f.*

phone /fəun/ *n.* téléphone *m.* —*v.t.* (*person*) téléphoner à; (*message*) téléphoner. —*v.i.* téléphoner. ~ **back,** rappeler. **on the** ~, au téléphone. ~ **book,** annuaire *m.* ~ **box,** ~ **booth,** cabine téléphonique *f.* ~ **call,** coup de fil *m.* ~**in** *n.* émission à ligne ouverte *f.*

phonecard /'fəunkɑ:d/ *n.* télécarte *f.*

phonetic /fə'netık/ *a.* phonétique.

phoney /'fəunı/ *a.* (**-ier, -iest**) (*sl.*) faux. —*n.* (*person: sl.*) charlatan *m.* **it's a** ~, (*sl.*) c'est faux.

phosphate /'fɒsfeıt/ *n.* phosphate *m.*

phosphorus /'fɒsfərəs/ *n.* phosphore *m.*

photo /'fəutəu/ *n.* (*pl.* **-os**) (*fam.*) photo *f.*

photocop|y /'fəutəukɒpı/ *n.* photocopie *f.* —*v.t.* photocopier. ~**ier** *n.* photocopieuse *f.*

photogenic /fəutəu'dʒenık/ *a.* photogénique.

photograph /'fəutəgrɑ:f/ *n.* photographie *f.* —*v.t.* photographier. ~**er** /fə'tɒgrəfə(r)/ *n.* photographe *m./f.* ~**ic** /-'græfık/ *a.* photographique. ~**y** /fə'tɒgrəfı/ *n.* (*activity*) photographie *f.*

phrase /freız/ *n.* expression *f.*; (*idiom & gram.*) locution *f.* —*v.t.* exprimer, formuler. ~**-book** *n.* guide de conversation *m.*

physical /'fızıkl/ *a.* physique. ~**ly** *adv.* physiquement.

physician /fı'zıʃn/ *n.* médecin *m.*

physicist /'fızısıst/ *n.* physicien(ne) *m.* (*f.*).

physics /'fızıks/ *n.* physique *f.*

physiology /fızı'ɒlədʒı/ *n.* physiologie *f.*

physiotherap|y /fızıəʊ'θerəpı/ *n.* kinésithérapie *f.* ~**ist** *n.* kinésithérapeute *m./f.*

physique /fı'zi:k/ *n.* constitution *f.*; (*appearance*) physique *m.*

pian|o /pı'ænəu/ *n.* (*pl.* **-os**) piano *m.* ~**ist** /'pıənıst/ *n.* pianiste *m./f.*

piazza /pı'ætsə/ *n.* (*square*) place *f.*

pick[1] /pık/ *n.* (*tool*) *n.* pioche *f.*

pick[2] /pık/ *v.t.* choisir; (*flower etc.*) cueillir; (*lock*) crocheter; (*nose*) se curer; (*pockets*) faire. ~ (**off**), enlever. —*n.* choix *m.*; (*best*) meilleur(e) *m.* (*f.*). ~ **a quarrel with,** chercher querelle à. ~ **holes in,** relever les défauts de. **the** ~ **of,** ce qu'il y a de mieux dans. ~ **off,** (*mil.*) abattre un à un. ~ **on,** harceler. ~ **out,** choisir; (*identify*) distinguer. ~ **up** *v.t.*

ramasser; (*sth. fallen*) relever; (*weight*) soulever; (*habit, passenger, speed, etc.*) prendre; (*learn*) apprendre; *v.i.* s'améliorer. **∼-me-up** *n.* remontant *m.* **∼-up** *n.* partenaire de rencontre *m./f.*; (*truck, stylus-holder*) pick-up *m.*

pickaxe /'pɪkæks/ *n.* pioche *f.*

picket /'pɪkɪt/ *n.* (*single striker*) gréviste *m./f.*; (*stake*) piquet *m.* **∼ (line)**, piquet de grève *m.* —*v.t.* (*p.t.* **picketed**) mettre un piquet de grève devant.

pickings /'pɪkɪŋz/ *n. pl.* restes *m. pl.*

pickle /'pɪkl/ *n.* vinaigre *m.*; (*brine*) saumure *f.* **∼s**, pickles *m. pl.*; (*Amer.*) concombres *m.pl.* —*v.t.* conserver dans du vinaigre *or* de la saumure. **in a ∼**, (*fam.*) dans le pétrin.

pickpocket /'pɪkpɒkɪt/ *n.* (*thief*) pickpocket *m.*

picnic /'pɪknɪk/ *n.* pique-nique *m.* —*v.i.* (*p.t.* **picnicked**) piqueniquer.

pictorial /pɪk'tɔːrɪəl/ *a.* illustré.

picture /'pɪktʃə(r)/ *n.* image *f.*; (*painting*) tableau *m.*; (*photograph*) photo *f.*; (*drawing*) dessin *m.*; (*film*) film *m.*; (*fig.*) description *f.*, tableau *m.* —*v.t.* s'imaginer; (*describe*) dépeindre. **the ∼s**, (*cinema*) le cinéma. **∼ book**, livre d'images *m.*

picturesque /pɪktʃə'resk/ *a.* pittoresque.

piddling /'pɪdlɪŋ/ *a.* (*fam.*) dérisoire.

pidgin /'pɪdʒɪn/ *a.* **∼ English**, pidgin *m.*

pie /paɪ/ *n.* tarte *f.*; (*of meat*) pâté en croûte *m.* **∼ chart**, camembert *m.*

piebald /'paɪbɔːld/ *a.* pie *invar.*

piece /piːs/ *n.* morceau *m.*; (*of currency, machine, etc.*) pièce *f.* —*v.t.* **∼ (together)**, (r)assembler. **a ∼ of advice/furniture/***etc.*, un conseil/meuble/ *etc.* **∼-work** *n.* travail à la pièce *m.* **go to ∼s**, (*fam.*) s'effondrer. **take to ∼s**, démonter.

piecemeal /'piːsmiːl/ *a.* par bribes.

pier /pɪə(r)/ *n.* (*promenade*) jetée *f.*

pierc|e /pɪəs/ *v.t.* percer. **∼ing** *a.* perçant; (*cold*) glacial.

piety /'paɪətɪ/ *n.* piété *f.*

piffl|e /'pɪfl/ *n.* (*sl.*) fadaises *f. pl.* **∼ing** *a.* (*sl.*) insignifiant.

pig /pɪg/ *n.* cochon *m.* **∼-headed** *a.* entêté.

pigeon /'pɪdʒən/ *n.* pigeon *m.* **∼-hole** *n.* casier *m.*; *v.t.* classer.

piggy /'pɪgɪ/ *a.* porcin; (*greedy: fam.*) goinfre. **∼-back** *adv.* sur le dos. **∼ bank**, tirelire *f.*

pigment /'pɪgmənt/ *n.* pigment *m.* **∼ation** /-en'teɪʃn/ *n.* pigmentation *f.*

pigsty /'pɪgstaɪ/ *n.* porcherie *f.*

pigtail /'pɪgteɪl/ *n.* natte *f.*

pike /paɪk/ *n. invar.* (*fish*) brochet *m.*

pilchard /'pɪltʃəd/ *n.* pilchard *m.*

pile /paɪl/ *n.* pile *f.*, tas *m.*; (*of carpet*) poils *m.pl.* —*v.t.* **∼ (up)**, (*stack*) empiler. —*v.i.* **∼ into**, s'empiler dans. **∼ up**, (*accumulate*) (s')accumuler. **a ∼ of**, (*fam.*) un tas de. **∼-up** *n.* (*auto.*) carambolage *m.*

piles /paɪlz/ *n. pl.* (*fam.*) hémorroïdes *f. pl.*

pilfer /'pɪlfə(r)/ *v.t.* chaparder. **∼age** *n.* chapardage *m.*

pilgrim /'pɪlgrɪm/ *n.* pèlerin *m.* **∼age** *n.* pèlerinage *m.*

pill /pɪl/ *n.* pilule *f.*

pillage /'pɪlɪdʒ/ *n.* pillage *m.* —*v.t.* piller. —*v.i.* se livrer au pillage.

pillar /'pɪlə(r)/ *n.* pilier *m.* **∼-box** *n.* boîte à *or* aux lettres *f.*

pillion /'pɪljən/ *n.* siège arrière *m.* **ride ∼**, monter derrière.

pillory /'pɪlərɪ/ *n.* pilori *m.*

pillow /'pɪləʊ/ *n.* oreiller *m.*

pillowcase /'pɪləʊkeɪs/ *n.* taie d'oreiller *f.*

pilot /'paɪlət/ *n.* pilote *m.* —*a.* pilote. —*v.t.* (*p.t.* **piloted**) piloter. **∼-light** *n.* veilleuse *f.*

pimento /pɪ'mentəʊ/ *n.* (*pl.* **-os**) piment *m.*

pimp /pɪmp/ *n.* souteneur *m.*

pimpl|e /'pɪmpl/ *n.* bouton *m.* **∼y** *a.* boutonneux.

pin /pɪn/ *n.* épingle *f.*; (*techn.*) goupille *f.* —*v.t.* (*p.t.* **pinned**) épingler, attacher; (*hold down*) clouer. **have ∼s and needles**, avoir des fourmis. **∼ s.o. down**, (*fig.*) forcer qn. à se décider. **∼-point** *v.t.* repérer, définir. **∼ up**, afficher. **∼-up** *n.* (*fam.*) pin-up *f. invar.*

pinafore /'pɪnəfɔː(r)/ *n.* tablier *m.*

pincers /'pɪnsəz/ *n. pl.* tenailles *f. pl.*

pinch /pɪntʃ/ *v.t.* pincer; (*steal:* sl.) piquer. —*v.i.* (*be too tight*) serrer. —*n.* (*mark*) pinçon *m.*; (*of salt*) pincée *f.* **at a ∼**, au besoin.

pincushion /'pɪnkʊʃn/ *n.* pelote à épingles *f.*

pine[1] /paɪn/ *n.* (*tree*) pin *m.* **∼-cone** *n.* pomme de pin *f.*

pine[2] /paɪn/ *v.i.* **∼ away**, dépérir. **∼ for**, languir après.

pineapple /'paɪnæpl/ *n.* ananas *m.*

ping /pɪŋ/ *n.* bruit métallique *m.*

ping-pong /'pɪŋpɒŋ/ *n.* ping-pong *m.*

pink /pɪŋk/ *a. & n.* rose (*m.*).

pinnacle /'pɪnəkl/ *n.* pinacle *m.*

pint /paɪnt/ n. pinte f. (imperial = 0.57 litre; Amer. = 0.47 litre).

pioneer /paɪə'nɪə(r)/ n. pionnier m. —v.t. être le premier à faire, utiliser, étudier, etc.

pious /'paɪəs/ a. pieux.

pip[1] /pɪp/ n. (seed) pépin m.

pip[2] /pɪp/ n. (sound) top m.

pipe /paɪp/ n. tuyau m.; (of smoker) pipe f.; (mus.) pipeau m. —v.t. transporter par tuyau. ~-cleaner n. cure-pipe m. ~ down, se taire. ~-dream n. chimère f.

pipeline /'paɪplaɪn/ n. pipeline m. in the ~, en route.

piping /'paɪpɪŋ/ n. tuyau(x) m. (pl.). ~ hot, très chaud.

piquant /'pi:kənt/ a. piquant.

pique /pi:k/ n. dépit m.

pira|te /'paɪərət/ n. pirate m. —v.t. pirater. ~cy n. piraterie f.

Pisces /'paɪsi:z/ n. les Poissons m. pl.

pistachio /pɪ'stæʃɪəʊ/ n. (pl. -os) pistache f.

pistol /'pɪstl/ n. pistolet m.

piston /'pɪstən/ n. piston m.

pit /pɪt/ n. fosse f., trou m.; (mine) puits m.; (quarry) carrière f.; (for orchestra) fosse f.; (of stomach) creux m.; (of cherry etc.: Amer.) noyau m. —v.t. (p.t. pitted) trouer; (fig.) opposer. ~ o.s. against, se mesurer à.

pitch[1] /pɪtʃ/ n. (tar) poix f. ~-black a. d'un noir d'ébène.

pitch[2] /pɪtʃ/ v.t. lancer; (tent) dresser. —v.i. (of ship) tanguer. —n. degré m.; (of voice) hauteur f.; (mus.) ton m.; (sport) terrain m. ~ed battle, bataille rangée f. a high-~ed voice, une voix aiguë. ~ in, (fam.) contribuer. ~ into, (fam.) s'attaquer à.

pitcher /'pɪtʃə(r)/ n. cruche f.

pitchfork /'pɪtʃfɔ:k/ n. fourche à foin f.

pitfall /'pɪtfɔ:l/ n. piège m.

pith /pɪθ/ n. (of orange) peau blanche f.; (essence: fig.) moelle f.

pithy /'pɪθɪ/ a. (-ier, -iest) (terse) concis; (forceful) vigoureux.

piti|ful /'pɪtɪfl/ a. pitoyable. ~less a. impitoyable.

pittance /'pɪtns/ n. revenu or salaire dérisoire m.

pity /'pɪtɪ/ n. pitié f.; (regrettable fact) dommage m. —v.t. plaindre. take ~ on, avoir pitié de. what a ~, quel dommage. it's a ~, c'est dommage.

pivot /'pɪvət/ n. pivot m. —v.i. (p.t. pivoted) pivoter.

pixie /'pɪksɪ/ n. lutin m.

pizza /'pi:tsə/ n. pizza f.

placard /'plækɑ:d/ n. affiche f.

placate /plə'keɪt, Amer. 'pleɪkeɪt/ v.t. calmer.

place /pleɪs/ n. endroit m., lieu m.; (house) maison f.; (seat, rank, etc.) place f. —v.t. placer; (an order) passer; (remember) situer. at or to my ~, chez moi. be ~d, (in race) se placer. change ~s, changer de place. in the first ~, d'abord. out of ~, déplacé. take ~, avoir lieu. ~-mat n. set m.

placenta /plə'sentə/ n. placenta m.

placid /'plæsɪd/ a. placide.

plagiar|ize /'pleɪdʒəraɪz/ v.t. plagier. ~ism n. plagiat m.

plague /pleɪg/ n. peste f.; (nuisance: fam.) fléau m. —v.t. harceler.

plaice /pleɪs/ n. invar. carrelet m.

plaid /plæd/ n. tissu écossais m.

plain /pleɪn/ a. (-er, -est) clair; (candid) franc; (simple) simple; (not pretty) sans beauté; (not patterned) uni. —adv. franchement. —n. plaine f. ~ chocolate, chocolat noir. in ~ clothes, en civil. ~ly adv. clairement; franchement; simplement. ~ness n. simplicité f.

plaintiff /'pleɪntɪf/ n. plaignant(e) m. (f.).

plaintive /'pleɪntɪv/ a. plaintif.

plait /plæt/ v.t. tresser, natter. —n. tresse f., natte f.

plan /plæn/ n. projet m., plan m.; (diagram) plan m. —v.t. (p.t. planned) prévoir, projeter; (arrange) organiser; (design) concevoir; (economy, work) planifier. —v.i. faire des projets. ~ to do, avoir l'intention de faire.

plane[1] /pleɪn/ n. (tree) platane m.

plane[2] /pleɪn/ n. (level) plan m.; (aeroplane) avion m. —a. plan.

plane[3] /pleɪn/ n. (tool) rabot m. —v.t. raboter.

planet /'plænɪt/ n. planète f. ~ary a. planétaire.

plank /plæŋk/ n. planche f.

plankton /'plæŋktn/ n. plancton m.

planning /'plænɪŋ/ n. (pol., comm.) planification f. family ~, planning familial m. ~ permission, permis de construire m.

plant /plɑ:nt/ n. plante f.; (techn.) matériel m.; (factory) usine f. —v.t. planter; (bomb) (dé)poser. ~ation /-'teɪʃn/ n. plantation f.

plaque /plɑ:k/ n. plaque f.

plasma /'plæzmə/ n. plasma m.

plaster /'plɑ:stə(r)/ n. plâtre m.; (adhesive) sparadrap m. —v.t. plâtrer; (cover) tapisser (with, de). in ~, dans

le plâtre. ~ **of Paris,** plâtre à mouler *m.*
~**er** *n.* plâtrier *m.*

plastic /'plæstɪk/ *a.* en plastique; (*art,
substance*) plastique. —*n.* plastique *m.*
~ **surgery,** chirurgie esthétique *f.*

Plasticine /'plæstɪsiːn/ *n.* (P.) pâte à
modeler *f.*

plate /pleɪt/ *n.* assiette *f.*; (*of metal*)
plaque *f.*; (*gold or silver dishes*)
vaisselle plate *f.*; (*in book*) gravure *f.*
—*v.t.* (*metal*) plaquer. ~**ful** *n.* (*pl.*
-fuls) assiettée *f.*

plateau /'plætəʊ/ *n.* (*pl.* **-eaux** /-əʊz/)
plateau *m.*

platform /'plætfɔːm/ *n.* (*in classroom,
hall, etc.*) estrade *f.*; (*for speaking*)
tribune *f.*; (*rail.*) quai *m.*; (*of bus &
pol.*) plate-forme *f.*

platinum /'plætɪnəm/ *n.* platine *m.*

platitude /'plætɪtjuːd/ *n.* platitude *f.*

platonic /plə'tɒnɪk/ *a.* platonique.

platoon /plə'tuːn/ *n.* (*mil.*) section *f.*

platter /'plætə(r)/ *n.* plat *m.*

plausible /'plɔːzəbl/ *a.* plausible.

play /pleɪ/ *v.t./i.* jouer; (*instrument*)
jouer de; (*record*) passer; (*game*) jouer
à; (*opponent*) jouer contre; (*match*)
disputer. —*n.* jeu *m.*; (*theatre*) pièce *f.*
~**-act** *v.i.* jouer la comédie. ~ **down,**
minimiser. ~**-group,** ~**-school** *ns.*
garderie *f.* ~**-off** *n.* (*sport*) belle *f.* ~
on, (*take advantage of*) jouer sur. ~ **on
words,** jouer de mots *m.* ~**ed out,** épuisé.
~**-pen** *n.* parc *m.* ~ **safe,** ne pas
prendre de risques. ~ **up,** (*fam.*) créer
des problèmes (à). ~ **up to,** flatter. ~**er**
n. joueur|r, -se *m.*, *f.*

playboy /'pleɪbɔɪ/ *n.* play-boy *m.*

playful /'pleɪfl/ *a.* enjoué; (*child*) joueur.
~**ly** *adv.* avec espièglerie.

playground /'pleɪgraʊnd/ *n.* cour de
récréation *f.*

playing /'pleɪɪŋ/ *n.* jeu *m.* ~**-card** *n.*
carte à jouer *f.* ~**-field** *n.* terrain de
sport *m.*

playmate /'pleɪmeɪt/ *n.* camarade *m./f.*,
copain, -ine *m.*, *f.*

plaything /'pleɪθɪŋ/ *n.* jouet *m.*

playwright /'pleɪraɪt/ *n.* dramaturge
m./f.

plc *abbr.* (*public limited company*) SA.

plea /pliː/ *n.* (*entreaty*) supplication *f.*;
(*reason*) excuse *f.*; (*jurid.*) défense *f.*

plead /pliːd/ *v.t./i.* (*jurid.*) plaider; (*as
excuse*) alléguer. ~ **for,** (*beg for*)
implorer. ~ **with,** (*beg*) implorer.

pleasant /'pleznt/ *a.* agréable. ~**ly** *adv.*
agréablement.

please /pliːz/ *v.t./i.* plaire (à), faire plaisir

(à). —*adv.* s'il vous *or* te plaît. ~ **o.s.,
do as one** ~**s,** faire ce qu'on veut. ~**d**
a. content (**with,** de). **pleasing** *a.*
agréable.

pleasur|e /'pleʒə(r)/ *n.* plaisir *m.* ~**able**
a. très agréable.

pleat /pliːt/ *n.* pli *m.* —*v.t.* plisser.

plebiscite /'plebɪsɪt/ *n.* plébiscite *m.*

pledge /pledʒ/ *n.* (*token*) gage *m.*; (*fig.*)
promesse *f.* —*v.t.* promettre; (*pawn*)
engager.

plentiful /'plentɪfl/ *a.* abondant.

plenty /'plentɪ/ *n.* abondance *f.* ~ (**of**),
(*a great deal*) beaucoup (de); (*enough*)
assez (de).

pleurisy /'plʊərəsɪ/ *n.* pleurésie *f.*

pliable /'plaɪəbl/ *a.* souple.

pliers /'plaɪəz/ *n. pl.* pince(s) *f.* (*pl.*).

plight /plaɪt/ *n.* triste situation *f.*

plimsoll /'plɪms(ə)l/ *n.* chaussure de gym
f.

plinth /plɪnθ/ *n.* socle *m.*

plod /plɒd/ *v.i.* (*p.t.* **plodded**) avancer
péniblement *or* d'un pas lent; (*work*)
bûcher. ~**der** *n.* bûcheu|r, -se *m.*, *f.*
~**ding** *a.* lent.

plonk /plɒŋk/ *n.* (*sl.*) pinard *m.* —*v.t.* ~
down, poser lourdement.

plot /plɒt/ *n.* complot *m.*; (*of novel etc.*)
intrigue *f.* ~ (**of land**), terrain *m.*
—*v.t./i.* (*p.t.* **plotted**) comploter; (*mark
out*) tracer.

plough /plaʊ/ *n.* charrue *f.* —*v.t./i.*
labourer. ~ **back,** réinvestir. ~ **into,**
rentrer dans. ~ **through,** avancer
péniblement dans.

plow /plaʊ/ *n. & v.t./i.* (*Amer.*) =
plough.

ploy /plɔɪ/ *n.* (*fam.*) stratagème *m.*

pluck /plʌk/ *v.t.* cueillir; (*bird*) plumer;
(*eyebrows*) épiler; (*strings: mus.*)
pincer. —*n.* courage *m.* ~ **up courage,**
prendre son courage à deux mains. ~**y**
a. courageux.

plug /plʌg/ *n.* (*of cloth, paper, etc.*)
tampon *m.*; (*for sink etc.*) bonde *f.*;
(*electr.*) fiche *f.*, prise *f.* —*v.t.* (*p.t.*
plugged) (*hole*) boucher; (*publicize:
fam.*) faire du battage autour de. —*v.i.*
~ **away,** (*work: fam.*) bosser. ~ **in,**
brancher. ~**-hole** *n.* vidange *f.*

plum /plʌm/ *n.* prune *f.* ~ **job,** travail en
or *m.* ~ **pudding,** (plum-)pudding *m.*

plumb /plʌm/ *adv.* tout à fait. —*v.t.*
(*probe*) sonder. ~**-line** *n.* fil à plomb *m.*

plumb|er /'plʌmə(r)/ *n.* plombier *m.*
~**ing** *n.* plomberie *f.*

plum|e /pluːm/ *n.* plume(s) *f.* (*pl.*).
~**age** *n.* plumage *m.*

plummet /'plʌmɪt/ *v.i.* (*p.t.* **plummeted**) tomber, plonger.

plump /plʌmp/ *a.* (**-er, -est**) potelé, dodu. —*v.i.* ～ **for**, choisir. ～**ness** *n.* rondeur *f.*

plunder /'plʌndə(r)/ *v.t.* piller. —*n.* (*act*) pillage *m.*; (*goods*) butin *m.*

plunge /plʌndʒ/ *v.t./i.* (*dive, thrust*) plonger; (*fall*) tomber. —*n.* plongeon *m.*; (*fall*) chute *f.* **take the** ～, se jeter à l'eau.

plunger /'plʌndʒə(r)/ *n.* (*for sink etc.*) ventouse *f.*, débouchoir *m.*

plural /'plʊərəl/ *a.* pluriel; (*noun*) au pluriel. —*n.* pluriel *m.*

plus /plʌs/ *prep.* plus. —*a.* (*electr. & fig.*) positif. —*n.* signe plus *m.*; (*fig.*) atout *m.* **ten** ～, plus de dix.

plush(y) /'plʌʃ(ɪ)/ *a.* somptueux.

ply /plaɪ/ *v.t.* (*tool*) manier; (*trade*) exercer. —*v.i.* faire la navette. ～ **s.o. with drink**, offrir continuellement à boire à qn.

plywood /'plaɪwʊd/ *n.* contreplaqué *m.*

p.m. /piː'em/ *adv.* de l'après-midi *or* du soir.

pneumatic /njuː'mætɪk/ *a.* pneumatique. ～ **drill**, marteau-piqueur *m.*

pneumonia /njuː'məʊnɪə/ *n.* pneumonie *f.*

PO *abbr. see* Post Office.

poach /pəʊtʃ/ *v.t./i.* (*game*) braconner; (*staff*) débaucher; (*culin.*) pocher. ～**er** *n.* braconnier *m.*

pocket /'pɒkɪt/ *n.* poche *f.* —*a.* de poche. —*v.t.* empocher. **be out of** ～, avoir perdu de l'argent. ～**-book** *n.* (*notebook*) carnet *m.*; (*wallet: Amer.*) portefeuille *m.*; (*handbag: Amer.*) sac à main *m.* ～**-money** *n.* argent de poche *m.*

pock-marked /'pɒkmɑːkt/ *a.* (*face etc.*) grêlé.

pod /pɒd/ *n.* (*peas etc.*) cosse *f.*; (*vanilla*) gousse *f.*

podgy /'pɒdʒɪ/ *a.* (**-ier, -iest**) dodu.

poem /'pəʊɪm/ *n.* poème *m.*

poet /'pəʊɪt/ *n.* poète *m.* ～**ic** /-'etɪk/ *a.* poétique.

poetry /'pəʊɪtrɪ/ *n.* poésie *f.*

poignant /'pɔɪnjənt/ *a.* poignant.

point /pɔɪnt/ *n.* point *m.*; (*tip*) pointe *f.*; (*decimal point*) virgule *f.*; (*meaning*) sens *m.*, intérêt *m.*; (*remark*) remarque *f.* ～**s**, (*rail.*) aiguillage *m.* —*v.t.* (*aim*) braquer; (*show*) indiquer. —*v.i.* indiquer du doigt (**at** *or* **to s.o.**, qn.). ～ **out that**, **make the** ～ **that**, faire remarquer que. **good** ～**s**, qualités *f. pl.* **make a** ～ **of doing**, ne pas manquer de faire. **on**

the ～ **of**, sur le point de. ～**-blank** *a. & adv.* à bout portant. ～ **in time**, moment *m.* ～ **of view**, point de vue *m.* ～ **out**, signaler. **to the** ～, pertinent. **what is the** ～**?**, à quoi bon?

pointed /'pɔɪntɪd/ *a.* pointu; (*remark*) lourd de sens.

pointer /'pɔɪntə(r)/ *n.* (*indicator*) index *m.*; (*dog*) chien d'arrêt *m.*; (*advice: fam.*) tuyau *m.*

pointless /'pɔɪntlɪs/ *a.* inutile.

poise /pɔɪz/ *n.* équilibre *m.*; (*carriage*) maintien *m.*; (*fig.*) assurance *f.* ～**d** *a.* en équilibre; (*confident*) assuré. ～**d for**, prêt à.

poison /'pɔɪzn/ *n.* poison *m.* —*v.t.* empoisonner. ～**ous** *a.* (*substance etc.*) toxique; (*plant*) vénéneux; (*snake*) venimeux.

poke /pəʊk/ *v.t./i.* (*push*) pousser; (*fire*) tisonner; (*thrust*) fourrer. —*n.* (petit) coup *m.* ～ **about**, fureter. ～ **fun at**, se moquer de. ～ **out**, (*head*) sortir.

poker[1] /'pəʊkə(r)/ *n.* tisonnier *m.*

poker[2] /'pəʊkə(r)/ *n.* (*cards*) poker *m.*

poky /'pəʊkɪ/ *a.* (**-ier, -iest**) (*small*) exigu; (*slow: Amer.*) lent.

Poland /'pəʊlənd/ *n.* Pologne *f.*

polar /'pəʊlə(r)/ *a.* polaire. ～ **bear**, ours blanc *m.*

polarize /'pəʊləraɪz/ *v.t.* polariser.

Polaroid /'pəʊlərɔɪd/ *n.* (P.) polaroïd (P.) *m.*

pole[1] /pəʊl/ *n.* (*fixed*) poteau *m.*; (*rod*) perche *f.*; (*for flag*) mât *m.* ～**-vault** *n.* saut à la perche *m.*

pole[2] /pəʊl/ *n.* (*geog.*) pôle *m.*

Pole /pəʊl/ *n.* Polonais(e) *m.* (*f.*).

polemic /pə'lemɪk/ *n.* polémique *f.*

police /pə'liːs/ *n.* police *f.* —*v.t.* faire la police dans. ～ **state**, état policier *m.* ～ **station**, commissariat de police *m.*

police|man /pə'liːsmən/ *n.* (*pl.* **-men**) agent de police *m.* ～**woman** (*pl.* **-women**) femme-agent *f.*

policy[1] /'pɒlɪsɪ/ *n.* politique *f.*

policy[2] /'pɒlɪsɪ/ *n.* (*insurance*) police (d'assurance) *f.*

polio(myelitis) /'pəʊlɪəʊ(maɪə'laɪtɪs)/ *n.* polio(myélite) *f.*

polish /'pɒlɪʃ/ *v.t.* polir; (*shoes, floor*) cirer. —*n.* (*for shoes*) cirage *m.*; (*for floor*) encaustique *f.*; (*for nails*) vernis *m.*; (*shine*) poli *m.*; (*fig.*) raffinement *m.* ～ **off**, finir en vitesse. ～ **up**, (*language*) perfectionner. ～**ed** *a.* raffiné.

Polish /'pəʊlɪʃ/ *a.* polonais. —*n.* (*lang.*) polonais *m.*

polite /pə'laɪt/ a. poli. **~ly** adv.
poliment. **~ness** n. politesse f.

political /pə'lɪtɪkl/ a. politique.

politician /pɒlɪ'tɪʃn/ n. homme politique
m., femme politique f.

politics /'pɒlətɪks/ n. politique f.

polka /'pɒlkə, Amer. 'pəʊlkə/ n. polka f.
~ dots, pois m. pl.

poll /pəʊl/ n. scrutin m.; (survey)
sondage m. —v.t. (votes) obtenir. **go to
the ~s**, aller aux urnes. **~ing-booth** n.
isoloir m. **~ing station**, bureau de vote
m.

pollen /'pɒlən/ n. pollen m.

pollut|e /pə'luːt/ v.t. polluer. **~ion** /-ʃn/
n. pollution f.

polo /'pəʊləʊ/ n. polo m. **~ neck**, col
roulé m. **~ shirt**, polo m.

polyester /pɒlɪ'estə(r)/ n. polyester m.

polygamy /pə'lɪgəmɪ/ n. polygamie f.

polytechnic /pɒlɪ'teknɪk/ n. institut
universitaire de technologie m.

polythene /'pɒlɪθiːn/ n. polythène m.,
polyéthylène m.

pomegranate /'pɒmɪgrænɪt/ n. (fruit)
grenade f.

pomp /pɒmp/ n. pompe f.

pompon /'pɒmpɒn/ n. pompon m.

pomp|ous /'pɒmpəs/ a. pompeux.
~osity /-'pɒsətɪ/ n. solennité f.

pond /pɒnd/ n. étang m.; (artificial)
bassin m.; (stagnant) mare f.

ponder /'pɒndə(r)/ v.t./i. réfléchir (à),
méditer (sur).

ponderous /'pɒndərəs/ a. pesant.

pong /pɒŋ/ n. (stink: sl.) puanteur f.
—v.i. (sl.) puer.

pony /'pəʊnɪ/ n. poney m. **~-tail** n.
queue de cheval f.

poodle /'puːdl/ n. caniche m.

pool[1] /puːl/ n. (puddle) flaque f.; (pond)
étang m.; (of blood) mare f.; (for
swimming) piscine f.

pool[2] /puːl/ n. (fund) fonds commun m.,
(of ideas) réservoir m.; (of typists) pool
m.; (snooker) billard américain m. **~s**,
pari mutuel sur le football m. —v.t.
mettre en commun.

poor /pɔː(r)/ a. (-er, -est) pauvre; (not
good) médiocre, mauvais. **~ly** adv.
mal; a. malade.

pop[1] /pɒp/ n. (noise) bruit sec m.
—v.t./i. (p.t. **popped**) (burst) crever; (put) mettre. **~ in/out/off**,
entrer/sortir/partir. **~ over**, faire un
saut (**to see s.o.**, chez qn.). **~ up**, surgir.

pop[2] /pɒp/ n. (mus.) musique pop f. —a.
pop invar.

popcorn /'pɒpkɔːn/ n. pop-corn m.

pope /pəʊp/ n. pape m.

poplar /'pɒplə(r)/ n. peuplier m.

poppy /'pɒpɪ/ n. pavot m.; (wild)
coquelicot m.

popsicle /'pɒpsɪkl/ n. (P.) (Amer.) glace
à l'eau f.

popular /'pɒpjʊlə(r)/ a. populaire; (in
fashion) en vogue. **be ~ with**, plaire à.
~ity /-'lærətɪ/ n. popularité f. **~ize** v.t.
populariser. **~ly** adv. communément.

populat|e /'pɒpjʊleɪt/ v.t. peupler. **~ion**
/-'leɪʃn/ n. population f.

populous /'pɒpjʊləs/ a. populeux.

porcelain /'pɔːsəlɪn/ n. porcelaine f.

porch /pɔːtʃ/ n. porche m.

porcupine /'pɔːkjʊpaɪn/ n. (rodent)
porc-épic m.

pore[1] /pɔː(r)/ n. pore m.

pore[2] /pɔː(r)/ v.i. **~ over**, étudier
minutieusement.

pork /pɔːk/ n. (food) porc m.

pornograph|y /pɔː'nɒgrəfɪ/ n. por-
nographie f. **~ic** /-ə'græfɪk/ a.
pornographique.

porous /'pɔːrəs/ a. poreux.

porpoise /'pɔːpəs/ n. marsouin m.

porridge /'pɒrɪdʒ/ n. porridge m.

port[1] /pɔːt/ n. (harbour) port m. **~ of
call**, escale f.

port[2] /pɔːt/ n. (left: naut.) bâbord m.

port[3] /pɔːt/ n. (wine) porto m.

portable /'pɔːtəbl/ a. portatif.

portal /'pɔːtl/ n. portail m.

porter[1] /'pɔːtə(r)/ n. (carrier) porteur m.

porter[2] /'pɔːtə(r)/ n. (door-keeper)
portier m.

portfolio /pɔːt'fəʊlɪəʊ/ n. (pl. -os) (pol.,
comm.) portefeuille m.

porthole /'pɔːthəʊl/ n. hublot m.

portico /'pɔːtɪkəʊ/ n. (pl. -oes) portique
m.

portion /'pɔːʃn/ n. (share, helping)
portion f.; (part) partie f.

portly /'pɔːtlɪ/ a. (-ier, -iest) corpulent
(et digne).

portrait /'pɔːtrɪt/ n. portrait m.

portray /pɔː'treɪ/ v.t. représenter. **~al** n.
portrait m., peinture f.

Portug|al /'pɔːtjʊgl/ n. Portugal m.
~uese /-'giːz/ a. & n. invar.
portugais(e) (m. (f.)).

pose /pəʊz/ v.t./i. poser. —n. pose f. **~
as**, (expert etc.) se poser en.

poser /'pəʊzə(r)/ n. colle f.

posh /pɒʃ/ a. (sl.) chic invar.

position /pə'zɪʃn/ n. position f.; (job,
state) situation f. —v.t. placer.

positive /'pɒzətɪv/ a. (test, help, etc.)
positif; (sure) sûr, certain; (real) réel,

vrai. **～ly** adv. positivement; (absolutely) complètement.
possess /pə'zes/ v.t. posséder. **～ion** /-ʃn/ n. possession f. **take ～ion of,** prendre possession de. **～or** n. possesseur m.
possessive /pə'zesɪv/ a. possessif.
possib|le /'pɒsəbl/ a. possible. **～ility** /-'bɪlətɪ/ n. possibilité f.
possibly /'pɒsəblɪ/ adv. peut-être. **if I ～ can,** si cela m'est possible. **I cannot ～ leave,** il m'est impossible de partir.
post¹ /pəʊst/ n. (pole) poteau m. —v.t. **～ (up),** (a notice) afficher.
post² /pəʊst/ n. (station, job) poste m. —v.t. poster; (appoint) affecter.
post³ /pəʊst/ n. (mail service) poste f.; (letters) courrier m. —a. postal. —v.t. (put in box) poster; (send) envoyer (par la poste). **catch the last ～,** attraper la dernière levée. **keep ～ed,** tenir au courant. **～box** n. boîte à or aux lettres f. **～ code** code postal m. **P～ Office,** postes f. pl.; (in France) Postes et Télécommunications f. pl. **～ office,** bureau de poste m., poste f.
post- /pəʊst/ pref. post-.
postage /'pəʊstɪdʒ/ n. tarif postal m., frais de port m.pl.
postal /'pəʊstl/ a. postal. **～ order,** mandat m. **～ worker,** employé(e) des postes m. (f.).
postcard /'pəʊstkɑːd/ n. carte postale f.
poster /'pəʊstə(r)/ n. affiche f.; (for decoration) poster m.
posterior /pɒ'stɪərɪə(r)/ n. postérieur m.
posterity /pɒ'sterətɪ/ n. postérité f.
postgraduate /pəʊst'grædʒʊət/ n. étudiant(e) de troisième cycle m. (f.).
posthumous /'pɒstjʊməs/ a. posthume. **～ly** adv. à titre posthume.
postman /'pəʊstmən/ n. (pl. -men) facteur m.
postmark /'pəʊstmɑːk/ n. cachet de la poste m.
postmaster /'pəʊstmɑːstə(r)/ n. receveur des postes m.
post-mortem /pəʊst'mɔːtəm/ n. autopsie f.
postpone /pə'spəʊn/ v.t. remettre. **～ment** n. ajournement n.
postscript /'pəʊskrɪpt/ n. (to letter) post-scriptum m. invar.
postulate /'pɒstjʊleɪt/ v.t. postuler.
posture /'pɒstʃə(r)/ n. posture f. —v.i. (affectedly) prendre des poses.
post-war /pəʊst'wɔː(r)/ a. d'après-guerre.
pot /pɒt/ n. pot m.; (for cooking) marmite f.; (drug: sl.) marie-jeanne f.

—v.t. (plants) mettre en pot. **go to ～,** (sl.) aller à la ruine. **～-belly** n. gros ventre m. **take ～ luck,** tenter sa chance. **take a ～-shot at,** faire un carton sur.
potato /pə'teɪtəʊ/ n. (pl. -oes) pomme de terre f.
poten|t /'pəʊtnt/ a. puissant; (drink) fort. **～cy** n. puissance f.
potential /pə'tenʃl/ a. & n. potentiel (m.). **～ly** adv. potentiellement.
pot-hol|e /'pɒthəʊl/ n. (in rock) caverne f.; (in road) nid de poule m. **～ing** n. spéléologie f.
potion /'pəʊʃn/ n. potion f.
potted /'pɒtɪd/ a. (plant etc.) en pot; (preserved) en conserve; (abridged) condensé.
potter¹ /'pɒtə(r)/ n. potier m. **～y** n. (art) poterie f.; (objects) poteries f.pl.
potter² /'pɒtə(r)/ v.i. bricoler.
potty /'pɒtɪ/ a. (-ier, -iest) (crazy: sl.) toqué.— n. pot m.
pouch /paʊtʃ/ n. poche f.; (for tobacco) blague f.
pouffe /puːf/ n. pouf m.
poultice /'pəʊltɪs/ n. cataplasme m.
poult|ry /'pəʊltrɪ/ n. volaille f. **～erer** n. marchand de volailles m.
pounce /paʊns/ v.i. bondir (on, sur). —n. bond m.
pound¹ /paʊnd/ n. (weight) livre f. (= 454 g.); (money) livre f.
pound² /paʊnd/ n. (for dogs, cars) fourrière f.
pound³ /paʊnd/ v.t. (crush) piler; (bombard) pilonner. —v.i. frapper fort; (of heart) battre fort; (walk) marcher à pas lourds.
pour /pɔː(r)/ v.t. verser. —v.i. couler, ruisseler (from, de); (rain) pleuvoir à torrents. **～ in/out,** (people) arriver/sortir en masse. **～ off or out,** vider. **～ing rain,** pluie torrentielle f.
pout /paʊt/ v.t./i. **～ (one's lips),** faire la moue. —n. moue f.
poverty /'pɒvətɪ/ n. misère f., pauvreté f.
powder /'paʊdə(r)/ n. poudre f. —v.t. poudrer. **～ed** a. en poudre. **～y** a. poudreux. **～-room** n. toilettes pour dames f. pl.
power /'paʊə(r)/ n. puissance f.; (ability, authority) pouvoir m.; (energy) énergie f.; (electr.) courant m. **～ cut,** coupure de courant f. **～ed by,** fonctionnant à; (jet etc.) propulsé par. **～less** a. impuissant. **～ point,** prise de courant f. **～-station** n. centrale électrique f.
powerful /'paʊəfl/ a. puissant. **～ly** adv. puissamment.

practicable /'præktɪkəbl/ a. praticable.
practical /'præktɪkl/ a. pratique. **~ity**
/-'kælətɪ/ n. sens or aspect pratique m.
~ joke, farce f.
practically /'præktɪklɪ/ adv. pratiquement.
practice /'præktɪs/ n. pratique f.; (of
profession) exercice m.; (sport)
entraînement m.; (clients) clientèle f. **be
in ~,** (doctor, lawyer) exercer. **in ~,**
(in fact) en pratique; (well-trained) en
forme. **out of ~,** rouillé. **put into ~,**
mettre en pratique.
practis|e /'præktɪs/ v.t./i. (musician,
typist, etc.) s'exercer (à); (sport)
s'entraîner (à); (put into practice)
pratiquer; (profession) exercer. **~ed** a.
expérimenté. **~ing** a. (Catholic etc.)
pratiquant.
practitioner /præk'tɪʃənə(r)/ n. prati-
cien(ne) m. (f.).
pragmatic /præg'mætɪk/ a. prag-
matique.
prairie /'preərɪ/ n. (in North America)
prairie f.
praise /preɪz/ v.t. louer. —n. éloge(s) m.
(pl.), louange(s) f. (pl.).
praiseworthy /'preɪzwɜːðɪ/ a. digne
d'éloges.
pram /præm/ n. voiture d'enfant f.,
landau m.
prance /prɑːns/ v.i. caracoler.
prank /præŋk/ n. farce f.
prattle /'prætl/ v.i. jaser.
prawn /prɔːn/ n. crevette rose f.
pray /preɪ/ v.i. prier.
prayer /preə(r)/ n. prière f.
pre- /priː/ pref. pré-.
preach /priːtʃ/ v.t./i. prêcher. **~ at or to,**
prêcher. **~er** n. prédicateur m.
preamble /priː'æmbl/ n. préambule m.
pre-arrange /priːə'reɪndʒ/ v.t. fixer à
l'avance.
precarious /prɪ'keərɪəs/ a. précaire.
precaution /prɪ'kɔːʃn/ n. précaution f.
~ary a. de précaution.
preced|e /prɪ'siːd/ v.t. précéder. **~ing** a.
précédent.
precedence /'presɪdəns/ n. priorité f.; (in
rank) préséance f.
precedent /'presɪdənt/ n. précédent m.
precept /'priːsept/ n. précepte m.
precinct /'priːsɪŋkt/ n. enceinte f.;
(pedestrian area) zone f.; (district:
Amer.) circonscription f.
precious /'preʃəs/ a. précieux. —adv.
(very: fam.) très.
precipice /'presɪpɪs/ n. (geog.) à-pic m.
invar.; (fig.) précipice m.

precipitat|e /prɪ'sɪpɪteɪt/ v.t. (person,
event, chemical) précipiter. —a. /-ɪtət/
précipité. **~ion** /-'teɪʃn/ n. précipitation
f.
précis /'preɪsiː/ n. invar. précis m.
precis|e /prɪ'saɪs/ a. précis; (careful)
méticuleux. **~ely** adv. précisément.
~ion /-'sɪʒn/ n. précision f.
preclude /prɪ'kluːd/ v.t. (prevent)
empêcher; (rule out) exclure.
precocious /prɪ'kəʊʃəs/ a. précoce.
preconc|eived /priːkən'siːvd/ a. pré-
conçu. **~eption** n. préconception f.
pre-condition /priːkən'dɪʃn/ n. condition requise f.
predator /'predətə(r)/ n. prédateur m.
~y a. rapace.
predecessor /'priːdɪsesə(r)/ n. prédécesseur m.
predicament /prɪ'dɪkəmənt/ n. mauvaise situation or passe f.
predict /prɪ'dɪkt/ v.t. prédire. **~able** a.
prévisible. **~ion** /-kʃn/ n. prédiction f.
predispose /priːdɪ'spəʊz/ v.t. prédisposer (**to do,** à faire).
predominant /prɪ'dɒmɪnənt/ a. prédominant. **~ly** adv. pour la plupart.
predominate /prɪ'dɒmɪneɪt/ v.i. prédominer.
pre-eminent /priː'emɪnənt/ a. pré-
éminent.
pre-empt /priː'empt/ v.t. (buy) acquérir
d'avance; (stop) prévenir. **~ive** a.
preventif.
preen /priːn/ v.t. (bird) lisser. **~ o.s.,**
(person) se bichonner.
prefab /'priːfæb/ n. (fam.) bâtiment
préfabriqué m. **~ricated** /-'fæbrɪk-
eɪtɪd/ a. préfabriqué.
preface /'prefɪs/ n. préface f.
prefect /'priːfekt/ n. (pupil) élève
chargé(e) de la discipline m.(f.);
(official) préfet m.
prefer /prɪ'fɜː(r)/ v.t. (p.t. **preferred**)
préférer (**to do,** faire). **~able**
/'prefrəbl/ a. préférable. **~ably** adv. de
préférence.
preferen|ce /'prefrəns/ n. préférence f.
~tial /-ə'renʃl/ a. préférentiel.
prefix /'priːfɪks/ n. préfixe m.
pregnan|t /'pregnənt/ a. (woman)
enceinte; (animal) pleine. **~cy** n. (of
woman) grossesse f.
prehistoric /priːhɪ'stɒrɪk/ a. préhistorique.
prejudge /priː'dʒʌdʒ/ v.t. préjuger de;
(person) juger d'avance.
prejudice /'predʒʊdɪs/ n. préjugé(s) m.
(pl.); (harm) préjudice m. —v.t.

(*claim*) porter préjudice à; (*person*) prévenir. **~d** *a.* partial; (*person*) qui a des préjugés.

preliminar|y /prɪ'lɪmɪnərɪ/ *a.* préliminaire. **~ies** *n. pl.* préliminaires *m. pl.*

prelude /'prelju:d/ *n.* prélude *m.*

pre-marital /pri:'mærɪtl/ *a.* avant le mariage.

premature /'premətjʊə(r)/ *a.* prématuré.

premeditated /pri:'medɪteɪtɪd/ *a.* prémédité.

premier /'premɪə(r)/ *a.* premier. *—n.* premier ministre *m.*

première /'premɪeə(r)/ *n.* première *f.*

premises /'premɪsɪz/ *n. pl.* locaux *m. pl.* **on the ~,** sur les lieux.

premiss /'premɪs/ *n.* prémisse *f.*

premium /'pri:mɪəm/ *n.* prime *f.* **be at a ~,** faire prime.

premonition /pri:mə'nɪʃn/ *n.* prémonition *f.,* pressentiment *m.*

preoccup|ation /pri:ɒkjʊ'peɪʃn/ *n.* préoccupation *f.* **~ied** /-'ɒkjʊpaɪd/ *a.* préoccupé.

prep /prep/ *n.* (*work*) devoirs *m.pl.* **~ school = preparatory school.**

preparation /prepə'reɪʃn/ *n.* préparation *f.* **~s,** préparatifs *m. pl.*

preparatory /prɪ'pærətrɪ/ *a.* préparatoire. **~ school,** école primaire privée *f.*; (*Amer.*) école secondaire privée *f.*

prepare /prɪ'peə(r)/ *v.t./i.* (se) préparer (**for,** à). **be ~d for,** (*expect*) s'attendre à **~d to,** prêt à.

prepay /pri:'peɪ/ *v.t.* (*p.t.* **-paid**) payer d'avance.

preponderance /prɪ'pɒndərəns/ *n.* prédominance *f.*

preposition /prepə'zɪʃn/ *n.* préposition *f.*

preposterous /prɪ'pɒstərəs/ *a.* absurde, ridicule.

prerequisite /pri:'rekwɪzɪt/ *n.* condition préalable *f.*

prerogative /prɪ'rɒgətɪv/ *n.* prérogative *f.*

Presbyterian /prezbɪ'tɪərɪən/ *a. & n.* presbytérien(ne) (*m.* (*f.*)).

prescri|be /prɪ'skraɪb/ *v.t.* prescrire. **~ption** /-ɪpʃn/ *n.* prescription *f.*; (*med.*) ordonnance *f.*

presence /'prezns/ *n.* présence *f.* **~ of mind,** présence d'esprit *f.*

present¹ /'preznt/ *a.* présent. *—n.* présent *m.* **at ~,** à présent. **for the ~,** pour le moment. **~-day** *a.* actuel.

present² /'preznt/ *n.* (*gift*) cadeau *m.*

present³ /prɪ'zent/ *v.t.* présenter; (*film, concert, etc.*) donner. **~ s.o. with,** offrir à qn. **~able** *a.* présentable. **~ation** /prezn'teɪʃn/ *n.* présentation *f.* **~er** *n.* présentalteur, -trice *m., f.*

presently /'prezntlɪ/ *adv.* bientôt; (*now: Amer.*) en ce moment.

preservative /prɪ'zɜ:vətɪv/ *n.* (*culin.*) agent de conservation *m.*

preserv|e /prɪ'zɜ:v/ *v.t.* préserver; (*maintain & culin.*) conserver. *—n.* réserve *f.*; (*fig.*) domaine *m.*; (*jam*) confiture *f.* **~ation** /prezə'veɪʃn/ *n.* conservation *f.*

preside /prɪ'zaɪd/ *v.i.* présider. **~ over,** présider.

presiden|t /'prezɪdənt/ *n.* président(e) *m.* (*f.*). **~cy** *n.* présidence *f.* **~tial** /-'denʃl/ *a.* présidentiel.

press /pres/ *v.t./i.* (*button etc.*) appuyer (sur); (*squeeze*) presser; (*iron*) repasser; (*pursue*) poursuivre. *—n.* (*newspapers, machine*) presse *f.*; (*for wine*) pressoir *m.* **be ~ed for,** (*time etc.*) manquer de. **~ for sth.,** faire pression pour avoir qch. **~ s.o. to do sth.,** pousser qn. à faire qch. **~ conference/cutting,** conférence/coupure de presse *f.* **~ on,** continuer (**with** sth., qch.). **~ release,** communiqué de presse *m.* **~-stud** *n.* bouton-pression *m.* **~-up** *n.* traction *f.*

pressing /'presɪŋ/ *a.* pressant.

pressure /'preʃə(r)/ *n.* pression *f.* *—v.t.* faire pression sur. **~-cooker** *n.* cocotte-minute *f.* **~ group,** groupe de pression *m.*

pressurize /'preʃəraɪz/ *v.t.* (*cabin etc.*) pressuriser; (*person*) faire pression sur.

prestige /pre'sti:ʒ/ *n.* prestige *m.*

prestigious /pre'stɪdʒəs/ *a.* prestigieux.

presumably /prɪ'zju:məblɪ/ *adv.* vraisemblablement.

presum|e /prɪ'zju:m/ *v.t.* (*suppose*) présumer. **~e to,** (*venture*) se permettre de. **~ption** /-'zʌmpʃn/ *n.* présomption *f.*

presumptuous /prɪ'zʌmptʃʊəs/ *a.* présomptueux.

pretence, (*Amer.*) **pretense** /prɪ'tens/ *n.* feinte *f.,* simulation *f.*; (*claim*) prétention *f.*; (*pretext*) prétexte *m.*

pretend /prɪ'tend/ *v.t./i.* faire semblant (**to do,** de faire). **~ to,** (*lay claim to*) prétendre à.

pretentious /prɪ'tenʃəs/ *a.* prétentieux.

pretext /'pri:tekst/ *n.* prétexte *m.*

pretty /'prɪtɪ/ *a.* (**-ier, -iest**) joli. *—adv.* assez. **~ much,** presque.

prevail /prɪ'veɪl/ v.i. prédominer; (win) prévaloir. ~ **on,** persuader (**to do,** de faire). ~**ing** a. actuel; (wind) dominant.

prevalen|t /'prevələnt/ a. répandu. ~**ce** n. fréquence f.

prevent /prɪ'vent/ v.t. empêcher (**from doing,** de faire). ~**able** a. évitable. ~**ion** /-enʃn/ n. prévention f. ~**ive** a. préventif.

preview /'priːvjuː/ n. avant-première f.; (fig.) aperçu m.

previous /'priːvɪəs/ a. précédent, antérieur. ~ **to,** avant. ~**ly** adv. précédemment, auparavant.

pre-war /priː'wɔː(r)/ a. d'avant-guerre.

prey /preɪ/ n. proie f. —v.i. ~ **on,** faire sa proie de; (worry) préoccuper. **bird of** ~, rapace m.

price /praɪs/ n. prix m. —v.t. fixer le prix de. ~**less** a. inestimable; (amusing: sl.) impayable.

pricey /'praɪsɪ/ a. (fam.) coûteux.

prick /prɪk/ v.t. (with pin etc.) piquer. —n. piqûre f. ~ **up one's ears,** dresser l'oreille.

prickl|e /'prɪkl/ n. piquant m.; (sensation) picotement m. ~**y** a. piquant; (person) irritable.

pride /praɪd/ n. orgueil m.; (satisfaction) fierté f. —v. pr. ~ **o.s. on,** s'enorgueillir de. ~ **of place,** place d'honneur f.

priest /priːst/ n. prêtre m. ~**hood** n. sacerdoce m. ~**ly** a. sacerdotal.

prig /prɪg/ n. petit saint m., pharisien(ne) m. (f.). ~**gish** a. hypocrite.

prim /prɪm/ a. (**primmer, primmest**) guindé, méticuleux.

primar|y /'praɪmərɪ/ a. (school, elections, etc.) primaire; (chief, basic) premier, fondamental. —n. (pol.: Amer.) primaire m. ~**ily** Amer. /-'merɪlɪ/ adv. essentiellement.

prime¹ /praɪm/ a. principal, premier; (first-rate) excellent. **P~ Minister,** Premier Ministre m. **the ~ of life,** la force de l'âge.

prime² /praɪm/ v.t. (pump, gun) amorcer; (surface) apprêter. ~**r**¹ /-ə(r)/ n. (paint etc.) apprêt m.

primer² /'praɪmə(r)/ n. (school-book) premier livre m.

primeval /praɪ'miːvl/ a. primitif.

primitive /'prɪmɪtɪv/ a. primitif.

primrose /'prɪmrəʊz/ n. primevère (jaune) f.

prince /prɪns/ n. prince m. ~**ly** a. princier.

princess /prɪn'ses/ n. princesse f.

principal /'prɪnsəpl/ a. principal. —n. (of school etc.) directeur, -trice m., f. ~**ly** adv. principalement.

principle /'prɪnsəpl/ n. principe m. **in/on** ~, en/par principe.

print /prɪnt/ v.t. imprimer; (write in capitals) écrire en majuscules. —n. (of foot etc.) empreinte f.; (letters) caractères m. pl.; (photograph) épreuve f.; (engraving) gravure f. **in** ~, disponible. **out of** ~, épuisé. ~**-out** n. listage m. ~**ed matter,** imprimés m. pl.

print|er /'prɪntə(r)/ n. (person) imprimeur m.; (comput.) imprimante f. ~**ing** n. impression f.

prior¹ /'praɪə(r)/ a. précédent. ~ **to,** prep. avant (de).

prior² /'praɪə(r)/ n. (relig.) prieur m. ~**y** n. prieuré m.

priority /praɪ'ɒrətɪ/ n. priorité f. **take** ~, avoir la priorité (**over,** sur).

prise /praɪz/ v.t. forcer. ~ **open,** ouvrir en forçant.

prism /'prɪzəm/ n. prisme m.

prison /'prɪzn/ n. prison f. ~**er** n. prisonnier, -ière m., f. ~ **officer,** gardien(ne) de prison m. (f.).

pristine /'prɪstiːn/ a. primitif; (condition) parfait.

privacy /'prɪvəsɪ/ n. intimité f., solitude f.

private /'praɪvɪt/ a. privé; (confidential) personnel; (lessons, house, etc.) particulier; (ceremony) intime. —n. (soldier) simple soldat m. **in** ~, en privé; (of ceremony) dans l'intimité. ~**ly** adv. en privé; dans l'intimité; (inwardly) intérieurement.

privation /praɪ'veɪʃn/ n. privation f.

privet /'prɪvɪt/ n. (bot.) troène m.

privilege /'prɪvəlɪdʒ/ n. privilège m. ~**d** a. privilégié. **be** ~**d to,** avoir le privilège de.

privy /'prɪvɪ/ a. ~ **to,** au fait de.

prize /praɪz/ n. prix m. —a. (entry etc.) primé; (fool etc.) parfait. —v.t. (value) priser. ~**fighter** n. boxeur professionnel m. ~**winner** n. lauréat(e) m. (f.); (in lottery etc.) gagnant(e) m. (f.).

pro /prəʊ/ n. **the** ~**s and cons,** le pour et le contre.

pro- /prəʊ/ pref. pro-.

probab|le /'prɒbəbl/ a. probable. ~**ility** /-'bɪlətɪ/ n. probabilité f. ~**ly** adv. probablement.

probation /prə'beɪʃn/ n. (testing) essai m.; (jurid.) liberté surveillée f. ~**ary** a. d'essai.

probe /prəʊb/ n. (device) sonde f.; (fig.)

enquête f. —v.t. sonder. —v.i. ∿ into, sonder.

problem /'prɒbləm/ n. problème m. —a. difficile. ∿atic /-'mætɪk/ a. problématique.

procedure /prə'si:dʒə(r)/ n. procédure f.; (way of doing sth.) démarche à suivre f.

proceed /prə'si:d/ v.i. (go) aller, avancer; (pass) passer (to, à); (act) procéder. ∿ (with), (continue) continuer. ∿ to do, se mettre à faire. ∿ing n. procédé m.

proceedings /prə'si:dɪŋz/ n. pl. (discussions) débats m. pl.; (meeting) réunion f.; (report) actes m. pl.; (jurid.) poursuites f. pl.

proceeds /'prəʊsi:dz/ n. pl. (profits) produit m., bénéfices m. pl.

process /'prəʊses/ n. processus m.; (method) procédé m. —v.t. (material, data) traiter. in ∿, en cours. in the ∿ of doing, en train de faire.

procession /prə'seʃn/ n. défilé m.

proclaim /prə'kleɪm/ v.t. proclamer. ∿amation /prɒklə'meɪʃn/ n. proclamation f.

procrastinate /prə'kræstɪneɪt/ v.i. différer, tergiverser.

procreation /prəʊkrɪ'eɪʃn/ n. procréation f.

procure /prə'kjʊə(r)/ v.t. obtenir.

prod /prɒd/ v.t./i. (p.t. prodded) pousser. —n. poussée f., coup m.

prodigal /'prɒdɪgl/ a. prodigue.

prodigious /prə'dɪdʒəs/ a. prodigieux.

prodigy /'prɒdɪdʒɪ/ n. prodige m.

produce[1] /prə'dju:s/ v.t./i. produire; (bring out) sortir; (show) présenter; (cause) provoquer; (theatre, TV) mettre en scène; (radio) réaliser; (cinema) produire. ∿er n. metteur en scène m.; réalisateur m.; producteur m. ∿tion /-'dʌkʃn/ n. production f.; mise en scène f.; réalisation f.

produce[2] /'prɒdju:s/ n. (food etc.) produits m. pl.

product /'prɒdʌkt/ n. produit m.

productive /prə'dʌktɪv/ a. productif. ∿ity /prɒdʌk'tɪvətɪ/ n. productivité f.

profane /prə'feɪn/ a. sacrilège; (secular) profane. ∿ity /-'fænətɪ/ n. (oath) juron m.

profess /prə'fes/ v.t. professer. ∿ to do, prétendre faire.

profession /prə'feʃn/ n. profession f. ∿al a. professionnel; (of high quality) de professionnel; (person) qui exerce une profession libérale; n. professionnel(le) m. (f.).

professor /prə'fesə(r)/ n. professeur (titulaire d'une chaire) m.

proficient /prə'fɪʃnt/ a. compétent. ∿cy n. compétence f.

profile /'prəʊfaɪl/ n. profil m.

profit /'prɒfɪt/ n. profit m., bénéfice m. —v.i. (p.t. profited). ∿ by, tirer profit de. ∿able a. rentable.

profound /prə'faʊnd/ a. profond. ∿ly adv. profondément.

profuse /prə'fju:s/ a. abondant. ∿e in, (lavish in) prodigue de. ∿ely adv. en abondance; (apologize) avec effusion. ∿ion /-ʒn/ n. profusion f.

progeny /'prɒdʒənɪ/ n. progéniture f.

program /'prəʊgræm/ n. (Amer.) = **programme**. (computer) ∿, programme m. —v.t. (p.t. programmed) programmer. ∿mer n. programmeur, -se m., f. ∿ming n. (on computer) programmation f.

programme /'prəʊgræm/ n. programme m.; (broadcast) émission f.

progress[1] /'prəʊgres/ n. progrès m. (pl.). in ∿, en cours. make ∿, faire des progrès. ∿ report, compte-rendu m.

progress[2] /prə'gres/ v.i. (advance, improve) progresser. ∿ion /-ʃn/ n. progression f.

progressive /prə'gresɪv/ a. progressif; (reforming) progressiste. ∿ly adv. progressivement.

prohibit /prə'hɪbɪt/ v.t. interdire (s.o. from doing, à qn. de faire).

prohibitive /prə'hɪbətɪv/ a. (price etc.) prohibitif.

project[1] /prə'dʒekt/ v.t. projeter. —v.i. (jut out) être en saillie. ∿ion /-kʃn/ n. projection f.; saillie f.

project[2] /'prɒdʒekt/ n. (plan) projet m.; (undertaking) entreprise f.; (schol.) dossier m.

projectile /prə'dʒektaɪl/ n. projectile m.

projector /prə'dʒektə(r)/ n. (cinema etc.) projecteur m.

proletariat /prəʊlɪ'teərɪət/ n. prolétariat m. ∿an a. prolétarien; n. prolétaire m./f.

proliferate /prə'lɪfəreɪt/ v.i. proliférer. ∿ion /-'reɪʃn/ n. prolifération f.

prolific /prə'lɪfɪk/ a. prolifique.

prologue /'prəʊlɒg/ n. prologue m.

prolong /prə'lɒŋ/ v.t. prolonger.

promenade /prɒmə'nɑːd/ n. promenade f. —v.t./i. (se) promener.

prominent /'prɒmɪnənt/ a. (projecting) proéminent; (conspicuous) bien en vue; (fig.) important. ∿ce n. proéminence f.; importance f. ∿ly adv. bien en vue.

promiscu|ous /prə'mɪskjʊəs/ a. qui a plusieurs partenaires; (*pej.*) de mœurs faciles. **~ity** /prɒmɪ'stjuːətɪ/ *n.* les partenaires multiples; (*pej.*) liberté de mœurs *f.*

promis|e /'prɒmɪs/ *n.* promesse *f.* —*v.t./i.* promettre. **~ing** *a.* prometteur; (*person*) qui promet.

promot|e /prə'məʊt/ *v.t.* promouvoir; (*advertise*) faire la promotion de. **~ion** /-'məʊʃn/ *n.* (*of person, sales, etc.*) promotion *f.*

prompt /prɒmpt/ *a.* rapide; (*punctual*) à l'heure, ponctuel. —*adv.* (*on the dot*) pile. —*v.t.* inciter; (*cause*) provoquer; (*theatre*) souffler (son rôle) à. **~er** souffleur, -se *m., f.* **~ly** *adv.* rapidement; ponctuellement. **~ness** *n.* rapidité *f.*

prone /prəʊn/ *a.* couché sur le ventre. **~ to**, prédisposé à.

prong /prɒŋ/ *n.* (*of fork*) dent *f.*

pronoun /'prəʊnaʊn/ *n.* pronom *m.*

pron|ounce /prə'naʊns/ *v.t.* prononcer. **~ouncement** *n.* déclaration *f.* **~unciation** /-ʌnsɪ'eɪʃn/ *n.* prononciation *f.*

pronounced /prə'naʊnst/ *a.* (*noticeable*) prononcé.

proof /pruːf/ *n.* (*evidence*) preuve *f.*; (*test, trial copy*) épreuve *f.*; (*of liquor*) teneur en alcool *f.* —*a.* **~ against**, à l'épreuve de.

prop[1] /prɒp/ *n.* support *m.* —*v.t.* (*p.t.* **propped**). **~ (up)**, (*support*) étayer; (*lean*) appuyer.

prop[2] /prɒp/ *n.* (*theatre, fam.*) accessoire *m.*

propaganda /prɒpə'gændə/ *n.* propagande *f.*

propagat|e /'prɒpəgeɪt/ *v.t./i.* (se) propager. **~ion** /-'geɪʃn/ *n.* propagation *f.*

propane /'prəʊpeɪn/ *n.* propane *m.*

propel /prə'pel/ *v.t.* (*p.t.* **propelled**) propulser. **~ling pencil**, porte-mine *m. invar.*

propeller /prə'pelə(r)/ *n.* hélice *f.*

proper /'prɒpə(r)/ *a.* correct, bon; (*seemly*) convenable; (*real*) vrai; (*thorough: fam.*) parfait. **~ noun**, nom propre *m.* **~ly** *adv.* correctement, comme il faut; (*rightly*) avec raison.

property /'prɒpətɪ/ *n.* propriété *f.*; (*things owned*) biens *m. pl.*, propriété *f.* —*a.* immobilier, foncier.

prophecy /'prɒfəsɪ/ *n.* prophétie *f.*

prophesy /'prɒfɪsaɪ/ *v.t./i.* prophétiser. **~ that**, prédire que.

prophet /'prɒfɪt/ *n.* prophète *m.* **~ic** /prə'fetɪk/ *a.* prophétique.

proportion /prə'pɔːʃn/ *n.* (*ratio, dimension*) proportion *f.*; (*amount*) partie *f.* **~al, ~ate** *adjs.* proportionnel.

proposal /prə'pəʊzl/ *n.* proposition *f.*; (*of marriage*) demande en mariage *f.*

propos|e /prə'pəʊz/ *v.t.* proposer. —*v.i.* **~e to**, faire une demande en mariage à. **~e to do**, se proposer de faire. **~ition** /prɒpə'zɪʃn/ *n.* proposition *f.*; (*matter: fam.*) affaire *f.*; *v.t.* (*fam.*) faire des propositions malhonnêtes à.

propound /prə'paʊnd/ *v.t.* (*theory etc.*) proposer.

proprietor /prə'praɪətə(r)/ *n.* propriétaire *m./f.*

propriety /prə'praɪətɪ/ *n.* (*correct behaviour*) bienséance *f.*

propulsion /prə'pʌlʃn/ *n.* propulsion *f.*

prosaic /prə'zeɪɪk/ *a.* prosaïque.

proscribe /prə'skraɪb/ *v.t.* proscrire.

prose /prəʊz/ *n.* prose *f.*; (*translation*) thème *m.*

prosecut|e /'prɒsɪkjuːt/ *v.t.* poursuivre. **~ion** /-'kjuːʃn/ *n.* poursuites *f. pl.* **~or** *n.* procureur *m.*

prospect[1] /'prɒspekt/ *n.* perspective *f.*; (*chance*) espoir *m.* **a job with ~s**, un travail avec des perspectives d'avenir.

prospect[2] /prə'spekt/ *v.t./i.* prospecter. **~or** *n.* prospecteur *m.*

prospective /prə'spektɪv/ *a.* (*future*) futur; (*possible*) éventuel.

prospectus /prə'spektəs/ *n.* prospectus *m.*; (*univ.*) guide *m.*

prosper /'prɒspə(r)/ *v.i.* prospérer.

prosper|ous /'prɒspərəs/ *a.* prospère. **~ity** /-'sperətɪ/ *n.* prospérité *f.*

prostate /'prɒsteɪt/ *n.* prostate *f.*

prostitut|e /'prɒstɪtjuːt/ *n.* prostituée *f.* **~ion** /-'tjuːʃn/ *n.* prostitution *f.*

prostrate /'prɒstreɪt/ *a.* (*prone*) à plat ventre; (*submissive*) prosterné; (*exhausted*) prostré.

protagonist /prə'tægənɪst/ *n.* protagoniste *m.*

protect /prə'tekt/ *v.t.* protéger. **~ion** /-kʃn/ *n.* protection *f.* **~or** *n.* protecteur, -trice *m., f.*

protective /prə'tektɪv/ *a.* protecteur; (*clothes*) de protection.

protégé /'prɒtɪʒeɪ/ *n.* protégé *m.* **~e** *n.* protégée *f.*

protein /'prəʊtiːn/ *n.* protéine *f.*

protest[1] /'prəʊtest/ *n.* protestation *f.* **under ~**, en protestant.

protest[2] /prə'test/ *v.t./i.* protester. **~er** *n.* (*pol.*) manifestant(e) *m.* (*f.*).

Protestant /'prɒtɪstənt/ *a. & n.* protestant(e) (*m.* (*f.*)).
protocol /'prəʊtəkɒl/ *n.* protocole *m.*
prototype /'prəʊtətaɪp/ *n.* prototype *m.*
protract /prə'trækt/ *v.t.* prolonger, faire traîner. ~**ed** *a.* prolongé.
protractor /prə'træktə(r)/ *n.* (*for measuring*) rapporteur *m.*
protrude /prə'truːd/ *v.i.* dépasser.
proud /praʊd/ *a.* (**-er, -est**) fier, orgueilleux. ~**ly** *adv.* fièrement.
prove /pruːv/ *v.t.* prouver. —*v.i.* ~ (**to be**) easy/*etc.*, se révéler facile/*etc.* ~ **o.s.**, faire ses preuves. ~**n** *a.* prouvé.
proverb /'prɒvɜːb/ *n.* proverbe *m.* ~**ial** /prə'vɜːbɪəl/ *a.* proverbial.
provide /prə'vaɪd/ *v.t.* fournir (**s.o. with sth.**, qch. à qn.). —*v.i.* ~ **for**, (*allow for*) prévoir; (*guard against*) parer à; (*person*) pourvoir aux besoins de.
provided /prə'vaɪdɪd/ *conj.* ~ **that**, à condition que.
providence /'prɒvɪdəns/ *n.* providence *f.*
providing /prə'vaɪdɪŋ/ *conj.* = **provided.**
province /'prɒvɪns/ *n.* province *f.*; (*fig.*) compétence *f.* ~**ial** /prə'vɪnʃl/ *a. & n.* provincial(e) (*m.* (*f.*)).
provision /prə'vɪʒn/ *n.* (*stock*) provision *f.*; (*supplying*) fourniture *f.*; (*stipulation*) disposition *f.* ~**s**, (*food*) provisions *f. pl.*
provisional /prə'vɪʒənl/ *a.* provisoire. ~**ly** *adv.* provisoirement.
proviso /prə'vaɪzəʊ/ *n.* (*pl.* **-os**) condition *f.*, stipulation *f.*
provoke /prə'vəʊk/ *v.t.* provoquer. ~**cation** /prɒvə'keɪʃn/ *n.* provocation *f.* ~**cative** /-'vɒkətɪv/ *a.* provocant.
prow /praʊ/ *n.* proue *f.*
prowess /'praʊɪs/ *n.* prouesse *f.*
prowl /praʊl/ *v.i.* rôder. —*n.* **be on the** ~, rôder. ~**er** *n.* rôdeur, -se *m.*, *f.*
proximity /prɒk'sɪmətɪ/ *n.* proximité *f.*
proxy /'prɒksɪ/ *n.* **by** ~, par procuration.
prude /pruːd/ *n.* prude *f.* ~**ish** *a.* prude.
prudent /'pruːdnt/ *a.* prudent. ~**ce** *n.* prudence *f.* ~**tly** *adv.* prudemment.
prune[1] /pruːn/ *n.* pruneau *m.*
prune[2] /pruːn/ *v.t.* (*cut*) tailler.
pry[1] /praɪ/ *v.i.* être indiscret. ~ **into**, fourrer son nez dans.
pry[2] /praɪ/ *v.t.* (*Amer.*) = **prise.**
psalm /sɑːm/ *n.* psaume *m.*
pseudo- /'sjuːdəʊ/ *pref.* pseudo-.
pseudonym /'sjuːdənɪm/ *n.* pseudonyme *m.*
psoriasis /sə'raɪəsɪs/ *n.* psoriasis *m.*

psyche /'saɪkɪ/ *n.* psyché *f.*
psychiatry /saɪ'kaɪətrɪ/ *n.* psychiatrie *f.* ~**ic** /-ɪ'ætrɪk/ *a.* psychiatrique. ~**ist** *n.* psychiatre *m./f.*
psychic /'saɪkɪk/ *a.* (*phenomenon etc.*) métaphysique; (*person*) doué de télépathie.
psychoanalyse /saɪkəʊ'ænəlaɪz/ *v.t.* psychanalyser. ~**t** /-ɪst/ *n.* psychanalyste *m./f.*
psychoanalysis /saɪkəʊə'næləsɪs/ *n.* psychanalyse *f.*
psychology /saɪ'kɒlədʒɪ/ *n.* psychologie *f.* ~**ical** /-ə'lɒdʒɪkl/ *a.* psychologique. ~**ist** *n.* psychologue *m./f.*
psychopath /'saɪkəʊpæθ/ *n.* psychopathe *m./f.*
psychosomatic /saɪkəʊsə'mætɪk/ *a.* psychosomatique.
psychotherapy /saɪkəʊ'θerəpɪ/ *n.* psychothérapie *f.* ~**ist** *n.* psychothérapeute *m./f.*
pub /pʌb/ *n.* pub *m.*
puberty /'pjuːbətɪ/ *n.* puberté *f.*
public /'pʌblɪk/ *a.* public; (*library etc.*) municipal. **in** ~, en public. ~ **address system,** sonorisation *f.* (*dans un lieu public*). ~ **house,** pub *m.* ~ **relations,** relations publiques *f. pl.* ~ **school,** école privée *f.*; (*Amer.*) école publique *f.* ~ **servant,** fonctionnaire *m./f.* ~**spirited** *a.* dévoué au bien public. ~ **transport,** transports en commun *m. pl.* ~**ly** *adv.* publiquement.
publican /'pʌblɪkən/ *n.* patron(ne) de pub *m.* (*f.*).
publication /pʌblɪ'keɪʃn/ *n.* publication *f.*
publicity /pʌb'lɪsətɪ/ *n.* publicité *f.*
publicize /'pʌblɪsaɪz/ *v.t.* faire connaître au public.
publish /'pʌblɪʃ/ *v.t.* publier. ~**er** *n.* éditeur *m.* ~**ing** *n.* édition *f.*
puck /pʌk/ *n.* (*ice hockey*) palet *m.*
pucker /'pʌkə(r)/ *v.t./i.* (se) plisser.
pudding /'pʊdɪŋ/ *n.* dessert *m.*; (*steamed*) pudding *m.* **black** ~, boudin *m.* **rice** ~, riz au lait *m.*
puddle /'pʌdl/ *n.* flaque d'eau *f.*
pudgy /'pʌdʒɪ/ *a.* (**-ier, -iest**) dodu.
puerile /'pjʊəraɪl/ *a.* puéril.
puff /pʌf/ *n.* bouffée *f.* —*v.t./i.* souffler. ~ **at,** (*cigar*) tirer sur. ~ **out,** (*swell*) (se) gonfler.
puffy /'pʌfɪ/ *a.* gonflé.
pugnacious /pʌg'neɪʃəs/ *a.* batailleur, combatif.
pug-nosed /'pʌgnəʊzd/ *a.* camus.
pull /pʊl/ *v.t./i.* tirer; (*muscle*) se

froisser. —*n.* traction *f.*; (*fig.*) attraction *f.*; (*influence*) influence *f.* **give a ~,** tirer. **~ a face,** faire une grimace. **~ one's weight,** faire sa part du travail. **~ s.o.'s leg,** faire marcher qn. **~ apart,** mettre en morceaux. **~ away,** (*auto.*) démarrer. **~ back** *or* **out,** (*withdraw*) (se) retirer. **~ down,** baisser; (*building*) démolir. **~ in,** (*enter*) entrer; (*stop*) s'arrêter. **~ off,** enlever; (*fig.*) réussir. **~ out,** (*from bag etc.*) sortir; (*extract*) arracher; (*auto.*) déboîter. **~ over,** (*auto.*) se ranger. **~ round** *or* **through,** s'en tirer. **~ o.s. together,** se ressaisir. **~ up,** remonter; (*uproot*) déraciner; (*auto.*) (s')arrêter.

pulley /'pʊlɪ/ *n.* poulie *f.*

pullover /'pʊləʊvə(r)/ *n.* pull(-over) *m.*

pulp /pʌlp/ *n.* (*of fruit*) pulpe *f.*; (*for paper*) pâte à papier *f.*

pulpit /'pʊlpɪt/ *n.* chaire *f.*

pulsate /pʌl'seɪt/ *v.i.* battre.

pulse /pʌls/ *n.* (*med.*) pouls *m.*

pulverize /'pʌlvəraɪz/ *v.t.* (*grind, defeat*) pulvériser.

pummel /'pʌml/ *v.t.* (*p.t.* **pummelled**) bourrer de coups.

pump[1] /pʌmp/ *n.* pompe *f.* —*v.t./i.* pomper; (*person*) soutirer des renseignements à. **~ up,** gonfler.

pump[2] /pʌmp/ *n.* (*plimsoll*) tennis *m.*; (*for dancing*) escarpin *m.*

pumpkin /'pʌmpkɪn/ *n.* potiron *m.*

pun /pʌn/ *n.* jeu de mots *m.*

punch[1] /pʌntʃ/ *v.t.* donner un coup de poing à; (*perforate*) poinçonner; (*a hole*) faire. —*n.* coup de poing *m.*; (*vigour: sl.*) punch *m.*; (*device*) poinçonneuse *f.* **~-drunk** *a.* sonné. **~-line,** chute *f.* **~-up** *n.* (*fam.*) bagarre *f.*

punch[2] /pʌntʃ/ *n.* (*drink*) punch *m.*

punctual /'pʌnktʃʊəl/ *a.* à l'heure; (*habitually*) ponctuel. **~ity** /-'æləti/ *n.* ponctualité *f.* **~ly** *adv.* à l'heure; ponctuellement.

punctuat|**e** /'pʌnktʃʊeɪt/ *v.t.* ponctuer. **~ion** /-'eɪʃn/ *n.* ponctuation *f.*

puncture /'pʌnktʃə(r)/ *n.* (*in tyre*) crevaison *f.* —*v.t./i.* crever.

pundit /'pʌndɪt/ *n.* expert *m.*

pungent /'pʌndʒənt/ *a.* âcre.

punish /'pʌnɪʃ/ *v.t.* punir (**for sth.,** de qch.). **~able** *a.* punissable (**by,** de). **~ment** *n.* punition *f.*

punitive /'pju:nɪtɪv/ *a.* punitif.

punk /pʌŋk/ *n.* (*music, fan*) punk *m.*; (*person: Amer., fam.*) salaud *m.*

punt[1] /pʌnt/ *n.* (*boat*) bachot *m.*

punt[2] /pʌnt/ *v.i.* (*bet*) parier.

puny /'pju:nɪ/ *a.* (**-ier, -iest**) chétif.

pup(py) /'pʌp(ɪ)/ *n.* chiot *m.*

pupil /'pju:pl/ *n.* (*person*) élève *m./f.*; (*of eye*) pupille *f.*

puppet /'pʌpɪt/ *n.* marionnette *f.*

purchase /'pɜ:tʃəs/ *v.t.* acheter (**from s.o.,** à qn.). —*n.* achat *m.* **~r** /-ə(r)/ *n.* acheteulr, -se *m., f.*

pur|**e** /pjʊə(r)/ *a.* (**-er, -est**) pur. **~ely** *adv.* purement. **~ity** *n.* pureté *f.*

purgatory /'pɜ:gətrɪ/ *n.* purgatoire *m.*

purge /pɜ:dʒ/ *v.t.* purger (**of,** de). —*n.* purge *f.*

purif|**y** /'pjʊərɪfaɪ/ *v.t.* purifier. **~ication** /-ɪ'keɪʃn/ *n.* purification *f.*

purist /'pjʊərɪst/ *n.* puriste *m./f.*

puritan /'pjʊərɪtən/ *n.* puritain(e) *m.* (*f.*). **~ical** /-'tænɪkl/ *a.* puritain.

purple /'pɜ:pl/ *a.* & *n.* violet (*m.*).

purport /pə'pɔ:t/ *v.t.* **~ to be,** (*claim*) prétendre être.

purpose /'pɜ:pəs/ *n.* but *m.*; (*fig.*) résolution *f.* **on ~,** exprès. **~-built** *a.* construit spécialement. **to no ~,** sans résultat.

purr /pɜ:(r)/ *n.* ronronnement *m.* —*v.i.* ronronner.

purse /pɜ:s/ *n.* porte-monnaie *m. invar.*; (*handbag: Amer.*) sac à main *m.* —*v.t.* (*lips*) pincer.

pursue /pə'sju:/ *v.t.* poursuivre. **~r** /-ə(r)/ *n.* poursuivant(e) *m.* (*f.*).

pursuit /pə'sju:t/ *n.* poursuite *f.*; (*fig.*) activité *f.*, occupation *f.*

purveyor /pə'veɪə(r)/ *n.* fournisseur *m.*

pus /pʌs/ *n.* pus *m.*

push /pʊʃ/ *v.t./i.* pousser; (*button*) appuyer sur; (*thrust*) enfoncer; (*recommend: fam.*) proposer avec insistance. —*n.* poussée *f.*; (*effort*) gros effort *m.*; (*drive*) dynamisme *m.* **be ~ed for,** (*time etc.*) manquer de. **be ~ing thirty/** *etc.*, (*fam.*) friser la trentaine/*etc.* **give the ~ to,** (*sl.*) flanquer à la porte. **~ s.o. around,** bousculer qn. **~ back,** repousser. **~-chair** *n.* poussette *f.* **~er** *n.* revendeulr, -se (de drogue) *m., f.* **~ off,** (*sl.*) filer. **~ on,** continuer. **~-over** *n.* jeu d'enfant *m.* **~ up,** (*lift*) relever; (*prices*) faire monter. **~-up** *n.* (*Amer.*) traction *f.* **~y** *a.* (*fam.*) autoritaire.

pushing /'pʊʃɪŋ/ *a.* arriviste.

puss /pʊs/ *n.* (*cat*) minet(te) *m.* (*f.*).

put /pʊt/ *v.t./i.* (*p.t.* **put,** *pres. p.* **putting**) mettre, placer, poser; (*question*) poser. **~ the damage at a million,** estimer les dégâts à un million; **I'd put it at a thousand,** je dirais un millier. ~ **sth. tactfully,** dire qch. avec tact. ~ **across,** communiquer. ~ **away,** ranger; (*fig.*) enfermer. ~ **back,** remettre; (*delay*) retarder. ~ **by,** mettre de côté. ~ **down,** (dé)poser; (*write*) inscrire; (*pay*) verser; (*suppress*) réprimer. ~ **forward,** (*plan*) soumettre. ~ **in,** (*insert*) introduire; (*fix*) installer; (*submit*) soumettre. ~ **in for,** faire une demande de. ~ **off,** (*postpone*) renvoyer à plus tard; (*disconcert*) déconcerter; (*displease*) rebuter. ~ **s.o. off sth.,** dégoûter qn. de qch. ~ **on,** (*clothes, radio*) mettre; (*light*) allumer; (*speed, accent, weight*) prendre. ~ **out,** sortir; (*stretch*) (é)tendre; (*extinguish*) éteindre; (*disconcert*) déconcerter; (*inconvenience*) déranger. ~ **up,** lever, remonter; (*building*) construire; (*notice*) mettre; (*price*) augmenter; (*guest*) héberger; (*offer*) offrir. ~**-up job,** coup monté *m.* ~ **up with,** supporter.

putt /pʌt/ *n.* (*golf*) putt *m.*
putter /'pʌtə(r)/ *v.i.* (*Amer.*) bricoler.
putty /'pʌti/ *n.* mastic *m.*
puzzle /'pʌzl/ *n.* énigme *f.*; (*game*) casse-tête *m. invar.*; (*jigsaw*) puzzle *m.* —*v.t.* rendre perplexe. —*v.i.* se creuser la tête.
pygmy /'pɪgmɪ/ *n.* pygmée *m.*
pyjamas /pə'dʒɑːməz/ *n. pl.* pyjama *m.*
pylon /'paɪlɒn/ *n.* pylône *m.*
pyramid /'pɪrəmɪd/ *n.* pyramide *f.*
Pyrenees /pɪrə'niːz/ *n. pl.* the ~, les Pyrénées *f. pl.*
python /'paɪθn/ *n.* python *m.*

Q

quack[1] /kwæk/ *n.* (*of duck*) coin-coin *m. invar.*
quack[2] /kwæk/ *n.* charlatan *m.*
quad /kwɒd/ (*fam.*) = **quadrangle, quadruplet.**
quadrangle /'kwɒdræŋgl/ (*of college*) *n.* cour *f.*
quadruped /'kwɒdrʊped/ *n.* quadrupède *m.*
quadruple /kwɒ'druːpl/ *a. & n.* quadruple (*m.*). —*v.t./i.* quadrupler. ~**ts** /-plɪts/ *n. pl.* quadruplé(e)s *m.* (*f.*) *pl.*
quagmire /'kwægmaɪə(r)/ *n.* (*bog*) bourbier *m.*
quail /kweɪl/ *n.* (*bird*) caille *f.*

quaint /kweɪnt/ *a.* (**-er, -est**) pittoresque; (*old*) vieillot; (*odd*) bizarre. ~**ness** *n.* pittoresque *m.*
quake /kweɪk/ *v.i.* trembler. —*n.* (*fam.*) tremblement de terre *m.*
Quaker /'kweɪkə(r)/ *n.* quaker(esse) *m.* (*f.*).
qualification /kwɒlɪfɪ'keɪʃn/ *n.* diplôme *m.*; (*ability*) compétence *f.*; (*fig.*) réserve *f.*, restriction *f.*
qualif|y /'kwɒlɪfaɪ/ *v.t.* qualifier; (*modify: fig.*) mettre des réserves à; (*statement*) nuancer. —*v.i.* obtenir son diplôme (**as,** de); (*sport*) se qualifier; (*fig.*) remplir les conditions requises. ~**ied** *a.* diplômé; (*able*) qualifié (**to do,** pour faire); (*fig.*) conditionnel; (*success*) modéré. ~**ying** *a.* (*round*) éliminatoire; (*candidates*) qualifiés.
qualit|y /'kwɒlətɪ/ *n.* qualité *f.* ~**ative** /-ɪtətɪv/ *a.* qualitatif.
qualm /kwɑːm/ *n.* scrupule *m.*
quandary /'kwɒndərɪ/ *n.* embarras *m.*, dilemme *m.*
quantit|y /'kwɒntətɪ/ *n.* quantité *f.* ~**ative** /-ɪtətɪv/ *a.* quantitatif.
quarantine /'kwɒrəntiːn/ *n.* (*isolation*) quarantaine *f.*
quarrel /'kwɒrəl/ *n.* dispute *f.*, querelle *f.* —*v.i.* (*p.t.* **quarrelled**) se disputer. ~**some** *a.* querelleur.
quarry[1] /'kwɒrɪ/ *n.* (*prey*) proie *f.*
quarry[2] /'kwɒrɪ/ *n.* (*excavation*) carrière *f.* —*v.t.* extraire.
quart /kwɔːt/ *n.* (*approx.*) litre *m.*
quarter /'kwɔːtə(r)/ *n.* quart *m.*; (*of year*) trimestre *m.*; (*25 cents: Amer.*) quart de dollar *m.*; (*district*) quartier *m.* ~**s,** logement(s) *m.* (*pl.*) —*v.t.* diviser en quatre; (*mil.*) cantonner. **from all** ~**s,** de toutes parts. ~**-final** *n.* quart de finale *m.* ~**ly** *a.* trimestriel; *adv.* trimestriellement.
quartermaster /'kwɔːtəmɑːstə(r)/ *n.* (*mil.*) intendant *m.*
quartet /kwɔː'tet/ *n.* quatuor *m.*
quartz /kwɔːts/ *n.* quartz *m.* —*a.* (*watch etc.*) à quartz.
quash /kwɒʃ/ *v.t.* (*suppress*) étouffer; (*jurid.*) annuler.
quasi- /'kweɪsaɪ/ *pref.* quasi-.
quaver /'kweɪvə(r)/ *v.i.* trembler, chevroter. —*n.* (*mus.*) croche *f.*
quay /kiː/ *n.* (*naut.*) quai *m.* ~**side** *n.* (*edge of quay*) quai *m.*
queasy /'kwiːzɪ/ *a.* (*stomach*) délicat. **feel** ~, avoir mal au cœur.
queen /kwiːn/ *n.* reine *f.*; (*cards*) dame *f.* ~ **mother,** reine mère *f.*

queer /kwɪə(r)/ *a.* (**-er, -est**) étrange; (*dubious*) louche; (*ill*) patraque. —*n.* (*sl.*) homosexuel *m.*

quell /kwel/ *v.t.* réprimer.

quench /kwentʃ/ *v.t.* éteindre; (*thirst*) étancher; (*desire*) étouffer.

query /ˈkwɪərɪ/ *n.* question *f.* —*v.t.* mettre en question.

quest /kwest/ *n.* recherche *f.*

question /ˈkwestʃən/ *n.* question *f.* —*v.t.* interroger; (*doubt*) mettre en question, douter de. **a ~ of money**, une question d'argent. **in ~**, en question. **no ~ of**, pas question de. **out of the ~**, hors de question. **~ mark**, point d'interrogation *m.*

questionable /ˈkwestʃənəbl/ *a.* discutable.

questionnaire /kwestʃəˈneə(r)/ *n.* questionnaire *m.*

queue /kjuː/ *n.* queue *f.* —*v.i.* (*pres. p.* **queuing**) faire la queue.

quibble /ˈkwɪbl/ *v.i.* ergoter.

quick /kwɪk/ *a.* (**-er, -est**) rapide. —*adv.* vite. —*n.* **a ~ one**, (*fam.*) un petit verre. **cut to the ~**, piquer au vif. **be ~**, (*hurry*) se dépêcher. **have a ~ temper**, s'emporter facilement. **~ly** *adv.* rapidement, vite. **~-witted** *a.* vif.

quicken /ˈkwɪkən/ *v.t./i.* (s')accélérer.

quicksand /ˈkwɪksænd/ *n.* **~(s)**, sables mouvants *m. pl.*

quid /kwɪd/ *n. invar.* (*sl.*) livre *f.*

quiet /ˈkwaɪət/ *a.* (**-er, -est**) (*calm, still*) tranquille; (*silent*) silencieux; (*gentle*) doux; (*discreet*) discret. —*n.* tranquillité *f.* **keep ~**, se taire. **on the ~**, en cachette. **~ly** *adv.* tranquillement; silencieusement; doucement; discrètement. **~ness** *n.* tranquillité *f.*

quieten /ˈkwaɪətn/ *v.t./i.* (se) calmer.

quill /kwɪl/ *n.* plume (d'oie) *f.*

quilt /kwɪlt/ *n.* édredon *m.* (**continental**) **~**, couette *f.* —*v.t.* matelasser.

quinine /ˈkwɪniːn, *Amer.* ˈkwaɪnaɪn/ *n.* quinine *f.*

quintet /kwɪnˈtet/ *n.* quintette *m.*

quintuplets /kwɪnˈtjuːplɪts/ *n. pl.* quintuplé(e)s *m.* (*f.*) *pl.*

quip /kwɪp/ *n.* mot piquant *m.*

quirk /kwɜːk/ *n.* bizarrerie *f.*

quit /kwɪt/ *v.t.* (*p.t.* **quitted**) quitter. —*v.i.* abandonner; (*resign*) démissionner. **~ doing**, (*cease: Amer.*) cesser de faire.

quite /kwaɪt/ *adv.* tout à fait, vraiment; (*rather*) assez. **~ (so)!**, parfaitement! **~ a few**, un assez grand nombre (de).

quits /kwɪts/ *a.* quitte (**with**, envers). **call it ~**, en rester là.

quiver /ˈkwɪvə(r)/ *v.i.* trembler.

quiz /kwɪz/ *n.* (*pl.* **quizzes**) test *m.*; (*game*) jeu-concours *m.* —*v.t.* (*p.t.* **quizzed**) questionner.

quizzical /ˈkwɪzɪkl/ *a.* moqueur.

quorum /ˈkwɔːrəm/ *n.* quorum *m.*

quota /ˈkwəʊtə/ *n.* quota *m.*

quotation /kwəʊˈteɪʃn/ *n.* citation *f.*; (*price*) devis *m.*; (*stock exchange*) cotation *f.* **~ marks**, guillemets *m. pl.*

quote /kwəʊt/ *v.t.* citer; (*reference*: *comm.*) rappeler; (*price*) indiquer; (*share price*) coter. —*v.i.* **~ for**, faire un devis pour. **~ from**, citer. —*n.* (*estimate*) devis; (*fam.*) = **quotation**. **in ~s**, (*fam.*) entre guillemets.

quotient /ˈkwəʊʃnt/ *n.* quotient *m.*

R

rabbi /ˈræbaɪ/ *n.* rabbin *m.*

rabbit /ˈræbɪt/ *n.* lapin *m.*

rabble /ˈræbl/ *n.* (*crowd*) cohue *f.* **the ~**, (*pej.*) la populace.

rabid /ˈræbɪd/ *a.* enragé.

rabies /ˈreɪbiːz/ *n.* (*disease*) rage *f.*

race¹ /reɪs/ *n.* course *f.* —*v.t.* (*horse*) faire courir; (*engine*) emballer. **~ (against)**, faire la course à. —*v.i.* courir; (*rush*) foncer. **~-track** *n.* piste *f.*; (*for horses*) champ de courses *m.*

race² /reɪs/ *n.* (*group*) race *f.* —*a.* racial; (*relations*) entre les races.

racecourse /ˈreɪskɔːs/ *n.* champ de courses *m.*

racehorse /ˈreɪshɔːs/ *n.* cheval de course *m.*

racial /ˈreɪʃl/ *a.* racial.

racing /ˈreɪsɪŋ/ *n.* courses *f. pl.* **~ car**, voiture de course *f.*

racis|t /ˈreɪsɪst/ *a. & n.* raciste (*m./f.*). **~m** /-zəm/ *n.* racisme *m.*

rack¹ /ræk/ *n.* (*shelf*) étagère *f.*; (*pigeon-holes*) casier *m.*; (*for luggage*) porte-bagages *m. invar.*; (*for dishes*) égouttoir *m.*; (*on car roof*) galerie *f.* —*v.t.* **~ one's brains**, se creuser la cervelle.

rack² /ræk/ *n.* **go to ~ and ruin**, aller à la ruine; (*building*) tomber en ruine.

racket¹ /ˈrækɪt/ *n.* raquette *f.*

racket² /ˈrækɪt/ *n.* (*din*) tapage *m.*; (*dealings*) combine *f.*; (*crime*) racket *m.* **~eer** /-əˈtɪə(r)/ *n.* racketteur *m.*

racy /'reɪsɪ/ a. (-ier, -iest) fougueux, piquant; (*Amer.*) risqué.

radar /'reɪdɑː(r)/ n. radar m. —a. (*system etc.*) radar invar.

radial /'reɪdɪəl/ a. (*tyre*) à carcasse radiale.

radian|t /'reɪdɪənt/ a. rayonnant. ∼ce n. éclat m. ∼tly adv. avec éclat.

radiat|e /'reɪdɪeɪt/ v.t. dégager. —v.i. rayonner (**from**, de). ∼ion /-'eɪʃn/ n. rayonnement m.; (*radioactivity*) radiation f.

radiator /'reɪdɪeɪtə(r)/ n. radiateur m.

radical /'rædɪkl/ a. radical. —n. (*person: pol.*) radical(e) m. (f.).

radio /'reɪdɪəʊ/ n. (*pl.* -os) radio f. —v.t. (*message*) envoyer par radio; (*person*) appeler par radio.

radioactiv|e /reɪdɪəʊ'æktɪv/ a. radioactif. ∼ity /-'tɪvɪtɪ/ n. radioactivité f.

radiographer /reɪdɪ'ɒgrəfə(r)/ n. radiologue m./f.

radish /'rædɪʃ/ n. radis m.

radius /'reɪdɪəs/ n. (*pl.* -dii /-dɪaɪ/) rayon m.

raffle /'ræfl/ n. tombola f.

raft /rɑːft/ n. radeau m.

rafter /'rɑːftə(r)/ n. chevron m.

rag[1] /ræg/ n. lambeau m., loque f.; (*for wiping*) chiffon m.; (*newspaper*) torchon m. **in** ∼**s**, (*person*) en haillons; (*clothes*) en lambeaux. ∼ **doll**, poupée de chiffon f.

rag[2] /ræg/ v.t. (*p.t.* ragged) (*tease: sl.*) taquiner. —n. (*univ., sl.*) carnaval m. (*pour une œuvre de charité*).

ragamuffin /'rægəmʌfɪn/ n. va-nu-pieds m. invar.

rage /reɪdʒ/ n. rage f., fureur f. —v.i. rager; (*storm, battle*) faire rage. **be all the** ∼, faire fureur.

ragged /'rægɪd/ a. (*clothes, person*) loqueteux; (*edge*) déchiqueté.

raging /'reɪdʒɪŋ/ a. (*storm, fever, etc.*) violent.

raid /reɪd/ n. (*mil.*) raid m.; (*by police*) rafle f.; (*by criminals*) hold-up m. invar. —v.t. faire un raid *or* une rafle *or* un hold-up dans. ∼**er** n. (*person*) bandit m., pillard m. ∼**ers** n. pl. (*mil.*) commando m.

rail /reɪl/ n. (*on balcony*) balustrade f.; (*stairs*) main courante f., rampe f.; (*for train*) rail m.; (*for curtain*) tringle f. **by** ∼, par chemin de fer.

railing /'reɪlɪŋ/ n. ∼**s**, grille f.

railroad /'reɪlrəʊd/ n. (*Amer.*) = **railway**.

railway /'reɪlweɪ/ n. chemin de fer m. ∼

line, voie ferrée f. ∼**man** n. (*pl.* -men) cheminot m. ∼ **station**, gare f.

rain /reɪn/ n. pluie f. —v.i. pleuvoir. ∼**forest**, forêt (humide) tropicale f. ∼**storm** n. trombe d'eau f. ∼**water** n. eau de pluie f.

rainbow /'reɪnbəʊ/ n. arc-en-ciel m.

raincoat /'reɪnkəʊt/ n. imperméable m.

rainfall /'reɪnfɔːl/ n. précipitation f.

rainy /'reɪnɪ/ a. (-ier, -iest) pluvieux; (*season*) des pluies.

raise /reɪz/ v.t. lever; (*breed, build*) élever; (*question etc.*) soulever; (*price etc.*) relever; (*money etc.*) obtenir; (*voice*) élever. —n. (*Amer.*) augmentation f.

raisin /'reɪzn/ n. raisin sec m.

rake[1] /reɪk/ n. râteau m. —v.t. (*garden*) ratisser; (*search*) fouiller dans. ∼ **in**, (*money*) amasser. ∼**off** n. (*fam.*) profit m. ∼ **up**, (*memories, past*) remuer.

rake[2] /reɪk/ n. (*man*) débauché m.

rally /'rælɪ/ v.t./i. (se) rallier; (*strength*) reprendre; (*after illness*) aller mieux. —n. rassemblement m.; (*auto.*) rallye m.; (*tennis*) échange m. ∼ **round**, venir en aide.

ram /ræm/ n. bélier m. —v.t. (*p.t.* rammed) (*thrust*) enfoncer; (*crash into*) emboutir, percuter.

RAM /ræm/ abbr. (*random access memory*) mémoire vive f.

rambl|e /'ræmbl/ n. randonnée f. —v.i. faire une randonnée. ∼**e on**, parler (sans cesse), divaguer. ∼**er** n. randonneur, -se, m., f. ∼**ing** a. (*speech*) décousu.

ramification /ræmɪfɪ'keɪʃn/ n. ramification f.

ramp /ræmp/ n. (*slope*) rampe f.; (*in garage*) pont de graissage m.

rampage[1] /ræm'peɪdʒ/ v.i. se livrer à des actes de violence, se déchaîner.

rampage[2] /'ræmpeɪdʒ/ n. **go on the** ∼ = **rampage**[1].

rampant /'ræmpənt/ a. **be** ∼, (*disease etc.*) sévir, être répandu.

rampart /'ræmpɑːt/ n. rempart m.

ramshackle /'ræmʃækl/ a. délabré.

ran /ræn/ see **run**.

ranch /rɑːntʃ/ n. ranch m.

rancid /'rænsɪd/ a. rance.

rancour /'ræŋkə(r)/ n. rancœur f.

random /'rændəm/ a. fait, pris, etc. au hasard, aléatoire (*techn.*). —n. **at** ∼, au hasard.

randy /'rændɪ/ a. (-ier, -iest) (*fam.*) excité, en chaleur.

rang /ræŋ/ see **ring**[2].

range /reɪndʒ/ n. (distance) portée f.; (of aircraft etc.) rayon d'action m.; (series) gamme f.; (scale) échelle f.; (choice) choix m.; (domain) champ m.; (of mountains) chaîne f.; (stove) cuisinière f. —v.i. s'étendre; (vary) varier.

ranger /reɪndʒə(r)/ n. garde forestier m.

rank[1] /ræŋk/ n. rang m.; (grade: mil.) grade m., rang m. —v.t./i. ∼ **among**, compter parmi. **the ∼ and file**, les gens ordinaires.

rank[2] /ræŋk/ a. (-er, -est) (plants: pej.) luxuriant; (smell) fétide; (complete) absolu.

rankle /ˈræŋkl/ v.i. ∼ **with s.o.**, rester sur le cœur à qn.

ransack /ˈrænsæk/ v.t. (search) fouiller; (pillage) saccager.

ransom /ˈrænsəm/ n. rançon f. —v.t. rançonner; (redeem) racheter. **hold to ∼**, rançonner.

rant /rænt/ v.i. tempêter.

rap /ræp/ n. petit coup sec m. —v.t./i. (p.t. rapped) frapper.

rape /reɪp/ v.t. violer. —n. viol m.

rapid /ˈræpɪd/ a. rapide. ∼**ity** /rəˈpɪdətɪ/ n. rapidité f. ∼**s** n. pl. (of river) rapides m. pl.

rapist /ˈreɪpɪst/ n. violeur m.

rapport /ræˈpɔː(r)/ n. rapport m.

rapt /ræpt/ a. (attention) profond. ∼ **in**, plongé dans.

raptur|e /ˈræptʃə(r)/ n. extase f. ∼**ous** a. (person) en extase; (welcome etc.) frénétique.

rar|e[1] /reə(r)/ a. (-er, -est) rare. ∼**ely** adv. rarement. ∼**ity** n. rareté f.

rare[2] /reə(r)/ a. (-er, -est) (culin.) saignant.

rarefied /ˈreərɪfaɪd/ a. raréfié.

raring /ˈreərɪŋ/ a. ∼ **to**, (fam.) impatient de.

rascal /ˈrɑːskl/ n. coquin(e) m. (f.).

rash[1] /ræʃ/ n. (med.) éruption f., rougeurs f. pl.

rash[2] /ræʃ/ a. (-er, -est) imprudent. ∼**ly** adv. imprudemment. ∼**ness** n. imprudence f.

rasher /ˈræʃə(r)/ n. tranche (de lard) f.

raspberry /ˈrɑːzbrɪ/ n. framboise f.

rasping /ˈrɑːspɪŋ/ a. grinçant.

rat /ræt/ n. rat m. —v.i. (p.t. ratted). ∼ **on**, (desert) lâcher; (inform on) dénoncer. ∼ **race**, foire d'empoigne f.

rate /reɪt/ n. (ratio, level) taux m.; (speed) allure f.; (price) tarif m. ∼**s**, (taxes) impôts locaux m. pl. —v.t. évaluer; (consider) considérer; (deserve: Amer.) mériter. —v.i. ∼ **as**, être

considéré comme. **at any ∼**, en tout cas. **at the ∼ of**, (on the basis of) à raison de.

ratepayer /ˈreɪtpeɪə(r)/ n. contribuable m./f.

rather /ˈrɑːðə(r)/ adv. (by preference) plutôt; (fairly) assez, plutôt; (a little) un peu. **I would ∼ go**, j'aimerais mieux partir. ∼ **than go**, plutôt que de partir.

ratif|y /ˈrætɪfaɪ/ v.t. ratifier. ∼**ication** /-ɪˈkeɪʃn/ n. ratification f.

rating /ˈreɪtɪŋ/ n. classement m.; (sailor) matelot m.; (number) indice m. **the ∼s**, (TV) l'audimat (P.).

ratio /ˈreɪʃɪəʊ/ n. (pl. -os) proportion f.

ration /ˈræʃn/ n. ration f. —v.t. rationner.

rational /ˈræʃənl/ a. rationnel; (person) raisonnable.

rationalize /ˈræʃənəlaɪz/ v.t. tenter de justifier; (organize) rationaliser.

rattle /ˈrætl/ v.i. faire du bruit; (of bottles) cliqueter. —v.t. agacer; (sl.) agacer. —n. bruit (de ferraille) m.; cliquetis m.; (toy) hochet m. ∼ **off**, débiter en vitesse.

rattlesnake /ˈrætlsneɪk/ n. serpent à sonnette m., crotale m.

raucous /ˈrɔːkəs/ a. rauque.

raunchy /ˈrɔːntʃɪ/ a. (-ier, -iest) (Amer., sl.) cochon.

ravage /ˈrævɪdʒ/ v.t. ravager. ∼**s** /-ɪz/ n. pl. ravages m. pl.

rav|e /reɪv/ v.i. divaguer; (in anger) tempêter. ∼**e about**, s'extasier sur. ∼**ings** n. pl. divagations f. pl.

raven /ˈreɪvn/ n. corbeau m.

ravenous /ˈrævənəs/ a. vorace. **I am ∼**, je meurs de faim.

ravine /rəˈviːn/ n. ravin m.

raving /ˈreɪvɪŋ/ a. ∼ **lunatic**, fou furieux m., folle furieuse f.

ravioli /rævɪˈəʊlɪ/ n. ravioli m. pl.

ravish /ˈrævɪʃ/ v.t. (rape) ravir. ∼**ing** a. (enchanting) ravissant.

raw /rɔː/ a. (-er, -est) cru; (not processed) brut; (wound) à vif; (immature) inexpérimenté. **get a ∼ deal**, être mal traité. ∼ **materials**, matières premières f. pl.

ray /reɪ/ n. (of light etc.) rayon m. ∼ **of hope**, lueur d'espoir f.

raze /reɪz/ v.t. (destroy) raser.

razor /ˈreɪzə(r)/ n. rasoir m. ∼**-blade** n. lame de rasoir f.

re /riː/ prep. concernant.

re- /riː/ pref. re-, ré-, r-.

reach /riːtʃ/ v.t. atteindre, arriver à; (contact) joindre; (hand over) passer. —v.i. s'étendre. —n. portée f. ~ for, tendre la main pour prendre. within ~ of, à portée de; (close to) à proximité de.

react /rɪ'ækt/ v.i. réagir.

reaction /rɪ'ækʃn/ n. réaction f. ~ary a. & n. réactionnaire (m./f.).

reactor /rɪ'æktə(r)/ n. réacteur m.

read /riːd/ v.t./i. (p.t. read /red/) lire; (fig.) comprendre; (study) étudier; (of instrument) indiquer. —n. (fam.) lecture f. ~ about s.o., lire un article sur qn. ~ out, lire à haute voix. ~able a. agréable or facile à lire. ~ing n. lecture f.; indication f. ~ing-glasses pl. n. lunettes pour lire f. pl. ~ing-lamp n. lampe de bureau f. ~-out n. affichage m.

reader /'riːdə(r)/ n. leciteur, -trice m., f. ~ship n. lecteurs m. pl.

readily /'redɪlɪ/ adv. (willingly) volontiers; (easily) facilement.

readiness /'redɪnɪs/ n. empressement m. in ~, prêt (for, à).

readjust /riːə'dʒʌst/ v.t. rajuster. —v.i. se réadapter (to, à).

ready /'redɪ/ a. (-ier, -iest) prêt; (quick) prompt. —n. at the ~, tout prêt. ~-made a. tout fait. ~ money, (argent) liquide m. ~ reckoner, barème m. ~-to-wear a. prêt-à-porter.

real /rɪəl/ a. vrai, véritable, réel. —adv. (Amer., fam.) vraiment. ~ estate, biens fonciers m. pl.

realis|t /'rɪəlɪst/ n. réaliste m./f. ~m /-zəm/ n. réalisme m. ~tic /-'lɪstɪk/ a. réaliste. ~tically /-'lɪstɪklɪ/ adv. avec réalisme.

reality /rɪ'ælətɪ/ n. réalité f.

realiz|e /'rɪəlaɪz/ v.t. se rendre compte de, comprendre; (fulfil, turn into cash) réaliser; (price) atteindre. ~ation /-'zeɪʃn/ n. prise de conscience f.; réalisation f.

really /'rɪəlɪ/ adv. vraiment.

realtor /'rɪəltə(r)/ n. (Amer.) agent immobilier m.

realm /relm/ n. royaume m.

reap /riːp/ v.t. (crop, field) moissonner; (fig.) récolter.

reappear /riːə'pɪə(r)/ v.i. réapparaître, reparaître.

reappraisal /riːə'preɪzl/ n. réévaluation f.

rear¹ /rɪə(r)/ n. arrière m., derrière m. —a. arrière invar., de derrière. ~-view mirror, rétroviseur m.

rear² /rɪə(r)/ v.t. (bring up, breed) élever. —v.i. (horse) se cabrer. ~ one's head, dresser la tête.

rearguard /'rɪəgɑːd/ n. (mil.) arrière-garde f.

rearm /riː'ɑːm/ v.t./i. réarmer.

rearrange /riːə'reɪndʒ/ v.t. réarranger.

reason /'riːzn/ n. raison f. —v.i. raisonner. it stands to ~ that, de toute évidence. we have ~ to believe that, on a tout lieu de croire que. there is no ~ to panic, il n'y a pas de raison de paniquer. ~ with, raisonner. everything within ~, tout dans les limites normales. ~ing n. raisonnement m.

reasonable /'riːznəbl/ a. raisonnable.

reassur|e /riːə'ʃʊə(r)/ v.t. rassurer. ~ance n. réconfort m.

rebate /'riːbeɪt/ n. remboursement (partiel) m.; (discount) rabais m.

rebel¹ /'rebl/ n. & a. rebelle (m./f.).

rebel² /rɪ'bel/ v.i. (p.t. rebelled) se rebeller. ~lion n. rébellion f. ~lious a. rebelle.

rebound /rɪ'baʊnd/ v.i. rebondir. ~ on, (backfire) se retourner contre. —n. /'riːbaʊnd/ n. rebond m.

rebuff /rɪ'bʌf/ v.t. repousser. —n. rebuffade f.

rebuild /riː'bɪld/ v.t. reconstruire.

rebuke /rɪ'bjuːk/ v.t. réprimander. —n. réprimande f., reproche m.

rebuttal /rɪ'bʌtl/ n. réfutation f.

recall /rɪ'kɔːl/ v.t. (to s.o., call back) rappeler; (remember) se rappeler. —n. rappel m.

recant /rɪ'kænt/ v.i. se rétracter.

recap /'riːkæp/ v.t./i. (p.t. recapped) (fam.) récapituler. —n. (fam.) récapitulation f.

recapitulat|e /riːkə'pɪtʃʊleɪt/ v.t./i. récapituler. ~ion /-'leɪʃn/ n. récapitulation f.

recapture /riː'kæptʃə(r)/ v.t. reprendre; (recall) recréer.

reced|e /rɪ'siːd/ v.i. s'éloigner. his hair is ~ing, son front se dégarnit. ~ing a. (forehead) fuyant.

receipt /rɪ'siːt/ n. (written) reçu m.; (of letter) réception f. ~s, (money: comm.) recettes f. pl.

receive /rɪ'siːv/ v.t. recevoir. ~r /-ə(r)/ n. (of stolen goods) receleulr, -se m., f.; (telephone) combiné m.

recent /'riːsnt/ a. récent. ~ly adv. récemment.

receptacle /rɪ'septəkl/ n. récipient m.

reception /rɪ'sepʃn/ n. réception f. give s.o. a warm ~, donner un accueil chaleureux à qn. **~ist** *n.* réceptionniste *m./f.*

receptive /rɪ'septɪv/ *a.* réceptif.

recess /rɪ'ses/ *n.* (*alcove*) renfoncement *m.*; (*nook*) recoin *m.*; (*holiday*) vacances *f. pl.*; (*schol.*, *Amer.*) récréation *f.*

recession /rɪ'seʃn/ *n.* récession *f.*

recharge /ri:'tʃɑːdʒ/ *v.t.* recharger.

recipe /'resəpɪ/ *n.* recette *f.*

recipient /rɪ'sɪpɪənt/ *n.* (*of honour*) récipiendaire *m.*; (*of letter*) destinataire *m./f.*

reciprocal /rɪ'sɪprəkl/ *a.* réciproque.

reciprocate /rɪ'sɪprəkeɪt/ *v.t.* offrir en retour. —*v.i.* en faire autant.

recital /rɪ'saɪtl/ *n.* récital *m.*

recite /rɪ'saɪt/ *v.t.* (*poem*, *lesson*, *etc.*) réciter; (*list*) énumérer.

reckless /'reklɪs/ *a.* imprudent. **~ly** *adv.* imprudemment.

reckon /'rekən/ *v.t./i.* calculer; (*judge*) considérer; (*think*) penser. **~ on/with**, compter sur/avec. **~ing** *n.* calcul(s) *m.* (*pl.*).

reclaim /rɪ'kleɪm/ *v.t.* (*seek return of*) réclamer; (*land*) défricher; (*flooded land*) assécher.

recline /rɪ'klaɪn/ *v.i.* être étendu. **~ing** *a.* (*person*) étendu; (*seat*) à dossier réglable.

recluse /rɪ'kluːs/ *n.* reclus(e) *m.* (*f.*), ermite *m.*

recognition /rekəg'nɪʃn/ *n.* reconnaissance *f.* **beyond ~**, méconnaissable. **gain ~**, être reconnu.

recognize /'rekəgnaɪz/ *v.t.* reconnaître.

recoil /rɪ'kɔɪl/ *v.i.* reculer (**from**, devant).

recollect /rekə'lekt/ *v.t.* se souvenir de, se rappeler. **~ion** /-kʃn/ *n.* souvenir *m.*

recommend /rekə'mend/ *v.t.* recommander. **~ation** /-'deɪʃn/ *n.* recommandation *f.*

recompense /'rekəmpens/ *v.t.* (ré)compenser. —*n.* récompense *f.*

reconcile /'rekənsaɪl/ *v.t.* (*people*) réconcilier; (*facts*) concilier. **~e o.s. to**, se résigner à. **~iation** /-sɪlɪ'eɪʃn/ *n.* réconciliation *f.*

recondition /riːkən'dɪʃn/ *v.t.* remettre à neuf, réviser.

reconnoitre /rekə'nɔɪtə(r)/ *v.t.* (*pres. p.* **-tring**) (*mil.*) reconnaître. **~aissance** /rɪ'kɒnɪsns/ *n.* reconnaissance *f.*

reconsider /riːkən'sɪdə(r)/ *v.t.* reconsidérer. —*v.i.* se déjuger.

reconstruct /riːkən'strʌkt/ *v.t.* reconstruire; (*crime*) reconstituer.

record[1] /rɪ'kɔːd/ *v.t./i.* (*in register, on*

tape, *etc.*) enregistrer; (*in diary*) noter. **~ that**, rapporter que. **~ing** *n.* enregistrement *m.*

record[2] /'rekɔːd/ *n.* (*report*) rapport *m.*; (*register*) registre *m.*; (*mention*) mention *f.*; (*file*) dossier *m.*; (*fig.*) résultats *m. pl.*; (*mus.*) disque *m.*; (*sport*) record *m.* (*criminal*) **~**, casier judiciaire *m.* —*a.* record *invar.* **off the ~**, officieusement. **~-holder** *n.* déten⸌teur, -trice du record *m.*, *f.* **~-player** *n.* électrophone *m.*

recorder /rɪ'kɔːdə(r)/ *n.* (*mus.*) flûte à bec *f.*

recount /rɪ'kaʊnt/ *v.t.* raconter.

re-count /riː'kaʊnt/ *v.t.* recompter.

recoup /rɪ'kuːp/ *v.t.* récupérer.

recourse /rɪ'kɔːs/ *n.* recours *m.* **have ~ to**, avoir recours à.

recover /rɪ'kʌvə(r)/ *v.t.* récupérer. —*v.i.* se remettre; (*med.*) se rétablir; (*economy*) se redresser. **~y** *n.* récupération *f.*; (*med.*) rétablissement *m.*

recreation /rekrɪ'eɪʃn/ *n.* récréation *f.* **~al** *a.* de récréation.

recrimination /rɪkrɪmɪ'neɪʃn/ *n.* contre-accusation *f.*

recruit /rɪ'kruːt/ *n.* recrue *f.* —*v.t.* recruter. **~ment** *n.* recrutement *m.*

rectangle /'rektæŋgl/ *n.* rectangle *m.* **~ular** /-'tæŋgjʊlə(r)/ *a.* rectangulaire.

rectify /'rektɪfaɪ/ *v.t.* rectifier. **~ication** /-ɪ'keɪʃn/ *n.* rectification *f.*

recuperate /rɪ'kjuːpəreɪt/ *v.t.* récupérer. —*v.i.* (*med.*) se rétablir.

recur /rɪ'kɜː(r)/ *v.i.* (*p.t.* **recurred**) revenir, se répéter.

recurrent /rɪ'kʌrənt/ *a.* fréquent. **~ce** *n.* répétition *f.*, retour *m.*

recycle /riː'saɪkl/ *v.t.* recycler.

red /red/ *a.* (**redder, reddest**) rouge; (*hair*) roux. —*n.* rouge *m.* **in the ~**, en déficit. **roll out the ~ carpet for**, recevoir en grande pompe. **Red Cross**, Croix-Rouge *f.* **~-handed** *a.* en flagrant délit. **~ herring**, fausse piste *f.* **~-hot** *a.* brûlant. **the ~ light**, le feu rouge *m.* **~ tape**, paperasserie *f.*, bureaucratie *f.*

redcurrant /red'kʌrənt/ *n.* groseille *f.*

redden /'redn/ *v.t./i.* rougir.

reddish /'redɪʃ/ *a.* rougeâtre.

redecorate /riː'dekəreɪt/ *v.t.* (*repaint etc.*) repeindre, refaire.

redeem /rɪ'diːm/ *v.t.* racheter. **~ing quality**, qualité qui rachète les défauts *f.* **redemption** *n.* /rɪ'dempʃn/ rachat *m.*

redeploy /riːdɪ'plɔɪ/ *v.t.* réorganiser; (*troops*) répartir.

redirect /ri:daɪə'rekt/ v.t. (letter) faire suivre.

redness /'rednɪs/ n. rougeur f.

redo /ri:'du:/ v.t. (p.t. **-did**, p.p. **-done**) refaire.

redolent /'redələnt/ a. ~ **of**, qui évoque.

redouble /rɪ'dʌbl/ v.t. redoubler.

redress /rɪ'dres/ v.t. (wrong etc.) redresser. —n. réparation f.

reduc|e /rɪ'dju:s/ v.t. réduire; (temperature etc.) faire baisser. ~**tion** /rɪ'dʌkʃn/ n. réduction f.

redundan|t /rɪ'dʌndənt/ a. superflu; (worker) licencié. **make** ~, licencier. ~**cy** n. licenciement m.; (word, phrase) pléonasme m.

reed /ri:d/ n. (plant) roseau m.; (mus.) anche f.

reef /ri:f/ n. récif m., écueil m.

reek /ri:k/ n. puanteur f. —v.i. ~ (**of**), puer.

reel /ri:l/ n. (of thread) bobine f.; (of film) bande f.; (winding device) dévidoir m. —v.i. chanceler. —v.t. ~ **off**, réciter.

refectory /rɪ'fektərɪ/ n. réfectoire m.

refer /rɪ'fɜ:(r)/ v.t./i. (p.t. **referred**). ~ **to**, (allude to) faire allusion à; (concern) s'appliquer à; (consult) consulter; (submit) soumettre à; (direct) renvoyer à.

referee /refə'ri:/ n. arbitre m.; (for job) répondant(e) m. (f.). —v.t. (p.t. **refereed**) arbitrer.

reference /'refrəns/ n. référence f.; (mention) allusion f.; (person) répondant(e) m. (f.). **in** or **with** ~ **to**, en ce qui concerne; (comm.) suite à. ~ **book**, ouvrage de référence m.

referendum /refə'rendəm/ n. (pl. **-ums**) référendum m.

refill[1] /ri:'fɪl/ v.t. remplir (à nouveau); (pen) recharger.

refill[2] /'ri:fɪl/ n. (of pen, lighter, lipstick) recharge f.

refine /rɪ'faɪn/ v.t. raffiner. ~**d** a. raffiné. ~**ment** n. raffinement m.; (techn.) raffinage m. ~**ry** /-ərɪ/ n. raffinerie f.

reflate /ri:'fleɪt/ v.t. relancer.

reflect /rɪ'flekt/ v.t. refléter; (of mirror) réfléchir, refléter. —v.i. réfléchir (**on**, à). ~ **on s.o.**, (glory etc.) (faire) rejaillir sur qn.; (pej.) donner une mauvaise impression de qn. ~**ion** /-kʃn/ n. réflexion f.; (image) reflet m. **on** ~**ion**, réflexion faite. ~**or** n. réflecteur m.

reflective /rɪ'flektɪv/ a. réfléchissant.

reflex /'ri:fleks/ a. & n. réflexe (m.).

reflexive /rɪ'fleksɪv/ a. (gram.) réfléchi.

reform /rɪ'fɔ:m/ v.t. réformer. —v.i. (person) s'amender. —n. réforme f. ~**er** n. réforma|teur, -trice m., f.

refract /rɪ'frækt/ v.t. réfracter.

refrain[1] /rɪ'freɪn/ n. refrain m.

refrain[2] /rɪ'freɪn/ v.i. s'abstenir (**from**, de).

refresh /rɪ'freʃ/ v.t. rafraîchir; (of rest etc.) ragaillardir, délasser. ~**ing** a. (drink) rafraîchissant; (sleep) réparateur. ~**ments** n. pl. rafraîchissements m. pl.

refresher /rɪ'freʃə(r)/ a. (course) de perfectionnement.

refrigerat|e /rɪ'frɪdʒəreɪt/ v.t. réfrigérer. ~**or** n. réfrigérateur m.

refuel /ri:'fju:əl/ v.t./i. (p.t. **refuelled**) (se) ravitailler.

refuge /'refju:dʒ/ n. refuge m. **take** ~, se réfugier.

refugee /refjʊ'dʒi:/ n. réfugié(e) m. (f.).

refund /rɪ'fʌnd/ v.t. rembourser. —n. /'ri:fʌnd/ remboursement m.

refurbish /ri:'fɜ:bɪʃ/ v.t. remettre à neuf.

refus|e[1] /rɪ'fju:z/ v.t./i. refuser. ~**al** n. refus m.

refuse[2] /'refju:s/ n. ordures f. pl.

refute /rɪ'fju:t/ v.t. réfuter.

regain /rɪ'geɪn/ v.t. retrouver (lost ground) regagner.

regal /'ri:gl/ a. royal, majestueux.

regalia /rɪ'geɪlɪə/ n. pl. (insignia) insignes (royaux) m. pl.

regard /rɪ'gɑ:d/ v.t. considérer. —n. considération f., estime f. ~**s**, amitiés f. pl. **in this** ~, à cet égard. **as** ~**s**, ~**ing** prep. en ce qui concerne.

regardless /rɪ'gɑ:dlɪs/ adv. quand même. ~ **of**, sans tenir compte de.

regatta /rɪ'gætə/ n. régates f. pl.

regenerat|e /rɪ'dʒenəreɪt/ v.t. régénérer. ~**ion** /-'reɪʃn/ n. régénération f.

regen|t /'ri:dʒənt/ n. régent(e) m. (f.). ~**cy** n. régence f.

regime /reɪ'ʒi:m/ n. régime m.

regiment /'redʒɪmənt/ n. régiment m. ~**al** /-'mentl/ a. d'un régiment. ~**ation** /-en'teɪʃn/ n. discipline excessive f.

region /'ri:dʒən/ n. région f. **in the** ~ **of**, environ. ~**al** a. régional.

regist|er /'redʒɪstə(r)/ n. registre m. —v.t. enregistrer; (vehicle) immatriculer; (birth) déclarer; (letter) recommander; (indicate) indiquer; (express) exprimer. —v.i. (enrol) s'inscrire; (fig.) être compris. ~**er office**, bureau d'état civil m. ~**ration** /-'streɪʃn/ n. enregistrement m.; inscription f.; (vehicle document) carte grise *f.* ~**ration (number),** (*auto.*) numéro d'immatriculation *m.*

registrar /redʒɪ'strɑː(r)/ *n.* officier de l'état civil *m.*; (*univ.*) secrétaire général *m.*

regret /rɪ'gret/ *n.* regret *m.* —*v.t.* (*p.t.* **regretted**) regretter (**to do,** de faire). ~**fully** *adv.* à regret. ~**table** *a.* regrettable, fâcheux. ~**tably** *adv.* malheureusement; (*small, poor, etc.*) fâcheusement.

regroup /riː'gruːp/ *v.t./i.* (se) regrouper.

regular /'regjʊlə(r)/ *a.* régulier; (*usual*) habituel; (*thorough*: *fam.*) vrai. —*n.* (*fam.*) habitué(e) *m.* (*f.*). ~**ity** /-'lærətɪ/ *n.* régularité *f.* ~**ly** *adv.* régulièrement.

regulat|e /'regjʊleɪt/ *v.t.* régler. ~**ion** /-'leɪʃn/ *n.* réglage *m.*; (*rule*) règlement *m.*

rehabilitat|e /riːə'bɪlɪteɪt/ *v.t.* réadapter; (*in public esteem*) réhabiliter. ~**ion** /-'teɪʃn/ *n.* réadaptation *f.*; réhabilitation *f.*

rehash[1] /riː'hæʃ/ *v.t.* remanier.

rehash[2] /'riːhæʃ/ *n.* réchauffé *m.*

rehears|e /rɪ'hɜːs/ *v.t./i.* (*theatre*) répéter. ~**al** *n.* répétition *f.*

re-heat /riː'hiːt/ *v.t.* réchauffer.

reign /reɪn/ *n.* règne *m.* —*v.i.* régner (**over,** sur).

reimburse /riːɪm'bɜːs/ *v.t.* rembourser.

rein /reɪn/ *n.* rêne *f.*

reindeer /'reɪndɪə(r)/ *n. invar.* renne *m.*

reinforce /riːɪn'fɔːs/ *v.t.* renforcer. ~**ment** *n.* renforcement *m.* ~**ments** *n. pl.* renforts *m. pl.* ~**d concrete,** béton armé *m.*

reinstate /riːɪn'steɪt/ *v.t.* réintégrer, rétablir.

reiterate /riː'ɪtəreɪt/ *v.t.* réitérer.

reject[1] /rɪ'dʒekt/ *v.t.* (*offer, plea, etc.*) rejeter; (*book, goods, etc.*) refuser. ~**ion** /-kʃn/ *n.* rejet *m.*; refus *m.*

reject[2] /'riːdʒekt/ *n.* (article de) rebut *m.*

rejoic|e /rɪ'dʒɔɪs/ *v.i.* se réjouir. ~**ing** *n.* réjouissance *f.*

rejuvenate /rɪ'dʒuːvəneɪt/ *v.t.* rajeunir.

relapse /rɪ'læps/ *n.* rechute *f.* —*v.i.* rechuter. ~ **into,** retomber dans.

relate /rɪ'leɪt/ *v.t.* raconter; (*associate*) rapprocher. —*v.i.* ~ **to,** se rapporter à; (*get on with*) s'entendre avec. ~**d** /-ɪd/ *a.* (*ideas etc.*) lié. ~**d to s.o.,** parent(e) de qn.

relation /rɪ'leɪʃn/ *n.* rapport *m.*; (*person*) parent(e) *m.* (*f.*). ~**ship** *n.* lien de parenté *m.*; (*link*) rapport *m.*; (*affair*) liaison *f.*

relative /'relətɪv/ *n.* parent(e) *m.* (*f.*). —*a.* relatif; (*respective*) respectif. ~**ly** *adv.* relativement.

relax /rɪ'læks/ *v.t./i.* (*less tense*) (se) relâcher; (*for pleasure*) (se) détendre. ~**ation** /riːlæk'seɪʃn/ *n.* relâchement *m.*; détente *f.* ~**ing** *a.* délassant.

relay[1] /'riːleɪ/ *n.* relais *m.* ~ **race,** course de relais *f.*

relay[2] /rɪ'leɪ/ *v.t.* relayer.

release /rɪ'liːs/ *v.t.* libérer; (*bomb*) lâcher; (*film*) sortir; (*news*) publier; (*smoke*) dégager; (*spring*) déclencher. —*n.* libération *f.*; sortie *f.*; (*record*) nouveau disque *m.* (*of pollution*) émission *f.*

relegate /'relɪgeɪt/ *v.t.* reléguer.

relent /rɪ'lent/ *v.i.* se laisser fléchir. ~**less** *a.* impitoyable.

relevan|t /'reləvənt/ *a.* pertinent. **be** ~**t to,** avoir rapport à. ~**ce** *n.* pertinence *f.*, rapport *m.*

reliab|le /rɪ'laɪəbl/ *a.* sérieux, sûr; (*machine*) fiable. ~**ility** /-'bɪlətɪ/ *n.* sérieux *m.*; fiabilité *f.*

reliance /rɪ'laɪəns/ *n.* dépendance *f.*; (*trust*) confiance *f.*

relic /'relɪk/ *n.* relique *f.* ~**s,** (*of past*) vestiges *m. pl.*

relief /rɪ'liːf/ *n.* soulagement *m.* (**from,** à); (*assistance*) secours *m.*; (*outline, design*) relief *m.* ~ **road,** route de délestage *f.*

relieve /rɪ'liːv/ *v.t.* soulager; (*help*) secourir; (*take over from*) relayer.

religion /rɪ'lɪdʒən/ *n.* religion *f.*

religious /rɪ'lɪdʒəs/ *a.* religieux.

relinquish /rɪ'lɪŋkwɪʃ/ *v.t.* abandonner; (*relax hold of*) lâcher.

relish /'relɪʃ/ *n.* plaisir *m.*, goût *m.*; (*culin.*) assaisonnement *m.* —*v.t.* savourer; (*idea etc.*) aimer.

relocate /riːləʊ'keɪt/ *v.t.* (*company*) déplacer; (*employee*) muter. —*v.i.* se déplacer, déménager.

reluctan|t /rɪ'lʌktənt/ *a.* fait, donné, *etc.* à contrecœur. ~**t to,** peu disposé à. ~**ce** *n.* répugnance *f.* ~**tly** *adv.* à contrecœur.

rely /rɪ'laɪ/ *v.i.* ~ **on,** compter sur; (*financially*) dépendre de.

remain /rɪ'meɪn/ *v.i.* rester. ~**s** *n. pl.* restes *m. pl.*

remainder /rɪ'meɪndə(r)/ *n.* reste *m.*; (*book*) invendu soldé *m.*

remand /rɪ'mɑːnd/ *v.t.* mettre en détention préventive. —*n.* **on** ~**,** en détention préventive.

remark /rɪ'mɑːk/ *n.* remarque *f.* —*v.t.*

remarquer. —*v.i.* ~ **on**, faire des commentaires sur. ~**able** *a.* remarquable.

remarry /riːˈmærɪ/ *v.i.* se remarier.

remed|y /ˈremədɪ/ *n.* remède *m.* —*v.t.* remédier à. ~**ial** /rɪˈmiːdɪəl/ *a.* (*class etc.*) de rattrapage; (*treatment*: *med.*) curatif.

rememb|er /rɪˈmembə(r)/ *v.t.* se souvenir de, se rappeler. ~**er to do**, ne pas oublier de faire. ~**rance** *n.* souvenir *m.*

remind /rɪˈmaɪnd/ *v.t.* rappeler (**s.o. of sth.**, qch. à qn.). ~ **s.o. to do**, rappeler à qn. qu'il doit faire. ~**er** *n.* (*letter, signal*) rappel *m.*

reminisce /remɪˈnɪs/ *v.i.* évoquer ses souvenirs. ~**nces** *n. pl.* réminiscences *f. pl.*

reminiscent /remɪˈnɪsnt/ *a.* ~ **of**, qui rappelle, qui évoque.

remiss /rɪˈmɪs/ *a.* négligent.

remission /rɪˈmɪʃn/ *n.* rémission *f.*; (*jurid.*) remise (de peine) *f.*

remit /rɪˈmɪt/ *v.t.* (*p.t.* **remitted**) (*money*) envoyer; (*debt*) remettre. ~**tance** *n.* paiement *m.*

remnant /ˈremnənt/ *n.* reste *m.*, débris *m.*; (*trace*) vestige *m.*; (*of cloth*) coupon *m.*

remodel /riːˈmɒdel/ *v.t.* (*p.t.* **remodelled**) remodeler.

remorse /rɪˈmɔːs/ *n.* remords *m.* (*pl.*). ~**ful** *a.* plein de remords. ~**less** *a.* implacable.

remote /rɪˈməʊt/ *a.* (*place*, *time*) lointain; (*person*) distant; (*slight*) vague. ~ **control**, télécommande *f.* ~**ly** *adv.* au loin; vaguement. ~**ness** *n.* éloignement *m.*

removable /rɪˈmuːvəbl/ *a.* (*detachable*) amovible.

remov|e /rɪˈmuːv/ *v.t.* enlever; (*lead away*) emmener; (*dismiss*) renvoyer; (*do away with*) supprimer. ~**al** *n.* enlèvement *m.*; renvoi *m.*; suppression *f.*; (*from house*) déménagement *m.* ~**al men**, déménageurs *m. pl.* ~**er** *n.* (*for paint*) décapant *m.*

remunerat|e /rɪˈmjuːnəreɪt/ *v.t.* rémunérer. ~**ion** /-ˈreɪʃn/ *n.* rémunération *f.*

rename /riːˈneɪm/ *v.t.* rebaptiser.

render /ˈrendə(r)/ *v.t.* (*give*, *make*) rendre; (*mus.*) interpréter. ~**ing** *n.* interprétation *f.*

rendezvous /ˈrɒndeɪvuː/ *n.* (*pl.* -**vous** /-vuːz/) rendez-vous *m. invar.*

renegade /ˈrenɪɡeɪd/ *n.* renégat(e) *m.* (*f.*).

renew /rɪˈnjuː/ *v.t.* renouveler; (*resume*) reprendre. ~**able** *a.* renouvelable. ~**al** *n.* renouvellement *m.*; reprise *f.*

renounce /rɪˈnaʊns/ *v.t.* renoncer à; (*disown*) renier.

renovat|e /ˈrenəveɪt/ *v.t.* rénover. ~**ion** /-ˈveɪʃn/ *n.* rénovation *f.*

renown /rɪˈnaʊn/ *n.* renommée *f.* ~**ed** *a.* renommé.

rent /rent/ *n.* loyer *m.* —*v.t.* louer. **for** ~, à louer. ~**al** *n.* prix de location *m.*

renunciation /rɪnʌnsɪˈeɪʃn/ *n.* renonciation *f.*

reopen /riːˈəʊpən/ *v.t./i.* rouvrir. ~**ing** *n.* réouverture *f.*

reorganize /riːˈɔːɡənaɪz/ *v.t.* réorganiser.

rep /rep/ *n.* (*comm.*, *fam.*) représentant(e) *m.* (*f.*).

repair /rɪˈpeə(r)/ *v.t.* réparer. —*n.* réparation *f.* **in good/bad** ~, en bon/mauvais état. ~**er** *n.* réparateur *m.*

repartee /repɑːˈtiː/ *n.* repartie *f.*

repatriat|e /riːˈpætrɪeɪt/ *v.t.* rapatrier. ~**ion** /-ˈeɪʃn/ *n.* rapatriement *m.*

repay /riːˈpeɪ/ *v.t.* (*p.t.* **repaid**) rembourser; (*reward*) récompenser. ~**ment** *n.* remboursement *m.*; récompense *f.* **monthly** ~**ments**, mensualités *f. pl.*

repeal /rɪˈpiːl/ *v.t.* abroger, annuler. —*n.* abrogation *f.*

repeat /rɪˈpiːt/ *v.t./i.* répéter; (*renew*) renouveler. —*n.* répétition *f.*; (*broadcast*) reprise *f.* ~ **itself**, ~ **o.s.**, se répéter.

repeatedly /rɪˈpiːtɪdlɪ/ *adv.* à maintes reprises.

repel /rɪˈpel/ *v.t.* (*p.t.* **repelled**) repousser. ~**lent** *a.* repoussant.

repent /rɪˈpent/ *v.i.* se repentir (**of**, de). ~**ance** *n.* repentir *m.* ~**ant** *a.* repentant.

repercussion /riːpəˈkʌʃn/ *n.* répercussion *f.*

repertoire /ˈrepətwɑː(r)/ *n.* répertoire *m.*

repertory /ˈrepətrɪ/ *n.* répertoire *m.* ~ (**theatre**), théâtre de répertoire *m.*

repetit|ion /repɪˈtɪʃn/ *n.* répétition *f.* ~**ious** /-ˈtɪʃəs/, ~**ive** /rɪˈpetətɪv/ *adjs.* plein de répétitions.

replace /rɪˈpleɪs/ *v.t.* remettre; (*take the place of*) remplacer. ~**ment** *n.* remplacement *m.* (**of**, de); (*person*) remplaçant(e) *m.* (*f.*); (*new part*) pièce de rechange *f.*

replay /ˈriːpleɪ/ *n.* (*sport*) match rejoué *m.*; (*recording*) répétition immédiate *f.*

replenish /rɪˈplenɪʃ/ *v.t.* (*refill*) remplir; (*renew*) renouveler.

replica /ˈreplɪkə/ *n.* copie exacte *f.*

reply /rɪ'plaɪ/ v.t./i. répondre. —n. réponse f.

report /rɪ'pɔːt/ v.t. rapporter, annoncer (**that**, que); (notify) signaler; (denounce) dénoncer. —v.i. faire un rapport. ~ (**on**), (news item) faire un reportage sur. ~ **to**, (go) se présenter chez. —n. rapport m.; (in press) reportage m.; (schol.) bulletin m.; (sound) détonation f. ~**edly** adv. selon ce qu'on dit.

reporter /rɪ'pɔːtə(r)/ n. reporter m.

repose /rɪ'pəʊz/ n. repos m.

repossess /riːpə'zes/ v.t. reprendre.

represent /reprɪ'zent/ v.t. représenter. ~**ation** /-'teɪʃn/ n. représentation f. **make ~ations to**, protester auprès de.

representative /reprɪ'zentətɪv/ a. représentatif, typique (**of**, de). —n. représentant(e) m. (f.).

repress /rɪ'pres/ v.t. réprimer. ~**ion** /-ʃn/ n. répression f. ~**ive** a. répressif.

reprieve /rɪ'priːv/ n. (delay) sursis m.; (pardon) grâce f. —v.t. accorder un sursis à; gracier.

reprimand /'reprɪmɑːnd/ v.t. réprimander. —n. réprimande f.

reprint /'riːprɪnt/ n. réimpression f.; (offprint) tiré à part m.

reprisals /rɪ'praɪzlz/ n. pl. représailles f. pl.

reproach /rɪ'prəʊtʃ/ v.t. reprocher (**s.o. for sth.**, qch. à qn.). —n. reproche m. ~**ful** a. de reproche, réprobateur. ~**fully** adv. avec reproche.

reproduc|e /riːprə'djuːs/ v.t./i. (se) reproduire. ~**tion** /-'dʌkʃn/ n. reproduction f. ~**tive** /-'dʌktɪv/ a. reproducteur.

reptile /'reptaɪl/ n. reptile m.

republic /rɪ'pʌblɪk/ n. république f. ~**an** a. & n. républicain(e) (m. (f.)).

repudiate /rɪ'pjuːdɪeɪt/ v.t. répudier; (treaty) refuser d'honorer.

repugnan|t /rɪ'pʌgnənt/ a. répugnant. ~**ce** n. répugnance f.

repuls|e /rɪ'pʌls/ v.t. repousser. ~**ion** /-ʃn/ n. répulsion f. ~**ive** a. repoussant.

reputable /'repjʊtəbl/ a. honorable, de bonne réputation.

reputation /repjʊ'teɪʃn/ n. réputation f.

repute /rɪ'pjuːt/ n. réputation f. ~**d** /-ɪd/ a. réputé. ~**dly** /-ɪdlɪ/ adv. d'après ce qu'on dit.

request /rɪ'kwest/ n. demande f. —v.t. demander (**of**, **from**, à). ~ **stop**, arrêt facultatif m.

requiem /'rekwɪem/ n. requiem m.

require rɪ'kwaɪə(r) v.t. (of thing) demander; (of person) avoir besoin de; (demand, order) exiger. ~**d** a. requis. ~**ment** n. exigence f.; (condition) condition (requise) f.

requisite /'rekwɪzɪt/ a. nécessaire. —n. chose nécessaire f. ~**s**, (for travel etc.) articles m. pl.

requisition /rekwɪ'zɪʃn/ n. réquisition f. —v.t. réquisitionner.

re-route /riː'ruːt/ v.t. dérouter.

resale /'riːseɪl/ n. revente f.

rescind /rɪ'sɪnd/ v.t. annuler.

rescue /'reskjuː/ v.t. sauver. —n. sauvetage m. (**of**, de); (help) secours m. ~**r** /-ə(r)/ n. sauveteur m.

research /rɪ'sɜːtʃ/ n. recherche(s) f.(pl.). —v.t./i. faire des recherches (sur). ~**er** n. chercheur, -se m., f.

resembl|e /rɪ'zembl/ v.t. ressembler à ~**ance** n. ressemblance f.

resent /rɪ'zent/ v.t. être indigné de, s'offenser de. ~**ful** a. plein de ressentiment, indigné. ~**ment** n. ressentiment m.

reservation /rezə'veɪʃn/ n. réserve f.; (booking) réservation f.; (Amer.) réserve (indienne) f. **make a ~**, réserver.

reserve /rɪ'zɜːv/ v.t. réserver. —n. (reticence, stock, land) réserve f.; (sport) remplaçant(e) m. (f.). **in ~**, en réserve. **the ~s**, (mil.) les réserves f. pl. ~**d** a. (person, room) réservé.

reservist /rɪ'zɜːvɪst/ n. (mil.) réserviste m.

reservoir /'rezəvwɑː(r)/ n. (lake, supply, etc.) réservoir m.

reshape /riː'ʃeɪp/ v.t. remodeler.

reshuffle /riː'ʃʌfl/ v.t. (pol.) remanier. —n. (pol.) remaniement (ministériel) m.

reside /rɪ'zaɪd/ v.i. résider.

residen|t /'rezɪdənt/ a. résidant. **be ~t**, résider. —n. habitant(e) m. (f.); (foreigner) résident(e) m. (f.); (in hotel) pensionnaire m./f. ~**ce** n. résidence f.; (of students) foyer m. **in ~ce**, (doctor) résidant; (students) au foyer.

residential /rezɪ'denʃl/ a. résidentiel.

residue /'rezɪdjuː/ n. résidu m.

resign /rɪ'zaɪn/ v.t. abandonner; (job) démissionner de. —v.i. démissionner. ~ **o.s. to**, se résigner à. ~**ation** /rezɪg'neɪʃn/ n. résignation f.; (from job) démission f. ~**ed** a. résigné.

resilien|t /rɪ'zɪlɪənt/ a. élastique; (person) qui a du ressort. ~**ce** n. élasticité f.; ressort m.

resin /'rezɪn/ *n*. résine *f*.

resist /rɪ'zɪst/ *v.t./i*. résister (à). ∼**ance** *n*. résistance *f*. ∼**ant** *a*. (*med*.) rebelle; (*metal*) résistant.

resolut|e /'rezəlu:t/ *a*. résolu. ∼**ion** /-'lu:ʃn/ *n*. résolution *f*.

resolve /rɪ'zɒlv/ *v.t*. résoudre (**to do**, de faire). —*n*. résolution *f*. ∼**d** *a*. résolu (**to do**, à faire).

resonan|t /'rezənənt/ *a*. résonnant. ∼**ce** *n*. résonance *f*.

resort /rɪ'zɔːt/ *v.i*. ∼ **to**, avoir recours à. —*n*. (*recourse*) recours *m*.; (*place*) station *f*. **in the last** ∼, en dernier ressort.

resound /rɪ'zaʊnd/ *v.i*. retentir (**with**, de). ∼**ing** *a*. retentissant.

resource /rɪ'sɔːs/ *n*. (*expedient*) ressource *f*. ∼**s**, (*wealth etc*.) ressources *f*. *pl*. ∼**ful** *a*. ingénieux. ∼**fulness** *n*. ingéniosité *f*.

respect /rɪ'spekt/ *n*. respect *m*.; (*aspect*) égard *m*. —*v.t*. respecter. **with** ∼ **to**, à l'égard de, relativement à. ∼**ful** *a*. respectueux.

respectab|le /rɪ'spektəbl/ *a*. respectable. ∼**ility** /-'bɪlətɪ/ *n*. respectabilité *f*. ∼**ly** *adv*. convenablement.

respective /rɪ'spektɪv/ *a*. respectif. ∼**ly** *adv*. respectivement.

respiration /respə'reɪʃn/ *n*. respiration *f*.

respite /'resp(a)ɪt/ *n*. répit *m*.

resplendent /rɪ'splendənt/ *a*. resplendissant.

respond /rɪ'spɒnd/ *v.i*. répondre (**to**, à) ∼ **to**, (*react to*) réagir à.

response /rɪ'spɒns/ *n*. réponse *f*.

responsib|le /rɪ'spɒnsəbl/ *a*. responsable: (*job*) qui comporte des responsabilités. ∼**ility** /-'bɪlətɪ/ *n*. responsabilité *f*. ∼**ly** *adv*. de façon responsable.

responsive /rɪ'spɒnsɪv/ *a*. qui réagit bien. ∼ **to**, sensible à.

rest[1] /rest/ *v.t./i*. (se) reposer; (*lean*) (s')appuyer (**on**, sur); (*be buried*, *lie*) reposer. —*n*. (*repose*) repos *m*.; (*support*) support *m*. **have a** ∼, se reposer; (*at work*) prendre une pause. ∼**-room** *n*. (*Amer*.) toilettes *f*. *pl*.

rest[2] /rest/ *v.i*. (*remain*) demeurer. —*n*. (*remainder*) reste *m*. (**of**, de). **the** ∼ (**of the**), (*others*, *other*) les autres. **it** ∼**s with him to**, il lui appartient de.

restaurant /'restərɒnt/ *n*. restaurant *m*.

restful /'restfl/ *a*. reposant.

restitution /restɪ'tjuːʃn/ *n*. (*for injury*) compensation *f*.

restive /'restɪv/ *a*. rétif.

restless /'restlɪs/ *a*. agité. ∼**ly** *adv*. avec agitation, fébrilement.

restor|e /rɪ'stɔː(r)/ *v.t*. rétablir; (*building*) restaurer. ∼**e sth. to s.o.**, restituer qch. à qn. ∼**ation** /restə'reɪʃn/ *n*. rétablissement *m*.; restauration *f*. ∼**er** *n*. (*art*) restaurateur, -trice *m*., *f*.

restrain /rɪ'streɪn/ *v.t*. contenir. ∼ **s.o. from**, retenir qn. de. ∼**ed** *a*. (*moderate*) mesuré; (*in control of self*) maître de soi. ∼**t** *n*. contrainte *f*.; (*moderation*) retenue *f*.

restrict /rɪ'strɪkt/ *v.t*. restreindre. ∼**ion** /-kʃn/ *n*. restriction *f*. ∼**ive** *a*. restrictif.

restructure /riː'strʌktʃə(r)/ *v.t*. restructurer.

result /rɪ'zʌlt/ *n*. résultat *m*. —*v.i*. résulter. ∼ **in**, aboutir à.

resum|e /rɪ'zjuːm/ *v.t./i*. reprendre. ∼**ption** /rɪ'zʌmpʃn/ *n*. reprise *f*.

résumé /'rezjuːmeɪ/ *n*. résumé *m*.; (*of career*: *Amer*.) CV *m*., curriculum vitae *m*.

resurgence /rɪ'sɜːdʒəns/ *n*. réapparition *f*.

resurrect /rezə'rekt/ *v.t*. ressusciter. ∼**ion** /-kʃn/ *n*. résurrection *f*.

resuscitate /rɪ'sʌsɪteɪt/ *v.t*. réanimer.

retail /'riːteɪl/ *n*. détail *m*. —*a*. & *adv*. au détail. —*v.t./i*. (se) vendre (au détail). ∼**er** *n*. détaillant(e) *m*. (*f*.).

retain /rɪ'teɪn/ *v.t*. (*hold back*, *remember*) retenir; (*keep*) conserver.

retaliat|e /rɪ'tælɪeɪt/ *v.i*. riposter. ∼**ion** /-'eɪʃn/ *n*. représailles *f*. *pl*.

retarded /rɪ'tɑːdɪd/ *a*. arriéré.

retch /retʃ/ *v.i*. avoir un haut-le-cœur.

retentive /rɪ'tentɪv/ *a*. (*memory*) fidèle. ∼ **of**, qui retient.

rethink /riː'θɪŋk/ *v.t*. (*p.t*. **rethought**) repenser.

reticen|t /'retɪsnt/ *a*. réticent. ∼**ce** *n*. réticence *f*.

retina /'retɪnə/ *n*. rétine *f*.

retinue /'retɪnjuː/ *n*. suite *f*.

retire /rɪ'taɪə(r)/ *v.i*. (*from work*) prendre sa retraite; (*withdraw*) se retirer; (*go to bed*) se coucher. —*v.t*. mettre à la retraite. ∼**d** *a*. retraité. ∼**ment** *n*. retraite *f*.

retiring /rɪ'taɪərɪŋ/ *a*. réservé.

retort /rɪ'tɔːt/ *v.t./i*. répliquer. —*n*. réplique *f*.

retrace /riː'treɪs/ *v.t*. ∼ **one's steps**, revenir sur ses pas.

retract /rɪ'trækt/ *v.t./i*. (se) rétracter.

retrain /riː'treɪn/ *v.t./i*. (se) recycler.

retread /riː'tred/ *n*. pneu rechapé *m*.

retreat /rɪ'triːt/ *v.i*. (*mil*.) battre en retraite. —*n*. retraite *f*.

retrial /riːˈtraɪəl/ n. nouveau procès m.
retribution /retrɪˈbjuːʃn/ n. châtiment
m.; (*vengeance*) vengeance f.
retriev|e /rɪˈtriːv/ v.t. (*recover*)
récupérer; (*restore*) rétablir; (*put right*)
réparer. ∼**al** n. récupération f.; (*of
information*) recherche documentaire f.
∼**er** n. (*dog*) chien d'arrêt m.
retrograde /ˈretrəgreɪd/ a. rétrograde
—v.i. rétrograder.
retrospect /ˈretrəspekt/ n. **in** ∼,
rétrospectivement.
return /rɪˈtɜːn/ v.i. (*come back*) revenir;
(*go back*) retourner; (*go home*) rentrer.
—v.t. (*give back*) rendre; (*bring back*)
rapporter; (*send back*) renvoyer; (*put
back*) remettre. —n. retour m.; (*yield*)
rapport m. ∼**s**, (*comm.*) bénéfices m. pl.
in ∼ **for**, en échange de. ∼ **journey**,
voyage de retour m. ∼ **match**, match
retour m. ∼ **ticket**, aller-retour m.
reunion /riːˈjuːnɪən/ n. réunion f.
reunite /riːjuːˈnaɪt/ v.t. réunir.
rev /rev/ n. (*auto.*, *fam.*) tour m. —v.t./i.
(*p.t.* **revved**). ∼ (**up**), (*engine*: *fam.*)
(s')emballer.
revamp /riːˈvæmp/ v.t. rénover.
reveal /rɪˈviːl/ v.t. révéler; (*allow to
appear*) laisser voir. ∼**ing** a. révélateur.
revel /ˈrevl/ v.i. (*p.t.* **revelled**) faire
bombance. ∼ **in**, se délecter de. ∼**ry** n.
festivités f. pl.
revelation /revəˈleɪʃn/ n. révélation f.
revenge /rɪˈvendʒ/ n. vengeance f.;
(*sport*) revanche f. —v.t. venger.
revenue /ˈrevənjuː/ n. revenu m.
reverberate /rɪˈvɜːbəreɪt/ v.i. (*sound,
light*) se répercuter.
revere /rɪˈvɪə(r)/ v.t. révérer. ∼**nce**
/ˈrevərəns/ n. vénération f.
reverend /ˈrevərənd/ a. révérend.
reverent /ˈrevərənt/ a. respectueux.
reverie /ˈrevərɪ/ n. rêverie f.
revers|e /rɪˈvɜːs/ a. contraire, inverse.
—n. contraire m.; (*back*) revers m.,
envers m.; (*gear*) marche arrière f.
—v.t. (*situation, bracket, etc.*) renverser; (*order*) inverser; (*decision*) annuler. —v.i. (*auto.*) faire marche
arrière. ∼**al** n. renversement m.; (*of
view*) revirement m.
revert /rɪˈvɜːt/ v.i. ∼ **to**, revenir à.
review /rɪˈvjuː/ n. (*inspection,
magazine*) revue f.; (*of book etc.*)
critique f. —v.t. passer en revue;
(*situation*) réexaminer; faire la critique
de. ∼**er** n. critique m.
revis|e /rɪˈvaɪz/ v.t. réviser; (*text*) revoir.
∼**ion** /-ɪʒn/ n. révision f.

revitalize /riːˈvaɪtəlaɪz/ v.t. revitaliser,
revivifier.
reviv|e /rɪˈvaɪv/ v.t. (*person, hopes*)
ranimer; (*play*) reprendre; (*custom*)
rétablir. —v.i. se ranimer. ∼**al** n.
(*resumption*) reprise f.; (*of faith*)
renouveau m.
revoke /rɪˈvəʊk/ v.t. révoquer.
revolt /rɪˈvəʊlt/ v.t./i. (se) révolter. —n.
révolte f.
revolting /rɪˈvəʊltɪŋ/ a. dégoûtant.
revolution /revəˈluːʃn/ n. révolution f.
∼**ary** a. & n. révolutionnaire (m./f.).
∼**ize** v.t. révolutionner.
revolv|e /rɪˈvɒlv/ v.i. tourner. ∼**ing
door**, tambour m.
revolver /rɪˈvɒlvə(r)/ n. revolver m.
revulsion /rɪˈvʌlʃn/ n. dégoût m.
reward /rɪˈwɔːd/ n. récompense f. —v.t.
récompenser (**for**, de). ∼**ing** a.
rémunérateur; (*worthwhile*) qui (en)
vaut la peine.
rewind /riːˈwaɪnd/ v.t. (*p.t.* **rewound**)
(*tape, film*) rembobiner.
rewire /riːˈwaɪə(r)/ v.t. refaire
l'installation électrique de.
reword /riːˈwɜːd/ v.t. reformuler.
rewrite /riːˈraɪt/ v.t. récrire.
rhapsody /ˈræpsədɪ/ n. rhapsodie f.
rhetoric /ˈretərɪk/ n. rhétorique f. ∼**al**
/rɪˈtɒrɪkl/ a. (de) rhétorique; (*question*)
de pure forme.
rheumati|c /ruːˈmætɪk/ a. (*pain*)
rhumatismal; (*person*) rhumatisant.
∼**sm** /ˈruːmətɪzəm/ n. rhumatisme m.
rhinoceros /raɪˈnɒsərəs/ n. (*pl.* -**oses**)
rhinocéros m.
rhubarb /ˈruːbɑːb/ n. rhubarbe f.
rhyme /raɪm/ n. rime f.; (*poem*) vers m.
pl. —v.t./i. (faire) rimer.
rhythm /ˈrɪðəm/ n. rythme m. ∼**ic(al)**
/ˈrɪðmɪk(l)/ a. rythmique.
rib /rɪb/ n. côte f.
ribald /ˈrɪbld/ a. grivois.
ribbon /ˈrɪbən/ n. ruban m. **in** ∼**s**, (*torn
pieces*) en lambeaux.
rice /raɪs/ n. riz m.
rich /rɪtʃ/ a. (-**er**, -**est**) riche. ∼**es** n. pl.
richesses f. pl. ∼**ly** adv. richement.
∼**ness** n. richesse f.
rickety /ˈrɪkətɪ/ a. branlant.
ricochet /ˈrɪkəʃeɪ/ n. ricochet m. —v.i.
(*p.t.* **ricocheted** /-ʃeɪd/) ricocher.
rid /rɪd/ v.t. (*p.t.* **rid**, *pres. p.* **ridding**)
débarrasser (**of**, de). **get** ∼ **of**, se
débarrasser de.
riddance /ˈrɪdns/ n. **good** ∼!, bon
débarras!
ridden /ˈrɪdn/ *see* ride.

riddle[1] /'rɪdl/ n. énigme f.

riddle[2] /'rɪdl/ v.t. ~ **with,** (bullets) cribler de; (mistakes) bourrer de.

ride /raɪd/ v.i. (p.t. **rode**, p.p. **ridden**) aller (à bicyclette, à cheval, etc.); (in car) rouler. ~ **(a horse),** (go riding as sport) monter (à cheval). —v.t. (a particular horse) monter; (distance) parcourir. —n. promenade f., tour m.; (distance) trajet m. **give s.o. a** ~, (Amer.) prendre qn. en voiture. **go for a** ~, aller faire un tour (à bicyclette, à cheval, etc.). ~**r** /-ə(r)/ n. cavalier, -ière m., f.; (in horse race) jockey m.; (cyclist) cycliste m./f.; (motorcyclist) motocycliste m./f.; (in document) annexe f.

ridge /rɪdʒ/ n. arête f., crête f.

ridicule /'rɪdɪkjuːl/ n. ridicule m. —v.t. ridiculiser.

ridiculous /rɪ'dɪkjʊləs/ a. ridicule.

riding /'raɪdɪŋ/ n. équitation f.

rife /raɪf/ a. be ~, être répandu, sévir. ~ **with,** abondant en.

riff-raff /'rɪfræf/ n. canaille f.

rifle /'raɪfl/ n. fusil m. —v.t. (rob) dévaliser.

rift /rɪft/ n. (crack) fissure f.; (between people) désaccord m.

rig[1] /rɪg/ v.t. (p.t. **rigged**) (equip) équiper. —n. (for oil) derrick m. ~ **out,** habiller. ~**-out** n. (fam.) tenue f. ~ **up,** (arrange) arranger.

rig[2] /rɪg/ v.t. (p.t. **rigged**) (election, match, etc.) truquer.

right /raɪt/ a. (morally) bon; (fair) juste; (best) bon, qu'il faut; (not left) droit. **be** ~, (person) avoir raison (**to,** de); (calculation, watch) être exact. —n. (entitlement) droit m.; (not left) droite f.; (not evil) le bien. —v.t. (a wrong, sth. fallen, etc.) redresser. —adv. (not left) à droite; (directly) tout droit; (exactly) bien, juste; (completely) tout (à fait). **be in the** ~, avoir raison. **by** ~**s,** normalement. **on the** ~, à droite. **put** ~, arranger, rectifier. ~ **angle,** angle droit m. ~ **away,** tout de suite. ~**-hand** a. à or de droite. ~**-hand man,** bras droit m. ~**-handed** a. droitier. ~ **now,** (at once) tout de suite; (at present) en ce moment. ~ **of way,** (auto.) priorité f. ~**-wing** a. (pol.) de droite.

righteous /'raɪtʃəs/ a. (person) vertueux; (cause, anger) juste.

rightful /'raɪtfl/ a. légitime. ~**ly** adv. à juste titre.

rightly /'raɪtlɪ/ adv. correctement; (with reason) à juste titre.

rigid /'rɪdʒɪd/ a. rigide. ~**ity** /rɪ'dʒɪdətɪ/ n. rigidité f.

rigmarole /'rɪgmərəʊl/ n. charabia m.; (procedure) comédie f.

rig|our /'rɪgə(r)/ n. rigueur f. ~**orous** a. rigoureux.

rile /raɪl/ v.t. (fam.) agacer.

rim /rɪm/ n. bord m.; (of wheel) jante f. ~**med** a. bordé.

rind /raɪnd/ n. (on cheese) croûte f.; (on bacon) couenne f.; (on fruit) écorce f.

ring[1] /rɪŋ/ n. anneau m.; (with stone) bague f.; (circle) cercle m.; (boxing) ring m.; (arena) piste f. —v.t. entourer; (word in text etc.) entourer d'un cercle. (wedding) ~, alliance f. ~ **road,** périphérique m.

ring[2] /rɪŋ/ v.t./i. (p.t. **rang**, p.p. **rung**) sonner; (of words etc.) retentir. —n. sonnerie f. **give s.o. a** ~, donner un coup de fil à qn. ~ **the bell,** sonner. ~ **back,** rappeler. ~ **off,** raccrocher. ~ **up,** téléphoner (à). ~**ing** n. (of bell) sonnerie f. ~**ing tone,** tonalité f.

ringleader /'rɪŋliːdə(r)/ n. chef m.

rink /rɪŋk/ n. patinoire f.

rinse /rɪns/ v.t. rincer. ~ **out,** rincer. —n. rinçage m.

riot /'raɪət/ n. émeute f.; (of colours) orgie f. —v.i. faire une émeute. **run** ~, se déchaîner. ~**er** n. émeutier, -ière m., f.

riotous /'raɪətəs/ a. turbulent.

rip /rɪp/ v.t./i. (p.t. **ripped**) (se) déchirer. —n. déchirure f. **let** ~, (not check) laisser courir. ~ **off,** (sl.) rouler. ~**-off** n. (sl.) vol m.

ripe /raɪp/ a. (-er, -est) mûr. ~**ness** n. maturité f.

ripen /'raɪpən/ v.t./i. mûrir.

ripple /'rɪpl/ n. ride f., ondulation f.; (sound) murmure m. —v.t./i. (water) (se) rider.

rise /raɪz/ v.i. (p.t. **rose**, p.p. **risen**) (go upwards, increase) monter, s'élever; (stand up, get up from bed) se lever; (rebel) se soulever; (sun, curtain) se lever; (water) monter. —n. (slope) pente f.; (of curtain) lever m.; (increase) hausse f.; (in pay) augmentation f.; (progress, boom) essor m. **give** ~ **to,** donner lieu à. ~ **up,** se lever. ~**r** /-ə(r)/ n. **be an early** ~**r,** se lever tôt.

rising /'raɪzɪŋ/ n. (revolt) soulèvement m. —a. (increasing) croissant; (price) qui monte; (tide) montant; (sun) levant. ~ **generation,** nouvelle génération f.

risk /rɪsk/ n. risque m. —v.t. risquer. **at**

~, menacé. **~ doing,** (*venture*) se risquer à faire. **~y** *a.* risqué.

rissole /'rɪsəʊl/ *n.* croquette *f.*

rite /raɪt/ *n.* rite *m.* **last ~s,** derniers sacrements *m. pl.*

ritual /'rɪtʃʊəl/ *a. & n.* rituel (*m.*).

rival /'raɪvl/ *n.* rival(e) *m.* (*f.*). —*a.* rival; (*claim*) opposé. —*v.t.* (*p.t.* **rivalled**) rivaliser avec. **~ry** *n.* rivalité *f.*

river /'rɪvə(r)/ *n.* rivière *f.*; (*flowing into sea & fig.*) fleuve *m.* —*a.* (*fishing, traffic, etc.*) fluvial.

rivet /'rɪvɪt/ *n.* (*bolt*) rivet *m.* —*v.t.* (*p.t.* **riveted**) river, riveter. **~ing** *a.* fascinant.

Riviera /rɪvɪ'eərə/ *n.* **the (French) ~,** la Côte d'Azur.

road /rəʊd/ *n.* route *f.*; (*in town*) rue *f.*; (*small*) chemin *m.* —*a.* (*sign, safety*) routier. **the ~ to,** (*glory etc.: fig.*) le chemin de. **~-block** *n.* barrage routier *m.* **~- hog** *n.* chauffard *m.* **~-map** *n.* carte routière *f.* **~-works** *n. pl.* travaux *m. pl.*

roadside /'rəʊdsaɪd/ *n.* bord de la route *m.*

roadway /'rəʊdweɪ/ *n.* chaussée *f.*

roadworthy /'rəʊdwɜːðɪ/ *a.* en état de marche.

roam /rəʊm/ *v.i.* errer. —*v.t.* (*streets, seas, etc.*) parcourir.

roar /rɔː(r)/ *n.* hurlement *m.*; rugissement *m.*; grondement *m.* —*v.t./i.* hurler; (*of lion, wind*) rugir; (*of lorry, thunder*) gronder. **~ with laughter,** rire aux éclats.

roaring /'rɔːrɪŋ/ *a.* (*trade, success*) très gros. **~ fire,** belle flambée *f.*

roast /rəʊst/ *v.t./i.* rôtir. —*n.* (*roast or roasting meat*) rôti *m.* —*a.* rôti. **~ beef,** rôti de bœuf *m.*

rob /rɒb/ *v.t.* (*p.t.* **robbed**) voler (**s.o. of sth.,** qch. à qn.); (*bank, house*) dévaliser; (*deprive*) priver (**of,** de). **~ber** *n.* voleur, -se *m.*, *f.* **~bery** *n.* vol *m.*

robe /rəʊb/ *n.* (*of judge etc.*) robe *f.*; (*dressing-gown*) peignoir *m.*

robin /'rɒbɪn/ *n.* rouge-gorge *m.*

robot /'rəʊbɒt/ *n.* robot *m.*

robust /rəʊ'bʌst/ *a.* robuste.

rock¹ /rɒk/ *n.* roche *f.*; (*rock face, boulder*) rocher *m.*; (*hurled stone*) pierre *f.*; (*sweet*) sucre d'orge *m.* **on the ~s,** (*drink*) avec des glaçons; (*marriage*) en crise. **~-bottom** *a.* (*fam.*) très bas. **~-climbing** *n.* varappe *f.*

rock² /rɒk/ *v.t./i.* (se) balancer; (*shake*) (faire) trembler; (*child*) bercer. —*n.* (*mus.*) rock *m.* **~ing-chair** *n.* fauteuil à bascule *m.*

rockery /'rɒkərɪ/ *n.* rocaille *f.*

rocket /'rɒkɪt/ *n.* fusée *f.*

rocky /'rɒkɪ/ *a.* (**-ier, -iest**) (*ground*) rocailleux; (*hill*) rocheux; (*shaky: fig.*) branlant.

rod /rɒd/ *n.* (*metal*) tige *f.*; (*for curtain*) tringle *f.*; (*wooden*) baguette *f.*; (*for fishing*) canne à pêche *f.*

rode /rəʊd/ *see* **ride.**

rodent /'rəʊdnt/ *n.* rongeur *m.*

rodeo /rəʊ'deɪəʊ, *Amer.* 'rəʊdɪəʊ/ *n.* (*pl.* **-os**) rodéo *m.*

roe¹ /rəʊ/ *n.* œufs de poisson *m. pl.*

roe² /rəʊ/ *n.* (*pl.* **roe** or **roes**) (*deer*) chevreuil *m.*

rogue /rəʊg/ *n.* (*dishonest*) bandit, voleur, -se *m.*, *f.*; (*mischievous*) coquin(e) *m.* (*f.*). **~ish** *a.* coquin.

role /rəʊl/ *n.* rôle *m.* **~-playing** *n.* jeu de rôle *m.*

roll /rəʊl/ *v.t./i.* rouler. **~ (about),** (*child, dog*) se rouler. —*n.* rouleau *m.*; (*list*) liste *f.*; (*bread*) petit pain *m.*; (*of drum, thunder*) roulement *m.*; (*of ship*) roulis *m.* **be ~ing (in money),** (*fam.*) rouler sur l'or. **~-bar** *n.* arceau de sécurité *m.* **~-call** *n.* appel *m.* **~ing-pin** *n.* rouleau à pâtisserie *m.* **~ out,** étendre. **~ over,** (*turn over*) retourner. **~ up** *v.t.* (*sleeves*) retrousser; *v.i.* (*fam.*) s'amener.

roller /'rəʊlə(r)/ *n.* rouleau *m.* **~-blind** *n.* store *m.* **~-coaster** *n.* montagnes russes *f. pl.* **~-skate** *n.* patin à roulettes *m.*

rollicking /'rɒlɪkɪŋ/ *a.* exubérant.

rolling /'rəʊlɪŋ/ *a.* onduleux.

ROM (*abbr.*) (*read-only memory*) mémoire morte *f.*

Roman /'rəʊmən/ *a. & n.* romain(e) (*m.* (*f.*)). **~ Catholic** *a. & n.* catholique (*m./f.*). **~ numerals,** chiffres romains *m. pl.*

romance /rə'mæns/ *n.* roman d'amour *m.*; (*love*) amour *m.*; (*affair*) idylle *f.*; (*fig.*) poésie *f.*

Romania /rəʊ'meɪnɪə/ *n.* Roumanie *f.* **~n** *a. & n.* roumain(e) (*m.* (*f.*)).

romantic /rə'mæntɪk/ *a.* (*of love etc.*) romantique; (*of the imagination*) romanesque. **~ally** *adv.* (*behave*) en romantique.

romp /rɒmp/ *v.i.* s'ébattre; (*fig.*) réussir. —*n.* **have a ~,** s'ébattre.

roof 431 rub

roof /ruːf/ *n.* (*pl.* **roofs**) toit *m.*; (*of tunnel*) plafond *m.*; (*of mouth*) palais *m.* —*v.t.* recouvrir. ~**ing** *n.* toiture *f.* ~**rack** *n.* galerie *f.* ~**-top** *n.* toit *m.*

rook[1] /rʊk/ *n.* (*bird*) corneille *f.*

rook[2] /rʊk/ *n.* (*chess*) tour *f.*

room /ruːm/ *n.* pièce *f.*; (*bedroom*) chambre *f.*; (*large hall*) salle *f.*; (*space*) place *f.* ~**-mate** *n.* camarade de chambre *m./f.* ~**y** *a.* spacieux; (*clothes*) ample.

roost /ruːst/ *n.* perchoir *m.* —*v.i.* percher. ~**er** /ˈruːstə(r)/ *n.* coq *m.*

root[1] /ruːt/ *n.* racine *f.*; (*source*) origine *f.* —*v.t./i.* (s')enraciner. ~ **out,** extirper. **take** ~, prendre racine. ~**less** *a.* sans racines.

root[2] /ruːt/ *v.i.* ~ **about,** fouiller. ~ **for,** (*Amer., fam.*) encourager.

rope /rəʊp/ *n.* corde *f.* —*v.t.* attacher. **know the** ~**s,** être au courant. ~ **in,** (*person*) enrôler.

rosary /ˈrəʊzərɪ/ *n.* chapelet *m.*

rose[1] /rəʊz/ *n.* (*flower*) rose *f.*; (*colour*) rose *m.*; (*nozzle*) pomme *f.*

rose[2] /rəʊz/ *see* **rise.**

rosé /ˈrəʊzeɪ/ *n.* rosé *m.*

rosette /rəʊˈzet/ *n.* (*sport*) cocarde *f.*; (*officer's*) rosette *f.*

roster /ˈrɒstə(r)/ *n.* liste (de service) *f.*, tableau (de service) *m.*

rostrum /ˈrɒstrəm/ *n.* (*pl.* **-tra**) tribune *f.*; (*sport*) podium *m.*

rosy /ˈrəʊzɪ/ *a.* (**-ier, -iest**) rose; (*hopeful*) plein d'espoir.

rot /rɒt/ *v.t./i.* (*p.t.* **rotted**) pourrir. —*n.* pourriture *f.*; (*nonsense: sl.*) bêtises *f. pl.*, âneries *f. pl.*

rota /ˈrəʊtə/ *n.* liste (de service) *f.*

rotary /ˈrəʊtərɪ/ *a.* rotatif.

rotat|e /rəʊˈteɪt/ *v.t./i.* (faire) tourner; (*change round*) alterner. ~**ing** *a.* tournant. ~**ion** /-ʃn/ *n.* rotation *f.*

rote /rəʊt/ *n.* **by** ~, machinalement.

rotten /ˈrɒtn/ *a.* pourri; (*tooth*) gâté; (*bad: fam.*) mauvais, sale.

rotund /rəʊˈtʌnd/ *a.* rond.

rouge /ruːʒ/ *n.* rouge (à joues) *m.*

rough /rʌf/ *a.* (**-er, -est**) (*manners*) rude; (*to touch*) rugueux; (*ground*) accidenté; (*violent*) brutal; (*bad*) mauvais; (*estimate etc.*) approximatif; (*diamond*) brut. —*adv.* (*live*) à la dure; (*play*) brutalement. —*n.* (*ruffian*) voyou *m.* —*v.t.* ~ **it,** vivre à la dure. ~-**and-ready** *a.* (*solution etc.*) grossier (mais efficace). ~-**and-tumble** *n.* mêlée *f.* ~ **out,** ébaucher. ~ **paper,** papier brouillon *m.* ~**ly** *adv.* rudement;

(*approximately*) à peu près. ~**ness** *n.* rudesse *f.*; brutalité *f.*

roughage /ˈrʌfɪdʒ/ *n.* fibres (alimentaires) *f. pl.*

roulette /ruːˈlet/ *n.* roulette *f.*

round /raʊnd/ *a.* (**-er, -est**) rond. —*n.* (*circle*) rond *m.*; (*slice*) tranche *f.*; (*of visits, drinks*) tournée *f.*; (*mil.*) ronde *f.*; (*competition*) partie *f.*, manche *f.*; (*boxing*) round *m.*; (*of talks*) série *f.* —*prep.* autour de. —*adv.* autour. —*v.t.* (*object*) arrondir; (*corner*) tourner. **go** *or* **come** ~ **to,** (*a friend etc.*) passer chez. **I'm going** ~ **the corner,** je vais juste à côté. **enough to go** ~, assez pour tout le monde. **go the** ~**s,** circuler. **she lives** ~ **here** elle habite par ici. ~ **about,** (*near by*) par ici; (*fig.*) à peu près. ~ **of applause,** applaudissements *m. pl.* ~ **off,** terminer. ~ **the clock,** vingt-quatre heures sur vingt-quatre. ~ **trip,** voyage aller-retour *m.* ~ **up,** rassembler. ~**-up** *n.* rassemblement *m.*; (*of suspects*) rafle *f.*

roundabout /ˈraʊndəbaʊt/ *n.* manège *m.*; (*for traffic*) rond-point (à sens giratoire) *m.* —*a.* indirect.

rounders /ˈraʊndəz/ *n.* sorte de baseball *f.*

roundly /ˈraʊndlɪ/ *adv.* (*bluntly*) franchement.

rous|e /raʊz/ *v.t.* éveiller; (*wake up*) réveiller. **be** ~**ed,** (*angry*) être en colère. ~**ing** *a.* (*speech, music*) excitant; (*cheers*) frénétique.

rout /raʊt/ *n.* (*defeat*) déroute *f.* —*v.t.* mettre en déroute.

route /ruːt/ *n.* itinéraire *m.*, parcours *m.*; (*naut., aviat.*) route *f.*

routine /ruːˈtiːn/ *n.* routine *f.* —*a.* de routine. **daily** ~, travail quotidien *m.*

rov|e /rəʊv/ *v.t./i.* errer (dans). ~**ing** *a.* (*life*) vagabond.

row[1] /rəʊ/ *n.* rangée *f.*, rang *m.* **in a** ~, (*consecutive*) consécutif.

row[2] /rəʊ/ *v.i.* ramer; (*sport*) faire de l'aviron. —*v.t.* faire aller à la rame. ~**ing** *n.* aviron *m.* ~**(ing)-boat** *n.* bateau à rames *m.*

row[3] /raʊ/ *n.* (*noise: fam.*) tapage *m.*; (*quarrel: fam.*) engueulade *f.* —*v.i.* (*fam.*) s'engueuler.

rowdy /ˈraʊdɪ/ *a.* (**-ier, -iest**) tapageur. —*n.* voyou *m.*

royal /ˈrɔɪəl/ *a.* royal. ~**ly** *adv.* (*treat, live, etc.*) royalement.

royalt|y /ˈrɔɪəltɪ/ *n.* famille royale *f.* ~**ies,** droits d'auteur *m. pl.*

rub /rʌb/ *v.t./i.* (*p.t.* **rubbed**) frotter.

—n. friction f. ~ **it in,** insister là-dessus. ~ **off on,** déteindre sur. ~ **out,** (s')effacer.

rubber /'rʌbə(r)/ n. caoutchouc m.; (*eraser*) gomme f. ~ **band,** élastique m. ~ **stamp,** tampon m. ~-**stamp** v.t. approuver. ~**y** a. caoutchouteux.

rubbish /'rʌbɪʃ/ n. (*refuse*) ordures f. pl.; (*junk*) saletés f. pl.; (*fig.*) bêtises f. pl. ~**y** a. sans valeur.

rubble /'rʌbl/ n. décombres m. pl.

ruby /'ru:bɪ/ n. rubis m.

rucksack /'rʌksæk/ n. sac à dos m.

rudder /'rʌdə(r)/ n. gouvernail m.

ruddy /'rʌdɪ/ a. (-**ier, -iest**) coloré, rougeâtre; (*damned: sl.*) fichu.

rude /ru:d/ a. (-**er, -est**) impoli, grossier; (*improper*) indécent; (*shock, blow*) brutal. ~**ly** adv. impoliment. ~**ness** n. impolitesse f.; indécence f.; brutalité f.

rudiment /'ru:dɪmənt/ n. rudiment m. ~**ary** /-'mentrɪ/ a. rudimentaire.

rueful /'ru:fl/ a. triste.

ruffian /'rʌfɪən/ n. voyou m.

ruffle /'rʌfl/ v.t. (*hair*) ébouriffer; (*clothes*) froisser; (*person*) contrarier. —n. (*frill*) ruche f.

rug /rʌg/ n. petit tapis m.

Rugby /'rʌgbɪ/ n. ~ (**football**), rugby m.

rugged /'rʌgɪd/ a. (*surface*) rude, rugueux; (*ground*) accidenté; (*character, features*) rude.

ruin /'ru:ɪn/ n. ruine f. —v.t. (*destroy*) ruiner; (*damage*) abîmer; (*spoil*) gâter. ~**ous** a. ruineux.

rule /ru:l/ n. règle f.; (*regulation*) règlement m.; (*pol.*) gouvernement m. —v.t. gouverner; (*master*) dominer; (*decide*) décider. —v.i. régner. **as a** ~, en règle générale. ~ **out,** exclure. ~**d paper,** papier réglé m. ~**r** /-ə(r)/ n. dirigeant(e) m. (f.), gouvernant m.; (*measure*) règle f.

ruling /'ru:lɪŋ/ a. (*class*) dirigeant; (*party*) au pouvoir. —n. décision f.

rum /rʌm/ n. rhum m.

rumble /rʌmbl/ v.i. gronder; (*stomach*) gargouiller. —n. grondement m.; gargouillement m.

rummage /'rʌmɪdʒ/ v.i. fouiller.

rumour (*Amer.*) **rumor** /'ru:mə(r)/ n. bruit m., rumeur f. **there's a** ~ **that,** le bruit court que.

rump /rʌmp/ n. (*of horse etc.*) croupe f.; (*of fowl*) croupion m.; (*steak*) romsteck m.

rumpus /'rʌmpəs/ n. (*uproar: fam.*) chahut m.

run /rʌn/ v.i. (p.t. **ran,** p.p. **run,** pres. p.

running) courir; (*flow*) couler; (*pass*) passer; (*function*) marcher; (*melt*) fondre; (*extend*) s'étendre; (*of bus etc.*) circuler; (*of play*) se jouer; (*last*) durer; (*of colour in washing*) déteindre; (*in election*) être candidat. —v.t. (*manage*) diriger; (*event*) organiser; (*risk, race*) courir; (*house*) tenir; (*blockade*) forcer; (*temperature, errand*) faire; (*comput.*) exécuter. —n. course f.; (*journey*) parcours m.; (*outing*) promenade f.; (*rush*) ruée f.; (*series*) série f.; (*in cricket*) point m. **have the** ~ **of,** avoir à sa disposition. **in the long** ~, avec le temps. **on the** ~, en fuite. ~ **across,** rencontrer par hasard. ~ **away,** s'enfuir. ~ **down,** descendre en courant; (*of vehicle*) renverser; (*production*) réduire progressivement; (*belittle*) dénigrer. **be** ~ **down,** (*weak etc.*) être sans forces or mal fichu. ~ **in,** (*vehicle*) roder. ~ **into,** (*hit*) heurter. ~ **off,** (*copies*) tirer. ~-**of-the-mill** a. ordinaire. ~ **out,** (*be used up*) s'épuiser; (*of lease*) expirer. ~ **out of,** manquer de. ~ **over,** (*of vehicle*) écraser; (*details*) revoir. ~ **through sth.,** regarder qch. rapidement. ~ **sth. through sth.,** passer qch. à travers qch. ~ **up,** (*bill*) accumuler. **the** ~-**up to,** la période qui précède.

runaway /'rʌnəweɪ/ n. fugitif, -ve m., f. —a. fugitif; (*horse, vehicle*) fou; (*inflation*) galopant.

rung[1] /rʌŋ/ n. (*of ladder*) barreau m.

rung[2] /rʌŋ/ see **ring**[2].

runner /'rʌnə(r)/ n. coureulr, -se m., f. ~ **bean,** haricot (grimpant) m. ~-**up** n. second(e) m. (f.).

running /'rʌnɪŋ/ n. course f.; (*of business*) gestion f.; (*of machine*) marche f. —a. (*commentary*) suivi; (*water*) courant. **be in the** ~ **for,** être sur les rangs pour. **four days/etc.** ~, quatre jours/etc. de suite.

runny /'rʌnɪ/ a. (*nose*) qui coule.

runt /rʌnt/ n. avorton m.

runway /'rʌnweɪ/ n. piste f.

rupture /'rʌptʃə(r)/ n. (*breaking, breach*) rupture f.; (*med.*) hernie f. —v.t./i. (se) rompre. ~ **o.s.,** se donner une hernie.

rural /'ruərəl/ a. rural.

ruse /ru:z/ n. (*trick*) ruse f.

rush[1] /rʌʃ/ n. (*plant*) jonc m.

rush[2] /rʌʃ/ v.i. (*move*) se précipiter; (*be in a hurry*) se dépêcher. —v.t. faire, envoyer, etc. en vitesse; (*person*) bousculer; (*mil.*) prendre d'assaut. —n.

ruée f.; (haste) bousculade f. **in a ~,**
pressé. **~-hour** n. heure de pointe f.
rusk /rʌsk/ n. biscotte f.
russet /'rʌsɪt/ a. roussâtre, roux.
Russia /'rʌʃə/ n. Russie f. **~n** a. & n.
russe (m./f.); (lang.) russe m.
rust /rʌst/ n. rouille f. —v.t./i. rouiller.
~-proof a. inoxydable. **~y** a. (tool,
person, etc.) rouillé.
rustic /'rʌstɪk/ a. rustique.
rustle /'rʌsl/ v.t./i. (leaves) (faire) bruire;
(steal: Amer.) voler. **~ up,** (food etc.:
fam.) préparer.
rut /rʌt/ n. ornière f. **be in a ~,** rester
dans l'ornière.
ruthless /'ruːθlɪs/ a. impitoyable. **~ness**
n. cruauté f.
rye /raɪ/ n. seigle m.; (whisky) whisky m.
(à base de seigle).

S

sabbath /'sæbəθ/ n. (Jewish) sabbat m.;
(Christian) dimanche m.
sabbatical /sə'bætɪkl/ a. (univ.) sab-
batique.
sabot|age /'sæbətɑːʒ/ n. sabotage m.
—v.t. saboter. **~eur** /-'tɜː(r)/ n.
saboteulr, -se m., f.
saccharin /'sækərɪn/ n. saccharine f.
sachet /'sæʃeɪ/ n. sachet m.
sack[1] /sæk/ n. (bag) sac m. —v.t. (fam.)
renvoyer. **get the ~,** (fam.) être
renvoyé. **~ing** n. toile à sac f.;
(dismissal: fam.) renvoi m.
sack[2] /sæk/ v.t. (plunder) saccager.
sacrament /'sækrəmənt/ n. sacrement
m.
sacred /'seɪkrɪd/ a. sacré.
sacrifice /'sækrɪfaɪs/ n. sacrifice m. —v.t.
sacrifier.
sacrileg|e /'sækrɪlɪdʒ/ n. sacrilège m.
~ious /-'lɪdʒəs/ a. sacrilège.
sad /sæd/ a. (**sadder, saddest**) triste.
~ly adv. tristement; (unfortunately)
malheureusement. **~ness** n. tristesse f.
sadden /'sædn/ v.t. attrister.
saddle /'sædl/ n. selle f. —v.t. (horse)
seller. **~ s.o. with,** (task, person) mettre
à qn. **in the ~,** bien en selle. **~-bag** n.
sacoche f.
sadis|t /'seɪdɪst/ n. sadique m./f. **~m**
/-zəm/ n. sadisme m. **~tic** /sə'dɪstɪk/
a. sadique.
safari /sə'fɑːrɪ/ n. safari m.
safe /seɪf/ a. (**-er, -est**) (not dangerous)

sans danger; (reliable) sûr; (out of
danger) en sécurité; (after accident)
sain et sauf; (wise: fig.) prudent. —n.
coffre-fort m. **to be on the ~ side,** pour
être sûr. **in ~ keeping,** en sécurité. **~
conduct,** sauf-conduit m. **~ from,** à
l'abri de. **~ly** adv. sans danger; (in safe
place) en sûreté.
safeguard /'seɪfɡɑːd/ n. sauvegarde f.
—v.t. sauvegarder.
safety /'seɪftɪ/ n. sécurité f. **~-belt** n.
ceinture de sécurité f. **~-pin** n. épingle
de sûreté f. **~-valve** n. soupape de
sûreté f.
saffron /'sæfrən/ n. safran m.
sag /sæɡ/ v.i. (p.t. **sagged**) s'affaisser,
fléchir. **~ging** a. affaissé.
saga /'sɑːɡə/ n. saga f.
sage[1] /seɪdʒ/ n. (herb) sauge f.
sage[2] /seɪdʒ/ a. & n. sage (m.).
Sagittarius /sædʒɪ'teərɪəs/ n. le Sagittaire.
said /sed/ see **say**.
sail /seɪl/ n. voile f.; (journey) tour en
bateau m. —v.i. naviguer; (leave)
partir; (sport) faire de la voile; (glide)
glisser. —v.t. (boat) piloter. **~ing-
boat, ~ing-ship** ns. bateau à voiles m.
sailor /'seɪlə(r)/ n. marin m.
saint /seɪnt/ n. saint(e) m. (f.). **~ly** a.
(person, act, etc.) saint.
sake /seɪk/ n. **for the ~ of,** pour, pour
l'amour de.
salad /'sæləd/ n. salade f. **~-dressing** n.
vinaigrette f.
salami /sə'lɑːmɪ/ n. salami m.
salar|y /'sælərɪ/ n. traitement m., salaire
m. **~ied** a. salarié.
sale /seɪl/ n. vente f. **~s,** (at reduced
prices) soldes m. pl. **~s assistant,**
(Amer.) **~s clerk,** vendeulr, -se m., f.
for ~, à vendre. **on ~,** en vente; (at a
reduced price: Amer.) en solde. **~-
room** n. salle des ventes f.
saleable /'seɪləbl/ a. vendable.
sales|man /'seɪlzmən/ n. (pl. **-men**) (in
shop) vendeur m.; (traveller) représentant m. **~woman** n. (pl. **-women**) ven-
deuse f.; représentante f.
salient /'seɪlɪənt/ a. saillant.
saline /'seɪlaɪn/ a. salin. —n. sérum
physiologique m.
saliva /sə'laɪvə/ n. salive f.
sallow /'sæləʊ/ a. (**-er, -est**)
(complexion) jaunâtre.
salmon /'sæmən/ n. invar. saumon m.
salon /'sælɒn/ n. salon m.
saloon /sə'luːn/ n. (on ship) salon m.;
(bar: Amer.) bar m., saloon m. **~ (car),**
berline f.

salt /sɔːlt/ n. sel m. —a. (culin.) salé; (water) de mer. —v.t. saler. **~-cellar** n. salière f. **~y** a. salé.

salutary /'sæljʊtrɪ/ a. salutaire.

salute /sə'luːt/ n. (mil.) salut m. —v.t. saluer. —v.i. faire un salut.

salvage /'sælvɪdʒ/ n. sauvetage m.; (of waste) récupération f.; (goods) objets sauvés m. pl. —v.t. sauver; (for re-use) récupérer.

salvation /sæl'veɪʃn/ n. salut m.

salvo /'sælvəʊ/ n. (pl. -oes) salve f.

same /seɪm/ a. même (as, que). —pron. the ~, le or la même, les mêmes. at the ~ time, en même temps. the ~ (thing), la même chose.

sample /'saːmpl/ n. échantillon m.; (of blood) prélèvement m. —v.t. essayer; (food) goûter.

sanatorium /sænə'tɔːrɪəm/ n. (pl. -iums) sanatorium m.

sanctify /'sæŋktɪfaɪ/ v.t. sanctifier.

sanctimonious /sæŋktɪ'məʊnɪəs/ a. (person) bigot; (air, tone) de petit saint.

sanction /'sæŋkʃn/ n. sanction f. —v.t. sanctionner.

sanctity /'sæŋktətɪ/ n. sainteté f.

sanctuary /'sæŋktjʊərɪ/ n. (relig.) sanctuaire m.; (for animals) réserve f.; (refuge) asile m.

sand /sænd/ n. sable m. **~s**, (beach) plage f. —v.t. sabler. **~-castle** n. château de sable m. **~-pit**, (Amer.) **~-box** n. bac à sable m.

sandal /'sændl/ n. sandale f.

sandpaper /'sændpeɪpə(r)/ n. papier de verre m. —v.t. poncer.

sandstone /'sændstəʊn/ n. grès m.

sandwich /'sænwɪdʒ/ n. sandwich m. —v.t. **~ed between**, pris en sandwich entre. **~ course**, stage de formation continue à mi-temps m.

sandy /'sændɪ/ a. sablonneux, de sable; (hair) blond roux invar.

sane /seɪn/ a. (-er, -est) (view etc.) sain; (person) sain d'esprit. **~ly** adv. sainement.

sang /sæŋ/ see **sing**.

sanitary /'sænɪtrɪ/ a. (clean) hygiénique; (system etc.) sanitaire. **~ towel**, (Amer.) **~ napkin**, serviette hygiénique f.

sanitation /sænɪ'teɪʃn/ n. hygiène (publique) f.; (drainage etc.) système sanitaire m.

sanity /'sænətɪ/ n. santé mentale f.; (good sense: fig.) bon sens m.

sank /sæŋk/ see **sink**.

Santa Claus /'sæntəklɔːz/ n. le père Noël m.

sap /sæp/ n. (of plants) sève f. —v.t. (p.t. **sapped**) (undermine) saper.

sapphire /'sæfaɪə(r)/ n. saphir m.

sarcas|m /'saːkæzəm/ n. sarcasme m. **~tic** /saː'kæstɪk/ a. sarcastique.

sardine /saː'diːn/ n. sardine f.

Sardinia /saː'dɪnɪə/ n. Sardaigne f.

sardonic /saː'dɒnɪk/ a. sardonique.

sash /sæʃ/ n. (on uniform) écharpe f.; (on dress) ceinture f. **~-window** n. fenêtre à guillotine f.

sat /sæt/ see **sit**.

satanic /sə'tænɪk/ a. satanique.

satchel /'sætʃl/ n. cartable m.

satellite /'sætəlaɪt/ n. & a. satellite (m.). **~ dish**, antenne parabolique f.

satin /'sætɪn/ n. satin m.

satir|e /'sætaɪə(r)/ n. satire f. **~ical** /sə'tɪrɪkl/ a. satirique.

satisfactor|y /sætɪs'fæktərɪ/ a. satisfaisant. **~ily** adv. d'une manière satisfaisante.

satisf|y /'sætɪsfaɪ/ v.t. satisfaire; (convince) convaincre. **~action** /-'fækʃn/ n. satisfaction f. **~ying** a. satisfaisant.

satsuma /sæt'suːmə/ n. mandarine f.

saturat|e /'sætʃəreɪt/ v.t. saturer. **~ed** a. (wet) trempé. **~ion** /-'reɪʃn/ n. saturation f.

Saturday /'sætədɪ/ n. samedi m.

sauce /sɔːs/ n. sauce f.; (impudence: sl.) toupet m.

saucepan /'sɔːspən/ n. casserole f.

saucer /'sɔːsə(r)/ n. soucoupe f.

saucy /'sɔːsɪ/ a. (-ier, -iest) impertinent; (boldly smart) coquin.

Saudi Arabia /saʊdɪə'reɪbɪə/ n. Arabie Séoudite f.

sauna /'sɔːnə/ n. sauna m.

saunter /'sɔːntə(r)/ v.i. flâner.

sausage /'sɒsɪdʒ/ n. saucisse f.; (pre-cooked) saucisson m.

savage /'sævɪdʒ/ a. (fierce) féroce; (wild) sauvage. —n. sauvage m./f. —v.t. attaquer férocement. **~ry** n. sauvagerie f.

sav|e /seɪv/ v.t. sauver; (money) économiser; (time) (faire) gagner; (keep) garder; (prevent) éviter (from, de). —n. (football) arrêt m. —prep. sauf. **~er** n. épargnant(e) m. (f.). **~ing** n. (of time, money) économie f. **~ings** n. pl. économies f. pl.

saviour, (Amer.) **savior** /'seɪvɪə(r)/ n. sauveur m.

savour, (Amer.) **savor** /'seɪvə(r)/ n.

saveur f. —v.t. savourer. ~y a. (tasty) savoureux; (culin.) salé.

saw¹ /sɔː/ see see¹.

saw² /sɔː/ n. scie f. —v.t. (p.t. sawed, p.p. sawn /sɔːn/ or sawed) scier.

sawdust /'sɔːdʌst/ n. sciure f.

saxophone /'sæksəfəʊn/ n. saxophone m.

say /seɪ/ v.t./i. (p.t. said /sed/) dire; (prayer) faire. —n. have a ~, dire son mot; (in decision) avoir voix au chapitre. I ~!, dites donc!

saying /'seɪɪŋ/ n. proverbe m.

scab /skæb/ n. (on sore) croûte f.; (blackleg: fam.) jaune m.

scaffold /'skæfəʊld/ n. (gallows) échafaud m. ~ing /-əldɪŋ/ n. (for workmen) échafaudage m.

scald /skɔːld/ v.t. (injure, cleanse) ébouillanter. —n. brûlure f.

scale¹ /skeɪl/ n. (of fish) écaille f.

scale² /skeɪl/ n. (for measuring, size, etc.) échelle f.; (mus.) gamme f.; (of salaries, charges) barème m. on a small/etc. ~, sur une petite/etc. échelle. ~ model, maquette f. —v.t. (climb) escalader. ~ down, réduire (proportionnellement).

scales /skeɪlz/ n. pl. (for weighing) balance f.

scallop /'skɒləp/ n. coquille Saint-Jacques f.

scalp /skælp/ n. cuir chevelu m. —v.t. (mutilate) scalper.

scalpel /'skælp(ə)l/ n. scalpel m.

scamper /'skæmpə(r)/ v.i. courir, trotter. ~ away, détaler.

scampi /'skæmpɪ/ n. pl. grosses crevettes f. pl., gambas f. pl.

scan /skæn/ v.t. (p.t. scanned) scruter; (quickly) parcourir; (poetry) scander; (of radar) balayer. —n. (ultrasound) échographie f.

scandal /'skændl/ n. (disgrace, outrage) scandale m.; (gossip) cancans m. pl. ~ous a. scandaleux.

scandalize /'skændəlaɪz/ v.t. scandaliser.

Scandinavia /skændɪ'neɪvɪə/ n. Scandinavie f. ~n a. & n. scandinave (m./f.).

scant /skænt/ a. insuffisant.

scant|y /'skæntɪ/ a. (-ier, -iest) insuffisant; (clothing) sommaire. ~ily adv. insuffisamment. ~ily dressed, à peine vêtu.

scapegoat /'skeɪpgəʊt/ n. bouc émissaire m.

scar /'skɑː(r)/ n. cicatrice f. —v.t. (p.t.

scarred) marquer d'une cicatrice; (fig.) marquer.

scarc|e /skeəs/ a. (-er, -est) rare. make o.s. ~e, (fam.) se sauver. ~ity n. rareté f., pénurie f.

scarcely /'skeəslɪ/ adv. à peine.

scare /'skeə(r)/ v.t. faire peur à. —n. peur f. be ~d, avoir peur. bomb ~, alerte à la bombe f.

scarecrow /'skeəkrəʊ/ n. épouvantail m.

scarf /skɑːf/ n. (pl. scarves) écharpe f.; (over head) foulard m.

scarlet /'skɑːlət/ a. écarlate. ~ fever, scarlatine f.

scary /'skeərɪ/ a. (-ier, -iest) (fam.) qui fait peur, effrayant.

scathing /'skeɪðɪŋ/ a. cinglant.

scatter /'skætə(r)/ v.t. (throw) éparpiller, répandre; (disperse) disperser. —v.i. se disperser. ~brain n. écervelé(e) m. (f.).

scavenge /'skævɪndʒ/ v.i. fouiller (dans les ordures). ~r /-ə(r)/ n. (vagrant) personne qui fouille dans les ordures f.

scenario /sɪ'nɑːrɪəʊ/ n. (pl. -os) scénario m.

scene /siːn/ n. scène f.; (of accident, crime) lieu(x) m. (pl.); (sight) spectacle m.; (incident) incident m. behind the ~s, en coulisse. to make a ~, faire un esclandre.

scenery /'siːnərɪ/ n. paysage m.; (theatre) décor(s) m. (pl.).

scenic /'siːnɪk/ a. pittoresque.

scent /sent/ n. (perfume) parfum m.; (trail) piste f. —v.t. flairer; (make fragrant) parfumer.

sceptic /'skeptɪk/ n. sceptique m./f. ~al a. sceptique. ~ism /-sɪzəm/ n. scepticisme m.

schedule /'ʃedjuːl, Amer. 'skedʒʊl/ n. horaire m.; (for job) planning m. —v.t. prévoir. behind ~, en retard. on ~, (train) à l'heure; (work) dans les temps. ~d flight, vol régulier m.

scheme /skiːm/ n. plan m.; (dishonest) combine f.; (fig.) arrangement m. —v.i. intriguer. pension ~, caisse de retraite f. ~r /-ə(r)/ n. intrigant(e) m. (f.).

schism /'sɪzəm/ n. schisme m.

schizophrenic /skɪtsəʊ'frenɪk/ a. & n. schizophrène (m./f.).

scholar /'skɒlə(r)/ n. érudit(e) m. (f.) ~ly a. érudit. ~ship n. érudition f.; (grant) bourse f.

school /skuːl/ n. école f.; (secondary) lycée m.; (of university) faculté f. —a. (age, year, holidays) scolaire. —v.t. (person) éduquer; (animal) dresser.

~**ing** n. (education) instruction f.; (attendance) scolarité f.

school|boy /'sku:lbɔɪ/ n. écolier m. ~**girl** n. écolière f.

school|master /'sku:lmɑːstə(r)/, ~**mistress**, ~**teacher** ns. (primary) instituteur, -trice m., f.; (secondary) professeur m.

schooner /'sku:nə(r)/ n. goélette f.

sciatica /saɪ'ætɪkə/ n. sciatique f.

scien|ce /'saɪəns/ n. science f. ~**ce fiction**, science-fiction f. ~**tific** /-'tɪfɪk/ a. scientifique.

scientist /'saɪəntɪst/ n. scientifique m./f.

scintillate /'sɪntɪleɪt/ v.i. scintiller; (person: fig.) briller.

scissors /'sɪzəz/ n. pl. ciseaux m. pl.

scoff[1] /skɒf/ v.i. ~ **at**, se moquer de.

scoff[2] /skɒf/ v.t. (eat: sl.) bouffer.

scold /skəʊld/ v.t. réprimander. ~**ing** n. réprimande f.

scone /skɒn/ n. petit pain au lait m., galette f.

scoop /sku:p/ n. (for grain, sugar) pelle (à main) f.; (for food) cuiller f.; (ice cream) boule f.; (news) exclusivité f. —v.t. (pick up) ramasser. ~ **out**, creuser. ~ **up**, ramasser.

scoot /sku:t/ v.i. (fam.) filer.

scooter /'sku:tə(r)/ n. (child's) trottinette f.; (motor cycle) scooter m.

scope /skəʊp/ n. étendue f.; (competence) compétence f.; (opportunity) possibilité(s) f. (pl.).

scorch /skɔːtʃ/ v.t. brûler, roussir. ~**ing** a. brûlant, très chaud.

score /skɔː(r)/ n. score m.; (mus.) partition f. —v.t. marquer; (success) remporter. —v.i. marquer un point; (football) marquer un but; (keep score) compter les points. **a** ~ **(of)**, (twenty) vingt. **on that** ~, à cet égard. ~ **out**, rayer. ~**board** n. tableau m. ~**r** /-ə(r)/ n. (sport) marqueur m.

scorn /skɔːn/ n. mépris m. —v.t. mépriser. ~**ful** a. méprisant. ~**fully** adv. avec mépris.

Scorpio /'skɔːpɪəʊ/ n. le Scorpion.

scorpion /'skɔːpɪən/ n. scorpion m.

Scot /skɒt/ n. Écossais(e) m. (f.). ~**tish** a. écossais.

Scotch /skɒtʃ/ a. écossais. —n. whisky m., scotch m.

scotch /skɒtʃ/ v.t. mettre fin à.

scot-free /skɒt'friː/ a. & adv. sans être puni; (gratis) sans payer.

Scotland /'skɒtlənd/ n. Écosse f.

Scots /skɒts/ a. écossais. ~**man** n. Écossais m. ~**woman** n. Écossaise f.

scoundrel /'skaʊndrəl/ n. vaurien m., bandit m., gredin(e) m. (f.).

scour[1] /'skaʊə(r)/ v.t. (pan) récurer. ~**er** n. tampon à récurer m.

scour[2] /'skaʊə(r)/ v.t. (search) parcourir.

scourge /skɜːdʒ/ n. fléau m.

scout /skaʊt/ n. (mil.) éclaireur m. —v.i. ~ **around (for)**, chercher.

Scout /skaʊt/ n. (boy) scout m., éclaireur m. ~**ing** n. scoutisme m.

scowl /skaʊl/ n. air renfrogné m. —v.i. faire la tête (**at**, à).

scraggy /'skrægɪ/ a. (-**ier**, -**iest**) décharné, efflanqué.

scram /skræm/ v.i. (sl.) se tirer.

scramble /'skræmbl/ v.i. (clamber) grimper. —v.t. (eggs) brouiller. —n. bousculade f., ruée f. ~ **for**, se bousculer pour avoir.

scrap[1] /skræp/ n. petit morceau m. ~**s**, (of metal, fabric, etc.) déchets m. pl.; (of food) restes m. pl. —v.t. (p.t. **scrapped**) mettre au rebut; (plan etc.) abandonner. ~**-book** n. album m. **on the** ~**-heap**, mis au rebut. ~**-iron** n. ferraille f. ~**-paper** n. brouillon m. ~**py**[2] a. fragmentaire.

scrap[2] /skræp/ n. (fight: fam.) bagarre f., dispute f.

scrape /skreɪp/ v.t. racler, gratter; (graze) érafler. —v.i. (rub) frotter. —n. raclement m.; éraflure f. **in a** ~, dans une mauvaise passe. ~ **through**, réussir de justesse. ~ **together**, réunir. ~**r** /-ə(r)/ n. racloir m.

scratch /skrætʃ/ v.t./i. (se) gratter; (with claw, nail) griffer; (graze) érafler; (mark) rayer. —n. éra flure f. **start from** ~, partir de zéro. **up to** ~, au niveau voulu.

scrawl /skrɔːl/ n. gribouillage m. —v.t./i. gribouiller.

scrawny /'skrɔːnɪ/ a. (-**ier**, -**iest**) décharné, émacié.

scream /skriːm/ v.t./i. crier, hurler. —n. cri (perçant) m.

scree /skriː/ n. éboulis m.

screech /skriːtʃ/ v.i. (scream) hurler; (of brakes) grincer. —n. hurlement m.; grincement m.

screen /skriːn/ n. écran m.; (folding) paravent m. —v.t. masquer; (protect) protéger; (film) projeter; (candidates) filtrer; (med.) faire subir un test de dépistage. ~**ing** n. projection f.

screenplay /'skriːnpleɪ/ n. scénario m.

screw /skruː/ n. vis f. —v.t. visser. ~ **up**, (eyes) plisser; (ruin: sl.) bousiller.

screwdriver /ˈskruːdraɪvə(r)/ n. tournevis m.

screwy /ˈskruːɪ/ a. (-ier, -iest) (crazy: sl.) cinglé.

scribble /ˈskrɪbl/ v.t./i. griffonner. —n. griffonnage m.

scribe /skraɪb/ n. scribe m.

script /skrɪpt/ n. écriture f.; (of film) scénario m.; (of play) texte m. **~-writer** n. scénariste m./f.

Scriptures /ˈskrɪptʃəz/ n. pl. the **~**, l'Écriture (sainte) f.

scroll /skrəʊl/ n. rouleau m. —v.t./i. (comput.) (faire) défiler.

scrounge /skraʊndʒ/ v.t. (meal) se faire payer; (steal) chiper. —v.i. (beg) quémander. **~ money from**, taper. **~r** /-ə(r)/ n. parasite m.; (of money) tapeur, -se m., f.

scrub[1] /skrʌb/ n. (land) broussailles f. pl.

scrub[2] /skrʌb/ v.t./i. (p.t. scrubbed) nettoyer (à la brosse), frotter. —n. nettoyage m.

scruff /skrʌf/ n. **by the ~ of the neck**, par la peau du cou.

scruffy /ˈskrʌfɪ/ a. (-ier, -iest) (fam.) miteux, sale.

scrum /skrʌm/ n. (Rugby) mêlée f.

scruple /ˈskruːpl/ n. scrupule m.

scrupulous /ˈskruːpjʊləs/ a. scrupuleux. **~ly** adv. scrupuleusement. **~ly clean**, impeccable.

scrutin|y /ˈskruːtɪnɪ/ n. examen minutieux m. **~ize** v.t. scruter.

scuba-diving /ˈskuːbədaɪvɪŋ/ n. plongée soumarine f.

scuff /skʌf/ v.t. (scratch) érafler.

scuffle /ˈskʌfl/ n. bagarre f.

sculpt /skʌlpt/ v.t./i. sculpter. **~or** n. sculpteur m. **~ure** /-tʃə(r)/ n. sculpture f.; v.t./i. sculpter.

scum /skʌm/ n. (on liquid) écume f.; (people: pej.) racaille f.

scurf /skɜːf/ n. pellicules f. pl.

scurrilous /ˈskʌrɪləs/ a. grossier, injurieux, venimeux.

scurry /ˈskʌrɪ/ v.i. courir (for, pour chercher). **~ off**, filer.

scuttle[1] /ˈskʌtl/ v.t. (ship) saborder.

scuttle[2] /ˈskʌtl/ v.i. **~ away**, se sauver, filer.

scythe /saɪð/ n. faux f.

sea /siː/ n. mer f. —a. de (la) mer, marin. **at ~**, en mer. **by ~**, par mer. **~-green** a. vert glauque invar. **~-level** n. niveau de la mer m. **~ shell**, coquillage m. **~shore** n. rivage m.

seaboard /ˈsiːbɔːd/ n. littoral m.

seafarer /ˈsiːfeərə(r)/ n. marin m.

seafood /ˈsiːfuːd/ n. fruits de mer m. pl.

seagull /ˈsiːgʌl/ n. mouette f.

seal[1] /siːl/ n. (animal) phoque m.

seal[2] /siːl/ n. sceau m.; (with wax) cachet m. —v.t. sceller; cacheter; (stick down) coller. **~ing-wax** n. cire à cacheter f. **~ off**, (area) boucler.

seam /siːm/ n. (in cloth etc.) couture f.; (of coal) veine f.

seaman /ˈsiːmən/ n. (pl. -men) marin m.

seamy /ˈsiːmɪ/ a. **~ side**, côté sordide m.

seance /ˈseɪɑːns/ n. séance de spiritisme f.

seaplane /ˈsiːpleɪn/ n. hydravion m.

seaport /ˈsiːpɔːt/ n. port de mer m.

search /sɜːtʃ/ v.t. fouiller; (study) examiner. —n. fouille f.; (quest) recherche(s) f. (pl.). **in ~ of**, à la recherche de. **~ for**, chercher. **~-party** n. équipe de secours f. **~-warrant** n. mandat de perquisition f. **~ing** a. (piercing) pénétrant.

searchlight /ˈsɜːtʃlaɪt/ n. projecteur m.

seasick /ˈsiːsɪk/ a. **be ~**, avoir le mal de mer.

seaside /ˈsiːsaɪd/ n. bord de la mer m.

season /ˈsiːzn/ n. saison f. —v.t. assaisonner. **in ~**, de saison. **~able** a. qui convient à la saison. **~al** a. saisonnier. **~ing** n. assaisonnement m. **~-ticket** n. carte d'abonnement f.

seasoned /ˈsiːznd/ a. expérimenté.

seat /siːt/ n. siège m.; (place) place f.; (of trousers) fond m. —v.t. (put) placer; (have seats for) avoir des places assises pour. **be ~ed**, **take a ~**, s'asseoir. **~-belt** n. ceinture de sécurité f.

seaweed /ˈsiːwiːd/ n. algues f. pl.

seaworthy /ˈsiːwɜːðɪ/ a. en état de naviguer.

secateurs /sekəˈtɜːz/ n. pl. sécateur m.

sece|de /sɪˈsiːd/ v.i. faire sécession. **~ssion** /-eʃn/ n. sécession f.

seclu|de /sɪˈkluːd/ v.t. isoler. **~ded** a. isolé. **~sion** /-ʒn/ n. solitude f.

second[1] /ˈsekənd/ a. deuxième, second. —n. deuxième m./f., second(e) m. (f.); (unit of time) seconde f. **~s**, (goods) articles de second choix m. pl. —adv. (in race etc.) en seconde place. —v.t. (proposal) appuyer. **~-best** a. de second choix, numéro deux invar. **~-class** a. de deuxième classe. **at ~ hand**, de seconde main. **~-hand** a. & adv. d'occasion; n. (on clock) trotteuse f. **~-rate** a. médiocre. **have ~ thoughts**, avoir des doutes, changer d'avis. **on ~ thoughts**, (Amer.) **on ~ thought**, à la réflexion. **~ly** adv. deuxièmement.

second² /sɪ'kɒnd/ v.t. (*transfer*) détacher (**to,** à). **~ment** n. détachement m.

secondary /'sekəndrɪ/ a. secondaire. **~ school,** lycée m., collège m.

secrecy /'siːkrəsɪ/ n. secret m.

secret /'siːkrɪt/ a. secret. —n. secret m. **in ~,** en secret. **~ly** adv. en secret, secrètement.

secretariat /sekrə'teərɪət/ n. secrétariat m.

secretar|y /'sekrətrɪ/ n. secrétaire m./f. **S~y of State,** ministre m.; (*Amer.*) ministre des Affaires étrangères m. **~ial** /-'teərɪəl/ a. (*work etc.*) de secrétaire.

secret|e /sɪ'kriːt/ v.t. (*med.*) sécréter. **~ion** /-ʃn/ n. sécrétion f.

secretive /'siːkrətɪv/ a. cachottier.

sect /sekt/ n. secte f. **~arian** /-'teərɪən/ a. sectaire.

section /'sekʃn/ n. section f.; (*of country, town*) partie f.; (*in store*) rayon m.; (*newspaper column*) rubrique f.

sector /'sektə(r)/ n. secteur m.

secular /'sekjʊlə(r)/ a. (*school etc.*) laïque; (*art, music, etc.*) profane.

secure /sɪ'kjʊə(r)/ a. (*safe*) en sûreté; (*in mind*) tranquille; (*psychologically*) sécurisé; (*firm*) solide; (*against attack*) sûr; (*window etc.*) bien fermé. —v.t. attacher; (*obtain*) s'assurer; (*ensure*) assurer. **~ly** adv. solidement; (*safely*) en sûreté.

security /sɪ'kjʊərətɪ/ n. (*safety*) sécurité f.; (*for loan*) caution f. **~ guard,** vigile m.

sedan /sɪ'dæn/ n. (*Amer.*) berline f.

sedate¹ /sɪ'deɪt/ a. calme.

sedat|e² /sɪ'deɪt/ v.t. donner un sédatif à. **~ion** /-ʃn/ n. sédation f.

sedative /'sedətɪv/ n. sédatif m.

sedentary /'sedntrɪ/ a. sédentaire.

sediment /'sedɪmənt/ n. sédiment m.

sedition /sɪ'dɪʃn/ n. sédition f.

seduce /sɪ'djuːs/ v.t. séduire. **~r** /-ə(r)/ n. séduclteur, -trice m., f.

seduct|ion /sɪ'dʌkʃn/ n. séduction f. **~ive** /-tɪv/ a. séduisant.

see¹ /siː/ v.t./i. (*p.t.* **saw,** *p.p.* **seen**) voir; (*escort*) (r)accompagner. **~ about** *or* **to,** s'occuper de. **~ through,** (*task*) mener à bonne fin; (*person*) deviner (le jeu de). **~ (to it) that,** veiller à ce que. **see you (soon)!,** à bientôt! **~ing that,** vu que.

see² /siː/ n. (*of bishop*) évêché m.

seed /siːd/ n. graine f.; (*collectively*) graines f. pl.; (*origin: fig.*) germe m.; (*tennis*) tête de série f. **go to ~,** (*plant*)

monter en graine; (*person*) se laisser aller. **~ling** n. plant m.

seedy /'siːdɪ/ a. (**-ier, -iest**) miteux.

seek /siːk/ v.t. (*p.t.* **sought**) chercher. **~ out,** aller chercher.

seem /siːm/ v.i. sembler. **~ingly** adv. apparemment.

seemly /'siːmlɪ/ adv. convenable.

seen /siːn/ *see* **see**¹.

seep /siːp/ v.i. (*ooze*) suinter. **~ into,** s'infiltrer dans. **~age** n. suintement m.; infiltration f.

see-saw /'siːsɔː/ n. balançoire f., tape-cul m. —v.t. osciller.

seethe /siːð/ v.i. **~ with,** (*anger*) bouillir de; (*people*) grouiller de.

segment /'segmənt/ n. segment m.; (*of orange*) quartier m.

segregat|e /'segrɪgeɪt/ v.t. séparer. **~ion** /-'geɪʃn/ n. ségrégation f.

seize /siːz/ v.t. saisir; (*take possession of*) s'emparer de. —v.i. **~ on,** (*chance etc.*) saisir. **~ up,** (*engine etc.*) se gripper.

seizure /'siːʒə(r)/ n. (*med.*) crise f.

seldom /'seldəm/ adv. rarement.

select /sɪ'lekt/ v.t. choisir, sélectionner. —a. choisi; (*exclusive*) sélect. **~ion** /-kʃn/ n. sélection f.

selective /sɪ'lektɪv/ a. sélectif.

self /self/ n. (*pl.* **selves**) (*on cheque*) moi-même. **the ~,** le moi m. *invar.* **your good ~,** vous-même.

self- /self/ *pref.* **~-assurance** n. assurance f. **~-assured** a. sûr de soi. **~-catering** a. où l'on fait la cuisine soi-même. **~-centred,** (*Amer.*) **~-centered** a. égocentrique. **~-coloured,** (*Amer.*) **~-colored** a. uni. **~-confidence** n. confiance en soi f. **~-confident** a. sûr de soi. **~-conscious** a. gêné, timide. **~-contained** a. (*flat*) indépendant. **~-control** n. maîtrise de soi f. **~-defence** n. autodéfense f.; (*jurid.*) légitime défense f. **~-denial** n. abnégation f. **~-employed** a. qui travaille à son compte. **~-esteem** n. amour-propre m. **~-evident** a. évident. **~-government** n. autonomie f. **~-indulgent** a. qui se permet tout. **~-interest** n. intérêt personnel m. **~-portrait** n. autoportrait m. **~-possessed** a. assuré. **~-reliant** a. indépendant. **~-respect** n. respect de soi m., dignité f. **~-righteous** a. satisfait de soi. **~-sacrifice** n. abnégation f. **~-satisfied** a. content de soi. **~-seeking** a. égoïste. **~-service** n. & a. libre-service (m.). **~-styled** a. soi-disant. **~-sufficient** a. indépendant. **~-willed** a. entêté.

selfish /'selfɪʃ/ a. égoïste; (*motive*) intéressé. ∼**ness** n. égoïsme m.

selfless /'selflɪs/ a. désintéressé.

sell /sel/ v.t./i. (*p.t.* **sold**) (se) vendre. ∼-**by date**, date limite de vente f. **be sold out of**, n'avoir plus de. ∼ **off**, liquider. ∼-**out**, n. trahison f. **it was a** ∼-**out**, on a vendu tous les billets. ∼ **up**, vendre son fonds, sa maison, *etc.* ∼**er** n. vendeur, -se m., f.

Sellotape /'seləuteɪp/ n. (P.) scotch m. (P.).

semantic /sɪ'mæntɪk/ a. sémantique. ∼**s** n. sémantique f.

semaphore /'seməfɔ:(r)/ n. signaux à bras m. pl.; (*device: rail.*) sémaphore m.

semblance /'sembləns/ n. semblant m.

semen /'si:mən/ n. sperme m.

semester /sɪ'mestə(r)/ n. (*univ., Amer.*) semestre m.

semi- /'semɪ/ *pref.* semi-, demi-.

semibreve /'semɪbri:v/ n. (*mus.*) ronde f.

semicirc|le /'semɪsɜ:kl/ n. demi-cercle m. ∼**ular** /-'sɜ:kjʊlə(r)/ a. en demi-cercle.

semicolon /semɪ'kəʊlən/ n. point-virgule m.

semiconductor /semɪkən'dʌktə(r)/ n. semi-conducteur n.

semi-detached /semɪ'dɪtætʃt/ a. ∼ **house,** maison jumelle f.

semifinal /semɪ'faɪnl/ n. demi-finale f.

seminar /'semɪnɑ:(r)/ n. séminaire m.

seminary /'semɪnərɪ/ n. séminaire m.

semiquaver /'semɪkweɪvə(r)/ n. (*mus.*) double croche f.

Semit|e /'si:maɪt, *Amer.* 'semaɪt/ n. Sémite m./f. ∼**ic** /sɪ'mɪtɪk/ a. sémite; (*lang.*) sémitique.

semolina /semə'li:nə/ n. semoule f.

senat|e /'senɪt/ n. sénat m. ∼**or** /-ətə(r)/ n. sénateur m.

send /send/ v.t./i. (*p.t.* **sent**) envoyer. ∼ **away,** (*dismiss*) renvoyer. ∼ (**away** *or* **off**) **for,** commander (par la poste). ∼ **back,** renvoyer. ∼ **for,** (*person, help*) envoyer chercher. ∼ **a player off,** renvoyer un joueur. ∼-**off** n. adieux chaleureux m. pl. ∼ **up,** (*fam.*) parodier. ∼**er** n. expéditeur, -trice m., f.

senil|e /'si:naɪl/ a. sénile. ∼**ity** /sɪ'nɪlətɪ/ n. sénilité f.

senior /'si:nɪə(r)/ a. plus âgé (**to,** que); (*in rank*) supérieur; (*teacher, partner*) principal. —n. aîné(e) m. (f.); (*schol.*) grand(e) m. (f.). ∼ **citizen,** personne âgée f. ∼**ity** /-'ɒrətɪ/ n. priorité d'âge

f.; supériorité f.; (*in service*) ancienneté f.

sensation /sen'seɪʃn/ n. sensation f. ∼**al** a. (*event*) qui fait sensation; (*wonderful*) sensationnel.

sense /sens/ n. sens m.; (*sensation*) sensation f.; (*mental impression*) sentiment m.; (*common sense*) bon sens m. ∼**s,** (*mind*) raison f. —v.t. (*pres.*)sentir. **make** ∼, avoir du sens. **make** ∼ **of,** comprendre. ∼**less** a. stupide; (*med.*) sans connaissance.

sensibilit|y /sensə'bɪlətɪ/ n. sensibilité f. ∼**ies,** susceptibilité f.

sensible /'sensəbl/ a. raisonnable, sensé; (*clothing*) fonctionnel.

sensitiv|e /'sensɪtɪv/ a. sensible (**to,** à); (*touchy*) susceptible. ∼**ity** /-'tɪvətɪ/ n. sensibilité f.

sensory /'sensərɪ/ a. sensoriel.

sensual /'senʃʊəl/ a. sensuel. ∼**ity** /-'ælətɪ/ n. sensualité f.

sensuous /'senʃʊəs/ a. sensuel.

sent /sent/ *see* **send**.

sentence /'sentəns/ n. phrase f.; (*decision: jurid.*) jugement m., condamnation f.; (*punishment*) peine f. —v.t. ∼ **to,** condamner à.

sentiment /'sentɪmənt/ n. sentiment m.

sentimental /sentɪ'mentl/ a. sentimental. ∼**ity** /-'tælətɪ/ n. sentimentalité f.

sentry /'sentrɪ/ n. sentinelle f.

separable /'sepərəbl/ a. séparable.

separate[^1] /'seprət/ a. séparé, différent; (*independent*) indépendant. ∼**s** n. pl. coordonnés m. pl. ∼**ly** adv. séparément.

separat|e[^2] /'sepəreɪt/ v.t./i. (se) séparer. ∼**ion** /-'reɪʃn/ n. séparation f.

September /sep'tembə(r)/ n. septembre m.

septic /'septɪk/ a. (*wound*) infecté. ∼ **tank,** fosse septique f.

sequel /'si:kwəl/ n. suite f.

sequence /'si:kwəns/ n. (*order*) ordre m.; (*series*) suite f.; (*of film*) séquence f.

sequin /'si:kwɪn/ n. paillette f.

serenade /serə'neɪd/ n. sérénade f. —v.t. donner une sérénade à.

seren|e /sɪ'ri:n/ a. serein. ∼**ity** /-enətɪ/ n. sérénité f.

sergeant /'sɑ:dʒənt/ n. (*mil.*) sergent m.; (*policeman*) brigadier m.

serial /'sɪərɪəl/ n. (*story*) feuilleton m. —a. (*number*) de série.

series /'sɪəri:z/ n. invar. série f.

serious /'sɪərɪəs/ a. sérieux; (*very bad, critical*) grave, sérieux. ∼**ly** adv. sérieusement, gravement. **take** ∼**ly,** prendre au sérieux. ∼**ness** n. sérieux m.

sermon /'sɜːmən/ n. sermon m.

serpent /'sɜːpənt/ n. serpent m.

serrated /sɪ'reɪtɪd/ a. (edge) en dents de scie.

serum /'sɪərəm/ n. (pl. -a) sérum m.

servant /'sɜːvənt/ n. domestique m./f.; (of God etc.) serviteur m.

serve /sɜːv/ v.t./i. servir; (undergo, carry out) faire; (of transport) desservir. —n. (tennis) service m. ~ as/to, servir de/à. ~ its purpose, remplir sa fonction.

service /'sɜːvɪs/ n. service m.; (maintenance) révision f.; (relig.) office m. ~s, (mil.) forces armées f. pl. —v.t. (car etc.) réviser. of ~ to, utile à. ~ area, (auto.) aire de services f. ~ charge, service m. ~ station, station-service f.

serviceable /'sɜːvɪsəbl/ a. (usable) utilisable; (useful) commode; (durable) solide.

serviceman /'sɜːvɪsmən/ n. (pl. -men) militaire m.

serviette /sɜːvɪ'et/ n. serviette f.

servile /'sɜːvaɪl/ a. servile.

session /'seʃn/ n. séance f.; (univ.) année (universitaire) f.; (univ., Amer.) semestre m.

set /set/ v.t. (p.t. set, pres. p. setting) mettre; (put down) poser, mettre; (limit etc.) fixer; (watch, clock) régler; (example, task) donner; (for printing) composer; (in plaster) plâtrer. —v.i. (of sun) se coucher; (of jelly) prendre. —n. (of chairs, stamps, etc.) série f.; (of knives, keys, etc.) jeu m.; (of people) groupe m.; (TV, radio) poste m.; (style of hair) mise en plis f.; (theatre) décor m.; (tennis) set m.; (mathematics) ensemble m. —a. fixe; (in habits) régulier; (meal) à prix fixe; (book) au programme. ~ against sth., opposé à. be ~ on doing, être résolu à faire. ~ about or to, se mettre à. ~ back, (delay) retarder; (cost: sl.) coûter. ~-back n. revers m. ~ fire to, mettre le feu à. ~ free, libérer. ~ in, (take hold) s'installer, commencer. ~ off or out, partir. ~ off, (mechanism, activity) déclencher; (bomb) faire éclater. ~ out, (state) exposer; (arrange) disposer. ~ out to do sth., entreprendre de faire qch. ~ sail, partir. ~ square, équerre f. ~ to, (about to) sur le point de. ~-to n. querelle f. ~ to music, mettre en musique. ~ up, (establish) fonder, établir; (launch) lancer. ~-up n. (fam.) affaire f.

settee /se'tiː/ n. canapé m.

setting /'setɪŋ/ n. cadre m.

settle /'setl/ v.t. (arrange, pay) régler; (date) fixer; (nerves) calmer. —v.i. (come to rest) se poser; (live) s'installer. ~ down, se calmer; (become orderly) se ranger. ~ for, accepter. ~ in, s'installer. ~ up (with), régler. ~r /-ə(r)/ n. colon m.

settlement /'setlmənt/ n. règlement m. (of, de); (agreement) accord m.; (place) colonie f.

seven /'sevn/ a. & n. sept (m.). ~th a. & n. septième (m./f.).

seventeen /sevn'tiːn/ a. & n. dix-sept (m.). ~th a. & n. dix-septième (m./f.).

seventy /'sevntɪ/ a. & n. soixante-dix (m.). ~ieth a. & n. soixante-dixième (m./f.).

sever /'sevə(r)/ v.t. (cut) couper; (relations) rompre. ~ance n. (breaking off) rupture f. ~ance pay, indemnité de licenciement f.

several /'sevrəl/ a. & pron. plusieurs.

sever|e /sɪ'vɪə(r)/ a. (-er, -est) sévère; (violent) violent; (serious) grave. ~ely adv. sévèrement; gravement. ~ity /sɪ'verətɪ/ n. sévérité f.; violence f.; gravité f.

sew /səʊ/ v.t./i. (p.t. sewed, p.p. sewn or sewed) coudre. ~ing n. couture f. ~ing-machine n. machine à coudre f.

sewage /'sjuːɪdʒ/ n. eaux d'égout f. pl., vidanges f. pl.

sewer /'suːə(r)/ n. égout m.

sewn /səʊn/ see sew.

sex /seks/ n. sexe m. —a. sexuel. have ~, avoir des rapports (sexuels). ~maniac, obsédé(e) sexuel(le) m. (f.). ~y a. sexy invar.

sexist /'seksɪst/ a. & n. sexiste (m./f.).

sextet /seks'tet/ n. sextuor m.

sexual /'sekʃʊəl/ a. sexuel. ~ intercourse, rapports sexuels m. pl. ~ity /-'ælətɪ/ n. sexualité f.

shabb|y /'ʃæbɪ/ a. (-ier, -iest) (place, object) minable, miteux; (person) pauvrement vêtu; (mean) mesquin. ~ily adv. (dress) pauvrement; (act) mesquinement.

shack /ʃæk/ n. cabane f.

shackles /'ʃæklz/ n. pl. chaînes f. pl.

shade /ʃeɪd/ n. ombre f.; (of colour, opinion) nuance f.; (for lamp) abat-jour m.; (blind: Amer.) store m. a ~ bigger/etc., légèrement plus grand/etc. —v.t. (of person etc.) abriter; (of tree) ombrager.

shadow /'ʃædəʊ/ n. ombre f. —v.t. (follow) filer. S~ Cabinet, cabinet fantôme *m.* **∼y** *a.* ombragé; *(fig.)* vague.

shady /'ʃeɪdɪ/ *a.* (**-ier, -iest**) *(dubious: fig.)* louche.

shaft /ʃɑ:ft/ *n.* *(of arrow)* hampe *f.*; *(axle)* arbre *m.*; *(of mine)* puits *m.*; *(of light)* rayon *m.*

shaggy /'ʃægɪ/ *a.* (**-ier, -iest**) *(beard)* hirsute; *(hair)* broussailleux; *(animal)* à longs poils.

shake /ʃeɪk/ *v.t.* (*p.t.* **shook**, *p.p.* **shaken**) secouer; *(bottle)* agiter; *(house, belief, etc.)* ébranler. —*v.i.* trembler. —*n.* secousse *f.* **∼ hands with,** serrer la main à. **∼ off,** *(get rid of)* se débarrasser de. **∼ one's head,** *(in refusal)* dire non de la tête. **∼ up,** *(disturb, rouse, mix contents of)* secouer. **∼-up** *n.* *(upheaval)* remaniement *m.*

shaky /'ʃeɪkɪ/ *a.* (**-ier, -iest**) *(hand, voice)* tremblant; *(table etc.)* branlant; *(weak: fig.)* faible.

shall /ʃæl/ *unstressed* ʃ(ə)l/ *v. aux.* **I ∼ do,** je ferai. **we ∼ do,** nous ferons.

shallot /ʃə'lɒt/ *n.* échalote *f.*

shallow /'ʃæləʊ/ *a.* (**-er, -est**) peu profond; *(fig.)* superficiel.

sham /ʃæm/ *n.* comédie *f.*; *(person)* imposteur *m.*; *(jewel)* imitation *f.* —*a.* faux; *(affected)* feint. —*v.t.* (*p.t.* **shammed**) feindre.

shambles /'ʃæmblz/ *n. pl.* *(mess: fam.)* désordre *m.*, pagaille *f.*

shame /ʃeɪm/ *n.* honte *f.* —*v.t.* faire honte à. **it's a ∼,** c'est dommage. **∼ful** *a.* honteux. **∼fully** *adv.* honteusement. **∼less** *a.* éhonté.

shamefaced /'ʃeɪmfeɪst/ *a.* honteux.

shampoo /ʃæm'puː/ *n.* shampooing *m.* —*v.t.* faire un shampooing à, shampooiner.

shandy /'ʃændɪ/ *n.* panaché *m.*

shan't /ʃɑːnt/ = **shall not.**

shanty /'ʃæntɪ/ *n.* *(shack)* baraque *f.* **∼ town,** bidonville *m.*

shape /ʃeɪp/ *n.* forme *f.* —*v.t.* *(fashion, mould)* façonner; *(future etc.: fig.)* déterminer. —*v.i.* **∼ up,** *(plan etc.)* prendre tournure *or* forme; *(person etc.)* faire des progrès. **∼less** *a.* informe.

shapely /'ʃeɪplɪ/ *a.* (**-ier, -iest**) *(leg, person)* bien tourné.

share /ʃeə(r)/ *n.* part *f.*; *(comm.)* action *f.* —*v.t./i.* partager; *(feature)* avoir en commun. **∼-out** *n.* partage *m.*

shareholder /'ʃeəhəʊldə(r)/ *n.* actionnaire *m./f.*

shark /ʃɑːk/ *n.* requin *m.*

sharp /ʃɑːp/ *a.* (**-er, -est**) *(knife etc.)* tranchant; *(pin etc.)* pointu; *(point)* aigu; *(acute)* vif; *(sudden)* brusque; *(dishonest)* peu scrupuleux. —*adv.* *(stop)* net. **six o'clock/etc. ∼,** six heures/etc. pile. —*n.* *(mus.)* dièse *m.* **∼ly** *adv.* *(harshly)* vivement; *(suddenly)* brusquement.

sharpen /'ʃɑːpən/ *v.t.* aiguiser; *(pencil)* tailler. **∼er** *n.* *(for pencil)* taille-crayon(s) *m.*

shatter /'ʃætə(r)/ *v.t./i.* *(glass etc.)* (faire) voler en éclats, (se) briser; *(upset, ruin)* anéantir.

shav|e /ʃeɪv/ *v.t./i.* (se) raser. —*n.* **have a ∼e,** se raser. **∼en** *a.* rasé. **∼er** *n.* rasoir électrique *m.* **∼ing-brush** *n.* blaireau *m.* **∼ing-cream** *n.* crème à raser *f.*

shaving /'ʃeɪvɪŋ/ *n.* copeau *m.*

shawl /ʃɔːl/ *n.* châle *m.*

she /ʃiː/ *pron.* elle. —*n.* femelle *f.*

sheaf /ʃiːf/ *n.* *(pl.* **sheaves**) gerbe *f.*

shear /ʃɪə(r)/ *v.t.* (*p.p.* **shorn** *or* **sheared**) *(sheep etc.)* tondre. **∼ off,** se détacher.

shears /ʃɪəz/ *n. pl.* cisaille(s) *f.* (*pl.*).

sheath /ʃiːθ/ *n.* *(pl.* **-s** /ʃiːðz/) gaine *f.*, fourreau *m.*; *(contraceptive)* préservatif *m.*

sheathe /ʃiːð/ *v.t.* rengainer.

shed[1] /ʃed/ *n.* remise *f.*

shed[2] /ʃed/ *v.t.* (*p.t.* **shed,** *pres. p.* **shedding**) perdre; *(light, tears)* répandre.

sheen /ʃiːn/ *n.* lustre *m.*

sheep /ʃiːp/ *n. invar.* mouton *m.* **∼-dog** *n.* chien de berger *m.*

sheepish /'ʃiːpɪʃ/ *a.* penaud. **∼ly** *adv.* d'un air penaud.

sheepskin /'ʃiːpskɪn/ *n.* peau de mouton *f.*

sheer /ʃɪə(r)/ *a.* pur (et simple); *(steep)* à pic; *(fabric)* très fin. —*adv.* à pic, verticalement.

sheet /ʃiːt/ *n.* drap *m.*; *(of paper)* feuille *f.*; *(of glass, ice)* plaque *f.*

sheikh /ʃeɪk/ *n.* cheik *m.*

shelf /ʃelf/ *n.* *(pl.* **shelves**) rayon *m.*, étagère *f.* **on the ∼,** *(person)* laissé pour compte.

shell /ʃel/ *n.* coquille *f.*; *(on beach)* coquillage *m.*; *(of building)* carcasse *f.*; *(explosive)* obus *m.* —*v.t.* *(nut etc.)* décortiquer; *(peas)* écosser; *(mil.)* bombarder.

shellfish /'ʃelfɪʃ/ *n. invar.* *(lobster etc.)* crustacé(s) *m.* (*pl.*); *(mollusc)* coquillage(s) *m.* (*pl.*).

shelter /'ʃeltə(r)/ *n.* abri *m.* —*v.t./i.* (s')abriter; *(give lodging to)* donner asile à. **∼ed** *a.* *(life etc.)* protégé.

shelve /ʃelv/ v.t. (plan etc.) laisser en suspens, remettre à plus tard.

shelving /ˈʃelvɪŋ/ n. (shelves) rayonnage(s) m. (pl.).

shepherd /ˈʃepəd/ n. berger m. —v.t. (people) guider. ~'s **pie**, hachis Parmentier m.

sherbet /ˈʃɜːbət/ n. jus de fruits m.; (powder) poudre acidulée f.; (water-ice: Amer.) sorbet m.

sheriff /ˈʃerɪf/ n. shérif m.

sherry /ˈʃerɪ/ n. xérès m.

shield /ʃiːld/ n. bouclier m.; (screen) écran m. —v.t. protéger.

shift /ʃɪft/ v.t./i. (se) déplacer, bouger; (exchange, alter) changer de. —n. changement m.; (workers) équipe f.; (work) poste m.; (auto.: Amer.) levier de vitesse m. **make** ~, se débrouiller. ~ **work**, travail par roulement.

shiftless /ˈʃɪftlɪs/ a. paresseux.

shifty /ˈʃɪftɪ/ a. (-ier, -iest) louche.

shilling /ˈʃɪlɪŋ/ n. shilling m.

shilly-shally /ˈʃɪlɪʃælɪ/ v.i. hésiter, balancer.

shimmer /ˈʃɪmə(r)/ v.i. chatoyer. —n. chatoiement m.

shin /ʃɪn/ n. tibia m.

shine /ʃaɪn/ v.t./i. (p.t. **shone** /ʃɒn/) (faire) briller. —n. éclat m., brillant m. ~ **one's torch** or **the light (on)**, éclairer.

shingle /ˈʃɪŋgl/ n. (pebbles) galets m. pl.; (on roof) bardeau m.

shingles /ˈʃɪŋglz/ n. pl. (med.) zona m.

shiny /ˈʃaɪnɪ/ a. (-ier, -iest) brillant.

ship /ʃɪp/ n. bateau m., navire m. —v.t. (p.t. **shipped**) transporter; (send) expédier; (load) embarquer. ~**ment** n. cargaison f., envoi m. ~**per** n. expéditeur m. ~**ping** n. (ships) navigation f., navires m. pl.

shipbuilding /ˈʃɪpbɪldɪŋ/ n. construction navale f.

shipshape /ˈʃɪpʃeɪp/ adv. & a. parfaitement en ordre.

shipwreck /ˈʃɪprek/ n. naufrage m. ~**ed** a. naufragé. **be** ~**ed**, faire naufrage.

shipyard /ˈʃɪpjɑːd/ n. chantier naval m.

shirk /ʃɜːk/ v.t. esquiver. ~**er** n. tire-au-flanc m. invar.

shirt /ʃɜːt/ n. chemise f.; (of woman) chemisier m. **in** ~**-sleeves**, en bras de chemise.

shiver /ˈʃɪvə(r)/ v.i. frissonner. —n. frisson m.

shoal /ʃəʊl/ n. (of fish) banc m.

shock /ʃɒk/ n. choc m., secousse f.; (electr.) décharge f.; (med.) choc m.

—a. (result) choc invar.; (tactics) de choc. —v.t. choquer. ~ **absorber**, amortisseur m. **be a** ~**er**, (fam.) être affreux. ~**ing** a. choquant; (bad: fam.) affreux. ~**ingly** adv. (fam.) affreusement.

shodd|y /ˈʃɒdɪ/ a. (-ier, -iest) mal fait, mauvais. ~**ily** adv. mal.

shoe /ʃuː/ n. chaussure f., soulier m.; (of horse) fer (à cheval) m.; (in vehicle) sabot (de frein) m. —v.t. (p.t. **shod** /ʃɒd/, pres. p. **shoeing**) (horse) ferrer. ~ **repairer**, cordonnier m. **on a** ~**string**, avec très peu d'argent.

shoehorn /ˈʃuːhɔːn/ n. chausse-pied m.

shoelace /ˈʃuːleɪs/ n. lacet m.

shoemaker /ˈʃuːmeɪkə(r)/ n. cordonnier m.

shone /ʃɒn/ see **shine**.

shoo /ʃuː/ v.t. chasser.

shook /ʃʊk/ see **shake**.

shoot /ʃuːt/ v.t. (p.t. **shot**) (gun) tirer un coup de; (missile, glance) lancer; (kill, wound) tuer, blesser (d'un coup de fusil, de pistolet, etc.); (execute) fusiller; (hunt) chasser; (film) tourner. —v.i. tirer (**at**, sur). —n. (bot.) pousse f. ~ **down**, abattre. ~ **out**, (rush) sortir en vitesse. ~ **up**, (spurt) jaillir; (grow) pousser vite. **hear** ~**ing**, entendre des coups de feu. ~**ing-range** n. stand de tir m. ~**ing star**, étoile filante f.

shop /ʃɒp/ n. magasin m., boutique f.; (workshop) atelier m. —v.i. (p.t. **shopped**) faire ses courses. ~ **around**, comparer les prix. ~ **assistant**, vendeur, -se m., f. ~**-floor** n. (workers) ouvriers m. pl. ~**per** n. acheteur, -se m., f. ~**-soiled**, (Amer.) ~**-worn** adjs. abîmé. ~ **steward**, délégué(e) syndical(e) m. (f.). ~ **window**, vitrine f.

shopkeeper /ˈʃɒpkiːpə(r)/ n. commerçant(e) m. (f.).

shoplift|er /ˈʃɒplɪftə(r)/ n. voleur, -se à l'étalage m., f. ~**ing** n. vol à l'étalage m.

shopping /ˈʃɒpɪŋ/ n. (goods) achats m. pl. **go** ~, faire ses courses. ~ **bag**, sac à provisions m. ~ **centre**, centre commercial m.

shore /ʃɔː(r)/ n. rivage m.

shorn /ʃɔːn/ see **shear**. —a. ~ **of**, dépouillé de.

short /ʃɔːt/ a. (-er, -est) court; (person) petit; (brief) court, bref; (curt) brusque. **be** ~ **(of)**, (lack) manquer (de). —adv. (stop) net. —n. (electr.) court-circuit m.; (film) court-metrage m. ~**s**, (*trousers*) short *m*. ~ **of money**, à court d'argent. **I'm two** ~, il m'en manque deux. ~ **of doing sth**, à moins de faire qch. **everything** ~ **of**, tout sauf. **nothing** ~ **of**, rien de moins que. **cut** ~, écourter. **cut s.o.** ~, couper court à qn. **fall** ~ **of**, ne pas arriver à. **he is called Tom for** ~, son diminutif est Tom. **in** ~, en bref. ~**-change** *v.t.* (*cheat*) rouler. ~ **circuit**, court-circuit *m*. ~**-circuit** *v.t.* court-circuiter. ~ **cut**, raccourci *m*. ~**-handed** *a*. à court de personnel. ~ **list**, liste des candidats choisis *f*. ~**-lived** *a*. éphémère. ~**-sighted** *a*. myope. ~**-staffed** *a*. à court de personnel. ~ **story**, nouvelle *f*. ~**-term** *a*. à court terme. ~ **wave**, ondes courtes *f*. *pl*.

shortage /'ʃɔ:tɪdʒ/ *n*. manque *m*.

shortbread /'ʃɔ:tbred/ *n*. sablé *m*.

shortcoming /'ʃɔ:tkʌmɪŋ/ *n*. défaut *m*.

shorten /'ʃɔ:tn/ *v.t.* raccourcir.

shortfall /'ʃɔ:tfɔ:l/ *n*. déficit *m*.

shorthand /'ʃɔ:thænd/ *n*. sténo(graphie) *f*. ~ **typist**, sténodactylo *f*.

shortly /'ʃɔ:tlɪ/ *adv*. bientôt.

shot /ʃɒt/ *see* **shoot**. —*n*. (*firing, attempt, etc*.) coup de feu *m*.; (*person*) tireur *m*.; (*bullet*) balle *f*.; (*photograph*) photo *f*.; (*injection*) piqûre *f*. **like a** ~, comme une flèche. ~**-gun** *n*. fusil de chasse *m*.

should /ʃʊd, *unstressed* ʃəd/ *v.aux.* devoir. **you** ~ **help me**, vous devriez m'aider. **I** ~ **have stayed**, j'aurais dû rester. **I** ~ **like to**, j'aimerais bien. **if he** ~ **come**, s'il vient.

shoulder /'ʃəʊldə(r)/ *n*. épaule *f*. —*v.t.* (*responsibility*) endosser; (*burden*) se charger de. ~**-bag** *n*. sac à bandoulière *m*. ~**-blade** *n*. omoplate *f*. ~**-pad** *n*. épaulette *f*.

shout /ʃaʊt/ *n*. cri *m*. —*v.t./i.* crier. ~ **at**, engueuler. ~ **down**, huer.

shove /ʃʌv/ *n*. poussée *f*. —*v.t./i.* pousser; (*put: fam.*) ficher. ~ **off**, (*depart: fam.*) se tirer.

shovel /'ʃʌvl/ *n*. pelle *f*. —*v.t.* (*p.t.* **shovelled**) pelleter.

show /ʃəʊ/ *v.t.* (*p.t.* **showed**, *p.p.* **shown**) montrer; (*of dial, needle*) indiquer; (*put on display*) exposer; (*film*) donner; (*conduct*) conduire. —*v.i.* (*be visible*) se voir. —*n*. démonstration *f*.; (*ostentation*) parade *f*.; (*exhibition*) exposition *f*., salon *m*.; (*theatre*) spectacle *m*.; (*cinema*) séance *f*. **for** ~, pour l'effet. **on** ~, exposé. ~**-down** *n*. épreuve de force *f*. ~**-jumping** *n*. con-

cours hippique *m*. ~ **off** *v.t.* étaler; *v.i.* poser, crâner. ~**-off** *n*. poseur, -se *m*., *f*. ~**-piece** *n*. modèle du genre *m*. ~ **s.o. in/out**, faire entrer/sortir qn. ~ **up**, (faire) ressortir; (*appear: fam.*) se montrer. ~**ing** *n*. performance *f*.; (*cinema*) séance *f*.

shower /'ʃaʊə(r)/ *n*. (*of rain*) averse *f*.; (*of blows etc*.) grêle *f*.; (*for washing*) douche *f*. —*v.t.* ~ **with**, couvrir de. —*v.i.* se doucher. ~**y** *a*. pluvieux.

showerproof /'ʃaʊəpru:f/ *a*. imperméable.

showmanship /'ʃəʊmənʃɪp/ *n*. art de la mise en scène *m*.

shown /ʃəʊn/ *see* **show**.

showroom /'ʃəʊrʊm/ *n*. salle d'exposition *f*.

showy /'ʃəʊɪ/ *a*. (**-ier, -iest**) voyant; (*manner*) prétentieux.

shrank /ʃræŋk/ *see* **shrink**.

shrapnel /'ʃræpn(ə)l/ *n*. éclats d'obus *m*. *pl*.

shred /ʃred/ *n*. lambeau *m*.; (*least amount: fig.*) parcelle *f*. —*v.t.* (*p.t.* **shredded**) déchiqueter; (*culin.*) râper. ~**der** *n*. destructeur de documents *m*.

shrew /ʃru:/ *n*. (*woman*) mégère *f*.

shrewd /ʃru:d/ *a*. (**-er, -est**) astucieux. ~**ness** *n*. astuce *f*.

shriek /ʃri:k/ *n*. hurlement *m*. —*v.t./i.* hurler.

shrift /ʃrɪft/ *n*. **give s.o. short** ~, traiter qn. sans ménagement.

shrill /ʃrɪl/ *a*. strident, aigu.

shrimp /ʃrɪmp/ *n*. crevette *f*.

shrine /ʃraɪn/ *n*. (*place*) lieu saint *m*.; (*tomb*) châsse *f*.

shrink /ʃrɪŋk/ *v.t./i.* (*p.t.* **shrank**, *p.p.* **shrunk**) rétrécir; (*lessen*) diminuer. ~ **from**, reculer devant. ~**age** *n*. rétrécissement *m*.

shrivel /'ʃrɪvl/ *v.t./i.* (*p.t.* **shrivelled**) (se) ratatiner.

shroud /ʃraʊd/ *n*. linceul *m*. —*v.t.* (*veil*) envelopper.

Shrove /ʃrəʊv/ *n*. ~ **Tuesday**, Mardi gras *m*.

shrub /ʃrʌb/ *n*. arbuste *m*. ~**bery** *n*. arbustes *m*. *pl*.

shrug /ʃrʌg/ *v.t.* (*p.t.* **shrugged**) ~ **one's shoulders**, hausser les épaules. —*n*. haussement d'épaules *m*. ~ **sth. off**, réagir avec indifférence à qch.

shrunk /ʃrʌŋk/ *see* **shrink**. ~**en** *a*. rétréci; (*person*) ratatiné.

shudder /'ʃʌdə(r)/ *v.i.* frémir. —*n*. frémissement *m*.

shuffle /'ʃʌfl/ *v.t.* (*feet*) traîner; (*cards*)

battre. —*v.i.* traîner les pieds. —*n.* démarche traînante *f.*

shun /ʃʌn/ *v.t.* (*p.t.* **shunned**) éviter, fuir.

shunt /ʃʌnt/ *v.t.* (*train*) aiguiller.

shush /ʃʊʃ/ *int.* (*fam.*) chut.

shut /ʃʌt/ *v.t.* (*p.t.* **shut**, *pres. p.* **shutting**) fermer. —*v.i.* se fermer; (*of shop, bank, etc.*) fermer. ∼ **down** *or* **up**, fermer. ∼**-down** *n.* fermeture *f.* ∼ **in** *or* **up**, ∼ **up** *v.i.* (*fam.*) se taire; *v.t.* (*fam.*) faire taire.

shutter /ʃʌtə(r)/ *n.* volet *m.*; (*photo.*) obturateur *m.*

shuttle /ʃʌtl/ *n.* (*bus etc.*) navette *f.* —*v.i.* faire la navette. —*v.t.* transporter. ∼ **service**, navette *f.*

shuttlecock /ʃʌtlkɒk/ *n.* (*badminton*) volant *m.*

shy /ʃaɪ/ *a.* (**-er**, **-est**) timide. —*v.i.* reculer. ∼**ness** *n.* timidité *f.*

Siamese /saɪə'miːz/ *a.* siamois.

sibling /'sɪblɪŋ/ *n.* frère *m.*, sœur *f.*

Sicily /'sɪsɪlɪ/ *n.* Sicile *f.*

sick /sɪk/ *a.* malade; (*humour*) macabre. **be** ∼, (*vomit*) vomir. **be** ∼ **of**, en avoir assez *or* marre de. **feel** ∼, avoir mal au cœur. ∼**-bay** *n.* infirmerie *f.* ∼**-leave** *n.* congé maladie *m.* ∼**-pay** *n.* assurance-maladie *f.* ∼**room** *n.* chambre de malade *f.*

sicken /'sɪkən/ *v.t.* écœurer. —*v.i.* **be** ∼**ing for**, (*illness*) couver.

sickle /'sɪkl/ *n.* faucille *f.*

sickly /'sɪklɪ/ *a.* (**-ier**, **-iest**) (*person*) maladif; (*taste, smell, etc.*) écœurant.

sickness /'sɪknɪs/ *n.* maladie *f.*

side /saɪd/ *n.* côté *m.*; (*of road, river*) bord *m.*; (*of hill*) flanc *m.*; (*sport*) équipe *f.* —*a.* latéral. —*v.i.* ∼ **with**, se ranger du côté de. **on the** ∼, (*extra*) en plus; (*secretly*) en catimini. ∼ **by side**, côte à côte. ∼**-car** *n.* side-car *m.* ∼**-effect** *n.* effet secondaire *m.* ∼**-saddle** *adv.* en amazone. ∼**-show** *n.* petite attraction *f.* ∼**-step** *v.t.* (*p.t.* **-stepped**) éviter. ∼**-street** *n.* rue laterale *f.* ∼**-track** *v.t.* faire dévier de son sujet.

sideboard /'saɪdbɔːd/ *n.* buffet *m.* ∼**s**, (*whiskers*: *sl.*) pattes *f. pl.*

sideburns /'saɪdbɜːnz/ *n. pl.* pattes *f. pl.*, rouflaquettes *f. pl.*

sidelight /'saɪdlaɪt/ *n.* (*auto.*) veilleuse *f.*, lanterne *f.*

sideline /'saɪdlaɪn/ *n.* activité secondaire *f.*

sidewalk /'saɪdwɔːk/ *n.* (*Amer.*) trottoir *m.*

side|ways /'saɪdweɪz/, ∼**long** *adv. & a.* de côté.

siding /'saɪdɪŋ/ *n.* voie de garage *f.*

sidle /'saɪdl/ *v.i.* avancer furtivement (**up to**, vers).

siege /siːdʒ/ *n.* siège *m.*

siesta /sɪ'estə/ *n.* sieste *f.*

sieve /sɪv/ *n.* tamis *m.*; (*for liquids*) passoire *f.* —*v.t.* tamiser.

sift /sɪft/ *v.t.* tamiser. —*v.i.* ∼ **through**, examiner.

sigh /saɪ/ *n.* soupir *m.* —*v.t./i.* soupirer.

sight /saɪt/ *n.* vue *f.*; (*scene*) spectacle *m.*; (*on gun*) mire *f.* —*v.t.* apercevoir. **at** *or* **on** ∼, à vue. **catch** ∼ **of**, apercevoir. **in** ∼, visible. **lose** ∼ **of**, perdre de vue.

sightsee|ing /'saɪtsiːɪŋ/ *n.* tourisme *m.* ∼**r** /-ə(r)/ *n.* touriste *m./f.*

sign /saɪn/ *n.* signe *m.*; (*notice*) panneau *m.* —*v.t./i.* signer. ∼ **language**, (*for deaf*) langage des sourds-muets *m.* ∼ **on**, (*when unemployed*) s'inscrire au chômage. ∼ **up**, (s')enrôler.

signal /'sɪgnəl/ *n.* signal *m.* —*v.t.* (*p.t.* **signalled**) communiquer (par signaux); (*person*) faire signe à. ∼**-box** *n.* poste d'aiguillage *m.*

signalman /'sɪgnəlmən/ *n.* (*pl.* **-men**) (*rail.*) aiguilleur *m.*

signatory /'sɪgnətrɪ/ *n.* signataire *m./f.*

signature /'sɪgnətʃə(r)/ *n.* signature *f.* ∼ **tune**, indicatif musical *m.*

signet-ring /'sɪgnɪtrɪŋ/ *n.* chevalière *f.*

significan|t /sɪg'nɪfɪkənt/ *a.* important; (*meaningful*) significatif. ∼**ce** *n.* importance *f.*; (*meaning*) signification *f.* ∼**tly** *adv.* (*much*) sensiblement.

signify /'sɪgnɪfaɪ/ *v.t.* signifier.

signpost /'saɪnpəʊst/ *n.* poteau indicateur *m.*

silence /'saɪləns/ *n.* silence *m.* —*v.t.* faire taire. ∼**r** /-ə(r)/ *n.* (*on gun, car*) silencieux *m.*

silent /'saɪlənt/ *a.* silencieux; (*film*) muet. ∼**ly** *adv.* silencieusement.

silhouette /sɪlu:'et/ *n.* silhouette *f.* —*v.t.* **be** ∼**d against**, se profiler contre.

silicon /'sɪlɪkən/ *n.* silicium *m.* ∼ **chip**, microplaquette *f.*

silk /sɪlk/ *n.* soie *f.* ∼**en**, ∼**y** *adjs.* soyeux.

sill /sɪl/ *n.* rebord *m.*

silly /'sɪlɪ/ *a.* (**-ier**, **-iest**) bête, idiot.

silo /'saɪləʊ/ *n.* (*pl.* **-os**) silo *m.*

silt /sɪlt/ *n.* vase *f.*

silver /'sɪlvə(r)/ *n.* argent *m.*; (*silverware*) argenterie *f.* —*a.* en argent, d'argent. ∼ **wedding**, noces d'argent *f. pl.* ∼**y** *a.* argenté; (*sound*) argentin.

silversmith /'sɪlvəsmɪθ/ n. orfèvre m.

silverware /'sɪlvəweə(r)/ n. argenterie f.

similar /'sɪmɪlə(r)/ a. semblable (**to**, à). ~**ity** /-ə'lærətɪ/ n. ressemblance f. ~**ly** adv. de même.

simile /'sɪmɪlɪ/ n. comparaison f.

simmer /'sɪmə(r)/ v.t./i. (soup etc.) mijoter; (water) (laisser) frémir; (smoulder: fig.) couver. ~ **down**, se calmer.

simper /'sɪmpə(r)/ v.i. minauder. ~**ing** a. minaudier.

simpl|e /'sɪmpl/ a. (-er, -est) simple. ~**e-minded** a. simple d'esprit. ~**icity** /-'plɪsətɪ/ n. simplicité f. ~**y** adv. simplement; (absolutely) absolument.

simplif|y /'sɪmplɪfaɪ/ v.t. simplifier. ~**ication** /-ɪ'keɪʃn/ n. simplification f.

simplistic /sɪm'plɪstɪk/ a. simpliste.

simulat|e /'sɪmjʊleɪt/ v.t. simuler. ~**ion** /-'leɪʃn/ n. simulation f.

simultaneous /sɪml'teɪnɪəs, Amer. saɪml'teɪnɪəs/ a. simultané. ~**ly** adv. simultanément.

sin /sɪn/ n. péché m. —v.i. (p.t. **sinned**) pécher.

since /sɪns/ prep. & adv. depuis. —conj. depuis que; (because) puisque. ~ **then**, depuis.

sincer|e /sɪn'sɪə(r)/ a. sincère. ~**ely** adv. sincèrement. ~**ity** /-'serətɪ/ n. sincérité f.

sinew /'sɪnjuː/ n. tendon m. ~**s**, muscles m. pl.

sinful /'sɪnfl/ a. (act) coupable, qui constitue un péché; (shocking) scandaleux.

sing /sɪŋ/ v.t./i. (p.t. **sang**, p.p. **sung**) chanter. ~**er** n. chanteur|r, -se m., f.

singe /sɪndʒ/ v.t. (pres. p. **singeing**) brûler légèrement, roussir.

single /'sɪŋgl/ a. seul; (not double) simple; (unmarried) célibataire; (room, bed) pour une personne; (ticket) simple. —n. (ticket) aller simple m.; (record) 45 tours m. invar. ~**s**, (tennis) simple m. ~**s bar**, bar pour les célibataires m.—v.t. ~ **out**, choisir. **in** ~ **file**, en file indienne. ~**-handed** a. sans aide. ~**-minded** a. tenace. ~ **parent**, parent seul m. **singly** adv. un à un.

singlet /'sɪŋglɪt/ n. maillot de corps m.

singsong /'sɪŋsɒŋ/ n. **have a** ~, chanter en chœur. —a. (voice) monotone.

singular /'sɪŋgjʊlə(r)/ n. singulier m. —a. (uncommon & gram.) singulier; (noun) au singulier. ~**ly** adv. singulièrement.

sinister /'sɪnɪstə(r)/ a. sinistre.

sink /sɪŋk/ v.t./i. (p.t. **sank**, p.p. **sunk**) (faire) couler; (of ground, person) s'affaisser; (well) creuser; (money) investir. —n. (in kitchen) évier m.; (wash-basin) lavabo m. ~ **in**, (fig.) être compris. ~ **into** v.t. (thrust) enfoncer dans; v.i. (go deep) s'enfoncer dans. ~ **unit**, bloc-evier m.

sinner /'sɪnə(r)/ n. péchleur, -eresse m., f.

sinuous /'sɪnjʊəs/ a. sinueux.

sinus /'saɪnəs/ n. (pl. -**uses**) (anat.) sinus m.

sip /sɪp/ n. petite gorgée f. —v.t. (p.t. **sipped**) boire à petites gorgées.

siphon /'saɪfn/ n. siphon m. —v.t. ~ **off**, siphonner.

sir /sɜː(r)/ n. monsieur m. **Sir**, (title) Sir m.

siren /'saɪərən/ n. sirène f.

sirloin /'sɜːlɔɪn/ n. faux-filet m., aloyau m.; (Amer.) romsteck m.

sissy /'sɪsɪ/ n. personne efféminée f.; (coward) dégonflé(e) m. (f.).

sister /'sɪstə(r)/ n. sœur f.; (nurse) infirmière en chef f. ~**-in-law** (pl. ~**s-in-law**) belle-sœur f. ~**ly** a. fraternel.

sit /sɪt/ v.t./i. (p.t. **sat**, pres. p. **sitting**) (s')asseoir; (of committee etc.) siéger. ~ (**for**), (exam) se présenter à. **be** ~**ting**, être assis. ~ **around**, ne rien faire. ~ **down**, s'asseoir. ~ **in on a meeting**, assister à une réunion pour écouter. ~**-in** n. sit-in m. invar. ~**ting** n. séance f.; (in restaurant) service m. ~**ting-room** n. salon m.

site /saɪt/ n. emplacement m. (**building**) ~, chantier m. —v.t. placer, construire, situer.

situat|e /'sɪtʃʊeɪt/ v.t. situer. **be** ~**ed**, être situé. ~**ion** /-'eɪʃn/ n. situation f.

six /sɪks/ a. & n. six (m.). ~**th** a. & n. sixième (m./f.).

sixteen /sɪk'stiːn/ a. & n. seize (m.). ~**th** a. & n. seizième (m./f.).

sixt|y /'sɪkstɪ/ a. & n. soixante (m.). ~**ieth** a. & n. soixantième (m./f.).

size /saɪz/ n. dimension f.; (of person, garment, etc.) taille f.; (of shoes) pointure f.; (of sum, salary) montant m.; (extent) ampleur f. —v.t. ~ **up**, (fam.) jauger, juger. ~**able** a. assez grand.

sizzle /'sɪzl/ v.i. grésiller.

skate[1] /skeɪt/ n. invar. (fish) raie f.

skat|e[2] /skeɪt/ n. patin m. —v.i. patiner. ~**er** n. patinelur, -se m., f. ~**ing** n. patinage m. ~**ing-rink** n. patinoire f.

skateboard /'skeɪtbɔːd/ n. skateboard m., planche à roulettes f.

skelet|on /'skelɪtən/ n. squelette m. ~**on crew** or **staff,** effectifs minimums m. pl. ~**al** a. squelettique.

sketch /sketʃ/ n. esquisse f., croquis m.; (theatre) sketch m. —v.t. faire un croquis de, esquisser. —v.i. faire des esquisses. ~ **out,** esquisser. ~ **pad,** bloc à dessins.

sketchy /'sketʃɪ/ a. (-**ier,** -**iest**) sommaire, incomplet.

skew /skju:/ n. **on the** ~, de travers. ~-**whiff** a. (fam.) de travers.

skewer /'skjʊə(r)/ n. brochette f.

ski /ski:/ n. (pl. -**is**) ski m. —a. de ski. —v.i. (p.t. **ski'd** or **skied,** pres. p. **skiing**) skier; (go skiing) faire du ski. ~ **jump,** saut à skis m. ~ **lift,** remonte-pente m. ~**er** n. skieulr, -se m., f. ~**ing** n. ski m.

skid /skɪd/ v.i. (p.t. **skidded**) déraper. —n. dérapage m.

skilful /'skɪlfl/ a. habile.

skill /skɪl/ n. habileté f.; (craft) métier m. ~**s,** aptitudes f. pl. ~**ed** a. habile; (worker) qualifié.

skim /skɪm/ v.t. (p.t. **skimmed**) écumer; (milk) écrémer; (pass or glide over) effleurer. —v.i. ~ **through,** parcourir.

skimp /skɪmp/ v.t./i. ~ (**on**), lésiner (sur).

skimpy /'skɪmpɪ/ a. (-**ier,** -**iest**) (clothes) étriqué; (meal) chiche.

skin /skɪn/ n. peau f. —v.t. (p.t. **skinned**) (animal) écorcher; (fruit) éplucher. ~-**diving** n. plongée sous-marine f. ~-**tight** a. collant.

skinflint /'skɪnflɪnt/ n. avare m./f.

skinny /'skɪnɪ/ a. (-**ier,** -**iest**) maigre, maigrichon.

skint /skɪnt/ a. (sl.) fauché.

skip¹ /skɪp/ v.i. (p.t. **skipped**) sautiller; (with rope) sauter à la corde. —v.t. (page, class, etc.) sauter. —n. petit saut m. ~**ping-rope** n. corde à sauter f.

skip² /skɪp/ n. (container) benne f.

skipper /'skɪpə(r)/ n. capitaine m.

skirmish /'skɜ:mɪʃ/ n. escarmouche f., accrochage m.

skirt /skɜ:t/ n. jupe f. —v.t. contourner. ~**ing-board** n. plinthe f.

skit /skɪt/ n. sketch satirique m.

skittle /'skɪtl/ n. quille f.

skive /skaɪv/ v.i. (sl.) tirer au flanc.

skivvy /'skɪvɪ/ n. (fam.) boniche f.

skulk /skʌlk/ v.i. (move) rôder furtivement; (hide) se cacher.

skull /skʌl/ n. crâne m. ~-**cap** n. calotte f.

skunk /skʌŋk/ n. (animal) mouffette f.; (person: sl.) salaud m.

sky /skaɪ/ n. ciel m. ~-**blue** a. & n. bleu ciel a. & m. invar.

skylight /'skaɪlaɪt/ n. lucarne f.

skyscraper /'skaɪskreɪpə(r)/ n. gratte-ciel m. invar.

slab /slæb/ n. plaque f., bloc m.; (of paving-stone) dalle f.

slack /slæk/ a. (-**er,** -**est**) (rope) lâche; (person) négligent; (business) stagnant; (period) creux. —n. **the** ~, (in rope) du mou —v.t./i. (se) relâcher.

slacken /'slækən/ v.t./i. (se) relâcher; (slow) (se) ralentir.

slacks /slæks/ n. pl. pantalon m.

slag /slæg/ n. scories f. pl. ~-**heap** n. crassier m.

slain /sleɪn/ see **slay.**

slake /sleɪk/ v.t. étancher.

slalom /'slɑ:ləm/ n. slalom m.

slam /slæm/ v.t./i. (p.t. **slammed**) (door etc.) claquer; (throw) flanquer; (criticize: sl.) critiquer. —n. (noise) claquement m.

slander /'slɑ:ndə(r)/ n. diffamation f., calomnie f. —v.t. diffamer, calomnier. ~**ous** a. diffamatoire.

slang /slæŋ/ n. argot m. ~**y** a. argotique.

slant /slɑ:nt/ v.t./i. (faire) pencher; (news) présenter sous un certain jour. —n. inclinaison f.; (bias) angle m. ~**ed** a. partial. **be** ~**ing,** être penché.

slap /slæp/ v.t. (p.t. **slapped**) (strike) donner une claque à; (face) gifler; (put) flanquer. —n. claque f.; gifle f. —adv. tout droit. ~-**happy** a. (carefree: fam.) insouciant; (dazed: fam.) abruti. ~-**up meal,** (sl.) gueuleton m.

slapdash /'slæpdæʃ/ a. fait, qui travaille etc. n'importe comment.

slapstick /'slæpstɪk/ n. grosse farce f.

slash /slæʃ/ v.t. (cut) taillader; (sever) trancher; (fig.) réduire (radicalement). —n. taillade f.

slat /slæt/ n. (in blind) lamelle f.; (on bed) latte f.

slate /sleɪt/ n. ardoise f. —v.t. (fam.) critiquer, éreinter.

slaughter /'slɔ:tə(r)/ v.t. massacrer; (animals) abattre. —n. massacre m.; abattage m.

slaughterhouse /'slɔ:təhaʊs/ n. abattoir m.

Slav /slɑ:v/ a. & n. slave (m./f.). ~**onic** /slə'vɒnɪk/ a. (lang.) slave.

slave /sleɪv/ n. esclave m./f. —v.i. trimer. ~-**driver** n. négrlier, -ière m., f. ~**ry** /-ərɪ/ n. esclavage m.

slavish /'sleɪvɪʃ/ a. servile.
slay /sleɪ/ v.t. (p.t. slew, p.p. slain) tuer.
sleazy /'sli:zɪ/ a. (-ier, -iest) (fam.) sordide, miteux.
sledge /sledʒ/ n. luge f.; (horse-drawn) traîneau m. ∼-hammer n. marteau de forgeron m.
sleek /sli:k/ a. (-er, -est) lisse, brillant; (manner) onctueux.
sleep /sli:p/ n. sommeil m. —v.i. (p.t. slept) dormir; (spend the night) coucher. —v.t. loger. go to ∼, s'endormir. ∼ in, faire la grasse matinée. ∼er n. dormeulr, -se m., f.; (beam: rail) traverse f.; (berth) couchette f. ∼ing-bag n. sac de couchage m. ∼ing pill, somnifère m. ∼less a. sans sommeil. ∼-walker n. somnambule m./f.
sleep|y /'sli:pɪ/ a. (-ier, -iest) somnolent. be ∼y, avoir sommeil. ∼ily adv. à moitié endormi.
sleet /sli:t/ n. neige fondue f.; (coat of ice: Amer.) verglas m. —v.i. tomber de la neige fondue.
sleeve /sli:v/ n. manche f.; (of record) pochette f. up one's ∼, en réserve. ∼less a. sans manches.
sleigh /sleɪ/ n. traîneau m.
sleight /slaɪt/ n. ∼ of hand, prestidigitation f.
slender /'slendə(r)/ a. mince, svelte; (scanty: fig.) faible.
slept /slept/ see sleep.
sleuth /slu:θ/ n. limier m.
slew¹ /slu:/ v.i. (turn) virer.
slew² /slu:/ see slay.
slice /slaɪs/ n. tranche f. —v.t. couper (en tranches).
slick /slɪk/ a. (unctuous) mielleux; (cunning) astucieux. —n. (oil) ∼, nappe de pétrole f., marée noire f.
slide /slaɪd/ v.t./i. (p.t. slid) glisser. —n. glissade f.; (fall: fig.) baisse f.; (in playground) toboggan m.; (for hair) barrette f.; (photo.) diapositive f. ∼ into, (go silently) se glisser dans. ∼-rule n. règle à calcul f. sliding a. (door, panel) à glissière, à coulisse. sliding scale, échelle mobile f.
slight /slaɪt/ a. (-er, -est) petit, léger; (slender) mince; (frail) frêle. —v.t. (insult) offenser. —n. affront m. ∼est a. moindre. ∼ly adv. légèrement, un peu.
slim /slɪm/ a. (slimmer, slimmest) mince. —v.i. (p.t. slimmed) maigrir. ∼ness n. minceur f.
slim|e /slaɪm/ n. boue (visqueuse) f.; (on

river-bed) vase f. ∼y a. boueux; vaseux; (sticky, servile) visqueux.
sling /slɪŋ/ n. (weapon, toy) fronde f.; (bandage) écharpe f. —v.t. (p.t. slung) jeter, lancer.
slip /slɪp/ v.t./i. (p.t. slipped) glisser. —n. faux pas m.; (mistake) erreur f.; (petticoat) combinaison f.; (paper) fiche f. give the ∼ to, fausser compagnie à. ∼ away, s'esquiver. ∼-cover n. (Amer.) housse f. ∼ into, (go) se glisser dans; (clothes) mettre. ∼ of the tongue, lapsus m. ∼ped disc, hernie discale f. ∼-road n. bretelle f. s.o.'s mind, échapper à qn. ∼-stream n. sillage m. ∼ up, (fam.) gaffer. ∼-up n. (fam.) gaffe f.
slipper /'slɪpə(r)/ n. pantoufle f.
slippery /'slɪpərɪ/ a. glissant.
slipshod /'slɪpʃɒd/ a. (person) négligent; (work) négligé.
slit /slɪt/ n. fente f. —v.t. (p.t. slit, pres. p. slitting) couper, fendre.
slither /'slɪðə(r)/ v.i. glisser.
sliver /'slɪvə(r)/ n. (of cheese etc.) lamelle f.; (splinter) éclat m.
slob /slɒb/ n. (fam.) rustre m.
slobber /'slɒbə(r)/ v.i. baver.
slog /slɒg/ v.t. (p.t. slogged) (hit) frapper dur. —v.i. (work) trimer. —n. (work) travail dur m.; (effort) gros effort m.
slogan /'sləʊgən/ n. slogan m.
slop /slɒp/ v.t./i. (p.t. slopped) (se) répandre. ∼s n. pl. eaux sales f. pl.
slop|e /sləʊp/ v.i. être en pente; (of handwriting) pencher. —n. pente f.; (of mountain) flanc m. ∼ing a. en pente.
sloppy /'slɒpɪ/ a. (-ier, -iest) (ground) détrempé; (food) liquide; (work) négligé; (person) négligent; (fig.) sentimental.
slosh /slɒʃ/ v.t. (fam.) répandre; (hit: sl.) frapper. —v.i. patauger.
slot /slɒt/ n. fente f. —v.t./i. (p.t. slotted) (s')insérer. ∼-machine n. distributeur automatique m.; (for gambling) machine à sous f.
sloth /sləʊθ/ n. paresse f.
slouch /slaʊtʃ/ v.i. avoir le dos voûté; (move) marcher le dos voûté.
slovenl|y /'slʌvnlɪ/ a. débraillé. ∼iness n. débraillé m.
slow /sləʊ/ a. (-er, -est) lent. —adv. lentement. —v.t./i. ralentir. be ∼, (clock etc.) retarder. in ∼ motion, au ralenti. ∼ly adv. lentement. ∼ness n. lenteur f.
slow|coach /'sləʊkəʊtʃ/, (Amer.) ∼poke ns. lambin(e) m. (f.).

sludge /slʌdʒ/ n. gadoue f., boue f.

slug /slʌg/ n. (mollusc) limace f.; (bullet) balle f.; (blow) coup m.

sluggish /'slʌgɪʃ/ a. lent, mou.

sluice /sluːs/ n. (gate) vanne f.

slum /slʌm/ n. taudis m.

slumber /'slʌmbə(r)/ n. sommeil. m. —v.i. dormir.

slump /slʌmp/ n. effondrement m.; baisse f.; (in business) marasme m. —v.i. (collapse, fall limply) s'effondrer; (decrease) baisser.

slung /slʌŋ/ see sling.

slur /slɜː(r)/ v.t./i. (p.t. slurred) (spoken words) mal articuler. —n. bredouillement m.; (discredit) atteinte f. (on, à).

slush /slʌʃ/ n. (snow) neige fondue f. ∼ fund, fonds servant à des pots-de-vin m. ∼y a. (road) couvert de neige fondue.

slut /slʌt/ n. (dirty) souillon f.; (immoral) dévergondée f.

sly /slaɪ/ a. (slyer, slyest) (crafty) rusé; (secretive) sournois. —n. on the ∼, en cachette. ∼ly adv. sournoisement.

smack¹ /smæk/ n. tape f.; (on face) gifle f. —v.t. donner une tape à; gifler. —adv. (fam.) tout droit.

smack² /smæk/ v.i. ∼ of sth., (have flavour) sentir qch.

small /smɔːl/ a. (-er, -est) petit. —n. ∼ of the back, creux des reins m. —adv. (cut etc.) menu. ∼ness n. petitesse f. ∼ ads, petites annonces f. pl. ∼ businesses, les petites entreprises. ∼ change, petite monnaie f. ∼ talk, menus propos m. pl. ∼-time a. petit, peu important.

smallholding /'smɔːlhəʊldɪŋ/ n. petite ferme f.

smallpox /'smɔːlpɒks/ n. variole f.

smarmy /'smɑːmɪ/ a. (-ier, -iest) (fam.) obséquieux, patelin.

smart /smɑːt/ a. (-er, -est) élégant; (clever) astucieux, intelligent; (brisk) rapide. —v.i. (of wound etc.) brûler. ∼ly adv. élégamment. ∼ness n. élégance f.

smarten /'smɑːtn/ v.t./i. ∼ (up), embellir. ∼ (o.s.) up, se faire beau; (tidy) s'arranger.

smash /smæʃ/ v.t./i. (se) briser, (se) fracasser; (opponent, record) pulvériser. —n. (noise) fracas m.; (blow) coup m.; (fig.) collision f.

smashing /'smæʃɪŋ/ a. (fam.) formidable, épatant.

smattering /'smætərɪŋ/ n. a ∼ of, des notions de.

smear /smɪə(r)/ v.t. (stain) tacher; (coat) enduire; (discredit: fig.) entacher. —n. tache f. ∼ test, frottis m.

smell /smel/ n. odeur f.; (sense) odorat m. —v.t./i. (p.t. smelt or smelled) sentir. ∼ of, sentir. ∼y a. malodorant, qui pue.

smelt¹ /smelt/ see smell.

smelt² /smelt/ v.t. (ore) fondre.

smil|e /smaɪl/ n. sourire. —v.i. sourire. ∼ing a. souriant.

smirk /smɜːk/ n. sourire affecté m.

smith /smɪθ/ n. forgeron m.

smithereens /smɪðə'riːnz/ n. pl. to or in ∼, en mille morceaux.

smitten /'smɪtn/ a. (in love) épris (with, de).

smock /smɒk/ n. blouse f.

smog /smɒg/ n. brouillard mélangé de fumée m., smog m.

smoke /sməʊk/ n. fumée f. —v.t./i. fumer. have a ∼, fumer. ∼d a. fumé. ∼less a. (fuel) non polluant. ∼r /-ə(r)/ n. fumeu|r, -se m., f. ∼-screen n. écran de fumée m.; (fig.) manœuvre de diversion f. smoky a. (air) enfumé.

smooth /smuːð/ a. (-er, -est) lisse; (movement) régulier; (manners, cream) onctueux; (flight) sans turbulence; (changes) sans heurt. —v.t. lisser. ∼ out, (fig.) faire disparaître. ∼ly adv. facilement, doucement.

smother /'smʌðə(r)/ v.t. (stifle) étouffer; (cover) couvrir.

smoulder /'sməʊldə(r)/ v.i. (fire, discontent, etc.) couver.

smudge /smʌdʒ/ n. tache f. —v.t./i. (se) salir, (se) tacher.

smug /smʌg/ a. (smugger, smuggest) suffisant. ∼ly adv. avec suffisance. ∼ness n. suffisance f.

smuggl|e /'smʌgl/ v.t. passer (en contrebande). ∼er n. contrebandi|er, -ière m., f. ∼ing n. contrebande f.

smut /smʌt/ n. saleté f. ∼ty a. indécent.

snack /snæk/ n. casse-croûte m. invar. ∼-bar n. snack(-bar) m.

snag /snæg/ n. difficulté f., inconvénient m.; (in cloth) accroc m.

snail /sneɪl/ n. escargot m. at a ∼'s pace, à un pas de tortue.

snake /sneɪk/ n. serpent m.

snap /snæp/ v.t./i. (p.t. snapped) (whip, fingers, etc.) (faire) claquer; (break) (se) casser net; (say) dire sèchement. —n. claquement m.; (photograph) instantané m.; (press-stud: Amer.) bouton-pression m. —a. soudain. ∼ at, (bite) happer; (angrily) être cassant avec. ∼ up, (buy) sauter sur.

snappy /'snæpɪ/ a. (-ier, -iest) (*brisk: fam.*) prompt, rapide. **make it ~,** (*fam.*) se dépêcher.

snapshot /'snæpʃɒt/ n. instantané m., photo f.

snare /sneə(r)/ n. piège m.

snarl /snɑːl/ v.i. gronder (en montrant les dents). —n. grondement m. **~-up,** n. embouteillage m.

snarl /snɑːl/ v.i. gronder (en montrant les dents). —n. grondement m. **~-up** n. embouteillage m.

snatch /snætʃ/ v.t. (*grab*) saisir; (*steal*) voler. **~ from s.o.,** arracher à qn. —n. (*theft*) vol m.; (*short part*) fragment m.

sneak /sniːk/ v.i. aller furtivement. —n. (*schol., sl.*) rapporteulr, -se m., f. **~y** a. sournois.

sneakers /'sniːkəz/ n. pl. (*shoes*) tennis m. pl.

sneaking /'sniːkɪŋ/ a. caché.

sneer /snɪə(r)/ n. ricanement m. —v.i. ricaner.

sneeze /sniːz/ n. éternuement m. —v.i. éternuer.

snide /snaɪd/ a. (*fam.*) narquois.

sniff /snɪf/ v.t./i. renifler. —n. reniflement m.

snigger /'snɪɡə(r)/ n. ricanement m. —v.i. ricaner.

snip /snɪp/ v.t. (*p.t.* snipped) couper. —n. morceau coupé m.; (*bargain: sl.*) bonne affaire f.

snipe /snaɪp/ v.i. canarder. **~r** /-ə(r)/ n. tireur embusqué m.

snippet /'snɪpɪt/ n. bribe f.

snivel /'snɪvl/ v.i. (*p.t.* snivelled) pleurnicher.

snob /snɒb/ n. snob m./f. **~bery** n. snobisme m. **~bish** a. snob invar.

snooker /'snuːkə(r)/ n. (*sorte de*) jeu de billard m.

snoop /snuːp/ v.i. (*fam.*) fourrer son nez partout. **~ on,** espionner.

snooty /'snuːtɪ/ a. (-ier, -iest) (*fam.*) snob invar., hautain.

snooze /snuːz/ n. petit somme m. —v.i. faire un petit somme.

snore /snɔː(r)/ n. ronflement m. —v.i. ronfler.

snorkel /'snɔːkl/ n. tuba m.

snort /snɔːt/ n. grognement m. —v.i. (*person*) grogner; (*horse*) s'ébrouer.

snotty /'snɒtɪ/ a. morveux.

snout /snaʊt/ n. museau m.

snow /snəʊ/ n. neige f. —v.i. neiger. **be ~ed under with,** être submergé de. **~-bound** a. bloqué par la neige. **~-drift** n. congère f. **~-plough** n. chasse-neige m.

invar. **~-shoe** n. raquette f. **~y** a. neigeux.

snowball /'snəʊbɔːl/ n. boule de neige f. —v.i. faire boule de neige.

snowdrop /'snəʊdrɒp/ n. perce-neige m./f. invar.

snowfall /'snəʊfɔːl/ n. chute de neige f.

snowflake /'snəʊfleɪk/ n. flocon de neige m.

snowman /'snəʊmæn/ n. (*pl.* -men) bonhomme de neige m.

snowstorm /'snəʊstɔːm/ n. tempête de neige f.

snub /snʌb/ v.t. (*p.t.* snubbed) (*person*) snober; (*offer*) repousser. —n. rebuffade f.

snub-nosed /'snʌbnəʊzd/ a. au nez retroussé.

snuff¹ /snʌf/ n. tabac à priser m.

snuff² /snʌf/ v.t. (*candle*) moucher.

snuffle /'snʌfl/ v.i. renifler.

snug /snʌɡ/ a. (**snugger, snuggest**) (*cosy*) comfortable; (*tight*) bien ajusté; (*safe*) sûr.

snuggle /'snʌɡl/ v.i. se pelotonner.

so /səʊ/ adv. si, tellement; (*thus*) ainsi. —conj. donc, alors. **so am I,** moi aussi. **so good/etc. as,** aussi bon/etc. que. **so does he,** lui aussi. **that is so,** c'est ça. **I think so,** je pense que oui. **five or so,** environ cinq. **so-and-so** n. un(e) tel(le) m. (f.). **so as to,** de manière à. **so-called** a. soi-disant invar. **~ far,** jusqu'ici. **so long!,** (*fam.*) à bientôt! **so many, so much,** tant (de). **so-so** a. & adv. comme ci comme ça. **so that,** pour que.

soak /səʊk/ v.t./i. (faire) tremper (**in,** dans). **~ in** or **up,** absorber. **~ing** a. trempé.

soap /səʊp/ n. savon m. —v.t. savonner. **~ opera,** feuilleton m. **~ powder,** lessive f. **~y** a. savonneux.

soar /sɔː(r)/ v.i. monter (en flèche).

sob /sɒb/ n. sanglot m. —v.i. (*p.t.* sobbed) sangloter.

sober /'səʊbə(r)/ a. qui n'est pas ivre; (*serious*) sérieux; (*colour*) sobre. —v.t./i. **~ up,** dessoûler.

soccer /'sɒkə(r)/ n. (*fam.*) football m.

sociable /'səʊʃəbl/ a. sociable.

social /'səʊʃl/ a. social; (*gathering, life*) mondain. —n. réunion (amicale) f., fête f. **~ly** adv. socialement; (*meet*) en société. **~ security,** aide sociale f.; (*for old age: Amer.*) pension (de retraite) f. **~ worker,** assistant(e) social(e) m. (f.).

socialist /'səʊʃəlɪst/ n. socialiste m./f. **~m** /-zəm/ n. socialisme m.

socialize /'səʊʃəlaɪz/ v.i. se mêler aux autres. **~ with,** fréquenter.

society /sə'saɪətɪ/ n. société f.

sociolog|y /səʊsɪ'ɒlədʒɪ/ n. sociologie f. **~ical** /-ə'lɒdʒɪkl/ a. sociologique. **~ist** n. sociologue m./f.

sock[1] /sɒk/ n. chaussette f.

sock[2] /sɒk/ v.t. (hit: sl.) flanquer un coup (de poing) à.

socket /'sɒkɪt/ n. cavité f.; (for lamp) douille f.; (electr.) prise (de courant) f.; (of tooth) alvéole f.

soda /'səʊdə/ n. soude f. **~(-pop)**, (Amer.) soda m. **~(-water)**, soda m., eau de Seltz f.

sodden /'sɒdn/ a. détrempé.

sodium /'səʊdɪəm/ n. sodium m.

sofa /'səʊfə/ n. canapé m., sofa m.

soft /sɒft/ a. (-er, -est) (gentle, lenient) doux; (not hard) doux, mou; (heart, wood) tendre; (silly) ramolli; (easy: sl.) facile. **~ drink**, boisson non alcoolisée f. **~ly** adv. doucement. **~ness** n. douceur f. **~ spot**, faible m.

soften /'sɒfn/ v.t./i. (se) ramollir; (tone down, lessen) (s')adoucir.

software /'sɒftweə(r)/ n. (for computer) logiciel m.

softwood /'sɒftwʊd/ n. bois tendre m.

soggy /'sɒgɪ/ a. (-ier, -iest) détrempé; (bread etc.) ramolli.

soil[1] /sɔɪl/ n. sol m., terre f.

soil[2] /sɔɪl/ v.t./i. (se) salir.

solar /'səʊlə(r)/ a. solaire.

sold /səʊld/ see **sell**. **—a. ~ out**, épuisé.

solder /'sɒldə(r)/, Amer. 'sɒdər/ n. soudure f. **—v.t.** souder. **~ing iron**, fer à souder m.

soldier /'səʊldʒə(r)/ n. soldat m. **—v.i. ~ on**, (fam.) persévérer.

sole[1] /səʊl/ n. (of foot) plante f.; (of shoe) semelle f.

sole[2] /səʊl/ n. (fish) sole f.

sole[3] /səʊl/ a. unique, seul. **~ly** adv. uniquement.

solemn /'sɒləm/ a. (formal) solennel; (not cheerful) grave. **~ity** /sə'lemnətɪ/ n. solennité f. **~ly** adv. solennellement; gravement.

solicit /sə'lɪsɪt/ v.t. (seek) solliciter. **—v.i.** (of prostitute) racoler.

solicitor /sə'lɪsɪtə(r)/ n. avoué m.

solid /'sɒlɪd/ a. solide; (not hollow) plein; (gold) massif; (mass) compact; (meal) substantiel. **—n.** solide m. **~s**, (food) aliments solides m. pl. **~state** a. à circuits intégrés. **~ity** /sə'lɪdətɪ/ n. solidité f. **~ly** adv. solidement.

solidarity /sɒlɪ'dærətɪ/ n. solidarité f.

solidify /sə'lɪdɪfaɪ/ v.t./i. (se) solidifier.

soliloquy /sə'lɪləkwɪ/ n. monologue m., soliloque m.

solitary /'sɒlɪtrɪ/ a. (alone, lonely) solitaire; (only, single) seul.

solitude /'sɒlɪtjuːd/ n. solitude f.

solo /'səʊləʊ/ n. (pl. -os) solo m. **—a.** (mus.) solo invar.; (flight) en solitaire. **~ist** n. soliste m./f.

solstice /'sɒlstɪs/ n. solstice m.

soluble /'sɒljʊbl/ a. soluble.

solution /sə'luːʃn/ n. solution f.

solv|e /sɒlv/ v.t. résoudre. **~able** a. soluble.

solvent /'sɒlvənt/ a. (comm.) solvable. **—n.** (dis)solvant m.

sombre /'sɒmbə(r)/ a. sombre.

some /sʌm/ a. (quantity, number) du, de l'*, de la, des; (unspecified, some or other) un(e), quelque; (a little) un peu de; (a certain) un(e) certain(e), quelque; (contrasted with others) quelques, certain(e)s. **—pron.** quelques-un(e)s; (certain quantity of it or them) en; (a little) un peu. **—adv.** (approximately) quelque. **pour ~ milk**, versez du lait. **buy ~ flowers**, achetez des fleurs. **~ people love them**, il y a des gens qui les aiment. **~ of my friends**, quelques amis à moi. **he wants ~**, il en veut. **~ book (or other)**, un livre (quelconque), quelque livre. **~ time ago**, il y a un certain temps.

somebody /'sʌmbədɪ/ pron. quelqu'un. **—n. be a ~**, être quelqu'un.

somehow /'sʌmhaʊ/ adv. d'une manière ou d'une autre; (for some reason) je ne sais pas pourquoi.

someone /'sʌmwʌn/ pron. & n. = **somebody**.

someplace /'sʌmpleɪs/ adv. (Amer.) = **somewhere**.

somersault /'sʌməsɔːlt/ n. culbute f. **—v.i.** faire la culbute.

something /'sʌmθɪŋ/ pron. & n. quelque chose (m.). **~ good**, quelque chose de bon/etc. **~ like**, un peu comme.

sometime /'sʌmtaɪm/ adv. un jour. **—a.** (former) ancien. **~ in June**, en juin.

sometimes /'sʌmtaɪmz/ adv. quelquefois, parfois.

somewhat /'sʌmwɒt/ adv. quelque peu, un peu.

somewhere /'sʌmweə(r)/ adv. quelque part.

son /sʌn/ n. fils m. **~-in-law** n. (pl. **~s-in-law**) beau-fils m., gendre m.

sonar /'səʊnɑː(r)/ n. sonar m.

sonata /sə'nɑːtə/ n. sonate f.

song /sɒŋ/ n. chanson f. **going for a ~**, à vendre pour une bouchée de pain.

sonic /ˈsɒnɪk/ a. ~ **boom**, bang supersonique m.

sonnet /ˈsɒnɪt/ n. sonnet m.

sonny /ˈsʌnɪ/ n. (fam.) fiston m.

soon /suːn/ adv. (-er, -est) bientôt; (early) tôt. **I would** ~**er stay**, j'aimerais mieux rester. ~ **after**, peu après. ~**er or later**, tôt ou tard.

soot /sʊt/ n. suie f. ~**y** a. couvert de suie.

soothe /suːð/ v.t. calmer. ~**ing** a. (remedy, words, etc.) calmant.

sophisticated /səˈfɪstɪkeɪtɪd/ a. raffiné; (machine etc.) sophistiqué.

sophomore /ˈsɒfəmɔː(r)/ n. (Amer.) étudiant(e) de seconde année m. (f.).

soporific /sɒpəˈrɪfɪk/ a. soporifique.

sopping /ˈsɒpɪŋ/ a. trempé.

soppy /ˈsɒpɪ/ a. (-ier, -iest) (fam.) sentimental; (silly: fam.) bête.

soprano /səˈprɑːnəʊ/ n. (pl. -os) (voice) soprano m.; (singer) soprano m./f.

sorcerer /ˈsɔːsərə(r)/ n. sorcier m.

sordid /ˈsɔːdɪd/ a. sordide.

sore /sɔː(r)/ a. (-er, -est) douloureux; (vexed) en rogne (**at, with**, contre). —n. plaie f.

sorely /ˈsɔːlɪ/ adv. fortement.

sorrow /ˈsɒrəʊ/ n. chagrin m. ~**ful** a. triste.

sorry /ˈsɒrɪ/ a. (-ier, -iest) (regretful) désolé (**to, de; that, que**); (wretched) triste. **feel** ~ **for**, plaindre. ~**!**, pardon!

sort /sɔːt/ n. genre m., sorte f., espèce f.; (person: fam.) type m. —v.t. ~ (**out**), (classify) trier. **what** ~ **of?**, quel genre de? **be out of** ~**s**, ne pas être dans son assiette. ~ **out**, (tidy) ranger; (arrange) arranger; (problem) régler.

SOS /esəʊˈes/ n. SOS m.

soufflé /ˈsuːfleɪ/ n. soufflé m.

sought /sɔːt/ see **seek**.

soul /səʊl/ n. âme f. ~**-destroying** a. démoralisant.

soulful /ˈsəʊlfl/ a. plein de sentiment, très expressif.

sound[1] /saʊnd/ n. son m., bruit m. —v.t./i. sonner; (seem) sembler (**as if**, que). ~ **a horn**, klaxonner. ~ **barrier**, mur du son m. ~ **like**, sembler être. ~**proof** a. insonorisé; v.t. insonoriser. ~**track** n. bande sonore f.

sound[2] /saʊnd/ a. (-er, -est) solide; (healthy) sain; (sensible) sensé. ~ **asleep**, profondément endormi. ~**ly** adv. solidement; (sleep) profondément.

sound[3] /saʊnd/ v.t. sonder. ~ **out**, sonder.

soup /suːp/ n. soupe f., potage m. **in the** ~, (sl.) dans le pétrin.

sour /ˈsaʊə(r)/ a. (-er, -est) aigre. —v.t./i. (s')aigrir.

source /sɔːs/ n. source f.

south /saʊθ/ n. sud m. —a. sud invar., du sud. —adv. vers le sud. **S**~ **Africa/America**, Afrique/Amérique du Sud f. **S**~ **African** a. & n. sud-africain(e) (m. (f.)). **S**~ **American** a. & n. sud-américain(e) (m. (f.)). ~**-east** n. sud-est m. ~**erly** /ˈsʌðəlɪ/ a. du sud. ~**ward** a. au sud. ~**wards** adv. vers le sud. ~**-west** n. sud-ouest m.

southern /ˈsʌðən/ a. du sud. ~**er** n. habitant(e) du sud m. (f.).

souvenir /suːvəˈnɪə(r)/ n. (thing) souvenir m.

sovereign /ˈsɒvrɪn/ n. & a. souverain(e) (m. (f.)). ~**ty** n. souveraineté f.

Soviet /ˈsəʊvɪət/ a. soviétique. **the** ~ **Union**, l'Union soviétique f.

sow[1] /səʊ/ v.t. (p.t. **sowed**, p.p. **sowed** or **sown**) (seed etc.) semer; (land) ensemencer.

sow[2] /saʊ/ n. (pig) truie f.

soya, soy /ˈsɔɪə, sɔɪ/ n. ~ **bean**, graine de soja f. ~ **sauce**, sauce soja f.

spa /spɑː/ n. station thermale f.

space /speɪs/ n. espace m.; (room) place f.; (period) période f. —a. (research etc.) spatial. —v.t. ~ (**out**), espacer.

space|**craft** /ˈspeɪskrɑːft/ n. invar. ~**ship** n. engin spatial m.

spacesuit /ˈspeɪssuːt/ n. scaphandre m.

spacious /ˈspeɪʃəs/ a. spacieux.

spade[1] /speɪd/ n. (large, for garden) bêche f.; (child's) pelle f.

spade[2] /speɪd/ n. (cards) pique m.

spadework /ˈspeɪdwɜːk/ n. (fig.) travail préparatoire m.

spaghetti /spəˈgetɪ/ n. spaghetti m. pl.

Spa|**in** /speɪn/ n. Espagne f. ~**niard** /ˈspænɪəd/ n. Espagnol(e) m. (f.). ~**nish** /ˈspænɪʃ/ a. espagnol; n. (lang.) espagnol m.

span[1] /spæn/ n. (of arch) portée f.; (of wings) envergure f.; (of time) durée f. —v.t. (p.t. **spanned**) enjamber; (in time) embrasser.

span[2] /spæn/ past see **spick**.

spaniel /ˈspænɪəl/ n. épagneul m.

spank /spæŋk/ v.t. donner une fessée à. ~**ing** n. fessée f.

spanner /ˈspænə(r)/ n. (tool) clé (plate) f.; (adjustable) clé à molette f.

spar /spɑː(r)/ v.i. (p.t. **sparred**) s'entraîner (à la boxe).

spare /speə(r)/ v.t. épargner; (do without) se passer de; (afford to give) donner, accorder; (use with restraint) ménager. —*a.* en réserve; (*surplus*) de trop; (*tyre*, *shoes*, *etc.*) de rechange; (*room*, *bed*) d'ami. —*n.* ~ **(part)**, pièce de rechange *f.* ~ **time**, loisirs *m. pl.* **are there any** ~ **tickets?** y a-t-il encore des places?

sparing /'speərɪŋ/ *a.* frugal. ~ **of**, avare de. ~**ly** *adv.* en petite quantité.

spark /spɑːk/ *n.* étincelle *f.* —*v.t.* ~ **off**, (*initiate*) provoquer. ~**(ing)-plug** *n.* bougie *f.*

sparkle /'spɑːkl/ *v.i.* étinceler. —*n.* étincellement *m.*

sparkling /'spɑːklɪŋ/ *a.* (*wine*) mousseux, pétillant; (*eyes*) pétillant.

sparrow /'spærəʊ/ *n.* moineau *m.*

sparse /spɑːs/ *a.* clairsemé. ~**ly** *adv.* (*furnished etc.*) peu.

spartan /'spɑːtn/ *a.* spartiate.

spasm /'spæzəm/ *n.* (*of muscle*) spasme *m.*; (*of coughing, anger, etc.*) accès *m.*

spasmodic /spæz'mɒdɪk/ *a.* intermittent.

spastic /'spæstɪk/ *n.* handicapé(e) moteur *m.* (*f.*).

spat /spæt/ *see* **spit**[1].

spate /speɪt/ *n.* **a** ~ **of**, (*letters etc.*) une avalanche de.

spatter /'spætə(r)/ *v.t.* éclabousser (**with**, de).

spatula /'spætjʊlə/ *n.* spatule *f.*

spawn /spɔːn/ *n.* frai *m.*, œufs *m. pl.* —*v.t.* pondre. —*v.i.* frayer.

speak /spiːk/ *v.i.* (*p.t.* **spoke**, *p.p.* **spoken**) parler. —*v.t.* (*say*) dire; (*language*) parler. ~ **up**, parler plus fort.

speaker /'spiːkə(r)/ *n.* (*in public*) orateur *m.*; (*pol.*) président; (*loudspeaker*) baffle *m.* **be a French/a good**/*etc.* ~, parler français/bien/*etc.*

spear /spɪə(r)/ *n.* lance *f.*

spearhead /'spɪəhed/ *n.* fer de lance *m.* —*v.t.* (*lead*) mener.

spearmint /'spɪəmɪnt/ *n.* menthe verte *f.* —*a.* à la menthe.

spec /spek/ *n.* **on** ~, (*as speculation: fam.*) à tout hasard.

special /'speʃl/ *a.* spécial; (*exceptional*) exceptionnel. ~**ity** /-ɪ'ælətɪ/, (*Amer.*) ~**ty** *n.* spécialité *f.* ~**ly** *adv.* spécialement.

specialist /'speʃəlɪst/ *n.* spécialiste *m.*/*f.*

specialize /'speʃəlaɪz/ *v.i.* se spécialiser (**in**, en). ~**d** *a.* spécialisé.

species /'spiːʃiːz/ *n. invar.* espèce *f.*

specific /spə'sɪfɪk/ *a.* précis, explicite. ~**ally** *adv.* explicitement; (*exactly*) précisément.

specif|y /'spesɪfaɪ/ *v.t.* spécifier. ~**ication** /-ɪ'keɪʃn/ *n.* spécification *f.*; (*details*) prescriptions *f. pl.*

specimen /'spesɪmɪn/ *n.* spécimen *m.*, échantillon *m.*

speck /spek/ *n.* (*stain*) (petite) tache *f.*; (*particle*) grain *m.*

speckled /'spekld/ *a.* tacheté.

specs /speks/ *n. pl.* (*fam.*) lunettes *f. pl.*

spectacle /'spektəkl/ *n.* spectacle *m.* ~**s**, lunettes *f. pl.*

spectacular /spek'tækjʊlə(r)/ *a.* spectaculaire.

spectator /spek'teɪtə(r)/ *n.* spectateur, -trice *m.*, *f.*

spectre /'spektə(r)/ *n.* spectre *m.*

spectrum /'spektrəm/ *n.* (*pl.* **-tra**) spectre *m.*; (*of ideas etc.*) gamme *f.*

speculat|e /'spekjʊleɪt/ *v.i.* s'interroger (**about**, sur); (*comm.*) spéculer. ~**ion** /-'leɪʃn/ *n.* conjectures *f. pl.*; (*comm.*) spéculation *f.* ~**or** *n.* spéculateur, -trice *m.*, *f.*

speech /spiːtʃ/ *n.* (*faculty*) parole *f.*; (*diction*) élocution *f.*; (*dialect*) langage *m.*; (*address*) discours *m.* ~**less** *a.* muet (**with**, de).

speed /spiːd/ *n.* (*of movement*) vitesse *f.*; (*swiftness*) rapidité *f.* —*v.i.* (*p.t.* **sped** /sped/) aller vite; (*p.t.* **speeded**) (*drive too fast*) aller trop vite. ~ **limit**, limitation de vitesse *f.* ~ **up**, accélérer; (*of pace*) s'accélérer. ~**ing** *n.* excès de vitesse *m.*

speedboat /'spiːdbəʊt/ *n.* vedette *f.*

speedometer /spiː'dɒmɪtə(r)/ *n.* compteur (de vitesse) *m.*

speedway /'spiːdweɪ/ *n.* piste pour motos *f.*; (*Amer.*) autodrome *m.*

speed|y /'spiːdɪ/ *a.* (**-ier, -iest**) rapide. ~**ily** *adv.* rapidement.

spell[1] /spel/ *n.* (*magic*) charme *m.*, sortilège *m.*; (*curse*) sort *m.*

spell[2] /spel/ *v.t./i.* (*p.t.* **spelled** *or* **spelt**) écrire; (*mean*) signifier. ~ **out**, épeler; (*explain*) expliquer. ~**ing** *n.* orthographe *f.* ~**ing mistake**, faute d'orthographe *f.*

spell[3] /spel/ *n.* (courte) période *f.*

spend /spend/ *v.t.* (*p.t.* **spent**) (*money*) dépenser (**on**, pour); (*time, holiday*) passer; (*energy*) consacrer (**on**, à). —*v.i.* dépenser.

spendthrift /'spendθrɪft/ *n.* dépenslier, -ière *m.*, *f.*

spent /spent/ *see* **spend**. —*a.* (*used*) utilisé; (*person*) épuisé.

sperm /spɜːm/ *n.* (*pl.* **sperms** *or* **sperm**)

(*semen*) sperme *m.*; (*cell*) spermatozoïde *m.* ~**icide** *n.* spermicide *m.*

spew /spju:/ *v.t./i.* vomir.

sphere /sfɪə(r)/ *n.* sphère *f.*

spherical /'sferɪkl/ *a.* sphérique.

spic|e /spaɪs/ *n.* épice *f.*; (*fig.*) piquant *m.* ~**y** *a.* épicé; piquant.

spick /spɪk/ *a.* ~ **and span**, impeccable, d'une propreté parfaite.

spider /'spaɪdə(r)/ *n.* araignée *f.*

spiel /ʃpiːl, (*Amer.*) spiːl/ *n.* baratin *m.*

spik|e /spaɪk/ *n.* (*of metal etc.*) pointe *f.* ~**y** *a.* garni de pointes.

spill /spɪl/ *v.t.* (*p.t.* **spilled** or **spilt**) renverser, répandre. —*v.i.* se répandre. ~ **over**, déborder.

spin /spɪn/ *v.t./i.* (*p.t.* **spun**, *pres. p.* **spinning**) (*wool, web, of spinner*) filer; (*turn*) (faire) tourner; (*story*) débiter. —*n.* (*movement, excursion*) tour *m.* ~ **out**, faire durer. ~**-drier** *n.* essoreuse *f.* ~**ning-wheel** *n.* rouet *m.* ~**-off** *n.* avantage accessoire *m.*; (*by-product*) dérivé *m.*

spinach /'spɪnɪdʒ/ *n.* (*plant*) épinard *m.*; (*as food*) épinards *m. pl.*

spinal /'spaɪnl/ *a.* vertébral. ~ **cord**, moelle épinière *f.*

spindl|e /'spɪndl/ *n.* fuseau *m.* ~**y** *a.* filiforme, grêle.

spine /spaɪn/ *n.* colonne vertébrale *f.*; (*prickle*) piquant *m.*

spineless /'spaɪnlɪs/ *a.* (*fig.*) sans caractère, mou, lâche.

spinster /'spɪnstə(r)/ *n.* célibataire *f.*; (*pej.*) vieille fille *f.*

spiral /'spaɪərəl/ *a.* en spirale; (*staircase*) en colimaçon. —*n.* spirale *f.* —*v.i.* (*p.t.* **spiralled**) (*prices*) monter (en flèche).

spire /'spaɪə(r)/ *n.* flèche *f.*

spirit /'spɪrɪt/ *n.* esprit *m.*; (*boldness*) courage *m.* ~**s**, (*morale*) moral *m.*; (*drink*) spiritueux *m. pl.* —*v.t.* ~ **away**, faire disparaître. ~**-level** *n.* niveau à bulle *m.*

spirited /'spɪrɪtɪd/ *a.* fougueux.

spiritual /'spɪrɪtʃʊəl/ *a.* spirituel. —*n.* (*song*) (negro-)spiritual *m.*

spit[1] /spɪt/ *v.t./i.* (*p.t.* **spat** or **spit**, *pres. p.* **spitting**) cracher; (*of rain*) crachiner. —*n.* crachat(s) *m.* (*pl.*) ~ **out**, cracher. **the** ~**ting image of**, le portrait craché or vivant de.

spit[2] /spɪt/ *n.* (*for meat*) broche *f.*

spite /spaɪt/ *n.* rancune *f.* —*v.t.* contrarier. **in** ~ **of**, malgré. ~**ful** *a.* méchant, rancunier. ~**fully** *adv.* méchamment.

spittle /'spɪtl/ *n.* crachat(s) *m.* (*pl.*).

splash /splæʃ/ *v.t.* éclabousser. —*v.i.* faire des éclaboussures. ~ (**about**), patauger. —*n.* (*act, mark*) éclaboussure *f.*; (*sound*) plouf *m.*; (*of colour*) tache *f.*

spleen /spliːn/ *n.* (*anat.*) rate *f.*

splendid /'splendɪd/ *a.* magnifique, splendide.

splendour /'splendə(r)/ *n.* splendeur *f.*, éclat *m.*

splint /splɪnt/ *n.* (*med.*) attelle *f.*

splinter /'splɪntə(r)/ *n.* éclat *m.*; (*in finger*) écharde *f.* ~ **group**, groupe dissident *m.*

split /splɪt/ *v.t./i.* (*p.t.* **split**, *pres. p.* **splitting**) (*se*) fendre; (*tear*) (se) déchirer; (*divide*) (se) diviser; (*share*) partager. —*n.* fente *f.*; déchirure *f.*; (*share: fam.*) part *f.*, partage *m.*; (*quarrel*) rupture *f.*; (*pol.*) scission *f.* ~ **up**, (*couple*) rompre. **a** ~ **second**, un rien de temps. ~ **one's sides**, se tordre (de rire).

splurge /splɜːdʒ/ *v.i.* (*fam.*) faire de folles dépenses.

splutter /'splʌtə(r)/ *v.i.* crachoter; (*stammer*) bafouiller; (*engine*) tousser; (*fat*) crépiter.

spoil /spɔɪl/ *v.t.* (*p.t.* **spoilt** or **spoiled**) (*pamper*) gâter; (*ruin*) abîmer; (*mar*) gâcher, gâter. —*n.* ~(**s**), (*plunder*) butin *m.* ~**-sport** *n.* trouble-fête *m./f. invar.*

spoke[1] /spəʊk/ *n.* rayon *m.*

spoke[2], **spoken** /spəʊk, 'spəʊkən/ *see* **speak.**

spokesman /'spəʊksmən/ *n.* (*pl.* **-men**) porte-parole *m. invar.*

sponge /spʌndʒ/ *n.* éponge *f.* —*v.t.* éponger. —*v.i.* ~ **on**, vivre aux crochets de. ~**-bag** *n.* trousse de toilette *f.* ~**-cake** *n.* génoise *f.* ~**r** /-ə(r)/ *n.* parasite *m.* **spongy** *a.* spongieux.

sponsor /'spɒnsə(r)/ *n.* (*of concert*) parrain *m.*, sponsor *m.*; (*surety*) garant *m.*; (*for membership*) parrain *m.*, marraine *f.* —*v.t.* parrainer, sponsoriser; (*member*) parrainer. ~**ship** *n.* patronage *m.*; parrainage *m.*

spontane|ous /spɒn'teɪnɪəs/ *a.* spontané. ~**ity** /-tə'niːətɪ/ *n.* spontanéité *f.* ~**ously** *adv.* spontanément.

spoof /spuːf/ *n.* (*fam.*) parodie *f.*

spool /spuːl/ *n.* bobine *f.*

spoon /spuːn/ *n.* cuiller *f.* ~**-feed** *v.t.* (*p.t.* **-fed**) nourrir à la cuiller; (*help: fig.*) mâcher la besogne à. ~**ful** *n.* (*pl.* **-fuls**) cuillerée *f.*

sporadic /spə'rædɪk/ *a.* sporadique.

sport /spɔːt/ *n.* sport *m.* (**good**) ~, (*person*: *sl.*) chic type *m.* —*v.t.* (*display*) exhiber, arborer. ~s **car/coat,** voiture/veste de sport *f.* ~**y** *a.* (*fam.*) sportif.

sporting /'spɔːtɪŋ/ *a.* sportif. **a** ~ **chance,** une assez bonne chance.

sports|man /'spɔːtsmən/ *n.* (*pl.* -**men**) sportif *m.* ~**manship** *n.* sportivité *f.* ~**woman** *n.* (*pl.* -**women**) sportive *f.*

spot /spɒt/ *n.* (*mark, stain*) tache *f.*; (*dot*) point *m.*; (*in pattern*) pois *m.*; (*drop*) goutte *f.*; (*place*) endroit *m.*; (*pimple*) bouton *m.* —*v.t.* (*p.t.* **spotted**) (*fam.*) apercevoir. **a** ~ **of,** (*fam.*) un peu de. **be in a** ~, (*fam.*) avoir un problème. **on the** ~, sur place; (*without delay*) sur le coup. ~ **check,** contrôle à l'improviste *m.* ~**ted** *a.* tacheté; (*fabric*) à pois. ~**ty** *a.* (*skin*) boutonneux.

spotless /'spɒtlɪs/ *a.* impeccable.

spotlight /'spɒtlaɪt/ *n.* (*lamp*) projecteur *m.*, spot *m.*

spouse /spaʊs/ *n.* époux *m.*, épouse *f.*

spout /spaʊt/ *n.* (*of vessel*) bec *m.*; (*of liquid*) jet *m.* —*v.i.* jaillir. **up the** ~, (*ruined*: *sl.*) fichu.

sprain /spreɪn/ *n.* entorse *f.*, foulure *f.* —*v.t.* ~ **one's wrist**/*etc.*, se fouler le poignet/*etc.*

sprang /spræŋ/ *see* **spring.**

sprawl /sprɔːl/ *v.i.* (*town, person, etc.*) s'étaler. —*n.* étalement *m.*

spray¹ /spreɪ/ *n.* (*of flowers*) gerbe *f.*

spray² /spreɪ/ *n.* (*water*) gerbe d'eau *f.*; (*from sea*) embruns *m. pl.*; (*device*) bombe *f.*, atomiseur *m.* —*v.t.* (*surface, insecticide*) vaporiser; (*plant etc.*) arroser; (*crops*) traiter.

spread /spred/ *v.t./i.* (*p.t.* **spread**) (*stretch, extend*) (s')étendre; (*news, fear, etc.*) (se) répandre; (*illness*) (se) propager; (*butter etc.*) (s')étaler. —*n.* propagation *f.*; (*of population*) distribution *f.*; (*paste*) pâte à tartiner *f.*; (*food*) belle table *f.* ~**-eagled** *a.* bras et jambes écartés.

spreadsheet /'spredʃiːt/ *n.* tableur *m.*

spree /spriː/ *n.* **go on a** ~, (*have fun*: *fam.*) faire la noce.

sprig /sprɪg/ *n.* (*shoot*) brin *m.*; (*twig*) brindille *f.*

sprightly /'spraɪtlɪ/ *a.* (-**ier, -iest**) alerte, vif.

spring /sprɪŋ/ *v.i.* (*p.t.* **sprang**, *p.p.* **sprung**) bondir. —*v.t.* faire, annoncer, *etc.* à l'improviste (**on,** à). —*n.* bond *m.*; (*device*) ressort *m.*; (*season*) printemps *m.*; (*of water*) source *f.* ~**-clean** *v.t.*

nettoyer de fond en comble. ~ **from,** provenir de. ~ **onion,** oignon blanc *m.* ~ **up,** surgir.

springboard /'sprɪŋbɔːd/ *n.* tremplin *m.*

springtime /'sprɪŋtaɪm/ *n.* printemps *m.*

springy /'sprɪŋɪ/ *a.* (-**ier, -iest**) élastique.

sprinkle /'sprɪŋkl/ *v.t.* (*with liquid*) arroser (**with,** de); (*with salt, flour*) saupoudrer (**with,** de). ~ **sand**/*etc.*, répandre du sable/*etc.* ~**r** /-ə(r)/ *n.* (*in garden*) arroseur *m.*; (*for fires*) extincteur (à déclenchement) automatique *m.*

sprinkling /'sprɪŋklɪŋ/ *n.* (*amount*) petite quantité *f.*

sprint /sprɪnt/ *v.i.* (*sport*) sprinter. —*n.* sprint *m.* ~**er** *n.* sprinteur/, -se *m., f.*

sprout /spraʊt/ *v.t./i.* pousser. —*n.* (*on plant etc.*) pousse *f.* (**Brussels**) ~**s,** choux de Bruxelles *m. pl.*

spruce¹ /spruːs/ *a.* pimpant. —*v.t.* ~ **o.s. up,** se faire beau.

spruce² /spruːs/ *n.* (*tree*) épicéa *m.*

sprung /sprʌŋ/ *see* **spring.** —*a.* (*mattress etc.*) à ressorts.

spry /spraɪ/ *a.* (**spryer, spryest**) alerte, vif.

spud /spʌd/ *n.* (*sl.*) patate *f.*

spun /spʌn/ *see* **spin.**

spur /spɜː(r)/ *n.* (*of rider, cock, etc.*) éperon *m.*; (*stimulus*) aiguillon *m.* —*v.t.* (*p.t.* **spurred**) éperonner. **on the** ~ **of the moment,** sous l'impulsion du moment.

spurious /'spjʊərɪəs/ *a.* faux.

spurn /spɜːn/ *v.t.* repousser.

spurt /spɜːt/ *v.i.* jaillir; (*fig.*) accélérer. —*n.* jet *m.*; (*at work*) coup de collier *m.*

spy /spaɪ/ *n.* espion(ne) *m.* (*f.*). —*v.i.* espionner. —*v.t.* apercevoir. ~ **on,** espionner. ~ **out,** reconnaître.

squabble /'skwɒbl/ *v.i.* se chamailler. —*n.* chamaillerie *f.*

squad /skwɒd/ *n.* (*of soldiers etc.*) escouade *f.*; (*sport*) équipe *f.*

squadron /'skwɒdrən/ *n.* (*mil.*) escadron *m.*; (*aviat.*) escadrille *f.*; (*naut.*) escadre *f.*

squal|id /'skwɒlɪd/ *a.* sordide. ~**or** *n.* conditions sordides *f. pl.*

squall /skwɔːl/ *n.* rafale *f.*

squander /'skwɒndə(r)/ *v.t.* (*money, time, etc.*) gaspiller.

square /skweə(r)/ *n.* carré *m.*; (*open space in town*) place *f.*; (*instrument*) équerre *f.* —*a.* carré; (*honest*) honnête; (*meal*) solide; (*fam.*) ringard. (**all**) ~, (*quits*) quitte. —*v.t.* (*settle*) régler. —*v.i.* (*agree*) cadrer (**with,** avec). ~ **up**

to, faire face à. **~ metre,** mètre carré *m.* **~ly** *adv.* carrément.

squash /skwɒʃ/ *v.t.* écraser; (*crowd*) serrer. —*n.* (*game*) squash *m.*; (*marrow: Amer.*) courge *f.* **lemon ~,** citronnade *f.* **orange ~,** orangeade *f.* **~y** *a.* mou.

squat /skwɒt/ *v.i.* (*p.t.* **squatted**) s'accroupir. —*a.* (*dumpy*) trapu. **~ in a house,** squatteriser une maison. **~ter** *n.* squatter *m.*

squawk /skwɔːk/ *n.* cri rauque *m.* —*v.i.* pousser un cri rauque.

squeak /skwiːk/ *n.* petit cri *m.*; (*of door etc.*) grincement *m.* —*v.i.* crier; grincer. **~y** *a.* grinçant.

squeal /skwiːl/ *n.* cri aigu *m.* —*v.i.* pousser un cri aigu. **~ on,** (*inform on: sl.*) dénoncer.

squeamish /'skwiːmɪʃ/ *a.* (trop) délicat, facilement dégoûté.

squeeze /skwiːz/ *v.t.* presser; (*hand, arm*) serrer; (*extract*) exprimer (**from,** de); (*extort*) soutirer (**from,** à). —*v.i.* (*force one's way*) se glisser. —*n.* pression *f.*; (*comm.*) restrictions de crédit *f. pl.*

squelch /skweltʃ/ *v.i.* faire flic flac. —*v.t.* (*suppress*) supprimer.

squid /skwɪd/ *n.* calmar *m.*

squiggle /'skwɪgl/ *n.* ligne onduleuse *f.*

squint /skwɪnt/ *v.i.* loucher; (*with half-shut eyes*) plisser les yeux. —*n.* (*med.*) strabisme *m.*

squire /'skwaɪə(r)/ *n.* propriétaire terrien *m.*

squirm /skwɜːm/ *v.i.* se tortiller.

squirrel /'skwɪrəl, *Amer.* 'skwɜːrəl/ *n.* écureuil *m.*

squirt /skwɜːt/ *v.t./i.* (faire) jaillir. —*n.* jet *m.*

stab /stæb/ *v.t.* (*p.t.* **stabbed**) (*with knife etc.*) poignarder. —*n.* coup (de couteau) *m.* **have a ~ at sth.,** essayer de faire qch.

stabilize /'steɪbəlaɪz/ *v.t.* stabiliser.

stab|le[1] /'steɪbl/ *a.* (-er, -est) stable. **~ility** /stə'bɪlətɪ/ *n.* stabilité *f.*

stable[2] /'steɪbl/ *n.* écurie *f.* **~-boy** *n.* lad *m.*

stack /stæk/ *n.* tas *m.* —*v.t.* **~ (up),** entasser, empiler.

stadium /'steɪdɪəm/ *n.* stade *m.*

staff /stɑːf/ *n.* personnel *m.*; (*in school*) professeurs *m. pl.*; (*mil.*) état-major *m.*; (*stick*) bâton *m.* —*v.t.* pourvoir en personnel.

stag /stæg/ *n.* cerf *m.* **have a ~-party,** enterrer sa vie de garçon.

stage /steɪdʒ/ *n.* (*theatre*) scène *f.*; (*phase*) stade *m.*, étape *f.*; (*platform in hall*) estrade *f.* —*v.t.* mettre en scène; (*fig.*) organiser. **go on the ~,** faire du théâtre. **~-coach** *n.* (*old use*) diligence *f.* **~ door,** entrée des artistes *f.* **~ fright,** trac *m.* **~-manage** *v.t.* monter, organiser. **~-manager** *n.* régisseur *m.*

stagger /'stægə(r)/ *v.i.* chanceler. —*v.t.* (*shock*) stupéfier; (*holidays etc.*) étaler. **~ing** *a.* stupéfiant.

stagnant /'stægnənt/ *a.* stagnant.

stagnat|e /stæg'neɪt/ *v.i.* stagner. **~ion** /-ʃn/ *n.* stagnation *f.*

staid /steɪd/ *a.* sérieux.

stain /steɪn/ *v.t.* tacher; (*wood etc.*) colorer. —*n.* tache *f.*; (*colouring*) colorant *m.* **~ed glass window,** vitrail *m.* **~less steel,** acier inoxydable *m.* **~ remover,** détachant *m.*

stair /steə(r)/ *n.* marche *f.* **the ~s,** l'escalier *m.*

stair|case /'steəkeɪs/, **~way** *ns.* escalier *m.*

stake /steɪk/ *n.* (*post*) pieu *m.*; (*wager*) enjeu *m.* —*v.t.* (*area*) jalonner; (*wager*) jouer. **at ~,** en jeu. **~ a claim to,** revendiquer.

stale /steɪl/ *a.* (-er, -est) pas frais; (*bread*) rassis; (*smell*) de renfermé; (*news*) vieux. **~ness** *n.* manque de fraîcheur *m.*

stalemate /'steɪlmeɪt/ *n.* (*chess*) pat *m.*; (*fig.*) impasse *f.*

stalk[1] /stɔːk/ *n.* (*of plant*) tige *f.*

stalk[2] /stɔːk/ *v.i.* marcher de façon guindée. —*v.t.* (*prey*) traquer.

stall /stɔːl/ *n.* (*in stable*) stalle *f.*; (*in market*) éventaire *m.* **~s,** (*theatre*) orchestre *m.* —*v.t./i.* (*auto.*) caler. **~ (for time),** temporiser.

stallion /'stæljən/ *n.* étalon *m.*

stalwart /'stɔːlwət/ *n.* (*supporter*) partisan(e) fidèle *m.* (*f.*).

stamina /'stæmɪnə/ *n.* résistance *f.*

stammer /'stæmə(r)/ *v.t./i.* bégayer. —*n.* bégaiement *m.*

stamp /stæmp/ *v.t./i.* **~ (one's foot),** taper du pied. —*v.t.* (*letter etc.*) timbrer. —*n.* (*for postage, marking*) timbre *m.*; (*mark: fig.*) sceau *m.* **~collecting** *n.* philatélie *f.* **~ out,** supprimer.

stampede /stæm'piːd/ *n.* fuite désordonnée *f.*; (*rush: fig.*) ruée *f.* —*v.i.* s'enfuir en désordre; se ruer.

stance /stæns/ *n.* position *f.*

stand /stænd/ *v.i.* (*p.t.* **stood**) être *or* se tenir (debout); (*rise*) se lever; (*be* *situated*) se trouver; (*rest*) reposer; (*pol.*) être candidat (**for,** à). —*v.t.* mettre (debout); (*tolerate*) supporter. —*n.* position *f.*; (*mil.*) résistance *f.*; (*for lamp etc.*) support *m.*; (*at fair*) stand *m.*; (*in street*) kiosque *m.*; (*for spectators*) tribune *f.*; (*jurid., Amer.*) barre *f.* **make a** ～, prendre position. ～ **a chance,** avoir une chance. ～ **back,** reculer. ～ **by** or **around,** ne rien faire. ～ **by,** (*be ready*) se tenir prêt; (*promise, person*) rester fidèle à. ～**-by** *a.* de réserve; *n.* **be a** ～**-by,** être de réserve. ～ **down,** se désister. ～ **for,** représenter; (*fam.*) supporter. ～ **in for,** remplacer. ～**-in** *n.* remplaçant(e) *m.* (*f.*). ～ **in line,** (*Amer.*) faire la queue. ～**-offish** *a.* (*fam.*) distant. ～ **out,** (*be conspicuous*) ressortir. ～ **to reason,** être logique. ～ **up,** se lever. ～ **up for,** défendre. ～ **up to,** résister à.

standard /ˈstændəd/ *n.* norme *f.*; (*level*) niveau (voulu) *m.*; (*flag*) étendard *m.* ～**s,** (*morals*) principes *m. pl.* —*a.* ordinaire. ～ **lamp,** lampadaire *m.* ～ **of living,** niveau de vie *m.*

standardize /ˈstændədaɪz/ *v.t.* standardiser.

standing /ˈstændɪŋ/ *a.* debout *invar.*; (*army, offer*) permanent. —*n.* position *f.*, réputation *f.*; (*duration*) durée *f.* ～ **order,** prélèvement bancaire *m.* ～ **room,** places debout *f. pl.*

standpoint /ˈstændpɔɪnt/ *n.* point de vue *m.*

standstill /ˈstændstɪl/ *n.* **at a** ～, immobile. **bring/come to a** ～, (s’)immobiliser.

stank /stæŋk/ *see* **stink**.

stanza /ˈstænzə/ *n.* strophe *f.*

staple[1] /ˈsteɪpl/ *n.* agrafe *f.* —*v.t.* agrafer. ～**r** /-ə(r)/ *n.* agrafeuse *f.*

staple[2] /ˈsteɪpl/ *a.* principal, de base.

star /stɑː(r)/ *n.* étoile *f.*; (*famous person*) vedette *f.* —*v.t.* (*p.t.* **starred**) (*of film*) avoir pour vedette. —*v.i.* ～ **in,** être la vedette de. ～**dom** *n.* célébrité *f.*

starboard /ˈstɑːbəd/ *n.* tribord *m.*

starch /stɑːtʃ/ *n.* amidon *m.*; (*in food*) fécule *f.* —*v.t.* amidonner. ～**y** *a.* féculent; (*stiff*) guindé.

stare /steə(r)/ *v.i.* ～ **at,** regarder fixement. —*n.* regard fixe *m.*

starfish /ˈstɑːfɪʃ/ *n.* étoile de mer *f.*

stark /stɑːk/ *a.* (**-er, -est**) (*desolate*) désolé; (*severe*) austère; (*utter*) complet; (*fact etc.*) brutal. —*adv.* complètement.

starling /ˈstɑːlɪŋ/ *n.* étourneau *m.*

starlit /ˈstɑːlɪt/ *a.* étoilé.

starry /ˈstɑːrɪ/ *a.* étoilé. ～**-eyed** *a.* naïf, (*trop*) optimiste.

start /stɑːt/ *v.t./i.* commencer; (*machine*) (se) mettre en marche; (*fashion etc.*) lancer; (*cause*) provoquer; (*jump*) sursauter; (*of vehicle*) démarrer. —*n.* commencement *m.*, début *m.*; (*of race*) départ *m.*; (*lead*) avance *f.*; (*jump*) sursaut *m.* ～ **to do,** commencer or se mettre à faire. ～ **off doing,** commencer par faire. ～ **out,** partir. ～ **up a business,** lancer une affaire. ～**er** *n.* (*auto.*) démarreur *m.*; (*runner*) partant *m.*; (*culin.*) entrée *f.* ～**ing point,** point de départ *m.* ～**ing tomorrow,** à partir de demain.

startle /ˈstɑːtl/ *v.t.* (*make jump*) faire tressaillir; (*shock*) alarmer.

starv|e /stɑːv/ *v.i.* mourir de faim. —*v.t.* affamer; (*deprive*) priver. ～**ation** /-ˈveɪʃn/ *n.* faim *f.*

stash /stæʃ/ *v.t.* (*hide*: *sl.*) cacher.

state /steɪt/ *n.* état *m.*; (*pomp*) apparat *m.* **S**～, (*pol.*) État *m.* —*a.* d’État, de l’État; (*school*) public. —*v.t.* affirmer (**that,** que); (*views*) exprimer; (*fix*) fixer. **the S**～**s,** les États-Unis. **get into a** ～, s’affoler.

stateless /ˈsteɪtlɪs/ *a.* apatride.

stately /ˈsteɪtlɪ/ *a.* (**-ier, -iest**) majestueux. ～ **home,** château *m.*

statement /ˈsteɪtmənt/ *n.* déclaration *f.*; (*of account*) relevé *m.*

statesman /ˈsteɪtsmən/ *n.* (*pl.* **-men**) homme d’État *m.*

static /ˈstætɪk/ *a.* statique. —*n.* (*radio, TV*) parasites *m. pl.*

station /ˈsteɪʃn/ *n.* station *f.*; (*rail.*) gare *f.*; (*mil.*) poste *m.*; (*rank*) condition *f.* —*v.t.* poster, placer. ～**ed at** or **in,** (*mil.*) en garnison à. ～ **wagon,** (*Amer.*) break *m.*

stationary /ˈsteɪʃnrɪ/ *a.* immobile, stationnaire; (*vehicle*) à l’arrêt.

stationer /ˈsteɪʃnə(r)/ *n.* papetier, -ière *m.*, *f.* ～**’s shop,** papeterie *f.* ～**y** *n.* papeterie *f.*

statistic /stəˈtɪstɪk/ *n.* statistique *f.* ～**s,** statistique *f.* ～**al** *a.* statistique.

statue /ˈstætʃuː/ *n.* statue *f.*

stature /ˈstætʃə(r)/ *n.* stature *f.*

status /ˈsteɪtəs/ *n.* (*pl.* **-uses**) situation *f.*, statut *m.*; (*prestige*) standing *m.* ～ **quo,** statu quo *m.*

statut|e /ˈstætʃuːt/ *n.* loi *f.* ～**es,** (*rules*) statuts *m. pl.* ～**ory** /-ʊtrɪ/ *a.* statutaire; (*holiday*) légal.

staunch /stɔːntʃ/ *a.* (**-er, -est**) (*friend etc.*) loyal, fidèle.

stave /steɪv/ n. (mus.) portée f. —v.t. ~ **off,** éviter, conjurer.

stay /steɪ/ v.i. rester; (spend time) séjourner; (reside) loger. —v.t. (hunger) tromper. —n. séjour m. ~ **away from,** (school etc.) ne pas aller à. ~ **behind/on/late/**etc., rester. ~ **in/out,** rester à la maison/dehors. ~ **up (late),** veiller, se coucher tard.

stead /sted/ n. **stand s.o. in good** ~, être bien utile à qn.

steadfast /'stedfɑːst/ a. ferme.

stead|y /'stedɪ/ a. (-ier, -iest) stable; (hand, voice) ferme; (regular) régulier; (staid) sérieux. —v.t. maintenir, assurer; (calm) calmer. **~ily** adv. fermement; régulièrement.

steak /steɪk/ n. steak m., bifteck m.; (of fish) darne f.

steal /stiːl/ v.t./i. (p.t. **stole,** p.p. **stolen**) voler (from s.o., à qn.).

stealth /stelθ/ n. **by** ~, furtivement. **~y** a. furtif.

steam /stiːm/ n. vapeur f.; (on glass) buée f. —v.t. (cook) cuire à la vapeur; (window) embuer. —v.i. fumer. **~-engine** n. locomotive à vapeur f. ~ **iron,** fer à vapeur m. **~y** a. humide.

steam|er /'stiːmə(r)/ n. (culin.) cuit-vapeur m.; (also **~ship**) (bateau à) vapeur m.

steamroller /'stiːmrəʊlə(r)/ n. rouleau compresseur m.

steel /stiːl/ n. acier m. —v. pr. ~ **o.s.,** s'endurcir, se cuirasser. ~ **industry,** sidérurgie f.

steep[1] /stiːp/ v.t. (soak) tremper. **~ed in,** (fig.) imprégné de.

steep[2] /stiːp/ a. (-er, -est) raide, rapide; (price: fam.) excessif. **~ly** adv. **rise ~ly,** (slope, price) monter rapidement.

steeple /'stiːpl/ n. clocher m.

steeplechase /'stiːpltʃeɪs/ n. (race) steeple(-chase) m.

steer[1] /stɪə(r)/ n. (ox) bouvillon m.

steer[2] /stɪə(r)/ v.t. diriger; (ship) gouverner; (fig.) guider. —v.i. (in ship) gouverner. ~ **clear of,** éviter. **~ing** n. (auto.) direction f. **~ing-wheel** n. volant m.

stem[1] /stem/ n. tige f.; (of glass) pied m. —v.i. (p.t. **stemmed**). ~ **from,** provenir de.

stem[2] /stem/ v.t. (p.t. **stemmed**) (check, stop) endiguer, contenir.

stench /stentʃ/ n. puanteur f.

stencil /'stensl/ n. pochoir m.; (for typing) stencil m. —v.t. (p.t. **stencilled**) (document) polycopier.

stenographer /ste'nɒgrəfə(r)/ n. (Amer.) sténodactylo f.

step /step/ v.i. (p.t. **stepped**) marcher, aller. —v.t. ~ **up,** augmenter. —n. pas m.; (stair) marche f.; (of train) marchepied m.; (action) mesure f. **~s,** (ladder) escabeau m. in ~, au pas; (fig.) conforme (with, à). ~ **down,** (resign) démissionner; (from ladder) descendre. ~ **forward,** (faire un) pas en avant. ~ **up,** (pressure) augmenter. ~ **in,** (intervene) intervenir. **~-ladder** n. escabeau m. **~ping-stone** n. (fig.) tremplin m.

step|brother /'stepbrʌðə(r)/ n. demi-frère m. **~daughter** n. belle-fille f. **~father** n. beau-père m. **~mother** n. belle-mère f. **~sister** n. demi-sœur f. **~son** n. beau-fils m.

stereo /'steriəʊ/ n. (pl. **-os**) stéréo f.; (record-player) chaîne stéréo f. —a. stéréo invar. **~phonic** /-ə'fɒnɪk/ a. stéréophonique.

stereotype /'steriətaɪp/ n. stéréotype m. **~d** a. stéréotypé.

steril|e /'steraɪl, Amer. 'sterəl/ a. stérile. **~ity** /stə'rɪlətɪ/ n. stérilité f.

steriliz|e /'sterəlaɪz/ v.t. stériliser. **~ation** /-'zeɪʃn/ n. stérilisation f.

sterling /'stɜːlɪŋ/ n. livre(s) sterling f. (pl.). —a. sterling invar.; (silver) fin; (fig.) excellent.

stern[1] /stɜːn/ a. (-er, -est) sévère.

stern[2] /stɜːn/ n. (of ship) arrière m.

steroid /'sterɔɪd/ n. stéroïde m.

stethoscope /'steθəskəʊp/ n. stéthoscope m.

stew /stjuː/ v.t./i. cuire à la casserole. —n. ragoût m. **~ed fruit,** compote f. **~ed tea,** thé trop infusé m. **~-pan** n. cocotte f.

steward /stjʊəd/ n. (of club etc.) intendant m.; (on ship etc.) steward m. **~ess** /-'des/ n. hôtesse f.

stick[1] /stɪk/ n. bâton m.; (for walking) canne f.

stick[2] /stɪk/ v.t. (p.t. **stuck**) (glue) coller; (thrust) enfoncer; (put: fam.) mettre; (endure: sl.) supporter. —v.i. (adhere) coller, adhérer; (to pan) attacher; (remain: fam.) rester; (be jammed) être coincé. **be stuck with s.o.,** (fam.) se farcir qn. **~-in-the-mud,** encroûté(e) m. (f.). ~ **at,** persévérer dans. ~ **out** v.t. (head etc.) sortir; (tongue) tirer; v.i. (protrude) dépasser. ~ **to,** (promise etc.) rester fidèle à. ~ **up for,** (fam.) défendre. **~ing-plaster** n. sparadrap m.

sticker /'stɪkə(r)/ n. autocollant m.

stickler /'stɪklə(r)/ *n.* **be a ~ for,** insister sur.

sticky /'stɪkɪ/ *a.* **(-ier, -iest)** poisseux; (*label, tape*) adhésif.

stiff /stɪf/ *a.* **(-er, -est)** raide; (*limb, joint*) ankylosé; (*tough*) dur; (*drink*) fort; (*price*) élevé; (*manner*) guindé. ~ **neck,** torticolis *m.* **~ness** *n.* raideur *f.*

stiffen /'stɪfn/ *v.t./i.* (se) raidir.

stifle /'staɪfl/ *v.t./i.* étouffer.

stigma /'stɪgmə/ *n.* (*pl.* **-as**) stigmate *m.* ~**tize** *v.t.* stigmatiser.

stile /staɪl/ *n.* échalier *m.*

stiletto /stɪ'letəʊ/ *a. & n.* (*pl.* **-os**) ~**s,** ~ **heels** talons aiguille.

still[1] /stɪl/ *a.* immobile; (*quiet*) calme, tranquille. —*n.* silence *m.* —*adv.* encore, toujours; (*even*) encore; (*nevertheless*) tout de même. **keep ~!,** arrête de bouger! **~ life,** nature morte *f.*

still[2] /stɪl/ *n.* (*apparatus*) alambic *m.*

stillborn /'stɪlbɔːn/ *a.* mort-né.

stilted /'stɪltɪd/ *a.* guindé.

stilts /stɪlts/ *n. pl.* échasses *f. pl.*

stimul|ate /'stɪmjʊleɪt/ *v.t.* stimuler. ~**ant** *n.* stimulant *m.* ~**ation** /-'leɪʃn/ *n.* stimulation *f.*

stimulus /'stɪmjʊləs/ *n.* (*pl.* **-li** /-laɪ/) (*spur*) stimulant *m.*

sting /stɪŋ/ *n.* piqûre *f.*; (*organ*) dard *m.* —*v.t./i.* (*p.t.* **stung**) piquer. ~**ing** *a.* (*fig.*) cinglant.

stingy /'stɪndʒɪ/ *a.* **(-ier, -iest)** avare (**with,** de).

stink /stɪŋk/ *n.* puanteur *f.* —*v.i.* (*p.t.* **stank** *or* **stunk,** *p.p.* **stunk**). ~ (**of**), puer. —*v.t.* ~ **out,** (*room etc.*) empester.

stinker /'stɪŋkə(r)/ *n.* (*thing: sl.*) vacherie *f.*; (*person: sl.*) vache *f.*

stint /stɪnt/ *v.i.* ~ **on,** lésiner sur. —*n.* (*work*) tour *m.*

stipulat|e /'stɪpjʊleɪt/ *v.t.* stipuler. ~**ion** /-'leɪʃn/ *n.* stipulation *f.*

stir /stɜː(r)/ *v.t./i.* (*p.t.* **stirred**) (*move*) remuer; (*excite*) exciter. —*n.* agitation *f.* ~ **up,** (*trouble etc.*) provoquer.

stirrup /'stɪrəp/ *n.* étrier *m.*

stitch /stɪtʃ/ *n.* point *m.*; (*in knitting*) maille *f.*; (*med.*) point de suture *m.*; (*muscle pain*) point de côté *m.* —*v.t.* coudre. **be in ~es,** (*fam.*) avoir le fou rire.

stoat /stəʊt/ *n.* hermine *f.*

stock /stɒk/ *n.* réserve *f.*; (*comm.*) stock *m.*; (*financial*) valeurs *f. pl.*; (*family*) souche *f.*; (*soup*) bouillon *m.* —*a.* (*goods*) courant. —*v.t.* (*shop etc.*) approvisionner; (*sell*) vendre. —*v.i.* ~

up, s'approvisionner (**with,** de). ~-**car** *n.* stock-car *m.* ~ **cube,** bouillon-cube *m.* **S~ Exchange,** ~ **market,** Bourse *f.* ~ **phrase,** cliché *m.* ~-**taking** *n.* (*comm.*) inventaire *m.* **in ~,** en stock. **we're out of ~,** il n'y en a plus. **take ~,** (*fig.*) faire le point.

stockbroker /'stɒkbrəʊkə(r)/ *n.* agent de change *m.*

stocking /'stɒkɪŋ/ *n.* bas *m.*

stockist /'stɒkɪst/ *n.* stockiste *m.*

stockpile /'stɒkpaɪl/ *n.* stock *m.* —*v.t.* stocker; (*arms*) amasser.

stocky /'stɒkɪ/ *a.* **(-ier, -iest)** trapu.

stodg|e /stɒdʒ/ *n.* (*fam.*) aliment(s) lourd(s) *m.* (*pl.*). ~**y** *a.* lourd.

stoic /'stəʊɪk/ *n.* stoïque *m./f.* ~**al** *a.* stoïque. ~**ism** /-sɪzəm/ *n.* stoïcisme *m.*

stoke /stəʊk/ *v.t.* (*boiler, fire*) garnir, alimenter.

stole[1] /stəʊl/ *n.* (*garment*) étole *f.*

stole[2], **stolen** /stəʊl, 'stəʊlən/ *see* **steal.**

stolid /'stɒlɪd/ *a.* flegmatique.

stomach /'stʌmək/ *n.* estomac *m.*; (*abdomen*) ventre *m.* —*v.t.* (*put up with*) supporter. ~-**ache** *n.* mal à l'estomac *or* au ventre *m.*

ston|e /stəʊn/ *n.* pierre *f.*; (*pebble*) caillou *m.*; (*in fruit*) noyau *m.*; (*weight*) 6.350 kg. —*a.* de pierre. —*v.t.* lapider; (*fruit*) dénoyauter. ~**e-cold-deaf,** complètement froid/sourd. ~**y** *a.* pierreux. ~**y-broke** *a.* (*sl.*) fauché.

stonemason /'stəʊnmeɪsn/ *n.* maçon *m.*, tailleur de pierre *m.*

stood /stʊd/ *see* **stand.**

stooge /stuːdʒ/ *n.* (*actor*) comparse *m./f.*; (*fig.*) fantoche *m.*, laquais *m.*

stool /stuːl/ *n.* tabouret *m.*

stoop /stuːp/ *v.i.* (*bend*) se baisser; (*condescend*) s'abaisser. —*n.* **have a ~,** être voûté.

stop /stɒp/ *v.t./i.* (*p.t.* **stopped**) arrêter (**doing,** de faire); (*moving, talking*) s'arrêter; (*prevent*) empêcher (**from,** de); (*hole, leak, etc.*) boucher; (*pain, noise, etc.*) cesser; (*stay: fam.*) rester. —*n.* arrêt *m.*; (*full stop*) point *m.* ~ **off,** s'arrêter. ~ **up,** boucher. ~**-over** *n.* (*port of call*) escale *f.* ~-**light** *n.* (*on vehicle*) stop *m.* ~-**watch** *n.* chronomètre *m.*

stopgap /'stɒpgæp/ *n.* bouche-trou *m.* —*a.* intérimaire.

stoppage /'stɒpɪdʒ/ *n.* arrêt *m.*; (*of work*) arrêt de travail *m.*; (*of pay*) retenue *f.*

stopper /'stɒpə(r)/ *n.* bouchon *m.*

storage /'stɔːrɪdʒ/ *n.* (*of goods, food, etc.*) emmagasinage *m.* ~ **heater,**

radiateur électrique à accumulation *m.*
~ **space,** espace de rangement *m.*

store /stɔː(r)/ *n.* réserve *f.*; (*warehouse*)
entrepôt *m.*; (*shop*) grand magasin *m.*;
(*Amer.*) magasin *m.* —*v.t.* (*for future*)
mettre en réserve; (*in warehouse, mind*)
emmagasiner. **have in ~ for,** réserver
à. **set ~ by,** attacher du prix à. ~**-room**
n. réserve *f.*

storey /ˈstɔːrɪ/ *n.* étage *m.*

stork /stɔːk/ *n.* cigogne *f.*

storm /stɔːm/ *n.* tempête *f.*, orage *m.*
—*v.t.* prendre d'assaut. —*v.i.* (*rage*)
tempêter. ~**y** *a.* orageux.

story /ˈstɔːrɪ/ *n.* histoire *f.*; (*in press*)
article *m.*; (*storey: Amer.*) étage *m.* ~
book, livre d'histoires *m.* ~**-teller** *n.*
conteu|r, -se *m.*, *f.*; (*liar: fam.*)
menteu|r, -se *m.*, *f.*

stout /staʊt/ *a.* (**-er, -est**) corpulent;
(*strong*) solide. —*n.* bière brune *f.*
~**ness** *n.* corpulence *f.*

stove /staʊv/ *n.* (*for cooking*) cuisinière
f.; (*heater*) poêle *m.*

stow /staʊ/ *v.t.* ~ **away,** (*put away*)
ranger; (*hide*) cacher. —*v.i.* voyager
clandestinement.

stowaway /ˈstaʊəweɪ/ *n.* passag|er, -ère
clandestin(e) *m.*, *f.*

straddle /ˈstrædl/ *v.t.* être à cheval sur,
enjamber.

straggle /ˈstrægl/ *v.i.* (*lag behind*)
traîner en désordre. ~**r** /-ə(r)/ *n.*
traînard(e) *m.* (*f.*).

straight /streɪt/ *a.* (**-er, -est**) droit; (*tidy*)
en ordre; (*frank*) franc. —*adv.* (*in
straight line*) droit; (*direct*) tout droit.
—*n.* ligne droite *f.* ~ **ahead** *or* **on,** tout
droit. ~ **away,** tout de suite. ~ **face,**
visage sérieux *m.* **get sth. ~,** mettre
qch. au clair. ~ **off,** (*fam.*) sans hésiter.

straighten /ˈstreɪtn/ *v.t.* (*nail, situation,
etc.*) redresser; (*tidy*) arranger.

straightforward /streɪtˈfɔːwəd/ *a.* honnête; (*easy*) simple.

strain[1] /streɪn/ *n.* (*breed*) race *f.*;
(*streak*) tendance *f.*

strain[2] /streɪn/ *v.t.* (*rope, ears*) tendre;
(*limb*) fouler; (*eyes*) fatiguer; (*muscle*)
froisser; (*filter*) passer; (*vegetables*)
égoutter; (*fig.*) mettre à l'épreuve.
—*v.i.* fournir des efforts. —*n.* tension
f.; (*fig.*) effort *m.* ~**s,** (*tune: mus.*)
accents *m. pl.* ~**ed** *a.* forcé; (*relations*)
tendu. ~**er** *n.* passoire *f.*

strait /streɪt/ *n.* détroit *m.* ~**s,** détroit *m.*;
(*fig.*) embarras *m.* ~**-jacket** *n.*
camisole de force *f.* ~**-laced** *a.* collet
monté *invar.*

strand /strænd/ *n.* (*thread*) fil *m.*, brin
m.; (*lock of hair*) mèche *f.*

stranded /ˈstrændɪd/ *a.* (*person*) en
rade; (*ship*) échoué.

strange /streɪndʒ/ *a.* (**-er, -est**) étrange;
(*unknown*) inconnu. ~**ly** *adv.* étrange-
ment. ~**ness** *n.* étrangeté *f.*

stranger /ˈstreɪndʒə(r)/ *n.* inconnu(e) *m.*
(*f.*).

strangle /ˈstræŋgl/ *v.t.* étrangler.

stranglehold /ˈstræŋglhəʊld/ *n.* **have a
~ on,** tenir à la gorge.

strap /stræp/ *n.* (*of leather etc.*) courroie
f.; (*of dress*) bretelle *f.*; (*of watch*)
bracelet *m.* —*v.t.* (*p.t.* **strapped**)
attacher.

strapping /ˈstræpɪŋ/ *a.* costaud.

stratagem /ˈstrætədʒəm/ *n.* stratagème
m.

strategic /strəˈtiːdʒɪk/ *a.* stratégique.

strategy /ˈstrætədʒɪ/ *n.* stratégie *f.*

stratum /ˈstrɑːtəm/ *n.* (*pl.* **strata**)
couche *f.*

straw /strɔː/ *n.* paille *f.* **the last ~,** le
comble.

strawberry /ˈstrɔːbrɪ/ *n.* fraise *f.*

stray /streɪ/ *v.i.* s'égarer; (*deviate*)
s'écarter. —*a.* perdu; (*isolated*) isolé.
—*n.* animal perdu *m.*

streak /striːk/ *n.* raie *f.*, bande *f.*; (*trace*)
trace *f.*; (*period*) période *f.*; (*tendency*)
tendance *f.* —*v.t.* (*mark*) strier. —*v.i.*
filer à toute allure. ~**y** *a.* strié.

stream /striːm/ *n.* ruisseau *m.*; (*current*)
courant *m.*; (*flow*) flot *m.*; (*in schools*)
classe (de niveau) *f.* —*v.i.* ruisseler
(**with,** de); (*eyes, nose*) couler.

streamer /ˈstriːmə(r)/ *n.* (*of paper*)
serpentin *m.*; (*flag*) banderole *f.*

streamline /ˈstriːmlaɪn/ *v.t.* rationaliser.
~**d** *a.* (*shape*) aérodynamique.

street /striːt/ *n.* rue *f.* ~ **lamp,** réverbère
m. ~ **map,** plan des rues *m.*

streetcar /ˈstriːtkɑː(r)/ *n.* (*Amer.*)
tramway *m.*

strength /streŋθ/ *n.* force *f.*; (*of wall,
fabric, etc.*) solidité *f.* **on the ~ of,** en
vertu de.

strengthen /ˈstreŋθn/ *v.t.* renforcer,
fortifier.

strenuous /ˈstrenjʊəs/ *a.* énergique;
(*arduous*) ardu; (*tiring*) fatigant. ~**ly**
adv. énergiquement.

stress /stres/ *n.* accent *m.*; (*pressure*)
pression *f.*; (*med.*) stress *m.* —*v.t.*
souligner, insister sur.

stretch /stretʃ/ *v.t.* (*pull taut*) tendre;
(*arm, leg*) étendre; (*neck*) tendre;
(*clothes*) étirer; (*truth etc.*) forcer.

—*v.i.* s'étendre; (*of person, clothes*) s'étirer. —*n.* étendue *f.*; (*period*) période *f.*; (*of road*) tronçon *m.* —*a.* (*fabric*) extensible. ~ **one's legs,** se dégourdir les jambes. **at a** ~, d'affilée.

stretcher /'stretʃə(r)/ *n.* brancard *m.*

strew /struː/ *v.t.* (*p.t.* **strewed,** *p.p.* **strewed** *or* **strewn**) (*scatter*) répandre; (*cover*) joncher.

stricken /'strɪkən/ *a.* ~ **with,** frappé *or* atteint de.

strict /strɪkt/ *a.* (**-er, -est**) strict. ~**ly** *adv.* strictement. ~**ness** *n.* sévérité *f.*

stride /straɪd/ *v.i.* (*p.t.* **strode,** *p.p.* **stridden**) faire de grands pas. —*n.* grand pas *m.*

strident /'straɪdnt/ *a.* strident.

strife /straɪf/ *n.* conflit(s) *m.* (*pl.*).

strike /straɪk/ *v.t.* (*p.t.* **struck**) frapper; (*blow*) donner; (*match*) frotter; (*gold etc.*) trouver. —*v.i.* faire grève; (*attack*) attaquer; (*clock*) sonner. —*n.* (*of workers*) grève *f.*; (*mil.*) attaque *f.*; (*find*) découverte *f.* **on** ~, en grève. ~ **off** *or* **out,** rayer. ~ **up a friendship,** lier amitié (**with,** avec).

striker /'straɪkə(r)/ *n.* gréviste *m./f.*; (*football*) buteur *m.*

striking /'straɪkɪŋ/ *a.* frappant.

string /strɪŋ/ *n.* ficelle *f.*; (*of violin, racket, etc.*) corde *f.*; (*of pearls*) collier *m.*; (*of lies etc.*) chapelet *m.* —*v.t.* (*p.t.* **strung**) (*thread*) enfiler. **the** ~**s,** (*mus.*) les cordes. ~ **bean,** haricot vert *m.* **pull** ~**s,** faire jouer ses relations, faire marcher le piston. ~ **out,** (s')échelonner. ~**ed** *a.* (*instrument*) à cordes. ~**y** *a.* filandreux.

stringent /'strɪndʒənt/ *a.* rigoureux, strict.

strip¹ /strɪp/ *v.t./i.* (*p.t.* **stripped**) (*undress*) (se) déshabiller; (*machine*) démonter; (*deprive*) dépouiller. ~**per** *n.* strip-teaseuse *f.*; (*solvent*) décapant *m.* ~**-tease** *n.* strip-tease *m.*

strip² /strɪp/ *n.* bande *f.* **comic** ~, bande dessinée *f.* ~ **light,** néon *m.*

stripe /straɪp/ *n.* rayure *f.*, raie *f.* ~**d** *a.* rayé.

strive /straɪv/ *v.i.* (*p.t.* **strove,** *p.p.* **striven**) s'efforcer (**to,** de).

strode /strəud/ *see* **stride**.

stroke¹ /strəuk/ *n.* coup *m.*; (*of pen*) trait *m.*; (*swimming*) nage *f.*; (*med.*) attaque *f.*, congestion *f.* **at a** ~, d'un seul coup.

stroke² /strəuk/ *v.t.* (*with hand*) caresser. —*n.* caresse *f.*

stroll /strəul/ *v.i.* flâner. —*n.* petit tour *m.* ~ **in**/*etc.*, entrer/*etc.* tranquillement. ~**er** *n.* (*Amer.*) poussette *f.*

strong /strɒŋ/ *a.* (**-er, -est**) fort; (*shoes, fabric, etc.*) solide. **be fifty**/*etc.* ~, être au nombre de cinquante/*etc.* ~**-box** *n.* coffre-fort *m.* ~**-minded** *a.* résolu. ~**-room** *n.* chambre forte *f.* ~**ly** *adv.* (*greatly*) fortement; (*with energy*) avec force; (*deeply*) profondément.

stronghold /'strɒŋhəuld/ *n.* bastion *m.*

strove /strəuv/ *see* **strive**.

struck /strʌk/ *see* **strike**. —*a.* ~ **on,** (*sl.*) impressionné par.

structur|e /'strʌktʃə(r)/ *n.* (*of cell, poem, etc.*) structure *f.*; (*building*) construction *f.* ~**al** *a.* structural; de (la) construction.

struggle /'strʌgl/ *v.i.* lutter, se battre. —*n.* lutte *f.*; (*effort*) effort *m.* **have a** ~ **to,** avoir du mal à.

strum /strʌm/ *v.t.* (*p.t.* **strummed**) (*banjo etc.*) gratter de.

strung /strʌŋ/ *see* **string**. —*a.* ~ **up,** (*tense*) nerveux.

strut /strʌt/ *n.* (*support*) étai *m.* —*v.i.* (*p.t.* **strutted**) se pavaner.

stub /stʌb/ *n.* bout *m.*; (*of tree*) souche *f.*; (*counterfoil*) talon *m.* —*v.t.* (*p.t.* **stubbed**). ~ **one's toe,** se cogner le doigt de pied. ~ **out,** écraser.

stubble /'stʌbl/ *n.* (*on chin*) barbe de plusieurs jours *f.*; (*remains of wheat*) chaume *m.*

stubborn /'stʌbən/ *a.* opiniâtre, obstiné. ~**ly** *adv.* obstinément. ~**ness** *n.* opiniâtreté *f.*

stubby /'stʌbɪ/ *a.* (**-ier, -iest**) (*finger*) épais; (*person*) trapu.

stuck /stʌk/ *see* **stick²**. —*a.* (*jammed*) coincé. **I'm** ~, (*for answer*) je sèche. ~**-up** *a.* (*sl.*) prétentieux.

stud¹ /stʌd/ *n.* clou *m.*; (*for collar*) bouton *m.* —*v.t.* (*p.t.* **studded**) clouter. ~**ded with,** parsemé de.

stud² /stʌd/ *n.* (*horses*) écurie *f.* ~**(-farm)** *n.* haras *m.*

student /'stjuːdnt/ *n.* (*univ.*) étudiant(e) *m.* (*f.*); (*schol.*) élève *m./f.* —*a.* (*restaurant, life, residence*) universitaire.

studied /'stʌdɪd/ *a.* étudié.

studio /'stjuːdɪəu/ *n.* (*pl.* **-os**) studio *m.* ~ **flat,** studio *m.*

studious /'stjuːdɪəs/ *a.* (*person*) studieux; (*deliberate*) étudié. ~**ly** *adv.* (*carefully*) avec soin.

study /'stʌdɪ/ *n.* étude *f.*; (*office*) bureau *m.* —*v.t./i.* étudier.

stuff /stʌf/ *n.* substance *f.*; (*sl.*) chose(s) *f.* (*pl.*). —*v.t.* rembourrer; (*animal*) empailler; (*cram*) bourrer; (*culin.*)

farcir; (*block up*) boucher; (*put*) fourrer. ~ing *n.* bourre *f.*; (*culin.*) farce *f.*

stuffy /'stʌfɪ/ *a.* (**-ier, -iest**) mal aéré; (*dull: fam.*) vieux jeu *invar.*

stumbl|e /'stʌmbl/ *v.i.* trébucher. ~e **across** *or* **on,** tomber sur. ~**ing-block** *n.* pierre d'achoppement *f.*

stump /stʌmp/ *n.* (*of tree*) souche *f.*; (*of limb*) moignon *m.*; (*of pencil*) bout *m.*

stumped /stʌmpt/ *a.* (*baffled: fam.*) embarrassé.

stun /stʌn/ *v.t.* (*p.t.* **stunned**) étourdir; (*bewilder*) stupéfier.

stung /stʌŋ/ *see* **sting.**

stunk /stʌŋk/ *see* **stink.**

stunning /'stʌnɪŋ/ *a.* (*delightful: fam.*) sensationnel.

stunt¹ /stʌnt/ *v.t.* (*growth*) retarder. ~**ed** *a.* (*person*) rabougri.

stunt² /stʌnt/ *n.* (*feat: fam.*) tour de force *m.*; (*trick: fam.*) truc *m.*; (*dangerous*) cascade *f.* ~**man** *n.* cascadeur *m.*

stupefy /'stju:pɪfaɪ/ *v.t.* abrutir; (*amaze*) stupéfier.

stupendous /stju:'pendəs/ *a.* prodigieux, formidable.

stupid /'stju:pɪd/ *a.* stupide, bête. ~**ity** /-'pɪdətɪ/ *n.* stupidité *f.* ~**ly** *adv.* stupidement, bêtement.

stupor /'stju:pə(r)/ *n.* stupeur *f.*

sturd|y /'stɜ:dɪ/ *a.* (**-ier, -iest**) robuste. ~**iness** *n.* robustesse *f.*

stutter /'stʌtə(r)/ *v.i.* bégayer. —*n.* bégaiement *m.*

sty¹ /staɪ/ *n.* (*pigsty*) porcherie *f.*

sty² /staɪ/ *n.* (*on eye*) orgelet *m.*

styl|e /staɪl/ *n.* style *m.*; (*fashion*) mode *f.*; (*sort*) genre *m.*; (*pattern*) modèle *m.* —*v.t.* (*design*) créer. **do sth. in** ~**e,** faire qch. avec classe. ~**e s.o.'s hair,** coiffer qn. ~**ist** *n.* (*of hair*) coiffeu|r, -se *m.*, *f.*

stylish /'staɪlɪʃ/ *a.* élégant.

stylized /'staɪlaɪzd/ *a.* stylisé.

stylus /'staɪləs/ *n.* (*pl.* **-uses**) (*of record-player*) saphir *m.*

suave /swɑːv/ *a.* (*urbane*) courtois; (*smooth: pej.*) doucereux.

sub- /sʌb/ *pref.* sous-, sub-.

subconscious /sʌb'kɒnʃəs/ *a.* & *n.* inconscient (*m.*), subconscient (*m.*). ~**ly** *adv.* inconsciemment.

subcontract /sʌbkən'trækt/ *v.t.* soustraiter.

subdivide /sʌbdɪ'vaɪd/ *v.t.* subdiviser.

subdue /səb'dju:/ *v.t.* (*feeling*) maîtriser; (*country*) subjuguer. ~**d** *a.*

(*weak*) faible; (*light*) tamisé; (*person, criticism*) retenu.

subject¹ /'sʌbdʒɪkt/ *a.* (*state etc.*) soumis. —*n.* sujet *m.*; (*schol., univ.*) matière *f.*; (*citizen*) ressortissant(e) *m.* (*f.*), sujet(te) *m.* (*f.*). ~**-matter** *n.* contenu *m.* ~ **to,** soumis à; (*liable to, dependent on*) sujet à.

subject² /səb'dʒekt/ *v.t.* soumettre. ~**ion** /-kʃn/ *n.* soumission *f.*

subjective /səb'dʒektɪv/ *a.* subjectif.

subjunctive /səb'dʒʌŋktɪv/ *a.* & *n.* subjonctif (*m.*).

sublet /sʌb'let/ *v.t.* sous-louer.

sublime /sə'blaɪm/ *a.* sublime.

submarine /sʌbmə'ri:n/ *n.* sousmarin *m.*

submerge /səb'mɜ:dʒ/ *v.t.* submerger. —*v.i.* plonger.

submissive /səb'mɪsɪv/ *a.* soumis.

submi|t /səb'mɪt/ *v.t./i.* (*p.t.* **submitted**) (se) soumettre (**to,** à). ~**ssion** *n.* soumission *f.*

subordinate¹ /sə'bɔ:dɪnət/ *a.* subalterne; (*gram.*) subordonné. —*n.* subordonné(e) *m.* (*f.*).

subordinate² /sə'bɔ:dɪneɪt/ *v.t.* subordonner (**to,** à).

subpoena /səb'pi:nə/ *n.* (*pl.* **-as**) (*jurid.*) citation *f.*, assignation *f.*

subroutine /'sʌbru:ti:n/ *n.* sousprogramme *m.*

subscribe /səb'skraɪb/ *v.t./i.* verser (de l'argent) (**to,** à). ~ **to,** (*loan, theory*) souscrire à; (*newspaper*) s'abonner à, être abonné à. ~**r** /-ə(r)/ *n.* abonné(e) *m.* (*f.*).

subscription /səb'skrɪpʃn/ *n.* souscription *f.*; abonnement *m.*; (*membership dues*) cotisation *f.*

subsequent /'sʌbsɪkwənt/ *a.* (*later*) ultérieur; (*next*) suivant. ~**ly** *adv.* par la suite.

subside /səb'saɪd/ *v.i.* (*land etc.*) s'affaisser; (*flood, wind*) baisser. ~**nce** /-əns/ *n.* affaissement *m.*

subsidiary /səb'sɪdɪərɪ/ *a.* accessoire. —*n.* (*comm.*) filiale *f.*

subsid|y /'sʌbsədɪ/ *n.* subvention *f.* ~**ize** /-ɪdaɪz/ *v.t.* subventionner.

subsist /səb'sɪst/ *v.i.* subsister. ~**ence** *n.* subsistance *f.*

substance /'sʌbstəns/ *n.* substance *f.*

substandard /sʌb'stændəd/ *a.* de qualité inférieure.

substantial /səb'stænʃl/ *a.* considérable; (*meal*) substantiel. ~**ly** *adv.* considérablement.

substantiate /səb'stænʃɪeɪt/ *v.t.* justifier, prouver.

substitut|e /'sʌbstɪtjuːt/ n. succédané m.; (*person*) remplaçant(e) m. (f.). —v.t. substituer (**for**, à). **~ion** /-'tjuːʃn/ n. substitution f.

subterfuge /'sʌbtəfjuːdʒ/ n. subterfuge m.

subterranean /sʌbtə'reɪnɪən/ a. souterrain.

subtitle /'sʌbtaɪtl/ n. sous-titre m.

subtle /'sʌtl/ a. (-**er**, -**est**) subtil. **~ty** n. subtilité f.

subtotal /sʌb'təʊtl/ n. total partiel m.

subtract /səb'trækt/ v.t. soustraire. **~ion** /-kʃn/ n. soustraction f.

suburb /'sʌbɜːb/ n. faubourg m., banlieue f. **~s**, banlieue f. **~an** /sə'bɜːbən/ a. de banlieue.

suburbia /sə'bɜːbɪə/ n. la banlieue.

subversive /səb'vɜːsɪv/ a. subversif.

subver|t /səb'vɜːt/ v.t. renverser. **~sion** /-ʃn/ n. subversion f.

subway /'sʌbweɪ/ n. passage souterrain m.; (*Amer.*) métro m.

succeed /sək'siːd/ v.i. réussir (**in doing**, à faire). —v.t. (*follow*) succéder à. **~ing** a. suivant.

success /sək'ses/ n. succès m., réussite f.

successful /sək'sesfl/ a. réussi, couronné de succès; (*favourable*) heureux; (*in exam*) reçu. **be ~ in doing**, réussir à faire. **~ly** adv. avec succès.

succession /sək'seʃn/ n. succession f. **in ~**, de suite.

successive /sək'sesɪv/ a. successif. **six ~ days**, six jours consécutifs.

successor /sək'sesə(r)/ n. successeur m.

succinct /sək'sɪŋkt/ a. succinct.

succulent /'sʌkjʊlənt/ a. succulent.

succumb /sə'kʌm/ v.i. succomber.

such /sʌtʃ/ a. & pron. tel(le), tel(le)s; (*so much*) tant (de). —adv. si. **~ a book**/etc., un tel livre/etc. **~ books**/etc., de tels livres/etc. **~ courage**/etc., tant de courage/etc. **~ a big house**, une si grande maison. **~ as**, comme, tel que. **as ~**, en tant que tel. **there's no ~ thing**, ça n'existe pas. **~-and-such** a. tel ou tel.

suck /sʌk/ v.t. sucer. **~ in** or **up**, aspirer. **~er** n. (*rubber pad*) ventouse f.; (*person: sl.*) dupe f.

suction /'sʌkʃn/ n. succion f.

sudden /'sʌdn/ a. soudain, subit. **all of a ~**, tout à coup. **~ly** adv. subitement, brusquement. **~ness** n. soudaineté f.

suds /sʌdz/ n. pl. (*froth*) mousse de savon f.

sue /suː/ v.t. (*pres. p.* **suing**) poursuivre (en justice).

suede /sweɪd/ n. daim m.

suet /'suːɪt/ n. graisse de rognon f.

suffer /'sʌfə(r)/ v.t./i. souffrir; (*loss, attack, etc.*) subir. **~er** n. victime f., malade m./f. **~ing** n. souffrance(s) f. (pl.).

suffice /sə'faɪs/ v.i. suffire.

sufficient /sə'fɪʃnt/ a. (*enough*) suffisamment de; (*big enough*) suffisant. **~ly** adv. suffisamment.

suffix /'sʌfɪks/ n. suffixe m.

suffocat|e /'sʌfəkeɪt/ v.t./i. suffoquer. **~ion** /-'keɪʃn/ n. suffocation f.; (*med.*) asphyxie f.

suffused /sə'fjuːzd/ a. **~ with**, (*light, tears*) baigné de.

sugar /'ʃʊgə(r)/ n. sucre m. —v.t. sucrer. **~y** a. sucré.

suggest /sə'dʒest/ v.t. suggérer. **~ion** /-tʃn/ n. suggestion f.

suggestive /sə'dʒestɪv/ a. suggestif. **be ~ of**, suggérer.

suicid|e /'suːɪsaɪd/ n. suicide m. **commit ~e**, se suicider. **~al** /-'saɪdl/ a. suicidaire.

suit /suːt/ n. costume m.; (*woman's*) tailleur m.; (*cards*) couleur f. —v.t. convenir à; (*of garment, style, etc.*) aller à; (*adapt*) adapter. **~ability** n. (*of action etc.*) à-propos m.; (*of candidate*) aptitude(s) f. (pl.). **~able** a. qui convient (**for**, à), convenable. **~ably** adv. convenablement. **~ed** a. (**well**) **~ed**, (*matched*) bien assorti. **~ed to**, fait pour, apte à.

suitcase /'suːtkeɪs/ n. valise f.

suite /swiːt/ n. (*rooms, retinue*) suite f.; (*furniture*) mobilier m.

suitor /'suːtə(r)/ n. soupirant m.

sulfur /'sʌlfər/ n. (*Amer.*) = **sulphur**.

sulk /sʌlk/ v.i. bouder. **~y** a. boudeur, maussade.

sullen /'sʌlən/ a. maussade. **~ly** adv. d'un air maussade.

sulphur /'sʌlfə(r)/ n. soufre m. **~ic** /-'fjʊərɪk/ a. **~ic acid**, acide sulfurique m.

sultan /'sʌltən/ n. sultan m.

sultana /sʌl'tɑːnə/ n. raisin de Smyrne m., raisin sec m.

sultry /'sʌltrɪ/ a. (-**ier**, -**iest**) étouffant, lourd; (*fig.*) sensuel.

sum /sʌm/ n. somme f.; (*in arithmetic*) calcul m. —v.t./i. (*p.t.* **summed**). **~ up**, résumer, récapituler; (*assess*) évaluer.

summar|y /'sʌmərɪ/ n. résumé m. —a. sommaire. **~ize** v.t. résumer.

summer /'sʌmə(r)/ n. été m. —a. d'été. **~-time** n. (*season*) été m. **~y** a. estival.

summit /'sʌmɪt/ n. sommet m. ∼ **(conference),** (pol.) (conférence f. au) sommet m.

summon /'sʌmən/ v.t. appeler; (meeting, s.o. to meeting) convoquer. ∼ **up,** (strength, courage, etc.) rassembler.

summons /'sʌmənz/ n. (jurid.) assignation f. —v.t. assigner.

sump /sʌmp/ n. (auto.) carter m.

sumptuous /'sʌmptʃʊəs/ a. somptueux, luxueux.

sun /sʌn/ n. soleil m. —v.t. (p.t. sunned). ∼ **o.s.,** se chauffer au soleil. ∼**-glasses** n. pl. lunettes de soleil f. pl. ∼**-roof** n. toit ouvrant m. ∼**-tan** n. bronzage m. ∼**-tanned** a. bronzé.

sunbathe /'sʌnbeɪð/ v.i. prendre un bain de soleil.

sunburn /'sʌnbɜːn/ n. coup de soleil m. ∼**t** a. brûlé par le soleil.

Sunday /'sʌndɪ/ n. dimanche m. ∼ **school,** catéchisme m.

sundial /'sʌndaɪəl/ n. cadran solaire m.

sundown /'sʌndaʊn/ n. = sunset.

sundr|y /'sʌndrɪ/ a. divers. ∼**ies** n. pl. articles divers m. pl. **all and ∼y,** tout le monde.

sunflower /'sʌnflaʊə(r)/ n. tournesol m.

sung /sʌŋ/ see sing.

sunk /sʌŋk/ see sink.

sunken /'sʌŋkən/ a. (ship etc.) submergé; (eyes) creux.

sunlight /'sʌnlaɪt/ n. soleil m.

sunny /'sʌnɪ/ a. (-ier, -iest) (room, day, etc.) ensoleillé.

sunrise /'sʌnraɪz/ n. lever du soleil m.

sunset /'sʌnset/ n. coucher du soleil m.

sunshade /'sʌnʃeɪd/ n. (lady's) ombrelle f.; (awning) parasol m.

sunshine /'sʌnʃaɪn/ n. soleil m.

sunstroke /'sʌnstrəʊk/ n. insolation f.

super /'suːpə(r)/ a. (sl.) formidable.

superb /suː'pɜːb/ a. superbe.

supercilious /suːpə'sɪlɪəs/ a. hautain, dédaigneux.

superficial /suːpə'fɪʃl/ a. superficiel. ∼**ity** /-ɪ'ælətɪ/ n. caractère superficiel m. ∼**ly** adv. superficiellement.

superfluous /suː'pɜːfluəs/ a. superflu.

superhuman /suːpə'hjuːmən/ a. surhumain.

superimpose /suːpərɪm'pəʊz/ v.t. superposer (**on,** à).

superintendent /suːpərɪn'tendənt/ n. direc|teur, -trice m., f.; (of police) commissaire m.

superior /suː'pɪərɪə(r)/ a. & n. supérieur(e) (m. (f.)). ∼**ity** /-'ɒrɪtɪ/ n. supériorité f.

superlative /suː'pɜːlətɪv/ a. suprême. —n. (gram.) superlatif m.

superman /'suːpəmæn/ n. (pl. **-men**) surhomme m.

supermarket /'suːpəmɑːkɪt/ n. supermarché m.

supernatural /suːpə'nætʃrəl/ a. surnaturel.

superpower /'suːpəpaʊə(r)/ n. superpuissance f.

supersede /suːpə'siːd/ v.t. remplacer, supplanter.

supersonic /suːpə'sɒnɪk/ a. supersonique.

superstiti|on /suːpə'stɪʃn/ n. superstition f. ∼**ous** a. superstitieux.

superstore /'suːpəstɔː(r)/ n. hypermarché m.

supertanker /'suːpətæŋkə(r)/ n. pétrolier géant m.

supervis|e /'suːpəvaɪz/ v.t. surveiller, diriger. ∼**ion** /-'vɪʒn/ n. surveillance f. ∼**or** n. surveillant(e) m. (f.); (shop) chef de rayon m.; (firm) chef de service m. ∼**ory** /-'vaɪzərɪ/ a. de surveillance.

supper /'sʌpə(r)/ n. dîner m.; (late at night) souper m.

supple /'sʌpl/ a. souple.

supplement[1] /'sʌplɪmənt/ n. supplément m. ∼**ary** /-'mentrɪ/ a. supplémentaire.

supplement[2] /'sʌplɪment/ v.t. compléter.

supplier /sə'plaɪə(r)/ n. fournisseur m.

suppl|y /sə'plaɪ/ v.t. fournir; (equip) pourvoir; (feed) alimenter (**with,** en). —n. provision f.; (of gas etc.) alimentation f. ∼**ies,** (food) vivres m. pl.; (material) fournitures f. pl. ∼**y teacher,** (professeur) suppléant(e) m. (f.).

support /sə'pɔːt/ v.t. soutenir; (family) assurer la subsistance de; (endure) supporter. —n. soutien m., appui m.; (techn.) support m. ∼**er** n. partisan(e) m. (f.); (sport) supporter m. ∼**ive** a. qui soutient et encourage.

suppos|e /sə'pəʊz/ v.t./i. supposer. **be ∼ed to do,** être censé faire, devoir faire. ∼**ing he comes,** supposons qu'il vienne. ∼**ition** /sʌpə'zɪʃn/ n. supposition f.

supposedly /sə'pəʊzɪdlɪ/ adv. soi-disant, prétendument.

suppress /sə'pres/ v.t. (put an end to) supprimer; (restrain) réprimer; (stifle) étouffer. ∼**ion** /-ʃn/ n. suppression f.; répression f.

suprem|e /suː'priːm/ a. suprême. ∼**acy** /-eməsɪ/ n. suprématie f.

surcharge /'sɜːtʃɑːdʒ/ n. prix supplémentaire m.; (tax) surtaxe f.; (on stamp) surcharge f.

sure /ʃɔː(r)/ a. (-er, -est) sûr. —adv. (Amer., fam.) pour sûr. **make ~ of**, s'assurer de. **make ~ that**, vérifier que. **~ly** adv. sûrement.

surety /ʃɔːrəti/ n. caution f.

surf /sɜːf/ n. (waves) ressac m. **~ing** n. surf m.

surface /'sɜːfɪs/ n. surface f. —a. superficiel. —v.t. revêtir. —v.i. faire surface; (fig.) réapparaître. **~ mail**, courrier maritime m.

surfboard /'sɜːfbɔːd/ n. planche de surf f.

surfeit /'sɜːfɪt/ n. excès m. (of, de).

surge /sɜːdʒ/ v.i. (of crowd) déferler; (of waves) s'enfler; (increase) monter. —n. (wave) vague f.; (rise) montée f.

surgeon /'sɜːdʒən/ n. chirurgien m.

surg|ery /'sɜːdʒərɪ/ n. chirurgie f.; (office) cabinet m.; (session) consultation f. **need ~ery**, devoir être opéré. **~ical** a. chirurgical. **~ical spirit**, alcool à 90 degrés m.

surly /'sɜːlɪ/ a. (-ier, -iest) bourru.

surmise /sə'maɪz/ v.t. conjecturer. —n. conjecture f.

surmount /sə'maʊnt/ v.t. (overcome, cap) surmonter.

surname /'sɜːneɪm/ n. nom de famille m.

surpass /sə'pɑːs/ v.t. surpasser.

surplus /'sɜːpləs/ n. surplus m. —a. en surplus.

surpris|e /sə'praɪz/ n. surprise f. —v.t. surprendre. **~ed** a. surpris (at, de). **~ing** a. surprenant. **~ingly** adv. étonnamment.

surrender /sə'rendə(r)/ v.i. se rendre. —v.t. (hand over) remettre; (mil.) rendre. —n. (mil.) reddition f.; (of passport etc.) remise f.

surreptitious /sʌrəp'tɪʃəs/ a. subreptice, furtif.

surround /sə'raʊnd/ v.t. entourer; (mil.) encercler. **~ing** a. environnant. **~ings** n. pl. environs m. pl.; (setting) cadre m.

surveillance /sɜː'veɪləns/ n. surveillance f.

survey¹ /sə'veɪ/ v.t. (review) passer en revue; (inquire into) enquêter sur; (building) inspecter. **~or** n. expert (géomètre) m.

survey² /'sɜːveɪ/ n. (inquiry) enquête f.; inspection f.; (general view) vue d'ensemble f.

survival /sə'vaɪvl/ n. survie f.; (relic) vestige m.

surviv|e /sə'vaɪv/ v.t./i. survivre (à). **~or** n. survivant(e) m. (f.).

susceptib|le /sə'septəbl/ a. sensible (to, à). **~le to**, (prone to) prédisposé à. **~ility** /-'bɪlətɪ/ n. sensibilité f.; prédisposition f.

suspect¹ /sə'spekt/ v.t. soupçonner; (doubt) douter de.

suspect² /'sʌspekt/ n. & a. suspect(e) (m. (f.)).

suspen|d /sə'spend/ v.t. (hang, stop) suspendre; (licence) retirer provisoirement. **~ded sentence**, condamnation avec sursis f. **~sion** n. suspension f.; retrait provisoire m. **~sion bridge**, pont suspendu m.

suspender /sə'spendə(r)/ n. jarretelle f. **~s**, (braces: Amer.) bretelles f. pl. **~ belt**, porte-jarretelles m.

suspense /sə'spens/ n. attente f.; (in book etc.) suspense m.

suspicion /sə'spɪʃn/ n. soupçon m.; (distrust) méfiance f.

suspicious /sə'spɪʃəs/ a. soupçonneux; (causing suspicion) suspect. **be ~ of**, (distrust) se méfier de. **~ly** adv. de façon suspecte.

sustain /sə'steɪn/ v.t. supporter; (effort etc.) soutenir; (suffer) subir.

sustenance /'sʌstɪnəns/ n. (food) nourriture f.; (quality) valeur nutritive f.

swab /swɒb/ n. (pad) tampon m.

swagger /'swægə(r)/ v.i. (walk) se pavaner, parader.

swallow¹ /'swɒləʊ/ v.t./i. avaler. **~ up**, (absorb, engulf) engloutir.

swallow² /'swɒləʊ/ n. hirondelle f.

swam /swæm/ see swim.

swamp /swɒmp/ n. marais m. —v.t. (flood, overwhelm) submerger. **~y** a. marécageux.

swan /swɒn/ n. cygne m. **~-song** n. (fig.) chant du cygne m.

swank /swæŋk/ n. (behaviour: fam.) épate f., esbroufe f.; (person: fam.) crâneu|r, -se m., f. —v.i. (show off: fam.) crâner.

swap /swɒp/ v.t./i. (p.t. swapped) (fam.) échanger. —n. (fam.) échange m.

swarm /swɔːm/ n. (of insects, people) essaim m. —v.i. fourmiller. **~ into or round**, (crowd) envahir.

swarthy /'swɔːðɪ/ a. (-ier, -iest) noiraud; (complexion) basané.

swastika /'swɒstɪkə/ n. (Nazi) croix gammée f.

swat /swɒt/ v.t. (p.t. swatted) (fly etc.) écraser.

sway /sweɪ/ v.t./i. (se) balancer; (influence) influencer. —n. balancement m.; (rule) empire m.

swear /sweə(r)/ v.t./i. (p.t. **swore**, p.p. **sworn**) jurer (**to sth.**, de qch.). ~ **at**, injurier. ~ **by sth.**, (fam.) ne jurer que par qch. ~**word** n. juron m.

sweat /swet/ n. sueur f. —v.i. suer. ~-**shirt** n. sweat-shirt m. ~**y** a. en sueur.

sweater /'swetə(r)/ n. pull-over m.

swede /swi:d/ n. rutabaga m.

Swed|e /swi:d/ n. Suédois(e) m. (f.). ~**en** n. Suède f. ~**ish** a. suédois; n. (lang.) suédois m.

sweep /swi:p/ v.t./i. (p.t. **swept**) balayer; (carry away) emporter, entraîner; (chimney) ramoner. —n. coup de balai m.; (curve) courbe f.; (mouvement) geste m., mouvement m.; (for chimneys) ramoneur m. ~ **by**, passer rapidement or majestueusement. ~ **out**, balayer. ~**er** n. (for carpet) balai mécanique m.; (football) arrière volant m. ~**ing** a. (gesture) large; (action) qui va loin; (statement) trop général.

sweet /swi:t/ a. (-er, -est) (not sour, pleasant) doux; (not savoury) sucré; (charming: fam.) gentil. —n. bonbon m.; (dish) dessert m.; (person) chéri(e) m. (f.). **have a ~ tooth,** aimer les sucreries. ~ **corn,** maïs m. ~ **pea,** pois de senteur m. ~ **shop,** confiserie f. ~**ly** adv. gentiment. ~**ness** n. douceur f.; goût sucré m.

sweeten /'swi:tn/ v.t. sucrer; (fig.) adoucir. ~**er** n. édulcorant m.

sweetheart /'swi:thɑ:t/ n. petit(e) ami(e) m. (f.); (term of endearment) chéri(e) m. (f.).

swell /swel/ v.t./i. (p.t. **swelled**, p.p. **swollen** or **swelled**) (increase) grossir; (expand) (se) gonfler; (of hand, face) enfler. —n. (of sea) houle f. —a. (fam.) formidable. ~**ing** n. (med.) enflure f.

swelter /'sweltə(r)/ v.i. étouffer. ~**ing** a. étouffant.

swept /swept/ see **sweep**.

swerve /swɜ:v/ v.i. faire un écart.

swift /swift/ a. (-er, -est) rapide. —n. (bird) martinet m. ~**ly** adv. rapidement. ~**ness** n. rapidité f.

swig /swig/ v.t. (p.t. **swigged**) (drink: fam.) lamper. —n. (fam.) lampée f., coup m.

swill /swil/ v.t. rincer; (drink) lamper. —n. (pig-food) pâtée f.

swim /swim/ v.i. (p.t. **swam**, p.p. **swum**, pres. p. **swimming**) nager; (be dizzy) tourner. —v.t. traverser à la nage; (distance) nager. —n. baignade f. **go for a ~,** aller se baigner. ~**mer** n.

nageur, -se m., f. ~**ming** n. natation f. ~**ming-bath**, ~**ming-pool** ns. piscine f. ~**suit** n. maillot (de bain) m.

swindle /'swindl/ v.t. escroquer. —n. escroquerie f. ~**r** /-ə(r)/ n. escroc m.

swine /swain/ n. pl. (pigs) pourceaux m. pl. —n. invar. (person: fam.) salaud m.

swing /swiŋ/ v.t./i. (p.t. **swung**) (se) balancer; (turn round) tourner; (of pendulum) osciller. —n. balancement m.; (seat) balançoire f.; (of opinion) revirement m. (**towards,** en faveur de); (mus.) rythme m. **be in full ~,** battre son plein. ~ **round,** (of person) se retourner.

swingeing /'swindʒiŋ/ a. écrasant.

swipe /swaip/ v.t. (hit: fam.) frapper; (steal: fam.) piquer. —n. (hit: fam.) grand coup m.

swirl /swɜ:l/ v.i. tourbillonner. —n. tourbillon m.

swish /swiʃ/ v.i. (hiss) siffler, cingler l'air. —a. (fam.) chic invar.

Swiss /swis/ a. suisse. —n. invar. Suisse(sse) m. (f.).

switch /switʃ/ n. bouton (électrique) m., interrupteur m.; (shift) changement m., revirement m. —v.t. (transfer) transférer; (exchange) échanger (**for,** contre); (reverse positions of) changer de place. ~ **trains/**etc., (change) changer de train/etc. —v.i. (go over) passer. ~ **off,** éteindre. ~ **on,** mettre, allumer.

switchback /'switʃbæk/ n. montagnes russes f. pl.

switchboard /'switʃbɔ:d/ n. (telephone) standard m.

Switzerland /'switsələnd/ n. Suisse f.

swivel /'swivl/ v.t./i. (p.t. **swivelled**) (faire) pivoter.

swollen /'swəʊlən/ see **swell**.

swoon /swu:n/ v.i. se pâmer.

swoop /swu:p/ v.i. (bird) fondre; (police) faire une descente, foncer. —n. (police raid) descente f.

sword /sɔ:d/ n. épée f.

swore /swɔ:(r)/ see **swear**.

sworn /swɔ:n/ see **swear**. —a. (enemy) juré; (ally) dévoué.

swot /swɒt/ v.t./i. (p.t. **swotted**) (study: sl.) bûcher. —n. (sl.) bûcheur, -se m., f.

swum /swʌm/ see **swim**.

swung /swʌŋ/ see **swing**.

sycamore /'sikəmɔ:(r)/ n. (maple) sycomore m.; (Amer.) platane m.

syllable /'siləbl/ n. syllabe f.

syllabus /'siləbəs/ n. (pl. **-uses**) (schol., univ.) programme m.

symbol /'sımbl/ *n.* symbole *m.* ∼**ic(al)** /-'bɒlık(l)/ *a.* symbolique. ∼**ism** *n.* symbolisme *m.*

symbolize /'sımbəlaız/ *v.t.* symboliser.

symmetr|y /'sımətrı/ *n.* symétrie *f.* ∼**ical** /sı'metrıkl/ *a.* symétrique.

sympathize /'sımpəθaız/ *v.i.* ∼ **with**, (*pity*) plaindre; (*fig.*) comprendre les sentiments de. ∼**r** /ə(r)/ *n.* sympathisant(e) *m.* (*f.*).

sympath|y /'sımpəθı/ *n.* (*pity*) compassion *f.*; (*fig.*) compréhension *f.*; (*solidarity*) solidarité *f.*; (*condolences*) condoléances *f. pl.* **be in** ∼**y with**, comprendre, être en accord avec. ∼**etic** /-'θetık/ *a.* compatissant; (*fig.*) compréhensif. ∼**etically** /-'θetıklı/ *adv.* avec compassion; (*fig.*) avec compréhension.

symphon|y /'sımfənı/ *n.* symphonie *f.* —*a.* symphonique. ∼**ic** /-'fɒnık/ *a.* symphonique.

symposium /sım'pəʊzıəm/ *n.* (*pl.* -**ia**) symposium *m.*

symptom /'sımptəm/ *n.* symptôme *m.* ∼**atic** /-'mætık/ *a.* symptomatique (**of**, de).

synagogue /'sınəgɒg/ *n.* synagogue *f.*

synchronize /'sıŋkrənaız/ *v.t.* synchroniser.

syndicate /'sındıkət/ *n.* syndicat *m.*

syndrome /'sındrəʊm/ *n.* syndrome *m.*

synonym /'sınənım/ *n.* synonyme *m.* ∼**ous** /sı'nɒnıməs/ *a.* synonyme.

synopsis /sı'nɒpsıs/ *n.* (*pl.* -**opses** /-sı:z/) résumé *m.*

syntax /'sıntæks/ *n.* syntaxe *f.*

synthesis /'sınθəsıs/ *n.* (*pl.* -**theses** /-sı:z/) synthèse *f.*

synthetic /sın'θetık/ *a.* synthétique.

syphilis /'sıfılıs/ *n.* syphilis *f.*

Syria /'sırıə/ *n.* Syrie *f.* ∼**n** *a.* & *n.* syrien(ne) (*m.* (*f.*)).

syringe /sı'rındʒ/ *n.* seringue *f.*

syrup /'sırəp/ *n.* (*liquid*) sirop *m.*; (*treacle*) mélasse raffinée *f.* ∼**y** *a.* sirupeux.

system /'sıstəm/ *n.* système *m.*; (*body*) organisme *m.*; (*order*) méthode *f.* ∼**s analyst**, analyste-programmeu|r, -se *m.*, *f.* ∼**s disk**, disque système *m.*

systematic /sıstə'mætık/ *a.* systématique.

T

tab /tæb/ *n.* (*flap*) languette *f.*, patte *f.*;

(*loop*) attache *f.*; (*label*) étiquette *f.*; (*Amer.*, *fam.*) addition *f.* **keep** ∼**s on**, (*fam.*) surveiller.

table /'teıbl/ *n.* table *f.* —*v.t.* présenter; (*postpone*) ajourner. —*a.* (*lamp, wine*) de table. **at** ∼, à table. **lay** *or* **set the** ∼, mettre la table. ∼**-cloth** *n.* nappe *f.* ∼**mat** *n.* dessous-de-plat *m. invar.*; (*cloth*) set *m.* ∼ **of contents**, table des matières *f.* ∼ **tennis**, ping-pong *m.*

tablespoon /'teıblspu:n/ *n.* cuiller à soupe *f.* ∼**ful** *n.* (*pl.* ∼**fuls**) cuillerée à soupe *f.*

tablet /'tæblıt/ *n.* (*of stone*) plaque *f.*; (*drug*) comprimé *m.*

tabloid /'tæblɔıd/ *n.* tabloïd *m.* **the** ∼ **press**, la presse populaire.

taboo /tə'bu:/ *n.* & *a.* tabou (*m.*).

tabulator /'tæbjʊleıtə(r)/ *n.* (*on typewriter*) tabulateur *m.*

tacit /'tæsıt/ *a.* tacite.

taciturn /'tæsıtɜ:n/ *a.* taciturne.

tack /tæk/ *n.* (*nail*) broquette *f.*; (*stitch*) point de bâti *m.*; (*course of action*) voie *f.* —*v.t.* (*nail*) clouer; (*stitch*) bâtir; (*add*) ajouter. —*v.i.* (*naut.*) louvoyer.

tackle /'tækl/ *n.* équipement *m.*, matériel *m.*; (*football*) plaquage *m.* —*v.t.* (*problem etc.*) s'attaquer à; (*football player*) plaquer.

tacky /'tækı/ *a.* (-**ier, -iest**) poisseux, pas sec; (*shabby, mean*: *Amer.*) moche.

tact /tækt/ *n.* tact *m.* ∼**ful** *a.* plein de tact. ∼**fully** *adv.* avec tact. ∼**less** *a.* qui manque de tact. ∼**lessly** *adv.* sans tact.

tactic /'tæktık/ *n.* tactique *f.* ∼**s** *n.* & *n. pl.* tactique *f.* ∼**al** *a.* tactique.

tactile /'tæktaıl/ *a.* tactile.

tadpole /'tædpəʊl/ *n.* têtard *m.*

tag /tæg/ *n.* (*label*) étiquette *f.*; (*end piece*) bout *m.*; (*phrase*) cliché *m.* —*v.t.* (*p.t.* **tagged**) étiqueter; (*join*) ajouter. —*v.i.* ∼ **along**, (*fam.*) suivre.

tail /teıl/ *n.* queue *f.*; (*of shirt*) pan *m.* ∼**s**, (*coat*) habit *m.* ∼**s!**, (*tossing coin*) pile! —*v.t.* (*follow*) filer. —*v.i.* ∼ **away** *or* **off**, diminuer. ∼**-back** *n.* (*traffic*) bouchon *m.* ∼**-end** *n.* fin *f.*, bout *m.* ∼**gate** *n.* hayon arrière *m.*

tailcoat /'teılkəʊt/ *n.* habit *m.*

tailor /'teılə(r)/ *n.* tailleur *m.* —*v.t.* (*garment*) façonner; (*fig.*) adapter. ∼**made** *a.* fait sur mesure. ∼**-made for**, (*fig.*) fait pour.

tainted /'teıntıd/ *a.* (*infected*) infecté; (*decayed*) gâté; (*fig.*) souillé.

take /teık/ *v.t./i.* (*p.t.* **took**, *p.p.* **taken**) prendre; (*carry*) (ap)porter (**to**, à);

(*escort*) accompagner, amener; (*contain*) contenir; (*tolerate*) supporter; (*prize*) remporter; (*exam*) passer; (*choice*) faire; (*precedence*) avoir. ~ sth. from s.o., prendre qch. à qn. ~ sth. from a place, prendre qch. d'un endroit. ~ s.o. home, ramener qn. chez lui. be ~n by or with, impressionné par. be ~n ill, tomber malade. it ~s time/courage/*etc.* to, il faut du temps/du courage/*etc.* pour. ~ after, ressembler à. ~ apart, démonter. ~ away, (*object*) emporter; (*person*) emmener; (*remove*) enlever (from, à). ~-away n. (*meal*) plat à emporter m.; (*shop*) restaurant qui fait des plats à emporter m. ~ back, reprendre; (*return*) rendre; (*accompany*) raccompagner; (*statement*) retirer. ~ down, (*object*) descendre; (*notes*) prendre. ~ in, (*object*) rentrer; (*include*) inclure; (*cheat*) tromper; (*grasp*) saisir. ~ it that, supposer que. ~ off v.t. enlever; (*mimic*) imiter; v.i. (*aviat.*) décoller. ~-off n. imitation f.; (*aviat.*) décollage m. ~ on, (*task, staff, passenger, etc.*) prendre; (*challenger*) relever le défi de. ~ out, (*stain etc.*) enlever. ~ over v.t. (*factory, country, etc.*) prendre la direction de; (*firm: comm.*) racheter; v.i. (*of dictator*) prendre le pouvoir. ~ over from, (*relieve*) prendre la relève de; (*succeed*) prendre la succession de. ~-over n. (*pol.*) prise de pouvoir f.; (*comm.*) rachat m. ~ part, participer (in, à). ~ place, avoir lieu. ~ sides, prendre parti (with, pour). ~ to, se prendre d'amitié pour; (*activity*) prendre goût à. ~ to doing, se mettre à faire. ~ up, (*object*) monter; (*hobby*) se mettre à; (*occupy*) prendre; (*resume*) reprendre. ~ up with, se lier avec.
takings /'teɪkɪŋz/ n. pl. recette f.
talcum /'tælkəm/ n. talc m. ~ **powder**, talc m.
tale /teɪl/ n. conte m.; (*report*) récit m.; (*lie*) histoire f.
talent /'tælənt/ n. talent m. ~**ed** a. doué, qui a du talent.
talk /tɔːk/ v.t./i. parler; (*say*) dire; (*chat*) bavarder. —n. conversation f., entretien m.; (*words*) propos m. pl.; (*lecture*) exposé m. ~ **into doing**, persuader de faire. ~ **over**, discuter (de). ~-**show** n. talk-show m. ~**er** n. causeur, -se m., f. ~**ing-to** n. (*fam.*) réprimande f.
talkative /tɔːkətɪv/ a. bavard.
tall /tɔːl/ a. (-er, -est) (*high*) haut;

(*person*) grand. ~ **story**, (*fam.*) histoire invraisemblable f.
tallboy /'tɔːlbɔɪ/ n. commode f.
tally /'tælɪ/ v.i. correspondre (**with**, à), s'accorder (**with**, avec).
tambourine /tæmbə'riːn/ n. tambourin m.
tame /teɪm/ a. (-er, -est) apprivoisé; (*dull*) insipide. —v.t. apprivoiser; (*lion*) dompter. ~**r** /-ə(r)/ n. dompteur, -se m., f.
tamper /'tæmpə(r)/ v.i. ~ **with**, toucher à, tripoter; (*text*) altérer.
tampon /'tæmpɒn/ n. (*med.*) tampon hygiénique m.
tan /tæn/ v.t./i. (p.t. **tanned**) bronzer; (*hide*) tanner. —n. bronzage m. —a. marron clair invar.
tandem /'tændəm/ n. (*bicycle*) tandem m. **in** ~, en tandem.
tang /tæŋ/ n. (*taste*) saveur forte f.; (*smell*) odeur forte f.
tangent /'tændʒənt/ n. tangente f.
tangerine /tændʒə'riːn/ n. mandarine f.
tangible /'tændʒəbl/ a. tangible.
tangle /'tæŋgl/ v.t. enchevêtrer. —n. enchevêtrement m. **become** ~**d**, s'enchevêtrer.
tango /'tæŋgəʊ/ n. (pl. -os) tango m.
tank /tæŋk/ n. réservoir m.; (*vat*) cuve f.; (*for fish*) aquarium m.; (*mil.*) char m., tank m.
tankard /'tæŋkəd/ n. chope f.
tanker /'tæŋkə(r)/ n. camion-citerne m.; (*ship*) pétrolier m.
tantaliz|**e** /'tæntəlaɪz/ v.t. tourmenter. ~**ing** a. tentant.
tantamount /'tæntəmaʊnt/ a. **be** ~ **to**, équivaloir à.
tantrum /'tæntrəm/ n. crise de colère or de rage f.
tap[1] /tæp/ n. (*for water etc.*) robinet m. —v.t. (p.t. **tapped**) (*resources*) exploiter; (*telephone*) mettre sur table d'écoute. **on** ~, (*fam.*) disponible.
tap[2] /tæp/ v.t./i. (p.t. **tapped**) frapper (doucement). —n. petit coup m. ~-**dance** n. claquettes f. pl.
tape /teɪp/ n. ruban m.; (*sticky*) ruban adhésif m. (**magnetic**) ~, bande (magnétique) f. —v.t. (*tie*) attacher; (*stick*) coller; (*record*) enregistrer. ~-**measure** n. mètre (à) ruban m. ~-**recorder**, magnétophone m.
taper /'teɪpə(r)/ n. (*for lighting*) bougie f. —v.t./i. (s')effiler. ~ **off**, (*diminish*) diminuer. ~**ed**, ~**ing** adjs. (*fingers etc.*) effilé, fuselé; (*trousers*) étroit du bas.

tapestry /'tæpɪstrɪ/ n. tapisserie f.

tapioca /tæpɪ'əʊkə/ n. tapioca m.

tar /tɑː(r)/ n. goudron m. —v.t. (p.t. **tarred**) goudronner.

tardy /'tɑːdɪ/ a. (-ier, -iest) (slow) lent; (belated) tardif.

target /'tɑːgɪt/ n. cible f.; (objective) objectif m. —v.t. prendre pour cible.

tariff /'tærɪf/ n. (charges) tarif m.; (on imports) tarif douanier m.

Tarmac /'tɑːmæk/ n. (P.) macadam (goudronné) m.; (runway) piste f.

tarnish /'tɑːnɪʃ/ v.t./i. (se) ternir.

tarpaulin /tɑː'pɔːlɪn/ n. bâche goudronnée f.

tarragon /'tærəgən/ n. estragon m.

tart¹ /tɑːt/ a. (-er, -est) acide.

tart² /tɑːt/ n. tarte f.; (prostitute; sl.) poule f. —v.t. ~ **up**, (pej., sl.) embellir (sans le moindre goût).

tartan /'tɑːtn/ n. tartan m. —a. écossais.

tartar /'tɑːtə(r)/ n. tartre m. ~ **sauce**, sauce tartare f.

task /tɑːsk/ n. tâche f., travail m. **take to** ~, réprimander. ~ **force**, détachement spécial m.

tassel /'tæsl/ n. gland m., pompon m.

taste /teɪst/ n. goût m. —v.t. (eat, enjoy) goûter; (try) goûter à; (perceive taste of) sentir le goût de. —v.i. ~ **of** or **like**, avoir un goût de. **have a** ~ **of**, (experience) goûter de. ~**less** a. sans goût; (fig.) de mauvais goût.

tasteful /'teɪstfl/ a. de bon goût. ~**ly** adv. avec goût.

tasty /'teɪstɪ/ a. (-ier, -iest) délicieux, savoureux.

tat /tæt/ see **tit²**.

tatter|s /'tætəz/ n. pl. lambeaux m. pl. ~**ed** /'tætəd/ a. en lambeaux.

tattoo¹ /tə'tuː/ n. (mil.) spectacle militaire m.

tattoo² /tə'tuː/ v.t. tatouer. —n. tatouage m.

tatty /'tætɪ/ a. (-ier, -iest) (shabby: fam.) miteux, minable.

taught /tɔːt/ see **teach**.

taunt /tɔːnt/ v.t. railler. —n. raillerie f. ~**ing** a. railleur.

Taurus /'tɔːrəs/ n. le Taureau.

taut /tɔːt/ a. tendu.

tavern /'tævn/ n. taverne f.

tawdry /'tɔːdrɪ/ a. (-ier, -iest) (showy) tape-à-l'œil invar.

tax /tæks/ n. taxe f., impôt m.; (on income) impôts m.—v.t. imposer; (put to test: fig.) mettre à l'épreuve. ~**able** a. imposable. ~**ation** /-'seɪʃn/ n. imposition f.; (taxes) impôts m. pl.

~**-collector** n. percepteur m. ~**-deductible** a. déductible d'impôts. ~ **disc**, vignette f. ~**-free** a. exempt d'impôts. ~**ing** a. (fig.) éprouvant. ~ **haven** paradis fiscal m. ~ **inspector**, inspecteur des impôts m. ~ **relief**, dégrèvement fiscal m. ~ **return**, déclaration d'impôts f.

taxi /'tæksɪ/ n. (pl. -is) taxi m. —v.i. (p.t. **taxied**, pres. p. **taxiing**) (aviat.) rouler au sol. ~**-cab** n. taxi m. ~ **rank**, (Amer.) ~ **stand**, station de taxi f.

taxpayer /'tækspeɪə(r)/ n. contribuable m./f.

tea /tiː/ n. thé m.; (snack) goûter m. ~**bag** n. sachet de thé m. ~**-break** n. pause-thé f. ~**-leaf** n. feuille de thé f. ~**-set** n. service à thé m. ~**-shop** n. salon de thé m. ~**-towel** n. torchon m.

teach /tiːtʃ/ v.t. (p.t. **taught**) apprendre (s.o. sth., qch. à qn.); (in school) enseigner (s.o. sth., qch. à qn.). —v.i. enseigner. ~**er** n. professeur m.; (primary) instituteur, -trice m., f.; (member of teaching profession) enseignant(e) m. (f.). ~**ing** n. enseignement m.; a. pédagogique; (staff) enseignant.

teacup /'tiːkʌp/ n. tasse à thé f.

teak /tiːk/ n. (wood) teck m.

team /tiːm/ n. équipe f.; (of animals) attelage m. —v.i. ~ **up**, faire équipe (with, avec). ~**-work** n. travail d'équipe m.

teapot /'tiːpɒt/ n. théière f.

tear¹ /teə(r)/ v.t./i. (p.t. **tore**, p.p. **torn**) (se) déchirer; (snatch) arracher (from, à); (rush) aller à toute vitesse. —n. déchirure f.

tear² /tɪə(r)/ n. larme f. **in** ~**s**, en larmes. ~**-gas** n. gaz lacrymogène m.

tearful /'tɪəfl/ a. (voice) larmoyant; (person) en larmes. ~**ly** adv. en pleurant, les larmes aux yeux.

tease /tiːz/ v.t. taquiner. —n. (person: fam.) taquin(e) m. (f.).

teaspoon /'tiːspuːn/ n. petite cuiller f. ~**ful** n. (pl. -**fuls**) cuillerée à café f.

teat /tiːt/ n. (of bottle, animal) tétine f.

technical /'teknɪkl/ a. technique. ~**ity** /-'kælətɪ/ n. détail technique m. ~**ly** adv. techniquement.

technician /tek'nɪʃn/ n. technicien(ne) m. (f.).

technique /tek'niːk/ n. technique f.

technolog|y /tek'nɒlədʒɪ/ n. technologie f. ~**ical** /-ə'lɒdʒɪkl/ a. technologique.

teddy /'tedɪ/ a. ~ **bear**, ours en peluche m.

tedious /'ti:dɪəs/ a. fastidieux.

tedium /'ti:dɪəm/ n. ennui m.

tee /ti:/ n. (golf) tee m.

teem[1] /ti:m/ v.i. (swarm) grouiller (**with**, de).

teem[2] /ti:m/ v.i. ~ (**with rain**), pleuvoir à torrents.

teenage /'ti:neɪdʒ/ a. (d')adolescent. ~**d** a. adolescent. ~**r** /-ə(r)/ n. adolescent(e) m. (f.).

teens /ti:nz/ n. pl. **in one's** ~, adolescent.

teeny /'ti:nɪ/ a. (**-ier, -iest**) (tiny: fam.) minuscule.

teeter /'ti:tə(r)/ v.i. chanceler.

teeth /ti:θ/ see **tooth**.

teeth|**e** /ti:ð/ v.i. faire ses dents. ~**ing troubles**, (fig.) difficultés initiales f. pl.

teetotaller /ti:'təʊtlə(r)/ n. personne qui ne boit pas d'alcool f.

telecommunications /telɪkəmju:nɪ'keɪʃnz/ n. pl. télécommunications f. pl.

telegram /'telɪgræm/ n. télégramme m.

telegraph /'telɪgrɑ:f/ n. télégraphe m. —a. télégraphique. ~**ic** /-'græfɪk/ a. télégraphique.

telepath|**y** /tɪ'lepəθɪ/ n. télépathie f. ~**ic** /telɪ'pæθɪk/ a. télépathique.

telephone /'telɪfəʊn/ n. téléphone m. —v.t. (person) téléphoner à; (message) téléphoner. —v.i. téléphoner. ~ **book**, annuaire m. ~**-box** n., ~ **booth**, cabine téléphonique f. ~ **call**, coup de téléphone m. ~ **number**, numéro de téléphone m.

telephonist /tɪ'lefənɪst/ n. (in exchange) téléphoniste m./f.

telephoto /telɪ'fəʊtəʊ/ a. ~ **lens**, téléobjectif m.

telescop|**e** /'telɪskəʊp/ n. télescope m. —v.t./i. (se) télescoper. ~**ic** /-'skɒpɪk/ a. télescopique.

teletext /'telɪtekst/ n. télétexte m.

televise /'telɪvaɪz/ v.t. téléviser.

television /'telɪvɪʒn/ n. télévision f. ~ **set**, poste de télévision m.

telex /'teleks/ n. télex m. —v.t. envoyer par télex.

tell /tel/ v.t. (p.t. **told**) dire (**s.o. sth.,** qch. à qn.); (story) raconter; (distinguish) distinguer. —v.i. avoir un effet; (know) savoir. ~ **of**, parler de. ~ **off**, (fam.) gronder. ~**-tale** n. rapporteu|r, -se m., f.; a. révélateur. ~ **tales**, rapporter.

teller /'telə(r)/ n. (in bank) caiss|lier, -ière m., f.

telling /'telɪŋ/ a. révélateur.

telly /'telɪ/ n. (fam.) télé f.

temerity /tɪ'merətɪ/ n. témérité f.

temp /temp/ n. (temporary employee: fam.) intérimaire m./f. —v.i. faire de l'intérim.

temper /'tempə(r)/ n. humeur f.; (anger) colère f. —v.t. (metal) tremper; (fig.) tempérer. **lose one's** ~, se mettre en colère.

temperament /'temprəmənt/ n. tempérament m. ~**al** /-'mentl/ a. capricieux; (innate) inné.

temperance /'tempərəns/ n. (in drinking) tempérance f.

temperate /'tempərət/ a. tempéré.

temperature /'temprətʃə(r)/ n. température f. **have a** ~, avoir (de) la fièvre or de la température.

tempest /'tempɪst/ n. tempête f.

tempestuous /tem'pestʃʊəs/ a. (meeting etc.) orageux.

template /'templ(e)ɪt/ n. patron m.

temple[1] /'templ/ n. temple m.

temple[2] /'templ/ n. (of head) tempe f.

tempo /'tempəʊ/ n. (pl. **-os**) tempo m.

temporal /'tempərəl/ a. temporel.

temporar|**y** /'tempərərɪ/ a. temporaire, provisoire. ~**ily** adv. temporairement, provisoirement.

tempt /tempt/ v.t. tenter. ~ **s.o. to do**, donner envie à qn. de faire. ~**ation** /-'teɪʃn/ n. tentation f. ~**ing** a. tentant.

ten /ten/ a. & n. dix (m.).

tenable /'tenəbl/ a. défendable.

tenac|**ious** /tɪ'neɪʃəs/ a. tenace. ~**ity** /-'æsətɪ/ n. ténacité f.

tenancy /'tenənsɪ/ n. location f.

tenant /'tenənt/ n. locataire m./f.

tend[1] /tend/ v.t. s'occuper de.

tend[2] /tend/ v.i. ~ **to**, (be apt to) avoir tendance à.

tendency /'tendənsɪ/ n. tendance f.

tender[1] /'tendə(r)/ a. tendre; (sore, painful) sensible. ~**ly** adv. tendrement. ~**ness** n. tendresse f.

tender[2] /'tendə(r)/ v.t. offrir, donner. —v.i. faire une soumission. —n. (comm.) soumission f. **be legal** ~, (money) avoir cours. **put sth. out to** ~, faire un appel d'offres pour qch.

tendon /'tendən/ n. tendon m.

tenement /'tenəmənt/ n. maison de rapport f., H.L.M. m./f.; (slum: Amer.) taudis m.

tenet /'tenɪt/ n. principe m.

tenner /'tenə(r)/ n. (fam.) billet de dix livres m.

tennis /'tenɪs/ n. tennis m. —a. de tennis ~ **shoes**, tennis m. pl.

tenor /'tenə(r)/ n. (meaning) sens général m.; (mus.) ténor m.

tense¹ /tens/ n. (*gram.*) temps m.

tense² /tens/ a. (**-er, -est**) tendu. —v.t. (*muscles*) tendre, raidir. —v.i. (*of face*) se crisper. **~ness** n. tension f.

tension /'tenʃn/ n. tension f.

tent /tent/ n. tente f.

tentacle /'tentəkl/ n. tentacule m.

tentative /'tentətɪv/ a. provisoire; (*hesitant*) timide. **~ly** adv. provisoirement; timidement.

tenterhooks /'tentəhʊks/ n. pl. **on ~,** sur des charbons ardents.

tenth /tenθ/ a. & n. dixième (m./f.).

tenuous /'tenjʊəs/ a. ténu.

tenure /'tenjʊə(r)/ n. (*in job, office*) (période de) jouissance f. **have ~,** être titulaire.

tepid /'tepɪd/ a. tiède.

term /tɜːm/ n. (*word, limit*) terme m.; (*of imprisonment*) temps; (*in school etc.*) trimestre m.; (*Amer.*) semestre m. **~s,** conditions f. pl. —v.t. appeler, nommer. **on good/bad ~s,** en bons/mauvais termes. **in the short/long ~,** à court/long terme **come to ~s,** arriver à un accord. **come to ~s with sth.,** accepter qch. **~ of office,** (*pol.*) mandat m.

terminal /'tɜːmɪnl/ a. terminal, final; (*med.*) en phase terminale. —n. (*oil, computer*) terminal m.; (*rail.*) terminus m.; (*electr.*) borne f. (**air**) **~,** aérogare f.

terminat|e /'tɜːmɪneɪt/ v.t. mettre fin à. —v.i. prendre fin. **~ion** /-'neɪʃn/ n. fin f.

terminology /tɜːmɪ'nɒlədʒɪ/ n. terminologie f.

terminus /'tɜːmɪnəs/ n. (pl. **-ni** /-naɪ/) (*station*) terminus m.

terrace /'terəs/ n. terrasse f.; (*houses*) rangée de maisons contiguës f. **the ~s,** (*sport*) les gradins m. pl.

terracotta /terə'kɒtə/ n. terre cuite f.

terrain /te'reɪn/ n. terrain m.

terrib|le /'terəbl/ a. affreux, atroce. **~y** adv. affreusement; (*very*) terriblement.

terrier /'terɪə(r)/ n. (*dog*) terrier m.

terrific /tə'rɪfɪk/ a. (*fam.*) terrible. **~ally** /-klɪ/ adv. (*very: fam.*) terriblement; (*very well: fam.*) terriblement bien.

terrif|y /'terɪfaɪ/ v.t. terrifier. **be ~ied of,** avoir très peur de.

territorial /terɪ'tɔːrɪəl/ a. territorial.

territory /'terɪtərɪ/ n. territoire m.

terror /'terə(r)/ n. terreur f.

terroris|t /'terərɪst/ n. terroriste m./f. **~m** /-zəm/ n. terrorisme m.

terrorize /'terəraɪz/ v.t. terroriser.

terse /tɜːs/ a. concis, laconique.

test /test/ n. examen m., analyse f.; (*of goods*) contrôle m.; (*of machine etc.*) essai m.; (*in school*) interrogation f.; (*of strength etc.: fig.*) épreuve f. —v.t. examiner, analyser; (*check*) contrôler; (*try*) essayer; (*pupil*) donner une interrogation à; (*fig.*) éprouver. **driving ~,** (épreuve f. du) permis de conduire m. **~ match,** match international m. **~ pilot** pilote d'essai m. **~-tube** n. éprouvette f.

testament /'testəmənt/ n. testament m. **Old/New T~,** Ancien/Nouveau Testament m.

testicle /'testɪkl/ n. testicule m.

testify /'testɪfaɪ/ v.t./i. témoigner (**to,** de). **~ that,** témoigner que.

testimony /'testɪmənɪ/ n. témoignage m.

testy /'testɪ/ a. grincheux.

tetanus /'tetənəs/ n. tétanos m.

tetchy /'tetʃɪ/ a. grincheux.

tether /'teðə(r)/ v.t. attacher. —n. **at the end of one's ~,** à bout.

text /tekst/ n. texte m.

textbook /'tekstbʊk/ n. manuel m.

textile /'tekstaɪl/ n. & a. textile (m.).

texture /'tekstʃə(r)/ n. (*of paper etc.*) grain m.; (*of fabric*) texture f.

Thai /taɪ/ a. & n. thaïlandais(e) (m. (f.)). **~land** n. Thaïlande f.

Thames /temz/ n. Tamise f.

than /ðæn, unstressed ðən/ conj. que, qu'*; (*with numbers*) de. **more/less ~ ten,** plus/moins de dix.

thank /θæŋk/ v.t. remercier. **~s** n. pl. remerciements m. pl. **~ you!,** merci! **~s!,** (*fam.*) merci! **~s to,** grâce à. **T~sgiving (Day),** (*Amer.*) jour d'action de grâces m. (*fête nationale*).

thankful /'θæŋkfl/ a. reconnaissant (**for,** de). **~ly** adv. (*happily*) heureusement.

thankless /'θæŋklɪs/ a. ingrat.

that /ðæt, unstressed ðet/ a. pl. **those**) ce or cet*, cette. **those,** ces. —pron. ce or c'*, cela, ça. **~ (one),** celui-là, celle-là. **those (ones),** ceux-là, celles-là. —adv. si, aussi. —rel. pron. (*subject*) qui; (*object*) que, qu'*. —conj. que, qu'*. **~ boy,** ce garçon (*with emphasis*) ce garçon-là. **~ is, c'est. ~ is (to say),** c'est-à-dire. **after ~,** après ça or cela. **the day ~,** le jour où. **the man ~ married her,** l'homme qu'i l'a épousée. **the man ~ she married,** l'homme qu'elle a épousé. **the car ~ I came in,** la voiture dans laquelle je suis venu. **~ big,** grand comme ça. **~ many, ~ much,** tant que ça.

thatch /θætʃ/ n. chaume m. **~ed** a. en chaume. **~ed cottage,** chaumière f.

thaw /θɔ:/ v.t./i. (faire) dégeler; (snow) (faire) fondre. —n. dégel m.

the /before vowel ði, before consonant ðə, stressed ði:/ a. le or l'*, la or l'*, pl. les. **of ~, from ~,** du, de l'*, de la, pl. des. **to ~, at ~,** au, à l'*, à la, pl. aux. **~ third of June,** le trois juin.

theatre /ˈθɪətə(r)/ n. théâtre m.

theatrical /θɪˈætrɪkl/ a. théâtral.

theft /θeft/ n. vol m.

their /ðeə(r)/ a. leur, pl. leurs.

theirs /ðeəz/ poss. pron. le or la leur, les leurs.

them /ðem, unstressed ðəm/ pron. les; (after prep.) eux, elles. **(to) ~,** leur. **I know ~,** je les connais.

theme /θi:m/ n. thème m. **~ song,** (in film etc.) chanson principale f.

themselves /ðəmˈselvz/ pron. eux-mêmes, elles-mêmes; (reflexive) se; (after prep.) eux, elles.

then /ðen/ adv. alors; (next) ensuite, puis; (therefore) alors, donc. —a. d'alors. **from ~ on,** dès lors.

theolog|y /θɪˈɒlədʒɪ/ n. théologie f. **~ian** /θɪəˈləʊdʒən/ n. théologien(ne) m. (f.).

theorem /ˈθɪərəm/ n. théorème m.

theor|y /ˈθɪərɪ/ n. théorie f. **~etical** /-ˈretɪkl/ a. théorique.

therapeutic /θerəˈpju:tɪk/ a. thérapeutique.

therapy /ˈθerəpɪ/ n. thérapie f.

there /ðeə(r)/ adv. là; (with verb) y; (over there) là-bas. —int. allez. **he goes ~,** il y va. **on ~,** là-dessus. **~ is, ~ are,** il y a; (pointing) voilà. **~, ~!,** allons, allons! **~abouts** adv. par là. **~after** adv. par la suite. **~by** adv. de cette manière.

therefore /ˈðeəfɔ:(r)/ adv. donc.

thermal /ˈθɜ:ml/ a. thermique.

thermometer /θəˈmɒmɪtə(r)/ n. thermomètre m.

thermonuclear /θɜ:məʊˈnju:klɪə(r)/ a. thermonucléaire.

Thermos /ˈθɜ:məs/ n. (P.) thermos m./f. invar. (P.).

thermostat /ˈθɜ:məstæt/ n. thermostat m.

thesaurus /θɪˈsɔ:rəs/ n. (pl. -ri /-raɪ/) dictionnaire de synonymes m.

these /ði:z/ see **this**.

thesis /ˈθi:sɪs/ n. (pl. theses /-si:z/) thèse f.

they /ðeɪ/ pron. ils, elles; (emphatic) eux, elles; (people in general) on.

thick /θɪk/ a. (-er, -est) épais; (stupid) bête; (friends: fam.) très lié. —adv. = **thickly.** —n. **in the ~ of,** au plus gros

de. **~ly** adv. (grow) dru; (spread) en couche épaisse. **~ness** n. épaisseur f.

~-skinned a. peu sensible.

thicken /ˈθɪkən/ v.t./i. (s')épaissir.

thickset /θɪkˈset/ a. trapu.

thief /θi:f/ n. (pl. thieves) voleur, -se m., f.

thigh /θaɪ/ n. cuisse f.

thimble /ˈθɪmbl/ n. dé (à coudre) m.

thin /θɪn/ a. (thinner, thinnest) mince; (person) maigre, mince; (sparse) clairsemé; (fine) fin. —adv. = **thinly.** —v.t./i. (p.t. thinned) (liquid) (s')éclaircir. **~ out,** (in quantity) (s')éclaircir. **~ly** adv. (slightly) légèrement. **~ner** n. diluant m. **~ness** n. minceur f.; maigreur f.

thing /θɪŋ/ n. chose f. **~s,** (belongings) affaires f. pl. **the best ~ is to,** le mieux est de. **the (right) ~,** ce qu'il faut (**for s.o.,** à qn.).

think /θɪŋk/ v.t./i. (p.t. thought) penser (**about, of,** à); (carefully) réfléchir (**about, of,** à); (believe) croire. **I ~ so,** je crois que oui. **~ better of it,** se raviser. **~ nothing of,** trouver naturel de. **~ of,** (hold opinion of) penser de. **I'm ~ing of going,** je pense que j'irai peut-être. **~ over,** bien réfléchir à. **~-tank** n. comité d'experts m. **~ up,** inventer. **~er** n. penseur, -se m., f.

third /θɜ:d/ a. troisième m./f.; (fraction) tiers m. **~ly** adv. troisièmement. **~-rate** a. très inférieur. **T~ World,** Tiers-Monde m.

thirst /θɜ:st/ n. soif f. **~y** a. **be ~y,** avoir soif. **make ~y,** donner soif à.

thirteen /θɜ:ˈti:n/ a. & n. treize (m.). **~th** a. & n. treizième (m./f.).

thirt|y /ˈθɜ:tɪ/ a. & n. trente (m.). **~ieth** a. & n. trentième (m./f.).

this /ðɪs/ a. (pl. these) ce or cet*, cette. **these,** ces. —pron. ce or c'*, ceci. **~ (one),** celui-ci, celle-ci. **these (ones),** ceux-ci, celles-ci. **~ boy,** ce garçon; (with emphasis) ce garçon-ci. **~ is a mistake,** c'est une erreur. **~ is the book,** voici le livre. **~ is my son,** je vous présente mon fils. **~ is Anne speaking,** c'est Anne à l'appareil. **after ~,** après ceci.

thistle /ˈθɪsl/ n. chardon m.

thorn /θɔ:n/ n. épine f. **~y** a. épineux.

thorough /ˈθʌrə/ a. consciencieux; (deep) profond; (cleaning, washing) à fond. **~ly** adv. (clean, study, etc.) à fond; (very) tout à fait.

thoroughbred /ˈθʌrəbred/ n. (horse etc.) pur-sang m. invar.

thoroughfare /'θʌrəfeə(r)/ *n.* grande artère *f.*

those /ðəʊz/ *see* that.

though /ðəʊ/ *conj.* bien que. —*adv.* (*fam.*) cependant.

thought /θɔːt/ *see* think. —*n.* pensée *f.*; (*idea*) idée *f.*

thoughtful /'θɔːtfl/ *a.* pensif; (*considerate*) attentionné. ∼ly *adv.* pensivement; avec considération.

thoughtless /'θɔːtlɪs/ *a.* étourdi. ∼ly *adv.* étourdiment.

thousand /'θaʊznd/ *a.* & *n.* mille (*m. invar.*). ∼s of, des milliers de.

thrash /θræʃ/ *v.t.* rosser; (*defeat*) écraser. ∼ about, se débattre. ∼ out, discuter à fond.

thread /θred/ *n.* (*yarn & fig.*) fil *m.*; (*of screw*) pas *m.* —*v.t.* enfiler. ∼ one's way, se faufiler.

threadbare /'θredbeə(r)/ *a.* râpé.

threat /θret/ *n.* menace *f.*

threaten /'θretn/ *v.t./i.* menacer (with, de). ∼ingly *adv.* d'un air menaçant.

three /θriː/ *a.* & *n.* trois (*m.*). ∼-dimensional *a.* en trois dimensions.

thresh /θreʃ/ *v.t.* (*corn etc.*) battre.

threshold /'θreʃəʊld/ *n.* seuil *m.*

threw /θruː/ *see* throw.

thrift /θrɪft/ *n.* économie *f.* ∼y *a.* économe.

thrill /θrɪl/ *n.* émotion *f.*, frisson *m.* —*v.t.* transporter (de joie). —*v.i.* frissonner (de joie). be ∼ed, être ravi. ∼ing *a.* excitant.

thriller /'θrɪlə(r)/ *n.* livre *or* film à suspense *m.*

thriv|e /θraɪv/ *v.i.* (*p.t.* thrived *or* throve, *p.p.* thrived *or* thriven) prospérer. he ∼es on it, cela lui réussit. ∼ing *a.* prospère.

throat /θrəʊt/ *n.* gorge *f.* have a sore ∼, avoir mal à la gorge.

throb /θrɒb/ *v.i.* (*p.t.* throbbed) (*wound*) causer des élancements; (*heart*) palpiter; (*fig.*) vibrer. —*n.* (*pain*) élancement *m.*; palpitation *f.* ∼bing *a.* (*pain*) lancinant.

throes /θrəʊz/ *n. pl.* in the ∼ of, au milieu de, aux prises avec.

thrombosis /θrɒm'bəʊsɪs/ *n.* thrombose *f.*

throne /θrəʊn/ *n.* trône *m.*

throng /θrɒŋ/ *n.* foule *f.* —*v.t.* (*streets etc.*) se presser dans. —*v.i.* (*arrive*) affluer.

throttle /'θrɒtl/ *n.* (*auto.*) accélérateur *m.* —*v.t.* étrangler.

through /θruː/ *prep.* à travers; (*during*) pendant; (*by means or way of, out of*) par; (*by reason of*) grâce à, à cause de. —*adv.* à travers; (*entirely*) jusqu'au bout. —*a.* (*train etc.*) direct. be ∼, (*finished*) avoir fini. come *or* go ∼, (*cross, pierce*) traverser. I'm putting you ∼, je vous passe votre correspondant.

throughout /θruː'aʊt/ *prep.* ∼ the country/*etc.*, dans tout le pays/*etc.* ∼ the day/*etc.*, pendant toute la journée/*etc.* —*adv.* (*place*) partout; (*time*) tout le temps.

throw /θrəʊ/ *v.t.* (*p.t.* threw, *p.p.* thrown) jeter, lancer; (*baffle: fam.*) déconcerter. —*n.* jet *m.*; (*of dice*) coup *m.* ∼ a party, (*fam.*) faire une fête. ∼ away, jeter. ∼-away *a.* à jeter. ∼ off, (*get rid of*) se débarrasser de. ∼ out, jeter; (*person*) expulser; (*reject*) rejeter. ∼ over, (*desert*) plaquer. ∼ up, (*one's arms*) lever; (*resign from*) abandonner; (*vomit:fam.*) vomir.

thru /θruː/ *prep., adv. & a.* (*Amer.*) = through.

thrush /θrʌʃ/ *n.* (*bird*) grive *f.*

thrust /θrʌst/ *v.t.* (*p.t.* thrust) pousser. —*n.* poussée *f.* ∼ into, (*put*) enforcer dans, mettre dans. ∼ upon, (*force on*) imposer à.

thud /θʌd/ *n.* bruit sourd *m.*

thug /θʌg/ *n.* voyou *m.*, bandit *m.*

thumb /θʌm/ *n.* pouce *m.* —*v.t.* (*book*) feuilleter. ∼ a lift, faire de l'auto-stop. ∼-index, répertoire à onglets *m.*

thumbtack /'θʌmtæk/ *n.* (*Amer.*) punaise *f.*

thump /θʌmp/ *v.t./i.* cogner (sur); (*of heart*) battre fort. —*n.* grand coup *m.* ∼ing *a.* (*fam.*) énorme.

thunder /'θʌndə(r)/ *n.* tonnerre *m.* —*v.i.* (*weather, person, etc.*) tonner. ∼ past, passer dans un bruit de tonnerre. ∼y *a.* orageux.

thunderbolt /'θʌndəbəʊlt/ *n.* coup de foudre *m.*; (*event: fig.*) coup de tonnerre *m.*

thunderstorm /'θʌndəstɔːm/ *n.* orage *m.*

Thursday /'θɜːzdɪ/ *n.* jeudi *m.*

thus /ðʌs/ *adv.* ainsi.

thwart /θwɔːt/ *v.t.* contrecarrer.

thyme /taɪm/ *n.* thym *m.*

thyroid /'θaɪrɔɪd/ *n.* thyroïde *f.*

tiara /tɪ'ɑːrə/ *n.* diadème *m.*

tic /tɪk/ *n.* tic (nerveux) *m.*

tick[1] /tɪk/ *n.* (*sound*) tic-tac *m.*; (*mark*) coche *f.*; (*moment: fam.*) instant *m.* —*v.i.* faire tic-tac. —*v.t.* ∼ (off), cocher. ∼ off, (*fam.*) réprimander. ∼

over, (*engine*, *factory*) tourner au ralenti.

tick² /tɪk/ *n*. (*insect*) tique *f*.

ticket /'tɪkɪt/ *n*. billet *m*.; (*for bus*, *cloakroom*, *etc*.) ticket *m*.; (*label*) étiquette *f*. **~-collector** *n*. contrôleuIr, -se *m*., *f*. **~-office** *n*. guichet *m*.

tickle /'tɪkl/ *v.t.* chatouiller; (*amuse*: *fig*.) amuser. —*n*. chatouillement *m*.

ticklish /'tɪklɪʃ/ *a*. chatouilleux.

tidal /'taɪdl/ *a*. qui a des marées. **~ wave**, raz-de-marée *m. invar.*

tiddly-winks /'tɪdlɪwɪŋks/ *n*. (*game*) jeu de puce *m*.

tide /taɪd/ *n*. marée *f*.; (*of events*) cours *m*. —*v.t*. **~ over**, dépanner.

tidings /'taɪdɪŋz/ *n. pl.* nouvelles *f. pl.*

tid|y /'taɪdɪ/ *a*. (**-ier**, **-iest**) (*room*) bien rangé; (*appearance*, *work*) soigné; (*methodical*) ordonné; (*amount*: *fam*.) joli. —*v.t./i.* ranger. **~y o.s.**, s'arranger. **~ily** *adv*. avec soin. **~iness** *n*. ordre *m*.

tie /taɪ/ *v.t.* (*pres. p* **tying**) attacher, nouer; (*a knot*) faire; (*link*) lier. —*v.i.* (*darts etc.*) finir à égalité de points; (*football*) faire match nul; (*in race*) être ex aequo. —*n*. attache *f*.; (*necktie*) cravate *f*.; (*link*) lien *m*.; égalité (de points) *f*.; match nul *m*. **~ down**, attacher; (*job*) bloquer. **~ s.o. down to**, (*date*) forcer qn. à respecter. **~ in with**, être lié à. **~ up**, attacher; (*money*) immobiliser; (*occupy*) occuper. **~-up** *n*. (*link*) lien *m*.; (*auto*., *Amer.*) bouchon *m*.

tier /tɪə(r)/ *n*. étage *m*., niveau *m*.; (*in stadium etc.*) gradin *m*.

tiff /tɪf/ *n*. petite querelle *f*.

tiger /'taɪgə(r)/ *n*. tigre *m*.

tight /taɪt/ *a*. (**-er**, **-est**) (*clothes*) étroit, juste; (*rope*) tendu; (*lid*) solidement fixé; (*control*) strict; (*knot*, *collar*, *schedule*) serré; (*drunk*: *fam.*) ivre. —*adv*. (*hold*, *sleep*, *etc.*) bien; (*squeeze*) fort. **~ corner**, situation difficile *f*. **~-fisted** *a*. avare. **~ly** *adv*. bien; (*squeeze*) fort.

tighten /'taɪtn/ *v.t./i.* (se) tendre; (*bolt etc.*) (se) resserrer; (*control etc.*) renforcer. **~ up on**, se montrer plus strict à l'égard de.

tightrope /'taɪtrəʊp/ *n*. corde raide *f*. **~ walker**, funambule *m./f.*

tights /taɪts/ *n. pl.* collant *m*.

tile /taɪl/ *n*. (*on wall*, *floor*) carreau *m*.; (*on roof*) tuile *f*. —*v.t*. carreler; couvrir de tuiles.

till¹ /tɪl/ *v.t*. (*land*) cultiver.

till² /tɪl/ *prep. & conj.* = until.

till³ /tɪl/ *n*. caisse (enregistreuse) *f*.

tilt /tɪlt/ *v.i./i.* pencher. —*n*. (*slope*) inclinaison *f*. **(at) full ~**, à toute vitesse.

timber /'tɪmbə(r)/ *n*. bois (de construction) *m*.; (*trees*) arbres *m. pl.*

time /taɪm/ *n*. temps *m*.; (*moment*) moment *m*.; (*epoch*) époque *f*.; (*by clock*) heure *f*.; (*occasion*) fois *f*.; (*rhythm*) mesure *f*. **~s**, (*multiplying*) fois *f. pl.* —*v.t*. choisir le moment de; (*measure*) minuter; (*sport*) chronométrer. **any ~**, n'importe quand. **behind the ~s**, en retard sur son temps. **for the ~ being**, pour le moment. **from ~ to time**, de temps en temps. **have a good ~**, s'amuser. **in no ~**, en un rien de temps. **in ~**, à temps; (*eventually*) avec le temps. **a long ~**, longtemps. **on ~**, à l'heure. **what's the ~?**, quelle heure est-il? **~ bomb**, bombe à retardement *f*. **~-honoured** *a*. consacré (par l'usage). **~-lag** *n*. décalage *m*. **~-limit** *n*. délai *m*. **~-scale** *n*. délais fixés *m. pl.* **~ off**, du temps libre. **~ zone**, fuseau horaire *m*.

timeless /'taɪmlɪs/ *a*. éternel.

timely /'taɪmlɪ/ *a*. à propos.

timer /'taɪmə(r)/ *n*. (*for cooker etc.*) minuteur *m*.; (*on video*) programmateur; (*culin.*) compte-minutes *m. invar.*; (*with sand*) sablier *m*.

timetable /'taɪmteɪbl/ *n*. horaire *m*.

timid /'tɪmɪd/ *a*. timide; (*fearful*) peureux. **~ly** *adv*. timidement.

timing /'taɪmɪŋ/ *n*. (*measuring*) minutage *m*.; (*moment*) moment *m*.; (*of artist*) rythme *m*.

tin /tɪn/ *n*. étain *m*.; (*container*) boîte *f*. **~(plate)**, fer-blanc *m*. —*v.t*. (*p.t* **tinned**), mettre en boîte. **~ foil**, papier d'aluminium *m*. **~ny** *a*. métallique. **~-opener** *n*. ouvre-boîte(s) *m*.

tinge /tɪndʒ/ *v.t*. teinter (**with**, de). —*n*. teinte *f*.

tingle /'tɪŋgl/ *v.i.* (*prickle*) picoter. —*n*. picotement *m*.

tinker /'tɪŋkə(r)/ *n*. rétameur *m*. —*v.i.* **~ (with)**, bricoler.

tinkle /'tɪŋkl/ *n*. tintement *m*.; (*fam.*) coup de téléphone *m*.

tinsel /'tɪnsl/ *n*. cheveux d'ange *m. pl.*, guirlandes de Noël *f. pl.*

tint /tɪnt/ *n*. teinte *f*.; (*for hair*) shampooing colorant *m*. —*v.t*. (*glass*, *paper*) teinter.

tiny /'taɪnɪ/ *a*. (**-ier**, **-iest**) minuscule, tout petit.

tip¹ /tɪp/ *n*. bout *m*.; (*cover*) embout *m*. **~ped cigarette**, cigarette (à bout) filtre *f*.

tip² /tɪp/ v.t./i. (p.t. **tipped**) (tilt) pencher; (overturn) (faire) basculer; (pour) verser; (empty) déverser; (give money) donner un pourboire à. —n. (money) pourboire m.; (advice) tuyau m.; (for rubbish) décharge f. ∼ **off**, prévenir. ∼**-off** n. tuyau m. (pour prévenir).

tipsy /'tɪpsɪ/ a. un peu ivre, gris.

tiptoe /'tɪptəʊ/ n. **on** ∼, sur la pointe des pieds.

tiptop /'tɪptɒp/ a. (fam.) excellent.

tir|e¹ /'taɪə(r)/ v.t./i. (se) fatiguer. ∼**e of**, se lasser de. ∼**eless** a. infatigable. ∼**ing** a. fatigant.

tire² /'taɪə(r)/ n. (Amer.) pneu m.

tired /'taɪəd/ a. fatigué. **be** ∼ **of**, en avoir assez de.

tiresome /'taɪəsəm/ a. ennuyeux.

tissue /'tɪʃuː/ n. tissu m.; (handkerchief) mouchoir en papier m. ∼**-paper** n. papier de soie m.

tit¹ /tɪt/ n. (bird) mésange f.

tit² /tɪt/ n. **give** ∼ **for tat**, rendre coup pour coup.

titbit /'tɪtbɪt/ n. friandise f.

titillate /'tɪtɪleɪt/ v.t. exciter.

title /'taɪtl/ n. titre m. ∼**-deed** n. titre de propriété m. ∼**-role** n. rôle principal m.

titter /'tɪtə(r)/ v.i. rigoler.

titular /'tɪtjʊlə(r)/ a. (ruler etc.) nominal.

to /tuː, unstressed tə/ prep. à; (towards) vers; (of attitude) envers. —adv. **push** or **pull to**, (close) fermer. **to France/etc.**, en France/etc. **to town**, en ville. **to Canada/etc.**, au Canada/etc. **to the baker's/etc.**, chez le boulanger/etc. **the road/door/etc. to**, la route/porte/etc. de. **to me/her/etc.**, me/lui/etc. **to do/ sit/etc.**, faire/s'asseoir/etc. **I wrote to tell her**, j'ai écrit pour lui dire. **I tried to help you**, j'ai essayé de t'aider. **ten to six**, (by clock) six heures moins dix. **go to and fro**, aller et venir. **husband/etc. -to-be** n. futur mari/etc.

toad /təʊd/ n. crapaud m.

toadstool /'təʊdstuːl/ n. champignon (vénéneux) m.

toast /təʊst/ n. pain grillé m., toast m.; (drink) toast m. —v.t. (bread) faire griller; (drink to) porter un toast à; (event) arroser. ∼**er** n. grille-pain m. invar.

tobacco /tə'bækəʊ/ n. tabac m.

tobacconist /tə'bækənɪst/ n. marchand(e) de tabac m. (f.). ∼**'s shop**, tabac m.

toboggan /tə'bɒgən/ n. toboggan m., luge f.

today /tə'deɪ/ n. & adv. aujourd'hui (m.).

toddler /'tɒdlə(r)/ n. tout(e) petit(e) enfant m.(f).

toddy /'tɒdɪ/ n. (drink) grog m.

toe /təʊ/ n. orteil m.; (of shoe) bout m. —v.t. ∼ **the line**, se conformer. **on one's** ∼**s**, vigilant. ∼**-hold** n. prise (précaire) f.

toffee /'tɒfɪ/ n. caramel m. ∼**-apple** n. pomme caramélisée f.

together /tə'geðə(r)/ adv. ensemble; (at same time) en même temps. ∼ **with**, avec. ∼**ness** n. camaraderie f.

toil /tɔɪl/ v.i. peiner. —n. labeur m.

toilet /'tɔɪlɪt/ n. toilettes f. pl.; (grooming) toilette f. ∼**-paper** n. papier hygiénique m. ∼**-roll** n. rouleau de papier hygiénique m. ∼ **water**, eau de toilette f.

toiletries /'tɔɪlɪtrɪz/ n. pl. articles de toilette m. pl.

token /'təʊkən/ n. témoignage m., marque f.; (voucher) bon m.; (coin) jeton m. —a. symbolique.

told /təʊld/ see **tell**. —a. **all** ∼, (all in all) en tout.

tolerab|le /'tɒlərəbl/ a. tolérable; (not bad) passable. ∼**y** adv. (work, play, etc.) passablement.

toleran|t /'tɒlərənt/ a. tolérant (**of**, à l'égard de). ∼**ce** n. tolérance f. ∼**tly** adv. avec tolérance.

tolerate /'tɒləreɪt/ v.t. tolérer.

toll¹ /təʊl/ n. péage m. **death** ∼, nombre de morts m. **take its** ∼, (of age) faire sentir son poids.

toll² /təʊl/ v.i. (of bell) sonner.

tom /tɒm/, ∼**-cat** ns. matou m.

tomato /tə'mɑːtəʊ, Amer. tə'meɪtəʊ/ n. (pl. **-oes**) tomate f.

tomb /tuːm/ n. tombeau m.

tombola /tɒm'bəʊlə/ n. tombola f.

tomboy /'tɒmbɔɪ/ n. garçon manqué m.

tombstone /'tuːmstəʊn/ n. pierre tombale f.

tomfoolery /tɒm'fuːlərɪ/ n. âneries f. pl., bêtises f. pl.

tomorrow /tə'mɒrəʊ/ n. & adv. demain (m.). ∼ **morning/night**, demain matin/soir. **the day after** ∼, après-demain.

ton /tʌn/ n. tonne f. (= 1016 kg.). **(metric)** ∼, tonne f. (= 1000 kg.). ∼**s of**, (fam.) des masses de.

tone /təʊn/ n. ton m.; (of radio, telephone, etc.) tonalité f. —v.t. ∼ **down**, atténuer. —v.i. ∼ **in**,

s'harmoniser (**with**, avec). ∼-**deaf** *a.*
qui n'a pas d'oreille. ∼ **up**, (*muscles*)
tonifier.

tongs /tɒŋz/ *n. pl.* pinces *f. pl.*; (*for
sugar*) pince *f.*; (*for hair*) fer *m.*

tongue /tʌŋ/ *n.* langue *f.* ∼-**tied** *a.* muet.
∼-**twister** *n.* phrase difficile à
prononcer *f.* **with one's** ∼ **in one's
cheek**, ironiquement.

tonic /'tɒnɪk/ *n.* (*med.*) tonique *m.* —*a.*
(*effect, accent*) tonique. ∼ (**water**),
tonic *m.*

tonight /tə'naɪt/ *n. & adv.* cette nuit (*f.*);
(*evening*) ce soir (*m.*).

tonne /tʌn/ *n.* (*metric*) tonne *f.*

tonsil /'tɒnsl/ *n.* amygdale *f.*

tonsillitis /tɒnsɪ'laɪtɪs/ *n.* amygdalite *f.*

too /tuː/ *adv.* trop; (*also*) aussi. ∼ **many**
a. trop de; *n.* trop. ∼ **much** *a.* trop de;
adv. & n. trop.

took /tʊk/ *see* **take**.

tool /tuːl/ *n.* outil *m.* ∼-**bag** *n.* trousse à
outils *f.*

toot /tuːt/ *n.* coup de klaxon *m.* —*v.t./i.*
∼ (**the horn**), klaxonner.

tooth /tuːθ/ *n.* (*pl.* **teeth**) dent *f.* ∼**less** *a.*
édenté.

toothache /'tuːθeɪk/ *n.* mal de dents *m.*

toothbrush /'tuːθbrʌʃ/ *n.* brosse à dents
f.

toothcomb /'tuːθkəʊm/ *n.* peigne fin *m.*

toothpaste /'tuːθpeɪst/ *n.* dentifrice *m.*,
pâte dentifrice *f.*

toothpick /'tuːθpɪk/ *n.* cure-dent *m.*

top[1] /tɒp/ *n.* (*highest point*) sommet *m.*;
(*upper part*) haut *m.*; (*upper surface*)
dessus *m.*; (*lid*) couvercle *m.*; (*of bottle,
tube*) bouchon *m.*; (*of beer bottle*)
capsule *f.*; (*of list*) tête *f.* —*a.* (*shelf
etc.*) du haut; (*floor*) dernier; (*in rank*)
premier; (*best*) meilleur; (*distinguished*) éminent; (*maximum*) maximum. —*v.t.* (*p.t.* **topped**) (*exceed*)
dépasser; (*list*) venir en tête de. **from** ∼
to bottom, de fond en comble. **on** ∼ **of**,
sur; (*fig.*) en plus de. ∼ **hat**, haut-de-
forme *m.* ∼-**heavy** *a.* trop lourd du haut.
∼-**level** *a.* du plus haut niveau. ∼-
notch *a.* excellent. ∼-**quality** *a.* de la
plus haute qualité. ∼ **secret**, ultra-
secret. ∼ **up**, remplir. ∼**ped with**,
surmonté de; (*cream etc.*: *culin.*) nappé
de.

top[2] /tɒp/ *n.* (*toy*) toupie *f.*

topic /'tɒpɪk/ *n.* sujet *m.*

topical /'tɒpɪkl/ *a.* d'actualité.

topless /'tɒplɪs/ *a.* aux seins nus.

topple /'tɒpl/ *v.t./i.* (faire) tomber, (faire)
basculer.

topsy-turvy /tɒpsɪ'tɜːvɪ/ *adv. & a.* sens
dessus dessous.

torch /tɔːtʃ/ *n.* (*electric*) lampe de poche
f.; (*flaming*) torche *f.*

tore /tɔː(r)/ *see* **tear**[1].

torment[1] /'tɔːment/ *n.* tourment *m.*

torment[2] /tɔː'ment/ *v.t.* tourmenter;
(*annoy*) agacer.

torn /tɔːn/ *see* **tear**[1].

tornado /tɔː'neɪdəʊ/ *n.* (*pl.* **-oes**) tornade
f.

torpedo /tɔː'piːdəʊ/ *n.* (*pl.* **-oes**) torpille
f. —*v.t.* torpiller.

torrent /'tɒrənt/ *n.* torrent *m.* ∼**ial**
/tə'renʃl/ *a.* torrentiel.

torrid /'tɒrɪd/ *a.* (*climate etc.*) torride;
(*fig.*) passionné.

torso /'tɔːsəʊ/ *n.* (*pl.* **-os**) torse *m.*

tortoise /'tɔːtəs/ *n.* tortue *f.*

tortoiseshell /'tɔːtəsʃel/ *n.* (*for orna-
ments etc.*) écaille *f.*

tortuous /'tɔːtʃʊəs/ *a.* tortueux.

torture /'tɔːtʃə(r)/ *n.* torture *f.*, supplice
m. —*v.t.* torturer. ∼**r** /-ə(r)/ *n.*
tortionnaire *m.*

Tory /'tɔːrɪ/ *n.* tory *m.* —*a.* tory (*f.
invar.*).

toss /tɒs/ *v.t.* jeter, lancer; (*shake*) agiter.
—*v.i.* s'agiter. ∼ **a coin**, ∼ **up**, tirer à
pile ou face (**for**, pour).

tot[1] /tɒt/ *n.* petit(e) enfant *m.(f.)*; (*glass:
fam.*) petit verre *m.*

tot[2] /tɒt/ *v.t.* (*p.t.* **totted**). ∼ **up**, (*fam.*)
additionner.

total /'təʊtl/ *a.* total. —*n.* total *m.* —*v.t.*
(*p.t.* **totalled**) (*find total of*) totaliser;
(*amount to*) s'élever à. ∼**ity** /-'tælətɪ/
n. totalité *f.* ∼**ly** *adv.* totalement.

totalitarian /təʊtælɪ'teərɪən/ *a.* totalitaire.

totter /'tɒtə(r)/ *v.i.* chanceler.

touch /tʌtʃ/ *v.t./i.* toucher; (*of ends,
gardens, etc.*) se toucher; (*tamper with*)
toucher à. —*n.* (*sense*) toucher *m.*;
(*contact*) contact *m.*; (*of colour*) touche
f.; (*football*) touche *f.* **a** ∼ **of**, (*small
amount*) un peu de. **get in** ∼ **with**,
contacter. **lose** ∼, perdre contact. **be
out of** ∼, n'être plus dans le coup. ∼-
and-go *a.* douteux. ∼ **down**, (*aviat.*)
atterrir. ∼-**line** *n.* (ligne de) touche *f.* ∼
off, (*explode*) faire partir; (*cause*)
déclencher. ∼ **on**, (*mention*) aborder.
∼ **up**, retoucher.

touchdown /'tʌtʃdaʊn/ *n.* atterrissage
m.; (*sport, Amer.*) but *m.*

touching /'tʌtʃɪŋ/ *a.* touchant.

touchstone /'tʌtʃstəʊn/ *n.* pierre de
touche *f.*

touchy /'tʌtʃi/ a. susceptible.

tough /tʌf/ a. (**-er, -est**) (*hard, difficult*) dur; (*strong*) solide; (*relentless*) acharné. —n. ~ (**guy**), dur m. ~ **luck!**, (*fam.*) tant pis! ~**ness** n. dureté f.; solidité f.

toughen /'tʌfn/ v.t. (*strengthen*) renforcer; (*person*) endurcir.

toupee /'tu:peɪ/ n. postiche m.

tour /tʊə(r)/ n. voyage m.; (*visit*) visite f.; (*by team etc.*) tournée f. —v.t. visiter. **on** ~, en tournée. ~ **operator**, voyagiste m.

tourism /'tʊərɪzəm/ n. tourisme m.

tourist /'tʊərɪst/ n. touriste m./f. —a. touristique. ~ **office**, syndicat d'initiative m.

tournament /'tɔ:nəmənt/ n. (*sport & medieval*) tournoi m.

tousle /'taʊzl/ v.t. ébouriffer.

tout /taʊt/ v.i. ~ (**for**), racoler. —v.t. (*sell*) revendre. —n. racoleur, -se m./f.; revendeur, -se m., f.

tow /təʊ/ v.t. remorquer. —n. remorque f. **on** ~, en remorque. ~ **away**, (*vehicle*) (faire) enlever. ~-**path** n. chemin de halage m. ~ **truck**, dépanneuse f.

toward(s) /tə'wɔ:d(z), *Amer.* tɔ:d(z)/ prep. vers; (*of attitude*) envers.

towel /'taʊəl/ n. serviette f.; (*teatowel*) torchon m. ~**ling** n. tissu-éponge m.

tower /'taʊə(r)/ n. tour f. —v.i. ~ **above**, dominer. ~ **block**, tour f., immeuble m. ~**ing** a. très haut.

town /taʊn/ n. ville f. **go to** ~, (*fam.*) mettre le paquet. ~ **council**, conseil municipal m. ~ **hall**, hôtel de ville m.

toxic /'tɒksɪk/ a. toxique.

toxin /'tɒksɪn/ n. toxine f.

toy /tɔɪ/ n. jouet m. —v.i. ~ **with**, (*object*) jouer avec; (*idea*) caresser.

toyshop /'tɔɪʃɒp/ n. magasin de jouets m.

trace /treɪs/ n. trace f. —v.t. suivre or retrouver la trace de; (*draw*) tracer; (*with tracing-paper*) décalquer; (*relate*) retracer.

tracing /'treɪsɪŋ/ n. calque m. ~-**paper** n. papier-calque m.

track /træk/ n. (*of person etc.*) trace f., piste f.; (*path, race-track & of tape*) piste f.; (*on disc*) plage f.; (*of rocket etc.*) trajectoire f.; (*rail.*) voie f. —v.t. suivre la trace or la trajectoire de. **keep** ~ **of**, suivre. ~ **down**, (*find*) retrouver; (*hunt*) traquer. ~ **suit**, survêtement m.; (*with sweatshirt*) jogging m.

tract[1] /trækt/ n. (*land*) étendue f.; (*anat.*) appareil m.

tract[2] /trækt/ n. (*pamphlet*) tract m.

tractor /'træktə(r)/ n. tracteur m.

trade /treɪd/ n. commerce m.; (*job*) métier m.; (*swap*) échange m. —v.i. faire du commerce. —v.t. échanger. ~ **deficit**, déficit commercial m. ~ **in**, (*used article*) faire reprendre. ~-**in** n. reprise f. ~ **mark**, marque de fabrique f.; (*name*) marque déposée f. ~-**off** n. (*fam.*) compromis m. ~ **on**, (*exploit*) abuser de. ~ **union**, syndicat m. ~-**unionist** n. syndicaliste m./f. ~**r** /-ə(r)/ n. négociant(e) m. (f.), commerçant(e) m. (f.).

tradesman /'treɪdzmən/ n. (*pl.* **-men**) commerçant m.

trading /'treɪdɪŋ/ n. commerce m. ~ **estate**, zone industrielle f.

tradition /trə'dɪʃn/ n. tradition f. ~**al** a. traditionnel.

traffic /'træfɪk/ n. trafic m.; (*on road*) circulation f. —v.i. (*p.t.* **trafficked**) trafiquer (**in**, de). ~ **circle**, (*Amer.*) rond-point m. ~ **cone**, cône de délimitation de voie m. ~ **jam**, embouteillage m. ~-**lights** n. pl. feux (de circulation) m. pl. ~ **warden**, contractuel(le) m. (f.).

tragedy /'trædʒədɪ/ n. tragédie f.

tragic /'trædʒɪk/ a. tragique.

trail /treɪl/ v.t./i. traîner; (*of plant*) ramper; (*track*) suivre. —n. (*of powder etc.*) traînée f.; (*track*) piste f.; (*beaten path*) sentier m. ~ **behind**, traîner.

trailer /'treɪlə(r)/ n. remorque f.; (*caravan: Amer.*) caravane f.; (*film*) bande-annonce f.

train /treɪn/ n. (*rail.*) train m.; (*underground*) rame f.; (*procession*) file f.; (*of dress*) traîne f. —v.t. (*instruct, develop*) former; (*sportsman*) entraîner; (*animal*) dresser; (*ear*) exercer; (*aim*) braquer. —v.i. recevoir une formation; s'entraîner. ~**ed** a. (*skilled*) qualifié; (*doctor etc.*) diplômé. ~**er** n. (*sport*) entraîneur, -se m., f. ~**ers**, (*shoes*) chaussures de sport f. pl. ~**ing** n. formation f.; entraînement m.; dressage m.

trainee /treɪ'ni:/ n. stagiaire m./f.

traipse /treɪps/ v.i. (*fam.*) traîner.

trait /treɪ(t)/ n. trait m.

traitor /'treɪtə(r)/ n. traître m.

tram /træm/ n. tram(way) m.

tramp /træmp/ v.i. marcher (d'un pas lourd). —v.t. parcourir. —n. pas lourds m. pl.; (*vagrant*) clochard(e) m. (f.); (*Amer., sl.*) dévergondée f.; (*hike*) randonnée f.

trample /'træmpl/ v.t./i. ~ **(on)**, piétiner; (fig.) fouler aux pieds.

trampoline /'træmpəli:n/ n. (canvas sheet) trampoline m.

trance /trɑ:ns/ n. transe f.

tranquil /'træŋkwɪl/ a. tranquille. ~**lity** /-'kwɪlətɪ/ n. tranquillité f.

tranquillizer /'træŋkwɪlaɪzə(r)/ n. (drug) tranquillisant m.

transact /træn'zækt/ v.t. traiter. ~**ion** /-kʃn/ n. transaction f.

transatlantic /trænzət'læntɪk/ a. transatlantique.

transcend /træn'send/ v.t. transcender. ~**ent** a. transcendant.

transcript /'trænskrɪpt/ n. (written copy) transcription f.

transfer[1] /træns'fɜ:(r)/ v.t. (p.t. **transferred**) transférer; (power) faire passer. —v.i. être transféré. ~ **the charges,** (telephone) téléphoner en PCV.

transfer[2] /'trænsfɜ:(r)/ n. transfert m.; (of power) passation f.; (image) décalcomanie f.; (sticker) autocollant m.

transform /træns'fɔ:m/ v.t. transformer. ~**ation** /-ə'meɪʃn/ n. transformation f. ~**er** n. (electr.) transformateur m.

transfusion /træns'fju:ʒn/ n. (of blood) transfusion f.

transient /'trænzɪənt/ a. transitoire, éphémère.

transistor /træn'zɪstə(r)/ n. (device, radio set) transistor m.

transit /'trænsɪt/ n. transit m.

transition /træn'zɪʃn/ n. transition f. ~**al** a. transitoire.

transitive /'trænsətɪv/ a. transitif.

transitory /'trænsɪtərɪ/ a. transitoire.

translat|e /trænz'leɪt/ v.t. traduire. ~**ion** /-ʃn/ n. traduction f. ~**or** n. tradu|cteur, -trice m., f.

translucent /trænz'lu:snt/ a. translucide.

transmi|t /trænz'mɪt/ v.t. (p.t. **transmitted**) (pass on etc.) transmettre; (broadcast) émettre. ~**ssion** n. transmission f.; émission f. ~**tter** n. émetteur m.

transparen|t /træns'pærənt/ a. transparent. ~**cy** n. transparence f.; (photo.) diapositive f.

transpire /træn'spaɪə(r)/ v.i. s'avérer; (happen: fam.) arriver.

transplant[1] /træns'plɑ:nt/ v.t. transplanter; (med.) greffer.

transplant[2] /'trænsplɑ:nt/ n. transplantation f.; greffe f.

transport[1] /træn'spɔ:t/ v.t. (carry, delight) transporter. ~**ation** /-'teɪʃn/ n. transport m.

transport[2] /'trænspɔ:t/ n. (of goods, delight, etc.) transport m.

transpose /træn'spəʊz/ v.t. transposer.

transverse /'trænzvɜ:s/ a. transversal.

transvestite /trænz'vestaɪt/ n. travesti(e) m. (f.).

trap /træp/ n. piège m. —v.t. (p.t. **trapped**) (jam, pin down) coincer; (cut off) bloquer; (snare) prendre au piège. ~**per** n. trappeur m.

trapdoor /træp'dɔ:(r)/ n. trappe f.

trapeze /trə'pi:z/ n. trapèze m.

trappings /'træpɪŋz/ n. pl. (fig.) signes extérieurs m. pl., apparat m.

trash /træʃ/ n. (junk) saleté(s) f. (pl.); (refuse) ordures f. pl.; (nonsense) idioties f. pl. ~**can** n. (Amer.) poubelle f. ~**y** a. qui ne vaut rien, de mauvaise qualité.

trauma /'trɔ:mə/ n. traumatisme m. ~**tic** /-'mætɪk/ a. traumatisant.

travel /'trævl/ v.i. (p.t. **travelled**, Amer. **traveled**) voyager; (of vehicle, bullet, etc.) aller. —v.t. parcourir. —n. voyage(s) m. (pl.). ~ **agent,** agent de voyage m. ~**ler** n. voyageur, -se m., f. ~**ler's cheque,** chèque de voyage m. ~**ling** n. voyage(s) m. (pl.). ~ **sickness,** mal des transports m.

travesty /'trævəstɪ/ n. parodie f., simulacre m. —v.t. travestir.

trawler /'trɔ:lə(r)/ n. chalutier m.

tray /treɪ/ n. plateau m.; (on office desk) corbeille f.

treacherous /'tretʃərəs/ a. traître. ~**ly** adv. traîtreusement.

treachery /'tretʃərɪ/ n. traîtrise f.

treacle /'tri:kl/ n. mélasse f.

tread /tred/ v.i. (p.t. **trod**, p.p. **trodden**) marcher (**on,** sur). —v.t. parcourir (à pied); (soil: fig.) fouler. —n. démarche f.; (sound) (bruit m. de) pas m. pl.; (of tyre) chape f. ~ **sth. into,** (carpet) étaler qch. sur (avec les pieds).

treason /'tri:zn/ n. trahison f.

treasure /'treʒə(r)/ n. trésor m. —v.t. attacher une grande valeur à; (store) conserver. ~**r** /-ə(r)/ n. trésorier, -ière m., f.

treasury /'treʒərɪ/ n. trésorerie f. **the T**~, le ministère des Finances.

treat /tri:t/ v.t. traiter; (consider) considérer. —n. (pleasure) plaisir m., régal m.; (present) gâterie f.; (food) régal m. ~ **s.o. to sth.,** offrir qch. à qn.

treatise /'tri:tɪz/ n. traité m.

treatment /'tri:tmənt/ n. traitement m.

treaty /'tri:tɪ/ n. (pact) traité m.

trebl|e /'trebl/ a. triple. —v.t./i. tripler. —n. (voice: mus.) soprano m. **~e clef**, clé de sol f. **~y** adv. triplement.

tree /tri:/ n. arbre m. **~-top** n. cime (d'un arbre) f.

trek /trek/ n. voyage pénible m.; (sport) randonnée f. —v.i. (p.t. **trekked**) voyager (péniblement); (sport) faire de la randonnée.

trellis /'trelɪs/ n. treillage m.

tremble /'trembl/ v.i. trembler.

tremendous /trɪ'mendəs/ a. énorme; (excellent: fam.) fantastique. **~ly** adv. fantastiquement.

tremor /'tremə(r)/ n. tremblement m. **(earth) ~**, secousse (sismique) f.

trench /trentʃ/ n. tranchée f.

trend /trend/ n. tendance f.; (fashion) mode f. **~-setter** n. lanceur, -se de mode m., f. **~y** a. (fam.) dans le vent.

trepidation /trepɪ'deɪʃn/ n. (fear) inquiétude f.

trespass /'trespəs/ v.i. s'introduire sans autorisation (**on**, dans). **~er** n. intrus(e) m. (f.).

tresses /'tresɪz/ n. pl. chevelure f.

trestle /'tresl/ n. tréteau m. **~-table** n. table à tréteaux f.

tri- /traɪ/ pref. tri-.

trial /'traɪəl/ n. (jurid.) procès m.; (test) essai m.; (ordeal) épreuve f. **go on ~**, passer en jugement. **~ and error**, tâtonnements m. pl. **~ run**, galop d'essai m.

triangle /'traɪæŋgl/ n. triangle m. **~ular** /-'æŋgjʊlə(r)/ a. triangulaire.

trib|e /traɪb/ n. tribu f. **~al** a. tribal.

tribulation /trɪbjʊ'leɪʃn/ n. tribulation f.

tribunal /traɪ'bju:nl/ n. tribunal m.; (mil.) commission f.

tributary /'trɪbjʊtərɪ/ n. affluent m.

tribute /'trɪbju:t/ n. tribut m. **pay ~ to**, rendre hommage à.

trick /trɪk/ n. astuce f., ruse f.; (joke, feat of skill) tour m.; (habit) manie f. —v.t. tromper. **do the ~**, (fam.) faire l'affaire.

trickery /'trɪkərɪ/ n. ruse f.

trickle /'trɪkl/ v.i. dégouliner. **~ in/out**, arriver or partir en petit nombre. —n. filet m.; (fig.) petit nombre m.

tricky /'trɪkɪ/ a. (crafty) rusé; (problem) délicat, difficile.

tricycle /'traɪsɪkl/ n. tricycle m.

trifle /'traɪfl/ n. bagatelle f.; (cake) diplomate m. —v.i. **~ with**, jouer avec. **a ~**, (small amount) un peu.

trifling /'traɪflɪŋ/ a. insignifiant.

trigger /'trɪgə(r)/ n. (of gun) gâchette f., détente f. —v.t. **~ (off)**, (initiate) déclencher.

trilby /'trɪlbɪ/ n. (hat) feutre m.

trim /trɪm/ a. (trimmer, trimmest) net, soigné; (figure) svelte. —v.t. (p.t. **trimmed**) (cut) couper légèrement; (hair) rafraîchir; (budget) réduire. —n. (cut) coupe légère f.; (decoration) garniture f. **in ~**, en bon ordre; (fit) en forme. **~ with**, (decorate) orner de. **~ming(s)** n. (pl.) garniture(s) f. (pl.).

Trinity /'trɪnətɪ/ n. Trinité f.

trinket /'trɪŋkɪt/ n. colifichet m.

trio /'tri:əʊ/ n. (pl. **-os**) trio m.

trip /trɪp/ v.t./i. (p.t. **tripped**) (faire) trébucher; (go lightly) marcher d'un pas léger. —n. (journey) voyage m.; (outing) excursion f.; (stumble) faux pas m.

tripe /traɪp/ n. (food) tripes f. pl.; (nonsense: sl.) bêtises f. pl.

triple /'trɪpl/ a. triple. —v.t./i. tripler. **~ts** /-plɪts/ n. (pl.) triplé(e)s m. (f.) pl.

tripod /'traɪpɒd/ n. trépied m.

trite /traɪt/ a. banal.

triumph /'traɪəmf/ n. triomphe m. —v.i. triompher (**over**, de). **~al** /-'ʌmfl/ a. triomphal. **~ant** /-'ʌmfənt/ a. triomphant, triomphal. **~antly** /-'ʌmfəntlɪ/ adv. en triomphe.

trivial /'trɪvɪəl/ a. insignifiant. **~ize** v.t. considérer comme insignifiant.

trod, trodden /trɒd, 'trɒdn/ see tread.

trolley /'trɒlɪ/ n. chariot m. **(tea-)~**, table roulante f. **~-bus** n. trolleybus m.

trombone /trɒm'bəʊn/ n. (mus.) trombone m.

troop /tru:p/ n. bande f. **~s**, (mil.) troupes f. pl. —v.i. **~ in/out**, entrer/sortir en bande. **~er** n. soldat de cavalerie m. **~ing the colour**, le salut au drapeau.

trophy /'trəʊfɪ/ n. trophée m.

tropic /'trɒpɪk/ n. tropique m. **~s**, tropiques m. pl. **~al** a. tropical.

trot /trɒt/ n. trot m. —v.i. (p.t. **trotted**) trotter. **on the ~**, (fam.) de suite. **~ out**, (produce: fam.) sortir; (state: fam.) formuler.

trouble /'trʌbl/ n. ennui(s) m. (pl.), difficulté(s) f. (pl.); (pains, effort) mal m., peine f. **~(s)**, ennuis m. pl.; (unrest) conflits m. pl. —v.t./i. (bother) (se) déranger; (worry) ennuyer. **be in ~**, avoir des ennuis. **go to a lot of ~**, se donner du mal. **what's the ~?**, quel est le problème? **~d** a. inquiet; (period)

agité. **~-maker** n. provocalteur, -trice
m., f. **~-shooter** n. personne appelée
pour désamorcer une crise.

troublesome /'trʌblsəm/ a. ennuyeux,
pénible.

trough /trɒf/ n. (drinking) abreuvoir m.;
(feeding) auge f. **~ (of low pressure)**,
dépression f.

trounce /traʊns/ v.t. (defeat) écraser;
(thrash) rosser.

troupe /truːp/ n. (theatre) troupe f.

trousers /'traʊzəz/ n. pl. pantalon m.
short ~, culotte courte f.

trousseau /'truːsəʊ/ n. (pl. **-s** /-əʊz/) (of
bride) trousseau f.

trout /traʊt/ n. invar. truite f.

trowel /'traʊəl/ n. (garden) déplantoir
m.; (for mortar) truelle f.

truan|t /'truːənt/ n. absentéiste m./f.;
(schol.) élève absent(e) sans permission
m.(f.). **play ~t**, sécher les cours. **~cy** n.
absentéisme m.

truce /truːs/ n. trève f.

truck /trʌk/ n. (lorry) camion m.; (cart)
chariot m.; (rail.) wagon m., plateforme
f. **~-driver** n. camionneur m.

truculent /'trʌkjʊlənt/ a. agressif.

trudge /trʌdʒ/ v.i. marcher péniblement,
se traîner.

true /truː/ a. (-er, -est) vrai; (accurate)
exact; (faithful) fidèle.

truffle /'trʌfl/ n. truffe f.

truly /'truːlɪ/ adv. vraiment; (faithfully)
fidèlement; (truthfully) sincèrement.

trump /trʌmp/ n. atout m. —v.t. **~ up**,
inventer. **~ card**, atout m.

trumpet /'trʌmpɪt/ n. trompette f.

truncate /trʌŋ'keɪt/ v.t. tronquer.

trundle /'trʌndl/ v.t./i. rouler bruyamment.

trunk /trʌŋk/ n. (of tree, body) tronc m.;
(of elephant) trompe f.; (box) malle f.;
(auto., Amer.) coffre m. **~s**, (for
swimming) slip de bain m. **~-call** n.
communication interurbaine f. **~-road**
n. route nationale f.

truss /trʌs/ n. (med.) bandage herniaire
m. —v.t. (fowl) trousser.

trust /trʌst/ n. confiance f.; (association)
trust m. —v.t. avoir confiance en. —v.i.
~ in or **to**, s'en remettre à. **in ~**, en
dépôt. **on ~**, de confiance. **s.o. with**,
confier à qn. **~ed** a. (friend etc.)
éprouvé, sûr. **~ful, ~ing** adjs. confiant.
~y a. fidèle.

trustee /trʌs'tiː/ n. administralteur, -trice
m., f.

trustworthy /'trʌstwɜːðɪ/ a. digne de
confiance.

truth /truːθ/ n. (pl. **-s** /truːðz/) vérité f.
~ful a. (account etc.) véridique;
(person) qui dit la vérité. **~fully** adv.
sincèrement.

try /traɪ/ v.t./i. (p.t. **tried**) essayer; (be a
strain on) éprouver; (jurid.) juger. —n.
(attempt) essai m.; (Rugby) essai m. **~
on** or **out**, essayer. **~ to do**, essayer de
faire. **~ing** a. éprouvant.

tsar /zɑː(r)/ n. tsar m.

T-shirt /'tiːʃɜːt/ n. tee-shirt m.

tub /tʌb/ n. baquet m., cuve f.; (bath:
fam.) baignoire f.

tuba /'tjuːbə/ n. tuba m.

tubby /'tʌbɪ/ a. (-ier, -iest) dodu.

tub|e /tjuːb/ n. tube m.; (railway: fam.)
métro m.; (in tyre) chambre à air f.
~ing n. tubes m. pl.

tuberculosis /tjuːbɜːkjʊ'ləʊsɪs/ n. tuber-
culose f.

tubular /'tjuːbjʊlə(r)/ a. tubulaire.

tuck /tʌk/ n. (fold) rempli m., (re)pli m.
—v.t. (put away, place) ranger; (hide)
cacher. —v.i. **~ in** or **into**, (eat: sl.)
attaquer. **~ in**, (shirt) rentrer; (blanket,
person) border. **~-shop** n. (schol.)
boutique à provisions f.

Tuesday /'tjuːzdɪ/ n. mardi m.

tuft /tʌft/ n. (of hair etc.) touffe f.

tug /tʌg/ v.t. (p.t. **tugged**) tirer fort (sur).
—v.i. tirer fort. —n. (boat) remorqueur
m. **~ of war**, jeu de la corde tirée m.

tuition /tjuː'ɪʃn/ n. cours m. pl.; (fee)
frais de scolarité m. pl.

tulip /'tjuːlɪp/ n. tulipe f.

tumble /'tʌmbl/ v.i. (fall) dégringoler.
—n. chute f. **~-drier** n. séchoir à linge
(à air chaud) m. **~ to**, (realize: fam.)
piger.

tumbledown /'tʌmbldaʊn/ a. délabré,
en ruine.

tumbler /'tʌmblə(r)/ n. gobelet m.

tummy /'tʌmɪ/ n. (fam.) ventre m.

tumour /'tjuːmə(r)/ n. tumeur f.

tumult /'tjuːmʌlt/ n. tumulte m. **~uous**
/-'mʌltʃʊəs/ a. tumultueux.

tuna /'tjuːnə/ n. invar. thon m.

tune /tjuːn/ n. air m. —v.t. (engine)
régler; (mus.) accorder. —v.i. **~ in**
(to), (radio, TV) écouter. **be in ~/out of
~**, (instrument) être accordé/désac-
cordé; (singer) chanter juste/faux. **~ful**
a. mélodieux. **tuning-fork** n. diapason
m. **~ up**, (orchestra) accorder leurs
instruments.

tunic /'tjuːnɪk/ n. tunique f.

Tunisia /tjuː'nɪzɪə/ n. Tunisie f. **~n** a. &
n. tunisien(ne) (m. (f.)).

tunnel /'tʌnl/ n. tunnel m.; (in mine)

galerie *f.* —*v.i.* (*p.t.* **tunnelled**) creuser un tunnel (**into,** dans).

turban /'tɜːbən/ *n.* turban *m.*

turbine /'tɜːbaɪn/ *n.* turbine *f.*

turbo /'tɜːbəʊ/ *n.* turbo *m.*

turbulen|t /'tɜːbjʊlənt/ *a.* turbulent. **~ce** *n.* turbulence *f.*

tureen /tjʊ'riːn/ *n.* soupière *f.*

turf /tɜːf/ *n.* (*pl.* **turf** *or* **turves**) gazon *m.* —*v.t.* **~ out,** (*sl.*) jeter dehors. **the ~,** (*racing*) le turf.

turgid /'tɜːdʒɪd/ *a.* (*speech, style*) boursouflé, ampoulé.

Turk /tɜːk/ *n.* Turc *m.*, Turque *f.* **~ey** *n.* Turquie *f.* **~ish** *a.* turc; *n.* (*lang.*) turc *m.*

turkey /'tɜːkɪ/ *n.* dindon *m.*, dinde *f.*; (*as food*) dinde *f.*

turmoil /'tɜːmɔɪl/ *n.* trouble *m.*, chaos *m.* **in ~,** en ébullition.

turn /tɜːn/ *v.t./i.* tourner; (*of person*) se tourner; (*to other side*) retourner; (*change*) (se) transformer (**into,** en); (*become*) devenir; (*deflect*) détourner; (*milk*) tourner. —*n.* tour *m.*; (*in road*) tournant *m.*; (*of mind, events*) tournure *f.*; (*illness: fam.*) crise *f.* **do a good ~,** rendre service. **in ~,** à tour de rôle. **speak out of ~,** commettre une indiscrétion. **take ~s,** se relayer. **~ against,** se retourner contre. **~ away** *v.i.* se détourner; *v.t.* (*avert*) détourner; (*refuse*) refuser; (*send back*) renvoyer. **~ back** *v.i.* (*return*) retourner; (*vehicle*) faire demi-tour; *v.t.* (*fold*) rabattre; (*reduce*) baisser. **~ in,** (*go to bed: fam.*) se coucher. **~ off,** (*light etc.*) éteindre; (*engine*) arrêter; (*tap*) fermer; (*of driver*) tourner. **~-off** *n.* (*auto.*) embranchement *m.* **~ on,** (*light etc.*) allumer; (*engine*) allumer; (*tap*) ouvrir. **~ out** *v.t.* (*light*) éteindre; (*empty*) vider; (*produce*) produire; *v.i.* (*transpire*) s'avérer; (*come: fam.*) venir. **~-out** *n.* assistance *f.* **~ over,** (se) retourner. **~ round,** (*person*) se retourner. **~-round** *n.* revirement *m.* **~ up** *v.i.* arriver; (*be found*) se retrouver; *v.t.* (*find*) déterrer; (*collar*) remonter. **~-up** *n.* (*of trousers*) revers *m.*

turning /'tɜːnɪŋ/ *n.* rue (latérale) *f.*; (*bend*) tournant *m.* **~-point** *n.* tournant *m.*

turnip /'tɜːnɪp/ *n.* navet *m.*

turnover /'tɜːnəʊvə(r)/ *n.* (*pie, tart*) chausson *m.*; (*money*) chiffre d'affaires *m.*

turnpike /'tɜːnpaɪk/ *n.* (*Amer.*) autoroute à péage *f.*

turnstile /'tɜːnstaɪl/ *n.* (*gate*) tourniquet *m.*

turntable /'tɜːnteɪbl/ *n.* (*for record*) platine *f.*, plateau *m.*

turpentine /'tɜːpəntaɪn/ *n.* térébenthine *f.*

turquoise /'tɜːkwɔɪz/ *a.* turquoise *invar.*

turret /'tʌrɪt/ *n.* tourelle *f.*

turtle /'tɜːtl/ *n.* tortue (de mer) *f.* **~-neck** *a.* à col montant, roulé.

tusk /tʌsk/ *n.* (*tooth*) défense *f.*

tussle /'tʌsl/ *n.* bagarre *f.*, lutte *f.*

tutor /'tjuːtə(r)/ *n.* précep|teur, -trice *m.*, *f.*; (*univ.*) direc|teur, -trice d'études *m.*, *f.*

tutorial /tjuː'tɔːrɪəl/ *n.* (*univ.*) séance d'études *or* de travaux pratiques *f.*

tuxedo /tʌk'siːdəʊ/ *n.* (*pl.* **-os**) (*Amer.*) smoking *m.*

TV /tiː'viː/ *n.* télé *f.*

twaddle /'twɒdl/ *n.* fadaises *f. pl.*

twang /twæŋ/ *n.* (*son: mus.*) pincement *m.*; (*in voice*) nasillement *m.* —*v.t./i.* (faire) vibrer.

tweed /twiːd/ *n.* tweed *m.*

tweezers /'twiːzəz/ *n. pl.* pince (à épiler) *f.*

twel|ve /twelv/ *a. & n.* douze (*m.*). **~fth** *a. & n.* douzième (*m./f.*). **~ve (o'clock),** midi *m. or* minuit *m.*

twent|y /'twentɪ/ *a. & n.* vingt (*m.*). **~ieth** *a. & n.* vingtième (*m./f.*).

twice /twaɪs/ *adv.* deux fois.

twiddle /'twɪdl/ *v.t./i.* **~ (with),** (*fiddle with*) tripoter. **~ one's thumbs,** se tourner les pouces.

twig[1] /twɪg/ *n.* brindille *f.*

twig[2] /twɪg/ *v.t./i.* (*p.t.* **twigged**) (*understand: fam.*) piger.

twilight /'twaɪlaɪt/ *n.* crépuscule *m.* —*a.* crépusculaire.

twin /twɪn/ *n. & a.* jumeau, -elle (*m.*, *f.*). —*v.t.* (*p.t.* **twinned**) jumeler. **~ning** *n.* jumelage *m.*

twine /twaɪn/ *n.* ficelle *f.* —*v.t./i.* (*wind*) (s')enlacer.

twinge /twɪndʒ/ *n.* élancement *m.*; (*remorse*) remords *m.*

twinkle /'twɪŋkl/ *v.i.* (*star etc.*) scintiller; (*eye*) pétiller. —*n.* scintillement *m.*; pétillement *m.*

twirl /twɜːl/ *v.t./i.* (faire) tournoyer.

twist /twɪst/ *v.t.* tordre; (*weave together*) entortiller; (*roll*) enrouler; (*distort*) déformer. —*v.i.* (*rope etc.*) s'entortiller; (*road*) zigzaguer. —*n.* torsion *f.*;

(*in rope*) tortillon *m.*; (*in road*) tournant *m.*; (*of events*) tournure *f.*, tour *m.*

twit /twɪt/ *n.* (*fam.*) idiot(e) *m.* (*f.*).

twitch /twɪtʃ/ *v.t./i.* (se) contracter nerveusement. —*n.* (*tic*) tic *m.*; (*jerk*) secousse *f.*

two /tuː/ *a. & n.* deux (*m.*). **in** *or* **of** ∼ **minds,** indécis. **put** ∼ **and two together,** faire le rapport. ∼**-faced** *a.* hypocrite. ∼**fold** *a.* double; *adv.* au double. ∼**-piece** *n.* (*garment*) deux-pièces *m. invar.*

twosome /ˈtuːsəm/ *n.* couple *m.*

tycoon /taɪˈkuːn/ *n.* magnat *m.*

tying /ˈtaɪɪŋ/ *see* **tie.**

type /taɪp/ *n.* (*example*) type *m.*; (*kind*) genre *m.*, sorte *f.*; (*person: fam.*) type *m.*; (*print*) caractères *m. pl.* —*v.t./i.* (*write*) taper (à la machine). ∼**cast** *a.* catégorisé (**as,** comme).

typescript /ˈtaɪpskrɪpt/ *n.* manuscrit dactylographié *m.*

typewrit|er /ˈtaɪpraɪtə(r)/ *n.* machine à écrire *f.* ∼**ten** /-ɪtn/ *a.* dactylographié.

typhoid /ˈtaɪfɔɪd/ *n.* ∼ (**fever**), typhoïde *f.*

typhoon /taɪˈfuːn/ *n.* typhon *m.*

typical /ˈtɪpɪkl/ *a.* typique. ∼**ly** *adv.* typiquement.

typify /ˈtɪpɪfaɪ/ *v.t.* être typique de.

typing /ˈtaɪpɪŋ/ *n.* dactylo(graphie) *f.*

typist /ˈtaɪpɪst/ *n.* dactylo *f.*

tyrann|y /ˈtɪrənɪ/ *n.* tyrannie *f.* ∼**ical** /tɪˈrænɪkl/ *a.* tyrannique.

tyrant /ˈtaɪərənt/ *n.* tyran *m.*

tyre /ˈtaɪə(r)/ *n.* pneu *m.*

U

ubiquitous /juːˈbɪkwɪtəs/ *a.* omniprésent, qu'on trouve partout.

udder /ˈʌdə(r)/ *n.* pis *m.*, mamelle *f.*

UFO /ˈjuːfəʊ/ *n.* (*pl.* **-Os**) OVNI *m.*

Uganda /juːˈɡændə/ *n.* Ouganda *m.*

ugl|y /ˈʌɡlɪ/ *a.* (**-ier, -iest**) laid. ∼**iness** *n.* laideur *f.*

UK *abbr. see* **United Kingdom.**

ulcer /ˈʌlsə(r)/ *n.* ulcère *m.*

ulterior /ʌlˈtɪərɪə(r)/ *a.* ultérieur. ∼ **motive,** arrière-pensée *f.*

ultimate /ˈʌltɪmət/ *a.* dernier, ultime; (*definitive*) définitif; (*basic*) fondamental. ∼**ly** *adv.* à la fin; (*in the last analysis*) en fin de compte.

ultimatum /ʌltɪˈmeɪtəm/ *n.* (*pl.* **-ums**) ultimatum *m.*

ultra- /ˈʌltrə/ *pref.* ultra-.

ultrasound /ˈʌltrəsaʊnd/ *n.* ultrason *m.*

ultraviolet /ʌltrəˈvaɪələt/ *a.* ultraviolet.

umbilical /ʌmˈbɪlɪkl/ *a.* ∼ **cord,** cordon ombilical *m.*

umbrella /ʌmˈbrelə/ *n.* parapluie *m.*

umpire /ˈʌmpaɪə(r)/ *n.* (*sport*) arbitre *m.* —*v.t.* arbitrer.

umpteen /ˈʌmptiːn/ *a.* (*many: sl.*) un tas de. ∼**th** *a.* (*fam.*) énième.

UN *abbr.* (*United Nations*) ONU *f.*

un- /ʌn/ *pref.* in-, dé(s)-, non, peu, mal, sans.

unabated /ʌnəˈbeɪtɪd/ *a.* non diminué, aussi fort qu'avant.

unable /ʌnˈeɪbl/ *a.* incapable; (*through circumstances*) dans l'impossibilité (**to do,** de faire).

unacceptable /ʌnəkˈseptəbl/ *a.* inacceptable, inadmissible.

unaccountabl|e /ʌnəˈkaʊntəbl/ *a.* (*strange*) inexplicable. ∼**y** *adv.* inexplicablement.

unaccustomed /ʌnəˈkʌstəmd/ *a.* inaccoutumé. ∼ **to,** peu habitué à.

unadulterated /ʌnəˈdʌltəreɪtɪd/ *a.* (*pure, sheer*) pur.

unaided /ʌnˈeɪdɪd/ *a.* sans aide.

unanim|ous /juːˈnænɪməs/ *a.* unanime. ∼**ity** /-əˈnɪmətɪ/ *n.* unanimité *f.* ∼**ously** *adv.* à l'unanimité.

unarmed /ʌnˈɑːmd/ *a.* non armé.

unashamed /ʌnəˈʃeɪmd/ *a.* éhonté. ∼**ly** /-ɪdlɪ/ *adv.* sans vergogne.

unassuming /ʌnəˈsjuːmɪŋ/ *a.* modeste, sans prétention.

unattached /ʌnəˈtætʃt/ *a.* libre.

unattainable /ʌnəˈteɪnəbl/ *a.* inaccessible.

unattended /ʌnəˈtendɪd/ *a.* (laissé) sans surveillance.

unattractive /ʌnəˈtræktɪv/ *a.* peu séduisant, laid; (*offer*) peu intéressant.

unauthorized /ʌnˈɔːθəraɪzd/ *a.* non autorisé.

unavailable /ʌnəˈveɪləbl/ *a.* pas disponible.

unavoidabl|e /ʌnəˈvɔɪdəbl/ *a.* inévitable. ∼**y** *adv.* inévitablement.

unaware /ʌnəˈweə(r)/ *a.* **be** ∼ **of,** ignorer. ∼**s** /-eəz/ *adv.* au dépourvu.

unbalanced /ʌnˈbælənst/ *a.* (*mind, person*) déséquilibré.

unbearable /ʌnˈbeərəbl/ *a.* insupportable.

unbeat|able /ʌnˈbiːtəbl/ *a.* imbattable. ∼**en** *a.* non battu.

unbeknown(st) /ʌnbɪˈnəʊn(st)/ *a.* ∼**(st) to,** (*fam.*) à l'insu de.

unbelievable /ʌnbɪ'liːvəbl/ a. incroyable.

unbend /ʌn'bend/ v.i. (p.t. **unbent**) (relax) se détendre.

unbiased /ʌn'baɪəst/ a. impartial.

unblock /ʌn'blɒk/ v.t. déboucher.

unborn /ʌn'bɔːn/ a. futur, à venir.

unbounded /ʌn'baʊndɪd/ a. illimité.

unbreakable /ʌn'breɪkəbl/ a. incassable.

unbridled /ʌn'braɪdld/ a. débridé.

unbroken /ʌn'brəʊkən/ a. (intact) intact; (continuous) continu.

unburden /ʌn'bɜːdn/ v. pr. ~ o.s., (open one's heart) s'épancher.

unbutton /ʌn'bʌtn/ v.t. déboutonner.

uncalled-for /ʌn'kɔːldfɔː(r)/ a. injustifié, superflu.

uncanny /ʌn'kænɪ/ a. (-ier, -iest) étrange, mystérieux.

unceasing /ʌn'siːsɪŋ/ a. incessant.

unceremonious /ʌnserɪ'məʊnɪəs/ a. sans façon, brusque.

uncertain /ʌn'sɜːtn/ a. incertain. be ~ whether, ne pas savoir exactement si (to do, on doit faire). ~ty n. incertitude f.

unchang|ed /ʌn'tʃeɪndʒd/ a. inchangé. ~ing a. immuable.

uncivilized /ʌn'sɪvɪlaɪzd/ a. barbare.

uncle /'ʌŋkl/ n. oncle m.

uncomfortable /ʌn'kʌmftəbl/ a. (thing) peu confortable; (unpleasant) désagréable. **feel** or **be** ~, (person) être mal à l'aise.

uncommon /ʌn'kɒmən/ a. rare. ~ly adv. remarquablement.

uncompromising /ʌn'kɒmprəmaɪzɪŋ/ a. intransigeant.

unconcerned /ʌnkən'sɜːnd/ a. (indifferent) indifférent (by, à).

unconditional /ʌnkən'dɪʃənl/ a. inconditionnel.

unconscious /ʌn'kɒnʃəs/ a. sans connaissance, inanimé; (not aware) inconscient (of, de) —n. inconscient m. ~ly adv. inconsciemment.

unconventional /ʌnkən'venʃənl/ a. peu conventionnel.

uncooperative /ʌnkəʊ'ɒpərətɪv/ a. peu coopératif.

uncork /ʌn'kɔːk/ v.t. déboucher.

uncouth /ʌn'kuːθ/ a. grossier.

uncover /ʌn'kʌvə(r)/ v.t. découvrir.

undecided /ʌndɪ'saɪdɪd/ a. indécis.

undefinable /ʌndɪ'faɪnəbl/ a. indéfinissable.

undeniable /ʌndɪ'naɪəbl/ a. indéniable, incontestable.

under /'ʌndə(r)/ prep. sous; (less than) moins de; (according to) selon. —adv. au-dessous. ~ **age**, mineur. ~ **it/there**, là-dessous. ~ **way**, (in progress) en cours; (on the way) en route.

under- /'ʌndə(r)/ pref. sous-.

undercarriage /'ʌndəkærɪdʒ/ n. (aviat.) train d'atterrissage m.

underclothes /'ʌndəkləʊðz/ n. pl. sous-vêtements m. pl.

undercoat /'ʌndəkəʊt/ n. (of paint) couche de fond f.

undercover /ʌndə'kʌvə(r)/ (agent, operation) a. secret.

undercurrent /'ʌndəkʌrənt/ n. courant (profond) m.

undercut /ʌndə'kʌt/ v.t. (p.t. **undercut**, pres. p. **undercutting**) (comm.) vendre moins cher que.

underdeveloped /ʌndədɪ'veləpt/ a. sous-développé.

underdog /'ʌndədɒg/ n. (pol.) opprimé(e) m. (f.); (socially) déshérité(e) m. (f.).

underdone /'ʌndədʌn/ a. pas assez cuit; (steak) saignant.

underestimate /ʌndər'estɪmeɪt/ v.t. sous-estimer.

underfed /ʌndə'fed/ a. sous-alimenté.

underfoot /ʌndə'fʊt/ adv. sous les pieds.

undergo /ʌndə'gəʊ/ v.t. (p.t. **-went**, pp. **-gone**) subir.

undergraduate /ʌndə'grædʒʊət/ n. étudiant(e) (qui prépare la licence) m. (f.).

underground¹ /ʌndə'graʊnd/ adv. sous terre.

underground² /'ʌndəgraʊnd/ a. souterrain; (secret) clandestin. —n. (rail.) métro m.

undergrowth /'ʌndəgrəʊθ/ n. sous-bois m. invar.

underhand /'ʌndəhænd/ a. (deceitful) sournois.

under|lie /ʌndə'laɪ/ v.t. (p.t. **-lay**, p.p. **-lain**, pres. p. **-lying**) sous-tendre. ~lying a. fondamental.

underline /ʌndə'laɪn/ v.t. souligner.

undermine /ʌndə'maɪn/ v.t. (cliff, society, etc.) miner, saper.

underneath /ʌndə'niːθ/ prep. sous. —adv. (en) dessous.

underpaid /ʌndə'peɪd/ a. sous-payé.

underpants /'ʌndəpænts/ n. pl. (man's) slip m.

underpass /'ʌndəpɑːs/ n. (for cars, people) passage souterrain m.

underprivileged /ʌndə'prɪvəlɪdʒd/ *a.* défavorisé.

underrate /ʌndə'reɪt/ *v.t.* sous-estimer.

undershirt /'ʌndəʃɜːt/ *n.* (*Amer.*) maillot (de corps) *m.*

undershorts /'ʌndəʃɔːts/ *n. pl.* (*Amer.*) caleçon *m.*

underskirt /'ʌndəʃkɜːt/ *n.* jupon *m.*

understand /ʌndə'stænd/ *v.t./i.* (*p.t.* -stood) comprendre. ～**able** *a.* compréhensible. ～**ing** *a.* compréhensif; *n.* compréhension *f.*; (*agreement*) entente *f.*

understatement /'ʌndəsteɪtmənt/ *n.* litote *f.* **that's an** ～, c'est en deçà de la vérité.

understudy /'ʌndəstʌdɪ/ *n.* (*theatre*) doublure *f.*

undertak|e /ʌndə'teɪk/ *v.t.* (*p.t.* -took, *p.p.* -taken) entreprendre; (*responsibility*) assumer. ～**e to,** s'engager à. ～**ing** *n.* (*task*) entreprise *f.*; (*promise*) promesse *f.*

undertaker /'ʌndəteɪkə(r)/ *n.* entrepreneur de pompes funèbres *m.*

undertone /'ʌndətəʊn/ *n.* **in an** ～, à mi-voix.

undervalue /ʌndə'væljuː/ *v.t.* sous-évaluer.

underwater /ʌndə'wɔːtə(r)/ *a.* sous-marin. —*adv.* sous l'eau.

underwear /'ʌndəweə(r)/ *n.* sous-vêtements *m. pl.*

underwent /ʌndə'went/ *see* **undergo**.

underworld /'ʌndəwɜːld/ *n.* (*of crime*) milieu *m.*, pègre *f.*

undeserved /ʌndɪ'zɜːvd/ *a.* immérité.

undesirable /ʌndɪ'zaɪərəbl/ *a.* peu souhaitable; (*person*) indésirable.

undies /'ʌndɪz/ *n. pl.* (*female underwear: fam.*) dessous *m. pl.*

undignified /ʌn'dɪgnɪfaɪd/ *a.* qui manque de dignité, sans dignité.

undisputed /ʌndɪ'spjuːtɪd/ *a.* incontesté.

undistinguished /ʌndɪ'stɪŋgwɪʃt/ *a.* médiocre.

undo /ʌn'duː/ *v.t.* (*p.t.* -did, *p.p.* -done /-dʌn/) défaire, détacher; (*a wrong*) réparer. **leave** ～**ne,** ne pas faire.

undoubted /ʌn'daʊtɪd/ *a.* indubitable. ～**ly** *adv.* indubitablement.

undreamt /ʌn'dremt/ *a.* ～ **of,** insoupçonné, inimaginable.

undress /ʌn'dres/ *v.t./i.* (se) déshabiller. **get** ～**ed,** se déshabiller.

undu|e /ʌn'djuː/ *a.* excessif. ～**ly** *adv.* excessivement.

undulate /'ʌndjʊleɪt/ *v.i.* onduler.

undying /ʌn'daɪɪŋ/ *a.* éternel.

unearth /ʌn'ɜːθ/ *v.t.* déterrer.

unearthly /ʌn'ɜːθlɪ/ *a.* mystérieux. ～ **hour,** (*fam.*) heure indue *f.*

uneasy /ʌn'iːzɪ/ *a.* (*ill at ease*) mal à l'aise; (*worried*) inquiet; (*situation*) difficile.

uneducated /ʌn'edʒʊkeɪtɪd/ *a.* (*person*) inculte; (*speech*) populaire.

unemploy|ed /ʌnɪm'plɔɪd/ *a.* en chômage. ～**ment** *n.* chômage *m.* ～**ment benefit,** allocations de chômage *f. pl.*

unending /ʌn'endɪŋ/ *a.* interminable, sans fin.

unequal /ʌn'iːkwəl/ *a.* inégal. ～**led** *a.* inégalé.

unerring /ʌn'ɜːrɪŋ/ *a.* infaillible.

uneven /ʌn'iːvn/ *a.* inégal.

uneventful /ʌnɪ'ventfl/ *a.* sans incident.

unexpected /ʌnɪk'spektɪd/ *a.* inattendu, imprévu. ～**ly** *adv.* subitement; (*arrive*) à l'improviste.

unfailing /ʌn'feɪlɪŋ/ *a.* constant, continuel; (*loyal*) fidèle.

unfair /ʌn'feə(r)/ *a.* injuste. ～**ness** *n.* injustice *f.*

unfaithful /ʌn'feɪθfl/ *a.* infidèle.

unfamiliar /ʌnfə'mɪlɪə(r)/ *a.* inconnu, peu familier. **be** ～ **with,** ne pas connaître.

unfashionable /ʌn'fæʃənəbl/ *a.* (*clothes*) démodé. **it's** ～ **to,** ce n'est pas à la mode de.

unfasten /ʌn'fɑːsn/ *v.t.* défaire.

unfavourable /ʌn'feɪvərəbl/ *a.* défavorable.

unfeeling /ʌn'fiːlɪŋ/ *a.* insensible.

unfinished /ʌn'fɪnɪʃt/ *a.* inachevé.

unfit /ʌn'fɪt/ *a.* (*med.*) peu en forme: (*unsuitable*) impropre (**for,** à). ～ **to,** (*unable*) pas en état de.

unflinching /ʌn'flɪntʃɪŋ/ *a.* (*fearless*) intrépide.

unfold /ʌn'fəʊld/ *v.t.* déplier; (*expose*) exposer. —*v.i.* se dérouler.

unforeseen /ʌnfɔː'siːn/ *a.* imprévu.

unforgettable /ʌnfə'getəbl/ *a.* inoubliable.

unforgivable /ʌnfə'gɪvəbl/ *a.* impardonnable, inexcusable.

unfortunate /ʌn'fɔːtʃʊnət/ *a.* malheureux; (*event*) fâcheux. ～**ly** *adv.* malheureusement.

unfounded /ʌn'faʊndɪd/ *a.* (*rumour etc.*) sans fondement.

unfriendly /ʌn'frendlɪ/ *a.* peu amical, froid.

ungainly /ʌn'geɪnlɪ/ *a.* gauche.

ungodly /ʌn'gɒdlɪ/ a. impie. ∼ **hour,** (*fam.*) heure indue *f.*

ungrateful /ʌn'greɪtfl/ a. ingrat.

unhapp|y /ʌn'hæpɪ/ a. (**-ier, -iest**) malheureux, triste; (*not pleased*) mécontent (**with,** de). ∼**ily** *adv.* malheureusement. ∼**iness** *n.* tristesse *f.*

unharmed /ʌn'hɑːmd/ a. indemne, sain et sauf.

unhealthy /ʌn'helθɪ/ a. (**-ier, -iest**) (*climate etc.*) malsain; (*person*) en mauvaise santé.

unheard-of /ʌn'hɜːdɒv/ a. inouï.

unhinge /ʌn'hɪndʒ/ v.t. (*person, mind*) déséquilibrer.

unholy /ʌn'həʊlɪ/ a. (**-ier, -iest**) (*person, act, etc.*) impie; (*great: fam.*) invraisemblable.

unhook /ʌn'hʊk/ v.t. décrocher; (*dress*) dégrafer.

unhoped /ʌn'həʊpt/ a. ∼ **for,** inespéré.

unhurt /ʌn'hɜːt/ a. indemne.

unicorn /'juːnɪkɔːn/ n. licorne *f.*

uniform /'juːnɪfɔːm/ n. uniforme *m.* —a. uniforme. ∼**ity** /-'fɔːmətɪ/ n. uniformité *f.* ∼**ly** *adv.* uniformément.

unif|y /'juːnɪfaɪ/ v.t. unifier. ∼**ication** /-ɪ'keɪʃn/ n. unification *f.*

unilateral /juːnɪ'lætrəl/ a. unilatéral.

unimaginable /ʌnɪ'mædʒɪnəbl/ a. inimaginable.

unimportant /ʌnɪm'pɔːtnt/ a. peu important.

uninhabited /ʌnɪn'hæbɪtɪd/ a. inhabité.

unintentional /ʌnɪn'tenʃənl/ a. involontaire.

uninterest|ed /ʌn'ɪntrəstɪd/ a. indifférent (**in,** à). ∼**ing** a. peu intéressant.

union /'juːnɪən/ n. union *f.*; (*trade union*) syndicat *m.* ∼**ist** n. syndiqué(e) *m. (f.).* **U∼ Jack,** drapeau britannique *m.*

unique /juː'niːk/ a. unique. ∼**ly** *adv.* exceptionnellement.

unisex /'juːnɪseks/ a. unisexe.

unison /'juːnɪsn/ n. **in ∼,** à l'unisson.

unit /'juːnɪt/ n. unité *f.*; (*of furniture etc.*) élément *m.*, bloc *m.* ∼ **trust,** (*equivalent d'une*) SICAV *f.*

unite /juː'naɪt/ v.t./i. (s')unir. **U∼d Kingdom,** Royaume-Uni *m.* **U∼d Nations,** Nations Unies *f. pl.* **U∼d States (of America),** États-Unis (d'Amérique) *m. pl.*

unity /'juːnətɪ/ n. unité *f.*; (*harmony: fig.*) harmonie *f.*

universal /juːnɪ'vɜːsl/ a. universel.

universe /'juːnɪvɜːs/ n. univers *m.*

university /juːnɪ'vɜːsətɪ/ n. université *f.*;

—a. universitaire; (*student, teacher*) d'université.

unjust /ʌn'dʒʌst/ a. injuste.

unkempt /ʌn'kempt/ a. négligé.

unkind /ʌn'kaɪnd/ a. pas gentil, méchant. ∼**ly** *adv.* méchamment.

unknowingly /ʌn'nəʊɪŋlɪ/ *adv.* sans le savoir, inconsciemment.

unknown /ʌn'nəʊn/ a. inconnu. —n. **the ∼,** l'inconnu *m.*

unleash /ʌn'liːʃ/ v.t. déchaîner.

unless /ən'les/ *conj.* à moins que.

unlike /ʌn'laɪk/ a. (*brothers etc.*) différents. —*prep.* à la différence de; (*different from*) très différent de.

unlikel|y /ʌn'laɪklɪ/ a. improbable. ∼**ihood** n. improbabilité *f.*

unlimited /ʌn'lɪmɪtɪd/ a. illimité.

unlisted /ʌn'lɪstɪd/ a. (*comm.*) non inscrit à la cote; (*Amer.*) qui n'est pas dans l'annuaire.

unload /ʌn'ləʊd/ v.t. décharger.

unlock /ʌn'lɒk/ v.t. ouvrir.

unluck|y /ʌn'lʌkɪ/ a. (**-ier, -iest**) malheureux; (*number*) qui porte malheur. ∼**ily** *adv.* malheureusement.

unmarried /ʌn'mærɪd/ a. célibataire, qui n'est pas marié.

unmask /ʌn'mɑːsk/ v.t. démasquer.

unmistakable /ʌnmɪ'steɪkəbl/ a. (*voice etc.*) facilement reconnaissable; (*clear*) très net.

unmitigated /ʌn'mɪtɪgeɪtɪd/ a. (*absolute*) absolu.

unmoved /ʌn'muːvd/ a. indifférent (**by,** à), insensible (**by,** à).

unnatural /ʌn'nætʃrəl/ a. pas naturel, anormal.

unnecessary /ʌn'nesəsərɪ/ a. inutile; (*superfluous*) superflu.

unnerve /ʌn'nɜːv/ v.t. troubler.

unnoticed /ʌn'nəʊtɪst/ a. inaperçu.

unobtainable /ʌnəb'teɪnəbl/ n. impossible à obtenir.

unobtrusive /ʌnəb'truːsɪv/ a. (*person, object*) discret.

unofficial /ʌnə'fɪʃl/ a. officieux.

unorthodox /ʌn'ɔːθədɒks/ a. peu orthodoxe.

unpack /ʌn'pæk/ v.t. (*suitcase etc.*) défaire; (*contents*) déballer. —v.i. défaire sa valise.

unpalatable /ʌn'pælətəbl/ a. (*food, fact, etc.*) désagréable.

unparalleled /ʌn'pærəleld/ a. incomparable.

unpleasant /ʌn'pleznt/ a. désagréable (**to,** avec).

unplug /ʌn'plʌg/ v.t. (electr.) débrancher; (unblock) déboucher.

unpopular /ʌn'pɒpjʊlə(r)/ a. impopulaire. ~ **with**, mal vu de.

unprecedented /ʌn'presidentid/ a. sans précédent.

unpredictable /ʌnprɪ'dɪktəbl/ a. imprévisible.

unprepared /ʌnprɪ'peəd/ a. non préparé; (person) qui n'a rien préparé. **be ~ for**, (not expect) ne pas s'attendre à.

unpretentious /ʌnprɪ'tenʃəs/ a. sans prétention(s).

unprincipled /ʌn'prinsəpld/ a. sans scrupules.

unprofessional /ʌnprə'feʃənl/ a. (work) d'amateur; (conduct) contraire au code professionel.

unpublished /ʌn'pʌblɪʃt/ a. inédit.

unqualified /ʌn'kwɒlɪfaɪd/ a. non diplômé; (success etc.) total. **be ~ to**, ne pas être qualifié pour.

unquestionabl|e /ʌn'kwestʃənəbl/ a. incontestable. **~y** adv. incontestablement.

unravel /ʌn'rævl/ v.t. (p.t. **unravelled**) démêler, débrouiller.

unreal /ʌn'rɪəl/ a. irréel.

unreasonable /ʌn'ri:znəbl/ a. déraisonnable, peu raisonnable.

unrecognizable /ʌnrekəg'naɪzəbl/ a. méconnaissable.

unrelated /ʌnrɪ'leɪtɪd/ a. (facts) sans rapport (**to**, avec).

unreliable /ʌnrɪ'laɪəbl/ a. peu sérieux; (machine) peu fiable.

unremitting /ʌnrɪ'mɪtɪŋ/ a. (effort) acharné; (emotion) inaltérable.

unreservedly /ʌnrɪ'zɜ:vɪdlɪ/ adv. sans réserve.

unrest /ʌn'rest/ n. troubles m. pl.

unrivalled /ʌn'raɪvld/ a. sans égal, incomparable.

unroll /ʌn'rəʊl/ v.t. dérouler.

unruffled /ʌn'rʌfld/ a. (person) qui n'a pas perdu son calme.

unruly /ʌn'ru:lɪ/ a. indiscipliné.

unsafe /ʌn'seɪf/ a. (dangerous) dangereux; (person) en danger.

unsaid /ʌn'sed/ a. **leave ~**, passer sous silence.

unsatisfactory /ʌnsætɪs'fæktərɪ/ a. peu satisfaisant.

unsavoury /ʌn'seɪvərɪ/ a. désagréable, répugnant.

unscathed /ʌn'skeɪðd/ a. indemne.

unscheduled /ʌn'ʃedju:ld, Amer. ʌn'skedju:ld/ a. pas prévu.

unscrew /ʌn'skru:/ v.t. dévisser.

unscrupulous /ʌn'skru:pjʊləs/ a. sans scrupules, malhonnête.

unseemly /ʌn'si:mlɪ/ a. inconvenant, incorrect, incongru.

unseen /ʌn'si:n/ a. inaperçu. —n. (translation) version f.

unsettle /ʌn'setl/ v.t. troubler. **~d** a. (weather) instable.

unshakeable /ʌn'ʃeɪkəbl/ a. (person, belief, etc.) inébranlable.

unshaven /ʌn'ʃeɪvn/ a. pas rasé.

unsightly /ʌn'saɪtlɪ/ a. laid.

unskilled /ʌn'skɪld/ a. inexpert; (worker) non qualifié.

unsociable /ʌn'səʊʃəbl/ a. insociable, farouche.

unsophisticated /ʌnsə'fɪstɪkeɪtɪd/ a. peu sophistiqué, simple.

unsound /ʌn'saʊnd/ a. peu solide. **of ~ mind**, fou.

unspeakable /ʌn'spi:kəbl/ a. indescriptible; (bad) innommable.

unspecified /ʌn'spesɪfaɪd/ a. indéterminé.

unstable /ʌn'steɪbl/ a. instable.

unsteady /ʌn'stedɪ/ a. (step) chancelant; (ladder) instable; (hand) mal assuré.

unstuck /ʌn'stʌk/ a. décollé. **come ~**, (fail. fam.) échouer.

unsuccessful /ʌnsək'sesfl/ a. (result, candidate) malheureux; (attempt) infructueux. **be ~**, ne pas réussir (**in doing**, à faire).

unsuit|able /ʌn'su:təbl/ a. qui ne convient pas (**for**, à), peu approprié. **~ed** a. inapte (**to**, à).

unsure /ʌn'ʃɔ:(r)/ a. incertain.

unsuspecting /ʌnsə'spektɪŋ/ a. qui ne se doute de rien.

unsympathetic /ʌnsɪmpə'θetɪk/ a. (unhelpful) peu compréhensif; (unpleasant) antipathique.

untangle /ʌn'tæŋgl/ v.t. démêler.

untenable /ʌn'tenəbl/ a. intenable.

unthinkable /ʌn'θɪŋkəbl/ a. impensable, inconcevable.

untid|y /ʌn'taɪdɪ/ a. (-ier, -iest) (person) désordonné; (clothes, hair, room) en désordre; (work) mal soigné. **~ily** adv. sans soin.

untie /ʌn'taɪ/ v.t. (knot, parcel) défaire; (person) détacher.

until /ən'tɪl/ prep. jusqu'à. **not ~**, pas avant. —conj. jusqu'à ce que; (before) avant que.

untimely /ʌn'taɪmlɪ/ a. inopportun; (death) prématuré.

untold /ʌn'təʊld/ a. incalculable.

untoward /ʌntə'wɔ:d/ a. fâcheux.

untrue /ʌn'tru:/ a. faux.

unused[1] /ʌn'ju:zd/ a. (new) neuf; (not in use) inutilisé.

unused[2] /ʌn'ju:st/ a. ～ to, peu habitué à.

unusual /ʌn'ju:ʒʊəl/ a. exceptionnel; (strange) insolite, étrange. ～ly adv. exceptionnellement.

unveil /ʌn'veɪl/ v.t. dévoiler.

unwanted /ʌn'wɒntɪd/ a. (useless) superflu; (child) non désiré.

unwelcome /ʌn'welkəm/ a. fâcheux; (guest) importun.

unwell /ʌn'wel/ a. indisposé.

unwieldy /ʌn'wi:ldɪ/ a. difficile à manier.

unwilling /ʌn'wɪlɪŋ/ a. peu disposé (to, à); (victim) récalcitrant. ～ly adv. à contrecœur.

unwind /ʌn'waɪnd/ v.t./i. (p.t. unwound /ʌn'waʊnd/) (se) dérouler; (relax: fam.) se détendre.

unwise /ʌn'waɪz/ a. imprudent.

unwittingly /ʌn'wɪtɪŋlɪ/ adv. involontairement.

unworkable /ʌn'wɜ:kəbl/ a. (plan etc.) irréalisable.

unworthy /ʌn'wɜ:ðɪ/ a. indigne.

unwrap /ʌn'ræp/ v.t. (p.t. unwrapped) ouvrir, défaire.

unwritten /ʌn'rɪtn/ a. (agreement) verbal, tacite.

up /ʌp/ adv. en haut, en l'air; (sun, curtain) levé; (out of bed) levé, debout; (finished) fini. **be up**, (level, price) avoir monté. —prep. (a hill) en haut de; (a tree) dans; (a ladder) sur. —v.t. (p.t. upped) augmenter. **come** or **go up**, monter. **up in the bedroom**, là-haut dans la chambre. **up there**, là-haut. **up to**, jusqu'à; (task) à la hauteur de. **it is up to you**, ça dépend de vous (to, de). **be up to sth.**, (able) être capable de qch.; (do) faire qch.; (plot) préparer qch. **be up to**, (in book) en être à. **be up against**, faire face à. **be up in**, (fam.) s'y connaître en. **feel up to doing**, (able) être de taille à faire. **have ups and downs**, connaître des hauts et des bas. **up-and-coming** a. prometteur. **up-market** a. haut-de-gamme. **up to date**, moderne; (news) récent.

upbringing /'ʌpbrɪŋɪŋ/ n. éducation f.

update /ʌp'deɪt/ v.t. mettre à jour.

upgrade /ʌp'greɪd/ v.t. (person) promouvoir; (job) revaloriser.

upheaval /ʌp'hi:vl/ n. bouleversement m.

uphill /ʌp'hɪl/ a. qui monte; (fig.) difficile. —adv. **go ～**, monter.

uphold /ʌp'həʊld/ v.t. (p.t. upheld) maintenir.

upholster /ʌp'həʊlstə(r)/ v.t. (pad) rembourrer; (cover) recouvrir. ～y n. (in vehicle) garniture f.

upkeep /'ʌpki:p/ n. entretien m.

upon /ə'pɒn/ prep. sur.

upper /'ʌpə(r)/ a. supérieur. —n. (of shoe) empeigne f. **have the ～ hand**, avoir le dessus. **～ class**, aristocratie f. **～most** a. (highest) le plus haut.

upright /'ʌpraɪt/ a. droit. —n. (post) montant m.

uprising /'ʌpraɪzɪŋ/ n. soulèvement m., insurrection f.

uproar /'ʌprɔ:(r)/ n. tumulte m.

uproot /ʌp'ru:t/ v.t. déraciner.

upset[1] /ʌp'set/ v.t. (p.t. upset, pres. p. upsetting) (overturn) renverser; (plan, stomach) déranger; (person) contrarier, affliger. —a. peiné.

upset[2] /'ʌpset/ n. dérangement m.; (distress) chagrin m.

upshot /'ʌpʃɒt/ n. résultat m.

upside-down /ʌpsaɪd'daʊn/ adv. (in position, in disorder) à l'envers, sens dessus dessous.

upstairs /ʌp'steəz/ adv. en haut. —a. (flat etc.) d'en haut.

upstart /'ʌpstɑ:t/ n. (pej.) parvenu(e) m. (f.).

upstream /ʌp'stri:m/ adv. en amont.

upsurge /'ʌpsɜ:dʒ/ n. recrudescence f.; (of anger) accès m.

uptake /'ʌpteɪk/ n. **be quick on the ～**, comprendre vite.

uptight /ʌp'taɪt/ a. (tense: fam.) crispé; (angry: fam.) en colère.

upturn /'ʌptɜ:n/ n. amélioration f.

upward /'ʌpwəd/ a. & adv., ～s adv. vers le haut.

uranium /jʊ'reɪnɪəm/ n. uranium m.

urban /'ɜ:bən/ a. urbain.

urbane /ɜ:'beɪn/ a. courtois.

urchin /'ɜ:tʃɪn/ n. garnement m.

urge /ɜ:dʒ/ v.t. conseiller vivement (to do, de faire). —n. forte envie f. **～ on**, (impel) encourager.

urgen|t /'ɜ:dʒənt/ a. urgent; (request) pressant. ～cy n. urgence f.; (of request, tone) insistance f. ～tly adv. d'urgence.

urinal /jʊə'raɪnl/ n. urinoir m.

urin|e /'jʊərɪn/ n. urine f. ～ate v.i. uriner.

urn /ɜ:n/ n. urne f.; (for tea, coffee) fontaine f.

us /ʌs, unstressed əs/ pron. nous. **(to) us**, nous.

US abbr. see **United States**.

USA *abbr. see* **United States of America**.

usable /'juːzəbl/ *a*. utilisable.

usage /'juːsɪdʒ/ *n*. usage *m*.

use[1] /juːz/ *v.t.* se servir de, utiliser; (*consume*) consommer. ∼ **up**, épuiser. ∼**r** /-ə(r)/ *n*. usager *m*. ∼**r-friendly** *a*. facile d'emploi.

use[2] /juːs/ *n*. usage *m*., emploi *m*. **in** ∼, en usage. **it is no** ∼ **shouting**/*etc.*, ça ne sert à rien de crier/*etc.* **make** ∼ **of**, se servir de. **of** ∼, utile.

used[1] /juːzd/ *a*. (*second-hand*) d'occasion.

used[2] /juːst/ *p.t.* **he** ∼ **to do**, il faisait (autrefois), il avait l'habitude de faire. —*a*. ∼ **to**, habitué à.

useful /'juːsfl/ *a*. utile. ∼**fully** *adv*. utilement. ∼**less** *a*. inutile; (*person*) incompétent.

usher /'ʌʃə(r)/ *n*. (*in theatre, hall*) placeur *m*. —*v.t.* ∼ **in**, faire entrer. ∼**ette** *n*. ouvreuse *f*.

USSR *abbr.* (*Union of Soviet Socialist Republics*) URSS *f*.

usual /'juːʒʊəl/ *a*. habituel, normal. **as** ∼, comme d'habitude. ∼**ly** *adv*. d'habitude.

usurp /juːˈzɜːp/ *v.t.* usurper.

utensil /juːˈtensl/ *n*. ustensile *m*.

uterus /'juːtərəs/ *n*. utérus *m*.

utilitarian /juːtɪlɪˈteərɪən/ *a*. utilitaire.

utility /juːˈtɪlətɪ/ *n*. utilité *f*. (**public**) ∼, service public *m*.

utilize /'juːtɪlaɪz/ *v.t.* utiliser.

utmost /'ʌtməʊst/ *a*. (*furthest, most intense*) extrême. **the** ∼ **care**/*etc.*, (*greatest*) le plus grand soin/*etc.* —*n*. **do one's** ∼, faire tout son possible.

Utopia /juːˈtəʊpɪə/ *n*. utopie *f*. ∼**n** *a*. utopique.

utter[1] /'ʌtə(r)/ *a*. complet, absolu. ∼**ly** *adv*. complètement.

utter[2] /'ʌtə(r)/ *v.t.* proférer; (*sigh, shout*) pousser. ∼**ance** *n*. déclaration *f*. **give** ∼**ance to**, exprimer.

U-turn /'juːtɜːn/ *n*. demi-tour *m*.

V

vacan|**t** /'veɪkənt/ *a*. (*post*) vacant; (*seat etc.*) libre; (*look*) vague. ∼**cy** *n*. (*post*) poste vacant *m*.; (*room*) chambre disponible *f*.

vacate /vəˈkeɪt, *Amer.* 'veɪkeɪt/ *v.t.* quitter.

vacation /veɪˈkeɪʃn/ *n*. (*Amer.*) vacances *f. pl*.

vaccinat|**e** /'væksɪneɪt/ *v.t.* vacciner. ∼**ion** /-'neɪʃn/ *n*. vaccination *f*.

vaccine /'væksiːn/ *n*. vaccin *m*.

vacuum /'vækjʊəm/ *n*. (*pl.* **-cuums** *or* **-cua**) vide *m*. ∼ **cleaner**, aspirateur *m*. ∼ **flask**, bouteille thermos *f*. (P.). ∼**-packed** *a*. emballé sous vide.

vagabond /'vægəbɒnd/ *n*. vagabond(e) *m*. (*f*.).

vagina /vəˈdʒaɪnə/ *n*. vagin *m*.

vagrant /'veɪgrənt/ *n*. vagabond(e) *m*. (*f*.), clochard(e) *m*. (*f*.).

vague /veɪg/ *a*. (**-er, -est**) vague; (*outline*) flou. **be** ∼ **about**, ne pas préciser. ∼**ly** *adv*. vaguement.

vain /veɪn/ *a*. (**-er, -est**) (*conceited*) vaniteux; (*useless*) vain. **in** ∼, en vain. ∼**ly** *adv*. en vain.

valentine /'væləntaɪn/ *n*. (*card*) carte de la Saint-Valentin *f*.

valet /'vælɪt, 'væleɪ/ *n*. (*manservant*) valet de chambre *m*.

valiant /'vælɪənt/ *a*. courageux.

valid /'vælɪd/ *a*. valable. ∼**ity** /vəˈlɪdətɪ/ *n*. validité *f*.

validate /'vælɪdeɪt/ *v.t.* valider.

valley /'vælɪ/ *n*. vallée *f*.

valour, (*Amer.*) **valor** /'vælə(r)/ *n*. courage *m*.

valuable /'væljʊəbl/ *a*. (*object*) de valeur; (*help etc.*) précieux. ∼**s** *n. pl*. objets de valeur *m. pl*.

valuation /væljʊˈeɪʃn/ *n*. expertise *f*.; (*of house*) évaluation *f*.

value /'væljuː/ *n*. valeur *f*. —*v.t.* (*appraise*) évaluer; (*cherish*) attacher de la valeur à. ∼ **added tax**, taxe à la valeur ajoutée *f*., TVA *f*. ∼**d** *a*. estimé. ∼**r** /-ə(r)/ *n*. expert *m*.

valve /vælv/ *n*. (*techn.*) soupape *f*.; (*of tyre*) valve *f*.; (*radio*) lampe *f*.

vampire /'væmpaɪə(r)/ *n*. vampire *m*.

van /væn/ *n*. (*vehicle*) camionnette *f*.; (*rail.*) fourgon *m*.

vandal /'vændl/ *n*. vandale *m./f.* ∼**ism** /-əlɪzəm/ *n*. vandalisme *m*.

vandalize /'vændəlaɪz/ *v.t.* abîmer, détruire, saccager.

vanguard /'vængɑːd/ *n*. (*of army, progress, etc.*) avant-garde *f*.

vanilla /vəˈnɪlə/ *n*. vanille *f*.

vanish /'vænɪʃ/ *v.i.* disparaître.

vanity /'vænɪtɪ/ *n*. vanité *f*. ∼ **case**, mallette de toilette *f*.

vantage-point /'vɑːntɪdʒpɔɪnt/ *n*. (*place*) excellent point de vue *m*.

vapour /'veɪpə(r)/ *n*. vapeur *f*.

vari|able /'veərɪəbl/ a. variable. **∼ation** /-'eɪʃn/ n. variation f. **∼ed** /-ɪd/ a. varié.

variance /'veərɪəns/ n. **at ∼,** en désaccord (**with,** avec).

variant /'veərɪənt/ a. différent. —n. variante f.

varicose /'værɪkəʊs/ a. **∼ veins,** varices f. pl.

variety /vəˈraɪətɪ/ n. variété f.; (entertainment) variétés f. pl.

various /'veərɪəs/ a. divers. **∼ly** adv. diversement.

varnish /'vɑːnɪʃ/ n. vernis m. —v.t. vernir.

vary /'veərɪ/ v.t./i. varier.

vase /vɑːz, Amer. veɪs/ n. vase m.

vast /vɑːst/ a. vaste, immense. **∼ly** adv. infiniment, extrêmement. **∼ness** n. immensité f.

vat /væt/ n. cuve f.

VAT /viːeɪˈtiː, væt/ abbr. (value added tax) TVA f.

vault[1] /vɔːlt/ n. (roof) voûte f.; (in bank) chambre forte f.; (tomb) caveau m.; (cellar) cave f.

vault[2] /vɔːlt/ v.t./i. sauter. —n. saut m.

vaunt /vɔːnt/ v.t. vanter.

VCR abbr. see **video cassette recorder.**

VDU abbr. see **visual display unit.**

veal /viːl/ n. (meat) veau m.

veer /vɪə(r)/ v.i. tourner, virer.

vegan /'viːgən/ a. & n. végétalien(ne) (m. (f.)).

vegetable /'vedʒtəbl/ n. légume m. —a. végétal. **∼ garden,** (jardin) potager m.

vegetarian /vedʒɪ'teərɪən/ a. & n. végétarien(ne) (m. (f.)).

vegetate /'vedʒɪteɪt/ v.i. végéter.

vegetation /vedʒɪ'teɪʃn/ n. végétation f.

vehement /'viːəmənt/ a. véhément. **∼ly** adv. avec véhémence.

vehicle /'viːɪkl/ n. véhicule m.

veil /veɪl/ n. voile m. —v.t. voiler.

vein /veɪn/ n. (in body, rock) veine f.; (on leaf) nervure f. (mood) esprit m.

velocity /vɪ'lɒsətɪ/ n. vélocité f.

velvet /'velvɪt/ n. velours m.

vending-machine /'vendɪŋməʃiːn/ n. distributeur automatique m.

vendor /'vendə(r)/ n. vendeulr, -se m., f.

veneer /və'nɪə(r)/ n. placage m.; (appearance: fig.) vernis m.

venerable /'venərəbl/ a. vénérable.

venereal /və'nɪərɪəl/ a. vénérien.

venetian /vəˈniːʃn/ a. **∼ blind,** jalousie f.

vengeance /'vendʒəns/ n. vengeance f. **with a ∼,** furieusement.

venison /'venɪzn/ n. venaison f.

venom /'venəm/ n. venin m. **∼ous** /'venəməs/ a. venimeux.

vent[1] /vent/ n. (in coat) fente f.

vent[2] /vent/ n. (hole) orifice m.; (for air) bouche d'aération f. —v.t. (anger) décharger (on, sur). **give ∼ to,** donner libre cours à.

ventilat|e /'ventɪleɪt/ v.t. ventiler. **∼ion** /-'leɪʃn/ n. ventilation f. **∼or** n. ventilateur m.

ventriloquist /ven'trɪləkwɪst/ n. ventriloque m./f.

venture /'ventʃə(r)/ n. entreprise f. —v.t./i. (se) risquer.

venue /'venjuː/ n. lieu de rencontre or de rendez-vous m.

veranda /vəˈrændə/ n. véranda f.

verb /vɜːb/ n. verbe m.

verbal /'vɜːbl/ a. verbal.

verbatim /vɜːˈbeɪtɪm/ adv. textuellement, mot pour mot.

verdict /'vɜːdɪkt/ n. verdict m.

verge /vɜːdʒ/ n. bord m. —v.i. **∼ on,** friser, frôler. **on the ∼ of doing,** sur le point de faire.

verif|y /'verɪfaɪ/ v.t. vérifier. **∼ication** /-ɪ'keɪʃn/ n. vérification f.

vermicelli /vɜːmɪ'selɪ/ n. vermicelle(s) m. (pl.).

vermin /'vɜːmɪn/ n. vermine f.

vermouth /'vɜːməθ/ n. vermouth m.

vernacular /vəˈnækjʊlə(r)/ n. langue f.; (regional) dialecte m.

versatil|e /'vɜːsətaɪl, Amer. 'vɜːsətl/ a. (person) aux talents variés; (mind) souple. **∼ity** /-'tɪlətɪ/ n. souplesse f. **her ∼ity,** la variété de ses talents.

verse /vɜːs/ n. strophe f.; (of Bible) verset m.; (poetry) vers m. pl.

versed /vɜːst/ a. **∼ in,** versé dans.

version /'vɜːʃn/ n. version f.

versus /'vɜːsəs/ prep. contre.

vertebra /'vɜːtɪbrə/ n. (pl. **-brae** /-briː/) vertèbre f.

vertical /'vɜːtɪkl/ a. vertical. **∼ly** adv. verticalement.

vertigo /'vɜːtɪgəʊ/ n. vertige m.

verve /vɜːv/ n. fougue f.

very /'verɪ/ adv. très. —a. (actual) même. **the ∼ day/etc.,** le jour/etc. même. **at the ∼ end,** tout à la fin. **the ∼ first,** le tout premier. **∼ much,** beaucoup.

vessel /'vesl/ n. (duct, ship) vaisseau m.

vest /vest/ n. maillot de corps m.; (waistcoat: Amer.) gilet m.

vested /'vestɪd/ a. **∼ interests,** droits acquis m. pl., intérêts m. pl.

vestige /'vestɪdʒ/ n. vestige m.

vestry /'vestrɪ/ n. sacristie f.

vet /vet/ n. (fam.) vétérinaire m./f. —v.t. (p.t. **vetted**) (candidate etc.) examiner (de près).

veteran /'vetərən/ n. vétéran m. (**war**) ∼, ancien combattant m.

veterinary /'vetərɪnərɪ/ a. vétérinaire. ∼ **surgeon**, vétérinaire m./f.

veto /'viːtəʊ/ n. (pl. **-oes**) veto m.; (right) droit de veto m. —v.t. mettre son veto à.

vex /veks/ v.t. contrarier, irriter. ∼**ed question**, question controversée f.

via /'vaɪə/ prep. via, par.

viable /'vaɪəbl/ a. (baby, plan, firm) viable.

viaduct /'vaɪədʌkt/ n. viaduc m.

vibrant /'vaɪbrənt/ a. vibrant.

vibrat|e /vaɪ'breɪt/ v.t./i. (faire) vibrer. ∼**ion** /-ʃn/ n. vibration f.

vicar /'vɪkə(r)/ n. pasteur m. ∼**age** n. presbytère m.

vicarious /vɪ'keərɪəs/ a. (emotion) ressenti indirectement.

vice[1] /vaɪs/ n. (depravity) vice m.

vice[2] /vaɪs/ n. (techn.) étau m.

vice- /vaɪs/ pref. vice-.

vice versa /'vaɪsɪ'vɜːsə/ adv. vice versa.

vicinity /vɪ'sɪnətɪ/ n. environs m. pl. **in the** ∼ **of**, aux environs de.

vicious /'vɪʃəs/ a. (spiteful) méchant; (violent) brutal. ∼ **circle**, cercle vicieux m. ∼**ly** adv. méchamment; brutalement.

victim /'vɪktɪm/ n. victime f.

victimiz|e /'vɪktɪmaɪz/ v.t. persécuter, martyriser. ∼**ation** /-'zeɪʃn/ n. persécution f.

victor /'vɪktə(r)/ n. vainqueur m.

Victorian /vɪk'tɔːrɪən/ a. & n. victorien(ne) (m. (f.)).

victor|y /'vɪktərɪ/ n. victoire f. ∼**ious** /-'tɔːrɪəs/ a. victorieux.

video /'vɪdɪəʊ/ a. (game, camera) vidéo invar. —n. (recorder) magnétoscope m.; (film) vidéo f. ∼ **cassette**, vidéocassette f. ∼ (**cassette**) **recorder**, magnétoscope m. —v.t. (programme) enregistrer.

videotape /'vɪdɪəʊteɪp/ n. bande vidéo f. —v.t. (programme) enregistrer; (wedding) filmer avec une caméra vidéo.

vie /vaɪ/ v.i. (pres. p. **vying**) rivaliser (**with**, avec).

view /vjuː/ n. vue f. —v.t. (watch) regarder; (consider) considérer (**as**, comme); (house) visiter. **in my** ∼, à mon avis. **in** ∼ **of**, compte tenu de. **on** ∼, exposé. **with a** ∼ **to**, dans le but de.

∼**er** n. (TV) téléspectateur, -trice m., f.; (for slides) visionneuse f.

viewfinder /'vjuːfaɪndə(r)/ n. viseur m.

viewpoint /'vjuːpɔɪnt/ n. point de vue m.

vigil /'vɪdʒɪl/ n. veille f.; (over sick person, corpse) veillée f.

vigilan|t /'vɪdʒɪlənt/ a. vigilant. ∼**ce** n. vigilance f.

vig|our, (Amer.) **vigor** /'vɪgə(r)/ n. vigueur f. ∼**orous** a. vigoureux.

vile /vaɪl/ a. (base) infâme, vil; (bad) abominable, exécrable.

vilify /'vɪlɪfaɪ/ v.t. diffamer.

villa /'vɪlə/ n. villa f., pavillon m.

village /'vɪlɪdʒ/ n. village m. ∼**r** /-ə(r)/ n. villageois(e) m. (f.).

villain /'vɪlən/ n. scélérat m., bandit m.; (in story etc.) méchant m. ∼**y** n. infamie f.

vindicat|e /'vɪndɪkeɪt/ v.t. justifier. ∼**ion** /-'keɪʃn/ n. justification f.

vindictive /vɪn'dɪktɪv/ a. vindicatif.

vine /vaɪn/ n. vigne f.

vinegar /'vɪnɪgə(r)/ n. vinaigre m.

vineyard /'vɪnjəd/ n. vignoble m.

vintage /'vɪntɪdʒ/ n. (year) année f., millésime m. —a. (wine) de grand cru; (car) d'époque.

vinyl /'vaɪnɪl/ n. vinyle m.

viola /vɪ'əʊlə/ n. (mus.) alto m.

violat|e /'vaɪəleɪt/ v.t. violer. ∼**ion** /-'leɪʃn/ n. violation f.

violen|t /'vaɪələnt/ a. violent. ∼**ce** n. violence f. ∼**tly** adv. violemment, avec violence.

violet /'vaɪələt/ n. (bot.) violette f.; (colour) violet m. —a. violet.

violin /vaɪə'lɪn/ n. violon m. ∼**ist** n. violoniste m./f.

VIP /viːaɪ'piː/ abbr. (very important person) personnage de marque m.

viper /'vaɪpə(r)/ n. vipère f.

virgin /'vɜːdʒɪn/ n. (woman) vierge f. —a. vierge. **be a** ∼, (woman, man) être vierge. ∼**ity** /və'dʒɪnətɪ/ n. virginité f.

Virgo /'vɜːgəʊ/ n. la Vierge.

viril|e /'vɪraɪl, Amer. 'vɪrəl/ a. viril. ∼**ity** /vɪ'rɪlətɪ/ n. virilité f.

virtual /'vɜːtʃʊəl/ a. vrai. **a** ∼ **failure/**etc., pratiquement un échec/etc. ∼**ly** adv. pratiquement.

virtue /'vɜːtʃuː/ n. (goodness, chastity) vertu f.; (merit) mérite m. **by** or **in** ∼ **of**, en raison de.

virtuos|o /vɜːtʃʊ'əʊsəʊ/ n. (pl. **-si** /-siː/) virtuose m./f. ∼**ity** /-'ɒsətɪ/ n. virtuosité f.

virtuous /'vɜːtʃʊəs/ a. vertueux.

virulent /'vɪrʊlənt/ a. virulent.

virus /'vaɪərəs/ n. (pl. **-uses**) virus m.
visa /'viːzə/ n. visa m.
viscount /'vaɪkaʊnt/ n. vicomte m.
viscous /'vɪskəs/ a. visqueux.
vise /vaɪs/ n. (Amer.) étau m.
visib|le /'vɪzəbl/ a. (discernible, obvious) visible. ∼**ility** /-'bɪlətɪ/ n. visibilité f. ∼**ly** adv. visiblement.
vision /'vɪʒn/ n. vision f.
visionary /'vɪʒənərɪ/ a. & n. visionnaire (m./f.).
visit /'vɪzɪt/ v.t. (p.t. **visited**) (person) rendre visite à; (place) visiter. —v.i. être en visite. —n. (tour, call) visite f.; (stay) séjour m. ∼**or** n. visiteur, -se m., f.; (guest) invité(e) m. (f.); (in hotel) client(e) m. (f.).
visor /'vaɪzə(r)/ n. visière f.
vista /'vɪstə/ n. perspective f.
visual /'vɪʒʊəl/ a. visuel. ∼ **display unit,** visuel m., console de visualisation f. ∼**ly** adv. visuellement.
visualize /'vɪʒʊəlaɪz/ v.t. se représenter; (foresee) envisager.
vital /'vaɪtl/ a. vital. ∼ **statistics,** (fam.) mensurations f. pl.
vitality /vaɪ'tælətɪ/ n. vitalité f.
vitally /'vaɪtəlɪ/ adv. extrêmement.
vitamin /'vɪtəmɪn/ n. vitamine f.
vivac|ious /vɪ'veɪʃəs/ a. plein d'entrain, animé. ∼**ity** /-'æsətɪ/ n. vivacité f., entrain m.
vivid /'vɪvɪd/ a. vif; (graphic) vivant. ∼**ly** adv. vivement; (describe) de façon vivante.
vivisection /vɪvɪ'sekʃn/ n. vivisection f.
vocabulary /və'kæbjʊlərɪ/ n. vocabulaire m.
vocal /'vəʊkl/ a. vocal; (person: fig.) qui s'exprime franchement. ∼ **cords,** cordes vocales f. pl. ∼**ist** n. chanteur, -se m., f.
vocation /və'keɪʃn/ n. vocation f. ∼**al** a. professionnel.
vociferous /və'sɪfərəs/ a. bruyant.
vodka /'vɒdkə/ n. vodka f.
vogue /vəʊg/ n. (fashion, popularity) vogue f. **in** ∼, en vogue.
voice /vɔɪs/ n. voix f. —v.t. (express) formuler.
void /vɔɪd/ a. vide (**of,** de); (not valid) nul. —n. vide m.
volatile /'vɒlətaɪl, Amer. 'vɒlətl/ a. (person) versatile; (situation) variable.
volcan|o /vɒl'keɪnəʊ/ n. (pl. **-oes**) volcan m. ∼**ic** /-ænɪk/ a. volcanique.
volition /və'lɪʃn/ n. **of one's own** ∼, de son propre gré.

volley /'vɒlɪ/ n. (of blows etc., in tennis) volée f.; (of gunfire) salve f. ∼**-ball** n. volley(-ball) m.
volt /vəʊlt/ n. (electr.) volt m. ∼**age** n. voltage m.
voluble /'vɒljʊbl/ a. volubile.
volume /'vɒljuːm/ n. volume m.
voluntar|y /'vɒləntərɪ/ a. volontaire; (unpaid) bénévole. ∼**ily** /-trəlɪ, Amer. -'terəlɪ/ adv. volontairement.
volunteer /vɒlən'tɪə(r)/ n. volontaire m./f. —v.i. s'offrir (**to do,** pour faire); (mil.) s'engager comme volontaire. —v.t. offrir.
voluptuous /və'lʌptʃʊəs/ a. voluptueux.
vomit /'vɒmɪt/ v.t./i. (p.t. **vomited**) vomir. —n. vomi(ssement) m.
voracious /və'reɪʃəs/ a. vorace.
vot|e /vəʊt/ n. vote m.; (right) droit de vote m. —v.t./i. voter. ∼ (**in**), (person) élire. ∼**er** n. électeur, -trice m., f. ∼**ing** n. vote m. (**of,** de); (poll) scrutin m.
vouch /vaʊtʃ/ v.i. ∼ **for,** se porter garant de, répondre de.
voucher /'vaʊtʃə(r)/ n. bon m.
vow /vaʊ/ n. vœu m. —v.t. (loyalty etc.) jurer (**to,** à). ∼ **to do,** jurer de faire.
vowel /'vaʊəl/ n. voyelle f.
voyage /'vɔɪɪdʒ/ n. voyage (par mer) m.
vulgar /'vʌlgə(r)/ a. vulgaire. ∼**ity** /-'gærətɪ/ n. vulgarité f.
vulnerab|le /'vʌlnərəbl/ a. vulnérable. ∼**ility** /-'bɪlətɪ/ n. vulnérabilité f.
vulture /'vʌltʃə(r)/ n. vautour m.

W

wad /wɒd/ n. (pad) tampon m.; (bundle) liasse f.
wadding /'wɒdɪŋ/ n. rembourrage m., ouate f.
waddle /'wɒdl/ v.i. se dandiner.
wade /weɪd/ v.i. ∼ **through,** (mud etc.) patauger dans; (book: fig.) avancer péniblement dans.
wafer /'weɪfə(r)/ n. (biscuit) gaufrette f.; (relig.) hostie f.
waffle[1] /'wɒfl/ n. (talk: fam.) verbiage m. —v.i. (fam.) divaguer.
waffle[2] /'wɒfl/ n. (cake) gaufre f.
waft /wɒft/ v.i. flotter. —v.t. porter.
wag /wæg/ v.t./i. (p.t. **wagged**) (tail) remuer.
wage[1] /weɪdʒ/ v.t. (campaign) mener. ∼ **war,** faire la guerre.

wage[2] /weɪdʒ/ n. (*weekly*, *daily*) salaire m. **~s**, salaire m. **~-earner** n. salarié(e) m. (f.).

wager /ˈweɪdʒə(r)/ n. (*bet*) pari m. —v.t. parier (**that**, que).

waggle /ˈwægl/ v.t./i. remuer.

wagon /ˈwægən/ n. (*horse-drawn*) chariot m.; (*rail.*) wagon (de marchandises) m.

waif /weɪf/ n. enfant abandonné(e) m.(f.).

wail /weɪl/ v.i. (*utter cry or complaint*) gémir. —n. gémissement m.

waist /weɪst/ n. taille f.

waistcoat /ˈweɪskəʊt/ n. gilet m.

wait /weɪt/ v.t./i. attendre. —n. attente f. **I can't ~**, je n'en peux plus d'impatience. **let's ~ and see**, attendons voir. **while you ~**, sur place. **~ for**, attendre. **~ on**, servir. **~ing-list** n. liste d'attente f. **~ing-room** n. salle d'attente f.

wait|er /ˈweɪtə(r)/ n. garçon m., serveur m. **~ress** n. serveuse f.

waive /weɪv/ v.t. renoncer à

wake[1] /weɪk/ v.t./i. (p.t. **woke**, p.p. **woken**). **~ (up)**, (se) réveiller.

wake[2] /weɪk/ n. (*track*) sillage m. **in the ~ of**, (*after*) à la suite de.

waken /ˈweɪkən/ v.t./i. (se) réveiller, (s')éveiller.

Wales /weɪlz/ n. pays de Galles m.

walk /wɔːk/ v.i. marcher; (*not ride*) aller à pied; (*stroll*) se promener. —v.t. (*streets*) parcourir; (*distance*) faire à pied; (*dog*) promener. —n. promenade f., tour m.; (*gait*) (dé)marche f.; (*pace*) marche f., pas m.; (*path*) allée f. **~ of life**, condition sociale f. **~ out**, (*go away*) partir; (*worker*) faire grève. **~-out** n. grève surprise f. **~ out on**, abandonner. **~-over** n. victoire facile f.

walker /ˈwɔːkə(r)/ n. (*person*) marcheur, -se m., f.

walkie-talkie /wɔːkɪˈtɔːkɪ/ n. talkie-walkie m.

walking /ˈwɔːkɪŋ/ n. marche (à pied) f. —a. (*corpse*, *dictionary*: *fig.*) vivant. **~-stick** n. canne f.

Walkman /ˈwɔːkmən/ n. (P.) Walkman (P.) m., baladeur m.

wall /wɔːl/ n. mur m.; (*of tunnel*, *stomach*, *etc.*) paroi f. —a. mural. —v.t. (*city*) fortifier. **go to the ~**, (*firm*) faire faillite.

wallet /ˈwɒlɪt/ n. portefeuille m.

wallflower /ˈwɔːlflaʊə(r)/ n. (*bot.*) giroflée f.

wallop /ˈwɒləp/ v.t. (p.t. **walloped**) (*hit*:

sl.) taper sur. —n. (*blow*: sl.) grand coup m.

wallow /ˈwɒləʊ/ v.i. se vautrer.

wallpaper /ˈwɔːlpeɪpə(r)/ n. papier peint m. —v.t. tapisser.

walnut /ˈwɔːlnʌt/ n. (*nut*) noix f.; (*tree*) noyer m.

walrus /ˈwɔːlrəs/ n. morse m.

waltz /wɔːls/ n. valse f. —v.i. valser.

wan /wɒn/ a. pâle, blême.

wand /wɒnd/ n. baguette (magique) f.

wander /ˈwɒndə(r)/ v.i. errer; (*stroll*) flâner; (*digress*) s'écarter du sujet; (*in mind*) divaguer. **~er** n. vagabond(e) m. (f.).

wane /weɪn/ v.i. décroître. —n. **on the ~**, (*strength*, *fame*, *etc.*) en déclin; (*person*) sur son déclin.

wangle /ˈwæŋgl/ v.t. (*obtain*: sl.) se débrouiller pour avoir.

want /wɒnt/ v.t. vouloir (**to do**, faire); (*need*) avoir besoin de (**doing**, d'être fait); (*ask for*) demander. —v.i. **~ for**, manquer de. —n. (*need*, *poverty*) besoin m.; (*desire*) désir m.; (*lack*) manque m. **I ~ you to do it**, je veux que vous le fassiez. **for ~ of**, faute de. **~ed** a. (*criminal*) recherché par la police.

wanting /ˈwɒntɪŋ/ a. **be ~**, manquer (**in**, de).

wanton /ˈwɒntən/ a. (*cruelty*) gratuit; (*woman*) impudique.

war /wɔː(r)/ n. guerre f. **at ~**, en guerre. **on the ~-path**, sur le sentier de la guerre.

ward /wɔːd/ n. (*in hospital*) salle f.; (*minor*: *jurid.*) pupille m./f.; (*pol.*) division électorale f. —v.t. **~ off**, (*danger*) prévenir; (*blow*, *anger*) détourner.

warden /ˈwɔːdn/ n. direct|eur, -trice m., f.; (*of park*) gardien(ne) m. (f.). (**traffic**) **~**, contractuel(le) m. (f.).

warder /ˈwɔːdə(r)/ n. gardien (de prison) m.

wardrobe /ˈwɔːdrəʊb/ n. (*place*) armoire f.; (*clothes*) garde-robe f.

warehouse /ˈweəhaʊs/ n. (pl. **-s** /-haʊzɪz/) entrepôt m.

wares /weəz/ n. pl. (*goods*) marchandises f. pl.

warfare /ˈwɔːfeə(r)/ n. guerre f.

warhead /ˈwɔːhed/ n. ogive f.

warily /ˈweərɪlɪ/ adv. avec prudence.

warm /wɔːm/ a. (**-er**, **-est**) chaud; (*hearty*) chaleureux. **be or feel ~**, avoir chaud. **it is ~**, il fait chaud. —v.t./i. **~ (up)**, (se) réchauffer; (*food*) chauffer; (*liven up*) (s')animer; (*exercise*) s'échauffer. **∼-hearted** a. chaleureux. **∼ly** adv. (wrap up etc.) chaudement; (heartily) chaleureusement. **∼th** n. chaleur f.

warn /wɔːn/ v.t. avertir, prévenir. **∼ s.o. off sth.**, (advise against) mettre qn. en garde contre qch.; (forbid) interdire qch. à qn. **∼ing** n. avertissement m.; (notice) avis m. **without ∼ing**, sans prévenir. **∼ing light**, voyant m. **∼ing triangle**, triangle de sécurité m.

warp /wɔːp/ v.t./i. (wood etc.) (se) voiler; (pervert) pervertir.

warrant /'wɒrənt/ n. (for arrest) mandat (d'arrêt) m.; (comm.) autorisation f. —v.t. justifier.

warranty /'wɒrəntɪ/ n. garantie f.

warring /'wɔːrɪŋ/ a. en guerre.

warrior /'wɒrɪə(r)/ n. guerrlier, -ière m., f.

warship /'wɔːʃɪp/ n. navire de guerre m.

wart /wɔːt/ n. verrue f.

wartime /'wɔːtaɪm/ n. **in ∼**, en temps de guerre.

wary /'weərɪ/ a. (-ier, -iest) prudent.

was /wɒz, unstressed wəz/ see **be**.

wash /wɒʃ/ v.t./i. (se) laver; (flow over) baigner. —n. lavage m.; (clothes) lessive f.; (of ship) sillage m. **have a ∼**, se laver. **∼-basin** n. lavabo m. **∼-cloth** n. (Amer.) gant de toilette m. **∼ down**, (meal) arroser. **∼ one's hands of**, se laver les mains de. **∼ out**, (cup etc.) laver; (stain) (faire) partir. **∼-out** n. (sl.) fiasco m. **∼-room** n. (Amer.) toilettes f. pl. **∼ up**, faire la vaisselle; (Amer.) se laver. **∼able** a. lavable. **∼ing** n. lessive f. **∼ing-machine** n. machine à laver f. **∼ing-powder** n. lessive f. **∼ing-up** n. vaisselle f.; **∼ing-up liquid**, produit pour la vaisselle m.

washed-out /wɒʃt'aʊt/ a. (faded) délavé; (tired) lessivé; (ruined) anéanti.

washer /'wɒʃə(r)/ n. rondelle f.

wasp /wɒsp/ n. guêpe f.

wastage /'weɪstɪdʒ/ n. gaspillage m. **some ∼**, (in goods, among candidates, etc.) du déchet.

waste /weɪst/ v.t. gaspiller; (time) perdre. —v.i. **∼ away**, dépérir. —a. superflu; (product) de rebut. —n. gaspillage m.; (of time) perte f.; (rubbish) déchets m. pl. **lay ∼**, dévaster. **∼ disposal unit**, broyeur d'ordures m. **∼ (land)**, (desolate) terre désolée f.; (unused) terre inculte f.; (in town) terrain vague m. **∼ paper**, vieux papiers m. pl. **∼-**

paper basket, corbeille (à papier) f. **∼-pipe** n. vidange f.

wasteful /'weɪstfl/ a. peu économique; (person) gaspilleur.

watch /wɒtʃ/ v.t./i. (television) regarder; (observe) observer; (guard, spy on) surveiller; (be careful about) faire attention à. —n. (for telling time) montre f.; (naut.) quart m. **be on the ∼**, guetter. **keep ∼ on**, surveiller. **∼-dog** n. chien de garde m. **∼ out**, (take care) faire attention (for, à). **∼ out for**, guetter. **∼-tower** n. tour de guet f. **∼ful** a. vigilant.

watchmaker /'wɒtʃmeɪkə(r)/ n. horlogier, -ère m., f.

watchman /'wɒtʃmən/ n. (pl. -men) (of building) gardien m.

water /'wɔːtə(r)/ n. eau f. —v.t. arroser. —v.i. (of eyes) larmoyer. **my/his/**etc. **mouth ∼s**, l'eau me/lui/etc. vient à la bouche. **by ∼**, en bateau. **∼-bottle** n. bouillotte f. **∼-closet** n. waters m. pl. **∼-colour** n. couleur pour aquarelle f.; (painting) aquarelle f. **∼ down**, couper (d'eau); (tone down) édulcorer. **∼ heater**, chauffe-eau m. **∼-ice** n. sorbet m. **∼-lily** n. nénuphar m. **∼-main** n. canalisation d'eau f. **∼-melon** n. pastèque f. **∼-pistol** n. pistolet à eau m. **∼ polo**, water-polo m. **∼ power**, énergie hydraulique f. **∼-skiing** n. ski nautique m.

watercress /'wɔːtəkres/ n. cresson (de fontaine) m.

waterfall /'wɔːtəfɔːl/ n. chute d'eau f., cascade f.

watering-can /'wɔːtərɪŋkæn/ n. arrosoir m.

waterlogged /'wɔːtəlɒgd/ a. imprégné d'eau; (land) détrempé.

watermark /'wɔːtəmɑːk/ n. (in paper) filigrane m.

waterproof /'wɔːtəpruːf/ a. (material) imperméable.

watershed /'wɔːtəʃed/ n. (in affairs) tournant décisif m.

watertight /'wɔːtətaɪt/ a. étanche.

waterway /'wɔːtəweɪ/ n. voie navigable f.

waterworks /'wɔːtəwɜːks/ n. (place) station hydraulique f.

watery /'wɔːtərɪ/ a. (colour) délavé; (eyes) humide; (soup) trop liquide; (tea) faible.

watt /wɒt/ n. watt m.

wav|e /weɪv/ n. vague f.; (in hair) ondulation f.; (radio) onde f.; (sign) signe m. —v.t. agiter. —v.i. faire signe (de la main); (*move in wind*) flotter. ∼y *a*. (*line*) onduleux; (*hair*) ondulé.

wavelength /'weɪvleŋθ/ *n*. (*radio & fig.*) longueur d'ondes *f*.

waver /'weɪvə(r)/ *v.i.* vaciller.

wax[1] /wæks/ *n*. cire *f*.; (*for skis*) fart *m*. —*v.t.* cirer; farter; (*car*) astiquer. ∼en, ∼y *adjs*. cireux.

wax[2] /wæks/ *v.i.* (*of moon*) croître.

waxwork /'wækswɜːk/ *n*. (*dummy*) figure de cire *f*.

way /weɪ/ *n*. (*road, path*) chemin *m*. (**to**, de); (*distance*) distance *f*.; (*direction*) direction *f*.; (*manner*) façon *f*.; (*means*) moyen *m*.; (*particular*) égard *m*. ∼s, (*habits*) habitudes *f. pl*. —*adv*. (*fam*.) loin. **be in the ∼**, bloquer le passage; (*hindrance: fig.*) gêner (qn.). **be on one's ∼ or the ∼**, être sur son *or* le chemin. **by the ∼**, à propos. **by the ∼side**, au bord de la route. **by ∼ of**, comme; (*via*) par. **go out of one's ∼**, se donner du mal pour. **in a ∼**, dans un sens. **make one's ∼ somewhere**, se rendre quelque part. **push one's ∼ through**, se frayer un passage. **that ∼**, par là. **this ∼**, par ici. **∼ in**, entrée *f*. **∼ out**, sortie *f*. **∼-out** *a*. (*strange: fam.*) original.

waylay /'weɪleɪ/ *v.t.* (*p.t.* **-laid**) (*assail*) assaillir; (*stop*) accrocher.

wayward /'weɪwəd/ *a*. capricieux.

WC /dʌb(ə)ljuː'siː/ *n*. w.-c. *m. pl*.

we /wiː/ *pron*. nous.

weak /wiːk/ *a*. (**-er, -est**) faible; (*delicate*) fragile. **∼ly** *adv*. faiblement; *a*. faible. **∼ness** *n*. faiblesse *f*.; (*fault*) point faible *m*. **a ∼ness for**, (*liking*) un faible pour.

weaken /'wiːkən/ *v.t.* affaiblir —*v.i.* s'affaiblir, faiblir.

weakling /'wiːklɪŋ/ *n*. gringalet *m*.

wealth /welθ/ *n*. richesse *f*.; (*riches, resources*) richesses *f. pl*.; (*quantity*) profusion *f*.

wealthy /'welθɪ/ *a*. (**-ier, -iest**) riche. —*n*. **the ∼**, les riches *m. pl*.

wean /wiːn/ *v.t.* (*baby*) sevrer.

weapon /'wepən/ *n*. arme *f*.

wear /weə(r)/ *v.t.* (*p.t.* **wore**, *p.p.* **worn**) porter; (*put on*) mettre; (*expression etc.*) avoir. —*v.i.* (*last*) durer. **∼ (out)**, (s')user. —*n*. usage *m*.; (*damage*) usure *f*.; (*clothing*) vêtements *m. pl*. **∼ down**, user. **∼ off**, (*colour, pain*) passer. **∼ on**, (*time*) passer. **∼ out**, (*exhaust*) épuiser.

wear|y /'wɪərɪ/ *a*. (**-ier, -iest**) fatigué, las; (*tiring*) fatigant. —*v.i.* **∼y of**, se lasser de. **∼ily** *adv*. avec lassitude. **∼iness** *n*. lassitude *f*., fatigue *f*.

weasel /'wiːzl/ *n*. belette *f*.

weather /'weðə(r)/ *n*. temps *m*. —*a*. météorologique. —*v.t.* (*survive*) réchapper de *or* à. **under the ∼**, patraque. **∼-beaten** *a*. tanné. **∼ forecast**, météo *f*. **∼-vane** *n*. girouette *f*.

weathercock /'weðəkɒk/ *n*. girouette *f*.

weave /wiːv/ *v.t./i.* (*p.t.* **wove**, *p.p.* **woven**) tisser; (*basket etc.*) tresser; (*move*) se faufiler. —*n*. (*style*) tissage *m*. **∼r** /-ə(r)/ *n*. tisserand(e) *m*. (*f*.).

web /web/ *n*. (*of spider*) toile *f*.; (*fabric*) tissu *m*.; (*on foot*) palmure *f*. **∼bed** *a*. (*foot*) palmé. **∼bing** *n*. (*in chair*) sangles *f. pl*.

wed /wed/ *v.t.* (*p.t.* **wedded**) épouser. —*v.i.* se marier. **∼ded to**, (*devoted to: fig.*) attaché à.

wedding /'wedɪŋ/ *n*. mariage *m*. **∼-ring** *n*. alliance *f*.

wedge /wedʒ/ *n*. coin *m*.; (*under wheel etc.*) cale *f*. —*v.t.* caler; (*push*) enfoncer; (*crowd*) coincer.

Wednesday /'wenzdɪ/ *n*. mercredi *m*.

wee /wiː/ *a*. (*fam*.) tout petit.

weed /wiːd/ *n*. mauvaise herbe *f*. —*v.t./i.* désherber. **∼-killer** *n*. désherbant *m*. **∼ out**, extirper. **∼y** *a*. (*person: fig.*) faible, maigre.

week /wiːk/ *n*. semaine *f*. **a ∼ today/tomorrow**, aujourd'hui/demain en huit. **∼ly** *adv*. toutes les semaines; *a*. & *n*. (*periodical*) hebdomadaire (*m.*).

weekday /'wiːkdeɪ/ *n*. jour de semaine *m*.

weekend /wiːk'end/ *n*. week-end *m*., fin de semaine *f*.

weep /wiːp/ *v.t./i.* (*p.t.* **wept**) pleurer (**for** s.o., qn.). **∼ing willow**, saule pleureur *m*.

weigh /weɪ/ *v.t./i.* peser. **∼ anchor**, lever l'ancre. **∼ down**, lester (avec un poids); (*bend*) faire plier; (*fig.*) accabler. **∼ up**, (*examine: fam.*) calculer.

weight /weɪt/ *n*. poids *m*. **lose/put on ∼**, perdre/prendre du poids. **∼lessness** *n*. apesanteur *f*. **∼-lifting** *n*. haltérophilie *f*. **∼y** *a*. lourd; (*subject etc.*) de poids.

weighting /'weɪtɪŋ/ *n*. indemnité *f*.

weir /wɪə(r)/ *n*. barrage *m*.

weird /wɪəd/ *a*. (**-er, -est**) mystérieux; (*strange*) bizarre.

welcome /'welkəm/ *a*. agréable; (*timely*) opportun. **be ∼**, être le *or* la bienvenu(e), être les bienvenu(e)s. **you're ∼!**, (*after thank you*) il n'y a pas de quoi! **∼ to do**, libre de faire. —*int*.

soyez le *or* la bienvenu(e), soyez les
bienvenu(e)s. —*n.* accueil *m.* —*v.t.*
accueillir; (*as greeting*) souhaiter la
bienvenue à; (*fig.*) se réjouir de.

weld /weld/ *v.t.* souder. —*n.* soudure *f.*
~er *n.* soudeur *m.* **~ing** *n.* soudure *f.*

welfare /'welfeə(r)/ *n.* bien-être *m.*; (*aid*)
aide sociale *f.* **W~ State,** État-
providence *m.*

well[1] /wel/ *n.* (*for water, oil*) puits *m.*; (*of
stairs*) cage *f.*

well[2] /wel/ *adv.* (**better, best**) bien. —*a.*
bien *invar.* **as ~,** aussi. **be ~,** (*healthy*)
aller bien. —*int.* eh bien; (*surprise*)
tiens. **do ~,** (*succeed*) réussir. **~-
behaved** *a.* sage. **~-being** *n.* bien-être
m. **~-built** *a.* bien bâti. **~-disposed** *a.*
bien disposé. **~ done!,** bravo! **~-
dressed** *a.* bien habillé. **~-heeled** *a.*
(*fam.*) nanti. **~-informed** *a.* bien
informé. **~-known** *a.* (bien) connu. **~-
meaning** *a.* bien intentionné. **~ off,**
aisé, riche. **~-read** *a.* instruit. **~-
spoken** *a.* qui parle bien. **~-to-do** *a.*
riche. **~-wisher** *n.* admiralteur, -trice
m., *f.*

wellington /'welɪŋtən/ *n.* (*boot*) botte de
caoutchouc *f.*

Welsh /welʃ/ *a.* gallois. —*n.* (*lang.*)
gallois *m.* **~man** *n.* Gallois *m.* **~
rabbit,** croûte au fromage *f.* **~woman**
n. Galloise *f.*

welsh /welʃ/ *v.i.* **~ on,** (*debt, promise*)
ne pas honorer.

welterweight /'weltəweɪt/ *n.* poids mi-
moyen *m.*

wench /wentʃ/ *n.* (*old use*) jeune fille *f.*

wend /wend/ *v.t.* **~ one's way,** se
diriger, aller son chemin.

went /went/ *see* **go.**

wept /wept/ *see* **weep.**

were /wɜ:(r), *unstressed* wə(r)/ *see* **be.**

west /west/ *n.* ouest *m.* **the W~,** (*pol.*)
l'Occident *m.* —*a.* d'ouest. —*adv.* vers
l'ouest. **the W~ Country,** le sud-ouest
(de l'Angleterre). **W~ Germany,**
Allemagne de l'Ouest *f.* **W~ Indian** *a.*
& *n.* antillais(e) (*m.* (*f.*)). **the W~
Indies,** les Antilles *f. pl.* **~erly** *a.*
d'ouest. **~ern** *a.* de l'ouest; (*pol.*) oc-
cidental; *n.* (*film*) western *m.* **~erner** *n.*
occidental(e) *m.* (*f.*). **~ward** *a.* à
l'ouest. **~wards** *adv.* vers l'ouest.

westernize /'westənaɪz/ *v.t.* occiden-
taliser.

wet /wet/ *a.* (**wetter, wettest**) mouillé;
(*damp, rainy*) humide; (*paint*) frais.
—*v.t.* (*p.t.* **wetted**) mouiller. —*n.* **the
~,** l'humidité *f.*; (*rain*) la pluie *f.* **get**

~, se mouiller. **~ blanket,** rabat-joie
m. invar. **~ness** *n.* humidité *f.* **~ suit,**
combinaison de plongée *f.*

whack /wæk/ *n.* (*fam.*) grand coup *m.*
—*v.t.* (*fam.*) taper sur.

whacked /wækt/ *a.* (*fam.*) claqué.

whacking /'wækɪŋ/ *a.* énorme.

whale /weɪl/ *n.* baleine *f.*

wham /wæm/ *int.* vlan.

wharf /wɔ:f/ *n.* (*pl.* **wharfs**) (*for ships*)
quai *m.*

what /wɒt/ *a.* (*in questions*) quel(le),
quel(le)s. —*pron.* (*in questions*)
qu'est-ce qui; (*object*) (qu'est-ce) que
or qu'*; (*after prep.*) quoi; (*that which*)
ce qui; (*object*) ce que, ce qu'*. —*int.*
quoi, comment. **~ date?,** quelle date?
~ time?, à quelle heure? **~ happened?,** qu'est-ce qui s'est passé? **~
did he say?,** qu'est-ce qu'il a dit? **~ he
said,** ce qu'il a dit. **~ is important,** ce
qui est important. **~ is it?,** qu'est-ce
que c'est? **~ you need,** ce dont vous
avez besoin. **~ a fool/***etc.***,** quel
idiot/*etc.*! **~ about me/him/***etc.***?,** et
moi/lui/*etc.*? **~ about doing?,** si on
faisait? **~ for?,** pourquoi?

whatever /wɒt'evə(r)/ *a.* **~ book/***etc.***,**
quel que soit le livre/*etc.* —*pron.* (*no
matter what*) quoi que, quoi qu'*;
(*anything that*) tout ce qui; (*object*) tout
ce que *or* qu'*. **~ happens,** quoi qu'il
arrive. **~ happened?,** qu'est-ce qui est
arrivé? **~ the problems,** quels que
soient les problèmes. **~ you want,** tout
ce que vous voulez. **nothing ~,** rien du
tout.

whatsoever /wɒtsəʊ'evər/ *a.* & *pron.* =
whatever.

wheat /wi:t/ *n.* blé *m.*, froment *m.*

wheedle /'wi:dl/ *v.t.* cajoler.

wheel /wi:l/ *n.* roue *f.* —*v.t.* pousser.
—*v.i.* tourner. **at the ~,** (*of vehicle*) au
volant; (*helm*) au gouvernail. **~ and
deal,** faire des combines.

wheelbarrow /'wi:lbærəʊ/ *n.* brouette *f.*

wheelchair /'wi:ltʃeə(r)/ *n.* fauteuil
roulant *m.*

wheeze /wi:z/ *v.i.* siffler (en respirant).
—*n.* sifflement *m.*

when /wen/ *adv.* & *pron.* quand. —*conj.*
quand, lorsque. **the day/moment ~,** le
jour/moment où.

whenever /wen'evə(r)/ *conj.* & *adv.* (*at
whatever time*) quand; (*every time that*)
chaque fois que.

where /weə(r)/ *adv.*, *conj.*, & *pron.* où;
(*whereas*) alors que; (*the place that*) là
où. **~abouts** *adv.* (à peu prés) où; *n.*

s.o.'s ~abouts, l'endroit où se trouve qn. ~by *adv.* par quoi. ~upon *adv.* sur quoi.

whereas /weər'æz/ *conj.* alors que.

wherever /weər'evə(r)/ *conj. & adv.* où que; (*everywhere*) partout où; (*anywhere*) (là) où; (*emphatic where*) où donc.

whet /wet/ *v.t.* (*p.t.* whetted) (*appetite, desire*) aiguiser.

whether /'weðə(r)/ *conj.* si. **not know ~,** ne pas savoir si. **~ I go or not,** que j'aille ou non.

which /wɪtʃ/ *a.* (*in questions*) quel(le), quel(le)s. —*pron.* (*in questions*) lequel, laquelle, lesquel(le)s; (*the one or ones that*) celui (celle, ceux, celles) qui; (*object*) celui (celle, ceux, celles) que *or* qu'*; (*referring to whole sentence,* = *and that*) ce qui; (*object*) ce que, ce qu'*; (*after prep.*) lequel/*etc.* —*rel. pron.* qui; (*object*) que, qu'*. **~ house?,** quelle maison? **~ (one) do you want?,** lequel voulez-vous? **~ are ready?,** lesquels sont prêts? **the bird ~ flies,** l'oiseau qui vole. **the hat ~ he wears,** le chapeau qu'il porte. **of ~, from ~,** duquel/*etc.* **to ~, at ~,** auquel/*etc.* **the book of ~,** le livre dont *or* duquel. **after ~,** après quoi. **she was there, ~ surprised me,** elle était là, ce qui m'a surpris.

whichever /wɪtʃ'evə(r)/ *a.* **~ book/***etc.***,** quel que soit le livre/*etc.* que *or* qui. **take ~ book you wish,** prenez le livre que vous voulez. —*pron.* celui (celle, ceux, celles) qui *or* que.

whiff /wɪf/ *n.* (*puff*) bouffée *f.*

while /waɪl/ *n.* moment *m.* —*conj.* (*when*) pendant que; (*although*) bien que; (*as long as*) tant que. —*v.t.* **~ away,** (*time*) passer.

whilst /waɪlst/ *conj.* = while.

whim /wɪm/ *n.* caprice *m.*

whimper /'wɪmpə(r)/ *v.i.* geindre, pleurnicher. —*n.* pleurnichement *m.*

whimsical /'wɪmzɪkl/ *a.* (*person*) capricieux; (*odd*) bizarre.

whine /waɪn/ *v.i.* gémir, se plaindre. —*n.* gémissement *m.*

whip /wɪp/ *n.* fouet *m.* —*v.t.* (*p.t.* whipped) fouetter; (*culin.*) fouetter, battre; (*seize*) enlever brusquement. —*v.i.* (*move*) aller en vitesse. **~-round** *n.* (*fam.*) collecte *f.* **~ out,** (*gun etc.*) sortir. **~ up,** exciter; (*cause*) provoquer; (*meal: fam.*) préparer.

whirl /wɜːl/ *v.t./i.* (faire) tourbillonner. —*n.* tourbillon *m.*

whirlpool /'wɜːlpuːl/ *n.* (*in sea etc.*) tourbillon *m.*

whirlwind /'wɜːlwɪnd/ *n.* tourbillon (de vent) *m.*

whirr /wɜː(r)/ *v.i.* vrombir.

whisk /wɪsk/ *v.t.* (*snatch*) enlever *or* emmener brusquement; (*culin.*) fouetter. —*n.* (*culin.*) fouet *m.*; (*broom, brush*) petit balai *m.* **~ away,** (*brush away*) chasser.

whisker /'wɪskə(r)/ *n.* poil *m.* **~s,** (*man's*) barbe *f.*, moustache *f.*; (*sideboards*) favoris *m. pl.*

whisky /'wɪskɪ/ *n.* whisky *m.*

whisper /'wɪspə(r)/ *v.t./i.* chuchoter. —*n.* chuchotement *m.*; (*rumour: fig.*) rumeur *f.*, bruit *m.*

whistle /'wɪsl/ *n.* sifflement *m.*; (*instrument*) sifflet *m.* —*v.t./i.* siffler. **~ at *or* for,** siffler.

Whit /wɪt/ *a.* **~ Sunday,** dimanche de Pentecôte *m.*

white /waɪt/ *a.* (-er, -est) blanc. —*n.* blanc *m.*; (*person*) blanc(he) *m.* (*f.*). **~ coffee,** café au lait *m.* **~-collar worker,** employé(e) de bureau *m.* (*f.*). **~ elephant,** objet, projet, *etc.* inutile *m.* **~ lie,** pieux mensonge *m.* **W~ Paper,** livre blanc *m.* **~ness** *n.* blancheur *f.*

whiten /'waɪtn/ *v.t./i.* blanchir.

whitewash /'waɪtwɒʃ/ *n.* blanc de chaux *m.* —*v.t.* blanchir à la chaux; (*person: fig.*) blanchir.

whiting /'waɪtɪŋ/ *n. invar.* (*fish*) merlan *m.*

Whitsun /'wɪtsn/ *n.* la Pentecôte *f.*

whittle /'wɪtl/ *v.t.* **~ down,** tailler (au couteau); (*fig.*) réduire.

whiz /wɪz/ *v.i.* (*p.t.* whizzed) (*through air*) fendre l'air; (*hiss*) siffler; (*rush*) aller à toute vitesse. **~-kid** *n.* jeune prodige *m.*

who /huː/ *pron.* qui.

whodunit /huː'dʌnɪt/ *n.* (*story: fam.*) roman policier *m.*

whoever /huː'evə(r)/ *pron.* (*no matter who*) qui que ce soit qui *or* que; (*the one who*) quiconque. **tell ~ you want,** dites-le à qui vous voulez.

whole /həʊl/ *a.* entier; (*intact*) intact. **the ~ house/***etc.***,** toute la maison/*etc.* —*n.* totalité *f.*; (*unit*) tout *m.* **on the ~,** dans l'ensemble. **~-hearted** *a.*, **~-heartedly** *adv.* sans réserve.

wholefoods /'həʊlfuːdz/ *n. pl.* aliments naturels et diététiques *m. pl.*

wholemeal /'həʊlmiːl/ *a.* **~ bread,** pain complet *m.*

wholesale /'həʊlseɪl/ n. gros m. —a. (firm) de gros; (fig.) systématique. —adv. (in large quantities) en gros; (buy or sell one item) au prix de gros; (fig.) en masse. ~r /-ə(r)/ n. grossiste m./f.

wholesome /'həʊlsəm/ a. sain.

wholewheat /'həʊlhwiːt/ a. = **wholemeal**.

wholly /'həʊlɪ/ adv. entièrement.

whom /huːm/ pron. (that) que, qu'*; (after prep. & in questions) qui. of ~, dont. with ~, avec qui.

whooping cough /'huːpɪŋkɒf/ n. coqueluche f.

whopping /'wɒpɪŋ/ a. (sl.) énorme.

whore /hɔː(r)/ n. putain f.

whose /huːz/ pron. & a. à qui, de qui. ~ hat is this?, ~ is this hat?, à qui est ce chapeau? ~ son are you?, de qui êtes-vous le fils? the man ~ hat I see, l'homme dont or de qui je vois le chapeau.

why /waɪ/ adv. pourquoi. —int. eh bien, ma parole, tiens. the reason ~, la raison pour laquelle.

wick /wɪk/ n. (of lamp etc.) mèche f.

wicked /'wɪkɪd/ a. méchant, mauvais, vilain. ~ly adv. méchamment. ~ness n. méchanceté f.

wicker /'wɪkə(r)/ n. osier m. ~work n. vannerie f.

wicket /'wɪkɪt/ n. guichet m.

wide /waɪd/ a. (-er, -est) large; (ocean etc.) vaste. —adv. (fall etc.) loin du but. **open ~**, ouvrir tout grand. ~ **open**, grand ouvert. ~-**angle lens** grand-angle m. ~ **awake**, éveillé. ~ly adv. (spread, space) largement; (travel) beaucoup; (generally) généralement; (extremely) extrêmement.

widen /'waɪdn/ v.t./i. (s')élargir.

widespread /'waɪdspred/ a. très répandu.

widow /'wɪdəʊ/ n. veuve. f. ~ed a. (man) veuf; (woman) veuve. be ~ed, (become widower or widow) devenir veuf or veuve. ~er n. veuf m.

width /wɪdθ/ n. largeur f.

wield /wiːld/ v.t. (axe etc.) manier; (power: fig.) exercer.

wife /waɪf/ n. (pl. **wives**) femme f., épouse f. ~ly a. d'épouse.

wig /wɪg/ n. perruque f.

wiggle /'wɪgl/ v.t./i. remuer; (hips) tortiller; (of worm) se tortiller.

wild /waɪld/ a. (-er, -est) sauvage; (sea, enthusiasm) déchaîné; (mad) fou; (angry) furieux. —adv. (grow) à l'état sauvage. ~s n. pl. régions sauvages f. pl. **run ~**, (free) courir en liberté. ~-**goose chase**, fausse piste f. ~ly adv. violemment; (madly) follement.

wildcat /'waɪldkæt/ a. ~ **strike**, grève sauvage f.

wilderness /'wɪldənɪs/ n. désert m.

wildlife /'waɪldlaɪf/ n. faune f.

wile /waɪl/ n. ruse f., artifice m.

wilful /'wɪlfl/ a. (intentional, obstinate) volontaire.

will[1] /wɪl/ v. aux. he ~ do/you ~ sing/etc., (future tense) il fera/tu chanteras/etc. ~ **you have a coffee?**, voulez-vous prendre un café?

will[2] /wɪl/ n. volonté f.; (document) testament m. —v.t. (wish) vouloir. at ~, quand or comme on veut. ~-**power** n. volonté f. ~ **o.s. to do**, faire un effort de volonté pour faire.

willing /'wɪlɪŋ/ a. (help, offer) spontané; (helper) bien disposé. ~ **to**, disposé à. ~ly adv. (with pleasure) volontiers; (not forced) volontairement. ~ness n. empressement m. (**to do**, à faire); (goodwill) bonne volonté f.

willow /'wɪləʊ/ n. saule m.

willy-nilly /'wɪlɪ'nɪlɪ/ adv. bon gré mal gré.

wilt /wɪlt/ v.i. (plant etc.) dépérir.

wily /'waɪlɪ/ a. (-ier, -iest) rusé.

win /wɪn/ v.t./i. (p.t. **won**, pres. p. **winning**) gagner; (victory, prize) remporter; (fame, fortune) acquérir, trouver. —n. victoire f. ~ **round**, convaincre.

wince /wɪns/ v.i. se crisper, tressaillir. **without ~ing**, sans broncher.

winch /wɪntʃ/ n. treuil m. —v.t. hisser au treuil.

wind[1] /wɪnd/ n. vent m.; (breath) souffle m. —v.t. essouffler. **get ~ of**, avoir vent de. **in the ~**, dans l'air. ~**cheater**, (Amer.) ~**breaker** ns. blouson m. ~ **instrument**, instrument à vent m. ~**swept** a. balayé par les vents.

wind[2] /waɪnd/ v.t./i. (p.t. **wound**) (s')enrouler; (of path, river) serpenter. ~ (**up**), (clock etc.) remonter. ~ **up**, (end) (se) terminer. ~ **up in hospital**, finir à l'hôpital. ~**ing** a. (path) sinueux.

windfall /'wɪndfɔːl/ n. fruit tombé m.; (money: fig.) aubaine f.

windmill /'wɪndmɪl/ n. moulin à vent m.

window /'wɪndəʊ/ n. fenêtre f.; (glass pane) vitre f.; (in vehicle, train) vitre f.; (in shop) vitrine f.; (counter) guichet m. ~-**box** n. jardinière f. ~-**cleaner** n.

laveur de carreaux *m*. ~**-dresser** *n*. étalagiste *m./f*. ~**-ledge** *n*. rebord de (la) fenêtre *m*.; ~**-shopping** *n*. lèche-vitrines *m*. ~**-sill** *n*. (*inside*) appui de (la) fenêtre *m*.; (*outside*) rebord de (la) fenêtre *m*.

windpipe /'wɪndpaɪp/ *n*. trachée *f*.

windscreen /'wɪndskriːn/, (*Amer*.) **windshield** /'wɪndʃiːld/ *n*. pare-brise *m*. *invar*. ~ **washer,** lave-glace *m*. ~ **wiper,** essuie-glace *m*.

windsurf|ing /'wɪndsɜːfɪŋ/ *n*. planche à voile *f*. ~**er** *n*. véliplanchiste *m./f*.

windy /'wɪndɪ/ *a*. (**-ier, -iest**) venteux. **it is** ~, il y a du vent.

wine /waɪn/ *n*. vin *m*. ~**-cellar** *n*. cave (à vin) *f*. ~**-grower** *n*. viticulteur *m*. ~**-growing** *n*. viticulture *f*.; *a*. viticole. ~ **list,** carte des vins *f*. ~**-tasting** *n*. dégustation de vins *f*. ~ **waiter,** sommelier *m*.

wineglass /'waɪnɡlɑːs/ *n*. verre à vin *m*.

wing /wɪŋ/ *n*. aile *f*. ~**s**, (*theatre*) coulisses *f. pl*. **under one's** ~, sous son aile. ~ **mirror,** rétroviseur extérieur *m*. ~**ed** *a*. ailé. ~**er** *n*. (*sport*) ailier *m*.

wink /wɪŋk/ *v.i*. faire un clin d'œil; (*light, star*) clignoter. —*n*. clin d'œil *m*.; clignotement *m*.

winner /'wɪnə(r)/ *n*. (*of game*) gagnant(e) *m*. (*f*.); (*of fight*) vainqueur *m*.

winning /'wɪnɪŋ/ *see* **win**. —*a*. (*number, horse*) gagnant; (*team*) victorieux; (*smile*) engageant. ~**s** *n. pl*. gains *m. pl*.

wint|er /'wɪntə(r)/ *n*. hiver *m*. —*v.i*. hiverner. ~**ry** *a*. hivernal.

wipe /waɪp/ *v.t*. essuyer. —*v.i*. ~ **up,** essuyer la vaisselle. —*n*. coup de torchon *or* d'éponge *m*. ~ **off** *or* **out,** essuyer. ~ **out,** (*destroy*) anéantir; (*remove*) effacer.

wir|e /'waɪə(r)/ *n*. fil *m*.; (*Amer*.) télégramme *m*. ~**e netting,** grillage *m*. ~**ing** *n*. (*electr*.) installation électrique *f*.

wireless /'waɪəlɪs/ *n*. radio *f*.

wiry /'waɪərɪ/ *a*. (**-ier, -iest**) (*person*) nerveux et maigre.

wisdom /'wɪzdəm/ *n*. sagesse *f*.

wise /waɪz/ *a*. (**-er, -est**) prudent, sage; (*look*) averti. ~ **guy,** (*fam*.) petit malin *m*. ~ **man,** sage *m*. ~**ly** *adv*. prudemment.

wisecrack /'waɪzkræk/ *n*. (*fam*.) mot d'esprit *m*., astuce *f*.

wish /wɪʃ/ *n*. (*specific*) souhait *m*., vœu *m*.; (*general*) désir *m*. —*v.t*. souhaiter, vouloir, désirer (**to do,** faire); (*bid*)

souhaiter. —*v.i*. ~ **for,** souhaiter. **I** ~ **he'd leave,** je voudrais bien qu'il parte. **best** ~**es,** (*in letter*) amitiés *f. pl*.; (*on greeting card*) meilleurs vœux *m. pl*.

wishful /'wɪʃfl/ *a*. **it's** ~ **thinking,** on se fait des illusions.

wishy-washy /'wɪʃɪwɒʃɪ/ *a*. fade.

wisp /wɪsp/ *n*. (*of smoke*) volute *f*.

wistful /'wɪstfl/ *a*. mélancolique.

wit /wɪt/ *n*. intelligence *f*.; (*humour*) esprit *m*.; (*person*) homme d'esprit *m*., femme d'esprit *f*. **be at one's** ~**'s** *or* ~**s' end,** ne plus savoir que faire.

witch /wɪtʃ/ *n*. sorcière *f*. ~**craft** *n*. sorcellerie *f*.

with /wɪð/ *prep*. avec; (*having*) à; (*because of*) de; (*at house of*) chez. **the man** ~ **the beard,** l'homme à la barbe. **fill**/*etc*. ~, remplir/*etc*. de. **pleased/ shaking**/*etc*. ~, content/frémissant/ *etc*. de. ~ **it,** (*fam*.) dans le vent.

withdraw /wɪð'drɔː/ *v.t./i*. (*p.t*. **withdrew,** *p.p*. **withdrawn**) (se) retirer. ~**al** *n*. retrait *m*. ~**n** *a*. (*person*) renfermé.

wither /'wɪðə(r)/ *v.t./i*. (se) flétrir. ~**ed** *a*. (*person*) desséché.

withhold /wɪð'həʊld/ *v.t*. (*p.t*. **withheld**) refuser (de donner); (*retain*) retenir; (*conceal, not tell*) cacher (**from,** à).

within /wɪ'ðɪn/ *prep. & adv*. à l'intérieur (de); (*in distances*) à moins de. ~ **a month,** (*before*) avant un mois. ~ **sight,** en vue.

without /wɪ'ðaʊt/ *prep*. sans. ~ **my knowing,** sans que je sache.

withstand /wɪð'stænd/ *v.t*. (*p.t*. **withstood**) résister à.

witness /'wɪtnɪs/ *n*. témoin *m*.; (*evidence*) témoignage *m*. —*v.t*. être le témoin de, voir; (*document*) signer. **bear** ~ **to,** témoigner de. ~ **box** *or* **stand,** barre des témoins *f*.

witticism /'wɪtɪsɪzəm/ *n*. bon mot *m*.

witt|y /'wɪtɪ/ *a*. (**-ier, -iest**) spirituel. ~**iness** *n*. esprit *m*.

wives /waɪvz/ *see* **wife**.

wizard /'wɪzəd/ *n*. magicien *m*.; (*genius: fig*.) génie *m*.

wobbl|e /'wɒbl/ *v.i*. (*of jelly, voice, hand*) trembler; (*stagger*) chanceler; (*of table, chair*) branler. ~**y** *a*. tremblant; branlant.

woe /wəʊ/ *n*. malheur *m*.

woke, woken /wəʊk, 'wəʊkən/ *see* **wake**[1].

wolf /wʊlf/ *n*. (*pl*. **wolves**) loup *m*. —*v.t*. (*food*) engloutir. **cry** ~, crier au loup. ~**-whistle** *n*. sifflement admiratif *m*.

woman /'wʊmən/ n. (pl. **women**) femme f. ~ **doctor,** femme médecin f. ~ **driver,** femme au volant f. ~ **friend,** amie f. ~**hood** n. féminité f. ~**ly** a. féminin.

womb /wu:m/ n. utérus m.

women /'wɪmɪn/ see **woman.**

won /wʌn/ see **win.**

wonder /'wʌndə(r)/ n. émerveillement m.; (thing) merveille f. —v.t. se demander (**if,** si). —v.i. s'étonner (**at,** de); (reflect) songer (**about,** à). **it is no** ~, ce or il n'est pas étonnant (**that,** que).

wonderful /'wʌndəfl/ a. merveilleux. ~**ly** adv. merveilleusement; (work, do, etc.) à merveille.

won't /wəʊnt/ = **will not.**

woo /wu:/ v.t. (woman) faire la cour à; (please) chercher à plaire à.

wood /wʊd/ n. bois m. ~**ed** a. boisé. ~**en** a. en or de bois; (stiff: fig.) raide, comme du bois.

woodcut /'wʊdkʌt/ n. gravure sur bois f.

woodland /'wʊdlənd/ n. région boisée f., bois m. pl.

woodpecker /'wʊdpekə(r)/ n. (bird) pic m., pivert m.

woodwind /'wʊdwɪnd/ n. (mus.) bois m. pl.

woodwork /'wʊdwɜːk/ n. (craft, objects) menuiserie f.

woodworm /'wʊdwɜːm/ n. (larvae) vers (de bois) m. pl.

woody /'wʊdɪ/ a. (wooded) boisé; (like wood) ligneux.

wool /wʊl/ n. laine f. ~**len** a. de laine. ~**lens** n. pl. lainages m. pl. ~**ly** a. laineux; (vague) nébuleux; n. (garment: fam.) lainage m.

word /wɜːd/ n. mot m.; (spoken) parole f., mot m.; (promise) parole f.; (news) nouvelles f. pl. —v.t. rédiger. **by** ~ **of mouth,** de vive voix. **give/keep one's** ~, donner/tenir sa parole. **have a** ~ **with,** parler à. **in other** ~**s,** autrement dit. ~ **processor,** machine de traitement de texte f. ~**ing** n. termes m. pl.

wordy /'wɜːdɪ/ a. verbeux.

wore /wɔː(r)/ see **wear.**

work /wɜːk/ n. travail m.; (product, book, etc.) œuvre f., ouvrage m.; (building etc. work) travaux m. pl. ~**s,** (techn.) mécanisme m.; (factory) usine f. —v.t./i. (of person) travailler; (shape, hammer, etc.) travailler; (techn.) (faire) fonctionner, (faire) marcher; (land, mine) exploiter; (of drug etc.) agir. ~ **s.o.,** (make work) faire

travailler qn. ~**-force** n. main-d'œuvre f. ~ **in,** (s')introduire. ~**-load** n. travail (à faire) m. ~ **off,** (get rid of) se débarrasser de. ~ **out** v.t. (solve) résoudre; (calculate) calculer; (elaborate) élaborer; v.i. (succeed) marcher; (sport) s'entraîner. ~**-station** n. poste de travail m. ~ **to-rule** n. grève du zèle f. ~ **up** v.t. développer; v.i. (to climax) monter vers. ~**ed up,** (person) énervé.

workable /'wɜːkəbl/ a. réalisable.

workaholic /wɜːkə'hɒlɪk/ n. (fam.) bourreau de travail m.

worker /'wɜːkə(r)/ n. travailleur, -se m., f.; (manual) ouvrlier, -ière m., f.

working /'wɜːkɪŋ/ a. (day, lunch, etc.) de travail. ~**s** n. pl. mécanisme m. ~ **class,** classe ouvrière f. ~**-class** a. ouvrier. **in** ~ **order,** en état de marche.

workman /'wɜːkmən/ n. (pl. **-men**) ouvrier m. ~**ship** n. maîtrise f.

workshop /'wɜːkʃɒp/ n. atelier m.

world /wɜːld/ n. monde m. —a. (power etc.) mondial; (record etc.) du monde. **best in the** ~, meilleur au monde. ~**-wide** a. universel.

worldly /'wɜːldlɪ/ a. de ce monde, terrestre. ~**-wise** a. qui a l'expérience du monde.

worm /wɜːm/ n. ver m. —v.t. ~ **one's way into,** s'insinuer dans. ~**-eaten** a. (wood) vermoulu; (fruit) véreux.

worn /wɔːn/ see **wear.** —a. usé. ~**-out** a. (thing) complètement usé; (person) épuisé.

worr|y /'wʌrɪ/ v.t./i. (s')inquiéter. —n. souci m. ~**ied** a. inquiet. ~**ier** n. inquiet, -iète m., f.

worse /wɜːs/ a. pire, plus mauvais. —adv. plus mal. —n. pire m. **be** ~ **off,** perdre.

worsen /'wɜːsn/ v.t./i. empirer.

worship /'wɜːʃɪp/ n. (adoration) culte m. —v.t. (p.t. **worshipped**) adorer. —v.i. faire ses dévotions. ~**per** n. (in church) fidèle m./f.

worst /wɜːst/ a. pire, plus mauvais. —adv. (**the**) ~, (sing etc.) le plus mal. —n. **the** ~ (**one**), (person, object) le or la pire. **the** ~ (**thing**), le pire (**that,** que). **get the** ~ **of it,** (be defeated) avoir le dessous.

worsted /'wʊstɪd/ n. worsted m.

worth /wɜːθ/ a. **be** ~, valoir. **it is** ~ **waiting/**etc., ça vaut la peine d'attendre/etc. —n. valeur f. **ten pence** ~ **of,** (pour) dix pence de. **it is** ~ (**one's**) **while,** ça (en) vaut la peine. ~**less** a. qui ne vaut rien.

worthwhile /wɜːθˈwaɪl/ a. qui (en) vaut la peine.

worthy /ˈwɜːðɪ/ a. (**-ier, -iest**) digne (**of,** de); (*laudable*) louable. —n. (*person*) notable m.

would /wʊd, *unstressed* wəd/ v. aux. he ∼ **do/you** ∼ **sing/***etc.*, (*conditional tense*) il ferait/tu chanterais/*etc.* **he** ∼ **have done,** il aurait fait. **I** ∼ **come every day,** (*used to*) je venais chaque jour. **I** ∼ **like some tea,** je voudrais du thé. ∼ **you come here?,** voulez-vous venir ici? **he** ∼**n't come,** il a refusé de venir. ∼**-be** a. soi-disant.

wound[1] /wuːnd/ n. blessure f. —v.t. blesser. **the** ∼**ed,** les blessés m. pl.

wound[2] /waʊnd/ see **wind**[2].

wove, woven /wəʊv, ˈwəʊvn/ see **weave**.

wow /waʊ/ int. mince (alors).

wrangle /ˈræŋgl/ v.i. se disputer. —n. dispute f.

wrap /ræp/ v.t. (p.t. **wrapped**). ∼ (**up**), envelopper. —v.i. ∼ **up,** (*dress warmly*) se couvrir. —n. châle m. ∼**ped up in,** (*engrossed*) absorbé dans. ∼**per** n. (*of book*) jaquette f.; (*of sweet*) papier m. ∼**ping** n. emballage m.; ∼**ping paper,** papier d'emballage m.

wrath /rɒθ/ n. courroux m.

wreak /riːk/ v.t. ∼ **havoc,** (*of storm etc.*) faire des ravages.

wreath /riːθ/ n. (pl. **-s** /-ðz/) (*of flowers, leaves*) couronne f.

wreck /rek/ n. (*sinking*) naufrage m.; (*ship, remains, person*) épave f.; (*vehicle*) voiture accidentée *or* délabrée f. —v.t. détruire; (*ship*) provoquer le naufrage de. ∼**age** n. (*pieces*) débris m. pl.; (*wrecked building*) décombres m. pl.

wren /ren/ n. roitelet m.

wrench /rentʃ/ v.t. (*pull*) tirer sur; (*twist*) tordre; (*snatch*) arracher (**from,** à). —n. (*tool*) clé f.

wrest /rest/ v.t. arracher (**from,** à).

wrestl|e /ˈresl/ v.i. lutter, se débattre (**with,** contre). ∼**er** n. lutteur, -se m., f.; catcheur, -se m., f. ∼**ing** n. lutte f. (**all-in**) ∼**ing,** catch m.

wretch /retʃ/ n. malheureu|x, -se m., f.; (*rascal*) misérable m./f.

wretched /ˈretʃɪd/ a. (*pitiful, poor*) misérable; (*bad*) affreux.

wriggle /ˈrɪgl/ v.t./i. (se) tortiller.

wring /rɪŋ/ v.t. (p.t. **wrung**) (*twist*) tordre; (*clothes*) essorer. ∼ **out of,** (*obtain from*) arracher à. ∼**ing wet,** trempé (jusqu'aux os).

wrinkle /ˈrɪŋkl/ n. (*crease*) pli m.; (*on skin*) ride f. —v.t./i. (se) rider.

wrist /rɪst/ n. poignet m. ∼**-watch** n. montre-bracelet f.

writ /rɪt/ n. acte judiciaire m.

write /raɪt/ v.t./i. (p.t. **wrote,** p.p. **written**) écrire. ∼ **back,** répondre. ∼ **down,** noter. ∼ **off,** (*debt*) passer aux profits et pertes; (*vehicle*) considérer bon pour la casse. ∼**-off** n. perte totale f. ∼ **up,** (*from notes*) rédiger. ∼**-up** n. compte rendu m.

writer /ˈraɪtə(r)/ n. auteur m., écrivain m. ∼ **of,** auteur de.

writhe /raɪð/ v.i. se tordre.

writing /ˈraɪtɪŋ/ n. écriture f. ∼(**s**), (*works*) écrits m. pl. **in** ∼, par écrit. ∼**-paper** n. papier à lettres m.

written /ˈrɪtn/ see **write**.

wrong /rɒŋ/ a. (*incorrect, mistaken*) faux, mauvais; (*unfair*) injuste; (*amiss*) qui ne va pas; (*clock*) pas à l'heure. **be** ∼, (*person*) avoir tort (**to,** de); (*be mistaken*) se tromper. —adv. mal. —n. injustice f.; (*evil*) mal m. —v.t. faire (du) tort à. **be in the** ∼, avoir tort. **go** ∼, (*err*) se tromper; (*turn out badly*) mal tourner; (*vehicle*) tomber en panne. **it is** ∼ **to,** (*morally*) c'est mal de. **what's** ∼?, qu'est-ce qui ne va pas? **what is** ∼ **with you?,** qu'est-ce que vous avez? ∼**ly** adv. mal; (*blame etc.*) à tort.

wrongful /ˈrɒŋfl/ a. injustifié, injuste. ∼**ly** adv. à tort.

wrote /rəʊt/ see **write**.

wrought /rɔːt/ a. ∼ **iron,** fer forgé m.

wrung /rʌŋ/ see **wring**.

wry /raɪ/ a. (**wryer, wryest**) (*smile*) désabusé, forcé. ∼ **face,** grimace f.

X

xerox /ˈzɪərɒks/ v.t. photocopier.

Xmas /ˈkrɪsməs/ n. Noël m.

X-ray /ˈeksreɪ/ n. rayon X m.; (*photograph*) radio(graphie) f. —v.t. radiographier.

xylophone /ˈzaɪləfəʊn/ n. xylophone m.

Y

yacht /jɒt/ n. yacht m. ∼**ing** n. yachting m.

yank /jæŋk/ v.t. tirer brusquement. —n. coup brusque m.

Yank /jæŋk/ *n.* (*fam.*) Américain(e) *m.* (*f.*), Amerloque *m./f.*

yap /jæp/ *v.i.* (*p.t.* **yapped**) japper.

yard¹ /jɑ:d/ *n.* (*measure*) yard *m.* (= *0.9144 metre*).

yard² /jɑ:d/ *n.* (*of house etc.*) cour *f.*; (*garden: Amer.*) jardin *m.*; (*for storage*) chantier *m.*, dépôt *m.*

yardstick /ˈjɑ:dstɪk/ *n.* mesure *f.*

yarn /jɑ:n/ *n.* (*thread*) fil *m.*; (*tale: fam.*) (longue) histoire *f.*

yawn /jɔ:n/ *v.i.* bâiller. —*n.* bâillement *m.* ~**ing** *a.* (*gaping*) béant.

year /jɪə(r)/ *n.* an *m.*, année *f.*; **school/tax**/*etc.* ~, année scolaire/fiscale/*etc.* **be ten**/*etc.* ~**s old,** avoir dix/*etc.* ans. ~**-book** *n.* annuaire *m.* ~**ly** *a.* annuel; *adv.* annuellement.

yearn /jɜ:n/ *v.i.* avoir bien *or* très envie (**for, to,** de). ~**ing** *n.* envie *f.*

yeast /ji:st/ *n.* levure *f.*

yell /jel/ *v.t./i.* hurler. —*n.* hurlement *m.*

yellow /ˈjeləʊ/ *a.* jaune; (*cowardly: fam.*) froussard. —*n.* jaune *m.*

yelp /jelp/ *n.* (*of dog etc.*) jappement *m.* —*v.i.* japper.

yen /jen/ *n.* (*desire*) grande envie *f.*

yes /jes/ *adv.* oui; (*as answer to negative question*) si. —*n.* oui *m. invar.*

yesterday /ˈjestədɪ/ *n. & adv.* hier (*m.*).

yet /jet/ *adv.* encore; (*already*) déjà. —*conj.* pourtant, néanmoins.

yew /ju:/ *n.* (*tree, wood*) if *m.*

Yiddish /ˈjɪdɪʃ/ *n.* yiddish *m.*

yield /ji:ld/ *v.t.* (*produce*) produire, rendre; (*profit*) rapporter; (*surrender*) céder. —*v.i.* (*give way*) céder. —*n.* rendement *m.*

yoga /ˈjəʊgə/ *n.* yoga *m.*

yoghurt /ˈjɒgət, *Amer.* ˈjəʊgərt/ *n.* yaourt *m.*

yoke /jəʊk/ *n.* joug *m.*

yokel /ˈjəʊkl/ *n.* rustre *m.*

yolk /jəʊk/ *n.* jaune (d'œuf) *m.*

yonder /ˈjɒndə(r)/ *adv.* là-bas.

you /ju:/ *pron.* (*familiar form*) tu, *pl.* vous; (*polite form*) vous; (*object*) te, t'*, pl.* vous; (*polite*) vous; (*after prep.*) toi, *pl.* vous; (*polite*) vous; (*indefinite*) on; (*object*) vous. (**to**) ~, te, t'*, pl.* vous; (*polite*) vous. **I gave** ~ **a pen,** je vous ai donné un stylo. **I know** ~, je te connais; je vous connais.

young /jʌŋ/ *a.* (**-er, -est**) jeune. —*n.* (*people*) jeunes *m. pl.*; (*of animals*) petits *m. pl.* ~**er** *a.* (*brother etc.*) cadet.

~**est** *a.* my ~**est brother,** le cadet de mes frères.

youngster /ˈjʌŋstə(r)/ *n.* jeune *m./f.*

your /jɔ:(r)/ *a.* (*familiar form*) ton, ta, *pl.* tes; (*polite form, & familiar form pl.*) votre, *pl.* vos.

yours /jɔ:z/ *poss. pron.* (*familiar form*) le tien, la tienne, les tien(ne)s; (*polite form, & familiar form pl.*) le *or* la vôtre, les vôtres. ~**s faithfully/sincerely,** je vous prie d'agréer/de croire en l'expression de mes sentiments les meilleurs.

yourself /jɔ:ˈself/ *pron.* (*familiar form*) toi-même; (*polite form*) vous-même; (*reflexive & after prep.*) te, t'*; vous. ~**ves** *pron. pl.* vous-mêmes; (*reflexive*) vous.

youth /ju:θ/ *n.* (*pl.* **-s** /-ðz/) jeunesse *f.*; (*young man*) jeune *m.* ~ **club,** centre de jeunes *m.* ~ **hostel,** auberge de jeunesse *f.* ~**ful** *a.* juvénile, jeune.

yo-yo /ˈjəʊjəʊ/ *n.* (*pl.* **-os**) (P.) yo-yo *m. invar.* (P.).

Yugoslav /ˈju:gəslɑ:v/ *a. & n.* Yougoslave (*m./f.*) ~**ia** /-ˈslɑ:vɪə/ *n.* Yougoslavie *f.*

yuppie /ˈjʌpɪ/ *n.* yuppie *m.*

Z

zany /ˈzeɪnɪ/ *a.* (**-ier, -iest**) farfelu.

zap /zæp/ *v.t.* (*fam.*) (*kill*) descendre; (*comput.*) enlever; (*TV*) zapper.

zeal /zi:l/ *n.* zèle *m.*

zealous /ˈzeləs/ *a.* zélé. ~**ly** *a.* zèle.

zebra /ˈzebrə, ˈzi:brə/ *n.* zèbre *m.* ~ **crossing,** passage pour piétons *m.*

zenith /ˈzenɪθ/ *n.* zénith *m.*

zero /ˈzɪərəʊ/ *n.* (*pl.* **-os**) zéro *m.* ~ **hour,** l'heure H *f.*

zest /zest/ *n.* (*gusto*) entrain *m.*; (*spice: fig.*) piment *m.*; (*of orange or lemon peel*) zeste *m.*

zigzag /ˈzɪgzæg/ *n.* zigzag *m.* —*a. & adv.* en zigzag. —*v.i.* (*p.t.* **zigzagged**) zigzaguer.

zinc /zɪŋk/ *n.* zinc *m.*

Zionism /ˈzaɪənɪzəm/ *n.* sionisme *m.*

zip /zɪp/ *n.* (*vigour*) allant *m.* ~**(-fastener),** fermeture éclair *f.* (P.). —*v.t.* (*p.t.* **zipped**) fermer avec une fermeture éclair (P.). —*v.i.* aller à toute vitesse. **Zip code,** (*Amer.*) code postal *m.*

zipper /ˈzɪpə(r)/ *n.* (*Amer.*) = **zip (-fastener).**

zither /'zɪðə(r)/ *n.* cithare *f.*
zodiac /'zəʊdɪæk/ *n.* zodiaque *m.*
zombie /'zɒmbɪ/ *n.* mort(e) vivant(e) *m.*
 (*f.*); (*fam.*) automate *m.*
zone /zəʊn/ *n.* zone *f.*
zoo /zuː/ *n.* zoo *m.*
zoolog|y /zəʊ'ɒlədʒɪ/ *n.* zoologie *f.*

~**ical** /-ə'lɒdʒɪkl/ *a.* zoologique. ~**ist**
 n. zoologiste *m./f.*
zoom /zuːm/ *v.i.* (*rush*) se précipiter. ~
 lens, zoom *m.* ~ **off** *or* **past,** filer
 (comme une flèche).
zucchini /zuː'kiːnɪ/ *n. invar.* (*Amer.*)
 courgette *f.*

French Verb Tables

Notes The conditional may be formed by substituting the following endings for those of the future: *ais* for *ai* and *as*, *ait* for *a*, *ions* for *ons*, *iez* for *ez*, *aient* for *ont*. The present participle is formed (unless otherwise indicated) by substituting *ant* for *ons* in the first person plural of the present tense (e.g. *finissant* and *donnant* may be derived from *finissons* and *donnons*). The imperative forms are (unless otherwise indicated) the same as the second persons singular and plural and the first person plural of the present tense. The second person singular does not take *s* after *e* or *a* (e.g. *donne, va*), except when followed by *y* or *en* (e.g. *vas-y*).

Regular verbs:

1. in *-er* (e.g. **donn|er**)

Present. ~e, ~es, ~e, ~ons, ~ez, ~ent.
Imperfect. ~ais, ~ais, ~ait, ~ions, ~iez, ~aient.
Past historic. ~ai, ~as, ~a, ~âmes, ~âtes, ~èrent.
Future. ~erai, ~eras, ~era, ~erons, ~erez, ~eront.
Present subjunctive, ~e, ~es, ~e, ~ions, ~iez, ~ent.
Past participle, ~é.

2. in *-ir* (e.g. **fin|ir**)

Pres. ~is, ~is, ~it, ~issons, ~issez, ~issent.
Impf. ~issais, ~issais, ~issait, ~issions, ~issiez, ~issaient.
Past hist. ~is, ~is, ~it, ~îmes, ~îtes, ~irent.
Fut. ~irai, ~iras, ~ira, ~irons, ~irez, ~iront.
Pres. sub. ~isse, ~isses, ~isse, ~issions, ~issiez, ~issent.
Past part. ~i.

3. in *-re* (e.g. **vend|re**)

Pres. ~s, ~s, ~, ~ons, ~ez, ~ent.
Impf. ~ais, ~ais, ~ait, ~ions, ~iez, ~aient.
Past hist. ~is, ~is, ~it, ~îmes, ~îtes, ~irent.
Fut. ~rai, ~ras, ~ra, ~rons, ~rez, ~ront.
Pres. sub. ~e, ~es, ~e, ~ions, ~iez, ~ent.
Past part. ~u.

Peculiarities of *-er* verbs:

In verbs in *-cer* (e.g. **commencer**) and *-ger* (e.g. **manger**), *c* becomes *ç* and *g* becomes *ge* before *a* and *o* (e.g. commença, commençons; mangea, mangeons).

In verbs in *-yer* (e.g. **nettoyer**), *y* becomes *i* before mute *e* (e.g. nettoie, nettoierai). Verbs in *-ayer* (e.g. **payer**) may retain *y* before mute *e* (e.g. paye or paie, payerai or paierai).

In verbs in *eler* (e.g. **appeler**) and in *-eter* (e.g. **jeter**), *l* becomes *ll* and *t* becomes *tt* before a syllable containing mute *e* (e.g. appelle, appellerai; jette, jetterai). In the verbs **celer, ciseler, congeler, déceler, démanteler, écarteler, geler, marteler, modeler,** and **peler,** and in the verbs **acheter, crocheter, fureter, haleter** and **racheter,** *e* becomes *è* before a syllable containing mute *e* (e.g. cèle, cèlerai; achète, achèterai).

In verbs in which the penultimate syllable contains mute *e* (e.g. **semer**) or *é* (e.g. **révéler**), both *e* and *é* become *è* before a syllable containing mute *e* (e.g. sème, sèmerai; révèle). However, in the verbs in which the penultimate syllable contains *é*, *é* remains unchanged in the future and conditional (e.g. révélerai).

Irregular verbs:

At least the first persons singular and plural of the present tense are shown. Forms not listed may be derived from these. Though the base form of the imperfect, future, and present subjunctive may be irregular, the endings of these tenses are as shown in the regular verb section. Only the first person singular of these tenses is given in most cases. The base form of the past historic may also be irregular but the endings of this tense shown in the verbs below fall (with few exceptions) into the 'u' category, listed under **être** and **avoir,** and the 'i' category shown under **finir** and **vendre** in the regular verb section. Only the first person singular of the past historic is listed in most cases.

Additional forms appear throughout when these cannot be derived from the forms given or when it is considered helpful to list them. Only those irregular verbs judged to be the most useful are shown in the tables.

abattre *as* BATTRE.

accueillir *as* CUEILLIR.

acquérir ● *Pres.* acquiers, acquérons, acquièrent. ● *Impf.* acquérais. ● *Past hist.* acquis. ● *Fut.* acquerrai. ● *Pres. sub.* acquière. ● *Past part.* acquis.

admettre *as* METTRE.

aller ● *Pres.* vais, vas, va, allons, allez, vont. ● *Fut.* irai. ● *Pres. sub.* aille, allions.

apercevoir *as* RECEVOIR.

apparaître *as* CONNAÎTRE.

appartenir *as* TENIR.

apprendre *as* PRENDRE.

asseoir ● *Pres.* assieds, asseyons, asseyent. ● *Impf.* asseyais. ● *Past hist.* assis. ● *Fut.* assiérai. ● *Pres. sub.* asseye. ● *Past part.* assis.

atteindre ● *Pres.* atteins, atteignons, atteignent. ● *Impf.* atteignais. ● *Past hist.* atteignis. ● *Fut.* atteindrai. ● *Pres. sub.* atteigne. ● *Past part.* atteint.

avoir ● *Pres.* ai, as, a, avons, avez, ont. ● *Impf.* avais. ● *Past hist.* eus, eut, eûmes, eûtes, eurent. ● *Fut.* aurai. ● *Pres. sub.* aie, aies, ait, ayons, ayez, aient. ● *Pres. part.* ayant. ● *Past part.* eu. ● *Imp.* aie, ayons, ayez.

battre ● *Pres.* bats, bat, battons, battez, battent.

boire ● *Pres.* bois, buvons, boivent. ● *Impf.* buvais. ● *Past hist.* bus. ● *Pres. sub.* boive, buvions. ● *Past part.* bu.

bouillir ● *Pres.* bous, bouillons, bouillent. ● *Impf.* bouillais. ● *Pres. sub.* bouille.

combattre *as* BATTRE.

commettre *as* METTRE.

comprendre *as* PRENDRE.

concevoir *as* RECEVOIR.

conclure ● *Pres.* conclus, concluons, concluent. ● *Past hist.* conclus. ● *Past part.* conclu.

conduire ● *Pres.* conduis, conduisons, conduisent. ● *Impf.* conduisais. ● *Past hist.* conduisis. ● *Pres. sub.* conduise. ● *Past part.* conduit.

connaître ● *Pres.* connais, connaît, connaissons. ● *Impf.* connaissais. ● *Past hist.* connus. ● *Pres. sub.* connaisse. ● *Past part.* connu.

construire *as* CONDUIRE.

contenir *as* TENIR.

contraindre *as* ATTEINDRE (except *ai* replaces *ei*).

contredire *as* DIRE, except ● *Pres.* vous contredisez.

convaincre *as* VAINCRE.

convenir *as* TENIR.

corrompre *as* ROMPRE.

coudre ● *Pres.* couds, cousons, cousent. ● *Impf.* cousais. ● *Past hist.* cousis. ● *Pres. sub.* couse. ● *Past part.* cousu.

courir ● *Pres.* cours, courons, courent. ● *Impf.* courais. ● *Past hist.* courus. ● *Fut.* courrai. ● *Pres. sub.* coure. ● *Past part.* couru.

couvrir ● *Pres.* couvre, couvrons. ● *Impf.* couvrais. ● *Pres. sub.* couvre. ● *Past part.* couvert.

craindre *as* ATTEINDRE (except *ai* replaces *ei*).

croire ● *Pres.* crois, croit, croyons, croyez, croient. ● *Impf.* croyais. ● *Past hist.* crus. ● *Pres. sub.* croie, croyions. ● *Past part.* cru.

croître ● *Pres.* crois, croît, croissons. ● *Impf.* croissais. ● *Past hist.* crûs. ● *Pres. sub.* croisse. ● *Past part.* crû, crue.

cueillir ● *Pres.* cueille, cueillons. ● *Impf.* cueillais. ● *Fut.* cueillerai. ● *Pres. sub.* cueille.

débattre *as* BATTRE.

décevoir *as* RECEVOIR.
découvrir *as* COUVRIR.
décrire *as* ÉCRIRE.
déduire *as* CONDUIRE.
défaire *as* FAIRE.
détenir *as* TENIR.
détruire *as* CONDUIRE.
devenir *as* TENIR.
devoir ● *Pres.* dois, devons, doivent. ● *Impf.* devais. ● *Past hist.* dus. ● *Fut.* devrai. ● *Pres. sub.* doive. ● *Past part.* dû, due.
dire ● *Pres.* dis, dit, disons, dites, disent. ● *Impf.* disais. ● *Past hist.* dis. ● *Past part.* dit.
disparaître *as* CONNAÎTRE.
dissoudre ● *Pres.* dissous, dissolvons. ● *Impf.* dissolvais. ● *Pres. sub.* dissolve. ● *Past part.* dissous, dissoute.
distraire *as* EXTRAIRE.
dormir ● *Pres.* dors, dormons. ● *Impf.* dormais. ● *Pres. sub.* dorme.
écrire ● *Pres.* écris, écrivons. ● *Impf.* écrivais. ● *Past hist.* écrivis. ● *Pres. sub.* écrive. ● *Past part.* écrit.
élire *as* LIRE.
émettre *as* METTRE.
s'enfuir *as* FUIR.
entreprendre *as* PRENDRE.
entretenir *as* TENIR.
envoyer ● *Fut.* enverrai.
éteindre *as* ATTEINDRE.
être ● *Pres.* suis, es, est, sommes, êtes, sont. ● *Impf.* étais. ● *Past hist.* fus, fut, fûmes, fûtes, furent. ● *Fut.* serai. ● *Pres. sub.* sois, soit, soyons, soyez, soient. ● *Pres. part.* étant. ● *Past part.* été. ● *Imp.* sois, soyons, soyez.
exclure *as* CONCLURE.
extraire ● *Pres.* extrais, extrayons. ● *Impf.* extrayais. ● *Pres. sub.* extraie. ● *Past part.* extrait.
faire ● *Pres.* fais, fait, faisons, faites, font. ● *Impf.* faisais. ● *Past hist.* fis. ● *Fut.* ferai. ● *Pres. sub.* fasse. ● *Past part.* fait.

falloir (impersonal) ● *Pres.* faut. ● *Impf.* fallait. ● *Past hist.* fallut. ● *Fut.* faudra. ● *Pres. sub.* faille. ● *Past part.* fallu.
feindre *as* ATTEINDRE.
fuir ● *Pres.* fuis, fuyons, fuient. ● *Impf.* fuyais. ● *Past hist.* fuis. ● *Pres sub.* fuie. ● *Past part.* fui.
inscrire *as* ÉCRIRE.
instruire *as* CONDUIRE.
interdire *as* DIRE, except ● *Pres.* vous interdisez.
interrompre *as* ROMPRE.
intervenir *as* TENIR.
introduire *as* CONDUIRE.
joindre *as* ATTEINDRE (except *oi* replaces *ei*).
lire ● *Pres.* lis, lit, lisons, lisez, lisent. ● *Impf.* lisais. ● *Past hist.* lus. ● *Pres. sub.* lise. ● *Past part.* lu.
luire ● *Pres.* luis, luisons. ● *Impf.* luisais. ● *Past hist.* luisis. ● *Pres. sub.* luise. ● *Past part.* lui.
maintenir *as* TENIR.
maudire ● *Pres.* maudis, maudissons. ● *Impf.* maudissais. ● *Past hist.* maudis. ● *Pres. sub.* maudisse. ● *Past part.* maudit.
mentir *as* SORTIR (except *en* replaces *or*).
mettre ● *Pres.* mets, met, mettons, mettez, mettent. ● *Past hist.* mis. ● *Past part.* mis.
mourir ● *Pres.* meurs, mourons, meurent. ● *Impf.* mourais. ● *Past hist.* mourus. ● *Fut.* mourrai. ● *Pres. sub.* meure, mourions. ● *Past part.* mort.
mouvoir ● *Pres.* meus, mouvons, meuvent. ● *Impf.* mouvais. ● *Fut.* mouvrai. ● *Pres. sub.* meuve, mouvions. ● *Past part.* mû, mue.
naître ● *Pres.* nais, naît, naissons. ● *Impf.* naissais. ● *Past hist.* naquis. ● *Pres. sub.* naisse. ● *Past part.* né.
nuire *as* LUIRE.

obtenir *as* TENIR.

offrir, ouvrir *as* COUVRIR.

omettre *as* METTRE.

paraître *as* CONNAÎTRE.

parcourir *as* COURIR.

partir *as* SORTIR (except *ar* replaces *or*).

parvenir *as* TENIR.

peindre *as* ATTEINDRE.

percevoir *as* RECEVOIR.

permettre *as* METTRE.

plaindre *as* ATTEINDRE (except *ai* replaces *ei*).

plaire ● *Pres.* plais, plaît, plaisons. ● *Impf.* plaisais. ● *Past hist.* plus. ● *Pres. sub.* plaise. ● *Past part.* plu.

pleuvoir (impersonal) ● *Pres.* pleut. ● *Impf.* pleuvait. ● *Past hist.* plut. ● *Fut.* pleuvra. ● *Pres. sub.* pleuve. ● *Past part.* plu.

poursuivre *as* SUIVRE.

pourvoir *as* VOIR, except ● *Fut.* pourvoirai

pouvoir ● *Pres.* peux, peut, pouvons, pouvez, peuvent. ● *Impf.* pouvais. ● *Past hist.* pus. ● *Fut.* pourrai. ● *Pres. sub.* puisse. ● *Past part.* pu.

prédire *as* DIRE, except ● *Pres.* vous prédisez.

prendre ● *Pres.* prends, prenons, prennent. ● *Impf.* prenais. ● *Past hist.* pris. ● *Pres. sub.* prenne, prenions. ● *Past part.* pris.

prescrire *as* ÉCRIRE.

prévenir *as* TENIR.

prévoir *as* VOIR, except ● *Fut.* prévoirai.

produire *as* CONDUIRE.

promettre *as* METTRE.

provenir *as* TENIR.

recevoir ● *Pres.* reçois, recevons, reçoivent. ● *Impf.* recevais. ● *Past hist.* reçus. ● *Fut.* recevrai. ● *Pres. sub.* reçoive, recevions. ● *Past part.* reçu.

reconduire *as* CONDUIRE.

reconnaître *as* CONNAÎTRE.

reconstruire *as* CONDUIRE.

recouvrir *as* COUVRIR.

recueillir *as* CUEILLIR.

redire *as* DIRE.

réduire *as* CONDUIRE.

refaire *as* FAIRE.

rejoindre *as* ATTEINDRE (except *oi* replaces *ei*).

remettre *as* METTRE.

renvoyer *as* ENVOYER.

repartir *as* SORTIR (except *ar* replaces *or*).

reprendre *as* PRENDRE.

reproduire *as* CONDUIRE.

résoudre ● *Pres.* résous, résolvons. ● *Impf.* résolvais. ● *Past hist.* résolus. ● *Pres. sub.* résolve. ● *Past part.* résolu.

ressortir *as* SORTIR.

restreindre *as* ATTEINDRE.

retenir, revenir *as* TENIR.

revivre *as* VIVRE.

revoir *as* VOIR.

rire ● *Pres.* ris, rit, rions, riez, rient. ● *Impf.* riais. ● *Past hist.* ris. ● *Pres. sub.* rie, riions. ● *Past part.* ri.

rompre *as* VENDRE (regular), except ● *Pres.* il rompt.

satisfaire *as* FAIRE.

savoir ● *Pres.* sais, sait, savons, savez, savent. ● *Impf.* savais. ● *Past hist.* sus. ● *Fut.* saurai. ● *Pres. sub.* sache, sachions. ● *Pres. part.* sachant. ● *Past part.* su. ● *Imp.* sache, sachons, sachez.

séduire *as* CONDUIRE.

sentir *as* SORTIR (except *en* replaces *or*).

servir ● *Pres.* sers, servons. ● *Impf.* servais. ● *Pres. sub.* serve.

sortir ● *Pres.* sors, sortons. ● *Impf.* sortais. ● *Pres. sub.* sorte.

souffrir *as* COUVRIR.

soumettre *as* METTRE.

soustraire *as* EXTRAIRE.

soutenir *as* TENIR.

suffire ● *Pres.* suffis, suffisons. ● *Impf.* suffisais. ● *Past hist.* suffis. ● *Pres. sub.* suffise. ● *Past part.* suffi.

suivre ● *Pres.* suis, suivons. ● *Impf.* suivais. ● *Past hist.* suivis. ● *Pres. sub.* suive. ● *Past part.* suivi.

surprendre *as* PRENDRE.
survivre *as* VIVRE.
taire
- *Pres.* tais, taisons.
- *Impf.* taisais. • *Past hist.* tus. • *Pres. sub.* taise.
- *Past part.* tu.

teindre *as* ATTEINDRE.
tenir
- *Pres.* tiens, tenons, tiennent. • *Impf.* tenais.
- *Past hist.* tins, tint, tînmes, tîntes, tinrent.
- *Fut.* tiendrai. • *Pres. sub.* tienne. • *Past part.* tenu.

traduire *as* CONDUIRE.
traire *as* EXTRAIRE.
transmettre *as* METTRE.
vaincre
- *Pres.* vaincs, vainc, vainquons. • *Impf.* vainquais. • *Past hist.* vainquis. • *Pres. sub.* vainque. • *Past part.* vaincu.

valoir
- *Pres.* vaux, vaut, valons, valez, valent. • *Impf.* valais. • *Past hist.* valus.
- *Fut.* vaudrai. • *Pres. sub.* vaille. • *Past part.* valu.

venir *as* TENIR.
vivre
- *Pres.* vis, vit, vivons, vivez, vivent. • *Impf.* vivais. • *Past hist.* vécus.
- *Pres. sub.* vive. • *Past part.* vécu.

voir
- *Pres.* vois, voyons, voient. • *Impf.* voyais.
- *Past hist.* vis. • *Fut.* verrai. • *Pres. sub.* voie, voyions. • *Past part.* vu.

vouloir
- *Pres.* veux, veut, voulons, voulez, veulent.
- *Impf.* voulais. • *Past hist.* voulus. • *Fut.* voudrai. • *Pres. sub.* veuille, voulions. • *Past part.* voulu. • *Imp.* veuille, veuillons, veuillez.